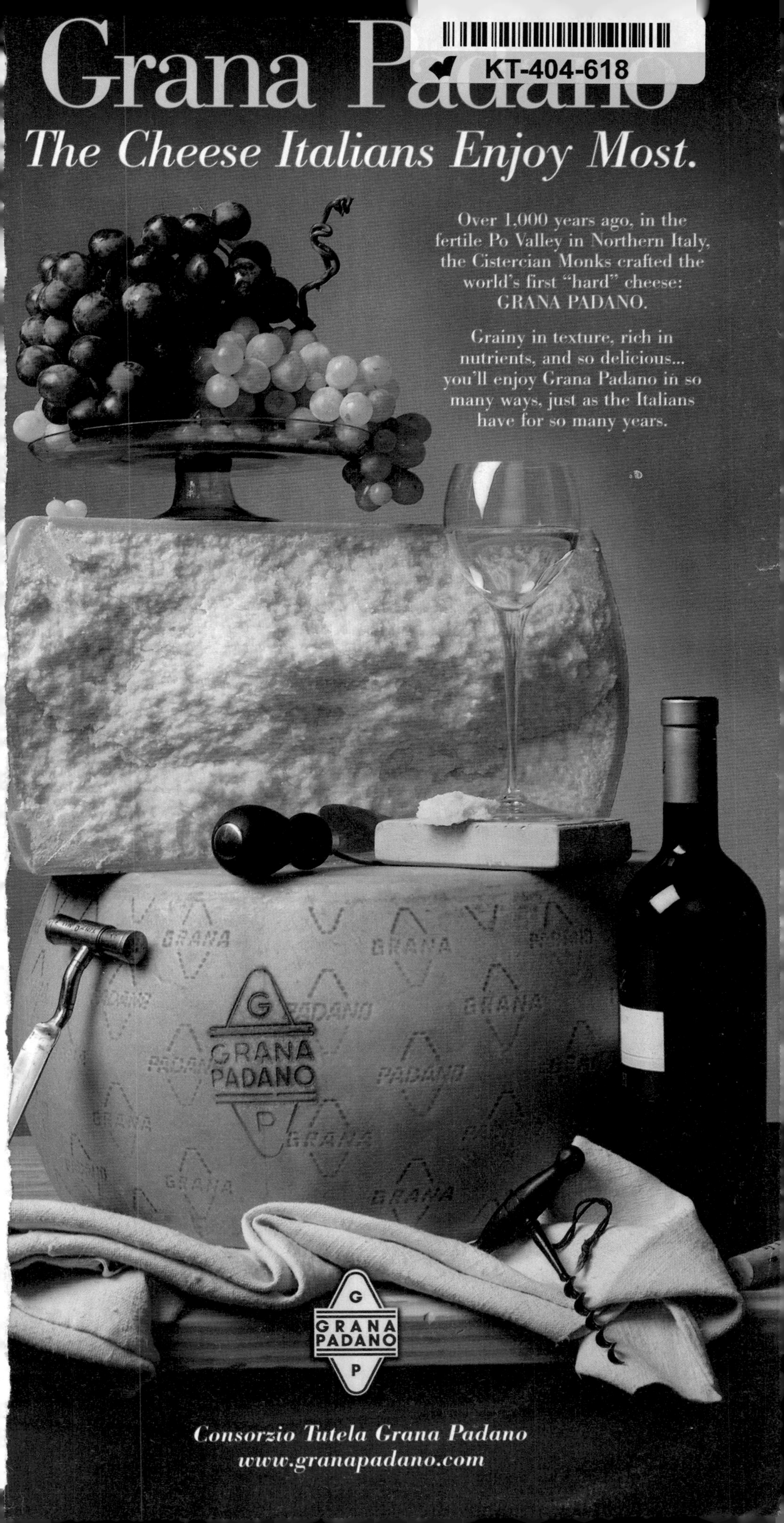
Grana Padano
The Cheese Italians Enjoy Most.
Over 1,000 years ago, in the fertile Po Valley in Northern Italy, the Cistercian Monks crafted the world's first "hard" cheese: GRANA PADANO.
Grainy in texture, rich in nutrients, and so delicious... you'll enjoy Grana Padano in so many ways, just as the Italians have for so many years.
G GRANA PADANO P
Consorzio Tutela Grana Padano
www.granapadano.com

Grana Padano

Its Versatility Is Unmatched

Both table and grating cheese, Grana Padano is never sliced, but rather chipped like an ice sculpture. A special knife with an almond-shaped blade is recommended for breaking the cheese into yellowish white granules. Use Grana Padano in your store to illustrate to your customers how to incorporate this versatile cheese into their meals. Some ideas include:

- *Shave over carpaccio*
- *Use in macaroni and cheese casseroles*
- *Grate over your favorite pasta dish*
- *Serve with fruit or nuts as an appetizer*
- *Use as part of a cheese plate for dessert*

Risotto with Vegetables & Grana Padano

Risotto con Verdure e Grana Padano

Recipe by Lidia Bastianich, New York, N

Makes 6 servings

- 1/2 pound broccoli (about 1 medium-size stalk)
- 1 cup blanched fava beans or frozen baby lima beans
- 3 tablespoons extra virgin olive oil
- 1/2 cup minced scallions, greens included (about 6)
- 1 tablespoon minced shallot
- 2 1/2 cups Arborio or Carnaroli rice
- 1/2 cup dry white wine
- 6 1/2 cups hot Chicken Stock or canned chicken broth
- 1/2 teaspoon salt, or as needed
- 2 tablespoons unsalted butter, cut into bits
- 1/2 cup freshly grated Grana Padano cheese
- Freshly ground black pepper

1. Cut broccoli florets from stems. Keep the florets small (about 1 1/4 cups). Peel th broccoli stems and then cut them into 2-inch pieces. Steam the florets just until bright green, about 1 minute. Reserve. Steam the stems until tender, about 4 minutes. Reserve the steaming liquid. Transfer the stems to a blender or food processor and process until smooth. If needed add some of the steaming liquid to make a smooth mixture. Scrape puree into a small bowl. Set florets and puree aside
2. If using the baby lima beans, cook them in boiling salted water for 2 minutes. Drai them thoroughly and set aside. (The blanched fava beans are ready as they are.)
3. In a 3- to 4-quart casserole or pot, heat the olive oil over medium heat. Add the scallion and shallot and sauté until translucent, stirring often, about 4 min utes. Add the rice and stir to coat with the oil. Toast the rice until the edges become translucent, 1 to 2 minutes.
4. Pour in the wine and stir well until evaporated. Add 1/2 cup of the hot stock and the salt. Cook, stirring constantly, until all the stock has been absorbed. Continue to add hot stock in small batches– about half a cup, just enough to completely moisten the rice– and cook until each successive batch has been absorbed. About 12 minutes after the first addition of stock, stir in the broccol puree and the favas or limas. About 3 minutes after that, stir in the broccoli florets. Stir constantly and adjust the level of heat so the rice is simmering ver gently while adding the stock until the rice mixture is creamy but al dente. This will take about 18 minutes from the first addition of stock.
5. Remove the casserole from the heat. Whip in the butter until melted, then the grated Grana Padano cheese. Adjust the seasoning with salt, if necessary, and pepper. Serve immediately, ladled into warm shallow bowls.

G GRANA PADANO P

Consorzio Tutela Grana Padano • www.granapadano.com

italianwines 2007

LE GUIDE
DEL GAMBERO ROSSO

Gambero Rosso®

Slow Food Editore

ITALIAN WINES 2007

GAMBERO ROSSO®- SLOW FOOD EDITORE

EDITORIAL STAFF FOR THE ORIGINAL EDITION
DANIELE CERNILLI AND GIGI PIUMATTI

SENIOR EDITORS
GIANNI FABRIZIO AND MARCO SABELLICO

TECHNICAL SUPERVISION
GILBERTO ARRU, DARIO CAPPELLONI, NICOLA FRASSON, TIZIANO GAIA, GIANCARLO GARIGLIO, FABIO GIAVEDONI, ELEONORA GUERINI, VITTORIO MANGANELLI, RICCARDO VISCARDI, PAOLO ZACCARIA

MEMBERS OF FINAL TASTING PANELS
BARBARA ANTOGNINI, ALESSANDRO BOCCHETTI, ANTONIO BOCO, GIULIO COLOMBA, PAOLO DE CRISTOFARO, EGIDIO FEDELE DELL'OSTE, GIACOMO MOJOLI, LEONARDO ROMANELLI

CONTRIBUTORS
NINO AIELLO, GILBERTO ARRU, STEFANO ASARO, VITTORIO BARBIERI, PAOLO BATTIMELLI, ENRICO BATTISTELLA, FRANCESCO BEGHI, ALESSANDRO BOCCHETTI, ANTONIO BOCO, SERGIO BONANNO, WALTER BORDO, MICHELE BRESSAN, PASQUALE BUFFA, PAOLO CAMOZZI, DARIO CAPPELLONI, DIONISIO CASTELLO, DANIELE CERNILLI, ROBERTO CHECCHETTO, ANTONIO CIMINELLI, GIULIO COLOMBA, PAOLO DE CRISTOFARO, FILIPPO DE GRANDI, GIANNI FABRIZIO, EGIDIO FEDELE DELL'OSTE, DARIO FERRO, FAUSTO FERRONI, CARLO FIORANI, NICOLA FRASSON, FABIO FUSINA, TIZIANO GAIA, PIETRO GARIBBO, GIANCARLO GARIGLIO, FABIO GIAVEDONI, ELEONORA GUERINI, VITO LACERENZA, MASSIMO LANZA, GIANCARLO LO SICCO, PATRIZIO MASTROCOLA, GIORGIO MELANDRI, GIACOMO MOJOLI, FABIO MONGARETTO, GIOVANNI NORESE, FRANCO PALLINI, DAVIDE PANZIERI, STEFANO PASTOR, ALESSANDRO PENNETTA, ANGELO PERETTI, ONORIO PERON, NICOLA PICCININI, GUIDO PIRAZZOLI, GIGI PIUMATTI, MARIO PLAZIO, FABIO PRACCHIA, FRANCESCO QUERCETTI, PIERPAOLO RASTELLI, LEONARDO ROMANELLI, FABRIZIO RUSSO, MARCO SABELLICO, DIEGO SORACCO, MAURIZIO STAGNITTO, HERBERT TASCHLER, RENATO TEDESCO, MASSIMO TOFFOLO, ANDREA VANNELLI, MASSIMO VOLPARI, PAOLO ZACCARIA

MEMBERS OF REGIONAL TASTING PANELS
BARBARA ANTOGNINI, ANTONELLA AMODIO, ARTEMIO ASSIRI, EMIDIO BACHETTI, ANTONELLA BAMBA, ANDREA BASSETTI, SALVATORE BASTA, MIRCO BERTAZZO, ALBERTO BETTINI, TEODOSIO BUONGIORNO, REMO CAMURANI, SERGIO CECCARELLI, VALERIO CHIARINI, ENZO CODOGNO, VALENTINA CONGIU, GOFFREDO D'ANDREA, MARIO DEMATTE, MARINO DEL CURTO, ROBERTO DE VITI, TIZIANA DI MICELI, KATHRIN FEHERVARY, ROSSANO FERRAZZANO, PIERO FIORENTINI, NATALE FIORINO, LAURA GIORGI, RAFFAELE GUZZON, TONI LABELLA, DARIO LAURENZI, CRISTIANA LAURO, ENRICO LUCARINI, LUCA MANZONI, MIRCO MARCONI, MINO MARTUCCI, GIACOMO MAZZAVILLANI, DANIELE MEREU, ENZO MERZ, FRANCESCO MONACO, DANNY MURARO, VANNI MURARO, UGO ONGARETTO, RENATO ORLANDO, ROBERTO PALMIERI, LINA PAOLILLO, PIERPAOLO PENCO, LIANO PETROZZI, SIMONE PETROZZI, MARGHERITA PIANCASTELLI, MAX PLETT, FILIPPO POLIDORI, RENZO PRIORI, SILVANO PROMPICAI, VALENTINO RAMELLI, HELMUT RIEBSCHLÄGER, MAURIZIO ROSSI, ALESSANDRA RUGGI, PAOLO TRIMANI, PAOLO VALDASTRI, ALBERTO ZACCONE, SIMONE ZOLI

EDITING
BARBARA ANTOGNINI, DARIO CAPPELLONI, ELEONORA GUERINI, BIANCA MINERDO, VITTORIO MANGANELLI, PAOLO ZACCARIA

EDITORIAL CO-ORDINATOR
GIORGIO ACCASCINA

TRANSLATIONS CO-ORDINATED AND EDITED BY
GILES WATSON

TRANSLATORS
MAUREEN ASHLEY, EDGAR BETTRIDGE, HELEN DONALD, DAVE HENDERSON, STEPHEN JACKSON, GILES WATSON, AILSA WOOD

PUBLISHER
GAMBERO ROSSO, INC.
PRESIDENT STEFANO BONILLI
636 BROADWAY - SUITE 1111 - NEW YORK, NY 10012
TEL. +1-212- 253-5653 FAX +1-212- 253-8349 - E-MAIL: gamberousa@aol.com

DISTRIBUTION
USA AND CANADA BY ANTIQUE COLLECTORS' CLUB, EASTWORKS, 116 PLEASANT ST # 18
EASTHAMPTON, MA 01027, USA;
UK AND AUSTRALIA BY ANTIQUE COLLECTORS' CLUB LTD - SANDY LANE, OLD MARTLESHAM
WOODBRIDGE, SUFFOLK IP12 4SD - UNITED KINGDOM
TEL. +44-1394-389950 - FAX. +44-1394-389999

ITALIAN WINES 2007 WAS CLOSED ON 20 SEPTEMBER 2006

PRINTED IN ITALY FOR G. R. H. SPA IN JANUARY 2007 BY
GRAFICHE PFG – VIA CANCELLERIA, 62 – 00040 ARICCIA - ROME

CONTENTS

INTRODUCTION

"Wine is a solution of alcohol and water obtained by the fermentation of the sugar contained in grapes. That might be a good way to start a treatise on oenology but luckily our subject is not restricted to such coldly technical matters. We cannot ignore, for example, all the cultural and social connotations that wine has acquired, especially in Mediterranean civilization". That was how the 1988 edition of the Guide opened. It was the first in a series that has now reached number 20. We quote it in translation because it surprised us to see that one of the main principles underpinning the project at that time is still as relevant as ever today, and is still a benchmark for our efforts. The primacy of culture and the social, not just the economic, role of wine are crucial to our approach. This means that the almost solipsistic organoleptic ritual of tasting is necessary, but not in itself sufficient, to determine the quality of a wine. For any agricultural product, quality also has to do with its symbolic value and ability to represent and respect a territory, including safeguarding the environment. That is why when our tasting panels meet to evaluate the wines from a specific area, they do not make their judgements solely on the basis of personal opinion, in other words the wine's organoleptic profile. Guide tasters also take into account various other considerations to assess the compliance of each product with the principles we have just listed. Is the wine typical or not? Is it representative of its origins? Is it so representative as to be instantly recognizable at blind tasting? There are such wines. Sassicaia, Valentini's Montepulciano and Trebbiano, Gravner's Breg and Ribolla, Barolo Monfortino by Roberto Conterno, the great reds from Angelo Gaja, the Passito di Pantelleria wines by Salvatore Murana, Gewürztraminer Nussbaumer from the Cantina Produttori di Termeno and Romano Dal Forno's Amarone are just a few. Wines like these have a truly distinctive character – a soul even – that goes beyond organoleptic considerations. They are thoroughbreds. Obviously, there are many more such products and for this 20th anniversary edition, we decided to give a special award to just one, the bottle we believe is the greatest we have ever had the privilege to uncork: Barolo Gran Bussia Riserva 1989 from Aldo Conterno. It is a monument to marriage of representativity and sensory values. But now, as every year, it is time to talk about Italian Wines 2007, about what we discovered and about how the Guide was compiled. There were some 282 Three Glass wines, the highest number ever, but we also tasted more wines than ever before – about 16,000 – and the 2,206 cellars reviewed are another record for the Guide. If we compare these figures with the first edition – 1,500 wines tasted, 500 cellars and 32 Three Glasses – this year's Guide has more than five times as many wineries than the 1988 Guide, more than 11 times as many wines and nine times as many top prizes. Only 23 people contributed to that first edition. It is interesting to note who is still with us today among the 130 who figure on the list of today's collaborators. Apart from the present writers, the only person who has contributed to all the editions of the Guide is Gilberto Arru, our man in Sardinia, a fine taster and a dear friend of many years' standing. We would like to thank Gilberto for his invaluable work, which has been crucial to the publication of the Guide over all these years. For the rest, we followed our usual pattern. We began in May, when the tasting panels in the various regions started to collect the samples that they would assess at blind comparative tastings. Wherever possible, we strove to involve protection consortia, chambers of commerce and anyone else who could act as neutral guarantors for the collection of wines and the organization of tasting sessions. Around 70,000 bottles were collected all over Italy for the Guide. They had to be sourced, conserved and masked for tasting after being divided into groups of similar wines. Readers can imagine how much work this involved. We also believe that the supervision of this phase by independent institutions is a very positive factor. Such bodies represent all the producers and scrutinize our operations to ensure they are carried out properly, safeguarding the interests of consumers and monitoring what we do, for which we are very grateful. We will thank all of them, in the hope that none are inadvertently omitted: the consortia of Chianti Classico, Brunello and Rosso di Montalcino, Nobile di Montepulciano, Bolgheri, Vernaccia di San Gimignano, Chianti Rufina, Morellino di Scansano, Montecucco, Monteregio di Massa Marittima, Franciacorta, Oltrepò Pavese, Valtellina, Soave and Valpolicella, the Enoteca Regionale del Roero, the Enoteca Regionale at Dozza, the Enoteca Regionale at Gattinara, the Istituto Agronomico Mediterraneo at Valenzano, Centro Agroalimentare Umbro at Foligno, the Bolzano Chamber of Commerce, the Avellino Chamber of Commerce, the Trento Chamber of Commerce, the Arezzo Chamber of Commerce, Assivip at Majolati Spontini, Vinea at Offida and the Anteprima group at Lucca. Then there are the Strada del Vino associations of Carmignano and Costa degli Etruschi, and Unioncamere at Matera. Private bodies include the Hotel Gallura at Olbia, the Reserve at Caramanico, the Vineria della Signora in Rosso at Nizza Monferrato, the Enoteca Grapes at Isernia and the Le Due Sorelle restaurant at Messina. If we add those who worked at the consortia to the roughly 130 tasters we deployed, it is obvious that a Guide like this requires the contribution of at least 250 individuals every year. In short, a whole lot of people. The 30 or so tasting panels, each comprising at least three judges, worked for about two months, tasting around 25,000 wines. Just under 10,000 wines were rejected outright, and the rest were awarded scores ranging from zero to Two Glasses. In this first phase, we awarded points out of 100 and selected the roughly 1,500 wines that would go forward to the Three Glass taste-offs. At the end of this huge task, the final awards committee met. Made up of prominent figures on local tasting panels, the committee scrutinized all the wines sent to the finals. Again, all tastings were blind. The judgement here was more drastic, a yes or a no. Each decision was carefully justified. Every wine was discussed and analysed by all the members of the commission, whose votes had equal weight. For this Guide, the following panellists joined Daniele Cernilli, Gigi Piumatti, Gianni Fabrizio and Marco Sabellico for at least one of the three final taste-offs over a total of 15 days: Vittorio Manganelli, Dario Cappelloni, Nicola Frasson, Eleonora Guerini, Giulio Colomba, Giacomo Mojoli, Egidio Fedele dell'Oste, Leonardo Romanelli, Paolo Zaccaria, Fabio Giavedoni, Riccardo Viscardi, Antonio Boco, Paolo De Cristofaro, Alessandro Bocchetti, Tiziano Gaia and Giancarlo Gariglio. Tastings were held at Città del Gusto in Rome, the University of Gastronomic Sciences at Pollenzo and the Là di Petros restaurant at Colloredo di Monte Albano. New developments this year include the Award for Sustainable Viticulture, which went to Peter Pliger, from Kuenhof at Bressanone/Brixen, one of the pioneers of organic winemaking in Alto Adige. A number of Three Glass awards went to areas that will be the new frontier of Italian wine over the next few years, such as northern Piedmont with its long-established designated areas like Gattinara, Ghemme, Lessona, Boca, Fara and Bramaterra. Then there are the small producers in the Colli Tortonesi with their Timorasso, an extremely interesting white that is still prevented from featuring on labels by exasperatingly complicated red tape. There is Valtellina, with Sfursat and other wines. There is Valle d'Aosta, with Italy's finest Chardonnays and Pinot Gris. Valle Isarco and Val Venosta in Alto Adige have varieties like veltliner, sylvaner and riesling, as well as widespread environmental awareness that has few equals up in Italy. Further south, Brunello di Montalcino is currently undergoing a major rethink and significant improvement in the average level of quality. There has been exciting quality progress for Montepulciano d'Abruzzo, partly thanks to the new DOCG zone for the Colline Teramane. Finally, we pass through Irpinia and Vulture to reach Etna and the rest of eastern Sicily, where there are some highly distinctive, characterful wines. Rarely do they come from high-yielding zones. Rarely are the cellar names famous. But this is the way forward for Italy's oenological avant-garde: these are the wineries that can push the envelope of fashion that held back Italian winemaking until a few years ago. Now we wish you an enjoyable read.

Daniele Cernilli and Gigi Piumatti

THREE GLASS AWARDS 2007

VALLE D'AOSTA

Valle d'Aosta Chardonnay Cuvée Bois Cuvée Frissonnière Les Crêtes '04	Les Crêtes	19
Valle d'Aosta Chardonnay Élevé en Fût de Chêne '05	Anselmet	22
Valle d'Aosta Pinot Gris Lo Triolet '05	Lo Triolet	20

PIEDMONT

Arcàss Passito '04	Cascina Chicco	55
Barbaresco '03	Cantina del Pino	35
Barbaresco Rabajà Ris. '01	Bruno Giacosa	132
Barbaresco S. Stefanetto '03	Piero Busso	130
Barbaresco S. Stefano Ris. '01	Castello di Neive	134
Barbaresco Vign. Brich Ronchi '03	Albino Rocca	40
Barbaresco Vign. Starderi Ris. '01	La Spinetta	64
Barbaresco Vigneti in Pajé Ris. '01	Produttori del Barbaresco	33
Barbaresco Vigneti in Rio Sordo Ris. '01	Produttori del Barbaresco	33
Barbera d'Alba Marun '04	Matteo Correggia	56
Barbera d'Alba Mulassa '04	Cascina Ca' Rossa	55
Barbera d'Alba Rocca delle Marasche '04	Deltetto	57
Barbera d'Alba Sup. '04	Filippo Gallino	57
Barbera d'Asti Ai Suma '04	Braida	147
Barbera d'Asti Pomorosso '04	Coppo	62
Barbera d'Asti Sup. Bionzo '04	La Spinetta	64
Barbera d'Asti Sup. Nizza La Court '03	Michele Chiarlo	53
Barbera d'Asti Sup. Nizza La Crena '03	Vietti	73
Barolo Bricco Boschis V. S. Giuseppe Ris. '00	F.lli Cavallotto	71
Barolo Bricco delle Viole '01	G. D. Vajra	49
Barolo Cannubi '01	Giacomo Brezza & Figli	43
Barolo Cerretta '01	Ettore Germano	158
Barolo Lazzarito V. La Delizia '01	Fontanafredda	157
Barolo Le Gramolere Ris. '00	Giovanni Manzone	121
Barolo Massara '01	Castello di Verduno	170
Barolo Monfortino Ris. '99	Giacomo Conterno	118
Barolo Monprivato '01	Giuseppe Mascarello e Figlio	115
Barolo Pernanno '01	Cascina Bongiovanni	71
Barolo Runcot '01	Elio Grasso	120
Barolo S. Lorenzo '01	F.lli Alessandria	168
Barolo V. dei Dardi Ris. '00	Alessandro e Gian Natale Fantino	119
Barolo V. Elena '01	Elvio Cogno	141
Barolo V. Rionda '01	Oddero	105
Barolo Vecchie Vigne in Mariondino Ris. '99	Armando Parusso	122
Carema Et. Nera '01	Ferrando	97
Colli Tortonesi Bianco Pitasso '04	Claudio Mariotto	165
Colli Tortonesi Bianco Sterpi '04	Vigneti Massa	125
Dogliani Papà Celso '05	Abbona	85
Dolcetto d'Alba Barturot '05	Ca' Viola	86
Dolcetto di Dogliani Sup. Bricco Botti '04	Pecchenino	87
Gattinara Podere dei Ginepri '01	Nervi	91
Gattinara Ris. '01	Giancarlo Travaglini	92
Gattinara Vign. Osso S. Grato '01	Antoniolo	90
Langhe Larigi '04	Elio Altare - Cascina Nuova	98
Langhe Nebbiolo Costa Russi '03	Gaja	37
Langhe Nebbiolo Sorì S. Lorenzo '03	Gaja	37
Lessona S. Sebastiano allo Zoppo '01	Sella	110
Monferrato Rosso Sonvico '03	Cascina La Barbatella	137

VENETO

Amarone della Valpolicella Cl. '01	Allegrini	328
Amarone della Valpolicella Cl. '99	Cav. G.B. Bertani	330
Amarone della Valpolicella Cl. Casa dei Bepi '01	Viviani	348
Amarone della Valpolicella Cl. Vign. Monte Ca' Bianca '01	Lorenzo Begali	355
Amarone della Valpolicella Cl. Villa Rizzardi '01	Guerrieri Rizzardi	321
Amarone della Valpolicella Proemio '03	Santi	332
Amarone della Valpolicella Vign. di Monte Lodoletta '01	Romano Dal Forno	331
Bianco di Custoza Sup. Amedeo '04	Cavalchina	368
Breganze Cabernet Sauvignon Palazzotto '04	Maculan	323
Breganze Cabernet Vign. Due Santi '04	Vigneto Due Santi	322
Capitel Croce '04	Roberto Anselmi	341
Montello e Colli Asolani Il Rosso dell'Abazia '03	Serafini & Vidotto	349
Recioto della Valpolicella Cl. '04	Tommaso Bussola	345
Relogio '04	Ca' Orologio	318
Soave Cl. Ca' Visco '05	Coffele	365
Soave Cl. Calvarino '04	Leonildo Pieropan	366
Soave Cl. La Froscà '05	Gini	342
Soave Cl. Le Bine '04	Tamellini	368
Soave Cl. Monte Carbonare '05	Suavia	367
Soave Cl. Monte Fiorentine '05	Ca' Rugate	341
Soave Cl. Monte Grande '05	Prà	344
Valpolicella Cl. Sup. '99	Giuseppe Quintarelli	346
Valpolicella Sup. '03	Corte Sant'Alda	337
Valpolicella Sup. Terre di S. Colombano '03	Trabucchi	332

FRIULI VENEZIA GIULIA

Arbis Blanc '05	Borgo San Daniele	406
Breg Anfora '02	Gravner	431
Calvari '02	Miani	396
COF Bianco Pomèdes '04	Roberto Scubla	447
COF Pignolo di Buttrio '03	Girolamo Dorigo	395
COF Refosco P. R. Romain '03	Paolo Rodaro	403
COF Rosazzo Bianco Terre Alte '04	Livio Felluga	410
COF Sauvignon Zuc di Volpe '05	Volpe Pasini	467
COF Tocai Friulano Vigneto Storico '05	Adriano Gigante	420
Collio Pinot Bianco '05	Doro Princic	413
Collio Pinot Bianco '05	Franco Toros	417
Collio Pinot Grigio '05	Branko	407
Collio Rosso della Castellada '99	La Castellada	430
Collio Sauvignon '05	Ronco dei Tassi	414
Collio Sauvignon '05	Russiz Superiore	398
Collio Sauvignon de La Tour '05	Villa Russiz	400
Collio Sauvignon Ronco delle Mele '05	Venica & Venica	423
Collio Tocai Friulano '05	Colle Duga	409
Collio Tocai Friulano '05	Mauro Drius	409
Collio Tocai Friulano '05	Edi Keber	410
Collio Tocai Friulano '05	Dario Raccaro	413
Collio Tocai Friulano '05	Castello di Spessa	399
Collio Tocai Friulano '05	Oscar Sturm	416
Friuli Grave Merlot Vistorta '04	Vistorta	455
Friuli Isonzo Rive Alte Sauvignon Vieris '04	Vie di Romans	438
Friuli Isonzo Rive Alte Tocai Friulano '05	Ronco del Gelso	415

Pinot Grigio Gris '04	Lis Neris	463
Ribolla Anfora '02	Gravner	431
Vespa Bianco '04	Bastianich	445
EMILIA ROMAGNA		
C. P. Cabernet Sauvignon Luna Selvatica '04	La Tosa	501
C. P. Malvasia Passito V. del Volta '04	La Stoppa	499
C. P. Vin Santo Albarola Val di Nure '96	Conte Otto Barattieri di San Pietro	501
Colli di Rimini Rosso Noi '04	San Patrignano	484
Diggioanni Cabernet Sauvignon '04	Vallona	482
Marzieno '03	Fattoria Zerbina	488
Sangiovese di Romagna Sup. Michelangiolo Ris. '03	Calonga	489
TUSCANY		
Anfiteatro '03	Vecchie Terre di Montefili	607
Avvoltore '04	Moris Farms	562
Bolgheri Rosso Sup. Grattamacco '03	Colle Massari	521
Bolgheri Sassicaia '03	Tenuta San Guido	518
Brancaia Il Blu '04	Brancaia	613
Brunello di Montalcino '01	Biondi Santi - Tenuta Il Greppo	565
Brunello di Montalcino '01	Cerbaiona	569
Brunello di Montalcino '01	Collemattoni	570
Brunello di Montalcino '01	Podere La Fortuna	573
Brunello di Montalcino '01	Il Palazzone	578
Brunello di Montalcino '01	La Rasina	583
Brunello di Montalcino Cerretalto '00	Casanova di Neri	566
Brunello di Montalcino Donna Olga '01	Donna Olga	572
Brunello di Montalcino Il Divasco '01	La Rasina	583
Brunello di Montalcino Prime Donne '01	Casato Prime Donne Donatella Cinelli Colombini	571
Brunello di Montalcino Ris. '99	Poggio di Sotto	582
Brunello di Montalcino Tenuta Nuova '01	Casanova di Neri	566
Brunello di Montalcino Terra Rossa '01	Il Poggiolo	582
Brunello di Montalcino Ugolaia '00	Lisini	576
Camartina '03	Querciabella	553
Casalferro '03	Barone Ricasoli	543
Castello del Terriccio '03	Castello del Terriccio	528
Cepparello '03	Isole e Olena	514
Chianti Cl. Bellavista '01	Castello di Ama	542
Chianti Cl. Castello di Ama '03	Castello di Ama	542
Chianti Cl. Castello di Brolio '03	Barone Ricasoli	543
Chianti Cl. Castello di Fonterutoli '03	Castello di Fonterutoli	523
Chianti Cl. I Massi Ris. '03	Il Colombaio di Cencio	544
Chianti Cl. La Selvanella Ris. '03	Melini	610
Chianti Cl. Rancia Ris. '03	Fattoria di Felsina	532
Chianti Cl. Vigna Casi Ris. '03	Castello di Meleto	545
Chianti Cl. Ris. '03	Villa Cafaggio	608
Colline Lucchesi Tenuta di Valgiano '03	Tenuta di Valgiano	560
Corbaia '03	Castello di Bossi	530
Flaccianello della Pieve '03	Tenuta Fontodi	604
Galatrona '04	Fattoria Petrolo	518
Giorgio Primo '03	La Massa	605
Gratius '04	Il Molino di Grace	605
Guidalberto '04	Tenuta San Guido	518
I Sodi di San Niccolò '02	Castellare di Castellina	522
Il Carbonaione '03	Podere Poggio Scalette	552

MOLISE		
Molise Aglianico Contado '03	Di Majo Norante	766
CAMPANIA		
Costa d'Amalfi Furore Bianco Fiorduva '05	Gran Furor Divina Costiera	775
Cupo '05	Cantine Pietracupa	777
Falerno del Massico Bianco Vigna Caracci '04	Villa Matilde	773
Fiano di Avellino '05	Colli di Lapio	776
Fiano di Avellino Radici '05	Mastroberardino	770
Fiano di Avellino Vigna della Congregazione '04	Villa Diamante	778
Montevetrano '04	Montevetrano	782
Pàtrimo '04	Feudi di San Gregorio	784
Pietraincatenata '04	Luigi Maffini	772
Serpico '04	Feudi di San Gregorio	784
Taurasi Radici Ris. '00	Mastroberardino	770
Taurasi Vigna Cinque Querce Ris. '01	Salvatore Molettieri	779
Terra di Lavoro '04	Galardi	783
BASILICATA		
Aglianico del Vulture Il Nibbio Grigio Et. Nera '03	Di Palma	797
Aglianico del Vulture V. Caselle Ris. '01	Cantine D'Angelo	797
PUGLIA		
Artas '04	Castello Monaci	811
Castel del Monte Nero di Troia Puer Apuliae '04	Rivera	807
Cotinone '05	Tenuta Coppadoro	819
Graticciaia '01	Agricole Vallone	814
Masseria Maime '04	Tormaresca	808
CALABRIA		
Scavigna Vigna Garrone '03	G.B. Odoardi	831
SICILIY		
Benuara '05	Cusumano	848
Cometa '05	Planeta	844
Contea di Sclafani Rosso del Conte '03	Tasca d'Almerita	847
Contessa Entellina Milleunanotte '03	Donnafugata	842
Duca Enrico '03	Duca di Salaparuta - Vini Corvo	838
Etna Bianco Sup. Pietramarina '02	Benanti	851
Etna Rosso Feudo di Mezzo Quadro delle Rose '04	Tenuta delle Terre Nere	849
Etna Rosso Serra della Contessa '03	Benanti	851
Faro Palari '04	Palari	845
Merlot '04	Planeta	844
Montenero '04	Abbazia Santa Anastasia	838
Moscato di Pantelleria Mueggen '04	Salvatore Murana	847
Passopisciaro '04	Passopisciaro	839
Ribeca '04	Firriato	846
Tenute Dorrasita Nero d'Avola '04	Cantine Foraci	844
SARDINIA		
Alghero Marchese di Villamarina '01	Tenute Sella & Mosca	862
Tenores '03	Tenute Dettori	871
Terras Rosso '04	Josto Puddu	868
Turriga '02	Antonio Argiolas	872

RETROSPECTIVE THREE GLASS AWARDS

PIEDMONT	
Barbaresco Camp Gros '97	Tenute Cisa Asinari dei Marchesi di Gresy
Barbaresco Valgrande '99	Ca' del Baio
Barolo Brunate '96	Poderi Marcarini
Barolo Bussia Dardi Le Rose '99	Poderi Colla
Barolo Monfortino Ris. '96	Giacomo Conterno
Caluso Passito Sulè '98	Orsolani
ALTO ADIGE	
A.A. Schiava Gschleier '90	Cantina Produttori Cornaiano
VENETO	
Amarone della Valpolicella Cl. '99	Brigaldara
Amarone della Valpolicella Cl. Capitel Monte Olmi '97	F.lli Tedeschi
Amarone della Valpolicella Cl. Sergio Zenato '95	Zenato
FRIULI VENEZIA GIULIA	
Breg '98	Gravner
Collio Bianco Ronco della Chiesa '02	Borgo del Tiglio
Where the Dreams Have no End '95	Vinnaioli Jermann
TUSCANY	
Brunello di Montalcino Ris. '95	Biondi Santi
Chianti Classico Bellavista '95	Ama
Chianti Classico La Selvanella Ris. '99	Melini
Flaccianello della Pieve '01	Tenuta Fontodi
I Sodi di San Niccolò '95	Castellare di Castellina
Le Pergole Torte '99	Montevertine
Percarlo '95	San Giusto a Rentennano
MARCHE	
Verdicchio dei Castelli di Jesi Cl. Serra Fiorese Ris. '96	Garofoli
Verdicchio dei Castelli di Jesi Cl. Villa Bucci Ris. '95	Bucci
UMBRIA	
Torgiano Rubesco Vigna Monticchio Ris. '88	Lungarotti
CAMPANIA	
Taurasi Radici Ris. '99	Mastroberardino
BASILICATA	
Aglianico del Vulture Don Anselmo '94	Paternoster
SICILY	
Etna Bianco Sup. Pietramarina '97	Benanti

THE WINE OF THE PAST 20 YEARS

BAROLO GRAN BUSSIA RISERVA '89 | PODERI ALDO CONTERNO

THE WINES OF THE YEAR

THE SPARKLER

FRANCIACORTA SATÈN '02 | GATTI

ITHE WHITE

CUPO '05 | PIETRACUPA

THE RED

BRUNELLO DI MONTALCINO '01 | CERBAIONA

THE SWEET

A. A. MOSCATO GIALLO PASSITO SERENADE '03 | CANTINA VITICOLTORI DI CALDARO

WINERY OF THE YEAR

BENANTI

OENOLOGIST OF THE YEAR

CASIMIRO MAULE

UP-AND-COMING WINERY

VILLA MEDORO

BEST PRICED WINE

SOAVE CLASSICO MONTE FIORENTINE '05 | CA' RUGATE

GROWER OF THE YEAR

JOSKO GRAVNER

AWARD FOR SUSTAINABLE VITICULTURE

PETER PLIGER

THE STARS

In the Guide's 20 years of existence, some 82 wineries have earned Three Glass awards at least ten times. Heading the list is Angelo Gaja, regarded by many as the most representative of Italian wine producers. Angelo has picked up an amazing 39 Three Glasses, which become 43 if we factor in those won by Ca' Marcanda, Pieve di Santa Restituta and Gromis, all of which have now been fully integrated into the group. Antinori has in fact done even better. The group's San Casciano, Castello della Sala, Prunotto, Guado al Tasso and Tomaresca properties have totted up 48 top awards, albeit split across five separately considered cellars. There is a third Star for Giorgio Rivetti and his family, from whom we had erroneously deducted a Three Glass award in our calculations, and a second for Castello di Ama and Fattoria di Felsina while there are several new faces on ten Three Glasses. We'll mention some of the most prestigious: Montevertine, Quintarelli, Venica, Tua Rita, Le Crêtes, Falesco and Garofoli. And there some equally well-known names waiting in the wings on nine top awards: Frescobaldi, Avignonesi, Walch, Vietti and many more. We look forward to welcoming them to our Star club.

★ ★ ★

39
GAJA (Piedmont)

30
LA SPINETTA (Piedmont)

★ ★

28
CA' DEL BOSCO (Lombardy)

25
ELIO ALTARE - CASCINA NUOVA (Piedmont)

22
ALLEGRINI (Veneto)
CASTELLO DI FONTERUTOLI (Tuscany)

21
CASTELLO DI AMA (Tuscany)

20
FATTORIA DI FELSINA (Tuscany)

★

18
MARCHESI ANTINORI (Tuscany)
DOMENICO CLERICO (Piedmont)
GIROLAMO DORIGO (Friuli Venezia Giulia)
JERMANN (Friuli Venezia Giulia)
POLIZIANO (Tuscany)
VALENTINI (Abruzzo)
VILLA RUSSIZ (Friuli Venezia Giulia)

17
CANTINA PRODUTTORI SAN MICHELE APPIANO (Alto Adige)
CASTELLO DELLA SALA (Umbria)
FEUDI DI SAN GREGORIO (Campania)
IOSKO GRAVNER (Friuli Venezia Giulia)
PLANETA (Sicily)
TENUTA SAN GUIDO (Tuscany)
VIE DI ROMANS (Friuli Venezia Giulia)

16
BELLAVISTA (Lombardy)
CASTELLO BANFI (Tuscany)
GIACOMO CONTERNO (Piedmont)
FERRARI (Trentino)
LIVIO FELLUGA (Friuli Venezia Giulia)

15
ROMANO DAL FORNO (Veneto)
TENUTA FONTODI (Tuscany)
ISOLE E OLENA (Tuscany)
CASCINA LA BARBATELLA (Piedmont)
GIANNI MASCIARELLI (Abruzzo)
TENIMENTI RUFFINO (Tuscany)
PAOLO SCAVINO (Piedmont)
SCHIOPETTO (Friuli Venezia Giulia)

14
CANTINA PRODUTTORI TERMENO (Alto Adige)
MATTEO CORREGGIA (Piedmont)
MIANI (Friuli Venezia Giulia)
TENUTA DELL'ORNELLAIA (Tuscany)
PIEROPAN (Veneto)
TASCA D'ALMERITA (Sicily)
ROBERTO VOERZIO (Piedmont)

13
ANTONIO ARGIOLAS (Sardinia)
CANTINA PRODUTTORI COLTERENZIO (Alto Adige)
CONTERNO FANTINO (Piedmont)
QUERCIABELLA (Tuscany)

12
ANSELMI (Veneto)
CAPRAI VAL DI MAGGIO (Umbria)
ALDO CONTERNO (Piedmont)
BRUNO GIACOSA (Piedmont)
LE VIGNE DI ZAMÒ (Friuli Venezia Giulia)
MACULAN (Veneto)
NINO NEGRI (Lombardy)
BARONE RICASOLI (Tuscany)
RONCO DEL GELSO (Friuli Venezia Giulia)

11
BRICCO ROCCHE - BRICCO ASILI (Piedmont)
CANTINA PRODUTTORI SANTA MADDALENA/ CANTINA DI BOLZANO (Alto Adige)
CASTELLO DEL TERRICCIO (Tuscany)
MICHELE CHIARLO (Piedmont)
FORADORI (Trentino)
LA MASSA (Tuscany)
MONTEVETRANO (Campania)
PRUNOTTO (Piedmont)
PODERE ROCCHE DEI MANZONI (Piedmont)
TENUTA SAN LEONARDO (Trentino)
UBERTI (Lombardy)

10
CA' VIOLA (Piedmont)
CANTINA VITICOLTORI DI CALDARO (Alto Adige)
CASANOVA DI NERI (Tuscany)
CASTELLO DEI RAMPOLLA (Tuscany)
LES CRÊTES (Valle d'Aosta)
FALESCO (Lazio)
GIOACCHINO GAROFOLI (Marche)
TENUTA J. HOFSTÄTTER (Alto Adige)
LE MACCHIOLE (Tuscany)
MONTEVERTINE (Tuscany)
GIUSEPPE QUINTARELLI (Veneto)
LUCIANO SANDRONE (Piedmont)
SERAFINI & VIDOTTO (Veneto)
TUA RITA (Tuscany)
VENICA & VENICA (Friuli Venezia Giulia)
FATTORIA ZERBINA (Emilia Romagna)

A GUIDE TO VINTAGES 1971 - 2003

	BARBARESCO	BRUNELLO DI MONTALCINO	BAROLO	CHIANTI CLASSICO	NOBILE DI MONTEPULCIANO	AMARONE
1971	●●●●	●●●	●●●●●	●●●●●	●●●●	●●●●
1974	●●●●	●●	●●●●	●●●	●●●	●●●●
1975	●●	●●●●●	●●	●●●●	●●●●	●●●
1977	●●	●●●●	●●	●●●●	●●●●	●●●
1978	●●●●●	●●●●	●●●●●	●●●●●	●●●●●	●●●
1979	●●●●	●●●●	●●●●	●●●●	●●●●	●●●●
1980	●●●●	●●●●	●●●●	●●●●	●●	●●●
1981	●●●	●●●	●●●	●●●	●●●	●●●
1982	●●●●●	●●●●●	●●●●●	●●●●	●●●●	●
1983	●●●●	●●●●	●●●●	●●●●	●●●●	●●●●●
1985	●●●●●	●●●●●	●●●●●	●●●●●	●●●●●	●●●●
1986	●●●	●●●	●●●	●●●●	●●●●	●●●
1987	●●	●●	●●	●●	●●	●●
1988	●●●●●	●●●●●	●●●●●	●●●●●	●●●●●	●●●●●
1989	●●●●●	●●	●●●●●	●	●	●●
1990	●●●●●	●●●●●	●●●●●	●●●●●	●●●●●	●●●●●
1991	●●●	●●●	●●●	●●●	●●●	●●
1993	●●●	●●●●	●●●	●●●●	●●●●●	●●●●
1994	●●	●●●	●●	●●	●●	●●
1995	●●●●	●●●●●	●●●●	●●●●●	●●●●●	●●●●
1996	●●●●●	●●●	●●●●●	●●●	●●●	●●●
1997	●●●●	●●●●●	●●●●	●●●●●	●●●●●	●●●●●
1998	●●●●	●●●●	●●●●	●●●●	●●●	●●●
1999	●●●●●	●●●●●	●●●●●	●●●●●	●●●●●	●●●
2000	●●●●	●●●	●●●●	●●●	●●●	●●●●
2001	●●●●●	●●●●●	●●●●●	●●●●●	●●●●●	●●●
2002	●●	●	●	●	●	●●
2003	●●●	●●●	●●●	●●●	●●●	●●●

HOW TO USE THE GUIDE

KEY
- ○ WHITE WINES
- ● RED WINES
- ⊙ ROSÉ WINES

RATINGS

LISTING WITHOUT A GLASS SYMBOL:
A WELL-MADE WINE OF AVERAGE QUALITY IN ITS CATEGORY

🍷
ABOVE AVERAGE TO GOOD IN ITS CATEGORY, EQUIVALENT TO 70-79/100

🍷🍷
VERY GOOD TO EXCELLENT IN ITS CATEGORY, EQUIVALENT TO 80-89/100

🍷🍷
VERY GOOD TO EXCELLENT WINE SELECTED FOR FINAL TASTINGS

🍷🍷🍷
EXCELLENT WINE IN ITS CATEGORY, EQUIVALENT TO 90-99/100

(🍷, 🍷🍷, 🍷🍷🍷) WINES RATED IN PREVIOUS EDITIONS OF THE GUIDE ARE INDICATED BY WHITE GLASSES, PROVIDED THEY ARE STILL DRINKING AT THE LEVEL FOR WHICH THE ORIGINAL AWARD WAS MADE

STAR ★

INDICATES WINERIES THAT HAVE WON TEN THREE GLASS AWARDS FOR EACH STAR

PRICE RANGES [1] [2]

1 UP TO $4.20 AND UP TO £2.45
2 FROM $4.21 TO $6.00 AND FROM £2.46 TO £3.50
3 FROM $6.01 TO $9.00 AND FROM £3.51 TO £5.25
4 FROM $9.01 TO $15.60 AND FROM £5.26 TO £9.10
5 FROM $15.61 TO $24.00 AND FROM £9.11 TO £14.00
6 FROM $24.01 TO $36.00 AND FROM £14.01 TO £21.00
7 FROM $36.01 TO $48.00 AND FROM £21.01 TO £28.00
8 MORE THAN $48.01 AND MORE THAN £28.01

[1]Approx. retail prices in USA and UK [2] 1,00 = $1.20 = £0.70

ASTERISK *

INDICATES ESPECIALLY GOOD VALUE FOR MONEY

NOTE

PRICES INDICATED REFER TO RETAIL AVERAGES. INDICATIONS OF PRICE NEXT TO WINES ASSIGNED WHITE GLASSES (AWARDS MADE IN PREVIOUS EDITIONS) TAKE INTO ACCOUNT APPRECIATION OVER TIME WHERE APPROPRIATE

ABBREVIATIONS

A. A.	Alto Adige
C.	Colli
Cl.	Classico
C.S.	Cantina Sociale
Cant.	Cantina
CEV	Colli Etruschi Viterbesi
Cast.	Castello
COF	Colli Orientali del Friuli
Cons.	Consorzio
Coop.Agr.	Cooperativa Agricola
C. B.	Colli Bolognesi
C. P.	Colli Piacentini
Et.	Etichetta
M.	Metodo
M.to	Monferrato
OP	Oltrepò Pavese
P.R.	Peduncolo Rosso
P.	Prosecco
Rif. Agr.	Riforma Agraria
Ris.	Riserva
Sel.	Selezione
Sup.	Superiore
TdF	Terre di Franciacorta
V.	Vigna
Vign.	Vigneto
V. T.	Vendemmia Tardiva

VALLE D'AOSTA

Last year, we wrote that it was the end of an era for Valle d'Aosta – the era in which only Costantino Charrère was awarded Three Glasses – and the beginning of a new one. We looked forward to developments in eager anticipation and one year on, our hopes have become reality. Both Giorgio Anselmet and Marco Martin received the highest accolade, as well as Les Crêtes, of course. These two 40-year-old friends, who studied together and now represent the winemaking future of Valle d'Aosta, both decided when quite young to work on their family estates, despite the problems posed by Valle d'Aosta's complicated territory. Anselmet's Chardonnay repeated last year's success and joins Italy's winemaking elite, where it found the familiar face of Costantino Charrère, whose Chardonnay Cuvée Bois won Three Glasses for the eighth time in a row and earned him a star. Marco Martin astonished our panels with an extremely good Pinot Gris at an unbeatable price. At this point, we might be accused of favouring non-native grapes when we have pushed for years to promote native varieties. Apart from the fact that chardonnay and pinot grigio have been grown in Valle d'Aosta since time immemorial, we should also point out that we will soon be seeing great wines from the two most promising local varieties, fumin and petite arvine. The Valle d'Aosta winemaking situation is in excellent health with more and more youngsters returning to the vineyards to work the land. We are delighted to mention Maurizio Fiorano of Château Feuillet and Michel Vallet of Feudo di San Maurizio, in particular. Once again, there was no outstanding performance from a co-operative but there are several positive straws in the wind. La Crotta di Chambave gave us another excellent dried-grape wine and there have been marked improvements in the quality of the basic bottles. The Cave di Morgex has invested time and resources in its classic-method sparkling wines. After our tasting of the early results, we fully support the ambitions to raise quality expressed by winemaker Gianluca Telloli and chairman Mauro Jaccod. The huge Cave des Onze Communes produces 500,000 bottles annually and quality is rising. The general upward trend of quality in Valle d'Aosta wines ought to encourage producers to venture outside their cramped regional confines more often and penetrate the national market to avoid saturating the local one. At this point, we can confidently state that Valle d'Aosta's winemaking has come of age. It's time the rest of the country took notice.

AOSTA

INSTITUT AGRICOLE RÉGIONAL
RÉGION LA ROCHERE, 1A
11100 AOSTA
TEL. 0165215811
www.iaraosta.it

The wines of the Institut Agricole Régional are a cut above the average standard for Valle d'Aosta, and we were impressed by the clean style and clear personality of the huge range we tasted – there were more than a dozen different wines. Credit for this goes to the winemaker Luciano Rigazio and his staff, including the highly competent Provino Lale Demoz. The reds aged in wood are very good indeed while the Petite Arvine is one of the region's best and maintained last year's high standard. The whites, vinified exclusively in stainless steel, are very pleasant. The only two wrong notes are the Comète and the barrique-aged Chardonnay, which is rather overwhelmed by oak-derived aromas. Let's start our analysis with the Petite Arvine, which is remarkably rich in pulp and fresh minerally hints, and move on to the Pinot Gris and the basic Chardonnay, which are both excellent. We would also point out the debut tasting of the Metodo Classico Brut Monchoisi, which is crafted in a very rigorous traditional style with lively aromas of yeast and croissants ennobling the very enjoyable palate. High scores went to the native Fumin red and the international Syrah Trésor du Caveau, the grenache-based Rouge du Prieur, Vin du Prévôt, from cabernet franc and sauvignon, and the pinot noir-only Sang des Salasses. The fruit-forward Cornalin, also from a native local variety, is just a step behind.

● Rouge du Prieur '04	▼▼	5
● Sang des Salasses '04	▼▼	5
● Valle d'Aosta Fumin '04	▼▼	5
● Valle d'Aosta Syrah Trésor du Caveau '04	▼▼	5
● Vin du Prévôt '04	▼▼	5
○ Valle d'Aosta Chardonnay '05	▼▼	4*
○ Valle d'Aosta Petite Arvine '05	▼▼	4*
○ Valle d'Aosta Pinot Gris '05	▼▼	4*
○ Monchoisi Brut	▼▼	5
● Valle d'Aosta Cornalin '04	▼	5
● Valle d'Aosta Syrah Trésor du Caveau '03	▽▽	5
○ Valle d'Aosta Petite Arvine '04	▽▽	4

AYMAVILLES (AO)

L'ATOUEYO
LOC. URBAINS, 8
11010 AYMAVILLES (AO)
TEL. 0165902550
www.atoueyo.vievini.it

Omar Jerusel is a perfect example of the small Valle d'Aosta producer, who very rarely devotes all his time to making wine. Omar, in fact, has another day job but most of his spare time is dedicated to wine. He is helped by his whole family in the fields and in the cellar: his wife Raffaella, and parents Fernanda Saraillon and Guido Jerusel who founded the winery in 2000. This team seems to work beautifully and the wines produced by L'Atoueyo are improving with every year that goes by. Only 20,000 bottles are produced annually from the two hectares of vineyards, split up into countless tiny plots, with additional fruit purchased from selected, cellar-monitored growers. The Chardonnay is again very good. Aged in stainless steel vats and then in bottle, it proffers apple and pear fruit that mingles with floral hints on the nose. The palate is juicy and flavoursome as it unfolds with delicious lingering length. The Fumin 2004 is equally good, giving very heady aromas over its dark ruby red. The Torrette is subtle and stylish. Blackcurrants and blueberries on the nose usher in a full-bodied, warm palate with light, delicate tannins. The fresh and very approachable Gamay and the Pinot Nero are a little straightforward but none the less enjoyable for that.

● Valle d'Aosta Fumin '04	▼▼	5
○ Valle d'Aosta Chardonnay '05	▼▼	4*
● Valle d'Aosta Torrette '05	▼▼	4*
● Valle d'Aosta Gamay '05	▼	4
● Valle d'Aosta Pinot Nero '05	▼	4
● Valle d'Aosta Fumin '02	▽▽	5
○ Valle d'Aosta Chardonnay '03	▽▽	4
● Valle d'Aosta Fumin '03	▽▽	5
○ Valle d'Aosta Chardonnay '04	▽▽	4

AYMAVILLES (AO)

★ LES CRÊTES
LOC. VILLETOS, 50
11010 AYMAVILLES (AO)
TEL. 0165902274
www.lescretesvins.it

We have grown used to surprises from Costantino Charrère, Valle d'Aosta's best-known and most widely admired producer outside the region, but this year's profile reports a real step change at his wineries. From summer 2006, the traditional family winery that bears his name no longer exists and the wines produced there will now be managed exclusively by Les Crêtes. The administrative structure remains unchanged, with Costantino as the absolute head and his daughter Eleonora now in charge of running of the cellar. The huge range of wines embraces practically all the types produced in Valle d'Aosta but for reasons of space we will only be able to mention some of those we tasted. Let's begin with the multiple award-winning Chardonnay Cuvée Bois 2004, from an excellent vintage that enhances the ripe pineapple and grapefruit aromas on the nose and the tangy, juicy, palate with its quite sumptuous length. Charrère's tenth Three Glass prize lights up a star in Valle d'Aosta region. The Fumin is also extremely fine, giving appealing fruity sensations, hints of cherries and chocolate and the stylish, harmonious palate of a true champion. The Coteau La Tour, from 100 per cent syrah, has very stylish tannic texture and the basic Chardonnay is exemplary. Very few other Italian producers are able to offer such complex, exciting sensory perceptions at such a moderate price. From the Costantino Charrère line we particularly liked the Vin Les Fourches and Vin de La Sabla 2004. The rest of the range does full justice to the well-deserved fame of Les Crêtes wines.

○	Valle d'Aosta Chardonnay Cuvée Bois Cuvée Frissonnière Les Crêtes '04	🍷🍷🍷	6
●	Coteau La Tour '04	🍷🍷	5
●	Valle d'Aosta Fumin Vigne La Tour '04	🍷🍷	6
○	Les Abeilles '04	🍷🍷	6
●	Vin de La Sabla '04	🍷🍷	4*
●	Vin Les Fourches '04	🍷🍷	5
○	Valle d'Aosta Chardonnay Cuvée Frissonnière Les Crêtes '05	🍷🍷	4*
○	Valle d'Aosta Petite Arvine Vigne Champorette '05	🍷🍷	4*
○	Valle d'Aosta Pinot Gris Vigne Brulant '05	🍷🍷	4*
●	Valle d'Aosta Torrette Vigne Les Toules '05	🍷🍷	3*

CHAMBAVE (AO)

LA CROTTA DI VEGNERON
P.ZZA RONCAS, 2
11023 CHAMBAVE (AO)
TEL. 016646670
www.lacrotta.it

La Crotta di Vegneron is the moscato winery and the co-operative identifies totally with this grape, which has found an ideal habitat here at Chambave. The work of 130 grower members, who farm 33 hectares in total, is coordinated by the talented winemaker Andrea Costa and chairman Elio Cornaz. News from the co-operative this year includes the inauguration of a new sales outlet, which will make visits even more enjoyable for the countless wine tourists who visit Chambave. We were presented with a very wide range of wines, although one of the most important reds, Nus Crème, was missing from the roll-call. The high point was Chambave Muscat, which our panel finally awarded Two Glasses. The nose is as lively nose with lovely hints of orange peel and melon preceding a confidently juicy initial impact on the subtle, harmonious palate. The leading wine did not disappoint its many admirers. Moscato Passito breezed through to our final tastings and was nominated the best sweet wine in the region. Its impressive golden yellow ushers in typical candied fruit aromas on the nose and a buttery, sugar-rich palate rescued from cloying by nice background acidity. The winery's two most important reds, the Quatre Vignobles and the Fumin Esprit Follet, put on good performances. The rest of the nicely interpreted range, consisting of reds Nus Rouge, Gamay and Cornalin and the white Müller Thurgau, is well typed.

○	Valle d'Aosta Chambave Moscato Passito '04	🍷🍷	6
●	Valle d'Aosta Chambave Sup. Quatre Vignobles '04	🍷🍷	4*
●	Valle d'Aosta Fumin Esprit Follet '04	🍷🍷	5*
○	Valle d'Aosta Chambave Muscat '05	🍷🍷	4*
●	Valle d'Aosta Nus Rouge '05	🍷🍷	4*
●	Valle d'Aosta Cornalin '05	🍷	4
●	Valle d'Aosta Gamay '05	🍷	4
○	Valle d'Aosta Müller Thurgau '05	🍷	4
○	Valle d'Aosta Chambave Moscato Passito '02	YY	6
○	Valle d'Aosta Chambave Moscato Passito '03	YY	6

INTROD (AO)

LO TRIOLET
LOC. JUNOD, 7
11010 INTROD (AO)
TEL. 016595437
www.lotriolet.vievini.it

In Valle d'Aosta, the pinot grigio grape was traditionally called malvoisie. It was extremely common and widely planted, although the wines made from it were not particularly impressive. Thirteen years ago, Marco Martin, helped by his mother Emilia and father Renato, started making Pinot Grigio. It was instantly clear that he had bags of potential which would be rewarded, sooner or later, by major critical acclaim. Years later, the estate has expanded. Instead of just a few thousand square metres, the Martins now have two and half hectares of vineyards and buy in a small quantity of selected grapes, bringing annual production to a total of 30,000 bottles. This year, Marco gave us an unforgettable version of his unoaked Pinot Grigio, which has earned him his first Three Glass award. The wine is pale straw yellow with attractive greenish highlights that herald an explosion of aromas on the nose, from Alpine herbs to tropical fruit and summer flowers. The palate is lingering, enjoyable and stylishly tangy. This is a real champ, sold at an incredibly reasonable price. The barrique-aged Pinot Grigio performed well and also reached our final tastings. A few more months' ageing in the bottle might have brought our highest accolade within its grasp. The juicy, flavoursome Coteau Barrage displays its pleasing ingredients in a profile of excellent personality. We also liked the Nus very much, and the fresh, very pleasant Gamay. The Pinot Noir was well up to the standard of the other wines presented.

○	Valle d'Aosta Pinot Gris Lo Triolet '05	🍷🍷🍷	4*
○	Valle d'Aosta Pinot Gris Élevé en Fût de Chêne '05	🍷🍷	5
●	Valle d'Aosta Coteau Barrage '05	🍷🍷	5
●	Valle d'Aosta Gamay '05	🍷🍷	4*
●	Valle d'Aosta Nus Rouge '05	🍷🍷	4*
●	Valle d'Aosta Pinot Noir '05	🍷	4
○	Valle d'Aosta Pinot Gris Élevé en Fût de Chêne '03	YY	5
●	Valle d'Aosta Coteau Barrage '04	YY	5
○	Valle d'Aosta Pinot Gris Élevé en Fût de Chêne '04	YY	5

MORGEX (AO)

CAVE DU VIN BLANC DE MORGEX ET DE LA SALLE - FRAZ. LA RUINE
CHEMIN DES ILES, 19
11017 MORGEX (AO)
TEL. 0165800331
www.caveduvinblanc.com

Cave de Morgex continues to win praise for its two main Blanc de Morgex selections: both Rayon and the Vini Estremi version walked away with Two Glasses. But the duo in charge of the co-operative, winemaker Gianluca Telloli and chairman Mauro Jaccod, refuse to slacken the pace even with such good reviews and sales, and have raised their sights higher. Heavy investments were made in 2005 and 2006 to provide modern equipment in the cellar that will make it suitable for ageing the various classic-method wines. The aim for 2008 is to release a first spumante with five years on the yeasts, and follow it up with another aged for ten years. The two spumantes produced today, a Brut and an Extra Brut, seemed a little simple because they had only been aged for 14 months but the improvements on last year's performance lead us to believe that the co-operative is on the right track. In Morgex, the 2005 growing year was generally considered typical in terms of the quantity of rainfall and average temperature, and this is another reason why the Rayon is less flavoursome than the previous version. The nose shows vibrant fruity aromas with the pleasant minerality typical of the grape. This is more marked in the Blanc de Morgex Vini Estremi, in which only local yeasts were used. The Chaudelune, an ice wine harvested in early December, has very unusual aromas and the basic Blanc de Morgex is as sound as usual.

○	Valle d'Aosta Blanc de Morgex et de La Salle Rayon '05	🍷🍷	4*
○	Valle d'Aosta Blanc de Morgex et de La Salle Vini Estremi '05	🍷🍷	4*
○	Chaudelune Vin de Glace '04	🍷	5
○	Valle d'Aosta Blanc de Morgex et de La Salle M. Cl. Brut '04	🍷	4
○	Valle d'Aosta Blanc de Morgex et de La Salle M. Cl. Extra Brut '04	🍷	4
○	Valle d'Aosta Blanc de Morgex et de La Salle '05	🍷	3
○	Chaudelune Vin de Glace '03	YY	5
○	Valle d'Aosta Blanc de Morgex et de La Salle Rayon '04	YY	4

QUART (AO)

F.LLI GROSJEAN
VILLAGGIO OLLIGNAN, 1
11020 QUART (AO)
TEL. 0165775791
www.grosjean.vievini.it

The Grosjean brothers' winery is one of the pillars of Valle d'Aosta winemaking so we are delighted to learn that the problems caused by a fungus that blighted their wines with mouldy aromas are now definitively solved. The wines presented this year were all interesting. We were particularly impressed by the Petite Arvine, which missed our finals by a hair's breadth, and by the Pinot Gris. Working alongside Vincent in the winery are his brothers, Eraldo, Fernando, Marco and Piergiorgio, and their father, the winery's founder Dauphin. The winery is situated on the border between the municipal areas of Quart and Saint Christophe, and this is the location of the vineyards: Tzeriat, Rovetta, Creton, Tourena Quart, Tzantè de Bagnère, Merletta and Castello di Pleod. The winery produces 60,000 bottles a year from the seven hectares of vineyards farmed with a respectful eye on the environment: no insecticides or acaricides have been used since 1975. Moving on to the wines, the Petite Arvine has vibrant minerally and floral aromas with a remarkably flavoursome, pulpy palate. The Pinot Gris, in its first year of production, is quite pleasant with generous, concentrated fruit. The Torrette is ruby red in colour with redcurrants and strawberries on the nose and a pleasant, very lingering palate. Just a step lower are the Fumin, Gamay and Prëmetta. The last wine is made from the native grape of the same name, which is now vinified by very few producers in Valle d'Aosta.

○ Valle d'Aosta Petite Arvine V. Rovetta '05	▼▼	4*
○ Valle d'Aosta Pinot Gris V. Creton '05	▼▼	4*
● Valle d'Aosta Torrette '05	▼▼	4*
● Valle d'Aosta Fumin Barrique '04	▼	4
● Valle d'Aosta Gamay '05	▼	4
● Valle d'Aosta Prëmetta '05	▼	4
● Valle d'Aosta Fumin '03	▽▽	4
○ Valle d'Aosta Petite Arvine '04	▽	4

SAINT-PIERRE (AO)

BRÉGY & GILLIOZ
VIA VERGNOD, 7
11010 SAINT-PIERRE (AO)
TEL. 016595217
www.grain-noble.ch

The winery owned by Swiss producers Brégy and Gillioz has been included in the Guide for three years. Though their involvement in the wine business began as a hobby, and their main aim was make a wine that conformed to their own tastes, it has turned into a small – three hectares under vine – winery that produces a very interesting dried-grape wine at a competitive price. Charles-André Brégy is more closely involved in the cellar and vineyard management for he is also a professional winemaker working at the Swiss Federal Winegrowing Research Centre in Changins. The vineyards are very densely planted at 10,000 plants per hectare with a drop-irrigation system that is indispensable on beautiful south-facing land in an area with low average annual rainfall. The wine is fermented and aged for one year in French oak barriques at a controlled temperature. The decision to make just one wine, a dried-grape passito, came about because the owners are unable to supervise cellar work on a daily basis. The 2004 vintage of Podium is a wine with strong personality and quite a pleasant nose that discloses candied fruit and orange peel, with hints of vanilla and liquorice from the period ageing in small oak barrels. The warm, richly sweet impact on the palate also reveals savouriness and beautiful balance, never lapsing into cloying sensations.

○ Podium '04	▼▼	6
○ Podium '01	▽▽	6
○ Podium '02	▽▽	6
○ Podium '03	▽▽	6

SAINT-PIERRE (AO)

DI BARRÒ
LOC. CHÂTEAU FEUILLET, 8
11010 SAINT-PIERRE (AO)
TEL. 016595260
www.dibarro.vievini.it

The wines made by husband and wife team Andrea Barmaz and Elvira Rini continue to improve in quality. This winery does not have a particularly long history but every year it takes another step forward thanks to the enthusiasm of the two owners. Last year, the small but functional new winery was inaugurated, which has also made an important contribution to the improved results. This year, there was a new wine, Fumin, which has earned generous approval from the tasting panel since its debut. The number of bottles produced annually is still 15,000 since the surface area under vine is only just over two and a half hectares. The Torrette Vigne di Torrette 2004 is again very good indeed and, like last year, it is made from grapes that were slightly raisined in a small drying room. This production technique gives the wine its lively aromas of red berries and, particularly, violets preceding a luscious, alcohol-rich, mouthfilling palate with lots of power. The 2004 Fumin earned a very high score for its aromas of leather, plums and cherries on the nose and a strong, dynamic palate. The petit rouge-based Torrette Supérieur is back in the Guide having shown itself to be a stylish, distinctly pleasant wine with a long-lingering finish. Andrea Barmaz has delayed release of the Mayolet because it was not ready for the market. The rest of the range was interesting, especially the stainless steel-aged Chardonnay, the Petit Rouge, the basic Torrette and Lo Flapì.

●	Valle d'Aosta Fumin '04	▼▼	5
●	Valle d'Aosta Torrette Sup. Clos de Château Feuillet '04	▼▼	5
●	Valle d'Aosta Torrette Sup. V. de Torrette '04	▼▼	7
○	Lo Flapì '03	▼	7
○	Valle d'Aosta Chardonnay '05	▼	4
●	Valle d'Aosta Petit Rouge '05	▼	4
●	Valle d'Aosta Torrette '05	▼	4
●	Valle d'Aosta Torrette Sup. V. de Torrette '03	▽▽	7
○	Valle d'Aosta Chardonnay '04	▽▽	4*

VILLENEUVE (AO)

ANSELMET
FRAZ. LA CRÊTE, 194
11018 VILLENEUVE (AO)
TEL. 016595419
www.maisonanselmet.vievini.it

Having won our highest accolade in last year's Guide, Giorgio Anselmet and his father Renato are continuing to release excellent wines. One piece of news is their decision to build a new cellar since the current one is difficult to move around in, which hinders the working process. Some of the new vineyards are now productive so numbers are slowly growing each year and the cellar now produces 35,000 bottles a year from over five hectares of vineyards. Chardonnay aged in barriques is the real Anselmet workhorse but their style is gradually changing and with better-judged use of wood it is becoming even more pleasant. The nose reveals tropical fruit aromas like mango and pineapple, with light hints of bananas, butter and vanilla. The palate is very buttery and succulent, taking you through to a long-lingering finish. Congratulations to the Anselmet family on repeating last year's Three Glass triumph. Turning to the reds, we particularly liked the Le Prisonnier 2004. This petit rouge, cornalin, mayolet and fumin blend is possibly in its best version ever, having developed from an experimental wine produced in limited numbers to a solid product with over 1,500 bottles a year. The bouquet is enhanced by the raisined grapes and the distinct residual sugar on the palate makes it wonderfully lingering. Also excellent are the Syrah Henry, a DOC wine as of this year, the basic Chardonnay, the Torrette and the Pinot Noir. The L'Arline is a little below par compared to past versions while the Müller Thurgau and Petit Rouge are again well typed and accurately styled.

○	Valle d'Aosta Chardonnay Élevé en Fût de Chêne '05	▼▼▼	6
●	Le Prisonnier '04	▼▼	8
●	Valle d'Aosta Syrah Henry '04	▼▼	6
○	Valle d'Aosta Chardonnay '05	▼▼	4*
●	Valle d'Aosta Pinot Noir '05	▼▼	5*
●	Valle d'Aosta Torrette '05	▼▼	5*
○	Arline Flètrì '04	▼	6
○	Valle d'Aosta Müller Thurgau '05	▼	4
●	Valle d'Aosta Petit Rouge '05	▼	4
○	Valle d'Aosta Chardonnay Élevé en Fût de Chêne '04	▽▽▽	5
○	Valle d'Aosta Chardonnay Élevé en Fût de Chêne '03	▽▽	5

OTHER WINERIES

COOPERATIVA LA KIUVA
FRAZ. PIED DE VILLE, 42
11020 ARNAD (AO)
TEL. 0125966351

La Kiuva wines were a little below par this time, especially the Chardonnays. The late-harvested La Perla has disappointing aromas and the body is lightweight, although the Arnad-Montjovet is still interesting and pleasant. The stainless steel-aged Chardonnay is fresh with quite good body.

●	Valle d'Aosta Arnad-Montjovet Sup. '04	🍷🍷	4*
○	Valle d'Aosta Chardonnay '05	🍷	3
○	Valle d'Aosta La Perla '04		7

COOPÉRATIVE DE L'ENFER
VIA CORRADO GEX, 65
11011 ARVIER (AO)
TEL. 016599238
www.coenfer.it

Aosta's smallest co-operative opened at Arvier in 1978, six years after the creation of the DOC. The only red, from petit rouge, vien de nus, neyret and dolcetto with splashes of pinot noir and gamay, has red berries and Alpine flowers on the nose and a succulent palate with well-measured tannin.

●	Valle d'Aosta Enfer d'Arvier '05	🍷🍷	4*

CAVE DES ONZE COMMUNES
LOC. URBAINS, 14
11010 AYMAVILLES (AO)
TEL. 0165902912
www.caveonzecommunes.it

The Valley's largest winery, which releases 500,000 bottles a year, repeated last year's excellent performance. There were Two easy Glasses for the firm, tannic Fumin, the fruity and elegant Torrette Supérieur and the international-style Pinot Noir. Just behind is the very nice Petite Arvine.

●	Valle d'Aosta Fumin '04	🍷🍷	4*
●	Valle d'Aosta Pinot Noir '04	🍷🍷	4*
●	Valle d'Aosta Torrette Sup. '04	🍷🍷	4*
○	Valle d'Aosta Petite Arvine '05	🍷	4

CAVES COOPÉRATIVES DE DONNAS
VIA ROMA, 97
11020 DONNAS (AO)
TEL. 0125807096
www.donnasvini.com

The Donnas basin is one of the loveliest wine zones in Valle d'Aosta, thanks to the commitment of the co-operative's growers and chairman Mario Dalbard. This year, we liked the Donnas Supérieur Vieilles Vignes and the Napoleone selection. The basic Donnas is also very good.

●	Valle d'Aosta Donnas Napoleone '03	🍷🍷	4*
●	Valle d'Aosta Donnas Sup.V. V. '02	🍷🍷	5
●	Valle d'Aosta Donnas '03	🍷	4

Diego Curtaz
Fraz. Viseran, 61
11020 Gressan (AO)
tel. 0165251079
www.diegocurtazvini.it

Diego Curtaz has a beautiful winery with over one hectare under vine and produces a maximum of 10,000 bottles a year of two different wines. The Torrette 2005 is pleasant and fragrant, with hints of red berry fruit and sweet spices, while the Dï Meun blend is warm and spicy.

●	Valle d'Aosta Torrette '05	ŸŸ	4*
●	Dï Meun	Ÿ	4

Costantino Praz
Fraz. Turille, 17
11020 Jovencan (AO)
tel. 0165250358
www.vievini.it

Costantino grows native grapes – petit rouge, prëmetta, fumin and cornalin – as well as the international gamay and pinot noir varieties on one hectare of land. His Torrette gives warm red berries and measured tannin, while the good Pinot Noir has violets and roses. The Gamay is fresh and moreish.

●	Valle d'Aosta Pinot Noir '05	ŸŸ	4*
●	Valle d'Aosta Torrette '05	ŸŸ	5
●	Valle d'Aosta Gamay '05	Ÿ	4

Marziano Vevey
V.le del Convento
11017 Morgex (AO)
tel. 0165808931
www.vievini.it

Marziano Vevey inherited this lovely winery from his father Marcello in 1981. It has grown from 2,000 to 16,000 square metres and produces over 7,000 bottles per year. Marziano and his wife Judith presented their minerally, elegant Blanc de Morgex, which is the best in the whole DOC.

○	Valle d'Aosta Blanc de Morgex et de La Salle '05	ŸŸ	4*

Maison Albert Vevey
Fraz. Villair
S.da del Villair, 57
11017 Morgex (AO)
tel. 0165808930 - www.vievini.it

Brothers Mario and Mirko Vevey run this family winery founded in 1968, making 5,000 bottles per year of just one wine from their hectare under vine, a Blanc de Morgex made from native prié blanc grapes. The pleasant 2005 is minerally and floral on the nose with a juicy, tangy palate.

○	Valle d'Aosta Blanc de Morgex et de La Salle '05	ŸŸ	4*

Le Château Feuillet
Loc. Château Feuillet
11010 Saint-Pierre (AO)
tel. 0165903905
www.chateaufeuillet.vievini.it

Maurizio Fiorano's cellar makes its Guide debut now that he has decided to devote himself full-time to making wine. Maurizio releases 20,000 bottles a year from two and a half hectares of vineyards. We liked the Fumin best, with its enfolding aromas, but the Petite Arvine is also excellent.

●	Valle d'Aosta Fumin '04	ŸŸ	4*
○	Valle d'Aosta Petit Arvine '05	ŸŸ	4*
○	Valle d'Aosta Chardonnay '05	Ÿ	4
●	Valle d'Aosta Torrette '05	Ÿ	4

Feudo di San Maurizio
Fraz. Maillod, 44
11010 Sarre (AO)
tel. 0165257498
www.feudo.vievini.it

For his debut in the Guide, Michel Vallet gave us an impressive range of wines in both type and quality. We liked the Fumin, which almost made it to the finals, the unusual sweet Pierrots, from petit rouge and fumin raisined till December, the excellent Saro Djablo and the pleasant Grapillon.

●	Pierrots '03	ŸŸ	6
●	Saro Djablo '04	ŸŸ	4*
●	Valle d'Aosta Fumin '04	ŸŸ	4*
○	Grapillon '05	Ÿ	4

PIEDMONT

Old Piedmont has shaken off some of its years and pops up in this edition of the Guide in sparkling form, brimming with new ideas and points of interest. We think there is every reason to be optimistic. The region may still be suffering the tensions of an unpredictable market, a style strategy that has still to be fully defined and a general need to tighten up organization but producers have refused to be cowed by challenging vintages. They have continued to invest and experiment where it was sensible to do so and above all they have rethought the astonishing heritage of biodiversity and terroirs that Piedmont's wine country puts at their disposal. Today, many are reaping the rewards of their intelligent tenacity. The pages that follow tell this story truthfully, and as passionately as professional detachment will allow. Piedmont's 2007 haul of full profiles and Other Wineries entries comes to 364 cellars, the highest number ever. That's almost one for every day of the year in a region that strives to promote the daily consumption of wine. There are 53 Three Glass wineries, which is not a record partly because of the low profile assumed by one of the region's signature products, Barolo. The king of wines is not infallible, and in an indifferent growing year like 2002 even Barolo has to face up to reality. We'll forget about last year's 37 Three Glass Barolos and enjoy the splendid 16 from 1999, 2000 and 2001 that took our prize this time. If Barolo weeps, Barbaresco is certainly not smiling. Forecasts of a far from memorable 2003 were fulfilled in many of the wines we tasted and in fact only three bottles from the type and vintage managed to earn Three Glasses. The other five winners are from the fantastic 2001 growing year. Roero put on its best performance ever, some ten cellars picking up top awards for Nebbiolo, Barbera and sweet wines. Barbera d'Alba speaks for the left bank of the Tanaro, threatening to displace its twin from Asti, which is still excellent nonetheless. But this year, the super territories are to be found elsewhere around Tortona, where the amazing Timorasso variety won its first top award, and in northern Piedmont, where Carema, Lessona and especially Gattinara swept up five Three Glass scores. There are ten newcomers to the Three Glass club, an encouraging sign of vitality, three double award-winners in Gaja, La Spinetta and the surprising Produttori del Barbaresco, and Ca' Viola won its first Star. But we can also look back on the Three retrospective Glass prizes that retastings convinced us to award the second time round. There are six of them. Adding all this to Vino del Ventennale, the Barolo Gran Bussia 1989 from Aldo Conterno that is a fitting lifetime achievement, we come to a total of 60. And that used to be the top score in the Italian school-leaving examination, the "maturità". For Piedmont, it represents the springboard to a shining future.

AGLIANO TERME (AT)

DACAPO

S.DA ASTI MARE, 4
14041 AGLIANO TERME (AT)
TEL. 0141964921
www.dacapo.it

Paolo Dania and Dino Riccomagno's estate has no ambitions to turn out big numbers but it does steadfastly pursue quality. The five hectares under vine are scattered across the municipalities of Agliano and Castagnole Monferrato, where they yield the raw material for about 50,000 bottles a year. We were unable to sample one of the cellar's signature wines, Barbera Riserva del Fondatore, which is only released in outstanding vintages so we will begin with Barbera Sanbastiàn 2004, whose ruby red shades into purple. Very pronounced, persistent fruit unfolds on the nose, hinting at raspberry, plum jam, mulberries and sweet spices, then the soft, mouthfilling palate shows plenty of lively acid grip and assertive tannins. Barbera Vigna Dacapo 2003 is excellent and very well made. Its dark, concentrated hue heralds complex aromatics that range from black cherries and plums to blackcurrants, tobacco, spice and chocolate in a succession of sensations. Firm texture and ripe tannins take you through to a long, satisfying finish. Monferrato Rosso Tre 2003 is a blend of merlot, barbera and nebbiolo that is elegant and harmonious on the palate after a characterful nose has displayed all its depth. Appeal and drinkability are the calling cards of the Ruché 2005, its cherry to pale ruby colour accompanied by rose and wild strawberry aromas.

● Barbera d'Asti Sup. Nizza V. Dacapo '03	🍷🍷	5
● Monferrato Rosso Tre '03	🍷🍷	5
● Barbera d'Asti Sanbastiàn '04	🍷🍷	4*
● Ruché di Castagnole M.to Bric Majoli '05	🍷🍷	4*
● Barbera d'Asti Sup. Nizza V. Dacapo '01	🍷🍷 (outline)	5
● Barbera d'Asti Sup. Nizza V. Dacapo '00	🍷🍷 (outline)	5
● Barbera d'Asti Sup. Nizza La Riserva del Fondatore '01	🍷🍷 (outline)	5
● Barbera d'Asti Sanbastiàn '03	🍷🍷 (outline)	4

AGLIANO TERME (AT)

ROBERTO FERRARIS

FRAZ. DOGLIANO, 33
14041 AGLIANO TERME (AT)
TEL. 0141954234

Roberto Ferraris has been looking for ways to improve in vineyard and cellar for years as he continues to crank up the quality levels of his wines. His estate is a one-variety affair: Roberto is a convinced Barbera man. His nine hectares under vine all lie in the municipality of Agliano and yield the fruit that goes into two selections and a standard-label Barbera. It was no easy task to differentiate the two estate flagbearers from the 2004 growing year. Barbera La Cricca has dark, spicy and evolved aromas of coffee, earth, leather, pencil lead and cocoa powder, layered over plum and morello cherry fruit. The palate is powerful and austere, its tannic weave close-woven and ripe, as the vigorous, mouthfilling weight drives through to a savoury, lingering finish. Barbera Nobbio, sourced from 60-year-old vines, is just a shade more complete and rounded, reflecting the territorial typicity of its vineyard. Dark ruby in the glass, it reveals a fruit-rich nose that embraces mulberries and cherries, mingling these with florality and vegetal nuances of wild herbs. All the wine's character comes out in the exceptional texture and personality of the palate, substantial alcohol working with serious acidity and rich extract to find a splendid point of equilibrium. The standard-label Barbera 2004 gives intense red fruit, a vibrantly balanced weave and chewy, velvet-smooth texture.

● Barbera d'Asti Nobbio '04	🍷🍷	4*
● Barbera d'Asti '04	🍷🍷	3*
● Barbera d'Asti Sup. La Cricca '04	🍷🍷	5
● Barbera d'Asti Sup. La Cricca '00	🍷🍷 (outline)	5
● Barbera d'Asti Sup. La Cricca '01	🍷🍷 (outline)	5
● Barbera d'Asti Sup. La Cricca '03	🍷🍷 (outline)	5
● Barbera d'Asti '01	🍷🍷 (outline)	3
● Barbera d'Asti Sup. Nobbio '01	🍷🍷 (outline)	4
● Barbera d'Asti '03	🍷🍷 (outline)	3
● Barbera d'Asti Nobbio '03	🍷🍷 (outline)	4

AGLIANO TERME (AT)

Garetto

s.da Asti Mare, 30
14041 Agliano Terme (AT)
tel. 0141954068
www.garetto.it

The decision to delay release of the Favà 2003 selection, Alessandro Garetto's flagship Barbera, to enable it to mature for another year in the cellar, has paid off. The wine's exuberant personality has been reined in and today it is harmonious, sumptuous and free of the youthful rough edges that were still in evidence 12 months ago. Solemn and inky in colour, it opens intense on the nose with concentrated hints of tobacco, black cherry, plum jam and pencil lead. Impressive extract is adequately offset by balanced acidity and sustained acidity but the wine is still utterly convincing overall. The back palate echoes the nose impeccably with wonderfully long length. Barbera In Pectore 2004 releases blackcurrant, cherry and mulberry aromas. The follow-through is exemplary and the palate's vibrant drinkability holds up to the lingering, beautifully balanced finish. The dark hue of the Barbera Tra Neuit e Dì 2005 contrasts with the ripe immediacy and crisp definition of the fragrances in the spectrum of aromatics. This splendidly made wine is an object lesson in drinkability, overshadowed only by the stature of its stablemates. Both whites are good but we preferred the flowery Cortese to the tidy, straightforward Chardonnay. It is more opulent if less crisp on the nose, which has yet to absorb its oak.

●	Barbera d'Asti Sup. Favà '03	▼▼	5
●	Barbera d'Asti Sup. In Pectore '04	▼▼	4
●	Barbera d'Asti Tra Neuit e Dì '05	▼▼	3*
○	Cortese dell'Alto M.to Le Due Cioche '05	▼▼	3*
○	Piemonte Chardonnay Diversamente '05	▼	4
●	Barbera d'Asti Sup. Favà '01	▽▽	5
●	Barbera d'Asti Sup. Favà '02	▽▽	5
●	Barbera d'Asti Sup. Favà '00	▽▽	5
●	Barbera d'Asti Sup. In Pectore '03	▽▽	4
●	Barbera d'Asti Tra Neuit e Dì '04	▽▽	3

AGLIANO TERME (AT)

Agostino Pavia e Figli

fraz. Bologna, 33
14041 Agliano Terme (AT)
tel. 0141954125

Our tastings of the wines presented this year by brothers Mauro and Giuseppe Pavia confirm the encouraging comments made last time about this lovely Asti winery. Production, which hinges on Barbera, has now achieved excellent standards of quality. Barbera Bricco Blina, from 50-year-old vines and vinified exclusively in steel, is a lustrous, moderately intense ruby red. The nose unveils marked plum and black berry fruit before the soft, pervasive palate, perked up by smooth tannins and lifted by a satisfying finish, mirrors the aromas with textbook consistency. Marescialla 2003 is noteworthy for its characterful, upfront nose of ripe cherry, blueberry and golden leaf tobacco, as well as for the dynamism of its rich, close-woven palate, which magisterially matches mouthfilling alcohol with acidity and tannins in a lingering finish of long length. Moliss 2003 is intriguing complex, revealing fruity nuances that meld elegantly with florality. The finesse and harmony in the mouth of the Grignolino d'Asti 2005 are convincing. It discloses elegant geraniums, raspberries and spices followed by balance and grip that the assertive tannins nicely highlight.

●	Barbera d'Asti Sup. La Marescialla '03	▼▼	5
●	Barbera d'Asti Sup. Moliss '03	▼▼	4
●	Barbera d'Asti Bricco Blina '04	▼▼	4
●	Grignolino d'Asti '05	▼▼	3*
●	Barbera d'Asti La Marescialla '00	▽▽	5
●	Monferrato Rosso Talin '00	▽▽	5
●	Barbera d'Asti Bricco Blina '01	▽▽	4
●	Barbera d'Asti Bricco Blina '03	▽▽	4

AGLIÈ (TO)

CIECK
FRAZ. SAN GRATO
VIA BARDESONO
10011 AGLIÈ (TO)
TEL. 0124330522
www.cieck.it

Cieck has a wide range of labels featuring various wine types. The metodo classico sparklers, obtained exclusively from erbaluce, are always very good indeed. For this edition of the Guide, we picked out Brut Calliope 2001, made by maturing part of the base wine in small wood. Dense and rich on the nose, where oak-derived notes peek through from time to time, it has structure on the palate enhanced by delicate effervescence. San Giorgio Brut matures in steel and then spends almost three years on the lees. But the 2001 edition did not reveal the customary, and indeed legendary, complexity. It is a little static, focusing on nonetheless subtle, well-defined spring flowers. A tad slender on the palate, it failed to reach the Three Glass finals, unlike the Calliope. Erbaluce is also vinified in still versions. But this year the Misobolo 2005 had a slightly muzzy nose that held it back, for this is generally an exemplary interpretation of the variety. Acidity also completely overwhelms the wine's minerality, knocking the palate out of kilter. The dried-grape Passito Alladium 2001 has well-defined honey and candied peel but it failed to excite in the mouth, and the slightly cloying finish took it no further than One Glass. The same fate befell the Neretto 2004, which lacks the focus of previous editions, while the Cieck Rosso 2003, a barbera-led blend, stands out for rather unusual nose of forest floor and aromatic herbs.

○ Caluso Brut Calliope '01	▼▼	5
○ Caluso Brut S. Giorgio '01	▼▼	4*
● Canavese Rosso Cieck '03	▼▼	4
○ Caluso Passito Alladium Vign. Runc '01	▼	6
● Canavese Rosso Neretto di S. Giorgio '04	▼	4
○ Erbaluce di Caluso V. Misobolo '05	▼	3
○ Caluso Brut Calliope '00	▽▽	5
○ Caluso Brut S. Giorgio '00	▽▽	4
● Canavese Rosso Cieck '01	▽▽	5
● Canavese Rosso Neretto di S. Giorgio '03	▽▽	4

ALBA (CN)

BOROLI
LOC. MADONNA DI COMO, 34
12051 ALBA (CN)
TEL. 0173365477
www.boroli.it

This edition of the Guide may not perhaps be the best occasion to point out the enormous work done in just a few years by Achille Boroli and his staff, who first restructured the cellar at Madonna di Como and then built a vat cellar at Villero near Castiglione Falletto. But the winery has fulfilled its promise. The 2002 Barolos were missing so Boroli played two almost new cards: his Barolo Bussia 2001, a trump that only appears now and again, and the Barolo Villero Riserva 1998, released for the first time. Both flew to within an ace of Three Glasses. Bussia 2001 has a broadish nose with clear aniseed and sweet tobacco followed by impressive tannins and excellent length on the palate, which only lacks a hint of acidity to be worthy of top honours. The Riserva Villero 1998 has a fairly evolved garnet hue introducing dried roses and liquorice as well as a warm, lingering palate that is still a touch astringent. It's a fine Barolo that opts for elegance and finesse. As is always the case with Achille Boroli, the other labels kept the cellar's standard flying high. The most interesting performances came as ever from the fruit-forward, beefy Dolcetto Madonna di Como and the fresh, drinkable Moscato Aureum. But the other wines are all Two Glass products, many offering excellent value for money.

● Barolo Bussia '01	▼▼	8
● Barolo Villero Ris. '98	▼▼	8
● Barbera d'Alba Quattro Fratelli '04	▼▼	4*
● Nebbiolo d'Alba '04	▼▼	6
● Dolcetto d'Alba Madonna di Como '05	▼▼	4*
● Langhe Anna '05	▼▼	4*
○ Langhe Chardonnay Bel Amì '05	▼▼	4
○ Moscato d'Asti Aureum '05	▼▼	4
● Barolo Villero '00	▽▽▽	8
● Barolo Villero '01	▽▽▽	8
● Barolo '01	▽▽	6
● Barolo Villero '99	▽▽	8

ALBA (CN)

Ceretto

Loc. San Cassiano, 34
12051 Alba (CN)
tel. 0173282582
www.ceretto.com

Barolo Zonchera and Barbaresco Asij were missing, a consequence of the challenging 2002 growing year, so the 2004 Langhe Bianco Arbarei was the most interesting bottle in the Ceretto family line-up this time. It is obtained from riesling grown in the upper Langhe, more specifically in the municipality of Albaretto Torre. Brothers Bruno and Marcello Ceretto were the first to believe in the potential of the soil in this part of the Langhe at considerably more than 500 metres above sea level. The Arbarei vineyard is the source of this splendid white with its deep yellow hue and benzene aromas that fuse with attractive fruit, showing taut and minerally yet elegant on the palate. Also well up the quality scale is the Langhe Rosso Monsordo, from cabernet sauvignon, merlot and nebbiolo. Even in a warm growing year like 2003, it managed to display nice finesse and attractive freshness. Thanks to the three great red grapes that go into the blend, the nose unveils spicy sensations that provide suitable contrast to its marked bell pepper and pepper. Breadth and harmony in the mouth are brought together on the back palate by robust alcohol. The Nebbiolo d'Alba Bernardina 2004 is a fine, pale ruby wine with the variety's trademark fragrance of roses. Elegance rather than power is the strong suit of the palate. The Barbera d'Alba has appreciable acidity on the back palate while the straightforward Dolcetto Rossana is nonetheless very pleasing. This leaves us with the Blangé, a white from the arneis grapes that have brought the Ceretto family such market visibility and success. It is very well made but offers nothing more than uncomplicated drinking pleasure.

○	Langhe Bianco Arbarei '04	🍷🍷	5
●	Langhe Rosso Monsordo '03	🍷🍷	6
●	Nebbiolo d'Alba Bernardina '04	🍷🍷	5
●	Barbera d'Alba Piana '05	🍷	5
●	Dolcetto d'Alba Rossana '05	🍷	4
○	Langhe Arneis Blangé '05	🍷	5
○	Langhe Arbarei '03	YY	5
●	Langhe Rosso Monsordo '00	YY	6
●	Barbaresco Asij '01	YY	7
●	Barolo Zonchera '01	YY	7
●	Langhe Rosso Monsordo '01	YY	6
●	Langhe Nebbiolo Lantasco '02	YY	6

ALBA (CN)

Poderi Colla

Loc. San Rocco Seno d'Elvio, 82
12051 Alba (CN)
tel. 0173290148
www.podericolla.it

The experience Beppe and Tino Colla can point to has few equals in the Langhe. Beppe was trained in no less a school than that of Alfredo Prunotto, at a time when you could count the number of Barolo and Barbaresco labels on your fingers. For more than two decades, they were trained at that much-decorated Alba cellar, today owned by the Antinori group, before Poderi Colla came into being. Today, they have almost 30 hectares under vine in three distinct plots at Cascine Drago, at San Rocco Seno d'Elvio, the Roncaglie vineyards at Barbaresco and the Dardi Le Rose estate at Bussia near Monforte d'Alba. Managing this little empire has never proved a problem for the Colla brothers, with the help of Beppe's daughter Federica. Poor weather in 2002 meant that the Barolo Bussia Dardi Le Rose did not go into bottle but the Barbaresco Roncaglie 2003 performed well. It sidestepped the problems of that dry, torrid vintage, conserving nice freshness on nose and palate and earning Two Glasses. The real surprise, however, is the Langhe Bricco del Drago, a trailblazing 85-15 blend of two native grapes –dolcetto and nebbiolo – created in the late 1960s by Luciano De Giacomi, which went through to the finals to vie for Three Glasses. It missed out by a whisper but the 2003 edition is without doubt one of the finest ever produced. It combines a very elegant fruit-led nose with a palate of sophisticated, close-woven tannins. In fact, it's a gem. Rounding off the range are a hefty Barbera Costa Bruna, a fruit-forward Dolcetto Pian Balbo and a refreshing Sanrocco, from a blend of pinot nero, chardonnay and riesling. Finally, we thought the Barolo Bussia Dardi Le Rose 1999 was superb and awarded it Three retrospective Glasses.

●	Langhe Rosso Bricco del Drago '03	🍷🍷	5
●	Barbaresco Roncaglie '03	🍷🍷	7
●	Barbera d'Alba Costa Bruna '04	🍷🍷	4*
●	Dolcetto d'Alba Pian Balbo '05	🍷🍷	4*
○	Langhe Bianco Sanrocco '05	🍷🍷	4*
●	Nebbiolo d'Alba '04	🍷	4
●	Barolo Bussia Dardi Le Rose '99	YYY	7
●	Barolo Bussia Dardi Le Rose '00	YY	7
●	Barolo Bussia Dardi Le Rose '01	YY	7
●	Barbaresco Roncaglie '00	YY	7
●	Barbaresco Roncaglie '01	YY	7
●	Langhe Bricco del Drago '01	YY	5
●	Barolo Bussia Dardi Le Rose '98	YY	7

ALBA (CN)

GIANLUIGI LANO

FRAZ. SAN ROCCO SENO D'ELVIO
S.DA BASSO, 38
12051 ALBA (CN)
TEL. 0173286958

Quite a few vintages have passed since their first bottlings in 1993 but the enthusiasm displayed by Gianluigi Lano and his wife Daniela has if anything increased. The quality of their generous, authentically territorial wines has also improved. All that is missing from the line-up is that final peak of excellence but if the Lanos continue as they are, it is sure to come soon. Their Barbaresco 2003 has depth and vitality on the nose, where complex fragrances of wild berries meld with earthier notes and hints of Mediterranean scrubland. These shade into balsamic eucalyptus and sweet spice, introducing a palate with decent tautness and a finish to match the nose. The standard Barbera 2004 gives morello cherry and plum followed by a supple, upfront palate of rich fruit and balanced drinkability. The two flagship Barberas, both from 2004, performed well. Fondo Prà spent a year in barrique, emerging with breadth on a nose that offers everything from prunes to wild berries, and a concentrated palate that progresses to a well-balanced finale. Barbera d'Alba Altavilla 2004 is very varietal. Intense morello cherry and blackcurrant fruit are nicely echoed on the warm palate, where serious structure takes you through to a finish that reprises the aromatics of the nose. The appealing Freisa Vivace is very moreish and from the Dolcettos, we note the Ronchella 2004 with its black fruit aromas, good concentration and decent breadth while the standard 2005 was designed to be an approachable easy drinker.

●	Barbera d'Alba Fondo Prà '04	🍷🍷	4*
●	Barbaresco '03	🍷🍷	6
●	Barbera d'Alba '04	🍷🍷	3*
●	Barbera d'Alba Altavilla '04	🍷🍷	4
●	Dolcetto d'Alba Ronchella '04	🍷🍷	4
●	Dolcetto d'Alba '05	🍷	3
○	Langhe Favorita '05	🍷	3
●	Langhe Freisa Vivace '05	🍷	3
●	Barbaresco '00	☖☖	6
●	Barbaresco '01	☖☖	6
●	Barbera d'Alba Fondo Prà '01	☖☖	5
●	Barbera d'Alba Fondo Prà '03	☖☖	5
●	Barbaresco '99	☖☖	6

ALBA (CN)

PIO CESARE

VIA CESARE BALBO, 6
12051 ALBA (CN)
TEL. 0173440386
www.piocesare.it

A visit to the Pio Cesare cellars, bounded in part by Roman walls, is a thrilling trip into the wine heritage and the long history of Alba. Pio Cesare continues to vinify in the traditional manner but without excluding the present altogether, and its wines are milestones in the oenology of Alba. Sadly, two famous labels were missing from this year's line-up, Barolo Ornato and Barbaresco Il Bricco, victims of the unmemorable 2002 vintage. Barbera Fides, a happy marriage of modernity and territory, offers sensory emotions that only the greatest bottles can convey. Its elegant spectrum of aromatics ranges from fruity blueberry, plum and blackberry jam to tempting spice that fuse together against a backdrop of pencil lead and tobacco, over satisfying deep balsam. There is body and depth in the mouth, where warm alcohol is offset by serious structure, superbly handled tannins and refreshing acidity. The lingering finish reprises the nose in exemplary fashion. The Barolo 2002 may not have the authority of the greatest vintages but it is nicely managed, well-orchestrated and balanced. The Barbaresco is less convincing, showing complexity on the nose but lacking a vital spark. PiodiLei, a Chardonnay that is admirably suited for the cellar, is as magnificent as ever. Finally, the sophisticated bouquet and attractive drinkability of the Nebbiolo 2003 make it a paragon of appeal.

●	Barolo '02	🍷🍷	8
●	Barbera d'Alba Fides '04	🍷🍷	6
●	Barbaresco '02	🍷🍷	8
●	Nebbiolo d'Alba '03	🍷🍷	4
●	Barbera d'Alba '04	🍷🍷	6
○	Langhe Chardonnay PiodiLei '04	🍷🍷	6
●	Langhe Rosso Il Nebbio '05	🍷🍷	4
○	Piemonte Chardonnay L'Altro '05	🍷🍷	4
●	Dolcetto d'Alba '05	🍷	4
●	Barolo Ornato '85	☖☖☖	8
●	Barolo Ornato '89	☖☖☖	8
●	Barbaresco Il Bricco '97	☖☖☖	8
●	Barolo Ornato '01	☖☖	8

ALBA (CN)

★ PRUNOTTO
REG. SAN CASSIANO, 4G
12051 ALBA (CN)
TEL. 0173280017
www.prunotto.it

The long-established Alba-based Prunotto winery was acquired in the mid-1990s by Antinori from Tuscany, one of Italy's most prestigious wine groups. With the new owners came a new philosophy. Production, previously based largely on fruit bought in from reliable growers, is now obtained almost entirely from estate-owned grapes grown on plots purchased in the Langhe and the Asti area. And Asti is the source of some of this season's most interesting wines, Barbera Costamiòle, from Agliano, and Monferrato Mompertone from Caliano. Barbera Costiamòle, back on our list with the 2001 vintage after a brief absence, is absolutely wonderful. It is made along the lines of most Barberas from the past decade, which have been softer and more complex than in the past thanks to barrique ageing. Costimòle has also benefited from leisurely maturing in bottle, which has smoothed away the rough edges characteristic of the variety. Intense ruby red introduces pencil lead, morello cherry and tobacco before the harmonious, velvet-smooth palate with a balsamic hint in the finish. Barbera and syrah are the varieties that go into the 60-40 blend of Mompertone 2004. Syrah is to the fore on the nose and then the barbera comes through in the mouth in the back palate's acidity. Although both the Barolo Bussia and Barbaresco Bric Turot were missing after the mediocre 2002 growing year, the other Alba wines were well up to the standards of Prunotto's historic vineyards. Dolcetto Mosesco is youthfully alcoholic and fruit-forward, Barbera Pian Romualdo is well rounded and Nebbiolo Occhetti is austere. Finally, the 2001 Barbaresco is well managed and the standard-label wines are attractive and uncomplicated.

●	Barbera d'Asti Costamiòle '01	▼▼	7
●	Barbaresco '01	▼▼	7
●	Barbera d'Alba Pian Romualdo '03	▼▼	6
●	Nebbiolo d'Alba Occhetti '03	▼▼	5
●	Monferrato Mompertone '04	▼▼	4*
●	Dolcetto d'Alba Mosesco '05	▼▼	4*
●	Barbera d'Asti Fiulòt '05	▼	4
●	Dolcetto d'Alba '05	▼	4
●	Barolo Bussia '01	▽▽▽	8
●	Barbera d'Asti Costamiòle '96	▽▽▽	6
●	Barolo Bussia '96	▽▽▽	8
●	Barbera d'Asti Costamiòle '97	▽▽▽	6
●	Barolo Bussia '98	▽▽▽	8
●	Barbera d'Asti Costamiòle '99	▽▽▽	6
●	Barolo Bussia '99	▽▽▽	8

ALBA (CN)

MAURO SEBASTE
FRAZ. GALLO
VIA GARIBALDI, 222BIS
12051 ALBA (CN)
TEL. 0173262148
www.maurosebaste.it

Mauro Sebaste's range this time was bereft of nebbiolo-based products from the 2002 growing year, a season that saw heavy rain first and then hailstorms. But the surviving labels show fine quality and an ever more recognizable winery personality. Centobricchi Rosso 2004 fermented in steel tanks and aged in barrique for 18 months, emerging purplish ruby red with a complex nose of coffee, vanilla and elegant florality. Soft on the palate, it has balance, polished tannins, cleanness and good length on the back palate. Nebbiolo d'Alba Parigi 2004 is almost garnet in the glass. It tempts the nose with a swath of aromatics that opens on balsamic notes to shade into fruit and the minerally nuances. The extract is rich but not over-assertive thanks to substantial supporting acidity that keeps the exuberant tannins in their place. We were less convinced by the Barbera d'Alba Santa Rosalia 2005, which has little to say on the nose and offers predictable progression in the mouth. The Dolcetto d'Alba Santa Rosalia 2005 is very reluctant to open, at least at first, but after aerating in the glass for a good long while, it expresses all the variety's characteristics precisely and very attractively. The Arneis, with its ripe tropical fruit, peach and acacia blossom, is well up to snuff and the sauvignon-based Centobricchi Bianco has good depth. The palate has plenty of energy and the broad, smoke-tinged spectrum of aromatics offers dried fruit, somewhat dominated by over-assertive oak.

●	Langhe Rosso Centobricchi '04	▼▼	5
●	Nebbiolo d'Alba Parigi '04	▼▼	5
●	Barbera d'Alba S. Rosalia '05	▼	4
●	Dolcetto d'Alba S. Rosalia '05	▼	4
○	Langhe Bianco Centobricchi '05	▼	4
○	Roero Arneis '05	▼	4
●	Barolo Brunate '01	▽▽	7
●	Barolo Brunate '00	▽▽	7
●	Barolo Monvigliero '00	▽▽	7
●	Barolo Monvigliero '01	▽▽	7
●	Barolo Prapò '01	▽▽	7
●	Barolo Prapò '99	▽▽	7

ALFIANO NATTA (AL)

TENUTA CASTELLO DI RAZZANO
FRAZ. CASARELLO
LOC. RAZZANO, 2
15021 ALFIANO NATTA (AL)
TEL. 0141922124 - 0141922426
www.castellodirazzano.it

As we mentioned in the last Guide, major restoration work on the castle has been completed and the country hotel is fully operational, thanks in no small measure to Rita Olearo. The structure includes the ancient cellars, which are now used for maturing wines. Here, Augusto Olearo and his children beaver away to produce bottles that are ever more intriguing and representative of their territory. We had confirmation of this approach when we tasted the wines that the Olearos put forward for this year's Guide. Barbera Superiore Valentino Caligaris 2004, fermented and matured in wood, is again the standard-bearer: 3,600 bottles were released. Barbera Superiore Eugenea 2003 also made a welcome comeback to our pages. Only 2,000 bottles were produced of this steel-fermented, barrique-aged wine. The 15,000 bottles of Barbera Superiore Vigna del Beneficio show intense ruby red, with fruit-forward aromas that hint only slightly at their time in oak. The last of the Barberas we uncorked, Superiore Campasso, is a very attractive, nicely balanced wine at every stage of tasting. Nor should its value for money be overlooked. To round off, we would point out two very pleasing wines, the fragrant Grignolino Pianaccio and the equally aroma-rich Chardonnay Costa al Sole.

●	Barbera d'Asti Sup. V. Valentino Caligaris '04	🍷🍷	5
●	Barbera d'Asti Sup. Eugenea '03	🍷🍷	4
●	Barbera d'Asti Sup. Campasso '04	🍷🍷	3*
●	Barbera d'Asti Sup. V. del Beneficio '04	🍷🍷	4
●	Grignolino del M.to Casalese Pianaccio '05	🍷	3
○	Monferrato Bianco Costa al Sole '05	🍷	3
●	Barbera d'Asti Sup. V. del Beneficio '03	🍸🍸	4
●	Barbera d'Asti Sup. V. del Beneficio '01	🍸🍸	4

ALICE BEL COLLE (AL)

CA' BIANCA
REG. SPAGNA, 58
15010 ALICE BEL COLLE (AL)
TEL. 0144745420
www.giv.it

Alice Bel Colle is a small municipality in the heart of upper Monferrato in the province of Alessandria. The area is spectacularly beautiful and vines have always been grown here. Barbera is the main grape type and most of the hillside vineyards around the village are planted to the variety. But there are also plenty of rows of moscato, the area's other great resource. Ca' Bianca, which was taken over by Gruppo Italiano Vini a few years ago, is right in the midst of the hills, where it has 42 hectares under vine. The main estate provides three Barberas and a Moscato d'Asti while two subsidiary plots enable vinification of Gavi from Novi Ligure and Barolo at La Morra. We tasted five wines, of which the most persuasive in terms of structure and fruit was the Barbera Chersì selection (the name means "grown" in Piedmontese), made with the best grapes from the Polsino farm. Barrique ageing has given this Barbera the opportunity to develop marvellous softness while retaining the nice vein of acidity typical of the variety. The nose gives ripe red fruit, interwoven with spice and attractive vanilla sensations. Fruit aromas and a chewy palate are the keynotes of the Antè selection while Teis is a very fine standard-label wine. The attractive line-up of this long-established winery is rounded off by a fresh-tasting Gavi and a Nebbiolo with a fruity nose and restrained tannins.

●	Barbera d'Asti Sup. Chersì '04	🍷🍷	5
●	Barbera d'Asti Antè '04	🍷🍷	4*
●	Barbera d'Asti Teis '05	🍷	4
○	Gavi '05	🍷	4
●	Langhe Nebbiolo Guardastelle '05	🍷	4
●	Barbera d'Asti Sup. Chersì '03	🍸🍸	5
●	Barolo '01	🍸🍸	6
●	Barbera d'Asti Antè '03	🍸🍸	4

ASTI

F.lli Rovero
Loc. Valdonata
Fraz. San Marzanotto, 218
14100 Asti
tel. 0141592460
www.rovero.it

The Rovero family comprises brothers Claudio, Franco and Michele, with Michele's son Enrico. Together they run a mixed-crop farm that grows fruit and vegetables, as well as cultivating grapes and distilling some very successful grappas. There is also a comfortable agriturismo on hand to offer Monferrato cooking and typical local products. The estate's 25 hectares – 20 planted to vine – are farmed organically and the grapes grown are the traditional ones, with occasional excursions into international territory. The range on offer is wide and includes young whites, mature whites, fruity reds and more complex versions. Having put the rainy 2002 growing year behind them, the Roveros had to face a 2003 that was hot and dry. Barbera Superiore Gustin is upfront and fruity while Monferrato Rocca Schiavino, from cabernet franc and sauvignon, is rich and warm. The pinot nero Lajetto is a nice version of the wine type, its pale ruby proffering exciting fruity sensations. The steel-fermented Sauvignon Villa Drago is attractively varietal while the barrique-aged Sauvignon Villa Guani is more concentrated and sweeter. The Grignolino is spicy and well typed.

●	Barbera d'Asti Sup. Vign. Gustin '03	🍷🍷	4*
●	Monferrato Rosso Rocca Schiavino '03	🍷🍷	4*
●	Monferrato Rosso Lajetto '04	🍷🍷	4*
●	Grignolino d'Asti Vign. La Casalina '05	🍷	3
○	Monferrato Bianco Villa Drago '05	🍷	3
○	Monferrato Bianco Villa Guani '05	🍷	4
●	Barbera d'Asti Sup. Rouvè '00	YY	5
●	Barbera d'Asti Sup. Rouvè '01	YY	5
●	Barbera d'Asti Sup. Rouvè '02	YY	5

BARBARESCO (CN)

Produttori del Barbaresco
via Torino, 54
12050 Barbaresco (CN)
tel. 0173635139
www.produttoridelbarbaresco.com

This is a cellar from wonderland. Produttori del Barbaresco is one of the few co-operatives that can compete on quality with its more famous peers from Alto Adige. The work that oenologist Gianni Testa and manager Aldo Vasca have been doing for many years is bearing fruit. Only nebbiolo from the Barberesco area is vinified in the cellar and all the wines are excellent, from the straightforward Langhe Nebbiolo to the celebrated Barbaresco vineyard selections and the standard Barbaresco. This year, the reward was two Three Glass awards, despite the fact that only five 2001 selections were presented, release of the remaining four having been delayed. Spreading the 2001 wines over time will help enthusiasts to wait with a little more patience for the 2004 selections: none will be released for 2002 or 2003. Both the Pajé and the Rio Sordo are absolutely stunning. The Pajé is a veritable hymn of praise to Barbaresco nebbiolo. Intriguing complexity on the nose comes out in heady liquorice, raspberry and dried flowers. The palate has quite massive body and sweet tannins that convey the perception of enormous pervasiveness and persistence. Equally stunning is the Rio Sordo, even though it is more restrained in character. Less open on the nose, it demands patience before it unveils all its cinchona and rain-soaked earth fragrance, lifted by nuances of rhubarb and liquorice. Powerful and long in the mouth, it has more austere tannicity than its partner, suggesting it might be longer lived. Close behind is a splendid Pora, which has much of Rio Sordo's personality. Finally, the Asili, Rabajà and Langhe Nebbiolo all earned Two comfortable Glasses.

●	Barbaresco Vigneti in Pajé Ris. '01	🍷🍷🍷	6*
●	Barbaresco Vigneti in Rio Sordo Ris. '01	🍷🍷🍷	6*
●	Barbaresco Vigneti in Pora Ris. '01	🍷🍷	6
●	Barbaresco Vigneti in Asili Ris. '01	🍷🍷	6
●	Barbaresco Vigneti in Rabajà Ris. '01	🍷🍷	6
●	Langhe Nebbiolo '04	🍷🍷	4
●	Barbaresco '02	🍷	5
●	Barbaresco Vigneti in Montefico Ris. '99	YYY	6
●	Barbaresco Vigneti in Montestefano Ris. '99	YYY	6

BARBARESCO (CN)

La Ca' Növa
Strada Ovello, 4
12050 Barbaresco (CN)
tel. 0173635123

It was another excellent performance from the cellar run by brothers Pietro, Giulio and Franco Rocca, with their assistants Ivano and Marco. The wines are good and crafted in the best Langhe tradition, with long macerations and maturing in large Slavonian oak barrels. With the poor 2002 vintage behind them, the Roccas turn out about 45,000 bottles from 14 hectares under vine in fine locations. The 5,000 bottles of Barbaresco Montestefano 2003 are very good. Their colour is deep and intense, the aromas give roses, raspberries and plum, mingling with tobacco and cinnamon spice, and the powerful palate shows fine equilibrium, closing with remarkable length. The standard Barbaresco 2003 did well. Its ruby red has a garnet rim, the nose gives plenty of fruit and chocolate and tobacco spice, and the broad palate impresses with its persistence. Barbaresco Bric Mentina 2003 is warm and rich in hue. Ripe fruit and spice introduce a palate that is soft and round on entry, signing off with a clean finish. Barbera d'Alba Loreto 2004, of which 5,000 units went into bottle, is very well made. The ruby red, still flecked with purple, heralds a fruit and flower nose and a refreshingly drinkable palate with an appealingly frank finish. The 10,000 bottles of Dolcetto d'Alba also impressed our tasters. The purple hue is typical Dolcetto and the cherry and raspberry nose ushers in good acidity in the mouth, kept nicely in place by alcohol, and a very fresh, moreish finish.

● Barbaresco Montestefano '03	▼▼	6
● Barbaresco Bric Mentina '03	▼▼	6
● Barbera d'Alba Loreto '04	▼▼	4
● Dolcetto d'Alba '05	▼▼	3*
● Barbaresco '03	▼	5
● Barbaresco Bric Mentina '01	▽▽▽	6
● Barbaresco Montestefano '01	▽▽	6
● Barbaresco Bric Mentina '02	▽▽	6

BARBARESCO (CN)

Ca' Rome' - Romano Marengo
s.da Rabajà, 86/88
12050 Barbaresco (CN)
tel. 0173635126
www.carome.com

Romano Marengo, helped by his son Giuseppe for winemaking and daughter Paola for marketing, runs the Ca' Rome' estate and its seven hectares under vine distributed equally between Serralunga and Barbaresco. Winemaking is traditional in style, with manual pump-overs and punching-down. This time the two Barolo selections, Ceretta and Rapet, were missing because they skipped 2002. The barrique-matured Barbaresco Maria di Brun, 3,200 bottles of which were released, did well, from its intense, garnet-flecked colour to the wild berries, sweet tobacco and well-integrated oak on the nose and the nicely intense, very persistent palate. Barbaresco Sorì Rio Sordo 2003, another barrique-aged wine with 4,000 units available, is sourced from 35-year-old vines. Deep ruby red, it flaunts fruit laced with cocoa powder and liquorice on the nose and then a full, pervasive palate with a long finish and extremely elegant after-aromas. The Riserva wine is Barbaresco Sorì Rio Sordo 2001, aged in small wood with 3,100 bottles available. Its intense garnet red introduces liqueur cherries, spicy tobacco and cocoa powder lifted by nuances of topsoil. The elegance of the palate is underlined by firm, but not aggressive, tannins and good persistence in the finale. The 3,300 bottles of Barbera La Gamberaja 2004 are remarkably well made. The ruby red is tinged with purple and the nose of dark fruit is laced with spice. Assertive on the palate, it unleashes plenty of alcohol that pervades the lingering finish.

● Barbaresco Sorì Rio Sordo Ris. '01	▼▼	7
● Barbaresco Maria di Brun '03	▼▼	8
● Barbaresco Sorì Rio Sordo '03	▼▼	7
● Barbera d'Alba La Gamberaja '04	▼▼	5
● Barbaresco Sorì Rio Sordo Ris. '00	▽▽	7
● Barolo Rapet '01	▽▽	7
● Barolo V. Cerretta '01	▽▽	7
● Barbaresco Maria di Brun '98	▽▽	8

BARBARESCO (CN)

CANTINA DEL PINO
VIA OVELLO, 31
12050 BARBARESCO (CN)
TEL. 0173635147

Cantina del Pino is managed by Renato Vacca, who looks after both vine stock and cellar. He extracts a remarkably fine range of 30,000 bottles each year from his five hectares at Ovello in Barbaresco and two at Neive. The 3,000 bottles of Barbaresco Ovello 2002, aged in new and used barriques, are very good. Deep in colour with dark fruit and spice aromas, it has perfectly absorbed oak laced with menthol notes. A broad front palate offers pervasive, elegant tannins, very good length and a clean, persistent after-aroma. But this year the best performance came from the standard Barbaresco 2003, of which 10,000 units went into bottle, again after maturing in new and used barriques. Its intense garnet red precedes a still-fruity nose with spiciness that already hints at liquorice and chocolate. The palate impresses, showing body and superior extract, to close harmonious and whistle-clean. Despite the very hot growing year, Renato managed to keep his wonderchild fresh-tasting and extremely inviting. In fact, it was so good it earned Cantina del Pino Three Glasses. The 3,000 bottles of Barbera 2004 are also very good. Aged for a few months in new barriques, it is still bright in colour and fruity on the nose, where there is a faint hint of vanilla, and the fresh palate unveils very nice length. The 7,000 bottles of tank-fermented Dolcetto 2005 are still purplish in colour. It's a fresh, drinkable wine with good length. The 3,000 bottles of semi-sparkling Freisa 2005 are well made. In short, this is a top rank line-up with a starry stand-out wine.

● Barbaresco '03	▼▼▼	6*
● Barbaresco Ovello '02	▼▼	6
● Barbera d'Alba '04	▼▼	5
● Dolcetto d'Alba '05	▼▼	4*
● Langhe Freisa '05	▼	3
● Barbaresco Ovello '99	▽▽▽	6
● Barbaresco Ovello '01	▽▽	6
● Barbaresco Ovello '00	▽▽	6
● Barbaresco Ovello '97	▽▽	6
● Barbaresco Ovello '98	▽▽	6

BARBARESCO (CN)

CASCINA BRUCIATA
S.DA RIO SORDO, 46
12050 BARBARESCO (CN)
TEL. 0173638826

Cascina Bruciata stands atop one of Barbaresco's most important vineyards, Rio Sordo. Nestling among the rows is the home of the Balbo family, who have seven hectares under vine where they grow two local varieties, nebbiolo and dolcetto. It was only in 2001 that 50-something Carlo Balbo decided to bottle the wine he produces and to go for quality. For help in achieving his ambitious objectives, he turned to oenologist Guido Martinetti and agronomist Federico Curtaz. Carlo's wife Franca and their children Marco and Alessandro also lend a hand. The cellar turns out about 40,000 bottles, split across five labels, including the excellent Barbaresco Rio Sordo 2003, which went through to the finals. It aged for 24 months in barrique, emerging with violet, cinchona and tobacco aromas and a full-bodied, impressively structured palate with lovely balance. We liked the other Barbaresco selection, Vigneto Balbo 2003, which matured for 12 months in barrique and as much again in large wood. Austere and elegant on the nose, it has slightly more rugged tannins than the preceding wine. Other Two Glass winners were the attractively fruity Langhe Nebbiolo Usignolo 2004 and the Dolcetto d'Alba Vigneti in Rio Sordo, which is clean and stylish on the nose before showing fresh and fruity in the mouth. The Dolcetto d'Alba Rian 2005 is juicy and very drinkable.

● Barbaresco Rio Sordo '03	▼▼	6
● Barbaresco Vigneto Balbo '03	▼▼	6
● Langhe Nebbiolo Vigneti dell'Usignolo '04	▼▼	4*
● Dolcetto d'Alba Vigneti in Rio Sordo '05	▼▼	4*
● Dolcetto d'Alba Rian '05	▼	4
● Barbaresco Vigneto Balbo '02	▽▽	6
● Langhe Nebbiolo Vigneti dell'Usignolo '03	▽▽	4

BARBARESCO (CN)

TENUTE CISA ASINARI
DEI MARCHESI DI GRESY
C.DA MARTINENGA, 21
12050 BARBARESCO (CN)
TEL. 0173635221 - 0173635222
www.marchesidigresy.com

It was an in-between year for Alberto Cisa Asinari di Gresy and the staff that assist him on his 35 hectares under vine. For this edition of the Guide, there was little contribution from the vineyards of Martinenga, the beautiful wine-friendly amphitheatre that surrounds the cellar at Barbaresco. The only Barbaresco on show was the 2003 since no selections were released for 2002 and the cellar "made do" with its plots at Cassine, in Acqui Terme and Alessandria. And there were some lovely surprises. On their second release with the 2003 vintage, Barbera d'Asti Monte Colombo and Monferrato Merlot da Solo put on convincing performances. The Barbera combines broad, opulent plum and cherry with more complex notes of rain-soaked earth, followed by a warm, soft palate. Its merlot-based stablemate has a fresh vegetal note as well as fruit-like sensations and the palate has 2003's robust tannins. Also from Cassine is the Passito L'Altro Moscato in one of its finest versions ever, flaunting dried apricots and ginger in a superbly balanced whole. The dry, austere Barbaresco Martinenga 2003 shows the influence of its growing year. Barbera in the blend of the Virtus 2003 brings the freshness and fullness that nebbiolo could not offer that year. Moving on to the whites, we liked the character and finesse of the Sauvignon 2005 but the Chardonnay and the chardonnay and sauvignon Villa Giulia also impressed. The Dolcetto and Langhe Nebbiolo are undemanding and agreeable. Finally, we were awed by our retasting of Barbaresco Camp Gros 1997, which earned Three retrospective Glasses.

● Langhe Rosso Virtus '03	🍷🍷	6
● Barbaresco Martinenga '03	🍷🍷	7
● Barbera d'Asti Monte Colombo '03	🍷🍷	6
● Monferrato Rosso Merlot da Solo '03	🍷🍷	6
○ Piemonte Moscato Passito L'Altro Moscato '03	🍷🍷	5
○ Langhe Sauvignon '05	🍷🍷	4*
● Dolcetto d'Alba Monte Aribaldo '05	🍷	4
○ Langhe Bianco Villa Giulia '05	🍷	4
○ Langhe Chardonnay '05	🍷	4
● Langhe Nebbiolo Martinenga '05	🍷	4
● Barbaresco Camp Gros '97	🍸🍸🍸	8

BARBARESCO (CN)

GIUSEPPE CORTESE
S.DA RABAJÀ, 80
12050 BARBARESCO (CN)
TEL. 0173635131
www.cortesegiuseppe.it

At last, Giuseppe and Piercarlo Cortese's winery was able to give us a full set of wines to taste, after the omissions imposed by the difficult 2002 growing year. We'll begin with the admirable Barbaresco Rabajà 1999 Riserva, of which 6,000 bottles were obtained from the 55-year-old vines. Deep garnet red introduces ripe fruit, cinnamon, cocoa powder and leather aromas before the assertive but elegant tannins on the mouthfilling palate take you through to a remarkably lingering finish. The 17,000 bottles of Barbaresco Rabajà 2003 are equally good. Its deep ruby ushers in still fruity aromas with spices, chocolate and tobacco peeking through. On the palate, the sunny ripeness of the vintage is evident and the finish is long and clean. Barbera d'Alba Morassina 2003 is good. Mulberry and plums on the nose precede an impressive entry on the broad, pervasive palate with its good length. The Barbera d'Alba 2004 also stands out for its fruit – wild berries, in this case – and attractive acidity in the mouth. The Dolcetto d'Alba Trifolera 2005 has a purple colour and a youthfully alcoholic, very drinkable palate: it's a well-made wine. The straw-yellow Langhe Chardonnay proffers tropical fruit-like aromas and a fresh-tasting palate with decent length. And the Langhe Nebbiolo 2003 is excellent, giving fruit and flowers with a full, well-balanced palate.

● Barbaresco Rabajà Ris. '99	🍷🍷	8
● Barbaresco Rabajà '03	🍷🍷	6
● Barbera d'Alba Morassina '03	🍷🍷	5
● Langhe Nebbiolo '03	🍷🍷	5
● Barbera d'Alba '04	🍷🍷	4*
● Dolcetto d'Alba Trifolera '05	🍷🍷	4*
○ Langhe Chardonnay '05	🍷	4
● Barbaresco Rabajà Ris. '96	🍸🍸🍸	8
● Barbaresco Rabajà '00	🍸🍸	6
● Barbaresco Rabajà '01	🍸🍸	6
● Barbaresco Rabajà '97	🍸🍸	6
● Barbaresco Rabajà '98	🍸🍸	6
● Barbaresco Rabajà '99	🍸🍸	6

BARBARESCO (CN)

★ ★ ★ GAJA
VIA TORINO, 18
12050 BARBARESCO (CN)
TEL. 0173635158

In recent years, Angelo Gaja's profile has featured none of the cellar's whites, which range from the sauvignon-based Alteni di Brassica to Gaja & Rey. This is not an editorial omission nor is it a result of negative evaluations by our tasting panel. Sadly, Angelo Gaja decided not to release wines for the poor 2002 growing year and his whites also skipped the very hot 2003 vintage. We will have to be patient and await new releases in the certainty that they will be amazingly good and wonderfully long-lived. This year's line-up is one of the best in Italy, despite the absence of all the 2002s that should have been obtained from nebbiolo from the Barolo area. There is no Langhe Nebbiolo Conteisa, nor is there a Langhe Nebbiolo Sperss. Darmagi, made with cabernet fruit from Barbaresco, was also missing. But the Barbaresco 2003 put on its usual fine performance, showing subtle and elegant notwithstanding the very warm, difficult to handle, year. The intense ruby red introduces fruity aromas that give way to spicy sensations. Massive on the palate, it flaunts sweet tannins that lift the long finale. And the three nebbiolo-based selections from the estate's top vineyards, Sorì San Lorenzo, Costa Russi and Sorì Tildin, are all excellent. All three are stand-outs and obtained similar scores, even though we liked the San Lorenzo best for its complexity, and the sheer balance of all its components, along with the pervasive, superbly refined Costa Russi, a textbook Gaja wine. Sorì Tildin was only a hair's breadth behind.

● Langhe Nebbiolo Costa Russi '03	▼▼▼	8
● Langhe Nebbiolo Sorì S. Lorenzo '03	▼▼▼	8
● Barbaresco '03	▼▼	8
● Langhe Nebbiolo Sorì Tildin '03	▼▼	8
● Langhe Nebbiolo Sorì Tildin '00	▽▽▽	8
● Barbaresco '00	▽▽▽	8
● Barbaresco '01	▽▽▽	8
● Langhe Nebbiolo Conteisa '01	▽▽▽	8
● Langhe Nebbiolo Sorì Tildin '97	▽▽▽	8
● Langhe Nebbiolo Sorì Tildin '98	▽▽▽	8
● Langhe Nebbiolo Sorì S. Lorenzo '99	▽▽▽	8

BARBARESCO (CN)

CARLO GIACOSA
S.DA OVELLO, 9
12050 BARBARESCO (CN)
TEL. 0173635116

The reins of this winery are now firmly in the hands of Maria Grazia Giacosa, still with help from her father Carlo and mother Carla. The five estate-owned hectares, planted to nebbiolo, barbera and dolcetto, yield an average of 35,000 bottles a year of very competitively priced wines. This year, we tasted a very good range indeed, including three 2003 Barbarescos that are as good as any. The 5,000 bottles of Narin contain a ruby red wine with a faintly orange-tinged rim. Intense fruit aromas introduce good structure, vigorous tannins and grace notes of liquorice and tobacco. The 2,500 bottles of Carla proffer spice and balsam aromas. Elegance and balance emerge on the palate, flanked by sweet, silky tannins. Some 5,500 units of Montefico went into bottle. It's still closed, opening slowly in the glass to reveal red fruits, dried roses and chocolate before vigorous tannins come through on a palate that signs off with elegant notes of chocolate and coffee. Both Barberas scored very well. Mucin 2005 is an admirable, deep purplish, standard-label wine with fruit-led aromatics and a chewy palate whose tannins and acidity complement each other well before the lingering finish. Barbera Lina 2004 is even richer and more complex, its spiciness melding with red berry fruit and its acidity contributing freshness. Nebbiolo Maria Grazia 2005 is a very well-managed version of the variety, showing soft tannins and fruity aromas. Last up was the attractively drinkable Dolcetto Cuchet.

● Barbaresco Carla '03	▼▼	6*
● Barbaresco Montefico '03	▼▼	6*
● Barbaresco Narin '03	▼▼	6*
● Barbera d'Alba Lina '04	▼▼	4
● Barbera d'Alba Mucin '05	▼▼	4
● Langhe Nebbiolo Maria Grazia '05	▼▼	4
● Dolcetto d'Alba Cuchet '05	▼	4
● Barbaresco Narin '01	▽▽	6
● Barbaresco Montefico '00	▽▽	6
● Barbaresco Narin '00	▽▽	6
● Barbaresco Montefico '01	▽▽	6
● Barbaresco '02	▽▽	5
● Barbaresco Montefico '02	▽▽	5
● Barbera d'Alba Lina '03	▽▽	4

BARBARESCO (CN)

Cascina Luisin

S.da Rabajà, 34
12050 Barbaresco (CN)
tel. 0173635154

We admired a fine performance by the wines from Cascina Luisin, which excelled despite their less than brilliant vintages, such as the notorious 2002 growing year. Luigi Minuto and his son Roberto tend seven hectares in the best parts of Barbaresco, to which they have added a plot at Barolo, for a total output of about 30,000 bottles. From the controversial 2002 vintage, we preferred the Barbaresco Rabajà to the Barolo Leon. The balsamic Barbaresco has an elegant, complex nose while the palate is slightly let down by its not terribly broad palate whereas the Barolo impresses on the already quite evolved nose, giving way to greenish and rather rugged tannins on the palate. The Barbera d'Alba Asili 2004 did well. From an excellent vintage, it shows good balance of alcohol and acidity on the palate, which reprises the jam and dried flowers of the nose. The gutsy, tannic Barbaresco Sorì Paolin 2003 is a fine wine. Our special compliments go to the Dolcetto d'Alba Bric Trifüla 2005. Eight months in large wood enhance the flowers and red fruits on the nose, also lending fullness and appeal to the palate. The 3,000 bottles of Langhe Nebbiolo Maggiur 2004 flaunt intense, vibrant aromatics while the well-crafted tannins are deliberately less concentrated, making this a very approachable bottle that you can uncork now. Freshness and drinkability are also the keynotes of the Barbera d'Alba Maggiur 2005.

● Barbera d'Alba Asili '04	🍷🍷	6
● Barbaresco Rabajà '02	🍷🍷	7
● Barolo Leon '02	🍷🍷	8
● Barbaresco Sorì Paolin '03	🍷🍷	7
● Langhe Nebbiolo Maggiur '04	🍷🍷	4*
● Barbera d'Alba Maggiur '05	🍷🍷	4*
● Dolcetto d'Alba Bric Trifüla '05	🍷🍷	4*
● Barbera d'Alba Asili '00	♀♀♀	6
● Barbera d'Alba Asili Barrique '97	♀♀♀	6
● Barbera d'Alba Asili '99	♀♀♀	6
● Barolo Leon '01	♀♀	8
● Barbera d'Alba Asili '03	♀♀	6
● Barbaresco Rabajà '00	♀♀	7
● Barbaresco Sorì Paolin '01	♀♀	7

BARBARESCO (CN)

Moccagatta

S.da Rabajà, 46
12050 Barbaresco (CN)
tel. 0173635228 - 0173635152

The 2003 vintage sees the return of the three Barbaresco selections, leading a production of about 60,000 bottles of which brothers Franco and Sergio Minuto can justly be proud. In fact, Barbaresco Cole 2003 flew straight through to the finals. What a shame that only 2,200 bottles were released. Colour and aromatics are impeccable, spices and cloves heralding a broad, sweet palate with a satisfyingly long finish. Not far behind are the rich, pulpy Barbaresco Bric Balin 2003, whose austere tannins need more cellar time, and the Barbaresco Basarin 2003, from 40-year-old vines at Neive. Its 18 months in barrique have given it a more approachable personality and a robust tobacco and leather-themed palate. We thought two of the vintage's best products were the Dolcetto d'Alba 2005, for its well-defined red berry nose and attractively fresh, balanced palate, and the Barbera d'Alba 2005, a standard-label wine whose steel vinification enables the fruit to emerge in all its splendour on a palate that finds a nice balance of freshness and alcohol. Violets, morello cherry and youthful tannins are the characteristics of the Langhe Nebbiolo 2005 but the two Chardonnays deserve closer attention. Langhe Chardonnay 2005 has elegant citrus and a fresh, savoury palate but the Langhe Chardonnay Buschet 2004 was the stand-out. Yellow gold, it has just enough wood to lift the yellow peach and melon aromas before the tangy, minerally palate finds a lovely point of equilibrium between oak and robust alcohol.

● Barbaresco Cole '03	🍷🍷	7
● Barbaresco Basarin '03	🍷🍷	8
● Barbaresco Bric Balin '03	🍷🍷	7
○ Langhe Chardonnay Buschet '04	🍷🍷	5
● Barbera d'Alba '05	🍷🍷	4*
● Dolcetto d'Alba '05	🍷🍷	4*
○ Langhe Chardonnay '05	🍷🍷	4*
● Langhe Nebbiolo '05	🍷	5
● Barbaresco Bric Balin '01	♀♀♀	8
● Barbaresco Bric Balin '90	♀♀♀	8
● Barbaresco Cole '97	♀♀♀	8
● Barbaresco Bric Balin '00	♀♀	8
● Barbaresco Cole '00	♀♀	8
● Barbaresco '02	♀♀	6
● Barbaresco Cole '01	♀♀	8

BARBARESCO (CN)

Montaribaldi

Fraz. Tre Stelle
s.da Nicolini Alto, 12/14
12050 Barbaresco (CN)
tel. 0173638220
www.ilturismo.com/montaribaldi.htm

Giuseppe can be proud of the job his two sons Luciano and Roberto are doing, with help from their wives Antonella and Franca. Their dozen wines, including new products like Barolo, are all good and the two Barbarescos are particularly admirable. Not for the first time, it was the Sörì Montaribaldi that stood out. It went through to our finals for its exemplary garnet red hue, intense forest floor, mint and talcum powder aromatics and a palate whose sweet tannins precede a long finish. The 5,500 bottles of Barbaresco Palazzina 2003 come from the Starderi vineyard at Neive, which has imbued it with an estery nose of dried flowers offset on the palate by the thrust of a whistle-clean tannic weave. We look forward to improvements from the newcomer, Barolo Borzoni 2002, whose 2,800 bottles are sourced from the vineyard of the same name at Grinzane Cavour. It pays the price of its vintage in a vegetal nose and a palate that lacks breadth but does show its texture and potential. Moving on to the Barberas, we noticed that the Barbera d'Asti La Consolina 2005 and Barbera d'Alba dü Gir 2004 complement each other. Their provenance is different, although both come from very old vines, and the former is vinified in concrete vats and large wood whereas the latter has 18 months in new barriques. What unites them is their quality, which comes out particularly in the broad, fresh-tasting and seriously good palate. It's a similar story with the Dolcetto d'Alba Vagnona 2005, steel-fermented and aged for pleasurable drinkability, and the Dolcetto d'Alba Nicolini 2005, whose oak adds completeness to nose and palate. Cleanness is the keynote of the Langhe Nebbiolo Gambarin 2004, and to round off there are two constantly improving whites, the Roero Arneis Capural 2005 and the Langhe Chardonnay Stissa d'le Favole 2005.

●	Barbaresco Sörì Montaribaldi '03	**YY**	6*
●	Barbaresco Palazzina '03	**YY**	5
●	Barbera d'Alba dü Gir '04	**YY**	4
●	Barbera d'Asti La Consolina '05	**YY**	3*
●	Dolcetto d'Alba Nicolini '05	**YY**	4
○	Langhe Chardonnay Stissa d'le Favole '05	**Y**	3
○	Roero Arneis Capural '05	**Y**	4
●	Barolo Borzoni '02	**Y**	6
●	Langhe Nebbiolo Gambarin '04	**Y**	4
●	Dolcetto d'Alba Vagnona '05	**Y**	3
●	Barbaresco Sörì Montaribaldi '00	YY	6
●	Barbaresco Sörì Montaribaldi '01	YY	6
●	Barbaresco Palazzina '01	YY	6

BARBARESCO (CN)

Cascina Morassino

s.da Bernino, 10
12050 Barbaresco (CN)
tel. 0173635149

Again this year, all the Cascina Morassino wines cruised past the Two Glass mark and Barbaresco Ovello went into the finals. It is all down to the work of Roberto Bianco and his father Marioi, with consultancy from Dino Bevione and Sergio Molino. They devote their energies to three and a half hectares under vine which provide them with about 20,000 bottles a year. When we tasted this year's line-up, we thought the best bottle was the Barbaresco Ovello from 2003. A dry growing year has given it exuberant structure, delightfully offset by acidity that will ensure a bright future in the cellar for several years. Sensations of wild berry fruit, violets and subtle balsam tempt the nose before the palate unfolds beefy tannins and well-defined cocoa powder, coffee and liquorice, signing off with a very leisurely finale. The Barbaresco Morassino is almost as good. It's readier for the corkscrew but less complex and less nuanced overall. The ruby red has a faint orange-tinged rim, the fruit-forward aromas are lifted by leather and tobacco and there is good balance in the mouth, as well as silky tannins. The Dolcetto has rich fruit, nice pulp and close-knit tannins, as well as lots of drinkability. The Barbera Vignot 2004 unveils plums and spices, backed up by varietal acidity with rich extract, alcohol and tannins. Vigna del Merlo 2004 is a single-variety Merlot that regales the nose with vanilla, cocoa powder and red fruits, showing soft and satisfying on the palate. Finally, the Nebbiolo 2004 is a classic interpretation of the variety.

●	Barbaresco Ovello '03	**YY**	7
●	Barbaresco Morassino '03	**YY**	6*
●	Barbera d'Alba Vignot '04	**YY**	5
●	Langhe Nebbiolo '04	**YY**	5
●	Langhe Rosso V. del Merlo '04	**YY**	5
●	Dolcetto d'Alba '05	**YY**	4*
●	Barbaresco Ovello '00	YY	7
●	Barbaresco Morassino '01	YY	6
●	Barbaresco Ovello '01	YY	7
●	Barbaresco Ovello '02	YY	7
●	Barbaresco Morassino '00	YY	6
●	Barbaresco Morassino '02	YY	6
●	Barbaresco Morassino '99	YY	6
●	Barbaresco Ovello '99	YY	7

BARBARESCO (CN)

I Paglieri - Roagna

Loc. Pajé
S.da Paglieri, 7
12050 Barbaresco (CN)
tel. 0173635109
www.roagna.com

To understand how the Roagna estate works, you really have to go and see for yourself. Alfredo and his son Luca look after everything. In fact, fans of biodiversity ought to go to Castiglione Falletto for an object lesson in the subject. Alfredo and Luca have kept the woodland around the property intact so that the growing environment enjoys optimal humidity and coolness. And even if they don't make a song and dance about it, the duo tend their lands in accordance with tradition and the precepts of organic farming. At the Roagna winery, nature and her fruits are respected. The cellar is equipped with valid technology and Alfredo was discussing barriques as long ago as the late 1970s. Wine is treated as it should be and Roagna bottles are only released to market when they are good and ready. That is also why the range presented for the Guide is not always complete and this time round, we only managed to taste four wines. We'll have to come back for the major nebbiolo-based Riservas. We'll begin with the 8,000 bottles of Barbaresco Pajé 2001. The lovely intense colour heralds spices that meld nicely with the fruit, a broad, austere palate and a tannin-rich finish that is perked up by juicy acidity. The Barolo La Rocca e La Pira 2000, of which 10,000 units went into bottle, stands out for its balsamic fragrances attractively supported by spices and chocolate. Rich and mouthfilling, it flaunts a weave of ripe, well-absorbed tannins. The Dolcetto has grip and the 2005 Langhe Bianco, from almost all chardonnay with five per cent nebbiolo fermented off the skins, is appealing.

● Barolo La Rocca e La Pira '00	▼▼	7
● Barbaresco Pajé '01	▼▼	7
● Dolcetto d'Alba '05	▼▼	4*
○ Langhe Bianco '05	▼▼	4*
● Barolo La Rocca e La Pira '99	▽▽	7
● Barbaresco Pajé '00	▽▽	7
● Langhe Rosso '01	▽▽	5
○ Langhe Solea '01	▽▽	5
● Barbaresco Crichët Pajé '98	▽▽	8
● Barbaresco Pajé Ris. '98	▽▽	8
● Barolo La Rocca e La Pira '98	▽▽	7
● Barbaresco Pajé '99	▽▽	7
● Opera Prima XV	▽▽	8

BARBARESCO (CN)

Albino Rocca

S.da Ronchi, 16/18
12050 Barbaresco (CN)
tel. 0173635145
www.roccaalbino.com

After bravely slashing his range for the poor 2002 vintage, which he handled very well by the way, Angelo Rocca is back with a full and formidable line-up. The estate's vineyards are at Barbaresco, Neive and at Alba in the outlying district of San Rocco Seno d'Elvio, for a total of 15 hectares that yield 70,000 bottles a year. The major news this year is the reduced use of barriques in favour of 20-hectolitre barrels to age Barbaresco Brich Ronchi and Barbera Gepin. The Barbaresco has great elegance and harmony. Dried flowers and violets precede a palate whose soft tannins are well absorbed thanks to skilful use of wood and a warm, muscular finish. Our Three Glass award was a formality. The other house Barbaresco selection, Vigneto Loreto, also did well, It's a more austere interpretation that needs more time in bottle to develop its potential to the full. But the standard Barbaresco is ready for the corkscrew now, having aged in oak for 18 months, and proffers intriguing fragrances of red fruit and spices. Barbera Gepin cruised through to the finals thanks to its intense red fruit and vanilla aromas complemented by freshness and acidity contributed by the superb 2004 growing year. The cortese-based Langhe Bianco La Rocca scored well, as did the Dolcetto Vignalunga and the soft-textured, aristocratic Rosso di Rocca, a blend of 80 per cent nebbiolo with barbera and cabernet franc. Just a neck behind is the Langhe Chardonnay da Bertü.

● Barbaresco Vign. Brich Ronchi '03	▼▼▼	7
● Barbaresco Vign. Loreto '03	▼▼	7
● Barbera d'Alba Gepin '04	▼▼	5
● Barbaresco '03	▼▼	6
● Dolcetto d'Alba Vignalunga '05	▼▼	4*
○ Langhe Bianco La Rocca '05	▼▼	5
● Rosso di Rocca '05	▼▼	4*
○ Langhe Chardonnay da Bertü '05	▼	4
● Barbaresco Vign.Brich Ronchi '00	▽▽▽	7
● Barbaresco Vign. Brich Ronchi '97	▽▽▽	7
● Barbaresco Vign. Loreto '98	▽▽▽	7

BARBARESCO (CN)

BRUNO ROCCA
S.DA RABAJÀ, 60
12050 BARBARESCO (CN)
TEL. 0173635112
www.brunorocca.it

After last year's success, the excellent Barbaresco Maria Adelaide was not produced in the 2002 vintage but we welcome the return of two other celebrated Bruno Rocca selections, Coparossa and Rabajà, which join the standard-label version. The news here is the release of a great Barbera d'Asti, obtained from three well-aspected hectares in the municipality of Vaglio Serra. Bruno is assisted in the cellar by his children, Francesco e Luisa, who help him to bottle about 65,000 units a year. When we tasted the wines, we sent three through to the finals. Barbaresco Rabajà has warm cinchona and wild berry aromas that close on notes of coffee and vanilla. In the mouth, it reveals all the energy and tannins of the very warm 2003 vintage. Barbaresco Coparossa is a more elegant, well-orchestrated offering, its subtly fruity nose enhanced by cocoa powder and pencil lead acquired from leisurely ageing in barriques and 25-hectolitre barrels. Right from its first release, the Barbera d'Asti 2004 delighted our panel with its cherry, plum, vanilla and chocolate fragrances, backed up by warm sensations on the palate. We were not disappointed by the standard-label Barbaresco and the excellent scores of the past were again awarded to the juicy, fresh-tasting Barbera d'Alba 2004, the concentrated, easy-drinking Dolcetto Trifolè 2005, the Chardonnay Cadet 2005, for its understated oak, and the cabernet sauvignon, nebbiolo and barbera-based Langhe Rosso Rabajolo 2004.

●	Barbaresco Coparossa '03	TT	8
●	Barbaresco Rabajà '03	TT	8
●	Barbera d'Asti '04	TT	5
●	Barbaresco '03	TT	7
●	Barbera d'Alba '04	TT	5
●	Langhe Rosso Rabajolo '04	TT	6
●	Dolcetto d'Alba V. Trifolè '05	TT	4*
○	Langhe Chardonnay Cadet '05	TT	5
●	Barbaresco Rabajà '00	YYY	8
●	Barbaresco Maria Adelaide '01	YYY	8
●	Barbaresco Rabajà '01	YYY	8
●	Barbaresco Rabajà '93	YYY	8
●	Barbaresco Rabajà '96	YYY	8
●	Barbaresco Coparossa '97	YYY	8
●	Barbaresco Rabajà '98	YYY	8

BARBARESCO (CN)

RONCHI
S.DA RONCHI
12050 BARBARESCO (CN)
TEL. 0173635156

Giancarlo Rocca is a 40-something wine man who for years has been running the family estate here among the vineyards of Barbaresco. Out in the rows, help is available from his father Alfonso, the elder brother of winemaker Albino Rocca. Giancarlo's property comprises almost six hectares under vine around the old family home. Annual production is rarely more than 30,000 bottles. We applaud Giancarlo's decision to use no herbicides in his vineyards to safeguard the integrity of the environment. As is fitting, given that we are in the area, the most interesting of the wines presented was the Barbaresco Ronchi 2003, of which 2,000 bottles were released. Aged for 20 months in new barriques, it cruised effortlessly into the Three Glass finals. A nose of pepper, tobacco, violets and cherries ushers in assertive, and still slightly drying, tannins on the palate, whose finish is long and appealing. The Langhe Nebbiolo 2003 is very much like the Barbaresco, although it offers a little more fruit and flowers. The palate is juicy and emphatically flavoursome. Also good is the Barbera d'Alba Terlé 2004, which spent 18 months in new and once-used barriques, emerging with vanilla, coffee, currant and blueberry fragrances. Two well-deserved Glasses went to the Langhe Chardonnay 2004, which has tropical fruit aromas and a rounded palate perked up by attractive supporting acidity. Finally, the bright Langhe Freisa 2004 and the muscular, full-bodied Dolcetto d'Alba Rosario 2004 also caught our eye.

●	Barbaresco Ronchi '03	TT	6*
●	Langhe Nebbiolo '03	TT	5
●	Barbera d'Alba Terlé '04	TT	4*
○	Langhe Chardonnay '04	TT	4*
●	Dolcetto d'Alba Rosario '04	T	4
●	Langhe Freisa '04	T	4
●	Barbaresco '02	YY	6

BARBARESCO (CN)

RINO VARALDO
VIA SECONDINE, 2
12050 BARBARESCO (CN)
TEL. 0173635160

Rino and Michele Varaldo run a good old-fashioned farm right in the middle of the Barbaresco DOCG zone. They have seven hectares under vine and release about ten labels, all rigorously red. Local varieties are the mainstays, with nebbiolo leading a pack that includes dolcetto, barbera and the odd merlot or cabernet vine. This year, there was no Barolo Vigna di Aldo. It's sad, because it is a wine that has always brought the cellar much satisfaction, but it simply wasn't made in the traumatic 2002 growing year. So we are focusing on Barbaresco, of which three selections were presented for 2003, Bricco Libero, Sorì Loreto and La Gemma. The best was Sorì Loreto, which comes from a vineyard at Barbaresco. The ruby colour introduces ripe fruit aromas and a warm, well-sustained palate that is just a shade too alcoholic. The finish drives on nicely, buoyed up by sweet tannins and good body. Bricco Libero, another warm, meaty wine, is good while La Gemma, from a vineyard at Treiso, has power but puts a little too much emphasis on oak and alcohol. Despite their concentration, the Barbera d'Alba Vigna delle Fate and the Langhe Fantasia 4.20, from nebbiolo, barbera, cabernet and merlot, 2004 selections also stand out for finesse. The Barbera d'Alba has ripe fruit over vanilla followed by a savoury, austere palate while its stablemate is mouthfilling and balsamic, showing sweet, well-integrated tannins. Finally, the standard-label Dolcetto and Barbera d'Alba are straightforward and well managed.

● Barbaresco Sorì Loreto '03	🍷🍷	7
● Barbaresco Bricco Libero '03	🍷🍷	7
● Barbaresco La Gemma '03	🍷🍷	7
● Barbera d'Alba V. delle Fate '04	🍷🍷	5
● Langhe Rosso Fantasia 4.20 '04	🍷🍷	5
● Barbera d'Alba '05	🍷	4
● Dolcetto d'Alba '05	🍷	4
● Barbaresco Bricco Libero '97	🍷🍷🍷	7
● Barolo V. di Aldo '00	🍷🍷	8
● Barbaresco Bricco Libero '01	🍷🍷	7
● Barolo V. di Aldo '01	🍷🍷	8
● Barolo V. di Aldo '99	🍷🍷	8
● Barbaresco Sorì Loreto '00	🍷🍷	7

BAROLO (CN)

GIACOMO BORGOGNO & FIGLI
VIA GIOBERTI, 1
12060 BAROLO (CN)
TEL. 017356108
www.borgogno-wine.com

A visit to the Borgogno cellar is an exciting affair now that restructuring is complete. As you stroll through the rooms, more than 200 years of history – the winery was founded in 1761 – are waiting around every corner in the ancient fermentation vats, today used for storing bottles, whose concrete walls are still encrusted with tartrates. The Boschis family is still in charge. Brothers Giorgio and Cesare, with their father Franco, have about 20 hectares under vine and turn out about 100,000 bottles a year. They gave us three Barolos. The Classico 2001, aged only in large wood like the other Barolos, is on top form. The ruby red is flecked with garnet, heralding dried violets, ripe fruit and spicy tobacco and chocolate sensations. The vigorous tannins are truly elegant and the finish is enviably long. Only a short distance behind is the intensely hued Barolo Liste 2001, which gives dark berry fruit and spice. Full and long on entry, the palate is pervasive and the tannins silky. The standard-label Barolo 2001 did well, too. An intense, lingering nose is offset by the nicely tannic palate that flows beautifully through to the finish. The Barbera d'Alba 2005 is purplish and intense in hue, with attractive still fresh red fruit perceptions, good roundness and lingering flavour. Last on the list was the Dolcetto d'Alba 2005,

● Barolo Cl. '01	🍷🍷	8
● Barolo Liste '01	🍷🍷	8
● Barolo '01	🍷🍷	8
● Barbera d'Alba '05	🍷🍷	4
● Dolcetto d'Alba '05	🍷	4
● Barolo Cl. '98	🍷🍷🍷	8
● Barolo Cl. '00	🍷🍷	8
● Barolo Cl. '99	🍷🍷	8
● Barolo Cl. '97	🍷🍷	8
● Barolo Cl. '96	🍷🍷	8
● Barolo Liste '00	🍷🍷	8

BAROLO (CN)

GIACOMO BREZZA & FIGLI
VIA LOMONDO, 4
12060 BAROLO (CN)
TEL. 0173560921 - 017356354
www.brezza.it

Discretion, a sense of proportion, a serious approach to their work and competence are qualities the Brezza family communicate when you visit their winery, or simply sit down at table in their Barolo restaurant, located right over their cellars. The Brezza philosophy is simple. It is closely linked to tradition in the best sense of the word, that is appropriately screened and adapted to modern needs for cleanness, definition and precision. Fermentation with long maceration, large wood and a light hand in the cellar combine with care in the vineyard to produce frank, austere wines with lots of stuffing and no flashy bells or whistles. Barolo Cannubi 2001 is an excellent example. It is ripe, earthy, broad and subtly shaded across wild berries, wild roses and cocoa powder with a hint of mint. The savoury palate has taut tannins and good depth, a faint note of iron-rich minerality and liquorice-like nuances peeking through in the finish. It has been a long time since we tasted such a superb wine from this cellar, which is another reason for congratulation on this Three Glass prize. The Barbera Cannubi Muscatel 2004 is very nice. Juicy fruit, flowers, chewiness and an attractively edgy palate come together with freshness, austerity and fine aromatic persistence. The more upfront, lean Barbera Santa Rosalia 2005, with its crunchy red fruit aromatics, signs off with a pleasant hint of almonds. And the Dolcetto San Lorenzo 2005 is uncomplicated and playfully bright, giving spice and dark cherries.

●	Barolo Cannubi '01	▼▼▼	7
●	Barbera d'Alba Cannubi Muscatel '04	▼▼	5
●	Barbera d'Alba Santa Rosalia '05	▼▼	4*
●	Dolcetto d'Alba S. Lorenzo '05	▼	4
●	Barolo Cannubi '96	▽▽▽	7
●	Barolo Sarmassa '00	▽▽	7
●	Barolo Bricco Sarmassa '01	▽▽	8
●	Barolo Sarmassa '01	▽▽	7
●	Barolo Bricco Sarmassa '97	▽▽	7
●	Barolo Cannubi '97	▽▽	7
●	Barolo Sarmassa '98	▽▽	7
●	Barolo Bricco Sarmassa '99	▽▽	8
●	Barolo Cannubi '99	▽▽	7

BAROLO (CN)

BRIC CENCIURIO
VIA ROMA, 24
12060 BAROLO (CN)
TEL. 017356317
www.briccenciurio.com

Bric Cenciurio has been based in Barolo for only a few years. Previously, the fruit was vinified at Magliano Alfieri, a Roero municipality that still supplies the winery's barbera, and the name Bric Cenciurio comes from the location at Castellinaldo where arneis, cabernet sauvignon and brachetto grow. The business is family run. Mother Fiorella Pittatore, her sons Alessandro and Alberto, and uncle Carlo Sacchetto share the work on 12 hectares of vineyards that yield about 40,000 bottles a year. Whites are much esteemed at Bric Cenciurio, and respond in grand style, emerging from the cellar with good structure, alcohol and colour, and warm, round palates. When we tasted the 2005 Arneis Sito dei Fossili selection, it actually still had some way to go. We predict it will improve in the cellar. And the two Barberas scored well. The Superiore 2004 is intriguing and drinking well now, its crisp aromas complementing a juicy palate. In contrast, Naunda 2004, barrique-aged and from older vines, has yet to evolve. It gives estery, balsamic aromas over very concentrated fruit. Two Glasses went to the well-made Nebbiolo 2004, from grapes sourced in the Langhe and Roero, for its character and equilibrium, but there was only One for the Langhe Rosso Rosso Di Caialupo 2003, a blend of cabernet sauvignon and nebbiolo that is still a tad tousled and tannin-heavy. Finally, the Barolo 2002, of which only 1,800 bottles were released, has very persuasive breadth on the nose and an elegant palate. Last up was an encouraging arneis-based Sito dei Fossili da Vendemmia Tardiva 2003. The colour of quartz, it gives honey, pear and liquorice before the sweet, fatty palate signs off on a caramel-like note.

●	Barolo Costa di Rose '02	▼▼	6
○	Sito dei Fossili V.T. '03	▼▼	6
●	Barbera d'Alba Sup. '04	▼▼	4*
●	Barbera d'Alba Sup. Naunda '04	▼▼	5
●	Langhe Nebbiolo '04	▼▼	5
○	Roero Arneis Sito dei Fossili '05	▼▼	4*
●	Langhe Rosso Rosso Di Caialupo '03	▼	5
○	Roero Arneis '05	▼	4
●	Barolo Costa di Rose '01	▽▽	6
●	Barolo Costa di Rose '00	▽▽	6
●	Barbera d'Alba Sup. Naunda '01	▽▽	5
●	Barbera d'Alba Sup. Naunda '03	▽▽	5

BAROLO (CN)

CASCINA ADELAIDE
VIA AIE SOTTANE, 14
12060 BAROLO (CN)
TEL. 0173560503
www.cascinaadelaide.com

The futuristic Cascina Adelaide cellar was designed by architect Ugo Dellapiana. Despite its ultra-modern looks, it blends perfectly into the countryside, just below the castle at Barolo. The cellar, like the estate itself, came into being thanks to the drive of Amabile Drucco, a dynamic local entrepreneur, with help from oenologist Sergio Molino and a wide range of children, in-laws and grandchildren that bodes well for the future. In all, the estate has seven hectares at Preda and Cannubi at Barolo, Fossati at La Morra and Costa Grillo and Costa Fiore at Diano for an overall output of 40,000 bottles. There were no 2002 Barolos, and two Barberas had not yet gone into bottle when we tasted, so we were only able to try three wines, all of which were good. We started with a juicy, concentrated Dolcetto Vigna Costa Fiore 2005, 4,000 bottles of which were released. Its blackberry jam aromas and silky-soft palate are never oppressive. The 3,400 bottles of Barbera Superiore Vigna Preda 2004 are stunning after more than a year in barrique. The deep colour heralds fruit and balsam aromas and a well-rounded, fresh-tasting palate with a close-knit weave of sweet tannins. The Barolo Riserva Per Elen 2000 is a selection of fruit from Preda and Cannubi. Still young on the palate, it has assertive tannins and very attractive raspberry on the nose. This is a winery on the way up. Watch this space.

●	Barolo Per Elen Ris. '00	🍷🍷	8
●	Barbera d'Alba Sup. V. Preda '04	🍷🍷	5
●	Diano d'Alba V. Costa Fiore '05	🍷🍷	4*
●	Barolo Cannubi '00	YY	7
●	Barolo Preda '00	YY	8
●	Barolo Cannubi '01	YY	7
●	Barolo Preda '01	YY	8
●	Barolo Cannubi '99	YY	7

BAROLO (CN)

DAMILANO
VIA ROMA, 31
12060 BAROLO (CN)
TEL. 017356265 - 017356105
www.cantinedamilano.it

Damilano is a long-established label at Barolo. Soon, work on the cellar, which stands near the fork for La Morra, will be complete. Meanwhile, the vine stock has expanded to the present 15 hectares, including plots in historic Barolo vineyards like Cannubi, Liste, Fossati and Brunate, and overall output hovers around 150,000 bottles a year. There was only one Barolo this year, Lecinquevigne, obtained from the best grapes that the cellar selected from 2002, plus the small amount of fruit sourced from Cannubi and Liste, whose grapes are normally vinified separately. The nose gives ripe fruit and a hint of spice before the still rugged tannins come through on a palate with good overall structure. This wine aged for 18 months in Allier barriques and then large ovals. Diano d'Alba was the source for the interesting Nebbiolo, whose elegant nose of broad fruit and balsam accompanies a faint green note on the attractive tannic weave that makes its presence felt without intruding. The nice Barbera has a broad, fruit-led nose and fresh acidity, showing good balance. We'll sign off with the early-drinking Dolcetto d'Alba and a light, fruity white from arneis, again sourced at Diano.

●	Barolo Lecinquevigne '02	🍷🍷	6
●	Barbera d'Alba '04	🍷🍷	5
●	Nebbiolo d'Alba '04	🍷🍷	4*
●	Dolcetto d'Alba '05	🍷	4
○	Langhe Arneis '05	🍷	4
●	Barolo Cannubi '01	YYY	8
●	Barolo Cannubi '00	YYY	8
●	Barolo Liste '00	YY	8
●	Barolo Cannubi '99	YY	8
●	Barolo Liste '99	YY	8
●	Barolo '97	YY	7
●	Barolo Cannubi '97	YY	7
●	Barolo Cannubi '98	YY	7
●	Barolo Liste '98	YY	7

BAROLO (CN)

Giacomo Grimaldi

via Luigi Einaudi, 8
12060 Barolo (CN)
tel. 017335256

It's fascinating to chat to Ferruccio Grimaldi about his land, his work, his passion for winemaking and his quality-focused philosophy, which aims to maintain a strong link with the territory. The vines extend over eight hectares in excellent sites that enable Ferruccio to imbue his wines with personality. Currently, the cellar offers two Barolos, one from the Le Coste vineyard at Barolo and the other from Sotto Castello at Novello, in addition to two Barberas and a Dolcetto. At this year's tasting, there were no Barolos because the 2002 vintage was not up to snuff for the top labels. So with no leading nebbiolo-based wines, attention shifted to Barbera d'Alba Pistìn 2005, obtained from 60 to 70-year-old vines in the Monforte area. Intense ruby red, it opens on broad black fruit with a spicy vein of alcohol. The palate is dry and attractively tannic, fruit and mulberry providing a sweet note. The other Barbera, Fornaci, is even better. Sourced from a range of separate plots, it aims for satisfying drinkability that is anything but uncomplicated. Now flowery, now fruit-led, it unveils perky acidity before signing off with an elegant back palate. Also intriguing is Nebbiolo Valmaggiore, a clean, classy wine with an occasionally vegetal nose, alcohol-laced tannins and a nice twist of bitterness in the finale. And the list was rounded off by a clean, straightforward Dolcetto.

● Barbera d'Alba Fornaci '04	🍷🍷	5
● Nebbiolo d'Alba Valmaggiore '04	🍷🍷	4*
● Barbera d'Alba Pistìn '05	🍷🍷	4*
● Dolcetto d'Alba '05	🍷	3
● Barolo Le Coste '00	YY	8
● Barolo Le Coste '99	YY	8
● Barolo Sotto Castello di Novello '00	YY	7
● Barbera d'Alba Fornaci '01	YY	6
● Barolo Le Coste '98	YY	7

BAROLO (CN)

Tenuta La Volta - Cabutto

via San Pietro, 13
12060 Barolo (CN)
tel. 017356168

Not far from La Volta castle, the Cabutto brothers ply their trade as growers, like their grandfather before them. The 18 hectares under vine are distributed over the nearby La Volta and Bricco delle Viole sites, as well as the outstanding Sarmassa vineyard and Bricco Bergera at Novello. All the grapes are rigorously local Piedmontese reds. Osvaldo has been an oenologist since 1976. He looks after the cellar while Bruno takes care of distribution, although he frequently heads off to the vineyards on his tractor. The cellar did not bottle a Barolo 2002 in order not to disappoint a clientele accustomed to quite another class of wine. Nevertheless, our panel was able to enjoy a great Barolo. It was a 2000 Riserva from old vines at Sarmassa, of which 2,500 bottles were released. Elegant with delicate, well-defined aromatics, it foregrounds spicy cocoa powder and liquorice in the mouth. The Barbera Superiore 2004, whose 15,000 bottles were sourced from the Bricco delle Viole vineyard, has a deep hue and traces of earth and leather on the nose. It seductive palate unveils superb equilibrium and upfront varietal character. Finally, the 30,000 bottles of the traditional Dolcetto La Volta 2005 put the accent on drinkability rather than muscle, as is the cellar's style. Pepper, liquorice and herbs tempt the nose.

● Barolo Riserva del Fondatore V. Sarmassa '00	🍷🍷	8
● Barbera d'Alba Sup. '04	🍷🍷	5
● Dolcetto d'Alba V. La Volta '05	🍷	3
● Barolo Ris. del Fondatore '99	YY	8
● Barolo V. La Volta '00	YY	7
● Barolo V. La Volta '01	YY	7
● Barolo Ris. del Fondatore '96	YY	8
● Barolo Ris. del Fondatore '97	YY	8
● Barolo V. La Volta '97	YY	7
● Barolo Ris. del Fondatore '98	YY	8
● Barolo V. La Volta '98	YY	7
● Barolo V. La Volta '99	YY	7

BAROLO (CN)

Marchesi di Barolo

via Alba, 12
12060 Barolo (CN)
tel. 0173564400
www.marchesibarolo.com

In the early 1990s, Marchesi di Barolo changed tack. The new direction is obvious at times like this year, when the poor 2002 vintage prevented the release of the cellar's Barolo selections. Barolo is everything for the Marchesi and in fact it was one of the first wineries to link its name to the production of the king of wines. Actually, the cellar did manage to present one Barolo. It was the Riserva Grande Annata from 2000 and although it is very good, it failed to achieve the peak of excellence that enabled the 1999 to earn Three Glasses in the last edition of the Guide. A pale garnet introduces distinct tertiary notes dominated by dried flowers and saddle leather. Juicy and austere in the mouth, it melds soft, mature tannins into its overall structure. After the Barolo, we can move on to the less celebrated wines, which include two Dolcettos and two equally interesting Barberas. Dolcetto d'Alba Boschetti 2005 impressed. Its intense purplish hue heralds fruity aromas with morello cherry to the fore. Great depth and inviting tannins take you through to a pervasive finale lifted by a pleasing note of bitter almonds. The fruit-forward, very drinkable Dolcetto Madonna di Como is almost as complex. Each Barbera has its own personality, too, the Paiagal selection showing slightly more weight than the Ruvei. The Paiagal has balsamic sensations and a rounded palate while the Ruvei brings out the acidulous vein characteristic of the variety. The palate of the Barbaresco Creja 2003 makes up for a slight lack of definition on the nose, a result of the particularly hot growing year. Finally, there were very positive performances from the Nebbiolo Michet, the Gavi, the Arneis and the Moscato d'Asti Zagara.

● Barolo Riserva Grande Annata '00	▼▼	8
● Dolcetto d'Alba Boschetti '05	▼▼	4*
● Barbaresco Creja '03	▼▼	6
● Barbera d'Alba Paiagal '04	▼▼	4
● Barbera d'Alba Ruvei '04	▼▼	4
● Dolcetto d'Alba Madonna di Como '05	▼▼	3*
● Nebbiolo d'Alba Michet '04	▼	4
○ Gavi del Comune di Gavi '05	▼	4
○ Moscato d'Asti Zagara '05	▼	4
○ Roero Arneis '05	▼	4
● Barolo Riserva Grande Annata '99	▽▽▽	8
● Barolo Sarmassa '01	▽▽	8

BAROLO (CN)

Bartolo Mascarello

via Roma, 15
12060 Barolo (CN)
tel. 017356125

For anyone who might not know, the Bartolo Mascarello winery is right in the heart of Barolo at number 15 Via Roma. Time seems to have stopped here, as you peek through the window of Bartolo's studio with its countless books, photographs and labels. After protracted renovation work, the new warehouse is ready, as are the offices and a delightful tasting room. We owe this last feature to the good taste of Maria Teresa, the cellar's driving spirit, and the help she has from her capable mother, Franca. Today, Maria Teresa is charge of vineyard, cellar and marketing. The vine stock is still the same five hectares and for years annual output has been stable at 30,000 bottles. When things go right, of course, because if nature is unco-operative, as she was in 2002, the figure can be considerably lower. There was no Barolo that year, but this time Maria Teresa had two fine wines to tempt us, Dolcetto 2005 and Barbera 2004. The 6,000 bottles of the former were made with fruit from the Monrobiolo and Ruè vineyards. It's a very well balanced wine, and in fact is rounder and juicier than usual, so we gave it Two resounding Glasses. Barbera Vigneto San Lorenzo, from the other side of the Cannubi hill, confirmed the status it has earned in previous vintages. Its balance and varietal typicity emerge through bitter cherry and almond aromatics perked up by vibrant acidity.

● Barbera d'Alba Vign. S. Lorenzo '04	▼▼	5
● Dolcetto d'Alba Monrobiolo e Ruè '05	▼▼	4*
● Barolo '83	▽▽▽	8
● Barolo '84	▽▽▽	8
● Barolo '85	▽▽▽	8
● Barolo '89	▽▽▽	8
● Barolo '98	▽▽▽	8
● Barolo '99	▽▽▽	8
● Barolo '01	▽▽▽	8
● Barolo '00	▽▽	8
● Barolo '96	▽▽	8
● Barbera d'Alba Vign. S. Lorenzo '03	▽▽	5

BAROLO (CN)

E. Pira & Figli
via Vittorio Veneto, 1
12060 Barolo (CN)
tel. 017356247
www.il-vino.com/pira/home.html

It's a pleasure to visit the estate owned by Chiara Boschis and talk to her about her vineyards and wines. Her love of winemaking and this territory is overwhelming, and it was for this that she tore herself away from her family – at least during working hours – years ago to devote her energies to crafting her ideal Barolo. Chiara's interpretation is in the modern idiom. She uses brief maceration times, thorough extraction of colour and ageing in small oak barrels, but she never loses sight of the Langhe sense of territory. Chiara was faced with lots of problems in 2002. In the end, she was able to release 3,000 bottles from the estate's plots in the Cannubi and Via Nuova vineyards, which she blended into Cuvée Chiara. The ruby red already has garnet tinges and the nose offers wild berries, violets and vanilla and cocoa powder spice. Nice acidity joins soft, well-absorbed tannins to take you through to the decently long, pervasive, back palate. The Barbera d'Alba 2004 is on excellent form. Its still purplish red accompanies fresh, intense fragrances of plum and liqueur cherries followed by alcohol offset by longevity-ensuring acidity and an attractive, very clean finish. Finally, the Dolcetto d'Alba 2005 also scored well. Its intense, purple red heralds a well-defined, youthfully alcoholic nose, fresh flavour and moreish drinkability.

● Barbera d'Alba '04	**YY**	5
● Dolcetto d'Alba '05	**YY**	4
● Barolo Cuvée Chiara '02	**Y**	7
● Barolo Cannubi '01	YYY	8
● Barolo Cannubi '00	YYY	8
● Barolo Cannubi '97	YYY	8
● Barolo Cannubi '96	YYY	8
● Barolo Ris. '90	YYY	8
● Barolo '94	YYY	8
● Barolo Cannubi '01	YY	8
● Barolo Via Nuova '01	YY	8
● Barolo Via Nuova '00	YY	8
● Barolo Via Nuova '99	YY	8

BAROLO (CN)

Giuseppe Rinaldi
via Monforte, 3
12060 Barolo (CN)
tel. 017356156

To enter Giuseppe Rinaldi's cellar is to step into the past. Fragrances and atmospheres take you back to a lost world of the countryside that is still very much alive in this intriguing Langhe personality. His wide-ranging conversation reveals a certain regret over a heritage – cultural, more than anything else – that is jealously preserved in Rinaldi's cellar but, if Beppe is to be believed, no longer exists elsewhere. Rinaldi's wines bespeak skills as ancient as the art that informs his two celebrated Barolos. These are not single-vineyard products but come instead from his plots in four vineyards, blended in two pairs: Cannubi San Lorenzo-Ravera and Brunate-Le Coste. The area under vine is six and a half hectares, which Beppe inherited from his father and grandfather before him. The 2002 growing year produced only one wine. This edition of the Barolo Brunate-Le Coste was vinified with fruit mainly from Brunate. Ordinarily, about 20,000 units go into bottle but the rain and hail-tormented 2002 vintage could only manage just over 6,000. The quality is excellent, though. A pale red introduces a broad, classy nose of liqueur fruit over warm alcohol before a clean palate reveals surprisingly soft tannins and spicy notes that round out a solidly mouthfilling experience.

● Barolo Brunate-Le Coste '02	**YY**	7
● Barolo Brunate-Le Coste '01	YYY	7
● Barolo Brunate-Le Coste '00	YYY	7
● Barolo Brunate-Le Coste '97	YYY	7
● Barolo Cannubi S. Lorenzo-Ravera '00	YY	7
● Barolo Brunate-Le Coste '99	YY	7
● Barolo Brunate-Le Coste '96	YY	7
● Barolo Brunate-Le Coste '98	YY	7
● Barolo Cannubi S. Lorenzo-Ravera '99	YY	7

BAROLO (CN)

★ LUCIANO SANDRONE
VIA PUGNANE, 4
12060 BAROLO (CN)
TEL. 0173560023
www.sandroneluciano.com

There is little to add to the universal admiration afforded to Luciano Sandrone in Italy and all over the world. His wines tell the story of tenacious effort to bring the finest grapes his vines can produce into the cellar, where he makes a further selection to ensure it is the best of the vintage's best that goes into bottle. For 2002, only Barolo Le Vigne was released, from fruit grown in the Conterni and Ceretta vineyards, vinified separately and then blended. Its brilliant red precedes a fruit and balsam nose of great breadth and depth followed by a well-rounded palate with serious tannins. Ripe liqueur fruit joins spicy sensations to complete the spectrum of aromatics. The fruit for Nebbiolo Valmaggiore came from the heart of Roero. Its aromatics speak eloquently and elegantly of ripe strawberries and currants before ripening tannins peek through on a mid-structured palate. The Barbera is a blend of fruit from several low-yielding plots at Novello and Monforte. The deep ruby red is redolent of fruit and balsam, the palate is well-balanced, offsetting alcohol with bracing acidity, and the long finish has a liquorice theme. The Dolcetto, too, is very enjoyable. It's an easy drinker but by no means predictable.

● Barolo Le Vigne '02	TT	8
● Barbera d'Alba '04	TT	5
● Nebbiolo d'Alba Valmaggiore '04	TT	6
● Dolcetto d'Alba '05	TT	4
● Barolo Cannubi Boschis '00	YYY	8
● Barolo '83	YYY	8
● Barolo '84	YYY	8
● Barolo Cannubi Boschis '86	YYY	8
● Barolo Cannubi Boschis '87	YYY	8
● Barolo Cannubi Boschis '89	YYY	8
● Barolo Cannubi Boschis '90	YYY	8
● Barolo Le Vigne '99	YYY	8
● Barolo Le Vigne '00	YY	8
● Barolo Cannubi Boschis '99	YY	8

BAROLO (CN)

GIORGIO SCARZELLO E FIGLI
VIA ALBA, 29
12060 BAROLO (CN)
TEL. 017356170
www.barolodibarolo.com

This small – only five hectares under vine – but beautiful estate, run by the Scarzello family, has a decades-long tradition of winemaking. The results obtained in recent years reward the hard work put in by the competent, enthusiastic and clear-headed Federico, with valid help from his parents. Their clean, well-made wines have an attractive sense of place. No Barolo was made in 2002 but an extra year in glass has done wonders for Barolo Vigna Merenda 2001, sourced from a plot in the Sarmassa vineyard and aged in 30-hectolitre barrels. Its intense, broad nose has serious, well-defined aromatics of dark cherries, plums, violets, cocoa powder and earth. Taut, thrusting tannins and good weight grace a palate that reprises the fruit of the nose to close savoury and deep. Barbera Superiore 2003 is a child of its vintage, warm, ripe and with generous florality, showing rich, mouthfilling and admirably deep on the palate. The steel-matured Barbera 2004 is agile and fresh-tasting, bringing together meaty fruit and a very attractive, refreshing progression in the mouth. Rounding off the range is a bright, juicy Dolcetto 2004 with forest fruit aromatics lifted by earthy and balsamic notes.

● Barolo Vigna Merenda '01	TT	7
● Barbera d'Alba Sup. '03	TT	5
● Barbera d'Alba '04	TT	4*
● Dolcetto d'Alba '04	TT	4*
● Barolo Vigna Merenda '99	YYY	6
● Barolo '01	YY	6
● Barolo '95	YY	6
● Barolo '96	YY	6
● Barolo '97	YY	6
● Barolo Vigna Merenda '98	YY	6
● Barolo '99	YY	6

GamberoRosso Città del gusto®
the only city devoted to taste
Rome Città del gusto
www.gamberorosso.it
> the Events
> the Shop
> the Osteria
> the Schools
> the Cooking Theatre
> the Television Studios
> the Wine Theatre Wine Bar
Roma Città del gusto | via Enrico Fermi, 161 | 00146 Italy | gambero@gamberorosso.it

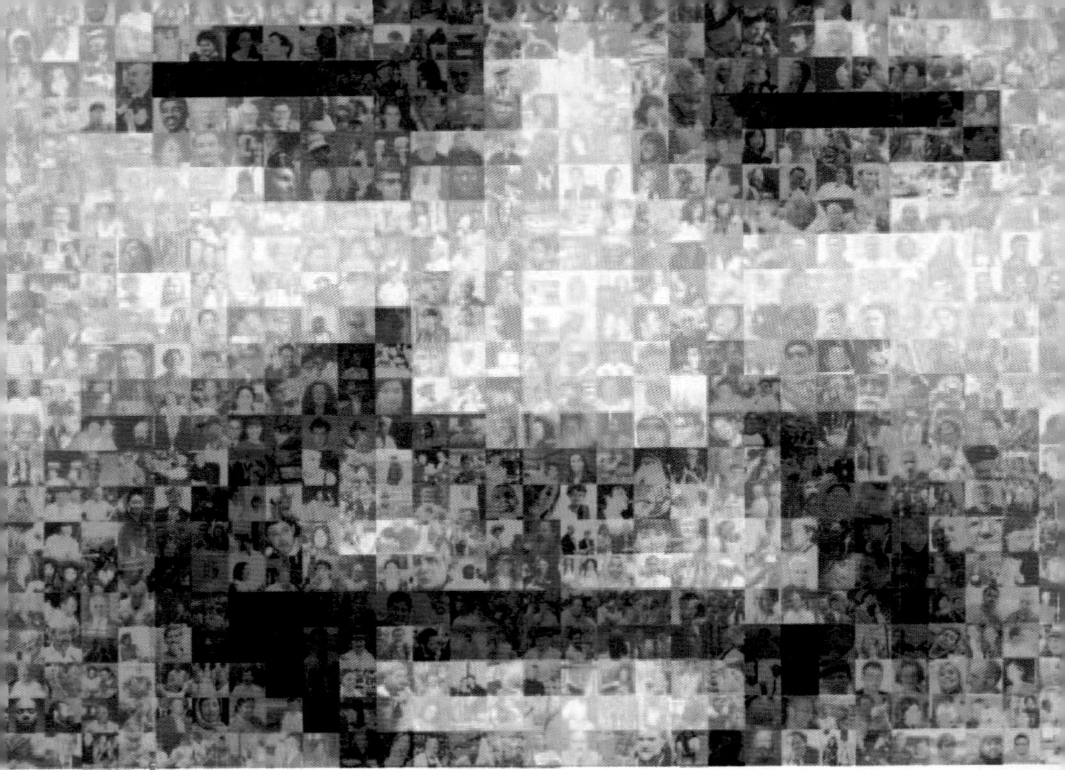

BAROLO (CN)

TERRE DA VINO
VIA BERGESIA, 6
12060 BAROLO (CN)
TEL. 0173564611
www.terredavino.it

Created in 1980 to distribute the wines of the small-scale producers in the co-operative, Terre da Vino has become one of the most prestigious such operations in the region and beyond. The initial objectives are fine-tuned each year and today Terre da Vino has several fine lines that cater for the demands of an increasingly complicated market. In the early years, quality was the goal and contributing growers were encouraged to deliver better grapes. Then in the late 1990s the Superbarbera project was launched to enhance the quality of the La Luna e i Falò selection. It is an exciting product and substantial numbers of bottles are available thanks to the 100 hectares devoted to the project by member growers who take part. From 2003, Terre da Vino has had another Barbera selection from the Nizza subzone while the most significant development for 2006 is the release to market of the 2001 Barolo Essenze. This is blended from grapes sourced from vineyards in six municipalities – Bussia at Monforte, Annunziata at La Morra, Ravera at Novello, La Volta at Barolo, Scarrone at Castiglione Falletto and Gianetto at Serralunga – which comprise the "essence" of the DOCG zone. The ruby colour is attractively intense and the nose offers fruit well supported by more complex liquorice and toastiness. Austerity, depth and pervasive, fine-grained tannins delight the palate. The Martlet selection stands out from the Barberas for its finesse and complexity but the Barbera d'Alba Croere is also impressive. And the rest of the line-up is good, especially the Barbaresco.

●	Barolo Essenze '01	🍷🍷	7
●	Barbera d'Asti Sup. Nizza Martlet '04	🍷🍷	5
●	Barbera d'Asti Sup. La Luna e i Falò '04	🍷🍷	5
●	Barbaresco La Casa in Collina '03	🍷🍷	6
●	Barbera d'Alba Sup. Croere '04	🍷🍷	4*
●	Langhe Nebbiolo La Malora '03	🍷	5
○	Piemonte Moscato Passito La Bella Estate '04	🍷	5
○	Gavi del Comune di Gavi Masseria dei Carmelitani '05	🍷	4
○	Roero Arneis La Villa '05	🍷	4
●	Barolo Podere Scarrone '01	🥂🥂	7

BAROLO (CN)

G. D. VAJRA
LOC. VERGNE
VIA DELLE VIOLE, 25
12060 BAROLO (CN)
TEL. 017356257

The modern, functional G.D. Vajra cellar is run by Aldo and Milena with help from their children. They are a lovely family who will welcome wine fans with the best of Barolo hospitality. There are lots of wines on the list. Barolo Bricco delle Viole 2001, with 10,000 bottles released after ageing in large wood, is exciting. Intense colour introduces dried flowers, plums and wild cherries laced with tobacco and cocoa powder spice before the balanced palate takes you through to a lingering finish. For the third year running, we gave it Three Glasses. Not quite so good is the Barolo Albe 2002. Its 11,000 bottles are less intense in colour and the nose is still closed, but nascent fruit and spice sensations emerge and the finale is lovely. The riesling renano-only Langhe Bianco 2005, whose 5,000 bottles were fermented and aged in steel, is a very fine wine. Pale straw yellow ushers in flowers, damsons and peaches mingling with the variety's trademark minerality. A hint of acidity melds with glycerine and alcohol in the mouth to offer sincere sensations and admirable persistence. There was another good performance from the Barbera Superiore 2004, whose 30,000 units briefly sojourned in new barriques. The colour is intense, the nose has fruit and flowers and the concentrated palate goes on forever. Dolcetto d'Alba Coste & Fossati 2005 is lovely. Purplish in colour, it proffers intense, upfront fragrances and a pleasant, already well-balanced palate. The 10,000 bottles of the fresh, well-structured Moscato d'Asti 2005 are moderately sweet and exceptionally successful. Some 15,000 bottles of Langhe Nebbiolo 2005 were released. Still vibrant in the glass, it gives roses and mulberries before the intense, close-knit flavours linger nicely on the palate. And the rest of the range is well worth investigating.

●	Barolo Bricco delle Viole '01	🍷🍷🍷	8
○	Langhe Bianco '05	🍷🍷	5
●	Barolo Albe '02	🍷🍷	7
●	Barbera d'Alba '04	🍷🍷	4*
●	Barbera d'Alba Sup. '04	🍷🍷	5
●	Langhe Freisa Kyè '04	🍷🍷	5
●	Dolcetto d'Alba Coste & Fossati '05	🍷🍷	4*
●	Langhe Nebbiolo '05	🍷🍷	5
○	Moscato d'Asti '05	🍷🍷	4*
●	Dolcetto d'Alba '05	🍷	4
●	Barolo Bricco delle Viole '00	🥂🥂🥂	8
●	Barolo Bricco delle Viole '99	🥂🥂🥂	8
○	Langhe Bianco '02	🥂🥂🥂	5
●	Barbera d'Alba Sup. '01	🥂🥂🥂	5

BASTIA MONDOVÌ (CN)

Bricco del Cucù
loc. Bricco, 10
12060 Bastia Mondovì (CN)
tel. 017460153
www.briccocucu.com

We are only about 20 kilometres from the Barolo country at Monforte d'Alba yet Bastia Mondovì seems to be on another planet, or at least on one where serious wine is unknown. It has to be said that up here, not far from Rocca Ciglié, we are light years from the single-crop farming that has afflicted so much of Langhe: most of Dario Sciolla's property is planted to hazelnuts or simply left as woodland. But when Dario bravely took the plunge into premium-quality winemaking, his life was transformed. Today, he and his family have a functional, well-equipped cellar and with help from consultant Luca Caramellino they release a range of excellent wines at very competitive prices. Langhe Bianco 2005 is a blend of arneis and sauvignon that shows how the cooler site climates of this part of Piedmont show the way forward for whites. Lemon and apple lifted by minerality introduce a savoury, well-orchestrated palate with vibrant acidity. The attractively drinkable Langhe Dolcetto has been joined by the new Langhe Dolcetto Vinot. It has less alcohol (11.5 per cent) than its big brother, fruit-led, youthfully alcoholic fragrances and a slim body with just the right touch of acidity. Dogliani 2005 is the archetype of a great Dolcetto, showing fruity and concentrated yet soft. Bricco San Bernardo 2004 has enormous structure that will need a few more years before it is at its peak. Finally, there is a new Langhe Rosso to look forward to next year.

●	Dolcetto di Dogliani '05	🍷🍷	3*
●	Dolcetto di Dogliani Sup. Bricco S. Bernardo '04	🍷🍷	4
○	Langhe Bianco '05	🍷🍷	3*
●	Langhe Dolcetto '05	🍷🍷	3*
●	Langhe Dolcetto Vinot '05	🍷	3
●	Dolcetto di Dogliani Sup. Bricco S. Bernardo '01	YY	4
●	Dolcetto di Dogliani '03	YY	3
●	Dolcetto di Dogliani '04	YY	3

BERZANO DI TORTONA (AL)

Terralba
fraz. Inselmina
15050 Berzano di Tortona (AL)
tel. 013180403

Last year, Terralba had to forgo its flagship wine because of the weather during the growing year, which could not guarantee a product that would meet the cellar's quality standards. This time round, the range is complete and all the wines we tasted were noteworthy. We'll begin with the Timorasso Stato, which always seems to stroll through to our Three Glass finals. The variety's signature minerality is even more apparent in this vintage, coming through strongly on both nose and palate. After the decision not to release the good Cortese any more, Timorasso is the only white still produced by Terralba. We'll move straight on to the reds, which account for the bulk of production as is often the case in the Colli Tortonesi. First up is Terralba 2003, from barbera only and first aged in barrique then slowly in glass before it leaves the cellar. A serious, well-structured wine, it has a dark hue and intriguing fragrances of red fruit laced with vanilla. The balance is impressive and the length very long indeed. We also very much liked the steel-vinified barbera-based L'Identità selection for its youthful alcohol and well-managed acidity on a palate that strikes a fine balance of structure and drinkability. In line with the cellar's philosophy, the Strà Loja blend of barbera, merlot and syrah is full bodied and very agreeable, as is the new La Vetta, an unusual blend of barbera and moradella.

○	Colli Tortonesi Bianco Stato '04	🍷🍷	5
●	Colli Tortonesi Rosso Terralba '03	🍷🍷	6
●	Colli Tortonesi Rosso Identità '05	🍷🍷	4*
●	Colli Tortonesi Rosso La Vetta '04	🍷	5
●	Colli Tortonesi Rosso Strà Loja '04	🍷	5
●	Colli Tortonesi Rosso Montegrande '01	YY	6
●	Colli Tortonesi Rosso Terralba '01	YY	6
○	Colli Tortonesi Bianco Stato '02	YY	5
○	Colli Tortonesi Bianco Stato '03	YY	5

BOCA (NO)

Le Piane
Loc. Le Piane
28010 Boca (NO)
tel. 0322866982
www.bocapiane.com

Christoph Künzli, his friends and his collaborators here in the hills at Boca have reached an important first turning point this year. Having invested considerable capital of passion, effort and skill, as well as material assets, in recovering Antonio Cerri's former cellar and vineyards, they spent a few years putting together the pieces of the puzzle that is a good territory-focused wine. The Le Piane Boca 2001 is their first evidence of absolute quality. The pure, deep nose offers a range of aromatics including well-defined and very varietal eucalyptus and bergamot as well as dried violets and currants. A sophisticated palate reveals subtle tannins that merge in depth with the supporting acidity, leaving room for pervasive savoury minerality as solo notes of white pepper, citrus and currants emerge from the chorus. This is a wine with an exciting future ahead of it and it will long be able to act as an ambassador for the DOC zone's potential. Le Piane 2004, from croatina with splashes of nebbiolo and vespolina, also impressed our tasters. Balsam and citrus emerge from croatina's characteristic concentration, already noted in the Boca. Here they fuse with denser, darker fruit led by ripe cherries and blueberries. The Maggiorina 2004, reviewed in error last year, is reminiscent on the nose of the two more noble wines. It has less structure but can still offer tempting drinkability.

●	Boca '01	▼▼	7
●	Colline Novaresi Le Piane '04	▼▼	6
●	Colline Novaresi La Maggiorina '04	▼	3
●	Boca '00	▽▽	5
●	Colline Novaresi Le Piane '03	▽▽	6
●	Boca '99	▽▽	7

BRA (CN)

Ascheri
via Piumati, 23
12042 Bra (CN)
tel. 0172412394
www.ascherivini.it

In the course of little more than a decade, the Ascheri cellar at Bra has been transformed. First, a comfortable new eatery appeared and then last year the Ascheris opened a large, modern hotel. At the helm of this enterprising operation is the capable Mattero Ascheri, helped by his determined mother Cristina. Every year, they turn out 300,000 bottles with the harvest from their splendid vine stock. In 2002, the Ascheris did not make any Barolos, which means this edition of the Guide is missing Barolo Sorano Coste & Bricco and Barolo Sorano. But there was a very impressive performance from the 2001 Barolo Vigna dei Pola, sourced from the Pisapola vineyard at Verduno. Aged for 24 months in large oak, it stays a further year in steel and one more in glass before release. The elegant nose has cinchona, autumn leaves and red fruit to introduce restrained, harmonious tannins and a long satisfyingly drinkable palate. Also very interesting is the Langhe Bianco Montelupa, from a viognier vineyard just outside Bra. Rich varietal aromas usher in its sweet entry on the palate and full progression. The fruit-forward Nebbiolo d'Alba Bricco San Giacomo is nice, as are the Verduno Pelaverga Do ut Des – a charity wine whose sales finance the projects of the St Vincent de Paul society – and two Dolcettos. The standard-label Barbera and Langhe Arneis picked up a Glass each.

●	Barolo V. dei Pola '01	▼▼	6*
○	Langhe Bianco Montalupa '04	▼▼	5
●	Nebbiolo d'Alba Bricco S. Giacomo '04	▼▼	5
●	Dolcetto d'Alba Nirane '05	▼▼	4*
●	Dolcetto d'Alba S. Rocco '05	▼▼	4*
●	Verduno Pelaverga Do ut Des '05	▼▼	4*
●	Barbera d'Alba V. Fontanelle '05	▼	4
○	Langhe Arneis Cristina Ascheri '05	▼	4
●	Barolo Sorano '00	▽▽▽	6
●	Barolo Sorano Coste & Bricco '00	▽▽	7
●	Barolo Sorano Coste & Bricco '99	▽▽	7
●	Barolo V. dei Pola '00	▽▽	6
●	Barolo Sorano '99	▽▽	6
●	Barolo Vigna dei Pola '99	▽▽	6

BRIGNANO FRASCATA (AL)

PAOLO POGGIO
VIA ROMA, 67
15050 BRIGNANO FRASCATA (AL)
TEL. 0131784929

There is a welcome return to a full profile for Paolo Poggio and his cellar. Located in the hamlet of Brignano Frascata, it was one of the first wineries in the area to bottle its wines and understand the potential of the local timorasso grape, which it developed and promoted. This year, the Ronchetto is even better than the excellent 2003 vintage. Its vibrant straw yellow is followed by crisp minerality and citrus. Good acidity on the palate then accompanies white peach and a tenuous hint of smokiness. Apart from the Timorasso, the wines that caught the panel's eye were Barbera Derio and Croatina Prosone. The Barbera is a banker, and one of the finest selections from the territory, but the Croatina is a welcome surprise. Its purple red proffers captivating spices and berry fruit before the palate's thrust takes you through to a sweetish but not cloying finale. In contrast, Prosone is vigorous and beefy, giving balsam with vanillaed sensations from its long stay in wood. The tannins are still very much to the fore but this is a bottle to lay down in your cellar. Less demanding but equally good value for money are the Cortese Campogallo and Barbera Campo la Bà, the former presenting attractive fragrances and the Barbera showing nicely alcohol-rich.

●	Colli Tortonesi Barbera Derio '04	**YY**	4
○	Colli Tortonesi Ronchetto '04	**YY**	3*
●	Colli Tortonesi Rosso Prosone '04	**YY**	4
●	Colli Tortonesi Campo la Bà '05	**Y**	3*
○	Colli Tortonesi Campogallo '05	**Y**	2*
●	Colli Tortonesi Barbera Derio '00	YY	4
●	Colli Tortonesi Barbera Derio '01	YY	4
●	Colli Tortonesi Barbera Derio '03	YY	4

BRUSNENGO (BI)

BARNI
VIA FORTE, 63
13862 BRUSNENGO (BI)
TEL. 015985977

Filippo Barni continues his endeavours as a grower and an artist. His bottles flaunt labels reproducing the canvases he likes to paint between harvests. Filippo moved to Brusnengo in the mid 1990s when he purchases the long-established Mesola vineyard in its splendid south-facing sun-trap. The six hectares were planted in the early 20th century using the old maggiorina training system and they yield croatina, nebbiolo, uva rara and erbaluce while the small plot at Brusnengo produces erbaluce and chardonnay. The products that emerge from the vineyards reflect the personality of their maker: they are characterful and have a strong link with the territory. The best of the range this year was the Passito Cantagal 2003, from erbaluce dried bunch by bunch for five months. The fruit lost 80 per cent of its weight and after a year's ageing in wood, the wine has strong sensations of dried apricots, pineapple and jam, but never threatens to cloy. It went through to the finals and was among the best in its category. Two Glasses went to the Bramaterra Doss Pilun 2002 and the Mesolone 2003. The former impressed our panel more thanks to spicy ginger, oak and an austere, tannin-heavy palate. Mesolone is the cellar's traditional flagship and confirmed its good track record, giving plums and red fruit in a rustic, territory-driven style. Albaciara Bianco 2005 is an interesting wine from erbaluce with a splash of international varieties. It has moderately complex aromatics and elegant vegetal notes.

○	Cantagal '03	**YY**	7
●	Bramaterra V. Doss Pilun '02	**YY**	5
●	Coste della Sesia Rosso Mesolone '03	**YY**	5
○	Albaciara Bianco '05	**Y**	5
●	Coste della Sesia Rosso Mesolone '02	YY	5
●	Coste della Sesia Rosso Torrearsa '02	YY	5
●	Bramaterra V. Doss Pilun '01	YY	6
●	Coste della Sesia Rosso Mesolone '01	YY	5
●	Coste della Sesia Rosso Torrearsa '01	YY	5

★ Michele Chiarlo

s.da Nizza-Canelli, 99
14042 Calamandrana (AT)
tel. 0141769030
www.chiarlo.it

Even though the dreadful weather of 2002 prevented production of the noblest Barolo selections, the intriguing, generous Barberas and Nebbiolos that did make it onto the shelves shot Michele Chiarlo to the top of our table. All the wines from this long-standing winery attracted attention, starting with the deep, well-structured, very complex Countacc!, from syrah, barbera and nebbiolo. The Barbaresco Asili 2003 has intense, concentrated fragrances of black fruits, sweet spices, dried roses and eucalyptus backed by a close-knit tannic weave and an endlessly long finish. The excellent Barolo Triumviratum Riserva 1999 comes from fruit sourced at the Cannubi, Cerequio and Brunate vineyards. Its deep, lustrous garnet red is accompanied by supremely elegant aromatics of sophisticated pipe tobacco, liquorice, liqueur cherries, cocoa powder and spring flowers. On the palate, the perfect equilibrium of structure, alcohol and bright acidity is very satisfying and the long finish is lifted by a precise reprise of the aromatics on the nose. Cipressi della Court 2004 is well defined and managed, but Barbera La Court 2003 has quite astounding personality that comes through on a deep nose of currants, morello cherry, cocoa powder and pencil lead set off by a thrilling balsamic backdrop. The warm palate echoes the nose with vigour and vitality driven by its massive extract, appealing, well-gauged tannins and nicely modulated acidity. Three resounding Glasses. And the other labels were well up to snuff.

●	Barbera d'Asti Sup. Nizza La Court '03	TTT	6
●	Barolo Triumviratum Ris. '99	TT	8
●	Monferrato Montemareto Countacc! '03	TT	6
●	Barbaresco Asili '03	TT	7
●	Barbera d'Asti Sup. Cipressi della Court '04	TT	4*
○	Moscato d'Asti Smentiò '04	TT	5
○	Gavi del Comune di Gavi Rovereto '05	TT	4*
●	Barbera d'Asti Sup. Nizza La Court '00	YYY	6
●	Barbera d'Asti Sup. Nizza La Court '01	YYY	6

CALAMANDRANA (AT)

La Giribaldina

reg. San Vito, 39
14042 Calamandrana (AT)
tel. 0141718043
www.giribaldina.com

Mariagrazia Macchi and her son Emanuele have help from agronomist Piero Roseo and oenologist Beppe Caviola. Together, they have built up La Giribaldini's image on a foundation of constant experimentation and territory focus. This year's range is excellent, starting with the Barbera Monte del Mare 2005. A steel-fermented wine, it has a purplish ruby red hue that heralds a ripe nose of finesse and elegance that opens on spice and crisp fruit aromas of morello cherry, plum, blueberry and liqueur fruit. The palate has textbook balance and its tannins enfold rich, highly drinkable fruit that never overdoes the opulence on its way through to a very satisfyingly persistent finish. Barbera Vigneti della Val Sarmassa 2004 has very complex aromas that range across a swath of flowers and fruit. Concentrated and well sustained in the mouth, it progresses gradually to its savoury finish over a velvet-soft tannic weave. Barbera d'Asti Cala delle Mandrie 2004 is another stand-out for the impeccable quality of its spectrum of aromatics, including currants, blueberries, morello cherries and sweet spice and its marvellous dried flower bouquet. Subtly woven supporting tannins and an intense finale round off the palate in a nice, well-defined reprise of the nose. The very good Sauvignon Ferro di Cavallo 2005 is entirely vinified in steel and the dried-grape Passito is very good.

●	Barbera d'Asti Sup. Cala delle Mandrie '04	TT	5
●	Barbera d'Asti Sup. Vign. della Val Sarmassa '04	TT	4
○	Piemonte Moscato Passito '04	TT	4
●	Barbera d'Asti Monte del Mare '05	TT	3*
○	Monferrato Bianco Ferro di Cavallo '05	T	4
●	Barbera d'Asti Sup. Cala delle Mandrie '03	YY	5
●	Barbera d'Asti Sup. Cala delle Mandrie '01	YY	5
●	Barbera d'Asti Sup. Vign. della Val Sarmassa '03	YY	4

CALOSSO (AT)

Tenuta dei Fiori

fraz. Rodotiglia
via Valcalosso, 3
14052 Calosso (AT)
tel. 0141853819
www.tenutadeifiori.com

Walter Bosticardo, the go-ahead owner of Tenuta dei Fiori, continues to make progress, as does the overall quality of his wines. The labels he presented are all modern in style but respect tradition and territoriality. We particularly liked the Monferrato Rosso Cinque File 2003 with its dark, purple-flecked ruby hue. Its deep, expressive nose flaunts intense cherry, strawberry, mulberry and plum fruit that melds seamlessly with spice and vegetal notes. The characterful palate has an unusual wealth of extract, combining power with finesse over a close-knit tannic weave through to thoroughly satisfying length on the back palate. Barbera Tulipanonero 2001 is a brilliant if not particularly deep ruby red. Juicy and succulent, with crunchy black fruit sensations that melt into a backdrop of pencil lead, liquorice, cinchona and sweet spice before attractive balance and a warm, full-bodied structure in the mouth. We were less persuaded by the Monferrato Rosso L'Ultimo, a blend of three native varieties – barbera, dolcetto and freisa. Its slightly forward colour introduces attractive fragrances but it is let down by nervy acidity, over-assertive tannins and a slightly drying back palate.

●	Monferrato Rosso Cinque File '03	2 glasses (black)	5
●	Barbera d'Asti Tulipanonero '01	2 glasses (black)	5
●	Monferrato Rosso L'Ultimo '04	1 glass (black)	4
●	Barbera d'Asti Rusticardi Castello di Calosso '01	2 glasses (white)	6
●	Monferrato Rosso Cinque File '01	2 glasses (white)	5
●	Barbera d'Asti Sup. Rusticardi 1933 '03	2 glasses (white)	6
●	Barbera d'Asti Tulipanonero '97	2 glasses (white)	5

CALOSSO (AT)

Scagliola

fraz. San Siro
via San Siro, 42
14052 Calosso (AT)
tel. 0141853183

The Scagliola family has been keeping this cellar firmly on the path of quality, investing to raise the quality of the wines even higher and purchasing new vineyards. Work is also under way on a new cellar and now Giovanni has joined the team, fresh from his studies at the Alba Institute of Oenology. The quality of the range this year was very impressive, starting with the Barbera d'Asti SanSì 2003 Selezione. Its concentrated aromatics and sweet, opulent palate are elegant and aristocratic, the structure is solid, the tannins are velvety and the length admirable. The SanSì 2004 has an attractive personality, offering intense, persistent fragrances that focus on sweeter notes, with subtle blackcurrant, plum and cocoa powder laced with spice. The Monferrato Rosso Azörd 2004, from barbera, nebbiolo and cabernet, is stunningly powerful, deep and rich in personality on its second release. The admirable sensations of eucalyptus, thyme, roses and black berry fruit herald a palate that underlines the stature of the wine with its sensual, mouthfilling tannic weave and remarkably enjoyable persistence. Two comfortable Glasses went to Barbera Frem 2005. Dolcetto Busiord is anything but predictable, as are the two versions of Chardonnay: we preferred the steel-fermented Casot dan Vian. Finally, Moscato d'Asti Volo di Farfalle 2005 is one of the finest interpretations of the type.

●	Barbera d'Asti Sup. SanSì Sel. '03	2 glasses (black)	7
●	Monferrato Rosso Azörd '04	2 glasses (black)	5
●	Barbera d'Asti Frem '05	2 glasses (black)	4
●	Barbera d'Asti Sup. SanSì '04	2 glasses (black)	5
○	Piemonte Chardonnay Casot dan Vian '05	2 glasses (black)	3*
○	Moscato d'Asti Volo di Farfalle '05	2 glasses (black)	3*
●	Monferrato Dolcetto Busiord '05	1 glass (black)	3*
○	Piemonte Chardonnay '04	1 glass (black)	5
●	Barbera d'Asti Sup. SanSì Sel. '00	3 glasses (white)	7
●	Barbera d'Asti Sup. SanSì Sel. '01	3 glasses (white)	7

CANALE (CN)

Cascina Ca' Rossa

Loc. Cascina Ca' Rossa, 56
12043 Canale (CN)
tel. 017398348
www.cascinacarossa.com

Angelo Ferrio is the living embodiment of a territory that has risen to wine prominence in a relatively short period of time and today is facing the consequences of this achievement. A new production profile has to be managed. Distribution and image have to be organized. A well-defined style has to be created and projected to the market. The Ferrios' small estate is tackling these new challenges with rigour, aiming for quality in a range with no frills. The family has rethought some of its thoroughbreds – the Roero Mompissano is kept in the cellar for a year longer and aged in large wood – and given the standard-label wines a new livery. These are major adjustments that have in no way altered Angelo's generous, passionate approach to winemaking. He is showing Roero the way forward. The range has never been this good. Never before have the Ferrios sent all three of their flagship reds to out finals but this year it was hard to decide which was best. Barbera Mulassa 2004 is fantastic. Elegant, fruit-forward yet sinewy, it is acidulous without slipping into rustic asperity and soft yet never predictable. We thought it deserved our top score of Three Glasses. This year's Roero wines offer two very different interpretations of the type. Mompissano has taken advantage of its leisurely ageing to emerge austere, earthy and supported by excellent raw material. Audinaggio 2004, in contrast, exploits the freshness of the growing year to produce fruit on the nose and impeccable consistency in the mouth. It, too, is a gem. The standard-label Langhe Nebbiolo is admirable and the Arneis is well made.

●	Barbera d'Alba Mulassa '04	▼▼▼	6
●	Roero Mompissano '03	▼▼	6
●	Roero Audinaggio '04	▼▼	6
●	Langhe Nebbiolo '05	▼▼	4*
○	Roero Arneis Merica '05	▼	4
●	Roero Audinaggio '01	▽▽▽	6
●	Roero Vigna Audinaggio '96	▽▽▽	6
●	Barbera d'Alba Mulassa '99	▽▽▽	6
●	Barbera d'Alba Mulassa '01	▽▽	6
●	Barbera d'Alba Mulassa '03	▽▽	6
●	Roero Audinaggio '03	▽▽	6
●	Roero Audinaggio '00	▽▽	6
●	Roero Mompissano '01	▽▽	6
●	Roero Audinaggio '99	▽▽	6

CANALE (CN)

Cascina Chicco

via Valentino, 144
12043 Canale (CN)
tel. 0173979411 - 0173979069
www.cascinachicco.com

Not many Roero cellars can put together an extensive range of wines that maintain excellent quality all along the line. One such winery is Cascina Chicco, an influential estate on the left bank of the Tanaro that combines a family dimension – the Faccenda parents, children and in-laws are all involved – with a shrewd entrepreneurial approach that has taken production to nearly 150,000 bottles a year, sourced from 20 hectares under vine and processed in the practical cellar just outside Canale. The stylistic differentiation of the various labels is achieved through sophisticated vineyard management and vinification techniques that focus on concentration without excess, structure that does not jeopardize elegance and longevity that is never at the expense of freshness or drinkability. The news this year is the exploit of the arneis-based dried-grape Passito. Arcàss 2004 represents a comeback for the wine type – its name comes from the word for "return" in the popular Piedmontese ball game of "pallone elastico" – and it astonishes with its candied peel, dried flowers and figs aromas and the power of a palate that never loses site of poised elegance. It is the best-ever version of the label and well worth Three Glasses. Not far behind are two long-established wines, Barbera Bric Loira 2004 and Roero Valmaggiore 2003. The Barbera is spicy and full bodied whereas the Roero is austere and monumental. Only slightly less complex are the Nebbiolo Mompissano and the 2004 Roero Montespinato. The standard-label Barbera is also good. Finally, the two whites put on a fine performance to round off a range that never dips below Two Glasses.

○	Arcàss Passito '04	▼▼▼	6
●	Roero Valmaggiore '03	▼▼	5
●	Barbera d'Alba Bric Loira '04	▼▼	5
●	Nebbiolo d'Alba Mompissano '04	▼▼	5
●	Roero Montespinato '04	▼▼	4*
●	Barbera d'Alba Granera Alta '05	▼▼	4*
○	Langhe Favorita '05	▼▼	4*
○	Roero Arneis Anterisio '05	▼▼	4*
●	Barbera d'Alba Bric Loira '97	▽▽▽	5
●	Barbera d'Alba Bric Loira '98	▽▽▽	5
●	Nebbiolo d'Alba Mompissano '99	▽▽▽	5
●	Roero Valmaggiore Sup. '01	▽▽	5
●	Barbera d'Alba Bric Loira '03	▽▽	5

CANALE (CN)

Cornarea

via Valentino, 150
12043 Canale (CN)
tel. 017365636 - 0173979091

Last year, we started the Cornarea profile by pointing out how enthusiastically the cellar had welcomed the promotion of Roero Arneis to DOCG status. The Bovone family was one of the first to invest in premium interpretations of the type, which is still all too often regarded as a second-rank wine in the Italian panorama. Those who remember past Cornarea Arneis wines will be able to testify to its potential, provided parameters for excellence are implemented in vineyard and cellar. Here, there is no lack of attention. We even noted further improvement in the overall standard of the range thanks to a surprising newcomer. Andrè 2003 is a table wine obtained solely from late-harvested arneis grapes. Our initial fears – an aged Arneis, from fruit harvested late in an already very hot year – vanished at first sniff, which revealed a complex minerally, almost iodine-like bouquet with petrolly notes that bring to mind some of the whites of Alsace. All that promise is maintained on the palate, which perfectly offsets the still bright acidity with subtle, restrained sweetness. It has loads of body and lingers remarkably, making an excellent impression overall. As we wait for the famous dried-grape Passito, which will be back on our tasting table next year, the Arneis 2005 is as ever one of the best of its category, showing savoury, sinewy and fragrant. Both reds, the Roero and the Nebbiolo, come from the 2003 growing year and have managed to tame the vintage's heat, preserving freshness over their crisp, fruity base.

○ Andrè '03	▼▼	5
● Nebbiolo d'Alba '03	▼▼	4
● Roero '03	▼▼	4
○ Roero Arneis '05	▼▼	4
○ Tarasco Passito '00	▽▽	6
○ Tarasco Passito '01	▽▽	6
○ Tarasco Passito '99	▽▽	6
● Roero Sup. '00	▽▽	5
● Roero Sup. '01	▽▽	5

CANALE (CN)

★ Matteo Correggia

loc. Case Sparse Garbinetto, 124
12043 Canale (CN)
tel. 0173978009
www.matteocorreggia.com

Year after year, Roero's celebrated Matteo Correggia cellar prompts reflection that goes beyond the undoubted excellence of its wines. Five years after Matteo's much-lamented passing, the winery is moved by two distinct but interdependent spirits. One is the tangible heritage of the brilliant founder and the other is the grace of Ornella Costa, who continues determinedly along the path of insights charted by her husband. We can say that Ornella is not alone. The top-flight agronomic and winemaking team is coordinated by Luca Rostagno and today has valuable input from Gian Piero Romana in the vineyard and Gianfranco Cordero in the cellar. Discreet advice is always on hand from old friend Giorgio Rivetti. And of course Ornella also enjoys the respect and affection of producers and lovers of the wines that have come to represent this territory. The range was finally complete this time, after the sacrifices imposed by the eminently forgettable 2002 vintage. Roero Ròche d'Ampsèj did marvellously, showing warm, doughy and austere in the 2003 edition. Langhe Le Marne Grigie 2003 may not be a territory wine but it is at the top of its class. Roero-grown merlot, cabernet and syrah fuse to produce an elegant, enviably balanced wine that lets all three varieties express themselves. And the trio of immense products is rounded off by the sumptuous Barbera Marun 2004, which finds a far from obvious balance of acidity and alcohol that take it back to the big time. In fact, our tasters gave this Barbera archetype Three Glasses. Nebbiolo La Val dei Preti is always good and the rest of the range is impeccable, with a special mention for the two interpretations of Anthos, a brachetto vinified both as a dry wine and from part-dried fruit.

● Barbera d'Alba Marun '04	▼▼▼	6
● Langhe Rosso Le Marne Grigie '03	▼▼	7
● Roero Ròche d'Ampsèj '03	▼▼	8
● Anthos Passito	▼▼	5
● Barbera d'Alba '04	▼▼	4*
○ Langhe Bianco Matteo Correggia '04	▼▼	6
● Nebbiolo d'Alba La Val dei Preti '04	▼▼	6
● Anthos	▼▼	4*
● Roero '04	▼	4
○ Roero Arneis '05	▼	4
● Roero Ròche d'Ampsèj '00	▽▽▽	8
● Roero Ròche d'Ampsèj '01	▽▽▽	8

CANALE (CN)

Deltetto

C.so Alba, 43
12043 Canale (CN)
tel. 0173979383
www.deltetto.com

There's no stopping Tonino Deltetto. For years, his profile has been one of the most exciting to write. New cellar areas, labels and organizational changes mean that there is always something to add to our previous reports in the Guide. If we had to sum up Tonino's passion in winemaking in a word, that word would be "bubbles". The fine quality and commercial success of the Extra Brut Riserva have encouraged Tonino to persevere with the wine. Actually, he has added a couple of variations to the theme and we will be able to toast from this year with Deltetto Brut, a slightly sweeter, more voluptuous version of the Riserva, and Extra Brut Rosé, a marriage of nebbiolo and pinot nero that has produced an attractive, not too challenging but superbly made, spumante. As we wait for Tonino to fine-tune his new toys, we can enjoy a remarkable, flowery Riserva 2003 with good fizz, breadth and persistence. The running-in period is over and on its fourth release, this is a great version of the wine. Skilful handling of whites is also evident in the still wines. Every version of Arneis and Favorita is a winner. But Deltetto can also make serious reds. Barbera Rocca delle Marasche 2004, from fruit harvested slightly later than usual, shot through to the finals where its monumental nose and magisterial combination of acidity, fruit and alcohol stunned the judges. Three Glasses was the verdict. Complex spice, autumn leaves and earth tempt on the Roero Braja 2004, and the tannins are silky. Barbera Bramé 2004 also did well.

●	Barbera d'Alba Rocca delle Marasche '04	TTT	6
●	Roero Braja '04	TT	5
○	Deltetto Extra Brut Ris. '03	TT	5
●	Barbera d'Alba Bramé '04	TT	4*
○	Langhe Favorita Sarvai '05	TT	4*
○	Roero Arneis S. Michele '05	TT	4*
○	Deltetto Brut	TT	5
○	Roero Arneis Daivej '05	T	4
⊙	Deltetto Extra Brut Rosé	T	5
●	Roero Braja '01	YY	5
●	Barbera d'Alba Rocca delle Marasche '03	YY	6
●	Roero Braja '00	YY	5
●	Roero Braja '03	YY	5

CANALE (CN)

Filippo Gallino

Fraz. Valle del Pozzo, 63
12043 Canale (CN)
tel. 017398112
www.filippogallino.com

For years, the Gallino family has been advocating authentic, rigorous viticulture firmly rooted in the territory. They shun any fripperies that might distract from the objective of supreme quality while respecting tradition in their vineyards of arneis, barbera and nebbiolo. In the cellar, the approach is shrewdly modern and the use of small wood never masks the full expression of aromas and fragrances. Every year, Filippo and Gianni Gallino engage in a duel over their bottling – and our tasting – period for the top-flight reds. The wines' youth, urgent work in the vineyard and the wrong phase of the moon (that's right!) extend this crucial operation beyond the deadline for our profiles. But when the wines do arrive, we have to admit that once again farming lore knows best. This time, the two Superiore 2004s maintain a standard of quality that is getting impressively consistent. The Barbera and Roero show good progression and unusually pulpy fruit in an elegant, refined style. These are two big wines that keep their exuberance under control with great class. Never excessive, they impress on tasting and – more important – drink quite beautifully. We just preferred the soft Barbera this time for its bright acidity and power. It's a Three Glass gem. The rest of this impeccably consistent range is made to the same standards. In all, the Gallinos obtain 60,000 bottles a year from their 12 hectares of vineyards.

●	Barbera d'Alba Sup. '04	TTT	5
●	Roero Sup. '04	TT	6
●	Barbera d'Alba '05	TT	4*
○	Roero Arneis '05	TT	4*
●	Langhe Nebbiolo '05	T	4
●	Roero Sup. '01	YYY	6
●	Roero Sup. '03	YYY	6
●	Barbera d'Alba Sup. '97	YYY	5
●	Roero Sup. '98	YYY	6
●	Roero Sup. '99	YYY	6
●	Barbera d'Alba Sup. '01	YY	5
●	Barbera d'Alba Sup. '03	YY	5
●	Barbera d'Alba Sup. '00	YY	5

CANALE (CN)

MALVIRÀ
LOC. CANOVA
VIA CASE SPARSE, 144
12043 CANALE (CN)
TEL. 0173978145
www.malvira.com

Take a glance at the table below: two points stand out clearly. One is a quantitative consideration because it tells us that the Malvirà range is at full strength. The 12 labels, equally distributed between whites and reds, represent the maximum potential ever presented at our tastings. The second point is qualitative for the cellar is performing at a quite extraordinary level. Brothers Massimo and Roberto Damonte have been working well. From their Villa Tiboldi hotel, they can gaze with satisfaction on the cellar below and on the neatly arranged rows of vines on the hillsides around. We'll get on with our review. Traditionally, the cellar favours whites, from the standard-label Arneis to the Saglietto 2004 via the Trinità and Renesio selections. All present the sensations typical of the variety: minerality, herbaceousness, fruit and savouriness. The Treuve 2004 from chardonnay, sauvignon and arneis and the Bianco 2005 are labelled Langhe but have all the marks of the Roero terroir. The Bianco in particular has impressive freshness and sauvignon's varietal typicity. On the red front, Roero 2003 was on form. Mombeltramo is softer and readier for the corkscrew but the austere, wonderfully elegant Trinità is a gem of a wine that earned Three Glasses. But the surprise came from the Barberas. The still very good 2003 paid the price of the very hot summer but the 2004 is riding high, having combined acidity, structure, finesse and body in a seamless whole. Finally, the two Langhe reds are excellent.

●	Roero Sup. Trinità '03	🍷🍷🍷	6
●	Roero Sup. Mombeltramo '03	🍷🍷	6
●	Barbera d'Alba S. Michele '04	🍷🍷	4*
○	Langhe Bianco '05	🍷🍷	4*
●	Barbera d'Alba Sup. S. Michele '03	🍷🍷	4
●	Langhe Rosso S. Guglielmo '03	🍷🍷	5
○	Langhe Bianco Treuve '04	🍷🍷	4
●	Langhe Nebbiolo '04	🍷🍷	4
○	Roero Arneis Saglietto '04	🍷🍷	4
○	Roero Arneis Renesio '05	🍷🍷	4
○	Roero Arneis Trinità '05	🍷🍷	4
○	Roero Arneis '05	🍷	3
●	Roero Sup. Mombeltramo '00	🍷🍷🍷	6
●	Roero Sup. Trinità '01	🍷🍷🍷	6

CANALE (CN)

MONCHIERO CARBONE
VIA SANTO STEFANO ROERO, 2
12043 CANALE (CN)
TEL. 017395568
www.monchierocarbone.com

There is no family news this time – two new babies in the last two Guides are enough for the time being – but there are plenty of new developments at the Monchiero Carbone winery in Canale. Francesco has this Roero estate well in hand, where very functional new fermentation cellars were recently opened and the vine stock was expanded to more than 12 hectares – there are new plots in the pipeline in the municipality of Priocca - bringing total production to 80,000 bottles. The rigorous style and personality that distinguish the range can be found in every bottle, from the territory-driven whites to the full-bodied reds and the moscato-based sweet wine. In the two Arneis 2005s, we liked the marked acidity of the long-established Re Cit and the streamlined flower and fruit elegance of the more recent Cecu d'la Biunda. The arneis and chardonnay Tamardì gets better with every vintage. And the reds were also on form, Barbera MomBirone putting on one of its finest performances ever. Intense, with spice, berry fruit, black cherry and rain-soaked earth, it unveils a taut, full-bodied palate with great thrust and length. The Roeros come from two vintages that could not have been more different. Srü captures all the freshness of 2004, showing round and delicious, while Printi tackled 2003's heat with a beautifully balanced nose of florality and tertiary notes followed by juicy pulp nicely honed to a polish by the oak. Finally, a round of applause for the well-gauged sweetness of the Passito, which is always a pleasure to taste.

●	Roero Printi '03	🍷🍷	6
●	Barbera d'Alba MonBirone '04	🍷🍷	5
○	Piemonte Moscato Passito Sorì di Ruchin '04	🍷🍷	5
●	Roero Srü '04	🍷🍷	5
○	Langhe Bianco Tamardì '04	🍷🍷	4*
○	Roero Arneis Cecu d'la Biunda '05	🍷🍷	4*
○	Roero Arneis Re Cit '05	🍷🍷	4*
●	Langhe Nebbiolo Regret '04	🍷	4
●	Barbera d'Alba Pelisa '05	🍷	4
●	Roero Printi '00	🍷🍷🍷	6
●	Roero Printi '99	🍷🍷🍷	6
●	Roero Printi '01	🍷🍷	6
●	Barbera d'Alba MonBirone '03	🍷🍷	5

CANALE (CN)

PACE

FRAZ. MADONNA DI LORETO
CASCINA PACE, 52
12043 CANALE (CN)
TEL. 0173979544

Yet another newcomer has emerged in the Roero territory on the left bank of the Tanaro river. It's a zone that is acquiring oenological visibility thanks mainly to family-run estates that may work with small numbers but keep quality in their sights. This little introduction brings us to the Negro brothers' winery. Dino and Pietro inherited their property from their father Giovanni, who recently passed away. Before him, grandfather Bernardo worked the farm at Madonna di Loreto, a village that looks as if it came straight out of an impressionist painting with its little church, verdant hills and cottages scattered among the vines. Negros have worked the land here since 1919, the year they moved from a neighbouring municipality and founded Cascina Pace, where the cellar is now located. Over the years, they have gradually acquired 20 hectares of vines, from which they obtain 25,000 bottles a year, selling off much of the harvest. Arneis, barbera and nebbiolo are Roero's oenological trinity and the Negros stay true to tradition, releasing only a few labels from a cellar where Enzo Quinterno consults. The vineyard, meanwhile, is the domain of agronomist Nicola Argamante. Both Barbera 2004s are excellent. The standard-label is a fresh-tasting early drinker while the Superiore is a classic serious, but not overwhelming, wine with lots of flavour and nice acidity. Best of the three nebbiolo-based wines is the fruity Roero 2004 with its well-gauged tannins. The well-managed 2003 is let down by the very hot growing year and the young Nebbiolo is all attractive freshness. The Arneis is very good.

●	Barbera d'Alba '04	**YY**	4
●	Barbera d'Alba Sup. '04	**YY**	4
●	Roero '04	**YY**	4
○	Roero Arneis '05	**YY**	3*
●	Roero Sup. '03	**Y**	5
●	Langhe Nebbiolo '05	**Y**	4
●	Barbera Sup. '03	YY	4
●	Roero Sup. '01	YY	4
●	Roero Sup. '02	YY	4
●	Roero '03	YY	4

CANALE (CN)

PORELLO

C.SO ALBA, 71
12043 CANALE (CN)
TEL. 0173979324 - 0173611147
www.porellovini.it

Now he is no longer a newcomer, Marco Porello can point to a well-earned track record of reliability. We had been aware of his serious approach for some time. All he lacked was the touch of maturity and the experience that today he has in spades. Marco has invested heavily in his impressive cellar next to the castle at Guarene and now he is concentrating on his range of wines. There are one or two new labels, as well as new developments among his established wines. For example, the Arneis has a new character and force deriving from drastic vineyard management, bold vinification – no stabilizing, inoculation with cultured yeasts – and a general desire to get as much as possible out of Roero's signature white. The 2005 edition shows the way forward. Clean white-fleshed fruit joins wild flowers and sweet almonds before the taut, acidic palate takes you through to a finale that reprises the fruit nicely. But the top of the range is still the Roero Torretta. In 2004, Marco turned out a perfect version. Intriguingly complex aromatics hint at spices and berry fruit, melding seamlessy into vanilla and evolved sensations. A soft, well-structured palate echoes the nose and lingers on the finish. It was so good that it earned Marco the first Three Glasses of his career. The rest of the line-up is good, with a special note of praise for the crunchy, well-rounded Barbera Filatura 2004, one of the best of its category.

●	Roero Torretta '04	YYY	5
●	Barbera d'Alba Filatura '04	YY	5
●	Nebbiolo d'Alba '04	**YY**	4
●	Barbera d'Alba Mommiano '05	**YY**	4
○	Roero Arneis Camestrì '05	**YY**	3*
○	Langhe Favorita '05	**Y**	3
●	Roero Torretta '01	YY	4
●	Roero Torretta '02	YY	5
●	Roero Torretta '03	YY	5
●	Barbera d'Alba Filatura '01	YY	4
●	Barbera d'Alba Filatura '03	YY	5

CANALE (CN)

Enrico Serafino
c.so Asti, 5
12043 Canale (CN)
tel. 0173967111
www.barbero1891.it

Roero's wine map is studded with a vast number of very different estates. In the popular imagination, Roero means small or medium-size family-run wineries but it would be wrong to exclude from this picture some much larger enterprises, in terms of volume, that are still very ambitious about quality. The story of Enrico Serafino is emblematic. The business was famous in the late 19th century for its sales of Piedmontese wines but fell out of favour in the course of the 20th century. Today, it is a jewel in the huge Barbero-Campari group's crown. We would single out from the winemaking team that has contributed to the estate's comeback the house oenologist, Daniele Saracco, and external consultant Beppe Caviola. Nor should we forget the foresight and enthusiasm of Emilio Barbero, a brilliant boss with very clear ideas. Gradually, the range of wines is settling down. Rationalizing the labels is sure to bring clearer focus and visibility to the wines in the shops. As we wait for the Spumante Alta Langa 2003 – the 2002 was excellent on retasting – the most complete wines appear to be the territory-based reds. Barbera Parduné 2003 has shaken off the torrid summer heat and shows very fresh. Its fruit has definition, complexity and depth. In the mouth, it is richly extracted, attractively alcoholic and enjoyably acidic. Just a mark or two below is the Roero 2004, which still has to mellow out its tannins. The panel liked the Barbaresco 2003 and the Barolo 2001, which already has excellent texture. We preferred the Arneis to the Chardonnay and the Dolcetto is well typed.

●	Barbera d'Alba Sup. Parduné '03	TT	4*
●	Barolo '01	TT	7
●	Barbaresco '03	TT	6
●	Roero Sup. '04	TT	4
○	Roero Arneis '05	TT	4
●	Dolcetto d'Alba '05	T	3
○	Langhe Chardonnay '05	T	3
●	Roero Sup. '03	YY	4
●	Roero Sup. Pasiunà '00	YY	4
●	Barbera d'Alba Sup. Parduné '01	YY	4
●	Roero Sup. Pasiunà '01	YY	4
○	Alta Langa M. Cl. '02	YY	5

CANELLI (AT)

L'Armangia
fraz. San Giovanni, 122
14053 Canelli (AT)
tel. 0141824947
www.armangia.it

Ignazio Giovine runs L'Armangia, a young, dynamic winery with a range of whistle-clean, modern wines sold at attractive prices. The three fresh-tasting 2005 whites from international varieties – Ignazio has no faith in cortese grown at Canelli – all earned One full Glass. We thought the citrussy, varietal Sauvignon EnneEnne was better than the two Chardonnays, Non, steel vinified and aged, and Pratorotondo, part of which goes into barrique to mature. The three Barberas deserve attention. Sopra Berruti 2005 is a dark wine that gives blueberry jam and a juicy, savoury palate, Titon 2003, which matures for 18 months in oak, is powerful, concentrated and very warm in the mouth, and the 2003 Vignali, the former Castello di Calosso 2003, comes from vines more than 70 years old, matures exclusively in new barriques and has emerged with a youthful personality and tannins that still have to get into step with the seriously dense, juicy structure. Monferrato Rosso Pacifico 2003, a blend of nebbiolo, cabernet, merlot, barbera and freisa, is very nice. The dark, deep hue introduces fresh raspberries and vanilla before the powerful, sweet entry on the palate shows good balance and takes you through to an appealing liquorice-tinged finish. We'll conclude with the sweet wines. The Moscato d'Asti Il Giai 2005 gives faint sage and mint and the 2004 Mesicaseu is obtained from very ripe moscato and chardonnay.

●	Barbera d'Asti Sup. Titon '03	TT	4
●	Barbera d'Asti Vignali '03	TT	6
●	Monferrato Rosso Pacifico '03	TT	4
●	Barbera d'Asti Sopra Berruti '05	TT	3*
○	Mesicaseu '04	T	4
○	Moscato d'Asti Il Giai '05	T	3
○	Monferrato Bianco EnneEnne '05	T	3
○	Piemonte Chardonnay Non '05	T	3
○	Piemonte Chardonnay Pratorotondo '05	T	3
●	Barbera d'Asti Vignali Castello di Calosso '01	YY	6
●	Barbera d'Asti Sup. Titon '01	YY	4
●	Monferrato Rosso Pacifico '01	YY	4

CANELLI (AT)

Cascina Barisel

reg. San Giovanni, 2
14053 Canelli (AT)
tel. 0141824848
www.barisel.it

As you head out of Canelli on the road for Moasca, you'll see on your right the Penna brothers' Cascina Barisel standing among the family vineyards. Annual production is around 30,000 bottles, most accounted for by Moscato and Barbera d'Asti. Our tasting revealed the cellar's aim of turning out territory-driven, original wines that fit no moulds, made while respecting the environment and the equilibrium of the vineyard. L'avìja means bee in Piedmontese and it is also the name of this rich, very sweet Moscato from grapes left to overripen on the vine and then part-dried on racks in the cellar. The 2004 edition is deep gold and gives tropical banana, honey and balsam before the palate unveils its sweetness from 13 per cent acquired alcohol and 23 per cent overall, taking the residual sugar into account. As ever, the 2005 Moscato d'Asti is very good. Some 13,000 bottles were released of this deep, vibrant-hued wine that gives quince, peach and sage preceding a fresh-tasting, juicy, creamy palate with a fragrant finish so dry it is almost tangy. The exemplary Barbera d'Asti 2004 comes from vines more than 40 years old, all at Canelli. The dense, balanced palate is marvellously drinkable and the price tag is more than honest. Barbera Superiore La Cappelletta 2004 is a more serious wine but still very young. It's sourced from a vineyard planted in 1955 on the crest of a well-aspected hill. Last up was a white called Foravìa, which means out of the ordinary in the local dialect. It's a straightforward, well-made Favorita.

○	L'avìja '04	▼▼	6
●	Barbera d'Asti '04	▼▼	4*
●	Barbera d'Asti Sup. La Cappelletta '04	▼▼	5
○	Moscato d'Asti '05	▼▼	4*
○	Monferrato Bianco Foravìa '05	▼	3
●	Barbera d'Asti Sup. La Cappelletta '01	▽▽	5
○	L'avìja '03	▽▽	6
●	Barbera d'Asti Sup. La Cappelletta '00	▽▽	5
●	Barbera d'Asti Sup. La Cappelletta '03	▽▽	5

CANELLI (AT)

Contratto

via G. B. Giuliani, 56
14053 Canelli (AT)
tel. 0141823349
www.contratto.it

The grandeur of Contratto is evident from the structure of the underground cellar named after the Sempione tunnel. In fact, it was constructed in the early 20th century at the same time as the link between Italy and Switzerland to bring lustre to this historic label. Since 1995, the winery has been owned by the Bocchino family and Carluccio has turned it inside out. The plots in the finest parts of Asti and Langhe wine country have done the rest, enabling the Bocchinos to achieve major success. This year, they gave us only four selections, two Metodo Classico sparklers and two Barbera d'Astis. Missing from the line-up were the Barolo from Cerequio at La Morra as the 2002 edition was judged not to be up to par, the Chardonnay Sabauda and the Moscato d'Asti De Miranda, both of which are still ageing. Back on top form is the Brut Riserva Giuseppe Contratto from 2002 and the 2003 Asti De Miranda Metodo Classico. The Brut Riserva is from equal parts of pinot nero and chardonnay and has better balanced oak aromas than other vintages. Its deep, bright straw yellow introduces a medley of fruit and flowers before more complex sensations of crusty bread, creaminess, pervasiveness and elegance inform the long finale. De Miranda performed well, its distinctive moscato aromatics ushering in a richer complexity in the mouth. It's an outstanding Asti, produced the old way using the Metodo Classico. From the reds, we liked the good Barbera Solus Ad 2004, which just needs to absorb the last of its oak, and the delightful Barbera Panta Rei 2005, an admirable combination of price and quality.

○	Spumante M. Cl. Brut Ris. Giuseppe Contratto '02	▼▼	6
○	Asti De Miranda M. Cl. '03	▼▼	6
●	Barbera d'Asti Solus Ad '04	▼▼	7
●	Barbera d'Asti Panta Rei '05	▼▼	4*
○	Asti De Miranda M. Cl. '00	▽▽▽	6
○	Spumante M. Cl. Brut Ris. Giuseppe Contratto '96	▽▽▽	6
○	Asti De Miranda M. Cl. '97	▽▽▽	6
●	Barolo Cerequio Tenuta Secolo '97	▽▽▽	8
●	Barolo Cerequio '99	▽▽▽	8
●	Barolo Cerequio '00	▽▽	8
○	Asti De Miranda M. Cl. '01	▽▽	6

CANELLI (AT)

Coppo

via Alba, 68
14053 Canelli (AT)
tel. 0141823146
www.coppo.it

The Coppo family runs a winery that is a major player on the Monferrato scene. We think they have won their wager to create a Canelli winery making mature still reds, great whites and spumantes of merit, but not many Moscatos. All this comes together in a range that brings to mind a Burgundy négociant more than a typical local winery. It is no coincidence that the Coppos were once leading importers of the wines of Burgundy and Champagne. The celebrated Riserva del Fondatore Piero Coppo was not released so we had to make do with the tropical aromas and warm palate of the soft, creamy Coppo Brut Riserva 2000. Our tasters thought the Gavi La Rocca was superior to the Chardonnay Costebianche. The Gavi is fresh and minerally while the Chardonnay foregrounds balsam and fruit. One of the best Chardonnays around is the Monteriolo 2004, of which 20,000 bottles were obtained from vineyards at Agliano and Castelnuovo Calcea. A particularly elegant wine, it shows minerality and spice laced with citrus. Both 2004 Barbera d'Astis are fine wines. Some 100,000 units of Camp du Rouss went into bottle and their attractively elegant close-knit texture offers toastiness and slight saltiness whereas the Pomorosso stands out for its concentration and finesse, giving minerality and richness before signing off with a warm, pervasive finish. Yet again, it was the best label on offer and yet again it won Three well-deserved Glasses. The enticing Alterego 2003, from cabernet and barbera, is soft yet acidic. Mondaccione 2003 is an impressive wine from the vineyard of the same name at Altavilla near Santo Stefano Belbo and the big, tannin-heavy Freisa has perky fragrances.

●	Barbera d'Asti Pomorosso '04	▼▼▼	7
●	Monferrato Alterego '03	▼▼	6
●	Barbera d'Asti Camp du Rouss '04	▼▼	4*
○	Coppo Brut Ris. '00	▼▼	6
●	Monferrato Mondaccione '03	▼▼	6
○	Piemonte Chardonnay Monteriolo '04	▼▼	6
●	Barbera d'Asti L'Avvocata '05	▼	4
○	Gavi La Rocca '05	▼	4
○	Piemonte Chardonnay Costebianche '05		4
●	Barbera d'Asti Pomorosso '03	▽▽▽	7
●	Barbera d'Asti Pomorosso '01	▽▽▽	7
●	Barbera d'Asti Pomorosso '00	▽▽▽	7

CANELLI (AT)

Gancia

c.so Libertà, 66
14053 Canelli (AT)
tel. 01418301
www.gancia.it

This year, there are two profiles for this large Canelli winery, one for the spumantes and one for still wines. The former, known as Cantine Gancia, is the core business and has been producing premium sparklers since 1850 while the other winery, Tenute dei Vallarino, was set up in the mid 1990s to concentrate on reds with strong links to the Asti area. Management of the new winery has passed to the younger generations, in the persons of brothers Lamberto and Max and their cousin Edoardo. In recent years, the most significant moves have been to differentiate the various production lines more clearly. Numbers of bottles released are very high but there is still space for the top-of-the-range wines we review here. Major restructuring is also under way, in the course of which part of the old cellars will be recovered and incorporated. This time, there was no Carlo Gancia Cuvée del Fondatore for us to taste, as it is only released in very good years, which was not the case in 2002. Instead, the top of the list was Camillo Gancia, an Asti produced using the Metodo Classico. Its yellow hue shades into gold, heralding complex fragrances laced with the variety's classic aromatics and a powerful, mouthfilling palate with a nice hint of acidity in the finish. Asti Modonovo is fresh, elegant and aroma-rich. Best of the dry wines on show were the chardonnay and pinot nero Carlo Gancia Brut and the new Rosé Integral.

○	Asti Camillo Gancia '04	▼▼	6
○	Asti Modonovo '05	▼▼	4
○	Piemonte Brut Carlo Gancia M. Cl.	▼▼	4
⊙	Piemonte Rosé Integral	▼▼	5
⊙	OP Pinot Nero Brut P.rosé	▼	3
○	P.rosé Blanc Extra Dry	▼	4
○	Alta Langa Carlo Gancia Cuvée del Fondatore '01	▽▽	5

CANELLI (AT)

VILLA GIADA
REG. CEIROLE, 4
14053 CANELLI (AT)
TEL. 0141831100
www.andreafaccio.it

Andrea Faccio has a degree in agriculture and puts it to good use on his 24 hectares of vineyard in the municipalities of Agliano, Calosso and Canelli, where he turns out about 180,000 bottles a year. It was Andrea's grandfather Giuseppe, one of the founder members and for years president of the historic Cantina Sociale di Canelli co-operative, who purchased Villa Giada at Ceirole, where it stands in the midst of long rows of moscato. When we started tasting, we liked all four of the Barberas. The fresh, carefree I Surì 2005 is a touch herbaceous. The very interesting Ajan 2005, from slowly macerated grapes, has raspberry fruit and a juicy, savoury palate. The elegant La Quercia 2004, aged only in large wood is dense and concentrated. And finally the muscular Bricco Dani 2004 emerged from small barrels with tannins, structure and great prospects for the future. Andrea also bottled 600 magnums of Barbera Superiore 2003, a super-selection that we'll be talking about next year. At the moment, Dolcetto San Pietro 2005 is a difficult wine, showing serious tannins and fruit along with herbaceousness and salty notes. But the nebbiolo and barbera Monferrato Rosso Treponti was the big surprise. Its subtle, well-defined aromas precede a concentrated but gutsy, smooth-flowing palate with nice length and elegance. PrimoVolo 2003 did well. It's a red from Piedmontese barbera, Veneto merlot from La Montecchia and Tuscan sangiovese from Rocca delle Macìe. The panel like the candied peel and dried rose sensations of the savoury Brachetto 2005, which also offers a nicely balanced palate. Finally, the Moscato 2005 is less interesting, perhaps because of the difficult vintage.

●	Barbera d'Asti Sup. Nizza Bricco Dani '04	TT	5
●	Barbera d'Asti Sup. Vign. La Quercia '04	TT	4*
●	Monferrato Rosso Treponti '04	TT	4*
●	PrimoVolo '03	TT	6
●	Barbera d'Asti Ajan '05	TT	4*
●	Piemonte Brachetto Amis '05	TT	4*
●	Barbera d'Asti I Surì '05	T	3
○	Moscato d'Asti Ceirole '05	T	4
●	Monferrato Dolcetto San Pietro '05	T	4
○	Monferrato Bianco I Surì '05		3
●	Barbera d'Asti Sup. Bricco Dani '03	YY	5

CAREMA (TO)

CANTINA DEI PRODUTTORI NEBBIOLO
DI CAREMA
VIA NAZIONALE, 32
10010 CAREMA (TO)
TEL. 0125811160

The Cantina dei Produttori is the only Carema producer whose base is actually in the tiny village that gives its name to the DOC zone. This stunningly beautiful setting is framed by the Alps and the river Dora and dotted with thousands of "tapiun", the characteristic stone supports for the small pergolas that cover every open space between the houses and snake up the mountainside. Here at the entrance to Valle d'Aosta the wines have a very strong, distinctively mountainous, territorial personality. Nebbiolo has adapted to the site with two local clones, picutener and pugnet. New vintages presented for tasting revealed one or two stylistic wobbles but quality was good overall. The standard 2002 has the usual range of dried flowers, currants and eucalyptus followed by a savoury palate and a classic minerally, coppery finish that is not entirely pure. The Riserva 2001 is darker and less brilliant than usual. There are notes of new wood on the nose that have yet to integrate with the classic overall style of the wine and jeopardize its performance. But attractive pomegranate, mint and rose helped it over the Two Glass threshold. Finally, the barriqued 2001 version, of which only a few thousand bottles were released, has a rich, oak-led nose of cocoa powder, liquorice, nutmeg and walnutskin. Dense structure backed up by good acidity take you through to a dried flower-themed finale.

●	Carema Barricato '01	TT	5
●	Carema Ris. '01	TT	4*
●	Carema Et. Nera '02	T	4
●	Carema Et. Nera '01	YY	4
●	Carema Et. Bianca Barricato '98	YY	4
●	Carema Barricato '99	YY	5
●	Carema Et. Bianca Ris. '99	YY	4
●	Carema Ris. '00	Y	4

CASTAGNOLE DELLE LANZE (AT)

★ ★ ★ La Spinetta

via Annunziata, 17
14054 Castagnole delle Lanze (AT)
tel. 0141877396 - 0173262291
www.la-spinetta.com

The Rivetti brothers are never still. Their significant investments in Tuscany, including a modern cellar at Casanova in the hinterland of Terriciola, have been followed by new Riseva versions of Barbaresco and Barolo. These wines – about 1,600 of each – are available only in magnums and come from rigorous selections in the vineyard. Only grapes from the oldest vines in the best-aspected rows were picked to make these jewels of oenology. Given the superb level overall, it was a challenge to choose one, although the Starderi is perhaps more convincingly full and sustained on the palate. We thought so, anyway, and gave it Three well-earned Glasses. Barbaresco Starderi 2001 has black berries in a subtle, estery weave before the assertive, full-bodied progression reveals its rare elegance and harmony. The Gallina is nearly as astounding while the Valeirano from the same vintage went through to our finals on the strength of its luscious, concentrated pulp. The 2003 Barbarescos are more tannin-heavy and intense after a growing year that was anything but balanced in its weather conditions. From the three, we liked the Starderi and the Valeirano. Barolo Riserva Campè 2000 offers warm raspberry, cherry and damson melding with perceptions contributed by its time in barrique. The nebbiolo and barbera Monferrato Rosso Pin 2004 and Barbera d'Alba Gallina 2004 went on to the finals while the Barbera d'Asti Bionzo 2004 put a wonderful seal on a stunning all-round performance with a fantastic Three Glass exploit. Our tasters also appreciated the Moscato Bricco Quaglia and Passito Oro while the rest of this marvellous list lived up to the cellar's amazing reputation.

● Barbaresco Vign. Starderi Ris. '01	🍷🍷🍷	8
● Barbera d'Asti Sup. Bionzo '04	🍷🍷🍷	8
● Barolo Campè della Spinetta Ris. '00	🍷🍷	8
● Barbaresco Vign. Gallina Ris. '01	🍷🍷	8
● Barbaresco Vign. Valeirano Ris. '01	🍷🍷	8
● Barbaresco Vign. Starderi '03	🍷🍷	8
● Barbaresco Vign. Valeirano '03	🍷🍷	8
● Monferrato Rosso Pin '04	🍷🍷	7
● Barbera d'Alba Vign. Gallina '04	🍷🍷	7
○ Piemonte Moscato Passito Oro '01	🍷🍷	7
● Barbaresco Vign. Gallina '03	🍷🍷	8
● Barbera d'Asti Ca' di Pian '04	🍷🍷	5
○ Langhe Bianco '04	🍷🍷	6
○ Langhe Chardonnay Lidia '04	🍷🍷	6
○ Moscato d'Asti Bricco Quaglia '05	🍷🍷	4*

CASTEL BOGLIONE (AT)

Araldica Vini Piemontesi

v.le Laudano, 2
14040 Castel Boglione (AT)
tel. 014176311
www.araldicavini.com

The Araldica quality project commenced in the late 1990s with the purchase of Il Cascinone. Today, it is taking shape in a highly respectable range based on wines that offer very attractive value for money. Alongside these products, the cellar has added two Gavis sourced from another purchase, the La Battistina estate. Production of these two premium labels hovers below half a million bottles a year while the selections are destined for the on-trade. These are very modest numbers in comparison with the total production of this co-operative winery, which has more than 250 members with about 900 hectares of vineyards. Currently, management is in the hands of Claudio Manera, who is assisted by Luigi Bertini and a technical team of seven oenologists and three agronomists. Our panel was pleased to note the good all-round quality of the range, which is best represented by the two Barbera selections. The excellent 2004 Barbera d'Asti Superiore Rive is sourced from old vines and some 50,000 bottles were released. Its intense ruby red accompanies fruit-forward aromas laced with rain-soaked earth and a rich, concentrated palate with a nicely acidic finish. D'Annona 2003 has more alcohol and concentration but is a little less elegant. Best of the whites are the Arneis Sorilaria and the standard-label Gavi. The Gavi Bricco and Sauvignon Camillona were less successful. Rounding off the Il Cascinone wines is the Nebbiolo Castellero, which has lashings of alcohol and decent finesse. Finally, the Brut Alasia, from a 60-40 blend of pinot nero and chardonnay, is intriguingly complex.

● Barbera d'Asti Sup. Rive '04	🍷🍷	4*
● Barbera d'Asti Sup. D'Annona '03	🍷🍷	4
○ Gavi '05	🍷🍷	3*
○ Roero Arneis Sorilaria '05	🍷🍷	4
○ Piemonte Brut Alasia '97	🍷🍷	4
● Langhe Nebbiolo Castellero '03	🍷	4
○ Gavi Bricco Battistina '05	🍷	4
○ Monferrato Bianco Camillona '05	🍷	4
● Barbera d'Asti Sup. D'Annona '01	🍸🍸	4
● Barbera d'Asti Sup. Rive '03	🍸🍸	4
● Monferrato Rosso Luce Monaca '03	🍸🍸	5

CASTEL BOGLIONE (AT)

CASCINA GARITINA
VIA GIANOLA, 20
14040 CASTEL BOGLIONE (AT)
TEL. 0141762162
www.cascinagaritina.it

Cascina Garitina has 20 hectares under vine at Castel Boglione supervised by Gianluca Morino. Its wines are very well made in a modern style that puts the accent on depth and finesse. Emblematic of the approach is the flagship Barbera Neuvsent 2003. A pleasingly dense ruby red, it unveils a complex bouquet ranging from red fruits in alcohol to hints of hay and coffee. The palate has power, well-sustained progression and faintly assertive sweetness before the long finish. Barbera Caranti 2003's ruby red shades into dense, slightly forward garnet. Its elegant nose is a little dominated by oak-derived tones and the warm palate has moderate structure. Barbera d'Asti Bricco Garitta 2005 is fresh-tasting. A vibrant ruby red and intense, exciting nose of ripe red fruit and spice provide an elegant introduction for the character and harmony of a palate that flaunts enjoyable acidity and a persistent finale. Fairly intense in colour, the Dolcetto Caranzano 2005 mingles wild berries with estery notes in a nicely intense spectrum of aromatics. In the mouth, it is concentrated and robust. Brachetto Niades 2005 elegantly hints at part-dried fruit and then gives depth and concentration in the mouth. And the Barbera Vivace Il Morinaccio 2005 is well typed.

●	Barbera d'Asti Sup. Caranti '03	▼▼	4*
●	Barbera d'Asti Sup. Nizza Neuvsent '03	▼▼	5
●	Barbera d'Asti Bricco Garitta '05	▼▼	4*
●	Barbera del M.to Vivace Il Morinaccio '05	▼	4
●	Brachetto d'Acqui Niades '05	▼	4
●	Dolcetto d'Asti Caranzano '05	▼	3
●	Barbera d'Asti Sup. Nizza Neuvsent '00	▽▽	5
●	Monferrato Rosso Amis '00	▽▽	5
●	Monferrato Rosso Amis '01	▽▽	5
●	Barbera d'Asti Sup. Neuvsent '99	▽▽	5

CASTELLETTO D'ORBA (AL)

LUIGI TACCHINO
VIA MARTIRI DELLA BENEDICTA, 26
15060 CASTELLETTO D'ORBA (AL)
TEL. 0143830115 - 0143830040
www.luigitacchino.it

Renovation work at Cascina Baudrano carries on apace and will soon be finished. This will make it possible to further the Tacchino family's plans – and Romina's in particular – to improve the quality of the wines. All this is going on with due respect for the territory, country traditions and local vine types. As we waited for the vineyards planted in recent years to come onstream, and for Dolcetto Du Riva and Monferrato Eresia to emerge from the cellar where they are ageing, we tasted the few wines that the Tacchinos were able to present. Barbera del Monferrato Albarola 2004 is ruby red, with intense, moderately complex aromatics that include red fruits, followed by a palate that finds a decent balance of acidity and full, elegant structure. There was another good performance from the Barbera del Monferrato 2005. Aged only in steel, it gives an upfront nose of youthful alcohol and a very fresh palate that makes it very enjoyable to drink. The standard-label Dolcetto 2005 is well made and there were good marks for the Gavi and Cortese Marsenca, both of which easily passed the One Glass threshold.

●	Barbera del M.to Albarola '04	▼▼	4
●	Barbera del M.to '05	▼▼	2*
○	Cortese dell'Alto M.to Marsenca '05	▼	2
●	Dolcetto di Ovada '05	▼	2
○	Gavi del Comune di Gavi '05	▼	4
●	Barbera del M.to Albarola '01	▽▽	4
●	Barbera del M.to Albarola '03	▽▽	4

CASTELLINALDO (CN)

RAFFAELE GILI
LOC. PAUTASSO, 7
12050 CASTELLINALDO (CN)
TEL. 0173639011

Raffale Gili is not a man to rest on his laurels. In just a few years, he has created a fine winery at one of Roero's most dynamic winemaking centres, Castellinaldo. His lovely home and cellar stand among the Gili vineyards just outside the village and recently the facilities have been made over and expanded. Now Raffaele and his wife Laura have plenty of space to handle their raw material, grapes from various sites around Castellinaldo, which each year yield about 40,000 bottles released under a few carefully crafted labels. Truth to tell, two were missing this year. Roero Bric Angelino and Langhe Rosso L'Assemblato 2004 will see the light of day next year after a further period of ageing. That means it was the two Barbera 2004 wines that attracted most attention. Pautasso foregrounds florality on the nose and nicely handled acidity on the palate whereas the Castellinaldo version is more sophisticated, its time in oak informing the nose without dominating and the taut, close-knit palate flaunting good progression and a leisurely finish. But the honour of the Nebbiolos was amply defended by the Sansivé selection. Here, too, Raffaele skilfully handled the generosity of an excellent growing year, creating a red that puts the accent on elegance rather than depth and is splendidly drinkable. The Roero Arneis is minerally, nicely acidic and has a hint of bitterness on the back palate and the Favorita is just as it should be: fresh, fruity and very well typed.

● Barbera d'Alba Pautasso '04	🍷🍷	4
● Castellinaldo Barbera d'Alba '04	🍷🍷	5
● Nebbiolo d'Alba Sansivé '04	🍷🍷	5
○ Roero Arneis '05	🍷🍷	4
○ Langhe Favorita '05	🍷	3
● Castellinaldo Barbera d'Alba '01	YY	5
● Roero Bric Angelino '03	YY	5
● Castellinaldo Barbera d'Alba '00	YY	5
● Roero Bric Angelino '01	YY	5
● Castellinaldo Barbera d'Alba '02	YY	5
● Castellinaldo Barbera d'Alba '03	YY	5

CASTELLINALDO (CN)

MARSAGLIA
VIA MADAMA MUSSONE, 2
12050 CASTELLINALDO (CN)
TEL. 0173213048
www.cantinamarsaglia.it

We welcome back to the Guide an estate that we have been monitoring in the intervening years, confident that the quality leap would come sooner or later. Marina Marsaglia has done a good job. This determined, articulate wine woman has never wavered from the pursuit of excellence while also promoting the image of her winery and its territory. With her well-motivated family team of husband Emilio and children Monica and Enrico, backed up by a highly competent oenologist like Gianfranco Cordero in the cellar, Marina was able to present us with one of the finest ranges in the area this year. There is one more piece of news. The vine stock now extends over 15 hectares, all in the municipality of Castellinaldo, and production is running at an average of 70,000 bottles a year. On the wine front, Roero Arneis Serramiana inaugurates the DOCG zone with convincingly well-defined aromatics and minerality. We preferred the 2005 Barbera San Cristoforo for its vigorous, immediate acidity to a 2004 that is already evolved on the nose but still commendable for its overall character. The Castellinaldo Barbera 2003 impressed. Neither the hot growing year nor slow maturation in small wood has affected the surprising fruit, flowers and spices that pervade nose and palate. When we tasted the Nebbiolos, the Alba version from 2004 was deliciously soft to drink and the Roero 2003 stood out for its nose of forest fruits, rain-soaked earth and leaf tobacco, as well as for its character in the mouth. The Langhe, from nebbiolo, barbera and syrah, is well managed.

● Castellinaldo Barbera d'Alba '03	🍷🍷	5
● Roero Sup. Brich d'America '03	🍷🍷	5
● Nebbiolo d'Alba San Pietro '04	🍷🍷	4*
● Barbera d'Alba S. Cristoforo '05	🍷🍷	4*
○ Roero Arneis Serramiana '05	🍷🍷	4*
● Langhe Complotto '03	🍷	5
● Barbera d'Alba S. Cristoforo '04	🍷	4
● Castellinaldo Barbera d'Alba '00	YY	5
● Castellinaldo Barbera d'Alba '01	YY	5
● Roero Sup. Brich d'America '01	YY	5
● Roero Sup. Brich d'America '02	YY	5

CASTELLINALDO (CN)

STEFANINO MORRA
VIA CASTAGNITO, 50
12050 CASTELLINALDO (CN)
TEL. 0173213489
www.morravini.it

The Roero wine map has a new landmark in Stefanino Morra. After a quiet start a few years ago, Stefanino has slowly converted the family wine estate. First, he brought it to acceptable levels of quality and then he invested in the vineyards and cellar before making a determined change of tack towards excellence in a range that today is extensive, territory-focused and even personal in style. Stefanino's ten hectares yield 65,000 bottles a year and his new hospitality and tasting facilities are a point of departure for the ever more ambitious goals that now seem to be within his grasp. On a more technical note, we observe that the range of labels is complete again after last year's absences and quality has never been so high. The Barbera di Castellinaldo and Roero Srai, both from 2003, astonished the panel and earned slots at the top of their respective categories. The Barbera in particular is amazingly compact on the nose, where the succession of fruit and spice perceptions comes straight out of the textbook. Acidity, sinew and soft texture are exemplary, showing that Castellinaldo is a favoured zone for the variety. Srai, too, is exceptional. Noble earthy, balsamic aromas are mirrored on the muscular, warm palate with its leisurely finish. The standard-label versions of Barbera and Roero echo the tasting profile of the flagship bottles in a minor key. The arneis-based dried-grape passito named after Stefanino's son is very good, as are the Arneis wines, although we preferred the 2005.

●	Castellinaldo Barbera d'Alba '03	**YY**	5
●	Roero Srai '03	**YY**	6
●	Barbera d'Alba '04	**YY**	4*
○	Luca Passito '04	**YY**	5
●	Roero Sup. '04	**YY**	4*
○	Roero Arneis '05	**YY**	4*
○	Roero Arneis Vign. S. Pietro '04	**Y**	4
●	Castellinaldo Barbera d'Alba '00	YY	5
●	Castellinaldo Barbera d'Alba '01	YY	5
●	Roero Sup. '03	YY	4
●	Roero Srai '01	YY	6
●	Roero Sup. '01	YY	4

CASTELLINALDO (CN)

FABRIZIO PINSOGLIO
FRAZ. MADONNA DEI CAVALLI, 8
12050 CASTELLINALDO (CN)
TEL. 0173213078

There is no news on the wine front at Fabrizio Pinsoglio's winery but he still managed to get into the newspapers. Early in the growing season, he had a nasty accident in the vineyard, reminiscent of other sad episodes in Roero's wine history, but luckily this time there was a happy ending. Then in the middle of August, Fabrizio married Andreina, the woman who for years has been at his side at work and in their private life. So much for human interest, which is of anything but secondary importance as it offers an insight into the true value and significance of the range of wines. And when we uncorked the samples, two reds scored high marks, Barbera Rondolina 2004 and Roero 2003. The Barbera offers spice, autumn leaves and earth, marked acidity and admirable length, backed up by a very favourable vintage. In contrast, the Roera opens austere and deep on a nose of blackcurrant, crushed roses and berry fruit before the seriously good palate complements its generous tannins with alcohol and structure. The Nebbiolo 2004 is less complex but deliciously moreish in a way few wines can match. A persuasively fruit-led nose precedes a soft, no-nonsense palate. The Arneis is exciting, but this is hardly news since the type has a fine track record here. And to finish off, the standard-label Giaconi Barbera is well handled and very drinkable.

●	Roero Sup. '03	**YY**	5
●	Barbera d'Alba Bric La Rondolina '04	**YY**	5
●	Nebbiolo d'Alba '04	**YY**	4
○	Roero Arneis Vign. Malinat '05	**YY**	3*
●	Barbera d'Alba Vign. Giaconi '05	**Y**	4
●	Barbera d'Alba Bric La Rondolina '01	YY	5
●	Roero Sup. '01	YY	5
●	Barbera d'Alba Bric La Rondolina '03	YY	5
●	Barbera d'Alba Bric La Rondolina '00	YY	5
●	Roero '00	YY	5
●	Roero '99	YY	5

CASTELLINALDO (CN)

Vielmin

via San Damiano, 16
12050 Castellinaldo (CN)
tel. 0173213298 - 0173611248

Vielmin is further proof that Castellinaldo is a dynamic, exciting wine territory. In recent years, we have watched young, motivated winemakers grow under the protective – professionally speaking – wing of families already well established in wine before taking their cue from leading Langhe and Roero producers and spreading wings of their own. Ivan Gili, aka Vielmin, is one such wine man. His brother Raffaele is a widely respected producer and his father Francesco continues to be active in the vineyards while Ivan, having slowly started up his own winery is now on course for greater things. And the new cellar is the symbolic but highly functional cherry on Ivan's cake. He only has a few hectares under vine, enough to give him just over 30,000 bottles a year plus a certain quantity of wine sold unbottled. Territory-driven is the only description for these wines, which make no concessions to fancy or experimentation. This year's range performed well overall, even though bottling, which coincided with our tastings, probably prevented some labels from expressing themselves to the full. The 2004 Castellinaldo Barbera and Roero La Rocca are the top scorers. The Barbera brings acidity, alcohol and oak together seamlessly whereas the nicely tannic Roero is more austere than soft. Another nice wine is the Arneis, which gives good, typical minerality and herbaceousness. Also well-made are the Favorita, Nebbiolo and Barbera from 2004.

●	Castellinaldo Barbera d'Alba '04	▼▼	5
●	Roero La Rocca '04	▼▼	5
○	Langhe Arneis '05	▼▼	3*
●	Barbera d'Alba Srëi '04	▼	4
●	Nebbiolo d'Alba '04	▼	5
○	Langhe Favorita '05	▼	3
●	Castellinaldo Barbera d'Alba '03	▽▽	5
●	Castellinaldo Barbera d'Alba '00	▽▽	5
●	Castellinaldo Barbera d'Alba '01	▽▽	5
●	Roero La Rocca '01	▽▽	5
●	Roero La Rocca '03	▽▽	5

CASTELLO DI ANNONE (AT)

Villa Fiorita

via Case Sparse, 2
14034 Castello di Annone (AT)
tel. 0141401231 - 0141401852
www.villafiorita-wines.com

Francesco Rondolino, the man who owns Villa Fiorita, gets his varied range of typical Monferrato wines from 12 hectares of vineyards on the hillsides a few kilometres to the east of Asti. Among the wines tasted for this edition of the Guide, we particularly liked the barbera and pinot nero Monferrato Rosso Maniero from 2004. Its deep, lustrous ruby red introduces attractive currant-like fruit well integrated into the oak. The palate is savoury and full bodied, braced by soft, close-knit tannins and appealingly rounded off by a lingering finish. The other 2004 reds, the Nero di Villa and the Abaco, were also interesting. Nero di Villa is an oak-aged single-variety Pinot Nero with penetrating, estery aromas in a fairly forward bouquet. The attractive body is slightly let down by exuberant tannins that tend to disturb the harmony. Abaco is another single-variety Pinot Nero, but steel-aged this time. Its moderately intense hue precedes rich, well-defined fruit and a powerful palate with impressive weight. Grignolino Pian delle Querce 2005 is pale in hue, its spicy aromas ushering in a savoury, slightly roughish palate. Barbera Superiore 2004's fruit tones are veined with green and entry on the palate is juicy and nicely poised. The tidy Chardonnay Le Tavole 2005 is refreshing. Sovrano, from sauvignon and chardonnay, is good, particularly in the varietal expression of the two grapes. Its best qualities come through on the palate, although it still needs to absorb its oak-derived component.

●	Monferrato Rosso Abaco '04	▼▼	3*
●	Monferrato Rosso Maniero '04	▼▼	5
●	Monferrato Rosso Nero di Villa '04	▼▼	6
●	Grignolino d'Asti Pian delle Querce '05	▼▼	3*
●	Barbera d'Asti Sup. '04	▼	4
○	Sovrano '04	▼	5
○	Piemonte Chardonnay Le Tavole '05	▼	4
●	Barbera d'Asti Sup. Il Giorgione '03	▽▽	5
●	Barbera d'Asti Sup. '03	▽▽	4
●	Monferrato Rosso Maniero '03	▽▽	4

CASTELNUOVO DON BOSCO (AT)

CASCINA GILLI
VIA NEVISSANO, 36
14022 CASTELNUOVO DON BOSCO (AT)
TEL. 0119876984 - 0119927656
www.cascinagilli.it

Over the years, Gianni Vergnano's wines have made his Castelnuovo Don Bosco-based cellar one of Asti's most reliable, and now they are getting better. This corner of Monferrato, where the eye begins to be drawn towards the hills of Turin, is the home of some native varieties critics often neglect, malvasia, freisa and bonarda. To help him look after his 20 hectares under vine, Gianni can count on Bruno Tamagnone, Giovanni Matteis, Marco Piovano and Germana Rosa Clot. This year, the vibrant ruby red Barbera Vigna delle More 2004 is excellent. An intense nose of beautifully expressed, elegant fruit lifted by hints of spice and minerals precedes the nicely gauged richness of the savoury, juicy palate, signing off with an utterly convincing finale that highlights just how stylish this lovely wine is. The youthful, almost impenetrable hue of the attractive Barbera Sebrì 2004 introduces assertively rustic aromas and a characterful palate that tends towards boisterousness but drinks emphatically well. As ever, the Malvasia di Castelnuovo is nice. Intriguing black cherry accompanies an appealingly creamy palate. The tidy, upfront Chardonnay Rafé 2005 has florality and a moderately complex palate. The serene agility of the dried-grape red Dlicà is worth investigating. Freisa Arvelé 2004 has an austere nose and plenty of substance in the mouth. Finally, there are several appealingly upfront semi-sparkling Bonardas and Freisas to enjoy.

●	Barbera d'Asti V. delle More '04	🍷🍷	4*
●	Barbera d'Asti Sebrì '04	🍷🍷	4
●	Malvasia di Castelnuovo Don Bosco '05	🍷🍷	3*
●	Freisa d'Asti Arvelé '04	🍷🍷	4
●	Freisa d'Asti Luna di Maggio '05	🍷	3
●	Freisa d'Asti Vivace '05	🍷	3
●	Piemonte Bonarda Vivace Moyé '05	🍷	3
○	Piemonte Chardonnay Rafé '05	🍷	3
●	Dlicà	🍷	5
●	Freisa d'Asti Arvelé '03	YY	4
●	Barbera d'Asti Sebrì '03	YY	4

CASTIGLIONE FALLETTO (CN)

AZELIA
FRAZ. GARBELLETTO
VIA ALBA-BAROLO, 53
12060 CASTIGLIONE FALLETTO (CN)
TEL. 017362859

Last time round, the Azelia cellar received Three Glasses for the 2001 Barolo Bricco Fiasco but in the subsequent vintage, Luigi and Lorella Scavino were unable to release their celebrated vineyard selections: 2002 was simply not good enough. All the nebbiolo grapes went into a single Barolo, which nonetheless did very well indeed at our tastings. The wine in question is pale ruby red and proffers dried flowers and violets on the nose. The tannic, but not too tannic, palate leads to a clean, well-managed finale. But the top of the range this time is an unusual Riserva, Voghera Brea 2000, which had our panel nodding in approval. The fragrant, complex nose of rain-soaked earth, leaf tobacco and sweet spices is followed by a weighty, well-controlled palate with shrewdly gauged tannins and plenty of length. The 6,600 bottles of Barbera d'Alba Vigneto Punta 2004 aged for 14 months in small oak barrels, having been sourced from vines more than 50 years old. An intense, purple-flecked red introduces morello cherries and currants laced with coffee and vanilla from the sojourn in barrique. The imposing structure, with lots of body and pulp, is braced by supporting acidity that adds considerable length on the palate. We enjoyed the Dolcetto d'Alba Bricco dell'Oriolo 2005, of which 18,000 units went into bottle. Its intense, lingering fruit is mirrored faithfully on the palate. Finally, the 4,900 bottles of Langhe Nebbiolo 2005 benefited from a short stay in oak.

●	Barolo Voghera Brea Ris. '00	🍷🍷	8
●	Barolo '02	🍷🍷	7
●	Barbera d'Alba Vign. Punta '04	🍷🍷	5
●	Dolcetto d'Alba Bricco dell'Oriolo '05	🍷🍷	4*
●	Langhe Nebbiolo '05	🍷	4
●	Barolo Bricco Fiasco '01	YYY	8
●	Barolo Bricco Fiasco '93	YYY	8
●	Barolo Bricco Fiasco '95	YYY	8
●	Barolo Bricco Fiasco '96	YYY	8
●	Barolo S. Rocco '99	YYY	8
●	Barolo Bricco Fiasco '00	YY	8
●	Barolo S. Rocco '01	YY	8
●	Barolo Bricco Fiasco '98	YY	8
●	Barolo Bricco Fiasco '99	YY	8

CASTIGLIONE FALLETTO (CN)

★ Bricco Rocche - Bricco Asili
via Monforte, 63
12060 Castiglione Falletto (CN)
tel. 0173282582
www.ceretto.com

There isn't very much news from this prestigious winery – long one of the benchmark estates in the Langhe – but it is important. Grapes from the renowned Barolo Cannubi vineyard will be going to a selection, although we cannot yet tell you exactly when. We do know that it will be released exclusively in magnums. This year, no Barolos at all emerged from the Bricco Rocche cellar at Castiglione Falletto in the aftermath of the forgettable 2002 growing year, but advance tastings of subsequent vintages revealed some thrilling wines that will certainly repay the patience of their many fans. Barbaresco Bernardot 2003 has an outstanding nose of spice and intriguing tobacco, mulberries, liqueur cherries, cocoa powder and white pepper laced with roses and dried flowers. It explodes onto the palate thanks to an assertively ripe tannic weave and austere personality to finish with a textbook reprise of the nose. Barbaresco Bricco Asili 2003 is concentrated and sensual on the nose, where intense red fruits, sweet spices, balsam, juniper and autumn leaves vie for attention. Velvet-smooth and impressive on entry, the palate is admirably complex and well balanced, beautifully weaving together its components through to a very long, pervasive finish.

● Barbaresco Bernardot Bricco Asili '03	🍷🍷	8
● Barbaresco Bricco Asili '03	🍷🍷	8
● Barbaresco Bricco Asili '96	ΥΥΥ	8
● Barbaresco Bricco Asili '97	ΥΥΥ	8
● Barbaresco Bricco Asili '99	ΥΥΥ	8
● Barolo Bricco Rocche '00	ΥΥΥ	8
● Barolo Bricco Rocche '89	ΥΥΥ	8
● Barolo Brunate Bricco Rocche '90	ΥΥΥ	8
● Barolo Prapò Bricco Rocche '83	ΥΥΥ	8
● Barbaresco Bricco Asili '01	ΥΥ	8
● Barolo Prapò Bricco Rocche '01	ΥΥ	8

CASTIGLIONE FALLETTO (CN)

Brovia
via Alba-Barolo, 54
12060 Castiglione Falletto (CN)
tel. 017362852
www.brovia.net

Barbera d'Alba Sorì del Drago 2004 has a vibrant hue, elegant morello cherry and red fruits aromas, a juicy palate, crunch acidity, great length and personality rounded off by a perfectly poised fruit finish. It's a magnificently drinkable wine in the finest Barbera tradition. Our thanks go to this increasingly extended family – hi, Tomàs and Jacopo – that so confidently interprets the diversity of its estate's terroirs in both Barolo and Barbera, even if this year not a single bottle of the former was released following disastrous 2002 hailstorms that cut production in half. It also means that the 2004 Brea, from a long-established Barolo nebbiolo vineyard at Serralunga, is a totally different Barbera, and not just because of the small wood in which half was matured. Its self-confident power faithfully reflects its provenance. Dolcetto Vignavillej is very nice. Typical almondy notes, attractive drinkability and freshness lead into a liquorice-themed finish. We are always impressed by Solatìo, from 50-year-old vines. Its vibrant, intense colour, assertive fruit and juicy, assured palate with attractive acidity tell you it still has a long way to go. So once again, despite the absence of the Barolos, it was an excellent performance from Brovia.

● Barbera d'Alba Sorì del Drago '04	🍷🍷	4*
● Barbera d'Alba Brea '04	🍷🍷	5
● Dolcetto d'Alba Solatìo '04	🍷🍷	5
● Dolcetto d'Alba Vignavillej '04	🍷🍷	4
● Barolo Ca' Mia '00	ΥΥΥ	8
● Barolo Monprivato '90	ΥΥΥ	8
● Barolo Ca' Mia '96	ΥΥΥ	8
● Barolo Ca' Mia '01	ΥΥ	8
● Barolo Rocche dei Brovia '01	ΥΥ	8
● Barolo Villero '01	ΥΥ	8

CASTIGLIONE FALLETTO (CN)

Cascina Bongiovanni

Fraz. Uccellaccio
via Alba-Barolo, 4
12060 Castiglione Falletto (CN)
tel. 0173262184

Davide Mozzone, who runs this estate, manages to get flattering results from the seven hectares that give him about 30,000 bottles a year. The cellar's flagship vineyard selection, Barolo Pernanno 2001, did well. Some 4,500 units went into bottle after ageing in small barrels of French oak, emerging dense in colour and intense on the interestingly complex nose. The palate is big on entry, long and lingering on mid palate and closes with attractively harmonious composure. We thought it was so good that we gave it Three Glasses. The 3,000 bottles of standard-label Barolo matured in new and pre-used barriques. Palish in hue, they release dried violets and red berry fruit aromas before the palate expands satisfyingly to close equally nicely with a long-lingering after-aroma. The 2004 Barbera aged in small, once-used barrels for nine months and 4,000 bottles were released. The colour is still purplish, the nose gives fresh fruit and the clean, well-defined finish is nice. The 2005 editions of the Dolcetto d'Alba and Dolcetto di Diano d'Alba – 4,000 and 3,000 bottles respectively – were both steel-vinified and aged, and are still fresh-tasting and youthfully alcoholic. The 3,000 units of Langhe Rosso 2004, from equal proportions of nebbiolo, barbera and cabernet sauvignon, saw barrique during maturation. They emerged dense in colour, giving mulberry and spice, and have a broad, satisfying finish. The 7,000 bottles of steel-vinified Langhe Arneis 2005 are a lovely rich yellow. Flowers and tropical fruits introduce an attractively elegant palate with decent persistence.

●	Barolo Pernanno '01	🍷🍷🍷	7
●	Barolo '02	🍷🍷	5*
●	Barbera d'Alba '04	🍷🍷	5
●	Langhe Rosso Faletto '04	🍷🍷	5
●	Dolcetto d'Alba '05	🍷🍷	4
●	Dolcetto di Diano d'Alba '05	🍷🍷	4
○	Langhe Arneis '05	🍷	4
●	Barolo Pernanno '00	🍷🍷 (white)	7
●	Barolo Pernanno '99	🍷🍷 (white)	7
●	Barolo Pernanno '98	🍷🍷 (white)	7
●	Barolo Pernanno '97	🍷🍷 (white)	7
●	Barolo '01	🍷🍷 (white)	6
●	Barbera d'Alba '03	🍷🍷 (white)	5
●	Langhe Rosso Faletto '04	🍷🍷 (white)	5

CASTIGLIONE FALLETTO (CN)

F.lli Cavallotto

loc. Bricco Boschis
s.da Alba-Monforte
12060 Castiglione Falletto (CN)
tel. 017362814
www.cavallotto.com

Laura, Alfio and Giuseppe, the competent Cavallotto family team, make a full range of typical Langhe wines, from Dolcetto to Barolo. This year's labels were well up to expectations, confirming that the Cavallottos, not content with what they have achieved so far, are aiming to entrench themselves in the front rank of Piedmontese winemaking. There was no Barolo Bricco Boschis 2002 after a fraught growing year so the Riserva wines stepped into the breach. Vignolo 2000 is excellent. An imperiously broad spectrum of aromatics takes you through dark coffee notes to tobacco and medicinal herbs. An overwhelmingly exuberant palate combines authority with elegance, flaunting textbook tannins that set the tempo before the deliciously long finish rounds things off. The crisp, well-defined Riserva Bricco Boschis Vigna San Giuseppe unveils liquorice, cloves, saddle leather, dried roses and spice. Soft and pervasive, the close-knit palate has ripe tannicity accompanying you through to a very long, satisfying finish. In fact, it was so good we gave it Three Glasses, which neatly reprises last year's award. Also excellent were the Dolcettos. Scot 2005 is more immediate, putting the accent on appealing drinkability, whereas Vigna Melera 2004 is meatier and more complex. Barbera Vigna del Cuculo 2003 is purple-flecked scarlet in the glass, releasing crisply defined fruit fragrances that introduce generous, velvety sensations in the mouth. And the headily aromatic 2004 Chardonnay has remarkable depth.

●	Barolo Bricco Boschis V. S. Giuseppe Ris. '00	🍷🍷🍷	8
●	Barolo Vignolo Ris. '00	🍷🍷	8
●	Barbera d'Alba V. del Cuculo '03	🍷🍷	5
●	Dolcetto d'Alba V. Melera '04	🍷🍷	4
○	Langhe Chardonnay '04	🍷🍷	4
●	Langhe Freisa '04	🍷🍷	4
●	Langhe Nebbiolo '04	🍷🍷	5
●	Dolcetto d'Alba V. Scot '05	🍷	4
●	Barolo V. S. Giuseppe Ris. '89	🍷🍷🍷 (white)	8
●	Barolo Bricco Boschis V. S. Giuseppe Ris. '99	🍷🍷🍷 (white)	8
●	Barolo Vignolo Ris. '99	🍷🍷 (white)	8
●	Barolo Bricco Boschis '01	🍷🍷 (white)	7

★ Paolo Scavino

fraz. Garbelletto
via Alba-Barolo, 59
12060 Castiglione Falletto (CN)
tel. 017362850

This cellar releases what we might call auteur wines, bottles that reveal all of Enrico Scavino's love of the land as well as his attention to detail at all stages of winemaking, from vineyard to cellar. Enrico's cellar was recently restructured and apart from flaunting some very impressive architecture, it is a happy synthesis of cutting-edge technology, from the heated flooring in the barrique cellar to encourage malolactic fermentation, to the steam jets that maintain humidity at just the right level. Although 2002 has deprived us of many of Enrico's famous labels, the superb quality of the wines he did present is very comforting. The surprising Barolo Bricco Ambrogio 2002 comes from rigorous thinning that has limited the quantity but not the character of the wine. Ripe fruit and spices introduce a mouthfilling palate with unexpectedly hefty structure. Barolo Riserva Rocche dell'Annunziata 2000 is well on its way to greater things with all its customary personality. Garnet red heralds elegant morello cherry, plum and leather, followed by a close-knit, well-modulated palate and a finale that lingers endlessly. Corale 2003, from nebbiolo, barbera and cabernet, constructs a mosaic of fragrances that usher in a palate that hangs together very satisfyingly. The Nebbiolo 2004 is a textbook interpretation of the variety. The Barbera 2005 is uncomplicated, the Barbera Affinata in Carati 2003 is elegant and the Dolcettos and whites are impeccable.

●	Barolo Rocche dell'Annunziata Ris. '00	🍷🍷	8
●	Barolo Bricco Ambrogio '02	🍷🍷	8
●	Langhe Corale '03	🍷🍷	5
○	Langhe Bianco Sorriso '04	🍷🍷	6
○	Langhe Bianco '05	🍷🍷	4*
●	Langhe Nebbiolo '04	🍷🍷	5
●	Barbera d'Alba Affinata in Carati '03	🍷🍷	6
●	Barbera d'Alba '05	🍷🍷	4*
●	Dolcetto d'Alba '05	🍷🍷	4*
●	Barolo Rocche dell'Annunziata Ris. '96	YYY	8
●	Barolo Rocche dell'Annunziata Ris. '97	YYY	8

CASTIGLIONE FALLETTO (CN)

Terre del Barolo

via Alba-Barolo, 5
12060 Castiglione Falletto (CN)
tel. 0173262053
www.terredelbarolo.com

Terre del Barolo has about 400 member growers who tend the 800 hectares of vineyards that enable this major co-operative winery to release a vast range of territorial products. This year, our tasting panels were presented with two very aristocratically complex, thoroughbred Barolos. We'll start with the top of the winery's range, Barolo Castello Riserva 1999. Elegant breadth on the fruit-led nose of blueberries, liqueur cherries and mulberries mingle with tempting balsam over golden leaf tobacco. The deep, characterful palate has lots of body, developing well, its alcohol balanced by muscular structure and ripe, polished tannins before the long, well-sustained finish. The Barolo Rocche Riserva 1998 is less explicit, presenting pale, rather forward garnet red and then unveiling ripe fruit aromas lifted by liquorice, leather and complex florality. Entry on the palate is warm, soft and velvety, with decent energy from a well-defined, close-knit tannic weave that leads to a satisfyingly persistent finish. As usual the Dolcettos are admirable, with Cascinotto 2004 standing out from the pack. From the Barberas, we liked the succulent, harmonious Valdisera 2004 and the Pelaverga is also nice. On the white front, the Chardonnay is well typed and the Favorita attractive.

●	Barolo Rocche Ris. '98	🍷🍷	8
●	Barolo Castello Ris. '99	🍷🍷	7
●	Barbera d'Alba Sup. '04	🍷🍷	3*
●	Barbera d'Alba Valdisera '04	🍷🍷	3*
●	Dolcetto di Diano d'Alba Cascinotto '04	🍷🍷	3*
●	Nebbiolo d'Alba '04	🍷🍷	4
●	Verduno Pelaverga '05	🍷🍷	4
●	Dolcetto d'Alba Castello '04	🍷	4
●	Barbera d'Alba '05	🍷	3
●	Dolcetto d'Alba '05	🍷	3
●	Dolcetto di Diano d'Alba '05	🍷	3
○	Langhe Bianco Favorita '05	🍷	3
○	Langhe Chardonnay '05	🍷	3

CASTIGLIONE FALLETTO (CN)

VIETTI

P.ZZA VITTORIO VENETO, 5
12060 CASTIGLIONE FALLETTO (CN)
TEL. 017362825
www.vietti.com

Vietti continues to deserve its reputation as one of the most prestigious wineries in Langhe and beyond. Luca Currado and Mario Cordero maintain commendable consistency of quality while turning out serious numbers: we are talking about an estate that releases more than 200,000 bottles a year. As a matter of policy, it was decided not to produce any nebbiolo-based selections from the difficult 2002 growing year. But Barbera d'Asti Superiore Nizza La Crena 2003 has thrilling depth, elegance, structure, length and complexity. Its dark hue heralds a concentrated, wide-ranging spectrum of aromatics including blackcurrants, plums and blackberry jam, and sweet spices that fuse with cocoa powder and dark tobacco. Progression in the mouth is remarkably powerful as the exuberant alcohol is tempered by fresh acidity and ripe, mouthfilling tannins. Three well-deserved Glasses. Both Barbera d'Alba wines are good, especially Scarrone Vigna Vecchia 2004, and the 2004 Scarrone is only a shade less concentrated on nose and palate. Langhe Nebbiolo Perbacco 2003 has the aromatics of a small-scale Barolo, standing out for finesse, imposing structure and soft, refined tannins. Barbaresco Masseria 2003 is deep garnet red, giving intense pipe tobacco, liquorice, coffee and cocoa powder nuanced with wild roses. On the well-sustained palate, which is well up to expectations, the perfect equilibrium of structure, alcohol and bright acidity is very satisfying indeed. Barbera Tre Vigne also scored well.

●	Barbera d'Asti Sup. Nizza La Crena '03	▼▼▼	6
●	Barbera d'Alba Scarrone V. Vecchia '04	▼▼	7
●	Barbaresco Masseria '03	▼▼	7
●	Langhe Nebbiolo Perbacco '03	▼▼	5
●	Barbera d'Alba Scarrone '04	▼▼	5
●	Barbera d'Asti Tre Vigne '04	▼▼	4*
●	Barbera d'Alba Scarrone V. Vecchia '00	▽▽▽	7
●	Barbera d'Alba Scarrone V. Vecchia '01	▽▽▽	7
●	Barolo Rocche '01	▽▽▽	8
●	Barbera d'Asti La Crena '99	▽▽▽	7
●	Barolo Brunate '01	▽▽	8

CASTIGLIONE TINELLA (CN)

LA CAUDRINA

S.DA BROSIA, 20
12053 CASTIGLIONE TINELLA (CN)
TEL. 0141855126
www.caudrina.it

For decades, Romano Dogliotti has been synonymous with premium Moscato and the man himself has been a beacon for lovers of the wine type. After years of hard work and substantial investment, Romano's new cellar is finally ready and the estate staff now has modern technology and renewed confidence in the future. This year's tasting yet again showed just how magnificently the Dogliottis handle Moscato and some of the cellar's new products shot straight to the top of the category. Particularly convincing is the spectrum of aromatics offered by La Galeisa 2005. Its deep straw yellow is flecked with gold and ushers in depth and finesse on the nose, where pears, home baking, candied citrus and moss come through clearly. The temptingly creamy palate is bright and fresh-tasting, its sweetness offset by restrained effervescence. Moscato La Caudrina is less concentrated in hue, its pale straw yellow showing greenish highlights and heralding elegant, grape, elderflower and tangy apple followed by a persistent, attractively savoury palate. The 2004 Barbera La Solista was vinified exclusively in steel, emerging with a moderately complex estery nose with a black berry fruit and cocoa powder theme. A smooth palate of moderate breadth offers balance and drinkability. Finally, Asti La Selvatica is as captivating as ever.

○	Moscato d'Asti La Galeisa '05	▼▼	4*
●	Barbera d'Asti La Solista '04	▼▼	4
○	Asti La Selvatica '05	▼▼	4
○	Moscato d'Asti La Caudrina '05	▼▼	4
●	Barbera d'Asti Sup. Montevenere '00	▽▽	5
●	Barbera d'Asti La Solista '03	▽▽	4
●	Barbera d'Asti Sup. Montevenere '99	▽▽	5

CASTIGLIONE TINELLA (CN)

ICARDI
LOC. SAN LAZZARO
VIA BALBI, 30
12053 CASTIGLIONE TINELLA (CN)
TEL. 0141855159

The major winery, founded in 1914, has scaled the heights of Italian winemaking thanks to the commitment and enthusiasm of Claudio and Maria Grazia Icardi. The wide range is characterized by its style, which strives for elegance and grace rather than power or big-league extract. The Icardis are two of the most determined supporters of harmony and balance in their relationship with the vineyard. This translates into the utmost respect for the vines, which are never placed under stress from extreme management techniques. Tastings this year have revealed further advances beginning with the Bricco del Sole 2003, a happy marriage of nebbiolo, barbera and cabernet. Apart from the clear advantage of enhancing the characteristics of the different varieties, the blend has a lively personality, stirs the emotions and satisfies the senses. All the Barberas were convincing but we were particularly intrigued by the refined grace of Nuj Suj 2004. The bouquet of sensations on the nose yields black berry fruit, cocoa powder and tobacco notes. The sensually soft palate opens up gradually on smooth tannins and then signs off with a persistent, refined finish. Our panel also liked the Surì di Mù with its well-defined, well-crafted profile on the nose. The Tabaren 2005 is harmonious and immediately pleasing. The Monferrato Bianco Pafoj 2005 is excellent, flaunting fruity peach and damson notes on a deep, intense floral background. The excellent Barbaresco Montubert 2003 is rich in well-gauged fruity shades. The other labels are exemplary.

●	Monferrato Rosso Cascina Bricco del Sole '03	🍷🍷	7
●	Barbera d'Asti Nuj Suj '04	🍷🍷	6
●	Barbaresco Montubert '03	🍷🍷	8
●	Barbera d'Alba Surì di Mù '04	🍷🍷	5
●	Langhe Rosso Nej '04	🍷🍷	6
○	Monferrato Bianco Pafoj '05	🍷🍷	6
●	Barbera d'Asti Tabaren '05	🍷	4
●	Dolcetto d'Alba Rousori '05	🍷	4
●	Barolo Parej '01	(🍷🍷)	8
●	Langhe Rosso Nej '03	(🍷🍷)	6
●	Barbera d'Alba Surì di Mù '03	(🍷🍷)	5
●	Barbera d'Asti Nuj Suj '03	(🍷🍷)	6

CASTIGLIONE TINELLA (CN)

LA MORANDINA
LOC. MORANDINI, 11
12053 CASTIGLIONE TINELLA (CN)
TEL. 0141855261
www.lamorandina.com

La Morandina is named for the Morando family, present in the village of Morandini since the 17th century. Giulio handles the cellar and Paolo the vineyards. The quality of their wines derives from these 21 hectares planted to moscato, barbera and nebbiolo. Production is about 100,000 bottles a year, released under eight labels, from Barbera to Barbaresco, Moscato and Chardonnay. All the wines tasted for this year's Guide were interesting. First, the fruity, intense Chardonnay 2005 flaunts tropical fruit and peaches. The excellent Moscato d'Asti is aromatic and creamy with a big, well-integrated palate and well-crafted acid in the finish. Moving on to the three Barbera selections, the heady, intense standard-label Barbera d'Asti finishes juicy and savoury in the mouth. Barbera d'Asti Zucchetto 2005 is more full-bodied and almost tannic. Impenetrable in colour, it gives damp earth and red fruit on the nose. The stylish, tidy palate shows a gutsy, gratifying minerally note. The quality goes up a notch with Varmat, a 2004 Barbera selection aged in small wood with a concentrated, smoke-tinged morello cherry nose. The juicy, integrated palate brings back the fruit in its broad spectrum of flavours. Barbaresco Bricco Spessa 2003 is slightly penalized by the growing year but shows warm and alcoholic with a lovely tannic structure. L'Insieme, from a meticulous selection of barbera, nebbiolo and syrah, shows vegetal and spicy notes. The Costa del Sole Passito from moscato and riesling is very good.

○	Costa del Sole Passito '03	🍷🍷	6
●	Barbera d'Asti Varmat '04	🍷🍷	6
○	Moscato d'Asti '05	🍷🍷	4*
●	Barbaresco Bricco Spessa '03	🍷🍷	8
●	L'Insieme '03	🍷🍷	8
●	Barbera d'Asti '05	🍷🍷	4
●	Barbera d'Asti Zucchetto '05	🍷🍷	4
○	Langhe Chardonnay '05	🍷	4
●	Barbera d'Asti Varmat '00	(🍷🍷)	5
●	Barbera d'Asti Varmat '01	(🍷🍷)	5
●	Barbera d'Asti Varmat '03	(🍷🍷)	5
●	Barbaresco '01	(🍷🍷)	7
●	L'Insieme '01	(🍷🍷)	8

CASTIGLIONE TINELLA (CN)

Elio Perrone

s.da San Martino, 3bis
12053 Castiglione Tinella (CN)
tel. 0141855803
www.elioperrone.it

Stefano Perrone is the enthusiastic owner of an estate he manages with help from his wife Giuliana and the tireless energy of his parents. Stefano works to bring out the best qualities in those native varieties he uses and produce modern wines with personality that can interpret the territory and the grape's typicity. News this year includes the absence of a major wine, Barbera d'Asti Grivò, which is currently enjoying more time in the cellar and will be evaluated in the next edition of the Guide, and the birth of a new Barbera aged in large wood. We will report on this wine in 2007 as well. Shining in density and depth, the Barbera Mongovone 2004 is the estate warhorse. Its purple hue ushers in a deep nose yielding fruity notes of morello cherry mingled harmoniously with spicy sensations and vegetality. The palate shows great character and remarkable extract, marrying power and elegance with perfect balance of taut, vigorous tannins and substantial yet composed acidity. Both the Moscatos from 2005 are convincing. The Clarté offers a clean, precise nose with floral notes of broom and intense aromas of tropical fruit, pear, pink grapefruit and sage followed by exciting freshness, length and measured sweetness in the mouth. The light straw-yellow Sourgal offers charming mango, citron, hedgerow, golden apple and moss, followed by a round, caressing mouthfeel. Finally, the attractive brachetto-based Bigarò has aromas of raspberries, roses and wild strawberries.

●	Barbera d'Asti Mongovone '04	▼▼	6
○	Moscato d'Asti Clarté '05	▼▼	4
○	Moscato d'Asti Sourgal '05	▼▼	4
●	Bigarò '05	▼	4
●	Barbera d'Asti Mongovone '01	▽▽	6
●	Barbera d'Asti Grivò '03	▽▽	4
●	Barbera d'Asti Mongovone '03	▽▽	6
●	Barbera d'Asti Grivò '04	▽▽	4

CASTIGLIONE TINELLA (CN)

Paolo Saracco

via Circonvallazione, 6
12053 Castiglione Tinella (CN)
tel. 0141855113

We are in the part of Piedmont called Langa Astigiana, a series of long, deep valleys with vineyards everywhere, on the slopes that catch the morning sun as well as the evening's rays. The vines stand in stratified chalky marl mixed with sand where man has toiled since classical times to cultivate the moscato grape that has adapted perfectly to this environment. Paolo Saracco loves all phases of his work, from managing the vineyard or vinification and the cellar, soon to be remodelled to meet future production needs. There are 40 hectares of vines on this family estate. Add to that grapes purchased from long-standing suppliers and production reaches 400,000 bottles a year, almost all moscato except for 10,000 bottles of still dry wines. Speaking of these, the long-awaited Pinot Nero 2003 has been released. Helped by a hot growing season, the wine shows more Langhe than Pinot, with robust yet sweet tannins, fruit jam and spice. The very convincing Prasuè 2004 is minerally and varietal, showing simple in the mouth yet enjoyable for its structure and rich flavour. Released in 380,000 bottles, the Moscato 2005 is very good with complex aromas of honey, sage and mint and a fresh, never cloying palate. The Moscato d'Autunno 2005 selection, released in 13,000 bottles, is fantastic with concentration and well-gauged aromas on the nose. The palate explodes with density and breadth, closing on vibrant acidity.

○	Piemonte Moscato d'Autunno '05	▼▼	4*
●	Monferrato Rosso Pinot Nero '03	▼▼	5
○	Langhe Chardonnay Prasuè '04	▼▼	4
○	Moscato d'Asti '05	▼▼	4
○	Piemonte Moscato d'Autunno '04	▽▽	4
○	Piemonte Moscato d'Autunno '03	▽▽	4
○	Piemonte Moscato d'Autunno '01	▽▽	4

CAVALLIRIO (NO)

ANTICO BORGO DEI CAVALLI

VIA DANTE, 54
28010 CAVALLIRIO (NO)
TEL. 016380115
www.vinibarbaglia.it

Sergio Barbaglia's small, well-managed winery is one of the best emerging producers in the province of Novara. Sergio is making a great effort to expand the product range, intelligently aiming to revive the best traditions while carrying out some excitingly original experiments. In the near future, look out for an erbaluce-based metodo classico we think will be very interesting. This year sees the debut of Boca 2001, a wine that contributes significantly to the reawakening of a DOC zone with a long history and great prestige. In this first edition, it's clear the style needs some fine-tuning but those citrus touches on the nose are quite promising, as is the rich, spacious palate of plum and cinnamon that closes out slightly astringent because of the wine's youth. Vespolina Ledi 2005 proved itself one of the best interpretations ever and underlines the variety's enormous aromatic potential by expressing the typical array of floral aromas, wild berries and spices in particularly fine, sweet tones, leading to a consistent, streamlined palate that is savoury and long. The Silente 2003 had a less felicitous growing season and has to deal with the hot vintage and unusually noticeable oak that detracts from the nobility of the nebbiolo sourced from a single, 90-year-old vineyard. The always pleasant Lea is a lovely monovarietal exercise in uva rara that foregrounds raspberry and a touch of cloves. The performance of the Lucino 2005 was instead less successful, even though this monovarietal Erbaluce is normally among the best labels from the province.

● Boca '01		6
● Colline Novaresi Nebbiolo Il Silente '03		5
● Colline Novaresi Vespolina Ledi '05		4*
○ Colline Novaresi Bianco Lucino '05		5
● Colline Novaresi Uva Rara Lea '05		3
● Colline Novaresi Vespolina Ledi '04		4
● Colline Novaresi Nebbiolo Il Silente '01		5
● Colline Novaresi Nebbiolo Il Silente '02		5

CERRINA MONFERRATO (AL)

IULI

FRAZ. MONTALDO
VIA CENTRALE, 27
15020 CERRINA MONFERRATO (AL)
TEL. 0142943894 - 3382566139
www.iuli.it

In the previous edition of the Guide, we sang the praises of the magnificent Universo Trattoria managed by the Iuli family. Unfortunately, we have to announce its closing this year. Fabrizio's mother, Maria, after many honourable years in the kitchen, has decided to hang up her pots and pans and devote herself exclusively to her family. Fortunately, the winery continues to turn out interesting and enjoyable products thanks to the labours of Fabrizio, his sister Cristina and Claudio Barzaghi. But those who follow the Guide will also be familiar with this estate's invaluable partners, the Lerner brothers, Dan and Gad. The 15 hectares under vine, nine of them leased, produce a total of nearly 50,000 bottles. Our review begins with the Barbera del Monferrato Barabba 2003, aged 18 months in French-oak barriques. The colour is an almost impenetrable ruby red. Complex notes of rain-soaked earth, leather, chocolate and ripe red fruit show on the nose before the warm, alcoholic palate finishes long and slightly bitterish. Its two siblings, Barbera Rossore and Umberta, both from 2004, also did well. The former ages for a much longer period in small, once-used oak barrels that enrich it with toasty, spicy nuances. Umberta is more immediate, minerally, supple and fresh. Just below this, the monovarietal pinot nero-based Monferrato Rosso Nino 2004 yields cherry and wild strawberry sensations.

● Barbera del M.to Sup. Barabba '03		6
● Barbera del M.to Rossore '04		4*
● Barbera del M.to Sup. Umberta '04		4*
● Monferrato Rosso Nino '04		5
● Barbera del M.to Sup. Barabba '01		6
● Barbera del M.to Rossore '03		4
● Barbera del M.to Barabba '00		6
● Monferrato Rosso Malidea '01		5
● Barbera del M.to Barabba '02		6
● Barbera del M.to Rossore '02		4
● Monferrato Rosso Malidea '02		5
● Monferrato Rosso Malidea '03		5

CHIERI (TO)

MARTINI & ROSSI
LOC. PESSIONE
P.ZZA LUIGI ROSSI, 2
10123 CHIERI (TO)
TEL. 0118108465
www.mymartini.it

Martini & Rossi is one of the oldest brands in Italian wines. Founded in 1863, it has always been renowned for its production of traditional Piedmont spumante and further established itself with the vermouth, in both the red and white versions, that became famous with the legendary Martini cocktail enjoyed by the biggest stars in Hollywood. After being acquired in the late 1990s by the American multinational Bacardi, Martini & Rossi went through an adjustment period but has now returned to its regular place in our Guide. The overall wine production is enormous but these numbers thin out in the top quality line reserved for restaurants, sold under the name Sigillo Blu Martini. There are four selections in this line. The Prosecco comes from Veneto, grapes for the Riesling from the hills of Oltrepò, those for the Moscato from the province of Asti and the hills of the upper Langhe supply fruit for the vintage Spumante Alta Langa Riserva Montelera. This star of the line-up is missing this year. The Alta Langa Riserva is not yet ready for commercial release and has been replaced with the classic non-vintage Riserva Montelera Talento. This Metodo Classico, from pinot nero and bianco sourced from Oltrepò, exemplifies the company's style. Fresh-tasting and dosed with restraint, it is an excellent aperitif. Tastings of the other wines from the Sigillo Blu brand were less convincing but they passed the One Glass threshold, the Prosecco and Riesling being easy to drink. The Moscato is a bit austere and heavy.

○	Montelera Brut Talento Ris.	▼▼	5
○	Moscato d'Asti Sigillo Blu '05	▼	4
○	OP Riesling Brut Sigillo Blu	▼	3
○	Prosecco di Valdobbiadene Extra Dry Sigillo Blu	▼	4
○	Alta Langa Montelera Brut Ris. Sigillo Blu '02	▽▽	5

COCCONATO (AT)

CANTINE BAVA
S.DA MONFERRATO, 2
14023 COCCONATO (AT)
TEL. 0141907083
www.bava.com

Paolo, Roberto and Giulio Bava, with their father Piero, have succeeded in the difficult task of combining large production numbers with high quality in their wines. The quality is all there in the Monferrato Rosso Vigneti di Cadodo 2005 and Barbera Libera 2004, both of which won Two Glasses in our tastings. The first shows a nice dense garnet red colour and a nose that recalls red fruit, such as morello cherry and redcurrants, and closes on minerally tones. The palate is rich with good fullness, barely perceptible tannins and a long back palate. The Barbera is a medium intense ruby red introducing aromas rich in wild berries, blueberries and raspberries, in a slightly alcoholic profile. The palate shows pleasant richness and a lingering finish. The pleasing Brut Toto Corde has a clear colour and sensations of fruit and flowers ushering in a delicate, balanced palate. The other classic method from the Giulio Cocchi line is Oro, an atypical spumante from grapes harvested when overripe. As a result, the aromas are warm and exuberant and entry on the palate is powerful and complex. The Chardonnay Thou Bianc is mature but goes no further than a mention. Delicate and gradual in disclosing its varietal aromatics, the Moscato Bass Tuba unfolds fresh and pleasant on the palate. The orange-tinged ruby red Malvasia di Castelnuovo Don Bosco Rosa Canina has layered flowers and fruit on the nose and a tidy palate with well-measured effervescence.

○	Alta Langa Toto Corde Giulio Cocchi '03	▼▼	5
●	Barbera d'Asti Libera '04	▼▼	4
●	Monferrato Rosso Vigneti di Cadodo '05	▼▼	4
○	Piemonte Alta Langa M. Cl. Brut Oro Giulio Cocchi '99	▼▼	5
●	Malvasia di Castelnuovo Don Bosco Rosa Canina '05	▼	4
○	Moscato d'Asti Bass Tuba '05	▼	4
○	Piemonte Chardonnay Thou Bianc '05		4
●	Barbera d'Asti Libera '03	▽▽	4
●	Monferrato Rosso Vigneti di Cadodo '04	▽▽	4

COSSOMBRATO (AT)

CARLO QUARELLO
VIA MARCONI, 3
14020 COSSOMBRATO (AT)
TEL. 0141905204

If the banner of grignolino, that prized but endangered variety, still waves over the imposing bastions of Piedmontese viticulture, then much credit goes to this small, excellent winery in Monferrato. Carlo Quarello, assisted by his dynamic son Valerio in the difficult art of vinification and the just as difficult job of commercial management, continues to work enthusiastically in his vineyards and cellar. In addition, and bureaucracy permitting, they should also open the doors of their new structure at Cardona in Alfiano Natta before the end of 2006. While waiting to review the new wines, Nebbiolo and Barbera, now in the cellar, we will comment on those submitted, beginning with the excellent Crebarné 2004. This little jewel is a purple-tinged ruby with an intense nose of spice, ripe red fruit, cocoa powder and golden tobacco. The light, juicy palate has perfectly balanced acidity and tannins, with a lingering finish that reprises the fruit from the nose. The always excellent Cré Marcaleone is one of the winery's warhorses. The 2005 version has textbook varietal sensations ranging from pepper and geranium to wild strawberry before the palate stands our for its balance of acidity and tannins. The Barbera d'Asti Vigna Cré 2004 is as good as the other wines and reveals a concentrated profile on the nose followed by a caressing, soft palate.

●	Barbera d'Asti V. Cré '04	TT	4*
●	Monferrato Rosso Crebarné '04	TT	5
●	Grignolino del M.to Casalese Cré Marcaleone '05	TT	4*
●	Barbera d'Asti V. Cré '03	YY	4
●	Grignolino del M.to Casalese Cré Marcaleone '03	YY	4
●	Grignolino del M.to Casalese Cré Marcaleone '04	YY	4
●	Monferrato Rosso Crebarné '99	YY	5

COSTA VESCOVATO (AL)

LUIGI BOVERI
FRAZ. MONTALE CELLI
VIA XX SETTEMBRE, 6
15050 COSTA VESCOVATO (AL)
TEL. 0131838165

The Tortona area is well known as the land of barbera. Proof of this comes in the wines of Luigi Boveri for all his red labels are produced from this variety. Boccanera, steel-fermented and sold young, has all the true, youthfully alcoholic fragrances of the variety. Luigi also makes this wine in a slightly sparkling "vivace" version for those who love this type. His Poggio delle Amarene version is probably unique in the Tortona district because it is a selection of barbera not vinified in oak, as would normally be the case for a cru. The result is a wine with very interesting sensory characteristics and quite a long finish that can offer very decent ageing prospects. The house champion, Vignalunga, never emerged from the cellar in the 2002 vintage because of weather problems during the growing connected year but it made a great comeback in '03 and reached our finals. This wine stature is in the poise with which it manages to splendidly link together a solid framework of body and structure and an acidity that shows yet never exceeds the limit. The result is a wine with captivating aromas and sensations on the palate that recall spices and chocolate. As he has for some years now, Luigi again presented one of the best selections of Timorasso and the 2004 vintage lived up to our expectations. Filari di Timorasso 2004 adds benzene notes to its minerality before the palate foregrounds apricot. Finally, pleasant Vigna del Prete is a cortese-based white.

●	Colli Tortonesi Barbera Vignalunga '03	TT	5
●	Colli Tortonesi Barbera Poggio delle Amarene '04	TT	4*
○	Colli Tortonesi Bianco Filari di Timorasso '04	TT	5
●	Colli Tortonesi Barbera Boccanera '05	T	3
○	Colli Tortonesi Cortese Vigna del Prete '05	T	3
●	Colli Tortonesi Barbera Vignalunga '01	YY	5
○	Colli Tortonesi Bianco Filari di Timorasso '03	YY	5
●	Colli Tortonesi Barbera Vignalunga '00	YY	5

COSTA VESCOVATO (AL)

CARLO DANIELE RICCI
VIA MONTALE CELLI, 9
15050 COSTA VESCOVATO (AL)
TEL. 0131838115

After last year's good results, the estate managed by Daniele Ricci showed it is one of the up and coming operations in this area with an array of interesting wines with great personality. This year, we were impressed by the Terre del Timorasso, theoretically the base Timorasso, rather than its big brother, San Leto. Both are good but the former has more refined characteristics and entry on the palate is enlivened by good acidity, fruity aromas and evolved nuances. San Leto is more concentrated and aims more for the variety's trademark minerality but last year yielded more intense sensations. The wines from red varieties are also very good, including the Barbera Castellania. Barrique-ageing and a long period in bottle have helped it achieve remarkable structure and body that never dominate the wine's nice sensory profile for this is a red with distinctive red berry fruit aromas and spicy notes. Rich in personality, the San Martino is a blend with some barbera added to the nebbiolo. The resulting wine has deep aromas and vigorous notes on a palate that recalls cocoa powder and cinnamon. The Bonarda 'L Mat is less challenging but definitely pleasing and invites a second sip with its fresh, heady aromas.

○	Colli Tortonesi Terre del Timorasso '04	▼▼	4*
○	Colli Tortonesi Bianco San Leto '04	▼▼	5
●	Colli Tortonesi Barbera Castellania '03	▼▼	5
●	Colli Tortonesi Rosso San Martino '04	▼▼	5
●	Piemonte Bonarda 'L Mat '04	▼	4
○	Colli Tortonesi Bianco San Leto '03	▽▽	5
●	Colli Tortonesi Barbera Castellania '01	▽▽	5
●	Colli Tortonesi Rosso Elso '01	▽▽	5

COSTIGLIOLE D'ASTI (AT)

BERTELLI
VIA SAN CARLO
14055 COSTIGLIOLE D'ASTI (AT)
TEL. 0258314153 - 0141966137

During our annual visit to Bertelli, we could feel a new wind blowing. Fans have no reason to fear: the style of the wines, which respects the territory and its personality before it seeks technical perfection, will not be changing. The 11 hectares under vine, all in the San Carlo di Costigliole area, and the winery are still managed by Elisabetta Bertelli and her father Aldo. Elisabetta's brother Alberto supervises vinification. The big news is that young oenology graduate Claudio Dacasto has joined the estate, guaranteeing a technical continuity undreamed-of only a short while ago. And finally, teamwork and especially the perseverance of Elisabetta's husband, Francesco Ferraro, have ensured the wines will be better distributed. Beyond the necessary work of cleaning and reorganizing the cellar, great effort was focused in 2004 and 2005 on renewing the vineyards, replacing dead or sick vines, top grafting chardonnay onto nebbiolo and cabernet, and updating the vineyard land registry. Luckily, all this expended energy has not jeopardized the quality of the wines, which still reflect the Bertelli philosophy and standard quality criteria for this brand. There is an irresistible poetry to the estate's whites. Chardonnay Giarone 2004 is complex and opulent, the traminer-based Plissé, fragrant and mouthfilling and the San Marsan Bianco, from a blend of Rhône valley grapes, is deep and minerally. Best of the reds is the MB 2001, an austere, powerful Piedmont Merlot.

○	Plissé Traminer '03	▼▼	6
○	Piemonte Chardonnay Giarone '04	▼▼	6
●	Monferrato Rosso MB '01	▼▼	6
○	San Marsan Bianco '03	▼▼	6
●	San Marsan Rosso '02	▼	6
●	Barbera d'Asti S. Antonio Vieilles Vignes '00	▽▽	6
○	San Marsan Bianco '02	▽▽	6
○	Piemonte Chardonnay Giarone '03	▽▽	6
●	Barbera d'Asti Montetusa '99	▽▽	6
●	Barbera d'Asti S. Antonio Vieilles Vignes '99	▽▽	6

COSTIGLIOLE D'ASTI (AT)

Cascina Castlet

s.da Castelletto, 6
14055 Costigliole d'Asti (AT)
tel. 0141966651
www.cascinacastlet.com

Mariuccia Borio's estate continues its steady ascent towards the heights of regional winemaking. Work is now almost finished on the new cellar that will give competent Cascina oenologist Giorgio Gozzelino the technology and conditions to bring out the best in the grapes harvested from 20 hectares under vine located in the heart of the barbera and moscato production zones. For some years now, Mariuccia and her staff, in collaboration with several university institutes, have directed their efforts to research and experimentation with the native uvalino variety. Tastings this year showed positive development for the entire production range and brought several labels back into the spotlight. Among these, a place of honour awaits the Policalpo 2003. This barbera blend with a moderate amount of cabernet is a dark ruby hue with a broad profile on a nose rich in fruity notes. The palate unveils a wonderfully dense texture that balances successfully generous alcohol and acidity. The finish is well sustained and long-lingering. The most significant Barbera, the Passum selection, is in no hurry and will remain for another year to age in the cellar. We'll be back for it in 2007. Although still finding its feet, the intriguing Litina is distinguished by intense echoes of fruit, coffee and liquorice and the search for a harmonious balance between of imposing extract and lively tannins. The other Barberas are juicy and enjoyable while the Moscatos are sound.

●	Monferrato Rosso Policalpo '03	TT	5
●	Barbera d'Asti Sup. Litina '04	TT	5
○	Moscato d'Asti '05	TT	4*
○	Piemonte Moscato Passito Avié '04	T	6
●	Barbera d'Asti '05	T	3
●	Barbera del M.to Goj '05	T	3
●	Barbera d'Asti Sup. Passum '01	YY	5
●	Barbera d'Asti Sup. Passum '03	YY	5
●	Monferrato Rosso Policalpo '00	YY	5
●	Monferrato Rosso Policalpo '01	YY	5
●	Barbera d'Asti Sup. Litina '03	YY	5
●	Monferrato Rosso Policalpo '98	YY	5

COSTIGLIOLE D'ASTI (AT)

Cascina Roera

fraz. Bionzo
via Bionzo, 32
14055 Costigliole d'Asti (AT)
tel. 0141968437

Claudio Rosso and Piero Nebiolo combined their two estates to rationalize management and deal as a team with the difficulties of the wine sector. Production aims at making the most of this area's main variety, barbera, used for making three selections. But there is no lack of good supporting actors, like Freisa d'Asti, Monferrato Rosso Vigna Piva and two whites, the more structured Chardonnay Le Aie and simpler Ciapin Bianco from chardonnay, arneis and cortese. This year, the whites from the new vintage were not yet bottled at the time of tasting so we settled for a sound selection of reds. Wines produced by Cascina Roera from barbera show all the flexibility of a grape that can be vinified fresh and fruity or made more complex and concentrated. The most convincing selection is the Superiore Cardin from 2003. An intense ruby, it gives aromas of damp earth and red fruit in syrup, and a soft, velvety palate with a nicely acidulous finish that sustains the substantial alcoholic impact. The San Martino 2003 is also very good and more linear in comparison with the previous bottle. The textbook La Roera selection is simple, fruity and easy to drink. The Monferrato Vigna Piva is austere and tannic while the Freisa is a little aggressive in the tannic, bitterish finish.

●	Barbera d'Asti Sup. Cardin '03	TT	4*
●	Barbera d'Asti Sup. S. Martino '03	TT	4*
●	Monferrato Rosso V. Piva '03	TT	4*
●	Barbera d'Asti La Roera '04	T	3
●	Freisa d'Asti '04	T	3
●	Barbera d'Asti Sup. Cardin Ris. '00	YY	5
●	Barbera d'Asti Sup. Cardin '01	YY	4
●	Barbera d'Asti Sup. Cardin Sel. '01	YY	5
●	Barbera d'Asti Sup. S. Martino '02	YY	4

COSTIGLIOLE D'ASTI (AT)

Cascina Ferro

via Nosserio, 14
14055 Costigliole d'Asti (AT)
tel. 0141966693 - 0141966737

Brothers Piero and Maggiorino Ferro, owners of Cascina Ferro, produce 25,000 bottles a year from around seven hectares under vine. This small production is distinguished by its quality and it was no surprise that this year the Barbera Bric 2004 went confidently through to our finals. An intense lively ruby red, it has a nose of great finesse that reveals splendid notes of plum, cherry and sweet spices in a general profile with great personality. The palate is enthralling, with broad body and a stimulatingly rich palate that closes unwaveringly on a long finish that recapitulates the aromas: a wine of remarkable class. The estate's signature label, Barbera Superiore Vanet, is pleasant on the nose and palate but not helped by the very hot 2003 growing year, which saw almost no precipitation during the summer. The Monferrato Rosso Cin 2004 is also very good, from a base of barbera, freisa and cabernet. Dense and bright to the eye, the nose offers intense, stylish aromas with lovely spicy notes that frame the fruity, tobacco tones. The palate is rich with good backbone and overall progression supported by powerful ripe tannins that reinforce and lengthen the mouthfeel. More balanced compared to the 2003 edition, the Chardonnay Realtà has a yellow colour of average intensity and gives clear varietal aromas, including clear echoes of ripe yellow and white-fleshed fruit in a very pleasing overall panorama.

●	Barbera d'Asti Bric '04	**YY**	4*
●	Barbera d'Asti Sup. Vanet '03	**YY**	5
●	Monferrato Rosso Cin '04	**YY**	5
○	Piemonte Chardonnay Realtà '04	**YY**	5
●	Barbera d'Asti Sup. Vanet '01	YY	5
●	Barbera d'Asti Bric '03	YY	4
●	Monferrato Rosso Cin '01	YY	5
●	Monferrato Rosso Cin '03	YY	5

COSTIGLIOLE D'ASTI (AT)

Sciorio

via Asti-Nizza, 87
14055 Costigliole d'Asti (AT)
tel. 0141966610

Brothers Giuseppe and Mauro Gozzelino submitted a very interesting array of wines this year. Their Barbera d'Asti Superiore Sciorio from 2003 stood out from this high-quality range thanks to a profile that marries majestic extract with elegance. The impenetrable lively ruby red with purple-flecked highlights introduces an exciting profile on a nose slightly marked by toasty oak sensations. It opens on pencil lead and liquorice notes, continuing with layered touches of tobacco, black berry fruit and balsam. The warm, opulent palate is wrapped in outstanding softness and perked up by bright acidity and a ripe, generous tannic weave right up to the long, consistent finish. The Barbera Vigna Beneficio 2001 is different and more mature, right from the visual examination, yielding dark notes of coffee, damp earth and leather before it reveals a rich, full-flavoured body with a clean, leisurely finish. The complex, expressive Antico Vitigno 2002, an estate classic from a cabernet sauvignon base, offers a nose of broad fruit, ripe cherry tones, new-mown hay and bell pepper framed in a sound, stylish structure. The Vigna Levi 2004, a tempting Chardonnay, has sweet aromas of ripe fruit, caramel, honey and vanilla followed by a sensuous, harmonious entry on the palate.

●	Barbera d'Asti Sup. Sciorio '03	**YY**	4*
●	Barbera d'Asti Sup. Vigna Beneficio '01	**YY**	5
●	Monferrato Rosso Antico Vitigno '02	**YY**	5
○	Piemonte Chardonnay Vigna Levi '04	**Y**	5
●	Barbera d'Asti Sup. Sciorio '01	YY	4
●	Barbera d'Asti Sup. Sciorio '00	YY	4
●	Barbera d'Asti Sup. Vigna Beneficio '00	YY	5
●	Barbera d'Asti Sup. Vigna Beneficio '98	YY	5
●	Barbera d'Asti Sup. Vigna Beneficio '99	YY	5

COSTIGLIOLE D'ASTI (AT)

VALFIERI
S.DA LORETO, 5
14055 COSTIGLIOLE D'ASTI (AT)
TEL. 0141966881
www.valfieri.it

The wines from this Costigliole d'Asti estate, managed by the brother and sister team of Maria Chiara and Angelo Clerici with help from oenologist Luca Caramellino and agronomist Gian Piero Romana, are as interesting as ever. The range submitted runs from fascinating interpretations of several international varieties to versions of the most widely planted and enjoyed native grape in the province of Asti, barbera. We'll begin our review with the Barbera Superiore 2004. It has an intense ruby red colour and a nose with good power and fruit presented in a slightly husky profile. The palate shows excellent body and taut tannins that make the wine confident and dry with a long, convincing finish. The standard-label Barbera has a purplish red colour and a nice, consistent nose of average elegance. The palate is succulent and smooth, staying fresh to close with a lingering finish. From a merlot base with ten per cent cabernet, the Rosso Matot has an intense colour and a deep, interesting nose enriched with nuances of black berry fruit, green tobacco and cinchona in a calm, elegant profile. The palate also reveals character, unwinding without wavering and closing with a remarkably pleasing finish. Finally, the chardonnay-sauvignon blend Bianco Barricello is gratifying with spicy, secondary tones on the nose, and the Rosso Cassabò, from 70 per cent barbera with the rest nebbiolo, is rather dry with average body.

●	Monferrato Rosso Matot '03	▼▼	5
●	Barbera d'Asti Sup. '04	▼▼	4*
●	Barbera d'Asti '05	▼▼	4*
●	Monferrato Rosso Cassabò '05	▼▼	4*
○	Langhe Bianco Barricello '05	▼	4
●	Barbera d'Asti Sup. I Filari Lunghi '03	▽▽	6
●	Barbera d'Asti Sup. I Filari Lunghi '00	▽▽	6
●	Barbera d'Asti Sup. I Filari Lunghi '01	▽▽	6
●	Barbera d'Asti Sup. I Filari Lunghi '99	▽▽	6

DIANO D'ALBA (CN)

CLAUDIO ALARIO
VIA SANTA CROCE, 23
12055 DIANO D'ALBA (CN)
TEL. 0173231808

Although less extensive than on other occasions, the array of wines submitted by Claudio Alario this year put on a good performance. Unfortunately, the Barolo did not see daylight since the awful weather in 2002 convinced this winery, as well as many others in the Langhe, not to produce it. Still a classic country estate with the entire family working in the vineyards and cellar, this winery boasts ten hectares under vine in some of the best vineyards: at Diano, Montagrillo and Costa Fiore for Dolcetto; Cascinotto for Nebbiolo; and Valletta for Barbera; at Verduno, Rive for Barolo; and at Serralunga d'Alba, Sorano again for Barolo. We'll begin the tasting notes for these wines with the two Diano d'Alba Dolcettos from 2005. Released in 20,000 bottles, the excellent Costa Fiore has a nose that gives red fruit sensations well sustained by a minerally note of pencil lead. The palate is rich and complex with a succulent finish. The Montagrillo is headier on the nose, and austere and tannic in the mouth with a pleasant almondy vein in the finish. The textbook Barbera Valletta from 2004 makes the most of the vintage and went through to our finals. The nose is run through with ripe red fruit, wet earth and smoky aromas before the palate shows its character and juicy, inviting acidity. The Nebbiolo Cascinotto 2004 is less convincing, turning out austere and tannic with the oak still too apparent.

●	Barbera d'Alba Valletta '04	▼▼	5
●	Diano d'Alba Costa Fiore '05	▼▼	4*
●	Nebbiolo d'Alba Cascinotto '04	▼▼	5
●	Diano d'Alba Montagrillo '05	▼▼	4
●	Barolo Riva '01	▽▽	7
●	Diano d'Alba Costa Fiore '04	▽▽	4
●	Barolo Riva '99	▽▽	7
●	Barolo Riva '00	▽▽	7
●	Barbera d'Alba Valletta '03	▽▽	5
●	Nebbiolo d'Alba Cascinotto '03	▽▽	5
●	Barolo Riva '97	▽▽	7
●	Barolo Riva '98	▽▽	7

DIANO D'ALBA (CN)

Bricco Maiolica

FRAZ. RICCA
VIA BOLANGINO, 7
12055 DIANO D'ALBA (CN)
TEL. 0173612049
www.briccomaiolica.it

For years now, Beppe Accomo has adopted a winemaking style that favours elegance and drinkability over power or opulence. His wines are clear and precise in the definition of their spectrum of aromatics and Beppe has never been one to follow market logic or the fashions of the moment. Finesse and harmony also distinguish the 2005 vintage of the Diano d'Alba Sörì Bricco Maiolica. Although obviously not lacking in extract, it charms the nostrils with the refinement of its aromas, from fruity wild cherry, strawberry and blackcurrants to floral notes of violet and wild rose, right through to balsamic sensations of mint and aniseed. The palate opens soft and balanced, progressing to a finish marked by varietal almonds and lingering, satisfying length. The base version is also sound, if just a bit less intense. At its second release, the Merlot Filius 2003 proffers an intriguing bouquet on a nose that releases sensations of cherry, plum, golden tobacco, wet earth and vegetality. The profile on the palate is vibrant, rounded and consistent. The Nebbiolo Cumot 2003 is a pleasant synthesis of the variety's character. While we wait for the Barbera Vigna Vigia, whose 2004 edition is benefiting from further bottle ageing, the base version offers an immediate, yet never dull, taste experience. The Langhe Bianco Rolando, with intriguing smoky touches, unleashes tropical fruit, sage and medicinal herb notes. The harmonious, tangy palate shows fullness and character, and nicely duplicates the sensations on the nose.

● Diano d'Alba Sörì Bricco Maiolica '05	▼▽	4*
● Langhe Rosso Filius '03	▼▼	6
● Nebbiolo d'Alba Cumot '03	▼▼	5
● Barbera d'Alba '04	▼▼	4
○ Langhe Bianco Rolando '04	▼▼	4
● Dolcetto di Diano d'Alba '05	▼▼	4
● Barbera d'Alba V. Vigia '98	▽▽▽	5
● Barbera d'Alba V. Vigia '03	▽▽	5
● Barbera d'Alba V. Vigia '00	▽▽	5
● Barbera d'Alba V. Vigia '01	▽▽	5
● Diano d'Alba Sörì Bricco Maiolica '01	▽▽	4
● Diano d'Alba Sörì Bricco Maiolica '03	▽▽	4

DIANO D'ALBA (CN)

Renzo Castella

VIA ALBA, 15
12055 DIANO D'ALBA (CN)
TEL. 017369203

After his studies at the oenological institute in Alba and experience at some of the major Langhe wineries, 30-year-old Renzo Castella decided to put his skills into practice by working the family estate. This small winery in the village of Lopiano, near Diano d'Alba, is equipped with all the latest technology. Renzo's mother Enza and father Simone give him a hand among the rows of vines and barrels. Together they cultivate ten hectares under vine and produce a total of 30,000 bottles, almost exclusively Dolcetto. The Castellas have presented their most successful and interesting wines from precisely this type. We should also point out that these wines are sold at very competitive prices, making the Castella range one of the most reasonable in the Langhe. At 17,000 bottles, the estate's top seller is the Dolcetto di Diano d'Alba Vigna della Rivolia 2005, sourced from grapes grown on the hillside looking onto the centre of La Morra. These marl-rich clayey terrains create ripe red fruit aromas like morello cherry and redcurrant as well as chestnut leaves and damp earth. The richness on the palate is very pleasant and enjoyable. The Dolcetto Vigna La Sorda 2005 is slightly simpler and easier to drink yet never boring. The nose gives clear sensations of blueberry, wild cherries and strawberries, preceding a soft, harmonious palate. A step below this, the Barbera d'Alba Vigna Piadvenza 2004 has not yet completely absorbed its oak-derived vanilla and coffee, and the Nebbiolo d'Alba Malìn 2003 reflects the unfavourable vintage for the variety.

● Dolcetto di Diano d'Alba V. della Rivolia '05	▼▼	3*
● Dolcetto di Diano d'Alba V. La Sorda '05	▼▼	3*
● Nebbiolo d'Alba Malìn '03	▼	4
● Barbera d'Alba V. Piadvenza '04	▼	3

DIANO D'ALBA (CN)

RIZIERI
CASCINA RICCHINO
12055 DIANO D'ALBA (CN)
TEL. 0173468540
www.rizieri.com

Giampiero Piazza has managed to create this lovely, reliable estate in Diano d'Alba in less than a decade. Since 1999, the year the first wine with the Rizieri label was released, the quality of his products has risen steadily. In addition to the winery, Piazza has also restored and opened a comfortable inn with four tastefully furnished rooms and 40 seats for dining, thanks to help from dynamic Ivan Milani and Silvio Porzionato. The cellar is under the supervision of consultant oenologist Beppe Caviola while agronomist Gian Piero Romana looks after the vineyards. The estate has seven hectares under vine and a production that, depending on the growing year, fluctuates around 25,000 bottles, released under three different labels. Let's move on to the wines. We liked the dolcetto-based Diano d'Alba 2005 with its impenetrable purple colour. The intense nose yields clear notes of plums bottled in alcohol, cinchona, violet and morello cherry. The palate is dense and warm against a backdrop of freshness guaranteed by sweet tannins. Also excellent is the Barbera d'Alba 2004, which gives cherry, sweet spice, coffee and vanilla. On the palate, there is confident acid backbone that lengthens the progression. The panel liked the Nebbiolo d'Alba 2004, which introduces itself with a lustrous ruby red and a nose rich in wild roses, currants, blueberry and raspberry sensations. The palate is enjoyably tannic with full structure, finishing attractively and remarkably long.

● Barbera d'Alba '04	▼▼	5
● Nebbiolo d'Alba '04	▼▼	5
● Diano d'Alba Rizieri '05	▼▼	4*
● Nebbiolo d'Alba '03	▽▽	5
● Diano d'Alba Rizieri '04	▽▽	4

DIANO D'ALBA (CN)

PODERI SINAGLIO
FRAZ. RICCA
VIA SINAGLIO, 5
12055 DIANO D'ALBA (CN)
TEL. 0173612209
www.poderisinaglio.it

Located right on the border of the municipalities of Alba and Diano, this family-sized estate is proving itself to be a reliable feature on the Langhe wine scene and a careful interpreter of the territory. Moving on to the wines we tasted this year, we'll begin with the Barbera. The completely stainless steel-fermented base version is cloaked in a purple-tinged ruby. The nose has decent complexity and shows red and black berry fruit with recognizable sweet spices. The structure is not massive but expands over the palate in a balanced array of pleasurable sensations. Its stablemate, Barbera Vigna Erta from 2004, is dark ruby and unveils a broad array of elegant, lingering aromas with echoes of blackcurrants and golden tobacco. Entry on the palate is warm and velvety and the close-knit tannins are well defined. Nicely made from barbera, nebbiolo and freisa, the Langhe Rosso Sinaij 2003 shows off a nose of flowers, vegetal echoes and balsamic sensations that usher in a full-bodied structure with great character and a long, leisurely finish. The estate has traditionally specialized in producing Dolcetto di Diano. Both of the 2005 versions, the base and the Sorì Bric Maiolica, effortlessly earned Two Glasses for their extraordinarily fresh drinkability, in the first case, and impressive complexity on nose and palate in the second. The rest of the range is well managed.

● Langhe Rosso Sinaij '03	▼▼	4
● Barbera d'Alba V. Erta '04	▼▼	4
● Diano d'Alba Sorì Bric Maiolica '05	▼▼	4
● Dolcetto di Diano d'Alba '05	▼▼	3*
● Nebbiolo d'Alba Giachét '04	▼	4
● Barbera d'Alba '05	▼	3
● Langhe Rosso Sinaij '00	▽▽	4
● Barbera d'Alba V. Erta '01	▽▽	4
● Barbera d'Alba V. Erta '03	▽▽	4
● Nebbiolo d'Alba Giachét '03	▽▽	4
● Dolcetto di Diano d'Alba Madonna di Como '04	▽▽	4

DOGLIANI (CN)

ABBONA
B.TA SAN LUIGI, 40
12063 DOGLIANI (CN)
TEL. 0173721317
www.abbona.com

Last year, we spoke of Marziano Abbona's psychological stress as he anxiously waited to see if his new cellar would be ready in time to vinify the 2005 vintage. Now, the structure can finally be considered ready as the official inauguration was held on 28 August 2006. If we base our judgements on this year's tastings, we note that luckily the chaos in the cellar till a few months ago has in no way penalized the wines from 2005. In an unfortunate edition of the Guide for Barolo and Barbaresco, which suffered in two difficult growing seasons in 2002 and 2003, Marziano immediately took the new Barolo Cerviano 2001 to our finals. This complex red nicely melds fruity raspberry aromas with cinchona and liquorice. Its power comes out on the palate, which flaunts majestically harmonious tannins of great class. The Barolo Terlo Ravera 2002 could not aspire to the same concentration and shows some leanness from an unexciting growing season. The Barbaresco Faset 2003 had better luck and is only flawed by a slight lack of freshness. In almost a photocopy of the situation in the last edition, the other major players are still the Dogliani Papà Celso 2005 – the correct name for the new DOCG – and the Barbera Rinaldi 2004. Fruity and complex, the former turned out to be at the top of its category and won Three Glasses. The Barbera repeated the fine performance of the 2003. The other wines also merited excellent scores although special mention goes to the Nebbiolo d'Alba Bricco Barone 2004.

●	Dogliani Papà Celso '05	🍷🍷🍷	4*
●	Barolo Cerviano '01	🍷🍷	7
●	Barbera d'Alba Rinaldi '04	🍷🍷	4*
●	Barbaresco Faset '03	🍷🍷	6
●	Nebbiolo d'Alba Bricco Barone '04	🍷🍷	4
○	Cinerino '05	🍷🍷	5
●	Barolo Vign. Terlo Ravera '02	🍷	7
●	Dolcetto di Dogliani San Luigi '05	🍷	4
●	Barolo Pressenda '00	🍸🍸🍸	7
●	Dolcetto di Dogliani Papà Celso '04	🍸🍸🍸	4
●	Dolcetto di Dogliani Papà Celso '00	🍸🍸🍸	4

DOGLIANI (CN)

FRANCESCO BOSCHIS
FRAZ. SAN MARTINO DI PIANEZZO, 57
12063 DOGLIANI (CN)
TEL. 017370574
www.marcdegrazia.com

Wines from Mario Boschis's small estate, with 11 hectares and an average production of 45,000 bottles, are making such giant steps that the cellar now has a full profile in the Guide. At the estate, Marco depends on the valued collaboration of his wife Simona and sons Marco and Paolo, who is also winery oenologist. The range submitted was very good, particularly the Dolcetto di Dogliani wines. The most interesting is Vigna dei Prey 2005, barrique-aged for ten months, which is an impenetrable ruby red and gives cinchona, morello cherry, blackberry and damson aromas on the nose. The palate is fresh, soft and has very long. Another Two Glass winner was the Dolcetto di Dogliani Superiore Vigna del Ciliegio 2004, which gives nuances of cocoa powder, sweet spices, black berry fruit and cinchona and is rich on the palate with sustained acidity and excellent alcohol. Our panel also praised the Barbera d'Alba Le Masserie 2004, which has coffee and toasty notes, from its time in barrique, over cherry and plum sensations. The palate is full and powerful with sustained supporting acidity. The simpler yet never boring Dolcetto di Dogliani Pianezzo 2005 is juicy and easy drinking while the sauvignon-based Langhe Bianco Vigna dei Garisin 2005 is fresh and satisfying. The rest of the range presented is very well managed.

●	Barbera d'Alba Le Masserie '04	🍷🍷	5
●	Dolcetto di Dogliani Sup. V. del Ciliegio '04	🍷🍷	4
●	Dolcetto di Dogliani Pianezzo '05	🍷🍷	3*
●	Dolcetto di Dogliani V. dei Prey '05	🍷🍷	4
●	Dolcetto di Dogliani V. Sorì San Martino '05	🍷	4
○	Langhe Bianco Vigna dei Garisin '05	🍷	4
●	Langhe Freisa Bosco delle Cicale '05	🍷	4

DOGLIANI (CN)

★ Ca' Viola

B.ta San Luigi, 11
12063 Dogliani (CN)
tel. 017370547
www.caviola.com

Sometimes we ask ourselves how one of the most famous, sought-after oenologists in our country can travel around Italy from north to south, to Alto Adige, Veneto, Liguria, Marche, Tuscany, Puglia and Sicily, not to mention Piedmont, and still manage to find time to brilliantly run his own estate. Although Beppe Caviola deserves respect for his successful career, the winery would never have taken off without the commitment of his wife, Simonetta, and trusted Maurizio Anselma. It also seems paradoxical that one of the most brilliant interpreters of dolcetto, with a great cellar in his chosen hometown of Dogliani, has no vineyards in the municipality. The nearly eight hectares under vine of Ca' Viola are mainly in Montelupo Albese and, after a recent modest acquisition, also in Novello. The Langhe Bric du Luv is from a mix of barbera, sourced from old vineyards in Montelupo, and a less than ten per cent Barolo nebbiolo harvested at Novello. It's a red with great harmony that shows how well new oak was administered and has excellent structure that never threatens to crowd out its elegant features. This year, the Dolcetto d'Alba Barturot 2005 is extraordinary with its main strengths lying in its sense of place and variety. Never before has it been so well defined or caressing and it was hardly surprising that it won Three Glasses. As usual the Barbera d'Alba Brichet, part fermented in pre-used small oak, offers carefree drinking without sacrificing structure. Beppe's list ends with Vilot, an extremely drinkable Dolcetto.

● Dolcetto d'Alba Barturot '05	▼▼▼	5
● Langhe Rosso Bric du Luv '04	▼▼	6
● Barbera d'Alba Brichet '05	▼▼	5
● Dolcetto d'Alba Vilot '05	▼▼	4*
● Dolcetto d'Alba Barturot '01	▽▽▽	5
● Langhe Rosso Bric du Luv '99	▽▽▽	6
● Dolcetto d'Alba Barturot '98	▽▽▽	5
● Dolcetto d'Alba Barturot '96	▽▽▽	5
● Langhe Rosso Bric du Luv '03	▽▽▽	6
● Langhe Rosso Bric du Luv '01	▽▽▽	6
● Langhe Rosso Bric du Luv '95	▽▽▽	6
● Langhe Rosso Bric du Luv '96	▽▽▽	6
● Langhe Rosso Bric du Luv '98	▽▽▽	6
● Dolcetto d'Alba Barturot '04	▽▽	5
● L'Insieme '01	▽▽	7

DOGLIANI (CN)

Quinto Chionetti & Figlio

B.ta Valdiberti, 44
12063 Dogliani (CN)
tel. 017371179
www.chionettiquinto.com

Faithful to habit, this grand old man of Dogliani looks after his vineyards as if they were gardens located on the most beautifully exposed plots in the entire Dogliani region. Could this be Quinto Chionetti's not particularly difficult-to-guess secret? Or maybe the simple fact is that although he uses modern equipment in the cellar, he continues with traditional methods that enable him to respect first the grape then the wine. There has never been room here for osmosis or vacuum concentrators or even oenological tannins or other products of the chemistry laboratory. Backed by his long experience, Quinto has never wavered even when popular Dolcettos were very different from his. He continued to work the way he has always worked and now he is being proved right. Those who buy Dolcetto at his cellar are looking for powerful wines, as it should be in Dogliani, but rich in fruity sensations, in memory of those childhood berry feasts. Above all, they are looking for wines that avoid excessive hardness. The estate's 14 hectares under vine are entirely planted to dolcetto and yield these now classic reds, Dolcetto di Dogliani San Luigi and Dolcetto di Dogliani Briccolero. The first offers an overview of the world according to Chionetti with all the freshness and fragrance of the variety. Blackberry and almond aromas show on a still pleasingly heady background. The fullness is almost dense, yet the wine never loses that easy-drinking quality. The second is, as usual, a stand-out.

● Dolcetto di Dogliani Briccolero '05	▼▼	4*
● Dolcetto di Dogliani S. Luigi '05	▼▼	4*
● Dolcetto di Dogliani Briccolero '04	▽▽▽	4
● Dolcetto di Dogliani Briccolero '03	▽▽	4

DOGLIANI (CN)

Einaudi
B.ta Gombe, 31
12063 Dogliani (CN)
tel. 017370191
www.poderieinaudi.com

This major estate has continued to acquire vineyards in different parts of the Langhe and now has a total of about 50 hectares. Its long, prestigious history has allowed it negotiate the challenges of the vintage under consideration almost unscathed. In fact, only a few bottles were produced in 2002 of a generic Barolo by blending the best fruit recovered from those vineyards not affected by hail. In further defence of the winery and consultant Beppe Caviola, we should say that the Langhe Rosso dedicated to the former president of Italy is from a harvest that could not actually be defined as bad but was certainly difficult. This explains why the Einaudi family did not hit the Three Glass target this year after a long, uninterrupted string of top awards. At any rate, two wines did make it to our finals, Langhe Rosso Luigi Einaudi 2003 and Dolcetto di Dogliani Vigna Tecc 2004. The Luigi Einaudi, a blend of nebbiolo, cabernet sauvignon, merlot and barbera, though still a great wine, lacks the depth and class of the best versions. The stifling 2003 season has brought out ripe blackberry and blackcurrant fruit, well balanced by the spiciness of the barrique, but it has curbed the freshness on the palate. The Dolcetto Vigna Tecc has all the characteristics of a great Dolcetto di Dogliani, including an almost impenetrable ruby colour, intense aromas of black berry jam and cocoa powder, irrepressible power on the palate and a very long finish. The rest of the range is well up to the outstanding Einaudi reputation.

● Langhe Rosso Luigi Einaudi '03	🍷🍷	6
● Dolcetto di Dogliani V. Tecc '04	🍷🍷	4*
● Barolo '02	🍷🍷	6
● Langhe Nebbiolo '04	🍷🍷	4
● Dogliani '05	🍷🍷	4
● Dolcetto di Dogliani '05	🍷🍷	4
● Piemonte Barbera '04	🍷	5
● Barolo nei Cannubi '00	🍷🍷🍷	8
● Barolo Costa Grimaldi '01	🍷🍷🍷	8
● Langhe Rosso Luigi Einaudi '97	🍷🍷🍷	6
● Barolo nei Cannubi '98	🍷🍷🍷	8
● Langhe Rosso Luigi Einaudi '98	🍷🍷🍷	6
● Barolo nei Cannubi '99	🍷🍷🍷	8
● Langhe Rosso Luigi Einaudi '99	🍷🍷🍷	6

DOGLIANI (CN)

Pecchenino
B.ta Valdiberti, 59
12063 Dogliani (CN)
tel. 017370686
www.pecchenino.com

After having worked long and hard to promote the dolcetto variety and Dogliani wines, and having been among the main campaigners for the DOCG, brothers Attilio and Orlando Pecchenino have realized their dream of making a Barolo. In fact, they have leased a hectare and a half in Monforte d'Alba in the Le Coste vineyard since 2004. We'll have to wait till 2008 to taste this first Barolo labelled Pecchenino. At any rate, at the moment Orlando's biggest worry is dolcetto that occupies a large section of the 25 hectares under vine managed by his family. For a couple of years now, as in many other operations in the area, Pecchenino has expended much energy on making it more elegant and appetizing abroad as well as in Italy. The results of our tastings speak clearly with three excellent scores for the house Dolcettos. The San Luigi opens on clear, refined fruit and ushers in a soft, juicy palate that illuminates a long finish with nicely stylish tannins. The Sirì d'Jermu is a gem of elegance that, through its complexity, manages to make its remarkable concentration seem natural and even light. The Bricco Botti 2004 is the result of a superior harvest and therefore offers great structure but also more austere tannins and more vibrant acidity. Compared to past versions, the impact of the oak has been strongly reduced. For us, this was very much a Three Glass wine. The Nebbiolo Vigna Botti and Barbera Quass showed their high quality though the latter fell short of last edition's exploits. The release of the Langhe Bianco has been postponed for a year.

● Dolcetto di Dogliani Sup. Bricco Botti '04	🍷🍷🍷	5
● Dogliani Sirì d'Jermu '05	🍷🍷	5
● Dolcetto di Dogliani S. Luigi '05	🍷🍷	4*
● Barbera d'Alba Quass '04	🍷🍷	5
● Langhe Nebbiolo V. Botti '04	🍷🍷	5
● Dolcetto di Dogliani S. Luigi '00	🍷🍷🍷	4
● Dolcetto di Dogliani Sirì d'Jermu '03	🍷🍷🍷	5
● Dolcetto di Dogliani Sirì d'Jermu '01	🍷🍷🍷	5
● Dolcetto di Dogliani Sirì d'Jermu '99	🍷🍷🍷	5
● Dolcetto di Dogliani Sirì d'Jermu '98	🍷🍷🍷	5

DOGLIANI (CN)

San Fereolo

Loc. San Fereolo
B.ta Valdibà, 59
12063 Dogliani (CN)
tel. 0173742075
www.sanfereolo.com

By now, Nicoletta Bocca is firmly installed on the Valdibà hillside and her time in the city is just a distant memory. The winemaking life becomes Ms Bocca. In the past, like many other enlightened Langhe farmers, Nicoletta always tended her 12 hectares under vine with special attention to the environment but since 2005, San Fereolo has been making the first steps to switch over to organic methods. Furthermore, Nicoletta is doing all she can for the new Dogliani DOCG that she and other long-established producers wanted so badly. So we should not be surprised to find the Dogliani leading this strong range of wines. The aromas of ripe black berry fruit on the mineral background lead into a full, long palate like a steel fist in a velvet glove. The Langhe Austri 2004, from barbera with a splash of nebbiolo, comes close to repeating last year's exploit. As always in the wines from San Fereolo, the use of wood is very discreet and serves to enhance the earthy and fruity plum component and balance the explosive structure of the palate. The excellent scores continued with the Dolcetto di Dogliani Superiore 2004, which has a broad, multi-faceted nose but a slightly dried palate. Down among the standard-label Dolcettos, the Valdibà 2005 is difficult to classify since it has the structure and length of a much more ambitious wine. For the first time in 2004, Nicoletta risked vinifying an almost monovarietal Nebbiolo, with only about five per cent barbera. It will carry Langhe Rosso Il Provinciale on the label and is a great new thoroughbred for her aristocratic stable.

● Langhe Rosso Il Provinciale '04	TT	5
● Langhe Rosso Austri '04	TT	5
● Dogliani '05	TT	4*
● Dolcetto di Dogliani Sup. '04	TT	5
● Dolcetto di Dogliani Valdibà '05	TT	4
● Langhe Rosso Austri '03	YYY	5
● Dolcetto di Dogliani S. Fereolo '97	YYY	4
● Langhe Rosso Brumaio '97	YYY	5
● Dolcetto di Dogliani Sup. '03	YY	5
● Dolcetto di Dogliani Sup. 1593 '99	YY	5
● Dolcetto di Dogliani Sup. 1593 '00	YY	5
● Langhe Rosso Brumaio '01	YY	5

DOGLIANI (CN)

San Romano

B.ta Giachelli, 8
12063 Dogliani (CN)
tel. 017376289
www.sanromano.com

Owned by businessman Giulio Napoli, San Romano seems to have got back into the swing of things since the departure just before the 2005 harvest of Bruno Chionetti, the man who for years had made San Romano famous. Enrico Durando is the new house factotum and has made the most of his long experience gained at the side of his predecessor. His clear preference for vineyard work has left ample room in the cellar for Beppe Caviola, who has for years watched over San Romano's oenological progress. Today, the estate includes around nine hectares under vine, most planted to dolcetto, and a very recently constructed cellar furnished with all the modern equipment necessary to guarantee a level of security during vinification. Unfortunately for Giulio Napoli, the first vintage of the new cycle was ill-starred. The dramatic hailstorm at the beginning of September that year ruined most of the estate's dolcetto, and with it most of their hopes. Dolcetto is the most difficult and frustrating of all Langhe varieties. Troublesome weather can block the ripening of the berries or even cause them to drop off the vine. This kind of bad luck had to leave its mark on the wines from 2005. The downbeat beginning with the new staff brought us just three premium wines. The leader is obviously Vigna del Pilone, which offers a good fruity nose that is just a bit too intense and a mid-bodied palate marked by a metallic note. The effects of the hail are even more tangible in the Bricco delle Lepri and the Ciancé, from dolcetto, merlot and pinot nero.

● Dolcetto di Dogliani V. del Pilone '05	TT	4*
● Dolcetto di Dogliani Bricco delle Lepri '05	T	3
● Langhe Rosso Ciancé '05		3
● Dolcetto di Dogliani V. del Pilone '97	YYY	4
● Dolcetto di Dogliani V. del Pilone '98	YYY	4
● Dolcetto di Dogliani V. del Pilone '99	YYY	4
● Dolcetto di Dogliani Sup. Dolianum '01	YY	5
● Dolcetto di Dogliani V. del Pilone '04	YY	4

FARA NOVARESE (NO)

LUIGI DESSILANI E FIGLIO
VIA CESARE BATTISTI, 21
28073 FARA NOVARESE (NO)
TEL. 0321829252
www.dessilani.it

For 30 years, the Lucca family has run the Dessilani estate with great success, but owner Enzio, who is always on the look-out for new challenges, is still not satisfied. This year, he finalized the purchase of an extremely good plot at Fara, which will probably see the creation of a new label. The long-established wines on offer include estate stalwart Fara Caramino, which offers typical notes of black cherry and brandied fruit with sophisticated minerality that lifts and highlights the nose. The over-generous alcohol is no doubt due to the growing year, 2003, which was a real scorcher. The aromas follow through nicely on the palate and the very pleasant richness of flavour tones down the sweet sensations in the finish. Fara Lochera does not seem to have suffered the effects of the great heat of 2003, probably because of the tolerance levels of the old vines to be found in the vineyard. Aromatically it is similar to the Caramino, but it lacks alcohol-derived tonalities and is therefore smoother on the palate. It may be less powerful, but it is undoubtedly more sensual and fulfilling. Ghemme and Sizzano, both from 2002, reveal technical mastery and knowledge of the territory. Of the two, we prefer red the Ghemme, which offers a fuller interpretation of nebbiolo. We gave One Glass to the Nebbiolo '03, which was penalized by the vintage: the fruit is very ripe and the acidity fails to achieve a complete balance.

● Fara Lochera '03	🍷🍷	5
● Ghemme '02	🍷🍷	5
● Sizzano '02	🍷🍷	6
● Fara Caramino '03	🍷🍷	5
● Colline Novaresi Nebbiolo '03	🍷	4
● Fara Caramino '99	🍷🍷🍷 (white)	6
● Fara Caramino '01	🍷🍷 (white)	5
● Fara Lochera '01	🍷🍷 (white)	6
● Sizzano '01	🍷🍷 (white)	6
● Fara Caramino '02	🍷🍷 (white)	6
● Ghemme '01	🍷 (white)	6

FARIGLIANO (CN)

ANNA MARIA ABBONA
FRAZ. MONCUCCO, 21
12060 FARIGLIANO (CN)
TEL. 0173797228
www.amabbona.com

Farigliano is a small municipality that separates the Langhe from the Mondovì area, a border territory that few outside Piedmont will have heard of. All the same, it boasts a handful of important estates. One of these is the one that belongs to Anna Maria Abbona and her husband, Franco Schellino. Established in 1989, its eight and a half hectares planted to vine extend across slopes so steep that the owners are forced to work them by hand. Almost all the vineyards are dedicated to the key variety of the territory, dolcetto, available in several versions, each boasting a confidently individual character. The Dolcetto di Dogliani Superiore '04, obtained from a plot planted in 1943, did particularly well at our tastings. Dark, almost opaque red in the glass, the nose hints at blackberry and cherry intermingled with notes of Peruvian bark and pepper left over from 12 months of ageing in big barrels. It is rich and firmly structured on the palate where its pleasant supporting acidity gives it length. The Dolcetto di Dogliani Maioli '05, matured exclusively in stainless steel vats, also scored high thanks to its concentrated fruitiness and overall harmony of flavour. The Langhe Rosso Cadò '04, a mix of barbera and dolcetto aged in 25-hectolitre barrels and 900-litre casks, did not disappoint. The Dolcetto di Dogliani Sorì dij But '05 and the elegant Langhe Nebbiolo '04 are both interesting, with the easy-drinking Langhe Dolcetto '05 a notch below.

● Dolcetto di Dogliani Sup. '04	🍷🍷	5
● Dolcetto di Dogliani Maioli '05	🍷🍷	4*
● Langhe Nebbiolo '04	🍷🍷	4
● Langhe Rosso Cadò '04	🍷🍷	5
● Dolcetto di Dogliani Sorì dij But '05	🍷🍷	4
● Langhe Dolcetto '05	🍷	3
● Dolcetto di Dogliani Sup. '01	🍷🍷 (white)	5
● Dolcetto di Dogliani Maioli '03	🍷🍷 (white)	4
● Dolcetto di Dogliani Sup. '03	🍷🍷 (white)	5
● Dolcetto di Dogliani Maioli '04	🍷🍷 (white)	4
● Langhe Rosso Cadò '01	🍷🍷 (white)	5
● Langhe Rosso Cadò '03	🍷🍷 (white)	5

FARIGLIANO (CN)

GIOVANNI BATTISTA GILLARDI

CASCINA CORSALETTO, 69
12060 FARIGLIANO (CN)
TEL. 017376306
www.gillardi.it

The ever brilliant Giacolino Gillardi is moving full steam ahead with plans to make his cellar more functional and better suited to the range of wines he produces. He has upped production of Harys, the estate's flagship offering, which finally earned the Langhe Rosso appellation in the 2005 vintage. Next year, Gillardi will release 3,500 bottles of this syrah-based wine to market, significantly more than the current 2,500. Also significant is the decision taken by Giacomo Gillardi and his father Giovanni Battista – a tower of strength in the vineyard – not to use the new DOCG for their Dolcetto di Dogliani. Their seven hectares of vineyards will give them a maximum of 35,000 bottles. Moving on to the wines themselves, the Harys '04 is on fine form after its 18-month sojourn in barriques. It flaunts an intense purplish colour and fruity aromas mingled with more complex notes of tobacco, cocoa powder and pepper. Surefooted and solidly built on the palate, it can with elegant, juicy phenolics. The Langhe Rosso Yeta '04 is from dolcetto with ten per cent cabernet sauvignon and aged for a year in oak. Its nose enchants with notes of mint and jam, while the harmonious palate nicely balances tannins and acidity. The two '05 Dolcettos are skilfully made in a fairly traditional style. The Vigneto Maestra is fruitier and fresher, and the Cursalet is less approachable, opening out gradually to reveal a complexity worthy of the great Dogliani Dolcettos.

●	Harys '04	🍷🍷	7
●	Dolcetto di Dogliani Cursalet '05	🍷🍷	4*
●	Langhe Rosso Yeta '04	🍷🍷	5
●	Dolcetto di Dogliani Vign. Maestra '05	🍷🍷	4
●	Harys '00	YYY	7
●	Harys '98	YYY	7
●	Harys '99	YYY	7
●	Harys '01	YY	7
●	Harys '02	YY	7
●	Harys '03	YY	7
●	Langhe Rosso Yeta '00	YY	5
●	Langhe Rosso Yeta '01	YY	5
●	Langhe Rosso Yeta '03	YY	5

GATTINARA (VC)

ANTONIOLO

C.SO VALSESIA, 277
13045 GATTINARA (VC)
TEL. 0163833612

This estate has come along in leaps and bounds since Alberto Antoniolo took the cellar in hand: continuously good sales, wide acclaim from wine enthusiasts in Italy and overseas, and a series of awards from the wine press. Antoniolo has also made some major investments in the vineyards and in particular in the cellar, where work to renovate and expand the available space is now almost complete. The old cellars bring us just two Gattinaras this year, the basic '02 and the Osso San Grato '01, which looks set to repeat the performance of the superlative 1999. Absolutely typical in its bright garnet red appearance and its nose of rhubarb root with hints of roses, rust and flint, it truly comes into its own on the palate, where the juicy, tannic body is accompanied by vibrant, perfectly integrated acidity. The never-ending finish is dominated by a salty sensation that hints at the sea. The Gattinara '02 also comes from the Osso San Grato plot. As a result of the problems of the vintage, the other two estate crus, San Francesco and Castelle, were withdrawn and the basic label was obtained from grapes grown in the most prestigious vineyard. This Gattinara shows tannic-acidic elements softened by an aromatic profile that is full, charming and unmistakably territorial. We also liked the Erbaluce di Caluso '05 with its pleasing notes of lime echoed in the citrus-like finish, and the fruity Nebbiolo Juvenia '05 for its refreshing vein of acidity.

●	Gattinara Vign. Osso S. Grato '01	🍷🍷🍷	7
●	Gattinara '02	🍷🍷	6
○	Erbaluce di Caluso '05	🍷🍷	4*
●	Coste della Sesia Nebbiolo Juvenia '05	🍷	4
●	Gattinara Vign. Castelle '00	YYY	7
●	Gattinara Vign. S. Francesco '01	YYY	6
●	Gattinara Vign. Castelle '99	YYY	7
●	Gattinara Vign. Osso S. Grato '00	YY	7
●	Gattinara Vign. S. Francesco '00	YY	6
●	Gattinara Vign. Castelle '01	YY	7
●	Gattinara Vign. Osso S. Grato '99	YY	7

GATTINARA (VC)

ANZIVINO
C.SO VALSESIA, 162
13045 GATTINARA (VC)
TEL. 0163827172
www.anzivino.net

Emanuele Anzivino is a Milan-based entrepreneur whose passion for wine brought him to the rugged Gattinara foothills. This year, Emanuele presented his fifth official range of wines after his debut with the Gattinara '99. The list of bottles on offer is now quite significant and has already received some impressive plaudits from our Guide. Anzivino is gaining quite a reputation for his rigorous, elegant style, credit for which must also go to Beppe Zatti, a capable and highly talented oenologist. The Gattinara skipped the '00 vintage but by way of compensation we tasted the brand new Riserva, obtained by selecting the best lots of the 2001 Gattinara and ageing it for longer than usual. The classic nose combines clear notes of medicinal herbs and currant with strong mineral tones as the prelude to a full-bodied, very lengthy palate that slackens off ever so slightly in the finish on a note of extremely ripe fruit. The Bramaterra '03 also put on a fine show, managing like few other wines to weave croatina's big personality into an elegant, complex texture, the perfect foil for noble nebbiolo. Its notes of orange peel and ginger are truly exciting. Tarlo '04, a nebbiolo and cabernet blend, is very good, consistent and tasty. But this year's real masterpiece is the Faticato '03, made from the estate's very best nebbiolo part-dried for a short time on racks. The nose is a veritable triumph of aromas that are at once sweet, well defined, warm and dense, blackcurrant, myrtle and green olives giving way to rhubarb and white pepper. The palate is gutsy, fruity and compact. Try it.

● Bramaterra '03	2 black glasses	5*
● Coste della Sesia Faticato '03	2 black glasses	7
● Gattinara Ris. '01	2 black glasses	6
● Il Tarlo '04	2 black glasses	4*
● Bramaterra '01	2 glasses	5
● Bramaterra '02	2 glasses	5
● Gattinara '00	2 glasses	6
● Coste della Sesia Faticato '01	2 glasses	7
● Gattinara '01	2 glasses	6
● Gattinara '99	2 glasses	6

GATTINARA (VC)

NERVI
C.SO VERCELLI, 117
13045 GATTINARA (VC)
TEL. 0163833228
www.gattinara-nervi.it

The Nervi estate has spent the last few years renovating its vineyards and cellar. In the magnificent natural amphitheatre formed by the Molsino plot, the vines have been partially replanted to comply with the most up-to-date techniques. In the cellar, meanwhile, barriques and 900-litre casks have appeared alongside the traditional large ovals in a move to combine traditional and modern processes. For this edition of the Guide, Nervi presented us with just one new label, the Gattinara Podere dei Ginepri '01. Molsino was not produced in the disappointing 2002 vintage so we shall have to wait until next year to taste it. Obtained from a special selection of the estate's cru aged at length in oak, the new offering has a gorgeous vibrancy in its brilliant garnet red. The nose offers aromas typical of the Gattinara terroir, a minerality that mingles iron and plant roots that merge with nebbiolo's dignified notes of roses and violets, all refreshed and ennobled by a lively hint of balsam. The soft palate mirrors the pleasant sensations of the nose, and its richness of flavour integrates well with the acidity to buttress the palate. The finish is exceptional for cleanliness and consistency. This is one of the best Gattinaras we tasted, every inch a Three Glass champion.

● Gattinara Podere dei Ginepri '01	3 black glasses	6
● Gattinara Vign. Molsino '00	3 glasses	6
● Gattinara Vign. Molsino '01	2 glasses	6
● Gattinara '01	2 glasses	5

GATTINARA (VC)

GIANCARLO TRAVAGLINI
VIA DELLE VIGNE, 36
13045 GATTINARA (VC)
TEL. 0163833588
www.travaglinigattinara.it

In his dynamic 40-year career, Giancarlo Travaglini succeeded in his arduous quest to earn Gattinara a place on the world wine stage, creating a vigorous, positive image for both the territory and the wine. His sad loss two years ago left a gap that his daughters Cinzia and Cristina must now try to fill. We salute Giancarlo at the beginning of our tasting notes because this year the estate has finally achieved its first Three Glass trophy for a monumental Gattinara Riserva '01, a fitting and splendid tribute to an extraordinary grower. We'll start at the top, with the champion itself. The Riserva is, quite simply, epic. It fills the glass, showing a typical, almost garnet edge and a nose redolent of roses and iron-bearing minerals. The palate reveals all the majesty of its fruit of origin on the way to achieving perfect harmony with the oak, and bowled us over with its aromas and complexity. A rare jewel indeed. In last year's edition of the Guide, we mistakenly reviewed the Gattinara Tre Vigne '01, but our words of praise hold true for this year. A berry fruit nose with balsamic undertones precedes a chewy, lip-smacking palate and an austere, tannic finish. The basic Gattinara is distinctive. Typical rooty sensations mingle with gamey, woodland aromas on the nose, but the palate's slight lack of succulence highlights hard, tannic-acid elements that are particularly noticeable in the finish. This year sees the addition of a new recruit to the line-up, the Coste della Sesia '04. Obtained exclusively from nebbiolo, it is varietal and well managed but has room for growth.

● Gattinara Ris. '01	▼▼▼	6
● Gattinara Tre Vigne '01	▼▼	6
● Gattinara '02	▼▼	6
● Coste della Sesia Nebbiolo '04	▼	4
● Gattinara Ris. '00	▽▽	6
● Gattinara '01	▽▽	5
● Gattinara Ris. '99	▽▽	6
● Gattinara Tre Vigne '00	▽▽	6
● Gattinara Tre Vigne '99	▽▽	6

GAVI (AL)

NICOLA BERGAGLIO
FRAZ. ROVERETO
LOC. PEDAGGERI, 59
15066 GAVI (AL)
TEL. 0143682195

This year the Guide celebrates its 20th anniversary and the Nicola Bergaglio estate has appeared in every single one of our 20 editions. The levels of quality achieved by this estate are all the more impressive if you consider that in the past two decades the Bergaglio family has done very little to change things. The country estate set up in the early 1980s remains fundamentally the same and the few changes they have made have done nothing to sway their philosophy. They have extended their cellar, introduced a new cru, Minaia, and for this edition of the Guide they presented us with a new Gavi label, Ciapon. The winery is fortunate enough to have 15 hectares of first-class vineyards in the heart of the small district of Rovereto, a zone well known for cortese. Gianluigi Bergaglio has run the estate for 20 years and was joined several years ago by his son, Diego. They gave us three superb Gavis to taste, all offering excellent quality and value for money given the extremely reasonable price. Well-balanced acidity makes the basic version very agreeable and refreshing on the palate. Ciapon is conditioned in small barrels to produce a lovely pale straw-yellow colour and flowery, vanilla aromas. The Minaia cru – obtained from vines over 30 years old – is top drawer and always stands out for its sensory profile. Straw-yellow, almost golden in appearance, it reveals flowery notes with exotic nuances, a harmonious, full-bodied palate and a pleasant lip-smacking finish. A gem of a Gavi.

○ Gavi del Comune di Gavi Minaia '05	▼▼	4*
○ Gavi del Comune di Gavi Ciapon '05	▼▼	4*
○ Gavi del Comune di Gavi '05	▼	3
○ Gavi del Comune di Gavi Minaia '04	▽▽	4

GAVI (AL)

GIAN PIERO BROGLIA
TENUTA LA MEIRANA
LOC. LOMELLINA, 22
15066 GAVI (AL)
TEL. 0143642998
www.broglia.eu

The Broglia family has its headquarters in a cascina, La Meriana, where there is evidence that wine has been produced and sold since as far back as AD 972. Today, the tradition of vine growing continues on this beautiful property situated in the centre of the Gavi DOCG. The estate totals over 100 hectares, 47 of which are planted to vine, mainly cortese. Gian Piero Broglia runs operations with the technical support of Donato Lanati, one of the best-known oenologists on the peninsula and a leading expert on the indigenous varieties of the Alessandria region. The wines they presented this year all performed very well. One of the three we tasted went as far as the final rounds for the Three Glass awards and the others sailed past the Two Glass level. First up we have the Gavi Bruno Broglia, a wine that over the years has proved its qualitative mettle in Gavi territory. Its cortese grapes are selected from an old plot that has been in production for over 100 years and the result is truly astonishing. Straw-yellow in the glass with almost golden highlights, it possesses a deep, captivating mineral nose. The body's excellent backbone ensures a rounded, full-flavoured palate whose overall balance is superb and the oaky nuances not at all invasive. The Gavi La Meirana is less concentrated but quite delightful. The fruity, dolcetto-based Monferrato Rosso Pernici '05 does well, its palate enhanced by the bitterish note that emerges in the finish.

○ Gavi del Comune di Gavi Bruno Broglia '04	🍷🍷	5
○ Gavi del Comune di Gavi La Meirana '05	🍷🍷	4
● Monferrato Rosso Le Pernici '05	🍷🍷	4
○ Gavi del Comune di Gavi Bruno Broglia '03	ΥΥ	5
● Monferrato Rosso Bruno Broglia '03	ΥΥ	5
○ Gavi del Comune di Gavi La Meirana '04	ΥΥ	4

GAVI (AL)

CASTELLARI BERGAGLIO
FRAZ. ROVERETO, 136
15066 GAVI (AL)
TEL. 0143644000

Since it was founded in 1890, the Castellari Bergaglio estate has grown nothing but cortese. Over the years this devotion to Gavi's most typical variety has paid off because today the estate enjoys a reputation as one of the DOCG's most important points of reference. In addition to making wine, Marco Bergaglio and his sister Barbara have made it their mission to promote the territory's development by organizing various cultural and food-and-wine events. The range of wines we tasted this time around excelled for its sheer quality. Gavi Fornaci '05, obtained from grapes cultivated on slopes in the Tassarolo zone, is particularly good. Its lovely straw-yellow colour with greenish lights in the glass is the prelude to a nice, fresh-tasting palate and a full-flavoured, lingering finish. The Gavi Rovereto '05 is obtained from fruit grown in vineyards that are over 80 years old and the result is a most intriguing, agreeable wine.
The nose offers hints of peach and citrus peel enhanced by notes of chamomile and wild flowers, while the palate's charming supporting acidity gives it refreshing drinkability. The Gavi Pilìn '01 is a very unusual selection obtained from the very finest bunches of certosina and aged in the cellar in small barrels. The Gavi Rolona '05 is not quite up to the same standards.

○ Gavi del Comune di Gavi Pilìn '01	🍷🍷	5
○ Gavi del Comune di Gavi Rovereto Vignavecchia '05	🍷🍷	4*
○ Gavi del Comune di Tassarolo Fornaci '05	🍷🍷	4*
○ Gavi del Comune di Gavi Rolona '05	🍷	4
○ Gavi del Comune di Gavi Rolona '04	ΥΥ	4
○ Gavi del Comune di Gavi Rovereto '04	ΥΥ	4

GAVI (AL)

La Giustiniana
Fraz. Rovereto, 5
15066 Gavi (AL)
tel. 0143682132

La Giustiniana belongs to the Lombardini family and has been managed for many years by the excellent Enrico Tomalino, who works very hard to ensure that the wines produced are invariably of the highest quality. This estate traces its roots all the way back to 1615, when the Republic of Genoa conferred the property on the Giustiniani family, who planted the first vines and built the splendid villa that still stands today. The estate totals around 110 hectares, 39 of which are planted to vine. Turning to the wines presented this year, we enjoyed Gavi Montessora '05 for its delightful straw-yellow appearance and a nose that recalls peach, apricot and wild flowers. The soft palate ends in a slightly bitterish finish. The Gavi Lugarara '05 offers clear notes of chamomile and a fresh-tasting, full-flavoured palate. The ruby red Monferrato Rosso Granciarossa '05 possesses elegant aromas of ripe fruit and a velvety entry on the palate. Compared to the previous versions we have tasted, the Monferrato Rosso Just '04, a blend of barbera and nebbiolo, is a tad below par. A further period of ageing in the bottle will do much to help it find balance.

○ Gavi del Comune di Gavi Lugarara '05	▼▼	4*
○ Gavi del Comune di Gavi Montessora '05	▼▼	5
● Monferrato Rosso Just '04	▼	5
● Monferrato Rosso Granciarossa '05	▼	3
● Monferrato Rosso Just '03	▽▽	5
○ Gavi del Comune di Gavi Lugarara '04	▽▽	4

GAVI (AL)

Morgassi Superiore
Case Sparse Sermoria, 7
15066 Gavi (AL)
tel. 0143642007
www.morgassisuperiore.it

More than 15 years have passed since Marino Piacitelli and his daughter Cecilia acquired this estate with its peerless position commanding a stunning view over the hills of Gavi. Although the duo each had a completely different professional background, their great passion for wine has been the catalyst for the recovery of old vine-growing plots that had been abandoned over the years. Marino and Cecilia's aspiration to achieve consistently high quality in the wines they produce knows no bounds, and to this end they have just planted an additional two hectares of cortese. As for the wines presented this year, we particularly liked the timorasso-based Monferrato Bianco Timorasso '04. Its big character is immediately discernible in the rich straw-yellow colour enhanced by golden highlights in the glass. The hue is a prelude to complex aromas of apple-like fruit and faint minerally nuances, followed by a generous, mouthfilling palate that reveals extraordinarily long-lingering aromas. The combination of all these characteristics earned it a place in our final tastings. We also like the Gavi '05, a straw-yellow wine with elegant greenish flecks. The nose suggests peach and apricot and the fresh, richly flavoured palate shows a typically bitterish finish. Finally, Gavi Etichetta Oro '04 was a little disappointing compared to previous vintages.

○ Monferrato Bianco Timorgasso '04	▼▼	5
○ Gavi del Comune di Gavi '05	▼▼	4*
○ Gavi del Comune di Gavi Et. Oro '04	▼	5
● Tamino '01	▽▽	6
● Sarastro '01	▽▽	5
○ Gavi del Comune di Gavi Et. Oro '03	▽▽	5

GAVI (AL)

Villa Sparina

Fraz. Monterotondo, 56
15066 Gavi (AL)
Tel. 0143633835
www.villasparina.it

In recent years, the Moccagatta family has concentrated its efforts on two important fronts: first and foremost, growing grapes and making wine; second, and also very important, tourist facilities. The latter aspect is a mark of the estate's strong emphasis on promoting the territory not only through the wines produced at Villa Sparina, but also through the Ostelliere hotel and the restaurant, La Gallina. This year's range of wines did very well and the honours were not just reserved for one product, but for almost all of those we tasted. We start with a magnificent Gavi Monterotondo '04, bottled in magnums only. This wine is obtained from a single plot, one of the most beautiful on the estate, planted with vines that are over 40 years old. Meticulous vinification is designed to produce a white as faithful as possible to cortese's varietal characteristics. which means complex but not overly intense aromas in which the mineral tones of the fruit clearly come through. Significantly lower oakiness gives the palate excellent balance. The Rivalta, the estate's other big wine, is also on good form. A dark red appearance with delicate garnet highlights ushers in rich, lingering aromas of blackberry and forest fruits intermingled with hints of vanilla and charred oak, and then a long, soft, balanced palate. The other house white, the Montej '05 from chardonnay, müller thurgau and sauvignon blanc, is also good. This year, the Barbera del Monferrato Montej '04 was also presented, a ruby red wine with frank, crisp aromas, decent backbone and refreshing acidity on the palate.

●	Monferrato Rosso Rivalta '03	▼▼	6
○	Gavi del Comune di Gavi Monterotondo '04	▼▼	5
●	Barbera del M.to Montej '04	▼▼	4*
○	Gavi del Comune di Gavi '05	▼▼	4*
○	Monferrato Bianco Montej '05	▼▼	4*
○	Villa Sparina Brut M. Cl.	▼▼	5
●	Monferrato Rosso Sampò '03	▼	4
●	Barbera del M.to Rivalta '97	▽▽▽	6
●	Monferrato Rosso Rivalta '00	▽▽▽	6
○	Gavi del Comune di Gavi Monterotondo '99	▽▽▽	5
●	Monferrato Rosso Rivalta '99	▽▽▽	6
●	Monferrato Rosso Rivalta '01	▽▽	6

GHEMME (NO)

Antichi Vigneti di Cantalupo

via Michelangelo Buonarroti, 5
28074 Ghemme (NO)
Tel. 0163840041
www.cantalupo.net

The Arlunno family, owners of Antichi Vigneti di Cantalupo, has made wine at Ghemme for almost two centuries. This zone is known for its nebbiolo, which is cultivated on the morainic slopes formed by the ancient Monte Rosa glaciers. The estate's vineyards extend over about 34 hectares and are divided into various plots. These are crus in the true sense of the word. Most face south and south-west and 80 per cent are planted to nebbiolo, known locally as spanna, the "uva spanea" mentioned by the natural historian Pliny. The remaining 20 per cent of the estate is given over to the indigenous varieties vespolina, uva rara, arneis and greco novarese, as well as an international presence in the form of chardonnay. Production focuses on nebbiolo, presented in various selections all originating in the Ghemme DOCG. None take advantage of the right to add vespolina allowed by regulations. The resulting wines are strongly territorial in character and also long-lived, needing time to reveal their full potential. We tasted two of them this year and our preference was for Ghemme Signore di Bayard '01, a pure nebbiolo sourced from a plot of morainic, gravelly soil and matured for three years in oak barrels and bottle. It presents a wonderful ruby red and a spicy nose of black pepper with a touch of oak that has not yet entirely been absorbed. The palate reveals typical earthy-salty aromas and a hint of cherry. Carolus '05, a white derived from a blend of greco novarese, arneis and chardonnay, is simpler and more drinkable with a peachy note on the reasonably long palate.

●	Ghemme Signore di Bayard '01	▼▼	6
○	Carolus '05	▼▼	3*
○	Carolus '04	▽▽	3
●	Ghemme '00	▽▽	5
●	Ghemme Collis Breclemae '98	▽▽	6
●	Ghemme '99	▽▽	5
●	Ghemme Collis Breclemae '99	▽▽	6
●	Ghemme Collis Carellae '99	▽▽	6

GHEMME (NO)

ROVELLOTTI
INTERNO CASTELLO, 22
28074 GHEMME (NO)
TEL. 0163840393
www.rovellotti.it

The magnificent fortified village of Ricetto in the heart of Ghemme is an added bonus for visitors to the cellars of the Rovellotti family estate. The Rovellotis' love of their territory is clearly evident in both the range of varieties they grow and the management policies they practise on the estate. The 15 hectares are planted exclusively to the indigenous grape types of northern Piedmont: nebbiolo, vespolina, uva rara and erbaluce. From the wines we tasted this year, we particularly liked the Vespolina, a local variety that does not get the attention it deserves. This interpretation made it to our finals, establishing the estate as a point of reference for the vinification of the variety. Lovely notes of white pepper, ginger and flowers render the nose unusually pleasant and elegant, while the palate is very long and full of flavour. All this comes at a price that makes it excellent value for money. The Ghemme Riserva '01 took home Two Glasses despite a faint oaky overtone and a touch too much alcohol. Notes of violets, roses and rich berry fruit are nicely buttressed by measured tannins. The Bianco is simple and easy-drinking with grassy, citrus-like aromas and is obtained from greco novarese, as erbaluce is known in these parts. This variety also went to make a Passito, Valdenrico '04, which offers agreeable apricot nuances and lingering sweetness. A step down from these, we have the Uva Rara '05, the local version of Bonarda. It's perky enough with nice strawberry sensations but perhaps a bit too predictable.

●	Colline Novaresi Vespolina '05	🍷🍷	3*
●	Ghemme Ris. '01	🍷🍷	6
○	Colline Novaresi Bianco '04	🍷	4
○	Valdenrico Passito '04	🍷	7
●	Colline Novaresi Uva Rara '05		3
○	Valdenrico Passito '01	YY	7
●	Colline Novaresi Vespolina '03	YY	3
○	Valdenrico Passito '03	YY	7
●	Colline Novaresi Vespolina '04	YY	3
●	Ghemme '99	YY	5
●	Ghemme Ris. '99	YY	6

INCISA SCAPACCINO (AT)

BREMA
VIA POZZOMAGNA, 9
14045 INCISA SCAPACCINO (AT)
TEL. 014174019

Once again, Alessandra and Ermanno Brema brought us a superb range of wines, several of which went home with a Two Glass accolade. One of the best products to come out of this Incisa-based cellar is its Barbera Bricco della Volpettona. It failed to repeat last year's sterling performance, which earned it a place in our final tastings, but it is still a first-class wine. The '04 shows a rich, bright ruby red appearance and aromas ranging from berry fruit jam to spicy notes in a nicely complex nose. The palate has good texture and close-knit tannins that follow its solid taste development through to a very lengthy finish. The fresh-tasting Barbera Ai Cruss '05 did very well with its brilliant ruby red colour and lively nose full of pleasant fruity tones with intriguing hints of tobacco and ethereal, minerally nuances. The rich, weighty palate is full and juicy with a soft, lingering finish. In place of the Bricconizza, we have Barbera Superiore Nizza '04, which presents fruity aromas and a palate of medium intensity ever so slightly in thrall to the oak. The Monferrato Rosso Il Fulvo '04 has a concentrated nose of sweet spices, leather and tobacco and a warm palate leading into a rather ethereal finish. The Brachetto Carlotta '05, is pleasant if a touch overripe.

●	Barbera d'Asti Sup. Bricco della Volpettona '04	🍷🍷	6
●	Barbera d'Asti Sup. Nizza '04	🍷🍷	5
●	Barbera d'Asti Ai Cruss '05	🍷🍷	4*
●	Monferrato Rosso Il Fulvo '04	🍷	5
●	Brachetto d'Acqui Carlotta '05	🍷	4
●	Barbera d'Asti Sup. Bricco della Volpettona '01	YY	6
●	Barbera d'Asti Sup. Bricco della Volpettona '03	YY	6
●	Barbera d'Asti Sup. Bricco della Volpettona '00	YY	6
●	Barbera d'Asti Sup. Bricconizza '03	YY	5

INCISA SCAPACCINO (AT)

TENUTA OLIM BAUDA
REG. PRATA, 50
14045 INCISA SCAPACCINO (AT)
TEL. 014174266
www.tenutaolimbauda.it

Gianni, Dino and Diana Bertolino obtain 50,000 bottles a year from their 25-hectare property and over the last few years we have seen a distinct rise in the quality of their products. After its enforced sabbatical in 2002, the estate's flagship Barbera Superiore Nizza '03 is back on fighting form and romped all the way to our final tastings. It shows a brilliant ruby red in the glass and the complex nose opens out slowly to reveal notes of wild berry jam layered over ethereal nuances and traces of leather. The full, juicy palate is well sustained right through to the warmly alcoholic finish. Excellent, too, is the Barbera Superiore del '04, which presents almost opaque red in the glass with aromas of rain-soaked earth and currant and a gutsy, flavoursome palate. The Chardonnay '04 is rich straw yellow verging on gold. Its rather mature nose is not overly fresh but the palate reveals itself to be simple and tidy and is rounded off by a very clean finish. The rather pale yellow Gavi '05 offers agreeable hints of peachy fruit and chamomile flowers. The palate is cool and well sustained with lively acidity that gives it agreeable length. The Moscato '05 reveals intense notes of peach and sage on the nose with deep aromatic tones in an overall framework of absolute candour, while the palate is dynamic and pleasant. We'll end our notes with a simple but fruity standard-label Barbera d'Asti.

●	Barbera d'Asti Sup. Nizza '03	🍷🍷	5
●	Barbera d'Asti Sup. '04	🍷🍷	5
○	Gavi del Comune di Gavi '05	🍷🍷	4*
○	Moscato d'Asti '05	🍷🍷	4*
●	Barbera d'Asti '05	🍷	4
○	Piemonte Chardonnay '04	🍷	5
●	Barbera d'Asti Sup. '00	🍷🍷 (white)	5
●	Barbera d'Asti Sup. Nizza '01	🍷🍷 (white)	6
●	Barbera d'Asti Sup. Nizza '00	🍷🍷 (white)	6
●	Barbera d'Asti Sup. '98	🍷🍷 (white)	5
●	Barbera d'Asti Sup. '99	🍷🍷 (white)	5

IVREA (TO)

FERRANDO
VIA TORINO, 599A
10015 IVREA (TO)
TEL. 0125633550 - 0125641176
www.ferrandovini.it

The Ferrando family has been producing wine since the late 1800s, concentrating on Erbaluce di Caluso for both their dry and sweet whites and the prestigious Nebbiolo di Carema for their reds. These form the basis for a full range of wines that this year is one of the best to come out of upper Piedmont. Credit for this goes largely to a truly spectacular Carema Etichetta Nera '01, the proud winner of a first Three Glass trophy. The refined, limpid nose releases sharp tones of geraniums and sweeter notes of cocoa powder followed by a complex spiciness – cardamom, cinnamon and white pepper to the fore – with clear rust-like undertones. The supple palate offers pomegranate and currant aromas and lively yet sweet acidity that invigorates the whole. The finish is elegant and lavish, revealing new aromatic nuances. Etichetta Bianca '02 bears the same stamp but has less powerful structure, a range of aromas strongly redolent of dried flowers, and an extremely pleasing and very varietal mineral vein. The Cariola '05 is a superb, elegant Erbaluce. Its mellow and highly complex nose recalls white pepper, pear and eucalyptus, while the sound, rich palate is enlivened by traces of lime and mineral acidity. Solativo, obtained from a late harvest of erbaluce grapes, scored high again this year. Elegant notes of tangerine, hazelnut and marzipan are the prelude to a consistent palate enhanced by measured residual sugar. The Passito di Caluso '01 is a classic, confident wine possessing a yellow apple and chestnut honey nose and a full, continuous palate that is supple and fulfilling.

●	Carema Et. Nera '01	🍷🍷🍷	6
○	Solativo V.T. '04	🍷🍷	5
○	Caluso Passito Vign. Cariola '01	🍷🍷	6
●	Carema Et. Bianca '02	🍷🍷	5
○	Erbaluce di Caluso Cariola '05	🍷🍷	4*
●	Carema Et. Nera '00	🍷🍷 (white)	6
○	Caluso Passito Vign. Cariola '00	🍷🍷 (white)	6
○	Solativo V.T. '03	🍷🍷 (white)	5
●	Carema Et. Nera '98	🍷🍷 (white)	6
●	Carema Et. Nera '99	🍷🍷 (white)	6

LA MORRA (CN)

★ ★ Elio Altare - Cascina Nuova

fraz. Annunziata, 51
12064 La Morra (CN)
tel. 017350835
www.elioaltare.com

Barolo is conspicuous by its absence this year. Not a man given to half measures or compromise, Elio Altare withheld all his major wines in the 2002 vintage. With 40 or so years of experience under his belt, he is a standard bearer for Langhe's noble farming tradition where people are proud of what they do, knuckle down and get their hands dirty in the vineyard and cellar every day yet always have time to make a visitor feel welcome. Today Elio is in two minds about his calling, happy with the results he has achieved but perturbed by the issues that plague the wine world. As for his wines, the three '04 Langhes we tasted were excellent, exemplary in their cleanness and rational, beautifully managed approach. The barbera-based Larigi '04 is complex and full, showing dark, flowery and balsamic on the nose and authoritatively dense and balanced on the tidy palate. It's a blue-blooded champ that fully deserved Three Glasses. The nebbiolo-based Arborina '04 is warm and mellow, sweet in its very ripe berry fruit and succulent, with a densely textured palate and a finish revealing alcohol and clear oaky notes. La Villa '04, obtained from nebbiolo and barbera, has pervasive, well-defined aromas of black cherry and violets, a consistent, fruity encore on the palate, well-balanced tannic weight and a flavoursome finish. We thoroughly enjoyed the Dolcetto '05's fruity, fresh approachability. The Barbera '05 is lip-smacking, clean and full-bodied with fascinating spicy, balsamic nuances. Finally, the new L'Insieme, from the excellent 2004 harvest, is first-class.

●	Langhe Larigi '04	▼▼▼	8
●	Langhe Arborina '04	▼▼	8
●	Langhe La Villa '04	▼▼	8
●	L'Insieme '04	▼▼	7
●	Barbera d'Alba '05	▼▼	4*
●	Dolcetto d'Alba '05	▼▼	4*
●	Barolo Vign. Arborina '00	▽▽▽	8
●	Barolo Vign. Arborina '01	▽▽▽	8
●	Langhe Larigi '95	▽▽▽	8
●	Langhe Arborina '96	▽▽▽	8
●	Langhe Arborina '97	▽▽▽	8
●	Langhe Larigi '97	▽▽▽	8
●	Barolo Vign. Arborina '98	▽▽▽	8
●	Barolo Vign. Arborina '99	▽▽▽	8
●	Langhe La Villa '99	▽▽▽	8

LA MORRA (CN)

Batasiolo

fraz. Annunziata, 87
12064 La Morra (CN)
tel. 017350130 - 017350131
www.batasiolo.com

In the Langhe, an area of country traditions that is home to many small wine estates, the Dogliani family has managed to create a colossus, Batasiolo, without disturbing the natural ambience. Their estate embraces over 110 hectares of vines and turns out approximately two and a half million bottles a year. Oenologist Giorgio Lavagna has run the technical side of things for many years now and keeps an eagle eye on Batasiolo's long tradition of quality. What is truly astonishing is that such a wide range of wines has been able to achieve such good overall standards and produce some real gems. This year, we were offered two Barolo '01 selections to taste, Boscareto and Bofani, and we weren't disappointed. The less well-known Bofani went all the way to our final Three Glass tastings, proof positive of its great quality and its close ties with the Langhe territory that are evident in its powerful tannic strength and rich liquorice and raspberry aromas. Boscareto, its better known sibling, did not entirely convince us as the rough edges typical of Serralunga Barolos are still all too obvious. The straightforward '02 completes the Barolo offering, but we preferred the complex, gutsy Barbaresco '03 and gave it Two Glasses. Dolcetto Bricco di Vergne and Barbera Sovrana are two labels that always offer excellent value. There was also a round of applause for the harmonious Chardonnay Morino '05, the fresh-tasting Gavi Granée and the Spumante Metodo Classico Batasiolo Dosage Zéro '02. The Chardonnay Serbato, Moscato Bosc dla Rei and Arneis are sound but show less personality.

●	Barolo Vign. Bofani '01	▼▼	8
●	Barolo Vign. Boscareto '01	▼▼	8
●	Barbaresco '03	▼▼	6
●	Barbera d'Alba Sovrana '05	▼▼	5
●	Dolcetto d'Alba Bricco di Vergne '05	▼▼	4*
●	Barolo '02	▼	6
○	Dosage Zéro M. Cl. '02	▼	5
○	Gavi di Gavi Granée '05	▼	4
○	Langhe Chardonnay Morino '05	▼	6
○	Moscato d'Asti Bosc dla Rei '05	▼	4
○	Langhe Chardonnay Serbato '05	▼	4
○	Roero Arneis '05		4
●	Barolo Corda della Briccolina '90	▽▽▽	8

LA MORRA (CN)

EUGENIO BOCCHINO
FRAZ. SANTA MARIA
LOC. SERRA, 2
12064 LA MORRA (CN)
TEL. 0173364226

Several years ago, Eugenio and Cinzia Bocchino launched themselves with youthful enthusiasm into their great winemaking adventure. The pair started out with a small plot of land left to them by their grandfather and have expanded over the years to their current five plus hectares, which are spread across the municipalities of Alba, Roddi, Verduno and La Morra. In 2001, they built a new cellar at Santa Maria in La Morra and soon after converted the adjacent rooms initially planned for visitors into their new home. They have progressed in leaps and bounds and today this small family estate is emerging as one of the most interesting in the territory. In the absence of the Barolo '02, the wine that made the greatest impression on us was Nebbiolo La Perucca '03. It is sourced from a vineyard in the municipality of Alba that shows great potential as the source of noble, austere wines. The warm alcohol is very well managed, the nose presents clean notes of ripe cherry with soft flowery undertones, and the adequately fluent, harmonious palate shows a well-gauged use of small wood. Langhe Suo di Giacomo '03, a nebbiolo and barbera blend, is full, dark and densely fruity, if somewhat dominated by the toastiness of the oak. The consistent palate remains balanced and drinkable, despite its massive presence. The Barbera '04 performed better. It's a full, chewy wine that is still a bit closed on the nose but shows flavoursome, full and mouthfilling. Strong florality, biting tannins and marked alcoholic warmth characterize the pleasant Nebbiolo '04.

● Langhe Rosso Suo di Giacomo '03	**YY**	6
● Nebbiolo d'Alba La Perucca '03	**YY**	6
● Barbera d'Alba '04	**YY**	4*
● Nebbiolo d'Alba '04	**Y**	4
● Barolo '01	YY	7
● Barolo '00	YY	7
● Langhe Rosso Suo di Giacomo '00	YY	6
● Nebbiolo d'Alba La Perucca '01	YY	6
● Langhe Rosso Suo di Giacomo '02	YY	5
● Nebbiolo d'Alba La Perucca '02	YY	5

LA MORRA (CN)

ENZO BOGLIETTI
VIA ROMA, 37
12064 LA MORRA (CN)
TEL. 017350330
www.langhe.net/enzoboglietti

The new cellar is now ready for the grapes that Enzo and Gianni Boglietti tend so lovingly in their vineyards, some of the finest in the Langhe. They have just bought Vigna Talpone and we had a preview tasting of the Merlot and Cabernet '03 from this plot. There were too few bottles available to pronounce judgement, but both wines promise well. The Bogliettis' courageous decision to forgo their '02 Barolo has undoubtedly affected this year's results, but careful readers will note the high level of the range's overall quality and the sterling performance of the Barbera d'Alba Roscaleto '04, which reached our final tastings. Its concentrated, lingering nose offers generous aromas of flowers, berry fruit and tobacco, while the caressing, harmonious palate ends in a long finish. This little gem outshone the Barbera d'Alba Vigna dei Romani '03, whose 12-month ageing in new barriques followed by eight months in large barrels has created an elegant, mouthfilling wine. But it's still a top-class Barbera and the Langhe Rosso Buio '04, from 80 per cent nebbiolo and 20 per cent barbera, is equally good. A stay in new casks has given both nose and palate a delightful softness that melds with just the right amount of tannic texture and a long, clean finish. The '05 reds are good, too. The Langhe Nebbiolo shows marked but not aggressive tannins; the Barbera d'Alba is well typed, juicy and fresh; the Dolcetto d'Alba offers pleasing cherry aromas; and the Dolcetto d'Alba Tigli Neri '05's complex flowery bouquet and full, enfolding palate mark it out as one of the best of the vintage.

● Barbera d'Alba Roscaleto '04	**YY**	6
● Barbera d'Alba V. dei Romani '03	**YY**	7
● Langhe Rosso Buio '04	**YY**	6
● Barbera d'Alba '05	**YY**	4*
● Dolcetto d'Alba '05	**YY**	4*
● Dolcetto d'Alba Tigli Neri '05	**YY**	4*
● Langhe Nebbiolo '05	**YY**	5
● Barolo Brunate '01	YYY	8
● Barbera d'Alba Vigna dei Romani '94	YYY	8
● Barolo Fossati '96	YYY	7
● Barolo Brunate '97	YYY	8
● Barolo Case Nere '99	YYY	8
● Barolo Case Nere '01	YY	8

LA MORRA (CN)

GIANFRANCO BOVIO

FRAZ. ANNUNZIATA
B.TA CIOTTO, 63
12064 LA MORRA (CN)
TEL. 017350667

Gianfranco Bovio has brought in Walter Porasso and Beppe Caviola to run his estate and the wisdom of this decision is borne out by its success. Despite the absence of the Barolo crus, which were not produced in 2002, this year's range is of very good overall quality. Stepping into the breach, the Barolo Riserva Bricco Parussi '00 romped straight through to our final tastings on its debut appearance in the Guide. Obtained from a long-established plot at Castiglione Falletto planted with old vines, it is notable for its splendid garnet red colour, an eloquent nose ranging from dried violets to tar that owes much to the wine's sojourn in large wood, and a palate with just the right amount of tannins and a long, long finish. In place of the Barbera d'Alba Regiaveja '04, which has not yet been released, we tasted the Barbera d'Alba Il Ciotto '05. Approachable and drinking now, it expresses rich, juicy agreeable fruitiness, characteristics mirrored in the Dolcetto d'Alba Dabbene '05. Once again we were impressed by the estate's two whites, of which only 2,000 bottles apiece are released but which are big on quality. Although the Langhe Chardonnay La Villa '05 sees no oak it nevertheless shows a complex nose of apple-like fruit and butter before unveiling a palate nicely buttressed by plenty of freshness. The Langhe Bianco '05, from 100 per cent sauvignon, offers lovely varietal notes of tomato leaf on the nose but realizes its full potential on the palate, where it is refreshing, flavoursome and full.

●	Barolo Bricco Parussi Ris. '00	🍷🍷	7
●	Barbera d'Alba Il Ciotto '05	🍷🍷	4*
○	Langhe Bianco '05	🍷🍷	4*
○	Langhe Chardonnay V. La Villa '05	🍷🍷	4*
●	Dolcetto d'Alba Dabbene '05	🍷	4
●	Barolo V. Arborina '90	🍷🍷🍷	8
●	Barolo Rocchettevino '00	🍷🍷	7
●	Barolo V. Arborina '00	🍷🍷	7
●	Barolo V. Gattera '00	🍷🍷	7
●	Barolo V. Arborina '01	🍷🍷	7
●	Barolo V. Gattera '01	🍷🍷	7
●	Barolo Rocchettevino '01	🍷🍷	7
●	Barolo Rocchettevino '98	🍷🍷	8

LA MORRA (CN)

CASCINA BALLARIN

FRAZ. ANNUNZIATA, 115
12064 LA MORRA (CN)
TEL. 017350365
www.cascinaballarin.it

Gianni and Giorgio Viberti run this lovely family estate and agriturismo with their parents and wives. Even without the two '02 Barolos, the quality of their wines is on the up and they reached the finals again this year with the Barolo Bricco Rocca Tistot Riserva '00. It hails from a vineyard that is more than 50 years old and is vinified traditionally with a month's maceration followed by ageing in Slavonian oak barrels. The estery nose has a bouquet of dried flowers and berry fruit, and the palate is notable for its wonderful chocolate finish with tannins and exuberant alcohol integrated by the oak. The two Dolcettos are vinified solely in stainless steel. Pilade is more approachable, but its south-facing plot gives the Bussia '05 greater backbone, warmth and complexity. Barbera d'Alba Giuli '04 also comes from an old plot and 18 months in barrique gives it a harmonious palate that echoes the notes of liqueur cherries evident on the nose. Right now it is more complex and cleaner than the Barbera d'Alba Pilade '04, which is matured in Slavonian oak barrels and needs longer to show its full potential. The two Langhe Rossos are even more individual. The Ultimi Grappoli '03, from overripe barbera and nebbiolo with some merlot and cabernet, has rather a muddled nose but improves on the nicely balanced palate. Cino, from barbera, nebbiolo and dolcetto, is very simple and very pleasant. The varietal Langhe Nebbiolo '05 has lively tannins. Langhe Bianco Ballarin '05, from chardonnay, pinot nero fermented off the skins and favorita, is fresh, leisurely and pleasant.

●	Barolo Bricco Rocca Tistot Ris. '00	🍷🍷	8
●	Langhe Rosso Ultimi Grappoli '03	🍷🍷	7
●	Barbera d'Alba Giuli '04	🍷🍷	5
●	Dolcetto d'Alba Bussia '05	🍷🍷	4*
○	Langhe Bianco Ballarin '05	🍷🍷	4*
●	Barbera d'Alba Pilade '04	🍷🍷	4*
●	Dolcetto d'Alba Pilade '05	🍷	4
●	Langhe Nebbiolo '05	🍷	5
●	Langhe Rosso Cino '05	🍷	3
●	Barolo Bricco Rocca '00	🍷🍷	7
●	Barolo Bricco Rocca '01	🍷🍷	7
●	Barolo Bussia '97	🍷🍷	8
●	Barolo Bricco Rocca '99	🍷🍷	8

LA MORRA (CN)

GIOVANNI CORINO
FRAZ. ANNUNZIATA, 24B
12064 LA MORRA (CN)
TEL. 0173509452

After dividing the estate with his brother, Renato, Giuliano Corino kept the old name and the traditional label so beloved of wine enthusiasts. Giuliano's seven hectares are planted half to nebbiolo for Barolo and half to barbera and dolcetto in equal parts for a total annual production of around 45,000 bottles. This year, he presented us with an excellent wine to taste, Barolo Vecchie Vigne '01. Its appearance enchants with its vitality and colour and serves as the prelude to gentle aromas of violets and roses enhanced by a hint of blackcurrant. The palate develops wonderfully to reveal sweet, spicy fruit and great elegance, signing off with a long, juicy finish enriched by a touch of liquorice. The two 2002 Barolos, Giachini and Arborina, fell victim to hailstorms and were not released. Produced in a quantity of 14,000 bottles, the Barbera '05 is rather good. Several months of oak conditioning has given it a brilliant hue and lively notes of plum and eucalyptus. The palate is fruity and full of flavour, showing delicate and not too powerful in the finish. Some 3,500 bottles of Nebbiolo '05 are available. It is pale in appearance and releases very clean violet and berry fruit notes. Solid and rather rustic on the palate, it flaunts robust tannins but avoids bitterness in the finish. The 10,000 bottles of Dolcetto '05 are quite intense in colour and give dried herbs and almonds, followed by a firmly structured palate with impressive alcohol and nice tanginess. Last but not least, the L'Insieme '03 is a powerful mix of nebbiolo, barbera, cabernet sauvignon and merlot.

● Barolo Vecchie Vigne '01	ŸŸ	8
● L'Insieme '03	ŸŸ	8
● Barbera d'Alba '05	ŸŸ	4*
● Dolcetto d'Alba '05	Ÿ	4
● Langhe Nebbiolo '05	Ÿ	4

LA MORRA (CN)

RENATO CORINO
B.TA POZZO, 49A
12064 LA MORRA (CN)
TEL. 017350349

Renato Corino set up his beautiful new estate following the friendly separation from his brother, Giuliano. The winery has a good position in the heart of La Morra and is tiny in size: five hectares planted to vine for a potential production of 30-35,000 bottles a year,12,000 of which will be dedicated to Barolo in those vintages that escape the ravages of hail. The vineyards lie on the right of the Arborina cru, just below the Pozzo plot. The house is joined to the cellar, which is already up and running. It commands a spectacular view of a range of hills dotted with the odd house, small villages, and the luxuriant slopes of vines that produce the great Langhe wines such as those in which Renato excels. The proof of the pudding is the magnificent Barolo Vecchie Vigne '01. A joyously vivacious colour in the glass precedes a touch of spice enhancing a violet and rose nose, while the palate develops tightly to reveal sweet fruit and sublime elegance. The finish is balanced and leisurely. The deeply hued Barbera Vigna Pozzo '03 is very good indeed. It offers concentrated aromas of very ripe fruit with hints of balsam and nuances of raspberry. The very solid palate is nicely acidic, powerfully alcoholic, full, flavoursome and capped by a spicy finish. The lively Barbera '05 performed well with its rich fruit and juicy, easy-drinking palate. The Dolcetto '05 is decent, showing very fragrant with good mouthfeel and fruit well-sustained by acidity. The Barolo '02 was withdrawn because of rain and the aforementioned hail.

● Barolo Vecchie Vigne '01	ŸŸ	8
● Barbera d'Alba Vigna Pozzo '03	ŸŸ	6
● Barbera d'Alba '05	ŸŸ	4*
● Dolcetto d'Alba '05	Ÿ	4

LA MORRA (CN)

F.LLI FERRERO
FRAZ. ANNUNZIATA, 12
12064 LA MORRA (CN)
TEL. 017350691
www.baroloferrero.com

If our tasting notes seem a little spartan this year, it has nothing to do with Renato Ferrero. For a small estate such as this, which produces at most 25,000 bottles, the decision not to produce either the Barolo Manzoni or the Gattera e Luciani in the 2002 vintage was a particularly difficult one to take. Not only that, Renato also didn't produce a Langhe Nebbiolo '05, and all these factors combine to explain why we only reviewed two wines for this edition of the Guide. By way of compensation, the Barbera d'Alba Goretta '04 put on its best ever performance and earned a place in our final tastings for the very first time. Renato can be justly proud, as can his companion, Nina Rasmussen, and their esteemed consultant, Beppe Caviola. Produced in the limited quantity of 9,000 bottles and aged for 12 months in barriques of French oak, this wine opens on flowery aromas before progressing to reveal notes of forest fruits and a tertiary nuance. On the palate, the barbera's typical acid vigour acts as the perfect foil to the high alcohol content, balancing it harmoniously. The Nebiosè is an interesting example of its type, an unusual blend of nebbiolo, barbera and pinot nero. It is a 2005, although the label doesn't say so because it is a table wine. Conditioning in stainless steel vats gives it a bright ruby red colour and a clean, fruity if not particularly generous nose. The barbera's lovely drinkability is enhanced by the touch of depth lent by the other two varieties on the palate.

● Barbera d'Alba Goretta '04	**YY**	5*
● Nebiosè	**Y**	5
● Barolo Manzoni '01	YY	7
● Barolo Gattera e Luciani '00	YY	6
● Barolo Manzoni '00	YY	7
● Barolo Gattera e Luciani '01	YY	6
● Barolo Gattera e Luciani '99	YY	6
● Barolo Manzoni '99	YY	7

LA MORRA (CN)

SILVIO GRASSO
FRAZ. ANNUNZIATA
CASCINA LUCIANI, 112
12064 LA MORRA (CN)
TEL. 017350322

In 1985 flanked by his wife, Marilena, and their sons, Silvio and Paolo, Federico Grasso embarked on his quest to produce wines of absolute quality. This aspiration has placed his ten-hectare estate with an annual production of around 70,000 bottles firmly at the forefront of wine, both in Langhe and beyond. Federico's philosophy is to remain faithful to the territory, a principle that firmly underpins his work and led him to take the drastic decision not to release any of the six Barolos he usually produces in the 2002 vintage. We have a new recruit to the ranks this year in the form of the Nebbiolo d'Alba '04 from the Diano d'Alba plots. Aged in used barriques, it expresses all the characteristics of the variety with wonderful freshness and drinkability. The jewel in the estate's crown, however, is the Barolo Pì Vigne '01. On the nose, this wine is remarkably harmonious in its melding of fruity and balsamic notes, while the palate shows body and good acidity with impressive cohesion of the oak. The Barbera Fontanile '03 also stands out. Its conditioning in new, once and twice-used barriques allows the typical aromas of the varietal to emerge without becoming too dominant. L'Insieme '03 is a fine example of the blending of indigenous with international varieties, combining barbera and nebbiolo with cabernet sauvignon and merlot. The Dolcetto and Barbera d'Alba '05, each true to its own varietal characteristics, are drinking now. Finally, we were pleasantly surprised by the mix of freshness and complexity expressed by the Langhe Nebbiolo Peirass '03.

● Barolo Pì Vigne '01	**YY**	6
● Barbera d'Alba Fontanile '03	**YY**	5
● Langhe Nebbiolo Peirass '03	**YY**	5
● L'Insieme '03	**YY**	5
● Nebbiolo d'Alba '04	**YY**	5
● Barbera d'Alba '05	**YY**	5
● Dolcetto d'Alba '05	**YY**	4*
● Barolo Bricco Luciani '01	YYY	8
● Barolo Bricco Luciani '90	YYY	8
● Barolo Bricco Luciani '95	YYY	8
● Barolo Bricco Luciani '96	YYY	8
● Barolo Ciabot Manzoni '00	YY	8
● Barolo Ciabot Manzoni '01	YY	8
● Barolo Ciabot Manzoni '99	YY	8

LA MORRA (CN)

PODERI MARCARINI

P.ZZA MARTIRI, 2
12064 LA MORRA (CN)
TEL. 017350222
www.marcarini.it

The 2006 growing year saw some big decisions for the Marcarini estate, reluctantly taken as a result of the short, challenging summer of 2002. The latter vintage has gone down in history for the belting rain and violent hailstorms in early September that hit the zone of La Morra where the estate has its best vineyards. For Luisa and Manuel Marchetti, this means no 2002 Barolos. Their plots extend across three municipalities, Neviglie, Montaldo Roero and La Morra, where the main holding lies. We'll start with a wine from the Roero vineyard, a Roero Arneis '05 with typical vegetal aromas and a palate captivating in its acidity. Some 3,000 units go into bottle each year. The Dolcetto Fontanazza '05 is wonderfully fresh and richly extracted, proffering typical notes of forest fruit. Obtained from pre-phylloxera vines, the Dolcetto Boschi di Berri '05 astounds with aromatic complexity concentrated around unusual notes of sage and a strong balsamic vein. Elegance and fullness unite harmoniously on the palate. The Langhe Nebbiolo Lasarin '05 derives from grapes grown in Roero and La Morra and vinified in stainless steel vats. It combines all the characteristics of the variety with marvellous drinkability. The well-balanced Barbera d'Alba Ciabot Camerano '04 owes its fascinating profile to La Morra fruit and its measured aromas to grapes from Neviglie, all rounded by a nine-month sojourn in big barrels of Slavonian oak. Our second tasting of the Barolo Brunate '96 revealed a magnificent wine that we felt compelled to give Three retrospective Glasses.

●	Dolcetto d'Alba Boschi di Berri '05	▼▼	5
●	Barbera d'Alba Ciabot Camerano '04	▼▼	5
●	Langhe Nebbiolo Lasarin '05	▼▼	4*
●	Dolcetto d'Alba Fontanazza '05	▼	4
○	Roero Arneis '05	▼	4
●	Barolo Brunate '96	▽▽▽	7
●	Barolo Brunate '01	▽▽▽	7
●	Barolo Brunate Ris. '85	▽▽▽	7
●	Dolcetto d'Alba Boschi di Berri '96	▽▽▽	5
●	Barolo Brunate '99	▽▽▽	7
●	Barolo Brunate '00	▽▽	7
●	Barolo La Serra '01	▽▽	7

LA MORRA (CN)

MARIO MARENGO

VIA XX SETTEMBRE, 34
12064 LA MORRA (CN)
TEL. 017350127 - 017350115

It is always a great pleasure to visit a small winery where everything is built on a human scale and find wines of consistently high quality. A prime example is this estate in the heart of La Morra run by Marco Marengo. A master in the vineyards and cellar, Marco produces a lean range of labels consistent with the territory. He is about to embark on an ambitious project to build a new cellar at Bricco Viole, right beside the Barolo plots. Beppe Caviola consults. The estate produces 25,000 bottles annually, a number sadly reduced this year owing to the absence of the two Barolos, victims of the bad weather that affected the entire 2002 vintage. As a result, we only tasted two wines for this edition of the Guide. We'll start with the 3,000 bottles of Nebbiolo d'Alba Valmaggiore '04 obtained from a rented plot in Roero's Vezza d'Alba. Now in its fourth edition, this wine comes from a good vintage. It offers a rich, elegant nose that promises to develop well, mingling notes of aniseed and vanilla with nuances of ripe fruit. The fresh-tasting palate possesses velvety tannins and a faintly toasty finish thanks to maturation in mostly used barriques. The Dolcetto d'Alba '05, vinified in stainless steel, performed well. Alcohol-rich and very fresh, it suggests violets, raspberries and ripe cherries.

●	Nebbiolo d'Alba Valmaggiore '04	▼▼	4*
●	Dolcetto d'Alba '05	▼▼	4*
●	Barolo Brunate '00	▽▽	7
●	Barolo Brunate '01	▽▽	7
●	Barolo Bricco Viole '01	▽▽	8
●	Barolo Brunate '96	▽▽	7
●	Barolo Bricco Viole '97	▽▽	8
●	Barolo Brunate '97	▽▽	7
●	Barolo Bricco Viole '98	▽▽	8
●	Barolo Brunate '99	▽▽	7

LA MORRA (CN)

Mauro Molino

Loc. Annunziata
B.ta Gancia, 111
12064 La Morra (CN)
tel. 017350814

Mauro Molino had very little choice but to take the sound, sensible decision to sacrifice his entire production of Barolo in the 2002 vintage. This infamous year hit hard in these parts, forcing Marco to withdraw all of the Barolo labels that have so delighted us in the past and often won our top awards. Kipling's advice, "If you can meet with triumph and disaster and treat those two impostors just the same", is appropriate for Langhe. Undaunted, the Molinos continue to work hard and put their faith in new vintages. Matteo, Mauro's 33-year-old son, is expanding his role within the company and is now jointly responsible for the estate's oenological successes. Beppe Caviola, a family friend, acts as consultant, offering advice and help with analyses in the cellar. Annual production totals around 55,000 bottles, which are obtained from almost ten hectares planted to vine in La Morra, Barolo and Monforte d'Alba. First up we have the Barbera Vigna Gattere '04, aged for 18 months in barrique. This elegant wine presents a fresh, fruity, nicely concentrated nose and a palate pleasing for the balance it shows between acidity and restrained tannins. The finish is warm and echoes the liquorice-like aromas. The Langhe Nebbiolo '05 is interesting with its strong flowery notes and caressing palate. The Barbera d'Alba '05 and the Dolcetto d'Alba '05 are agreeable and well made. Both bear the clear stamp of their vintage and varieties and are fresh, easy-drinking pleasers.

●	Barbera d'Alba V. Gattere '04	🍷🍷	6
●	Barbera d'Alba '05	🍷🍷	4*
●	Langhe Nebbiolo '05	🍷🍷	4*
●	Dolcetto d'Alba '05	🍷	4
●	Barbera d'Alba V. Gattere '00	YYY	6
●	Barolo Vigna Conca '00	YYY	8
●	Barolo V. Gallinotto '01	YYY	8
●	Barbera d'Alba V. Gattere '96	YYY	6
●	Barolo V. Conca '96	YYY	8
●	Barbera d'Alba V. Gattere '97	YYY	6
●	Barolo V. Conca '97	YYY	8
●	Barolo V. Conca '01	YY	8
●	Barolo V. Gancia '01	YY	7

LA MORRA (CN)

Monfalletto - Cordero di Montezemolo

fraz. Annunziata, 67
12064 La Morra (CN)
tel. 017350344
www.corderodimontezemolo.com

We always enjoy our visits to this cellar. Gianni and Enrico Cordero, ably supported by their children, Alberto and Elena, make us feel very welcome as we drink in the view and, more important, the superb wines. The terrible vintage of 2002 prevented production of the Corderos' most noble crus, taking its toll on those Barolos that have done so well in the past. This time around it was the Barbera d'Alba Funtanì '04 that earned a place in the finals. The generous, estery, elegant nose suggests tobacco with the merest hint of spice. Tannins complement acidity on the palate, both splendidly balanced by the alcohol. Given the vintage, the Barolo '02 put on a brave show. The 12,000 bottles offer notes of flowers, balsam and liquorice, and a reasonably full, if rather brief, palate. The very characterful Barolo Riserva Gorette '00 is available direct from the cellar in magnums only. Confident tertiary aromas with hints of coffee and tobacco fill the nose, while the austere palate is smoothed by the dense tannic texture. In the Langhe Nebbiolo '05, lovely notes of berry fruit announce a palate that is less powerfully tannic and nicely astringent. The Barbera d'Alba and Dolcetto d'Alba, both from 2005, are similar in style. Varietal on the nose and easy to drink, they are not very full on the palate. The two whites are very interesting. Langhe Chardonnay Elioro '04 is one of the best interpretations of the variety in the zone and the Langhe Arneis '05 is a pleasant surprise. We gave it Two Glasses for its excellent nose-palate consistency and tangy minerality on the palate.

●	Barbera d'Alba Sup. Funtanì '04	🍷🍷	6
●	Barolo Gorette Ris. '00	🍷🍷	8
○	Langhe Chardonnay Elioro '04	🍷🍷	5
○	Langhe Arneis '05	🍷🍷	4*
●	Langhe Nebbiolo '05	🍷🍷	5
●	Barolo Monfalletto '02	🍷	6
●	Barbera d'Alba '05	🍷	4
●	Dolcetto d'Alba '05	🍷	4
●	Barolo V. Enrico VI '00	YYY	8
●	Barolo V. Enrico VI '96	YYY	8
●	Barolo V. Enrico VI '97	YYY	8
●	Barolo V. Bricco Gattera '99	YYY	8
●	Barolo Monfalletto '01	YY	6
●	Barolo V. Bricco Gattera '01	YY	8
●	Barolo V. Enrico VI '01	YY	8

ANDREA OBERTO

B.TA SIMANE, 11
12064 LA MORRA (CN)
TEL. 017350104

Andrea Oberto and his son, Fabio, own 16 hectares of vineyards in the municipalities of La Morra, Cherasco, Alba and Barolo. Despite this territorial spread, the Obertos did not produce a Barolo in the 2002 vintage because they considered the fruit to be below their usual standards. As a result, we were unable to taste last year's Three Glass champ, the Albarella selection, the Rocche or even the basic Barolo. Their absence has made quite a dent in total production numbers, which are much lower than the 80,000 the estate usually produces. But we did welcome another winner from the house of Oberto back to the pages of the Guide, Barbera d'Alba Giada, which reached our final tastings. Even in the face of a hot, dry year like 2003, Andrea and Fabio have succeeded in producing a complex, deeply fascinating wine. Vinification in stainless steel vats and barrique-ageing for 18 months have coaxed out aromas of black cherry, liquorice and cassis, and a full, fresh, flavoursome palate. Release of the Langhe Rosso Fabio '04, a nebbiolo and barbera blend, has been delayed as it is not yet deemed ready for bottling. The agreeably fruity Barbera d'Alba Bricco San Giuseppe '05 scored very high with our panel. A stay in oak has lent nuances of currant, blueberry, vanilla and coffee. Every bit its equal, the Dolcetto d'Alba Vigneto Vantrino Albarella is always one of the best of its category, as is the standard Langhe Nebbiolo. The Dolcetto and basic Barbera do not quite scale these dizzy heights.

●	Barbera d'Alba Giada '03	🍷🍷	6
●	Barbera d'Alba Bricco San Giuseppe '05	🍷🍷	4*
●	Dolcetto d'Alba Vigneto Vantrino Albarella '05	🍷🍷	4*
●	Langhe Nebbiolo '05	🍷🍷	4*
●	Barbera d'Alba '05	🍷	4
●	Dolcetto d'Alba '05	🍷	4
●	Barbera d'Alba Giada '00	🍷🍷🍷	6
●	Barolo V. Albarella '01	🍷🍷🍷	8
●	Barbera d'Alba Giada '96	🍷🍷🍷	6
●	Barolo V. Rocche '96	🍷🍷🍷	8
●	Barbera d'Alba Giada '97	🍷🍷🍷	6
●	Barolo V. Albarella '00	🍷🍷	8
●	Barolo V. Rocche '01	🍷🍷	8

LA MORRA (CN)

ODDERO

FRAZ. SANTA MARIA
VIA TETTI, 28
12064 LA MORRA (CN)
TEL. 017350618
www.odderofratelli.it

The old cellars of the Oddero estate are steeped in Barolo history. It is only recently that barriques have been introduced alongside the old barrels of Slavonian oak through which countless hectolitres of Barolo have passed before being bottled and labelled by Oddero, a procedure that started at the beginning of the 1960s. Over the generations, the Oddero family has gradually expanded its vineyards to today's impressive 60 hectares, many of which lie in the illustrious Barolo vineyards of Vigna Rionda, Rocche di Castiglione, Rivera di Castiglione and Mondoca di Bussia Soprana. While a quick glance at the list of wines presented for this edition of the Guide might suggest a low-key year for Luigi and Cristina Oddero, the estate has in fact pulled off one of its usual coups to bag another Three Glass trophy. The wine in question is the Vigna Rionda '01, released a year late to give it time to smooth out its youthful rough edges. Today, it offers complex fruity, salty aromas with notes of tar, and very soft tannins that fill the mouth and leave the finish long and pervasive. Of the other wines on offer, the two '04 Barberas and the Langhe Nebbiolo '03 did very well. Compared to the more approachable Barbera d'Alba, which is fruity and sublimely soft on the palate, the Barbera d'Asti is more complex and gamey, but it also shows more alcohol supported by lively acidity. The Nebbiolo '03 resembles a basic Barolo in the breadth of its aromas and its elegant austerity. The Dolcetto and Chardonnay Collaretto are simpler but very sound.

●	Barolo V. Rionda '01	🍷🍷🍷	8
●	Langhe Nebbiolo '03	🍷🍷	4
●	Barbera d'Alba '04	🍷🍷	4
●	Barbera d'Asti '04	🍷🍷	4
○	Langhe Chardonnay Collaretto '04	🍷	4
●	Dolcetto d'Alba '05	🍷	4
●	Barolo V. Rionda '00	🍷🍷🍷	8
●	Barolo V. Rionda '89	🍷🍷🍷	8
●	Barolo V. Rionda '98	🍷🍷🍷	8
●	Barolo Mondoca di Bussia Soprana '00	🍷🍷	8
●	Barolo Rocche di Castiglione '00	🍷🍷	7
●	Barolo Rivera di Castiglione '01	🍷🍷	7
●	Barolo V. Rionda '99	🍷🍷	8

LA MORRA (CN)

Renato Ratti

Fraz. Annunziata, 7
12064 La Morra (CN)
tel. 017350185
www.renatoratti.com

The estate that used to belong to Renato Ratti has completed work on its new cellar and what a cellar it is. Nestling harmoniously on the hillside in the small village of Annunziata in La Morra beneath the bell tower of the ancient church, it looks out over Langhe's most prestigious vineyards. That the new building blends so well into the local surroundings is thanks to Pietro Ratti and Massimo Martinelli, the amiable, intelligent duo that runs this important winery. The line-up is missing three of its Barolos this year after the poor weather conditions suffered in 2002. Of the wines we did taste, the high spot was the Monferrato Rosso Villa Pattono '04 that went all the way to the finals. The grapes for this barbera, nebbiolo, merlot and cabernet sauvignon blend are grown on one of the Rattis' ancestral properties in Costigliole d'Asti. Malolactic fermentation takes place in barriques, where the wine stays for 12 months. It displays most intriguing aromas of very complex, generous fruit rendered elegant by measured notes of vanilla and coffee from its oak-conditioning. Entry on the palate is powerful and well rounded and the finish is long-lingering. A fine showing, too, from the sauvignon-based Monferrato Bianco I Cedri di Villa Pattono '05, varietal on the nose with a creamy, pleasantly acidic palate. Obtained from grapes harvested in the municipality of Monteu Roero, the Nebbiolo d'Alba Ochetti '04 has elegant, delicate aromas. The fresh, drinkable Barbera d'Alba Torriglione and the Dolcetto d'Alba Colombè, both from '05, are good.

●	Monferrato Rosso Villa Pattono '04	🍷🍷	5
●	Nebbiolo d'Alba Ochetti '04	🍷🍷	5
●	Barbera d'Alba Torriglione '05	🍷🍷	4*
●	Dolcetto d'Alba Colombè '05	🍷🍷	4*
○	Monferrato Bianco I Cedri di Villa Pattono '05	🍷🍷	4*
●	Barolo Rocche Marcenasco '83	ΨΨΨ	8
●	Barolo Rocche Marcenasco '84	ΨΨΨ	8
●	Barolo Conca Marcenasco '00	ΨΨ	8
●	Barolo Rocche Marcenasco '00	ΨΨ	8
●	Barolo Conca Marcenasco '01	ΨΨ	8
●	Barolo Rocche Marcenasco '01	ΨΨ	8

LA MORRA (CN)

F.lli Revello

Fraz. Annunziata, 103
12064 La Morra (CN)
tel. 017350276
www.revellofratelli.it

This estate was founded by brothers Enzo and Carlo Revello in 1990. Their cellar looks out over one of the most spectacular views in Langhe: the famous Gattera vineyard dominated by the cedar of Lebanon planted 150 years ago by the Montezemolos. The estate has grown over the years and now totals 11 hectares planted to vine that give the Revellos a production of 60,000 bottles in a normal year. But in September 2002, one of the worst hailstorms in living memory hit Annunziata, destroying every single bunch of the nebbiolo grapes cultivated by Enzo and Carlo for their Barolos. As a result, all their best-known selections are missing from this year's edition of the Guide: Rocche dell'Annunziata, Vigna Gattera, Vigna Giachini, Vigna Conca and even the standard Barolo. We were well compensated, however, by a stupendous version of Barbera d'Alba Ciabot du Re '04, of which 6,000 bottles were released. Aged for 18 months in French oak barriques, it is purplish red with a complex nose of pencil lead, forest fruits and liquorice. The dynamic, characterful palate is fruity and firm-bodied and the finish refreshingly acidic. There was a fine showing from the Langhe Nebbiolo '04, a fruity, flowery wine with intriguing notes of dried roses, violets and tobacco. The standard Barbera d'Alba is fresh-tasting and easy-drinking and although the Dolcetto d'Alba is not quite up to the same standard we liked its intensely fruity character.

●	Barbera d'Alba Ciabot du Re '04	🍷🍷	6
●	Langhe Nebbiolo '04	🍷🍷	5
●	Barbera d'Alba '05	🍷🍷	4*
●	Dolcetto d'Alba '05	🍷	4
●	Barbera d'Alba Ciabot du Re '00	ΨΨΨ	7
●	Barolo Rocche dell'Annunziata '00	ΨΨΨ	8
●	Barolo Rocche dell'Annunziata '01	ΨΨΨ	8
●	Barolo '93	ΨΨΨ	8
●	Barolo Rocche dell'Annunziata '97	ΨΨΨ	8
●	Barolo V. Conca '99	ΨΨΨ	8

LA MORRA (CN)

MICHELE REVERDITO

FRAZ. RIVALTA
B.TA GARASSINI, 74B
12064 LA MORRA (CN)
TEL. 017350336
www.reverdito.it

This estate belonging to the Reverdito family makes it debut appearance in the pages of our Guide this year. It is run by 37-year-old Michele with the help of his father, Silvano, mother, Maria, and sister, Sabrina. This dauntless team works 18 hectares in the municipalities of Serralunga and La Morra for an annual production of 60,000 bottles. Their most important Barolo is obtained from grapes grown in Rivalta in La Morra, a tiny village that until now had little in terms of top labels to rival the more prestigious La Morra villages of Annunziata and Santa Maria. We start our notes with the jewel in the house's crown, the Barolo Bricco Cogni '01. Thirty months of barrique-ageing has given this little gem complex, very impressive aromas and smoothed out its robust tannins. The other two 2002 Barolos are both good, if completely different. The Serralunga is an austere wine, tannic and powerful, while the Moncucco, obtained from plots in Rivalta, is more scented and rounded. The Reverditos produced three Barberas but we only tasted two as the Delia isn't ready and its release has consequently been delayed. The Barbera d'Alba Butti '04's superb drinkability took in to within a hair's breadth of our final tastings. The very reasonably priced basic Barbera '04 offers excellent value for money, as indeed do all the wines on the list. The Verduno Pelaverga put on a fine show, displaying clear nuances of rain-soaked earth and pepper. The Langhe Nebbiolo Simane '03 is elegant and stylish; the Dolcetto d'Alba Formica '04 cool and easy-drinking.

●	Barolo Bricco Cogni '01	🍷🍷	6*
●	Barolo Moncucco '02	🍷🍷	5
●	Barolo Serralunga '02	🍷🍷	5
●	Langhe Nebbiolo Simane '03	🍷🍷	4*
●	Barbera d'Alba '04	🍷🍷	3*
●	Barbera d'Alba Butti '04	🍷🍷	4*
●	Verduno Pelaverga '05	🍷🍷	3*
●	Dolcetto d'Alba Sup. Formica '04	🍷	3

LA MORRA (CN)

ROCCHE COSTAMAGNA

VIA VITTORIO EMANUELE, 8
12064 LA MORRA (CN)
TEL. 0173509225
www.rocchecostamagna.it

Situated in the historic centre of La Morra, Rocche Costamagna is a town winery. It was founded 150 years ago and its long tradition has been enriched over the last decade by the contributions of the dynamic Alessandro Locatelli. His influence extends beyond his own cellar to the entire cultural scene of La Morra, where he organizes successful book fairs. In the ongoing quest to improve the quality of his wines, Alessandro calls on the support of two highly regarded professionals, oenologist Beppe Caviola and fruitmaker Gian Piero Romana. He did not present either of his Barolos for this edition of the Guide, both withdrawn as a result of 2002's appalling weather conditions. Of the wines he did present, we particularly liked the Barbera d'Alba Rocche delle Rocche '04 which aged for 15 months in barriques. Its irresistibly fascinating nose releases notes of raspberry and cherry that meld perfectly with the nuances of coffee, vanilla and cinchona from its maturation in oak. Simpler, but no less agreeable for it, is the Barbera d'Alba Annunziata '04, a fresh, fruity wine whose palate echoes the nose and is lifted by good acidity. Of the two Dolcettos on offer we preferred the Rùbis '05, a solidly built, fruity wine with a clean, leisurely finish. The Langhe Nebbiolo Roccardo is elegant and harmonious and the Langhe Arneis '05, with its flowery, delicately fruity sensations, is an early drinker. Finally, the Dolcetto Murrae '05 has an intense nose with ripe fruit to the fore.

●	Langhe Nebbiolo Roccardo '03	🍷🍷	4*
●	Barbera d'Alba Annunziata '04	🍷🍷	4*
●	Barbera d'Alba Rocche delle Rocche '04	🍷🍷	4*
●	Dolcetto d'Alba Rùbis '05	🍷🍷	4*
●	Dolcetto d'Alba Murrae '05	🍷	4
○	Langhe Arneis '05	🍷	4
●	Barolo Bricco Francesco Rocche dell'Annunziata '00	🍷🍷 (outline)	7
●	Barolo Bricco Francesco Rocche dell'Annunziata '01	🍷🍷 (outline)	7
●	Barolo Bricco Francesco Rocche dell'Annunziata '99	🍷🍷 (outline)	8
●	Barolo Rocche dell'Annunziata '01	🍷🍷 (outline)	7

LA MORRA (CN)

MAURO VEGLIO
FRAZ. ANNUNZIATA
CASCINA NUOVA, 50
12064 LA MORRA (CN)
TEL. 0173509212
www.mauroveglio.com

Our tasting notes for the estate owned by Daniela and Mauro Veglio feel the effects of 2002's bad weather, which treated Annunziata particularly harshly. On 3 September a hailstorm hit the area, ruining the entire production of what was already a poor vintage thanks to the rain that fell almost continuously throughout the month of August. The estate's final line-up is therefore missing the Barolo selections that in the past have so thrilled enthusiasts of this DOCG. In normal years, the cellar obtains 55,000 bottles from its 11 hectares of vineyards. The highest-scoring label at our tasting table was the Barbera d'Alba Cascina Nuova. A product of the balanced 2004 vintage, it sailed through to our finals. Its rich ruby red appearance is flecked with purple and ushers in a wealth of aromas ranging from ripe cherry to Peruvian bark, vanilla and tobacco. The palate is extremely fruity and very fleshy with a long, lingering finish. The Langhe Nebbiolo Angelo '04, dedicated to the memory of Veglio senior, Mauro, also shows very well. It combines notes of violets and dried roses with hints of berry fruit and pepper. Since 2004, the L'Insieme has been released as a Langhe DOC and we shall taste the Veglios' version next year as it was not ready for this round of tastings. Up last, the Barbera d'Alba and the vintage Dolcetto gave a classy performance, showing character and excellent drinkability.

● Barbera d'Alba Cascina Nuova '04	▼▼	5
● Langhe Nebbiolo Angelo '04	▼▼	6
● Barbera d'Alba '05	▼▼	4*
● Dolcetto d'Alba '05	▼▼	4*
● Barolo Vign. Arborina '00	▽▽▽	7
● Barolo Vign. Arborina '01	▽▽▽	7
● Barolo V. Rocche '99	▽▽▽	8
● Barbera d'Alba Cascina Nuova '96	▽▽▽	5
● Barbera d'Alba Cascina Nuova '99	▽▽▽	5
● Barolo Vign. Castelletto '00	▽▽	7
● Barolo Vign. Castelletto '01	▽▽	7
● Barolo Vign. Arborina '96	▽▽	6

LA MORRA (CN)

ERALDO VIBERTI
FRAZ. SANTA MARIA
B.TA TETTI, 53
12064 LA MORRA (CN)
TEL. 017350308

One of our greatest satisfactions in the Guide is to reward a small producer with high, well-deserved marks at our tastings. One such producer is Eraldo Viberti, and we are doubly happy in his case because he works hard and unstintingly, with no help from anyone else. He has just four hectares, one of which is rented, and his annual production is below 23,000 bottles. In spite of these limited resources, Eraldo continues to present us with a range of excellent quality. He maintains a balanced relationship with the land, refusing, for example, to use chemical fertilizers or pesticides among his vines. Of the wines he offered us this year, we very much liked the Barbera d'Alba Vigna Clara '03 which is aged for 20 months in once and twice-used barriques. The richly fruity nose is well supported by a clear mineral note that lends it elegance and nobility. The aromas of strawberry, tobacco and liquorice are echoed on the very fresh palate, which is capped by a long, agreeable finish. The Barolo '02, vinified in stainless steel vats and matured for 30 months in barrels, hardly suffered from the poor vintage. The soft tannins are expertly managed by Eraldo, while the nose offers fascinating aromas of flowers and fruit. We also note a fine performance from the Langhe Nebbiolo '05, oak-aged for 10 months, and the easy-drinking, pleasant Dolcetto d'Alba, vinified in stainless steels vats.

● Barbera d'Alba V. Clara '03	▼▼	6
● Barolo '02	▼▼	7
● Langhe Nebbiolo '05	▼▼	4*
● Dolcetto d'Alba V. Vaglio '05	▼	4
● Barolo '93	▽▽▽	8
● Barolo '00	▽▽	7
● Barolo '01	▽▽	7
● Barbera d'Alba V. Clara '01	▽▽	6
● Barolo '97	▽▽	7
● Barbera d'Alba V. Clara '98	▽▽	6
● Barolo '98	▽▽	7
● Barbera d'Alba V. Clara '99	▽▽	6

LA MORRA (CN)

OSVALDO VIBERTI
FRAZ. SANTA MARIA
B.TA SERRA DEI TURCHI, 95
12064 LA MORRA (CN)
TEL. 017350374
www.vibertiosvaldo.it

Osvaldo Viberti embarked on his adventure in the wine world in 1993 when he decided to dedicate himself full-time to cultivating his vines. Step by step, he has succeeded in raising the quality of his wines and the dimensions of his small estate, which now totals six hectares, three his own and three rented. This compact area gives him a maximum of 20,000 bottles a year, assuming that the weather works in his favour. The 2002 growing year has gone down in history as a meteorological disaster and put paid to one of the Viberti champions, the Barolo Serra dei Turchi. Osvaldo's father, Luigi, and wife, Carla, work alongside him in the cellar where Sergio Molino offers invaluable advice as consultant oenologist. Moving on to the wines presented this year, the Barbera d'Alba Mancine '04 showed very well. Twelve months of maturation in barriques and medium-sized barrels produce 2,500 bottles of an intense ruby red wine with purplish highlights. Fruity sensations such as morello cherry and currant blend superbly with hints of balsam and coffee on the nose. The fruity palate is leisurely and agreeable thanks to its rich flesh and refreshing acidity. The 2005 version of the Dolcetto d'Alba Galletto is well made and easily earned Two Glasses. The basic Barbera d'Alba, easy-drinking and correct, is not quite up to the same standard.

●	Barbera d'Alba Mancine '04	🍷🍷	5
●	Dolcetto d'Alba Galletto '05	🍷🍷	3*
●	Barbera d'Alba '04	🍷	4
●	Barolo Serra dei Turchi '00	🍷🍷	6
●	Barbera d'Alba Mancine '01	🍷🍷	5
●	Barolo Serra dei Turchi '01	🍷🍷	6
●	Barbera d'Alba Mancine '03	🍷🍷	5
●	Barolo Serra dei Turchi '97	🍷🍷	6
●	Barolo Serra dei Turchi '98	🍷🍷	6
●	Barolo Serra dei Turchi '99	🍷🍷	6

LA MORRA (CN)

GIANNI VOERZIO
S.DA LORETO, 1
12064 LA MORRA (CN)
TEL. 0173509194

Like so many of his La Morra compatriots, Gianni Voerzio was hit very badly in 2002 by the hailstorms in early September. One in a long list of victims, the Barolo La Serra was withdrawn and we were therefore unable to taste a superb wine that has always performed very well in the past. We consoled ourselves with the rest of Gianni's extensive range. His 14 hectares planted to vine give him an annual production of up to 70,000 bottles. The Barbera d'Alba Ciabot della Luna '04 romped through to our final tastings. On the nose, deep, austere aromas of cherry and prune meld perfectly with sensations of vanilla and coffee left over from maturation in new and used barriques. Every bit its equal, the Langhe Rosso Serrapiù '04 is obtained from nebbiolo and barbera grapes also matured in barriques. The nose hints at sweet spice and tobacco, while the full, fresh-tasting palate ends in a long, lingering finish. We noted an outstanding performance from the Langhe Nebbiolo Ciabot della Luna '04, whose stay in new 900-litre casks has produced aromas of dried flowers and berry fruit. There was a fine showing, too, from the basic wines: the Dolcetto Rocchettevino is complex and richly extracted; the Freisa Sotto I Bastioni is alcohol-rich and fragrant; and the Arneis Bricco Cappellina, obtained from grapes grown in the municipality of Castellinaldo in Roero, is fruity and easy-drinking. Not quite as impressive but still very interesting, the Moscato Vignasergente has a rich, creamy palate and a fragrant, elegant nose.

●	Barbera d'Alba Ciabot della Luna '04	🍷🍷	5
●	Langhe Rosso Serrapiù '04	🍷🍷	6
●	Langhe Nebbiolo Ciabot della Luna '04	🍷🍷	6
●	Dolcetto d'Alba Rocchettevino '05	🍷🍷	4*
●	Langhe Freisa Sotto I Bastioni '05	🍷🍷	4*
○	Roero Arneis Bricco Cappellina '05	🍷🍷	4*
○	Moscato d'Asti Vignasergente '05	🍷	5
●	Barolo La Serra '96	🍷🍷🍷	8
●	Barolo La Serra '97	🍷🍷🍷	8
●	Barolo La Serra '98	🍷🍷🍷	8

LA MORRA (CN)

★ ROBERTO VOERZIO
LOC. CERRETO, 1
12064 LA MORRA (CN)
TEL. 0173509196

This year, the mighty line-up usually presented by Roberto Voerzio and his wife Pinuccia is sadly decimated. Blame 2002's terrible weather conditions, which took a particularly hard toll on La Morra, where the Voerzios have their vineyards. As result, we were unable to taste the Barolo Brunate, Cerequio, La Serra, Rocche dell'Annunziata Torriglione or Sarmassa. By way of compensation, we sampled a magnificent version of the Barolo Vecchie Viti dei Capalot e delle Brunate Riserva '01, released in magnums only. Vinified with ambient yeasts and aged for two years in small barrels, it presents a dark garnet red with aromas of cherry, chocolate and eucalyptus. The palate displays perfect acid-tannic balance and is rounded off by an extremely concentrated finish. We found the Barbera Vigneto Pozzo dell'Annunziata '03, from an exceptionally hot, dry year, very interesting. Notes of morello cherry and strawberry blend wonderfully well with the nuances of coffee and vanilla left by its lengthy stay in oak and the palate is fruity, full and impressive. Langhe Fontanazza-Pissotta '04, based on merlot as indicated on the label, possesses an explosive nose offering a cornucopia of aromas ranging from plums to wild berries and from minerally tones to tobacco. Entry on the palate reveals supple, even tannins. Barbera Vigneti Cerreto '04 and the Dolcetto Priavino '05 are proof positive that Roberto devotes the same care and seriousness to his everyday wines as he does to his nobler labels.

● Barolo Vecchie Viti dei Capalot e delle Brunate Ris. '01	🍷🍷	8
● Barbera d'Alba Vign. Pozzo dell'Annunziata Ris. '03	🍷🍷	8
● Langhe Fontanazza-Pissotta '04	🍷🍷	8
● Barbera d'Alba Vign. Cerreto '04	🍷🍷	5
● Dolcetto d'Alba Priavino '05	🍷🍷	4*
● Barolo Rocche dell'Annunziata Torriglione '00	YYY	8
● Barolo Brunate '96	YYY	8
● Barolo Cerequio '96	YYY	8
● Barolo Brunate '98	YYY	8
● Barbera d'Alba Vign. Pozzo dell'Annunziata Ris. '99	YYY	8
● Barolo Brunate '99	YYY	8

LESSONA (BI)

SELLA
VIA IV NOVEMBRE
13060 LESSONA (BI)
TEL. 01599455

The Sella family traces its wine traditions back to 1671, when records attest the first production in Lessona territory. The cellars still contain bottles from the late 1800s when the great statesman, Quintino Sella, began to vinify wines at Bramaterra. With such an illustrious history, it is only natural that the estate's wines are strongly territorial in character. This plus exceptional elegance is the hallmark of Sella wines, faithful expressions of the terroir of northern Piedmont. This year's range is extraordinarily good. Of the four wines we tasted, three featured in our final tastings and the last was an easy Two Glass winner. In the absence of the Quintino Sella selection, the house's most important product is Lessona San Sebastiano allo Zoppo '01, sourced from a splendid plot over 80 years old with a southwest-facing aspect and sandy soil. Fascinating, complex notes of spice, geranium and medicinal herbs fill the nose, while the deep, balsamic palate shows very fine-grained tannins buttressed by wonderful richness of flavour and minerality. This outstanding wine earned a first Three Glass crown for this long-established estate. Bramaterra and Lessona are flavoursome, minerally '03s, also aged slowly in large wood and have little to envy their sibling. The first offers a thrilling, deliciously spicy nose led by white pepper and dark berry fruit while the second has a deep, complex palate with sweeter notes of berry fruit and gorgeous earthy, flowery nuances. Two full Glasses go to the Orbello '04 for its strawberry notes and pleasant, very territorial palate.

● Lessona S. Sebastiano allo Zoppo '01	🍷🍷🍷	6*
● Bramaterra '03	🍷🍷	5
● Lessona '03	🍷🍷	5
● Coste della Sesia Rosso Orbello '04	🍷🍷	4*
● Bramaterra '00	YY	5
● Lessona S. Sebastiano allo Zoppo '00	YY	6
● Lessona '01	YY	5
● Lessona Omaggio a Quintino Sella Ris. '99	YY	7
● Lessona S. Sebastiano allo Zoppo '99	YY	6
● Bramaterra '01	YY	5

LOAZZOLO (AT)

Borgo Maragliano

Reg. San Sebastiano, 2
14050 Loazzolo (AT)
tel. 014487132
www.borgomaragliano.com

Carlo and Silvia Galliano run one of the best estates in this zone. Particularly famed for the production of one of Piedmont's most outstandingly elegantly passitos, Borgo Maragliano is also known for its high-quality spumantes and its range of Moscatos. The sparkling wines the Gallianos offered us for tasting this year included the very attractive Giovanni Galliano Brut Rosé Metodo Classico '03. Its very rich, vibrant rosé is the prelude to notes of berry fruit and flowers with faint aromatic undertones. The full, invigorating palate ends in a pleasant finish with a slightly almondy vein. The Giuseppe Galliano Brut '02 is also bottle-fermented and presents a lovely, lively yellow. The nose suggests citrus and apple-like fruit as well as yeast and the palate follows through, building up to a clean and pleasant finish. The straw-yellow Chardonnay Crevoglio '05 performed very well. Flower and fruit aromas precede a restrained, balanced entry on the palate. As usual, Loazzolo is round and full of personality. Its amber colour and notes of fruit and summer flowers with unusual minerally undertones announce an elegant, balanced palate that keeps the aromatic tone lively and fresh right through to the long finish. Moscato La Caliera '05 offers grassy, fruity nuances in an overall framework of elegance while the supple, tidy palate never threatens to disappoint. The El Calié '05, another moscato-based wine, is simple and easy drinking.

⊙ Giovanni Galliano Brut Rosé M. Cl. '03	TT	5
○ Loazzolo Borgo Maragliano V.T. '03	TT	6
○ Piemonte Chardonnay Crevoglio '05	TT	3*
○ Giuseppe Galliano Chardonnay Brut '02	TT	5
○ El Calié '05	T	3
○ Moscato d'Asti La Caliera '05	T	3
○ Giuseppe Galliano Brut M. Cl. '00	YY	5
○ Loazzolo Borgo Maragliano V.T. '00	YY	6
○ Giuseppe Galliano Brut M. Cl. '01	YY	5
○ Loazzolo Borgo Maragliano V.T. '98	YY	6

LOAZZOLO (AT)

Forteto della Luja

Reg. Candeletta, 4
14050 Loazzolo (AT)
tel. 0141831596

This small estate run by Giancarlo Scaglione and his children, Silvia and Gianni, produces an interesting array of labels including distinctive three dessert wines and an elegant red. The area of Loazzolo is particularly well suited to cultivating moscato and the Scaglione family brings us two versions, Moscato d'Asti and Loazzolo, a complex, agreeable Passito. The first of these, Piasa San Maurizio '05, is a little overripe in its aromas, although the palate is tidy and harmonious. Piasa Rischei '03, the estate's flagship product, presents an intense yellow enhanced by amber highlights in the glass. The nose reveals complex notes of dried fruit and golden leaf tobacco in an evolved, intriguing bouquet, while the palate displays potent fullness and a generous finish with all the myriad nuances that this aromatic grape can offer. The other dessert wine, the distinctive, inviting Brachetto Passito Pian dei Sogni '04, is pale ruby red with a nose rich in sensations of fruit and wild roses overlaid with spice. The palate is fluent without being shallow, showing silky and pleasing. The finish simply bursts with personality. The Monferrato Rosso Le Grive '04, from pinot nero and barbera, has a dense, lively ruby red appearance and complex, delicate notes of cinnamon, coffee and vanilla that merge with the fruit. The palate's tight-knit, juicy, lip-smacking, succulent texture is rounded off by a flawless finish.

○ Loazzolo Piasa Rischei '03	TT	7
● Monferrato Rosso Le Grive '04	TT	5
● Piemonte Brachetto Forteto Pian dei Sogni '04	TT	6
○ Moscato d'Asti Piasa San Maurizio '05	T	4
○ Loazzolo Piasa Rischei '93	YYY	7
○ Loazzolo Piasa Rischei '94	YYY	7
○ Loazzolo Piasa Rischei '95	YYY	7
○ Loazzolo Piasa Rischei '96	YYY	7
○ Loazzolo Piasa Rischei '97	YYY	7
○ Loazzolo Piasa Rischei '00	YY	7
○ Loazzolo Piasa Rischei '98	YY	7
● Piemonte Brachetto Forteto Pian dei Sogni '00	YY	6

LU (AL)

CASALONE

VIA MARCONI, 100
15040 LU (AL)
TEL. 0131741280
www.casalone.com

The Casalone family's production of around 50,000 bottles a year is spread across a lot of labels. Each year we find ourselves tasting them in rotation according to the bottling period. This well-organized system enables the Casalones to release their wines with a certain sense of confidence. The wines that are not reviewed in this edition of the Guide will, therefore, be presented next year with the exception of the Monferrato Rosso Arnest. This 100 per cent Pinot Nero is produced only in better years and did not appear in the 2004 vintage. The Barbera d'Asti Rubermillo '04 stands out for its deep, lively ruby red colour, its stylish, elegant nose, and its harmonious palate sustained by good alcoholic content. Monferrato Rosso Rus '04 is a blend of barbera, merlot and pinot nero with rather a pale ruby red appearance and aromas of morello cherry and plum. Twelve months of oak-ageing fail to mask its flowery notes, while the palate shows tannins that are still developing and impressive aromatic length. Monemvasia is an interesting table wine sourced from aromatic malvasia greca grapes. It proffers intense varietal notes with hints of peach, sage and almond and a balanced palate supported by refreshing acidity. The Chardonnay Munsrët '05 came close to the Two Glass mark. It underwent alcoholic and malolactic fermentation in the oak casks where the wine remained for six months on the fine lees.

● Barbera d'Asti Rubermillo '04	🍷🍷	4*
● Monferrato Rosso Rus '04	🍷🍷	4*
○ Monemvasia '05	🍷	3
○ Monferrato Bianco Munsrët '05	🍷	3
● Monferrato Rosso Rus '01	🍷🍷 (white)	5
● Monferrato Rosso Rus '00	🍷🍷 (white)	5
● Monferrato Rosso Rus '03	🍷🍷 (white)	5
● Monferrato Rosso Rus '99	🍷🍷 (white)	5

LU (AL)

TENUTA SAN SEBASTIANO

CASCINA SAN SEBASTIANO, 41
15040 LU (AL)
TEL. 0131741353
www.dealessi.it

The road embarked upon by Roberto De Alessi continues to bring him success. Today, his estate is one of the most important around Alessandria and the range of wines Roberto presented this year is yet further proof of how his efforts in the vineyard and cellar are paying off. The Barbera del Monferrato Mepari in 7,000 bottles is the estate's flagship product. Intense ruby red in appearance, it releases notes of berry fruit, sweet spices and vanilla. Roberto only produced 4,000 bottles of his cabernet sauvignon and merlot blend, Monferrato Rosso Dalera '03. Its very dark ruby colour is the prelude to a complex aromatic framework and wonderful balance on the palate. LV is a moscato-based Passito aged for a year in oak and stainless steel and was released in a quantity of 2,000 bottles. Its notes of apricot and acacia honey are echoed on the palate in well-defined nose-palate harmony. The pale ruby Grignolino del Monferrato Casalese also showed well, offering delicate, elegant spiciness on the nose and fullness of flavour on the palate where the tannins are kept well in check and the acidity impresses. Sol-Do, a Monferrato Rosso based on pinot nero and cabernet franc, neared the Two Glass level in the '04 version, missing out because of its all too brief ageing. We conclude our Tenuta San Sebastiano tasting notes with the Barbera '05, released in 18,000 bottles, a wine rich in acidity with a refreshing, very agreeable palate.

● Barbera del M.to Mepari '04	🍷🍷	4*
● Monferrato Rosso Dalera '03	🍷🍷	6
○ LV Passito '04	🍷🍷	5
● Grignolino del M.to Casalese '05	🍷🍷	3*
● Monferrato Rosso Sol-Do '04	🍷	4
● Barbera del M.to '05	🍷	3
● Barbera del M.to Mepari '03	🍷🍷 (white)	4
● Barbera del M.to Mepari '00	🍷🍷 (white)	4
● Barbera del M.to Mepari '01	🍷🍷 (white)	4
● Monferrato Rosso Dalera '01	🍷🍷 (white)	6
● Barbera del M.to Mepari '99	🍷🍷 (white)	4

MANGO (CN)

CASCINA FONDA

LOC. CASCINA FONDA, 45
12056 MANGO (CN)
TEL. 0173677156
www.cascinafonda.com

With 11 labels in production and a Spumante Metodo Classico soon to be released, brothers Massimo and Marco Barbero are anything but averse to experimentation. The Moscato remains the estate's flagship product and we start our tasting notes with an Asti Spumante, a paper white wine with a sweet citrus-like fragrance, typical aromas and sweetness sustained by nice fizz. We also liked the Moscato Vigna Il Piano for its uncompromising nose and ebullient sweetness supported by lively acidity. The much-awaited Driveri Metodo Classico makes its debut appearance among our pages. Obtained from moscato refermented in the bottle for 12 months, it is straw yellow in colour with sweet, fruity aromas. The big palate has sparkle and reasonably balanced acidity, while the finish mirrors the nose and offers good length. The golden yellow Moscato Passito '03 is excellent. It unveils notes of aromatic herbs, strong minerally tones and just the right amount of sweetness on the clean palate where hints of tropical fruit emerge, lacking only a bit of acidity in the finish. The Brachetto is interesting with its aromatic nuances of strawberry and pleasantly soft finish. Aged in small barrels for 18 months, the Barbaresco Bertola stands out among the reds. Its red shades into garnet and introduces reasonable nose-palate harmony and lovely long length. We end our notes with the Dolcetto Brusalino, which is clean and fruity and drinking now.

○	Piemonte Moscato Passito '03	ŸŸ	5
○	Asti Driveri M. Cl. '04	ŸŸ	6
○	Asti '05	ŸŸ	4
○	Moscato d'Asti V. Il Piano '05	ŸŸ	4
●	Piemonte Brachetto '05	ŸŸ	4
●	Barbaresco Bertola '03	Ÿ	6
●	Dolcetto d'Alba Brusalino '05	Ÿ	4

MANGO (CN)

SERGIO DEGIORGIS

VIA CIRCONVALLAZIONE, 3
12056 MANGO (CN)
TEL. 014189107
www.degiorgis-sergio.com

The estate belonging to Sergio and Patrizia Degiorgis is situated on the outskirts of Mango and its ten hectares of vineyards lie in one of the best zones in the district. One of their most interesting Moscatos takes its name from a farmhouse situated on one of the properties, Cascina del Re. Low yields per hectare and elderly vines combine to create a wine with a deep straw-yellow colour and a complex nose of tropical fruit and medicinal herbs. The full palate's explosion of sweetness is buttressed by a fine acid vein and a fruity encore. The basic Moscato is very good, showing varietal in its captivating fruitiness with a sweet but never cloying palate. The estate also offers a moscato-based Passito, Essenza '03. It is richer in both its colour and aroma which, although typical, also offer exotic, sugary notes. The big, generous finish clearly mirrors the sensations of the nose. We also liked the reds we tasted, first and foremost the deep ruby red Barbera d'Alba '04. Its nose releases notes of black berry fruit, while the elegant palate shows nice acidity and a firm, dry finish of good length. The Barbera Luna Nuova and Dolcetto Bricco Peso, both from '05, are fair.

○	Essenza '03	ŸŸ	5
○	Moscato d'Asti Sorì del Re '05	ŸŸ	4*
●	Barbera d'Alba '04	ŸŸ	4
○	Moscato d'Asti '05	ŸŸ	4
●	Barbera d'Alba Luna Nuova '05	Ÿ	3
●	Dolcetto d'Alba Bricco Peso '05	Ÿ	3
●	Barbera d'Alba '01	ΥΥ	5
○	Essenza '01	ΥΥ	5
●	Langhe Rosso Riella '01	ΥΥ	5

MOASCA (AT)

La Ghersa

v.le San Giuseppe, 19
14050 Moasca (AT)
tel. 0141856012
www.laghersa.it

In the space of a few short years, Massimo Pastura Barbero has succeeded in building up a modern estate with great potential. His 15 hectares of vineyards, in part owned and in part rented, plus the fruit he buys in from a group of reliable producers, give him a total production of 250,000 bottles. The stand-out wine he presented for tasting this year was the deep ruby red Barbera Camparò '04. The intense nose opens out gradually to reveal fruity, spicy notes in an overall framework of pleasing rusticity, while the full, deep palate has a lovely entry and a leisurely finish. The Barbera Vignassa always does well but this year it seems to be feeling the effects of the rather unbalanced 2003 vintage. While the nose lacks the freshness it needs to be really impressive, the palate shows body, dry character and a good long finish. Rosso La Ghersa '03, a blend of barbera, merlot and cabernet, is excellent. It is dense in appearance, giving complex aromas of brandied fruit, spice and autumn leaves followed by a full body. The standard-label Barbera, Piagè, is fruity and pleasantly drinkable with notes of cherry and earth and a certain ruggedness on the inviting palate. Obtained from cortese, chardonnay and sauvignon, the Bianco Sivoy '05 offers notes of fruit and spring flowers and a fleshy, fabulously soft palate. The Moscato Giorgia is pale in colour with pleasant, typical aromas and a balanced, mouthfilling palate.

●	Barbera d'Asti Sup. Nizza Vignassa '03	TT	6
●	Monferrato Rosso La Ghersa '03	TT	5
●	Barbera d'Asti Sup. Camparò '04	TT	4*
○	Moscato d'Asti Giorgia '05	TT	4*
●	Barbera d'Asti Piagè '05	T	4
○	Monferrato Bianco Sivoy '05	T	4
●	Barbera d'Asti Sup. Nizza Vignassa '00	YY	6
●	Barbera d'Asti Sup. Nizza Vignassa '01	YY	6
●	Monferrato Rosso La Ghersa '01	YY	5

MOMBARUZZO (AT)

Malgrà

loc. Bazzana
via Nizza, 8
14046 Mombaruzzo (AT)
tel. 0141725055 - 0141726377
www.malgra.it

The estate belonging to Nico Conta, Massimiliano Diotto and brothers Ezio and Giorgio Chiarle goes from strength to strength. Despite its substantial dimensions – 140 hectares and annual production of 950,000 bottles – it monitors the quality of its wines very carefully and has delayed release of several labels that are does not yet considered ready for bottling. That meant we did not taste the Barbera Mora di Sassi, Brut Col dei Ronchi or Chardonnay Innuce. The range on offer, however, was more than worthy of the renowned Malgrà name. We'll start with Barbera Fornace di Cerreto '04, a deep ruby red wine with brilliant highlights. Its concentrated nose opens gradually to reveal perceptions of berry fruit, cherry and currant, mingling with vegetal nuances in an overall framework of supreme elegance. The palate is muscular and tasty, with good character and a long finish. Barbera Gaiana '03, also dark in appearance, offers aromas of plum jam with undertones of vanilla and coffee preceding a soft, round palate with light alcohol. The rather pale Briga della Mora '05 is a coherent wine with a simple nose and a tidy palate. The Monferrato Rosso Treviri '04 is from barbera, dolcetto and cabernet that give dense colour and an intensely fruity nose with elegant spicy tones and hints of Peruvian bark. The palate is very full and agreeably long. Monferrato Rosso Malgrà '04 from barbera and cabernet sauvignon is not far behind with its sweet, pleasant aromas and full-bodied, well-sustained palate. The stylish, fruity Gavi Poggio Basco '05 is solid and tempting on the palate.

●	Barbera d'Asti Sup. Fornace di Cerreto '04	TT	4*
●	Barbera d'Asti Sup. Gaiana '03	TT	4
●	Monferrato Rosso Malgrà '04	TT	4
●	Monferrato Rosso Treviri '04	TT	5
●	Barbera d'Asti Briga della Mora '05	T	3*
○	Gavi del Comune di Gavi Poggio Basco '05	T	4
●	Barbera d'Asti Sup. Nizza Mora di Sassi '03	YY	6
●	Barbera d'Asti Sup. Nizza Mora di Sassi '00	YY	6
●	Monferrato Rosso Treviri '03	YY	5
●	Monferrato Rosso Emmerosso '99	YY	5
●	Barbera d'Asti Sup. Gaiana '01	Y	5

MOMBERCELLI (AT)

LUIGI SPERTINO
VIA LEA, 505
14047 MOMBERCELLI (AT)
TEL. 0141959098
www.luigispertino.it

Mauro Spertino is the archetypal grower: he works incredibly hard in his vineyards, tends his vines meticulously, and ensures that his wines faithfully express the characteristics of the terroir. Flanked by his father, Luigi, who lends an invaluable hand in the vineyards, he works four hectares of his own and two he rents out for a maximum annual production of 45,000 bottles. Barbera is the Spertinos' passion and every year they take this wine to new levels of quality, offering value for money that is hard to beat. For this edition of the Guide, we tasted a Metodo Classico '01, Lunà, which impressed us greatly. It is obtained from grapes grown on the slopes of the Oltrepò Pavese near Santa Maria della Versa at an altitude of 300 metres. It flaunts an elegant straw-yellow colour and moderate perlage, the aromas of croissants and yeast well sustained by fruity, flowery sensations. The palate is dynamic and powerful and the finish superlative. The Barbera d'Asti '04, with 12,000 bottles released, repeated last year's performance to earn a place in our final tastings for a richly balsamic nose that suggests red peppers and berry fruit. Entry on the palate is fruity and progression taut. Mauro is also one of the best interpreters of the much underrated grignolino variety. His 2005 version expresses all the characteristics of the grape type in an exceedingly fresh, agreeable wine. We also loved the complex, spicy Monferrato Rosso La Mandorla '04, which is 100 per cent pinot nero.

●	Barbera d'Asti '04	TT	4*
○	Lunà Brut M. Cl. '01	TT	5
●	Monferrato Rosso La Mandorla '04	TT	6
●	Grignolino d'Asti '05	TT	4
●	Barbera d'Asti '02	YY	4
●	Barbera d'Asti '03	YY	4
●	Barbera d'Asti '01	YY	4
●	Monferrato Rosso La Mandorla N° 1 '01	YY	6

MONCHIERO (CN)

GIUSEPPE MASCARELLO E FIGLIO
S.DA DEL GROSSO, 1
12060 MONCHIERO (CN)
TEL. 0173792126
www.mascarello1881.com

Mauro Mascarello likes to refer to himself as a master cellarman, not because he wants to cock a snook at oenologists but because he learned his craft in the vineyard and especially in the cellar. The strength of the historic house of Monchiero lies in the experience Mauro has accumulated in over 30 years of meticulous work, experience that his son, Giuseppe, is now building on. Over his long career, Mauro has learned to take fashions and overnight successes with a pinch of salt. You will find no oaky or ingratiating wines in Mauro's range; his preference is for full-bodied, austere reds that mellow out over time developing extraordinary fragrances that pay tribute to the noble nebbiolo grape. His efforts and passion for his work have paid off this year in the shape of three finalists and a Three Glass champion. After taking a backseat for many years, Barolo Monprivato '01, flagship wine of the Mascarello family, returns to claim our top prize. This magnificent, traditional-style Barolo presents intoxicating notes of dried roses, medicinal herbs, tobacco and tar introducing a palate caressed by the sweetness of the tannins. The Villero has little to envy it, although it shows a shade less complexity and a bit more freshness. The Riserva di Monprivato '96, Cà d' Morissio, has a more evolved nose but the palate is buttressed by good acidity. We'll end our review of the Barolos with an austere Santo Stefano di Perno '01. The rest of the range is just as good, including the splendid Dolcetto Bricco '04 whose complexity and depth transcend the grape's usual ambitions.

●	Barolo Monprivato '01	TTT	8
●	Barolo Villero '01	TT	8
●	Barolo Monprivato Cà d' Morissio Ris. '96	TT	8
●	Barolo S. Stefano di Perno '01	TT	8
●	Langhe Nebbiolo '03	TT	5
●	Dolcetto d'Alba Bricco '04	TT	4*
●	Langhe Rosso Status '99	TT	5
●	Langhe Freisa Toetto '03	T	4
●	Dolcetto d'Alba S. Stefano di Perno '04	T	4
●	Barolo Monprivato '85	YYY	8
●	Barolo Villero '96	YYY	8
●	Barolo S. Stefano di Perno '98	YYY	8
●	Barolo Monprivato '00	YY	8

MONDOVÌ (CN)

Il Colombo - Barone Riccati

via dei Sent, 2
12084 Mondovì (CN)
tel. 017441607
www.ilcolombo.com

In last year's edition of the Guide, we described Il Colombo as one of the most spectacularly beautiful estates in Italy and we find ourselves wondering if Norwegians Britt and Theo Holm read our review before they decided to take it over. What we do know is that we are sorry to lose Carlo Riccati and his wife, Adriana Giusta, who are retiring from the wine world. In a few short years, they managed to create a peaceful, sophisticatedly elegant oasis in the hills of Mondovì that produced very charming, complex wines. The Scandinavian couple have not yet moved to Italy and for the moment rely on Sabina Bosio and her husband, Bruno Chionetti, to look after the estate on a day-to-day basis. Both caretakers have extensive experience working for cellars in the Dogliano area. Il Colombo has three and a half hectares planted to vine that give it an annual production of almost 15,000 bottles. As for the wines themselves, the Dolcetto delle Langhe Monregalesi Superiore Il Colombo '04 earned a place in our final tastings. Its opaque ruby red appearance announces aromas of cinnamon-led sweet spice intermingled with notes of ripe fruit, notably plum and cherry. The dense, tight-knit palate reveals robust tannins that promise good ageing potential. The Dolcetto La Chiesetta '05 is fresher, offering elegant vegetal and fruity nuances followed by a juicy palate with compact, silky phenolics.

● Dolcetto delle Langhe Monregalesi Sup. Il Colombo '04	TT	4*
● Dolcetto delle Langhe Monregalesi La Chiesetta '05	TT	3*
● Dolcetto delle Langhe Monregalesi Il Colombo '97	YYY	4
● Dolcetto delle Langhe Monregalesi Il Colombo '98	YYY	4
● Dolcetto delle Langhe Monregalesi Sup. Il Colombo '03	YY	4
● Dolcetto delle Langhe Monregalesi Il Colombo '00	YY	4
● Dolcetto delle Langhe Monregalesi Il Colombo '01	YY	4

MONFORTE D'ALBA (CN)

Gianfranco Alessandria

loc. Manzoni, 13
12065 Monforte d'Alba (CN)
tel. 017378576
www.gianfrancoalessandria.com

No 2002 versions of the basic Barolo or Barolo San Giovanni from Gianfranco Alessandria this year after his decision not to bottle the nebbiolo grapes ravaged by this dreadful vintage. Not for the first time, the title of best estate wine goes to the Barbera Vittoria '04, a superlative interpretation of all the grape's potential. It proffers a deep purplish colour, concentrated aromas of berry fruit, spice and vanilla and a full, complex palate sustained by good acidity. All in all, it's a more balanced and probably more cellarable Barbera Vittoria than the '03, which is nevertheless excellent. The basic Barbera '05 also did well. Fresh and fruity, it has good drinkability and finds a good balance of tannins and acidity. The Langhe Nebbiolo '04 presents a lovely ruby colour verging on garnet, raspberry and violet aromas and a full palate with soft, elegant tannins. The intensely purple-hued Dolcetto is a heady, fruity wine with a fulfilling palate showing robust tannins and a reasonably long finish. Rounding off the range we have L'Insieme, the result of an exciting joint effort by eight Langhe producers. This year, Gianfranco also created a fascinating wine based on 40 per cent nebbiolo and 30 per cent each barbera and cabernet sauvignon grapes harvested in 2003. Aged for 18 months in new oak, it has a dark purple appearance and fruity, vanilla aromas that combine with intriguing notes of coffee and chocolate on the palate, perfectly fusing the typical notes of the three varieties with a shrewdly gauged dose of oak.

● Barbera d'Alba Vittoria '04	TT	6
● L'Insieme '03	TT	7
● Langhe Nebbiolo '04	TT	5
● Barbera d'Alba '05	TT	4*
● Dolcetto d'Alba '05	TT	4*
● Barolo S. Giovanni '00	YYY	8
● Barolo S. Giovanni '01	YYY	8
● Barolo '93	YYY	8
● Barbera d'Alba Vittoria '97	YYY	6
● Barolo S. Giovanni '97	YYY	8
● Barbera d'Alba Vittoria '98	YYY	6
● Barolo S. Giovanni '98	YYY	8
● Barolo S. Giovanni '99	YYY	8
● Barbera d'Alba Vittoria '03	YY	6

MONFORTE D'ALBA (CN)

★ Domenico Clerico

Loc. Manzoni, 67
12065 Monforte d'Alba (CN)
tel. 017378171

It is in the difficult years that a producer shows his true mettle and Domenico Clerico and Massimo Conterno have triumphed over the setbacks of the 2002 vintage to bring us an excellent Barolo. They obtained just 14,000 bottles from a careful selection of the best grapes from the estate's three crus whose names are blazoned on their labels. Ruby with an orange edge, the wine displays elegant aromas of rose and berry fruit with faint balsamic nuances, confident tannins and taste sensations that end on a note of coffee and liquorice. The 12,500 bottles of Arte '04 perform very well. Obtained from 90 per cent nebbiolo and the rest barbera, it finds a perfect balance of nebbiolo's firm structure and tannins and barbera's fruit and acidity. Its deep, almost opaque purple heralds a nose of berry fruit, tobacco and chocolate, aromas that are mirrored on the palate where tannins and impressive backbone are followed by an elegantly balsamic finish. The fruity Barbera Trevigne '04 has spicy aromas before the palate unveils its lovely richness of flavour and big body to finish on notes of cocoa powder and vanilla. Ageing in small casks gives the Dolcetto Visadì '05 a purplish colour, intense, alcohol-rich aromas of fruit and vanilla, and a juicy palate with silky tannins and an enjoyable finish. Domenico has a long list of projects for the future, chief among these the building of a new, more efficient cellar over the next three years.

● Langhe Rosso Arte '04	TT	6
● Barolo '02	TT	7
● Barbera d'Alba Trevigne '04	TT	5
● Langhe Dolcetto Visadì '05	TT	4*
● Barolo Ciabot Mentin Ginestra '01	YYY	8
● Barolo Pajana '90	YYY	8
● Barolo Pajana '93	YYY	8
● Barolo Pajana '95	YYY	8
● Barolo Percristina '95	YYY	8
● Barolo Percristina '96	YYY	8
● Barolo Percristina '97	YYY	8
● Barolo Percristina '98	YYY	8
● Barolo Ciabot Mentin Ginestra '99	YYY	8
● Barolo Percristina '99	YYY	8
● Langhe Rosso Arte '03	YY	6

MONFORTE D'ALBA (CN)

★ Aldo Conterno

Loc. Bussia, 48
12065 Monforte d'Alba (CN)
tel. 017378150

The story of Aldo Conterno, born in 1931, and Monforte Barolo are one and the same. He is among the last Langhe patriarchs and his work has shown many of the territory's producers the way to quality, making the king of Italian wines a household name around the world. We gave his Barolo Gran Bussia '89 a special award for the finest wine ever tasted for the Guide, the Best Wine of The Last 20 Years. Aldo's sons, Franco, Giacomo and Stefano, work alongside him and together they run 25 hectares of stunning vineyards located in world-famous crus such as Bussia, Colonnello and Cicala. The Conternos did not produce a Barolo in the 2002 vintage and the range this year is therefore rather depleted. Two wines reached our final selections. The first is the Langhe Nebbiolo Il Favot '03, which impressed us with its elegance and harmony. Pale ruby red in the glass, it offers delicately fruity notes of dried roses, ripe cherry and cassis. The palate is fresh-tasting, dynamic and full with silky tannins and a long, agreeable finish. The Barolo Gran Bussia Riserva '00 performed well. It is obtained from grapes grown in the Romirasco, Cicala and Colonnello vineyards, vinified in stainless steel vats and aged for 36 months in barrels of Slavonian oak. The nose suggests torrefaction and liquorice with a touch of berry fruit bringing up the rear before the palate presents firm-bodied and full. Langhe Rosso Quartetto from nebbiolo, barbera, cabernet sauvignon and merlot is modern and pleasing while the toasty Barbera d'Alba Conca Tre Pile '03 feels the impact of the dry growing year.

● Barolo Gran Bussia Ris. '00	TT	8
● Langhe Nebbiolo Il Favot '03	TT	7
● Langhe Rosso Quartetto '03	TT	6
● Barbera d'Alba Conca Tre Pile '03	T	5
● Barolo Gran Bussia Ris. '82	YYY	8
● Barolo Gran Bussia Ris. '88	YYY	8
● Barolo Gran Bussia Ris. '89	YYY	8
● Barolo Gran Bussia Ris. '90	YYY	8
● Barolo V. del Colonnello '90	YYY	8
● Barolo Gran Bussia Ris. '95	YYY	8
● Barolo Cicala '01	YY	8
● Barolo Colonnello '01	YY	8
● Barolo Gran Bussia Ris. '99	YY	8
● Barolo Bussia '01	YY	8

★ Giacomo Conterno

Loc. Ornati, 2
12065 Monforte d'Alba (CN)
tel. 017378221

In the previous edition of our Guide, we awarded Three Glasses to a monumental Barolo Cascina Francia '01. This year, we lament the absence of the 2002 version, which was not released. Instead, the grapes went to produce its elder brother, the multiple prizewinning Monfortino. So, Langhe's most famous Barolo will be released in the challenging 2002 vintage but not in 2003, which Roberto Conterno considered less suitable for the long ageing required by this selection. We'll start our notes with the Barbera d'Alba '04, which is vinified in oak vats and aged for 22 months in large wood of various sizes. Intense ruby red in the glass, it offers notes of blackberry and cassis with an elegant, grassy, almost minerally tone. The fruity, nicely balanced, lip-smacking palate ends on a long-lingering finish. The Barolo Monfortino Riserva '99 comes from of an exceptional vintage for Langhe nebbiolo and it shows: we put it at the top of its category. Also vinified in oak vats, it undergoes an impressive 82 months of maturation in large barrels. A ruby red appearance heralds a nose of rare complexity with aromas ranging from cherries to violets, dried roses and Mediterranean scrub. The palate luxuriates in perfectly ripe tannins, elegant length of flavour and remarkable balance. This magnificent wine will only improve with cellaring and is destined to become of one of the all-time greats. Today, it more than deserves a resounding Three Glasses. A retasting of the Monfortino '96 was revelatory: a decade in the cellar earned it Three retrospective Glasses.

● Barolo Monfortino Ris. '99	**YYY**	8
● Barbera d'Alba '04	**YY**	5
● Barolo Monfortino Ris. '96	YYY	8
● Barolo Monfortino Ris. '97	YYY	8
● Barolo Monfortino Ris. '90	YYY	8
● Barolo Monfortino Ris. '88	YYY	8
● Barolo Monfortino Ris. '87	YYY	8
● Barolo Monfortino Ris. '85	YYY	8
● Barolo Monfortino Ris. '82	YYY	8
● Barolo Cascina Francia '01	YYY	8
● Barolo Cascina Francia '00	YYY	8
● Barolo Cascina Francia '97	YYY	8
● Barolo Cascina Francia '89	YYY	8
● Barolo Cascina Francia '87	YYY	8
● Barolo Cascina Francia '85	YYY	8

Paolo Conterno

via Ginestra, 34
12065 Monforte d'Alba (CN)
tel. 017378415
www.paoloconterno.com

Nestling among the vines of Ginestra, one of the most prestigious vineyards in the entire Barolo DOCG, lies Paolo Conterno's estate. His is one of those classic family-run properties that continue to form the backbone of Langhe winemaking. Paolo and his wife are helped by their children, Marisa and Giorgio. Giorgio looks after the technical side of things and, with the help of Beppe Caviola, seeks to mature the estate's wines in the Piedmont tradition. Paolo Conterno produces exclusively red wines from local varieties, immune to the trends that have infected the zone over the last 15 years. Although the 2002 Barolo comes entirely from Ginestra grapes, it does not bear the vineyard's name on the label. Happily this cru escaped the ravages of the hailstorm on 3 September and offers us a fine example of Barolo from '02. Elegant notes of raspberry and pepper introduce a supple, rather immature body that still has plenty of style. The Barolo Ginestra Riserva '00, Langhe Nebbiolo Bric Ginestra '04 and Barbera Ginestra '04 all benefit from generous harvests and serve as the estate's standard bearers. The Barolo is full and estery with notes of brandied fruit and a potent palate showing rather rugged tannins that act as a foil for the extraordinarily generous alcohol. The Nebbiolo offers a complex, elegant personality with mint, raspberry and tobacco aromas and is an absolute gem of its type. The elegant, fresh-tasting Barbera '04 also has character while the Dolcetto is still young and edgy.

● Barolo Ginestra Ris. '00	**YY**	8
● Barolo '02	**YY**	7
● Barbera d'Alba Ginestra '04	**YY**	5
● Langhe Nebbiolo Bric Ginestra '04	**YY**	6
● Dolcetto d'Alba Ginestra '05	**Y**	4
● Barolo Ginestra Ris. '98	YY	8
● Barolo Ginestra '99	YY	8
● Barolo Ginestra Ris. '99	YY	8
● Barolo Ginestra '00	YY	8
● Barolo Ginestra '96	YY	8
● Barolo Ginestra Ris. '96	YY	8
● Barolo Ginestra Ris. '97	YY	8

MONFORTE D'ALBA (CN)

★ Conterno Fantino

via Ginestra, 1
12065 Monforte d'Alba (CN)
tel. 017378204
www.conternofantino.it

We always enjoy our visits to Claudio Conterno and Guido Fantino, first of all for the 360-degree view that delights the eye and second for the wines that thrill our other senses. Even without the Barolo selections – including Barolo Mosconi, due to replace the Parussi, which has gone out of production – the range performed well. The Langhe Rosso Monprà '03 shot back into our finals. This blend of equal parts of barbera and nebbiolo with ten per cent cabernet spent18 months in barrique and is still developing, although the cabernet's grassy tones are yielding to notes of forest fruit and spice. On the palate the nebbiolo's sweet, leisurely tannins lead the way. The Barolo '02 is obtained from the few grapes harvested from the various vineyards and only 13,000 bottles are available. It has the austere nose of a great Barolo but the structure is inevitably more lightweight and the tannins are still green. Still, it is well styled and satisfyingly drinkable. The Barbera d'Alba Vignota '05 from the Ginestra vineyard stands out from the other reds for its rich, already enjoyable fruit and will balance out more with cellaring. On their customary form are the Dolcetto d'Alba Bricco Bastia '05 with its flowery aromas and, notably, the Langhe Nebbiolo Ginestrino '05, young and inviting in appearance with a clean flowery nose and pleasantly tannic palate. Finally, hats off to the Langhe Chardonnay Bastia '03, which is excellent despite its hot vintage. Elegant aromas hint at tropical fruit, peach and vanilla and the palate's tangy freshness sustains the strong alcohol.

●	Langhe Rosso Monprà '03	🍷🍷	6
●	Barolo '02	🍷🍷	7
○	Langhe Chardonnay Bastia '03	🍷🍷	5
●	Barbera d'Alba Vignota '05	🍷🍷	5
●	Langhe Nebbiolo Ginestrino '05	🍷🍷	4*
●	Dolcetto d'Alba Bricco Bastia '05	🍷	4
●	Barolo Sorì Ginestra '00	🍸🍸🍸	8
●	Barolo V. del Gris '01	🍸🍸🍸	8
●	Barolo V. del Gris '96	🍸🍸🍸	8
●	Barolo V. del Gris '97	🍸🍸🍸	8
●	Langhe Rosso Monprà '97	🍸🍸🍸	8
●	Barolo Sorì Ginestra '98	🍸🍸🍸	8
●	Langhe Rosso Monprà '98	🍸🍸🍸	8
●	Barolo Sorì Ginestra '99	🍸🍸🍸	8

MONFORTE D'ALBA (CN)

Alessandro e Gian Natale Fantino

via G. Silvano, 18
12065 Monforte d'Alba (CN)
tel. 017378253

Hard work and determination always pay off and the Fantino brothers are living proof. This year, they slipped another award into their trophy case for the stunning Barolo Vigna dei Dardi Riserva '00. This sumptuous, harmonious wine presents an ethereal nose with balsamic, flowery aromas announcing a generous, consistent palate with sweet tannins and perfectly tempered oak before the long-lingering finish ranges from liquorice to chocolate. This absolutely magnificent performance brought the estate its first, fully deserved Three Glass crown. Not quite at the same level – but then again, what is? – we have the Barolo Vigna dei Dardi '02. Rich garnet red, it offers fruity aromas well supported by oak. The balance in the mouth is considerable but it pays the price of a difficult vintage in terms of breadth and depth. The same eight-hectare Bussia plot planted in 1945 brings us the Barbera d'Alba Vigna dei Dardi '04. Vinified without the use of oak, it is a clean, elegant wine that echoes the nose's cherry and plum aromas on the palate. Overall, it was an impressive showing from this array of wines and our only complaint is their limited availability. The estate's scant 40,000 bottles are sold almost exclusively to the overseas markets or directly at the cellar door. Still, if you find the cellars empty at least you will have had the chance to visit the Fantinos' in their lovely, expertly restored winery in Monforte's historic centre.

●	Barolo V. dei Dardi Ris. '00	🍷🍷🍷	7
●	Barbera d'Alba V. dei Dardi '04	🍷🍷	4*
●	Barolo V. dei Dardi '02	🍷🍷	6
●	Barolo V. dei Dardi Ris. '98	🍸🍸	7
●	Barolo V. dei Dardi Ris. '99	🍸🍸	7
●	Barolo V. dei Dardi '00	🍸🍸	6
●	Barolo V. dei Dardi '01	🍸🍸	6
●	Barolo V. dei Dardi '96	🍸🍸	6
●	Barolo V. dei Dardi '97	🍸🍸	6
●	Barolo V. dei Dardi '98	🍸🍸	6
●	Barolo V. dei Dardi '99	🍸🍸	6

MONFORTE D'ALBA (CN)

ATTILIO GHISOLFI
LOC. BUSSIA, 27
12065 MONFORTE D'ALBA (CN)
TEL. 017378345
www.ghisolfi.com

Much of what has been said about the 2002 vintage is full of sound and fury, signifying nothing. The truth is that those producers who managed it well, reducing their yields and, yes, also their prices, have obtained some very good wines, hail permitting. Gianmarco Ghisolfi's Barolo Bricco Visette '02 is a prime example and won a place in our finals. The barely 3,500 bottles offer a lovely, lustrous garnet red and typical, concentrated aromas ranging from plum to tar. The palate has good balance but lacks a bit of fullness and backbone. But there is lots of backbone to be found in the other finalist, Barolo Riserva Fantini '00. Its 2,500 bottles are obtained from an old vineyard extending over less than a hectare. Impressive tertiary notes are already emerging on the nose, while the palate is notable for the sweetness of its still rather exuberant tannins. The two Langhe Rosso blends, Alta Bussia '04 and Carlin '02, are very much on a par. The first, from 60 per cent barbera and 40 per cent nebbiolo, is well managed on both nose and palate with unusual grassy notes, a hint of tobacco and strong toastiness. The second exchanges freisa for the barbera. Almost three years of maturing in barrique and stainless steel have left it with notes of berry fruit and spice and sweet, ripe tannins. Concentrated aromas of flowers and berry fruit are the calling card of the Barbera d'Alba Vigna Lisi '04, whose palate is appropriately fresh and long. The pinot nero-based Langhe Pinay '04 came close to Two Glasses for its varietal currant nose and young, agreeable palate.

● Barolo Fantini Ris. '00	2 glasses (black)	7
● Barolo Bricco Visette '02	2 glasses (black)	7
● Langhe Rosso Carlin '02	2 glasses (black)	5
● Barbera d'Alba V. Lisi '04	2 glasses (black)	5
● Langhe Rosso Alta Bussia '04	2 glasses (black)	5
● Langhe Rosso Pinay '04	1 glass (black)	4
● Langhe Rosso Alta Bussia '00	3 glasses (white)	6
● Barolo Bricco Visette '01	3 glasses (white)	7
● Langhe Rosso Alta Bussia '01	3 glasses (white)	6
● Langhe Rosso Alta Bussia '99	3 glasses (white)	6
● Barolo Bricco Visette '00	2 glasses (white)	7
● Langhe Rosso Alta Bussia '03	2 glasses (white)	6
● Barolo Bricco Visette '99	2 glasses (white)	7
● Barolo Bricco Visette '98	2 glasses (white)	7

MONFORTE D'ALBA (CN)

ELIO GRASSO
LOC. GINESTRA, 40
12065 MONFORTE D'ALBA (CN)
TEL. 017378491
www.eliograsso.it

Elio Grasso's dream is coming true: the long gallery dug into the hillside to avoid impact on the landscape is ready for his barriques and bottles. While the project was under way, it was business as usual in the vineyard and cellar. Helped by his son, Gianluca, and Enrico Marchisio, Elio presented us with his usual excellent range despite the absence of the 2002 Barolo selections. As always, Barolo Runcot excelled. The '01 revels in aromas of brandied cherries, walnut and chocolate and a warm, generous, jammy palate with harmonious tannins. Savour every drop of this sumptuous Three Glass wonder because it wasn't bottled in the '02 and '03 vintages and the '04 will be released as a Riserva so it won't hit the shops until 2010! The Barbera d'Alba Vigna Martina '03 was a surprise finalist. Its very intense nose recalls wild cherries, blackberry and tobacco, while the harmony between alcohol and acid backbone make the palate both impressive and pleasing. Cru grapes harvested in 2002 went into the basic Barolo, which showed well. We particularly liked its liquorice and dried fruit nose. On the palate the tannins are still rather immature, but the finish is reasonably long. Stainless steel has brought out the fruit in the coherent, pleasing Dolcetto d'Alba dei Grassi '05. The same approach was used for Langhe Nebbiolo Gavarini '05, which lacks clarity at the moment. The nose is a bit closed and the palate very young. A round of applause for the Langhe Chardonnay Educato '05 and its notes of chamomile, fragrant oak and peach, introducing a fresh, tangy palate that lingers.

● Barolo Runcot '01	3 glasses (black)	8
● Barbera d'Alba V. Martina '03	2 glasses (black)	5
● Barolo '02	2 glasses (black)	7
● Dolcetto d'Alba dei Grassi '05	2 glasses (black)	4*
○ Langhe Chardonnay Educato '05	2 glasses (black)	5
● Langhe Nebbiolo Gavarini '05	1 glass (black)	4
● Barolo Gavarini V. Chiniera '00	3 glasses (white)	8
● Barolo Gavarini V. Chiniera '01	3 glasses (white)	8
● Barolo Ginestra V. Casa Maté '93	3 glasses (white)	8
● Barolo Runcot '96	3 glasses (white)	8
● Barolo Gavarini V. Chiniera '98	3 glasses (white)	8
● Barolo Gavarini V. Chiniera '99	3 glasses (white)	8

Giovanni Manzone

via Castelletto, 9
12065 Monforte d'Alba (CN)
tel. 017378114

With just eight hectares and a little under 40,000 bottles a year, Giovanni Manzone's estate is not particularly well-known to the public or Langhe wine enthusiasts. Giovanni has a retiring character and is not given to hogging the limelight, preferring to devote his energies to his vineyards and cellar. And yet his wines have always been quite excellent. It may be that in the past a slight air of healthy rusticity clung to them, preventing them from winning the recognition they deserve, but no more. Today, the Manzone Barolos have attained enviable levels of elegance and balance. The only Barolo '02 bottled by the estate derives from a blend of grapes harvested in all the vineyards and is one of the best to come out of that wretched vintage. For sure it's no heavyweight, but it does have lovely clean fruit, reasonable fullness and length that is impressive for the vintage. Barolo Le Gramolere Riserva '00 is a worthy successor to the 1999 version. Its big personality perfectly expresses the characteristics of the hotter growing year and it fully deserves its Three Glasses. Concentrated aromas of spice and balsam pave the way for notes of violet and liquorice. Entry on the palate is overwhelming, almost voluptuous, and the finish closes on a long, invigorating, astringent sensation. Barbera La Serra '04 merited a place on our final tasting table for its intense vanilla aromas perfectly offset by notes of ripe cherry, and its full-flavoured, concentrated palate. The Rosserto, a powerful white from the rare rossese bianco grape, is the cellar's misunderstood gem.

●	Barolo Le Gramolere Ris. '00	TTT	8
●	Barbera d'Alba La Serra '04	TT	5
●	Barolo '02	TT	6
○	Rosserto Bianco '04	TT	4*
●	Barbera d'Alba '05	TT	4*
●	Dolcetto d'Alba La Serra '05	TT	4*
●	Dolcetto d'Alba Le Ciliegie '05	T	3
●	Langhe Nebbiolo '05	T	4
●	Barolo Le Gramolere Ris. '99	YYY	8
●	Barolo Le Gramolere '01	YY	7
●	Barolo Le Gramolere Bricat '01	YY	7
●	Barolo Le Gramolere Bricat '99	YY	7
●	Barolo Le Gramolere Bricat '97	YY	7
●	Barolo Le Gramolere Ris. '97	YY	8
●	Barolo Le Gramolere Ris. '98	YY	7

Monti

fraz. Camia
loc. San Sebastiano, 39
12065 Monforte d'Alba (CN)
tel. 017378391
www.paolomonti.com

The quality of Pier Paolo Monti's wines is now a given. Much of the credit for this goes to the care with which he looks after his 11 hectares of vineyards and his newly renovated cellar. Thanks to the bad weather that put paid to his 2002 Barolos, Pier Paolo's already limited production of 50,000 bottles was down to 32,000 this year but they all show the level of quality that we have come to expect in recent years. From 40 per cent each cabernet and merlot and 20 per cent nebbiolo, the Langhe Rosso Dossi Rossi '03 almost made it to our finals. The three varieties were handled to bring out their distinctive characteristics, having been harvested at different times and then aged in new barriques for the cabernet and used for the other grapes. The result is a harmonious blend that gives voice to each of the component varieties: the nose is merlot, the backbone cabernet, and the elegant tannins nebbiolo. Next up we tasted the Barbera d'Alba '04, obtained from vines in the Bussia vineyard that have an average age of 40 years. Maturing in new Allier barriques has given it lovely lively aromas rich in nuances of flowers, rhubarb, tobacco and cinnamon, and a stylish palate capped by a long finish that hints at coffee. The 5,000 bottles of Langhe Bianco L'Aura '05 performed very well. From an unusual blend of 70 per cent chardonnay fermented in medium to well-toasted barrels and 30 per cent riesling renano fermented in stainless steel. The riesling's lemony aromas merge to perfection with the chardonnay's notes of butter and tropical fruit.

●	Langhe Rosso Dossi Rossi '03	TT	6
●	Barbera d'Alba '04	TT	6
○	Langhe Bianco L'Aura '05	TT	5
●	Barolo Bussia '00	YY	8
●	Barolo Bussia '01	YY	8
●	Barolo Bussia '99	YY	8
●	Langhe Rosso '01	YY	8
●	Langhe Rosso Dossi Rossi '01	YY	6
●	Barbera d'Alba '99	YY	6
●	Langhe Rosso Dossi Rossi '99	YY	6

MONFORTE D'ALBA (CN)

ARMANDO PARUSSO
LOC. BUSSIA, 55
12065 MONFORTE D'ALBA (CN)
TEL. 017378257
www.parusso.com

Since 1985, Marco and Tiziana Parusso have been the proud owners of 20 hectares planted to vine, most of which lie in Bussia, one of the top Barolo subzones. Given the meteorological havoc wreaked in 2002, the Parussos have opted not to produce their best selections of Langhe's big red. From a tasting or, to be more accurate, not-tasting perspective, this is their year of reckoning and the range they offered was much leaner than usual. The Barolo Vecchie Vigne in Mariondino Riserva '99 kept the estate's flag flying with a Three Glass performance. Its garnet red announces a balsamic, minty nose and a palate that has good texture, enormous backbone and lovely balance of oak and fruit followed by a long, leisurely finish. The Barbera d'Alba Superiore '03 and Barbera d'Alba Ornati '04 are also extremely well made. The former has suffered none of the effects of its dry vintage, presenting deep ruby red with an estery nose and a palate that starts of with acidity to the fore and then unfurls raspberry and strawberry sensations. The Ornati has a richly fruity bouquet whose aromas echo across the palate. The Dolcetto offers complex notes of bay leaf, cherry and plum followed by vegetal and balsamic sensations on the palate. The Langhe Nebbiolo '04 is a wine that commands attention, displaying spicy aromas on both nose and the easy-drinking, extremely agreeable palate. Of the whites on offer, we liked the pure sauvignon Bricco Rovella '03. It is a tad oaky but has nice vanilla notes with hints of caramel. The Langhe Bianco '05 is simpler but still highly enjoyable.

●	Barolo Vecchie Vigne in Mariondino Ris. '99	🍷🍷🍷	8
●	Barbera d'Alba Sup. '03	🍷🍷	6
○	Langhe Bianco Bricco Rovella '03	🍷🍷	6
●	Barbera d'Alba Ornati '04	🍷🍷	4*
●	Langhe Nebbiolo '04	🍷🍷	5
●	Dolcetto d'Alba Piani Noci '05	🍷🍷	4*
○	Langhe Bianco '05	🍷	4
●	Barbera d'Alba Sup. '00	ҮҮҮ	6
●	Barolo Bussia V. Munie '96	ҮҮҮ	8
●	Langhe Rosso Bricco Rovella '96	ҮҮҮ	6
●	Barolo Bussia V. Munie '97	ҮҮҮ	8
●	Barolo Bussia V. Munie '99	ҮҮҮ	8

MONFORTE D'ALBA (CN)

FERDINANDO PRINCIPIANO
VIA ALBA, 19
12065 MONFORTE D'ALBA (CN)
TEL. 0173787158
www.ferdinandoprincipiano.it

Americo's experience and his son Ferdinando's ideas are a match made in heaven. Americo has spent a lifetime in the vineyards and cellar while Ferdinando is a constant source of ideas who aspires to make quality wines without too much interference from technology. Machinery has undoubtedly brought many advantages but occasionally something important is lost along the way, such as the relationship between product and nature. The environment is everything around us, so why not work with it rather than against it? This means sustainable farming methods in the vineyard and to that end Nando has done away with plant protection products and introduced thinning techniques that don't overstress the vine. Similarly, he has implemented a clear basic process for the fruit when it arrives in the cellar: manual pumping over, alcoholic fermentations at flexibly controlled temperatures, almost homeopathic quantities of sulphites and the use of natural ambient yeasts. The first wine from Ferdinando's new approach is Barbera d'Alba La Romualda '04 and it's one of the best in its category. It presents a rich ruby red with notes of blackberry, raspberry and strawberry, and a deep, crisp palate ending in a long, lingering finish. Excellent, too, is the Langhe Nebbiolo Coste '05 with its spicy nose and soft tannins combined with berry fruit and a hint of coffee on the palate. Finally, the well-made Dolcetto d'Alba Sant'Anna '05 offers balsamic, fruity aromas, a soft entry on the palate, taut progression and a lengthy finish.

●	Barbera d'Alba La Romualda '04	🍷🍷	6
●	Dolcetto d'Alba S. Anna '05	🍷🍷	4*
●	Langhe Nebbiolo Coste '05	🍷🍷	4*
●	Barolo Boscareto '93	ҮҮҮ	8
●	Barolo Boscareto '01	ҮҮ	8
●	Barolo Boscareto '99	ҮҮ	8
●	Barolo Boscareto '00	ҮҮ	8
●	Barbera d'Alba La Romualda '01	ҮҮ	5
●	Barbera d'Alba La Romualda '03	ҮҮ	5
●	Barolo Boscareto '98	ҮҮ	8
●	Barolo Le Coste '98	ҮҮ	8
●	Barolo Le Coste '99	ҮҮ	8

MONFORTE D'ALBA (CN)

★ PODERE ROCCHE DEI MANZONI

LOC. MANZONI SOPRANI, 3
12065 MONFORTE D'ALBA (CN)
TEL. 017378421
www.roccheddeimanzoni.it

Valentino Migliorini's estate is one of the best in Langhe, boasting 40 beautiful hectares of vines and an average production of 250,000 bottles a year. For this edition of the Guide, neither of the Spumante Metodo Classicos, Riserva Elena or Valentino Brut Zero, were available for tasting as their release has been postponed until next year. We particularly liked the Quatr Nas '01, a blend of 50 per cent nebbiolo with equal parts cabernet sauvignon, merlot and pinot nero. Its wide-ranging, complex nose flits across sensations of forest fruits, dried roses, mint and cocoa powder while the full, velvety palate exhibits mouthfilling tannins and nuances of coffee and tobacco through the extremely long finish. We also liked Bricco Manzoni from 80 per cent nebbiolo and 20 per cent barbera, a prototype of this kind of grape mix in the Langhe. Ruby in the glass, it unveils violet and spice aromas and then well-balanced tannins and acidity accompanied by fruity, pleasantly vanillaed notes. The Barolo Rocche '02, available in just 15,000 bottles, is a sound interpretation of a difficult vintage. Ruby verging on garnet in colour, its notes of violets, tobacco and berry fruit are the prelude to a harmonious palate that is more elegant than powerful, with soft tannins and traces of leather and liquorice in the finish. The Barbera Sorito Mosconi '03 comes from vines that are over 70 years old. Intense in colour, it gives fruit, spice and vanilla ushering in a full, fruity palate of impressive length. The L'Angelica '04 is a very nice Chardonnay with concentrated ripe fruit tones.

●	Langhe Rosso Quatr Nas '01	▼▼	7
●	Langhe Rosso Bricco Manzoni '01	▼▼	6
●	Barbera d'Alba Sorito Mosconi '03	▼▼	6
○	Langhe Chardonnay L'Angelica '04	▼▼	7
●	Barolo Rocche '02	▼	7
●	Barolo V. Cappella di S. Stefano '01	▽▽▽	8
●	Barolo V. Big Ris. '89	▽▽▽	8
●	Barolo V. d'la Roul Ris. '90	▽▽▽	8
●	Barolo V. Cappella di S. Stefano '96	▽▽▽	8
○	Valentino Brut Zero Ris. '98	▽▽▽	6
●	Barolo V. Big 'd Big '99	▽▽▽	8

MONFORTE D'ALBA (CN)

FLAVIO RODDOLO

FRAZ. BRICCO APPIANI
LOC. SANT'ANNA, 5
12065 MONFORTE D'ALBA (CN)
TEL. 017378535

Flavio Roddolo is a lovely person to be around and a visit to his estate is one of our greatest pleasures. He is shy by nature and weighs every word before he speaks, but if you know him well you will have seen him on occasion get carried away when talking about his work and the Langhe. Flavio's opinions on Langhe winemaking and his own wines are based on the solid common sense of one who has spent his life on the land. He has very clear priorities regarding the management of his small six-hectare estate and the approximately 20,000 bottles he obtains from it, from dormant pruning to how to deliver the product to the customer. He is one of the territory's last remaining genuine growers and, although not officially organic, eschews chemicals and limits the use of plant protection products to a minimum. He has banned from his cellar cultured yeasts, enzymes and all unnatural, sophisticated substances or contraptions that add nothing to the winemaking process. We are inclined to agree with him if this year's superb range is anything to go by. We'll start with a simple Dolcetto d'Alba '05 that is more drinkable than usual. Moving on and up, we have a wine that symbolizes the estate, an astonishingly powerful, vital Dolcetto Superiore '04 with a long life ahead of it. Next, two very well-made products, a warm Barbera '03 and a harmonious Barolo Ravera '02 that surpasses the mediocre standards of its vintage. We end with two absolute little gems, a Nebbiolo '03 of extraordinary complexity and length, and an explosive Bricco Appiani that in the 2003 vintage becomes a Langhe Rosso DOC.

●	Barolo Ravera '02	▼▼	6
●	Langhe Rosso Bricco Appiani '03	▼▼	6
●	Nebbiolo d'Alba '03	▼▼	5
●	Dolcetto d'Alba Sup. '04	▼▼	4*
●	Barbera d'Alba '03	▼▼	4
●	Dolcetto d'Alba '05	▼▼	3*
●	Barolo Ravera '01	▽▽▽	6
●	Barolo Ravera '97	▽▽▽	6
●	Bricco Appiani '99	▽▽▽	6
●	Barolo Ravera '00	▽▽	6
●	Barolo Ravera '99	▽▽	6
●	Barolo '96	▽▽	6
●	Bricco Appiani '97	▽▽	6

MONFORTE D'ALBA (CN)

PODERE RUGGERI CORSINI

LOC. BUSSIA CORSINI, 106
12065 MONFORTE D'ALBA (CN)
TEL. 017378625

Loredana Addari and Nicola Argamante are very thorough in the running of their six hectares, which give them an annual production of 45,000 bottles. Their vineyards lie in Corsini, not one of the more famous parts of Barolo territory but one which, for that very reason, represents an exciting challenge. Ruggeri Corsini wines are always sound and the quality improves significantly every year. Interestingly, Loredana and Nicola are cultivating some experimental varieties in their vineyards, including nascetta and albarossa, grape types that are limited to just a few plots in the Langhe. As for the wines themselves, we were greatly impressed by the Barolo Corsini '02 despite the difficult vintage. Elegant, pervasive aromas of roasted coffee beans herald a fruity palate balanced by the oak and a medium-long finish with a bitterish after-aroma. The Barolo San Pietro has a clean, fruity nose and a well-rounded, leisurely palate. After rather an oaky beginning, the Barbera d'Alba Superiore Armujan reveals pleasant notes of balsam, eucalyptus and blackberry. The Langhe Rosso Argamakow '04 is very well made, unfurling the typical aromas of a pinot nero and albarossa blend. The palate is warm and alcohol-rich with earthy sensations permeating the finale. The other reds are good too, notably the austere, varietal Nebbiolo '04. The estate's only white is obtained from a blend of sauvignon, chardonnay and nascetta in equal parts. Its notes of sage and stewed apple make it a pleasing easy drinker.

●	Barolo Corsini '02	TT	6
●	Barbera d'Alba Sup. Armujan '04	TT	4*
●	Langhe Nebbiolo '04	TT	4*
●	Langhe Rosso Argamakow '04	TT	5
●	Barolo San Pietro '02	T	6
●	Barbera d'Alba '05	T	4
●	Dolcetto d'Alba '05	T	3
○	Langhe Bianco '05	T	4
●	Barolo Corsini '00	YY	6
●	Barolo Corsini '01	YY	6
●	Langhe Rosso Argamakow '01	YY	5
●	Langhe Rosso Argamakow '03	YY	5
●	Barolo Corsini '99	YY	6

MONFORTE D'ALBA (CN)

F.LLI SEGHESIO

LOC. CASTELLETTO, 19
12065 MONFORTE D'ALBA (CN)
TEL. 017378108

Aldo and Riccardo Seghesio have a production style that is reflected in the way they manage their ten-hectare family estate and in their aspiration to produce nothing but the wines of the territory. The only exception they make is the Langhe Rosso Bouquet, a merlot, cabernet sauvignon and nebbiolo blend. Output is 55,000 bottles a year and the two great warhorses are Barbera d'Alba Vigneto della Chiesa '04 and Barolo La Villa '02. The Barbera was a clear contender for our final tastings thanks to its concentrated nose of charred oak, cherry and jam. The palate is generous, powerful, perfectly acidic and extremely long with an aftertaste of brandied fruit. The Barolo is one of the best we tasted from this unhappy vintage. Deep garnet red in appearance, it offers notes of earth, leather and dried flowers. The palate has strong backbone and overcomes the limits of the vintage to display impressive length. The ever so elegant Bouquet '03 shows aromas of spice and dried flowers on the nose that correspond perfectly with the palate's warm, fruity sensations. The oak is skilfully gauged, staying in the background, and the finish is quite long with a typical merlot-derived tone. The Dolcetto Vigneto della Chiesa also showed well in our tastings with its complex nose, fruity palate and sweet finish. The Langhe Nebbiolo Sugli is comparably good and displays a complex array of flowery, earthy aromas that are mirrored on the palate. The standard Barbera is, as usual, sound.

●	Barbera d'Alba Vign. della Chiesa '04	TT	6
●	Barolo Vign. La Villa '02	TT	7
●	Langhe Rosso Bouquet '04	TT	6
●	Dolcetto d'Alba Vign. della Chiesa '05	TT	4*
●	Langhe Nebbiolo '05	TT	4*
●	Barbera d'Alba '05	T	4
●	Barbera d'Alba Vign. della Chiesa '00	YYY	6
●	Barolo Vign. La Villa '91	YYY	7
●	Barbera d'Alba Vign. della Chiesa '97	YYY	6
●	Barolo Vign. La Villa '99	YYY	7

MONLEALE (AL)

RENATO BOVERI
VIA XXV APRILE, 1
15059 MONLEALE (AL)
TEL. 013180560

This year is a bit of a watershed for the Renato Boveri estate. Renato has decided to give some of his most important labels extra cellar time to let them fulfil their potential. This is both a courageous and a wise decision that will enable him to release the wines to market when they are ready for the corkscrew. But it means that this year we must be content with tasting only three of the many reds produced by this cellar plus a white from cortese. The best of the line-up has to be the croatina-based Colli Tortonesi Costa '05. Its splendid, bright ruby red is the prelude to aromas of berry fruit and faint traces of spice. Entry on the palate is enhanced by the alcohol, which is well sustained by the structure, and warm nuances of blueberries and plum jam subsequently emerge. When we tasted the Barbera Sant'Ambrogio '04 it had yet to reach its peak but we had a hint of its promise in the firm backbone and alcohol-rich aromas. The Colli Tortonesi Rosso La Nà '05 is obtained from a vinification of freisa grapes that brings out all the typical freshness of the variety. The fresh-tasting, enjoyable Cortese Cappelletta '05 is worth uncorking, not least for the good value for money it offers.

●	Colli Tortonesi Barbera S. Ambrogio '04	TT	4
●	Colli Tortonesi Rosso Costa '05	TT	5
○	Colli Tortonesi Cortese Cappelletta '05	T	3
●	Colli Tortonesi Rosso La Nà '05	T	4
●	Colli Tortonesi Barbera Monleale '99	YY	5
●	Colli Tortonesi Barbera Monleale '00	YY	5
●	Colli Tortonesi Barbera Monleale '98	YY	5
●	Colli Tortonesi Rosso Madai! '99	YY	5

MONLEALE (AL)

VIGNETI MASSA
P.ZZA G. CAPSONI, 10
15059 MONLEALE (AL)
TEL. 013180302

Timorasso dei Colli Tortonesi finally became a DOC with the 2005 vintage, a much deserved tribute for a wine that Walter Massa rediscovered and raised to such high standards. As is right and even logical, Massa the prophet played a leading role in the historic performance that earns this typology its first Three Glass prize. The Sterpi '04 selection is a giant of a wine: mineral, fruity, balsamic and as elegant as it is powerful on the palate, which is capped by a long finish. It's an absolute jewel. This year we tasted no less than three Timorasso selections including this mighty champion. The historic Costa del Vento '04 selection impressed for the way it sets body and acidity in a perfect harmony of enchanting aromas and taste sensations. Obtained from younger vines, Derthona is also superb, showing fresher and more approachable. This is Barbera territory, however, and Walter is a renowned master of the variety. In anticipation of the Cerreta that is due to be released next year, he brought us two '03 selections, Bigolla and Monleale. Bigolla blends barbera and other grapes to offer intense sensations. Great concentration, structure and vigorous body promise outstanding longevity. Monleale is a 100 per cent barbera-based wine already capable of satisfying even the most exacting palate. The stainless steel-aged Barbera Sentieri '05, the splendid Croatina Pertichetta and the Freisa Pietra del Gallo round off the reds. As ever, the Colli Tortonesi Casareggio '05 from cortese is fresh and fragrant. We also point out the delightful Moscato Muscatè.

○	Colli Tortonesi Bianco Sterpi '04	TTT	7
○	Colli Tortonesi Bianco Costa del Vento '04	TT	7
●	Colli Tortonesi Rosso Monleale '03	TT	6
●	Colli Tortonesi Rosso Bigolla '03	TT	7
●	Colli Tortonesi Rosso Pertichetta '04	TT	5
●	Colli Tortonesi Rosso Sentieri '05	TT	5
○	Muscatè '05	TT	3*
○	Colli Tortonesi Bianco Derthona '04	TT	6
○	Colli Tortonesi Bianco Casareggio '05	T	4
●	Colli Tortonesi Freisa Pietra del Gallo '05	T	4

MONTÀ (CN)

GIOVANNI ALMONDO
VIA SAN ROCCO, 26
12046 MONTÀ (CN)
TEL. 0173975256
www.giovannialmondo.com

We admired yet another triumphant showing from this Roero cellar which has toiled for years to achieve quality and recognition for the typical wines of the territory. Domenico Almondo heads the family-run estate and refuses to let critical or market acclaim turn his head.
Whenever we visit him in his cellar and well-tended vineyards, or simply run down the list of wines he proposes at the bottom of the page, the artisanal bent of this small estate is clear to see. His ten or so hectares give him an annual production that varies from 50,000 to 60,000 bottles depending on the vintage. Arneis, Barbera and Roero are all here in force and their hallmark is rigour. Two reds stand out this year and they are no strangers to us: Roero Bric Valdiana and the Barbera Valbianchera, both '04s. The first opens on intriguing, varietal notes led by berry fruit, forest floor and tea leaves. The palate combines muscular body with suppleness and good control, while the excellent finish clearly echoes the fruit. The Barbera More tends more to elegance and finesse, giving one of the best performances we can remember. Strong acidity is nicely offset by alcohol in an overall nose-palate framework of graceful, flawless tonality. The Roero '04 is more drinkable than powerful but still very sound. Of the two Arneis on offer our preference is for the Vigne Sparse, whose aromas and energy are almost on a par with those of its elder sibling, the famous Bricco delle Ciliegie selection, which is also very good this year.

● Barbera d'Alba Valbianchera '04	▼▼	5
● Roero Bric Valdiana '04	▼▼	6
● Roero '04	▼▼	5
○ Roero Arneis Bricco delle Ciliegie '05	▼▼	4*
○ Roero Arneis V. Sparse '05	▼▼	4*
● Roero Bric Valdiana '00	▽▽▽	6
● Roero Bric Valdiana '01	▽▽▽	6
● Roero Bric Valdiana '03	▽▽▽	6
● Barbera d'Alba Valbianchera '01	▽▽	5
● Barbera d'Alba Valbianchera '03	▽▽	5
● Barbera d'Alba Valbianchera '00	▽▽	5
● Roero Sup. Giovanni Almondo '97	▽▽	7

MONTÀ (CN)

MICHELE TALIANO
C.SO A. MANZONI, 24
12046 MONTÀ (CN)
TEL. 0173976512

Softly, softly, step by step, brothers Alberto and Ezio Taliano have built up a solid estate that today enjoys a well-deserved reputation as one of the most reliable in the district of Roero. They produce around 60,000 bottles a year from their dozen hectares of vines. Most of their plots are situated in Roero but a few lie ambitiously over the Tanaro in Langhe and it is these that bring us one of the best wines from the Talianios' range this year. The grapes that go to make the Barbaresco Ad Altiora '03 are obtained from a beautiful Langhe vineyard at San Rocco Seno d'Elvio. It is deep garnet red in appearance with a nicely gauged nose suggesting sweet spices, rain-soaked earth and autumn leaves. The well-developed palate is both robust and elegant. The Roero Ròche dra Bòssora, also '03, can claim to be one of the very best we tasted from that torrid vintage. Although the alcohol is very powerful, it is perfectly offset by the deep, succulent mouthfeel that brings harmony to the overall framework. The tannins make their presence felt but never overwhelm and add a fresh note of fruit in the finish. A little edgy and short on acid backbone, the Barbera Laboriosa seems to feel the effects of the vintage. The last of the 2003s on offer is also sound, the Langhe Rosso obtained from a mix of grapes native to the territory. The standard-label wines are all well typed, fresh and enjoyable, from the Arneis to the Barbera, Dolcetto and Nebbiolo.

● Barbaresco Ad Altiora '03	▼▼	6
● Roero Ròche dra Bòssora '03	▼▼	5
● Barbera d'Alba Laboriosa '03	▼▼	4*
● Langhe Rosso '03	▼▼	4*
● Barbera d'Alba A Bon Rendre '05	▼▼	4*
○ Roero Arneis Sernì '05	▼▼	4*
● Dolcetto d'Alba Ciabot Vigna '05	▼	4
● Langhe Nebbiolo Blagheur '05	▼	4
● Barbaresco Ad Altiora '01	▽▽	6
● Roero Ròche dra Bòssora '01	▽▽	5
● Barbera d'Alba Laboriosa '00	▽▽	4
● Roero Ròche dra Bòssora '00	▽▽	5
● Barbera d'Alba Laboriosa '01	▽▽	4

MONTEGROSSO D'ASTI (AT)

TENUTA LA MERIDIANA
VIA TANA BASSA, 5
14048 MONTEGROSSO D'ASTI (AT)
TEL. 0141956172 - 0141956250

Over the years, Giampiero Bianco has considerably improved the quality of the wines he obtains from his 12-hectare estate and the range he presents to us for tasting is always excellent. The rich red Barbera Bricco Sereno '03 offers a warm nose with lovely notes of cherry jam and brandied fruit in a clean overall framework. The powerful, alcoholic palate ends in a leisurely finish. A fine showing also came from the Barbera Tra La Terra e Il Cielo '03, which is vibrant and almost opaque in appearance. Very delicate aromas of mint, berry fruit and leather fill the nose, before the thickly flavoursome palate lingers generously. Barbera Vitis '04 has a pale ruby colour and aromas ranging from fruit to nuances of cinchona in a coherent framework. The very tasty, reasonably well-sustained palate shows balance and tempting drinkability. The Barbera Le Gagie '04 is pleasant with a robust, satisfying palate. Monferrato Rosso Rivaia '03 from nebbiolo, barbera and cabernet is garnet red in the glass. Its leisurely nose has bags of personality and the palate impresses with the fullness of its body and remarkable extract. Passito Sol '03 is from chardonnay grapes partially dried on racks to produce a warm, concentrated wine whose rich palate is buttressed by refreshing supporting acidity. The Bianco Puntet '05, a chardonnay, cortese and favorita blend, has wild flower aromas and a reasonably harmonious palate. Up last, the red La Malaga '05, is soundly crafted.

● Barbera d'Asti Sup. Nizza Tra La Terra e Il Cielo '03	YY	5
● Barbera d'Asti Sup. Bricco Sereno '03	YY	4
● Monferrato Rosso Rivaia '03	YY	5
○ Passito Sol '03	YY	6
● Barbera d'Asti Vitis '04	YY	3*
● La Malaga '05	YY	4
● Barbera d'Asti Le Gagie '04	Y	4
○ Monferrato Bianco Puntet '05	Y	4
● Monferrato Rosso Rivaia '01	YY (white)	5
● Barbera d'Asti Sup. Tra Terra e Cielo '98	YY (white)	5
● Barbera d'Asti Sup. Bricco Sereno '99	YY (white)	5

MONTELUPO ALBESE (CN)

DESTEFANIS
VIA MORTIZZO, 8
12050 MONTELUPO ALBESE (CN)
TEL. 0173617189
www.marcodestefanis.com

Marco Destefanis' estate is a wholly family affair. In the post-war years, Marco's grandfather Francesco built the foundations of a business that he handed on to Marco's father, Beppe, who ran it from the 1970s and still works in the vineyard and cellar today. The Destefanis women are equally involved, with wife Silvia and mother Rosangela lending invaluable support in managing the agricultural and commercial sides of things. The estate has 12 hectares planted to vine, three of which are rented. The range of wines offered is wide and very competitive in price. Once again, the stand-out on the Destefanis list is the Dolcetto d'Alba Vigna Monia Bassa '05. It is obtained from grapes grown in vineyards that are more than 50 years old and lie at an altitude of 430 metres. Matured for 11 months in stainless steel vats and used 900-litre casks, it presents a nose of ripe berry fruit and sweet cinnamon-led spice. The palate combines impressive backbone with silky tannins and extremely agreeable length. The 15,000 bottles of Dolcetto Bricco Galluccio '05 are a bit simpler and easier to drink but nevertheless of absolute quality. Both the elegant, harmonious Nebbiolo d'Alba '04 and the Barbera d'Alba Bricco Galluccio '04, barrique-aged for 12 months, performed outstandingly. The Langhe Chardonnay '05, matured exclusively in stainless steel, and the drinkable, agreeable Barbera d'Alba '05 are fair.

● Dolcetto d'Alba V. Monia Bassa '05	YY	3*
● Barbera d'Alba Bricco Galluccio '04	YY	4
● Nebbiolo d'Alba '04	YY	4
● Dolcetto d'Alba Bricco Galluccio '05	YY	2*
● Barbera d'Alba '05	Y	3
○ Langhe Chardonnay '05	Y	3
● Dolcetto d'Alba V. Monia Bassa '03	YY (white)	3
● Dolcetto d'Alba V. Monia Bassa '04	YY (white)	3

MONTEU ROERO (CN)

ANGELO NEGRO & FIGLI
FRAZ. SANT'ANNA, 1
12040 MONTEU ROERO (CN)
TEL. 017390252
www.negroangelo.it

Three Glasses is the maximum prize we give to a wine of absolute quality. On occasion, however, we also award it in tribute to the significant growth shown by an estate, the attainment of full maturity or a producer that plays a leading role in his territory. The house of Negro is just such a case. Roero Sudisfà '03 shows the best form we have ever seen in this label, but our praise goes beyond the wine to the decades of effort put in by this family team, which has few rivals in the whole district of Roero. So we take our hats off to the Negros: Giovanni, indefatigable at the helm, his wife Marisa and their children Gabriele, Angelo, Emanuela and Giuseppe, all of whom hold various positions and contribute to the smooth running of the estate. The vine stock extends over more than 50 hectares and there are plots beyond the borders of Roero. Annual production totals 250,000 bottles. The range of labels presented for tasting is long and boasts impressive overall quality, but by unanimous vote this year's out and out winner is the Sudisfà. Obtained from a super selection of Roero's best nebbiolo, this is a fresh, fruity wine in spite of its torrid vintage. The nose is pervasive and well defined and the palate reveals austerity and impressive power: a real champion. Hot on its heels comes the Barbera Bric Bertu '04 with a perfect display of spicy notes on the nose and balanced acidity and alcohol on the palate. The other reds are all good. Negro has always been a standard bearer for Roero whites: Perdaudin is sound and the Brut pleasing.

●	Roero Sudisfà '03	▼▼▼	6
●	Barbera d'Alba Bric Bertu '04	▼▼	5
●	Barbaresco Basarin '03	▼▼	6
●	Roero Prachiosso '03	▼▼	5
●	Barbera d'Alba Nicolon '04	▼▼	4*
○	Perdaudin Passito '04	▼▼	6
●	Roero '04	▼▼	4*
○	Roero Arneis Perdaudin '05	▼▼	4*
●	Barbera d'Alba '05	▼	3
○	Roero Arneis Brut M. Cl. Perdaudin '04	▼	5
○	Roero Arneis Gianat '05	▼	4
●	Roero Sudisfà '00	▽▽	6
●	Roero Sudisfà '01	▽▽	6
●	Barbera d'Alba Bric Bertu '03	▽▽	5

MONTEU ROERO (CN)

CASCINA PELLERINO
LOC. SANT'ANNA, 93
12040 MONTEU ROERO (CN)
TEL. 0173978171
www.cascinapellerino.com

Today, Cascina Pellerino enjoys a solid reputation around Roero. Cristian Bono, the 30-year-old owner who will become a father around the time our Guide is published, has brought the estate along in leaps and bounds in recent years. He is ably supported by his partner, Roberto Ghione, and after finding their feet and setting up the winery, the two now enjoy a strong working relationship and share the running of the estate. Cristian manages the vineyards and the functional, well-equipped cellar where the estate's impressive quantity and quality of grapes are processed while Roberto looks after the business and marketing side of things. Production is forecast to reach almost 100,000 bottles a year within the near future. Our main concern is the quality of the wines and we must confess to being more than satisfied with this year's tastings. The Roero Leoni '03 emerged unscathed from the great heat of the growing year and is in fine fettle. A fascinating nose reveals notes of wild roses, faint spice and rain-soaked earth, and a leisurely, lip-smacking palate. It outshines the Vicot '04, which is still very interesting with intense nuances of leather and tobacco leaf and a vibrantly enfolding palate. The big red triumvirate is completed by a Barbera Gran Madre '04 of fabulous fragrance and aromatic length. The whites show encouraging progress too. The Boneur selection is flanked by a new Arneis, Desiré '05, which is very good and varietal on its first outing. The rest of the range performed well.

●	Roero Leoni '03	▼▼	6
●	Barbera d'Alba Sup. Gran Madre '04	▼▼	5
●	Roero Vicot '04	▼▼	5
○	Langhe Favorita '05	▼▼	3*
●	Roero '05	▼▼	4
○	Roero Arneis Desiré '05	▼▼	3*
○	Roero Arneis Boneur '05	▼▼	3*
●	Dolcetto d'Alba '05	▼	3
●	Roero Leoni '01	▽▽	6
●	Roero Vicot '01	▽▽	5
●	Roero Vicot '03	▽▽	5
●	Barbera d'Alba Sup. Gran Madre '03	▽▽	5

MORSASCO (AL)

LA GUARDIA
PODERE LA GUARDIA, 74
15010 MORSASCO (AL)
TEL. 014473076
www.laguardiavini.it

The Priarone family runs the La Guardia estate with great devotion and passion, reliably turning out wines of high quality. Over the years, they have experimented widely and presented new labels, but their real strength lies in the vineyards that surround the beautiful Villa Delfini. The estate's 30 hectares are planted to a range of varieties, from the indigenous dolcetto, barbera, brachetto and cortese to the international cabernet sauvignon and chardonnay grapes. Turning to the wines, Dolcetto Villa Delfini has undoubtedly benefited from its extra year in glass. The nose is concentrated and lingering with notes of forest fruits and sweet spices while the palate shows soft, enjoyable tannins. The Dolcetto Bricco Riccardo has a particularly brilliant ruby red appearance and pervasive aromas of blackberry with faint nuances of spice. The Dolcetto di Ovada Il Gamondino '04 stands out for its vivacious, reasonably complex palate. The Barbera del Monferrato Ornovo '04 also impressed. Ruby with lovely garnet red lights in the glass, it has refreshing acidity and decent backbone on the palate. The Monferrato Rosso Sacroeprofano's aromas of hay and red fruit announce rather a rough palate. A few more months of ageing will doubtless leave it balanced and agreeable. We enjoyed the Figlio di un Bacco Minore, a Brachetto Passito which is very well made and pleasing on the palate. Good, too, is the Piemonte Chardonnay Butàs '04. The Monferrato Rosso Leone was not deemed ready and so was not presented; neither was the Barbera Vigna di Dante.

●	Dolcetto di Ovada Sup. Villa Delfini '03	🍷🍷	4*
●	Monferrato Rosso Sacroeprofano '03	🍷🍷	5
●	Barbera del M.to Ornovo '04	🍷🍷	4
●	Dolcetto di Ovada Sup. Il Gamondino '04	🍷🍷	4
●	Dolcetto di Ovada Sup. Vign. Bricco Riccardo '04	🍷🍷	4
●	Figlio di un Bacco Minore	🍷🍷	4
○	Piemonte Chardonnay Butàs '04	🍷	5
○	Cortese dell'Alto M.to La Vigna di Lena '05	🍷	4
○	Piemonte Chardonnay Il Delfino '05	🍷	4

MURISENGO (AL)

ISABELLA
FRAZ. CORTERANZO
VIA GIANOLI, 64
15020 MURISENGO (AL)
TEL. 0141693000

It was business as usual in Corteranzo despite the high temperatures and scant rain that characterized the harvest. Gabriele Calvo and his family are putting the finishing touches to the new structure they have built next to the cellar and which they inaugurate in autumn 2006. This space is dedicated to wine tourists in the area and offers a range of facilities including a gymnasium and an indoor swimming pool. Of the array of wines offered to us by the Isabella estate, two were conspicuous by their absence, Barbera d'Asti Bric Stupui and Chardonnay Carpe Diem. The first will be presented next year as it is not yet ready, and the second will not be released for another two years or so because it was not produced in either 2004 or 2005. One of the labels that made the biggest impression on us is the Barbera del Monferrato Bricco Montemà Tardivo '04. The pleasing palate is enhanced by a range of very tempting cherry and blackberry-led aromas and goes on to reveal strong grip and personality. The Barbera d'Asti Truccone presents a deep ruby red, with hints of fruit and vague vegetal notes on the nose, and excellent acidity and aromatic length on the palate. We enjoyed a fine showing from the Grignolino del Monferrato Casalese Montecastello '05, a balanced, full-flavoured wine with just the right amount of tannins. Last but not least, a Glass went to the Freisa Vivace Sobric '05, a typical Monferrato product that is not overly challenging but is very approachable and pleasing to drink.

●	Barbera d'Asti Truccone '04	🍷🍷	4
●	Barbera del M.to Bricco Montemà Tardivo '04	🍷🍷	3*
●	Grignolino del M.to Casalese Montecastello '04	🍷🍷	4
●	Monferrato Freisa Vivace Sobric '05	🍷	3
●	Barbera d'Asti Bric Stupui '00	☐☐	6
●	Barbera d'Asti Bric Stupui '01	☐☐	5
●	Barbera d'Asti Bric Stupui '03	☐☐	5

NEIVE (CN)

PIERO BUSSO
VIA ALBESANI, 8
12052 NEIVE (CN)
TEL. 017367156
www.bussopiero.com

The dynamic family team headed by Piero Busso works hard and determinedly to maintain the levels of quality they have achieved on this small Neive estate. The range of wines presented includes three 2003 Barbaresco selections, each differently nuanced, which attest to skill in the cellar. Obtained from a plot in Treiso that has produced superb results over the last few years, Barbaresco Santo Stefanetto rises head and shoulders above the rest. It starts out full and warm on ripe cherry-led aromas with minerally, earthy undertones. The lingering, deeply harmonious palate has well-modelled tannins and confirms the wine as a fine interpretation of the vintage. We gave it Three full Glasses. The austere, flowery Barbaresco Borgese has a more evolved, mellow profile showing lovely aromas of citrus peel. The hot vintage has taken more of a toll here, however, curbing its excessive verve on the palate and leaving it with rather rough tannins. The Barbaresco Gallina '03 is graceful, captivating, warm and well-balanced with crisp, crystal-clear fruit aromas. The consistent palate is softer and readier overall. It may not be particularly deep but it is exceptionally clean. We round off the reds with the excellent Barbera d'Alba Santo Stefanetto '04, which impressed us with the fullness, fruity chewiness and flowery freshness of its nose. Combine this with the balanced aromas on the palate and it adds up to very satisfying drinkability. The Langhe Bianco '05, a blend of chardonnay and sauvignon in equal parts, is refreshing, dry and dependable.

●	Barbaresco S. Stefanetto '03	🍷🍷🍷	8
●	Barbera d'Alba S. Stefanetto '04	🍷🍷	6
●	Barbaresco Borgese '03	🍷🍷	7
●	Barbaresco Gallina '03	🍷🍷	8
○	Langhe Bianco '05	🍷	4
●	Barbaresco S. Stefanetto '00	YYY	8
●	Barbaresco S. Stefanetto '01	YYY	8
●	Barbaresco V. Borgese '97	YYY	7
●	Barbaresco '02	YY	6
●	Barbaresco Borgese '01	YY	7
●	Barbaresco Gallina '03	YY	8
●	Barbaresco Mondino '01	YY	6
●	Barbera d'Alba V. Majano '04	YY	4

NEIVE (CN)

F.LLI CIGLIUTI
VIA SERRABOELLA, 17
12052 NEIVE (CN)
TEL. 0173677185

The Cigliuti family works six hectares in an excellent position in the eastern part of the municipality of Neive with a passion and determination that bring us an array of very well-made wines. As a result of the disastrous growing year of 2002, they decided to produce just one Barbaresco with no vineyard indication instead of the usual two estate crus. As the Serraboella wasn't ready, we tasted the Barbaresco Vigne Erte '03, which impressed us with a well-gauged interpretation of the vintage. The warm, evolved nose offers hints of ripe cherry, liquorice and dried flowers without the slightest trace of overripeness. The broad palate unbends gradually to show nice depth and serious tannins sustained by good acid backbone, all of which bodes well for its future progress in the cellar. Overall, the same goes for the other two wines from that vintage, the Langhe Briccoserra '03 and the Barbera d'Alba Campass '03. The first, an equal blend of nebbiolo and barbera, has a more modern slant with black berry fruit, spice and aromatic herbs, and a warm, embracing if not particularly deep palate. The second presents intense notes of ripe dark berry fruit and black berry jam, balsam and flower tones, and a juicy, full palate quite well supported by acidity. The Barbera d'Alba Serraboella '04 also did very well, showing refreshing notes of clean red berry fruit, flowers, spices and chocolate. The succulent palate is firmly structured and nicely balanced.

●	Barbaresco V. Erte '03	🍷🍷	6
●	Barbera d'Alba Campass '03	🍷🍷	5
●	Barbera d'Alba Serraboella '04	🍷🍷	5
●	Langhe Rosso Briccoserra '03	🍷🍷	6
●	Barbaresco Serraboella '90	YYY	8
●	Barbaresco Serraboella '96	YYY	8
●	Barbaresco Serraboella '97	YYY	8
●	Barbaresco V. Erte '00	YY	6
●	Barbaresco V. Erte '01	YY	6
●	Barbaresco '02	YY	6
●	Barbera d'Alba Serraboella '00	YY	5
●	Barbera d'Alba Serraboella '01	YY	5
●	Barbera d'Alba Serraboella '03	YY	5

NEIVE (CN)

COLLINA SERRAGRILLI
VIA SERRAGRILLI, 30
12057 NEIVE (CN)
TEL. 0173677010
www.serragrilli.it

At first glance, Collina Serragrilli seems like the stereotypical Langhe winery: a medium-size, family-run farm that has been passed down through four generations of farmers and growers who have all worked hard in their vineyards. A closer examination, however, reveals who owns and manages the estate today and shows it to be anything but stereotypical. At the helm of Collina Serragrilli we have the well-matched team of Lequio sisters, Antonella, Daniela and Rosanna, who is flanked by her husband Piernicola Bruno. This almost all-female estate consists of 16 hectares planted to vine and has a maximum annual production of 90,000 bottles. Oenologists Beppe Rattazzo and Giuliano Noè offer their invaluable support in the cellar. The best of the wines presented, we thought, were the Barbaresco Basarin '01 and the Barbaresco Serragrilli '03. The first stands out for its cherry and strawberry aromas with nuances of leather, rain-soaked earth and tobacco while velvety tannins and fine elegance mark of the palate. The second, from a very hot growing year, offers a ripe nose and tannins that are assertive but not invasive on the palate. The round, fruity Barbera d'Alba Grillaia '04 is quite excellent. We awarded Two Glasses to the Langhe Grillobianco '04, a chardonnay and sauvignon blend, for its enjoyable freshness. Slightly lower in the rankings come the Dolcetto d'Alba '04 and the Langhe Grillorosso '02 from nebbiolo, barbera and cabernet sauvignon.

●	Barbaresco Basarin '01	🍷🍷	6
●	Barbaresco Serragrilli '03	🍷🍷	6
●	Barbera d'Alba Grillaia '04	🍷🍷	4*
○	Langhe Grillobianco '04	🍷🍷	4*
●	Langhe Grillorosso '02	🍷	4
●	Dolcetto d'Alba '04	🍷	4
●	Barbaresco Basarin '00	YY	6
●	Barbaresco Serragrilli '01	YY	6

NEIVE (CN)

FONTANABIANCA
VIA BORDINI, 15
12057 NEIVE (CN)
TEL. 017367195
www.fontanabianca.it

Passion and enthusiasm, delight in the consistently excellent results achieved to date, and a good dose of humility that enables him to maintain a sense of balance: these are the qualities that distinguish Aldo Pola. Flanked by partner Bruno Ferro and assisted by his son, Davide, Aldo makes a range of excellent wines in the district of Neive. Oenologist Beppe Caviola offers invaluable support in the cellar, which produces more than 60,000 bottles a year from the estate's 13 hectares of vineyards. After sacrificing the 2002 vintage, a decision that served to show just how serious this cellar is – no quality fruit, no wine – we are happy to welcome the Barbarescos back in this edition of the Guide. Sorì Burdin '03 is consistent with its vintage, showing a warm, complex nose of ripe fruit and aniseed, and no-nonsense tannins on the full palate where hints of spice emerge. The basic Barbaresco also showed very well, It's a refreshing wine with unmistakable notes of liquorice and dried flowers. But it was the Barbera d'Alba Brunet '04 that stood out from the range of wines presented. Fifteen months of barrique-conditioning have given it an immediate impact of intense aromas including black cherry and chocolate on the nose, and a soft, elegant palate. The other wines are all interesting and a special mention goes to the tannic but supple Dolcetto d'Alba Bordini. The Nebbiolo '04 and Arneis '05 are both clean and fresh.

●	Barbera d'Alba Brunet '04	🍷🍷	4*
●	Barbaresco '03	🍷🍷	7
●	Barbaresco Sorì Burdin '03	🍷🍷	7
●	Dolcetto d'Alba Bordini '05	🍷🍷	4
●	Langhe Nebbiolo '04	🍷	4
○	Langhe Arneis '05	🍷	4
●	Barbaresco Sorì Burdin '01	YYY	7
●	Barbaresco Sorì Burdin '98	YYY	7
●	Barbaresco Sorì Burdin '00	YY	8
●	Barbera d'Alba Brunet '01	YY	5
●	Barbera d'Alba Brunet '03	YY	5
●	Barbaresco Sorì Burdin '97	YY	7
●	Barbaresco Sorì Burdin '99	YY	7

NEIVE (CN)

GASTALDI

via Albesani, 20
12057 Neive (CN)
tel. 0173677400

Reviewing Dino Gastaldi's wines is an almost impossible task. Last year we noted how difficult it was to write a full critique based solely on the two wines presented, but we expected that the release of two more labels would swell the ranks for our 2007 edition. Alas, no. Only the Langhe Bianco Gastaldi 2002 is ready for the market now in Dino's opinion. The estate has almost 13 hectares planted to vine in zones that differ widely in terms of site climate and position. Several years ago, Dino added a property in Monforte d'Alba to his historic vineyards in Neive and Rodello. In previous years, the estate has featured fine performances by the following wines: Dolcetto d'Alba Moriolo; Gastaldi Rosso which became Langhe Rosso Gastaldi; a Sauvignon and a Chardonnay that then went to make the Langhe Bianco Gastaldi; Barbaresco and Langhe Rosso Castlé. But Dino Gastaldi's approach does not permit us to follow up all his releases on a regular basis. He produces wines for a few vintages and then abandons them, releases products erratically or quite simply changes their names over the years. All of this complicates his customers' lives, to say nothing of ours. But we have nothing but unstinting admiration for this creative winemaker who has opened up new horizons, set the quality bar for new wine types and has the courage to bottle and sell only his very best wines. This year, we were delighted to uncork a Langhe Bianco with concentrated hazelnut and butter aromas and a palate that is exemplary in its fullness and balanced acidity.

○	Langhe Bianco Gastaldi '02	▼▼	6
●	Gastaldi Rosso '88	ΥΥΥ	8
●	Gastaldi Rosso '89	ΥΥΥ	8
●	Dolcetto d'Alba Sup. Moriolo '90	ΥΥΥ	5
●	Barbaresco '01	ΥΥ	7
○	Langhe Bianco Gastaldi '01	ΥΥ	6
●	Langhe Rosso Gastaldi '98	ΥΥ	7
●	Barbaresco '99	ΥΥ	7
○	Langhe Bianco Gastaldi '00	ΥΥ	6
●	Barbaresco '97	ΥΥ	7
●	Langhe Rosso Castlé '97	ΥΥ	7
●	Langhe Rosso Castlé '98	ΥΥ	7

NEIVE (CN)

★ BRUNO GIACOSA

via XX Settembre, 52
12057 Neive (CN)
tel. 017367027
www.brunogiacosa.it

Together with Aldo Conterno, Bruno Giacosa is the embodiment of the great Langhe heritage. His head and his hands have created wines that have built and continue to promote the superlative international reputation that Barolo and Barbaresco enjoy today. A lifetime spent in the zone's most prestigious vineyards assessing their real qualitative potential has given Bruno a knowledge of this territory second to none. When it was time to buy land he brought his wealth of experience to bear and, sellers permitting, selected plots in the three magnificent vineyards of Falletto at Serralunga d'Alba and Asili and Rabajà at Barbaresco. This year, he presented us with two selections in their mythical red labels: Barolo Le Rocche del Falletto '00 and Barbaresco Rabajà '01. Bruno and his oenologist-cellarman Dante Scaglione opt to mature all the estate's big reds for 24 to 36 months in big barrels of French oak. Our tastings reveal 2001's slight superiority over 2000, and in fact we awarded the Barbaresco Rabajà Riserva Three Glasses. It flaunts a complex nose with aromas of raspberry, rain-soaked earth, dried flowers and tobacco, followed by a flavoursome palate of impeccable breeding. Although balanced and elegant, the Asili '01 lacks the Rabajà's depth. The Barolo Le Rocche del Falletto '00 displays riper notes on nose and palate. Neither the fresh Barbera Falletto '04 nor the powerful Spumante Extra Brut '03 disappoints.

●	Barbaresco Rabajà Ris. '01	▼▼▼	8
●	Barolo Le Rocche del Falletto Ris. '00	▼▼	8
●	Barbaresco Asili '01	▼▼	8
○	Bruno Giacosa Extra Brut '03	▼▼	6
●	Barbera d'Alba Sup. Falletto '04	▼▼	7
●	Nebbiolo d'Alba Valmaggiore '04	▼	5
○	Roero Arneis '05	▼	5
●	Barbaresco Santo Stefano '00	ΥΥΥ	8
●	Barolo Falletto '00	ΥΥΥ	8
●	Barbaresco Santo Stefano '01	ΥΥΥ	8
●	Barolo Falletto '01	ΥΥΥ	8
●	Barbaresco Asili Ris. '96	ΥΥΥ	8
●	Barolo Falletto '96	ΥΥΥ	8
●	Barbaresco Asili '99	ΥΥΥ	8

NEIVE (CN)

F.lli Giacosa

via XX Settembre, 64
12052 Neive (CN)
tel. 017367013
www.giacosa.it

Founded in 1895, F.lli Giacosa is today run by brothers Valerio and Renzo. They are ably supported by their sons, Maurizio and Paolo, whose ideas ensure that the estate continues to flourish the way it has for generations. The Giacosas' 40 hectares extend across five different municipalities in the zones of Barolo, Barbaresco and upper Langhe. The cellar offered us several new wines to taste for this edition of the Guide. Before we commence our review of the labels, a nod to oenologist Beppe Zatti from Pavia who plays a key role in putting the Giacosa brothers' production philosophy into practice. As for the wines, we note that the Barbaresco changed name in the 2003 vintage and from now on will be known as Basarin. It is dense garnet red and proffers notes of fruit and sweet spice, with vanilla and pepper to the fore. The substantial palate shows aromatic complexity and very pleasing drinkability. Barbera Madonna di Como '04, a new recruit to the estate's ranks, was aged in large wood that has refined its varietal profile. The sole wine to emerge from the difficult 2002 vintage, Barolo Vigna Mandorlo, took home Two brimming Glasses for its unexpected elegance and cleanliness. Rounding off the range we have two Chardonnays, the stainless steel-matured Roera '05 and the oak-aged Ca' Lunga '04, a Dolcetto d'Alba '05 and Barbera Maria Gioana '03.

● Barbaresco Basarin '03	▼▼	6
● Barolo V. Mandorlo '02	▼▼	6
● Barbera d'Alba Maria Gioana '03	▼▼	4
● Barbera d'Alba Madonna di Como '04	▼▼	4
● Dolcetto d'Alba Madonna di Como '05	▼▼	4
○ Langhe Chardonnay Ca' Lunga '04	▼	4
○ Langhe Chardonnay Roera '05	▼	4
● Barolo V. Mandorlo '01	▽▽	6
● Barbaresco Rio Sordo '00	▽▽	7
● Barolo V. Mandorlo '00	▽▽	7
● Barbaresco Rio Sordo '01	▽▽	7
● Barolo Bussia '01	▽▽	7

NEIVE (CN)

Ugo Lequio

via del Molino, 10
12057 Neive (CN)
tel. 0173677224
www.ugolequio.it

Since the early 1980s, Ugo Lequio has been expertly selecting the grapes he buys from a group of dependable growers. This fruit forms the basis for a range of wines that is always extremely interesting. In terms of vinification, Ugo ironically defines himself a hybrid who upholds the old Piedmont traditions but keeps a weather eye on new processes and techniques. He produces around 28,000 bottles a year split across four different, rigorously single-varietal wines: Barbaresco, Barbera, Dolcetto and Arneis. We start our notes with the last of these, Langhe Arneis '05. The typical vegetal nose is enhanced by notes of acacia honey and pear, while the palate shows good density and acidity and is rounded off by a charming, leisurely finish redolent of sage. The Barbera d'Alba Gallina '04 aged for 15 months in 25-hectolitre barrels, emerging with rich fruit and spice sensations and intriguing balance. The Barbaresco Gallina '03 combines balsamic and fruity sensations on the nose with roundness on the palate enhanced by ripe tannins and a liquorice finish. Eucalyptus, strawberry jam and faint traces of tar emerge on the Barbaresco Gallina Riserva '01, of which 3,500 units went into bottle. The palate entices with elegant tannins and complex aromas of spice worthy of a great vintage and a great wine. Last up we have the ruby red Dolcetto whose aromas are a fine expression of the variety's sensory profile.

● Barbaresco Gallina Ris. '01	▼▼	7
● Barbaresco Gallina '03	▼▼	6
● Barbera d'Alba Sup. Gallina '04	▼▼	4
○ Langhe Arneis '05	▼▼	4
● Dolcetto d'Alba '05	▼	4
● Barbaresco Gallina '00	▽▽	6
● Barbaresco Gallina '01	▽▽	6
● Barbera d'Alba Gallina '01	▽▽	4
● Barbera d'Alba Sup. Gallina '03	▽▽	4
● Barbaresco Gallina Ris. '99	▽▽	7

NEIVE (CN)

CASTELLO DI NEIVE
VIA CASTELBORGO, 1
12052 NEIVE (CN)
TEL. 017367171

This estate is named after the beautiful castle in the historic centre of Neive that once belonged to the local aristocracy. The splendid cellar is probably the place where the first modern-style – that is, not sweet – wine was made in 1857 from nebbiolo grapes. Today, this lovely estate, the property of the Stupino family since 1964, has much more than its illustrious history going for it. Italo, an engineer, runs it with passion and a staff supported by the University of Turin. The estate's 25 hectares occupy some of the best positions in the territory. One of these, in the Santo Stefano vineyard, gave us the Barbaresco Riserva '01, which displays its weight above all on the austere, solidly built, deep palate. The nose is spicy, earthy and very complex and although still youthful, is guaranteed to become colossal with further cellaring. That is certainly the case with the Riserva 1999, which on second tasting revealed itself to be truly extraordinary on all counts. But the Santo Stefano already deserves Three resounding Glasses. The Barbaresco Santo Stefano '03 clearly reflects the characteristics of its vintage: warmth, fruity ripeness, nuances of dried flowers and aromatic herbs, reasonable elegance and balance. The Barbera Santo Stefano '05 displays fine backbone and we preferred it to the more powerful Mattarello '04. The lovely Dolcetto '05 is fresh, fruity and juicy, offering further proof of the Basarin vineyard's affinity with this variety. The pinot nero-based I Cortini '05 is interesting and the Arneis Montebertotto '05 is young, tangy and austere.

●	Barbaresco S. Stefano Ris. '01	TTT	8
●	Barbaresco S. Stefano '03	TT	7
●	Barbera d'Alba S. Stefano '05	TT	4*
●	Dolcetto d'Alba Basarin '05	TT	4*
●	Langhe Rosso I Cortini '05	TT	5
●	Barbera d'Alba Mattarello '04	T	4
○	Castello di Neive V.T. '04	T	5
○	Langhe Arneis Montebertotto '05	T	4
●	Barbaresco S. Stefano Ris. '99	YYY	8
●	Barbaresco S. Stefano '01	YY	6
●	Barbaresco S. Stefano '00	YY	7
●	Barbaresco S. Stefano Ris. '98	YY	8

NEIVE (CN)

PAITIN
LOC. BRICCO
VIA SERRA BOELLA, 20
12052 NEIVE (CN)
TEL. 017367343
www.paitin.it

The Pasquero faThe Pasquero family business is a respected, long-standing winery in the municipality of Neive. Today, Giovanni and Silvano flank their father, Secondo, at the helm. The estate includes 17 hectares, most of which lie in Bricco di Neive next to the headquarters in one of the most scenic and best-positioned spots in the wine country around Barbaresco. And it is, in fact, on this wine that the estate concentrates its efforts, consistently producing excellent products that win it great acclaim. This year, Paitin presented a broad array of wines despite the absence of its regular champion Barbaresco Sorì Paitin Vecchie Vigne, which was not produced in 2002. We'll start with Barbaresco Sorì Paitin '03 and a performance reflecting a vintage that was not particularly fresh, notably on the palate where the wine is warm, alcoholic and strongly tannic. By way of contrast, the nose offers very restrained notes of sweet spice, violets and berry fruit. Of the Barberas on offer, the more structured Campolive '04 emerged in pole position. Aged in new large wood, it has a first-class nose of cherry and forest fruits and a faint trace of vanilla on the deeply generous, acidic palate. Not far behind we have the Serra Boella '05, fresh-tasting and nicely spicy after a sojourn in used barriques. The Langhe Paitin '04, from 100 per cent cabernet sauvignon, and the Nebbiolo d'Alba never disappoint. The rest of the range is pleasant.

●	Barbaresco Sorì Paitin '03	TT	6
●	Barbera d'Alba Campolive '04	TT	5
●	Langhe Paitin '04	TT	6
●	Nebbiolo d'Alba Ca Veja '04	TT	5
○	Langhe Arneis V. Elisa '05	TT	4*
●	Barbera d'Alba Serra Boella '05	TT	4*
●	Dolcetto d'Alba Sorì Paitin '05	T	4
●	Barbaresco Sorì Paitin Vecchie Vigne '01	YYY	8
●	Barbaresco Sorì Paitin '95	YYY	7
●	Barbaresco Sorì Paitin '97	YYY	7
●	Langhe Paitin '97	YYY	6
●	Barbaresco Sorì Paitin Vecchie Vigne '99	YYY	8

NEIVE (CN)

PRINSI

VIA GAIA, 5
12052 NEIVE (CN)
TEL. 017367192
www.prinsi.it

Daniele Lequio runs this lovely estate with the help of his father, Franco, and grandfather, Ottavio. Given that the overall level of wines presented is very good, we are assuming that this year's ups and downs are nothing more than a passing phase. We must confess to being a little disappointed by the estate flagship wines: Barbaresco Gallina '03 shows an aggressive, almost acidulous nose and unbalanced alcohol on the palate, and although the Barbera d'Alba Superiore Vigneto Much '04 displays nicely concentrated fruit, it is rather too oak-influenced. As we said, we prefer to look on the bright side and turn our attention to the other Barbaresco, Fausone Riserva '01. Bright garnet red in appearance, it has dried flowers, balsam and cloves, a soft entry on the full palate and a long finish. Next up was Calvario Zerotre, a 2003, which is a table wine although it does not say so on the label. This 50-50 blend of nebbiolo and barbera exhibits pleasant aromas and well-integrated tannins. Equally nice is the Dolcetto d'Alba San Cristoforo '04 with its morello and wild cherry aromas, and the Langhe Freisa A Cristina '05 with its far from dull berry fruit nose and hint of sparkle that perks up the palate. We end with some unexpected praise for the whites: the Langhe Chardonnay Vigneto Tre Fichi '05 has a flowery nose and rather a fresh, leisurely palate, and the Camp 'd Pietru Zerocinque from steel-vinified sauvignon stands out for its crisp varietal aromas of tomato leaf and balanced palate with nice minerality and freshness.

●	Barbaresco Fausone Ris. '01	▼▼	6
●	Calvario Zerotre	▼▼	4
○	Camp 'd Pietrù Zerocinque	▼▼	5
○	Langhe Chardonnay Vign. Tre Fichi '05	▼▼	4*
●	Barbaresco Gallina '03	▼	6
●	Barbera d'Alba Sup. Vign. Much '04	▼	5
●	Dolcetto d'Alba San Cristoforo '04	▼	4
●	Langhe Freisa A Cristina '05	▼	4
●	Barbaresco Gaia Principe '00	▽▽	6
●	Barbaresco Gaia Principe '01	▽▽	6
●	Barbaresco Gallina '00	▽▽	6
●	Barbaresco Gallina '99	▽▽	6

NEIVE (CN)

SOTTIMANO

FRAZ. COTTÀ, 21
12052 NEIVE (CN)
TEL. 0173635186
www.sottimano.it

A visit to the Sottimano estate on the border of the municipalities of Neive and Barbaresco, and a chat with young Andrea and his father, Rino, reveal the clear-headedness, care, research and enthusiasm that they bring to their work in vineyard and cellar. They have 14 hectares planted to vine that they run with the help of the rest of the family. But proof of the Sottimano pudding is in our tastings. This year, the wines presented were excellent and revealed a technical expertise based on skilful use of small barrels and exemplary stylistic precision and cleanliness. The four 2003 Barbarescos all offer fine interpretations of this hot vintage in their crisply defined aromas. It is hard to choose between them and, to be honest, a lot comes down to personal taste in the end. Currà stands out for its density, fruity fullness and grandeur and although still clenched, it has great potential. Pajoré is more subdued, with notes of spice and aromatic herbs. It has elegance, depth and is drinking now. Cottà is more mature, dark, brooding and earthy. Very intriguing and loath to open up as yet, it has serious body that will need time to unbend. Fausoni exhibits more balsamic, refreshingly flowery notes and a consistent, complex if not particularly deep palate. The very fragrant Langhe Nebbiolo '04 promises well, the Barbera Pairolero '04 is powerful and solidly built and the young Dolcetto Bric del Salto '05 is fresh-tasting and clean.

●	Barbaresco Cottà '03	▼▼	7
●	Barbaresco Currà '03	▼▼	7
●	Barbaresco Pajoré '03	▼▼	7
●	Barbaresco Fausoni '03	▼▼	7
●	Barbera d'Alba Pairolero '04	▼▼	5
●	Langhe Nebbiolo '04	▼▼	5
●	Dolcetto d'Alba Bric del Salto '05	▼▼	4*
●	Maté '05	▼	4
●	Barbaresco Pajoré '00	▽▽▽	7
●	Barbaresco Pajoré '01	▽▽▽	7
●	Barbaresco Fausoni V. del Salto '96	▽▽▽	7
●	Barbaresco Cottà V. Brichet '97	▽▽▽	7
●	Barbaresco Cottà '98	▽▽▽	7
●	Barbaresco Pajoré '98	▽▽▽	7

NEVIGLIE (CN)

BERA
VIA CASTELLERO, 12
12050 NEVIGLIE (CN)
TEL. 0173630194 - 0173630500
www.bera.it

Over the years, we have come to expect a reassuringly consistent level of quality from Walter Bera's wines that allows him to tackle a range of wine types, from Spumante Metodo Classico to Barbaresco. Our tastings this year highlighted once again the absolute class of the Barbera La Lena, a 2004 obtained from grapes grown in a vineyard that is more than 40 years old. The nose releases clear notes of cherry, forest fruits, spice and tobacco. The palate owes its fullness and density to explosive extract and its refreshing acidity and tight-knit tannic texture give it a fine vein of edginess that is extraordinarily elegant. The finish is sumptuous and lingering. One tiny step below this, the harmonious, elegant Barbaresco '01 displays deep, concentrated flowery aromas and a fabulous follow-through on the palate. The complex, eloquent Langhe Sassisto '03 is a deep ruby red wine with purplish highlights that integrates and enhances the characteristics of the three varieties that go into it: barbera, nebbiolo and merlot. The Moscato d'Asti Su Reimond has a complex, very expressive nose with generous flowery notes and fruity nuances of peach and melon. The basic Moscato also earned Two Glasses. The other wines we tasted had little to envy the big boys: the Dolcetto, basic Barbera and Asti Spumante are all impeccable. A special mention goes to the soft, appealing Brut Metodo Classico. And the Langhe Nebbiolo '02 is flawless.

●	Barbera d'Alba Sup. La Lena '04	🍷🍷	4*
●	Barbaresco '01	🍷🍷	6
●	Langhe Sassisto '03	🍷🍷	5
○	Moscato d'Asti '05	🍷🍷	4
○	Moscato d'Asti Su Reimond '05	🍷🍷	4
○	Bera Brut M. Cl.	🍷🍷	5
●	Langhe Nebbiolo Alladio '02	🍷	5
○	Asti '05	🍷	4
●	Barbera d'Alba '05	🍷	3
●	Dolcetto d'Alba '05	🍷	3
●	Barbera d'Alba Sup. La Lena '03	ΥΥ	5
●	Barbaresco '00	ΥΥ	7
●	Barbera d'Alba Sup. La Lena '01	ΥΥ	4

NEVIGLIE (CN)

ROBERTO SAROTTO
VIA RONCONUOVO, 13
12050 NEVIGLIE (CN)
TEL. 0173630228

Roberto Sarotto, oenologist and mayor of Neviglie, produces wines that share a common style and a strong territorial stamp. His more than 50 hectares of vineyards are located in four different districts and give him an impressive annual production of over 150,000 bottles ranging from Gavi to Barolo. This year we report a fine showing from the Barbera d'Alba Elena Sugli, which is aged in new and used barriques. Its clear, vivid nose bursts with personality and offers intense aromas of cherry, plum and sweet spice. Entry on the palate is assertive and progresses slowly and harmoniously to reveal polished tannins. The Barbera Bricco Macchia '04 matured in large barrels and although good, does not come close to scaling the sensory heights of its stablemate. We liked the Barolo Audace Riserva '00, a caressing, forward yet charming wine that exhibits more elegance and drinkability than power. Of the other big wines, the Barolo Bricco Bergera '02 is traditional in style but suffered the ravages of the vintage. The Dolcetto Giot, obtained from vineyards that are over 70 years old, throws a full, elegant nose suggesting blueberry-like fruit tones. The Moscato Sorì Ciabot '05 is reasonably dense, while the flavoursome Moscato Passito Paiass '03 presents notes of dried figs and raisins. From the Gavi di Gavi L'Aurora to the Arneis, the whites are sound, fresh and perked up by a hint of prickle.

●	Barolo Audace Ris. '00	🍷🍷	7
●	Barbera d'Alba Elena '04	🍷🍷	4
○	Gavi del Comune di Gavi Bric Sassi '05	🍷🍷	4
●	Barbera d'Alba Bricco Macchia '04	🍷🍷	4*
●	Barolo Bricco Bergera '02	🍷	6
●	Dolcetto d'Alba Giot '04	🍷	5
○	Moscato Passito Paiass '03	🍷	5
○	Gavi del Comune di Gavi L'Aurora '05	🍷	4
○	Langhe Arneis Runcneuv '05	🍷	4
○	Moscato d'Asti Sorì Ciabot '05	🍷	4
●	Barbaresco Gaia Principe '01	ΥΥ	6
●	Barolo Audace '01	ΥΥ	6
●	Barolo Bricco Bergera '01	ΥΥ	6
●	Barbaresco Gaia Principe '02	ΥΥ	7

NIZZA MONFERRATO (AT)

ANTONIO BALDIZZONE
CASCINA LANA
C.SO ACQUI, 187
14049 NIZZA MONFERRATO (AT)
TEL. 0141726734

A visit to Cascina Lana gives you one of the most spectacular views across hillside vineyards in the whole of southern Piedmont. The estate's 20 hectares are located in a single block practically on the border of the municipal districts of Nizza Monferrato and Acqui Terme. Aided by his father, Davide, and wife, Graziana Rizzoli, Antonio Baldizzone produces 70,000 bottles released under several labels. Some of these are dedicated to a faithful clientele that still likes to buy their wines ready to drink or unbottled. From this year's fairly wide range we selected a few products that are of particular interest and quality. The cream of the crop is the Barbera d'Asti Superiore Nizza, whose 12 months in barrique have left it with generous notes of red berry fruit, currant and morello cherry mingling with sweet spice. The juicy palate is richly extracted and well rounded. This Nizza cellar's top seller, Barbera d'Asti La Cirimela '05, offers excellent value for money at an unbeatable price and is appreciable for its sweetness and wonderful simplicity on the palate. Care and passion have gone into the making of the Monferrato Rosso Vën ëd Michen '04, a blend of barbera, cabernet sauvignon and nebbiolo. The nose reveals capsicum-led varietal nuances that merge to perfection with notes of sweet spice and blueberry, the palate showing substantial backbone and impressive length. Dolcetto d'Asti La Milana '05 is straightforward and agreeable, as is the fragrant and never cloying Moscato 2005.

● Barbera d'Asti Sup. Nizza '04	▼▼	5
● Monferrato Rosso Vën ëd Michen '04	▼▼	5
● Barbera d'Asti La Cirimela '05	▼▼	3*
● Dolcetto d'Asti La Milana '05	▼	3
○ Moscato d'Asti '05	▼	3
● Barbera d'Asti Sup. Nizza '03	▽▽	5
● Barbera d'Asti La Cirimela '04	▽▽	4

NIZZA MONFERRATO (AT)

★ CASCINA LA BARBATELLA
S.DA ANNUNZIATA, 55
14049 NIZZA MONFERRATO (AT)
TEL. 0141701434

For many years now, Angelo Sonvico's prestigious estate has been a bright star in the Asti firmament, producing wines of rare elegance. The estate's five hectares of vines yield just over 20,000 bottles a year. It is often said that structure counts for little in a wine if it has no elegance and this is what comes to mind when you taste Angelo's wines. The Barbera d'Asti Superiore Nizza Vigna dell'Angelo '03 has a charming, dense ruby red appearance that is slightly evolved. The nose opens out gradually, not explosively, to reveal clear notes of fruit and pepper with delicately forward undertones. The palate's fullness, fruitiness and richness of flavour make its development stimulating while the substantial power and character are never excessive or unbalanced. The basic Barbera is extremely enjoyable. Its bright ruby red is the prelude to green, balsamic aromas that form the perfect framework for gorgeous fruity tones. The palate is full and tempting with a long, lip-smacking finish. Monferrato Rosso Sonvico '03 is a barbera and cabernet sauvignon blend aged for 12 months in barriques of French oak. It took home a resounding Three Glasses for its nuances of blueberry, rose, pencil lead and tobacco, and velvety, gently tannic palate. Actually, this is one of the best versions we have ever tasted. The simpler Monferrato Rosso Aldar '05 is obtained from barbera, cabernet and pinot nero matured exclusively in stainless steel, and is a pleasant wine with a fresh, satisfying palate. The agreeable Monferrato Bianco Noè '05 from cortese and sauvignon is aromatic and varietal.

● Monferrato Rosso Sonvico '03	▼▼▼	7
● Barbera d'Asti Sup. Nizza Vigna dell'Angelo '03	▼▼	7
● Barbera d'Asti '05	▼▼	4*
● Monferrato Rosso Aldar '05	▼	4
○ Monferrato Bianco Noè '05	▼	4
● Barbera d'Asti Sup. Nizza Vigna dell'Angelo '01	▽▽▽	7
● Monferrato Rosso Mystère '01	▽▽▽	7
● La Vigna di Sonvico '95	▽▽▽	7
● La Vigna di Sonvico '96	▽▽▽	7
● Monferrato Rosso Sonvico '97	▽▽▽	7
● Monferrato Rosso Sonvico '98	▽▽▽	7

BERSANO

P.ZZA DANTE, 21
14049 NIZZA MONFERRATO (AT)
TEL. 0141720211
www.bersano.it

Bersano made its name in the early 1960s with the Antichi Conti della Cremosina brand and boasts a long history in the wine sector. The array of bottles on offer is wide and ranges from sparklers to still whites, young reds and more structured interpretations, all the way through to dessert wines. Of the labels we tasted for this edition of the Guide, we particularly liked the Barbera Cremosina '04. Its ruby red colour shades into fairly intense garnet and the nose offers subtle notes of very ripe fruit and interesting vegetal tones. The palate is temptingly drinkable and impressively balanced while the finish is very long. Not quite up to its usual standards, the Barbera Generala '04 is intensely red in the glass with delicate orange highlights. Hints of slightly evolved fruit emerge in the nose, but the palate is notable for its lovely harmony and enjoyable finish. The excellent Barbaresco Mantico '03 is a pale purple red revealing refined notes suggestive of balsam, fruit and flowers. The palate shows fullness and warmth and a long, leisurely, convincing finish. The pale straw-yellow Moscato San Michele offers nuances of melon, peach and violet in an overall framework of nice finesse. The Ruché di Castagnole Monferrato San Pietro '05 is a poised essay in varietal aromas and the Brachetto d'Acqui Castelgaro is a pleasant dessert wine.

●	Barbaresco Mantico '03	▼▼	7
●	Barbera d'Asti Sup. Cremosina '04	▼▼	6
●	Barbera d'Asti Sup. Generala '04	▼▼	6
○	Moscato d'Asti S. Michele '05	▼▼	3*
●	Brachetto d'Acqui Castelgaro '05	▼	4
●	Ruché di Castagnole Monferrato S. Pietro '05	▼	4
●	Barbera d'Asti Sup. Generala '97	▽▽▽	7
●	Barbera d'Asti Sup. Generala '01	▽▽	6
●	Barbera d'Asti Sup. Generala '03	▽▽	6

NIZZA MONFERRATO (AT)

EREDE DI ARMANDO CHIAPPONE

LOC. SAN MICHELE, 51
14049 NIZZA MONFERRATO (AT)
TEL. 0141721424
www.eredechiappone.com

We visited the Chiappones' cellar on the feast of St Michael, the patron saint of the small village where the family lives. We were welcomed by young Daniela, the heart and soul of this estate, who was preparing for the community dinner and laying the floor for dancing. Despite her commitments, she showed us round her small cellar and gave us a pleasant, informative tour. The estate comprises ten hectares planted to vine and produces a maximum of 30,000 bottles a year, mainly Barbera. Daniela joined the family business in 2001 when she left Sinergo, a wine consultancy company in Nizza. She is supported by her sister, Michela, and parents Franco and Domenica. The most interesting wine we tasted this year was Barbera d'Asti Ru '03, which stayed for 12 months in 900-litre casks and earned a place in our finals for its richly extracted nose and fruity, lingering palate. Barbera d'Asti Brentura '04 matured for a year in stainless steel and offers notes of red berry fruit and a remarkably generous palate. Aged in small barrels and stainless steel, Freisa d'Asti Sanpedra '02 is very distinctive and we liked it for its refreshing tannins and elegant, bitterish finish. The fresh-tasting, fruity Dolcetto d'Asti Mandola '04 showed well, but the citrus-like Monferrato Bianco Valbeccara '04 from cortese and favorita is not quite as good.

●	Barbera d'Asti Sup. Nizza Ru '03	▼▼	5
●	Dolcetto d'Asti Mandola '04	▼▼	3*
●	Freisa d'Asti Sanpedra '02	▼▼	3*
●	Barbera d'Asti Brentura '04	▼▼	4
○	Monferrato Bianco Valbeccara '04	▼	3
●	Barbera d'Asti Brentura '03	▽▽	4

NIZZA MONFERRATO (AT)

Cascina Giovinale
s.da San Nicolao, 102
14049 Nizza Monferrato (AT)
tel. 0141793005
www.cascinagiovinale.com

In 1980, Bruno Ciocca, then a manager at Olivetti, and his wife Anna Solaini bought seven hectares of vines on the splendid San Nicolao hill just outside Nizza Monferrato. Although they lived in Ivrea, they are both originally from Nizza and for them this was a return to their roots. For several years, they sold the grapes they cultivated but in 1998 they decided to put their land to the test and started to vinify the fruit themselves. They brought in expert oenologist Giuliano Noè who, together with fruitmaker Piero Roseo, laid the foundations for the production of wines strongly influenced by local traditions. This means barbera and moscato with a small amount of dolcetto and an international variety, cabernet. Today, the estate produces around 20,000 bottles a year released under five labels: two Barberas, two Moscatos, a Passito, a standard cork Passito, and a blend called Trinum. In the absence of the Barbera Anssèma '04, which is still ageing, and the Moscato Passito Fleur, we tasted three selections this year. From a good vintage, the deep ruby basic Barbera '04 in 10,000 bottles put on an excellent performance. The concentrated nose of fruity aromas hints at rain-soaked earth and the powerful palate has just the right amount of acidity and minerality in the finish. The warm, mouthfilling Monferrato Trinum '03 from barbera, dolcetto and cabernet is also very good. The Moscato '05 has notes of sage and candied peel and a big palate that keeps a light touch in the sweet finish.

● Monferrato Trinum '03	🍷🍷	5
● Barbera d'Asti '04	🍷🍷	4*
○ Moscato d'Asti '05	🍷🍷	4*
● Barbera d'Asti Sup. Nizza Anssèma '00	YY	5
● Barbera d'Asti '01	YY	4
● Barbera d'Asti Sup. Nizza Anssèma '03	YY	5
● Barbera d'Asti Sup. Ansèmma '99	YY	5

NIZZA MONFERRATO (AT)

La Gironda
s.da Bricco, 12
14049 Nizza Monferrato (AT)
tel. 0141701013
www.lagironda.com

Known throughout the wine world for the production of precision winemaking machinery (Robino & Galandrino of Canelli, wire hood and capping machines), Agostino Galandrino retired from the business several years ago and bought a farm in the Nizza Monferrato hills. On the advice of friend and oenologist Giuliano Noè, the patriarch of top-quality Barbera, he invested in a beautiful property in the zone of Bricco Cremosina in Nizza Monferrato, a historic area and one of the best for growing barbera. After acquiring five hectares around the winery itself and a further two on the terraced slopes of upper Calamandrana, Agostino built a simple but functional cellar with several features he designed himself to assist the cellarhands in their work. Today, Susanna Galandrino and her husband, Alberto Adamo, run the estate alongside Susanna's father, with support from consultants Beppe Rattazzo in the cellar and Piero Roseo in the vineyards. The array of wines the Galandrinos offered us for tasting this year was very interesting, with the Barbera d'Asti Superiore Nizza Le Nicchie '03 going all the way to our final Three Glass tastings. Deep ruby in colour, it has notes of rain-soaked earth followed by ripe red berry fruit and faint oaky undertones. The palate's lovely chewiness is not affected by the refreshing acidulous note that enhances the superb finish. The La Gena '04 selection is fruity and dynamic, La Lippa is simple but never dull, and the Brachetto d'Acqui '05 is aromatic and agreeable.

● Barbera d'Asti Sup. Nizza Le Nicchie '03	🍷🍷	5
● Barbera d'Asti La Gena '04	🍷🍷	4*
● Barbera d'Asti La Lippa '05	🍷	3
● Brachetto d'Acqui '05	🍷	4
● Barbera d'Asti La Gena '03	YY	4
● Barbera d'Asti La Lippa '04	YY	3

NIZZA MONFERRATO (AT)

CLEMENTE GUASTI
C.SO IV NOVEMBRE, 80
14049 NIZZA MONFERRATO (AT)
TEL. 0141721350
www.clemente.guasti.it

This famous Nizza Monferrato estate run by brothers Alessandro and Andrea Guasti produces a series of very good wines. As is to be expected in this zone, Barbera d'Astis take pride of place. One of the best to emerge from this year's tastings is the rather pale ruby red Barbera Superiore Fonda San Nicolao '03. It has a nicely concentrated, somewhat rustic nose with interesting notes of brandied fruit. Entry on the palate is excellent with crisp follow-through and an impressively long finish. Barcarato '03 bears the Nizza subzone on the label. It has a very bright, intense ruby red appearance and a compact nose that opens out slowly to reveal elegant notes of fruit and spice. The very full palate follows through consistently to end in a warm, leisurely finish. The vividly coloured Cascina Boschetto Vecchio '03 has a more mature, less explosive nose than the Barcarato but it is still very intense. The palate exhibits austere balance and is easy drinking. The youthful Barbera Desideria '05 possesses a brilliant colour and a generous nose with lovely fruity notes and attractive earthy tones. The agreeable, inviting palate echoes the initial aromas of fresh fruit. The quite pale Barbera Superiore '03 presents notes of fruit and oak and a palate of medium weight and moderate balance. Finally, the Barbera Vivace Clementina and the Grignolino, both '05s, are pleasant.

● Barbera d'Asti Cascina Boschetto Vecchio '03	🍷🍷	5
● Barbera d'Asti Sup. Nizza Barcarato '03	🍷🍷	6
● Barbera d'Asti Sup. '03	🍷🍷	4*
● Barbera d'Asti Sup. Cascina Fonda San Nicolao '03	🍷🍷	5
● Barbera d'Asti Desideria '05	🍷	4
● Barbera del M.to Vivace Clementina '05	🍷	4
● Grignolino d'Asti '05	🍷	4
● Barbera d'Asti Sup. Nizza Barcarato '01	🍷🍷 (white)	6
● Barbera d'Asti Sup. Nizza Barcarato '00	🍷🍷 (white)	6

NIZZA MONFERRATO (AT)

ANTICA CASA VINICOLA SCARPA
VIA MONTEGRAPPA, 6
14049 NIZZA MONFERRATO (AT)
TEL. 0141721331
www.scarpavini.it

This historic Nizza estate has recently been restructured and expanded. Its staff consists of Maria Piera Zola, Vincenzo Munì, and Carlo and Mario Castino. Several key products were absent from the line-up this year, including the Barbera d'Asti La Bogliona, the Barbaresco Tettineive, the Monferrato RossoScarpa and the Rouchet Passito. But the wines we tasted were all very good nonetheless. We'll start our notes with Barbera Bricchi di Castelrocchero '01. It is a deep, intense red with warm aromas of cherry and spice in rather an evolved framework. The palate shows lots of flesh and solid backbone and follows through superbly to end in a lingering finish. The Barolo Tettimorra '01 offers notes of roasted coffee beans, dried flowers and red berry fruit in an elegant framework. The concentrated palate is nicely buttressed by tight-knit phenolics and flaunts a long finish. The attractive, pleasing Brachetto Secco La Selva di Moirano '05 possesses delicate aromas and a rich, gutsy palate. Rouchet Briccorosa is a well-made wine with tidy aromas and an agreeably dry palate. Barbera CasaScarpa '04 has a deep, vivid colour and a fairly uncomplicated nose. Entry on the palate is sincere and assured. We liked Dolcetto La Selva di Moirano, whose tannins and strong acidity give it a bitterish note. Obtained exclusively from albarossa, the Rosso Super has lovely fruity notes and a crisp, generous palate. Up last, the Nebbiolo d'Alba Bric du Nota exhibits classic, elegant flowery nuances and a lip-smacking palate with delicate tannins.

● Barbera d'Asti Bricchi di Castelrocchero '01	🍷🍷	5
● Barolo Tettimorra '01	🍷🍷	8
● Nebbiolo d'Alba Bric du Nota '01	🍷🍷	5
● Brachetto Secco La Selva di Moirano '05	🍷🍷	6
● Monferrato Rosso Rouchet Briccorosa '05	🍷🍷	6
● Rosso Super '04	🍷	5
● Barbera d'Asti CasaScarpa '04	🍷	5
● Dolcetto d'Acqui La Selva di Moirano '05	🍷	4
● Rouchet Briccorosa '90	🍷🍷🍷 (white)	8
● Barbaresco Tettineive '01	🍷🍷 (white)	8
● Barbera d'Asti La Bogliona '03	🍷🍷 (white)	6

NIZZA MONFERRATO (AT)

Franco e Mario Scrimaglio
via Alessandria, 67
14049 Nizza Monferrato (AT)
tel. 0141721385 - 0141727052
www.scrimaglio.it

Francesco and Piergiorgio Scrimaglio run this 18-hectare estate that offers consumers an interesting range of wines, first and foremost numerous versions of Barbera d'Asti. Top of our tastings this year come Sant'Ippolito '04 and Acsé '03. The former presents a deep, almost opaque ruby red and offers a concentrated, fragrant nose showing clear notes of berry fruit with harmonious minerally undertones. The palate is impressive for its substantial backbone, full body and remarkable length. The brilliant red Acsé unveils a charming nose with pleasant hints of cherry, blackberry and spice in a clear, elegant framework. The classy, full palate also has a wonderfully clean finish. The intensely coloured Barbera Crôutin '04 has vanilla and ripe black berry fruit aromas followed by a palate that combines harmony and consistency with temptingly easy drinkability. The coherent Rocca Nivo '04 possesses a delicate nose and medium weight in the mouth. The No Cork '04 is pleasantly rustic on the nose with a simple but agreeable palate. The Barbera Il Sogno '03 shows excellent balance on the palate and nuances of blueberry, currant and raspberry. The barbera and cabernet sauvignon-based Rosso Tantra '04 did very well. Monferrato Bianco No Cork '04 is well-managed and Futuro '05, a white table wine from a blend of several traditional Piedmont varieties, has attractive peaches and apricots followed by a tidy, lingering palate.

●	Barbera d'Asti Sup. Acsé '03	🍷🍷	6
●	Barbera d'Asti Sup. Bricco S. Ippolito '04	🍷🍷	4*
●	Barbera d'Asti Sup. Crôutin '04	🍷🍷	6
●	Monferrato Rosso Tantra '04	🍷🍷	6
●	Barbera d'Asti Sup. Il Sogno '03	🍷	4
●	Barbera d'Asti No Cork '04	🍷	4
●	Barbera d'Asti Sup. Vign. Rocca Nivo '04	🍷	4
○	Futuro '05	🍷	4
○	Monferrato Bianco No Cork '04		3
●	Barbera d'Asti Sup. Nizza Acsé '00	ΥΥ	6
●	Monferrato Rosso Tantra '01	ΥΥ	6

NOVELLO (CN)

Elvio Cogno
via Ravera, 2
12060 Novello (CN)
tel. 0173744006
www.elviocogno.com

Walter Fissore is one of the brightest rising stars in the Langhe firmament. Every year, Walter, his wife Nadia Cogno and oenologist Beppe Caviola present wines full of character and personality. The estate obtains 65,000 bottles a year from its nine hectares plus two that are leased. The Vigna Elena was not produced in 2002 and its grapes have been combined with those of the Ravera to produce a Barolo that showed very well despite the challenges of the vintage. A brick red colour introduces notes of red berry fruit, dried violets and cinchona. Entry on the palate is surefooted and tannic, and the finish is long and leisurely. The jewel in the estate's crown is Barolo Vigna Elena '01, aged for 36 months in 30-hectolitre barrels. Aromas of liquorice, golden leaf tobacco and currants announce a superlative palate that bowled our tasting panel over with its full flavour, tannins and fruit. Last year, it was the Ravera '01; this year the Vigna Elena earned Three Glasses. These two magnificent wines seem to continue to take turns in claiming our top prize. Langhe Rosso Montegrilli '04, a nebbiolo and barbera blend, possesses a delicately fruity nose with flowery nuances. High marks went to the Dolcetto d'Alba Vigna del Mandorlo '05 for its intense, fresh aromas and full, elegantly tannic palate. The Langhe Bianco also scored well. It is vinified from nascetta, an interesting local variety that Walter has helped to rescue from oblivion. Barbera d'Alba Bricco dei Merli, conditioned for 12 months in barriques of French oak, is a step below.

●	Barolo V. Elena '01	🍷🍷🍷	8
●	Langhe Rosso Montegrilli '04	🍷🍷	5
●	Dolcetto d'Alba V. del Mandorlo '05	🍷🍷	4*
○	Langhe Bianco Anas-Cetta '05	🍷🍷	4*
●	Barolo '02	🍷	6
●	Barbera d'Alba Bricco dei Merli '04	🍷	5
●	Barolo Ravera '01	ΥΥΥ	7
●	Barolo V. Elena '99	ΥΥΥ	8
●	Barolo Ravera '00	ΥΥ	7
●	Barolo Ravera '99	ΥΥ	7
●	Barolo Ravera '96	ΥΥ	7
●	Barolo V. Elena '97	ΥΥ	8
●	Barolo V. Elena '98	ΥΥ	8

NOVI LIGURE (AL)

IL VIGNALE
LOC. LOMELLINA
VIA GAVI, 130
15067 NOVI LIGURE (AL)
TEL. 014372715
www.ilvignale.it

Eighty per cent of this ten-hectare estate is planted to cortese and almost all of its vineyards lie on the slopes of Monte Mesima in the municipalities of Novi and Gavi. Piero and Vilma Cappelletti have run Il Vignale for ten years or so and a visit to their cellar shows just how much effort and passion they put into their work. It has all paid off in the consistently excellent results achieved by their wines. Giuseppe Bassi offers invaluable technical support in the cellar. Turning to the wines, we were particularly impressed by Gavi Vilma Cappelletti '05, a lively straw-yellow in the glass with attractive golden highlights. Intense, lingering aromas suggest apple and wild flowers and are lifted by delicate lemony, balsamic nuances. Well-gauged supporting acidity gives the very agreeable palate wonderful harmony and enhances its drinkability. All this combines to make the label one of the best from the 2005 vintage, winning it a place on our final tasting table. The house's other Gavi, the Vigne Alte, is less complex but very well made. Its flowery nose introduces a very pleasant palate whose balanced acidity enhances its freshness. The Monferrato Rosso di Malì, which scored very high in previous editions of the Guide, was not presented this year as it is not yet considered ready for bottling.

○	Gavi Vilma Cappelletti '05	🍷🍷	4*
○	Gavi Vigne Alte '05	🍷	4
○	Gavi Vigne Alte '04	YY	4
●	Monferrato Rosso Rosso di Malì '02	YY	4
○	Gavi Vilma Cappelletti '04	YY	4

OTTIGLIO (AL)

CAVE DI MOLETO
LOC. MOLETO
REG. MOLETO, 4
15038 OTTIGLIO (AL)
TEL. 0142921468
www.moleto.it

The estate belonging to the Bottinelli family extends over no less than 110 hectares, 25 of which are planted to vine. This year production was up to about 120,000 bottles, almost all 2003s. The infamously variable weather made this a difficult vintage, but Cave di Moleto rose above its challenges to produce some truly fabulous bottles. The two Monferratos gave a convincing performance. Rosso Mulej and Pieve di San Michele are both obtained from the same proportions of cabernet and merlot grapes but are distinguished by their ageing processes: Mulej enjoys longer oak-ageing and stays in barrique for no less than 24 months. Both labels are balanced and offer tempting, pleasing vegetal aromas typical of the varieties on which they are based. Moving on to the Barberas, Procchio excels for the intense fruity nuances and overall balance that earned it Two Glasses. Bricco della Prera is not quite up to the same standard, requiring more time in the cellar to smooth out its still rather dominant oakiness. The Grignolino debuted very well. We thought it was one of the best we tasted thanks to its notes of flower and spice that alternate with fruity aromas in a very pleasant crescendo. The Barbera del Monferrato '03 rounds off the range. This pleasant, firmly structured wine is available in approximately 40,000 bottles.

●	Barbera del M.to Procchio '03	🍷🍷	4*
●	Monferrato Rosso Mulej '03	🍷🍷	5
●	Monferrato Pieve di San Michele '03	🍷🍷	5
●	Grignolino del M.to Casalese '05	🍷🍷	3*
●	Barbera del M.to '03	🍷	3
●	Barbera del M.to Bricco della Prera '03	🍷	5
●	Barbera del M.to Procchio '00	YY	4
●	Barbera del M.to Procchio '01	YY	4
●	Monferrato Pieve di San Michele '01	YY	5

OVADA (AL)

BONDI
S.DA CAPPELLETTE, 73
15076 OVADA (AL)
TEL. 0143821369
www.bondivini.it

Bosco Marengo is famous as the birthplace of Antonio Ghisleri, who became Pope Pius V, and the site of the monumental Santa Croce complex. It is here that the Bondi family runs the Locanda dell'Olmo, a renowned inn serving traditional Alessandrian fare. It used to be the custom in this zone for each innkeeper to produce a house wine that he served with the food from the kitchen. The Bondis have revived this tradition by acquiring the Banaia farmstead in Cappellette, Ovada, where they produce high-quality wines exclusively from the zone's main varieties, barbera and dolcetto. In just a few short years, the Bondis have made a name for themselves in the local wine world, presenting increasingly good wines acclaimed by critics and enthusiasts alike. Their most representative label, Barbera Ruvrin, is missing from the line-up this year because the 2004 has been left to age longer to allow it to smooth out the edginess of an extremely rich vintage. Dolcetto di Ovada Du'ien '04 keeps the quality flag flying, however. Obtained from a vineyard planted more than 50 years ago, it offers fairly intense, lingering aromas with pervasive notes of blackberry and red berry fruit. The almost austere palate is generous and balanced. Monferrato Rosso Le Guie '04 derives from barbera and dolcetto grapes conditioned partly in twice-used barrels and partly in stainless steel. Fruity and spicy on the nose, it displays a harmonious palate of medium structure.

● Dolcetto di Ovada Sup. Du'ien '04	**YY**	4*
● Monferrato Rosso Le Guie '04	**Y**	4
● Barbera del M.to Ruvrin '03	YY	5
● Dolcetto di Ovada Sup. Du'ien '03	YY	4
● Monferrato Rosso Le Guie '03	YY	4

PEROSA ARGENTINA (TO)

COUTANDIN
B.TA CIABOT, 12
10063 PEROSA ARGENTINA (TO)
TEL. 0121803473

This tiny estate was founded in 1997 thanks to the efforts of Giuliano and Laura Coutandin. They came from very different professional backgrounds but made the joint decision to devote themselves to the country life and grow grapes. This was no small challenge for them, as they set about recovering several vineyards that had been abandoned – and by abandoned we mean left to run completely wild – in the zone. The small pockets of land planted to vine that they work lie in the municipalities of Perosa Argentina and Pomaretto, where the slopes are so steep that the Turin provincial authority has built a monorail to facilitate access to the fields. As if this weren't enough, the Coutandins have set themselves the task of salvaging a series of indigenous varieties that are almost extinct: avanà, avarengo, neretto and bequet. For the moment, they produce only 5,000 bottles that they release under two labels. Ramìe '04 was obtained from the vinification of the above grape types and aged in both stainless steel and 900-litre casks. It presents a deep ruby red in the glass, releasing notes of ripe fruit and sweet spice, such as cinnamon, vanilla and cloves, on the nose. The palate has assertive but not overwhelming tannins, lovely freshness and extremely agreeable length in the finish. Barbichè '03, a table wine, has undergone longer ageing in oak and this is evident particularly on the nose, which is toastier and richer in hints of chocolate powder. The confident palate unveils elegance and attractive harmony.

● Barbichè '03	**YY**	4*
● Pinerolese Ramìe '04	**YY**	5
● Pinerolese Ramìe '03	YY	5

PIOBESI D'ALBA (CN)

TENUTA CARRETTA
LOC. CARRETTA, 2
12040 PIOBESI D'ALBA (CN)
TEL. 0173619119
www.tenutacarretta.it

The Miroglio-Dracone family can be proud. They have taken over a historic label, risen to new challenges, faced a new era and turned it into a leading name in Roero. No mean feat, for this required resources, organization and above all ideas. Today, Tenuta Carretta has transformed all of this into a charming country hotel, an award-winning restaurant and – the part that we like best – a big, functional cellar that has been designed to have almost no impact at all on the environment. Overseen by the dynamic Giandomenico Negro, this year's range of wines is missing one of its major players, the Barolo sourced from Cannubi. It, too, fell victim to the 2002 growing year and we shall have to wait until next time, when it will be back in another vintage. By way of compensation, Barbaresco Bordino is back after a sabbatical from last year's edition of the Guide when it was replaced by a simple Barbaresco '02. The '03 inevitably felt the effects of the hot growing year and shows slightly too much alcohol as well as big tannins that are not altogether smooth. It came close to Three Glasses but failed to go that final inch. It's a magnificent wine, though, with depth, a pervasive palate and sumptuous body. The Roero, also '03, is even better, with a fresher, already well-defined nose hinting at earth and spice. The palate is warm but harmonious, the finish long and tidy. The other two reds showed well. Among the whites, the Cayega is approachable and enjoyable and the Canorei '04, erroneously reviewed last year, is more ambitious and refined.

●	Barbaresco Cascina Bordino '03	**YY**	7
●	Roero Sup. Bric Paradiso '03	**YY**	5
●	Barbera d'Alba Sup. Bric Quercia '04	**YY**	5
○	Roero Arneis V. Canorei '04	**YY**	5
○	Roero Arneis Cayega '05	**Y**	4
●	Nebbiolo d'Alba V. Tavoleto '04	**Y**	5
●	Barolo Vign. in Cannubi '00	YYY	8
●	Barbaresco Cascina Bordino '00	YY	7
●	Barbaresco Cascina Bordino '01	YY	7
●	Barolo Vign. in Cannubi '01	YY	8
●	Roero Sup. Bric Paradiso '02	YY	5
●	Barolo Vign. in Cannubi '99	YY	8
●	Barolo Vign. in Cannubi '98	YY	8

PORTACOMARO (AT)

CASTELLO DEL POGGIO
LOC. POGGIO, 9
14038 PORTACOMARO (AT)
TEL. 0141202543
www.poggio.it

The Zonin family owns one of the largest wine companies in Italy with headquarters at Gambellara in Veneto. They have no less than 130 hectares planted to vine at Castello del Poggio on the Portacomaro slopes, which they bought around ten years ago. The vineyards are in an amphitheatre centred around the magnificent Valle del Tempio, where the ruins of an ancient fortress bear witness to a Templar settlement. The estate's production is based on the indigenous local varieties, primarily grignolino and barbera, although merlot, an international grape type that goes to make the Bunéis selection, is also present. The best labels produced by Castello del Poggio are part of the Gianni Zonin Vineyards line, which was created especially to focus on the great care that goes into the making of these wines. This year, the Portacomaro cellars brought us four selections. Several of the historic labels, including Grignolino '05 and Barbera Bunéis '04, have been left to age for an extra year before release. To our minds, the most interesting and representative of the four is Barbera d'Asti Masaréj '03. It is warm and chewy but has plenty of thrust, as well as an acidulous note that keeps the generous alcohol typical of the vintage in check. The Moscato d'Asti is big and aromatic, while the Dolcetto is spicy and fruity. The Brachetto shows pleasant sensations of rose.

●	Barbera d'Asti Masaréj Gianni Zonin Vineyards '03	**YY**	6
○	Moscato d'Asti '05	**YY**	4*
●	Monferrato Dolcetto '05	**Y**	4
●	Piemonte Brachetto Spumante '05	**Y**	4
●	Barbera d'Asti Masaréj Gianni Zonin Vineyards '01	YY	6
●	Piemonte Barbera Bunéis Gianni Zonin Vineyards '01	YY	6
●	Piemonte Barbera Bunéis Gianni Zonin Vineyards '03	YY	6
●	Grignolino d'Asti Gianni Zonin Vineyards '04	YY	4

PRIOCCA (CN)

HILBERG - PASQUERO
VIA BRICCO GATTI, 16
12040 PRIOCCA (CN)
TEL. 0173616197
www.vinipiemonte.com

Tasting is not the only way to get to know and appreciate a wine's virtues. Occasionally, simply talking to the grower can give us a very good profile of the wine that we are about to discover in the glass. At Bricco Gatti, a steep, isolated hill in Priocca, we witness this producer-wine symbiosis every time we visit. Michelangelo Pasquero and Annette Hilberg have such clarity of vision about their work and its implications – its relationship with the environment, links to the territory and distinctive characteristics – that when it finally comes to uncorking the bottle, we feel as if we have already drunk its contents through their images and words. The six wines presented this year are quite simply the souls of their creators become nectar. And what nectar! The Nebbiolo d'Alba '04 is the best of its category with its light, balanced explosion of fruity freshness and juicy palate whose taut progression is tannic to just the right degree and very long. For lovers of statistics, this is the fifth Three Glass champion from this estate in six years; only the 2002 missed out. The Barbera Superiore and Langhe Pedrocha, a nebbiolo and barbera blend, both came to within a hair's breadth of the top prize. The first is caressing and acidulous, the second austere, vigorous and powerful. The standard Barbera and the Vareij from brachetto and barbera are solid winners. Then we have a newcomer and it's not the much-requested Roero but a Langhe Nebbiolo. This first edition is a flawless, thoroughly enjoyable '04 that perfectly mirrors the style of the rest of the range.

●	Nebbiolo d'Alba '04	🍷🍷🍷	6
●	Barbera d'Alba Sup. '04	🍷🍷	6
●	Langhe Rosso Pedrocha '04	🍷🍷	5
●	Langhe Nebbiolo '04	🍷🍷	5
●	Barbera d'Alba '05	🍷🍷	4*
●	Vareij Rosso '05	🍷🍷	4*
●	Nebbiolo d'Alba '00	YYY	6
●	Nebbiolo d'Alba '01	YYY	6
●	Nebbiolo d'Alba '03	YYY	6
●	Barbera d'Alba Sup. '97	YYY	6
●	Barbera d'Alba Sup. '98	YYY	6
●	Nebbiolo d'Alba '99	YYY	6
●	Barbera d'Alba Sup. '01	YY	6
●	Barbera d'Alba Sup. '03	YY	6

PRIOCCA (CN)

CASCINA VAL DEL PRETE
S.DA SANTUARIO, 2
12040 PRIOCCA (CN)
TEL. 0173616534 - 0173616624

This year we welcome back a full array of wines from Mario Roagna. Last year's ravages, the aftermath of the infamous 2002 vintage that took its toll on the Roero label, are behind him now. With more favourable vintages at his disposal Mario has takes his entire range a firm step up the quality ladder. He makes a very manageable 50,000 bottles, the classic Roero level of production. As soon as you set foot on Mario's Val del Prete estate you can feel its spirit. The cellar is not particularly big but highly functional and stands in the midst of vineyards that form an amphitheatre around it. The rows are tended like a garden and for some time now have been cultivated to biodynamic principles. High quality, respect for the environment and good value for money are all characteristics that help turn a wine into a winner and Marioi's Roero '03 has them in abundance. Its nose impresses with a cornucopia of perfectly mingled fruity sensations integrated with a hint of oak that never overwhelms. Entry on the palate is rather austere but it unbends nicely to reveal echoes of the fruit, strong tannins and a very leisurely finish. It all adds up to another Three Glasses for Mario's trophy case. The other two serious reds performed very well. Nebbiolo Vigna di Lino '04, perfect in the role of "deuxième vin", is younger and drinking now, while the Barbera Carolina's no-nonsense acidity and character put it at the top of its typology. The standard Barbera and white Arneis round off a remarkable range.

●	Roero '03	🍷🍷🍷	7
●	Barbera d'Alba Sup. Carolina '04	🍷🍷	6
●	Nebbiolo d'Alba V. di Lino '04	🍷🍷	6
●	Barbera d'Alba Serra de' Gatti '05	🍷🍷	4*
○	Roero Arneis Luet '05	🍷	4
●	Nebbiolo d'Alba V. di Lino '00	YYY	5
●	Roero '00	YYY	6
●	Roero '01	YYY	6
●	Barbera d'Alba Sup. Carolina '03	YY	6
●	Nebbiolo d'Alba V. di Lino '03	YY	6
●	Barbera d'Alba Sup. Carolina '01	YY	6
●	Roero '98	YY	6
●	Roero '99	YY	6

QUARGNENTO (AL)

Colle Manora

S.da Bozzole, 4
15044 Quargnento (AL)
tel. 0131219252
www.collemanora.it

This estate run by Mauro Burighel produces around 70,000 bottles a year that are released under six labels. The grapes come from the estate's 20 hectares of Guyot-trained vineyards planted to a density of 4-5,000 vines per hectare. As for the array of wines presented for tasting this year, the sauvignon blanc-based Monferrato Bianco Mimosa '04 is as interesting as ever. It shows typical primary aromas and balance that few can rival in this part of the province of Alessandria. Palo Alto '03 is a Monferrato Rosso obtained from a blend of pinot nero, cabernet sauvignon, merlot and barbera. It presents a ruby red with garnet highlights in the glass and notes of vanilla and balsam left over from its oak-ageing. Entry on the palate is soft and the alcohol leaves a sweet nuance. The Manora, a Monferrato Barbera, benefits from long, meticulous vinification in the cellar but the problematical summer of 2003 still managed to leave its mark in the form of faintly overripe, not terribly fresh, sensations that we have never noted before in this splendid label. The Barbera del Monferrato Pais '04 lacks its customary harmony, exhibiting fairly strong acidity in the finish. We end our review of Colle Manora's offering with the Mila, a table wine derived from sauvignon blanc and chardonnay grapes that in the 2003 version is a little too oak-dominated.

● Monferrato Rosso Palo Alto '03	🍷🍷	4*
○ Monferrato Bianco Mimosa '04	🍷🍷	4*
● Barbera del M.to Manora '03	🍷	5
○ Mila Bianco '03	🍷	4
● Barbera del M.to Pais '04	🍷	4
● Barbera del M.to Manora '00	YY	5
● Monferrato Rosso Palo Alto '00	YY	6
● Barbera del M.to Manora '01	YY	5
● Monferrato Rosso Palo Alto '01	YY	6

ROCCA GRIMALDA (AL)

Cascina La Maddalena

loc. Piani del Padrone, 257
15078 Rocca Grimalda (AL)
tel. 0143876074
www.cascina-maddalena.com

Anna Poggio, Cristina Bozzano and Marilena De Gasperi run this beautiful estate with passion and a firm, all-female hand. Their philosophy is to produce quality wines that are strongly linked to the local tradition of using only the indigenous varieties found in the Ovada area, dolcetto and barbera. To forge an even stronger bond with the territory, they have opened a cosy bed and breakfast that is perfectly positioned for lovely walks through the charming hills on the Ligurian border. The trio combine tradition with a touch of technology that allows them to present sound wines appropriate for a market that is increasingly demanding and well-informed. Giovanni Bailo, an expert oenologist from this part of Alessandria's wine country, is technical consultant. The estate's five hectares planted to vine all lie in the municipal territory of Rocca Grimalda. The Cascina La Maddalena line offers a total of just five labels; the Barbera Rossa d'Ocra selection has been left to age and is therefore missing from the line-up this year. We tasted two Dolcettos and our preference is for the Migulle selection. It is obtained from an old plot with naturally low yields that produce extremely elegant, richly flavoured wines. Good, but not quite as good as the Migulle, is the Dolcetto Bricco del Bagatto '04, which takes its name from the old group of farmhouses where the estate's headquarters is now located. The standard-label Barbera is pleasing on the palate and the Monferrato Rosso Bricco della Maddalena from 100 per cent barbera is full and concentrated.

● Monferrato Rosso Bricco della Maddalena '03	🍷🍷	5
● Dolcetto di Ovada Migulle '04	🍷🍷	4*
● Dolcetto di Ovada Bricco del Bagatto '04	🍷	4
● Barbera del M.to '05	🍷	4
● Barbera del M.to Rossa d'Ocra '03	YY	4

ROCCHETTA TANARO (AT)

Braida

via Roma, 94
14030 Rocchetta Tanaro (AT)
tel. 0141644113
www.braida.it

Giuseppe Bologna, founder of this dynasty, was nicknamed Braida back when he used to spend Sunday playing "pallone a pugno", a traditional southern Piedmontese and western Ligurian sport. This soubriquet has been a theme for this cellar, which has built its reputation on barbera, the chief variety of the whole Asti area. Today, the estate is run by Giuseppe's grandchildren, oenologists Raffaella and Beppe, and their mother, Anna, with the support of their respective spouses, Norbert and Cristina. The production philosophy laid out in the early 1980s by the late Giacomo Bologna still holds true: to produce excellent Barbera selections, from the simple, fruity Monella to the more challenging Ai Suma, Bricco dell'Uccellone and Bricco della Bigotta, without neglecting the zone's other typical grape types, grignolino, moscato and brachetto. The estate grows only a small amount of international varieties, mainly chardonnay for the Serra dei Fiori line, and just one red, pinot nero, that goes into the Bacialé. The three Barbera selections have pride of place, each diverse in terms of length of oak-ageing and harvest time. This year, the magnificent Ai Suma selection swept the boards to take Three Glasses. First produced in 1989, it is the youngest of the three crus, its grapes having been allowed to overripen slightly for 15 extra days. It stayed in barrique for 12 months, emerging as an extraordinarily full but fruity wine, with good freshness and balance. Hot on its heels come the Uccellone and the Bigotta. Il Bacialé and Barbera Montebruna are solid second leads.

●	Barbera d'Asti Ai Suma '04	3 glasses (black)	7
●	Barbera d'Asti Bricco della Bigotta '04	2 glasses (black)	7
●	Barbera d'Asti Bricco dell'Uccellone '04	2 glasses (black)	7
●	Barbera d'Asti Montebruna '04	2 glasses (black)	4*
●	Monferrato Rosso Il Bacialé '04	2 glasses (black)	4*
○	Langhe Chardonnay Asso di Fiori '04	1 glass (black)	4
●	Brachetto d'Acqui '05	1 glass (black)	4
●	Grignolino d'Asti '05	1 glass (black)	4
○	Langhe Bianco Il Fiore '05	1 glass (black)	4
●	Barbera d'Asti Bricco dell'Uccellone '01	3 glasses (white)	7
●	Barbera d'Asti Bricco dell'Uccellone '03	3 glasses (white)	7

ROCCHETTA TANARO (AT)

Marchesi Incisa della Rocchetta

via Roma, 66
14030 Rocchetta Tanaro (AT)
tel. 0141644647
www.lacortechiusa.it

The Incisa della Rocchetta family can trace its roots back to before the year 1000, when the Aleramico marquisate was founded. Winemaking is in the blood of this noble family, for centuries steeped in a tradition that was probably started by the Benedictine monks who cultivated vines on the hills of the Incisas' property. The monks left behind a chapel dedicated to Sant'Emiliano, which stands in the family vineyard of the same name. One final note: in the mid-1800s, Marchese Leopoldo played a key role in improving oenological knowledge and defining the ampelography of the era. The estate has dedicated a wine to him. Backed by this illustrious history, Marchesi Incisa produce superb wines and offer charming accommodation on their beautiful farm to those seeking a relaxing natural break. The wines we tasted were extremely interesting, comprising five labels obtained from just three varieties: the traditional barbera and grignolino having been joined by aristocratic pinot nero. The cream of the crop is the Barbera Sant'Emiliano '03, which marched confidently into our finals. Ripe fruit aromas mingled with toasty notes left over from its oak-ageing announce a full, chewy palate and a finish well-managed by alcohol and acid sensations. We also admired fine performances from the pinot nero-based Marchese Leopoldo '03, a fruity, characterful wine, and the Barbera Valmorena '04 with its very elegant palate. Barbera and pinot nero lend backbone and elegance to the Rollone '04, while the Grignolino '05 shows a spicy nose and rather a tannic palate.

●	Barbera d'Asti Sup. Sant'Emiliano '03	2 glasses (black)	5
●	Monferrato Rosso Marchese Leopoldo '03	2 glasses (black)	5
●	Barbera d'Asti Valmorena '04	2 glasses (black)	4*
●	Monferrato Rosso Rollone '04	2 glasses (black)	4*
●	Grignolino d'Asti '05	1 glass (black)	4
●	Barbera d'Asti Sup. Sant'Emiliano '02	2 glasses (white)	5
●	Barbera d'Asti Valmorena '03	2 glasses (white)	4
●	Monferrato Rosso Rollone '03	2 glasses (white)	4

RODELLO (CN)

F.lli Mossio

via Montà, 12
12050 Rodello (CN)
tel. 0173617149
www.mossio.com

For this edition of the Guide, the Mossio brothers presented us with two new wines to taste, a Barbera and a Langhe Nebbiolo, having ceased production of the Langhe Rosso that was obtained from two local varieties. We roundly applaud this clear, courageous decision made with consumers in mind. Remo, Valerio, Claudio, Guido and Mauro form a tight-knit family team that for many years now has worked the estate's ten hectares to produce around 40,000 bottles. As for the wines, the Dolcetto d'Alba Bricco Caramelli'05 released in 5,000 bottles dominates as usual. This wine shows its strong character in its deep ruby red appearance with purplish highlights. The nose's pronounced, pervasive mineral note is enhanced by hints of forest fruit and eucalyptus, and the palate is also full and flavoursome, well buttressed by an exceedingly pleasant fresh vein. A touch of almond in the finish lends the mouthfeel extra elegance. The readier Dolcetto d'Alba Piano delli Perdoni '05 is the cellar's best seller and is available in 30,000 bottles. It is a bona fide everyday wine in the best sense of the word: obtained from fruit of exceptional quality, it is easy-drinking with invigorating tannins. And all this comes at a reasonable price. Moving on to the new labels, we particularly liked the Langhe Nebbiolo '04 with its fragrant in its fruity nuances. The Barbera d'Alba '04 is not quite as good but still hovers on the Two Glass threshold.

●	Dolcetto d'Alba Bricco Caramelli '05	🍷🍷	4*
●	Langhe Nebbiolo '04	🍷🍷	4*
●	Dolcetto d'Alba Piano delli Perdoni '05	🍷🍷	4*
●	Barbera d'Alba '04	🍷	4
●	Dolcetto d'Alba Bricco Caramelli '00	YYY	4
●	Dolcetto d'Alba Bricco Caramelli '03	YY	4
●	Dolcetto d'Alba Bricco Caramelli '04	YY	4
●	Langhe Rosso '01	YY	5
●	Langhe Rosso '02	YY	5
●	Langhe Rosso '03	YY	5

ROSIGNANO MONFERRATO (AL)

Vicara

loc. Madonna
cascina Madonna delle Grazie
15030 Rosignano Monferrato (AL)
tel. 0142488054
www.vicara.it

The Vicara estate was founded in 1992. This year, the range of labels on offer impressed us with its stylistic cleanliness and impeccable character. Credit for this goes to the skilled team of Edoardo Monticelli and Alberto Pansecchi in the vineyard and Domenico Ravizza and Mario Ronco in the cellar. Together they manage around 50 hectares planted to vine for an annual production of approximately 200,000 bottles. For several years now the Monferrato Superiore Cantico della Crosia has reigned supreme and the 2004 version is as complex on the nose as it is balanced on the palate. Monferrato Rosso Rubello '04 from 80 per cent barbera, 15 per cent cabernet sauvignon and nebbiolo, also performed very well, as did L'Uccelletta '03, an interesting blend of grignolino and pinot nero matured for 24 months first in barrique and then in bottle. For those who like their Barberas young, we recommend Volpuva '05. Its purple colour attests to its youth and lovely freshness, while the nose is full of fruity aromas and entry on the palate is very dense. We had a fine showing from the Barbera Vadmò, which stayed in large barrels for 12 months. The long list of Two Glass champions ends with the Grignolino del Monferrato Casalese, one of the best of its type and released in 12,000 bottles. Finally, we have Barbera Vivace, an easy-drinking wine that still has a large following, and Monferrato Bianco Airales, an assemblage of cortese, chardonnay and sauvignon.

●	Monferrato Rosso L'Uccelletta '03	🍷🍷	5
●	Barbera del M.to Sup. Cantico della Crosia '04	🍷🍷	5
●	Barbera del M.to Sup. Vadmò '04	🍷🍷	5
●	Monferrato Rosso Rubello '04	🍷🍷	5
●	Grignolino del M.to Casalese '05	🍷🍷	3*
●	Barbera del M.to Volpuva '05	🍷	3*
●	Barbera del M.to Vivace '05	🍷	3
○	Monferrato Bianco Airales '05	🍷	4
●	Barbera del M.to Sup. Cantico della Crosia '01	YY	5
●	Barbera del M.to Sup. Cantico della Crosia '00	YY	5

SAN GIORGIO CANAVESE (TO)

ORSOLANI
VIA MICHELE CHIESA, 12
10090 SAN GIORGIO CANAVESE (TO)
TEL. 012432386
www.orsolani.it

Orsolani may be a long-established label in the Canavese area, but this does not prevent it from being one of the most dynamic and innovative. Gigi Orsolani is largely responsible for the success of the Spumante version of Erbaluce di Caluso and has set up a national association that brings together the best Metodo Classicos obtained from native Italian varieties with the objective of promoting this small but valuable national asset. In the absence of the Gran Riserva, which was not ready for tasting in the new vintage, the Cuvée Tradizione '01 stepped into the breach as house standard-bearer with typical aromas of ripe citrus fruit, yellow apple and honey. The two still Erbaluces are also very good. Vignot Sant'Antonio '04 sojourns in small barrels but its oaky tones are barely discernible and leave lots of room for faintly peppery aromas and good backbone. La Rustìa '05 exhibits a flowery, aromatic nose and a palate brimming with pineapples and almonds. Caluso Passito Sulé never disappoints and the '01 shows fabulous body and very intriguing oxidized notes. Obtained from a selection of some of the best Carema vineyards, Carema Le Tabbie '01 weds a strongly territorial character with precise, meticulous vinification. The result is a nose that combines the clearest flowery nuances with deep chewy notes and tangy, almost ferrous mineral tones. The fluent, fruity palate roundly echoes the mineral tones in the finish. The barbera-based Acini Sparsi '04 is nice and a retasting of the Caluso Passito Sulé '98 revealed a splendid wine that merited Three retrospective Glasses.

○ Erbaluce di Caluso Vignot S. Antonio '04	🍷🍷	5
○ Caluso Passito Sulé '01	🍷🍷	6
○ Caluso Spumante Brut Cuvée Tradizione '01	🍷🍷	5
● Carema Le Tabbie '01	🍷🍷	6
○ Erbaluce di Caluso La Rustìa '05	🍷🍷	4
● Canavese Rosso Acini Sparsi '04	🍷	4
○ Caluso Passito Sulé '98	🍷🍷🍷 (retrospective)	6
○ Caluso Passito Sulé '00	🍷🍷 (retrospective)	6
○ Caluso Spumante Brut Gran Ris. '99	🍷🍷 (retrospective)	6

SAN MARTINO ALFIERI (AT)

MARCHESI ALFIERI
P.ZZA ALFIERI, 28
14010 SAN MARTINO ALFIERI (AT)
TEL. 0141976015
www.marchesialfieri.it

Sisters Giovanna, Antonella and Emanuela San Martino di San Germano never cease to surprise us with the reliability of their wines, which year after year show unfailingly good quality and great character. We'll start our notes with the estate's most important Barbera and the wine that has won it the most awards, the Alfiera. Nuances of plum, blackberry and vanilla emerge on the nose before entry on the palate manages to be both powerful and harmonious at the same time. The Barbera d'Asti La Tota '04 presents a dense, lively ruby appearance with purplish highlights and a concentrated, very elegant nose that superbly balances aromas of charred oak and fruit. The palate is enthralling, powerful and rich. The Monferrato Rosso dei Marchesi changed its name in the 2004 vintage to become the Rosso Sostegno, but its composition remains the same: pinot nero and barbera. Deep ruby red in the glass, it offers an extremely intense nose in which very clear notes of currant-led fruit meld elegantly with hints of spice. The palate is potent and full and the excellent finish very leisurely. The Grignolino Sansoero '05, a pale but very bright ruby red wine, has a typical varietal nose full of character and elegance. We particularly liked the hints of pepper and dried roses that mingle with faint, complex vegetal notes. Up last, the Monferrato Rosso San Germano '04 from 100 per cent pinot nero has delicate aromas of wild strawberry, currant, blueberry and raspberry leading into a full, lip-smacking palate.

● Barbera d'Asti La Tota '04	🍷🍷	4*
● Barbera d'Asti Sup. Alfiera '04	🍷🍷	6
● Monferrato Rosso S. Germano '04	🍷🍷	5
● Monferrato Rosso Sostegno '04	🍷🍷	4*
● Piemonte Grignolino Sansoero '05	🍷🍷	4
● Barbera d'Asti Sup. Alfiera '00	🍷🍷🍷 (retrospective)	6
● Barbera d'Asti Sup. Alfiera '01	🍷🍷🍷 (retrospective)	6
● Barbera d'Asti Sup. Alfiera '99	🍷🍷🍷 (retrospective)	6
● Barbera d'Asti Sup. Alfiera '03	🍷🍷 (retrospective)	6
● Monferrato Rosso S. Germano '01	🍷🍷 (retrospective)	5
● Monferrato Rosso S. Germano '03	🍷🍷 (retrospective)	5

SAN MARZANO OLIVETO (AT)

TENUTA DELL' ARBIOLA

LOC. ARBIOLA
REG. SALINE, 67
14050 SAN MARZANO OLIVETO (AT)
TEL. 0141856194
www.arbiola.it

Domenico Terzano and his son Riccardo embarked on their winemaking venture over 15 years ago when they started to vinify the grapes produced on their beautiful property at San Marzano Oliveto. Over the last few years, they have made rapid progress thanks to the excellent people they have brought on board for technical advice, first and foremost fruitmaker Federico Curtaz. The Terzanos obtain 100,000 bottles a year from their 20 hectares, planted mainly to barbera and moscato, although in recent years they have made space for international varieties such as chardonnay, sauvignon, cabernet sauvignon, pinot nero and merlot. Their sound production philosophy focuses on a limited number of labels: two Barberas, one a standard-label and the other more challenging, a Monferrato Rosso Arbiola based on barbera, cabernet and pinot, and three whites, Moscato, Arbiola Bianco from chardonnay and sauvignon, and Chardonnay. Monferrato Rosso Arbiola is missing from this year's line-up so our top marks go to Barbera d'Asti Superiore Nizza Romilda IX '04. Deep ruby red in the glass, it offers aromas of red berry fruit, rain-soaked earth and nice minerality. The full, balanced palate is gutsy and enfolding with acidity well supported by the alcohol. The basic Barbera d'Asti, Carlotta, is more vegetal than fruity. From the whites on offer, we preferred the fruity, characterful sauvignon-chardonnay blend to the simple Chardonnay. Finally, the first-rate Moscato Ferlingot '05 shows concentrated aromas and a full, complex palate nicely buttressed by acidity.

●	Barbera d'Asti Sup. Nizza Romilda IX '04	two black glasses	5
○	Moscato d'Asti Ferlingot '05	two black glasses	3*
○	Monferrato Bianco Arbiola '05	two black glasses	4
●	Barbera d'Asti Carlotta '05	one black glass	3
○	Piemonte Chardonnay '05	one black glass	3
●	Barbera d'Asti Sup. Nizza Romilda VII '01	two white glasses	6
●	Barbera d'Asti Sup. Nizza Romilda VIII '03	two white glasses	6
●	Monferrato Rosso Arbiola '00	two white glasses	5
○	Monferrato Bianco Arbiola '04	two white glasses	5

SAN MARZANO OLIVETO (AT)

GUIDO BERTA

LOC. SALINE, 53
14050 SAN MARZANO OLIVETO (AT)
TEL. 0141856193

Born in 1972, Guido Berta built up his experience working in several of the big Asti cellars before returning full-time to the family vineyards in 2001. Most of his 12 hectares are given over to barbera and he has taken production from a scant 2,000 bottles to the current 30,000 in just a few short years. His father, Giuseppe, lends a hand in the cellar where he brings his considerable expertise as a viticulturist to bear. The estate's thoroughbred champ is Barbera d'Asti Superiore Nizza Canto di Luna '03. Matured for 18 months in barrique, it presents a ruby appearance and notes of red berry fruit, notably morello cherries and currants, that merge perfectly with the notes of vanilla and coffee left over from its oak-ageing. Entry on the palate is sweet and harmonious, enhanced by a very, very long finish. Reviewed by mistake in the 2006 edition of the Guide, the Barbera d'Asti Le Rondini '04 performed exceptionally well. It unveils notes of blueberry and fresh fruit on the nose and then a juicy palate with lots of stuffing. The Piemonte Chardonnay '04 also passed the Two Glass mark. Obtained from fruit overripened on the vine, it is a rich straw yellow with golden highlights. The nose suggests ripe peach and banana and its ten-month sojourn in oak has left it with discreet nuances of vanilla and roasted hazelnuts. Simpler but by no means less agreeable, the Chardonnay Le Rondini '05 is fresh and easy-drinking with just the right amount of acidity.

●	Barbera d'Asti Sup. Nizza Canto di Luna '03	two black glasses	5
●	Barbera d'Asti Le Rondini '04	two black glasses	3*
○	Piemonte Chardonnay '04	two black glasses	4
○	Piemonte Chardonnay Le Rondini '05	one black glass	3
●	Barbera d'Asti Sup. '03	two white glasses	4

SAN MARZANO OLIVETO (AT)

Alfiero Boffa
via Leiso, 50
14050 San Marzano Oliveto (AT)
tel. 0141856115
www.alfieroboffa.com

Alfiero Boffa grows almost exclusively barbera on his estate, where he was joined in the early 1990s by sons Rossano and Simone. Alfiero's philosophy is to produce wines from individual vineyards and to this end he seeks the best fruit from San Marzano Oliveto. To lend his project more prestige, in the mid 1980s Alfiero developed the Vigne Uniche line consisting of high-quality wines obtained from vineyards that are at least 40 years old. Our hero has also added to the charm of his estate by renovating the San Marzano castle cellars, the perfect environment for ageing these wines in barrels. This year, we tasted no less than five Barberas – three '04s and two '03s – two reds from the Monferrato DOC zone, and a pleasant Rosé based on pinot nero. Although we deemed all the Barbera selections worthy of Two Glasses, the most interesting is the Superiore Nizza La Riva, of which 4,250 bottles were released. The complex nose and fullness of the fruit combine to give this red extraordinary character, and it has emerged unscathed from the dry harvest of 2003 to show remarkable freshness and fruitiness. The 6,500 bottles of Superiore Collina della Vedova are warmer and more austere. The 2004 selections are not as juicy on the palate but are nicely acidulous. The 9,800 bottles of More are mature and minerally, Muntrivé is dry and fruity and Cua Longa in 7,500 bottles is spicy and gamey. Velo di Maya '03 from 70 per cent barbera is firm and tannic while Ombra del Ciliegio '04, from freisa, dolcetto, pinot nero and a little barbera, is light and rich in red fruit.

● Barbera d'Asti Sup. Collina della Vedova '03	🍷🍷	5
● Barbera d'Asti Sup. Nizza Vigna La Riva '03	🍷🍷	5
● Monferrato Rosso Velo di Maya '03	🍷🍷	5
● Barbera d'Asti Sup. V. Cua Longa '04	🍷🍷	5
● Barbera d'Asti Sup. V. More '04	🍷🍷	5
● Barbera d'Asti Sup. V. Muntrivé '04	🍷🍷	5
● Monferrato Rosso Ombra del Ciliegio '04	🍷	4
⊙ Monferrato Ciaret Gran Buchet '05		4

SAN MARZANO OLIVETO (AT)

Franco Mondo
reg. Mariano, 33
14050 San Marzano Oliveto (AT)
tel. 0141834096

The Mondo family estate has 13 hectares of vineyards in the Asti municipality of San Marzano Oliveto and an annual production of around 60,000 bottles. The range presented for tasting this year is of good quality and several of the versions of barbera, the zone's most important variety, excelled. Vigna del Salice '04 is first-class. It has an impenetrable ruby red appearance with youthful crimson lights and a pervasive nose revealing nuances of plum, Peruvian bark, toastiness and cocoa powder. The full, powerful palate is well sustained by the acid backbone and closes splendidly in a lip-smacking, exceedingly long finish with a faintly bitterish tail. We also very much liked the Barbera Superiore Vigna delle Rose Selezione '01, of which 1,900 magnums were released. Notes of blackberry and black pepper are the prelude to pleasant acid backbone that lengthens the palate's progression. The basic Barbera '05 presents a dense ruby red and a nose impressive for its concentration and freshness with hints of black berry fruit. The mid-weight palate is well-balanced and very agreeable overall. The Dolcetto Tre Vigne, a ruby colour of medium intensity, has a no-nonsense nose suggesting earth and wild berries and a palate slightly dominated by the uncompromising extract but the finish is full and invigorating. The pale straw-yellow Cortese exhibits aromas of yeast and banana and a light sweet vein with delicate, consistent progression on the palate.

● Barbera d'Asti Sup. V. delle Rose Sel. '01	🍷🍷	7
● Barbera d'Asti V. del Salice '04	🍷🍷	4*
● Barbera d'Asti '05	🍷	3
○ Cortese dell'Alto Monferrato '05	🍷	3
● Dolcetto d'Asti Tre Vigne '05	🍷	3
● Barbera d'Asti Sup. V. delle Rose '00	🍸🍸	5
● Barbera d'Asti Sup. V. delle Rose '01	🍸🍸	5
● Barbera d'Asti Sup. V. delle Rose '03	🍸🍸	5
● Barbera d'Asti V. del Salice '03	🍸🍸	4

SAN MARZANO OLIVETO (AT)

Tenute dei Vallarino

reg. Valle Asinari, 20
14050 San Marzano Oliveto (AT)
tel. 0141823048

In 2001, the Gancia family turned its sights on Monferrato in Asti. They bought a lovely estate of around 15 hectares in Valle Asinari and set about improving the quality of their reds, the symbol of the territory. After the triumphs of the mid 1980s when Vittorio Vallarino Gancia acquired the famous Cannubi vineyard at Barolo, Edoardo Gancia and his brothers Lamberto and Max are once more producing red wines of absolute quality. In 2003 they added 20 hectares at Casalese in Vignale Monferrato to the Valle Asinari property. Here they have planted local varieties, such as barbera, albarossa, bussanello and barbera bianca, plus the international grape types merlot, syrah, chardonnay and sauvignon. At Valle Asinari they cultivate barbera, nebbiolo, cabernet sauvignon and merlot and they also obtain some moscato from a property belonging to Edoardo below the castle of Canelli. Right from the start the wines produced by this estate have shown how good they are and this year two selections reached our Three Glass finals. Wines and vines enjoy the attentions of an expert staff: Piergiorgio Cane is technical director and oenologist Beppe Caviola and fruitmaker Federico Curtaz consult. The wines have improved significantly and show a better defined style. Sourced from older plots, the superb Barbera d'Asti Nizza Bricco Asinari '04 has a dark ruby red colour, morello cherry and rain-soaked earth aromas, followed by a deep, elegant palate. The Dialogo from cabernet sauvignon, merlot, barbera and nebbiolo is slightly less sumptuous and the Barbera La Ladra offers good value for money.

●	Barbera d'Asti Sup. Nizza Bricco Asinari '04	🍷🍷	6
●	Monferrato Rosso Dialogo '04	🍷🍷	6
●	Barbera d'Asti Sup. La Ladra '04	🍷🍷	4*
●	Monferrato Rosso Inter Nos '04	🍷🍷	4*
○	Moscato d'Asti Castello Gancia '05	🍷🍷	4*
●	Barbera d'Asti La Ladra '03	YY	4
●	Barbera d'Asti Sup. Nizza Bricco Asinari '03	YY	6
●	Monferrato Rosso Dialogo '03	YY	6

SANTO STEFANO BELBO (CN)

Ca' d' Gal

fraz. Valdivilla
s.da Vecchia di Valdivilla, 1
12058 Santo Stefano Belbo (CN)
tel. 0141847103
www.ca-d-gal.com

As you climb the San Maurizio hill, before you reach the small village of Valdivilla you will come to the Ca' d' Gal estate. The winery has recently opened some charming accommodation and a small restaurant and offers a spectacular view across the moscato-clad slopes. From an old vineyard situated right below the cellar, Alessandro Boido obtains a Moscato of exceptional quality that will undoubtedly raise the profile of this wine type if he keeps going in this direction. Alessandro has 11 hectares planted to vine, half his own and half rented, and production is growing. This year, he bottled 65,000 bottles of Moscato, but decided to forgo house red Pian del Gäje in the 2002 vintage. For several years now, he has produced Asti in response to the interest shown by the market. The 2005, available in 12,000 bottles, exhibits aromas of apple and honey and a fresh, clean, faintly vegetal palate buttressed by substantial effervescence. The 45,000 bottles of Moscato d'Asti Lumine '05 live up to expectations. The nose has yet to develop fully but hints at honey, fresh herbs and liquorice, while the palate offers very gratifying creaminess, freshness and balance. In short, it's an easy-drinking wine that is perfect for the table. Finally, the magnificent golden Vigna Vecchia '05 in 5,300 bottles impressed us with its generosity and sweetness, and the silkiness of its mousse. A tasting of older vintages confirmed that we were right to put our money on this prestigious Moscato selection.

○	Moscato d'Asti V. Vecchia '05	🍷🍷	5
○	Moscato d'Asti Lumine '05	🍷🍷	4*
○	Asti '05	🍷	4
○	Moscato d'Asti V. Vecchia '04	YY	5

SANTO STEFANO BELBO (CN)

TENUTA IL FALCHETTO

FRAZ. CIOMBI
VIA VALLE TINELLA, 16
12058 SANTO STEFANO BELBO (CN)
TEL. 0141840344
www.ilfalchetto.com

After performing well to return to the Other Wineries section last year, Tenuta Il Falchetto scored high again and regained a full profile. Supported by their family, Forno brothers Giorgio, Fabrizio, Roberto and Adriano run this beautiful estate located in Langhe and Monferrato. They produce 250,000 bottles a year of the typical wines of these two zones, ranging from sweet Moscatos to Barbera d'Astis, Nebbiolos and Barbera d'Albas. The estate extends over 34 hectares planted to vine and consists of no less than five properties: Tenuta Il Falchetto, Tenuta dei Ciombi and Cascina Moncucco in Santo Stefano, Tenuta Bricco del Paradiso in Agliano and Tenuta del Fant in Calosso. The range of labels produced is extensive and we tasted some of those that we consider more ambitious and important. We start with a fine version of Barbera d'Asti Superiore Bricco Paradiso '03 that we reviewed by mistake last year. Sensations of ripe fruit on the nose are nicely supported by notes of sweet spice and coffee. The fruity, full-flavoured palate displays excellent balance between alcohol and acid. Also from '03, the Monferrato Rosso La Mora from 60 per cent barbera and 40 per cent cabernet shows no ill effects from the hot, dry growing year. The nose combines lovely vegetal notes with fruity sensations and the tannins on the powerful, gutsy palate enhance the lip-smacking finish. The sweet wines are excellent and two Moscatos in particular, the Tenuta del Fant and Ciombi, are on top form. We'll end with a flavoursome Moscato Passito '03 that has candied peel and an elegant palate.

●	Barbera d'Asti Sup. Bricco Paradiso '03	ΥΥ	4*
●	Monferrato Rosso La Mora '03	🍷🍷	4
○	Piemonte Moscato Passito '03	🍷🍷	6
○	Moscato d'Asti Ciombi '05	🍷🍷	3*
○	Moscato d'Asti Tenuta del Fant '05	🍷🍷	3*
●	Barbera d'Asti Sup. La Rossa '03	ΥΥ	4
●	Barbera d'Asti Sup. Lurèi '03	ΥΥ	4

SANTO STEFANO BELBO (CN)

PIERO GATTI

LOC. MONCUCCO, 28
12058 SANTO STEFANO BELBO (CN)
TEL. 0141840918
www.vinigatti.it

This estate on the slopes of the Moncucco hill near Santo Stefano was founded in 1988 by Piero Gatti, who sadly passed away prematurely. It is now run by his wife, Rita, with the support of oenologist Sergio Stella and her daughter, Barbara, who has finished her studies and come to work full-time in the family business. Production totals around 50,000 bottles a year and focuses on Moscato, the estate's trusty warhorse, which has been at the top of its category for years. It is obtained from a blend of grapes grown in various vineyards scattered across the hills around Santo Stefano, each differing in terms of soil and position to ensure that the quality remains constant throughout each harvest. The 40,000 bottles of Moscato '05 display a lively straw-yellow colour and fragrant aromas of yeast, honey and peach. The palate is sweet, creamy and well-balanced, signing off with a dry, leisurely finish. In comparison, the Brachetto '05, available in 10,000 bottles, seems to have a bit of an inferiority complex. Fruity and grassy on the nose, it is fresh and clean on the palate but considerably less smooth than the Moscato. The young Freisa '05 is pure Piedmont, drinking well and bigger on the palate than you might expect; very impressive. Its 2,800 bottles offer fine, elegant aromas of raspberry and spice and tannins worthy of its nebbiolo-based cousin. All told, it's a coherent, full-flavoured wine that would go well with a wide range of dishes.

●	Langhe Freisa '05	🍷🍷	4*
○	Piemonte Moscato '05	🍷🍷	4*
●	Piemonte Brachetto '05	🍷	4
○	Piemonte Moscato '04	ΥΥ	4
●	Verbeia '04	ΥΥ	4

Sergio Grimaldi - Ca' du Sindic

Loc. San Grato, 15
12058 Santo Stefano Belbo (CN)
tel. 0141840341

The small Ca' du Sindic estate in the village of San Grato in Santo Stefano Belbo has eight hectares of vineyards and annual production of around 50,000 bottles. As you would expect, Moscato d'Asti accounts for the lion's share but a small percentage is reserved for a decent Barbera d'Asti. With the help of his wife, Angela, and son, Paolo, who has just finished studying to be an oenologist, Sergio produces strongly territorial wines at very competitive prices. We'll start our notes with the wines that make this part of Piedmont unique and unrivalled. For years, Stefano has bottled two Moscatos whose packaging and name differ only in the colour of their capsules: Argento (Silver) and Oro (Gold). The first is obtained from grapes grown in vineyards on the slopes of San Grato that surround the cellar. The 35,000 bottles of the 2005 version present a rich golden appearance and sweet aromas of orange blossom, apple and mint. The palate is big and sweet with a crunchy finish. The second, an '05 released in 5,000 bottles, derives from a 50-year-old plot on the nearby San Maurizio hill. More closed on the nose, it offers notes of sage and mint and a palate full of sweetness and creaminess for an absolute winner. The Barbera San Grato '04 in 4,000 bottles is up to its usual standards. It displays woodland aromas of herbs and fresh pepper supported by consistent flesh balanced by acidity. Produced in 5,000 bottles, the Barbera d'Asti '04 is simpler and rather vegetal, and the Brachetto '05, in 4,000 bottles, releases honey and red fruit but is lean on the palate.

○	Moscato d'Asti Ca' du Sindic Capsula Oro '05	▼▼	4*
●	Barbera d'Asti San Grato '04	▼▼	4
○	Moscato d'Asti Ca' du Sindic Capsula Argento '05	▼▼	3*
●	Barbera d'Asti '04	▼	3
●	Piemonte Brachetto '05	▼	4
●	Barbera d'Asti San Grato '03	▽▽	4
○	Montaldi '03	▽▽	6
○	Moscato d'Asti Ca' du Sindic Capsula Oro '04	▽▽	4

SANTO STEFANO BELBO (CN)

I Vignaioli di Santo Stefano

Loc. Marini, 26
12058 Santo Stefano Belbo (CN)
tel. 0141840419
www.ceretto.com

I Vignaioli di Santo Stefano is celebrating its 30th anniversary. Founded in 1976, this private cellar was one of the first in the zone to show that it is possible to produce and sell excellent wines without succumbing to the pressures of the big industrial wineries. Back then, Moscato and other wines derived from this variety were the prerogative of large wineries and co-operatives that squeezed out the smaller cellars. Four growers from the slopes at Marini in Santo Stefano joined forces and, with the help of the Ceretto family who provided technical and business know-how, set about conquering one of the most difficult markets in the wine world. Within a few short years, they had won their challenge and the wines of I Vignaioli di Santo Stefano earned a reputation and wide acclaim in Italy and overseas. The wines are obtained by vinifying the grapes grown on the estate's 32 hectares and production totals around 170,000 bottles a year. The estate started out with a few hectares in Marini, but added to this in 1995 when it rented the beautiful San Maurizio property belonging to Carlo Vittorio Incisa Beccaria, complete with 30 hectares boasting one of the most spectacular positions in the whole designated area. The wines we were offered for tasting this year are all excellent. The Moscato d'Asti '05 shows very typical aromas of quince and apricot, while the Asti, also '05, is more delicate and has a pleasant, creamy mousse. The Passito, also from moscato, is sound. Its intoxicating notes of candied fruit are well sustained by smoky nuances left over from its oak-ageing.

○	Piemonte Moscato Passito IL '02	▼▼	5
○	Asti '05	▼▼	4
○	Moscato d'Asti '05	▼▼	4
○	Piemonte Moscato Passito IL '00	▽▽	5
○	Piemonte Moscato Passito IL '01	▽▽	5

SAREZZANO (AL)

MUTTI
LOC. SAN RUFFINO, 49
15050 SAREZZANO (AL)
TEL. 0131884119

If Walter Massa is known for having rescued timorasso from the jaws of oblivion, then Andrea Mutti certainly deserves equal recognition as a pioneer in this challenging quest and the first to undertake agronomic research into this indigenous variety. The overriding quality of his Timorasso selection, Castagnoli, is its finesse. This wine distinguishes itself from many of the others for the way in which Andrea succeeds in bringing out such elegant characteristics from a grape type that has fullness as one of its chief qualities. This finesse is also evident in the other white, Sull'Aia, obtained from sauvignon blanc. Varietal notes of white peach and a lovely acid vein always make this an agreeable wine, perfect as an aperitif or to serve with fish and even fresh cheese. We'll end our review of the whites with the Cortese Noceto, which is less challenging but far from dull. Of the reds on offer, we particularly liked the Barbera San Ruffino. Derived from 100 per cent barbera aged for 12 months in small oak barrels, it balances acidity nicely against body and backbone, allowing all of its varietal attributes to emerge. The Rivadestra is also rather good but needs a bit of time to breathe before it will reveal its complex characteristics. Barbera Boscobarona is pleasant and alcohol-rich with fragrant aromas.

○ Colli Tortonesi Bianco Castagnoli '04	🍷🍷	5
● Colli Tortonesi Rosso Rivadestra '03	🍷🍷	5
● Colli Tortonesi Rosso S. Ruffino '03	🍷🍷	5
○ Colli Tortonesi Bianco Sull'Aia '05	🍷🍷	4*
○ Colli Tortonesi Bianco Noceto '05	🍷	3
● Colli Tortonesi Rosso Boscobarona '05	🍷	3
○ Colli Tortonesi Bianco Castagnoli '03	🍷🍷 (outline)	5

SCURZOLENGO (AT)

CANTINE SANT'AGATA
REG. MEZZENA, 19
14030 SCURZOLENGO (AT)
TEL. 0141203186
www.santagata.com

Castagnole Monferrato has always been considered the home of Ruché, but it is only in recent years that the wine has earned a reputation beyond the borders of the region, thanks in large part to the Sant'Agata estate. Informed wine lovers were already familiar with a sound Ruché that rose to fame because it was produced by the village priest, Fr Giacomo Cauda. The turning point came, however, in 1987 when Ruché di Castagnole became a DOC. Among the first to produce and bottle this red wine were the Cavallero brothers, Franco and Claudio, who founded the Sant'Agata cellars in the early 1990s. They share the estate's management between them: Franco looks after the domestic and overseas markets, while Claudio takes care of production in vineyard and cellar. The estate focuses almost exclusively on varieties native to Monferrato – ruché, barbera, grignolino and cortese – but has an international presence in the form of chardonnay that goes to make Eliseo, a white. On the downside, the range is too broad, embracing fully 15 labels, two whites and the rest reds. On the upside, the wines are always of very good quality and the brothers' marketing ploys are more imaginative every year. In chronological order, the most recent labels are a Ruché, which carries the recommended selling price of 9.99 euros on its label, a selection available in half-litre bottles, Il Cavaliere, and a wine dedicated to Ducati Corse. The Ruché Pro Nobis leads the pack. Selections Vota, a Ruché, Cavalé, a Barbera d'Asti, and Genesi, from barbera and ruché, are all worth trying.

● Ruché di Castagnole M.to Pro Nobis '05	🍷🍷	5
● Monferrato Rosso Genesi '03	🍷🍷	5
● Barbera d'Asti Sup. Cavalé '04	🍷🍷	5
● Ruché di Castagnole M.to 'Na Vota '05	🍷🍷	4*
● Barbera d'Asti Sup. Altea '04	🍷	4
● Ruché di Castagnole M.to Il Cavaliere '05	🍷	4
● Ruché di Castagnole M.to 9.99 '05	🍷	4
● Barbera d'Asti Baby '05		3
● Grignolino d'Asti Miravalle '05		3
● Ruché di Castagnole M.to Pro Nobis '04	🍷🍷 (outline)	5

SERRALUNGA D'ALBA (CN)

SERRALUNGA D'ALBA (CN)

Luigi Baudana

Fraz. Baudana, 43
12050 Serralunga d'Alba (CN)
tel. 0173613354
www.baudanaluigi.com

Luigi Baudana and his wife, Fiorina, have just over four hectares planted to vine in the district of Serralunga from which they obtain an average of 25,000 bottles a year. The Baudanas have opted not to present any 2002 Barolos owing to the poor quality of the grapes harvested in that catastrophic growing year. However, they have released 4,500 bottles of the estate's thoroughbred, Barolo Cerretta Piani '01. It exhibits a ruby red colour verging on garnet, pervasive aromas of earth, leather, tobacco and dried flowers, and a palate that unbends to reveal mouthfilling tannins, good acidity and nuances of balsam and mint. It's a typical example of a Serralunga Barolo, powerful and long-lived. The Lorenso '03 derives from a blend of 50 per cent nebbiolo, 30 per cent barbera and merlot. It has a deep ruby appearance and a nose full of fruity, vanilla sensations. The three varietals are perfectly integrated on the palate where robust tannins, refreshing acidity and faint vegetal aromas lead into a delightful finish suggesting cocoa powder and tobacco. The Barbera Donatella '04 presents purplish highlights in the glass and notes of black cherry, cherry and spice. Evidence of the wine's oak-ageing comes through but never dominates the palate, notes of vanilla merging nicely with the varietal acidity and the fruit. The pale yellow Chardonnay shows intense notes of apple and banana and a harmonious, fulfilling palate with good body and length. The Dolcetto '05 is a classic everyday wine in the Langhe tradition, alcohol-rich and fruity.

● Barolo Cerretta Piani '01	▼▼	7
● Langhe Rosso Lorenso '03	▼▼	5
● Barbera d'Alba Donatella '04	▼▼	5
○ Langhe Chardonnay '05	▼▼	4*
● Dolcetto d'Alba '05	▼	4
● Barolo Cerretta Piani '00	▽▽	7
● Barolo Baudana '01	▽▽	7
● Barolo Cerretta Piani '99	▽▽	7
● Barolo Baudana '00	▽▽	7
● Barbera d'Alba Donatella '01	▽▽	5
● Langhe Rosso Lorenso '01	▽▽	5
● Barbera d'Alba Donatella '03	▽▽	5
● Barolo Cerretta Piani '96	▽▽	7
● Barolo Cerretta Piani '97	▽▽	7
● Barolo Cerretta Piani '98	▽▽	7

Cascina Cucco

Loc. Cucco
via Mazzini, 10
12050 Serralunga d'Alba (CN)
tel. 0173613003
www.cascinacucco.com

This estate belonging to the Stroppiana family comprises 11 hectares of vines, most of which are situated in Serralunga's famed Cucco and Cerrati vineyards. The Stroppianas grow their barbera grapes in the municipality of Roddi. Work in the vineyard and cellar is overseen by consultants fruitmaker Gian Piero Romana and oenologist Beppe Caviola. Like so many other estates, in 2002 Cascina Cucco opted not to produce the Barolo that is usually presented in three versions. So we tasted a reduced number of wines this year but they are all of very high quality. We start with the Langhe Rosso Mondo '04, a barbera and nebbiolo blend with a splash of cabernet sauvignon. Its ruby appearance with purplish highlights is the prelude to aromas of rose and forest fruits. The palate is at once powerful and harmonious, displaying a fine balance of acidity and tannins with elegant notes of liquorice and chocolate. There are two versions of Barbera on offer this year. We liked the '05 for its freshness and drinkability but the Superiore '04 is more complex and powerful, skilful use of oak imbuing it with intense fruity, spicy sensations that echo across nose and palate. The heady, fruity Dolcetto Vughera '05 shows good backbone and length on the palate. The rich straw-yellow Chardonnay offers notes of hawthorn, apple and pineapple-led fruit and flowers, and a refreshing, enjoyable palate with perfect supporting acidity.

● Barbera d'Alba Sup. '04	▼▼	5
● Langhe Rosso Mondo '04	▼▼	5
● Dolcetto d'Alba Vughera '05	▼▼	4*
○ Langhe Chardonnay '05	▼▼	4*
● Barbera d'Alba '05	▼	4
● Barolo V. Cerrati '00	▽▽	7
● Barolo V. Cucco '00	▽▽	7
● Barolo V. Cerrati '01	▽▽	7
● Barolo V. Cucco '01	▽▽	7
● Barolo '01	▽▽	7
● Barolo V. Cucco '97	▽▽	7
● Barolo V. Cerrati '98	▽▽	7
● Barolo V. Cucco '98	▽▽	7
● Barolo V. Cerrati '99	▽▽	7
● Barolo V. Cucco '99	▽▽	7

Fontanafredda

via Alba, 15
12050 Serralunga d'Alba (CN)
tel. 0173626111
www.fontanafredda.it

The 2006 growing year was an exceptional one for Fontanafredda. Its wines graced the evening award ceremonies, parties and celebrations of the Turin Olympics, winning praise from athletes of every nationality and the horde of international celebrities who had gathered in the Piedmontese capital to participate in this great sporting event. In fact, this Serralunga-based winery, owned by the Monte dei Paschi di Siena bank, sponsored the 20th Winter Olympics as an official partner. Management of the estate remains in the capable hands of president Giovanni Minetti and oenologist Danilo Drocco and production tops 6,000,000 bottles a year. Fontanafredda buys in some of its fruit from a pool of reliable producers, but has an impressive 90 hectares of its own under the care of fruitmaker Alberto Grasso. As for the wines themselves, Barolo Lazzarito '01 romped home to a resounding Three Glasses. Elegant notes of red berry fruit and dried flowers announce a full palate with well-gauged tannins that enabled this Barolo of enormous character to continue its winning streak. The fruity Barbera d'Alba Raimonda '04 also did very well, revealing notes of cherry, currant and cassis and fabulous length on the palate. Barolo Vigna La Rosa '01 is austere and balanced, Nebbiolo Marne Brune '04 is easy drinking with extremely enjoyable aromas, Moscato Moncucco is sweet but not too sweet, Barbera Papagena and Pamina '03 are powerful and rounded, and Alta Langa Brut Metodo Classico Vigna Gatinera '02 is well made with croissant-like aromas. The rest of this fine range is sound.

●	Barolo Lazzarito V. La Delizia '01	🍷🍷🍷	8
●	Barolo Fontanafredda V. La Rosa '01	🍷🍷	8
●	Barbera d'Alba Raimonda '04	🍷🍷	4*
●	Barolo Paiagallo V. La Villa '01	🍷🍷	7
○	Alta Langa V. Gatinera Brut '02	🍷🍷	5
●	Barbaresco Coste Rubìn '03	🍷🍷	6
●	Barbera d'Alba Sup. Papagena e Pamina '03	🍷🍷	4*
●	Nebbiolo d'Alba Marne Brune '04	🍷🍷	4*
○	Moscato d'Asti Moncucco '05	🍷🍷	4*
●	Diano d'Alba La Lepre '05	🍷	4
○	Roero Arneis Pradalupo '05	🍷	3

SERRALUNGA D'ALBA (CN)

Gabutti - Franco Boasso

b.ta Gabutti, 3a
12050 Serralunga d'Alba (CN)
tel. 0173613165
www.gabuttiboasso.com

With the help of his wife Marina and sons Claudio and Ezio, Franco Boasso transforms the grapes from his five and half hectares into an average of 30,000 bottles a year. Franco's plots all occupy good positions in the municipality of Serralunga. After the poor harvest of 2002, this year's line-up is missing the Barolos but the rest of the range more than makes up for their absence. Two interesting new table wines made their debut. Grappoli White and the Grappoli Red, both '05s, share their name with the farm holiday centre next to the cellar. Grappoli White is a pure Chardonnay with a pale straw-yellow colour and nuances of apple and citrus fruit. The palate is fresh and full of flavour with pleasant acidity. Grappoli Red is obtained from a blend of 50 per cent nebbiolo, 40 per cent barbera and merlot. The nebbiolo offers notes of rose and violet on the nose and big tannins and aromas of coffee and liquorice on the palate, the fruity barbera contributes hints of spice and acidity, and the merlot adds elegance and softness. We gave Two full Glasses to both Grappolis and to the other two wines proposed by the Boassos. The barrel-aged Barbera '05 flaunts a dark purplish colour, charming aromas of red berry fruit and spice, and a silky, elegant palate. Dolcetto Meriame '05 is fruity and heady with lots of tannins and nice length on the palate.

●	Barbera d'Alba '05	🍷🍷	4
●	Dolcetto d'Alba Meriame '05	🍷🍷	4
●	Grappoli Red	🍷🍷	5
○	Grappoli White	🍷	3*
●	Barolo Gabutti '00	ΥΥ	7
●	Barolo Serralunga '00	ΥΥ	7
●	Barolo Gabutti '01	ΥΥ	7
●	Barolo Serralunga '01	ΥΥ	7
●	Barolo Gabutti '97	ΥΥ	7
●	Barolo Gabutti '98	ΥΥ	7
●	Barolo Gabutti '99	ΥΥ	7

SERRALUNGA D'ALBA (CN)

Ettore Germano

Loc. Cerretta, 1
12050 Serralunga d'Alba (CN)
tel. 0173613528 - 0173613593
www.germanoettore.com

Sergio Germano's estate is finally up to a comfortable cruising speed. His spacious, well-equipped cellars facilitate work in the cellar and he has completely reorganized the vineyards to fill the huge gap left when his father, Ettore, passed away. Finally, the hail that has afflicted this zone of Serralunga all too often in recent years seems to have called a truce, allowing the family time to draw breath. Today, the estate totals around 12 hectares planted to vine located in Serralunga and Mondovì. Sergio has given full rein to his passion for whites, in particular riesling, that has led him to seek cooler site climates suitable for the cultivation of white grapes. If the results are anything to go by, his instinct is spot on and he is showing quite a talent for the vinification of both whites and reds. For the moment, the Barolo Cerretta remains top dog on the estate. With an extra year's bottle ageing under its belt, this majestic red presents close-knit tannic texture and concentrated aromas of aniseed and liquorice and make it every inch a Three Glass wine. The Barbera Vigna della Madre '04 reached our final tastings thanks to sensations of fruity fullness followed by long, refreshing after-aromas. But we were most surprised by the wonderful minerality of the two whites, the Chardonnay and Binel, a 50-50 blend of chardonnay and riesling. We are willing to bet that the pure Riesling soon to be released will also be a winner. In the meantime, sit back and enjoy this excellent range of wines.

●	Barolo Cerretta '01	🍷🍷🍷	7
●	Barbera d'Alba V. della Madre '04	🍷🍷	5
○	Langhe Bianco Binel '04	🍷🍷	4*
●	Langhe Rosso Balàu '04	🍷🍷	5
○	Langhe Chardonnay '05	🍷🍷	4*
●	Dolcetto d'Alba Vign. Lorenzino '05	🍷	4
●	Barolo Cerretta '98	🍸🍸🍸	7
●	Barolo Cerretta '00	🍸🍸	8
●	Barolo Prapò '00	🍸🍸	8
●	Barolo Prapò '01	🍸🍸	7

SERRALUNGA D'ALBA (CN)

Bruna Grimaldi

via Roddino
12050 Serralunga d'Alba (CN)
tel. 0173262094

Bruna Grimaldi and her husband Franco Fiorino met at the Institute of Oenology in Alba and in 1989 began to cultivate eight hectares in several of Langhe's municipalities. The estate's registered office is in Serralunga but the modern vinification cellars are located on the Grinzane Cavour plain. Beppe Caviola is consultant oenologist and Gian Piero Romana contributes his expertise as fruitmaker. The pair bottle almost all of their annual production for a total of 45,000 units released under a limited number of labels. From next year, a second Barolo based on the grapes from Grinzane Cavour will go into production. The estate's most interesting product is Barolo Badarina Vigna Regnola '01. Matured for 24 months in barriques and a further six in the bottle, it mingles notes of violet and dried flowers with nuances of vanilla, chocolate and coffee. The full-flavoured, elegant palate is capped by a richly textured finish. Two Glasses went to the Nebbiolo d'Alba Briccola '03, obtained from fruit grown in the municipal district of Diano d'Alba. It flaunts a blueberry and currant nose, velvety tannins and measured acidity. We also admired the fine performance from the Barbera d'Alba Superiore Scassa '04, aged for 15 months in new and used 900-litre casks. The nose offers estery, alcoholic sensations and the palate develops to reveal very minerally aromas and a long, agreeable finish. Good but not quite as good is the Dolcetto d'Alba Vigna San Martino '05, released in 12,000 easy-drinking bottles, and the Langhe Chardonnay Valscura '05, which has clear apricot and peach.

●	Barolo Badarina V. Regnola '01	🍷🍷	6
●	Nebbiolo d'Alba Briccola '03	🍷🍷	4*
●	Barbera d'Alba Sup. Scassa '04	🍷🍷	4*
●	Dolcetto d'Alba V. S. Martino '05	🍷	3
○	Langhe Chardonnay Valscura '05	🍷	3

SERRALUNGA D'ALBA (CN)

Paolo Manzone

Loc. Meriame, 1
12050 Serralunga d'Alba (CN)
tel. 0173613113 - 0173285527
www.barolomeriame.com

The view from the road that leads to Paolo Manzone's winery is so beautiful that you need to be careful not to drive off the edge. Here in Serralunga at Meriame, a handful of houses overlook the spectacular village of Castiglione Falletto where, surrounded by Barolo nebbiolo vineyards, we can make out the soft red silhouette of Manzone's recently renovated farmhouse, which is also a bed and breakfast with five rooms and a lovely pool for guests. Paolo's father Armando and his wife Luisella help him in the four hectares of vineyards at Serralunga and six at Sinio, which are planted to barbera, dolcetto and nebbiolo. The winery is comparatively new since its first harvest was in 1999. The more ambitious wines are aged mainly in 350-litre and 25-hectolitre oak barrels. Meriame, a Barolo selection, was not produced in 2002 but the Barolo Serralunga is well structured with marked flower and fruit aromas. We also tasted the 2001 version, which wasn't presented for last year's Guide, and were impressed by its aromas of leather, pipe tobacco and cherries. The palate has succulent chewy fruit and a pleasantly tannic finish. The rounded, elegant Nebbiolo d'Alba Mirinè 2004 is well made, as is the fresh, pleasantly sharp Barbera d'Alba Fiorenza 2005, which aged in wood for six months. Just one step lower is the delicious steel-aged Dolcetto d'Alba Magna 2005.

● Barolo Serralunga '01	two black glasses	6
● Nebbiolo d'Alba Mirinè '04	two black glasses	4*
● Barbera d'Alba Fiorenza '05	two black glasses	4*
● Barolo Serralunga '02	one black glass	6
● Dolcetto d'Alba Magna '05	one black glass	3
● Barolo Meriame '01	two white glasses	7
● Nebbiolo d'Alba Mirinè '03	two white glasses	4

SERRALUNGA D'ALBA (CN)

Luigi Pira

via XX Settembre, 9
12050 Serralunga d'Alba (CN)
tel. 0173613106

The winery is enthusiastically run by brothers Giampaolo and Romolo, assisted by their father Luigi, and is rightly considered one of the most interesting in the Serralunga area. But how could it be otherwise, with plots in some of the area's most prestigious vineyards – Marenca, Margheria and Rionda? But when the weather is bad, not even the finest technical expertise in the cellar will obtain results to satisfy a winery's ambitions and expectations. This is why no Barolos were made in 2002 and in consequence the range is somewhat reduced. The Barbera Ròche du Tarpùn 2004 is thick, dense, dark, meaty and intense. The wood is perceptible above all in the hints of charred oak, coffee and chocolate but it doesn't hamper the dynamic flavour, which is nicely supported by vibrant acidity. The complex Nebbiolo Le Ombre 2004 has mature, powerful aromas starting with hints of violets and very ripe red berry fruit over light vanilla sensations. A soft, submissive initial impact on the palate is followed by acidity and dryness and a touch of vegetality in the finish. The Dolcetto 2005 is chocolatey and richly textured but still shows freshness, with edgy tannins that will require more time to settle and a nice hint of almonds in the finish.

● Barbera d'Alba Ròche du Tarpùn '04	two black glasses	5
● Langhe Nebbiolo Le Ombre '04	two black glasses	5
● Dolcetto d'Alba '05	one black glass	4
● Barolo V. Rionda '00	three white glasses	8
● Barolo Vign. Marenca '01	three white glasses	8
● Barolo Vign. Marenca '97	three white glasses	8
● Barolo Vign. Marenca '00	two white glasses	8
● Barolo Vign. Margheria '00	two white glasses	7
● Barolo V. Rionda '01	two white glasses	8
● Barolo Vign. Margheria '01	two white glasses	7
● Barolo V. Rionda '99	two white glasses	8
● Barolo Vign. Marenca '99	two white glasses	8
● Barolo '01	two white glasses	6
● Barolo Vign. Margheria '99	two white glasses	7

Giovanni Rosso

Loc. Baudana, 6
12050 Serralunga d'Alba (CN)
tel. 0173613142
www.giovannirosso.com

Davide Rosso is the driving force who manages and symbolizes this winery, though no slight is implied to his parents Giovanni and Ester, who certainly do their bit behind the scenes, as in any self-respecting family business. You're unlikely to drop by the winery for a quick visit – a far more likely scenario is that you'll be driven by Davide himself across the nine hectares of vineyards in a four-wheel-drive Panda, weaving confidently through the rows of vines as he explains the details of each row according to its aspect, grape variety and age in an educational tour of some of the best vineyards in Serralunga. Behind Davide's infectious passion and enthusiasm are years of study, various stints elsewhere and an ongoing dialogue with anything better and different that the rest of the winemaking world produces. The result is a lucid and only superficially obvious production philosophy that calls for maximum effort in the vineyard and restraint in the cellar. The results are clear from the limited range of wines presented this year. The 2002 vintage was not good enough for a Barolo Ceretta to be made, and all the grapes were used in the Barolo Serralunga 2002, a good choice, judging by its quality. For a lesser wine, it is very coherent with warm aromas of bottled cherries and minerally earthy hints followed by an understated, fairly approachable, balanced palate and muted tannins. The Barbera Donna Margherita 2004 is good. Vibrant with dark fruit, it is generous and still quite tight on the nose but has nice weight and a meaty texture on the savoury palate.

● Barolo Serralunga '02	▼▼	6*
● Barbera d'Alba Donna Margherita '04	▼▼	4*
● Barolo Cerretta '01	▽▽	7
● Barolo Cerretta '00	▽▽	7
● Barolo Serralunga '00	▽▽	6
● Barolo Serralunga '01	▽▽	6
● Barolo Cerretta '97	▽▽	6
● Barolo Cerretta '98	▽▽	7
● Barolo Cerretta '99	▽▽	7

SERRALUNGA D'ALBA (CN)

Vigna Rionda - Massolino

P.zza Cappellano, 8
12050 Serralunga d'Alba (CN)
tel. 0173613138
www.massolino.it

The Massolino brothers always buck the trend. Nearly all the most important Langhe producers featured in this edition of the Guide decided not to produce a Barolo 2002 selection. Some were hit hard by the hailstorm in September of that year and were unable even to bottle a basic wine. Franco and Roberto, however, decided to release their best-known selections, Parafada and Margheria, as well as the Vigna Rionda Riserva. But it is quite probable that the 2003 version of their most famous award-winning wine will not see the light because it was not up to scratch. Let's start our review with the Barolo Parafada 2002, which is one of the best of that year. Red berry fruit, pipe tobacco, leather and vanilla on the nose precede well-judged tannins on the powerful, full-bodied palate with its long pleasant finish. The Barbera d'Alba Gisep also made it to the final tastings. It shows no ill effects from the heat of 2003 and is very concentrated in colour and on the nose, with aromas of blackcurrant, morello cherries and coffee. The palate is full-bodied and mouthfilling with a fresh, drinkable flavour. The Barolo Vigna Rionda Riserva 2000 is excellent, as usual. It aged in large oak barrels for 40 months and shows a very complex aroma profile including floral and fruity notes on a pleasantly spicy background. The juicy, tangy palate has ripe, harmonious tannins. The basic Barolo, austere Barolo Margheria, Chardonnay, Barbera d'Alba and Dolcetto all earned a well-deserved Two Glasses. One step behind are the Moscato d'Asti and Langhe Nebbiolo 2002.

● Barolo V. Rionda Ris. '00	▼▼	8
● Barolo Parafada '02	▼▼	7
● Barbera d'Alba Gisep '03	▼▼	5
● Barolo '02	▼▼	6
● Barolo Margheria '02	▼▼	7
○ Langhe Chardonnay '04	▼▼	4*
● Barbera d'Alba '05	▼▼	4*
● Dolcetto d'Alba '05	▼▼	4*
● Langhe Nebbiolo '02	▼	5
○ Moscato d'Asti di Serralunga '05	▼	4
● Barolo V. Rionda Ris. '90	▽▽▽	8
● Barolo V. Rionda Ris. '96	▽▽▽	8
● Barolo V. Rionda Ris. '97	▽▽▽	8
● Barolo V. Rionda Ris. '98	▽▽▽	8
● Barolo V. Rionda Ris. '99	▽▽▽	8

SPIGNO MONFERRATO (AL)

TRAVERSA - CASCINA BERTOLOTTO
VIA PIETRO PORRO, 70
15018 SPIGNO MONFERRATO (AL)
TEL. 014491223 - 014491551

Barbera Monferrato I Cheini 2005 is missing from the range of wines presented by Fabio Traversa because it has not been bottled yet, so we will be reviewing it in next year's Guide. The moscato-based Passito Surì di Bertolotto 2003 has an intense straw-yellow colour with golden highlights, hints of apricot and candied fruit on the nose and a palate with a harmonious finish free of any cloying. This is one of the best sweet wines in the province of Alessandria, and just 2,000 bottles are made each year. Neither of the Dolcetto d'Acqui wines was awarded Two Glasses this year. La Cresta 2005 lacks the overall harmony we have become used to while La Muïètte 2004, a Cascina Bertoletto vineyard selection, has vibrant fruity aromas but the palate is too challenging, with rugged tannins and imperfectly balanced acidity.
The La Tia table wine, from dried brachetto grapes, put on a good show with the classic brachetto aromas on the nose and a juicy, full-bodied, lingering palate with nice acidity. The Monferrato Bianco Il Barigi 2005, from favorita and cortese, is deep straw-yellow in colour with aromas of citrus and tropical fruit. In the mouth, deliciously tangy acidity adds interest and length.

○	Surì di Bertolotto '03	▼▼	6
●	Dolcetto d'Acqui La Muïètte '04	▼	4
●	La Tia '04	▼	5
●	Dolcetto d'Acqui La Cresta '05	▼	4
○	Monferrato Bianco Il Barigi '05	▼	4
●	La Tia '01	▽▽	5
●	La Tia '03	▽▽	5

STREVI (AL)

MARENCO
P.ZZA VITTORIO EMANUELE, 10
15019 STREVI (AL)
TEL. 0144363133 - 0144364942
www.marencovini.com

Michela, Patrizia and Doretta Marenco are a phenomenal team and have taken this Strevi winery to the front rank of upper Monferrato wineries. Much attention is devoted to the cultivation of native grape varieties, with full respect for the local area, in the 65 impeccably farmed hectares of this large estate. Moving on to our review of the wines tasted, we'll begin with the Barbera d'Asti Ciresa 2003. Its purple-red, almost inky colour with warm, bright highlights introduces rich, persistent aromas of blackberries and cherries that blend perfectly with hints of vanilla and sweet spices. The well-structured palate has beautifully judged acidity. The Dolcetto d'Acqui Marchesa 2005 has a nice intense red colour, elegant fruit and herbaceous aromas and a well-structured palate. The Moscato Scrapona 2005 has an attractive golden colour and the broad nose is rich in varietal aromas from the grape with hints of peaches and apricots. The palate is sweet but free of cloying sensations. The Moscato Passito Passrì di Scrapona is intriguingly full-bodied and mature. We also recommend the MuMa – from the names of the grapes, Muscaté, which is dialect for moscato, and Marenco – a dry moscato with a particularly enjoyable palate. Carialoso is another interesting white made from the rare native caricalasino grape.

●	Barbera d'Asti Ciresa '03	▼▼	6
○	Piemonte Moscato Passito Passrì di Scrapona '04	▼▼	6
○	MuMa '05	▼▼	4*
●	Brachetto d'Acqui Pineto '05	▼	5
○	Carialoso '05	▼	4
●	Dolcetto d'Acqui Marchesa '05	▼	4
○	Moscato d'Asti Scrapona '05	▼	4
●	Barbera d'Asti Ciresa '00	▽▽	5
●	Barbera d'Asti Ciresa '01	▽▽	6
○	Piemonte Moscato Passito Passrì di Scrapona '01	▽▽	6
○	Piemonte Moscato Passito Passrì di Scrapona '03	▽▽	6

STREVI (AL)

Vigne Regali
via Vittorio Veneto, 76
15019 Strevi (AL)
tel. 0144362600
www.vigneregali.com

Vigne Regali is just one of the wineries that make up the galaxy of Montalcino giant Banfi. The winery owns 50 of the 80 hectares of vineyards available, mainly planted to native Piedmontese grapes like barbera, dolcetto and cortese, although there are also international varieties such as chardonnay, sauvignon blanc and pinot, both nero and bianco. The international grape varieties are used in the winery's traditional Spumante production while in recent years Vigne Regali has also worked hard on still reds. The Barbera Banin 2003 is an intense red in colour with hints of black cherries, vanilla and hints of charred oak on the nose. The acidity is nicely supported by structure on the palate, with a long, enjoyable finish. The Dolcetto Argusto 2003 still has slightly rugged tannins in the mouth but the fresh acidity makes it particularly drinkable. The Dolcetto L'Ardì 2005 is more approachable on the palate and flaunts a lively ruby red colour as well as heady aromas on the nose. We also enjoyed the Brachetto Vigneto La Rosa, with its aromas of roses and raspberries, beautifully drinkable palate and fresh-tasting finish. The Gavi Principessa Gavia is fresh and harmonious and we also recommend the Moscato Strevi which has vibrant, delicate aromas and a beautifully sweet, but not cloying, palate. Turning to the sparklers, we liked the harmonious, well-made Banfi Brut Talento from chardonnay, pinot nero and bianco as well as the Tener. The other wines in the range are all good.

●	Barbera d'Asti Vign. Banin '03	🍷🍷	5
●	Dolcetto d'Acqui Argusto '03	🍷🍷	4*
○	Talento Banfi Brut M. Cl.	🍷🍷	4*
●	Brachetto d'Acqui Vign. La Rosa '05	🍷	4
●	Dolcetto d'Acqui L'Ardì '05	🍷	4
○	Gavi Principessa Gavia '05	🍷	4
○	Moscato d'Asti Strevi '05	🍷	4
○	Tener Spumante Brut	🍷	4
○	Alta Langa Cuvée Aurora '02	🍸🍸	5
○	Alta Langa Cuvée Aurora '99	🍸🍸	5

SUNO (NO)

Francesco Brigatti
via Olmi, 31
28019 Suno (NO)
tel. 032285037
www.vinibrigatti.it

We've been following this winery with interest in recent years, and it now makes its debut with a full profile, having made progress along the path of quality and territory focus. Traditionally, Brigatti's most important labels are the Colline Novaresi Motfrei and Motziflon, and this year we are reviewing the 2003 vintage of these wines. Motfrei, aged in small oak barrels, has warm aromas of bottled fruit reflected with evolved sensations on the palate, which is enlivened by bright savouriness and the wood is very nicely judged. The winery's long-standing top wine, Motziflon, is rather better. The nose shows the typical features of great Nebbiolos – violets and mint – and the palate has crisp fruit as well as lively but not over-assertive tannins. The winery's commitment to the local area is reflected in the fact that the two typical grape varieties of the Novara area, uva rara and vespolina, are fermented separately. The vespolina-based wine breezed away with Two Glasses, showing a lovely blend of spicy varietal aromas and hints of oak from the ageing vessels. The Uva Rara 2005 is the best wine of its type we tasted this year. Delicious aromas of roses, black cherries, redcurrants and spices are perfectly reflected on the palate that leads to a long, typically bitterish finish. Lastly, the erbaluce-based white Mottobello 2005 has a distinctively fresh, appetizing nose and interesting palate, and the Barbera 2005 is no more than well typed.

●	Colline Novaresi Rosso Motziflon '03	🍷🍷	4
○	Colline Novaresi Bianco V. Mottobello '05	🍷🍷	3*
●	Colline Novaresi Vespolina '05	🍷🍷	4
●	Colline Novaresi Nebbiolo V. Motfrei '03	🍷	4
●	Colline Novaresi Uva Rara '05	🍷	3
●	Colline Novaresi Barbera '05	🍷	4
●	Colline Novaresi Rosso Motziflon '01	🍸	4
○	Colline Novaresi Bianco V. Mottobello '04	🍸	3
●	Colline Novaresi Vespolina '04	🍸	4

TAGLIOLO MONFERRATO (AL)

CASTELLO DI TAGLIOLO
VIA CASTELLO, 1
15070 TAGLIOLO MONFERRATO (AL)
TEL. 014389195 - 014389197
www.castelloditagliolo.com

The headquarters of Castello di Tagliolo is inside the ancient residence, documented as long ago as 976, which has been owned by the Gentile family since 1498. In 1750, after the marriage of Teresa Gentile and Costantino Pinelli, the estate passed to the Pinelli Gentile family and today Oberto Pinelli Gentile and his son Luca run the winery with Franco Ferrero's help on the technical side. The very impressive range of wines presented for this year's Guide includes a particularly enjoyable Dolcetto di Ovada La Castagnola 2001, aged for a year in small wooden barrels and another three years in bottle before release. The result is a very fine wine, as the intense ruby red colour suggests. A rich swath of attractively fruity aromas with hints of vanilla and chocolate precede a full-bodied, harmonious palate with a long, lingering finish. The Dolcetto di Ovada Superiore 2003 is bright ruby red with heady, penetrating aromas and well-judged tannins on the palate, signing off with a bitterish finish. The Monferrato Rosso Nobile 2003, from barbera and cabernet sauvignon, is almost inky red in colour, with hints of bell peppers, black pepper, plums and morello cherries on the nose and a powerful, succulent palate. Lastly, the chardonnay, pinot bianco and riesling italico Bianco Nobile aged in tonneaux for several months.

●	Dolcetto di Ovada La Castagnola '01	TT	4*
●	Dolcetto di Ovada Sup. '03	TT	4
●	Monferrato Rosso Nobile '03	TT	3*
○	Bianco Nobile '04	T	3
●	Dolcetto di Ovada La Castagnola '00	YY	3

TASSAROLO (AL)

CINZIA BERGAGLIO
VIA GAVI, 29
15060 TASSAROLO (AL)
TEL. 0143342203

Wine has been made at Bergaglio for several generations but in the past, the seven hectares of vineyards in the Tassarolo and Rovereto areas produced grapes for direct sales or to go into unbottled wine. Only very small quantities of wine were bottled for family consumption. The turning point was 2002 when Elda placed the wheel in the sure hands of her daughter, Cinzia. With the help of her mother, her father Modesto, her husband Massimo and consultant Agostino Berruti, Cinzia began to sell a larger proportion of the overall production. The first wine released on the market was the Gavi Fornaci, followed by Gavi Grifone delle Roveri, which reached our final tastings with the 2005 vintage. The wine is obtained from cortese grapes grown in the Rovereto vineyards, Straw yellow in colour with greenish hues, it is nicely vibrant and lingering on the nose with floral hints and light tropical sensations that lead into a beautifully delicate, complex palate with pleasant, well-blended supporting acidity and a lingering, typically bitterish finish. The grapes in the Gavi Fornaci 2005, which takes its name from the old brickworks in these clayey hills, are grown in vineyards in the Tassarolo area. This wine is slightly less complicated than the Grifone, with floral and fruity aromas on the nose followed by a savoury, lingering palate.

○	Gavi del Comune di Gavi Grifone delle Roveri '05	TT	3*
○	Gavi del Comune di Tassarolo Fornaci '05	TT	3*
○	Gavi del Comune di Tassarolo Fornaci '03	YY	3

TORINO

Franco M. Martinetti
via San Francesco da Paola, 18
10123 Torino
tel. 0118395937

Over the years, we have described Franco Maria Martinetti's class, style and determination, all of which have enabled him to make great wines. But until now, we have barely mentioned his two young sons, who are playing an increasingly important role in their father's activity. Guido, the elder son, is involved in winemaking as well as in a substantial high-quality ice cream business. Michele works on the marketing and sales of the many wines produced here. Eleven wines were presented to us this year, ranging across all the most important Piedmont types and designated areas. Five of these made it to the final selection in this year's Guide, which indicates a very high standard of quality. Let's begin with the Barolo Marasco. Even in a difficult year like 2002, its aristocratic character comes through in aromas of redcurrants, cherries and chocolate on the nose and a subtly tannic, full-bodied palate with a long, enjoyable finish. The Barbera d'Asti Montruc and Monferrato Sul Bric 2004 both performed very well indeed. Both are rich in fruity pulp and juice, with a long, satisfying, fresh-tasting palate. The two whites are on top form, both the fragrant Gavi Minaia, and the Colli Tortonesi Bianco Martin made from timorasso grapes, which improves every year and meets with increasing approval. The other wines are all very good, with a special mention for the Brut Quarantatre, freisa-based Colli Tortonesi Rosso Lauren and croatina-based Colli Tortonesi Georgette.

●	Barolo Marasco '02	▼▼	8
●	Barbera d'Asti Sup. Montruc '04	▼▼	6
○	Colli Tortonesi Bianco Martin '04	▼▼	7
○	Gavi Minaia '04	▼▼	6
●	Monferrato Rosso Sul Bric '04	▼▼	6
○	Brut M. Cl. Quarantatre '02	▼▼	6
●	Colli Tortonesi Rosso Georgette '04	▼▼	6
●	Colli Tortonesi Rosso Lauren '04	▼▼	6
●	Barbera d'Asti Bric dei Banditi '05	▼▼	4*
○	Alcedo	▼▼	7
●	Barolo Marasco '00	▽▽▽	8
●	Monferrato Rosso Sul Bric '00	▽▽▽	6
●	Barolo Marasco '01	▽▽▽	8

TORTONA (AL)

La Colombera
fraz. Vho
s.da Comunale per Vho, 7
15057 Tortona (AL)
tel. 0131867795
www.lacolomberavini.it

If anyone had told Pier Carlo Semino a few years ago that his son Lorenzo would take part in the Olympics and his daughter Elisa would be running the winery, he would probably have laughed and carried on with his usual labours in the vineyard and cellar. But this year Lorenzo was part of the national snowboard team, and for some time Elisa has been the driving force behind La Colombera sales, and much more. Since she graduated in oenology, this motivated young woman has supervised the winemaking and commercial and promotional side of the winery. This year, the red wine called Elisa is back in the spotlight after an absence brought on by the fraught 2002 vintage. It's a monovarietal Barbera aged in barrique for 12 months with warm red berry fruit and spices on the nose. As usual, the steel-aged Barbera Vegia Rampana 2004 is very good indeed, with a bright purple-red colour and all the finest sensory perceptions of the grape. The nibiò-based Suciaja – the grape is related to dolcetto – is aged in wood and has striking balance with good nose-palate consistency. The white made from timorasso grapes lived up to our expectations and went through to the finals. This year, it is one of the best in the Tortona area, where this gem of a native variety is particularly widely planted. We also liked the croatina-based red and the cortese-based white, Bricco Bartolomeo 2005.

○	Colli Tortonesi Bianco '04	▼▼	5
●	Piemonte Barbera Elisa '03	▼▼	5
●	Colli Tortonesi Rosso Suciaja '03	▼▼	5
●	Colli Tortonesi Rosso Vegia Rampana '04	▼▼	4*
●	Colli Tortonesi Croatina '04	▼	5
○	Colli Tortonesi Bianco Bricco Bartolomeo '05	▼	2*
●	Piemonte Barbera Elisa '01	▽▽	5
●	Piemonte Barbera Elisa '00	▽▽	5
●	Piemonte Barbera Elisa '99	▽▽	5
●	Colli Tortonesi Rosso Suciaja '02	▽▽	5

TORTONA (AL)

Claudio Mariotto
fraz. Vho
s.da per Sarezzano, 29
15057 Tortona (AL)
tel. 0131868500
www.claudiomariotto.it

Tortona has been a wine-producing area for centuries and unlike other places, where growers have become managers, here the producers have remained farmers. Claudio Mariotto is one such. He supervises the whole production process for his wines from vineyard, to cellar, to sales. The two 2004 Timorassos are both excellent. Pitasso is a selection from Claudio's oldest vineyards and is recognized as one of the best wines made with this native grape variety, which is carving an increasingly large niche for itself on Italy's winemaking scene. The most distinctive features of this great white, which is also very suitable for ageing, are very minerally sensations, warm fruity aromas and an outstandingly lingering palate. It's another Three Glass wine for Piedmont. Derthona shares some of these distinctive traits, although it is grassier on the nose. The cortese-based Profilo 2005 is another leading white that shows fragrant with a pleasant drinkable flavour. The reds are all of a high standard, from the Poggio del Rosso 2003, a barbera selection aged in small oak barrels, which is powerful and rich in extract with clear red berry fruit and cocoa powder on the nose, to the Vho, also barbera-based and aged in wood, with its unique combination of structure and drinkability. The pleasantly fragrant Territorio, a steel-aged barbera, and Dolcetto Campo del Gatto, are both good and both from 2005.

○	Colli Tortonesi Bianco Pitasso '04	🍷🍷🍷	5
○	Colli Tortonesi Bianco Derthona '04	🍷🍷	5
●	Colli Tortonesi Rosso Vho '04	🍷🍷	5
●	Colli Tortonesi Rosso Poggio del Rosso '03	🍷🍷	6
●	Colli Tortonesi Rosso Campo del Gatto '05	🍷🍷	4*
●	Colli Tortonesi Rosso Territorio '05	🍷🍷	4*
○	Colli Tortonesi Bianco Coccalina '05	🍷	4
○	Colli Tortonesi Bianco Profilo '05	🍷	4

TREISO (CN)

Orlando Abrigo
fraz. Cappelletto, 5
12050 Treiso (CN)
tel. 0173630232
www.orlandoabrigo.it

Giovanni Abrigo grows mainly traditional local grape varieties, with a small amount of merlot, chardonnay and sauvignon, on his 12-hectare estate. The vineyards are situated in prestigious zones of the Treiso municipal area. Giovanni presented many wines this year, including 6,000 bottles of an outstanding garnet-red Barbaresco Rongallo 2003 that has loads of power and elegance. The nose gives plums, violets and pipe tobacco while the palate is very well-structured with vigorous, ripe tannins and clear hints of chocolate and liquorice in the finish. The Barbaresco Montersino 2003 is more austere and slower to open out but once it does, it is extremely impressive with fruity and floral sensations and evidence of shrewd barrique ageing. The Barbera Roreto 2004 is fresh and fruity with a satisfying palate. Barbera Mervisano 2004 is made from late-harvested grapes. More complex and powerful, it gives clearly defined aromas of ripe red fruit, spices, chocolate, an edge of acidity and alluring tannins. Nebbiolo Settevie has aromas of plums, violets and balsamic hints on the nose introducing glossy tannins in a pleasantly drinkable palate with fresh-tasting acidity. The elegant Livraie 2003 is 100 per cent merlot and shows well balanced with nice fruit and discreet oak from the barriques. The basic Barbaresco, fruity and heady Dolcetto are good, as are the two whites, D'Amblè and Très, which provide a good illustration of the sensory perceptions from sauvignon and chardonnay grapes respectively.

●	Barbaresco V. Rongallo '03	🍷🍷	6
●	Barbaresco V. Montersino '03	🍷🍷	6
●	Langhe Rosso Livraie '03	🍷🍷	6
●	Barbera d'Alba Mervisano '04	🍷🍷	5
●	Langhe Nebbiolo Settevie '04	🍷🍷	4*
●	Barbaresco '03	🍷	6
●	Barbera d'Alba V. Roreto '04	🍷	4
●	Dolcetto d'Alba V. dell'Erto '05	🍷	4
○	Langhe Bianco D'Amblè '05	🍷	4
○	Langhe Chardonnay Très '05	🍷	4
●	Barbaresco V. Rongallo '00	▽▽	6
●	Barbaresco V. Rongallo '01	▽▽	6
●	Barbaresco '02	▽▽	6
●	Barbaresco V. Montersino '00	▽▽	6
●	Barbaresco V. Montersino '01	▽▽	6

TREISO (CN)

Ca' del Baio

via Ferrere, 33
12050 Treiso (CN)
tel. 0173638219
www.cadelbaio.com

The Grasso family's wines have taken giant steps in recent years. The commitment of Giulio, his wife Luciana and elder daughter Paola is now yielding highly satisfactory results in the standard of quality achieved and encouraging sales figures. The owners' production policy has always been tempered by healthy country caution, which recommends taking one small step forward at a time. This explains why a winery with about 21 hectares of vineyards, some in famous Barberesco crus like Asili, Pora, Marcarini and Valgrande, has not made more of a name for itself in the past. The cellar is at last operating and, with the help of consultant Beppe Caviola, Giulio has decided to take the final, ambitious step and processing all the estate's grapes himself. So there are two new Barberescos on the list this year, Marcarini 2003, available now, and Pora 2004, for which we'll have to wait two more years. The highest accolade was not forthcoming this year but the three 2003 Barbarescos came very close. We liked the velvety, elegant Asili while the Marcarini has good personality based on deep fruit. The Valgrande, aged in once-used wooden barrels, is a little more edgy but very complex. The quality of the range is demonstrated by the fact that many of the wines were awarded Two Glasses and are sold at very affordable prices, especially the very fragrant Moscato. The Barbaresco Valgrande 1999 is excellent and deserved Three retrospective Glasses.

●	Barbaresco Asili '03	2 glasses (grey)	6*
●	Barbaresco Macarini '03	2 glasses (grey)	6*
●	Barbaresco Valgrande '03	2 glasses	6
●	Langhe Nebbiolo Bric del Baio '04	2 glasses	4
●	Langhe Rosso Incanto '04	2 glasses	4
●	Dolcetto d'Alba Lodoli '05	2 glasses	4
○	Langhe Chardonnay Sermine '05	2 glasses	5
○	Moscato d'Asti '05	2 glasses	4
○	Langhe Chardonnay Luna d'Agosto '05	1 glass	4
●	Barbaresco Valgrande '99	3 glasses (white)	6
●	Barbaresco Valgrande '01	2 glasses (white)	6
●	Barbaresco Asili '01	2 glasses (white)	6

TREISO (CN)

Ada Nada

loc. Rombone
via Ausario, 12b
12050 Treiso (CN)
tel. 0173638127
www.barbaresco.com

Giancarlo and Ada Nada skilfully process the grapes from their nine hectares of vineyards in Rombone, in the municipal area of Treiso, helped by their daughters Annalisa and Sara. The varieties are those typical of the area – nebbiolo, barbera and dolcetto – and annual production is around 50,000 bottles per year. After missing the 2002 vintage, the Barbarescos from 2003 have now been released. Cichin is intense ruby red with garnet hues and broad, lingering aromas of red berry fruit, spices and pipe tobacco. The palate reveals hints of fruit, chocolate and spices and the tannins blend well with the acidity. Valeirano opens out more slowly and after aeration releases its aromas of plums and dried roses with spices and balsam. Both wines were awarded Two Glasses, as were the Barbera Salgà 2003 and the Langhe La Bisbetica 2003. The former is deep purple in colour with aromas of black cherries and pepper on the nose. Its acidity offers good support on the palate to the tannins and the pleasant flavour lingers. The Bisbetica is a perfect marriage of two grape varieties and in fact the blend of nebbiolo and barbera is now a classic in the Langhe. The tannins and heady aromas of the nebbiolo fuse seamlessly with barbera's fruit and acidity. Finally, the purplish Dolcetto Autinot has heady fruit aromas and a satisfying palate.

●	Barbaresco Cichin '03	2 glasses	7
●	Barbaresco Valeirano '03	2 glasses	7
●	Barbera d'Alba Salgà '03	2 glasses	5
●	Langhe Rosso La Bisbetica '03	2 glasses	6
●	Dolcetto d'Alba Autinot '05	1 glass	4
●	Barbaresco Valeirano '00	2 glasses (white)	7
●	Barbaresco Cichin '01	2 glasses (white)	7
●	Barbaresco Cichin '00	2 glasses (white)	7
●	Barbaresco Elisa '00	2 glasses (white)	7
●	Barbaresco Valeirano '01	2 glasses (white)	7
●	Barbaresco Cichin '99	2 glasses (white)	7
●	Barbaresco Valeirano '99	2 glasses (white)	7

TREISO (CN)

FIORENZO NADA
LOC. ROMBONE
VIA AUSARIO, 12C
12050 TREISO (CN)
TEL. 0173638254
www.nada.it

Nada is a small but well-established country winery in the Barbaresco DOCG. The winery headquarters and six hectares of vineyards are at Treiso, in two of the designated area's classic subzones, Rombone and Manzola. Bruno and his father Fiorenzo produce just a few wines with scrupulous care, a winning formula adopted to appeal to real Barbaresco enthusiasts. The wines show consistently high quality every year, which they maintain through experience in the vineyards, a touch of traditional wisdom and a good dose of respect for the local area. The two 2003 Barberescos are excellent, both the Rombone selection and the standard-label, which combines the grapes from five different plots. The Rombone is almost garnet ruby red with a vigorous nose of fruit and spice aromas. The well-structured palate has prominent tannins and black berry fruit echoing the nose, alongside a hint of black tea leaves, which lingers through the long finish. The basic Barbaresco shows a slight youthful boisterousness but the aromas are warm and broad with well-rounded tannins, acidity and alcohol nicely blended and a good lingering flavour. The Seifile 2003 is a blend of barbera with a dash of nebbiolo. The colour hints at its powerful structure, the nose has concentrated black berry fruit and the fruity palate is weighty with alcohol and tannins, closing in a lingering finish. The Barbera is delicate and distinctively drinkable while the Dolcetto is very true to type, showing fruity and heady on the nose with a gutsy, almond-veined palate.

●	Barbaresco Rombone '03	🍷🍷	8
●	Langhe Rosso Seifile '03	🍷🍷	8
●	Barbaresco '03	🍷🍷	7
●	Barbera d'Alba '04	🍷🍷	5
●	Dolcetto d'Alba '05	🍷🍷	4*
●	Barbaresco '01	YYY	7
●	Langhe Rosso Seifile '01	YYY	8
●	Langhe Rosso Seifile '96	YYY	8
●	Langhe Rosso Seifile '95	YYY	8
●	Seifile '93	YYY	8
●	Barbaresco Rombone '97	YYY	8
●	Barbaresco Rombone '99	YYY	8
●	Barbaresco Rombone '00	YY	8
●	Langhe Rosso Seifile '00	YY	8
●	Barbaresco Rombone '01	YY	8

TREISO (CN)

PELISSERO
VIA FERRERE, 10
12050 TREISO (CN)
TEL. 0173638430
www.pelissero.com

The splendid Barbaresco winery expertly run by Giorgio and Cristina Pelissero offers a cloudless sky of quality. Their ten wines are a sumptuous calling card that tells the story of a dream come true: to make a range of top-quality wines. From the three 2003 Barbarescos, Vanotu and Tulin jostle for first place on our scale of preference. The former is dense garnet red in colour with broad aromas, including balsamic hints and black berry fruit. The palate is well-rounded, mouthfilling, tannic and nicely crafted with good balance of wood, acidity and alcohol. Tulin is equally good. Its colour is more austere, and the aromas have hints of spices and blackcurrants, while the elegant palate has powerful tannic impact and a long lingering finish. The third Barbaresco, Nubiola, is nicely drinkable overall and just a little less complex and structured than the other two. The winery's other pedigree wine is the Langhe Long Now 2004, a blend of barbera and nebbiolo from Neviglie. Dense ruby red introduces an enthralling nose with juicy fruit and hints of vanilla before intriguing tannins meld on the palate with warm alcohol to sign off with a very long finish. The Barbera Piani 2005 and the Dolcetto Augenta are both very good indeed while the Nebbiolo, Dolcetto Munfrina, Favorita and Fresia are more than just well typed.

●	Barbaresco Tulin '03	🍷🍷	7
●	Barbaresco Vanotu '03	🍷🍷	8
●	Langhe Rosso Long Now '04	🍷🍷	6
●	Barbaresco Nubiola '03	🍷🍷	6
●	Barbera d'Alba Piani '05	🍷🍷	4*
●	Dolcetto d'Alba Augenta '05	🍷🍷	4*
●	Langhe Nebbiolo '05	🍷	4
●	Dolcetto d'Alba Munfrina '05	🍷	3
○	Langhe Favorita '05	🍷	2*
●	Langhe Freisa '05	🍷	2*
●	Barbaresco Vanotu '01	YYY	8
●	Barbaresco Vanotu '95	YYY	8
●	Barbaresco Vanotu '97	YYY	8
●	Barbaresco Vanotu '99	YYY	8
●	Barbaresco Vanotu '00	YY	8

TREISO (CN)

Vignaioli Elvio Pertinace

Loc. Pertinace, 2
12050 Treiso (CN)
tel. 0173442238
www.pertinace.it

The Cantina Pertinace co-operative was set up in the early 1970s. The 15 member growers own a total of 70 hectares, almost all of which are in the municipal area of Treiso. The many wines presented are all well typed and excellent value for money. Since this year they all easily earned at least One Glass, let's move quickly on to an analysis of the bottles that most impressed our tasters, starting with the Barbaresco Nervo 2003, which made it through to the Three Glass finals. The colour is ruby red with garnet flecks and introduces red berry fruit and spices on the nose before a silky, tannic palate unveils considerable intensity and a long finish. The Barbaresco Marcarini, which has hints of spice and chocolate, and the fruity, elegant Castellizzano with its sweet, glossy tannins, are both very good. The Langhe Pertinace, from cabernet sauvignon, nebbiolo and barbera, combines complex aromas with powerful structure. The Barbera d'Asti 2003, from excellent vineyards at Agliano, is lively with ripe fruit, robust alcohol and rich extract attractively offset acidity. The two 2005 Dolcettos, Nervo and Castellizzano, have pleasant fruity aromas and appealingly bitterish, almond-like notes in the finish. The rest of the wines are enjoyable and very well made.

●	Barbaresco Nervo '03	▼▼	6
●	Barbaresco Castellizzano '03	▼▼	6
●	Barbaresco Marcarini '03	▼▼	6
●	Langhe Pertinace '03	▼▼	5
●	Barbera d'Asti Gratia Plena '03	▼▼	4*
●	Dolcetto d'Alba Castellizzano '05	▼▼	4*
●	Dolcetto d'Alba Vigneto Nervo '05	▼▼	4*
●	Barbaresco '03	▼	6
●	Langhe Nebbiolo '04	▼	4
●	Barbera d'Alba '05	▼	4
●	Dolcetto d'Alba '05	▼	4
○	Langhe Chardonnay '05	▼	4
○	Langhe Chardonnay S. Stefanetto '05	▼	4

VERDUNO (CN)

F.lli Alessandria

via B. Valfré, 59
12060 Verduno (CN)
tel. 0172470113
www.fratellialessandria.it

Few Piedmontese wineries can boast such charmingly aristocratic headquarters as Fratelli Alessandria, situated close to the historic centre of this small Langhe town. The elegant, noble lines of the house reveal its 18th-century origins and the cellars date back to the 19th century. The wines produced here quickly acquired an international reputation. Gian Alessandria runs the winery helped by his son, Vittore, and winemaker Franco Alessandria. Together they manage the 12 hectares of vineyards and obtain 60,000 bottles a year. The leading wine in the range is the Barolo San Lorenzo 2001, which is in a class of its own. The interesting nose, with aromas of red berry fruit, violets and quinine, is followed by a harmonious, stylish palate with full body and engaging succulence. In fact, it is so good we gave it Three Glasses. The 2002 vintage Barolo Monvigliero and Gramolere were not released so the grapes from those vineyards were used in the basic Barolo, which picked up Two Glasses. The Barbera d'Alba La Priora 2004 made it through to our finals. Lively ripe red berry fruit on the nose ushers in a well-rounded palate refreshed by nice acidity. The Langhe Rosso Luna 2004, a blend of nebbiolo, barbera and freisa, is the only wine to be aged in barrique, where it stays for 15 months. We would also point out the care taken over less demanding wines, of which the most remarkable is the characterful Verduno Pelaverga, which has bags of personality. The Dolcetto d'Alba and the Barbera, both from 2005, are good.

●	Barolo S. Lorenzo '01	▼▼▼	7
●	Barbera d'Alba Sup. La Priora '04	▼▼	4*
●	Barolo '02	▼▼	6
●	Langhe Rosso Luna '04	▼▼	4
●	Verduno Pelaverga '05	▼▼	4
●	Dolcetto d'Alba '05	▼	4
●	Barbera d'Alba '05	▼	4
●	Barolo Monvigliero '95	▽▽▽	7
●	Barolo Monvigliero '01	▽▽	7
●	Barolo S. Lorenzo '00	▽▽	7
●	Barolo Gramolere '01	▽▽	7
●	Barolo Monvigliero '97	▽▽	7
●	Barolo Monvigliero '99	▽▽	7
●	Barolo S. Lorenzo '99	▽▽	7

VERDUNO (CN)

Bel Colle
fraz. Castagni, 56
12060 Verduno (CN)
tel. 0172470196

The Bel Colle winery is situated on a lovely hill on the scenic road from La Morra to Verduno. The modern cellar is equipped with all the latest vinification technology for processing the grapes from the extensive, varied vineyards in Langhe and Roero. Total production is 150,000 bottles per year. The range of wines presented for this year's Guide met with our general approval and credit is due above all to skilled winemaker Paolo Torchio, the cellar manager. The Barolo Monvigliero 2001 made it to our final tastings thanks to a ruby red colour and unusually stylish, complex aromas of quinine, violets, dried flowers, blackcurrants and blueberries. The hints of fruit reappear on the palate, nicely supported by rich texture and full-bodied structure, with well-gauged extract harmoniously contributing to the long, broad finish. The Barbaresco Roncaglie 2003 also performed very well, with its enthralling spicy, estery nose and tannin-forward, savoury hints on the palate set against background freshness, which will undoubtedly extend its ageing potential. The Verduno Pelaverga 2005 is very fragrant, showing prominent white pepper and damp earth on the nose and a succulent, stylish palate. The moreish Dolcetto d'Alba 2005 is just a step behind the two Bel Colle whites, Roero Arneis and Favorita, both from 2005.

● Barolo Monvigliero '01	🍷🍷	6*
● Barbaresco Roncaglie '03	🍷🍷	6
● Dolcetto d'Alba '05	🍷🍷	4*
● Verduno Pelaverga '05	🍷🍷	4*
○ Langhe Favorita '05	🍷	4
○ Roero Arneis '05	🍷	4
● Barolo Monvigliero '00	YY	6
● Barbaresco Roncaglie '00	YY	6
● Barolo Monvigliero '97	YY	6
● Barolo Monvigliero '98	YY	6
● Barolo Monvigliero '99	YY	6

VERDUNO (CN)

G. B. Burlotto
via Vittorio Emanuele, 28
12060 Verduno (CN)
tel. 0172470122
www.burlotto.com

After the unfavourable weather of summer 2002, Marina Burlotto and her son Fabio Alessandria, who has been the family's brilliant winemaker for several years now, decided not to bottle any Barolos from that vintage. The Barolo Monvigliero 2001, which is still maturing, will not be officially released for another year. So in the absence of the bigger fish, Fabio demonstrated his considerable skills by taking the Barbera d'Alba Aves 2004 to the Three Glass finals. It is a very deep ruby red with purplish tinges and the typical features of the 2004 growing year – intensity, fresh fruit aromas and palate-trimming acidity – as well as power and length in the mouth accompanied by good, rounded body. Over the years, Fabio has enjoyed particular success with sauvignon and he presented us with two versions: Langhe Viridis, fermented in stainless steel, and Langhe Dives, which spends more than ten months in 500-litre tonneaux during fermentation and maturation. The more structured Dives 2004 can hold its own against the best Sauvignons in Italy. The rich varietal aromas of smoke-nuanced gooseberries and redcurrants are never excessive and the palate opens with full body and a nice buttery texture, leading to a slow finish supported all the way by good acidity. The Viridis 2005 has simpler aromas with clearly defined herbaceousness, and the palate is sharper and rangier, although no less interesting. Finally, we also liked the warm Langhe Mores 2003, a 50-50 blend of barbera and nebbiolo, the complex Nebbiolo 2004 and the excellent still Freisa 2004.

● Barbera d'Alba Aves '04	🍷🍷	5
○ Langhe Bianco Dives '04	🍷🍷	4*
● Langhe Mores '03	🍷🍷	5
● Langhe Freisa '04	🍷🍷	4
● Langhe Nebbiolo '04	🍷🍷	4
○ Langhe Bianco Viridis '05	🍷🍷	4
⊙ Rosato Teres '05	🍷	4
● Verduno Pelaverga '05	🍷	4
● Barolo Vign. Cannubi '00	YY	7
● Barolo Vign. Monvigliero '00	YY	7
● Barolo Acclivi '00	YY	7
● Barolo Acclivi '01	YY	7
● Barolo Vign. Cannubi '01	YY	7
● Barolo Vign. Cannubi '99	YY	7
● Barolo Vign. Monvigliero '99	YY	7

VERDUNO (CN)

CASTELLO DI VERDUNO
VIA UMBERTO I, 9
12060 VERDUNO (CN)
TEL. 0172470284
www.castellodiverduno.com

The Burlotto sisters have created an oasis of food, drink and accommodation that is practically unparalleled in the Langhe: a restaurant, a charming hotel in the fortress residence overlooking the town of Verduno, a holiday centre and a beautiful ageing and bottling cellar run by Gabriella Burlotto and her husband Franco Bianco. The wines are fermented in a pretty farmhouse in Barbaresco. Three of the wines from the castle made it to the final tastings this year. We particularly liked the superlative version of Barolo Massara 2001, aged in large oak barrels for 28 months and in glass for a dozen more. The colour is pale ruby red and the nose reveals all the class of a traditional Barolo. Aromas of red berry fruit and dried flowers mingle with quinine and roses. The palate is stylish and harmonious, taking you through to a long finish, softened by subtle extract. At last, Castello di Verduno can savour the long-awaited satisfaction of Three Glasses, thanks to this Massara 2001. The Barbaresco Rabajà 2001, with hints of green herbs, black pepper and pipe tobacco, is excellent, like the Barolo Monvigliero from a 30-year-old plot in the Verduno vineyard of the same name. The Barbaresco Faset 2001 lived up to expectations. Traditional in style with raspberries and violets on the nose, it shows full-bodied and succulent on the front palate. We never tire of praising the work this winery puts into promoting the pelaverga grape and Basadone is one of our favourite everyday wines: peppery, minerally and very drinkable. The Barbera is good and the other wines are enjoyable.

● Barolo Massara '01	TTT	7
● Barbaresco Rabajà '01	TT	6
● Barolo Monvigliero '01	TT	7
● Barbaresco Faset '01	TT	6
● Barbera d'Alba Bricco del Cuculo '04	TT	4*
● Langhe Nebbiolo '05	TT	4*
● Verduno Basadone '05	TT	4*
● Dolcetto d'Alba Campot '05	T	4
● Barbaresco Faset '00	YY	7
● Barolo Massara Ris. '97	YY	8
● Barolo Massara '99	YY	7
● Barolo Massara Ris. '96	YY	8
● Barbaresco Faset '98	YY	7
● Barolo Massara '98	YY	7

VEZZA D'ALBA (CN)

PIOIERO
CASCINA PIOIERO, 1
12040 VEZZA D'ALBA (CN)
TEL. 017365492
www.pioiero.com

Roero's small wineries are just waiting to be discovered. Nearly all the local towns have a dynamic winemaking scene which is growing fast in quality and renown. We have been keeping our eye on the Rabino family's winery. Remember we are not in Valmaggiore, the most famous nebbiolo vineyard in Roero, at Vezza, but heading towards Castellino. After a kilometre of unmade road through orchards and hazelnut trees, a characteristic, tastefully restored farmhouse comes into view.
It has been adapted for use as a house and winery in a lush hollow surrounded by well cared-for vineyards and a pond, the home of heron and many kinds of fish. In this little Eden, skilled grower Antonio Rabino is helped by his wife Bruna and occasionally by their sons Danilo, Emanuele and Gianluca. The six hectares of vineyards produce 30,000 bottles a year under the supervision of consultants Elio Ressia and Giuseppe Cavallo in the vineyard, and Gianfranco Cordero in the cellar. The wines produced all have strong territorial links and are sold at very reasonable prices. Our tasters were particularly impressed by the Roero Superiore 2004 which flaunts generous fresh fruit streaked with spices on the nose and a powerful, stylish palate. The Barbera 2004 is also excellent, showing a glorious nose of blackberries, morello cherries and blackcurrants followed by an acidic palate. Both of these wines aged mainly in large oak barrels. The Arneis is fresh-tasting with crisp floral aromas and a minerally palate. The Nebbiolo and Favorita are both well typed and appetizing.

● Roero Sup. '04	TT	4*
● Barbera d'Alba Sup. '04	TT	4
○ Roero Arneis '05	TT	4
● Nebbiolo d'Alba '04	T	3
○ Langhe Favorita '05	T	3
● Roero Sup. '01	YY	4
● Roero Sup. '02	YY	4
● Barbera d'Alba Sup. '03	YY	4
● Roero Sup. '03	YY	4

VIGNALE MONFERRATO (AL)

Giulio Accornero e Figli

Ca' Cima, 1
15049 Vignale Monferrato (AL)
tel. 0142933317
www.accornerovini.it

This winery is consistently in the front rank of Alessandria winemaking and is a sure guarantee of quality for the consumer. Many producers were wrong-footed by unfavourable years like 2003, which was unusually hot, and their results therefore may fluctuate in quality. But producers who showed more expertise in managing the harvest and fermentation succeeded in producing remarkable wines. Talented Ermanno Accornero presented us with two excellent 2003s, the Barbera Superiore Bricco Battista and the Monferrato Rosso Centenario. Some 12,000 units of the Barbera go into bottle each year. Inky in colour, it gives a vibrant, complex nose and a smooth entry on the palate followed by a lingering finish. The Centenario is a blend of 80 per cent cabernet sauvignon and the rest barbera, and 4,500 bottles were produced. It, too, made it to our final tastings for its astonishing balance. The nose has red berry fruit and sweet spices from its long stay in oak, which serve as a prelude to the unusually stylish impact on the palate. Ermanno decided to delay release of the Barbera del Monferrato Giulin 2005 because he does not consider it ready for sale. The Grignolino Bricco del Bosco 2005 and the non-sparkling Freisa La Bernardina 2005 both faithfully reflect the Monferrato terroir that the Accornero winery interprets so wonderfully well. Finally, we were not disappointed by the sweet, fragrant malvasia-based Casorzo Brigantino 2005 or the Monferrato Bianco Fonsìna 2005.

●	Barbera del M.to Sup. Bricco Battista '03	TT	6
●	Monferrato Rosso Centenario '03	TT	6
●	Grignolino del M.to Casalese Bricco del Bosco '05	TT	4*
●	Monferrato Freisa La Bernardina '05	TT	3*
●	Casorzo Brigantino '05	T	4
○	Monferrato Bianco Fonsìna '05	T	4
●	Barbera del M.to Sup. Bricco Battista '98	YYY	6
●	Barbera del M.to Sup. Bricco Battista '99	YYY	6

VIGNALE MONFERRATO (AL)

Bricco Mondalino

reg. Mondalino, 5
15049 Vignale Monferrato (AL)
tel. 0142933204
www.briccomondalino.it

This year, we were not able to taste the two leading wines from the talented Mauro Gaudio. The Barbera d'Asti Selezione Gaudium Magnum was not released because Mauro did not consider the 2002 vintage good enough and the Grignolino Bricco Mondalino had not been bottled at the time of going to press so we will taste and review it next year. Of the wines that have been released, we particularly liked the Barbera del Monferrato Superiore 2004. Its 25,000 bottles contain a wine with a deep ruby red colour introducing a vibrantly generous nose subtly laced with hints of morello cherries and wild berries. The palate is fruity, rounded and lingering, signing off with a long, complex finish. The basic Grignolino also gave a good account of itself. The pale ruby red is tinged with orangey hues and the nose shows well-defined hints of sweet spice, flowers and red berries. The tannins are nicely extracted and perceptible but not over-assertive on the harmonious, well-balanced palate. The Barbera del Monferrato Zerolegno is a little below par in comparison with its usual form, showing quite vibrant fruity aromas and a frank, simple palate. Finally, we liked the Monferrato Casalese Cortese and the Freisa La Monferrina, both from 2005, for their charming freshness.

●	Barbera del M.to Sup. '04	TT	3*
●	Grignolino del M.to Casalese '05	TT	3*
●	Barbera del M.to Zerolegno '04	T	4
○	Monferrato Casalese Cortese '05	T	3
●	Monferrato Freisa La Monferrina '05	T	3
●	Grignolino del M.to Casalese Bricco Mondalino '03	YY	4
●	Barbera d'Asti Sel. Gaudium Magnum '01	YY	5

VIGNALE MONFERRATO (AL)

MARCO CANATO
FRAZ. FONS SALERA
LOC. CA' BALDEA, 18/2
15049 VIGNALE MONFERRATO (AL)
TEL. 0142933653 - 0142933678
www.canatovini.it

The consistency that Marco Canato has accustomed us to in recent years is a clear sign of his maturity in estate management and the maintenance of quality. This year, he turned out just over 20,000 bottles, even though there is potential for much more. But Marco has decided to grow step by step, with the clear objective of not upsetting his production methods and above all of avoiding any negative impact on the quality of the range. Absent from our tastings was the 2004 Barbera del Monferrato Superiore Rapet, which was still ageing in the cellar. It will be on parade next year. But Barbera del Monferrato Superiore La Baldea 2004 was on song, and still manages to offer value for money that is unrivalled anywhere else in Piedmont. Its intense ruby red and very intense, fruit-forward nose usher in a wonderfully balance palate with a lingering finish. Grignolino del Monferrato Casalese Celio 2005 is attractively well orchestrated and the fresh-tasting finish features nicely discreet tannins. Marco's flagship white, Chardonnay Bric di Bric 2004, matures in barrique for a few months. What comes out is a gold-flecked straw-yellow wine with a nose of tropical fruit and oak-derived vanilla. The palate is soft, juicy and intense. Finally, we would also like to mention the Chardonnay Piasì and the young, moreish Barbera Gambaloita.

● Barbera del M.to Sup. La Baldea '04	TT	3*
○ Piemonte Chardonnay Bric di Bric '04	TT	4
● Grignolino del M.to Casalese Celio '05	TT	3*
● Barbera del M.to Gambaloita '05	T	3
○ Piemonte Chardonnay Piasì '05	T	3
● Barbera del M.to Sup. La Baldea '03	YY	3
● Barbera del M.to Sup. Rapet '03	YY	4

VINCHIO (AT)

CANTINA SOCIALE
DI VINCHIO VAGLIO SERRA
S.P. 40, KM 3,650
REG. SAN PANCRAZIO, 1
14040 VINCHIO (AT)
TEL. 0141950903 - www.vinchio.com

This co-operative winery again confirmed its skills at combining big numbers with big quality to match. Mauro Cazzola and Giuliano Noè consult in the cellar, which yet again lived up to expectations by presenting a range of wines that stand out for vigour, sincerity and sense of place. Two labels caught our eye in particular, Barbera d'Asti Vigne Vecchie 2004 and Barbera d'Asti Insynthesis 2003. The first of these opens slowly to unfold a broad, lingering range of aromas that hint at strawberries, plums and morello cherries. The palate mirrors the nose nicely, taking you through a full, structured and attractively soft progression. Insynthesis offers a broad range of mulberry, blueberry and ripe fruits that meld attractively with the cocoa powder. A full, warm front palate progresses to a lingering, well-defined finale that echoes the nose precisely. Monferrato Rosso Tutti per Uno 2004 is a Bordeaux blend with barbera. Its fruit interweaves with darker, more evolved notes of coffee and cassis that meld with the restrained, nicely handled oak. Generous, but far from inelegant, tannins stand out on the front palate. The other Barberas are also very respectable. The very attractive Grignolino 2005 is true to the sensory profile of its variety, tempting the nose with geraniums and pepper. The 2005 whites include Lipiai, a blend of müller thurgau, chardonnay and cortese, and the well put together single-variety Chardonnay, which has more to say for itself.

● Barbera d'Asti Sup. Sei Vigne Insynthesis '03	TT	7
● Barbera d'Asti Sup. I Tre Vescovi '04	TT	3*
● Barbera d'Asti Sup. Nizza Bricco Laudana '04	TT	4
● Barbera d'Asti Sup. Vigne Vecchie '04	TT	5
● Monferrato Rosso Tutti per Uno '04	TT	5
○ Monferrato Bianco Lipiai '05	TT	3*
● Barbera d'Asti '05	T	3
● Monferrato Rosso Frusté '05	T	5
○ Piemonte Chardonnay '05	T	3
● Grignolino dì Asti '05	T	3

OTHER WINERIES

La Luna del Rospo
fraz. Salere, 38
14041 Agliano Terme (AT)
tel. 0141954222

Michael Schaffer and Renate Schütz's organic estate, founded in 1995, releases 80,000 bottles. The interesting Barbera d'Asti Bric Rocche 2003 gives jam, cinchona and cocoa powder. Barbera d'Asti Solo per Laura 2003 is also nice with its cherry and vanilla touches. The rest of the range is sound.

●	Barbera d'Asti Bric Rocche '03	🍷🍷	4*
●	Barbera d'Asti Solo per Laura '03	🍷🍷	5
●	Monferrato Rosso Gli Storni '03	🍷	5
●	Grignolino d'Asti '05	🍷	3

Poderi Rosso
p.zza Roma, 1
14041 Agliano Terme (AT)
tel. 0141954006
www.poderirossogiovanni.it

Poderi Rosso submitted two interesting versions of the area's main variety, barbera. The Cascina Perno 2004 has red fruit and sweet spice aromas, a juicy, full entry on the palate and great balance of acid and fruit. The Vigna del Carlinet 2004 is just a step below this.

●	Barbera d'Asti Sup. Cascina Perno '04	🍷🍷	4*
●	Barbera d'Asti Sup. V. del Carlinet '04	🍷	4

Giovanni Silva
cascine Rogge, 1b
10011 Aglie (TO)
tel. 012433356
www.silvavini.com

The broad range of this long-standing Canavese producer includes the dried-grape Poetica, with clear dried fruit and apricot. Just behind is Canavese Rosso Cantagrì, a blend of classic local grapes. Erbaluce di Caluso, Tre Cioché and Dry Ice stop at One Glass for freshness problems on the nose.

○	Caluso Passito Poetica '01	🍷🍷	6
●	Canavese Rosso Cantagrì '04	🍷	4
○	Erbaluce di Caluso Dry Ice '05	🍷	4
○	Erbaluce di Caluso Tre Cioché '05	🍷	3

Tenuta Langasco
fraz. Madonna di Como, 10
12051 Alba (CN)
tel. 0173286972

Claudio Sacco's wines continue to improve. Madonna di Como hill in Alba is one of the most interesting areas for Dolcetto and Miclet is confirmation. It's impenetrable to the eye, fruity on the nose and rich and almondy in the mouth. The gutsy Nebbiolo Sorì Coppa never lets you down.

●	Nebbiolo d'Alba Sorì Coppa '04	🍷🍷	4
●	Dolcetto d'Alba Madonna di Como V. Miclet '05	🍷🍷	3*

VECCHIA POSTA
VIA MONTEBELLO, 2
15050 AVOLASCA (AL)
TEL. 0131876254

Vecchia Posta is an example of far-sighted vineyard management as well as good food since the country inn is never disappointing. Outstanding among the labels we tasted is Rebelot, which is definitely worth mentioning, and the Timorasso gets better every year.

- ○ Colli Tortonesi Bianco Il Selvaggio '04 — 🍷🍷 4
- ● Colli Tortonesi Rosso Rebelot '04 — 🍷🍷 3*
- ● Colli Tortonesi Rosso Teraforta '04 — 🍷 3

LE MARIE
VIA CARDÉ, 5
12032 BARGE (CN)
TEL. 0175345159 - 0175346900

Giorgio Beltramo and Valerio Raviolo make quality wines from native varieties in a previously declining subzone at Barge. Spice and liquorice permeate the Debàrges from nebbiolo, barbera and local varieties. Barbera Colombè gives red fruit and minerality. The Dolcetto and Bonarda are pleasant.

- ● Pinerolese Barbera Colombè '04 — 🍷🍷 4*
- ● Pinerolese Debàrges '04 — 🍷🍷 4*
- ● Pinerolese Bonarda '05 — 🍷 3
- ● Pinerolese Dolcetto '05 — 🍷 3

VIRNA
VIA ALBA, 73
12060 BAROLO (CN)
TEL. 017356120
www.virnabarolo.it

This year, Lodovico Borgogno gave us top-quality wines, especially the two Barolos, a 2000 and 2001. Preda Sarmassa 2001, aged in Slavonian oak barrels and tonneaux, has a warm, elegant palate. The Cannubi Boschis 2000 has soft, pleasing tannins. The Barolo 2002 is just below this.

- ● Barolo Cannubi Boschis '00 — 🍷🍷 6
- ● Barolo Preda Sarmassa '01 — 🍷🍷 7
- ● Barolo '02 — 🍷 6

CA' NOVA
VIA SAN ISIDORO, 1
28020 BOGOGNO (NO)
TEL. 0322863406

This winery in the province of Novara makes its Guide debut, presenting an interesting range of Nebbiolos. The Melchiòr and San Quirico 2003 are both good and share a modern style carried with restrained elegance. The Bocciolo 2004 is a small gem of aromatic purity.

- ● Colline Novaresi Nebbiolo Melchiòr '03 — 🍷🍷 4
- ● Colline Novaresi Nebbiolo V. San Quirico '03 — 🍷🍷 5
- ● Colline Novaresi Nebbiolo Bocciolo '04 — 🍷🍷 3*

CARLOTTA
VIA CONDOVE, 61
10050 BORGONE SUSA (TO)
TEL. 0119646150

With vines 1,000 metres above sea level, this Val Susa estate returns to the Guide thanks to the nice Valsusa Costa Oro 2005, from neretta cuneese, ciliegiolo, barbera and other rare cultivars. The pleasant Rocca del Lupo 2005 comes from avanà and barbera. Vigna Combe 2005 is just below these.

- ● Valsusa Costa Oro '05 — 🍷🍷 4*
- ● Valsusa Rocca del Lupo '05 — 🍷🍷 4*
- ● Valsusa Vigna Combe '05 — 🍷 4

LA CAPLANA
VIA CIRCONVALLAZIONE, 4
15060 BOSIO (AL)
TEL. 0143684182

The Guido family makes excellent wines. One of the best in its category, the Gavi Vigna Vecchia 2005 did well at our tastings. The Gavi del Comune di Gavi 2005 offers a stylish nose and fresh drinkability. The Dolcetto di Ovada Barricco 2004 is sound. Barbera d'Asti Rubis del 2004 is just behind.

- ○ Gavi Vigna Vecchia '05 — 🍷🍷 3*
- ● Dolcetto di Ovada Barricco '04 — 🍷🍷 3*
- ○ Gavi del Comune di Gavi '05 — 🍷🍷 3*
- ● Barbera d'Asti Rubis '04 — 🍷 3

Domenico Ghio e Figli

via Circonvallazione, 2
15060 Bosio (AL)
tel. 0143684117 - 0143684320
www.ghiovini.it

The Ghio family submitted a good set of wines this year. Dolcetto di Ovada L'Arciprete is intense ruby, with red fruit on the nose and a good palate with already soft tannins. The base Dolcetto is also nice. As for the Gavis, the La Cascina label is fresh and easy drinking.

●	Dolcetto di Ovada Sup. L'Arciprete '04	🍷	4
●	Dolcetto di Ovada '05	🍷	3
○	Gavi '05	🍷	3
○	Gavi La Cascina '05	🍷	4

La Smilla

via Garibaldi, 7
15060 Bosio (AL)
tel. 0143684245
www.lasmilla.it

Talented, enthusiastic Danilo Guido is the latest member of a family that has made wine for decades. We liked his Gavi I Bergi 2004 that gives very elegant citrus-like nuances. The Gavi 2005, Dolcetto di Ovada Nsè Pesa and Barbera del Monferrato Scarlatta 2004 are all enjoyable.

○	Gavi del C. di Gavi I Bergi '04	🍷🍷	4*
●	Barbera del M.to Scarlatta '04	🍷	3
●	Dolcetto di Ovada Nsè Pesa '04	🍷	4
○	Gavi del Comune di Gavi '05	🍷	3

Fabio Fidanza

via Rodotiglia, 55
14052 Calosso (AT)
tel. 0141826921
www.castellodicalosso.it

After a year off, Barbera d'Asti Sterlino 2003 returns with an impenetrable ruby-red hue, a nose with powerful toast and coffee, an alcohol-rich, structured palate and a long finish. The Monferrato, from nebbiolo and cabernet sauvignon, impressed. The Barbera d'Asti 2004 is well typed.

●	Barbera d'Asti Sterlino Castello di Calosso '03	🍷🍷	5
●	Monferrato Rosso Que Duàn '04	🍷🍷	4*
●	Barbera d'Asti '04	🍷	3

Podere Macellio

via Roma, 18
10014 Caluso (TO)
tel. 0119833511
www.erbaluce-bianco.it

This estate grows mainly the native Caluso erbaluce, making dry, sparkling and dried-grape versions. The Erbaluce 2005 stopped short of Two Glasses but the Spumante's finesse took it over the threshold. The Passito failed to repeat last year's brilliant performance and earned only a mention.

○	Caluso Spumante M. Cl. Pas Dosé	🍷🍷	4*
○	Erbaluce di Caluso '05	🍷	3
○	Caluso Passito '02		5

Funtanin

via Torino, 191
12043 Canale (CN)
tel. 0173979488

The series submitted by this major Canale winery is missing its most important wines, Roero Bricco Barbisa and Barbera Ciabot Pierin. But Arneis Pierin di Soc and the base Barbera d'Alba passed the Two Glass mark. The Langhe Favorita and Langhe Nebbiolo 2005 are a step below these.

●	Barbera d'Alba '04	🍷🍷	4*
○	Roero Arneis Pierin di Soc '05	🍷🍷	4*
○	Langhe Favorita '05	🍷	3
●	Langhe Nebbiolo '05	🍷	4

Malabaila di Canale

loc. cascina Pradvaj
via Madonna dei Cavalli, 19
12043 Canale (CN)
tel. 017398381 - www.malabaila.com

This historic Canale estate is constantly improving. For this edition, we tasted two excellent Roeros. The first is the elegant, structured Castelletto 2003 and the second is the fragrant, stylish Bric Volta 2004. The Barbera Mezzavilla 2004 and Arneis Pradvaj 2005 are nicely made and well crafted.

●	Roero Sup. Castelletto '03	🍷🍷	5
●	Roero Sup. Bric Volta '04	🍷🍷	5
●	Barbera d'Alba Mezzavilla '04	🍷	4
○	Roero Arneis Pradvaj '05	🍷	4

Giacomo Scagliola e Figlio
reg. Santa Libera, 20
14053 Canelli (AT)
tel. 0141831146
www.scagliolagiacomo.it

The Scagliola family makes characterful wines from 13 hectares under vine. We liked the sweet Moscato d'Asti Santa Libera 2005, with its refreshing supporting acidity, and the fruity, complex steel-aged Barbera d'Asti 2003. There is a mention for the Monferrato Dolcetto Cascina Valdirosa 2004.

●	Barbera d'Asti '03	🍷🍷	3*
○	Moscato d'Asti Santa Libera '05	🍷🍷	3*
●	Monferrato Dolcetto Cascina Valdirosa '04		3

Karin e Remo Hohler
reg. Bricco Bosetti, 85
14050 Cassinasco (AT)
tel. 0141851209
www.hohler.it

Karin and Remo Hohler patiently follow Mother Nature's rhythms and this year only released the selection of steel-aged Barbera Pian Bosco, an intense ruby wine with ripe fruit aromas and a savoury, attractively nuanced palate. The barrique-aged selection and barbera-croatina blend were missing.

●	Barbera d'Asti Pian Bosco '04	🍷🍷	4*
●	Barbera d'Asti Pian Bosco '03	🍸🍸	4
●	Barbera d'Asti Pian Bosco Barrique '03	🍸🍸	5

Gianni Doglia
fraz. Annunziata, 56
14054 Castagnole delle Lanze (AT)
tel. 0141878359

Gianni Doglia's wines performed well. The merlot Monferrato Rosso "!" 2003 is muscular and rich on the palate while the Moscato d'Asti 2005 is sweet with nice supporting acidity that lengthens the progression. The Barbera d'Asti Boscodonne 2005 is nice and Barbera d'Asti Superiore 2004 correct.

●	Monferrato Rosso "!" '03	🍷🍷	5
●	Barbera d'Asti Boscodonne '05	🍷🍷	4*
○	Moscato d'Asti '05	🍷🍷	4*
●	Barbera d'Asti Sup. '04	🍷	5

Noceto Michelotti
s.da Bogliona, 15/17
14040 Castel Boglione (AT)
tel. 0141762170
www.nocetomichelotti.com

This lovely winery with its large vineyards in Castel Boglione makes a Guide debut. We particularly liked the Barbera d'Asti Strada del Sole 2004, as well as the Barbera d'Asti Superiore Montecanta 2003. The Moscato d'Asti 2005 is decent and nicely typed.

●	Barbera d'Asti Sup. Montecanta '03	🍷🍷	5
●	Barbera d'Asti Strada del Sole '04	🍷🍷	4*
○	Moscato d'Asti '05	🍷	4

Ca' dei Mandorli
via IV Novembre, 15
14010 Castel Rocchero (AT)
tel. 0141760131
www.cadeimandorli.com

The admirable Ca' dei Mandorli winery gave us an excellent range for this edition of the Guide, beginning with the convincingly fruity Barbera d'Asti La Bellalda Oro 2003 with its rich spice. The Brachetto d'Acqui Le Donne dei Boschi 2005 is always good.

●	Barbera d'Asti Sup. La Bellalda Oro '03	🍷🍷	5
●	Brachetto d'Acqui Le Donne dei Boschi '05	🍷🍷	4*

Clemente Cossetti
via Guardie, 1
14043 Castelnuovo Belbo (AT)
tel. 0141799803
www.cossetti.it

The Clemente Cossetti winery makes nice wines. A young, easy-drinking, well-crafted Barbera d'Asti VentidiMarzo 2005 won Two Glasses hands down. The more structured, mouthfilling Barbera d'Asti La Vigna Vecchia 2004 is interesting. The Brachetto d'Acqui Theo 2005 always lives up to expectations.

●	Barbera d'Asti La Vigna Vecchia '04	🍷🍷	3*
●	Barbera d'Asti VentidiMarzo '05	🍷🍷	3*
●	Brachetto d'Acqui Theo '05	🍷	4

Giovanni Daglio

via Montale Celli, 10
15050 Costa Vescovato (AL)
tel. 0131838262

Giovanni Daglio is always friendly and helpful. If you visit, remember to stock up on his wines since quality at these prices is hard to find. The Basinas was missing, so this year we enjoyed the steel-aged Barbera Pias. The Cortese is well made but the real champion is the structured, long Nibiò.

●	Colli Tortonesi Rosso Nibiò '04	🍷🍷	4*
●	Colli Tortonesi Barbera Pias '04	🍷	3
○	Colli Tortonesi Cortese Vigna del Re '05	🍷	3

Alfonso Boeri

fraz. Bionzo
via Bricco Quaglia, 10
14055 Costigliole d'Asti (AT)
tel. 0141968171 - www.boerivini.it

The three generations on the Alfonso Boeri estate began as grape growers and became winemakers over time. The barbera-nebbiolo blend Monferrato Barbòlo 2003 is very good, as is the Barbera Pörlapà 2003, aged in barrique for 18 months. The nice Chardonnay Bevion 2004 gives vanilla and butter.

●	Barbera d'Asti Sup. Pörlapà '03	🍷🍷	6
●	Monferrato Rosso Barbòlo '03	🍷🍷	6
○	Piemonte Chardonnay Bevion '04	🍷	4

Cantina Sociale del Canavese

via Montalenghe, 9
10090 Cuceglio (TO)
tel. 012432034 - 0124492731
www.cantinacanavese.it

Wines from the Cantina Sociale del Canavese showed good overall quality this year. We particularly liked the Erbaluce di Caluso Passito Morenico 2001 with its golden-flecked amber hue. The Barbera 2004 is good. The two decent Erbaluces stand out for their floral aromas and easy drinking palate.

○	Erbaluce di Caluso Passito Morenico '01	🍷🍷	6
●	Canavese Barbera '04	🍷🍷	4*
○	Erbaluce di Caluso Crio '05	🍷	4
○	Erbaluce di Caluso La Traccia '05	🍷	3

Benotto

via San Carlo, 52
14055 Costigliole d'Asti (AT)
tel. 0141966406

The Barbera crus are still ageing so Benotto has moved into the Other Wineries. But there were interesting wines among the selections we tasted. The Nebieul 2003 is rich and austere, if a bit evolved on the nose. The Cortese Lacrime di Gioia is fruity, the Bonarda spicy, and the Barbera coherent.

●	Monferrato Rosso Nebieul '03	🍷🍷	5
●	Barbera d'Asti '04	🍷	3
●	Piemonte Bonarda '05	🍷	4
○	Piemonte Cortese Lacrime di Gioia '05	🍷	4

Giuseppe Stella

s.da Bossola, 8
14055 Costigliole d'Asti (AT)
tel. 0141966142 - 0141878385

Beppe Stella's wines scored well, though we found some a bit too marked by sweetness. The pleasant Barbera Bricco Fubine Il Vino del Maestro has fruit and sweet spice. The interesting Barbera d'Asti Giaiet is minerally and savoury, and the Piemonte Chardonnay 2005 is a nice easy drinker.

●	Barbera d'Asti Bricco Fubine Il Vino del Maestro '04	🍷🍷	4*
●	Barbera d'Asti Giaiet '04	🍷🍷	4*
○	Piemonte Chardonnay Cascina Stella '05	🍷	3

F.lli Abrigo

via Moglia Gerlotto, 2
12055 Diano d'Alba (CN)
tel. 017369104
www.abrigofratelli.com

This lovely Diano winery has expanded the cellar and continues to raise the quality of its wines. Two Glasses went to the Sörì dei Berfi Vigna Pietrìn 2005 and base Sörì dei Berfi. Both are pleasing and fruity with soft, measured tannins. The Bric Tumlìn 2005 is well managed and easy to drink.

●	Diano d'Alba Sörì dei Berfi '05	🍷🍷	3*
●	Diano d'Alba Sörì dei Berfi V. Pietrìn '05	🍷🍷	4
●	Diano d'Alba Bric Tumlìn '05	🍷	3

Casavecchia

via Roma, 2
12055 Diano d'Alba (CN)
tel. 017369321

The Casavecchia brothers' winery did well. We liked the ruby red Nebbiolo d'Alba Piadvenza 2004 with currant, morello cherry and sweet spice and a succulent, nicely tannic palate. The firm, complex Diano Sörì Bruni 2005 is also good. The Barbera d'Alba San Quirico 2004 and Barolo are sound.

● Nebbiolo d'Alba Piadvenza '04	🍷🍷	4*
● Diano d'Alba Sörì Bruni '05	🍷🍷	4*
● Barolo Piantà '01	🍷🍷	7
● Barbera d'Alba San Quirico '04	🍷	4

Cascina Flino

via Abelloni, 7
12055 Diano d'Alba (CN)
tel. 017369231

Paolo Monte runs a nice country inn surrounded by vineyards. In addition, his winery has produced several very interesting and enjoyable labels this year. The Diano Vigna Vecchia 2005 and Nebbiolo d'Alba 2004 are excellent. The Barbera d'Alba Flin 2004 has yet to absorb its oak.

● Nebbiolo d'Alba '04	🍷🍷	4*
● Diano d'Alba V. Vecchia '05	🍷🍷	4*
● Barbera d'Alba Flin '04	🍷	4

Osvaldo Barberis

b.ta Valdibà, 42
12063 Dogliani (CN)
tel. 017370054

Osvaldo Barberis has again made some of the best Dolcetto di Dogliani wines around. The missing Barbera had not yet been bottled when we tasted. The good Dolcetto Puncin 2005 is an impenetrable ruby with a fruity, concentrated palate. The San Lorenzo 2005 has a pleasant yet less powerful mouthfeel.

● Dolcetto di Dogliani Puncin '05	🍷🍷	4*
● Dolcetto di Dogliani San Lorenzo '05	🍷🍷	3*

Cascina Corte

b.ta Valdiberti, 33
12063 Dogliani (CN)
tel. 0172411641
www.cascinacorte.it

Wines from Sandro Barosi and his wife Amalia continue to grow in quality. All four earned excellent scores and showed outstanding rich personality and excellent craftsmanship. We particularly like the deep Dolcetto di Dogliani Vigna Pirochetta 2005 and elegant Langhe Nebbiolo 2005.

● Dolcetto di Dogliani '05	🍷🍷	3*
● Dolcetto di Dogliani V. Pirochetta '05	🍷🍷	4*
● Langhe Nebbiolo '05	🍷🍷	4*
● Piemonte Barbera '05	🍷	3

Eraldo Revelli

loc. Pianbosco, 29
12060 Farigliano (CN)
tel. 0173797154
www.eraldorevelli.com

The Revelli family presented three Dolcetto di Doglianis. San Matteo has remarkably rich extract. Autin Lungh is fruity and pleasant drinking and the simpler Otto Filari is made with grapes from the youngest vines. The Langhe La Basarisca, from barbera and nebbiolo, is worth a try.

● Langhe Rosso La Basarisca '04	🍷🍷	4*
● Dolcetto di Dogliani Autin Lungh '05	🍷🍷	4*
● Dolcetto di Dogliani S. Matteo '05	🍷🍷	4*
● Dolcetto di Dogliani Otto Filari '05	🍷	4

Castello di Lignano

via Lignano, 1
15035 Frassinello Monferrato (AL)
tel. 0142925326
www.castellodilignano.com

Castello di Lignano returns to the Guide after a brief absence and some changes at the estate, beginning with new winery management. Oenologist Gabriele Moro is manager and Mario Ronco oversees vinification. Among the wines tasted, we particularly like the two Barberas.

● Barbera d'Asti Sup. V. Stramba '03	🍷🍷	5
● Barbera del M.to Sup. Valisenda '03	🍷🍷	5
● Monferrato Rosso Lhennius '03	🍷	5

Cantina Sociale di Gattinara

via Monte Grappa, 7
13045 Gattinara (VC)
tel. 0163833568

This winery has been replacing its barrels since 2001. If the results are those seen in the Gattinara 2001, with its majestic typicity, expressiveness and elegance, then we hope all the old barrels go soon. The Riserva 2000 still clearly shows limits on the nose from the old oak.

● Gattinara '01	🍷🍷	4*
● Gattinara Ris. '00	🍷	5

La Chiara

loc. Vallegge, 24
15066 Gavi (AL)
tel. 0143642293
www.lachiara.it

La Chiara's owner Roberto Bergaglio again submitted good wines for the Guide. The excellent, straw-yellow Gavi has nicely intense aromas with floral notes. Vigneto Groppella is slightly below par and the cabernet, barbera and dolcetto Monferrato Rosso Nabarì is decent.

○ Gavi del C. di Gavi La Chiara '05	🍷🍷	3*
● Monferrato Rosso Nabarì '04	🍷	4
○ Gavi del Comune di Gavi Vign. Groppella '05	🍷	4

Produttori del Gavi

via Cavalieri di Vittorio Veneto, 45
15066 Gavi (AL)
tel. 0143642786

Cantina Produttori del Gavi includes a hundred or so member growers and confirmed the improvement in quality we have been observing for some time. We particularly like the Aureliana, which reached our taste-offs. The Gavi La Maddalena is simpler on both nose and palate.

○ Gavi Cascine dell'Aureliana '05	🍷🍷	4*
○ Gavi del Comune di Gavi La Maddalena '05	🍷🍷	4
○ Gavi del Comune di Gavi '05	🍷	3

La Ghibellina

fraz. Monterotondo, 61
15066 Gavi (AL)
tel. 0143686257
www.laghibellina.it

Founded a few years ago, and capably managed by Alberto and Marina Ghibellini, La Ghibellina has become one of the most promising producers in Gavi. Two Glasses went to both the Monferrato Rosso 2003, from barbera, dolcetto dal raspo rosso, merlot and ciliegiolo, and the Gavi 2005.

● Monferrato Rosso '03	🍷🍷	4*
○ Gavi del Comune di Gavi '05	🍷🍷	4*
○ Gavi del Comune di Gavi '04	🍷🍷 (white)	4

Torraccia del Piantavigna

via Romagnano, 69a
28074 Ghemme (NO)
tel. 0163840040 - 0163844711
www.torracciadelpiantavigna.it

Alessandro Francoli forges ahead. His Gattinara 2001 reached the finals for its classically crafted aromatic profile of roots, minerals and eucalyptus. Two Glasses went to the exemplary Vespolina Maretta 2005, and the Tre Confini 2004, a succulent, powerful Nebbiolo. The Ghemme 2001 is sound.

● Gattinara '01	🍷🍷	6
● Ghemme '01	🍷🍷	6
● Colline Novaresi Nebbiolo Tre Confini '04	🍷🍷	4*
● Colline Novaresi Vespolina Maretta '05	🍷🍷	4*

Gianni Gagliardo

b.ta Serra dei Turchi, 88
12064 La Morra (CN)
tel. 017350829
www.gagliardo.it

Gagliardo will now release two lines: Gianni Gagliardo for wines from estate-grown grapes, and Gagliardo for those from bought-in fruit. Oenologist Stefano's line-up is good: the charming, rich Favorita is macerated on the skins, Nebbiolo San Ponzio is dense and Zerodue 2002, a mini-Barolo, is nice.

○ Langhe Favorita Casà '03	🍷🍷	5
● Nebbiolo d'Alba San Ponzio '04	🍷🍷	5
● Langhe Nebbiolo Zerodue '02	🍷	5
● Barolo Cannubi '01	🍷🍷 (white)	8

ROCCOLO DI MEZZOMERICO
CASCINA ROCCOLO BELLINI, 4
28040 MEZZOMERICO (NO)
TEL. 0321920407

Two wines submitted. The modern-style Nebbiolo Valentina has an intriguing nose and slightly less exuberant alcohol would have won it Two Glasses. The same goes for the late-harvest chardonnay Mataccio 2005, which has interesting aromatics but was blocked at One Glass by a bitterish finish.

● Colline Novaresi Nebbiolo Valentina '02	Y	4
○ Il Mataccio '05	Y	4

BUSSIA SOPRANA
LOC. BUSSIA, 81
12065 MONFORTE D'ALBA (CN)
TEL. 039305182

Last year, Bussia Soprana released three excellent Barolos from 2001: Bussia, Vigna Colonnello and Mosconi. The terrible 2002 season ruled out any Barolos worthy of the name so we only tasted two wines, the warm, evolved Langhe Rosso 2003 and the Barbera Vin del Ross 2003.

● Barbera d'Alba Vin del Ross '03	YY	5
● Langhe Rosso '03	YY	5
● Barolo Bussia '01	(YY)	8
● Barolo Mosconi '01	(YY)	8

JOSETTA SAFFIRIO
FRAZ. CASTELLETTO, 32
12065 MONFORTE D'ALBA (CN)
TEL. 017378660
www.josettasaffirio.com

Sara Vezza did not submit any wines from the dreadful 2002 harvest, which was ravaged by hail. We settled for the Langhe Nebbiolo 2003, a mini-Barolo with an attractive pale ruby red colour and complex leather and tobacco aromas. The palate has docile tannins that set off the alcohol.

● Langhe Nebbiolo '03	YY	4*
● Barolo '88	(YYY)	8
● Barolo '89	(YYY)	8
● Barolo '01	(YY)	6

VALERIO ALOI
VIA PIETRO FISSORE, 6
12046 MONTÀ (CN)
TEL. 0173975604

Nicoletta, wife of the late Valerio Aloi, continues her skilful efforts determinedly. This year, she submitted a wonderful Roero Bricco Morinaldo 2004 that went through to our final taste-offs. The fruity, juicy Barbera d'Alba 2004 is also good and Roero Arneis 2005 is fresh and quaffable.

● Roero Bricco Morinaldo '04	YY	5
● Barbera d'Alba '04	YY	3*
○ Roero Arneis '05	Y	4

CASCINA SALICETTI
VIA CASCINA SALICETTI, 2
15050 MONTEGIOCO (AL)
TEL. 0131875192

Here is a fine example of the new advancing at an appropriate pace. All the wines tasted were sound but we were particularly impressed by the oak-aged Barbera, Punta del Sole, for its great balance of structure and finesse. The Montarlino, a white from cortese, was also very good.

● Colli Tortonesi Punta del Sole '04	YY	4*
○ Colli Tortonesi Cortese Montarlino '05	YY	4
● Colli Tortonesi Rosso Morganti '04	Y	4

CANTINA DEL BRICCHETTO
VIA BRICCHETTO, 4
12057 NEIVE (CN)
TEL. 0173677307
www.cantinadelbricchetto.com

The wines submitted by the tenacious Franco Rocca were once again well up to snuff. The elegant, harmonious Barbaresco Albesani 2003 scored Two Glasses for its violets and dried flower aromas and soft, gratifying tannins. The full, succulent Barbera d'Alba Bricco Sterpone 2003 is just as good.

● Barbaresco Albesani '03	YY	6
● Barbera d'Alba Bricco Sterpone '03	YY	4*

COCITO
LOC. MICCA, 25
12057 NEIVE (CN)
TEL. 017367052

Despite the hot, dry growing year, Ezio Cocito managed to make a very interesting wine. The ruby red Barbaresco Baluchin 2003 has violets, cinchona and wild roses on the nose that meld nicely with coffee from oak ageing. The attractively tannic palate has good length and a harmonious finish.

●	Barbaresco Baluchin '03	▼▼	8
●	Barbaresco Baluchin '01	▽▽	8
●	Barbaresco Baluchin '02	▽▽	8

CANTINA DEL GLICINE
VIA GIULIO CESARE, 1
12052 NEIVE (CN)
TEL. 017367215
www.cantinadelglicine.it

The spectacular Cantina del Glicine is back in the Guide thanks to two Barbarescos. The Curà 2003 has a close-knit yet pleasant tannic texture with a full, solidly built finish. The Marcorino 2003 gives aromas of violets and dried flowers lifted by ripe red fruit and cinchona.

●	Barbaresco Curà '03	▼▼	6
●	Barbaresco Marcorino '03	▼▼	6

CECILIA MONTE
VIA SERRACAPELLI, 17
12052 NEIVE (CN)
TEL. 017367454

Cecilia Monte has two hectares under vine planted only to nebbiolo and dolcetto. Consultants Giorgio Gozzellino and Beppe Caviola are on hand. The interesting Barbaresco Serracapelli 2003 has tight-knit, well-defined tannins, as does the fruity, quaffable Dolcetto d'Alba Montubert 2005.

●	Barbaresco Serracapelli '03	▼▼	6
●	Dolcetto d'Alba Montubert '05	▼▼	4*

CASCINA BARICCHI
VIA TINELLA, 15
12050 NEVIGLIE (CN)
TEL. 0173630141

Natale Simonetta's Cascina Baricchi is known for its Solenne ice wine and Guardo dried-grape wine. Both scored well at our tastings thanks to their outstanding character and personality. The pinot nero-only Langhe Brigante in Fuga 2000 is intriguing and the Langhe Nebbiolo 2001 is good.

●	Langhe Brigante in Fuga '00	▼▼	6
○	Solenne '00	▼▼	8
○	Guardo '03	▼▼	8
●	Langhe Nebbiolo '01	▼	5

CANTINA SOCIALE DI NIZZA
VIA ALESSANDRIA, 57
14049 NIZZA MONFERRATO (AT)
TEL. 0141721348
www.nizza.it

Cantina di Nizza, managed by oenologist Giovanni Chiarle, released only one Barbera selection, Ceppi Vecchi. The absence of the rich Magister and gutsy 50 Vendemmie meant that this major winery moved down to the Other Wineries. Ceppi Vecchi 2003 is fruity, succulent and well structured.

●	Barbera d'Asti Sup. Ceppi Vecchi '03	▼▼	4*
●	Barbera d'Asti Sup. Magister '03	▽▽	4
●	Barbera d'Asti Sup. 50 Vendemmie '03	▽▽	4

CASCINA DEGLI ULIVI
S.DA MAZZOLA, 14
15067 NOVI LIGURE (AL)
TEL. 0143744598
www.cascinadegliulivi.it

A Guide fixture for many years, this biodynamic estate alternates good years with others that are less convincing. The decent Monferrato Dolcetto Nibiô has good balance on the palate and intense red fruit aromas. The Gavi Filagnotti, Monferrato Bianco Montemarino, and Barbera Mounbé scored well.

●	Monferrato Dolcetto Nibiô '04	▼	4
●	Piemonte Barbera Mounbé '04	▼	4
○	Gavi Filagnotti '05	▼	4
○	Monferrato Bianco Montemarino '05	▼	4

LAURA VALDITERRA
S.DA MONTEROTONDO, 75
15067 NOVI LIGURE (AL)
TEL. 0143321451

Laura Valditerra supervises first hand all the work in cellar and vineyard. This dedication has enabled her make interesting, pleasant wines. We liked the Gavi Vigna del Lago 2005. The nose has floral sensations followed by a fresh palate and is ready to drink. The rest of the range is good.

●	Monferrato Rosso FiorDesAri '04	🍷🍷	4*
○	Gavi V. del Lago '05	🍷🍷	4*
●	Piemonte Barbera '04	🍷	4

GAGGINO
S.DA S. EVASIO, 29
15076 OVADA (AL)
TEL. 0143822345

This year, Gaggino released an excellent Dolcetto di Ovada, Il Convivio 2005. It's intense ruby red with elegant red fruit and a harmonious, tannic palate. The complex, structured Dolcetto di Ovada Sant'Evasio 2004 is also good. Just below are the Monferrato Rosso Il Ticco and Barbera La Lazzarina.

●	Dolcetto di Ovada Sup. S. Evasio '04	🍷🍷	4*
●	Dolcetto di Ovada Il Convivio '05	🍷🍷	3*
●	Monferrato Rosso Il Ticco '04	🍷	4
●	Barbera del M.to La Lazzarina '05	🍷	3

BECCARIA
VIA GIOVANNI BIANCO, 3
15039 OZZANO MONFERRATO (AL)
TEL. 0142487321
www.beccaria-vini.it

A new entry in the Guide, Davide Beccaria's winery makes around 20,000 bottles a year of mostly Barbera del Monferrato. From the range presented, we particularly liked the Convivium with its rich nose of fruit and sweet spices, succulent palate and long-lingering finish.

●	Barbera del M.to '04	🍷🍷	3*
●	Barbera del M.to Sup. Convivium '04	🍷🍷	4
●	Grignolino del M.to Casalese '05	🍷	3

CANTINE VALPANE
CASCINA VALPANE, 10/1
15039 OZZANO MONFERRATO (AL)
TEL. 0142486713
www.cantinevalpane.com

Pietro Arditi presented three wines of excellent overall quality. The well-gauged oak in the Barbera Valpane 2001 never masks the fruit on either nose or palate. The Perlydia 2003 is intense and long in every phase of tasting. The Barbera Rosso Pietro 2005 is fresh, young and enjoyable.

●	Barbera del M.to Valpane '01	🍷🍷	5
●	Barbera del M.to Perlydia '03	🍷🍷	4*
●	Barbera del M.to Rosso Pietro '05	🍷	3

RENATO BUGANZA
LOC. CASCINA GARBINOTTO, 4
12040 PIOBESI D'ALBA (CN)
TEL. 0173619370

A new Guide entry, Renato Buganza is assisted on the estate by his son Emanuele. Their Roero Bric Paradis 2003 and Barbera d'Alba Gerbole 2003 both scored Two Glasses. The fresh, easy-drinking Roero Arneis dla Trifula 2005 and the Langhe 2003, from barbera and nebbiolo, are both decent.

●	Barbera d'Alba Gerbole '03	🍷🍷	4*
●	Roero Bric Paradis '03	🍷🍷	5
●	Langhe '03	🍷	4
○	Roero Arneis dla Trifula '05	🍷	4

FAVARO
S.DA CHIUSURE, 1BIS
10010 PIVERONE (TO)
TEL. 012572606

Neither the dried-grape Sole d'Inverno nor the red Basy were released this year. We tasted two Erbaluce di Caluso wines, the steel-vinified base 2005, with complex aromas and structure but too much alcohol, and the 13 Mesi 2004, aged in new barriques, which has found a good rapport with the oak.

○	Erbaluce di Caluso 13 Mesi '04	🍷	4
○	Erbaluce di Caluso '05	🍷	4

La Gioia

Loc. Trionzo, 43
15078 Rocca Grimalda (AL)
tel. 0143831966

Alberto Malaspina and his sister Simona own this nice estate with vineyards in Trionzo, the homeland of Dolcetto di Ovada. The excellent Dolcetto Sole Dentro 2005 is fruity, balsamic, tannic and caressing. On retasting, the 2003 version is also enjoyable and still very compact.

- ● Dolcetto di Ovada Il Sole Dentro '05 — 🍷🍷 4*
- ● Dolcetto di Ovada Il Sole Dentro '03 — 🍷🍷 (white) 4

Daniele Saccoletto

s.s. Casale-Asti, 82
15020 San Giorgio Monferrato (AL)
tel. 0142806509
www.saccolettovini.com

The Saccoletto estate has 14 hectares just outside Casale Monferrato and produces 25,000 bottles a year. The striking new Krasis is a blend of 60 per cent nebbiolo with barbera, freisa and syrah. Passito Brina, from part-dried moscato scored high. The Grignolino Vigna in Cornalasca 2005 is sound.

- ○ Brina — 🍷🍷 5
- ● Monferrato Rosso Krasis '05 — 🍷🍷 4*
- ● Grignolino del M.to Casalese Vigna in Cornalasca '05 — 🍷 3

Carussin

reg. Mariano, 27
14050 San Marzano Oliveto (AT)
tel. 0141831358
www.carussin.it

Luca, Luigi, Bruna and Matteo Ferro run the Carussin winery. The most interesting wine they submitted is Barbera d'Asti Superiore Nizza Ferro Carlo 2003, aged 18 months in barrique and large oak. Barbera d'Asti Asinoi 2005 is decent, as is the sweet, well-made Moscato d'Asti Filari Corti 2005.

- ● Barbera d'Asti Sup. Nizza Ferro Carlo '03 — 🍷🍷 6
- ● Barbera d'Asti Asinoi '05 — 🍷 3
- ○ Moscato d'Asti Filari Corti '05 — 🍷 2*

Schiavenza

via Mazzini, 4a
12050 Serralunga d'Alba (CN)
tel. 0173613115
www.schiavenza.com

There was no Schiavenza Barolo Riserva or Barbera d'Alba 2004 this year. We took consolation in a good Barolo Prapò 2002, which is complex and firmly structured with violets and dried flower aromas. The three Dolcettos submitted were also nice, especially Vughera and Sorì, both from 2005.

- ● Barolo Prapò '02 — 🍷🍷 7
- ● Dolcetto d'Alba Sorì '05 — 🍷🍷 4*
- ● Dolcetto d'Alba Vughera '05 — 🍷🍷 4*
- ● Dolcetto d'Alba '05 — 🍷 4

Tenuta La Tenaglia

s.da Santuario di Crea, 5c
15020 Serralunga di Crea (AL)
tel. 0142940252
www.latenaglia.com

The Bianchi estate is certified organic. It's one of the few producers in the Sizzano DOC and presented a simple 2001. The two bigger DOCs were more exciting. Though not terribly precise, the Ghemme is rich, dense and alcoholic. The Gattinara is typical and acid-forward with complex tertiary notes.

- ● Grignolino del M.to Casalese '05 — 🍷🍷 3*
- ○ Piemonte Chardonnay '05 — 🍷🍷 3*
- ● Barbera d'Asti Bricco Crea '05 — 🍷 3

Bianchi

via Roma, 37
28070 Sizzano (NO)
tel. 0321810004 - 0321820823
www.bianchibiowine.it

Massimiliana Spinola's Castello di Tassarolo estate gave us two characterful Gavis. Castello di Tassarolo has citrus and spring flowers on the nose then a pleasantly fresh palate that finishes slightly bitterish. This well-crafted Gavi reached our final taste-offs. The S version was just behind.

- ● Gattinara '01 — 🍷🍷 4*
- ● Ghemme '01 — 🍷🍷 4*
- ● Sizzano '01 — 🍷 4

CASTELLO DI TASSAROLO
CASCINA ALBORINA, 1
15060 TASSAROLO (AL)
TEL. 0143342248

With 35 hectares under vine, Ernesto Dellapiana's estate has one of the most attractive and extensive vineyard properties in the Langhe. The wines submitted were interesting. The Barbaresco Riserva 2001 and Barbaresco Boito 2003 both earned Two Glasses. The Barbera d'Alba 2004 is pleasant.

○ Gavi del Comune di Tassarolo Castello di Tassarolo '05	🍷🍷	4*
○ Gavi del Comune di Tassarolo S '05	🍷	3

RIZZI
VIA RIZZI, 15
12050 TREISO (CN)
TEL. 0173638161
www.cantinarizzi.it

This estate's 30 hectares under vine use certified organic farming methods. The wines submitted for tasting stand out for their good overall quality, starting with the Barbera Minola 2003, aged in barriques and tonneaux. The Grignolino 2005 also performed very well.

● Barbaresco Ris. '01	🍷🍷	6
● Barbaresco Boito '03	🍷🍷	6
● Barbera d'Alba '04	🍷	3

NUOVA CAPPELLETTA
CA' CAPPELLETTA, 9
15049 VIGNALE MONFERRATO (AL)
TEL. 0142933135
www.nuovacappelletta.it

Founded three decades ago, La Scamuzza released 15,000 bottles this year under just a few labels, partly because Barbera Vigneto della Amorosa 2004 was missing. The good barbera and cabernet sauvignon Monferrato San Tomaso is mellow and round. Barbera Baciamisubito is fresh and easy drinking.

● Barbera del Monferrato Minola '03	🍷🍷	4*
● Grignolino del M.to Casalese '05	🍷	3
● Monferrato Freisa '05	🍷	3

LA SCAMUZZA
CASCINA POMINA, 17
15049 VIGNALE MONFERRATO (AL)
TEL. 0142926214 - 0142401414
www.lascamuzza.it

Founded three decades ago, La Scamuzza released 15,000 bottles this year under just a few labels, partly because Barbera Vigneto della Amorosa 2004 was missing. The good barbera and cabernet sauvignon Monferrato San Tomaso is mellow and round. Barbera Baciamisubito is fresh and easy drinking.

● Monferrato Rosso Bricco San Tomaso '04	🍷🍷	5
● Barbera del M.to Baciamisubito '05	🍷	4

CASCINA MONTAGNOLA
S.DA MONTAGNOLA, 1
15058 VIGUZZOLO (AL)
TEL. 0131898558
www.cascinamontagnola.com

Again, it was the whites that impressed from this estate managed by Donatella Gianotti with help from her husband Bruno. The outstanding barrique-aged Chardonnay Risveglio sets off attractive aromas against vanilla. Cortese Dunin is delicate but Barbera Rodeo has not yet reached its full potential.

○ Colli Tortonesi Cortese Dunin '05	🍷🍷	4
○ Colli Tortonesi Risveglio '05	🍷🍷	5
● Colli Tortonesi Rosso Rodeo '03	🍷	5

COSTA OLMO
VIA SAN MICHELE, 18
14040 VINCHIO (AT)
TEL. 0141950423
www.costaolmo.com

Vittorio Limone and his wife Paola have five hectares under vine. The Barbera d'Asti 2003 is good, giving intense red fruit and sweet spice. The palate has energy and power with a nice long, pleasant finish. The Barbera La Madrina also picked up Two Glasses. Chardonnay A Paola 2004 is just behind.

● Barbera d'Asti Sup. '03	🍷🍷	5
● Barbera d'Asti La Madrina '04	🍷🍷	4*
○ Piemonte Chardonnay A Paola '04	🍷	4

LIGURIA

The weather this year helped Liguria, pushing up average standards and consolidating quality, but there are also signs that producers are changing focus. Having started by restructuring their vineyards for quality, more and more wineries are modernizing production with close, technology-assisted monitoring of fermentation while agronomists and oenologists have become familiar figures even in the smallest businesses. The fruits of these efforts are now in the glass and we note them with pleasure. Nevertheless, some thought should be given to changes in market requirements and tastes as consumers become more sophisticated. There is perceptibly more interest in native grape varieties and in wines with the sort of terroir-driven character that can only be captured by skilful winemakers. Another topical issue is the current batch of Ligurian reds, in particular those from the Ponente area, an increasingly crowded new frontier. Having decided on grenache as a core variety – it has been present in western Liguria for some centuries and is blended with other varieties according to the preferences of each individual producer – growers are moving towards greater concentration and softness; but no wine, not even a great wine, should sacrifice drinkability. If we accept this, producers should attempt to comply. Besides, consumers are becoming less reverential when presented with muscular wines: they want variety, personality and elegance. Riccardo Bruna is a passionate grower and knows how to rise to the challenge. His Pigato, Baccan, achieves the highest levels of expression through drastic selection in the oldest vineyards at Russeghine and Garascin, traditional maceration on the skins for 48 hours at cellar temperature, fermentation with ambient yeasts, maturation on fine lees with stirring for six months, bottling one year after harvest and three months in glass. It's a memorable wine indeed. Ponente is leading the charge, then, but the Levante end of Liguria is not standing still. The stream of Two Glass wines, many of them brimming, shows that the winemakers are performing at their best. In addition to familiar names like Emanuele Trevia, Vladimiro Galluzzo, Massimo Alessandri, Ottaviano Lambruschi, Valter De Battè, Kurt Wachter and Stefano Salvetti, we also found excellent new producers like Gianni Arlotti (Alta Via), Rossana Zappa and her husband Roberto (Vis Amoris), Bonanini and Bonanni-Fellegara, just to mention a few. So come on, visit the wineries, enjoy these wines and allow yourselves to be fascinated by this region of sea and mountains.

ALBENGA (SV)

Anfossi

Fraz. Bastia
via Paccini, 39
17031 Albenga (SV)
tel. 018220024
www.aziendaagrariaanfossi.it

This small winery is in Bastia, which is at the confluence of the torrential Arroscia and Neva rivers. It is based in a fortified manor house built under the Genoese Republic at the turn of the 14th and 15th centuries and the building appears on all the labels. Mario Anfossi and Paolo Grossi are the owners. They are business partners and friends who have invested much energy and money in improving the estate's activities, which range from market gardening – their basil is superb – to viticulture. The wines have always been good, but they are improving further and have gone up a gear for this edition. Tasting 2004 Pigato Le Caminate is a stimulating experience. This selection from the Campochiesa hills has an intensely perfumed ripe peach and pineapple nose; on the palate it is rich but lively with fascinating aromatic expression and a nice long finish with a twist of bitterness. The 2005 Vermentino is just as good. A fine, delicate nose with precise notes of citrus fruits and aromatic herbs precedes a refreshing, balanced, full-bodied and mouthfilling palate leading to a long controlled finish. The basic Pigato almost achieved Two Glasses. It is inviting on the nose with aromas of sage and rosemary followed by fruit tones. Development in the mouth is supported by good weight, tangy freshness and an almondy finish. The Rossese is well behaved, giving cheerfully youthful with notes reminiscent of meadow flowers and Mediterranean scrubland. It is reasonably structured with a pleasantly fruity taste and clean finish.

○	Riviera Ligure di Ponente Pigato Le Caminate '04	🍷🍷	4*
○	Riviera Ligure di Ponente Vermentino '05	🍷🍷	4
○	Riviera Ligure di Ponente Pigato '05	🍷	4
●	Riviera Ligure di Ponente Rossese '05	🍷	4

ALBENGA (SV)

Calleri

Fraz. Salea
reg. Fratti, 2
17031 Albenga (SV)
tel. 018220085

This reliable winery, which is now in the capable hands of Marcello Calleri, has again come up with a range of high quality across the board, living up to its track record of professionalism and determination. The grapes are bought from trusted suppliers in the best areas around Albenga, and are grown with respect for the environment in accordance with the criteria laid down by Marcello. The products tasted were all technically well made, but also showed backbone and character. The standard Pigato is particularly good. The intense straw-yellow colour is followed by subtle pineapple and lychee smells, and a complex, balanced, full-bodied palate uniting lively aromatics with good development and length. The I Muzazzi Vermentino displays inviting, well-defined perfumes ranging from citron to golden delicious apples and almonds. These are precisely reflected on the palate, where they show concentration, good development and appealing richness of flavour. The other two wines, Saleasco Pigato and the basic Vermentino, are sound without being surprising. The first has a straw colour and mainly fruit aroma with peach foremost, then a lighter apricot note with a touch of balsam. The strong points on the palate, which is not particularly rich, are balance, aromatics and composure. The Vermentino opens with clean no-nonsense scents of meadow flowers and aromatic herbs followed by a medium-weight crisp body and good balance of acidity and alcohol.

○	Riviera Ligure di Ponente Pigato '05	🍷🍷	4
○	Riviera Ligure di Ponente Vermentino I Muzazzi '05	🍷🍷	4*
○	Riviera Ligure di Ponente Pigato Saleasco '05	🍷	4
○	Riviera Ligure di Ponente Vermentino '05	🍷	4

ALBENGA (SV)

LE ROCCHE DEL GATTO
FRAZ. SALEA
REG. RUATO, 4
17031 ALBENGA (SV)
TEL. 3355223547 - 018221175
www.lerocchedelgatto.it

Le Rocche del Gatto made its debut in the wine world with the 2002 harvest. The production philosophy behind the wines of this estate, which is run by Fausto De Andreis, Chiara Crosa di Vergagni and her father Gigi, is to vinify using the best elements of ancient tradition and modern technology with the aim of achieving typicity and flavour expression. Spigau Crociata 2004 is a fine example. It is made with a selection of pigato grapes which are given long temperature-controlled maceration. The intense straw colour presages a complex nose with emphatic floral and herbal aromas that develop into hints of ripe peach and pineapple. The fruit flavours are even more pronounced on the palate, where the wine shows concentration and good development, backed up by warm alcohol offset by sufficient acidity. Last year's Pigato also showed enjoyably, with fresh, delicate spring flowers and Mediterranean scrubland fragrances. The aroma profile gains an enjoyable almondy undertone as it flows across the palate and develops well. Neither is Macajolo shamed by the lack of a prestigious DOC label. It is made exclusively from ormeasco grapes and this means that it cannot be included in the DOC since the introduction of the new regulations. Aromatic and spicy, it offers fruit-led, blackberry preserve notes and hints of white pepper before showing warm and uncomplicated on the palate, and the development is remarkable for its balance and for the precision of the taste sensations. Intin, though, is less focused. It's a Vermentino with decidedly herbaceous aromas and not much mouthfeel.

○ Spigau Crociata '04	🍷🍷	4*
● Macajolo '05	🍷🍷	4*
○ Riviera Ligure di Ponente Pigato '05	🍷	4
○ L'Intin '05		4

ALBENGA (SV)

LA VECCHIA CANTINA
FRAZ. SALEA
VIA CORTA, 3
17031 ALBENGA (SV)
TEL. 0182559881

Umberto Calleri has deep roots in the wine world reaching back as far as his great-grandparents, who also grew grapes and made their own wine. Around 25 years ago, Umberto followed in their footsteps, refitting the old family cellars as a business venture. Since then, he has worked patiently and achieved constant improvements in quality. The estate's winemaking expertise is applied exclusively to grapes grown on-site from vines on the best-aspected hillside sites at Salea, just outside Albenga. The best of the small range of wines is the Pigato. It has an intense straw-yellow colour and envelops the nose in fruity aromas with hints of undergrowth, almonds and honey. On the palate, it is soft and balanced with good body and development, underpinned by a pleasant, marked aromatic almondy note. After a year's hiatus when the 2000 version was not released, Pigato Passito made a comeback. Its gold is tinted with amber, introducing a caressing waft of honey, ripe apricots, walnuts and fruits preserved in alcohol. In the mouth, the marked alcohol is balanced by brisk acidity, which also keeps the sweetness in check as it signs of with a harmonic finish. The Vermentino is equally encouraging. On the nose, it gives grass, meadow flowers and a note of apples before the fresh, lively palate delivers good fruit, moderate structure and a long finish.

○ Riviera Ligure di Ponente Pigato '05	🍷🍷	4*
○ Colline Savonesi Passito '01	🍷	6
○ Riviera Ligure di Ponente Vermentino '05	🍷	4

ANDORA (SV)

Cascina Praié

Loc. Colla Micheri
17051 Andora (SV)
tel. 019602377

Massimo Viglietti and his wife Anna Maria Corrent are single-minded workers. Since they set up their winery in 2001, these two well-matched agronomists have been applying some very clear principles: low environmental impact vineyard management, maximum focus on the fruit and spraying only with copper and sulphur. In the cellar, they are increasingly using ambient yeasts while gradually reducing the use of filtration, enzymes and sulphur. The results have come quickly and very flattering they are, too. Vermentino Le Cicale 2004 has a finely perfumed floral nose scented with Mediterranean scrubland and there is an intriguing minerality on the elegantly developing palate. A delicate vein of acidity adds to drinkability. Pigato Il Canneto is also successful in its first year of production. An intensely fruity nose develops into notes of mossy undergrowth. Full-bodied fruity and honeyed characters show well on the palate, and there is a pleasant warming sensation through to the finish. The 2004 reds, Ardesia and Sciurbì, are both praiseworthy. Ardesia is a cabernet and rossese blend with a ripe nose redolent of fruit preserved in alcohol, jam and an elegant use of wood. The palate has good body and complexity, underpinned by a successful combination of smoothness and power. Sciurbì, which is mainly granaccia with some sangiovese, shows a range of aromas from tobacco to spices and dried flowers. We liked its balanced palate, persistent fruit and smooth development. Vermentino Colla Micheri is fresh and drinkable.

●	Ardesia '04	▼▼	5
○	Riviera Ligure di Ponente Vermentino Le Cicale '04	▼▼	4*
●	Sciurbì '04	▼▼	4*
○	Riviera Ligure di Ponente Pigato Il Canneto '05	▼▼	4*
○	Riviera Ligure di Ponente Vermentino Colla Micheri '05	▼	5

CAMPOROSSO (IM)

Tenuta Giuncheo

Loc. Giuncheo
18033 Camporosso (IM)
tel. 0184288639 - 0184287056
www.tenutagiuncheo.it

We have been following architect Arnold Schweizer's winery and its rather good products for some time. Recently, it has achieved further excellence thanks to Marco Romagnoli's rigorous approach in vineyard and cellar. We'll start with the Vermentino. There are inviting fragrances of Mediterranean scrubland, meadow flowers, apples and pears. In the mouth, it has finesse, weight, fruit and a long warming finish. Le Palme is also good. Its fruit comes through the oak, developing smoothly on the palate with freshness and balance. Eclis 2004 is a high-flyer with fine spicy aromas mingling with ripe tropical fruit, honey, white chocolate and balsam before the full-flavoured palate signs off with a long finish. Rossese Pian del Vescovo 2004 has an intense, warming nose that shows notes of esters, balsam, aromatic herbs and forest fruits. On the palate, there is elegance, body, and an enjoyable fruitiness over almonds. The basic Rossese is simpler but well structured. It develops well, balancing vigour and length. Lunico, a rossese and syrah blend in its first year of production, is much more demanding. The nose has fruit aromas, spicy wood notes, minerality and balsam which are all mirrored on the palate. The development is nice, despite slightly assertive tannins that prevent the wine from achieving full roundness. Syrah Sirius 2004 is an attention grabber, with aromas ranging from smoky notes to spiciness, coffee and ripe fruit. In the mouth, the decidedly tannic character melds with fruity notes, showing reasonable concentration and seamless development.

●	Lunico '04	▼▼	5
○	Riviera Ligure di Ponente Vermentino Eclis '04	▼▼	6
●	Rossese di Dolceacqua Vigneto Pian del Vescovo '04	▼▼	5
●	Sirius '04	▼▼	7
○	Riviera Ligure di Ponente Vermentino '05	▼▼	4*
○	Riviera Ligure di Ponente Vermentino Le Palme '05	▼	4
●	Rossese di Dolceacqua '05	▼	4
●	Sirius '03	▽▽	7
●	Rossese di Dolceacqua Vigneto Pian del Vescovo '03	▽▽	5

CASTELNUOVO MAGRA (SP)

Ottaviano Lambruschi

via Olmarello, 28
19030 Castelnuovo Magra (SP)
tel. 0187674261

This estate's history goes back to the beginning of the 1960s, which was not a great time to be going into the world of wine. But the Lambruschi family took on the challenge, and it proved to be a winning move. They have five hectares of vineyard on the Lunigiana hillsides, surrounded by the characteristic Mediterranean scrubland that can be tasted in the wines themselves. These slopes may well be inaccessible and difficult to work, but the Lambruschis still aim unswervingly for quality. Hard work in the vineyard and respect for the grapes in the winery is the philosophy which has guided the business for more than half a century, starting with Ottaviano Lambruschi and continuing with his son Fabio. Sarticola 2005 is a striking straw yellow. Its spectrum of aromatics is reminiscent of juniper and yellow-fleshed fruit, introducing medium body, good acidity and length. In contrast, Costa Marina 2005 has nuances of ripe fruit, apricots, almonds and meadow flowers on the nose. On the palate, it is rich, with a balsam and citrus finish. Last but not least is Vermentino Alessandro, the newest wine. It has a complex nose with herbaceous notes, spring flowers and thyme preceding a well-balanced, nicely persistent palate with a good finish hinting at walnutskin.

○	Colli di Luni Vermentino Alessandro '05	🍷🍷	4*
○	Colli di Luni Vermentino Costa Marina '05	🍷🍷	4*
○	Colli di Luni Vermentino Sarticola '05	🍷	4

Il Torchio

via Provinciale, 202
19030 Castelnuovo Magra (SP)
tel. 0187674075

Giorgio Tendola is a man who has close ties to his birthplace, Colli di Luni, in the south of Liguria where it shades into Tuscany. Here his father used to manage an olive press producing good extra virgin oil, as well as a cellar just large enough to turn out a little wine for sale in demijohns. Now the estate stretches over six hectares, mostly planted to the vine. It releases around 45,000 bottles a year and the facilities also include a neat little cellar, an olive press and a very welcoming farm holiday centre run by Giorgio's daughter and son-in-law with six tastefully decorated rooms and strictly local food. We tasted three wines, Rosso Riserva 2003, a successful blend of merlot, sangiovese and other red-skinned varieties, and two whites, the classic Vermentino and a fresh wine made with albarola, malvasia and vermentino. The Riserva has a vivacious, fruity bouquet with notes of balsam, toast and woodland introducing an enjoyably well-crafted palate with good harmony that fully justifies its award of Two Glasses. The Vermentino has good intensity of colour and a fine spectrum of aromatics themed around acacia blossom, citrus fruits, moss and sage. The linear palate is soft and enveloping. Il Torchio is fresh and drinkable; in short, an excellent aperitif wine.

●	Colli di Luni Rosso Ris. '03	🍷🍷	5
○	Colli di Luni Vermentino '05	🍷	4
○	Il Torchio	🍷	3

CHIAVARI (GE)

ENOTECA BISSON
C.SO GIANELLI, 28
16043 CHIAVARI (GE)
TEL. 0185314462
www.bissonvini.it

Piero Lugano – known to everyone as Bisson – continues to devote his energies to enhancing the image of Genoese viticulture. His success in this role is such that his town centre winery is acknowledged as an oenological beacon for the whole province. Having achieved recognition for its white wines, this year the estate also won Two Glasses for Makallé, which is made entirely from granaccia, demonstrating that Liguria is well suited to growing this ancient variety. Three versions were on parade: a standard vinification, a late harvest and a barrique-aged. The first two of these were convincing, but the wood-aged one was weak, and has not been reviewed. Granaccio 2005, the version vinified normally with skin contact, has an intense ruby colour with spicy, fruity aromas. On the palate, it is well-rounded with the same aroma profile as the nose. These sensory responses are magnified in the barrel-fermented late-harvest version, Makallé 2005. Here, the aromas of cherry, strawberry and blackberry are intense and well defined. The palate lives up to this promise with balanced structure and a long finish. On the white front, Vigna Intrigoso Vermentino 2005 is excellent. Its floral nose has green notes then silky development on the palate is complemented by good length. Vigna Erta was a little below this level, whilst U Pastine, made with the typical bianchetta grape of the Genoese hills, is as enjoyable as ever.

●	Colline del Genovesato Rosso Makallé '05	▼▼	5
●	Colline del Genovesato Rosso Makallé Il Granaccio '05	▼▼	5
○	Golfo del Tigullio Vermentino Vigna Intrigoso '05	▼▼	4*
○	Golfo del Tigullio Bianchetta Genovese U Pastine '05	▼	4
○	Golfo del Tigullio Vermentino Vigna Erta '05	▼	4
○	Acini Rari Passito '02	▽▽	5

CHIUSANICO (IM)

LA ROCCA DI SAN NICOLAO
FRAZ. GAZZELLI
VIA DANTE, 10
18027 CHIUSANICO (IM)
TEL. 018352850
www.roccasannicolao.com

This estate in the hamlet of Gazzelli takes its name from a 13th-century chapel dedicated to Saint Nicholas, the last surviving building of what used to be a monastery in the hinterland of Imperia, surrounded by nature where the Maritime Alps meet the sea. The area under vine is typical of the region in that it is planted on terraces hewn out of the mountain at 350 to 600 metres above sea level. As for the wines, the basic Vermentino is straw-coloured, with fine floral notes of juniper and hawthorn, fruit notes of apples, damsons and hints of citrus. The palate is enjoyable and develops well, with a clean, fresh finish. Vigna Proxi, in contrast, is a bright straw yellow with herby and meadow flower notes backed up by soft fruit. On the palate it is dry, with a nicely gauged balance of alcohol and acidity, showing an almond-themed flavour, medium body and reasonable development. Moving on to the Pigatos, the basic wine has balsamic aromas and well defined peach on the nose and palate. It is pleasantly fresh and the finish is almondy and long. Vigna Proxi Pigato is very varietal and repeats last year's success. An intense, fruit-led nose reveals peaches, apricots and whitecurrants before the soft, full-flavoured palate unveils its body and length.

○	Riviera Ligure di Ponente Pigato Vigna Proxi '05	▼▼	4
○	Riviera Ligure di Ponente Vermentino '05	▼▼	3*
○	Riviera Ligure di Ponente Pigato '05	▼	3
○	Riviera Ligure di Ponente Vermentino Vigna Proxi '05	▼	4

DIANO CASTELLO (IM)

MARIA DONATA BIANCHI
VIA DELLE TORRI, 16
18010 DIANO CASTELLO (IM)
TEL. 0183498233

This estate is rightly seen as a benchmark in Liguria. Its owner, Emanuele Trevia, is recognized as one of the most dedicated winemakers in the Ponente. This year, she again presented us with an extremely successful range. The property comprises four and a half hectares of vines centred on Diano Aretino, with outposts at Diano Castello, and production totals 40,000 bottles a year. Our tasting notes start with the Vermentino, which was a success from every point of view. It entices the nostrils with a delicately persistent bouquet of floral aromas, woodland notes and, more subtly, pears. In the mouth, it manages to be expressive, full-flavoured, fruity and delicately warming, with good concentration and a long, tidy finish. Vermentino Antico Sfizio was next up, its deep straw-yellow colour tinged with amber. On the nose, it is substantial with ripe fruit and balsamic notes before the palate shows good structure, backbone, enjoyable development and attractive dried fruit with pleasantly bitterish undertones. The Pigato, on the other hand, is characterized by aromas of citrus, peaches and Mediterranean scrubland. Entry on the palate is assured, unfolding into a rich, fruity body lifted by crisp acidity and a long finish. La Mattana 2004 is an excellent syrah and grenache blend. Its credentials are immediately obvious in its bright ruby red, which ushers in an intense, complex nose with coffee, forest fruit jam, plums and spices. The palate is equally impressive, giving a densely woven web of fruit and oak with just the right level of tannins and an enjoyable finish.

● La Mattana '04	🍷🍷	6
○ Antico Sfizio '05	🍷🍷	4*
○ Riviera Ligure di Ponente Pigato '05	🍷🍷	4*
○ Riviera Ligure di Ponente Vermentino '05	🍷🍷	4*
● La Mattana '03	🍷🍷 (outline)	6
○ Antico Sfizio '04	🍷🍷 (outline)	4
○ Riviera Ligure di Ponente Vermentino '04	🍷🍷 (outline)	4

DIANO MARINA (IM)

POGGIO DEI GORLERI
FRAZ. DIANO GORLERI
VIA SAN LEONARDO
18013 DIANO MARINA (IM)
TEL. 0183495207
www.poggiodeigorleri.com

This year, the Merano family estate made another positive showing. Although Giampiero and his sons Davide and Matteo are not from wine backgrounds, they have clear ideas about how to go about achieving results. Passion and experimentation have encouraged those results while input from oenologist Beppe Caviola and agronomist Gian Piero Romana has also helped. The property now comprises four hectares under vine, which may be supplemented by a further two hectares around Albenga in the near future. They produce 7,000 bottles of Pigato Cycnus, named after a king of the Western Ligurian tribes. It is straw yellow in appearance and opens on an inviting note of juniper with hints of yellow-fleshed fruit, principally peaches and apricots. The palate confirms the attractive fruit of the nose, enhancing it with a well-structured frame, good acidity and freshness. Vermentino Apricus has fairly intense elderflower, pears and apple aromas on the nose leading into a clean, very well balanced palate that shows attractive evidence of a period of wood-ageing. Vigna Sorì is named after a road which winds through the well-aspected hills of one of the best zones for vermentino, in Diano Marina and Diano Gorleri. On the nose, it has citron, hints of yellow apples and damson which reappear on the full-flavoured harmonious palate. The finish is warm and clean.

○ Riviera Ligure di Ponente Pigato Cycnus '05	🍷🍷	4*
○ Riviera Ligure di Ponente Vermentino Apricus '05	🍷🍷	5
○ Riviera Ligure di Ponente Vermentino V. Sorì '05	🍷🍷	4*
○ Riviera Ligure di Ponente Vermentino Apricus '05	🍷🍷 (outline)	5

DOLCEACQUA (IM)

ALTA VIA

LOC. ARCAGNA
18035 DOLCEACQUA (IM)
TEL. 0184488230

When you arrive here, you notice the harmony of the landscape and the elegant buildings, which blend perfectly into their surroundings. The vine stock covers five hectares, three planted to rossese. The hectare of syrah is at Col di Rodi and there is the same area again of vermentino at Poggio di San Remo, although this is not yet in production. Savino Formentini and Gianni Arlotti have taken their first, important step. The future holds plans for the acquisition of other vineyards in the area as well as accommodation for guests. The trio is completed by the able agronomist and entrepreneurial winemaker Federico Curtaz and the results of this partnership have been impressive from the outset. We'll begin with the Rossese Superiore 2004 with its soft aroma profile showing notes of wood, fruit, spice and hints of quinine. Pleasantly fresh in the mouth, it develops nicely on the palate over a very enjoyable almondy undertone. The 2005 is even more successful. Concentrated aromas are laced with stylish oak fading into ripe fruits of the forest and balsamic notes. The palate is taut, offering significant weight, softness and good fruit. Skip Intro 2004 is a Syrah and shows blackberry, morello cherry, blackcurrant, black pepper and some balsam on the nose. In the mouth, it has solid structure with intense softness and a compact finish. Finally, the rossese and syrah Dapprimo 2005 is extremely good, giving concentrated aromas of ripe fruit, spices and tobacco fusing with a smoky undertone. The palate is warm, silky, energetic and intensely fruity and the finish has good depth.

● Dapprimo '05	🍷🍷	4*
● Rossese di Dolceacqua Sup. '04	🍷🍷	5
● Skip Intro '04	🍷🍷	5
● Rossese di Dolceacqua Sup. '05	🍷🍷	5

DOLCEACQUA (IM)

GIOBATTA MANDINO CANE

VIA ROMA, 21
18035 DOLCEACQUA (IM)
TEL. 0184206120

Mandino Cane draws strength from his bond with his land and he wears his 77 years with nonchalance. Mandino continues to follow his star undaunted, fully aware of just how important the vineyard is, effecting rigorous selections with the aim of raising quality ever higher. Concrete results and hard work are the watchwords that have allowed him to attain the status of a respected master winemaker. Mandino's wines have the fascinating quality of artisanal products whose every detail is scrupulously crafted. His Rossese Superiore Vigneto Arcagna, sourced from an excellently aspected hillside that looks down on Dolceacqua, easily picked up Two Glasses. The wine's appeal and elegance is immediately evident on the nose, which has aromatic herb notes, wild berries and hints of spice. It is harmonious on the palate with a deliciously intense fruit and almonds flavour, leading to a clean, long finish. Vigneto Morghe 2005 is another fine bottle. Its ruby colour complements intense Mediterranean scrubland aromas and wild strawberries with subtle hints of pepper. The well-structured palate has good concentration, attractive nose-palate consistency and excellent balance. The white vermentino and viognier blend, Vervionè, is highly drinkable and will keep well. It has a direct impact, richness and well-structured aromas before developing with attractive complexity on the palate, which is full-bodied, full-flavoured, balanced, well sustained and clean. This year L'Intruso was not presented as it is still maturing in barrel.

● Rossese di Dolceacqua Sup. Vign. Arcagna '05	🍷🍷	5
● Rossese di Dolceacqua Sup. Vign. Morghe '05	🍷🍷	5
○ Vervionè '05	🍷🍷	3*
● Rossese di Dolceacqua Sup. Vign. Arcagna '04	🍷🍷 (white)	5
● Rossese di Dolceacqua Sup. Vign. Morghe '04	🍷🍷 (white)	5
● L'Intruso '03	🍷🍷 (white)	5

DOLCEACQUA (IM)

TERRE BIANCHE
LOC. ARCAGNA
18035 DOLCEACQUA (IM)
TEL. 018431426
www.terrebianche.com

The Arcagna zone, which is home to Terre Bianche, is truly magnificent with its vineyards, olive groves and verdant Mediterranean scrubland. Filippo Rondelli and Franco Laconi have no doubts about the land's calling as a wine-producing area and support predominantly local varieties like rossese di Dolceacqua. The basic version of this varietal wine has a nose of ripe fruit and aromatic herbs that then reappear on the palate with good progression, silkiness and balance. Moving up a gear, Bricco Arcagna 2004 is a Rossese of seductive drinkability with an intense nose of forest fruits, spices and a dash of balsamic menthol. On the palate, it flaunts elegance, length and a powerful body with rich flavour, warming alcohol, fruit and a delicious twist of almonds. Arcana Rosso 2003 is a very good cabernet and rossese blend. The deep ruby red is followed by aromas of cassis, blackberries and chocolate. In the mouth, the energy of the fruit is well matched to the structure of the wine, leading to a long, intense finish. The quality of the estate's range is ensured by attention to each product in equal measure, as is demonstrated by the Vermentino, which has a charming nose leading to a long palate with a nice flesh and attractive fruity, almondy notes. The Pigato is also very good, giving intense Mediterranean scrubland, peach and sage aromas overlaid on a fresh linear palate and a long finish. Finally, Arcana Bianco 2004 easily earned Two Glasses with rich fruit and notes of almond, honey and vanilla ushering in a harmonious palate with a long, well-sustained finish.

●	Arcana Rosso '03	2 black glasses	5
○	Arcana Bianco '04	2 black glasses	5
●	Rossese di Dolceacqua Bricco Arcagna '04	2 black glasses	5
○	Riviera Ligure di Ponente Pigato '05	2 black glasses	4*
○	Riviera Ligure di Ponente Vermentino '05	2 black glasses	4*
●	Rossese di Dolceacqua '05	1 black glass	4
●	Arcana Rosso '01	2 white glasses	5
●	Rossese di Dolceacqua Bricco Arcagna '03	2 white glasses	5
●	Rossese di Dolceacqua Bricco Arcagna '01	2 white glasses	5

FINALE LIGURE (SV)

CASCINA DELLE TERRE ROSSE
VIA MANIE, 3
17024 FINALE LIGURE (SV)
TEL. 019698782

The Cascina delle Terre Rosse estate is ably steered by helmsman Vladimiro Galluzzo, who is supported by oenologist Giuliano Noè. Careful selection allows them to pick white grapes at levels of potential alcohol and dry extract on a par with serious reds. It is no coincidence that their Pigato is an excellent wine with a rich aroma profile of peach, damson, bananas and acacia blossom. The concentrated, flavoursome palate develops with great complexity into a long, clean finish. Apogeo was equally good and in fact was one of the best Pigatos we tasted. The whistle-clean aromas of peach, honey, apricot and moss introduce a flavoursome, perfectly expressed palate that has heft without sacrificing elegance. In Le Banche 2005, Vladimiro has created a truly remarkable wine. The oak is very well-judged and never masks a nose of white peaches, damsons, acacia honey, resin and woodland herbs. It is marvellously balanced on the palate, showing soft, round and well sustained all the way through to a long finish. The Vermentino was a little less good than usual, but easily earned One Glass, as did the varietal lumassina-based L'Acerbina. As ever, Solitario scored well with its blend of grenache, barbera and a dash of rossese. The entry is clean and intense, the fruit revealing notes of undergrowth and blackcurrant along with sweet spices. The palate is gloriously expressive and beautifully melded together, the warming flavour, softness, elegant fruit and balsam all backed up by plenty of stuffing.

●	Solitario '04	2 black glasses	6
○	Le Banche '05	2 black glasses	5
○	Apogeo '05	2 black glasses	5
○	Riviera Ligure di Ponente Pigato '05	2 black glasses	5
○	L'Acerbina '05	1 black glass	4
○	Riviera Ligure di Ponente Vermentino '05	1 black glass	5
○	Riviera Ligure di Ponente Pigato '99	3 white glasses	5
●	Solitario '03	2 white glasses	6
○	Apogeo '04	2 white glasses	5

MONTEROSSO AL MARE (SP)

Buranco
via Buranco, 72
19016 Monterosso al Mare (SP)
tel. 0187817677
www.buranco.info

We had mixed feelings of anticipation and regret when we compiled this year's profile on Buranco. Anticipation because the estate, which used to belong to Kurt Wachter and his wife Sonja, has been sold to new owners, who we hope will be able to manage it as well as the impassioned couple from Liechtenstein; regret because we already know that we will miss their dreams, lucidity and calm elegance. Our thoughts went to them when we tasted perhaps the best ever version of Sciacchetrà they ever produced. This 2004 is big, aromatic and deep with honey, elegance, fat mouthfeel, extreme length and a phenomenal sweetness which never cloyed at any point of the tasting. It is a minor monument of a wine and although time may swallow it up as the bottles come to an end, it will stay chiselled on our memories for very many years to come. Slipstreaming in the wake of the sweet wine, the Cinque Terre and Buranco are both at very high quality levels. The former shows clear notes of iodine and sea salt combined with intense floral and white fruit aromas leading into a focused, minerally and distinctly long palate. The Buranco, from mainly cabernet sauvignon with some merlot and syrah, has a nose of wild berries and raspberries then an austere, full-flavoured palate with good harmony. Finally came Sonjare, the well made and enjoyable white blend based on vermentino which Kurt dedicated to his wife.

○	Cinque Terre Sciacchetrà '04	🍷🍷	8
●	Buranco '04	🍷🍷	6
○	Cinque Terre '05	🍷🍷	5
○	Sonjare	🍷	5
○	Cinque Terre Sciacchetrà '03	🍷🍷 (outline)	8
●	Buranco '03	🍷🍷 (outline)	6

ORTONOVO (SP)

La Pietra del Focolare
fraz. Isola di Ortonovo
via Dogana, 209
19034 Ortonovo (SP)
tel. 0187662129
www.lapietradelfocolare.it

After many years of receiving prestigious testimonials, La Pietra del Focolare is acknowledged as one of the most exciting estates in the Colli di Luni. It has only a few hectares, part estate-owned and part leased, but all are managed with scrupulous care, particularly when it comes to ensuring the grapes reach optimum ripeness. Most of the vine stock is Guyot-trained and most of the varieties are local. Total production fluctuates around the 25,000 bottle mark and is mainly Vermentino, sold in three versions. Viva Luce 2005 is well made, enjoyable and will accompany a wide range of foods. Straw yellow, it unveils floral, yellow plum and honey aromas and then balance on the palate characterized by a marked, albeit typical, almondy finish. Villa Linda is also good and shows attractive Mediterranean scrubland aromas and tart acidity. Hot on its heels comes Solarancio, made with grapes from the highly rated vineyards at Sarticola and Bacchiano. The meadow flower and yellow-fleshed fruit nose is reticent, but there is good balance on the palate with a subtle and characteristic almondy finish. Saltamasso 2004 is a well-behaved blend of sangiovese, merlot and massaretta. It is intense, garnet-streaked ruby red and the nose shows attractive prune and cassis notes. The tannins are still stalky but otherwise there is good consistency. La Merla dal Becco 2004 only just manages to keep up, expressing its terroir attractively with aromas of flowers and red fruit overlaid on vanilla and woodland notes. On the palate it is warm with a well-defined finish.

○	Colli di Luni Vermentino Villa Linda '05	🍷🍷	4*
○	Colli di Luni Vermentino Viva Luce '05	🍷🍷	4*
●	Colli di Luni Rosso La Merla dal Becco '04	🍷	5
●	Colli di Luni Rosso Saltamasso '04	🍷	4
○	Colli di Luni Vermentino Solarancio '05	🍷	5

PIEVE DI TECO (IM)

TOMMASO LUPI & C.
VIA MAZZINI, 9
18026 PIEVE DI TECO (IM)
TEL. 018336161
www.vinilupi.it

With his track record of producing carefully made, elegantly drinkable wines since the 1960s, one of the things that have given Tommaso Lupi most satisfaction must be seeing his three children follow him on the same path. The division of labour means Tiziana looks after the business side, Fabio handles viticulture and Massimo vinification in a close-knit family team that has shown it can continue their father's work. The best of the whites we tasted was the excellent Pigato Le Petraie. Rich and full on the nose, it has balsamic hints alongside lighter fruity notes and then shows weighty and full bodied in the mouth, its softness balanced by delicious acidity, attractive aromatics and a long finish. The basic Vermentino is also very good, its delicate aromas reminiscent of Mediterranean scrubland, citrus fruits and apples before the well-sustained palate unfolds to reveal good fruit, balanced by fresh acidity, and lovely persistence. Vignamare 2003 combines a slightly gold-tinged colour with aromas of ripe peaches, apricots and pineapple that have been lifted by their period in wood. In the mouth, it is attractively warm and balanced. Vermentino Le Serre is on a par, flaunting intense quince-like aromas, good body, structure and aromatic fruit. The basic Pigato is very drinkable, showing well rounded and charming, with subtle hints of sweetness and honey. Finally, Ormeasco Sciac-trà and Ormeasco Superiore Le Braje are as focused and enjoyable as ever.

○ Riviera Ligure di Ponente Pigato Le Petraie '05	🍷🍷	5
○ Riviera Ligure di Ponente Vermentino '05	🍷🍷	4*
○ Vignamare '03	🍷	5
● Ormeasco di Pornassio Sup. Le Braje '04	🍷	5
⊙ Ormeasco di Pornassio Sciac-trà '05	🍷	4
○ Riviera Ligure di Ponente Pigato '05	🍷	4
○ Riviera Ligure di Ponente Vermentino Le Serre '05	🍷	5
○ Vignamare '02	🍷	5

PONTEDASSIO (IM)

LAURA ASCHERO
P.ZZA V. EMANUELE, 7
18027 PONTEDASSIO (IM)
TEL. 0183710307

During the last century, Laura Aschero's grandfather used to vinify his grapes in the cellar of the family home. In the 1980s, Laura took this work one step further by setting up a winery in her own name and planting selected vermentino, pigato and rossese clones in well-aspected hillside sites at Monti and Posai, near Pontedassio. Laura was ahead of her time because she completely restructured the cellar and installed modern functional equipment. This unforgettable, straightforward and single-minded lady was one of the few female figures in the Ligurian wine world, and sadly she passed away in spring 2006. Her son Marco has taken up the baton, having been involved with the company for over 20 years, during which time he shared his mother's plans and philosophy. It is a philosophy that has given us an intriguing, well-gauged 2005 Vermentino that is highly enjoyable. The brilliant straw colour is pleasing and the nose is fascinating, showing intense floral notes including acacia blossom, honey and ripe fruits. The palate is warming and elegant, reprising the aromas perceived on the nose in a vibrant kaleidoscope of flavours that ends on an attractively bitterish, long finish. The Pigato 2005 fell slightly short of our expectations but overall the wine is nevertheless very respectable. The nose is fragrant, showing aromatic peach and pineapple fruit together with subtle musky notes, and the palate is warming, smooth and balanced with full, well-defined flavours.

○ Riviera Ligure di Ponente Vermentino '05	🍷🍷	4*
○ Riviera Ligure di Ponente Pigato '05	🍷	4

RANZO (IM)

A Maccia

fraz. Borgo
via Umberto I, 54
18020 Ranzo (IM)
tel. 0183318003
www.amaccia.it

The Valle Arroscia hillsides overlooking the Albenga plain are one of the best areas for the production of pigato. For over 150 years, this long-established farm estate has been producing good-quality wines that respect tradition and environment. The name A Maccia derives from the local dialect word meaning scrubland and in the past, the estate consisted of vineyards interspersed with other crops. These days, the area under vine is much more uniform and totals three hectares. The current grower and, for that matter owner, Loredana Faraldi, is youthfully and enthusiastically driving forward the work started by her great-grandfather Giovanni. The resulting products successfully combine the characteristics of the land with reliable quality. The estate's flagship is Pigato, of which 15,000 bottles are produced. It is straw yellow in the glass, with a marked citrus nose accompanied by yellow peaches and meadow flowers before the palate shows silky and attractively fruity, uniting softness with freshness. Solid structure and balance are followed up by a good, long finish. The Rossese is a slightly pale ruby red with a nose ranging from aromatic herbs to dried roses and even wild strawberries. There is a faint almondy vein on the palate, which is balanced, full flavoured, tannic and well defined through to the finish.

○	Riviera Ligure di Ponente Pigato '05	🍷🍷	4*
●	Riviera Ligure di Ponente Rossese '05	🍷	4

RANZO (IM)

Massimo Alessandri

fraz. Costa Parrocchia
18028 Ranzo (IM)
tel. 018253458
www.massimoalessandri.it

Thanks to the nature of the soil and generous sunlight, the municipality of Ranzo is one of the best-suited subzones for viticulture in the area around Imperia. This is where, year after year, Massimo Alessandri has been producing increasingly good wines with the help of oenologist Valter Bonetti and agronomist Diego Passaniti. The two whites presented cruised off with Two Glasses and the red even reached our final tastings. Pigato Costa de Vigne is a high-quality wine with well-defined aromatic herbs and Mediterranean scrubland aromas. Its palate is taut, elegant, aromatic and well sustained, its confident progression in the mouth lifted by an almondy twist. Aromatic finesse is the strong point of Costa de Vigne Vermentino, which combines apples and citrus with subtle florality. The palate is full and fresh, with attractive balance, good development in the mouth and a long finish. Ligustico 2004 has a strong, decisive personality from its blend of syrah and granaccia fermented in steel and matured for 12 months in 600-litre French oak barrels. The swath of aromas on the nose is deep and layered, with forest fruits, hints of oak, spicy pepper and anise mingling with leather and bitter chocolate. The palate manages to be both concentrated and supple, showing intense, fleshy fruit that closely mirrors the nose.

●	Ligustico '04	🍷🍷	6
○	Riviera Ligure di Ponente Pigato Costa de Vigne '05	🍷🍷	4*
○	Riviera Ligure di Ponente Vermentino Costa de Vigne '05	🍷🍷	4*
●	Vigne Vegie Rosso '03	🍸🍸	5

RANZO (IM)

BRUNA
VIA UMBERTO I, 81
18020 RANZO (IM)
TEL. 0183318082

Riccardo Bruna's rule is that all production decisions have to be made with quality in mind: he brooks no exceptions. Riccardo's small team, consisting of his family and Valter Bonetti, is right behind him. This year, that quality has been complemented by a new graphic design for, as Riccardo's daughter Francesca says, attention to detail is critical to effective communication. Il Baccan 2004 continues to be a byword for great, cellarable Pigato. At first, the aromas are reminiscent of riesling then over time the full intense complexity of the wine unfolds in ripe peaches, ripe apricots, hints of dried fruit, subtle minerality and balsamic undertones. Solid in structure, full in flavour, high in concentration and long in the finish, this wine dances elegantly across the palate in time to the warm energetic beat of its alcohol and acidity. And it earned Three Glasses, as it did last year. Then comes Le Russeghine. On the nose, it gives aromas of broom, meadow flowers, white peaches and hints of woodland resin before unfolding elegantly in the mouth with tidy fruit structure. Villa Torrachetta 2005 just missed Two Glasses. A sweet note on the nose accentuates the aromas of ripe fruit and faint balsam and in the mouth it progresses well with softness and decent length. The grenache, barbera, syrah and cinsault Pulin 2004 is another jewel in the Bruna crown. Its complex nose of fruit, spices and a touch of mint is echoed with intensity of flavour on the palate, which has sweet pervasive tannins and excellent alcohol. Finally came the Rossese, which is long and moreish.

○ Riviera Ligure di Ponente Pigato U Baccan '04	🍷🍷🍷	5
● Rosso Pulin '04	🍷🍷	5
○ Riviera Ligure di Ponente Pigato Le Russeghine '05	🍷🍷	4*
○ Riviera Ligure di Ponente Pigato Villa Torrachetta '05	🍷	4
● Riviera Ligure di Ponente Rossese '05	🍷	4
○ Riviera Ligure di Ponente Pigato U Baccan '03	🍷🍷🍷 (outline)	5
● Rosso Pulin '03	🍷🍷 (outline)	5

RIOMAGGIORE (SP)

BONANNI FELLEGARA
VIA DI LOCA, 189
19017 RIOMAGGIORE (SP)
TEL. 3384063383

The Cinque Terre has a split personality that looks very different, depending on your point of view. On the one hand, it is tourist-driven, glossy and international but also slightly false and a tad unauthentic. And then there is the true soul of the place, less superficial and harder to discover. You need to leave the crowded cafés and busy Via dell'Amore in Riomaggiore, walk to the terraces perched dizzily over the sea, go past olive trees and rows of vines trained up dry-stone walls, and breathe in the salty tang of the breeze that gives the land its soul. It was this Cinque Terre that Paolo Fellegara fell in love with, prompting him to move from Crema to set up his winery. Paolo has involved local man Tonino Bonanni as a partner in the business, which consists currently of a hectare of vines and a tiny cellar. Getting to the cellar takes patience and a willingness to climb up a vertigo-inducing stone stairway. Fellegara has invested all his dedication into this venture, as well as the knowledge he has picked up from a great Langhe winemaker, Elio Altare, who set him on the road to quality production. Paolo grows bosco, albarola and vermentino to produce wines which speak the same language as this extreme land. Cinque Terre 2004 has got amazing personality: Mediterranean scrubland and hints of sea salt on the nose and an acid and tannin-heavy palate make it a white you have to think about, not just taste. The Sciacchetrà has aromas of honey, walnuts and caramel, its sweetness restrained on the warming, elegant palate. It's very interesting and very good.

○ Cinque Terre Sciacchetrà '04	🍷🍷	8
○ Cinque Terre '04	🍷🍷	6

RIOMAGGIORE (SP)

WALTER DE BATTÉ
VIA TRARCANTU, 25
19017 RIOMAGGIORE (SP)
TEL. 0187920127

Walter De Batté shows his love for the land by getting involved in winemaking projects that most people would think were practically madness. Having faith in the flavour potential of varieties which are often written off as also-rans is a challenge that drives him on to strive for quality. The two hectares of vines in more than 20 different plots produce grapes that yield wines that are always exciting. Vinifying whites as if they were reds, long maceration on the skins and the use of techniques like lees stirring lend his wines unique character. Sciacchetrà 2003 is amber-gold with delicate aromas of dried grapes and hints of dried almonds with honey. On the palate, the good acidity offsets the sweetness and highlights the apricot jam fruitiness. There is good structure, determined thrust and clean finish. The new development this year was the first harvest of Cerricò 2004, which is named after a vineyard 500 metres above sea level inland from Riomaggiore. The wine is mainly grenache with a tiny dash of syrah. It gains enormously in aroma complexity through maceration for three weeks on the skins, followed by lees stirring for a month and then maturation on the lees in stainless steel for a year. Cooked fruit and balsam show on the nose and then the palate has slightly stalky, green tannins, which will need more time to soften. Unfortunately, the Cinque Terre was not produced this year because wild boar ate the entire crop.

○ Cinque Terre Sciacchetrà '03	🍷🍷	8
● Rosso Cerricò '04	🍷	7
○ Cinque Terre '04	🍷🍷 (white)	6

SARZANA (SP)

SANTA CATERINA
VIA SANTA CATERINA, 6
19038 SARZANA (SP)
TEL. 0187629429

With eight hectares spread over five farms of small orchards, vineyards and olive groves, Andrea Kihlgren is slowly realizing his objectives. The principle at the root of the project is respect for nature, and production is therefore organic. The aim is to preserve the soil by natural means, planting cover crops and applying animal fertilizer. In these hills, the vermentino grape is undisputed king, but Kihlgren has also decided to plant other varieties which are not strictly local, using tocai, sauvignon blanc and merlot for new blends. Giuncàro is a successful assemblage of tocai, sauvignon blanc and vermentino with fruit characters, Mediterranean scrubland and hints of balsam followed by a delicately warming palate. This is clearly an original wine for the area. Ghiarètolo 2003 is an interesting single-variety Merlot with plums, bark and cherries on the nose. It is aged for a year in 350-litre oak barrels and has emerged with good follow-through and personality. Moving on to the Vermentinos, the basic Colli di Luni is very fresh, with notes of peach and meadow flows and a soft finish in the mouth. Finally, Poggi Alti 2005 lived up to the expectations raised by the previous vintage, repeating the structure, and floral honeyed notes that characterized the earlier version. Annual production is around 32,000 bottles.

○ Colli di Luni Vermentino '05	🍷🍷	4*
● Ghiarètolo '03	🍷	4
○ Colli di Luni Vermentino Poggi Alti '05	🍷	4
○ Giuncaro '05	🍷	4

SPOTORNO (SV)

Sancio

via Laiolo, 73
17028 Spotorno (SV)
tel. 019743255

Step by step, this family-run winery is slowly asserting itself on the Ligurian wine scene. It was founded at the beginning of the 1980s but had to wait until 2000 for the turning point when the Sancio family's love for their land made them decide to change course and boost quality. They obtain around 40,000 bottles a year from their seven hectares of vineyard, which are all in the Savona area at Spotorno and Celle Ligure, to be precise. The vines are those typical of the area: rossese, pigato, vermentino and lumassina. The basic Vermentino 2005 has an attractive straw-yellow colour and fresh aromas of meadow flowers, golden delicious apples, oranges and mandarins. Fresh and supple in the mouth, it unveils a linear, balanced and very enjoyable progression. The basic Pigato has aromas of meadow flowers, fruit and Mediterranean scrubland with an undertone of moss. What distinguishes the palate is the way the marked fruit complements the balance of alcohol and acidity with good structure and an enjoyable finish. Cappellania is a nice surprise. It is straw in colour and has intense, inviting aromas of Mediterranean scrubland and aromatic herbs over a background of fresh fruit. A well-sustained palate with sufficient acidity and softness shows good character and a warming finish. Finally, the Rossese has enjoyable black cherry and herby fruit, a full-flavoured, well-balanced palate and a dry finish.

○	Riviera Ligure di Ponente Pigato Cappellania '05	🍷🍷	5
○	Riviera Ligure di Ponente Pigato '05	🍷	4
●	Riviera Ligure di Ponente Rossese '05	🍷	4
○	Riviera Ligure di Ponente Vermentino '05	🍷	4

VENDONE (SV)

Claudio Vio

fraz. Crosa, 16
17032 Vendone (SV)
tel. 018276338

This family-run estate is at 300 metres above sea level in the small village of Vendone over the Albenga plain. Despite his youth, Claudio Vio is a winemaker who is clear about the arduous path to be followed in order to make quality wines. He would already have changed career if he were not so in love with his work and, especially, his land. It is only thanks to this deep passion that he manages to find the strength to go on working such harsh, unforgiving terrain. The Vio winery has been advised for some time by oenologist Valter Bonetti, who succeeds in coaxing it into expressing its full potential every vintage. The two hectares of vineyards are all owned by the family and produce an average of 15,000 bottles a year of the classic varieties of the area, pigato and vermentino. The Pigato 2005 is straw yellow with flashes of gold in the glass. On the nose, it has striking floral and fruit aromas with hints of broom preceding a fresh palate with acidity present, suppleness and light structure. The Vermentino 2005 emphasizes slightly ripe pears, peaches, white plums and pineapple. Vivacious on the palate, it is long and very well balanced with an enjoyable thrust focused on soft tones.

○	Riviera Ligure di Ponente Vermentino '05	🍷🍷	4*
○	Riviera Ligure di Ponente Pigato '05	🍷	4

OTHER WINERIES

BioVio
FRAZ. BASTIA
VIA CROCIATA, 24
17031 ALBENGA (SV)
TEL. 018220776 - www.biovio.it

This small winery continues in the right direction. The Bacilò rossese and granaccia blend continues to be enjoyable with good nose-palate consistency. Vermentino Regione Marixe has Mediterranean scrubland on the nose and well-defined fruit notes on the palate leading into a round, soft finish.

●	Bacilò '05	🍷	4
○	Riviera Ligure di Ponente Vermentino Regione Marixe '05	🍷	4

Il Chioso
LOC. BACCANO
19038 ARCOLA (SP)
TEL. 0187986620 - 0187625147

Conte Picedi Benettini makes reliably good wines and this year was no exception. The straw Vermentino gives Mediterranean scrubland and moss before unveiling its warm, soft palate. On the other hand, the Rosso has ripe fruit notes and a good seam of acidity, nice tannins, warmth and elegance.

●	Colli di Luni Rosso Gran Baccano '05	🍷	4
○	Colli di Luni Vermentino Il Chioso '05	🍷	4

Giacomelli
VIA PALVOTRISIA, 134
19030 CASTELNUOVO MAGRA (SP)
TEL. 0187674155

Roberto Petacchi aims to bring out the character of the local grapes in his high-quality range. Boboli impressed us with its personality, mineral notes and ripe white fruit aromas. The basic wine has focused aromas of meadow flowers and citrus notes with a reasonably long finish.

○	Colli di Luni Vermentino Boboli '05	🍷🍷	5
○	Colli di Luni Vermentino '05	🍷	5

Enoteca Andrea Bruzzone
VIA BOLZANETO, 94/96
16162 GENOVA
TEL. 0107455157
www.andreabruzzonevini.it

The Polcèvera valley's Andrea Bruzzone fights a wine crusade to recover the area's native varieties. This year's offerings include the enjoyable Treipaexi red, a heady, fruity, easy drinker and the Bianchetta from a local grape is fresh and balanced with notes of bread on the nose.

○	Val Polcèvera Bianchetta Genovese '05	🍷	3
●	Val Polcèvera Rosso Treipaexi '05	🍷	3

Colle dei Bardellini

loc. Bardellini
via Fontanarosa, 12
18100 Imperia
tel. 0183291370 - www.colledeibardellini.it

This estate has four hectares planted to vermentino and pigato. The Vermentino Vigna U Munte has grass and meadow flowers on the nose, good fruit and a balanced palate. Pigato Vigna La Torretta has Mediterranean scrubland and citrus aromas with a full-flavoured, supple palate, freshness and length.

- ○ Riviera Ligure di Ponente Pigato V. La Torretta '05 — 🍷 5
- ○ Riviera Ligure di Ponente Vermentino V. U Munte '05 — 🍷 4

Fontanacota

via Dolcedo, 121
18100 Imperia
tel. 0183293457

Founded in 2001 by Marina Antonella Berta, Fontanacota has three hectares of vines around Pornassio and in the Dolcedo valley. The Vermentino gives banana and apple-like fruit, good character and a balanced palate. The Pigato has peach and citrus laced with meadow flowers, warmth and a long finish.

- ○ Riviera Ligure di Ponente Pigato '05 — 🍷🍷 4
- ○ Riviera Ligure di Ponente Vermentino '05 — 🍷🍷 4

Vis Amoris

s.da privata Molino Jave, 23
18100 Imperia
tel. 3483959569

Take a small parcel of vines at Caramagna, a young couple's enthusiasm and an oenologist like Giuliano Noè and hey presto: Pigato Vigna Domè. Intense Mediterranean scrubland, summer flowers, peaches, plums and bananas precede an elegant, full-flavoured palate with temptingly rich aromatics.

- ○ Riviera Ligure di Ponente Pigato V. Domè '05 — 🍷🍷 4*

Cooperativa Agricoltori della Vallata di Levanto

loc. Ghiare, 20
19015 Levanto (SP)
tel. 0187800867

This is a good start for a small, territory-focused enterprise that uses modern techniques to control vinification. Costa di Mattelun is a vermentino, albarola and bosco blend with an attractive straw-yellow appearance, delicate Mediterranean herb and mineral notes and a juicy, balanced palate.

- ○ Colline di Levanto Costa di Mattelun '05 — 🍷 4

La Felce

via Bozzi, 36
19034 Ortonovo (SP)
tel. 018766789

Andrea Marcesini has less than three hectares of vines. His Vermentino has varietal fruit and meadow flowers with good flavour and acidity. Pian di Sabbia is reliable. The red Re di Macchi has clearly-defined ripe red fruit and herbaceous notes, but the tannins are a little green and aggressive.

- ○ Colli di Luni Vermentino '05 — 🍷 4
- ○ Pian di Sabbia '05 — 🍷 3
- ● Re di Macchia '05 — 4

Durin

via Roma, 202
17037 Ortovero (SV)
tel. 0182547007
www.durin.it

This is a first Guide entry for the Basso family and their territory-driven wines. Lunghera Vermentino has citron, apple and broom on the nose, a full palate and a fruity, warm finish. I Matti 2004 gives spice, ripe mulberries and cherries that are echoed on the elegant palate. Ormeasco is reliable.

- ● Colli Savonesi I Matti '04 — 🍷🍷 5
- ○ Riviera Ligure di Ponente Vermentino Lunghera '05 — 🍷🍷 4*
- ● Ormeasco di Pornassio '05 — 🍷 4

NIRASCA
FRAZ. NIRASCA - VIA ALPI, 3
18026 PIEVE DI TECO (IM)
TEL. 018336071
www.cascinanirasca.com

Gabriele Maglio and Marco Temesio manage an excellent balance of winemaking techniques from past and present. The good 70-30 syrah and sangiovese Senso 2004 red is soft with notes of balsam. The basic Ormeasco is intense, supple and warming. The Superiore 2004 and Pigato 2005 are also reliable.

●	Senso '04	🍷🍷	5
●	Ormeasco di Pornassio '05	🍷🍷	4*
●	Ormeasco di Pornassio Sup. '04	🍷	4
○	Riviera Ligure di Ponente Pigato '05	🍷	4

GIAMPAOLO RAMÒ
VIA S. ANTONIO, 9
18020 PORNASSIO (IM)
TEL. 018333097

Lorenzo Ramò is a competent oenologist who runs the family estate which is exclusively planted to ormeasco, aka dolcetto a raspo verde. The variety yields around 25,000 bottles split between a Sciac-trà and Ormeasco. The wines are enjoyable and have a high-quality flavour palette.

●	Ormeasco di Pornassio '05	🍷🍷	4*
⊙	Ormeasco di Pornassio Sciac-trà '05	🍷	4

SAMUELE HEYDI BONANINI
VIA DI LOCA, 189
19017 RIOMAGGIORE (SP)
TEL. 3483162470

This young winery produces 1,000 good quality bottles, a few hundred of which are Cinque Terre Sciacchetrà 2004. This is amber with warm aromas of honey and dried fruits, good structure, warmth and enjoyable length. The full-flavoured dry version shows vine flowers and almonds.

○	Cinque Terre Sciacchetrà '04	🍷	8
○	Cinque Terre '05	🍷	5

LUCIANO CAPELLINI
VIA MONTELLO, 240B
19010 RIOMAGGIORE (SP)
TEL. 0187920632
www.vinbun.it

Make a note of Luciano Capellini's wines, Cinque Terre 2005 and Vino di Buccia 2004. The former has the terroir's signature warmth and iodine character while the second is a dessert wine made with "ripasso" – post-fermentation contact with sciacchetrà skins – to emerge honeyed, juicy and enveloping.

○	Cinque Terre '05	🍷🍷	5
○	Vino di Buccia '04	🍷🍷	6

FORLINI CAPPELLINI
LOC. MANAROLA
VIA RICCOBALDI, 45
19010 RIOMAGGIORE (SP)
TEL. 0187920496

The Forlini Cappellini estate has historic status in Cinque Terre. This year, there was only one wine, Cinque Terre 2005 from bosco, albarola and vermentino grapes. The elderflower, aniseed and Mediterranean scrubland aromas are well defined and the delightful finish is warm.

○	Cinque Terre '05	🍷	5
○	Cinque Terre Sciacchetrà Ris. '00	ΥΥ	8

IL MONTICELLO
VIA GROPPOLO, 7
19038 SARZANA (SP)
TEL. 0187621432
www.ilmonticello.vai.li

This year, Il Monticello released only two wines as major work goes on to expand facilities and improve quality. The basic Vermentino gives fruit and broom that precede a fresh, elegant palate. Rupestro is a sangiovese, canaiolo, pollera nera and ciliegiolo blend of intensity and pervasiveness.

●	Colli di Luni Rosso Rupestro '05	🍷	4
○	Colli di Luni Vermentino '05	🍷	4

LOMBARDY

With ten Three Glass awards, Lombardy chalked up impressive results this year. It did so despite the unevenness of the past few growing seasons, which alternated between drought and constant rain, with one or two hailstorms for good measure in some zones. In other words, Lombardy came through all this with head held high, demonstrating the organization and know-how that make it an important part of the Italian winemaking landscape. This is even truer when you focus on sparklers, given that five out of ten award-winning wines were excellent Franciacorta cuvées. Ca' del Bosco presented an Annamaria Clementi '99 that is up there with the best vintages. The same goes for Bellavista with its Gran Cuvée Brut '02. Uberti again stood out with an excellent Comarì del Salem '01, and Gatti at Erbusco swept up the Sparkler of the Year award with its sensual, seductive Satèn '02. Alongside these big names, the enthusiastic, determined Marcello Monzio Compagnoni finally hit the mark after his sacrifices and investment with a spectacular Extra Brut '03. There's no need to tell you that our final taste-offs were particularly busy. The same goes for Valtellina, a small wine zone with extraordinary quality that has pulled out four top wines, the Valtellina Numero Uno '01 from Plozza for its first Three Glass award, Sfursat Albareda '04 from Mamete Prevostini, confirming its quality, and then Nino Negri, a long-standing benchmark in Lombardy thanks to its excellent vineyards and the talent of oenologist Casimiro Maule, won two prizes this year, one for Sfursat '03 and the other for the celebrated Sfursat 5 Stelle '03. Add to this the fact that Vigneto Fracia and Sassella Le Tense, both '03, were in the finals and you will see how the utterly professional Maule more than deserved the Oenologist of the Year award. The list of prizewinners closes with a modern classic, Garda Cabernet Le Zalte '04 from Ruggero Brunori's Cascina la Pertica. As always, this great red is proof that biodynamic agriculture, far from imposing limits on growers, is actually a fascinating key to interpreting the territory. What's more several different wines, above all Lugana, showed they were just a step away from the goal. The Oltrepò Pavese won no trophies this year but sent quite a few wines to the finals, in addition to the excellent cuvées from Monsupello. Growers in Oltrepò still lack a little clarity about how they are going to get there but the DOC is moving decisively towards high-end production and away from big numbers. Alongside the most famous designated areas, other smaller zones are emerging. They may not have the numbers and market penetration of the DOCs mentioned above, they do have dozens of producers dedicated to quality. This goes for Valcalepio, Botticino, San Colombano al Lambro and the province of Mantua.

ADRO (BS)

Battista Cola
via Sant'Anna, 22
25030 Adro (BS)
tel. 0307356195
www.colabattista.it

The performance of wines from father and son team Battista and Stefano Cola was a tad less brilliant this year. From the ten hectares of terraced vineyards on the slopes of Monte Alto at Adro, they have obtained a standard Franciacorta Brut with a well-expressed, pleasant character revealing rich mineral and oak tones that never mask the fruit on the nose. There's also a lively note of citrus. Though the palate is less succulent than the version tasted last year, we enjoyed it for its freshness and great overall harmony. On the other hand, the Brut '02 convinced us with its complex bouquet where sensations of ripe white-fleshed fruit provide the background for more complex balsamic, oaky tones. Then comes a palate that shows style and solid structure, caressing effervescence and good length. The Franciacorta Satèn has appealing aromas of honey, toasty bread and coffee, and a fresh, tangy palate that brings back the sensations on the nose but closes out a bit too fast. For its part, the Franciacorta Extra Brut has a complex minerally character but the nose is less than perfectly clear and the character is a tad over-developed. While we are waiting for the new vintage of the red Tamino, we would point out the Terre di Franciacorta Bianco '05 with its pleasant tropical fruit tones. Other well-managed wines include the fresh, consistent Terre di Franciacorta Rosso '04 and the Terre di Franciacorta Bianco Tinazza '04, from chardonnay with small amounts of pinot bianco, which is less fragrant and full than previous editions.

○ Franciacorta Brut '02	**YY**	6
○ Franciacorta Brut	**YY**	4
○ Franciacorta Extra Brut	**Y**	5
○ TdF Bianco V. Tinazza '04	**Y**	4
● TdF Rosso '04	**Y**	4
○ TdF Bianco '05	**Y**	4
○ Franciacorta Satèn	**Y**	6
○ Franciacorta Brut '01	YY	6
● TdF Rosso Tamino '03	YY	4*
○ TdF Bianco '04	YY	5

ADRO (BS)

Contadi Castaldi
loc. Fornace Biasca
via Colzano, 32
25030 Adro (BS)
tel. 0307450126
www.contadicastaldi.it

This lovely Adro winery, owned by Vittorio Moretti, is part of the family agricultural corporation, Terre Moretti. In contrast to Bellavista, which only uses fruit from its own vineyards, this cellar, skilfully and enthusiastically managed by oenologist Mario Falcetti, purchases grapes and directly oversees around 60 hectares under vine, 18 of them estate-owned. The well-managed annual production runs to about 450,000 bottles and stands out for its excellent value for money. Specialists in Satèn, Falcetti presented us this year with two interesting versions. Soul '99 has a nice bright straw-yellow hue and tiny bubbles. The nose opens complex and elegant on notes of cakes, yeast and vanilla, perked up by fresh white-fleshed fruit and grapefruit. The palate is fresh, round, appealingly soft and well balanced with remarkable length. The Satèn '02 is just a bit less complex but still enjoyable for its overall freshness and softness, and the butter and cake sensations that support the clear floral note. From the numerous estate labels, we would mention an excellent Terre di Franciacorta Bianco '05 with an inviting peach bouquet and zesty, invigoratingly full palate. Finally, the good Franciacorta Brut has nice fullness, Zéro is dry and spirited and the Rosé '02 has red berry fruit and aromatic herb tones.

○ Franciacorta Satèn '02	**YY**	6
○ TdF Bianco Curtefranca '05	**YY**	4
○ Franciacorta Soul Satèn '99	**YY**	7
⊙ Franciacorta Brut Rosé '02	**Y**	6
● TdF Rosso Curtefranca '03	**Y**	4
○ Franciacorta Brut	**Y**	5
○ Franciacorta Zéro	**Y**	5
○ Franciacorta Satèn '01	YY	6
○ Franciacorta Satèn '99	YY	6

ADRO (BS)

FERGHETTINA

VIA SALINE, 11
25030 ADRO (BS)
TEL. 0307451212
www.ferghettina.it

By now perfectly settled into their wonderful new winery in Adro, Roberto Gatti and his family are dedicating themselves with their customary enthusiasm to perfecting and expanding the range of Franciacortas and wines that have earned them such well-deserved success. The Extra Brut '99 missed by a hairsbreadth an encore of the previous vintage's success but we are certain the near future will bring much satisfaction to this family of winemakers and growers. Roberto and his wife Andreina have for some time been assisted by their daughter Laura, who studied oenology at the University of Milan, and son Matteo. The Extra Brut '99 has a lovely bright greenish straw-yellow hue. The nose opens broad and complex with a bouquet that melds ripe peach and damson-led fruit with elegant aromatic herbs and hedgerow. The palate is rich, succulent and well coordinated, a fresh acid vein and caressing effervescence providing support. But the revelation this time is the Brut Rosé '02, a cuvée that opens up great new prospects for developing the wine type in Franciacorta. Its bright coral introduces great depth on the nose, which is marked by fruit and aromatic herbs, with notes of flowers and again vanilla. The solid, rich palate unfolds zestily with very good persistence. The other great labels from Ferghettina include an excellent, well-profiled Satèn '02 and a Chardonnay Favento '04 that is as good as its best vintages.

⊙	Franciacorta Rosé '02	🍷🍷	6
○	Franciacorta Extra Brut '99	🍷🍷	6
○	Franciacorta Satèn '02	🍷🍷	6
○	TdF Bianco Favento '04	🍷🍷	4*
○	TdF Bianco '05	🍷🍷	4*
○	Franciacorta Brut	🍷	5
●	TdF Rosso '04	🍷	4
○	Franciacorta Satèn '97	🍸🍸🍸	5*
○	Franciacorta Extra Brut '98	🍸🍸🍸	6
○	Franciacorta Satèn '98	🍸🍸🍸	5
○	Franciacorta Satèn '99	🍸🍸🍸	6

ADRO (BS)

MONZIO COMPAGNONI

VIA NIGOLINE, 18
25030 ADRO (BS)
TEL. 0307457803
www.monziocompagnoni.com

This year, Marcello Monzio Compagnoni presented us with a range of extraordinarily good Franciacortas. His Extra Brut '03 swept first into the final taste-offs and then to a Three Glass award. This excellent cuvée from separately fermented chardonnay grapes found just the right way to interpret the hot 2003 growing year with a brilliant greenish straw yellow that accompanies a perlage of rare finesse. The nose opens elegant, fresh and well coordinated on tones of crisp, fresh fruit brightened up by citron, veering to complex minerality. The palate shows a full, solid structure and lovely tanginess, consistently reprising the fruity notes of the nose before fading out long on echoes of vanilla. In other words, this small wonder justifies the intense efforts Marcello has made since the late 1980s at his two wineries, the original one in Valcalepio and this more recent one in Franciacorta. The rest of the range is up there with the Extra Brut and includes a Satèn '03, showing outstandingly elegant notes of acacia honey and cakes, and a Brut '03 fragrant with fruit and aromas and rich in fruity pulp. We thought the black cherry and white chocolate Rosé '03 was slightly less exciting because of its excessive softness and opulence. Ronco della Seta Bianco '05 shows structure and freshness while the Rosso '04 is pleasant and well balanced. Moscato di Scanzo Don Quijote '03 is as good as it has always been.

○	Franciacorta Extra Brut '03	🍷🍷🍷	6
○	Franciacorta Satèn '03	🍷🍷	6
○	Franciacorta Brut '03	🍷🍷	6
●	Moscato di Scanzo Don Quijote '03	🍷🍷	6
○	TdF Bianco Ronco della Seta '05	🍷🍷	4*
⊙	Franciacorta Brut Rosé '03	🍷	6
●	TdF Rosso Ronco della Seta '04	🍷	4
○	Franciacorta Extra Brut '01	🍸🍸	5
○	Franciacorta Satèn '01	🍸🍸	6
○	Franciacorta Brut '02	🍸🍸	6

ADRO (BS)

VILLA CRESPIA - F.LLI MURATORI
VIA VALLI
25031 ADRO (BS)
TEL. 0307451051
www.fratellimuratori.com

The Muratori brothers' ambitious project has now taken shape with the setting up of a series of wineries in various different areas, each specialized in the production of one wine. So they make a meditation wine in Ischia, full-bodied reds in Maremma, Tuscany, and rich complex whites in Sannio. And where better to make distinguished cuvées than Franciacorta? Here, under the expert guidance of oenologist and researcher Francesco Iacono, this Adro cellar makes a wonderful range of DOCG wines with grapes sourced from 60 hectares of estate vineyards, divided into various parcels. From the Brolese vineyard comes the Rosé '02, an Extra Brut with clear tones of raspberry-led red berry fruit that veers towards minerality and vanilla notes. The palate shows nice fullness and elegant balance before fading out long on shades of ripe fruit. The Brut Miolo offers a bouquet marked by white-fleshed fruit and Alpine flowers, and a well-balanced, harmonious palate with caressing effervescence and good length. The Numerozero has a pleasant fruity character that develops elegantly on the palate and signs off with balsamic hints. The Brut Novalia offers up floral aromas and a pleasantly pulpy, harmonious palate that ends on vanilla notes. But we felt the Satèn Cesonato was less balanced than in previous editions and a tad too marked by wood.

⊙	Franciacorta Brolese Rosé Extra Brut '02	YY	8
○	Franciacorta Brut Miolo	YY	5
○	Franciacorta Brut Novalia	YY	6
○	Franciacorta Dosaggio Zéro Numerozero	YY	7
○	Franciacorta Satèn Brut Cesonato	Y	7
○	Franciacorta Brut Miolo	(YY)	5

BEDIZZOLE (BS)

CANTRINA
FRAZ. CANTRINA
VIA COLOMBERA, 7
25081 BEDIZZOLE (BS)
TEL. 0306871052
www.cantrina.it

By now Cantrina is one of the most reliable benchmarks in Garda winemaking. The estate is named after a tiny district in the deepest hinterland of the Garda area. In the late 1980s, Dario Dattoli decided to plant little more than six hectares of vineyard not far from the town, on a hill dominated by a small Lombard-style villa, selecting French varieties as a tribute to his passion for wines from across the Alps. Following him in this tenacious effort was Cristina Inganni, accompanied by her husband Diego Lavo and Verona winemaker Celestino Gaspari. The new edition of the Nepomuceno, their showcase Merlot, is still ageing in the new underground cellar. The '03 shows great promise but further cellar time is all to the good. The wines we tasted were still quite interesting, starting with the elegant Rinè '04, a white from chardonnay and riesling renano with a splash of sauvignon. It unveils juicy fruit, lovely floral notes and delicately recalls medicinal herbs. Sole di Dario, a passito from part-dried sauvignon, sémillon and riesling, is as engaging as ever. Though the '03 edition will probably offer its best after further bottle ageing, it is already satisfying with deep sensations of candied fruit and honey. The '01 edition of Corteccio, a Pinot Nero with well-calibrated tones of berry fruit, is among the best ever. The other red, Zerdì, is well made.

●	Corteccio '01	YY	6
○	Sole di Dario '03	YY	6
○	Rinè '04	YY	4
●	Benaco Bresciano Zerdì '04	Y	4
●	Nepomuceno '01	(YY)	5
●	Garda Merlot Nepomuceno '00	(YY)	6
○	Riné '00	(YY)	4
○	Sole di Dario '01	(YY)	6
○	Rinè '03	(YY)	4
○	Sole di Dario '99	(YY)	6

CANEVINO (PV)

Caseo

Fraz. Caseo, 9
27040 Canevino (PV)
tel. 038599937 - 038599392
www.caseowines.com

Every year, Caseo manages to submit a range of better than good wines that earn much praise. The winery could be criticized for a lack of overall cohesion, considering there may be too many labels and the best results come in rotation, making it difficult to identify what could be defined as a flagship wine of consistently high quality. Having said this, we couldn't help notice that this year the classic method sparklers did better all round. The Grande Cuvée Pas Dosé from the '00 vintage is long and complex with a lovely dark colour and nice, stylish nose that gives clear ripe golden apple. The Extra Dry, from only chardonnay, has a golden colour, overripe but not tired tropical fruit, a broad range of aromas from roasted hazelnut to vanilla and remarkable structure. The Pinot Nero Rosé was also convincing this year. It's lighter and less orangey in colour than usual puts the accent on strawberry-led fruit. After the spectacular '01 version and disappointing '03 version, Sauvignon I Crocioni made a comeback with the '04, which is overripe in keeping with Marco Goia's style. Many other wines racked up interesting scores, beginning with the Chardonnay I Ronchi '03, which will be much better in a year or two when it has absorbed its generous dose of oak.

○	OP Spumante Cl. Caseo Grande Cuvée Pas Dosé '00	🍷🍷	5
○	OP Sauvignon Blanc I Crocioni '04	🍷🍷	4
○	Extra Dry Cl. Chardonnay	🍷🍷	5
⊙	OP Pinot Nero Spumante Cl. Caseo Rosé	🍷🍷	5
○	Gioiacaseo Brut	🍷	5
●	OP Barbera Donna Clarizia '01	🍷	6
○	OP Chardonnay I Ronchi '03	🍷	5
○	OP Riesling Renano Le Segrete '03	🍷	4
○	OP Moscato La Dote '05	🍷	4

CANNETO PAVESE (PV)

F.lli Giorgi

Fraz. Camponoce, 39a
27044 Canneto Pavese (PV)
tel. 0385262151
www.giorgi-wines.it

The loss of oenologist Gianfranco Giorgi, one of the co-owner brothers, was difficult but now this great winery in Valle Versa has set its sights on an ever more convincing top line. Although the so-called base range is one of the best and most reliable in Oltrepò, starting with the long-standing semi-sparkling Pinot Nero fermented off the skins. Buttafuoco Casa del Corno is the best of its type we tasted this year. Credit for this goes to the estate since the wine comes from the difficult 2002 growing year. With a bit more finesse and breadth in the aromas, this product could aspire to even better results. The Brut Metodo Classico Gianfranco Giorgi from the '03 vintage is also fairly good. Elegant, clean and zesty, it could gain in complexity from more time on the yeasts. With its pleasingly generous wild red berry fruit, the Vigalòn '05 IGT is made from the zone's traditional red varieties, croatina, barbera, uva rara and pinot nero. Nice tannins join good softness and balance on the palate. The Bonarda La Brughera '05 is again one of the best from Oltrepò, with its dark, purple ruby colour, upfront wild berry fruit and very soft palate. The same goes for the fragrant, clean Sangue di Giuda '05. This year also saw the first release of two rosé sparklers, a Metodo Classico and a Martinotti Extra Dry. The first shows outstanding elegance while the second goes down deliciously well. The Pinot Nero and Chardonnay from the '04 vintage are pleasant, varietal and well made.

●	OP Buttafuoco Casa del Corno '02	🍷🍷	4
○	OP Pinot Nero Brut Cl. Gianfranco Giorgi '03	🍷🍷	6
●	OP Bonarda Vivace La Brughera '05	🍷🍷	4
●	Vigalòn '05	🍷🍷	3*
⊙	OP Pinot Nero Gianfranco Giorgi Rosé Pas Dosé '03	🍷	5
○	OP Chardonnay Mesdì '04	🍷	5
●	OP Pinot Nero Monteroso '04	🍷	5
●	OP Sangue di Giuda Frizzante '05	🍷	4
⊙	OP Pinot Nero Extra Dry Martinotti Cuvée Eleonor Rosé	🍷	4
●	OP Bonarda Vivace La Brughera '04	🍷🍷 (previous edition)	4

CANNETO PAVESE (PV)

Bruno Verdi
via Vergomberra, 5
27044 Canneto Pavese (PV)
tel. 038588023
www.verdibruno.it

Fifteen years after its creation, Paolo Verdi's Rosso Riserva Cavariola is still one of the best from Oltrepò for its consistency of quality and style. The vineyard is located in such a particularly fortunate position that last year the Cavariola '02 made it to our finals, in spite of a distinctly unfavourable vintage. But it takes skill in the cellar to transform the grape into this sort of wine. Since Verdi began vinifying by punching down the cap manually in upright tonneaux, there has been further improvement in terms of finesse and complexity on the nose, leaving the balsamic component, Cavariola's calling card, intact. The palate has beautiful tannic weight and harmoniously fruity pulp. It will be interesting to follow its maturation curve over the next few years. The Brut Classico Vergomberra is well balanced and tangy. On its third release, the Pinot Nero is coming on nicely with the growing maturity of a still very young vineyard. Clean and fragrant in the '04 version, it gives a foretaste of extremely interesting developments in the near future. The series of best wines ends with the Bonarda Vivace Possessione di Vergombera and Sangue di Giuda Dolce Paradiso, both from '05 and both with fragrant, clean and very enjoyable aromas of violets and wild berry fruit. The Riesling Vigna Costa '05 is slightly under par but it really needs two or three years in bottle. The Pinot Grigio, Buttafuoco and Moscato '05 are consistent and well made.

●	OP Rosso Cavariola Ris. '03	▾▾	5
○	OP Brut Cl. Vergomberra '03	▼▼	5
●	OP Pinot Nero '04	▼▼	4
●	OP Bonarda Vivace Possessione di Vergombera '05	▼▼	3*
●	OP Sangue di Giuda Dolce Paradiso '05	▼▼	3*
●	OP Buttafuoco '05	▼	3
○	OP Moscato Volpara '05	▼	3
○	OP Pinot Grigio '05	▼	3
○	OP Riesling Renano V. Costa '05	▼	4*
●	OP Rosso Cavariola Ris. '02	▽▽	5
●	OP Pinot Nero '03	▽▽	4
●	OP Bonarda Vivace Possessione di Vergomberra '04	▽▽	3

CAPRIOLO (BS)

Lantieri de Paratico
loc. Colzano
via Simeone Paratico, 50
25031 Capriolo (BS)
tel. 030736151
www.lantierideparatico.it

For years now, Fabio Lantieri de Paratico has presented us with a fine range of Franciacortas and still wines that testify to his diligent efforts, even though he also has another career. Today, this estate whose name has been familiar in Franciacorta for centuries, owns 17 hectares under vine and a lovely cellar in a 14th-century palazzo at Capriolo. Oenologists Cesare Ferrari, who consults, and Alessandro Santini oversee production and Pierluigi Donna manages the vineyards. This estate's showcase wine, Franciacorta Arcadia '02, opens on the nose with lovely complex fruity tones, lifted by notes of medicinal herbs, subtle balsamic shades and a touch of vanilla. The palate is fresh, rich, pulpy and has pleasantly caressing effervescence. The Franciacorta Brut, Extra Brut and Satèn form a well-matched that shows a major step forward in quality compared to previous editions. The Brut has a rich nose marked by lavender and ripe fruit, and lovely freshness on the palate. The Satèn shows solid body and nice acid backbone. Finally, the Extra Brut has the vibrant richness of white-fleshed fruit, tanginess and decent, elegant structure. The vintage Satèn debuted with the '02, but we found it a little evolved and marked by fairly intrusive liqueur. While waiting for the new vintages of Terre di Franciacorta Rosso and Bianco from the Colzano vintage, we would point out the good Terre di Franciacorta Bianco '05 and Rosso '04.

○	Franciacorta Brut Arcadia '02	▾▾	6
○	Franciacorta Brut	▼▼	5*
○	Franciacorta Extra Brut	▼▼	5
○	Franciacorta Satèn	▼▼	5
○	Franciacorta Satèn '02	▼	6
●	TdF Rosso '04	▼	4
○	TdF Bianco '05	▼	4
○	Franciacorta Brut Arcadia '01	▽▽	6
○	Franciacorta Brut Arcadia '97	▽▽	5
○	Franciacorta Brut Arcadia '98	▽▽	5
○	Franciacorta Brut Arcadia '99	▽▽	6

CAPRIOLO (BS)

RICCI CURBASTRO
VIA ADRO, 37
25031 CAPRIOLO (BS)
TEL. 030736094
www.riccicurbastro.it

Riccardo Ricci Curbastro manages a family estate that sprawls across more than 30 hectares, 25 of them under vine, and produces around 230,000 bottles a year of Franciacortas and still wines. Franciacorta, in all its various guises, is the centre of attention at this family winery and Riccardo gives us a rather personal interpretation aimed at bringing out the best in the type and territory, with no technical excesses and a non-interventionist style. The Franciacorta Extra Brut '02 is exemplary in this sense, with its lovely straw yellow flecked with golden highlights. The nose opens rich and complex on notes of yeast and baked cakes, well ripened fruit and again floral notes that finally veer into fresh citrus. The broad, well-coordinated palate shows solid structure and succulent fruity tones sustained by a fresh acid vein that accompanies it to a long finish. Flowers and acacia honey emerge on the back palate. A similar wine that made a good showing in our finals because of its solid profile and intact fruit is the fresh non-vintage Brut, which has pleasant tropical touches and a long finish veined with aromatic herbs. The soft, pulp-rich Satèn has a round, vanillaed character and unfolds softly across the palate. From the still wines, a special mention goes to the nicely structured Rosso Santella del Gröm '03, the currant-led Sebino Rosso '04 and the Brolo dei Passoni '04, an elegant passito from part-dried chardonnay.

○	Franciacorta Extra Brut '02	♥♥	5
●	TdF Rosso Santella del Gröm '03	♥♥	4*
○	Brolo dei Passoni '04	♥♥	5
●	Sebino Rosso '04	♥♥	3*
○	Franciacorta Brut	♥♥	5
○	Franciacorta Satèn Brut	♥♥	5
○	TdF Bianco V. Bosco Alto '03	♥	4
●	TdF Rosso Curtefranca '04	♥	3
○	TdF Bianco Curtefranca '05	♥	3
○	Franciacorta Demi Sec	♥	5
○	Franciacorta Extra Brut '00	♡♡	5
○	Franciacorta Extra Brut '01	♡♡	6
○	Franciacorta Extra Brut '99	♡♡	5

CASTEGGIO (PV)

RICCARDO ALBANI
LOC. CASONA
S.DA SAN BIAGIO, 46
27045 CASTEGGIO (PV)
TEL. 038383622 - 038383345
www.vinialbani.it

The Albani family estate has quickly regained its rightful place in the Guide with two wines that went through to our finals. Credit goes to organic management that, among other things, involves little or no use of sulphur dioxide even if the risk of undesired oxidation is always just around the corner. Barbera and Riesling are two wines that should be understood and appreciated for their unique qualities. The former has a practically impenetrable ruby colour and after uncorking yields touches of reduction that slowly vanish as it aerates in the glass to reveal deep tones of printer's ink and wild berries. The palate is a parade of sensations. The impressive entry shows enough structure to make light of the 14.5 per cent alcohol declared. High acidity, typical of barbera, and a subtle tannic weave do not prevent the palate from being soft and the finish is long. No less original is the Riesling '04, drinks more like a Treviri wine than a Casteggio product. The golden hue introduces an evolved, almost oxidative style with unfolding minerality and intact fruit that is broad and richly shaded but not opulent. Easier to understand, although still very distinctive, is the Bonarda Vivace '05, which offers gamey and forest floor aromas as well as blackberry, blueberry and gooseberry. The soft, fragrant palate has a nice open finish. The Oltrepò Pavese Rosso Costa del Morone '03 shows cherry sensations and overripe fruit.

●	OP Barbera '04	♥♥	4*
○	OP Riesling Renano '04	♥♥	4*
●	OP Bonarda Vivace '05	♥♥	4*
●	OP Rosso Costa del Morone '03	♥	4
●	OP Rosso Vigne della Casona Ris. '98	♡♡	5
●	OP Rosso Costa del Morone '99	♡♡	4
●	OP Rosso Vigne della Casona Ris. '99	♡♡	5
●	OP Bonarda Vivace '03	♡♡	4

CASTEGGIO (PV)

Bellaria

fraz. Mairano
via Castel del Lupo, 28
27045 Casteggio (PV)
tel. 038383203
www.vinibellaria.it

Paolo Massone's enthusiasm and professionalism mean that, since grapes from the difficult 2002 harvest were considered unfit, the two estate jewels were not produced: there is no La Macchia Merlot or cabernet sauvignon and barbera Bricco Sturnèl. But on the other hand, Paolo always has high quality wines in a fairly limited range of labels for Oltrepò Pavese. The Barbera Olmetto '03 is among the best from the vintage. Not intended to be a powerful wine, it uses a vinification strategy that keeps oak to a minimum and gives some complexity without weakening the integrity of the fruit. A deep ruby colour, its aromas recall chocolate-covered liqueur cherries. On tasting, it shows good pulp and fruit, as well as freshness, so the acidity was not entirely penalized by the sweltering weather. We could talk forever about the Chardonnay Costa Soprana '03, not so much about its quality as the wine type it belongs to. It has a bright golden colour and at first the dose of new oak and toast is overwhelming. Slowly, a range of aromas then emerges and expands, including sweet spices, overripe bananas, wild flowers and honey. The full, fairly broad palate shows the value of the good acidity that supports it through to the long, leisurely finish. Finally, the Bonarda Vivace La Bria '05 has a deep ruby colour, hints of blackberry and blueberry with almost gamey notes of forest floor, nice ripe tannins and good fruit. It's expressive and soft, without overdoing the residual sugar.

●	OP Barbera Olmetto '03	🍷🍷	4
○	OP Chardonnay Costa Soprana '03	🍷🍷	5
●	OP Bornarda Vivace La Bria '05	🍷🍷	4*
●	La Macchia '00	🍷🍷 (outline)	5
●	Bricco Sturnèl '01	🍷🍷 (outline)	5
●	La Macchia '01	🍷🍷 (outline)	5
●	OP Barbera Olmetto '01	🍷🍷 (outline)	4

CASTEGGIO (PV)

Cantina di Casteggio

via Torino, 96
27045 Casteggio (PV)
tel. 0383806311
www.cantinacasteggio.it

With the Vite, Ambiente, Qualità (Vine, Environment, Quality) project, supervised by Riccardo Cotarella, Cantina di Casteggio aims to ensure future production will continue along the road to higher quality. The most interesting wine this year is Barbera Console Marcello '04, which went straight to the Three Glass finals. An almost impenetrable ruby colour, it is well constructed with oak that, although evident, never masks the balsamic notes and intact wild berry aromas. Tasting shows it to be powerful yet well balanced, modern and sure to improve with a year or two in bottle. The Longobardo '04 is an IGT from croatina, barbera, cabernet sauvignon and pinot nero. The remarkable pulp shows blackberry and blueberry upfront, and although it still has slightly exuberant tannins, everything is in place to round out the rough edges in bottle. Excellent scores also went to both the white and rosé versions of the classic method Pinot Nero Postumio, both impressing more with the cleanliness and finesse of their aromas than their structure. The Bianco is fuller and the Rosé softer and more of a charmer. These wines cost little more than six euros at the cellar door and it's almost impossible to find a top quality classic method sparkler at that sort of price. The Riesling Italico Clefi, Sauvignon, Mallowsia and Pinot Grigio '05 are well managed and varietal, with Clefi earning a special mention.

●	OP Barbera Console Marcello '04	🍷🍷	4*
●	Il Longobardo '04	🍷🍷	4
○	OP Pinot Nero Brut Postumio	🍷🍷	4*
⊙	OP Pinot Nero Brut Postumio Rosé	🍷🍷	4*
○	OP Malvasia '05	🍷	3
○	OP Pinot Grigio '05	🍷	3
○	OP Riesling Italico Clefi '05	🍷	3
○	OP Sauvignon '05	🍷	3
●	Il Longobardo '02	🍷🍷 (outline)	4
●	OP Barbera Console Marcello '03	🍷🍷 (outline)	4
○	OP Riesling Italico Clefi '03	🍷🍷 (outline)	3*

CASTEGGIO (PV)

LE FRACCE
FRAZ. MAIRANO
VIA CASTEL DEL LUPO, 5
27045 CASTEGGIO (PV)
TEL. 038382526

There is no Bohemi from '02. Although the base wine was rather good, the decision not to release the showcase label from this splendid estate was purely commercial. The same goes for Cirgà. On the still red front, we have Garboso '04, from this year on no longer an Oltrepò Pavese Rosso but a single-variety Barbera IGT. It has a lovely, clean nose with cherries emerging confidently then a well-balanced palate with proper acidity, lovely softness and a nice finish. Though it is not, and never aspires to being, a complex wine, it is still extremely enjoyable. Even better, the Bonarda La Rubiosa '05 is one of the best from the vintage to come out of Oltrepò. Fragrant and scented, it explodes with wild berries and shows perfect balance of its extract and restrained residual sugar. The Riesling Landò '05 is very good. Alongside its customary elegance, in line with the style of Roberto Gerbino, this year it adds better tanginess, minerality and structure compared to recent years. The Pinot Nero '03 comes from a very young vineyard. For now it is fragrant, varietal and clear, and needs only to acquire some complexity and depth. Cuvée Bussolera '04 is the best Martinotti method from Oltrepò. Fine and elegant, with broad and rather complex aromas because of its 12 months on the lees, it could almost be mistaken for classic method wine. Finally, the Pinot Grigio Levriere '05 has precise nose-palate consistency.

●	OP Pinot Nero '03	🍷🍷	6
●	Garboso '04	🍷🍷	4*
○	OP Pinot Nero Cuvée Bussolera Extra Brut '04	🍷🍷	4
●	OP Bonarda La Rubiosa '05	🍷🍷	4
○	OP Riesling Landò '05	🍷🍷	4
○	OP Pinot Grigio Levriere '05	🍷	4
●	OP Bonarda La Rubiosa '03	🍷🍷 (outline)	4
○	OP Pinot Nero Cuvée Bussolera Extra Brut '03	🍷🍷 (outline)	4

CASTEGGIO (PV)

FRECCIAROSSA
VIA VIGORELLI, 141
27045 CASTEGGIO (PV)
TEL. 0383804465
www.frecciarossa.com

Drought-plagued, sweltering 2003 was not the best growing season for a delicate variety like pinot nero, which needs a wide range of temperatures to bring out its marvellous aromatics. But at Frecciarossa, they know how to manage the weather. For years, Giorgio Odero has constantly been one of the best Pinot Neros from Oltrepò and this year it was the only one to reach the finals. Its lovely, pale garnet colour ushers in a remarkable bouquet where balsamic notes mingle with small wild berries and the elegant spice contributed by well-gauged oak The forthright palate offers wonderfully smooth, stylish tannins, verve and depth. The Francigeno IGT has replaced Villa Odero in the estate's range and the formula has been changed. The blend now calls for 50 per cent merlot plus croatina and barbera. This '03, though easily racking up a high score, still needs a bit more bottle time to integrate the oak. The spice, cake and wild berry aromas are intriguing but the palate still has to find a length. We gave a good score to the Riesling Renano Gli Orti '05 for its forthright bouquet where fruit and flower aromas overshadow the mineral component. The Uva Rara '05 is as pleasant as ever while the Bonarda Dardo, full and dark on the nose, would be excellent if its tannins were a shade less assertive.

●	OP Pinot Nero Giorgio Odero '03	🍷🍷	5
●	Francigeno '03	🍷🍷	5
●	OP Rosso Le Praielle '03	🍷	4
●	OP Bonarda Vivace Dardo '05	🍷	3
○	OP Riesling Renano Gli Orti '05	🍷	3
●	Uva Rara '05	🍷	3*
●	OP Pinot Nero Giorgio Odero '00	🍷🍷 (outline)	5
●	OP Rosso Le Praielle '02	🍷🍷 (outline)	4
●	OP Bonarda Vivace Dardo '03	🍷🍷 (outline)	3

CASTELLI CALEPIO (BG)

IL CALEPINO

VIA SURRIPE, 1
24060 CASTELLI CALEPIO (BG)
TEL. 035847178
www.ilcalepino.it

Sparklers are the main focus here at Calepino. Already mentioned in last year's Guide, Riserva Fra' Ambrogio '00 confirmed its quality with the new disgorgement. We also give similar scores to the other three sparkling wines presented this year. We felt the best was the Brut '02, mature in its overripe tropical fruit aromas and blessed with good backbone, remarkable length and nice overall balance. The Extra Brut '01 is also evolved and more hesitant on the nose, but dry and spirited in the mouth, with a slightly bitterish close. The family has expanded to include a well-made, pleasing Rosé with an orange-tinged colour and notes of raspberry and toast. Kalòs '03 is a nice Cabernet Sauvignon with sweetish aromas and echoes of almond biscuits. It has structure and some residual sugar that makes it a natural match for desserts. The Valcalepio Rosso Riserva Surìe '02, aged 18 months in mainly large barrels, has spice, toast and coffee with tertiary aromas that dominate the wild berry fruit. The palate is fairly full and harmonious, even though it closes rather abruptly. Another unusual wine is the Epias – the name should be read "Ergas" as in Ancient Greek – a full, sweet chardonnay with chestnut honey aromas and a bitterish finish. The Valcalepio Rosso and Bianco are well made, correct and varietal, and come respectively from the 2004 and 2005 vintages.

○	Extra Brut Cl. Il Calepino '01	🍷🍷	5
○	Brut Cl. Il Calepino '02	🍷🍷	4
⊙	Brut Cl. Rosé Il Calepino '02	🍷	4
●	Valcalepio Rosso Surìe Ris. '02	🍷	4
●	Kalòs '03	🍷	6
●	Valcalepio Rosso '04	🍷	3
○	Valcalepio Bianco '05	🍷	3
○	Chardonnay Epias	🍷	6
○	Brut Cl. Fra' Ambrogio Ris. '00	YY	5

CAZZAGO SAN MARTINO (BS)

CASTELFAGLIA

FRAZ. CALINO
LOC. BOSCHI, 3
25046 CAZZAGO SAN MARTINO (BS)
TEL. 059812411
www.cavicchioli.it

The Cavicchioli family from Modena produces more than just excellent Lambruscos. Their interests in the wine world, and sparklers in particular, have expanded over the years. In the late 1980s, they acquired this beautiful estate in Cazzago San Martino and more recently another sparkling wine brand, Francesco Bellei at Bomporto. In Franciacorta, CastelFaglia now owns 20 hectares under vine and, with expert guidance from oenologist Sandro Cavicchioli, the cellar currently produces 250,000 good-quality bottles a year. This year's tastings provided confirmation in the Franciacorta Brut Monogram '97, which spent eight years on the lees. It shows great elegance, tiny bubbles and elegant aromas of ripe fruit with shades of aromatic herbs and a stylish minerally character we find again on the harmonious, long palate. We liked Franciacorta Brut, which is rich on the nose with fresh notes of white-fleshed fruit shading to sage, and good backbone, as well as the Satèn, with tones of flowers and peach, and a soft, inviting palate. Also enjoyable is the Extra Brut, with complex sensations on nose and palate edged with elegant boisé shades. The Brut and Satèn from the Monogram line were less appealing. They're a bit rustic on the nose, but still pleasant to drink. We were impressed by the Rosé Brut, which is fresh, clean and supple with fresh tones of wild strawberry and vanilla.

○	Franciacorta Monogram Brut '97	🍷🍷	7
○	Franciacorta Brut	🍷🍷	5
○	Franciacorta Extra Brut	🍷🍷	5
○	Franciacorta Satèn	🍷🍷	5
●	TdF Rosso '04	🍷	4
○	TdF Bianco '05	🍷	4
○	Franciacorta Monogram Brut	🍷	4
⊙	Franciacorta Rosé Brut	🍷	6
○	Franciacorta Monogram Satèn	🍷	6
○	Franciacorta Monogram Brut '98	YY	6
○	Franciacorta Monogram Brut '99	YY	7

CAZZAGO SAN MARTINO (BS)

MONTE ROSSA

FRAZ. BORNATO
VIA LUCA MARENZIO, 14
25040 CAZZAGO SAN MARTINO (BS)
TEL. 030725066 - 0307254614
www.monterossa.com

Emanuele Rabotti courageously decided to leave his signature wine, Franciacorta Cabochon, which has won more than one Three Glass award, for another year on the yeasts. But we are patient and will console ourselves by drinking its rosé twin, Cabochon Rosé '01, which came near to repeating the success of the white version. For some years now, Emanuele has been at the helm and he is used to taking drastic decisions when it comes to quality. For example, how can we forget he was the first, several seasons ago, to eliminate still wines from his range to concentrate exclusively on Franciacortas? Well, the Cabochon Rosé is part of the new wave in Franciacorta rosés that has really delighted us this year. It has a lovely bright salmon pink colour preceding elegant, intriguing aromas of red berry fruit and aromatic herbs with a hint of vanilla. The palate is elegant, fresh, harmonious and caressingly long with touches of currant. Alongside this, the Franciacorta Rosé is not quite as concentrated and rich but every bit as elegant, and the basic Brut Franciacorta Prima Cuvée shows a bright golden straw yellow and deep, elegantly evolved tone we have rarely encountered in this category of wines. Finally, the Satèn is as good as ever, showing elegant tones of butter, cakes and flowers to fade out fresh, elegant and long in a cloud of vanilla.

⊙	Franciacorta Brut Cabochon Rosé '01	▼▼	8
○	Franciacorta Prima Cuvée Brut	▼▼	5
⊙	Franciacorta Rosé Brut	▼▼	6
○	Franciacorta Satèn Brut	▼▼	6
○	Franciacorta Brut Cabochon '01	YYY	7
○	Franciacorta Brut Cabochon '97	YYY	6
○	Franciacorta Brut Cabochon '98	YYY	6
○	Franciacorta Brut Cabochon '99	YYY	8

CAZZAGO SAN MARTINO (BS)

MONTENISA

FRAZ. CALINO
VIA PAOLO VI, 62
25046 CAZZAGO SAN MARTINO (BS)
TEL. 0307750838
www.antinori.it

The Antinoris have a long-standing affinity with sparklers. Consider that early in the last century, they hired an oenologist from Champagne, one Lucien Charlemagne, and began classic method production in their San Casciano cellars. This was in 1905, and since that time the Florentine label has always produced excellent sparklers. But it wasn't enough. So in 1999 the family acquired a 60-hectare estate in Franciacorta, at Cazzago San Martino, and completely restored the vineyards and buildings. Once owned by the Maggi family, the estate is now up and running and makes excellent wines, overseen by expert oenologist and production manager Giorgio Oddi. While waiting for the new release of the prestige cuvée, the elegant vintage Brut Contessa Camilla Maggi, the estate gave us an excellent Brut and Satèn. Our preference is for the Franciacorta Brut, a bright greenish straw-yellow colour, whose intense, fresh, clear aromas of white-fleshed fruit are perked up by citrus and shade into elegant minerality. The palate is close-knit, pulpy, full and rich in fresh acidity, flaunting vigorously fragrant notes of apricot, damson and pear. It closes out long on vanillaed tones. The Satèn has good concentration and remarkably rich pulp but develops less positively on the palate and shades into evolved sensations that indicate a heavy hand with the liqueur.

○	Franciacorta Brut	▼▼	5
○	Franciacorta Satèn	▼	7
○	Franciacorta Brut Contessa Camilla Maggi '00	YY	7
○	Franciacorta Satèn	YY	7

CHIURO (SO)

★ Nino Negri
via Ghibellini
23030 Chiuro (SO)
tel. 0342485211
www.giv.it

If wine production in Valtellina has today reached excellent quality, much of the credit goes to Casimiro Maule who, with 36 harvests behind him, has set the standards for the winemaking renaissance in the valley. Just take a look at the results for his wines to see why he was nominated Oenologist of the Year. First off, the '03 vintage of the Sforzato 5 Stelle joins the club of wines that have earned ten consecutive Three Glass awards. Balsamic and spicy in its aromas, it has a close-knit, steadily unfolding palate that offers more elegance than power, finishing rich and consistent. The standard Sforzato '03 is a great wine with a nose that recalls morello cherry jam. The palate flaunts wonderful texture, showing dense and harmonious with a long, well-balanced finish. Although it just missed a Third Glass, the monovarietal nebbiolo Vigneto Fracia '03 shows aromas of rare finesse and beautifully portrays the variety from which it is made. The smooth palate has a rich, dense texture and a soft, very harmonious finish. The Mazer '03 and Grumello Sassorosso '03 are both good and show a nice sense of place with spice and fruit aromas and a round, lingering palate. The Sassella Le Tense '03 is something else entirely. The complex aromas show black cherry notes and the silky palate has fine-grained tannins that denote a great terroir. From chiavennasca fermented off the skins, sauvignon and chardonnay, the Ca' Brione '05 performs well with complex, stylish aromas and a tangy, progressive, dry palate with a long, balanced finish.

●	Valtellina Sfursat '03	🍷🍷🍷	7
●	Valtellina Sfursat 5 Stelle '03	🍷🍷🍷	8
●	Valtellina Sup. Sassella Le Tense '03	🍷🍷	5
●	Valtellina Sup. Vigneto Fracia '03	🍷🍷	6
●	Valtellina Sup. Grumello Vigna Sassorosso '03	🍷🍷	5
●	Valtellina Sup. Mazer '03	🍷🍷	5
○	Ca' Brione '05	🍷🍷	5
●	Valtellina Sfursat 5 Stelle '01	YYY	7
●	Valtellina Sfursat 5 Stelle '02	YYY	7
●	Valtellina Sfursat 5 Stelle '96	YYY	5
●	Valtellina Sfursat 5 Stelle '97	YYY	6
●	Valtellina Sfursat 5 Stelle '98	YYY	6
●	Valtellina Sfursat 5 Stelle '99	YYY	6

CHIURO (SO)

Aldo Rainoldi
via Stelvio, 128
23030 Chiuro (SO)
tel. 0342482225
www.rainoldi.com

The Rainoldi cellar showed why it is in the front rank of Valtellina winemaking with a string of labels that positively grabbed our attention. The wines presented this year derive from a production philosophy that respects vintages and types, aiming for the best from nebbiolo and the territory. Take the Sforzato '02, for example, with its very intense aromas showing notes of leather and roasted hazelnut. The palate is all elegance and balance with soft, ripe, spicy fruit. Showing remarkable personality inspired by the nebbiolo grape, Inferno Riserva '02 is complex on the nose, with notes of leather and tobacco leaf. The caressing, harmonious palate has a long, dry finish. Sassella Riserva '02 is good and brings out the best in the grape with a complex nose over a backdrop of forest floor. The soft palate finishes with good acidity and length. The Crespino '02 is again a major wine. This monovarietal nebbiolo emphasizes aromatic finesse and notes of spice and red berry fruit. The savoury, rich palate shows all the weight and softness of the tannins. The truly unique Grumello '03 has clear aromas of dried fruit and cherry and a racy, fresh, balanced palate with a long, lip-smacking finish. The pleasant Prugnolo '03 is characterized by classic nebbiolo aromas of hazelnut, cherry and plum and has a fruity palate with a pleasant mouthfeel.

●	Valtellina Sfursat '02	🍷🍷	6
●	Valtellina Sup. Inferno Ris. '02	🍷🍷	5
●	Valtellina Sup. Crespino '02	🍷🍷	5
●	Valtellina Sup. Sassella Ris. '02	🍷🍷	5
●	Valtellina Sup. Grumello '03	🍷🍷	4
●	Valtellina Sup. Prugnolo '03	🍷	4
●	Valtellina Sfursat Fruttaio Ca' Rizzieri '00	YYY	7
●	Valtellina Sfursat Fruttaio Ca' Rizzieri '95	YYY	5
●	Valtellina Sfursat Fruttaio Ca' Rizzieri '97	YYY	6
●	Valtellina Sfursat Fruttaio Ca' Rizzieri '98	YYY	6
●	Valtellina Sfursat Fruttaio Ca' Rizzieri '01	YY	7

COCCAGLIO (BS)

BONOMI - TENUTA CASTELLINO

VIA SAN PIETRO, 46
25030 COCCAGLIO (BS)
TEL. 0307721015
www.tenutabonomi.it

Last year, the Bonomi family wisely decided to delay release of Franciacorta Brut '00 and at the time submitted the younger, less imposing Brut '01 for tasting. Now the '00 vintage is here and it's a dazzler with bright colour, tiny bubbles and complex, deep aromas of ripe damson, hedgerow and acacia honey. The dry, meaty palate has great elegance and a rich medley of fruit. The caressing effervescence reflects long, well-managed bottle fermentation. Tenuta Castellino's excellent cellar management is coordinated by Professor Leonardo Valenti from the University of Milan and the 16 hectares under vine at the foot of Monte Orfano are just as professionally managed by agronomist Pierluigi Donna. If a winery's quality can be judged by its base products, then here is an exemplary non-vintage Brut with floral, citrus-like aromas, softness and a succulent, zesty palate. The Terre di Franciacorta Bianco '05 also amazed us with the intensity of its ripe apple tones, freshness and good structure, qualities it shares with the '04 white from the Solicano vineyard, which has deeper vanillaed and boisé tones. Outstanding among the reds is the Curtefranca Cordelio '03, known in previous vintages as Solicano Rosso. It has a garnet ruby colour, aromas of tobacco and red berry fruits, good structure and a caressing mouthfeel. Finally, the Terre di Franciacorta Rosso '04 came close to the same score, with its fresh blackberry and blueberry tones, and both the Satèn and Rosé Extra Brut are good.

○	Franciacorta Brut '00	🍷🍷	6
●	TdF Rosso Curtefranca Cordelio '03	🍷🍷	6
○	TdF Bianco Curtefranca Solicano '04	🍷🍷	4
○	Franciacorta Brut	🍷🍷	5
⊙	Franciacorta Rosé Extra Brut '03	🍷	6
○	Franciacorta Satèn '03	🍷	6
●	TdF Rosso '04	🍷	4
○	TdF Bianco '05	🍷	4
○	Franciacorta Brut '01	YY	5
○	Franciacorta Brut '98	YY	6
○	Franciacorta Extra Brut Gran Cru Lucrezia '99	YY	8

CODEVILLA (PV)

MONTELIO

VIA D. MAZZA, 1
27050 CODEVILLA (PV)
TEL. 0383373090

First, we should clarify something here. Last year, we gave poor marks to Pinot Nero Costarsa '01, which had only just gone into bottle. Subsequent tastings led us to upgrade our estimations, so we will make amends the Brazzola sisters and oenologist Mario Maffi. Having said that, let's move on to this year's wines, beginning with the Solarolo '01, an Oltrepò Pavese Rosso Riserva designed around overripe fruit tones, with nice pulp, lively, velvety tannins and remarkable depth. The interesting Noblerot '03 is packaged in a clear, octagonal bottle that shows off its golden highlights. With 40 grams of residual sugar per litre, this sweet wine is intended not so much as a dessert wine but rather as an accompaniment for tangy cheeses. The monovarietal merlot Comprino Mirosa '03 is one to look forward to. For now, the tertiary notes contributed by the oak, tobacco and spice in particular, are still overwhelming but the remarkable base is all there. The nice bright ruby Rosso '04 is fresh, fragrant, simple and pleasant with smooth tannins. The Rosato '05 is also attractive and soft-textured. The Cortese '05 and Martinotti sparkler La Stroppa, from a cortese and chardonnay base, are both good and well typed.

●	OP Rosso Solarolo Ris. '01	🍷🍷	5
●	Comprino Mirosa '03	🍷🍷	6
○	Noblerot '03	🍷🍷	4
●	OP Rosso '04	🍷	4
●	OP Bonarda Frizzante '05	🍷	3*
○	OP Cortese '05	🍷	3
⊙	OP Rosato '05	🍷	3
○	Brut Martinotti La Stroppa	🍷	4
●	OP Rosso Solarolo Ris. '00	YY	5
●	Comprino Mirosa '01	YY	6
●	OP Pinot Nero Costarsa '01	YY	5
●	OP Bonarda Frizzante '03	YY	3

CORTE FRANCA (BS)

Barone Pizzini

fraz. Timoline
via Brescia, 3a
25050 Corte Franca (BS)
tel. 0309848311
www.baronepizzini.it

Managed with a firm hand by Silvano Brescianini, this estate is owned by a group of businessmen from Brescia who some years ago acquired the property from Barone Giulio Pizzini Piomarta. Wine has been produced here since 1870. With the collaboration of a close team, including oenological consultant Paolo Caciorgna and vineyard manager Pierluigi Donna, Barone Pizzini is now one of the best estates in the territory. Its strong point lies is the 40 hectares under vine, excellently positioned and organically managed. This estate is part of a group that also includes Poderi di Ghiaccioforte in Maremma, Tuscany, Pievalta in Le Marche and Tenuta del Barco in Puglia. We thought the main cuvée, Franciacorta Bagnadore '02, was excellent this year. This Extra Brut has a rich, fresh, intense nose that elegantly mingles fruity tones and notes of mallow and marjoram. The soft, full, invigorating palate closes out long on elegant echoes of thyme and sage. The Satèn from the same vintage is enjoyable for its bright colour, butter and acacia honey aromas and great overall harmony. We thought the Franciacorta Brut was as good as ever, driven as it is by lovely acid verve with fresh apple-like aromas and rich fruit with a dense, caressing palate. The Franciacorta Rosé is also sound, though it shows slightly more evolved and ripe tones than usual and the nose is not perfectly sharp. From the still wine list, the Terre di Franciacorta Bianco '05 has apricot tones and remarkable texture. We found the Terre di Franciacorta Rosso '04, with violet aromas, to be well made and pleasant.

○	Franciacorta Extra Brut Bagnadore '02	▼▼	6
○	Franciacorta Satèn '02	▼▼	6
○	TdF Bianco Curtefranca '05	▼▼	4
○	Franciacorta Brut	▼▼	5
⊙	Franciacorta Rosé Extra Dry	▼	6
●	TdF Rosso Curtefranca '04	▼	4
○	Franciacorta Satèn '00	▽▽	6
○	Franciacorta Satèn '01	▽▽	6

CORTE FRANCA (BS)

F.lli Berlucchi

loc. Borgonato
via Broletto, 2
25040 Corte Franca (BS)
tel. 030984451
www.berlucchifranciacorta.it

Fratelli Berlucchi is one of the most beautiful properties in Franciacorta. Spread over 100 hectares, 70 under vine, it releases every year around 400,000 bottles of excellent wines. Credit clearly goes to energetic Pia Donata Berlucchi at the helm, with skilled help from consulting oenologist Cesare Ferrari. Our tasting panel particularly enjoyed the Franciacorta Casa delle Colonne '01, a cuvée of 80 per cent chardonnay and the rest pinot nero, aged over five years on the lees before disgorgement. Its rich, complex character mingles yeast and ripe fruit aromas. The nose shows more complex shades of antique wood, honey and spices, hints we find again on a palate that instead expresses freshness, structure and an invigorating vitality. We also liked the fragrant Rosé '02 with limpid notes of red berry fruit and flowers. The palate is tangy, full, firmly structured, rich in fruit and balanced. Just as interesting is the Satèn, which focuses on complex minerally, boisé tones and displays considerable balance with a nice soft tone overall. The dryer, leaner Brut '02 is a bit too evolved. The Pas Dosé from the same vintage is full and gratifying on the attack yet flags later on. From the still wine list, the non-vintage Bordeaux Casa delle Colonne Rosso offers structure and fullness with elegant tannins and fresh grassy and pencil lead tones on both nose and palate. Terre di Franciacorta Bianco Dossi delle Querce is pleasant for the richness of its fruit and vanillaed nuances. The other Terre di Franciacorta labels are interesting and well made.

○	Franciacorta Casa delle Colonne '00	▼▼	6
⊙	Franciacorta Brut Rosé '02	▼▼	5
○	Franciacorta Satèn '02	▼▼	6
○	TdF Bianco Dossi delle Querce '04	▼▼	4
●	Casa delle Colonne	▼▼	8
●	TdF Rosso Dossi delle Querce '01	▼	4
○	Franciacorta Brut '02	▼	5
○	Franciacorta Pas Dosé '02	▼	6
●	TdF Rosso '04	▼	3
○	TdF Bianco '05	▼	3
○	Franciacorta Casa delle Colonne '97	▽▽	6

CORTE FRANCA (BS)

Guido Berlucchi & C.
loc. Borgonato
p.zza Duranti, 4
25040 Corte Franca (BS)
tel. 030984381
www.berlucchi.it

In 1961, young, talented oenologist Franco Ziliani and Guido Berlucchi created this estate and the Franciacorta phenomenon. Now with over 5,000,000 bottles produced each year and worldwide exports, Berlucchi is a leading name in Italian wine. Franco still runs the estate with the able assistance of his sons, Arturo in production and Paolo in the commercial sector. Most of the production goes out under the Cuvée Imperiale label, made with grapes sourced from various designated areas in Oltrepò, Alto Adige, Trentino and Gavi, where Berlucchi has several crushing centres. Alongside these are the two Cellarius labels, the Bianco and Rosé from '02. The first shows cakes on the nose and nice backbone. The Rosé has rich wild berry notes on the nose as well as a zesty, vibrant palate. But the most interesting label tasted this year was the Franciacorta Cuvée Storica, with its tiny bubbles and rich stylish notes of aromatic herbs and fruit on the nose. The succulent, invigorating palate is elegant, soft and long. The Cuvée Imperiale Vintage '01, from an equal blend of chardonnay and pinot nero, has a pleasing bright straw-yellow colour and elegant, clear aromas of vanilla, white-fleshed fruit and flowers. The tangy palate has good backbone yet caresses at the same time. From the Cuvée Imperiale line, we should not neglect the Brut, of which 3,400,000 units are released each year. It's fragrant with yeast and fruit then pleasantly soft and full on the palate. The Max Rosé Extra Dry gives wild strawberries and blueberries and a round, balanced palate.

○	Cuvée Imperiale Brut Vintage '01	🍷🍷	6
○	Cellarius Brut '02	🍷🍷	6
⊙	Cellarius Brut Rosé '02	🍷🍷	6
○	Franciacorta Cuvée Storica	🍷🍷	5
○	TdF Bianco Le Arzelle '03	🍷	5
○	TdF Curtefranca '05	🍷	4
○	Cuvée Imperiale Brut	🍷	5
○	Cuvée Imperiale Brut Extrême	🍷	5
⊙	Cuvée Imperiale Max Rosé	🍷	5
○	Franciacorta Cuvée Storica	ΥΥ	5

CORVINO SAN QUIRICO (PV)

Tenuta Mazzolino
via Mazzolino, 26
27050 Corvino San Quirico (PV)
tel. 0383876122
www.tenuta-mazzolino.com

With major investments, a beautiful estate and model cellar, Tenuta Mazzolino should have all it takes to achieve an excellence that is slow in coming. Not that the wines are indifferent – far from it – but things never seem to lift off or make that great leap. The best wine this year is the Pinot Nero Noir '04 although we thought it needed more bottle time to express itself. A pale garnet colour, it has coffee and minerally tones with good ripe wild berry fruit, nice, smooth tannins and drinks fresh and clean with an unwavering finish. An excellent score also went to the Terrazze '05, an IGT red from a blend of cabernet sauvignon, croatina and pinot nero. The last of these varieties seems to dominate in the medium dark ruby colour and lovely aromas of flowers and wild black berry fruit. In the mouth, it is fresh, well made and pleasant. But the Chardonnay Blanc '04 was not completely satisfying. In previous years, it had another density entirely. The wine is well made, with a nice bright straw-yellow colour, well-measured oak, aromas of hazelnut, flowers, citrus and tropical fruit. The palate shows proper balance but is a little simple and closes out fairly quickly. Not bad, especially as regards value for money, is the IGT white Camarà '05, from chardonnay, riesling and sauvignon blanc, which shows stylish, fresh and agreeable. The Bonarda Mazzolino '05 has a purple ruby colour and blackberry sensations but still rather astringent tannins.

●	OP Pinot Nero Noir '04	🍷🍷	6
●	Terrazze '05	🍷🍷	3*
○	OP Chardonnay Blanc '04	🍷	4
○	Camarà '05	🍷	3
●	OP Bonarda Mazzolino '05	🍷	4
●	OP Pinot Nero Noir '00	ΥΥ	6
●	OP Pinot Nero Noir '01	ΥΥ	6
●	OP Pinot Nero Noir '02	ΥΥ	6
●	OP Cabernet Sauvignon Corvino '03	ΥΥ	4
○	OP Chardonnay Blanc '03	ΥΥ	4

DESENZANO DEL GARDA (BS)

Provenza
via dei Colli Storici
25015 Desenzano del Garda (BS)
tel. 0309910006
www.provenzacantine.it

Walter Contato founded the Provenza estate in the mid 1960s near Desenzano, actually a stone's throw from Sirmione in the heart of Lugana. Over the past few years, his children have accelerated the estate's growth both in terms of size, reaching almost 100 hectares under vine, and more important quality. In fact, this operation is now rightly considered one of the benchmark estates on the western shore of Lake Garda. Almost as if to put his seal on this exciting progress, Fabio Contato has given his name to two wines, a white and a red. The white Lugana is a textbook interpretation in the '04 vintage, managing to meld and balance the essential qualities of trebbiano grown in the clay of this subzone. With its ripe yellow-fleshed fruit, vegetal veins, minerally echoes and well-crafted freshness on very decent body, it tells the story of the variety and terrain in every detail. The other two Luganas also did very well. The Superiore Molin '04 charmed with its dense fruit and expressive length, while the Tenuta Maiolo '05 won us over with its spirited freshness run through with vegetal notes. The other Selezione signed by Fabio Contato, the Garda Classico Rosso '03, is an elegant wine with caressing ripe fruit sensations. An excellent score also went to the Negresco, another Garda Classico Rosso as velvety and fragrant with fruit as ever. All the other labels were sound.

○ Lugana Sup. Molin '04	🍷🍷	5
○ Lugana Sup. Sel. Fabio Contato '04	🍷🍷	6
● Garda Cl. Rosso Sel. Fabio Contato '03	🍷🍷	6
● Garda Cl. Rosso Negresco '04	🍷🍷	5
○ Sol Doré '04	🍷🍷	6
○ Lugana Tenuta Maiolo '05	🍷🍷	3
⊙ Garda Cl. Chiaretto Tenuta Maiolo '05	🍷	4
● Garda Cl. Groppello Tenuta Maiolo '05	🍷	4
● Giomè '05	🍷	4
○ Lugana Brut Cl. Ca' Maiol	🍷	5
○ Lugana Brut Sebastian	🍷	3
○ Lugana Sup. Sel. Fabio Contato '03	🍸🍸	6
○ Lugana Sup. Sel. Fabio Contato '01	🍸🍸	6

ERBUSCO (BS)

★ Bellavista
via Bellavista, 5
25030 Erbusco (BS)
tel. 0307762000
www.terramoretti.it

In 1977 Vittorio Moretti, a successful businessman from Franciacorta, decided to start production of still wines and Franciacorta, at that time the rising star in Italy's sparkling wine firmament. After 30 years, the venture's eventful history would be difficult to summarize but today, Bellavista is the crowning jewel of Terra Moretti, the umbrella company for the various family estates, including Petra in Tuscany and Contadi Castaldi in Franciacorta. Now general manager, skilled oenologist Mattia Vezzola has worked alongside Moretti since the early 1980s and helped shape the unmistakable style of these cuvées. Currently an icon of Franciacorta worldwide, Bellavista picked up another Three Glass award this year with an excellent Franciacorta Gran Cuvée Brut '02. It shows great elegance, fullness and rich clear tones of fruit, citrus and aromatic herbs on the nose. The appealing palate has fresh, rich fruity pulp, elegant effervescence and great length. While waiting for the release of the Pas Operé, which is spending another year on the yeasts, here is the Gran Cuvée Rosé to flaunt its perfect balance and fragrant tones of red berry fruit. Excellent as always, the Gran Cuvée Satèn shows pear and white peach tones and fresh vitality. The standard Franciacorta Brut Cuvée is rich in freshness, soft vanilla tones, citrus and fresh fruit. From the still wines, special mention goes to the Chardonnay Convento dell'Annunciata '03, which is structured, spicy, juicy, rich in minerality and one of the best in Italy. The other labels were all good.

○ Franciacorta Gran Cuvée Brut '02	🍷🍷🍷	7
⊙ Franciacorta Gran Cuvée Brut Rosé '02	🍷🍷	7
○ TdF Bianco Convento dell'Annunciata '03	🍷🍷	6
● Solesine '01	🍷🍷	6
○ TdF Bianco Uccellanda '03	🍷🍷	6
○ TdF Curtefranca Bianco '05	🍷🍷	4
○ Franciacorta Cuvée Brut	🍷🍷	6
○ Franciacorta Gran Cuvée Satèn	🍷🍷	7
○ Franciacorta Gran Cuvée Pas Operé '00	🍸🍸🍸	7
○ Franciacorta Gran Cuvée Brut '98	🍸🍸🍸	6
○ Franciacorta Gran Cuvée Brut '99	🍸🍸🍸	6

ERBUSCO (BS)

★ ★ Ca' del Bosco

via Case Sparse, 20
25030 Erbusco (BS)
tel. 0307766111
www.cadelbosco.it

A wine buff going round Ca' del Bosco tends to marvel like a child in Willy Wonka's chocolate factory. This state-of-the-art structure surrounded by forests and vineyards produces some of Italy's very finest wines. Here president and founder Maurizio Zanella has collected works by major contemporary artists and created walking paths throughout his 22,000-square metre sprawl for the delight of those who come for a visit or a tasting. The 28th Three Glass award to Ca' del Bosco this year goes to the 1999 edition of the extraordinary Cuvée Annamaria Clementi. This Franciacorta has a rarefied elegance and reveals an impressive repertory of aromas that come together in an incomparable bouquet. The palate shows structure, fruit and fullness with everything in perfect balance. Just a step below this, there is a series of still wines in numbers few wineries can match. The Rosé '02 is without a doubt the best version ever. A lovely deep coral, it is zesty and pulpy in its shades of fresh red and black berry fruit. The Satèn '01 has character, elegance and structure that make it a benchmark for the type. The Dosage Zéro '02 caresses your palate with hints of white peach, vanilla and aromatic herbs. And so on and so forth down a long, fascinating procession of still wines and Franciacortas with some of the major labels, such as the Chardonnay, Carmenèro and Pinèro, still ageing another year in the cellar. We can wait.

○	Franciacorta Cuvée Annamaria Clementi '99	🍷🍷🍷	8
○	Franciacorta Satèn '01	🍷🍷	7
○	Franciacorta Dosage Zéro '02	🍷🍷	7
⊙	Franciacorta Rosé '02	🍷🍷	7
●	TdF Rosso Curtefranca '03	🍷🍷	5
○	Elfo 15 '05	🍷🍷	6
○	TdF Bianco Curtefranca '05	🍷🍷	5
●	Rosso Merlot '01	🍷	8
○	Franciacorta Brut '02	🍷	7
○	TdF Chardonnay '02	🍷🍷🍷	8
○	Franciacorta Cuvée Annamaria Clementi '97	🍷🍷🍷	8
○	Franciacorta Cuvée Annamaria Clementi '98	🍷🍷🍷	8

ERBUSCO (BS)

Cavalleri

via Provinciale, 96
25030 Erbusco (BS)
tel. 0307760217
www.cavalleri.it

The end of 2005 saw the sudden passing of Giovanni Cavalleri. Since the 1960s, he had managed the family estate and transformed it into a star of the first magnitude in the firmament of Franciacorta winemaking. He dedicated his greatest effort specifically to Franciacorta and also contributed to making it what it is today in his role as president of the Consorzio Vini della Franciacorta. His children Giovanni, Giulia and Maria are now in charge of this beautiful winery, which includes 43 hectares under vine and a very modern cellar. They are assisted by a competent estate staff that includes commercial manager Aldo Pagnoni, production manager Giampaolo Turra and cellarman Pierluigi Calabria. Our tastings this year spotlighted the Franciacorta Collezione Brut '01. With tiny bubbles and a lovely pale golden colour, it has a charmingly complex bouquet of minerally notes and roasted coffee beans that never mask the clean fruit component and floral shades. The clear, invigorating palate shows great finesse and balance. The Collezione Rosé from the same vintage pleases with its finesse and delicate, soft tones of vanilla and red berry fruit on both the nose and the whistle-clean, long palate. The Franciacorta Brut, Satèn '02 and Pas Dosé '02 have their customary fruit, softness and elegance. Moving onto still wines, we liked Rampaneto '04, one of the best whites tasted this year, and the Rosso Tajardino '03, with blackberry aromas and solid structure.

○	Franciacorta Collezione Brut '01	🍷🍷	6
⊙	Franciacorta Collezione Rosé '01	🍷🍷	6
○	Franciacorta Pas Dosé '02	🍷🍷	6
○	Franciacorta Satèn '02	🍷🍷	6
●	TdF Rosso Tajardino '03	🍷🍷	5
○	TdF Bianco Rampaneto '04	🍷🍷	4
○	Franciacorta Brut	🍷🍷	5
●	TdF Rosso '04	🍷	4
○	TdF Bianco '05	🍷	4
○	Franciacorta Collezione Brut '93	🍷🍷🍷	6
○	Franciacorta Collezione Brut '94	🍷🍷🍷	6
○	Franciacorta Collezione Brut '99	🍷🍷🍷	6
○	Franciacorta Satèn '01	🍷🍷	6

ERBUSCO (BS)

ENRICO GATTI
VIA METELLI, 9
25030 ERBUSCO (BS)
TEL. 0307267999
www.enricogatti.it

The Franciacorta Satèn '02 from Gatti is so good it won the estate not only its third Three Glass award but also our prize for Sparkler of the Year. In other words, hearty congratulations to Roberto Gatti, his sister Paola and her husband Enzo Balzarini, a close-knit team that has given us excellent still wines and Franciacortas since the early 1990s. Those who knew the estate back then, when it was little more than a boutique winery, can only celebrate with them this award and the achievement of their production goal of more than 120,000 bottles a year from 17 hectares under vine, all thanks to incredible commitment and a great spirit of sacrifice. But let's get back to the Satèn with its bright golden straw-yellow colour and tiny bubbles. The nose opens up elegant, deep, complex and rich on ripe fruit tones mingled with spice, hedgerow and an engaging minerality we find again on the palate, where it is succulent, tight-knit and caressing but lifted by a fresh acid vein that sustains the long finish of vanilla and apricot. This wonderful wine is partnered by a Franciacorta Brut with a caressing, floral character and a tangy, full, fresh and supple palate. Among the other labels is Gatti Rosso '03, a Bordeaux blend with a rather grassy character, two sound Terre di Franciacorta wines, Bianco '05 and Rosso '04, and a very decent Extra Brut.

○ Franciacorta Satèn '02	🍷🍷🍷	6
○ Franciacorta Brut	🍷🍷	5
● Gatti Rosso '03	🍷	4
● TdF Rosso Curtefranca '04	🍷	4
○ TdF Bianco Curtefranca '05	🍷	4
○ Franciacorta Extra Brut	🍷	5
○ Franciacorta Satèn '00	YYY	6
○ Franciacorta Satèn '01	YYY	5

ERBUSCO (BS)

SAN CRISTOFORO
VIA VILLANUOVA, 2
25030 ERBUSCO (BS)
TEL. 0307760482

Bruno Dotti and Claudia Cavalleri farm a dozen or so hectares under vine and, with consultancy from oenologist Massimo Gigola, make around 100,000 bottles annually of Franciacortas and still wines from the territory. The estate warhorse is Franciacorta Brut, produced in around 35,000 bottles. It has a lovely bright straw-yellow colour, an elegant nose that adds tones of aromatic herbs and liquorice to notes of ripe fruit, and an opulently soft, well-structured palate supported by a lively acid vein. The Re Probus '03 is a full-bodied red exclusively from barbera, a variety that always been grown in Franciacorta. It is part of the blend for the Terre di Franciacorta Rosso but is now yielding more and more terrain to international varieties such as cabernet and merlot. The Dottis have dedicated a wine to this reprobate "worthy king" and it shows rich fruit on both the nose and palate, where there are blackberry, blackcurrants and elegant oaky shades as well as soft, smooth extract. Too bad there are barely a thousand magnums. But there are around 3,000 bottles of the San Cristoforo Uno '03, a juicy Merlot with fresh, vegetal tones and good body. The Terre di Franciacorta Bianco '05 is correct, supple and fresh with white peach tones.

● Re Probus '03	🍷🍷	8
○ Franciacorta Brut	🍷🍷	5
● San Cristoforo Uno '03	🍷	5
○ TdF Curtefranca Bianco '05	🍷	4*
● Re Probus '01	YY	8
○ Franciacorta Brut	YY	5

ERBUSCO (BS)

★ Uberti

loc. Salem
via E. Fermi, 2
25030 Erbusco (BS)
tel. 0307267476
www.ubertivini.it

With the excellent Comarì del Salem '01 again a Three Glass award winner, and a new cuvée, Sublimis '00, which fell just short, Uberti has become a leading estate in Franciacorta and a major label on the national winemaking scene. The family's oenologist daughter, Silvia, now holds a permanent position alongside Agostino and Eleonora at the helm of the estate. Cesare Ferrari, one of the greatest Italian professionals especially when it comes to sparklers, continues his historic role as consultant. The '01 is absolutely one of the best vintages ever of Comarì. It shows opulence and rich fruit yet at the same time a solid, almost austere profile that foreshadows elegant development over the next few years. But it is already very appealing, right from its tiny bubbles and highly complex bouquet with its incredible repertory of aromatic herbs and tropical fruit followed by coffee, vanilla and elegant minerally nuances. The palate is tangy, powerful, assertive and gratifying. An elegantly crafted Pas Dosé, Sublimis '00, gives intense minerality on the nose with tones that resemble the Comarì although more along lines the French would call "empyreumatic". But it's a thoroughbred. The Satèn Magnificentia plays off the usual cake, vanilla and tropical aromas but maintains great control and freshness. Not surprisingly, we also found the Brut and Extra Brut from the Francesco I line very sound. The Chardonnay Maria Medici '04 and Cabernet Rosso dei Frati Priori '03 stand out among the still wines.

○ Franciacorta Extra Brut Comarì del Salem '01	▼▼▼	7
○ Franciacorta Non Dosato Sublimis '00	▼▼	7
● Rosso dei Frati Priori '03	▼▼	6
○ TdF Bianco Maria Medici '04	▼▼	5
○ Franciacorta Brut Francesco I	▼▼	5
○ Franciacorta Extra Brut Francesco I	▼▼	5
○ Franciacorta Satèn Magnificentia	▼▼	6
● TdF Curtefranca Rosso '04	▼	4
○ TdF Bianco Curtefranca '05	▼	4
⊙ Franciacorta Brut Rosé Francesco I	▼	5
○ Franciacorta Brut Comarì del Salem '00	▽▽▽	7
○ Franciacorta Extra Brut Comarì del Salem '98	▽▽▽	7

ERBUSCO (BS)

Giuseppe Vezzoli

via Costa Sopra, 22
25030 Erbusco (BS)
tel. 0307267579

A touch more fullness and length and Giuseppe Vezzoli's Brut Rosé would have become one of the Guide's prizewinners. In any case, we liked his Franciacorta Rosé '02 very much. It has a bright, deep salmon pink colour and the intense nose is full and tight-knit with ripe red berry fruit tones that veer toward more evolved and complex notes of mineral and charred oak, with a pinch of oriental spice. The palate is dense and rich in fruit and flaunts a nice acid backbone like a true "blanc de noirs". This is one of those wines that signal a sea change in how wine is considered and made in Franciacorta. There is willingness here to risk making this type with the best-suited variety, pinot nero. An energetic winemaker, Giuseppe has in just a few years expanded this estate from family-size to 150,000 bottles a year and 30 hectares under vine and we are happy to acknowledge that the Rosé is not his only good cuvée. Assisted by oenologist Cesare Ferrari, his whole range is top-notch, beginning with the Brut Nefertiti '00, a monovarietal chardonnay that after five years on the lees shows rich structure, juicy, elegant and complex in its vanilla, coffee and candied citrus peel notes. The Franciacorta Brut '02 is one of the best of the vintage, with engaging tones of white peach, crusty bread and yeast on the nose, and a fresh, vital, invigoratingly fruit-themed palate. From the '02 vintage, we found the Satèn a bit less alluring. It's a tad too evolved and dominated by vanilla notes, though still interesting. Sec Nausicaa is fragrant with gooseberry and mixed flower honey.

⊙ Franciacorta Brut Rosé '02	▼▼	6
○ Franciacorta Brut Nefertiti '00	▼▼	7
○ Franciacorta Brut '02	▼▼	6
○ Franciacorta Satèn '02	▼	6
○ Franciacorta Sec Nausicaa '02	▼	5
○ Franciacorta Brut '01	▽▽	6
⊙ Franciacorta Brut Rosé '01	▽▽	6
○ Franciacorta Satèn '01	▽▽	6
○ Franciacorta Brut Nefertiti '99	▽▽	7

MESE (SO)

MAMETE PREVOSTINI
VIA LUCCHINETTI, 63
23020 MESE (SO)
TEL. 034341003
www.mameteprevostini.com

As punctual as a Japanese train, the Three Glass award goes for the third time this year to the Sforzato Albareda '04. It is as if Mamete Prevostini, having acquired the technique and refined his style, has now concentrated on getting the absolute best out of nebbiolo, and is doing the needful from the standpoint of vineyard management and the relationship with the terrain. With very low yields per hectare, grape bunches are meticulously selected then masterfully part-dried to obtain this elegant Albareda, with its warm nose, fine sensations of dried flowers and opulent, juicy notes of red berry fruit. The pure palate is vigorous and well styled with a long, lip-smacking finish showing well-measured oak. Dense in its raspberry jam-led aromas, the Corte di Cama '04 has a soft, commanding palate with a deep ripe fruit finish. One of the best Sassellas tasted this year was Sommarovina '04, which veers on the nose towards jam and tar and has a round, characterful, rich, expressive palate. Simpler yet still supple, the Sassella '04 is fresh with good drinkability. The interesting Inferno Riserva '02 has complex aromas with balsamic notes, the solid palate showing velvety tannins and good length. The Botonero '05 and Santarita '05 are both from nebbiolo, pleasant, intensely fruity and both good value for money. The Opera '05 is from a base of 80 per cent chardonnay with some sauvignon and müller thurgau. Its complex bouquet shows off flowers and white-fleshed fruit, and the palate is dense and full with a long finish.

●	Valtellina Sforzato Albareda '04	▼▼▼	7
●	Valtellina Sup. Sassella Sommarovina '04	▼▼	5
●	Valtellina Sup. Inferno Ris. '02	▼▼	4
●	Valtellina Sup. Corte di Cama '04	▼▼	6
○	Opera Bianco '05	▼▼	5
●	Valtellina Sup. Sassella '04	▼	4
●	Botonero '05	▼	3
●	Valtellina Santarita '05	▼	3
●	Valtellina Sforzato Albareda '00	▽▽▽	7
●	Valtellina Sforzato Albareda '03	▽▽▽	7
●	Valtellina Sup. Corte di Cama '02	▽▽	6
●	Valtellina Sup. Corte di Cama '03	▽▽	6

MONIGA DEL GARDA (BS)

COSTARIPA
VIA COSTA, 1A
25080 MONIGA DEL GARDA (BS)
TEL. 0365502010 - 0365503716
www.costaripa.it

The estate managed by Mattia and Imer Vezzola on the western shore of Lake Garda is achieving great results. Projects in the vineyards and cellar are coming to fruition and the cellar's decision to adopt an elegant interpretation of Valtenesi tradition in is a winning one. For example, the native Groppello variety finds is beautifully handled in the exuberant, youthful Le Castelline '05, which recalls juicy strawberry and berry fruit. The '04 vintage of the other Groppello, Maim, is still ageing in the cellar. The choice of longer ageing seems completely understandable in light of the positive development shown till now by previous vintages of this wine, one of the most interesting expressions of the area's main variety. Two Glasses also went to Le Mazane '05, a well-interpreted, fruity, tannic Marzemino. Then there are the rosés, another estate warhorse. Molmenti is a charming, unusual Chiaretto, oak-aged and released much later than is customary locally. It flaunts complexity and spice, without losing fruity fragrance or fresh tanginess. The other Chiaretto, Rosamara '05, is more easy-drinking. Mattia Vezzola's long experience with sparkling wines is reflected in two excellent Bruts. Our preference is for the non-vintage version, a dense, creamy, buttery chardonnay-based wine that is remarkably pleasing but the '99 vintage is also very fine.

⊙	Garda Cl. Chiaretto Molmenti '04	▼▼	5
●	Garda Cl. Groppello Vign. Le Castelline '05	▼▼	4
●	Marzemino Le Mazane '05	▼▼	4
○	Costaripa Brut '99	▼▼	6
○	Costaripa Brut	▼▼	5
●	Garda Cabernet Sauvignon Pradamonte '03	▼	5
●	Garda Cl. Rosso Campostarne '04	▼	4
⊙	Garda Cl. Chiaretto Rosamara '05	▼	4
○	Lugana Pievecroce '05	▼	4
●	Garda Cl. Groppello Maim '01	▽▽	5
●	Garda Cl. Groppello Maim '03	▽▽	5

MONTALTO PAVESE (PV)

DORIA

LOC. CASA TACCONI, 3
27040 MONTALTO PAVESE (PV)
TEL. 0383870143
www..vinidoria.com

The Doria family always submits top-quality wines from the estate managed by that non-local oenologist Daniele Manini. The Barbera A.D. '04 has been postponed till next year. Aged in chestnut barriques, it is emblematic of an estate management style aimed at rediscovering ancient traditions but it has just been bottled and is not yet ready for release. A place in the Three Glass finals went to Roncorosso '03, with intense, fragrant aromas of red berry fruit and pepper-led spice, followed by a full, harmonious, long palate. The very good Querciolo Bianco '04 is from pinot nero vinified off the skins and fermented in wood. A golden straw-yellow colour, it has yellow-fleshed fruit, vanilla and spice aromas, and good backbone. The forthright Pinot Nero Riserva Querciolo Rosso '04 shows a varietal dark garnet colour and cassis and flower aromas, but still needs time to find better harmony. The pinot nero-based Brut Metodo Martinotti Querciolo is not bad at all, its deep, golden straw yellow preceding a soft, fruity palate. The Bonarda Vivace '05 is correct and well executed. The A.D. Bianco is a passito from part-dried moscato. It has honeyed notes and intrigues with its vigorous acid vein and fairly restrained sweetness.

● OP Rosso Roncorosso '03	🍷🍷	4
○ OP Pinot Nero in bianco Querciolo '04	🍷🍷	4
● OP Pinot Nero Querciolo Ris. '04	🍷	6
● OP Bonarda Vivace '05	🍷	4
○ Bianco A.D.	🍷	4
○ OP Pinot Nero Brut Querciolo	🍷	4
○ OP Pinot Nero in bianco Querciolo '03	YY	4
○ Bianco A.D.	YY	4

MONTALTO PAVESE (PV)

MARCHESI DI MONTALTO

LOC. COSTA GALLOTTI
27040 MONTALTO PAVESE (PV)
TEL. 3394982856
www.marchesidimontalto.it

The Marchesi family submitted a fine range of wines from the grapes harvested off their nearly 200 hectares of estate-owned vineyards. After the impressive '02 version, the Riesling Italico Monsaltus '03 was back in the finals. Though this wine has little or nothing to do with Oltrepò in style, given that it drinks more like a Mosel Riesling, it still amazed us right from its bright golden colour and explosion of aromas that run from honey to sage, perked up by minerality. On the palate, richness and depth play counterpoint to a vigorous acid backbone. The very good Moscato Passito Pasirè '04 has aromas of butter biscuits, citron peel, dates and dried fruits and shows opulent and full in the mouth. An excellent score also went to the Barbera Cascina Bellaria '03 that nicely expresses its terrain with almond and cherry aromas and lovely freshness, despite the very hot growing season. The Pinot Nero Ca' Nuè '04 has a rather dark garnet colour, wild flower and spice aromas, and a palate with velvety tannins. The Pinot Grigio Boschetto di Mezzo '05 is varietal, well made and fragrant with flowers but less intense than the '04 version. There are lovely wild berry fruit aromas in the lively, acidulous Bonarda Vivace Cascina Francone '05, which shows good balance of extract and residual sugar.

○ OP Riesling Italico Monsaltus '03	🍷🍷	4
● OP Barbera Cascina Bellaria '03	🍷🍷	4*
○ OP Moscato Passito Pasirè '04	🍷🍷	5
● OP Pinot Nero Ca' Nuè '04	🍷🍷	5
● OP Bonarda Vivace Cascina Francone '05	🍷	4
○ OP Pinot Grigio Boschetto di Mezzo '05	🍷	4
● OP Barbera Cascina Bellaria '01	YY	5
○ OP Riesling Italico Monsaltus '02	YY	6*
○ OP Pinot Grigio Boschetto di Mezzo '04	YY	4

MONTEBELLO DELLA BATTAGLIA (PV)

Tenuta La Costaiola

via Costaiola, 25
27054 Montebello della Battaglia (PV)
tel. 038383169 - 038382069

Production was limited this year for the Oltrepò Pavese Rosso Riserva Vigna Bricca and Barbera Auriga. The difficult '02 growing season forced the Rossetti and Scrivani families to carry out meticulous selection of the raw material, to the extent not even the Pinot Nero Aiole was released, since it was not considered up to snuff. In its place, Vigna Bricca still earned impressive marks for its dark, ruby colour, aromas of wild berries with overripe tones, its pulp and substance. The Barbera Auriga has a nice close-knit nose of hazelnut and overripe cherry, lovely succulent fruit in the mouth and a remarkably long finish. The long tank-fermented method Brut, Haris, is very well made and earned a good score for its nice tiny, persistent bubbles, stylish, elegant nose of flowers and wild berries with balsamic notes and aromatic herbs, not to mention a very soft, full, satisfying palate. The series of wines from the '05 vintage opens with the Riesling Attimo, a green-flecked straw-yellow wine fragrant with aromatic herbs. It shows good juicy fruit and a fairly sustained finish. The Barbera I Due Draghi '05 has a deep, purple ruby colour, nice red berry fruit, pulp and rather high acidity. The Giada and Massona are both slightly sparkling Bonardas, the first a DOC and the second an IGT. We just preferred Massona for its more complex, intense aromas but the Giada is also pleasant and well made. The Barbera Vivace Padron '05 is decent and uncomplicated.

●	OP Barbera Auriga '02	▼▼	5
●	OP Rosso V. Bricca Ris. '02	▼▼	4
○	OP Pinot Nero Brut Martinotti Haris	▼▼	4
●	Croatina Vivace Massona '05	▼	3
●	OP Barbera I Due Draghi '05	▼	4*
●	OP Bonarda Vivace Giada '05	▼	3
○	OP Riesling Renano Attimo '05	▼	3
●	OP Barbera Vivace Padron '05		3
●	Auriga '01	▽▽	5
●	OP Rosso V. Bricca Ris. '01	▽▽	4

MONTICELLI BRUSATI (BS)

La Montina

via Baiana, 17
25040 Monticelli Brusati (BS)
tel. 030653278
www.lamontina.it

The Bozza brothers submitted another excellent range of labels to our tastings this year. This is not surprising, given this beautiful estate at Monticelli Brusati boasts around 50 hectares of vineyards and a production of over 400,000 bottles a year. For some time, it has been firmly established as one of the best wineries in the area. Technical consultancy comes from Cesare Ferrari and Alceo Totò oversees the vineyards with the collaboration of agronomist Rocco Marino. La Montina's benchmark label is the vintage Brut. Even if the '01 cannot boast the same deep complexity as previous vintages, it makes one of the best showings from the year. It has a bright greenish straw-yellow colour and delicate perlage. The clear, full nose opens on ripe white-fleshed fruit with elegant shades of yeast and vanilla. The palate is clear and succulent, supported by fresh acidity and pleasantly long. In some ways, the non-vintage Franciacorta Brut is even more convincing, with a rich bouquet where tropical and white-fleshed fruit meld with croissant tones that never mask the complex sensation of flowers and delicate minerality. The palate flaunts lovely acid tension that bolsters the soft fruit. The soft, creamy Extra Brut is excellent and develops nice weight on the palate. We enjoyed the Satèn for its elegant coffee, toast and oaky tones that caress the fruit. The Bianco Palanca '05 is also excellent, showing tangy and structured, and the other house labels are as good as ever.

○	Franciacorta Brut '01	▼▼	5
○	TdF Bianco Vign. Palanca '05	▼▼	3*
○	Franciacorta Brut	▼▼	5
○	Franciacorta Extra Brut	▼▼	5
○	Franciacorta Satèn	▼▼	5
⊙	Franciacorta Rosé Demi Sec	▼	5
●	TdF Rosso dei Dossi '03	▼	4
●	TdF Rosso '04	▼	3
○	Franciacorta Brut '00	▽▽	6
○	Franciacorta Brut '97	▽▽	5
○	Franciacorta Brut '98	▽▽	6
○	Franciacorta Brut '99	▽▽	6

MONTICELLI BRUSATI (BS)

VILLA
VIA VILLA, 12
25040 MONTICELLI BRUSATI (BS)
TEL. 030652329 - 030652100
www.villa-franciacorta.it

At the foot of the hill of Madonna della Rosa at Monticelli Brusati, there lies a perfectly restored Renaissance village surrounded by vineyards. This is Villa, the wonderful Bianchi family estate whose pride and joy is the beautiful Gradoni vineyard that lies just behind it, a charming sequence of terraced vineyards supported by perfectly preserved, centuries-old, dry stone walls. Alessandro Bianchi saved Villa from abandonment in the early 1960s and gave it a fine reputation in the wine world. Paolo Pizziol now manages it even though Alessandro very much present. Technical management in the cellar comes from Corrado Cugnasco and Ermes Vianelli tends the 35 hectares of vineyards. Excellent raw material is grown and painstakingly transformed here. Proof of this is the estate's Franciacorta Brut '02, one of the best from this vintage. Though it just missed Three Glasses, it has an enjoyable nice pale, bright greenish straw-yellow colour, delicate perlage and captivating aromas of ripe damson, white chocolate and vanilla. The fresh, caressing, invigorating palate closes out long on soft of tones of pear and flowers. The Extra Dry Cuvette '01 is zesty and complex, clear in its fruit, rounded and balsamic. The Pas Dosé Cuvette Diamant '01 shows deep minerality, pulp and freshness while the Rosé Demi Sec '02 is pleasantly sweetish and fragrant with blueberry and currants. Less immediate but still sound, the Selezione '00 and Satèn '02 have over-evolved tones. The two Terre di Franciacortas, the Bianco Pian della Villa '04 and Rosso Gradoni '03, are excellent.

○	Franciacorta Brut '02	TT	5*
○	Franciacorta Cuvette Diamant Pas Dosé '01	TT	6
○	Franciacorta Extra Dry Cuvette '01	TT	5*
⊙	Franciacorta Rosé Demi Sec '02	TT	6
●	TdF Rosso Gradoni '03	TT	5
○	TdF Bianco Pian della Villa '04	TT	4
○	Franciacorta Brut Sel. '00	T	6
○	Franciacorta Satèn '02	T	6
○	Franciacorta Extra Brut '98	YYY	5*
○	Franciacorta Brut '01	YY	5*
○	Franciacorta Extra Brut '99	YY	5
○	Franciacorta Cuvette Diamant Pas Dosé '00	YY	6

MONTÙ BECCARIA (PV)

VERCESI DEL CASTELLAZZO
VIA AURELIANO, 36
27040 MONTÙ BECCARIA (PV)
TEL. 038560067

The Rosso del Castellazzo '03 from the Vercesi brothers is a great wine. Fruit, spice and secondary and tertiary aromas meld harmoniously in a mix of remarkable finesse, softness and density. With a dash more complexity, it would have prised open the doors to the Three Glass finals. The Gugiarolo, a pinot nero vinified off the skins, is surprising for it has decent cellarability although it wasn't designed that way. The '05 amazed us with intense fruity aromas of peach, raspberry and ripe tropical fruit, the density backed up by nice acid backbone and the nose-palate length. We hated not to give a high score to the Pinot Nero Luogo dei Monti '03, one of the most representative in the entire Oltrepò and a wine that has yielded extraordinary results in years like the legendary '95. Sadly, this vineyard faces due south and suffers particularly from heat. Actually, it is at its best in in-between growing years characterized by good temperature ranges. Something 2003 was absolutely not. Don't misunderstand us. The wine is good, structured and solid but the overripeness of the fruit has already partially taken away one of its special characteristics, that freshness and finesse on the nose and palate. The Pezzalunga '05 is well made, fruity and while it lacks any special complexity it is still very enjoyable. The Bonarda Vivace Luogo della Milla '05 is good with violet and raspberry aromas and a nice palate, even though it closes out a little too quickly. The spicy Vespolino '05 is as pleasant as ever.

●	Rosso del Castellazzo '03	TT	5
○	OP Pinot Nero in bianco Gugiarolo '05	TT	3*
●	OP Pinot Nero Luogo dei Monti '03	T	4
●	OP Bonarda Luogo della Milla '05	T	3
●	OP Rosso Pezzalunga '05	T	3*
●	Vespolino '05	T	3*
●	Rosso del Castellazzo '01	YY	6
●	OP Pinot Nero Luogo dei Monti '02	YY	5
●	Rosso del Castellazzo '02	YY	5
●	OP Barbera Clà '04	YY	4
●	OP Bonarda Vivace Luogo della Milla '04	YY	3

MORNICO LOSANA (PV)

CA' DI FRARA

VIA CASA FERRARI, 1
27040 MORNICO LOSANA (PV)
TEL. 0383892299
www.cadifrara.it

It is hard to find adequate words of praise for the Bellani family's efforts over the years, under the guidance of young Luca. The Frater '03, Oltrepò Pavese Rosso Riserva, from a substantial croatina base, deserves attention. Just bringing it near the nose unleashes a whirlwind of sensations since the blackberry and blueberry-led wild berry fruit is wonderful, clear and well integrated with the tertiary notes. The palate also shows breadth, depth, elegance, balance, softness and vitality. Faced with a champion of this calibre, even an excellent wine like Io Rosso '03, which also went straight to our finals, risked being overshadowed. From mostly barbera and pinot nero, it makes elegance its strength. The fruit is dense, intact, complex and well supported by a pattern of spices. Above all, it is a wine that brings out the characteristics of its own terroir. Although missing out on the finals, where it has already been many times, the Pinot Grigio Raccolta Tardiva '05 has a golden straw-yellow colour and the customary aromas of hedgerow, with honeysuckle upfront, and an even fullness in the mouth. The Cento '03 is a wine from a base of non-native varieties and celebrates the estate's centenary. The style is more international but Luca's hand is also obvious. Though very good, the Pinot Nero Il Raro Nero '03 suffered from the hot growing season with the development of very marked fruit. The Io Bianco '04 and Riesling Apogeo '05 are always elegant and would deserve further comment if only we had more space.

●	Io Rosso '03	▼▼	5
●	OP Rosso Il Frater Ris. '03	▼▼	6
●	Cento '03	▼▼	5
●	OP Pinot Nero Il Raro Nero '03	▼▼	5
○	Io Bianco '04	▼▼	5
○	OP Pinot Grigio Raccolta Tardiva '05	▼▼	4
○	OP Riesling Renano Apogeo '05	▼▼	4*
●	OP Rosso Il Frater Ris. '01	▽▽	6
○	Io Bianco '02	▽▽	5
○	OP Pinot Grigio Raccolta Tardiva '02	▽▽	4
○	OP Pinot Grigio Raccolta Tardiva '04	▽▽	4
●	Io Rosso '01	▽▽	5

OME (BS)

MAJOLINI

LOC. VALLE
VIA MANZONI, 3
25050 OME (BS)
TEL. 0306527378
www.majolini.it

Ezio Majolini passionately, skilfully manages his family's 20 hectares of lovely vineyards in the best positions around the municipality of Ome, with assistance from his nephew Simone and invaluable oenological consultancy from Jean-Pierre Valade. Ezio is also president of the Consorzio di Tutela del Franciacorta. This year, the Majolini cellar submitted a series of wonderfully good wines. Two cuvées, the Pas Dosé Aligi Sassu '00 and Electo '01, distinguished themselves at our finals though they fell just short of a Three Glass award this year. The Aligi Sassu is dedicated to the great Milanese artist whose latest sculpture graces the entrance to the estate. After three years on the lees, this monovarietal Chardonnay is introduced by a bright straw-yellow colour and rich ripe fruit, yeast and vanilla aromas with a delicate shade of barley sugar. The palate has backbone, pulp and elegance, and closes out long and caressing. With 20 per cent pinot nero blended into the chardonnay, the Electo '01 Brut is elegant and full, rich in seductive, juicy, clear fruit tones and backbone, and very long. From chardonnay with ten per cent pinot nero and after six years on the lees, the Valentino Majolini '94 now shows elegant and complex with notes of aromatic wood, flowers and dried fruit on the nose, where it also reveals a mineral tone that returns on the elegant palate, which expands harmoniously and finishes long. The vanilla and aromatic herb Franciacorta Brut is simply one of the best from the DOCG zone. We thought Rosé Altèra was well typed but unexciting.

○	Franciacorta Pas Dosé Aligi Sassu '00	▼▼	7
○	Franciacorta Electo Brut '01	▼▼	7
○	Franciacorta Brut Valentino Majolini '94	▼▼	7
○	Franciacorta Brut	▼▼	6
⊙	Franciacorta Altèra Rosé	▼	7
○	Franciacorta Electo Brut '00	▽▽▽	7
○	Franciacorta Electo Brut '97	▽▽▽	6
○	Franciacorta Brut Electo '99	▽▽▽	6
○	Franciacorta Ante Omnia Satèn '01	▽▽	6
○	Franciacorta Pas Dosé Aligi Sassu '99	▽▽	6

PASSIRANO (BS)

LE MARCHESINE
VIA VALLOSA, 31
25050 PASSIRANO (BS)
TEL. 030657005
www.lemarchesine.it

While waiting for the new releases of his prized vintage sparklers, this year Giovanni Biatta presented us with an excellent Satèn '02 that powered its way into our final taste-offs. This is a nice accomplishment for an estate that started up about 20 years ago and now turns out 32,000 bottles a year,. Teaming up with Giovanni are his son Loris and oenological consultant Jean-Pierre Valade. The brilliant Satèn '02 has a fine perlage and a well-defined nose with elegant tones of white-fleshed fruit, aromatic herbs and vanilla edged with stylish minerality. It expands across the rich palate with good fruit, freshness, harmony and caressing length. The base Brut is enjoyable for its overall fresh invigorating quality, floral hints on the nose and a full finish on a theme of citrus peel and vanilla. We found the Brut Rosé '02, with its insistent citrus note, and the Extra Brut, which has slightly over-evolved tones, both less fascinating. The excellent Cabernet Sauvignon Alice '01 is firmly structured and rich in elegant fruit and smooth tannins, and the Pinot Nero Il Podere '01 is varietal and elegant. The two Terre di Franciacortas, the Bianco '05 and Rosso '04, are both sound products.

○	Franciacorta Satèn '02	🍷🍷	6
●	Cabernet Sauvignon Alice '01	🍷🍷	6
●	Il Podere Pinot Nero '01	🍷🍷	6
○	Franciacorta Brut	🍷🍷	5
⊙	Franciacorta Brut Rosé '02	🍷	6
○	Franciacorta Extra Brut	🍷	5
●	TdF Rosso Curtefranca '04	🍷	4
○	TdF Bianco '05	🍷	4
●	Cabernet Sauvignon Alice '00	YY	6
⊙	Franciacorta Brut Rosé '01	YY	6
○	Franciacorta Brut Secolo Novo '99	YY	7

PASSIRANO (BS)

IL MOSNEL
LOC. CAMIGNONE
VIA BARBOGLIO, 14
25040 PASSIRANO (BS)
TEL. 030653117
www.ilmosnel.com

Emanuela Barboglio's lovely estate is now one of the top brands in Franciacorta. Its roughly 40 hectares, almost all in the DOCG zone, are divided into 16 plots surrounding the beautiful renaissance headquarters of the estate and winery. Her children, Giulio and Lucia Barzanò, have assisted her for some years now. Giulio handles technical, commercial and production aspects in collaboration with estate oenologists and consultants while Lucia deals with administration and marketing the wines, as well as public and press relations. Their excellent production now runs at 250,000 bottles annually, overseen by oenologists Alberto Musatti and Luigi Biemmi. The top Il Mosnel label is the vintage Brut, which in the '01 version earned a place in our finals thanks to complex aromas that interweave floral tones with spice and balsamic hints, and the lovely fruity pulp proffered on a palate that unfolds in soft, caressing, complexity with tones of ripe fruit, medicinal herbs and vanilla. The Satèn '02 is fresh, soft, rich in white-fleshed fruit and delicately aromatic with great harmony. As always, the estate's workhorse non-vintage Brut earned flattering reviews for its good density, floral and delicately citrus tones and overall harmony. The Parosé '02, with red berry fruit and medicinal herb tones, and the soft Pas Dosé, which is fragrant with white peach, are also sound. The chardonnay-based Passito '04 is very sound, the Terre di Franciacorta Bianco '05 and Rosso '04 are as good as ever and the Campolarga '05 is excellent.

○	Franciacorta Brut '01	🍷🍷	6
⊙	Franciacorta Pas Dosé Parosé '02	🍷🍷	6
○	Franciacorta Satèn '02	🍷🍷	6
○	Sebino Passito '04	🍷🍷	6
○	TdF Bianco Campolarga '05	🍷🍷	4*
○	Franciacorta Brut	🍷🍷	5
○	Franciacorta Pas Dosé	🍷🍷	5
●	TdF Rosso '04	🍷	4
○	TdF Bianco '05	🍷	4
○	Franciacorta Brut '00	YY	6
○	Franciacorta Satèn '00	YY	6
○	Franciacorta Brut '99	YY	6
○	Sebino Passito '03	YY	6
○	TdF Bianco Campolarga '04	YY	4*

POLPENAZZE DEL GARDA (BS)

Cascina La Pertica
loc. Picedo
via Rosario, 44
25080 Polpenazze del Garda (BS)
tel. 0365651471

Though the property was acquired in the late 1960s, it took around 20 years for Cascina La Pertica to launch the real revolution that took this estate into the front rank of winemaking in the Garda area. Some time in the late 1990s, Ruggero Brunori and Andrea Salvetti decided to convert their vineyards in Polpenazze – around 16 hectares in all, densely planted and tended like a garden – to organic methods, still an unusual choice in this zone. The results have been successful. In particular, Zalte, a blend of 60 per cent cabernet sauvignon with cabernet franc and merlot, took flight on wings of lightness and elegance, stringing together one success after another. The '04 vintage is as good as ever in terms of cleanness of fruit, aromatic charm, succulent drinkability and expressive length. Vineyard yields are low at around 5,000 kilograms per hectare, ageing is done in small wood and the resulting wine fully deserved its Three Glasses. There was a good performance from the Colombaio '05, a Groppello with a stylish profile and satisfying drinkability. The new vintages of the other two reds, the Garda Classico and the IGT Il Rosso, are still ageing in the cellar and the choice of postponing their release seems more than justified considering the positive development shown in previous vintages. These wines need time to express themselves. The pleasant, distinctive Chardonnay is vinified entirely in stainless steel. The Chiaretto '05 is well made.

●	Garda Cabernet Le Zalte '04	🍷🍷🍷	7
●	Garda Cl. Groppello Il Colombaio '05	🍷🍷	4
○	Garda Chardonnay Le Sincette '05	🍷	4
⊙	Garda Cl. Chiaretto Le Sincette '05	🍷	4
●	Garda Cabernet Le Zalte '00	🍸🍸🍸	7
●	Garda Cabernet Le Zalte '01	🍸🍸🍸	7
●	Garda Cabernet Le Zalte '03	🍸🍸🍸	7
●	Garda Cabernet Le Zalte '99	🍸🍸🍸	5

POZZOLENGO (BS)

Tenuta Roveglia
loc. Roveglia, 1
25010 Pozzolengo (BS)
tel. 030918663
www.tenutaroveglia.it

There is a breath of fresh air blowing through Roveglia. The courageous choices made over the past two years are bearing fruit and the Zweifel Azzone family's historic estate is back at the top of Lugana area production. The trebbiano di Lugana variety is king here, occupying 55 out of a total 60 hectares under vine, relegating red varieties to marginal positions. The painstaking labours of Paolo Fabiani in the vineyard and cellar and Flavio Prà's consultancy are bringing out the best characteristics of the various terroirs. This clear, convincingly solid growth in quality comes from harvesting that is staggered to capture all the details and shadings these vineyards are capable of producing. About 45 days separate the first pass from the last. An excellent example of the new operation here is the zesty, spirited Lugana '05, which is rich in fruit but also has satisfying veins of chlorophyll, making it drinkable yet complex at the same time. The two Superiore wines also scored well. They are sourced from the oldest vineyards on the estate, part planted during the 1950s, and harvested at low yields of 6-7,000 kilograms per hectare. Resting on the fine lees until June, these two whites already reveal the potential for expression the estate's Lugana selections will have in the future. The Vigna di Catullo '04, aged entirely in stainless steel, and Filo d'Arianna '03, aged in oak, flaunt fruit and minerality. The two Garda DOCs are sound.

○	Lugana Sup. Filo di Arianna '03	🍷🍷	4
○	Lugana Sup. Vigna di Catullo '04	🍷🍷	4
○	Lugana '05	🍷🍷	3
●	Garda Cabernet Sauvignon Ca' d'Oro '03	🍷	5
●	Garda Merlot '04	🍷	4
○	Lugana '04	🍸🍸	3

PROVAGLIO D'ISEO (BS)

BERSI SERLINI
LOC. CERETO
VIA CERRETO, 7
25050 PROVAGLIO D'ISEO (BS)
TEL. 0309823338
www.bersiserlini.it

There is an air of enthusiasm and something new at this lovely estate, energetically and skilfully managed by Maddalena Bersi Serlini. Remodelling work on the cellar and welcome centre has been finished and today the estate flaunts a fascinating mix of centuries-old structures and cutting-edge architecture. Antonietta Zandomeneghi has joined the estate staff as head of marketing and Paola Bersi Serlini is in charge of image and communications. But technical management of the house cuvées continues to rest on the shoulders of Corrado Cugnasco, an oenologist specialized in Franciacorta, who has presented some remarkably good labels this year. The Franciacorta Extra Brut '01, a Three Glass finalist, is a bright, pale straw yellow and complex on the nose, where alongside clear fruit tones it gives complex aromatic herb, floral and boisé nuances. The palate unfolds with broad, elegant hints of fruit then closes out long on minerally notes. The cuvée Vintage Brut '00 made an excellent debut. It's a single-varietal Chardonnay from the best-aspected plots on the estate. Aged over five years on the lees, it has an elegantly floral character on the nose and solid, well-layered structure on the palate. We also mention the juicy, fragrant Cuvée n. 4 Brut, and a base Brut designed around freshness and soft fruit tones. The Satèn is round and as complex as you'd expect. The Nuvola, with sweet hints of cakes, and the two Terre di Franciacortas, the Bianco '05 and Rosso '04, are all pleasant and inviting.

○	Franciacorta Extra Brut '01	🍷🍷	6
○	Franciacorta Brut Vintage '00	🍷🍷	7
○	Franciacorta Brut	🍷🍷	6
○	Franciacorta Brut Cuvée n. 4	🍷🍷	6
○	Franciacorta Satèn	🍷🍷	6
●	TdF Rosso Curtefranca '04	🍷	5
○	TdF Bianco Curtefranca '05	🍷	4
○	Nuvola Demi Sec	🍷	6
○	Franciacorta Brut '00	🍷🍷 (outline)	6
○	Franciacorta Extra Brut '00	🍷🍷 (outline)	6

PUEGNAGO SUL GARDA (BS)

PASINI - SAN GIOVANNI
FRAZ. RAFFA
VIA VIDELLE, 2
25080 PUEGNAGO SUL GARDA (BS)
TEL. 0365651419
www.pasiniproduttori.com

Pasini Produttori is changing its name to Azienda Agricola Pasini – San Giovanni, combining the family name with the name of the place where the beautiful, modern winery is located. We mention this change with pleasure because it is more than a face-lift. In fact, the move marks a decisive and even courageous emphasis on a chosen strategy that puts marketing in second place to invest resources and energy in the vineyards, production and the promotion of Valtenesi. The estate has just under 40 hectares overall, 15 in Raffa di Puegnago, the same number in Picedo di Polpenazze and ten in Lugana. The number of bottles has been cut almost in half, the vineyards are more densely planted and quality has swung sharply up. Convincing proof of this change of pace comes with the Groppello selection from the Arzane vineyard, two hectares on the small hill of Picedo. The Riserva '03 recalls dense echoes of berry fruit on an almost grassy texture. The rediscovery of Groppello is also apparent in San Gioan '01, a lovely red that mixes this typical variety from Valtenesi with cabernet sauvignon, a blend that ages two years in large oak. The cabernet from the Montezalto vineyard finds expression in another interesting red. The '01 version, all from small barrels, will express itself better after further bottle ageing, but now already offers up nice fruit and pleasant vegetal sensations. The well-made Lugana is rich in yellow-fleshed fruit sensations and other wines are all sound.

●	Garda Cabernet Sauvignon Vign. Montezalto '01	🍷🍷	5
●	San Gioan Rosso I Carati '01	🍷🍷	4
●	Garda Cl. Groppello Vign. Arzane Ris. '03	🍷🍷	4
●	Garda Cl. Rosso Sup. Cap del Priù '03	🍷	4
○	Garda Cl. Bianco Il Renano '05	🍷	4
○	Lugana Il Lugana '05	🍷	4
○	Brut Cl. Ceppo 326	🍷	5
○	Lugana Brut	🍷	4
●	Garda Cl. Groppello Il Groppello '05		4
●	Garda Cl. Groppello Vign. Arzane Ris. '00	🍷🍷 (outline)	4
●	Garda Cl. Groppello Vign. Arzane Ris. '01	🍷🍷 (outline)	4

RETORBIDO (PV)

MARCHESE ADORNO
VIA CORIASSA, 4
27050 RETORBIDO (PV)
TEL. 0383374404
www.marcheseadorno-wines.it

We were correct last year when we predicted major results would arrive soon at this estate after the significant investments made by the owner. Right on schedule, here is a lovely line-up of bottles that have helped Marchese Marcello Cattaneo Adorno earn a full Guide profile. We'll begin with Rugla, a Bordeaux blend that went through to the Three Glass finals. Its dark, ruby red colour precedes a nose that opens slowly on notes of bell pepper, aromatic herbs and coffee before the palate reveals fruity pulp, softness, balance and great length. Though still young, it is already enjoyable. The Barbera Vigna del Re '03 also made a great leap forward compared to the previous vintage. With its intense bouquet of coffee, spice and wild berries, it has well-measured wood, a pleasing style, some edges that are more tannic than acid and a long liquorice finish. It will be on top form after another year or so in bottle. The Pinot Nero '04 should also be left patiently to develop, and is also characterized by coffee notes from the new oak that let the variety's signature cassis and forest floor emerge. It has structure, lively tannins and a finish marked by liquorice. The Bonarda Frizzante '05 is deep, fruity and well crafted. An excellent score also went to the Arcolaio '05 and Cliviano '04. The first is a full cortese-chardonnay blend well supported by acidity and Cliviano is a fresh, fruity Bordeaux blend not without complexity. The Pinot Grigio '05 and Barbera '04 are correct and varietal.

●	OP Barbera V. del Re '03	🍷🍷	6
●	Rugla '03	🍷🍷	4
●	Cliviano '04	🍷🍷	4
●	OP Pinot Nero '04	🍷🍷	5
○	Arcolaio '05	🍷🍷	4*
●	OP Bonarda Frizzante '05	🍷🍷	4*
●	OP Barbera '04	🍷	4
○	OP Pinot Grigio '05	🍷	4

ROCCA DE' GIORGI (PV)

ANTEO
LOC. CHIESA
27040 ROCCA DE' GIORGI (PV)
TEL. 038599073 - 0385951057
www.anteovini.it

We appreciated the excellent performance from this estate managed by Antonella Cribellati and her brother Piero. The priority given to sparkling wine production is obvious as soon as you enter the cellar, where a vast underground space is dedicated to housing an expanse of wooden riddling racks for manual remuage. After the '98 edition, the Riserva del Poeta '99 also makes it to the Three Glass finals. This spumante has great class and intense, intriguing aromas of cakes, meringue, ripe tropical fruit, peach, golden apples and more. The palate is chewy, harmonious, full and complex with a long-lasting finish. The Rosé is the best ever and made it through to the finals. The onionskin hue glows, the rich red berry fruit and aromatic herb aromas seduce, and the elegance of the clear, precise palate wins you over as the softness melds with the acid vein. The Nature Ecru '01 is also very good, with all the style and liveliness of an undosed sparkler, the fruit supported by great acid backbone. Rounding off the sparklers is a high-scoring base Brut, which is simpler even though it spends around 30 months on the lees. The croatina and pinot nero Coste del Roccolo '05 is fruity, approachable and pleasant, the Bonarda Frizzante Staffolo '05 is very well made, the Chardonnay Quattro Marzo '05 is lovely and redolent of tropical fruit and the Moscato di Volpara La Volpe e L'Uva '05 is varietal and citrus-like.

○	OP Pinot Nero Brut Cl. Riserva del Poeta '99	🍷🍷	6
○	OP Anteo Pinot Nero Brut Cl. Nature Ecru '01	🍷🍷	5
●	Coste del Roccolo '05	🍷🍷	4*
●	OP Bonarda Staffolo '05	🍷🍷	4*
○	OP Chardonnay Quattro Marzo '05	🍷🍷	4*
⊙	OP Anteo Brut Cl. Anteo Rosé	🍷🍷	5
○	OP Moscato La Volpe e L'Uva '05	🍷	4
○	OP Pinot Nero Cl. Anteo Brut	🍷	5
○	OP Pinot Nero Brut Cl. Nature Ecru '00	🍷🍷 (outline)	5
○	OP Anteo Nature Ecru Mill. '99	🍷🍷 (outline)	5
●	OP Bonarda Staffolo '04	🍷🍷 (outline)	4

ROCCA DE' GIORGI (PV)

CONTE CARLO GIORGI DI VISTARINO
VILLA FORNACE
27040 ROCCA DE' GIORGI (PV)
TEL. 038585117 - 0385241171
www.contevistarino.it

After some ups and downs, this estate seems at last to have found the right path to fulfilling its enormous potential, under the guidance of young Ottavia. But then again, an 806-hectare property with 180 hectares under vine and an 18th-century villa almost has a moral duty to aim to be a benchmark for all of Oltrepò wine production. The Pinot Nero Pernice has turned out to be one of the very best from the scorching 2003 growing year. It has the deep garnet colour typical of the zone, fresh, clear intact fruit, lovely coffee notes, good acidity and balance. With a bit more complexity, it could have aspired to the finals. The Sorbe '04 is also very good. It's a single-variety croatina with the classic purple ruby colour, forthright fresh aromas of wild berries, nice mellow fruit, tannins that are lively and abundant yet fine-grained and velvet-smooth. It's a wonderful example of the still partially unexplored potential of the variety when vinified as a still wine. The Brut Metodo Classico from the '03 vintage shows a fairly evolved style right from its golden straw yellow and tropical fruit notes. It is fresh and pleasant though not particularly complex. The Pinot Nero Costa del Nero '04 also earned a good review. Simpler with respect to the Pernice, it is harmonious in its aromas and softness. The Bonarda Vivace L'Alcova '05 has touches of violets and red berry fruit. The Buttafuoco Monte Selva '04 has slightly stewed fruit. The Brut Metodo Martinotti and Sangue di Giuda Costiolo '05 are both well made.

○ OP Pinot Nero Brut Cl. '03	TT	3
● OP Pinot Nero Pernice '03	TT	4
● OP Pinot Nero Costa del Nero '04	TT	3*
● Sorbe '04	TT	4
● OP Buttafuoco Monte Selva '04	T	4
● OP Bonarda L'Alcova '05	T	3
○ OP Pinot Nero Brut Martinotti	T	3*
● OP Sangue di Giuda Costiolo '05	T	3

RODENGO SAIANO (BS)

MIRABELLA
VIA CANTARANE, 2
25050 RODENGO SAIANO (BS)
TEL. 030611197
www.mirabellavini.it

Since 1979, this dynamic estate has been synonymous with Franciacorta in Italy and beyond. Over more than 25 years, manager Francesco Bracchi and oenologists Teresio and Alessandro Schiavi have worked toward quality, creating a broad, carefully made range of products. This year, after tasting the excellent Franciacorta Non Dosato '98, we had the distinct sensation that the estate had shifted up a gear and was making a determined run for absolute quality. Made from an extreme selection of wines sourced from Mirabella's 30 hectares under vine, it missed our highest prize by only a hair's breadth. The cuvée is 50 per cent Chardonnay, 20 per cent Pinot Bianco and the rest Pino Nero and the wine itself is a bright straw yellow with tiny bubbles and aromas of rare complexity where fruit and yeast mingle with florality and oaky shades. A delicate minerally background shows through, returning on the broad palate with its rich structure and soft development. From the other cuvées, we would mention an excellent Franciacorta Brut with subtle ageing aromas that mingle with rich fruit, and the Rosé Brut, which is fragrant with blueberry and currants then zesty, fruity and supple on the palate. The Terre di Franciacorta Rosso Maniero '04 is structured, soft and stylishly tannic, and all the other labels are sound, such as the Nero d'Ombra, a Bordeaux blend with a dash of nebbiolo. The Satèn seemed slightly under par this time in comparison with previous editions.

○ Franciacorta Non Dosato '98	TT	5*
● TdF Rosso Maniero '04	TT	4*
○ Franciacorta Brut	TT	4*
⊙ Franciacorta Brut Rosé	TT	4*
○ Franciacorta Satèn	T	5
● Nero d'Ombra '02	T	6
○ TdF Bianco Palazzina '04	T	4
⊙ Franciacorta Brut Rosé '01	YY	4*
● Nero d'Ombra '01	YY	6
○ Franciacorta Non Dosato '97	YY	5

ROVESCALA (PV)

Agnes

via Campo del Monte, 1
27040 Rovescala (PV)
tel. 038575206
www.fratelliagnes.it

Brothers Sergio and Cristiano Agnes always extract high overall quality from this "croatina factory", which practically has only that one variety on the estate. This year, we were most impressed by the Vignazzo '04. Its inky-black ruby colour heralds ripe, dense fruit with tertiary notes of spice, liquorice, toast and abundant yet excellent quality wood. On the palate there is everything you would expect: concentration, abundant yet velvety tannins, depth and length. Although still young, it promises very interesting development. The Poculum '04, the other IGT from bonarda pignolo, a croatina clone characterized by a clearly smaller bunch shaped like a pine cone, hinted at in the name ("pigna" means pine cone). The wine runs more or less along the same lines in colour and intensity, with blackberry and blueberry aromas, but is a bit behind the Vignazzo in its development. In fact, it might be better to release these wines after another year in bottle. The scores in the Guide might even be higher since they have everything there to aspire to the finals. Among the slightly sparkling Bonardas from the '05 vintage, it was a stand-off between the Cresta del Ghiffi and Campo del Monte. Both are fragrant with well-gauged tannins and a chewy palate but the former has more residual sugar. The Possessione del Console is less convincing but still well made.

● Rosso Poculum '04	TT	5*
● Rosso Vignazzo '04	TT	4
● OP Bonarda Campo del Monte '05	TT	3*
● OP Bonarda Cresta del Ghiffi '05	TT	3*
● OP Bonarda Possessione del Console '05	T	3
● OP Bonarda Possessione del Console '03	YY	3
● Rosso Poculum '03	YY	5
● OP Bonarda Campo del Monte '04	YY	4
● OP Bonarda Cresta del Ghiffi '04	YY	3

SAN DAMIANO AL COLLE (PV)

Bisi

loc. Cascina San Michele
fraz. Villa Marone, 70
27040 San Damiano al Colle (PV)
tel. 038575037
www.aziendagricolabisi.it

With the favourable '03 growing season, Claudio Bisi has regained his full Guide profile. This seemed only fitting given the remarkable array of wines he presented. The most impressive, and a benchmark for what Barbera can be in Oltrepò if managed properly with green harvests and low yields, is the Roncolongo '03, which went straight to the finals. A beautiful dark, almost impenetrable ruby, it has an aromatic bouquet that immediately won us over with whispers of almonds, berries, cherry wood and fine spices, all linked together in exemplary harmony. In keeping with this, the palate reprises the chewy fruit with the cherry right up front, backing it with crisp acidity, never cloying softness, powerful yet never excessive structure and a finish with great length. Also very good is the dark ruby Cabernet Sauvignon Primm '03, which has lovely aromas that nicely blend the varietal quality of mature hay with sensations of chocolate, wild berries and balsamic herbs. The palate is big and opulent, revealing fine-grained, velvet-smooth tannins, good length and attractive harmony. On its first release, the Pinot Nero Calonga '03 reveals the winemaker's style in its marriage of power and elegance. It may lack a little typicity but the sheer quality of the wine is beyond discussion with its rather deep garnet colour, aromas of wild berries, tar, forest floor and balsamic notes, nice close-knit tannins, intact fruit and a great finish. The Bonarda Frizzante '05 is also very good, showing broad and fragrant on the nose and good balance on the meaty palate.

● OP Barbera Roncolongo '03	TT	5
● Calonga '03	TT	5
● OP Cabernet Sauvignon Primm '03	TT	5
● OP Bonarda Frizzante '05	TT	3*
● OP Cabernet Sauvignon Primm '00	YY	5
● OP Barbera Roncolongo '01	YY	5
● OP Cabernet Sauvignon Primm '01	YY	5
● OP Barbera Roncolongo '00	YY	5
● OP Bonarda Frizzante '04	YY	3

SAN DAMIANO AL COLLE (PV)

VANZINI
FRAZ. BARBALEONE, 7
27040 SAN DAMIANO AL COLLE (PV)
TEL. 038575019
www.vanzini-wine.com

The Bonarda Frizzante '05 from the Vanzini brothers continues to be one of the best in the Oltrepò, despite the major production numbers. It has a lovely bright purple ruby colour, forthright aromas of blackberry, raspberry and almond, nice fruity pulp with perfectly gauged tannins and nice verve in the finish. The very appealing Pinot Nero Extra Dry Metodo Martinotti has a bright straw-yellow colour, a lovely nose of peach and citrus, good finesse, softness and a long finish. The Sangue di Giuda '05 is also very good, with a violet, cherry and wild red berry fruit bouquet and soft, measured tannins. The Pinot Nero '03 was good and promising well when tasted from the vat. Though it's still a good wine, bottle maturation has penalized the nose in particular, with slightly tired overripe fruit. But it picks up again on the palate with close-knit, velvety tannins, good balance and a long finish. The sparkling Extra Dry Martinotti Rosé is pleasant, its bright rose colour introducing clear aromas of flowers and red fruit, and good softness from 16 grams per litre residual sugar. The Barbera, Riesling Italico and Moscato from the '05 vintage are correct, precise in their varietal sensations, clean and well made.

● OP Bonarda Frizzante '05	🍷🍷	4*
● OP Sangue di Giuda '05	🍷🍷	4*
○ OP Pinot Nero Extra Dry	🍷🍷	4*
● OP Pinot Nero '03	🍷	5
● OP Barbera '05	🍷	3*
○ OP Moscato '05	🍷	3
○ OP Riesling Italico '05	🍷	3
⊙ OP Pinot Nero Rosé Extra Dry	🍷	4
● OP Sangue di Giuda '01	ΨΨ	3*
● OP Bonarda Frizzante '04	ΨΨ	4
● OP Sangue di Giuda '04	ΨΨ	4

SAN PAOLO D'ARGON (BG)

CANTINA SOCIALE BERGAMASCA
VIA BERGAMO, 10
24060 SAN PAOLO D'ARGON (BG)
TEL. 035951098
www.cantinabergamasca.it

The best wine from Cantina Sociale Bergamasca this year is Valcalepio Rosso Riserva Vigna del Conte '03. It needs to mature more but, young as it is, it still flaunts all its potential starting with a lovely intense nose with outstanding balsamic notes, spices, vanilla, cocoa powder and blueberry. The palate is dense and soft, the velvety tannins accompanying remarkable depth. The Valcalepio Rosso Riserva Akros '02 nicely expresses the grassy notes of hay and bell pepper contributed by the cabernet and merlot. It has well-measured wood, with discreet spice, good fullness on the palate and a liquorice echo in the finish. The '02 version of the Valcalepio Moscato Passito Perseo is good as always, showing candid, intense, pulpy and harmonious, characterized by nice verve in the finish. The Valcalepio Rosso Orologio '04 is inexpensive and simple yet very well made with a nice balance of fruit and vegetal notes. The Aureo '03, a passito from part-dried moscato giallo, has sensations of box hedge, lemon and citron, residual sugar that does not cloy, good backbone and balance. The Merlot '05 is nice and simple yet not without elegance. Two new labels made a good debut. The fragrant Solivo is a vino da tavola from rosé-fermented schiava. The Manzoni IGT is in fact a pleasant Incrocio Manzoni with distinct aromas of sage and pennyroyal. The two Valcalepio Biancos are good, the Orologio '05 showing simpler and more immediate and the Leukos '05 more complex, although it still needs to find balance.

● Valcalepio Moscato Passito Perseo '02	🍷🍷	6
● Valcalepio Rosso Akros Ris. '02	🍷🍷	4
● Valcalepio Rosso Vigna del Conte Ris. '03	🍷🍷	5
● Valcalepio Rosso Orologio '04	🍷🍷	3*
○ Moscato Giallo Aureo '03	🍷	5
○ Manzoni Bianco '05	🍷	3
● Merlot '05	🍷	2
○ Valcalepio Bianco Leukos '05	🍷	3
○ Valcalepio Bianco Orologio '05	🍷	3
⊙ Solivo	🍷	3
● Valcalepio Rosso Orologio '03	ΨΨ	3

SANTA MARIA DELLA VERSA (PV)

CANTINA SOCIALE LA VERSA
VIA F. CRISPI, 15
27047 SANTA MARIA DELLA VERSA (PV)
TEL. 0385798411
www.laversa.it

The long-established Cantina Sociale in Santa Maria della Versa gave us a thoroughly decent array of wines, flattering results for a 6,000,000-bottle estate that under the direction of Francesco Cervetti has not only managed to create a top product line, I Roccoli, but also improved the rest of the range, for example the commendably priced Terre d'Alteni line. The new IGT red Casale del Re '03, from a blend of barbera and pinot nero, is fragrant on the nose with strawberry and cherry aromas. It has nice fruity pulp with well-gauged tannins and a remarkably long finish. Among the sparklers, there was the customary good score for the fresh, fruity Carta Oro with its well-defined nose-palate profile. The same goes for the Testarossa Principio '99, a special edition of this historic label. The deep colour ushers in yeast and cakes, and good backbone. The standard Testarossa is also good but a tad less expressive. The Bonarda Ca' Bella '05 is well made, harmonious and characteristic. On its first release, Pinot Nero Liutajo del Re '03 is a bit behind schedule on its maturation curve. The nice background reveals woodland aromas of berry fruit and rain-soaked earth and the palate lacks a little balance. The Riesling Renano Roccolo delle Fate '05 is stylish and varietal. The Moscato di Volpara '05 from the I Roccoli series is pleasant with its characteristic citrus notes. The Brut Martinotti Monte Calvo is well made while the Bonarda Frizzante and Pinot Grigio from the Terre d'Alteni line are forthright and well typed, as is the Sangue di Giuda, all from the '05 vintage.

●	Casale Del Re '03	▼▼	6
●	OP Bonarda Frizzante Ca' Bella '05	▼▼	4
●	OP Bonarda Frizzante Terre d'Alteni '05	▼▼	4*
○	Cuvée Testarossa Principio '99	▼▼	8
○	OP Pinot Nero Brut Carta Oro	▼▼	4*
○	Cuvée Testarossa Brut	▼	5
●	OP Pinot Nero Liutajo Del Re '03	▼	6
○	OP Moscato di Volpara '05	▼	4
○	OP Pinot Grigio Terre D'Alteni '05	▼	5
○	OP Riesling Roccolo delle Fate '05	▼	5
●	OP Sangue di Giuda '05	▼	4
○	OP Pinot Nero Monte Calvo	▼	4

SIRMIONE (BS)

CA' DEI FRATI
FRAZ. LUGANA
VIA FRATI, 22
25019 SIRMIONE (BS)
TEL. 030919468
www.cadeifrati.it

If Lugana winemakers have become aware of the potential of their white, much of the credit has to go to the Dal Cero brothers and their Lugana I Frati. Considered the estate's base wine until just a few years ago, it has shown an enviable ability to stand the test of time, developing an engaging minerality over the years. Painstaking selection in the vineyard, later and later harvests and an almost maniacal attention to detail in the cellar have helped the latest vintages of I Frati to move into the limelight as one of the best interpretations of the Garda territory. The '05 probably marks a fundamental turning point. Its typical, fresh young aromas of yellow-fleshed fruit and chlorophyll are accompanied by those subtle benzene veins that until now Lugana trebbiano developed almost exclusively with the passage of time. The mix turns out to be truly captivating. The Lugana Brolettino is always good and the '04 vintage has made it zesty and pulpy. The same goes for the Brolettino Grande Annata, which in the '02 edition has a somewhat lower contribution from oak to focus attention on the vibrant fruit. The Pratto '04 is also very fruity. The density of the overripe trebbiano melds with the aromas of the chardonnay and sauvignon. But the entire production marked Ca' dei Frati is convincing. The Ronchedone '03 is rich in red berry fruit, the Chiaretto '05 is pleasing, the dried-grape Tre Filer '03 shows caressing sweetness and the Lugana Metodo Classico is elegant.

○	Lugana I Frati '05	▼▼	4
○	Lugana Brolettino Grande Annata '02	▼▼	5
○	Lugana Brut Cuvée dei Frati '03	▼▼	4
●	Ronchedone '03	▼▼	4
○	Tre Filer '03	▼▼	5
○	Lugana Brolettino '04	▼▼	4
○	Pratto '04	▼▼	4
⊙	Riviera del Garda Bresciano I Frati Chiaretto '05	▼▼	4
○	Pratto '96	▽▽▽	4
○	Lugana I Frati '04	▽▽	4
○	Lugana Brolettino '03	▽▽	5
○	Pratto '03	▽▽	5

SIRMIONE (BS)

CA' LOJERA
LOC. ROVIZZA
VIA 1886, 19
25019 SIRMIONE (BS)
TEL. 0457551901 - 030919550
www.calojera.com

It's hard for us to swallow Franco Tiraboschi's story when he says he feels old and doesn't know how much longer he'll be able to make wine. We don't believe him for at least two reasons. First, he has a young boy's twinkle in his eye when he speaks and second because he admits he is planting new vines with a clear view to maintaining high quality. We should also add that he and his wife Ambra are never in a hurry to release their wines, arguing that Luganas give their best only after sufficient ageing, Actually, this is one of the few wineries in the zone where you can find several vintages on sale. From the cellar in Rovizza near Sirmione, on the border of Lombardy and Veneto, we tasted three Luganas this time: the Superiore '03, the Riserva del Lupo '04 and the base '05. The second edition of the Riserva was the most convincing of the trio. Although it did not hit the impressive heights of the '03 version, which is probably destined to make history in Lugana territory, it is still a satisfyingly drinkable wine with powerful structure and good freshness, as well as fruit steeped in minerally sensations. The Superiore shows it is a white with a sound profile and considerable body. The Lugana '05 is more immediate and easy drinking. The dried-grape Ravel '03 did well, showing sweet yet never cloying and saturated with touches of candied fruit and dried apricot. The Chardonnay '04 shows remarkable texture. The reds are well made but not particularly complex.

○	Lugana Sup. '03	🍷🍷	5
○	Ravel '03	🍷🍷	5
○	Lugana Riserva del Lupo '04	🍷🍷	5
○	Lugana '05	🍷🍷	4
●	Garda Cabernet '04	🍷	4
○	Garda Chardonnay '04	🍷	4
●	Garda Merlot '04	🍷	4
○	Lugana Sup. Riserva del Lupo '03	YY	5
○	Lugana Sup. '00	YY	4
○	Lugana Sup. '01	YY	4

TEGLIO (SO)

SANDRO FAY
LOC. SAN GIACOMO DI TEGLIO
VIA PILA CASELLI, 1
23030 TEGLIO (SO)
TEL. 0342786071

Sandro Fay's estate is destined to leave a mark on Valtellina winemaking: not just for its wines, but also its serious investment in improving the vineyards and replanting the areas under vine. Furthermore, Sandro, an oenologist, has also strategically involved his children Marco and Elena in his project. They now work full-time on the front lines in various estate activities. One of the most interesting submissions this year was an original Valgella Carterìa '03, sourced from a lovely vineyard. The nose gives clear sensations of red berry fruit and spices. The palate is soft, rich and pleasantly fresh with convincing length. Unmistakeable style and personality mark out the Sforzato Ronco del Picchio '04, which has a rich, layered profile on the nose that runs from ripe fruit to cocoa powder and sweet oaky shades. The palate is compact and warm with a harmonic finish. The Valgella Ca' Morèi '03 is good proffering a spicy, broad nose with notes of ripe plums. The palate shows solid body with a dense, meaty texture. The Sassella Il Glicine '03 enhances all the best features of the nebbiolo variety. The aromas are stylish and complex with notes of cherry and the juicy palate is savoury with long, harmonious fruit.

●	Valtellina Sup. Valgella Carterìa '03	🍷🍷	5
●	Valtellina Sforzato Ronco del Picchio '04	🍷🍷	7
●	Valtellina Sup. Sassella Il Glicine '03	🍷🍷	5
●	Valtellina Sup. Valgella Ca' Morèi '03	🍷🍷	5
●	Valtellina Sforzato Ronco del Picchio '02	YYY	7
●	Valtellina Sforzato Ronco del Picchio '01	YY	6
●	Valtellina Sup. Valgella Ca' Morèi '02	YY	5
●	Valtellina Sforzato Ronco del Picchio '03	YY	7
●	Valtellina Sforzato Ronco del Picchio '99	YY	6
●	Valtellina Sup. Valgella Ca' Morèi '01	YY	5

TIRANO (SO)

PLOZZA
VIA SAN GIACOMO, 22
23037 TIRANO (SO)
TEL. 0342701297
www.plozza.com

It is very satisfying to reward an estate that has wisely grown slowly, year after year, and understands how to appreciate its past while looking to the future. Credit goes to the perspicuity of Marco Zanolari, oenologist and long-standing owner of this estate who, alongside his son Andrea, has skilfully invested in the cellar and in the obvious potential there is for nebbiolo in Valtellina. The result is a Numero Uno not just in name but also in fact. This complex, elegant wine from the '01 vintage won Three well-deserved Glasses. Made from slightly dried nebbiolo, selected from half century-old vines, it is the expertly crafted embodiment of the uniqueness of a terrain and its favourite variety. Rich, balsamic and spicy in its aromas, it offers a dense, juicy palate with excellent progression based on the balance in the wine's various components. Also nebbiolo-based, Passione '01 is very good with aromas of forest floor and plum. Its palate is soft with fruit to the fore and a long, leisurely finish. The Riserva La Scala '02 gives dried flower, almond and tobacco sensations on the nose. The palate is warm with a fresh, pleasant acid backbone. The Grumello Riserva '02 shows compact, typical aromas and a dry, linear palate, well sustained by the almondy note in the finish. The elegant Sforzato '02, with intense aromas of plums and damp earth, is definitely coming on. The palate is caressing, lingering and well sustained by pleasant fullness.

●	Valtellina Numero Uno '01	▼▼▼	8
●	Passione Barrique '01	▼▼	7
●	Valtellina Sforzato Vin da Ca' '02	▼▼	6
●	Valtellina Sup. Grumello Ris. '02	▼▼	4
●	Valtellina Sup. La Scala Ris. '02	▼▼	4
●	Valtellina Sup. Grumello Ris. '00	▽▽	5
●	Valtellina Sup. La Scala Ris. '00	▽▽	5
●	Valtellina Sforzato Vin da Ca' '01	▽▽	6
●	Valtellina Sup. La Scala Ris. '01	▽▽	5
●	Valtellina Sfurzat Vin da Ca' '98	▽▽	6

TIRANO (SO)

CONTI SERTOLI SALIS
P.ZZA SALIS, 3
23037 TIRANO (SO)
TEL. 0342710404
www.sertolisalis.com

The Sertoli Salis winery structure has changed. After the sudden passing of Cesare Sertoli Salis, his brother Francesco took over estate management, ably assisted by his wife Paola. Technical management remains in the expert hands of oenologist Claudio Introini, who again gave us a line-up of top-quality wines, beginning with the Capo di Terra '03 made from slightly dried nebbiolo grapes. The nose is dense with the intact fruit to the fore. The palate is juicy and round with good intensity and length. Among the best from the vintage, Sforzato Canua '03 deserved its place in the taste-offs. It has a powerful personality, a long lifespan, warm spicy aromas and a dense palate with soft tannins and a lingering finish. The Grumello '03 put on an interesting performance with fruity, morello cherry-led aromas. The palate is broad with well-resolved tannins and a balanced richness of flavour. We thought the classic interpretation of the Sassella '03 was good, with sweet plum aromas and a nicely acidic palate that drinks warm, full and long. The supple Saloncello '05 has fruity aromas, but we felt it was slightly lean. The Rosso di Valtellina '05 is pleasant to drink, fresh in its aromas and honestly priced. The well-crafted Torre della Sirena '05, from native pignola and rossola grapes, shows peach and hedgerow aromas and a taut palate with a precise, minerally, savoury finish.

●	Valtellina Sforzato Canua '03	▼▼	7
●	Valtellina Sup. Capo di Terra '03	▼▼	5
●	Valtellina Sup. Grumello '03	▼▼	4
●	Valtellina Sup. Sassella '03	▼▼	4
○	Torre della Sirena '05	▼▼	4
●	Il Saloncello '05	▼	4
●	Rosso di Valtellina '05	▼	3
●	Valtellina Sforzato Canua '00	▽▽▽	6
●	Valtellina Sforzato Canua '01	▽▽▽	7
●	Valtellina Sforzato Canua '02	▽▽▽	7
●	Valtellina Sforzato Canua '99	▽▽▽	6

TORRICELLA VERZATE (PV)

MONSUPELLO
VIA SAN LAZZARO, 5
27050 TORRICELLA VERZATE (PV)
TEL. 0383896043
www.monsupello.it

Producing 240,000 bottles from around 50 hectares of vineyards in production means harvesting more or less 5,000 kilograms of fruit per hectare. Considering the Monsupello vineyards have an average density of 5,000 plants per hectare, each plant, on average, produces one kilogram of grapes. This is achieved through quality-oriented training systems, such as Guyot, very short pruning and bunch thinning. In addition, only the first-pressing must is used for fermentation of the still and sparkling wines. This is just to explain why this particular estate stands apart on the crowded winemaking scene in Oltrepò, where big yields and big numbers are the norm. Father and son team, Carlo and Pierangelo Boatti each year give us a range of wines with great character that are always excellent and at times unforgettable. This year, two labels went into our finals. The Brut Ca' del Tava, from 60 per cent pinot nero with some chardonnay, and Pinot Nero Brut Classese '00, both just missed a third Glass. The soft yet assertive Ca' del Tava boasts structure, fruity pulp and elegant oaky notes. The Pinot Nero may offer greater expressive finesse in this phase, with a floral, yeasty nose sustained by a nice acid backbone, but it lacks a little length. A parade of excellent still and sparkling wines follows with the deep, complex Chardonnay Senso '04 in the lead, then the delicious, varietal Riesling Renano '05 and solid Barbera Vigna Pivena '03, with its morello cherry, boisé and balsamic notes.

○	OP Pinot Nero Brut Cl. Classese '00	▼▼	5
○	OP Brut Cl. Cuvée Ca' del Tava	▼▼	8
●	OP Barbera V. Pivena '03	▼▼	5
○	OP Chardonnay Senso '04	▼▼	6
●	OP Barbera Vivace Magenga '05	▼▼	4*
●	OP Bonarda Vivace Vaiolet '05	▼▼	4*
○	OP Chardonnay '05	▼▼	4*
○	OP Pinot Grigio '05	▼▼	4*
○	OP Pinot Nero Brut Cl.	▼▼	5
○	OP Riesling Renano '05	▼▼	4*
○	OP Sauvignon '05	▼▼	4*
○	OP Pinot Nero Cl. Nature	▼▼	5
●	OP Barbera I Gelsi '04	▼	4
○	OP Brut Cl. Cuvée Ca' del Tava	▽▽▽	8
○	OP Pinot Nero Cl. Nature	▽▽▽	5

VILLA DI TIRANO (SO)

TRIACCA
VIA NAZIONALE, 121
23030 VILLA DI TIRANO (SO)
TEL. 0342701352
www.triacca.com

Because they were still ageing, several showcase wines were missing from this major Valtellina estate which, over the past few years, has concentrated its attention on experimenting in the vineyards above all to make nebbiolo great in Valtellina. Despite the absences, the wines submitted this year earned very positive reviews. This was the case with the Riserva La Gatta '01 whose fruity aromas on the nose mingle well with tobacco and spice notes. The palate shows energy with supporting acidity and a pleasant finish. The very good Grumello '03 is one of the best in this type, its floral aromas showing fresh yet intense at the same time. The palate has character but never loses its suppleness to finish long and invigorating. Intense aromas of red berry fruit with hints of spice introduce the Sassella '03. The palate is balanced and soft with almond-like shades in the finish. The Inferno '03 put on a good performance with its elegantly distinctive plum-led nose and a soft palate with exemplary texture. Casa La Gatta '03 has well-typed aromas with fruity notes preceding a supple palate with a tangy freshness. The Sauvignon Del Frate '04 shows confident aromas that are streaked by new wood. The dense palate has a lingering finish.

●	Valtellina Sup. La Gatta Ris. '01	▼▼	6
●	Valtellina Sup. Grumello '03	▼▼	5
●	Valtellina Sup. Inferno '03	▼▼	5
●	Valtellina Sup. Sassella '03	▼▼	5
●	Valtellina Sup. Casa La Gatta '03	▼	5
○	Sauvignon Del Frate '04	▼	5
●	Valtellina Sforzato '00	▽▽▽	7
●	Valtellina Sforzato San Domenico '01	▽▽▽	7
●	Valtellina Prestigio Millennium '97	▽▽▽	5
●	Valtellina Sforzato '99	▽▽▽	6
●	Valtellina Sforzato San Domenico '02	▽▽	7

OTHER WINERIES

CORNALETO
VIA CORNALETTO, 2
25030 ADRO (BS)
TEL. 0307450507
www.cornaleto.it

The Lancinis personally tend 18 hectares under vine on Monte Alto at Adro. Estate production has been excellent for years. Proof of this is the Brut with elegant, complex aromas of white-fleshed fruit, honey and chamomile. The juicy, balanced, supple palate leads to a long, graceful close.

○ Franciacorta Brut	🍷🍷	5

RONCO CALINO
LOC. QUATTRO CAMINI
FRAZ. TORBIATO - VIA FENICE
25030 ADRO (BS)
TEL. 0307451073 - www.roncocalino.it

Paolo Radici's estate has for years presented excellent wines and elegantly styled Franciacortas. We liked the Brut with soft aromas of cake and barley sugar and a round, supple palate, and the sound Terre di Franciacorta Bianco '05 with fresh, fruity aromas, and a lean yet harmonious body.

○ Franciacorta Brut	🍷🍷	5
○ TdF Bianco '05	🍷	3

LURANI CERNUSCHI
VIA CONVENTO, 3
24031 ALMENNO SAN SALVATORE (BG)
TEL. 035642576 - 035640102

The Cabernet Sauvignon Umbriana '03 has intense colour, ripe red fruit and spice aromas, lively tannins and good structure. Valcalepio Rosso '03 shows slightly overripe fruity notes with abundant and fairly velvety tannins. The simple Valcalepio Bianco '05 has notes of citrus and tropical fruit.

● Umbriana '03	🍷🍷	3
● Valcalepio Rosso '03	🍷	3
○ Valcalepio Bianco '05	🍷	2

TENUTA CÀ BOFFENISIO
VIA BOFFENISIO, 3
27040 BORGO PRIOLO (PV)
TEL. 0383871149

The top wines from Mariele Galanti's estate were missing this year. The red Disperato '04 from barbera and croatina is a deep ruby colour with cherry aromas, and a bit short in the finish. The Ghiaia del Monte '01 is an evolved, riesling-based white with marked minerality and an oxidized note.

○ Ghiaia del Monte '01	🍷	3
● Disperato '04	🍷	3

OLMO ANTICO
VIA MARCONI, 8
27040 BORGO PRIOLO (PV)
TEL. 0383872672
www.olmoantico.it

Merlot Giorgio Quinto '03 is dark ruby with intense, slightly overripe, tight-knit cherry and wild berry fruit, and smooth, plentiful tannins. The Barbera '03 has broad tobacco and spice with balsamic notes, and a rich, satisfying palate. The IGT Riesling Olmo Bianco '05 is well made and varietal.

●	Barbera '03	🍷🍷	5
●	Giorgio Quinto '03	🍷🍷	6
○	Olmo Bianco '05	🍷	4

MONTENATO GRIFFINI
VIA SPARANO, 13/14
27049 BOSNASCO (PV)
TEL. 0385272904
www.montenatogriffini.it

These reds come from soils that give abundant tannicity. So the Rosso Riserva '01 failed to repeat the score from '00. With clean, mature aromas of spice and jam, the tannins on the palate tend to dry the fruit. Much the same could be said of the barrique-aged Bonarda Puntofermo '03.

●	OP Rosso Riserva '01	🍷	4
●	OP Bonarda Puntofermo Barricato '03	🍷	4

TENUTA SCARPA COLOMBI
VIA GROPPALLO, 26
27049 BOSNASCO (PV)
TEL. 0385272081
www.colombiwines.com

Pinot Nero Ariolo '03 is good and varietal with precise flower, wild berry and spice aromas and a fairly intense palate. The still Bonarda Marubbio '04 is mature, redolent of blackberry jam, solid, soft and pleasant. The well-made Pinot Nero Brut Metodo Martinotti is pleasant and uncomplicated.

●	OP Pinot Nero Ariolo '03	🍷🍷	4
●	OP Bonarda Marubbio '04	🍷🍷	4
○	OP Pinot Nero Brut Martinotti	🍷	4

ANTICA TESA
LOC. MATTINA
VIA MERANO, 28
25080 BOTTICINO (BS)
TEL. 0302691500

Alessandra Noventa continues to experiment with vineyard selections. Different vine ages and market release dates distinguish the two wines from the Ulivi vineyard and two others from Pià della Tesa. The Vigna del Gobbio '03 is good, with nice extract and rich berry fruit.

●	Botticino Vigna del Gobbio '03	🍷🍷	6
●	Botticino Pià della Tesa Sel V. Vecchia '03	🍷	5
●	Botticino Vigna degli Ulivi Sel. V. Nuova '03	🍷	4
●	Botticino Cà del Roccolo '04	🍷	6

CANTINA SOCIALE DI BRONI
VIA SANSALUTO, 81
27043 BRONI (PV)
TEL. 038551505

The Pinot Nero '04 is not bad. Slow to open, it then shows forthright, varietal aromas with nicely handled wood. The Classese is fresh and well crafted, though a bit simple. The Sangue di Giuda and Bonarda Vivace '05 are fragrant with well-typed wild berry aromas and well-controlled tannins.

●	OP Pinot Nero '04	🍷🍷	3
●	OP Bonarda Vivace '05	🍷	2
●	OP Sangue di Giuda '05	🍷	3
○	OP Pinot Nero Brut Classese	🍷	4

CA' TESSITORI
VIA MATTEOTTI, 15
27043 BRONI (PV)
TEL. 038551495

The Barbera Vignamarona '03 has remarkable texture and typicity. The Brut Metodo Classico Ca' Tessitori is well made and enjoyable with a peach, citrus and aromatic herb nose. The Rosso Borghesia '05 is interesting and very pleasant thanks to uncomplicated black cherry and blackberry fruit.

●	OP Barbera Vignamarona '03	🍷🍷	4
○	OP Pinot Nero Cl. Brut	🍷🍷	5
●	OP Rosso Borghesia '05	🍷	4

Montagna
via Cairoli, 67
27043 Broni (PV)
tel. 038551028
www.cantinemontagna.it

The pleasing Berté & Cordini '05 Sauvignon has a bright, deep straw yellow colour with peach and box hedge aromas then a palate that lingers. The golden dried-grape Mufi shows peach, apricot and dried fruit supported by good acidity. The Pinot Nero Viti di Luna '02 is varietal and pleasant.

○	OP Sauvignon Berté & Cordini '05	🍷🍷	3
○	Mufì	🍷🍷	5
●	OP Pinot Nero Viti di Luna '02	🍷	3

La Torre
fraz. Mocasina di Calvagese
25080 Calvagese della Riviera (BS)
tel. 030601034
www.pasini-latorre.com

Attilio Pasini knows how to present western Garda wines. Products from his inland vineyards have a rustic yet always pleasant impact. The best this year, the white Rossetto, is blessed with vibrant citrus and spirited freshness. The reds show a solid profile. The Chiaretto is pleasant.

○	Garda Cl. Bianco Rossetto '05	🍷🍷	3
●	Garda Cl. Rosso Sup. Rosso del Cuntì '01	🍷	4
●	Garda Cl. Rosso Barbeta '04	🍷	3
⊙	Garda Cl. Chiaretto '05	🍷	3

Travaglino
loc. Travaglino, 6
27040 Calvignano (PV)
tel. 0383872222
www.travaglino.it

The pennyroyal and sage aromas of Riesling Campo della Fojada '05 recall Spätlese from the Rhine. The Classese '01 is mature with robust structure. Of the two Pinot Neros fermented on the skins, we prefer the fresh, fragrant Pernero '05. Poggio della Buttinera '02 comes from an indifferent vintage.

○	OP Pinot Nero Brut Classese '01	🍷🍷	5
○	OP Riesling Campo della Fojada '05	🍷🍷	4
●	OP Pinot Nero Poggio della Buttinera '02	🍷	5
●	OP Pinot Nero Pernero '05	🍷	4

Calvi
fraz. Vigalone, 13
27044 Canneto Pavese (PV)
tel. 038560034
www.andreacalvi.it

Andrea Calvi submitted a nice, full-bodied Barbera Tre '00 showing lovely spicy fruit with balsamic, cinchona and citrus notes, fruity pulp and a nice finish. The Bonarda Vivace '05 foregrounds floral aromas, good fruit and lively tannins only partially offset by residual sugar.

●	OP Barbera Tre '00	🍷🍷	4
●	OP Bonarda Vivace '05	🍷	3

Fiamberti
via Chiesa, 17
27044 Canneto Pavese (PV)
tel. 038588019
www.fiambertivini.it

Fiamberti's best wine is the clean, well-typed Bonarda Frizzante Bricco della Sacca '05. Buttafuoco Storico Vigna Solenga shows nice substance and frank almond and wild berry aromas but rather hard tannins. The Buttafuoco Poderi Fiamberti '02 is well made, the Riesling Italico varietal.

●	OP Bonarda Frizzante Bricco della Sacca '05	🍷🍷	4
●	OP Buttafuoco Storico V. Solenga '01	🍷	5
●	OP Buttafuoco Poderi Fiamberti '02	🍷	4
○	OP Riesling Italico V. Croce Monteveneroso '04	🍷	3

Andrea Picchioni
loc. Camponoce, 8
27044 Canneto Pavese (PV)
tel. 0385262139
www.picchioniandrea.it

Andrea Picchioni gave us a nice Buttafuoco '02 with fragrant red berry fruit and liquorice followed by smooth tannins. The frank, soft Bonarda '05 is good. The Pinot Nero Soleluna, fermented off the skins, is pleasant and fruity. Buttafuoco Luogo della Cerasa '05 has balance and finesse.

●	OP Buttafuoco '02	🍷🍷	4
●	OP Bonarda Vivace '05	🍷🍷	3
●	OP Buttafuoco Luogo della Cerasa '05	🍷	4
○	OP Soleluna '05	🍷	4

QUAQUARINI
LOC. MONTEVENEROSO
VIA CASA ZAMBIANCHI, 26
27044 CANNETO PAVESE (PV)
TEL. 038560152

The Sangue di Giuda Vigna Acqua Calda '05 is excellent. Magister '04 is good, full and fruity. The well-typed Buttafuoco Vigna La Guasca '04 gives black cherry and liquorice, and abundant tannins. The Pinot Nero Blau '03 shows nice wild berries with sweet spices, marked tannins and good fullness.

●	OP Sangue di Giuda V. Acqua Calda '05	🍷🍷	4
●	OP Pinot Nero Blau '03	🍷	4
●	OP Buttafuoco V. La Guasca '04	🍷	4
●	OP Rosso Magister '04	🍷	4

TENUTA DEGLI ANGELI
FRAZ. SANTO STEFANO - VIA FARA, 2
24060 CAROBBIO DEGLI ANGELI (BG)
TEL. 035687130 - 035951489
www.tenutadegliangeli.it

The good Valcalepio Bianco Triplok '04 has white peach, tropical fruit and floral aromas, and a balanced, juicy palate. The two metodo classico sparklers, Brut and Extra Brut, are both a tad over-evolved on the nose. We just preferred the rather full Brut. The Extra Brut is simpler.

○	Valcalepio Bianco Triplok '04	🍷🍷	4
○	Spumante Brut Cl. degli Angeli	🍷	5
○	Spumante Extra Brut Cl. degli Angeli	🍷	5

TENUTA PEGAZZERA
LOC. PEGAZZERA
VIA VIGORELLI
27045 CASTEGGIO (PV)
TEL. 0383804646 - www.pegazzera.it

The always interesting golden Brut Classico di Pegazzera has honey and cake aromas. The Cabernet Sauvignon Ligna '03 yields varietal aromas and well-centred balance. The pleasant Barbera '04 shows violets and blueberry. The well-made Riesling Italico Brut Martinotti is nicely evolved.

○	OP Pinot Nero Brut Cl.	🍷🍷	4
●	OP Cabernet Sauvignon Ligna '03	🍷	4
●	OP Barbera '04	🍷	3
○	OP Riesling Italico Brut Martinotti	🍷	3*

RUIZ DE CARDENAS
LOC. MAIRANO - VIA MOLLIE, 35
27045 CASTEGGIO (PV)
TEL. 038382301 - 024045805
www.ruizdecardenas.it

We expected something more from Ruiz de Cardenas, especially the sparklers, since the Pinot Nero crus were not released in '02, only a pleasant varietal base version. The Blanc de Blanc is better, with elegant floral aromas and a bit more structure compared to the stylish yet very simple Galanta.

○	Blanc de Blanc '02	🍷	4
○	Galanta Brut Cl. '02	🍷	5
●	OP Pinot Nero '02	🍷	4

CONTI BETTONI CAZZAGO
VIA MARCONI, 6
25046 CAZZAGO SAN MARTINO (BS)
TEL. 0307750875 - 3394422255
www.contibettonicazzago.it

We thought the most interesting cuvée from Vincenzo Bettoni Cazzago this year was the Satèn with damson and white peach on the nose, and a fresh, solid, round palate with great length. With its touches of tropical fruit, the Brut Santa Giulia is more complex yet lighter in weight on the palate.

○	Franciacorta Brut Satèn	🍷🍷	6
○	Franciacorta Brut Santa Giulia	🍷	5

CASCINA SAN PIETRO
FRAZ. CALINO
VIA SAN PIETRO, 30
25040 CAZZAGO SAN MARTINO (BS)
TEL. 035912448 - www.cascinaspietro.it

We liked the Franciacorta Brut by Giuseppe Pecis. It has a bright straw-yellow colour and intense aromas of new-mown hay, honey and ripe fruit. The palate is full, juicy and oaky. The Satèn is also interesting for its clear floral echoes and cake on the back palate.

○	Franciacorta Brut	🍷🍷	4
○	Franciacorta Satèn	🍷	5

VIGNA DORATA
LOC. CALINO
VIA SALA, 80
25040 CAZZAGO SAN MARTINO (BS)
TEL. 0307254275 - www.vignadorata.it

Luciana Mingotti proposed two excellent cuvées this year. The Brut has complex aromas with intact fruit and tones of coffee, croissant and vanilla while the Satèn is rich in ripe fruit and apricot preserves then a fresh, gentle palate that offers good backbone and overall balance.

○	Franciacorta Brut	🍷🍷	5
○	Franciacorta Satèn	🍷🍷	6

CAMINELLA
VIA DANTE ALIGHIERI, 13
24069 CENATE SOTTO (BG)
TEL. 035941828
www.caminella.it

The cabernet, merlot and pinot nero Luna Rossa has an elegant nose and harmonious palate. The well-balanced Verde Luna, from chardonnay, sauvignon blanc and pinot bianco, gives herbs and chamomile. Valcalepio Rosso Ripa di Luna '04 is well made and overripe. Brut Ripa di Luna is quite simple.

●	Luna Rossa '04	🍷🍷	5
○	Verde Luna Bianco	🍷🍷	4
●	Valcalepio Rosso Ripa di Luna '04	🍷	4
○	Ripa di Luna Brut	🍷	5

PIETRO NERA
VIA IV NOVEMBRE, 43
23030 CHIURO (SO)
TEL. 0342482631
www.neravini.com

Although the most important labels were missing, the Inferno Riserva '02 has complex aromas with tobacco leaf. The tannins are in place and the palate is vibrant, fresh and savoury. A step below this, the Sassella Riserva '00 has spicy aromas, medium structure and soft tannins.

●	Valtellina Sup. Sassella Ris. '00	🍷🍷	5
●	Valtellina Sup. Inferno Ris. '02	🍷🍷	5

CA' MONTEBELLO
LOC. MONTEBELLO, 10
27040 CIGOGNOLA (PV)
TEL. 038585182
www.camontebello.it

The well-made Classese has fragrant flowers and crusty bread. The Pinot Nero '05 yields stylish, pleasant floral varietal tones. The Barbera from the same vintage has a dark ruby colour, frank, enjoyable cherry aromas and nice fruity pulp. The Bonarda Frizzante '05 is well made, typical and soft.

○	OP Pinot Nero Brut Classese	🍷🍷	4
●	OP Barbera '05	🍷	3
●	OP Bonarda Frizzante '05	🍷	3
●	OP Pinot Nero '05	🍷	3

CASTELLO DI CIGOGNOLA
P.ZZA CASTELLO, 1
27040 CIGOGNOLA (PV)
TEL. 038585601

Gianmarco and Letizia Moratti, with consulting oenologist Riccardo Cotarella and agronomist Emilio De Filippi, make an excellent Barbera at Cigognola. The dark '03 has complex aromas of red and black berry fruit and spices. The palate is concentrated, deep, fruity elegantly tannic and very long.

●	OP Barbera '03	🍷🍷	6

MONTERUCCO
VALLE CIMA, 38
27040 CIGOGNOLA (PV)
TEL. 038585151 - 038585411
www.monterucco.it

The Malvasia IGT Valentina '05 has a bright straw-yellow colour, peach and pennyroyal aromas, good fruit and an interesting finish. The Buttafuoco Sanluigi '03 has a garnet-tinged ruby colour and a lot of pulp with slightly over-evolved, overripe wild berries.

●	OP Buttafuoco Sanluigi '03	🍷	3
○	Valentina '05	🍷	3

LORENZO FACCOLI & FIGLI
VIA CAVA, 7
25030 COCCAGLIO (BS)
TEL. 0307722761

This small Coccaglio estate makes well-crafted wines from its own vineyards. The outstanding Extra Brut shows floral aromas, a delicate balsamic vein that never masks the fruit and nice structure on the palate. The excellent Brut has tropical fruit tones on the nose and a soft, fresh palate.

○ Franciacorta Brut	🍷🍷	5
○ Franciacorta Extra Brut	🍷🍷	5*

LA BOSCAIOLA
VIA RICCAFANA, 19
25033 COLOGNE (BS)
TEL. 0307156386 - 030715596
www.laboscaiola.com

The Brut from Nelson and Giuliana Cenci is golden straw yellow with intense crusty bread, yeast and coffee aromas that let the fruit come through. The palate boasts decent density, good acid backbone and nice overall harmony. The sound Ritorno '02 Bordeaux blend has good wild berry aromas.

○ Franciacorta Brut '00	🍷🍷	5
● Sebino Rosso Il Ritorno '02	🍷🍷	5

RICCAFANA
VIA FACCHETTI, 91
25033 COLOGNE (BS)
TEL. 0307156797
www.riccafana.com

Riccardo Fratus, in collaboration with Cesare Ferrari, makes excellent Franciacortas at his beautiful estate in Cologne. We preferred the fragrant Rosé, which is bright salmon with wild berries on both the nose and soft, satisfying palate. The vanilla-toned Brut is also sound.

⊙ Franciacorta Rosé	🍷🍷	4
○ Franciacorta Brut	🍷	5

BARBOGLIO DE GAIONCELLI
FRAZ. COLOMBARO
VIA NAZARIO SAURO
25040 CORTE FRANCA (BS)
TEL. 0309826831

Guido Costa owns this old estate in Corte Franca. From his 15 hectares under vine, he makes well-crafted wines like the Franciacorta Brut with its ripe apple aromas, balsamic notes and a juicy, fresh palate, and the soft, slim-bodied Rosé Extra Dry, fragrant with red berry fruit.

○ Franciacorta Brut	🍷🍷	5
⊙ Franciacorta Rosé Extra Dry	🍷	5

BOSIO
LOC. TIMOLINE - VIA MARIO GATTI
25040 CORTE FRANCA (BS)
TEL. 030984398
www.bosiofranciacorta.it

Cesare Bosio manages around 20 hectares under vine. His interesting array of products features a Franciacorta Brut with a complex nose of fruit, flowers and minerals and a dense, elegant, spirited palate. The fragrant Satèn gives floral, citrus and vanilla tones.

○ Franciacorta Brut	🍷🍷	6
○ Franciacorta Satèn	🍷🍷	6

LA FIÒCA
FRAZ. NIGOLINE
VIA VILLA, 13B
25040 CORTE FRANCA (BS)
TEL. 0309826313 - www.lafioca.com

The Gatti family's La Fiòca offers some interesting labels from the estate vineyards. The Franciacorta Brut has a fresh nose of white-fleshed fruit with elegant floral notes. The palate shows good structure, fruit and freshness. The less expressive Satèn boasts spicy tones and a fairly lean body.

○ Franciacorta Brut	🍷🍷	5
○ Franciacorta Satèn	🍷	5

Togni Rebaioli

Fraz. Erbanno
via Rossini, 19
25047 Darfo Boario Terme (BS)
tel. 0364529706

Created in 2003, the Valcamonica IGT already has a standard-bearer. From his six hectares, young Enrico Togni makes characterful reds destined to become more elegant with age. We preferred the Millesettecentotre from marzemino and barbera. We also tasted a very promising, recently bottled Merlot.

● Valcamonica Millesettecentotre '04	🍷🍷	4
● Valcamonica Lambrù '04	🍷	4
● Valcamonica Merlot Rebaioli Cav. Enrico '04	🍷	5

Cantine Colli a Lago

loc. San Martino della Battaglia
Cascina Capuzza
25010 Desenzano del Garda (BS)
tel. 0309910279 - 03099100381

With the Campo del Soglio '04, fragrant with floral and citrus notes, the Formentini family pays homage to the DOC zone named after San Martino della Battaglia, where the estate is headquartered. We gave a good score to the red Madèr '03. The current Lugana and Brut Metodo Classico are pleasant.

● Garda Cl. Sup. Rosso Madèr '03	🍷🍷	4
○ San Martino della Battaglia Campo del Soglio '04	🍷🍷	4
○ Lugana '05	🍷	3
○ Lugana Brut M. Cl. Hirundo	🍷	4

Olivini

loc. San Martino della Battaglia
Demesse Vecchie, 2
25015 Desenzano del Garda (BS)
tel. 0309910268 - www.olivini.net

The Olivini family estate can no longer be considered up-and-coming. This sound operation is capable of consistent high quality. The Merlot Notte a San Martino '03 is very good and dense with fruit. The Brut Metodo Classico '03 stands out in the flawless series of three Luganas.

○ Lugana Brut '03	🍷🍷	4
● Notte a San Martino '03	🍷🍷	5
○ Lugana '05	🍷🍷	3
○ Lugana Sup. Demesse Vecchie '03	🍷	4

Boschi

via Iseo, 76
25030 Erbusco (BS)
tel. 03077245
www.agricolaboschi.it

From Franco Timoteo Metelli's broad range of wines and Franciacortas, we picked out a Brut rich in ripe fruit and toasted oak aromas with a round, juicy, well-balanced palate. The sound Dosaggio Zéro shows complex honey and beeswax aromas, and is dry and zesty with good acid backbone.

○ Franciacorta Brut	🍷🍷	5
○ Franciacorta Brut Dosage Zéro	🍷	5

Podere della Cavaga

via Gafforelli, 1
24060 Foresto Sparso (BG)
tel. 035930939
www.vinicavaga.it

The Brut Classico Clamor is fragrant. Valcalepio Bianco Adamante '05 shows ripe tropical fruit with good pulp. Franconia Selezione Mario Acerbis '03 is ruby with spice and vanilla aromas, and shows agreeably full. Valmeluna IGT Cabernet Sauvignon has clear varietal notes and good fruit.

○ Brut Cl. Clamor	🍷🍷	5
● Franconia Sel. Mario Acerbis '03	🍷	6
○ Valcalepio Bianco Adamante '05	🍷	3
● Valmeluna '05	🍷	3

Vincenzo Tallarini

via Fontanile, 7/9
24060 Gandosso (BG)
tel. 035834003 - 3357559628
www.tallarini.com

The Serafo Bordeaux blend is intense and structured. Satiro '01 is a lively Cabernet Sauvignon, varietal in its aromas and juicy in the mouth. Valcalepio Moscato Passito di Gandosso '01 is complex and spicy. The Valcalepio Bianco Fabula '04 is fresh and unusual with wild fennel touches.

● Satiro '01	🍷🍷	6
● Valcalepio Rosso Moscato di Gandosso '01	🍷🍷	7
● Serafo '03	🍷🍷	5
○ Valcalepio Bianco Fabula '04	🍷	4

TREVISANI
LOC. SOPRAZOCCO - VIA GALUZZO, 2
25087 GAVARDO (BS)
TEL. 0365373154 - 036532825
www.trevisanionline.it

Trevisani's best is Benacus '03, a blend of native and international varieties dense with red berry fruit. The chardonnay-based white Balì '05 is elegant and citrus-like. Cabernet Due Querce '03 came near Two Glasses. The rustic yet interesting Berzamina '05 bears the name of a local variety.

●	Benacus '03	🍷🍷	6
○	Balì '05	🍷🍷	4
●	Rosso Due Querce '03	🍷	4
●	Berzamina '05	🍷	4

CARLOZADRA
VIA GANDOSSI, 13
24064 GRUMELLO DEL MONTE (BG)
TEL. 035830244 - 035832066

Carlo Zadra's Bruts were better than the Extra Drys this year. Properly evolved, the very good Nondosato '00 is dry, full and long on the palate. The elegant Brut from the '02 vintage has good backbone and a long finish. The always pleasant Extra Dry Liberty is a bit less intense than usual.

○	Carlozadra Cl. Brut Nondosato '00	🍷🍷	5
○	Carlozadra Cl. Brut '02	🍷🍷	5
○	Carlozadra Extra Dry Liberty	🍷	5

LE CORNE
LOC. CORNE
VIA SAN PANTALEONE, 4
24064 GRUMELLO DEL MONTE (BG)
TEL. 035830215 - www.lecorne.it

Torcularia '03 Cabernet Sauvignon IGT is juicy and broad. The Pinot Grigio Buldesicho '05 has clear aromatic herb, peach and pineapple aromas and good backbone. Both the barrique-aged Valcalepio Bianco Messerbianco '04 and Valcalepio Rosso Gonzaghesco '04, with its notes of prunes, are evolved.

●	Torcularia '03	🍷🍷	4*
○	Pinot Grigio Buldesicho '05	🍷🍷	2*
○	Valcalepio Bianco Messerbianco '04	🍷	4
●	Valcalepio Rosso Gonzaghesco '04	🍷	3

GATTA
VIA SAN ROCCO, 33
25064 GUSSAGO (BS)
TEL. 0302772950
www.paginegialle.it/agricolagatta

Mario Gatta makes a well-crafted range of wines and Franciacortas from his vineyards in Gussago. This year, we mention a pleasing Satèn with clear fruit tones and a lean body. The Terre di Franciacorta Rosso '03 is also interesting for its soft wild berry tones on both nose and palate.

●	TdF Rosso '03	🍷	4
○	Franciacorta Satèn	🍷	5

AVANZI
LOC. S.S. DESENZANO-SALÒ
VIA TREVISAGO, 32
25080 MANERBA DEL GARDA (BS)
TEL. 0365551013 - www.avanzi.net

The showcase wine from Avanzi, a major producer on the Lombardy shore of Lake Garda at Manerba, is Cabernet Vigna Bragagna. The '02 vintage is good with dense ripe red berry fruit and elegant spices. The two Luganas, the Vigna Bragagna '05 and Sirmione '04, are well managed.

●	Garda Cabernet Sauvignon Vigna Bragagna '02	🍷🍷	4
○	Lugana Sup. Sirmione '04	🍷	4
○	Lugana di Sirmione Vigna Bragagna '05	🍷	3

MONTE CICOGNA
VIA DELLE VIGNE, 6
25080 MONIGA DEL GARDA (BS)
TEL. 0365503200
www.montecicogna.it

In the '01 vintage, the Don Lisander was again one of the most interesting reds from the Lombardy shore of Lake Garda, capable of evolving elegantly in bottle for several years. The rustically interpreted Groppello Beana '04 is fruity and herbaceous. The Lugana and Chiaretto are pleasant.

●	Garda Cl. Rosso Sup. Don Lisander '01	🍷🍷	5
●	Garda Cl. Rosso Groppello Beana '04	🍷	4
⊙	Garda Cl. Chiaretto Il Torrione '05	🍷	4
○	Lugana Il Torrione '05	🍷	4

Ca' del Gè
fraz. Ca' del Gè, 3
27040 Montalto Pavese (PV)
tel. 0383870179
www.cadelge.it

The still Bonarda La Fidela '03 has a dark ruby colour, aromas of wild berries and aromatic herbs. Marinoni from barrique-fermented riesling renano offers minerally tones and a full, long palate. Barbera Vigna Varmasì '03 has a very evolved style with overripe red berry fruit.

● O. P. Barbera V. Varmasì '03	🍷🍷	4
● OP Bonarda La Fidela '03	🍷🍷	5
○ OP Riesling Renano V. Marinoni '04	🍷🍷	5

Ca' del Santo
loc. Campolungo, 4
27040 Montalto Pavese (PV)
tel. 0383870545 - 038551026

Sangue di Giuda Trepoderi and Bonarda Vivace Grand Cuvée, both from '05, scored high. Their purple ruby precedes fragrant upfront aromas and a nice balance of softness and freshness. The Barbera Campo dei Frati '05 and Riesling Italico Rivalunga '05 are pleasant, simple and enjoyable.

● OP Bonarda Vivace Grand Cuvée '05	🍷🍷	4
● OP Sangue di Giuda Trepoderi '05	🍷🍷	3
● OP Barbera Campo dei Frati '05	🍷	3
○ OP Riesling Italico Rivalunga '05	🍷	3

Tenimenti Castelrotto - Torti
fraz. Castelrotto, 6
27047 Montecalvo Versiggia (PV)
tel. 0385951000
www.tortiwinepinotnero.com

The Brut Castelrotto sparkler by Dino and Giusi Torti, with daughters Patrizia and Laura, has a nice bright colour, good bubbles and clean flower and peach aromas. The Bonarda Vivace Brioso '04 has a lovely dark ruby colour, well-controlled tannins, nice fruity pulp and softness.

● OP Bonarda Vivace Brioso '04	🍷	4
○ OP Pinot Nero Brut Cl. Castelrotto	🍷	5

Pietro Torti
fraz. Castelrotto, 9
27047 Montecalvo Versiggia (PV)
tel. 038599763 - 038599344
www.pietrotorti.it

The Pinot Nero '03 is among the year's best from Oltrepò, having suffered less from the heat. The Bonarda Vivace '05 is well made, fragrant and fruity. The Chardonnay Fagù '05 is harmonious with tropical fruit aromas. The Verzello is a soft, pleasant, simple red from a croatina-barbera blend.

● OP Pinot Nero '03	🍷🍷	5
○ Fagù '05	🍷🍷	3
● OP Bonarda Vivace '05	🍷🍷	3
● Verzello '05	🍷	3

Castelveder
via Belvedere, 4
25040 Monticelli Brusati (BS)
tel. 030652308
www.castelveder.it

Renato Alberti makes 100,000 bottles a year of still wines and Franciacortas from his 12 hectares under vine. His excellent Brut gives clear apple, damson and flowers on the nose and good body on the harmonious palate. The Terre di Franciacorta Bianco '05 has a nice, simple profile.

○ Franciacorta Brut	🍷🍷	5
○ TdF Curtefranca Bianco '05	🍷	4

Antica Cantina Fratta
via Fontana, 11
25040 Monticelli Brusati (BS)
tel. 030652068
www.anticafratta.it

Cristina Ziliani energetically manages this estate, part of the Guido Berlucchi organization. We liked an excellent Brut, which is supple with clear white-fleshed fruit, and a soft, balanced Satèn with chestnut honey aromas. The succulent Rosé Extra Dry is sound.

○ Franciacorta Brut	🍷🍷	5
○ Franciacorta Satèn	🍷🍷	6
⊙ Franciacorta Rosé Extra Dry	🍷	6

LO SPARVIERE
VIA COSTA, 2
25040 MONTICELLI BRUSATI (BS)
TEL. 030652382
www.losparviere.com

The Gussalli Beretta family produces sound wines and Franciacortas at this lovely estate. The excellent Franciacorta Extra Brut '00 is enjoyable for its lovely structure and the elegant, fresh intensity of its fruit. The equally good Brut shows clear notes of peach and a harmonious palate.

○ Franciacorta Extra Brut '00	🍷🍷	5
○ Franciacorta Brut	🍷🍷	4

LUCIANO BREGA
FRAZ. BERGAMASCO, 7
27040 MONTÙ BECCARIA (PV)
TEL. 038560237 - 038561176

Luciano Brega's purple ruby Bonarda Vivace '05 has a nose of wild berry fruit notes and a soft, warm palate showing plums. The still Bonarda Casapiana '03 has a bright ruby colour, good fruit, fairly smooth tannins and softness, though it lacks a bit of supporting acidity.

● OP Bonarda Vivace '05	🍷🍷	3
● OP Bonarda Casapiana '03	🍷	3

IL MONTÙ
VIA MARCONI, 10
27040 MONTÙ BECCARIA (PV)
TEL. 0385262252
ww.ilmontu.com

The garnet Bonarda '02 has rather an evolved nose and a palate with good fruity pulp and well-controlled tannins. The golden, straw-yellow Millesimato '02 gives tea and aromatic herbs but suffers from heavy liqueur d'expédition. The Pinot Nero Vigna Rosara '01 is varietal but not quite balanced.

● OP Pinot Nero V. Rosara '01	🍷	5
● OP Bonarda '02	🍷	3
○ OP Pinot Nero Brut Cl. Il Millesimato '02	🍷	6

PICCOLO BACCO DEI QUARONI
FRAZ. COSTAMONTEFEDELE
27040 MONTÙ BECCARIA (PV)
TEL. 038560521 - 3391402381
www.piccolobaccodeiquaroni.it

The typical, well-made Pinot Nero Vigneto La Fiocca '03 has upfront aromas. The dark ruby Bonarda Vivace Mons Acutus '05 has wild black berry and forest floor aromas and well-controlled tannins. The red Gustavo '04, from stainless steel-fermented barbera and croatina, is flavourful and pleasant.

● OP Pinot Nero Vign. La Fiocca '03	🍷🍷	3*
● Gustavo '04	🍷🍷	2
● OP Bonarda Vivace Mons Acutus '05	🍷🍷	2

RICCHI
VIA FESTONI, 13D
46040 MONZAMBANO (MN)
TEL. 0376800238
www.cantinaricchi.it

The dried-grape Le Cime shows honey, flowers and citrus with a mellow palate. The elegant, well-made Chardonnay Meridiano '05 has tropical fruit, backbone and balance. The Cabernet Ribò '03 is varietal with grassy notes. The Carpino '02 has stylish wild berry aromas and a soft, harmonious palate.

○ Passito Le Cime '04	🍷🍷	5
○ Garda Chardonnay Meridiano '05	🍷🍷	4
● Garda Merlot Carpino '02	🍷	5
● Garda Cabernet Ribò '03	🍷	4

CASCINA GNOCCO
FRAZ. LOSANA, 20
27040 MORNICO LOSANA (PV)
TEL. 0383892280
www.cascinagnocco.it

The bright semi-sparkling Moscato IGT Adagetto has nice citrus and apple aromas and a structured, mellow palate. Another IGT, the pleasant and harmonic Rosso del Moro-Nico, shows a hay and bell pepper aromatic base from the cabernet sauvignon, and frank wild berry aromas.

○ Moscato Adagetto '05	🍷🍷	4
● Rosso del Moro-Nico '05	🍷	3

La Guarda
Fraz. Castrezzone
via Zanardelli, 49
25080 Muscoline (BS)
tel. 0365372948 - www.laguarda.com

Gigi Negri always hits the spot. His small estate near Lake Garda makes wines with a pleasant impact, substantial personality and good ageing prospects. The Garda Classico Rosso '00 and Sabbioso '01 did well. Both have good fruit and balanced tannins. The Bianco is pleasant and easy drinking.

●	Garda Cl. Rosso Sup. '00	YY	4
●	Garda Cl. Rosso Sabbioso '01	YY	5
○	Garda Cl. Bianco '05	Y	4

Riviere
via Moniga del Bosco, 61
25080 Muscoline (BS)
tel. 0365374432

Riviere makes its Guide debut. Wines from this tiny inland estate near Lake Garda mix expressive power and elegance. From old vines of chardonnay, Derio Podavini makes Cobèi, a long-lived white. The Sangioviale, from rebo and cabernet sauvignon, and the Groppello Castelà are both very pleasant.

●	Sangioviale Rosso '01	YY	5
○	Cobèi '04	YY	4*
●	Garda Cl. Groppello Castelà '04	Y	4

Ugo Vezzoli
loc. San Pancrazio
via G. B. Vezzoli, 20
25030 Palazzolo sull'Oglio (BS)
tel. 030738018

From his five hectares, Ugo Vezzoli produces a small array of territorial wines with consultancy from Cesare Ferrari. The quality is exemplified by the dense, elegant Brut '01, with its fragrant flower and fruit tones and soft palate. The Brut is also sound with slightly evolved tones.

○	Franciacorta Brut '01	YY	5
○	Franciacorta Brut	Y	5

Monte Delma
loc. Valenzano
25050 Passirano (BS)
tel. 0306546161
www.montedelma.it

The Berardi family has 20 hectares under vine at Passirano and produces 50,000 bottles a year of wines and Franciacortas. The excellent Brut shows fresh fruit aromas with a delicate vegetal hint, and a pleasingly zesty, full palate. The interesting Satèn has intense vanilla aromas.

○	Franciacorta Brut	YY	5
○	Franciacorta Satèn	Y	5

La Costa
fraz. Costa
via Curone, 15
22050 Perego (LC)
tel. 0395312218 - www.la-costa.it

The chardonnay and riesling renano Solesta '04 has floral aromas with pink grapefruit and a minerally palate. From merlot, cabernet and syrah, the Serìz '04 has a concentrated nose and soft palate. The pinot nero San Giobbe '04 has red fruit and tobacco aromas and a juicy palate with iodine notes.

●	San Giobbe '04	YY	5
●	Serìz '04	YY	5
○	Solesta '04	YY	4

Scuropasso
fraz. Scorzoletta, 40/42
27043 Pietra de' Giorgi (PV)
tel. 038585143
www.scuropasso.it

Sangue di Giuda '05 is frank and pleasant. The Bonarda Vivace Palatinus '05 is typical, soft and well made. Buttafuoco Lunapiena '03 has nice fruity pulp but still rather hard tannins. The Brut Metodo Classico has nice bubbles and green aromas, and is fresh and pleasant if slightly simple.

●	OP Sangue di Giuda '05	YY	2
●	OP Buttafuoco Lunapiena '03	Y	5
●	OP Bonarda Vivace Palatinus '05	Y	3
○	OP Pinot Nero Brut Cl.	Y	6

CHIARA ZILIANI
VIA FRANCIACORTA, 7
25050 PROVAGLIO D'ISEO (BS)
TEL. 030981661
www.cantinazilianichiara.it

Chiara Ziliani makes good wines and Franciacortas from 12 hectares of vineyards in Provaglio. The Brut Conte di Provaglio has a nose of decent complexity and finesse that shows toasted bread, white-fleshed fruit and aromatic herbs. The palate is solid, elegant and long. The Satèn is also good.

○ Franciacorta Brut Conte di Provaglio	🍷🍷	5
○ Franciacorta Satèn	🍷	5

COMINCIOLI
LOC. CASTELLO
VIA ROMA, 10
25080 PUEGNAGO SUL GARDA (BS)
TEL. 0365651141 - www.comincioli.it

Gianfranco Comincioli continues his successful work with native varieties from Valtenesi. Alongside the distinctive Groppello and rustic Chiaretto, he amazed us this year with a white from trebbiano Valtenesi and erbamàt, Perlì '05, which has great character and ageing prospects.

● Riviera del Garda Bresciano Gropèl '03	🍷🍷	5
● Riviera del Garda Bresciano Sulèr '03	🍷🍷	7
○ Perlì '05	🍷🍷	4
⊙ Riviera del Garda Bresciano Chiaretto '05	🍷	4

LEALI DI MONTEACUTO
FRAZ. MONTEACUTO
VIA DOSSO, 4
25080 PUEGNAGO SUL GARDA (BS)
TEL. 0365651291

Antonio Leali decided to extend the ageing for the new vintage of his flagship wine, Simut. But he still offered us a nice red, Groppello '04 which has solid structure and rich berry fruit and spice. The subtly fragrant Garda Riesling and rustic Chiaretto are as good as ever.

● Garda Bresciano Groppello '04	🍷🍷	4
⊙ Garda Bresciano Chiaretto '05	🍷	4
○ Garda Riesling '05	🍷	4

FORTESI
FRAZ. CÀ NOVA
27040 ROVESCALA (PV)
TEL. 038575093
www.fortesi.com

The soft, purple ruby Uva Rara '05 gives flowers and wild berries. The Bonarda Vivace '05 is initially closed on the nose but the palate shows well-measured tannins and good pulp. The part-dried Croatina Ludus Vendemialis '04 IGT has interesting aromas but still lacks balance in the mouth.

● Uva Rara '05	🍷🍷	4
● Ludus Vendemialis '04	🍷	4
● OP Bonarda Vivace '05	🍷	4

CASTELLO DI LUZZANO
LOC. LUZZANO, 5
27040 ROVESCALA (PV)
TEL. 0523863277
www.castelloluzzano.it

The good, lively Bonarda Carlino '05 has plum and violet aromas and well-controlled tannins. The Pinot Nero Umore Nero '05 is fresh and pleasant. The Barbera Oreste '04 is good and fruity but lacks the explosiveness of the '03. The tannins in the merlot Merloblù '05 are a bit too marked.

● OP Bonarda Carlino '05	🍷🍷	4
● OP Pinot Nero Umore Nero '05	🍷🍷	4
● OP Barbera Oreste '04	🍷	4
● Merloblù '05	🍷	4

MARTILDE
FRAZ. CROCE, 4A1
27040 ROVESCALA (PV)
TEL. 0385756280
www.martilde.it

The ever-reliable Barbera '05 is juicy, soft and pleasant. The IGT Mantissa '05 has hay and bell pepper notes, nice pulp and a liquorice finish. The frank, varietal Pinot Nero Nina '05 shows nice tannins and pleasant fruit. The well-made, dark ruby Bonarda Vivace Gianna '05 has a meaty palate.

● OP Barbera '05	🍷🍷	3
● OP Bonarda Vivace Gianna '05	🍷	3
● OP Pinot Nero Nina '05	🍷	4
● Rosso Mantissa '05	🍷	4

Tenuta San Francesco
via Scazzolino, 55
27040 Rovescala (PV)
tel. 029085141

There is a lot of body and extract in the slightly rugged wines produced by Annibale Alziati. Gaggiarone is a Bonarda di Rovescala with plentiful tannins, almondy notes, pulp and a clear bitterish finish. The Bonarda Riserva '01 has evolved tones, lively tannins and a nice long finish.

●	OP Bonarda Ris. '01	🍷	4
●	Gaggiarone '03	🍷	4

Nettare dei Santi
via Capra, 17
20078 San Colombano al Lambro (MI)
tel. 0371897371 - 0371200523
www.nettaredeisanti.it

The pleasant, well made Passito di Verdea is bright gold with honey and peach tea aromas. The IGT red Podere Roverone '05, from barbera, croatina, uva rara, cabernet and merlot, is fruity, simple and fragrant. The Domm '00, a chardonnay-based metodo classico, is rather evolved.

○	Spumante Domm Brut '00	🍷	4
●	Podere Roverone '05	🍷	2
○	Passito di Verdea	🍷	4

Panigada - Banino
via della Vittoria, 13
20078 San Colombano al Lambro (MI)
tel. 037189103

The still young San Colombano Vigna La Merla Riserva '03 is dark ruby with mouthfilling tannins, showing spicy, warm and juicy. It's softer than usual and will improve in bottle. The riesling IGT Bianco '05 has a bright golden colour, light vanilla notes, a nice floral bouquet and satisfying pulp.

●	San Colombano V. La Merla Ris. '03	🍷🍷	5
○	Banino Bianco '05	🍷🍷	3*

Pietrasanta
via Sforza, 55/57
20078 San Colombano al Lambro (MI)
tel. 0371897540

The well-made San Colombano '04 from Pietrasanta shows raspberry and cherry, smooth tannins and good fruit. The riesling and sauvignon Bianco della Costa '04 is bright straw yellow with coppery highlights and a warm, full palate but the slightly masking oak pushes the fruit into the background.

●	San Colombano '04	🍷	3
○	San Colombano Bianco della Costa '04	🍷	4

Isimbarda
loc. Castello - Cascina Isimbarda
27046 Santa Giuletta (PV)
tel. 0383899256
www.tenutaisimbarda.com

The best wine this year is the purple ruby Monplò '03 with intense wild berries, balance and pleasant length. The Vigna Martina '05 has nice flower and citrus aromas with light minerally notes. The Barbera Vivace '05 is fragrant and fruity and the Bonarda Frizzante '05 well made and typical.

●	OP Rosso Monplò '03	🍷🍷	4
○	OP Riesling Renano Vigna Martina '05	🍷🍷	4
●	OP Barbera Vivace '05	🍷	3
●	OP Bonarda Vivace '05	🍷	3

Podere San Giorgio
loc. Castello, 1
27046 Santa Giuletta (PV)
tel. 0383899168
www.poderesangiorgio.it

The good Bonarda Vivace Rebecca '05 has violet and wild berry aromas. The fragrant, simple, balanced Barbera Ceresino '05 puts pleasure before complexity. The well-made Pinot Grigio Argento Vivo '05 is full and varietal. The Rosé Metodo Classico starts well on the nose but falls off in the finish.

●	OP Barbera Ceresino '05	🍷🍷	3
●	OP Bonarda Vivace Rebecca '05	🍷🍷	3
⊙	OP Castel San Giorgio Brut Rosé	🍷	5
○	OP Pinot Grigio Argento Vivo '05	🍷	3

FATTORIA GAMBERO
FRAZ. CASE NUOVE
27045 SANTA MARIA DELLA VERSA (PV)
TEL. 038579268 - 3356084692
www.fattoriailgambero.it

The entire series of wines this year has finesse and varietal tones, with a special mention for the clean Riesling Italico Kafir '04, part fermented in maple tonneaux, and the soft Bonarda Frizzante Alborada '05. Both the Tinterosse '04 and Bobinò '05 are precise and well crafted.

○	OP Riesling Italico Kafir '04	🍷🍷	4
●	OP Bonarda Frizzante Alborada '05	🍷🍷	3
●	OP Pinot Nero Tinterosse '04	🍷	4
○	OP Chardonnay Bobinò '05	🍷	4

LA BRUGHERATA
FRAZ. ROSCIATE
VIA G. MEDOLAGO, 47
24020 SCANZOROSCIATE (BG)
TEL. 035655202 - www.labrugherata.it

The well-typed, intense Moscato di Scanzo Doge '03 is mellow and long on the palate. The fruity, spicy, rich and juicy Valcalepio Rosso Riserva Doglio '02 scored well. Valcalepio Bianco Vescovado del Feudo Riserva '04 shows stylish, elegant aromas, good backbone and decent fullness.

●	Valcalepio Rosso Doglio Ris. '02	🍷🍷	5
●	Moscato di Scanzo Passito Doge '03	🍷🍷	8
○	Valcalepio Bianco Vescovado del Feudo Ris. '04	🍷	4

IL CIPRESSO
VIA CERRI, 2
24020 SCANZOROSCIATE (BG)
TEL. 0354597005 - 335206131
www.ilcipresso.info

Next to Serafino '03, one of the most interesting, complex and intense Moscato di Scanzos, we find the Valcalepio Rosso Riserva Bartolomeo '03, fragrant with alpine herbs, Valcalepio Rosso Dionisio '04, with jammy tones, and Valcalepio Bianco Melardo '05, with tropical fruit sensations.

●	Moscato di Scanzo Serafino '03	🍷🍷	7
●	Valcalepio Rosso Bartolomeo Ris. '03	🍷🍷	4
●	Valcalepio Rosso Dionisio '04	🍷🍷	4*
○	Valcalepio Bianco Melardo '05	🍷	4

EMILIO PASETTO
VIA ALBARONE, 9
25019 SIRMIONE (BS)
TEL. 0309904943 - 3334632417

Emilio Pasetto moved to Lugana in 1977 and manages this estate with his children. The family presented two well-made Luganas. We preferred the I Calmi '05 selection for its seductive fruit and flower fragrances mingled with elegant medicinal herbs. The Cascina Albarone shows enjoyable typicity.

○	Lugana I Calmi '05	🍷🍷	4
○	Lugana Cascina Albarone '05	🍷	3

BONALDI - CASCINA DEL BOSCO
LOC. PETOSINO - VIA GASPAROTTO, 96
24010 SORISOLE (BG)
TEL. 035571701 - 0354532711
www.cascinadelbosco.it

From chardonnay and pinot bianco, the Cantoalto '03 has a stylish nose and fruity pulp. The Brut Classico Bonaldi is fairly intense and complex. The good Valcalepio Rosso Riserva Cantoalto '02 foregrounds overripe notes. Valcalepio Bianco '05 shows bergamot and apple aromas and is fresh and soft.

○	Cantoalto Bianco '03	🍷🍷	5
○	Bonaldi Brut M. Cl.	🍷🍷	5
●	Valcalepio Rosso Cantoalto Ris. '02	🍷	5
○	Valcalepio Bianco '05	🍷	3

F.LLI BETTINI
LOC. SAN GIACOMO
VIA NAZIONALE, 4A
23036 TEGLIO (SO)
TEL. 0342786068 - 0342786096

The Sforzato '03 is interesting. A complex nose ushers in a warm palate with spicy, ripe fruit shades. The good Inferno '03 is intense on the nose with a concentrated palate and long, dry finish. The nebbiolo-based Sant'Andrea '03 has stylish aromas, good structure and balance.

●	Valtellina Sup. Inferno Prodigio '03	🍷🍷	5
●	Valtellina Sup. Sant'Andrea '03	🍷🍷	5
●	Valtellina Sup. Sforzato Vigneti di Spina '03	🍷🍷	7

Caven Camuna
via Caven, 1
23036 Teglio (SO)
tel. 0342484330
www.cavencamuna.it

The two wines we tasted are representative of their territory. The first is a good Sassella '02 with floral, fruity aromas, then a soft palate and velvety finish. The Inferno '03 has red fruit and freshness on the nose, a harmonic palate with a pleasant savoury note and a long almondy finish.

●	Valtellina Sup. Inferno Al Carmine '03	🍷🍷	5
●	Valtellina Sup. Sassella La Priora '02	🍷🍷	5

Torrevilla
via Emilia, 4
27050 Torrazza Coste (PV)
tel. 038377003 - 038377520
www.torrevilla.it

The Spumante Brut Metodo Classico La Genisia '00 is pleasant, full and soft with forthright aromas. The Classese is also well made, its bright colour introducing clear aromas. The interesting Cortese La Genisia Garlà '05 is fruity and soft. Bonarda Frizzante La Genisia '05 is nice and typical.

○	Brut Cl. La Genisia '00	🍷🍷	4
○	OP Pinot Nero Brut Classese	🍷🍷	4
●	OP Bonarda Frizzante La Genisia '05	🍷	3
○	OP La Genisia Garlà '05	🍷	3

La Tordela
via Torricelli, 1
24060 Torre de' Roveri (BG)
tel. 035580172
www.latordela.it

Valcalepio Rosso Riserva Campo Roccoli Vecchi '01 is good, elegant and spicy, with balsamic notes and dark gamey tones, then a big, long palate. The well-made Valcalepio Moscato Passito di Torre de' Roveri '03 is direct, precise, soft and full. The IGT Merlot '03 is simple and pleasant.

●	Valcalepio Rosso Campo Roccoli Vecchi Ris. '01	🍷🍷	6
●	Valcalepio Moscato Passito di Torre de' Roveri '03	🍷🍷	7
●	Merlot '03	🍷	2

Il Bisserino
via Dordi, 17
27010 Torrevecchia Pia (PV)
tel. 038268245

This is Claudio Pozzi's debut. His purple ruby San Colombano Vin de Milan '04 opens on raspberry and cherry notes and then a warm palate with good fruit and abundant tannins. The merlot-led IGT red Torrevecchia '04 shows clear fruit enhanced by spicy notes, but the tannins have yet to ripen fully.

●	San Colombano Vin de Milan '04	🍷🍷	4
●	Torrevecchia '04	🍷	4

Medolago Albani
via Redona, 12
24069 Trescore Balneario (BG)
tel. 035942022
www.medolagoalbani.it

Valcalepio I Due Lauri Riserva '02 has balsamic aromas with spice and wild berries and a solid, balanced palate. Valcalepio Rosso '04 is well made with nice florality. The Brut Classico is evolved on the nose and zesty on the palate. Cabernet Sauvignon Villa Redona '02 is spicy and flavoursome.

●	Valcalepio I Due Lauri Ris. '02	🍷🍷	4
●	Villa Redona '02	🍷	4
●	Valcalepio Rosso '04	🍷	3
○	Brut M. Cl.	🍷	4

Tenuta Il Bosco
loc. Il Bosco
27049 Zenevredo (PV)
tel. 0385245326
www.ilbosco.com

The good Brut Il Bosco '98 has a golden colour, nice apple, peach, citrus and tropical fruit aromas and a full palate. The stylish, soft Bonarda '05 has fruity pulp and wild berry, violet aromas. The Pinot Nero '04 is varietal yet simple. The tank-method Brut Philèo sparkler is nicely crafted.

●	OP Bonarda Vivace '05	🍷🍷	3
○	OP Brut Cl. Il Bosco '98	🍷🍷	5
●	OP Pinot Nero '04	🍷	4
○	OP Pinot Nero Brut Martinotti Philèo	🍷	4

TRENTINO

Trentino won seven Three Glass awards this year. This major milestone also came with a long string of second places. There are actually around 40 red Glasses, showing how well Trentino's co-operatives, wineries and growers are doing. This year, the region's winemaking means above all classic method sparklers and the ever more influential Trento DOC zone, which is no longer just synonymous with top quality spumante but has also found its own typicity. For some time, the prizewinners have been a class apart. Giulio Ferrari, Methius and Altemasi Graal are joined this year by the Riserva from Abate Nero, a Trentino sparkling winemaker that is as small as it is solid and has been in the front rank for some time, even beyond the region. Then come another two wines from equally famous and reliable wineries, Granato from Elisabetta Foradori and Villa Gresti from Tenuta San Leonardo. With "her Teroldego", Elisabetta Foradori continues to be an established member of the top group. But Marchese Guerrieri Gonzaga did the same. While waiting for the 2003 vintage of his legendary San Leonardo to mature, we tasted Villa Gresti, a red from merlot with a pinch of carmenère that foregrounds finesse and elegance. The list of the seven Trentino chart-toppers closes with a still white, a type that had not won Three Glasses for four years now. Vinified in 2001 by Pojer & Sandri, it was left to age in the cellar before being uncorked for our tasting panel, whose approval was unanimous. There were also excellent scores for many other wines that reached our finals, beginning with the sparklers and ending with a few Teroldegos of proven reliability and typicity. And there is some exciting news. The L'Ora project involves several estates in the Vallagarina, particularly Pravis, all of which are striving to make a unique, territory-driven white, produced exclusively in the variety's native zone, by leaving nosiola grapes to dry in special lofts and then vinifying them in acacia barrels. The variety and the zone are the classic ones for Vino Santo, which confirms Trentino's oenological status, as do many other excellent wines. Some are from international varieties; others have a distinctly "dolomitic" style. Discover both types and more besides as you browse through the following pages.

ALA (TN)

BORGO DEI POSSERI
LOC. POZZO BASSO, 1
38061 ALA (TN)
TEL. 0464671899 - 3358390501

The Pilati-Mainenti family manages this new estate on the hills above Ala, a zone that had not produced high quality wines until now, and submitted wines beyond all our expectations. With the enthusiasm of the self-taught, Margherita and Martin Mainenti gave us good, characteristic wines, starting with Quaron, a Müller Thurgau that finds a lot to say for itself in this area south of Rovereto. It is the estate's showcase wine again this year thanks to a broad, complex bouquet with outstanding notes of wild herbs, sage, medicinal plants and alpine flowers, and a fresh palate with nice acidity and a certain richness marked by the typical minerality of Vallagarina. Alongside their white wine production, Martin Mainenti and oenologist Michele Waissler have been working for years on a soft, velvety red. The preview tasting of the Rocol '04, a monovarietal Merlot, told us they are heading in the right direction. It may be a bit too concentrated in its colour, but shows fruity and red berry notes and is pleasant on the palate, although there is slightly excessive alcoholic richness. The other two whites are not bad, either. The Sauvignon Furiel '05 and Chardonnay Malusel '05 are both pleasant and varietal. Furiel is tangy and slightly peppery while Malusel is in the classic Trentino idiom.

●	Merlot Rocol '04	🍷🍷	4
○	Müller Thurgau Quaron '05	🍷🍷	4*
○	Chardonnay Malusel '05	🍷	4
○	Sauvignon Furiel '05	🍷	4
○	Müller Thurgau Quaron '04	YY	4*

ARCO (TN)

MADONNA DELLE VITTORIE
VIA LINFANO, 81
38062 ARCO (TN)
TEL. 0464505432
www.madonnadellevittorie.it

That very satisfying lakeshore sparkler, the Trento Classico from Madonna delle Vittorie, won our tasters over. Trento Brut '01 is a bright spumante with straw-yellow highlights, an appealing spectrum of aromatics and a caressing palate that leaves the mouth with a pleasant after-aroma of apricot jam. At their constantly expanding estate, whose vineyards sprawl across the Trento shore of Lake Garda, the Mandelli family has invested in viticultural research and experimentation with the aim of bringing out the most of the Garda terroir. Oenologist Massimo Azzolini, assisted by Matteo Santoni, supervises the long list of wines. The most interesting is the Trentino Bianco Summolaco, from chardonnay, pinot bianco and pinot grigio. In the 2004 version, this white has the evolved sensations of mountain apples and mixed flower honey while the structure on the palate is as good as it is supple. Though perhaps a bit less convincing than previous versions, the Trentino Rosso Summolaco '03, from cabernet, teroldego and lagrein, still shows very decent structure on the palate. The Trentino Chardonnay '05, Trentino Pinot Grigio '05 and a fresh Trentino Riesling '05 are correct, pleasant, immediate and released at very reasonable prices. Finally, the Moscato Frizzante '05 is unusual and delicate. The wines from teroldego, lagrein and rebo were all still ageing when we tasted.

○	Trento Brut '01	🍷🍷	4
○	Trentino Bianco Summolaco '04	🍷🍷	4
●	Trentino Rosso Summolaco '03	🍷	4
○	Moscato Frizzante '05	🍷	3
○	Trentino Chardonnay '05	🍷	4
○	Trentino Pinot Grigio '05	🍷	3
○	Trentino Riesling '05	🍷	4
●	Trentino Rosso Summolaco '02	YY	4
○	Trentino Bianco Summolaco '03	YY	4
○	Trentino Traminer '04	YY	3

AVIO (TN)

CANTINA SOCIALE DI AVIO
VIA DANTE, 14
38063 AVIO (TN)
TEL. 0464684008
www.viticoltoriinavio.it

This dependable co-operative winery has made some radical changes in its operational structure by completely remodelling the building used for vinification and cellaring. All this, however, has yet to show in the character of the wines, which are good but still finding their feet, even though the grapes are harvested in one of the best areas in the entire region, Campi Sarni. The cellar's representative wine remains the Trentino Rosso, a Bordeaux blend of cabernet and merlot that again in the 2003 version is slim-bodied, elegant and beautifully drinkable. Fresh-tasting and nicely mature, it carries a very attractive price tag. The winery staff, managed by Alfonso Iannielli, also makes Enantio from lambrusco a foglia frastagliata, a variety that has been grown for centuries at the Verona end of Vallagarina. Dark in colour, the wine has an almost rustic fragrance with blackberry-led berry fruit sensations. It is supple, flavourful and effortlessly easy to drink. From the rest of the extensive range, we would mention the Pinot Grigio selection, which is well made, tangy and juicy, with nice acidity, showing the potential of Avio territory and the way forward for the co-operative to return to the top level now that reorganization is over.

● Trentino Rosso '03	🍷🍷	4
● Valdadige Terra dei Forti Enantio '03	🍷🍷	3*
○ Trentino Pinot Grigio '05	🍷	3
● Trentino Rosso Ris. '00	YY	4
● Trentino Rosso '01	YY	4*
● Valdadige Terra dei Forti Enantio '01	YY	3*
● Trentino Rosso '02	YY	4
● Valdadige Terra dei Forti Enantio '02	YY	3*

AVIO (TN)

★ TENUTA SAN LEONARDO
FRAZ. BORGHETTO ALL'ADIGE
LOC. SAN LEONARDO
38060 AVIO (TN)
TEL. 0464689004
www.sanleonardo.it

Marchese Carlo Guerrieri Gonzaga and his son Anselmo dedicate all their time and energy to this estate at Borghetto. They continue to wait patiently for time to do its work and never try to upset the growing season's progress or force the rhythm and tempo of nature. Hence the decision to wait a few more months before releasing the San Leonardo '03, already in bottle and still slowly maturing. The cellar's attention turned to Villa Gresti, from merlot vinified with a dash of carmenère and what has emerged is a wine with class, crafted unmistakeably in the Guerrieri Gonzaga style, thanks to the winemaking intuition of much-respected oenologist Carlo Ferrini, the vineyard management of estate manager Luigino Tinelli and above all to the patience and insight of Marchese Carlo, who has never swerved from his belief in the importance of restoring a focus on absolute quality to merlot cultivation. The 2003 growing year yielded a Villa Gresti that foregrounds elegance. Its impenetrable ruby precedes a nose with fresh red fruit notes and balsamic, earthy, spicy tones. The impact on the palate is soft, round and mouthfilling thanks to splendidly integrated, never aggressive tannins. Sensations of white pepper and cardamom accompany the finish. It was a performance by Villa Gresti that won a first Three Glass prize for the wine. The traditional, approachable Merlot '03 is also more than just sound.

● Villa Gresti '03	🍷🍷🍷	7
● Merlot '03	🍷🍷	4
● San Leonardo '00	YYY	8
● San Leonardo '01	YYY	8
● San Leonardo '90	YYY	5
● San Leonardo '93	YYY	5
● San Leonardo '94	YYY	5
● San Leonardo '95	YYY	5
● San Leonardo '96	YYY	5
● San Leonardo '97	YYY	5
● San Leonardo '99	YYY	8
● Villa Gresti '00	YY	7
● Villa Gresti '01	YY	7

AVIO (TN)

VALLAROM

FRAZ. MASI, 21
38063 AVIO (TN)
TEL. 0464684297
www.vallarom.it

The place name Valerom appears on 15th-century maps indicating the small valley below the hill of Avio, directly in front of Sabbionara castle, which was used for centuries as an observation point during wartime. Over the past half century, the Scienza family has transformed the Valerom hill into a splendid wine estate, preserving its history and projecting its future. The two current owners, winemakers Barbara and Filippo Scienza, understand all this and continue the family management style that produces wines with such great personality. First of all, we would like to say that these wines need time and may have reached us just a bit too young. If you have the patience and good luck to retaste an old vintage, you will understand their potential for development. Again, the most convincing wine was the Syrah '04 for its fullness, overall freshness and gunflint tones on both the nose and the spicy, flavourful palate. The Pinot Nero shows pleasant, flavoursome notes of morello cherry and blueberry jam. The Cabernet Sauvignon seemed less expressive than usual, perhaps because the 2004 vintage has yet to unveil its true character. The Marzemino is light, bitterish and slightly atypical. Vadum Caesaris '05, a white blend from chardonnay, pinot bianco, riesling and sauvignon, is as pleasant and charming as ever.

●	Syrah '04	▼▼	6
●	Pinot Nero '04	▼▼	5
○	Vadum Caesaris '05	▼▼	4
●	Cabernet Sauvignon '04	▼	4
●	Marzemino '05	▼	4
●	Pinot Nero '03	▽▽	5
●	Syrah '03	▽▽	6
○	Vadum Caesaris '04	▽▽	4

CALAVINO (TN)

TOBLINO

FRAZ. SARCHE
VIA LONGA, 1
38070 CALAVINO (TN)
TEL. 0461564168
www.toblino.it

This year Toblino became Produttori Toblino, underlining in the name the importance of the member growers. The growers themselves are spread across Vallagarina, the area adjacent to scenic Lake Toblino between Trento, Garda and the Brenta Dolomites. Under the tireless management of Carlo Filiberto Bleggi, Produttori Toblino has over the past few years rethought the style of the wines, tying them even closer to the territory but taking into account market preferences for some international appeal. That's why the cellar has become involved in the L'Ora project. Acacia barrels are used to ferment nosiola grapes previously left to dry on special racks, in line with a set of rules drafted by a number of winemakers in the valley, to produce a full-bodied, mouthfilling white. L'Ora '03 is a great wine, showing mature, full and very convincing. In some ways, it recalls Trentino Vino Santo Puro Selezione '97, just as sound a wine and as rich and deep as this winery has ever created. Credit for these excellent results goes to the management of a close-knit group of oenologists, Gian Antonio Pombeni, Lorenzo Tomazzoli and Marco Pederzolli. They have presented us with a lovely line-up of wines. The traditional Nosiola '05 is fresh, acidulous and easy-drinking, the top-range sparkler Trento Brut Antares '00 is as always sound and satisfying, the Trentino Rebo '04 is easy and versatile while the tangy, minerally Kerner '05 is sourced from a mountain vineyard in the Giudicarie valley near Madonna di Campiglio.

○	Nosiola Sel. L'Ora '03	▼▼	5
○	Trentino Vino Santo Puro Sel. '97	▼▼	6
○	Trento Brut Antares '00	▼▼	4
○	Kerner '05	▼▼	4*
●	Trentino Rebo '04	▼	3
○	Trentino Nosiola '05	▼	3
○	Trentino Vino Santo Puro Sel. '96	▽▽	6
●	Teroldego '03	▽▽	3
○	Kerner '04	▽▽	3*
○	Trentino Vino Santo '96	▽▽	6
○	Trento Brut Antares '99	▽▽	4

CALLIANO (TN)

VIVALLIS
VIA VALENTINI, 37
38060 CALLIANO (TN)
TEL. 0464834113
www.vivallis.it

This year, Vivallis submitted a splendid array of Marzeminos in three excellent interpretations. This co-operative winery for years now has been completely reorganizing its vineyards, convincing member growers to focus on quality. We can see the results. The Trentino Marzemino dei Ziresi Superiore, sourced from the area of the same name along the river Adige between Volano and Calliano, might be the best Marzemino 2004 we have tasted so far. A dense, almost purple ruby, this wine has great style and class. The nose immediately releases blackberry and violet sensations over slightly spicy shades before the austere palate shows its determination and backbone. It's invigorating and long, something you'd never expect from a Marzemino, which is usually lighter and simpler. But there is more. The other Superiore, Marzemino d'Isera, from the Isera vineyard in the town of the same name near Volano on the opposite side of the river, shows strawberry and raspberry followed by slightly vanillaed notes leading to a palate with body and fullness, nicely mellowed tannins – again, rare for the type – and a long, pleasantly bitterish finish. Although not a Superiore, the third Marzemino, Vigna Fornas, is just as impressive and on a par with its two bigger brothers. Outstanding among the other wines is Vigna Carbonera, a selection of cabernet sauvignon. The Traminer Vigna San Biagio is sincere, flavourful and as sound as ever, just like the Merlot Vigna Borgo Sacco '03 and Paris '04, a lagrein-merlot blend.

●	Trentino Cabernet Sauvignon Vigna Carbonera '04	🍷🍷	4
●	Trentino Marzemino dei Ziresi Sup. '04	🍷🍷	5
●	Trentino Marzemino di Isera Sup. '04	🍷🍷	4
●	Trentino Marzemino Vigna Fornas '04	🍷🍷	4
●	Trentino Merlot Borgo Sacco '03	🍷	4
○	Trentino Traminer Vigna San Biagio '05	🍷	4
○	Trentino Bianco Vigna Pra' dei Frati '03	🍷🍷 (white)	4
●	Trentino Marzemino dei Ziresi Sup. '03	🍷🍷 (white)	4
●	Trentino Marzemino di Isera Sup. '03	🍷🍷 (white)	4

CAVEDINE (TN)

GINO PEDROTTI
FRAZ. LAGO DI CAVEDINE
VIA CAVEDINE, 7
38073 CAVEDINE (TN)
TEL. 0461564123
www.ginopedrotti.it

Wine depends on many factors, including the personality of the winemaker. At this winery on the shore of Lake Cavedine, the Pedrotti family could be taken as a direct example of how growing grapes can become a way of life. Three young siblings, Giuseppe, Clara and Tullia, carry on this operation with their father Gino, a shrewd interpreter of Trentino's wines and one of the first producers of Vino Santo. The youngsters are learning their craft well. Although their wines are uncomplicated and a bit rustic, they have the power of immediacy. This takes nothing away from the charm and significance of the Pedrotti Vino Santo, which is always excellent and a leading representative of the type, despite the fact the 1996 version has less concentration than usual. To make up for this, the Nosiola '05 shows spontaneous grace and backbone. This fresh, immediate white is less bitterish than usual and more versatile in its aromatics, sustained by touches of green hazelnut and new-mown mountain hay. The interesting Rebo '03 is from a variety Rebo Rigotti created many years ago from by crossing marzemino and teroldego. This intense red shows slightly grassy and red berry fruit aromas with an unusual note of cinnamon on the nose, and a soft, savoury, supple palate. Uncomplicated but still capable of maturing over the years, the Cabernet '03, from mostly cabernet franc, is also served by the Pedrottis as the house wine at their small distillery-cum-osteria (restaurant).

●	Rebo '03	🍷🍷	4
○	Nosiola '05	🍷🍷	4
○	Trentino Vino Santo '96	🍷🍷	7
●	Cabernet '03	🍷	4
○	Trentino Vino Santo '95	🍷🍷 (white)	7
○	Trentino Vino Santo '90	🍷🍷 (white)	7
○	Trentino Vino Santo '91	🍷🍷 (white)	7
○	Trentino Vino Santo '94	🍷🍷 (white)	7

FAEDO (TN)

Bellaveder

Loc. Maso Belvedere
38010 Faedo (TN)
tel. 0461650171
www.bellaveder.it

The name already says it all. This genuine belvedere, situated on a knoll just above the Istituto Agrario di San Michele on the hillside facing Faedo, has sweeping views over the river Adige and the Piana Rotaliana. Since its ten or so hectares of vineyards were planted in the late 1990s, the estate is really just starting out. The brand new cellar has been built completely underground to preserve the charm of a wine estate that is considered one of the best in Trentino. Founded years ago by Doctor Mario Seppi, father-in-law of current owner businessman Tranquillo Lucchetta, who is assisted by oenologist Lorenzo Baldo, Bellaveder has been expanded with the acquisition of adjacent parcels of land and the construction of the cellar. Only a few varieties are planted, exploiting the composition of the various soil types, some morainic and marly, some limestone and dolomitic. The different terroirs create equally different wines, sourced from vines that are perhaps still a bit young. The purplish Rosso Bellaveder is a lagrein-led blend with some teroldego and merlot. The fresh, clean nose shows notes of fruit and plum jam. Although the structure may be a bit lightweight, the mouthfeel is pleasant. The Chardonnay '05 is rich in white-fleshed fruit sensations. The Traminer '05 shows good aromatics. The Schiava '05 is zesty, acidulous and easy drinking.

●	Rosso Bellaveder '04	🍷🍷	4
○	Trentino Chardonnay '05	🍷🍷	4
●	Schiava '05	🍷	4
○	Trentino Traminer '05	🍷	4
○	Trentino Chardonnay '04	🍸🍸	4

FAEDO (TN)

Graziano Fontana

via Case Sparse, 9
38010 Faedo (TN)
tel. 0461650400

Graziano Fontana is a winemaker of few words who lets his wines do the talking for him. Forthright and apparently rustic, in reality they are small winemaking treats, intensified by the growing season's progress and characterized by many factors, including Graziano's experience. This time the Trentino Sauvignon '05 amazed everyone. It proving its worth at every contest, from the one organized by the long-established Confraternita della Vite e del Vino Trentino to various national and local shows and finally our tastings. One of the best Sauvignons in the region, it is designed around aromatic richness that borders on excess, with touches of ripe tomato as well as pear and pineapple. The palate has good body, nice acidity and stylish length with nectarine notes. The other whites are also very good. The fragrant Müller Thurgau is very much in the style of Faedo, the town where this variety has been planted since the mid 20th century, showing backbone and perhaps less fruit than usual but much more concentration in its mineral tanginess. The Chardonnay '05 is ripe but perhaps a bit too evolved, with echoes of acacia honey, apples and the yellow dandelions that blossom beneath the hillside vines in spring. The Traminer Aromatico '05 is less exciting and still closed. But the two house reds made a great showing: the velvety, long Pinot Nero '04 and Graziano Fontana's special favourite, the Lagrein '04. Vinified in the hills, it is well structured, flavoursome, rich in fruit on the palate and long but it should be left in the cellar for a few more years.

●	Trentino Lagrein di Faedo '04	🍷🍷	5
●	Trentino Pinot Nero di Faedo '04	🍷🍷	5
○	Trentino Müller Thurgau di Faedo '05	🍷🍷	4
○	Trentino Sauvignon di Faedo '05	🍷🍷	4
○	Trentino Chardonnay di Faedo '05	🍷	4
○	Trentino Traminer Aromatico di Faedo '05	🍷	4
●	Trentino Lagrein di Faedo '00	🍸🍸	4
●	Trentino Lagrein di Faedo '02	🍸🍸	5
○	Trentino Müller Thurgau di Faedo '03	🍸🍸	4

FAEDO (TN)

Pojer & Sandri

Loc. Molini, 4
38010 Faedo (TN)
tel. 0461650342
www.pojeresandri.it

Faye Bianco '01 must be one of the best whites our panel has tasted recently and thoroughly deserves its Three Glass award. After careful vinification of the chardonnay and pinot bianco fruit the wine, produced only in the best vintages, is allowed to age for several months in the cellar. Its fabulously entrancing golden colour introduces exciting depth and gentle, caressing sensations on both nose and palate. It's a wine that is symbolic of the maturity and evolution of the best viticulture in Trentino. Just as good is Faye Rosso '03, from cabernet, merlot and lagrein, which fell just short of our highest award again this year but did show plenty of character and generosity. The fragrant richness on nose and palate ranges from candied fruit, orange peel and honey to cocoa powder and spice sensations in the long finish. Pojer & Sandri also produces excellent sparklers. The simply exquisite new Spumante Rosé, from chardonnay and pinot nero, is immediate and easy drinking. Among the other wines produced, we'll mention Essenzia '04, an excellent example of a late-harvest wine from the Dolomites, as well as the white and red Beslers, the Sauvignon, Nosiola and Müller Thurgau, all from '05, which are all complex and very well typed.

○	Bianco Faye '01	**YYY**	5
●	Rosso Faye '03	**YY**	6
○	Besler Biank '03	**YY**	5
●	Besler Ross '03	**YY**	5
○	Essenzia '04	**YY**	6
○	Nosiola '05	**YY**	4
○	Sauvignon '05	**YY**	5
○	Trentino Müller Thurgau '05	**YY**	4
⊙	Spumante Brut Rosé	**YY**	5
○	Essenzia '02	YY	6
○	Sauvignon '04	YY	5
○	Spumante Brut '99/'00	YY	6

FAEDO (TN)

Arcangelo Sandri

via Vanegge, 4
38010 Faedo (TN)
tel. 0461650935

Last year, they debuted in the main section of the Guide. This time, their place has been confirmed. Now finishing their agricultural degrees after their diplomas in oenology, the talented Nadia and Sonia Sandri manage their small estate above Faedo with their father Arcangelo. The Trentino Chardonnay I Canopi '05 stood out at our tastings. A golden colour with greenish highlights, it yields touches of hazelnut and tropical fruit on the nose that usher in a broad, well-crafted, succulent palate with notes of apple that shows fresh and gently astringent before fading out on a full, tangy finish. This is one of the best Chardonnays in Trentino, thanks to its finesse and forthright immediacy, as well as very cellarable structure. A Lagrein from the hills, the Trentino Lagrein Capòr '03, has the style of a real thoroughbred. Perhaps not even the Sandris thought they could produce a wine with such structure and concentration, although it is still young and developing, without recourse to high technology or extreme vinification. This splendid red is awesome and inviting with a fragrant, fruity nose beautifully mirrored on the palate. It may achieve mineral complexity in a few years but it is already more satisfying and convincing than any other Trentino Lagrein we have tasted. The two other wines are sound. Trentino Müller Thurgau Cosler '05 is intense and fruity and Trentino Traminer Razer '05 is round and full, although it has yet to develop.

●	Trentino Lagrein Capòr '03	**YY**	5
○	Trentino Chardonnay I Canopi '05	**YY**	4
○	Trentino Müller Thurgau Cosler '05	**Y**	4
○	Trentino Traminer Razer '05	**Y**	4
●	Trentino Lagrein '01	YY	5
○	Trentino Müller Thurgau Cosler '04	YY	4
○	Trentino Traminer Razer '04	YY	4

GIOVO (TN)

VILLA CORNIOLE
FRAZ. VERLA
VIA AL GREC', 23
38030 GIOVO (TN)
TEL. 0461695067
www.villacorniole.com

The Pellegrini brothers are building contractors as well as enthusiastic winemakers who some years ago decided to bottle the fruits of their efforts. Grapes are harvested from estate property, each variety cultivated in a specific area on plots scattered across the valley floor and along the banks of the rivers Adige or Noce as well as the steep Cembra hillsides. They are then brought to Verla, at Giovo, to the new cellar carved into the red porphyry rock that characterizes the Cembra valley, where Maddalena Nardin Pellegrini works with consultancy from oenologist Walter Webber. The Teroldego Rotaliano may be the best example of Villa Corniole's approach to winemaking and the 7 Pergole selection gets better every year. Opening with currants on the nose, it is most convincing on the palate where a powerful fruity note melds with chocolate and liquorice. The Teroldego '04 has a similar tasting profile, showing a nice balance of rich of the extract and excellently crafted freshness. But there is more equally pleasant news. Trentino Cabernet Sauvignon Gregiòti '03 is also good, if perhaps a little light-bodied because of the youth of the vines, but very intriguing for its broad aromatic range and remarkable richness of flavour. We found no fault with the Trentino Müller Thurgau '05, a wine born right at the cellar door among the vines planted on the porphyry terraces across the hills between Giovo and Cembra. The other wines, the Chardonnay and a copper-coloured Pinot Grigio, both from '05, are well managed.

●	Teroldego Rotaliano 7 Pergole '03	TT	6
●	Trentino Cabernet Sauvignon Gregiòti '03	TT	6
●	Teroldego Rotaliano '04	TT	4
○	Trentino Müller Thurgau '05	TT	4
○	Trentino Chardonnay '05	T	4
○	Trentino Pinot Grigio Ramato '05	T	4
●	Teroldego Rotaliano 7 Pergole '02	YY	6
●	Teroldego Rotaliano '03	YY	4
○	Trentino Chardonnay Lukin '03	YY	5

ISERA (TN)

CANTINA D'ISERA
VIA AL PONTE, 1
38060 ISERA (TN)
TEL. 0464433795
www.cantinaisera.it

Marzemino d'Isera is one of the best-known, best-loved wines in Trentino, eagerly sought out by masses of consumers who appreciate its simple fragrance. The town of Isera is rightly proud of being the capital of Marzemino and every year promotes the wine's charms through shows, debates and competitions with Marzeminos from other areas such as Veneto or the Brescia shore of Lake Garda. The progress of the growing season and in particular the unpredictable weather during the months before the harvest obviously have to be taken into account. So we should say that the 2005 harvest for the member growers of this long-established co-operative was generous in quantity but not outstanding in terms of quality. Despite the weather, Marzemino in every version made here, Superiore included, confirmed its versatility as a reliable, easy-going and very appealing wine for carefree drinking. Even the Etichetta Verde selection, though not as fragrant or structured as usual, is well managed and fresh. It also has to be said that the almost 100,000 bottles released are on sale at a very reasonable price. Another quaffable red is the upfront and slightly acerbic Schiava Costa Felisa. The unusual Teroldego '05, from vines grown among marzemino vineyards, is so fragrant and fresh it is almost a vin nouveau. The whites are all up to scratch, with the frank, fruity Pinot Grigio Agiato '05 standing out.

●	Teroldego Vign. delle Dolomiti '05	T	3
●	Trentino Marzemino '05	T	3
○	Trentino Pinot Grigio Agiato '05	T	4
●	Trentino Sup. Marzemino Etichetta Verde '05	T	4
⊙	Valdadige Schiava Costa Felisa '05	T	3
●	Trentino Sup. Marzemino Etichetta Verde '03	YY	4
●	Trentino Marzemino Sup. d'Isera Etichetta Verde '04	YY	4
⊙	Valdadige Schiava Costa Felisa '04	YY	3
○	Trentino Pinot Grigio Agiato '04	Y	4

ISERA (TN)

DE TARCZAL
FRAZ. MARANO D'ISERA
VIA G. B. MIORI, 4
38060 ISERA (TN)
TEL. 0464409134
www.detarczal.com

Winemaker Ruggero Dell'Adami de Tarczal boasts some illustrious ancestors. The estate belonged to the noble Alberti di Poja family until the marriage of Irma Alberti to Géza Dell'Adami de Tarczal, admiral of the Austro-Hungarian imperial fleet and direct ancestor of Ruggero. So we should not be surprised at this estate's attention to tradition in producing their wines. Not coincidentally, the property won a recent prize from the municipality of Isera for the best-tended vineyard of marzemino. This determined maker of red wines releases his best-known, most characteristic wines, the Marzeminos, in a base version and the Husar selection, named after the Hapsburg soldier that features on the label. But this year, the wines are not ready so the estate decided to leave them in the cellar for further ageing. Despite this, Ruggero managed to amaze us with an absolutely wonderful Pinot Bianco '05. Its intense straw yellow ushers in apple sensations overlaid with toasted hazelnut and a finish with excellent length. We also enjoyed the Schiava Gentile '05, a wine too frequently ignored but one that, at least in this case, is not just supple and wonderfully pleasing but also marked by nice deep spicy and minerally notes. Outstanding among the other wines are the Merlot '03 and Cabernet Franc '04, both showing round and lightly tannic.

⊙	Schiava gentile '05	🍷🍷	3
○	Trentino Pinot Bianco '05	🍷🍷	4
●	Trentino Merlot '03	🍷	4
●	Trentino Cabernet Franc '04	🍷	4
●	Trentino Marzemino d'Isera Husar '03	🍸🍸	4
●	Trentino Marzemino d'Isera '04	🍸🍸	4
●	Trentino Marzemino d'Isera Husar '04	🍸🍸	4
○	Brut de Tarczal '99	🍸🍸	5

LASINO (TN)

PISONI
LOC. SARCHE
FRAZ. PERGOLESE DI LASINO
VIA SAN SIRO, 7A
38070 LASINO (TN)
TEL. 0461564106 - www.pisoni.net

Sparkling wines are the most interesting products from the Pisoni family estate this year for they presented some particularly good Trentos. Their experience in sparkling winemaking is certainly not recent, considering they began in the late 1960s when Arrigo, Gino and Vittorio Pisoni attempted to make sparklers out of a few hundred bottles filled with chardonnay for that purpose in the caverns of an old Second World War air-raid shelter. Though their children now manage the estate, recent disgorgements have confirmed the wisdom of their choice. Both the Trento Brut '02 and Trento Extra Brut Riserva '01 are a deep straw yellow with tiny bubbles, floral tones on the nose and white-fleshed fruit that shades elegantly into oaky nuances. The Extra Brut has a palate that is stylish yet powerful and progresses with the typical fragrance of a Trento Classico. The Brut is fruitier with a finish that echoes traces of damson and just ripened golden apples. The pleasant, easy-going Trento Rosé is fresh and quaffable. The still wines are also good. The Pisoni Vino Santo '97, from nosiola grapes left to dry on rush mats and crushed at Easter, is one of the symbols of the category, showing majestic on the nose and then full and delicate on the palate. The Sarica Rosso '03 is also coming along nicely. This unusual blend of shiraz and pinot nero is light in its spicy aromas and full on the palate, with rich morello cherry-led fruit. The nicely executed Nosiola '05 is simple and generous.

○	Trentino Vino Santo '97	🍷🍷	7
○	Trento Extra Brut Ris. '01	🍷🍷	5
○	Trento Brut '02	🍷🍷	4
●	Sarica Rosso '03	🍷	5
○	Trentino Nosiola '05	🍷	4
⊙	Trento Brut Rosé	🍷	5
○	Trentino Vino Santo '95	🍸🍸	7
○	Trentino Vino Santo '96	🍸🍸	7
●	Sarica Rosso '99	🍸🍸	5
○	Trento Extra Brut Ris. '99	🍸🍸	5

LASINO (TN)

PRAVIS
LOC. LE BIOLCHE, 1
38076 LASINO (TN)
TEL. 0461564305
www.pravis.it

Respect the earth, the life force, the spontaneity of wine and its ties with the culture of the people from the villages in this valley. Make wine as your life's choice and revive country customs by cultivating many small plots with rows that are never planted against the wind. These three craftsmen from Pravis, Gianni Chisté, Domenico Pedrini and Mario Zambarda, have been quietly working away for three decades, oblivious to fashion. One visit to their lovely winery below Castel Madruzzo is enough to understand the honesty and spontaneous frankness of the owners, as well as that of their wines. They say never plant against the wind because the Ora, the breeze off Lake Garda, ripens the grapes perfectly, especially the nosiola variety that Pravis uses to make two awesome wines. L'Ora '04 comes from overripe bunches dried on special rush mats then vinified and aged in acacia barrels until it becomes a pure gold wine that is full, savoury, very minerally and citrus-like, with a sweet close. The rare Vino Santo '97, called Arèle, the local name for the rush mats, is rich, intense and full yet never cloys. It's a genuine meditation wine. But there is more. The cabernet-based red Fratagranda '02 also scored very well, fascinating our tasters with its almost rustically assertive class. The Nosiola Le Frate '05 is typical, the monovarietal Merlot Enfin '03 convinces and the Soliva '04, also from overripe grapes, is delicious.

● Fratagranda '02	▼▼ (grey)	5
○ L'Ora '04	▼▼ (grey)	5
○ Trentino Vino Santo Arèle '97	▼▼ (grey)	7
● Enfin '03	▼▼	5
○ Soliva '04	▼▼	6
○ Nosiola Le Frate '05	▼▼	5
○ Stravino di Stravino '01	YY	7
● Syrae '02	YY	6
○ Soliva '03	YY	5
○ Stravino di Stravino '03	YY	6
○ Trentino Vino Santo Arèle '95	YY	7
○ Müller Thurgau St. Thomà '04	YY	4
○ Nosiola Le Frate '04	YY	4

LAVIS (TN)

BOLOGNANI
VIA STAZIONE, 19
38015 LAVIS (TN)
TEL. 0461246354
www.bolognani.com

Here's a wine you can bank on. The Bolognani brothers proudly present their cabernet-heavy Bordeaux blend Gabàn, the greatest product of their recent winemaking activities. The Bolognanis actually started out as cellarmen but over the past few years their attention has shifted more and more to production from their small family estate of around four hectares owned and another four rented. But they still work as sought-after cellarmen at major estates in Trentino and beyond. In other words, the Gabàn is the beginning of a new challenge and results are exciting to say the least. In the 2003 version, this explosive red breezed into our finals. Outstandingly silky overall, it gives a remarkably intense palate with echoes of ripe plums and mature, nicely textured tannins. The teroldego-based Armilo '04 is also juicy and immediate with a finish rich in youthful grip, good backbone and structure. From the white wines, the Müller Thurgau '05 has full aromas with touches of hay and chamomile. The body may be a tad too slim but there is still good ageing potential. The stylish, intense Sauvignon '05 has a varietal timbre on both nose and palate with notes of bell pepper and gunflint, a pleasant finish and good staying power.

● Gabàn '03	▼▼ (grey)	6
● Teroldego Armilo '04	▼▼	4
○ Trentino Müller Thurgau '05	▼▼	4
○ Trentino Sauvignon '05	▼	4
● Gabàn '00	YY	6
● Gabàn '01	YY	6
● Teroldego Armilo '02	YY	4
● Teroldego Armilo '03	YY	4
○ Trentino Müller Thurgau '03	YY	4*
○ Trentino Müller Thurgau '04	YY	4*
○ Trentino Traminer Aromatico Sanròc '04	YY	4

LAVIS (TN)

Cesconi

Fraz. Pressano
via Marconi, 39
38015 Lavis (TN)
tel. 0461240355

Patience is the virtue of the strong. The Cesconis are young winemakers with the shrewdness of old farmers and theirs is a dynasty of growers who have never been in a hurry to amaze anyone. This time, they decided to leave their prized whites in the cellar and submitted only a couple of reds, Pivier '03 and the more immediate Moratél '04. The Pivier is a single-variety Merlot that caresses nose and palate. Dark ruby, it shows elegant aromas of plain chocolate, vanilla, white spice and smoked juniper followed by a powerful, long palate with an elegantly expressive tannic weave and very pleasant close. In other words, the Pivier is enchanting, despite the youth of the vines growing in Vallagarina near Drò, on the Trentino shore of Lake Garda, in an especially mild, almost Mediterranean climate, pleasantly reflected in this truly delightful wine. The other family red, Moratél, happily brings together several different varieties. From a merlot and cabernet base, it also has some teroldego, lagrein and syrah from the Cesconis' vineyards in Pressano, above Lavis, as well as the plot on the Garda side, home of the powerful Pivier. Apparently simple and easy drinking, Moratél is actually as heady as it is elegant, showing soft yet vigorous with enjoyable acidity and robust tannins. We will have to wait for the whites, as well as the other red, a lagrein-teroldego blend, since they won't be ready until mid 2007.

● Rosso del Pivier '03	**ΨΨ**	6
● Moratel '04	**ΨΨ**	4
● Rosso del Pivier '01	ΨΨ	6
○ Olivar '02	ΨΨ	5
○ Olivar '03	ΨΨ	5
● Rosso del Pivier '02	ΨΨ	6
○ Traminer Aromatico '02	ΨΨ	5
● Moratel '03	ΨΨ	4
○ Chardonnay '04	ΨΨ	5
○ Nosiola '04	ΨΨ	4
○ Olivar '04	ΨΨ	5
○ Pinot Grigio '04	ΨΨ	5
○ Traminer Aromatico '04	ΨΨ	5

LAVIS (TN)

Vignaiolo Giuseppe Fanti

Fraz. Pressano
P.zza della Croce, 3
38015 Lavis (TN)
tel. 0461240809

In autumn, the hill of Lavis, between Pressano and Faedo, resembles some of the villages in Alsace. The landscape is dotted with vineyards, country wineries where you can taste the must, and friendly winemakers, rightfully proud of their efforts. You also get a vaguely Alsatian feeling as you taste the wines of Alessandro Fanti, an enthusiastic grower, skilled oenologist and cellarman who was born to the trade. His Incrocio Manzoni '05 has backbone and stylish aromatic notes. The broad, mouthfilling palate has a caressing acidity that gives it length and staying power. Alessandro always makes a mark with this wine, of which he releases fewer than 3,000 bottles. It can stand comparison with the best in the region. Alessandro's skill can also be seen in the Nosiola, as well as the other major white from the estate, Pritianum, from the ancient place name for Pressano, the town where generations of Fantis have tended vineyards. The Nosiola '05 is fragrant, uncompromising and nicely bitterish, with touches of wild flowers on nose and palate. The blend for Pritianum '05 includes chardonnay, incrocio Manzoni, riesling and nosiola to created an invigorating, full wine, much more convincing on the palate despite a first-class spectrum of aromatics that has yet to unfold entirely. Finally, the blend of teroldego, cabernet and merlot, Portico Rosso '04, is less aggressive than usual, with good concentration and notes of leather and tobacco followed by ripe cherry jam sensations. Uncork it in a few years' time.

○ Incrocio Manzoni '05	**ΨΨ**	4
○ Pritianum '05	**ΨΨ**	5
○ Trentino Nosiola '05	**ΨΨ**	4
● Portico Rosso '04	**Ψ**	4
● Portico Rosso '01	ΨΨ	5
○ Incrocio Manzoni '02	ΨΨ	5
○ Trentino Chardonnay Robur '02	ΨΨ	5
○ Incrocio Manzoni '03	ΨΨ	5
○ Trentino Chardonnay Robur '03	ΨΨ	5
○ Incrocio Manzoni '04	ΨΨ	4
○ Pritianum '04	ΨΨ	5
○ Trentino Nosiola '04	ΨΨ	4

LAVIS (TN)

LA VIS/VALLE DI CEMBRA
VIA DEL CARMINE, 7
38015 LAVIS (TN)
TEL. 0461246325
www.la-vis.com

Although La Vis failed to win Three Glasses this year, the winemaking group managed by Fausto Peratoner has again confirmed its reputation as one of the most influential in Italy thanks to the overall results. Four of their wines reached our finals, just a whisper away from top marks. We'll begin with the Ritratto Rosso. This lagrein-teroldego blend perhaps lacks the extra something that comes from a great growing season, since 2004 in Trentino was a difficult year for red grapes. Next comes the Ritratto Bianco '05, a blend of chardonnay, pinot grigio and riesling renano, which is even better than its red stablemate and shows full and elegant with lovely minerality. Despite the vintage, the Trentino Pinot Nero Vigna di Saoisent '04 has the backbone, grace, fruit and length of a real thoroughbred and is one of the best Pinot Neros from Trentino. Mandolaia '05 is an increasingly convincing blend of late-harvested chardonnay, riesling and traminer that shows sweet but has gutsy acidity and is technically perfect with intriguing aromas and a satisfying finish. The other wines are difficult to summarize in just a few lines. The Trentino Müller Thurgau '05, a classic released in almost a half million bottles, continues to improve. Credit for this goes to the growers in the Valle di Cembra who plant it only the best vineyard plots in the high mountains. A special mention goes to the Ritratti version of Cabernet Sauvignon '04, as powerful on the palate as it is gentle and inviting on the nose, and the Pinot Grigio '05, by now a model of quality and personality.

●	Ritratto Rosso '04	🍷🍷 (2 black glasses)	5
●	Trentino Pinot Nero Vigna di Saoisent '04	🍷🍷 (2 black glasses)	4*
○	Mandolaia '05	🍷🍷 (2 black glasses)	5
○	Ritratto Bianco '05	🍷🍷 (2 black glasses)	5
●	Trentino Cabernet Sauvignon Ritratti '04	🍷🍷 (2 black glasses)	4
○	Trentino Müller Thurgau '05	🍷🍷 (2 black glasses)	3
○	Trentino Pinot Grigio Ritratti '05	🍷🍷 (2 black glasses)	4
●	Ritratto Rosso '03	3 white glasses	5
○	Ritratto Bianco '03	2 white glasses	5
○	Mandolaia '04	2 white glasses	5

LAVIS (TN)

MASO FURLI
LOC. FURLI
VIA FURLI, 32
38015 LAVIS (TN)
TEL. 0461240667

The overall output of barely 15,000 bottles has not increased but the already high quality of the wines has clearly grown at this microscopic estate located at the first bend in the road running from Lavis to the Valle di Cembra and hill of Pressano. The sunny hollow seems tailor made for growing grapes. For Marco Zanoni and his family, making wine is a natural consequence of a way of life. Despite the fact he is not an oenologist, in just a few years Marco has become an innovative and much imitated cellarman. His Trentino Traminer Aromatico '05 convinced us right away with the incredible richness of its aromas and a consistent palate that flows from aniseed to citrus and minerally tones, then on to a long, deep, lingering finish. The equally powerful Bordeaux-blend Maso Furli Rosso is immediate in its black berry fruit on the nose and then long and complex on the palate. Rich pulp combines with well-integrated tannins and great personality. Finally, what can we say about the Trentino Chardonnay '04 and Trentino Sauvignon '05? They are great, as usual. The Chardonnay is deep straw yellow with golden highlights, giving golden apples and a mature, succulent palate. Perhaps a bit less elegant than usual, the Sauvignon has a certain huskiness that does however make it interesting. With a nose that focuses on elderflower and walnutskin, it is as satisfying as only a savoury country-crafted wine can be.

●	Maso Furli Rosso '03	🍷🍷 (2 black glasses)	5
○	Trentino Traminer Aromatico '05	🍷🍷 (2 black glasses)	5
○	Trentino Chardonnay '04	🍷🍷 (2 black glasses)	5
○	Trentino Sauvignon '05	🍷🍷 (2 black glasses)	5
○	Trentino Sauvignon '03	2 white glasses	5
○	Trentino Sauvignon '04	2 white glasses	5
●	Maso Furli Rosso '01	2 white glasses	5
●	Maso Furli Rosso '02	2 white glasses	5
○	Trentino Chardonnay '02	2 white glasses	5
○	Trentino Chardonnay '03	2 white glasses	5
○	Trentino Traminer Aromatico '03	2 white glasses	5
○	Trentino Traminer Aromatico '04	2 white glasses	5

LAVIS (TN)

CASATA MONFORT

VIA CARLO SETTE, 21
38015 LAVIS (TN)
TEL. 0461246353
www.cantinemonfort.it

Lorenzo Simoni is a young winemaking entrepreneur who some time ago reorganized the family estate, founded just after the Second World War by his grandfather Giovanni. Lorenzo has been gradually expanding the property by purchasing good plots and working to bring back older varieties that were on the verge of extinction, planting them on the hills around Castel Pergine in Valsugana. He has just purchased the Maso Cantanghel estate at the entrance to Valsugana near the Forti di Civezzano. Meanwhile, the grapes crushed at the historic Palazzo Monfort in the heart of Lavis have produced some interesting wines. The Blanc de Sers '05 is a blend of six old varieties, including wanderbara or vernaza, sourced from vineyards cultivated on various tiny plots near Serso. This wine is getting increasingly interesting with unusual aromas of wild flowers, jasmine and field gladiolus. The invigorating, minerally palate gives attractively clean-tasting acidity. The acerbic yet pulp-rich Pinot Grigio '05 is a carefully crafted wine with a flavoursome varietal, rather than aromatic, elegance. The Pinot Nero '04 is savoury and in the mainstream Trentino tradition. Its oak slightly masks its potential but there are marked notes of cherry jam and currants, rounded off by a velvety finish. In contrast, the Lagrein '03 is still closed on the nose. The other wines are well typed. The extensive range embraces all the traditional Trentino wines, including Marzemino and Teroldego.

○ Blanc de Sers '05	🍷🍷	4
○ Trentino Pinot Grigio '05	🍷🍷	4
● Trentino Lagrein '03	🍷	4
● Trentino Pinot Nero '04	🍷	5
● Teroldego Rotaliano '05	🍷	4
● Trentino Marzemino '05	🍷	4
○ Blanc de Sers '04	🍷🍷 (empty)	4
● Teroldego Rotaliano '04	🍷 (empty)	4

MEZZOCORONA (TN)

MARCO DONATI

VIA CESARE BATTISTI, 41
38016 MEZZOCORONA (TN)
TEL. 0461604141

There's no point repeating that Marco Donati is one of the finest interpreters of Teroldego Rotaliano. This is a matter of production style as well as his family's centuries-old tradition of cultivating vineyards at their Mezzocorona estate along the Noce mountain stream in the vine-growing heart of the Piana Rotaliana. Again this year, Teroldego Sangue del Drago is one of the best reds from Trentino. The 2004 version shows intensity and fullness from every point of view and has a vigorously bracing drinkability laced with pepper and oriental spices. The fruity palate has a length few other Teroldegos can boast. The winemaker's expert hand is also evident in the vinification of Teroldego Rotaliano Bagolari '05, a wine that is immediate yet anything but simple. Syrah Costa dei Sauri '03 is very sound. Just a few thousand bottles are made of this warm, round red that progresses nicely to a finish rich in peppery, jammy notes. As for the whites, all from the 2005 vintage, the Nosiola Sole Alto is an early drinker, showing bitterish with notes of wild hazelnuts lifted by a tanginess. The interesting Riesling Stellato '05 is an unusual wine made in an almost experimental microvinification by a Teroldego-maker who loves the challenge of working with other varieties. Finally, the good Traminer Tramonti '05 is outstandingly fragrant on the nose and decently rich on the palate.

● Teroldego Rotaliano Sangue del Drago '04	🍷🍷	6
● Syrah Costa dei Sauri '03	🍷🍷	5
● Teroldego Rotaliano Bagolari '05	🍷🍷	4
○ Trentino Nosiola Sole Alto '05	🍷	4
○ Trentino Riesling Stellato '05	🍷	4
○ Trentino Traminer Tramonti '05	🍷	4
● Teroldego Rotaliano Sangue del Drago '02	🍷🍷 (empty)	6
● Teroldego Rotaliano Sangue del Drago '03	🍷🍷 (empty)	6
● Teroldego Rotaliano Bagolari '03	🍷🍷 (empty)	4
● Teroldego Rotaliano Bagolari '04	🍷🍷 (empty)	4

MEZZOCORONA (TN)

F.LLI DORIGATI
VIA DANTE, 5
38016 MEZZOCORONA (TN)
TEL. 0461605313
www.dorigati.it

Five generations of Dorigati cellarmen have developed the family estate while still respecting the rhythms and methods of their country origins. The winery has not moved its headquarters from the centre of Mezzocorona, perhaps out of respect for the viticultural traditions of their home town, once filled with the countless private "caneve", or wine shops, that were part of the identity of this Piana Rotaliana community. The Dorigatis have reached the top in regional production while keeping their dual identity as makers of sparkling wines and Teroldego. Once again, they picked up the Three Glass award for their Trento Methius Brut Riserva '00, confirming that this wine is in a class by itself. Its vitality, fine perlage and nose of wood resin and citrus set it apart and make it delightfully complex and satisfying. But this is not all, for the Dorigatis came close to another top prize for their Teroldego Rotaliano Diedri '04, an ever more fascinating, concentrated and reliable product. Alongside the Diedri, there is the more straightforward and accessible Teroldego Rotaliano '04, which is savoury and succulent with rich fruit. The restrained, almost sweetish, lightly structured Rebo '04 is made from the variety of the same name created in the 1950s by the Trentino researcher Rebo Rigotti. We close with the Lagrein Kretzer '05. Even though it is almost an eccentric foible in this range, it is actually a well-structured, pleasantly acerbic rosé.

○	Trento Methius Brut Ris. '00	▼▼▼	7
●	Teroldego Rotaliano Diedri '04	▼▼	6
●	Teroldego Rotaliano '04	▼	4
●	Trentino Rebo '04	▼	4
⊙	Lagrein Kretzer '05	▼	4
○	Trento Methius Brut. Ris. '98	▽▽▽	7
●	Teroldego Rotaliano '02	▽▽	4*
●	Teroldego Rotaliano Diedri '03	▽▽	6
○	Trento Methius Brut Ris. '99	▽▽	7
●	Teroldego Rotaliano Diedri Ris. '01	▽▽	6
●	Teroldego Rotaliano '03	▽▽	4*
●	Trentino Cabernet Grener '03	▽▽	6
⊙	Lagrein Kretzer '04	▽▽	4

MEZZOCORONA (TN)

MEZZACORONA
VIA DEL TEROLDEGO, 1
38016 MEZZOCORONA (TN)
TEL. 0461616399
www.mezzacorona.it

MezzaCorona is one of Italy's major winemaking groups with a series of cellars operating in various parts of the country. Though most of its more than 30,000,000 bottles are intended for the international market, the company is attentive to the qualities of each of its production environments, which stretch from Trentino to Sicily. For some years now, the Trentino managers have been attempting to make a Superteroldego. Considering the reviews for the Teroldego Rotaliano Nòs '01, this time they have succeeded. The barely 10,000 bottles of Nòs reveal a certain reversal of trends in the group's production plans. Very well made, it has a dark, intense ruby colour and a lovely nose of blackberry jam. The convincing palate is dense and rich in fruit with a stylish finish on a vaguely almondy note. The series of classic sparkers is also good. The chardonnay-led Trento Rotari Brut Riserva '01 shows fragrant apple and pear aromas and a fruity palate with light mineral tones and good length. The Trento Rotari Cuvée 28 is not bad either. A million units went into bottle after at least 28 months on the lees. Fresh with an easy impact, subtle texture and lovely fruit, it is nicely acidulous and very food-friendly. The Trento Rotari Brut Rosé also shows refined class and technique with its crusty bread aromas and a fruity palate with outstanding strawberry notes, slight sweetness and a doughy texture. From the whites released under the new Castel Firmian line, the Pinot Grigio Riserva '04 is particularly sound.

●	Teroldego Rotaliano Nòs '01	▼▼	6
○	Trento Rotari Brut Ris. '01	▼▼	5
○	Trentino Pinot Grigio Castel Firmian Ris. '04	▼▼	5
○	Trento Rotari Cuvée 28	▼▼	5
⊙	Trento Rotari Brut Rosé	▼	5
○	Trento Rotari Brut Ris. '00	▽▽	5
●	Teroldego Rotaliano Ris. '01	▽▽	5*

MEZZOLOMBARDO (TN)

★ Foradori

via Damiano Chiesa, 1
38017 Mezzolombardo (TN)
tel. 0461601046
www.elisabettaforadori.com

Elisabetta Foradori had a great year in 2004. Her three Trentino wines are delicious, a necessary distinction in view of her new Tuscan commitment with Ampeleja. We'll set aside for the moment the prizewinning Granato and look first at the fragrant Myrto, a white from a blend of sauvignon, incrocio Manzoni and pinot bianco so captivating we were bewitched by its oriental-style aroma, succulent mouthfeel and warm, sunny Mediterranean vitality, quite a combination in a wine from the Dolomites. Next came the Teroldego Rotaliano, sourced from the outstanding vineyards of Mezzolombardo that surround the winery owned by Elisabetta and her mother Gabriella. The wine offers ripe fruit sensations that guarantee compactness on the soft, dynamic palate with close-knit, well-integrated tannins and a long finale that reprises the intense aromas of red fruit. With almost 150,000 bottles available, this is also a major wine in terms of numbers, reflecting the skills of a dedicated winemaker. Finally we come to that Three Glass Granato. No need to underline its one-of-a-kind character for this is a textbook Teroldego. The colour enchants, as do the equally ravishing nose and palate. Vigorous on entry, the palate progresses assertively unveiling a powerful tannic weave and a finish that expands on sensations of blackberry, raspberry and ripe pomegranate seeds. To call it splendid is an understatement.

●	Granato '04	🍷🍷🍷	7
○	Myrto '04	🍷🍷	5
●	Teroldego Rotaliano '04	🍷🍷	5
●	Granato '01	YYY	7
●	Granato '02	YYY	7
●	Granato '03	YYY	7
○	Myrto '02	YY	5
●	Teroldego Rotaliano '02	YY	5
○	Myrto '03	YY	5
●	Teroldego Rotaliano '03	YY	5

MEZZOLOMBARDO (TN)

Cantina Rotaliana

via Trento, 65b
38017 Mezzolombardo (TN)
tel. 0461601010
www.cantinarotaliana.it

Confidently, dependably, combining experimentation with the revival of traditional growing practices to make wines with greater personality and identity, Cantina Rotaliana has again turned out a fine range. Thanks for this go to 320 member growers, farmers who are proud to be team players for this co-operative winery in Mezzolombardo and all comply with strict production protocols to ensure top-quality grape harvests. All four versions of Teroldego Rotaliano earned unanimous consensus, the best being the excellently crafted and altogether wonderful Clesurae '04. Though the aromatics may still be a bit closed, the palate has the powerful bite of a singular wine. The other Teroldegos are also good, starting with the Riserva 2003. Although more slim-bodied, it is anything but simple, showing a lovely array of fruit aromas, spicy tones on both nose and palate, and a long, persuasive finish. The Superiore '04 introduces aromatic notes that recall the Clesurae, although they're a tad less rich. The palate is close-knit and full. Etichetta Rossa, produced in 520,000 bottles a year, shows exemplary quality, production consistency, good ageing prospects and good value for money. The Lagrein and Pinot Nero are both elegant and savoury overall. Finally, the whites are pleasant, from the Pinot Grigio, as usual floral and tangy in the mouth, to the Chardonnay, Moscato Giallo, Traminer and Müller Thurgau.

●	Teroldego Rotaliano Clesurae '04	🍷🍷	6
●	Teroldego Rotaliano Ris. '03	🍷🍷	4
●	Teroldego Rotaliano Sup. '04	🍷🍷	4
●	Teroldego Rotaliano Etichetta Rossa '05	🍷🍷	3*
○	Trentino Chardonnay '05	🍷	3
●	Trentino Lagrein '05	🍷	3*
○	Trentino Moscato Giallo '05	🍷	3
○	Trentino Müller Thurgau '05	🍷	3
○	Trentino Pinot Grigio '05	🍷	3
●	Trentino Pinot Nero '05	🍷	4
●	Trentino Traminer Aromatico '05	🍷	4

MORI (TN)

MORI - COLLI ZUGNA
VIA DEL GARDA, 35
38065 MORI (TN)
TEL. 0464918154
www.cantinamoricollizugna.it

At Mori - Colli Zugna, they reduced the number of wines produced, insisted on territorial specificity, increased controls on vineyard management and limited yields per hectare in order to adhere to the regulations for the Trentino Superiore DOC. Positive results were quick to come. This great co-operative winery was founded in Mori during the 1950s, recently expanded through the merger with Colli Zugna, and includes more than 600 member growers with the same number of hectares under vine scattered around Rovereto and Vallagarina. In the space of a couple of harvests, all their wines have taken a clear step forward in quality. The most representative product is a Marzemino Superiore, Terre di San Mauro '04. It's a really good Marzemino, a textbook purple in colour with fruity aromas followed by hints of Parma violets. Entry in the mouth is nicely bitterish and the mid palate spreads out soft, elegant and pleasantly spicy, especially in the finish. The fragrant, straw-yellow Trentino Müller Thurgau Pendici del Baldo '05 is very floral and curiously astringent on the nose, showing lovely flavours of sage and still unripe white plums on the palate. The equally floral Pinot Grigio Vigna del Gelso is straw yellow with coppery shades. The other three red wines are more than convincing. The Rosso Reale '04 is a savoury, cellarable Bordeaux blend with nice round tannins. The Lagrein Vigna del Gelso '04 is mature and powerful, just like the Teroldego Vigna del Gelso '04, despite the fact both are still experimental varieties in this part of Trentino.

● Terodelgo V. del Gelso '04	TT	3
● Trentino Lagrein V. del Gelso '04	TT	4*
● Trentino Rosso Reale '04	TT	3
● Trentino Sup. Marzemino d'Isera Terre di San Mauro '04	TT	4
○ Trentino Müller Thurgau Pendici del Baldo '05	TT	4*
○ Trentino Pinot Grigio V. del Gelso '04	T	4
● Trentino Sup. Marzemino d'Isera Terre di San Mauro '03	YY	4

NOGAREDO (TN)

CASTEL NOARNA
FRAZ. NOARNA DI NOGAREDO
VIA CASTELNUOVO, 19
38060 NOGAREDO (TN)
TEL. 0464413295 - 0464435222
www.castelnoarna.com

Marco Zani only presented three wines but what delicious wines they are! Marco has put into practice his belief of doing little but well. At his splendid castle, with help from an experienced Trentino technician, oenologist Francesco Polastri, he not only vinifies the grapes harvested from vineyards along the medieval fortress walls but he also promotes wine-related meetings, conferences and international tastings. His flagship wine is still Bianco di Castelnuovo, dedicated to the fortress where it is made from a blend of riesling, traminer, chardonnay and sauvignon. Though the wine still needs time to express all its potential, it still swept straight through to our final taste-offs. A golden colour – you'd never guess it was fermented in oak – introduces a complex spectrum of aromatics that run from fruit in syrup to oriental spices. The palate is big and caressing with a rich, floral finish. Dedicated to one of the women burned at the stake in the castle courtyard after a summary trial by the Inquisition, the imposing, austere Mercuria '03, from cabernet, lagrein and merlot, is concentrated and dense with great suppleness. To round off, the Lagrein '04 shows more fruit than savouriness with a note of juniper and black spices, boosted by appealing alcohol. These three wines have everything to gain from further time in bottle.

○ Bianco di Castelnuovo '04	TT	5
● Mercuria Rosso '03	TT	5
● Lagrein '04	T	4
○ Bianco di Castelnuovo '02	YY	5
○ Salvanèl '02	YY	3*
○ Trentino Nosiola '02	YY	4
○ Bianco di Castelnuovo '03	YY	5
○ Nosiola '03	YY	4
○ Salvanèl '03	YY	4*
○ Nosiola '04	YY	4
● Romeo '99	YY	5

NOMI (TN)

GRIGOLETTI
VIA GARIBALDI, 12
38060 NOMI (TN)
TEL. 0464834215
www.grigoletti.com

The Grigoletti winemaking dynasty from Nomi has intimate links with this village on the right bank of the river Adige. The area is well suited to the red grape varieties that flourish in the alluvial terrain of the Adige and rather Mediterranean climate created by the sheltering Bondone mountain group on one side and Mount Baldo in front. In fact, the Grigolettis have been able to make the best of these merlot grapes even from recent harvests. The fruit from their historic vineyard has created a velvety, soft-textured wine with remarkable complexity on the palate in the Trentino Merlot Antica Vigna di Nomi '04, which is modern on entry and stylish, long and mouthfilling. It could be the best of the Merlots we have tasted recently in Trentino. The San Martin Vendemmia Tardiva '04 is also excellent. From a blend of five varieties left to raisin on the vine till November, this fragrant white is evolved and intriguing with notes of flowers and ripe fruit before the dynamic palate shows nice drinkability despite its richness. Named for the ancient guild of carriers who transported the still-fermenting must in wooden containers, the attractive cabernet and merlot Gonzalier '03 is a dark ruby with notes of spice and fruit on the nose, good consistency, nice acidity and balance on the palate rounded off by an enjoyably lingering finish. The other wines are sound. The Trentino Marzemino '05 is fresh and bitterish, as is Retiko '04, a pleasant blend of chardonnay and sauvignon.

● Trentino Merlot Antica Vigna di Nomi '04	ꝎꝎ (2 black glasses)	5
○ San Martin V.T. '04	2 black glasses	4
● Gonzalier '03	1 black glass	5
○ Retiko '04	1 black glass	5
● Trentino Marzemino '05	1 black glass	4
● Maso Federico Passito Rosso '01	2 white glasses	5
● Trentino Merlot Antica Vigna di Nomi '01	2 white glasses	4
● Trentino Merlot Antica Vigna di Nomi '02	2 white glasses	5
● Trentino Merlot Antica Vigna di Nomi '03	2 white glasses	5

ROVERÈ DELLA LUNA (TN)

GAIERHOF
VIA IV NOVEMBRE, 51
38030 ROVERÈ DELLA LUNA (TN)
TEL. 0461658514
www.gaierhof.com

The Togn family's new winemaking challenge is Maso Poli, located above the town of Lavis on the Faedo side, and now merged with Gaierhof at Roveré della Luna. These two distinct operations are deliberately diversified though they share the same philosophy: good-quality production that respects the grape varieties to bring out their characters and create wines for a range of markets. For some years now, Luigi Togn has managed the estate with the help of daughters Romina, Martina and Valentina with her husband, wine technician Goffredo Pasolli, in charge respectively of commercial, production and technical matters. The most outstanding wine bottled under the Gaierhof label is a traditional Teroldego Rotaliano, which stands out for its rustic, powerful energy, full colour and length. The other high quality products start with the Müller Thurgau dei Settecento, because the vines are 700, or "settecento", metres above sea level. This wine is itself one of the most aromatic of its type. The unusual standard-label Syrah is satisfying, young and pleasantly spicy. Now we come to Maso Poli. Now work on the new cellar is complete, attention has turned to the wines that spotlight greater concentration on the nose with notes of white-fleshed fruit and jasmine, especially in the Costa Erta, a fine Trentino Chardonnay that offers a fresh, well-sustained palate, rich in citrus, vanilla and mineral notes. Finally, the chardonnay, nosiola and müller thurgau Sorni Bianco is a typical wine from the Lavis hillside and offers approachability, fragrant aromas and good acid backbone.

● Teroldego Rotaliano '04	2 black glasses	4
○ Trentino Chardonnay Costa Erta '04	2 black glasses	4
● Syrah '05	2 black glasses	4
○ Trentino Müller Thurgau Sup. dei Settecento '05	2 black glasses	4
○ Trentino Sorni Bianco Maso Poli '05	1 black glass	4
● Teroldego Rotaliano Sup. '03	2 white glasses	4
○ Trentino Chardonnay Costa Erta '03	2 white glasses	4
● Trentino Moscato Rosa '04	2 white glasses	5
○ Trentino Müller Thurgau Sup. dei Settecento '04	2 white glasses	4

ROVERETO (TN)

NICOLA BALTER
VIA VALLUNGA II, 24
38068 ROVERETO (TN)
TEL. 0464430101

Two refined classic sparklers, two graceful white wines, three red blends and the Barbanico scene-stealer: that sums up the estate of Nicola Balter, a committed red winemaker who has also proved himself skilled at making sparklers. The Trento Brut Riserva '00 is enchanting. The intensity and richness on the nose immediately won our panel over with notes of peach and apricot wrapped in floral sensations. The palate is consistent and full with a dry freshness and lovely lingering finish. In other words, this exemplary Trento is absolutely reliable and increasingly convincing. The traditional Brut with its fine perlage is also good, offering an elegant, aroma-rich nose of bread yeast, acacia honey and apple that recalls the orchards bordering Balter's lovely estate on the Rovereto hillside. It's an area that environmental organizations are attempting to have declared an educational woodland. The Sauvignon '05 is simpler, as is the Clarae '04, a blend of aromatic varieties in clear development. The Barbanico '03 blend of cabernet, merlot and lagrein came close to Three Glasses for its explosive fruit coupled with the finesse of aromas that reveal sensations of incense and liquorice after notes of currant jam. The spicy, savoury palate has refined balance and a long finish. The Lagrein-Merlot '05 is forthright and frank, and the Cabernet Sauvignon '03 is, as always, powerful.

○	Trento Brut Ris. '00	🍷🍷	6
●	Barbanico '03	🍷🍷	5
●	Cabernet Sauvignon '03	🍷🍷	4
○	Clarae '04	🍷🍷	4
○	Trento Brut	🍷🍷	4
●	Lagrein-Merlot '05	🍷	4
○	Sauvignon '05	🍷	4
●	Barbanico '00	YY	5
●	Barbanico '01	YY	5
○	Trento Brut Riserva '99	YY	6
○	Trento Brut Ris. '01	YY	6

ROVERETO (TN)

CONTI BOSSI FEDRIGOTTI
VIA UNIONE, 43
38068 ROVERETO (TN)
TEL. 0464439250
www.bossifedrigotti.com

Isabella Bossi Fedrigotti is a writer who loves wine and not just the wine from the family estate. She has often written about the importance of safeguarding vineyard culture because of the ancient bond of land, vines, eye and heart. Entering the Conti Bossi Fedrigotti estate is like travelling back along the evolution of vines. The future of the family is now entrusted to three siblings who have taken up the reins of the estate with immediately positive results. Maria José is at the helm, assisted by her brother Giampaolo and also the famous writer, Isabella, with collaborators Fabrizio Giacomini and Denis Dalpiaz supervising the oenological side. The results show that Marzemino, Rovereto's symbolic wine, is held in high esteem. There are two convincing 2005 versions but the traditional Marzemino may have the edge on the Superiore. The former is more immediately fragrant, delicate and heady. We thought the second was a little too concentrated, though it is mouthfilling. The legendary Bordeaux blend created in the 1960s, Fojaneghe, is again in the '04 version well made and velvety, foregrounding elegance with a nice attack on the broad, juicy palate. It does fall apart slightly in the finish but there is nice length, although vegetal notes are still there. The unusual Trecento '04 offers complex red berry sensations and has a solid body with confident, well-developed tannins. Altogether delicious.

●	Fojaneghe Rosso '04	🍷🍷	5
●	Trecento '04	🍷🍷	4
●	Trentino Marzemino '05	🍷🍷	4
●	Trentino Sup. Marzemino Sel. Campobove '05	🍷	5
●	Trecento '03	YY	4
●	Trentino Marzemino '03	YY	4
●	Trentino Sup. Marzemino Sel. Campobove '03	YY	4
●	Trentino Marzemino '04	YY	4*
●	Trentino Sup. Marzemino Sel. Campobove '04	YY	4

ROVERETO (TN)

LETRARI
VIA MONTE BALDO, 13/15
38068 ROVERETO (TN)
TEL. 0464480200
www.letrari.it

With almost 60 harvests behind him, Leonello Letrari still encourages his children to manage the family estate innovatively, release new wines and improve the ones that are already well established. Here is a sparkler left on the lees for almost eight years, a Riserva dedicated to the founder of this winery that is now in the hands of his children, oenologist Lucia and manager Paolo Emilio. The powerful Trento Riserva del Fondatore '98 has a deep golden colour with fascinating ripe apple aromas, nice smooth-flowing bubbles, as creamy in appearance as they are in substance, and a well-balanced palate. The Trentino Moscato Rosa '03 is also high quality. Sourced from low-yield vineyards, it is only made during particularly good growing years. The rose petal jam aromas are intense and palate, long and marked by rich spicy notes. On the other hand, Ballistarius suffers from the ups and downs of the 2002 vintage and this time lacks its usual distinguishing fullness and silkiness. The Trentino Cabernet Franc Riserva '02 is more correct with its classic bell pepper and wild fruit notes. The Trentino Marzemino Selezione '05 has good quality and, although firmly in keeping with tradition, tends more towards Parma violets than the typically vinous fragrances of the variety. The exquisite Dulce Vitae '04 is a late-harvest wine from chardonnay and sauvignon. Finally, the new wine, Pinot Grigio Ramato Aes '05, is onionskin hued, acidulous, fruit-forward and tangy yet also very approachable thanks to minerality that gives it thrust and linearity.

●	Trentino Moscato Rosa '03	🍷🍷	7
○	Trento Riserva del Fondatore '98	🍷🍷	6
○	Trento Brut Ris. '01	🍷🍷	6
●	Ballistarius '02	🍷🍷	6
○	Trentino Dulce Vitae '04	🍷🍷	5
○	Pinot Grigio Aes '05	🍷🍷	3
●	Trentino Marzemino Sel. '05	🍷🍷	5
●	Trentino Cabernet Franc Ris. '02	🍷	5
●	Ballistarius '00	YY	6
●	Ballistarius '01	YY	6
○	Trento Brut Ris. '99	YY	6
○	Trento Brut Ris. '00	YY	6
●	Trentino Marzemino Sel. '02	YY	5
●	Trentino Moscato Rosa '02	YY	7
●	Trentino Marzemino Sel. '04	YY	5

ROVERETO (TN)

LONGARIVA
FRAZ. BORGO SACCO
VIA R. ZANDONAI, 6
38068 ROVERETO (TN)
TEL. 0464437200
www.longariva.it

Winemaker Marco Manica is almost obsessive about his vineyards yet he never overdoes intervention in the vineyard, respecting the vines' natural potential. Each vineyard is planted to a single variety to give the individual wines greater character. His Trentino Pinot Bianco Pergole '05 is the best in the region. It's a beautiful wine, from the crystal-clear golden colour with greenish highlights to the broad, floral nose and dynamic palate with remarkable structure thanks to good acid backbone and an unusual softness for Trentino interpretations of the type. Longariva celebrated its 30th anniversary by producing a pair of special Riservas. Marognon '02 is one of the best monovarietal Cabernet Sauvignons we tasted in Trento and embodies the Manica style, his quest for complex, evolved products intended for near meditative drinking. The same approach is obvious in the other 30th-anniversary wine, Tre Cesure '02, a Bordeaux blend red with a dark colour, broad aromas and a fascinatingly sweet palate of red berry fruit, vanilla, coffee and chocolate. As for the other wines, the Trentino Pinot Grigio Graminé '05 is always pleasant, the Trentino Sauvignon Cascari '04 is fresh yet powerful and the Trentino Marzemino Ai Dossi '04 is subtle and delicate. To round off, the prodigious late-harvest Migoléta '04 is intriguing with arresting sweetness played off against substantial acidity.

●	Trentino Cabernet Sauvignon Marognon 30° Anniversario '02	🍷🍷	6
○	Trentino Pinot Bianco Pergole '05	🍷🍷	5
●	Trentino Rosso Tre Cesure 30° Anniversario '02	🍷🍷	6
○	Migoléta '04	🍷🍷	6
○	Trentino Sauvignon Cascari '04	🍷🍷	4
○	Trentino Pinot Grigio Graminé '05	🍷🍷	5
●	Trentino Marzemino Ai Dossi '04	🍷	4
●	Trentino Pinot Nero Zinzèle '00	YY	7
●	Trentino Cabernet Sauvignon Marognon '02	YY	6
●	Trentino Merlot Tovi '02	YY	4
○	Trentino Sauvignon Cascari '03	YY	4

ROVERETO (TN)

Armando Simoncelli
via Navicello, 7
38068 Rovereto (TN)
tel. 0464432373

Armando Simoncelli, assisted by his wife Silvia and their children Anna and Paolo, manages this estate along the Adige riverbed in an ancient alluvial area just outside Rovereto. The well-tended vineyards are in the Marzemino heartland. For a couple of years, Armando has concentrated on improving the land and cellar, leaving just a few parcels of wine to age, but now he is showing off his signature wines. The Trento Brut '02 was first up. Made exclusively from chardonnay in just a few thousand bottles, this sparkler recalls golden apples on both the nose and in the rich fruity notes in the finish. Dry and complex, it has a racy, supple structure but is still young and will improve over the next few years. In contrast, the 2005 growing season was unfavourable for the wine that has made this estate's reputation in the region, Trentino Marzemino. It's no more than good, dry and bitterish but will satisfy those who love this variety. The very interesting Navesèl '03 is not so much a surprise as a confirmation. This Bordeaux blend is sourced from 30-year-old vines and after long barrique-ageing shows a garnet red colour with raspberry and currant notes on the nose. The palate is slightly vegetal, as is frequently the case with Trentino Cabernets, revealing ripe tannins, savouriness and a caressing mouthfeel. The Trentino Chardonnay '05 is good. Again, it comes from old vines and was stainless-steel fermented to enhance the fruity notes of pineapple and banana, with lovely acidity on the consistent palate where there are rich echoes of golden delicious apples.

○	Trento Brut '02	🍷🍷	5
●	Trentino Rosso Navesèl '03	🍷🍷	5
○	Trentino Chardonnay '05	🍷🍷	4
●	Trentino Marzemino '05	🍷	4
●	Trentino Marzemino '00	YY	3*
●	Trentino Rosso Navesèl '00	YY	5
●	Trentino Rosso Navesèl '97	YY	4
●	Trentino Rosso Navesèl '98	YY	4
●	Trentino Rosso Navesèl '99	YY	4

SAN MICHELE ALL'ADIGE (TN)

Endrizzi
loc. Masetto, 2
38016 San Michele all'Adige (TN)
tel. 0461650129
www.endrizzi.it

The Teroldego Rotaliano made with grapes from Maso Camorz is truly great. This enchanting red embodies the production philosophy of Endrizzi, a winery located beneath Castel Monreale, near San Michele all'Adige, and owned by the Endrici family: the name is usually pronounced "Endrizzi" in Trentino. Founded in 1885 and recently expanded, this winery is a splendid balance of ancient and modern. The wines have always had a typically Trentino character that puts the accent on pleasure. Intended mainly for a foreign market, the range aims to bring out the best in the varieties from this zone. Maso Camorz '03 is not the only wine that makes a good showing. Masetto Nero '03, a blend of merlot, cabernet, lagrein and teroldego, has remarkable concentration, lovely silkiness and a powerful palate. Grace and harmony are the strong suits of the Masetto Dulcis '04, a wine from overripe chardonnay, riesling and traminer. The other wines are good, although we had higher expectations for the Gran Masetto '03, a special selection of Teroldego. The whites are fragrant, especially the acidulous, easy-drinking Trentino Müller Thurgau '05, which is always outstanding for its substantial fruit. Both the Trentino Chardonnay '05 and Trentino Pinot Grigio '05 are tangy, juicy, well-made easy drinkers that are ready for the corkscrew.

●	Masetto Nero '03	🍷🍷	5
●	Teroldego Rotaliano Maso Camorz '03	🍷🍷	4
○	Masetto Dulcis '04	🍷🍷	5
●	Gran Masetto '03	🍷	6
○	Trentino Chardonnay Tradizione '05	🍷	4
○	Trentino Müller Thurgau '05	🍷	4
○	Trentino Pinot Grigio Tradizione '05	🍷	4
●	Masetto Nero '02	YY	5
●	Teroldego Rotaliano Maso Camorz '02	YY	4

SAN MICHELE ALL'ADIGE (TN)

Istituto Agrario Provinciale San Michele all'Adige
via Edmondo Mach, 1
38010 San Michele all'Adige (TN)
tel. 0461615252
www.ismaa.it

The Magnificent 15 could be the title for this profile after the scores we awarded to the wines from this outstanding Trentino teaching winery. All 15 wines in our tastings were superb in their absolute typicity, great technique, extreme balance and, for two in particular, impressive complexity. The Trento Mach Riserva del Fondatore, dedicated to Edmondo Mach, who founded the school in 1874, proved to be one of Italy's best sparklers. That could be because it is supervised by cellar manager Enrico Paternoster, who is very attentive to sparkling wine production. The 2002 growing season has given this spumante fruity tones, apple and wisteria fragrances and support to the full, harmonious structure. It never quite manages to assert itself perhaps because of a certain youthful vigour but time can only add to the wine's appeal. We found the monovarietal cabernet franc Trentino Rosso Monastero '04 to be just as good. Wild berry-led fruit follow spices, medicinal herbs and minty shades, and the palate is full and well managed but still too young to show all its potential. From the other excellent bottles, the late-harvest Prepositura is intriguing even though the 2005 lacks the succulence of other vintages. The Bordeaux blend Trentino Rosso Castel San Michele '04 is invitingly ready, the pleasant Moscato Rosa '02 is the pride of the school, and the other wines are absolutely typical, the Nosiola and Pinot Bianco in particular.

○	Trento Mach Riserva del Fondatore '02	TT	5
●	Trentino Rosso Monastero '04	TT	6
●	Trentino Moscato Rosa '02	TT	5
●	Trentino Rosso Castel San Michele '04	TT	5
○	Prepositura '05	TT	5
○	Trentino Nosiola '05	TT	5
○	Trentino Pinot Bianco '05	TT	4
○	Trento Mach Riserva del Fondatore '01	YY	5
●	Trentino Rosso Monastero '03	YY	6
○	Prepositura '04	YY	5
○	Trentino Bianco Monastero '03	YY	5
○	Trentino Pinot Grigio '04	YY	4

SAN MICHELE ALL'ADIGE (TN)

Roberto Zeni
fraz. Grumo
via Stretta, 2
38010 San Michele all'Adige (TN)
tel. 0461650456
www.zeni.tn.it

The 2005 vintage was an important one for this estate on the banks of the Adige, with vineyards sprawling across the valley sides and the Piana Rotaliana in San Michele, Mezzocorona and Lavis. The vintage was particularly important for Sortì – the name means "well done" in the Trentino dialect – a white from an expert blend of pinot bianco, riesling renano and sauvignon skilfully vinified by the Zeni brothers, Roberto and Andrea, after much experimentation. The resulting wine is complex, appealing and intense on the nose. The deep, succulent palate is big and well integrated, showing minerality and notes of tropical fruit as well as golden delicious apple, grapefruit and remarkable acid backbone. It's a product that can stand the test of time. Despite the fact they are committed red winemakers, the Zenis also submitted an excellent, copper-flecked Pinot Grigio Fontane with broad aromas and a juicy palate well sustained by fresh acidity. But the red wines also show quality. The Teroldego Rotaliano Le Albere '04 is fresh and immediate and the Trentino Moscato Rosa '05 is very good indeed. The Zenis have produced this wine for years and it is a benchmark for comparing different interpretations of this challenging variety. Finally, there is a Teroldego from grapes left to dry on rush mats until Christmas Eve. It is the alcohol-rich Ororosso '03, an impenetrably dark vino da meditazione with a dense, full palate. For Trentino, it's a pioneering wine.

○	Sortì '05	TT	5
●	Ororosso '03	TT	5
●	Teroldego Rotaliano Vign. Le Albere '04	TT	4
⊙	Pinot Grigio Vign. Fontane '05	TT	4
●	Trentino Moscato Rosa '05	TT	7
○	Trento Brut Ris. '95	YY	6
●	Teroldego Rotaliano Pini '01	YY	7
●	Trentino Moscato Rosa '04	YY	7
○	Sortì '03	YY	5
○	Sortì '04	YY	5

TRENTO

Abate Nero

Fraz. Gardolo
Sponda Trentina, 45
38014 Trento
tel. 0461246566
www.abatenero.it

This calls for a toast. The Cuvée dell'Abate Riserva spumante won Three Glasses by a landslide, rewarding the dedication of oenologist Luciano Lunelli, former cellarman at Mezzolombardo and founder of this small sparkling wine cellar which for years has been among the best in Trentino. The Riserva has come close to a top award many times thanks to its typically Trentino make-up with complex, consistent aromas and flavours. The 2001 growing season helped create a special base from chardonnay, pinot bianco and pinot nero, guaranteeing excellent, slow second fermentation in bottle. Powerful and complex, it still shows lovely finesse and elegance with an array of aromas as close-knit as they are clear with ripe white-fleshed fruit to the fore. The front palate has fine effervescence splendidly complemented by the solid, almost austere, structure that underlines the calibre of this wine. Our congratulations to Luciano Lunelli, Eugenio de Castel Terlago and their friends and collaborators. Aside from the Cuvée dell'Abate, a round of applause also goes to the other three house sparklers, monovarietal Chardonnays from the 2003 vintage. Accounting for the bulk of the cellar's production, which amounts to fewer than 70,000 bottles overall, the traditional Brut is quaffable, always flavourful and designed for carefree, festive drinking. The ever-dependable Extra Brut is dry and acidulous with lovely mousse and perlage. The Extra Dry is simple and round with a touch of sweetness. But the number one wine is that superb Riserva, which has now received its just reward.

○ Trento Brut Cuvée dell'Abate Ris. '01	▼▼▼	6
○ Trento Abate Nero Brut '03	▼▼	5
○ Trento Abate Nero Extra Brut '03	▼▼	5
○ Trento Abate Nero Extra Dry '03	▼	5
○ Trento Brut Ris. '96	YY	5
○ Trento Cuvée dell'Abate '98	YY	6
○ Trento Brut Cuvée dell'Abate Ris. '99	YY	5

TRENTO

Cavit

via del Ponte di Ravina, 31
38040 Trento
tel. 0461381711
www.cavit.it

Good things come in threes, so they say, and for the third time in a row, Altemasi Graal Brut Riserva has lifted our top prize. This well deserved award is for its fresh notes of white-fleshed fruit on the nose and the elegance of the texture and creaminess on the palate, where all its vitality shines. And remember it's a 1997 wine! Three Glasses also pay tribute to Cavit's commitment to quality across the entire production range from this winemaking colossus. We found this tangibly high quality in practically all the 28 wines submitted to our tasting, some of which earned scores that put them in the finals, like the Quattro Vicariati '03, a Bordeaux blend red from cabernet and merlot. It's well integrated, showing great balance and exquisite drinkability as well as pleasant vegetal notes of bell pepper mingling with cocoa power. We found more quality in the exciting Aréle, a 1996 Vino Santo with light citrus tones, sweetness on the palate and length that left our tasters yearning for more. It's quite unforgettable. There was an honourable mention for the Trento Cantus, a monovarietal Chardonnay with a new name but made to a tried and tested winemaking technique that ensures attractive, and anything but boring, bubbly. The Marzeminos are convincing, the one from the Bottega Vinai line and especially the two crus, Farfossi and Vaioni. The Chardonnay, Pinot Grigio and the rest of the range are all good but we'll have to skip them for lack of space.

○ Trento Altemasi Graal Brut Ris. '97	▼▼▼	6
● Trentino Rosso Quattro Vicariati '03	▼▼	5
○ Trentino Vino Santo Aréle '96	▼▼	8
● Trentino Marzemino Bottega Vinai '04	▼▼	4*
● Trentino Marzemino dei Ziresi Farfossi Sup. '04	▼▼	4
● Trentino Marzemino D'Isera Vaioni Sup. '04	▼▼	4
○ Trentino Chardonnay Bottega Vinai '05	▼▼	4
○ Trentino Pinot Grigio Bottega Vinai '05	▼▼	4
○ Trento Cantus Brut	▼▼	5
○ Trento Altemasi Graal Brut Ris. '95	YYY	6
○ Trento Altemasi Graal Brut Ris. '96	YYY	7
○ Trentino Pinot Grigio Bottega Vinai '04	YY	4
○ Trentino Vendemmia Tardiva Rupe Re '04	YY	4

TRENTO

★ FERRARI
VIA PONTE DI RAVINA, 15
38100 TRENTO
TEL. 0461972311
www.ferrarispumante.it

That symbol of the best in Italian sparkling winemaking, the Giulio Ferrari by the Lunelli brothers, has spent ten years on the lees to give it even more lustre, as if any were needed. The 1997 vintage is a powerful one for a supreme wine that has held onto pole position on the top-quality sparkler grid thanks not just to its aromatic appeal but also to a powerful palate. This spumante-wine has the character, longevity, fullness, energy, elegance, dynamism and sheer drinkability that you only find in a great bottle. There is no mention of Perlé this year since it is still ageing on the lees. The Lunellis have decided to extend its time in bottle to at least five years. It means the place of honour goes to the Perlé Rosé '02, from pinot nero with some chardonnay. This sparkler is the result of years of experimentation to create a significant product and confirms the reliability of this Trentino winery. Its lovely colour introduces peach on the nose, followed by strawberry-like notes. Entry on the palate reveals vibrant, well-gauged effervescence with sensations that are acidulous yet soft at the same time and take you through to a fresh, inviting cherry finish. The other three Ferrari sparklers show classic style and tasting profiles. The delicate Maximum Brut is bubbly and round on the palate while the Brut is fresh and distinctive, even though it's produced in 3,200,000 units. Soft with more than a hint of sugar, the Maximum Demi Sec will satisfy those who like to toast with a touch of sweetness.

○ Trento Giulio Ferrari '97	▼▼▼	8
⊙ Trento Brut Perlé Rosé '02	▼▼	7
○ Trento Brut	▼▼	6
○ Trento Maximum Brut	▼▼	6
○ Trento Démi Sec	▼	5
○ Giulio Ferrari '88	▽▽▽	8
○ Giulio Ferrari '89	▽▽▽	8
○ Giulio Ferrari '90	▽▽▽	8
○ Giulio Ferrari '91	▽▽▽	8
○ Giulio Ferrari '92	▽▽▽	8
○ Giulio Ferrari '93	▽▽▽	8
○ Giulio Ferrari '94	▽▽▽	8
○ Trento Giulio Ferrari '95	▽▽▽	8
○ Trento Giulio Ferrari '96	▽▽▽	8

TRENTO

MASO MARTIS
LOC. MARTIGNANO
VIA DELL'ALBERA, 52
38040 TRENTO
TEL. 0461821057
www.masomartis.it

In just a few years, Maso Martis sparklers have become firm favourites with young people in Trento, thanks to classic method vinification that puts the accent on approachability, immediacy, softness and a soupçon of sweetness. Recent disgorgements of selections carefully monitored by Roberta and Antonio Stelzer also show the top quality of their traditional sparklers and confirm the cellar's youth-friendly style. The Trento Brut is a 2003 vintage chardonnay-pinot nero blend with golden highlights that are slightly more intense than usual. The nose suggests crusty bread and there is a creamy note we find also on the palate. The same format is also clear in the Trento Rosé '03, which is almost entirely from pinot nero, hand-crafted in every detail from the beautiful bright rose colour to the rich, full palate that closes out on a soft, creamy finish. It's convincing and easy to drink. Alongside the two Trentos, there are another two Trentino Chardonnays, the base 2005, vinified for a ready-to-drink white, and the Incanto '04 from a much more careful field selection, vinification and overall ageing to create a significant wine with outstanding vanilla and white-fleshed fruit notes.

○ Trento Brut '03	▼▼	5
⊙ Trento Brut Rosé '03	▼▼	6
○ Trentino Chardonnay L'Incanto '04	▼▼	4
○ Trentino Chardonnay '05	▼	4
○ Trento Brut Ris. '00	▽▽	6
● Trentino Cabernet Sauvignon '00	▽▽	5
○ Trentino Chardonnay L'Incanto '01	▽▽	4
○ Trentino Chardonnay L'Incanto '02	▽▽	4
○ Trento Brut '02	▽▽	5
○ Trentino Chardonnay L'Incanto '03	▽▽	4
● Moscato Rosa '04	▽▽	5

TRENTO

CONTI WALLENBURG
LOC. MARTIGNANO
VIA BASSANO, 3
38100 TRENTO
TEL. 045913399 - 0461821513
www.vinimontresor.it

The Verona-based Montresor family, one of the most celebrated dynasties in the wine sector, has just finished planting new vines across the Martignano hillside, which has excellent exposure to sunlight beneath Monte Calisio. Their products, sparklers as well as still wines, are all finding exciting levels of quality and all are vinified by estate technicians with consultancy from oenologist Enrico Paternoster. The Marquardo '04 is made from a teroldego-lagrein base with splashes of cabernet and merlot and develops a dark ruby colour after slow oak fermentation. The lovely fragrance on the nose, with red berry fruit and ripe blueberries upfront, leads to a close-knit, pleasant palate with a long, complex finish. The Maria Adelaide '05, a blend of chardonnay, pinot bianco, sauvignon and incrocio Manzoni, shows style and aromatic fullness but needs further ageing. And what about their sparklers? The Trento Brut Corte Imperiale has a good bouquet, even though it may be a tad simple in the finish. The pleasant, unusual Cuvée Costantinopoli is a classic rosé from pinot nero that shows acidulous, immediate and is definitely ready for uncorking.

● Marquardo '04	🍷🍷	6
○ Maria Adelaide '05	🍷	6
⊙ Cuvée Costantinopoli Rosé	🍷	5
○ Trento Corte Imperiale Brut	🍷	5
○ Trento Corte Imperiale Brut '02	🥂🥂	5
● Marquardo '03	🥂🥂	6

VILLA LAGARINA (TN)

VILÀR
VIA CAVOLAVILLA, 35
38060 VILLA LAGARINA (TN)
TEL. 0461946012 - 3407243016

Founded by Luigi Spagnolli, the Vilàr estate is constantly evolving from an oenological as well as logistical standpoint. A new structure is going up at Sasso, in Nogaredo, to help solve the problems caused by having headquarters in Villa Lagarina, vineyards scattered across the valley and vinification done at the family cellar in Isera. In the meantime, the wines are improving, the Morela '03 even coming close to Three Glasses. This major red immediately yields sensations of ripe red fruit, cherries to the fore, and also shows quite unusual aromatic timbre and length. This is not just from the varieties used – lagrein, teroldego, merlot and cabernet – but also comes from the nature of the soil, vineyard management techniques that put the vines first and the absence of any invasive technology. In other words, this wine is light in character and deliberately aims for a Villa Lagarina style. Luigi Spagnolli and his companion Ivana Ferrari reserve the same dedication for their Marzemino. On tasting, the 2005 version shows heady, Parma violet notes in the aromas. The palate is full and broad, balanced and enhanced by rich fruity notes that reprise the attractive sweetness. The Cabernet Sauvignon '03 is also good, showing harmonious and spicy with notes of cloves and that vaguely vegetal timbre typical of Cabernets from Trentino. The two white wines, the Nosiola '05 and Traminer '05, are fragrant and flavourful. The latter is still on its way, perhaps because it is sourced from young vines.

● Morela '03	🍷🍷	6
● Cabernet Sauvignon '03	🍷🍷	4
● Trentino Marzemino '05	🍷🍷	4
○ Trentino Nosiola '05	🍷	5
○ Trentino Traminer '05	🍷	5
● Morela '02	🥂🥂	6
● Trentino Marzemino '03	🥂🥂	5
● Trentino Marzemino '04	🥂🥂	5

VOLANO (TN)

CONCILIO
ZONA INDUSTRIALE, 2
38060 VOLANO (TN)
TEL. 0464411000
www.concilio.it

Three wineries in one make up this group, which produces over 8,000,000 bottles a year from more than 500 hectares under vine. The cellars for vinification and ageing at company headquarters in Volano are in continuous expansion and equipped with state-of-the-art winemaking technology, including some of the most advanced computerized microfiltration and bottling plants in Europe. The Concilio motto is quality, style and personality and the group diversifies its efforts by developing its other wineries, some even in Sicily, while never neglecting to respect for the Trentino tradition. Proof of this comes from the Chardonnay '05, which immediately stood out at our tastings. The range of aromatic shadings is so broad it seems like an apple orchard on the nose. The aromas are boosted by a good attack on the tangy palate, rich in pulp and long with a balanced acidity that gives a glimpse of further development in the cellar. To sum up, this Chardonnay is in a Trentino-style yet also has an international side to its character. The Sauvignon is the result of a particularly meticulous selection and shows off varietal notes of pineapple and grapefruit with lovely floral shades and fullness on the palate. Only one red wine was submitted, the delicate, quaffable Pinot Nero Riserva '03, which is aimed at a market segment looking for an immediately enjoyable wine. The other whites are all well typed, with the usual special mention going to the Traminer Aromatico.

○	Trentino Chardonnay '05	🍷🍷	4
●	Trentino Pinot Nero Ris. '03	🍷	4
○	Trentino Sauvignon '05	🍷	4
○	Trentino Traminer Sel. '05	🍷	4
●	Trentino Rosso Mori Vecio '01	YY	5
●	Teroldego Rotaliano Braide '03	YY	4
●	Trentino Marzemino Mozart '03	YY	4

VOLANO (TN)

EUGENIO ROSI
VIA TAVERNELLE, 3B
38060 VOLANO (TN)
TEL. 0464461375 - 3400611047
www.vignaioli.trentino.it

Although Esegesi is his best wine, artisan-winemaker Eugenio Rosi's touch is particularly obvious in the Dòron. As its Greek name suggests, the Dòron '03 is a gift of nature. Though produced in less than 2,000 half bottles, it is exquisite, rare, striking, sweet yet never cloying and a true delight for those few wine lovers who will manage to get hold of a glass. The Trentino Marzemino Poiema '04, from marzemino gentile, shows an elegance and power seldom seen in a marzemino. Its purple hue precedes a full, intense nose and savoury palate with nice thrust and length. Trentino Rosso Esegesi '02 is a blend of mainly cabernet with a splash of merlot. Rosi has been striving to achieve a wine like this for years. He knows that to make a great product starting with just a few estate vines and difficult cellar logistics, considering he vinifies and ages in locations that are far apart from one another, you have to be able to interpret what the growing season has to offer. Eugenio harvests in several different passes, leaving some parcels of grapes to dry on rush mats and puts off bottling for as long as possible. In this way, he has managed to make a top-quality wine even from a challenging harvest like 2002. That takes skill. Esegesi has body to spare and the elegant, supple palate reveals a remarkable tannic structure. After an almost aggressive attack, it slowly wins you over with a lingering, velvet-smooth finish.

●	Trentino Rosso Esegesi '02	🍷🍷	5
●	Dòron '03	🍷🍷	6
●	Trentino Marzemino Poiema '04	🍷🍷	5
●	Trentino Rosso Esegesi '00	YY	5
●	Dòron '01	YY	6
●	Trentino Marzemino Poiema '01	YY	5
●	Trentino Rosso Esegesi '01	YY	5
●	Dòron '02	YY	6
●	Trentino Marzemino Poiema '02	YY	5
●	Trentino Marzemino Poiema '03	YY	5

OTHER WINERIES

Alessandro Secchi

Fraz. Serravalle di Ala
loc. Coleri, 10
38060 Ala (TN)
tel. 0464696647 - www.secchivini.it

Alessandro Secchi produces a sound range of Vallagarina-style wines named after minerals as if they were precious stones. The Berillo d'Oro, a chardonnay-based blend, shows good concentration, stylish, structured texture and nice long finish. The Bordeaux-style red Corindone is as full as usual.

● Corindone Rosso '03	TT	5
○ Berillo d'Oro '05	T	4
● Corindone Rosso '02	YY	5
● Realgar '04	YY	4

Bongiovanni

loc. Sabbionara
via Sant' Antonio, 28
38063 Avio (TN)
tel. 0464684388

A small estate in the Avio hills, Bongiovanni releases well-made, upfront wines at reasonable prices for carefree everyday drinking. The Enantio '04 from lambrusco a foglia frastagliata is always sound. The Merlot '04 slips down easily and the Pinot Grigio '05 is well typed an uncomplicated.

● Trentino Enantio Terra dei Forti '04	TT	5
● Trentino Merlot '04	T	4
○ Trentino Pinot Grigio '05	T	4

Spagnolli

via G. B. Rosina, 4a
38060 Isera (TN)
tel. 0464409054
www.vinispagnolli.it

The Spagnolli family has always made wine seriously and offers a nice selection. Outstanding as usual is the Marzemino, with its austere impact and attractive mouthfeel. The unique yet convincing, dry Moscato Giallo is ideal as an aperitif, the Tebro reliable and the Nosiola savoury.

● Trentino Marzemino '05	TT	4
● Trentino Rosso Tebro '02	T	5
○ Trentino Moscato Giallo '05	T	4
○ Trentino Nosiola '05	T	4

De Vescovi Ulzbach

P.zza Garibaldi, 12
38016 Mezzocorona (TN)
tel. 0461605648
www.devescoviulzbach.it

Growers since 1708, De Vescovi Ulzbach have bottled their wines for a couple of harvests now with brilliant results. The base Teroldego is excellent and Riserva Vigilius is also very good. Both are opulent in style. Production is still small, but we think the wines are promising. We'll be back.

● Teroldego Rotaliano Vigilius Ris. '03	TT	6
● Teroldego Rotaliano '04	TT	5

CIPRIANO FEDRIZZI
VIA 4 NOVEMBRE, 1
38017 MEZZOLOMBARDO (TN)
TEL. 0461602328

A convinced Rotaliano red wine man, Giovanni Fedrizzi produces fewer than 35,000 bottles of only Teroldego and Lagrein. He makes two Teroldegos, with the Due Vigneti selection even richer and more concentrated than usual. The current Teroldego is good and the Lagrein fresh.

● Teroldego Rotaliano Due Vigneti '04	5
● Trentino Lagrein '04	4
● Teroldego Rotaliano '05	4

REDONDÈL
VIA ROMA, 28
38017 MEZZOLOMBARDO (TN)
TEL. 0461601618

A self-taught Teroldego maker, Paolo Zanini continues along his personal production path. The base Teroldego is an immediate, easy-drinking wine. Produced only in the best growing seasons, Mezum is complex and deep, yet also manages to be pleasant and very drinkable.

● Teroldego Rotaliano Mezum '04	5
● Teroldego Rotaliano '04	5
● Teroldego Rotaliano '02	5
● Teroldego Rotaliano Mezum '03	5

LUIGI ZANINI
VIA ROMA, 24 - VIA DE GASPERI, 42
38017 MEZZOLOMBARDO (TN)
TEL. 0461601496
www.zaniniluigi.com

Teroldego and Teroldego: Oscar Zanini always manages to hit the bull's-eye with the two wines he presents. They are excellent, albeit perhaps less powerful this time than in other years, but still pleasant and flavourful. The late-harvest chardonnay Gocce di Sole is good.

● Teroldego Rotaliano Le Cervare '04	5
○ Gocce di Sole '03	6
● Teroldego Rotaliano '05	3

RICCARDO BATTISTOTTI
VIA 3 NOVEMBRE, 21
38060 NOMI (TN)
TEL. 0464834145
www.battistotti.com

Expert cellarman Luciano Battistotti skilfully runs his family's estate, known for its typical wines, above all Marzemino. The Selezione Verdini is stylish and elegant; the base Marzemino is traditional and pleasant. The Moscato Rosa, always sound, is released in 900 top-quality half bottles.

● Trentino Marzemino Verdini '04	5
● Trentino Moscato Rosa '04	6
● Trentino Marzemino '05	4
● Trentino Marzemino Verdini '02	5

CANTINA SOCIALE DI NOMI
VIA ROMA, 1
38060 NOMI (TN)
TEL. 0464834195
www.athesiavini.it

This long-standing co-operative winery has shifted its production strategies to tradition, diversified commercial efforts, set up export companies and expanded its Sicilian winery. Selected from the best plots in Vallagarina, the Merlot and Marzemino are reliable and very good.

● Trentino Merlot Le Campagne '03	4
● Trentino Marzemino Le Fornas '05	4
● Trentino Merlot Antichi Portali '02	4

CANTINA RIVA DEL GARDA
VIA LUTTI, 10
38066 RIVA DEL GARDA (TN)
TEL. 0464522133
www.agririva.it

The new structure will start up in a few months, offering appealing wines from the Trentino shore of Lake Garda. The good-quality range is sensibly priced. The well-made classic method sparkler is full and convincing. The Merlot Créa, Chardonnay Lorè and Bordeaux Gére are all ready to drink.

○ Trento Cuvée D'Antan	4
● Gére '05	4
○ Trentino Chardonnay Lorè '05	4
● Trentino Merlot Créa '05	4

CESARINI SFORZA
FRAZ. RAVINA - VIA STELLA, 9
38040 TRENTO
TEL. 0461382200
www.cesarinisforza.com

This winery is in the Other Wineries only for reasons of space. The ambitious new sparklers from Cesarini Sforza, now under new management, will be ready in a few years. Meanwhile, the Trento Tridentum '02 and Brut Rosé are excellent. The other major products will have to wait for the next Guide.

○ Trento Tridentum '02	🍷🍷	5
⊙ Trento Cuvée Brut Rosé	🍷🍷	4
○ Trento Cuvée Brut	YY	5
⊙ Trento Cuvée Brut Rosé	YY	4

LUNELLI
VIA PONTE DI RAVINA, 15
38100 TRENTO
TEL. 0461972311
www.ferrarispumante.it

The Lunellis have diversified production with wineries in Tuscany and Umbria. They only grow white grapes in Trento and this year only presented Trentino Superiore Chardonnay Villa Margon '04, a wine with the customary class and style of all the famous sparklers from Ferrari.

○ Trentino Chardonnay Villa Margon '04	🍷🍷	5
● Trentino Rosso Maso Le Viane '00	YY	6
● Trentino Rosso Maso Le Viane '01	YY	6
● Trentino Pinot Nero Maso Montalto '03	YY	6

DIEGO E FRANCESCO MOSER
LOC. MEANO
38040 TRENTO
TEL. 0461990786 - 3497325879

Cycling champion Francesco Moser built this winery, with its splendid estate and country inn, in the Gardolo hills between Trento and Lavis. The Lagrein and Müller Thurgau already show personality. The Lagrein is fruity and full, the Müller Thurgau, pleasantly acidulous and very easy to drink.

● Lagrein Deamater '05	🍷🍷	5
○ Müller Thurgau '05	🍷	4

GIOVANNI POLI
LOC. SANTA MASSENZA
VIA VEZZANO S. MASSENZA, 37
38070 VEZZANO (TN)
TEL. 0461864119 - www.poligiovanni.it

Father and son team Giovanni and Graziano Poli are Nosiola makers as well as expert distillers. The Nosiola Goccia d'Oro '05 is good, if not very typical. The same goes for Vino Santo Emblemi d'Amor '00, again from nosiola, which is rich and mellow yet with a promising young vigorous tone.

○ Trentino Vino Santo Emblemi d'Amor '00	🍷🍷	6
○ Trentino Nosiola Goccia d'Oro '05	🍷🍷	3
○ Trentino Nosiola Goccia d'Oro '04	YY	4
○ Trentino Vino Santo '99	YY	6

FRANCESCO POLI
LOC. SANTA MASSENZA
VIA AL LAGO
38070 VEZZANO (TN)
TEL. 0461340090 - www.francescopoli.it

Expert distillers and competent winemakers, Poli make a white Maiano '04, from nosiola left to overripen on the vine and rush mats as part of the Ora Project. It's very good, warm and harmonious. The rich, appealing Vino Santo '98 is clearly a major wine and the Nosiola Sottovi '05 is fragrant.

○ Maiano Bianco '04	🍷🍷	5
○ Trentino Vino Santo '98	🍷🍷	7
○ Trentino Nosiola V. Sottovi '05	🍷	4

VOLANO
VIA ZUCCHELLI, 5
38060 VOLANO (TN)
TEL. 0464410455

The Volano Marzemino dei Ziresi follows the ups and downs of its growing year and there were good scores for the 2004 vintage. The Bordeaux red Salengo '03 is full and flavourful. It's named after Salenghi, the area along the shore of the Adige where the Raffaelli family vineyards are located.

● Trentino Marzemino dei Ziresi Sup. '04	🍷🍷	5
● Salengo '03	🍷	4

ALTO ADIGE

When even a major region with as much potential as Alto Adige goes from 18 to 23 – or rather 24, as we'll explain later – Three Glass awards, when the number of estate profiles rises from 80 to 87 and when there are also two national awards – one to Produttori di Caldaro's Serenade for Sweet Wine of the Year and the other to Peter Pliger for Sustainable Viticulture – some might call it a triumph. But given the technical capabilities and overall organization of Alto Adige's winemaking, "si può dare di più" – they could give more – as the popular song goes. We are not exaggerating. Alto Adige winemaking has for some time been more than just large co-operative wineries producing nice wines at a good price plus a few private estates here and there. One look at the Three Glass awards shows how things have changed for the better, both for Alto Adige wines and consumers. Eight awards went to co-operative wineries, seven to private estates and eight to small producers. We think this is all to the good and offers another real chance for the whole sector at a difficult time when the sector's economy is in the doldrums but showing encouraging signs of recovery. In fact, Alto Adige producers are the first to see how important it is to be able to go to market with a range of products that are different in terms of style, numbers and prices, yet all with the common denominators of typicity and quality. In consequence, they have put petty differences behind them. The big co-operatives are not resting on their laurels and have garnered a nice series of Three Glass awards beginning with the long-established Termeno, San Michele Appiano, Colterenzio, Bolzano, Terlano, Caldaro and Valle Isarco wineries. Results from private estates were impressive, to say the least, with the clear success of Elena Walch and Abbazia di Novacella, which won two Three Glass awards each, the triumph of Cantina Muri and Haas and the welcome return of Tiefenbrunner and its signature Feldmarschall von Fenner zu Fennberg. Major results also came from small producers, adding spice to the Alto Adige scene. Valle Isarco is proving to be one of the most dynamic areas with Three Glasses for young Christian Kerschbaumer from Garlider and for Obermairlhof from Haderburg's owner, Alois Ochsenreiter. But there was also a strong showing from Valle Venosta and the Bolzano area with the Riesling from Falkenstein, the magnificent Lagrein Riserva from Georg Ramoser and new Three Glass winner Loacker. As for the reds, the Lagreins are very good, flaunting more definition, elegance and a distinct sense of place. The whites are more balanced and at last generally have less alcohol after years of constant, worrying increases. The 2005 Schiavas were simply delicious, a fact underlined by the retrospective number 24 Three Glass award to the Gschleier '90 from Cornaiano.

ANDRIANO/ANDRIAN (BZ)

CANTINA PRODUTTORI ANDRIANO

VIA DELLA CHIESA, 2
39010 ANDRIANO/ANDRIAN (BZ)
TEL. 0471510137
www.andrianer-kellerei.it

Cantina Produttori Andriano presented us with a wonderful series of wines this year. Oenologist Alber Sinn has managed this small winery for more than 20 years and although is not a man who loves to be the centre of attention, he amazes us year after year with good quality wines. Nor are these restricted to the premium lines, Tor di Lupo and Sonnengut, which Andriano has always sold at more than reasonable prices. Contributing to this success are the 105 member growers, who farm a total of 102 hectares under the guiding hand of its president, Hansjörg Hafner. The complex Lagrein Sonnengut Riserva '03 shows a lot of extract on the palate, with notes of pepper and cocoa powder. Deep, dynamic and long, it thoroughly deserved to go through to the finals. A bit below this is the Lagrein Tor di Lupo '04, which shows full, spicy, balsamic and mineral. The other two reds are also top quality. Merlot Sonnengut Riserva '03 shows great concentration and a long, powerful finish while Cabernet Tor di Lupo '03 is intense, mineral, juicy and dynamic. The well-typed Schiava Sonnengut Justiner '05, one of the best from the zone, is fruity, intense, full, elegant and easy drinking. Whites not to miss include the Traminer Aromatico Tor di Lupo '05, a fresh, mineral wine with elegant with touches of aromatic herbs and roses, the long, enjoyable Terlano Sauvignon '05 with its aromas of aniseed and tomato, and the Terlano Pinot Bianco Sonnengut '05, which is well made but a bit woody. The winery made the right decision to let the '04 Merlot Tor di Lupo age another year.

●	A. A. Lagrein Ris. Sel. Sonnengut '03	TT	5
●	A. A. Cabernet Tor di Lupo '03	TT	5
●	A. A. Merlot Sonnengut Ris. '03	TT	5
●	A. A. Lagrein Scuro Tor di Lupo '04	TT	6
○	A. A. Gewürztraminer Tor di Lupo '05	TT	5
●	A. A. Schiava Sonnengut Justiner '05	TT	4
○	A. A. Terlano Sauvignon '05	TT	4
○	A. A. Terlano Pinot Bianco Sonnengut '05	T	4
●	A. A. Cabernet Tor di Lupo '00	YYY	5
●	A. A. Lagrein Scuro Tor di Lupo '00	YYY	5
●	A. A. Lagrein Scuro Tor di Lupo '02	YY	6
○	A. A. Gewürztraminer Sel. Tor di Lupo '04	YY	6

APPIANO/EPPAN (BZ)

JOSEF BRIGL

LOC. SAN MICHELE
VIA MADONNA DEL RIPOSO, 3
39057 APPIANO/EPPAN (BZ)
TEL. 0471662419
www.brigl.com

This is one of the biggest, longest established wineries in Alto Adige, producing 2,000,000 bottles from 50 estate-owned hectares in the region's finest wine country. There is a great heritage here for the earliest reports of the winery go back to the 14th century, but there is also an ability to adapt to the needs of an ever more demanding market. Ignaz and Josef Brigl should be satisfied with this year's achievements. All the wines tasted earned better than positive scores beginning with the estate's trademark product, Lagrein Briglhof Riserva '03. Intense fruity aromas with balsamic shades usher in a palate with sturdy tannins balanced against a solid backbone vibrant with fragrant acidity. The long, extended finish makes it a real classic. The fresh, well-typed Sauvignon '05 expresses vibrant dynamism and pronounced minerality on medium-dense structure. The Gewürztraminer Windegg '05 has clear tropical fruit and acacia honey aromas before offering a balanced profile on the palate that only lacks a bit of thrust in the finish. From the difficult 2003 growing year, the Pinot Bianco Haselhof '05 and Pinot Nero Kreuzbichler are true to type and well made. These results are more than just creditable.

●	A. A. Lagrein Briglhof Ris. '03	TT	5
○	A. A. Gewürztraminer Windegg '05	TT	4
○	A. A. Sauvignon '05	TT	4*
●	A. A. Pinot Nero Kreuzbichler '03	T	5
○	A. A. Pinot Bianco Haselhof '05	T	4*
●	A. A. Lagrein Scuro Briglhof '01	YY	5
●	A. A. Lagrein Scuro Briglhof '02	YY	5
●	A. A. Lagrein Scuro Briglhof '03	YY	5
○	A. A. Pinot Bianco Haselhof '04	YY	4*

★ Cantina Produttori Colterenzio

Loc. Cornaiano/Girlan
strada del Vino, 8
39050 Appiano/Eppan (BZ)
tel. 0471664246
www.colterenzio.com

Colterenzio made an impressive show of strength this year, winning Three Glasses for a phenomenal '05 version of Gewürztraminer Cornell, plus another two wines in the finals and another ten wines that received the better than respectable Two Glass rating. This outcome matches the historic and economic importance of a winery that this year presented a new Kellermeister, Martin Lemayr, originally from Hofstätter. Martin seems to have fitted in straight away, much to the joy of the stern, demanding president, Luis Raifer. The Gewürztraminer we admired manages to marry typicity, significant extractive weight, acidity and alcohol, in a wine that makes balance its greatest feature. This was not easy, given that the type in years past has produced bottles that were too concentrated and heavy. But what can we say about another classic that won Three Glasses in its '97 version, the Pinot Bianco Weisshaus '05, one of the best from the vintage. We found it tangy, almost a little salty and nicely dynamic. We would stress that a winery's true worth comes mostly from its simpler, standard-label wines. Taste for example the vibrant Sauvignon Prail '05, which went through to our finals, or the Chardonnay Altkirch, Pinot Grigio Puiten or Pinot Bianco from the classic line, all 2005s. The Sauvignon Lafoa, Chardonnay Cornell and Pinot Bianco Cornell, all from 2004, are better than good. While awaiting next year's release of the Cabernet Sauvignon Lafoa '03, wisely left to age another year, our compliments go to Schreckbichl/Colterenzio.

○ A. A. Gewürztraminer Cornell '05	🍷🍷🍷	5
○ A. A. Pinot Bianco Weisshaus '05	🍷🍷	4*
○ A. A. Sauvignon Prail '05	🍷🍷	4*
● A. A. Cabernet Sauvignon Kastèlt Ris. '03	🍷🍷	5
● A. A. Cornelius '03	🍷🍷	6
● A. A. Merlot Siebeneich Ris. '03	🍷🍷	4*
○ A. A. Chardonnay Cornell '04	🍷🍷	5
○ A. A. Gewürztraminer Passito Cornell '04	🍷🍷	6
○ A. A. Pinot Bianco Cornell '04	🍷🍷	5
○ A. A. Sauvignon Lafoa '04	🍷🍷	6
○ A. A. Chardonnay Altkirch '05	🍷🍷	4*
○ A. A. Pinot Bianco '05	🍷🍷	4*
○ A. A. Pinot Grigio Puiten '05	🍷🍷	4*

APPIANO/EPPAN (BZ)

Cantina Produttori Cornaiano

Loc. Cornaiano/Girlan
via San Martino, 24
39050 Appiano/Eppan (BZ)
tel. 0471662403
www.girlan.it

Gherard Kofler's arrival at Girlan last year was more of a homecoming, since he was born and still lives in Cornaiano, but he has shifted quality up a notch. Credit also goes to winery management beginning with the director Helmut Meraner and marketing manager Christian Oberdöfer. Although the six wines in our finals were a reassuring sign, there was also the impeccable all-round performance. One of the most famous wines in Alto Adige, the near legendary Schiava Gschleier, was back, surprising us by being released as a standard label. Changing style might seem risky but Gherard has skilfully managed to preserve all the wine's established characteristics, great minerality, dense tannic weight and depth, adding extraordinary freshness both on the nose, where the spicy, floral elements are crystal clear, and the palate, where there is remarkable style and complexity. We had the good fortune to taste a '90 that was so simply spectacular we enthusiastically awarded it Three retrospective Glasses. The two '05 Sauvignons, the SelectArt Flora selection and the attractive base Indra, are both good. The Pinot Bianco Plattenriegl '05, Moscato Rosa Passito Pasithea '04 and Cabernet Sauvignon '03 selection are well typed. The Gewürztraminer SelectArt Flora '05 is austere, fresh and minerally. Bianco '05, a pinot grigio-led blend with added pinot bianco and sauvignon, is perfect, like the other Schiava, the Fass N.9, again from the same vintage. They haven't seen such a well-deserved collection of Glassware like this for some time at Cornaiano.

● A. A. Cabernet Sauvignon SelectArt Flora '03	🍷🍷	5
● A. A. Moscato Rosa Passito Pasithea Rosa '04	🍷🍷	6
○ A. A. Pinot Bianco Plattenriegl '05	🍷🍷	4*
○ A. A. Sauvignon Indra '05	🍷🍷	4*
○ A. A. Sauvignon SelectArt Flora '05	🍷🍷	5
● A. A. Schiava Gschleier SelectArt Flora '05	🍷🍷	4*
○ Pasithea Oro '04	🍷🍷	6
○ A. A. Bianco '05	🍷🍷	4
○ A. A. Gewürztraminer SelectArt Flora '05	🍷🍷	5
● A. A. Schiava Fass N. 9 '05	🍷🍷	4*
● A. A. Schiava Gschleier '90	🍷🍷🍷 (retrospective)	4

APPIANO/EPPAN (BZ)

K. Martini & Sohn

Loc. Cornaiano/Girlan
via Lamm, 28
39050 Appiano/Eppan (BZ)
tel. 0471663156
www.martini-sohn.it

K. Martini & Sohn has established itself as one of the most solid, reliable wineries in the region. Founded in 1976 by Karl Martini and his son Gabriel, it obtains around 350,000 bottles a year from 30 estate hectares, some owned and some rented. This mid-sized property performs well across the entire range presented and has understood how to marry tradition with technological innovation. Sauvignon Palladium '05 is particularly good although it fails to reach the levels that led to a Three Glass award last year. It is still among the best in its type, especially for the elegance of aromas that avoid the "sauvage" notes that so often coarsen Sauvignons. The zesty, minerally and very expressive palate shows a particularly dynamic finish. The singular Riesling '05 has spicy, vegetal notes on the nose and a taut, balanced palate with good progression. The Chardonnay Maturum '05 is also convincing with notes of tropical fruit and pink grapefruit and a balanced, pleasantly drinkabile palate. Lagrein Rueslhof Gurnzan '04 is dense and powerful yet fresh and stylish at the same time. The Pinot Bianco Lamm, Chardonnay Palladium and Lago di Caldaro Felton, all from the 2005 vintage, are extremely competently made.

●	A. A. Lagrein Scuro Rueslhof Gurnzan '04	▼▼	4*
○	A. A. Chardonnay Maturum '05	▼▼	4
○	A. A. Riesling '05	▼▼	4*
○	A. A. Sauvignon Palladium '05	▼▼	4
●	A. A. Lagrein-Cabernet Coldirus Palladium '04	▼	4
○	A. A. Chardonnay Palladium '05	▼	4
●	A. A. Lago di Caldaro Cl. Felton '05	▼	3
○	A. A. Pinot Bianco Lamm '05	▼	4
○	A. A. Sauvignon Palladium '04	▽▽▽	4*
●	A. A. Lagrein Scuro Rueslhof Gurnzan '03	▽▽	4*
○	A. A. Chardonnay Maturum '04	▽▽	4
○	A. A. Chardonnay Palladium '04	▽▽	4*

APPIANO/EPPAN (BZ)

Josef Niedermayr

Loc. Cornaiano/Girlan
via Casa di Gesù, 15
39050 Appiano/Eppan (BZ)
tel. 0471662451
www.niedermayr.it

A quick snapshot of Josef Niedermayr's estate would show a reliable winery, managed with extreme professionalism and one of the leading actors on the viticultural scene in Alto Adige with 16 hectares and around 350,000 bottles a year. In this edition of the Guide, which has seen substantial progress in the region's winemaking sector, this estate put two wines in our finals and missed our highest prize by just a hair. Aureus is always the leader, but it is accompanied by a series of completely respectable wines. A white from part-dried chardonnay and sauvignon with a little gewürztraminer, the Aureus '04 is now a classic. It is hard to resist the charms of its delicately musty, citron peel aromas and sweet yet never cloying flavour well supported by generous acidity. Lagrein Blacedelle '05 has great backbone and, although only a standard-label, shows intense fruit and minerally, spicy notes. The palate is full and tannins are robust, yet never rough, and supported by good acidity. The typical, fragrant Gewürztraminer Lage Doss '05 shows floral and tropical fruit aromas. What struck us was the taut, tight weave from nose to back palate. One of the estate's historic wines, the concentrated, juicy Euforius '04, is from 60 per cent cabernet with equal parts of lagrein and merlot. Not surprisingly, the Lagrein Riserva '04, the delicious Schiava Ascherhof '05, the Sauvignon Allure '05 and the classic Santa Maddalena '05 are all very well made.

○	A. A. Aureus '04	▼▼	7
●	A. A. Lagrein Gries Blacedelle '05	▼▼	5
●	Euforius '04	▼▼	6
○	A. A. Gewürztraminer Lage Doss '05	▼▼	6
●	A. A. Lagrein Aus Gries Ris. '04	▼	6
●	A. A. Santa Maddalena '05	▼	4
○	A. A. Sauvignon Allure '05	▼	5
●	A. A. Schiava Ascherhof '05	▼	4
○	A. A. Aureus '98	▽▽▽	6
○	A. A. Aureus '99	▽▽▽	6
○	A. A. Sauvignon Allure '04	▽▽	5
●	Euforius '99	▽▽	5

APPIANO/EPPAN (BZ)

IGNAZ NIEDRIST
LOC. CORNAIANO/GIRLAN
VIA RONCO, 5
39050 APPIANO/EPPAN (BZ)
TEL. 0471664494

Ignaz Niedrist is one of the most serious, reliable producers in the entire province of Bolzano. A professional, intelligent winemaker and grower, he refuses to produce caricatured, showy wines, always looking for balance and elegance. It is no accident Ignaz has always tackled difficult varieties like riesling, pinot nero and sauvignon. From his six and a half hectares near Appiano, he produces around 30,000 bottles of always well-made, typical wines that this year perhaps lacked that pinch more personality to be completely successful. We were most convinced by Terlano Pinot Bianco '05, sourced from the Prantzoll and Guggen vineyards at around 500 metres above sea level. Introduced by subtle floral and wild strawberry aromas, the palate shows a perfect Niedrist-style, spirited, minerally take, well supported by dynamic acidity. The Lagrein Berger Gei '04 is again among the best in its vintage. Sourced from the vineyard of the same name in Gries and barrique-aged for 14 months, this red has an intense spice and tobacco bouquet. Its dense palate shows a confident almost earthy minerality and a finish with a confident progression. The concentrated Terlano Sauvignon '05 shows rich ripe fruit notes and expresses customary grip in its development on the palate. The Pinot Nero '04 is fresh and quaffable though the slightly dusty tannins disturb its enjoyment. Frankly we expected more from the Riesling '05 and found it a bit too lean though still pleasant. But we always expect the best from Ignaz.

●	A. A. Lagrein Berger Gei '04	▼▼	5
○	A. A. Terlano Pinot Bianco '05	▼▼	4*
○	A. A. Terlano Sauvignon '05	▼▼	5
●	A. A. Pinot Nero '04	▼	5
○	A. A. Riesling Renano '05	▼	4
○	A. A. Riesling Renano '00	▽▽	4
○	A. A. Terlano Pinot Bianco '04	▽▽	4*
●	A. A. Lagrein Berger Gei '01	▽▽	5
●	A. A. Lagrein Berger Gei '02	▽▽	5
○	A. A. Terlano Pinot Bianco '02	▽▽	4
●	A. A. Lagrein Berger Gei '03	▽▽	5
●	A. A. Merlot Mühlweg '03	▽▽	5
○	A. A. Riesling Renano '04	▽▽	5
○	A. A. Terlano Sauvignon '04	▽▽	5

APPIANO/EPPAN (BZ)

★ CANTINA PRODUTTORI
SAN MICHELE APPIANO
VIA CIRCONVALLAZIONE, 17/19
39057 APPIANO/EPPAN (BZ)
TEL. 0471664466
www.stmichael.it

Writing the profile for the Cantina Produttori San Michele Appiano is never easy. This is the winery that sparked the explosion and success, both critical and commercial, of Alto Adige wines in Italy and worldwide. We also find an equally massive personality in Hans Terzer, who literally revolutionized winemaking methods in the region during the 1990s. A lot of water has passed under the bridge but this co-operative winery and its Kellermeister are always at the top, in spite of ever-tougher competition. There may be no need to mention that Sauvignon Sanct Valentin '05 has again won Three Glasses, as it has every year since 1994, simply because it is always the best Alto Adige Sauvignon despite being regularly produced in over 100,000 bottles. Rich yet elegant, concentrated yet fresh and minerally: that is Sanct Valentin. The name says it all. Just to show Hans may now be running on automatic pilot with this type, the second line Sauvignon Lahn '05 is simply delicious. But even the sweet wines always show high quality. Just taste the Bianco Passito Comtess '04, from 70 per cent gewürztraminer and equal parts sauvignon and riesling, all part-dried, with its citrus-like aromas and perfect balance of sweetness and acidity. As usual, the best wines include Gewürztraminer Sanct Valentin '05 and Pinot Bianco Schulthauser '05 is again utterly typical. What can we say about reds like the Cabernet '03, Pinot Nero '03 and Lagrein '03, all from the Sanct Valentin line and all with impeccable style? The old lion's claws are still sharp.

○	A. A. Sauvignon St. Valentin '05	▼▼▼	5
○	A. A. Bianco Passito Comtess '04	▼▼	6
○	A. A. Gewürztraminer St. Valentin '05	▼▼	5
●	A. A. Cabernet St. Valentin '03	▼▼	6
●	A. A. Lagrein St. Valentin '03	▼▼	6
●	A. A. Merlot St. Valentin '03	▼▼	6
●	A. A. Pinot Nero St. Valentin '03	▼▼	6
○	A. A. Chardonnay St. Valentin '04	▼▼	5
○	A. A. Pinot Bianco St. Valentin '04	▼▼	5
○	A. A. Pinot Grigio St. Valentin '04	▼▼	5
○	A. A. Chardonnay Merol '05	▼▼	4
○	A. A. Pinot Bianco Schulthauser '05	▼▼	4*
○	A. A. Riesling Montiggl '05	▼▼	4*
○	A. A. Sauvignon Lahn '05	▼▼	4*

APPIANO/EPPAN (BZ)

CANTINA SOCIALE SAN PAOLO
LOC. SAN PAOLO
VIA CASTEL GUARDIA, 21
39050 APPIANO/EPPAN (BZ)
TEL. 0471662183
www.cantinasanpaolo.com

Splendid vineyards in the heart of the Alto Adige frame the town of San Paolo. In such a picturesque landscape, the local co-operative winery, a mid-sized operation producing around 600,000 a year, feels obliged to carry on the centuries-old winemaking tradition. Recent news was the acquisition of the major Kössler estate. Again this year, we preferred the Pinot Bianco Plötzner Exclusiv '05, a leader in its type for years now and a banker for consumers. But we have to say all this estate's wines are well made and reliable. Credit for this high quality goes to management and the technical staff that have understood how to create positive synergy over the past few years. The truly special red Verlab Exclusiv '04, from half schiava with added lagrein and pinot nero, has intense blackberry and morello cherry aromas. The palate shows sweet tannins and well-defined minerality with a long, expansive finish. The equally good Merlot DiVinus Riserva '03 has clear notes of ripe blackberry. The palate opens dense but with a lovely freshness that confidently leads us right up to the nicely long finish. The absolutely delicious Schiava Sarnerhof Exclusiv '05 shows outstanding character. The Sauvignon Gfillhof Exclusiv '05 and Lagrein DiVinus Riserva'03 are marked by balance although the latter is slightly betrayed by dusty tannins. The Pinot Grigio Eggleiten '05 and Gewürztraminer St. Justina '05 from the Exclusiv line are well made.

●	A. A. Lagrein Scuro DiVinus Ris. '03	▼▼	6
●	A. A. Merlot DiVinus Ris. '03	▼▼	6
●	Verlab Exclusiv Vign. delle Dolomiti '04	▼▼	4*
○	A. A. Pinot Bianco Exclusiv Plötzner '05	▼▼	4*
○	A. A. Sauvignon Exclusiv Gfillhof '05	▼▼	4
●	A. A. Schiava Sarnerhof Exclusiv '05	▼▼	4*
○	A. A. Gewürztraminer St. Justina Exclusiv '05	▼	5
○	A. A. Pinot Grigio Exclusiv Egg Leiten '05	▼	4
●	A. A. Lagrein Scuro DiVinus Ris. '02	▽▽	6
○	A. A. Pinot Bianco Exclusiv Plötzner '03	▽▽	4*

APPIANO/EPPAN (BZ)

STROBLHOF
LOC. SAN MICHELE
VIA PIGANO, 25
39057 APPIANO/EPPAN (BZ)
TEL. 0471662250 - 3285774992
www.stroblhof.it

We recommend you pay a visit to Stroblhof near Appiano for various reasons. The estate spreads magnificently across forest-clad hills and vineyards particularly well suited to white wines. The estate-owned hotel is one of the most comfortable in the area and the wines produced at this small winery, managed by the brilliant Andreas Nicolussi-Leck since 1995, are excellent. Stroblhof boasts a long grape growing and winemaking tradition and, from its four hectares of vineyards, produces around 30,000 bottles every year divided equally between whites and reds. Scores are more than flattering again this year. The wines are elegant, fresh and show good personality, starting with the classic Pinot Bianco Strahler '05. Aromas of hawthorn and peach on the nose are accompanied by full, supple structure that shows a precise minerally vein and spirited acidity to supports it right through to the rather long finish. The Pinot Nero Riserva '03 has surprising freshness and shows very fine, elegant tannins, decent acidity and unusual backbone for the vintage. The progression is well sustained and balance stays firm on the long finish. Sourced from very young vineyards, the Sauvignon Nico '05 is also interesting. Though still unable to show great complexity, it is fresh, pleasant and has very good grip. We find the same feature in the elegant Chardonnay Schwarzhaus '05 with its supple, harmonious development. A retasting of the Pinot Nero Riserva '02 confirmed we were not mistaken last year when we called it one of the best in Italy.

●	A. A. Pinot Nero Ris. '03	▼▼	6
○	A. A. Chardonnay Schwarzhaus '05	▼▼	4
○	A. A. Pinot Bianco Strahler '05	▼▼	4
○	A. A. Sauvignon Nico '05	▼▼	5
●	A. A. Pinot Nero Ris. '02	▽▽	6
○	A. A. Pinot Bianco Strahler '03	▽▽	4*
●	A. A. Pinot Nero Ris. '01	▽▽	6
●	A. A. Pinot Nero Pigeno '02	▽▽	5
○	A. A. Chardonnay Schwarzhaus '03	▽▽	4
○	A. A. Chardonnay Schwarzhaus '04	▽▽	4
○	A. A. Pinot Bianco Strahler '04	▽▽	4

BOLZANO/BOZEN

ANDREAS BERGER - THURNHOF

LOC. ASLAGO
VIA CASTEL FLAVON, 7
39100 BOLZANO/BOZEN
TEL. 0471288460 - 0471285446
www.thurnhof.com

We have never heard Andreas Berger raise his voice. This reflects his unassuming character, reserved but determined. He makes around 20,000 bottles from his small estate of three and a half hectares under vine at the edge of Bolzano. They are modern-style wines somewhat resemble their producer. This year we tasted a series of very well-made wines of balance and outstanding character. We particularly enjoyed the Lagrein Merlau '05 which, despite being a so-called "base" wine, has personality to spare. The intense ripe blackberry as well as minerally and earthy aromas are typical of Lagrein and especially of Thurnhof wines. On the palate, the attack has clear spice. The tannins are close-knit and development continuous.
Uncoincidentally, this wine went straight to our finals. While waiting for the Lagrein Riserva '04 that Andreas has rightly decided to leave in the cellar for another year, we enjoyed a Cabernet Riserva '03 with sound structure, good balance and a dose of oak that is distinct but not intrusive. Moscato Giallo is always one of Andreas' best wines and the '05 is varietal, carefree and minerally with a fresh drinkability. The Cabernet '05 is still young, the Santa Maddalena '05 as fragrant and fruity as ever and the Sauvignon '05 pleasant.
We are convinced that Thurnhof is close to scaling the heights of quality and that the talented Andreas will not keep us waiting long.

●	A. A. Lagrein Scuro Merlau '05	▼▼	4*
●	A. A. Cabernet Sauvignon Ris. '03	▼▼	5
●	A. A. Cabernet '05	▼▼	4
○	A. A. Moscato Giallo '05	▼▼	4
●	A. A. Santa Maddalena '05	▼▼	4*
○	A. A. Sauvignon '05	▼	4
●	A. A. Lagrein Scuro '99	▽▽▽	4*
●	A. A. Lagrein Scuro Ris. '02	▽▽	5
●	A. A. Cabernet Sauvignon Ris. '00	▽▽	5
●	A. A. Cabernet Merlot Wienegg '01	▽▽	6
●	A. A. Cabernet Sauvignon Ris. '02	▽▽	5
●	A. A. Lagrein Scuro Ris. '03	▽▽	5
●	A. A. Cabernet '04	▽▽	5
○	A. A. Sauvignon '04	▽▽	4

BOLZANO/BOZEN

CANTINA GRIES/CANTINA DI BOLZANO

FRAZ. GRIES
P.ZZA GRIES, 2
39100 BOLZANO/BOZEN
TEL. 0471270909 - 0471972944
www.kellereibozen.com

This performance had elements of light and shade. Paradoxically, Cantina di Gries/Bolzano actually convinced us more this year with its white wines than its classic reds, including the renowned Lagreins. Let's start with the positive notes. In particular, the Pinot Bianco Dellago '05 has improved so much in personality and definition it can now be considered one of the best in its category. Despite its youth, it already has complex, well-coordinated aromas. The palate has good structure, harmonic development and traction to spare in the finish. The Moscato Giallo Vinalia '04 is a star with its appealing touches of citron and dried apricot. The palate is sweet and concentrated, yet animated by a refreshing acidity, and finishes dynamically long. It's a wine with great balance. We confess we were somewhat disappointed by the two Lagreins, the Riserva Prestige Line '03 and the Collection Baron Carl Eyrl '04. The first is slightly clenched with somewhat dusty, mouth-drying tannins. The second has very interesting aromas of spice and cinchona but is a little simple in the mouth and lacks that dynamism that makes a wine really great. We return to the usual standards with the succulent, elegant Merlot Collection Otto Graf Huyn Riserva '04. The standard-label Lagrein Grieser '05, Moscato Rosa Rosis '05 and Lagrein Merlot Mauritius '04 are also delicious. We are sure that Stephan Filippi will bounce back next year.

○	A. A. Pinot Bianco Collection Dellago '05	▼▼	4*
●	A. A. Lagrein Merlot Mauritius '04	▼▼	6
●	A. A. Merlot Otto Graf Huyn Ris. '04	▼▼	5*
○	A. A. Moscato Giallo Vinalia '04	▼▼	6
●	A. A. Lagrein Grieser '05	▼▼	4*
●	A. A. Moscato Rosa Rosis '05	▼▼	6
●	A. A. Lagrein Grieser Prestige Line Ris. '03	▼	6
●	A. A. Lagrein Grieser Baron Carl Eyrl '04	▼	4
●	A. A. Lagrein Scuro Grieser Prestige Line Ris. '00	▽▽▽	6
○	A. A. Moscato Giallo Vinalia '03	▽▽▽	6

BOLZANO/BOZEN

GARLIDER

FRAZ. VELTURNO/FELDTHURNS
VIA UNTRUM, 20
39040 BOLZANO/BOZEN
TEL. 0472847296

A Three Glass winner has been declared. We refer here to the Veltliner '05 created by Christian Kerschbaumer, born in 1974, who just two years ago we called a "rising star in Valle Isarco and Alto Adige viticulture". The man comes from Velturno, where he lives with his charming family and produces around 15,000 bottles, and has really amazed us this year. His Veltliner '05 is an absolutely great wine that, in our humble opinion, can stand up to many of its celebrated Austrian cousins. It already shows complex aromas of citron and aromatic herbs. The palate is a real delight with concentration, balance and energy, the precise opposite of a standardized wine. A skilled and unusual winemaker, Christian over the past two years has been converting to organic growing as well as experimenting with the use of native yeasts with his award-winning Veltliner and other wines. He is also a real enthusiast who travels around Italy tasting wines and meeting other producers. But Garlider is not just Veltliner. We tasted a series of wines with a very personal style that puts the emphasis on definition. For proof, just taste his Sylvaner '05, which distances itself from the others in Valle Isarco not just because it originates from a slightly lower area but also for its very special character. The same goes for the remarkable Pinot Nero '04, which is unique in Valle Isarco. The Gewürztraminer, Pinot Grigio and Müller Thurgau, all from the 2005 vintage, are delicious and in true Garlider style. To sum up, an excellent result, well deserved and one that bodes well for the future.

○	A. A. Valle Isarco Veltliner '05	🍷🍷🍷	4*
○	A. A. Valle Isarco Sylvaner '05	🍷🍷	4*
●	A. A. Pinot Nero '04	🍷🍷	5
○	A. A. Valle Isarco Gewurztraminer '05	🍷🍷	5
○	A. A. Valle Isarco Müller Thurgau '05	🍷🍷	4
○	A. A. Valle Isarco Pinot Grigio '05	🍷🍷	4
○	A. A. Valle Isarco Sylvaner '04	♀♀	4*
○	A. A. Valle Isarco Veltliner '04	♀♀	4*
○	A. A. Valle Isarco Sylvaner '03	♀♀	4
○	A. A. Valle Isarco Veltliner '03	♀♀	4*
○	A. A. Valle Isarco Gewurztraminer '04	♀♀	5

BOLZANO/BOZEN

FRANZ GOJER GLÖGGLHOF

FRAZ. SANTA MADDALENA
VIA RIVELLONE, 1
39100 BOLZANO/BOZEN
TEL. 0471978775
www.gojer.it

Franz Gojer is the ideal companion at the dinner table. He is congenial, cheerful, witty and loves to eat and drink in company. We add to this that since he inherited this estate in 1982, he has produced some of the best, classic wines in the Bolzano area. Glögglhof is in fact located on the Santa Maddalena hill north of Bolzano and his four hectares yield around 40,000 bottles a year of always highly characteristic wines, beginning with the one that takes its name from the designated area. Franz is a true maestro of Santa Maddalena and has made some truly mouthwatering versions, a standard-label and the Rondell selection, from 2005, a great year for schiava. The former is intensely floral and fruity with a scrumptious, juicy, minerally palate. The Rondell '05 is still a bit young but already expresses all the elegance and personality that make it one of the representative wines of its type. The Lagrein Riserva '04 easily reached our final taste-offs despite the fact it is a bit young and marked by the wood. Still, it is already showing perfectly decent structure. The standard-label Lagrein is typical and fresh and foregrounds attractive drinkability. The same goes for the Merlot Spitz '04 with very typical vegetal notes and supple, refreshing palate.

●	A. A. Lagrein Scuro Ris. '04	🍷🍷	5
●	A. A. Merlot Spitz '04	🍷🍷	5
●	A. A. Lagrein '05	🍷🍷	4*
●	A. A. Santa Maddalena Cl. '05	🍷🍷	4*
●	A. A. Santa Maddalena Rondell '05	🍷🍷	4*
●	A. A. Lagrein Scuro Ris. '03	♀♀	5
●	A. A. Santa Maddalena Rondell '04	♀♀	4*
●	A. A. Lagrein '04	♀♀	4*
●	A. A. Santa Maddalena Cl. '04	♀♀	4*

BOLZANO/BOZEN

GEORG MUMELTER GRIESBAUERHOF
VIA RENCIO, 66
39100 BOLZANO/BOZEN
TEL. 0471973090
www.tirolensisarsvini.it

Getting noticed is not one of Georg Mumelter's priorities. For him, only his vineyard of just over three hectares exists, along with the cellar near Rencio where he produces around 30,000 bottles a year of very well made wines. The bottles are as austere as the man who makes them but still have a distinctive charm and personality. These wines always need time to express themselves but they never disappoint in the long term and are always reliable. Let's start this brief review of the estate's products with the surprising Isarcus '04, a wine from 95 per cent schiava with lagrein, a sort of Super Santa Maddalena, barrique-aged for ten months. It gives the lie to all that talk about the "simplicity" of schiava, or rather vernatsch. In fact, this wine shows elegant aromas of spice and mulberry. The sweet, fine-grained tannins on the palate are accompanied by a clear spicy vein and a minerally finish for which aristocratic is the word. Although still quite young and slightly marked by oak, the Lagrein Riserva '03 shows close-knit, smooth tannins and a lively dynamism. As delicious as ever, the Santa Maddalena '05 has a fragrance in the mouth that reinforced our predilection for the type. Although a bit austere and closed, the Cabernet Sauvignon '03 still has loads of body even if the tannins are a bit dusty. The only estate white, Pinot Grigio '05, is varietal and well made.

● A. A. Cabernet Sauvignon '03	TT	5
● A. A. Lagrein Scuro Ris. '03	TT	5
● Isarcus '04	TT	4*
● A. A. Santa Maddalena '05	TT	3*
○ A. A. Pinot Grigio '05	T	4
● A. A. Lagrein Scuro Ris. '99	YYY	5
● A. A. Cabernet Sauvignon '01	YY	5
● A. A. Lagrein Scuro Ris. '01	YY	5
● A. A. Lagrein Scuro Ris. '02	YY	5
● Isarcus '03	YY	4

BOLZANO/BOZEN

LOACKER SCHWARHOF
LOC. SANTA GIUSTINA, 3
39100 BOLZANO/BOZEN
TEL. 0471365125
www.loacker.net

The Loackers play a special role in the winemaking world of Alto Adige as artists and philosophers of viticulture artists. These pioneers have for decades followed a biodynamic, minimum-intervention route in their cellars and vineyards, including the Corte Pavone estate in Montalcino and Valdifalco in Maremma, along with the 14th-century Schwarhof estate above Bolzano, where there are seven hectares under vine. Rainer and Hayo Loacker's philosophy is based on the principle that their duty is to "support and encourage the land, allowing the nature of the terrain to emerge alive and strong". Wines from the Loacker estate are a true expression of this concept, interpreting and reflecting the nature of grape and terrain. Not always easy to understand on first impact, sometimes they need a bit of time to open up but they are always full of character. Absolutely one of the best Italian Merlots from the vintage, the Merlot Iwain '04 is a great wine, minerally and stylish, almost aristocratic on the palate where it is full, long and very young with a lovely acidity and soft tannins. We are pleased to award it the Loackers' first and truly well-deserved Three Glasses. The Pinot Nero Norital '04 is still marked by a bit of oak, yet shows good, fruity aromatics. Though the tannins are slightly green, it is full flavoured and minerally with a nice length. The Santa Maddalena Morit '05 is concentrated and complex. The Sauvignon Tasnim '05 is also very varietal, juicy, fairly elegant and fresh.

● A. A. Merlot Iwain '04	TTT	5*
● A. A. Cabernet Lagrein Kastlet '03	TT	5
● A. A. Pinot Nero Norital '04	TT	5
● A. A. Santa Maddalena Morit '05	TT	4*
○ A. A. Sauvignon Blanc Tasmin '05	TT	5
○ A. A. Gewürztraminer Atagis '05	T	5
● A. A. Cabernet Lagrein Kastlet '01	YY	5
○ A. A. Valle Isarco Gewürztraminer Atagis '02	YY	5
○ A. A. Valle Isarco Sylvaner Ysac '04	YY	4
○ A. A. Sauvignon Blanc Tasmin '04	YY	4

BOLZANO/BOZEN

Josephus Mayr

Erbhof Unterganzner
loc. Cardano
via Campiglio, 15
39053 Bolzano/Bozen
tel. 0471365582

So utterly distinctive are Josephus Mayr's wines that it is hardly worth the bother of masking them. They are branded by the distinct trademark of Unterganzner, the splendid family estate in the extreme eastern part of the broad hollow of Bolzano. Two wines reached our finals and the others were interesting to say the least. Controversial is a better word for they divide both enthusiasts and experts. We are somewhat perplexed by a few of the more extreme choices made by Josephus Mayr but he is rightly committed to following his own path. More precisely, although these wines are good, characteristic and anything but boring, we feel a pinch less concentration would not hurt. Let's start with a great house classic, the Lagrein Riserva '03. Still very young, the nose is austere but shows clear notes of cinchona and spice. The palate is concentrated, dense and very minerally. The tannins are a bit powdery but the finish is very long. The Lamarein '04 is something else entirely. From part-dried lagrein, this is clearly an unusual wine, right from its impenetrable colour. The confident aromas are a bit marked by oak and then the creamy palate shows imposing tannins and well-balanced acidity. Though not for everyone, this is a wine with charm. But Josephus never fails to amaze us. This year, it was with two white wines, the dynamic, juicy, vibrant Chardonnay '05 and the elegantly varietal, minerally Sauvignon '05. The other winery workhorse, Santa Maddalena '05, is fresh and fruity. Though still quite young, the austere Cabernet Riserva '03 is sound.

●	A. A. Lagrein Scuro Ris. '03	TT	5
●	Lamarein '04	TT	7
●	A. A. Cabernet Ris. '03	TT	5
○	A. A. Chardonnay '05	TT	4
●	A. A. Santa Maddalena '05	TT	4*
○	A. A. Sauvignon '05	TT	4
⊙	A. A. Lagrein Rosato '05	T	4
●	A. A. Lagrein Scuro Ris. '00	YYY	5
●	A. A. Lagrein Scuro Ris. '01	YYY	5
●	A. A. Lagrein Scuro Ris. '98	YYY	5
●	A. A. Lagrein Scuro Ris. '99	YYY	5
●	A. A. Cabernet Ris. '02	YY	5
●	A. A. Lagrein Scuro Ris. '02	YY	5

BOLZANO/BOZEN

Cantina Convento Muri-Gries

p.zza Gries, 21
39100 Bolzano/Bozen
tel. 0471282287
www.muri-gries.com

Over the past ten years, Lagrein has taken some giant steps, from being a wine consumed almost exclusively in the province of Bolzano to a popular type with consumers everywhere. One of the driving forces behind this phenomenon is Cantina Convento Muri-Gries and its long-serving Kellermeister Christian Werth, who took his father's place in the cellar in 1988. Christian was one of the first to concentrate on Lagrein, restore the old vineyards and experiment in the cellar with fantastic results. We recommend a visit to this history-soaked winery, where in 1407 Archduke Leopold of Tyrol gave some homeless monks the castle of Gries, which they later transformed into a monastery. The old chapel was made into the cellar where the great Muri Lagreins age in small and large oak barrels. The Three Glass award is now almost a formality for Lagrein Abtei Riserva '03, austere and aristocratic on the nose with spicy, flinty notes. The density on the palate is as unmistakable as the impeccable balance and the finish is dynamic and deep. It will be at its best in a few years. We have tried for years to convince Christian to submit his Santa Maddalena for tasting. We finally managed this year and it swept into our finals thanks to a charm and complexity that now no longer surprise us. The Lagrein '05 is typical, fragrant and ready to drink. Other well-made wines include the Bianco Abtei '04, from 70 per cent pinot bianco and the rest pinot grigio, and the Terlano Pinot Bianco, the Lagrein Rosato and the Pinot Grigio, all three from 2005.

●	A. A. Lagrein Abtei Ris. '03	TTT	5
●	A. A. Santa Maddalena '05	TT	3*
●	A. A. Lagrein '05	TT	4*
○	A. A. Terlano Pinot Bianco '05	TT	4
○	A. A. Bianco Abtei Muri '04	T	4
⊙	A. A. Lagrein Rosato '05	T	3
○	A. A. Pinot Grigio '05	T	4
●	A. A. Lagrein Abtei Ris. '00	YYY	5
●	A. A. Lagrein Abtei Ris. '01	YYY	5
●	A. A. Lagrein Abtei Ris. '02	YYY	5
●	A. A. Lagrein Abtei Ris. '98	YYY	5
●	A. A. Lagrein Abtei Ris. '99	YYY	5

BOLZANO/BOZEN

Johannes Pfeifer Pfannenstielhof

via Pfannestiel, 9
39100 Bolzano/Bozen
tel. 0471970884 - 3388116623
www.pfannenstielhof.it

The affable Johannes Pfeifer is a real winemaker with every reason to be satisfied because this year he has created some noteworthy wines with a very precise style and skilfully handled wood. From his four hectares under vine located right in the heart of Lagrein country, Johannes produces around 40,000 bottles, all reds and all very well crafted. We'll start with our weakness, the Santa Maddalena that virtually no one makes better than Johannes here at Pfannenstielhof. The juicy, fragrant palate has a finish that always tempts us to drink more. Though still very young, the Lagrein Riserva '03 is already expressive and typical with just a slightly powdery finish. The Lagrein '05 is an explosion of exuberant youth that assails the nose with abundant spice and cinchona. The elegant, stylish palate leads to a deep, juicy finish. The latest wine created at the estate, the Pinot Nero '03 is also a surprise and, despite a growing season for this type that was unfortunate to say the least, has still managed to preserve more than respectable freshness, but with slightly drying tannins. In any case, wines from this definitely reliable estate are never boring even though we are convinced Johannes and his lovely wife will soon reach greater heights.

●	A. A. Lagrein Scuro Ris. '03	TT	5
●	A. A. Pinot Nero '03	TT	5
●	A. A. Lagrein Scuro '05	TT	4*
●	A. A. Santa Maddalena Cl. '05	TT	3*
●	A. A. Lagrein Scuro Ris. '00	YY	5
●	A. A. Lagrein Scuro Ris. '01	YY	5
●	A. A. Lagrein Scuro Ris. '02	YY	5
●	A. A. Pinot Nero '02	YY	5
●	A. A. Lagrein Scuro '04	YY	4*
●	A. A. Santa Maddalena Cl. '04	YY	3*

BOLZANO/BOZEN

Stefan Ramoser - Fliederhof

loc. Santa Maddalena
di Sotto, 33
39100 Bolzano/Bozen
tel. 0471979048

Stefan Ramoser is the classic Alto Adige winemaker, a bit timid with a sincere smile, rough hands and great love for his work. His area is the heart of Santa Maddalena wine production, translated into classic local types along with a small production of Moscato Giallo. Thanks to its very typical, characterful wines, this small estate – only 2.4 hectares under vine and around 25,000 bottles produced on average – has become a significant presence on the ever more varied, and in certain ways difficult, growing and winemaking landscape in Alto Adige. Let's start with the most representative wine, the Lagrein Riserva '03. Still very young, this product of a great vintage proffers ripe fruit and great concentration yet also confidently embodies elegance and overall balance. The short time in small oak never compromises its distinct typicity, which comes through in rich spices and minerality supported by firm, fresh fruit. The fresh, juicy, easy-drinking, standard-label Lagrein Scuro expresses all its youthful enthusiasm. Fragrant and mouthwatering, the Santa Maddalena '05 shows all the best characteristics of the type along with a special richness of flavour. We close with the fresh and floral Pfefferer '05 from moscato giallo, which makes allure its calling card. Finally, we should also mention Fliederhof's very competitive prices.

●	A. A. Lagrein Ris. '03	TT	5
●	A. A. Lagrein Scuro '05	TT	4*
●	A. A. Santa Maddalena Cl. '05	TT	4*
○	Pfefferer '05	T	4
●	A. A. Lagrein Ris. '00	YY	5
●	A. A. Lagrein Ris. '01	YY	5
●	A. A. Lagrein Ris. '02	YY	5
●	A. A. Lagrein Scuro '04	YY	4*
●	A. A. Santa Maddalena Cl. '04	YY	4*

BOLZANO/BOZEN

Georg Ramoser - Untermoserhof

via Santa Maddalena, 36
39100 Bolzano/Bozen
tel. 0471975481

"I want to keep the Lagrein Riserva '03 another year in the cellar because it is not ready yet", Georg Ramoser told us in the spring of 2005. His words now seem almost prophetic in light of the resounding Three Glass award. We use the term resounding because this wine aroused unanimous appreciation in the tasting panel, something that is never easy for a Lagrein. This version has a modern style yet great typicity and stylistic definition. The use of oak is practically perfect, just like the balance and elegance. It is fragrant, complex, vibrant and layered in every phase of tasting, a minor miracle considering the intrinsically rustic nature of the grape. In other words, six years after winning with his Lagrein Riserva '97, Georg brings home another eminently well-deserved Three Glass prize. He is a tenacious, intelligent winemaker and it is a real pleasure to honour him. But Untermoserhof also produces some other very interesting wines from its four hectares under vine yielding around 40,000 bottles here in the heart of Santa Maddalena. The Lagrein '05 is less complex than the Riserva but it has that immediately recognizable estate style. The outstanding Merlot Riserva '03 shows pencil lead and black berry fruit on the nose and a taut, complex, austere yet long palate with a very dynamic finish. The Santa Maddalena '05 is fragrant and juicy. Now we await the first organic experiments and, knowing this winery, we're certain they'll be a success.

●	A. A. Lagrein Scuro Ris. '03	**YYY**	5*
●	A. A. Merlot Ris. '03	**YY**	5
●	A. A. Lagrein Scuro '05	**YY**	4*
●	A. A. Santa Maddalena Cl. '05	**YY**	4*
●	A. A. Lagrein Scuro Ris. '97	YYY	5
●	A. A. Lagrein Scuro Ris. '00	YY	5
●	A. A. Lagrein Scuro Ris. '01	YY	5
●	A. A. Lagrein Scuro '04	YY	4*
●	A. A. Lagrein Scuro Ris. '99	YY	5
●	A. A. Lagrein Scuro Ris. '02	YY	5
●	A. A. Merlot Ris. '02	YY	5
●	A. A. Santa Maddalena Cl. '03	YY	4*

BOLZANO/BOZEN

Hans Rottensteiner

via Sarentino, 1a
39100 Bolzano/Bozen
tel. 0471282015
www.rottensteiner-weine.com

Founded in 1956 by Hans Rottensteiner, this small winery at the entrance to Val Sarentino, northwest of the city of Bolzano, is today managed by Anton Rottensteiner, one of the outstanding winemaking personalities in Alto Adige, and his son Hannes. Special attention is given to the grapes on the ten hectares of estate vineyards in the heart of the zone for Lagrein and Santa Maddalena Classico. While waiting for the release of the Lagrein Riserva '03, this year we enjoyed a splendid version of the Gewürztraminer Passito Cresta '04, an extraordinary sweet wine and among the best in its type from Alto Adige. A golden amber colour, it won us over with aromatic, intense honey and rose aromas and fullness on the palate where it shows concentrated, powerful and creamy with very refreshing acidity. The elegant, minerally Sauvignon '05 convinced us with its depth and finesse. Prem '04 from 85 per cent schiava and the rest lagrein aged six months in large wood is a characterful wine that gives intense aromas of cinchona, red berry fruits and delicate spicy shades. The subtle palate has sweet tannins and consistent finesse. As usual, the Santa Maddalena Premstallerhof '05 is one of the best around with floral aromas, a fragrant palate and very appealing drinkability. The Cabernet Riserva Select '03, Pinot Bianco Carnol '04, Sylvaner '05 and Pinot Nero Mazon Riserva Select '03 are all well made. All in all, with its 400,000 bottles, this winery is one consumers can bank on.

○	A. A. Gewürztraminer Passito Cresta '04	**YY**	6
●	Prem '04	**YY**	4
●	A. A. Santa Maddalena Cl. Premstallerhof '05	**YY**	4*
○	A. A. Sauvignon '05	**YY**	4
●	A. A. Cabernet Select Ris '03	**Y**	5
●	A. A. Pinot Nero Mazon Select Ris. '03	**Y**	5
○	A. A. Pinot Bianco Carnol '05	**Y**	4
○	A. A. Valle Isarco Sylvaner '05	**Y**	4
●	A. A. Lagrein Ris. '02	YYY	4*
●	A. A. Santa Maddalena Cl. Premstallerhof '04	YY	4*

BOLZANO/BOZEN

★ Cantina Produttori Santa Maddalena/ Cantina di Bolzano
via Brennero, 15
39100 Bolzano/Bozen
tel. 0471270909 - 0471972944
www.cantinabolzano.com

We can only say that by now Stephan Filippi runs on automatic with Lagrein, particularly what may be the Lagrein par excellence, Taber. What is most impressive is his ability to regularly maintain absolutely excellent quality year after year. Even in a vintage we feel was not marvellous for the type, here is another jewel. It might all seem very simple considering this historic Kellermeister, at the estate since 1988, can choose the best parcels from a massive production. But his ability to interpret Lagrein is still clearly extraordinary. If you haven't already guessed, Taber '04 won Three Glasses. If such a thing is possible, this Lagrein has further refined its best features of typicity, concentration and elegance. The use of wood is very shrewdly handled, the aromas spicy and balsamic with almost earthy shades, and the palate creamy and minerally with a perfectly measured acidity. The finish is endless and even has a minty note. We could patiently wait for it another year or so but it is drinking beautifully now. But man does not live on Lagrein alone and so here at the court of King Taber is an excellent Chardonnay Kleinstein, another of our finalists, a classic Sauvignon Mock, two Gewürztraminers – the base and the Kleinstein – the Valle Isarco Müller Thurgau and the unmissable Santa Maddalena Huck am Bach, all from the 2005 vintage, followed by an elegant Pinot Nero Riserva, Cabernet Riserva Mumelter and Lagrein Riserva Perl from 2004. Let's just say these results are pretty impressive.

●	A. A. Lagrein Scuro Taber Ris. '04	TTT	6
○	A. A. Chardonnay Kleinstein '05	TT	4
●	A. A. Cabernet Mumelter Ris. '04	TT	6
●	A. A. Lagrein Scuro Perl '04	TT	4
●	A. A. Pinot Nero Ris. '04	TT	5
○	A. A. Gewürztraminer '05	TT	4
○	A. A. Gewürztraminer Kleinstein '05	TT	5
●	A. A. Santa Maddalena Cl. Huck am Bach '05	TT	4
○	A. A. Sauvignon Mock '05	TT	4
○	A. A. Valle Isarco Müller Thurgau '05	TT	4*
●	A. A. Lagrein Scuro Taber Ris. '03	YYY	6

BOLZANO/BOZEN

Anton Schmid - Oberrautner
fraz. Gries
via M. Pacher, 3
39100 Bolzano/Bozen
tel. 0471281440
www.schmid.bz

Schmid Oberrautner is a typical Alto Adige family-run winemaking estate. In fact, Andreas Schmid's son Florian assists him in every phase of production. Located in Gries, the heart of the Lagrein production zone, its history goes all the way back to 1411. Over the past few years, Andreas has proven himself with unswervingly high-quality wines and an extremely consumer-friendly pricing policy. Let's begin with the Lagrein Scuro Riserva Oro '03, the estate's showcase wine that still shows a little wood on the nose but whose well-balanced palate has great body and very refreshing acidity. The tannins are nicely textured and there are typical spicy notes on the very deep, minerally finish. The Pinot Bianco '05 is also excellent and shows intense ripe fruit aromas and a fresh, dynamic palate with a clear minerally vein. We stress that the price tag is wonderfully honest. Another great value for money wine is the fresh, easy-drinking Lagrein '05, which has lovely grip. A bit below this is the Lagrein Villa Schmid '03. It is elegant enough but loses a bit of verve in the finish. Moving up again to the Pinot Nero '03, we should mention its balance and freshness, despite the truly unfortunate growing season for this variety. The Lagrein Rosato '05 is floral, juicy and deliciously quaffable. These results are very reassuring and confirmation Schmid Oberrautner's status.

●	A. A. Lagrein Scuro Grieser Oro Ris. '03	TT	5
●	A. A. Pinot Nero '03	TT	5
⊙	A. A. Lagrein Rosato '05	TT	3*
●	A. A. Lagrein Scuro Grieser '05	TT	3*
○	A. A. Pinot Bianco '05	TT	4*
●	A. A. Lagrein Scuro Villa Schmid '03	T	4
●	A. A. Lagrein Scuro Gries Ris. '00	YY	4
●	A. A. Lagrein Scuro Grieser Ris. '01	YY	4*
●	A. A. Pinot Nero '01	YY	4*
●	A. A. Cabernet Ritsch '02	YY	4
●	A. A. Lagrein Scuro Grieser '04	YY	3*

BOLZANO/BOZEN

TENUTA WALDGRIES
CHRISTIAN PLATTNER
LOC. SANTA GIUSTINA, 2
39100 BOLZANO/BOZEN
TEL. 0471323603
www.waldgries.it

Christian Plattner is one of the greatest interpreters of Alto Adige's best-known and most important red, Lagrein. We say this with no fear of contradiction because his wines have character, stylistic definition and above all a sense of place few others can equal. Let's start by saying this splendid old farm is located on the lovely Santa Maddalena hillside and is well worth a visit. The five estate hectares are managed with rare expertise and began converting to organic methods a couple of years ago. The wines are always very elegant with balanced components and great personality, beginning with the selection Mirell '03, an aristocratic Lagrein with dense structure combined with dynamism and a minerally, balsamic finish. It's a one-of-a-kind with a great future. Just as good is the Riserva '04, which has a leaner profile but great character and depth. The standard-label '05 is fresh, lively and deliciously drinkable yet shows very decent backbone. But one of the Waldgries wines we love best is the Santa Maddalena. In such a favourable year for schiava, what has always been an excellent product has acquired a touch of aristocratic elegance that puts it on a par with many of the best Beaujolais. This simply marvellous wine is penalized only by the fact it is called Santa Maddalena. The Cabernet Laurenz '04, Moscato Rosa '04 and Sauvignon '05 are absolutely flawless in the true Waldgries style.

●	A. A. Lagrein Scuro Mirell '03	▼▼	7
●	A. A. Lagrein '05	▼▼	4*
●	A. A. Santa Maddalena Cl. '05	▼▼	4*
●	A. A. Cabernet Sauvignon Laurenz '04	▼▼	6
●	A. A. Lagrein Scuro Ris. '04	▼▼	6
●	A. A. Moscato Rosa '04	▼▼	6
○	A. A. Sauvignon '05	▼▼	4
●	A. A. Lagrein Scuro Mirell '01	▽▽▽	7
●	A. A. Cabernet Sauvignon '99	▽▽▽	6
●	A. A. Lagrein Scuro Mirell '02	▽▽	7
●	A. A. Lagrein Scuro Ris. '03	▽▽	6
●	A. A. Santa Maddalena Cl. '04	▽▽	4*

BRESSANONE/BRIXEN (BZ)

KUENHOF - PETER PLIGER
LOC. MARA, 110
39042 BRESSANONE/BRIXEN (BZ)
TEL. 0472850546

There is a lot of frequently silly talk about organic, biodynamic or even "natural" wines as well-known and less well-known personalities try to elbow their way into the limelight of fashion. Then we come to Kuenhof, a couple of kilometres south of Bressanone in Valle Isarco, uncork a few bottles in the old farmhouse and start chatting to Peter Pliger and his wife Brigitte. The chasm separating substance from appearance, and trends from a way of life, becomes all too obvious. After discussing the magnetic balance of the soil and homeopathic products for treating the vineyards, we took a tour of the vines and rediscovered the meaning of Peter's words and his way of living life, nature and wine. Kuenhof more than deserves the first award given for Sustainable Viticulture. We should add that over the years Peter's wines have gradually shed their baroque trappings and achieved a distinctive personality. They are deep, reserved wines yet possess explosive energy: these wines of being, not appearing. The portrait of the Three Glass winner, Riesling Kaiton '05, shows it as austere, still young but brilliant and dynamic in the attack on a palate that continues persuasively right up to the spirited, almost salty finish. Just as good, in perhaps its best version ever, is the very Valle Isarcoesque Sylvaner '05, whose aromatic herb and damson aromas meld into a vibrant, taut palate. The wine Peter perhaps loves least, Gewürztraminer, is great in 2005, and the excellent Veltliner from the same vintage shows rare finesse. People like Peter make our job worthwhile.

○	A. A. Valle Isarco Riesling Kaiton '05	▼▼▼	5*
○	A. A. Valle Isarco Sylvaner '05	▼▼	5*
○	A. A. Valle Isarco Gewürztraminer '05	▼▼	4
○	A. A. Valle Isarco Veltliner '05	▼▼	4*
○	Kaiton '01	▽▽▽	4
○	A. A. Valle Isarco Sylvaner '02	▽▽▽	4*
○	A. A. Valle Isarco Sylvaner '03	▽▽▽	4*
○	A. A. Valle Isarco Sylvaner V.T. '04	▽▽▽	4*
○	Kaiton '99	▽▽▽	4

BRESSANONE/BRIXEN (BZ)

Manfred Nössing - Hoandlhof

Fraz. Kranebih
via dei Vigneti, 66
39042 Bressanone/Brixen (BZ)
tel. 0472832672

One thing is certain, there is no risk of getting bored with Manni Nössing. You might think a small producer, with his third consecutive Three Glass award and a new cellar just finished, would calm down and continue on the road that has earned him fame and fortune. That might be the case if the above-mentioned producer were not Manni Nössing. This year's surprises start with the elimination of acacia wood barrels. "They make the wine too soft and I'd rather have them a little firmer. If they are ready later then who cares." The second is giving up the small production of the rare red Espan. "It dirtied my new cellar". This gives the measure of the man. We have to admit that Manni was right at least on the first point. His wines have acquired a brightness and energy that may in years past have been concealed by the wood. Advancing by subtracting, he has improved their elegance and vigour, perhaps achieving a new stylistic maturity that opens up as yet unexplored possibilities. We only reviewed three wines since the Gewürztraminer '05 had not yet been bottled at the time of our tastings and the production of the very good Müller Thurgau was too limited. But what wines these are. The Three Glass winner, Kerner '05, is less opulent than usual. Actually, it is austere and still edgy yet has the vigour and energy that show Manni's distinctive touch. The Sylvaner '05 is very much in the Valle Isarco style and shows still quite youthful but already has complexity and an overwhelming finish. The Veltliner '05 scintillates like Luke Skywalker's sword. Awesome.

○ A. A. Valle Isarco Kerner '05	▼▼▼	4*
○ A. A. Valle Isarco Sylvaner '05	▼▼	4*
○ A. A. Valle Isarco Veltliner '05	▼▼	4*
○ A. A. Valle Isarco Kerner '02	▽▽▽	4
○ A. A. Valle Isarco Kerner '03	▽▽▽	4*
○ A. A. Valle Isarco Sylvaner '04	▽▽▽	4*
○ A. A. Valle Isarco Sylvaner '02	▽▽	4
○ A. A. Valle Isarco Kerner '04	▽▽	4*
○ A. A. Valle Isarco Sylvaner '03	▽▽	4
○ A. A. Valle Isarco Veltliner '04	▽▽	4*
○ Manni Gewürztraminer '04	▽▽	4*

BRESSANONE/BRIXEN (BZ)

Taschlerhof

loc. Mara, 107
39042 Bressanone/Brixen (BZ)
tel. 0472851091 - 3356914480
www.taschlerhof.com

Taschlerhof makes a great return to the front ranks with four thoroughly decent wines. Two of them even reached our finals. We are very happy for this small estate at Mara/Mahr, a small village south of Bressanone, and for Peter Wachtler, one of the young lions from the valley who is pushing Alto Adige viticulture on to greater things. The two and a half hectares under vine yield around 15,000 bottles a year and the new cellar is nearly finished. The vineyards among the woods are around 550 metres above sea level and aspected to southwest. The wines are very typical and show great character, with slightly less forced acidity in comparison with those from other producers in the zone but with the typical Valle Isarco white wine minerality. We were most impressed by the Sylvaner Lahner '05, obtained from a special selection of fruit from the oldest vines. It has complex aromas of Mediterranean herbs and balsamic tones on the nose before the tangy, expansive palate shows great development. This is almost a model Sylvaner. Instead, the superb Kerner '05 has notes of benzene and tropical fruit and the palate has traction to spare, a taut but well-gauged acidity and a very deep finish. The other two wines, the base Sylvaner and Gewürztraminer both from 2005, are varietal and pleasing.

○ A. A. Valle Isarco Kerner '05	▼▼	4*
○ A. A. Valle Isarco Sylvaner Lahner '05	▼▼	5*
○ A. A. Valle Isarco Gewürztraminer '05	▼▼	5
○ A. A. Valle Isarco Sylvaner '05	▼▼	4*
○ A. A. Valle Isarco Gewürztraminer '02	▽▽	4
○ A. A. Valle Isarco Sylvaner '02	▽▽	4
○ A. A. Valle Isarco Gewürztraminer '03	▽▽	5
○ A. A. Valle Isarco Sylvaner '03	▽▽	4

CALDARO/KALTERN (BZ)

CANTINA SOCIALE ERSTE & NEUE
VIA DELLE CANTINE, 5/10
39052 CALDARO/KALTERN (BZ)
TEL. 0471963122
www.erste-neue.it

Caldaro's Erste & Neue is one of the leading co-operative wineries in Alto Adige in more than just size and, despite a slightly difficult year from the corporate point of view, has not presented a range of such top quality wines in some time. In fact, four of them reach our Three Glass finals, better than good results for this winery located in the heart of the classic Caldaro zone. The Pinot Bianco Prunar '05 is rich and full with fresh notes on the nose and a long, elegant palate. The Bianco Passito Anthos '03 is also a really great wine, with aromas of figs, dates and citron peel on the nose, and a palate that is deep, concentrated, well balanced and long. The Lagrein Puntay Riserva '03 shows striking elegance and freshness and is balsamic and rich in backbone. Instead, the Merlot Puntay '03 shows minerally and elegant, with soft tannins and lovely texture, acidity and length. The Gewürztraminer Puntay '05 is as good as ever, balsamic and floral with almond notes on the nose. The stylish, elegant palate is fresh with minerally notes. The Pinot Bianco Puntay '05 is a tad less successful. Though nice and rich, it falls a bit flat. The appealing winery workhorse, the Lago di Caldaro Scelto Puntay '05 is intense, fruity, floral, zesty, juicy and soft, and drinks beautifully.

○	A. A. Anthos Bianco Passito '03	**YY**	6
●	A. A. Lagrein Puntay Ris. '03	**YY**	5
●	A. A. Merlot Puntay '03	**YY**	6
○	A. A. Pinot Bianco Prunar '05	**YY**	4*
○	A. A. Gewürztraminer Puntay '05	**YY**	5
●	A. A. Lago di Caldaro Scelto Puntay '05	**YY**	4*
○	A. A. Pinot Bianco Puntay '05	**Y**	4
○	A. A. Gewürztraminer Puntay '01	YYY	5
○	A. A. Anthos Bianco Passito '01	YY	6
○	A. A. Anthos Bianco Passito '02	YY	6
○	A. A. Gewürztraminer Puntay '04	YY	5
●	A. A. Cabernet Puntay '01	YY	6
●	A. A. Lagrein Puntay Ris. '02	YY	5
○	A. A. Pinot Bianco Prunar '04	YY	4*

CALDARO/KALTERN (BZ)

TENUTA RITTERHOF
STRADA DEL VINO, 1
39052 CALDARO/KALTERN (BZ)
TEL. 0471963298
www.ritterhof.it

Ritterhof was one of those typical Alto Adige winemaking estates. The wines were pleasant and well made at good prices, though perhaps a bit limited from the standpoint of personality. This year's results make us think it has taken a new path and credit goes to manager Ludwig Kaneppele and skilled oenologist Bernard Hannes. Vineyards at this reliable estate, owned by the Roner family, stretch across the best grape growing terrains between Caldaro and Termeno. Along with the seven hectares both owned and rented, grapes from forty or so regular growers bring annual production to around 250,000 bottles. Let's start with one of the best Gewürztraminers from the vintage year. The Crescendo '05 stunned us with the complexity of its aromas and a palate so concentrated yet with such a fresh attack and deep, elegant development. The broad, creamy, well-typed Lagrein Manus Riserva '03 shows refreshing and balanced acidity. The other two whites that reached our finals, the base line Pinot Grigio and Sauvignon, both from the 2005 vintage, were typical, elegant and characterful. The standard Gewürztraminer was also flawless and only a tad less concentrated than its big brother. But what was impressive was the number of wines that made better than respectable scores. A glance at the chart below shows that Ritterhof is just one step short of achieving great success.

●	A. A. Lagrein Manus Ris. '03	**YY**	5
○	A. A. Gewürztraminer Crescendo '05	**YY**	5
○	A. A. Pinot Grigio '05	**YY**	4*
○	A. A. Sauvignon '05	**YY**	4*
●	A. A. Cabernet Merlot Crescendo Ris. '03	**YY**	5
○	A. A. Gewürztraminer '05	**YY**	4*
○	A. A. Pinot Bianco '05	**YY**	4
●	A. A. Santa Maddalena Perlhof '05	**YY**	4
●	Perlhof Crescendo '05	**YY**	4
○	A. A. Sauvignon '04	YY	4*

CALDARO/KALTERN (BZ)

JOSEF SÖLVA - NIKLASERHOF

LOC. SAN NICOLO
VIA BRUNNER, 31A
39052 CALDARO/KALTERN (BZ)
TEL. 0471963432
www.niklaserhof.it

Surrounded by vineyards in the small village of San Nicolò above Caldaro, the Niklaserhof estate is a reliable address for great quality wines with character and originality. Josef and Dieter Sölva energetically and professionally work their family's five hectares under vine. But their general enthusiasm for wine is found in the old private Sölva family cellar and the collection of thousands of mainly regional bottles with labels that go back to the 1950s. Wooden barrels are found in the new stonewalled cellar, proof that tradition fits nicely with new technology and innovation. Over the past few years, Niklaserhof has submitted some excellent whites from its vineyards located in the highest parts of the zone. The Kerner '05 went through to the Three Glass finals, having convinced the panel with its fragrant aromas of flowers and bell pepper. The palate is juicy, zesty and elegant, proffering lovely acidity and fantastic grip. The two Pinot Bianco '05s from the estate are also great. The fresh, fruity Klaser has notes of pear and banana. The standard version is tangy and full of character. Bianco Mondevinum '04 still shows very young with lovely oak and notes of ripe fruit. The Sauvignon '05 is fruity, exotic and intense on the nose, then mineral and juicy in the mouth with nice acidity and length. The Lago di Caldaro Scelto Classico '05 is floral, spicy and fresh as well as very drinkable. The two 2003 reds, the Merlot and Lagrein-Cabernet Klaser, are mature, slightly marked by the oak and show somewhat dusty tannins.

○	A. A. Kerner '05	🍷🍷	4*
○	A. A. Bianco Mondevinum '04	🍷🍷	5
●	A. A. Lago di Caldaro Scelto Cl. '05	🍷🍷	3*
○	A. A. Pinot Bianco '05	🍷🍷	4*
○	A. A. Pinot Bianco Klaser '05	🍷🍷	4
○	A. A. Sauvignon '05	🍷🍷	4
●	A. A. Lagrein-Cabernet Klaser '03	🍷	5
●	A. A. Merlot Klaser '03	🍷	5
○	A. A. Bianco Mondevinum '03	🍷🍷 (prev.)	5
○	Kerner Mondevinum '03	🍷🍷 (prev.)	4
●	A. A. Lago di Caldaro Scelto Cl. '04	🍷🍷 (prev.)	3*
○	A. A. Pinot Bianco '04	🍷🍷 (prev.)	4*
○	A. A. Pinot Bianco Klaser '04	🍷🍷 (prev.)	4

CALDARO/KALTERN (BZ)

PETER SÖLVA & SÖHNE

VIA DELL'ORO, 33
39052 CALDARO/KALTERN (BZ)
TEL. 0471964650
www.soelva.com

The Peter Sölva & Söhne winery is one of the oldest in Caldaro. Viticultural activities at the estate have been documented as far back as 1731, one reason the president of the provincial council gave the estate an award a few months ago for 275 years of activity. This led Stephan Sölva, the proud, young powerhouse force of the estate, to jokingly define himself as a "true autochthonous variety". The Sölva family produces roughly 60,000 bottles a year, released under the Desilvas and Amistar lines. They are excellent, technically well-made wines that have loads of varietal typicity and character. Lagrein Desilvas '05 has intense fruit on the nose. The rich, full-bodied palate shows juicy, long, powerful and dynamic. As usual, the Lago di Caldaro Desilvas Peterleiten '05 has cherry and almond fragrances and a very intense, full-flavoured, soft palate with depth and beautiful progression. The Amistar Rosso '03, from a base of lagrein, merlot and cabernet, is powerful and well structured with ripe fruit, very clear tannins and an intense, sweet finish. Outstanding whites this year include the Sauvignon Desilvas '05, with asparagus and aniseed notes, minerality, elegance and length on the palate, and the Gewürztraminer Amistar '05, which is fragrant, full and intense. Terlano Pinot Bianco Desilvas '05 is pleasing thanks to its fruity nose and lovely freshness but the Lagrein Desilvas Edizione '03 lacks a bit of energy because of overripe notes and a slightly dusty palate.

●	A. A. Lagrein Scuro Desilvas '05	🍷🍷	4
●	Amistar Rosso '03	🍷🍷	6
○	A. A. Gewürztramimer Amistar '05	🍷🍷	5
●	A. A. Lago di Caldaro Scelto Cl. Sup. Desilvas Peterleiten '05	🍷🍷	4
○	A. A. Sauvignon Desilvas '05	🍷🍷	5
●	A. A. Lagrein Scuro Desilvas '03	🍷	5
○	A. A. Terlano Pinot Bianco Desilvas '05	🍷	5
○	A. A. Gewürztramimer Amistar '04	🍷🍷 (prev.)	5
●	Amistar Edizione S '02	🍷🍷 (prev.)	7
○	Amistar Bianco '03	🍷🍷 (prev.)	5
●	A.A. Lago di Caldaro Cl. Sup. Desilvas Peterleiten '04	🍷🍷 (prev.)	4

CALDARO/KALTERN (BZ)

★ Cantina Viticoltori di Caldaro

via Cantine, 12
39052 Caldaro/Kaltern (BZ)
tel. 0471963149
www.kellereikaltern.com

Cantina Produttori Caldaro is a major Alto Adige winemaking estate that has never lacked a spirit of initiative. A few years ago, it converted around 20 hectares of vineyards to biodynamic farming and we tasted the interesting first wines from there. Kellermeister Helmuth Zozin, one of Italy's most competent, cultured oenologists, now has two reasons to be satisfied, having won a Three Glass award and our prize for the best sweet wine in Italy with the Moscato Giallo Passito Serenade '03. The nose proffers candied orange peel, dates and Mediterranean herbs. The consistent, balanced palate is concentrated yet refreshed by lively acidity and the finish echoes the citrus. All of this is presented with great balance. This co-operative is also famous for its Cabernet Sauvignons and two selections reached our finals, the Campaner Riserva '03 and Pfarrhof Riserva '03. The former, still slightly marked by the wood, has intense pencil lead aromas and a concentrated, austere palate that has great balance and thrust. We just preferred the latter, sourced from the historic Pfarrhof vineyard, especially for the quality of its sweet, ripe tannins. The two Sauvignons, Premstaler '05 and Castel Giovanelli '04, also performed very well, revealing concentration and character. The classic Chardonnay Wadleith '05, Pinot Nero Saltner '04, the excellent Lago di Caldaro Pfarrhof '05 and Lagrein Spigel '04 are all built along the same lines. As we said at the start, the first biodynamic wine produced, the juicy, caressing Lago di Caldaro Solos '05, is interesting.

○ A. A. Moscato Giallo Passito Serenade '03	YYY	6
● A. A. Cabernet Sauvignon Campaner Ris. '03	YY	5
● A. A. Cabernet Sauvignon Pfarrhof Ris. '03	YY	6
● A. A. Lagrein Spigel '04	YY	5
● A. A. Pinot Nero Saltner '04	YY	4
○ A. A. Sauvignon Castel Giovanelli '04	YY	6
○ A. A. Chardonnay Wadleith '05	YY	4*
○ A. A. Gewürztraminer Campaner '05	YY	5
● A. A. Lago di Caldaro Pfarrhof '05	YY	4*
● A. A. Lago di Caldaro Solos '05	YY	4
○ A. A. Sauvignon Premstaler '05	YY	4*

CASTELBELLO CIARDES/KASTELBELL TSCHARS (BZ)

Köfelgut - Martin Pohl

rione ai Tre Canti, 12
39020 Castelbello Ciardes/
Kastelbell Tschars (BZ)
tel. 0473624634 - 0473624142

The first commandment at Köfelgut in Castelbello, Val Venosta, is respect nature in the vineyard and cellar. First mentioned in 1333, this ancient property has been owned by the Pohl family since 1786. Hubert Pohl has been one of the pioneers of viticulture in the valley over the past decade. In 1973, he planted the first vines of pinot nero in Val Venosta and that same year was one of the first to bottle and market his own wines. Today, his son Martin enthusiastically carries on his labours. Pinot nero, schiava, pinot bianco, pinot grigio, chardonnay and riesling are all cultivated on the estate's four and a half hectares of vineyards that yield around 30,000 bottles. A wine that shows the special character of Val Venosta, Pinot Nero Fleck Riserva '03 is fruity and very elegant with wild berry aromas, lovely freshness and long, sweet finish. Another characteristic and well-typed wine is the Gewürztraminer '05, which gives roses, honey and apricot. On the powerful, broad palate, we found intensity, freshness and elegance. Crafted in the perfect Valle Venosta style of finesse and minerality, the assertive Riesling '05 unveils lovely notes of citrus and flint. The Valle Venosta Bianco Cuvée '05, from a base of 70 per cent pinot grigio with some pinot bianco and chardonnay, has a convincing minerally structure, stylish aromatics and tanginess. We close with the delightfully drinkable Pinot Bianco '05, a classic from the zone, with fresh apple aromas and lovely acidity.

● A. A. Valle Venosta Pinot Nero Fleck Ris. '03	YY	6
○ A. A. Valle Venosta Bianco Cuvée '05	YY	5
○ A. A. Valle Venosta Gewürztraminer '05	YY	5
○ A. A. Valle Venosta Pinot Bianco '05	YY	4*
○ A. A. Valle Venosta Riesling '05	YY	4*
○ A. A. Valle Venosta Gewürztraminer '03	ΥΥ (white)	5
○ A. A. Valle Venosta Pinot Grigio '03	ΥΥ (white)	4
● A. A. Valle Venosta Pinot Nero Fleck '03	ΥΥ (white)	5
○ A. A. Valle Venosta Pinot Bianco '04	ΥΥ (white)	4*
○ A. A. Valle Venosta Riesling '04	ΥΥ (white)	4*

CASTELBELLO CIARDES/KASTELBELL TSCHARS (BZ)

TENUTA UNTERORTL - CASTEL JUVAL

FRAZ. JUVAL, 1B
39020 CASTELBELLO CIARDES/
KASTELBELL TSCHARS (BZ)
TEL. 0473667580 - 3474013858
www.unterortl.it

The Unterortl estate is owned by Reinhold Messner. A place of dizzying beauty, it has been run for some years now by Martin and Gisela Aurich, partners in work and life. Martin also teaches oenology at the San Michele all'Adige wine school and is one of the best wine technicians in the region. Working conditions are demanding to say the least with inclines that reach up to 45 per cent, but the results are so rewarding that thanks to the Aurichs, and a small band of growers you can count on one hand, wines from Valle Venosta have achieved major results. In fact, the Riesling '05 even this young came close to Three Glasses. The nose is still closed but the palate is elegant and well sustained with great minerality, dynamic development and a finish that is actually minty. We'll just have to be patient. The same goes for the Riesling Windbichel '04, from grapes harvested in a small vineyard just above the cellar and aged exclusively in stainless steel. It has a more robust structure without losing any of its freshness or depth. The Pinot Bianco '05 is all elegance and fragrance. This apparently simple wine is complex and layered, minerally and deep. The stylish, slightly smoky Pinot Nero '04 is in the Valle Venosta style. There is also an unusual wine in the pleasant, minerally, fresh-drinking Glimmert '05, a white from a cuvée of fraueler, blaterle and riesling.

○	A. A. Valle Venosta Riesling '05	🍷🍷	5
●	A. A. Valle Venosta Pinot Nero '04	🍷🍷	5
○	A. A. Valle Venosta Riesling Windbichel '04	🍷🍷	5
○	A. A. Valle Venosta Pinot Bianco '05	🍷🍷	4*
○	Juval Glimmet '05	🍷	4*
○	A. A. Valle Venosta Riesling '03	🍷🍷🍷	5*
○	A. A. Valle Venosta Riesling '04	🍷🍷🍷	5*
○	A. A. Valle Venosta Riesling '02	🍷🍷	5
○	A. A. Valle Venosta Pinot Bianco '04	🍷🍷	4*

CERMES/TSCHERMS (BZ)

GRAF PFEIL WEINGUT KRÄNZL

VIA PALADE, 1
39010 CERMES/TSCHERMS (BZ)
TEL. 0473564549

Graf Franz Pfeil is a special personality even in Alto Adige wine, a world with more than a few interesting types. A man of few words, a bit distant yet polite, Franz has his own ideas about producing wine and pays no attention to fads, market trends or, well, wine guides. A strictly organic producer since 1985 at his splendid estate in Tscherms, he makes the wines he likes best and they resemble him. His final products may not please everyone because of their slightly old-fashioned aura, but they stand apart on the Alto Adige winemaking scene, at times too dominated by technique. Anyway, we like Weingut Kränzl wines, of which around 35,000 bottles are produced, precisely because of their light style. They set us talking but we consider this an added value. Let's begin by introducing a magnificent version of Meranese Baslan '04, a great, elegant Schiava. It's a bit atypical because of its density but it has extraordinary minerality and freshness. It's a wine that stands outside categories. Pinot Bianco Helios '04 is as special as ever, with intense aromatic herb and ripe fruit aromas. The apparently lightweight palate is compact, vivid, minerally and elegant. The floral, spicy Meranese '04 is fragrant, supple and very drinkable. In the same style, the Gewürztraminer Passito Dorado '03 shows lovely citrus and floral notes followed by a stylish, balanced palate. The Cabernet Sauvignon-Merlot Sagittarius '03 and Pinot Nero '03 are both well made. The latter manages to preserve some integrity in spite of the unavoidable difficulties of the growing year.

●	A. A. Meranese Hügel Ris. Baslan '04	🍷🍷	4
○	A. A. Gewürztraminer Passito Dorado '03	🍷🍷	6
●	A. A. Meranese Hügel '04	🍷🍷	3*
○	A. A. Pinot Bianco Helios '04	🍷🍷	5
●	A. A. Cabernet Sauvignon-Merlot Sagittarius '03	🍷	6
●	A. A. Pinot Nero '03	🍷	5
○	A. A. Pinot Bianco Helios '02	🍷🍷	5
●	A. A. Cabernet Sauvignon-Merlot Sagittarius '01	🍷🍷	6
○	A. A. Pinot Bianco Helios '01	🍷🍷	5
●	A. A. Pinot Nero Ris. '02	🍷🍷	5

CHIUSA/KLAUSEN (BZ)

CANTINA PRODUTTORI VALLE ISARCO
VIA COSTE, 50
39043 CHIUSA/KLAUSEN (BZ)
TEL. 0472847553
www.cantinavalleisarco.it

If we were to list all the wines from Cantina Produttori Valle Isarco that scored at least Two Glasses, this entire profile would not be long enough. And that may be the best tribute a winery could receive. The cellar won Three Glasses for a particularly elegant – no easy thing – '05 version of Kerner Aristos. But we feel this award represents the classic icing on the cake for the extraordinarily competent work of legendary estate oenologist Thomas Dorfmann, a man who was born to the trade. In fact, our finals this year included the Gewürztraminer, Sylvaner, Riesling and even the delicious Müller Thurgau, all from the 2005 vintage of the Aristos line. Add to this the excellent performance of the Pinot Grigio and Veltliner, again Aristos and again '05. But we must emphasize that a standard line of these wines also exists. If they were submitted for tasting, many would achieve surprisingly high scores. We feel there few operations wineries in Alto Adige, or indeed Italy, can boast results as consistent as those achieved by this fairly new co-operative winery with very clear ideas. But let's return to the award-winner, a Kerner with typical citrus and tropical fruit aromas and a concentrated palate that is embellished by a fresh, elegant style and a classic minerally finish of wet stone. There is really little else to add, except a mention for the extraordinary Laitacher '05, a red from a schiava base with splashes of lagrein, pinot nero and portoguieser, which is very fresh and very drinkable.

○	A. A. Valle Isarco Kerner Aristos '05	🍷🍷🍷	4*
○	A. A. Valle Isarco Gewürztraminer Aristos '05	🍷🍷	5
○	A. A. Valle Isarco Müller Thurgau Aristos '05	🍷🍷	4*
○	A. A. Valle Isarco Riesling Aristos '05	🍷🍷	4*
○	A. A. Valle Isarco Sylvaner Aristos '05	🍷🍷	4*
○	A. A. Sauvignon Aristos '05	🍷🍷	4
●	A. A. Valle Isarco Klausener Laitacher '05	🍷🍷	4*
○	A. A. Valle Isarco Pinot Grigio Aristos '05	🍷🍷	4
○	A. A. Valle Isarco Veltliner Aristos '05	🍷🍷	4*

CORTACCIA/KURTATSCH (BZ)

CANTINA PRODUTTORI CORTACCIA
STRADA DEL VINO, 23
39040 CORTACCIA/KURTATSCH (BZ)
TEL. 0471880115
www.kellerei-kurtatsch.it

This by now customary outstanding performance from Cantina Produttori di Cortaccia is no surprise. Four wines reached our finals, which is no small feat. Founded in 1900 and located downhill from the village, its more than 200 member growers cultivate 240 hectares under vine that extend to 900 metres above sea level. This zone is perfect for producing great white wines as well as complex, characterful reds. The special site climates, the excellent properties of the terrain and the great skill of the entire staff including President Arnold Terzer, a leading figure in Alto Adige wine, and Kellermeister Othmar Donà, all help create high-calibre wines. Let's start with one of the cellar's historic wines. The Gewürztraminer Freienfeld '05 has over the years lost certain slightly heavy notes, improving in finesse and balance, as in this vintage, where elegant notes of tropical fruits usher in a concentrated yet slim-bodied palate with citrus-like and flinty notes. Another significant white, the Sauvignon Fohrhof '05 shows benzene and elegant acidity on the palate. Two more long-established reds are among the best from their respective types, Cabernet Freienfeld '03 and Merlot Brenntal from the same vintage. The former flaunts a palate with the usual density and elegant tannins and a finish with great progression. The second has aromas of pencil lead and ripe blackberry that introduce the juicy palate with its racy freshness. The Lagrein Freienfeld '04, Schiava Sonntaler '05, Chardonnay Felsenhof '05 and Cabernet Kirchhügel '04 are all excellent.

●	A. A. Cabernet Freienfeld '03	🍷🍷	7
●	A. A. Merlot Brenntal '03	🍷🍷	6
○	A. A. Gewürztraminer Freienfeld '05	🍷🍷	5
○	A. A. Sauvignon Fohrhof '05	🍷🍷	4
●	A. A. Cabernet Kirchhügel '04	🍷🍷	5
●	A. A. Lagrein Freienfeld '04	🍷🍷	5
○	A. A. Chardonnay Felsenhof '05	🍷🍷	4*
●	A. A. Schiava Grigia Sonntaler '05	🍷🍷	4*
●	A. A. Cabernet Freienfeld '97	YYY	6
●	A. A. Merlot Brenntal '97	YYY	5
○	A. A. Bianco Freienfeld '04	YY	5

Tiefenbrunner

Fraz. Niclara
via Castello, 4
39040 Cortaccia/Kurtatsch (BZ)
tel. 0471880122
www.tiefenbrunner.com

Tiefenbrunner is one of the most famous wineries in Alto Adige and its best-known wine is the Müller Thurgau sourced from a vineyard over a thousand metres above sea level. This extreme wine is dedicated to Feldmarschall von Fenner, founder of the Austro-Hungarian Empire's Alpine troops. This symbol of the winery, and indeed one of Alto Adige's legendary whites, has finally won Three Glasses. This makes us happy because, after a fairly depressed spell, this old, must-visit Cortaccia estate has over the last few years experienced a general increase in quality while maintaining its style of elegant, never excessive wines. For example, the "Feld" is apparently uncomplicated but just leave it in the glass a minute. Mineral and benzene notes will start to show through the varietal fruity aromas. The wonderfully characterful palate is spirited, vibrant and long, promising exceedingly well for its life in the cellar. The Gewürztraminer Castel Turmhof, Sauvignon Kirchleiten and Cuvée Anna, from equal parts of pinot bianco and grigio, are all from 2005 and all went through to our finals. We would also like to mention one of the best '03 Pinot Neros from Alto Adige. Riserva Linticlarus '03 has managed to preserve a certain freshness and shows elegant tannins and outstanding overall integrity. The Chardonnay and Schiava Grigia, both from the Castel Turmhof line and the 2005 vintage, are pictures of finesse and elegance. But then the whole range submitted this year by Christof and Herbert Tiefenbrunner won our applause.

○	Feldmarschall von Fenner zu Fennberg '05	TTT	5
○	A. A. Cuvée Anna Castel Turmhof '05	TT	4*
○	A. A. Gewürztraminer Castel Turmhof '05	TT	5
○	A. A. Sauvignon Kirchleiten '05	TT	4*
●	A. A. Cabernet Sauvignon Linticlarus Ris. '03	TT	6
●	A. A. Cuvée Linticlarus '03	TT	5
●	A. A. Lagrein Linticlarus Ris. '03	TT	5
●	A. A. Pinot Nero Linticlarus Ris. '03	TT	5
○	A. A. Chardonnay Linticlarus '04	TT	5
○	A. A. Chardonnay Castel Turmhof '05	TT	4*
●	A. A. Schiava Grigia Castel Turmhof '05	TT	4*
○	A. A. Gewürztraminer Castel Turmhof '02	YYY	5

CORTACCIA/KURTATSCH (BZ)

Baron Widmann

Endergasse, 3
39040 Cortaccia/Kurtatsch (BZ)
tel. 0471880092
www.baron-widmann.it

Baron Widmann makes a welcome and impressive return. This outstanding Adige Valley winery has been absent from the Guide for years, because of owner Andreas Widmann's excessive reserve, so to speak. Producing wine since 1824, the cellar alone is worth a visit to the charming village of Cortaccia, where you will find simple graciousness at the farmhouse and wines characterized by elegance and wonderful drinkability. Around 35,000 bottles are produced from the 15 estate-owned hectares under vine. The word elegance immediately brings to mind the Rot '04, from cabernet sauvignon, franc and merlot grown in the Auhof vineyard. The aromas are intense and the full, stylish palate offers silky tannins, confident progression, harmony and depth. Our tasters sent it on to the Three Glass finals. The simply delightful Schiava '05 shows florality with a fragrant palate. The Weiss '05 is also quite interesting. It's a blend of pinot bianco and chardonnay, sourced from the Milla and Sulzhof vineyards, with a spectrum of aromatics that shows acacia honey and summer flowers. The palate is elegant, fresh and deep with dynamic progression that makes this a stylish, gutsy white. The Sauvignon from the same vintage shows almost aggressive aromas but then we rediscover that elegance in the mouth that characterizes all the house wines, combined with clear minerality and a taut, vibrant finish. The Gewürztraminer '05 is a classic, showing concentrated and intense but unfolding harmoniously along the entire vibrant progression. We can only call this a return in grand style.

●	A. A. Cabernet-Merlot Rot '04	TT	5
○	A. A. Gewürztraminer '05	TT	4
○	A. A. Sauvignon '05	TT	4
●	A. A. Schiava '05	TT	4*
○	A. A. Weiss '05	TT	4*
●	A. A. Cabernet Feld '91	YYY	5
●	A. A. Cabernet-Merlot Auhof '97	YYY	5

CORTINA/KURTINIG (BZ)

Peter Zemmer

Strada del Vino, 24
39040 Cortina/Kurtinig (BZ)
tel. 0471817143
www.zemmer.com

Managed with a sure hand by Helmuth Zemmer, this estate's quality standards have remained better than just good for several years now. And it is not easy to stay in front in a region like Alto Adige, where competition is always getting tougher. This is a major winery in numbers as well, considering production has now reached around 650,000 bottles a year. Among the most interesting wines is Cortinie Bianco '05, from 60 per cent chardonnay and pinot bianco with small amounts of pinot grigio, sauvignon and a splash of gewürztraminer. It gives intense fruit on the nose and power, rich depth and harmony in its development on the palate. The flawless Pinot Bianco La Lot '05 shows elegant tones of white-fleshed fruit and a dynamic, spirited palate with a truly enjoyable mouthfeel. The varietal, well-balanced Pinot Grigio '05 has a juicy palate although it may lack a pinch of finesse. The robust Lagrein Reserve '03 reveals solid backbone and well-gauged acidity that sustains the clear, fresh fruit. The Chardonnay and Sauvignon, both from 2005, are technically very well made but lack a little personality.

●	A. A. Lagrein Reserve '03	🍷🍷	5
○	A. A. Pinot Bianco La Lot '05	🍷🍷	4*
○	A. A. Pinot Grigio '05	🍷🍷	4
○	Cortinie Bianco '05	🍷🍷	5
○	A. A. Chardonnay '05	🍷	4
○	A. A. Sauvignon '05	🍷	4
○	A. A. Chardonnay '03	ΥΥ	4*
○	A. A. Chardonnay Reserve '03	ΥΥ	5
○	Cortinie Bianco '03	ΥΥ	4
○	A. A. Pinot Bianco La Lot '04	ΥΥ	4*
○	A. A. Pinot Grigio '04	ΥΥ	4*

EGNA/NEUMARKT (BZ)

H. Lun

loc. Villa, 22/24
39044 Egna/Neumarkt (BZ)
tel. 0471813256
www.lun.it

Wines from the Lun estate take us back to 35 years to when our first tasting of Alto Adige wines included whites from this estate, a historic name in Alto Adige viticulture, founded in 1840. In 2006, it is still at the forefront even in the constantly shifting conditions of Alto Adige, where life is hard even for the most skilled producers. For some years now, it has been part of the Cornaiano co-operative and this year, it again submitted a respectable range of wines. They may not have tremendous personality but they are all well made, balanced and great value for money. Among the most interesting of them is the intensely fruity Bianco Sandbichler '05, from 50 per cent pinot bianco, 30 per cent chardonnay and the rest riesling with a pinch of sauvignon. It's a wine that shows a gutsy palate with minerally notes and a positively juicy finish. Notes of grilled bell pepper and wild fennel announce the Cabernet Sauvignon Albertus Riserva '03 before the palate unveils fine-grained tannins and an elegant profile. The Santa Maddalena Föhrner '05 is fresh and minerally. The two '05 Sauvignons, the standard and the Albertus selection, are very typical and elegant. The first is fresher and more dynamic, the second more concentrated. The Gewürztraminer Albertus and Riesling, both from '05, and the Lagrein Albertus Riserva '03, are all impeccable.

●	A. A. Cabernet Sauvignon Albertus Ris. '03	🍷🍷	5
○	A. A. Bianco Sandbichler '05	🍷🍷	4
●	A. A. Santa Maddalena Föhrner '05	🍷🍷	4*
○	A. A. Sauvignon '05	🍷🍷	4
○	A. A. Sauvignon Albertus '05	🍷🍷	5
●	A. A. Lagrein Scuro Albertus Ris. '03	🍷	5
○	A. A. Gewürztraminer Albertus '05	🍷	5
○	A. A. Riesling '05	🍷	3*
○	A. A. Bianco Sandbichler '03	ΥΥ	4
●	A. A. Lagrein Scuro Albertus Ris. '02	ΥΥ	5
○	A. A. Bianco Sandbicher '04	ΥΥ	4

FIÈ ALLO SCILIAR/VÖLS AM SCHLERN (BZ)

Gumphof - Markus Prackwieser

LOC. NOVALE DI PRESULE, 8
39050 FIÈ ALLO SCILIAR/
VÖLS AM SCHLERN (BZ)
TEL. 0471601190
www.gumphof.it

This year, Markus Prackwieser failed to win another Three Glass award with his Sauvignon Praesulis '05. Nonetheless, it is still one of the best around, with aniseed and damson notes that open up on a full, juicy yet taut palate with vibrant acidity and a long, expansive finish. It's a pity because this likeable young winemaker has for some years now always submitted characterful, personal bottles from the 30,000 units he bottles at his four-hectare estate clinging to a steep cliff on the slopes of the Sciliar range, at the entrance to Valle Isarco. Seen from the valley floor, the estate makes your head spin. To reach it, you take a small, narrow, winding road up to the insanely steep vineyards. At around 400 metres above sea level, the area has a lot of light and good daytime temperatures that help proper ripening of the grapes, dropping significantly in the evening as air currents arrive from the valley. Markus is not just a skilled winemaker, he is also an enthusiast. His eyes flash when he talks about his projects. This year, he submitted an interesting Pinot Nero '04. Actually, the small selection presented by Gumphof is always respectable, starting with the two Pinot Biancos, the standard wine and the Praesulis selection, both from '05. The former is simpler but drinks beautifully while the second is richer, varietal and dynamic. The Gewürztraminer '05 is minerally, progressive, crisp and elegant. We confess a weakness for Markus's Schiava and think the 2005 is absolutely one of the best for its typicity and enjoyable drinkability, along with a modest price tag.

○	A. A. Sauvignon Praesulis '05	🍷🍷	5
●	A. A. Pinot Nero '04	🍷🍷	5
○	A. A. Gewurztraminer Praesulis '05	🍷🍷	5
○	A. A. Pinot Bianco '05	🍷🍷	4*
○	A. A. Pinot Bianco Praesulis '05	🍷🍷	4*
●	A. A. Schiava '05	🍷🍷	3*
○	A. A. Sauvignon Praesulis '04	🍸🍸🍸	5*
○	A. A. Pinot Bianco Praesulis '02	🍸🍸	4
○	A. A. Sauvignon Praesulis '02	🍸🍸	4
○	A. A. Pinot Bianco Praesulis '04	🍸🍸	4*
○	A. A. Gewurztraminer Praesulis '04	🍸🍸	4*

MARLENGO/MARLING (BZ)

Cantina Produttori Burggräfler

VIA PALADE, 64
39020 MARLENGO/MARLING (BZ)
TEL. 0473447137
www.burggraefler.it

Our compliments to Burggräfler Kellerei, which submitted a range of very sound wines this year. The vast experience and skill of oenologist Hansjörg Donà and the constant efforts of the 210 member growers of the winery, founded in 1901 at Marlengo near Merano, are bearing fruit. Two wines made it to the Three Glass finals. This excellent result rewards all the small growers that supply the winery with select grapes. Though only 25 per cent of the vines bear white grapes, we really liked the Pinot Bianco Vendemmia Tardiva MerVin '05, which convinced us with a rich bouquet of fig, apricot and aromatic herbs. The palate is fruity, fresh, concentrated and long with lovely acidity. The complex, intense Merlot-Lagrein Privat '04 is combines fruit and pepper on the nose, then unveils a juicy, elegantly minerally palate. The excellent Pinot Bianco Privat '05 has great body, concentration and freshness. Chardonnay Privat '05 is full, minerally and dynamic but still marked by slightly oaky notes on the palate. The two Gewürztraminers, the Privat '05 and the new MerVin '05, both of which are simplish, and the Sauvignon Privat '05 were all a bit less convincing this year. The Moscato Giallo Schickenburg '05 is well typed with aromatic tones of honey and broom. The pleasantly drinkable Schiava Meranese Schickenburg '05, from the variety that makes up almost half the winery's vine stock, is fruity, fresh, spicy, juicy and supple. The Meranese Algunder Rosengarten '05 is also invitingly delicious.

●	A. A. Merlot-Lagrein Privat '04	🍷🍷	5
○	A. A. Pinot Bianco V. T. MerVin '05	🍷🍷	6
○	A. A. Chardonnay Privat '05	🍷🍷	4
○	A. A. Pinot Bianco Privat '05	🍷🍷	4
●	A. A. Schiava Meranese Schickenburg '05	🍷🍷	4*
○	A. A. Gewürztraminer MerVin '05	🍷	5
○	A. A. Gewürztraminer Privat '05	🍷	4
○	A. A. Moscato Giallo Schickenburg '05	🍷	4
○	A. A. Sauvignon Privat '05	🍷	4
●	A. A. Schiava Meranese Algunder Rosengarten '05	🍷	4
●	A. A. Pinot Nero MerVin '02	🍸🍸	5
○	A. A. Gewürztraminer Privat '04	🍸🍸	4
○	A. A. Pinot Bianco Privat '04	🍸🍸	4

MELTINA/MÖLTEN (BZ)

VIVALDI - ARUNDA
VIA CENTRO, 53
39010 MELTINA/MÖLTEN (BZ)
TEL. 0471668033
www.arundavivaldi.it

Joseph Reiterer is a legendary figure among sparkling winemakers in Alto Adige. An excellent oenologist, he is president and one of the founders of the Alto Adige Metodo Classico association. His winery is managed in tandem with his wife Marianna and is located at Meltina. At 1,200 metres above sea level, it is one of the highest sparkling wineries in Europe, if not the world. Arunda, or Vivaldi, depending whether the product is for the German or Italian-speaking market, produces 70,000 bottles a year of numerous cuvées that are always chardonnay-led when not actual blanc de blancs. Long periods of ageing on the lees give these spumante sparklers their identifying features of finesse and delicate elegance. We were most persuaded by the Spumante Extra Brut Cuvée Marianna, which shows lovely tones of apricot, flowers and aromatic herbs. The palate is elegant, zesty and full, and after developing well closes out delicately on almonds and minerals. Just as good is the Spumante Extra Brut Blanc de Blancs, which has delicately floral tones, crusty bread and light notes of citrus. The palate is supple, soft and spirited, and has decent length. Just a step below this are the pleasant Spumante Extra Brut Riserva '01 and Spumante Rosé Brut.

○ A. A. Spumante Extra Brut Cuvée Marianna	🍷🍷	6
○ A. A. Spumante Talento Blanc de Blancs Extra Brut	🍷🍷	5
○ A. A. Spumante Talento Extra Brut Ris. '01	🍷	6
⊙ A. A. Spumante Rosé Brut	🍷	5
○ A. A. Spumante Vivaldi Ris. '97	ΥΥ	5
○ A. A. Spumante Extra Brut Arunda Ris. '98	ΥΥ	6
○ A. A. Spumante Brut Vivaldi '99	ΥΥ	4
○ A. A. Spumante Extra Brut Cuvée Marianna	ΥΥ	6

MERANO/MERAN (BZ)

CANTINA VINI MERANO
LOC. MAIA BASSA
VIA SAN MARCO, 11
39012 MERANO/MERAN (BZ)
TEL. 0473235544
www.meranerkellerei.com

The fashion for Gewürztraminer knows no bounds, just as the habit of drinking the current vintage shows no signs of decreasing. Once Christmas has arrived, it disappears from shops and wine lists. This is a pity since this wine actually gives its best with the slow passing of time. This little introduction is to call attention to Gewürztraminer Graf von Meran '05, one of the best and most cellarable from Alto Adige. The intense aromas of candied citron peel and alfalfa return in the mouth, where the structure is dense but elegant and minerally with well-balanced acidity and no-nonsense freshness. But the standard Gewürztraminer, with its amazing complexity, character and elegance, shows the winery's skill with the type. Credit goes to the Cantina Produttori di Merano, a small co-operative winery for Alto Adige releasing around 350,000 bottles from 142 hectares of splendidly positioned vineyards. Under the guidance of Kellermeister Stefan Kapfinger, the cellar puts together a range of, to say the least, spectacular wines that still, however, lacks a Three Glass award. But as you can see, the Glassware collection is impressive. The standard Sauvignon '05 actually left us open-mouthed with its elegant star anise and aromatic herbs, and a vibrant, stylish, supple palate. But the house Kellermeister also shows he can handle Schiava, with three completely different wines, all well-defined and full of personality. The Sauvignon '05, Pinot Bianco '05 and Cabernet Sauvignon Riserva '03, all from the Graf von Meran selection, show great expertise.

○ A. A. Gewürztraminer Graf Von Meran '05	🍷🍷	5*
○ A. A. Sauvignon '05	🍷🍷	4*
● A. A. Cabernet Sauvignon Graf Von Meran Ris. '03	🍷🍷	5
○ A. A. Gewürztraminer '05	🍷🍷	4*
● A. A. Meraner Eines Fürsten Traum '05	🍷🍷	4*
● A. A. Meraner St. Valentin '05	🍷🍷	3*
○ A. A. Pinot Bianco Graf von Meran '05	🍷🍷	4*
○ A. A. Sauvignon Graf Von Meran '05	🍷🍷	5
● A. A. Val Venosta Schiava Sonnenberg '05	🍷🍷	3*
○ A. A. Gewürztraminer Graf Von Meran '03	ΥΥ	5
○ A. A. Gewürztraminer Graf Von Meran '04	ΥΥ	5*

MONTAGNA/MONTAN (BZ)

FRANZ HAAS
VIA VILLA, 6
39040 MONTAGNA/MONTAN (BZ)
TEL. 0471812280
www.franz-haas.it

When we saw the wines Franz Haas submitted for tasting this year, we thought he had little hope of winning Three Glasses. The estate's two stars, Pinot Nero Schweizer '03 and Moscato Rosa '05, were in fact missing, the former because it had been sold out for some time and the second because Franz felt it was not yet ready. The real surprise here was Manna '04 for this blend of 50 per cent riesling with added chardonnay, sauvignon and gewürztraminer won our highest award hands down. It has an interesting story to tell. Franz Haas and Luisa Manna had only recently married when they went out to dinner at a famous restaurant in Val Pusteria. Between bottles and dishes, they began to discuss a white that would be concentrated yet fresh and mineral, with good grip: in short, a wine like Luisa herself, a woman with loads of character. This was in 1990 and 1995 saw release of the first vintage of Manna, the wine Franz dedicated to his wife. We believe both must be especially happy about this success. As we said, the wine is gutsy, dense yet dynamic. It has minerality, caressing texture, balance and a very dynamic finish. Having said this, the other estate wines are as well crafted as ever. But then Franz Haas is a technician as refined as he is meticulous and when the new cellar is finished and certain vineyards he showed us go into production, we will see great things. His Pinot Bianco '05 is varietal and dynamic, the Müller Thurgau '05 is particularly fragrant and the Lagrein '04 and Gewürztraminer '05 are pleasant. Congratulations to Luisa.

○ Manna '04	▼▼▼	5
○ A. A. Gewürztraminer '05	▼▼	5
○ A. A. Müller Thurgau '05	▼▼	4*
○ A. A. Pinot Bianco '05	▼▼	4
● A. A. Lagrein '04	▼	5
● A. A. Moscato Rosa Schweizer '00	▽▽▽	5
● A. A. Pinot Nero Schweizer '01	▽▽▽	6
● A. A. Pinot Nero Schweizer '02	▽▽▽	6
● A. A. Moscato Rosa Schweizer '99	▽▽▽	5
○ A. A. Gewürztraminer '04	▽▽	5*

NALLES/NALS (BZ)

CANTINA NALS MARGREID
VIA HEILIGENBERG, 2
39010 NALLES/NALS (BZ)
TEL. 0471678626
www.kellerei.it

Nalles Magré is one of those wineries you can trust. Year in and year out, it presents excellent wines that outstandingly reflect the character of their terroir, at better than honest value for money. The dynamic, innovative managerial group includes commercial director Gottfried Pollinger and oenologist Harald Schraffl. The 150 hectares under vine belonging to 140 members, in Nalles near Merano and Magré in the Adige valley, have everything it takes to produce high-quality fruit and even though not all the products convinced us entirely this year, our faith in the cellar remains unshaken. One great Three Glass final wine is the Chardonnay Baron Salvadori '04. Its tropical fruits aromas mingle with well-integrated wood before the palate shows off sensations of confectioner's cream backed up by nice acidity and minerality. Also one of the best in its category, the Terlano Pinot Bianco Sirmian '05 has hedgerow aromas, a full, lively palate with nice minerality and – best of all – is great value for money. The appealing Pinot Grigio Punggl '05 is concentrated and fresh. The Moscato Giallo Passito Baronesse '04 is also dynamic and shows good body. Terlano Sauvignon Mantele '05 and Gewürztraminer Baron Salvadori '05 are very true to type and well made. The Galea '05 is as always a great Schiava. It is fruity and spicy on the nose and then juicy, supple, stylish and elegant in the mouth. As for the Riserva reds, the Lagrein, Cabernet Sauvignon and Cabernet-Merlot Anticus, all from the Baron Salvadori line, are a little marked by the hot weather of the 2003 growing season.

○ A. A. Chardonnay Baron Salvadori '04	▼▼	5
● A. A. Cabernet Sauvignon Baron Salvadori Ris. '03	▼▼	6
○ A. A. Moscato Giallo Passito Baronesse '04	▼▼	6
○ A. A. Pinot Grigio Punggl '05	▼▼	4
● A. A. Schiava Galea '05	▼▼	4*
○ A. A. Terlano Pinot Bianco Sirmian '05	▼▼	4*
● A. A. Cabernet-Merlot Anticus Baron Salvadori Ris. '03	▼	6
● A. A. Lagrein Baron Salvadori Ris. '03	▼	5
○ A. A. Gewürztraminer Baron Salvadori '05	▼	5
○ A. A. Terlano Sauvignon Cl. Mantele '05	▼	4
○ A. A. Chardonnay Baron Salvadori '00	▽▽▽	5

NALLES/NALS (BZ)

Castello Schwanburg
via Schwanburg, 16
39010 Nalles/Nals (BZ)
tel. 0471678622
www.schwanburg.com

After a couple of difficult seasons, the Castel Schwanburg estate has this year returned to levels more befitting the status we were accustomed to some years ago. A symbol of quality wines from Alto Adige since 1556, this ancient estate boasts 27 hectares under vine on the high ground above the village of Nalles, where everything is in place for making great wine. One sign of improvement is the fact that two Schwanburg wines reached our Three Glass finals this year. The Pinot Bianco Pitzon '05 has varietal aromas and distinct florality, showing minerally and assertive with fresh notes of citron peel on the long, dynamic palate. The classic Bordeaux blend Cabernet Sauvignon Riserva '03 shows lovely freshness and finesse, as well as elegance and good depth. The well-made Riesling Bacher '05 is very minerally, intense and fruity. Sauvignon Engl '05 is zesty and long. The Bianco Pallas '05 is pleasant, with lovely notes of white-fleshed fruit, but it is a bit lean. The fresh Lagrein Riserva '03 shows good structure and nice dynamism. The Cabernet Sauvignon Privat '03 is balsamic with notes of black cherry. The Cabernet Sauvignon-Merlot Geierberg '03 is a tad green and a little out of kilter. These thoroughly decent results bode well for an auspicious return to the top for this major winery.

●	A. A. Cabernet Sauvignon Ris. '03	🍷🍷	5
○	A. A. Pinot Bianco Pitzon '05	🍷🍷	4*
●	A. A. Lagrein Scuro Ris. '03	🍷🍷	5
○	A. A. Sauvignon Engl '05	🍷🍷	4*
●	A. A. Cabernet Sauvignon Privat '03	🍷	7
○	A. A. Bianco Pallas '05	🍷	4
○	A. A. Riesling Bacher '05	🍷	4
●	A. A. Cabernet Sauvignon Ris. '01	🍸🍸	5
●	A. A. Lagrein Scuro Ris. '02	🍸🍸	5
○	A. A. Pinot Bianco Pitzon '04	🍸🍸	4*

NATURNO/NATURNS (BZ)

Falkenstein
via Castello, 15
39025 Naturno/Naturns (BZ)
tel. 0473666054
www.falkenstein.bz

After five years, Franz Pratzner has finally recaptured Three Glasses with his splendid Riesling '05. He came very close last year but problems with bottling times and Guide deadlines kept us from awarding him his prize. What can we say about this Riesling? Even though it is still young – a babe in swaddling clothes, as it were – it already has complex, minerally aromas with slightly smoky tones. But it really starts to lift off on the palate. Apparently restrained, little by little its remarkable stamina shines through as tasting continues. It is minerally and elegant with deeply spaced length, hefty acidity of 7.8 grams per litre and a literally overwhelming finish.
One recommendation, though. It is true that this wine is already drinking superbly but have the patience to wait for it. Wait maybe just a year, but wait. Almost as good, the Valle Venosta-style Pinot Bianco '05 puts finesse first, even revealing notes of rosemary and a very minerally finish. On the contrary, the Sauvignon '05 is concentrated and powerful yet at the same time stylish and gutsy, with intense Mediterranean herbs. The Pinot Nero '04 is special, like all wines from Valle Venosta, and the Gewürztraminer Vendemmia Tardiva '04 is also enjoyable. To sum up, a trip to "Falcon's Rock" is well worth it to buy a few bottles, if you can still find them, to meet Franz, a real winemaker, and to visit his vineyards. Unless, of course, you suffer from vertigo.

○	A. A. Valle Venosta Riesling '05	🍷🍷🍷	6
○	A. A. Valle Venosta Pinot Bianco '05	🍷🍷	5
○	A. A. Valle Venosta Sauvignon '05	🍷🍷	5
○	A. A. Valle Venosta Gewürztraminer V. T. '04	🍷🍷	6
●	A. A. Valle Venosta Pinot Nero '04	🍷🍷	6
○	A. A. Valle Venosta Riesling '00	🍸🍸🍸	5
○	A. A. Valle Venosta Riesling '98	🍸🍸🍸	5
○	A. A. Valle Venosta Pinot Bianco '04	🍸🍸	5
○	A. A. Valle Venosta Riesling '04	🍸🍸	5
○	A. A. Valle Venosta Sauvignon '04	🍸🍸	5

SALORNO/SALURN (BZ)

HADERBURG
FRAZ. BUCHOLZ
LOC. POCHI, 30
39040 SALORNO/SALURN (BZ)
TEL. 0471889097 - 3384049785
www.haderburg.it

Alois Ochsenreiter's personality may not always be easy to deal with, but the Three Glass award for the Sylvaner '05 clearly shows how good a winemaker he is. Produced at his small biodynamically managed Obermairlhof estate at Chiusa, Valle Isarco, this, like all his other wines, is aged exclusively in stainless steel and inoculated only with native yeasts. In a perfect Valle Isarco style, it introduces itself with a spectrum of emerging aromatics that is already complex despite its youth. The overwhelming palate shows concentration perfectly offset by no-nonsense acidity and implacable grip, signing off with a remarkably dynamic finish. But the Riesling '05 also impressed us with elegance and a surprising complexity for a wine from a vineyard only four years old. Also crafted along the same lines are an energetic Gewürztraminer '05 and the Cuvée Obermairl '04, produced from a blend of 50 per cent sylvaner, 30 per cent gewürztraminer and the rest pinot grigio and müller thurgau. But Obermairlhof's great success should not overshadow the results from the Haderburg estate. The Spumante Brut '01, from 90 per cent chardonnay with some pinot nero, has round, elegant aromas of great clarity. The Pas Dosé from the same vintage is a Riserva made from the same cuvée, aged five years on the lees. It has undeniable class and shows structure, freshness and complex toast and minerally notes that never mask the vibrant fruit. Also interesting are the two Pinot Neros, the Hausmannhof '04 and the Riserva '03, which hangs together surprisingly well.

○	A. A. Valle Isarco Sylvaner Obermairlhof '05	🍷🍷🍷	4*
○	A. A. Spumante Pas Dosé '01	🍷🍷	5
●	A. A. Pinot Nero Hausmannhof Ris. '03	🍷🍷	6
○	A. A. Riesling Obermairlhof '05	🍷🍷	5*
○	A. A. Valle Isarco Gewürztraminer Obermairlhof '05	🍷🍷	4*
○	A. A. Spumante Brut '01	🍷🍷	5
●	A. A. Pinot Nero Hausmannhof '04	🍷🍷	5
○	A. A. Spumante Hausmannhof Brut Ris. '95	🥂🥂	7

TERLANO/TERLAN (BZ)

TENUTA KORNELL
LOC. SETTEQUERCE
VIA BOLZANO, 23
39018 TERLANO/TERLAN (BZ)
TEL. 0471917507
www.kornell.it

Last year, Tenuta Kornell was one of the most interesting new items in Alto Adige. This year, only a Three Glass award was missing to crown the performance of this very young estate, which has only been bottling its own wines since 2003. Four out of six wines produced reached our finals so we need say nothing more about the quality of the work from Florian Brigl's estate. Ten hectares on family property around the splendid farm, loose-packed sand and clay soil, rich in porphyry, a Mediterranean climate, vines planted between 1985 and 2005, a committed owner and an intense relationship with nature are all elements that come through in Florian's wines, bottles that are, to use an abused term, very natural. But this is wine territory, especially for cabernet. We might add that the range is very good value for money. The dense, creamy Merlot Staves '03 shows sweet tannins, good balance between fruit and acidity, and great minerality. The black olive and balsamic tones of the Merlot-Cabernet Sauvignon Staves '03 usher in a caressing, concentrated yet pleasantly fresh palate, sweet tannins and a long, elegant finish. Austere and aristocratic on the nose, the Cabernet Sauvignon Staves '03 projects an elegant profile with great minerality and wonderful thrust. The Lagrein Greif '04 is fresh, mouthfilling and very drinkable, yet at the same time complex and well coordinated. The Sauvignon '05 is floral and elegant with tangerine notes and a fresh, minerally, determined palate. Not a bad showing for almost first outing.

●	A. A. Cabernet Sauvignon Staves '03	🍷🍷	6
●	A. A. Merlot Staves '03	🍷🍷	6
●	A. A. Merlot-Cabernet Sauvignon Staves '03	🍷🍷	6
●	A. A. Lagrein Greif '04	🍷🍷	4*
○	A. A. Sauvignon Staves '05	🍷🍷	4*
●	A. A. Zeder '04	🍷	4
●	A. A. Cabernet Sauvignon Staves '02	🥂🥂	6
●	A. A. Merlot Staves '02	🥂🥂	6
●	A. A. Lagrein Greif '03	🥂🥂	4*

TERLANO/TERLAN (BZ)

CANTINA TERLANO
VIA COLLI D'ARGENTO, 7
39018 TERLANO/TERLAN (BZ)
TEL. 0471257135
www.cantina-terlano.com

This winery picked up its usual Three Glasses this year for a dazzling, crystalline Chardonnay '94, sent another five wines to the finals and arrayed a series of what are becoming cult wines for their distinct style, a mix of austerity, pleasing drinkability and almost legendary lifespan. This one-of-a-kind character is the trademark of Cantina Terlano. Credit goes to the exceptional technical and executive staffs that understand how to create a highly effective collaborative relationship with member growers. The results of these efforts are obvious. The Chardonnay '94 has aromatic herbs and tropical fruit aromas, yet shows a certain austerity. The stylish, zesty, minerally palate shows lively energy. We'd recommend leaving it in the glass for a few minutes so it can unveil all its complexity. We rather enjoyed the Lagrein Porphyr '03 with its very individual style and great minerality. The Pinot Bianco Vorberg Riserva '03 is powerful and rich, but the growing year may have taken away a bit of verve. The Terlano Sauvignon Quartz '04 is still too young but what character and class. In contrast to some boring, heavy Chardonnays made elsewhere, Kreuth '04 is minerally and even spicy. And the Pinot Grigio '05 is typical and gutsy. These are the Magnificent Six from Rudi Kofler, a young but self-assured oenologist. The array of Glassware that follows is impressive to say the least and puts Cantina Terlano right at the top of Italian winemaking.

○	A. A. Terlano Chardonnay '94	🍷🍷🍷	8
●	A. A. Lagrein Porphyr '03	🍷🍷	6
○	A. A. Terlano Pinot Bianco Vorberg Ris. '03	🍷🍷	4*
○	A. A. Terlano Chardonnay Kreuth '04	🍷🍷	4*
○	A. A. Terlano Sauvignon Quarz '04	🍷🍷	6
○	A. A. Pinot Grigio '05	🍷🍷	4*
○	A. A. Terlano Nova Domus Ris. '02	🍷🍷	6
●	A. A. Lagrein Gries Ris. '03	🍷🍷	4*
●	A. A. Pinot Nero Montigl '03	🍷🍷	4
○	A. A. Gewürztraminer Lunare '04	🍷🍷	6
○	A. A. Terlano Cl. '05	🍷🍷	4*
○	A. A. Terlano Pinot Bianco Cl. '05	🍷🍷	4*
○	A. A. Terlano Sauvignon Winkl '05	🍷🍷	4*

TERMENO/TRAMIN (BZ)

ELENA WALCH
VIA A. HOFER, 1
39040 TERMENO/TRAMIN (BZ)
TEL. 0471860172
www.elenawalch.com

Winning Three Glasses in Alto Adige has become quite a task as more and more good wines and aggressive new wineries appear on the market. Earning two top awards happens once in a blue moon. With her distinctive class, the energetic owner of this beautiful estate, Elena Walch has this year joined the exclusive double winners' club. But Castel Ringberg, which dominates Lake Caldaro from above, and Kastelaz, with its enchanting steep slopes in the heart of Termeno, are ideal places for producing great wines. Gewürztraminer Kastelaz '05 is a great wine and confirms last year's success, introducing itself with clear aromas of candied citron peel laced with iodine. The complex, dry palate has characteristic finesse and dynamic development as well as great depth. The Three Glass encore comes from a wine we particularly love, the varietal, spice and mineral-themed Lagrein Castel Ringberg Riserva '03. The palate is chewy and succulent with sweet, tight-knit tannins and the consistent finish shows pencil lead and clear minerality. But another three wines reached our finals: Bianco Beyond the Clouds '04, which has never before been this streamlined, an exemplary version of the vibrant, minerally Chardonnay Cardellino '05, and the best interpretation yet of Bianco Passito Chachmere '04, from gewürztraminer and sauvignon, with aristocratic citrus and talc aromas and a palate of great concentration yet at the same time fresh, balanced and complex. The success of this female-run estate is rounded off by a series of better than good wines.

●	A. A. Lagrein Castel Ringberg Ris. '03	🍷🍷🍷	6
○	A. A. Gewürztraminer Kastelaz '05	🍷🍷🍷	6
○	A. A. Bianco Beyond the Clouds '04	🍷🍷	6
○	A. A. Cashmere Passito '04	🍷🍷	7
○	A. A. Chardonnay Cardellino '05	🍷🍷	5
●	A. A. Cabernet Sauvignon Castel Ringberg Ris. '03	🍷🍷	7
●	Kermesse '03	🍷🍷	7
○	A. A. Chardonnay Castel Ringberg '04	🍷🍷	5
○	A. A. Sauvignon Castel Ringberg '05	🍷🍷	5
○	A. A. Gewürztraminer Kastelaz '00	🍸🍸🍸	5
○	A. A. Gewürztraminer Kastelaz '04	🍸🍸🍸	6

★ Tenuta J. Hofstätter

p.zza Municipio, 7
39040 Termeno/Tramin (BZ)
tel. 0471860161
www.hofstatter.com

This estate managed by Martin Foradori is one of the most modern and dynamic in Italy. Scrupulous care in vineyards and cellar, special attention for traditional varieties, without losing sight of new market trends, and aggressive, broad-scale marketing strategies have resulted in a range of wines with high overall quality that has been rewarded with well-deserved commercial success. The Three Glasses were missing this year but four wines from some of the most representative varieties in Alto Adige reached our finals: Pinot Nero, Lagrein and Gewürztraminer. Gewürztraminer Kolbenhof '05 is a classic cru, sourced from one splendid vineyard on the hills above Termeno. Its intense, elegant aromas usher in a caressing, dynamic attack on the palate that closes out concentrated and balanced on lovely notes of mineral and fresh almond. Despite the unlucky growing season for the variety, Pinot Nero Barthenau Vigna Sant'Urbano '03 shows all its class, revealing lovely integrity and above all elegant tannic weight and a fairly dynamic finish. The Lagrein '05 shows intense aromas of cinchona and a fragrant palate. A complex aromatic spectrum of cinchona, leather and delicate vegetal notes introduces the Yngram '03, from 70 per cent cabernet and the rest petit verdot and syrah. The palate is concentrated and dense, yet harmonious with sweet tannins and a complex finish. This great performance signs off with the two late-harvest Gewürztraminers, Maria '05 and Joseph '04, the Lagrein Steinraffler '03, the Pinot Bianco '05 and the Bianco Barthenau Vigna San Michele '05.

●	A. A. Pinot Nero Barthenau V. S. Urbano '03	YY	8
●	Yngram '03	YY	7
○	A. A. Gewürztraminer Kolbenhof '05	YY	5
●	A. A. Lagrein '05	YY	4*
●	A. A. Lagrein Scuro Steinraffler '03	YY	6
○	A. A. Gewürztraminer Joseph V. T. '04	YY	6
○	A. A. Barthenau V. S. Michele '05	YY	5
○	A. A. Maria V. T. '05	YY	4
○	A. A. Pinot Bianco '05	YY	4*
○	De Vite '05	YY	4
○	A. A. Gewürztraminer Kolbenhof '03	yyy	5
○	A. A. Gewürztraminer Kolbenhof '04	yyy	5
●	A. A. Pinot Nero Barthenau V. S. Urbano '02	yy	8

★ Cantina Produttori Termeno

strada del Vino, 144
39040 Termeno/Tramin (BZ)
tel. 0471860126
www.tramin-wine.it

It's always difficult to talk about results from Cantina Produttori Termeno, not least because it seems to achieve them with disarming ease. But knowing Willi Stürz and his constant drive for improvement, we know those results come from a great effort that involves all this co-operative winery's structures and nearly 300 member growers. If we say the "usual" Three Glasses, we risk trivializing everything and so kudos to the Gewürztraminer Nussbaumer '05 and Gewürztraminer Passito V.T. Terminum '04. The first, of which more than 50,000 bottles were released, is the usual show of absolute superiority built on complexity, concentration and, we might add, increasing definition and elegance. We have the impression that each year, Willi Stürz proceeds with this wine by exclusion, refining yet at the same time giving it more character. With the Terminum '04, he has succeeded in the difficult exercise of marrying concentration, sweetness and freshness within a framework where balance reaches near perfection. We'll add a great Lagrein Urban '04, the other Gewürztraminer V.T., Roan '04, the best Pinot Grigio from Alto Adige, Unterebner '05, the award-winning Termeno white, the Stoan '05 from 65 per cent chardonnay, 20 per cent sauvignon and a splash of gewürztraminer and pinot bianco, and the well-typed Moscato Rosa Terminum '04. But there is more. The Schiava Freisinger '05 is simply delightful, the Cabernet-Merlot Rungg '03 is juicy and complex and the Sauvignon '05 has elegance and freshness. We should mention that five hectares of vines are now managed organically.

○	A. A. Gewürztraminer Passito Terminum V. T. '04	YYY	8
○	A. A. Gewürztraminer Nussbaumer '05	YYY	5
○	A. A. Gewürztraminer Roan V. T. '04	YY	6
●	A. A. Lagrein Urban '04	YY	6
●	A. A. Moscato Rosa Terminum '04	YY	6
○	A. A. Pinot Grigio Unterebner '05	YY	5*
○	A. A. Stoan '05	YY	5*
●	A. A. Rosso Rungg '03	YY	4
○	A. A. Sauvignon '05	YY	4
●	A. A. Schiava Freisinger '05	YY	4
○	A. A. Gewürztraminer Nussbaumer '03	yyy	5
○	A. A. Gewürztraminer Nussbaumer '04	yyy	5

VADENA/PFATTEN (BZ)

Cantina Laimburg
Loc. Laimburg, 6
39040 Vadena/Pfatten (BZ)
tel. 0471969700
www.laimburg.bz.it

The Laimburg winery in Vadena is part of the experimental agricultural and forestry centre of the Bolzano provincial authority. The basic duties of the estate are research and experimentation in the viticultural and oenological sectors, as well as releasing the resulting wines to market. The 50 hectares under vine are spread around the best vineyard zones in Alto Adige on various terrains and at different altitudes. Two lines are produced, one of traditional current-vintage wines the other of wines with special characteristics, mostly barrique-aged, with names taken from the Ladin legends of the Dolomites. The base line Pinot Bianco '05 is excellent this year. Fresh, elegant, minerally and zesty with good structure and length, it more than deserved a place in the Three Glass finals. Gewürztraminer Elyònd '05 is intense and exotic with a rich, full, deep palate while Sauvignon Oyèll '05 is simpler. But the Lagrein Riserva Barbagòl '03 went through to the finals with its intense, elegant style and long, juicy, minerally palate. The red IGT Col de Réy '03 shows lovely fullness and drinks dynamically and long with good freshness. Finally, the Cabernet Riserva Sass Roà '03 is still a tad woody, with a good mouthfeel but slightly dusty tannins and a drying finish.

● A. A. Lagrein Scuro Barbagòl Ris. '03	▼▼	6
○ A. A. Pinot Bianco '05	▼▼	4*
● Col de Réy '03	▼▼	6
○ A. A. Gewürztraminer Elyònd '05	▼▼	5
● A. A. Cabernet Sass Roà Ris. '03	▼	5
○ A. A. Sauvignon Oyèll '05	▼	5
● A. A. Lagrein Scuro Barbagòl Ris. '00	▽▽▽	6
● A. A. Lagrein Scuro Barbagòl Ris. '01	▽▽	6
● A. A. Pinot Nero Selyèt Ris. '01	▽▽	5
○ A. A. Sauvignon Passito Saphir '03	▽▽	8
○ A. A. Pinot Bianco '04	▽▽	4*

VARNA/VAHRN (BZ)

Abbazia di Novacella
fraz. Novacella
via dell'Abbazia, 1
39040 Varna/Vahrn (BZ)
tel. 0472836189
www.abbazianovacella.it

As the crowning touch on unprecedented results from Valle Isarco, the historic Abbazia di Novacella winery swept up two rousing Three Glass awards. This is the first time for Valle Isarco and a feather in the cowl, as it were, of the Augustinians who own the estate. This success is no coincidence. It comes from efforts concentrated on the quality and appreciation of Valle Isarco's typical varieties. Credit goes to the energetic Urban von Klebelsberg, who is assisted by oenologist Celestino Lucin. The portrait is completed by a series of high-scoring wines in both the premium Praepositus line and the standard range, something we think is important for establishing the worth of any estate. So Three Glasses go to the Sylvaner and Kerner '05, both from the Praepositus line. These two wines have very varietal characteristics but they also embody the style Celestino Lucin attempts to give all products in this line: complexity, coordination, concentration on the palate, freshness, balance, pressure and minerality. Another two wines also reached our finals. The more typical than ever Lagrein Praepositus Riserva '03 is fragrant and creamy with splendid acidity, and the Gewürztraminer Praepositus '05 is concentrated yet elegant and spirited. High scores also went to the Veltliner, Pinot Grigio, Müller Thurgau, Sylvaner and Kerner, all from 2005 and all from the standard line.

○ A. A. Valle Isarco Kerner Praepositus '05	▼▼▼	5*
○ A. A. Valle Isarco Sylvaner Praepositus '05	▼▼▼	4*
● A. A. Lagrein Praepositus Ris. '03	▼▼	6
○ A. A. Valle Isarco Gewürztraminer Praepositus '05	▼▼	5
○ A. A. Valle Isarco Kerner '05	▼▼	4*
○ A. A. Valle Isarco Kerner Praepositus Passito '05	▼▼	6
○ A. A. Valle Isarco Müller Thurgau '05	▼▼	4*
○ A. A. Valle Isarco Pinot Grigio '05	▼▼	4*
○ A. A. Valle Isarco Sylvaner '05	▼▼	4*
○ A. A. Valle Isarco Veltliner '05	▼▼	4*

VARNA/VAHRN (BZ)

KÖFERERHOF
FRAZ. NOVACELLA
VIA PUSTERIA, 3
39040 VARNA/VAHRN (BZ)
TEL. 0472836649

This year, Günther Kershbaumer sent four wines to our finals. That's no mean feat for a small estate like Köfererhof, little more than five hectares under vine in magnificent positions around the cellar slightly north of Bressanone. It produces 30,000 bottles of wines with a very personal style: a tad severe, especially when young, and with almost aggressive minerality. These whites need time to express themselves and this is the only reason Köfererhof will not be able to toast its first Three Glass award this year. But we are convinced it is on the right path. We notice that all the wines have acquired elegance and certain slightly rustic notes have disappeared. But the wine that amazed us most of all is the Riesling '05, with its very personal aromas of pink pepper and aromatic herbs. The palate, still a little tight, is very stylish, minerally and taut with a dynamic finish. The Gewürztraminer '05 is very much in the Valle Isarco style, showing minerally with surprising acidity for this variety but still backed up by an outstanding structure. The aromas from the Sylvaner '05 are not perfectly expressed but the palate is gutsy and elegant with a truly vibrant finish. The well-typed Kerner '05 is concentrated, minerally and taut. Closing the range are a surprisingly complex Müller Thurgau '05, a typical Pinot Grigio '05 and the distinctive Gewürztraminer Passito Liebelei '03, a powerful yet balanced wine with good progression, better than ever in this edition.

○ A. A. Valle Isarco Gewürztraminer '05	2 black glasses	5
○ A. A. Valle Isarco Kerner '05	2 black glasses	5
○ A. A. Valle Isarco Riesling '05	2 black glasses	5
○ A. A. Valle Isarco Sylvaner '05	2 black glasses	4*
○ A. A. Valle Isarco Liebelei Passito '03	2 black glasses	6
○ A. A. Valle Isarco Müller Thurgau '05	2 black glasses	4*
○ A. A. Valle Isarco Pinot Grigio '05	2 black glasses	4*
○ A. A. Valle Isarco Pinot Grigio '04	2 white glasses	4
○ A. A. Valle Isarco Riesling '04	2 white glasses	5
○ A. A. Valle Isarco Gewürztraminer '04	2 white glasses	5
○ A. A. Valle Isarco Kerner '04	2 white glasses	5
○ A. A. Valle Isarco Müller Thurgau '04	2 white glasses	4
○ A. A. Valle Isarco Sylvaner '04	2 white glasses	4*

VARNA/VAHRN (BZ)

PACHERHOF
FRAZ. NOVACELLA
V.LO PACHER, 1
39040 VARNA/VAHRN (BZ)
TEL. 0472835717
www.pacherhof.com

As well as being recognized last year as the Guide's Up-and-Coming Winery, Pacherhof received a Three Glass award for a splendid Riesling '04. This was no flash in the pan. Andreas Huber not only did well with the Sylvaner Alte Reben '05 but also put another two wines in the finals and showed top quality across the rest of his range. The vineyards enjoy splendid exposure to the south and southwest, at around 700 metres above sea level, and yield lively, aromatic wines, rich in elegance and backbone, that Andreas ferments in stainless steel and large barrels. But the cellar has ambitions. Two years ago, Andreas began converting his six hectares of vineyards to biodynamic farming. Obtained from 30-year-old vines, a rarity in Valle Isarco, the Sylvaner Alte Reben '05 shows a complex, floral nose with fresh almond hints and light smokiness. The rich, austere attack on the palate has great elegance, stylishly restrained minerality and an aristocratic bearing. Although still quite young, it sweeps through to an endless finish that is all grip and grace. The crystalline Riesling '05 comes from a young vineyard yet shows surprising complexity with ripe fruit, aromatic herbs and minerally notes, an elegant palate and a finish of rare fullness. It's still young but already very expressive. An incredible Müller Thurgau '05 also went into the finals. We say "incredible" because in Valle Isarco, this sadly underrated variety is producing surprising results. The Kerner, Pinot Grigio and standard Sylvaner, all from 2005, are very good. All in all, a very fine performance.

○ A. A. Valle Isarco Sylvaner Alte Reben '05	3 black glasses	5
○ A. A. Valle Isarco Müller Thurgau '05	2 black glasses	4*
○ A. A. Valle Isarco Riesling '05	2 black glasses	5
○ A. A. Valle Isarco Kerner '05	2 black glasses	4*
○ A. A. Valle Isarco Pinot Grigio '05	2 black glasses	4
○ A. A. Valle Isarco Sylvaner '05	2 black glasses	4*
○ A. A. Valle Isarco Riesling '04	3 white glasses	5*
○ A. A. Valle Isarco Kerner '04	2 white glasses	4*
○ A. A. Valle Isarco Sylvaner Alte Reben '04	2 white glasses	5
○ A. A. Valle Isarco Müller Thurgau '04	2 white glasses	4
○ A. A. Valle Isarco Pinot Grigio '04	2 white glasses	4*

OTHER WINERIES

Alois Warasin

loc. Cornaiano
via Colterenzio, 1
39057 Appiano/Eppan (BZ)
tel. 0471662462

This small Cornaiano estate, producing around 10,000 bottles from four hectares, debuts in the Guide. The Sauvignon '05 convinced us with its delicate aniseed and lightly vegetal notes. The assertive palate shows good backbone and dynamism. The Pinot Nero '03 and Pinot Bianco '05 are well typed.

○	A.A. Sauvignon '05	YY	3*
●	A.A. Pinot Nero '03	Y	3
○	A.A. Pinot Bianco '05	Y	2*

Ebnerhof

loc. Renon - fraz. Cardano
Laste Basse, 21
39053 Bolzano/Bozen
tel. 0471365120 - www.ebnerhof.it

Johannes Plattner did well again with two wines in the finals. The superb Sauvignon '05 shows fragrant, minerally sensations, tanginess and an elegant finish. The merlot and lagrein Merleum '03 is powerful yet supple and dynamic at the same time. The Santa Maddalena '05 and Pinot Nero '04 are nice.

●	Merleum '03	YY	6
○	A. A. Sauvignon '05	YY	4*
●	A. A. Santa Maddalena '05	YY	3*
●	A. A. Pinot Nero '04	Y	5

Egger-Ramer

via Guncina, 5
39100 Bolzano/Bozen
tel. 0471280541
www.egger-ramer.com

Skilled Bolzano-based growers Toni and Peter Egger are back in the Guide with a series of good Lagreins. At the top, the Tenuta Kristan '04 opens with notes of cinchona, blackberry and minerality that return on the dense, gutsy palate. The base '05 and Riserva Kristan '03 are not bad at all.

●	A. A. Lagrein Scuro Gries Kristan '04	YY	4*
●	A. A. Lagrein Gries Tenuta Kristan Ris. '03	YY	5
●	A. A. Lagrein Gries '05	YY	4*
⊙	A. A. Lagrein Kretzer Gries '05	Y	3*

R. Malojer Gummerhof

via Weggestein, 36
39100 Bolzano/Bozen
tel. 0471972885
www.malojer.it

The historic estate managed by Elisabeth, Urban and Alfred Malojer Gummerhof performed very well. The Sauvignon Gur zu Sand and Pinot Bianco are from 2005 and both are excellent. The Cabernet Merlot Bautzanum Riserva '03 and fruity Müller Thurgau '05 show character.

●	A. A. Cabernet-Lagrein Bautzanum Ris. '03	YY	5
○	A. A. Pinot Bianco '05	YY	4*
○	A. A. Sauvignon Gur zu Sand '05	YY	4*
○	A. A. Muller Thurgau '05	Y	3*
●	A. A. Lagrein Scuro Gummerhof zu Gries '02	YY	5

MESSNERHOF
LOC. SAN PIETRO, 7
39100 BOLZANO/BOZEN
TEL. 0471977162
www.messnerhof.net

Bernhard Pichler has run this small estate since 1993, producing around 10,000 bottles a year of classic Bolzano wines. The floral Santa Maddalena '05 shows fresh and velvety but the Lagrein Riserva '04 failed to repeat last year's success. Its lack of weight reveals an adverse growing season.

● A. A. Santa Maddalena '05	🍷🍷	4
● A. A. Lagrein Ris. '04	🍷	5

NUSSERHOF
VIA MAYR NUSSER, 72
39100 BOLZANO/BOZEN
TEL. 0471978388

Expert taster Heinrich Mayr, the genial owner of Nusserhof, has made organic wines for years. We have a real weakness for his Lagrein Riserva, which in the '02 version has grip and character to spare. The rare white Blaterle '05 is pleasant and the Lagrein Rosato '05 is as good as ever.

● A. A. Lagrein Scuro Ris. '02	🍷🍷	4*
○ A. A. Blaterle '05	🍷🍷	3*
⊙ A. A. Lagrein Rosato '05	🍷🍷	3*

ROTTENSTEINER H. & T. - OBERMOSER
FRAZ. RENCIO
VIA SANTA MADDALENA, 35
39100 BOLZANO/BOZEN
TEL. 0471973549 - www.obermoser.it

Space constraints robbed Obermoser of a full profile. Owner Heinrich Rottensteiner and his son Thomas submitted four wines that all scored well but we preferred the Sauvignon '05. The other three are Cabernet-Merlot Putz Riserva, Lagrein Grafenleiten Riserva, both from 2004, and Santa Maddalena '05.

● A. A. Cabernet-Merlot Putz Ris. '04	🍷🍷	5
● A. A. Lagrein Scuro Grafenleiten Ris. '04	🍷🍷	5
● A. A. Santa Maddalena Cl. '05	🍷🍷	4*
○ A. A. Sauvignon '05	🍷🍷	4*

HARTMANN LENTSCH
VIA NAZIONALE, 71
39051 BRONZOLO/BRANZOOL (BZ)
TEL. 0471596017

The lovely Adige valley estate run by Hartmann and Klaus Lentsch returns to the Guide. The Lagrein '02 has typical aromas of wild berry fruit and a fresh, enjoyable palate. The Merlot and Cabernet from 2002 and Moscato Giallo '05 are all very pleasant.

● A. A. Cabernet '02	🍷🍷	5
● A. A. Lagrein '02	🍷🍷	5
● A. A. Merlot '02	🍷🍷	5
○ A. A. Moscato Giallo '05	🍷🍷	4

BARON DI PAULI
VIA CANTINE, 12
39052 CALDARO/KALTERN (BZ)
TEL. 0471963696
www.barondipauli.com

Skilfully managed by Helmuth Zozin, this beautiful Caldaro estate impressed our tasters. The well-typed Lagrein Carano '04 has confident aromatics, structure, elegance and character. The Lago di Caldaro Kalkofen '05 is juicy and enjoyable and the Cabernet Merlot Arzio '03 has elegant poise.

● Arzio '03	🍷🍷	7
● A. A. Carano Lagrein '04	🍷🍷	5
● A. A. Lago di Caldaro Cl. Sup. Kalkofen '05	🍷🍷	4

KETTMEIR
VIA DELLE CANTINE, 4
39052 CALDARO/KALTERN (BZ)
TEL. 0471963135 - 0471963518
www.kettmeir.com

This historic Caldaro estate has produced positive results. The excellent Spumante Brut shows chamomile, aromatic herbs and acacia honey then good thrust on the long palate. The Cabernet Sauvignon Maso Castello '03, Spumante Rosé Brut and Lagrein Athesis Riserva '03 are all very good.

● A. A. Cabernet Sauvignon Maso Castello '03	🍷🍷	5
● A. A. Lagrein Athesis Ris. '03	🍷🍷	6
○ A. A. Spumante Brut	🍷🍷	5*
⊙ Brut Rosé Cl.	🍷🍷	5*

Lieselehof
via Kardatsch, 6
39052 Caldaro/Kaltern (BZ)
tel. 0471965060 - 3299011593
www.lieselehof.com

Werner Morandell's small, organically farmed Liesele estate at Caldaro produces around 10,000 bottles from two hectares. Maximilian '03 is from half cabernet sauvignon with added merlot, cabernet franc and carmenère.
The white Julian '05 and Lago di Caldaro Amadeus '05 are interesting.

● Maximilian '03	🍷🍷	5
○ Julian '05	🍷🍷	5
● A. A. Lago di Caldaro Amadeus '05	🍷	3

Castel Sallegg
v.lo di Sotto, 15
39052 Caldaro/Kaltern (BZ)
tel. 0471963132
www.castelsallegg.it

Castel Sallegg at Caldaro is a major Alto Adige estate. The nice Pinot Bianco '04 is powerful and rich on the palate. The Pinot Grigio '05 is concentrated and well typed. The Chardonnay '05 is simple with a bit too much wood but decent body.
The Merlot Riserva '02 has concentration and balance.

● A. A. Merlot Ris. '02	🍷🍷	5
○ A. A. Pinot Bianco '04	🍷🍷	4
○ A. A. Pinot Grigio '05	🍷🍷	4*
○ A. A. Chardonnay '05	🍷	4

Steflhof
via Pfleganger, 9
39052 Caldaro/Kaltern (BZ)
tel. 0471964955
www.steflhof.it

Georg Andergassen's two and a half hectare estate releases around 20,000 bottles. It did well again, its fragrant, traditional-style Lagrein '04 offering personality and finesse. The concentrated Chardonnay '05 shows nice ripe apple notes but misses a pinch of freshness. The Merlot '04 is decent.

● A. A. Lagrein '04	🍷🍷	4
○ A. A. Chardonnay '05	🍷🍷	4
● A. A. Merlot '04	🍷	5

Biedermannhof
via Lebenberger, 1
39010 Cermes/Tscherms (BZ)
tel. 0473563097
www.biedermannhof.it

On his tiny estate – little more than a hectare – founded in 2001, Josef Innerhofer produces 6,000 bottles here at Cermes. His Lagrein '04 is juicy and fragrant. A step below is the Cuvée Gallus '04 from merlot and lagrein. All in all, it wasn't bad for a first showing.

● A. A. Lagrein '04	🍷🍷	5*
● A. A. Cuvèe Gallus '04	🍷	6

Kupelwieser
strada del Vino, 24
39040 Cortina/Kurtinig (BZ)
tel. 0471809240
www.kupelwieser.it

Wines from Kupelwieser always make a good showing. We'll start with the Lagrein Intenditore '04, which deservedly went on to our Three Glass finals thanks to truly superior typicity and elegance.
The Pinot Bianco, Chardonnay and Sauvignon Intenditore, all from 2005, are very well made.

● A. A. Lagrein Intenditore '04	🍷🍷	5*
○ A. A. Pinot Bianco '05	🍷🍷	4
○ A. A. Sauvignon Intenditore '05	🍷🍷	5
○ A. A. Chardonnay '05	🍷	4

Brunnenhof
fraz. Mazzon - via degli Alpini, 5
39044 Egna/Neumarkt (BZ)
tel. 0471820687
www.brunnenhof-mazzon.it

After a year off, the Guide welcomes back Kurt Rottensteiner's small estate, which produces just 10,000 bottles split between the very pleasant Gewürztraminer '05 and a fresh, well-typed Pinot Nero Mazzon Riserva '04 that has plenty to say for itself.

● A. A. Pinot Nero Ris. '04	🍷🍷	6
○ A. A. Gewürztraminer '05	🍷	5

GOTTARDI
LOC. MAZZON - VIA DEGLI ALPINI, 17
39044 EGNA/NEUMARKT (BZ)
TEL. 0471812773
www.gottardi-mazzon.com

Pinot Neros from Bruno Gottardi's legendary estate are very hard to find in Italy but we managed to get hold of a few. The Pinot Nero Riserva '02 reached our finals thanks to its sheer elegance and typicity. We found the same finesse in the Pinot Nero '04, which flaunts a juicy, fresh palate.

● A. A. Pinot Nero Ris. '02	🍷🍷	7
● A. A. Pinot Nero '04	🍷🍷	5

BESSERERHOF
NOVALE DI PRESULE, 10
39050 FIÈ ALLO SCILIAR/
VÖLS AM SCHLERN (BZ)
TEL. 0471601011 - 3383230550

Otmar Mair's estate near Novale di Presule is one of many new entries this year. Production runs to 30,000 bottles of remarkable overall quality with some interesting high points such as the Pinot Bianco '05 and Chardonnay '04. The Gewurztraminer '05 and Moscato Giallo 2004 are also interesting.

○ A. A. Chardonnay '04	🍷🍷	4
○ A. A. Moscato Giallo '04	🍷🍷	4
○ A. A. Gewurztraminer '05	🍷🍷	4
○ A. A. Pinot Bianco '05	🍷🍷	4*

CASTELLO RAMETZ
FRAZ. MAIA ALTA - VIA LABERS, 4
39012 MERANO/MERAN (BZ)
TEL. 0473211011 - 0473290187
www.rametz.com

Stanislaus Schmid's historic estate releases around 400,000 bottles a year and makes a deserved return to the Guide. The nice Chardonnay '05 has good structure. The Cabernet '03 is fresh and well balanced while the Riesling '05 offers typicity. They could get even better: the potential is there.

○ A. A. Chardonnay '05	🍷🍷	3*
● A. A. Cabernet '03	🍷	6
○ A. A. Riesling '05	🍷	3

UNTERBERGER SIEGFRIED STEGERHOF
VIA LABERS, 14
39012 MERANO/MERAN (BZ)
TEL. 0473272300
www.stegerhof.info

Owned by Siegfried Unterberger, this beautiful, small estate with six hectares under vine in Merano has earned its spurs. Again this year, we enjoyed a Riesling '04 with rare definition and elegance, tropical fruit aromas and a solid, determined palate.

○ A. A. Riesling '04	🍷🍷	4*

TENUTA PFITSCHERHOF
VIA GLENO, 9
39040 MONTAGNA/MONTAN (BZ)
TEL. 0471819773
www.pfitscher.it

Klaus Pfitscher's Lagrein Kotznloater '04 is good and deserved its place in the finals. Well typed right from the caressing spice aromas, the palate shows grand finesse with smooth tannins and a lively, refreshing acidity. The Pinot Nero Matan is decent but penalized by the vintage.

● A. A. Lagrein Kotznloater '04	🍷🍷	5
● A. A. Pinot Nero Matan '03	🍷	5

ISTITUTO TECNICO AGRARIO ORA
VIA DEL CASTELLO, 10
39040 ORA/AUER (BZ)
TEL. 0471810538
www.ofl-auer.it

Some of the wines here are very good, others less so. Owned by the Bolzano provincial authority, this small estate at Ora turns out 20,000 bottles a year and this time submitted a dense, juicy Merlot '04, an elegantly harmonious Merlot-Cabernet Sauvignon Riserva '03 and a decent Chardonnay '05.

● A. A. Merlot-Cabernet Sauvignon Ris. '03	🍷🍷	4*
● A. A. Merlot '04	🍷🍷	4*
○ A. A. Chardonnay '05	🍷	5

BARON VON KRIPP STACHLBURG
VIA MITTERHOFER, 2
39020 PARCINES/PARTSCHINS (BZ)
TEL. 0473968014
www.stachlburg.com

Barone Von Kripp's Stachlburg estate makes a great return to the Guide with a series of remarkable wines. In the Three Glass finals, the Pinot Nero '04 has a floral nose and delicate, elegant, stylish, deep palate. There are two good Chardonnays, a fresh steel-aged 2005 and a barrique-aged 2003.

● A. A. Valle Venosta Pinot Nero '04	🍷🍷	5*
○ Vign. Dolomiti Chardonnay '03	🍷🍷	4
○ A. A. Valle Venosta Chardonnay '05	🍷🍷	4

BRAUNBACH
LOC. SETTEQUERCE
VIA PADRE ROMEDIUS, 5
39018 TERLANO/TERLAN (BZ)
TEL. 0471910184 - www.braunbach.it

There are ups and downs at Braunbach in San Genesio, the heart of Santa Maddalena Classico country. Well-crafted wines such as Cabernet-Lagrein Calldiv Prestige Riserva '01 and Merlot Siebeneich '04 sit alongside others we found less convincing.

● A. A. Cabernet Lagrein Prestige Calldiv '01	🍷🍷	5
● A. A. Merlot Siebeneich '04	🍷🍷	5

WILHELM WALCH
VIA A. HOFER, 1
39040 TERMENO/TRAMIN (BZ)
TEL. 0471860172
www.elenawalch.com

This historic Termeno estate brilliantly confirmed its reputation. The magnificent Pinot Bianco '05 is dense, minerally and dynamic, the Bordeaux-style Cabernet Merlot Jaras '03 has elegance and Pinot Grigio Marat '05 is balanced, varietal and very stylish.

● A. A. Cabernet-Merlot Jeras '03	🍷🍷	4*
○ A. A. Pinot Bianco Premium '05	🍷🍷	4*
○ A. A. Pinot Grigio Marat '05	🍷🍷	4*
● A. A. Schiava Plattensteig '05	🍷	4*

HANNES BAUMGARTNER STRASSERHOF
FRAZ. NOVACELLA - UNTERRAIN, 8
39040 VARNA/VAHRN (BZ)
TEL. 0472830804
www.strasserhof.info

Our good opinion of Strasserhof, and Hannes Baumgartner who cultivates the three hectares, was confirmed. These elegant wines have a clear Valle Isarco timbre and would be some of the best with a bit more grip. But the four wines produced are still good, especially the Sylvaner '05.

● Thurner '04	🍷🍷	4
○ A. A. Valle Isarco Kerner '05	🍷🍷	4
○ A. A. Valle Isarco Sylvaner '05	🍷🍷	4*
○ A. A. Valle Isarco Gewurztraminer '05	🍷	4

RÖCKHOF
VIA SAN VALENTINO, 9
39040 VILLANDRO/VILLANDERS (BZ)
TEL. 0472847130

Konrad Augschöll's small estate near Villandres has is proving reliable. The fresh, juicy Müller Thurgau '05 is consistently among the best in its type. Caruess has never been better than in this 2005 edition.

○ A. A. Valle Isarco Müller Thurgau '05	🍷🍷	4
○ Caruess '05	🍷🍷	4

VENETO

At a time when neglected values like elegance, territoriality and sheer drinkability are regaining importance over structure and softness at all costs, the Veneto region has no intention of being caught napping. Quite the opposite. As ever, Veneto is one of the most relevant parts of Italy since wine has always been part and parcel of daily life here. Over the years, this homely relationship has ensured that competition wines – not even the most fashionable – have never gained the upper hand over the enduring preference for quality and a drinker-friendly style. Even a zone like Valpolicella, where wines tend to be sweet and rich in extract, there is a new preference for lighter products, particularly among Valpolicella Superiores, achieved by cutting residual sugar in the Amarones. The observations made in last year's Guide on the 2004 and 2003 vintages have held true while the white wines from the Verona area performed particularly well in 2005. The cool growing year has endowed the wines with unusually delicate aromas along with a tangy flavour and grip we have not experienced for a long time. Important accomplishments came this year from newcomers with the success of Colli Euganei, an area which has brought many new wineries into the spotlight in just a few years. The newcomers are all committed to promoting the zone, as is demonstrated by the first Three Glass prize to be awarded to Maria Gioia Rosellini and her Ca' Orologio. The neighbouring Colli Berici zone is working to recover the tocai rosso grape, and new interpretations of this variety are bound to generate plenty of interest. The western part of Verona is struggling for success although Luciano and Franco Piona's classy Bianco di Custoza points the way with fine quality, character and style. Valpolicella is literally bursting with talent. Three wineries won top accolades, Corte Sant'Alda, Quintarelli, who has earned a Star, and Trabucchi for the first time. There's also news from Amarone. A first Three Glass award went to Guerrieri Rizzardi, a winery with products from all Verona's wine types but particularly adept at Valpolicella. Alongside are many other repeat successes, including Bussola's Recioto, which help paint an overall picture of considerable excitement. But Soave is the zone that stands above the rest this year, thanks to the extraordinary performance of two great vintages, 2004 and 2005. Eight wines received the highest accolade including Gini, again, and the Tamellini brothers, who saw their hard work duly rewarded. Eastern Veneto had cause to celebrate with the undisputed leader, Ca' Orologio, Serafini & Vidotto, who picked up a coveted Star, a third Three Glass prize for Stefano and Adriano Zonta, and Maculan. All these wineries demonstrate that it is possible to make characterful wines that reflect the terroir, even with international varieties like merlot and cabernet.

ANNONE VENETO (VE)

Bosco del Merlo

via Postumia, 14
30020 Annone Veneto (VE)
tel. 0422768167
www.boscodelmerlo.it

We ended our comments in last year's Guide with the announcement that Tocai Juti would be released a year late so it would be on top form when it hit the shelves. It is rare for intuition to pay off so well but the wine is now redolent of carefree fragrant youth, with interwoven floral and lightly balsamic hints floating elegantly up to tempt the nostrils. On the palate the wine is both confident and stylishly sophisticated, dry with assertive acidity reminiscent of sea breezes, Mediterranean scrubland and apple and pear fruit right up to the pleasant finish. The other products are no less impressive, starting with Tocai's usual companion hereabouts, Refosco. Roggio dei Roveri exploits the warm weather of 2003 with a fruitily approachable and sensual nose revealing floral notes in the background over spices and hints of medicinal herbs. The palate is as supple as usual, framed in sweet tannins and refreshing acidity. The winery's own outstanding Bordeaux blend, 360, melds fruit and flowers on the nose with mineral and vegetal hints, all perfectly reflected on the subtle, creamy palate. At a time when the clouds over the market have yet to disperse, it is a pleasure to see a large winery like this – 600,000 bottles released each year – prepared to make sacrifices to be able to offer wines of outstanding quality with strong territorial links.

● Lison-Pramaggiore Refosco P. R. Roggio dei Roveri '03	🍷🍷	6
● 360 Ruber Capitae '03	🍷🍷	5
○ Lison-Pramaggiore Cl. Tocai Juti '04	🍷🍷	5
○ Lison-Pramaggiore Sauvignon Turranio '05	🍷🍷	4*
○ Priné '04	🍷	5
○ Verduzzo Soandre '04	🍷	4
○ Lison-Pramaggiore Pinot Grigio '05	🍷	4
● 360 Ruber Capitae '01	🍸🍸	5
● Lison-Pramaggiore Refosco P. R. Roggio dei Roveri '02	🍸🍸	6

BAONE (PD)

Ca' Orologio

via Ca' Orologio, 7a
35030 Baone (PD)
tel. 042950099
www.caorologio.com

Ca' Orologio only presented three wines this year, but what wines they are! We are getting a clearer and increasingly interesting picture of Maria Gioia Rosellini's project with each passing year and can now glimpse the ultimate purpose of the decisions she has taken as the pieces of this – fortunately – never-ending puzzle fall into place. "My ambitious project is to perfect a mouthfilling red wine which represents the best possible expression of the territory I love and work in – the Colli Euganei". That's why the puzzle will never really be complete, but let's enjoy it unfolding. The Relogio, from 100 per cent carmenère, made an excellent impression on the panel. It embodies the noble nature of the fresh-tasting Bordeaux grape through the filter of a volcanic, sun-kissed terroir. Wild berry aromas interweave with spices and balsamic hints, leaving the vegetal notes in the background and a flavoursome palate that reveals itself austere and firm-bodied. This performance earned this young winery its first Three Glass prize. The red Calaone is even more youthful in the glass. It's a blend of merlot and cabernet that benefits from the surge of freshness provided by the barbera grapes added to the blend instead of being used for a single-variety wine. Red berry fruit, forest floor, cyclamen and damp leaves are released in the nose to be perfectly reflected on the supple, elegant palate. Salarola is a good Pinot Bianco with apple and pear fruit on the nose and a tangy, vibrant palate.

● Relogio '04	🍷🍷🍷	5
● Colli Euganei Rosso Calaone '04	🍷🍷	4*
○ Salarola '05	🍷	4
● Colli Euganei Rosso Calaone '03	🍸🍸	5
● Relogio '03	🍸🍸	5

BAONE (PD)

GIORDANO EMO CAPODILISTA
VIA VILLA RITA
35030 BAONE (PD)
TEL. 049637294
www.classica.it

The outstanding 2004 vintage plus one of the region's most interesting, vine-friendly terroirs yield an unusually complex, elegant wine which is almost a summary of everything the area has to offer. On the hills furthest south in Veneto, cabernet sauvignon grapes ripen perfectly, rich in red berry aromas and minerally hints from the volcanic soil, which penetrate into the skins thanks to the excellent temperature range in this area. Here, among the tracks of wild boar and lush vegetation – remember that we are in the Colli Euganei regional park – Giordano Emo Capodilista has created a small but functional cellar that blends perfectly into the landscape in both architectural and strictly environmental terms. The arrangement of the south-facing, light-filled vineyards provides a breathtaking view today as it gradually gives way to woods and olive groves. Thanks to the working relationship with Andrea Boaretti, whose knowledge of this land is extensive, the 2004 vintage was fully exploited in a wine with dark ruby red colour, vibrant, stylish aromas of plums and morello cherries, minerally hints and aromatic herbs entwined with violets that lead in to a perfectly harmonious palate. The sweet fruit blends beautifully with the vibrant freshness and fine-grained tannins on a long, elegant finish. The Fior d'Arancio Passito Donna Daria is once again extraordinarily generous and flavoursome, intriguing both nose and palate.

●	Colli Euganei Cabernet Sauvignon Ireneo '04	▼▼	6
○	Colli Euganei Fior d'Arancio Passito Donna Daria '04	▼▼	6
●	Colli Euganei Cabernet Sauvignon Ireneo '01	▽▽	6
○	Colli Euganei Fior d'Arancio Passito Donna Daria '01	▽▽	6
●	Colli Euganei Cabernet Sauvignon Ireneo '02	▽▽	6
○	Colli Euganei Fior d'Arancio Passito Donna Daria '02	▽▽	6
●	Colli Euganei Cabernet Sauvignon Ireneo '03	▽▽	6

BAONE (PD)

IL FILÒ DELLE VIGNE
VIA TERRALBA, 14
35030 BAONE (PD)
TEL. 042956243
www.ilfilodellevigne.it

Overlooking the last slopes of the Baone area is Filò delle Vigne, apparently undecided between the muggy atmosphere of the plain and the cooler climes and excellent temperature variation of the hills. This south-facing vineyard suffers in hotter years even more than you might expect. Then, as if by magic, along comes a terrible year that practically everyone else has written off after the heavens have done their worst and it gives Gino Giordani and Niccolò Voltan's estate, not to mention their wines, commendable balance. The extraordinary leap forward in quality is already clear from the winery's first red wine, Vigna Cecilia di Baone, entirely aged in concrete, which won our tasters over with its fragrant aromas and ripe, crisp red fruit. The house champ is still Borgo delle Casette, a blend of cabernet sauvignon and franc with a generous, intriguingly complex range of aromas in which the fruit and spices allow glimpses of vibrant minerally notes. The taut, firmly structured palate is beautifully supple and bewitchingly drinkable. Calto delle Fate is a chardonnay-based white aged in barrique that has emerged generous and mouthfilling thanks to the excellent growing year. The best version yet of Luna del Parco, from late-harvested fior d'arancio, has vibrant, subtle aromas of candied citrus fruit, as well as floral and minerally notes. The palate copes admirably with the sweetness and acidity, closing with a very long, juicy finish.

●	Colli Euganei Cabernet Borgo delle Casette Ris. '02	▼▼	5
○	Colli Euganei Fior d'Arancio Luna del Parco '04	▼▼	6
●	Colli Euganei Cabernet Vigna Cecilia di Baone Ris. '02	▼▼	5
○	Il Calto delle Fate '04	▼	5
●	Colli Euganei Cabernet Borgo delle Casette Ris. '00	▽▽	5
●	Colli Euganei Cabernet Vigna Cecilia di Baone Ris. '00	▽▽	5
●	Colli Euganei Cabernet Borgo delle Casette Ris. '01	▽▽	5
●	Colli Euganei Cabernet Vigna Cecilia di Baone Ris. '01	▽▽	5

BAONE (PD)

IL MOTTOLO
LOC. LE CONTARINE
VIA COMEZZARE
35030 BAONE (PD)
TEL. 049632185

From Baone, there is a beautiful view of the volcanic uplands that form the Colli Euganei regional park. They come to an almost abrupt end, relegating the vineyards to the valley known as Piana delle Contarine. This is where Il Mottolo is located, a new winery that has made its entrance into the rich variety of Colli Euganei winemaking with a clear focus on quality. Almost uniquely, the first wines to be released are those the winery produced before the cellar was built, thanks to the friendship of owner Sergio Fortin with Franco Zanovello of Ca' Lustra. There are just four hectares of vineyards, all at Baone, to which another two will be added after the next harvest. Production has yet to top 20,000 bottles a year and the three reds take the lion's share in the cellar. The Serro 2004 made an excellent impression. Product specifications require a prevalence of merlot in this blend, with the addition of cabernet sauvignon and franc. Serro has pronounced aromas of red berry fruit and fresh herbs on the nose, with a pinch more pizzazz from its hint of pepper, followed by a firm, very fresh-tasting palate. The Merlot Comezzara is not far behind, playing on sturdier mouthfeel rather than complexity. Le Contarine 2005 is an interesting dry moscato-based white. Its fresh, vibrant aromas introduce a tangy and remarkably pleasant palate. The Cabernet Vigna Marè 2004 is more approachable and accessible, with herb and berry fruit sensations typical of Veneto wines.

●	Colli Euganei Merlot Comezzara '04	🍷🍷	3*
●	Colli Euganei Rosso Serro '04	🍷🍷	4*
●	Colli Euganei Cabernet V. Marè '04	🍷	3
○	Le Contarine '05	🍷	3

BAONE (PD)

VIGNALE DI CECILIA
LOC. FORNACI
VIA CROCI, 14
35030 BAONE (PD)
TEL. 042951420
www.vignaledicecilia.it

It is always a pleasure to visit Paolo Brunello's winery, located in a natural amphitheatre that resembles a Roman arena with the vines surrounding the ideal stage where, unsurprisingly, the protagonist is cabernet sauvignon. But don't be fooled into thinking that this winery has followed the usual pattern of investing all its hopes of success in merlot and cabernet. As we continually assure readers, Bordeaux varieties came to the Colli Euganei over 150 years ago and adapted so marvellously that they have become an outstanding vehicle for the expression of different territories. Growing year after growing year, the Baone subzone provides an increasingly accomplished demonstration of its special characteristics within the Colli Euganei, a DOC zone where Bordeaux grapes ripen perfectly to yield vibrant red berry fruit and minerally hints that become more and more evident over the years. The warm growing years in 2003 has endowed Passacaglia with sensations of fruit-led ripeness. If you are patient, subtle notes of medicinal herbs, autumn leaves and pencil lead appear on the nose to enhance the spectrum of aromatics, exploding on the palate with abundant but not excessive softness. Covolo is the opposite, not in style – aged in concrete vats, it lacks the full body of its big brother – so much as in the way it interprets the following vintage with subtler, lighter notes overall. It's a perfect example of a fine Veneto wine. Folia 2003, in contrast, hints at the ripeness of the growing year with generous, enthralling sweetness.

●	Colli Euganei Rosso Passacaglia '03	🍷🍷	5
○	Folia '03	🍷🍷	5
●	Colli Euganei Rosso Covolo '04	🍷	4
●	Colli Euganei Rosso Passacaglia '01	🍸🍸	5
●	Colli Euganei Rosso Passacaglia '02	🍸🍸	5
○	Folia '02	🍸🍸	5

Guerrieri Rizzardi

via Verdi, 4
37011 Bardolino (VR)
tel. 0457210028
www.guerrieri-rizzardi.it

Giuseppe Rizzardi knows his own mind. The family's vineyard selection, Calcarole, must be an individual Amarone, which means not every vintage is suitable. In fact, the next version to be released will be the 2003. With the agreement of his brother Agostino, who manages the winery, and mother Maria Cristina Loredan, Giuseppe used the 2001 Calcarole grapes together with those from Poiega in a new experimental Amarone called Villa Rizzardi. It's excellent. This is a characterful, dry and assertive red with plenty of fruit and spices, lifted by the subtle handling of its huge body. We liked it so much that we awarded the winery its first ever Three Glass prize with a well-deserved "bravo" to all concerned. The winery takes its name from two ancient Veronese families, the Guerrieris of Bardolino and the Rizzardis from Negrar. In the early 20th century, Carlo Rizzardi's marriage to Giuseppina Guerrieri united the properties in Valpolicella and Garda and land was subsequently purchased in Valdadige and Soave, taking the total vine stock to about 100 hectares. The main winery headquarters is in the old palazzo in Bardolino and there are crushing facilities in Soave and Negrar. Leading the lakeside products is the Bardolino Classico Superiore Munus 2004, which succeeds in balancing a supple palate against juicy fruit. The excellent Valpolicella Superiore Poiega 2004 comes from the vineyards at Negrar. Half of the fruit by weight underwent a second fermentation on the Amarone skins. The Valdadige white, Chardonnay Vignaunica, is interesting and potentially ageworthy.

●	Amarone della Valpolicella Cl. Villa Rizzardi '01	🍷🍷🍷	7
●	Bardolino Cl. Sup. Munus '04	🍷🍷	5
●	Valpolicella Cl. Sup. Poiega '04	🍷🍷	4
●	Castello Guerrieri Rosso '03	🍷	5
⊙	Bardolino Chiaretto Cl. '05	🍷	3
●	Bardolino Cl. Tacchetto '05	🍷	4
○	Castello Guerrieri Bianco '05	🍷	4
○	Dogoli Bianco '05	🍷	4
○	Soave Cl. Sup. Costeggiola '05	🍷	4
○	Valdadige Chardonnay Vignaunica '05	🍷	4
●	Amarone della Valpolicella Cl. Calcarole '00	(🍷🍷)	8

BARDOLINO (VR)

Vigneti Villabella

fraz. Calmasino
loc. Canova, 2
37011 Bardolino (VR)
tel. 0457236448 - 0456260655
www.vignetivillabella.com

The products of this large winery are always impressive. Although the main cellar and the core vineyards are in the Bardolino zone, the range includes wines from all the Verona zones, from flavoursome Amarone to fresh-tasting Custoza and Lugana. Selection of the best grapes from the 300-plus hectares of part-owned, part-leased vineyards make it possible for the estate to maintain a high standard of quality even in their less complicated wines. Amarone Fracastoro 2001 gave an excellent performance. In the strikingly complex bouquet, wild berries interweave with spices and pencil lead while the mature aromas are refreshed by aromatic herbs. The palate is still youthful and requires further ageing, given its hefty body and dense tannic weave. The standard-label Amarone is only a step behind, showing livelier and sunnier on the nose with hints of cherry jam and cocoa powder, aromas that are beautifully reflected on the warm, mouthfilling palate. The leading red, Villa Cordevigo, needs further ageing and we'll be tasting it next year. The Lugana Ca' del Lago is excellent and easily earned Two Glasses thanks to its clear, generous aromas and firm but very supple palate. The rest of the products are all of a very high standard, especially the Valpolicella Ripasso 2003 and the Pinot Grigio Vigna di Pesina 2005, which missed a second Glass by a hair's breadth.

●	Amarone della Valpolicella Cl. '01	🍷🍷	6
●	Amarone della Valpolicella Cl. Fracastoro '01	🍷🍷	7
○	Lugana Ca' del Lago '05	🍷🍷	4*
●	Valpolicella Cl. Sup. Ripasso '03	🍷	4
●	Bardolino Cl. Sup. Terre di Cavagion '04	🍷	4
⊙	Bardolino Chiaretto Cl. Pozzo dell'Amore '05	🍷	3
○	Bianco di Custoza Fiordaliso '05	🍷	3
○	Pinot Grigio V. di Pesina '05	🍷	4
○	Soave Cl. La Torretta '05	🍷	3
●	Valpolicella Cl. I Roccoli '05	🍷	4
●	Villa Cordevigo Rosso '01	(🍷🍷)	6

BARDOLINO (VR)

F.lli Zeni

via Costabella, 9
37011 Bardolino (VR)
tel. 0457210022
www.zeni.it

At a time when the market is rediscovering the pleasures of light, drinkable wines, how could we miss tasting the products of this great winery on the eastern side of Lake Garda? Annual production is just under a million bottles, spread across a wide range that will satisfy the demands of all enthusiasts. The grapes used in the Bardolinos are all from vineyards owned by the winery, while the grapes for the other wines are bought in from growers who are monitored continually throughout the year. Gaetano, or "Nino", is also trying to purchase vineyards in nearby Valpolicella to further improve monitoring of the grapes for the more prestigious wines. At last the Bardolino Superiore 2004 is on top form, having succeeded in the difficult task of combining lightness and fragrance with depth, rich extract and generous aromas. The results are excellent both on the subtle nose, rich in fruit and hints of autumn leaves, and on the taut, rangy and nicely tangy palate. The Cruino 2004 will please wine fans. It's a refreshing, vibrant monovarietal Corvina with an edge of acidity. The surprising Valpolicella Superiore Vigne Alte juxtaposes youthful, heady aromas and a firm, nicely complex palate which promises well for the future. The Amarone 2003 is approachable, reliable and definitely appealing, with plenty of fruit and softness.

●	Amarone della Valpolicella Cl. '03	🍷🍷	6
●	Bardolino Cl. Sup. '04	🍷🍷	4*
●	Cruino Rosso '04	🍷🍷	5
●	Valpolicella Cl. Sup. Vigne Alte '04	🍷🍷	4*
●	Corvar Rosso '04	🍷	6
●	Costalago Rosso '04	🍷	5
○	Lugana Marogne '04	🍷	4
●	Merlar Rosso '04	🍷	6
○	Soave Cl. Marogne '04	🍷	4
⊙	Bardolino Chiaretto Cl. Vigne Alte '05	🍷	3*
●	Bardolino Cl. Vigne Alte '05	🍷	3*
○	Bianco di Custoza '05	🍷	3*
○	Lugana V. Alte '05	🍷	3*
○	Soave Cl. Vigne Alte '05	🍷	3*

BASSANO DEL GRAPPA (VI)

Vigneto Due Santi

v.le Asiago, 174
36061 Bassano del Grappa (VI)
tel. 0424502074

Just a glance at the foot of the page will prove the standard of quality achieved by Stefano and Adriano Zonta's winery, but this does not do full justice to the facts. Before reading reviews or tasting the wines, you should take a trip to meet these two cousins and spend a day with them in their vineyards before you taste the range of products in the simple, recently extended cellar. You'll realise at once that their project focuses on the vineyard and the promotion of the local area. The cellar comes next, as the place where the grapes are processed into a wine that speaks volumes about this corner of Veneto. So let's start with the most distant wine, Prosecco, in an interpretation typical of a red wine expert that has prevalently ripe fruit aromas and a firm, satisfying palate. The two more accessible whites are along the same lines. Breganze Bianco handles its considerable structure with ease while the Malvasia's appeal is in its fragrant aromas and relaxed palate. The Sauvignon is still very youthful, with delicate but full aromas on the nose and a generous, promising palate. Lastly come the three 2004 reds. The Cabernet is typical of the area, showing fresh, well-structured and nicely drinkable, and the Breganze Rosso is a Merlot with refreshing aromas and a tangy palate. The Three Glass winner is a great Cabernet Vigneto Due Santi 2004 with extraordinarily clear, generous aromas of wild berries, medicinal herbs and mint on its enthralling nose, followed by excellent mouthfeel with sweet tannins on a juicy and very drinkable palate.

●	Breganze Cabernet Vign. Due Santi '04	🍷🍷🍷	5
●	Breganze Cabernet '04	🍷🍷	4*
●	Breganze Rosso '04	🍷🍷	4*
○	Breganze Bianco Rivana '05	🍷🍷	4*
○	Breganze Sauvignon Vign. Due Santi '05	🍷🍷	4*
○	Malvasia Campo di Fiori '05	🍷🍷	4*
○	Prosecco	🍷	3
●	Breganze Cabernet Vign. Due Santi '00	🍸🍸🍸	5
●	Breganze Cabernet Vign. Due Santi '03	🍸🍸🍸	5
●	Breganze Cabernet Vign. Due Santi '01	🍸🍸	5

BREGANZE (VI)

★ Maculan

via Castelletto, 3
36042 Breganze (VI)
tel. 0445873733 - 0445873124
www.maculan.net

One Three Glass wine and another two wines in the finals was this year's haul for the great Breganze winery. Last year, we emphasized how Fausto Maculan has improved the quality of his mid-range wines and this year we can confirm that these products are in no way inferior to the others. They are quite excellent wines at competitive prices, starting with the successful Palazzotto 2004, a Cabernet Sauvignon that can hold its own against the best Italian labels and to which we awarded Three Glasses. In some ways, Palazzotto is the most interesting Maculan wine, since it has less extreme extract than the winery's two biggies, Fratta and Crosara. For this reason and also because of to its flawless quality, Palazzotto's enviable character and sense of place are very evident. Madoro made an excellent debut. A Passito with generous cherry jam, chocolate and Mediterranean scrubland aromas, it flaunts tannins that succeed in the difficult task of conserving austerity and density on a bewitchingly sweet palate. Fratta and Crosara are both of an extraordinarily high standard, the former deep and austere, the latter more mature and mouthfilling. Torcolato almost made it to the finals, thanks to its intriguingly floral, spicy nose and the customary crystal-clear palate. Brentino and Speaia are both outstanding value for money as is the Breganze di Breganze, a tangy Tocai poised on the threshold of a second Glass.

●	Breganze Cabernet Sauvignon Palazzotto '04	🍷🍷🍷	5
●	Breganze Rosso Crosara '04	🍷🍷	8
●	Fratta '04	🍷🍷	8
○	Breganze Torcolato '04	🍷🍷	7
●	Brentino '04	🍷🍷	4*
●	Madoro Passito '04	🍷🍷	7
●	Speaia '04	🍷🍷	4*
●	Breganze Cabernet '04	🍷	4
○	Breganze di Breganze '05	🍷	4
○	Breganze Vespaiolo '05	🍷	3
○	Dindarello '05	🍷	5
○	Ferrata '05	🍷	5
○	Pino & Toi '05	🍷	3
●	Fratta '01	🍸🍸🍸	8

BREGANZE (VI)

Firmino Miotti

via Brogliati Contro, 53
36042 Breganze (VI)
tel. 0445873006
www.firminomiotti.it

Firmino Miotti has been very fortunate in having a daughter like Franca, who has enthusiastically taken over the running of this small but important winery. Such good fortune is not bestowed by chance but comes from perseverance, determination and a good deal of sacrifice, so we are convinced that credit for the rosy future we can look forward to today goes partly to Firmino, who set Franca an example of strong values and love for the land. With this solid background, Franca seems determined to set her sights ambitiously high and her wines compete increasingly successfully with the elite of the Veneto and beyond. Valletta 2003 is the most shining example. A Bordeaux blend aged in barriques, it is one of the most interesting versions of its type thanks to generous aromas – particularly wild berries, jam and mint – and an austerely powerful, mouthfilling, confidently lingering palate. It's a wine that will surely be at its best in a few years' time. The Cabernet 2004 is also good, showing pleasant vegetal hints alongside wild berries on the nose and a taut, elegant progression on the palate. The main grape varieties used in the Le Colombare 2005 are tocai and riesling and the wine is characterful, impressively generous on the nose and palate and nicely balanced. The tropical fruit Torcolato 2003 is livelier and suppler than previous versions.

●	Rosso Valletta '03	🍷🍷	6
○	Breganze Torcolato '03	🍷🍷	7
●	Breganze Cabernet '04	🍷🍷	4
○	Le Colombare '05	🍷🍷	3
○	Breganze Pinot Bianco '05	🍷	3
○	Breganze Vespaiolo '05	🍷	3
●	Rosso Valletta '01	🍸🍸	6
●	Rosso Valletta '02	🍸🍸	6
●	Rosso Valletta '00	🍸🍸	6

CASTELNUOVO DEL GARDA (VR)

Giovanna Tantini

Loc. Oliosi
via Goito, 10
37014 Castelnuovo del Garda (VR)
tel. 0457575070
www.giovannatantini.it

The small village of Oliosi is in the countryside near Castelnuovo, on one of the last ridges of morainic hills to the south-east of Lake Garda. A plaque on one of its houses commemorates 24 June 1866, when a handful of soldiers lost their lives defending their infantry regiment against bandits. Oliosi's one historical monument is just a stone's throw from the headquarters of a young, energetic wine producer, Giovanna Tantini, who has invested in Bardolino and the corvina grape grown in the Garda area. Giovanna took a bachelor's degree in law and a master's in winery management before calling in expert consultant winemakers Attilio Pagli and Laura Zuddas and agronomist Federico Curtaz to help redesign the family's 12 hectares of vineyards. Only five of these, situated at Mischi, are currently productive but the results are remarkable. The Bardolino 2004 manages to avoid stereotypes and is at its best after a year's ageing in bottles, which in no way deprives it of a delightful fruity palate and subtle spicy hints. The Chiaretto is stylishly fragrant with floral and berry fruit aromas, while the Bardolino 2005 is generously mouthfilling. The 2003 vintage brought a newcomer, Ettore, a serious red made mainly from corvina grapes, with small quantities of cabernet and merlot. The grapes undergo two brief partial drying periods, first on the vine, using the shoot cutting technique, and then in wooden boxes for a week. The result is full-bodied, juicy ripe fruit sensations. The unusual label shows the graph of the heartbeat of Giovanna's baby, Ettore, when he was born.

●	Ettore '03	TT	5
●	Bardolino '04	TT	4
⊙	Bardolino '05	TT	4
⊙	Bardolino Chiaretto '05	TT	3*
●	Bardolino '03	YY	4

CAVAION VERONESE (VR)

Le Fraghe

Loc. Colombara, 3
37010 Cavaion Veronese (VR)
tel. 0457236832
www.fraghe.it

What we particularly like about Matilde Poggi, who owns this traditional winery in the area inland of Lake Garda, is her absolute determination to pursue her objective: to give the wines a highly personal style that is unaffected by passing trends. She is aided in this endeavour by the nature of the land, which is rich in contrasting soft and harsh features, and by a climate that hovers between mildness from the lake and colder climes from the nearby mountains. The unstoppable Matilde loves to experiment with anything new and this year she presented a new white alongside the usual range. Vendemmia a San Goffredo 2004 is from late-harvested garganega grapes, some aged for a few months in stainless steel and some in large oak barrels. The debut version of this wine is immediately impressive, with overripe fruit leading the range of aromas and a full-bodied, gutsy palate perhaps just lacking a little freshness. Quaiare 2003 is the winery's leading product, a blend of cabernet sauvignon and cabernet franc with a rather edgy character. The acidity on the palate is assertive but intriguing, offering encouraging hints of red berry fruit and subtler, ethereal hints of unusual gamey aromas. The other wines, Garganega Camporengo and two Bardolinos, are well styled and pleasant overall.

●	Quaiare Cabernet '03	TT	5
○	Camporengo Garganega Vendemmia a San Goffredo '04	TT	4
●	Bardolino '05	T	3
⊙	Bardolino Chiaretto Ròdon '05	T	3
○	Camporengo Garganega '05	T	3
●	Quaiare Cabernet '00	YY	5
●	Quaiare Cabernet '01	YY	5
●	Quaiare Cabernet '96	YY	5
●	Quaiare Cabernet '97	YY	5
●	Quaiare Cabernet '98	YY	5

CINTO EUGANEO (PD)

CA' LUSTRA

LOC. FAEDO
VIA SAN PIETRO, 50
35030 CINTO EUGANEO (PD)
TEL. 042994128 - 0429644111
www.calustra.it

Pioneer wineries like Ca' Lustra are responsible for the ferment in the Colli Euganei zone today. Franco has built up the winery he runs today with Ivano Giacomin gradually, focusing on essentials, and the wines are obtained from 35 hectares of vineyards in various prestigious areas of the local DOC zone. The annual production of 180,000 bottles is split into two lines, basic wines released as Ca' Lustra and the Villa Alessia selections, named after the estate which is also a centre of wine culture. Work is humming on the cellar renovations to cater for new production requirements. Let's begin with the delightful Cabernet 2004, which is excellent value for money. The Moscato Secco 'A Cengia 2005 confidently repeated its success: it's an important local variety that is gradually earning the approval of producers and enthusiasts alike. The Manzoni Bianco and Chardonnay Roverello are both very good and some bottle-ageing will further enhance their qualities. The Moscato Fior d'Arancio Passito made a remarkable debut alongside the other Moscato, La Betia. The Pinot Bianco and Merlot are both dependable examples of their respective categories. The happy ending to this story comes from the two winery champions: Cabernet Girapoggio 2003, with warm, herbal aromas, generous fruit and a fresh-tasting palate of chocolate, leather and coffee in the finish, and the Merlot Sassonero 2004 which clearly expresses the minerally Colli Euganei terroir with plenty of blackberry, plum and blackcurrant sensations. This very stylish wine should age extremely well.

●	Colli Euganei Cabernet Girapoggio Villa Alessi '03	🍷🍷	5
●	Colli Euganei Merlot Sassonero Villa Alessi '04	🍷🍷	5
●	Colli Euganei Cabernet '04	🍷🍷	4*
○	Colli Euganei Passito Fior d'Arancio Villa Alessi '04	🍷🍷	5
○	Moscato La Betia Villa Alessi '04	🍷🍷	4*
○	Colli Euganei Chardonnay Roverello Villa Alessi '05	🍷🍷	4*
○	Manzoni Bianco Pedevenda V A '05	🍷🍷	4*
○	Moscato Secco 'A Cengia Villa Alessi '05	🍷🍷	4*
●	Colli Euganei Merlot '04	🍷	3
○	Colli Euganei Pinot Bianco '05	🍷	3

CINTO EUGANEO (PD)

MONTE FASOLO

LOC. FAEDO
VIA MONTE FASOLO, 2
35030 CINTO EUGANEO (PD)
TEL. 0429634030
www.montefasolo.com

Fattoria Monte Fasolo certainly made an explosive appearance but it was rather a foregone conclusion that the winemaking heritage of Maria Grazia and Gabrielle Mazzuccato would bring it up to the front rank of Colli Euganei winemaking in just a few short years. The winery's history began over 30 years ago but for a long time it restricted itself to well-typed but ordinary products. The desire to excel was fulfilled in 2004 with a technical shake-up and the important input of agronomist Filippo Giannone and wine technician Andrea Boaretti, both acknowledged professionals but also, and more importantly, experienced connoisseurs of the territory the grapes grown here. The numbers speak for themselves: 70 of the estate's 200 hectares are used for vineyards, with an average yield per hectare of 60 quintals – 40 for the selections – and an annual production of about 150,000 bottles. From a generally high quality range, the outstanding wine is the Cabernet Le Tavole 2004, from the splendid Baone vineyard. Pronounced aromas of fines herbes and pepper join juicy fruit and the full-bodied palate has extraordinarily sweet tannins. The Rusta, a Bordeaux blend of mainly merlot grapes, is well made with strikingly good body and a supple palate. Turning to the whites, the Spumante di Fior d'Arancio is very good while the Passito from the same grapes and the Colli Euganei Bianco Milante 2004 just missed a second Glass by a whisker.

●	Colli Euganei Cabernet Podere Le Tavole '04	🍷🍷	4*
●	Colli Euganei Rosso Rusta '04	🍷🍷	3*
○	Colli Euganei Fior d'Arancio Spumante	🍷🍷	4
○	Colli Euganei Bianco Milante '04	🍷	3
○	Colli Euganei Fior d'Arancio Passito Solone '04	🍷	5
○	Colli Euganei Serprino '05	🍷	3

COLOGNOLA AI COLLI (VR)

Fasoli

fraz. San Zeno
via C. Battisti, 49
37030 Colognola ai Colli (VR)
tel. 0457650741
www.fasoligino.com

The Fasoli brothers own a good solid winery working in both the Valpolicella and Soave zones. Natalino and Amadio have transformed this farm, whose crops once included everything produced in the area, into a winery focusing on fine quality wines. The grapes are those typical of the two key zones, garganega for the whites, corvina and rondinella for the reds. A passion for experimentation and careful management of the land have also prompted the brothers to plant non-traditional grapes to give the various varieties an opportunity to express the different types of soil to best advantage. Hence the presence of merlot, used to make two very dense wines, and pinot nero, planted almost as a joke, which has yielded extremely interesting results in favourable years. All the wines show the estate's typical stylistic features of generosity and soft sensations, without distorting the identity of the grape. The best-made wine this year is the Merlot Calle. Although it requires further ageing, it already has very appealing aromas and a lively, juicy palate. The Soave Borgoletto is completely different in style, translating the cool weather of 2005 into a lean, clearly defined wine with apple and pear fruit alongside the vegetal aromas on the nose and a balance of fresh acidity and tangy flavour on the palate. Of the two La Corte del Pozzo Valpolicellas, the Ripasso was the less impressive while the Soave Pieve Vecchia is generous and mouthfillingly soft.

●	Calle Merlot '04	🍷🍷	6
○	Soave Pieve Vecchia '04	🍷🍷	5
●	Valpolicella Cl. La Corte del Pozzo '04	🍷🍷	5
○	Soave Borgoletto '05	🍷🍷	4
●	Recioto della Valpolicella Cl. La Corte del Pozzo '01	🍷	6
●	Valpolicella Cl. Ripasso La Corte del Pozzo '04	🍷	5
○	Recioto di Soave S. Zeno '02	🍷🍷 (white)	6
○	Soave Sup. Pieve Vecchia '02	🍷🍷 (white)	4
●	Calle Merlot '03	🍷🍷 (white)	6
○	Recioto di Soave S. Zeno '03	🍷🍷 (white)	6
○	Soave Borgoletto '04	🍷🍷 (white)	4
○	Soave Pieve Vecchia '03	🍷 (white)	4

COLOGNOLA AI COLLI (VR)

Agostino Vicentini

fraz. San Zeno
via C. Battisti, 62c
37030 Colognola ai Colli (VR)
tel. 0457650539

This lovely Colognola ai Colli winery confirmed its Guide-worthy status with a range of high quality products that express the typical features of the local area and the different wine types made. The small but functional cellar creates wines from both the Soave and Valpolicella designated areas at invariably interesting prices. The estate has about 15 hectares of vineyards and only the best grapes are used in the blends with the Vicentini label. The rest of the products are usually sold wholesale to keep the quality in the house brand high. The stand-out white again this year is Vigneto Terrelunghe, a standard-label Soave with subtle aromas of flowers and aromatic herbs on the nose. The palate maintains its grip, showing enviably tangy and lingering. The Superiore Il Casale, on the other hand, does not quite live up to the production effort required, doe it has very mature aromas and the palate lacks acidity. The generous, very fresh Recioto gives a good performance, though, with hints of white peaches in the finish. Turning to the reds, while we wait for the new vintage of Idea Bacco, we tasted Valpolicella Superiore 2002, whose traditional aromas hint at dried fruit and crushed flowers before the dry palate unveils a creamy tannic texture.

○	Recioto di Soave '04	🍷🍷	6
○	Soave Vign. Terrelunghe '05	🍷🍷	3*
●	Valpolicella Sup. '02	🍷	3
○	Soave Sup. Il Casale '04		4
●	Valpolicella Sup. Idea Bacco '03	🍷🍷 (white)	4
○	Soave Vign. Terrelunghe '04	🍷🍷 (white)	3

FARRA DI SOLIGO (TV)

Andreola Orsola

Loc. Col San Martino
via Cal Longa, 52
31010 Farra di Soligo (TV)
tel. 0438989379
www.andreolaorsola.it

Farra di Soligo is a small town between Valdobbiadene and Conegliano. Although the main local activity is growing grapes for wine, it has never really made a name for itself, unlike neighbouring towns. And yet the wines made here reflect the area. They are halfway between the fragrant lightness of Valdobbiadene and the structure and dynamism of Conegliano, in a logical combination of these two profiles. The Andreola Orsola winery has been active here for many years, a little off the beaten track but always present nonetheless, vintage after vintage. Production obviously focuses on prosecco, as well as verdiso and the red Bordeaux varieties. The typical feature of the juicy, stylish Cartizze is generous ripe yellow peach, apricot and apple fruit. The Prosecco Extra Dry Vigneto Dirupo, which made an excellent impression on our panel, is still very approachable on the nose but performs best on the taut, dry palate, backed up by the strength of the fruit rather than by sugar, a sure sign of good winemaking technique. The rest of the line-up of well-balanced Proseccos more or less repeat the style. All are made from good quality grapes and have not undergone excessively severe winemaking procedures. The Cabernet Franc 2005 is fresh and peppery while the red Valbone 2003 is a Bordeaux blend with generous fruit and a nice tangy palate.

○	Cartizze	🍷🍷	5
○	Prosecco di V. Extra Dry Vign. Dirupo	🍷🍷	4
●	Valbone Rosso '03	🍷	4
●	Cabernet Franc '05	🍷	3
○	Prosecco di V. Dry Mill. '05	🍷	4
○	Prosecco di V. Frizzante	🍷	4
○	Verdiso Frizzante	🍷	4
○	Prosecco di V. Tranquillo Romit	🍷	3
○	Verdiso '05		3

FOSSALTA DI PIAVE (VE)

De Stefani

via Cadorna, 92
30020 Fossalta di Piave (VE)
tel. 042167502
www.de-stefani.it

The De Stefani family are originally from Refrontolo, near Conegliano, the home of marzemino and prosecco. Tiziano, founder of this winery, left Refrontolo in 1960 for Fossalta on the river Piave. Today his son Alessandro, who studied at the oenology school in Conegliano, runs the large winery with him, turning out 250,000 bottles a year. The 29-hectare property comprises the Le Ronche estate at Fossalta and Prà Longo at Monastier, in the provinces of Venice and Treviso, and the gentle hills of Refrontolo where the Colvendrame farmstead is situated. The vineyards were planted between 1973 and 1987 and are therefore perfectly able to ensure the steady results that have earned the winery a place in the front rank of local producers. The wide range of wines includes just about everything, from whites to spumantes, young reds, mature reds and sweet wines. This time the whites shone for their freshness. The Olmera 2005 from tocai and sauvignon grapes has prominent aromatic herbs on the nose with pronounced fresh fruit. The tocai and chardonnay-based Vitalys 2005 is fragrant with a juicy citrus note and the Pinot Grigio is very sound. But it is the sweet wines that have made a leap forward in quality. The Passito di Refrontolo (marzemino) is excellent and the Passut 2000 is just a little sugary. The reds are all reliably well made but lack the verve we expect from the leading selections, which are more about extract than finesse.

●	Colli di Conegliano Refrontolo Passito '03	🍷🍷	6
○	Olmera Le Ronche '05	🍷🍷	5
○	Vitalys '05	🍷🍷	4*
○	Passito Passut '00	🍷	6
●	Soler '02	🍷	4
●	Piave Cabernet '04	🍷	4
●	Refosco P. R. Kreda '04	🍷	6
●	Terre Nobili Rosso Le Ronche '04	🍷	5
●	Merlot '05	🍷	4
○	Pinot Grigio Prà Longo '05	🍷	4
●	Terre Nobili Rosso Le Ronche '03	YY	6
○	Olmera Le Ronche '04	YY	5

FOSSALTA DI PORTOGRUARO (VE)

Santa Margherita

via Ita Marzotto, 8
30025 Fossalta di Portogruaro (VE)
tel. 0421246111
www.santamargherita.com

As it was last year, the Malbech is the most striking wine in the range presented by the large group led by the Marzotto family. While last time the most interesting feature of this wine was its old-fashioned style, the 2004 version marks a different trend with a surge of freshness and a modern style and the quality of the wine is even better. It is no coincidence that there is also new artwork, and the Laudato has disappeared to make room for a new label. So here is a red from the estate's vineyards in Lison with vibrant blackberry and blueberry aromas alongside hints of minerals and aromatic herbs. The palate is impressively creamy on entry with sweet silky tannins and succulence from the pronounced acidity. Merlot Verdato is only a step behind on the same path, for it is still very young and requiring further ageing. The 2004 Merlot Lison-Pramaggiore is more traditionally made, with subtler, less approachable fruit and a full-bodied, harmoniously tangy palate. The wines from the Alto Adige estates are all reliably good. Pinot Bianco, Sauvignon and Pinot Grigio Impronta del Fondatore all express their territory of origin and grape variety very well, as does the Pinot Grigio Valdadige. The Luna dei Feldi is an enjoyable and original blend of chardonnay, müller and gewürztraminer with intriguing aromas.

●	Malbech '04	▼▼	5
●	Versato '04	▼▼	4*
●	Lison-Pramaggiore Cabernet Franc '04	▼	4
●	Lison-Pramaggiore Merlot '04	▼	4
●	Lison-Pramaggiore Refosco P. R. '04	▼	3
○	A. A. Pinot Bianco '05	▼	4
○	A. A. Pinot Grigio Impronta del Fondatore '05	▼	4
○	A. A. Sauvignon '05	▼	4
○	Luna dei Feldi '05	▼	4
○	Valdadige Pinot Grigio '05	▼	4
○	Prosecco di V. Extra Dry	▼	4
●	Laudato di Malbech '01	▽▽	5

FUMANE (VR)

★★ Allegrini

via Giare, 9/11
37022 Fumane (VR)
tel. 0456832011
www.allegrini.it

A winery that produces over half a million bottles a year, sends three out of four wines to the finals and whose fourth is a Two Glass winner costing about five euros a bottle wholesale – what more can we say? Allegrini is actually something of an iceberg. The above-water part is here in these positive reviews but the more important invisible part consists of almost 90 hectares of specialized vineyards, respect for the territory, quality traditional wines with a modern feel and well-trained personnel with close links to the local area. Replanting in an area where viticulture has never flourished particularly has slowed down a little so as not to lose the heritage of old vineyards indispensable to the Allegrini production philosophy. Turning to the wines themselves, we just have to begin with a sumptuous Amarone. A year's ageing has endowed it with complex aromas and a stunningly balanced palate typical of the very finest vintages. It earned Three delicious Glasses, trophy number 22 for the winery showcase. The Recioto is outstanding with lively ripe, juicy wild berry fruit aromas and fresh minerally hints of aromatic herbs leading into a succulent, lingering, very stylish palate. La Poja is conspicuous by its absence but La Grola 2003 went a long way towards helping us get over it. Clearly defined, enthralling aromas of black berry fruit and spices are beautifully reflected on the juicy, taut palate. Finally, the approachable Valpolicella Classico is anything but ordinary, offering generous fruit on the nose and refreshing drinkability.

●	Amarone della Valpolicella Cl. '01	▼▼▼	8
●	La Grola '03	▼▼	5
●	Recioto della Valpolicella Cl. Giovanni Allegrini '03	▼▼	7
●	Valpolicella Cl. '05	▼▼	4*
●	Amarone della Valpolicella Cl. '00	▽▽▽	8
●	Recioto della Valpolicella Cl. Giovanni Allegrini '00	▽▽▽	6
●	La Poja '01	▽▽▽	8
●	Amarone della Valpolicella Cl. '95	▽▽▽	8
●	Amarone della Valpolicella Cl. '96	▽▽▽	8
●	La Poja '96	▽▽▽	8
●	Amarone della Valpolicella Cl. '97	▽▽▽	8
●	La Poja '97	▽▽▽	8
●	Amarone della Valpolicella Cl. '98	▽▽▽	8

FUMANE (VR)

LE SALETTE
VIA PIO BRUGNOLI, 11C
37022 FUMANE (VR)
TEL. 0457701027
www.lesalette.it

The proof of a winery's professionalism is found not just in the bottles themselves but also in the reasons for their creation. This is why, in an unfavourable vintage like 2002, the Scamperles did not bring out the most important wines from the best vineyards. This is true professionalism, an ability to acknowledge that the harvest did not yield fruit of sufficient quality to justify making the winery's top bottles. We applaud Monica and Franco for this decision. But there are plenty of fine wines here. We'll start with Recioto Pergole Vece 2003. Strikingly fresh floral aromas mingle aromatic herbs with ripe fruit, finally giving way to subtler spicy, mineral hints. Lively sweetness on the sumptuous palate is accompanied by nicely gauged acidity and tannins. The two Valpolicella Superiores also performed very well. Ca' Carnocchio is still rather youthful and needs ageing, while I Progni, made using the "ripasso" technique of adding unpressed Amarone skins to the fermented wine, is ready to charm us with mouthfilling silkiness. Amarone La Marega makes the best of the 2002 vintage year by playing on subtle aromas more than structure and the standard-label Valpolicella is making great progress. Fresh, appetizing fruit is followed by a relaxed, fragrant palate that nicely brings together weighty extract and lightness.

●	Recioto della Valpolicella Cl. Pergole Vece '03	▼▼	6
●	Amarone della Valpolicella Cl. La Marega '02	▼▼	6
●	Valpolicella Cl. Sup. Ca' Carnocchio '03	▼▼	5
●	Valpolicella Cl. Sup. I Progni '03	▼▼	4
●	Valpolicella Cl. '05	▼▼	3*
○	Cesare Passito Bianco '04	▼	5
●	Amarone della Valpolicella Cl. Pergole Vece '95	▽▽▽	8
●	Amarone della Valpolicella Cl. Pergole Vece '01	▽▽	8
●	Valpolicella Cl. Sup. I Progni '02	▽▽	4

GAMBELLARA (VI)

LA BIANCARA
FRAZ. SORIO
C.DA BIANCARA, 14
36053 GAMBELLARA (VI)
TEL. 0444444244

The explosive Angiolino Maule is not a man to make compromises. Having followed a professional and – dare we add, ethical – path that embraced biodynamics and minimum intervention in the cellar, he has now decided to change course. Separation from his old travelling companions was painful but now he has founded an association – VinNatur – which aims to take his project even further, without spiralling into pointless dogmatism. His wines seem to express themselves more freely every year, which is perhaps also due to reduced maceration. The white Masieri is starting to be very sound, fruity and minerally. A certain underlying fragility is the price paid by Sassaia for an inclement year, although considering the unfavourable weather the result is very good. We prefer the sulphur-free version which is more enjoyable, lingering and tangy. Pico 2004 is less extreme than usual, with benzene and ripe peaches on the nose followed by a stylishly put-together palate with glimpses of spices, liquorice, rue and more fruit in the finish. Turning to the reds, the Masieri is fragrant, the Canà fruity and the unusually floral and minerally Merlot 2003 shows breeding, nicely reflecting the volcanic local soil of Gambellara. The Recioto impressed our tasting panel for its character, wide range of aromas and stylish palate. Lastly, sweetness pervades the late-harvested Taibane.

○	Recioto di Gambellara '02	▼▼	7
○	Pico '04	▼▼	5
○	Sassaia '05	▼▼	4*
○	Sassaia Senza Solforosa '05	▼▼	4*
●	Merlot '03	▼▼	5
●	Canà Rosso '04	▼	4
○	Masieri Bianco '05	▼	3
●	Masieri Rosso '05	▼	4
○	Taibane '99	▼	7
○	Pico '02	▽▽▽	4
○	Pico '01	▽▽	4
○	Pico '03	▽▽	4
○	Sassaia '03	▽▽	4
○	Sassaia '04	▽▽	4

GAMBELLARA (VI)

ZONIN
VIA BORGOLECCO, 9
36053 GAMBELLARA (VI)
TEL. 0444640111
www.zonin.it

The best wineries on the Italian scene are undoubtedly those which monitor the productive process from start to finish, and as often as not are involved in protecting the environment as much as promoting the vineyards. But we do tend to forget that there is a restricted circle of négociant-style wine merchants whom we might describe as far-sighted. They are able to give the best possible interpretation of the grapes they often monitor from the vineyard on, not simply profiting from the work of farmers to make ordinary wines. This is true of Zonin, a cellar that releases two Valpolicella wines of indisputable quality even though it owns no actual vineyards. The wines are almost identical in their high quality although we preferred the Amarone. Its generous hints of cherry jam and chocolate on the nose are followed by an unexpectedly fresh palate with aromatic herbs and forthright, very pleasant flavour. The Valpolicella has more subdued fruit with vegetal aromas and crushed flowers, while the husky palate is very well typed. Recioto di Gambellara Aristòs is as good as ever. It's a wine that aims to astound with its style and balance rather than strength, and these features keep the alluring sweetness in check. The other wines are all good, whether Veronese, like the Valpolicella and Soaves, or from the Aquileia DOC, and express the varietal features of their grapes.

●	Amarone della Valpolicella '03	🍷🍷	6
○	Recioto di Gambellara Podere il Giangio Aristòs '03	🍷🍷	6
●	Valpolicella Sup. Ripasso '03	🍷🍷	4*
●	Friuli Aquileia Cabernet '04	🍷	3
●	Friuli Aquileia Merlot '04	🍷	3
●	Valpolicella Cl. '04	🍷	3
○	Friuli Aquileia Pinot Grigio '05	🍷	3
○	Gambellara Cl. Podere Il Giangio '05	🍷	3
○	Soave Cl. '05	🍷	3
●	Friuli Aquileia Refosco P. R. '04		3
○	Prosecco Special Cuvée	🍷	3
●	Amarone della Valpolicella '00	🍷🍷 (empty)	6

GREZZANA (VR)

CAV. G.B. BERTANI
FRAZ. ARBIZZANO
LOC. NOVARE
37023 GREZZANA (VR)
TEL. 0458658444
www.bertani.net

Often the meaning of the term "tradition" is not really clear, because presenting the past in a modern light at every harvest tends to be associated with an image of something archaic, static and unable to keep pace with the times. But at this large Grezzana winery, tradition is given its noblest interpretation. The ancient skills and knowledge of winemaking are translated into modern, fine quality wines. It would be a mistake to simplify matters by thinking of the usual contrasts of barrique and barrel, stainless steel and concrete, or in the vineyard context, of rows and pergolas. The reality is much more complex. The above contrasts are simply a means to an end, and the end result is a wine of indisputable quality, anchored in values like elegance, the faithful reflection of terroir and vintage, and drinkability. Amarone Classico 1999 is a great, complex wine with generous ripe red berry fruit mingling on the nose with aromatic herbs, Mediterranean scrubland and dried roses. Entry on the palate is classy and sophisticated, showing taut, juicy fruit with tannins so sweet they practically melt away. Let's drink to this Three Glass award and stop talking about it. Next comes a younger, more bouncy Amarone Villa Arvedi 2002, a tangy, more drinkable Secco Bertani and a Soave with amazing balance of sweetness from the oak and freshness from the garganega grapes. Just taste these wines, and forget about trying to pigeon-hole them. You are unlikely to do them justice.

●	Amarone della Valpolicella Cl. '99	🍷🍷🍷	8
○	Soave Sereole '05	🍷🍷	4*
●	Amarone della Valpolicella Valpantena Villa Arvedi '02	🍷🍷	7
●	Albion Cabernet Sauvignon Villa Novare '03	🍷🍷	6
●	Valpantena Secco Bertani '03	🍷🍷	4*
●	Valpolicella Cl. Sup. Vigneto Ognisanti '03	🍷🍷	5
●	Valpolicella Cl. Sup. Ripasso Villa Novare '04	🍷🍷	4*
○	Le Lave '04	🍷	4
●	Valpolicella Cl. Villa Novare '05	🍷	4
●	Amarone della Valpolicella Cl. '97	🍷🍷🍷 (empty)	8
●	Amarone della Valpolicella Cl. '98	🍷🍷🍷 (empty)	8

GREZZANA (VR)

La Costa di Romagnano

loc. La Costa
37034 Grezzana (VR)
tel. 0458650111
www.agricosta.it

In just three years, Lorenzo Zampieri's winery has earned itself an enviably solid reputation. This is not due to overblown marketing techniques or stratagems but to simple dedication and shrewd management of this little corner of Valpolicella. This relatively new winery consists of two old converted farmhouses, one now a holiday centre and the other the cellar, and 20 or so hectares of vineyards at the edge of a wood of nearly a hundred. Only Amarone and Valpolicella wines are made. Despite the unfavourable vintages presented for inspection this time, the wines won us over with their clear definition and faithful rendering of territoriality and vintage, qualities unfortunately not always present in even the most prestigious bottles. This Amarone Calandra di Romagnano is from the rain-ravaged 2002 growing year, and the nose is dominated by aromas of ripe fruit, minerally notes and aromatic herbs. The palate highlights the problems of the vintage and the residual sugar which usually characterizes this type of wine is a little excessive. The palate finishes with a deep minerally note. The Valpolicella Superiore from the same vineyard is completely different in style. A warm year has endowed it with almost excessively ripe aromas and the palate appears to need further ageing to allow the alcohol, acidity and tannin to settle into a more harmonious balance. A little bottle ageing will do nothing but good.

● Amarone della Valpolicella Vign. Calandra di Romagnano '02	▼▼	6
● Valpantena Sup. Vign. Calandra di Romagnano '03	▼	4
● Amarone della Valpolicella Vign. Calandra di Romagnano '01	▽▽	6
● Amarone della Valpolicella Valpantena Vign. Timarol '01	▽▽	6
● Valpantena Sup. Vign. Calandra di Romagnano '01	▽▽	4
● Valpantena Sup. Vign. Calandra di Romagnano '02	▽▽	4

ILLASI (VR)

★ Romano Dal Forno

fraz. Cellore
loc. Lodoletta, 1
37030 Illasi (VR)
tel. 0457834923
www.dalforno.net

It is tricky to talk about Romano Dal Forno, his winery or his wines without falling into a well-worn litany of great passion, scrupulous care in vineyards and cellar, outstanding wines, scarce availability, prices and so on and so forth. But that's how things actually are. When just 30,000 bottles are obtained from 25 hectares of vineyards, it's impossible to ignore the work in the fields or the meticulous care taken over the planting, pruning and harvesting. Not to mention the shrewdly calculated, gently administered drying period to make sure that that fruit receives a concentrated dose of the classy Illasi terroir and the contribution of the growing year. This is followed by long ageing requiring both time and space, hence the extension of a cellar which, although very large, was no longer sufficiently spacious. New vineyards will also soon be productive. Finally comes the wine, or rather, The Wine, Amarone, a bottle that needs to be opened well before tasting to free itself of oak-derived notes and liberate the fruit. Red, indeed black, it is ripe and appetizing on the seemingly endlessly nose in a frame of spices and minerality. The rigid palate slowly melts into a mouthfillingly confident flavour and our Three Glasses were a formality. The Valpolicella Superiore is built on the same lines and has rarely been so good. Again, it needs to free itself of oakiness but then proceeds with class and determination, clearly defined fruit melding with mint and dried flowers to close with a long taut finish.

● Amarone della Valpolicella Vign. di Monte Lodoletta '01	▼▼▼	8
● Valpolicella Sup. Vign. di Monte Lodoletta '02	▼▼	8
● Amarone della Valpolicella Vign. di Monte Lodoletta '00	▽▽▽	8
● Amarone della Valpolicella Vign. di Monte Lodoletta '96	▽▽▽	8
● Amarone della Valpolicella Vign. di Monte Lodoletta '97	▽▽▽	8
● Amarone della Valpolicella Vign. di Monte Lodoletta '98	▽▽▽	8
● Amarone della Valpolicella Vign. di Monte Lodoletta '99	▽▽▽	8

ILLASI (VR)

SANTI
VIA UNGHERIA, 33
37031 ILLASI (VR)
TEL. 0456520077
www.giv.it

There was another remarkably good performance from the Santi winery of Illasi. The charming, elegant Amarone Proemio 2003 and Valpolicella Solane 2004 confirm the winery's leading position in Valpolicella. Founded by Carlo Santi in 1843, the winery has a history that unfolds in three stages. First there was a pioneering stage, which lasted until the early 1970s, when the winery entered the Gruppo Italiano Vini. Second came the progressive extension of the vineyards to 40 hectares in Valpolicella and 30 in the Lake Garda area. The third and most recent phase has seen Emilio Pedron press to promote his wines and follow a development route which culminates in the performances we see today. In confirmation of this trend, winemaker Christian Scrinzi and manager Pierluigi Borgna presented another two very pleasant wines. Proemio 2003, a modern, juicy, dynamic Amarone blends strength and approachability that brought home the coveted Three Glasses and the Solane 2004 is firm-structured with nice fruit, a satisfying palate and a reasonable price, which is equally important. The whole range appears to have come on with the two leading wines. The standard-label Amarone 2003, aged in large barrels and traditional in style, has good texture while the Lugana Melibeo 2005 is nicely harmonious with apple and pear fruit and hints of chamomile. Soave Monteforte is more complex. It undergoes long maceration and benefits from a splash of partially dried garganega grapes.

●	Amarone della Valpolicella Proemio '03	🍷🍷🍷	7
●	Valpolicella Cl. Sup. Ripasso Solane '04	🍷🍷	4*
●	Amarone della Valpolicella '03	🍷🍷	6
○	Lugana Melibeo '05	🍷🍷	4
○	Soave Cl. Monteforte '05	🍷🍷	3
●	Valpolicella Cl. Le Caleselle '05	🍷	3
●	Amarone della Valpolicella Proemio '00	🍷🍷🍷 (outline)	7
●	Amarone della Valpolicella Proemio '01	🍷🍷 (outline)	7
●	Valpolicella Cl. Sup. Solane '02	🍷🍷 (outline)	4
●	Valpolicella Cl. Sup. Solane '03	🍷🍷 (outline)	4

ILLASI (VR)

TRABUCCHI
LOC. MONTE TENDA
37031 ILLASI (VR)
TEL. 0457833233
www.trabucchivini.it

The Trabucchi winery owns 21 hectares of well-aspected vineyards with a good temperature range in Val d'Illasi, in Valpolicella and Soave. The modern, well-equipped cellar is situated below the vineyards and is practically invisible from the outside. The wines reflect this innovative spirit, while eloquently expressing their territory and the history that produced them. Of the wines presented, the Valpolicella Superiore Terre di San Colombano 2003 made a particularly good impression. Its generous fragrant nose with heady ripe red fruit is followed by subtler minerality and floral sensations. The palate is taut, juicy, firm and intense, showing suppleness, elegance and sophistication. In fact, it earned Trabucchi its first Three Glass award. The Recioto della Valpolicella 2004 is also very good, rich in dried red berry fruit, it is at its best on the palate, which shows a refined balance of sweetness and well-judged acidity. The Amarone from the difficult growing year of 2002 requires further ageing to achieve its best expression. Its nose is fresh with floral, fruity and spicy sensations while the palate is supple and well-balanced without being excessively powerful. The Valpolicella Superiore Terre del Cereolo 2002 is outstanding with juicy fruit, a fresh-tasting palate and good structure. Finally, the Recioto di Soave 2004 is balsamic, creamy and full of Mediterranean high spirits.

●	Valpolicella Sup. Terre di S. Colombano '03	🍷🍷🍷	5
●	Recioto della Valpolicella '04	🍷🍷	8
●	Amarone della Valpolicella '02	🍷🍷	8
●	Valpolicella Sup. Terre del Cereolo '02	🍷🍷	6
○	Recioto di Soave '04	🍷🍷	7
●	Amarone della Valpolicella '01	🍷🍷 (outline)	8
●	Recioto della Valpolicella '03	🍷🍷 (outline)	7
●	Amarone della Valpolicella '00	🍷🍷 (outline)	8
●	Amarone della Valpolicella '96	🍷🍷 (outline)	8
●	Amarone della Valpolicella '97	🍷🍷 (outline)	8
●	Amarone della Valpolicella '98	🍷🍷 (outline)	8
●	Amarone della Valpolicella '99	🍷🍷 (outline)	7

LONGARE (VI)

COSTOZZA
FRAZ. COSTOZZA
P.ZZA DA SCHIO, 4
36023 LONGARE (VI)
TEL. 0444555099
www.costozza-villadaschio.it

The nexus of history, culture and wine is an ancient, much respected value in the town of Costozza. The famous caves, or "covoli", are carved with Etruscan graffiti, and the stone quarried here was of sufficiently high quality to be used for the works of the Romans and later of Palladio. This delightful corner of Veneto along the Riviera Berica is full of churches and lavish villas, a real discovery which adds charm to the winery owned by the Conti da Schio. In the late 19th century the family gave local winemaking a strong thrust, planting new vineyards and bringing in noble grape varieties from France like cabernet and pinot noir. Today, Giulio supervises production with the invaluable help of winemaker Claudio De Bortoli. The vineyard is situated on clayey-sandy hillside land, covering 12 of the property's 50 hectares and is spread across plots in Montecchio and Casetta. The cabernet sauvignon Rosso Costozza 2004 is an elegant wine with subtle aromatic herbs on the nose and captivating hints of rosemary and tobacco. The juicy cherry fruit blends delightfully with acidity and pronounced tannins. The Cabernet Colli Berici 2004, cabernet franc-based, also amply fulfilled our expectations, its unquestionable virtues being vibrant black pepper, fresh sour cherries and raspberries, fragrant juice and a lingering finish. The Pinot Nero Rosato 2005, on the other hand, is youthful and approachable. Cherry red with grassy aromas alongside red berry fruit and plums, it is an uncomplicated and delightfully drinkable wine.

●	Rosso Costozza '04	🍷🍷	5
●	Colli Berici Cabernet '04	🍷🍷	4
⊙	Pinot Nero Rosato '05	🍷	3
●	Rosso Costozza '03	ΥΥ	5
●	Colli Berici Cabernet '01	ΥΥ	5
●	Rosso Costozza '01	ΥΥ	5
●	Colli Berici Cabernet '02	ΥΥ	5
●	Colli Berici Cabernet '03	ΥΥ	5

MARANO DI VALPOLICELLA (VR)

CA' LA BIONDA
FRAZ. VALGATARA
LOC. BIONDA, 4
37020 MARANO DI VALPOLICELLA (VR)
TEL. 0456801198
www.calabionda.it

Helped by his sons Alessandro and Nicola, not to mention the considerable production potential available in the form of an efficient, recently renovated cellar and beautiful hillside vineyards, owner Pietro Castellani continues unperturbed on the route taking his winery up the quality ladder. The favourable position of the vineyards and unusual limestone and clay composition of the soil have always given Ca' La Bionda wines a nice mix of style and sophistication, bolstered increasingly over the years by generous fruit. The Amarone Vigneti di Ravazzol 2001 tasted this year impressed us enough to rank it among the best expressions of the type. We liked the nose and palate for their balance and the grace with which all that texture is handled, for it never slips back into dull predictability. All the component parts combine to produce a harmonious, highly complex and enjoyable bouquet. The Recioto Vigneti Le Tordare is a little tart but equally impressive, although it still needs more ageing, but the residual sugar is well handled. The two Valpolicellas confirmed the positive impression made by the preceding two wines. We just preferred the Campo Casal Vegri 2003 for its juicy flavour and excellent structure.

●	Amarone Cl. Vign. di Ravazzol Ris. Pietro Castellani '01	🍷🍷	8
●	Valpolicella Cl. Sup. Campo Casal Vegri '03	🍷🍷	5
●	Recioto della Valpolicella Cl. Vign. Le Tordare '04	🍷🍷	6
●	Valpolicella Cl. Sup. Vign. di Ravazzol '04	🍷	4
●	Amarone Cl. Vign. di Ravazzol Ris. Pietro Castellani '00	ΥΥ	8
●	Amarone della Valpolicella Cl. '00	ΥΥ	6
●	Amarone della Valpolicella Cl. Vign. di Ravazzol '00	ΥΥ	7
●	Amarone della Valpolicella Cl. '01	ΥΥ	6

MARANO DI VALPOLICELLA (VR)

Giuseppe Campagnola

loc. Valgatara
via Agnella, 9
37020 Marano di Valpolicella (VR)
tel. 0457703900
www.campagnola.com

In 1907, the Verona Chamber of Commerce awarded the Campagnola winery a prize for its Recioto. This is why Beppe Campagnola considers that date to be the official beginning of the winery's business, although his family had obviously been working in the wine sector for some years previously. But this important anniversary deserves due recognition so an Amarone will be released to mark the centenary of the prize. It is Amarone del Centenario, a wine that falls between the traditional and the modern stools, rich in juicy, ripe, almost jammy red fruit aromas of cherries and plums accompanied by hints of balsam and dried flowers, which are reflected on the palate with depth and austerity. These are 40,000 bottles of huge class and character. The Amarone Classico 2003 is also wonderful, showing taut and subtle from the nose onwards, and outstandingly generous yet supple and drinkable in the mouth. The Valpolicella Caterina Zardini 2004 has pronounced wild berry fruit on the nose, lifted by mint and fresh flowers. The perfectly defined palate reveals skilled use of wood, the tannins are sweet and the acidity lively. The two wines produced in serious numbers, Valpolicella Vigneti di Purano and Soave Monte Foscarino, are also both good. Although they come from different areas and grapes, the clean, richly aromatic style and the balanced flavour are identical.

●	Amarone della Valpolicella Cl. del Centenario '03	🍷🍷	8
●	Valpolicella Cl. Sup. Caterina Zardini '04	🍷🍷	4*
●	Amarone della Valpolicella Cl. '03	🍷🍷	6
●	Recioto della Valpolicella Cl. Casotto del Merlo '04	🍷🍷	5
●	Valpolicella Cl. Sup. Ripasso Vign. di Purano Le Bine '04	🍷🍷	4*
○	Soave Cl. Vign. Monte Foscarino Le Bine '05	🍷🍷	4
●	Corte Agnella Corvina Veronese '05	🍷	4
●	Amarone della Valpolicella Cl. Caterina Zardini '01	YYY	7

MARANO DI VALPOLICELLA (VR)

Michele Castellani

fraz. Valgatara
via Granda, 1
37020 Marano di Valpolicella (VR)
tel. 0457701253
www.castellanimichele.it

Sergio Castellani knows Valpolicella better than most other people and forges doggedly ahead to consolidate his large family winery. Another 13 hectares of vineyards at Negrar have now joined the almost 50 hectares owned or rented by the winery. The new vineyards are ideally situated on a hillside at 400 metres above sea level, planted mainly to corvina and corvinone, the objective being to obtain high quality fruit. The extensive range of wines is complete and although a top note is perhaps lacking, the average level is very high. We are pleased to note that there is no pointless proliferation of labels, since we have always maintained that simplifying the range helps the client and saves wasted effort on the part of the producer. There are two versions of Amarone. The more approachable Campo Casalin 2001 is soft without being languid, while the Le Vigne Ca' del Pipa is from a different soil type and appears more closed and difficult to decipher. It has undeniable potential and is probably just regrouping, as it were. In the meantime, you could uncork a well-made Valpolicella Costamaran 2003. Like the Amarones, there are also two versions of Recioto: Monte Fasenara 2004, which has youthful sensations despite its strong hints of crushed fruit, and the mature Le Vigne Ca' del Pipa, which is richer in extract and easily the winery's most interesting product.

●	Amarone della Valpolicella Cl. Campo Casalin I Castei '01	🍷🍷	8
●	Amarone della Valpolicella Cl. Le Vigne Ca' del Pipa '01	🍷🍷	8
●	Recioto della Valpolicella Cl. Le Vigne Ca' del Pipa '03	🍷🍷	7
●	Valpolicella Cl. Sup. Ripasso I Castei Costamaran '03	🍷🍷	5
●	Recioto della Valpolicella Cl. Monte Fasenara I Castei '04	🍷🍷	7
●	Recioto della Valpolicella Cl. Le Vigne Ca' del Pipa '99	YYY	7
●	Recioto della Valpolicella Cl. Campo Casalin I Castei '00	YY	7

MARANO DI VALPOLICELLA (VR)

Corte Rugolin

Fraz. Valgatara
loc. Rugolin
37020 Marano di Valpolicella (VR)
tel. 0457702153
www.corterugolin.it

The small winery owned by Elena and Federico Coati never ceases to amaze us. Every year, small but important changes bring this lovely estate closer to the highest peaks of quality. Inside the old courtyard, the rooms used for tastings today have gradually been renovated like, of course, the cellar, which although small is spacious enough to accommodate all the barrels required to age the wines. The grapes are grown on the winery's ten hectares of vineyards in the municipal areas of Marano, Sant'Ambrogio and San Pietro in Cariano. The Amarone Monte Danieli 2002 is missing from the roll-call because of the unfavourable growing year but another wine of considerable weight and class captured our attention, the Valpolicella Ripasso 2003. The very generous aromas are dominated by wild berry fruit, blackberries, cyclamen, blueberries and mint, which gradually give way to spices and minerals. The powerful palate is supple and harmonious with densely woven tannins and fresh acidity, giving it a juicy and very persistent flavour. The Recioto 2003 is even more unusual, combining fruity jam and balsam on the nose with an intriguing flavour nicely supported by sharp acidity. The garganega-based Passito Aresco is a beautifully balanced and textured sweet wine. The standard-label Valpolicella is fresh-tasting, approachable and very enjoyable, with genuine fruit that helps make it easily and satisfyingly drinkable.

●	Recioto della Valpolicella Cl. '03	🍷🍷	6
●	Valpolicella Cl. Sup. Ripasso '03	🍷🍷	5
○	Aresco Passito '03	🍷🍷	6
●	Valpolicella Cl. '05	🍷	3
●	Amarone della Valpolicella Cl. Monte Danieli '01	YY	7
●	Amarone della Valpolicella Cl. Monte Danieli '00	YY	7
●	Amarone della Valpolicella Cl. Monte Danieli '97	YY	7
●	Amarone della Valpolicella Cl. Monte Danieli '98	YY	7
●	Amarone della Valpolicella Cl. Monte Danieli '99	YY	7

MARANO DI VALPOLICELLA (VR)

F.lli Degani

Fraz. Valgatara
via Tobele, 3a
37020 Marano di Valpolicella (VR)
tel. 0457701850

If you are looking for uncompromising wines with no frills, and are more interested in what's in the glass than the architectural distraction afforded by the cellar, then look no further. The Degani brothers' small family winery owns six hectares of vineyards at Marano and Fumane. The cellar is basic, with no flashy modern devices or advanced technology. Plenty of care is lavished on the vineyard and the wines are strongly traditional in style. We feel able to say that a little more care over the vinification and ageing phases wouldn't go amiss, since a few of the wines were lacking in aroma. After our tastings, we can recommend the perky, drinkable standard-label Valpolicella. The Cicilio, a homage to the Deganis' progenitor, undergoes the "ripasso" technique of adding unpressed Amarone skins to the fermented wine. The grassy aromas are offset by a soft palate marked with uncomplicated fruit. The Recioto 2004 is old-fashioned in style and more interesting on the palate than on the nose. We were less impressed by the vegetal, rather tousled Superiore 2003 and the Amarone La Rosta 2003 which is over-evolved and lacks freshness, despite the good quality of the fruit. The best results come from the standard-label Amarone 2003 which is gutsy, dry and fragrant with herbal infusions and liquorice, and shows nice continuity on the palate, as well as the jovial Recioto La Rosta 2003.

●	Amarone della Valpolicella Cl. '03	🍷🍷	5
●	Recioto della Valpolicella Cl. La Rosta '03	🍷🍷	5
●	Amarone della Valpolicella Cl. La Rosta '03	🍷	6
●	Valpolicella Cl. Sup. '03	🍷	4
●	Valpolicella Cl. Sup. Ripasso Cicilio '03	🍷	4
●	Recioto della Valpolicella Cl. '04	🍷	5
●	Valpolicella Cl. '05	🍷	2*
●	Amarone della Valpolicella Cl. '01	YY	6
●	Recioto della Valpolicella Cl. La Rosta '02	YY	6

MARANO DI VALPOLICELLA (VR)

La Giaretta

Fraz. Valgatara
via del Platano, 12
37020 Marano di Valpolicella (VR)
tel. 0457701791
www.cantinalagiaretta.com

Francesco Vaona's winery is small but capable of some very fine interpretations of the classic Valpolicella wines. The estate's ten hectares of vineyards produce two different lines. One is more traditional in style and the other, I Quadretti, reflects Francesco's quest for greater strength and extract. You might actually expect greater finesse and less structure from the vineyards in Val di Marano but the rest of the products, from Arbizzano, show strength and generosity that you would be unlikely to find elsewhere. The most impressive wine of all was definitely the Recioto 2002. It's very generous yet uncomplicated, with red berry fruit and spices on the nose, and an even more impressive palate with overwhelming sweetness kept in check by the dense tannic weave that lends austerity. The Valpolicella I Quadretti 2003 is not far behind in quality. Underneath the still rather forward oak is a world of red berry fruit, cocoa powder and spices that just keep on coming. The palate is nice and fresh, with plenty of vigour and sweet silky tannins. The Amarone I Quadretti 2000 is not quite so impressive. The aromas give beautifully generous cherry jam, chocolate and spices, and the palate shows considerable structure, but the components lack harmony and finesse. Only time will point this wine back towards a closer coherence with its terroir.

● Recioto della Valpolicella Cl. '02	TT	6
● Valpolicella Cl. Sup. I Quadretti '03	TT	5
● Amarone della Valpolicella Cl. I Quadretti '00	T	8
● Valpolicella Cl. Sup. '01	YY	4
● Valpolicella Cl. Sup. I Quadretti '01	YY	5
● Amarone della Valpolicella Cl. I Quadretti '99	YY	8

MARANO DI VALPOLICELLA (VR)

Novaia

via Novaia
37020 Marano di Valpolicella (VR)
tel. 0457755129
www.novaia.it

The Marano valley is probably the most successful Veneto zone at expressing its terroir, with enormously fresh aromas, an edge of pronounced acidity and not too excessive structure. One of the reasons why the Vaona brothers' lovely winery is so popular is that they understood and promoted these features from the beginning, abandoning the traditional pergola training in favour of the more functional, quality-promoting vertical trellis system which also enabled their wines to take a different path from most Valpolicella products. The 2002 growing year was unfavourable in this area too, so none of the most important selections were made. But there is a generous, charming Recioto 2003 with still rather uncomplicated aromas hinting at ripe juicy fruit as well as medicinal herbs and floral notes that try delicately to peep through. The extremely sweet palate is rendered more mouth-wateringly approachable by sharp acidity. The Valpolicella Superiore I Cantoni is only a step behind in quality. Its aromas of crushed fruit and spices are more mature and discreet and the palate is subtly characterful, closing with a tangy, promising finish. The Valpolicella Classico is impressive as ever. The wine is released after a year in glass as a link between the younger wines and the Valpolicella Superiores.

● Recioto della Valpolicella Cl. Le Novaje '03	TT	5
● Valpolicella Cl. Sup. I Cantoni '03	TT	4*
● Valpolicella Cl. Sup. Ripasso '03	T	4
● Valpolicella Cl. '04	T	3
● Amarone della Valpolicella Cl. Le Balze '01	YY	8
● Amarone della Valpolicella Cl. Le Balze '00	YY	8
● Amarone della Valpolicella Cl. Le Balze '98	YY	8
● Amarone della Valpolicella Cl. Le Balze '99	YY	8

MEZZANE DI SOTTO (VR)

CORTE SANT'ALDA

LOC. FIOI
VIA CAPOVILLA, 28
37030 MEZZANE DI SOTTO (VR)
TEL. 0458880006
www.cortesantalda.it

Marinella Camerani seems to possess a clear, far-sighted view of the wine sector and its events from her winery near Mezzane and appears as a result to be able to take very clear, far-sighted decisions: protecting her woodland by giving up a few hectares of vineyards so as not to tamper with the site climate; gradually abandoning chemicals; allowing the wines to express themselves in new ways and rejecting accepted stereotypes. These choices might seem unremarkable but at the time of making them they required intelligence and, yes, courage. Today, however, the wines are here to show how valid Marinella's decisions were. Their level of quality is high, their links with the territory close and they have much more personality than in the past. The Amarone Mithas 2000 is magnificent, the great growing year having endowed it with generous ripe aromas of cherries and plums over deeper hints of pencil lead and medicinal herbs and exotic spices. The powerful palate is held in place by the tannins and the lively backbone of acidity. The Valpolicella Superiore 2003 is even more striking in character with generous, stylish aromas of forest floor, cyclamen and dried roses on the nose followed by unexpected delicacy alongside the strength of the palate, which has rich, elegant flavour. A very classy Three Glasses, we thought. The spirited Valpolicella Ca' Fiui 2005 and the Recioto 2004 with its well-judged, perfectly blended sweetness are both excellent, despite their very different characteristics. The tangy, sturdy Soave Vigne di Mezzane just missed a second Glass.

●	Valpolicella Sup. '03	▼▼▼	6
●	Amarone della Valpolicella Mithas '00	▼▼	8
●	Recioto della Valpolicella '04	▼▼	7
●	Valpolicella Ca' Fiui '05	▼▼	4*
○	Soave Vigne di Mezzane '05	▼	4
●	Amarone della Valpolicella '00	▽▽▽	8
●	Amarone della Valpolicella '90	▽▽▽	8
●	Amarone della Valpolicella '95	▽▽▽	8
●	Amarone della Valpolicella Mithas '95	▽▽▽	8
●	Amarone della Valpolicella '98	▽▽▽	8
●	Valpolicella Sup. Mithas '01	▽▽	6
●	Valpolicella Sup. '02	▽▽	6
●	Valpolicella Sup. Mithas '00	▽▽	6

MEZZANE DI SOTTO (VR)

ROCCOLO GRASSI

VIA SAN GIOVANNI DI DIO, 19
37030 MEZZANE DI SOTTO (VR)
TEL. 0458880089

The name Roccolo Grassi derives from the vineyard in the village of San Briccio, in the Mezzane valley. This area has long been one of the best in Valpolicella, as it forms a kind of watershed between this zone and Soave, allowing growers to produce both types of wine. The Sartori family began working in this business in 1960 and the winery took the name it uses today in 1996, when the new generation, Marco and Francesca, joined the business. In just a short time, they have defeated the competition and brought their winery to the top of the ladder. Their commitment to quality is very obvious from the number of bottles they obtain – about 32,000 each year – from their 13.5 hectares. The reds have plenty of personality and a good combination of finesse and strength. This year, there is no Amarone to review because Marco did not consider the 2002 good enough to be bottled. The Recioto 2003 is a quintessential example of its type. It's subtle, mouthfilling, fresh and velvety. The lingering, harmonious palate has rich spices, flowers, blackberry and plum jam. The Valpolicella 2003 is a classic example of a truly noble interpretation of its wine type. Enviably elegant, it has sweet fruit and silky tannins, with a beautifully light palate. The equally prestigious whites are grown on the gravelly soil of Broia and the Soave Superiore 2004 has subtle aromatic herbs and apple and pear fruit on the nose leading into a fresh, full-bodied palate with stylish smoke and mineral sensations.

●	Recioto della Valpolicella Roccolo Grassi '03	▼▼	6
●	Valpolicella Sup. Roccolo Grassi '03	▼▼	6
○	Soave Sup. La Broia '04	▼▼	4*
●	Amarone della Valpolicella Roccolo Grassi '00	▽▽▽	8
●	Amarone della Valpolicella Roccolo Grassi '99	▽▽▽	8
●	Amarone della Valpolicella Roccolo Grassi '01	▽▽	8
●	Amarone della Valpolicella Roccolo Grassi '98	▽▽	8

MEZZANE DI SOTTO (VR)

TENUTA SANT'ANTONIO
FRAZ. SAN BRICCIO
VIA VALFREDDA
37030 MEZZANE DI SOTTO (VR)
TEL. 0457650383 - 04587406282
www.tenutasantantonio.it

Faced with an impressive range of wines like those presented every year by the Castagnedi brothers, it becomes clear that luck has nothing to do with success. The plan was clear from the very beginning. The vineyards are planted at high densities on poor soil, the grapes from each destined for one wine. The quest for the utmost quality is extreme at all stages of production and typicity is at a premium. It is therefore no surprise that in just a few years this winery has scaled the heights of regional production. La Bandina has long shown it has the stature of a first-class wine and the 2003 edition maintains the tradition. Although very young, it is juicy and rich in extract and although less subtle than the 2001, it is definitely more forceful. The tangy, minerally Monti Garbi is a grassier, no-nonsense version of Valpolicella. The Amarone Antonio Castagnedi 2003 is elegant and enjoyable, indeed almost a textbook example of this type. It aims not to be a second Amarone but to offer more approachability than the Campo dei Gigli, which is in a class of its own. The extended ageing of the 2000 has focused the aromas to better effect and the palate gives an impression of unlimited strength, held in check by acidity and fine-grained tannins. Herbs, dried flowers and the usual mineral notes reappear in the highly enjoyable finish. Lastly, we were also impressed by the Soave Monte Ceriani 2004.

● Amarone della Valpolicella Campo dei Gigli '00	🍷🍷	8
● Valpolicella Sup. La Bandina '03	🍷🍷	5
● Cabernet Sauvignon Capitel del Monte '02	🍷🍷	5
● Amarone della Valpolicella Sel. Antonio Castagnedi '03	🍷🍷	7
● Valpolicella Sup. Ripasso Monti Garbi '03	🍷🍷	4*
○ Soave Monte Ceriani '04	🍷🍷	4*
● Valpolicella Sup. La Bandina '01	🍷🍷🍷	6
● Amarone della Valpolicella Campo dei Gigli '98	🍷🍷🍷	8
● Amarone della Valpolicella Campo dei Gigli '99	🍷🍷🍷	8

MIANE (TV)

GREGOLETTO
FRAZ. PREMAOR
VIA SAN MARTINO, 83
31050 MIANE (TV)
TEL. 0438970463
www.gregoletto.com

With over 60 harvests behind him, Luigi Gregoletto is undoubtedly the most charismatic figure in the Conegliano-Valdobbiadene area and is renowned locally for his excellent memory, abilities as a storyteller and dedication to his profession, which has again resulted in an outstanding performance. The wines range from good to excellent, following a style that remains unaffected by trends. The Miane estate, halfway between Conegliano and Valdobbiadene, consists of 15 hectares located in Miane and San Pietro di Feletto. Some of the grapes are bought in from trusted growers, and overall production is around 250,000 bottles each year. Luigi's Prosecco Spumante is bang on target, showing intensely fruity, fresh, creamy and fragrant. The Manzoni Bianco 2005 is no less impressive. A blend of riesling renano and pinot bianco, it gives aromas of wild flowers, citrus fruit and gunflint on the nose and a minerally palate that is as sharp as a knife. The Colli di Conegliano Bianco Albio 2005, the first wine of this type and still the best, is a blend of mainly Manzoni bianco with chardonnay, pinot bianco, riesling and sauvignon. On a par with it is the Colli di Conegliano Rosso 2002, from cabernet, merlot and marzemino. Dark, dense and gamey, it has hints of morello cherries, mint and tobacco that lead into a spicy, fresh, stylish palate. The Cabernet 2004 is also very well typed with pronounced aromas of fines herbes and red berry fruit. The Merlot is almost as good and the rest of the range is well up to snuff.

● Colli di Conegliano Rosso '02	🍷🍷	6
● Cabernet '04	🍷🍷	3*
○ Colli di Conegliano Bianco Albio '05	🍷🍷	3*
○ Manzoni Bianco '05	🍷🍷	3*
○ Prosecco di Conegliano V. Extra Dry	🍷🍷	4
● Merlot '04	🍷	3
○ Chardonnay '05	🍷	3
○ Prosecco di Conegliano V. Tranquillo '05	🍷	3
○ Pinot Bianco '05	🍷	3
○ Sauvignon '05	🍷	3
○ Verdiso '05	🍷	3
○ Verdiso Frizzante '05	🍷	3

MONSELICE (PD)

Borin Vini & Vigne
fraz. Monticelli
via dei Colli, 5
35043 Monselice (PD)
tel. 042974384
www.viniborin.it

If one part of Veneto is emerging strongly as high-potential wine country, it is the volcanic Euganei hills that rise sharply from the flatlands of the Po valley. A sleepy backwater for many years, the Colli Euganei have woken up with a bang, thanks in part to wineries like the one owned by Gianni Borin, who has been wise enough to aim for quality even when tourism and the Padua metropolitan area absorbed all his products. Today, his sons Francesco and Giampaolo work alongside Gianni and his wife Teresa with increasing skill and passion in both vineyard and cellar. Once again the two leading reds – Cabernet Sauvignon Mons Silicis and Merlot Rocca Chiara – are on top form. The former comes from the hot growing year of 2003 and has ripe red berry fruit on a nose that relegates spices and minerals to a marginal role before the aromas are beautifully reflected on the broad, mouthfilling palate. The Merlot, from 2004, has complex aromas in which the fruit, spices and floral hints blend perfectly. The palate is nicely tangy and beautifully harmonious with a sturdy body. The Fiore di Gaia 2004, a new Moscato Giallo, aged slowly in stainless steel on the fine lees, came close to Two Glasses on its debut. The Corte Borin, a Manzoni Bianco, is outstandingly good and has never come so close to the finals. The aromas are still uncomplicated and varietal, but the palate shows character and unexpected grip. The Fior d'Arancio Passito 2002 is also very sound.

○	Colli Euganei Fior d'Arancio Passito '02	🍷🍷	5
●	Colli Euganei Cabernet Sauvignon Mons Silicis Ris. '03	🍷🍷	5
●	Colli Euganei Merlot Rocca Chiara Ris. '04	🍷🍷	5
○	Corte Borin '05	🍷🍷	4*
●	Colli Euganei Cabernet Sauvignon V. Costa '04	🍷	4
○	Fiore di Gaia '04	🍷	4
○	Colli Euganei Fior d'Arancio '05	🍷	4
○	Colli Euganei Pinot Bianco Monte Archino '05	🍷	4
●	Colli Euganei Cabernet Sauvignon Mons Silicis Ris. '02	🍷🍷 (outline)	5

MONSELICE (PD)

Castello di Lispida
via IV Novembre, 4
35043 Monselice (PD)
tel. 0429780530
www.lispida.com

It's tempting to say that there is nothing new at Lispida. Since Nature rules supreme here, what news could there be, except for the new fruits of Nature herself? Nature as a running theme, a nurturer, growing and shaping, and a mother who bears and loves her children. Hence the 15 hectares on volcanic Euganean trachyte are cultivated with full respect for the origins of this area's extraordinarily high potential. There are now four wines, not three, and a surprise fifth as a pure expression of winemaking genius. First the mainly tocai Terralba 2002 is vibrant yellow with amber hues and penetrating sensations of flowers and aromatic herbs. Endless aromas of honey, apricots, peaches and spice tempt the nose and there is a warm mixture of both fresh and dried fruit on the sharply defined palate, deftly backed up by fine-grained tannins. Next is the tocai-only Amphora 2004 which, like the two reds, is made with a technique that requires the contribution of the taster. It spends six months on the skins and 15 ageing in terracotta and then glass. After this come the reds, which are also unconventional in their aromas, sensations and flavours. Unusual wines like the gamey Terraforte 2001 and the luscious Merlot Montelispida 2001 are bound to provoke discussion. Last is the Amphora Rosso. Only 700 bottles were made, so obviously we are not awarding a score at such an early stage in development, but this wine is a new concept and an adventure that goes beyond the frontiers of everyday winemaking.

○	Terralba '02	🍷🍷	6
●	Montelispida '01	🍷🍷	6
●	Terraforte '01	🍷🍷	6
○	Amphora '04	🍷🍷	7
○	Terralba '00	🍷🍷 (outline)	7
○	Amphora '01	🍷🍷 (outline)	7
○	Terralba '01	🍷🍷 (outline)	7
○	Amphora '02	🍷🍷 (outline)	7
○	Terralba '99	🍷🍷 (outline)	7

MONTEBELLO VICENTINO (VI)

Domenico Cavazza & F.lli

Contrada Selva, 22
36054 Montebello Vicentino (VI)
tel. 0444649166
www.cavazzawine.com

The two hearts of the Cavazza winery beat with reassuring steadiness and although they have not yet scaled the absolute regional heights, they have helped raise general production standards. At Gambellara, work continues on improving the garganega clones and finding out which training systems are best suited to this variety. As usual, La Bocara opens the range, which is dependably good if somewhat predictably technical. The grapes used in the Creari 2005 are grown on the better-aspected Gambellara hills and make a wine that appears at last to have opened new horizons for this winery. The terroir's typical minerality is nicely focused and depth is certainly not lacking. The Recioto 2004 is fragrant and well balanced. Tenuta Cicogna's 50 hectares of vineyards have given us some new wines, among which we recommend the minerally, earthy and spicy Tocai Rosso 2003 and the velvety, juicily stylish Syrhae 2004. The cellar has invested heavily in these wines, funding new vineyards and vinification techniques so as to preserve as much elegance as possible. The Merlot Cicogna 2004 has plenty of strength and appealing depth. Lastly, there are 12,000 bottles of San Martino Cicogna 2003, made from lightly raisined merlot and cabernet and designed to please those who like their wines extract-rich. The earthy aromas of rosemary express the terroir while the palate is still settling into place.

●	Colli Berici Tocai Rosso '03	TT	5
●	Colli Berici Cabernet Costiera Capitel S. Libera '04	TT	4
●	Colli Berici Merlot Cicogna '04	TT	5
○	Recioto di Gambellara Cl. Capitel S. Libera '04	TT	5
●	Syrhae Cicogna '04	TT	5
○	Gambellara Cl. Creari Capitel S. Libera '05	TT	4
●	Vicenza Rosso San Martino Cicogna '03	T	5
●	Fornetto Capitel S. Libera '04	T	4
○	Gambellara Cl. La Bocara '05	T	4
●	Colli Berici Cabernet Cicogna '03	YY	5
●	Colli Berici Merlot Cicogna '03	YY	5

MONTEBELLO VICENTINO (VI)

Luigino Dal Maso

loc. Selva
via Selva, 62
36054 Montebello Vicentino (VI)
tel. 0444649104
www.dalmasovini.com

As we mentioned last year, Nicola Dal Maso believes deeply in the Vicenza area and invests generous amounts of time, energy and finance to achieve his ambitious goals. He bought old hillside garganega vineyards at Giambellara in the hope of making a very characterful white wine. Riva del Molino 2005 is less expressive than it could be. The trademark rustic character of the garganega grape is too prominent, probably a result of a growing year that had nothing more to give. The Ca' Fischele is built on the same lines and turns out to be a reliable basic wine. The Cabernet and Merlot Casara Roveri are still ageing but we liked the firm-structured, varietal Cabernet Montebelvedere. We are pleased to welcome the debut of a new wine made from tocai rosso grapes picked in the Colli Berici, Colpizzarda 2004. Although the local practice is to give this variety a vinification process halfway between a red and rosé, some producers are trying to change this and release the wine as a serious red for the cellar. The oak is carefully judged so as not to mask the tannins and the flower and fruit nose ranges through minerally and herbal aromas. The texture of the palate has stylish personality that promises well for ageing. Terra dei Rovi 2004 is stronger and better structured, but too young to be able to unleash all its potential. The Recioto Riva dei Perari 2004 is one of the best in its category.

●	Colli Berici Tocai Rosso Colpizzarda '04	TT	4*
●	Colli Berici Cabernet Montebelvedere '04	TT	4
○	Recioto di Gambellara Cl. Riva dei Perari '04	TT	5
●	Terra dei Rovi Rosso '04	TT	6
○	Gambellara Cl. Ca' Fischele '05	T	3
○	Gambellara Cl. Riva del Molino '05	T	4
●	Terra dei Rovi Rosso '03	YY	6
●	Colli Berici Cabernet Casara Roveri '03	YY	5
●	Colli Berici Merlot Casara Roveri '03	YY	5

MONTECCHIA DI CROSARA (VR)

Ca' Rugate

via Pergola, 72
37030 Montecchia di Crosara (VR)
tel. 0456176328
www.carugate.it

Since we were surprised to find so many good wines at the Tessari cellar last year, we have been waiting to see whether it was a coincidence or whether the winery really had moved forward. Not that Ca' Rugate's wines weren't already of a sound standard – they had been awarded Three Glasses more than once – but we just weren't expecting such a generally high level throughout the range. Well, the results are even more impressive this year, thanks to work that is starting to benefit the longer-lived wines, too. Amedeo, Gianni and Michele, assisted by Gian Piero Romana and Beppe Caviola, are a close-knit team who share the same ideas on winemaking, from the vineyard to distribution strategies. Let's start with the Monte Fiorentine, now subtler than ever on the nose. Floral aromas interweave with ripe, juicy apple and pear fruit, and together with confident grip on the palate, earned it Three Glasses. The Recioto La Perlara 2004 is excellent. It has rich aromas of citrus fruit, ginger and liquorice on the nose and a buttery, mouthfilling palate streaked through with fresh, very lingering acidity. This same freshness characterizes the progression of the great Valpolicella Campo Lavei – a veritable explosion of fruit and minerality – while the perfectly blended oak in the Monte Alto achieves its goal of lifting the texture and harmony. The Bucciato is once again of a high standard. It is a vibrant Garganega with hints of oriental spices, citrus fruit and aromatic herbs on the nose, and a taut, beautifully structured palate.

○	Soave Cl. Monte Fiorentine '05	🍷🍷🍷	4*
○	Bucciato '04	🍷🍷	4*
○	Recioto di Soave La Perlara '04	🍷🍷	5
●	Valpolicella Sup. Campo Lavei '04	🍷🍷	5
●	Amarone della Valpolicella '02	🍷🍷	7
●	Recioto della Valpolicella L'Eremita '04	🍷🍷	5
○	Soave Cl. Monte Alto '04	🍷🍷	4
○	Soave Cl. San Michele '05	🍷🍷	3*
●	Valpolicella Rio Albo '05	🍷	3
○	Soave Cl. Sup. Monte Alto '00	YYY	4
○	Soave Cl. Monte Fiorentine '04	YYY	4
○	Soave Cl. Sup. Monte Alto '96	YYY	4
○	Soave Cl. Sup. Bucciato '99	YYY	4
●	Amarone della Valpolicella '01	YY	7

MONTEFORTE D'ALPONE (VR)

★ Roberto Anselmi

via San Carlo, 46
37032 Monteforte d'Alpone (VR)
tel. 0457611488
www.robertoanselmi.com

Roberto Anselmi is a manager and a grower with a vision of wine that is both no-nonsense and complex. In the 1980s, he revolutionized this winery, founded in 1948, and transformed it into a jewel of Veneto winemaking. The 70 hectares of owned and rented vineyards and a production capacity of 600,000 bottles a year, sold all over the world. Alongside this sage, skilful leader are his children Lisa and Tommaso, whose youthful freshness contributes to the work of the cellar. Roberto has chosen not to adhere to any DOC regulations and his wines are an excellent expression of his own whirlwind personality, leaning heavily on the garganega grape, which is a basic, traditional element of the local area. Let's start with the San Vincenzo 2005, perhaps in its best-ever version, the subtle grassy hints on the nose mingling with delicate almonds, peaches and yellow plums. These are generously reflected on the palate with its long, enjoyable finish. It takes expert winemaking to produce 450,000 bottles of this standard. Then comes the Capitel Foscarino 2005 with its delightful green apple-like hints and distinct gunflint on the nose followed by a fresh clean palate. Capitel Croce 2004, from 100 per cent garganega, fermented and aged in used barriques, discloses sophistication and elegance in the magical timbre of its bouquet. It picked up Three Glasses again for the umpteenth time. Finally, the sweet I Capitelli 2004 was the wine that took Anselmi into the big league, opening new horizons for the type. It's fragrant, vibrant and rich in sensations of apricots, honey and dates.

○	Capitel Croce '04	🍷🍷🍷	5
○	I Capitelli '04	🍷🍷	6
○	Capitel Foscarino '05	🍷🍷	4*
○	San Vincenzo '05	🍷🍷	4*
○	Capitel Croce '00	YYY	5
○	Capitel Croce '01	YYY	5
○	Capitel Croce '02	YYY	5
○	Capitel Croce '03	YYY	5
○	Capitel Croce '99	YYY	5
○	Capitel Foscarino '04	YY	4
○	I Capitelli '00	YY	7
○	I Capitelli '02	YY	7
○	Capitel Foscarino '03	YY	4
○	I Capitelli '03	YY	7

La Cappuccina

Fraz. Costalunga
via San Brizio, 125
37030 Monteforte d'Alpone (VR)
tel. 0456175036 - 0456175840
www.lacappuccina.it

The Tessari brothers' winery takes its name from the tiny chapel next to Villa Buri, which is now the new winery headquarters. The tastefully renovated little church is depicted on some of the La Cappuccina labels. The cellar itself is on the basalt that reveals the volcanic origins of the Monteforte area. The style of these wines eschews modernist trends in favour of a traditional feel with ample use of advanced technology. For example, since 1985 the vineyards have been replanted in line with more severe quality criteria, without losing sight of the aim to make elegant, drinkable wines. The basic Soave is never too alcoholic and thus all the more enjoyable. The Fontégo is higher in minerally components, with sensations of green apples, chlorophyll and spring flowers on the nose and a light, stylish flavour. The San Brizio 2004, from 100 per cent garganega, fermented and aged in medium oak barrels, is richer in extract and here is in its most clearly defined version ever. Again, the palate is restrained and the acidity nicely balanced by ripe, almost sweet fruit, while the imperceptible oak helps harmonize the various sensations and gives the wine ageing potential. The Madégo 2005 is a young and absolutely drinkable red wine – ready now – while the Passito Arzìmo 2004 is a vibrant, enjoyable fortified wine with nicely integrated sweetness that never cloys.

○	Soave San Brizio '04	🍷🍷	4*
○	Arzìmo Passito '04	🍷🍷	5
○	Soave Fontégo '05	🍷🍷	4
●	Madégo '05	🍷	4
○	Sauvignon '05	🍷	4
○	Soave '05	🍷	3
●	Cabernet Franc Campo Buri '95	🍸🍸🍸	5
○	Arzìmo Passito '02	🍸🍸	5
●	Campo Buri '02	🍸🍸	5
○	Soave San Brizio '02	🍸🍸	4
○	Soave Fontégo '03	🍸🍸	4
○	Soave San Brizio '03	🍸🍸	4
○	Soave Fontégo '04	🍸🍸	4

Gini

via Matteotti, 42
37032 Monteforte d'Alpone (VR)
tel. 0457611908
www.ginivini.com

Dependability. If we were to sum up the winery owned by brothers Claudio and Sandro Gini in a word, it would be dependability – the ability to repeat the same very high quality year after year without fail. Of course, every vintage has its own particular features but the skill of these two growers lies in understanding how the wine must interpret them each time, and which routes to follow in order to scale the heights of a great DOC like Soave. A couple of difficult harvests in 2002 and 2003 were followed by two extraordinary years that gave generous aromas, acidity and tangy flavour. The result is the gems called La Froscà and Salvarenza that flank a great Soave Classico 2005. We'll begin with the Soave Classico. Approachable and uncomplicated, it is beautifully fruity, with an enjoyable but never commonplace palate. Salvarenza shows more clarity than in recent years, disarming class and uncomplicated floral, spicy and green apple-like aromas, followed by a firm-structured, harmonious and outrageously drinkable palate. The same standard in a different key for the La Froscà, which timidly hides and then delicately proffers its floral aromas, which are nicely reflected on a palate that is equally graceful and elegant. Our Three Glasses went to this star. Recioto Col Foscarin 2004 is also very good, with a lively nose and alluring, perfectly assimilated sweetness.

○	Soave Cl. La Froscà '05	🍷🍷🍷	5
○	Soave Cl. Contrada Salvarenza Vecchie Vigne '04	🍷🍷	5
○	Recioto di Soave Cl. Col Foscarin '04	🍷🍷	6
○	Soave Cl. '05	🍷🍷	4
○	Soave Cl. Sup. Contrada Salvarenza Vecchie Vigne '00	🍸🍸🍸	5
○	Soave Cl. Sup. Contrada Salvarenza Vecchie Vigne '96	🍸🍸🍸	5
○	Soave Cl. Sup. Contrada Salvarenza Vecchie Vigne '98	🍸🍸🍸	5
○	Soave Cl. Sup. La Froscà '99	🍸🍸🍸	5
○	Soave Cl. Contrada Salvarenza Vecchie Vigne '03	🍸🍸	5

 MONTEFORTE D'ALPONE (VR)

Le Mandolare

Loc. Brognoligo
via Fontana Nuova, 1
37030 Monteforte d'Alpone (VR)
tel. 0456175083 - 0456175507
www.cantinalemandolare.com

For years, Renzo Rodighiero and his wife Germana had the opposite problem of most Veneto wineries: they owned 25 hectares of vineyards but the cellar layout was too complex, the various close, but not adjoining, rooms making endless acrobatics necessary for the owners to work in them. At last, with this harvest, they have moved to the new, more functional cellar in Mandolare along the headland access path leading from the centre of Brognoligo to Le Rugate and this has facilitated Renzo and Germana's work considerably. This is not all the news, though. There is also a great wine, a Soave Superiore aged in oak barrels which captures all the potential of the soil and the garganega grape. The aromas are delicate but generous, with peaches and apples embracing the subtler floral hints and finally yielding sensations of spices and citrus fruit. The structure is nicely supported by acidity and freshness on the classy, taut palate. The Soave Il Roccolo is just a step behind, with aromas that are still youthful but hint at a generosity that is revealed on the tangy, harmonious palate. The Soave Corte Menini is less complicated, but pleasant and vibrantly drinkable. Recioto Le Schiavette 2004 is very good, with generous sensations ranging from dried apricots to pineapple and liquorice, and characteristically lively but perfectly balanced sweetness.

○	Soave Cl. Sup. Monte Sella '04	▼▼	4*
○	Recioto di Soave Cl. Le Schiavette '04	▼▼	5
○	Soave Cl. Il Roccolo '05	▼▼	3*
○	Soave Cl. Corte Menini '05	▼	3
○	Recioto di Soave Cl. Le Schiavette '03	▽▽	5

Cantina Sociale di Monteforte d'Alpone

via XX Settembre, 24
37032 Monteforte d'Alpone (VR)
tel. 0457610110
www.cantinadimonteforte.it

There are many winemaking co-operatives in the Soave area and, as often happens, they have their pros and cons. From a social point of view, they have guaranteed an income for members over the years, particularly in difficult times, but on the other hand, they have not always given the area a favourable quality image in both growing and winemaking terms. The history of this large Monteforte co-operative is a little different, because it has only bottled wines for a few years and most of the products are still sold by the truckload to other bottlers. With 1,200 hectares of vineyards and 600 members, Gaetano Tobin has settled annual production at around a million bottles, which makes it possible to effect careful selection of the grapes and the best vineyards. The two Soaves are on top form. Classico Clivus 2005 is very enjoyable with fresh aromas and Classico Superiore Vigneto di Castellaro 2004 is very striking indeed, giving apple and pear fruit and floral aromas led by roses on the nose, with a harmonious, tangy and very long palate. The Durello Metodo Classico also performed well, making excellent use of the variety's considerable acidity. From nearby Valpolicella comes a lively Recioto with nicely integrated sweetness.

●	Recioto della Valpolicella '03	▼▼	5
○	Soave Cl. Sup. Vign. di Castellaro '04	▼▼	4
○	Soave Cl. Clivus '05	▼▼	3*
●	Amarone della Valpolicella Re Teodorico '03	▼	6
○	Recioto di Soave Il Sigillo '03	▼	5
○	Soave Cl. Il Vicario '05	▼	4
○	Lessini Durello Brut	▼	4

Umberto Portinari

fraz. Brognoligo
via Santo Stefano, 2
37032 Monteforte d'Alpone (VR)
tel. 0456175087

We've been waiting for a wine like this since the 1998 edition of the Guide, when we reviewed that extraordinary, territory-focused Soave Albare that so impressed enthusiasts. But wine – especially Umberto Portinari's – is unpredictable. It can be very good year after year without ever making such a profound impression again. This unpredictability is what makes it great, and makes the waiting worthwhile, because when it comes it's like a bolt of lightning, erasing previous vintages so we only remember this new surge of emotion. And so here it is: straw yellow in colour, subdued at first and then becoming more generous and intriguing. First there is apple and pear fruit, giving way gradually to rustic vegetal notes and subtle minerality that will become stronger with time. The palate has astounding grip and lightness yet sturdy body and a very long, pleasantly bitterish finish. The Ronchetto is more rugged, with approachably ripe, crunchy apple and pear fruit standing out against a background of spring flowers and spices. The tangy, well-structured palate is supported by assertive, but not aggressive, acidity. The Soave Santo Stefano from 2002 has ripe, juicy peach fruit and the oak is rather unbalanced. Three wines, all with excellent quality and character, and all of which have something to say about the terroir and the winery.

○	Soave Albare Doppia Maturazione Ragionata '05	**YY**	4*
○	Soave Cl. Ronchetto '05	**YY**	4*
○	Soave Santo Stefano '02	**YY**	5
○	Soave Sup. V. Albare Doppia Maturazione Ragionata '97	YYY	4
○	Soave Albare Doppia Maturazione Ragionata '04	YY	4
○	Recioto di Soave Oro '01	YY	6
○	Soave Sup. V. Albare Doppia Maturazione Ragionata '01	YY	4
○	Soave Cl. Ronchetto '04	YY	4

MONTEFORTE D'ALPONE (VR)

Prà

via della Fontana, 31
37032 Monteforte d'Alpone (VR)
tel. 0457612125

If today Soave has been restored to its former splendour, credit is due to wineries like this one, run by Graziano, Flavio and Sergio Prà. Since 1983, Prà has been committed to steady improvement of quality and has produced some of the best Soaves ever. The 20 hectares of hillside vineyards yield about 200,000 bottles a year and are situated in the Soave Classico DOC zone on clayey, volcanic soil which allows the local garganega grape to develop all its potential. This is very evident in the latest Prà wine, Staforte, the medieval name of Monteforte d'Alpone. The 2004 vintage has produced a breathtakingly generous wine with bags of personality. It's very subtle and stylish with vibrant floral and fruit aromas on the nose that meld with splendid spice and intriguing minerally sensations. The Monte Grande 2005 is its usual thoroughbred self, perhaps in its most elegant version to date. A broad, well-defined spectrum of aromatic herbs, peaches, apples, bananas and citrus fruit comes together in an alluringly fresh bouquet to pick up another Three Glasses. The Colle Sant'Antonio 2004 is luscious with muted, delicate boisé hints before the aromas of herbs, flowers, aniseed, citrus fruit, orange liqueur and coffee cream: in short, it's delicious. The Recioto is buttery with pronounced aromas of cream, dates, figs and apricot jam. A touch more freshness would have earned a higher score. Last up was the standard-label Soave, an absolutely magnificent wine of which every wine enthusiast should have few bottles tucked away.

○	Soave Cl. Monte Grande '05	**YYY**	5
○	Soave Cl. Staforte '04	**YY**	4*
○	Soave Cl. Colle S. Antonio '04	**YY**	5
○	Soave Cl. '05	**YY**	4
○	Recioto di Soave Le Fontane '04	**Y**	6
○	Soave Cl. Sup. Monte Grande '00	YYY	5
○	Soave Cl. Monte Grande '02	YYY	5
○	Soave Cl. Monte Grande '03	YYY	5
○	Soave Cl. Monte Grande '04	YYY	5
○	Soave Cl. Colle S. Antonio '02	YY	5
○	Soave Cl. Colle S. Antonio '01	YY	5
○	Soave Cl. Monte Grande '01	YY	5

NEGRAR (VR)

Tommaso Bussola
Loc. San Peretto
via Molino Turri, 30
37024 Negrar (VR)
tel. 0457501740
www.bussolavini.com

There's a lot going on at the Bussola cellar. Having purchased new vineyards, Tommaso is dividing his energies between looking after the new plantings and building a new, spacious cellar that will adjoin the existing buildings to give him more functional spaces and facilitate winemaking. There are now 16 hectares of vineyards producing about 120,000 bottles a year. Tommaso's wines reflect his personality – passionate, enthusiastic, determined – and have close links with tradition in their strength, extract and liveliness. As we have often noted, the Recioto expresses these sensations most eloquently and is a real champion of its type. The nose is an explosion of wild berries, blending into spices and mint to create a sophisticated spectrum of aromatics that precedes a juicy, very sweet, long-lingering palate. It walked away with Three Glasses. Errante 2003 also conforms to Tommaso's style. A blend of part-raisined merlot and cabernet, fermented on the Recioto skins, it underwent lengthy ageing in wood. The palate is taut, juicy and still a little tannic, while the aromas could be sharper and fresher. The Valpolicella Superiore TB 2003 combines traditional aromas with a generous, juicily structured palate. The Amarone TB 2001 flaunts a wide range of aromas and a sweet, silky palate with a pleasantly bitterish finish.

● Recioto della Valpolicella Cl. '04	🍷🍷🍷	7
● Amarone della Valpolicella Cl. TB '01	🍷🍷	8
● L'Errante '03	🍷🍷	7
● Valpolicella Cl. Sup. TB '03	🍷🍷	6
● Recioto della Valpolicella Cl. BG '03	🍷🍷🍷	7
● Recioto della Valpolicella Cl. TB '95	🍷🍷🍷	8
● Recioto della Valpolicella Cl. TB '97	🍷🍷🍷	8
● Recioto della Valpolicella Cl. TB '98	🍷🍷🍷	8
● Recioto della Valpolicella Cl. TB '99	🍷🍷🍷	8
● Amarone della Valpolicella Cl. TB Vign. Alto '00	🍷🍷	8
● Amarone della Valpolicella Cl. BG '02	🍷🍷	8

NEGRAR (VR)

Roberto Mazzi
Loc. San Peretto
via Crosetta, 8
37024 Negrar (VR)
tel. 0457502072 - 0458266150
www.robertomazzi.it

With the inauguration of the new cellar, the Mazzi family has achieved the balance between area under vine and vinification and ageing space that they were looking for. Showing the thrift typical of country folk, they have kept the work to a necessary minimum, limiting the architectural impact of the buildings on the environment and employing plenty of good taste in harmoniously matching the renovated parts with the new buildings. The wines seem to have come on as well. The Valpolicella 2004 fully reflects the Mazzi style of releasing clean, fresh, drinkable, concentrated wines. These features are further enhanced in the 2003 version of the Poiega, which is more impressive than ever before. The typically vegetal nature of the grapes grown in this corner of Valpolicella blends with spicy floral features and the structure is invigorated by light raisining, although the tannins have yet to be completely absorbed. Amarone Punta di Villa 2003 is still reticent in yielding up its qualities, partly because it is young. But what we were able to experience made us fall in love with this wine. The usual alcohol and fruit are balanced by a subtle, measured palate without excessive sugariness. The particular nature of the soil in this vineyard makes it possible to manage the vines whether the growing year is rainy or hot, like 2003. This wine has an intriguing minerally finish with plenty of grip. Finally, the Recioto 2003 is gutsy, fruity, high in extract and powerful.

● Amarone della Valpolicella Cl. Punta di Villa '03	🍷🍷	7
● Recioto della Valpolicella Cl. Le Calcarole '03	🍷🍷	6
● Valpolicella Cl. Sup. Vign. Poiega '03	🍷🍷	5
● Valpolicella Cl. Sup. '04	🍷🍷	4
● Amarone della Valpolicella Cl. Punta di Villa '00	🍷🍷	7
● Amarone della Valpolicella Cl. Punta di Villa '01	🍷🍷	7
● Recioto della Valpolicella Cl. Le Calcarole '01	🍷🍷	6
● Valpolicella Cl. Sup. Vign. Poiega '02	🍷🍷	4

NEGRAR (VR)

★ Giuseppe Quintarelli

via Cere, 1
37024 Negrar (VR)
tel. 0457500016

Indelibly printed on our memory is the image of the patient skill with which Bepi Quintarelli placed the fruit destined to become Recioto in the cases, bunch by bunch. His actions made clear his attitude to wine: calm, clear-headed patience that will continue until his creations are ready for the highly selected enthusiasts of this wine. Leaving Bepi to his task, we were accompanied by his loyal assistants Nadia and Nicola on a journey into the innermost essence of Valpolicella. Because that is what a tasting of Quintarelli wines is: a subtle dialogue with the land itself. The Alzero 1997 is a "cabernet-based Amarone", perhaps the only product of its kind. The wine's finesse, elegance and strength work in unison to create a rising tide of sensations. The Rosso del Bepi 1999 and the Primo Fiore 2003 try to live up to this very tough standard, the former darkly austere and the latter showing more youthful and playful. But the champion this year is the splendid Valpolicella Classico 1999, mouthfilling and velvety, it gives gamey, warm aromas rich in red berry fruit and so aristocratic you would almost think it was an Amarone. All in all, it's a peerless, starry wine that won our tasting panel over unreservedly and was awarded Three resounding Glasses.

● Valpolicella Cl. Sup. '99	TTT	8
● Alzero Cabernet Franc '97	TT	8
● Rosso del Bepi '99	TT	8
● Primo Fiore '03	T	6
● Amarone della Valpolicella Cl. Ris. '83	YYY	8
● Amarone della Valpolicella Cl. '84	YYY	8
● Amarone della Valpolicella Cl. Ris. '85	YYY	8
● Amarone della Valpolicella Cl. '86	YYY	8
● Alzero Cabernet Franc '90	YYY	8
● Recioto della Valpolicella Cl. '95	YYY	8
● Rosso del Bepi '96	YYY	8
● Amarone della Valpolicella Cl. '97	YYY	8

NEGRAR (VR)

Le Ragose

fraz. Arbizzano
via Le Ragose, 1
37020 Negrar (VR)
tel. 0457513241
www.leragose.com

In the late 1960s, Arnaldo Galli took the view that traditional Veronese wines were indivisibly linked to their territory, and this vision is upheld in the products presented by his sons Paolo and Marco. The high hillside location of the vineyards, the use of the simple pergola training system, full respect for the vine and the time it takes the wine in the cellar to reach its full potential are all elements that translate into products that are never extreme or excessively powerful but convinced our tasters with their dignified elegance and distinctive character. Valpolicella Superiore Le Sassine 2003 is a magnificent example of this type, showing very fresh and supple despite the hot year. The generous, deep nose expresses its ripe fruit with clarity, alternating with mineral and spicy hints as well as aromatic herbs that extend the range of aromas. The perfectly balanced palate is lingering and harmonious. Just behind it are the Amarone and the Valpolicella Superiore Marta Galli, both from 2002. The former has complex aromas in which dried fruit and aromatic herbs blend into earthy tobacco sensations, and a polished, silky palate which is still youthful and fresh with unexpected depth. The Valpolicella is juicy, creamy and drinkable with a nice balanced flavour. The Cabernet Sauvignon 2001 is impressive with well-handled texture, overripe fruit blending with pleasant minerality.

● Valpolicella Cl. Sup. Le Sassine '03	TT	4*
● Garda Cabernet Sauvignon '01	TT	5
● Amarone della Valpolicella Cl. '02	TT	8
● Valpolicella Cl. Sup. Marta Galli '02	TT	6
● Amarone della Valpolicella Cl. '86	YYY	8
● Amarone della Valpolicella Cl. '88	YYY	8
● Amarone della Valpolicella Marta Galli '00	YY	8
● Amarone della Valpolicella '01	YY	8
● Amarone della Valpolicella '99	YY	8
● Amarone della Valpolicella '98	YY	8

NEGRAR (VR)

CASA VINICOLA SARTORI

FRAZ. SANTA MARIA
VIA CASETTE, 2
37024 NEGRAR (VR)
TEL. 0456028011
www.sartorinet.com

The new wines from I Saltari estate confirm the good impression made last year, starting with an Amarone released after well-gauged ageing. Sharply defined, complex aromas on the nose precede the classy balanced palate that all great wines should have. The Valpolicella is brighter and more approachable, translating the heat of the 2003 vintage into heady fruit and softness. Turning to the Sartori wines, the house champions are still of course the two Amarones. Reius 2001 is approachable and impressive, giving cherry jam, chocolate and spices on the nose and a soft but light palate. The Corte Brà 2000 is even more interesting and polished, with clearly defined wild berries and aromatic herbs against a background of oak with muted minerality. The dry, high-spirited palate is unusually mouthfilling with sweet tannins. The Valpolicella Montegradella 2004 is very good. Its nose is still youthful while the extract and finesse on the palate should take it far. The same applies to the Soave Vigneti di Sella 2005, which missed a second Glass by a hair's breadth. The two Reciotos, Vernus and Rerum, are obviously different from one another but both absorb their highly concentrated sugar component with suppleness and a light touch. Finally, the Valpolicella Classico 2004 plays on attractive harmony and is very competitively priced.

- ● Amarone della Valpolicella Le Vigne di Turano I Saltari '01 — 🍷🍷 8
- ● Amarone della Valpolicella Cl. Corte Brà '00 — 🍷🍷 7
- ● Amarone della Valpolicella Cl. Reius '01 — 🍷🍷 7
- ● Valpolicella Sup. Le Vigne di Turano I Saltari '03 — 🍷🍷 6
- ● Recioto della Valpolicella Cl. Rerum '04 — 🍷🍷 6
- ○ Recioto di Soave Vernus '04 — 🍷🍷 5
- ● Valpolicella Cl. '04 — 🍷🍷 3*
- ● Valpolicella Cl. Sup. Vign. di Montegradella '04 — 🍷🍷 4
- ○ Soave Cl. Vign. di Sella '05 — 🍷 3

NEGRAR (VR)

CANTINA SOCIALE VALPOLICELLA

VIA CA' SALGARI, 2
37024 NEGRAR (VR)
TEL. 0456014300
www.cantinanegrar.it

As we have said before, Negrar is the best co-operative in the Veneto region. The statistics speak for themselves – the 500 hectares of vineyards yield over 6,000,000 bottles a year – but the quality of the wine and, even more so, of the viticulture is what makes the difference. Over ten years ago, the co-operative began to impose on its members a hitherto unimaginable standard of quality in the vineyards. The results are more impressive every year in both the most ambitious wines and those for everyday consumption, which account for the greater part of production. This is true of the Valpolicella Classico Superiore Domini Veneti 2004. Approachably enjoyable, generous with juicy fruit, the 300,000 bottles released each year are sold at a very competitive price. The house champion is still, as often happens, the Recioto Vigneti di Moron, which takes its rightful place in the front rank of the category. The nose is an explosion of red berry fruit, cherries and black cherries, with cocoa powder and a surge of aromatic herbs. Extraordinarily sweet on the palate as ever, it is also beautifully balanced showing suppleness and drinkability. One step down are the Valpolicella La Casetta and the Vigneti di Torbe. The former has a subtle, harmonious palate while the latter has undergone the "ripasso" technique of adding unpressed Amarone skins to the fermented wine and seems a tad more rustic, although it is also outrageously juicy. The Amarone Vigneti di Jago is very good. Its nose is still rather closed but the palate is sound, giving rich extract and sweet tannins.

- ● Recioto della Valpolicella Cl. Vign. di Moron Domini Veneti '04 — 🍷🍷 5
- ● Amarone della Valpolicella Cl. Vign. di Jago Domini Veneti '01 — 🍷🍷 7
- ● Valpolicella Cl. Sup. La Casetta di Ettore Righetti Domini Veneti '03 — 🍷🍷 4
- ● Valpolicella Cl. Sup. Vign. di Torbe Domini Veneti '03 — 🍷🍷 4
- ● Valpolicella Cl. Sup. Domini Veneti '04 — 🍷🍷 2*
- ● Amarone della Valpolicella Cl. Domini Veneti '02 — 🍷 6
- ○ Soave Cl. Vign. di Ca' de Napa Domini Veneti '05 — 🍷 4

NEGRAR (VR)

VILLA SPINOSA
LOC. JAGO
37024 NEGRAR (VR)
TEL. 0457500093
www.villaspinosa.it

Enrico Cascella, who has owned the Villa Spinosa winery for about 20 years, has never tried to make easy wines with rich extract and softness, which appeal to many critics and consumers. His style is more traditional and based on principles that put more complex sensations above approachability. Enrico's wines undergo a long ageing period which undoubtedly helps give them character, finesse and depth that would otherwise be difficult to obtain. The 30,000 bottles produced each year are divided into four types: one Amarone, the Recioto Francesca Finato Spinosa and two Valpolicellas, a Classico and a Superiore made using the "ripasso" technique of adding unpressed Amarone skins to the fermented wine (Jago, named after the local area). As we can see, the range includes no wines made from international grapes, which is indicative of the close links with tradition. This year, we were especially impressed by the Amarone 1999 with its elusively ethereal aromas highlighting uncommon finesse and a charming, complex personality of fines herbes, dried fruit and minerals. The Recioto 2004 is not as good as the previous version and the sugar content needs work. At the moment, there is too much and it tends to cover the good texture. The Valpolicella Classico 2005 is rugged but nicely intense.

●	Amarone della Valpolicella Cl. '99	🍷🍷	7
●	Recioto della Valpolicella Cl. Francesca Finato Spinosa '04	🍷	6
●	Valpolicella Cl. '05	🍷	4
●	Valpolicella Cl. Sup. Jago '00	YY	5
●	Valpolicella Cl. Sup. Jago '01	YY	5
●	Amarone della Valpolicella Cl. '95	YY	6
●	Amarone della Valpolicella Cl. '96	YY	6
●	Amarone della Valpolicella Cl. '97	YY	7
●	Amarone della Valpolicella Cl. '98	YY	8

NEGRAR (VR)

VIVIANI
LOC. MAZZANO
VIA MAZZANO, 8
37020 NEGRAR (VR)
TEL. 0457500286
www.cantinaviviani.com

Claudio Viviani is a top quality grower whose private sanctuary is situated in the upper Negrar valley, in the Mazzano vineyard to be precise. In this uncommonly good terroir, polished style blends beautifully with opulent fruit. From his 14 hectares of exemplary vineyards, as befits one of the gems of Valpolicella, he obtains 80,000 bottles a year, sought after by enthusiasts from all over the world and served in the best restaurants. The foundation of the range is the delicious standard-label Valpolicella, purplish ruby red in colour with clear red berry fruit and a youthful, tasty, lingering florality. Next up is the Campo Morar 2003, one of the great Valpolicellas. Dense and broodingly dark in colour, it offers subtle aromas of blackcurrants, blackberries and cherries on the nose. The full-bodied palate lingers endlessly with forward youthful tannins and plenty of freshness. The Amarone Casa dei Bepi 2001 is on its best form ever. Intense ripe cherry red, it is the very soul of Amarone, unfolding polished aromas that include grassy notes mingling with warm tobacco and fresh, juicy red berry fruit. The palate is streaked through with fine chocolate, fading into velvety, unusually complex coffee. Once again, it stepped up for its annual Three Glasses. The Recioto 2003 is deep purple in colour with very elegant spicy aromas in the extremely delicate, lush bouquet where black cherry and plum jam take the lead. The silky tannins enhance the flavour and will preserve this wine at length for those who can wait for its glorious evolution to unfold.

●	Amarone della Valpolicella Cl. Casa dei Bepi '01	🍷🍷🍷	8
●	Recioto della Valpolicella Cl. '03	🍷🍷	7
●	Valpolicella Cl. Sup. Campo Morar '03	🍷🍷	6
●	Valpolicella Cl. '05	🍷	3*
●	Amarone della Valpolicella Cl. Casa dei Bepi '00	YYY	8
●	Valpolicella Cl. Sup. Campo Morar '01	YYY	6
●	Amarone della Valpolicella Cl. Casa dei Bepi '97	YYY	8
●	Amarone della Valpolicella Cl. Tulipano Nero '97	YYY	8
●	Amarone della Valpolicella Cl. Casa dei Bepi '98	YYY	8

NEGRAR (VR)

Zymè

v.le Europa, 3
37024 Negrar (VR)
tel. 0457501305
www.zyme.it

Zymè's history revolves around Celestino Gaspari, a connoisseur of Valpolicella and its wines with plenty of experience amassed at the home of his father-in-law, Giuseppe Quintarelli. Since 2000, Celestino has been busy on a new venture, mainly as a consultant, collaborating with two friends, Francesco Parisi and Flavio Peroni. But the call of the land is strong and consultancy work does not entirely satisfy what used to be the Team Zymè. So the partners set up a winery of the same name with just eight hectares of vineyards producing fewer than 20,000 bottles a year, released under three prestigious labels. Celestino is still at the helm, with Francesco helping in the cellar and Flavio concentrating on the administrative side. But mere production figures fail to illustrate the winery's guiding philosophy: the promotion of a forgotten grape variety, oseleta, on the one hand, and of the territory on the other. This translates as two wines made using 15 different grape varieties. While waiting for Harlequin, the more ambitious wine, we tasted the excellent Kairos, the blend of the aforementioned 15 black and white grapes, which were partly raisined. The generous aromas are echoed by an enviably sturdy palate that can only improve with a few years' ageing. After allowing it sufficient time to breathe, the 100 per cent oseleta Oz reveals good fruit and a flavoursome, juicy palate.

● Kairos '03	🍷🍷	8
● Oseleta Oz '03	🍷🍷	6

NERVESA DELLA BATTAGLIA (TV)

★ Serafini & Vidotto

via Carrer, 8/12
31040 Nervesa della Battaglia (TV)
tel. 0422773281

At Nervesa, work is never finished and when Antonello Vidotto and Francesco Serafini are not worrying about the vineyards or the new cellar, Francesco is keeping his brain active running the Consorzio di Tutela del Montello e Colli Asolani. Following revision of the production regulations, Rosso dell'Abazia has become a DOC wine, which is no mean feat, since in this part of Veneto the best wines are nearly always IGTs. The desire to enter the DOC is a clear indication of the partners' attachment to the local area, despite the huge critical and market success they already enjoy. Just taste any one of their bottles and you will understand how closely the wines are linked to this area. The wines have never followed preconceived models, trying instead to bring out the best in the qualities Montello can give: supple body and vibrant acidity. So from a hot year like 2003, here's a Rosso dell'Abazia – at last a DOC – with very mature aromas on the nose while conserving its grip on the palate, making it fresh and lingering as well as a very fine expression of territoriality. A great Three Glass wine that celebrates the new designated area and a Star honouring ten top awards. Phigaia 2003 continues to impress. This blend is of a lesser wine on paper only because the distance separating it from its elder brother is narrowing every year. The Pinot Nero is excellent with very ripe red berry fruit. The two sparklers both did well, one a fresh rosé and the other a delicious Prosecco, while the sauvignon-based Bianco 2005 is tangy and dry.

● Montello e Colli Asolani Il Rosso dell'Abazia '03	🍷🍷🍷	7
● Phigaia After the Red '03	🍷🍷	4*
● Pinot Nero '03	🍷🍷	7
○ Il Bianco '05	🍷🍷	4*
○ Bollicine di Prosecco	🍷🍷	4*
⊙ Bollicine di Prosecco Rosé	🍷	4
● Il Rosso dell'Abazia '00	🍷🍷🍷	7
● Il Rosso dell'Abazia '01	🍷🍷🍷	7
● Il Rosso dell'Abazia '02	🍷🍷🍷	7
● Il Rosso dell'Abazia '94	🍷🍷🍷	7
● Il Rosso dell'Abazia '95	🍷🍷🍷	7
● Il Rosso dell'Abazia '96	🍷🍷🍷	7
● Il Rosso dell'Abazia '97	🍷🍷🍷	7
● Il Rosso dell'Abazia '98	🍷🍷🍷	7

ORMELLE (TV)

ITALO CESCON
FRAZ. RONCADELLE
P.ZZA DEI CADUTI, 3
31024 ORMELLE (TV)
TEL. 0422851033
www.cesconitalo.it

This estate is one of the oldest in the Piave area. It was founded 50 years ago by Italo Cescon and immediately carved a niche in local winemaking. Today, his children Domenico, Gloria and Graziella honour their father's legacy and are committed to keeping their wines on a par with the most aristocratic wineries, with expertise and no little ambition. This has become clear in the tastings of the last few years and this edition of the Guide records a further step ahead. The most impressive wine was the Amaranto 72, a blend of four grape varieties – cabernet sauvignon, merlot, cabernet franc and marzemino – fermented separately in oak barrels. The wines obtained are then blended into a single product, which is aged in medium-sized oak barrels and barriques. The wood is very evident on the nose with coffee and toasty aromas jostling with fragrant fruit. The palate is succulent, potent and flavoursome, lacking only a little elegance. We are pleased to note the success of the Raboso La Cesura 2002, which demonstrates a desire to promote this native grape variety. Fresh wild berries with nice minerally notes are the principal aromas, followed by a stylish, lingering palate. The Cabernet La Cesura Riserva 2003 is also nicely characterful.

● Piave Raboso La Cesura Ris. '02	🍷🍷	5
● Amaranto 72 '03	🍷🍷	6
● Piave Cabernet La Cesura Ris. '03	🍷🍷	5
● Piave Merlot La Cesura Ris. '03	🍷	5
○ Italo 06 '04	🍷	5
○ Manzoni Bianco La Cesura '05	🍷	4
○ Piave Chardonnay La Cesura '05	🍷	4
○ Piave Müller Thurgau La Cesura '05	🍷	4
○ Piave Pinot Grigio La Cesura '05	🍷	4
○ Prosecco di V. Extra Dry	🍷	4
● Piave Raboso La Cesura Ris. '01	ΥΥ	5

PESCHIERA DEL GARDA (VR)

OTTELLA
FRAZ. S. BENEDETTO DI LUGANA
LOC. OTTELLA
37019 PESCHIERA DEL GARDA (VR)
TEL. 0457551950

The trebbiano di Lugana grape produces excellent fruit on the clayey soil south of Lake Garda. This is the grape most commonly grown hereabouts but older local growers have always had a special affection for merlot which, so they say, grows well on this difficult terrain. Francesco Montresor, his brother Michele and his father Lodovico believe in the two-sided nature of this strip of the Garda zone, so much so that over two-thirds of the 30 hectares of vineyards owned by Ottella are planted to trebbiano di Lugana and the rest with red grape varieties. This time a red was the most impressive of their products, as good as any around here. Campo Sireso 2004, from 50 per cent merlot with corvina veronese and cabernet in equal proportions, is an approachable, appetizing wine with deliciously juicy red berry fruit. The trio of Luganas is outstanding, although we just preferred Superiore Molceo 2004, which has the generous peach fruit typical of Luganas from around Lake Frassino. The palate is taut, dry and resolute. There were excellent performances from the Le Creete, which needs a few months' ageing in bottles as usual before it will be at its best, and the edgy, vibrant standard-label Lugana 2005. We'll have to wait another year to taste the sweet wine because 2003 did not give Passito Prima Luce enough freshness, so the winery showed excellent judgement in deciding not to bottle it.

● Campo Sireso '04	🍷🍷	5
○ Lugana Sup. Molceo '04	🍷🍷	5
○ Lugana '05	🍷🍷	4
○ Lugana Le Creete '05	🍷🍷	4*
● Rosso Ottella '05	🍷	4
○ Lugana Sup. Molceo '01	ΥΥ	5
○ Prima Luce Passito '01	ΥΥ	6
○ Prima Luce Passito '02	ΥΥ	6
● Campo Sireso '02	ΥΥ	5
○ Lugana Sup. Molceo '02	ΥΥ	5
● Campo Sireso '03	ΥΥ	5
○ Lugana Sup. Molceo '03	ΥΥ	5

PESCHIERA DEL GARDA (VR)

La Sansonina

Loc. Sansonina
37019 Peschiera del Garda (VR)
tel. 0457551905
www.sansonina.it

At last, the long-awaited permits are forthcoming for the construction of a new cellar at this beautiful winery in the Lake Garda basin. It's somewhat unusual since along the Veronese shore of the lake, the most commonly grown varieties are those which provide the raw material for the most widely made wines – corvina above all for the reds, and garganega and trebbiano di Lugana for the whites. But since 1997, the first vintage, Carla Prospero has focused on merlot, which has found a natural habitat over the years on the clay soil of the vineyards located in the southern part of this strip of land in the provinces of Verona and Brescia. High quality winegrowing and respect for the environment have always brought superior results that reflect the weather of the growing year. Here is the 2003 version with vibrant, ripe red berry fruit aromas as well as livelier hints of blueberries and aromatic herbs vying to contribute greater freshness. The heat of the year comes through on the palate in alluringly soft sensations, spiced up by a dense tannic weave that holds the wine firmly on its well mapped out track to a beautifully long, lingering finish.

● Sansonina '03	**YY**	7
● Sansonina '00	YY	7
● Sansonina '01	YY	7
● Sansonina '97	YY	7
● Sansonina '98	YY	7

PESCHIERA DEL GARDA (VR)

Zenato

fraz. S. Benedetto di Lugana
via S. Benedetto, 8
37019 Peschiera del Garda (VR)
tel. 0457550300
www.zenato.it

Two passions prevail here, corvina and trebbiano di Lugana. The former is the grape of the great Valpolicella reds, while trebbiano di Lugana is the main variety grown to the south of Lake Garda where the family winery is located. Yes the family, the foundation of this famous house of wine. Although it has grown to a considerable size, Zenato is still run as a family business. Sergio supervises the vineyards, including 30 hectares in Valpolicella and 40 in Lugana, and the blends, his wife Carla watches over everything and children Alberto and Nadia work in the cellar and sales department, respectively. Turning to the wines, we'll risk repeating ourselves as we describe the magnificent new performance of the Amarone Sergio Zenato. The 2001 vintage took our breath away with its combination of expressive strength and aristocratic drinkability. This is a great wine today and will remain great over time. The Valpolicella Superiore continues to astonish and the 2003 is on great form, showing youthful, with dense, appetizing fresh fruit and a good tannic weave. This is a gem of a wine at an affordable price. The trio of Luganas is as enjoyable as ever. Vigneto Massoni 2005 reminds us what classic peach fruit is like while San Benedetto shows edgy vegetal features and the Sergio Zenato 2004 selection confidently aims for overripe fruity sweetness. The Alberto 2003 gave an excellent performance. It's a modern red blend of corvina veronese, merlot and cabernet. We tasted the Amarone Sergio Zenato 1995 again and found it splendid, a great wine which deserves Three retrospective Glasses.

● Amarone della Valpolicella Cl. Sergio Zenato '01	**YY**	8
● Valpolicella Cl. Sup. '03	**YY**	4*
● Alberto '03	**YY**	5
○ Lugana Sergio Zenato '04	**YY**	4
○ Lugana S. Benedetto '05	**YY**	3*
○ Lugana Vign. Massoni Santa Cristina '05	**YY**	4
○ Rigoletto Passito '04	**Y**	6
● Amarone della Valpolicella Cl. Sergio Zenato '95	YYY	8
● Amarone della Valpolicella Cl. Sergio Zenato '00	YYY	8
● Amarone della Valpolicella Cl. Sergio Zenato Ris. '98	YYY	8

SALGAREDA (TV)

ORNELLA MOLON TRAVERSO
FRAZ. CAMPO DI PIETRA
VIA RISORGIMENTO, 38
31040 SALGAREDA (TV)
TEL. 0422804807
www.molon.it

Ornella and Giancarlo Molon's winery has always been a benchmark for the Piave DOC. Ever since their winemaking adventure began, they have worked to make wines of absolute quality, and they continue to adhere to this philosophy today, working with winemaker Simone Casazza and their elder son, Stefano. The estate owns 22 hectares of vineyards and rents 20, producing half a million bottles a year. The excess is sold unbottled, as tradition and good sense dictate. The main winemaking centre, where the wines are aged and marketed, is a particularly beautiful 1652 Venetian villa, which once belonged to the Venetian Doge Giustinian, and more recently to the Podestà (governor) Carretta. The leading wine is the Rosso di Villa 2003, a Merlot that shows a strong palate with silky tannins and hints of red berry fruit and coffee. The Piave Merlot 2003 is similar to its big brother though the fruit is much sweeter and it is less challenging to drink. The Vite Rossa 2002 does not seem to have suffered from the unfavourable vintage and is nicely elegant, especially on the palate, with ripe red berry fruit, full body and an exceptionally lingering, complex finish. The Traminer may not be traditional but it has adapted well to the Piave plain and deserves our attention. It is mature and full-bodied, with floral and citrus aromas streaked with more unusual saltiness and Mediterranean scrubland. The Vite Bianca 2004 is a blend of chardonnay and pinot bianco aged in small wooden barrels and came close to a second Glass.

● Vite Rossa Ornella '02	▼▼	6
● Piave Merlot Ornella '03	▼▼	5
● Piave Merlot Rosso di Villa '03	▼▼	6
○ Sauvignon Ornella '05	▼▼	4
○ Traminer Ornella '05	▼▼	4
● Piave Raboso Ornella '01	▼	5
● Piave Cabernet Ornella '03	▼	4
○ Vite Bianca Ornella '04	▼	5
○ Piave Chardonnay Ornella '05	▼	4
● Piave Merlot Rosso di Villa '01	▽▽	6
● Piave Merlot Rosso di Villa '02	▽▽	6
● Piave Merlot Rosso di Villa '00	▽▽	6
● Piave Merlot Ornella '02	▽▽	5
● Piave Merlot Rosso di Villa '98	▽▽	6
● Piave Merlot Rosso di Villa '99	▽▽	6

SAN BONIFACIO (VR)

INAMA
LOC. BIACCHE, 50
37047 SAN BONIFACIO (VR)
TEL. 0456104343
www.inamaaziendaagricola.it

It is not easy to manage two environments and soil types as different from each other as Soave and Colli Berici in the same winery. The history, climate, soil and grape varieties do not seem to have anything in common, but they do come together in the ideas and aspirations of Stefano Inama, who has passed on the task of dealing with these two separate entities to two separate teams who are experts in their respective areas. This is the crucial issue: bending technical knowledge to the sensitive interpretation of different terroirs and the grapes that have adapted to them. Today the huge improvements at the Inama cellar are obvious in the way the vineyards are managed. Scrupulous attention is given to older plantings, where failed grafts are carefully replaced to avoid dispersal of the enormous heritage of old plants. Meanwhile in the Colli Berici, most of the vineyards are new and organically run. International grape varieties are used, but less productive clones have been sought out, particularly those best suited to this area. While we wait for the two great reds, which are still ageing in glass, we'll have to make do as it were with the best ever version of the Bradisismo. This is an elegant cabernet sauvignon-based red with rich extract and a taut, supple palate. The Soave Vigneti di Foscarino 2004 is wonderful, with subtly vibrant aromas that are elegantly reflected on the palate. Lastly, the Vin Soave 2005 is a very fine white at an almost unbeatable price.

● Bradisismo '03	▼▼	6
○ Soave Cl. Vign. di Foscarino '04	▼▼	5
○ Soave Cl. Vin Soave '05	▼▼	4*
○ Sauvignon Vulcaia Fumé '04	▼▼	6
○ Chardonnay '05	▼	4
○ Sauvignon Vulcaia '05	▼	5
○ Soave Cl. Vign. Du Lot '00	▽▽▽	5
○ Soave Cl. Vign. Du Lot '01	▽▽▽	5
○ Soave Cl. Vign. Du Lot '96	▽▽▽	5
○ Soave Cl. Vign. Du Lot '99	▽▽▽	5
○ Soave Cl. Vign. Du Lot '02	▽▽	5
○ Soave Cl. Vign. di Foscarino '03	▽▽	5
○ Soave Cl. Vign. Du Lot '03	▽▽	5

SAN FIOR (TV)

MASOTTINA
LOC. CASTELLO ROGANZUOLO
VIA BRADOLINI, 54
31020 SAN FIOR (TV)
TEL. 0438400775
www.masottina.it

Masottina is owned by the Dal Bianco brothers and has gradually emerged as an important winery in the Treviso area while maintaining a good standard of quality. The range of wines is extensive in origin, ambition and price, comprising over 2,000,000 bottles a year, which are sold to a varied clientele. The Ai Palazzi line gave a stronger performance at our tastings. The Cabernet Sauvignon Riserva 2003 has wild berries and balsam on the nose, and a nicely austere, lingering palate with close-knit, sweet tannins. Very ripe fruit appears in the sweet, juicy aromas of the Merlot, also from 2003, while the palate is firm and flavoursome, although extra time in bottle should improve the balance. The Cartizze has vibrant fruity and floral aromas and beautifully integrated fizz that caresses the palate throughout the tasting. The Pinot Grigio, also from the Ai Palazzi line, is interesting, giving floral aromas, with hints of roses, and a tangy, well-structured, elegant palate. The oak has not yet settled in the Colli di Conegliano Bianco Rizzardo 2004 and the Rosso Montesco lacks a touch of verve that would have given it a higher score. The Chardonnay Ai Palazzi is mature, complex and mouthfilling.

● Piave Cabernet Sauvignon Ai Palazzi Ris. '03	🍷🍷	5
● Piave Merlot Ai Palazzi Ris. '03	🍷🍷	5
● Colli di Conegliano Rosso Montesco '03	🍷	6
○ Colli di Conegliano Bianco Rizzardo '04	🍷	5
○ Incrocio Manzoni 6.0.13 '05	🍷	4
○ Piave Chardonnay Ai Palazzi '05	🍷	4
○ Piave Pinot Grigio '05	🍷	4
○ Piave Pinot Grigio Ai Palazzi '05	🍷	4
○ Cartizze	🍷	6

SAN MARTINO BUON ALBERGO (VR)

MARION
LOC. MARCELLISE
VIA BORGO, 1
37036 SAN MARTINO BUON ALBERGO (VR)
TEL. 0458740021
www.marionvini.it

We are delighted to report the excellent performance of the wines produced by this young winery, demonstrating the soundness of the policy they have followed for several years of going for higher quality. We do not often find ourselves faced with such a large number of products at such an excellent level. Credit is certainly due to Stefano Campedelli and his wife Nicoletta, who have maintained a balance between modern and traditional styles, making elegant wines which are the result of great care and attention in the vineyards, rather than extreme technical efforts in the cellar. Although young, the Amarone 2000 has considerable personality and gives fruit-led, ripe cherry aromas as well as more tantalizing hints of dried fruit, dates and chocolate leading at last to complex balsamic and mineral sensations. The palate is strong with plenty of sweet tannins and the substantial body is handled with unusual delicacy. The 2002 Teroldego and Valpolicella are more or less on a par. The very elegant Teroldego shows an appreciable array of berry fruit aromas on the nose along with subtle hints of liquorice before the nicely succulent palate reveals distinctive and prestigious balance of the tannins. The Valpolicella is more evolved in style, with almost decadent aromas of overripe fruit and tobacco. The palate is taut, succulent and extremely drinkable.

● Amarone della Valpolicella '00	🍷🍷	8
● Teroldego '02	🍷🍷	6
● Valpolicella Sup. '02	🍷🍷	6
○ Passito Bianco '01	🍷	6
● Valpolicella Sup. '00	🍷🍷 (white)	6
● Cabernet Sauvignon '01	🍷🍷 (white)	6
● Cabernet Sauvignon '00	🍷🍷 (white)	6
● Teroldego '00	🍷🍷 (white)	6
● Teroldego '01	🍷🍷 (white)	6
● Valpolicella Sup. '01	🍷🍷 (white)	6
● Cabernet Sauvignon '98	🍷🍷 (white)	6
● Cabernet Sauvignon '99	🍷🍷 (white)	6

SAN MARTINO BUON ALBERGO (VR)

MUSELLA

VIA FERRAZZETTE, 2
37036 SAN MARTINO BUON ALBERGO (VR)
TEL. 045973385
www.musella.it

The Musella estate has a rich winemaking heritage but also has a wealth of land. The 27 hectares of vineyards are part of a total of 220 hectares of natural greenery. The existing buildings have been intelligently restored and adapted to their new functions, so the fermentation cellar and rooms used for drying grapes are part of the old hayloft, while the former stable block, with columns dating back to the 17th century and a vaulted ceiling, has become the ageing cellar. Emilio Pasqua, his daughter Maddalena and their invaluable helper and winemaker cousin Enrico have managed to give the range of wines better definition in recent years. The Amarone Senza Titolo deserves special attention. After long maceration in open vats and three years ageing in large wooden barrels, it is a sort of experiment that year after year assesses the potential of the wine type. The 2000 version is not too dark in colour with a generous nose rich in ripe fruit and cocoa powder alongside fresh sensations, creating an overall impression of remarkable polish. The Valpolicella Ripasso 2003, whose fruit interweaves with toasty and mineral aromas, and the sweet but beautifully balanced Recioto 2003, are both outstanding. Also excellent are the Monte del Drago 2002, a blend of corvina and cabernet with a modern take on flavour and the Bianco del Drago 2003, made from garganega and chardonnay grapes. The Valpolicella Vigne Nuove di Musella is succulent, lingering and harmonious.

● Amarone della Valpolicella Senza Titolo '00	🍷🍷	8
● Monte del Drago Rosso '02	🍷🍷	6
○ Bianco del Drago '03	🍷🍷	5
● Recioto della Valpolicella '03	🍷🍷	6
● Valpolicella Sup. Ripasso '03	🍷🍷	6
● Valpolicella Sup. Vigne Nuove di Musella '04	🍷🍷	4*
● Amarone della Valpolicella '00	🍷🍷 (white)	7
● Amarone della Valpolicella '01	🍷🍷 (white)	7
● Monte del Drago Rosso '01	🍷🍷 (white)	6
● Valpolicella Sup. Vign. Palazzine '01	🍷🍷 (white)	5
● Amarone della Valpolicella '99	🍷🍷 (white)	7

SAN PIETRO IN CARIANO (VR)

STEFANO ACCORDINI

FRAZ. PEDEMONTE
VIA ALBERTO BOLLA, 9
37020 SAN PIETRO IN CARIANO (VR)
TEL. 0457701733 - 0457725376
www.accordinistefano.it

The Accordini family has always had a close relationship with the land and the cycles of nature. This means being able to wait patiently and calmly for the new vineyards in Mazzurega, located 400 metres above sea level in the municipality of Fumane, to find their feet, and so provide a wider choice of grapes rich in the delicate aromas they develop in the high hills. In the meantime, we can enjoy a splendid version of the winery's leading product, the 2000 Il Fornetto. This wine is intended to be a summary of the territory's potential and is only made in really outstanding growing years. An explosion of aromas on the nose embraces dried fruit to jam and chocolate, developing into delicate aromatic herbs. Rather assertive tannins on the silky, mouthfilling palate take you to a long harmonious finish. The Passo 2004 blend of lightly raisined corvina, cabernet and merlot is very good indeed. Vibrant and complex on the nose, with crisp ripe fruit and pleasant spice, it proffers a warm, quite soft palate whose sweetness is offset by minerality. The Valpolicella Superiore, made using the "ripasso" technique of adding unpressed Amarone skins to the fermented wine is very concentrated and the oak has not yet been fully absorbed. The standard Valpolicella is only a step away from a second Glass, showing nice grip on the palate and interesting floral notes.

● Amarone della Valpolicella Vign. Il Fornetto '00	🍷🍷	8
● Passo Rosso '04	🍷🍷	6
● Valpolicella Cl. Sup. Ripasso Acinatico '04	🍷🍷	5
● Valpolicella Cl. '05	🍷	4
● Recioto della Valpolicella Cl. Acinatico '00	🍷🍷🍷 (white)	7
● Amarone della Valpolicella Cl. Vigneto Il Fornetto '93	🍷🍷🍷 (white)	8
● Amarone della Valpolicella Cl. Vigneto Il Fornetto '95	🍷🍷🍷 (white)	8
● Passo Rosso '03	🍷🍷 (white)	6
● Recioto della Valpolicella Cl. Acinatico '03	🍷🍷 (white)	7

SAN PIETRO IN CARIANO (VR)

Lorenzo Begali

via Cengia, 10
37020 San Pietro in Cariano (VR)
tel. 0457725148
www.begaliwine.it

The decision to delay release of the Amarone Monte Ca' Bianca 2001 has yielded results, not so much in terms of Glasses, although this wine has once again earned our highest accolade for this Valpolicella winery, as in the fuller expressive of the wine that is only possible after longer ageing. This year, the Recioto was given the same treatment, a far-sighted decision by Lorenzo and Giordano Begali that came from their professional attitude to wine and its consumers. Following small purchases around the winery, there are now eight hectares of vineyards producing on average 50,000 bottles a year. Let's go back to the Amarone Monte Ca' Bianca, the jewel in the Begali family's crown. Vibrant, clearly defined ripe, crunchy fruit streaked through with floral, minerally and spicy sensations precede an even better palate with silky tannins and a long life in the cellar ahead of it. Considering the difficult year, the Amarone 2002 is excellent. The vegetal notes are sharper on the nose and the palate is firm and well coordinated. The fruit in the Tigiolo 2003 is more approachable and clearly defined, followed up by a beautifully crafted, harmonious palate. Although not up to the standard of previous vintages, this wine is a lighter, more modern expression of the part-drying tradition. The Valpolicella Superiore La Cengia 2004 has that attractively upfront rusticity often found in the type while the standard-label Valpolicella is uncomplicated and fragrantly drinkable.

●	Amarone della Valpolicella Cl. Vign. Monte Ca' Bianca '01	🍷🍷🍷	8
●	Amarone della Valpolicella Cl. '02	🍷🍷	7
●	Tigiolo '03	🍷🍷	6
●	Valpolicella Cl. Sup. Ripasso Vign. La Cengia '04	🍷🍷	5
●	Valpolicella Cl. '05	🍷	4
●	Amarone della Valpolicella Cl. Vign. Monte Ca' Bianca '00	YYY	8
●	Recioto della Valpolicella Cl. '00	YYY	7
●	Amarone della Valpolicella Cl. Vign. Monte Ca' Bianca '97	YYY	8
●	Amarone della Valpolicella Cl. Vign. Monte Ca' Bianca '99	YYY	8

Brigaldara

fraz. San Floriano
via Brigaldara, 20
37020 San Pietro in Cariano (VR)
tel. 0457701055
www.valpolicella.it/brigaldara

Brigaldara wines have the gift of reflecting their territory with uncomplicated sincerity. Stefano Cesari's devotion to his land is obvious from a glance at the vineyards, laid out as if they were protecting the villa and cellar, which is as spare as it is functional. There are more vineyards at Fumane, Grezzana and Marcellise, reinforcing the link with the wider Valpolicella area. The only white produced here is a simple, straightforward Garda Garganega. The Valpolicella is aged in both stainless steel and wood and then blended, with a brief stay on the Amarone skins if the growing year permits, to make it more accessible and complex, and improve ageing potential. The Recioto 2003 has vegetal and blackberry jam aromas on the nose followed by nice sweetness on a palate whose mouthwatering acidity makes it ideal with mature or marbled cheeses. The Amarones vie for first place on the list this year. The grapes for the splendid Case Vecie 2001 come from the young Grezzana vineyards and offer a medley of fruit jam, chocolate and spicy aromas. The palate is initially ripe, luscious and soft with a lingering, dry, floral finish. The Classico 2003 is completely different in style, showing austere aromas of crunchy fruit, pepper and earthy sensations while the progression is a mirror image of the Case Vecie, opening on a dry, minerally note and leading into a rounded creamy finish. Even more interesting was a retasting of the 1999 Amarone, a great red that proves the ageing potential of this winery's products. It earned Three well-deserved retrospective Glasses.

●	Amarone della Valpolicella Case Vecie '01	🍷🍷	7
●	Amarone della Valpolicella Cl. '03	🍷🍷	7
●	Recioto della Valpolicella Cl. '03	🍷🍷	7
●	Valpolicella Cl. '04	🍷	4
○	Garda Garganega '05	🍷	4
●	Amarone della Valpolicella Cl. '99	YYY	7
●	Amarone della Valpolicella Case Vecie '00	YYY	7
●	Amarone della Valpolicella Cl. '97	YYY	7
●	Amarone della Valpolicella Cl. '98	YYY	7
●	Amarone della Valpolicella Cl. '01	YY	7
●	Valpolicella Cl. '03	YY	4

SAN PIETRO IN CARIANO (VR)

Luigi Brunelli
via Cariano, 10
37029 San Pietro in Cariano (VR)
tel. 0457701118
www.brunelliwine.com

The horseshoe-shaped farm complex of Corte Cariano, just outside San Pietro, encloses a beautiful, well-preserved yard where Luigi Brunelli continues the family tradition, helped by his wife Luciana and son Alberto. The old house has been painstakingly renovated and a new cellar built, so now the Brunellis can focus their attention on organizing the ten or so hectares of vineyards, some in rows and some in pergolas, while giving the vines time to achieve balance. This year, the champion Campo del Titari 2001 is back on the team. This Amarone is made from grapes grown in the old pergola vineyards with an average age of 30 years. This vintage shows considerable extract and is weighty, powerful and lively on the palate with overripe red berry fruit, chocolate and coffee sensations and rigorous tannins giving way to hints of leather and spices. The Valpolicella Superiore Campo Praesel 2004 is also good. Fruity aromas laced with herbaceousness are followed by a harmonious, well-structured palate. The sweetness of the fruit in the Recioto 2003 reflects the hot growing year, and the slightly over-emphatic oak is offset by tangy freshness. The Valpolicella Ripasso Pa' Riondo and the corvina-based Corte Cariano are well-made and appealing while the standard-label Valpolicella is approachably moreish.

● Amarone della Valpolicella Cl. Campo del Tìtari '01	▼▼	8
● Recioto della Valpolicella Cl. '03	▼▼	5
● Valpolicella Cl. Sup. Campo Praesel '04	▼▼	4*
● Corte Cariano Rosso '04	▼	4
● Valpolicella Cl. Sup. Ripasso Pa' Riondo '04	▼	4
● Valpolicella Cl. '05	▼	4
● Amarone della Valpolicella Cl. Campo del Tìtari '96	▽▽▽	8
● Amarone della Valpolicella Cl. Campo del Tìtari '97	▽▽▽	8
● Amarone della Valpolicella Cl. Campo Inferi '01	▽▽	8

SAN PIETRO IN CARIANO (VR)

Buglioni
fraz. Corrubio
via Campagnole, 55
37029 San Pietro in Cariano (VR)
tel. 0456760681
www.buglioni.it

The Corrubio area seems detached from Valpolicella as its gentle slopes descend gradually towards the Adige, where the grapes begin to jostle with peaches forspace. There are some prestigious vineyards among these gentle folds and the Buglionis are promoting them as best they can. The winery was founded in 1993 and owns around 16 hectares of vineyards, three around the Carrubio winery, three in Bardolino and ten at Ca' Vegri, producing an annual total of about 70,000 bottles. Alfredo Buglioni is at the helm with the help of his son Mariano on the commercial side and Diego Bertoni in the cellar. The full range of wines is dependably good and led by the excellent Valpolicella Il Bugiardo 2003. This is made using the "ripasso" technique of adding unpressed Amarone skins to the fermented wine and has vibrant ripe fruit and chocolate aromas that lead into a firm, balanced palate. The Amarone 2001 is also very good, showing powerful rather than delicate with lively fruit, while the Valpolicella Il Ruffiano 2004 is more harmonious and polished with varietal expression of blueberries, mint and forest floor on the nose and a deep finish on the palate. The Bardolino is uncomplicated and fresh-tasting while the Recioto 2004 is very sweet but lacks a pinch of verve on the nose and freshness in the flavour.

● Amarone della Valpolicella Cl. '01	▼▼	7
● Valpolicella Cl. Sup. Ripasso Il Bugiardo '03	▼▼	5
● Valpolicella Cl. Sup. Il Ruffiano '04	▼▼	4*
● Recioto della Valpolicella Cl. '04	▼	6
● Bardolino '05	▼	3
● Recioto della Valpolicella Cl. '03	▽▽	6

SAN PIETRO IN CARIANO (VR)

MARCHESI FUMANELLI

FRAZ. SAN FLORIANO
LOC. SQUARANO
37029 SAN PIETRO IN CARIANO (VR)
TEL. 0457704875
www.squarano.com

This San Pietro in Cariano winery has almost 40 hectares located in some of the best areas of Valpolicella like Mezzane and San Floriano. Although annual production of just 100,000 bottles is still based on a small proportion of the vineyards, there are plenty of possibilities for future expansion given the total area. The estate has one golden rule – the quality of the grapes must be outstanding. This is immediately clear in the Amarone Pralongo 2003, which is evidently superb although it has not aged sufficiently in the bottles so far. Its youthfulness is especially perceptible on the nose, where the aromas of ripe red berry fruit, medicinal herbs and grassier vegetal hints remind us of an enduring tradition, although they yet to find harmony. The wine is closer to squaring the circle on the palate, where very concentrated fruit is supported by mouthfilling silky tannins. The standard-label Valpolicella came close to Two Glasses, thanks to clearly defined varietal aromas and a very enjoyable tangy palate. The two whites also performed well. Flora is fresh and, as the name suggests, flowery and Terso, a blend of trebbiano and garganega, reflects the warm growing year of 2003 with mouthfilling complexity.

●	Amarone della Valpolicella Cl. Pralongo '03	🍷🍷	6
○	Terso Bianco '03	🍷	5
○	Flora '05	🍷	3
●	Valpolicella Cl. '05	🍷	3
●	Amarone della Valpolicella Cl. Pralongo '01	YY	6
●	Valpolicella Cl. Sup. Squarano '01	YY	5

SAN PIETRO IN CARIANO (VR)

TENUTE GALTAROSSA

VIA ANDREA MONGA, 9
37029 SAN PIETRO IN CARIANO (VR)
TEL. 0456838307
www.tenutegaltarossa.com

Villa Pullè, one the most elegant historic buildings in the Valpolicella area, has been owned by the Galtarossa family for almost 80 years. To reach this beautiful complex, follow the cross-country road from San Pietro in Cariano to Pescantina, where you'll see the huge entrance with its long avenue flanked by ancient cypress trees. On one side are the rural buildings that house the Tenute Galtarossa offices. This farm and winery has a total of 130 hectares, of which 80 are planted to vine, and the quality of its products has improved considerably over the last few years. Tradition is at home here – in 1682 Lorenzo Pullè described his estate as comprising farmland, vineyards and mulberry trees – but the owner Giacomo Galtarossa has chosen to promote the Valpolicella territory with expert consultancy from winemaker Christian Scrinzi. The Amarone 2003 gives a clear demonstration of the quality of the wines. Weighty with enthralling flavour and steady grip, it gives generous fruit aromas streaked with minerality and aromatic herbs. The Corte Colombara 2004, once again a truly excellent Valpolicella Superiore, also has a remarkable array of aromas with lingering, juicy ripe fruit sensations. The Massabò 2004, from 50 per cent corvina valpolicellese and 50 per cent cabernet and merlot, is less challenging but pleasantly drinkable.

●	Amarone della Valpolicella Cl. '03	🍷🍷	7
●	Valpolicella Cl. Sup. Corte Colombara '04	🍷🍷	5
●	Massabò '04	🍷	4
●	Amarone della Valpolicella Cl. '01	YY	7
●	Valpolicella Cl. Sup. Corte Colombara '01	YY	5
●	Valpolicella Cl. Sup. Corte Colombara '02	YY	5
●	Amarone della Valpolicella Cl. '00	YY	7
●	Valpolicella Cl. Sup. Corte Colombara '03	YY	5

MANARA

FRAZ. SAN FLORIANO
VIA DON CESARE BIASI, 53
37020 SAN PIETRO IN CARIANO (VR)
TEL. 0457701086
www.manaravini.it

A winery's professionalism and dependability are clear not just from the quality of its wines but also from the decisions made at important junctures. The Manara brothers may not have a particularly long track record in the business but they have proved they have a steady hand when it comes to taking big decisions. Here are two examples. The Three Glasses awarded for the 2000 vintage have not entailed a revision of the price list and in 2002, only the Amarone Classico was made, not the Postera selection. These apparently secondary issues actually reveal just how scrupulously serious the Manara winery is and it's the kind of approach that the market is looking for today. A new wine was created with the 2003 vintage, Guido Manara, named after the cellar's founder. This blend of part-raisined cabernet sauvignon, merlot and croatina has vibrant, complex aromas of wild berries, cocoa powder and spices on the nose. The oak has not been completely absorbed on the palate but the texture is so rich that small details like this do not detract from its quality. The Amarone is excellent, its nicely rustic aromas redolent of herbaceousness and stewed fruit before a refreshing vein of acidity lends the dry palate lightness and agility. Recioto El Rocolo 2003 is in a different key entirely with lively overripe fruit, chocolate and aromatic herbs on the nose and well-judged, perfectly integrated sweetness.

	Wine	Glasses	Price
●	Amarone della Valpolicella Cl. '02	🍷🍷	6
●	Guido Manara '03	🍷🍷	6
●	Recioto della Valpolicella Cl. El Rocolo '03	🍷🍷	5
●	Recioto della Valpolicella Cl. Moronalto '04	🍷	5
●	Amarone della Valpolicella Cl. '00	YYY	6
●	Amarone della Valpolicella Cl. '01	YY	6
●	Amarone della Valpolicella Cl. Postera '00	YY	6
●	Amarone della Valpolicella Cl. Postera '01	YY	6
●	Valpolicella Cl. Sup. Le Morete '03	YY	4

SAN PIETRO IN CARIANO (VR)

ANGELO NICOLIS E FIGLI

VIA VILLA GIRARDI, 29
37029 SAN PIETRO IN CARIANO (VR)
TEL. 0457701261
www.vininicolis.com

Having invested heavily in extending the estate's vineyards, which are now scattered across most of Valpolicella, some outside the Classico zone, Beppe and Giancarlo Nicoli have realized that the wiggle room in what seemed like an adequately sized cellar will soon be insufficient. So the need arose to extend it discreetly. During building work, there was a terrifying chasm next to the existing cellar but once the walls had been built, the new constructions turned out to be more harmoniously sited than we had initially feared. The new space will make it easier to manage the barrel stock, consisting of both small oak barrels and the larger, more traditional version, and also make room for the leading wines, which need to age in bottle before release. The Amarone Ambrosan 2001 is on good form. Complex, vibrant and fruity in colour and on the nose, it has ripe red berry fruit aromas and subtle hints of cocoa powder and thyme. The close-knit tannins and acidity on the lively, full-bodied palate reflect great balance and texture. The Recioto 2004 gave a good account of itself with pronounced aromas of ripe cherries and chocolate followed by an enthralling palate with crunchy, juicy fruit. Just a step behind is the Valpolicella Superiore, while the standard-label version is fragrant and uncomplicatedly drinkable.

	Wine	Glasses	Price
●	Amarone della Valpolicella Cl. Ambrosan '01	🍷🍷	8
●	Recioto della Valpolicella Cl. '04	🍷🍷	6
●	Valpolicella Cl. Sup. '04	🍷🍷	4*
●	Valpolicella Cl. '05	🍷	3
●	Amarone della Valpolicella Cl. Ambrosan '93	YYY	8
●	Amarone della Valpolicella Cl. Ambrosan '98	YYY	8
●	Amarone della Valpolicella Cl. '00	YY	7
●	Amarone della Valpolicella Cl. Ambrosan '00	YY	8
●	Amarone della Valpolicella Cl. '01	YY	7
●	Amarone della Valpolicella Cl. '98	YY	7

Santa Sofia

FRAZ. PEDEMONTE
VIA CA' DEDÉ, 61
37020 SAN PIETRO IN CARIANO (VR)
TEL. 0457701074
www.santasofia.com

A glance at the list of wines below might suggest that not much has changed here at Begnoni. But our tasting of the wines revealed there has been an important improvement, which took the Amarone to the finals. In addition, and perhaps more significantly, it has had positive repercussions on the rest of the range, which were much more impressive than previously, albeit without reaching the highest peaks of quality. In particular, these wines show cleaner, better defined aromas and are exactly right for the current market. Santa Sofia has long produced wines that focus more on personality than structure. But to go back to the Amarone 2001, the aromas of wild berries, rain-soaked leaves and cyclamen are vibrant and whistle-clean, and the dry rigorous palate is set in a frame of sweet silky tannins. This wine missed our highest accolade by a whisker. The Soave Montefoscarino 2005 performed well. We liked the elegant floral, apple fruit aromas and understated, beautifully tangy succulence of the palate. The Arleo suffers a little from an unfavourable year. The palate is stylishly supple but lacks length and complexity. All the other products are good, earning One Glass and more often than not coming close to a second. We recommend in particular the Recioto di Soave 2004 and the Lugana 2005.

●	Amarone della Valpolicella Cl. '01	**YY**	7
○	Soave Cl. Montefoscarino '05	**YY**	3*
●	Arleo Rosso '02	**Y**	6
○	Recioto di Soave Cl. '04	**Y**	6
○	Soave Cl. Costalta '04	**Y**	4
⊙	Bardolino Chiaretto Cl. '05	**Y**	3
●	Bardolino Cl. '05	**Y**	3
○	Lugana '05	**Y**	3
○	Valdadige Pinot Grigio Le Fratte '05	**Y**	3
○	Bianco di Custoza Montemagrin '05		3
●	Amarone della Valpolicella Cl. '00	YY	7
●	Amarone della Valpolicella Cl. Gioé '98	YY	8

SAN PIETRO IN CARIANO (VR)

F.lli Speri

FRAZ. PEDEMONTE
VIA FONTANA, 14
37020 SAN PIETRO IN CARIANO (VR)
TEL. 0457701154
www.speri.com

Sometimes the concept of tradition is actually masking the fact that a winery refuses to face up to the inevitability of constant evolution, or does not know how. But when we are talking about wineries that have been in business for over a century, tradition means something else. It means remembering your origins and an eye for the detail that are additional values for winemakers with so many harvests behind them. Innovation is thus not a break with the past but adds continuity to the experience. There have been no world-shaking revolutions at the Speri winery but a number of innovations have crept in: a newly organized cellar, new 20 and 40-hectolitre barrels, new harvesting and selection techniques and new smaller fermenting vats to enable plot-by-plot vinification. The Amarone 2002 was not released so the winery flagship is the sumptuous Recioto La Roggia 2003, an assertive reminder of the splendid 1994 version. Its symphony of ripe, figs, wild berries and citrus fruit on the nose precedes a hefty but elegant palate, lifted by well-judged sweetness. The Valpolicella Sant'Urbano benefits from a welcome element of freshness from the hillside location of the vineyards that offsets the ripeness of the 2003 vintage. The follow-through is very good, considering this wine still has a way to go. La Roverina is fairly uncomplicated but the 2004 is gutsier than usual. The basic 2005 Valpolicella is as supple and pleasant as ever.

●	Recioto della Valpolicella Cl. La Roggia '03	**YY**	7
●	Valpolicella Cl. Sup. Sant'Urbano '03	**YY**	5
●	Valpolicella Cl. Sup. La Roverina '04	**YY**	4
●	Valpolicella Cl. '05	**Y**	4
●	Amarone della Valpolicella Cl. Vign. Monte Sant'Urbano '00	YYY	8
●	Amarone della Valpolicella Cl. Vign. Monte Sant'Urbano '01	YYY	8
●	Amarone della Valpolicella Cl. Vign. Monte Sant'Urbano '95	YYY	8
●	Amarone della Valpolicella Cl. Vign. Monte Sant'Urbano '97	YYY	8

SAN PIETRO IN CARIANO (VR)

F.lli Tedeschi

fraz. Pedemonte
via G. Verdi, 4
37020 San Pietro in Cariano (VR)
tel. 0457701487
www.tedeschiwines.com

It's well-known that in Valpolicella, the 2002 vintage will go down on record as one of the worst in living memory, both for the very rainy summer and the unexpected hailstorm which compromised most of the fruit right before the harvest. The Tedeschi family was not exempt from these calamitous events and consequently had to cancel the release of the Amarone Monte Olmi 2002, which should have been presented for this edition of the Guide. Thanks to long experience and a profound sense of place, this firmly rooted winery achieved satisfactory results, even in an indifferent growing year. The basic Amarone 2003 may not have the same ambition as the Monte Olmi selection but it performed well. Despite one or two flaws attributable to youth, like the closed nose and forward tannins, there is substantial weight in the close-knit texture. The Valpolicella Superiore Capitel dei Nicalò 2004 impressed us with its lively aromas of dried and overripe fruits, and its complex, juicy palate. The Capitel San Rocco 2004, made using the "ripasso" technique of adding unpressed Amarone skins to the fermented wine, is sound if slightly inferior in quality to the two preceding wines. The nose expresses typical chocolate-like aromas while the palate is nicely concentrated, firm and well defined. The standard-label Valpolicella Lucchine is well typed. We retasted the Amarone della Valpolicella Classico Capitel Monte Olmi 1997, which was excellent, and unquestionably worthy of Three retrospective Glasses.

●	Amarone della Valpolicella Cl. '03	🍷🍷	6
●	Valpolicella Cl. Sup. Capitel dei Nicalò '04	🍷🍷	4
●	Capitel S. Rocco '04	🍷🍷	4
●	Valpolicella Cl. Lucchine '05	🍷	3*
●	Amarone della Valpolicella Cl. Capitel Monte Olmi '97	🍸🍸🍸	8
●	Amarone della Valpolicella Cl. Capitel Monte Olmi '01	🍸🍸🍸	8
●	Amarone della Valpolicella Cl. Capitel Monte Olmi '99	🍸🍸🍸	8
●	Amarone della Valpolicella Cl. Capitel Monte Olmi '00	🍸🍸	8
●	Amarone della Valpolicella Cl. '01	🍸🍸	6

SAN PIETRO IN CARIANO (VR)

Viticoltori Tommasi

fraz. Pedemonte
via Ronchetto, 2
37020 San Pietro in Cariano (VR)
tel. 0457701266
www.tommasiwine.it

The fortunes of the Tommasi family are closely bound up with the history of wine in Valpolicella. The estate, now in the hands of the fourth generation, has grown in size thanks to purchases all around the Verona area from Bardolino to Soave, Custoza and Lugana. The heart of the winery beats in Valpolicella, however, with 95 hectares of vineyards in the best locations, made over in 1997 to allow each vineyard to specialize according to the wine to be made. Consequently the range now shows highly respectable average quality. We only have space to mention some of the many wines. Among the whites, we recommend the very enjoyable, well-defined florality of the Lugana San Martino 2005, while from the reds we liked the Valpolicella Ripasso 2004 with black cherry, herb and earth aromas on the nose reflecting the terroir, and a mature, fresh-tasting palate. The basic Amarone is designed to combine complexity and drinkability without overdoing the extract, and it succeeds. This wine will please those who like the more classic, evolved side of Amarone. Ca' Florian 2003 is a selection of the best grapes which follows a wholly traditional procedure, including drying the grapes on mats. The austere, minerally palate expresses strength and warmth, with a salty note alongside the sweet tannins. The Crearo della Conca d'Oro 2004 is made from corvina, cabernet franc and oseleta grapes that dried for a month. Aged in 35-hectolitre barrels, it is a characterful wine with sumptuous concentrated fruit and spicy, earthy, sensations that mingle with herbaceousness.

●	Crearo della Conca d'Oro '04	🍷🍷	5
●	Amarone della Valpolicella Cl. '03	🍷🍷	7
●	Amarone della Valpolicella Cl. Ca' Florian '03	🍷🍷	8
●	Valpolicella Cl. Sup. Ripasso '04	🍷🍷	5
○	Lugana Vign. San Martino Il Sestante '05	🍷	4
●	Amarone della Valpolicella Cl. Monte Masua Il Sestante '01	🍸🍸	8
●	Crearo della Conca d'Oro '03	🍸🍸	5
●	Recioto della Valpolicella Cl. Fiorato '03	🍸🍸	6
●	Valpolicella Cl. Sup. Ripasso '03	🍸🍸	5

SAN PIETRO IN CARIANO (VR)

Massimino Venturini

Fraz. San Floriano
via Semonte, 20
37020 San Pietro in Cariano (VR)
tel. 0457701331 - 0457703320
www.viniventurini.com

The fascination of Amarone forces us to look beyond our preconceived ideas about great wines. Some criteria are of course universal, like finesse, elegance, complex aromas or even just persistence of flavour. In the case of this great Veronese red, we need to read the wine from a new perspective, which is no easy thing. We need to accept that the wine may have evident residual sugar and walk the tightrope of oxidation, always apparently about to fall but never actually doing so. This can bring about one of two reactions: diffidence or love. We love this wine and Daniele and Mirco Venturini's Amarone is a perfect example of the type. The aromas sweep from ripe, almost jammy fruit to vegetal and metallic sensations, with cocoa powder and spices peeping through. The very solid palate is refreshed by acidity and well-judged sweetness. The Recioto 2004 is fresher and sunnier. Its aromas of must, cherries and plums are still very youthful and the palate is soft, succulent and approachable. The Semonte Alto, a Valpolicella Superiore made using the "ripasso" technique of adding unpressed Amarone skins to the fermented wine, pays the price for a very hot year in very ripe aromas of red berries and forest floor, and a palate with a broad mouthfeel that just lacks a touch of freshness. The standard-label Valpolicella is simple but very enjoyable.

● Recioto della Valpolicella Cl. '04	🍷🍷	5
● Amarone della Valpolicella Cl. '01	🍷🍷	6
● Valpolicella Cl. Sup. '03	🍷	4
● Valpolicella Cl. Sup. Ripasso Semonte Alto '03	🍷	4
● Valpolicella Cl. '05	🍷	3
● Recioto della Valpolicella Cl. Le Brugnine '97	YYY	6
● Amarone della Valpolicella Cl. '00	YY	7
● Amarone della Valpolicella Cl. Campomasua '00	YY	7
● Valpolicella Cl. Sup. Semonte Alto '02	YY	4
● Amarone della Valpolicella Cl. '99	YY	7
● Amarone della Valpolicella Cl. '98	YY	7

SAN PIETRO IN CARIANO (VR)

Villa Bellini

loc. Castelrotto di Negarine
via dei Fraccaroli, 6
37020 San Pietro in Cariano (VR)
tel. 0457725630
www.villabellini.com

Last winter when Cecilia Trucchi told us she would no longer be making Amarone, we thought it was one of those things people say out of frustration. But the convincing explanations that followed can be summed up as follows: her property is very small and it was frankly too much to divide production into four or five different labels, each in very limited numbers. Even more important, the Castelrotto vineyards are an especially attractive location that is best suited to two wines, Recioto and Valpolicella. At this point, we realized she was serious. So here is Il Taso 2003, a Valpolicella Superiore which uses lightly raisined grapes. From the first sniff onwards it is obvious that this wine is different from others, and that the difference immediately translates into character. The floral aromas are vibrant, indeed almost bewitching, with nicely compact dried roses followed by hints of blackcurrants and ripe raspberries as aromatic herbs peep out from behind subtle hints of oak. The palate emphasizes this wine's individuality even more. All elegant, silky sensations, it is generous, with sweet fruit and fills the mouth with unassertively robust tannicity. This is a very courageous yet modern choice. We wish Cecilia luck.

● Valpolicella Cl. Sup. Il Taso '03	🍷🍷	5
● Amarone della Valpolicella Cl. '00	YY	7
● Amarone della Valpolicella Cl. '01	YY	7
● Valpolicella Cl. Sup. Il Taso '01	YY	4
● Valpolicella Cl. Sup. Il Taso '02	YY	4
● Amarone della Valpolicella Cl. '97	YY	7
● Amarone della Valpolicella Cl. '98	YY	7
● Amarone della Valpolicella Cl. '99	YY	7

SAN POLO DI PIAVE (TV)

Casa Roma

via Ormelle, 19
31020 San Polo di Piave (TV)
tel. 0422855339
www.casaroma.com

Raboso is a tricky wine, all sharp edges and not so much roundness. Its best qualities are to be found in its lively assertiveness, not lightness or mouthfilling sensations. This is due to a grape variety that is uncommonly rustic, as well as an area where viticulture has never really flourished. Adriano and Gigi Peruzzetto embody the spirit of this land and this grape, not so much in terms of character, since they are polite and very hospitable, as in their determination to achieve their goals. And luck would have it that for them the most important goal is Raboso. Everything at Casa Roma revolves around this grape and chatting with Gigi, its importance becomes clear: it is the only opportunity for the local area to make a name for itself. The 2002 growing year was difficult in most of Italy, but it was a good one for Raboso, which ripens very late and therefore benefited from favourable early autumn weather. The complex, charming wine from that year is one of the best ever made, giving rich aromas of fruit and aromatic herbs streaked through with a restless feral note. The backbone of acidity on the palate is vibrant and succulent while the tannins are a little more restrained than usual. San Dordi 2004 is also very interesting. Fresher and more assertive than previous vintages, it is dry and lingers beautifully. The Manzoni Bianco gave a good performance, just missing out on a second Glass, and is very competitively priced.

●	Piave Raboso '02	🍷🍷	5
○	San Dordi '04	🍷🍷	4
●	Cabernet Franc '05	🍷	3
○	Manzoni Bianco '05	🍷	3
○	Vinegia Marzemina Bianca '05	🍷	3
○	Sauvignon '05	🍷	3
●	Piave Raboso '00	🍷🍷 (white)	5
●	Piave Raboso '01	🍷🍷 (white)	5
●	Piave Raboso '99	🍷🍷 (white)	5

SANT'AMBROGIO DI VALPOLICELLA (VR)

Masi

fraz. Gargagnago
via Monteleone, 2
37020 Sant'Ambrogio di Valpolicella (VR)
tel. 0456832500
www.masi.it

Sandro Boscaini's winery is prominent on the national scene but here, on Veronese soil, it really comes into its own in terms of bottles produced, image and quality. The shrewd decision to develop the business elsewhere, like Latisana in Friuli or Mendoza in Argentina, has avoided compromising the winery's strong connection to Valpolicella. It is from Valpolicella and its grapes that the most interesting wines come, like the Osar from 100 per cent oseleta. This variety has gradually been abandoned and if it is on form today it is thanks to the interest shown by Masi. The deep colour has bluish hues and the aromas are vibrant and gamey, giving rich wild berries and vegetal hints. Considerable structure on the palate is sustained by the significant weight of tannins and succulent fruit. The Amarone Campolongo di Torbe is very similar to the excellent 2000 version. It's built in the same style, with well-behaved fruit and very interesting iodine sensations mingling with Mediterranean scrubland. The progression is steady and gradual as the light, harmonious palate develops. From the other Amarones, we were impressed by the complex Vaio Armaron 2001, with its harmonious and well-coordinated flavour, and the Costasera 2003, which is more approachable and exuberant on the nose, with aromas of red berry jam and chocolate. The mature but very fresh Brolo di Campofiorin 2003 made an excellent impression, as did the Grandarella, which was just a step away from a second Glass.

●	Amarone della Valpolicella Cl. Campolongo di Torbe '01	🍷🍷	8
●	Amarone della Valpolicella Cl. Vaio Armaron '01	🍷🍷	8
●	Osar '01	🍷🍷	7
●	Amarone della Valpolicella Cl. Costasera '03	🍷🍷	6
●	Il Brolo di Campofiorin '03	🍷🍷	5
●	Campofiorin '03	🍷	4
●	Grandarella '03	🍷	6
○	Masianco '05	🍷	4
○	Possessioni Bianco Serègo Alighieri '05	🍷	4
●	Amarone della Valpolicella Cl. Campolongo di Torbe '00	🍷🍷🍷 (white)	8

SANT'AMBROGIO DI VALPOLICELLA (VR)

VILLA MONTELEONE

FRAZ. GARGAGNAGO
VIA MONTELEONE, 12
37020 SANT'AMBROGIO DI VALPOLICELLA (VR)
TEL. 0457704974 - 0456800533
www.villamonteleone.com

It is always exciting to visit the winery owned by Lucia Duran and the sadly missed Professor Raimondi: it is like a journey beyond vineyards and barrels into the ideas of the founder, which now inspire those involved in this adventure, Lucia, winemaker Federico Giotto and all the vineyard and cellar personnel. The few hectares of vineyards are scrupulously cared for with the greatest respect for both the vineyard itself and the surrounding natural environment, limiting the use of pesticides as much as possible. All the cellar procedures follow the same philosophy. Native yeasts are used, sulphites are limited and the wine is allowed to "choose" its own path. This means it is not straitjacketed by fashion but follows its own, memorably distinctive route. The wines are accessible to all, not being designed to astonish, and bear the mark of the winemaker. They stand at the opposite end of the spectrum from competition wines vinified only to astound. The Valpolicella Campo San Vito 2003 made an excellent impression on the panel. It is a characterful red, rich in cherry and blackberry fruit on a background of minerally hints and scrubland. Even fresher and more vibrant on the palate than the aromas suggest, it is sustained by close-knit, sweet tannins and a very long finish. The standard-label Campo Santa Lena is enjoyable and approachable with fresh fruit and floral aromas, while we'll have to wait another year for the Amarone Campo San Paolo.

●	Valpolicella Cl. Sup. Campo S. Vito '03	TT	5
●	Valpolicella Cl. Campo S. Lena '05	T	4
●	Amarone della Valpolicella Cl. '00	YY	8
●	Valpolicella Cl. Sup. Campo S. Vito '01	YY	5
●	Amarone della Valpolicella Cl. Campo S. Paolo '98	YY	8
●	Valpolicella Cl. Sup. Campo S. Vito '02	YY	5
●	Amarone della Valpolicella Cl. '98	YY	8
●	Amarone della Valpolicella Cl. '99	YY	8

SANTO STINO DI LIVENZA (VE)

MOSOLE

FRAZ. CORBOLONE
VIA ANNONE VENETO, 62
30029 SANTO STINO DI LIVENZA (VE)
TEL. 0421310404
www.mosole.com

Winemaking in Lison-Pramggiore has always been hard to assess because the cellars usually try to produce almost exclusively wines from the latest vintage, and if possible in all the numerous varieties permitted by the regulations. Obviously the overview that emerges is unfocused. If we do have a somewhat clearer image today, it is thanks to wineries like Lucio Mosole's, which have understood that forward in this DOC zone is through a few, well-defined types which are good expressions of the local area and its history. So here we find two varieties that have found a home on this clayey soil – merlot and tocai – as well as cabernet and chardonnay, partly as a challenge and partly out of passion. The remaining products are quite rightly fresh-tasting and excellent value for money. The house champion is definitely Merlot Ad Nonam, which does not seem to have suffered from the heat of 2003. The flower and forest floor aromas are vibrant and the palate is strikingly elegant, closing on well-defined, lively tannins. Eleo Rosso 2004 is only a step behind. It's is a well-made blend of merlot, carmenère and refosco that represents a link with tradition, playing on appealing fresh aromas and a free and easy palate. The tocai-only white of the same name is also very good with very youthful aromas, while on the palate the generous tangy flavour hints at interesting ageing prospects.

●	Lison-Pramaggiore Merlot Ad Nonam '03	TT	5
●	Lison-Pramaggiore Rosso Eleo '04	TT	4*
○	Lison-Pramaggiore Tocai Eleo '05	TT	4*
●	Lison-Pramaggiore Cabernet Hora Sexta '03	T	4
○	Hora Sexta '04	T	4
○	Lison-Pramaggiore Chardonnay '05	T	3
●	Lison-Pramaggiore Refosco P. R. '05	T	3
●	Lison-Pramaggiore Cabernet Hora Sexta '02	YY	5
●	Lison-Pramaggiore Rosso Eleo '03	YY	4

SELVAZZANO DENTRO (PD)

LA MONTECCHIA
VIA MONTECCHIA, 16
35030 SELVAZZANO DENTRO (PD)
TEL. 049637294
www.lamontecchia.it

Vineyards have stood on the hill of Montecchia, at the foot of the Colli Euganei range, for centuries enjoying the warm sunny weather, good temperature range and the unusual geological conformation of the landscape. Giordano Emo Capodilista, who is committed to the ongoing promotion of this area, is quite right to say that grapes like merlot and cabernet take on a "Euganean" personality here. The Villa Capodilista 2003 is once again an absolutely excellent Bordeaux blend with dark colour and a rich, very mature array of aromas, including pleasant hints of red berries and spices. These are nicely reflected on the palate, which is soft and elegant with a long, well-defined finish. The classy, supple Cà Emo 2004 is in a different style. The nose opens with aromas ranging from ripe red berry fruit to fresh floral hints before the taut, succulent palate follows through nicely. The last of the reds to be reviewed is the Godimondo 2005, an unexpected Cabernet Franc with spicy floral aromas and a tangy palate. The Fior d'Arancio is an interesting, well-made spumante with vibrant citrus fruit and floral aromas introducing a succulent, magnificently balanced palate. The dried-grape version is enjoyable, showing sweet jammy aromas and light minerally hints. The Pinot Bianco is uncomplicated and well typed.

●	Colli Euganei Rosso Villa Capodilista '03	🍷🍷	6
●	Colli Euganei Rosso Cà Emo '04	🍷🍷	3*
○	Colli Euganei Moscato Fior d'Arancio Spumante '05	🍷🍷	4
○	Colli Euganei Moscato Fior d'Arancio Passito '04	🍷	6
○	Colli Euganei Pinot Bianco '05	🍷	3
●	Godimondo Cabernet Franc '05	🍷	4
●	Colli Euganei Rosso Villa Capodilista '00	🍸🍸	6
●	Colli Euganei Rosso Villa Capodilista '01	🍸🍸	6
○	Colli Euganei Moscato Fior d'Arancio Passito '03	🍸🍸	6

SOAVE (VR)

BALESTRI VALDA
VIA MONTI, 44
37038 SOAVE (VR)
TEL. 0457675393 - 04577680015
www.vinibalestrivalda.com

We are really delighted to welcome Guido Rizzotto's winery to the full profile section of the Guide. In a well-developed designated area like Soave, it is not easy to find space for your wines, either in the market or in the specialized press. Of course, the product must be good but you also need determination, passion and strong links to the local area. These qualities are all part of Guido's discreet character and are obvious when you visit the estate. A dozen hectares of beautifully cultivated vineyards along the spurs leading to Castelcerino in the west of the Soave zone, and winery buildings in perfect harmony with the landscape and the architectural history of the area, are Guido's calling card of good taste and love for the land. There are two high-calibre Soaves. Sengialta 2004, aged in oak barrels, is flavoursome and fruity, with the healthy rusticity that is at the heart of the garganega grape. The Soave Classico 2005 is even more impressive, showing vibrant, sharply defined floral and green apple aromas, and mineral hints that emerge with each successive sip, and a gutsy, well-structured palate. The Scaligio is an interesting Cabernet Sauvignon from the nearby Colli Berici while Lunalonga 2004 is a well-made, flavoursome and mouthfillingly drinkable Soave.

●	Scaligio '03	🍷🍷	5
○	Soave Cl. Sengialta '04	🍷🍷	4
○	Soave Cl. '05	🍷🍷	3*
○	Soave Cl. Lunalonga '04	🍷	4
○	Soave Cl. '00	🍸	4

SOAVE (VR)

CANTINA DEL CASTELLO
CORTE PITTORA, 5
37038 SOAVE (VR)
TEL. 0457680093
www.cantinacastello.it

It's nothing new that Soave is one of the most exciting Italian whites. We should bear in mind, though, that along the way to this success, Soave has experienced moments of euphoria during which its nature has been distorted with excess wood, structure, sweetness or aromas, always in an attempt to find a way forward. Arturo Stocchetti's winery is one of the ones that have never wavered from the beaten track, staying true to a concept of Soave anchored in fragrance and fresh sensations. Of course, this winery has always aimed high but the basic starting point has remained the same. The sound, dynamic Carniga 2004 is on top form with white peaches and floral hints on the nose and a firm-structured palate with vibrant, tangy acidity leading to a long, dry, very classy finish. The Pressoni 2005 is just a step behind, with delicate flower and fruit aromas. Today, the palate is slim and succulent but speaking from direct experience, we are sure that in a couple of years it will have acquired considerable depth. Castello is the archetypal Soave, a relaxed, refreshing, appetizing white with a captivating flavour. The winery's one deviation from its well-trodden track is Acini Soavi, a flavoursome, mature wine with good fruit and forward hints of oak.

O Soave Cl. Carniga '04	ΨΨ	4*
O Soave Cl. Pressoni '05	ΨΨ	4*
O Soave Cl. Acini Soavi '04	ΨΨ	5
O Soave Cl. Castello '05	ΨΨ	4
O Recioto di Soave Cl. Corte Pittora '04	Ψ	5
O Soave Cl. Sup. Monte Pressoni '01	ΥΥΥ	4
O Soave Cl. Carniga '02	ΥΥ	4
O Soave Cl. Carniga '03	ΥΥ	4
O Soave Cl. Pressoni '03	ΥΥ	4
O Soave Cl. Pressoni '04	ΥΥ	4
O Soave Cl. Acini Soavi '02	ΥΥ	5
O Soave Cl. Acini Soavi '03	ΥΥ	5

SOAVE (VR)

COFFELE
VIA ROMA, 5
37038 SOAVE (VR)
TEL. 0457680007
www.coffele.it

The Coffele family has played a leading role in Soave winemaking for several years, albeit without a great deal of fuss and keeping a very low profile. This is the territory of great, classy Italian white wines. The beautifully tended vineyards at Castelcerino yield the ingredients for Alberto the cellar manager to process without the minimum of intervention. This is also made possible by scrupulous vineyard management and meticulous selection of the grapes. Many bunches were discarded in 2005 so that the wines produced would be really outstanding. The standard-label Soave is a textbook example of freshness and cleanness, even showing quite complex aromas of pears, orange-blossom honey, acacia flowers and fresh herbs. The plate is tangy and pleasantly bitterish. Ca' Visco is enjoyably tangy, elegant and spunky. Coherent rather than powerful on the palate, it persuaded the panel to award Three well-deserved Glasses. The spectrum of aromatics hinges on a no-nonsense note of minerality, followed by citrus and then tropical fruit, before the elegant palate is refreshed with a pleasant rush of acidity to balance the mature, deep texture that leads into a finish of kiwi fruit, mint and honeysuckle. Our congratulations to Alberto and his sister Chiara, who works on the sales side of the business. Alzari 2004 is pervaded with sweet fruit mingling with mineral and acidic hints on the palate. As ever, the generous, stylish Recioto Le Sponde reflects the huge efforts expended on its creation in well-gauged sweetness.

O Soave Cl. Ca' Visco '05	ΨΨΨ	4*
O Recioto di Soave Cl. Le Sponde '04	ΨΨ	6
O Soave Cl. Alzari '04	ΨΨ	5
O Chardonnay Castrum Icerini '04	Ψ	3
O Soave Cl. '05	Ψ	3
O Soave Cl. Ca' Visco '03	ΥΥΥ	4
O Soave Cl. Ca' Visco '04	ΥΥΥ	4
O Soave Cl. Ca' Visco '02	ΥΥ	4
O Recioto di Soave Cl. Le Sponde '03	ΥΥ	6
O Soave Cl. Ca' Visco '01	ΥΥ	4
O Soave Cl. Alzari '03	ΥΥ	5
O Soave Cl. '04	ΥΥ	3

SOAVE (VR)

MONTE TONDO

LOC. MONTE TONDO
VIA S. LORENZO, 89
37038 SOAVE (VR)
TEL. 0457680347
www.montetondo.it

The special feature, and at the same time the main reason for the success, of this winery is its commitment to continually believe and invest in what it is doing. Anyone who has watched its development over the last few years will have noticed the huge innovations, both aesthetic and functional, in the cellar and purchases in some of the area's most important vineyards. This is the reason for the steady improvement in quality and its constant high level, even in more challenging years. Credit for having pursued these ambitious results with determination and a spirit of sacrifice goes to owner Gino Magnabosco and his family. From the wines tasted this year, we thought the Casette Foscarin 2005 was very impressive. A mainly garganega-based Soave with some trebbiano di Soave, it is sourced in the hillside vineyard from which the wine takes its name. Fermentation is in tonneaux and barriques, both used and new. The lively, generous and complex aromas prepare the way for the palate, with its rustic, powerful structure and pleasantly sharp, tangy flavour. The Monte Tondo Soave is from garganega only, fermented in stainless steel, and it is just as impressive. Less powerful and flavoursome than the previous wine, it still shows great elegance and austerity, with a dry confident finish.

○ Soave Cl. Casette Foscarin '05	🍷🍷	4*
○ Soave Cl. Monte Tondo '05	🍷🍷	4
○ Recioto di Soave Nettare di Bacco '03		5
○ Soave Cl. Casette Foscarin '03	YY	4
○ Soave Cl. Sup. Foscarin Slavinus '03	YY	5
○ Soave Cl. Sup. Vign. in Casette Foscarin '01	YY	4
○ Soave Cl. Sup. Foscarin Slavinus '02	YY	5

SOAVE (VR)

★ LEONILDO PIEROPAN

VIA CAMUZZONI, 3
37038 SOAVE (VR)
TEL. 0456190171
www.pieropan.it

A chat with Leonildo Pieropan about how the latest harvest went, and the care he puts into his wines, goes a long way towards explaining how he manages to astonish us every year with the personality of his wines. It is almost like a father describing his growing son, attempting to glimpse his potential, and lavishing care on him as part of a greater plan. Nino's ability to read the land and weather conditions, limited intervention in the cellar, the use of ambient yeasts and fibreglass-lined cement fermentation vats are just some of the components of Nino's close relationship with his wines. The results are tangible throughout the range, starting with the simple Soave Classico with its big personality. The floral aromas and elegant hints of apples and pears on the nose are followed by a creamy, tangy palate with a nice almondy finish. Turning to the winery's two thoroughbreds, the version from the La Rocca cru has very complex aromas and an enthralling palate that is powerful, flavoursome and weighty yet dry, supple and succulent, with style and sophistication in the flavour. The Calvarino is even better. This wine is grown on basaltic soil, which gives it a naturally minerality. Delicate floral and apple fruit on the nose precede a dry, gutsy, tangy and impressively long palate. It is so long on the palate that we simply couldn't deny Three Glasses. Finally, Passito della Rocca 2001 is mouthfillingly sweet and generously fresh with a charming finish.

○ Soave Cl. Calvarino '04	🍷🍷🍷	5
○ Passito della Rocca '01	🍷🍷	7
○ Soave Cl. La Rocca '04	🍷🍷	6
○ Soave Cl. '05	🍷🍷	4*
○ Soave Cl. Sup. La Rocca '00	YYY	6
○ Soave Cl. Calvarino '02	YYY	5
○ Soave Cl. La Rocca '02	YYY	6
○ Soave Cl. Calvarino '03	YYY	5
○ Soave Cl. Sup. La Rocca '95	YYY	6
○ Soave Cl. Sup. La Rocca '96	YYY	6
○ Soave Cl. Sup. Calvarino '98	YYY	5
○ Soave Cl. Sup. La Rocca '98	YYY	6
○ Soave Cl. Sup. La Rocca '99	YYY	6

SOAVE (VR)

CANTINA DI SOAVE
V.LE VITTORIA, 100
37038 SOAVE (VR)
TEL. 0456139811
www.cantinasoave.it

After several editions of the Guide in which we noted how this large Soave co-operative was more successful at making wines from nearby Valpolicella than those from its own area, we were at last presented with a Soave that does this excellent designated area justice. It is almost as if the acquisition of important properties to the west of Verona had given the co-operative's morale a boost and inspired everyone – growers and cellar personnel alike – to make a fine white. Soave Classico Superiore Castelcerino 2004 has vibrant aromas of apples and flowers on the nose and a palate that satisfies both in structure and in its mouthwatering finesse. Turning to the reds, we have to report a setback this year: many labels weren't presented and even some of the wines we could taste didn't seem especially well focused. Of the two Amarones presented, we preferred the Selezione 1998 with its good complex aromas. It is more generous in fruit than in finesse, and shows power and softness on the palate. Although the Rocca Sveva is from the favourable year of 2000, it wasn't particularly impressive. The Valpolicella Superiore Ripasso 2003 is decently structured but lacks the verve on the nose. The red Fulvo and the Soave Rocca Sveva are both uncomplicated, relaxed and eminently drinkable wines.

○	Équipe 5 Brut '02	🍷🍷	5
○	Soave Cl. Sup. Castelcerino Rocca Sveva '04	🍷🍷	4*
●	Amarone della Valpolicella Rocca Sveva Sel. '98	🍷🍷	7
●	Amarone della Valpolicella Rocca Sveva '00	🍷	7
●	Fulvo Rocca Sveva '03	🍷	5
○	Lycos Bianco Rocca Sveva '03	🍷	5
●	Valpolicella Sup. Ripasso Rocca Sveva '03	🍷	4
○	Soave Cl. Rocca Sveva '05		4
●	Amarone della Valpolicella Rocca Sveva '99	YY	7

SOAVE (VR)

SUAVIA
FRAZ. FITTÀ DI SOAVE
VIA CENTRO, 14
37038 SOAVE (VR)
TEL. 0457675089
www.suavia.it

Suavia wines breathe the air of tidy vineyards geometrically arranged on the gentle hillsides of the rolling Soave designated area, absorbing the volcanic sensations from the rocks through roots that struggle to penetrate the ungenerous Foscarino terrain. This is a grand cru that you can glimpse from the plain but will only really discover by climbing the steep lanes leading to Fittà. So in such an attractive context it comes as no surprise that absolute priority is given to the vineyards, where the garganega grape finds perfect conditions to ripen and express its generous array of subtle aromas. The harmony between ethereal and solid components is fully realized in the Monte Carbonare 2005, which is as succulent, vibrant, minerally and well defined as only a truly characterful wine can be. The vineyards are up to 50 years old, which perhaps explains the particularly subtle organoleptic profile. It is a wine destined to become even greater with ageing, but already fully deserves Three Glasses. Le Rive 2004 is at the opposite end of the spectrum with well-judged oak and striving for greater ripeness that have made it a sunnier, softer wine but by no means less elegant in texture. The simple basic version is a real surprise, showing qualities that are somewhat unexpected in this category: its strength, fine texture and lingering flavour are all outstanding, making this wine unbeatable value for money.

○	Soave Cl. Monte Carbonare '05	🍷🍷🍷	4*
○	Soave Cl. Le Rive '04	🍷🍷	5
○	Soave Cl. '05	🍷🍷	4
○	Soave Cl. Sup. Le Rive '00	YYY	5
○	Soave Cl. Le Rive '02	YYY	5
○	Soave Cl. Monte Carbonare '02	YYY	4
○	Soave Cl. Monte Carbonare '04	YYY	4
○	Soave Cl. Sup. Le Rive '98	YYY	5
○	Recioto di Soave Acinatium '03	YY	6
○	Soave Cl. Le Rive '03	YY	5
○	Soave Cl. Monte Carbonare '03	YY	4

SOAVE (VR)

TAMELLINI
VIA TAMELLINI, 4
37038 SOAVE (VR)
TEL. 0457675328

Only three wines are made at Tamellini, which is almost ironic in comparison with the endless barrage of labels presented by some other wineries. Yet these three wines encapsulate the history and future of Soave. Here we a fine example of an everyday wine, another more flavoursome, complex product, representing ambition, and lastly a Recioto that exalts the voluptuous nature of the garganega grape. There is no need for anything else, just a family that believes in working the land and skilfully transforming its precious fruit into wine. Naturally this journey, which took just a few years, might not have been made without Federico Curtaz and Paolo Caciorgna. They have helped Gaetano and Piofrancesco Tamellini not so much simply to make good wines but rather to understand which aspects of their property to emphasize and which to play down. So here is the Soave 2005, making the best of an excellent year with vibrant, floral and nicely fruity aromas and good flavour perfectly sustained by acidity and tanginess. These features are obviously present in spades in the Le Bine 2004, which has very ripe, generous and juicy fruit on the nose and a firm-bodied, beautifully harmonious palate. A new star is born in the Soave sky, shining with the first ever Three Glass award for Tamellini. Lastly, the Recioto is an explosion of citrus and candied fruit and spices, transforming the rustic rough edges of the garganega grape into character. The very forward sweetness on the palate is countered by pronounced acidity, making this a succulent, supple wine.

○	Soave Cl. Le Bine '04	▼▼▼	4*
○	Recioto di Soave V. Marogne '02	▼▼	6
○	Soave '05	▼▼	4
○	Recioto di Soave V. Marogne '01	▽▽	5
○	Soave Cl. Le Bine '02	▽▽	5
○	Soave Cl. Le Bine '03	▽▽	5
○	Recioto di Soave V. Marogne '00	▽▽	5
○	Recioto di Soave V. Marogne '99	▽▽	5

SOMMACAMPAGNA (VR)

CAVALCHINA
LOC. CAVALCHINA - FRAZ. CUSTOZA
VIA SOMMACAMPAGNA, 7
37066 SOMMACAMPAGNA (VR)
TEL. 045516002
www.cavalchina.com

We had never encountered a Bianco di Custoza like this before and are not surprised that this first for the Garda DOC comes from Cavalchina. It was here, about 40 years ago, that Giulietto Piona first bottled a wine that bore the name of this little place on the label, a place made famous by two battles during the Risorgimento. Now his sons Luciano and Franco have made the leap in quality. Custoza Superiore Amedeo 2004, brimming with ripe fruit, captivating floral sensations and delightful flavour, is the result of a selection of garganega grapes, grown in the 25 hectares of vineyards on the morainic soil of Custoza, with some fernanda – as the cortese grape is known locally – and a dash of trebbiano. Could this be the beginning of a renaissance for lakeside whites? For the time being, it earned a stupendous first Three Glasses. A good all-round performance also came from the leading red, originating from the 40 hectares at Monzambano, La Prendina, on gentle hills in the province of Mantua. The Merlot Faial 2003 has generous aromatic herbs and black berry fruit, followed by a weighty, mouthfilling, austere palate. Also from Monzambano are the lovely trio of single-variety wines, Garganega Paroni, Sauvignon Valbruna and Garda Corvina, which have considerable personality and structure. Bardolino Superiore Santa Lucia 2004 is one of the best exponents of this DOCG in the province of Verona. The rosé Passito La Rosa is an fascinating, well-balanced blend of molinara and moscato bianco. All the other wines are dependably good.

○	Bianco di Custoza Sup. Amedeo '04	▼▼▼	4*
●	Garda Merlot Faial La Prendina '03	▼▼	6
●	Bardolino Sup. S. Lucia '04	▼▼	4
●	Garda Corvina La Prendina '04	▼▼	4
○	Garda Garganega Paroni La Prendina '04	▼▼	4
○	Garda Sauvignon Valbruna La Prendina '04	▼▼	4
⊙	La Rosa Passito '05	▼▼	4
●	Bardolino '05	▼	4
⊙	Bardolino Chiaretto '05	▼	4
○	Bianco di Custoza '05	▼	4
●	Garda Merlot La Prendina '05	▼	3
●	Garda Merlot Faial La Prendina '02	▽▽	6

SOMMACAMPAGNA (VR)

Le Vigne di San Pietro

via S. Pietro, 23
37066 Sommacampagna (VR)
tel. 045510016
www.levignedisanpietro.it

Carlo Nerozzi is a man of myriad ideas. You might find him designing a showroom for food events, organizing a film, or trading with the East. He devotes the same feverish brilliance to his wine, making choices that might seem rebellious in the Garda context, to the extent that he had decided to abandon the local DOCs except for the Custoza, to which he has a sentimental attachment. In this case, he immediately embraced the new abbreviated appellation allowed by the regulations. The winery is small, with four hectares on the San Pierin hill where the winery buildings are located and six at Balconi Rossi. This is also the source of the grapes used in the highly enjoyable Balconi Rossi 2003, which mingles nicely balanced complexity and succulent fruit with interesting streaks of aromatic herbs and dried flowers. Above all, this red wine indicates a new way to promote the Garda corvina grape, which accounts for 70 per cent of this blend, the remainder being equal quantities of merlot and cabernet sauvignon. The Centopercento 2004 is made exclusively from corvina. This is the red that Carlo Nerozzi and winemaker Federico Giotto created when the stopped producing Bardolino wines and it is very enjoyable, fruity and rich in spice. The Sanpietro 2004 is a very good white, made mainly from garganega with a splash of riesling. CorDeRosa is a lovely floral rosé. Finally, Custoza 2005 is fragrant and has bags of personality.

●	I Balconi Rossi '03	YY	6
○	Sanpietro '04	YY	4*
●	Centopercento '04	YY	4*
○	Custoza '05	Y	4
⊙	CorDeRosa '05	Y	4
○	Sud '95	(YYY)	7
●	Refolà Cabernet Sauvignon '00	(YY)	7
●	Refolà Cabernet Sauvignon '01	(YY)	7

SUSEGANA (TV)

Conte Collalto

via 24 Maggio, 1
31058 Susegana (TV)
tel. 0438738241
www.collalto.it

At last, after many profiles which dwelt on descriptions of the beautiful hills, the restored hamlet, and the plans for Collalto estate, we are delighted to be able to focus on the wines themselves, because they are excellent. It might seem easy to get a wine through to the finals in some areas, but here on the banks of the Piave there is a traditional approach to farming to contend with, as well as the inevitable comparisons with the rest of the world's Merlots and Cabernets. The house champion, which most impressed our panel, was the Cabernet Torrai 2000. The wine is obviously Bordeaux in style with intertwining red berry fruit and vegetal hints and plenty of room for spicy and floral aromas. It makes an elegant impact on the palate, where it fills the mouth delicately yet confidently, with exemplary harmony, length and persistence. Rambaldo VIII 2002 is in a different style. Generous hints of fruit on the nose and still rather forward oak precede a nicely balanced, concentrated palate. Colli di Conegliano Vinciguerra I 2001 falls somewhere between the two with vibrant wild berries, printer's ink and mint on the nose and a well-rounded palate where the considerable extract is managed with a light touch. The two Proseccos are both excellent. The new specialized vineyards are now productive, adding firmness to the palate as well as stylish aromas.

●	Piave Cabernet Torrai Ris. '00	YY	5
●	Colli di Conegliano Rosso Vinciguerra I '01	YY	4*
●	Rambaldo VIII '02	YY	5
○	Prosecco di Conegliano Brut San Salvatore	YY	4*
○	Prosecco di Conegliano Extra Dry	YY	4*
●	Incrocio Manzoni 2.15 '04	Y	4
●	Piave Cabernet '04	Y	3
●	Wildbacher '04	Y	4
○	Manzoni Bianco '05	Y	3
○	Pinot Grigio '05	Y	2
○	Verdiso '05	Y	2
○	Prosecco di Conegliano Tranquillo	Y	3
●	Piave Cabernet Torrai Ris. '99	(YY)	5

TORREGLIA (PD)

Vignalta

Fraz. Luvigliano
via dei Vescovi, 5
35038 Torreglia (PD)
tel. 0499933105 - 0429777225
www.vignalta.it

The 2003 Gemola, an emblematic Colli Euganei wine, was well worth the wait. It was a bizarre, stiflingly hot year, which gave all winegrowers a hard time and stretched to the limit their ability to make the best of a very unusual vintage. But Gemola is a thrilling wine in which freshness, elegance and full body blend in exemplary fashion, stylishly proffering grassy, spicy and red berry aromas and a very long finish. Congratulations to owners Lucio Gomiero and Graziano Cardin and their team, from winemaker Francesco Polastri to the excellent cellar manager Marco Michele Montecchio. The 55 hectares of vineyards are located in some of the best-aspected areas, like Monte Gemola, and produce around 240,000 bottles a year, enabling the winery to amply satisfy an enthusiastic worldwide clientele. Let's move on from the feather in the winery's cap to another wine we liked, which represents the cellar's willingness to research and experiment, one of the best ever versions of the Agno Tinto 2004. From the purplish-black colour onwards, this is a compelling wine with aromatic herbs, spices and mint on the nose opening out into fruity aromas, and a fresh, full-bodied palate with close-knit tannins. The Fior d'Arancio Passito Alpianae is another outstanding wine and surely one of the best sweet white wines in Veneto. The stylish, elegant Il Nero 2004 is on top form with hints of roses, freshly mown hay and subtle jammy aromas.

●	Colli Euganei Rosso Gemola '03	🍷🍷	6
○	Colli Euganei Fior d'Arancio Passito Alpianae '04	🍷🍷	5
●	Agno Tinto '04	🍷🍷	6
●	Il Nero '04	🍷🍷	6
○	Colli Euganei Chardonnay '04	🍷	5
●	Colli Euganei Rosso Venda '04	🍷	4
○	Colli Euganei Pinot Bianco '05	🍷	4
○	Sirio '05	🍷	4
●	Colli Euganei Rosso Gemola '00	🍸🍸🍸	6
●	Colli Euganei Rosso Gemola '01	🍸🍸🍸	6
●	Colli Euganei Rosso Gemola '98	🍸🍸🍸	6
●	Colli Euganei Rosso Gemola '99	🍸🍸🍸	6
○	Colli Euganei Fior d'Arancio Passito Alpianae '03	🍸🍸	5

VALDAGNO (VI)

Masari

loc. Maglio di Sopra
via Masetto, 18
36078 Valdagno (VI)
tel. 0445410780
www.masari.it

Some people nurture a dream their whole life long without ever really trying to make it come true. Others employ all possible methods and take personal risks to see their objectives fulfilled. Massimo Del Lago's dream has always been to make wine in the Agno valley, recovering old vineyards hidden away in the furthest corners or planting new ones in the best-aspected areas. Following the addition of Arianna Tessari to the team, Masari has begun to get down to business and the wines have taken on a definite character, which led to their debut in the Guide last year. Massimo has left his job as winemaker at the Maculan winery in Breganze to devote himself full-time to his own property. This has made it possible to improve and increase the range of wines, which includes a dry white, Agnobianco, an original blend of garganega and durella with interesting potential. The cabernet sauvignon and merlot San Martino comes from the same soil. It is minerally and gamey on the nose with elderflower aromas and a delightful acidic sensation on the palate. The Masari 2004 is still very young but has all it takes to absorb its two years in small oak barrels. Classic Bordeaux aromas of blackcurrant, black pepper and pencil lead greet the nose, and there is a typically edgy, territory-focused sensation in the finish. Finally, the Doro 2003 is excellent, its robust sugar content – 250 grams per litre – 11 per cent alcohol and considerable acidity making comparisons with Eiswein inevitable.

○	Doro Passito Bianco '03	🍷🍷	5
●	Masari '04	🍷🍷	6
○	Agnobianco '05	🍷	4
●	San Martino '05	🍷	4
○	Doro Passito Bianco '01	🍸🍸	5
○	Doro Passito Bianco '02	🍸🍸	5
●	Masari '02	🍸🍸	6
●	Masari '03	🍸🍸	6
●	San Martino '04	🍸🍸	4

VALDOBBIADENE (TV)

DESIDERIO BISOL & FIGLI
FRAZ. SANTO STEFANO
VIA FOLLO, 33
31040 VALDOBBIADENE (TV)
TEL. 0423900138 - 0438975809
www.bisol.it

The best way to define the set-up at the Bisol winery is to call it a team of older and younger generations who form the middle management at one of the big names in Prosecco. We have fond memories of when the current team captain, Gianluca Bisol, joined the group some time ago, and if history repeats itself, the new generations will in turn show their mettle. They will have to run a well-established estate of 60 hectares along the hills joining Valdobbiadene, Conegliano and Vittorio Veneto. Here the prosecco grape reigns supreme, expressing its many, often unacknowledged qualities to their best effect. It is grown on poor soil, consisting of marl, clayey limestone, marine sandstone and rough clay, which gives the wine its unique qualities of finesse and fragrance. The Cartizze, the top prosecco-based wine, is the best of the well-stocked batch, for its intense, generous and creamy qualities. Salis has delicate hints of wisteria, citrus fruit and williams pears while the Vigneti del Fol releases crisp apple, crusty bread and acacia flower aromas. After unhurried ageing, the Garnei made an excellent impression with its compelling mix of freshness and complexity. The Colmei is very flavoursome with a pleasant almondy finish and the Crede is an excellent wine to drink through the meal. The complex, intriguing Passito Duca di Dolle, dedicated to great poet Andrea Zanzotto, is a blend of 13 different vintages. All the other products are dependably good.

O Prosecco di V. Dry Garnei '04	🍷🍷	5
O Cartizze Dry '05	🍷🍷	6
O Prosecco di V. Brut Crede '05	🍷🍷	4
O Prosecco di V. Dry Salis '05	🍷🍷	4
O Prosecco di V. Extra Dry Vigneti del Fol '05	🍷🍷	5
O Duca di Dolle Prosecco Passito	🍷🍷	8
O Prosecco di V. Extra Dry Colmei Jeio	🍷🍷	4
O Prosecco di V. Tranquillo Molera '05	🍷	4
O Prosecco di V. Brut Jeio	🍷	4

VALDOBBIADENE (TV)

F.LLI BORTOLIN SPUMANTI
FRAZ. SANTO STEFANO
VIA MENEGAZZI, 5
31049 VALDOBBIADENE (TV)
TEL. 0423900135
www.bortolin.com

Fratelli Bortolin can definitely be counted among the benchmark wineries for spumante production in Valdobbiadene. Valeriano has passed on his knowledge of Prosecco-making, which comes from generations of family heritage, with passion and determination to his children Andrea, Claudia and Diego. Their profound connection with the local area translates into absolutely dependable quality in all 300,000 bottles produced each year. You are not likely to get any unpleasant surprises when you taste the wines in the range. The grapes are grown on 15 hectares of vineyards owned by the estate, a couple on the hills in the Cartizze subzone and the rest located around Felettano and Follina. In addition to this, fruit is bought in from trusted winegrowers with about another 15 hectares all in the municipal area of Valdobbiadene. The winery therefore has complete control over the sources of its grapes, offering a further guarantee of constant quality. The Cartizze and Prosecco Extra Dry are the best-defined examples. The Cartizze has an array of fruity aromas ranging from pears to apples and even tropical fruit, while the typical sweetness of this type stands out on the palate alongside lovely fruit. The Extra Dry Rù seems more complex. Nice fruity aromas come out on the nose to be followed by lovely floral sensations and the palate has impressively creamy mousse. The other Proseccos in the range are all sound.

O Cartizze Dry	🍷🍷	5
O Prosecco di V. Extra Dry Rù	🍷🍷	4*
O Prosecco di V. Brut	🍷	4
O Prosecco di V. Dry	🍷	4
O Prosecco di V. Extra Dry	🍷	4

VALDOBBIADENE (TV)

BORTOLOMIOL
VIA GARIBALDI, 142
31049 VALDOBBIADENE (TV)
TEL. 0423974911
www.bortolomiol.com

This large Valdobbiadene winery has always been at the top of the local spumante production ladder and its extensive knowledge of the area and expertise are recognized by colleagues. A few years after the death of its founder, the cellar is now undergoing changes to the range of wines, not only in the labels but also in the creation of a new line, with a standardized presentation that is easily distinguishable from the traditional line. Once again the Cartizze is the most interesting bottle, with floral and tropical fruit aromas and a sensationally fresh-tasting palate. Two of the new wines, the Dry Maior and the Extra Dry Senior, are almost as good. The former is full of lively fruit while Extra Dry Senior has a more rustic personality typical of the grape variety, nicely brought out in the aromas by a hint of apples and pears that is as pleasant as it is uncomplicated. As ever, the Banda Rossa put on an excellent performance, for it never misses an opportunity to display its class. The two Bruts are a different kettle of fish. Prior is uncomplicatedly, frankly drinkable while Motus Vitae, released after an extra year's ageing, does not make the most of its generous flavour notwithstanding interesting aromas on the nose. Finally, we recommend the very good Demi Sec, Suavis, with its emphatic sweetness and taut, succulent palate.

○	Cartizze	🍷🍷	6
○	Prosecco di V. Dry Maior	🍷🍷	4
○	Prosecco di V. Extra Dry Banda Rossa	🍷🍷	4
○	Prosecco di V. Extra Dry Senior	🍷🍷	4
○	Prosecco di V. Brut Motus Vitae '04	🍷	5
●	Piave Cabernet Sauvignon Mormorò '04	🍷	4
○	Prosecco di V. Brut Prior	🍷	4
○	Prosecco di V. Demi Sec Suavis	🍷	4
○	Prosecco di V. Frizzante Il Ponteggio	🍷	4

VALDOBBIADENE (TV)

CANEVEL SPUMANTI
LOC. SACCOL
VIA ROCCAT E FERRARI, 17
31049 VALDOBBIADENE (TV)
TEL. 0423975940
www.canevel.it

Canevel is representative of the whole Prosecco production zone, processing grapes from both Valdobbiadene and Conegliano. More specifically it owns about 15 hectares, almost all at Refrontolo in the Conegliano hills, and just one hectare – the San Biagio vineyard – in the municipality of Valdobbiadene at Saccol, which is also where the winery building is located. But the cellar also processes grapes bought in from growers, mainly in Valdobbiadene. These resources and continual technological updating allow the winery to maintain a high standard of quality in its wines even in challenging years like 2005, when the frequent rainfall coincided largely with the tricky harvest period. Our tastings show a good performance from all the spumantes including this year's new wine, Prosecco Demi Sec. It may lack a little complexity but it makes up for it with excellent balance of the sugars and came close to Two Glasses on its debut, already demonstrating that it is on the right track. The Cartizze is very good, showing considerable finesse and creamy fizz. The same can be said for the range's two mainstay Extra Drys, the basic and the Millesimato, which are both impressive in structure and elegance.

○	Prosecco di Conegliano V. Extra Dry Il Millesimato '05	🍷🍷	4
○	Cartizze	🍷🍷	5
○	Prosecco di Conegliano V. Brut	🍷🍷	4
○	Prosecco di V. Extra Dry	🍷🍷	4
○	Prosecco di V. Demi Sec	🍷	4
○	Prosecco di V. Tranquillo	🍷	4
●	Colli di Conegliano Rosso Vigna Levina '01	YY	5

VALDOBBIADENE (TV)

Col Vetoraz

Fraz. Santo Stefano
s.da delle Tresiese, 1
31040 Valdobbiadene (TV)
tel. 0423975291
www.colvetoraz.it

The road leading from the centre of Valdobbiadene to Vittorio Veneto is really delightful, surrounded by vines you can admire the steep prosecco-clad slopes, slightly tamed by the work of men. Near the small district of Santo Stefano is the Col Vetoraz winery, named after the vineyard. Although it is not all that old, Col Vetoraz has acquired a recognizable style that has become firmly established over the years, putting the accent on finesse, elegance and generous aromas. Once again this year, the Millesimato is a well-made spumante with vibrant floral hints and fresh aromas of pears and citrus fruit. These are beautifully reflected on the palate together with delicate fizz that gives the flavour lingering persistence and additional style. The Brut version is almost as good. Thanks to its lower sugar content, it displays pleasant acidity and a vibrant palate. The Extra Dry and Cartizze are both dependably good. The former has fresh, elegant floral sensations while the latter is fruitier, soft and fresh, with an interesting balance of acidity, sugars and fizz. The Prosecco Tranquillo is light and very drinkable while the Frizzante is attractively tangy.

○	Prosecco di Conegliano V. Dry Millesimato '05	🍷🍷	4*
○	Cartizze	🍷🍷	6
○	Prosecco di V. Extra Dry	🍷🍷	4*
○	Prosecco di V. Tranquillo Tresiese '05	🍷	4
○	Prosecco di V. Brut	🍷	4
○	Prosecco di V. Frizzante	🍷	4

VALDOBBIADENE (TV)

Le Colture

Fraz. Santo Stefano
via Follo, 5
31049 Valdobbiadene (TV)
tel. 0423900192

Unlike the average Valdobbiadene producer, Le Colture maintains strong links with the land, thanks in part to a substantial 40 hectares or so of vineyards. Most of the wine is therefore made from grapes grown on the estate. The vineyards are situated in various parts of Valdobbiadene and Conegliano so that different wines can be created to bring out the best characteristics of both zones: finesse and expressive aromas on the one hand and chewy structure on the other. The Dry Cruner is a cut above the other wines presented, with generous mouthfilling fruit – ripe, juicy apples and pears – enfolding the palate in nicely balanced sweetness that is tempered by fresh acidity. The Cartizze is also very interesting, opening with subtle, slow-to-emerge aromas that reveal their class gradually as they range from light floral hints to a more substantial sensation of white peaches. The fizz accompanies the palate through to a pleasant finish with hints of bitter almonds. Classic green apple aromas characterize the very nice Frizzante Mas, alongside fresh vegetal sensations and a tangy, succulent palate. The Extra Dry Pianer has sharply defined apple and pear aromas and emphatic charm and balance. Brut Fagher is lively and piquant, and the Tranquillo Masaré is very supple.

○	Cartizze	🍷🍷	5
○	Prosecco di V. Dry Cruner	🍷🍷	4*
○	Prosecco di V. Brut Fagher	🍷	4
○	Prosecco di V. Extra Dry Pianer	🍷	4
○	Prosecco di V. Frizzante Mas	🍷	4
○	Prosecco di V. Tranquillo Masaré	🍷	4
●	Colli di Conegliano Rosso Salera '02	🍷 (white glass)	5

VALDOBBIADENE (TV)

SILVANO FOLLADOR
LOC. FOLLO - FRAZ. SANTO STEFANO
VIA CALLONGA, 11
31040 VALDOBBIADENE (TV)
TEL. 0423900295
www.silvanofollador.it

Sometimes we fall into the trap of thinking that a wine like Prosecco can be put together purely by cellar techniques, with no influence from the countryside. Then, luckily, a vintage comes along to bring us back down to earth in one way or another, reminding us that each vintage is different from the last and needs to be interpreted accordingly. Who can forget the heat of 2003, which produced buttery, weighty wines? The 2005 vintage was something of a challenge, too, with a cool summer and very rainy autumn. Once again, Silvano and Alberta Follador have perfectly interpreted the grapes from that harvest and made the most of their fresh aromas and very rich flavour in vibrant, floral wines that are rounded yet free of excess sugar. The best example of this comes from the most important vineyard, which is no surprise. It's the Cartizze with pears and wisteria on the nose and a flavoursome palate pervaded with understated sweetness. The Extra Dry reveals aromas of lime blossom and jasmine alongside the apple fruit, and these are nicely reflected on the dry, gutsy palate. The Brut is slimmer-bodied and appears a little too simple without the contribution of sugar, although this feature also makes it an ideal table wine. The Passito made from prosecco grapes is interesting, giving faint aromas and perfectly balanced sweetness.

O Bianco Passito '03	🍷🍷	7
O Cartizze	🍷🍷	5
O Prosecco di V. Extra Dry	🍷🍷	4*
O Prosecco di V. Brut	🍷	4

VALDOBBIADENE (TV)

NINO FRANCO
VIA GARIBALDI, 147
31049 VALDOBBIADENE (TV)
TEL. 0423972051
www.ninofranco.it

The 2005 growing year yielded supple, fresh, sharp wines that are deliciously drinkable but not overly rich in texture. With the discreet, invaluable assistance of his wife Annalisa, Primo Franco could not miss the chance to give his personal and as ever outstanding interpretation of such a year. His Primo Franco 2005 – and we emphasize the possessive – is a characterful, complex wine with a dazzling bouquet of ripe apples, peaches and pears, fragrant hints of bananas and kiwi fruit and appealing cake aromas. The Cartizze, the Prosecco cru par excellence, is classy with frank, sharply defined, fresh aromas and mouthfilling crunchy fruit on a silky palate true to the winery's style. The Rive di San Floriano 2005 is very good, its sparkling greenish hues and very delicate flower and fruit aromas of apples, pears and hazelnuts impressing the panel. Prosecco Brut is a lovely wine to drink from starter to sweet for its aromatic herbs, wisteria, crusty bread, citrus fruit and almonds, light, gentle palate and extremely good balance. Some 750,000 bottles, out of an annual total of about 1,000,000, are made each year of the Rustico, the winery's workhorse, and it again earned our praise for its pleasant and very drinkable character. The Sassi Bianchi is back, one of the best Prosecco Tranquillos as always. Lastly, the second vintage of the Rosé Faìve, from mainly merlot with some cabernet, scintillates like the sparks – "faìve" in the local dialect – it is named for, giving almond-laced red berry fruit, and hints of medlar, plums and kermes. Simply delicious.

O Prosecco di V. Dry Primo Franco '05	🍷🍷	4*
O Cartizze	🍷🍷	5
O Prosecco di V. Brut Rive di S. Floriano '05	🍷🍷	4
O Prosecco di V. Brut	🍷🍷	4
O Prosecco di V. Tranquillo Sassi Bianchi '05	🍷	3
⊙ Brut Rosé Faìve	🍷	4
O Prosecco Brut Rustico	🍷	4

VALDOBBIADENE (TV)

Ruggeri & C.

via Prà Fontana
31049 Valdobbiadene (TV)
tel. 04239092
www.ruggeri.it

This large Valdobbiadene winery never fails to present a substantial range of wines combining excellent quality with nice expression of both the local area and the aroma-rich grape. The well-established production set-up is the result of a close working relationship with over 130 growers and is accompanied by two interesting Prosecco-related projects. The first is already under way: extremely scrupulous selection of grapes from very old vines – some around a century old – from the whole of the Valdobbiadene area, for use in a new wine, Brut Vecchie Viti. More than an attempt to produce a really outstanding spumante, this is an act of love for the grape and the terroir, using vines that have witnessed wars and agricultural revolutions, blisteringly hot summers and devastating storms but are still standing, twisted and clinging to the soil, yielding their fruit every autumn. The other project, centred on Montello, concerns older red grape varieties in the Treviso area and involves close work with the experimental viticultural institute in Conegliano. This is at an early stage but some old grape varieties are already showing interesting potential. Turning to the more traditional products, how could we fail to mention yet again the excellent quality throughout the range? The Extra Dry Giustiniano B. took centre stage, showing light, silky and powerful, with the fascinatingly tangy flavour typical of its vintage.

○	Prosecco di V. Brut Vecchie Viti '05	🍷🍷	5
○	Prosecco di V. Extra Dry Giustino B. '05	🍷🍷	5
○	Cartizze	🍷🍷	5
○	Prosecco di V. Dry S. Stefano	🍷🍷	4
○	Prosecco di V. Extra Dry Giall'Oro	🍷🍷	4
○	Prosecco di V. Tranquillo La Bastia '05	🍷	4
○	Pinot Grigio Vign. Cornuda '05	🍷	4
○	Prosecco di V. Brut Quartese	🍷	4

VALEGGIO SUL MINCIO (VR)

Corte Gardoni

loc. Gardoni, 5
37067 Valeggio sul Mincio (VR)
tel. 0457950382
www.cortegardoni.it

When Gianni Piccoli moved to Valeggio sul Mincio in the early 1970s, he intended to grow apples. For a long time fruit-growing was his main activity and half of the 50-hectare property is still used for that purpose. But since 1980, Gianni's passion for the vine took over and today the whole family is involved. His sons Mattia, Stefano and Andrea work alongside their father in the winery, though they are sent off to gain experience in France every so often. The immaculate vineyards are located on gentle, gravelly, morainic hills south of Lake Garda. Corvina, rondinella and garganega grapes, those most extensively grown at Corte Gardoni, are stored in cold stores originally built for the apples before crushing, to help preserve their aromas intact. The winery aims to create fragrant products that are comparatively long-lived yet also have a supple, racy flavour. This is nicely demonstrated by the Bardolino Superiore. The 2004 is one of the most interesting versions of the lakeside DOCG, giving vibrant, succulent wild berry fruit streaked with aromatic herbs and supported by a nice edgy acidity. The corvina-based Becco Rosso 2004 is similar in style, with dense berry fruit and developing very classy spicy veins over time. We enjoyed the nicely balanced sweetness of the Custoza Passito Fenili 2004. The Bardolino and Chiaretto are both pleasantly drinkable.

●	Bardolino Sup. '04	🍷🍷	4*
●	Becco Rosso '04	🍷🍷	4*
○	Bianco di Custoza Passito Fenili '04	🍷🍷	6
⊙	Bardolino Chiaretto '05	🍷	3
●	Bardolino Le Fontane '05	🍷	3
●	Bardolino Sup. '01	🍷🍷	4
●	Bardolino Sup. '02	🍷🍷	4
●	Bardolino Sup. '03	🍷🍷	4

VERONA

Cecilia Beretta

Loc. San Felice Extra
via Belvedere, 135
37131 Verona
tel. 0458432101
www.ceciliaberetta.it

Over the years, we have grown used to a significant standard of quality, steadily maintained, from Cecilia Beretta, one of the leading wineries of the Pasqua group. But the outstanding feature we noticed this year was the ability to extend these results to the whole range, and not just the flagship bottles. As we announced in last year's edition, a further year's ageing has been good for the Amarone Terre di Cariano 2001. Its ripe fruit aromas are juicy and clearly defined, and the weighty, mouthfilling palate has hints of cocoa powder and liquorice with rigorous, elegant tannins. The Valpolicella Superiore Terre di Cariano 2003 is also very good, showing vibrant on the nose where berry fruit blends with mint and interesting hints of forest floor. The Picàie 2003, a blend of lightly raisined corvina, cabernet and merlot, has taken a confident step forward and is weightier and more scrupulous now, with a deep, generous, concentrated nose. The aromas range from ripe fruit to earthy mineral notes and there is a vibrant final hint of pencil lead. The palate shows a good balance of mouthfilling softness and austere tannins. Turning to the whites, the Soave Brignoligo 2005 is uncomplicated yet attractive. Ripe fruit and flowers on the nose, with the faint vegetal hints typical of the variety, usher in a harmonious, enjoyable palate. We also recommend the very pleasant, fresh-tasting Recioto Case Vecie.

●	Amarone della Valpolicella Cl. Terre di Cariano '01	ΥΥ	8
●	Picàie '03	🍷🍷	5
●	Valpolicella Cl. Sup. Terre di Cariano '03	🍷🍷	4*
○	Soave Cl. Brognoligo '05	🍷🍷	4
○	Recioto di Soave Case Vecie '03	🍷	5
●	Amarone della Valpolicella Cl. Terre di Cariano '99	ΥΥΥ	7
●	Amarone della Valpolicella Cl. Terre di Cariano '00	ΥΥ	7
●	Valpolicella Cl. Sup. Terre di Cariano '01	ΥΥ	4
●	Amarone della Valpolicella Cl. Terre di Cariano '98	ΥΥ	7

VERONA

F.lli Bolla

P.zza Cittadella, 3
37122 Verona
tel. 0458090911
www.bolla.it

Bolla is back in the front rank of high quality production in the Verona area. There has been some outstanding work from the estate team both in the vineyards and in the cellar but credit must also go to the less visible, but equally indispensable, efforts of Maurizio Ferri, chairman of Bolla, who has skilfully and passionately convinced the large Brown-Forman Corporation to invest in this Piazza Cittadella-based winery. Giampaolo Vaona has set up a new network from growers to bottling and the average quality is now very high indeed. Although several million bottles are produced every year, the procedures adopted for the more ambitious line as well as all the classic Veronese wines is practically the same as in a small winery. Scrupulous care in the vineyards as well as during the drying of the grapes and subsequent ageing of the wine provides us with products like the three Amarones presented today, which are able to satisfy all the cellar's price and style parameters. The simple, beautifully balanced Classico is excellent, Le Origini is the most traditional of the three and a perfect example of what an Amarone should be while Capo di Torbe is vibrant, flavoursome and extraordinarily fresh-tasting, a great territory-dedicated wine that is well worth uncorking. The Valpolicella of the same name is also excellent, as are the Soaves, Le Maddalene 2004, aged in oak, and the fresher, more vibrant Tufaie 2005.

●	Amarone della Valpolicella Cl. Capo di Torbe '03	ΥΥ	8
●	Amarone della Valpolicella Cl. Le Origini '03	ΥΥ	7
●	Valpolicella Cl. Sup. Capo di Torbe '03	ΥΥ	5
●	Amarone della Valpolicella Cl. '03	🍷🍷	7
○	Soave Cl. Sup. Le Maddalene '04	🍷🍷	4*
●	Valpolicella Cl. Sup. Le Pojane '03	🍷	4
○	Soave Cl. Tufaie '05	🍷	4
●	Valpolicella Cl. Sup. Capo di Torbe '01	ΥΥ	5
●	Amarone della Valpolicella Cl. Capo di Torbe '01	ΥΥ	8

VERONA

Giacomo Montresor
via Ca' di Cozzi, 16
37124 Verona
tel. 045913399
www.vinimontresor.it

There is an increasingly impressive range of wines from the Montresor family, who understood years ago that Veneto wine must follow a path that emphasized territory and its traditions, reinterpreting them in a modern key. So there's one very modern-style Amarone, Castelliere delle Guaiate, and another, the Cantina Privata del Fondatore, which is much more traditional. Both are of excellent and offer a cross-section of the history of this great wine. Castelliere delle Guaiate is dark in colour with vibrant ripe fruit and spicy aromas followed by a very generous, firm-structured palate where the oak makes a perceptible but not intrusive reappearance. Cantina Privata del Fondatore has a broader, more mature nose with crushed flowers, vegetal hints and aromatic herbs mingling with the overripe fruit. The palate follows the typical progression of a traditional-style Amarone. The initial impact is supported by the sweetness of the residual sugar, progression is drier and the finish almost burning. The Lugana Gran Guardia 2005 is very good, in fact one of the best of its type. The nice generous aromas are followed by a flavoursome, beautifully harmonious palate. The alluringly sweet Recioto Re Teodorico 2003 and the well-typed, tangy and drinkable Soave Capitel Alto both earned a second Glass. The Sauvignon Sansaia 2005 and the Brut Regina Nera are both well crafted.

●	Amarone della Valpolicella Cl. Castelliere delle Guaite '01	TT	8
●	Amarone della Valpolicella Cl. Cantina Privata del Fondatore '02	TT	7
●	Recioto della Valpolicella Cl. Re Teodorico '03	TT	6
○	Lugana Gran Guardia '05	TT	4
○	Soave Cl. Capitel Alto '05	TT	5
○	Sauvignon Sansaia '05	T	5
○	Regina Nera Brut	T	5
●	Amarone della Valpolicella Cl. Castelliere delle Guaite '00	YY	8
●	Amarone della Valpolicella Cl. Castelliere delle Guaite '99	YY	8

VERONA

Vigneti e Cantine Pasqua
via Belviglieri, 30
37131 Verona
tel. 0458402111
www.pasqua.it

At last, building work is finished at San Felice and now that all the products have been transferred into the extended cellar, the administration of this large winery will also leave the offices in Borgo Venezia and move here. The whole Pasqua operation will be under one roof. Remember we are talking about a group that produces just under 20,000,000 bottles a year and sheer size brings its own problems. The range of wines presented for tasting by Giorgio Pasqua and his team, with input from consultant Luca d'Attoma, was limited in quantity but very impressive in quality: one Amarone, three Valpolicellas and a corvina-based red indicating, once again, this winery's desire to remember its origins at all times, and make tradition its distinguishing feature. The Amarone Villa Borghetti 2002 has not suffered from the difficult year, but brims with vibrant aromas of cherry jam, white chocolate and spices, while the palate is tauter and better defined than we might have expected, with a dry and dynamic flavour. The two Valpolicella Sagramosos are of the same high standard, the lively 2003 giving a ripe, warm flavour and the Ripasso 2004 a very firm, austere nose, with aromas of blackberries and forest floor, and a well-structured, fresh-tasting palate. The sturdy, lively corvina-based Kòrae 2004 and the Valpolicella Villa Borghetti, with its light florality, both came close to a second Glass.

●	Amarone della Valpolicella Cl. Villa Borghetti '02	TT	7
●	Valpolicella Sup. Sagramoso '03	TT	5
●	Valpolicella Sup. Ripasso Sagramoso '04	TT	5
●	Kòrae Rosso '04	T	4
●	Valpolicella Cl. Villa Borghetti '04	T	4
●	Amarone della Valpolicella Sagramoso '00	YY	7
●	Amarone della Valpolicella Cl. Villa Borghetti '01	YY	7
●	Valpolicella Sup. Ripasso Sagramoso '02	YY	5

VERONA

Tezza
Loc. Poiano di Valpantena
via Maioli, 4
37030 Verona
tel. 045550267
www.tezzawines.it

After crossing the Illasi and Mezzane valleys from the east, you reach Valpantena, which is perhaps the least known of the three but the only one that is officially a subzone. This is a fairly wide valley with a flat floor where the thin layer of soil hides gravelly subsoil below, the ideal habitat for vines. The Tezza cousins work here with good results, devoting their efforts to the classic Valpolicella wines, which are divided into two lines according to the slightly different interpretations: the traditional Monte delle Fontane and the more modern Brolo delle Giare. The Recioto Monte delle Fontane gave a good performance. Despite the heat of 2003, the aromas are fresh and still very youthful with plenty of time ahead to mature and acquire complexity. The palate is already nicely harmonious with pervasive, perfectly integrated sweetness offset by prominent acidity. The Amarone Brolo delle Giare 2001 has generous, very ripe, evolved fruit, with a rather decadent feel from the spices and hints of iodine. This sensation is echoed on the broad, soft palate. The Valpantena Superiore Monte delle Fontane is interesting and rich in ripe fruit and spices on the nose, while the palate is firm and dynamic. The Amarone 2002 from the same line does not manage to handle the challenging year. The nose is unexciting and the palate is over-evolved.

●	Amarone della Valpolicella Valpantena Brolo delle Giare '01	▼▼	7
●	Valpolicella Valpantena Sup. Ripasso Monte delle Fontane '02	▼▼	4
●	Recioto della Valpolicella Valpantena Monte delle Fontane '03	▼▼	5
●	Valpantena Sup. Brolo delle Giare '01	▼	4
●	Amarone della Valpolicella Valpantena Monte delle Fontane '02	▼	6
●	Recioto della Valpolicella Valpantena Brolo delle Giare '02	▽▽	5
●	Amarone della Valpolicella Valpantena Brolo delle Giare '00	▽▽	7

VERONA

Cantina Sociale della Valpantena
fraz. Quinto
via Colonia Orfani di Guerra, 5b
37034 Verona
tel. 045550032
www.cantinavalpantena.it

Co-operatives like this one skilfully run by Luca Degani are always very significant for the local economy because they provide income for a wide range of members and also help maintain the good reputation of Valpolicella. If, as in this particular case, they can also keep the price list firmly under control, this is all to the good, enabling all enthusiasts to afford wines like Amarone and Recioto without scaring the bank manager. Although the range of wines produced is very broad, few wineries can offer such an impressive standard of quality. This year, the champion is Amarone Valpantena 2003, which has vibrant, approachable aromas of black cherries, plums and aromatic herbs, and a palate that is not especially complex but won us over with its harmonious, firm body and dynamic acidity. The Recioto Tesauro is almost as good. The aromas are still simple and varietal but the palate is brimming with succulent sweetness. The Amarone Falasco 2002 is fruity and approachable, with a strong element of sweetness on the palate while the Valpolicella Superiore Ripasso Falasco 2004 is more austere and well defined. The nose opens out slowly into ripe crunchy fruit to be followed by a dry, characterful palate. The non-"ripasso" Valpolicella Superiore Falasco is fresher and slimmer-bodied, while the Valpantena Ritocco is enjoyably tangy. The Corvina Falasco 2005 deserves a special mention as a very pleasant wine at an unbeatable price.

●	Amarone della Valpolicella Falasco '02	▼▼	6
●	Amarone della Valpolicella Valpantena '03	▼▼	5
●	Recioto della Valpolicella Tesauro '03	▼▼	6
●	Valpantena Ritocco '04	▼▼	4*
●	Valpolicella Sup. Falasco '04	▼▼	4*
●	Valpolicella Sup. Ripasso Falasco '04	▼▼	4*
●	Recioto della Valpolicella Valpantena '04	▼	5
○	Chardonnay Baroncino '05	▼	4
●	Corvina Falasco '05	▼	2*
○	Garganega Falasco '05	▼	3

VIDOR (TV)

ADAMI

FRAZ. COLBERTALDO
VIA ROVEDE, 27
31020 VIDOR (TV)
TEL. 0423982110
www.adamispumanti.it

The fact that Franco Adami accepted the position as chairman of the Prosecco consortium a few years ago has not deprived this winery of his input. In fact Franco and Armando seem to have increased their commitment to the local area and its features. What else are we to think of the recent purchase of vineyards in the Col San Martino area? These comprise over two hectares where the land meets the sky, clinging to gravity-defying slopes where the days are very sunny but the temperature drops at night, guaranteeing optimum ripening and thus also generous aromas. For the moment, the grapes are used in the Extra Dry and Brut versions but the brothers have not ruled out the possibility of creating a new wine specially for these grapes. The Giardino vineyard has also been slightly extended with the purchase of a new plot, which has brought about a small increase in production of the winery's most representative wine. It is once again the best wine too, the very essence of Prosecco, aromatic, light and elegant, the palate caressed by gentle fizz. All the Adami products are excellent, but particular praise goes to the two top-selling wines, the delicious, harmonious Brut Bosco di Gica and Extra Dry dei Casel. The Cartizze is silky and mouthfillingly creamy while the still wines are forthright and have lively grip. The Incrocio Manzoni 2005 offers beautifully fresh aromas.

○	Prosecco di V. Dry Vign. Giardino '05	▼▼	4*
○	Cartizze Dry	▼▼	5
○	Prosecco di V. Bosco di Gica Brut	▼▼	4
○	Prosecco di V. Extra Dry dei Casel	▼▼	4
○	Incrocio Manzoni 6.0.13 Le Portelle '05	▼	4
○	Prosecco di V. Tranquillo Giardino '05	▼	4
○	P. Frizzante '05	▼	3
○	Waldaz Brut Ris.	▼	4

VIDOR (TV)

SORELLE BRONCA

FRAZ. COLBERTALDO
VIA MARTIRI, 20
31020 VIDOR (TV)
TEL. 0423987201 - 0423985369
www.sorellebronca.com

Piero Balcon shows great determination and patience in the pursuit of his objective: to create wines that combine quality with identifiable links to the local area. These features are quite unusual in this production zone, but year by year the wines Piero presents confirm the success of his quest. The two Colli di Coneglianos from the Rua di Feletto area made a significant contribution to this result. The characterful Colli di Conegliano Rosso Ser Bele 2003, a classic blend of cabernet, merlot and marzemino, is one of the best versions ever. Despite the hot growing year, it presents a very wide range of aromas with elegant ripe red berry fruit melding into spices and fresh vegetal notes, lifted by fascinatingly deep minerality, cyclamen and forest floor. The progression on the palate is delicious, weighty and reflects the aromas well, with an even more pronounced floral sensation. Last year, we reported that release of the Colli di Conegliano Bianco Delico would be delayed in order to allow it to age longer. It was a good decision. The 2004 shows vibrant ripe apple and pear fruit, followed by a mouthfilling, tangy palate nicely backed up by the fresh, juicy fruit. Outstanding among the Spumantes are the Extra Dry Particella 68, with stylish apple and pear fruit and floral aromas, and the lively, tropical fruit Brut version.

●	Colli di Conegliano Rosso Ser Bele '03	▼▼	6
○	Colli di Conegliano Bianco Delico '04	▼▼	4*
○	Prosecco di V. Brut	▼▼	4*
○	Prosecco di V. Extra Dry Particella 68	▼▼	4*
●	Ardesco '03	▼	4
○	Prosecco di V. Extra Dry	▼	4
●	Colli di Conegliano Rosso Ser Bele '01	▽▽	6
●	Colli di Conegliano Rosso Ser Bele '02	▽▽	6
●	Colli di Conegliano Rosso Ser Bele '00	▽▽	6

VILLAGA (VI)

Piovene Porto Godi

fraz. Toara
via Villa, 14
36020 Villaga (VI)
tel. 0444885142
www.piovene.com

Every year, Tommaso Piovene discreetly, modestly proves that his is the only winery in the Colli Berici that can confidently turn its hand to the entire range of wines in the DOC zone. Although this area is prevalently suited for the production of red wines, Porto Godi's whites have always shown particular features which enable them to stand out from a crowd of otherwise anonymous wines. The truth of this is demonstrated in our analysis of the 2005 vintage, which was complicated by bad weather. The Pinot Bianco shows no adverse effects, indeed it is one of the nicest we have ever tasted, with sharply defined aromas of almonds and flowers. The one Sauvignon selection, Fostine, has textbook aromas of nettles, peaches and tropical fruit, although the palate is a little lean. The Tocai Rosso 2005 from the Riveselle vineyard enjoyed a mild year and this is evident in its intriguing complexity and relaxed, eminently drinkable palate. Do take the trouble to discover this native Italian wine. The Polveriera Rosso is slimmer in body and more supple. The star of the show this time is the Cabernet Pozzare, at its very best in the 2003 version. The oak is very nicely absorbed, yielding faint hints of spices, followed by glimpses of blackcurrants, citrus fruit, black pepper, green herbs and a salty sensation. The palate is free of vegetal sensations, with very stylishly handled ripe fruit and a lovely lingering finish.

●	Colli Berici Cabernet Vign. Pozzare '03	2 black glasses	5
○	Colli Berici Pinot Bianco Polveriera '05	2 black glasses	4*
●	Colli Berici Tocai Rosso Vign. Riveselle '05	2 black glasses	3
○	Colli Berici Sauvignon Vign. Fostine '05	1 black glass	4
●	Polveriera Rosso '05	1 black glass	4
●	Colli Berici Merlot Fra i Broli '03	2 white glasses	5
●	Colli Berici Tocai Rosso Thovara '03	2 white glasses	6
○	Sauvignon Campigie '04	2 white glasses	4

VOLPAGO DEL MONTELLO (TV)

Conte Loredan Gasparini

fraz. Venegazzù
via Martignago Alto, 23
31040 Volpago del Montello (TV)
tel. 0423870024
www.venegazzu.com

An attractive setting and proximity to the plains have made Montello a popular tourist spot over the decades, resulting in a considerable increase in the number of restaurants. But the real soul of this area is winemaking, as Conte Loredan Gasparini clearly understood when he made one of the first and best Italian Bordeaux blends. Today, the Palla family runs the winery with passionate determination and the results have once again taken the cellar to the very apex of quality. Because of the heat in 2003, the more ambitious wines did not show any peaks of quality but even so the products overall are generally very interesting indeed. Venegazzù della Casa is on top form. Cooler ageing in large wooden barrels has endowed it with wild berry and aromatic herb fragrances on the nose, and the unfavourable year is hinted at only in the somewhat over-assertive tannins. The Capo di Stato, on the other hand, is very good but has suffered more from the hot weather. The aromas are very evolved and veined with a hint of chocolate that emerges into a generous, juicy palate. The Prosecco Extra Dry is good and the Manzoni Bianco and Falconera are varietal, simple and fragrant in style.

●	Capo di Stato '03	2 black glasses	6
●	Venegazzù della Casa '03	2 black glasses	5
●	Falconera Rosso '04	1 black glass	4
○	Manzoni Bianco '05	1 black glass	4
○	Montello e Colli Asolani Prosecco Extra Dry	1 black glass	4
●	Capo di Stato '02	2 white glasses	6
●	Capo di Stato '00	2 white glasses	6
●	Venegazzù della Casa '02	2 white glasses	5

OTHER WINERIES

GIORGIO POGGI

VIA POGGI, 7
37010 AFFI (VR)
TEL. 0457236222
www.cantinepoggi.com

Poggi, in the northernmost part of the Bardolino DOC, makes an interesting chardonnay-based Garda Le Tortone with vibrant citrus and floral aromas and nicely blended oak on a firm palate. Famaloso is a pleasant blend of corvina, croatina and lightly raisined rondinella. The Bardolino is good.

○	Garda Le Tortone '03	🍷🍷	4*
●	Famaloso '01	🍷	5
●	Bardolino Sup. Campi Regi '04	🍷	4

PALADIN & PALADIN

VIA POSTUMIA, 12
30020 ANNONE VENETO (VE)
TEL. 0422768167
www.paladin.it

The Paladin brothers can be considered the ambassadors of the Lison-Pramaggiore zone, on the Adriatic in the province of Venice. Malbech Gli Aceri is a very good red which needs time in bottle and glass to express itself fully.
The Traminer and the Refosco are only a step behind.

●	Malbech Gli Aceri '02	🍷🍷	5
●	Lison-Pramaggiore Refosco P. R. '05	🍷	4
○	Traminer '05	🍷	4

TENUTA S. ANNA

LOC. LONCON
VIA MONS. P. L. ZOVATTO, 71
30020 ANNONE VENETO (VE)
TEL. 0422864511 - 0422864503

This large winery is part of the Generali group with 140 hectares of vineyards all in the Lison-Pramaggiore DOC. Winemaker Luca Zuccarello and consultant Donato Lanati have worked together to give the range a quality boost. Podere 47, a well-structured Cabernet Sauvignon, is very good.

●	Lison-Pramaggiore Podere 47 Ris. '03	🍷🍷	5
●	Lison-Pramaggiore Refosco P. R. '05	🍷	4
○	Lison-Pramaggiore Tocai Cl. '05	🍷	3*

LENOTTI

VIA S. CRISTINA, 1
37011 BARDOLINO (VR)
TEL. 0457210484
www.lenotti.com

The wide range of this Garda estate includes wines from the lake and from Valpolicella. Capo Mastro is an interesting blend of corvina and merlot with vibrant aromas and a tangy, sturdy palate. Valpolicella Le Crosare is lovely and soft while the Bardolino Le Olle is generous and enjoyable.

●	Capo Mastro '05	🍷🍷	3*
●	Valpolicella Cl. Sup. Ripasso Le Crosare '03	🍷	4
●	Bardolino Cl. Sup. Le Olle '04	🍷	4

Luigi Valetti
loc. Calmasino di Bardolino
via Pragrande, 8
37010 Bardolino (VR)
tel. 0457235075

Valetti makes wines that are flavoursome and concentrated, yet light and accessible. Try the Bardolino Superiore for its strikingly fragrant aromas and tangy palate. The Chiaretto is more approachable, as is the fresh and jolly Valpolicella. The Amarone is more challenging.

● Amarone della Valpolicella Cl. '01	🍷🍷	7
● Bardolino Cl. Sup. '04	🍷🍷	3*
⊙ Bardolino Cl. Chiaretto '05	🍷	2*
● Valpolicella Cl. '05	🍷	2*

Cantina Beato Bartolomeo da Breganze
via Roma, 100
36042 Breganze (VI)
tel. 0445873112

This co-operative has moved quality significantly forward in the Breganze area. The premium label is Bosco Grande, and the Cabernet its leading wine. It's a cabernet franc clone rich in black berry fruit and minerality with a firmly structured palate, dry flavour and a long, clear finish.

● Breganze Cabernet Sup. Bosco Grande '04	🍷🍷	4*
● Breganze Cabernet Sup. Savardo '04	🍷	4

Roeno
via Mama, 5
37020 Brentino Belluno (VR)
tel. 0457230110
www.cantinaroeno.com

Few Italian wineries can offer a sweet wine like this: late-harvested trebbiano with splashes of sauvignon, pinot grigio and chardonnay, give strikingly generous aromas and nice sweetness that meld perfectly on the palate through to a long, enthralling finish. The other products are all good.

○ Passito Cristina Roeno '03	🍷🍷	5
● Teroldego '05	🍷	3*
○ Valdadige Chardonnay '05	🍷	3*
○ Valdadige Pinot Grigio Roeno '05	🍷	4

Cambrago
loc. San Zeno
via Cambrago, 7
37030 Colognola ai Colli (VR)
tel. 0457650745 - 0456150062

The Colognola ai Colli valley may lack a precise identity but the quality of Cambrago's Soaves expresses the garganega grape and the terroir well. Cerceni has clear apple fruit and florality followed by a dry tangy flavour. The Recioto's lively exotic sensations and sweetness are good.

○ Recioto di Soave I Cerceni '03	🍷🍷	6
○ Soave Cl. I Cerceni '05	🍷🍷	4*
○ Soave Vigne Maiores '05	🍷	3

Villa Canestrari
via Danta Broglio, 2
37030 Colognola ai Colli (VR)
tel. 0457650074
www.villacanestrari.com

This traditional winery has 18 hectares of vineyards in Val d'Illasi and Soave. We liked the Valpolicella di Ripasso I Lasi with its generous overripe fruit. Its vigorous style is maintained on the palate through to the almost burning finish. The Amarone and Recioto are also enjoyable.

● Valpolicella Sup. Ripasso I Lasi '03	🍷🍷	5
● Amarone della Valpolicella Plenum '01	🍷	8
● Recioto della Valpolicella '03	🍷	6

Villa Sandi
via Erizzo, 112
31035 Crocetta del Montello (TV)
tel. 0423665033
www.villasandi.it

Villa Sandi has worked with Prosecco for years, but its most representative wine is a Bordeaux blend from merlot and cabernet, Corpore, of which about 15,000 bottles are released. Avitus is a Manzoni Bianco aged entirely in oak. The Metodo Classico Riserva 2000 is also interesting.

○ Opere Trevigiane Brut Ris. '00	🍷🍷	6
● Corpore '04	🍷🍷	6
○ Avitus '04	🍷	6
○ Cartizze	🍷	5

ALBINO ARMANI
VIA CERADELLO, 401
37020 DOLCE (VR)
TEL. 0457290033
www.albinoarmani.com

For years, Armani has been a benchmark for Valdadige winegrowers and fans of foja tonda, a forgotten grape that this winery has brought back into the spotlight. The Foja Tonda is the most striking wine with floral aromas and aromatic herbs streaked through with crunchy red berry fruit.

●	Foja Tonda Rosso '04	▼▼	4*
●	Corvara Rosso '03	▼	5
○	Valdadige Pinot Grigio Vign. Corvara '05	▼	4

MEROTTO
LOC. COL SAN MARTINO
VIA TREVISET, 86
31010 FARRA DI SOLIGO (TV)
TEL. 0438989000 - www.merotto.it

Graziano Merotto's spumante-focused winery is in Col San Martino, a hamlet near Valdobbiadene. The Cartizze is good. It's uncomplicated but faithful to its grape with aromas of pears and golden delicious apples preceding a soft, mouthfilling palate. La Primavera di Barbara is generous and juicy.

○	Prosecco di V. Dry La Primavera di Barbara	▼▼	4*
○	Cartizze	▼▼	6
○	Prosecco di V. Brut Barreta	▼	4

VALENTINA CUBI
LOC. CASTERNA, 60
37022 FUMANE (VR)
TEL. 0457725199

The gradual renovations on this estate, founded in 1970, concern the vineyards, winery buildings and cellar. The Amarone Morar is excellent, rich in appealing fruit and toasty aromas on the palate. Ripasso Arusnatico is just as good with enfolding aromas and a dry, pleasantly husky palate.

●	Amarone della Valpolicella Cl. Morar '01	▼▼	8
●	Valpolicella Cl. Sup. Ripasso Arusnatico '03	▼▼	6

DAVID STERZA
LOC. CASTERNA
VIA CASTERNA, 37
37022 FUMANE (VR)
TEL. 0457704201

Although Valpolicella is now established as a wine zone, plenty of new estates are still making their name. One such is Sterza, which obtains a sound range from its four hectares. As we wait for the Amarone and Valpolicella, we enjoyed a flavoursome, vibrant Recioto with well-judged sweetness.

●	Recioto della Valpolicella Cl. '03	▼▼	6
●	Amarone della Valpolicella Cl. '01	▽▽	7
●	Valpolicella Cl. Sup. Ripasso '03	▽▽	5

VILLA BRUNESCA
VIA SERENISSIMA, 12
31040 GORGO AL MONTICANO (TV)
TEL. 0422800026
www.villabrunesca.it

Villa Brunesca is situated in the Piave DOC at Gorgo al Monticano. The winery, with 45 hectares of vineyards, is firmly focused on quality. Merlot Vigna Mora gave an excellent performance with salty and minerally notes alongside fruity aromas and an even more impressive palate.

●	Piave Merlot V. Mora '04	▼▼	5
●	Refosco P. R. V. Olinda '04	▼	5
●	Cabernet '05	▼	4
○	Traminer '05	▼	3*

MONTE TABOR
LOC. MONTE TABOR
VIA SAMMONTE, 45
37031 ILLASI (VR)
TEL. 0457830548

This beautiful estate in eastern Illasi is owned by Milan's San Raffaele hospital and produces flavoursome, well-textured wines. The good Valpolicella has complex fresh fruit and medicinal herb aromas and a distinctive strong, dry, rigorous palate. The Amarone is more mature and mouthfilling.

●	Amarone della Valpolicella San Raffaele '00	▼▼	8
●	Valpolicella Sup. San Raffaele '04	▼▼	6
●	Valpolicella Sup. San Raffaele '03	▽▽	5

GROTTA DEL NINFEO
VIA BOSCHETTO, 6
37030 LAVAGNO (VR)
TEL. 0458980154
www.grottadelninfeo.it

Tiziano Fraccaroli's 26-hectare estate is in the hills outside the classic DOC zone. His sons Domenico and Luca have brought a breath of fresh, forward-looking air into the winery. All the products are good, especially the two Valpolicellas and the Ripasso.

● Valpolicella Sup. '03	🍷🍷	5
● Valpolicella Sup. Ripasso '03	🍷🍷	5
● Amarone della Valpolicella '02	🍷	7

ANTOLINI
VIA PROGNOL, 22
37020 MARANO DI VALPOLICELLA (VR)
TEL. 0457755351
www.antolinivini.it

Valpolicella is a special DOC because at least four different wines can be made from the same vineyard and grapes. Antolini obtains a balanced range of products in all the types, and we particularly liked the flavoursome Amarone with its very expressive fruit.

● Amarone della Valpolicella Cl. '03	🍷🍷	7
● Recioto della Valpolicella Cl. '04	🍷	6
● Valpolicella Cl. '04	🍷	4
● Valpolicella Cl. Sup. Ripasso '04	🍷	4

LUIGINO E MARCO PROVOLO
VIA SAN CASSIANO, 2
37030 MEZZANE DI SOTTO (VR)
TEL. 0458880106
www.viniprovolo.com

This winery's fairly limited range nonetheless embraces all the Valpolicella types. The most impressive, once again, is the Amarone: it is multi-layered and slow to reveal its qualities, first fruit, then aromatic herbs and finally minerals. The palate is taut and elegant.

● Amarone della Valpolicella '01	🍷🍷	7
● Valpolicella Sup. Campotorbian '02	🍷	5
● Valpolicella Sup. Gino '03	🍷	5

VILLA ERBICE
VIA VILLA, 22
37030 MEZZANE DI SOTTO (VR)
TEL. 0458880086

The Erbice family owns 15 hectares of vineyards and makes both Valpolicella and Soave wines. The Amarone is brimming with generous fruit and chocolate aromas preceding a warm, mouthfilling palate. The Soave 2004 is interesting and pleasantly husky but with a taut, dry palate.

● Amarone della Valpolicella Vign. Tremenel '01	🍷🍷	7
○ Soave Sup. Vign. Panvinio '03	🍷	4
○ Soave Sup. '04	🍷	3

LE ALBARE
VIA PERGOLA, 69
37030 MONTECCHIA DI CROSARA (VR)
TEL. 0456175131 - 0456175953
www.vignadellostefano.it

On the Italian white wine scene, there aren't so many types that capture the full depth of their terroir with complexity, austerity, appeal and character. Soave is one such wine, as Le Albare's Vigna dello Stefano amply demonstrates.

○ Soave Cl. Vigna dello Stefano '05	🍷🍷	4*
○ Soave Cl. V. Vecia '04	🍷	4

CANTINA DI MONTECCHIA
VIA ALPONE, 53
37030 MONTECCHIA DI CROSARA (VR)
TEL. 0457450094
www.cantinadimontecchia.com

Cantina di Montecchia is one of the four co-operatives in the Soave DOC. Most of the vineyards are actually in Lessinia and planted with durello vines. The two Recioto di Soaves, Colli Neri and the I Fossili, are very striking, both of them showing fragrant and uncomplicated.

○ Recioto di Soave Colli Neri '03	🍷🍷	5
○ Recioto di Soave La Bastia I Fossili '04	🍷	5

Giovanni Fattori

via S. Pertini, 21d
37032 Monteforte d'Alpone (VR)
tel. 0457460041 - 0456100973
www.fattoriandgraney.it

This pleasant winery only bottles a small proportion of the wine from its 30 hectares. Most of it is Soave, although Pinot Grigio and the owner's passion – Sauvignon – are also made. The latter was really striking with fresh, green apple-like and tropical aromas returning on a firm, spare palate.

○	Sauvignon '05	🍷🍷	3*
○	Soave Cl. '05	🍷🍷	3*
○	Pinot Grigio '05	🍷	4
○	Soave Motto Piane '05	🍷	4

Tenuta Solar

via Dante, 125
37032 Monteforte d'Alpone (VR)
tel. 0456100550

One of the most promising emerging Soave wineries is Tenuta Solar, which earned a space in the Guide on its first try. The Soaves were impressive: Superiore Le Caselle for its tangy palate, La Posta for its well-managed balance and Le Barcole for its expression of the garganega grape.

○	Soave Cl. La Posta '04	🍷🍷	4*
○	Soave Cl. Sup. Le Caselle '04	🍷🍷	4*
○	Recioto di Soave Cl. El Re '04	🍷	5
○	Soave Cl. Le Barcole '05	🍷	4

I Stefanini

via Crosara, 21
37032 Monteforte d'Alpone (VR)
tel. 0456175249

Sometimes nature works even harder than man and a less complicated wine can overtake the more ambitious versions, as has happened here. The two selections, Monte di Fice and Monte de Toni, are concentrated and complex but the Il Selese impresses even more with its integrity, freshness and tanginess.

○	Soave Cl. Il Selese '05	🍷🍷	4*
○	Soave Cl. Sup. Monte de Toni '04	🍷	4
○	Soave Cl. Sup. Monte di Fice '04	🍷	4

La Di Motte

via Callunga, 9
31045 Motta di Livenza (TV)
tel. 0422863815
www.ladimotte.it

La Di Motte makes wine in the Piave zone from 100 hectares of vines. The wide range of products includes one or two prestigious wines, one of which is Mondaresca, a blend of merlot and cabernet sauvignon with a stylish palate. The other is the flavoursome, mouthfilling Cabernet Sauvignon Jugero.

●	Mondaresca Rosso '03	🍷🍷	4*
●	Piave Cabernet Sauvignon Jugero Ris. '03	🍷🍷	4*
●	Piave Merlot '04	🍷	2*

F.lli Recchia

loc. Jago
via Ca' Bertoldi, 30
37024 Negrar (VR)
tel. 0457500584 - www.recchiavini.it

Jago is one of the most famous areas of Valpolicella and its wines are typically deep and austere. The Amarone Ca' Bertoldi is very good, showing deep but also taut and elegant on the palate. The softer, mouthfilling Valpolicella Le Muraie is just a step behind.

●	Amarone della Valpolicella Cl. Vigneto Ca' Bertoldi '01	🍷🍷	6
●	Valpolicella Cl. Sup. Ripasso Le Muraie '03	🍷	4

Tessere

loc. Santa Teresina
via Bassette, 51
30020 Noventa di Piave (VE)
tel. 0421320438

Emanuela Bincoletto has kept the family winery concentrated on quality, even if production is limited and a little unconventional. Her results are increasingly impressive. Flavio Prà has worked with the winery to create a luscious, high calibre Merlot Galiòn, which is mature and flavoursome.

●	Piave Merlot Galiòn '03	🍷🍷	4*
●	Piave Raboso Barbarigo '02	🍷	7
●	Raboso Passito Rebecca '02	🍷	6
●	Piave Cabernet Matapan '03	🍷	4

BAROLLO
VIA BELLUDI, 30
35123 PADOVA
TEL. 049650813
www.barollo.com

Despite the office address, this winery is situated between Venice and Treviso at Preganziol, on the fertile plains where there is not much grape growing activity. The Merlot is very good with generous aromas and a silky, alluringly harmonious palate. The firm-structured Pinot Grigio is also good.

● Piave Merlot '03	🍷🍷	5
○ Pinot Grigio '05	🍷🍷	4*
○ Piave Chardonnay '04	🍷	5
● Frater Rosso '05	🍷	4

FRACCAROLI
LOC. BERRA VECCHIA, 4
37019 PESCHIERA DEL GARDA (VR)
TEL. 0457550949
www.fraccarolivini.it

The DOC zone south of the Lake Garda basin has been cranking up quality and Fraccaroli wines demonstrate this with their excellent territorial character.
The most impressive is Lugana Superiore Campo Serà with spring flowers and ripe fruit on the nose and a mouthfilling, tangy palate.

○ Lugana Sup. V. Campo Serà '04	🍷🍷	4*
○ Lugana Vegne Vecie '03	🍷	4
○ Lugana Vign. Pansere '05	🍷	3
○ Lugana Brut	🍷	4

MARTINO ZANETTI
VIA CHISINI, 79
31053 PIEVE DI SOLIGO (TV)
TEL. 0438841608

The products of Martino Zanetti's winery are split across two lines: Case Bianche for more accessible, single-variety wines and Col Sandango for the more ambitious products, including the vibrant Wildbacher and the polished Bordeaux blend Camoi. The Passito is also good.

● Wildbacher Col Sandago '03	🍷🍷	6
● Camoi Col Sandago '03	🍷	5
● Merlot Case Bianche '04	🍷	4
○ Passito Bianco Col Sandago	🍷	6

TENUTA TERACREA
LOC. LISON - VIA ATTIGLIANA, 61
30026 PORTOGRUARO (VE)
TEL. 0421287041 - 0421287900
www.tenutateracrea.it

When you taste Antonio Bigai's wines, it's like going back in time. The Tocai won't settle for just aromas of fruit or fermentation but also reveals minerally, salty sensations and Mediterranean scrubland. The palate is sturdy and tangy. The tocai-heavy A Mi Manera shows greater finesse on the nose.

○ A Mi Manera '05	🍷🍷	4
○ Lison-Pramaggiore Cl. Tocai Italico '05	🍷🍷	3*
○ Malvasia '05	🍷	3

LE CARLINE
VIA CARLINE, 24
30020 PRAMAGGIORE (VE)
TEL. 0421799741
www.lecarline.com

Daniele Piccinin's winemaking philosophy is driven by elegance and close links to the terroir and the growing year. He also respect s the environment and his winery has been organic for years. Carline Rosso is very good and the verduzzo-based Dogale Passito is a step away from a second Glass.

● Carline Rosso '02	🍷🍷	5
● Lison-Pramaggiore Cabernet Franc '05	🍷	3*
○ Dogale Passito	🍷	5

ASTORIA VINI
VIA CREVADA, 44
31020 REFRONTOLO (TV)
TEL. 04236699 - 0438980463
www.astoria.it

Working with a winemaker as good as Donato Lanati is starting to yield results. Fragrant Proseccos and juicy red and white Colli di Coneglianos are coming out of the cellar. The Crevada is a dry white with perfectly blended oak, whereas Mina is a lighter, jollier version.

○ Colli di Conegliano Crevada Bianco '04	🍷🍷	4
○ Colli di Conegliano Bianco Mina '05	🍷	4

MARCATO
VIA PRANDI, 10
37030 RONCÀ (VR)
TEL. 0457460070
www.marcatovini.it

Marcato's products come from several DOCs in both Verona and Vicenza. There's a mouthfilling Cabernet Pianalto from the Colli Berici, brimming with ripe red berry fruit. The two Passitos, Durello and Recioto di Soave, are both lively and sweet, though we preferred the former.

●	Colli Berici Cabernet Pianalto Ris. '01	▼▼	7
○	Lessini Durello Passito '02	▼▼	5
○	Recioto di Soave il Duello '03	▼	5

MONTEGRANDE
VIA TORRE, 2
35030 ROVOLON (PD)
TEL. 049 5226276
www.vinimontegrande.it

The Colli Euganei renaissance has swept through Rovolon into the Montegrande winery. Rosso Vigna delle Roche gave an excellent performance, with vibrant, fresh, penetrating aromas and a taut, juicy palate. Fior d'Arancio Passito is very good, showing lively aromas and a tasty, harmonious palate.

○	Colli Euganei Fior d'Arancio Passito '03	▼▼	4*
●	Colli Euganei Rosso V. delle Roche '04	▼▼	4*

SUTTO
VIA SAN LORENZETTO, 9
31040 SALGAREDA (TV)
TEL. 0422744063
www.sutto.it

This delightful Piave-based winery has a wide range of mainly current vintage wines plus two very interesting reds to lay down. The first of these is Dogma, a Bordeaux blend full of softness and ripeness. The Merlot Riserva is more polished with mature aromas yet a palate that is taut and graceful.

●	Dogma Rosso '03	▼▼	5
●	Piave Merlot Ris. '03	▼	5
○	Pinot Grigio '05	▼	4
○	Sauvignon '05	▼	4

VILLA DAL FERRO LAZZARINI
LOC. VILLA DEL FERRO
VIA CHIESA, 23
36040 SAN GERMANO DEI BERICI (VI)
TEL. 0444868025

For many years, Villa dal Ferro was the most representative winery in Colli Berici. Today, production is lower but the passion and quality of the wines remain the same. The Massi, from merlot with some cabernet franc, is very good. The Pinot Bianco Blatià is simpler but equally satisfying.

●	Il Massi '02	▼▼	5
○	Pinot Bianco Blatià '03	▼	5
●	Cabernet Le Rive Rosse '00	▽▽	5
●	Il Massi '01	▽▽	5

IGINO ACCORDINI
VIA BOLLA, 7
37020 SAN PIETRO IN CARIANO (VR)
TEL. 0456020604
www.accordini.it

Numbers are limited here but quality is exciting. The most striking wines in this wide range are the Amarone Le Bessole and the Recioto Le Viole. The former is ripe and lively with sweet fruit and a soft flavour. The latter is fresher, fragrant and mouthfilling.

●	Amarone della Valpolicella Cl. Le Bessole '03	▼▼	8
●	Recioto della Valpolicella Cl. Le Viole '03	▼▼	8

MONTE FAUSTINO
VIA BURE ALTO
37029 SAN PIETRO IN CARIANO (VR)
TEL. 0457701651
www.montefaustino.com

The Monte Faustino winery has six hectares of vineyards and is run by brothers Fabiano, Giorgio, Massimiliano and Paolo Fornaser. The focus is on classic local wines, including a white Passito. The taut, stylish Amarone is very good. The Recioto and Valpolicella Superiore are both attractive.

●	Amarone della Valpolicella Cl. '01	▼▼	8
●	Recioto della Valpolicella Cl. '01	▼▼	6
●	Valpolicella Cl. Sup. La Traversagna '02	▼	5

Villa Giona
loc. Cengia, 8
37029 San Pietro in Cariano (VR)
tel. 0456855011
www.villagiona.it

Villa Giona is more than a hotel. It is a wine, and even more it is a challenge – to demonstrate that Valpolicella means more than just raisining. This Bordeaux blend is rich in aromas of ripe fruit, spices and tobacco with a full, rounded palate that avoids the trap of excessive softness.

● Villa Giona '03	🍷🍷	7
● Villa Giona '00	ΥΥ	7
● Villa Giona '01	ΥΥ	7

Carlo Boscaini
via Sengia
37010 Sant'Ambrogio di Valpolicella (VR)
tel. 0457731412 - www.boscainicarlo.it

This winery was founded just after the Second World War and today is run by Carlo and Mario Boscaini. The wines are made only from grapes grown on the estate's 14 hectares. The Valpolicella di Ripasso Zane is very good with tasty dried fruit and aromatic herbs on the attractive, rustic palate.

● Valpolicella Cl. Sup. Ripasso Zane '04	🍷🍷	4*
● Amarone della Valpolicella Cl. San Giorgio '01	🍷	6

Casa Geretto
via Vanoni, 3
30029 Santo Stino di Livenza (VE)
tel. 0421460253 - 0421312248
www.geretto.it

The winery is in Veneto but the Geretto family use grapes from their vineyards in Friuli's Aquileia DOC for their most ambitious wines, the Merk line. Tre Uve is a very good blend of merlot, refosco and cabernet franc in equal quantities. The Tocai has typical aromas and a good husky palate.

● Friuli Aquileia Rosso Tre Uve Merk '04	🍷🍷	5
○ Friuli Aquileia Tocai Friulano Merk '05	🍷🍷	4*

Filippi
loc. Castelcerino
via Libertà, 55
37038 Soave (VR)
tel. 0457675005 - www.cantinafilippi.it

Castelcerino is one of the finest wine areas in the Soave zone. Add to this environment-friendly vineyard management and gentle fermentation techniques, and you will see why Filippi wines have always been popular. The Soave Colli Scaligeri and the Recioto di Soave Calprea are both excellent.

○ Recioto di Soave Calprea '04	🍷🍷	5
○ Soave Colli Scaligeri Castelcerino '05	🍷🍷	3*
○ Passito Bianco Scapà '03	🍷	5

Monte del Frà
via Strada per Custoza, 35
37066 Sommacampagna (VR)
tel. 045510490
www.montedelfra.it

This large Sommacampagna winery has been on a very laudable course for some years, promoting the local wine areas and pushing up the quality of the wines. There are two very sound wine types, Bardolino and Custoza. The more ambitious Custoza selection is still searching for harmony.

● Bardolino '05	🍷🍷	3*
○ Bianco di Custoza '05	🍷🍷	3*
○ Bianco di Custoza Sup. Ca' del Magro '05	🍷	4

Albino Piona
fraz. Custoza - via Bellavista, 48
37066 Sommacampagna (VR)
tel. 045516055
www.albinopiona.it

The Piona family's wines are always dependably good. They make the classic Garda wines and also devote their attention to corvina and merlot. The firm, fragrant Corvina Campo Massimo is exciting and the Passito La Rabitta is sweet and nicely balanced. The Bardolino just missed a second Glass.

● Campo Massimo Corvina Veronese '04	🍷🍷	3*
○ Bianco di Custoza Passito La Rabitta '03	🍷	5
● Bardolino '05	🍷	2

F.LLI FABIANO
VIA VERONA, 6
37060 SONA (VR)
TEL. 0456081111
www.fabiano.it

In recent years, Fabiano has revised its range, cutting the number of bottles released and boosting quality. Vajo, made from raisined corvina, cabernet sauvignon and merlot, is a deep, nicely complex red. Lugana I Fondatori is generous and mature while Argillaia is tangily fresh-tasting.

●	Vajo '03	🍷🍷	5
○	Lugana Argillaia I Fondatori '03	🍷	4
●	Cabernet Sauvignon Intenso '04	🍷	4
○	Lugana Argillaia '05	🍷	4

LE BELLERIVE - ANGELO RUGGERI
FRAZ. SANTO STEFANO
VIA FOLLO, 26
31040 VALDOBBIADENE (TV)
TEL. 0423900235 - www.lebellerive.it

We tasted four wines here, all very representative of Prosecco di Valdobbiadene. Brut is fresh-tasting and vibrant, Extra Dry has well-judged sweetness and the lively Funer Dry has tropical fruit fragrances. Finally, the Cartizze combines explosive aromas with a classy palate.

○	Cartizze	🍷🍷	5
○	Prosecco di V. Extra Dry	🍷🍷	4*
○	Prosecco di V. Brut	🍷	4
○	Prosecco di V. Dry Funer	🍷	4

LE BERTOLE
VIA EUROPA, 20
31049 VALDOBBIADENE (TV)
TEL. 0423975332
www.lebertole.com

The wide range of wines focuses on Prosecco in all its incarnations. The most interesting is the Cartizze, with its generous, varietal aromas and beautifully integrated fizz on the palate. The Dry Spumante version is only a step behind in quality, with lovely sweet fruit. The Extra Dry is stylish.

○	Cartizze	🍷🍷	5
○	Prosecco di V. Dry Supreme	🍷🍷	4*
○	Prosecco di V. Brut	🍷	4
○	Prosecco di V. Extra Dry	🍷	3

CASA COSTE PIANE
FRAZ. SANTO STEFANO
VIA COSTE PIANE, 2
31040 VALDOBBIADENE (TV)
TEL. 0423900219

Prosecco that has undergone a second fermentation in bottle has almost vanished these days. If it is made, less interesting grapes tend to be used. But Loris Follador devotes a great deal of attention to this product. In fact, it is his best wine and accounts for the majority of his total range.

○	Prosecco di V. Frizzante Sur Lie	🍷🍷	3*
○	Prosecco di V. Extra Dry San Venanzio	🍷	4
○	Prosecco di V. Tranquillo	🍷	3

MARSURET
LOC. GUIA - VIA SPINADE, 41
31040 VALDOBBIADENE (TV)
TEL. 0423900139
www.marsuret.it

Since the 1980s, brothers Valter and Ermes Marsura have run their family winery with good results. Production focuses on Prosecco and in 2005 the great Cartizze terroir proved its class in a well-rounded, polished wine. Extra Dry is distinctive and the Dry version is complex and mouthfilling.

○	Cartizze	🍷🍷	5
○	Prosecco di V. Extra Dry	🍷🍷	4*
○	Prosecco di V. Dry Cuvée Agostino '04	🍷	4

SANTA EUROSIA
FRAZ. SAN PIETRO DI BARBOZZA
VIA DELLA CIMA, 8
31040 VALDOBBIADENE (TV)
TEL. 0423973236 - www.santaeurosia.it

Giuseppe Geronazzo is a skilled maker of sparklers with a particular talent for bottle fermentation. His wines are always striking for their elegance and length, enhanced by the stylish fizz that gracefully accompanies them. The Prosecco Dry Millesimato and the Cartizze are both excellent.

○	Prosecco di V. Dry Mill. '05	🍷🍷	4*
○	Cartizze	🍷🍷	5
○	Prosecco di V. Brut	🍷	4
○	Prosecco di V. Extra Dry	🍷	4

Tanorè
Fraz. San Pietro di Barbozza
via Mont di Cartizze, 3
31040 Valdobbiadene (TV)
tel. 0423975770 - www.tanore.it

The classic range of wines is classified according to residual sugar, starting with a tangy, fresh-tasting Brut, followed by an Extra Dry that nimbly combines acidity and sugar. The Cartizze is polished and creamy. The range is rounded off by the Millesimato, which has pronounced sweetness.

○	Cartizze	🍷🍷	5
○	Prosecco di V. Extra Dry	🍷🍷	3*
○	Prosecco di V. Dry '05	🍷	4
○	Prosecco di V. Brut	🍷	4

Giorgio Cecchetto
Fraz. Tezze di Piave
via Piave, 67
31020 Vazzola (TV)
tel. 043828598 - www.rabosopiave.com

The renewed interest in the raboso grape is due in large part to Giorgio Cecchetto. His Gelsaia is made from raisined grapes which produce a superbly soft wine. The Raboso 2002 is simpler, while the Incrocio Manzoni and the Pinot Grigio are tangy and fragrant.

●	Piave Raboso Gelsaia '03	🍷🍷	6
●	Piave Raboso '02	🍷	4
○	Incrocio Manzoni 6.0.13 '05	🍷	3
○	Piave Pinot Grigio '05	🍷	3

Vigna Roda
loc. Cortelà
via Monte Versa, 1569
35030 Vo (PD)
tel. 0499940228 - www.vignaroda.com

Gianni Strazzacappa's leading position among emerging Colli Euganei wineries is not down to the quality of his wines but also to the way they interpret the territory and growing year. In 2005, Gianni's Merlot was unable to repeat the exploits of the previous vintage but we like the Scarlatto.

●	Colli Euganei Scarlatto '04	🍷🍷	4*
○	Colli Euganei Fior d'Arancio Passito '03	🍷	5
●	Colli Euganei Merlot '05	🍷	3

Ida Agnoletti
loc. Selva del Montello
via Saccardo, 55
31040 Volpago del Montello (TV)
tel. 0423620947

The Montello area is making more people aware of its huge potential every year through its better known wineries but also thanks to smaller estates like Ida Agnolotti's. Of her two Bordeaux blends we preferred the Seneca. The Ludwy has huge potential but needs more cellar time.

●	Seneca '03	🍷🍷	4*
●	Ludwy '03	🍷	4
○	Manzoni Bianco '05	🍷	3

Case Paolin
via Madonna Mercede, 53
31040 Volpago del Montello (TV)
tel. 0423871433

The Pozzobon family has worked in the Montello area for many years. The grapes for the very interesting red Superiore San Carlo, a classic Bordeaux blend, are picked only when overripe. The Manzoni Bianco and Rosèr, a merlot and cabernet-based rosé, are simpler but fresh-tasting.

●	Montello e Colli Asolani Sup. San Carlo '03	🍷🍷	5
○	Manzoni Bianco '05	🍷	3
⊙	Rosèr '05	🍷	3

Emilio Sartor
loc. Venegazzu
via Monte Grappa, 19
31040 Volpago del Montello (TV)
tel. 0423620567 - www.vinisartor.it

Carlo and Paolo Sartor own this interesting winery in the Montello area. The Merlot is sound, mature and well defined with a succulent palate. The peppery Cabernet Franc is fresher while the international-style Campo di Prà may have scored higher but has lost its link with the territory.

●	Montello e Colli Asolani Rosso Campo del Prà '03	🍷🍷	4
●	Montello e Colli Asolani Merlot '04	🍷	2*
●	Cabernet Franc '05	🍷	2*

FRIULI VENEZIA GIULIA

The 2005 growing year was very Friulian: neither too hot nor particularly cold, and rather changeable. Early spring rain and low temperatures until the end of April slowed vegetative growth. Late flowering and then warm weather during fruit set kept yield per vine low. In July and then August, heavy rainfall led to strong canopy growth, requiring constant leaf removal and thinning in the vineyards. Luckily, meteorological conditions took a turn for the better in early September, but the good weather lasted for only a couple of weeks, which did not always allow the grapes to reach full ripeness. One or two growers decided to bring the harvest forward for fear of losing the crop, which resulted in tighter acidity and thinner wines. But in the first few weeks after vinification, it became clear that the vintage had produced excellent results, at least in the cellars that had had the courage to wait. Others paid a price, especially the wineries that had bought in a significant proportion of the fruit used. A number of aromatic or semi-aromatic varieties were on top form, starting with sauvignon and continuing with its cousin, tocai friulano, and the little traminer grown. Varieties like chardonnay, however, were yielding undistinguished wines. For red grapes, the situation was looking patchy, with early drinkers punching well below their weight. In the meantime, a number of reds from the hot, dry 2003 vintage arrived for tasting. We were hoping for bags of structure but, alcohol apart, the wines often failed to live up expectations. This was the last vintage for the name Tocai Friulano, which is due to disappear from labels on 1 April 2007. The next edition of the Guide will feature plain Friulano, the name that will be adopted for the variety in Friuli Venezia Giulia. Only wines bottled before the fateful day will carry the traditional name. The variety will still be one of Friuli's standard bearers, not least because it gives excellent results in both dry years and very wet ones, a sure sign that the vine has adapted perfectly to the territory. There are quite a few new wineries in the Guide, and among the Three Glass winners, proof that local growers are unfailingly attentive to quality. Prices in general have been adjusted only very slightly, despite the rising cost of just about everything needed for winemaking, from glass to cardboard, transport and other items, indicating that the benchmark markets – domestic, Germany, Austria and the United States – are gradually picking up.

AQUILEIA (UD)

Ca' Tullio & Sdricca di Manzano

via Beligna, 41
33051 Aquileia (UD)
tel. 0431919700
www.catullio.it

Under Paolo Calligaris, the Ca' Tullio winery is focusing and differentiating its range on uncompromisingly high levels of quality. It is no easy job, for the 33 hectares under vine in the Aquileia DOC zone have been joined by 39 more in the Colli Orientali del Friuli, whose wines are sold under the Sdricca label. The cellar stands on the Grado road, which favours a lively cellar-door trade from holidaymakers on their way to the well-known coastal resort. It should be said that public relations, often handled by Patrizia Sepulcri, are made easier by the beautiful winery building, a large restored tobacco drying facility. The Calligaris family has created a space for convivial, often themed, occasions that have enjoyed remarkable success. Husband and wife Francesco Visintin and Roberta Bassi, both oenologists, have started to employ maceration techniques that give their whites an unexpected intensity of colour. Ca' Tullio's most serious wines come from hillside plots. The Tocai Friulano stands out for its elegant, multi-faceted, fruit-led nose and a palate of red apples and pears laced with boiled sweets leading to a refreshing finish. We noted the ripe fruit and creamy banana aromas of the Pinot Grigio Casaforte, followed by exciting freshness and appreciable length. Stylish green apple aromas on the nose of the Ribolla Gialla usher in a fresh, persistent palate with flower and fruit tones. Finally, the refosco, cabernet sauvignon and merlot Patriarca d'Aquileia 2004 flaunts a combination of red fruits and silky tannins that more than justifies the price tag.

●	Friuli Aquileia Rosso Il Patriarca d'Aquileia '04	🍷🍷	4*
○	COF Pinot Grigio Casaforte Sdricca '05	🍷🍷	5
○	COF Ribolla Gialla Sdricca '05	🍷🍷	4*
○	COF Tocai Friulano Sdricca '05	🍷🍷	4*
●	COF Rosso L'Ardito Sdricca '03	🍷	5
●	COF Pignolo Sdricca '04	🍷	4
●	COF Refosco P. R. Sdricca '04	🍷	4
○	COF Tocai Friulano Casaforte Sdricca '05	🍷	5
○	Friuli Aquileia Pinot Grigio '05	🍷	3
●	Friuli Aquileia Refosco P. R. '05	🍷	3
○	Friuli Aquileia Traminer Aromatico '05	🍷	3

AQUILEIA (UD)

Giovanni Donda

via Manlio Acidinio, 4
33051 Aquileia (UD)
tel. 043191185
www.vinidonda.it

The soil of the Aquileia DOC zone often mixes clay and gravel with sand, and vegetation cover is sparse. Vines have been grown in the area since the days of Ancient Rome, which pensioned off its army commanders with a lump sum and a few plants. The countryside gravitated around Aquileia, a settlement whose commercial importance – it stood on the salt route – elevated it to the status of second most populous city in the empire. All that remains today is archaeological remains but Aquileia's winemaking tradition lives on. On the site of the former circus of Aquileia is the winery of Giovanni Donda, whose family began to build it in 1924. Giovanni tends six hectares of vines but bottles only part of his production. On hand for consultancy is a local oenologist and producer, Giorgio Bertossi. This year's most satisfying bottle was the Sauvignon, which unveils classic tomato leaf and rue, breadth and weight in the mouth and a wealth of citrus that opens out in the finish. The Pinot Grigio, too, is more impressive on the palate than the nose, thanks to fresh acidity well backed up by firm fruit. The Merlot Riserva is closed on the nose at first but the palate is more accessible. Green notes mingle with the fruit, reprising in a minor key some of the classic French interpretations.

○	Friuli Aquileia Sauvignon '05	🍷🍷	4*
○	Friuli Aquileia Pinot Grigio '05	🍷	4
●	Friuli Aquileia Merlot Ris. '04	🍷	4
○	Friuli Aquileia Chardonnay '05	🍷	4
●	Friuli Aquileia Refosco P. R. '04	🍷	4
○	Friuli Aquileia Bianco Tàlis '05		4
○	Friuli Aquileia Chardonnay '04	🍸🍸	4

BAGNARIA ARSA (UD)

Tenuta Beltrame

FRAZ. PRIVANO
LOC. ANTONINI, 4
33050 BAGNARIA ARSA (UD)
TEL. 0432923670
www.tenutabeltrame.it

As you drive from Udine to Grado, you will see a beautifully tended expanse of vines along the way. This is Tenuta Beltrame. You will find the same care and attention at the winery itself, particularly in the old cellar, which has retained the charm of its ancient features after restoration, and in the atmospheric barrique cellar. Tenuta Beltrame wines, which this year have had an image and label makeover, also reveal the same precision and style. We knew that the enterprising Cristian Beltrame had a knack with reds and his decision last year not to release the 2002 had us looking forward to what we hoped would be truly exciting 2003 and 2004 products. Cristian didn't let us down for there are three excellent red Riservas at the top of a long list of Glass-winners. We'll start with the Merlot Riserva 2003. Its impenetrable, concentrated red introduces gamey and coffee-like sensations, along with liqueur fruits and candied citrus peel. The striking thing about the Cabernet Sauvignon Riserva 2003 is the way the soft blackberry jam fruit mellows the powerful tannicity. The Tazzelenghe Riserva 2003 has a characteristically rustic, almost aggressive, varietal note on the nose before the palate relaxes into a lingering fruit finish. One very full Glass went to the Refosco 2004, which opens slowly before showing all its concentration on the palate. This is a wine to watch as it matures. From the whites, our panel enjoyed the typicity of the Tocai, the fruit salad theme of the Pinot Grigio and the restrained green notes of the Sauvignon.

●	Friuli Aquileia Cabernet Sauvignon Ris. '03	🍷🍷	4*
●	Friuli Aquileia Merlot Ris. '03	🍷🍷	4*
●	Tazzelenghe Ris. '03	🍷🍷	5
●	Friuli Aquileia Cabernet Franc '04	🍷	4
●	Friuli Aquileia Merlot '04	🍷	4
●	Friuli Aquileia Refosco P. R. '04	🍷	4
○	Friuli Aquileia Chardonnay '05	🍷	4
○	Friuli Aquileia Pinot Grigio '05	🍷	4
○	Friuli Aquileia Sauvignon '05	🍷	4
○	Friuli Aquileia Tocai Friulano '05	🍷	4
●	Friuli Aquileia Cabernet Sauvignon '04		4
○	Friuli Aquileia Pinot Bianco '05		4

BAGNARIA ARSA (UD)

Mulino delle Tolle

FRAZ. SEVEGLIANO
VIA MULINO DELLE TOLLE, 15
33050 BAGNARIA ARSA (UD)
TEL. 0432928113
www.mulinodelletolle.it

It now seems certain that the vine arrived in Aquileia straight from southern Asia in pre-Roman times and the large numbers of wine amphorae that have come to light bear eloquent witness to the area's ancient vocation for winemaking. But we also know that without human intervention, little will improve. Individual skills and ingenuity are vital to differentiate the results of one context from another. The skills of the Bertossi cousins – Giorgio, who looks after vinification, and Eliseo – who own Mulino delle Tolle, must be remarkable, given the steady improvement in the quality of their wines, underlined this year by the admission of their Malvasia 2005 to the final Three Glass selections. Despite the commitment demanded by the construction of the new cellar, the Bertossi cousins managed to present us with a wine that might never have seen oak, although a small proportion did ferment in large wood. Peach, orange and crusty bread tempt the nose and then the alluring palate shows balance and a long citrus-themed finish. Also good are the malvasia, chardonnay and sauvignon Bianco Palmade 2005, which hints at tobacco, medicinal herbs and apples, and the very varietal Sauvignon 2005, with its elegant, restrained green notes of sage and tomato leaf.

○	Friuli Aquileia Malvasia '05	🍷🍷	3*
○	Friuli Aquileia Sauvignon '05	🍷🍷	4
○	Friuli Aquileia Bianco Palmade '05	🍷🍷	4
●	Friuli Aquileia Merlot '04	🍷	3
●	Friuli Aquileia Refosco P. R. '04	🍷	4
●	Friuli Aquileia Rosso Sabellius '04	🍷	4
●	Friuli Aquileia Rosso Sabellius '01	🍷🍷	3
●	Friuli Aquileia Rosso Sabellius '03	🍷🍷	4
○	Friuli Aquileia Bianco Palmade '04	🍷🍷	3
○	Friuli Aquileia Malvasia '04	🍷🍷	3

BICINICCO (UD)

Pradio

Loc. Felettis
via Udine, 17
33050 Bicinicco (UD)
tel. 0432990123
www.pradio.it

The Grave is generous with its yields, which often militate against quality, but wineries like Pradio are steadily bringing the DOC up to speed. The Cielos spare no effort in their scrupulous attention to vineyard and cellar management, striving to reflect the character of the territory. Situated at Felettis near Bicinicco, the estate extends over 30 hectares with a total production of around 200,000 bottles, half white and half red. From the 2005 vintage, the best of the whites was the Pinot Grigio in Rose, which we awarded Two Glasses. Its colour is an intriguingly pale, almost pink, onionskin. Fresh fruit and flowers regale the nose before the soft, long and pleasantly tangy palate unfolds its length. We thought the cellar's second-best product was the Refosco dal Peduncolo Rosso Tuaro, which has come on apace since last year. An intense ruby red introduces hints of forest fruits and tobacco while roughish tannins and herbaceousness on the finish are typical of the variety. Another very decent wine is the Plui Vignis 2004, from chardonnay, pinot grigio, tocai and sauvignon. Its pale straw and tropical fruit nose complement the full, soft palate.

○	Friuli Grave Pinot Grigio In Rose '05	🍷🍷	4
○	Friuli Grave Bianco Plui Vignis '04	🍷	4
●	Friuli Grave Cabernet Sauvignon Crearo '04	🍷	4
○	Friuli Grave Pinot Grigio Priara '05	🍷	4
●	Friuli Grave Refosco P. R. Tuaro '05	🍷	4
○	Friuli Grave Sauvignon Sobaja '05	🍷	4
●	Friuli Grave Rosso Rok '01	🍸🍸	5
●	Friuli Grave Cabernet Sauvignon Crearo '02	🍸🍸	4
●	Friuli Grave Rosso Rok '03	🍸🍸	5
○	Friuli Grave Sauvignon Sobaja '03	🍸🍸	4

BUTTRIO (UD)

Livio e Claudio Buiatti

via Lippe, 25
33042 Buttrio (UD)
tel. 0432674317
www.buiattivini.it

Claudio and Viviana Buiatti were very concerned about their wines from 2005 after the vineyards were devastated last year by a disastrous hailstorm. Thankfully, Claudio's experience and the invaluable professional skills of Valdino Dust turned out an intriguing line-up of whites well worthy of the reputation of this small – eight hectares – Buttrio winery. But the biggest surprises came from the reds and the cellar's new release, Verduzzo Momon d'Aur 2005. We'll start our round-up with this, a wine obtained from mat-dried fruit. It is quite delicious, revealing varietal baked apple and candied citrus. Good depth and weight on the palate, as well as very decent complexity, take you through to a long finish. Two Glasses, then, a fine result for a newcomer. The Bordeaux blend – merlot and cabernet sauvignon – Momon Ros 2003 made a very good impression with its elegant hay, sweet spices and ripe blackberries. Impressive structure and a chocolate nuance are the Merlot 2004's distinguishing characteristics, along with beefy tannins. Striking pepper, vanilla, currant and blueberry aromas fuse in the Refosco 2004 with an elegance that the variety does not always manage to deliver. From the whites, we liked the flowery Pinot Bianco and the fruit-led Tocai, both from 2005.

●	COF Rosso Momon Ros Ris. '03	🍷🍷	5
●	COF Merlot '04	🍷🍷	4*
●	COF Refosco P. R. '04	🍷🍷	4*
○	COF Verduzzo Friulano Momon d'Aur '05	🍷🍷	5
●	COF Cabernet '04	🍷	4
○	COF Pinot Bianco '05	🍷	4
○	COF Tocai Friulano '05	🍷	4
○	COF Pinot Grigio '05		4
○	COF Sauvignon '05		4
○	COF Tocai Friulano '04	🍸🍸	4
●	COF Rosso Momon Ros Ris. '02	🍸🍸	5
○	COF Sauvignon '04	🍸🍸	4

BUTTRIO (UD)

Conte D'Attimis-Maniago

via Sottomonte, 21
33042 Buttrio (UD)
tel. 0432674027

Dynamic Alberto D'Attimis-Maniago is the man in charge of this winery in the hills at Buttrio. Not satisfied with the seriously good results he has consistently obtained in recent years, Alberto is always ready to seek out new initiatives. He has also been busy replanting many vineyards, with a distinct preference for native varieties. Among the new releases for 2006 that favourably impressed our tasters were an appealing ribolla gialla-based Spumante Charmat and a successful red from one of Friuli's historic varieties, pignolo. Another first for the Conte D'Attimis-Maniago winery, and Friuli in general, was the appearance in the national finals of the 2002 Tazzelenghe, from a notoriously difficult native grape. Our tasting notes reveal that the Pignolo needs a little fine-tuning, especially as regards the palate, but the Ribula Brut was spot-on at the first attempt, both in terms of fragrance and for the tanginess that makes this Spumante a particularly delicious wine. Excellent winemaking and well-gauged ageing have knocked the rough edges off the Tazzelenghe, bringing out the fruit, which fuses successfully with the oak-derived balsamic notes. The palate is rich, warm and chewy. The other Two Glass winners, Malvasia, Refosco and Verduzzo Tore, are all very well made. Finally, the Sauvignon is nicely fragrant, offering long sensations of tropical fruit salad.

●	COF Tazzelenghe '02	🍷🍷	6
○	COF Malvasia '05	🍷🍷	4*
●	COF Refosco P. R. '05	🍷🍷	5
○	COF Sauvignon '05	🍷🍷	4*
○	Ribula Brut	🍷🍷	4*
○	COF Verduzzo Friulano Tore delle Signore '05	🍷🍷	4*
○	COF Bianco Ronco Broilo '03	🍷	6
●	COF Pignolo '03	🍷	5
●	COF Merlot '04	🍷	4
○	COF Picolit '04	🍷	8
●	COF Tazzelenghe '01	YY	6
○	COF Picolit '03	YY	8
○	COF Verduzzo Friulano Tore delle Signore '04	YY	4

BUTTRIO (UD)

★ Girolamo Dorigo

loc. Vicinale
via del Pozzo, 5
33042 Buttrio (UD)
tel. 0432674268
www.montsclapade.com

Girolamo Dorigo has many merits. He was the first to plant Guyot-trained vines at very high densities, and to do so acquired a row-straddling tractor. He was also the first to reproduce grafts from the pignolo vines that were gradually dying out at the abbey of Rosazzo. It was at Girolamo's cellar that the truth emerged about pignolo's two varieties, one dubbed "prezzemolata" for its dissected, parsley-like leaves and the other with a five-lobed leaf: the superb qualities of the former risked being swamped by the astonishing tannicity of the latter. Girolamo's son Alessio has refocused strategy so that while the cellar continues to release its flagship bottles, it also offers a range of great-value younger products. Two of these are the outstanding, traditional-style Pinot Grigio and a surprisingly good Traminer. A special mention must also go to Dorigo Brut, a metodo classico from pinot nero and chardonnay. But now back to the top wines. Montsclapade is a blend of cabernet sauvignon and merlot. The bunches are picked when slightly overripe and stay in wood for 30 months. Manual selection of the grapes ensures the end product is complex and mouthfilling, with hints of autumn leaves and plums, as well as serious tannins. Finally, the Pignolo took our top award. Late harvesting, manual selection of the fruit, 30 months ageing in new barriques have worked in harmony to produce a concentrated, elegant wine with a delightfully intense nose and an austere palate lifted by sensations of pencil lead, plum, endless fruit and generous spiciness. A hands-down winner.

●	COF Pignolo di Buttrio '03	🍷🍷🍷	8
●	COF Rosso Montsclapade '03	🍷🍷	7
●	COF Merlot '05	🍷🍷	4
○	COF Pinot Grigio '05	🍷🍷	4
○	COF Traminer '05	🍷🍷	4
○	Dorigo Brut M. Cl.	🍷🍷	5
○	COF Ribolla Gialla '05	🍷	4
○	COF Sauvignon '05	🍷	4
●	COF Schioppettino '05	🍷	5
●	COF Pignolo di Buttrio Vign. Ronc di Juri '00	YYY	8
●	COF Pignolo di Buttrio '01	YYY	8
●	COF Rosso Montsclapade '01	YYY	7
●	COF Pignolo di Buttrio '02	YYY	8
●	COF Pignolo di Buttrio '03	YYY	8

BUTTRIO (UD)

Davino Meroi
via Stretta, 7
33042 Buttrio (UD)
tel. 0432674025

The Meroi estate is increasingly important on the Friulian premium wine scene. When you chat with Paolo Meroi, you notice how keen he is to achieve ever more ambitious results. His long-standing friendship with Enzo Pontoni of Miani means that the two cellars co-operate closely, and in fact Enzo helps Paolo make the Meroi wines. Every year, our hero adds a few hectares to the vine stock he tends. Currently, he has about 13, which give him a total of roughly 15,000 bottles. The jewel in the crown is Dominin, a merlot-based red with a dash of refosco. Its excellent quality derives from the age of the vines, which are now anything from 40 to 60 years old. The intense ruby red is flecked with purple and the complex, concentrated nose melds spice and fruit seamlessly with the balsamic notes, as befits a wine of such elegance. The lingering, beautifully weighted palate echoes the nose. Ros di Buri 2004 is equally impressive. Morello cherry and blackcurrant fragrances precede sweet tannins on the pervasive palate. This year, Meroi presented us with a superb Tocai Friulano 2004, wonderfully made from impeccably handled raw material. We found apples, white-fleshed fruits and flowers that signed off with extremely stylish almonds. We'll round off with the excellent gold-coloured Picolit 2004. Estery, disclosing figs and faint hints of cream on the nose, it gives marked candied peel on the slightly sweet palate.

● COF Rosso Dominin '02	ΥΥ	8
● COF Merlot Ros di Buri '04	ΥΥ	6
○ COF Tocai Friulano '04	ΥΥ	6
○ COF Picolit '04	ΥΥ	7
○ COF Chardonnay '04	ΥΥ	6
○ COF Verduzzo Friulano '04	ΥΥ	6
● COF Rosso Dominin '01	ΥΥ	8
● COF Rosso Ros di Buri '01	ΥΥ	6
○ COF Tocai Friulano '02	ΥΥ	6
○ COF Chardonnay '03	ΥΥ	7
○ COF Tocai Friulano '03	ΥΥ	6
○ COF Picolit '03	ΥΥ	7

BUTTRIO (UD)

★ Miani
via Peruzzi, 10
33042 Buttrio (UD)
tel. 0432674327

Enzo Pontoni is a man who conveys a distinct sense of Friulianness. It's hard to pin down, but if you ever get the chance to chat with him, you'd agree. Enzo may have one or two rough edges, but you can see how thrilled he is as he listens to compliments on the quality he has achieved with his Refosco Calvari 2002, one of the most astonishing wines we were privileged to taste this year. He told us that using old-fashioned winemaking techniques was giving him excellent results and we were not going to contradict him: we gave this marvellous wine Three well-deserved Glasses. Fantastically complex, chewy and sumptuously rich, Calvari somehow manages to combine power with irresistible drinkability. Tar and liquorice mingle in the glass with abundant spice and ripe red fruit to tell you at once that this is a very superior red. There were two Sauvignons from the 2004 vintage. They are made the same way but the fruit comes from different vineyards, both named after the families that once farmed them. Sauvignon Banel has upfront aromas of peach and ripe fruit that follow through powerfully on the palate. Much the same can be said of the Sauvignon Saurint, which has very stylish sage, peach and flowers. It will not be easy to find these wines in the usual distribution channels. Very little Calvari in particular is available. But those lucky wine lovers who do find a bottle will remember it for a very long time.

● Calvari '02	ΥΥΥ	8
○ COF Sauvignon Banel '04	ΥΥ	8
○ COF Sauvignon Saurint '04	ΥΥ	8
○ COF Tocai Friulano '00	ΥΥΥ	7
● COF Merlot '02	ΥΥΥ	8
● COF Merlot '94	ΥΥΥ	6
● COF Rosso '96	ΥΥΥ	8
○ COF Sauvignon '96	ΥΥΥ	6
○ COF Bianco '97	ΥΥΥ	7
● COF Rosso '97	ΥΥΥ	8
● COF Merlot '98	ΥΥΥ	8
● COF Merlot '99	ΥΥΥ	8

BUTTRIO (UD)

FLAVIO PONTONI
VIA PERUZZI, 8
33042 BUTTRIO (UD)
TEL. 0432674352
www.pontoni.it

Flavio Pontoni's small winery was founded in 1904 when his grandfather Luigi signed a sharecropping contract for the Morpurgo family vineyards. Viticulture and winemaking continued when his son Giuseppe took over and now Flavio is the third generation of Pontonis to tend the vines. There are five hectares, one of which is leased, and they yield an annual production of around 30,000 bottles. Flavio's consultant oenologist is Giovanni Munisso and he bottles thanks to Giuseppe Lipari's mobile unit from the Centro di riferimento eonologico. The small cellar and its miscellany of containers may not look impressive but when you taste the wines, you soon realize just how good they are. The Chardonnay offers pineapple and citrus fruits then a broad, intriguing palate, gaining momentum as the wine opens up. Elegant violets tinged with lavender characterize both nose and palate of the Malvasia. The Tocai Friulano is remarkably well-balanced, intense, showing stylish and fruit-forward, especially on the lingering finish. A touch of acidity thins out the Sauvignon, knocking a few marks off, but the generous elderflower aromas are very elegant.

○ COF Chardonnay '05	🍷🍷	3*
○ COF Malvasia Istriana '05	🍷🍷	3*
○ COF Tocai Friulano '05	🍷🍷	3*
● COF Merlot '04	🍷	3
● COF Cabernet Franc '05	🍷	4
○ COF Picolit '05	🍷	6
○ COF Pinot Grigio '05	🍷	3
○ COF Sauvignon '05	🍷	4
○ COF Verduzzo Friulano '05	🍷	4
○ COF Pinot Grigio '04	YY	3

CAPRIVA DEL FRIULI (GO)

RONCÙS
VIA MAZZINI, 26
34070 CAPRIVA DEL FRIULI (GO)
TEL. 0481809349
www.roncus.it

The working partnership that saw Marco Perco, Gabriella De Marco and Loris Micelli managing the Roncùs winery together for a couple of years has been amicably broken up. Now Marco Pera is again running the 12-hectare estate on the Capriva hillsides on his own. There is no denying that this wine enterprise has an original range and lots of personality, deriving from its owner's approach to farming and oenology. Marco has opted to go for greater complexity by delaying release of his whites for a year, a difficult decision that has borne fruit. As a great believer in territory, Marco aims to make wines that will increase awareness of the Collio around the world, so he has flanked his complex, much-lauded Vecchie Vigne 2003 with a Collio Bianco 2004 from young tocai, sauvignon and pinot grigio vines. The wine is fresh and flowery with marked minerality and a citrus note that lingers on the back palate. We liked this debut edition very much. The Bianco Vecchie Vigne is very different. A blend of malvasia, tocai and ribolla, it has a broad swath of aromatics, which range from peach tea to vanilla, banana, wisteria and ripe melon and follow through on the palate to the attractively flavoursome finish. Also excellent are the elegant apple-themed Pinot Bianco 2004 and the buttery Tocai 2004 with its rue and williams pears.

○ Collio Bianco Vecchie Vigne '03	🍷🍷	6
○ Collio Bianco '04	🍷🍷	5
○ Pinot Bianco '04	🍷🍷	5
○ Collio Tocai Friulano '04	🍷🍷	5
○ Sauvignon '04	🍷	5
● Val di Miez '03	🍷	6
○ Roncùs Bianco Vecchie Vigne '01	YYY	6
○ Collio Bianco Vecchie Vigne '02	YY	6
○ Roncùs Bianco Vecchie Vigne '99	YY	6
○ Collio Pinot Bianco '03	YY	5
○ Collio Tocai Friulano '03	YY	5

CAPRIVA DEL FRIULI (GO)

Russiz Superiore

via Russiz, 7
34070 Capriva del Friuli (GO)
tel. 048199164
www.marcofelluga.it

Roberto Felluga, Marco's son, often observes that "wine is like a work of literature, or a painting, or music. It can express and communicate emotions and manages to transmit not just colour, fragrance and flavour but also the sensitivity, knowledge and labour of those who interpret it". Russiz Superiore wines certainly express quality, balance, elegance, respect for the variety and consequently for the territory, all attributes of the Felluga family itself. The Sauvignon 2005 adds a solar dimension of citrus and tropical fruit sensations as well as typicity in refreshing hints of tomato leaf and sage. A full, rich palate echoes these perceptions beautifully, rounding off with tempting tanginess for Three resounding Glasses. Bianco Coldisôre 2004 is a successful blend of pinot bianco, tocai, sauvignon and ribolla gialla that sets out its stall with intense petits fours, banana and apple. It holds up well in the mouth to a minerally finish that is gratifyingly refreshing. Another Russiz Superiore flagship is the classic Bordeaux blend Rosso degli Orzoni. The 2002 has finesse, complexity and staying power, not to mention beefy tannins. From the rest of the list, we would point out the upfront, well-rounded Tocai 2005, the intense fruit of the Merlot 2003, the elegantly varietal Cabernet Franc 2003 and the typicity of the Pinot Bianco 2005.

○	Collio Sauvignon '05	🍷🍷🍷	6
○	Collio Bianco Coldisôre '04	🍷🍷	6
●	Collio Rosso Ris. degli Orzoni '02	🍷🍷	8
●	Collio Cabernet Franc '03	🍷🍷	6
●	Collio Merlot '03	🍷🍷	6
○	Collio Pinot Bianco '05	🍷🍷	6
○	Collio Tocai Friulano '05	🍷🍷	6
○	Collio Bianco Russiz Disôre '00	YYY	5
○	Collio Bianco Russiz Disôre '01	YYY	6
○	Collio Sauvignon '04	YYY	6
●	Collio Rosso Ris. degli Orzoni '93	YYY	6
●	Collio Rosso Ris. degli Orzoni '94	YYY	7
○	Collio Sauvignon '98	YYY	5
○	Collio Pinot Bianco '03	YY	5

CAPRIVA DEL FRIULI (GO)

★ Schiopetto

via Palazzo Arcivescovile, 1
34070 Capriva del Friuli (GO)
tel. 048180332
www.schiopetto.it

It is no easy thing to inherit the name and legacy of a man like Mario Schiopetto, perhaps the most influential wine man in Friuli's oenological history. Comparison of present and past is unceasing and the tiniest glitch or unlucky incident is enough to attract the unwelcome attentions of those who fail to understand that time passes and the world moves on. But Mario's children, Maria Angela, Carlo and Giorgio, are doing their utmost to preserve, and if possible enhance, the Schiopetto winery's image. Maria Angela looks after administration, Carlo takes care of marketing and Giorgio manages vineyards and cellar. The trio has plenty of serious support, in the shape of pruning consultant Marco Simonit and Donato Lanati for red winemaking. Yet something failed to click during the past growing year. Perhaps the fear of imminent rain pushed the team into harvesting too early. Whatever the case, a couple of Schiopetto classics, Tocai Friulano and Sauvignon, are punching well below their weight. But the Mario Schiopetto Bianco, made with chardonnay from the Colli Orientali and tocai from the Collio is as outstanding as ever. Intense, elegant ripe apple and pear introduce an equally sumptuous, warm palate whose weight never falters. The seriously good Podere dei Blumeri 2003, a complex, concentrated blend of merlot, cabernet sauvignon and refosco, reveals beautifully managed tannins. Finally, the merlot, cabernet franc and cabernet sauvignon Rivarossa 2004 also has magnificent structure but is a little cramped by its tannins.

○	Mario Schiopetto Bianco '05	🍷🍷	6
●	Podere dei Blumeri Rosso '03	🍷🍷	6
●	Rivarossa '04	🍷🍷	5
○	Blanc des Rosis '05	🍷🍷	5
○	Collio Pinot Bianco '05	🍷🍷	5
○	Collio Pinot Grigio '05	🍷	5
○	Collio Sauvignon '05	🍷	5
○	Collio Tocai Friulano '05	🍷	5
○	Collio Pinot Bianco '00	YYY	5
○	Collio Tocai Friulano '00	YYY	5
○	Mario Schiopetto Bianco '02	YYY	6
○	Mario Schiopetto Bianco '03	YYY	6
○	Blanc des Rosis '04	YY	5
○	Collio Tocai Friulano '04	YY	5

CAPRIVA DEL FRIULI (GO)

CASTELLO DI SPESSA

VIA SPESSA, 1
34070 CAPRIVA DEL FRIULI (GO)
TEL. 0481639914 - 0481808124
www.paliwines.com

Sample tastings in late spring in the attentive and of course interested presence of owner Lorenzo Pali had hinted that great things were to come when Castello di Spessa sent its wines to the Guide's panel. At the original tasting were estate oenologist Domenico Lovat and consultant Gianni Menotti, but agronomist Marco Simonit was unable to attend. Together they make up a group that has worked in synergy to manage the 30 hectares, located around the estate's ageing cellar, to the best possible effect. Ageing, by the way, is carried out in a former military bunker, excavated between the two world wars and used by the various armies that have passed through the area. Now it has found more peaceful employment and does sterling work preserving Castello di Spessa's finest wines. The well-appointed rooms of the castle supplement accommodation at the neighbouring hotel for the recently opened golf course. On the wine front, the best of the whites is a superb Tocai Friulano with an uncompromising nose of pears, almond milk and rue. Elegant in the mouth, it unveils great density and concentration, lifted by hints of citrus and baked pears to end with astonishing persistence. A Three Glass wine. Sauvignon Segrè tempts the nose with gentle elderflower, sandalwood and candied citrus peel, leading into a structured, complex yet tight-knit palate with buttery fullness and a citrus theme. The close-knit weave, complexity and faint tarry note of the Merlot Torriani 2004 tell you that this is a wine that will cellar comfortably. To round off, the Pinot Grigio flaunts elegant tropical fruit.

○	Collio Tocai Friulano '05	🍷🍷🍷	5
●	Collio Merlot Torriani '02	🍷🍷	6
○	Collio Pinot Grigio '05	🍷🍷	5
○	Collio Sauvignon '05	🍷🍷	5
○	Collio Sauvignon Segrè '05	🍷🍷	6
○	Collio Pinot Bianco '05	🍷🍷	5
○	Collio Pinot Bianco di Santarosa '03	🍷🍷	5
○	Collio Ribolla Gialla '05	🍷🍷	5
●	Collio Rosso Conte di Spessa '02	🍷🍷	6
●	Collio Pinot Nero Casanova '03	🍷	6
○	Collio Pinot Bianco '01	(🍷🍷🍷)	4
○	Collio Sauvignon Segrè '03	(🍷🍷🍷)	6
○	Collio Sauvignon Segrè '04	(🍷🍷)	6

CAPRIVA DEL FRIULI (GO)

GESTIONI AGRICOLE VIDUSSI

VIA SPESSA, 18
34070 CAPRIVA DEL FRIULI (GO)
TEL. 048180072
www.vinimontresor.it

The hollow of Capriva where most of the Vidussi vines are located enjoys particularly favourable conditions for growing grapes. With some minor local differences, the other vineyards at Croce Alta at Pradis, near Cormons, and Ipplis, in the Colli Orientali del Friuli, are also excellently aspected on good vine-growing soil. It is these factors that explain the very high quality level of the Vidussi cellar's wines. Since 2000, the Verona-based Montresor family has managed the Vidussi vine stock, distributing much of its output from the Colli Orientali under the Borgo di Fradis label. Winemaking is carried out under the watchful eye of Luigini De Giuseppe, whose skills are also appreciated by the several local growers for whom he consults. Last year, it was the Tocai Friulano Croce Alta that went forward to the national finals but this time we chose the native red Schioppettino 2004 for the honour. A nose of sweet red fruit and spice ushers in a palate that reveals overripeness and sensation of softness on entry before opening onto very varietal peppery notes and a finish perked up by bracingly refreshing tannins. Typical tomato leaf and elderflower characterize the nose of the Sauvignon, which has a sweet, complex palate of citrus and, again, tomato leaf. Finally, the only moderately sweet Picolit Soreli a Mont faithfully reflects the variety's profile, proffering baked apple-like aromas.

●	COF Schioppettino Borgo di Fradis '04	🍷🍷	5
○	Collio Sauvignon '05	🍷🍷	4
○	COF Picolit Soreli a Mont '05	🍷🍷	5
●	Collio Rosso Are di Miute '04	🍷	5
○	Collio Chardonnay '05	🍷	4
○	Collio Malvasia '05	🍷	4
○	Collio Pinot Grigio '05	🍷	4
○	Collio Bianco Ronchi di Ravéz '05	🍷	6
○	Collio Tocai Friulano Croce Alta '05	🍷	4
○	Collio Traminer Aromatico '05	🍷	4

CAPRIVA DEL FRIULI (GO)

★ VILLA RUSSIZ
VIA RUSSIZ, 6
34070 CAPRIVA DEL FRIULI (GO)
TEL. 048180047
www.villarussiz.it

Villa Russiz has a noble history, having been founded after the Great War when Gräfin (Countess) Elvine von Zahoni decided to return to Austria. She was the widow of Count Théodore de La Tour en Voivre, a French nobleman who in the mid 19th century introduced into Friuli vine types such as merlot and the cabernets, not grown in the Collio at that time. The estate was entrusted to Adele Cerruti, a benefactress who had set up an orphanage. When she died, the property remained in public hands and today, as in the past, income from farming – wine, fruit and cereal crops – maintains a small community of nuns who look after children from disadvantaged homes. For some years, the foundation's president, Silvano Stefanutti, and estate manager Gianni Menotti have been working in perfect synergy. Sauvignon de La Tour, dedicated to the memory of Count Théodore, stands out from the other great wines in the range, as it has in past vintages. A complex, close-woven nose of attractive citrus, tomato leaf and peach is followed up by breadth and freshness on the fruit-forward, lazily lingering palate. This is a Three Glass wine with character. The Tocai Friulano has pear-like tones and signs off with almond milk on the back palate. All of Pinot Bianco's trademark elegance comes through in the Villa Russiz version of a wine that most consumers tend to underrate. Rich, substantial fruit quickly reins in the oak of the Chardonnay Gräfin de La Tour 2004 and the Merlot Graf de La Tour 2003 i s as good as it has always been in recent vintages. The rest of the list is well up to snuff.

○ Collio Sauvignon de La Tour '05	TTT	6
● Collio Merlot Graf de La Tour '03	TT	7
○ Collio Chardonnay Gräfin de La Tour '04	TT	6
○ Collio Pinot Bianco '05	TT	5
○ Collio Tocai Friulano '05	TT	5
● Collio Cabernet '04	TT	5
● Collio Merlot '04	TT	5
○ Collio Malvasia Istriana '05	TT	5
○ Collio Pinot Grigio '05	TT	5
○ Collio Ribolla Gialla '05	TT	5
○ Collio Sauvignon '05	TT	5
○ Collio Chardonnay Gräfin de La Tour '02	YYY	6
○ Collio Sauvignon de La Tour '02	YYY	6

CARLINO (UD)

CAV. EMIRO BORTOLUSSO
VIA OLTREGORGO, 10
33050 CARLINO (UD)
TEL. 043167596
www.bortolusso.it

The Bortolusso winery continues to be the best of the bunch in Friuli Annia, the region's smallest and most recent DOC zone. Brother and sister Sergio and Clara are serious about the way they run their 50 hectares under vine. The cellar has been renovated again and given a capacious warehousing facility that enables winemaking to go ahead in appropriate spaces. The Bortolussos can call on consultancy from Luigino De Giuseppe, an oenologist who works with a number of estates in Friuli and further afield. We should also point out that Sergio and Clara are immensely hospitable: visitors are able to taste the wide range of wines in a relaxed family atmosphere. The Malvasia 2005 may not have been as good as recent editions but the elegant Pinot Bianco, with its rich fruit-led aromatics offers good weight on the palate and refreshing length, is on form. Also up to par is the Chardonnay. Bright in colour and subtly deep on the nose, it is elegant and fat yet brightly fresh-tasting. Pear and almond are the Tocai Friulano's keynotes while the Pinot Grigio offers breadth of fruit and marked acidity. Finally, the Refosco is surprisingly complexity on both nose and palate.

○ Friuli Annia Pinot Bianco '05	TT	3*
○ Friuli Annia Chardonnay '05	TT	3*
○ Friuli Annia Malvasia '05	T	3
○ Friuli Annia Pinot Grigio '05	T	3
● Friuli Annia Refosco P. R. '05	T	3
○ Friuli Annia Tocai Friulano '05	T	3
● Friuli Annia Merlot '05		3
○ Friuli Annia Malvasia '04	YY	3
○ Friuli Annia Pinot Bianco '04	YY	3
○ Friuli Annia Tocai Friulano '04	YY	3
○ Friuli Annia Chardonnay '05	YY	3

CERVIGNANO DEL FRIULI (UD)

CA' BOLANI
VIA CA' BOLANI, 2
33052 CERVIGNANO DEL FRIULI (UD)
TEL. 043132670 - 043130904
www.cabolani.it

The Zonin family arrived in Friuli about 35 years ago and since then this estate has been turned inside out. Without doubt, Ca' Bolani is the region's largest wine property, extending over 550 hectares under vine. Tenuta Ca' Bolani comprises three separate vineyards, Ca' Bolani, Molin di Ponte and Ca' Vescovo, located in the Aquileia DOC in the municipalities of Cervignano del Friuli, Terzo di Aquileia and Strassoldo. Substantial investment has brought about the replanting of the vine stock and greater attention to hospitality facilities. During the week, the estate can be toured by bicycle or jeep starting from the vineyard and ending at the cellar, where the entire production process is explained. Visitors are given a guided tasting and much useful information on the world of wine. This year, Marco Rabino was appointed cellar manager and oenologist. The Pinot Bianco 2005 and Pinot Grigio 2005 were the wines that caught our tasters' attention. Spring flowers, peach and lingering apple on the Pinot Bianco's palate mirror the nose satisfyingly whereas its partner offers flowers and spice on the nose and a fresh, tangy palate. We were hoping for a little more from the very pleasant Opimio 2004, a 50-50 blend of tocai friulano and chardonnay. The rest of the range drinks beautifully.

○ Friuli Aquileia Pinot Bianco '05	🍷🍷	4*
○ Friuli Aquileia Pinot Grigio '05	🍷🍷	4*
● Friuli Aquileia Cabernet Franc '04	🍷	4
● Friuli Aquileia Refosco P. R. '04	🍷	4
○ Opimio Gianni Vineyards '04	🍷	4
○ Friuli Aquileia Sauvignon '05	🍷	4
○ Friuli Aquileia Sauvignon Tamànis Gianni Vineyards '05	🍷	4
○ Friuli Aquileia Tocai Friulano '05	🍷	4
○ Friuli Aquileia Pinot Bianco '04	🍷🍷 (outline)	4
○ Friuli Aquileia Pinot Grigio '04	🍷🍷 (outline)	4
○ Friuli Aquileia Sauvignon '04	🍷🍷 (outline)	4

CHIOPRIS VISCONE (UD)

VILLA CHIOPRIS
LOC. VISCONE
33048 CHIOPRIS VISCONE (UD)
TEL. 0432757173
www.livon.it

Villa Chiopris was set up recently – in 1992 – and is one of the jewels in the crown of brothers Tonino and Valneo Livon. The 110 hectares yield the fruit for almost half a million bottles each year. All the wines are released in serious numbers and are easy to find in the shops. The vine stock has been completely replanted to quality-focused criteria but investment has gone beyond the vineyards to include some of the large buildings that belonged to the previous estate. Two of these have been converted to create a stunning agriturismo complex by restoring the best of the previous buildings' ceilings, fireplaces and floors. Set among the tall trees of the estate's generous parkland, the complex is a stone's throw from the old cellar, which has also been carefully restored. This year's wines performed marvellously, particularly if we remember the heavy rain that hampered operations during harvesting. Freshness on the nose of the Chardonnay is dominated by distinct green apple before the palate unveils unexpected substance and exciting length. Bell pepper dominates the Cabernet Sauvignon but it is still a very drinkable, well-made wine. Outstanding nose-palate consistency and attractive fruit aromas characterize the Pinot Grigio.

○ Friuli Grave Chardonnay '05	🍷🍷	4*
● Friuli Grave Cabernet Sauvignon '05	🍷	4
○ Friuli Grave Pinot Grigio '05	🍷	4
○ Friuli Grave Tocai Friulano '05	🍷	4
● Friuli Grave Merlot '05		4
○ Friuli Grave Sauvignon '05		4
● Friuli Grave Merlot '03	🍷🍷 (outline)	4
○ Friuli Grave Sauvignon '04	🍷🍷 (outline)	4

CIVIDALE DEL FRIULI (UD)

DAL FARI

LOC. GAGLIANO
VIA DARNAZZACCO, 44/2
33100 CIVIDALE DEL FRIULI (UD)
TEL. 0432731219 - 0432706726
www.dalfari.it

This will be the last profile for the Dal Fari estate, which will no longer appear in the Guide. The cellar founded by Renzo Toffolutti and his wife Laura Largajolli was purchased recently by the Bastianich group, which already owns a major wine estate at Premariacco. The 2006 harvest was overseen by oenologist Valentino Giurato in collaboration with Emilio Del Medico. As it turned out, the departing owners left in style, uncorking for us a superb range of wines starting with a Tocai 2005 that puts the accent on varietal typicity. Sensation on nose and palate are very well-defined, revealing almonds, crusty bread and peach. The Chardonnay Etichetta Oro 2004 has yet to absorb the last of its oak but can still flaunt attractive citrus that mingles with butter and vanilla. In contrast, the standard-label Chardonnay is fresher and readier for the corkscrew, with perky supporting acidity. Bianco delle Grazie 2004 is a blend of chardonnay, sauvignon, tocai and riesling renano that presents flower and fruit aromas suggesting pear and white peach, signing off with a very minerally finish. The williams pear and gunflint Pinot Grigio is decent and the aromas of the Merlot 2003 promise well. Generous cinchona, mulberry, black cherry jam, chocolate and coffee tempt the nose but the tannins on the front palate are a little too incisive. Power is the keynote of the Cabernet 2004, which has a rich nose of leather, cocoa powder and bell peppers followed up by good development and structure on the palate.

●	COF Merlot '03	🍷🍷	4
○	COF Bianco delle Grazie '04	🍷🍷	4
●	COF Cabernet '04	🍷🍷	4
○	COF Chardonnay Et. Oro '04	🍷🍷	4
○	COF Chardonnay '05	🍷🍷	4
○	COF Pinot Grigio '05	🍷🍷	4
○	COF Tocai Friulano '05	🍷🍷	4
●	COF Schioppettino Rutilium '04	🍷	6
●	COF Schioppettino Rutilium '02	🍷🍷 (white)	6
○	COF Tocai Friulano '03	🍷🍷 (white)	4
○	COF Bianco delle Grazie '03	🍷🍷 (white)	4
○	COF Chardonnay Et. Oro '03	🍷🍷 (white)	4

CIVIDALE DEL FRIULI (UD)

MOSCHIONI

LOC. GAGLIANO
VIA DORIA, 30
33043 CIVIDALE DEL FRIULI (UD)
TEL. 0432730210

When Michele Moschioni joined his father in 1987, the estate was growing equal quantities of white and red grapes. Since then, there has been a radical change: picolit apart, all the vine stock now comprises red varieties. Michele wanted to focus especially on native varieties such as pignolo, refosco, schioppettino and tazzelenghe. He does also have a couple of international grapes, merlot and cabernet sauvignon, which go into the blends. The Moschionis have 13 hectares under vine, which yield 30-35,000 bottles a year. Ruthless thinning keeps the yield per hectare below 40 quintals a hectare and then mat-drying of part of the harvest for ten days or so pushes the yield in hectolitres even lower. The Moschionis threw out pesticides and insecticides years ago and cultivated yeasts went the same way. Natural vinification concludes when the wines go into bottle unfiltered, as all the labels now clearly state. Top of the range is Rosso Celtico 2003, a 50-50 blend of merlot and cabernet sauvignon. It could be the slightly higher yield of one kilogram per vine that gives this wine its elegance and suppleness without detracting from the close-knit weave or concentrated fruit with their hint of austerity. Overripeness is more evident in the Pignolo than the Schioppettino but both are impressively substantial native-grape wines.

●	COF Pignolo Non Filtrato '03	🍷🍷	8
●	COF Rosso Celtico Non Filtrato '03	🍷🍷	6
●	COF Schioppettino Non Filtrato '03	🍷🍷	7
●	COF Rosso Reâl Non Filtrato '03	🍷🍷	6
●	COF Refosco P. R. Non Filtrato '03		5
●	COF Rosso Celtico '00	🍷🍷 (white)	6
●	COF Rosso Celtico '01	🍷🍷 (white)	6
●	COF Rosso Celtico '02	🍷🍷 (white)	6
●	COF Schioppettino '02	🍷🍷 (white)	7
●	COF Pignolo '02	🍷🍷 (white)	8
●	COF Rosso Reâl '02	🍷🍷 (white)	6

CIVIDALE DEL FRIULI (UD)

Paolo Rodaro
fraz. Spessa
via Cormons, 60
33040 Cividale del Friuli (UD)
tel. 0432716066

Eclectic extrovert Paolo Rodaro is now one of the leading figures in Friulian wine. His determination has taken the Rodaro winery well up the scale in terms of both quality and quantity so that today Paolo works 45 hectares under vine to produce about 250,000 bottles a year. This year, the wines from the extensive range that caught our eye were the Refosco dal Peduncolo Rosso Romain 2003 and the Picolit 2004. The Romain is made to an ancient technique. In the 16th century, nobles from the Bosco Romagno area used to pick their grapes and leave them for about a month on mats in the loft. Paolo attempts to reproduce that wine in a modern idiom, obtaining an intense ruby red nectar with complex spice, ripe red fruit and mulberries that return on the palate, encouraged by the evident part-drying. This is a great wine and we gave it Three Glasses. The Picolit 2004 is almost as impressive. Prominent but not aggressive crusty bread and yeasty notes regale the nose before the palate unveils marmalade, a rich concentration of citrus, good thrust and superb overall elegance. Paolo's other sweet wine is Verduzzo Friulano Pra Zenar, which features distinct dried figs and jam. Ronc 2004 is a blend of pinot bianco and chardonnay nuanced with confectioner's cream and ripe fruit. And the rest of the range is consistently good, too.

●	COF Refosco P. R. Romain '03	🍷🍷🍷	7
○	COF Picolit '04	🍷🍷	7
○	COF Verduzzo Friulano Pra Zenar '04	🍷🍷	6
○	Ronc '04	🍷🍷	4
○	COF Ribolla Gialla Romain '05	🍷🍷	4
○	COF Sauvignon '05	🍷	4
○	COF Tocai Friulano '05	🍷	4
●	COF Schioppettino Romain '04	🍷	6
○	Ronc '00	🍸🍸🍸	4
○	COF Sauvignon Bosc Romain '96	🍸🍸🍸	5
○	COF Picolit '02	🍸🍸	7
●	COF Schioppettino Romain '02	🍸🍸	6

CIVIDALE DEL FRIULI (UD)

Giordano Sirch
via Fornalis, 277
33043 Cividale del Friuli (UD)
tel. 0432709835

Giordano Sirch, who farms on the municipal border between Cividale and Prepotto, has been bottling for only five years. He started out with 10,000 units and has now reached 50,000. Giordano has six hectares, to which he adds a further two hectares he has leased. After having the opportunity to taste a couple of his wines last year, we asked Giordano for a few bottles for the Guide: these earned the fantastic results in the table below. Of course, our heroes are no strangers to wine, although one of Giordano's sons, Luca, only joined the family farm four years ago. But Luca's great good fortune is to have at his side his brother Pierpaolo, one of Italy's top fruitmakers, and Alessio Dorigo, the oenologist who has been the revelation of recent years. The varieties grown are tocai friulano, ribolla gialla, pinot grigio and sauvignon, vinified exclusively in steel. Pierpaolo also buys in locally grown from old vines to bring out the sensory characteristics that the territory imparts. The citrussy Tocai Friulano 2005 has intensity and breadth on the nose. Almost soft on entry, the palate follows candied grapefruit and citrus with concentrated, lingering pear. The Pinot Grigio's spectrum of aromatics ranges from citrus to tropical fruits before an elegantly refreshing palate unveils well-sustained fruit. Elegance, intensity and typicity in the shape of sage and tomato leaf aromas all come together in the Sauvignon. Finally, the Tocai Mis Mas – the name means "mix" in Friulian – has this name because its vineyard of provenance has a small proportion of ribolla and malvasia vines.

○	COF Pinot Grigio '05	🍷🍷	4*
○	COF Sauvignon '05	🍷🍷	4*
○	COF Tocai Friulano '05	🍷🍷	4*
○	COF Tocai Friulano Mis Mas '05	🍷🍷	3*

CODROIPO (UD)

Vigneti Pittaro

via Udine, 67
33033 Codroipo (UD)
tel. 0432904726
www.vignetipittaro.com

Piero Pittaro's winery is next to the Rivolto airfield, home of Italy's Frecce Tricolori aerobatic team, and receives a constant stream of visitors. One reason for this is the owner's reputation as an oenologist and former chair of the category's international association but there are also other attractions. We refer to the winery's architecture, reminiscent of California's celebrated cellars with one part set aside for the production and storage of Pittaro's excellent metodo classico sparkling wines. The collection of wine-related glass, ranging from bottles to drinking vessels, is another reason for popping in. The main vineyards, comprising 85 hectares in a single plot, surround the winery while a small cellar at Tarcento vinifies grapes from the Ramandolo DOCG, which go into bottle as Ronco Vieri. Pittaro stands out on the Friulian wine scene as one of the few wineries to vinify unusual varieties like moscato rosa and incrocio Manzoni. And it was the first of these that produced the best of this year's Pittaro wines. Wild roses and citrus tempt the nose and the slight sweetness of the fresh-tasting palate is complemented by nice intensity and hints of honey and raspberry. The Brut wines are well worth uncorking and the Ramandolo came close to a second Glass.

●	Moscato Rosa Valzer in Rosa '05	🍷🍷	4
○	Apicio '04	🍷	4
●	COF Refosco P. R. '04	🍷	4
○	Friuli Grave Bianco '04	🍷	4
○	Ramandolo Ronco Vieri '04	🍷	5
○	Friuli Grave Chardonnay Mousqué '05	🍷	4
○	Manzoni '05	🍷	4
○	Talento Brut Etichetta Oro '98	🍷	6
○	Talento Brut Etichetta Argento	🍷	5
●	Moscato Rosa Valzer in Rosa '04	🍷🍷 (outline)	4

CORMONS (GO)

Tenuta di Angoris

loc. Angoris, 7
34071 Cormons (GO)
tel. 048160923
www.angoris.com

History can be a funny thing. This estate was founded in 1648, when the emperor of Austria gave 300 fields to one of his officers, Locatello Locatelli, who had distinguished himself in battle. Three hundred and twenty years later, another Locatelli – Luciano, this time and apparently no relation – purchased the property, having decided to abandon manufacturing industry for the world of farming. For many years, the Angoris farm combined viticulture with livestock breeding and today it is one of Friuli's biggest wine estates, sprawling over 640 hectares, of which 150 are under vine. Most of the stock stands around the superb villa where Claudia Locatelli, Luciano's daughter and the estate's manager, lives but there are also significant holdings in the hills at Rocca Bernarda, in the Colli Orientali del Friuli, and at Ca' delle Vallate, in the Collio. The oenologist is Alessandro Dal Zovo, a young professional who is flanked by consultant Riccardo Cotarella, while Marco Simonit manages the vine stock. Year after year, the results of their joint efforts are cause for satisfaction. There are two excellent Sauvignons, the fresher Villa Angoris with a sage, tomato and grapefruit nose whose elegance and finesse set it above the palate, and the Vôs da Vigne, which is slower to open, but impresses in the mouth where sage is joined by elderflower and grapefruit. Apples and pears take turns in the Tocai whereas the breadth of the Pinot Grigio comes at the expense of concentration, but both easily earned Two Glasses.

○	COF Sauvignon Vôs da Vigne '05	🍷🍷	4*
○	Collio Pinot Grigio Vôs da Vigne '05	🍷🍷	4*
○	Collio Tocai Friulano Vôs da Vigne '05	🍷🍷	4*
○	Friuli Isonzo Sauvignon Villa Angoris '05	🍷🍷	4
●	COF Merlot Vôs da Vigne '04	🍷	4
●	COF Refosco P. R. Vôs da Vigne '04	🍷	4
○	COF Chardonnay Vôs da Vigne '05	🍷	4
○	COF Ribolla Gialla Vôs da Vigne '05	🍷	4
○	Friuli Isonzo Pinot Bianco Villa Angoris '05	🍷	4
○	Friuli Isonzo Tocai Friulano Villa Angoris '05	🍷	4

CORMONS (GO)

La Boatina
via Corona, 62
34071 Cormons (GO)
tel. 048160445 - 0481639914
www.paliwines.com

La Boatina is the largest of the cellars in the Pali Wines group, owned by Loretto Pali. The vine holdings include 32 hectares in the Collio DOC zone and about 40 in Isonzo. Current annual production is 350,000 bottles but the cellar's sights are set considerably higher. Wines are released under the La Boatina label, which was joined a couple of years ago by I Roncati for more approachable, easy-drinking products. La Boatina's staff is the same as at Castello di Spessa, Loretto Pali's other winery. Domenico Lovat, who has been the oenologist for many years, was not long ago joined by consultant Gianni Menotti and in the vineyards Marco Simonit directs pruning operations. It should be remembered that the delightful winery complex also features a dining and tasting facility for hams, cheeses and processed meats. The Pinot Grigio from the Collio gives an intriguing medley of fruits with tropical notes that return on the elegantly well-sustained palate. The Isonzo Pinot Grigio has an equally impressive wealth of fruit but lost marks for excessive softness. But the best of the range this time was the Verduzzo 2004, obtained by carefully drying the grapes. The colour of old gold, it has almondy and dried fig aromas and sweet palate tautened by just the right note of volatile acidity backing tones of caramel and baked fruit.

○	Friuli Isonzo Verduzzo '04	TT	4*
○	Collio Pinot Grigio '05	TT	5
○	Collio Chardonnay '05	T	5
○	Collio Ribolla Gialla '05	T	4
○	Friuli Isonzo Pinot Grigio '05	T	4
○	Friuli Isonzo Tocai Friulano '05	T	4
●	Collio Rosso Picol Maggiore Ris. '01	YY	5
●	Collio Rosso Picol Maggiore '99	YY	5
●	Collio Merlot '03	YY	4
○	Collio Sauvignon '04	YY	4

CORMONS (GO)

Borgo del Tiglio
fraz. Brazzano
via San Giorgio, 71
34070 Cormons (GO)
tel. 048162166

Nicola Manferrari's great virtue is his consistency. You can spot his wines at a glance. When young, they have milky, vanilla-like perceptions that can on occasion be a tad too marked but then with time, they regain their balance. Texture and well-extracted fruit emerge to create irresistibly complex sensations. This time round, we sampled seven wines. We really liked the standard-label 2004 Chardonnay, one of the finest in the region and better even than the Selezione, which has rather marked acidity. Flowers, dried fruit and citrus pave the way for a broad, pervasive palate that is soft yet very full-bodied. Ronco della Chiesa 2004, a single-variety Tocai from old vines over the cellar, is warm and stylish, if still a little green and oaky. The standard version, which has an interesting spectrum of aromatics, is more convincing. Milk, butter and fruit are the keynotes of the Malvasia 2004, whose expansive, fresh-tasting palate promises well for the future. Nicola has also managed to make a couple of his dreams come true. One is his magnificent new underground cellar and the other is the release of the first wines from his Contrada Tenna vineyard, which is now productive. It is situated in the province of Fermo, in the heart of the Marche, and planted to two of central Italy's most characteristic varieties, sangiovese and montepulciano. Now Nicola presents a single-variety Montepulciano under a historic winery label, Milleuve. We were also very impressed by the 2002 Ronco della Chiesa on retasting. In fact, we gave it Three retrospective Glasses.

○	Collio Chardonnay '04	TT	6
○	Collio Studio di Bianco '04	TT	7
●	Milleuve Rosso '02	TT	4*
○	Collio Bianco Ronco della Chiesa '04	TT	7
○	Collio Malvasia Sel. '04	TT	7
○	Collio Tocai Friulano '04	TT	6
○	Collio Chardonnay Sel. '04	T	7
○	Collio Bianco Ronco della Chiesa '02	YYY	7
○	Collio Bianco Ronco della Chiesa '01	YYY	7
○	Collio Chardonnay Sel. '99	YYY	6
○	Collio Tocai Friulano Ronco della Chiesa '90	YYY	7

CORMONS (GO)

Borgo San Daniele

via San Daniele, 16
34071 Cormons (GO)
tel. 048160552
www.borgosandaniele.it

The Borgo San Daniele philosophy aims to produce wines of outstanding quality with a strong sense of belonging to their territory of provenance. Wines released by brother and sister Mauro and Alessandra Mauri need a certain amount of cellar time before they are at their very best, which is why the cellar has embarked on a new initiative to further enhance the quality of Borgo San Daniele bottles. At each vintage, they select one wine for release a year later than the others, allowing it an extra 12 months in glass. The programme started in 2005 with Arbis Ros 2003 and for 2006 the Mauris have chosen Tocai Friulano. Mauro maintains that "the cellar is the best place for wines and maturation can only give them even more structure and personality". Consumers will be pleased to note that the extra cellar time has not been accompanied by a rise in price. We'll start our report with the cellar's top wine, which is a Three Glass monster. Arbis Blanc 2005, from tocai friulano, pinot bianco, chardonnay and sauvignon, is a wonderful bottle. Extremely elegant, it combines fruit and spring flower aromas with notes of acacia honey and the buttery softness on the palate leaves plenty of room for the marked lingering minerality. The Pinot Grigio 2005 has a warm nose of pear and roasted almonds that return in the mouth. The pignolo and cabernet Arbis Ros 2003 flaunts bags of character and a stylish, wide-ranging nose that foregrounds red fruits and pencil lead.

○ Arbis Blanc '05	🍷🍷🍷	5
● Arbis Ros '03	🍷🍷	5
○ Friuli Isonzo Pinot Grigio '05	🍷🍷	5
○ Friuli Isonzo Arbis Blanc '02	🍷🍷🍷	5
○ Friuli Isonzo Tocai Friulano '03	🍷🍷🍷	5
○ Friuli Isonzo Pinot Grigio '04	🍷🍷🍷	5
○ Friuli Isonzo Pinot Grigio '99	🍷🍷🍷	5
● Arbis Ros '02	🍷🍷	5
○ Arbis Blanc '03	🍷🍷	5
○ Arbis Blanc '04	🍷🍷	5
○ Friuli Isonzo Tocai Friulano '04	🍷🍷	5

CORMONS (GO)

Borgo Savaian

via Savaian, 36
34071 Cormons (GO)
tel. 048160725

We were right to believe in Borgo Savaian, a winery that first appeared in the Guide only last year. That performance was no flash in the pan, but a portent of real quality. It was no surprise, as the family has a wine tradition that stretches back to grandfather Bruno, continued under his son Mario and is today being consolidated by Stefano Bastiani, who has absorbed and applied their lessons. That alone is enough to guarantee dependability. One of the most important things for a cellar is to maintain constancy of quality. It can only be done with vines of the right age, planted in favourable locations in harmony with the site environment, and of course it takes an experienced vineyard manager. All this comes together at Borgo Savaian in particular with the Pinot Bianco, which again went through to the finals. We liked the 2005's fresh nose of spring flowers, oranges, delicious apples and subtle hints of minerality. The breadth in the mouth is exemplary, as is the nose-palate consistency and the perfect balance of freshness and soft sensations. Similar results were achieved by the Pinot Grigio 2005, which stands out for its complex nose of gunflint, dried flowers and pears lifted by a twist of citrus in the finish. Progression on the palate, focusing on well-rounded fruit, is impressive. Tobacco and vanilla mingling with ripe banana and peach tell you that the Chardonnay 2005 was part-fermented in wood. But whites are not all that Borgo Savaian has to offer. Tolrem Sot Mont 2003, a fine red with creamy chocolate sensations and assertive tannins, is also on the list.

○ Collio Pinot Bianco '05	🍷🍷	4*
○ Collio Pinot Grigio '05	🍷🍷	4*
● Collio Tolrem Sot Mont Ris. '03	🍷🍷	5
○ Collio Chardonnay '05	🍷🍷	4
● Friuli Isonzo Cabernet Franc '04	🍷	4
● Collio Merlot '04	🍷	4
○ Friuli Isonzo Verduzzo Friulano '04	🍷	4
○ Collio Sauvignon '05	🍷	4
○ Collio Tocai Friulano '05	🍷	4
○ Friuli Isonzo Traminer Aromatico '05	🍷	4
○ Collio Chardonnay '04	🍷🍷	4
○ Collio Pinot Bianco '04	🍷🍷	4

CORMONS (GO)

BRANKO
LOC. ZEGLA, 20
34071 CORMONS (GO)
TEL. 0481639826

Igor Erzetic is a young wine technician who has come on apace thanks to the experience he acquired at various cellars in Friuli, his exceptional intuition and an appetite for hard work. His small cellar is named after his father Branko, another tireless worker. Further support comes from Igor's mother Daniela, who provides tempting traditional snacks to accompany tastings. Major refitting has been done over the past year and there is now a very practical tasting room. Cellar space has also been expanded. At present, Igor has six hectares in production and another hectare and a half, replanted last year, will come onstream in a couple of years' time. As in previous years, the entire range presented was excellent with the Pinot Grigio providing a Three Glass high note. Elegance is the keynote of the 13,000 bottles released, which give mixed fruits and tropical aromas and firmness, intensity, freshness and persistence in the mouth. It is a well-deserved award for a young producer who has lifted the quality of his range in a very short time. The Chardonnay is part-conditioned in large ovals, emerging with stylish tones of very ripe yellow-fleshed fruits. Igor has also managed to combine intensity with elegance, fullness and breadth in the Tocai Friulano. The steel-fermented and aged Sauvignon starts with bell pepper and rue before unveiling very varietal tomato leaf. Finally, Red is firm-textured, coffee and chocolate-themed and flaunts well-managed tannins before its long, rich finish.

○	Collio Pinot Grigio '05	TTT	5
●	Red Branko '03	TT	5
○	Collio Sauvignon '05	TT	5
○	Collio Tocai Friulano '05	TT	5
○	Collio Chardonnay '05	TT	5
○	Collio Chardonnay '02	YY	5
○	Collio Tocai Friulano '02	YY	5
○	Collio Tocai Friulano '03	YY	5
○	Collio Pinot Grigio '04	YY	5

CORMONS (GO)

MAURIZIO BUZZINELLI
LOC. PRADIS, 20
34071 CORMONS (GO)
TEL. 048160902
www.buzzinelli.com

Maurizio Buzzinelli is putting the final touches to his cellar makeover, which has taken much longer than was originally forecast. All the confusion did not stop Maurizio vinifying the 2006 harvest in the best possible conditions as the facilities are already fully functional. The cellar takes fruit from eight hectares in the Friuli Isonzo DOC and 16 in the Collio, including one or two rented plots. In recent years, replanting in flatlands vineyards has favoured red varieties, which now account for 40 per cent of total production. Since last year, Maurizio has been replanting his malvasia, one of the winery's leading products in past vintages. That's why there was no Malvasia at our tasting. The 2004 reds are still maturing in barrique, so we were unable to review them either. This summer, Maurizio's wife Marzia gave birth to Jacopo, another incentive for his father to excel. The most exciting of the wines presented was the Tocai Friulano 2005, of which 21,000 units went into bottle. Intense baked apples precede an elegant, full-bodied palate with a fresh taste and a pear-themed finish. The very tangy, elegantly fresh Chardonnay has loads of personality. Green apple is the keynote of the Ribolla Gialla while the Pinot Grigio has a broader range of fruit. Finally, the Sauvignon has bitter orange and citrus aromas as well as fine nose-palate consistency.

○	Collio Tocai Friulano '05	TT	4*
○	Collio Chardonnay '05	T	4
○	Collio Pinot Grigio '05	T	4
○	Collio Ribolla Gialla '05	T	3
○	Collio Sauvignon '05	T	4
○	Collio Tocai Friulano '04	YY	4

CORMONS (GO)

PAOLO CACCESE
LOC. PRADIS, 6
34071 CORMONS (GO)
TEL. 048161062

Every year, Paolo Caccese presents us with a very broad range of labels – despite the fact that he only has six hectares under vine – with an encouragingly high overall level of quality. That said, there are still year-to-year variations that developments during the growing year cannot always explain. This unpredictability veered in a positive direction this time in a vintage that brought problems for most growers but a rich haul of Glassware for Paolo, whose vines are on the hillslopes of Pradis at Cormons in a beautifully aspected site. The leading light this year turned out to be the Malvasia, which gives varietal lavender and violet, a full-bodied front palate followed by concentrated, unhurried progression. We thought the Pinot Bianco was more successful on the nose than in the mouth. Well-matched ripe golden delicious apples and aromatic herbs precede an unexpected tanginess. On the nose, the Pinot Grigio displays fruit salad over a subtle hint of camphor with a genuinely satisfying progression on the palate, right from the rich, appealing entry with a swath of fruit whose citrus and tropical fruit conjure up a very inviting spectrum of aromatics. Paolo is one of Friuli's last remaining local producers of Müller Thurgau, which again earned a very full Glass.

○ Collio Malvasia '05	🍷🍷	4*
○ Collio Pinot Bianco '05	🍷🍷	4*
○ Collio Pinot Grigio '05	🍷🍷	4*
○ Collio Müller Thurgau '05	🍷	4
○ Collio Sauvignon '05	🍷	4
○ Collio Tocai Friulano '05	🍷	4
● Collio Cabernet Franc '04	🍷	4
● Collio Merlot '04		4
○ Collio Tocai Friulano '01	YY	4
○ Collio Malvasia '03	YY	4
○ Collio Malvasia '04	YY	4

CORMONS (GO)

CARLO DI PRADIS
LOC. PRADIS, 22BIS
34071 CORMONS (GO)
TEL. 048162272
www.carlodipradis.it

A few years ago, Carlo Buzzinelli handed over management of the family cellar to his sons Boris and David after taking it steadily up the quality ladder. In acknowledgement of their father's contribution, Boris and Davide decided to name the winery after him, adding to it the hill that is one of the finest crus in Cormons. The two brothers have seven hectares around the cellar at Pradis with another eight on the lowlands near Cormons in the Friuli Isonzo DOC zone. We gave highest marks to the Collio Tocai Friulano for its deep, elegant, pervasive aromas, depth on the front palate and elegant ripe fruit veined with chamomile and sage. This is a bright, upfront wine that avoids becoming over-assertive. The gold-flecked Tocai Friulano Scusse was a tad below par. Jasmine-like vegetal aromas precede the rich, well-sustained warmth of the palate with its attractive oak-derived backdrop. The Collio Sauvignon also impresses. Its sage and elderflower are lifted by citrus and the close-woven, elegant palate adds bell pepper and rue to the sage. Comparisons with the fresh-tasting, varietal Isonzo Sauvignon reveal a considerable gap. Finally, the Collio Pinot Grigio 2005 gives pear, banana and summer flowers, and substance, good fruit and length on the palate.

○ Collio Tocai Friulano '05	🍷🍷	4*
○ Collio Tocai Friulano Scusse '04	🍷🍷	4
○ Collio Pinot Grigio '05	🍷🍷	4
○ Collio Sauvignon '05	🍷🍷	4
○ Friuli Isonzo Chardonnay BorDavi '05	🍷	4
○ Friuli Isonzo Sauvignon BorDavi '05	🍷	4
○ Collio Tocai Friulano '02	YY	4
○ Collio Pinot Grigio '04	YY	4
○ Friuli Isonzo Pinot Grigio BorDavi '04	YY	4

CORMONS (GO)

Colle Duga

Loc. Zegla, 10
34071 Cormons (GO)
tel. 048161177

Well, we had plenty of warning. For years, Damian Princic's seven hectares have been turning out wines that regularly earn Two very full Glasses from our panels. This time there was an embarrassment of riches as Damian notched up two finalists with his Tocai Friulano and Pinot Grigio. We preferred the Tocai Friulano 2005, which flaunts intense, elegant aromas on the almost overwhelmingly rich nose. These are mirrored faithfully on the irresistibly fruit-rich, very varietal palate, which hinges on pear. Fresh acidity reins in the alcohol in the finish. A surprisingly complex, elegant Pinot Grigio tempts with pear, citrus and hints of tropical fruits. Damian is the main artificer of these wines, helped particularly in the vineyards by his father Luciano and by Giorgio Bertossi, an oenologist as competent as he is modest. From the four hillside vineyards around the cellar, the Princic team last year obtained 38,000 bottles, including 12,000 of that starry Tocai. The two champions are accompanied by a fine clutch of Two Glass winners, starting with the fruit-forward Merlot that has a vein of sweetness to offset the tannins. The sauvignon, tocai and chardonnay Collio Bianco reveals its oak conditioning on the nose but there is plenty of fruit to ensure excellent ageing prospects. Sage and peach dominate the nose of the Sauvignon and the Chardonnay is drinking perfectly now.

○ Collio Tocai Friulano '05	▼▼▼	4*
○ Collio Pinot Grigio '05	▼▼	4*
● Collio Merlot '04	▼▼	4
○ Collio Bianco '05	▼▼	4
○ Collio Chardonnay '05	▼▼	4
○ Collio Sauvignon '05	▼▼	4
○ Collio Bianco '03	▽▽	5
○ Collio Bianco '04	▽▽	4
● Collio Merlot '03	▽▽	4
○ Collio Tocai Friulano '04	▽▽	4

CORMONS (GO)

Mauro Drius

via Filanda, 100
34071 Cormons (GO)
tel. 048160998

Last year, we said that Mauro Drius is a genuine wine man, the kind who achieves the goals he sets himself. True to form, Mauro's Tocais are now wines to bank on. The more exciting Collio version is sourced from a couple of hectares at Brazzano that Mauro wants to plant exclusively to the variety. It is a rich, mouthfilling white that is so thrillingly consistent that it is almost an archetype of Tocai. Whistle-clean apple, acacia blossom, honey and medlars usher in a pervasive, appealingly bitterish palate with plenty of alcohol, acidity and extract. And the everlasting finish is perked up by a refreshing twist of almonds: Three resounding Glasses to a great winemaker. The Isonzo version of the same variety is more immediate, fading in the finish in comparison with its stablemate, although it is equally impeccably crafted. The Sauvignon also convinces. Softness and freshness are nicely brought together against a backdrop of apricot and sage tones. Contributions from the tocai, sauvignon and pinot bianco, braced by savoury minerality, provide the framework for the Vignis di Sìris 2004. The Pinot Bianco is very traditional, showing yeasts and jasmine backed up by a concentrated, ripe palate. Crusty bread, spring flowers and apples characterize the Pinot Grigio and the pleasant Malvasia intrigues with gooseberry and faint aniseed-like aromas. Also worth investigating is the Merlot 2003.

○ Collio Tocai Friulano '05	▼▼▼	4*
○ Collio Sauvignon '05	▼▼	4*
○ Friuli Isonzo Bianco Vìgnis di Sìris '04	▼▼	4
○ Friuli Isonzo Pinot Bianco '05	▼▼	4
○ Friuli Isonzo Pinot Grigio '05	▼▼	4
○ Friuli Isonzo Tocai Friulano '05	▼▼	4
● Friuli Isonzo Merlot '03	▼	4
○ Friuli Isonzo Malvasia '05	▼	4
● Friuli Isonzo Cabernet '03		4
○ Friuli Isonzo Pinot Bianco '00	▽▽▽	4
○ Collio Tocai Friulano '02	▽▽▽	4
○ Friuli Isonzo Bianco Vìgnis di Sìris '02	▽▽▽	4
○ Collio Tocai Friulano '04	▽▽	4

★ LIVIO FELLUGA
FRAZ. BRAZZANO
VIA RISORGIMENTO, 1
34070 CORMONS (GO)
TEL. 048160203
www.liviofelluga.it

Recently, the Livio Felluga winery celebrated the 50th anniversary of the Map Label, the symbol that has made the cellar's wines instantly identifiable giving rise to an extremely successful brand. As luck would have it, the anniversary coincides with the return to top form of Terre Alte, a blend of the finest sauvignon, tocai friulano and pinot bianco grapes from the historic vineyards at Rosazzo. It is well-known that Terre Alte has been one of Friuli's flagship wines in world markets for some time: it has earned its spurs over the years, maintaining its superb quality for more than two decades since its first release, the 1981 vintage. Our congratulations to Livio and Maurizio Felluga, who lovingly shape a wine of which 40,000 units are distributed every year. The 2004 Terre Alte is stunningly rich and concentrated on the nose, where the spectrum of aromatics ranges from vanilla to banana and tomato. All these sensations return on the harmonious progression in the mouth, through to the finesse and sheer pleasure of the amazingly long, balanced finish. The elegant, refined Picolit 2003 drinks very cleanly, keeping its sweetness in check and proffering an aromatic weave with a candied citrus peel theme. Shàrjs, a successful blend of an international variety – chardonnay – with the native ribolla gialla, raised admiring eyebrows for its rich white chocolate and peach aromas ushering in a fresh, dynamic palate. The Refosco is very fruity and the Bianco Rosenplatz is tangy while the rest of this marvellous range is unfailingly good.

○ COF Rosazzo Bianco Terre Alte '04	▼▼▼	7
○ COF Rosazzo Picolit Ris. '03	▼▼	8
● COF Refosco P. R. '04	▼▼	5
○ COF Pinot Grigio '05	▼▼	5
○ COF Tocai Friulano '05	▼▼	5
○ Collio Bianco Rosenplatz '05	▼▼	5
○ Shàrjs '05	▼▼	4
○ COF Bianco Illivio '04	▼	5
○ COF Sauvignon '05	▼	5
● Vertigo '04	▼	4
○ COF Rosazzo Bianco Terre Alte '01	▽▽▽	6
○ COF Rosazzo Bianco Terre Alte '02	▽▽▽	6

CORMONS (GO)

EDI KEBER
LOC. ZEGLA, 17
34071 CORMONS (GO)
TEL. 048161184

Intelligent, sociable and a tireless worker, Edi Keber is a charismatic leader of Cormons winemakers. Now his son Kristjan is following in his footsteps, turning his hand to all the winery's tasks and eager to gain new experience in cellar's outside the region. Edi's wife Silvana runs the lovely agriturismo facility that has been created by careful restoration of the Keber family home. The cellar, too, has been skilfully restored and a number of spaces created in a faux antique style for which we will forgive Edi. We would like to stress Edi's courageous policy, one he has implemented for several years, to drastically reduce the number of labels. Most of the 70,000 bottles are Tocai Friulano, Collio Bianco and Collio Rosso: Edi only releases his Merlot in exceptional years. The Kebers are currently experimenting with a macerated, unfiltered white, which we will be reporting in future years. The merlot and cabernet franc Collio Rosso has strawberry and raspberry juice laced with cherry-like hints. The Collio Bianco is blended from tocai, ribolla and malvasia, with dashes of pinot bianco and pinot grigio. Melon and pear on the nose are complemented by a palate with good supporting alcohol. Once the Tocai Friulano has shaken off its initial reduction, it offers intensity, elegant and breadth, good nose-palate consistency, concentration, stylish williams pear and apple wrapped up in firm structure and satisfyingly long length. It's a splendid Tocai and yet again picked up Three Glasses.

○ Collio Tocai Friulano '05	▼▼▼	5
○ Collio Bianco '05	▼▼	5
● Collio Rosso '05	▼	5
○ Collio Tocai Friulano '01	▽▽▽	4
○ Collio Bianco '02	▽▽▽	4
○ Collio Tocai Friulano '03	▽▽▽	4
○ Collio Bianco '04	▽▽▽	5
○ Collio Tocai Friulano '04	▽▽	5

CORMONS (GO)

MAGNÀS
VIA CORONA, 47
34071 CORMONS (GO)
TEL. 048160991
www.magnas.it

The last growing year was a little harsh on the wines of these two very likeable producers, Luciano Visintin, aka Magnàs, and his son Andrea. They farm ten hectares and only some of their wine goes into bottle. To the delight of his many appreciative friends, Magnàs continues to make a small number of "caciotta" cheeses every day. In winter, he also makes cold meat products from the four pigs he raises during the year. Now that the old farmhouse has been restored, the property can boast attractive agriturismo accommodation run by Luciano's wife, Sonia. Magnàs' hospitality and approachable personality make tastings here particularly enjoyable. But blind tastings do not the producer's personal qualities into account, nor can our sincere regard for Magnàs influence the marks given. So it was that this year only the Pinot Grigio cleared the Two Glass hurdle, effortlessly as it turned out, thanks to a fruit-forward nose and an immensely generous palate with citrus-like nuances to bring out its freshness in the long finish. The 2005 Sauvignon has varietal sage and elderflower but lacks the sheer passion of the marvellous 2004. Elegance is common trait of all these wines, and it emerges especially in the Tocai Friulano and Chardonnay, both of which are more persuasive on the nose than in the mouth.

○ Friuli Isonzo Pinot Grigio '05	▼▼	5
○ Friuli Isonzo Chardonnay '05	▼	5
○ Friuli Isonzo Sauvignon '05	▼	5
○ Friuli Isonzo Tocai Friulano '05	▼	5
○ Friuli Isonzo Sauvignon '04	▽▽	5
○ Friuli Isonzo Pinot Grigio '03	▽▽	4
○ Friuli Isonzo Pinot Grigio '04	▽▽	5

CORMONS (GO)

ROBERTO PICÉCH
LOC. PRADIS, 11
34071 CORMONS (GO)
TEL. 048160347
www.picech.it

Work on the dream cellar is finally over. Roberto Picéch can now devote all his attention to the seven hectares under vine he tends at Pradis, a cru if ever there was one in the hills at Cormons. Results are starting to come through as quality improves across the board. We know Roberto is a modest chap, given to saying "I hope my dream of being a good grower can come true one day", but wines like Bianco Jelka are products that only a great winemaker can release. Named after Roberto's mother, it is a blend of ribolla gialla, tocai and malvasia fermented and aged in wood of different sizes and bottled without clarification or filtering. The 2004 edition has depth and personality from the start, proffering intense cream, banana and yellow peach fragrances. An assertive front palate expands with attractive softness, signing off with a lingering fruit-themed finish that echoes the nose. Roberto's Malvasia 2005 has power in its intense mineral, juniper and ripe pear aromas and in the softness of the palate, which closes with elegant creamy sensations. Lingering, concentrated fruit is the keynote of the equally good Pinot Bianco 2005. The standard Collio Rosso has nice ripe fruit while the 2005 Tocai, some of which aged in large wood, gives varietal almond aromas and a pleasantly tangy back palate.

○ Collio Bianco Jelka '04	▼▼	5
○ Collio Malvasia '05	▼▼	4
○ Collio Pinot Bianco '05	▼▼	4
● Collio Rosso '05	▼	4
○ Collio Tocai Friulano '05	▼	4
○ Collio Bianco Jelka '99	▽▽▽	4
○ Collio Pinot Bianco '03	▽▽	4
○ Collio Bianco Jelka '03	▽▽	5
● Collio Rosso Ris. '01	▽▽	6

CORMONS (GO)

Aldo Polencic

Loc. Plessiva, 13
34071 Cormons (GO)
tel. 048161027

Aldo Polencic has his own approach to wines, one that always involves serious structure and plenty of alcohol. Over the past two years, he has been restructuring and extending the cellar, a project that should be over before the end of the 2006 harvest. But this commitment has not stopped Aldo from producing excellent wine. He has had crucial assistance from his sister Marinka, a young oenologist who is gaining experience in Tuscany with Attilio Pagli. Aldo continues along the path traced out years ago by his father Ferdinando, although he has extended the use of wood in the cellar, which only the Pinot Grigio seems to have avoided. The names given to the various wines do not appear to follow a single plan. Last year, the Merlot bore the word Unico on the label whereas this year it is reserved for one of the Tocais. The phrase "degli Ulivi", reserved for wines that have been wood-fermented, is absent from the label of the Tocai Friulano, a wine in which the use of barriques is very evident. But let's leave labels to one side and look at the wines. Both Tocais are thoroughbreds, with the Unico much more concentrated and the standard version fruit-forward. Both flaunt distinct oak-derived vanilla. A similar sensation penalized the Pinot Bianco degli Ulivi a little but the fruit has no trouble in shining through. And the elegance and freshness of the Pinot Grigio were a very pleasant surprise.

○	Collio Pinot Bianco degli Ulivi '05	2 black glasses	5
○	Collio Pinot Grigio '05	2 black glasses	5
○	Collio Tocai Friulano '05	2 black glasses	5
○	Collio Tocai Friulano Unico '05	2 black glasses	5
●	Collio Merlot degli Ulivi '04	1 black glass	6
○	Collio Tocai Friulano '03	3 white glasses	5
○	Collio Tocai Friulano '03	2 white glasses	4
○	Collio Pinot Bianco '04	2 white glasses	6
●	Collio Merlot '02	2 white glasses	5
●	Collio Merlot Unico '03	2 white glasses	5

CORMONS (GO)

Isidoro Polencic

Loc. Plessiva, 12
34071 Cormons (GO)
tel. 048160655
www.polencic.com

There name Polencic has been present in the valley of the "three districts", where Plessiva lies, for more than four centuries. Isidoro Polencic has worked this land vigorously, passing on to his eldest son Michele all the culture and experience that is not written in books but has to be learned by working every day in vineyard and cellar. Michele may be young but he has absorbed these lessons, adding modern techniques he has acquired from his studies. His impact on the estate has been considerable and the cellar's wines are now some of the finest in the region. Investments also continue in the spacious cellar and out in the vineyards, where a further hectare and half of vines has been purchased, part of it in the neighbouring Isonzo DOC zone. The combination of experience and innovation has enabled the Polencic team, even in a challenging vintage like 2005, to present us with a remarkable range of wines, including a Tocai that sailed through to the final tastings. The stylish fragrances are led by sensations of apple, the palate is elegant, intense and beautifully poised, and the finish is lifted by refreshing minerality on the back palate. The Ribolla Gialla is fruit-forward and fresh, the ideal partner for fish. There are attractive smoky notes on the Pinot Bianco and the fruity softness of the Chardonnay is equally appealing. The buttery Pinot Grigio has good fruit and the Sauvignon is redolent of bell peppers and tomato leaf. Finally the muscular, spicy Bordeaux blend Oblin Ros 2003 shows reassuringly positive development.

○	Collio Tocai Friulano '05	2 black glasses	4*
●	Oblin Ros '03	2 black glasses	6
○	Collio Chardonnay '05	2 black glasses	4
○	Collio Pinot Bianco '05	2 black glasses	4
○	Collio Pinot Grigio '05	2 black glasses	4
○	Collio Ribolla Gialla '05	2 black glasses	4
○	Collio Bianco '05	1 black glass	4
○	Collio Sauvignon '05	1 black glass	4
○	Collio Tocai Friulano '04	3 white glasses	4
○	Collio Pinot Grigio '98	3 white glasses	4
○	Collio Pinot Grigio '03	2 white glasses	4
○	Collio Pinot Grigio '04	2 white glasses	4
○	Collio Pinot Bianco '04	2 white glasses	4

Doro Princic

Loc. Pradis, 5
34071 Cormons (GO)
tel. 048160723

Over the past few years, Sandro Princic has managed to give his wines a little extra tweak but this year's line-up is something else. You won't get much information out of Sandro if you interview him because he thinks it's quite normal to get results like these. He reminds us of the calm spontaneous disposition of his father Doro, one of the first to see the quality potential of wine from Cormons. Today, Sandro has more than ten hectares under vine and annual production hovers around 50,000 bottles. The hospitality of Sandro and his talented cook of a wife Grazia is legendary: we suspect that quite a lot of those bottles are uncorked at table for their guests. Prospective purchasers should not imagine that they can buy Princic wines without tasting them first in quantity, accompanied by the wide range of dishes that Grazia serves without respite. Top of the line again is the Pinot Bianco with its penetratingly elegant apple, substantial body and structure, minerality, good alcohol and freshness, all of which come together amazingly well. The Tocai Friulano is only a notch or two below: intense, immediate and shot through with pear and apple. A hint of aniseed veins the sweet tropical fruit of the Malvasia before pineapple emerges on the very attractive palate. And the sauvignon, too, is on target with its bell pepper and sage tones. Fresh fruit salad and substantial alcohol are the keynotes of the Pinot Grigio and the Cabernet 2004 is excellent while the Merlot 2004 provides the only less than brilliant note from an otherwise fantastic range of wines.

○	Collio Pinot Bianco '05	▼▼▼	5
○	Collio Malvasia '05	▼▼	5
○	Collio Pinot Grigio '05	▼▼	5
○	Collio Sauvignon '05	▼▼	5
○	Collio Tocai Friulano '05	▼▼	5
●	Collio Cabernet '04	▼▼	5
●	Collio Merlot '04	▼	5
○	Collio Pinot Bianco '95	▽▽▽	5
○	Collio Pinot Bianco '02	▽▽▽	5
○	Collio Pinot Bianco '04	▽▽▽	5
○	Collio Tocai Friulano '93	▽▽▽	5
○	Collio Pinot Bianco '01	▽▽	5
○	Collio Tocai Friulano '02	▽▽	5
○	Collio Tocai Friulano '04	▽▽	5
○	Collio Malvasia '03	▽▽	5

Dario Raccaro

Fraz. Rolat
via San Giovanni, 87
34071 Cormons (GO)
tel. 048161425

Halfway between Cormons and Brazzano is the historic Rolat vineyard with tocai vines that according to local legend are direct descendents of the plants that came from Hungary. What is beyond doubt is that extensions and replantings after the First World War were carried out with grafts of shoots taken from the two original rows. A few years ago, Dario Raccaro managed to gain access to this vineyard and it has added extra lustre to the already excellent tocai he was growing. Raccaro loves wines, provided they are white, but his passion for his Tocai knows no bounds. It is the emblematic Tocai Friulano. Our tasters recognized its merits, even in a year when other wines from the same variety were also scoring very high marks. Rarely do you encounter such intense, elegant pear and almond aromas, such complex, citrus-lifted fruit on the palate, such thrust or such persistence. The Three Glass award was a formality. Equally predictable was the quality of the fresh, clean-tasting Malvasia, its spring flowers mingling with elderflower and the generous palate revealing a hint of tannins. The Collio Bianco performed well. From tocai friulano, sauvignon and pinot grigio in almost exactly equal proportions, it was steel-fermented, like all the other Raccaro whites. Broad pear and apple sensations dominate the aromatics and fresh acidity in the finish offsets the substantial alcohol. Only the Merlot 2004 was below the standards we have come to expect from this very fine cellar.

○	Collio Tocai Friulano '05	▼▼▼	5
○	Collio Malvasia '05	▼▼	5
○	Collio Bianco '05	▼▼	5
●	Collio Merlot '04	▼	6
○	Collio Tocai Friulano '00	▽▽▽	4
○	Collio Tocai Friulano '01	▽▽▽	4
○	Collio Bianco '02	▽▽▽	4
○	Collio Bianco '03	▽▽▽	5
○	Collio Tocai Friulano '04	▽▽▽	5
●	Collio Merlot '03	▽▽	6
○	Collio Bianco '04	▽▽	5
○	Collio Malvasia '04	▽▽	5

CORMONS (GO)

Roncada

Loc. Roncada, 5
34071 Cormons (GO)
tel. 048161394
www.roncada.34x.com

The Gorizia-based Mattioni family have owned this historic winery since 1956 so they have just celebrated their 50th anniversary. As if to underline the special event, they chose this moment to present us with one of the best wines Roncada has ever released, a Pinot Bianco 2005 that we sent through to the Three Glass finals. After all, the potential of this estate is enormous thanks to 25 hectares of entirely south-facing vines. On top of the Roncada hill, as if standing guard over the rows, is the austere estate villa, erected in 1882 by the owners of the day, Angelo and Alberto Levi from Villanova di Farra. All of the many wines we tasted were interesting but the best, as predicted, was the successful Pinot Bianco with its very varietal aromas. Spring flowers and citrus delight the nose before the palate expands elegantly to finish off with a reprise of the florality. The steel-fermented Chardonnay is very well made, opening on spring flowers, melon and citrus. Full and well balanced, the palate progresses to a deliciously lingering finish. The Franconia 2004 is obtained from a variety planted by the previous owners, who were of German origin, and it impresses with its spicy tones and good fruit base. Finally, the Pinot Grigio lacks a little weight in the mouth but is more satisfying on the nose, where varietal fruit and minerals come through.

○	Collio Pinot Bianco '05	▼▼	4*
○	Collio Chardonnay '05	▼▼	4
●	Collio Cabernet Franc '04	▼	4
●	Franconia '04	▼	4
○	Collio Müller Thurgau '05	▼	4
○	Collio Pinot Grigio '05	▼	4
○	Collio Tocai Friulano '05	▼	4
●	Collio Cabernet Sauvignon '04		4
○	Collio Malvasia Istriana '05		4
○	Collio Pinot Bianco '02	▽▽	4
○	Collio Pinot Bianco '03	▽▽	4
○	Collio Sauvignon '04	▽▽	4

CORMONS (GO)

Ronco dei Tassi

Loc. Monte, 38
34071 Cormons (GO)
tel. 048160155
www.roncodeitassi.it

"There's a dream behind my wish to create this wine estate", said Fabio Coser recently in an interview. Now his dream has come true in the quality of his wines and the unity of his family, which underpins the cellar's very high standards. We know that Fabio is a man with his feet firmly on the ground. He is not the type to rest on his laurels for he is his own most severe critic and knows how to leverage his experience. It would be tempting for him just to freewheel for a while. Fosarin 2004 was the White of the Year in Italian Wines 2006 and now his magnificent Sauvignon 2005 has won another Three Glass award. But we can be sure that Fabio is already looking ahead to new goals. A proportion of the Sauvignon 2005 aged in oak barrels and the wine that came out is very elegant, a quality shared by all Fabio's products. Its subtle citrus and tropical fruits mingle with elderflower and mineral sensations. The fascinating palate hinges on the softness of the fruit and the freshness of the long finale. Bianco Fosarin, a blend of tocai, malvasia and pinot bianco, is impressive in the 2005 edition, nicely bringing together apple, almond and crusty bread. And Rosso Cjarandon 2003, a classic Bordeaux blend, is back on top form with a rich bouquet of balsamic fragrances, blackberry tart and blackcurrant. The palate has good structure and a close-knit weave of mellow tannins.

○	Collio Sauvignon '05	▼▼▼	4*
●	Collio Rosso Cjarandon '03	▼▼	5
○	Collio Bianco Fosarin '05	▼▼	4*
○	Collio Picolit '04	▼▼	6
○	Collio Malvasia '05	▼▼	4
○	Collio Tocai Friulano '05	▼▼	4
○	Collio Pinot Grigio '05	▼	4
●	Collio Rosso Cjarandon '00	▽▽▽	5
●	Collio Rosso Cjarandon '01	▽▽▽	5
○	Collio Bianco Fosarin '04	▽▽▽	4
○	Collio Bianco Fosarin '96	▽▽▽	4
○	Collio Sauvignon '98	▽▽▽	4
○	Collio Sauvignon '03	▽▽	4
○	Collio Tocai Friulano '04	▽▽	4

CORMONS (GO)

★ Ronco del Gelso

via Isonzo, 117
34071 Cormons (GO)
tel. 048161310

Year after year, Giorgio Badin uncorks a large number of good to very good wines and we always have difficulty in picking out the best. We'll start with his Pinot Bianco. It is object proof that this variety can achieve a finesse and elegance in its balance of savouriness and fruit sweetness that few other grapes can match. There were equally delicious sensations from the Pinot Grigio 2005. Wood ageing has given it an intriguing spectrum of aromatics and completed malolactic fermentation has lent it sweetness without compromising its vitality. Giorgio's Tocai Friulano is textbook stuff although when we tasted in the summer, just after bottling, it was slightly reduced, as it always is at that time. Summer over, it opens to reveal its full personality in mouthfilling fruit and mineral perceptions that linger deliciously. It's an outstanding white and this year again earned our top award: Three Glasses. Currently, the Merlot is the wine that is receiving most attention in the cellar. The 2004 seems straightforward at first but then tempts the palate with rich fruit and a gutsy attitude. It's a shame that the tannins are just a little intractable. Riesling is not a Friulian variety but Giorgio's version is always attractive and cellarable. The concentrated, very refreshing Latimis, from tocai, riesling and pinot bianco, is still youngish and the eminently drinkable Chardonnay is well typed and well balanced. The Cabernet Franc is creamy, fruity and spicy while the nicely balanced Sauvignon is a little more dilute than usual.

○	Friuli Isonzo Rive Alte Tocai Friulano '05	🍷🍷🍷	4*
○	Friuli Isonzo Pinot Bianco '05	🍷🍷	4*
○	Friuli Isonzo Rive Alte Pinot Grigio Sot lis Rivis '05	🍷🍷	4*
●	Friuli Isonzo Rive Alte Merlot '04	🍷🍷	5
●	Friuli Isonzo Cabernet Franc '05	🍷🍷	4
○	Friuli Isonzo Bianco Latimis '05	🍷🍷	4
○	Friuli Isonzo Rive Alte Chardonnay '05	🍷🍷	4
○	Friuli Isonzo Riesling '05	🍷🍷	4
○	Friuli Isonzo Rive Alte Sauvignon '05	🍷	4
○	Friuli Isonzo Rive Alte Tocai Friulano '04	🍸🍸🍸	4

CORMONS (GO)

Simon di Brazzan

fraz. Brazzano
via San Rocco, 17
34070 Cormons (GO)
tel. 048161182

Daniele Drius, the man who owns this small winery, does almost everything himself. He tends the vines, runs the cellar and even distributes the finished product, braced by the experience of four generations of winemakers. Autumn rain meant that 2005 was not an easy vintage. The right moment to harvest the fruit had to be selected with great care, an even more critical situation when the winery is small with few resources of its own. But despite these challenges, the wines we tasted maintained the standards of the previous vintage. All the wines are steel-vinified and given extended lees contact with the exception of the Merlot, which matures for 12 months in small and large wood, and still needs fine tuning. Blanc di Simon is a single-variety Tocai with distinct rue on the nose, and then green notes and substantial alcohol in the mouth. The Sauvignon is similar, although it has sweeter fruit and a slightly more abrupt finish. The Malvasia is one of the cellar's most successful wines. This year, however, it is penalized by residual carbon dioxide and sulphur, even though it is still very fresh and aroma-rich. We liked the Pinot Grigio and its gunflint, apple and mint aromas, reflected on the attractively long palate. Finally, the Cabernet Franc was made to be drunk young. Soft notes accompany the fresh-tasting fruit, mellowing the variety's "sauvage" woodland notes.

○	Pinot Grigio '05	🍷🍷	4*
○	Blanc di Simon '05	🍷	4
●	Cabernet Franc '05	🍷	4
○	Malvasia '05	🍷	4
○	Sauvignon '05	🍷	4
●	Friuli Isonzo Merlot '03		5
○	Blanc di Simon '04	🍸🍸	4

CORMONS (GO)

OSCAR STURM
LOC. ZEGLA, 1
34071 CORMONS (GO)
TEL. 048160720
www.sturm.it

Last year, we reported that Oscar Sturm was talking about handing over the reins to his son Patrick, and that he was optimistic about the winery's future. Denis has also come back to the nest with a degree from the Bocconi university in Milan but with every intention of helping out, and Oscar's wife Dunja and his young daughter Tajrin are on hand. All this convinced Oscar to make major new investments in the family home-cum-cellar, where there is now a splendid hospitality room and more space for stocking wine. The family farms about ten hectares, turning out 70,000 bottles every year. Much of the output goes to Germany and other non-domestic markets. Patrick excelled himself this time with the Tocai Friulano, a wine that was already excellent in its previous release. Intense apple and pear mingle with hawthorn on the nose, introducing a warm, broad palate with citrussy nuances and unrelenting thrust. It all came together and Three Glasses were delivered to the Sturm household for the very first time. Sauvignon is another Strum specialty. Varietal sage and tomato leaf usher in a palate lent softness by its rich glycerine before the fruit pushes through with a balsamic note. The finish is rounded and refreshing. Rosso Andritz 2003 is dedicated to the town in Styria that the Sturms left behind in the 19th century. A blend of merlot and cabernet sauvignon, it flaunts outstanding concentration and persistence with jammy red fruit. The Chardonnay will be even more attractive when it has had a few more months in bottle and the Pinot Grigio is very sound.

○ Collio Tocai Friulano '05	▼▼▼	4*
● Collio Rosso Andritz '03	▼▼	5
○ Collio Sauvignon '05	▼▼	4*
○ Chardonnay Andritz '05	▼▼	4
○ Collio Pinot Grigio '05	▼▼	4
○ Collio Tocai Friulano '02	▽▽	4
○ Collio Pinot Grigio '03	▽▽	4
○ Collio Sauvignon '03	▽▽	4
○ Chardonnay Andritz '04	▽▽	4
○ Collio Sauvignon '04	▽▽	4

CORMONS (GO)

SUBIDA DI MONTE
LOC. MONTE, 9
34071 CORMONS (GO)
TEL. 048161011
www.subidadimonte.it

Brothers Cristian and Andrea Antonutti continue along the successful path of renewal that they chose a few years ago. Faithful to the maxim that good wine is made in the vineyard, they are following Marco Simonit's expert advice and replanting their entire ten-hectare vine stock to a modern pattern of about 7,000 vines per hectare while aiming for moderate yields. Their father Gigi is one of the grand old men of Friulian wine. He must have raised an eyebrow at his sons' decision but gave them a free hand, trusting their ideas and showing remarkable far-sightedness. In the near future, they will probably expand their plantings of native vines. For the time being, we can report excellent results, particularly on the white front. We were amazed at the Tocai 2005, which earned a place in the Three Glass finals. It is in no hurry to open but then unveils lovely varietal apple fruit laced with almonds. Progression on the palate echoes the nose, enhancing the aromatics with citrus hints. Another big hitter was the Sauvignon 2005, with appealing yellow peach and apricot-led fruit that melds into varietal sage and elderflower. Varietal typicity is also the calling card of the Pinot Grigio 2005, which offsets rich, ripe fruit with elegant minerality. Best of the reds was the Bordeaux blend Rosso Poncaia 2003, an elegant, velvety wine with blackberry tart fruit and still boisterous tannins, but the 2004 Merlot and Cabernet Franc were below par.

○ Collio Tocai Friulano '05	▼▼	4*
● Collio Rosso Poncaia '03	▼▼	5
○ Collio Pinot Grigio '05	▼▼	4
○ Collio Sauvignon '05	▼▼	4
○ Valeas Vincas '05	▼	4
● Collio Cabernet Franc '04		4
● Collio Merlot '04		4
○ Collio Pinot Grigio '04	▽▽	4
○ Valeas Vincas '04	▽▽	4

CORMONS (GO)

Franco Toros

Loc. Novali, 12
34071 Cormons (GO)
tel. 048161327
www.vinitoros.com

Not for the first time, it is our pleasure to sing the praises of this small winery and its owner, Franco Toros, who luckily for us has kept his feet firmly on the ground he tends and cossets with such peerless skill. This time round, we were stunned by his Pinot Bianco, a wine underrated by the vagaries of fashion but which is no less elegant or complete than the ubiquitous Chardonnay with which some superficial nurserymen have often confused it.
Despite its non-local origins, Pinot Bianco is one of the varieties that most fully characterizes Friulian wine. Franco's 2005 is mouthfilling and broad, revealing yellow plums, crusty bread and vine blossom on the nose. The palate has all you could ask of a great Three Glass Pinot Bianco: perfect consistency with the nose, structure, persistence, softness and well-balanced acid freshness. The Tocai, a Toros banker, was almost as good. Fruit-led, warm and very long on the palate, it has a barely perceptible bitterish vein that is nicely balanced by gutsy, glycerine-rich flesh with lots of alcohol. Franco's Merlot is back on form. The 2003 has blackcurrant, mulberry, coffee and chocolate followed by a dense, doughy palate that still manages to flow. The no-nonsense Pinot Grigio is very attractive and the fresh-tasting Sauvignon fills the mouth.
Finally, the intense, well-managed Chardonnay is a tad less exciting than the rest of the range.

○ Collio Pinot Bianco '05	▼▼▼	5
● Collio Merlot Sel. '03	▼▼	7
○ Collio Tocai Friulano '05	▼▼	5
○ Collio Pinot Grigio '05	▼▼	5
○ Collio Sauvignon '05	▼▼	5
○ Collio Chardonnay '05	▼	5
● Collio Merlot Sel. '97	YYY	6
○ Collio Pinot Bianco '00	YYY	4
○ Collio Pinot Bianco '01	YYY	4
○ Collio Tocai Friulano '02	YYY	5
○ Collio Pinot Bianco '03	YYY	5
○ Collio Tocai Friulano '03	YYY	5
○ Collio Tocai Friulano '04	YYY	5
○ Collio Pinot Grigio '03	YY	5
○ Collio Pinot Bianco '04	YY	5

CORMONS (GO)

Vigna del Lauro

Loc. Monte, 38
34071 Cormons (GO)
tel. 048160155

Vigna del Lauro is a joint venture of respected oenologist and producer Fabio Coser and Eberhard Spangenberg, a German importer of Italian wines. The philosophy embodied in the wines, sourced from eight hectares in the Collio and Isonzo DOC zones, is we think oriented towards very good value varietal wines of no great complexity but with plenty of sincere drinkability. In short, the Fabio Coser style. But with vineyards that are well-aspected, mature vines and highly experienced technical supervision, it is no surprise that every so often a superstar emerges. One such is the Ribolla Gialla 2005, which went through to our final Three Glass tastings. The secret of this product is that it comes from 40-year-old vines. They are at the peak of maturity and their roots sink deep, ensuring perfect harmony with the soil and surrounding environment. All of Ribolla Gialla's aromatics are there, from the subtle notes of rennet apple, gunflint and sage to orange. These return on the full-bodied palate before the tangy finish unfurls all its length. Another very fine wine is the Pinot Grigio 2005, which like its stablemate comes from old vines. It stands out for its balance of fruit and the variety's mineral sensations. Entry on the palate is soft, expansive and well sustained as it moves through to a finish of almonds and apples. We would point out the fragrant palate of the Tocai 2005 and the creamy texture of the Chardonnay 2005. And to round off, there was a very fruity Sauvignon 2005.

○ Collio Ribolla Gialla '05	▼▼	4*
○ Collio Pinot Grigio '05	▼▼	4*
○ Collio Sauvignon '05	▼	4
○ Collio Tocai Friulano '05	▼	4
○ Friuli Isonzo Chardonnay '05	▼	4
○ Collio Sauvignon '99	YYY	4
○ Collio Bianco '02	YY	4
○ Collio Ribolla Gialla '04	YY	4
○ Collio Tocai Friulano '04	YY	4
○ Friuli Isonzo Chardonnay '04	YY	4

CORMONS (GO)

Francesco Vosca

fraz. Brazzano
via Sottomonte, 19
34070 Cormons (GO)
tel. 048162135

It's not easy to find Francesco Vosca's winery, even though Brazzano is hardly a metropolis. But when you get there, the owner is as unfussy as his cellar. Francesco is a serious, reflective wine man who takes a prudent approach to the market, bottling only when he is sure he can sell. Last year, we enjoyed a stunning Tocai Friulano 2004, which had no difficulty in finding customers. The Vosca holding includes two and a half hectares in the Collio, with a further three on the Isonzo flatlands, a fairly typical distribution in the Cormons area. Different varieties are grown in the two zones so there is no possibility of confusion. The vines are double-arch trained, called "alla cappuccina" in Friuli, and vineyard management is perforce manual. Francesco is continuing a family tradition but he can also call on advice from oenologist Luigino De Giuseppe and his good friend Mauro Mauri. Average annual production is roughly 15,000 bottles, released as we said in accordance with demand. Again Francesco uncorked a great Tocai Friulano with crisp williams pear on the nose and a fresh, tangy palate with nice fruit, minerality and elegance. The Pinot Grigio reveals citrus notes and impeccable nose-palate consistency. Concentration is the keynote of the Malvasia, which takes its time opening in the glass. Finally, the Friuli Isonzo Sauvignon and Chardonnay were a notch lower.

○	Collio Malvasia '05	🍷🍷	4*
○	Collio Pinot Grigio '05	🍷🍷	4*
○	Collio Tocai Friulano '05	🍷🍷	4*
○	Friuli Isonzo Sauvignon '05	🍷	4
○	Friuli Isonzo Chardonnay '05	🍷	4
○	Collio Malvasia '04	🍷🍷 (white)	4
○	Collio Tocai Friulano '04	🍷🍷 (white)	4
○	Friuli Isonzo Chardonnay '04	🍷🍷 (white)	4
○	Friuli Isonzo Sauvignon '04	🍷🍷 (white)	4

CORNO DI ROSAZZO (UD)

Alberice

via Bosco Romagno, 4
33044 Corno di Rosazzo (UD)
tel. 0422765571
www.tenutealeandri.it

The Tenute Aleandri group includes four distinct estates that operate in different geographical areas. One is the Alberice property, which lies in the heart of the Colli Orientali del Friuli DOC zone. The 25 hectares are located next to the Bosco Romagno nature reserve in the hills of the municipality of Corno di Rosazzo. Cellar policy is to produce premium wines from the area's classic varieties, starting with scrupulously tended vineyards. In recent years, the estate has engaged outside collaborators of the first order, both in the vineyard – Marco Simonit and Pierpaolo Sirch – and the cellar, Gianni Menotti. The consultants work in close contact with Francesco Carpené and Luciano Coden, who have been running the estate for as long as anyone can remember. This year's wines bear witness to these changes as four of the six presented won Two Glasses. Rosso Tango 2003, from merlot and cabernet sauvignon, is international in style, having matured for 12 months in barrique. Rich chocolate and cinchona aromas accompany serious structure that is nicely balanced by soft fruit. We like the spring flowers and tobacco aromas of the Pinot Grigio, which stand out against a backdrop of fruit. The steel-fermented Chardonnay has tempting banana and melon as well as good thrust on the very fresh palate. Malvasia is a new product. We enjoyed its sophisticated, well-defined chamomile, white peach and citrus nose, as well as the contrast of soft sensations and fresh acidity.

●	COF Rosso Tango '03	🍷🍷	5
○	COF Chardonnay '05	🍷🍷	4*
○	COF Pinot Grigio '05	🍷🍷	4*
○	COF Malvasia '05	🍷🍷	4*
○	COF Sauvignon '05	🍷	4
○	COF Tocai Friulano '05	🍷	4
○	COF Chardonnay '04	🍷🍷 (white)	4
○	COF Pinot Grigio '04	🍷🍷 (white)	4
○	COF Tocai Friulano '04	🍷🍷 (white)	4

Valentino Butussi

via Prà di Corte, 1
33040 Corno di Rosazzo (UD)
tel. 0432759194
www.butussi.it

It's always a pleasure to talk about estates when the people who work there live on site. In the case of the Butussis, we have a family business in the full sense of the term. After years of sacrifice, the gruff but profoundly genuine Angelo and his wife Pierina set up their 16-hectare wine estate on the marl and sandstone of Prà di Corte. One after the other, their four children Erika, Filippo, Tobia and Mattia have gradually taken on active roles in the business, which in the meantime has acquired a lovely agriturismo facility in an 18th-century villa. We imagine they are celebrating together over their latest Tocai, which went through to our finals. Butussi teamwork has brought us a wine with fresh citrus and spring flower sensations that meld attractively with varietal bitter almonds, preceding a well-balanced palate of mirror-like consistency with the nose. The Pinot Grigio is fragrant, clean and invitingly rich in citrus, peach and delicious apple notes. What we liked about the Picolit 2004 was the breadth and richness of the palate, with its never-ending finish of honey and candied citrus peel. The robustly structured Rosso di Corte, a cabernet sauvignon-heavy blend with smaller proportions of merlot and refosco, came close to a second Glass. From the rest of the range, we picked out the attractive minerality of the chardonnay, pinot bianco and ribolla Bianco di Corte, the varietal baked apple of the Verduzzo and the finesse of the Ribolla.

○	COF Tocai Friulano '05	🍷🍷	4*
○	COF Picolit '04	🍷🍷	7
○	COF Pinot Grigio '05	🍷🍷	4
○	COF Bianco di Corte '04	🍷	4
●	COF Cabernet Sauvignon '04	🍷	4
●	COF Rosso di Corte '04	🍷	5
○	COF Verduzzo Friulano '04	🍷	4
●	COF Cabernet Franc '05	🍷	4
○	COF Chardonnay '05	🍷	4
○	COF Ribolla Gialla '05	🍷	4
○	COF Sauvignon '05	🍷	4
○	Friuli Grave Pinot Bianco '05	🍷	4
●	Friuli Grave Refosco P. R. '05		4
○	COF Verduzzo Friulano '03	YY	4

Ca di Bon

via Casali Gallo, 1
33040 Corno di Rosazzo (UD)
tel. 0432759316
www.cadibon.com

Gianni and Ameris Bon are showing commendable far-sightedness by involving their children Luca and Francesca more and more in both the production and the distribution sides of the business. Some of the wine obtained from their 11 hectares is sold unbottled but the rest goes into almost 60,000 bottles, many sold in the attractive outlet that the Bons own at San Giovanni al Natisone. Most of the vineyards are in the Colli Orientali DOC, with just a small proportion in Grave del Friuli and Collio. Tocai Friulano was the wine that came out on top this time, its nose showing very ripe pear and baked apples before the warm, broad palate unleashes its generous fruit. The Ribolla Gialla came close to a second Glass for its nose of freshly squeezed citrus juice and attractive complexity in the mouth, where the freshness is nicely contrasted by a sweetish note that gives the long final considerable appeal. We found sweet apples and acacia blossom on its truly intriguing nose. These sensations return in the mouth but the acidity is a little over-assertive. Cherry, black cherry and plum jam delight both nose and palate as the Merlot opens out, losing none of its intensity. Finally, the golden Verduzzo Friulano gives varietal ripe apple before the sweet palate's dried apricots and caramel perhaps cloy slightly.

○	COF Tocai Friulano '05	🍷🍷	4
●	COF Merlot '05	🍷	4
○	COF Pinot Bianco '05	🍷	4
○	COF Pinot Grigio '05	🍷	4
○	COF Ribolla Gialla '05	🍷	4
○	COF Verduzzo Friulano '05	🍷	4
○	Friuli Grave Sauvignon '05		4
●	COF Refosco P. R. '05		4
●	COF Schioppettino '05		4
○	COF Tocai Friulano '03	YY	4

CORNO DI ROSAZZO (UD)

EUGENIO COLLAVINI

LOC. GRAMOGLIANO
VIA DELLA RIBOLLA GIALLA, 2
33040 CORNO DI ROSAZZO (UD)
TEL. 0432753222
www.collavini.it

Once again, Manlio Collavini's winery has lived up to the expectations of fine wine fans and released an extensive range of first-rate products. Our various tastings over recent months confirmed that the Collavini cellar was as dependable as ever and would offer consumers top-notch wines at fair prices. Manlio has the assistance of his sons Luigi, an irrepressible communicator who is in charge of marketing, and Giovanni, who keeps a supportive eye on the work of oenologist Walter Bergnach in the cellar. Output is roughly one and a half million bottles a year, obtained from fruit grown on 173 estate-owned or contracted hectares. In the cellar you will find everything needed to ensure the constancy of quality that can defy the vagaries of the growing year. Cask conditioning, raisining and freezing are just some of the processes that contribute to the excellent overall results. This year, the tocai, chardonnay and sauvignon-based Bianco Broy has an intensely creamy, elegant nose and a buttery palate of very ripe fruit and lingering citrus. Merlot dal Pic 2003 has a complex nose of cherries and black cherries, overripe fruit softening the flavour of the generous tannic weave. Finally, the onionskin-veined hue of the Pinot Grigio heralds an elegant, concentrated wine with tangy freshness and a broad swath of intriguing fruit.

●	Collio Merlot dal Pic '03	▼▼	6
○	Collio Bianco Broy '05	▼▼	5
○	Collio Pinot Grigio Canlungo '05	▼▼	4*
○	COF Ribolla Gialla Turian '05	▼▼	5
○	Collio Tocai Friulano T '05	▼▼	4
○	Friuli Isonzo Bianco Cuccanea '05	▼▼	5
○	Collio Bianco Broy '03	▽▽▽	5
○	Collio Bianco Broy '04	▽▽▽	5
●	Collio Merlot dal Pic '00	▽▽	6
●	Collio Merlot dal Pic '01	▽▽	6
○	Collio Pinot Grigio Canlungo '04	▽▽	4

CORNO DI ROSAZZO (UD)

ADRIANO GIGANTE

VIA ROCCA BERNARDA, 3
33040 CORNO DI ROSAZZO (UD)
TEL. 0432755835
www.adrianogigante.it

It's always refreshing to chat with Adriano Gigante. His fluent mode of conversation brims with enthusiasm for his work, but also with remarkable modesty. Actually, might not realize you were talking to one of Friuli's finest winemakers, and we do not say this out of friendship. We are simply stating the facts, confirmed this year by the stellar range Adriano presented. Yet again, his Tocai Vigneto Storico walked off with Three Glasses. The vines in the Vigneto Storico vineyard itself are more than 70 years old and they have brought us this clean, well-defined Tocai with varietal bitter almonds and crusty bread lifted by spring flowers. It explodes onto the palate with full, rich fruit that give way in the finish to the almond-like notes of the bouquet. Even better, the 10,000 bottles released offer great value for money. Only a step behind is the Pignolo 2002, which has warm gamey sensations fusing attractively with oak-derived perceptions. It's also long and very spicy on the lingering finish. The Merlot Riserva 2003 is another very fine red. Only released in exceptional vintages, it stands out for its prominent fruit and rounded, silky tannins. Two whites from the standard range also caught our tasters' attention, the Sauvignon and Pinot Grigio 2005. The Sauvignon opens slowly to reveal varietal green notes of rue and sage, highlighted against background minerality, while the Pinot Grigio has great thrust on the palate and a tangy finish. We would also point out the delicacy and finesse of the 2005 Tocai.

○	COF Tocai Friulano Vigneto Storico '05	▼▼▼	5*
●	COF Pignolo '02	▼▼	6
●	COF Merlot Ris. '03	▼▼	6
○	COF Sauvignon '05	▼▼	4*
●	COF Refosco P. R. '04	▼▼	4
●	COF Schioppettino '04	▼▼	5
○	COF Chardonnay '05	▼▼	4
○	COF Pinot Grigio '05	▼▼	4
○	COF Tocai Friulano '05	▼▼	4
○	COF Picolit '03	▼	7
○	COF Verduzzo Friulano '04	▼	4
●	COF Merlot '04		4
○	COF Tocai Friulano Storico '00	▽▽▽	5
○	COF Tocai Friulano Vigneto Storico '03	▽▽▽	5

CORNO DI ROSAZZO (UD)

PERUSINI

LOC. GRAMOGLIANO
VIA TORRIONE, 13
33040 CORNO DI ROSAZZO (UD)
TEL. 0432675018
www.perusini.com

The name Perusini looms large in the cultural and oenological history of Friuli. In the early 20th century, Giacomo Perusini wrote a treatise entitled "Il Piccolit", about a vine type that his winery was recovering and selecting. About half a century ago, Giuseppina Perusini Antonini published her book "Mangiare e ber Friulano", even today a key text on the region's food and wine. Her son Gaetano was a distinguished agricultural anthropologist and her other son Giampaolo continued selection of ribolla gialla and merlot, which Teresa Perusini has recently started again in collaboration with the University of Udine. Teresa (Resi) is an art historian but she and her husband Giacomo De Pace devote much of their time to running the family estate, which includes the Al Postiglione restaurant and a number of well-restored, attractively furnished accommodations, as well as the vineyards and cellar. There is also a large, striking truncated pyramid tower, built to plans by the University of Venice, which houses the estate offices, a Foucault's pendulum and an underground barrique cellar. The vines are the responsibility of Pierpaolo Sirch and Alessio Dorigo looks after vinification. Pinot Grigio is Resi Perusini's top wine again, thanks to broad fruit aromatics enhanced by citrus. We would also point out the fresh, varietal acidity of the Ribolla Gialla and the rich fruit of the Rosso del Postiglione 2004, a nicely balanced Bordeaux blend.

○	COF Pinot Grigio '05	▼▼	4
●	COF Merlot '04	▼	4
●	COF Rosso del Postiglione '04	▼	4
○	COF Chardonnay '05	▼	4
○	COF Ribolla Gialla '05	▼	4
○	COF Sauvignon '05	▼	4
●	COF Merlot '03	▽▽	4
○	COF Ribolla Gialla '03	▽▽	4
○	COF Pinot Grigio '04	▽▽	4

CORNO DI ROSAZZO (UD)

LEONARDO SPECOGNA

VIA ROCCA BERNARDA, 4
33040 CORNO DI ROSAZZO (UD)
TEL. 0432755840
www.specogna.it

Graziano Specogna and his sons, Cristian and Michele, deserve credit for having managed over the years to give their wines a distinctive style that is full-bodied, wonderfully expressive and very original. This is particularly true of the Pinot Grigio and Tocai. No one could accuse them of being swayed by the fashions of the moment. Instead, they have tenaciously continued along the route they mapped out long ago. The Specogna style is achieved through vinification techniques that include maceration on the skins – not too long for whites, more for reds – and the exclusive use of ambient yeasts. There can be no doubt about the stature of this year's vintage, although there is no great champion that would enable us to call it exceptional. But the Merlot Oltre 2002, a broad-shouldered, austere, wine from slightly raisined grapes that has lots of complexity, the Chardonnay 2004, with alluringly intense tropical fruit, and the very varietal Sauvignon 2005 all easily earned very high scores. The same is true of the Pignolo 2003 with its faint gaminess and attractive spice. The Pinot Grigio 2005 has a classic onionskin hue and lovely fragrances of apple, williams pear, melon and citrus and finally the Tocai 2005 as usual has the variety's trademark vegetality.

●	COF Merlot Oltre '02	▼▼	6
●	COF Pignolo '03	▼▼	5
○	COF Chardonnay '04	▼▼	4
○	COF Sauvignon '05	▼▼	4
○	COF Tocai Friulano '05	▼▼	4
○	Pinot Grigio '05	▼▼	4
●	COF Merlot '04	▼	4
○	COF Picolit '04	▼	7
●	COF Refosco P. R. '04	▼	4
○	COF Verduzzo Friulano '05	▼	4
●	COF Cabernet Franc '05		4
●	COF Merlot Oltre '01	▽▽	6
○	COF Chardonnay '03	▽▽	4
○	COF Tocai Friulano '04	▽▽	4

CORNO DI ROSAZZO (UD)

Andrea Visintini

via Gramogliano, 27
33040 Corno di Rosazzo (UD)
tel. 0432755813
www.vinivisintini.com

Andrea Visintini set up his winery in 1973. A few years ago, his children took over production and distribution, although Andrea is still on hand to help out. Oliviero and the twins Palmira and Cinzia are impossible to dislike and work very well together as a team. You can't miss the winery, thanks to the tower, dating from 1560, which the Visintinis have restored. A historical artefact with an ancient history, the original structure was actually part of the defence system created by the Romans to watch over the road from Aquileia to Forum Julii, today's Cividale. Obviously, the tower is a listed building, and for years this prevented the winery from expanding its working area. But the Visintinis are nothing if not enterprising. Over the years, the put together the finance to build their new cellar completely underground. Now the spaces they have to work in are sufficient and distinctly eye-catching, as visitors will be able to appreciate. The Visintinis also have more vine stock, which now extends over 25 hectares, and their production runs to about 100,000 bottles of competitively priced wines. The elegant, violet-fragranced Malvasia is back in the spotlight and the well-structured, savoury Tocai has well-gauged freshness. The other wines we tasted are well-managed and interesting, as well as delightfully easy to drink.

○	COF Tocai Friulano '05	🍷🍷	3*
○	Collio Malvasia '05	🍷🍷	4
○	COF Bianco '05	🍷	4
○	COF Pinot Bianco '05	🍷	4
○	COF Pinot Grigio '05	🍷	4
○	COF Ribolla Gialla '05	🍷	4
○	COF Sauvignon '05	🍷	4
○	COF Tocai Friulano '02	ΥΥ	3
○	COF Bianco '03	ΥΥ	3
○	COF Tocai Friulano '03	ΥΥ	3
○	COF Pinot Bianco '04	ΥΥ	4
○	COF Sauvignon '04	ΥΥ	4

CORNO DI ROSAZZO (UD)

Zof

fraz. Sant'Andrat del Judrio
via Giovanni XXIII, 32a
33040 Corno di Rosazzo (UD)
tel. 0432759673
www.zof.it

Just over 20 years ago, Alberto Zof decided to turn his hand to grape growing, flanking this activity with a busy agriturismo. But it was Alberto's son Daniele who cranked up the quality of the wines enough to earn a profile in the Guide. What happened was that Daniele met Donato Lanati at university and managed to persuade his father to hire the highly rated Piedmontese consultant. It was only a few years after Alberto's decision that the estate found itself in the front rank of Friulian wineries. Today, Alberto and his wife concentrate on the agriturismo and it is Daniele who devotes all his energies to tending the nine estate-owned and four rented hectares, producing about 60,000 bottles a year. The 2005 growing year was interrupted by heavy rain, which has left its mark on the Zof wines. Only the Ribolla Gialla managed to pick up a second Glass. Complex and elegantly intense on the melon and apple-led nose, it has varietal acidity in the mouth and a lingering finish. Bianco Sonata 2004 is from chardonnay and sauvignon. It is juicy and appealing, but let down a little by the vanilla and coffee it has acquired from the oak.

○	COF Ribolla Gialla '05	🍷🍷	4*
○	COF Picolit '03	🍷	6
○	COF Bianco Sonata '04	🍷	4
●	COF Cabernet Franc '04	🍷	4
○	COF Pinot Grigio '05	🍷	4
○	COF Tocai Friulano '05		4
○	COF Picolit '01	ΥΥ	6
●	COF Cabernet Franc '03	ΥΥ	4
○	COF Pinot Grigio '04	ΥΥ	4
○	COF Ribolla Gialla '04	ΥΥ	4

DOLEGNA DEL COLLIO (GO)

Ca' Ronesca

Loc. Lonzano
Casali Zorutti, 2
34070 Dolegna del Collio (GO)
tel. 048160034
www.caronesca.it

Davide Alcide Setten is a Veneto-based businessman with interests in football. He is also the new owner of Ca' Ronesca, an estate created in 1972 on the hills at Ipplis and Dolegna, with plots in the Collio and Colli Orientali del Friuli DOC zones. Some 52 of the estate's 100 acres are planted to vine, the rest being left as woodland to maintain the surrounding ecosystem alive and intact. The new owner's ideas are founded on the principles that have always underpinned Ca' Ronesca: to make excellent wines while respecting the territory's vocation and nature. That continuity is also present in the estate staff, under the guidance of long-standing winery oenologist Franco Della Rosa. The wines we tasted were all up to the standards displayed in previous editions of the Guide, and come from the vinification of healthy fruit grown in vineyards planted more than 30 years ago. The top products are the Bianco Marnà 2003, from pinot bianco and malvasia istriana aged for 15 months in barrique, the 2001 Cabernet Franc Podere San Giacomo selection and the Tocai Friulano. Bianco Marnà has complex mint, apricot and tea on the nose followed by a tangy, attractively creamy-textured palate. Delicious balsam pervades the Cabernet San Giacomo whereas the Tocai is headily redolent of flowers. Both the fruit-forward Pinot Grigio and the flower-themed Ribolla Gialla earned very full Glasses.

●	Collio Cabernet Franc Podere San Giacomo '01	🍷🍷	6
○	Collio Bianco Marnà '03	🍷🍷	5
○	Collio Tocai Friulano '05	🍷🍷	4*
○	Collio Chardonnay '05	🍷	4
○	Collio Pinot Grigio '05	🍷	4
○	Collio Ribolla Gialla '05	🍷	4
○	Collio Sauvignon '05		4
○	Collio Bianco Marnà '01	YY	4
○	COF Picolit '02	YY	6
○	COF Sauvignon Podere di Ipplis '04	YY	5
○	Collio Chardonnay '04	YY	4

DOLEGNA DEL COLLIO (GO)

★ Venica & Venica

Loc. Cero, 8
34070 Dolegna del Collio (GO)
tel. 048161264 - 048160177
www.venica.it

The family winery run by Gianni and Giorgio Venica was founded in 1930 and now farms 29 hectares, plus a further five that are rented. For some time, the two brothers have been investing in Calabria, where they produce wine and monocultivar olive oil. Wine production each year is about 250,000 bottles and their modern cellar is rationally laid out. Gianni's son, Giampaolo, has been taking on more and more responsibility in the cellar, although he, like the rest of the family, is never slow to lend a hand in the vineyard. Pruning at Venica & Venica is orchestrated by Marco Simonit and Pierpaolo Sirch, who ensure that the best fruit goes for vinification. Before we move on to the wines, we should note that Gianni's wife Ornella Venica is the tireless president of the prestigious Consorzio Collio. Back among the prizes is the classic Sauvignon Ronco delle Mele, a wine that has always been a benchmark for producers of the variety. Less aggressively assertive than in some recent vintages, it gives satisfying tomato leaf, bell pepper, sage and tropical fruit aromatics. Entry on the palate is stunning, opening elegantly in mid palate to suggest sweet citrus before the peach-veined finale. Tocai Ronco delle Cime offers remarkable intensity and richness, hinting at baked apple and pear, and the Pinot Bianco has all the variety's trademark elegance. A special mention goes to the Refosco Bottaz 2003. At last, the Venicas have a red worthy of their great whites.

○	Collio Sauvignon Ronco delle Mele '05	🍷🍷🍷	6
○	Collio Pinot Bianco '05	🍷🍷	5
○	Collio Tocai Friulano Ronco delle Cime '05	🍷🍷	5
●	Refosco P. R. Bottaz '03	🍷🍷	6
○	Collio Bianco Tre Vignis '04	🍷🍷	6
○	Collio Malvasia '05	🍷🍷	5
○	Collio Pinot Grigio Jesera '05	🍷🍷	5
○	Collio Ribolla Gialla '05	🍷🍷	5
○	Collio Traminer Aromatico '05	🍷🍷	5
○	Collio Sauvignon Ronco delle Mele '02	YYY	6

DUINO AURISINA (TS)

KANTE

FRAZ. PELAGIO
LOC. PREPOTTO, 1A
34011 DUINO AURISINA (TS)
TEL. 040200255

Edi Kante's wines are back, and with them the Guide profile that is his by right. Edi delayed release of his selections to give them time to mature. Wines from this part of the world, where the grapes grow on difficult-to-work soil wrested from the rock, need plenty of time to age. Nature must take its course, whatever the dictates of fashion. Edi has worked hard to give this less well-known corner of Friuli's wine map a role appropriate to its potential. In only a few short years, he has obtained recognition of his wines' quality both in Italy and abroad. He has won his wager to give the Carso DOC greater visibility and today, as you admire the eye-catching cellar carved out of the rock, Edi's incredible efforts now seem a thing of the past. This year, the Kante wines come in one-litre and half-litre bottles, both with an unusual, very small neck. The stoppers, from hillside cork oak plantations, are tiny and much denser than ordinary corks. The reliability of Edi's wines and his chosen strategy are underlined by the amazing Chardonnay 2003. Intense, sophisticated fragrances fuse citrus with white-fleshed fruits before the balance of freshness and soft perceptions on the palate takes you through to a long, tangy finish that makes the wine extremely tempting. The Malvasia has good thrust and breadth while the enjoyable Vitovska is very well-balanced. Spice, gamey aromas and more subtle sensations of blackberry tart pervade the Terrano, obtained from the Carso variety of the same name. Last up was the Sauvignon, a ripe, sunny white with tropical fruit sensations.

○	Carso Chardonnay '03	▼▼	6
●	Carso Terrano '02	▼▼	5
○	Carso Malvasia '03	▼▼	6
○	Carso Sauvignon '03	▼▼	6
○	Carso Vitovska '03	▼▼	6
○	Carso Malvasia '98	▽▽▽	6
○	Carso Chardonnay '94	▽▽▽	6
○	Carso Sauvignon '92	▽▽▽	6
○	Carso Sauvignon '91	▽▽▽	6
○	Carso Sauvignon '01	▽▽	6
○	Carso Chardonnay '02	▽▽	6
○	Carso Chardonnay Sel. '99	▽▽	6
○	Carso Malvasia '02	▽▽	6
○	Carso Vitovska '02	▽▽	6

DUINO AURISINA (TS)

SKERK

FRAZ. PELAGIO
LOC. PREPOTTO, 20
34011 DUINO AURISINA (TS)
TEL. 040200156 - 0402025098
www.skerk.com

Skerk is back in the Guide. The small Carso winery is run by Boris Skerk and – especially – by is son Sandi, a self-taught wine man who has accumulated a fine store of experience. Sandi has never lost his taste for experimenting, although he does prefer to do things one step at a time. Currently, only three and a half hectares out of six are in production, most replanted at a density of 8,000 vines per hectare. The small cellar deserves a brief description. The upper floor looks ordinary enough but the space underneath has been literally carved out of the Carso rock, because it turned out to be too rough for traditional drills. The walls are mostly smooth but here and there can be seen the famous karst cavities, one of which is apparently bottomless. It is here that the Skerks have put the large and small wood where the wines stay on the lees for almost a year. About 15,000 bottles are released each year under four labels. The intense fruit and classic elderflower aromas of the Sauvignon 2004 are accompanied by a marked milky note. Skilful use of wood is obvious in the Carso Vitovska 2004, from a native variety, where golden delicious apples and yeasts are picked up on the fresh-tasting palate. Finally, the Malvasia 2004 has good structure, its oak-derived confectioner's cream attractively complementing the fruit.

○	Carso Malvasia Non Filtrato '04	▼▼	4*
○	Carso Sauvignon Non Filtrato '04	▼▼	4*
○	Carso Vitovska Non Filtrato '04	▼▼	4*
●	Carso Terrano Non Filtrato '04	▼	4
○	Carso Sauvignon '02	▽▽	4
○	Carso Malvasia '02	▽▽	4
○	Carso Vitovska '02	▽▽	4

DUINO AURISINA (TS)

ZIDARICH
LOC. PREPOTTO, 23
34011 DUINO AURISINA (TS)
TEL. 040201223
www.zidarich.it

Beniamino Zidarich's approach to winemaking is meticulous and extremely respectful of nature, something that in the Carso zone is practically de rigueur. Vine density per hectare is high, ranging from 8-10,000 plants, and the fruit is destemmed before fermentation and maceration on the skins in open vats, with the cap punched down several times a day. There is no temperature control, ambient yeasts are used, ageing is in large Slavonian oak and Beniamino shuns filtering and stabilization. The same procedures are used for all the selections, whether white or red. Beniamino's new strategy is bearing fruit, as the last range of wines presented amply demonstrates. They are characterful wines that do not reveal their secrets easily but they do show just how good this small winery's environment-friendly products can be. First on our list was the excellent Prulke 2004, from sauvignon, vitovska and malvasia. Subtle almonds and dried flowers are the prelude to a palate that lives up to expectations. Ripe fruit, roses and elderflower are the keynotes of the Vitovska 2004, which has lovely balance in the mouth where the marked freshness is a counterpoint to faintly astringent sensations. But the ripe fruit and wisteria blossom Malvasia 2004 lacks a little balance, especially on the palate. Finally, the Terrano 2004 is a little muffled, and the raisining-derived notes are at odd with the rustic texture, but the spice and ripe-cherry aromas are true to type.

○	Prulke '04	▼▼	6
○	Carso Vitovska '04	▼▼	6
○	Carso Malvasia '04	▼	6
●	Carso Terrano '04	▼	6
○	Prulke '02	▽▽	6
●	Carso Terrano '00	▽▽	5
○	Prulke '01	▽▽	6
○	Prulke '03	▽▽	6
○	Carso Malvasia '99	▽▽	5

FAEDIS (UD)

MARCO CECCHINI
LOC. CASALI DE LUCA
VIA COLOMBANI
33040 FAEDIS (UD)
TEL. 0432720563
www.cecchinimarco.com

For several years, we have been following with great interest the winemaking career of Marco Cecchini, who has a degree in economics. Now 30 years old, Marco started out with a small plot his grandfather gave him, expanding his property to three hectares and renting a further seven. The location is not one of the best for red wines, and again this year his Refosco and Rosso Careme, from 70 per cent merlot with refosco and cabernet, went no further than a mention. The contributions of agronomist Gibil Crespan and technicians Fabio Narozzi in the vineyard and Sonia Dell'Oste in the cellar, together with Alessio Dorigo's Terra e Vino group, enable the small cellar to turn out about 25,000 bottles, with some well-established peaks. We refer in particular to Tovè, a white originally blended from tocai and verduzzo, which today is virtually a single-variety Tocai Friulano. The nose gives apple, pear and hints of peach, which follow through on the fruit-forward, fresh-tasting palate where sage and pear drops come through, lingering attractively. Verduzzo Verlit 2004 has varietal baked apples lifted after part-drying by dried figs and candied orange peel. On the nose of the Pinot Grigio we find apples, pears and damsons before williams pears takes over on a palate marked down by too much softness. Lemon and citrus characterize the Riesling Pietrevolte, from a variety that has no track record in Friuli.

○	COF Bianco Tovè '05	▼▼	4*
○	COF Verduzzo Friulano Verlit '04	▼	6
○	Pinot Grigio Bellagioia '05	▼	4
○	Riesling Pietrevolte '05	▼	4
●	COF Refosco P. R. '05		4
●	COF Rosso Careme '05		4
○	COF Bianco Tovè '02	▽▽	4
○	COF Picolit '03	▽▽	6
○	COF Verduzzo Friulano Verlit '03	▽▽	6
○	COF Verduzzo Friulano Verlit '02	▽▽	6
○	COF Pinot Grigio Vign. Bellagioia '04	▽▽	4

FAEDIS (UD)

PAOLINO COMELLI
FRAZ. COLLOREDO DI SOFFUMBERGO
VIA DELLA CHIESA, 8
33019 FAEDIS (UD)
TEL. 0432711226
www.comelli.it

It has to be said that the weather in Friuli during the 2005 growing year could have been better. Heavy summer rain was only partially offset by a dry, sunny September. That sort of weather pattern could have had a serious effect on the quality of fruit at this lovely estate, nestling in the cool, wooded hills at Faedis. But Pierluigi Comelli and oenologist Eros Zanini managed to pull yet another positive vintage out of their hat, presenting us with some very convincing, well-defined wines. The Comelli estate is tended like a garden and an old Friulian house with guest accommodation adds an extra touch. Production focuses on whites, although it has to be said that much effort has gone into improving the reds. Proof of this attention comes in the form of a lovely Tocai Friulano, a white with a great heritage, and a gutsy Merlot, both of which picked up Two Glasses. The Tocai stands out for rich aromatic herbs and gunflint before unfolding confidently on the almond-themed palate. Our tasters were impressed by the Merlot's blackberry tart and vanilla, which combine to give a sensation of creaminess. From the rest of the range, we would note the soft Cabernet Sauvignon 2004, the progression in the mouth of the Pinot Grigio, a fresh-tasting Chardonnay and the vegetal Sauvignon.

● COF Merlot '04	🍷🍷	4*
○ COF Tocai Friulano '05	🍷🍷	4*
● COF Cabernet Sauvignon '04	🍷	4
○ COF Chardonnay '05	🍷	4
○ COF Pinot Grigio '05	🍷	4
○ COF Sauvignon '05	🍷	4
○ COF Tocai Friulano '03	YY	4
○ COF Tocai Friulano '04	YY	4
○ COF Tocai Friulano '02	YY	4
● COF Merlot '03	YY	4
○ COF Pinot Grigio '04	YY	4

FARRA D'ISONZO (GO)

BORGO CONVENTI
S.DA DELLA COLOMBARA, 13
34070 FARRA D'ISONZO (GO)
TEL. 0481888004
www.borgoconventi.it

Borgo Conventi was set up in 1975 and soon became on of Friuli's most interesting wine estates. After many years at the top, the cellar went through a difficult period that coincided with its sale in 2001. The new owners of the lovely property were Tuscany-based Tenimenti Ruffino, which at the time was looking to expand its horizons. The branch of the Folonari family in charge of Tenimenti Ruffino decided that the Friuli's Collio and Isonzo were DOC zones that held potential for their winemaking ambitions. Now, Borgo Conventi has 42 hectares under vine and an annual production of 350,000 bottles split between two lines, Borgo Conventi for the wines from the Collio and I Fiori del Borgo for Friuli Isonzo DOC products. The wines we tasted in 2006 reflect the style established by the new owners, although positive input has come from consultant oenologist Gianni Menotti and vineyard selections are now on the agenda. The most interesting wines are the ones from the Collio, some of which earned Two Glasses, the Pinot Grigio 2005, Bianco Colle Russian 2004 from cask-conditioned chardonnay and malvasia, and the merlot and refosco Braida Nuova 2004. The Pinot Grigio is slow to open but then reveals elegant varietal gunflint, citrus and pears, a nicely concentrated palate and a warm almondy finale. Colle Russian strikes a fine balance of vanilla and citrus, following these up with a well-sustained palate. Lastly, Braida Nuova, has green notes on the nose and a satisfyingly dynamic palate. The rest of the range is up to snuff.

● Braida Nuova '04	🍷🍷	6
○ Collio Bianco Colle Russian '04	🍷🍷	5
○ Collio Pinot Grigio '05	🍷🍷	4*
○ Collio Chardonnay '05	🍷	4
○ Collio Ribolla Gialla '05	🍷	4
○ Collio Sauvignon '05	🍷	4
○ Collio Tocai Friulano '05	🍷	4
○ Friuli Isonzo Chardonnay '05	🍷	4
○ Friuli Isonzo Pinot Grigio '05	🍷	4
● Friuli Isonzo Refosco P. R. '05	🍷	4
○ Friuli Isonzo Sauvignon '05	🍷	4
○ Friuli Isonzo Tocai Friulano '05	🍷	4
○ Collio Pinot Grigio '04	YY	4

FARRA D'ISONZO (GO)

Casa Zuliani

via Gradisca, 23
34070 Farra d'Isonzo (GO)
tel. 0481888506
www.casazuliani.com

Federico Frumento has every right to be satisfied that he has taken his family estate into the front rank of Friulian wine in just a few short years. In the 1970s, his grandmother Bruna Zuliani expanded the property to its current 17 hectares but it took Federico's enthusiasm to put together a first-rate team of consultants like agronomists Marco Simonit and Pierpaolo Sirch, and oenologist Gianni Menotti, to flank long-standing estate manager Claudio Tomadin. It is Federico's optimism and energy that have driven Casa Zuliani to the extraordinary results achieved this year, continuing recent growth. Replanting the vine stock at higher densities – a major task – rigorous pruning and scrupulously meticulous vinification lie behind the extremely high quality evident in the various wines we tasted. Malvasia is a Casa Zuliani flagship, not for the first time. It may not be intense but its elegant spring flowers on the nose usher in a tasty, well-structured palate. In the Sauvignon Winter, we detected green apples, sage and rue, which are echoed on the palate and lifted by citrus and bell pepper. The Bordeaux blend Winter Rosso 2003 has complexity, shrewdly gauged wood, hints of tar, red fruits tart and an expansive palate of meaty fruit, dark chocolate and upfront tannins.

● Winter Rosso '03	🍷🍷	5
○ Collio Malvasia '05	🍷🍷	4*
○ Winter Sauvignon '05	🍷🍷	5
○ Winter Chardonnay '04	🍷🍷	5
○ Collio Pinot Bianco '05	🍷🍷	4
○ Collio Tocai Friulano '05	🍷🍷	4
○ Collio Chardonnay '05	🍷	4
○ Collio Pinot Grigio '05	🍷	4
○ Collio Sauvignon '05	🍷	4
○ Collio Malvasia '03	🍸🍸	4
○ Collio Sauvignon Blanc '04	🍸🍸	4
○ Sauvignon Blanc Bruna Zuliani	🍸🍸	4
○ Collio Tocai Friulano '04	🍸🍸	4

FARRA D'ISONZO (GO)

Colmello di Grotta

loc. Villanova
via Gorizia, 133
34070 Farra d'Isonzo (GO)
tel. 0481888445 - 0481888162
www.colmello.it

The 17 hectares on the south-facing hills at Farra, in the Collio and Isonzo DOC zones, yield 90,000 bottles a year of wine that continues to hover around the middle of the table. None of the wines is mediocre but equally there are no stars, even if these are products that will grow with the passage of time. This time around, most of the labels we were offered came from 2005, a less than marvellous vintage in these parts. As if to underline the point, the top scorer was the Cabernet Sauvignon 2003. Its deep ruby frames aromas of pencil lead and cherry, introducing a lingering, creamy palate pervaded by a sweet tannic weave. The Sauvignon starts off a little reduced but then cleans itself up and leaves the palate refreshed, although it is slightly dilute. The Tocai is impressive on the nose, ranging from acacia blossom to crusty bread, pear and sage but the palate fails to find a balance of almondiness with soft alcohol and residual sugar. This is only the second year the Ribolla has been released. It can improve further even if this version is much better than the first edition. The Chardonnay Collio convinces on nose and palate while we preferred the less noble of the two Pinot Grigio selections, the Isonzo, over the Collio wine. We'll round off with the warm Merlot 2003, which has a twist of bitterness in the finish.

● Friuli Isonzo Cabernet Sauvignon '03	🍷🍷	4*
● Friuli Isonzo Merlot '03	🍷	4
○ Collio Chardonnay '05	🍷	4
○ Collio Pinot Grigio '05	🍷	4
○ Collio Ribolla Gialla '05	🍷	4
○ Collio Sauvignon '05	🍷	4
○ Collio Tocai Friulano '05	🍷	4
○ Friuli Isonzo Chardonnay '05	🍷	4
○ Friuli Isonzo Pinot Grigio '05	🍷	4
○ Collio Chardonnay '01	🍸🍸	4
○ Friuli Isonzo Pinot Grigio '04	🍸🍸	4

FARRA D'ISONZO (GO)

★ JERMANN
LOC. VILLANOVA
VIA MONTE FORTINO, 21
34070 FARRA D'ISONZO (GO)
TEL. 0481888080
www.jermann.it

We do not know whether Silvio Jermann underestimated how much time and money, his new estate complex at Ruttars would demand. What is certain is that the effort to complete the spectacular new winery has jeopardized the serenity required to make wines of true excellence. Nevertheless, Silvio's skills have again produced three wines that went through to our final Three Glass tastings. We would also note the fine performances of the standard-label wines like Chardonnay, Vinnae, Sauvignon and Müller Thurgau. Chardonnay and Vinnae come with screwcaps and were bottled in the new cellar. Vinnae is a blend of ribolla gialla, riesling and tocai, part-matured in Slavonian oak, whereas the Chardonnay is steel-vinified only. Vintage Tunina is another blend, this time of sauvignon, chardonnay, malvasia, ribolla and picolit, part fermented and matured in 60-80 hectolitre barrels. Its elegance and complexity are givens but this year the excitement of previous editions seemed to be missing. But Dreams 2004, a single-variety Chardonnay fermented in three-hectolitre barrels, is fantastic: creamy, rich and complex with a warm, harmonious palate and impressive persistence. Capo Martino is another great white, from tocai, malvasia, picolit and ribolla gialla aged in Slavonian oak for ten months. Broad and fat, it offers cream, apricots and yellow peaches. Pignacolusse, a monovarietal pignolo, is spicy and concentrated, giving plum, chocolate, coffee and oak aromas that have in part still to be absorbed. And Three retrospective Glasses went to the superb Where the Dreams from 1995.

●	Pignacolusse '03	▼▼	6
○	Capo Martino '04	▼▼	7
○	W... Dreams... '04	▼▼	7
●	Blau&Blau Mjzzu '04	▼▼	7
○	Vintage Tunina '04	▼▼	7
○	Chardonnay '05	▼	5
○	Müller Thurgau '05	▼	5
○	Sauvignon '05	▼	5
○	Vinnae '05	▼	5
○	Where the Dreams Have no End '95	▽▽▽	8
○	Vintage Tunina '01	▽▽▽	7
○	Vintage Tunina '00	▽▽▽	7
○	Vintage Tunina '99	▽▽▽	7
●	Pignacolusse '00	▽▽▽	6

FARRA D'ISONZO (GO)

TENUTA VILLANOVA
LOC. VILLANOVA
VIA CONTESSA BERETTA, 29
34070 FARRA D'ISONZO (GO)
TEL. 0481889311
www.tenutavillanova.com

Tenuta Villanova is well known both for its many varied agriturismo activities and for its very extensive range of wines. Our round-up starts with the Chardonnay Ronco Cucco, of which 3,000 bottles were released. Fermented and matured in new barriques, it gives the initial sensations typical of oak-matured wines: vanilla, baked apple and ripe fruit on the nose and then structure and sweetness, as well as thrusting acidity, on the palate. It's a different story with the Pinot Grigio (48,000 bottles), which underwent brief maceration in the press, emerging with rich fruit and lots of appeal. The Isonzo Chardonnay, of which 24,000 units were bottled, has melon and yellow plum aromas and a fresh, upfront palate with good acidity to back up the fruit. Next on the list was a varietal Sauvignon selection, Ronco Cucco, whose 7,000 bottles reveal "sauvage" woodland notes that meld into the tropical fruit and a nice hint of citrus that veins the back palate. The well-balanced range has much else to offer from the Collio and Friuli Isonzo DOCs, embracing all these zones' classic wine types. The Collio brings us an attractive Friulano – the new name for Tocai – of which 7,000 bottles were released, a sweet, far from banal Picolit and a bright, fruit-forward Ribolla (10,000 bottles). The list of Isonzo wines is concluded by a classic Malvasia (6,000 bottles) and an aromatic Sauvignon (25,000 bottles). Barriques are on call again with Fraja, a Bordeaux blend whose 3,000 bottles flaunt red fruit, assertive tannins and decent length.

○	Collio Chardonnay Ronco Cucco '05	▼▼	5
○	Collio Pinot Grigio '05	▼▼	4*
○	Collio Sauvignon Ronco Cucco '05	▼▼	5
○	Friuli Isonzo Chardonnay '05	▼▼	4*
●	Fraja '03	▼	6
○	Collio Picolit Ronco Cucco '04	▼	6
○	Collio Ribolla Gialla '05	▼	4
○	Collio Friulano '05	▼	4
○	Friuli Isonzo Malvasia '05	▼	4
○	Friuli Isonzo Sauvignon '05	▼	4
○	Collio Ribolla Gialla '04	▽▽	4
○	Collio Sauvignon Ronco Cucco '04	▽▽	5

GONARS (UD)

DI LENARDO
FRAZ. ONTAGNANO
P.ZZA BATTISTI, 1
33050 GONARS (UD)
TEL. 0432928633
www.dilenardo.it

If we bear in mind that Massimo Di Lenardo's vineyards are in the Grave DOC zone, then we can safely say that he has won his personal wager. Even though he bottles about 500,000 units from his 47 hectares, year after year the Di Lenardo cellar shows that it can do quality as well as quantity. Massimo's next objective is to reach 50 hectares under vine. Most of the winery's output goes to the United States, with the Italian market absorbing about 30 per cent of the total. The man himself is dynamic to a fault, always looking for new ideas to develop. Nor can you ignore the imagination he puts into naming his wines. Just Me, for example, is a single-variety Merlot aged in American oak for 18 months and chock full of ripe red fruit, currants and briary fruit. The depth of this wine is incredible as it enters assertively and then opens on the palate into a wealth of pleasurable sensations. It's a product of undeniable drinkability. Also good is the Ronco Nolè 2004, from merlot, refosco and cabernet. Dry, austere and very complex on the nose, it is all fragrance in the mouth. The other bottles tasted included Pinot Grigio Vigne dai Vieris 2005, one of the cellar's big hitters. Flowers and banana-like fruit take you slowly through to the soft finish. Refosco dal Peduncolo Rosso 2005 is another characterful wine. Fermented on the skins for ten days in steel tanks, it has a deep ruby hue, red fruit aromas and a prolonged, agreeably taut progression on the palate.

●	Merlot Just Me '04	▼▼	5
●	Ronco Nolè Rosso '04	▼▼	4
●	Friuli Grave Refosco P. R. '05	▼▼	3*
○	Friuli Grave Pinot Grigio Vigne dai Vieris '05	▼▼	3*
●	Friuli Grave Cabernet Vigne dai Vieris '05	▼	4
○	Friuli Grave Pinot Bianco Vigne dai Vieris '05	▼	4
○	Friuli Grave Sauvignon Blanc Vigne dai Vieris '05	▼	3
○	Verduzzo Pass the Cookies '05	▼	4
○	Friuli Grave Chardonnay '05		3
○	Friuli Grave Tocai Friulano Toh! '05		4

GORIZIA

CONTI ATTEMS
FRAZ. LUCINICO
VIA GIULIO CESARE, 36A
34070 GORIZIA
TEL. 0481393619
www.attems.it

We'll start this profile with a bit of history. The noble Attems family originally came from central Europe in the early Middle Ages to settle in what is now known as Friuli. The family's ancient associations with viticulture are well documented. In 1506, Leonardo Attems was farming land owned by the abbey at Rosazzo, paying the rent in wine. Equally memorable is the work done by Sigismondo Douglas Attems in the 20th century. In the 1960s, he helped to set up the Consorzio del Collio, of which he was elected president in 1964. Today, the estate is managed by Tuscany's Frescobaldi cellar while Sigismondo's daughter Virginia looks after public relations. The winery headquarters are at Lucinico, in the municipality of Gorizia, and the vines actually run along the border with Slovenia between the Isonzo and Judrio rivers. Whites from a nice selection of native and international varieties account for most of the cellar's production. Pinot Bianco 2005, sourced from the marl and sandstone soil of the Collio Goriziano, is straw yellow and offers aromatics that range from citrus-led fruit to spring flowers. Assertive and mouthfilling, it teases the back palate with a hint of tanginess. The Merlot 2003 excellent, showing attractive fruit on the nose and an elegant, deep palate. We thought the rest of the range was good, too.

●	Collio Merlot '03	▼▼	4*
○	Collio Pinot Bianco '05	▼▼	4*
○	Collio Bianco Cicinis '04	▼	5
●	Refosco P. R. '04	▼	4
○	Collio Pinot Grigio '05	▼	5
○	Collio Sauvignon '05	▼	4
○	Collio Tocai Friulano '05	▼	4
○	Ribolla Gialla '05	▼	4
●	Collio Merlot '02	▽▽	5
○	Collio Pinot Grigio '04	▽▽	5
○	Collio Ribolla Gialla '04	▽▽	4

La Castellada

Fraz. Oslavia, 1
34170 Gorizia
tel. 048133670

La Castellada is a long-established winery but that doesn't prevent it from constantly trying out new things. Now and again, this means that the cellar's schedule fails to coincide with the Guide's deadlines. For example, this time we are reviewing the 2002 wines released over a year ago because the 2003s were still maturing when we were tasting. They will hit the market only in late spring 2007 and we will include them in the next Guide. By the way, our advance tastings at the cellar hinted that the 2003 range will be exciting. From the winemaking point of view, the cellar is using higher proportions of macerated grapes. In the past, small quantities of skins were used to activate the ambient yeasts before starting fermentation of the juice but the cellar is now using up to 30 per cent, a figure that is likely to increase. Our tasters were particularly impressed by the Rosso 1999, which swept the competition aside with its austere breeding, still bright orange-ruby hue and nose of spice, cherries, forest floor and tobacco. The close-knit, creamy texture of the palate is lifted superbly by well-integrated tannins. As a result, Three well-deserved Glasses again went to La Castellada, one of Friuli's top wineries. The Ribolla fascinates with its honey, ripe apple and dried fruit and the Bianco also gives honey, as well as hazelnut cream, as nose and palate establish a close-woven balanced consistency. Wisteria and pear are the keynotes of the Tocai, vinified as a monovarietal only in the best vintages, which has almost as much weight on the palate as the preceding wines.

●	Collio Rosso della Castellada '99	▼▼▼	8
○	Collio Bianco della Castellada '02	▼▼	6
○	Collio Ribolla Gialla '02	▼▼	6
○	Collio Tocai Friulano '02	▼▼	6
○	Collio Bianco della Castellada '98	▽▽▽	6
○	Collio Bianco della Castellada '99	▽▽▽	6
○	Collio Bianco della Castellada '00	▽▽	6

GORIZIA

Fiegl

Fraz. Oslavia
Loc. Lenzuolo Bianco, 1
34070 Gorizia
tel. 0481547103
www.fieglvini.com

Site climates that are unlike those anywhere else and the marl and clay soil known locally as "ponca" make Oslavia an ideal zone for making wines of superb quality, as the Fiegl winery amply demonstrates. Founded in 1782, Fiegl is run today by brothers Alessio (Ales), Giuseppe (Josko) and Rinaldo (Rado), who are assisted by Giuseppe's wife, Silvana, and their son, Martin. The 26 hectares that the family farm produce about 120,000 bottles split into two lines: Leopold, for wines that released a year later because they are oak-aged, and Classica. We thought the best of the Leopold wines were the Merlot 2001 and the Cuvée Rouge 2001. The Merlot gives marked black cherry syrup fragrances that meld with briary fruit, raspberries and vanilla. The merlot and cabernet sauvignon Cuvée Rouge is a characterful wine that fills the nostrils with red fruits and notable complexity that come back on the palate. Outstanding elegance and intensity are the distinguishing features of the pear, apple and spring flower Pinot Grigio 2005. Its fresh palate has lots of complexity, great thrust and attractive drinkability. Also excellent is the Malvasia 2003, its deep straw yellow introducing elegant confectioner's cream, hints of aniseed and a generous palate.

○	Collio Pinot Grigio '05	▼▼	4*
●	Collio Merlot Leopold '01	▼▼	4
●	Rosso Cuvée Rouge Leopold '01	▼▼	6
○	Collio Malvasia Leopold '03	▼▼	4
○	Collio Cuvée Blanc Leopold '04	▼	4
○	Collio Ribolla Gialla '05	▼	4
○	Collio Sauvignon '05	▼	4
○	Collio Tocai Friulano '05	▼	4
○	Collio Pinot Grigio '04	▽▽▽	4
●	Rosso Leopold '00	▽▽	6

GORIZIA

★ Gravner
Fraz. Oslavia
Loc. Lenzuolo Bianco, 9
34070 Gorizia
tel. 048130882
www.gravner.it

Josko Gravner is a leader with many followers in the wine world. But now, after two years of Gravner wines made exclusively in amphorae, we can take stock. Josko's philosophy, or ideal, is rigorous respect for the land. He knows that this land is the only one we have and that future generations will have to live on it after us. So Josko set himself a few straightforward rules to combine respect for the environment with the approachability of his wines. He keeps an eagle eye on yields: in 2002, a damp and unexceptional growing year, he obtained 270 hectolitres of wine from his 17 hectares. Josko has also gone back to ancient winemaking techniques, the only ones that can coax from the fruit all the elements that ensure is healthfulness, longevity, varietal typicity and territorial character. It is clear today that Josko's quest has taken him a long way with matchless results. That is why this master's wines are so exciting and earned two Three Glass prizes. Josko manages to combine naturalness with quite extraordinary wines, totally free of extraneous odours, rough edges or harsh notes. He has squared the oenological circle, as this year's wines show. We have little space here to describe them, but at the end of the day it is probably better for enthusiasts to discover them for themselves. We were stunned. We do recommend, though, that you should set preconceived ideas to one side. This was an unforgettable year for a winemaker who also picked up Three retrospective Glasses for Breg 1998.

○	Breg Anfora '02	▼▼▼	8
○	Ribolla Anfora '02	▼▼▼	8
●	Rosso Gravner '01	▼▼	8
○	Breg '98	▽▽▽	8
○	Breg '00	▽▽▽	8
○	Ribolla Anfora '01	▽▽▽	8
○	Collio Chardonnay '91	▽▽▽	8
○	Collio Chardonnay Ris. '91	▽▽▽	8
○	Chardonnay '92	▽▽▽	5
○	Chardonnay '93	▽▽▽	5
○	Sauvignon '93	▽▽▽	5
○	Breg '99	▽▽▽	8
○	Breg Anfora '01	▽▽	8
●	Rosso Gravner '00	▽▽	8

GORIZIA

Damijan Podversic
via Brigata Pavia, 61
34170 Gorizia
tel. 048178217

We'll start by expressing our admiration for Damijan. He is a man who knows his own mind, even though he is the first to acknowledge his debt to the peerless oenological inspiration of Josko Gravner, but we also admire him for producing his results in such precarious working conditions. Damijan has seven and a half hectares of high-density vines on the southern slopes of Monte Calvario, about 20 kilometres from his home, and produces just 15,000 bottles a year in a makeshift cellar a further 30 kilometres away. He is also admirable for the way he abandoned a path that seemed to be bearing fruit to take up a new, unconventional approach – some claim his wines are over-oxidized – and above all for the results he has achieved. Damian's vines are tended like a kitchen garden: the environment is always the first consideration. The wines are made using leisurely fermentation on the skins, with no cultured yeasts or temperature control, before they age for two years in large wood and then six or seven months in bottle. These, then, are assertively tannic whites, with deep colour and heady aromas of dried flowers, dried fruit, aniseed, mint and sage, characterized by a very immediate relationship with their vine type. The Ribolla 2003 is fresh-tasting and minerally while the malvasia, tocai and chardonnay Kaplja 2003 is complex, rounded and persistent. Damijan's merlot and cabernet sauvignon Rosso Prelit 2003 is garnet in hue and a tad forward, but still exciting, its aromatics revealing a concentrated array of tobacco, forest floor and walnutskin.

○	Kaplja '03	▼▼	6
○	Ribolla Gialla '03	▼▼	6
●	Rosso Prelit '03	▼▼	6
○	Collio Bianco '00	▽▽	5
●	Collio Rosso '00	▽▽	5
●	Collio Rosso Prelit '01	▽▽	6
○	Kaplja '02	▽▽	6

GORIZIA

Primosic
fraz. Oslavia
loc. Madonnina di Oslavia, 3
34070 Gorizia
tel. 0481535153
www.primosic.com

In 1967, the first-ever bottle bearing the label of the newly created Consorzio del Collio was released by the Primosic winery. At the time, the cellar was run by Silvestro Primosic, who had started bottling in 1956, but in later years, Silvestro hand the reins over to his sons Marko and Boris. Marko looks after the cellar and distribution while his brother handles administration and helps out in the cellar. Today, the Primosic estate extends over 26 hectares in the Collio, ten of them leased, and produces about 180,000 bottles a year. A few years ago, a new line called Palmadina was launched for wines from the five Primosic hectares in the Isonzo DOC. Some of the wines from the Collio line bear their vineyards of origin on the label. The cellar's best product again is the Chardonnay Gmajne 2004, a golden wine with typical yeast, crusty bread, banana and melon aromas preceding an elegant palate enhanced by minerality. Grapes from sauvignon, chardonnay, ribolla and tocai vines with just two per cent picolit, from the Klin vineyard, are the ingredients for the Bianco 2003 of the same name. Barrique maturing has left vanilla and cream that give way to baked apples. Very ripe citrus is the keynote of the luxurious, well-gauged palate. The Sauvignon Gmajne is resoundingly varietal with opulent citrus in the mouth. Rosso Riserva Metamorfosis 2001, a Bordeaux blend with five per cent refosco, combines freshness and complexity, hinting at forest fruits nuanced with tar. Finally, the oak-fermented Ribolla Gialla di Oslavia 2004 is already fantastic but will improve even further.

○	Collio Bianco Klin Ris. '03	🍷🍷	6
○	Collio Chardonnay Gmajne '04	🍷🍷	5
○	Collio Sauvignon Gmajne '05	🍷🍷	5
●	Collio Rosso Metamorfosis Ris. '01	🍷🍷	6
●	Collio Merlot Murno '04	🍷🍷	4
○	Collio Ribolla Gialla di Oslavia '04	🍷🍷	5
○	Collio Pinot Grigio Murno '05	🍷🍷	4
○	Collio Ribolla Gialla '05	🍷	4
○	Collio Bianco Klin Ris. '00	♡♡	5
○	Collio Chardonnay Gmajne '03	♡♡	5
○	Collio Pinot Grigio Murno '04	♡♡	4

GRADISCA D'ISONZO (GO)

Marco Felluga
via Gorizia, 121
34072 Gradisca d'Isonzo (GO)
tel. 048199164
www.marcofelluga.it

We might call this the estate on which rests the success of all the other properties in the extensive group so assertively led by Marco Felluga, one of the people who has written the history of wine in Friuli. The vine stock extends over 120 hectares and more fruit is bought in from long-serving growers who are followed at every stage by Felluga's technical staff. It all adds up to a yearly production of about 600,000 bottles. Castello di Buttrio is a superb wine estate around an imposing edifice dating from the 11th century. The vine stock has been subjected to scrupulous mass selection and replanting with native varieties, among other things. Marco's children, Roberto and Alessandra, direct the dynamic estate staff, who include the thoroughly competent pair oenologist Raffaela Bruno and agronomist Edi Fabbro, giving the group its defining traits of modernity and innovation. The numbers may be significant but the quality of the wines is equally impressive. The Ribolla Gialla is tangy and fresh-tasting while the Pinot Grigio Riserva is a successful marriage of subtle florality and richer citrus notes. The Sauvignon is intense in hue with sunny tropical fruit aromas and the fruit-led Bianco Molamatta is attractively rich while the Moscato Rosa 2003 is even more tempting for its black cherry tart tones. Best of the bunch from Castello di Buttrio were, we thought, the Chardonnay Ovestein 2004 and the Pignolo 2003. The Chardonnay is rigorously varietal and the Pignolo offers delicate balsamic notes with concentrated fruit.

○	Castello di Buttrio Pignolo '03	🍷🍷	6
●	Moscato Rosa '03	🍷🍷	6
○	Castello di Buttrio Ovestein Chardonnay '04	🍷🍷	6
○	Collio Pinot Grigio Ris. '04	🍷🍷	5
○	Collio Bianco Molamatta '05	🍷🍷	5
○	Collio Ribolla Gialla '05	🍷🍷	4
○	Collio Sauvignon '05	🍷🍷	4
●	Collio Merlot '04	🍷	4
●	Refosco P.R. Ronco dei Moreri '04	🍷	4
○	COF Tocai Friulano Castello di Buttrio '05	🍷	5
○	Collio Pinot Grigio '05	🍷	4
○	Collio Chardonnay '05		4

GRADISCA D'ISONZO (GO)

SANT'ELENA

VIA GASPARINI, 1
34072 GRADISCA D'ISONZO (GO)
TEL. 048192388

There are still some marketing puzzles to solve here, such as whether to go for an extensive range of labels or restrict production to a few well-defined wines, but on all other fronts Dominic Nocerino's estate knows where it is going. The 35 hectares are managed by Maurizio Drascek and the 120,000 bottles released are mainly for the United States market. Few varieties are planted, the flagship grapes being pinot grigio, merlot and in the future pignolo, and yields are only one bottle per plant. And results are coming. We very much liked the standard Merlot 2003, a variety of which the estate has nine clones. Its elegant nose gives black cherry jam, coffee and cocoa powder, followed by a bracing vegetal vein on the palate that perks up the very dense texture. Ròs di Rôl Merlot 2003 is only a step or two behind. It has greater concentration and breadth but doesn't quite come together. The other 2003 reds line up behind this pair. The Cabernet 2003 has juicy black cherries and a supple, yet intense structure whereas the Bordeaux blend Tato Rosso 2003 has evident notes of ripe red berries and a lingering, very attractive follow-through on the palate. From the whites, we enjoyed the Pinot Grigio and the Bianco JN 2004, from barrique-fermented chardonnay and steel-vinified sauvignon. Balance and complex tropical and citrus fruit are the Pinot Grigio's calling cards while Bianco JN is elegant and understated but not unexciting in its weight and spectrum of aromatics.

● Merlot '03	🍷🍷	5
● Cabernet '03	🍷🍷	5
● Ròs di Rôl Merlot '03	🍷🍷	7
● Tato Rosso '03	🍷🍷	6
○ Bianco JN '04	🍷🍷	5
○ Pinot Grigio '05	🍷🍷	5
○ Chardonnay '05		4
● Tato Rosso	♀♀	6

GRADISCA D'ISONZO (GO)

FRANCO VISINTIN

VIA ROMA, 37
34072 GRADISCA D'ISONZO (GO)
TEL. 048199974

Franco Visintin has an eight-hectare estate in the Friuli Isonzo DOC and Franco himself is much admired for some of his oenological trump cards, such as his hospitality, the quality of his ever-dependable wines, even in lesser vintages, and his very attractive pricing policies. Franco Visintin and his collaborator Saverio Di Giacomo presented us with a fine range of wines, the best of which is the Stàngja Bordeaux blend. The 2003 edition has subtle pencil lead, cherry, briary fruit and pepper. The palate is a little tousled at first but then opens onto marked tannicity that leaves a clean sensation in harmony with the nose. The rue and aniseed notes of the Sauvignon are faint but very pleasant. What stands out in the Tocai is the bitter almond note and the warm alcohol that nicely offsets the acidity. Peanut butter and pineapple tempt the nose in the whistle-clean Chardonnay with its uncomplicated finish. The slightly pale Pinot Grigio has savouriness and minerality that would have been better served by more depth of body. The sweet, spicy and slightly dilute Cabernet Franc 2004 is very similar in style to the Cabernet Sauvignon 2004. Both need clearer varietal focus to justify release under two separate labels. Finally, there was a lovely surprise in the shape of the Moscato, an unusual type for this area, which is perfect for sipping on a warm summer's evening.

● Stàngja Rosso '03	🍷🍷	4*
● Friuli Isonzo Cabernet Franc '04	🍷	4
● Friuli Isonzo Cabernet Sauvignon '04	🍷	4
○ Friuli Isonzo Chardonnay '05	🍷	3
○ Friuli Isonzo Pinot Grigio '05	🍷	3
○ Friuli Isonzo Sauvignon '05	🍷	3
○ Friuli Isonzo Tocai Friulano '05	🍷	3
○ Moscato '05	🍷	4
● Friuli Isonzo Merlot '04		3

MANZANO (UD)

GIANPAOLO COLUTTA
VIA ORSARIA, 32A
33044 MANZANO (UD)
TEL. 0432510654 - 0432751208
www.coluttagianpaolo.com

The quality of the wines released by Gianpaolo Colutta and his daughter Elisabetta improves all the time. After last year's fine performance, which enabled the winery to return to the main section of the Guide, we now have emphatic confirmation with a wine that went through to the finals and nearly earned Three Glasses. The cellar's policy is to focus on promoting local varieties through the I Magnifici Autoctoni project while still growing the international grapes that have found an appropriate habitat in Friuli. The range of wines we tasted was very exciting, starting with the Pinot Grigio 2005. The rich tropical fruit of the nose is nicely offset by peach, cream and citrus, introducing a tangy, mouthfilling palate that reprises the nose on the long finish. Equally good was the Pinot Bianco, which stands out for sweet hints of acacia honey and an elegant progression with just the right touch of almondiness. From the reds, our tasters liked the Refosco 2004. Gaminess on the nose is balanced by more subtle notes of black cherry and chocolate before the round, silky palate unveils its close-knit tannins. The fruit-led Bianco Prarion from ribolla gialla, chardonnay and picolit), the rounded Merlot, the full-bodied Cabernet and the complex Picolit all picked up One Glass.

○	COF Pinot Grigio '05	🍷🍷	4*
●	COF Refosco P. R. '04	🍷🍷	4
○	COF Pinot Bianco '05	🍷🍷	4
○	COF Bianco Prarion '05	🍷	5
○	COF Picolit '05	🍷	8
●	COF Cabernet '04	🍷	4
●	COF Merlot '04	🍷	4
●	COF Schioppettino '05		5
○	COF Sauvignon '03	🍸🍸	3
○	COF Bianco Prarion '04	🍸🍸	5
○	COF Pinot Bianco '04	🍸🍸	4
●	COF Schioppettino '04	🍸🍸	5

MANZANO (UD)

GIORGIO COLUTTA
VIA ORSARIA, 32
33044 MANZANO (UD)
TEL. 0432740315
www.colutta.it

Last year, we reported the completion of restructuring in the estate's 18th-century villa, where further cellar space has been created for fermentation in steel and in wood. But a wine man's work is never done, and Giorgio is already pencilling in further extensions to the building for use as offices, a cellar door outlet and hospitality facility. In the meantime, the vine stock has now risen to 23 hectares, five replanted at 5,600 vines per hectare and already in production. In charge of the vineyards is Antonio Maggio, while Marco Simonit consults. In the cellar, Trentino-born oenologist Clizia Zambiasi is still on hand. Production this year rose by 10,000 units to reach a total of 130,000. We very much enjoyed the Chardonnay Selezione 2004, from vines with a yield of only one kilogram per plant, of which only 1,650 bottles were released. The fruit is harvested and selected by hand before the must ferments in new French oak barriques, where it stays for about a year. This very stylish wine gives elegant petits fours, progressing delightfully on the palate. For the time being, the Pignolo 2002 is only an experiment, with 600 bottles produced, but we look forward to reporting on its progress in coming years. The other native red, Schioppettino 2004, is growing visibly and shows raspberry nuances in the after-aroma.

○	COF Chardonnay Sel. Giorgio Colutta '04	🍷🍷	5
●	COF Merlot Sel. Giorgio Colutta '04	🍷	6
●	COF Schioppettino '04	🍷	5
○	COF Bianco Nojâr '05	🍷	5
○	COF Pinot Grigio '05	🍷	4
○	COF Tocai Friulano '05	🍷	4
●	COF Refosco P. R. '04		4
○	COF Picolit '03	🍸🍸	7
○	COF Verduzzo Friulano '03	🍸🍸	7
○	COF Tocai Friulano '04	🍸🍸	4

MANZANO (UD)

RONCHI DI MANZANO
VIA ORSARIA, 42
33044 MANZANO (UD)
TEL. 0432740718
www.ronchidimanzano.com

We were impressed by the performance of the wines from Roberta Borghese's cellar, where this timid but tenacious wine woman has built up a very fine winery. The three plots at Ronc di Subule, Ronc di Scossai and Ronco di Rosazzo give Roberta a tidy 55 hectares under vine. With her, Boris the oenologist, technicians Ivan and Aldo and vineyard manager Raiko help to create the wines that are released under two labels, Ronco di Manzano and the very decent Vigne della Rocca. Hillside terrain, planting densities of up to 9,000 vines per hectare, great aspects and a cellar equipped with modern technology all contribute to the final result, but it is Roberta's sheer passion that makes the difference. A special mention must also go to the labels of the Pignolo 2004 and the Traminer Aromatico Fatato 2005, which are both works of art by any standards. The Pignolo is intense and varietal, giving wild roses and citrus whereas the Traminer is invitingly fresh-tasting. After fermentation in 45-hectolitre barrels and steel, the Chardonnay is on top form. The variety's signature yeasts and crusty bread are there, lifted by ripe apple that mingles with banana, apricot and peach. What we liked about the Pinot Grigio was the breadth of the fruit, which is reminiscent of fruit salad, while the Merlot Ronc di Subule 2003 gives hints of tar and liquorice on the nose and then red fruit structure and good alcohol on the palate. Finally, there is plenty of body in the Cabernet Sauvignon 2004.

●	COF Merlot Ronc di Subule '03	🍷🍷	5
●	COF Pignolo '04	🍷🍷	5
○	COF Chardonnay '05	🍷🍷	4
○	COF Pinot Grigio '05	🍷🍷	4
○	COF Rosazzo Bianco '05	🍷🍷	4
○	COF Traminer Aromatico Fatato '05	🍷🍷	5
●	COF Cabernet Franc '04	🍷	4
●	COF Cabernet Sauvignon '04	🍷	4
●	COF Refosco P. R. '04	🍷	4
○	COF Sauvignon '05	🍷	4
●	COF Merlot Ronc di Subule '99	YYY	5
●	COF Merlot Ronc di Subule '01	YY	5
○	COF Chardonnay '04	YY	4
○	COF Sauvignon '04	YY	4

MANZANO (UD)

RONCO DELLE BETULLE
LOC. ROSAZZO
VIA ABATE COLONNA, 24
33044 MANZANO (UD)
TEL. 0432740547
www.roncodellebetulle.it

Ivana Adami is the determined woman who for 17 years has been running the Ronco delle Betulle winery, set up in the late 1960s. Situated near the abbey, the estate has 14 hectares under vine on the marl and sandstone soil – the legendary "ponca" – at Rosazzo, which yield an average of 65,000 bottles a year. We approved of Ivana's decision not to present for tasting this year her Vanessa 2005, from pinot bianco and tocai friulano with a dash of ribolla gialla. It will age for a further 12 months in bottle and we will be back to report next year. We also agree with her that Narciso 2001 is the big hitter this time. It's an elegant, merlot-heavy Bordeaux blend with attractive softness and a rich bouquet of sweet, liquorice-veined spices. The Tocai Friulano 2005 is another wine with great prospects. Markedly aromatic apple and white peach tempt the nose to return in the velvet-textured mouth. Our panel enjoyed the Cabernet Franc 2004, from a mix of cabernet franc clones with some carmenère, an elegantly fruit-forward wine with a faint hint of raspberries. In the mouth, it has very nice red fruits and plums. Also good is the Franconia 2004, a varietally full-bodied, tannic wine with a characteristic purple-flecked ruby red colour and marked acidity.

●	COF Rosazzo Rosso Narciso '01	🍷🍷	6
●	COF Cabernet Franc '04	🍷🍷	5
●	Franconia '04	🍷🍷	5
○	COF Tocai Friulano '05	🍷🍷	4
○	COF Rosazzo Ribolla Gialla '05	🍷	7
○	COF Sauvignon '05	🍷	4
●	Narciso Rosso '94	YYY	6
●	COF Rosazzo Rosso Narciso '00	YY	6

MANZANO (UD)

Torre Rosazza

fraz. Oleis
loc. Poggiobello, 12
33044 Manzano (UD)
tel. 0422864511
www.borgomagredo.it

Genagricola is the Assicurazioni Generali company that manages the group's two estates in Friuli, one in the Grave DOC at Spilimbergo and the other in the hills at Rosazzo. Here, the vine stock sprawls over as much as 110 hectares, yielding 200,000 bottles for the Poggiobello label and 350,000 released as Torre Rosazza. The amphitheatre on which most of the vines stand is breathtakingly beautiful and a veritable sun-trap. It's a shame that at least 30 per cent of the vine stock is still Casarsa-trained, a system that is hard to reconcile with truly high-quality fruit. Since 2001, the estate oenologist has been Luca Zuccarello, who can call on input from the Piedmontese consultant, Donato Lanati. The estate's intentions of boosting quality are clearly stated, but results will only come with the passage of time, so we must wait. In this past, less than exciting, growing year, the top scorer was the Sauvignon Poggiobello, from the more accessible line of easy drinkers. Its fresh nose offers marked elderflower, which returns on the palate with hints of citrus. The Tocai Friulano scored One full Glass for its peaches and almonds, backed up by nicely balanced fruit and acidity. There is the same balance in the Pinot Grigio, which has fine breadth of fruit. To round off, the Pinot Nero Ronco del Palazzo has only moderate fruit but plenty of length and a bitterish twist in the finish.

○	COF Sauvignon Poggiobello '05	ΨΨ	4*
●	COF Pinot Nero Ronco del Palazzo '03	Ψ	5
●	COF Merlot Poggiobello '04	Ψ	4
○	COF Verduzzo Friulano Poggiobello '03	Ψ	4
○	COF Tocai Friulano '05	Ψ	4
○	COF Pinot Grigio '05	Ψ	4
○	COF Riesling Poggiobello '05	Ψ	4
○	COF Sauvignon '05	Ψ	4
○	COF Picolit '03		6
●	COF Refosco P. R. '04		4
○	COF Picolit '02	YY	6
○	COF Sauvignon '04	YY	4
○	COF Tocai Friulano '04	YY	4

MANZANO (UD)

★ Le Vigne di Zamò

loc. Rosazzo
via Abate Corrado, 4
33044 Manzano (UD)
tel. 0432759693
www.levignedizamo.com

Brothers Pierluigi and Silvano Zamò are on the right track to broaden the quality base of their range, thanks to input from the entire technical squad led by oenologist Emilio Del Medico and consultant Franco Bernabei, who has been collaborating with the cellar for more than ten years. True, a stand-out failed to emerge, but it is equally fair to say that it is hardly every day that a cellar chalks up six Two Glass wines and fully four finalists with Two coloured Glasses. It all points to across-the-range quality, from the whites to the reds and the single sweet wine. There are 60 hectares under vine and output fluctuates around 300,000 bottles a year, spread over more than 20 different labels, which is perhaps too many. The Tocai Friulano Vigne Cinquant'Anni 2004 shimmers quality from its lovely golden yellow. Beeswax, dried flowers, peaches and pears enliven the elegant, compact nose to be mirrored on a rich, complex palate. The Friulano 2005 – from 1 April 2007 the new name for Tocai Friulano – is every bit as elegant and full but has more freshness and hints of almond leaves on the palate. Ronco delle Acacie 2004, from chardonnay, pinot bianco and tocai, is intense and elegant, alternating flowers and fruit, and signing off with an amazingly long finish. Slightly bitterish tannins prevented the Pignolo 2003 from repeating the success last year of the preceding vintage and Vola...Vola... 2004, from 50 per cent-dried verduzzo and sauvignon with 100 per cent-dried picolit, is a wonderfully balanced sweet wine that never threatens to cloy.

●	COF Rosazzo Pignolo '03	ΨΨ	8
○	COF Rosazzo Bianco Ronco delle Acacie '04	ΨΨ	5
○	COF Tocai Friulano V. Cinquant'Anni '04	ΨΨ	6
○	COF Friulano '05	ΨΨ	5
●	COF Merlot V. Cinquant'Anni '03	ΨΨ	6
●	COF Refosco P. R. Re Fosco '03	ΨΨ	6
○	COF Pinot Bianco Tullio Zamò '04	ΨΨ	5
○	Vola... Vola... '04	ΨΨ	5
○	COF Malvasia '05	ΨΨ	5
○	COF Pinot Grigio '05	ΨΨ	5
○	COF Sauvignon '05	Ψ	5
●	COF Rosazzo Pignolo '01	YYY	8

MANZANO (UD)

Vinài dell'Abbàte

Loc. Rosazzo
P. zza Abbazia, 15
33044 Manzano (UD)
tel. 0432759429
www.tenutealeandri.it

Documentation relating to this winery dates back to 1341. The estate has had its ups and downs in recent years, changing management several times while remaining the property of the archiepiscopal curia of Udine. Tenuta Aleandri, a Veneto-based group with other interests in Friuli, is in charge today and has decided to entrust the cellar to the capable hands of Marco Simonit for vineyard management and Gianni Menotti as consultant oenologist. And it is only fair to point out that credit for a couple of the leading products should go to the previous management of Walter Filiputti. But the cellar's top wine is Pignolo Riserva 2000, with its dry, intense, tar-veined nose and well-defined entry on the palate, whose progression surprises with hints of prunes, warm black cherry and mixed spices. Another wine that came within an ace of going on to the finals was the Picolit 2003, a golden-hued wine with a nose of dried figs and apricots, candied citrus peel and almond paste leading into a sweet, creamy palate that hints at attractive candied peel. The hand of Gianni Menotti is evident in the Sauvignon 2005, where elegant apple gives way to citrus-like nuances that return in the mouth with citron, grapefruit and orange. Finally, Ronco degli Agostiniani, from chardonnay and tocai, could do with more personality.

●	COF Pignolo Ris. '00	🍷🍷	7
○	COF Picolit '03	🍷🍷	6
○	COF Sauvignon '05	🍷🍷	4
○	COF Bianco Ronco degli Agostiniani '04	🍷	4
○	COF Chardonnay '05	🍷	4
○	COF Pinot Grigio '05	🍷	4
○	COF Ribolla Gialla '05	🍷	4

MARIANO DEL FRIULI (GO)

Tenuta Luisa

fraz. Corona
via Cormons, 19
34070 Mariano del Friuli (GO)
tel. 048169680
www.viniluisa.com

Viticulture in the Isonzo zone is slow to reveal itself but if you go up to the first floor of the cellar run by Eddi Luisa and his sons Michele and Davide, you will realize that while wine may not be quite everything here, it is enormously important. Tenuta Luisa is a fine example of the DOC, with its 60 hectares under vine. Part of production is sold unbottled to an eager local market but the better wines go into about 250,000 bottles in the standard line - already in effect a selection – and the top of the range I Ferretti line. The Tocai is a wine to bank on, and once again went through to our finals. Appealingly themed around pears and apples, it shows warm and well structured, with good length and superb drinkability thanks to perky acidity. Other wines worthy of note are the minerally, fresh Pinot Grigio with its good nose-palate consistency and length, the Chardonnay, which is beautifully made and richly fruity, and the austere plum, cherry and cocoa Cabernet Franc I Ferretti. The thoroughly dependable list goes on. We pass from an elegant apple and yellow plum Pinot Bianco to a Sauvignon themed around peaches in syrup, apple and sage to end on a deliciously chewy Cabernet Franc. From the One Glass wines, we liked the standard-label Refosco better than its slightly edgier, more austere I Ferretti counterpart while the Merlot is fresh-tasting and attractive.

○	Friuli Isonzo Tocai Friulano '05	🍷🍷	4*
●	Friuli Isonzo Cabernet Franc '05	🍷🍷	4
●	Friuli Isonzo Cabernet Franc I Ferretti '05	🍷🍷	5
○	Friuli Isonzo Chardonnay '05	🍷🍷	4
○	Friuli Isonzo Pinot Bianco '05	🍷🍷	4
○	Friuli Isonzo Pinot Grigio '05	🍷🍷	4
○	Friuli Isonzo Sauvignon '05	🍷🍷	4
●	Friuli Isonzo Refosco P. R. I Ferretti '02	🍷	5
●	Friuli Isonzo Merlot '05	🍷	4
●	Friuli Isonzo Refosco P. R. '05	🍷	4
○	Friuli Isonzo Tocai Friulano '03	🍸🍸🍸	4
●	Friuli Isonzo Refosco P. R. I Ferretti '01	🍸🍸	5

Masut da Rive

via Manzoni, 82
34070 Mariano del Friuli (GO)
tel. 048169200
www.masutdarive.com

Brothers Marco and Fabrizio Gallo know exactly what they want from viticulture and winemaking. Faithful to the oft-quoted but not always applied adage that says "wine is made in the vineyard, not the cellar", they began a decade ago to completely overhaul the way their 20-hectare estate was managed, eliminating over-productive training systems and replacing them with Guyot pruning, much more conducive to low yields and high quality. In the older vineyards, the rows were planted more densely without disturbing the existing vines, which ensured continuity of results. Again this year, the entire range is extremely good, with two stand-outs in the Tocai, an estate banker, and the Merlot. The Tocai, a 2005, is a paragon of typicity and integrity of varietal aromas. The classic fragrances of almonds, crusty bread and dried spring flowers are all there. An assertive entry is followed by softer progression supported by balanced acidity, almond notes returning to accompany the rich tanginess and linger on the back palate. The Merlot 2004 is opulent and austere, its robust tannins tempered by hints of blackberry jam and cinchona. The Pinot Bianco 2005 is subtle and very delicate while the Chardonnay 2005 has varietal melon and cream. Fruit is the keynote of the Pinot Grigio 2005 and the Sauvignon from the same vintage is fragrant and moderately fat. Last up was the Cabernet Sauvignon 2004, which flaunts a convincingly rich palate.

● Friuli Isonzo Rive Alte Merlot '04	🍷🍷	4*
○ Friuli Isonzo Rive Alte Tocai Friulano '05	🍷🍷	4*
● Friuli Isonzo Cabernet Sauvignon '04	🍷🍷	4
○ Friuli Isonzo Rive Alte Chardonnay '05	🍷🍷	4
○ Friuli Isonzo Pinot Bianco '05	🍷🍷	4
○ Friuli Isonzo Rive Alte Pinot Grigio '05	🍷🍷	4
○ Friuli Isonzo Rive Alte Sauvignon '05	🍷🍷	4
● Friuli Isonzo Cabernet Franc '04	🍷	4
○ Friuli Isonzo Tocai Friulano '04	🍷🍷🍷 (white)	4

★ Vie di Romans

vie di Romans, 1
34070 Mariano del Friuli (GO)
tel. 048169600
www.viediromans.it

It's important to know what philosophy lies behind a wine: you may like it or not, but it would be superficial and wrong to discard it as an intellectual exercise. Gianfranco Gallo has no compunction about going against the flow, be it the fashion for barriques or, today, minerality, which is almost a tasting parameter for white wines, in particular. In fact, minerality is savouriness and coolness, but also a metallic sensation if it does not serve to support the fruit, and the older the wine, the truer this is. Gianfranco strives to combine everything at the very highest level with no concessions on the ripeness of the fruit or concentration, characteristics bolster a long-lived wine. Whether he is right or wrong remains to be seen. What is certain is his track record of wines that ages exceptionally well with tasting sensations that bear witness to raw material and winemaking technique that are second to none. We now have little space left for the wines, but they speak for themselves. The stand-out is a spectacular Sauvignon Vieris 2004, with an ever-changing array of sensory perceptions that develop sonata-like on the nose to be recapitulated on the palate. It is a superb example of the Gallo philosophy and a superb Three Glass wine. The rest of the range is exquisite but we would single out the Dolée 2004, a very personal interpretation of Tocai, and Dis Cumieris 2004, an equally individual Malvasia. There is also a successful newcomer, the merlot-based Rosé.

○ Friuli Isonzo Rive Alte Sauvignon Vieris '04	🍷🍷🍷	5
○ Dut'Un '03	🍷🍷	7
○ Friuli Isonzo Bianco Dolée '04	🍷🍷	5
○ Friuli Isonzo Chardonnay Ciampagnis Vieris '04	🍷🍷	5
○ Friuli Isonzo Chardonnay Vie di Romans '04	🍷🍷	5
○ Friuli Isonzo Pinot Grigio Dessimis '04	🍷🍷	5
○ Friuli Isonzo Sauvignon Piere '04	🍷🍷	5
○ Friuli Isonzo Dis Cumieris '04	🍷🍷	5
○ Friuli Isonzo Flors di Uis '04	🍷🍷	5
⊙ Friuli Isonzo Rosé Ciantons '04	🍷🍷	5
○ Dut'Un '02	🍷🍷🍷 (white)	7

MOIMACCO (UD)

ROSA BOSCO
VIA ROMA, 5
33040 MOIMACCO (UD)
TEL. 0432722461

There has been a minor revolution in Moimacco. Rosetta has recently signed a commercial agreement with Valfredo and Caterina De Puppi to set up the new Rosa Bosco company. She will continue to run the cellar, deciding winemaking strategies, while the technical side will be in the hands of her extremely competent son, Alessio Dorigo. It would be superfluous to note that care, dedication and a focus on the very highest overall quality are still the winery's strong suits. Who knows, the new alliance with the De Puppis might bring new labels to the Rosa Bosco range. Total output is still around 11,000 bottles and the two flagship wines are Sauvignon Blanc and the merlot-based Boscorosso. In her search for longer-lived wines, Rosetta has opted to age the Sauvignon Blanc 2005 in new barriques with the result, in our judgement, that vanilla aromas dominate. But despite the wood, flowers and fruit are there in abundance, white peaches and ripe fruit prevailing. All this is echoed on the complex and very long palate. It is a wine, we are sure, that will be at its peak in a couple of years' time. Yet again this year, Boscorosso 2004 has much to admire and be inspired by. It is a wine of character, showing red fruits, plum, spiciness and length that confirm the extraordinary quality we have come to expect from this product.

●	COF Rosso Il Boscorosso '04	🍷🍷	7
○	COF Sauvignon Blanc '05	🍷🍷	6
○	COF Sauvignon Blanc '02	ΥΥΥ	6
●	COF Rosso Il Boscorosso '01	ΥΥ	7
○	COF Sauvignon Blanc '03	ΥΥ	6
●	COF Rosso Il Boscorosso '00	ΥΥ	7
●	COF Rosso Il Boscorosso '02	ΥΥ	7

NIMIS (UD)

ANNA BERRA
VIA RAMANDOLO, 29
33045 NIMIS (UD)
TEL. 0432790296
www.annaberra.it

This lovely winery was set up by Anna Berra and is currently managed by her son, Ivan Monai, who personally takes care of all sides of the business, from viticulture to winemaking and distribution. The estate is modest in size, comprising seven hectares under vine, almost all within the bounds of the newly created Ramandolo DOCG. Obviously, attention is focused on the zone's leading variety, verduzzo friulano, but the cellar is doing interesting things with reds, too, especially refosco, which has always given good results around here. Ivan still has to find a consistent length with his reds but astonished the panel with the quality of his whites, first and foremost the Ramandolo Anno Domini 2002 selection, which almost claimed a third Glass. Obtained from overripe grapes dried in the drying room, it ferments in new barriques and stays there for 36 months. This laborious winemaking procedure lends it rich, well-defined sensations of caramelized figs, apricots and candied orange peel. The wine's sweetness is nicely offset by a remarkably full, lingering back palate perked up by refreshing acidity. The standard-label Ramandolo 2002 from late-harvested fruit is uncomplicated but progresses well on the palate. Another outstanding wine typical of this part of Friuli's hill country is Picolit. The Riserva 2003 is ripe, sunny and citrus-like with elegant hints of petits fours on the nose. An elegant wine, it flaunts plenty of breadth and good complexity.

○	Ramandolo Anno Domini '02	🍷🍷	5
○	COF Picolit Ris. '03	🍷🍷	6
○	Ramandolo '02	🍷	4
○	Ramandolo Anno Domini '01	ΥΥ	5
○	COF Picolit Ris. '02	ΥΥ	6

NIMIS (UD)

DARIO COOS
LOC. RAMANDOLO
VIA RAMANDOLO, 5
33045 NIMIS (UD)
TEL. 0432790320
www.dariocoos.it

Ramandolo is the most northerly part of the Colli Orientali del Friuli DOC. The morphology of soil and the climate have produced a variation of the verduzzo friulano grape that has its own specific profile, earning it the name of verduzzo dorato. The average temperature at Ramandolo is lower than in neighbouring areas and provokes frequent hailstorms. In fact, growers here use protective netting. Dario Coos is the long-serving champion of this great wine. In addition to turning out some very fine interpretations of the type, he has also secured a well thought-out delimitation of its production area. The Coos family has been living at Ramandolo for at least five generations. The outstanding Romandus 2002 is obtained from overripe grapes picked in several passes from late October to mid November, and then dried on racks until December or January. This means very low yields of 15-20 litres per quintal of fruit. The golden colour offers elegant, intense dates and melons then the sweet, creamy-textured palate, redolent of dried figs and sultanas, is stunningly persistent. Ramandolo 2003 is from overripe but not part-dried grapes and the Longhino 2003 matures exclusively in steel.

○ Ramandolo Romandus '02	two black glasses	7
○ Ramandolo '03	two black glasses	6
○ Ramandolo Il Longhino '03	two black glasses	5
● Refosco P. R. '03		5
○ Vindos '05		4
○ Ramandolo '01	two white glasses	6
○ COF Picolit '03	two white glasses	7

NIMIS (UD)

LA RONCAIA
FRAZ. CERGNEU
VIA VERDI, 26
33045 NIMIS (UD)
TEL. 0432790280
www.laroncaia.com

La Roncaia was established a few years ago by the Fantinel family in the persons of cousins Marco and Stefano. They took over from an existing small family business that today extends over 22 hectares, including the region's largest picolit vineyard, a six-hectare plot at Attimis. The other vineyards are at Nimis and Ramandolo, where site climates favour native varieties that have adapted over the centuries to the cold winds from the north east. There are about 500 barriques in the cellar, which also has special areas for drying grapes. Oenologist Massimo Vidoni presented us with a good selection, for which some of the credit must go to the consulting skills of the late Tibor Gal. For example, Gal's hand is evident in the Merlot 2002, from part-dried grapes and aged in oak for more than a year. Its overripe red fruit aromas are lifted by a hint of violet and the very complex palate foregrounds concentrated fruit and fine-grained tannins. The fresh, elegant Bianco Eclisse is a 90-10 blend of sauvignon and picolit that proffers intense Mediterranean scrubland, peach, apple and pear aromatics. The characterful Ramandolo 2003 is very sweet on the palate, where hazelnut and almond tones come through. Fusco 2002, from refosco, merlot, cabernet franc and tazzelenghe in decreasing proportions, fuses the softness of merlot with the rustic tannins of tazzelenghe.

● COF Merlot '02	two black glasses	4*
○ COF Bianco Eclisse '05	two black glasses	4
● COF Rosso Il Fusco '02	one black glass	4
○ COF Picolit '03	one black glass	7
○ Ramandolo '03	one black glass	4
○ COF Picolit '01	two white glasses	8
● Il Fusco '00	two white glasses	6
● COF Cabernet Sauvignon '01	two white glasses	4

NIMIS (UD)

IL RONCAT - GIOVANNI DRI
LOC. RAMANDOLO
VIA PESCIA, 7
33045 NIMIS (UD)
TEL. 0432790260
www.drironcat.com

Giovanni Dri's new cellar is at the foot of the steep hill on top which stands the unpretentious little church of Ramandolo. The cellar, though, is a substantial building that combines imaginative design with practical functionality. Considerable space is set aside for visitors and the cellar itself is striking for its minimal approach to technology, for the aim here is to enhance the wine's naturalness. It was Giovanni Dri who introduced the world to Ramandolo in the early 1970s but his progress in terms of production has not been all roses: it took him many years to get the cellar built and operational. Today, Giovanni has a mature business and he now flanks wine with grappas distilled from pomace or grapes, as well as olive oil production. The nine Dri hectares yield around 45,000 bottles a year. Ramandolo Uve Decembrine is obtained from fruit raisined on the vine, a process encouraged by cutting the shoot, which causes the leaves to fall but impedes nourishment from the vine. In late November or early December, the grapes are pressed and their wine is deep golden yellow, giving elegant baked apple and then a moderately sweet entry on the palate, which echoes the nose nicely, and varietal tannins. The Picolit 2004 foregrounds liqueur apricots and candied citrus peel, its sweet palate refreshed by appealing acidity. Roncat Rosso 2004 is from 50 per cent refosco and decreasing proportions of schioppettino, cabernet sauvignon and merlot.

○	COF Picolit '04	🍷🍷	8
○	COF Ramandolo Uve Decembrine '04	🍷🍷	7
●	COF Rosso Il Roncat '04	🍷	6
●	COF Cabernet '03	🍷	5
●	COF Refosco '04	🍷	5
○	Ramandolo Il Roncat '04	🍷	6
○	COF Picolit '03	🍷🍷 (outline)	8
○	COF Ramandolo Uve Decembrine '03	🍷🍷 (outline)	7

PASIAN DI PRATO (UD)

ANTONUTTI
FRAZ. COLLOREDO DI PRATO
VIA D'ANTONI, 21
33030 PASIAN DI PRATO (UD)
TEL. 0432662001
www.antonuttivini.it

Winemaking usually takes time, a limit dictated by the vine's unchanging biological schedule, and often even the most capable of winemakers may have to wait patiently to achieve the results he or she set out to obtain. That is the situation in which Adriana Antonutti and her husband Lino find themselves in after setting out, about three years ago, on an ambitious project of renewal for the estate they run with their children. The seesaw results of the past are now only a memory and the far-sighted project, in combination with the family's undoubted winemaking prowess, is beginning to bear fruit even though the vintage was a challenging one across the region. We have again given the Antonuttis a full Guide profile for their range of wines, which are good overall and include one or two excellent products. Best of the bunch as usual is the Sauvignon Blanc Poggio Alto 2005, a small proportion of which saw oak. The nose offers varietal tomato leaf that melds nicely with crisp notes of oranges and wild roses. The elegant entry on the palate leads on to a finish dominated by citrus notes. The Pinot Grigio 2005 is convincingly varietal, showing gunflint and pear laced with tobacco. And the third stand-out is the Chardonnay Poggio Alto 2004. Part of the must is barrique-fermented and the complex palate reprises the nose, alternating creamy white chocolate with fresher citrus and banana-like sensations.

○	Friuli Grave Chardonnay Poggio Alto '04	🍷🍷	4
○	Friuli Grave Pinot Grigio '05	🍷🍷	3*
○	Friuli Grave Sauvignon Blanc Poggio Alto '05	🍷🍷	4
●	Friuli Grave Cabernet Sauvignon Poggio Alto '02	🍷	4
●	Friuli Grave Merlot Poggio Alto '03	🍷	4
●	Friuli Grave Merlot '04	🍷	3
○	Friuli Grave Chardonnay '05	🍷	3
○	Friuli Grave Sauvignon '05	🍷	3
○	Friuli Grave Tocai Friulano '05	🍷	3
●	Friuli Grave Refosco P. R. '03		3
●	Friuli Grave Cabernet '04		3

PAVIA DI UDINE (UD)

PIGHIN
FRAZ. RISANO
V.LE GRADO, 1
33050 PAVIA DI UDINE (UD)
TEL. 0432675444
www.pighin.com

The past growing year seems to have been a lesser one for Pighin, even if our notes show marked improvement in the two standard-label Terre di Risano wines, the white and the red. For the past few years, Fernando Pighin has been in charge of the winery, founded more than 40 years ago, with his children Roberto and Raffaela. Roberto looks after non-domestic sales while his sister handles public relations. Fernando has started to renew the 30 hectares of vine stock in the Collio DOC, most of which is trained to a low-density Casarsa system, by replacing this with single Guyot pruning. The grapes obtained are vinified at the small cellar in Capriva, after which ageing is carried out at Risano in the facility designed by the architect Gino Valle. This is the heart of the winery, which for many years has entrusted winemaking to Paolo Valdesolo, recently joined by Cristian Peres. Annual production hovers around 1,300,000 bottles, some 60 per cent of which is sold abroad. The Collio Sauvignon has distinct bell pepper and sage on nose and palate, a hint of liquorice and marked softness on the finish. Terre di Risano Bianco is obtained from tocai, pinot grigio and sauvignon, separately fermented in steel only and subsequently blended. The sauvignon comes out on top in the wine's rue, sage and fresh-tasting minerality. Finally, the refosco, merlot and cabernet sauvignon-based red also pleased our tasters, its fruit keeping the oak well under control.

○	Collio Sauvignon '05	▼▼	4*
●	Friuli Grave Rosso Villa Agricola Ris. '01	▼	5
●	Collio Merlot '04	▼	4
●	Friuli Grave Rosso Terre di Risano '04	▼	3
○	Collio Pinot Grigio '05	▼	4
○	Friuli Grave Bianco Terre di Risano '05	▼	3
○	Friuli Grave Sauvignon '05	▼	3
●	Friuli Grave Refosco P. R. '04		3
○	Friuli Grave Tocai Friulano '03	▽▽	4
○	Collio Pinot Grigio '04	▽▽	4

PINZANO AL TAGLIAMENTO (PN)

ALESSANDRO VICENTINI ORGNANI
FRAZ. VALERIANO
VIA SOTTOPLOVIA, 2
33094 PINZANO AL TAGLIAMENTO (PN)
TEL. 0432950107
www.vicentiniorgnani.com

In recent years, Alessandro Vicentini Orgnani and his cellar have made great strides forward. When Alessandro took over, the 20 hectares were planted with only 24,000 vines, many belonging to not very profitable local varieties. Now one third of the vine stock has been replanted, there are 80,000 vines, the most recent planted at a density of 6,000 vines per hectare, and the cellar releases 80,000 bottles a year. Native varieties have been rigorously selected and in practice the only one left is ucelut. The 2006 growing year saw all the vineyards replanted to modern criteria come onstream and this can only boost the quality of the range even further. As we moved onto the wines, we tried Merlot Rosso di Valeriano 2001 first, a product that Alessandro plans to turn into a territory-focused red blend. For the time being, we like it the way it is. Rosso di Valeriano, from one fifth part-dried grapes, has lashings of personality after fermenting in large wood for 24 months and maturing in bottle for another year. The colour is as deep as the fragrances, which suggest blackberry tart, blueberries and liqueur cherries, before the palate unfolds with austere complexity on balsamic notes and caressingly soft tannins. Alessandro's elegant Pinot Grigio is also impressive, giving orange peel, williams pears and minerality. A firm entry on the palate soon gains momentum to sign off with attractive freshness. The Chardonnay's nose is intriguing as are the subtle fresh citrus and wild herb aromas of the Tocai.

●	Rosso di Valeriano Merlot '01	▼▼	5
○	Friuli Grave Pinot Grigio '05	▼▼	3*
○	Friuli Grave Chardonnay '05	▼	3
○	Friuli Grave Tocai Friulano '05	▼	3
○	Friuli Grave Sauvignon '05		3
●	Friuli Grave Cabernet Sauvignon '04		3
●	Friuli Grave Merlot '04		3
●	Friuli Grave Merlot '03	▽▽	3
○	Ucelut '01	▽▽	7
○	Ucelut '03	▽▽	7
○	Friuli Grave Chardonnay '04	▽▽	3

PORCIA (PN)

San Simone

Loc. Rondover
via Prata, 30
33080 Porcia (PN)
tel. 0434578633
www.sansimone.it

Wine tourists and others who visit San Simone are always impressed by the unity of the Brisotto family, as well as by their lovely winery which boasts a 14th-century chapel dedicated to St Simon. After Gino's untimely passing, Liviana and her children Chiara, Anna and Antonio have become if anything even more united. They continue along the path traced out by Gino, keeping a firm hand on a 40-hectare estate that can offer a number of very interesting products. The difficult 2005 growing year merely underlined the quality and competence of the San Simone winery, which from any point of view is a family business. After a year in barrique and six months in bottle, Merlot Evante 2004 has emerged in fine form. The almost impenetrably dense red introduces a broad spectrum of aromatics that ranges from briary fruit to liqueur cherries, cloves and chocolate, giving an opulent feel to the nose. The palate mirrors the nose, bolstered by robust tannins. Highlights of the long list of wines tasted included the inviting white fruit salad and flowers of the chardonnay and sauvignon Nòstos, which are not however matched by sufficient richness on the palate, the decent breadth of the Refosco Re Sugano, and the pleasing spice and hay of Rosso Bris, a blend of cabernet sauvignon and merlot.

●	Friuli Grave Merlot Evante '04	▼▼	6
●	Friuli Grave Refosco P. R. Re Sugano '04	▼	4
○	Friuli Grave Chardonnay '05	▼	3
○	Friuli Grave Pinot Grigio '05	▼	3
○	Friuli Grave Sauvignon '05	▼	3
○	Friuli Grave Tocai Friulano '05	▼	3
○	Nòstos '05	▼	4
●	Rosso Bris '05	▼	3
●	Friuli Grave Cabernet Sauvignon Nexus '03		4
●	Friuli Grave Cabernet Franc '05		3
●	Friuli Grave Cabernet Sauvignon Nexus '02	▽▽	4
●	Friuli Grave Merlot Evante '03	▽▽	6

POVOLETTO (UD)

Teresa Raiz

via Kennedy, 5
33040 Povoletto (UD)
tel. 0432679556
www.teresaraiz.it

For the past four years, Paolo Tosolini has been the sole owner of the winery his grandmother Teresa founded in 1971. An oenologist himself, Paolo has engaged the Terra e Vino group headed by Alessio Dorigo, a winemaker who is increasingly admired for the results he has achieved in a number of cellars while respecting the territoriality of each. The estate has 13 hectares in a single plot around the cellar at Marsure and a further seven in neighbouring Faedis, in the heart of the Colli Orientali del Friuli DOC zone. Paolo also selects and buys in quantities of fruit, enabling him to release a total of 250,000 bottles a year. Much of the vine stock has been restructured with the help of the French nurseryman Guillaume and planting density is now as high as 5,000 vines per hectares. Sovrej, an 80-15-5 blend of chardonnay, sauvignon and picolit, is delightfully complex, despite its still evident oak-derived vanilla, elegantly evoking banana and caramel in the finish. The Colli Orientali Pinot Grigio, too, stands out for its elegance. Fresh and creamy on both nose and palate, it signs off with delicious softness. This year, the Ribolla Gialla is less substantial than usual and failed to win a second Glass. Finally, it is always a pleasure to uncork Decano Rosso. From a blend of more than 50 per cent merlot with cabernet sauvignon and franc, it has lots of spicy structure. It's a pity that a green note knocked a few points off the score.

○	Sovrej '04	▼▼	5
○	COF Pinot Grigio '05	▼▼	4
●	COF Rosso Decano Rosso '02	▼	6
●	COF Cabernet '04	▼	4
●	Refosco P. R. Vign. Le Marsure '04	▼	4
○	Chardonnay Vign. Le Marsure '05	▼	4
○	COF Ribolla Gialla '05	▼	4
○	COF Tocai Friulano '05	▼	4
○	Pinot Grigio Vign. Le Marsure '05	▼	4
○	Sauvignon Vign. Le Marsure '05	▼	4

PRATA DI PORDENONE (PN)

Vigneti Le Monde

loc. Le Monde
via Garibaldi, 2
33080 Prata di Pordenone (PN)
tel. 0434622087
www.vignetilemonde.com

In the last edition of the Guide, we talked about the serene image of Le Monde, the almost idyllic calm that enfolds the area and the human pace of life it evokes. Then out of a clear blue sky came a complete reorganization of the estate. Building has begun on the new cellar, the vineyards are being modernized and replanted and the splendid 18th-century villa is undergoing restoration that will convert it into a sophisticated agriturismo. Piergiovanni Pistoni, the man behind this substantial investment, has always liked a challenge so we hope that all this will lead to further improvement in overall standards of quality. For the time being, we have another fine year to report for this ambitious outfit on the flatlands of Pordenone. Ca' Salice, a red blend, and Giacò, a plains Picolit that attracted favourable comments a few years ago, lead the list of invariably well-managed wines. Ca' Salice is a blend of refosco and cabernet. It's a tad slow to open but then shows convincing pipe tobacco and blackcurrant tart aromas that are echoed precisely in the mouth, where they are backed up by robust tannins. Giacò is named after Piergiovanni's son Giacomo and confirmed the excellent impression it made last time round. Delicate hints of stewed apple and candied citrus peel, clean sensations and a sweet but not cloying palate leading to a long candied apricot and caramel finish earned it Two resounding Glasses. The Pinot Nero with its balsam and wild berry flavours is back on form while the Pinot Bianco needs more weight on the palate to score higher.

● Friuli Grave Rosso Ca' Salice '04	🍷🍷	4*
○ Giacò	🍷🍷	5
● Friuli Grave Pinot Nero '02	🍷	4
○ Friuli Grave Chardonnay '05	🍷	3
○ Friuli Grave Pinot Bianco '05	🍷	3
○ Friuli Grave Bianco Pujà '03		4
● Friuli Grave Refosco P. R. '04		3
● Friuli Grave Cabernet Franc '05		3
○ Friuli Grave Pinot Grigio '05		3
○ Friuli Grave Sauvignon '05		3

PRATA DI PORDENONE (PN)

Villa Frattina

fraz. Ghirano
via Palazzetto, 68
33080 Prata di Pordenone (PN)
tel. 0434605911
www.villafrattina.it

After a disappointing year in the last Guide, the Averna brothers' estate emphatically claimed a full profile this time. We are pleased for the owners and for Ivan Molaro, the long-serving cellar oenologist. Needless to say, it has been important in recent years that consultancy was available from the noted university teacher of oenology, Donato Lanati. The 60 hectares under vine around the lovely Villa Frattina, built in the 17th century, are located in three different provinces that meet here, Pordenone, Treviso and Venice. The cellar is not content to vinify estate-grown fruit and buys in at least 5,000 quintals to supplement its own grapes. Annual production is in excess of 1,000,000 bottles and average quality is good. From this year, still wines are labelled simply Frattina whereas the Spumante retains the Villa Frattina name. The elegantly complex Pinot Grigio has fruit salad, fresh fruit and hints of tropical fruits before the intense, fresh-tasting palate unfolds all its length. We were unconvinced by a first sniff of the Tocai Italico but then it made up for this amply on the rich, pear and apple palate. The Refosco, the Cabernet Sauvignon and the chardonnay and pinot grigio DiGale are also all more convincing in the mouth than on the nose.

○ Lison-Pramaggiore Pinot Grigio '05	🍷🍷	3*
● Lison-Pramaggiore Refosco P. R. '04	🍷	3
○ DiGale '05	🍷	4
● Lison-Pramaggiore Cabernet Sauvignon '05	🍷	4
○ Lison-Pramaggiore Tocai Italico '05	🍷	3
● Corte dell'Abbà Rosso '01	🍷🍷 (outline)	6
● Lison-Pramaggiore Cabernet Franc Faè '01	🍷🍷 (outline)	5
● Robbio '02	🍷🍷 (outline)	4

PRAVISDOMINI (PN)

Terre di Ger

fraz. Frattina
s.da della Meduna
33076 Pravisdomini (PN)
tel. 0434644452
www.terrediger.it

Gianni Spinazzè is an entrepreneur who is well known to growers in the Triveneto regions and beyond because his post manufacturing business brings him into contact with a wide range of producers. It was hard not to fall under the spell of all those enthusiastic winemakers and in 1986 he purchased a small property that was sending grapes to a co-operative winery. In 1999, Gianni's son Robert, also bitten by the wine bug, decided to join the business. He reorganized the winery, bringing in expert agronomists in the vineyard, leading oenologists in the cellar and experts for the commercial side. The most recent acquisition is Alessio Dorigo from the Terra e Vino group, a winemaker like his father and a new point of reference for Friulian wine. In the meantime, the estate's old name, Podere del Ger, has been replaced by Terre del Ger, to reflect the growth in the vine stock to 38 hectares, with a further ten being replanted. The cellar has been extended again and can now handle 10,000 hectolitres. In short, everything is in place for Terre del Ger to become one of the region's most important wine estates. As usual, the 70-30 verduzzo trevigiano and chardonnay Limine is excellent. It ferments in barrique and ages on the lees in the same containers, without racking, for eight months. Cream, apricot and yellow peach fuse with vanilla in its spectrum of aromatics. The Chardonnay and Pinot Grigio are very well typed and the Refosco is spicy.

○ Limine '05	▼▼	4*
● Refosco '04	▼	4
○ Friuli Grave Chardonnay '05	▼	3
○ Friuli Grave Pinot Grigio '05	▼	4
● El Masut '01	▽▽	5
● Lison-Pramaggiore Cabernet Franc '03	▽▽	3
○ Friuli Grave Pinot Grigio '04	▽▽	3
○ Verduzzo Limine '04	▽▽	4

PREMARIACCO (UD)

Bastianich

via Casali Ottelio, 7
33040 Premariacco (UD)
tel. 0432655363
www.bastianich.com

The estate owned by Lidia Bastianich and her son Giuseppe doubled its area under vine a few months ago and today has 28 hectares. The heirs of the late Renzo Toffolutti sold the Dal Fari estate to the Italian-American Bastianiches, who now at last have a cellar to call their own. Valter Scarbolo and Denis Lepore are busy in the cellar, where the wines are supervised by oenologist Andrea Brunisso, with consultancy input from Emilio Del Medico and Maurizio Castelli. The Bastianiches intend to renew the newly purchased vineyards by increasing planting density. Recent growing years have been very different from each other and far from easy to interpret, which has prompted the winery to trim the range. This year, there are only three labels. There is a huge difference between two classic Bastianich wines, the Tocai Friulano 2005 and the Tocai Friulano Plus 2005. The Tocai is fresh and citrussy whereas its stablemate gives intense, elegant pear, apple, liquorice, melon and citrus fruits on the nose. Warm and fat on the palate, it is almost too fruit-forward and the soft finish takes nothing away from the overall experience. The Tocai Plus may be excellent but the Vespa Bianco 2004, from chardonnay, sauvignon and ten per cent picolit, is even better. In the winery's philosophy, it is very similar to the Tocai selection. Superbly complex, and veined with cream and banana, it is lifted by fresh fruit to heights of elegance. The supremely balanced, gutsy palate is textbook stuff, making this a particularly sophisticated Three Glass champion.

○ Vespa Bianco '04	▼▼▼	5
○ COF Tocai Friulano Plus '05	▼▼	5
○ COF Tocai Friulano '05	▼	4
○ Vespa Bianco '00	▽▽▽	5
○ Vespa Bianco '01	▽▽▽	5
○ Vespa Bianco '03	▽▽▽	5
○ Vespa Bianco '99	▽▽▽	5
○ COF Tocai Friulano Plus '02	▽▽▽	5
○ COF Tocai Friulano Plus '03	▽▽	5

PREMARIACCO (UD)

Dario e Luciano Ermacora

fraz. Ipplis
via Solzaredo, 9
33040 Premariacco (UD)
tel. 0432716250
www.ermacora.com

Dario and Luciano Ermacora are keeping up their string of fine performances. This time they may not have earned Three Glasses but they confirmed the dependability of their entire range. Three – Pignolo, Pinot Bianco and Pinot Grigio – out of the nine wines we tasted went through to the finals, three – Refosco, Sauvignon and Tocai – cruised off with Two Glasses while the remaining three – Merlot, Picolit and Verduzzo Friulano – went no further than One Glass. But apart from the results, we should remember the family's investments. The estate has been extended by four hectares purchased in the Buttrio area, in the heart of the Colli Orientali DOC. In the cellars, the Ermacoras take advice from Flavio Zuliani, a consultant who is much respected around here. The house Pignolo is a wine to bank on and went to our final taste-offs again this year. The 2002 selection has complex spice and aromatic herbs mingling with sweeter notes of damson jam and coffee cream. Well-structured and assertive in the mouth, it has beefy but well-integrated tannins. The Ermacoras' Pinot Bianco 2005 is one of Friuli's best. Rich and well-rounded, it enhances varietal apples with citrus and pears before the dynamic palate alternates fatty sensations with freshness. In contrast, the Pinot Grigio is strikingly clean with great breadth and the variety's elegant mineral notes. We will conclude by pointing out the flowery finesse of the Tocai, the Sauvignon's typicity and the attractive gamey notes of the Refosco.

●	COF Pignolo '02	TT	6
○	COF Pinot Bianco '05	TT	4*
○	COF Pinot Grigio '05	TT	4*
●	COF Refosco P. R. '04	TT	4
○	COF Sauvignon '05	TT	4
○	COF Tocai Friulano '05	TT	4
○	COF Picolit '04	T	7
○	COF Verduzzo Friulano '05	T	4
●	COF Merlot. '04	T	4
●	COF Pignolo '00	YYY	5
○	COF Picolit '02	YY	7
○	COF Pinot Bianco '04	YY	4

PREMARIACCO (UD)

Rocca Bernarda

fraz. Ipplis
via Rocca Bernarda, 27
33040 Premariacco (UD)
tel. 0432716914 - 0432716273
www.roccabernarda.com

It is remarkable to think that this winery was founded in 1559, and even more impressive that the Rocca complex, a superb country residence, was actually erected after the cellar in 1567. The estate belonged to two noblemen, Bernardo and Jacopo di Valvason-Maniago, and passed from generation to generation to Gaetano Perusini, who left it to the Sovereign Military Order of Malta. The Order is not exactly a flexible organization but Sandro Pistucchia's tenure as administrator brought with it a series of initiatives that in a just a few years restored Rocca Bernarda to its former glory. The estate has 200 hectares, of which 55 are under vine, and releases 180,000 bottles a year. Paolo Dolce is the estate manager and oenological consultancy is provided by Piedmont-born Marco Monchiero. Again, Picolit was one of Rocca Bernarda's big hitters, if not quite as good as last year's version, and in fact the wine type was relaunched by the estate in the early 20th century. Baked apple, almond paste, caramel and noble rot are the keynotes. Vineis, from 80 per cent tocai friulano and the remainder chardonnay and sauvignon, is a wine whose strong suit is elegant persistence. The Sauvignon has citrus while the palate of the Merlot Centis is held back by assertive tannins.

○	COF Picolit '04	TT	8
○	COF Bianco Vineis '05	TT	4*
○	COF Sauvignon '05	TT	4*
●	COF Merlot Centis '04	T	5
○	COF Chardonnay '05	T	4
○	COF Pinot Grigio '05	T	4
○	COF Tocai Friulano '05	T	4
○	COF Picolit '03	YYY	8
○	COF Picolit '01	YY	8
○	COF Picolit '02	YY	8
○	COF Chardonnay '04	YY	4
●	COF Merlot Centis '03	YY	5
●	COF Merlot Centis '02	YY	5

PREMARIACCO (UD)

ROBERTO SCUBLA
FRAZ. IPPLIS
VIA ROCCA BERNARDA, 22
33040 PREMARIACCO (UD)
TEL. 0432716258
www.scubla.com

We'll start by reporting a new development at Scubla. Fifteen years after the cellar was set up, it is to undergo a complete image makeover. Roberto has decided to change the labels of his wines and we like the new ones. On the organizational front, production went up this year by about 15,000 bottles to 60,000 from an area under vine covering 12 hectares, most estate-owned. Value for money is a major feature of these wines. The new purchases of old vines of tocai, merlot, ribolla gialla and malvasia are sure to bring the good results that Roberto hopes for. After a few years in the doldrums, Pomèdes shines again. Three well-deserved Glasses went to this wine for its tropical aromas mingling with confectioner's cream and faint vanilla. The flavour is complex, very aromatic and fruit-led with a long, lingering, acidity-braced finish. Pomèdes 2004 from tocai, pinot bianco, chardonnay and riesling renano ferments entirely in wood for about seven months. It does not undergo malolactic fermentation and is given frequent lees stirring. Verduzzo Friulano Cràtis 2003 confirmed its status as a great Friulian sweet wine. Intense amber introduces aromas of almond paste, dried fruit, figs and candied apricots, bolstered by the grapes natural tannins. The new Scubla jewel is the Sauvignon 2005, where we find intense peach-like aromas and ripe fruit that return satisfyingly in the mouth. The rest of the range is excellent.

○	COF Bianco Pomèdes '04	🍷🍷🍷	5
○	COF Verduzzo Friulano Cràtis '03	🍷🍷	6
○	COF Sauvignon '05	🍷🍷	4*
●	COF Rosso Scuro '03	🍷🍷	5
●	COF Cabernet Sauvignon '04	🍷🍷	5
●	COF Merlot '04	🍷🍷	5
○	COF Bianco Speziale '05	🍷🍷	4
○	COF Pinot Bianco '05	🍷🍷	4
○	COF Tocai Friulano '05	🍷🍷	4
○	COF Bianco Pomèdes '98	🍷🍷🍷	5
○	COF Bianco Pomèdes '99	🍷🍷🍷	5
○	COF Verduzzo Friulano Graticcio '99	🍷🍷🍷	6

PREMARIACCO (UD)

LA TUNELLA
FRAZ. IPPLIS
VIA DEL COLLIO, 14
33040 PREMARIACCO (UD)
TEL. 0432716030
www.latunella.it

The Zorzettig family's bachelor, Massimo, is such no longer since he married Romina in summer 2006, to the delight of his mother Gabriella. We can never heap too much praise on this indomitable woman, widowed when her children were barely teenagers, who has guided the estate to where, thanks to the efforts of Massimo and Marco, it is today, with a vine stock of about 70 hectares plus a further ten that are rented. The impressive new cellar manages to combine aesthetic appeal and practicality, enabling oenologist Luigino Zamparo to give full rein to his knack for experimentation. In the past, we have had doubts about the La Tunella reds but we were forced to change our minds by the excellent performances of the native Schioppettino and Refosco in particular. The Schioppettino, labelled Selènze (Friulian for excellence) is one of the best interpretations of the variety, its typically spicy nose offering elegant black cherry before the complex, lingering palate mirrors the nose. Apparently sweetish, it is in fact glycerine-rich. Grapes for the Picolit 2004 were left to overripen on the vine and part-dried in the cellar before ageing in wood. Almond paste and dried figs usher in a creamy, dense palate redolent of dates, dried apricots and almond milk. The Sauvignon flaunts direct notes of rue, sage, bell pepper and peach. Finally Biancosesto, from tocai and ribolla matured in large wood, proffers citrus, noble rot, pears and balsam.

●	COF Schioppettino Selènze '03	🍷🍷	5
○	COF Picolit '04	🍷🍷	7
○	COF Biancosesto '05	🍷🍷	4*
○	COF Sauvignon '05	🍷🍷	4*
○	COF Pinot Grigio '05	🍷🍷	4
○	COF Tocai Friulano Selènze '05	🍷🍷	4
○	COF Bianco Campo Marzio '04	🍷	5
●	COF Refosco P.R. '04	🍷	4
○	COF Ribolla Gialla Selènze '05	🍷	4
○	COF Picolit '02	🍷🍷	6
○	Noans '03	🍷🍷	5
○	COF Biancosesto '04	🍷🍷	4
○	COF Ribolla Gialla Selènze '04	🍷🍷	4
○	COF Sauvignon '04	🍷🍷	4

PREMARIACCO (UD)

VIGNE FANTIN NODÀR

LOC. ORSARIA
VIA CASALI OTTELIO, 4
33170 PREMARIACCO (UD)
TEL. 043428735
www.fantinnodar.it

Attilio Pignat bought this lovely estate in the rolling hills between Buttrio and Premariacco in 1991. The 20 hectares were largely renovated in 1993 and 1994, with planting densities raised to 5,000 vines per hectare and Guyot training introduced to improve the quality of the grapes harvested. Following the Friulian tradition of producing as many different grapes as possible, eight white varieties and four red are planted, which enables the cellar to release about 15 labels. Vineyard management is in the hands of Stefano Bortolussi while winemaking is the responsibility of Francesco Spitaleri. The best of the range again was the Sauvignon, confirming the validity of the clones selected, vineyard techniques employed and vinification procedures used. It's a refreshing wine with distinct peach, sage and bell pepper in a well-sustained whole. The cask-conditioned version, Sauvignon Auràtus 2004, has distinct toastiness, a milky vein, hints of citrus and a captivating after-aroma. The oak of the Refosco Auràtus 2004 has also yet to be fully absorbed but its structure and fullness shine through in a spicy, tar-veined whole. The Tocai Friulano is a wine to follow as it evolves and the Ribolla Gialla earned a mention.

●	COF Refosco P. R. Auràtus '04	YY	5
○	COF Sauvignon '05	YY	4*
○	COF Sauvignon Auràtus '04	Y	4
○	COF Tocai Friulano '05	Y	4
○	COF Ribolla Gialla '05		4
○	COF Bianco Carato '00	YY	5
○	COF Sauvignon '04	YY	4

PREPOTTO (UD)

LE DUE TERRE

VIA ROMA, 68B
33040 PREPOTTO (UD)
TEL. 0432713189

One of the most charismatic, capable winemakers around Prepotto is Flavio Basilicata, a man who is always ready to take on all-comers and stand up for the potential of his own terroir. The first harvest for Le Due Terre was 1984. "The winery came out of nothing", Flavio likes to say. Indeed, he gets so emotional about it that one well-known journalist was moved to write about "bottles born of a dream". Most people think the estate's name, which means The Two Lands, was chosen because the vine stock lies in two different production zones but the real reason is geological. Flavio grows some vines on marl and others on red earth. We had a long chat with Flavio about his Sacrisassi Bianco 2004, which was without doubt the wine that sparked off the liveliest debate among our tasters. On tasting some past vintages, we have concluded that more time in bottle will make it a truly memorable wine. Moving on to the reds, all of our panel members agreed that we had two fantastic wines on the table. Sacrisassi Rosso 2004, from refosco and schioppettino, has bramble and red fruit laced with plenty of spice in a very elegant product. Complex to a fault, the Merlot 2004 reveals attractive liquorice, blackcurrant and cherry, closing on confectioner's cream that comes back on the pervasive, persistent palate.

●	COF Merlot '04	YY	7
●	COF Rosso Sacrisassi '04	YY	6
○	COF Bianco Sacrisassi '04	YY	6
●	COF Merlot '00	YYY	7
●	COF Merlot '02	YYY	7
●	COF Rosso Sacrisassi '97	YYY	7
●	COF Rosso Sacrisassi '98	YYY	7
●	COF Pinot Nero '02	YY	7

PREPOTTO (UD)

Iole Grillo

via Albana, 60
33040 Prepotto (UD)
tel. 0432713201
www.vinigrillo.it

Anna Muzzolini has good reason to feel satisfied. Years ago, she abandoned her successful business in Ferrara to return, husband and son in tow, to Prepotto and take over the family wine estate. Today, she is reaping the well-deserved fruits of her commitment to the land. For Anna's impressive line-up includes a stand-out Merlot that was already delivering the goods last year, as we noted. Overall, the winery is growing and has recently planted two hectares exclusively to native varieties. There are also new developments in the cellar, where winemaking consultancy this year comes from Giuseppe Tosoratti. We were talking about that Merlot. It matures for two years in large wood and impresses with its austere nose of briary fruit, hay and intensely gamey nuances. On the palate, there is a fine balance of close-knit tannins and subtle fruit softness. Guardafuoco, a 50-50 blend of cabernet sauvignon and merlot, is another admirable red with a rich, full nose of chocolate and cinchona followed by nice progression in the mouth. Best of the whites – we are in Friuli, after all – was the Tocai, which has ripe, sunny citrus and tropical fruit and a lively palate. The Sauvignon is built along similar line, even if it does lack a little thrust that would take it further up the scale.

●	COF Merlot '03	🍷🍷	5
●	COF Rosso Guardafuoco '03	🍷🍷	5
○	COF Tocai Friulano '05	🍷🍷	4
●	COF Refosco P. R. '04	🍷	4
○	COF Pinot Grigio '05	🍷	4
○	COF Sauvignon '05	🍷	4
●	COF Schioppettino '04		5
●	COF Merlot '01	YY	5
○	COF Sauvignon '04	YY	4

PREPOTTO (UD)

Valerio Marinig

via Brolo, 41
33040 Prepotto (UD)
tel. 0432713012
www.marinig.it

Valerio Marinig is showing that he fully deserves his father Sergio's faith in him when he passed over to Valerio full responsibility for the management of the family estate. Sergio is still his son's main collaborator, particularly out in the vineyard, while wife Marisa is always on hand to welcome customers and visitors with a smile. Extension and rationalization of the cellar were completed a couple of years ago, enabling Valerio to move with a little more freedom among the tanks and barrels, although the new spaces are already beginning to look insufficient for future needs. Most of the wine obtained from eight hectares under vine goes into bottle, with the remainder sold unbottled, and despite the not inconsiderable success achieved in recent years, prices have remained very attractive. The Picolit 2004 is the colour of old gold. Figs, dried apricots, almond milk and apricot jam regale the nose, returning triumphantly on the palate, where they are joined by candied citrus peel. Yet again, Sauvignon is one of the highlights from this small cellar's list, offering tomato leaf, elderflower and citrus followed up by a refreshing, persistent palate. The Tocai Friulano missed out on a second Glass for its slight lack of weight in the mouth but it is nevertheless refreshing and very enjoyable.

○	COF Picolit '04	🍷🍷	6
○	COF Sauvignon '05	🍷🍷	4*
●	COF Cabernet Franc '04	🍷	4
●	COF Schioppettino '04	🍷	4
○	COF Chardonnay '05	🍷	4
○	COF Pinot Bianco '05	🍷	4
○	COF Tocai Friulano '05	🍷	4
●	Biel Cûr Rosso '03		4
●	COF Merlot '04		4
○	COF Verduzzo Friulano '04		4

PREPOTTO (UD)

PETRUSSA
FRAZ. ALBANA, 49
33040 PREPOTTO (UD)
TEL. 0432713192
www.petrussa.it

Slowly but surely, Paolo and Gianni Petrussa continue to expand their winery. Currently, they have eight hectares under vine and supplement these with a further two that they manage. Annual output is around 60,000 bottles and the Petrussas' next objectives are expanding their cellar space with a new section that will double capacity. Prepotto is the homeland of schioppettino, aka ribolla nera, a variety that is particularly well suited to the valley's climate. Like other local wineries, Petrussa is committed to increasing production of this wine and aims to reach 10,000 units a year. Tocai Friulano 2005, was steel-fermented only and 8,000 units went into bottle. A characterful wine, it gives broad pear and citrus that hold up well, signing off with a lingering finish. It is unarguably superior to the Tocai Sant'Elena, whose time in oak has partially muzzled the fruit. Typical sage and bell pepper are in evidence in the Sauvignon, which adds peach and citrus on the palate. Pensiero 2003 is a single-variety Verduzzo. Old gold in hue, it leaves persistent tears on the glass to let you know about its sweetness and rich glycerine. Baked apple, with dried and liqueur apricots, dominate the spectrum of aromatics against a backdrop of oak-derived vanilla.

○	Pensiero '03	▼▼	5
○	COF Sauvignon '05	▼▼	4
○	COF Tocai Friulano '05	▼▼	4
○	COF Tocai Friulano S. Elena '05	▼▼	5
●	COF Rosso Petrussa '03	▼	6
●	COF Schioppettino '03	▼	6
●	COF Cabernet '05	▼	4
○	COF Pinot Bianco '05		4
○	Pensiero '02	▽▽	5
○	COF Pinot Bianco '04	▽▽	4
○	COF Tocai Friulano '04	▽▽	4

PREPOTTO (UD)

RONCO DEI PINI
VIA RONCHI, 94
33040 PREPOTTO (UD)
TEL. 0432713239
www.roncodeipini.com

A winery that buys in much of its grapes inevitably has to face the vagaries of the weather, and when it is inclement, there is a price to pay. That is what has happened to Giuseppe and Claudio Novello's cellar. The range is still sound overall but only one wine earned a second Glass. Ronco dei Pini has four and a half hectares at Prepotto and manages a ten-hectare vineyard at Zegla, near Cormons, also buying in fruit from small-scale growers. Vineyard management is the job of Damiano Stramare while the cellar is the responsibility of oenologist Renato De Doni. Part-drying of the fruit has given the Verduzzo Riccovino a deep golden yellow hue and the tears in the glass that denote glycerine and substantial alcohol. Given this introduction, it is no surprise to find well-defined dried figs and caramel on the nose, or sweetness and concentration on the palate, which concludes with a milk of almonds finale. The Pinot Bianco is the best of the One Glass wines, its elegant apple and herb nose followed by a savoury, fresh-tasting palate with very decent fruit. Vanilla and toastiness come through on the Chardonnay but the principal sensation is dried flowers.

○	Verduzzo Friulano Riccovino '05	▼▼	5
●	COF Merlot '04	▼	4
○	COF Pinot Bianco '05	▼	4
○	COF Tocai Friulano '05	▼	4
○	Collio Chardonnay '05	▼	4
●	COF Cabernet '04		4
○	Collio Pinot Grigio '05		4
○	Collio Sauvignon '05		4
○	COF Tocai Friulano '04	▽▽	4
○	Collio Sauvignon '04	▽▽	4
○	Verduzzo Friulano Riccovino '04	▽▽	5

PREPOTTO (UD)

Ronco di Prepotto

via Brolo, 45
33040 Prepotto (UD)
tel. 0432281118
www.roncodiprepotto.com

After the progress we have seen in recent years, we believe the time has come to give the Macorig family winery a place in the Guide with a full profile. The surname is absolutely typical of the zone so Annibale and his son Giampaolo decided to name their winery after the town. The main estate dates from 1901 and is situated next to the cellar, building on which was started in the same year. Today, Annibale and Giampaolo farm ten hectares under vine, eight of them estate-owned. Production is split 60-40 between reds and whites, a choice determined by the alluvial nature of the soil, which favours the former type. The entire vine stock has been renewed since 2002: the plants have been lowered to 80 centimetres off the ground and are now Guyot-trained. The rows, which are grassed over, are kept tidy by Annibale manually, using a grass trimmer. Most of the time, Giampaolo, 34, looks after the cellar with consultancy from Emilio Del Medico. Zeus is a blend of 40 per cent each of refosco and schioppettino, with the rest merlot. Enough fruit is part-dried from each variety to make a single barrique. The wine itself is a harmonious mix of red fruits that shows no trace of overripeness. Part-drying is also employed for the tocai and malvasia that join riesling in Lavinia, a concentrated, fatty, fresh-tasting white. Finally, there is a very long pear-like note on the finish of the fairly untypical but complex Tocai.

○	COF Bianco Lavinia '03	🍷🍷	6
●	COF Rosso Zeus '03	🍷🍷	6
○	COF Tocai Friulano Vigneti dei Monti Sacri '05	🍷🍷	4*
●	COF Schioppettino Vigneti dei Monti Sacri '04	🍷	4

PREPOTTO (UD)

La Viarte

via Novacuzzo, 51
33040 Prepotto (UD)
tel. 0432759458
www.laviarte.it

The winery managed by Giulio Ceschin is perched on a hilltop between Ruttars and Prepotto. On a clear day, you can see the Adriatic from up here. In fact, the cellar set among its terraced vineyards is a panoramic treat for the eyes. Even the new cellar door sales outlet is pretty to look at and tastefully furnished. Giulio's passion for native vines prompted him to join about 30 other growers in the Prepotto Schioppettino producers' association. The recently formed body aims to give the schioppettino grape the dignity it deserves by complying with a demanding set of production regulations. After we tasted the wines Giulio uncorked for us, we can safely say that quality at La Viarte has taken a big step in the right direction. There was only one disappointment in the Tocai Friulano 2005, from which we were hoping for more. But we loved the Merlot 2003 with its red fruits, mulberries and raspberries. The nose is mirrored on the palate, which signs off with a lovely touch of caramel. The Sauvignon 2005 also went through to the finals. Its wealth of varietal aromatics offers an intriguing sequence of fruit. The Schioppettino 2003 has cherry jam, black cherry and warm alcohol and the Siùm 2003, a blend of picolit and verduzzo friulano, reveals honey, jam, candied peel and apricot. A sweet, well-rounded palate discloses verduzzo's keynote attractive tannins.

●	COF Merlot '03	🍷🍷	5
○	COF Sauvignon '05	🍷🍷	5
●	COF Schioppettino '03	🍷🍷	5
○	Siùm '03	🍷🍷	6
●	COF Tazzelenghe '02	🍷	5
●	COF Refosco P.R. '03	🍷	5
○	COF Bianco Lĭende '04	🍷	5
○	COF Pinot Grigio '05	🍷	4
○	COF Ribolla Gialla '05	🍷	4
○	COF Tocai Friulano '05	🍷	4
○	COF Tocai Friulano '04	🍷🍷 (outline)	5

PREPOTTO (UD)

Vigna Petrussa

Fraz. Albana, 47
33040 Prepotto (UD)
tel. 0432713021
www.vignapetrussa.it

After a lifetime spent in an office, Hilde Petrussa is now a fully fledged wine woman. Her enthusiasm for the recovery and promotion of schioppettino never threatens to flag. The variety, also known as ribolla nera, is most at home in the hills and alluvial flatlands at Prepotto and Albana. Everyone is agreed that the sweet version has no future but there is still plenty of debate involving supporters of the beefy interpretation of the dry wine and those who opt for elegance. Whatever the final preference, and despite the diffidence that is typical of growers everywhere, at Prepotto people are willing to discuss the issue thanks to Hilde's promptings. The lady herself has a satisfied smile as she shows us round her small but charming cellar, where her daughter's design and decoration skills have been put to good use, as they have in the tasting room. The intensely hued Tocai Friulano is outstanding. Concentrated and well-structured, it reveals slow-emerging but full pear and peach fruit. Richenza is a blend of riesling, malvasia, verduzzo, tocai and picolit part-dried in cases and fermented in barrique. It has absorbed the oak well, although touches of toastiness still peek through. After the initial moments, it is fruit that comes through in citrus and overripe banana, followed by a generously fatty, glycerine-rich palate.

○	Richenza '04	▼▼	5
○	COF Tocai Friulano '05	▼▼	4*
●	COF Cabernet Franc '04	▼	4
●	COF Schioppettino '04	▼	5
○	COF Picolit '02	▽▽	6
●	COF Cabernet Franc '03	▽▽	4
○	COF Picolit '03	▽▽	6
●	COF Schioppettino '03	▽▽	5

PREPOTTO (UD)

Vigna Traverso

via Ronchi, 73
33040 Prepotto (UD)
tel. 0422804807
www.molon.it

The Traverso-Molon family own about 45 hectares in this corner of the Colli Orientali del Friuli, just over one third of which is planted to vine. Stefano Traverso, the man who looks after business here, reinforced his links with Friuli in the summer by marrying Erika Butussi. Obviously, the family has not left Stefano on his own. His father Giancarlo is always on hand when he is needed and the cellar is watched over by Simone Casazza, the oenologist who works at the family's main Ornella Molon winery. For the past couple years, Stefano has had advice from Alessio Dorigo, who has made available all his invaluable knowledge of Friuli's wine territory. The new plantings and vineyard restructuring have been entrusted to fruitmakers Marco Simonit and Pierpaolo Sirch, who complete the Vigna Traverso team. With names like these on board, it was no great surprise for us to taste a range of wines that touched peaks of real excellence. Best of the bunch is the harmonious, supremely elegant Tocai Friulano. Intense and rich with ripe fruit and citrus, it has lashings of personality. Not far behind is the broad Pinot Grigio, which enhances its already rich fruit with mango and pineapple. Sottocastello Rosso 2004, a single-variety Merlot from selected grapes, has well-handled toastiness on the nose with concentrated fruit, vegetal hints and a hint of tar. All this follows through on the rich palate with well-integrated tannins.

●	COF Sottocastello Rosso '04	▼▼	6
○	COF Pinot Grigio '05	▼▼	4*
○	COF Tocai Friulano '05	▼▼	4*
●	COF Merlot '04	▼▼	5
●	COF Refosco P. R. '04	▼▼	5
●	COF Schioppettino '04	▼▼	5
○	COF Sottocastello Bianco '05	▼▼	5
○	COF Ribolla Gialla '05	▼▼	4
○	COF Sauvignon '05	▼▼	4
●	COF Cabernet Franc '04	▼	5
●	COF Sottocastello Rosso '01	▽▽	5
●	COF Refosco P. R. '02	▽▽	5
●	COF Refosco P. R. '03	▽▽	5
○	COF Tocai Friulano '02	▽▽	4
○	COF Tocai Friulano '04	▽▽	4

RIVE D'ARCANO (UD)

Bidoli

Fraz. Arcano Superiore
via Fornace, 19
33030 Rive d'Arcano (UD)
tel. 0432810796 - 0432810793
www.bidolivini.com

After Bidoli's confident entry into the Guide last year, we were looking forward to the new range from this big-numbers producer, which releases 1,200,000 bottles a year. In Friuli, the 2005 growing year was challenging, to put it mildly, especially for whites. Wineries like Bidoli, which we should remember buys in all its grapes from outside growers, were likely to feel the negative impact of the weather more than most. But instead, we found an excellent range in which the whites actually stood out. Our congratulations go to brother and sister Margherita and Arrigo Bidoli for their care in selecting the fruit. There are three fine standard-label whites and a Merlot Briccolo 2004 to lead the pack. We'll begin with the Pinot Grigio Fornâs dai Fradis. Fragrances of orange mingle with wild flowers and chamomile before the palate's excellent progression takes you through to a very minerally finish. The graceful orange blossom, apple and rue aromas of the Sauvignon return on the palate with impressive consistency. We liked the Pinot Bianco Fornâs dai Fradis for its complex aromas and juicy palate, where distinct fresh fruit comes through. Finally, Merlot Briccolo is a wine to bank on.
Nor did it let us down this year with its fragrances of blackberry tart, cinnamon, nutmeg and fresh cakes, backed up by full structure and attractively muscular tannins on the palate.

●	Friuli Grave Merlot Briccolo '04	🍷🍷	4
○	Friuli Grave Pinot Bianco Fornâs dai Fradis '05	🍷🍷	4
○	Friuli Grave Pinot Grigio Fornâs dai Fradis '05	🍷🍷	4
○	Friuli Grave Sauvignon '05	🍷🍷	3*
●	Friuli Grave Refosco P. R. Fornâs dai Fradis '03	🍷	4
○	Friuli Grave Chardonnay '05	🍷	2
○	Friuli Grave Tocai Friulano '05	🍷	2
○	Ramandolo '05	🍷	6
●	Friuli Grave Cabernet Franc Fornâs dai Fradis '05		3
○	Friuli Grave Traminer Aromatico Fornâs dai Fradis '05		3

RONCHI DEI LEGIONARI (GO)

Tenuta di Blasig

via Roma, 63
34077 Ronchi dei Legionari (GO)
tel. 0481475480
www.tenutadiblasig.it

Tenuta di Blasig is a woman-oriented winery. Elisabetta Bortolotto Sarcinelli is the owner and commercial manager while Erica Orlandino follows production in vineyard and cellar. The estate itself has 16 hectares under vine, which yield 60,000 bottles a year. Tenuta di Blasig has two lines, the classic range and the degli Affreschi label, which is intended for prestigious selections but which has not been bottled for a couple of years. After our tastings of the wines on the market, we can report a clear improvement in quality overall, even though there are one or two hiccups regarding individual products. The Tocai and Merlot disappointed, and failed to earn One Glass. But the Malvasia is good. Steel-fermented and aged, it has varietal honey and aniseed followed by a subtly elegant, minerally palate. Le Lule, a dried-grape verduzzo, is back on form, showing sweet but not cloying and foregrounding sensations of orange blossom, figs and hazelnuts. We stay on an excellent level with the Refosco 2004, an assertive wine with intense liqueur fruit and yeast aromas whose close-woven palate is nicely complemented by juicy varietal fruit acidity. The Chardonnay is a traditional, no-nonsense easy-drinker while the Pinot Grigio is fresh and fruity and the beefy Cabernet 2004 has balsamic notes.

○	Le Lule '03	🍷🍷	5
●	Friuli Isonzo Rive di Giare Refosco P. R. '04	🍷🍷	4*
○	Friuli Isonzo Malvasia '05	🍷🍷	4*
●	Friuli Isonzo Cabernet '04	🍷	4
○	Friuli Isonzo Chardonnay '05	🍷	4
○	Friuli Isonzo Pinot Grigio '05	🍷	4
●	Friuli Isonzo Merlot '04		4
○	Friuli Isonzo Tocai Friulano '05		4

RUDA (UD)

ALTRAN

LOC. CORTONA, 19
33050 RUDA (UD)
TEL. 0431970356

The Altran family set up this farm in 1964 and in 1998 it was purchased by Luciano Pinat and Guido Lanzellotti. Guido spends most of his time running a successful restaurant while Luciano supervises the 30 hectares under vine with the determined assistance of Marco Diamante, who is in charge of production. Much of the vine stock has been replanted in recent years to higher densities per hectare, the aim being to provide the cellar with better-quality grapes. A crucial role has been played by Igor Erzetic, the Cormons-based technician who also makes his own wines. Only part of Altran's output goes into bottle to be sold at extremely attractive prices. The most impressive wine from the last growing year comes from a variety that has established itself in the Aquileia DOC zone, traminer. An attractively elegant nose hints at wild roses and moss before the delicious, salty palate reveals fruit and plenty of personality. The Altran Tocai Friulano is good, its ripe pear nose reflected in the mouth against a very soft, tangy backdrop. Cabernet Sauvignon 2004 has concentration and breadth on the substantial nose. Entry on the palate is full and very fruity but the fresh citrus tends to bring out the tannins, which are a little over the top. The 2005 standard-label wines shows marked acidity from the growing year.

○	Friuli Aquileia Traminer Aromatico '05	🍷🍷	3*
●	Cabernet Sauvignon '04	🍷	3
●	Friuli Aquileia Merlot '05	🍷	3
○	Friuli Aquileia Pinot Bianco '05	🍷	3
○	Friuli Aquileia Tocai Friulano '05	🍷	3
○	Friuli Aquileia Chardonnay '05		3
○	Pinot Grigio '05		3
●	Cabernet Sauvignon '03	YY	3
○	Friuli Aquileia Tocai Friulano '04	YY	3

SACILE (PN)

VILLA RONCHE

LOC. VISTORTA
VIA VISTORTA, 82
33077 SACILE (PN)
TEL. 043471135
www.villaronche.it

The Villa Ronche cellar is on the eye-catching Cordignano estate, just on the far side of the Veneto-Friuli border, as are most of the vineyards, which belong to the Friuli Grave DOC. The estate sprawls over 150 hectares, with 36 under vine: Brandino Brandolini D'Adda is in charge. This explains why the administration is at Vistorta near Sacile, and also why the wines of that prestigious estate are created at this winery. The oenologist is Alec Ongaro, a technician who works in complete synergy with Brandino, and just as enthusiastically. Part of the vine stock is supervised by fruitmakers Marco Simonit and Pierpaolo Sirch, whose skilled pruning ensures that the raw material is as good as possible. Technology in the cellar leans towards the traditional, including concrete vats, as well as steel tanks. Output tops 200,000 bottles a year. The wine we liked best this year was the Sauvignon, of which 22,000 bottles were released. Minerally, with upfront elderflower and sage aromas, it adds grapefruit, citron and a trace of bell pepper on the palate. The Traminer Aromatico also stays true to type, expanding over the palate without sacrificing continuity. Evident pear characterizes the broad, fresh nose of the Tocai Friulano, adding a hint of peachskin before the palate shows an attractive savouriness with hints of almonds.

○	Friuli Grave Sauvignon '05	🍷🍷	3*
○	Friuli Grave Tocai Friulano '05	🍷🍷	3*
○	Friuli Grave Traminer Aromatico '05	🍷🍷	4
○	Friuli Grave Chardonnay '05	🍷	3
○	Friuli Grave Pinot Grigio '05	🍷	3
●	Primavigna '03		4
○	Friuli Grave Pinot Grigio '04	YY	3
○	Friuli Grave Sauvignon '04	YY	3
○	Friuli Grave Tocai Friulano '04	YY	3

SACILE (PN)

VISTORTA
VIA VISTORTA, 82
33077 SACILE (PN)
TEL. 043471135
www.vistorta.it

The Brandolini d'Adda family has owned the Vistorta estate since 1780 and in 1850, Guido Brandolini built the splendid stately home that stands in the beautiful parkland. The rose collection is fantastic and the bamboos are if anything even more stunning. Today, the estate's activities are managed by the skilled, enthusiastic Brandino Brandolini, who is happy to commute every day from Venice to supervise the vineyards and cellar. Overall, the estate has 200 hectares, of which 37 are under vine. Apart from 6 hectares planted to white grapes, the stock is almost entirely merlot. Brandino's background prompted him to choose Bordeaux's most significant variety in the knowledge that the latitude and soil type of his property are very similar to French terroirs. In the cellar, he has invaluable help from consultants George Pauli and Samuel Tinon, who have been instrumental for the professional progress of house oenologist Alec Ongaro. For a couple of years, Marco Simonit has been supervising the vineyards, which can only improve the quality of the grapes harvested. Carefully selected blending of wines from different barriques enables Brandino to release a stunning product. Elegant and intense on the nose, where smokiness mingles with currants and blackberry, cherry and blueberry preserves, it picks up all of this on a palate whose well-defined tannins underpin powerful, but restrained, with spices and coffee to lift the flavours. Some 66,000 bottles and 2,500 magnums released mean this wine is readily available to wine aficionados everywhere.

●	Friuli Grave Merlot Vistorta '04	🍷🍷🍷	5
●	Friuli Grave Merlot Vistorta '03	ΥΥΥ	5
●	Friuli Grave Merlot Vistorta '00	ΥΥ	5
●	Friuli Grave Merlot Vistorta '02	ΥΥ	5
●	Friuli Grave Merlot Vistorta '95	ΥΥ	5
●	Friuli Grave Merlot Vistorta '97	ΥΥ	5
●	Friuli Grave Merlot Vistorta '98	ΥΥ	5
●	Friuli Grave Merlot Vistorta '99	ΥΥ	5

SAGRADO (GO)

CASTELVECCHIO
VIA CASTELNUOVO, 2
34078 SAGRADO (GO)
TEL. 048199742
www.castelvecchio.com

The Castelvecchio brochure opens with a well-chosen slogan that talks about delicate roots sinking into a harsh land. It's a fair summary of the extreme viticulture practised here in an unyielding environment that demands massive structural intervention to permit competitive levels of production. Production specializes in red varieties, which this year again came up with fine performances, and is attentive to native varieties. And it was Terrano, a wine as difficult as the soil it comes from, was the bottle we liked best. Its classic style, cleanness and spicy red fruit make it the best of its type from the vintage. Also convincing, if still a little young, is the Cabernet Sauvignon 2003. A deep colour introduces a nose of mulberry, coffee and tar. Coherence and length characterize the palate, which is attractively pervaded by sweet, well-balanced tannins. From the whites, we enjoyed the Malvasia, a native variety that thrives on the hillside of the Carso DOC. Savoury minerality and a well-defined territorial personality mark out the Sauvignon. A slightly tousled balance holds back the substantial fruit of the Pinot Grigio. Sagrado Bianco 2004, a blend of malvasia, traminer and sauvignon, has attractive aromatics followed by a tangy, minerally palate. The Refosco is purplish, youthfully alcoholic and attractively rustic. Spicy fruit and gamey notes emerge from the Cabernet Franc 2003 and finally the Turmino did not quite live up to expectations, given that it is a 2003.

●	Carso Cabernet Sauvignon '03	🍷🍷	5
●	Carso Terrano '05	🍷🍷	4*
●	Carso Cabernet Franc '03	🍷	5
●	Carso Refosco P. R. '03	🍷	5
●	Carso Turmino '03	🍷	4
○	Sagrado Bianco '04	🍷	5
○	Carso Malvasia Istriana '05	🍷	4
○	Carso Pinot Grigio '05	🍷	4
○	Carso Sauvignon '05	🍷	4
○	Carso Traminer Aromatico '05	🍷	4
●	Carso Turmino '02	ΥΥ	4
●	Sagrado Rosso '02	ΥΥ	6

SAN FLORIANO DEL COLLIO (GO)

Ascevi - Luwa

Loc. Uclanzi, 24
34070 San Floriano del Collio (GO)
tel. 0481884140
www.asceviluwa.it

Ascevi - Luwa has been making fine wines in the hills at San Floriano since 1972. Ascevi comes from the name of the vineyard at Asci while Luwa, appended to the original winery name in 1990, is a conflation of Luana and Walter, Mariano and Loredana Pintar's children. The management style is traditional, involving all the family in the entire production process from vineyard to cellar to distribution. Overall, the vine stock covers 30 hectares, which yield an annual production of 150,000 bottles. Sauvignon Ronco dei Sassi is the cellar's leading wine and in 2005 it was again a notch or two better than the rest of the range. Obtained from grapes picked when slightly overripe and macerated for 24-30 hours, it is then fermented in steel and aged for two months in bottle, emerging frank and elegant. Two full Glasses went to this excellent Sauvignon with its green-flecked straw, aromas of white peach and tomato leaf lifted by intriguing aromatic nuances and a nicely acidic palate that mirrors the nose well. The standard-label Sauvignon is a shade less balanced, if comparable to its big brother, and reveals a bitterish note in the finish. Finally, the Pinot Grigio, Chardonnay and Ribolla Gialla are all well made.

○ Collio Sauvignon Ascevi '05	🍷🍷	5
○ Collio Sauvignon Ronco dei Sassi Ascevi '05	🍷🍷	5
○ Collio Chardonnay Luwa '05	🍷	4
○ Collio Pinot Grigio Ascevi '05	🍷	4
○ Ribolla Gialla Ronco de Vigna Vecia Ascevi '05	🍷	4
○ Col Martin Luwa '04	YY	6
○ Collio Pinot Grigio Ascevi '04	YY	4

SAN FLORIANO DEL COLLIO (GO)

Il Carpino

Loc. Sovenza, 14a
34070 San Floriano del Collio (GO)
tel. 0481884097
www.ilcarpino.com

Il Carpino was set up in 1987 and has about 15 hectares under vine, most in the Collio but part on the Isonzo flatlands. Owners Anna and Franco Sosol release their wines under two labels, Carpino and Vigna Runc. The Carpino wines are selections, fermented in large and small wood, which undergo complete malolactic fermentation and mature in oak for at least ten months to a year. Vigna Runc wines, in contrast, are exclusively steel-vinified, with the sole exception of the pinot grigio, chardonnay and sauvignon-based blend. That most dependable of agronomists, Marco Simonit, strives to achieve top quality in the vineyard and we were happy to find that quality back in the wines, after a few years in the doldrums. The flagship wine is Bianco Carpino 2003, an oak-matured blend of sauvignon, ribolla gialla and chardonnay. Its deep yellow colour heralds a well-structured wine whose sweet, fruit-led aromatics are veined with a milky note. Alcohol merges with remarkable elegance on the palate, which was marked down only by oak that has yet to be absorbed.
The Chardonnay is one of the best in the region and offers varietal yeasts, confectioner's cream, banana and melon. The Sauvignon Vigna Runc has varietal elderflower, nettle and citrus whereas the premium-label version discloses tertiary notes from its time in oak.

○ Bianco Carpino '03	🍷🍷	5
○ Collio Chardonnay Carpino '03	🍷🍷	5
○ Collio Ribolla Gialla Carpino '03	🍷	5
○ Collio Sauvignon Carpino '03	🍷	5
○ Bianco V. Runc '05	🍷	4
○ Collio Chardonnay V. Runc '05	🍷	4
○ Collio Pinot Grigio V. Runc '05	🍷	4
○ Collio Ribolla Gialla V. Runc '05	🍷	4
○ Collio Sauvignon V. Runc '05	🍷	4
○ Collio Chardonnay '02	YY	5
○ Collio Sauvignon V. Runc '03	YY	4
○ Collio Pinot Grigio V. Runc '02	YY	4

SAN FLORIANO DEL COLLIO (GO)

Conti Formentini

via Oslavia, 5
34070 San Floriano del Collio (GO)
tel. 0481884131
www.giv.it

Officially, the Conti Formentini estate dates from 1520. A few years ago, it was acquired by the Gruppo Italiano Vini and the technical side of things is in the hands of Marco Del Piccolo. The winemaking consultant is Marco Monchiero, the well-known Piedmontese oenologist. Some scholars maintain that it was the Formentini family that gave its name to the Hungarian furmint grape. Others note that in 1632, Contessa Aurora Formentini took to Hungary as part of her dowry 200 vines of "toccai" grapes. This is the basis for the defence of the name Tocai Friulano, which following a European Union agreement, can no longer use the name after 1 April 2007. History and modernity fuse at the Conti Formentini winery, at whose entrance you will find a small but intriguing museum of winemaking in Friuli. And history comes back in the cellar's flagship white, Rylint, named after an abbess from the family who devoted much attention to promoting local viticulture in the 16th century. Each year, at least 10,000 bottles of this wine are produced from chardonnay, pinot grigio and sauvignon grapes. The nose opens on elegant florality, immediately followed by fresh fruit, all of which is picked up in the very elegant mouth with its perceptions of fresh-picked fruit salad. We preferred the standard-label Chardonnay to the Torre di Tramontana 2004, mainly for its superior complexity of flavour. The Sauvignon gives elegant green tea and the Pinot Grigio has marked acidity, thanks to the growing year.

○	Collio Bianco Rylint '05	🍷🍷	4
○	Collio Chardonnay Torre di Tramontana '04	🍷	5
○	Collio Chardonnay '05	🍷	4
○	Collio Pinot Grigio '05	🍷	4
○	Collio Sauvignon '05	🍷	4
●	Collio Merlot Tajut '01	YY	6
○	Collio Bianco Rylint '03	YY	4
○	Collio Chardonnay Torre di Tramontana '03	YY	5

SAN FLORIANO DEL COLLIO (GO)

Gradis'ciutta

loc. Giasbana, 10
34070 San Floriano del Collio (GO)
tel. 0481390237

Robert Princic is maturing fast. Despite his lack of years, he takes care of all aspects of the business, with effective back-up from his father Doro. During the last growing year, it has to be said, Robert was busy building a new, up-to-date cellar with plenty of space. It was probably that major effort, which is sure to bear fruit in the shape of enhanced quality in the near future, that may have taken his eye off the ball in the vineyard and cellar. Poor weather will also have hindered Robert from giving us the usual starry wines. That said, this is still a very fine range. Apart from the Sauvignon, which nearly went through to the finals, we enjoyed a solid range of Two Glass wines that speak volumes for Robert's skills and the potential of the soil. They included a fresh-tasting Ribolla Gialla and a fragrant, fruit-forward Tocai, as well as a subtle Pinot Grigio with a very long, citrus finish. The Chardonnay successfully combines a soft texture and freshness while the Bianco Tùzz, from chardonnay, tocai and malvasia, offers a wealth of citrus, yellow peach and white chocolate. The only concession to reds this year was the Bordeaux blend Rosso dei Princic 2003, which gives elegant, well-defined hay and blueberry tart. Like all young growers, Robert is always looking for a challenge. He found one in a dried-grape passito, which he has called Rebus (puzzle). The result is a wine with candied peel aromas, nicely gauged sweetness and a clean, elegant back palate. Not bad for a first try.

●	Collio Rosso dei Princic '03	🍷🍷	5
○	Collio Bianco Tùzz Ris. '04	🍷🍷	4
○	Rebus '04	🍷🍷	4
○	Collio Chardonnay '05	🍷🍷	4
○	Collio Pinot Grigio '05	🍷🍷	4
○	Collio Ribolla Gialla '05	🍷🍷	4
○	Collio Tocai Friulano '05	🍷🍷	4
○	Collio Sauvignon '05	🍷🍷	4
○	Collio Ribolla Gialla '03	YY	4
○	Collio Sauvignon '03	YY	4
○	Collio Pinot Grigio '04	YY	4
○	Collio Ribolla Gialla '04	YY	4

 SAN FLORIANO DEL COLLIO (GO)

Marcello e Marino Humar

Loc. Valerisce, 2
34070 San Floriano del Collio (GO)
tel. 0481884094
www.humar.it

The Humar winery is redolent of tradition as the family of the late Marcello and his brother Marino continue to work with the one aim of quality. Underlying the family's strong bond was Loretta Humar's decision ten years ago to give up her previous job and devote herself entirely to the world of wine. It was certainly Loretta who decided, as announced last year, to cut down the number of wines produced to rationalize and focus work in the vineyards and cellar. Loretta's determination and singlemindedness are well known so already this year we are looking at a reduced range. Many other Friulian wineries would do well to copy this courageous, and very shrewd, move. As we were saying, the range of wines is small but good, only the disappointing growing year preventing it from bringing out the estate's full potential. Particularly good are the Pinot Grigio 2005 and the Cabernet Franc Rogoves 2002. The Pinot Grigio has well-defined dried flowers, apple and gunflint but performs best on the palate, which reveals thrust, elegance and plenty of savour. Rogoves' appealing spectrum of intense, complex aromatics is reminiscent of blackberry tart and coffee before it signs off with nice balsam. In the mouth, there is lovely balance of fruit sensations and toasty oak. Perceptible minerality and almonds are the keynotes of the Ribolla Gialla 2005 while the Tocai from the same vintage is uncomplicated and flower-themed.

●	Collio Cabernet Franc Rogoves '02	▼▼	6
○	Collio Pinot Grigio '05	▼▼	4
●	Collio Cabernet Franc '05	▼	4
○	Collio Ribolla Gialla '05	▼	4
○	Collio Tocai Friulano '05	▼	4
○	Collio Chardonnay '05		4
●	Friuli Grave Refosco P. R. '05		4
○	Collio Tocai Friulano '03	▽▽	4
○	Collio Ribolla Gialla '04	▽▽	4

Muzic

Loc. Bivio, 4
34070 San Floriano del Collio (GO)
tel. 0481884201
www.cantinamuzic.it

Here on the gentle hills of San Floriano del Collio is superb country for growing grapes and making wine, as is testified by documents and historical events that stretch back into the mists of time. For example, in 1616 the armies of Venice overran the area and carried off 300 cartloads of "very exquisite wine". Four hundred years have passed, and today life partners and work associates Ivan and Orietta tenaciously, ambitiously, continue to produce that "very exquisite wine" with their own very personal approach, which informs every stage of production. In Friuli, 2005 was an outstanding growing year for pinot grigio and tocai, an opportunity that Ivan Muzic was not slow to seize. His Pinot Grigio opens on bitter almonds that make way for more subtle dried flower and orange peel aromas. The palate finds a successful balance of acidity and fruity softness before the finish unleashes lingering citrus. The tocai may not be complex but it is invitingly fresh-tasting, persistent bitter almonds pervading the back palate. Lining up with these two whites is a Merlot whose attractive balsam melds into hay and cinchona. Bianco Bric, from tocai, malvasia and ribolla gialla, is very fruity and the Sauvignon Vigna Pàjze is more convincing on the fresh, smooth-flowing palate mouth than it is on the nose. Finally, the Ribolla Gialla arranges a beautiful marriage of minerality and richer fruit sensations, although it lacks the complexity of flavour that would have enhanced its score.

●	Friuli Isonzo Merlot '04	▼▼	4*
○	Collio Pinot Grigio '05	▼▼	4*
○	Collio Tocai Friulano '05	▼▼	4*
○	Collio Bianco Bric '05	▼	4
○	Collio Chardonnay '05	▼	4
○	Collio Ribolla Gialla '05	▼	4
○	Collio Sauvignon V. Pàjze '05	▼	4
●	Collio Cabernet Sauvignon '04		4
●	Friuli Isonzo Merlot '03	▽▽	4
○	Collio Chardonnay '04	▽▽	4

SAN FLORIANO DEL COLLIO (GO)

Evangelos Paraschos

Loc. Bucuje, 13a
34070 San Floriano del Collio (GO)
tel. 0481884154
www.paraschos.it

Evangelos Paraschos continues to experiment with mixed results. Sometimes the wines are fabulous and on other occasions they disappoint. El Grego, as they call him at San Floriano, has had a large cellar at his disposal for a couple of years, which means he can mature his wines at leisure and release them to market when the time is right. The estate has just over five hectares under vine and low yields gave Evangelos a production of 120 hectolitres of wine in 2004. Both white and red fruit from the 2004 harvest were left to ferment on the skins for more than two weeks in open wood vats, with no cultured yeasts or temperature control. Later, the wine was racked into barrels with capacities ranging from five to 25 hectolitres, where it stayed on the lees for 22 months. Evangelos risks not adding sulphur dioxide before bottling, which according to the experts will jeopardize its longevity. Only time will tell. The Bianco Riserva 2004 is a chardonnay and sauvignon-heavy blend with dashes of pinot bianco, malvasia, ribolla, picolit and verduzzo. Amber in the glass, it gives citrus and gooseberry echoed on the broad palate, a hint of bitterness rounding things off. Some 4,000 units went into bottle. Kaj, a single-variety Tocai, is veiled in the glass with serious citrus-like aromas. There are plum and carob aromas on the nose of the Merlot and then the well-defined palate has concentration and only slightly mouth-puckering tannins. The Sauvignon earned no more than a mention.

○	Bianco Ris. '04	▼▼	6
○	Kaj '04	▼▼	6
●	Merlot '04	▼▼	5
○	Sauvignon '04		6
○	Collio Bianco Ris. '03	▽▽	6
○	Collio Bianco Kaj '03	▽▽	6

SAN FLORIANO DEL COLLIO (GO)

Edi Skok

Loc. Giasbana, 15
34070 San Floriano del Collio (GO)
tel. 0481390280
www.skok.it

After years in the Other Wineries section, the Skok winery has made the big leap. Named after the family that owns it, the estate features a beautiful 16th-century stately home set amid the vines. Built by aristocrats from Salzburg, it was extended and restored in 1757 by Sigismund Attems, ancestor of the man who founded the Consorzio Collio. Sigismund sold the property to the Teuffenbach family, from whom the Skoks, a local family of farmers, finally purchased it. Today, there are 12 hectares under vine, out of a total of 18, managed by Edi Skok and his sister Orietta. While Edi looks after the vineyard and cellar, Orietta supervises sales and takes part in the tastings that enable Edi to decide on winemaking strategies. Only some of the production, amounting to 35,000 units a year, goes into bottle. Pinot Grigio has always been a standard-bearer at the Skok winery. The intriguing nose has complex fruit and the palate is well-defined. It may not have particular depth but it holds up well in the mouth and is very tempting. The Sauvignon has varietal elderflower sensations that mingle with nice fresh golden delicious apples. Pe Ar, dedicated to the Skoks' father Pepi and Uncle Armando, is a blend of 60 per cent chardonnay, almost half fermented overripe and matured in oak, with 30 per cent pinot grigio and the remainder sauvignon. The oak is still very prominent but there is temptingly refreshing acidity on the finish.

○	Collio Pinot Grigio '05	▼▼	4*
○	Collio Sauvignon '05	▼▼	4*
○	Collio Bianco Pe Ar '04	▼	4
○	Collio Chardonnay '05	▼	4
○	Collio Bianco Pe Ar '02	▽▽	4
○	Collio Pinot Grigio '04	▽▽	4

Matijaz Tercic

Loc. Bukuje, 9
34070 San Floriano del Collio (GO)
tel. 0481884193

Tercic is one of those family-run wineries where the rhythms of farming still dictate the pace of life. There are no sudden changes, just constant, unflagging effort to improve by renewing the vineyards, a job that should be completed soon, and by modernizing the cellar. The rest is up to the location, in the heart of the Collio, and to the skills of Matijaz. The Pinot Bianco is very good. The Tercic version of this unjustly neglected wine has apple, confectioner's cream and fresh bread on a nose that introduces a rich, ripe and very long palate. The Sauvignon is equally good. Elegantly understated on the nose, it has nice weight on the front palate where peaches, apricots and macaroons set the pace. Vino degli Orti, a 50-50 blend of malvasia and tocai, is improving all the time. Concentrated, lingering sensations of liquorice mingle with wild flowers as the palate progresses seamlessly. The 2003 vintage produced one of the best versions of Merlot Seme. Its smooth-flowing palate, sweet tannins and ripe red fruits make it a particularly appealing red. Planta 2004 is from chardonnay with ten per cent pinot bianco, fermented and matured in barrique. Its yellow-fleshed fruit, tobacco and honey are persuasive but milky and oak-derived aromas detract from its performance. The Ribolla is concentrated and never misses a beat, although there is a faint hint of bitterness. Finally, the Pinot Grigio deserves more complexity of structure but offers good fruit, flowers and minerally freshness.

● Collio Merlot Seme '03	🍷🍷	5
○ Collio Pinot Bianco '05	🍷🍷	4*
○ Collio Sauvignon '05	🍷🍷	4*
○ Vino degli Orti '05	🍷🍷	4
○ Collio Bianco Planta '04	🍷	5
○ Collio Pinot Grigio '05	🍷	4
○ Collio Ribolla Gialla '05	🍷	5
● Collio Merlot '01	🍸🍸	5

Franco Terpin

Loc. Valerisce, 6a
34070 San Floriano del Collio (GO)
tel. 0481884215

The absence of the Terpin winery from the last edition of the guide was due to Franco's financially onerous decision to delay release of his wines for a year to allow them to age. All of Franco's choices aim to promote a viticulture that respects the environment, free of chemical fertilizers, pesticides and insecticides. Only wild local yeasts are used in the cellar and fermentation is exclusively in wood, sometime large and sometimes small. In compliance with this rigorous approach, the wines go into bottle unfiltered. We are well aware that this style of winemaking creates products with loads of character but they may occasionally present one or two imperfections. This is the case with the two single-variety wines, Pinot Grigio Sialis 2005 and Ribolla Gialla 2003, which we thought were a tad below par. But it is a different story with the two blends. Rosso Stamas 2003, a merlot-heavy Bordeaux blend, has lovely aromas of ripe mulberries, blackcurrants and hay. Juicy in the mouth, it has great softness and a long dark chocolate and briary fruit finish. Stamas Bianco 2003 is a blend of sauvignon, tocai, pinot grigio and chardonnay that shows complex with peach, confectioner's cream, banana and tropical fruit sensations that are reprised harmoniously on the palate.

○ Collio Bianco Stamas '03	🍷🍷	5
● Collio Rosso Stamas '03	🍷🍷	5
○ Pinot Grigio Sialis '05	🍷	6
○ Ribolla Gialla '03		5
○ Collio Bianco '01	🍸🍸	5
○ Collio Bianco '02	🍸🍸	5
○ Pinot Grigio Sialis '02	🍸🍸	4

SAN FLORIANO DEL COLLIO (GO)

ZUANI

LOC. GIASBANA, 12
34070 SAN FLORIANO DEL COLLIO (GO)
TEL. 0481391432
www.zuanivini.it

Patrizia Felluga stays true to her brave production policy of releasing only two labels. Today, the estate has ten hectares but only distributes 50,000 bottles, one third under the black label of Zuani and the rest with the orange-leather livery of Zuani Vigne. Patrizia's original plan was to create a Zuani vineyard selection but that would have meant cutting down the size of the vine stock. Plots purchased in recent years have been renewed cautiously, with changes to planting densities and training systems. The estate's facilities have also been restored, significantly enhancing the functionality of the vinification areas. Patrizia's son Antonio, who has a degree in oenology, has been assisting his mother in the cellar for some time and daughter Caterina also helps with promotional events when her university studies permit. Grapes for the two Zuani wines contain the same varieties: tocai friulano, chardonnay, sauvignon and pinot grigio. What is different is the harvest period – grapes for Zuani are picked later – and the winemaking technique employed. Vigne 2005 is aged exclusively in stainless steel and offers lemony and citrus sensations. In the Zuani 2004, aged in barrique and matured in glass, the breadth of the palate is set off by rich peach and apricot fruit tinged with candied orange peel, signing off with excellent minerality.

○	Collio Bianco Zuani '04	🍷🍷	5
○	Collio Bianco Zuani Vigne '05	🍷	4
○	Collio Bianco Zuani '02	YY	5
○	Collio Bianco Zuani '03	YY	5
○	Collio Bianco Zuani Vigne '03	YY	4
○	Collio Bianco Zuani Vigne '04	YY	4

SAN GIORGIO DELLA RICHINVELDA (PN)

FORCHIR

FRAZ. PROVESANO
VIA CIASUTIS, 1B
33095 SAN GIORGIO DELLA RICHINVELDA (PN)
TEL. 042796037
www.forchir.it

The Forchir estate owned by Gianfranco Bianchini and Enzo Deana has 220 hectares under vine on either side of the river Tagliamento, right in the middle of the Friuli Grave DOC. Three vineyards in different locations – at Felettis, near Bicinicco, Camino al Tagliamento and Barbeano – enable the cellar to exploit the full potential of a DOC zone that can produce excellent wines, despite being generally considered inferior to wine country in the hills. That excellence is evident from the table below, which demonstrates the high quality of many of the wines we sampled. The two labels under which Forchir wines are released comprise one for selections and the other for traditional bottles. It is among the selections that we find the estate's most interesting wine, Pinot Bianco dei Gelsi, which was so good that it came very close to a place in the national finals. A white from ancient vines planted in the late 19th century, it is subtle on the nose of spring flowers, apples and aromatic herbs and in the mouth, where there is attractively fresh acidity in the finish. Traminer Aromatico has striking candied citrus peel sensations and the Pinot Grigio impresses with the minerality of the fruit. The varietal, juicy Sauvignon is very good and the Refoscone, obtained from a local variety of refosco, is intriguing.

○	Friuli Grave Pinot Bianco Campo dei Gelsi '05	🍷🍷	4
○	Friuli Grave Pinot Grigio '05	🍷🍷	3*
○	Friuli Grave Sauvignon '05	🍷🍷	3*
○	Friuli Grave Traminer Aromatico '05	🍷🍷	3*
●	Friuli Grave Refoscone '04	🍷	5
○	Bianco Un Blanc '05	🍷	4
○	Friuli Grave Friulano '05	🍷	3
●	Friuli Grave Refosco P. R. '05	🍷	4
○	Friuli Grave Sauvignon L'Altro '05	🍷	4
●	Rosso Un Neri '05		4
●	Friuli Grave Refoscone '03	YY	5

SAN GIOVANNI AL NATISONE (UD)

ALFIERI CANTARUTTI

VIA RONCHI, 9
33048 SAN GIOVANNI AL NATISONE (UD)
TEL. 0432756317
www.cantaruttialfieri.it

After returning to the Guide last year, the Alfieri Cantarutti winery consolidated its position with a range of organoleptically interesting wines. Antonella Cantarutti and her husband Fabrizio have 54 hectares planted to vine. Meanwhile in the cellar, they are experimenting with innovative vinification techniques with results that will become apparent in the wines to be released next year. This time, we were amazed at the edgy Tocai The Spirit of Ghost 2003, almost a tribute to the great Friulian native vine which in a year's time will no longer be able to use its present name. This is a label that will excite controversy. Available only in magnums, it is golden yellow proffering honey, candied orange peel, lime blossom and vanilla. Its full-bodied palate flaunts a wealth of soft apricot jam and citrus sensations. We also liked the classic Bianco Canto 2005, from tocai, pinot bianco and sauvignon, with its appealing contrast of fatty fruit and fresh-tasting finish on the palate. Equally good is the Tocai Friulano 2005, its Mediterranean ripeness lush with tropical fruit and subtle hints of lavender. And to round off the range, there are two fine reds. One is the very spicy, discreetly soft Schioppettino 2001 and the other is the Rosso Carato 1999, a single-variety Cabernet Sauvignon, with lots of personality, upfront herbaceousness and hints of black pepper. Finally, there is a very nice spumante metodo classico from pinot nero, Epilogo di Cantalfieri 1996.

●	COF Schioppettino '01	▼▼	6
○	COF Tocai Friulano The Spirit of Ghost '03	▼▼	6
○	COF Bianco Canto '05	▼▼	4*
○	COF Tocai Friulano '05	▼▼	4*
●	COF Rosso Carato '99	▼▼	6
●	COF Merlot '03	▼	4
●	COF Cabernet Sauvignon '04	▼	4
○	COF Ribolla Gialla '05	▼	4
○	COF Sauvignon '05	▼	4
○	Friuli Grave Chardonnay '05	▼	3
○	Epilogo di Cantalfieri Brut Blanc de Noir M. Cl. '96	▼	6
○	COF Bianco Canto '04	▽▽	4

SAN GIOVANNI AL NATISONE (UD)

LIVON

FRAZ. DOLEGNANO
VIA MONTAREZZA, 33
33048 SAN GIOVANNI AL NATISONE (UD)
TEL. 0432757173
www.livon.it

Brothers Valneo and Tonino Livon manage a series of wine estates scattered up and down Italy yet still manage to maintain a "family-run" style. Apart from the properties purchased by their father, Dorino, the two also have in Friuli Tenuta Roncalto, acquired in 1997 and located in the heart of the Collio, and Villa Chiopris, discussed in a separate profile. For several years, the Livons have also owned Borgo Salcetino at Radda in Chianti and Fattoria Colsanto at Bevagna in Umbria. Winemaking in all the cellars is in the hands of Rinaldo Stocco, the Livons' long-standing oenologist. At the Dolegnano winery, about 600,000 units go into bottle under the Livon label while Tenuta Roncalto turns out about 30,000 more. The Livon range distinguishes standard wines from selections by giving the latter names in Friulian. Despite the excellence of BraideAlte and TiareBlù, we have to say that the overall performance was not outstanding by Livon standards. BraideAlte is a blend of chardonnay, sauvignon, picolit and moscato giallo. Complex, balanced and fresh, it mingles pears with tropical fruits revealing a palate that is drinking now but deserves another couple of years in bottle. TiareBlù, from 80 per cent merlot with cabernet sauvignon, is intense, concentrated and attractively complex, with assertive tannins.

●	TiareBlù '03	▼▼	6
○	BraideAlte '04	▼▼	6
○	COF Verduzzo Friulano Casali Godia '04	▼	5
○	Collio Chardonnay BraideMate '04	▼	6
○	Collio Picolit Cumins '04	▼	7
○	Collio Bianco Vign. di Ruttars '05	▼	5
○	Collio Pinot Grigio Braide Grande '05	▼	5
○	Collio Ribolla Gialla Roncalto '05	▼	5
○	Collio Sauvignon Valbuins '05	▼	5
○	Collio Tocai Friulano Ronc di Zorz '05	▼	5
○	BraideAlte '00	▽▽▽	6
●	TiareBlù '00	▽▽▽	6

SAN GIOVANNI AL NATISONE (UD)

VIGNAI DA DULINE
LOC. VILLANOVA
VIA IV NOVEMBRE, 136
33048 SAN GIOVANNI AL NATISONE (UD)
TEL. 0432758115

Lorenzo Mocchiutti and Federica Magrini share their working and their private lives, and will look back happily on the 2005 vintage for many years to come. Federica told us, "Sofia was born on 1 October with the vintage in full swing. She waited patiently until we had picked the whites and some of the reds, and was born in our house, where the windows look onto the Duline". The new arrival inspired a special selection of refosco that will probably be released in three years' time. Yet the happy event does not seem to have distracted our heroes, for yet again their wines are good and the range has two peaks of excellence in the Chardonnay 2004 and the Refosco Morus Nigra from the same vintage. The Chardonnay fermented in barrique and its deep colour tells you it has serious structure. A complex nose of vanilla, tobacco, yeasts and ripe banana heralds a palate that opens out into a perfect fusion of toastiness and fruit sensations. Refosco Morus Nigra 2004 is named after the scientific name for the black mulberry. It's a complete wine offering a broad swath of fresh mulberry and currant sensations veined with complex nuances of leather, tobacco, hay and dark chocolate. The fruit sensations are echoed on the front palate before the progression discloses the tannic weave and a warm finish of chocolate and mulberries. The subtle standard-label Pinot Grigio is distinctly good, showing varietal sensations with a long, savoury finish. Finally, we liked the concentrated ripe fruit of the Bordeaux blend Viburnum 2004.

○ COF Chardonnay '04	TT	5
● Morus Nigra Refosco P. R. '04	TT	6
● COF Rosso Viburnum '04	TT	5
○ COF Pinot Grigio '05	TT	4*
○ COF Bianco Morus Alba '04	T	5
● Viburnum '01	YY	5
● COF Rosso Viburnum '02	YY	5
○ COF Chardonnay '03	YY	5
○ COF Bianco Morus Alba '02	YY	5

SAN LORENZO ISONTINO (GO)

LIS NERIS
VIA GAVINANA, 5
34070 SAN LORENZO ISONTINO (GO)
TEL. 048180105
www.lisneris.it

Once, we heard Alvaro Pecorari say, "When I was at high school, I often thought I would like sit down at table one day with my family in the sure knowledge that, at that precise moment, other families were sitting down to dinner with a bottle of my wine on the table. The thought gave me enormous motivation". We do not know if that was the only thought that motivated Alvaro, but his dream came true quite a few years ago. Yet again, we can look back on our tasting and report that Alvaro's wines are excellent. His Pinot Grigio earned Three Glasses and nor were the other wines far off the mark: none scored fewer that 80 points out of 100. Some of the wine for Gris 2004 was fermented in barrique and the lovely resulting vanilla and white chocolate fuse perfectly with the yellow peach and apricot fruit. We could say exactly the same thing about the palate, so faithfully does it reflect the nose before signing off with a lingering finish. Outstanding complexity is the keynote of the Chardonnay Jurosa 2004, which we reviewed by error last year. It's not an immediately approachable wine but it does have depth. We might even call it a meditation wine. The Bordeaux blend Lis Neris 2003 is stunningly elegant. Subtly appealing and admirably elegant, it proffers tannins of rounded silkiness. Finally, the verduzzo and riesling Tal Lùc 2004 is fatty and sweet yet never cloys, thanks to well-gauged freshness in a finish that echoes the nose's attractively long notes of candied citrus peel, caramel-covered figs and petits fours.

○ Pinot Grigio Gris '04	TTT	5
● Lis Neris '03	TT	7
○ Chardonnay Jurosa '04	TT	5
○ Tal Lùc '04	TT	8
○ Confini '04	TT	6
○ Sauvignon Picòl '04	TT	4
○ Lis '04	TT	6
○ Chardonnay '05	TT	4
○ Pinot Grigio '05	TT	4
○ Sauvignon '05	TT	4
○ Tal Lùc '02	YYY	7
○ Lis '03	YYY	6

SAN LORENZO ISONTINO (GO)

Pierpaolo Pecorari

via Tommaseo, 36c
34070 San Lorenzo Isontino (GO)
tel. 0481808775
www.pierpaolopecorari.it

The estate run by Pierpaolo Pecorari and his son Alessandro extends over 30 hectares and produces 130,000 bottles a year. The range of wines is excellent – some are Three Glass finalists - and they are split across three not always easy to distinguish lines. We'll try to clear things up so here are the criteria for the selections. The standard wines, with no particular reference to type, are generally obtained from younger vineyards and are fresh-tasting easy drinkers. Altis selections are more mature and may have undergone maceration; they are bottled later after a period of maturation. Finally, the vineyard selections stand out for complexity; they will have seen oak and are never dull. Two wines rise above the rest, the Pinot Bianco Altis 2004 and the Merlot Baolar 2003. The Pinot Bianco hints at medlar, rennet apple and yeast before the tidy, assertive palate offers mouthfilling sensations. The Merlot Baolar is a Pecorari classic that opens on cherry, currants and cocoa powder that are nicely reflected on the elegant, full-bodied palate. Another classic is Tao, a well-managed Refosco with attractive jamminess and good texture. Confident tannins dry the lingering finish. We thought the best of the Pinot Grigio selections was the Altis, even if the Olivers has structure that nicely contrasts the sweet, oak-derived sensations. Finally, it was the standard-label Sauvignon that scored higher of the two versions. Its green note is appealing and combines well with the variety's classic acidity.

●	Merlot Baolar '03	YY	7
○	Pinot Bianco Altis '04	YY	5
○	Pinot Grigio Altis '04	YY	5
○	Pinot Grigio Olivers '04	YY	6
●	Refosco P. R. Tao '02	YY	8
○	Sauvignon Altis '04	Y	5
○	Pinot Grigio '05	Y	4
○	Sauvignon '05	Y	4
○	Sauvignon Kolaus '04	Y	6
●	Merlot '04		6
●	Refosco P. R. Tao '01	YY (white)	8
○	Friuli Isonzo Tocai Friulano Vign'Alba '04	YY (white)	4

SAN MARTINO AL TAGLIAMENTO (PN)

Tenuta Pinni

via Sant'Osvaldo, 3
33096 San Martino al Tagliamento (PN)
tel. 0434899464
www.tenutapinni.com

Last year's Other Wineries appearance for Tenuta Pinni, a recently founded (1997) winery run by the young duo of Francesco and Roberto Pinni, was dictated only by the short list of wines presented. Intelligently, the Pinnis held back their reds and their Ucelut. But this time they are back with a fine, and very well-balanced, range of products. Rosso della Tenuta 2003, from cabernet sauvignon and refosco, is complex. Balsamic notes, dried roses, blackcurrant jam and mulberries tempt the nose and the full, broad palate flaunts silky tannins in an elegant whole. And we should bear in mind that it comes from the stony, unfertile plains around Pordenone. Another great wine is the Sauvignon della Tenuta 2004. Released two years after the harvest, it is an explosion of yellow peach, melon and apricot fruit, beautifully integrated into the vanilla that tells you it was oak-matured. Nicely balanced progression on the palate alternates softness with toasty notes. Ucelut 2001, from the variety of the same name, is sourced from the hills at Spilimbergo. Intense amber introduces varietal sensation of caramel-covered figs, confectioner's cream, camphor and mint that meld attractively to linger long on the back palate. From the rest of the range, we liked the smokiness of the Sauvignon, the varietal typicity of the Refosco and the complex gaminess of the Cabernet Franc. But elegance and finesse characterize the whole line-up.

○	Ucelut '01	YY	5
●	Friuli Grave Rosso della Tenuta '03	YY	4*
○	Sauvignon della Tenuta '04	YY	4*
●	Friuli Grave Cabernet Franc '04	Y	3
●	Friuli Grave Refosco P. R. '04	Y	3
○	Chardonnay '05	Y	3
○	Pinot Grigio '05	Y	3
○	Sauvignon '05	Y	3

SAN QUIRINO (PN)

RUSSOLO

VIA SAN ROCCO, 58A
33080 SAN QUIRINO (PN)
TEL. 0434919577
www.russolo.it

We are always impressed when we look over the table of wines and scores for Russolo after our tastings. We know the cellar has been active for more than three decades and that it is run by the skilled Iginio Russolo. We also know that he was one of the first in Friuli to age his wines in barrique, and that his son Rino has brought new energy to the winery. But maintaining such high quality over such a wide range of wines is no easy matter, especially in growing years as difficult as 2005. We are confident that the future, when the cellar will be focusing on native varieties, will bring new developments and reassuring confirmation. How could we not be favourably impressed by the consistency of the Müller Thurgau Mussignaz and the white Doi Raps? The Müller Thurgau's nose has wild roses, ginger and peach that are mirrored on the full, fragrant and well-balanced palate. From overripe sauvignon, pinot grigio and moscato, Doi Raps is fresh and flowery, disclosing citrus and rennet apple. The whistle-clean Chardonnay has distinct pear, banana, apple and in the fresh citrus-like finish. But the whites weren't the only wines to impress. The classic Grifo Nero, a very varietal Pinot Nero with hints of berries lifted by confectioner's cream and dried roses, is excellent. The Cabernet 2001's aromas are very ripe and the balsam, hay and plum jam of the Refosco 2003 are intriguing before the palate opens assertively and progresses with confidence.

●	Cabernet '01	🍷🍷	4
●	Pinot Nero Grifo Nero '03	🍷🍷	5
●	Refosco P. R. I Legni '03	🍷🍷	4
○	Doi Raps '04	🍷🍷	4
○	Chardonnay Ronco Calaj '05	🍷🍷	4
○	Müller Thurgau Mussignaz '05	🍷🍷	4
●	Borgo di Peuma '02	🍷	5
○	Bianco Jacot Ronco Calaj '05	🍷	3
○	Malvasia Istriana '05	🍷	4
●	Moscato Rosa Prato delle Rose '05	🍷	4
○	Pinot Grigio Ronco Calaj '05	🍷	4
●	Merlot Massarac '04		3
○	Doi Raps '03	🍸🍸	4
○	Müller Thurgau Mussignaz '04	🍸🍸	4

SPILIMBERGO (PN)

FANTINEL

FRAZ. TAURIANO
VIA TESIS, 8
33097 SPILIMBERGO (PN)
TEL. 0427591520
www.fantinel.com

Fantinel is a long-established presence on the Friulian winemaking scene, having been founded in 1969 by Mario Fantinel, a well-known restaurateur and hotelier with a passion for oenology. Currently, the estate extends over 250 hectares in the Collio, Colli Orientali and Friuli Grave DOC zones and produces some three and a half million bottles a year. Borgo Tesis is the label for wines from the Grave, la Santa Caterina identifies Collio bottles and Sant'Helena is a medley of three Collio whites and two from the Grave. About 30 years ago, the cellar introduced the signature bottle with the twisted neck, an imaginative move that left its mark on the winery and is still used for the Paron Mario wines. Three Fantinel wines picked up Two Glasses this year. Rosso Platinum 2002, from merlot, refosco, cabernet franc and cabernet sauvignon grapes, has a ripe, elegant nose that gives chocolate, red fruits and raspberries. All these sensations come back on the nicely rounded and very long palate. We also liked the Merlot Borgo Tesis 2004. It, too, has distinct raspberry, mulberry and ripe red fruits mingling with attractive spice and a grace note of herbaceousness on the finish. In the mouth, it is full and pervasive. Finally, the Pinot Grigio Sant'Helena 2005 is attractive and intriguing, revealing williams pears and quince that take you through to a long, easy-drinking finish.

●	Friuli Grave Merlot Borgo Tesis '04	🍷🍷	4
●	Barone Rosso Platinum '02	🍷🍷	5
○	Collio Pinot Grigio Sant'Helena '05	🍷🍷	5
●	Friuli Grave Cabernet Sauvignon Borgo Tesis '04	🍷	4
○	Collio Bianco Santa Caterina '05	🍷	4
○	Friuli Grave Pinot Grigio Borgo Tesis '05	🍷	4
○	Collio Sauvignon Sant'Helena '05		5
○	Collio Tocai Friulano Santa Caterina '05		4

SPILIMBERGO (PN)

Plozner

via delle Prese, 19
33097 Spilimbergo (PN)
tel. 04272902
www.plozner.it

We knew that there were major changes under way at the Plozner winery, and that both vine stock and cellar were involved. What surprised us was the latest line with its unusual name – Piedi per terra testa per aria (Feet on the Ground Head in the Air) – for selected recently planted varieties vinified using innovative techniques. The new range comes with a new-look bottle, sealed with a glass stopper and resplendent in an artistic label. The Sauvignon Quattroperuno Uno, in particular, is graced by different labels for each vintage from the well-known British artist Jonathan Monk. New ventures can often be tentative at first but this move has started on the right foot, with a line-up of excellent wines. Sauvignon Quattroperuno Uno even went through to the final taste-offs. From three different sauvignon clones and a splash of viognier, it stands out for its sincerity, elegance and the perfect balance of green notes and fruit. Pinot Grigio Malpelo is vinified on the skins, which explains the lustrous colour of a wine that reveals subtlety and a lovely alternation of minerality and understated sensations of apples and williams pears. Moscabianca, from an old estate clone of tocai, tempts the nose with wisteria, orange and delicious apples. The cellar vinified Refosco Bastiano in such a way as to bring out its varietal acidity. Finally, the rest of the range is good, especially the classic bell pepper and tomato Sauvignon.

○	Sauvignon Quattroperuno Uno '05	🍷🍷	4
○	Bianco Moscabianca '05	🍷🍷	4
○	Friuli Grave Sauvignon '05	🍷🍷	3*
○	Pinot Grigio Malpelo '05	🍷🍷	4
●	Friuli Grave Merlot '04	🍷	3
○	Friuli Grave Chardonnay '05	🍷	3
○	Friuli Grave Pinot Grigio '05	🍷	4
●	Refosco P. R. Bastiano '05	🍷	3
○	Friuli Grave Tocai Friulano '05		3
○	Friuli Grave Traminer Aromatico '05		3
○	Friuli Grave Pinot Grigio '04	YY	3
○	Friuli Grave Sauvignon '04	YY	3

TORREANO (UD)

Jacùss

fraz. Montina
v.le Kennedy, 35a
33040 Torreano (UD)
tel. 0432715147
www.jacuss.com

In an interview, Andrea Iacuzzi said, "The biggest wager that Sandro and I have won was not making the best wine in Friuli or becoming major producers. It was managing to build up a winery when the task looked impossible". His words convey the difficulties that the Iacuzzi brothers had to face when, at the start of their adventure, running ten hectares scattered over the hills at Montina was no joke. But passion counts, especially when it is combined with skill and careful stewardship of the assets available. Which is why we are here to comment on yet another brilliant performance from this ambitious duo. By now, Pinot Bianco is a Jacùss banker. This year's version is subtle, with pear, dried flowers and delicious apples on the nose followed by a bright, fresh-tasting palate and a long finish that reprises the fruit. Another traditionally fine wine is the Jacùss Sauvignon, whose standard-label version has elegant yellow peach and elderflower lifted by appealing minerality. Completing the round-up of estate classics is the Picolit. Very concentrated, fatty and rich, it delights with its honey and plum sensations. Rosso Lindi Uà 2001, a blend of merlot, cabernet and refosco, reveals attractive spice and from the rest of the range, we picked out the berry fruit of the Refosco 2003 and the typicity of the Tocai 2005 and the Verduzzo 2004.

○	COF Picolit '03	🍷🍷	8
○	COF Pinot Bianco '05	🍷🍷	4*
○	COF Sauvignon '05	🍷🍷	4*
●	COF Rosso Lindi Uà '01	🍷	4
●	COF Refosco P. R. '03	🍷	4
○	COF Verduzzo Friulano '04	🍷	4
○	COF Tocai Friulano '05	🍷	4
●	Tazzelenghe '02		4
●	COF Merlot '03		4
○	COF Pinot Bianco '04	YY	4
○	COF Picolit '00	YY	8
●	COF Rosso Lindi Uà '00	YY	4
○	COF Picolit '01	YY	8

TORREANO (UD)

Valchiarò

Fraz. Togliano
via dei Laghi, 4c
33040 Torreano (UD)
tel. 0432715502
www.valchiaro.it

There's important news from Valchiarò. For those who may not know, this winery was created by the union of the plots and passions of five friends. Recently, the original Armando, Emilio, Galliano, Giampaolo and Lauro have been joined by Doris and Stefano. A new cellar is also now operating at Togliano, where the winery has moved its base. Finally, new vine stock has been purchased, bringing the total area under vine to 20 hectares. After all this excitement, let's come back down to earth, which at Valchiarò means turning out superb wines from what we could justifiably call a cru, the hills at Torreano. Again this year, we particularly liked the Verduzzo Friulano 2004, a complex wine hinting at honey, figs and candied peel that return on a palate offering crisply defined flavours and graceful sweetness. We thought the more convincing of the latest vintage's Tocais was the standard-label version, preferring it to the Nexus. The former offers fresh wild herbs and apples while the Nexus has varietal bitter almonds and a richness that is nicely complemented by savoury sensations. The Pinot Grigio has varietal minerality and a very convincing palate that expands seamlessly and with confidence. The Refosco has a very attractive fusion of tartness with black cherry and mulberry fragrances and the Merlot Riserva still has a little way to go. Currently, it lacks a touch of complexity.

○	COF Verduzzo Friulano '04	▼▼	4*
●	COF Merlot Ris. '03	▼▼	4
●	COF Refosco P. R. '03	▼▼	4
○	COF Pinot Grigio '05	▼▼	4
○	COF Tocai Friulano '05	▼▼	4
○	COF Tocai Friulano Nexus '05	▼▼	4
●	COF Cabernet '04		4
○	COF Tocai Friulano Nexus '03	▽▽	4
○	COF Verduzzo Friulano '03	▽▽	4
○	COF Tocai Friulano Nexus '04	▽▽	4

Volpe Pasini

Fraz. Togliano
via Cividale, 16
33040 Torreano (UD)
tel. 0432715151
www.volpepasini.net

Ten years ago, physician and real estate entrepreneur Emilio Rotolo took over the Volpe Pasini cellar, which was on the brink of bankruptcy. Courageously, he kept the by then devalued name and opted to promote the existing distribution network. Obviously, Emilio had to revamp the crumbling cellar, the neglected vine stock and obsolete training systems that militated against quality. But in a few years, he changed the estate team and created an increasingly well-matched squad. He invested in staff and technology. And his reward was that soon Volpe Pasini was turning out excellent results and a million bottles a year, thanks in part to selected purchases of fruit that enabled the cellar to maintain high standards at competitive prices. The 52-hectare estate can count on the input of fruitmakers Pierpaolo Sirch and Marco Simonit, while in the cellar Alessio Dorigo's contribution is flanked by consultancy from no less than Riccardo Cotarella. Sauvignon Zuc di Volpe again amazed out panel and walked away with Three Glasses. Complex, rich and redolent of citrus and sage, it has lovely structure on the well-sustained palate, where a tempting hint of grapefruit emerges in the finish. We also enjoyed the Tocai Friulano from the same line. It's intense, fresh-tasting and elegant, just like the Pinot Grigio, a wine with an intense, sophisticated nose of mixed fruits and hawthorn. The easy-drinking palate has breadth and satisfyingly long length. And the rest of the Volpe Pasini range is seriously good.

○	COF Sauvignon Zuc di Volpe '05	▼▼▼	5
○	COF Pinot Grigio Zuc di Volpe '05	▼▼	4*
○	COF Tocai Friulano Zuc di Volpe '05	▼▼	4*
○	COF Pinot Grigio Ipso '04	▼▼	6
●	Focus Merlot Zuc di Volpe '04	▼▼	6
○	COF Pinot Bianco Zuc di Volpe '05	▼▼	5
○	COF Tocai Friulano Volpe Pasini '05	▼▼	4
●	Refosco P. R. Zuc di Volpe '04	▼	5
○	COF Pinot Grigio Grivò '05	▼	4
○	COF Ribolla Gialla Zuc di Volpe '05	▼	4
○	COF Sauvignon Zuc di Volpe '04	▽▽▽	5

VALVASONE (PN)

Borgo delle Oche

via Borgo Alpi, 5
33098 Valvasone (PN)
tel. 0434899398
www.borgodelleoche.it

After last year's fine performance, which enabled Borgo delle Oche to enter the Guide with a full profile, we had confirmation this time round. Actually, in a growing year – 2005 – that was particularly difficult for flatlands wineries, Luisa Menini and Nicola Pittini managed to turn out some very good products, even better than last year's assortment. The winery aims to get the best from its ten hectares under vine while respecting nature and the plant's vegetative cycle. The cellar shares this commitment and only releases the wines to market when they have aged sufficiently. The most interesting of the seven wines we sampled was the Bianco Alba, from traminer picked when overripe and dried in well-ventilated rooms. It sailed through to the finals. A complex nose foregrounds rich sensations for dried roses, ginger and candied citrus peel, all precisely reflected on the palate, where they are complemented by figs and hazelnuts. In contrast, the standard-label version flaunts nicely melded fruit and aromatic notes. There is richness and distinct ripe fruit on the new Bianco Lupi Terrae 2004, from barrique-fermented tocai and verduzzo friulano, while the Merlot is complex and the Bordeaux blend Svual 2003, from equal amounts of cabernet sauvignon and merlot, has appealing spiciness.

○	Bianco Alba '05	YY	5
○	Traminer Aromatico '05	YY	4*
●	Rosso Svual '03	Y	5
○	Bianco Lupi Terrae '04	Y	4
○	Chardonnay '04	Y	4
●	Merlot '05	Y	4
○	Pinot Grigio '05	Y	4
○	Bianco Alba '04	(YY)	5
○	Pinot Grigio '04	(YY)	4

VILLA VICENTINA (UD)

Valpanera

via Trieste, 5a
33059 Villa Vicentina (UD)
tel. 0431970395
www.valpanera.it

Giampietro Del Vecchio has invested heavily in this flatlands winery. The four vineyards have distinct agronomic profiles and extend over a total of 55 hectares of densely planted vines with an average age of ten years. Giampietro's new cellar is state-of-the-art stuff. We know that he nurtures the ambition to release a superb Refosco like the one Giacomo Casanova described in his "Histoire de ma vie" as exquisite. Actually, the Refosco Riserva 2003 comes very close. Obtained from late-harvested fruit, a small proportion of which was part-dried, it is an object lesson in concentration and rich sensations of liqueur black cherries, confectioner's cream, chocolate and red fruit jam. The balance of these perceptions with the robust tannins is particularly well gauged, and the finish is admirably long. For some time now, the cellar has been adding other strings to its bow. As well as Refosco, there is a fine Sauvignon 2005 that delights the nose with fruity melon and yellow peach that gradually give way to florality and elderflower. Progression on the palate is fresh, with rue peeking through the other aromas. From the rest of the range, we preferred the standard-label Chardonnay 2005 to the oak-aged Carato 2005. The standard-label Refosco 2004 is well managed but not particularly complex while the Rosso di Valpanera 2004, from cabernet, merlot and – inevitably – refosco, is youthfully alcoholic.

●	Friuli Aquileia Refosco P. R. Ris. '03	YY	5
○	Friuli Aquileia Sauvignon '05	YY	4
●	Friuli Aquileia Refosco P. R. '04	Y	3
●	Rosso di Valpanera '04	Y	3
○	Bianco di Valpanera '05	Y	3
○	Friuli Aquileia Chardonnay '05	Y	4
○	Friuli Aquileia Chardonnay Carato '05	Y	4
●	Friuli Aquileia Cabernet Sauvignon '04		3
●	Friuli Aquileia Refosco P. R. Ris. '02	(YY)	5
●	Rosso di Valpanera '03	(YY)	3
○	Friuli Aquileia Chardonnay '04	(YY)	4

OTHER WINERIES

PETRUCCO
via Morpurgo, 12
33042 Buttrio (UD)
tel. 0432674387
www.vinipetrucco.it

Paolo and Lina Petrucco, the owners of this 25-hectare estate, are dependable wine people who focus firmly on excellence. The candied citrus, almond milk, figs and dried apricots of the Picolit 2004 stand out in this minor vintage while the Tocai Friulano and Sauvignon are true to type.

○	COF Picolit '04	🍷🍷	7
○	COF Pinot Grigio '05	🍷	4
○	COF Sauvignon '05	🍷	4
○	COF Tocai Friulano '05	🍷	4

VALLE
via Nazionale, 3
33042 Buttrio (UD)
tel. 0432674289
www.valle.it

There were no real stand-outs on the 20-hectare property set up in 1952 by Gigi Valle, where he releases 200,000 bottles a year. Even the fresh, elegantly fruity Ribolla Gialla San Blâs, failed to pick up a second Glass. Tocai Friulano San Blâs, the standard Tocai and the Chardonnay are well made.

○	COF Ribolla Gialla Sel. San Blâs '05	🍷	4
○	COF Tocai Friulano Sel. San Blâs '05	🍷	4
○	COF Tocai Friulano Valle '05	🍷	4
○	Collio Chardonnay '05	🍷	4

GIOVANNI PUIATTI
via Aquileia, 30
34070 Capriva del Friuli (GO)
tel. 0481809922
www.puiatti.com

The winery that Giovanni and Elisabetta Puiatti inherited from their father, Vittorio, vinifies more and more estate-grown fruit. The best bottle is the Isonzo DOC Tocai Friulano, a clean elegant wine whose pear and apple notes are lifted by acidity. Chardonnay Archetipi 2001 is drinking perfectly.

○	Collio Chardonnay Archetipi '01	🍷	5
○	Collio Sauvignon Ruttars '05	🍷	4
○	Friuli Isonzo Tocai Friulano Le Zuccole '05	🍷	4

VILLA VITAS
fraz. Strassoldo
via San Marco, 5
33050 Cervignano del Friuli (UD)
tel. 043193083 - www.vitas.it

The Vitas family estate covers about 43 hectares, ten or so under vine. It owes this Guide debut to an excellent Chardonnay that mingles cake-like aromas with soft melon. The Merlot holds up well on the palate and the Sauvignon reveals penetrating elderflower aromas.

●	Friuli Aquileia Merlot '04	🍷🍷	4
○	Friuli Aquileia Chardonnay '05	🍷🍷	4
○	Friuli Aquileia Sauvignon Blanc '05	🍷	4

Brunner
P.zza de Senibus, 5
33048 Chiopris Viscone (UD)
tel. 0432991184
www.aziendagricolabrunner.it

Paolo and Monica Antonutti's cellar turns out 160,000 bottles a year from its 15 hectares. The couple offered us a fine 2003 Merlot, redolent of hay, chocolate and coffee with a warm finale. The merlot, cabernet and refosco Rosso Senibus Roos 2003 is austere and the Pinot Grigio fruit-led.

● Friuli Grave Merlot '03	🍷🍷	5
● Friuli Grave Rosso Senibus Roos '03	🍷	5
○ Friuli Grave Chardonnay '05	🍷	4
○ Friuli Grave Pinot Grigio '05	🍷	4

Il Roncal
via Fornalis, 148
33043 Cividale del Friuli (UD)
tel. 0432730138
www.ilroncal.it

The sad death of Roberto Zorzettig has had an undeniable impact on this winery's quality but Roberto's wife Martina is a determined woman. The Pinot Grigio has tasty, concentrated fruit and the upfront Sauvignon reveals a palate of citrus, sage and elderflower.

● COF Rosso Civon '03	🍷	5
○ COF Pinot Grigio '05	🍷	5
○ COF Sauvignon '05	🍷	5
● COF Schioppettino '05	🍷	5

Rubini
loc. Spessa
via Case Rubini, 4
33043 Cividale del Friuli (UD)
tel. 0432716141 - www.villarubini.net

This long-established winery can look back on 190 vintages from its base in the historic villa at Spessa, in the heart of the Colli Orientali del Friuli DOC. We liked the Pignolo and the Cabernet Franc. The Pinot Grigio PG has lively fruit.

● COF Cabernet Franc '03	🍷🍷	4*
● COF Pignolo '03	🍷🍷	7
● COF Refosco P.R. '04	🍷	4
○ Pinot Grigio PG '05	🍷	3

La Sclusa
loc. Spessa
via Strada di S. Anna, 7/2
33043 Cividale del Friuli (UD)
tel. 0432716259 - www.lasclusa.it

A deserved Guide debut for the winery that Gino Zorzettig has run for half a century, now with sons Germano and Luciano. They get 140,000 bottles from the 23 hectares, the flagship wine being a fruity, fresh Pinot Grigio. But the native Picolit and Verduzzo Friulano sweet wines are excellent.

○ COF Pinot Grigio '05	🍷🍷	4*
○ COF Picolit V. del Torrione '03	🍷	7
○ COF Ribolla Gialla '05	🍷	4
○ COF Verduzzo Friulano '05	🍷	4

Giulio Manzocco
via C. Battisti, 61
34071 Cormons (GO)
tel. 048160590

This year, the Manzoccos have hit the spot with two excellent wines, Pinot Bianco and Sauvignon. The former offers pineapple and citrus that return on the palate, which has good intensity and length. And the white peach and ripe fruit Sauvignon Isonzo is just as good.

○ Collio Pinot Bianco '05	🍷🍷	4*
○ Friuli Isonzo Sauvignon '05	🍷🍷	4*

Renzo Sgubin
via Faet, 15/1
34070 Cormons (GO)
tel. 0481630297

The roughly ten hectares of vines are tended like a garden by Renzo Sgubin, who inherited his determination from his father, Bruno. Renzo's range of wines is more than just well-managed and is led by a superb Tocai Friulano. The Pinot Grigio and Chardonnay are very tempting.

○ Friuli Isonzo Rive Alte Tocai Friulano '05	🍷🍷	4*
○ Friuli Isonzo Chardonnay '05	🍷	4
○ Friuli Isonzo Pinot Grigio '05	🍷	4

Blason
via Roma, 32
34072 Gradisca d'Isonzo (GO)
tel. 048192414
www.vinidocisonzo.it

Giovanni Blason's winery continues steadily on its course of growth. We were surprised by the concentration of the Merlot 2005 but the fine Tocai Friulano Bianco in Bruma 2005 paid the price of its vintage in marked acidity. Sauvignon Bruma, another 2005, is fresh, stylish and hints at bell peppers.

●	Friuli Isonzo Merlot '05	🍷	3
○	Friuli Isonzo Sauvignon Bruma '05	🍷	3
○	Friuli Isonzo Tocai Friulano Bianco in Bruma '05	🍷	3

Ronco Blanchis
fraz. Blanchis - via Blanchis, 70
34070 Mossa (GO)
tel. 0423870024
www.venegazzu.com

The Palla family's Ronco Blanchis estate, known as the Loredan Gasparin di Venegazzù winery, extends over 23 well-aspected hectares on the hill at Blanchis, in the town of Mossa. Not for the first time, we liked the Tocai 2005, which offsets fresh flowery aromas with rich peach.

○	Collio Tocai Friulano '05	🍷🍷	4*
○	Collio Chardonnay '05	🍷	4
○	Collio Pinot Grigio '05	🍷	4
○	Collio Sauvignon '05	🍷	4

Toblâr
loc. Ramandolo, 17
33045 Nimis (UD)
tel. 0432755840
www.specogna.it

Michele and Cristian Specogna have a small but excellent range. In fact, they're only in the Other Wineries because they release so few labels. We loved the fruit-rich base of the intense Sauvignon. The equally fruity Pinot Grigio Gris shows stylish minerality. Last up was a well-made Ramandolo.

○	Sauvignon Sauvignonas '05	🍷🍷	4*
○	Ramandolo '04	🍷	4
○	Pinot Grigio Gris '05	🍷	4

Aquila del Torre
fraz. Savorgnano del Torre
via Attimis, 25
33040 Povoletto (UD)
tel. 0432666428 - www.aquiladeltorre.it

Father and son Claudio and Michele Ciani have 25 hectares and make consistently good wines, as we noted from vat tastings and from the stunning Picolit, an intense fusion of dates, caramelized almonds and confectioner's cream. The refreshing, raspberry-themed merlot and refosco Canticum is good.

○	COF Picolit '03	🍷🍷	8
●	COF Rosso Canticum '03	🍷	5
○	COF Picolit Oasipicolit '02	🍷🍷 (white)	8

Antico Broilo
via Broilo, 42
33040 Prepotto (UD)
tel. 0432713082
www.anticobroilo.com

The Dri family has been making wine for at least four generations. Since Massimo took over the cellar, they have also bottled. The six hectares yield only 20,000 units but the small,scenic cellar is worth a visit. We enjoyed the spiciness of the Schioppettino and the structure of the Merlot.

●	COF Merlot Ris. '03	🍷🍷	5
●	COF Schioppettino '04	🍷🍷	4*
●	COF Refosco P. R '04	🍷	4
○	COF Tocai Friulano '04		4

Colli di Poianis
via Poianis, 34a
33040 Prepotto (UD)
tel. 0432713185
www.collidipoianis.com

The 11 hectares of this estate yield 40,000 bottles, many going to Austria, Germany and South Africa. The Sauvignon gives intense bell pepper, rue and tomato. Warm alcohol sustains the Tocai's lovely pear notes and trademark almondiness. The Chardonnay, too, is good, but lacks a touch of finesse.

○	COF Sauvignon '05	🍷🍷	4
○	COF Tocai Friulano '05	🍷🍷	4
●	COF Rosso Ronco della Poiana '04	🍷	5
○	COF Chardonnay '05	🍷	4

Ronco dei Folo
via di Novacuzzo, 46
33040 Prepotto (UD)
tel. 0552002811
www.tenutefolonari.com

Ronco dei Folo, the new name of Tenuta di Novacuzzo, is the first half of owners Ambrogio and Giovanni Folonari's surname. Production is currently 44,000 bottles, half Pinot Grigio. The Tocai Friulano is the best of the whites, holding up well with intriguing notes of honey and acacia blossom.

○	COF Pinot Grigio '05	▼▼	4*
○	COF Tocai Friulano '05	▼▼	4*
○	COF Pinot Grigio '04	▽▽	4

Do Ville
via Mitraglieri, 2
34077 Ronchi dei Legionari (GO)
tel. 0481775561
www.doville.it

Every year, brothers Paolo and Gianni Bonora present us with a very wide range under their Do Ville label and the fresher Ars Vivendi line. We loved the typicity and the violet, lavender and apple notes of the Malvasia Ars Vivendi. The Cabernet Sauvignon is close-knit but could do with more depth.

●	Cabernet Sauvignon Do Ville '03	▼	5
○	Chardonnay Barrique '03	▼	3
○	Friuli Isonzo Tocai Friulano '05	▼	3
○	Malvasia Istriana Ars Vivendi '05	▼	3

Conte Guido De Puppi
loc. Villanova dello Judrio
via 4 Novembre, 33
33048 San Giovanni al Natisone (UD)
tel. 0432758348

A new Guide entry with 18 hectares under vine out of a total of 90. Reds prevail here, especially the clean, utterly typical Refosco. The Pinot Grigio is luscious and there are intriguing aromas of white pepper and wild roses in the Oselot, an ancient native Friulian vine type.

●	Friuli Grave Refosco P.R. '03	▼▼	4
○	Friuli Grave Pinot Grigio '05	▼▼	3*
●	Rosso Oselot '03	▼	5
●	Friuli Grave Refosco P.R. '05	▼	3

Ronco del Gnemiz
via Ronchi, 5
33048 San Giovanni al Natisone (UD)
tel. 0432756238

Serena Palazzolo has opted to skip a vintage, having decided that her wines are slow to mature and cannot be fully appreciated if drunk too young. We are fully in agreement with this wise decision, taken after consultation with oenologist Andrea Pittana.

○	Bianco Bianco '03	▽▽	6
○	COF Bianco di Jacopo '03	▽▽	4
○	COF Pinot Grigio '04	▽▽	5
○	COF Sauvignon '04	▽▽	5

Ca' Selva
Strada di Sequals, 11a
33090 Sequals (PN)
tel. 0421274704
www.caselva.it

The estate stands on the stony flatlands around Sequals, birthplace of heavyweight boxing champion Primo Carnera. It entered the Guide thanks to a fine clutch of wines, especially an elegant, smoky, banana-led Chardonnay. The Pinot Grigio is well executed and the Sauvignon has nice fruity structure.

○	Friuli Grave Chardonnay '05	▼▼	4*
○	Friuli Grave Pinot Grigio '05	▼	4
○	Friuli Grave Sauvignon '05	▼	4

Brojli - Franco Clementin
via G. Galilei, 5
33050 Terzo d'Aquileia (UD)
tel. 043132642
www.fattoriaclementin.it

Challenging weather left its mark on the organic wines Franco Clementin uncorked for us. The range as a whole is very creditable but the usual stand-outs are missing. The Cabernet Franc 2005 is vegetal and flowery, the Refosco 2004 has rich fruit aromas and the Pinot Bianco 2005 is well-typed.

●	Refosco Campo della Stafula '04	▼	4
●	Friuli Aquileia Cabernet Franc '05	▼	3
○	Friuli Aquileia Pinot Bianco '05	▼	3
○	Friuli Aquileia Traminer Aromatico '05	▼	3

EMILIA ROMAGNA

In past editions of the Guide we have often dwelt on the disparity, assessed more often than not in terms of Three Glass awards, between wine production in Emilia and Romagna. But a glance at this year's results appears to show the opposite because the final score was Emilia 4, Romagna 3. But it would be a mistake to look at this figure in isolation. Closer analysis reveals a very different situation. Romagna has far more forward momentum and more widespread quality than Emilia. This does not mean that the Colli Piacentini and Bolognesi are unable to offer wines of extremely high quality. They can, and for this we must thank in particular the focused efforts of a few small-scale producers. For example, we have La Stoppa's Malvasia Vigna del Volta 2004, a Guide classic, and Otto Barattieri's Vin Santo Albarola 1996, which best embodies the Piacenza area's historic heritage of sweet wines, a tradition that finds its highest expression in the few, rare Vigoleno Vin Santos. The Three Glasses awarded to two Cabernet Sauvignons, La Tosa's Luna Selvatica 2004 and Maurizio Vallona's Diggioanni 2004, might seem to buck the general trend of giving more attention to native Italian grape varieties but in this case one very simple rule applies. Our awards are given to outstandingly good wines, whatever the grape variety may be. On the other hand French grape varieties have been widely planted in Emilia for a very long time, and are second in numbers only to lambrusco, while to the east of the Sillaro river, which many consider to be the winemaking boundary between the two areas, traditional varieties prevail, particularly albana, trebbiano and sangiovese. In fact, sangiovese has proved to be a strong suit for Romagna so the fact that only one Sangiovese di Romagna was awarded Three Glasses confirms the pessimistic predictions that accompanied the hot, difficult 2003 harvest. Most of the Riservas and other flagship versions are from this vintage. Calonga's fantastic Michelangiolo 2003 is a rare and welcome exception, like Fattoria Zerbina's Marzieno 2003. Perhaps the presence of a small quantity of cabernet alongside the sangiovese helped this wine to successfully maintain its distinctively elegant, austere style. Further celebration of the happy marriage of sangiovese and cabernet, with a splash of merlot for luck this time, is forthcoming in San Patrignano's Noi 2004. This nicely modulated wine shows yet again that the Rimini area is a very fine place to grow grapes for red wines.

BERTINORO (FC)

Raffaella Alessandra Bissoni
loc. Casticciano
via Colecchio, 280
47032 Bertinoro (FC)
tel. 0543460382
www.vinibissoni.com

The Bertinoro area, with its widespread presence of limestone soil and site climates influenced by the absence of surrounding hills, is unique of its kind in Romagna. The many local producers large and small enable us to analyse it in increasing detail. Raffaella Bissoni and her husband run an estate consisting of about five hectares of vineyards on the slopes facing the Bidente valley in Fratta Terme and Monte Maggio, providing further evidence of the difference between this zone and the area overlooking the sea, which produces tangy, soft wines. The winery's real strength is its vineyards, which have extraordinarily mature, biodiverse cover cropping between the rows while more precision is required in the cellar: investments are being made to ensure that precision is achieved. The Sangiovese Riserva 2003 made it through to the final tastings for Three Glasses. In this unfocused yet generous, charming and original wine good quality and texture rub shoulders with minor, forgivable flaws. Its best features come out on the palate, which is very soft, mouthfilling and slightly rugged with a dry finish and huge personality. The Albana Passito 2003 also performed well. Not recommended for fans of super-smooth wines, since it too is husky and unyielding, it does offer lots of interest and authenticity. The quintessential feature of the Albana is a generous, complex nose with the hint of fruit peel prized generations of Romagna's winemakers. The palate is dry, buttery and long with plenty of fruit.

●	Sangiovese di Romagna Sup. Ris. '03	🍷🍷	4*
○	Albana di Romagna Passito '03	🍷🍷	4

BERTINORO (FC)

Campodelsole
via Cellaimo, 121
47032 Bertinoro (FC)
tel. 0543444562
www.campodelsole.it

Following the inauguration of the magnificent new cellar designed by architect Fiorenzo Valbonesi, and the arrival of Fabio Fossi as sales manager and Stefano Salvini in charge of winemaking, Campodelsole is ready to fulfil all its potential and pursue the ambitious dual objective of quality and quantity. With great patience and far-sightedness the Isoldi family have created the conditions for well-deserved success. Gabriele Isoldi has followed the project from the beginning with utmost dedication and despite his youth he is a solid, reliable reference point for the family as well as for the winery staff. The winery's consultant winemaker Paolo Caciorgna was asked to interpret the terroir within the framework of a modern, enjoyable identity which is also evident in the artwork and in the architectural style of the very modern cellar. Starting from the features of the grapes themselves, Paolo has skilfully put together a clean, modern and original style that can be recognized throughout the range. The Vertice 2003 made it to the Three Glasses finals: despite the hot weather of that year, this is a stylish Sangiovese with expressive, original and very fruity aromas on the nose and a very smooth, dynamic, characterful palate with well-measured strength. Two Glasses go to the Sangiovese Palpedrigo 2004, a modern, clean wine rich in fruit and more mouthfilling than complex. Lastly One Glass for the San Maglorio 2005 which is simpler than the other Sangioveses but similar in style.

●	Sangiovese di Romagna Vertice Ris. '03	🍷🍷	6
●	Sangiovese di Romagna Sup. Palpedrigo '04	🍷🍷	4*
○	Albana di Romagna Selva '05	🍷	2
○	Pagadebit di Romagna San Pascasio '05	🍷	3
●	Sangiovese di Romagna Sup. San Maglorio '05	🍷	3
●	Sangiovese di Romagna Sup. Palpedrigo '03	🍸🍸	4

BERTINORO (FC)

CELLI

VIA CARDUCCI, 5
47032 BERTINORO (FC)
TEL. 0543445183
www.celli-vini.com

New winemakers continue to emerge around Bertinoro for the boundless resources offered by the area's hills have encouraged a dense fabric of production. A number of wineries have been in the spotlight for some time and defend their position honourably and tirelessly, deftly dealing with the problems of each season and continuing to guarantee wines of great interest. This is the case of the winery owned by the Sirri and Casadei families, better known by their nicknames of Bron and Rusèval. Every season has its difficulties but even the most challenging can also reserve pleasant surprises. This is true of the Albana Secco I Croppi 2005, a velvety wine of wonderful texture with strength and elegance from the rich alcohol content. The 2005 Chardonnay Bron & Rusèval was a confirmation, not a surprise. The palate is warm and mouthfilling with generous sweet, ripe fruit sensations and well-judged freshness to add complexity and appeal. The red 2004 version of the same name, from sangiovese and cabernet sauvignon, is seductively rounded on the almost overwhelming palate, where the sweet red berry fruit mingles with liquorice and spice. The finish is a little dry, which suggests that a balance with the powerful tannins has yet to be achieved. The Sangiovese Riserva Le Grillaie 2003 shows typical features of tradition and an orthodox approach to winemaking, with its rustic nose and full-bodied cherry and cocoa powder-led flavour.

●	Bron & Rusèval Sangiovese-Cabernet '04	🍷🍷	4
○	Albana di Romagna Secco I Croppi '05	🍷🍷	3*
○	Bron & Rusèval Chardonnay '05	🍷🍷	4
●	Sangiovese di Romagna Sup. Le Grillaie Ris. '03	🍷	4
●	Sangiovese di Romagna Sup. Le Grillaie '05		3
●	Sangiovese di Romagna Sup. Le Grillaie Ris. '01	YY	3
●	Bron & Rusèval Sangiovese-Cabernet '03	YY	4
○	Albana di Romagna Passito Solara '03	Y	4

BERTINORO (FC)

TENUTA LA VIOLA

VIA COLOMBARONE, 888
47032 BERTINORO (FC)
TEL. 0543445496
www.tenutalaviola.it

Stefano Gabellini has this land in his blood. He is always talking about ways to improve the wines from his neat, well-ordered vineyards, devoting the same energy to major decisions and small details with impressive help in the vineyards from his hard-working mother. Franco Calini arrived at La Viola as consultant winemaker and immediately struck up a harmonious relationship. There is still work to be done on the vines and the reduction of the wine's alcohol content, which should lead to a less warm and more elegant expression of this Romagna territory looking out to the sea 20 kilometres away. The Sangiovese Riserva Petra Honorii 2004 made it through to the final Three Glass tastings. A sound, full-bodied wine, it has bags of blackberry and wild berry jam fruit and a very dynamic palate, where the texture is as close-knit as the tannins. The finish is obscured by a slightly drying alcohol sensation. One Glass went to the Oddone 2005, a fresh-tasting Sangiovese made from grapes grown in the youngest vineyards and intelligently managed to slightly increase the yield, which has produced a wine with more moderate structure and more simplicity. The more ambitious standard-label Sangiovese, Il Colombarone 2005, is missing from the roll-call because Gabellini has decided to let it age longer in the bottles before release.

●	Sangiovese di Romagna Sup. Petra Honorii Ris. '04	🍷🍷	5
●	Sangiovese di Romagna Oddone '05	🍷	3
●	Sangiovese di Romagna Sup. La Badia Ris. '03	YY	5
●	Sangiovese di Romagna Sup. Il Colombarone '04	YY	4

BERTINORO (FC)

Giovanna Madonia

Loc. Villa Madonia
via de' Cappuccini, 130
47032 Bertinoro (FC)
tel. 0543444361 - 0543445085
www.giovannamadonia.it

At last we have a vintage that gives us some measure of this winery's true productive potential. The cellar's full repertoire is on show, spared from the misadventures that have dogged the vineyards in the past and hindered the cellar work of brilliant winemaker Attilio Pagli. The result of this all-round assessment is simple: Giovanna Madonia is right in the front rank of winemaking in the area. How else can we describe a wine like the Sangiovese Riserva Ombroso 2003, except as a minor – exclusively in terms of numbers of bottles released – masterpiece? Spicy hints from the oak lend elegance to the nose before the palate reveals its excellence in a beautifully rounded entry, with complex flavours ranging from ripe red berry fruit to liquorice, vanilla and chocolate. The other Sangiovese, Fermavento 2004, is also very good indeed with delicate aromas that conceal a sturdy, complex texture combining fresh, grassy sensations with sweeter, chewier hints and leading to a long, very stylish, lingering finish. The winery's last red, the merlot-based Sterpigno 2003, is brilliantly made. Elegant wild berry fruit tempts the nose and the velvety, dense, mouthfilling palate is backed up by fine-textured tannins that dry the finish a little. The Albana Passito Chimera 2003 has stylish botrytis aromas on the nose and complex sweetness on the palate, proffering a broad array of sensations, from honey to candied apricots and vanilla.

●	Sangiovese di Romagna Sup. Ombroso Ris. '03	🍷🍷	5
○	Albana di Romagna Passito Chimera '03	🍷🍷	5
●	Sterpigno Merlot '03	🍷🍷	6
●	Sangiovese di Romagna Sup. Fermavento '04	🍷🍷	4*
●	Sangiovese di Romagna Sup. Ombroso Ris. '01	YYY	5
●	Sterpigno Merlot '00	YY	6
●	Sangiovese di Romagna Sup. Ombroso Ris. '00	YY	5

BERTINORO (FC)

Fattoria Paradiso

Loc. Capocolle
via Palmeggiana, 285
47032 Bertinoro (FC)
tel. 0543445044
www.fattoriaparadiso.com

Fattoria Paradiso owes its name to a custom that has been popular since the Middle Ages: indicating in extravagant terms particularly beautiful locations with a mild climate. Often they actually were a paradise for particular species of animal or plants. This beautiful, ideally situated Fattoria Paradiso, where peacocks welcome you, has now paradoxically become the stage for a challenge between well-established traditions and an ambition to take the winery to the top of Romagna's winemaking league table. Jacopo Lupo Melia, grandson of the founder, Mario Pezzi, represents the new part of this equation and the future of this estate with all its huge potential revolves around him. Winemaker Carlo Ferrini, who is usually reluctant to leave his Tuscan homeland, has joined Jacopo to take up the challenge and nurture this ambition, probably convinced by the potential this location offers. Today's results include three wines that scored Two Glasses. These are generally based on good grapes although they still lacking personality of their own. We are sure that this will not be long in coming. The Sangiovese Vigna delle Lepri 2004 is undoubtedly one of the winery's most impressive wines with good fresh fruit, lively alcohol and substantial texture. The Barbarossa 2004 is more close-knit and austere, its nose being rather unfocused, but the aromatics are echoed nicely on the soft, reasonably long-lingering palate. The uncomplicated, fairly harmonious Mito 2004 is made from merlot, cabernet, barbarossa and syrah grapes, and reveals very approachable fruit.

●	Barbarossa Il Dosso '04	🍷🍷	5
●	Mito '04	🍷🍷	7
●	Sangiovese di Romagna Sup. V. delle Lepri Ris. '04	🍷🍷	5
○	Frutto Proibito '05	🍷	6
●	Sangiovese di Romagna Sup. Maestri di Vigna '05	🍷	4
●	Mito '00	YY	7
●	Barbarossa Il Dosso '01	YY	5
●	Barbarossa Il Dosso '03	YY	5
●	Mito '03	YY	7

BERTINORO (FC)

Villa Trentola

Loc. Capocolle di Bertinoro
via Molino Bratti, 1305
47032 Bertinoro (FC)
tel. 0543741389
www.villatrentola.it

This old winery has a recently acquired a new lease of life since Federica and Elisabetta Prugnoli took over management. The good grapes from the estate's 20 hectares, almost entirely planted with sangiovese, used to be swallowed up by the vats of a neighbouring co-operative but for the last few years, they have been fermented here in the winery's own new cellar. Thanks in part to the help of a winemaker of proven skill, Attilio Pagli, some selections have been created to embody the new production philosophy, focusing on research and respect for the integrity of the environment and the terroir. The young owners' confidence has grown hand-in-hand with their achievements and the range of wines has expanded accordingly. The new Sangiovese Placidio 2004 – the name of the Roman empress Galla Placidia often pops up in these parts – has seductive aromas of pencil lead, quinine and vanilla on the nose. The surprisingly soft, elegantly velvety palate opens broad and mouthfilling, dominated by sweet, persistent black cherry fruit, with close-knit tannins and outstandingly long-lingering flavour. Il Moro 2004 is brilliantly executed with ripe red berry fruit and nice oak aromas. The fruit is astonishingly generous and complex on the palate, as is the length of the very stylish aftertaste. The winery's last Sangiovese, Il Prugnolo 2004, is less complicated and rich in extract than the others but well-balanced with nicely judged freshness.

●	Sangiovese di Romagna Sup. Placidio '04	TT	6
●	Sangiovese di Romagna Sup. Il Moro di Villa Trentola '04	TT	5
●	Sangiovese di Romagna Sup. Il Prugnolo di Villa Trentola '04	T	4
●	Sangiovese di Romagna Sup. Il Moro di Villa Trentola '02	YY	5
●	Sangiovese di Romagna Sup. Il Moro di Villa Trentola '03	YY	5

BOMPORTO (MO)

Francesco Bellei

via per Modena, 80
41030 Bomporto (MO)
tel. 059812449
www.francescobellei.it

Christian Bellei has been carrying on the work begun by his unforgettable father, Beppe, who had the ingenious inspiration some years ago to make great classic method spumante from chardonnay and pinot nero grapes in an area almost exclusively devoted to the production of sparkling Lambrusco. The Cavicchioli family, who own the large San Prospero winery, are working alongside him to market the wines. The mutual respect of Christian and Sandro Cavicchioli, technical manager of the family winery, can only help both businesses develop. Rifermentazione Ancestrale is a Lambrusco made using the traditional method of second fermentation in bottle without disgorgement. It's therefore a little cloudy in the glass with a confident, hard flavour, perceptible acidity and hints of grapefruit in the finish. The Rosso Extra Cuvée is a classic method wine from lambrusco di Sorbara grapes. The lively cherry-red, stylishly lingering perlage and fragrant, fresh fruit usher in a generously complex flavour. The Speciale Cuvée 1999 spent a long time on the yeasts, which has given the wine stylish, very complex aromas, including wild flowers and herbs, and then a palate whose soft, mouthfilling impact takes you through to a full-bodied, lingering finish. The Rosé Extra Cuvée 2001 has a mature bouquet with ethereal hints of brandy, and a stiffish palate with an excessively bitter finish. The Brut Extra Cuvée is fragrant, generous and floral, and the palate is beautifully fresh and drinkable thanks to a substantial proportion of chardonnay grapes.

●	Brut Extra Cuvée Rosso '03	TT	4*
○	Bellei Brut Cuvée Speciale '99	TT	5
○	Brut Extra Cuvée	TT	5
⊙	Bellei Brut Rosé Extra Cuvée '01	T	6
●	Lambrusco Rifermentazione Ancestrale '05	T	4
○	Bellei Brut Cuvée Speciale '97	YY	5
⊙	Bellei Brut Rosé Extra Cuvée '98	YY	6

BORGONOVO VAL TIDONE (PC)

Castelli del Duca

via Moretta, 58
29011 Borgonovo Val Tidone (PC)
tel. 0522942135
www.medici.it

It was not a particularly brilliant year for Castelli di Duca, the brand name that indicates the partnership of Reggio winery Medici Ermete and Terre dei Farnese. The latter is a consortium of producers from the Piacenza area, especially Cantina Valtidone, where all the vinification procedures are carried out. The range, as usual, consists of exclusively non-sparkling wines made from local grape varieties, except for sauvignon. The products presented this year were all well made but, although the overall standard was good, they lacked that extra thrust which has made them benchmark wines for the designated area in the past. The Gutturnio Riserva Sigillum 2003 presents slightly evolved aromas, and develops a powerful spicy palate that tends to clench in the finish, which is marked by rather bitter tannin. The Gutturnio Classico Duca Augusto 2004 is simpler and tidier while the Sauvignon Duchessa Vittoria 2005 is clean and varietal with nicely put-together vegetal and tropical fruit aromas, a supple palate and a tangy, lingering finish. The Malvasia Passito Soleste is as fascinating as ever and the 2005 version makes a ripe, nicely rounded impact on the palate, pervaded with sweet, lingering sensations of citrus marmalade and apricots.

●	C. P. Gutturnio Sigillum Ris. '03	▼▼	5
○	C. P. Malvasia Passito Soleste '05	▼▼	5
●	C. P. Gutturnio Cl. Duca Augusto '04	▼	4
○	C. P. Sauvignon Duchessa Vittoria '05	▼	4
●	C. P. Barbera Duca Ranuccio '04		3
●	C. P. Bonarda Duca Ottavio '04		3
●	C. P. Gutturnio Sigillum Ris. '00	▽▽	5
●	C. P. Gutturnio Cl. Duca Augusto '03	▽▽	3
●	C. P. Gutturnio Sup. Duca Alessandro '03	▽▽	4

BORGONOVO VAL TIDONE (PC)

Cantina Sociale Valtidone

via Moretta, 58
29011 Borgonovo Val Tidone (PC)
tel. 0523862168 - 0523864086
www.cantinavaltidone.it

The numbers alone will provide an idea of how important this co-operative is for the Val Tidone area and the Colli Piacentini as a whole: over 330 grower members, 1,200 hectares of vineyards for a total of over 90,000 quintals of grapes, about a quarter of the total production for the Piacenza area. Sergio and Marcello Galetti are in charge of winemaking while Professor Boselli is responsible for the vineyards. The large, varied range includes a reliably excellent wine, Luna di Candia. The 2005 version of this Malvasia Passito has clear, nicely articulated aromas of candied citrus fruit and a soft, sweet palate that manages not to cloy. The surprise this year is a spumante, the Brut Perlage from chardonnay and pinot nero. This classic-method sparkler is released only in magnums and is excellent value for money. The initial impact is confident and fresh-tasting and there is good balance on the palate and well-judged sparkle, which smooths the flavour without creating heaviness. From the Vinum Merum line, we recommend the appealing Gutturnio Classico Julius 2003 and the Superiore Bollo Rosso 2003, whose ripe fruit on the palate is freshened up by nice acidity in the finish. In the Borgo del Conte line, the Gutturnio Superiore Flerido 2003 is again good , with assertive tannins and sensations that range from ripe, juicy fruit to balsamic hints on a satisfyingly smooth background. Slightly below par is the Gutturnio Giannone Riserva 2003, which offers very mature aromas, warmth and fullness but lacks freshness and integrity.

●	C. P. Gutturnio Sup. Borgo del Conte Flerido '03	▼▼	4
●	C. P. Gutturnio Sup. Bollo Rosso '03	▼▼	3*
○	C. P. Malvasia Passito Luna di Candia '05	▼▼	4
○	Brut Perlage	▼▼	5
●	C. P. Gutturnio Borgo del Conte Giannone Ris. '03	▼	5
●	C. P. Gutturnio Cl. Julius '03	▼	4
●	C. P. Cabernet Sauvignon Borgo di Rivalta Mabilia '03	▽▽	5
○	C. P. Malvasia Passito Luna di Candia '04	▽▽	4

BRISIGHELLA (RA)

La Berta

via Berta, 13
48013 Brisighella (RA)
tel. 054684998

Constantino Giovannini is one of the pioneers of quality winemaking in Romagna. His 27 hectares of vineyards are in a beautiful location among the gullies of the hills separating Faenza from Brisighella. Every year, he takes up the challenge of making wines to bring out all the territory's potential. The never-ending struggle of farmer and land over the years forges deep relationships, as in Conrad's "The Duellists", and Costantino is assisted in his confrontation by the winery's longstanding Tuscan-based oenologist, Stefano Chioccioli. Production is usually very good but each year the duel is wide open. Sometimes not all of our expectations are fulfilled. Solano 2005 put on an excellent performance. La Berta's basic Sangiovese won Two Glasses for its lovely fruit and clean, balanced profile. The Sangiovese Riserva Olmatello 2004 will need time to develop. Its good weighty texture is close-knit with fairly good structure and length. The Floresco is a different story. It's an ingenious invention of Costantino's that has not yet settled into a recognizable style. The project is a sophisticated and innovative one for Romagna and focuses on using trebbiano to achieve mature aromas through long ageing. The Floresco 2004 has generous aromas but the good minerality is not backed up by refreshing acidity and as a result the spectrum is dominated by almond and hazelnut sensations.

●	Sangiovese di Romagna Olmatello Ris. '04	🍷🍷	5
●	Sangiovese di Romagna Sup. Solano '05	🍷🍷	4*
○	Trebbiano di Romagna Floresco '04	🍷	4
○	Infavato Vino da Uve Stramature '04		5
●	Sangiovese di Romagna Olmatello Ris. '01	YY	5
●	Sangiovese di Romagna Olmatello Ris. '03	YY	5
●	Ca' di Berta Cabernet Sauvignon '01	YY	5

BRISIGHELLA (RA)

Consorzio Produttori di Brisighella

loc. Campiume - via Campiume, 6
48010 Brisighella (RA)
tel. 054680112
www.campiume.com

San Lorenzo in Campiume is an extraordinarily beautiful and one of the most attractive spots in the Lamone valley. This magical place is the setting for the fascinating tale of three young growers, Paolo Babini, Andrea Bragagni and Filippo Manetti. They all work in the upper part of the valley sharing a philosophy of harmony between man and the earth and working in partnership while keeping their individual production identities distinct. Andrea, Filippo and Paolo work all the land that reasonably can be worked on their own. Farmers and intellectuals, the three have a deep-rooted identity that they have brought forward into the modern age. The Vigne dei Boschi logo identifies the wines of Paolo Babini, from which we recommend the 100 per cent sangiovese Poggio Tura 2003, sourced from a bush-trained vineyard. It's very soft and fruity on the nose with a generous, somewhat rugged palate. We usually love Settepievi 2004, mainly from malbo gentile and merlot. This version is interesting, if a little lighter than usual. Turning to Andrea Bragagni's wines, the well-made, balanced Gheppio 2004 has good depth and is one of the most interesting Trebbianos in Romagna while Casa I Frati 2004 is a mellow, expressive Sangiovese with a long, flavoursome palate. Finally, Filippo Manetti's Vigne di San Lorenzo line offers a sangiovese Campiume 2004 that is characterful to the point of ruggedness and will settle down more harmoniously with cellar time. San Lorenzo 2004, made from cabernet sauvignon and merlot, has good rich texture.

●	Poggio Tura '03	🍷🍷	5
●	Campiume '04	🍷🍷	5
●	San Lorenzo '04	🍷🍷	5
●	Sangiovese di Romagna Casa I Frati '04	🍷🍷	4
○	Trebbiano di Romagna Gheppio '04	🍷🍷	3*
●	Settepievi '04	🍷	5
●	Campiume '03	YY	5
●	Settepievi '03	YY	5

BRISIGHELLA (RA)

Villa Liverzano
via Valloni, 47
48013 Brisighella (RA)
tel. 054680565
www.liverzano.it

Swiss citizen Marco Montanari, originally from Romagna, dropped into this corner of the region in the small plane he pilots himself and which he used to fly back and forth across the Apennines from Villa Livernano in Tuscany, where he spent an exciting and important period of in his life. He glimpsed this estate in the hills near Brisighella from the sky, fell in love with the beautiful surroundings and the villa hidden among the cypress trees, and decided to buy it. When he stood at the gate and read the name Villa Liverzano, he realized destiny had brought him there: the property was calling to something deep inside him. At the moment, the three hectares of vineyards are partly planted with bush-trained vines of mainly international varieties, right on the vein of chalky soil that makes this area a unique, original environment and one particularly well-suited to the production of extremely elegant wines. The Don 2004 is unusually packaged with two labels, one male and one female, that use the same design in different colours. This blend of cabernet sauvignon and carmenère grapes is vibrant and expressive with clearly defined, pervasive varietal aromas. The tannins are impressively compact on the rounded, velvety, lingering and weighty palate. Don made it to the Three Glass finals, as did the merlot and sangiovese Rebello 2004. It has bags of elegance and is warm yet austere, with an impressively generous palate. The merlot-led drift into sweetness is headed off on the palate by interesting rugged sensations.

●	Don '04	🍷🍷 (black)	6
●	Rebello '04	🍷🍷 (black)	6
●	Rebello '03	🍷🍷 (white)	5

CASALECCHIO DI RENO (BO)

Tizzano
via Marescalchi, 13
40033 Casalecchio di Reno (BO)
tel. 051571208 - 051577665

Gracious, pragmatic Luca Visconti di Modrone has run his estate increasingly proactively in recent years, implementing an effective policy of small steps that is achieving steady results. Luca is fortunate enough to be able to count on the collaboration of Gabriele Forni, the winery's long-serving manager and an expert in vineyard matters both technical field and above all cultural aspects, the ones that take the best of traditional farming lore and use it to improve the quality of the wines. But there are also new elements in this solid framework of tradition. It's the first edition of a new wine, Merlot 2004, long pondered and created without haste. We were very impressed by the generous, chewy fruit and the flavoursome, velvety palate with its nice, if slightly tannic and dry, progression. The whole range of whites is well made as usual and the Sauvignon 2005 stands out for its sharply defined, fresh varietal aromas, lovely texture and lingering tastiness. The pignoletto-based Spumante Brut is a mainstay of the winery's range. Dry and fragrant with continuous fizz, it flaunts long, dry flavour. Tizzano has made sparkling wines from pignoletto grapes for some time, with dependably good results, but inexplicably remains alone in this venture. Very few Colli Bolognesi producers have spotted the huge oenological and commercial huge potential of the type.

●	C. B. Merlot '04	🍷🍷 (black)	4
○	C. B. Sauvignon '05	🍷🍷 (black)	3*
○	C. B. Pignoletto Brut	🍷🍷 (black)	4
○	C. B. Pignoletto Frizzante '05	🍷 (black)	3
○	C. B. Pignoletto Sup. '05	🍷 (black)	4
○	C. B. Riesling Italico '05	🍷 (black)	3
●	C. B. Cabernet Sauvignon '01	🍷🍷 (white)	4
●	C. B. Cabernet Sauvignon Ris. '01	🍷🍷 (white)	5
●	C. B. Cabernet Sauvignon '02	🍷🍷 (white)	4

CASTEL BOLOGNESE (RA)

STEFANO FERRUCCI
VIA CASOLANA, 3045/2
48014 CASTEL BOLOGNESE (RA)
TEL. 0546651068
www.stefanoferrucci.it

Ilaria Ferrucci's 26 years are a huge resource for this traditional Romagna winery. They translate into energy, ambition and new ideas for at 26, you put intensity into fulfilling a dream that is difficult to find later on in life. Ilaria's dream is to take the winery founded by her father Stefano, who sadly passed away recently, to higher levels, keeping alive the desire to develop and grow that has always been a part of the family spirit. The challenge – to renovate the winery while hold onto its history – is difficult but there is every indication that it Ilaria is equal to it. She has already shown she can run the estate with intelligence. The good result of the Domus Caia 2003 is an important milestone for it pointed the way to our Three Glass finals. This Sangiovese is made, in compliance with tradition, using slightly raisined grapes but in this case the raisining process was very limited, not least because it was a hot growing year, and the wine is fragrant with fresher fruit. The nose has depth and complexity, introducing a mouthfilling, fruit-led palate, with progressively increasing clarity of focus as it heads into the long finish. The albana-based Passito Domus Aurea is also interesting, elegant and complex, especially on the nose. The winery's simplest wine, the Sangiovese Auriga 2005, also performed well. It's pleasingly genuine, offering a well-made, sharply defined interpretation of the territory. The Centurione 2005 is less successful as the "ripasso" addition of Domus Caia skins has detracted from its freshness and cleanness.

- ● Sangiovese di Romagna Sup. Domus Caia Ris. '03 — 6
- ○ Albana di Romagna Passito Domus Aurea '04 — 6
- ● Sangiovese di Romagna Auriga '05 — 3
- ○ Stefano Ferrucci Vino da Uve Stramature — 6
- ○ Albana di Romagna Dolce Lilaria '05 — 4
- ● Sangiovese di Romagna Sup. Centurione '05 — 4
- ● Sangiovese di Romagna Domus Caia Ris. '00 — 6
- ● Sangiovese di Romagna Domus Caia Ris. '01 — 6

CASTEL SAN PIETRO TERME (BO)

UMBERTO CESARI
VIA STANZANO, 1120
40050 CASTEL SAN PIETRO TERME (BO)
TEL. 051941896 - 051940234
www.umbertocesari.it

At Umberto Cesari's winery, there is no lack of inspiration or imagination – remember the packaging of the Polvere di Stelle, with the Swarovski crystals? The latest creation of this restless spirit is Moma, a wine whose name is an acronym of My Own MAsterpiece. But Umberto has added a pinch of mischievous ambiguity for the masterpiece in this case is meant to be the one shown on the label. The 2004 edition has a drawing by the Bolognese painter Giorgio Morandi. In the future, a panel of experts will select a new artist for the label every three years. But again, Umberto has focused on substance as well as style for the wine presented by the prestigious artist is actually very well made. The blend is cabernet sauvignon, sangiovese and merlot, with well-judged use of wood, and clearly considerable technical skill has gone into making it. Vanilla and almond aromas usher in a broad palate that ranges from wild berries to cocoa powder, spices and liquorice. The fine-grained tannins support but do not eclipse the dense, flavoursome fruit and ensure smooth lingering sensations. The Liano 2003, from sangiovese and cabernet sauvignon, is almost too powerfully structured and softly alluring before it signs off with a pervasive, full-flavoured finale. The stylishly made Sangiovese Riserva Laurento 2003 shows better balance and excellent fruit while the Riserva Umberto Cesari 2003 is, as usual, an enjoyable traditional Sangiovese sold at a reasonable price.

- ● Moma '04 — 4*
- ● Liano '03 — 5
- ● Sangiovese di Romagna Laurento Ris. '03 — 4
- ● Sangiovese di Romagna Umberto Cesari Ris. '03 — 4
- ○ Albana di Romagna Passito Colle del Re '03 — 5
- ○ Albana di Romagna Secco Colle del Re '05 — 3
- ○ Malise Pignoletto-Chardonnay '05 — 4
- ● Tauleto Sangiovese '00 — 6
- ● Tauleto Sangiovese '01 — 6
- ● Liano '02 — 5

CASTELL'ARQUATO (PC)

CARDINALI

POD. MONTEPASCOLO
29014 CASTELL'ARQUATO (PC)
TEL. 0523803502
www.cardinalidoc.it

The small, neat winery run by Laura Cardinali and her brother Alberto covers about ten hectares on the Arquato hills in the heart of the Arda valley. The wines presented this year speak eloquently of the dependability that this dynamic, constantly developing winery has achieved. One indication of professionalism is the Cardinalis' courage in refusing to release leading wines from less exciting vintages. Having skipped the 2002 growing year, Gutturnio Riserva Torquata is back with the 2003 vintage. Again, it's an exemplary specimen of the type, showing complex, nicely defined aromas of ripe fruit and a succulent palate with pronounced tannins and good nose-palate consistency. The Gutturnio Classico Nicchio 2005 is fermented in stainless steel vats and shows nice generous fruit on the nose, though a slight initial pungency leads it astray. The palate is supple, giving fruit with good body and smooth flavour. The cabernet sauvignon Ronchello 2001 is garnet red with complex aromas of very ripe fruit on the nose and a mouthfilling palate with glossy, well-integrated tannins. The white Monterosso Solata 2005 is from malvasia and sauvignon. It shows subtle and delicate on the nose before the nicely fresh-tasting palate reveals its coherent flavour. The Dolce Montepascolo is from moscato grapes and the 2005 version has lemon and honey on the nose and a sweet, juicy palate with a bitterish finish.

●	C. P. Gutturnio Cl. Torquato Ris. '03	🍷🍷	5
●	C. P. Cabernet Sauvignon Ronchello '01	🍷🍷	5
●	C. P. Gutturnio Cl. Nicchio '05	🍷🍷	4*
○	Dolce Montepascolo '05	🍷🍷	5
○	C. P. Monterosso Val d'Arda Solata '05	🍷	4
○	Dolce Montepascolo '03	🍸🍸	5
●	C. P. Gutturnio Cl. Nicchio '04	🍸🍸	4

CASTELLO DI SERRAVALLE (BO)

VALLONA

FRAZ. FAGNANO
VIA SANT'ANDREA, 203
40050 CASTELLO DI SERRAVALLE (BO)
TEL. 0516703058 - 0516703333

It is no surprise that one of Maurizio Vallona's wines should have won Three Glasses again. If anything, it's a shame that for one reason or another he has not received this sought-after accolade every year, since his approach has never varied. He is scrupulous, indeed almost obsessive, in the vineyard and keeps his intervention in the cellar to a few, shrewd procedures. Add to this simple recipe Maurizio's thirst for knowledge, which prompts him to constantly question what he does and seek dialogue beyond the borders of the Colli Bolognesi. It was the Cabernet Diggioanni 2004 that won Maurizio his Three Glasses this time. It's austere, slightly grassy aromas are in typical Bordeaux style, introducing perfectly ripe, fresh fruit and a flavoursome but nicely crafted palate that expands with character and elegance. The Merlot Affederico 2004 missed a similar award by a hair's breadth. The blackberry and blueberry fruit, in particular, is dense and chewy and the long finish is velvet-smooth. The Pignoletto 2005 is a very pleasant, drinkable wine that shows vibrantly fruity with a stylish mineral vein. The Pignoletto Permartina 2004 from late-harvested grapes is unusually sweet, given that it is usually soft and mouthfilling yet crisp and dry. On the one hand, the considerable residual sugar in the 2004 lifts the very ripe fruit but on the other it weighs the wine down and threatens to cloy. The Primedizione Cuvée, labelled 2006 from the year it was blended, is immediately captivating with broad, pervasive aromas.

●	Diggioanni Cabernet Sauvignon '04	🍷🍷🍷	5
●	Affederico Merlot '04	🍷🍷	5
○	C. B. Pignoletto '05	🍷🍷	3*
○	Permartina Pignoletto '04	🍷🍷	4
○	Pignoletto Vivace '05	🍷🍷	3*
○	Primedizione Cuvée 2006	🍷🍷	4
●	C. B. Cabernet Sauvignon '04	🍷	4
○	C. B. Sauvignon '05	🍷	4
●	C. B. Merlot Affederico '01	🍸🍸🍸	5
●	C. B. Cabernet Sauvignon Sel. '97	🍸🍸🍸	5
●	C. B. Cabernet Sauvignon Sel. '99	🍸🍸🍸	5
●	Affederico Merlot '03	🍸🍸	5
●	Diggioanni Cabernet Sauvignon '03	🍸🍸	5

CASTELVETRO DI MODENA (MO)

Corte Manzini

loc. Cà di Sola
via Modena, 131/3
41014 Castelvetro di Modena (MO)
tel. 059702658
www.cortemanzini.it

The continuity shown by this small winery in its output of increasingly good Lambruscos is becoming very impressive. This shows that the vineyards are managed competently, partly thanks to the attention the many members of the extended Manzini family devote to them. Above all, continuity shows that that all the praise heaped on young Stefano Manzini's running of the winery was justified. The wines in the range, which are almost all made exclusively from lambrusco grasparossa grapes, have a shared style based on a few, essential concepts: very clean aromas, ripe, fresh fruit, extremely fragrant and full-bodied flavour. It is the vines themselves that make the difference between one product and another: the younger plants produce grapes for the Bolla Rossa, which has a slightly more traditional nose than the other wines and a fairly hard, no-nonsense palate. Mid-aged vineyards give fruit for L'Acino, which again scaled the heights of regional winemaking in the 2005 version. This Lambrusco is almost too rich in cherry-led fruity aromas and chewy fruit pulp that softly fills the palate over a nice vein of acidity and considerable tannin. Finally, the grapes of the older vines, which are more than 40 years old, are used for Grasparossa Secco and Amabile. The former is well crafted and skilfully rounded, with plenty of texture, while the Amabile is extremely pleasant, generous, densely textured, flavoursome and perfectly balanced.

●	Lambrusco Grasparossa di Castelvetro Amabile '05	🍷🍷 (grey)	3*
●	Lambrusco Grasparossa di Castelvetro L'Acino '05	🍷🍷 (grey)	4
●	Lambrusco Grasparossa di Castelvetro Secco '05	🍷🍷	3*
●	Lambrusco Grasparossa di Castelvetro Secco Bolla Rossa '05	🍷🍷	3*
⊙	Brut Rosé Bollicina	🍷	4
⊙	Lambrusco Grasparossa di Castelvetro Secco Fior di Lambrusco	🍷	3
○	Malvasia dell'Emilia Dolce Incanto	🍷	3

CIVITELLA DI ROMAGNA (FC)

Poderi dal Nespoli

loc. Nespoli
villa Rossi, 50
47012 Civitella di Romagna (FC)
tel. 0543989637
www.poderidalnespoli.com

This traditional Romagna winery is run proficiently by Fabio Ravaioli, his cousins Valerio and Celita Ravaioli and Gianni Romanini. The grapes from 30 hectares are vinified with input from consultant winemaker Beppe Caviola. The Ravaioli family clearly has a profound knowledge of the area. They have made wine in the Bidente valley since the early 20th century and were selling it as long ago as 1929, although originally only in their osteria at Cusercoli. The grapes grown in the three vineyards, located in different parts of the valley but all around Cusercoli itself, are fermented separately in order to highlight their individual features. Although the vineyards are at different altitudes, they are all on clay and sandstone soil since their position is higher than the crosswise division of the valley marking the boundary between clay-only soil and clay and sandstone. The considerable temperature variation and local climate enable the grapes to ripen fully while keeping down strength and alcohol, which translates into elegant, balanced wines. Il Nespoli 2004 earned a well-deserved Two Glasses. This Sangiovese has deep, sound fruit with hints of pencil lead and mineral sensations. It is modern in style with an interestingly austere character. The Prugneto 2005 is a genuine wine: a genuine Sangiovese genuinely rooted in the land. The nose is expressive and palate is enjoyably fresh-tasting and clean. Finally, Poderi dal Nespoli has decided that its leading product, Borgo dei Guidi 2004, needs longer in bottle so we will be able to enjoy it in a year's time.

●	Il Nespoli Sangiovese '04	🍷🍷	5
●	Sangiovese di Romagna Prugneto '05	🍷🍷	4*
○	Damaggio Chardonnay '05	🍷	3
●	Sangiovese di Romagna Sup. Santodeno '05		3
●	Borgo dei Guidi '03	🍷🍷 (outline)	6
●	Borgo dei Guidi '01	🍷🍷 (outline)	6
●	Borgo dei Guidi '00	🍷🍷 (outline)	6
●	Il Nespoli Sangiovese '03	🍷🍷 (outline)	5

COLLECCHIO (PR)

MONTE DELLE VIGNE
LOC. OZZANO TARO
VIA COSTA, 27
43046 COLLECCHIO (PR)
TEL. 0521809105
www.montedellevigne.it

The makeover at Monte delle Vigne, which began some time ago, is making swift progress. By the end of this year, the new cellar will be completed and by the end of 2008 the last 20 hectares of vineyards will have been planted, bringing the total surface area to almost 60 hectares. With assistance from consultants Attilio Pagli and Federico Curtaz, Andrea Ferrari this year presented a range of wines that confirms the high level of quality we have come to expect from this winery. The white Callas 2005, made from malvasia grapes, is aged on the yeasts for six months in stainless steel vats. Fresh grassy aromas dominate the nose, while the equally fruity and fresh palate has balanced structure streaked through with nicely judged acidity. Nabucco 2004, the winery's flagship wine, is a 70-30 blend of barbera and merlot aged in barriques for 12 months. It lacks a little of the oomph that took it to the Three Glass finals last year but is still elegant and characterful with considerable structure and a prevalently fruity palate where solid tannins add a slightly astringent feel to the finish. The Monte delle Vigne Rosso, from barbera and bonarda, has rather a closed nose and a fresh-tasting, medium-textured palate with a refreshing, nicely lingering finale. Turning to the sparkling wines, the Lambrusco 2005 has a nice vein of acidity that keeps it fresh through the palate while the Colli di Parma Rosso 2005 has upfront fruit and lively continuous prickle.

● Nabucco '04	2 black glasses	5
○ Callas Malvasia '05	2 black glasses	5
● Colli di Parma Rosso Monte delle Vigne '05	1 black glass	4
● Colli di Parma Rosso Frizzante '05	1 black glass	3
● Lambrusco '05	1 black glass	3
● Nabucco '03	2 white glasses	5
● Nabucco '01	2 white glasses	5
● Nabucco '02	2 white glasses	5
● Monte delle Vigne Rosso '04	2 white glasses	4

CORIANO (RN)

SAN PATRIGNANO
VIA SAN PATRIGNANO, 53
47852 CORIANO (RN)
TEL. 0541362362
www.sanpatrignano.org

At San Patrignano, the focal value is the individual, around whom all things on the estate rotate. Naturally enough, heavy investment has been made on human skills, with one of the best teams around. Federico Rainero is in charge of non-domestic sales, Piero Prenna coordinates marketing for wine and food products, Stefano Bariani runs public relations, agronomist Roberto Dragoni manages the 100-plus hectares of vineyards, Mario Monaco is cellar manager and Luca Marcheselli looks after all farming and food processing activities, including milk and meat. There is also external consultancy from winemaker Riccardo Cotarella and agronomists Marco Simonit and Pierpaolo Sirch. Andrea Muccioli's well thought-out project for the estate focuses as ever on absolute quality. It was unsurprising, then, that three wines reached the Three Glass finals nor should it astonish anyone that our highest accolade was won by Noi 2004, from 60 per cent sangiovese with equal parts of cabernet and merlot. A wonderfully balanced, elegant wine, it is austere, dark and deep though to the pencil lead-nuanced aromas and complex, fruity palate. Montepirolo 2003 and Avi 2003 pay the price for the very hot year. The former is a classic Bordeaux blend with close-knit, austere aromas and a robust, unbending palate with sound, fresh fruit. Avi is a modern, warm Sangiovese with a very well defined, smooth palate.

● Colli di Rimini Rosso Noi '04	3 black glasses	6
● Colli di Rimini Cabernet Montepirolo '03	2 black glasses	6
● Sangiovese di Romagna Sup. Avi Ris. '03	2 black glasses	6
● Aulente Sangiovese '05	2 black glasses	4*
○ Vintàn '05	2 black glasses	4*
● Sangiovese di Romagna Sup. Avi Ris. '00	3 white glasses	6
● Colli di Rimini Cabernet Montepirolo '01	3 white glasses	6
● Sangiovese di Romagna Sup. Avi Ris. '01	3 white glasses	6
● Montepirolo '99	3 white glasses	6

CORIANO (RN)

Tenuta Santini

Fraz. Passano
via Campo, 33
47853 Coriano (RN)
tel. 0541656527
www.tenutasantini.com

The Rimini area is a Bolgheri in miniature where cabernet sauvignon and merlot find a fresh, elegant expression that is both appealing and complex. The nearby sea warms the colder days and tempers the hotter ones with a constant salty breeze that blows over the beautiful rolling hills of an area that has the landscape of Marche but Romagna's language and culture. Tenuta Santini is the southernmost quality winery and is very near to San Patrignano, so close that it shares certain characteristics. The winery is run by Sandro Santini, who generously dedicates his energy, passion and a great deal of time to the project, along with winemaker Lorenzo Landi and agronomist Remigio Bordini. The merlot and cabernet sauvignon Battarreo 2004 made it to the Three Glass finals. It is the winery's most impressive wine, with generous, sound and chewy fruit on the deep, attractive nose and a soft-flavoured, fruity palate with plenty of velvety texture that lingers unhurriedly. The Cornelianum 2004 from sangiovese reflects the features of the area in a profile that is smooth and mouthfilling rather than complex. This version lacks a little texture, which shortens the palate enough to highlight the slight dryness in the finish. Lastly, the Sangiovese Beato Enrico 2005 is a simpler wine with a warm, alluring and very fruity nose, although slightly penalized by the difficult vintage.

● Battarreo '04	🍷🍷	4*
● Sangiovese di Romagna Sup. Cornelianum Ris. '04	🍷🍷	5
● Sangiovese di Romagna Sup. Beato Enrico '05	🍷	4
● Battarreo '03	♡♡	4
● Sangiovese di Romagna Sup. Cornelianum Ris. '03	♡♡	5

FAENZA (RA)

Leone Conti

loc. Santa Lucia
via Pozzo, 1
48018 Faenza (RA)
tel. 0546642149
www.leoneconti.it

Leone Conti runs his winery with his partner Coral McGill, and his work can be viewed as a creative, even poetic, exploration that may linger on various aspects according to the stimuli that the sensitive Leone picks up. This sensitivity is shared by Coral, and her contribution is important not least because of the contrast she is able to provide. The winery's production is very diverse but there is a clear tendency to experiment and work with native grape varieties, from centesimino to longanesi and uva ruggine. The most interesting wine we tasted for this edition of the Guide was the centesimino-based Arcolaio 2004, a project close to Leone and Coral's hearts. The aromatic nose led by candied fruit and roses is followed by a vibrant, flavoursome, palate of balance and depth. The Albana Progetto 1 2005 is also very interesting for it is dynamic, with grapefruit and pineapple-led fruit and a fresh, lingering palate. Lastly, a couple of words about the Le Goduriose project, which winemaker Giancarlo Soverchia is working on with this winery. The idea is to enhance the wine with extended contact with the fine lees. Unfortunately, the wines often seem to emerge a little tired with evolved sensations that disturb the clarity of the nose. For example, this is the case with Il Mio Sangiovese 2003.

● Arcolaio '04	🍷🍷	5
○ Albana di Romagna Secco Progetto 1 '05	🍷🍷	4*
● Arcolaio Le Goduriose '03	🍷	5
● Sangiovese di Romagna Il Mio Sangiovese '03	🍷	6
● Colli di Faenza Rosso Le Ghiande '04	🍷	4
● Sangiovese di Romagna Sup. Le Betulle '04	🍷	4
○ Trebbiano di Romagna '05	🍷	3
● Arcolaio '03	♡♡	5
● RossoNero '03	♡♡	5
○ Tu Chiamale se Vuoi Emozioni Lato B '03	♡♡	6

FAENZA (RA)

PAOLO FRANCESCONI
LOC. SARNA
VIA TULIERO, 154
48018 FAENZA (RA)
TEL. 054643213

Few people interpret Romagna better than Paolo Francesconi. This is rich farming country with a generous production fabric woven from mainly small, enthusiastic enterprises. It is a culture in which new philosophies are beginning to emerge, focusing on gathering the fruits of the earth without disturbing its balance. So it is no coincidence that it was here that, a few years ago, Paolo decided to put his project into operation and began to make wine in compliance with the principles of organic farming. The heterodox route he chose was challenging so unsurprisingly there have occasionally been little moments of uncertainty and modest flaws, but they have not compromised the overall quality of Paolo's products. That is probably what we are now seeing this year. The price for the naturalness of the wines is aromas that are not perfectly sound and require further attention. This distinctive feature can be seen, for example, in the winery's leading product, the merlot-based Impavido 2004. Careful tasting does, however, reveal the great qualities of this wine, including rich extract, and therefore very dense texture, backed up by smooth tannins in a context of chewy, elegant softness, where a lovely hint of cherry fruit stands out. The sturdy Sangiovese Riserva Le Iadi 2004 is enriched by stylish oak while the slimmer Limbecca 2005 is dry, consistent and fruity.

●	Impavido Merlot '04	▼▼	5
●	Sangiovese di Romagna Sup. Le Iadi Ris. '04	▼▼	5
●	Sangiovese di Romagna Sup. Limbecca '05	▼▼	3*
●	Colli di Faenza Rosso Miniato '04	▼	4
●	Impavido Merlot '03	▽▽	5
●	Sangiovese di Romagna Sup. Le Iadi Ris. '03	▽▽	4
●	Impavido Merlot '02	▽▽	5

FAENZA (RA)

ANTONIO GALLEGATI
VIA ISONZO, 4
48018 FAENZA (RA)
TEL. 0546621149
www.aziendaagricolagallegati.it

Many small wineries, like this one owned by the Gallegati brothers, are currently flourishing in the Faenza area. Cesare and Antonio Gallegati are particularly well prepared with two degrees in agriculture and one in oenology between them, great sensitivity and motivation. The resulting knowledge is a resource for the whole Faenza area. The Gallegati project begins in the vineyards and the vegetative balance of the plants is the mainstay of their wines, which are always well made since they always come from fine quality grapes. The vineyards are situated in the Senio and Lamone valleys in the hills marked by ravines, a typical geological feature of this clay-rich area. The Sangiovese Corallo Nero 2004 is very elegant and fresh-tasting, beautifully put together, broad and mature. The lovely varietal character of the nose gives way to a supple palate with good follow-through. The Albana Passito Regina di Cuori 2004 gave an excellent performance. It was the first wine to be released in Romagna in the new Riserva category. The grapes come from a 40-year-old vineyard that was patiently recovered and the wine maintains the varietal features of the albana grape in combination with extraordinary complexity on the nose of quinces, dried figs, dates, apricots, spices, thyme. The palate is perfectly dry, concentrated and lingering with an echo of the aromas in the finish, which fades to allow the rich fruit to emerge. Corallo Rosso is no longer included on the winery list. At one time it was their second-label Sangiovese but now the Gallegatis have stopped making it.

○	Albana di Romagna Passito Regina di Cuori Ris. '04	▼▼	6
●	Sangiovese di Romagna Sup. Corallo Nero '04	▼▼	5
●	Sangiovese di Romagna Sup. Corallo Nero '03	▽▽	5
○	Colli di Faenza Bianco Corallo Bianco '04	▽▽	4
●	Sangiovese di Romagna Sup. Corallo Rosso '04	▽▽	4

FAENZA (RA)

PODERI MORINI
LOC. ORIOLO DEI FICHI
VIA GESUITA
48018 FAENZA (RA)
TEL. 0546634257

There was a tiny stop on the road for Alessandro Morini, driven by the decision to make top-quality wines. Many other decisions have followed, including extensive work on facilities, investment in technological equipment and a focus on native, even obsolete, grape varieties. This year's pause should not discourage. In fact, it's an opportunity to contemplate a future that can only get better. A platitude? Anything but, judging by the winery's most interesting product, a dried-grape red with an evocative name, Rubacuori (heartbreaker), made from centesimino grapes which are known hereabouts by the name of sâvignon rosso. The 2004 is a silky, dense-textured wine with stylish hints of dried figs and candied fruit. Its sweetness is anything but cloying and is backed up by smooth tannins on a soft, mouthfilling palate. Nonno Rico 2003 is an old-school Sangiovese with a mature, sturdy flavour in which blackberries, plums and cherries all feature. The remaining reds are not up to the standards of previous versions. The Nadèl 2003, a blend of sangiovese, merlot, longanesi and centesimino, is a little too mature, its weighty body a little overwhelmed by the oak in the finish. The two wines from sâvignon rosso share pleasant hints of varietal roses. Ilsavignone 2005 is rather predictable but the Traicolli 2004 has a sturdier, firmer structure. Lastly, we would mention a good Trebbiano, Brivido 2005, which is fresh-tasting and well balanced.

●	Rubacuori da Uve Stramature '04	🍷🍷	5
●	Sangiovese di Romagna Sup. Nonno Rico Ris. '03	🍷🍷	5
●	Augusto '03	🍷	4
●	Nadèl '03	🍷	5
●	Stravizio Merlot '04	🍷	4
●	Traicolli '04	🍷	5
○	Albana di Romagna Secco Sette Note '05	🍷	3
●	Ilsavignone '05	🍷	4
●	Sangiovese di Romagna Sup. Beccafico '05	🍷	3
○	Trebbiano di Romagna Brivido '05	🍷	3
●	Traicolli '03	🍷🍷 (white)	5

FAENZA (RA)

TRERÈ
LOC. ZONA MONTICORALLI
VIA CASALE, 19
48018 FAENZA (RA)
TEL. 054647034
www.trere.com

Wine is a strange thing. A winery of proven quality, supported by input from skilled consultants, is not always able to overcome the obstacles of unfavourable weather. Yet the impossibility of complete control is one of the reasons for wine's infinite charm. It is probably also the explanation for the situation at the winery owned by Morena Treré, whose willingness to work hard and strive for the best are beyond question. The wines presented this year, which is definitely something of a parenthesis, lack some of the subtler, more typical features that boost their charm and give them more personality: rich fruity pulp, subtle hints of peaches in the reds and sweet freshness in the whites. It's a parenthesis, as we said, but certainly not all negative. The Sangiovese Riserva Amarcord d'un Ross 2004 holds its own against past versions with plenty of appeal in its purple colour, rich extract and soft, mouthfillingly sweet plum, cherry and blackberry fruit. The long flavour is appropriate for such an austere, noble wine. The flavoursome, dense Montecorallo 2004 is a pleasant blend of cabernet, merlot and sangiovese. It does not lack texture although its generosity and strength find a less than loyal ally in the oak, which dries out the finish. The youthful Sangiovese Renero 2005 has a full-bodied, fleshy palate with distinctive ripe red berry fruit. The Sperone is a simpler, less powerful standard-label Sangiovese with good balance.

●	Colli di Faenza Rosso Montecorallo Ris. '04	🍷🍷	4*
●	Sangiovese di Romagna Amarcord d'un Ross Ris. '04	🍷🍷	4*
○	Colli di Faenza Rebianco '05	🍷	3
●	Colli di Faenza Sangiovese Renero '05	🍷	4
●	Sangiovese di Romagna Sup. Sperone '05	🍷	3
●	Colli di Faenza Rosso Montecorallo Ris. '03	🍷🍷 (white)	4
●	Sangiovese di Romagna Amarcord d'un Ross Ris. '03	🍷🍷 (white)	4

FAENZA (RA)

★ FATTORIA ZERBINA
FRAZ. MARZENO
VIA VICCHIO, 11
48018 FAENZA (RA)
TEL. 054640022
www.zerbina.com

Sometimes the impact of a winery is so positive that it enriches a whole area with its quality, consistency and continuity. This is true of Fattoria Zerbina, and Cristina Geminani, who has given so much – even more than she realizes – to Romagna and continues to do so. To Cristina, winemaking is a total commitment, the steady weaving of a network of exchanges, reasoning, comparisons, encounters – a route that has brought her very close to the boundaries of what a producer can do to interpret a specific area. Further proof of this is to be found in the ease with which the Marzieno 2003 has returned to the heights of Italian winemaking following the inevitable sacrifice of the 2002 vintage. This is a blend of sangiovese with small additions of cabernet and merlot. Tidy and low-key, it focuses directly on the texture of plentiful, stylish tannins and confidently austere fruit, with a dynamic palate and long finish. Welcome back to this wine and its splendid Three Glasses. The sweet Scacco Matto 2004 made from raisined albana grapes is also extraordinarily complex and deep with a nose that flows seamlessly and generously into the palate. Scacco Matto is only made in years when the grapes are attacked by noble rot and can be harvested in several passes. Torre di Ceparano 2004 also performed well It's an enjoyable wine from sangiovese grapes that reflects the winery's signature elegant style. Lastly the Sangiovese Pietramora 2004 was not presented because it was not regarded as ready for release yet.

● Marzieno '03	▼▼▼	6
○ Albana di Romagna Passito Scacco Matto '04	▼▼	7
● Sangiovese di Romagna Sup. Torre di Ceparano '04	▼▼	4*
○ Albana di Romagna Passito Arrocco '04	▼	6
● Sangiovese di Romagna Sup. Ceregio '05	▼	3
○ Trebbiano di Romagna Dalbiere '05	▼	3
● Marzieno '00	ΥΥΥ	6
● Marzieno '01	ΥΥΥ	6
● Sangiovese di Romagna Sup. Pietramora Ris. '03	ΥΥΥ	7

FORLÌ

STEFANO BERTI
LOC. RAVALDINO IN MONTE
VIA LA SCAGNA, 18
47100 FORLÌ
TEL. 0543488074

Stefano Berti is exactly what we all imagine a winegrower to be. He works his few hectares of vineyards alone, trusting in the growing year and the land without forcing things, working calmly in the knowledge that each of the many years ahead will have something to teach him. The well-established style reflected in the cellar's two wines owes a great deal to Stefano's philosophy of respecting the fruits of the land and the constancy of Ravaldo and Calisto is the most tangible proof of this. Differences pertaining to the vintage aside, both wines are mellow and expressive with plenty of texture, thrust, depth and fruit. The extraordinary Calisto 2004 made it to our final tastings for its outstanding quality. The massive extract and powerful fruit are handled with such beautiful balance that the wine is simply elegant with chewy, dark, velvety fruit pulp. The supple character of the long, eloquent palate is in no way inhibited by its alcoholic fullness. The less complicated Ravaldo 2005 perfectly reflects the cool, problematic growing year with a lighter palate than previous editions, although it is nicely put together with good texture leading to quite a long finish.

● Sangiovese di Romagna Sup. Calisto '04	▼▼	5
● Sangiovese di Romagna Sup. Ravaldo '05	▼▼	4*
● Sangiovese di Romagna Sup. Calisto '01	ΥΥΥ	5
● Sangiovese di Romagna Sup. Calisto '03	ΥΥ	5
● Sangiovese di Romagna Sup. Calisto '00	ΥΥ	5

FORLÌ

CALONGA

LOC. CASTIGLIONE
VIA CASTEL LEONE, 8
47100 FORLÌ
TEL. 0543753044

The fact that so many leading wineries can now count on skilled consultants, well-organized vineyards and well-equipped cellars means that in years to come it will be location that makes the difference. Maurizio Baravelli's winery holds a very important position in this geography of quality built on land and site climate. The characteristics of the place combine with the contribution of human endeavour – Maurizio's vineyard management is very careful. In this area, the sangiovese grape acquired extraordinary complexity and virtues, interpreting the vintage exceptional coherence. Given his context, the ease with which Sangiovese Michelangiolo Riserva 2003 picked up its Three Glasses is unsurprising. Deep and flavoursome, with impressively dense texture and bags of character, it is a wonderful interpretation of the sangiovese grape and this special terroir. An extremely clean profile and warm austerity exalt its depth and the excellent raw material is confidently handled. The immense but soft palate opens out very slowly, closing on yet more aromas and fullness in the finale. The Albana Secco 2005 made its debut this year. It comes from a courageous choice by winemaker Fabrizio Moltard. Fermented without any sulphur at all, it is designed to mature gradually over time. The complex nose is subtly, elegantly balanced while the palate is dry and velvety, warm and mature, with good length. Lastly, the sangiovese-based Ordelaffo 2004 is well made with a fresh, approachable palate.

● Sangiovese di Romagna Sup. Michelangiolo Ris. '03	🍷🍷🍷	5
○ Albana di Romagna Secco '05	🍷🍷	4*
● Ordelaffo Sangiovese '04	🍷	4
● Castellione Cabernet Sauvignon '01	🍷🍷	6
● Sangiovese di Romagna Sup. Michelangiolo Ris. '01	🍷🍷	6
● Castellione Cabernet Sauvignon '00	🍷🍷	6
● Sangiovese di Romagna Sup. Michelangiolo Ris. '00	🍷🍷	6

FORLÌ

DREI DONÀ TENUTA LA PALAZZA

LOC. MASSA DI VECCHIAZZANO
VIA DEL TESORO, 23
47100 FORLÌ
TEL. 0543769371
www.dreidona.it

In Romagna, the various sangiovese terroirs are gradually acquiring precise identities but to bring them out, the wine must be interpreted in a way that does not mask the deeper contribution of the land. Claudio and Enrico Drei Donà represent the determined, skilled type of wine producers who can provide an accurate interpretation of both territory and vintage every year. Once again their best results come from the Sangioveses, especially the Pruno 2003, which has maintained its varietally austere, profound style despite the difficult hot growing year. The nose is almost hesitant, with plenty of alcohol acting as a barrier, but it opens out to reveal a wealth of fruit and well-measured spice leading to a mature, nicely made and very long palate built around close-knit tannins that do not intrude. The sangiovese Notturno 2004, one of the region's best wines in terms of value for money, also gave a good performance. Expressive on the nose, it has a nicely constructed palate and a broad, lingering finish, although slightly dried by tannins. The Cabernet Sauvignon Magnificat 2003 is full-bodied and dynamic. Its slightly rigid nose is dominated by fresh red berry fruit while the lingering, dense palate is backed up by plenty of tannins that prolong the very characterful finish. The Chardonnay Il Tornese 2004 has good texture and is more in balanced style than previous versions, while the time-defying Graf Noir 2000 is sharp, accurate and close-knit with good follow-through on the palate and a slightly rugged finish.

● Magnificat Cabernet Sauvignon '03	🍷🍷	5
● Sangiovese di Romagna Sup. Pruno Ris. '03	🍷🍷	5
● Graf Noir '00	🍷🍷	8
○ Il Tornese Chardonnay '04	🍷🍷	5
● Notturno Sangiovese '04	🍷🍷	4*
○ Varenne '05	🍷	3
● Sangiovese di Romagna Sup. Pruno Ris. '00	🍷🍷🍷	5
● Sangiovese di Romagna Sup. Pruno Ris. '01	🍷🍷🍷	5
● Magnificat Cabernet Sauvignon '94	🍷🍷🍷	6

GAZZOLA (PC)

LURETTA
LOC. CASTELLO DI MOMELIANO
29010 GAZZOLA (PC)
TEL. 0523971070 - 0523971589
www.luretta.com

Lucio Salamini's estate of over 50 hectares is divided into four separate plots, part in Val Luretta and part in Val Nure. One wine accounts for just under half the total annual production of over 200,000 bottles, the pleasant and uncomplicated Spumante Principessa, made from chardonnay and trebbiano grapes. This is a modern interpretation of the traditional sparkling wines which undergo a second fermentation in bottle. The new spumante, called On Attend les Invités, is in a different class. Obtained from pinot nero grapes from the 2001 vintage, it is what the French call a "rosé de saignée", a sparkling rosé whose colour is not obtained from the addition of red wine during disgorgement but from contact of the must with the skins. The faint onionskin colour is enlivened by creamy foam and subtle aromas of red berry fruit enhance the dynamic palate with its tangy edge. The winery also presented two whites, the varietal Sauvignon I Nani and Le Ballerine 2005, which lacks the powerful aromas of the 2004 but progresses stylishly and coherently, and Malvasia Boccadirosa 2005, which flaunts well-defined aromas and a fruity palate of exemplary balance. Among the reds, the Pinot Nero Achab 2004 stands out for its crushed red fruit, glossy tannins and soft flavour progression. The Cabernet Sauvignon Corbeau 2004 is impressively broad and sound but less gutsy than previous vintages, while after six months ageing in barrique, the Barbera Carabas 2005 has florality in a fresh-tasting structure.

⊙	C. P. Brut On Attend les Invités '01	ΥΥ	5
●	C. P. Cabernet Sauvignon Corbeau '04	ΥΥ	7
●	C. P. Pinot Nero Achab '04	ΥΥ	6
○	C. P. Malvasia Boccadirosa '05	ΥΥ	4*
○	C. P. Sauvignon I Nani e Le Ballerine '05	ΥΥ	4*
●	C. P. Barbera Carabas '05	Υ	5
○	Principessa Brut	Υ	4
●	C. P. Cabernet Sauvignon Corbeau '00	ΥΥΥ	6
●	C. P. Cabernet Sauvignon Corbeau '03	ΥΥ	6
○	C. P. Malvasia Dolce Le Rane '04	ΥΥ	6

IMOLA (BO)

TENUTA CA' LUNGA
VIA CA' LUNGA BUORE, 5
40026 IMOLA (BO)
TEL. 0542609257
www.tenutacalunga.it

Paolo Cassetta is certainly not a man who lacks passion. He has relaunched the winery owned by his family since the 1960s and under his enthusiastic management, the 19 hectares of vineyards have begun to turn out undeniably excellent products. Some of the credit must go to agronomist Remigio Bordini and winemaker Lorenzo Landi, as well as the crucial contribution of Paolo's father, Angelo. Paolo is, above all, someone who knows how to learn. He is sure to get the most out of this year's wine and they show good continuity with the recent past. The Sangiovese Incantesimo 2005 is perhaps not quite as complex as other recent versions but it is uncomplicated, fruit-forward and has good texture. The very interesting Sangiovese Riserva Regale reveals all its strength with good, strong flavour. The aromas are more than typical, ranging from blackberries to cherries, and the excellent structure is harmonious and well-balanced, with a cheeky hint of charred oak. The Imperius 2004 is made from cabernet sauvignon and aged for some time in small oak barrels. The aromas are a little closed but the palate is subtle, very stylish, complex and flavoursome. If it lacks anything, it is the extra length to match its lovely softness. The typical features of the chardonnay-based Euforia 2005 are balance, freshness and cleanness while the Diadema 2005 is a subtler and more graceful blend of chardonnay and sauvignon.

●	Colli d'Imola Cabernet Sauvignon Imperius Ris. '04	ΥΥ	5
●	Colli d'Imola Sangiovese Regale Ris. '04	ΥΥ	5
●	Colli d'Imola Sangiovese Incantesimo '05	ΥΥ	3*
○	Colli d'Imola Bianco Euforia '05	Υ	3
○	Colli d'Imola Bianco Sup. Diadema '05	Υ	4
●	Colli d'Imola Cabernet Sauvignon Imperius Ris. '03	ΥΥ	5
●	Colli d'Imola Sangiovese Regale Ris. '03	ΥΥ	5
●	Sangiovese di Romagna Sup. Mistero '04	ΥΥ	4

IMOLA (BO)

Fattoria Monticino Rosso

via Montecatone, 7
40026 Imola (BO)
tel. 054240577 - 054242687
www.fattoriadelmonticinorosso.it

Brothers Gianni and Luciano Zeoli are one of the few examples from Romagna of premium-quality producers who have succeeded in making the move up from farming. Their links with the land and territory are obvious from the large and loyal clientele who buy still buy their wine unbottled for everyday use at table. The estate has a total of 20 hectares of vineyards, all modern in conception and managed with the greatest care and commitment. Since 2000, Gianni and Luciano have also worked with consultant winemaker Giancarlo Soverchia, who has prompted them to follow a path that is leading to excellent results today. This area, one of the most northerly in Romagna, is particularly well-suited to growing albana grapes and it was the Albana Codronchio 2004 that took the winery to the Three Glass finals this year. The grapes used in this wine are harvested late so they can botrytize. The wine is very broad, complex and almost citrus-like on the nose, which introduces a buttery, fresh and very tangy palate with a lingering, slightly bitterish finish. The Albana 2005 is also good, impressive and authentic. There was a fine performance from the stylish Albana Passito 2003, with its well-measured sweetness, and the Riserva di Cabernet Sauvignon 2003, which is tasty and dynamic on the palate despite slightly heavy fruit. The other wines in the wide range are all good and well typed.

○	Albana di Romagna Secco Codronchio '04	YY	4*
○	Albana di Romagna Passito '03	YY	5
●	Colli d'Imola Cabernet Sauvignon Pradello Ris. '03	YY	5
○	Albana di Romagna Secco '05	YY	3*
○	Malvasia Passito '02	Y	5
●	Sangiovese di Romagna Sup. '04	Y	3
○	Colli d'Imola Pignoletto '05	Y	2
●	Colli d'Imola Cabernet Sauvignon Pradello '03	YY (white)	4
●	Sangiovese di Romagna Sup. Le Morine '03	YY (white)	4

IMOLA (BO)

Tre Monti

loc. Bergullo
via Lola, 3
40026 Imola (BO)
tel. 0542657116
www.tremonti.it

Solid roots are the Navacchia family's strength. Unshaken by events, the family steadfastly continues its quest for well-built quality without recourse to shortcuts. Their experience has become a benchmark for the whole area and is an added value for the winery's projects. The estate, which has grown steadily, is now embarking on a major new project: to completely renew the 26 hectares of vineyards at Petrignone, in the hills between Faenza and Forlì. The Navacchias also own almost 30 hectares around the winery in the Imola hills, which are to be planted with new red grape vines. Vittorio Navacchia and his wife Roberta, who are in charge of vinification, can be very satisfied with the two reds, which both made it to the Three Glass finals. Although Vittorio is usually considered a white wine specialist, he showed himself on this occasion to be proficient in both types. The Sangiovese Thea 2004 is a very stylish wine with a personal style that has been coherently expressed over the years in a tangy supple palate with a good lingering finish. The Sangiovese Riserva 2003 is both subtle and deep, with a well-balanced, pleasantly authentic style that is territory-driven and opens up new horizons for Romagna. The standard-label whites, in their different styles, are all excellent as usual. The Chardonnay Ciardo is very international, fruity and creamy, while the sauvignon and chardonnay Salcerella is attractively aromatic and the Albana Vigna della Rocca is assertive.

●	Sangiovese di Romagna Sup. Ris. '03	YY	4*
●	Sangiovese di Romagna Sup. Thea '04	YY	5
○	Albana di Romagna Passito '04	YY	5
○	Colli d'Imola Chardonnay Ciardo '05	YY	4
○	Colli d'Imola Salcerella '05	YY	5
●	Colli d'Imola Boldo '04	Y	5
○	Colli d'Imola Thea '04	Y	5
○	Albana di Romagna Secco Vigna della Rocca '05	Y	3
○	Trebbiano di Romagna Vigna del Rio '05	Y	4
●	Colli d'Imola Boldo '03	Y (white)	5

MODENA

Chiarli 1860

via Daniele Manin, 15
41100 Modena
tel. 0593163311
www.chiarli.it

This large historic Lambrusco winery has produced 24,000,000 bottles since it was founded by Cleto Chiarli back in 1860. Let's begin our analysis with a newcomer to the range, the Pignoletto Spumante Cletò. We liked its ripe peach aromas, creamy foam and long, soft flavour with nice fruity sensations that linger on the palate. It's another hunch that has paid off for the Chiarli brothers, with their shrewd entrepreneurial skill for protecting traditions and their willingness to adapt to the market's ever-changing demands. They have luck on their side in the winery's longstanding winemaker, Franco De Biasio, who has extensive experience in sparkling wine production. At last, a Lambrusco di Sorbara has been awarded Two Glasses and we know how happy this will make the Chiarli brothers, who are particularly fond of the type. The Vecchia Modena Premium 2005 is subtle and stylish, as tradition dictates, but also tangy and mouthfilling. Nivola, one of the winery's leading bottles, is not a typical Lambrusco. Fairly subdued in its effervescence, it has smooth glossy tannins and a generous texture that echoes the vibrant cherry aromas on the nose. But Grasparossa Vigneto Enrico Cialdini is a very traditional Lambrusco with a floral nose, dry palate and nice satisfying finish. Finally, we enjoyed the Lambrusco del Fondatore 2004, made using the traditional procedure of second fermentation in bottle without disgorgement. The palate is rustic but clean and a nice vein of acidity lengthens the flavour.

●	Nivola Lambrusco Scuro '05	🍷🍷	2*
●	Lambrusco di Sorbara Vecchia Modena Premium MH '05	🍷🍷	3*
●	Lambrusco Grasparossa di Castelvetro Vign. Enrico Cialdini '05	🍷🍷	3*
○	Pignoletto Extra Dry Cletò	🍷🍷	3*
●	Lambrusco di Sorbara del Fondatore '04	🍷	3
●	Lambrusco Grasparossa di Castelvetro Pruno Nero '05	🍷	3
●	Lambrusco Grasparossa di Castelvetro Villa Cialdini '05	🍷	3
●	Lambrusco Grasparossa di Castelvetro Amabile Centenario	🍷	2

MODENA

Villa di Corlo

loc. Baggiovara
s.da Cavezzo, 200
41100 Modena
tel. 059510736
www.villadicorlo.com

The far-sighted, highly professional project that Maria Antonia Munari Giacobazzi began some time ago in the Reggio hills is taking shape. The two different vineyards of the Cà del Vento estate, both situated at 300 to 500 metres above sea level, are organically farmed. They are now fully productive, and the wines are meticulously made and well defined. Giaco di Viano 2004, from cabernet sauvignon with small quantities of cabernet franc and merlot, is soft yet austere in style, with strong aromas of garden vegetables on the nose and ripe fruit on a palate that builds to a crescendo in a finish veined with spice and vanilla. The estate's second wine, Gelsomoro di Viano 2005, was not considered ready so we will review it in next year's Guide. Meanwhile the 25 hectares of vineyards on the Baggiovara estate in the Modena countryside continue to yield good lambrusco grapes for the Grasparossa di Castelvetro, which is rather hard and sharp in flavour, the new Lambrusco Rosso Estella, with fresh cherries on the nose, subtle fruit and good acidity on the palate, and the slimmer-built Lambrusco di Sorbara, which is fresh and delicately fruity on the nose and has good breadth and acidity in the mouth. The Corleto 2005 is an unusual Lambrusco. It's always better a year after the harvest and improves even more after ageing in bottle. The structure is rigid, tannic and very dense.

●	Giaco di Viano '04	🍷🍷	4
●	Corleto Lambrusco '05	🍷🍷	3*
●	Lambrusco di Sorbara '05	🍷	3
●	Rosso Estella Lambrusco '05	🍷	3
●	Lambrusco Grasparossa di Castelvetro '05		3
●	Corleto Lambrusco '04	ΥΥ	3

MODIGLIANA (FC)

Castelluccio

Loc. Poggiolo
via Tramonto, 15
47015 Modigliana (FC)
tel. 0546942486
www.ronchidicastelluccio.it

Castelluccio was founded in 1974 at the initiative of Gian Vittorio Baldo. He and Vittorio Fiore had envisaged something that seemed very unlikely at the time – a great red wine produced in Romagna. Castelluccio soon became a front-rank cellar whose history has been both extraordinary and troubled but after each setback, it has found its way back on course, as if guided by the sheer quality of the project. Today, the Fiore family runs the winery. Vittorio's son Claudio is directly involved, as is his wife Veruska, and in recent years they have been carrying out a revolution, replanting the vineyards and increasing capacity while at the same time working on the wines to raise the winery's image. The leading bottles are modern and well-made, although the 2003 vintage seems to lack the cellar's distinctive deep relationship with the local area and tradition. The austere Ronco dei Ciliegi 2003, made entirely from sangiovese grapes, is nicely put together and well structured, if more eloquent on the palate than on the nose. Its twin, Ronco delle Ginestre 2003, is stiffer and offers impressive fruit but is a little dry. The deliciously spicy, mouthfilling Massicone 2003, a blend of sangiovese and cabernet, is international in style while Ronco del Re 2004 from, sauvignon aged in wood, is light and varietal.

● Massicone '03	🍷🍷	6
● Ronco dei Ciliegi '03	🍷🍷	6
● Ronco delle Ginestre '03	🍷🍷	6
○ Ronco del Re '04	🍷	6
● Sangiovese di Romagna Le More '05	🍷	4
● Ronco dei Ciliegi '00	YYY	6
● Massicone '01	YYY	6
● Ronco dei Ciliegi '02	YYY	6
● Ronco delle Ginestre '90	YYY	6
● Ronco delle Ginestre '01	YY	6

MODIGLIANA (FC)

Villa Papiano

via Ibola, 24
47015 Modigliana (FC)
tel. 0546941790
www.villapapiano.it

Villa Papiano is located at about 500 metres above sea level, making it one of the highest in Romagna, and the vines benefit from good temperature variation and the beautiful, unspoilt natural environment. Agronomist Remigio Bordini, with his plentiful experience and knowledge of Romagna, with consultant winemaker Lorenzo Landi, helped here by the promising young Francesco Bordini, have helped Villa Papiano gradually establish itself as a firmly rooted, well-run winery that will also be able to rack up the number of bottles released when all the vineyards become productive. The wines offer a good interpretation of the features of the Modigliana area. They are generally austere, elegant and rich in tidily expressed fruit and tannin. Remigio Bordini, who has planted vineyards in every corner of Romagna, believed in this beautiful spot because he wanted to take up the challenge of a complicated area that could offer exceptional expressions of the sangiovese grape. And Sangiovese Riserva I Probi di Papiano 2003 reached our Three Glass finals. Close-knit and well-balanced, it has a long fruity finish. A lot of energy and expectations have been invested in the Tregenda 2004, made from raisined albana grapes. It gave a good performance, showing quite complex on the nose, which extends to aromas of candied fruit, and a well-balanced palate, which is slightly dry and fairly sweet.

● Sangiovese di Romagna I Probi di Papiano Ris. '03	🍷🍷	4*
○ Tregenda '04	🍷🍷	5
● Papiano di Papiano '02	YY	6
● Papiano di Papiano '03	YY	6
● Sangiovese di Romagna I Probi di Papiano Ris. '02	YY	4
● Sangiovese di Romagna Le Papesse di Papiano '04	YY	4

MONTE SAN PIETRO (BO)

TENUTA BONZARA

VIA SAN CHIERLO, 37A
40050 MONTE SAN PIETRO (BO)
TEL. 0516768324 - 051225772
www.bonzara.it

The torrid summer of 2003 was anything but favourable for the grapes that went into Cabernet Sauvignon Bonzarone. But despite the weather, the wine made it to the Three Glass final thanks to its usual rigid, austere style, with sound, flavoursome fruit, dense, nicely put-together structure and powerful, steady follow-through on the palate. It would certainly have won its third Glass, too, were it not for some slight weather-induced flaws. Credit goes to Mario Carboni, the winery's longstanding cellar manager, for turning out such a good wine in such a difficult year. Mario knows better than anyone how to farm and interpret the San Chierlo area, though his work undoubtedly benefits from the contributions of winemaker Lorenzo Landi, who shows amazing sensitivity in his reading of the wineries he works for. The Le Carrate 2005 was once again nominated the best Sauvignon in the region. The excellent location of the vineyards has endowed it with the varietal features of the grape, particularly assertive yet subtle sage and tomato leaves, as well as broad, juicy, well-coordinated structure. The Pignoletto Vigna Antica 205 is beautifully made with a confident, dry flavour and nice development. Lastly, there is a word of praise for the sauvignon-based Passito Û Pâsa, which made a particularly good impression thanks to an elegant, well-adjusted style enhanced by subtle hints of botrytis to intensify the complexity of the sweet, generously fruity pulp.

●	C. B. Cabernet Sauvignon Bonzarone '03	🍷🍷	5
○	C. B. Pignoletto Cl. Vigna Antica '05	🍷🍷	3*
○	Colli Bolognesi Sauvignon Le Carrate '05	🍷🍷	3*
○	Passito Û Pâsa	🍷🍷	4
●	C. B. Merlot Rosso del Poggio '04	🍷	4
○	Monte Severo '04	🍷	4
○	C. B. Pignoletto Frizzante '05	🍷	3
○	Angelo Lambertini Spumante	🍷	4
●	C. B. Cabernet Sauvignon Bonzarone '97	YYY	5

MONTE SAN PIETRO (BO)

ISOLA

FRAZ. MONGIORGIO
VIA G. BERNARDI, 3
40050 MONTE SAN PIETRO (BO)
TEL. 0516768428

It is unusual to find such a virtuous family relationship - in winemaking terms - as that shared by Marco Franceschini and his son Gianluca. While Marco represents the solid traditions and firmly rooted knowledge of a true country farming family, Gianluca has tried to place more emphasis on the relationship with the land, enriching it with innovative input. His growing interest in biodynamic farming techniques practices is no secret and Gianluca applies them to his own vineyards with excellent judgment and restraint, shunning blind adherence to the precepts of some sacred text and seeking to work out how to make the precepts fit his requirements. This particular aspect of the work is still at an early stage but will certainly lead to an improvement in the already high quality and authenticity of Isola wines. The Cabernet Sauvignon Monte Gorgii 2004 is initially rather closed and dark on the nose but soon opens out into ripe, sound fruit. The palate is even more generously fruity with a long velvety finish and the wine is a successful combination of full body and freshness, austerity and fruitiness. The Chardonnay Monte Gorgii 2005 has charming, clearly defined aromas of ripe peaches, pears and pineapple, in particular, and a soft, weighty palate with only a hint of dryness in the finish to signal ageing in barrique. The steel-fermented Chardonnay is uncomplicated and slightly vegetal while the Pignoletto Superiore 2005 has fleshy, stylish structure and the Frizzante 2005 is impressively lean and hard on the palate.

●	C. B. Cabernet Sauvignon Monte Gorgii '04	🍷🍷	4
○	C. B. Chardonnay Monte Gorgii '05	🍷🍷	4
○	C. B. Pignoletto Sup. '05	🍷🍷	3*
○	C. B. Chardonnay '05	🍷	3
○	C. B. Pignoletto Frizzante '05	🍷	3
●	Barbera Monte Gorgii '03	YY	4
○	C. B. Pignoletto Sup. '04	YY	3

MONTE SAN PIETRO (BO)

SANTAROSA
FRAZ. SAN MARTINO IN CASOLA
VIA SAN MARTINO, 82
40050 MONTE SAN PIETRO (BO)
TEL. 051969203
www.santarosavini.com

In the last few years, the wines produced by Giovanna Della Valentina have settled into a recognizable style that focuses on generous fruit and a modern overall feel. It may be that their bond with the territory is not so tightly forged and they are more open than other wines to echoing features from other regions or countries, with the necessary differences. An "international style" is how it is generally described in the wine world. Pignoletto aside, the products are made using the main three international grape varieties, cabernet sauvignon, merlot and chardonnay, so the strategy is perfectly understandable and also supported by consistently excellent results. In this round of tastings, the most interesting wine was the Merlot Giòtondo 2004, which is soft and creamy on the palate, rich in fruity sensations and has close-knit, forward tannins. The Cabernet Sauvignon Giòrosso 2004 has striking aromas of blackberries and blueberries that are almost too emphatic on the nose, but the rich fruit is dried and compressed on the palate by the oak in which the wine aged. This also gives the finish a sweetish flavour. The Santarosa Rosso 2005, from cabernet and merlot in equal quantities, is fresher and more approachable, with generous juicy fruit, and a very drinkable, nicely dynamic palate. The Chardonnay Giòcoliere 2005 has smoky, toasty aromas that mingle with the fruit while the Pignoletto 2005 has a soft enjoyable palate with a dry, bitterish finish.

●	C. B. Merlot Giòtondo '04	**YY**	4*
●	C. B. Cabernet Sauvignon Giòrosso '04	**YY**	4
○	C. B. Chardonnay Giòcoliere '05	**YY**	4
○	C. B. Pignoletto Cl. '05	**YY**	3*
●	Santarosa Rosso '05	**YY**	3*
●	C. B. Merlot Giòtondo '00	YYY	4
●	C. B. Cabernet Sauvignon Giòrosso '02	YY	4
●	C. B. Cabernet Sauvignon Giòrosso '03	YY	4
●	C. B. Merlot Giòtondo '03	YY	4

MONTEVEGLIO (BO)

CORTE D'AIBO
VIA MARZATORE, 15
40050 MONTEVEGLIO (BO)
TEL. 051832583
www.cortedaibo.it

Corte d'Aibo is a firmly established, professional winery which is earning itself an increasingly numerous list of admirers attracted by the good quality of the wines, as well as the guarantee that they are unadulterated – the vineyards have been organically farmed for some time. Year after year, Antonio Capelli in the vineyard and Mario Pirondini in the cellar have steadily eliminated the less impressive features of their wines, particularly in view of the fact that they have to face different problems every year, and we don't suppose they are planning to stop now. The Cabernet Sauvignon Orfeo is back to its high standard in the 2003 version, which made its way to the Three Glass finals. It's a hard, austere wine with firm, ripe fruit and nice complexity. After a confident entry on the palate, the finish is very long and enhanced with nice balsamic hints. The Merlot Roncovecchio 2004 is a little below par in comparison with other versions. It's well structured but a little too acidic, with rather grassy fruit. But the Cabernet Sauvignon Le Borre 2004 is very well typed and varietal with a tangy, dry, very lingering palate. Lastly, the Barbera Cucherla 2005 has fresh, well-crafted fruit, nicely managed acidity and a lingering flavour. It's a pity though that the oak is rather too forward on the nose.

●	C. B. Cabernet Sauvignon Orfeo Ris. '03	**YY**	6
●	C. B. Cabernet Sauvignon Le Borre '04	**YY**	4
●	C. B. Barbera Cucherla '05	**YY**	3*
●	C. B. Merlot Roncovecchio '04	**Y**	4
○	C. B. Sauvignon Spungola '05		3
●	C. B. Cabernet Sauvignon Orfeo Ris. '00	YY	6
●	C. B. Merlot Roncovecchio '03	YY	4
●	C. B. Cabernet Sauvignon Orfeo Ris. '01	YY	6
●	C. B. Cabernet Sauvignon Le Borre '03	YY	4

MONTEVEGLIO (BO)

Gradizzolo

via Invernata, 2
40050 Monteveglio (BO)
tel. 051830265
www.gradizzolo.it

When you are wandering through the Montebudello hills, it's easy to spot Antonio Ognibene's vineyards. Just head for the scrupulously tended, east-facing plots at altitudes of 200 to 300 metres where the vines are obviously treated well. Some of the vineyards are almost 40 years old and planted with barbera, the variety Antonio loves best and which he uses in various interpretations, all of which make the best of the grape's fruitiness and structure. So it's no surprise that the Barbera Riserva Garò 2003 gave an excellent performance, showing austere and well-structured as usual with healthy, creamy fruit and smooth, close-knit tannins that lead to a slightly dry finish. The Barbera Bricco dell'Invernata 2004 is similar in style, if less weighty, with fresh, well-judged fruit slightly obscured by sweeter sensations from the oak in which it aged. Still, this is an impressive wine with a good dynamic palate. The Merlot Calastrino 2004 is a little below par compared to previous versions. Despite the firm structure, it tends to be predictable on the palate with persistent grassy hints. Lastly, the idea of making a Spumante with pignoletto grapes is an intelligent one. Pign'Oro has a pleasantly fragrant, rounded, mature and dynamic flavour.

● C. B. Barbera Garò Ris. '03	🍷🍷	5
● C. B. Barbera Bricco dell'Invernata '04	🍷🍷	3*
● C. B. Merlot Calastrino '04	🍷	5
○ Pignoletto Spumante Pign'Oro	🍷	3
● Rovo Nero Cabernet Sauvignon '04		4
● C. B. Barbera Ris. '01	🍷🍷 (white)	4
● C. B. Merlot Calastrino '02	🍷🍷 (white)	4
● C. B. Barbera Bricco dell'Invernata '03	🍷🍷 (white)	3
● C. B. Merlot Calastrino '03	🍷🍷 (white)	4

MONTEVEGLIO (BO)

La Mancina

fraz. Montebudello
via Motta, 8
40050 Monteveglio (BO)
tel. 051832691
www.lamancina.it

Francesca Zanetti's is a confident, dynamic hand at the helm of the family winery. She is now focusing her efforts on necessary cellar renovations after extensive replanting of the vineyards. Now that these jobs are done, all the pieces of the puzzle have fallen into place and we can therefore expect a future improvement in the quality of the wines as a result. This may take a while, since we are all aware that haste is not helpful in winemaking, so we will just have to wait and hope. Further proof that our hopes are not unfounded lies in the presence of the talented Piedmontese winemaker Giandomenico Negro. Meanwhile we enjoyed the current wines. Let's begin with the most impressive. The Cabernet Sauvignon Comandante della Guardia 2004 has lovely generous, healthy fruit on the nose and a rounded, austere and hard but well-crafted palate. The Merlot Lanciotto 2005 has uncomplicated, fresh, well-balanced fruit and a persistently fragrant, nicely drinkable palate. The Barbera Il Foriere 2005, fermented in stainless steel and aged in large barrels, is very well typed but lacks weight and is not especially mouthfilling. The Pignoletto Frizzante 2005 Condivisibile is a little too hard and dry. The winery decided to delay release of the Pignoletto Terre di Montebudello 2005 to allow it sufficient ageing time, so you'll find it in next year's Guide.

● C. B. Cabernet Sauvignon Comandante della Guardia '04	🍷🍷	4
● C. B. Merlot Lanciotto '05	🍷🍷	3*
● C. B. Barbera Il Foriere '05	🍷	4
● C. B. Cabernet Sauvignon '05	🍷	4
○ C. B. Pignoletto Frizzante '05	🍷	3
⊙ Chiosa '05		4
● C. B. Cabernet Sauvignon Comandante della Guardia '01	🍷🍷 (white)	4
● C. B. Barbera Il Foriere '03	🍷🍷 (white)	3
● C. B. Cabernet Sauvignon Comandante della Guardia '03	🍷🍷 (white)	4

PIANORO (BO)

Podere Riosto
via di Riosto, 12
40065 Pianoro (BO)
tel. 051777109 - 051774888
www.podereriosto.it

The steady improvements noted in past editions of the Guide have helped propel this winery to a prestigious position on the regional scene. The whole Galletti family lends a hand running their winery, engineer Alessandro supervising the cellar and his energetic daughter Cristiana managing the rest, and the projects they have put in place are very professional. But how could they be otherwise? Look at the team of consultants on call: Federico Curtaz for vineyard management and Beppe Caviola and Giambattista Zanchetta in the cellar, one for reds and the other for whites. The 15 hectares of vineyards surround the cellar in an area which is almost entirely abandoned, despite its ancient grape-growing traditions. In fact, Podere Riosto is the only operative winery in the whole hillside area southeast of Bologna. The winery focuses its attention on the white pignoletto grape, an intelligent choice judging by the good results obtained. The Frizzante 2005 has good foam, generous aromas of fresh flowers and fruit and a well-crafted, nicely dry palate, while the Superiore Vigna della Torre 2005 has a floral nose with attractive hints of thyme and rosemary, followed by and a nice, satisfying flavour. Turning to the reds, we found the Barbera Vigna della Valle 2003 selection especially good, showing fruity and true to type with well-judged use of wood. The Merlot 2004 from the same vineyard is simple and very drinkable, although the finish is a little dry. The other products are all well crafted.

●	C. B. Barbera Sel. Vigna della Valle '03	🍷🍷	4
○	C. B. Pignoletto Frizzante Vigna della Torre '05	🍷🍷	3*
○	C. B. Pignoletto Sup. Vigna della Torre '05	🍷🍷	3*
●	C. B. Cabernet Sauvignon Sel. Vigna Bel Poggio '03	🍷	4
○	Stilla '03	🍷	5
●	C. B. Merlot Sel. Vigna della Valle '04	🍷	5
●	C. B. Barbera Frizzante Vigna della Valle '05	🍷	3
○	C. B. Sauvignon V. del Pino '05	🍷	4
●	C. B. Merlot Vigna della Valle '03	🍸🍸	4

PONTE DELL'OLIO (PC)

Perinelli
loc. I Perinelli
29028 Ponte dell'Olio (PC)
tel. 0523571610
www.perinelli.it

This winery continues to move steadily forward through the crowded Colli Piacentini scene, acting quietly but with the right dose of ambition. The 17 hectares of vineyards produce around 60,000 bottles annually of six wines that are taking on a clearer identity with each passing year. Let's begin with the two sparklers. Ortrugo 2005 and Gutturnio 2005 are both simple and technically well made, walking away with One Glass each and confirming their place among the best of their type. Turning to the four non-sparkling wines, the Malvasia Torre della Ghiacciaia 2005 underwent cold maceration and aged partly in wood for five months. An elegant bouquet of flowers and aromatic herbs on the nose is a lively, well-coordinated introduction to the palate with its slightly minerally finish. On the red front, Vigna Vecchia 2004 is a blend of pinot nero, cabernet and a dash of barbera aged in barrique for a year. It performed well, showing slightly closed initially but opening out effortlessly into a very respectable crescendo with a hint of balsam in the finish. The Gutturnio Costa dei Salina 2005 is purple-tinged with fresh fruit aromas and grassy hints that are harmoniously enhanced on the palate over a soft, coherent texture. The Anno Tre is a sweet wine made from raisined sémillon, malvasia and viognier grapes from the 2003 harvest. It is golden yellow in colour with typical aromas from the malvasia grape mingling with hints of williams pears and tropical fruit. The palate is slender, fresh-tasting and subtly aromatic.

○	Anno Tre '03	🍷🍷	4*
●	Vigna Vecchia '04	🍷🍷	4*
●	C. P. Gutturnio Costa dei Salina '05	🍷🍷	4*
○	C. P. Malvasia Torre della Ghiacciaia '05	🍷🍷	4*
●	C. P. Gutturnio Vivace '05	🍷	3
○	C. P. Ortrugo Vivace '05	🍷	3
○	Anno Due '02	🍸🍸	4
●	Vigna Vecchia '02	🍸🍸	4
●	Vigna Vecchia '03	🍸🍸	4
●	C. P. Gutturnio Costa dei Salina '04	🍸🍸	4

REGGIO EMILIA

Ermete Medici & Figli

loc. Gaida
via Newton, 13a
42040 Reggio Emilia
tel. 0522942135
www.medici.it

When we talk about the Medici family, we run the risk of becoming boring. We are always saying how their good fortune is essentially due to the fact that long ago they understood that to make good wine you need good grapes, and - especially as far as Lambrusco is concerned - adequate technology in the cellar. But there isn't much we can add – this actually is their secret – except perhaps that their production method and concept of Lambrusco, with its generous fruit, extremely clean aromas and well-rounded flavour, should be an example for everyone else. The Assolo 2005 is once again one of the best red sparkling wines in Italy, showing vibrant and clearly defined on the nose with healthy, fresh fruit. It's not a typical Lambrusco, being neither particularly bubbly nor very weighty in texture, and the generous fruity pulp and firm softness on the palate give it the feel of a still wine. The Concerto 2005 is not quite as good but still beautifully made with generously rounded fruit and clear cherry aromas on the nose, followed by a dry tangy palate with rigid, well-coordinated, attractively dense structure. The first edition of the Lambrusco I Quercioli has vibrant aromas of wild strawberries and a soft, creamy palate while the Libesco, another new wine, has a broad palate with clean, simple fruit. The classic method Brut Rosé Unique Spumante has a fragrant nose and subtle flavour with a slightly bitterish finish. The other wines are all well made and excellent value for money.

●	Reggiano Assolo '05	🍷🍷	3*
●	Reggiano Lambrusco Secco Concerto '05	🍷🍷	3*
●	Reggiano Lambrusco Secco I Quercioli	🍷🍷	3*
●	Antica Osteria Lambrusco	🍷	2
⊙	Brut Rosé M. Cl. Unique '04	🍷	4
○	Colli di Scandiano e di Canossa Grasparossa Bocciolo '05	🍷	3
○	Colli di Scandiano e di Canossa Malvasia Daphne '05	🍷	3
○	Nebbie d'Autunno Dolce '05	🍷	3
●	Reggiano Lambrusco Secco	🍷	2
●	Reggiano Lambrusco Secco Libesco	🍷	3

RIMINI

San Valentino

fraz. San Martino in Venti
via Tomasetta, 11
47900 Rimini
tel. 0541752231
www.vinisanvalentino.com

San Valentino is a well-established, forward-looking estate, thanks to the commitment of Roberto Mascarin and the many ideas that subtly change the lovely face of this winery every year. One example is the small holiday centre, Acini, which offers accommodation to tempt wine enthusiasts and travellers wishing to discover this wonderful area. Turning to the wines, the range presented for this year's edition of the Guide is of a high general standard as usual although there is one item of news: the release of Sangiovese Terra di Covignano 2004 has been delayed because it will benefit from further ageing. The Luna Nuova 2003 made from 60 per cent cabernet sauvignon and merlot is finally available for tasting after ageing in bottle and it has emerged in distinctly fine fettle, proving how well-suited this area is to Bordeaux grape varieties. Luna Nuova is fresh and stylish despite the hot year, with a deep, austere nose and healthy, succulent fruit. The palate is complex and dynamic with mature, close-knit tannins and weighty, nicely handled texture. Eclissi di Sole 2005 sums up the features of Sangiovese wines from the Rimini area: mouthfilling, enjoyable, expressive and generous, if occasionally at the cost of complexity. Lastly, the Sangiovese Scabi 2005 may be the product of a less than outstanding year but it is still one of the best standard-label Sangioveses in Romagna. The two 2005 chardonnay-based whites are both well-made. Fiore has generous tropical fruit sensations and well-judged wood while Alta Marea is simpler and lighter.

●	Luna Nuova '03	🍷🍷	6
●	Eclissi di Sole '05	🍷🍷	5
●	Sangiovese di Romagna Sup. Scabi '05	🍷🍷	3*
○	Alta Marea '05	🍷	4
○	Fiore Chardonnay '05	🍷	5
●	Sangiovese di Romagna Sup. Terra di Covignano Ris. '01	🍸🍸🍸	5
●	Sangiovese di Romagna Sup. Terra di Covignano Ris. '02	🍸🍸🍸	5
●	Sangiovese di Romagna Sup. Terra di Covignano Ris. '03	🍸🍸🍸	5
●	Colli di Rimini Cabernet Sauvignon Luna Nuova '02	🍸🍸	5

RIVERGARO (PC)

La Stoppa

Loc. Ancarano
29029 Rivergaro (PC)
tel. 0523958159
www.lastoppa.it

We are delighted to begin this profile by announcing that Malvasia Passito Vigna del Volta has once again been awarded Three Glasses. Not only does this pay tribute to the wine's superb standard of quality, it confirms the aromatic malvasia di Candia variety's suitability for vinification as a dried-grape wine and the vocation of the territory for producing top-notch sweet wines, which La Stoppa has been doing for several years. The Vigna del Volta 2004 is dynamic and fresh-tasting, with unmistakably generous qualities of sunny sweetness and aromatic expression. The malvasia, trebbiano and ortrugo Ageno 2004 is less approachable. Its colour is old gold, thanks to prolonged skin contact, and the aromas are in continual evolution, gradually unveiling apples, aromatic herbs, honey and peach fruit. It opens confidently on the palate with unexpectedly dry and astringent sensations. This unusual wine requires unconventional interpretation and raises as many questions as it offers opportunities for reflection. Turning to the reds, the surprising Gutturnio 2005 has intense colour, sharply defined red berry and pencil lead aromas and a close-knit texture on the palate with plenty of acidity and grip. The merlot-based I Padri 2004 has warm aromas with gamey hints, and ripe generous fruit on the palate which lacks a little thrust. Lastly the Barbera 2004 has strong evolved aromas which affect the overall profile, but the palate is dynamic, lingering and rich in acidity. This wine needs to be uncorked in advance so that its qualities can be fully appreciated.

○	C. P. Malvasia Passito V. del Volta '04	▼▼▼	6
○	Ageno '04	▼▼	5
●	I Padri '04	▼▼	5
●	C. P. Gutturnio '05	▼▼	3*
●	C. P. Barbera della Stoppa '04	▼	5
○	C. P. Malvasia Passito V. del Volta '03	▽▽▽	5
●	Stoppa '96	▽▽▽	5
○	C. P. Malvasia Passito V. del Volta '97	▽▽▽	5
●	C. P. Barbera della Stoppa '00	▽▽	4
●	C. P. Cabernet Sauvignon Stoppa '03	▽▽	5

SASSO MARCONI (BO)

Floriano Cinti

fraz. San Lorenzo
via Gamberi, 48
40037 Sasso Marconi (BO)
tel. 0516751646
www.collibolognesi.com

Floriano Cinti's winery at Sasso Marconi is, once again, one of the most dependable wineries in the Colli Bolognesi DOC. Year after year, it releases wines of very good quality at affordable prices. Floriano has had to make sacrifices to achieve this enviable status, through steady, patient work that has seen him personally involved in the management of his magnificent vineyards and in the cellar, where he can call on consultant winemaker Giovanni Fraulini, with whom he shares very productive and mutually satisfactory relationship. Once again the Pignoletto Classico 2005 is one of the best wines in the region, with clean, stylish aromas of wild flowers and fresh fruit on the nose followed by a well-structured, savoury palate. The nice citrus acidity is set alongside rich extract in the lingering finish. The Cabernet Selezione 2003 is balanced despite the very hot growing year. It is lovely, soft and plush, its ripe, fleshy fruit not at all obscured by the oak it aged in. The impressive, well-crafted Chardonnay 2005 has toasty vanilla sensations to lift its tropical fruit. All the other wines are good but we particularly liked the dry, pleasantly drinkable Pignoletto Frizzante 2005 and the Rubrum Cor Laetificans 2003, made from raisined pinot nero, merlot and cabernet. The well-judged sweetness is beautifully dried on the palate by the smooth tannins.

●	C. B. Cabernet Sauvignon Sel. '03	▼▼	4*
○	C. B. Pignoletto Cl. '05	▼▼	4*
○	C. B. Chardonnay '05	▼▼	4
●	Rubrum Cor Laetificans '03	▼	5
●	C. B. Barbera '05	▼	4
●	C. B. Merlot '05	▼	4
○	C. B. Pignoletto Frizzante '05	▼	3
○	C. B. Sauvignon '05	▼	3
●	C. B. Merlot Sel. '03	▽▽	4
○	C. B. Pignoletto Cl. '04	▽▽	3
●	C. B. Cabernet Sauvignon Sel. '01	▽▽	4
●	C. B. Merlot Sel. '02	▽▽	4

SAVIGNANO SUL RUBICONE (FC)

Colonna - Vini Spalletti

loc. Castello di Ribiano
via Sogliano, 100
47039 Savignano sul Rubicone (FC)
tel. 0541945111 - 0541943446
www.spalletticolonnadipaliano.com

We are delighted to welcome back to these pages a winery whose history and tradition are among the richest in Romagna. This confident leap forward in quality is due to one event in particular, the construction of a new, larger and better-equipped cellar about three years ago, which allows skilled winemaker Leonardo Conti to make the best of the huge potential of the winery's vineyards. The traditional expertise and talent we have glimpsed at intervals in the recent past now have enough support to erase the memories of imprecise aromas and the unpredictable successes of the past. The new, courageous product line is nicely summed up in the Principe di Ribano, a 2005 Sangiovese of which 140,000 bottles were made. It's ingeniously simple with charming fresh character and seductive fruit that unfolds in a perfect continuum of sweet aromas on the nose and an appetizingly drinkable palate. The other wines, aged for longer and a tad more ambitious, also have plenty of appeal. Villa Rasponi 2003 is a Sangiovese Riserva whose subtle aromas belie its rounded but weighty texture, showing complex and stylishly creamy with ripe, sweet red berry fruit alongside hints of spice and pipe tobacco. The Cabernet Il Monaco di Ribano 2003 is a characterful wine with generous sweetness and robust oak sensations while the other Cabernet, Sabinio 2004, has less extract but shows loads of finesse. The Sangiovese Rocca di Ribano 2003 conforms to its traditional role as a sturdy, satisfying Sangiovese.

●	Il Monaco di Ribano Cabernet '03	ΨΨ	5
●	Sangiovese di Romagna Sup. Rocca di Ribano '03	ΨΨ	4
●	Sangiovese di Romagna Sup. Villa Rasponi Ris. '03	ΨΨ	4
●	Sabinio Cabernet '04	ΨΨ	3*
●	Sangiovese di Romagna Sup. Principe di Ribano '05	ΨΨ	3*
○	Albana di Romagna Passito Maolù '03	Ψ	5
●	Il Gianello Merlot '04	Ψ	4
○	Albana di Romagna Secco Duchessa di Montemar '05	Ψ	3
○	Principessa Ghika '05	Ψ	3

TRAVO (PC)

Il Poggiarello

loc. Scrivellano di Statto
29020 Travo (PC)
tel. 0523957241 - 0523571610
www.ilpoggiarellovini.it

We have long admired this winery for its consistent results, overall quality throughout the range and competitive prices. This year's tastings again revealed all-round quality and flawless technical performances. As far as the whites are concerned, we were particularly impressed by the Sauvignon Perticato Il Quadri 2005, which underwent cold maceration on the skins and then aged in stainless steel vats. It is a fresh, balanced, no-nonsense wine with seductively well-defined fruit and citrus notes dominating the palate, and a lively mineral sensation as a finishing touch. The Malvasia Perticato Beatrice Quadri 2005 is aromatic with vibrant fruit on the nose and spreads softly over the palate thanks to nicely balanced acidity and residual sugar. The winery's best wine this year is – yet again – Gutturnio La Barbona Riserva 2004, a skilful blend of barbera and bonarda grapes. It has weighty structure and perceptible tannins already integrated into the fruity texture to ensure a steady and lingering dynamism on the palate. Its younger brother, Gutturnio Perticato Valandrea 2005, has also has good weight and texture, the well-crafted palate refreshed in the finish by just the right amount of acidity. The slightly evolved initial sensation of the Cabernet Sauvignon Perticato del Novarei 2004 does not detract from its close-knit progression on the palate, where ripe fruit flanks sweet tannins and light hints of garden vegetables. The Perticato Le Giastre 2005 made from pinot nero has an approachably fresh-tasting, even palate with hints of raspberries and peaches.

●	C. P. Gutturnio La Barbona Ris. '04	ΨΨ	5
●	C. P. Cabernet Sauvignon Perticato del Novarei '04	ΨΨ	5
○	C. P. Malvasia Perticato Beatrice Quadri '05	ΨΨ	4*
○	C. P. Sauvignon Perticato Il Quadri '05	ΨΨ	4*
●	C. P. Gutturnio Perticato Valandrea '05	Ψ	4
●	C. P. Pinot Nero Perticato Le Giastre '05	Ψ	5
●	C. P. Gutturnio La Barbona Ris. '01	ΥΥ	5
●	C. P. Gutturnio La Barbona Ris. '03	ΥΥ	5
●	C. P. Barbera 'L Pistòn '04	ΥΥ	4

VIGOLZONE (PC)

Conte Otto Barattieri di San Pietro

via dei Tigli, 100
29020 Vigolzone (PC)
tel. 0523875111

Conte Barattieri's old winery in an aristocratic 17th-century residence in Albarola, a small hamlet in the heart of Val Nure, has been included in the Guide since the very first edition. One of the finest examples of the noble tradition of dessert wines is to be found here, Vin Santo Albarola, always produced in very limited quantities but only recently sold on general release because of problems with production regulations. Such limited production figures have in the past prevented us from awarding it our highest accolades but the extraordinary quality of the 1996 vintage and a small increase in output have changed our minds. Albarola is made from malvasia di Candia grapes partially dried in a drying room. After crushing, the wine is racked into small oak barrels in contact with a yeast-rich devatting residue dating from 1823, known as a "mother", for the very slow fermentation procedure. The wine is bottled after nine years' ageing without any other procedure, when its volume is reduced by almost half. It has a rich amber colour and a nose laden with fine evolved sensations with a huge spectrum of aromatics from honey to candied fruit, tea leaves and sweet pipe tobacco. These are echoed on the broad, velvety palate and enhanced with fresh balsamic hints. A distinct note of zabaglione seals the endless finish of this old-world nectar. The remaining products have, unfortunately, fallen back – we hope temporarily – from being generous, strong and rounded wines into one-dimensional products that are not much more than well made.

○	C. P. Vin Santo Albarola Val di Nure '96	▼▼▼	6
●	C. P. Gutturnio Frizzante '05	▼	3
●	C. P. Gutturnio Traversini '05	▼	3
●	C. P. Gutturnio Montesprello '04	▼	4
○	C. P. Vin Santo Albarola Val di Nure '95	▽▽	6
●	C. P. Gutturnio '03	▽▽	4
●	Il Faggio '03	▽▽	5

VIGOLZONE (PC)

La Tosa

loc. La Tosa
29020 Vigolzone (PC)
tel. 0523870727
www.latosa.it

Having come close to Three Glasses many times in recent years with Gutturnio Vignamorello, La Tosa has at last brought home our top award for Cabernet Sauvignon Luna Selvatica 2004. This is a particularly significant achievement given the recent drop in popularity of international varieties. Luna Selvatica 2004 is a very well-made wine, aged in barrique for 12 months and bottled without filtration. This version is less brawny than usual but unusually stylish, showing slightly closed initially then giving way immediately to a wide range of aromas including black berry fruit, pencil lead and tobacco with a hint of garden vegetables. Sweet fruit and freshness mingle on the mouthfilling palate, enhanced by the even-textured, very deep flavour. The fragrant, juicy Gutturnio Vignamorello 2005 is also on good form with the usual generous mouthfilling palate and rich array of red fruit and spicy aromas. On the white front, the Sauvignon 2005 has benefited from a cool year with nice healthy fruit, revealing its considerable potential and clearly defined aromas, especially on the palate. The Malvasia Sorriso di Cielo 2005 shows the usual lively, generous fruit on the nose while the perceptible residual sugar on the soft, broad palate is nicely offset by lovely natural acidity. A new product, L'Ora Felice 2005, is a subtle dried-grape wine made from aromatic malvasia di Candia grapes raisined in a drying room and vinified without oak. It shows sweet aromas of pears, white peaches, citrus peel and gooseberries on the nose and the palate is vibrant, elegant and very drinkable.

●	C. P. Cabernet Sauvignon Luna Selvatica '04	▼▼▼	6
●	C. P. Gutturnio Vignamorello '05	▼▼	5
○	C. P. Malvasia Passito L'Ora Felice '05	▼▼	5
○	C. P. Malvasia Sorriso di Cielo '05	▼▼	4*
○	C. P. Sauvignon '05	▼▼	4*
●	C. P. Gutturnio '05	▼	3
○	C. P. Valnure Frizzante '05	▼	3
●	C. P. Cabernet Sauvignon Luna Selvatica '97	▽▽▽	5
●	C. P. Gutturnio Vignamorello '04	▽▽	4

ZIANO PIACENTINO (PC)

GAETANO LUSENTI

LOC. CASE PICCIONI, 57
29010 ZIANO PIACENTINO (PC)
TEL. 0523868479
www.lusentivini.it

Lodovica Lusenti and her husband Giuseppe Ferri farm about 15 hectares of vineyards near Vicobarone in Val Tidone, pursuing a concept of winemaking that focuses on promoting local grape varieties, first and foremost croatina. Their characterful wines are more powerful than stylish and require patience from the taster before fully they will reveal their full potential. For this reason, the winery has decided to delay release of the Bonarda La Picciona 2004, an extract-rich wine from 100 per cent croatina. Moving on to the other wines, the Malvasia Bianca Regina 2004 macerated briefly on the skins and has confident colour with ripe apple and peach fruit on the nose alongside varietal citrus hints. The tannins on the well-structured, spirited palate are well gauged and refresh without weighing down as they lead to a clean, bitterish finish. The Gutturnio Superiore Cresta al Sole 2004 is ruby red with purple hints. Ripe fruit on the nose is followed by a well-structured, close-knit palate that lingers nicely showing good balance of tannins and acidity. The Cabernet Sauvignon Villante 2003 is almost garnet red in colour and the nose opens with vegetal aromas and spicy hints. The broad, mature palate reveals powerful tannins that slightly dry the finish. Lastly, the Gutturnio Frizzante 2005 is fresh and nicely put together with generous fruit and hints of spice.

●	C. P. Cabernet Sauvignon Villante '03	TT	4*
●	C. P. Gutturnio Sup. Cresta al Sole '04	TT	4*
○	C. P. Malvasia Bianca Regina '04	TT	4*
●	C. P. Gutturnio Frizzante '05	T	3
●	C. P. Bonarda La Picciona '02	YY	4
●	C. P. Cabernet Sauvignon Villante '01	YY	5
●	C. P. Cabernet Sauvignon Villante '02	YY	5
●	C. P. Bonarda La Picciona '03	YY	4

ZIANO PIACENTINO (PC)

TORRE FORNELLO

LOC. FORNELLO
29010 ZIANO PIACENTINO (PC)
TEL. 0523861001
www.torrefornello.it

Back in 1998, Enrico Sgorbati decided to restructure the old buildings at the heart of his 85-hectare estate – 60 planted to vine – and thus created one of the largest and most important wine estates in the Colli Piacentini DOC. This should be clear from the good impression made this year by Torre Fornello's wines, despite the absence of the more important reds. In fact, the only red presented was the Gutturnio Superiore Sinsäl 2005. Garnet in colour, it gives stylish ripe aromas with vegetal sensations and a well-proportioned, supple palate with a good, sweet, lingering finish. The whites have returned after a brief absence caused by hailstorms. Pratobianco 2005 is a very impressive blend of malvasia, sauvignon and chardonnay with nice personality. Slightly tropical fruit and mineral sensations on the nose reflect the varietal aromas of the sauvignon grape, emphasizing the lively, softly fresh palate where the fruit makes a leisurely reappearance. Donna Luigia 2005 is made entirely from malvasia di Candia. The nose has hints of pine resin and sage with the aromatic notes from the grape while the palate is harmonious with hints of citrus fruit and spices. The Sauvignon Cà del Rio 2005 is less impressive. Straw yellow with greenish hues, its grassy fragrant nose precedes a sharp, somewhat simple palate. The 2005 sparkling wines are technically flawless, as ever. We particularly liked the fresh Ortrugo for its well-judged softness and the Malvasia, in which the fresh fruity, aromatic sensations are slightly muted by a pleasant bitterish finish.

●	C. P. Gutturnio Sup. Sinsäl '05	TT	4*
○	C. P. Malvasia Donna Luigia '05	TT	4*
○	Pratobianco '05	TT	4*
○	C. P. Malvasia Frizzante '05	T	3
○	C. P. Ortrugo Frizzante '05	T	3
○	C. P. Sauvignon Cà del Rio '05	T	4
●	C. P. Bonarda Latitudo 45 '02	YY	5
●	C. P. Cabernet Sauvignon Ca' Bernesca '03	YY	5
●	C. P. Gutturnio Sup. Sinsäl '03	YY	4

ZOLA PREDOSA (BO)

Maria Letizia Gaggioli

via Raibolini detto il Francia, 55
40069 Zola Predosa (BO)
tel. 051753489 - 0516189198
www.gaggiolivini.it

With help from his daughter Maria Letizia, who is increasingly involved in the running of the family business, retired veterinary surgeon and founder Carlo Gaggioli continues the project he drew up some time ago for his winery. The good, if not outstanding, wines are very enjoyable and laudably affordable. Consultant winemaker Giovanni Fraulini ably manages the cellar, where the talented young Daniele Borsari is on hand. This is not an easy task given the extensive range of wines requiring fine-tuning: 15 different labels currently, which is perhaps rather too many for a winery with an overall annual production of 160,000 bottles. The quality of the red wines generally seems better than the whites, and the high point is the Cabernet Sauvignon Il Francia Rosso 2003, which made it to the Three Glass finals for the first time. The nose is a little closed but very subtle and sound in Bordeaux style while the palate is impeccably austere with generous fruit and holds a steady course to the long finish. The Merlot 2005 is nicely put together with ripe, well-measured fruit and a light, subtle palate while the Rosso Bagazzana 2005, from cabernet sauvignon and merlot, has nice fresh fruit on the nose and a more flavoursome, well-crafted palate. The white wines aren't bad, though. We particularly liked the two Charmat method spumantes, Brut Carlet from pignoletto, sauvignon and chardonnay with its thick foam and fruity, substantial palate and Francia Brut from pignoletto, chardonnay and pinot bianco, which has lighter body but is even more elegant and confident in character.

●	C. B. Cabernet Sauvignon Il Francia Rosso Ris. '03	▼▼	4*
●	C. B. Merlot '05	▼▼	4*
●	Rosso Bagazzana '05	▼▼	4*
●	C. B. Cabernet Sauvignon '05	▼	4
○	C. B. Pignoletto Frizzante '05	▼	3
○	C. B. Pignoletto Sup. '05	▼	3
○	C. B. Pinot Bianco Crilò '05	▼	3
○	Il Francia Bianco '05	▼	4
○	Brut Carlet	▼	3
○	Il Francia Brut	▼	4
●	C. B. Cabernet Sauvignon Il Francia Rosso Ris. '02	▽▽	4
●	C. B. Merlot '04	▽▽	4

ZOLA PREDOSA (BO)

Vigneto delle Terre Rosse

via Predosa, 83
40069 Zola Predosa (BO)
tel. 051755845 - 051759649
www.terrerosse.com

It's unusual to find three generations of a family drawn together by such a strong passion for wine, and particularly so when all the members of the family are involved in running the business in various capacities but Adriana, wife of founder Enrico Vallania, works harmoniously with her children Elisabetta and Giovanni, and grandson Enrico, Giovanni's son. Some time ago, Tuscan winemaker Luca D'Attoma also arrived to lend the Vallanias a hand, wisely refraining from changing the style of the wines, which are typically elegant after long ageing exclusively in stainless steel vats. Among the wines presented this year for the Guide we particularly took to the Cabernet Sauvignon Il Rosso di Enrico Vallania 2003. Even though it comes from a very hot growing year, it has not lost its distinctive sober, subtle character and gives fresh fruit with a dry flavour. But the Chardonnay Cuvée Speciale 2003 has suffered a little from the heat. Its aromas are over-evolved and don't have enough to say for themselves. The palate is well-structured, albeit with a touch too little acidity. The Pinot Bianco 2005 is full-bodied with delicate aromas on a stylish fruity nose and an even, efficient palate. The Riesling Malagò 2005 is fresh and subtle while the first edition of the Perditempo 2005, the standard-label Merlot that flanks Petroso, which is still ageing, is rather too simple and lean.

●	C. B. Cabernet Sauvignon Il Rosso di Enrico Vallania '03	▼▼	4*
○	C. B. Pinot Bianco '05	▼▼	4*
○	C. B. Chardonnay Cuvée Speciale '03	▼	4
○	C. B. Riesling Malagò '05	▼	5
●	Perditempo '05	▼	5
●	Grannero Pinot Nero '03		5
●	C. B. Cabernet Sauvignon Cuvée '00	▽▽	6
●	Grannero Pinot Nero '00	▽▽	4
●	Petroso Merlot '00	▽▽	5

OTHER WINERIES

DANIELE LONGANESI
VIA BONCELLINO, 114
48012 BAGNACAVALLO (RA)
TEL. 054560289

Small-scale producer Daniele Longanesi uses the grape with which he shares his surname to produce the dense-textured, austere, solid Bursôn Etichetta Nera. Etichetta Blu is simpler and more approachable. The Passito Anemo, from Longanesi and balsamina, is very fruity, fresh, dry and perfectly sweet.

● Bursôn Etichetta Nera '03	🍷🍷	4*
● Anemo Passito	🍷🍷	4*
● Bursôn Etichetta Blu '04	🍷	3

ERIOLI
LOC. SAN GIUSEPPE
VIA MONTEVEGLIO, 64
40053 BAZZANO (BO)
TEL. 051830103

Giorgio Erioli has kept us waiting for a year for his Cabernet Sauvignon but it was worth it. The 2003 has aged for nearly two years in barrique and the nose has fresh fruit blending nicely with its vegetal hints. The soft, weighty palate would be perfect with a bit more acidity.

● C. B. Cabernet Sauvignon Samodia Ris. '03	🍷🍷	4*

FATTORIA CA' ROSSA
VIA CELLAIMO, 735
47032 BERTINORO (FC)
TEL. 0543445130
www.fattoriacarossa.it

Welcome back to the Guide for Massimo Masotti with two well-made Sangioveses. Artusiano 2004 has ripe cherry aromas, good follow-through and a fresh, well-crafted, flavoursome palate. The velvety, austerely fruit-rich Riserva Costa del Sole 2003 has close-knit tannins. Cavalcaonte is approachable.

● Sangiovese di Romagna Sup. Costa del Sole Ris. '03	🍷🍷	4
● Artusiano Sangiovese '04	🍷🍷	3*
● Cavalcaonte '04	🍷	3

UVE DELLE MURA
VIA CÀ GNANO, 231
47032 BERTINORO (FC)
TEL. 0543743700

This year, Massimo Rocchi has an Albana Passito Roccaia, which we'll look at next time, alongside his two Sangioveses, the Trepastori 2004, with fresh fruit, well-handled weight, firm, close-knit tannins and a dryish finish, and the mid-bodied, uncomplicated, sweetly fruity Selva d'Olmo 2005.

● Sangiovese di Romagna Sup. Trepastori Ris. '04	🍷🍷	5
● Sangiovese di Romagna Sup. Selva d'Olmo '05	🍷	4

LA COLLINA
VIA PAGLIA, 19
48013 BRISIGHELLA (RA)
TEL. 054682110
www.lacollina-vinicola.com

This new small estate owned by Swiss André Eggli already has been beautifully laid out by expert agronomist Remigio Bordini. The only wine produced is the Sangiovese Cupola. The well-made 2003 is very stylish and lingering, showing modern and full-flavoured.

- ● Sangiovese di Romagna Sup. Cupola '03 — ΨΨ 5

RONTANA
VIA RONTANA, 50
48013 BRISIGHELLA (RA)
TEL. 030736094
www.rontana.it

The Romagna winery owned by Franciacorta-based Ricci Curbastro gave us a nice blend of cabernet, sangiovese and merlot, Colle Torre Monte 2003. It has firm structure and is a tad evolved but still fresh. The Sangiovese 2004 is frank and fruity while Col Mora 2003 is mature and slightly flabby.

- ● Colle Torre Monte '03 — ΨΨ 5
- ● Colli di Faenza Sangiovese Col Mora '03 — Ψ 4
- ● Colli di Faenza Sangiovese '04 — Ψ 3

FRANCESCO MONTESISSA
FRAZ. REZZANO - LOC. BUFFALORA, 91
29013 CARPANETO PIACENTINO (PC)
TEL. 0523850123
www.vinimontesissa.it

This Val Chero winery confirmed its status with a good range despite the absence of the still-maturing Il Ladro 2005. There are two high points: the Case Ronchi 2004 is a spicy Cabernet Sauvignon with good tannic structure and Gutturnio Classico Superiore 2004 is warm, soft and nicely savoury.

- ● C. P. Cabernet Sauvignon Case Ronchi '04 — ΨΨ 4*
- ● C. P. Gutturnio Cl. Sup. '04 — ΨΨ 4*
- ● C. P. Bonarda Il Ladro '04 — YY 4

TENUTA PENNITA
LOC. TERRA DEL SOLE
VIA PIANELLO, 34
47011 CASTROCARO TERME (FC)
TEL. 3482333510 - www.lapennita.it

The EdMeo 2004 and Sangiovese TerreDelSol 2004 were not ready so the Tenuta Pennita standard was held high by the Albana Passito Nedda 2003, which has unusual spicy aromas, well-measured sweetness and coffee and cream in the finish, and the simple, fresh, fruity Sangiovese La Pennita 2004.

- ○ Albana di Romagna Passito Nedda '03 — ΨΨ 5
- ● Sangiovese di Romagna La Pennita '04 — Ψ 3

TENUTA AMALIA
LOC. DIEGARO DI CESENA
VIA EMILIA PONENTE, 2619
47023 CESENA (FC)
TEL. 0547347037 - www.tenutaamalia.it

Tenuta Amalia intelligently presented two Sangioveses, both very good but quite different in style. The Riserva Pergami 2003 is subtle, dry and very traditional while the Case Rosse Superiore 2004 is soft and mature with juicy fruit.

- ● Sangiovese di Romagna Pergami Ris. '03 — ΨΨ 4*
- ● Sangiovese di Romagna Sup. Le Case Rosse '04 — Ψ 4

TERRE DELLA PIEVE
FRAZ. DIEGARO
VIA EMILIA PONENTE, 2412
47023 CESENA (FC)
TEL. 0547611535

The Sangiovese A Virgilio 2005 is not ready but Sergio Lucchi astounded us with an excellent Nobis selection. The 2004 is lovely and flavoursome with compact, crunchy fruit and close-knit, delicate, tannins on the palate. The albana-based Stil Nuovo 2005 is crisp, sweet and very alcoholic.

- ● Sangiovese di Romagna Sup. Nobis '04 — ΨΨ 4*
- ○ Stil Novo '05 — Ψ 5

Podere Vecciano

via Vecciano, 23
47852 Coriano (RN)
tel. 0541658388
www.poderevecciano.it

Podere Vecciano makes fine reds and an unusual white from rebola grapes. This year, we tasted the simple, vigorous Sangiovese D'Enio 2003, which is dry and not too expressive, and the hard, austere Vignala Volta 2004 from sangiovese, cabernet and merlot, whose tannins slightly upset the finish.

- ● Sangiovese di Romagna Sup. D'Enio Ris. '03 — 🍷🍷 5
- ● C. di Rimini Rosso VignalaVolta '04 — 🍷 4

Tenuta Godenza

fraz. San Lorenzo in Noceto
via dell'Appennino, 654
47010 Forlì
tel. 0543488424 - www.tenutagodenza.it

The gutsy, austere Sangiovese Riserva Mirus 2003 is penetrating and rather hard with restrained fruit. The Rubiano 2004 has a flowing dynamic flavour and sound, rich fruit. These two delicious wines are also excellent value for money.

- ● Sangiovese di Romagna Sup. Mirus Ris. '03 — 🍷🍷 4
- ● Sangiovese di Romagna Sup. Rubiano '04 — 🍷🍷 3*

Vigneti delle Rosenere

via del Tesoro, 23
47100 Forlì
tel. 0543769371
www.dreidona.it

Well-judged, focused style and prices from the Drei Donà family's new winery. The Albana Passito 2004 has sweet, balsamic aromas with hints of medicinal herbs and thyme and a nicely balanced, fragrant palate. The Sangiovese 2005 has a generous nose, good close-knit structure and a dryish palate.

- ○ Albana di Romagna Passito '04 — 🍷🍷 4*
- ● Sangiovese di Romagna Sup. '05 — 🍷 2

Tenuta Valli

loc. Ravaldino in Monte
via delle Caminate, 38
47100 Forlì
tel. 054524393 - www.tenutavalli.it

There was a slight dip in quality for Tenuta Valli wines but we recommend the good traditional Sangiovese Riserva della Beccaccia 2003, with good texture if a little dry on the palate. Sangiovese di Romagna Superiore Il Tibano 2005 has spicy varietal aromas on the nose and a fresh, fruity palate.

- ● Sangiovese di Romagna Sup. Riserva della Beccaccia Ris. '03 — 🍷🍷 4*
- ● Sangiovese di Romagna Sup. Il Tibano '05 — 🍷 3

Carra

loc. Casatico - via la Nave, 10b
43010 Langhirano (PR)
tel. 0521863510
www.carradicasatico.com

Bonfiglio Carra's sparkling wines are generally characterful and good, while the well-made still products have always offered breadth and dynamic flavour. The red Arcòl 2004 is well balanced and lingers. The Passito Eden is even and aromatic, just like Malvasia Acuto.

- ● Arcòl '04 — 🍷🍷 4*
- ○ Eden Passito '04 — 🍷 5
- ○ Colli di Parma Malvasia Acuto Extra Dry '05 — 🍷 4

Lamoretti

fraz. Casatico - s.da della Nave, 6
43013 Langhirano (PR)
tel. 0521863590
www.lamorettivini.com

Lamoretti always gives us characterful, high-calibre wines. The barbera and cabernet Serbato 2004 has ripe fruit and a good pulpy palate while the aromas of the Vinnalunga '71 2004 Bordeaux blend are less defined and still developing. The Malvasia Frizzante 2005 is aromatic and well typed.

- ● Serbato '04 — 🍷🍷 4*
- ● Vinnalunga '71 '04 — 🍷 4
- ○ Colli di Parma Malvasia Frizzante '05 — 🍷 3

Rocca Le Caminate

s.da Rocca delle Caminate
47014 Meldola (FC)
tel. 0545493482
www.roccalecaminate.it

Wines from Michele Fabbri get better every year, which means he's on course. Michele gave us two Sangioveses to review, a lovely, rounded Vitignano 2004, with good alcohol and prominent close-knit tannins and Sgarboleto 2004, which offers healthy, well-crafted fruit and a vibrant dry palate.

- Sangiovese di Romagna Sup. Sbargoleto '04 — ΨΨ 3*
- Sangiovese di Romagna Sup. Vitignano '04 — ΨΨ 4

Balìa di Zola

via Casale, 11
47015 Modigliana (FC)
tel. 0546948654

This is a new winery owned by Veruska Eluci, who works with her husband Claudio Fiore at Castelluccio. They release 10,000 bottles of just two Sangioveses. Redinoce 2004 is more structured with generous fleshy fruit and a balanced palate, while Balitore 2005 is lighter and simpler but well made.

- Redinoce '04 — ΨΨ 5
- Sangiovese di Romagna Balitore '05 — Ψ 4

Il Pratello

via Morana, 14
47015 Modigliana (FC)
tel. 0546942038
www.ilpratello.net

Emilio Placci's winery had a so-so year but there are two good wines. Sangiovese Mantignano 2003 has red berry fruit and spice followed by a fresh, simple, effectively styled palate with restrained body. The Riserva Badia Raustignolo 2001 has good texture, though it's a little dry and resiny.

- Colli di Faenza Sangiovese Badia Raustignolo Ris. '01 — ΨΨ 4*
- Colli di Faenza Sangiovese Mantignano Ris. '03 — ΨΨ 4*

Tenimenti San Martino in Monte

via San Martino in Monte
47015 Modigliana (FC)
tel. 3292984507

This small gem of a winery is owned by four friends from Faenza. One bush-trained vineyard planted in 1922 yields a rounded velvety Sangiovese with confident character. Vigna alle Querce 2003, from cabernet franc, merlot and carmenère, is richly textured, close-knit, flavoursome and nicely judged.

- Vigna alle Querce '03 — ΨΨ 6
- Sangiovese di Romagna Vigna 1922 '03 — ΨΨ 7

Terragens

via Provinciale Faentina, 46
47015 Modigliana (FC)
tel. 0546675611
www.terragens.com

This interesting project organized by the Caviro winemaking group with winemaker Attilio Pagli makes three different Sangioveses, all in a solid, modern style. Romio 2004 is softer and more mouthfilling, the Riserva 2003 is hard and lean and the standard-label Superiore is simple and fruity.

- Romio '04 — ΨΨ 5
- Sangiovese di Romagna Sup. Ris. '03 — Ψ 4
- Sangiovese di Romagna Sup. '05 — Ψ 3

Aldrovandi

via Marzatore, 36
40050 Monteveglio (BO)
tel. 0516810296

Federico Aldrovandi's experience, acquired in various parts of the world, has borne fruit. The debut product of his small merlot vineyard is 3,000 excellent bottles of Alto Vanto, a well-structured, soft, characterful wine that finds a nice good balance of extract and drinkability.

- C. B. Merlot Alto Vanto '04 — ΨΨ 5

ORSI - SAN VITO
VIA MONTE RODANO 6
40050 MONTEVEGLIO (BO)
TEL. 051964521

Federico Orsi's new direction begins with Pignoletto. The Superiore 2005 has healthy, fresh fruit and a well-crafted, flavoursome palate with a tangy finish. The Frizzante 2005 is soft, fresh and fragrant while the cheaper Bianco Frizzante 2005, also a pignoletto, is simple and approachable.

○	C. B. Pignoletto Sup. '05	🍷🍷	4*
○	C. B. Pignoletto Frizzante Vigneto San Vito '05	🍷	3
○	Bianco San Vito Frizzante '05	🍷	3

TENUTA SANTA CROCE
VIA ABE, 33
40050 MONTEVEGLIO (BO)
TEL. 0516702069 - 051670104

The Chiarli winery of Modena owns this Bolognese estate. The nicely typical Barbera 2004 has a rounded nose and fresh-tasting palate. The Merlot Camerlò 2004 is full-bodied but the fruit is a little too ripe. The Pignoletto Superiore 2005 has a nice tangy palate and a fruity but predictable nose.

●	C. B. Barbera '04	🍷🍷	3*
●	C. B. Merlot Camerlò '04	🍷	3
○	C. B. Pignoletto Sup. '05	🍷	3

CASETTO DEI MANDORLI
LOC. PREDAPPIO ALTA
VIA UMBERTO I, 21
47016 PREDAPPIO (FC)
TEL. 0543922361 - www.vini-nicolucci.it

As well as the Riserva Vigna del Generale 2001, a hard, austere and characterful Sangiovese, Alessandro Nicolucci gave us a new wine, Nero di Predappio 2003. This blend of sangiovese, refosco and merlot has strikingly fresh, rounded fruit and a firmly structured, drinkable palate.

●	Sangiovese di Romagna V. del Generale Ris. '01	🍷🍷	5
●	Nero di Predappio '03	🍷🍷	5

TENUTA PANDOLFA
FRAZ. FIUMANA - VIA PANDOLFA, 35
47010 PREDAPPIO (FC)
TEL. 0543940073
www.pandolfa.it

There were two good reds from this winery. Sangiovese Villa degli Spiriti 2004 is the more impressive with its meaty, opulent style and sweet, lingering ripe fruit. Cabernet Sauvignon Pezzolo 2004 is more restrained with vanilla aromas and a rather dry finish.

●	Sangiovese di Romagna Sup. Villa degli Spiriti Ris. '04	🍷🍷	4*
●	Pezzolo Cabernet Sauvignon '04	🍷	4

CA' DE' MEDICI
LOC. CADE - VIA DELLA STAZIONE, 32
42040 REGGIO EMILIA
TEL. 0522942141 - 0522941089
www.cademedici.it

As usual, Terra Calda was the most successful wine for Marica Medici. It's a modern, well-textured Lambrusco with a dark colour, vibrant fruity aromas and an austere, slightly dry and tannic flavour. Piazza San Prospero is simpler and more approachable and Malvasia Rubigalia is nicely fragrant.

●	Terra Calda Frizzante	🍷🍷	3*
○	Malvasia Dolce Rubigalia	🍷	2
●	Reggiano Lambrusco Piazza San Prospero	🍷	2

TENUTA UCCELLINA
VIA GARIBALDI, 51
48026 RUSSI (RA)
TEL. 0544580144

Alberto Rusticali's long experience with Albana Passito, which represents 50 per cent of the winery's overall production, has brought us a very typical 2003 with ripe fruit aromas, well-judged acidity, restrained sweetness and a nice dry finish on the palate.

○	Albana di Romagna Passito '03	🍷🍷	4*
●	Bursôn Et. Nera '02	🍷🍷 (white)	4
●	Ruchetto dell'Uccellina '01	🍷🍷 (white)	4

Cantine Cavicchioli & Figli

via Canaletto, 52
41030 San Prospero (MO)
tel. 059812411
www.cavicchioli.it

All the products of this large traditional winery are getting better and Lambrusco di Sorbara wines are its strongpoint. Vigna del Cristo 2005 has hints of cherry and apple fruit on the nose with a nicely dry, subtle flavour. The Lambrusco di Sorbara Tre Medaglie is lighter and very typical.

●	Lambrusco di Sorbara Vigna del Cristo '05	🍷	4
●	Lambrusco di Sorbara Tre Medaglie	🍷	3*

Moro - Rinaldini

fraz. Calerno
via Andrea Rivasi, 27
42040 Sant'Ilario d'Enza (RE)
tel. 0522679190 - www.rinaldinivini.it

Well-made still lambrusco-based wines are Paola Rinaldini's calling card. Vigna del Picchio 2002 is balsamic and generously fruity on the nose with a soft, very pleasant and drinkable palate. Moro del Moro 2001 is mellow and flabbier on the palate. The simple Rinaldo Brut has a buttery finish.

●	Moro del Moro '01	🍷🍷	6
●	Vigna del Picchio '02	🍷🍷	4
○	Rinaldo Brut Chardonnay	🍷	3

Cantina di Arceto

via Pagliani, 27
42019 Scandiano (RE)
tel. 0522989107

Among Cantina di Arceto's good Passitos are the intensely aromatic, nicely sweet Malvasia Passito with a well-balanced palate and slightly dry finish. The fragrant Marzemino Passito has candied fruit aromas and restrained sweetness. The Spumante Brut is good, lightly aromatic, soft and good value.

○	Malvasia Passito V. di Grazia	🍷🍷	5
●	Marzemino Passito V. di Grazia	🍷🍷	5
○	Colli di Scandiano e di Canossa Spumante Brut	🍷	2*

Ceci

via Provinciale, 99
43030 Torrile (PR)
tel. 0521810252

The Otello line is the feather in Ceci's cap and includes the very fragrant Lambrusco Etichetta Nera and NerodiLambrusco, which is more modern and velvety. Spumante Tre is made from malvasia, sauvignon and pinot nero grapes, which give it florality on the nose and a satisfyingly soft palate.

●	Otello Lambrusco Et. Nera	🍷🍷	3*
○	Tre	🍷🍷	4
●	Otello NerodiLambrusco	🍷	3

Alberto Lusignani

loc. Vigoleno
via Case Orsi, 9
29010 Vernasca (PC)
tel. 0523895178

Lusignani is the biggest producer of Vin Santo di Vigoleno. The 1998 was obtained from local grape varieties – santa maria, melara, ortrugo and bervedino – that have given it a husky, confident style and classic walnutskin aromas. Gutturnio Superiore 2004 is nicely drinkable but slightly evolved.

○	C. P. Vin Santo di Vigoleno '98	🍷🍷	6
●	C. P. Gutturnio Sup. '04	🍷	4

Massina

via Massina, 1
29010 Vernasca (PC)
tel. 0523895384

We can recommend Paolo Loschi's small winery and its excellent 2000 Vin Santo, of which only a few characterful bottles were produced. The nose is not flawless but the palate is weighty with good viscosity, depth and complexity, the hallmarks of great dessert wines.

○	C. P. Vin Santo di Vigoleno '00	🍷🍷	6

Pavolini

fraz. Bacedasco Alto
loc. Paolini, 3
29010 Vernasca (PC)
tel. 0523895407

The explosive Graziano Terzoni's family winery earned a well-deserved place in the Guide. The nicely made Malvasia Acquapazza 2005 has well-defined rose and lavender aromas with a deliciously soft flavour. The Ortrugo Bigarola 2004 is elegant and well-structured with good nose-palate consistency.

○	C. P. Malvasia Acquapazza '05	▼▼	4*
○	C. P. Ortrugo Bigarola '04	▼	4

Mattarelli

via Marconi, 35
44049 Vigarano Mainarda (FE)
tel. 053243123
www.mattarelli-vini.it

Congratulations to Emanuele Mattarelli, who works in the less fashionable Bosco Eliceo are, where he makes fine versions of the leading local wine, Fortana. From 2005, the fresh, fairly sweet Frizzante is joined by Frizzante Dolce, which is drier with fragrant fruit, and the innovative still Baba.

●	Bosco Eliceo Fortana Baba '05	▼	3
●	Bosco Eliceo Fortana Frizzante Dolce '05	▼	3
●	Bosco Eliceo Fortana Frizzante '05	▼	3

Podere Casale

loc. Vico Barone - via Creta
29010 Ziano Piacentino (PC)
tel. 0523868302
www.poderecasale.it

We are pleased to recommend Nicolas Rigamonti's Ortrugo, voted the best from 2005. The aromas are well defined, thanks to well-judged use of wood, and the good fruity flavour lingers. The Gutturnio Riserva 2003 has a mature nose and the palate is marked by very prominent tannins.

○	C. P. Ortrugo Fermo '05	▼▼	4*
●	C. P. Gutturnio Ris. '03	▼	5
○	C. P. Malvasia V. T. Gocce di Memoria '04	▽▽	5

Manara

fraz. Vicomarino
29010 Ziano Piacentino (PC)
tel. 0523860209

The Pradà 2003, from late-harvested and then raisined malvasia, has an amber colour, warm, evolved aromas and a nicely buttery palate. The Gutturnio Superiore 2003 is rounded, ripe and fruity while the enjoyably clean, fresh Ortrugo Frizzante 2005 is at the top of its category.

●	C. P. Gutturnio Sup. '03	▼▼	4*
○	Pradà Passito '03	▼▼	5
○	C. P. Ortrugo Frizzante '05	▼	3

Molinelli

v.le dei Mille, 21
29010 Ziano Piacentino (PC)
tel. 0523863230
www.molinelli.it

This year, eclectic Ginetto Molinelli's winery unveiled its Malvasia Vigna Borgo 2005. Attractive and fruity, with citrus and lavender on the nose, it has a fresh, even flavour. The Molinelli Vendemmia Tardiva from molinelli grape is sweet, uncomplicated, flavoursome and nicely drinkable.

○	C. P. Malvasia V. Borgo '05	▼▼	4*
○	Molinelli V. T. '05	▼	4
●	C. P. Barbera La Polveriera '04	▽▽	4

Il Negrese

loc. Il Negrese
29010 Ziano Piacentino (PC)
tel. 0523864804

The very well-made 2004 version of Malvasia Passito is flavoursome and varietal with apricot and peach fruit on the nose and a lively, racy palate. The barbera and croatina Rosso 2005 is firmly structured, balanced and powerful with aromas of ripe fruit and spice.

○	C. P. Malvasia Passito '04	▼▼	5
●	Rosso '05	▼	4

TUSCANY

After a few years with Piedmont leading the pack, Tuscany has now reclaimed the role of leading region in the Three Glass rankings for the 2007 Guide. We awarded Tuscany fully 55 trophies, thanks to the fact that many wineries presented wines from vintages that when not outstanding were at least sound. One could say that this is an edition in which Brunello di Montalcino looms large. The 2001 season did at times yield lean, somewhat tannic wines, but it was the best vintage in recent years and many of its Brunellos will in all likelihood enjoy enviable lifespans. Yes, these are wines that can be imposing. They can be difficult to appreciate by those who prefer immediate drinkability and softness but Brunello is a wine that exhibits leanness and even a youthful edginess, certainly not the jamminess some would demand. Regarding 2003, on the other hand, there are factors that must be borne in mind. It was a very hot, dry year when the ripening sometimes lost momentum and when sugar levels often did not develop at the same pace as polyphenols. It yielded high-alcohol wines but with immature, bitter tannins and low acidities. There were quite a few exceptions, for instance in the higher elevations of Chianti Classico and in Montepulciano. Many producers did know how to work with a vintage like that, assisted by favourable soils or climate. One thinks immediately of Sassicaia, above all, but also of Le Macchiole's Paleo and Grattamacco, all wines that have been able to retain their distinctiveness and identity even in a very anomalous year. But in discussing Tuscany, we cannot avoid treating a subject that preoccupies many professionals as well as wine writers over much of the world. In recent years, conversation seems always to centre on the crisis besetting the Tuscan wine identity, on the abandonment of the concept of the Supertuscans, those non-DOC wines often made with varieties other than sangiovese and matured, sometimes for too long, in French barriques. A rethink is currently in progress. Those who went too far are turning back and we ourselves are trying to follow and support this process. Thus, with more care than in preceding editions, we have almost always tried to favour those wines and those wineries that are pursuing, in an increasingly conscious manner, the goal of consistently and accurately expressing their unique local terroir. There are already many of these. The idea is taking hold, particularly in Chianti Classico, that the wine of a specific area should be recognizable as such. It should not be simply an excellent wine that could also be produced elsewhere. Origin bests aesthetics, in other words, and faithfulness to provenance becomes a kind of consumer's compass. This is certainly the correct direction, one that sees wines as the offspring of a particular place and particular winemakers proud to express their territory.

ALBINIA (GR)

TENUTA LA PARRINA
S.DA VICINALE DELLA PARRINA
58010 ALBINIA (GR)
TEL. 0564862636 - 0564862626
www.parrina.it

La Parrina is back with a full profile. Enjoying a long history in the southern Maremma, La Parrina is a winery with its own denomination. Franca Spinola owns the 57 hectares and produces some 250,000 bottles a year. His Radaia is never a plumped-up Merlot fruit-bomb. The '04 displays distinctive character with its first aromas, which release hints of slaty mineral over a base of elegant fruit. It expands with admirable energy in the mouth, developing a crispness and tangy sapidity that beg for another sip. Parrina Riserva '04 and Parrina Muraccio '04 exhibit the same qualities, although in a somewhat more minor key of course. Both are largely sangiovese, with modest amounts of cabernet sauvignon and merlot. The Riserva shows impressive, complex aromas, and a racy acidity that gives it lively progression and a lengthy finish. Muraccio develops an emphatic balsamic character on the nose and a concentrated, near chewy, palate with sweet tannins and a fruit-edged finale. Completing the line-up is Parrina Rosso '05, a simple, well-crafted sangiovese with straightforward fragrances and smooth drinkability. The whites performed well, too. Parrina Bianco '05, from trebbiano, sauvignon blanc and chardonnay, is delicate and well done. Ansonica Costa dell'Argentario '05, all ansonica, is a tad clumsy on the nose but clean, fresh, and enjoyable on the palate.

●	Parrina Rosso Muraccio '04	▼▼	4
●	Parrina Rosso Ris. '04	▼▼	5
●	Radaia '04	▼▼	7
○	Ansonica Costa dell'Argentario '05	▼	3
○	Parrina Bianco '05	▼	3
●	Parrina Rosso '05	▼	3
●	Radaia '00	▽▽	7
●	Radaia '01	▽▽	7
●	Parrina Rosso Muraccio '00	▽▽	4*
○	Ansonica Costa dell'Argentario '01	▽▽	3*
●	Parrina Rosso Ris. '02	▽▽	5
●	Radaia '02	▽▽	7
●	Parrina Rosso Ris. '03	▽▽	5

AREZZO

FATTORIA SAN FABIANO - BORGHINI BALDOVINETTI
LOC. SAN FABIANO, 33
52100 AREZZO
TEL. 057524566
www.fattoriasanfabiano.it

Fattoria di San Fabiano lies a bare kilometre from the walls of Arezzo. Its agricultural operations reach back centuries, even though its production of bottled wine is relatively recent, dating from the 1960s. Vineyards on the estate are documented as early as 1370, and one transaction relates to the sale of a vineyard by Francesco de' Bacci, an ancestor of the current owners, to finance frescoes by Piero della Francesca, which still adorn the family chapel in the basilica of San Francesco in Arezzo. Neither history nor the family coat-of-arms has determined the winery's return to the full profile section, however. Merit for that goes to the unrelenting effort that has ensured this year's terrific performance. In the lead is Armaiolo '03, from sangiovese and cabernet, which went to the national finals for its well-gauged expression of the vintage. The Bordeaux contribution is obvious in the nose, bringing nuances of ripe dark fruit and jam, plus cigar leaf and a touch of black pepper. Good depth and already supple tannins characterize the palate, where the sangiovese, brandishing its typical acid grip, emerges triumphant and contributes mightily to the wine's breadth and complexity. Very fine too is Nobile '03, made at Tenuta Poggio Uliveto, its nose an appealing duet of the earthy and the floral, with hints of spicy balsam. It's a tasty, well-balanced offering. Chianti '05, with a hefty production run of 250,000 bottles, is pleasant, straightforward, crisp and well crafted. The white Chiaro '05 is sound and an easy quaffer.

●	Armaiolo '03	▼▼	5
●	Nobile di Montepulciano Poggio Uliveto '03	▼▼	4
●	Chianti '05	▼	2
○	Chiaro '05	▼	2
●	Armaiolo '00	▽▽	6
●	Nobile di Montepulciano Poggio Uliveto '02	▽▽	4
●	Armaiolo '97	▽▽	5
●	Armaiolo '98	▽▽	5
●	Armaiolo '99	▽▽	6

BAGNO A RIPOLI (FI)

PETRETO
VIA ROSANO, 196A
50012 BAGNO A RIPOLI (FI)
TEL. 0556519021

According to an old saw, the cobbler always wears the worst shoes. With a bit of licence, we could say much the same of Alessandro Fonseca, winery owner and talented viticulturalist, insofar as he forgets at times to present his wines for our tastings, perhaps because he is caring for his neighbours' vineyards. But Petreto always merits serious attention, as does Pourriture Noble, the wine that has made it famous, produced from sémillon and sauvignon blanc infected with noble rot. The wine was the brainchild of Nicolò D'Afflitto, the oenologist who has assisted the operation from its earliest years. He believed that this area near to the Arno would prove to have a site climate similar to Sauternes. This '03 shows pale amber, the nose laden with honey and pine resin supported by orange peel and citrus and by very peach-like fruit essences. It enters the mouth creamy, rich and fat, a wonderfully seductive wine with a finish that is not huge but respectably long. The other wines are less exciting. The merlot-heavy Bocciolè '03 has a somewhat closed nose of leather and animal skin followed by red berry fruit. It is smooth and juicy enough on the palate, although its tannins are just a mite too noticeable, and the savoury finale is medium long. Podere Sassaie, a Sauvignon Blanc, debuted with the '05. It releases delectable lemon and mint on the nose, with the palate showing a tasty zest and medium length. Finally, Chianti Colli Fiorentini '03 issues fresh, crisp fruit and a dash of black pepper to introduce a lean, dynamic wine that is both juicy and delicious.

●	Bocciolè '03	TT	5
○	Pourriture Noble '03	TT	6
●	Chianti Colli Fiorentini '04	T	3
○	Podere Sassaie '05	T	4
○	Pourriture Noble '00	YY	6
●	Bocciolè '01	YY	5
○	Pourriture Noble '01	YY	6
○	Pourriture Noble '02	YY	6
○	Pourriture Noble '99	YY	6

BAGNO A RIPOLI (FI)

LE SORGENTI
LOC. VALLINA
VIA DI DOCCIOLA, 8
50012 BAGNO A RIPOLI (FI)
TEL. 055696004
www.fattoria-lesorgenti.com

After a year's absence, good overall performances bring the Ferrari family back to the Guide. And we expect even better in the future. Each Le Sorgenti team member has a particular responsibility. Public relations are the domain of mother Elizabeth, and the vineyards of father Gabriele, while son Filippo takes care of winemaking and sales. There's certainly enthusiasm and dedication to spare, although not all the arrows have hit the mark. Still, there's potential aplenty here, particularly in an area as dynamic as the Colli Fiorentini. Scirus '03, a 50-50 blend of cabernet and merlot, came out on top. Opaque to the eye, it offers spice-veined chocolate and conserves, although toasty oak tones still predominate. It enters warm and smooth, seems to hesitate a bit and then regains its momentum, aided by fine-grained tannins. The finale may not be particularly lengthy but it is appealingly smooth. Equally fine is Gaiaccia '04, made of sangiovese and merlot. It shows off wild berry nicely edged with mineral, pencil lead, and a light touch of mint. Tangy acidy and supple tannins are well in evidence on a self-confident palate that builds to an impressive finish. Sghiras '05 is a chardonnay with a dollop of sauvignon blanc. The nose exhibits a spicy complexity over a base of fleshy, white peach-based fruit. The palate is equally tasty and the finish impressive and full-flavoured. Chianti Colli Fiorentini Respiro '04 remains somewhat low-keyed throughout and Vin Santo '99, though pleasant enough, lacks concentration and length. The Calicò sparkler has a rather simple structure.

●	Scirus '03	TT	6
●	Gaiaccia '04	TT	4
●	Chianti Colli Fiorentini Respiro '04	T	4
○	Sghiras '05	T	4
○	Vin Santo '99	T	6
○	Calicò Brut	T	6
●	Scirus '01	YY	6
●	Scirus '00	YY	6
●	Gaiaccia '02	YY	4
○	Vin Santo '97	YY	6
●	Scirus '98	YY	5
●	Scirus '99	YY	5

 BARBERINO VAL D'ELSA (FI)

I BALZINI

LOC. PASTINE, 19
50021 BARBERINO VAL D'ELSA (FI)
TEL. 0558075503 - 0556580484
www.ibalzini.it

The 2002 weather struck less forcefully in this area than elsewhere, or so it seems from tasting the consistently good wines made by Vincenzo and Antonella D'Isanto. Excellent balance is the principal trait they all share, with good, emphatic aromas and acidities that are judicious and never excessive. The I Balzini operation celebrates its 30th anniversary this year since it was in 1977 that Vincenzo D'Isanto acquired a modest four-hectare property in Barberino Val d'Elsa and brought in Giulio Gambelli to work with him. Fully ten years had to pass until their first harvest, in 1987. Today, Antonella is in charge of sales and the estate has grown to more than ten hectares, with over half in vineyard. Merlot and cabernet sauvignon are planted in clayey soils, while alberese-rich soils are reserved for sangiovese. Of the two wines, White Label, a sangiovese and cabernet sauvignon blend, held the edge. A deep ruby leads off, followed by decisive fruit and crisp mint over herbal nuances. The body is sturdy but balanced, with a nice integrated acid, and the flavours build to a truly delicious finish. The merlot and cabernet sauvignon Black Label displays an extremely dense tonality and a suitably complex nose, where cinnamon and clove spice background wild red berry fruit, with a clean minerality obvious throughout. Following on, we note a dense body with plenty of tannin support, sinewy acidity and a finish that is a tad drying but overall lengthy and quite savoury.

● I Balzini White Label '02	▼▼	5
● I Balzini Black Label '02	▼	6
● I Balzini Black Label '01	▽▽	6
● I Balzini Black Label '00	▽▽	7
● I Balzini White Label '00	▽▽	6
● I Balzini White Label '01	▽▽	5
● I Balzini Black Label '99	▽▽	7

★ ISOLE E OLENA

LOC. ISOLE, 1
50021 BARBERINO VAL D'ELSA (FI)
TEL. 0558072763 - 0558072283

It is quite a challenge to find new words to convey the importance of the role played by Paolo De Marchi and Cepparello in the advancement of sangiovese. Once again it came away with a fully merited Three Glasses. Without actually being a clone of this obstinate Piedmontese, it would be hard to comprehend the scale of the challenge he faced when upon his arrival in Tuscany he decided to exploit the full potential of a variety in which few at that time had much faith. He also strove to do this without neglecting the international varieties, which form the core of the Collezione De Marchi. Cepparello '03 exhibits an incredible freshness on the nose, largely clean, straightforward fruit with just an intriguing touch of balsamic spiciness. Simply delectable on the palate, its suppleness is judiciously supported by rounded tannins and a tasty acidic grip, with a solid thrust towards a finale impressive as it is long. But all of this year's wines won plaudits. The Chardonnay '04 showed resplendent mineral and mint, which give way to ripe fruit, followed by a velvety, alluring mouthfeel with crisp edges and a savoury, toothsome finale. The Cabernet Sauvignon '01 leads with dense, blackberry-like fruit accompanied by nuances of spice and rich cocoa powder. Mellow tannins temper its sturdiness on the palate and the finish is as expansive as you could wish. We liked the generous aromatics of the Syrah '03, with nice game and spice, as well as its firm structure and vitality, overall a very compelling wine. Chianti Classico '04 is terroir-perfect and a true siren in the glass.

● Cepparello '03	▼▼▼	8
● Cabernet Sauvignon Collezione De Marchi '01	▼▼	8
● Syrah Collezione De Marchi '03	▼▼	7
○ Chardonnay Collezione De Marchi '04	▼▼	6
● Chianti Cl. '04	▼▼	5
○ Vin Santo '99	▼	7
● Cepparello '00	▽▽▽	7
● Cepparello '01	▽▽▽	7
● Cabernet Sauvignon '96	▽▽▽	6
● Cabernet Sauvignon '97	▽▽▽	6
● Cepparello '97	▽▽▽	5
● Cepparello '98	▽▽▽	6
● Cepparello '99	▽▽▽	6
● Syrah '99	▽▽▽	7

BARBERINO VAL D'ELSA (FI)

Castello di Monsanto

fraz. Monsanto
via Monsanto, 8
50021 Barberino Val d'Elsa (FI)
tel. 0558059000 - 0558059057
www.castellodimonsanto.it

Fabrizio Bianchi runs the winery with his daughter Laura. Their wines turned in good performances, although we expected better, given the area's superb terroir and the fact that Fabrizio sets great store by its qualities. Castello di Monsanto began winemaking immediately after purchase in 1962 but it was only after restructuring Il Poggio vineyard that the winery released in 1968 its first Chianti Classico, made exclusively with red varieties, sangiovese, colorino and canaiolo. They still focus on the same varieties although 1974 saw the first sangiovese-only wine, from the Scanni vineyard, and Nemo came out in 1981, a Cabernet Sauvignon from Il Mulino vineyard. Half their soils are galestro and half tufaceous. After very careful research into their climate and soils, it was decided to grow international varieties as well and chardonnay was planted in 1974. The estate comprises 206 hectares, half woodland. Some 72 hectares are in vines with 56 dedicated to sangiovese. Andrea Giovannini has looked after winemaking since 2001. Turning to the range, Riserva Il Poggio '03 is well executed, showing mineral, tanned leather and tobacco leaf, with bright cherry, succeeded by good balance and finesse on the palate, good juicy fruit and a nice finale. Nemo '03 has more bramble jelly and spice on the nose before opening onto a velvety palate with well-behaved tannins and concluding with a very tasty finale. Bright cherry and floral impressions introduce Chianti Classico '04, which opens generously to tangy acidity. Riserva '03 is more subdued, with dense, upfront tannins.

●	Chianti Cl. Il Poggio Ris. '03	🍷🍷	7
●	Nemo '03	🍷🍷	7
●	Chianti Cl. Ris. '03	🍷	5
●	Chianti Cl. '04	🍷	4
●	Nemo '01	YYY	7
●	Chianti Cl. Il Poggio Ris. '88	YYY	7
●	Nemo '00	YY	7
●	Tinscvil '00	YY	6
●	Fabrizio Bianchi Sangiovese '99	YY	7
○	Fabrizio Bianchi Chardonnay '00	YY	5
●	Chianti Cl. Ris. '01	YY	5
●	Chianti Cl. '03	YY	4
○	Fabrizio Bianchi Chardonnay '03	YY	5

BARBERINO VAL D'ELSA (FI)

Castello della Paneretta

loc. Monsanto
s.da della Paneretta, 35
50021 Barberino Val d'Elsa (FI)
tel. 0558059003 - 0558059050

All of Stefano Miniati's wines turned in excellent performances. Sangiovese is his variety of choice but he works with all the grapes traditional to the area, striving to bring out the qualities peculiar to the terroir. Castello della Paneretta is located in the Monsanto area, long famous for its wines, on a secondary road that threads through the valley. Its origins go back to a 15th-century fortress that replaced an earlier castle located farther down the valley, which the Florentines destroyed in the 13th century. Various historic Florentine families, such as the Capponi and the Strozzi, succeeded each other as owners over the centuries. This year, we particularly liked Vin Santo '01. An impressive amber, it is redolent of classic dried fruit, with dates in generous evidence and pungent orange zest. The very inviting palate shows good heft and unctuous mouthfeel, and the lengthy finish offers exemplary sweetness. Chianti Classico Torre a Destra Riserva '03 shows good body, too, after a complex, well-evolved bouquet with ripe fruit and an edge of spice. It is firm and fleshy, with perhaps a touch of roughness, but beautifully expansive on the finish. A fragrant florality lends much appeal to the sangiovese-only Solimpia '04, which develops into a lively, well-balanced quaffer. Chianti Classico '04 is straightforward and pleasurable while the all-sangiovese Quattrocentenario '03 comes across as somewhat awkward and drying.

○	Vin Santo del Chianti Cl. '01	🍷🍷	6
●	Chianti Cl. Torre a Destra Ris. '03	🍷🍷	6
●	Solimpia '04	🍷🍷	4
●	Quattrocentenario '03	🍷	7
●	Chianti Cl. '04	🍷	4
●	Le Terrine '00	YY	6
●	Le Terrine '01	YY	6
●	Quattrocentenario '01	YY	7
●	Chianti Cl. Torre a Destra '02	YY	6
●	Chianti Cl. '03	YY	4
●	Solimpia '03	YY	4
●	Chianti Cl. Torre a Destra Ris. '99	YY	5

BOLGHERI (LI)

CAMPO ALLA SUGHERA
LOC. CACCIA AL PIANO, 280
57020 BOLGHERI (LI)
TEL. 0565766936 - 0565766911
www.campoallasughera.com

The Knauf company's winery merits a full profile this year for the sustained quality improvements in the line-up over the years we have been tasting their wines. Beginning with 14 hectares of vineyard in the first year, 1998, Campo alla Sughera has built up to 20 today. They are planted at a density of 9,500 vines per hectare and yield some 60 quintals per hectare. All are in the Bolgheri denomination, where the winery borders the course of the Fosso di Bolgheri on one side. Weather in this area is typically quite warm but relieved by cooling breezes from the nearby Mediterranean, creating conditions for superb fruit quality. Bolgheri Superiore Arnione '03 is outstanding and reached the national taste-offs. The nose immediately betrays the characteristics of its vintage: fully ripe fruit, dried plum preserves and a satisfyingly pungent vein of balsamic spiciness. The acidic liveliness on the palate is a welcome surprise, enlivening a juicy mid palate. Tannins are still somewhat green and hard, though, impacting the finale so some more time in the bottle will definitely help. A good vintage lent a hand to the excellent Bolgheri Rosso Adeo '04. Not exactly huge, it is nonetheless a crisp, fruity, refreshing wine at all stages, with elegant red berry fruit and some appealing grassy notes. The sauvignon blanc and viognier Arioso '05 is a pleaser, exuding intriguing hedgerow and passion fruit, succulent, but somewhat simple. Bolgheri Bianco Achenio '05 shows over-use of oak.

● Bolgheri Superiore Arnione '03	🍷🍷	7
● Bolgheri Rosso Adeo '04	🍷🍷	5
○ Arioso '05	🍷	4
○ Bolgheri Bianco Achenio '05	🍷	5
● Arnione '01	ΥΥ	7
● Arnione '02	ΥΥ	6

BOLGHERI (LI)

TENUTA GUADO AL TASSO
LOC. BELVEDERE, 140
57020 BOLGHERI (LI)
TEL. 0565749735
www.antinori.it

Tenuta Guado al Tasso, Antinori's Bolgheri operation, covers some 1,000 hectares, of which fully 300 are in vine, and includes extensive woodland known as Macchia del Bruciato. The flagship wine, Guado al Tasso, is a blend of cabernet sauvignon, merlot and a small amount of syrah. It emerges again with the '03 vintage, having skipped '02 because of its unfavourable conditions. Neither was '03 among the best in recent memory, however, as this year's wine reminds us. It is far from the superlative '01. Although soundly made, the traits common to the '03 vintage leave their mark on this wine, too. Well-ripened fruit is evident, typified by notes of dried plum preserves but oak is obvious too, perhaps to excess. The palate is an improvement, and although the tannins remain tight, a lively acidity forges good progression. More time in the bottle, however, will harness its powerful but presently undisciplined components. Bruciato '04 presents the same varietal blend but in a decidedly modern key. An oak-laden nose is wedded to nice balsamic spice, followed by succulent, dense fruit that widens out in mid-palate, to close on a slightly bitterish note and with a dry, tannic edge. Vermentino '05 is a pleasure, crisp and ready to enjoy, as is the winery's rosé, Scalabrone.

● Bolgheri Rosso Sup. Guado al Tasso '03	🍷🍷	8
● Bolgheri Rosso Bruciato '04	🍷	5
⊙ Bolgheri Rosato Scalabrone '05	🍷	4
○ Bolgheri Vermentino '05	🍷	4
● Bolgheri Rosso Sup. Guado al Tasso '01	ΥΥΥ	8
● Bolgheri Rosso Sup. Guado al Tasso '90	ΥΥΥ	8
● Bolgheri Rosso Sup. Guado al Tasso '00	ΥΥ	8
● Bolgheri Rosso Sup. Guado al Tasso '98	ΥΥ	8
● Bolgheri Rosso Sup. Guado al Tasso '99	ΥΥ	8

★ LE MACCHIOLE
VIA BOLGHERESE, 189A
57020 BOLGHERI (LI)
TEL. 0565766092
www.lemacchiole.it

After a year of transition, Cinzia Campolmi obviously has a firm grip on the reins now. Sensitive and firm-handed, she exhibits all the qualities needed to keep quality at its currently high level at this winery, which has contributed so much to Bolgheri. With modest beginnings in 1974 as a project cherished by her husband Eugenio, Le Macchiole has produced some of the finest wines made in this area, in particular from the 1990s on. Three wines are the stars of the operation, of which Paleo is perhaps the most iconic in its expression of the area's impressive qualities. The '03 vintage captured Three Glasses this year. Powerful and dense, it shows at the same time elegance and finesse. This all-cabernet franc wine is a veritable showcase of this variety's distinctive characteristics. It opens to dense berry fruit, bright and dark alike, accompanied by an appealing, ultra-refined herbaceousness and then touches of coffee and chocolate. The palate exhibits the Platonic ideal of balance with exemplary length and depth, luxuriant, already integrated tannins and subtle yet lively acidity. Simply masterful. Equally fine are the other two benchmark offerings. Scrio '03, a syrah, leads with red berry fruit edged with vibrant notes of pungent white pepper and opens to a smooth, close-woven mouthfeel, although the tannins are still a bit restrictive. The merlot-based Messorio '03, in contrast, impresses with a splendidly structured palate, with power and breadth to spare, after blackberry and balsam on the nose. Bolgheri Rosso '04 is pleasurable, if somewhat oaky.

● Paleo Rosso '03	▼▼▼	8
● Messorio '03	▼▼	8
● Scrio '03	▼▼	8
● Bolgheri Rosso '04	▼	5
● Messorio '01	▽▽▽	8
● Paleo Rosso '01	▽▽▽	8
● Scrio '01	▽▽▽	8
● Bolgheri Rosso Sup. Paleo '95	▽▽▽	8
● Bolgheri Rosso Sup. Paleo '96	▽▽▽	8
● Bolgheri Rosso Sup. Paleo '97	▽▽▽	8
● Messorio '97	▽▽▽	8
● Messorio '98	▽▽▽	8
● Messorio '99	▽▽▽	8
● Bolgheri Rosso Sup. Paleo '00	▽▽	8

BOLGHERI (LI)

★ TENUTA DELL'ORNELLAIA
VIA BOLGHERESE, 191
57020 BOLGHERI (LI)
TEL. 056571811
www.ornellaia.it

Many years have passed since Tenuta dell'Ornellaia's has failed to win Three Glasses. But even the best suffer an occasional setback and no one doubts that this superb operation in Bolgheri figures among the best, not only in Tuscany but in all of Italy. Seriousness of purpose, professionalism, great talent and a sensitivity that few others can match have enabled Ornellaia's wines to march onto the world stage to merited applause. But Nature bats last, and the vintage in the spotlight, at least for the winery's top performers, is not one that will rank high in the history books. Too heavy and too much ultra-ripe fruit are the overall impressions conveyed by the two '03s, with Ornellaia showing a bit better than Masseto. Perhaps the torrid summer penalized less the almost all-cabernet sauvignon wine. The nose does in fact still display those characteristic smoky and herbaceous nuances with just a trace of ripe fruit. It is superlative on the palate, where its hallmark elegance is in full view right from the outset. But that distinctive touch, which tasters lovingly recall from the '01, has gone missing here. The all-merlot Masseto seems more laboured. It opens to emphatic dried plum jam, and the acidity, in a somewhat minor key, is not up to supporting its density and balance suffers. Serre Nuove '04, the winery's second wine, demonstrates that a different year can change the game. Crisp, succulent and leisurely, it turns in a fine performance. And Le Volte '04 is as enjoyable as ever.

● Bolgheri Sup. Ornellaia '03	▼▼	8
● Masseto '03	▼▼	8
● Bolgheri Rosso Serre Nuove '04	▼▼	7
● Le Volte '04	▼	4
● Masseto '00	▽▽▽	8
● Bolgheri Sup. Ornellaia '01	▽▽▽	8
● Masseto '01	▽▽▽	8
● Bolgheri Sup. Ornellaia '02	▽▽▽	8
● Masseto '95	▽▽▽	8
● Bolgheri Sup. Ornellaia '97	▽▽▽	8
● Masseto '97	▽▽▽	8
● Bolgheri Sup. Ornellaia '98	▽▽▽	8
● Masseto '98	▽▽▽	8
● Bolgheri Sup. Ornellaia '99	▽▽▽	8
● Masseto '99	▽▽▽	8

BOLGHERI (LI)

★ TENUTA SAN GUIDO
LOC. CAPANNE, 27
57020 BOLGHERI (LI)
TEL. 0565762003
www.sassicaia.com

It seems hard to believe, but even Sassicaia, perhaps one of the greatest Italian reds ever produced, does have a detractor or two. Forward ego seems to be the usual culprit, with those who dismiss such a celebrated wine possibly doing so to pump wind into their personal sails. And if one tastes a Sassicaia in its callow youth one can easily misjudge it, somewhat akin to assessing a marathoner at the two-kilometre mark: some competitors may well be metres ahead. But after 35 kilometres, the situation is decidedly different. When the '88 is tasted today, or the unpropitious '96, which the press around the world so pilloried, or the '02, which we alone seemed to appreciate, then certain critics find themselves beating an ignominious retreat. Will the same happen for the '03? Possibly, even though it is hard to spare the superlatives about a wine that we believe exhibits all of the compelling qualities of its most illustrious predecessors, beginning with the '85. At this moment, we have an incomparably seductive, very full-bodied Sassicaia, one that releases spicy, near-toasty nuances and then develops a rich palate with length and finesse. Here is a great Sassicaia, its Bolgheri terroir ably transforming the varietal traits of cabernet. It is flanked for the first time by the superb Guidalberto '04, a cabernet sauvignon-merlot blend, with perhaps a soupçon of sangiovese. Though lacking the denseness of its teammate, Guidalberto is very approachable and may even pull ahead in the middle stretch, but not for long, never fear.

● Bolgheri Sassicaia '03	▼▼▼	8
● Guidalberto '04	▼▼▼	7
● Bolgheri Sassicaia '00	▽▽▽	8
● Bolgheri Sassicaia '01	▽▽▽	8
● Bolgheri Sassicaia '02	▽▽▽	8
● Sassicaia '85	▽▽▽	8
● Sassicaia '88	▽▽▽	8
● Sassicaia '90	▽▽▽	8
● Sassicaia '92	▽▽▽	8
● Sassicaia '93	▽▽▽	6
● Bolgheri Sassicaia '95	▽▽▽	8
● Bolgheri Sassicaia '96	▽▽▽	8
● Bolgheri Sassicaia '97	▽▽▽	8
● Bolgheri Sassicaia '98	▽▽▽	8
● Bolgheri Sassicaia '99	▽▽▽	8

BUCINE (AR)

FATTORIA PETROLO
LOC. GALATRONA
FRAZ. MERCATALE VALDARNO
VIA PETROLO, 30
52021 BUCINE (AR)
TEL. 0559911322 - www.petrolo.it

The 2004 growing year was one to cherish at Fattoria Petrolo, with a picture-perfect season. But the estate added near-obsessive management of each step in vineyard and cellar, beginning with ultra-low yields per vine. Our tastings can only second the enthusiasm of the staff for the results achieved. We cannot be very far off the mark in saying that the '04 versions of Torrione and Galatrona, from 100 per cent sangiovese and 100 per cent merlot respectively, are the best Petrolo has ever made. Torrione '04 unfolds a broad spectrum of aromatics ranging from clean-edged red berry fruit to mineral essences of pencil lead and gunpowder. Although the oak is nice, the style is very modern, unleashing considerable power, well-crafted tannins and full flavours to create an overall impression of balance and expansiveness. The stature of Galatrona '04 comes not from muscle but from its finely tuned elegance and finesse. Dark, well-ripened fruit makes for a smooth opening, which merges into pungent herbs and olive pulp, cocoa powder and minerally, earthy notes, with a light hint of oak still present. Contrasting that is a compelling, succulent palate, with dense, rich tannins, that develops remarkable breadth and depth and achieves superlative balance. It won an amply merited Three Glasses in fitting tribute to the Sanjust family's commitment. Completing the line-up is the appealing Vinsanto '98, its sweetness concentrated and expressive and whose long, dynamic progression continues the toasted almond, dried nuts and zest of citrus encountered on the nose.

● Galatrona '04	▼▼▼	7
● Torrione '04	▼▼	5
○ Vin Santo del Chianti '98	▼▼	6
● Galatrona '00	▽▽▽	8
● Galatrona '01	▽▽▽	8
● Galatrona '97	▽▽▽	7
● Galatrona '98	▽▽▽	7
● Galatrona '99	▽▽▽	7
● Galatrona '02	▽▽	8
● Galatrona '03	▽▽	8

BUCINE (AR)

VILLA LA SELVA
LOC. MONTEBENICHI
52021 BUCINE (AR)
TEL. 055998203
www.villalaselva.it

This year brings a more than decent overall performance for Villa La Selva. True, they did not repeat last year's coup of sending two wines to the national finals but in their defence, it must be admitted that 2003 was a more challenging year than 2001. The winery is quite dynamic and growing steadily, pushing ahead determinedly with the renewal of the vineyards they began some years ago, which included new plantings just this past year. Rigorous vineyard practices and meticulous attention paid to every step in production have combined to bring them to a quality level they can be proud of and their '03 vintages prove just that. The all-sangiovese Felciaia '03 shows a deep, dense ruby and a nose still in development, with ripe dark cherry slowly yielding to notes of toasty oak. Those characteristics continue onto a sturdy, impressive palate with good progression and savoury flavours, even though still immature tannins and somewhat embryonic aromas augur further development. Selvamaggio '03, from cabernet sauvignon only, is more open and expressive. Blackcurrant and blueberry accompany floral and balsam-menthol essences and compose a rich, imposing nose. That power is matched on the palate, where the smooth, warm attack builds to an expansive, dense mid palate, although emphatic tannins emerge to render the finish somewhat stiff. Vinsanto Vigna del Papa '01 is lean and judiciously sweet, offering lovely florality and delicious candied fruit.

●	Felciaia '03	🍷🍷	5
●	Selvamaggio '03	🍷🍷	5
○	Vin Santo del Chianti V. del Papa '01	🍷	5
●	Selvamaggio '00	🍸🍸	6
●	Felciaia '01	🍸🍸	5
●	Selvamaggio '01	🍸🍸	5
●	Felciaia '00	🍸🍸	5
●	Merlo Rosso '01	🍸🍸	6
●	Selvamaggio '96	🍸🍸	5
●	Selvamaggio '97	🍸🍸	5
○	Vin Santo del Chianti V. del Papa '97	🍸🍸	5
●	Felciaia '99	🍸🍸	5
●	Selvamaggio '99	🍸🍸	5

CAPRAIA E LIMITE (FI)

TENUTA CANTAGALLO
VIA VALICARDA, 35
50056 CAPRAIA E LIMITE (FI)
TEL. 0571910078
www.enricopierazzuoli.com

The important news from the Pierazzuoli family is that they have recently sold their Matroneo winery in Chianti Classico to concentrate all their energies on their other operations in Montalbano, Le Farnete and Cantagallo. The line-up they presented is as good as ever, with wine styles in a judiciously modern key demonstrating full respect for location as well as tradition. Carmignano Le Farnete Riserva '03 is superlative, introduced by dense ruby and a nose to match, its spice-enriched wild red berry fruit appealing and complex. Good alcohol bolsters a generous palate, assisted by dense, fine-grained tannins, and the finish, though a tad stiff, is leisurely and satisfying. Gioveto '03, a blend of 60 per cent sangiovese plus merlot and syrah, comes across as more self-confident than earlier vintages. Dense ruby leads off, while the nose opens to notes of crisp, peppery spice over an intriguing mix of fruit and roasted coffee. Power and finesse are in admirable balance in the mouth and the finale is lengthy and aromatic. Equally fine is Chianti Montalbano Riserva '03. Crisp cherry and floral notes are followed by a body of decent heft, smoothness and warm alcohol, while tannins are slightly drying on the finish. Somewhat off the mark this time is Carmignano Le Farnete '03. The attack is smooth enough but the nose comes across rather undefined and tannins impede its progression. Millarium '00 staged a fairish performance, releasing macaroons and toasted hazelnuts then building a smooth, well-crafted palate.

●	Carmignano Le Farnete Ris. '03	🍷🍷	7
●	Chianti Montalbano Ris. '03	🍷🍷	4
●	Gioveto '03	🍷🍷	5
○	Millarium '00	🍷	5
●	Carmignano Le Farnete '03	🍷	6
●	Carmignano Le Farnete Ris. '97	🍸🍸🍸	5
●	Carmignano Le Farnete '01	🍸🍸	6
●	Carmignano Le Farnete Ris. '01	🍸🍸	7
●	Gioveto '01	🍸🍸	5
●	Carmignano Le Farnete '02	🍸🍸	6
●	Carmignano Le Farnete Ris. '96	🍸🍸	4

CARMIGNANO (PO)

TENUTA DI CAPEZZANA
LOC. SEANO
VIA CAPEZZANA, 100
59015 CARMIGNANO (PO)
TEL. 0558706005 - 0558706091
www.capezzana.it

Tenuta di Capezzana is perched on the ridge overlooking the village of Seano and the wines presented this year do full honours to its long-standing. The Contini Bonaccossi family is to be praised for its unstinting efforts at keeping quality so high. Carmignano Villa di Capezzana '04, which reached the national finals, is introduced by a deep ruby and elegant fragrances of well-ripened fruit, with spices and pencil lead lurking attractively in the background. There is plenty of succulent fruit on the palate, nicely supported by lively, but judicious acidity and a dense suite of silky tannins. The progression may be somewhat short but time will in all likelihood improve this in the 80,000 bottles produced. Vin Santo upholds the esteem paid to preceding vintages. The Riserva '00 opens to a lovely amber and to compelling honey and candied fruit aromas that meld into toasted almond and dried nuts. The palate is supple, luscious and fat, concluding with an extra dollop of candied fruit. Carmignano Villa di Trefiano '03 shows a bit less vigorous than usual. The ruby exhibits some evolution on the rim while a touch of spice and fresh grass spruces up ripe fruit on the nose. It develops smoothly, with good breadth, glossy tannins and a fluid, though not particularly lengthy, finish. Trebbiano '03 is delicious, with plenty of ripe peach and pear on the nose, plus wild herbs. Tasty acidity enlivens a rich, alluring palate, which finishes long.

○	Trebbiano '03	▼▼	6
●	Carmignano Villa di Capezzana '04	▼▼	5
○	Vin Santo di Carmignano Ris. '00	▼▼	6
●	Carmignano Villa di Trefiano '03	▼	5
●	Ghiaie della Furba '01	▽▽▽	6
●	Ghiaie della Furba '98	▽▽▽	5
●	Carmignano Villa di Capezzana '99	▽▽▽	5
●	Carmignano Villa di Capezzana '00	▽▽	5*
●	Carmignano Villa di Trefiano '00	▽▽	6
●	Ghiaie della Furba '00	▽▽	6
●	Carmignano Villa di Capezzana '01	▽▽	5

CASTAGNETO CARDUCCI (LI)

CA' MARCANDA
LOC. SANTA TERESA, 272
57022 CASTAGNETO CARDUCCI (LI)
TEL. 0173635158

Ca' Marcanda's standard bearer, the Bolgheri Rosso Superiore that bears the same name as the winery, was missing from the line-up again this year. The '03 vintage simply needs more time in the bottle to be ready for release. The Bolgheri operation that Angelo Gaja launched a few years ago is marked by nothing less than an absolute obsession for quality. Perfect, meticulously groomed vineyards spread out from the winemaking facility and its striking cellar, though large, blends into its environment, thanks to the use of building materials that harmonize with the tonalities of the soil. Such loving care exercised on the outside mirrors the scrupulous attention focused on what is produced inside. So we must simply wait. Magari '04 is good, though not as sensational as it was last year. A blend of merlot, cabernet sauvignon and cabernet franc, it offers ripe fruit and emphatic, pungent greens. The palate is succulent and appealing, with well-sustained acidity and it just seems a bit too lightweight to satisfy more demanding expectations. Promis '04 offers blackcurrant and some grassy notes on the nose. The structure is somewhat modest, and its tannins feel clenching, particularly on the finish, which seems a little bitterish.

●	Magari '04	▼▼	8
●	Promis '04	▼	7
●	Bolgheri Camarcanda '01	▽▽▽	8
●	Magari '03	▽▽▽	7
●	Magari '01	▽▽	8
●	Promis '03	▽▽	6
●	Promis '01	▽▽	6
●	Magari '02	▽▽	8

CASTAGNETO CARDUCCI (LI)

Colle Massari

Loc. Lungagnano
57022 Castagneto Carducci (LI)
tel. 0565765069
www.collemassari.it

Claudio Tipa's Grattamacco '03 won its umpteenth Three Glass prize. Colle Massari thus demonstrates Tipa's commitment and competence, beginning in the Montecucco zone and now in fine evidence at Castagneto Carducci. His strong points are his sensitivity to the local environment and terroirs and his patient understanding of every moment in the yearly cycle in the vineyard. The wines of each location are outstanding, but it is the historic Grattamacco that stands out. Despite the vintage, among the hottest in recent years, the wine embodies the distinctiveness and qualities possible in a vineyard at a certain elevation, one that enjoys breezes and favourable temperatures. Ripe red berry fruit, moist earth and a lovely, delicate herbaceousness compose an appealing nose, matched by rich depth in the mouth. Tannins show fairly stiff at the moment, but some more time will work to their advantage, while the acidity works well, right through to the finish. Grattamacco Bianco '04 is fine, as expected, although the oak shows through at the moment. Bolgheri '04 is appealing. From the Montecucco area, Montecucco Riserva '03 went to the national taste-offs. Dense, fleshy and tannic, it will shine with some patient waiting. All the other wines are admirable, from Montecucco Rigoleto '04 to the whites, Irisse and Melacce, and the rosé Gròttolo '05.

●	Bolgheri Rosso Sup. Grattamacco '03	TTT	8
●	Montecucco Ris. '03	TT	5
○	Bolgheri Bianco Grattamacco '04	TT	6
●	Bolgheri Rosso '04	T	5
○	Irisse '04	T	5
●	Montecucco Rigoleto '04	T	4
⊙	Gròttolo '05	T	4
●	Montecucco Melacce '05	T	4
●	Bolgheri Rosso Sup. Grattamacco '01	YYY	8
●	Grattamacco '85	YYY	8
●	Bolgheri Rosso Sup. Grattamacco '99	YYY	8

CASTAGNETO CARDUCCI (LI)

Michele Satta

Loc. Casone Ugolino, 23
57022 Castagneto Carducci (LI)
tel. 0565773041 - 0565773349
www.michelesatta.com

After a less than outstanding performance last year, Michele Satta once again presents the superlative wines that we have become used to over the years. The winery emerged as the child of a love affair – for the Bolgheri area, of course – and since then its accomplishments have made it the benchmark for the area. Meticulous vineyard practices yield superb fruit, which in turn is metamorphosed into uncompromising, beautifully structured wines in the modern style. The '03 version of Bolgheri Rosso Superiore I Castagni, largely cabernet sauvignon with some syrah and teroldego, is a fine effort. The nose is a bit closed and presents balsamic impressions over ultra-ripe fruit. The mouth shows a good vein of acidity and a lengthy finish, stiff tannins restricting the mid palate, but this is a powerful wine and some more time should resolve that. Diambra Rosso '04, predominantly sangiovese, is excellent, opening to crisp, tasty red and dark berry fruit nicely edged with fresh greens and following through with more fruit on a nice expansive, very juicy palate. Lively acidity drives through the long, full finish. The 2004 vintage shows every sign of being a propitious one in the area. We also liked Bolgheri Bianco '05, which conjures up spring blossoms, pear and peach, showing full in the mouth but with no loss of crispness. Piastraia '03, from merlot, syrah, sangiovese and cabernet sauvignon, is less successful. Oak seems to have contributed to over-clenched tannins. The vermentino and sauvignon Costa di Giulia '05 is delicious.

●	Bolgheri Rosso Sup. I Castagni '03	TT	8
●	Diambra Rosso '04	TT	4
○	Bolgheri Bianco '05	TT	4
●	Bolgheri Rosso Piastraia '03	T	7
○	Costa di Giulia '05	T	5
●	Bolgheri Rosso Piastraia '01	YYY	7
●	Bolgheri Rosso Piastraia '02	YYY	7
●	Bolgheri Rosso Piastraia '00	YY	7
●	Bolgheri Rosso Sup. I Castagni '00	YY	8
●	Bolgheri Rosso Sup. I Castagni '01	YY	8
●	Cavaliere '01	YY	7
●	Cavaliere '00	YY	7

CASTELLARE DI CASTELLINA

LOC. CASTELLARE
53011 CASTELLINA IN CHIANTI (SI)
TEL. 0577742903
www.castellare.it

Ask Paolo Panerai if he is more attached to his Class Editore publishing empire or to his lovely, though modest-sized, wine operation, and he will almost certainly indicate the latter, since for over three decades now he has been devoting as much passion to the winery as he does to journalism. In fact, Castellare di Castellina has for many years now been one of the fixed stars in the Chianti firmament. Panerai's deeply rooted beliefs have made its wines one of the benchmarks for fans of those great reds made of sangiovese at 100 per cent, or close to it, that so well express the qualities of both the variety and the territory. I Sodi di San Niccolò is precisely that kind of wine and even in a difficult year like 2002 it emerges blissfully unscathed. This is no pumped-up competition wine: this is a product that has just the right elegance and judicious structure to merit Three Glasses, the only red in this zone and vintage that turned in such a performance. For this reason, and after repeated tastings, we returned to an earlier vintage, the 1995, which we had previously, and perhaps a bit hastily, undervalued. Now the passage of a few years has revealed it as a magnificent wine so we went back over our notes and awarded it a retrospective Three Glasses. Among the other wines, we would point out the excellent Chianti Classico Vigna il Poggiale Riserva '03, the surprising, elegant Chianti Classico '04, a simpler Chianti Classico Riserva '03 and Governo di Castellare '05, a fragrant, accessible wine at a thankfully accessible price.

● I Sodi di San Niccolò '02	🍷🍷🍷	8
● Chianti Cl. V. il Poggiale Ris. '03	🍷🍷	6
● Chianti Cl. '04	🍷🍷	4
● Chianti Cl. Ris. '03	🍷	5
● Governo di Castellare '05	🍷	4
● Chianti Cl. V. il Poggiale Ris. '00	YYY	6
● Chianti Cl. V. il Poggiale Ris. '01	YYY	6
● I Sodi di San Niccolò '01	YYY	8
● I Sodi di San Niccolò '95	YYY	8
● Chianti Cl. V. il Poggiale Ris. '97	YYY	6
● I Sodi di San Niccolò '97	YYY	8
● I Sodi di San Niccolò '98	YYY	8

CASTELLINA IN CHIANTI (SI)

FAMIGLIA CECCHI

LOC. CASINA DEI PONTI, 56
53011 CASTELLINA IN CHIANTI (SI)
TEL. 057754311
www.cecchi.net

The Cecchi brothers' winery returns to a full profile. Some years ago, Andrea and Cesare set their sights on improving their entire line. Even though they have a way to go, they can be proud of the results thus far and will undoubtedly achieve excellent results shortly. The winery, founded in 1893, forms an important part of Chianti Classico history and still has an impressive presence worldwide. The statistics are eloquent. Production tops 7,000,000 bottles and the estate owns 400 hectares, 300 of those under vine. Giuseppe Mezzedimi has been managing viticulture for 20 years now, and Riccardo Perriccioli and Miria Bracali take care of the winemaking. They do produce Supertuscans, such as the all-sangiovese Spargolo and the cabernet sauvignon La Gavina, but Chianti Classico is obviously iconic, with three versions presented this year. Riserva di Famiglia '03 first displays animal skin and leather on a slightly muddled nose before opening up to ripened fruit. The palate is self-confident and spirited but the tannins constrain the finish. Of the two Supertuscans, Spargolo '03 enjoys overall good balance although it seems a bit on the light side, while La Gavina '04 is full bodied with succulent fruit, but a tad too green on the nose. Messer Pietro di Teuzzo '04 is enjoyable, though somewhat short, and the standard Chianti Classico is supple and savoury.

● Chianti Cl. Riserva di Famiglia '03	🍷	5
● Spargolo '03	🍷	7
● Chianti Cl. '04	🍷	4
● Chianti Cl. Messer Pietro di Teuzzo '04	🍷	5
● La Gavina '04	🍷	6
● Spargolo '00	YY	7
● Chianti Cl. Riserva di Famiglia '01	YY	6
● Chianti Cl. Villa Cerna Ris. '01	YY	5
● Spargolo '01	YY	7
● Vigneto La Gavina '01	YY	6
● Chianti Cl. Riserva di Famiglia '02	YY	5

COLLELUNGO
LOC. COLLELUNGO
53011 CASTELLINA IN CHIANTI (SI)
TEL. 0577740489
www.collelungo.com

The Cattelans, husband and wife, can be proud of their results, particularly since their Chianti Classico Riserva '03 went to the national finals. What struck us most in the tastings was the stylistic turnabout in the wines. Where they had previously hewn to the international style, they are now turning more in the direction of territory focus. The estate takes in some 92 hectares, 19 of those in vineyard, of which all but one dedicated to Chianti Classico. The above-mentioned Riserva boasts real elegance on the nose, where pencil lead and mint yield quickly to lively and emphatic redcurrant and sour cherry. The entry is enchanting and bursting with fruit, as is the finish, which though only moderately lengthy, has good tannins to knit everything together. Beautifully delineated fruit distinguishes Chianti Classico '04, caressed by subtle balsamic notes. A lively vein of acidity provides just the right amount of lift to the good, medium body and animates the expanding finish. Merlot '04 was the first we had tasted. The nose has lots of interest, sporting redcurrant and minerally slate, but the palate seemed a trifle light and the tannins a bit forward. The finish is not outstandingly long but it is smooth and savoury. Vin Santo Invidia '03 followed the numbers: dried fruit and citrus zest, but we missed the necessary fatness, and roundedness, in the mouth and wished for a lengthier conclusion.

●	Chianti Cl. Ris. '03	🍷🍷	5
●	Chianti Cl. '04	🍷🍷	4
○	Vin Santo del Chianti Cl. Invidia '03	🍷	6
●	Merlot '04	🍷	4
●	Chianti Cl. '00	♀♀	5
●	Chianti Cl. Campo ai Cerchi Ris. '00	♀♀	8
●	Chianti Cl. '01	♀♀	6
●	Chianti Cl. Ris. '99	♀♀	8
●	Chianti Cl. Roveto '99	♀♀	6
●	Chianti Cl. Campo Cerchi Ris. '01	♀♀	7
●	Chianti Cl. Ris. '01	♀♀	6
●	Chianti Cl. Ris. '98	♀♀	8
●	Chianti Cl. '99	♀♀	4

★ ★ CASTELLO DI FONTERUTOLI
LOC. FONTERUTOLI
VIA OTTONE III, 5
53011 CASTELLINA IN CHIANTI (SI)
TEL. 057773571
www.fonterutoli.it

The first of two important news items from Fonterutoli is that Siepi '04 will not be released until the second half of 2007, so its review will appear in next year's Guide. The second is that Ezio Rivella has acquired Il Caggio, a magnificent property adjacent to Fonterutoli. It comprises almost 30 hectares of vineyard, all sangiovese, and has yielded wines such as Chianti Classico Riserva Il Vanto and Chianti Classico Selve Scure, top performers in previous Guides. It must be said, though, that Fonterutoli has already shown its determination to change course stylistically. Some of its recent wines have been superb, but they have shown little in common with their terroir. We are not referring to Chianti Classico Castello di Fonterutoli, whose '03 version shows its usual thoroughbred qualities. Its a wine in a class by itself, even when it shows excess of body and concentration. Our remarks are directed at the standard wine, Chianti Classico Fonterutoli. The nose always contains some rather esoteric impressions and the colour is not the ruby red that you expect from 100 per cent sangiovese. But these are precisely what we find in the '04, to an even greater extent than in preceding vintages. Returning to Castello di Fonterutoli '03, whether one considers it typical or not, it is certainly a superlative wine, highly regarded by critics and consumers alike around the globe. Dense ruby precedes rich, alluring aromas that have an almost mineral quality and it develops an assertive, somewhat tannic, palate but with generous acidity that will see it through many years.

●	Chianti Cl. Castello di Fonterutoli '03	🍷🍷🍷	7
●	Chianti Cl. '04	🍷	5
●	Chianti Cl. Castello di Fonterutoli '00	♀♀♀	8
●	Siepi '00	♀♀♀	8
●	Chianti Cl. Castello di Fonterutoli '01	♀♀♀	7
●	Siepi '01	♀♀♀	8
●	Siepi '03	♀♀♀	8
●	Chianti Cl. Castello di Fonterutoli Ris. '95	♀♀♀	5
●	Siepi '95	♀♀♀	8
●	Siepi '96	♀♀♀	8
●	Chianti Cl. Castello di Fonterutoli '97	♀♀♀	8
●	Siepi '97	♀♀♀	8
●	Siepi '98	♀♀♀	8
●	Chianti Cl. Castello di Fonterutoli '99	♀♀♀	8
●	Siepi '99	♀♀♀	8

GAGLIOLE

LOC. GAGLIOLE, 42
53011 CASTELLINA IN CHIANTI (SI)
TEL. 0577740369 - 3341209185
www.gagliole.com

The winery of the Bar-Bettschart husband and wife team seems to have their compass pointing in the right direction since the sangiovese and cabernet sauvignon Pecchia '04, one of their Supertuscans, found its way to the national taste-offs. Tobias Fromann and Stefano Chioccioli are in charge respectively of vineyards and cellar, and their close collaboration is producing good results. Since the winery has only eight hectares under vine, achieving consistency is a challenge. Pecchia '04 is thoroughly appealing, releasing clean-edged redcurrant and sour cherry, smoothed a bit by a cinnamon and vanilla spiciness. The entry is impressive, rounded and expansive, and tannins are perfectly in line. If it drops off just a tad at the end, the finish is nevertheless a pleasurable one. Gagliole '04, from all sangiovese, is more straightforward on the nose, with some evolved leather-like notes alongside wild cherry. Firmly structured, it shows a magisterial equilibrium of tannin, acidity and alcohol, signing off with a savoury flourish. Chianti Classico Rubiolo '04 is less satisfying. The fragrances are inviting enough, centred on a pleasant florality, but the palate is muddled, with somewhat harsh tannins and a finale only medium long.

● Pecchia '04	▼▼	8
● Gagliole Rosso '04	▼▼	6
● Chianti Cl. Rubiolo '04	▼	4
● Gagliole Rosso '00	▽▽	6
● Gagliole Rosso '01	▽▽	6
● Chianti Cl. Rubiolo '03	▽▽	5
● Gagliole Rosso '03	▽▽	6
● Pecchia '03	▽▽	6
● Gagliole Rosso '95	▽▽	5
● Gagliole Rosso '97	▽▽	5
● Gagliole Rosso '98	▽▽	5
● Gagliole Rosso '99	▽▽	5

CASTELLINA IN CHIANTI (SI)

CASTELLO LA LECCIA

LOC. LA LECCIA
53011 CASTELLINA IN CHIANTI (SI)
TEL. 0577743148
www.castellolaleccia.com

Francesco Daddi's winery returns to the full profile section, one more confirmation of the excellence their efforts have achieved, even in 2003, a year that drove many a Tuscan winegrower to distraction. Francesco and his oenologist Paolo Salvi have long committed intense effort to perfecting their mastery of every operational phase, first in their vineyards and then in the cellar. The castle rises where once a fortress served as a Florentine outpost, seriously damaged during the Florence-Siena wars. The Daddi family acquired it in 1919. It is surrounded by a medieval hamlet, a section of which now provides guest accommodation. The winery farms some 20 hectares of vineyards, 13 of which are dedicated to Chianti Classico. Chianti Classico Bruciagna '03 yielded the most impressive results this year. Intense strawberry, wild berry and cherry animate an emphatic nose, then supple tannins contribute to a subtle entry. A lovely, crisp acidity ensures pleasurable leanness, with a medium-long but delicious finish. Chianti Classico '04 builds on generous fruit aromas that underpin nuances of spice and wild herbs. The palate eschews power, displaying a barely noticeable suite of well-judged tannins that usher in a velvety finish, although one might wish for a bit more length.

● Chianti Cl. Bruciagna '03	▼▼	6
● Chianti Cl. '04	▼▼	4
● Chianti Cl. Bruciagna '01	▽▽▽	6
● Chianti Cl. '01	▽▽	4
● Chianti Cl. '02	▽▽	4
● Bruciagna '97	▽▽	4
● Chianti Cl. '97	▽▽	3
● Chianti Cl. '98	▽▽	3
● Chianti Cl. '99	▽▽	4

TENUTA DI LILLIANO
LOC. LILLIANO, 8
53011 CASTELLINA IN CHIANTI (SI)
TEL. 0577743070
www.lilliano.com

The Ruspoli family returns to the Guide this year. Among other newsworthy events is a change of winemakers, with duties entrusted to Lorenzo Landi, and all of the estate's 50 hectares of vineyards is being replanted. Lilliano boasts a venerable history and its villa resides in a 19th-century hamlet. The area has always enjoyed an excellent reputation for growing sangiovese, so much so that it is regarded as a benchmark for Chianti traditions. Efforts made in the past few years have now come to fruition, and the wines presented this year compare with the best from the past. For instance, they no longer show the excessive hardness that has been their primary characteristic but they still retain their own individual identity. Chianti Classico '04 is representative and turned in a terrific performance. A sparkling ruby, it offers clean, nicely sculpted aromas with pungent herbs enriching generous impressions of fruit, largely wild cherry. The palate is elegant and supple, in perfect step with judicious alcohol and well-integrated tannins. Even acidity supports throughout and a tasty finale caps an admirable offering. Riserva '03 presents a more evolved bouquet, with leather and animal skin predominating over some well-ripened fruit, such as dried plum. The alcohol keeps a solid charge of tannins well in check and finishes long. Anagallis '03 is less satisfactory, showing well structured but with tannins that are too drying.

●	Chianti Cl. Ris. '03	▼▼	5
●	Chianti Cl. '04	▼▼	4
●	Anagallis '03	▼	6
●	Chianti Cl. E. Ruspoli Berlingieri Ris. '85	▽▽▽	6
●	Chianti Cl. Ris. '94	▽▽	4
●	Anagallis '95	▽▽	5
●	Chianti Cl. Ris. '95	▽▽	4
●	Anagallis '99	▽▽	6

CASTELLINA IN CHIANTI (SI)

FATTORIA NITTARDI
LOC. NITTARDI
53011 CASTELLINA IN CHIANTI (SI)
TEL. 0577740269
www.chianticlassico.com

The winemaking operation of Peter Fenfert and Stefania Canali continues in the promising direction set by their new Maremma estate, although quality seems to have slipped a notch from the levels achieved in the Chianti zone. But the potential is indisputable, and we believe that after putting behind them a series of difficult vintages they will be on the rebound. The Chianti winery includes 120 hectares of protected woods, 12 hectares of vineyards dedicated to Chianti Classico plus another four to olives. One of the significant features of the winery is its strong ties to contemporary art. Each year a limited edition of Chianti Classico Casanuova di Nittardi carries a label designed by a prestigious artist, and luminaries of the stature of Igor Mitoraj and Emilio Tadini have adorned past editions. In our tastings, there was an initial hesitation on the nose of Ad Astra '04, a blend of international varieties, but ample fruit did open out, followed by a combination of verve and easy accessibility in the mouth. The cabernet sauvignon and merlot Nectar Dei '04 showed well, developing bright red berry fruit cosseted by spice and chocolate but good weight on the palate was marred by somewhat excessive oak. Chianti Classico Casanuova di Nittardi '04 shone with an elegant nose flaunting rich floral and fruit essences. Confident and focused in the mouth, it presents tasty tannins and a lovely, medium-long finish. The nose on Riserva '03, on the other hand, is muddled. There is enough complexity on the palate but it comes across unbalanced and the finish seems stiff.

●	Ad Astra '04	▼▼	5
●	Chianti Cl. Casanuova di Nittardi '04	▼▼	5
●	Nectar Dei '04	▼▼	7
●	Chianti Cl. Ris. '03	▼	7
●	Chianti Cl. Ris. '98	▽▽▽	7
●	Chianti Cl. Ris. '00	▽▽	7
●	Nectar Dei '03	▽▽	6
●	Chianti Cl. Ris. '99	▽▽	7
●	Chianti Cl. Casanuova di Nittardi '01	▽▽	5
●	Chianti Cl. Ris. '01	▽▽	7
●	Chianti Cl. Casanuova di Nittardi '02	▽▽	5

Poggio Amorelli

loc. Poggio Amorelli
53011 Castellina in Chianti (SI)
tel. 0571668733

Once again, Marco Mazzarrini's Oracolo reached the national finals. Poggio Amorelli is a one-man show, with Mazzarrini as manager, sales director, viticulturalist and winemaker all rolled into one. Oracolo '04 is modern in style, as are all of the Poggio Amorelli wines, and even though it didn't capture Three Glasses, it was a stand-out and is beautifully made. A blend of sangiovese and colorino, it is a wine written in the key of density, from its opaque appearance to the nose with jammy red berry fruit, livened by toasty oak and a medley of spices, and onto the compelling palate, which shows an impressive melding of tannins and alcohol. The finish is not particularly lengthy but it is pleasurable and rounded. Everything else is down a rung, beginning with Gode II '04, showing uncomplicated fruit, even progression, refreshing acidity and a medium finale. Chianti Classico '04 is only fairish, suggesting wild flowers and cherry, with a supple enough body but emphatic tannins and a somewhat sluggish finish. Riserva '03 shows a confused mixture of animal fur, leather and greens, concluding with dried plum. A hefty acidity combines with forceful tannins, but the result is not harmonious, and the finish seems tired. An impressive hue introduces Morellino Poggio Barbone '04 to be followed by smooth fruit, preserves and sugared almond. The acidity is not quite the equal of the prominent oak and the finish is clean though not outstandingly long.

● Oracolo '04	🍷🍷	6
● Chianti Cl. Ris. '03	🍷	5
● Chianti Cl. '04	🍷	4
● Gode II '04	🍷	4
● Morellino di Scansano Poggio Barbone '04	🍷	3
● Oracolo '01	YYY	6
● Chianti Cl. Ris. '00	YY	5
● Chianti Cl. '00	YY	4
● Oracolo '03	YY	6

CASTELLINA IN CHIANTI (SI)

Querceto di Castellina

loc. Querceto, 9
53011 Castellina in Chianti (SI)
tel. 0577733590
www.querceto.com

Jacopo Di Battista's winery turned in an impressive performance, even though we believe his best results are yet to come. Querceto di Castellina can boast an impressive history as well, since its properties figure on the 16th-century Mappe dei Capitani di Parte Guelfa. Its estate totals some 50 hectares, with 11 in vines and three in olives. Jacopo's father acquired the farm in the1940s and it functioned as a vacation farm till the end of the 1980s. The first change was the transformation of the farm residence into an agriturismo and at first the vineyards were leased out. Then the Di Battista family took over the reins, and they began making wine in 1997. Eventually they restructured everything, both the vineyard and the cellar, with the constant assistance of oenologist Gioia Cresti. Turning to the wines now, we were impressed by Chianti Classico L'Aura '04, by its impenetrable colour and concentrated aromas, showcasing judicious oak influence, variegated ripe fruit and nuances of smooth spice. We liked the weight in the mouth, its good tannin-alcohol integration, measured acidity and expansive finish. A fine overall balsamic pungency characterizes the sangiovese and merlot Podalirio '04, intertwined with a delicate spiciness and a medley of wild berry. The palate is marked by fluidity and balance rather than energy, including well-measured tannins, and it finishes tasty and long.

● Chianti Cl. L'Aura '04	🍷🍷	4
● Podalirio '04	🍷🍷	6
● Podalirio '01	YYY	6
● Chianti Cl. L'Aura '01	YY	4
● Chianti Cl. L'Aura '03	YY	4
● Podalirio '00	YY	5
● Chianti Cl. L'Aura '02	YY	4
● Podalirio '03	YY	6
● Podalirio '99	YY	5

Rocca delle Macìe

Loc. Macìe, 45
53011 Castellina in Chianti (SI)
tel. 05777321
www.roccadellemacie.com

Sergio Zingarelli's winery staged another impressive performance. Zingarelli is both a successful businessman and a patron of young musicians, sponsoring an annual competition on his wine estate. His father Sergio, a well-known film producer with a passion for wine, founded the winery 30 years ago. Today, it covers more than 600 hectares, with six holdings: Le Macìe, Sant'Alfonso, Fizzano and Le Tavolelle in Chianti Classico, Campomaccione and Casamaria in the Morellino di Scansano DOC zone. This year, he presented the two Supertuscans as well, the sangiovese Ser Gioveto and Roccato, from sangiovese and cabernet sauvignon. The challenging 2003 vintage took its toll and the results were not quite as good as we had hoped. Ser Gioveto shows ripeness, even stewed fruit, on the nose with subtle spice but a full body still allows lively tannins and crisp acidity to shine and it concludes very well. Roccato unfolds berry fruit preserves enriched with subtle cinnamon and clove, opening to excellent breadth and depth, and develops well into an appealing, medium-long finale. Borgo Cennina '04, from sangiovese, cabernet and merlot, encored last year's performance, contrasting pencil lead and leather with mixed fruit, followed by juicy fruit on the palate and a superlative finish. Chianti Classico Riserva '03 showed well, as did Morellino '05, opening crisp and smooth, with a fine, savoury palate exhibiting fine aromatics. Vermentino Occhio a Vento '05 opens to tropical fruit and concludes with a good mineral-laced finish. The remaining wines are all excellent.

●	Chianti Cl. Ris. '03	🍷🍷	5
●	Roccato '03	🍷🍷	6
●	Ser Gioveto '03	🍷🍷	7
●	Borgo Cennina '04	🍷🍷	6
●	Morellino di Scansano Campomaccione '05	🍷🍷	4
●	Chianti Cl. Tenuta Fizzano Ris. '03	🍷	6
●	Chianti Cl. '04	🍷	4
●	Chianti Cl. Tenuta S. Alfonso '04	🍷	4
●	Chianti dei Colli Senesi Rubizzo '04	🍷	4
○	Vermentino Occhio a Vento '05	🍷	4
●	Roccato '00	🍸🍸🍸	7
●	Roccato '99	🍸🍸🍸	7

CASTELLINA IN CHIANTI (SI)

San Fabiano Calcinaia

Loc. Cellole
53011 Castellina in Chianti (SI)
tel. 0577979232
www.sanfabianocalcinaia.com

Guido Serio's Castellina operation resembles a meticulously kept garden with its magnificent vineyards, Cellole in particular. The winery is located in what was once an early 11th-century settlement. Of its approximately 40 hectares of vineyard, 24 are in Chianti Classico country. What impressed us most was the high quality of the entire line. Every wine is well made, clear evidence that the team of viticulturalist Rocco Giorgio and oenologist Carlo Ferrini is yielding good results. This year, both of Guido's icons, Chianti Classico Riserva Cellole and Cerviolo, went through to the national finals. Cellole '03 opens to a well-crafted nose displaying ripe fruit, spice and slaty mineral. An assertive entry yields to tasty, pulpy fruit, an attractive duet of zesty acidity and just noticeable tannins, plus an expansive, dynamic finish. Cerviolo '03, a blend of sangiovese, merlot and cabernet sauvignon, intrigues with generous toasty oak and spice married to bright red berry fruit and then builds the palate to considerable dimensions yet remaining crisp and vibrant right through a lengthy finish. Casa Boschino debuted with the '04 vintage. The blend is similar to Cerviolo, but it is sourced from younger vineyards. Supple and crisp, it is a most pleasurable quaffer. Chianti Classico '04 is enjoyable, not particularly huge but balanced and juicy. Vin Santo '98 seduces from the word go with orange zest and dried fruit. The palate is fat and silky, developing a sweet, lingering finish that crowns a very satisfying offering.

●	Cerviolo Rosso '03	🍷🍷	7
●	Chianti Cl. Cellole Ris. '03	🍷🍷	6
●	Casa Boschino '04	🍷🍷	4
●	Chianti Cl. '04	🍷🍷	4
○	Vin Santo del Chianti Cl. '98	🍷🍷	6
○	Cerviolo Bianco '04	🍷	5
●	Cerviolo Rosso '00	🍸🍸🍸	7
●	Chianti Cl. Cellole Ris. '00	🍸🍸🍸	6
●	Cerviolo Rosso '96	🍸🍸🍸	6
●	Cerviolo Rosso '97	🍸🍸🍸	6
●	Cerviolo Rosso '98	🍸🍸🍸	6
●	Cerviolo Rosso '99	🍸🍸🍸	6
●	Cerviolo Rosso '01	🍸🍸	7
●	Chianti Cl. Cellole Ris. '01	🍸🍸	6

CASTELLINA IN CHIANTI (SI) CASTELLINA MARITTIMA (PI)

Villa Cerna

Loc. Cerna
53011 Castellina in Chianti (SI)
tel. 057754311
www.villacerna.it

Excellent performances win this winery, owned by the Cecchi family, a full profile. The origins of the villa go back to the eleventh century when contemporary documents indicate that it was built by Benedictine monks. The estate consists of more than 205 hectares, with 80 under vine, trained to spurred cordon and Guyot, and over 70 of those go to Chianti Classico. Efforts focus on sangiovese, with use of other varieties as well, such as colorino and canaiolo. The staff is the same as for all other Cecchi group's production, so Giuseppe Mezzedimi directs the vineyard operations, and Riccardo Pericciolі and Miria Bracali the winemaking. Chianti Classico '04 showed very well with a lovely, deep ruby introducing textbook fragrances of cherry-like red berry, complemented by violets and floral notes, and by a subtle minerality. The entry begins a consistent progression with impressive dynamics, well-distributed tannins, and tangy acidity, with a medium-length finish that is still satisfying and pleasurable. The nose on Riserva '03 is more complex and evolved, suggesting tanned leather and animal fur, intermixed with dried plum preserve. It opens out very impressively, with decent weight, tannins that are lively and spacious, and well-integrated acidity. A lingering, sustained finale caps a fine effort.

●	Chianti Cl. Ris. '03	▼▼	5
●	Chianti Cl. '04	▼▼	4

★ Castello del Terriccio

Loc. Terriccio
56040 Castellina Marittima (PI)
tel. 050699709 - 050699792
www.terriccio.it

Confronting the wines of Terriccio presents the taster with a kind of professional paradox. On the one hand, they so clearly reflect their terroir that you can mistake them for no other. On the other, they are enigmatic and indefinable, made up of a myriad of tesserae that the artist has used to confuse the eye of the beholder. This, with only some exaggeration, sums up the wines of Castello del Terriccio, an estate that seems to hang in the air between the Tuscan archipelago and the forested hills that rise towards Volterra. Its 1,700 hectares attest to the hand of man operating in harmony with a wonderfully preserved environment. Their 50 hectares of vineyard flourish in the local terriccio, a mineral and ferruginous soil that is responsible for the distinctive fragrances and bouquet structure. Three Glasses went to Castello del Terriccio '03, a wine whose tremendous power is obvious right from its initial dense ruby. The nose is stunningly complex, with herbaceous fragrances of fresh-mown hay in harmony with pungent, spicy essences of liquorice, cinnamon and cardamom that shade into more evolved leather and tar. Magnificent depth in the mouth is perfectly complemented by vibrant flavours reflecting the wine's splendid fruit. Superb as it is, Lupicaia '03 lacks perhaps just this sensory equilibrium. After an exuberant nose that blends spicy balsam with rich dark fruit, the luscious palate seems not to be fully supported by an appropriate acidity. Tassinaia '03 needs more time to reach its best. The clean, classy chardonnay-based Rondinaia '05 is superlative.

●	Castello del Terriccio '03	▼▼▼	8
●	Lupicaia '03	▼▼	8
○	Rondinaia '05	▼▼	5
●	Tassinaia '03	▼	7
●	Castello del Terriccio '00	▽▽▽	8
●	Lupicaia '00	▽▽▽	8
●	Castello del Terriccio '01	▽▽▽	8
●	Lupicaia '01	▽▽▽	8
●	Lupicaia '93	▽▽▽	8
●	Lupicaia '95	▽▽▽	8
●	Lupicaia '96	▽▽▽	8
●	Lupicaia '97	▽▽▽	8
●	Lupicaia '98	▽▽▽	8
●	Lupicaia '99	▽▽▽	8

Fattoria dell' Aiola

fraz. Vagliagli
53010 Castelnuovo Berardenga (SI)
tel. 0577322615
www.aiola.net

Maria Grazia Malagodi's winery turned in a slightly disappointing performance this year. Nothing serious, of course, since Fattoria dell' Aiola's production is nicely consistent. But it never seems to reach the top step. In fact, we note a slight regression, despite what we believe is terrific potential. The winery has always sought to stay true to the traditional styles and to turn out the best possible versions, spurning trends. But we would suggest a bit more attention to cellar practices. The wine that impressed us most was Logaiolo '03, a blend of sangiovese and cabernet sauvignon. Crisp menthol does a good job of livening up dark cherry and dried plum, although the ripeness of the fruit presented some resistance. It starts off tasty enough in the mouth and develops good depth, and you can't quibble at the length of the finish, but the tannins, dense as they are, are not evenly distributed. Chianti Classico '04 shows a mite too simple and seems to dry out. We were disappointed by both of the 2003 Riservas. The hot year did not make picking decisions easy, and perhaps that was a contributing factor to the lack of balance on the nose, which appear muddled and overripe. Nor does the acidity quite find a length, resulting in an uncharacteristic lack of crispness and balance. Vin Santo '02 however displays textbook qualities, particularly those lovely essences of date and dried fruit, but it is also a tad awkward on the palate and fails to achieve the roundedness you would hope for.

●	Logaiolo '03	TT	4
○	Vin Santo del Chianti Cl. '02	T	5
●	Chianti Cl. Cancello Rosso Ris. '03	T	7
●	Chianti Cl. Ris. '03	T	5
●	Chianti Cl. '04	T	4
●	Chianti Cl. Cancello Rosso Ris. '00	YY	7
●	Chianti Cl. Ris. '00	YY	5
●	Chianti Cl. Ris. '01	YY	5
●	Rosso del Senatore '01	YY	6
●	Rosso del Senatore '03	YY	6

Tenuta di Arceno

loc. San Gusmé
Arceno
53010 Castelnuovo Berardenga (SI)
tel. 0577359346
www.tenutadiarceno.com

It comes as a welcome surprise that Jess Jackson has confounded our complaints last year about a lack of territoriality. The California wine mogul, who also has properties in Bordeaux, this time presented us with a Chianti Classico, and Riserva to boot. Pity it is not the flagship of the winery but that may take some more time, since sangiovese's complexities are not quickly mastered. The history of Arceno stretches back to the Etruscans and the 7th century BC, with the name itself derived from the Etruscan word "Archè", or point of origin. The estate is huge, taking in more than 1,000 hectares, of which some 90 are in vineyard, divided into 59 parcels. Soils range from clay to basalt and granite. Pierre Seillan directs winemaking, together with Lawrence Cronin. Arcanum II '04 went as far as the national taste-off round. Largely merlot with some cabernet sauvignon and sangiovese, it displays generous red berry fruit and nice forward spiciness on the nose. Its smooth, juicy palate is delicious and it drives along impressively to a very vibrant finale. In the Arcanum I '04 blend, cabernet franc predominates, with help from cabernet sauvignon and merlot. Menthol essences contribute to a crisp, fresh nose, followed by a supple palate with well-woven tannins, matching overall the appealing characteristics of the nose and finishing impressively long. Prima Voce '04, primarily merlot and cabernet, is a tasty treat, showing crisp and mouthfilling. An excess of tannins clenches up Riserva '03.

●	Arcanum II '04	TT	5
●	Arcanum I '04	TT	8
●	Prima Voce '04	TT	7
●	Chianti Cl. Ris. '03	T	6
●	Arcanum III '03	YY	8
●	Pozzo di San Donato '99	YY	6
●	Arcanum II '02	YY	8
●	Arcanum I '03	YY	8

CASTELNUOVO BERARDENGA (SI)

Castello di Bossi

Loc. Bossi in Chianti
53019 Castelnuovo Berardenga (SI)
tel. 0577359330
www.castellodibossi.it

Marco Bacci's performance was impressive, particularly since his Corbaia '03 took a richly merited Three Glasses. But he has determinedly slaved away over many years and he now has very decent, and consistent, results to show for it. The family-owned castle saw more use as a rural getaway than as a winemaking operation but intense interest by the two brothers, Marco and Maurizio, led to a complete overhaul in the 1990s, with new plantings and up-to-date equipment. This work bore quick fruit and this year fully three of the wines went into the national finals. Corbaia '03, a sangiovese and cabernet sauvignon pairing, shows a lovely combination of smooth balsam and generous fruit. On the palate, both attack and finish are wonderful, the first delicious and perfectly rounded, exhibiting solid sinew and structure, and the second seemingly endless, spacious and temptingly savoury. The all-merlot Girolamo '03 flaunts a spectrum of aromas that include fruit, pungent spice and tobacco leaf. Performance in the mouth is also impressive, with succulent fruit, tannins that are tamped-down but still effective and an alluring, lingering finish. The opaque hue of Berardo Riserva '03 finds its complement in the blackcurrant and dried plum of the nose. The wine then expands, with supple tannins contributing to a beautifully balanced mid palate and concludes with a tasty flourish. The Maremma estate yielded a delicious Vermentino Vento '05, marked by tempting aromas and toothsome flavours, while its Morellino Tempo '03 is distinctive, showing good grip and appealing drinkability.

●	Corbaia '03	▼▼▼	7
●	Chianti Cl. Berardo Ris. '03	▼▼	6
●	Girolamo '03	▼▼	7
○	Vento Vermentino '05	▼▼	4
●	Chianti Cl. '04	▼	5
●	Morellino di Scansano Tempo Terra di Talamo '05	▼	4
●	Corbaia '99	▽▽▽	8
●	Chianti Cl. Berardo Ris. '00	▽▽	6
●	Girolamo '00	▽▽	7
●	Corbaia '01	▽▽	7
●	Girolamo '01	▽▽	7
●	Girolamo '99	▽▽	8
●	Chianti Cl. Berardo Ris. '01	▽▽	6

CASTELNUOVO BERARDENGA (SI)

Canonica a Cerreto

Loc. Canonica a Cerreto
53019 Castelnuovo Berardenga (SI)
tel. 0577363261
www.canonicacerreto.it

The Lorenzi family should certainly be proud of the results this year from their two Chianti Classico versions, even if they were not able to present their iconic Sandiavolo, a blend of sangiovese, cabernet sauvignon, and merlot. The Riserva '03 was the version that climbed to the national taste-offs, although the standard '04 was not far behind. The source of the fruit is certainly of some consequence. Castelnuovo Berardenga is widely considered one of the best subzones in Chianti Classico, so much so that some importers, in the past, used to ask wineries to highlight that name on the label. Canonica a Cerreto has 20 hectares of vineyard, all dedicated to Chianti Classico production. This year's wines impressed us as scrupulously made and quite distinctive in style. The Riserva '03 displays a vibrant ruby, followed by aromas that show at once finesse and complexity, with piquant notes of wilds herbs an appealing foil to cherry-like berry fruit. These characteristics carry through nicely onto the palate, with a lively acidity and well-layered tannins, although the finish is perhaps not quite as long as one would expect. Subtle balsamic essences pervade the ripe fruit evidenced by Chianti Classico '04 and a firm, solid body is relieved from excess by judiciously gauged acidity. A tasty finish caps an inviting, pleasurable offering.

●	Chianti Cl. Ris. '03	▼▼	5
●	Chianti Cl. '04	▼▼	4
●	Chianti Cl. '00	▽▽	4*
●	Sandiavolo '00	▽▽	5
●	Sandiavolo '03	▽▽	5
●	Sandiavolo '01	▽▽	5
●	Chianti Cl. '03	▽▽	4

Fattoria Carpineta Fontalpino

FRAZ. MONTEAPERTI
LOC. CARPINETA
53019 CASTELNUOVO BERARDENGA (SI)
TEL. 0577369219
www.carpinetafontalpino.it

Filippo and Gioia Cresti's wine estate lies close to the Chianti Classico zone, in the municipality of Castelnuovo Berardenga. The estate vineyards, which you can glimpse from the road that leads to the village of Montaperti, cover 11 hectares and the Crestis lease three more. They are densely planted at some 6,000 vines per hectare, and trained largely to spurred cordon. Sangiovese predominates, with modest parcels of merlot, cabernet sauvignon, alicante and gamay. Masterful vineyard management is the reason behind this operation's success but meticulous attention is also devoted to winemaking practices, which are no-nonsense and as natural as possible, such as the use of ambient yeasts. The fruits of these efforts are wines that are characteristically forthright. Once again, Do ut Des, a blend of sangiovese, merlot, and cabernet sauvignon in equal amounts, went to the national finals, which it has done with stunning regularity right from its release in 1997. The '04 features optimally ripe fruit, perfect weight and nicely judged oak. It's a pity that it lacks just that ounce more complexity that would lift it to another level. Montaperto '05 too displays luxurious texture. From sangiovese, gamay and alicante, it is a winner showing crisp, generous, assertive, and completely delicious. Chianti Colli Senesi '05 is straightforward and delectable. Total production is some 50,000 bottles a year.

● Do Ut Des '04	**TT**	6
● Montaperto '05	**TT**	5
● Chianti Colli Senesi '05	**T**	4
● Do Ut Des '00	YY	6
● Do Ut Des '01	YY	6
● Do Ut Des '02	YY	6
● Do Ut Des '03	YY	6
● Do Ut Des '99	YY	6
● Do Ut Des '98	YY	6

CASTELNUOVO BERARDENGA (SI)

Fattoria di Dievole

VIA DIEVOLE, 6
53010 CASTELNUOVO BERARDENGA (SI)
TEL. 0577322613 - 0577322632
www.dievole.it

Another full profile confirms the success of the Schwenn family. Their news includes a gorgeous new facility, conscientiously presided over by Kathrin Puff, who is of German extraction. Last year, we remarked upon a more clearly recognizable style and that still remains true. It co-exists peacefully with hospitality to wine tourists, who are welcomed here very professionally. Among the wines we enjoyed the most is Plenum Quartus '01, which as it name indicates has now reached its fourth vintage. This is a wine that, by design, includes 50 per cent Dievole sangiovese while the other half always from some other European Union country. This year is Portugal's turn and the complementary variety is touriga franca, from the Quinta do Ramozeiros winery in the Ribera do Douro district. Such exotic products normally leave us underwhelmed, but this blend turned out to be organoleptically successful. Bright red berry fruit folded into wild cherry preserves makes for an intriguing nose before well-placed tannins and a nice charge of acidity provide the right support and energy for considerable heft in the mouth. The all-sangiovese Broccato '01 impressed us as well. Crisp mineral impressions emerge first, gradually acquiring a more fruit-like character, along with undertones of tobacco leaf and tanned leather. The palate shows good, but not excessive, fruit, and builds to a savoury, expansive finale. Chianti Classico '04 is simpler but more than decent.

● Broccato '01	**TT**	5
● Plenum Quartus '01	**TT**	7
● Chianti Cl. '04	**T**	4
● Chianti Cl. Dieulele Ris. '01	YY	5
● Broccato '00	YY	5
● Chianti Cl. '00	YY	4
● Chianti Cl. Dieulele '00	YY	5
● Chianti Cl. '03	YY	4
● Chianti Cl. Ris. '95	YY	4
● Chianti Cl. Novecento '96	YY	4
● Chianti Cl. Novecento '97	YY	4
● Chianti Cl. Novecento '98	YY	5

★ ★ Fattoria di Felsina

via del Chianti, 101
53019 Castelnuovo Berardenga (SI)
tel. 0577355117
www.felsina.it

Three Glasses come to this historic winery with the regularity of thunderbolts in a storm. Chianti Classico Rancia Riserva '03 takes this year's honours, bringing the overall total to 20, and thus earning a second star. Even more surprising, however, is the superb quality of all of the wines. After a slow start and some oxygen, Rancia reveals evolved tones of leather and tobacco, which then fold into well-ripened fruit. The altitude of the vineyard permitted vibrant acidity even in a hot year such as 2004. This and the alcohol keep upfront tannins in check. The palate builds to a succulent, powerful finale, which lingers on and on, with that mineral edge typical to this wine. The all-sangiovese Fontalloro '03, a winery classic, was another finalist. Beguiling redcurrant, raspberry and cherry are caressed by smooth spice. Entry on the palate is equally smooth, with well-modulated tannins that become slightly more evident in mid palate, while the finish is as luscious and crisp as you could want. The other icon, Maestro Raro, was not presented this year but we loved I Sistri '03. It showed a perfect chardonnay minerality, enriched with banana and tropical fruit. A tasty vein of acidity seems to dance on its succulent palate and contributes to an alluring finish. Chianti Classico Riserva '03 is delicious. With velvety mouthfeel, a lingering finish and supple fruit, it's ready for the table. Chianti Classico '04 is harmonious and pleasurable. Vin Santo '98 shows impressive progress, a fat, rounded, luscious palate following bewitching essences of orange and dried fruit.

● Chianti Cl. Rancia Ris. '03	▼▼▼	6
● Fontalloro '03	▼▼	6
● Chianti Cl. Ris. '03	▼▼	5
○ I Sistri '03	▼▼	4
● Chianti Cl. '04	▼▼	4
○ Vin Santo del Chianti Cl. '98	▼▼	5
● Chianti Cl. Rancia Ris. '00	▽▽▽	6
● Fontalloro '01	▽▽▽	6
● Maestro Raro '01	▽▽▽	6
● Chianti Cl. Rancia Ris. '93	▽▽▽	5
● Fontalloro '93	▽▽▽	6
● Maestro Raro '93	▽▽▽	6
● Fontalloro '97	▽▽▽	6
● Fontalloro '98	▽▽▽	6
● Fontalloro '99	▽▽▽	6

Castello di Monastero

loc. Monastero d'Ombrone, 19
53019 Castelnuovo Berardenga (SI)
tel. 0577355789
www.castellodimonastero.com

That wine-impassioned businessman, Lionello Marchesi, continues his efforts apace. Having involved himself with various wine operations in Tuscany over the years, he has now made Castello di Monastero his hub, subsequently bringing together the two properties in Montalcino and in the Maremma. The estate in Castelnuovo Berardenga has some 12 hectares of vineyards, largely planted in galestro soils. In our tastings, we do notice a certain consistency but we also believe that the potential is there for truly stellar performances. Brunello di Montalcino Coldisole '01 layers toasty oak and coffee over a textbook base of rich, well-delineated sour cherry. While not huge on the palate, it develops impressive progression, satisfying tannins and a leisurely finale. Infinito '03 is a sangiovese-cabernet sauvignon partnership. The cinnamon and spice that enliven its base of blackberry and dried plum confer an appealing complexity while exuberant but well-distributed tannins and a tasty acidity shine on the palate. Succulent fruit is there aplenty and the finish is dynamic. The remainder of the line-up strikes a more average note. Assertive tannins somewhat clench both Chianti versions, although both display good body. Chianti Superiore '05 is an inviting quaffer, showing clean fruit and a crisp, vibrant palate. Vin Santo Lunanuova '00 releases the classic hazelnut and date fragrances. Texture and finale are certainly up to par but the palate lacks that seductive hook.

● Infinito '03	▼▼	6
● Brunello di Montalcino Coldisole '01	▼▼	7
○ Vin Santo del Chianti Lunanuova '00	▼	7
● Chianti Cl. Ris. '03	▼	5
● Chianti Cl. '04	▼	4
● Chianti Sup. Castello di Montetondo '05	▼	3
● Brunello di Montalcino Coldisole '00	▽▽	7
● Chianti Cl. Ris. '01	▽▽	5
● Infinito '01	▽▽	6

CASTELNUOVO BERARDENGA (SI)

Fattoria di Petroio

loc. Quercegrossa
via di Mocenni, 7
53010 Castelnuovo Berardenga (SI)
tel. 0577328045 - 0644265210
www.chianticlassico.com

Rebounding from a rather lacklustre performance last year, the Lenzi family returns to the full profile section. Lenzis have owned this farm for over a century and their 14 hectares of vineyard are more than capably cared for, with 13 hectares dedicated to Chianti Classico. The history of their piece of land goes back to Roman times while the main villa dates to the Middle Ages. Its tower served in fact as a guard station on the Siena-Florence road. Petroio boasts an enviable wine heritage, seeing that it has been a member of the Consorzio Vino Chianti Classico since 1927. Chianti Classico Riserva '03 boasts an impressive mosaic of aromatics, with wild berry preserve grounding spicy cinnamon and clove, and intriguing hints of toasty oak throughout. A rounded, inviting palate offers tangy, refreshing acid and judicious tannins, both well integrated with the alcohol. The finale is medium long and smooth. Chianti Classico '04 is no less fine, although the nose seems a tad less rich, leaning more to wild red berries, spiced with some balsam essences. Good balance reigns in the mouth, with pleasing weight, tannins well in the background and a pleasurable, tasty finish with plenty of life to it.

● Chianti Cl. Ris. '03	**YY**	5
● Chianti Cl. '04	**YY**	4
● Chianti Cl. Ris. '97	YYY	5
● Chianti Cl. Ris. '00	YY	5
● Chianti Cl. Ris. '99	YY	6
● Chianti Cl. Ris. '01	YY	5
● Chianti Cl. Ris. '98	YY	5

CASTELNUOVO BERARDENGA (SI)

Poggio Bonelli

loc. Poggio Bonelli
53019 Castelnuovo Berardenga (SI)
tel. 0577355382 - 0577352045
www.poggiobonelli.it

The wine estate owned by the Monte dei Paschi bank and directed by Giovanni Bazzini turned in its usual top-drawer performance. In fact, the Supertuscan, Tramonto d'Oca '03, a sangiovese and merlot partnership, went through to the national finals. But all of the wines are admirable. Fifteen of the 56 hectares are in vineyard, dense-planted and trained to both Guyot and spurred cordon. They have carried out an extensive modernization project over the last few years, both in the vineyard and in the cellar, and good results emerged right from the outset. The all but impenetrable tonality of Tramonto d'Oca promises good complexity on the nose, which delivers appealing balsam and chocolate impressions over a solid base of wild red berry fruit. Tannins are silk smooth on an equally rounded palate, which exhibits a tasty vein of acidity and marches on to an expansive finish. Chianti Classico '04 releases a pleasurable spice box of mixed herbs, cinnamon and clove, fetchingly underpinned by wild cherry. The structure is as good as one should expect and tannins are just where they should be. The finish is tasty and long. Riserva '03 summons up an evolved complex of tanned leather and tobacco leaf twinned with dried-plum fruit and pungent notes of menthol. Supple tannins and a zesty acidity add to a strapping structure and the finish is satisfyingly lengthy.

● Tramonto d'Oca '03	**YY**	6
● Chianti Cl. Ris. '03	**YY**	6
● Chianti Cl. '04	**YY**	4
● Chianti Cl. Ris. '01	YY	6
● Tramonto d'Oca '01	YY	6
● Tramonto d'Oca '00	YY	6

San Felice

Loc. San Felice
53019 Castelnuovo Berardenga (SI)
tel. 05773991
www.agricolasanfelice.it

Agricola San Felice debuted a particularly intriguing wine this year, the result of years of experimentation in the vineyard. Pugnitello '03 is made from the variety of the same name and exhibits a sensory profile that is one of a kind. This is not through happenstance, since the winery launched a viticultural experimentation project back in 1968, under the then estate manager Enzo Morganti. The experiments have continued since then, along with another project, the restructuring of the ancient residential settlement, which eventually became an elegant hotel. Owned by the RAS insurance group, the estate covers 600 hectares, of which 180 are in vineyard and 115 are dedicated to Chianti Classico. The experimental vineyard, comprising some two hectares, is of prime importance. A collaborative project with the Tuscan regional authority and the University of Florence, it involves intense study of 270 different varieties, 161 of them red. The new wine offers great complexity on the nose, displaying tanned leather and animal skin, well interwoven with ripe dried plum and subtle herbaceous notes. Good, lively tannins, warm alcohol and a tangy acidity combine to build a palate of impressive assertiveness and the progression continues unimpeded into a rich, dynamic finale. Il Grigio Riserva '03 is a fine offering, with wild black berry fruit, good weight and a tasty finish. The smooth, juicy, vivacious Chianti Classico '04 is delicious and approachable.

● Pugnitello '03	▼▼	6
● Chianti Cl. Il Grigio Ris. '03	▼▼	5
● Chianti Cl. '04	▼▼	4
● Chianti Cl. Poggio Rosso Ris. '00	▽▽▽	6
● Vigorello '88	▽▽▽	5
● Chianti Cl. Poggio Rosso Ris. '90	▽▽▽	6
● Chianti Cl. Poggio Rosso Ris. '95	▽▽▽	5
● Vigorello '97	▽▽▽	5
● Chianti Cl. Poggio Rosso Ris. '01	▽▽	6
● Vigorello '98	▽▽	6
● Vigorello '99	▽▽	7
● Vigorello '01	▽▽	7

Castello di Selvole

Fraz. Vagliagli
Loc. Selvole, 1
53019 Castelnuovo Berardenga (SI)
tel. 0577322662
www.selvole.com

The winery of Guido Busetto and his wife Nobuko Hashimoto has graduated to a full profile. The results of this year's tastings are good but we admit that we expected better. Guido had a glorious past in France as a journalist, where he developed a love for wine. We have seen at first hand the passion that drives him and the almost maniacal attention he devotes to what he does. He and Nobuko studied at the Institute of Oenology at the University of Bordeaux, where they struck up a friendship with the dean, Yves Glories. After they acquired Selvole, Glories began working with them. The estate now has 40 hectares of vines and nine of olives, all managed by Stefano Porcinai. Extensive restructuring of both vineyards and cellar has quickly afforded them admirable results. The castle, built in the eleventh century, was considered by Siena to be one of its most crucial outlying strongholds. Of the wines, the sangiovese Barullo '03 impressed us most. A forthright ruby precedes subtle spice tones that nicely lift fruit that is well delineated. A gorgeous, leisurely finish caps its succulent, elegant development. We were less enthusiastic about Chianti Classico '04, which we found a tad simple on the nose and short on the end, but it does offer an attractive vein of acidity. Sangiovese '04 exhibits a quite decent structure, fine-grained tannins and tasty crispness.

● Barullo '03	▼▼	6
● Chianti Cl. '04	▼	4
● Sangiovese '04	▼	3
● Barullo '00	▽▽	6
● Chianti Cl. '00	▽▽	3*
● Chianti Cl. '01	▽▽	4*
● Chianti Cl. '99	▽▽	3
● Chianti Cl. Ris. '99	▽▽	5
● Barullo '01	▽▽	6
● Chianti Cl. '03	▽▽	4
● Chianti Cl. Ponte Rosso '03	▽▽	4
● Sangiovese '03	▽▽	3
● Chianti Cl. Ris. '96	▽▽	5

TOLAINI

s. p. 9 di Pievasciata, 28
53019 Castelnuovo Berardenga (SI)
tel. 0577356972
www.tolaini.it

Pierluigi Tolaini merits a full profile this year. Tolaini emigrated to Canada from Tuscany's Garfagnana area and built that country's largest transportation firm. But the pull from his native land was irresistible and he returned in 1998 to enter the wine business. He purchased the Montebello and San Giovanni properties, with their 108 hectares, 65 of them under vine. In 1999, he began total restructuring of the vineyards then launched construction of a new ageing cellar. Much study was focused on the potential of the local soil, with the result that international varieties such as cabernet sauvignon, merlot and petit verdot were added to complement sangiovese. Michel Rolland, consultant to the winery, may have a hand in this as well. Although Tolaini lies in the heart of the Chianti zone, it produces no Chianti Classico, only its own three blends. Picconero, the winery flagship, was still maturing in large wood but the remaining two wines did well. Due Santi '03 is made from cabernet franc, cabernet sauvignon and merlot. All but opaque, it offers a dense mélange of chocolate, toasty oak and blackcurrant preserve, with some subtle balsam hovering about. It opens to a spacious palate, with a very dense, tight-textured mouthfeel and a good tannin-alcohol marriage, achieving a smooth, well-leisured finish. Al Passo '03, of sangiovese and merlot, is keyed to more immediate enjoyment. Spice and fruit highlight the nose, followed by a palate marked by finesse, yet with appreciable acidic grip. The finale is as delicious and lengthy as one could wish for.

● Al Passo '03	🍷🍷	5
● Due Santi '03	🍷🍷	6
● Due Santi '02	🍷🍷 (white)	5

CASTELNUOVO BERARDENGA (SI)

VILLA A SESTA

loc. Villa a Sesta
p.zza del Popolo,1
53019 Castelnuovo Berardenga (SI)
tel. 0577359014
www.villasesta.com

While Riccardo Tattoni did not reprise last year's terrific performance, one of his wines did go all the way to the national taste-offs. The estate, located in the hamlet of Villa a Sesta, which seems to have Etruscan roots, comprises almost 100 hectares, with 16 in vineyard, all dedicated to Chianti Classico. Marco Mazzarrini directs vineyards and winemaking. The house style aims for soft texture and roundedness, and it has certainly struck a chord in the international market. The wine that stood out in our tastings was Chianti Classico Riserva '03. It displays a pleasing medley of fruit well-laced with pungent menthol and mineral essences, then delightful acidity and good heft in the mouth, noticeable but well-behaved tannins and an ambitious, expansive finish. Vas '04 is largely sangiovese, with a helping hand from merlot and colorino. Opaque to the eye, it certainly offers a gift to the nose, with a multi-faceted package of cinnamon and clove spice wrapped around ripe blueberry and blackcurrant, and emitting toasty nuances of oak. On entry, it broadens out impressively, exhibiting tucked-in tannins, velvety mouthfeel, vibrant acidity and a well-crafted finale. Chianti Classico Il Palei '04 steps down a rung in complexity and is simpler both on the nose and palate, with a medium-long finale, but drinks well enough at the present. Chianti Colli Aretini Ripaltella '04 is a consumer's find, well worth its price. Lovely floral-fruit aromas are followed by succulent fruit and good balance on this straightforward but tasty bottle.

● Chianti Cl. Ris. '03	🍷🍷	4
● Vas '04	🍷🍷	5
● Chianti Cl. Il Palei '04	🍷	4
● Chianti Colli Aretini Ripaltella '04	🍷	4
● Chianti Cl. Ris. '01	🍷🍷 (white)	4
● Chianti Cl. Il Palei '03	🍷🍷 (white)	4
● Vas '03	🍷🍷 (white)	5
● Chianti Colli Aretini Ripaltella '03	🍷🍷 (white)	3

CASTIGLION FIBOCCHI (AR)

TENUTA SETTE PONTI
LOC. VIGNA DI PALLINO
VIA SETTE PONTI,71
52029 CASTIGLION FIBOCCHI (AR)
TEL. 055477857
www.tenutasetteponti.it

Tenuta Sette Ponti maintains its quality edge even though no wine really stood out this year. In general, the wines made at the Arezzo estate impressed us more than those from the new Poggio al Lupo holding in the Maremma. For instance Oreno '04, predominantly sangiovese and merlot with a dash of cabernet sauvignon, is as well executed as ever. It is by design a dense, highly extracted wine but spicy balsamic notes and toasty oak lighten somewhat the dark, ripe, full fruit on the nose. The palate is in the same mould, quite compelling for its densely-woven texture, with gobs of tannins, but it shows low-key aromatics and is a touch bitterish on the finish. Crognolo '04 is made from sangiovese with a dollop of merlot. The nose, somewhat dumb at the moment, is more varietal, with a subtle florality contrasting nicely with earthiness and tobacco leaf. These echo on a palate that exhibits crisp savouriness, appreciable depth and good acidity that keeps everything well knit together. From the Maremma offerings, Poggio al Lupo '04, a blend of cabernet, alicante and petit verdot, opens with very ripe fruit but too much oak besets the palate, leaving it drying and astringent. Morellino di Scansano '05 exhibits smooth impressions on the nose and while structurally rather slender, it is a lively, crisp enough quaffer that will go down quite nicely.

●	Crognolo '04	**YY**	5
●	Oreno '04	**YY**	8
●	Poggio al Lupo '04	**Y**	6
●	Morellino di Scansano Poggio al Lupo '05	**Y**	4
●	Oreno '00	YYY	6
●	Oreno '01	YY	6
●	Poggio al Lupo '01	YY	6
●	Oreno '03	YY	7
●	Poggio al Lupo '03	YY	6
●	Oreno '99	YY	6

CASTIGLIONE D'ORCIA (SI)

PODERE FORTE
LOC. PETRUCCI, 13
53023 CASTIGLIONE D'ORCIA (SI)
TEL. 05778885100
www.podereforte.it

This year saw a performance that was not quite up to expectations for a winery that over the last few years has stood out as the most innovative and dynamic in the young Orcia DOC. The 2004 wines are technically well put together but they seem to lack the extra quality and distinctiveness that sets apart a thoroughbred. In our tastings, we had the feeling that these wines smacked too much of cellar technique, with too much extraction from the barrel and too little character from the terroir. Guardavigna '04, a team of sangiovese, cabernet sauvignon, merlot and petit verdot, arrives dark and dense to the eye, offering copious aromas of toast and smokiness. Massive structure and great weight develop on the palate, the tannins showing tight-textured but somewhat abrasive. Overall, the wine comes across as sluggish and the finish is bitterish but more time in the bottle may smooth everything out. The sangiovese Petrucci '04 shows softer contours, floral notes and red berry, though it is not as clean as one might wish. The attack is smooth enough but it soon clenches and loses energy amidst an excess of oak. We found Petruccino '04, within its more modest dimensions, to be better balanced. A sangiovese-cabernet sauvignon blend, it has a palate of succulent fruitiness and echoes the dark fruit, smooth spice and blossoms of the nose. There is nice breadth, dynamic progression and a more judicious contribution from the barrel.

●	Orcia Guardiavigna '04	**YY**	8
●	Orcia Petrucci '04	**Y**	8
●	Orcia Petruccino '04	**Y**	5
●	Orcia Guardiavigna '01	YYY	8
●	Orcia Guardiavigna '02	YY	8
●	Orcia Guardiavigna '03	YY	8
●	Orcia Petrucci '01	YY	8
●	Orcia Petrucci '02	YY	8

CERRETO GUIDI (FI)

VILLA PETRIOLO
VIA DI PETRIOLO, 7
50050 CERRETO GUIDI (FI)
TEL. 057155284
www.villapetriolo.com

Silvia Maestrelli's operation is back to a full profile with some excellent results. The winery is located in the municipality of Cerreto Guidi, an area already noted in the 19th century for the quality of its wines, even if its earlier fame was for the pomp of its gardens and villas. We might also note that one of Villa Petriolo's wines bears the name of the Golpaja estate, whose kilns furnished the bricks to build the Cerreto Guidi's Villa Medici in the mid-16th century. Moreno Maestrelli acquired the villa 40 years ago and for long used as his country retreat. Some eight years ago, his daughter Silvia launched an ambitious modernization project that involved replanting the vineyards and establishing an estate winery in the full sense of the term. The management is all-female, with Silvia's sister Simona directing the hospitality programme. We found Golpaja '04 excellent. Largely sangiovese, it spreads a base of dense, succulent fruit and then adds intriguing pencil lead and pungent herbs. Sound and balanced in the mouth, it offers judicious, even tannins and a toothsome, savoury finish. Vin Santo '00 is every bit as good, with the expected evolved impressions of apricot, dried peach and hazelnut enriched with nuances of honey. Everything is as it should be in the mouth as well. Dense, creamy texture, seductive, non-cloying sweetness and a leisurely, compelling finale. The fine Chianti '05 is one of the best value wines in the category.

○	Vin Santo del Chianti '00	ΨΨ (black)	5
●	Golpaja '04	ΨΨ (black)	5
●	Chianti Villa Petriolo '05	Ψ (black)	3*
●	Golpaja '00	ΨΨ	4
●	Golpaja '01	ΨΨ	5
●	Golpaja '03	ΨΨ	5
●	Golpaja '99	ΨΨ	4

CINIGIANO (GR)

SCHIACCIONAIA
LOC. POGGI DEL SASSO
58044 CINIGIANO (GR)
TEL. 0564967202
www.schiaccionaia.it

We welcome the Schiaccionaia to the Guide. The winery, owned by Riccardo Rolla and Marcella Turziani, is located in the centre of the Montecucco DOC zone. It has six hectares in vineyards, planted from 2001 onwards to a high density of 6,450 vines per hectare. They are cultivated organically and yield an annual production of just over 18,000 bottles. Alfredo Veronesi is the consulting viticulturalist. The variety of wines is impressive, as is their overall quality, and each merits a description. Let's open with the surprising Velis Passis '05, which went through to the national taste-offs. A passito from dried traminer grapes, it releases luscious draughts of sweet candied orange on a well-focused nose, and the palate, not at all cloying, is every bit as delicious and well balanced. The reds performed well too, particularly Poggio Le Mandrie '04, whose gorgeously textured, spicy bouquet betrays a judicious blend of cabernet sauvignon, merlot and sangiovese. Equally splendid is Montecucco Sangiovese Trasubie '04, mostly sangiovese with some merlot, which offers smoky notes and dark earth preceding a vibrant, bracing progression. Venuste '05, from 100 per cent viognier, is a masterpiece of craftsmanship with judicious aromas and crisp, intense flavours on the palate. Finally, the all-syrah Isistro '04 shows marked pepperiness, and solid weight in the mouth, tailing off just a little too light on the conclusion.

○	Vino Passito Velis Passis '05	ΨΨ (grey)	6
●	Montecucco Sangiovese Trasubie '04	ΨΨ (black)	4
●	Poggio Le Mandrie '04	ΨΨ (black)	5
○	Venuste '05	ΨΨ (black)	4
●	Isistro '04	Ψ (black)	5

CORTONA (AR)

Tenimenti Luigi D'Alessandro

via di Manzano, 15
52042 Cortona (AR)
tel. 0575618667 - 0575618636
www.tenimentidalessandro.it

Those who were looking forward to assessments of the new vintages from Tenimenti D'Alessandro will have to wait until next year's edition. They provided us this year with only the Vin Santo, having decided to postpone for a year the presentation of their wines. We compliment them on their courage in making this well thought-out move. By not following the usual practice of presenting the wines right after bottling, allowing them additional maturation in the bottle instead, they are ensuring that the wines perform better at a later date. The cellar also intends to get release dates into step with the publication schedule of the annual wine guides. So no Cortona Il Bosco '04, Cortona Syrah '05 or Fontarca '05, all of which we will look forward to at next year's tastings. We will respect this admirable position and make do, as it were, with the superlative Cortona Vin Santo '00. An opulent amber prepares us for an alluring array of complex impressions and fragrances, ranging from dried nuts and candied apricots and figs to yeasted dough and even an intriguing suggestion of pungent rust. The sweetness on the palate is measured, with all components impressively balanced, and its savoury flavours and rich aromas carry though into a long-lingering, tasty finale.

○	Cortona Vin Santo '00	🍷🍷	6
●	Cortona Il Bosco '01	YYY	7
●	Cortona Il Bosco '03	YYY	7
●	Podere Il Bosco '95	YYY	5
●	Podere Il Bosco '97	YYY	5
●	Cortona Il Bosco '00	YY	6
●	Podere Il Bosco '99	YY	6
●	Podere Il Bosco '96	YY	5
●	Podere Il Bosco '98	YY	5

DICOMANO (FI)

Frascole

loc. Frascole, 27a
50062 Dicomano (FI)
tel. 0558386340
www.frascole.it

The winery owned by Elisa Santoni and Enrico Lippi deservedly earned a full profile this year. They certainly have enthusiasm and pluck to spare. First, they decided to take up grape growing in an unusual area where there are no other wineries. Second, they worked out a well-nigh magical formula for making Vin Santo, which has yielded truly knockout results. And they have done so without orphaning their Chianti Rufina, which remains their iconic offering. The 1996 vintage of the Vin Santo emerged as one of the best anywhere. The expected amber hue introduces subtle but pungent medicinal herbs that act as an attractive foil to dried date and fig. The palate shows luscious and fat, with a tasty acidic zest, expanding impressively into a remarkably long, lip-smacking finale. Chianti Rufina Riserva '03 gives a more than capable performance, richly laden with jammy red berry fruit lifted by tones that suggest slaty mineral and spicy balsam. It satisfies easily with good weight, barely perceptible, fine-grained tannins and a dynamic and delicious finish. Chianti Rufina '04 relies on more straightforward fruit and herbal notes but is certainly lively enough. The tannins, though, are still a bit indigestible and tamp down the finish a little.

○	Vin Santo del Chianti Rufina '96	🍷🍷	8
●	Chianti Rufina Ris. '03	🍷🍷	5
●	Chianti Rufina '04	🍷	4
○	Vin Santo del Chianti Rufina '95	YY	8
●	Chianti Rufina '00	YY	4
●	Chianti Rufina Il Santo Ris. '00	YY	5
●	Chianti Rufina '01	YY	4*
●	Chianti Rufina Ris. '01	YY	5

EMPOLI (FI)

PIAZZANO
VIA DI PIAZZANO, 5
50053 EMPOLI (FI)
TEL. 0571994032

We are most pleased that Piazzano has made a return to our full pages after somewhat tentative appearances in 1994 and 1995. Piazzano, located in the hills south of Empoli, has seen many changes. Vineyard coverage has increased to 34 hectares, dedicated largely to sangiovese, with a few concessions to the internationals. Ilaria and Rolando Bettarini took over the reins from their father Riccardo in 1999 and have more than maintained the family tradition of commitment and wide-ranging proficiency. The wine style, too, has evolved gradually over the past few years, now clearly showing the hallmarks of a deep respect for local traditions, as well as up-to-date winemaking practices. Syrah '04 stood out from the other wines. After a deep, rich ruby, there is a slight wait but the nose gradually opens to a clean, varietal pepperiness, well laced with cinnamon and spice, over wild red berry. The palate shows an excellent combination of firm structure, rounded mouthfeel and a judicious tannic charge while the finish is as smooth and leisurely as one would want. Sangiovese '04 comes across beautifully, even if it is still a tad closed in. There is plenty of smooth, tasty fruit in the mouth, framed by dense, fleshy tannins and a bracing acidity supporting a long, delicious finale. On the same quality rung is Chianti '05, exhibiting exemplary balance and a well-fruited progression. Likewise appealing are the self-confident and harmonious Chianti Rio Camerata '05 and the supple, crisp, approachable Ventoso '05, an 80-20 blend of sangiovese and canaiolo.

● Piazzano Sangiovese '04	🍷🍷	6
● Piazzano Syrah '04	🍷🍷	5
● Chianti '05	🍷🍷	3*
● Chianti Rio Camerata '05	🍷	4
● Ventoso '05	🍷	3
● Piazzano '94	YY	5
● Chianti Ris. '98	YY	4

FAUGLIA (PI)

I GIUSTI E ZANZA
VIA DEI PUNTONI, 9
56043 FAUGLIA (PI)
TEL. 058544354
www.igiustiezanza.it

Fauglia, where gentle hills flank the left bank of the Arno just before it empties to the sea, was the spot where the passion for wine of Paolo Giusti and Fabio Zanza took root. Although their fervour is intense, it has always been expressed with intelligence and judiciousness, in sober terms we would say and always in step with the rhythms of the vine, which are irreconcilable with hurry and cash flow. These traits have led to our appreciation not just of their work but also of the two men themselves so we are doubly pleased to draw attention to the top-drawer performance this year of their winery near Pisa. Although this is just the second vintage for PerBruno '04, it reached the national finals. We found impressive both its deep ruby hue and its truly appealing bouquet, built up with dark blackcurrant and dried plum around a varietally faithful black pepper core. The palate is seduction incarnate, giving wonderful depth and texture with silk-smooth tannins and crisp, acidic vibrancy. The opera-inspired labels are just as magisterial. Dulcamara '03 is its usual superlative self, ably folding oak tones into wild red berry and spice, and developing an opulent palate afforded rich support by mature and supple tannins. Belcore '04 shows slight over-extraction from its sangiovese and merlot. But Nemorino Rosso and Bianco '05 are tone-perfect, lovely straightforward creations to be enjoyed full-tilt, worthy accompaniments to Donezetti's "Elisir d'amore", a splendid example of the 19th-century melodrama that inspired the wine names.

● PerBruno '04	🍷🍷	5
● Dulcamara '03	🍷🍷	6
● Belcore '04	🍷	4
● Nemorino Bianco '05	🍷	3
● Nemorino Rosso '05	🍷	3
● Dulcamara '00	YY	6
● Dulcamara '01	YY	6
● Dulcamara '98	YY	6
● Dulcamara '99	YY	6

FIESOLE (FI)

Bibi Graetz

via di Vincigliata, 19
50014 Fiesole (FI)
tel. 055597289 - 055597222
www.bibigraetz.com

One must know Bibi Graetz personally to fully appreciate how completely the wines he creates mirror the man. We find him imaginative, eclectic and imbued with a healthy dose of folly that was perhaps his inspiration to produce wines in a locality that no one else would have considered. But there is nothing capricious about his approach to viticulture. Quite the opposite. One of the wines that have always impressed us did in fact go to the national finals this year, Bugia '04. It is made from ansonica grapes grown on the Isola del Giglio, perhaps not Italy's most prestigious viticultural area. But Graetz's presence there seems to have spurred his local growers to ever better quality, and it shows. Sporting a lovely amber, Bugia releases an intriguingly citrus-edged medley of aromas ranging from earthy mineral to well-ripened fruit. It builds impressive volume in the mouth, but tangy, well-adjusted acidity holds it well within bounds and the tasty finale matches everything that precedes it. Testamatta '04, the other finalist, is an assemblage of sangiovese, colorino, canaiolo and moscato nero whose proportions vary according to the vintage. Pleasant spice gins up good fruit on the nose while a juicy finish nicely caps the rounded, smooth progression that shows appreciable energy. The Canaiolo '04, a 100 per cent varietal, releases crisp, pungent herb essences and a lively, charged development but exuberant tannins choke off the finale somewhat. Colore '04, all colorino, boasts solid structure that merits attention.

○	Bugia '04	🍷🍷	7
●	Testamatta '04	🍷🍷	8
●	Canaiolo '04	🍷🍷	8
●	Colore '04	🍷🍷	8
●	Testamatta '00	ΥΥ	8
●	Testamatta '01	ΥΥ	8
●	Testamatta '02	ΥΥ	8
●	Colore '03	ΥΥ	8
●	Testamatta '03	ΥΥ	8
○	Bugia '02	ΥΥ	6
○	Bugia '03	ΥΥ	7
●	Canaiolo '03	ΥΥ	8

FIRENZE

★ Marchesi Antinori

p.zza degli Antinori, 3
50123 Firenze
tel. 05523595
www.antinori.it

Solaia '03, one of the classics among Supertuscans, and made as always of 80-20 cabernet sauvignon and sangiovese, sparked some observations at our tastings. It confirmed, first, that 2003 was not an easy year for this is not the best version ever of Solaia. But neither is it one of the poorest. Far from being green or aggressive, its tannins rival in suppleness those of the '01 version, from a far more favourable growing season. All this demonstrates that the '03 benefited from carefully selected grapes and little manipulation in the cellar. Not only do we have a superb wine but it bears no signs of the overripe fruit and hard tannins that so obviously mark some of its fellow 2003s elsewhere. Flanking it is a good version of Tignanello. This '03 has 20 per cent cabernet sauvignon added to sangiovese and a couple more years in bottle will prove helpful. Likewise impressive are the Chianti Classico Riserva '03s, both Badia a Passignano and Tenute del Marchese. We found two surprises. Villa Antinori '03, predominantly sangiovese, seems to have regained youthfulness when it shook off its Chianti Classico label, as did Santa Cristina '05, it too once in the same category. Still largely sangiovese, it is by design a simpler product but no less delicious for that. All in all, this is a fine group of wines from the largest privately owned Italian winery, with an annual production of almost 18,000,000 bottles and a turnover of 120,000,000 euros.

●	Solaia '03	🍷🍷🍷	8
●	Chianti Cl. Badia a Passignano Ris. '03	🍷🍷	6
●	Chianti Cl. Tenute del Marchese Ris. '03	🍷🍷	6
●	Tignanello '03	🍷🍷	8
●	Villa Antinori Rosso '03	🍷🍷	4*
●	Santa Cristina '05	🍷	3
●	Solaia '00	ΥΥΥ	8
●	Solaia '01	ΥΥΥ	8
●	Solaia '90	ΥΥΥ	8
●	Solaia '94	ΥΥΥ	6
●	Solaia '95	ΥΥΥ	8
●	Solaia '96	ΥΥΥ	6
●	Solaia '97	ΥΥΥ	8
●	Solaia '98	ΥΥΥ	8
●	Solaia '99	ΥΥΥ	8

FIRENZE

MARCHESI DE' FRESCOBALDI
VIA SANTO SPIRITO, 11
50125 FIRENZE
TEL. 05527141
www.frescobaldi.it

No top trophy this year for Frescobaldi, but all the wines presented were of admirable quality. This is a tribute to Frescobaldi's talented organization and dedicated hard work since the cellar achieves sterling results even at high production levels. The team of Lamberto Frescobaldi and Niccolò D'Afflitto, responsible respectively for viticulture and oenology, obviously functions smoothly. This time, we particularly liked Vin Santo Castello di Pomino '01. Serving up a luscious medley of honey, vanilla, orange zest and medicinal herbs, it opens to a stunningly textured palate that boasts impressive depth and breadth, with every component neatly in balance. Alcoholic warmth is pronounced and only the finish a tad limited. Chianti Rufina Montesodi '04, too, went to the national finals. Opaque to the eye, it marries lively red fruit to dusky chocolate and spicy vanilla and oak, matched by good depth and texture, which fall off slightly at mid palate. The finale is smooth but only medium long. Mormoreto '03, a blend of cabernet sauvignon, cabernet franc and merlot, did not quite rise to our expectations. It has rich succulent fruit in the mouth but prominent tannins slow down the progression, and the nose seems muddled. Chianti Rufina Nipozzano Riserva '03 impresses with generous draughts of ripe plum and other fruit, shot through with spicy balsam. A splendid, lengthy finish concludes a smooth, balanced palate of pulpy fruit. The remaining wines are first-rate, with special mentions for Pater '04 and Albizzia '05, both excellent value for money.

○	Castello di Pomino Vin Santo '01	🍷🍷	6
●	Chianti Rufina Montesodi '04	🍷🍷	7
●	Chianti Rufina Nipozzano Ris. '03	🍷🍷	4
●	Mormoreto '03	🍷🍷	7
○	Pomino Il Benefizio '04	🍷🍷	6
●	Pater '04	🍷	3*
○	Albizzia '05	🍷	3*
●	Morellino di Scansano Santa Maria '05	🍷	4
○	Pomino Bianco '05	🍷	4
●	Chianti Rufina Montesodi '01	YYY	7
●	Mormoreto '01	YYY	7
●	Chianti Rufina Montesodi '90	YYY	7
●	Chianti Rufina Montesodi '96	YYY	7
●	Chianti Rufina Montesodi '97	YYY	7
●	Chianti Rufina Montesodi '99	YYY	7

FUCECCHIO (FI)

FATTORIA MONTELLORI
VIA PISTOIESE, 1
50054 FUCECCHIO (FI)
TEL. 0571260641
www.fattoriamontellori.it

Alessandro Nieri is not one to rest on his laurels. After gaining a well-consolidated foothold in the premium-wine market, he has for several years now been pushing towards more ambitious targets, showing an even deeper commitment to his operation. For his top wines, he has been meticulously following the advice of agronomist Andrea Paoletti regarding minimal yield per vine, low production and winemaking practices aimed at maximum exploitation of superb quality fruit. A good example is his stellar Salamartano '04. Its component varieties, cabernet sauvignon and merlot, show through at every stage, beginning with a complex suite of aromas that has spice and roast coffee over raspberry and blackberry veined with subtle oak nuances. Vigorous but velvety tannins help build a full body and drive development through to a lengthy finish. The all-syrah Tuttosole '04 performed equally well, displaying a rich, luminous tonality and an appealing combination of black pepper, well-ripened fruit and subtle spice. Here, too, we liked the smooth, rounded depth in the mouth, even progression and long, peppery finish. Chianti Fattoria le Caselle '05 is right on the mark, with a subtle florality behind emphatic red berry fruit, both of which go on to infuse the palate. Montellori Brut '01 is creamy, with a delicate mousse, and equally fine are Moro '04, marked by a well-crafted, even structure, and Chianti '05, fragrant and ready to enjoy. Sant'Amato and Vigna del Mandorlo, both '05s, are well-executed whites, crisp, refreshing and pleasurable.

●	Salamartano '04	🍷🍷	6
○	Montellori Brut '01	🍷🍷	5
●	Tuttosole '04	🍷🍷	5
●	Chianti Fattoria le Caselle '05	🍷🍷	3
●	Moro '04	🍷	4
●	Chianti '05	🍷	3
○	Sant'Amato '05	🍷	4
○	V. del Mandorlo '05	🍷	3
●	Salamartano '00	YY	6
●	Salamartano '01	YY	6
●	Dicatum '03	YY	5
●	Salamartano '03	YY	6
●	Tuttosole '03	YY	6

GAIOLE IN CHIANTI (SI)

AGRICOLTORI DEL CHIANTI GEOGRAFICO
LOC. MULINACCIO
VIA MULINACCIO, 10
53013 GAIOLE IN CHIANTI (SI)
TEL. 0577749489
www.chiantigeografico.it

It is gratifying to witness the unfolding of a programme whose goal is to achieve high quality spread equally over a production of millions of bottles, and to do so without any economic sacrifices. The Agricoltori winery has in the past defined itself as a co-operative, whereas today it reflects the more modern face of a viticulture that focuses on small vineyard owners, encouraging them to utilize better vineyard practices to improve the fruit brought to the cellar. Merit for this progress goes above all to director Carlo Salvadori, who has succeeded brilliantly in motivating his entire staff. Chianti Classico Contessa di Radda '04 is an outstanding example of a wine that has both typicity and fine sensory appeal, and as such it won a place in our national finals. It displays terrific depth of fruit on the nose and magisterial balance through a progression crowned with a resounding finish. We were most impressed by Riserva Montegiachi '03. Its tannins have smoothed out and are now nicely layered and well integrated with the alcohol while the finish is leisurely and silky. We didn't taste Ferraiolo, a blend of sangiovese and cabernet sauvignon. It is wisely being given another year's maturation in the cellar. The 100 per cent merlot Pulleraia '04 did well, offering fragrant wild berry and a rounded texture. It's not an especially complex wine but well done. The quality of Chianti Classico '04 represents excellent value for the consumer. Finally, Vin Santo '02 is a lovely foretaste of what is still slumbering in the barrels. Good news will emerge soon.

●	Chianti Cl. Contessa di Radda '04	▼▼	4
●	Chianti Cl. Montegiachi Ris. '03	▼▼	5
●	Pulleraia '04	▼▼	5
○	Vin Santo del Chianti Cl. '02	▼	6
●	Chianti Cl. '04	▼	4
●	Pulleraia '03	▽▽	5
●	Ferraiolo '02	▽▽	6
●	Pulleraia '02	▽▽	6
●	Ferraiolo '03	▽▽	5

GAIOLE IN CHIANTI (SI)

★ ★ CASTELLO DI AMA
FRAZ. LECCHI IN CHIANTI
LOC. AMA
53013 GAIOLE IN CHIANTI (SI)
TEL. 0577746031
www.castellodiama.com

If we had to pick the winery that in the past five years has impressed us most for sustained quality, Castello di Ama is the obvious choice. Nine Three Glass awards in the last four editions, 2005 Winery of the Year, Marco Pallanti Oenologist of the Year a couple of years before and a retrospective Three Glasses for Chianti Classico Bellavista '95, tasted again this year, for a grand total of 21 Three Glasses over 20 editions and a second Star. No cellar has turned in a better performance over the last few years. These achievements probably had a part in Marco Pallanti's recent election to the presidency of the Consorzio di Tutela del Chianti Classico, a prestigious position for a man of talent and balance who manages to avoid getting caught up in political games. But back to Ama, and to Marco and to Lorenza Sebasti, both colleagues and spouses, and to the wines they continue to offer. Chianti Classico Castello di Ama '03 is fairly expensive for a Chianti Classico with a production of almost 200,000 bottles but quibbles fade when you consider its quality, particularly in such a difficult vintage. At an elevation of almost 500 metres, Ama succeeds in fashioning wines that display elegance in even the hottest of seasons. Chianti Classico Bellavista is made of sangiovese with a dollop of malvasia nera. This year's version, the '01, is truly magisterial, one of the best ever, balanced and refined. Chardonnay Al Poggio '04 is excellent and much more elegant than the '03. Rosato '05 is a purely delicious quaffer and very affordable. Vigna Apparita '02 was not produced.

●	Chianti Cl. Bellavista '01	▼▼▼	8
●	Chianti Cl. Castello di Ama '03	▼▼▼	6
○	Al Poggio Chardonnay '04	▼▼	5
⊙	Rosato '05	▼	4*
●	Chianti Cl. Castello di Ama '00	▽▽▽	6
●	V. l'Apparita Merlot '00	▽▽▽	8
●	Chianti Cl. Castello di Ama '01	▽▽▽	6
●	Chianti Cl. La Casuccia '01	▽▽▽	8
●	V. l'Apparita Merlot '01	▽▽▽	8
●	Chianti Cl. Bellavista '90	▽▽▽	8
●	V. l'Apparita Merlot '92	▽▽▽	8
●	Chianti Cl. Bellavista '95	▽▽▽	6
●	Chianti Cl. La Casuccia '97	▽▽▽	8
●	Chianti Cl. Bellavista '99	▽▽▽	8
●	Chianti Cl. Castello di Ama '99	▽▽▽	5

BADIA A COLTIBUONO

LOC. BADIA A COLTIBUONO
53013 GAIOLE IN CHIANTI (SI)
TEL. 0577746110 - 0577744832
www.coltibuono.com

This year's results were not the most rewarding for this Gaiole-area operation. But Emanuela Stucchi Prinetti knows that it is better to let one year go in order to bring into better form all of the winery's flagship wines. We can review no Sangioveto, no Riserva '03 and just one standard-bearer, Cultus Boni, a thoroughly modern Chianti Classico. We can be sure that the decision was far from easy but it attests to a determination to provide the consumer only the highest-quality wines. And following the winery reorganization that Stucchi Prinetti carried out a few years ago, patience is absolutely necessary to ensure the desired results. Further, everything turns on bringing out the full potential of the area's signature variety, sangiovese, a source of joy and torment for all winegrowers and a grape that only in this area yields spectacular results. And it certainly helps to have as a consulting oenologist Maurizio Castelli when winemaking decisions have to be taken. In this year's tastings, Cultus Boni '03 yielded a generous spectrum of berry fragrances enriched by pencil lead and mineral earth, then a rounded, succulent palate supported by low-key tannins and a measured acidity. Chianti Classico '04 presents a lively layering of red berry fruit and slaty mineral but the palate could stand a tad more heft. Traditionalists are going to love Vin Santo '01 but we would prefer more complexity. The nose shows the expected dried fruit but seems to stop there while we expect more roundedness on the palate. Chianti Cetamura '05 and Trappoline '05 are both lovely.

●	Chianti Cl. Cultus Boni '03	YY	5
○	Vin Santo del Chianti Cl. '01	Y	6
●	Chianti Cl. '04	Y	5
●	Chianti Cetamura '05	Y	4
○	Trappoline '05	Y	4
●	Sangioveto '95	YYY	6
●	Chianti Cl. Cultus Boni '01	YY	5
●	Sangioveto '01	YY	7
●	Sangioveto '00	YY	7

GAIOLE IN CHIANTI (SI)

★ BARONE RICASOLI

CANTINE DEL CASTELLO DI BROLIO
53013 GAIOLE IN CHIANTI (SI)
TEL. 05777301
www.ricasoli.it

The wines that Barone Ricasoli presented this year put on a bravura performance, bringing this historic Chianti winery, with its more than a century and a half of history, straight back to the role it deserves. Little more than a decade ago, Francesco Ricasoli set out to relaunch the winery, following a period of dimmed reputation, and he continues to reap success. The renewal of the vineyards is all but complete. Fully 200 of the 240 hectares have been replanted at high densities and to new clones of sangiovese. Chianti Classico Castello di Brolio '03 perfectly demonstrates how it is possible, even in a torrid year, to produce a wine that is powerful but not overripe, thanks to sangiovese cultivars appropriate to the Brolio climate. Modern it may be but it is above all a wine that mirrors the traits of its terroir, which has always been considered ideally suited to making reds of impressive structure and great ageing potential. We tasted a Casalferro such as we have not seen for years. This '03, from sangiovese with 25 per cent cabernet sauvignon, unleashes power but nothing is out of balance and it even offers a marked spiciness on the nose. The remaining wines are excellent. Both 100 per cent sangioveses, Campo Ceni and Formulae '04, augur well for the winery stars of the same vintage. Chianti Classico Rocca Guicciarda Riserva '03 is superb and Chianti Classico Brolio '04 well executed. Torricella, a Chardonnay this time in the '05 version, continues to show way too much new oak.

●	Casalferro '03	YYY	6
●	Chianti Cl. Castello di Brolio '03	YYY	7
●	Chianti Cl. Rocca Guicciarda Ris. '03	YY	5
●	Campo Ceni '04	YY	4
●	Chianti Cl. Brolio '04	YY	4*
●	Formulae '04	YY	3*
○	Torricella '05	Y	5
●	Chianti Cl. Castello di Brolio '00	YYY	7
●	Chianti Cl. Castello di Brolio '01	YYY	7
●	Casalferro '97	YYY	6
●	Chianti Cl. Castello di Brolio '97	YYY	6
●	Casalferro '98	YYY	6
●	Chianti Cl. Castello di Brolio '98	YYY	6
●	Casalferro '99	YYY	6
●	Chianti Cl. Castello di Brolio '99	YYY	7

Castello di Cacchiano

Fraz. Monti in Chianti
loc. Cacchiano
53010 Gaiole in Chianti (SI)
tel. 0577747018
www.chianticlassico.com

Giovanni Ricasoli Firidolfi's winery seems to have regained its groove after a few years of lacklustre performance. Riserva Millennio, which has in the past won our Three Glasses, hasn't been seen for some time but we note with pleasure that the Castello di Cacchiano wines have developed a coherent stylistic bent and that they are very good expressions of their terroir, with all wines exhibiting real distinctiveness. The winery estate, located in the commune of Gaiole in Chianti, covers 200 hectares with 30 in vineyards, and enjoys a superlative climate and exposure. The winery's iconic offering remains Vin Santo, although it must be admitted that this '99 is not one of its best editions. It is still a benchmark, however, particularly for its bewitching aromas, which meld orange zest into luscious dried date and fig. The palate is creamy textured and well rounded, seducing at first sip, but the finale doesn't quite fulfil expectations. Chianti Classico '03 is redolent of intriguing mineral essences, of tanned leather and well-ripened dried plum. Entry is lively and juicy, tannins all in the right place, and a tangy acidity enlivens everything, making this a first-class quaffer. Rosso '03 is your perfect everyday tipple with a fruit-laden nose, stylish, supple structure, vibrant flavours and just the right amount of finish.

● Chianti Cl. '03	YY	5
○ Vin Santo '99	YY	6
● Rosso di Cacchiano '03	Y	4
● Chianti Cl. Millennio Ris. '90	(YYY)	5
● Chianti Cl. '02	(YY)	4
● Chianti Cl. Ris. '01	(YY)	5
● Chianti Cl. Millennio Ris. '97	(YY)	5
○ Vin Santo '97	(YY)	8
○ Vin Santo '98	(YY)	6

Il Colombaio di Cencio

loc. Cornia
53013 Gaiole in Chianti (SI)
tel. 0577747178 - 0577747303

The star did not quite reach the high note but overall the performances all of the wines presented at Werner Wilhelm's winery were outstanding. This is a crucial point since it underlines the producer's attention across the range, as opposed to one single winery icon. Il Colombaio di Cencio, located in a viticulturally prestigious area of Gaiole, comprises over 130 hectares with 25 under vine, and of those, ten or so are dedicated to Chianti Classico. The team of director Jacopo Morganti and consulting oenologist Paolo Vagaggini meshes perfectly. This year's finalist is Chianti Classico I Massi Riserva '03, with a dense ruby and a multi-faceted array of subtle but intriguing fragrances. Notes of red fruit, cinnamon and clove all blend well together. After a smooth attack, the palate develops delicious acidity and smooth, tucked-in tannins, concluding not long perhaps but tastily enough. Futuro '03, an assemblage of sangiovese, cabernet sauvignon and merlot, did not reach its usual heights. There's no quarrel with a fine complex of pencil lead, tobacco leaf and chocolate that segues seamlessly into tasty wild red berry fruit, nor with the rounded, full texture, decent acidity and a spacious weave of tannins, but the finish drops off somewhat quickly. The fragrant, leisurely Monticello '03 is a delight while Chianti Classico I Massi '04 impressed us with its overall equilibrium, pulpy fruit and expansive, dynamic conclusion.

● Chianti Cl. I Massi Ris. '03	YYY	6
● Il Futuro '03	YY	7
● Monticello '03	YY	4
● Chianti Cl. I Massi '04	YY	4
● Il Futuro '95	(YYY)	7
● Il Futuro '97	(YYY)	7
● Il Futuro '99	(YYY)	7
● Chianti Cl. I Massi '00	(YY)	6
● Chianti Cl. I Massi Ris. '99	(YY)	6
● Chianti Cl. I Massi '01	(YY)	6
● Chianti Cl. I Massi Ris. '01	(YY)	6
● Chianti Cl. I Massi '03	(YY)	5
● Chianti Cl. I Massi Ris. '98	(YY)	6

Castello di Meleto

Loc. Meleto
53013 Gaiole in Chianti (SI)
tel. 0577749217
www.castellomeleto.it

Admirable dedication has finally been rewarded at the winery directed by Roberto Garcea, as his Chianti Classico Vigna Casi Riserva '03 carried off Three Glasses. It is no small feat to manage 1,000 hectares, which include 166 in vineyard, particularly if one's goal is relentlessly high quality. Results have finally come from the vineyard replanting programme, carried out together with oenologist Stefano Chioccioli, who also tends the viticultural side of things. We also review here the wines made at Pieve di Spaltenna, the second estate, whose ten hectares include seven and a half dedicated to Chianti Classico. Vigna Casi Riserva '03 has great distinctiveness over its entire development, from a rich, classic red berry and moist earth to its fabulous, well-knit structure and pitch-perfect balance of tannin and acidity. Only a whisper behind is Reinero '03, a blend of merlot, cabernet sauvignon and sangiovese in equal proportions. Animal skins and leather blend with clean-edged berry fruit lifted by delicate notes of spice. It enters self-confidently and expands steadily, tannins and fruit woven beautifully together, a leisurely finale crowning a compelling offering. Chianti Classico Pieve di Spaltenna '04 is also a winner. Centred first on cherry and dried plum fragrances, it then quickly opens to a supple, well-weighted palate animated by crisp acidity. The finish is impressively rounded. Chianti Classico '04 could be a bit fatter in the mouth but shows good balance, while Sangiovese Merlot Pieve di Spaltenna '04, although just medium-bodied, is tasty and accessible.

● Chianti Cl. Vigna Casi Ris. '03	▼▼▼	5
● Rainero '03	▼▼	7
● Chianti Cl. Pieve di Spaltenna '04	▼▼	4
● Chianti Cl. '04	▼	4
● Sangiovese Merlot Pieve di Spaltenna '04	▼	3
● Chianti Cl. Ris. '01	▽▽	5
● Chianti Cl. Ris. '99	▽▽	4
● Rainero '99	▽▽	5

GAIOLE IN CHIANTI (SI)

Podere Il Palazzino

Fraz. Monti in Chianti
Pod. Il Palazzino
53013 Gaiole in Chianti (SI)
tel. 0577747008 - 3337545227
www.podereilpalazzino.it

We were perplexed by the wines offered by Podere Il Palazzino, whose labels over the years have always impressed us. True, the two thoroughbreds were not in the lists this time. There was no Chianti Classico Grosso Sanese, sourced from the oldest vineyard, two hectares planted originally in 1793, or Chianti Classico La Pieve, from a three-hectare block of vines with an average age of 25 years. But this hardly explains the listless performance of the other wines, particularly when you consider the meticulous care lavished on the vineyards by owners Alessandro and Andrea Sderci, and by oenologist Luciano Bandini. Their production philosophy has always been to reflect the traits of their local area and this is precisely what their wines have often done extremely well, all the while eschewing technical interventionism or grape varieties extraneous to local traditions. Of the two wines we tasted, Chianti Classico Argenina '04, sporting a luminous ruby, disappointed with a rather one-dimensional nose that restricts itself to raw leather and a few nugatory notes of fruit. The palate seems still to be inching towards equilibrium, showing very assertive tannins, somewhat incoherent acidity and a tasty but sluggish finale. Casina Girasole '04, sourced from the youngest sangiovese blocks, is pleasurable, straightforward and a good offering precisely because of its unpretentiousness. It displays upfront fruit layered with subtle menthol, the well-fruited progression flows well with well-crafted tannins and the finish shows generous sapidity and length.

● Casina Girasole '04	▼	3
● Chianti Cl. Argenina '04	▼	4
● Chianti Cl. Grosso Sanese '00	▽▽▽	8
● Chianti Cl. Grosso Sanese '01	▽▽▽	8
● Chianti Cl. Grosso Sanese '03	▽▽	6
● Chianti Cl. Grosso Sanese Ris. '95	▽▽	5
● Chianti Cl. Grosso Sanese Ris. '96	▽▽	5
● Chianti Cl. Argenina '00	▽▽	5
● Chianti Cl. Argenina '01	▽▽	5
● Chianti Cl. Argenina '03	▽▽	4
● Chianti Cl. Grosso Sanese Ris. '97	▽▽	5
● Chianti Cl. Grosso Sanese '98	▽▽	5

GAIOLE IN CHIANTI (SI)

Riecine

Loc. Riecine
53013 Gaiole in Chianti (SI)
tel. 0577749098 - 0577744046
www.riecine.com

Although La Gioia '03 didn't walk off with the top trophy, it is still a superb example of a single-variety Sangiovese. After all, the express objective of owner Gary Bauman is the absolutely highest quality possible. Bauman, an American living in Milan, purchased from founder John Dunkley in 1996 the winery with its 30 hectares of vineyard, olives and woods. Gary cultivates his grapes organically and in 1998 he completed the acquisition of a new vineyard near Montecucco. In 1997, the purchase of nine additional hectares allowed him to expand his clonal repertoire. These vineyards are planted to high densities, with the goal of increasing still further the complexity and distinctiveness of the wines. Sean O'Callaghan, who has directed vineyards and cellar since 1992, knows every piece of land like the back of his hand and has succeeded in crafting the wines to mirror the qualities of the terroir. La Gioia '03 boasts a magnificent, elegantly nuanced medley on the nose. Ripe fruit predominates with wild cherry and dried plum in the lead, all beautifully laced with pencil lead and tanned leather. The initial impact is intensely savoury and the wine expands judiciously with well-orchestrated tannin and alcohol, crisp, tasty acidity and a succulent, lingering finish. Chianti Classico Riserva '03 is equally impressive. The fragrances are woven into a fine texture that leads with wild cherry, aromatic herbs and wild berry fruit, presenting elegant, controlled structure and a sensuous finish.

● La Gioia '03	TT	7
● Chianti Cl. Ris. '03	TT	7
● La Gioia '01	YYY	7
● Chianti Cl. Ris. '86	YYY	5
● Chianti Cl. Ris. '88	YYY	6
● La Gioia '95	YYY	8
● La Gioia '98	YYY	8
● Chianti Cl. Ris. '99	YYY	8
● La Gioia '00	YY	8
● Chianti Cl. Ris. '98	YY	5
● Chianti Cl. Ris. '01	YY	6

Rocca di Castagnoli

Loc. Castagnoli
53013 Gaiole in Chianti (SI)
tel. 0577731004
www.roccadicastagnoli.com

Chianti Classico Capraia Riserva '03 turned in a sterling performance, which is good news for Calogero Calì, owner of this large, well-organized winemaking operation. The figures we reported last year were a bit off. The estate actually covers 1,200 hectares, with 99 of the 132 hectares planted to vineyard dedicated to Chianti Classico production. The hamlet of Castagnoli itself dates back to the Middle Ages, the earliest sources from the tenth century mentioning a farm known as Stielle. When it later became part of the territory of Florence, it also entered the Lega del Chianti in 1203. In the 18th century, the property developed into a model agricultural operation and was mentioned as such by the Grand Duke of Tuscany, among others, showing that the area's exceptional suitability for viticulture has long been known. The news this year is the big jump in quality for the denomination wines. The Riserva presents a well-executed medley of largely fruit-derived fragrances, with intriguing hints of autumn leaves and raw leather. An expansive finish crowns steady, dynamic progression accompanied by succulent fruit, expressive tannins and measured acidity. We liked the vibrant fruit in Chianti Classico '04, which is intensely redolent of wild berry fruit, and we found the palate spirited and supple. It signs off with an appealing, full-flavoured finish. Stielle '03 was disappointing, showing over-oaked and somewhat untogether. There is too much of the barrique in the all-chardonnay Molino delle Balze '04, although the palate is crisp and fresh and the finale delicious.

● Chianti Cl. Capraia Ris. '03	TT	5
● Chianti Cl. '04	TT	4
● Stielle '03	T	7
○ Molino delle Balze '04	T	4
● Stielle '00	YYY	8
● Buriano '00	YY	8
● Le Pratola '00	YY	8
● Buriano '01	YY	8
● Le Pratola '01	YY	8
● Stielle '01	YY	8
● Chianti Cl. Capraia Ris. '00	YY	6
● Chianti Cl. Capraia Ris. '01	YY	6

GAIOLE IN CHIANTI (SI)

ROCCA DI MONTEGROSSI

LOC. MONTI IN CHIANTI
53010 GAIOLE IN CHIANTI (SI)
TEL. 0577747977

Marco Ricasoli Firidolfi's winery achieved enviable results, with two of his wines going to the national finals, and those results are even more impressive because the winery's top Vin Santo was missing. La Rocca was founded by one of Marco's ancestors, Geremia, the man who founded the family and after whom one of the wines is named. The 18 hectares are planted largely to sangiovese. Ricasoli Firidolfi himself, together with Roberto Bandinelli, directs vineyard operations with Attilio Pagli watching over winemaking. Over the year, about half of the vine stock has been replanted at a density of some 6,000 vines per hectare. What has always impressed us has been the almost preternatural ability of these wines to reflect the qualities of the local territory with unfailing elegance and style. Chianti Classico Vigneto San Marcellino Riserva '03 exhibits crisp-edged complexity, with pungent herbs, tobacco leaf and leather infusing generous blackberry and dark cherry. It develops an elegantly-structured, sinewy palate of considerable dimensions, juicy acidity that drives a steady progression, subtle tannins and a long, savoury conclusion. Geremia '03, from cabernet sauvignon and merlot, is on the same level, releasing a refined, clove and cinnamon-enriched combination of ripe fruit and toasty oak. Once again, we see good depth and expansion in the mouth and multi-layered, fine-grained tannins. The balsam-scented finale lingers nicely. Chianti Classico '04, showing good body, is nonetheless held down by still roughish tannins.

●	Chianti Cl. Vigneto S. Marcellino Ris. '03	TT	6
●	Geremia '03	TT	6
●	Chianti Cl. '04	T	4
●	Chianti Cl. Vigneto S. Marcellino Ris. '99	YYY	5
○	Vin Santo del Chianti Cl. '97	YY	8
○	Vin Santo del Chianti Cl. '98	YY	8
●	Geremia '99	YY	6
●	Chianti Cl. Vigneto S. Marcellino Ris. '01	YY	6
●	Geremia '01	YY	6

GAIOLE IN CHIANTI (SI)

SAN GIUSTO A RENTENNANO

FRAZ. MONTI IN CHIANTI
LOC. SAN GIUSTO, 20
53013 GAIOLE IN CHIANTI (SI)
TEL. 0577747121
www.fattoriasangiusto.it

In its desire to faithfully interpret its terroir, San Giusto is one of those wineries that is naturally exposed to the vagaries of growing seasons. The brothers Martini di Cigala put out wines of uncompromising style and recognizable traits that nicely reflect their local area. They own 160 hectares, with over 30 in grapes and 11 in olives. Soils are uniquely variable and the climate is continental, with wide diurnal temperature swings. The vineyards are replanted on a regular basis with cultivars of sangiovese and canaiolo propagated from the oldest vines, some 40 years old. Since 1990, half the vineyards have been renewed and the current philosophy is totally organic. Percarlo '03, which went through to the final taste-off, shows an appreciable range of impressions from wild cherry and red berry fruit to aromatic herbs and heady spice. It opens well, showing good heft and an admirable distribution of tannins. Although it seems to hesitate in mid palate, it finishes clean and rounded. La Ricolma '03, from merlot only, puts together an interesting mosaic of balsam, menthol and mineral on the nose and then shows very spirited in the mouth, only slightly held back by a massive suite of tannins, and the finish is eminently sapid. Chianti Classico '04 flaunts delicious cherry and strawberry with touches of spring blossoms and a toothsome, vivacious palate that is a real pleaser. Repeated retastings over the years of Percalo '95 have convinced us that it is a wine worthy of Three Glasses. Though recognition is late in arriving, that's what we award it today.

●	Percarlo '03	TT	8
●	La Ricolma '03	TT	7
●	Chianti Cl. '04	TT	5
●	Percarlo '88	YYY	8
●	Percarlo '95	YYY	8
●	Percarlo '97	YYY	8
●	Percarlo '99	YYY	8
●	Percarlo '01	YY	8
●	La Ricolma '98	YY	8
●	Chianti Cl. Ris. '99	YY	6
●	La Ricolma '01	YY	7

GAIOLE IN CHIANTI (SI)

San Vincenti

Loc. San Vincenti
Pod. di Stignano, 27
53013 Gaiole in Chianti (SI)
tel. 0577734047
www.sanvincenti.it

The San Vincenti winery turned in solid results this year, even if the husband and wife Pucci team's Riserva didn't earn the high marks we expected. Of course, the 2003 season may have been a contributory factor. It was a difficult season with torrid temperatures in that area, which sapped the fruit. San Vincenti comprises some 60 hectares in the commune of Gaiole, eight planted to vines, with little more than six dedicated to Chianti Classico production. The soils are predominantly sandy with rocky galestro, a friable marl of limestone and sandstone, and the vines are trained to spurred cordon. We were not able to taste the winery's sangiovese-based Supertuscan, Stignano, since it needs another year of maturation in the cellar. Of the two wines we did taste, the better was Riserva '03. A deep ruby, it is a bit hesitant initially, but then opens to pungent menthol overlaid with rich blackcurrant and blackberry fruit and completed by a touch a spice. We were impressed by the power in the mouth and by acidity that takes charge. It shows a subtle, spacious tannic weave and an appealing, dynamic finish. Chianti Classico '04 builds on a base of good fruit, adding layers of pungent herbs and delicate florality. While not massive, it does have good depth. We found it an agile, vibrant wine, unified throughout by crisp acidity into a smooth but expansive finish.

●	Chianti Cl. Ris. '03	▼▼	6
●	Chianti Cl. '04	▼▼	5
●	Stignano '00	▽▽▽	7
●	Chianti Cl. Ris. '01	▽▽▽	6
●	Chianti Cl. Ris. '99	▽▽▽	5
●	Stignano '01	▽▽	7
●	Stignano '99	▽▽	7
●	Chianti Cl. Ris. '00	▽▽	6
●	Stignano '03	▽▽	6

GAIOLE IN CHIANTI (SI)

Vistarenni

Loc. Vistarenni
53013 Gaiole in Chianti (SI)
tel. 0577738186
www.vistarenni.com

The Santa Margherita group should be proud of the overall performance of their Tuscan facilities. Although we saw no sensational star, consistent, all-round high quality remains one of the most positive characteristics of the group's wineries located in some of the best areas of Chianti. Pile e Lamole, with 46 of its 141 hectares under vine, is in the Greve area, close to the hamlet of Lamole. The ageing cellar, used also for Vin Santo, is ancient. Vistarenni, located between Radda and Gaiole in Chianti, has 32 hectares of vineyard and a subterranean cellar. Lamole's wines turned in better performances. Chianti Classico Lamole di Lamole '03 is great value for money. It presents a rich ruby and delivers delicious wild cherry and blackberry while hinting at hedgerow. In the mouth, it is assertive and tannic, but well within bounds, developing a tangy acidity and a medium-long, compelling finish. Lamole di Lamole Etichetta Blu '03 is also fine, with similar blackberry characteristics, but here some menthol spice peeks round the edges. Subtle-textured tannins perfectly complement its measured weight and rising finish. Codirosso '04 is impressive. This blend of sangiovese and cabernet sauvignon yields balsamic and herbaceous nuances that go nicely with its ripe red berry fruit. Fresh acidity enlivens pulpy fruit in the mouth and the tannins are smooth but the finish is perhaps a tad short. Chianti Classico di Villa Vistarenni is a bit lacking in character. Cherry and floral essences compose a classic nose, but the palate lacks breadth and it seems slightly dried out.

●	Chianti Cl. Lamole di Lamole '03	▼▼	4*
●	Chianti Cl. Lamole di Lamole Etichetta Blu '03	▼▼	4
●	Codirosso '04	▼▼	3
●	Lam'oro '01	▼	7
●	Chianti Cl. '03	▼	4
●	Chianti Cl. Villa Vistarenni '03	▼	4
●	Chianti Cl. Campolungo Ris. '97	▽▽	5
●	Chianti Cl. Campolungo Ris. '99	▽▽	5
●	Chianti Cl. Campolungo Ris. '00	▽▽	7
○	Vin Santo del Chianti Cl. '00	▽▽	6
●	Chianti Cl. Campolungo Ris. '01	▽▽	5
●	Chianti Cl. Lamole di Lamole Ris. '01	▽▽	5

GAMBASSI TERME (FI)

Villa Pillo

via Volterrana, 24
50050 Gambassi Terme (FI)
tel. 0571680212
www.villapillo.com

There was a very successful series of tastings again this year for the wines of Villa Pillo, a cellar that has for some time now kept up an impressive pace. Even though we couldn't taste the winery flagship, Syrah, or the Vin Santo, the rest of the wines did very well indeed. We were most impressed by Merlot Sant'Adele '04, with its rich, upfront fruit, nicely delineated and foregrounding toasty oak and an intriguing, subtle herbaceousness. Good weight in the mouth finds its complement in a steady progression and lingering finish, with plenty of dense, supple tannins to enjoy along the way. No less enjoyable is Vivaldaia '04, all cabernet franc and probably the best version to date. It offers well-ripened, classically varietal fruit without resorting to vegetal or oaky clichés. In the mouth, it builds solid but not bloated structure that is cloaked by an elegant, silky texture. A leisurely, pepper-spice finish completes a superlative, elegant wine. Borgoforte '04 also offered a fine performance. It is an assemblage of 50 per cent sangiovese, 40 per cent cabernet sauvignon and the rest merlot, produced in 100,00 bottles. Crisp, clean aromas of fruit and spice abound and the palate, while not offering great depth, concentration or emphatic tannins, calmly relies on succulent flavours and balance, and succeeds.

●	Borgoforte '04	TT	4
●	Merlot Sant'Adele '04	TT	6
●	Vivaldaia '04	TT	6
●	Syrah '97	YYY	5
●	Syrah '99	YY	5
●	Merlot Sant'Adele '00	YY	6
●	Syrah '00	YY	6
●	Merlot Sant'Adele '01	YY	6
●	Syrah '01	YY	6
●	Merlot Sant'Adele '03	YY	6
●	Vivaldaia '03	YY	6
●	Syrah '98	YY	5

GAVORRANO (GR)

Poggio ai Lupi

loc. Giuncarico
loc. Bartolina
58023 Gavorrano (GR)
tel. 3392838006
www.poggioailupi.com

This edition of the Guide brings both corroboration of past results and news regarding Matteo and Marco Galtarossa's young operation. They have 20 hectares of estate vineyards, planted to high density and trained to spurred cordon. Production currently hovers at a bit more than 20,000 bottles. Their well-fashioned winemaking programme continues to yield consistently impressive results. The wine line-up evidences some changes, however. Chardonnay joins the team while Petit Verdot and Merlot-Cabernet are for the moment resting on the bench. As to the wines we tasted, past versions of Alicante have displayed good typicity and character and the '05 would be welcome in any squad. A full-fruited base offers good support for emphatic spice and lovely whiffs of smooth vanilla and pungent Mediterranean underbrush. Smooth on the palate, it develops impressive progression and an almost pepper-laden finish. Chardonnay makes a fine debut with the '05, exhibiting crisp peach and pear on the nose, a savoury palate and good length. Syrah '05 is a decent effort, offering crackling-fresh fruit along with a slight pepperiness. Delicious flavours flow across a palate that is just the slightest bit thin. Monteregio di Massa Marittima '05, from sangiovese with a dollop of alicante, does not aspire to complexity but offers rounded, smooth fragrances lead right to a supple, enjoyable palate.

●	Alicante '05	TT	5
○	Chardonnay '05	TT	3
●	Monteregio di Massa Marittima '05	T	4
●	Syrah '05	T	4
●	Alicante '04	YY	5
●	Syrah '04	YY	4

GAVORRANO (GR)

ROCCA DI FRASSINELLO

LOC. GIUNCARICO
58040 GAVORRANO (GR)
TEL. 0577742903

The foundations of Rocca di Frassinello winery rest upon two names, Paolo Panerai and Eric de Rothschild. Panerai is a publisher and financier, as well as owner of Castellare di Castellina, while de Rothschild directs the great banking family's viticultural operations, beginning with Château Lafite. The vine stock, currently just shy of 80 hectares, is situated on the hills facing the village of Giuncarico on the east side of the Via Aurelia. The 2004 wines mark the first releases and amount to some 130,000 bottles. Alessandro Cellai, director of Castellare di Castellina, oversees winemaking, with Christian Le Sommer, oenologist for Domaines Barons de Rothschild. The final touch is provided by architect Renzo Piano, who designed the cellar presently under construction. The wines from sangiovese, merlot and cabernet follow the French model. Poggio alla Guardia, the standard wine, is made only in steel and the winery name does not appear on its logo. Half of the second-tier wine, Le Sughere di Frassinello, is aged in new barriques and its label bears part of the winery name, making it equivalent to Carruades de Lafite. The cellar's iconic wine is Rocca di Frassinello, entirely matured in new oak, and our tastings confirmed this hierarchy. Poggio alla Guardia shows slender, crisp and eminently accessible, Le Sughere di Frassinello succulent and better layered, and Rocca di Frassinello is complex, full-bodied and vibrantly youthful.

● Rocca di Frassinello '04	🍷🍷	7
● Le Sughere di Frassinello '04	🍷🍷	6
● Poggio alla Guardia '04	🍷🍷	5

GREVE IN CHIANTI (FI)

I FABBRI

LOC. LAMOLE
VIA CASALE, 52
50022 GREVE IN CHIANTI (FI)
TEL. 0552345719 - 3394122622
www.agricolaifabbri.it

We have not yet listed renaming wine producers on our job description, even if it does happen occasionally in these pages. Last year, we attributed to I Fabbri's personable owner, Susanna Grassi, the name of her winery. It sounded so right that it went right by us! Having thus made amends, we can note how well Ms Grassi has in just a few years succeeded in turning around the family winery, transforming it from a bulk producer into a real gem. All this while she continues to live in Ferrara while the winery is located in Lamole, a charming village not far from Greve. Her operation shows great promise, well beyond what it has achieved this far. The year's stand-out was Chianti Classico Riserva '03. Despite the hot weather, we have crisp, lively aromas, with an ethereal florality and layers of balsam and earthy mineral interleaving emphatic cherry and dried plum. Succulent fruit continues in nice progression in the mouth to a rising finish, accompanied by firm, chewy tannins. The nose on Chianti Classico '04 is of more reduced dimension but well delineated and the palate too is measured and well balanced with noticeable acidity, signing off with a smooth, savoury conclusion. Terra di Lamole '04 is simpler – a kind of second wine – produced from the grapes that do not go into Chianti Classico. It delivers an appealing, floral nose and expressive tannins. The finish is medium long and the structure somewhat slender.

● Chianti Cl. Ris. '03	🍷🍷	5
● Chianti Cl. '04	🍷🍷	4
● Chianti Cl. Terra di Lamole '04	🍷	4
● Chianti Cl. Ris. '01	YY	5
● Chianti Cl. '03	YY	4
● Chianti Cl. Terra di Lamole '03	YY	4

GREVE IN CHIANTI (FI)

TENUTE AMBROGIO E GIOVANNI FOLONARI
LOC. PASSO DEI PECORAI
VIA DI NOZZOLE, 12
50022 GREVE IN CHIANTI (FI)
TEL. 055859811 - 055859811
www.tenutefolonari.com

This year brings overall good results for the Chianti operation belonging to Ambrogio and Giovanni Folonari. The estate at Nozzole comprises some 100 hectares devoted largely to sangiovese. It represents for the Folonaris, father and son, the flagship for all of their properties in Tuscany, not least because of the magnificent villa, used for visitors and guests. The sangiovese and cabernet sauvignon Cabreo Il Borgo '03 was the top performer. The nose offers a quite splendid bouquet that includes pencil lead, leather and pungent nuances of menthol over ripe blackberry and blueberry. Although the palate starts out somewhat sluggish, it grows to an expansive, appealing finish after exhibiting pulpy fruit and tannins that are dense and well calibrated. Chianti Classico La Forra Riserva '03 offers subtle spice and jammy red berry fruit but also intriguing pungency, suggesting herbs and fresh greens. It shows good concentration in the mouth and lively acidity melding with mellowed tannins animate a leisurely, juicy finish. Vin Santo '01 is a delicious treat, with its crisp, honey-smooth nose where orange zest and hazelnut stand out. It is just what we hoped for in the mouth, which shows fat, creamy and embracing with just a touch of acidity to lift the sweetness. The largely chardonnay Le Bruniche '05 shows clean, refreshing and delicious, capped by a full-flavoured finish. Cabreo La Pietra '04, however, is less successful. We found muddled aromas and a body somewhat in need of building.

○	Vin Santo del Chianti Cl. Nozzole '01	**YY**	5
●	Cabreo Il Borgo '03	**YY**	6
●	Chianti Cl. La Forra Ris. '03	**YY**	5
○	Cabreo La Pietra '04	**Y**	6
○	Le Bruniche '05	**Y**	4
●	Il Pareto '00	YYY	8
●	Il Pareto '01	YYY	8
●	Il Pareto '88	YYY	7
●	Chianti Cl. La Forra Ris. '90	YYY	5
●	Il Pareto '90	YYY	7
●	Il Pareto '93	YYY	7
●	Il Pareto '97	YYY	7
●	Il Pareto '98	YYY	7

GREVE IN CHIANTI (FI)

MONTECALVI
VIA CITILLE, 85
50022 GREVE IN CHIANTI (FI)
TEL. 0558544665
www.montecalvi.com

Fine performances for both Montecalvi wines consolidate the role in the Guide of Jacqueline Bolli and Daniel O'Byrne. This modest operation, launched in 1989, possesses ten hectares with three in vine. The surroundings are gorgeous and the area is propitious for premium growing, offering optimal exposure for the vineyards, which are all managed organically. The vines are planted at a density of 6,500 per hectare and trained to Guyot. Beginning in 2002, both Bolli and O'Byrne have been jointly managing both vineyard and cellar. We thought the Montecalvi '03 was the better of the two wines. Sangiovese predominates in the blend, helped by cabernet sauvignon with dabs of merlot, syrah and canaiolo. An almost opaque ruby inveigles the eye, followed by a veritable fruit-basket of aromas, including wild red berry laced with spice and smooth vanilla, and culminating in crisp balsamic essences. Succulent fruit rules in the mouth as well, complemented by well tucked-in tannins and a zesty acidity, and it finishes with good length. The all-sangiovese Chianti Classico '04 opens to a lovely flower-fruit duet that privileges wild cherry and raspberry, then makes a tasty debut in the mouth, marked by vigorous tannins and a confidant vein of acidity. The conclusion is savoury and appealing.

●	Montecalvi '03	**YY**	6
●	Chianti Cl. '04	**YY**	5
●	Montecalvi '98	YYY	8
●	Montecalvi '01	YY	6
●	Montecalvi '99	YY	8
●	Montecalvi '00	YY	6
●	Montecalvi '94	YY	8
●	Montecalvi '95	YY	8
●	Montecalvi '96	YY	8
●	Montecalvi '97	YY	8

GREVE IN CHIANTI (FI)

Podere Poggio Scalette

loc. Ruffoli
via Barbiano, 7
50022 Greve in Chianti (FI)
tel. 0558546108 - 0558546281
www.poggioscalette.it

Right on the heels of a somewhat disappointing performance last year, caused by a difficult vintage, Carbonaione picked itself up and breezed off with Three Glasses, as it has so often before. Accompanying it into the national finals was the all-merlot Piantonaia '03. It was back in 1991 that Vittorio Fiore, an oenologist already well regarded in Tuscany, and his wife Adriana Assjé di Marcorà, acquired Podere Poggio Scalette, a fairly modest operation near Greve in Chianti. The winery has expanded over the years and it currently possesses about 18 hectares of vineyard. Now working alongside his father in the vineyards is Jurij, an oenology degree from the University of Beaune tucked in his pocket. Turning back to the sangiovese Carbonaione '03, we were impressed by the wealth of clean, emphatic wild cherry-led fruit. The palate is simply superlative, with a terrific texture of the finest-grained tannins culminating in a finish that is long and velvet smooth, making this gem a total charmer. Piantonaia '03 is an intriguing, atypical merlot, which seems to think it is a Chianti and succeeds in eloquently expressing its local terroir. On the nose, pencil lead and leather ably interweave with red berry fruit. It opens generously on the palate to spacious tannins and a captivating acidity, closing on length and depth of flavour that make for a fine, complex wine.

● Il Carbonaione '03	▼▼▼	8
● Piantonaia '03	▼▼	8
● Il Carbonaione '00	▽▽▽	8
● Il Carbonaione '01	▽▽▽	8
● Il Carbonaione '96	▽▽▽	8
● Il Carbonaione '98	▽▽▽	8
● Il Carbonaione '99	▽▽	8
● Il Carbonaione '92	▽▽	8
● Il Carbonaione '93	▽▽	8
● Il Carbonaione '94	▽▽	8
● Il Carbonaione '95	▽▽	8
● Il Carbonaione '97	▽▽	8

GREVE IN CHIANTI (FI)

Castello di Querceto

loc. Querceto - fraz. Lucolena
via Dudda, 61
50020 Greve in Chianti (FI)
tel. 05585921
www.castellodiquerceto.it

It is sad that the Francois husband and wife team again fell just short of the ultimate trophy. Still, Castello di Querceto remains among the most impressive operations in the Greve area, with its entire line of wines riding high. The Cento marks the fact that the family has owned the castle for over 100 years and today, they carefully manage vineyards that now extend over 65 hectares out of their total of almost 200. Their many wines always stand out as individuals and even the internationals shed their varietal traits to better express the characteristics of the local terroir, traditions to which the Francois have always clung. Both Riservas went to the national tasting round. Il Picchio '03 showcases balsamic essences that enhance dense, complex fruit. It enters impressively with solid, succulent weight and finishes velvet smooth, just a touch held back by tannins. Chianti Classico Riserva '03 relies more on cherry and blackberry fruit lifted by light spice, followed by impressive tannic grip that adds complexity and there is good length. Cignale '03, a 50-50 cabernet sauvignon and merlot mix, releases a captivating balsamic infusion then builds to just the right weight and density. Slightly aggressive tannins close in somewhat the sangiovese and cabernet sauvignon Querciolaia '01 and shorten its conclusion. Appealing spice on the nose characterizes the all cabernet sauvignon Il Sole di Alessandro '01, as does a plush, leisurely palate. La Corte '01, from 100 per cent sangiovese, is tasty, as is Chianti Classico '04, although it could show more heft.

● Chianti Cl. Il Picchio Ris. '03	▼▼	6
● Chianti Cl. Ris. '03	▼▼	5
● Il Sole di Alessandro '01	▼▼	8
● Querciolaia '01	▼▼	6
● Cignale '03	▼▼	7
● La Corte '01	▼	7
● Chianti Cl. '04	▼	4
● Chianti Cl. Ris. '01	▽▽	5
● Querciolaia '00	▽▽	6
● Chianti Cl. Il Picchio Ris. '01	▽▽	6
● Cignale '01	▽▽	7

★ QUERCIABELLA
VIA BARBIANO, 17
50022 GREVE IN CHIANTI (FI)
TEL. 05585927777
www.querciabella.com

Sebastiano Cossia Castiglioni's winery has a good grip on the Three Glass award and doesn't relinquish it for very long. Last year's dearth of champions was due to the inauspicious 2002 growing year but here is his Camartina back with a vengeance this year to win another trophy. Such consistent quality is hardly surprising, given what we know of the dedication and painstaking attention that marks the entire staff and particularly the crucial figure of Cesare Turini. The biodynamic philosophy that reigns here is, according to Querciabella, the reason behind the improved quality of its fruit. Camartina '03 certainly supports that conviction. A blend of sangiovese and cabernet sauvignon, it obviously shrugged off the effects of the challenging growing year in 2003. It opens to a rich base of ripe fruit supporting an intriguing medley of tobacco leaf, leather and nuances of pencil lead. The entry is confident with verve to spare on a juicy palate marked by plenty of zesty acidity and it takes its leave with an intensely savoury finale. The tasty combination of crisp fruit and menthol that introduces Chianti Classico '04 impressed us, as did the pulpy, lively fruit on its palate. It shows just the right complexity and a compelling finish. We liked Batàr '04, a pinot bianco-chardonnay partnering. Spicy oak and slaty mineral are a good foil for crisp peach and pear while tangy acidity animates easy-drinking flavours. But this is no lightweight and it has plenty of length.

●	Camartina '03	3 black glasses	8
○	Batàr '04	2 black glasses	7
●	Chianti Cl. '04	2 black glasses	5
●	Camartina '00	3 glasses	8
●	Camartina '01	3 glasses	8
●	Camartina '88	3 glasses	8
●	Camartina '90	3 glasses	8
●	Camartina '94	3 glasses	8
●	Camartina '95	3 glasses	8
●	Chianti Cl. '95	3 glasses	4
●	Chianti Cl. Ris. '95	3 glasses	5
○	Batàr '97	3 glasses	7
●	Camartina '97	3 glasses	8
○	Batàr '98	3 glasses	7
●	Camartina '99	3 glasses	8

SAVIGNOLA PAOLINA
VIA PETRIOLO, 58
50022 GREVE IN CHIANTI (FI)
TEL. 0558546036
www.savignolapaolina.it

We should point out how the Savignola Paolina winery, owned by the Fabbri family, has been on the right path for some years and has been able to keep overall quality well up to snuff. Its modest five hectares in vineyard makes careful management of the vines and vigilant attention in the cellar imperative, and this is precisely what is provided by input in the vineyard from Remigio Bordini and for winemaking from Lorenzo Landi. We were unable to taste the all-sangiovese Supertuscan Granaio but the superb Riserva di Chianti kept us more than happy. Despite the hot 2003 season, with its attendant problems of overripeness, we found a refreshing crispness throughout the wine. The rich red berry fruit and dried plum, for example, were marked by exemplary cleanness and enriched by some dusky chocolate. The entry is confident and it unveils a fine-textured mouthfeel with rounded tannins and tasty acidity that girders it nicely. There is also plenty of length. Although its floral notes are more than appealing, the Chianti Classico '04 lacks a complex structure and its tannins seem somewhat drying. Still, we found it an enjoyable pleaser with a rounded, though not particularly long, finale.

●	Chianti Cl. Ris. '03	2 black glasses	5
●	Chianti Cl. '04	1 black glass	4
●	Granaio '01	2 glasses	6
●	Granaio '00	2 glasses	6
●	Granaio '02	2 glasses	6
●	Chianti Cl. '03	2 glasses	4
●	Granaio '03	2 glasses	5
●	Chianti Cl. Ris. '99	2 glasses	5

Castello di Tizzano

loc. San Polo in Chianti
via di Tizzano, 8
50020 Greve in Chianti (FI)
tel. 0558555040
www.selecru.it

After its debut last year in the Other Wineries section, Roberto Pandolfini's Castello di Tizzano winery has graduated to a full profile. The acquisition of the Greve-area fortress by the present family dates back to 1895, when Conte Pandolfini purchased the property with his own money and that of his wife Beatrice Corsini. The estate today takes in a substantial 250 hectares, of which 20 are in vineyard and 12 are officially dedicated to Chianti Classico production. Methods of viticulture are traditional, aiming to produce wines that will be a faithful expression of their territory. Terre del Castello di Tizzano '04 presents a garnet-tinged, deep ruby and the nose appears at first somewhat closed. Initial moist earth and slaty mineral soon give way, however, to well-ripened fruit with dried plum preserve in the lead. The palate flaunts plenty of succulent fruit as well, with a wealth of dense, expressive tannins joined to very perky acidity. The markedly savoury finish lingers and expands. Chianti Classico '04 is a luminous ruby and seems undeveloped on the nose, offering indistinct, somewhat blurred fruit. It develops impressive power in the mouth but here the problem is the tannins, which are rough and unruly, tending to dry out the finish.

● Chianti Cl. '04	▼▼	4
● Terre del Castello di Tizzano '04	▼▼	5
● Terre del Castello di Tizzano '01	▽▽	5

GREVE IN CHIANTI (FI)

Torraccia di Presura

loc. Strada in Chianti
via della Montagnola, 130
50027 Greve in Chianti (FI)
tel. 0558588656 - 055490563
www.torracciadipresura.it

The Osti family continues to feature in the Guide with commendable regularity. The estate is located on the road through the Chianti area that connects Siena and Florence, and the present villa took the place of an ancient watchtower. The Osti family acquired it in 1986 and launched a general restructuring that focused particularly on the vineyards. Soils and climate are optimal, as is the vineyard exposure. The estate includes about 24 hectares of vineyard with 13 dedicated to Chianti Classico production. Giovanni Cappelli directs activities in both vineyard and cellar. This year one of the wines, the all-sangiovese Chianti Classico Il Tarocco Riserva '03, graduated to the national finals. Produced for the first time in 1990, it is sourced from vines averaging 20 years old. The nose exhibits ripe fruit but this is appreciably enriched with some evolved nuances of tanned leather and tobacco leaf. It turns appealingly assertive in the mouth and shows quite zesty acid, although the tannins remain subdued. There is a drop in energy along the finish but it nonetheless concludes with a pleasurable fruitiness. Chianti Classico Il Tarocco '04, from largely sangiovese with some canaiolo, is less impressive. The nose is fairly straightforward but cherry and violets emerge. The finish comes up shortish but a refreshing vein of acidity keeps a lean, lively palate marching along.

● Chianti Cl. Il Tarocco Ris. '03	▼▼	5
● Chianti Cl. Il Tarocco '04	▼	4
● Lucciolaio '00	▽▽	6
● Chianti Cl. Il Tarocco Ris. '01	▽▽	5
● Chianti Cl. Il Tarocco '02	▽▽	4
● Chianti Cl. '03	▽▽	4
● Chianti Cl. Il Tarocco '03	▽▽	4

GREVE IN CHIANTI (FI)

Castello di Vicchiomaggio

Loc. Le Bolle
via Vicchiomaggio, 4
50022 Greve in Chianti (FI)
tel. 055854079
www.vicchiomaggio.it

John Matta's winery turned in a decent enough performance this year, even though we are convinced that he can easily better the results of the past few years. The local conditions are certainly outstanding and a more focused attention to style would possibly allow the operation to regain the consistently high quality that we used to see. Its location goes back to the fifth century, although the original place name, Vicchio dei Longobardi, was changed in the Renaissance to refer to the Florentine Calendimaggio festivities. Its strategic position made it an ideal defensive structure for the Florentines during their wars with Siena. Turning to the wines, we liked Ripa della Mandorle '04, from sangiovese and cabernet sauvignon. Opaque to the eye, it layers pungent underbrush and wild herbs into well-ripened fruit and then displays warm alcohol and velvety tannins that complement a firmly-structured, powerful palate. We were equally impressed by the finish. Chianti Classico Petri Riserva '03 hesitates on the nose but it soon releases evolved nuances of tobacco and leather over a base of blackberry preserve. Confidence marks the palate, with luscious tannins, crisp acidity and a leisurely, toothsome finale. Riserva La Prima '03 drops a rung with a dull nose and an awkward, though fairly rich, palate. Semifonte di Semifonte '03, an assemblage of cabernet sauvignon, merlot and sangiovese, can offer well-executed fragrances, including some earthy minerality, and tasty, pulpy fruit on a palate that seems a tad tight. It is simpler than the other wines but nonetheless delicious.

●	Chianti Cl. Petri Ris. '03	🍷🍷	6
●	Ripa delle Mandorle '04	🍷🍷	5
●	Chianti Cl. La Prima Ris. '03	🍷	7
●	Merlot '03	🍷	4
●	Semifonte di Semifonte '03	🍷	7
●	Chianti Cl. San Jacopo '04	🍷	5
●	Ripa delle More '94	🍷🍷🍷	5
●	Ripa delle More '97	🍷🍷🍷	6
●	Chianti Cl. La Prima Ris. '00	🍷🍷	7
●	Ripa delle More '01	🍷🍷	7
●	Semifonte di Semifonte '01	🍷🍷	6
●	Ripa delle More '99	🍷🍷	6
●	Chianti Cl. La Prima Ris. '01	🍷🍷	7

GREVE IN CHIANTI (FI)

Villa Vignamaggio

via di Petriolo, 5
50022 Greve in Chianti (FI)
tel. 055854661 - 0558546653
www.vignamaggio.com

Giovanni Battista Nunziante's winery made a good showing this year but on past performance we had reason to expect better. Specifically, we were quite disappointed by the 2003 edition of Obsession, his most famous wine, a blend of merlot, syrah and cabernet sauvignon. The nose is fine, giving an intriguing mix of fresh leather and pungent greens, but it seems to fall apart in the mouth and to run into some pretty hard patches there. The central core of the villa was designed by Gherardini in the 14th century. The complex was purchased in 1988 by Nunziante, who restored both gardens and buildings to their former glory. He then rebuilt from scratch the vineyards and the cellar. The 50 hectares of vines are in the hands of Francesco Naldi, who also oversees winemaking, together with Giorgio Marone. From the wines we tasted, Chianti Classico '04 turned in the best performance. Everything about it is delicious. It shows bright, crisp fruit on the nose, decent weight, lively acidity and supple tannins. Vin Santo '01 has allure to spare. On the nose, pungent medicinal herbs nicely enliven textbook dried dates, figs and jam. It then unveils magnificent volume on the palate, developing an opulent mouthfeel that is well served by a nervy acidity and the leisurely finish is perfect. Riserva Monna Lisa '03 offers evolved characteristics over rather simple fruit and obstreperous tannins hobble an otherwise powerful palate. Chianti Classico Terre di Prenzano '04 shows a slender structure but it is sound and tasty.

○	Vin Santo del Chianti Cl. '01	🍷🍷	6
●	Chianti Cl. '04	🍷🍷	5
●	Chianti Cl. Monna Lisa Ris. '03	🍷	6
●	Obsession '03	🍷	7
●	Chianti Cl. Terre di Prenzano '04	🍷	4
●	Vignamaggio '00	🍷🍷🍷	7
●	Vignamaggio '01	🍷🍷🍷	7
●	Chianti Cl. Monna Lisa Ris. '95	🍷🍷🍷	4
●	Chianti Cl. Monna Lisa Ris. '99	🍷🍷🍷	6
●	Obsession '00	🍷🍷	7
●	Obsession '01	🍷🍷	7
●	Vignamaggio '03	🍷🍷	7
●	Vignamaggio '99	🍷🍷	6
●	Chianti Cl. Ris. '01	🍷🍷	6

GREVE IN CHIANTI (FI)

Viticcio

via San Cresci, 12a
50022 Greve in Chianti (FI)
tel. 055854210
www.fattoriaviticcio.com

A good overall performance brings Alessandro Landini's Viticcio back into the full profile section, although we thought his Chianti Classico versions would do even better than they did. Alessandro's father Lucio, an engineer with a passion for wine, founded the winery and it has always enjoyed a reputation for innovation, both in viticulture and in oenology. The estate has more than 30 hectares of high-quality vineyards while Gabriella Tani consults on winemaking. We felt that both Supertuscans fell short of their considerable potential. The all-cabernet Monile '03 sports an impenetrable hue and then imparts intriguing hints of chocolate and spicy balsam that permeate well-ripened fruit to good effect. Spacious tannins carpet a generous, dense palate. Despite a slight hesitation in mid development, it recovers and the finale is exemplary. Prunaio'03 is 100 per cent sangiovese and it treats us to red berry fruit centred on cherry and strawberry with a broad draught of spice hovering in the background. Pronounced acidity and well-layered tannins contribute to good length and it concludes smooth and leisurely. We liked the Chianti Classico '04, too, particularly for the violet-led florality that elegantly balances crisp wild berry. It is an elegant, supple pleaser and concludes on a very appetizing note. On the other hand, we found the two '03 versions of Riserva Chianti Classico too dense and concentrated, and constricted by excessive tannins.

● Monile '03	🍷🍷	6
● Prunaio '03	🍷🍷	7
● Chianti Cl. '04	🍷🍷	4
● Chianti Cl. Beatrice Ris. '03	🍷	6
● Chianti Cl. Ris. '03	🍷	5
● Prunaio '99	YYY	7
● Chianti Cl. Beatrice Ris. '00	YY	6
● Prunaio '01	YY	8
● Chianti Cl. Ris. '99	YY	6
● Prunaio '00	YY	7
● Chianti Cl. Beatrice Ris. '01	YY	6
● Chianti Cl. '03	YY	5

GROSSETO

Tenuta Belguardo

loc. Montebottigli - VIII Zona
58100 Grosseto
tel. 057773571
www.belguardo.it

The Mazzei family, which used to own Castello di Fonterutoli in Chianti Classico, acquired Tenuta Belguardo in the 1990s. Situated in the hills between Grosseto and Montiano, the estate totals 70 hectares and relies on 32 hectares of vineyard, which are currently being increased. Following the recent purchase of a contiguous 40 hectares, the total area under vine will reach 60 hectares. All of the vineyards are at altitudes of 70 to 130 metres and face south or southwest. The varieties are largely sangiovese, cabernet sauvignon, alicante, merlot, cabernet franc and petit verdot, planted to high densities of 5,550 to 6,600 vines per hectare and trained mostly to spurred cordon. The final phase of the expansion project, in 2008, includes construction of a new cellar. Turning to the wines, we missed Tenuta Belguardo but it is gaining additional complexity in the cellar, so we will see it next year. We consoled ourselves with the excellent Morellino di Scansano Bronzone '04, mostly sangiovese with some alicante, in a production run of some 40,000 bottles. It opens classy, complex and fragrant, remaining vibrant throughout, constrained only slightly by a drying sensation on the finish. The cellar turns out 100,000 bottles of Serrata di Belguardo '04. Composed of sangiovese, cabernet sauvignon and merlot, it opens to spacious, crisp aromas that develop into a succulent palate of appreciable finesse and beautifully crafted equilibrium.

● Morellino di Scansano Bronzone '04	🍷🍷	5
● Serrata di Belguardo '04	🍷🍷	4
● Tenuta Belguardo '00	YY	6
● Serrata di Belguardo '01	YY	5
● Tenuta Belguardo '01	YY	8
● Tenuta Belguardo '02	YY	8
● Serrata di Belguardo '03	YY	5
● Tenuta Belguardo '03	YY	7
● Morellino di Scansano Poggio Bronzone '01	YY	6
● Serrata di Belguardo '02	YY	5
● Morellino di Scansano Bronzone '03	YY	5

Poggio Argentiera

Loc. Banditella di Alberese
58010 Grosseto
tel. 0564405099
www.poggioargentiera.com

Poggio Argentiera now has some 70 hectares of vineyards that yield almost 200,000 bottles a year. The wines have settled into a recognizable, characteristic style that privileges impressive structure side by side with delicious drinkability and clean-edged crispness with rich complexity. This seems to be the profile Giampaolo Paglia is trying to achieve and the results are heartening. Morellino Capatosta '04 is once again ahead by a length, winning entry to the national final round. Largely sangiovese with a little alicante, it flaunts a superlatively balsam-laced nose, dark-fruited and complex, well matched by a rich, powerful development in the mouth, displaying judiciously disposed tannins. The conclusion reveals exemplary length and sapidity. The 50-50 alicante-syrah Finisterre '04 performs expressively on the nose and offers crisp, full flavours on the palate but a slight excess of oak hobbles the finish to a degree. Morellino Bellamarsilia '05 is a partnering of sangiovese, ciliegiolo and alicante that shows sturdy and straightforward but no less delicious for its simplicity. Turning to the whites, Guazzo '05 is a crisp, uncomplicated ansonica-vermentino blend. Fonte 40 '05 is new, basically chardonnay with a bit of fiano fermented and aged in once-used barriques. It exudes banana and tropical fruit, and exhibits a lot of nice fatness on the palate. We found it well made but without any real distinctiveness to make it stand out.

● Morellino di Scansano Capatosta '04	TT	6
● Finisterre '04	TT	7
● Morellino di Scansano Bellamarsilia '05	TT	4
○ Fonte 40 '05	T	4
○ Guazzo '05	T	3
● Morellino di Scansano Capatosta '00	YYY	6*
● Finisterre '01	YY	7
● Morellino di Scansano Capatosta '01	YY	6
● Finisterre '02	YY	7
● Morellino di Scansano Capatosta '02	YY	6
● Finisterre '03	YY	7
● Morellino di Scansano Capatosta '03	YY	6

GROSSETO

Fattoria Le Pupille

Loc. Piagge del Maiano
58040 Grosseto
tel. 0564409518
www.elisabettageppetti.com

We missed the standard-bearer, Saffredi, but the '04 edition needs another year in the cellar. This absence hardly hurt the performance of Elisabetta Geppetti's winery, however, since her Morellino di Scansano Poggio Valente '04 confidently took home its Three Glasses and Solalto '04 went to the national finals. All of which is simply one more confirmation of the leading role that Le Pupille plays in the Maremma. Poggio Valente, produced in 45,000 bottles, is mostly sangiovese with a soupçon of alicante, and the '04 vintage is one of the best versions ever. The nose is gorgeously expressive, releasing a train of fragrances as smooth spice and aromatic herbs layer into rich, tasty fruit. The palate shows impressive breadth and supple tannins, developing energetic, lengthy progression. Solalto '04 is a late-picked assemblage of sauvignon, traminer and sémillon, of which 15,000 bottles were made. We found this a particularly well-executed version, displaying tasty, well-delineated candied citrus fruit on the nose and a seductive richness in the mouth, to finish long. Morellino is from sangiovese with touches of malvasia nera and alicante, produced this year in 360,000 bottles. It rarely disappoints. Nor did this '05, with aromas that are markedly crisp and refreshing, and a palate that shows vibrant and savoury. The last wine is far from least. Poggio Argentato '05, from traminer and sauvignon, unveils a delicate florality then displays a sapid, self-confident palate, all in all a quite appealing offering.

● Morellino di Scansano Poggio Valente '04	TTT	6
○ Solalto '04	TT	5
● Morellino di Scansano '05	TT	4
○ Poggio Argentato '05	TT	4
● Saffredi '00	YYY	8
● Saffredi '01	YYY	8
● Saffredi '02	YYY	8
● Saffredi '03	YYY	8
● Saffredi '90	YYY	8
● Saffredi '97	YYY	8
● Morellino di Scansano Poggio Valente '01	YY	6
● Morellino di Scansano Poggio Valente '03	YY	6

IMPRUNETA (FI)

Fattoria di Bagnolo

Loc. Bagnolo-Cantagallo
via Imprunetana per Tavarnuzze, 48
50023 Impruneta (FI)
tel. 0552313403
www.bartolinibaldelli.it

We are always delighted by the good performances from Marco Bartolini Baldelli's estate, which reward his efforts to produce the highest quality wines. Fattoria di Bagnolo does produce other agricultural products, but Marco's passion for wine is such that it constantly spurs him to reach ever higher levels of achievement. Being in a relatively untested viticultural area is far from being a disadvantage for it acts as a stimulus to demonstrate the particular local qualities in the context of a region as extensive and diverse as Tuscany. The Colli Fiorentini zone in particular, over the last few years, has shown itself to be one of the most dynamic of the emerging areas. Turning to the wines, we found them all impressive, although we liked Capro Rosso '04 best. In fact, it went on to the national finals. A partnership of sangiovese, colorino and cabernet sauvignon, it is a style that is eminently enjoyable now but at the same time demonstrates complexity and full body. The nose offers those qualities in spades, as does a smooth, leisurely finish. Showing less horsepower but just as much allure is Chianti Colli Fiorentini '04, which demonstrates the satisfaction a good partnership of alcohol and acidity can bring. We also like the way it integrates its tannins into a streamlined structure. Riserva '03 is another fine offering. Its nose goes in a different direction, unveiling nuances of spice and pungent, fresh leather. It builds to a sturdy structure, which becomes a tad stiff in mid palate but recovers and concludes with a full-flavoured flourish.

● Capro Rosso '04	**YY**	5
● Chianti Colli Fiorentini Ris. '03	**YY**	5
● Chianti Colli Fiorentini '04	**YY**	3
● Capro Rosso '00	YY	5
● Capro Rosso '01	YY	5
● Capro Rosso '02	YY	5
● Capro Rosso '03	YY	5
● Capro Rosso '99	YY	4

IMPRUNETA (FI)

Fattoria Collazzi

Loc. Tavarnuzze
via Colleramole, 101
50029 Impruneta (FI)
tel. 0552022528 - 0552374902
www.collazzi.com

Results amply justify our full profile for Fattoria Collazzi. The Marchi brothers are owners, while Lamberto Frescobaldi and Nicolò D'Afflitto team up to take care of the vineyards and the cellar respectively. The area around Impruneta has had quite a fillip over the last few years, ever since a group of producers from varying professional backgrounds concentrated their efforts on the area, to resoundingly good effect. The estate here covers a considerable area, almost 400 hectares. Some 20 are in vineyard, planted on sandy, limestone-rich soils. Wine production began only in 1999, after renewal of the olive oil production led to a re-examination of the property's viticultural potential. From the wines, Collazzi '04 put on a very good show. A blend of cabernet franc, cabernet sauvignon and merlot, it flaunts a deep, saturated tonality and gorgeous blackcurrant and raspberry fruit supporting spice and cinnamon. If the finish is a just tad less than full, it does unfold a rounded, velvety mouthfeel, assisted by a successful marriage of alcohol and tannins. Collazzi produces an all-sangiovese Chianti Classico, I Bastioni, sourced from vineyards located in the DOCG zone. The '04 edition is a fine effort, redolent of classic cherry aromas and complemented by a delicate florality. Incisive but appealing tannins team with savoury acidity to support the lively, supple palate and generous, savoury flavours on the finish.

● Collazzi '04	**YY**	7
● Chianti Cl. I Bastioni '04	**Y**	4
● Collazzi '00	YY	7
● Collazzi '01	YY	6
● Collazzi '02	YY	7
● Collazzi '03	YY	6
● Collazzi '99	YY	5

IMPRUNETA (FI)

La Querce

via Impruneta per Tavarnuzze, 41
50023 Impruneta (FI)
tel. 0552011380 - 3282423844
www.laquerce.com

Massimo Marchi repeated last year's good results, with one of his wines going to the finals and the rest close behind. The direction set by director Marco Ferretti some years ago continues to pay dividends. La Querce, near Impruneta and not far from Florence, owes its name to an oak that grew near the chapel that is part of the villa. The tree itself was destroyed in the Second World War. Vineyards and olive groves are ancient here, dating back to 1042, as attested by a sales deed for a house with adjoining vineyards. The Marchi family bought the property in 1962 and immediately set about restructuring the buildings and then restoring agricultural activities. They redoubled their efforts in the 1990s and dramatically improved the quality of all of their products. Currently, there are 42 hectares, of which eight are in vines and 12 in olives, the rest being wooded. Our tastings this year included the sangiovese and colorino La Querce '04, which did very well. Inky black in colour, it presents an intriguing bouquet that melds balsam and delicate spice into red berry preserves. Apart from slight hesitation in mid progression, the palate offers good density and breadth, finishing smooth and succulent. Chianti Colli Fiorentini La Torretta '04 is a lively pleaser, leading off with black pepper and cinnamon that enliven rich, dark berry fruit and then unfurling an energy-laden progression helped by delicious fruit and fine-grained tannins. The finish is a delicious treat. Chianti Sorrettole '05, a straightforward but enjoyable quaffer, shows appealing blossoms and spice.

● La Querce '04	**YY**	5
● Chianti Colli Fiorentini La Torretta '04	**YY**	4
● Chianti Sorrettole '05	**Y**	3
● La Querce '03	YY	5
● La Querce '00	YY	5
● La Querce '01	YY	5

LORO CIUFFENNA (AR)

Il Borro

fraz. San Giustino Valdarno
loc. Il Borro,1
52020 Loro Ciuffenna (AR)
tel. 0559772921
www.ilborro.it

The Ferragamo family presented a group of wines that all performed very well. Other wineries out on the market for the same few years would consider these results more than sufficient but not the staff of Il Borro. The massive efforts that went into restructuring the winery, from the fermentation and maturation facilities to the vineyards, augured a big jump up in quality. Our tastings did not reveal a quantum leap – perhaps one of the inhibiting factors was the nature of the 2004 growing season – but we are still convinced that such a bound is well within the winery's capacity. Il Borro '04 is a blend largely of merlot and cabernet sauvignon, plus a little syrah, and it puts out smooth aromas centred on dark wild berry, roasted coffee and notes of toasty oak. The impressively dense palate comes across as very tannin-clenched and the finish is disturbed by a slightly bitterish edge. The all-sangiovese Polissena '04 needs some aeration to open but it then reveals lovely varietal character, red berry fruit and spring blossoms, completed by a delicate spiciness. The palate evidences some energy but remains stiff and muddled, needing more time to develop fully. Pian di Nova '04, on the other hand, is a syrah with a hand from sangiovese that shows vivacious and expressive. A hefty charge of ripe fruit and pungent spice nicely holds its own against the smooth talc of oak. It continues distinctive and delicious in the mouth, with good expansion and pulpy fruit, even though the finish shows some warm alcohol.

● Il Borro '04	**YY**	7
● Pian di Nova '04	**Y**	4
● Polissena '04	**Y**	6
● Il Borro '00	YY	8
● Il Borro '01	YY	8
● Il Borro '02	YY	8
● Il Borro '03	YY	7
● Polissena '02	YY	6
● Il Borro '99	YY	8

LUCCA

TENUTA DI VALGIANO
FRAZ. VALGIANO
VIA DI VALGIANO, 7
55018 LUCCA
TEL. 0583402271
www.tenutadivalgiano.it

A sublime Tenuta di Valgiano '03 brings to the winery, Moreno Petrini and Laura di Collobiano, the second Three Glass prize after the first that was awarded two years ago. This is an impressive accomplishment for this pirate ship-like winery prowling the high seas of Italian wine, for they have eschewed compromises and uniformity and kept the business side of wine at arm's length. What they do rely upon is love of the land and this may help explain the very high-quality fruit they succeeded in harvesting in the torrid 2003, which ensured them luxurious freedom of choice in assembling their blends of sangiovese, syrah, and merlot. And we repeat: that '03 vintage of Tenuta di Valgiano exhibits amazing elegance. From the enthrallingly complex initial tangle, the nose begins to unpeel layers of blackberry preserves and spice, all intriguingly veined with delicate tobacco leaf. Then it delivers a truly aristocratic palate and tannins extracted to just the right degree support a full but weighty body, with the acidity caressing every component into equilibrium. This version is less instinctive than previous vintages but more mature and self-aware, a sign that this sustained improvement is a product of design, the direct consequence of the health of the Valgiano ecosystem. Palistorti '04, as usual, offers wondrous red berry fruit lightly caressed with a subtle herbaceousness and black pepper, then unfurls a compellingly alluring palate that is right on the mark. Giallo dei Muri '05, on the other hand, is just the slightest bit tight.

● Colline Lucchesi Tenuta di Valgiano '03	▼▼▼	7
● Colline Lucchesi Palistorti '04	▼▼	5
○ Colline Lucchesi Bianco Giallo dei Muri '05	▼	4
● Colline Lucchesi Tenuta di Valgiano '01	▽▽▽	8
● Colline Lucchesi Tenuta di Valgiano '00	▽▽	8
● Colline Lucchesi Tenuta di Valgiano '99	▽▽	8
● Colline Lucchesi Tenuta di Valgiano '02	▽▽	7

MAGLIANO IN TOSCANA (GR)

COL DI BACCHE
S.DA DI CUPI
58010 MAGLIANO IN TOSCANA (GR)
TEL. 0577738526 - 0564589538
ww.coldibacche.com

Col di Bacche certainly gives every indication of having set out determinedly along the path that leads to uninterrupted high wine quality. To mix metaphors, the proof is in the pudding, or more precisely in the tasting of the wines, which here are the very mirror image of last year's. In Alberto Carnasciali, we have a dedicated, serious winegrower who is not likely to be tempted by facile enthusiasms, who knows his direction and who works his vineyards with unceasing commitment. He now has ten hectares of vines, which yield him some 45,000 bottles. But let's get on to what we tasted, beginning with Rovente '04 from sangiovese with some syrah. It practically danced into the national finals, confirming its status as one of the best Morellinos around. Expressive, luxuriant, perfectly ripe fruit sets this wine apart, with low-key toasty oak to complete an elegant aromatic package. The palate is concentrated, and its tannins dense-packed, but tangy acidity runs through it and builds to a vital, distinctive finish, which displays just a hint of a burr. The merlot-only Cupinero '04 parades confident berry fruit that here and there allows somewhat emphatic oak to peek through, while youthful vigour marks the mostly steady progression accompanied by fine fruit and packed tannins. Morellino '05, from sangiovese and syrah, is the model of an enjoyable, accessible wine, flaunting a refreshing, juicy and balanced profile.

● Morellino di Scansano Rovente '04	▼▼	5
● Cupinero '04	▼▼	6
● Morellino di Scansano '05	▼▼	4
● Cupinero '02	▽▽	6
● Morellino di Scansano Rovente '03	▽▽	5
● Cupinero '01	▽▽	5
● Morellino di Scansano Rovente '02	▽▽	5
● Cupinero '03	▽▽	6
● Morellino di Scansano '03	▽▽	4
● Morellino di Scansano '04	▽▽	4

MAGLIANO IN TOSCANA (GR)

FATTORIA DI MAGLIANO
LOC. STERPETI, 10
58051 MAGLIANO IN TOSCANA (GR)
TEL. 0564593040
www.fattoriadimagliano.it

Fattoria di Magliano, owned by Agostino Lenci, has not been around very long but it has managed to carve out quite a reputation for itself not only within the industry but, far more important, among consumers. It farms 47 hectares of vineyard and produces about 200,000 bottles a year, with the assistance of consulting oenologist Graziana Grassini. The winery champion, Poggio Bestiale, is a 50-50 merlot-cabernet sauvignon blend and the reason for much of this success. The '04 edition performed very well right from its initial well-crafted amalgam of ultra-generous fruit and toasty oak. The tannins are distinctly exuberant and still young, but the palate is themed around deliciously savoury fruit. Perenzo '04 is all syrah and all sinewy pleasure. It leads off cleanly with fresh herbaceous and black pepper nuances before revealing a delicious nip of acidity and an impressive, compact tannic package, with just a touch too much oak that cinches development a bit. There's smooth vanilla on Morellino Heba '05, a blend of sangiovese and syrah, but it unfortunately tamps the fruit down somewhat. The deliciously full-flavoured palate does shine, though. Pagliatura '05, a 100 per cent vermentino, is well executed. Appealing floral notes emerge cleanly on the nose while the crisp, straightforward palate is markedly herbaceous.

● Poggio Bestiale '04	(2 black glasses)	6
● Perenzo '04	(2 black glasses)	6
● Morellino di Scansano Heba '05	(1 black glass)	4
○ Pagliatura '05	(1 black glass)	4
● Poggio Bestiale '01	(2 white glasses)	6
● Poggio Bestiale '02	(2 white glasses)	6
● Perenzo '03	(2 white glasses)	7
● Morellino di Scansano Heba '02	(2 white glasses)	4
● Morellino di Scansano Heba '03	(2 white glasses)	4

MAGLIANO IN TOSCANA (GR)

MANTELLASSI
LOC. BANDITACCIA, 26
58051 MAGLIANO IN TOSCANA (GR)
TEL. 0564592037
www.fatt-mantellassi.it

Mantellassi is one of the benchmark producers in the Morellino di Scansano denomination, whether in terms of history or size. It relies on 165 hectares of vineyard and produces up to 500,000 bottles. The cellar's long-time involvement in viticulture in the local area has meant that the wines demonstrate both a strong bond with tradition as well as an unmistakable style, even for the less complicated products. Morellino San Giuseppe '05 is a case in point. Predominantly sangiovese with some alicante and cabernet sauvignon, it sculpts very delicate aromas, tending to floral over fruit, and builds an upfront, tasty palate that makes this an extremely appealing quaffer. We have always found Morellino Le Sentinelle Riserva, from largely sangiovese with a soupçon of alicante, to be intriguing. The '03 version is all about power. Generous, warm fragrances pour out, the emphatic spice edged with fresh liquorice and sour cherry, to be succeeded by good grip on the palate, as well as by juicy flavours and slightly earthy tannins. The all-alicante Querciolaia '04 comes across as sturdy but by no means simple. Classy fruit marks the nose and it expands to good fullness in the mouth, helped by a tasty vein of acidity and discreet oak. Morellino Mentore '05 is a new Mantellassi offering, from alicante and a little cabernet sauvignon. We thought it charming and accessible, with clean-edged aromas. The all-vermentino Scalandrino '05, is well crafted and characterized by delicate lime blossom and a slender, crisp palate.

● Morellino di Scansano Le Sentinelle Ris. '03	(2 black glasses)	5
● Querciolaia '04	(2 black glasses)	5
● Morellino di Scansano San Giuseppe '05	(2 black glasses)	4
● Morellino di Scansano Mentore '05	(1 black glass)	4
○ Vermentino Scalandrino '05	(1 black glass)	4
● Querciolaia '01	(2 white glasses)	5
● Morellino di Scansano Le Sentinelle Ris. '01	(2 white glasses)	5
● Morellino di Scansano San Giuseppe '03	(2 white glasses)	4
● Morellino di Scansano San Giuseppe '04	(2 white glasses)	4*

MASSA MARITTIMA (GR)

La Cura

Loc. Cura Nuova, 12
58024 Massa Marittima (GR)
tel. 0566918094

The wines presented this year impressed us greatly with their genuineness and overall high quality. La Cura, owned by Enrico Corsi, is a modest operation in the heart of the Monteregio di Massa Marittima DOC zone. Corsi farms, and cares for personally, five hectares of vineyards, three of which are planted at 5,500 vines per hectares, the rest at 3,300. He makes 20,000 bottles, with Alessandro Biancolin assisting with the winemaking. Our opening remarks certainly apply to La Cura's Merlot '04, which came close to absolute quality and of course went forward to our final round of tastings. Fermented in barriques and tonneaux, it then matures for 18 months in the same vessels. It's an elegant wine that offers an interactive trio of red berry, deep spice and lovely herbaceousness, exhibiting exemplary balance in the mouth, where an alluring vein of acidity goes to create a wonderfully vibrant impression overall. Chardonnay, malvasia and trebbiano go into the blend for Trinus '05. The chardonnay is fermented in barrique and the malvasia and trebbiano in steel before maturation for eight months in oak. Trinus is an interesting wine for its blend of tropical fruit and pronounced minerality on the nose, lively progression and savouriness on the palate and a nice, bitter-almond finish. Monteregio di Massa Marittima Breccerosse '05 is a well-made, tasty blend of sangiovese, cabernet sauvignon and merlot while Valdemàr '05 is a straightforward, refreshing malvasia-trebbiano duo.

●	La Cura Merlot '04	▼▼	5
○	Trinus '05	▼▼	4
●	Monteregio di Massa Marittima Rosso Breccerosse '05	▼	4
○	Valdemàr '05	▼	3
●	La Cura Merlot '02	▽▽	5
●	La Cura Merlot '03	▽▽	5

MASSA MARITTIMA (GR)

Moris Farms

Loc. Cura Nuova
Fattoria Poggetti
58024 Massa Marittima (GR)
tel. 0566919135
www.morisfarms.it

Adolfo Parentini has guided Moris Farms to success with clear vision and a firm hand. His operation relies on some 70 hectares of vineyard, split between Fattoria Poggetti, located in the Monteregio di Massa Marittima DOC zone, and Poggio la Mozza in the Morellino di Scansano DOC area. Much of the success is due to Avvoltore, by which Parentini has always set much store. First released in 1988, it is a blend of sangiovese, cabernet sauvignon and syrah and it is also a wine that has, in a real sense, grown stylistically along with its source vineyard, Poggio all'Avvoltore, to acquire a self-confident identity. The '04, produced in the considerable number of 50,000 bottles, embodies in exemplary fashion all of Avvoltore's distinctive traits, and justly carried off Three Glasses. A multi-faceted spiciness caresses luscious fruit that expands right onto a palate of remarkable depth. There could be a tad more complexity perhaps but the tannins are admirably dense and do their work magisterially. The other wines performed well. Monteregio di Massa Marittima '05 is made of sangiovese and cabernet sauvignon in a production of 30,000 bottles. The fragrances are crisp and clean, and it drinks satisfactorily, but the palate lacks heft. Morellino di Scansano '05, made in 260,000 bottles, is sangiovese with some cabernet sauvignon. Supple and drinkable enough, it offers little clarity on the nose. Morellino Riserva '03 in 30,000 bottles releases warm, smooth aromas and is flavoursome in the mouth, although its tannins are quite incisive.

●	Avvoltore '04	▼▼▼	6
●	Morellino di Scansano Ris. '03	▼	5
●	Monteregio di Massa Marittima Rosso '04	▼	4
●	Morellino di Scansano '05	▼	4
●	Avvoltore '00	▽▽▽	6
●	Avvoltore '01	▽▽▽	6
●	Avvoltore '99	▽▽▽	6
●	Avvoltore '02	▽▽	6
●	Avvoltore '03	▽▽	6
●	Morellino di Scansano Ris. '00	▽▽	5
●	Morellino di Scansano Ris. '01	▽▽	5
●	Morellino di Scansano '03	▽▽	4
●	Morellino di Scansano Ris. '99	▽▽	5

MERCATALE VALDARNO (AR)

Podere Il Carnasciale

loc. Podere Il Carnasciale
52020 Mercatale Valdarno (AR)
tel. 0559911142

Caberlot is a wine of great character, and by its very nature, destined for just a handful of aficionados. Even though the vineyards were recently replanted, only a tiny amount is made, and only in large-format bottles – about 2,000 units are released in magnums and double magnum. Prices are not what you could call moderate. It's a garage wine, then, in almost the literal sense since while the wine is undergoing malolactic fermentation, the barriques practically take over part of owner Bettina Rogosky's house. For Caberlot devotees, the '03 could be a version that will generate discussion. Whereas the '02 was the child of a less favourable vintage, and exhibited uncharacteristic simplicity, a suppleness, a readiness even, the '03 is almost at the antipodes. Imposing and majestically structured, it hews to Caberlot's recognizable, distinctive aromatic profile of insistent spice, notes of fresh greens and black pepper, juniper berry and wild red berry fruit. Here those characteristics are on the warmer and riper side, more Mediterranean, the fruit jammier, the greens reminiscent of sweet peperonata, the spices more from the Orient and their expression is now richer and denser, less expansive and less layered. As to the palate, the tannic structure is dense and compact, if just slightly tight. This is a version that will be treasured by those who value full-bodied, mouthfilling muscular creations, although those traits jeopardize to some extent the wine's vibrancy and complexity. Now we wait for the '04 version, which barrel tastings hint will be fantastic.

● Caberlot '03	▼▼	8
● Caberlot '00	ΨΨΨ	8
● Caberlot '01	ΨΨ	8
● Caberlot '02	ΨΨ	8
● Caberlot '98	ΨΨ	6
● Caberlot '99	ΨΨ	8
● Caberlot '96	ΨΨ	6
● Caberlot '97	ΨΨ	6

MONTALCINO (SI)

Argiano

loc. Sant'Angelo in Colle
53020 Montalcino (SI)
tel. 0577844037
www.argiano.net

Returning to claim a full profile is Argiano, a long-standing Montalcino winery known throughout the world. Work goes on in a splendid palazzo that was once one of the fortified farming estates located around Montalcino and it gives a valuable idea of how cellars were build in the past. The new cellar was completed recently, with low impact on the environment and respect for the local landscape. Inside, all is perfectly organized and climate controlled, with spacious areas for fermentation, barrel ageing and bottle binning. Equipment is first-rate, with particular attention given to the various-sized barrels, and the well-furnished tasting room is very comfortable. Two important news items emerged from our tastings this year. The more important is that the Brunello went once again to our national finals, thanks to a fine '01 version. The second is the debut of Non Confunditur, a blend of cabernet sauvignon, merlot and syrah. The inaugural '04 is felicitous, with a crisp, lean nose and an impressive palate, offering good length, complexity and approachability. Solengo '04, its prestigious precursor at a more prestigious price, is similar in varietal make-up but flaunts the unique traits and texture that have always distinguished it. Brunello '01 is superlative and a nice stylistic compromise between tradition and innovation, where the judicious contribution of the oak does nothing to hamper its graceful oleander and red berry florality. We appreciated the nervy progression, well-fashioned tannins and compelling finish. Rosso '04 is pleasurable.

● Brunello di Montalcino '01	▼▼	7
● Non Confunditur '04	▼▼	4
● Solengo '04	▼▼	8
● Rosso di Montalcino '04	▼	4
● Brunello di Montalcino Ris. '85	ΨΨΨ	5
● Brunello di Montalcino Ris. '88	ΨΨΨ	6
● Solengo '95	ΨΨΨ	8
● Solengo '97	ΨΨΨ	8
● Solengo '00	ΨΨ	8
● Solengo '02	ΨΨ	8
● Solengo '03	ΨΨ	8
● Brunello di Montalcino '95	ΨΨ	8
● Brunello di Montalcino '97	ΨΨ	8
● Brunello di Montalcino '98	ΨΨ	8
● Brunello di Montalcino '99	ΨΨ	8

MONTALCINO (SI)

★ Castello Banfi
loc. Sant'Angelo Scalo
Castello di Poggio alle Mura
53024 Montalcino (SI)
tel. 0577840111
www.castellobanfi.com

Once again, the Mariani family winery can take satisfaction in fine results that place their winery in the company of Italy's best. Unremitting viticultural and oenological research under winery director Enrico Viglierchio has led to high levels of quality for all of the wines, from the simplest to the most complex. Sant'Antimo Excelsus '03 won the lion's share of the applause, returning to its former glory and again capturing our Three Glass award. A blend of cabernet sauvignon and merlot, it unfurls an aromatic spectrum of appreciable complexity, ranging from dark and red berry fruit to pungent pencil lead and orange zest, and weaves in subtle draughts of toasty oak. A multi-layered, rounded palate is saved from sweetness by a dense suite of bolstering tannins. A fabulous finish crowns a finely crafted effort. The all-cabernet sauvignon Tavernelle '03 exhibits enviable elegance and structure, eschewing razzle-dazzle for understatement. It expresses itself through a fabric of dense tannins, steady progression and a lengthy finish, and at a surprisingly good price. The '03 editions of Cum Laude and Summus are both impressive, as is Moscadello Florus '04. Among the Brunellos, we preferred Poggio alle Mura '01. It is true that the oak raises its head a bit too much but its right-on structure and body will eventually get this proportioned nicely. Brunello '01 is more straightforward but well crafted, showing lots of red berry fruit and a tight-knit, full structure. Rosso di Montalcino '04 is a pleasurable offering.

● Sant'Antimo Excelsus '03	3 glasses	7
● Sant'Antimo Tavernelle '03	2 glasses	5
○ Moscadello di Montalcino Florus '04	2 glasses	5
● Brunello di Montalcino '01	2 glasses	7
● Brunello di Montalcino Poggio alle Mura '01	2 glasses	8
● Sant'Antimo Cum Laude '03	2 glasses	4
● Sant'Antimo Summus '03	2 glasses	7
● Rosso di Montalcino '04	1 glass	4
● Brunello di Montalcino Poggio alle Mura '99	3 glasses (white)	8
● Brunello di Montalcino Poggio all'Oro Ris. '99	3 glasses (white)	8
● Sant'Antimo Excelsus '99	3 glasses (white)	8

MONTALCINO (SI)

Fattoria dei Barbi
loc. Podernovi, 170
53024 Montalcino (SI)
tel. 0577841111
www.fattoriadeibarbi.it

The historic Fattoria dei Barbi winery in Montalcino figures among the world's most well-known producers. The reason is not hard to find since its founder's philosophy was to produce a good-quality Brunello at an affordable price, enabling a large number of consumers to enjoy Brunello. The winery still follows this policy after almost a century of history, proving that successful innovations become valuable traditions. Stefano Cinelli Colombini directs the winery with enviable energy, firmly anchoring it to tradition, particularly regarding the Brunello production code. The wines we tasted all received high marks, with the top denomination wines showing the most marked improvements compared to past years. We were impressed by both Brunellos, particularly the Riserva '00. It leads off with a strikingly dense ruby and we liked the intriguing hint of rhubarb that accompanies well-focused, jammy red berry fruit. The tannins poke through a bit and slow down the entry but they are supple enough and contribute to a fine body. It expands nicely on the finish and some time in the bottle will bring good results. Brunello '01 goes in a different direction, its subtle oak tones still evident over a base of red berry and brambly fruit. Everything is in balance on the palate but for an acidity that, if it presently shortens somewhat the finish, will contribute to its long-term cellarability. Brusco dei Barbi '05 and Morellino Vivaio dei Barbi '04 were both delicious and both represent good value for the consumer.

● Brunello di Montalcino Ris. '00	2 glasses	8
● Brunello di Montalcino '01	2 glasses	6
● Morellino di Scansano Vivaio dei Barbi '04	1 glass	4
● Brusco dei Barbi '05	1 glass	3*
● Brunello di Montalcino '00	2 glasses (white)	6
● Brunello di Montalcino Ris. '95	2 glasses (white)	8
● Brunello di Montalcino Ris. '97	2 glasses (white)	8
● Brunello di Montalcino V. del Fiore '97	2 glasses (white)	8
● Brunello di Montalcino Ris. '99	2 glasses (white)	8

MONTALCINO (SI)

BIONDI SANTI - TENUTA IL GREPPO
LOC. VILLA GREPPO, 183
53024 MONTALCINO (SI)
TEL. 0577848087
www.biondisanti.it

A certain amount of technical tweaking has been taking place at the most famous Montalcino winery, with positive results. No, the wine style has not changed, which of course would be sacrilege on a national scale. But attention to small details is obvious and is bringing more to the fore the true greatness of these wines, a stature everyone has always recognized but now free of a certain asperity that made the Brunellos of the 1990s fairly off-putting, particularly in their youth. This may have had something to do with our not fully appreciating, in our tastings back then, the true character of the Riserva '95. At any rate, we do now finally appreciate its superb qualities and therefore assign it, on the Guide's 20th anniversary, Three retrospective Glasses. We can point to Brunello '01 as a benchmark and a top-of-the-class Three Glass wine that enthused all our tasters. Both eye and nose are classic Il Greppo, with ruby and just a touch of garnet at the rim followed by nuances of tobacco leaf and tanned leather emerging to immediately infuse generous yellow peach and subtle ripe cherry. The attack is magisterial, where a smooth alcohol and an acidity that is absolutely textbook drive an elegant development. Tannins are superlative, close-packed but already fairly supple, and the finale is generous and well nigh endless. Rosso di Montalcino '03 overcomes an infelicitous year, exhibiting tangy acidity and appealing mouthfeel. Rosato '04 is straightforward and delicious but too slender for the Biondi Santi price tag.

●	Brunello di Montalcino '01	🍷🍷🍷	8
●	Rosso di Montalcino '03	🍷🍷	6
⊙	Rosato Di Toscana '04	🍷	7
●	Brunello di Montalcino '83	🍸🍸🍸	6
●	Brunello di Montalcino Ris. '95	🍸🍸🍸	6
●	Brunello di Montalcino Ris. '99	🍸🍸🍸	8
●	Brunello di Montalcino '97	🍸🍸	8
●	Brunello di Montalcino '99	🍸🍸	8
●	Brunello di Montalcino Il Greppo Ris. '98	🍸🍸	8

MONTALCINO (SI)

TENUTA CAPARZO
LOC. CAPARZO
S.P. DEL BRUNELLO
53024 MONTALCINO (SI)
TEL. 0577848390
www.caparzo.com

Caparzo is one of Montalcino's best-known and most representative producers. Its vineyards figure among the area's most prestigious crus. Montosoli lies in the north and yields Brunello La Casa while Rosso di Montalcino La Caduta is sourced from Castelgiocondo, in the southwest. Property has recently been acquired in the Sesta zone, a dream location for every Brunello producer. Elisabetta Gnudi has been the owner for several years now and she merits kudos for the efforts she has expended. The status of what she took over, with respect to both the cellar and vineyard management, was unfortunately not good and certainly not up to the reputation of this prominent operation. That situation explains the extremely variable results of our tastings, depending on the period in which each wine was made. The wines that performed the best were those produced following the acquisition, which means the younger, more attractively priced wines. But the older wines also did well, such as Brunello Riserva '99, presented for the first time this year. It offers a very dense tonality and then a compelling nose, attractively crisp and fruity. It builds a fine body, and masterfully crafted tannins add considerably to its development on the palate. Although 2001 was a good year, the two Brunello '01 versions stumble somewhat, turning out to be muddled on the nose and too slender on the palate. Rosso di Montalcino La Caduta '03, however, impresses with well-balanced oak and fruit, and with its rich mouthfeel. All of the other wines are pleasurable.

●	Rosso di Montalcino La Caduta '03	🍷🍷	5
●	Brunello di Montalcino Ris. '99	🍷🍷	8
●	Brunello di Montalcino '01	🍷	7
●	Brunello di Montalcino La Casa '01	🍷	8
●	Sant'Antimo Ca' del Pazzo '03	🍷	6
●	Rosso Caparzo Sangiovese '04	🍷	4
●	Rosso di Montalcino '04	🍷	4
●	Rosso Caparzo '05	🍷	3*
●	Brunello di Montalcino La Casa '88	🍸🍸🍸	7
●	Brunello di Montalcino La Casa '93	🍸🍸🍸	7
●	Brunello di Montalcino '00	🍸🍸	7
●	Brunello di Montalcino La Casa '00	🍸🍸	8
●	Brunello di Montalcino '98	🍸🍸	7
●	Brunello di Montalcino '99	🍸🍸	7

MONTALCINO (SI)

TENUTA CARLINA
LOC. TAVERNELLE
S.DA DI ARGIANO - POD. PODERUCCIO
53024 MONTALCINO (SI)
TEL. 0668803000
www.brunellolatogata.com

This prominent Montalcino producer's performances see-sawed this year, and only a few of the wines presented did well. Owner Danilo Tonon is a lawyer in Rome, with the Consorzio del Brunello di Montalcino as a client. Following his taking up this adventure about 15 years ago, he expanded the operation considerably over the years, acquiring properties in various areas around Montalcino. The winery also created new wines to utilize the fruit from vineyards too young to go into the Brunello blend. With the roster of properties complete and the vineyards in, Tonon began construction of a partially underground cellar in order to improve winemaking, and it now houses some "botti" and a wide range of barriques and tonneaux. Turning to the wines we tasted, Brunello di Montalcino '01 put in its usual excellent performance, with well-delineated berry fruit and attractive oak, followed by a balanced duet between savoury fruit and fine-grained tannins, all leading to a finish that is decently lengthy. On a par is Barengo '04, but here we liked the berry preserves and fragrant balsam that beautifully matched the chewy tannins on the palate, complementing each other to create a delicious offering.

● Brunello di Montalcino La Togata '01	▼▼	7
● Barengo '04	▼▼	6
● Brunello di Montalcino '97	▽▽▽	7
● Brunello di Montalcino Ris. '95	▽▽	7
● Brunello di Montalcino Ris. '97	▽▽	8
● Brunello di Montalcino '99	▽▽	8
● Brunello di Montalcino La Togata '00	▽▽	8
● Barengo '02	▽▽	5
● Barengo '03	▽▽	5
● Brunello di Montalcino '98	▽▽	7

MONTALCINO (SI)

★ CASANOVA DI NERI
POD. FIESOLE
53024 MONTALCINO (SI)
TEL. 0577834455
www.casanovadineri.com

Consistent quality over the years has made Giacomo Neri's winery a benchmark for Montalcino. His three-storey cellar, underground and climate-conditioned, is now in operation, thus completing a growth and rationalization programme that has lasted some ten years now. The vineyards are numerous and diverse, with high-density plantings in different Montalcino zones. Some of the best crus are in prestigious areas such as Sesta, in the south, and those near the Castenuovo dell'Abate onyx quarry. Even the historic estate vineyards in the Torrenieri area are being renewed. For the wines tasted this year, the numbers of glasses awarded could almost replace descriptions. In first place are the Three Glasses captured by Brunello Cerretalto '00, from the historic estate cru in the western area, and Brunello Tenuta Nuova '01. Cerretalto displays a wealth of morello cherry preserve and blackberry fruit haunted by pungent spice. In the mouth, it shows complex and dense, yet energy laden, amply supported by luxuriant tannins and demonstrating surprising acidity considering the vintage. The finale is a masterpiece. The more modern-styled Tenuta Nuova '01 is no less remarkable. Here we see more barrel influence on the ripe fruit while the palate flaunts terrific component balance. It too builds a superbly luxurious, endless finish. Brunello '01 is excellent, with unexpected but well-focused oak on the nose and an elegant, leisurely palate. Rosso di Montalcino '04 is soundly made, and Pietradonice '03 shows very concentrated and tannic.

● Brunello di Montalcino Cerretalto '00	▼▼▼	8
● Brunello di Montalcino Tenuta Nuova '01	▼▼▼	7
● Brunello di Montalcino '01	▼▼	6
● Sant'Antimo Pietradonice '03	▼▼	8
● Rosso di Montalcino '04	▼	5
● Brunello di Montalcino '00	▽▽▽	6
● Sant'Antimo Pietradonice '00	▽▽▽	8
● Sant'Antimo Pietradonice '01	▽▽▽	8
● Brunello di Montalcino Cerretalto Ris. '88	▽▽▽	8
● Brunello di Montalcino Cerretalto '95	▽▽▽	8
● Brunello di Montalcino Tenuta Nuova '97	▽▽▽	7
● Brunello di Montalcino Cerretalto '99	▽▽▽	8
● Brunello di Montalcino Tenuta Nuova '99	▽▽▽	7

MONTALCINO (SI)

CASANUOVA DELLE CERBAIE
LOC. CASANOVA DELLE CERBAIE, 335
53024 MONTALCINO (SI)
TEL. 0577849284
www.casanuovadellecerbaie.com

The motto for Casanuova delle Cerbaie's wines could very well be "from the north with character". The traits regarded as typical of northern Montalcino are so blurred here, in fact, that one has to put aside the stereotype of wines produced in the area. There is a trick, though, and it goes to prove how masterfully the Morandini family manage their operation. They own some seven hectares in southern Montalcino, in fact, near Castello della Velona, and it is this fruit that probably accounts for the complexity of the wines. Another factor, surely, is their meticulous – nay, almost obsessive – selection of the grapes they use, and their overall vineyard yields are far below the minimum set by the production code. They did not produce Brunello Riserva in 2000, but we consoled ourselves with the superb Cerbaione '04, a blend of sangiovese and merlot that competed in the national finals. It beguiles with a very dense ruby and then serves up a duet of red and dark berry fruit beautifully enhanced by some pungent herbaceous and toasty oak essences. Lively but well-integrated tannins contribute to a body that is impressive and firmly structured. We certainly can't cavil with Brunello '01, either, even though it shows its youth with some expressive oak tones and tannins that straiten the palate somewhat. Rosso di Montalcino '04 is well crafted and fruity.

● Cerbaione '04	▼▼	6
● Brunello di Montalcino '01	▼▼	6
● Rosso di Montalcino '04	▼	5
● Brunello di Montalcino Ris. '97	▽▽▽	7
● Brunello di Montalcino Ris. '99	▽▽▽	8
● Brunello di Montalcino '00	▽▽	6
● Cerbaione '01	▽▽	6
● Brunello di Montalcino '97	▽▽	7
● Cerbaione '02	▽▽	6
● Cerbaione '03	▽▽	6
● Brunello di Montalcino '99	▽▽	7

MONTALCINO (SI)

CASTELGIOCONDO
LOC. CASTELGIOCONDO
53024 MONTALCINO (SI)
TEL. 057784131
www.frescobaldi.il

The results from this splendid estate belonging to Marchesi Frescobaldi represent a curious lapse in the wines most representative of the denomination. We found this most perplexing, since recent vintages have brought commendable performances from the winery. But Brunello di Montalcino '01 appears far too dense in hue. The nose is appealing and complex, releasing spicy balsam and layering on lots of dark and red berry fruit, reminding one particularly of preserves and brandied fruit. We were less impressed with its performance in the mouth, finding it quite out of balance with acidity and tannins neither in proportion nor cooperating, so much so that it materially detracts from the wine's fine extractive components. More ageing will no doubt help to improve the situation. Brunello Ripa al Convento Riserva '00 exhibits an unusual nose of crusted bread and cherry preserves, with slightly overripe notes betraying the hot vintage. Here, too, the palate was anything but supple. On the other hand, Rosso di Montalcino Campo ai Sassi '04 is delightful, boasting crisp, multi-layered fruit and then good weight and balance in the mouth. We liked Lamaione '03 as well, for its concentrated blackberry fragrance and measured oak tones, as well as for the suppleness of its palate and the lengthy conclusion.

● Lamaione '03	▼▼	8
● Rosso di Montalcino Campo ai Sassi '04	▼▼	4
● Brunello di Montalcino Ripa al Convento Ris. '00	▼	8
● Brunello di Montalcino '01	▼	7
● Brunello di Montalcino '00	▽▽▽	7
● Brunello di Montalcino Ris. '88	▽▽▽	6
● Brunello di Montalcino Ris. '90	▽▽▽	6
● Lamaione '01	▽▽	8
● Brunello di Montalcino '98	▽▽	7
● Brunello di Montalcino '99	▽▽	7
● Brunello di Montalcino Ripa al Convento '99	▽▽	8
● Lamaione '00	▽▽	8
● Brunello di Montalcino '97	▽▽	7

CENTOLANI

LOC. FRIGGIALI
S.DA MAREMMANA
53024 MONTALCINO (SI)
TEL. 0577849454

Centolani boasts an impressive 40 hectares of vineyards dedicated to Brunello production, divided equally between their Friggiali and Pietranera estates. The two areas differ significantly in both climate and soils, which is the reason for two different Brunellos. The soils in the Pietranera area, on Montalcino's southeast border, right beneath the recently restored Castello della Velona, are of volcanic basalt, which is rather unusual in Montalcino. Friggiali, in the west, is an area with tighter-textured clays and galestro limestone marls. The winemaking facility, located there, has been enlarged, and it hosts the classic "botti", as well as growing stocks of barriques. Brunello Pietranera '01 is a truly fine offering, whose origin in southern part of the zone is evidenced already on the nose by luscious fragrances of blackberry and raspberry preserve that work nicely as a tasty foil to sour cherry and oleander. On the palate, acidity and tannins are in fine evidence and work well to support the wine's appreciable weight and breadth. It concludes with plenty of succulent length. Its brother, Tenuta Friggiali '01, is behind only by a hair's breadth. Aromas of oak and roasted coffee betray a more modern bent but there is no lack of elegance on the palate, which shows good heft and progression as well. Rosso di Montalcino '04 comes across too tight in the mouth.

● Brunello di Montalcino Pietranera '01	▽▽	7
● Brunello di Montalcino Tenuta Friggiali '01	▼▼	6
● Rosso di Montalcino Tenuta Friggiali '04	▼	4
● Brunello di Montalcino Tenuta Friggiali Ris. '99	▽▽▽	8
● Brunello di Montalcino Tenuta Friggiali '00	▽▽	6
● Brunello di Montalcino Pietranera '99	▽▽	7
● Brunello di Montalcino Pietranera '00	▽▽	7
● Brunello di Montalcino Tenuta Friggiali '98	▽▽	8

MONTALCINO (SI)

LA CERBAIOLA

P.ZZA CAVOUR, 19
53024 MONTALCINO (SI)
TEL. 0577848499 - 335357456

This year's release of La Cerbaiola's Brunello unfortunately fell short of what we have come to expect from one of the most respected houses in Montalcino. Giulio and Mirella Salvioni have offered over the years wines of great distinction and character, and we are confident that such will be the case again quite soon. Their Brunello '01, showing a deep ruby, hesitates a moment on the nose but then reveals spicy notes of oak masterfully melded into well-ripened fruit and preserves. It enters confidently, developing impressive weight and complexity, the alcohol well under control and the tannins not yet smooth but getting there nicely, which is a trait of Salvioni Brunellos in the better years. With a finish that is a tad stiff and thus not as long as expected, we end up with a wine that evidences character but lacks refinement. Rosso di Montalcino '04 is superlative, practically a Brunello in miniature. It leads off with a rich ruby and clean cherry fruit and then unfurls a gorgeously complex, satisfyingly balanced palate. We eagerly look forward to next year's releases, knowing that the Salvioni talents and the incredible potential of one of the denomination's finest zones will bring forth new masterpieces.

● Brunello di Montalcino '01	▼▼	8
● Rosso di Montalcino '04	▼▼	6
● Brunello di Montalcino '00	▽▽▽	8
● Brunello di Montalcino '85	▽▽▽	8
● Brunello di Montalcino '87	▽▽▽	8
● Brunello di Montalcino '88	▽▽▽	8
● Brunello di Montalcino '89	▽▽▽	8
● Brunello di Montalcino '90	▽▽▽	8
● Brunello di Montalcino '97	▽▽▽	8
● Brunello di Montalcino '99	▽▽▽	8

CERBAIONA

LOC. CERBAIONA
53024 MONTALCINO (SI)
TEL. 0577848660

Right on schedule, with the reliability of a long-haul airliner, captain Molinari, ably assisted by co-pilot Nora, his life partner, and accompanied by their ever-present crew of cellar hands, touched down to claim our Three Glass award. The Brunello '01 is simply stupendous, impressing every member of the tasting panel and winning the award for the Best Red of the Year to boot. The winery style, sinewy and unmistakable, is obvious right from the appearance, a deep ruby that goes just far enough. A hedonistically expressive nose reveals the classic morello cherry foregrounding a subtle florality, as well as that vein of dark liquorice characteristic of the best vintages of Cerbaiona Brunello. But the best is yet to come. A warm, appealingly self-confident attack and authoritative progression bolstered by creamy, dense-packed tannins are accompanied by enthralling acidity that wraps everything together. The finish rises and goes on and on. In short, as Molinari himself would probably say, it's a little stunner. Cerbaiona '03, although it offers a satisfying texture, lacks balance and disappointed. As a preview, we can reveal that the Rosso di Montalcino will soon be back in production.

● Brunello di Montalcino '01	🍷🍷🍷	8
● Cerbaiona '03	🍷	6
● Brunello di Montalcino '85	🍷🍷🍷	8
● Brunello di Montalcino '88	🍷🍷🍷	8
● Brunello di Montalcino '90	🍷🍷🍷	8
● Brunello di Montalcino '97	🍷🍷🍷	8
● Brunello di Montalcino '99	🍷🍷🍷	8
● Brunello di Montalcino '98	🍷🍷	8
● Brunello di Montalcino '00	🍷🍷	8

CIACCI PICCOLOMINI D'ARAGONA

FRAZ. CASTELNUOVO DELL'ABATE
LOC. MOLINELLO
53024 MONTALCINO (SI)
TEL. 0577835616
www.ciaccipiccolomini.com

Paolo Bianchini, with the reins of his family winery now firmly in hand, has definitely shifted the winery into a higher gear, even though improvements in the wines will be fully appreciated only over the next few years. In the meantime, he has finished some phases of restructuring, such as the construction of a new cellar, which was designed to minimize impact on the environment. Its climate-controlled interior is strikingly functional, with spacious, well-organized areas for vinification and ageing. Fermentation is in wood vats and glass-lined cement while the barrel room comprises the traditional medium-sized Slavonian oak barrels of between 25 and 40 hectolitres, as well as smaller barriques for the production of the two Sant'Antimo wines. The splendid 15th-century edifice in the village Castelnuovo dell'Abate, which houses the winery offices, has been preserved. All of the wines we tasted performed well. First past the finish line was Brunello Pianrosso '01, a lean, beautifully structured wine in the traditional style and just what one would expect from a winery of this pedigree. A deep but judicious ruby, it yields clean, generous aromas of yellow peach and dark cherry on the nose, with delicate florality all along the line. A considerable charge of alcohol powers a lean, sinewy palate, which derives significant character from a magisterial complex of tannins. We liked the all-syrah Sant'Antimo Fabius '03 for its admirable complexity and elegantly perfumed nose, as well as Sant'Antimo Ateo '03, Rosso di Montalcino '04, and Montecucco Sangiovese '04.

● Brunello di Montalcino V. di Pianrosso '01	🍷🍷	8
● Sant'Antimo Fabius '03	🍷🍷	7
● Sant'Antimo Ateo '03	🍷	6
● Montecucco Sangiovese '04	🍷	6
● Rosso di Montalcino '04	🍷	6
● Brunello di Montalcino V. di Pianrosso '90	🍷🍷🍷	8
● Brunello di Montalcino V. di Pianrosso Ris. '95	🍷🍷🍷	6
● Brunello di Montalcino V. di Pianrosso '98	🍷🍷🍷	7
● Brunello di Montalcino V. di Pianrosso Ris. '99	🍷🍷🍷	8

MONTALCINO (SI)

Tenuta Col d'Orcia

Loc. Sant'Angelo in Colle
53020 Montalcino (SI)
tel. 057780891
www.coldorcia.it

Sadly, Brunello Poggio al Vento Riserva '99, Tenuta Col d'Orcia's standard-bearer, won't be out until next year. Its absence presented no serious negative effects, however, since the wines that were presented this year all acquitted themselves admirably. Edoardo Virano, from Piedmont but transplanted to Montalcino decades ago, has had swift success in achieving his objective of bringing improvements to his standard-level wines. His top-of-the-line wines, of course, needed no fiddling with, and in witness, Brunello '01 is the best version produced to date. Relying on classic floral-fruity essences, it also suggests winning nuances of oleander and green tea, which continue onto the palate. Here, supple, elegant structure is coupled with leisurely progression and a tasty suite of tannins contributes to a fine finish. The new sangiovese plantings, from cultivars sourced from long-established vineyards, have just come into production and are making their quality felt. Olmaia is all cabernet sauvignon and seems to have shrugged off the difficulties of 2002. It is a fine offering, its varietal herbaceousness well tempered by redcurrant and blueberry, while glossy, complex tannins support a development that is steady and well proportioned. Nearco '02, a cabernet, merlot and syrah assemblage, is an affordable delight, with good volume and appealing fruit. Rosso di Montalcino '04 and Rosso degli Spezieri '05 are both pleasurable and fantastic value.

● Brunello di Montalcino '01	TT	6
● Olmaia '02	TT	7
● Nearco '02	TT	7*
● Rosso di Montalcino '04	T	4
● Rosso degli Spezieri '05	T	3*
● Olmaia '01	YYY	7
● Brunello di Montalcino Poggio al Vento Ris. '88	YYY	8
● Brunello di Montalcino Poggio al Vento Ris. '90	YYY	8
● Brunello di Montalcino Poggio al Vento Ris. '95	YYY	8
● Brunello di Montalcino Poggio al Vento Ris. '97	YYY	8

Collemattoni

fraz. Sant'Angelo in Colle
pod. Collemattoni, 100
53020 Montalcino (SI)
tel. 0577844127
www.collemattoni.it

The relentless improvement in quality that has marked Collemattoni has led finally to the capture of a Three Glass trophy. Plaudits go to Marcello Bucci, who in just a few years has revolutionized this family winery located just outside Sant'Angelo in Colle. Brunello '01 is a champion through and through. A lovely rich ruby hue announces an equally appealing complexity on the nose, where slightly evolved essences of Peruvian bark, dark liquorice and medicinal herbs yield gradually to textbook wild cherry. In the mouth, rather than a massive blockbuster, we have a finely muscled thoroughbred. It is stunning for the magisterial proportion of its components, which show perfect definition and no excess, its tannins of exemplary suppleness weaving well into the texture. The finish, driven by perfectly crafted acidity, seems endless and expands to reprise in masterly fashion the qualities on the nose. We would also like to draw attention to the very reasonable price, although its limited production means that few will see it. No Riserva '00 was produced. It is sourced from the estate's Fontelontana vineyard, an old, well-aspected plot at Sant'Angelo in Colle, and the fruit was simply not up to Riserva quality. Rosso di Montalcino '04 is another fine effort, showing classic ruby and loads of morello and sour cherry, followed by a palate that is supple, leisurely and absolutely delightful.

● Brunello di Montalcino '01	TTT	6
● Rosso di Montalcino '04	TT	4
● Brunello di Montalcino '00	YY	6
● Brunello di Montalcino Fontelontano Ris. '99	YY	7
● Brunello di Montalcino '99	YY	6

TENUTA DI SESTA

FRAZ. CASTELNUOVO DELL'ABATE
LOC. SESTA
53020 MONTALCINO (SI)
TEL. 0577835612 - 0577596014
www.tenutadisesta.it

Ask growers in the Montalcino zone where they would prefer to acquire vineyards and the almost unanimous answer will be Sesta. Located between Sant'Angelo in Colle and Castelnuovo dell'Abate, Sesta presents many unique features. Although it lies in the southern reaches of Montalcino, ventilation is almost ideal and a layer of clay in the soil profile maintains a water reserve for vines in hot, dry conditions. Giovanni Ciacci's operation has been investing over several years to modernize the winemaking facility and ensure that their wines faithfully reflect their local terroir. That project is complete, and Giovanni is now beginning to see the results. We were impressed with the quality of all of the wines presented, as represented by Brunello '01, which competed in the national final round. A classic, intense ruby is followed by leisured aromas of cherries and other red fruit. The palate hews conscientiously to the Brunello canons, with a judicious charge of tannins perfectly folded into the fruit and a finish that is expansive and intensely satisfying, making this a truly elegant wine. Poggio d'Arna '04, from sangiovese, cabernet franc and merlot, is the new arrival, and it is a winner. Complex and well balanced, it is fruity all the way through, a charming, easy quaffer sold at an equally attractive price. We found Rosso di Montalcino '04 somewhat stiff but time should limber it up.

● Brunello di Montalcino '01	2 red glasses	7
● Poggio d'Arna '04	2 red glasses	4*
● Rosso di Montalcino '04	1 red glass	4
● Brunello di Montalcino Ris. '95	2 white glasses	8
● Brunello di Montalcino '00	2 white glasses	6
● Brunello di Montalcino Ris. '97	2 white glasses	8
● Brunello di Montalcino '99	2 white glasses	7
● Brunello di Montalcino Ris. '99	2 white glasses	8

CASATO PRIME DONNE

DONATELLA CINELLI COLOMBINI
LOC. CASATO
53024 MONTALCINO (SI)
TEL. 0577849421 - 0577662108
www.cinellicolombini.it

The programme that Donatella Cinelli Colombini set herself reveals the seriousness of its design in the wines presented for this edition of the Guide. The long-awaited champion has arrived to crown all Cinelli Colombini's efforts for Brunello Prime Donne '01 took our Three Glasses and two other wines went to the final taste-offs. Casato Prime Donne places so much faith in what women have to offer that it dedicated this wine to women. In fact, the blend itself was determined by a tasting panel composed exclusively of women wine professionals. After a dense ruby, it is a feast of cherries with ripe cherry fruit, sour cherry preserve and liqueur cherries laced with just the right infusion of oak tones, vanilla and balsam to keep everything in proportion. Tangy acidity and already integrated tannins help to create an impressive palate, completing an offering that is modern in inspiration but still bears the traits of local tradition. Brunello Riserva '00 hits all the right notes, too. It's a bit more classic in execution and we appreciated the tanned leather, tobacco leaf and pungent herbs that enliven the morello cherry, as well as the velvety tannic complex and generous acidity that perk up the palate. Orcia Cenerentola '03 is very well crafted whereas Brunello '01 and Rosso di Montalcino '04 are competently put together but too straightforward to offer much interest.

● Brunello di Montalcino Prime Donne '01	3 red glasses	7
● Brunello di Montalcino Ris. '00	2 red glasses	7
● Orcia Cenerentola '03	2 red glasses	6
● Brunello di Montalcino '01	1 red glass	6
● Rosso di Montalcino '04	1 red glass	5
● Brunello di Montalcino Ris. '98	2 white glasses	7
● Brunello di Montalcino '00	2 white glasses	6
● Brunello di Montalcino Prime Donne '00	2 white glasses	7
● Brunello di Montalcino '98	2 white glasses	7
● Brunello di Montalcino '99	2 white glasses	6
● Brunello di Montalcino Prime Donne '99	2 white glasses	7
● Brunello di Montalcino Ris. '99	2 white glasses	7

DONNA OLGA

LOC. FRIGGIALI
S.DA MAREMMANA
53024 MONTALCINO (SI)
TEL. 0577849454
www.donnaolga.com

The Donna Olga operation was launched with the 1997 vintage Brunello and has as its architect Olga Peluso, who was already a player in Montalcino, at the historic Centolani winery. Peluso's goal has remained that of squeezing every possible bit of potential out of viticultural experimentation in Montalcino. She has only four hectares, all dedicated to Brunello production and all dense-planted to the extreme. Her use of oak is fairly modern, utilizing various sizes of cask but predominantly small-capacity containers. After inspiring performances in the early years, Donna Olga evidenced a slight relaxation in style and quality, particularly in terms of typicity and expression of local conditions but it probably just took time to fine-tune the programme. This Brunello '01 is quite simply fabulous. It attracts with a deep ruby and the nose offers a rich panoply of classic components, ranging from cherry preserve and the more ethereal liqueur cherries, to delicate floral notes of violets and toasty oak nuances. It is exceptional in the mouth, showing very full and pulpy with spacious, well-distributed tannins and a vivacious acidity that animates a development notable for its breadth and energy. Few finishes demonstrate such multi-layered complexity and refinement. Rosso di Montalcino '04 is also impressive, with well-fruited aromas and a supple, rich palate. Worth noting is that a percentage of the proceeds from sales go to charity.

● Brunello di Montalcino Donna Olga '01	▼▼▼	7
● Rosso di Montalcino '04	▼▼	4
● Brunello di Montalcino Donna Olga '98	▽▽	8
● Brunello di Montalcino Donna Olga '97	▽▽	7
● Brunello di Montalcino Donna Olga '99	▽▽	7

FANTI - SAN FILIPPO

FRAZ. CASTELNUOVO DELL'ABATE
POD. PALAZZO
53020 MONTALCINO (SI)
TEL. 0577835795 - 0577835759

The dynamic president of the Consorzio di Tutela of Montalcino wines, now unfortunately at the end of his term, is quite adept at keeping numerous balls in the air at once, and has shown quite a flare as wine producer. A committed promoter of the qualities of the Castelnuovo dell'Abate area, Baldassarre Filippo Fanti has aimed over the years to embody this terroir in his wines, which have been lean structured and powerful. Past vintages, in fact, needed significant cellaring to begin to reveal their charms. We have noticed lately, however, an increased accessibility in the wines. The winery has just concluded fairly thorough-going renovation, with new vineyards as well as a new cellar, now functional and boasts some impressive technical innovations, particularly in the fermenter department. Work areas are spacious and include a handsome tasting room and an expansive barrel room that privileges small-capacity oak. Turning to the wines we tasted, we found Brunello '01 so impressive that it competed in the national finals. Made in a no-nonsense style that showcases its terroir, it begins with multi-faceted aromas that betray Peruvian bark and brambly essences suggesting blackberry in particular. In the mouth, it is concentrated with an admirable mouthfeel. If the palate seems a bit tight and the tannins a tad coarse at the moment, some more time in bottle will certainly smooth that out. The other wines, Rosso di Montalcino '04 and Sant'Antimo Rosso '05, are both pleasurable.

● Brunello di Montalcino '01	▼▼	7
● Rosso di Montalcino '04	▼	4
● Sant'Antimo Rosso '05	▼	4
● Brunello di Montalcino '00	▽▽▽	7
● Brunello di Montalcino Ris. '95	▽▽▽	7
● Brunello di Montalcino '97	▽▽▽	7
● Brunello di Montalcino '98	▽▽	7
● Brunello di Montalcino '95	▽▽	6
● Brunello di Montalcino '96	▽▽	6
● Brunello di Montalcino '99	▽▽	7

MONTALCINO (SI)

PODERE LA FORTUNA
LOC. LA FORTUNA, 83
53024 MONTALCINO (SI)
TEL. 0577848308
www.tenutalafortuna.it

For quite a few years now, the dedicated, outgoing Gioberto Zannoni has been presenting wines that offer more than interesting characteristics. They've always lacked that extra touch of distinctiveness that the 2001 vintage has finally provided. And so we now have the champion we have been waiting for, Brunello di Montalcino '01, a superb creation that relaunches the fortunes of Montalcino's northeast area. Podere La Fortuna is a family operation, with Zannoni's son directing the recently enlarged and rationalized cellar, which contains the traditional "botti", all of 30 hectolitres or less, as well as French oak barriques and tonneaux. Gioberto's future daughter-in-law, an agronomist, is charge of some nine hectares of estate vineyards, which yielded their finest Brunello. It impresses right off the bat, with a fine, deep ruby and then presents refined suggestions of balsam and medicinal herbs that cosset ripe cherry and blackberry over ethereal hints of bottled fruit. Excellent tannins and acid help form an alluring texture and allow the palate to expand impressively, developing evenly into a broad finish that exhibits remarkable harmony and length. Rosso di Montalcino '04 is quite appealing. The acidity is still a tad rough, lending the wine a nice crispness but shortening progression somewhat.

● Brunello di Montalcino '01	🍷🍷🍷	7
● Rosso di Montalcino '04	🍷	5
● Sant'Antimo La Fortuna '01	🍷🍷 (white)	6
● Brunello di Montalcino Ris. '97	🍷🍷 (white)	7
● Brunello di Montalcino '00	🍷🍷 (white)	6
● Sant'Antimo La Fortuna '02	🍷🍷 (white)	5
● Brunello di Montalcino '97	🍷🍷 (white)	7
● Brunello di Montalcino '98	🍷🍷 (white)	6
● Brunello di Montalcino '99	🍷🍷 (white)	6
● Brunello di Montalcino Ris. '99	🍷🍷 (white)	7

MONTALCINO (SI)

TENUTA LA FUGA
LOC. CAMIGLIANO
53024 MONTALCINO (SI)
TEL. 055859811
www.tenutefolonari.com

Owned by Tenute Ambrogio e Giovanni Folonari, Tenuta La Fuga is located near Camigliano, in the southwest section of the Montalcino area. The fruit ripens here considerably in advance of the rest of the Montalcino denomination. This means that the problem in the vineyards is often overripeness, which can lead to stunting of aromas in the wines as well as to high alcohol levels. Growers in this area, then, must be not only good winemakers but talented vineyard managers as well. Giovanni Folonari is personally involved in the management of the ten hectares of estate vineyards, most of those dedicated to production of Brunello and Rosso di Montalcino. The results have been most satisfactory, as amply demonstrated by the wines presented in our tastings, which show significant quality leaps year after year. Brunello '01 is splendid, and went through to compete in the national finals. The nose was very impressive, with crisp, well-focused fragrances of red berry fruit and blackberry, also flaunting admirable cleanness and judicious use of oak. It boasts tasty, smooth tannins that go to make up a finely woven texture, and perfectly calibrated alcohol that contributes to a spacious palate, unfolding with admirable rhythm. Rosso di Montalcino '04 was among the best we tasted of the vintage. White and morello cherry are fragrant, crisp and refreshing, followed by well-balanced alcohol and acidity that make for a delicious palate.

● Brunello di Montalcino '01	🍷🍷	7
● Rosso di Montalcino '04	🍷🍷	5
● Brunello di Montalcino '97	🍷🍷 (white)	7
● Brunello di Montalcino '99	🍷🍷 (white)	7
● Brunello di Montalcino La Due Sorelle Ris. '99	🍷🍷 (white)	8
● Brunello di Montalcino '00	🍷🍷 (white)	7
● Brunello di Montalcino Ris. '95	🍷🍷 (white)	6

MONTALCINO (SI)

EREDI FULIGNI
VIA SALONI, 33
53024 MONTALCINO (SI)
TEL. 0577848039 - 0577848127

Eredi Fuligni, managed by Roberto Guerrini, continues to make wines of uncompromising character and good fidelity to their origin. The estate vineyards lie at an altitude of about 400 metres on a ridge northeast of Montalcino. This area yields wines of marked equilibrium and refinement, as this producer demonstrates, and with an understated elegance that some mistake for simplicity. As a result of rigorous harvest-time selection of fruit, the wines show intense fruitiness and great concentration, with the acidity generally more prominent than the tannin component. Brunello '01 follows these canons and is most expressive of its terroir, and it was easily promoted to our final tasting round. Aromas of spice, cinnamon and vanilla abound, smoothing out the crisp essences of cherry fruit. Both acidity and tannins are as excellent and judicious as we have come to expect. They contribute to a balanced structure that enables a good, self-confident progression, finally capped by a rich, complex finale. We think Rosso di Montalcino Ginestreto '04 among the most appealing of the vintage, releasing copious draughts of morello cherry and then striking a magisterial balance of depth and a spirited crispness. S.J. '04, a sangiovese-merlot blend, is fine, with plentiful blossoms and yellow peach, and a delicious palate.

● Brunello di Montalcino '01	**YY**	7
● Rosso di Montalcino Ginestreto '04	**YY**	5
● S. J. '04	**YY**	4
● Brunello di Montalcino Ris. '97	YYY	8
● S. J. '01	YY	5
● Brunello di Montalcino Vigneti dei Cottimelli '97	YY	7
● Brunello di Montalcino '99	YY	7
● Brunello di Montalcino Vigneti dei Cottimelli Ris. '95	YY	7
● Brunello di Montalcino Vigneti dei Cottimelli '96	YY	7
● Brunello di Montalcino Vigneti dei Cottimelli '98	YY	7
● Brunello di Montalcino Ris. '99	YY	8

MONTALCINO (SI)

LA GERLA
LOC. CANALICCHIO
POD. COLOMBAIO, 5
53024 MONTALCINO (SI)
TEL. 0577848599
www.lagerla.it

La Gerla appears year after year because of the solid, consistent quality of the wines, which are always reliable, always well executed and rarely disappoint expectations. In addition, they also reflect the quality of the particular vintage. extremely well. The winery is owned by the Rossi family, who have a successful track record in advertising in Milan. Located in the northern sector of the denomination, the cellar stands on hills whose soils show significant limestone-based galestro and little clay. The estate recently acquired and planted new vineyards in the Castelnuovo dell'Abate area that are now in production. Having vineyards in two zones contributes to more complex wines and the improvements have been marked. It also makes for less complicated harvest periods, since picking dates in the two areas can vary by as much as two weeks. The two '01 Brunello versions, both of which went into the national tasting finals, display the improvements mentioned, although in different ways, particularly with respect to use of oak. Brunello '01 displays rich, crisp, cherry-led fruit with some notes of slightly underripe blackberry, then is all elegance on the palate, thanks to the calibrated acidity characteristic of the northern vineyards. Brunello Gli Angeli '01, on the other hand, presents a warmer profile on the nose, with some spicy oak and subtle notes of roasted coffee over a base of wild cherry jam. It shows good extractive qualities, helped by straightforward, fleshy tannins. Rosso '04 is enjoyable.

● Brunello di Montalcino '01	**YY**	6
● Brunello di Montalcino Gli Angeli '01	**YY**	8
● Rosso di Montalcino '04	**Y**	4
● Brunello di Montalcino '00	YY	6
● Brunello di Montalcino Gli Angeli Ris. '99	YY	8
● Brunello di Montalcino Ris. '97	YY	8
● Brunello di Montalcino Ris. '98	YY	8

MONTALCINO (SI)

Greppone Mazzi
Tenimenti Ruffino
loc. Greppone
53024 Montalcino (SI)
tel. 05583605

After last year's splendid performance, we expected more from the Ruffino group's winery in Montalcino. The Greppone Mazzi property is dominated by the striking Villa Leopoldina, whose loggia looks out over the newly planted vineyards. These ten hectares dedicated to Montalcino's leading variety represent the true treasure of the winery. They lie in eastern Montalcino, next to the state road that rises from Torrenieri towards Montalcino, not very far from the town. The vineyards are thus at a significant altitude, which contributes important elements to the profile of the winery's Brunellos. On the nose, this translates into crisp notes of red berry fruit and on the palate into a healthy acidity. Riserva '00 stands out immediately for a markedly intense, clean-edged nose, with fragrances of wild dark berry fruit and blackberry appetizingly accompanied by a pungent herbaceousness, a tempting nuance of oak and just the right level of spice. It is full bodied, nicely mirroring the nose, but the tannins are a little too noticeable and crimp the finish. Brunello '01 is not quite up to snuff and doesn't have all that we look for in a Montalcino Brunello. Here, too, we find plenty of dark blackberry fruit lifted by a subtle herbaceousness. The entry is self-confident, the tannins supple and the finish not excessively assertive.

●	Brunello di Montalcino Ris. '00	▼▼	8
●	Brunello di Montalcino '01	▼	7
●	Brunello di Montalcino '99	YYY	8
●	Brunello di Montalcino Ris. '99	YYY	6
●	Brunello di Montalcino '00	YY	8
●	Brunello di Montalcino '98	YY	8
●	Brunello di Montalcino '97	YY	8

MONTALCINO (SI)

Villa Le Prata
loc. Le Prata, 261
53024 Montalcino (SI)
tel. 0577848325
www.villaleprata.com

After a year out, Villa Le Prata has regained a full profile, thanks to two wines that easily went into our national final round. It's another all-woman operation in a denomination that is becoming well known for its many women winemakers releasing top-quality products. Benedetta Losapio energetically directs the winery founded by her father in the 1980s while Gioia Cresti gives her valiant assistance on the technical side. Villa Le Prata is a modest operation, with vineyards well placed throughout the denomination. This philosophy is a big plus since it facilitates vineyard management and ensures a range of characteristics in fruit sourced from various areas. The winery itself, along with the historic estate vineyard, is situated at a medium high elevation in western Montalcino, where the grapes display refined qualities that make a big contribution to concentration and well-focused aromas. The winery has four other hectares of vines south of Castello della Velona, near Castelnuovo dell'Abate. Brunello '01 is superlative, releasing generous red and black fruit aromas. The palate opens complex and spacious with fleshy tannins amplifying those qualities and an impressive finish crowns a very appealing offering. We were also impressed with the all-merlot Le Prata '03, which is quite a distinctive wine. After layering balsam and menthol over rich bilberry fragrances, it features a rich, multi-faceted palate and a finale lightly edged with toasty oak. Rosso di Montalcino Tirso '04 is one of the best of its category.

●	Brunello di Montalcino '01	▼▼	6
●	Le Prata '03	▼▼	5
●	Rosso di Montalcino Tirso '04	▼▼	5
●	Brunello di Montalcino '97	YY	7
●	Brunello di Montalcino '98	YY	6
●	Brunello di Montalcino '00	YY	6
●	Le Prata '00	YY	5
●	Le Prata '01	YY	5
●	Brunello di Montalcino '99	YY	6
●	Le Prata '99	YY	5

MONTALCINO (SI)

LISINI

LOC. SANT'ANGELO IN COLLE
53020 MONTALCINO (SI)
TEL. 0577844040
www.lisini.com

Top marks go to the wines of Lisini, one of Montalcino's historic producers, located in one of the most prestigious subzones of the denomination. Improvements in quality were becoming obvious in recent vintages but this year puts the cherry on the cake and there can be no doubt that the winery has returned to its former glory. The 2000 version of Brunello di Montalcino Ugolaia is superb. It is sourced from a splendid vineyard in the heart of the estate, located in the enclave of Sesta, whose distinctive characteristics emerge clearly in the wine. Although 2000 was a season marked by high temperatures and dry conditions, the terroir made the difference, allowing for optimal, even ripening of the fruit. After a typical dense ruby, Ugolaia '00 serves up a scrumptious, classic medley of tanned leather and rhubarb, a lovely admixture of subtle floral notes and ripe wild cherry aromas while hovering in the background are intriguing suggestions of moist earth. We were delighted by the expected velvety fabric of smooth tannins, and in the unrivalled complexity of the palate, well supported by perfect acidity that is so well integrated that we hardly notice it. The finish offers a beautiful flourish of tasty wild herbs. Brunello '01 too is an excellent effort, with rich depth in the mouth and a finish that ends on a harmonious note. Both Rosso di Montalcino '04 and the reasonably-priced San Biagio '04 are aromatic and delicious.

● Brunello di Montalcino Ugolaia '00	🍷🍷🍷	8
● Brunello di Montalcino '01	🍷🍷	7
● Rosso di Montalcino '04	🍷	5
● San Biagio '04	🍷	4
● Brunello di Montalcino '88	☐☐☐ (3 empty glasses)	6
● Brunello di Montalcino '90	☐☐☐ (3 empty glasses)	6
● Brunello di Montalcino Ugolaia '91	☐☐☐ (3 empty glasses)	8
● Brunello di Montalcino '00	☐☐ (2 empty glasses)	7
● Brunello di Montalcino Ugolaia '98	☐☐ (2 empty glasses)	8
● Brunello di Montalcino '99	☐☐ (2 empty glasses)	7
● Brunello di Montalcino Ugolaia '99	☐☐ (2 empty glasses)	8

MONTALCINO (SI)

IL MARRONETO

LOC. MADONNA DELLE GRAZIE, 307
53024 MONTALCINO (SI)
TEL. 0577849382
www.ilmarroneto.it

Alessandro Mori, a personable lawyer, has been devoting meticulous attention to his family winery since the 1970s. Year in and year out, he lavishes his considerable talent on his wines and this year they have responded with a very marked leap forward in quality. Perhaps the 2001 growing season lent a hand since it was up there with the most favourable. The operation is fairly modest in size and aficionados quickly snap up the few bottles released. Mori prefers a traditional style that renders the local terroir as closely as possible. His vineyards, amounting to little more than five hectares, lie in the northern area of the denomination, which favours the development of wines displaying harmony and elegance, qualities that Il Marroneto has in spades. The past few years have witnessed new developments at the winery. The 2004 vintage saw the debut of Ignaccio, a Rosso di Montalcino that displays dense red berry fruit and vigorous acidity. A new cru was also produced in the shape of Madonna delle Grazie '01, sourced from a vineyard parcel that Moro had noticed over the years for its exceptional Brunello fruit. Brunello '01 is the best wine Mori has ever presented and it intrigued us with its suggestion of smooth caramel over the rich, ripe red berry fruit. It then expands in all directions on the palate, unleashing a steady progression in a fine, elegant creation overall. Equally excellent is Brunello Madonna delle Grazie '01, its only blemish a slight contraction in the tannins.

● Brunello di Montalcino '01	🍷🍷	7
● Brunello di Montalcino Madonna delle Grazie '01	🍷🍷	8
● Rosso di Montalcino Ignaccio '04	🍷	5
● Brunello di Montalcino Madonna delle Grazie '00	☐☐ (2 empty glasses)	8
● Brunello di Montalcino '95	☐☐ (2 empty glasses)	6
● Brunello di Montalcino '97	☐☐ (2 empty glasses)	8
● Brunello di Montalcino '98	☐☐ (2 empty glasses)	8
● Brunello di Montalcino '99	☐☐ (2 empty glasses)	7

MASTROJANNI
FRAZ. CASTELNUOVO DELL'ABATE
POD. LORETO SAN PIO
53024 MONTALCINO (SI)
TEL. 0577835681
www.mastrojanni.com

This venerable winery in the Castelnuovo dell'Abate area continues to turn out wines marked by solid quality and – always important – quite competitive prices. We must confess, though, we are beginning to miss the star-quality Brunello that Mastrojanni achieved in past years. Talented Andrea Machetti still directs operations with his customary diligence and the consistent overall quality in the wines is due to his efforts. The general winery restructuring, which was starting to show good results, has been suspended for the moment. But the vineyards still yield outstanding fruit, thanks both to their superb position as well as to rigorous grape selection during harvest. All of the wines we tasted were impressive, results all the more praiseworthy for the absence of the Schiena d'Asino vineyard selection, which will come out next year. A Riserva was not produced in 2000, nor will a 2002 appear, since neither vintage was considered to be of good enough quality. But all of the Mastrojanni characteristics are in fine evidence in Brunello '01. The nose exhibits generous, well-focused white cherry and yellow peach while a terroir-faithful palate offers tannins that are insistent but never bitter. At the moment, they tamp down the expression and the finish comes across as somewhat stiff. Rosso di Montalcino '04 is fine, opening both floral and fruity, and developing a pleasurable mouthfeel and tannins that are perceptible but supple. San Pio '02, a sangiovese and cabernet blend, shows appealing balsam, balance and finesse.

● Brunello di Montalcino '01	TT	7
● San Pio '02	TT	5
● Rosso di Montalcino '04	TT	5
● Brunello di Montalcino Ris. '88	YYY	7
● Brunello di Montalcino '90	YYY	7
● Brunello di Montalcino Schiena d'Asino '90	YYY	7
● Brunello di Montalcino Schiena d'Asino '93	YYY	7
● Brunello di Montalcino '97	YYY	7
● Brunello di Montalcino '00	YY	7

TENUTE SILVIO NARDI
LOC. CASALE DEL BOSCO
53024 MONTALCINO (SI)
TEL. 0577808269
www.tenutenardi.com

There are a few figures who leave a deep imprint on the wineries they are involved with, and Emilia Nardi is certainly one of them. When she took over the tiller of her family operation, Tenute Silvio Nardi was known more for its extremely attractive prices than for the excellence of the wines. Over ten years, Nardi turned that on its head, making risky but courageous decisions that brought changes to distribution and production. The introduction of Brunello Manachiara was the most brilliant example. The latest development is a 100 per cent merlot and Sant'Antimo '04 is so good that in its first year it went to our final taste-offs. It grabs your attention right from the deep, saturated appearance and then develops multi-layered red and dark berry fruit integrated nicely with spicy oak. The palate betrays the wine's origin in vineyards in Montalcino's northern district, with an elegance and balance that characterize even the merlot fruit grown there. All of the other wines we tasted were fine. We must confess we expected a tad more out of Brunello Manachiara '01. It shows somewhat uncertain on the nose and after a smooth enough entry, tannins and acidity are still a bit in excess, which carries through to a stiffish finale. We found Brunello '01 admirably typical and well built, and Rosso di Montalcino '04 fragrant, complex and harmonious. Vin Santo '99 is pleasurable.

● Sant'Antimo Merlot '04	TT	5
● Brunello di Montalcino '01	TT	7
● Brunello di Montalcino Manachiara '01	TT	8
● Rosso di Montalcino '04	TT	5
● Vin Santo '99	T	4
● Brunello di Montalcino Manachiara '97	YYY	7
● Brunello di Montalcino Manachiara '99	YYY	8
● Brunello di Montalcino Manachiara '00	YY	8
● Brunello di Montalcino '98	YY	6
● Brunello di Montalcino '99	YY	6

MONTALCINO (SI)

SIRO PACENTI
LOC. PELAGRILLI, 1
53024 MONTALCINO (SI)
TEL. 0577848662

Giancarlo Pacenti's winery is among the most representative in the entire Montalcino denomination. Among the numerous reasons is Pacenti's intuition, some 15 years ago when Montalcino was still nascent, that it would be to the advantage of the zone to follow the French château model. The consequences of taking this direction are hard to miss today, namely, limited-production runs that are snapped up immediately. Siro Pacenti vineyards lie in two zones along a north-south axis, each with very different characteristics. That variety, plus meticulous vineyard management, ensures terrific quality fruit. A final quality grading of the grapes is carried out as they arrive in the cellar. The new cellar is now in full operation boasting custom-built fermenters, designed to Pacenti's specifications, which minimize the amount of pips present during fermentation. The wines we tasted this year were delicious and Brunello '01 actually went on to compete in the national finals. It leads off with dense ruby and then harmonizes a lovely florality with smooth notes of tobacco leaf while the palate is impressively complex, its tannins still just slightly incisive. Rosso di Montalcino '04 is full-bodied, crisp and exhibits good grip.

● Brunello di Montalcino '01	**YY**	8
● Rosso di Montalcino '04	**Y**	5
● Brunello di Montalcino '88	YYY	8
● Brunello di Montalcino '95	YYY	8
● Brunello di Montalcino '96	YYY	8
● Brunello di Montalcino '97	YYY	8
● Brunello di Montalcino '99	YY	8
● Brunello di Montalcino '00	YY	8
● Brunello di Montalcino '98	YY	8

MONTALCINO (SI)

IL PALAZZONE
LOC. DUE PORTE, 245
53024 MONTALCINO (SI)
TEL. 0577835764
www.ilpalazzone.com

It is worth pointing out that Il Palazzone's improvement in quality and consistency is now reaching remarkable levels, thanks perhaps to the solid relationship between owner Richard Parsons and consulting oenologist Paolo Vagaggini. The winery makes only Brunello di Montalcino, the grapes being sourced from estate vineyards located in two zones of Montalcino, which are quite different in character but also very complementary. The historic estate vineyards lie near the winery headquarters, Il Palazzone, just outside Montalcino, and at the fairly high elevation of 500 metres. Anticipating that grapes planted here could encounter difficulties in ripening fully in cooler years, some hectares were purchased years back in a more easterly part of Montalcino, looking towards Val d'Orcia, in the lower-down area of San Polo. Il Palazzone's Brunello, then, is a combination of fruit from these two zones. The '01 is a first-class version and easily walked away with our Three Glasses. A confident, medium ruby, it offers an absolutely classic array of complex dark and wild cherry fruit, clean and well focused, veined with notes of well-evolved tobacco leaf. Everything on the palate impresses, from a dense, well-extracted mouthfeel to a virtually endless finish that exhibits compelling breadth and depth. The tannin-acidity relationship is masterful and well proportioned. The winery thought the 2000 vintage was not up to snuff and made no Riserva '00. The future promises wines from additional varieties, including the internationals.

● Brunello di Montalcino '01	**YYY**	7
● Brunello di Montalcino Ris. '99	YYY	7
● Brunello di Montalcino '00	YY	7
● Rosso di Montalcino '00	YY	5
● Brunello di Montalcino Ris. '97	YY	8
● Brunello di Montalcino '99	YY	7
● Brunello di Montalcino Ris. '95	YY	7
● Brunello di Montalcino '97	YY	8
● Brunello di Montalcino '98	YY	8

MONTALCINO (SI)

Pieve Santa Restituta

Loc. Chiesa di Santa Restituta
53024 Montalcino (SI)
tel. 0173635158

In the last few years, we have noticed a change in direction in Angelo Gaja's Montalcino enterprise. Pieve Santa Restituta, located in one of the classic growing zones in Montalcino, has received much attention from Gaja, with a general restructuring programme affecting both the vineyards and the winemaking facility. The renewal of the vineyards, involving new high-density plantings, has been complete for a few years now. Work is still continuing on the cellar and some areas have still to be enlarged. Attilio Pagli, who has a comprehensive, nuanced knowledge of the Montalcino denomination, directs winemaking. The wonderful news on the wine front is that both of the Brunellos we tasted, Rennina and Sugarille, competed in the national finals, a clear sign that efforts over the last few years are paying off. Brunello Rennina '01 is most interesting, with an exuberant mélange of spicy oak, floral nuances and subtle eucalyptus infusing generous draughts of rich red berry fruit. Tannins are tasty and well fashioned, standing up forcefully to a vibrant acidity, and it concludes in elegance and finesse. Spicy oak and Peruvian bark give the blackberry fruit on Brunello Sugarille an attractive pungency while a full body is nicely matched by nervy acidity, which nonetheless succeeds in retaining its balance.

● Brunello di Montalcino Rennina '01	TT	8
● Brunello di Montalcino Sugarille '01	TT	8
● Brunello di Montalcino Rennina '99	YY	8
● Brunello di Montalcino Rennina '00	YY	8
● Brunello di Montalcino Sugarille '00	YY	8

MONTALCINO (SI)

Il Pinino

Loc. Pinino, 327
53024 Montalcino (SI)
tel. 0577849381
www.pinino.com

Il Pinino debuted in the Guide with a full profile, thanks to the good performance of its line-up as well as to the many improvements at the winery that we have observed taking place over recent years. Responsible for this achievement is a prominent Spanish industrialist, well known in the fashion world. Some years ago, he developed a passion for Brunello and purchased Il Pinino, a small Montalcino-area operation with a few hectares that went into Brunello, and renewal began immediately. New plantings brought the total hectares to 20, not all fully in production yet, and the vineyards are for the most part in the Torrenieri area, a zone now much in vogue. Fermentations were initially carried out at a friend's facility and the original small cellar was converted into an ageing cellar. It features various-sized casks in both French and Slavonian oak, reflecting plans to develop two different kinds of wine, which is indicated as well by Il Picino's two versions of Rosso di Montalcino. Brunello '01 is a fine effort, exhibiting textbook morello cherry and a luxurious palate composed of polished tannins and fine, ripe fruit. Rosso '04 is on the same level. Leather, tobacco leaf and subtle violets delight on the nose and then the rest is leisurely and seductive, making this delicious wine one of the best in its category. Rosso di Montalcino Clandestino '04 betrays a tad too much oak on the nose and the same goes for the tannins.

● Brunello di Montalcino '01	TT	7
● Rosso di Montalcino '04	TT	4
● Rosso di Montalcino Clandestino '04	T	5

MONTALCINO (SI)

Podere Brizio

Loc. Podere Brizio, 67
53024 Montalcino (SI)
tel. 0577846004
www.poderebrizio.it

Roberto Bellini, along with a group known as "I Lombardi", the Lombards, contributed substantially to the growth of Brunello, in the late 1970s and 1980s. In the 1990s, Angelo Gaja purchased his winery but Bellini couldn't stay away from the world of wine and he resurfaced with Podere Brizio. This year, the quality of his wines has brought him a full profile. The enterprise is far from modest with over 20 hectares of vines located near Chiesa di Santa Restituta and at Tavernelle. Roberto has an imposing, very well organized winemaking facility where his Brunello and other wines are matured both in traditional large Slavonian oak as well as in smaller oak casks of different origins. Brunello '01 performed beautifully and went to the national finals. Blackberry jam, dark cherry and wild red berry fruit compose a complex, classically clean lead-off and a masterfully textured palate benefits from bright acidity and dense-packed, elegant tannins. Cherry fruit returns deliciously on a finish that is as supple as it is generous. Pupà Pepu '03 is a very elegant wine, dedicated to Roberto's father. On the nose, delicate toasted almond serves as a delicious foil to blueberry, sour cherry preserve and redcurrant, and it finishes long to make this a wine with considerable distinctiveness overall. Both Rosso and Sant'Antimo Leonensis are pleasurable, well-made offerings.

● Brunello di Montalcino '01	🍷🍷	7
● Pupà Pepu '03	🍷🍷	8
● Rosso di Montalcino '04	🍷	4
● Sant'Antimo Leonensis '04	🍷	5
● Brunello di Montalcino '99	YY	7
● Pupà Pepu '00	YY	6
● Pupà Pepu '01	YY	8

MONTALCINO (SI)

Podere Salicutti

Pod. Salicutti, 174
53024 Montalcino (SI)
tel. 0577847003
www.poderesalicutti.it

Francesco Leanza always manages to offer fascinating wines, brimming with interesting characteristics and other traits still developing. Cellar construction is now over so clutter has been succeeded by calm order and careful attention to winemaking details. Maturation is carried out largely in tonneaux and barriques but oak influence is kept strictly subservient to typicity and tradition. Vineyard management practices border on the obsessive, which is understandable since Leanza farms organically. Turning now to the wines we tasted, we were delighted to see Rosso di Montalcino high flying again with the '04 vintage, a complex, elegant offering with great-quality fruit and a supple, delicious palate. Brunello '01 certainly sparked out interest and we appreciated the diminution of oak in favour of well-developed fruit, morello cherry and wild red berry, along with smooth notes of vanilla. It builds imposing depth of flavour in the mouth, which suffers just a bit from tannins that are somewhat assertive but not bitter, before that wonderful fruit returns to infuse a superlative finish. Dopoteatro '04 exhibits cabernet's typical green pepper notes on the nose, along with some oak, and it is a bit grippy and tight on the palate, although it concludes long.

● Brunello di Montalcino '01	🍷🍷	8
● Rosso di Montalcino '04	🍷🍷	5
● Dopoteatro '04	🍷	6
● Brunello di Montalcino '97	YYY	8
● Brunello di Montalcino '00	YY	8
● Brunello di Montalcino '99	YY	8

La Poderina

Fraz. Castelnuovo dell'Abate
Loc. Poderina
53022 Montalcino (SI)
tel. 0577835737
www.saiagricola.it

The Saiagricola group's Montalcino operation is located on the road leading to Castelnuovo dell'Abate. This is an area with its own characteristics, where average temperatures are lower than they are farther south and temperature differences between day and night are greater. Soil profiles too differ markedly, with generous amounts of sand and lower proportions of clay and gravel. All these elements combine to yield wines marked by aromatic complexity and overall elegance. The wines La Poderina presented this year were good expressions of the terroir, having renounced the rather obstreperous stylistic traits of recent vintages. Kudos to the production staff, headed by Lorenzo Landi. They will be pleased to see at last the completion of the new cellar, now in its final phases. Moscadello di Montalcino is the winery's standard-bearer, for many years now the absolute benchmark for the entire category. The '04 shows a compelling gold and releases tempting floral notes of wisteria and verbena that meld perfectly into orange and citrus fruit. Vibrant acidity girders the residual sugar to provide a crisp, rich tasting experience. Brunello '01 is right on the mark. Toasty oak and red berry fruit fragrances predominate, followed by an upfront, confident palate that unfurls vivacious tannins and splendid, pulpy fruit. Brunello Poggio Banale '00 offers more evolution on the nose in tanned leather and tobacco but these are freshened nicely by balsam and medicinal herbs. The mouth is dense and rich, and the tannins are masterful. Rosso '04 is a fine, pleasurable offering.

○	Moscadello di Montalcino '04	▼▼	6
●	Brunello di Montalcino Poggio Banale '00	▼▼	8
●	Brunello di Montalcino '01	▼▼	7
●	Rosso di Montalcino '04	▼	5
●	Brunello di Montalcino Poggio Banale '97	▽▽▽	8
●	Brunello di Montalcino '98	▽▽	7
●	Brunello di Montalcino '00	▽▽	7
●	Brunello di Montalcino Poggio Banale '98	▽▽	8
●	Brunello di Montalcino '99	▽▽	7

MONTALCINO (SI)

Poggio Antico

Loc. Poggio Antico
53024 Montalcino (SI)
tel. 0577848044
www.poggioantico.com

Paola Gloder's winery is among Montalcino's best known, partly for its extremely high quality and partly because of the reasonable prices. In fact, competitive prices have enabled Poggio Antico to weather the economic crisis that has beset the Italian wine industry over the past few years. It seems Paola can't produce enough Poggio Antico to satisfy demand. One reason is that production is limited as vineyard yields are kept well below those laid out in the denomination production code. The house thoroughbred was not presented this year but we were not too disappointed since all the wines we tasted were excellent. The new development at the winery is that Paolo Vagaggini has taken over winemaking duties, with results that we will see over the next few years, naturally. Paolo can build on sound foundations for huge investments have been made in the last few years both in the winemaking cellar and in the vineyards. All of the Brunellos we tasted were very good but it was the Brunello '01 that impressed us most. A dense ruby in appearance and a bit slow to open, it steadily reveals textbook ripe, fresh red berry fruit with notes of denser fruit jam. We didn't expect to find tannins tamping down the palate but ageing will cure this. We liked the complexity provided by some grassy notes in Brunello Altero '01, as well as its velvety texture. Riserva '00 is a fine effort but here too we noted somewhat coarse tannins that slowed down the progression. It's a shame since this is such an impressive wine but a bit of time will set things to rights here as well.

●	Brunello di Montalcino Ris. '00	▼▼	7
●	Brunello di Montalcino '01	▼▼	7
●	Brunello di Montalcino Altero '01	▼▼	7
●	Rosso di Montalcino '04	▼	5
●	Brunello di Montalcino '85	▽▽▽	7
●	Brunello di Montalcino Ris. '85	▽▽▽	8
●	Brunello di Montalcino '88	▽▽▽	7
●	Brunello di Montalcino Altero '99	▽▽▽	7
●	Brunello di Montalcino '99	▽▽	7
●	Brunello di Montalcino '00	▽▽	7
●	Brunello di Montalcino Altero '00	▽▽	7
●	Brunello di Montalcino Altero '98	▽▽	7

MONTALCINO (SI)

Poggio di Sotto

Fraz. Castelnuovo dell'Abate
Loc. Poggio di Sotto
53020 Montalcino (SI)
tel. 0577835502
www.poggiodisotto.com

After a motoring mishap, Piero Palmucci is back in fine form. For everybody's benefit, we might add, since his keen wit was much missed as well as his energetic defence of Montalcino's winemaking traditions, his great cause. This Castelnuovo dell'Abate winery continues its tradition of fine releases. Palmucci's credo is that the vineyard makes the wine and the winemaker's principal care is not to ruin good fruit. All of Poggio di Sotto's vineyards lie in Castelnuovo dell'Abate, at elevations that vary between 200 and 400 metres. They are located close to the winery so that the harvested grapes can be brought to the cellar quickly. Only 20 to 30-hectolitre Slavonian oak barrels are used and they are replaced fairly frequently so the wood is largely new. Palmucci's philosophy has yielded the superb Brunello Riserva '99, which amply repaid our patient wait. Ruby tending to garnet precedes confident, complex fragrances of leather, tobacco and medicinal herbs that still allow a lovely violet-infused florality to shine though. The glossiest of tannins and the lengthiest finish imaginable, plus its sheer elegance, call to mind a fine Burgundy. Brunello '01 is equally successful, showing abundant yellow peach and cherry, followed by already supple tannins and a ringingly vibrant palate, the contribution of acidity that is crisp and agile. Rosso di Montalcino '03 is very well executed.

● Brunello di Montalcino Ris. '99	ΨΨΨ	8
● Brunello di Montalcino '01	ΨΨ	8
● Rosso di Montalcino '03	ΨΨ	6
● Brunello di Montalcino Ris. '95	YYY	8
● Brunello di Montalcino '99	YYY	8
● Brunello di Montalcino '00	YY	8
● Brunello di Montalcino '94	YY	8
● Brunello di Montalcino '95	YY	8
● Brunello di Montalcino '96	YY	8
● Brunello di Montalcino '97	YY	8

MONTALCINO (SI)

Il Poggiolo

Loc. Poggiolo, 259
53024 Montalcino (SI)
tel. 0577848412
www.ilpoggiolomontalcino.com

Il Poggiolo, ably directed by Rudy Cosimi, always presents us with an embarrassment of riches in its line-up. Cosimi is an ex-motorcycle champion who has transferred his passion to motor racing. His operation is located in the medium elevations of the Montalcino hill country, in soil conditions that show significant variety. He produces three different Brunellos from them, convinced that each of these diverse terroirs deserves expression. We can only agree with him since in a denomination such as Montalcino, a wealth of different environments translates into a spectrum of distinctive wines. The quality of the wines we tasted this year was exceptional and two 2001 Brunellos actually went through to the national final round, one of them winning our top Three Glasses award. Terra Rossa was the favourite. Sourced from a vineyard lying in iron-rich soils, it yields dark aromas of cherry and blackberry sweetened with some smooth tobacco leaf. A generous partnership of acidity and tannins is a good foil to impressive extraction and the finish is both expansive and lengthy. Brunello Beato betrays a more modern interpretation but is still expressive of its terroir and a fine offering. It displays resplendent fruit, with lovely jammy notes, in a fabric of balsam and spicy oak nuances. The attack is vigorous and exuberant but the well-crafted tannins know their place and do not hamper the masterly development. Brunello Poggiolo '01 is elegant, with good body and an overall good interpretation.

● Brunello di Montalcino Terra Rossa '01	ΨΨΨ	7
● Brunello di Montalcino Beato '01	ΨΨ	8
● Brunello di Montalcino Poggiolo '01	ΨΨ	7
● Brunello di Montalcino Poggiolo Ris. '97	YY	8
● Brunello di Montalcino Beato Ris. '97	YY	8
● Brunello di Montalcino Five Stars '97	YY	7
● Brunello di Montalcino Terra Rossa Ris. '97	YY	8

MONTALCINO (SI)

Tenuta Il Poggione

Fraz. Sant'Angelo in Colle
P.zza Castello, 14
53020 Montalcino (SI)
tel. 0577844029
www.tenutailpoggione.it

The range of wines presented this year by Il Poggione just failed to catch fire, much to our amazement. Owned by Leopoldo and Livia Franceschi, and directed with great competence by Fabrizio Bindocci, this long-established winery at Sant'Angelo in Colle has turned in terrific performances in past years. What particularly surprised us were the disappointing results from the two denomination wines, Brunello '01 and Rosso '04. After a brief pause for air, the Brunello leads off well enough with dense ruby and evolved notes of cinchona melding with red berry fruit preserve. We like its good extraction but the acid-tannin component is ramped up much too high and tends to brake the progression and finale. The 2000 season was not up to winery expectations so no Riserva '00 was made. Rosso '04 performed a little better. Bottled cherries appear on the nose accompanied by a touch of oak, which is something new for Il Poggione. And although the acidity is bright and tasty, the palate comes up a bit short on length and depth. Both IGTs are good. After rich dark fruit, Poggione '04 develops appreciable balance and progression while San Leopoldo '03 begins with an appealing hint of green pepper over wild cherry, then opens to an impressive body nicely support by lively acidity.

● San Leopoldo '03	▼▼	5
● Il Poggione '04	▼▼	3*
● Brunello di Montalcino '01	▼	6
● Rosso di Montalcino '04	▼	4
● Brunello di Montalcino Ris. '97	▽▽▽	8
● Brunello di Montalcino Ris. '99	▽▽	7
● Brunello di Montalcino Ris. '95	▽▽	6
● Brunello di Montalcino '97	▽▽	6
● Brunello di Montalcino '99	▽▽	6

MONTALCINO (SI)

La Rasina

loc. Rasina, 132
53024 Montalcino (SI)
tel. 0577848536
www.larasina.it

A star is born in Montalcino. Double Three Glass winner La Rasina has made a stunning leap forward in quality over the last few years and Marco Mantengoli deserves applause. He directs this small operation in the eastern district of Montalcino along the road leading to Torrenieri. Marco's straightforwardness, youth and uncompromising philosophy augur well for the future of the estate. He has produced a new wine, which we tasted for the first time. Il Divasco, a Brunello, is sourced from a separate vineyard parcel and matured in small oak, largely barriques and tonneaux. A sparkling ruby, it opens out into a generous array of well-focused fruit, wild cherry preserve and bottled black cherries, temptingly enriched with a bit of white chocolate and spicy cinnamon. The entry is confident and masterful with a progression of rare perfection, buttressed by well-constructed tannins and tasty acidity that moves it into a terrific finish. A fabulous Brunello '01 will enthuse traditionalists. It certainly won over our tasting panel and earned itself our Three Glasses. Rich ruby is followed by a nose of eloquent complexity and suppleness, releasing a spectrum of dense fruit ranging from yellow peach to dark cherry. Everything is clean and in place, and accompanied by a compelling florality. It opens massive, deep and rich on the palate, with a complement of dense-textured tannins already showing admirable fluidity. They help shape a finish that is somewhat less sinewy than that of Il Divasco but certainly its equal in intensity and equilibrium. Rosso '04 is pleasurable.

● Brunello di Montalcino '01	▼▼▼	7
● Brunello di Montalcino Il Divasco '01	▼▼▼	7
● Rosso di Montalcino '04	▼	5
● Brunello di Montalcino '00	▽▽▽	6
● Brunello di Montalcino '98	▽▽	7

Sesti - Castello di Argiano

Loc. Sant'Angelo in Colle
Loc. Castello di Argiano
53024 Montalcino (SI)
tel. 0577843921

This is one of Montalcino's most reliable and consistent producers. It occupies the handsome tower of Argiano, which maps as early as the 13th century indicate as a fortress in the area of Camigliano. The cellar's portfolio of wines is quite broad, perhaps excessively so. Sauvignon is one of its most striking offerings, particularly considering its area of origin. After the classic varietal tomato leaf and sage, the '05 continues with a palate that is straightforward and pleasurable, although not overly complex. But Brunello is, as it should be, the standard-bearer here and both versions we tasted went to our national final round, each ably expressing the local terroir. Actually, very little separated Brunello Phenomena Riserva '00 from our top award. It builds a generous, multi-layered array of aromas that open with an expected, but very alluring, floral nuance. This quickly gives way to dried hay, tanned leather and tobacco leaf, all of which continue their impact throughout the subsequent development. The palate is warm and spacious, bright acidity contributing to its considerable energy assisted by tannins of masterful consistency. Textbook tobacco leaf and crisp morello cherry characterize Brunello '01. Compelling depth, sinew and tannic structure that is dense without becoming obstructive make for a very impressive offering. Grangiovese '04 is fine and a bit more complex than Sant'Antimo Terre di Siena '03 while Rosato '05 comes across as crisp, refreshing and delicious.

●	Brunello di Montalcino Phenomena Ris. '00	TT	8
●	Brunello di Montalcino '01	TT	7
●	Grangiovese '04	TT	4
●	Sant'Antimo Terra di Siena '03	T	6
⊙	Rosato '05	T	4
○	Sauvignon '05	T	4
●	Brunello di Montalcino Phenomena Ris. '99	YY	8
●	Brunello di Montalcino '00	YY	7
●	Brunello di Montalcino '99	YY	8

MONTALCINO (SI)

Solaria - Cencioni

pod. Capanna, 102
53024 Montalcino (SI)
tel. 0577849426
www.solariacencioni.com

Patrizia Cencioni is among Montalcino's most able producers and fiercely dedicated to her vineyards. She makes wines of austerity and complexity, with qualities that are hard to appreciate while the wines are young. The upshot is that it is difficult for this talented winemaker to win the top prize that her wines deserve, since just a few points can keep a wine under the Three Glasses threshold. Cencioni seems not to take this amiss. She is a wine woman in the tradition of Madame Bollinger, even if she beetles round the vineyard on a tractor, not a bicycle. As she says in her down-to-earth manner, you can't really apply pesticides from a bicycle. Now Patrizia's straightforwardness has produced a new wine: Brunello Solaria 123 '01. The fruit comes from the youngest vineyards in the lower sections of the property, albeit still at 350 metres. Right from fermentation, this fruit showed characteristics that Cencioni felt were not a good match with the current house style so she decided to make it a separate label. We preferred the classic-style Brunello, with its deep ruby and richly-faceted fragrances of tanned leather and fruit jam. Compact tannins are just one component of the well-crafted palate, where vivacious acidity animates the progression and portends long ageing. Brunello 123 is an impressive effort, even though the oak-derived aromas still stick out somewhat from the cherry preserve. There's enough rich complexity on the palate but it is stiffened slightly by assertive tannins, as is the finale. Rosso di Montalcino '04 is tasty.

●	Brunello di Montalcino '01	TT	7
●	Brunello di Montalcino Solaria 123 '01	TT	6
●	Rosso di Montalcino '04	T	5
●	Brunello di Montalcino '97	YYY	7
●	Brunello di Montalcino '00	YY	6
●	Brunello di Montalcino '98	YY	8
●	Brunello di Montalcino '99	YY	7
●	Brunello di Montalcino '95	YY	7
●	Brunello di Montalcino '96	YY	7

TENIMENTI ANGELINI

LOC. VAL DI CAVA
53024 MONTALCINO (SI)
TEL. 057780411 - 0577804229
www.tenimentiangelini.it

As in past editions, this profile combines the wines produced by Val di Suga in Montalcino and those of Tre Rose di Montepulciano. Mario Calzolari's Brunello '01 is a top-quality, absolute delight. This is no muscle-bound show-off but a traditionally-styled wine of considerable austerity and sincerity. A bit of aeration brings out a panoply of tantalizing aromas ranging from tobacco and leather to wild cherry and black berry fruit, lifted by a subtle spice that hovers considerately in the background. Although it displays impressive depth and solid structure, it also shows great suppleness on the palate and masterful equilibrium, making it a Brunello that brings sheer pleasure. We did not taste Brunello Vigna Spuntali, which will come out next year. Vigna del Lago Brunello will be absent for a lengthier period, since its vineyard and many others in the northern section, the nearest to the winery itself, have been replanted and have yet to return to production. Tre Rose di Montepulciano has put out a fine Nobile '03, redolent of autumn leaves and moist earth, along with the expected and enjoyable floral essences. The palate displays lovely, succulent fruit but the tannins are not yet as tamped in as they should be. Busillis '04 and Tuttobene '05, two whites standard to Tre Rose, don't seem to rise above the merely pleasant. The first is well-focused on the nose but lacks personality while the second shows crisp enough, with pleasant citrus fragrances.

● Brunello di Montalcino '01	🍷🍷	6
● Nobile di Montepulciano '03	🍷🍷	4*
○ Busillis '04	🍷	4
○ Tuttobene Bianco '05	🍷	3
● Brunello di Montalcino V. del Lago '90	🍷🍷🍷	8
● Brunello di Montalcino V. del Lago '93	🍷🍷🍷	8
● Brunello di Montalcino V. Spuntali '93	🍷🍷🍷	8
● Brunello di Montalcino V. del Lago '95	🍷🍷🍷	8
● Brunello di Montalcino V. Spuntali '95	🍷🍷🍷	8

TERRALSOLE

PIAN BASSOLINO
53024 MONTALCINO (SI)
TEL. 0577835678

Terralsole is an impressive new operation that for several years now has been releasing terrifically good wines. Directing it is an old friend, Mario Bollag, of Swiss origins and one-time owner of Il Palazzone. The winery relies on some 20 hectares of vineyards planted to high densities and all now in production, lying in the eastern area of Montalcino, looking towards Val d'Orcia. Bollag is being assisted by consulting winemaker Paolo Vagaggini, whose familiarity with the Montalcino denomination is legendary. The winemaking facility is substantial in size but nonetheless flawlessly integrated into its surroundings. Although only recently constructed, it is modelled on the traditional Tuscan farming settlement, the cascina, both in form and materials. As to the wines, Brunello '01 shows a lovely ruby and then forthright blackberry and well-ripened cherry, enlivened by a light whiff of green pepper. A dense, well-integrated array of tannins and appealing acidity masterfully support a structure of considerable proportions. Rosso di Montalcino '04 takes a completely different tack, displaying more evolved, emphatic notes of tobacco leaf and medicinal herbs but its tannins are fairly rough and crimp the finish.

● Brunello di Montalcino '01	🍷🍷	7
● Rosso di Montalcino '04	🍷	4

MONTALCINO (SI)

La Torraccia

Loc. Torraccia
53024 Montalcino (SI)
tel. 05777848156

We admired the very fine performance from this estate on the second showing of its Brunello di Montalcino. It was in the mid 1990s that Stefania Funari moved here to join the colony of exiles from Rome who have set up in Montalcino. The estate is small – not much more than two hectares – and lies in the northern part of the territory on the slopes leading down to Buonconvento. The view it commands is breathtaking, with the towers of Siena visible in the distance. The cellar is equipped with modern temperature-controlled vats for the fermentation processes and barriques for maturation. All the wines presented were very good, a major result for such a young estate that shows every sign of maintaining these standards. The Brunello '01 is impressive right from its deep, dark ruby appearance and the clear, lingering aromas that reveal its barrique-ageing. Notes of ripe red berry fruit and blackcurrant jam complete the picture. Entry on the palate is full and dense, showing lively, fragrant tannins and a good finish. The Canalone '04, obtained mainly from sangiovese, is interesting with its hints of printer's ink, black berry fruit and candied citron ushering in a deep, harmonious palate. Clean cherry-led aromas emerge on the nose of the Rosso di Montalcino '04, whose delightful palate is balanced and very drinkable.

● Brunello di Montalcino '01	ΨΨ	7
● Canalone '04	ΨΨ	4
● Rosso di Montalcino '04	ΨΨ	5

MONTALCINO (SI)

Uccelliera

fraz. Castelnuovo dell'Abate
pod. Uccelliera, 45
53020 Montalcino (SI)
tel. 0577835729
www.uccelliera-montalcino.it

Andrea Cortonesi has renovated his cellar to create a fully temperature-controlled environment with large, very elegant working spaces and a beautiful adjoining tasting room. It's nothing too grand, just very functional. The rooms have been created from the old structure, which blends perfectly into the new. In many ways, the new cellar reflects the simplicity of its owner. Andrea is a man of few words but he has very clear ideas and is a firm advocate of both the sangiovese variety and a traditional approach. He tends his vines with the utmost care and selects the oak-ageing technique to be used according to the fruit produced. His Brunello di Montalcino '01 is first-rate and very much in line with the estate's style. The reasonably full nose releases aromas of tobacco and liquorice with faint traces of fruit and an attractive oaky note that smooths out when the wine left to breathe for a while in the glass. The palate is elegant, not too big, and the well-managed tannins will balance out fully with cellaring. The finish is mellow and confident. The Rapace '03 is another well-made wine obtained from a blend of sangiovese with a dash of cabernet sauvignon. Maturing in 900-litre casks and big barrels has left notes of blackberry and briary fruit on the nose, along with fairly strong hints of jam, while the palate's fine body is well sustained by good acidity. The Rosso di Montalcino '04 starts out rather hesitantly on the nose but goes on to reveal nuances of fresh red berry fruit. The palate is fruity, elegant, fulfilling and very tempting.

● Brunello di Montalcino '01	ΨΨ	7
● Rapace '03	ΨΨ	6
● Rosso di Montalcino '04	Ψ	5
● Brunello di Montalcino Ris. '97	ΨΨΨ	8
● Brunello di Montalcino '00	ΨΨ	7
● Brunello di Montalcino '98	ΨΨ	7
● Brunello di Montalcino '99	ΨΨ	7
● Brunello di Montalcino Ris. '99	ΨΨ	8

MONTALCINO (SI)

TENUTA VAL DI CAVA
LOC. VAL DI CAVA
53024 MONTALCINO (SI)
TEL. 0577848261

In previous editions of the Guide, we have been greatly impressed by the progress of Vincenzo Abbruzzese's estate and the wines it offers, which show a perfect balance of technical precision and respect for the territory. It is for this reason that we were rather surprised by Val di Cava's Brunello '01: given the vintage, we expected a typical, big wine. It presents a very concentrated colour with dark highlights, while notes of dark berry fruit and cherry dominate on the palate. This was a new experience for us as we were used to more complexity and fuller aromas from this estate. The innovative slant continues on the palate, which we found to be over-rich, in fact almost overwhelmingly so. This leaves the progression a bit rigid, mainly because the young tannins are bitterish and not very well integrated. Although it is technically well made, we were not very keen. To our minds, its modern style subverts the austere elegance and the strong link with this zone north of Montalcino. We anxiously await next year's release of the Madonna del Piano selection, another '01. By contrast, the Rosso di Montalcino '04 is a very coherent, traditional wine. The full nose suggests morello cherry and the body is supported by strong acidity that renders the palate fresh and lively.

● Brunello di Montalcino '01	**YY**	7
● Rosso di Montalcino '04	**Y**	4
● Brunello di Montalcino Madonna del Piano Ris. '96	YY	8
● Brunello di Montalcino '99	YY	8
● Brunello di Montalcino Madonna del Piano Ris. '99	YY	3
● Brunello di Montalcino '00	YY	7
● Brunello di Montalcino Madonna del Piano Ris. '98	YY	8

MONTALCINO (SI)

LA VELONA
LOC. CASTELNUOVO DELL'ABATE
PODERE PIETRANERA, 30
53024 MONTALCINO (SI)
TEL. 0577835508 - 0577835525
www.lavelona.com

A steady improvement in quality earned La Velona a place in our national finals with an exceedingly well-made Brunello '01. The highly complex nose offers notes of balsam and eucalyptus that blend nicely with the warm fruity vein of blackberry and wild cherry jam. These wonderful aromas are mirrored on the palate, which develops very tidily, supported by acid-extract balance. The tannins are still a bit edgy but will smooth out over time. This is a Brunello that bears the hallmark of its zone of origin in its maturity and power. The estate lies in the far south-east of the slopes at Montalcino on the road that runs from Castelnuovo dell'Abate to Amiata. Here, the terrain is made up of dark basalt in very odd formations that are not found in anywhere else in the area. Notable for its impressive balance, the Rosso di Montalcino '04 also performed very well. The classic nose tells you it was oak-aged, there are hints of raspberry and raspberry jam and the harmonious palate has well-gauged acidity. The finish is unhurried and consistent. The Sant'Antimo Mefysto '03 is also nicely complex, its very intense appearance announcing notes of red and black berry fruit. The palate is held back a bit by the tannins.

● Brunello di Montalcino '01	**YY**	8
● Sant'Antimo Rosso Mefysto '03	**YY**	7
● Rosso di Montalcino '04	**YY**	6
● Brunello di Montalcino '99	YY	8
● Brunello di Montalcino '00	YY	8

MONTALCINO (SI)

VILLA POGGIO SALVI

LOC. POGGIO SALVI
53024 MONTALCINO (SI)
TEL. 0577848486

An engineer by trade, Pierluigi Tagliabue has owned the splendid Villa Poggio Salvi for years, an estate overlooking this north-west, rather out-of-the-way, pocket of Montalcino. He is the majority partner in Biondi Santi SpA and because the wines produced by his estate have always been distributed by this company, they have not attracted much attention until now. Recent events have more or less forced Pierluigi to return to the fray and put Villa Poggio Salvi more clearly under the spotlight. He offered us wines for tasting that are fairly traditional in style and number among them a fine Brunello Riserva '99 and a very impressive Brunello '01 whose class and varietal stamping earned it a place in our finals. Winemaking is overseen by consultant oenologist Vittorio Fiore, one of the best Brunello men around, and maturation is exclusively in big barrels. The result is a nose-palate profile centred around notes of black cherry, tobacco and those faintly smoky aromas that are so typical of the Brunellos produced in this particular subzone. But that's not all. When we visited the estate we discovered and tasted a "forgotten" Brunello that our panel of judges was consequently unable to evaluate. The wine is question is the '79, around 50,000 bottles of which have been quietly ageing in the cellar for all these years. It is a magnificent, garnet-coloured Brunello with complex, enfolding aromas and a palate of rare elegance. We begged Pierluigi to release it to market but he didn't seem very convinced. Perhaps if you were to try twisting his arm too…

● Brunello di Montalcino '01	▼▼	7
● Brunello di Montalcino Ris. '99	▼▼	8
● Brunello di Montalcino '99	▽▽	7
● Brunello di Montalcino '93	▽▽	6
● Brunello di Montalcino '96	▽▽	6
● Brunello di Montalcino '97	▽▽	7
● Brunello di Montalcino '98	▽▽	7

MONTALCINO (SI)

VITANZA

POD. BELVEDERE, S.P. KM 2,050
53024 MONTALCINO (SI)
TEL. 0577846031 - 3479731898
www.tenutavitanza.it

Work is finally complete on this picturesque cellar with its lofty spaces distributed over two storeys, a beautiful staircase and an exposed goods lift. The whole thing brings to mind a cathedral. Everything here, however, has been designed for maximum functionality. The first floor houses the fermentation zone where the grapes arrive. It is equipped with temperature-controlled stainless steel vats in which pump-overs can be carried out and exposure to oxygen regulated. The ground floor is where the wines are matured in barriques and the more traditional barrels of Slavonian oak that vary in capacity from 30 to 40 hectolitres. Owner Rosalba Vitanza has every right to be proud of this building and the 20 hectares of new vineyards that have just gone into production, ten of which are destined for Brunello. In addition to the cellar at Torrenieri, the estate has various plots scattered across the slopes of the Montalcino district. This year, it presented a new wine offering excellent value for money, a Chianti Colline Senesi '05 derived mainly from sangiovese. The Brunello '01 is first-rate. It displays generous notes of morello cherry, black cherry and blackberry jam and a heavyweight palate well-sustained by acidity with tannins that are already balancing out. The superb Rosso di Montalcino '04 is one of the best on offer this year. Its fresh nose of red berry fruit and aromatic herbs and fruity, well-developed, lingering palate make this a thoroughly enjoyable wine.

● Brunello di Montalcino '01	▼▼	7
● Rosso di Montalcino '04	▼▼	4
● Chianti Colli Senesi '05	▼	3*
● Brunello di Montalcino '00	▽▽▽	7
● Brunello di Montalcino '98	▽▽	8
● Brunello di Montalcino '99	▽▽	7

MONTECARLO (LU)

FATTORIA DEL BUONAMICO
LOC. CERCATOIA
VIA PROVINCIALE DI MONTECARLO, 43
55015 MONTECARLO (LU)
TEL. 058322038
www.buonamico.it

Once again it is the Fattoria del Buonamico that represents Montecarlo wines in the main section of our Guide. Perhaps we ought to look more closely into why such an important production area for the wine sector – one with such tradition and quality – has been gradually sidelined. But in the meantime, these notes are dedicated to Buonamico and its wines, which year after year steadily and very determinedly shift their quality up another notch. We take our hats off to manager Vasco Sassetti and his staff who have made some very astute investments over the last few years. In the absence of the Fortino Syrah, which was unavailable for tasting this year, the Cercatoja Rosso '03 made the biggest impression. Ruby red with purplish highlights, it has concentration on a nose that offers a perfect marriage of compact fruit and complex aromas. Initial deep blackberry notes give way to fascinating vegetal, spicy nuances in a pleasant, harmonious framework. Above all, the palate displays elegance, the true hallmark of this estate. Entry in the mouth is silky and the tannic weave is perfectly set off by the wine's character, giving it exquisite finesse. The only criticism we could make of this majestic wine is its slightly abrupt finish. The Montecarlo Bianco '05 is fresh with delicate notes of white-fleshed fruit that reflect its territory of origin. We also liked the eminently drinkable Cercatoja Rosato '05.

●	Cercatoja Rosso '03	■■	5
⊙	Cercatoja Rosato '05	■	3
○	Montecarlo Bianco '05	■	3
●	Montecarlo Rosso '05	■	4
●	Il Fortino Syrah '00	□□	7
●	Cercatoja Rosso '99	□□	6
●	Cercatoja Rosso '00	□□	6
●	Il Fortino Syrah '03	□□	7
●	Cercatoja Rosso '97	□□	6
●	Cercatoja Rosso '98	□□	6

MONTE SAN SAVINO (AR)

GIACOMO MARENGO
FRAZ. CAPRAIE
LOC. PALAZZUOLO
52048 MONTE SAN SAVINO (AR)
TEL. 0575847083
www.marengo.it

This estate run by Emilio Marengo presented us with a range of good quality wines, although there are no outstanding performances to report. The enormous property extends over about 2,500 hectares, 80 of which are planted to vine. It extends across the hills dividing Valdichiana and Valdambra all the way to the edge of the Crete Senesi hills. We are still convinced that this winery yet to achieve its full potential. It always offers us at least two or three first-rate products to taste but the range overall and the different vintages tend to lack consistency. Having said that, let's take a look at the wines that excelled among those we tasted this year. The Elena '03, obtained primarily from merlot with a little sangiovese, possesses a fresh fruit nose with hints of spice, and a consistent, full-flavoured palate that is firmly structured and complex. The Stroncoli '01 from sangiovese and cabernet is rather muddled on the nose but the sangiovese contributes nice florality and earthy aromas. The palate is reasonably full with sound tannins and well-balanced progression leading into a dry, rigorous finish. Another of the estate's trusty old warhorses is Chianti Riserva La Commenda. The '01 version flags a bit, showing an evolved profile with tertiary aromas. Nevertheless, it still manages to muster vitality and good acid backbone. The performance is below par but solid, dignified and austere, with strong but smooth tannins and a lip-smacking finish. The Chianti Le Tornaie '04 is nice.

●	Stroncoli '01	■■	6
●	Elena '03	■■	7
●	Chianti La Commenda Ris. '01	■	6
●	Chianti Le Tornaie '04	■	4
●	Elena '01	□□	7
●	Elena '02	□□	7
●	Chianti La Commenda Ris. '99	□□	5
●	Stroncoli '99	□□	6

MONTE SAN SAVINO (AR)

San Luciano

loc. San Luciano, 90
52048 Monte San Savino (AR)
tel. 0575848518
www.sanlucianovini.it

The Ziantoni family had high expectations of the new version of its flagship wine, D'Ovidio, following its sabbatical in 2002. We are happy to report that these expectations were well-founded because the D'Ovidio '03 put on a fine show to achieve its first appearance in our finals. Obtained from a blend of equal parts sangiovese and montepulciano with some merlot and cabernet, it unveils a well-defined, almost Bordeaux-like nose with notes of dark berry fruit, pencil lead, gorgeous spice and perfectly dosed oak. The warm, velvety palate shows well-made, balanced tannins. The heat of the growing year emerges only as the palate unfolds to display more breadth and pervasiveness than depth, with a note of alcohol in the finish. If it is true that an estate's quality can be judged not just by its flagship wines but above all by its basic products, then San Luciano has nothing to worry about. The Colle Carpito '04 from sangiovese and montepulciano was a wonderful surprise. It gives clear notes of sweet fruit and flowers with hints of spice and a lean, full-flavoured, fresh palate with complexity, smooth texture and lots of appeal. Almost up to the same standard is the Boschi Salviati '04, from sangiovese, montepulciano and cabernet. This lively wine offers notes of ripe red berry fruit and a round, succulent palate. The two San Luciano whites are always dependable. The Resico '05 from chardonnay, vermentino and trebbiano is dynamic and fragrant with firm body, and the Luna di Monte '05 from trebbiano, chardonnay and grechetto, is refreshing, tangy and pleasingly flowery.

●	D'Ovidio '03	🍷🍷	6
●	Colle Carpito '04	🍷🍷	4*
●	Boschi Salviati '04	🍷	4
○	Resico '05	🍷	3
○	Valdichiana Luna di Monte '05	🍷	3
●	D'Ovidio '99	🍷🍷 (outline)	5
●	D'Ovidio '00	🍷🍷 (outline)	7
●	D'Ovidio '01	🍷🍷 (outline)	6
●	D'Ovidio '98	🍷🍷 (outline)	5

MONTELUPO FIORENTINO (FI)

Tenuta San Vito

loc. San Vito, 32
50056 Montelupo Fiorentino (FI)
tel. 057151411
www.san-vito.com

An excellent range of wines from Roberto Drighi's Tenuta San Vito in Fior di Selva earned this estate a well-deserved return to the Guide. During the 1990s, Tenuta San Vito was a regular in these pages and in fact was one of the first wineries in the province of Florence to adopt organic farming methods in its vineyards. The estate has changed its image dramatically over the last few years, starting with a makeover of both the vineyards and cellar, where modern, functional processes have been introduced. The property currently totals around 30 hectares and the wines presented show character, personality and a decidedly modern slant. A prime example is the pure merlot Colli dei Mandorli '04, deep, rich ruby in colour with a pervasive nose of ripe fruit, sweet spice and balsam. The fruity, succulent palate possesses tight-knit, silky tannins and lovely long length. It's a seriously well-made wine. Every bit as good is the intensely ruby Madiere '04, which reveals notes of jam with hints of spice on the nose. The palate is full and well-balanced but slightly marred in the finish by the rigid tannins that will no doubt smooth out with bottle age. The excellent Chianti Colli Fiorentini Darno '05 is a little gem with a mouthfilling, savoury palate. We'll end our notes with the charming Amantiglio '05 and the fruity, easy-drinking Chianti '05.

●	Colle dei Mandorli '04	🍷🍷	6
●	Madiere '04	🍷🍷	5
○	Amantiglio '05	🍷🍷	4
●	Chianti dei Colli Fiorentini Darno '05	🍷🍷	4*
●	Chianti '05	🍷	3

MONTEMURLO (PO)

Tenuta di Bagnolo
fraz. Bagnolo
via Montalese, 156
50045 Montemurlo (PO)
tel. 0574652439 - 3356916329
www.pancrazi.it

For several years now, the noble Pancrazi family has divided its energies between the Tenuta di San Donato and the prestigious Tenuta di Bagnolo, which is known for its pinot nero-based wines. The second estate has six hectares planted to vine and an average production of 20,000 bottles, released under the Villa di Bagnolo and Vigna Baragazza labels. Not all of the San Donato estate's 14 hectares are in production but it obtains around 20,000 bottles a year its flagship wine, the colorino-based Casaglia, and the very reasonably priced San Donato. This year, our panel of judges gave excellent marks to Vigna Baragazza '03, a selection aged for a minimum of 12 months in barrique. Its confident aromas run the gamut of red forest fruits, charred oak, spice and liquorice. The palate unveils firm body, nice complexity and faint oaky notes in the finish. The Casaglia '04 from colorino is a tad below par. Dark in appearance, with purplish highlights, it offers pervasive aromas of blackberry and raspberry intermingled with nuances of spice and mint. The robust, vigorous palate gives assertive tannins and lovely long length but is rather austere in the finish. We were less enthusiastic about the Villa di Bagnolo '03, whose colour is a bit evolved. The flowery nose has undertones of liquorice and tar while the palate is fresh, agreeable and fluid, if short and slightly bitter in the finish. The simple San Donato '05 is pleasant to drink and on its debut appearance the Rosato '05 from pinot nero is well-made.

●	Pinot Nero V. Baragazza '03	▼▼	8
●	Casaglia '04	▼▼	6
●	Pinot Nero Villa di Bagnolo '03	▼	7
⊙	Pinot Nero Villa di Bagnolo Rosato '05	▼	4
●	San Donato '05	▼	4
●	Casaglia '02	▽▽	5
●	Casaglia '03	▽▽	5
●	Casaglia '01	▽▽	5
●	Pinot Nero V. Baragazza '01	▽▽	8
●	Pinot Nero Villa di Bagnolo '01	▽▽	6
●	Pinot Nero Villa di Bagnolo '97	▽▽	5
●	Pinot Nero Villa di Bagnolo '98	▽▽	5

MONTEPULCIANO (SI)

Podere Le Berne
loc. Cervognano
via Poggio Golo, 7
53040 Montepulciano (SI)
tel. 0578767328 - 3477966127
www.leberne.it

Our faith in the wines produced by Andrea Natalini's estate grows every year. They are well-made, balanced, eminently drinkable and have great character, all of which point to their deep-rooted links with their territory of origin. The Nobile Riserva, the wine that perhaps best represents Podere Le Berne, is missing from the ranks this year but this is perfectly understandable, as the poor growing year in 2002 was unable to deliver the necessary quality. The decision to withdraw the wine is yet further proof of the store the estate sets by quality. The Nobile is obtained primarily from prugnolo gentile with small amounts of canaiolo and colorino and was aged in large barrels. It is extremely good, despite the scorching summer of 2003 that certainly didn't spare Montepulciano. The nose is free of any excessive alcohol or overripe sensations, leaving lots of room for the clean, concentrated notes of red berry fruit and characterful smokiness. The palate shows good body, lip-smacking tannins and strong acid backbone, while the finish is deep but slightly marred by a mouth-drying sensation that fortunately does not detract from its drinkability. The Rosso di Montepulciano '05 is also very good and perhaps even one of the best editions. The nose is not terribly clear but the palate is very powerful and lively. The estate obtains 25,000 bottles a year from its 16 hectares of vines, most of which are at Cervognano, widely recognized as one of the best subzones around Montepulciano.

●	Nobile di Montepulciano '03	▼▼	4
●	Rosso di Montepulciano '05	▼▼	4
●	Nobile di Montepulciano Ris. '01	▽▽	6
●	Nobile di Montepulciano Ris. '00	▽▽	6
●	Rosso di Montepulciano '04	▽▽	4
●	Nobile di Montepulciano '98	▽▽	4

MONTEPULCIANO (SI)

BINDELLA

FRAZ. ACQUAVIVA
VIA DELLE TRE BERTE, 10A
53040 MONTEPULCIANO (SI)
TEL. 0578767777
www.bindella.it

Bindella, a well-established estate here at Montepulciano, was founded in the early 1960s by Rudi Bindella, a noted Swiss entrepreneur who created the structure that still survives today. It is run by Matteo Mazzamurro, a figure of long standing in the Montepulciano wine world and a man who has recently been appointed president of the board of control of the Vino Nobile di Montepulciano DOCG. The estate's 30 hectares planted to vine give an annual production of just over 100,000 bottles. Bindella's wines are not always the easiest to define, particularly when they are young, but after a few years in bottle, they can achieve very impressive quality. Derived from 100 per cent prugnolo gentile oak-aged for 18 months, the Nobile I Quadri '03 put on a solid, convincing performance. Its well-defined nose offers aromas of red berry fruit jam enhanced by abundant spicy notes and smoky nuances. Close-knit, flavoursome tannins emerge on the palate and the wine shows nice complexity, despite its rather dominant oakiness. The Nobile '03, from sangiovese with a little canaiolo and colorino, outshone the selection in terms of drinkability when we held our tastings. Its palate is fresher and more vibrant, but obviously less complex, while the aromas are led by harmonious fruity notes with characterful earthy tones. The well-made Rosso di Montepulciano Fosso Lupaio '05 has ripe aromas and a supple palate that is drinking now. The Nobile Riserva '01 shows signs of being a little forward.

● Nobile di Montepulciano I Quadri '03	🍷🍷	5
● Nobile di Montepulciano '03	🍷🍷	5
● Nobile di Montepulciano Ris. '01	🍷	5
● Rosso di Montepulciano Fosso Lupaio '05	🍷	4
● Nobile di Montepulciano I Quadri '01	🍷🍷	5
● Nobile di Montepulciano I Quadri '00	🍷🍷	5
● Vallocaia '98	🍷🍷	6
● Nobile di Montepulciano '99	🍷🍷	4

MONTEPULCIANO (SI)

PODERI BOSCARELLI

FRAZ. CERVOGNANO
VIA DI MONTENERO, 28
53040 MONTEPULCIANO (SI)
TEL. 0578767277 - 0578767608
www.poderiboscarelli.com

Podere Boscarelli's reds have a stylistic rigour all of their own based on naturalness, authenticity and character. Once again this year, the Nobile Nocio emerged as one of the best reds in Tuscany and won Three brimming Glasses. The '03 eschews sweet, fruity nuances in favour of big personality and a vibrant, complex palate. The nose mingles elegant fruit with notes of balsam, spice and faint earthy sensations and the odd minerally touch. On the palate there is wonderful acidity, tasty tannins and a lip-smacking, crystal-clear finish. The Nobile '03 also shows well, offering intense, spicy aromas. It unfurls full, elegant and well-sustained on the palate but flags a bit in the finish. The De Ferrari '04, from prugnolo gentile and canaiolo matured in oak and cement, was in some respects surprising. Extremely pleasant notes of fresh red berry fruit announce a supple, agile palate of excellent drinkability. We enjoyed the Rosso di Montepulciano Prugnolo '04 for its sweet, spicy nose and fresh, easy-drinking if somewhat lightweight palate. Poderi Boscarelli was established in 1962 by Paola and Ippolito De Ferrari and is now run by Paola De Ferrari with the help of her sons, Luca and Nicolò. It has 18 hectares of vineyards at Cervognano, perhaps the most important subzone in the entire territory of Montepulciano, and produces around 60,000 bottles a year. Maurizio Castelli is consultant oenologist.

● Nobile di Montepulciano Nocio dei Boscarelli '03	🍷🍷🍷	7
● Nobile di Montepulciano '03	🍷🍷	5
● De Ferrari '04	🍷	4
● Rosso di Montepulciano Prugnolo '04	🍷	4
● Nobile di Montepulciano Nocio dei Boscarelli '01	🍷🍷🍷	7
● Nobile di Montepulciano Ris. '88	🍷🍷🍷	5
● Nobile di Montepulciano V. del Nocio Ris. '91	🍷🍷🍷	7
● Nobile di Montepulciano V. del Nocio '99	🍷🍷	7
● Nobile di Montepulciano V. del Nocio '00	🍷🍷	7
● Rosso di Montepulciano Prugnolo '03	🍷🍷	4

Fattoria La Braccesca

Fraz. Gracciano
via Stella di Valiano, 10
53040 Montepulciano (SI)
tel. 0578724252
www.antinori.it

Antinori first started to buy up parcels for La Braccesca in 1990. The estate now totals approximately 379 hectares and is divided into two main bodies, the larger consisting of 264 hectares. Of these, 151 distributed across the municipalities of Montepulciano and Cortona are currently planted to vine. The second plot comprises 86 hectares, almost all of which are given over to the cultivation of vines and are distributed over the subzones that are best-known for the production of big Montepulciano reds, Cervognano, Gracciano and Santa Pia. The pure sangiovese Nobile Santa Pia '03 showed well. It is barrique-aged for 15 months and some 20,000 bottles are available. The nose has nice ripe fruitiness and notes of lavender and vanilla. The palate is very oaky but shows dynamic thrust mid palate and a long finish that is on the whole tasty. The Nobile '03 in 200,000 bottles is more approachable. Based mainly on sangiovese with small additions of merlot and cabernet sauvignon, it offers aromas of black berry fruit and sweet spice and a concentrated, lingering palate. The pure syrah Cortona Bramasole '03, released in around 18,000 bottles, goes to town with its extract. The oaky notes on the nose almost conceal the fruit at times while the palate lacks elegance and shows virtually no energy at all. The 300,000 bottles of the very pleasant Rosso di Montepulciano Sabazio '04 has a concentrated, approachable nose and a full, coherent palate.

● Nobile di Montepulciano '03	▼▼	5
● Nobile di Montepulciano Santa Pia '03	▼▼	6
● Cortona Bramasole '03	▼	5
● Rosso di Montepulciano Sabazio '04	▼	4
● Cortona Bramasole '00	▽▽	6
● Cortona Bramasole '01	▽▽	6
● Nobile di Montepulciano Santa Pia '01	▽▽	6
● Cortona Bramasole '02	▽▽	6
● Aleatico '04	▽▽	5
● Nobile di Montepulciano '96	▽▽	4
● Nobile di Montepulciano '97	▽▽	5
● Rosso di Montepulciano Sabazio '97	▽▽	3
● Merlot '98	▽▽	6
● Nobile di Montepulciano '98	▽▽	5

MONTEPULCIANO (SI)

La Calonica

Fraz. Valiano di Montepulciano
via della Stella, 27
53040 Montepulciano (SI)
tel. 0578724119
www.lacalonica.com

The estate belonging to Ferdinando Cattani, president of the young Cortona DOC, lies in Le Capezzine, partly on the slopes of Valiano in the municipal district of Montepulciano and partly in the municipality of Cortona. Of its approximately 50 hectares, some 38 are planted to vine. La Calonica's wines are well-managed, very consistent, unpretentious and stylistically recognizable for their strong character. We liked the Nobile '03, which is derived from sangiovese with small amounts of merlot and canaiolo and released in around 40,000 bottles. Its fruity aromas are full and ripe, pleasantly capped by notes of coffee and chocolate. The tasty palate is warm and rich, showing very lively grip all the way to the lip-smacking, leisurely finish. Obtained mainly from sangiovese with a little cabernet sauvignon and merlot, the Cortona Girifalco '04 is also interesting. A reasonably complex nose with notes of very clean red berry fruit and nice grassy tones is supported by smoky nuances and hints of sweet spice. On the palate, it has good fruit and savouriness, firm body and edgy tannins, signing off with a confident finish. There are 15,000 bottles available. The 30,000 bottles of Rosso di Montepulciano '05 and 20,000 of Cortona Sangiovese '04 are solid and unfussy. Of the two, we rather preferred the Rosso di Montepulciano with its fresh, concentrated nose and sweet, lively palate.

● Nobile di Montepulciano '03	▼▼	5
● Cortona Girifalco '04	▼▼	6
● Cortona Sangiovese '04	▼	4
● Rosso di Montepulciano '05	▼	4
● Cortona Girifalco '00	▽▽	6
● Signorelli '00	▽▽	7
● Nobile di Montepulciano Ris. '01	▽▽	6
○ Vin Santo di Montepulciano '98	▽▽	7
● Nobile di Montepulciano '99	▽▽	5
● Nobile di Montepulciano Ris. '99	▽▽	6
● Signorelli '99	▽▽	7

MONTEPULCIANO (SI)

Canneto

via dei Canneti, 14
53045 Montepulciano (SI)
tel. 0578757737
www.canneto.com

Lying on the western slope of Montepulciano near the famous church of San Biagio, the Canneto estate is a point of reference for this DOCG zone. In the early 1970s, before the designated area became a DOCG, a group of friends from Zurich began to import Nobile di Montepulciano on a regular basis. Over the years, they decided to buy a winery and in 1987 they set up Canneto. Today, it extends over 26 hectares and total production is just over 100,000 bottles. The wines it produces are solid and full of character. They are aged exclusively in five-hectolitre casks and stylistically have little in common with soft, round products. The Nobile '03 from prugnolo gentile with small amounts of merlot and cabernet sauvignon showed well. The nose starts out rather hesitantly but goes on to reveal perfectly ripe, eloquently expressed fruit followed by lovely spicy notes. But it is on the palate that the wine really comes into its own, displaying good extract, tanginess and energy. The Vendemmia Tardiva '02 is also extremely good. Obtained from a blend of malvasia, trebbiano and grechetto, it is released in about 7,000 bottles. Notes of citrus fruit render the nose fresh while the palate shows just the right density, enlivened by a strong acid vein that acts as the perfect foil for the measured sweetness. The Rosso di Montepulciano '05 is a simple but well-made wine with confident smoky tones on the nose and a full, smooth palate.

○	Vendemmia Tardiva '02	▼▼	5
●	Nobile di Montepulciano '03	▼▼	4
●	Rosso di Montepulciano '05	▼	4
●	Nobile di Montepulciano Ris '01	▽▽	5
○	Vendemmia Tardiva '01	▽▽	5
●	Nobile di Montepulciano '02	▽▽	4
●	Nobile di Montepulciano Ris. '99	▽▽	5

MONTEPULCIANO (SI)

Fattoria del Cerro

fraz. Acquaviva
via Grazianella, 5
53040 Montepulciano (SI)
tel. 0578767722 - 0577767700
www.saiagricola.it

The Fattoria del Cerro, owned by the Saiagricola group, is one of the most important estates in Montepulciano. First of all, it is very large, comprising 170 hectares of vineyards and a total production of almost 800,000 bottles. Its real strength, however, lies not just in numbers but in its ability to offer a very high overall quality in all its wines. Credit for this goes to a modern, competent management system that combines quantity and quality with ease. The wide range of wines on offer is well made, full of character and personality. The superb Nobile Antica Chiusina selection rises head and shoulders above the rest. This '03 went all the way to our finals thanks to its clear nose that is intense and sweet, its lovely fruitiness enhanced by mineral notes with bags of personality. The deep, harmonious palate reveals tight-knit, lively tannins and a long, juicy finish. The pure merlot Poggio Golo '04 did very well, showing dense, pervasive fruitiness on the nose and a substantial, full-bodied palate whose tannins leave the finish ever so slightly dry. The Nobile '03 is on top form, with a concentrated, flavoursome palate full of fine, delicate aromas. The charming Vin Santo di Montepulciano Sangallo '01, from trebbiano, malvasia and grechetto, is a well-made marriage of tradition and modernity featuring dried fruit aromas and a creamy but never cloying palate. The Rosso di Montepulciano '05 is simple but well-made.

●	Nobile di Montepulciano Vign. Antica Chiusina '03	▼▼	7
○	Vin Santo di Montepulciano Sangallo '01	▼▼	5
●	Nobile di Montepulciano '03	▼▼	4
●	Poggio Golo '04	▼▼	7
●	Rosso di Montepulciano '05	▼	4
●	Nobile di Montepulciano Vign. Antica Chiusina '00	▽▽▽	7
●	Nobile di Montepulciano '90	▽▽▽	4*
●	Nobile di Montepulciano Vign. Antica Chiusina '98	▽▽▽	7
●	Nobile di Montepulciano Vign. Antica Chiusina '99	▽▽▽	7
●	Nobile di Montepulciano Ris. '01	▽▽	5

MONTEPULCIANO (SI)

LA CIARLIANA
FRAZ. GRACCIANO
VIA CIARLIANA, 31
53040 MONTEPULCIANO (SI)
TEL. 0578758423
www.laciarliana.it

La Ciarliana possesses eight hectares planted to vine in Montepulciano. Generally speaking, the wines produced by Luigi Frangiosa's estate are clean, well-made and balanced with strong but not overwhelming oakiness. Backing up these positive elements are several additional characteristics that have emerged this year, particularly regarding personality, and these deserve a detailed review. La Ciarliana's wines are showing greater weight, clarity and authority. The Nobile '03 is a superbly drinkable wine with crisp notes of red berry fruit on the nose with secondary aromas of spice and incense. On the palate, it is solid and tasty with very elegant tannins and is sustained by an oakiness that never threatens to detract from its personality. The more complex Nobile Vigna Scianello '03 flaunts a layered profile. After rather a closed start, it opens out to reveal wonderfully limpid, fruity aromas with subdued vegetal tones and gorgeous minerality. The palate's harmonious, well-balanced complexity and mouthfilling acid freshness render it vibrant and intense. Another very interesting wine is the Nobile Riserva '01. Elegant and still extremely eloquent, it has a subtle spectrum of aromatics tending more to the flowery than the fruity, enhanced by the occasional pleasant smoky and spicy sensation. This full, lingering wine has close-knit tannic texture on the palate.

● Nobile di Montepulciano Ris. '01	2 black glasses	5
● Nobile di Montepulciano '03	2 black glasses	5
● Nobile di Montepulciano V. Scianello '03	2 black glasses	6
● Nobile di Montepulciano V. Scianello '01	2 glasses	6
● Santo Pellegrino '01	2 glasses	6
● Nobile di Montepulciano '98	2 glasses	4
● Nobile di Montepulciano '99	2 glasses	5

MONTEPULCIANO (SI)

MARIA CATERINA DEI
VIA DI MARTIENA, 35
53045 MONTEPULCIANO (SI)
TEL. 0578716878
www.cantinedei.com

Caterina Dei's estate belongs in the front rank of Montepulciano wineries, having released its first bottle of Nobile in 1985. The property extends over 38 hectares under vines that yield an annual production of about 120,000 bottles. This year, the estate's flagship product, Nobile Riserva Bossona, was absent from our tasting table as the powers that be wisely decided not to produce it in the poor 2002 vintage. This is yet further proof of Niccolò D'Afflitto and the technical staff's refusal to compromise. The Nobile '03 is, as always, a solid, convincing wine. It has rather a rich but not overripe nose with luxuriant, healthy fruity notes and undertones of sweet spice. Harmonious on the palate, it follows through well, supported by interesting acid freshness and dense, lip-smacking tannins. The deep finish is only slightly marred by an oaky, mouth-drying sensation. Sancta Catharina '04 is difficult to define. It exhibits texture and character and promises to cellar well, but it is still very young. The nose remains in thrall to the toasty notes of the oak, every now and then allowing much more complex aromas to emerge. The palate has big body but struggles to unbend. Without a doubt, further ageing in bottle will permit this blend of prugnolo gentile, cabernet sauvignon, syrah and petit verdot to attain perfect balance. The Rosso di Montepulciano '05 is harmonious and fresh.

● Nobile di Montepulciano '03	2 black glasses	5
● Sancta Catharina '04	2 black glasses	6
● Rosso di Montepulciano '05	1 black glass	4
● Nobile di Montepulciano '01	2 glasses	5
● Nobile di Montepulciano Bossona Ris. '01	2 glasses	6
● Nobile di Montepulciano Ris. '97	2 glasses	5
● Nobile di Montepulciano '99	2 glasses	5
● Nobile di Montepulciano Bossona Ris. '99	2 glasses	6
● Sancta Catharina '00	2 glasses	6
● Sancta Catharina '01	2 glasses	6
● Sancta Catharina '03	2 glasses	6
● Nobile di Montepulciano Ris. '98	2 glasses	5

MONTEPULCIANO (SI)

Fassati

Fraz. Gracciano
via di Graccianello, 3a
53040 Montepulciano (SI)
tel. 0578708708 - 06844311
www.fazibattaglia.com

Fassati, a venerable Tuscan winery founded in 1913, was taken over in 1969 by the Sparaco family, owners of Fazi Battaglia. Today, it is one of the leading estates in the district of Montepulciano with around 70 hectares planted to vine and an annual production of just under 1,000,000 bottles. The results of this year's tastings confirmed the overall high quality of Fassati's wines, which adhere closely to the main types in the zone and stylistically well managed. The Nobile Pasiteo and the Nobile Gersemi, both from the '03 vintage, are similar in terms of their solid, convincing sensory profile although they differ in their approach. The first is the estate's basic Nobile, obtained from sangiovese and colorino matured in large barrels. The nose is rather rustic but the wine has great character, displaying nice sensations, fragrance and edgy tannins on the palate. The Gersemi is a selection obtained from sangiovese with small amounts of merlot and cabernet sauvignon aged in barriques. The fruity notes on the nose are pleasantly ripe and enhanced by faint minerally hints and toastiness. The palate is well coordinated with round, tasty tannins and a warm, deep finish. We liked the Rosso di Montepulciano Selciaia '05, which is fresh and smooth on the palate.

●	Nobile di Montepulciano Pasiteo '03	▼▼	5
●	Nobile di Montepulciano Gersemi '03	▼▼	6
●	Rosso di Montepulciano Selciaia '05	▼	4
●	Nobile di Montepulciano Gersemi '00	▽▽	6
●	Nobile di Montepulciano Pasiteo '02	▽▽	5
●	Nobile di Montepulciano Gersemi '01	▽▽	6
●	Nobile di Montepulciano Salarco Ris. '01	▽▽	6

MONTEPULCIANO (SI)

Icario

via delle Pietrose, 2
53045 Montepulciano (SI)
tel. 0578758845
www.icario.it

We can report a good showing all round from the wines produced by this estate belonging to the Cecchetti family. The whole range is well crafted but gets an extra boost from a new product, the Vitaroccia Nobile selection. The estate started planting its 20 hectares to vine in 1998 in compliance with state-of-the-art vineyard management techniques. A new cellar is under construction and has been designed to allow gravity-fed processing of the fruit and must, eliminating the need for pumps. The Nobile Vitaroccia '03 is based primarily on sangiovese with a little canaiolo and is currently released in 5,000 bottles. Above all, it impresses for the wonderful energy it reveals on the palate. Balanced with tasty tannins, this wine has lovely freshness, good complexity and an intense, lip-smacking finish. Its aromas are consistent, clean and ripe and the oak's toasty notes are very well integrated. Although not quite as complex, the Nobile '03 displays the same basic characteristics and reveals a stylistic bias towards balance and elegance rather than power and concentration. Produced in approximately 20,000 bottles, it comes from sangiovese with a splash of canaiolo and has flowery notes and a racy, tasty palate. The just over 15,000 bottles of Rosso di Montepulciano '05 are light and fluent. Rubì delle Pietrose '05 is from an unusual blend of sangiovese, teroldego and merlot. Some 15,000 bottles of this very simple, well-made wine were released to market.

●	Nobile di Montepulciano '03	▼▼	5
●	Nobile di Montepulciano Vitaroccia '03	▼▼	5
●	Rosso di Montepulciano '05	▼	4
●	Rubì delle Pietrose '05	▼	3
●	Nobile di Montepulciano '01	▽▽	5

MONTEPULCIANO (SI)

Nottola

loc. Gracciano
via Bivio di Nottola, 9a
53040 Montepulciano (SI)
tel. 0578707060
www.cantinanottola.it

In the absence of the Vigna del Fattore selection, we tasted Nottola's two signature products, the Rosso and the Nobile. Giuliano Giomarelli's estate produces exceptionally well-made, very clean wines, although they fall a bit short in terms of character and relationship with their territory of origin. The grapes are carefully nurtured in the estate's 25 hectares of vineyards and the cellar is up-to-date but definitely basic with no frills. The Nobile '03 is based mainly on sangiovese with some canaiolo and merlot and matures in large barrels. Produced in 100,000 bottles, this is a solid, dependable wine. On the nose, clear notes of red and black berry fruit merge with sweet nuances of vanilla and hints of torrefaction. It is very well crafted on the palate, showing balanced and soft with creamy tannins that have absolutely no sign of roughness. The finish is long and sweet with slightly mouth-drying sensations but these do not detract from the excellent overall drinkability. Also extremely well made is the Rosso di Montepulciano '05, released in 50,000 bottles. Its nose is fresh and pleasantly spicy and the palate is very agreeable, lean and fluent with a finish that echoes the peppery notes. Riccardo Cotarella is consultant oenologist.

● Nobile di Montepulciano '03	TT	5
● Rosso di Montepulciano '05	TT	4
● Nobile di Montepulciano V. del Fattore '01	YY	6
● Nobile di Montepulciano '02	YY	5
● Nobile di Montepulciano V. del Fattore '02	YY	5
● Nobile di Montepulciano V. del Fattore '97	YY	5
● Nobile di Montepulciano '98	YY	4
● Nobile di Montepulciano V. del Fattore '98	YY	5
● Nobile di Montepulciano V. del Fattore '99	YY	5

MONTEPULCIANO (SI)

★ Poliziano

loc. Montepulciano Stazione
via Fontago, 1
53040 Montepulciano (SI)
tel. 0578738171
www.carlettipoliziano.com

We can barely contain our excitement when we find ourselves writing yet another glowing review of Federico Carletti's wines and the incredible results they have achieved. The '03 version of the Nobile Asinone romped home with glee and relentless reliability to win Three Glasses. This wine stands out not only for its exceptionally eloquent elegance, deep colour, clear aromas and full palate but also for the unique, slightly earthy tannins and mineral tones that are almost iron-like in their inner depths and serve to highlight the wine's distinct character and close ties with the territory. Hot on its heels come the ever so elegant Le Stanze '04, a cabernet sauvignon and merlot blend with a few rough edges still needing to be smoothed out, and the Mandrone di Lhosa '04, a mix of cabernet sauvignon, alicante and petit verdot from the Maremma that is peppery and tasty but still needs to develop its full personality. The reliable Nobile '03 is a masterpiece of balance with a nice mineral character and succulent, velvety tannins. The new Cortona Merlot In Violas '04 takes its name from the title of one Angelo Poliziano's "Latin Elegies". It did very well, impressing with its stylish, racy palate. For the moment, it is released in just 4,000 bottles. The lesser labels, Rosso di Montepulciano and Morellino di Scansano, both '05, are spot on, fresh and approachable. The winery extends over 120 hectares of vines in Montepulciano and 20 in the Maremma on the Magliano estate. Total production is just under 600,000 bottles.

● Nobile di Montepulciano Asinone '03	TTT	7
● Le Stanze '04	TT	7
● Mandrone di Lohsa '04	TT	6
● Nobile di Montepulciano '03	TT	5
● Cortona Merlot In Violas '04	TT	4
● Morellino di Scansano '05	T	4
● Rosso di Montepulciano '05	T	4
● Le Stanze '00	YYY	7
● Nobile di Montepulciano Asinone '01	YYY	7
● Le Stanze '03	YYY	7
● Le Stanze '97	YYY	7
● Le Stanze '98	YYY	7
● Nobile di Montepulciano Asinone '98	YYY	6
● Nobile di Montepulciano Asinone '99	YYY	6

MONTEPULCIANO (SI)

Massimo Romeo

fraz. Gracciano di Montepulciano
loc. Nottola, s.s. 326, 25
53040 Montepulciano (SI)
tel. 0578708599
www.massimoromeo.it

In addition to his role chairing the Consorzio del Vino Nobile di Montepulciano, Massimo Romeo runs this small four and a half hectare estate mostly by choice and just a little by chance, as he likes to say. Annual production is around 20,000 bottles. Given the limited size of his estate, Romeo oversees each individual phase of production himself, methodically putting his ideas into practice. The end result is a sort of high-level oenological craftsmanship that enables him to produce wines that reflect the clarity of his intentions. His products are characterful, restrained, at times austere and very consistent. They offer a fine interpretation of the personality of the prugnolo gentile variety and do not aim merely to respond to the demands of the market. With its alcohol well in check, the Nobile '03 is a very interesting wine, particularly on the palate where the slightly hard tannins are offset by impressive fullness and verve that make it very drinkable. It's a little less determined on the nose where rather rustic sensations emerge. The Nobile Lipitiresco is always inspired and rigorous. The '03 displays a complex nose dominated by notes of red berry fruit jam that meld nicely with the toasty tones of the oak and are enhanced by earthy, minerally aromas. The palate has good body, lively energy and sweet, tasty tannic texture. In line with its type, the Rosso di Montepulciano '05 is crisp and coherent.

● Nobile di Montepulciano '03	▼▼	5
● Nobile di Montepulciano Lipitiresco '03	▼▼	5
● Rosso di Montepulciano '05	▼	4
● Nobile Lipitiresco '01	♀♀	5
● Nobile di Montepulciano Ris. '95	♀♀	5

MONTEPULCIANO (SI)

Tenuta Valdipiatta

via della Ciarliana, 25a
53040 Montepulciano (SI)
tel. 0578757930
www.valdipiatta.it

Tenuta Valdipiatta's wines overcome the difficulties of a very hot growing year like 2003 with flying colours. Miriam Caporali runs the estate and obtains over 100,000 bottles from 30 hectares planted to vine. Around 20,000 of these are taken up by Nobile Vigna d'Alfiero, which was on splendid form at our tastings, living up to its privileged role as the estate's flagship wine. A 100 per cent sangiovese-based wine, it displays enviable freshness and lovely complexity on the nose. The fruit is luxuriant and ripe, the toasty tones of the oak are well integrated and the enriching earthy notes are full of personality. The palate shows rather lively grip and acid backbone, ending in a juicy, tasty finish. The 60,000 bottles of Nobile '03 from sangiovese and canaiolo also performed well. Its aromas are limpid if very warm, while the palate is full, solid and complex without being in the least rough, and there is supple, fluid progression. The Rosso di Montepulciano '05, released in 30,000 bottles, is also from sangiovese and canaiolo and is true to type. Its simple, sweet aromas are mirrored perfectly on the palate, giving the wine very approachable drinkability. The Trincerone '03 is a bit below par. Derived from merlot with a little canaiolo, it is fairly well made but falters a bit in terms of complexity and character.

● Nobile di Montepulciano '03	▼▼	5
● Nobile di Montepulciano V. d'Alfiero '03	▼▼	6
● Trincerone '03	▼	6
● Rosso di Montepulciano '05	▼	4
● Nobile di Montepulciano Ris. '90	♀♀♀	5
● Nobile di Montepulciano V. d'Alfiero '99	♀♀♀	6
● Nobile di Montepulciano V. d'Alfiero '01	♀♀	6
● Trincerone '01	♀♀	6
● Nobile di Montepulciano '98	♀♀	5
● Nobile di Montepulciano '99	♀♀	5

MONTESPERTOLI (FI)

TENUTA CASTIGLIONI

FRAZ. MONTAGNANA VAL DI PESA
VIA MONTEGUFONI, 35
50020 MONTESPERTOLI (FI)
TEL. 0571671387
www.frescobaldi.it

The results obtained by Tenuta Castiglioni's wines at this year's tastings mirror those achieved in the last edition of the Guide. The wines are good but they lack that extra-special something we expect from top performers. This is particularly true of sangiovese and merlot blend Giramonte. Yet the Frescobaldi family, who own Tenuta Castiglioni, deserves credit for believing in the potential of a territory whose wine production was for many years notably mainly for quantity. With Nicolò D'Afflitto and Lamberto Frescobaldi at the head of the staff, the production process is nothing if not well defined. The '04 Giramonte presents a bright colour and a full nose with notes of spice, cinnamon and cloves to the fore, combined with pervasively fruity, almost jammy, aromas of blackcurrant and raspberry. Entry on the palate is charming, round and creamily soft with well-integrated tannins and alcohol. The finish is good, although not quite as long as we would have liked. The Cabernet Sauvignon '04 starts out on notes of vanilla and chocolate but these give way to aromas of jam and faint traces of spice. The solid palate shows lots of backbone and strong tannins distributed well across the nice soft body. Measured acidity leaves the palate fresh and the finish is good, building up in a tasty crescendo. The Chianti '05 is very good value for money. It has clear fruit-led aromas, smooth, supple body and a convincing finish.

● Cabernet Sauvignon '04	🍷🍷	5
● Giramonte '04	🍷🍷	8
● Chianti '05	🍷	3
● Giramonte '00	YYY	8
● Giramonte '01	YY	8
● Giramonte '02	YY	8
● Cabernet Sauvignon '02	YY	5
● Cabernet Sauvignon '03	YY	5
● Giramonte '03	YY	8
● Giramonte '99	YY	6

MONTESPERTOLI (FI)

CASTELLO DI POPPIANO

FRAZ. POPPIANO
VIA DI FEZZANA, 45
50025 MONTESPERTOLI (FI)
TEL. 05582315
www.conteguicciardini.it

There was a good overall showing from Ferdinando Guicciardini's estate, the only sour note coming from the Maremma, where the wines did not perform brilliantly. Castello di Poppiano has 130 hectares planted to vine plus 50 hectares of olive groves. The castle dates back to medieval times and was built around the year 1000 to defend the city of Florence. Records show that it has been in the Guicciardini family since 1199. Wine and oil production first started in the 14th and 15th centuries, bearing witness to the zone's ancient winemaking traditions. The current owner took over in 1962 and immediately embarked upon a radical programme of modernization in the vineyards and cellar, acquiring the Maremma estate in the 1990s. The Syrah '04 is good with a complex nose mingling notes of pepper with hints of ripe cherry, game, leather and animal skins. The palate is gutsy, juicy and soft with a lovely continuous finish. Obtained from a blend of sangiovese, cabernet sauvignon and merlot, the Tricorno '03 presents notes of mint and balsam with undertones of ripe fruit, plum to the fore. The body is full, fruity and nicely dense with well-integrated acidity and a pleasant finish. The Toscoforte '04 derives from sangiovese with a small dash of syrah. Its delightful nose combines notes of forest fruits with touches of spice, notably cloves, and the finish is nice and long. The Chianti '04 and Riserva '03 are, as usual, decent and the Morellino '04 and Riserva '03 are enjoyable.

● Tricorno '03	🍷🍷	6
● Syrah '04	🍷🍷	4
● Chianti Colli Fiorentini Il Cortile Ris. '03	🍷	5
● Morellino di Scansano Massi di Mandorlaia Ris. '03	🍷	5
● Chianti Colli Fiorentini Il Cortile '04	🍷	4
● Morellino di Scansano Massi di Mandorlaia '04	🍷	4
● Toscoforte '04	🍷	4
● Tricorno '00	YY	6
● Tricorno '01	YY	6
● Syrah '03	YY	4
● Toscoforte '03	YY	4

MONTEVARCHI (AR)

La Rendola
loc. Rendola, 85
52025 Montevarchi (AR)
tel. 0559707594
www.renideo.com

La Rendola is back in the Guide after a year's absence following its decision not to produce any wines from the poor 2002 vintage. To be honest, it should have made its comeback last year but owing to an error in page layout at our head office the printers omitted the finished review from the final version. We apologize to both the estate and our readers and hope to make amends by assuring everyone of the estate's fine interpretation of the '03 vintage. The flagship Merlot is particularly successful. Its deep, dark aromatic profile reveals black berry fruit amidst notes ranging from coffee to rain-soaked earth and balsam. Although extremely well made, its oak ageing is very evident. The palate is consistent, full and tasty with deep, leisurely complexity that is almost cowed by the majestic body and tannins that harden to dry the finish. L'Incanto '03, a pure sangiovese, has an altogether different weight and style. Its mellow, generous nose suggests very ripe red berry fruit, flowers and herbs. It is immediately enjoyable for its lean, firm, supple structure, very smooth tannins and reasonable length. The Tardiva '03 is obtained from a traditional Chianti blend of sangiovese, canaiolo and colorino but it undergoes an unusual vinification process using partially dried grapes. The heat of the growing year has had a greater impact on this wine's nose-palate profile, giving it impressive concentration and density but an excess of overripe sensations, strong notes of alcohol and rather immature, aggressive tannins.

● La Rendola Merlot '03	▼▼	6
● L'Incanto '03	▼▼	4
● Tardiva '03	▼	5
● La Rendola Merlot '00	▽▽	6
● La Rendola Merlot '01	▽▽	6
● L'Incanto '01	▽▽	5

ORBETELLO (GR)

La Selva
loc. San Donato
via Pod. La Selva, 138
58015 Orbetello (GR)
tel. 0564885669 - 0564885799
www.bioselva.it

In the increasingly rich range of products coming out of the Maremma, it is quite difficult to find wines that stand out for originality. La Selva's wines, however, impressed us for just this quality. They have strong personality, interesting nose and palate profiles and very good quality. The estate belongs to Karl Egger, who cultivates his 17 hectares according to organic agricultural methods. The vines are cordon-trained and spur-pruned and planted at a density of between 4,000 and 5,200 vines per hectare. Production comes to around 60,000 bottles a year. The Vermentino La Selva '05 is an extremely interesting wine with gorgeous, fresh, crisp notes of flowers and lime blossom and a concentrated, vibrant, mineral palate. We very much enjoyed the Morellino '05 from sangiovese with a little merlot. It starts out rather closed on the nose but gradually opens up to reveal fresh notes of red berry fruit, elegantly enhanced by an intense spiciness. The palate displays lovely complexity with lively fruit supported by strong acid backbone. Obtained from a blend of cabernet sauvignon and merlot barrique-aged for 12 months, the Prima Causa '04 is characterful, balanced and unpretentious. Notes of black berry fruit combine harmoniously with hints of ground coffee on the nose, lending the wine lovely aromatic complexity. The palate is solid and full, vigorous and fruity. The approachable, easy-drinking Ciliegiolo '04 has subdued aromas and is still rather green on the palate.

● Prima Causa '04	▼▼	6
● Morellino di Scansano '05	▼▼	3
○ Vermentino La Selva '05	▼▼	3
● Ciliegiolo '04	▼	5
● Prima Causa '01	▽▽	5
○ Vermentino La Selva '04	▽▽	3

PANZANO (FI)

LE BOCCE
VIA CASE SPARSE, 76
50020 PANZANO (FI)
TEL. 055852153

The Farina family's estate gave an excellent performance and one of its most representative wines, Il Paladino '04, went through to the finals. Stefano Farina, a native of Como, started producing wine in the 1930s and passed the tradition on to his sons Bruno, Giancarlo and Gino. Today, the brothers' headquarters remain in Como but they own properties in Piedmont – Tenuta San Quirico and Cascina la Traversa – Tuscany – Le Bocce and Albereto – and Puglia, with La Rosa del Salice. Le Bocce in Panzano consists of 70 hectares, half of which is planted to vine. The Albereto estate is in Subbiano in the province of Arezzo near Casentino and has 20 of its 46 hectares under vine. This year's finalist is a pure Sangiovese whose confident fruity cherry and blackberry aromas mingle with pleasant flowery, balsamic notes. Entry on the palate is flavoursome, not too full but solid with well-distributed, elegant tannins and impressive acid backbone. The finish is lip-smacking and tasty. Sassaia di Albereto '04 from the Arezzo estate is still 100 per cent sangiovese. Its rather rustic nose suggests game, animal skins and leather followed by nuances of ripe fruit. Entry on the palate is gutsy, dynamic and chewy. The finish builds up impressively. San Leonino '04, another sangiovese-only wine, offers ripe notes led by jam and stewed fruit. Spicy nuances of cinnamon and cloves emerge in the bouquet while the structure is supple, dynamic and balanced and the finish gives leisurely satisfaction. The Chianti Classico '04 is agreeable but the Riserva '03 is dried out by its tannins.

● Il Paladino '04	🍷🍷	5
● San Leonino '04	🍷🍷	5
● Sassaia di Albereto '04	🍷🍷	5
● Chianti Cl. Ris. '03	🍷	5
● Chianti Cl. '04	🍷	4
● Chianti Cl. '00	🍷🍷 (outline)	4
● Il Paladino '00	🍷🍷 (outline)	4
● Chianti Cl. Ris. '01	🍷🍷 (outline)	5

PANZANO (FI)

CANDIALLE
VIA SAN LEOLINO, 71
50020 PANZANO (FI)
TEL. 055852201
www.candialle.com

This estate belonging to Jarkko Peranen and Josephin Cramer debuts in the Guide with a bang, immediately placing one of its wines in our finals. The property lies in the valley south of Panzano, a territory that boasts a high concentration of first-class estates. Candialle extends over an area of approximately 25 hectares, almost six of which are planted to vine, mainly sangiovese. The rest consist of small parcels of petit verdot, syrah and merlot. The terrain is largely clay and limestone galestro with some clay, lime and rock alberese. Remigio Bordini is vineyard manager and Vittorio Fiore is oenologist. The vines are cultivated without the use of fertilizers or any other chemicals. The proud finalist is the Ciclope '04, a blend of merlot and sangiovese with a small amount of syrah. It presents an extremely dense colour and a nose that luxuriates in aromas of forest fruits such as raspberry and blackcurrant ennobled by elegant nuances of spice. Entry on the palate is soft and silky with very layered tannic texture, well-developed acid backbone and a sweet, lingering finish. The Chianti Classico '04 offers notes of cherries and violets, faint traces of pepper-led spice and hints of balsam. Its lean body has good acid backbone, well-managed tannins and a pleasant, tasty finish.

● Ciclope '04	🍷🍷	5
● Chianti Cl. '04	🍷	4

PANZANO (FI)

CAROBBIO

VIA SAN MARTINO IN CECIONE, 26
50020 PANZANO (FI)
TEL. 0558560133

The Novarese family's estate obtained good results this year, but not as good as usual. This was partly owing to the absence of their two Supertuscans, the pure sangiovese Leone and the Pietraforte, obtained exclusively from cabernet sauvignon. In addition, the Chianti Riserva that has always thrilled us in the past was below par in comparison with previous vintages. The estate is small – just under ten hectares of vines – and occupies an excellent position. Remigio Bordini is consultant fruitmaker and Lorenzo Landi offers valuable advice as oenologist. To our mind, this year's range could have done with longer bottle ageing, which would have given the wines better balance. A case in point is the Riserva '03, which lacks clarity on the nose, its fruity aromas struggling to emerge as notes of tobacco and leather holding sway. Conversely, the body is full, powerful and very round with complex tannins that meld seamlessly with the alcohol. The finish is a bit short. At the moment, the Chianti Classico '04 is more enjoyable. Its aromas are better defined, the concentrated cherry and blackberry-led fruitiness enlivened by fascinating minty tones. The palate is rich in extract and manages to keep its tannins reasonably under control, ending in a mouth-watering finish. Although pleasant and extremely drinkable, the Vin Santo '97 is a bit dull on the nose and the palate is dominated by alcohol.

●	Chianti Cl. Ris. '03	**YY**	5
●	Chianti Cl. '04	**YY**	4
○	Vin Santo del Chianti Cl. '97	**Y**	5
●	Chianti Cl. Ris. '99	YYY	5*
●	Leone di Carobbio '00	YY	6
●	Pietraforte del Carobbio '00	YY	6
●	Chianti Cl. Ris. '01	YY	5
●	Leone di Carobbio '01	YY	6
●	Pietraforte del Carobbio '99	YY	6
●	Pietraforte del Carobbio '01	YY	6
●	Leone di Carobbio '99	YY	6

PANZANO (FI)

FATTORIA CASALOSTE

VIA MONTAGLIARI, 32
50020 PANZANO (FI)
TEL. 055852725
www.casaloste.com

The estate of Giovan Battista and Emilia d'Orsi failed to repeat last year's performance. Having said this, its most representative wine, Riserva Don Vincenzo, was missing from the line-up as it was not produced in 2002 for all the obvious reasons. The results are still good, though, and prove – as if proof were necessary – that the excellent work carried out over the years has paid off. Quality has always been the estate's main objective and for this reason it selected the highly prestigious zone of Panzano as its location in preference to other areas. Giovan Battista left his Campania roots behind to launch himself in a profession that at the time – and we're talking about 20 years ago – was very risky. Such a decision could only be based on a great passion for wine, a passion that has never waned as we can see from the quality of his products. Today, the estate consists of around 18 hectares, ten of which are planted to vine and lie in the Chianti Classico zone. Giovan himself runs the vineyards and Gabriella Tani is consultant oenologist. The Inversus '03 has a lovely ruby colour and an attractive nose that harmoniously combines notes of fruit and oak. The palate proffers balanced body with measured tannins and follows through well to reveal pleasing length. We also liked the Chianti Classico '04, which offers notes of ripe fruit, aromatic herbs and minerals, a gutsy body with clear tannic texture, delectable savouriness and consistent length.

●	Inversus '03	**YY**	6
●	Chianti Cl. '04	**YY**	5
●	Chianti Cl. Don Vincenzo Ris. '01	YYY	7
●	Chianti Cl. Don Vincenzo Ris. '00	YY	8
●	Chianti Cl. '03	YY	5
●	Chianti Cl. Ris. '95	YY	4
●	Chianti Cl. Don Vincenzo Ris. '96	YY	5
●	Chianti Cl. Don Vincenzo Ris. '97	YY	8
●	Chianti Cl. Don Vincenzo Ris. '99	YY	8
●	Chianti Cl. Ris. '99	YY	7

PANZANO (FI)

Cennatoio Intervineas

via di San Leolino, 35
50020 Panzano (FI)
tel. 0558963230
www.cennatoio.it

The Alessi family estate is back with a full profile in the Guide thanks to a good overall performance. The Chianti Classico takes a bit of a backseat compared to the other labels which are, as usual, very solid. We have come to expect nothing less from this now historic estate, which prefers to produce small quantities of different varieties and blends rather than focusing on just a few wines. The estate has 43 hectares, ten of which are planted to vine. Davide Picci is vineyard manager and Gabriella Tani is consultant oenologist. We'll start our notes with the pure sangiovese Etrusco '03, whose nose offers substantial sensations, notably of autumn leaves, combined with clean, cherry-led fruitiness. It displays lots of backbone thanks mainly to the tight-knit tannins that are not very well distributed. The finish is sweet and pleasant. The Rosso Fiorentino '03 from 100 per cent cabernet sauvignon presents a range of fruity aromas led by notes of blueberry and blackcurrant with faint undertones of aromatic herbs. The juicy palate shows good body that is refreshed but not held back by the supporting acidity and well-integrated tannins and alcohol. Obtained from merlot, the Mammolo '03 is also good. Its fascinating nose hints at vanilla and raspberry then opens out to reveal further spicy notes. Entry on the palate is charming and well coordinated with less obvious tannins and a well-made finish. The lean-bodied Chianti Classico '04 is dominated by powerful tannins and peters out in the finish. The Riserva O'Leandro '03 is a bit muddled and lacks balance.

● Etrusco '03	🍷🍷	6
● Mammolo '03	🍷🍷	6
● Rosso Fiorentino '03	🍷🍷	8
● Chianti Cl. O'Leandro Ris. '03	🍷	5
● Chianti Cl. '04	🍷	5
● Etrusco '94	🍸🍸🍸	5
● Rosso Fiorentino '01	🍸🍸	6
● Arcibaldo '99	🍸🍸	7
● Arcibaldo '01	🍸🍸	7
● Chianti Cl. Ris. '01	🍸🍸	5
● Etrusco '01	🍸🍸	6

PANZANO (FI)

Le Cinciole

via Case Sparse, 83
50020 Panzano (FI)
tel. 055852636
www.lecinciole.it

Le Cinciole belongs to Luca Orsini and Valeria Viganò and this year's performance was again very good. They didn't go home with the top prize but two of the wines presented went all the way to our final tastings. Last year's Three Glass champion, Riserva Petresco, is missing because it was not produced in 2002. The well-matched team is supported by consultant oenologist Stefano Chioccioli. Estate management procedures put in place over the years are producing the desired results. We have a new recruit to the ranks, the Camalaione '03 obtained from a blend of cabernet sauvignon, syrah and merlot. This may seem odd, coming from an estate that flies the sangiovese flag, but Luca and Valeria have great faith in the potential of a territory whose wine-friendly zones bring out the very best in the variety. In this case, the wine derives from plots planted at a density of 9,000 vines per hectare so that the plants compete with each other for nourishment and yield a limited amount of fruit per vine quite naturally, without recourse to bunch thinning. The result is excellent. The wine's aromas of mint and minerals are enhanced by notes of forest fruits before the enfolding palate displays fine, well-distributed tannic texture with consistent acidity and a lingering finish that builds in a crescendo. The Chianti Classico '04 also showed well. Its spectrum of aromatics includes fruit and aromatic herbs ennobled by hints of spice. The palate is lean and fruity with silky tannins and a smooth, agreeable finish.

● Camalaione '03	🍷🍷	7
● Chianti Cl. '04	🍷🍷	5
● Chianti Cl. Petresco Ris. '01	🍸🍸🍸	6
● Chianti Cl. '01	🍸🍸	4
● Chianti Cl. Petresco Ris. '00	🍸🍸	6
● Chianti Cl. Valle del Pozzo Ris. '95	🍸🍸	4
● Chianti Cl. Valle del Pozzo Ris. '96	🍸🍸	4
● Chianti Cl. Petresco Ris. '97	🍸🍸	4
● Chianti Cl. Petresco Ris. '98	🍸🍸	5

★ Tenuta Fontodi

fraz. Greve in Chianti
via San Leolino, 89
50020 Panzano (FI)
tel. 055852005
www.fontodi.com

Giovanni Manetti seems to have taken out a subscription to our Three Glass award. Yet again this year, the estate's magnificent classic, Flaccianello della Pieve '03, took our top prize. The estate consists of over 100 hectares, 68 of which are planted to vine with 53 registered as Chianti Classico. Franco Bernabei has for many years been Tenuta Fontodi's oenologist. The Three Glass winner has a truly fascinating nose whose range of aromas offers tertiary sensations at first, with leather and tobacco combining with complex fruitiness, lovely clean notes of plum and cherry in the lead. The palate is compact and harmonious, with very fine, well-distributed tannic texture, balanced acidity and a finish offering full, long satisfaction. The Syrah Case Via '03 is also very good. Rustic animal aromas give way to hints of forest fruits and spice, notably pepper and cinnamon. The dynamic, juicy palate ends in an excellent lip-smacking finish. The '04 version of the Chianti Classico is extremely enjoyable, displaying a complex nose of fruity, flowery nuances. The body is lean but very well-balanced and the finish is long and sweet. Giovanni has wisely decided to mature the Chianti Classico Vigna del Sorbo '03 for an extra year so we look forward to sampling it next year. We also gave a retrospective Three Glass award to the Flaccianello della Pieve '01. Recent retastings reveal that ageing has cleaned up the nose, which two years ago failed to impress us. By contrast the palate, then as now, is quite extraordinary and one of the best versions ever.

● Flaccianello della Pieve '03	🍷🍷🍷	7
● Syrah Case Via '03	🍷🍷	7
● Chianti Cl. '04	🍷🍷	5
● Flaccianello della Pieve '00	🍷🍷🍷	7
● Chianti Cl. V. del Sorbo Ris. '01	🍷🍷🍷	7
● Flaccianello della Pieve '01	🍷🍷🍷	7
● Flaccianello della Pieve '88	🍷🍷🍷	6
● Chianti Cl. V. del Sorbo Ris. '90	🍷🍷🍷	7
● Flaccianello della Pieve '90	🍷🍷🍷	7
● Flaccianello della Pieve '91	🍷🍷🍷	7
● Chianti Cl. V. del Sorbo Ris. '94	🍷🍷🍷	7
● Syrah Case Via '95	🍷🍷🍷	7
● Flaccianello della Pieve '97	🍷🍷🍷	7
● Syrah Case Via '98	🍷🍷🍷	7

Renzo Marinai

loc. S. Martino a Cecione, 6
50022 Panzano (FI)
tel. 0558560237
www.renzomarinai.it

Renzo Marinai earned his first full profile in the 2007 Guide with grand style. Last year's performance had already sown the seeds, his wines making a good impression at our tastings. Renzo's is an interesting story; passion led him to take up viticulture but at the same time he is a fierce custodian of local traditions. The heart of his estate lies on an ancient site and he has carried out a very careful recovery programme to ensure that none of the artistic wealth accumulated over the years is lost. His vineyards and overall production are rigorously organic, and he has even rediscovered and started to cultivate a variety of durum wheat that had almost disappeared. Renzo also has quite a few olive trees. The vineyards are cordon-trained and spur-pruned and planted mainly to sangiovese, with some canaiolo and other minor traditional grape types. The estate has also begun to cultivate chardonnay for its whites. Giovanni Cappelli lends support in both the vineyard and the cellar. The wine that made the biggest impression on our panel this year is the Chianti Classico Riserva '03. It presents a confident, powerful ruby appearance, fascinating notes of ripe fruit and faint spicy nuances redolent of cinnamon. The palate is nice and fleshy, juicy with a long, lip-smacking finish. The Chianti Classico '04 is a simpler wine, bright ruby in colour with a variety of aromas that range from cherry and plum to faint hints of mint. On the palate, the body is lean and supple with well-integrated tannins and a lovely finish that is not particularly long but sweet.

● Chianti Cl. Ris. '03	🍷🍷	5
● Chianti Cl. '04	🍷	4

PANZANO (FI)

★ La Massa

via Case Sparse, 9
50020 Panzano (FI)
tel. 055852722

We have a first from La Massa: the Giorgio Primo is no longer a Chianti Classico. Giampaolo Motta, a genial, inspired producer originally from Naples, has very clear ideas and single-mindedly pursues his objectives, even if this means creating controversy along the way for Giorgio Primo has come out of the DOCG to win another Three Glasses in the challenging growing year of 2003. We take our hats off to Giampaolo for his masterful handling of this very difficult vintage. Giampaolo obtained this champion from a blend primarily of sangiovese and merlot that offers a fascinating range of aromas combining a good dose of oak with notes of blackberry and blackcurrant-led forest fruits. Faint nuances of spice, notably cloves and cinnamon, complete the picture. Entry on the palate is substantial with well-integrated tannins of fine, crisply defined texture. Alcohol and acidity are mutually sustaining and the finish is long and tasty. The house's second wine, Massa '04, derives from the same blend. It is smooth and entirely enjoyable, the captivating nose mixing fruity notes with hints of spice. The soft body is buoyed up by a lively, vital acid vein and well-distributed tannins. Although not particularly long, the finish is full of lovely sensations.

● Giorgio Primo '03	🍷🍷🍷	8
● La Massa '04	🍷🍷	5
● Chianti Cl. Giorgio Primo '00	🍸🍸🍸	7
● Chianti Cl. Giorgio Primo '01	🍸🍸🍸	8
● La Massa '01	🍸🍸🍸	5
● Chianti Cl. Giorgio Primo '93	🍸🍸🍸	7
● Chianti Cl. Giorgio Primo '94	🍸🍸🍸	7
● Chianti Cl. Giorgio Primo '95	🍸🍸🍸	7
● Chianti Cl. Giorgio Primo '96	🍸🍸🍸	7
● Chianti Cl. Giorgio Primo '97	🍸🍸🍸	7
● Chianti Cl. Giorgio Primo '98	🍸🍸🍸	7
● Chianti Cl. Giorgio Primo '99	🍸🍸🍸	7

PANZANO (FI)

Il Molino di Grace

loc. Il Volano
50022 Panzano (FI)
tel. 0558561010
www.ilmolinodigrace.com

With amazing regularity, given its relative youth, Frank Grace's estate has taken home yet another Three Glasses for its trophy case. The wine in question is a superlative Gratius '04, a Supertuscan obtained from sangiovese. Estate manager Gerard Hirmer oversees the day-to-day work while wine guru Franco Bernabei looks after the oenological side of things on a consultancy basis. The estate lies on the road leading from Panzano in Chianti towards Radda, the galestro clay and limestone soil of its plots facing south and southeast. Gratius presents quite a range of aromas featuring various fruits, wild berries to the fore, and faint nuances of balsam. Entry on the palate is superb, enfolding and juicy, warm and powerful with extremely elegant tannins, well-integrated acidity and a very, very, long, sweet finish. The Riserva '03 also shows well, its nose luxuriating in hints of cherry-led ripe and brandied fruit that merge with notes of tobacco and leather. The structure is big but not hard, the tannins are good and the finish is pleasantly long. The Chianti Classico '04 is a light wine with a fine, elegant bouquet redolent of flowers, followed by a lean, fresh-tasting body. Il Volano offers excellent value for money in the '04 version with its delightful nose and tasty palate. We were rather disappointed by the Riserva Il Margone '03, which is a bit murkier on the nose and flags on the palate owing to its very rigid tannins.

● Gratius '04	🍷🍷🍷	7
● Chianti Cl. Ris. '03	🍷🍷	5
● Chianti Cl. '04	🍷🍷	4
● Il Volano '04	🍷🍷	3*
● Chianti Cl. Il Margone Ris. '03	🍷	6
● Gratius '00	🍸🍸🍸	7
● Chianti Cl. Ris. '01	🍸🍸🍸	5
● Chianti Cl. Il Margone Ris. '01	🍸🍸	6
● Gratius '01	🍸🍸	7
● Gratius '03	🍸🍸	7
● Chianti Cl. Il Margone Ris. '99	🍸🍸	5
● Chianti Cl. Il Margone Ris. '00	🍸🍸	6

PANZANO (FI)

Monte Bernardi

via Chiantigiana
50020 Panzano (FI)
tel. 055852400 - 055852305
www.montebernardi.com

We are delighted to have the chance to review this estate again after a long absence during which internal restructuring hampered its potential. Michael Schmelzer has taken over from previous owner Stak Aivaliotis, who had a career in the cinema. Of the estate's 53 hectares, six are planted to vine and five of these lie in the Chianti Classico area. Valerio Barbieri is vineyard manager and Giorgio Marone is oenologist. We have come to expect wines of a modern slant from this estate but this style has been eclipsed somewhat in the quest for a more territorial character. The deep ruby Chianti Classico '04 alternates between minty notes and ripe wild berry aromas. Tannins tend to dominate the solid palate but they are well-integrated with the alcohol and the finish has appeal. The densely coloured Tzingana '04 opens on notes of balsam and minerals that give way to compact, juicy sensations of fruit. The concentrated palate exhibits fairly tight-knit tannins. Warm and full, it tends to falter mid palate but picks up again to end on a fruity, lip-smacking finish. The Sa'etta '04 has yet to find full definition on its nose, tertiary aromas of animal skins and leather coming through strongly and then giving way to spicy notes of cinnamon. The palate is tempting and dynamic with well-distributed, tasty tannins and momentum that builds up impressively.

● Chianti Cl. Sa'etta '04	▼▼	6
● Tzingana '04	▼▼	7
● Chianti Cl. '04	▼	5
● Tzingana '97	∇∇∇	6
● Chianti Cl. '03	∇∇	5
● Sa'etta '97	∇∇	6
● Sa'etta '98	∇∇	6
● Tzingana '98	∇∇	6
● Chianti Cl. Paris '99	∇∇	5
● Sa'etta '99	∇∇	6
● Tzingana '99	∇∇	6

PANZANO (FI)

Panzanello

via Case Sparse, 86
50020 Panzano (FI)
tel. 055852470
www.panzanello.it

The estate belonging to Iole and Andrea Sommaruga did well this year, especially in light of the fact that the Manuzio, their sangiovese-based Supertuscan, was missing from the line-up. The range offered for tasting was good, if a little muddled at times in its aromas. Still, the quality of the grapes here is such that this is nothing a bit of fine-tuning in the cellar won't resolve. The estate extends over more than 100 hectares and 16 of these are dedicated to Chianti Classico. It can trace its roots back several centuries to at least 1427 when documents record the farm of Panzanello and describe the wine and oil it produced. Today, the owners rigorously apply organic techniques in the vineyards and have brought in Gioia Cresti as consultant fruitmaker and oenologist. The wine that appealed most to our tasting panel was the Chianti Classico Riserva '03. It presents a very concentrated ruby colour, disclosing aromas of wild berries and jam, faint traces of clove-dominated spice and delicate touches of tobacco. Entry on the palate is round with tannins that integrate well with the alcohol. The finish is a tad short but enjoyable nonetheless. The Chianti Classico '04 takes time to open up on the nose, first revealing aromas of game, animal skins and leather then giving way to fruity notes of plum followed by simple, cherry-led fruitiness. The warm, well-sustained palate shows slightly dominant but refreshing tannins. Le Piazzole '05 has a fruity nose and a simple, smooth body that is pleasantly drinkable.

● Chianti Cl. Panzanello Ris. '03	▼▼	5
● Chianti Cl. Panzanello '04	▼▼	4
● Le Piazzole '05	▼	4
● Il Manuzio '01	∇∇	6
● Il Manuzio '00	∇∇	6
● Chianti Cl. Panzanello Ris. '98	∇∇	4
● Chianti Cl. Panzanello Ris. '99	∇∇	5
● Il Manuzio '99	∇∇	5

PANZANO (FI)

★ **Castello dei Rampolla**
via Case Sparse, 22
50020 Panzano (FI)
tel. 055852001

No wines were presented this year by the Di Napoli estate, as the family has decided to delay release of their products to give them time to mature. We'll take the opportunity to pay tribute to a winery that has played a leading role in the recent history of Chianti Classico. Castello dei Rampolla occupies a superb position in Panzano's famous Conca d'Oro, a subzone that is one of the most prestigious vineyards in Italy. The castle has been in the Di Napoli Rampolla family since 1739 and it was Alceo Di Napoli, father of the current owners, who began to focus greater attention on the vineyard and cellar processes. The estate had its first harvest in 1970 and is now run by Alceo's children, Maurizia and Luca. The vineyards occupy 42 hectares but not all of them are in production. The very stony terrain is chalk-based and faces south-east and south-west at an altitude of 280 to 380 metres above sea level. In 1994, the estate went over to organic agricultural methods. Sangiovese and cabernet sauvignon form the basis of the Sammarco fruit, and in addition to these varieties merlot and petit verdot are cultivated. For white wine, Castello dei Rampolla grows traminer, sauvignon blanc, malvasia and chardonnay, all of which go into the late-harvested Trebianco. The wine that best represents the cellar is the D'Alceo, a blend of cabernet sauvignon and petit verdot named in honour of Di Napoli senior. We look forward to next year, confident that consumers will be as patient as we are with the prospect of tasting the estate's wines to look forward to.

● D'Alceo '00	ΥΥΥ	8
● D'Alceo '01	ΥΥΥ	8
● D'Alceo '03	ΥΥΥ	8
● Sammarco '85	ΥΥΥ	8
● Sammarco '86	ΥΥΥ	8
● Sammarco '94	ΥΥΥ	8
● La Vigna di Alceo '96	ΥΥΥ	8
● La Vigna di Alceo '97	ΥΥΥ	8
● La Vigna di Alceo '98	ΥΥΥ	8
● La Vigna di Alceo '99	ΥΥΥ	8

PANZANO (FI)

Vecchie Terre di Montefili
via San Cresci, 45
50022 Panzano (FI)
tel. 055853739
www.vecchieterredimontefili.com

Roccaldo Acuti's estate gave its customary fine performance at our tastings this year, placing its two most representative wines in the finals and winning Three Glasses for the pure sangiovese Anfiteatro '03. The Acuti family, entrepreneurs from Prato, acquired the estate in 1979 at a crucial moment when Chianti Classico was making its slow upward move in the direction of quality. Documents date the property back to 1200 when it was granted to the monks of the abbey of Passignano by an important Florentine family who owned the castle of Montefili. The estate's coat of arms, a vine with a bunch of grapes, pays tribute to the territory's wine potential. Of the 15 hectares, almost 13 are planted to vine and seven of these are registered as Chianti Classico. Vittorio Fiore has been consultant oenologist for many years and Remigio Bordini is vineyard manager. The Bruno di Rocca '03 from cabernet sauvignon and sangiovese offers a broad swath of aromas on the nose, including balsamic, minty notes, faint mineral sensations and vivid, wild berry-led fruitiness. Entry on the palate is confident and full with good tannic texture, lively freshness and a pleasantly long finish. The Three Glass winner offers aromas of red berry fruit, notably cherry and raspberry, with the odd tobacco nuance. The backbone is solid, the taste is deep and concentrated, the body is smooth and weighty and the finish develops wonderfully. This is every inch a superlative wine. The Chianti Classico '03 is simple and agreeable with a charming nose and enjoyable mouthfeel.

● Anfiteatro '03	🍷🍷🍷	8
● Bruno di Rocca '03	🍷🍷	8
● Chianti Cl. '03	🍷	5
● Chianti Cl. Ris. '85	ΥΥΥ	6
● Chianti Cl. Anfiteatro Ris. '88	ΥΥΥ	6
● Anfiteatro '94	ΥΥΥ	8
● Anfiteatro '01	ΥΥ	8
● Bruno di Rocca '01	ΥΥ	8
● Bruno di Rocca '99	ΥΥ	8
● Bruno di Rocca '02	ΥΥ	8
● Anfiteatro '98	ΥΥ	8
● Bruno di Rocca '98	ΥΥ	8

VIGNOLE

VIA CASE SPARSE, 14
50022 PANZANO (FI)
TEL. 0574592025 - 055852197

The estate belonging to the Nistri brothers has returned to the full profile section of the Guide. These Prato entrepreneurs with a passion for wine have 21 hectares, 12 of them planted to vine and all registered in the Chianti Classico area. Franco Gabbrielli acts as vineyard manager while Giorgio Marone looks after things in the cellar. The production zone in Panzano has a very good pedigree, lying just a stone's throw from the famous Conca d'Oro, one of the best vineyards in Chianti Classico. They offered us two versions of Chianti Classico to taste this year, the standard label and the Riserva. The estate's Supertuscan Congius, which also contains some cabernet, was missing from the line-up. The Riserva '03 has a lovely, dense ruby colour and a complex range of aromas showing balsamic notes flanked by hints of aromatic herbs and ripe fruit. In terms of profile, the body is lean and nicely invigorated by the acidity and well-defined tannins. It is crunchy but never aggressive and the finish builds up into appealing fruit. The Chianti Classico '04 also showed well, its nose releasing agreeable flowery aromas that immediately give way to notes of cherry-led berry fruit. The palate tends more to freshness than power and is capped by a pleasant finish enlivened by savoury tanginess.

● Chianti Cl. Ris. '03	▼▼	5
● Chianti Cl. '04	▼▼	4
● Congius '00	▽▽	6
● Chianti Cl. Ris. '95	▽▽	4
● Chianti Cl. Ris. '96	▽▽	4
● Congius '98	▽▽	6
● Congius '99	▽▽	6

VILLA CAFAGGIO

VIA SAN MARTINO A CECIONE, 5
50020 PANZANO (FI)
TEL. 0558549094 - 055852949
www.villacafaggio.it

Following last year's change of ownership when Stefano Farkas sold his property to the Lavis group, Villa Cafaggio returned to our tasting tables on splendid form. The Chianti Classico Riserva '03 picked up Three Glasses and the Cortaccio '03, a cabernet sauvignon-based Supertuscan, gave a fine performance. The estate's other Supertuscan, San Martino, is absent however. The estate takes its name from the ancient place name Cahago, meaning an enclosed cultivated field. The earliest documentary evidence dates back to the 15th century and the Florentine hospital of Santa Maria Nuova numbers among its previous owners. It was only in 1967 that the estate underwent its first radical transformation when the vineyards and olive groves were completely replanted. Subsequent work has always been carried out with the utmost respect for the territory. In the 1980s and 1990s almost all of the vineyards were replanted to the most suitable sangiovese clones. The Riserva '03 is a very good wine with an extremely dense, almost opaque ruby appearance. Its wide array of aromas runs the gamut from spicy nuances of cinnamon and cloves and well-dosed oak to assorted fruits. Its fine profile flaunts well-distributed, tasty tannins and a long, lip-smacking finish. The Cortaccio '03 has balsamic tones and notes of autumn leaf with undertones of cocoa powder and tobacco. The palate is full, the tannins are ever so slightly hard, but the finish is nevertheless lengthy. The Chianti Classico '04 is fluent and enjoyable.

● Chianti Cl. Ris. '03	▼▼▼	6
● Cortaccio '03	▼▼	8
● Chianti Cl. '04	▼	4
● San Martino '00	▽▽▽	8
● Cortaccio '01	▽▽▽	8
● Cortaccio '93	▽▽▽	6
● Cortaccio '97	▽▽▽	6
● San Martino '97	▽▽▽	5
● San Martino '98	▽▽▽	6
● San Martino '99	▽▽▽	7

PECCIOLI (PI)

Tenuta di Ghizzano

Fraz. Ghizzano
via della Chiesa, 19
56030 Peccioli (PI)
tel. 0587630096
www.tenutadighizzano.com

Once again this year it falls to Nambrot to wear the Three Glass crown, making this the fifth year in a row that Ginevra Venerosi Pesciolini has won our top award. Sometimes it's this wine, sometimes it's the Veneroso, but one thing is clear: it's no coincidence. Ginevra runs this paragon of an estate herself. Her rigorous, meticulous approach combined with that great passion that distinguishes all well-made, exceptional products have made this the most influential, representative estate in the territory of Pisa. Obtained from merlot and cabernet, Nambrot '04 possesses extraordinary elegance and personality. Coming from a growing year that was notable for the freshness and perfect ripeness of its grapes, Nambrot offers notes of ripe red berry fruit with hints of balsam and spice. The palate is fruity and very smooth and the seamless melding of acidity and tannins is absolutely superb. The finish is endlessly long and seductive. It's a wine that expresses all the charm and determination of its producer. The Veneroso '03 is also proof positive of the territory's great potential for it is no mean feat to obtain such a complex wine in a torrid growing year like this. The fruit and acidity survived the extreme heat thanks largely to the breeze that comes off the sea. Notes of cherry and aromatic herbs emerge on the nose, while the palate is austere and severe, if anything slightly curbed by oak-derived tannins that have not yet integrated fully. The Ghizzano '05 as always showed well, a very moreish wine that is a pleasure to drink.

●	Nambrot '04	YYY	7
●	Veneroso '03	YY	6
●	il Ghizzano '05	YY	4
●	Nambrot '00	YYY	8
●	Nambrot '01	YYY	8
●	Veneroso '01	YYY	6
●	Nambrot '03	YYY	7
●	Veneroso '00	YY	7
●	Nambrot '99	YY	8
●	Veneroso '99	YY	7
●	Nambrot '02	YY	6

PERGINE VALDARNO (AR)

Fattoria di Presciano

Loc. Pieve a Presciano
via Giovanni XXIII, 2
52020 Pergine Valdarno (AR)
tel. 0575897160
www.fattoriadipresciano.it

In recent years, Fattoria di Presciano has achieved good quality and manages to keeps it up. The property lies in the hills of the municipality of Pergine Valdarno that extend from the Arno valley to the Valdambra and Siena. Twenty-three of the more than 30 hectares are estate-owned. Running the show is Pasquale Cometti, who moved to Tuscany from Veneto and acts as consultant oenologist for several local estates. Serious and competent, he is a man of few words but clear ideas. Pasquale offers a broad range and the cream of the crop is Priscus '03, obtained mainly from sangiovese with some merlot. It presents warm, ripe aromas of berry fruit with earthy, flowery notes, a balanced, full-flavoured palate that is attractively dense and reasonably smooth despite its still rigid tannins. The Rosso Veleno '03 failed to match the '01 but showed well nevertheless. From sangiovese with small amounts of merlot and ciliegiolo, it is released under a different estate brand, Marina Mouritch, named after Pasquale's wife. It starts out rather closed and hesitant and offers a mellow, slightly evolved profile with peppery notes accompanying very ripe fruit. The palate is consistent, solid, soft and embracing with good close-knit texture. Among the '05s released under the new Pietraviva DOC, the Rosso from merlot with some sangiovese has a medium structure and good balance, and the Rosato from sangiovese, chardonnay and other red grapes is very fragrant and pleasant. The Alfiere Nero '05 is fresh and approachable while the Vinsanto Vinum Passum '00 is austere.

●	Priscus '03	YY	5
●	Rosso Veleno Vigneti di Marina Mouritch '03	YY	6
○	Vinsanto Vinum Passum '00	Y	6
●	Alfiere Nero '05	Y	2
⊙	Pietraviva Rosato '05	Y	4
●	Pietraviva Rosso '05	Y	4
●	Rosso Veleno Vigneti di Marina Mouritch '01	YY	6
●	Priscus '01	YY	5
●	Primadonna Vigneti di Marina Mouritch '03	YY	5

POGGIBONSI (SI)

Melini

Loc. Gaggiano
53036 Poggibonsi (SI)
tel. 0577998511
www.cantinemelini.it

In Tuscany's ongoing, occasionally crusade-like, war between modernists and traditionalists, it is rare that a wine meets with the approval of both factions. For several years now, Melini's Chianti Classico Vigneto La Selvanella has managed to pull off that very miracle. And how has it achieved this feat, you may well ask. First and foremost, the wine is obtained from just one vineyard of approximately 46 hectares and from almost 100 per cent sangiovese. This plot is managed to a rigorously modern approach, with more than 5,000 plants per hectare producing around one kilogram of fruit per plant. The vines stand an altitude of 450 to 500 metres above sea level on top of a hill in Lucarelli between Panzano and Radda, which extends a few hundred metres into the province of Siena. The wine is matured in large 50-hectolitre barrels to give a Chianti Classico of enormous character that is concentrated without being heavy or jammy, even in such torrid vintages as 2003. The altitude and position of the vineyard undoubtedly play an important role but credit must also go to owner Gruppo Italiano Vini's ingenious technicians, who are highly skilled at managing the vagaries of the climate. Their skills were also on parade in the very fine '99, which did not win any prizes at the time. We retasted it this year and awarded it Three retrospective Glasses, humbly begging pardon for this oversight. Melini also produces an interesting white, Vernaccia di San Gimignano Le Grillaie. The '05 is quite good but we've tasted better.

● Chianti Cl. La Selvanella Ris. '03	🍷🍷🍷	5
○ Vernaccia di S. Gimignano Le Grillaie '05	🍷	4
● Chianti Cl. La Selvanella Ris. '00	ΨΨΨ	5
● Chianti Cl. La Selvanella Ris. '01	ΨΨΨ	5
● Chianti Cl. La Selvanella Ris. '86	ΨΨΨ	6
● Chianti Cl. La Selvanella Ris. '90	ΨΨΨ	5
● Chianti Cl. La Selvanella Ris. '99	ΨΨΨ	6
● Chianti Cl. La Selvanella Ris. '95	ΨΨ	6
● Chianti Cl. La Selvanella Ris. '96	ΨΨ	6
● Chianti Cl. La Selvanella Ris. '97	ΨΨ	6
● Chianti Cl. La Selvanella Ris. '98	ΨΨ	6

POGGIBONSI (SI)

Fattoria Ormanni

Loc. Ormanni, 1
53036 Poggibonsi (SI)
tel. 0577937212
www.ormanni.it

The estate belonging to the Brini Batacchi family has kept its full profile in this edition of the Guide, even if the results of this year's tastings are not up to the levels achieved last time. The estate lies on the road that runs from Poggibonsi to Castellina in Chianti and takes its name, Ormanni, from the very first owners, a family that appears in Dante's Divine Comedy. The forebearers of the Brini Batacchis acquired the property at the beginning of the 1800s. Thirty-five of the 65 hectares planted to vine are registered as Chianti Classico and the vines are bush-trained. Our tasters thought that the best of the wines we were offered for tasting was the Chianti Classico '04. It presents superb fruity aromas of ripe cherry and plum intermingled with sensations of aromatic herbs that bring to mind the scents of Mediterranean scrubland. Entry on the palate is good, showing smooth tannins and enjoyable drinkability. The Riserva Borro del Diavolo '01 offers tertiary notes of leather, tobacco and animal skins that give way to hints of plum-led ripe fruit. Despite its age, the palate starts out still in thrall to the tannins but manages to move on to end in a long, agreeable finish.

● Chianti Cl. Borro del Diavolo Ris. '01	🍷🍷	5
● Chianti Cl. '04	🍷🍷	4
● Chianti Cl. Borro del Diavolo Ris. '00	ΨΨ	5
● Julius '00	ΨΨ	5
● Chianti Cl. '03	ΨΨ	4
● Chianti Cl. Ris. '95	ΨΨ	4
● Chianti Cl. Ris. '96	ΨΨ	4
● Julius '98	ΨΨ	5
● Julius '99	ΨΨ	6

POGGIO A CAIANO (PO)

PIAGGIA

LOC. POGGETTO
VIA CEGOLI, 47
59016 POGGIO A CAIANO (PO)
TEL. 0558705401

Mauro Vannucci continues to attract our attention with modern wines whose overall style is quite unique and easily recognizable. Prime examples are the Carmignano Riserva, the Sasso that this year enters the Carmignano DOC, and the new Poggio dè Colli. Carmignano Riserva '03 is a real thoroughbred and romps home to win a place in our finals. It presents an intense ruby colour and a rich, complex nose with a range of aromas that takes in red berry fruit, spice, charred oak and aromatic herbs. The confident character of the tight-knit, assertive tannins is sustained by the alcohol on the concentrated palate. The finish is convincing as it unfolds long and fruity. The Carmignano Sasso '04 is a little disappointing. Its dense colour is the prelude to a pervasive bouquet of dark berry fruit, blackberry and blueberry to the fore, with notes of mint and liquorice. The sweet, full palate has rich tannic texture and delectable savouriness. The finish is concentrated and complex but slightly dried by the hefty tannins. The impenetrable ruby Poggio dè Colli '04 from cabernet franc alone performed well if not quite so splendidly. The nose starts out rather closed and medicinal in tone but then opens to embrace notes of pepper and forest fruit. The palate shows nice flesh, soft character and an oak-dominated finish.

●	Carmignano Ris. '03	▼▼	6
●	Carmignano Sasso '04	▼▼	5
●	Poggio dè Colli '04	▼▼	8
●	Il Sasso '01	▽▽▽	5
●	Carmignano Ris. '97	▽▽▽	5
●	Carmignano Ris. '98	▽▽▽	6
●	Carmignano Ris. '99	▽▽▽	6
●	Carmignano Ris. '00	▽▽	6
●	Il Sasso '00	▽▽	5
●	Carmignano Ris. '01	▽▽	6
●	Carmignano Ris. '02	▽▽	6
●	Il Sasso '03	▽▽	5
●	Il Sasso '02	▽▽	5

PONTASSIEVE (FI)

GRIGNANO

FRAZ. GRIGNANO
VIA DI GRIGNANO, 22
50065 PONTASSIEVE (FI)
TEL. 0558398490 - 3391578008
www.fattoriadigrignano.com

The estate belonging to the Inghirami family has ancient roots. The original structure was built by the Marchesi Gondi and dates back to the 15th century. It was completely restructured in the 1700s when it assumed the appearance it still has today. The Inghirami family took over the property in 1972. Grignano includes over 600 hectares of vineyards, olive groves, arable farmland and woods. The varieties cultivated are mainly the traditional ones, which means sangiovese and canaiolo reds and the trebbiano and malvasia whites that are used to produce the Vin Santo. The estate also gives a nod to new cultivars in the form of merlot and chardonnay. Marco Bernabei acts as both vineyard manager and oenologist. This year, we have a new recruit to the ranks in the form of the Supertuscan Salicaria, obtained from sangiovese and merlot. Its modern style is immediately apparent in the fairly dense colour and aromas of spice and forest fruits, notably raspberry. The soft profile is a tad dominated by the oak but the tannins are well integrated with the alcohol and the finish is nice and long. The Chianti Rufina '04 has a lively, well-defined palate with aromas suggesting autumn leaves and aromatic herbs that lead to a lip-smacking finish, ever so slightly dried by the tannins. The Riserva '03 gives a ripe nose of jam with spicy hints of cinnamon and cloves. On the palate, the tannins dominate, the acidity is marked and the finish is long but dried by the extract. The Vin Santo '00 is pleasant but rather one-dimensional.

●	Salicaria '03	▼▼	6
○	Vin Santo del Chianti '00	▼	5
●	Chianti Rufina Ris. '03	▼	4
●	Chianti Rufina '04	▼	4
●	Chianti Rufina '03	▽▽	3

PONTASSIEVE (FI)

LAVACCHIO

VIA DI MONTEFIESOLE, 55
50065 PONTASSIEVE (FI)
TEL. 0558317472
www.fattorialavacchio.com

Several years ago, the Lavacchio estate belonging to the Lottero family made its Guide debut with a short profile. This year, it is promoted to the full profile section thanks to a very fine all round performance. The estate totals 109 hectares and 19 of these are planted to vine. When the Lotteros acquired the property in 1977, it was completely run down and they have spent the intervening years restoring it. Work is now almost complete and most of the buildings have been renovated for use as an agriturismo. The 44 hectares of olive trees also produce very good oil. Alberto Antonini is oenologist and the entire grape crop is cultivated according to organic methods. Two of the wines presented stood out at our tastings, the Oro del Cedro '01 from late-harvested traminer, and the Fontegalli '03, a blend of merlot, cabernet sauvignon and sangiovese. The first presents a faintly golden appearance and sweet sensations on the nose that recall honey, chamomile and dried fruits like apricot. Entry on the palate is sweet, creamy, full and enfolding, sustained by freshness all the way through the long, delicate finish. The Fontegalli offers aromas of wild berry jam and spice. Its embracing palate displays fine tannic texture and refreshing acidity, signing off with a good finish of just the right length. The Pachar '04 from a blend of chardonnay, viognier and sauvignon has a charming nose and good mouthfeel. The Chianti Rufina '04 and Riserva '03 are simpler, as is the Vin Santo '99.

○ Oro del Cedro V. T. '01	🍷🍷	5
● Fontegalli '03	🍷🍷	6
● Chianti Rufina Cedro Ris. '03	🍷	5
● Chianti Rufina Cedro '04	🍷	4
○ Pachar '04	🍷	4
○ Chianti Rufina Vin Santo '99	🍷	5
● Cortigiano '00	YY	6
● Chianti Rufina '01	YY	4
○ Oro del Cedro '98	YY	3

PONTASSIEVE (FI)

★ TENIMENTI RUFFINO

P.LE RUFFINO, 1
50065 PONTASSIEVE (FI)
TEL. 05583605
www.ruffino.it

This year, Tenimenti Ruffino gave a bit of a lacklustre performance. The vintages are not particularly interesting and the Chianti Classico Riserva Ducale Oro is missing in the 2002 version. All told, rather a poor showing but when the '04 reds are released, they will surely make up for it. We've already previewed them and we liked what we tasted. This is not to say that there wasn't a hidden gem or two this time. The Chianti Classico Santedame '04 was a very pleasant surprise, a truly excellent wine that anticipates the release of a Riserva that will be sensational. Although not terribly complex, this elegant red is engaging and very pleasing to drink. Then there is the Modus '03 in what may be one of the most interesting versions to come out of the cellar in the last few years. Obtained from a blend of sangiovese and cabernet sauvignon, this red finally proves a worthy successor to the legendary '99 and is probably the best yet. The Romitorio di Santedame '03 from sangiovese, colorino and merlot is a tad under par and pays the price of the torrid growing year, showing rather overripe notes on the nose and quite hard tannins that prevent it from achieving its usual harmony. La Solatia '05, a chardonnay-based white, is decent but serves to confirm our opinion that, with rare exceptions, Tuscany is not a territory that brings out the best in white grapes.

● Modus '03	🍷🍷	6
● Chianti Cl. Santedame '04	🍷🍷	4
● Romitorio di Santedame '03	🍷🍷	7
○ Chardonnay La Solatia '05	🍷	6
● Chianti Cl. Ris. Ducale Oro '00	YYY	6
● Romitorio di Santedame '00	YYY	7
● Chianti Cl. Ris. Ducale Oro '01	YYY	6
● Chianti Cl. Ris. Ducale Oro '88	YYY	5
● Chianti Cl. Ris. Ducale Oro '90	YYY	5
● Romitorio di Santedame '96	YYY	6
● Romitorio di Santedame '97	YYY	6
● Romitorio di Santedame '98	YYY	6
● Romitorio di Santedame '99	YYY	7

RADDA IN CHIANTI (SI)

Castello d' Albola

Loc. Pian d'Albola, 31
53017 Radda in Chianti (SI)
tel. 0577738019
www.albola.it

When it comes to assessing the results of this Zonin group estate, it's a bit like being on a seesaw. Ups like last year's performance are followed by downs like this. Fair enough, the estate's Supertuscan, Acciaiolo '03, made it to our final tastings but the rest of the wines presented were less than inspiring. In our opinion, this is not merely a problem of vintage because a zone as high as Castello di Albola should have escaped the worst of 2003's scorching heat. It's almost as if the estate has yet to find its style, perhaps requiring greater care in vineyard management and closer monitoring of the wines ageing in the cellar. But there can be no doubt that if the Zonins put their minds to it, they will achieve these objectives. As for the wines themselves, the sangiovese and cabernet sauvignon blend that reached our finals releases generous notes of plum and cherry jam intermingled with gamey tones of leather and vague hints of spice. The full palate displays solid body that is restrained and well-distributed, if not entirely smooth, tannins that curtail the finish. The Chianti Classico Riserva '03 alternates fresh nuances of autumn leaves with hints of red berry fruit on the nose. Entry on the palate is gutsy but the wine struggles to unbend and this holds the finish back. The Chianti Classico Le Ellere '03 is an undemanding wine but the Vin Santo '97 is devoid of personality, lacking life on the nose or complexity on the palate. The Monteregio Sassabruna '04 is pleasant.

●	Acciaiolo '03	▼▼	7
●	Chianti Cl. Le Ellere '03	▼	4
●	Chianti Cl. Ris. '03	▼	5
●	Monteregio di Massa Marittima Sassabruna '04	▼	4
●	Le Focaie Rocca di Montemassi '05	▼	4
○	Vin Santo del Chianti Cl. '97	▼	7
●	Acciaiolo '01	▽▽▽	7
●	Acciaiolo '95	▽▽▽	6
●	Acciaiolo '00	▽▽	7
●	Chianti Cl. Ris. '00	▽▽	5
●	Chianti Cl. Ris. '01	▽▽	5
●	Chianti Cl. Ris. '97	▽▽	5
●	Chianti Cl. Ris. '99	▽▽	5

RADDA IN CHIANTI (SI)

Brancaia

Loc. Poppi, 42b
53017 Radda in Chianti (SI)
tel. 0577742007
www.brancaia.it

Our congratulations again to the Widmer family, who took home Three Glasses for their top-of-the-range Blu '04, a wine known to consumers for its quality. The rest of the line-up also showed very well, proof that the success of this estate has been worked for by its well-structured team and not merely accidental. The style of the wines is thoroughly modern, although they also manage to convey a strong personality closely linked to their zone of origin. The top-prize winner is a blend of sangiovese and merlot with a dash of cabernet sauvignon. It is bright ruby with a nose that combines hints of mixed spice with notes of forest fruits. Entry on the palate is delightful, round and enveloping with well-integrated tannins and alcohol. The finish is leisurely, sweet and long. Another excellent wine is the Chianti Classico '04, whose cornucopia of red berry fruit aromas and well-defined profile earn it a place on our final tasting table. The tannins are perfectly integrated and the finish is long and tasty. The Tre '04 is obtained predominantly from sangiovese with some cabernet sauvignon and merlot. It's fresh and lively on both nose and palate and has an elegant style. The Ilatraia '04 is compact and solid.

●	Brancaia Il Blu '04	▼▼▼	7
●	Chianti Cl. '04	▼▼	6
●	Brancaia Tre '04	▼▼	5
●	Ilatraia '04	▼▼	7
●	Brancaia Il Blu '00	▽▽▽	7
●	Brancaia Il Blu '01	▽▽▽	7
●	Brancaia Il Blu '03	▽▽▽	7
●	Brancaia '94	▽▽▽	6
●	Brancaia '97	▽▽▽	6
●	Brancaia '98	▽▽▽	6
●	Brancaia '99	▽▽▽	8

RADDA IN CHIANTI (SI)

COLLE BERETO

LOC. COLLE BERETO
53017 RADDA IN CHIANTI (SI)
TEL. 0554299330 - 0577738083
www.collebereto.it

The two Chianti Classicos presented by the estate belonging to the Pinzauti family made a big impression on our judges. Indeed, they outshone the two Supertuscans, Il Tocco '04 from mainly merlot, and Il Cenno '04 from 100 per cent pinot nero. It's early days yet to say whether this denotes a new trend but we like the fact that the best wines are those with the deepest roots in the territory. Enthusiastic vineyard manager Bernardo Bianchi is also head of staff and Nicolò D'Afflitto is consultant oenologist. Although busy with other things, Lorenzo Pinzauti takes a personal interest in the estate, a property that is a lot more than a simple country retreat. It consists of ten hectares planted to vine, eight of which are in the Chianti Classico zone. We liked the Riserva '03 for its balsamic tones that merge with complex fruity notes of plum, blackberry and cherry on the nose. Entry on the palate is enveloping, vivid and fruity and manages to display freshness without sacrificing fullness. The finish is full-flavoured and enjoyable. The Chianti Classico '04 offers fine notes of pencil lead and fruit with undertones of spice and aromatic herbs. Entry on the palate is light and pleasant while the body is balanced and very drinkable, thanks to a lip-smacking finish. Il Tocco '04 reveals sweet, appealing sensations of fruit and spice on the nose but seems to peter out mid palate, signing off with a leisurely finish. Il Cenno '04 throws a fascinating array of complex aromas, with forest fruits to the fore. The body is supple and lean but it is a bit short on length.

● Chianti Cl. Ris. '03	▼▼	5
● Chianti Cl. '04	▼▼	4
● Il Cenno '04	▼	5
● Il Tocco '04	▼	6
● Il Tocco '03	▽▽	6
● Il Tocco '00	▽▽	6
● Il Tocco '01	▽▽	6
● Il Tocco '02	▽▽	6
● Il Cenno '03	▽▽	5
● Il Tocco '99	▽▽	5

RADDA IN CHIANTI (SI)

LIVERNANO

LOC. LIVERNANO, 67A
53017 RADDA IN CHIANTI (SI)
TEL. 0577738353
www.livernano.it

The estate founded by Marco Montanari has a new owner, Robert Cuillo, an American theatre producer. Robert has kept the same team, picking up where Marco left off. Stefano Chioccioli is consultant oenologist and Remigio Bordini is in charge of the vineyard, a winning combination if this debut performance is anything to go by. The Livernano '03, from cabernet sauvignon, merlot and sangiovese, waltzed away with Three Glasses. Livernano has an ancient history and occupies a site that was home to first Etruscan then Roman settlements. It was totally abandoned in the 1950s and didn't resurface until the 1990s, when Montanari set about restoring the property. The estate totals around 70 hectares, 12.5 of which are given over to specialized vineyards, and over the last 15 years the vine stock has been completely replanted at high density. We very much appreciated the wine's complex aromas of balsam and mint with their faint grassy, fruity nuances. The very fleshy, fruit-led palate has fine tannins and a finish that develops impressively. The pure sangiovese Puro Sangue '03 also shows well. It has a concentrated ruby appearance, lively aromas of red berry fruit with hints of tobacco and leather. The elegant palate reveals firm body and spirited freshness, ending in a tasty finish. The Chianti Classico '04 is fresh and agreeable on the nose, where notes of fruit and flowers emerge, and the palate is pleasant and enjoyable. The excellent Anima '04 is a blend of chardonnay, sauvignon, viognier and traminer with a fragrant nose, a tangy palate and a wonderful lingering finish.

● Livernano '03	▼▼▼	8
● Puro Sangue '03	▼▼	7
○ Anima '04	▼▼	7
● Chianti Cl. '04	▼▼	5
● Livernano '97	▽▽▽	8
● Livernano '98	▽▽▽	8
● Livernano '99	▽▽▽	8
● Puro Sangue '00	▽▽	7
● Puro Sangue '99	▽▽	7
● Puro Sangue '01	▽▽	7
○ Anima '03	▽▽	7

RADDA IN CHIANTI (SI)

★ MONTEVERTINE
LOC. MONTEVERTINE
53017 RADDA IN CHIANTI (SI)
TEL. 0577738009
www.montevertine.it

Absolutely perfect. That's all we have to say about the Pergole Torte, the flagship wine of this Radda in Chianti estate. Fair enough, the '03 is not the best version of all time but considering that the vintage wasn't fantastic, we can safely say that Martino Manetti and his family have every right to be satisfied. We gave it Three very well-deserved Glasses in tribute to the unremitting hard work and great professionalism demonstrated by this estate. The nose offers notes of ripe red berry fruit, rain-soaked earth and gamey tones with a very intriguing smoky nuance. The palate is extraordinary, showing intense and full, yet graceful and charming, with the typical acidity that distinguishes Montevertine's wines. The long, concentrated finish is enhanced by a hint of dried flowers. The real tour de force, however, is the sweet, perfectly integrated extract, by no means a foregone conclusion in an '03. We also liked the Montevertine '03. It's a bit simpler than its stablemate but this is as it should be. The nose is fresh and inviting and the palate is long, fruity, smooth and highly enjoyable. We enjoyed the very fine '04 version of Pian del Ciampolo, which shows off the vintage to it best advantage. It's fresh, clean and very well made. As we noted not too long ago, there is one Pergole Torte in particular that stands out among the ranks of very good vintages. We're talking about the '99, which was overlooked when we handed out our Three Glass awards. In this, the 20th edition of the Guide, we would like to make amends. As they say, better late than never.

●	Le Pergole Torte '03	■■■	8
●	Montevertine '03	■■	5
●	Pian del Ciampolo '04	■■	4
●	Le Pergole Torte '01	☐☐☐	8
●	Montevertine '01	☐☐☐	6
●	Le Pergole Torte '83	☐☐☐	8
●	Le Pergole Torte '86	☐☐☐	8
●	Le Pergole Torte '88	☐☐☐	8
●	Le Pergole Torte '90	☐☐☐	8
●	Le Pergole Torte '92	☐☐☐	8
●	Le Pergole Torte '99	☐☐☐	8

RADDA IN CHIANTI (SI)

TERRABIANCA
LOC. SAN FEDELE A PATERNO
53017 RADDA IN CHIANTI (SI)
TEL. 057754029
www.terrabianca.com

The Guldener family is back in the Guide with a decent all-round performance but we still feel they haven't achieved their full potential for quality. Roberto Guldener's story as a wine man started in 1988, when he sold his fashion boutique in Zurich and moved to Tuscany, inspired in part by the memory of his maternal grandfather who owned a small restaurant that obtained its wine from the Chianti area. His wife and daughters share his enthusiasm. Vittorio Fiore has been oenologist since day one and Remigio Bordini acts as vineyard manager. Roberto has recently bought an estate in Maremma, Il Tesoro, where he produces the wine of the same name. His Chianti estate extends over 230 hectares, of which 52 are planted to vine and 14 of these are registered as Chianti Classico. The cream of this year's crop is Ceppate '03, a cabernet sauvignon and merlot blend. It gives notes of vanilla, forest fruit jam, cinnamon and cloves, and a soft, round palate with smooth body and an enjoyably long finish. The Chianti Classico '04 did well with its fresh notes of aromatic herbs and flowers, gutsy palate, juicy tannins, tasty acid vein and captivating finish. The rest of the range failed to attain these dizzy heights. Il Tesoro '03, a pure merlot from the Maremma, has a simple nose and lightweight body, the 100 per cent sangiovese Piano del Cipresso '03 has a rich profile but lacks balance and the Campaccio '03 from sangiovese and cabernet is held back on the palate by its over-abundant extract. The Riserva Croce '03 lacks harmony while La Fonte '04 is easier and more enjoyable.

●	Ceppate '03	■■	7
●	Chianti Cl. Scassino '04	■■	4
●	Campaccio '03	■	5
●	Chianti Cl. V. della Croce Ris. '03	■	5
●	Il Tesoro '03	■	7
●	Piano del Cipresso '03	■	5
●	La Fonte '04	■	4
●	Campaccio '00	☐☐	5
●	Ceppate '01	☐☐	7
●	Ceppate '99	☐☐	7
●	Piano del Cipresso '00	☐☐	5
●	Campaccio '01	☐☐	5
●	Piano del Cipresso '01	☐☐	5
●	Chianti Cl. V. della Croce Ris. '99	☐☐	5
●	Piano del Cipresso '99	☐☐	5

RADDA IN CHIANTI (SI)

CASTELLO DI VOLPAIA

LOC. VOLPAIA
P.ZZA DELLA CISTERNA, 1
53017 RADDA IN CHIANTI (SI)
TEL. 0577738066
www.volpaia.com

The Mascheroni family chalked up some good results this year, even if they failed to produce an absolute winner. The Chianti Classico Coltassala Riserva '03 made it into our final tasting rounds but it was the overall level of performance that really impressed us. The new direction undertaken following the arrival of oenologist Riccardo Cotarella has improved the quality of the wines. The castle of Volpaia and the surrounding village have their origins in the 11th century, when they served as a fortified town halfway between the provinces of Siena and Florence. Cultivating vines and olives have always been the main activities here. The estate takes its name from the Florentine Dei della Volpaia family, the earliest owners whose members included expert watch makers. The finalist has an impenetrable colour and a nose enhanced by aromas of blackberry and forest fruit jam that give way to nuances of mixed spice. The good entry is followed by a big, soft mid palate with well-integrated tannins. The finish is rather curtailed by the tannins but is enjoyable nevertheless. The basic version of the Riserva '03 showed well. Notes of toasty oak emerge clearly on the nose together with hints of ripe fruit, such as plum, and minty tones. The palate is balanced but not huge with delicate acid backbone and a sweet finish. We enjoyed the Chianti Classico '04's eloquent fruit, sweetened by notes of vanilla. The body is lean and complex and the finish refreshes. The Vin Santo '99 is a bit disappointing. It's simple on the nose and the body rather insubstantial.

●	Chianti Cl. Coltassala Ris. '03	**YY**	7
●	Chianti Cl. Ris. '03	**YY**	6
●	Chianti Cl. '04	**YY**	4
○	Vin Santo del Chianti Cl. '99	**Y**	6
●	Balifico '00	YYY	7
●	Chianti Cl. Coltassala Ris. '01	YYY	7
●	Chianti Cl. Coltassala Ris. '00	YY	7
●	Chianti Cl. Coltassala Ris. '99	YY	6
●	Balifico '01	YY	7
●	Balifico '03	YY	7

RUFINA (FI)

FATTORIA DI BASCIANO

V.LE DUCA DELLA VITTORIA, 159
50068 RUFINA (FI)
TEL. 0558397034
www.renzomasibasciano.it

Renzo Masi's estate never fails to offer us wines of good quality. Meticulous work in the vineyard and cellar produces consistently good results. Most of the credit must go to Renzo's son, Paolo, who is both oenologist and fruitmaker. This year, we detected a change in style, particularly in the two Chianti Rufinas which are aiming to express the territory more fully. We also admired the skill brought to bear on handling the grapes bought in to produce the Erta, China and Chianti Riserva. Again, we liked the value-for-money Erta best of the three. Obtained from sangiovese and cabernet sauvignon in equal parts, it proffers delicious aromas of forest fruit and spice, a smooth, supple body, superb drinkability and a finish that unfolds satisfyingly. The other IGTs did well, too. Il Corto '04 from sangiovese with some cabernet sauvignon exhibits generous aromas of cherry and blueberry, juicy body with well-defined tannic texture and a lip-smacking finish. Derived from equal parts of cabernet sauvignon and syrah, I Pini '04 sets its stall with aromas that include pepper, leather and ripe fruitiness. The vibrant, dynamic body unbends in the finish to reveal a tasty acid vein. The Chianti Rufina Riserva '03 has a balsamic nose and a layered body in which extract and alcohol find a perfect match. The finish is clean and tasty. The Chianti Rufina '04 has crisp fruity notes, a simple, fluent body and wonderful drinkability. The Rosato is simple and enjoyable and the Vin Santo shows traditional oxidized characteristics but is shortish in the finish.

●	Chianti Rufina Ris. '03	**YY**	5
●	Erta e China '04	**YY**	3*
●	I Pini '04	**YY**	5
●	Il Corto '04	**YY**	5
○	Vin Santo Rufina '00	**Y**	4
●	Chianti Ris. '03	**Y**	3
●	Chianti Rufina '04	**Y**	3
⊙	Rosato '05	**Y**	2
●	Chianti Rufina Ris. '01	YY	5
●	Erta e China '02	YY	3
●	Il Corto '02	YY	4
●	Chianti Rufina '03	YY	3
●	Erta e China '03	YY	3
●	I Pini '03	YY	5
●	Il Corto '03	YY	5

RUFINA (FI)

FATTORIA SELVAPIANA
LOC. SELVAPIANA, 43
50068 RUFINA (FI)
TEL. 0558369848
www.selvapiana.it

Silvia and Federico Giuntini Masseti scored highly again this year despite the absence of the Riserva and the Fornace, which is from international varieties. We expect great things of these two wines next year now that the new cellar is up and running and work seems to have settled into a comfortable groove. Fattoria di Selvapiana is a typical Tuscan complex with a main villa, a cellar and other facilities. The two towers that are part of the structure bring to mind a look-out post and for many years the villa was in fact used as a summer retreat for Florentine bishops. The Giuntini family acquired the property in 1827 and current owner Francesco Giuntini Antinori is one of the strongest advocates of the wine potential of the Chianti Rufina zone. The estate comprises almost 250 hectares, 60 of which are planted to vine and 30 to olive trees. Selvapiana also oversees the Petrognano estate in the Pomino DOC. Franco Bernabei is consultant oenologist and next year celebrates 30 years of collaboration with the estate. The Vin Santo '99 is, as usual, excellent. It has a lovely golden colour, generous, complex aromas of apple, lemon and orange peel and dried apple-like fruit. The palate is sweet, round, big and enfolding, signing off in a long, pleasantly lingering finish. We also liked the Pomino Rosso '04, which offers fruity notes of cherry and forest fruits, dense body with well-integrated tannins, and a fresh, enjoyable finish. The Chianti Rufina '04 is a bit simple, but the Niccolò '05, a rosé, is tasty with wonderful mouthfeel.

●	Pomino Fattoria di Petrognano '04	🍷🍷	4
○	Vin Santo della Rufina '99	🍷🍷	6
●	Chianti Rufina '04	🍷	4
⊙	Niccolò '05	🍷	3
●	La Fornace '00	ΥΥ	7
●	La Fornace '01	ΥΥ	7
●	La Fornace '03	ΥΥ	6

SAN CASCIANO IN VAL DI PESA (FI)

CASTELVECCHIO
LOC. SAN PANCRAZIO
VIA CERTALDESE, 30
50026 SAN CASCIANO IN VAL DI PESA (FI)
TEL. 0558248032 - 0558248921
www.castelvecchio.it

We'll start the Rocchi family's tasting notes by correcting an error made in the 2006 edition of the Guide. The Chianti Santa Caterina we tasted last year was in fact the 2003, so this year's is the 2004. Overall, the results attained were good but they are not quite up to the standard we have come to expect from Filippo Rocchi. Filippo is the driving force of this estate and an avid worker in both vineyard and cellar, where he is extremely meticulous about every process. However, things don't always go as planned and this year the wines failed to take that qualitative step forward we had anticipated. Brecciolino '03, the estate's Supertuscan based on sangiovese, petit verdot and merlot, is in colour and throws a fruity nose with fascinating spicy notes of cinnamon and cloves. Entry on the palate is sweet and enveloping, developing soft with well-integrated tannins. The finish is sweet and of good length. We were less convinced by the Chianti Colli Fiorentini selection Vigna la Quercia '04. The nose starts off rather muddled then goes on to reveal gamey notes of animal skins and leather. The palate is a bit confused, although it is fruity and the tannins make their presence felt. The Numero Otto '05 from pure canaiolo shows fresh, even minty tones and a lean body that is well sustained by tasty acid backbone. The Chianti Colli Fiorentini '04 is as agreeable as ever, showing simple but nicely harmonious overall. The Chianti Santa Caterina '04 is slightly dried by the tannins but has good texture and a lip-smacking finish.

●	Il Brecciolino '03	🍷🍷	6
●	Chianti Colli Fiorentini '04	🍷	4
●	Chianti Colli Fiorentini V. La Quercia '04	🍷	4
●	Chianti Santa Caterina '04	🍷	3*
●	Numero Otto '05	🍷	5
●	Chianti Colli Fiorentini Ris. '00	ΥΥ	5
●	Il Brecciolino '00	ΥΥ	6
●	Chianti Colli Fiorentini Ris. '01	ΥΥ	5
●	Il Brecciolino '01	ΥΥ	6
●	Il Brecciolino '02	ΥΥ	6
●	Numero Otto '03	ΥΥ	5

SAN CASCIANO IN VAL DI PESA (FI)

Fattoria Le Corti

loc. Le Corti
via San Piero di Sotto, 1
50026 San Casciano in Val di Pesa (FI)
tel. 055829301
www.principecorsini.com

Le Corti has been in the Corsini family since 1427. The farm extends over approximately 250 hectares and 50 or so of these are given over to vines. The estate embarked on its quest for quality in 1992 when Duccio Corsini and consultant oenologist Carlo Ferrini joined forces. In addition to sangiovese, merlot and colorino are cultivated plus malvasia and trebbiano for the Vin Santo. Once again this year, it was Marsiliana from the Maremma estate of the same name that stood out at our tastings. This blend of cabernet sauvignon, merlot and sangiovese has a dense colour that introduces an array of aromas including red berry fruit jam and mixed spice with nuances of chocolate. Entry on the palate is firm, round and very enveloping, the tannins mid palate are restrained and the finish is pleasant if not overly long. The Chianti Classico Don Tommaso '03 is good but not as good as in previous years. Its concentrated nose combines notes of ripe fruit with hints of leather and pencil lead but the palate struggles a bit to unbend owing to the big tannins. The finish is nice and long. The Chianti Classico '04 is a simpler wine combining fresh aromas of cherry and blackberry with flowery sensations. The palate is smooth, lively and fruity and capped by a finish that unfolds very nicely. The Birillo '04 is another Maremma product. Simple but enjoyable, it offers notes of pepper and mixed fruit and a coherent, round palate.

● Marsiliana '03	▼▼	6
● Chianti Cl. Don Tommaso '03	▼▼	6
● Chianti Cl. '04	▼▼	4
● Birillo '04	▼	4
● Chianti Cl. Don Tommaso '99	▽▽▽	5
● Chianti Cl. Don Tommaso '00	▽▽	5
● Marsiliana '01	▽▽	6
● Marsiliana '02	▽▽	6
● Chianti Cl. Don Tommaso '01	▽▽	5

SAN CASCIANO IN VAL DI PESA (FI)

Fattoria Corzano e Paterno

fraz. San Prancazio
via Paterno, 8
50020 San Casciano in Val di Pesa (FI)
tel. 0558248179
www.corzanoepaterno.it

The Fattoria Corzano e Paterno has consolidated its position in our Guide with a range of wines that seeks above all to interpret the territory. Quality is good across the board and not just restricted to a couple of high-profile labels that lead the way for a lesser range of products. The Corzano '03, a blend of sangiovese with small amounts of cabernet and merlot, is a powerful wine. It has yet to develop fully but already bears the hallmark of its Tuscan origins, as revealed recently when we retasted some of the older versions. The nose is rather complex, showing attractive oaky and earthy aromas set against a backdrop of fruit and spice. Entry on the palate is full, concentrated and soft, the tannins are tight-knit and a little clenched but tasty nonetheless. The finish is fairly long and rigid, showing bitterish from time to time. The Chianti Terre di Corzano '04 is reasonably well made. It has a hesitant nose in which notes of fruit and geranium leaf emerge followed by a tangy, tannic palate with a marked acid vein. Il Corzanello '05 isn't bad at all, showing fruity aromas and an acidulous but very well-balanced palate. We'd like to mention that Alioscia Goldschmidt also makes excellent cheeses.

● Il Corzano '03	▼▼	6
● Chianti Terre di Corzano '04	▼	4
○ Il Corzanello '05	▼	4
● Il Corzano '97	▽▽▽	5
● Il Corzano '99	▽▽	6
● Il Corzano '00	▽▽	7
● Il Corzano '01	▽▽	6
● Il Corzano '02	▽▽	5

SAN CASCIANO IN VAL DI PESA (FI)

Castello di Gabbiano

fraz. Mercatale Val di Pesa
via Gabbiano, 22
50024 San Casciano in Val di Pesa (FI)
tel. 055821053
www.castellogabbiano.it

It's always difficult to follow a performance like that given by Castello di Gabbiano on its debut in our Guide last year but the important thing is that it has kept up the pace. The estate is owned by Beringer Blass, a Californian company that belongs to the Australian Foster group. Owing to the American market's passion for Chianti Classico, for many years it was almost impossible to find Castello di Gabbiano's wines in Italy. Then several years ago, the estate changed its distribution policy to give widespread coverage to the Italian market. We were offered three wines to taste this year. The Chianti Classico Riserva '03 is a lovely bright ruby colour accompanying fruity notes of cherry and blackberry that give way to meaty sensations. Entry on the palate is pervasive yet not excessive, the tannins are nice and weighty, the acidity is well dosed and the finish is agreeably long. The Alleanza '03 is a blend of sangiovese, merlot and cabernet sauvignon whose name refers to the marriage of the Tuscan variety with the two international grapes. It's no accident that Italian oenologist Giancarlo Roman and Californian Ed Sbragia work together. Sweet nuances of spice and vanilla merge with notes of forest fruits on the nose. The round palate owes its nice mouthfeel to good acid backbone and the finish builds up nicely. The Bellezza '03 from pure sangiovese is less convincing, its tannins tending to stunt the palate's development.

● Alleanza '03	▼▼	6
● Chianti Cl. Ris. '03	▼▼	5
● Bellezza '03	▼	6
● Alleanza '01	▽▽	7
● Bellezza '01	▽▽	7
● Chianti Cl. Ris. '01	▽▽	5

SAN CASCIANO IN VAL DI PESA (FI)

Castelli del Grevepesa

fraz. Mercatale in Val di Pesa
via Grevigiana, 34
50024 San Casciano in Val di Pesa (FI)
tel. 055821911
www.castellidelgrevepesa.it

Castelli del Grevepesa is a major force in Chianti Classico. Last year we mentioned the 40th-anniversary celebrations but these are in fact due to take place in 2008. The estate has come a long way since a small group of producers set up the co-operative in 1968. Today, it can count on around 180 members and has the equivalent of 1,000 hectares of vineyards, 650 of which are registered as Chianti Classico. Paolo Catarzi is vineyard manager and oenologist Stefano Mosele works in tandem with Gabriella Tani. The two Supertuscans were conspicuous by their absence this year because it was wisely decided not to produce them in 2002. The Chianti Classico Clemente VII did very well in both the standard-label '04 and Riserva '03 versions. The Riserva offers classic notes of ripe, slightly mature fruit flanked by complex spiciness. The palate shows elegant backbone, not too much complexity, silky tannins and a balanced acid vein, signing off with a pleasant, tasty finale. The '04 also showed well, displaying lively notes of red berry fruit mingled with aromatic herbs. The lean body develops good acid backbone and has nice tanginess as it progresses to an enjoyable finish. The Lamole '04 selection has an agreeable flowery nose but the body is a bit lean. The Chianti Classico Castelgreve '04 is easy and very drinkable. The Merlot Aprile '05 is an everyday, fresh-tasting wine while the Morellino Terramara '05 offers a rustic nose and a dynamic, fruity palate. It's not very tidy but the finish is long enough.

● Chianti Cl. Clemente VII Ris. '03	▼▼	5
● Chianti Cl. Clemente VII '04	▼▼	4
● Chianti Cl. Castelgreve '04	▼	4
● Chianti Cl. Lamole '04	▼	4
● Merlot Aprile '05	▼	3
● Morellino di Scansano Terramara '05	▼	4
● Chianti Cl. Clemente VII Ris. '00	▽▽	5
● Coltifredi '00	▽▽	6
● Coltifredi '01	▽▽	6
● Gualdo al Luco '01	▽▽	6
● Chianti Cl. Clemente VII Ris. '01	▽▽	5
● Chianti Cl. Clemente VII Ris. '99	▽▽	5

ISPOLI

FRAZ. MERCATALE VAL DI PESA
VIA SANTA LUCIA, 2
50024 SAN CASCIANO IN VAL DI PESA (FI)
TEL. 055821613

This estate belonging to the Mattheis husband and wife team is back with a full profile this year. It is located in a zone that is extremely well-adapted to vine cultivation not far from San Casciano, one of the Chianti Classico's most northerly outreaches. In spite of its limited dimensions, the winery manages to maintain a consistently high level of quality. We're happy to say that we detect more care and attention in the DOCG wines and it is no coincidence that the two Chianti Classicos scored highest with our judges this year. The deep ruby Riserva '03 opens on the nose with lovely fruity aromas of cherry and forest fruits. The palate shows an exceptionally well-balanced profile with silky, well-integrated tannins and a delightful, extended finish. The Chianti Classico '04 also performed well. Its aromas are less than generous but very lively with clear nuances of red berry fruit and the odd hint of flowers. The palate is smooth and fresh-tasting with a nice acid vein and well-defined tannic texture. The finish is not particularly long but pleasant. The Podere Ispoli '03, a sangiovese and merlot blend, is not quite so interesting. Notes of spicy fruit and nuances of vanilla and cinnamon emerge on the nose. The body is rather lean and rough in places, but the finish is sweet if a tad short.

● Chianti Cl. Ris. '03	ΨΨ	5
● Chianti Cl. '04	ΨΨ	4
● Podere Ispoli Rosso '03	Ψ	6
● Chianti Cl. Ris. '00	YY	6
● Ispolaia Rosso '00	YY	6
● Ispolaia Rosso '98	YY	4
● Ispolaia Rosso '99	YY	5

SAN CASCIANO IN VAL DI PESA (FI)

PERSETO DEL POZZO

VIA DI PERSETO, 11-13
50026 SAN CASCIANO IN VAL DI PESA (FI)
TEL. 0571608638
www.aziendapiazzini.florencewine.it

Perseto del Pozzo earned a full profile thanks to a fine performance from its Chianti Classicos. The estate is relatively new for the Piazzini brothers acquired it in 1999 and immediately set about a careful renovation of both the vineyards and the cellar. It consists of 23 hectares and just over 13 are planted to vine with around eight of these registered as Chianti Classico. The vines are between eight and 25 years old and are cordon-trained and spur-pruned. Fabio Burroni oversees work in the vineyards while Claudio Gori acts as consultant oenologist and Francesca Piazzini manages the estate. Despite the challenges of the 2003 growing year that produced both versions tasted of the Chianti Classico, the harvest has been masterfully managed. The basic Chianti Classico presents a lovely ruby colour and a clean if not particularly generous nose centred on ripe fruit with cherry and plum to the fore. Faint undertones of aromatic herbs complete the picture. The palate shows good flesh and marked tannins, a fresh acid vein and a lip-smacking finish that develops nicely. The deep ruby Riserva mingles tertiary aromas of leather and tobacco with notes of blackberry jam. The palate possesses solid body and confident backbone with close-knit, layered tannic texture offset by the balanced alcohol. The acid vein is refreshing and the finish is tasty.

● Chianti Cl. '03	ΨΨ	4
● Chianti Cl. Ris. '03	ΨΨ	4
● Viscardo '01	YY	5

SAN CASCIANO IN VAL DI PESA (FI)

POGGIO TORSELLI
VIA SCOPETI, 10
50026 SAN CASCIANO IN VAL DI PESA (FI)
TEL. 0558290241
www.poggiotorselli.it

Poggio Torselli stretches across the slopes in the municipality of San Casciano in Val di Pesa. Since 1427 the old villa that now houses the company headquarters has been known as Regina delle Ville (Queen of Villas). The current owners have returned it to its former glory after long, painstaking restoration, devoting equal care and attention to revamping the winemaking operations, with the support of vineyard managers Giovanni Colugnati and Maurizio Santoni, who also manages the estate. The highly experienced Vittorio Fiore acts as consultant oenologist. Of the estate's almost 42 hectares, 23 are planted to vine and 17 are registered as Chianti Classico. Sangiovese is the primary variety cultivated and yields the best selections. But from the wines presented for tasting this year, the ones that made the biggest impression are the Tieri del Fula '04, from pure cabernet sauvignon, and the 100 per cent merlot Ranieri '04. The first presents a lovely rich ruby colour and a wide array of aromas led by sensations of red berry fruit enhanced by touches of spice. Entry on the palate is good and progression substantial with well-integrated tannins, a refreshing acid vein and a strong finish. The Ranieri has a very dense appearance and mingles notes of forest fruits with hints of mixed spice such as cinnamon and vanilla. Entry on the palate is round, the tannins are fine and delicate and the finish lingers pleasantly. The Chianti Classico Riserva '03 is not so good, held back as it is by its tannic structure.

● Ranieri '04	🍷🍷	5
● Tieri del Fula '04	🍷🍷	5
● Chianti Cl. Ris. '03	🍷	5
● Tieri del Fula '03	YY	5

SAN CASCIANO IN VAL DI PESA (FI)

FATTORIA POGGIOPIANO
VIA DI PISIGNANO, 28/30
50026 SAN CASCIANO IN VAL DI PESA (FI)
TEL. 0558229629
www.fattoriapoggiopiano.it

The consistency with which the Bartoli family estate manages to win Three Glasses for Rosso di Sera is quite astonishing, especially given the relative size of the area planted to vine. This year, it is the turn of the '04. Hats off to all those who have done such a thorough job in the vineyards and the cellar, where oenologist Attilio Pagli oversees things with an eagle eye. The estate lies in the northern zone of Chianti Classico. In 1993, Stefano and Alessandro Bartoli acquired a semi-derelict farmhouse built at the end of the 19th century. The land that came with it was in equally parlous condition and the main task was first to restore the vineyards and then build a modern, efficient cellar. Today, the estate possesses nine hectares planted to vine, five of which are registered as Chianti Classico. The Rosso di Sera is obtained from a blend of sangiovese and colorino. Its opaque colour is the prelude to a wide-ranging, generous nose in which notes of forest fruits are followed by hints of mint, nuances of pencil lead and elegant sensations of medicinal herbs. Entry on the palate is gutsy and backed up by a dynamic, powerful body and rich tannic texture. Acid backbone adds savour and the finish is deeply satisfying. The Chianti Classico '04 also showed well, offering a variety of cherry-led ripe fruit with vague undertones of spice on the nose. The supple palate has sound character, smooth tannins, decent freshness and a sweet, lingering finish.

● Rosso di Sera '04	🍷🍷🍷	7
● Chianti Cl. '04	🍷🍷	4
● Rosso di Sera '03	YYY	7
● Rosso di Sera '95	YYY	5
● Rosso di Sera '97	YYY	5
● Rosso di Sera '98	YYY	6
● Rosso di Sera '99	YYY	6
● Rosso di Sera '00	YY	8
● Rosso di Sera '01	YY	8
● Chianti Cl. '99	YY	4*
● Chianti Cl. '01	YY	5
● Chianti Cl. '02	YY	4
● Chianti Cl. '03	YY	4

SAN CASCIANO IN VAL DI PESA (FI)

La Sala

Loc. Ponterotto
via Sorripa, 34
50026 San Casciano in Val di Pesa (FI)
tel. 055828111
www.lasala.it

Laura Baronti's estate regains its full profile with a mixed performance. The Chianti Classico Riserva '03 is excellent but the rest of the range is a bit disappointing. Still, this dependable winery simply needs to find its way back to the path of qualitative consistency from which it recently seems to have strayed. La Sala consists of 20 hectares, including 15 planted to vine, and around 12 of these are registered as Chianti Classico. Gabriella Tani looks after the cellar and Luca Socci takes care of things in the vineyards. The wine that reached our finals has an intense ruby colour and a nose that mingles notes of ripe fruit, notably blackberry and cherry, with fresh nuances of aromatic herbs and the odd touch of spice. The palate is round with well-made tannins, balanced acidity and rather a short but tasty finish. The Campo all'Albero '03, a blend of sangiovese and cabernet sauvignon, did not live up to expectations. Aromas centre on vegetal sensations, mingling grassy notes with rather muddled fruitiness. The palate is big with very lively tannins, quite pronounced freshness and a finish of decent length. The Chianti Classico '04 lacks clarity on the nose where sensations of cherry and faint flowery hints of violets emerge. It's too smooth on the palate and the hard elements are too assertive.

●	Chianti Cl. Ris. '03	TT	6
●	Campo all'Albero '03	T	6
●	Chianti Cl. '04	T	4
●	Campo all'Albero '00	YY	6
●	Campo all'Albero '01	YY	6
●	Chianti Cl. Ris. '97	YY	4
●	Chianti Cl. Ris. '98	YY	4
●	Chianti Cl. Ris. '99	YY	5

SAN GIMIGNANO (SI)

Baroncini

Loc. Casale, 43
53037 San Gimignano (SI)
tel. 0577940600
www.baroncini.it

The estate belonging to Bruna and Stefano Baroncini is probably one of the best-known and most successful in Tuscany and San Gimignano. It earned its place in this year's Guide with yet another consistent, well-made series of labels that pay tribute above all to Tuscany's great traditional varieties. We'll start our notes with a fine performance from Vernaccia Dometaia Riserva '04. A straw-yellow colour with golden lights, it offers a complex nose whose frank, fruity notes are lifted by tempting hints of vanilla and attractive oaky nuances. The full, velvety palate displays a refreshing acid vein and a leisurely, faintly bitterish finish. La Faina '04, a white obtained 100 per cent from slightly overripe trebbiano grapes, is always interesting. Lovely complex aromas emerge on the nose to suggest citrus fruit, candied fruit and flowers. The palate is reasonably full and develops softly with good acid backbone to end in a finish of medium length. The Vernaccia Poggio ai Cannicci Sovestro '05 did very well indeed. Straw yellow with green highlights in the glass, it displays notes of green apple with vegetal and flowery nuances. The palate is fresh and well-balanced but the finish is a bit weak. As for the reds, we again found them rather unassuming. The San Gimignano Rosso Il Casato '04 possesses good mouthfeel on the palate but lacks complexity. Of the Chianti Colli Senesi on offer, the San Domenico '05 is clean, fresh and fruity but the Brunello di Montalcino '01 from the Poggio Castellare estate is very good.

●	Brunello di Montalcino Poggio Castellare '01	TT	6
○	Vernaccia di S. Gimignano Dometaia Ris. '04	TT	4
○	La Faina '04	T	4
●	Rosso di Montalcino Poggio Castellare '04	T	4
●	S. Gimignano Rosso Il Casato '04	T	5
●	Chianti Colli Senesi Sup. V. S. Domenico Sovestro '05	T	3
○	Vernaccia di S. Gimignano Poggio ai Cannici Sovestro '05	T	3*
●	S. Gimignano Rosso Il Casato '00	YY	4
●	S. Gimignano Rosso Il Casato '01	YY	5
○	Vernaccia di S. Gimignano Dometaia Ris. '02	YY	4

SAN GIMIGNANO (SI)

TENUTA LE CALCINAIE
LOC. SANTA LUCIA, 32
53037 SAN GIMIGNANO (SI)
TEL. 0577943007

The stories of Simone Santini's genius and his growing fame as an outstanding producer of Vernaccia have inspired the wags among his friends to hang a notice proclaiming him the King of Vernaccia next to the signpost for his estate. Simone takes the joke in good spirit but does not allow it to go to his head, quite the contrary, in fact. He still strives to improve, setting his sights on ever more ambitious results. Simone cultivates his seven hectares of vineyard managed scientifically to rigorous organic methods, obtaining grape selections that undergo macerations on the skins and extended sojourns on the yeasts to produce wines full of personality. The Vernaccia Vigna ai Sassi '04 scored highest at our tastings this year. Its elegant complex nose offers hints of peach, flowers and citrus fruit with faint mineral tones. The weighty palate shows good consistency and the finish is fruity and lingering. Another well-made wine is the Vernaccia '05. Citrus-like aromas and notes of country herbs and green almonds herald a palate of medium density with a pleasant acid vein and good nose-palate consistency, rounded off by a long finish. Agreeable and easy to drink, the Chianti Colli Senesi '05 gives vegetality and hints of fresh fruit followed by a full-flavoured, supple palate. Last but not least, the Teodoro '03 from sangiovese and merlot starts out rather hesitantly with aromas of ripe fruit and dried flowers but then goes on to impress with its fine balance and captivating softness.

○	Vernaccia di S. Gimignano V. ai Sassi '04	▼▼	4
○	Vernaccia di S. Gimignano '05	▼▼	3
●	Teodoro '03	▼	5
●	Chianti Colli Senesi '05	▼	3
○	Vernaccia di S. Gimignano V. ai Sassi '03	▽▽	4
○	Vernaccia di S. Gimignano V. ai Sassi '00	▽▽	4
○	Vernaccia di S. Gimignano V. ai Sassi '02	▽▽	4
●	Teodoro '98	▽▽	4
●	Teodoro '99	▽▽	5

SAN GIMIGNANO (SI)

CASA ALLE VACCHE
FRAZ. PANCOLE
LOC. LUCIGNANO, 73A
53037 SAN GIMIGNANO (SI)
TEL. 0577955103
www.casaallevacche.it

We have nothing new to report from this estate, property of Fratelli Ciappi. The results of our tastings are identical to those from previous years and attest a level of quality that is good across the board. In short, we can't see a quality in either the wines belonging to the classic San Gimignano typologies like Vernaccia, or in the estate's most important products, for example the San Gimignano Rosso Acantho and Aglieno IGT, which are permitted to include international varieties such as cabernet and merlot. We'll start our notes with San Gimignano Rosso Acantho '03, a blend of sangiovese, cabernet and colorino that continues in pole position ahead of the other bottles from the cellar. Clean notes of black berry fruit, pepper and aromatic herbs characterize the nose. The soft, harmonious plate has smooth tannins and develops gradually but steadily to sign off in a medium-length finish. Aglieno '04, from sangiovese and merlot, is reasonably well made. It presents a lovely deep, compact ruby and the nose, although veiled at first, reveals aromas of fruit jam. The palate is sweet and full with balanced body and ends in a short, peppery finish. As for the Vernaccias, the best of the bunch is the I Macchioni '05 selection. It has musky aromas and notes of spring flowers followed by a fresh, lip-smacking palate with subtle hints of minerality. The Riserva Crocus '04 has a fruity, citrus nose and a round, not very dense palate. Finally, the standard-label Chianti Colli Senesi is a well-made wine that shows fruity, fresh and drinkable.

●	S. Gimignano Rosso Acantho '03	▼▼	4
●	Aglieno '04	▼▼	4
○	Vernaccia di S. Gimignano Crocus Ris. '04	▼	4
●	Chianti Colli Senesi '05	▼	2
○	Vernaccia di S. Gimignano I Macchioni '05	▼	2
●	S. Gimignano Rosso Acantho '00	▽▽	6
●	Chianti Colli Senesi Cinabro Ris. '01	▽▽	5
●	S. Gimignano Rosso Acantho '01	▽▽	6
●	Chianti Colli Senesi Cinabro Ris. '02	▽▽	4
○	Vernaccia di S. Gimignano Crocus Ris. '02	▽▽	4

SAN GIMIGNANO (SI)

Vincenzo Cesani

Fraz. Pancole
via Piazzetta, 82d
53037 San Gimignano (SI)
tel. 0577955084
www.agriturismo-cesani.com

Vincenzo Cesani gave us further proof of his skills this year, consolidating the quality of his wines, which maintain their solid links with their territory of origin. The estate's flagship bottle, Luenzo '03, gave a very satisfactory performance. Obtained from sangiovese and colorino, it is a very dark ruby with warm aromas of ripe fruit mingling with toasty undertones and hints of spice. The palate is soft and full but has a hard time unbending owing to the dense, rather ebullient tannins that curtail the length of the intense finale. The San Gimignano Rosso Cellori '03, a blend of sangiovese and merlot, is as reliable as ever. Clean, concentrated aromas on the nose recall forest fruits fused with notes of sweet oak. The palate shows good overall balance and a convincing, fruity finish. The estate's new wine, the Serisè '04 made from pure ciliegiolo, is well made. Its rich ruby red colour is the prelude to aromas of cherry jam and faint vegetal notes. The palate displays medium body, acidulous, juicy progression and a dry finish that is not terribly long. The Chianti Colli Senesi '05 is surprisingly good, showing fragrant fruit and a pleasantly enjoyable palate. Last year, we reviewed the Vernaccia Sanice '04 by mistake but this year it showed well on tasting. The palate is weighty and balanced, even if the finish is a tad short.

● Luenzo '03	🍷🍷	5
● San Gimignano Rosso Cellori '03	🍷🍷	6
○ Vernaccia di S. Gimignano Sanice '04	🍷🍷	4
● Chianti Colli Senesi '05	🍷🍷	3*
● Serisè '04	🍷	4
○ Vernaccia di S. Gimignano '05	🍷	3
● Luenzo '97	🍸🍸🍸	5
● Luenzo '99	🍸🍸🍸	5
● Luenzo '00	🍸🍸	6
● Luenzo '01	🍸🍸	6
● Luenzo '02	🍸🍸	6
● Cellori '01	🍸🍸	6
● Luenzo '98	🍸🍸	5

SAN GIMIGNANO (SI)

Il Colombaio di Santa Chiara

loc. San Donato, 1
53037 San Gimignano (SI)
tel. 0577942004
www.colombaiosantachiara.it

After some interesting results over the last few years, Il Colombaio di Santa Chiara put on a fine performance to earn a well-deserved place in our Guide. The Logi brothers, Alessio on the technical side and Stefano in the office, benefit from their father's experience and work under the supervision of expert consultant Paolo Caciorgna. They offered us a range of good-quality labels to try, chief among which are two fine interpretations of Vernaccia, the main variety grown in the hills of San Gimignano. Their 15,000 bottles of Vernaccia Selvabianca '05 have a straw-yellow colour with flecked with green. The nose alternates aromas of apple and flowers with faint mineral notes before the caressing palate offers attractive, edgy acidity and unbends to reveal agreeable almondy sensations. The Vernaccia Albereta '05 is matured in barrique and has a colour of medium intensity accompanied by lovely fruity tones on the nose. The palate achieves its full potential thanks to wonderful acid energy that acts as a foil to the balanced softness. In the finish, there is a varietal bitterish vein. The reds also show a skilled hand. Il Priore '04 from sangiovese and canaiolo is a well-made wine whose fruity bouquet is enhanced by spicy sensations. The palate is juicy and full-flavoured although the finish is not very long. The San Gimignano Rosso Colombaio '03 is from sangiovese with small amounts of canaiolo and colorino. It's not quite up to the same standard, however. The rather evolved nose has red berry fruit while the palate is reasonably fleshy with drying tannins.

● Il Priore '04	🍷🍷	4
○ Vernaccia di S. Gimignano Albereta '05	🍷🍷	4
○ Vernaccia di San Gimignano Selvabianca '05	🍷🍷	3*
● S. Gimignano Rosso Colombaio '03	🍷	5

SAN GIMIGNANO (SI)

Guicciardini Strozzi

Fattoria Cusona
loc. Cusona, 5
53037 San Gimignano (SI)
tel. 0577950028
www.guicciardinistrozzi.it

It's becoming increasingly difficult to squeeze the entire production of the Tenute Guicciardini Strozzi into just one profile. In addition to the ancient Fattoria Cusona in San Gimignano, the estate has production sites in the Maremma: Villa Le Pavoniere in Bolgheri in the north; Tenuta I Massi in Massa Marittima in the centre; Poggio Moreto in Scansano in the south; and Coste di Kuddìa in Pantelleria. Of the labels presented by the main San Gimignano farm, we particularly liked the sangiovese-based Sodole '03, which tends more towards elegance than extract-driven power. The medium-weight palate shows well-gauged tannins, acidity and alcohol. But although the Guicciardini Strozzi flagship wine is good, it is not outstanding. Obtained from sangiovese, cabernet sauvignon and merlot, Millanni '03 is a bit reticent on the nose, despite its prolonged ageing. It's more rewarding on the palate, where it shows good backbone and softness with tannins emerging in the medium-length finish. Both the Vernaccia Titolato '05 and the Vernaccia Riserva '04 put on a good performance. The former is firmly structured, nicely balanced and has a reasonably long finish while the second has a palate that is weighty and soft but a bit supple. As for the Maremma wines, the Arabesque '05 from vermentino is good, fresh and fruity on the palate.

● Millanni '03	🍷🍷	7
● Sodole '03	🍷🍷	6
○ Vernaccia di S. Gimignano Ris. '04	🍷🍷	4
○ Vernaccia di S. Gimignano Titolato '05	🍷🍷	3
○ Arabesque '05	🍷	4
● Millanni '99	YYY	7
● Millanni '00	YY	7
● Selvascura '01	YY	6
● Millanni '01	YY	8
● Sodole '01	YY	6
● Millanni '02	YY	7

SAN GIMIGNANO (SI)

Montenidoli

loc. Montenidoli
53037 San Gimignano (SI)
tel. 0577941565
www.montenidoli.com

When, over a glass of Vernaccia, Elisabetta Fagiuoli recounts the odyssey that led her into wine and her theories on winemaking, which go against the trend for standardization, what shines through most clearly is the passion she pours into vinifying the grapes from her vineyards to obtain wines that express the territory. In this task, Elisabetta does not have the support of that now ubiquitous figure, the winemaker. For her, the most important quality for a wine producer is the ability to understand and know how to interpret the vintage. This perhaps explains why her wines are different from everyone else's and display a typicity on nose and palate that may not be accessible but is certainly unique. The range of Vernaccias presented for tasting this year is very good indeed. The oak-aged Carato '02 caused quite a stir with our judges, who awarded it Three Glasses. The fascinating, concentrated nose offers sweet, fruity sensations and notes of honey set against a backdrop of flowers and hints of minerality. The sweet, silky palate has a measured profile and good follow-through, ending in a very long, lip-smacking finish. The Vernaccia Fiore '04 has notes of country herbs and ripe fruit before the palate shows decent acid backbone, balance and pleasantly bitterish undertones. The Vernaccia Tradizionale '04 is less invigorating. It reveals vegetal notes and chamomile followed by an agreeable if rather too fluid palate. The Chianti Colli Senesi Il Garrulo '03 is well made, soft and warm on the palate, which unveils tasty tannins.

○ Vernaccia di S. Gimignano Carato '02	🍷🍷🍷	5
○ Vernaccia di S. Gimignano Fiore '04	🍷🍷	4
● Chianti Colli Senesi Il Garrulo '03	🍷	3
○ Vernaccia di S. Gimignano Tradizionale '04	🍷	3
○ Vernaccia di S. Gimignano Carato '00	YY	5
○ Vernaccia di S. Gimignano Carato '01	YY	5
○ Vernaccia di S. Gimignano Fiore '01	YY	4
○ Vernaccia di S. Gimignano Fiore '03	YY	4

SAN GIMIGNANO (SI)

La Mormoraia

loc. Sant'Andrea, 15
53037 San Gimignano (SI)
tel. 0577940096 - 3482253904
www.mormoraia.it

La Mormoraia at Sant'Andrea has 90 hectares, 25 of which are planted to vine. The property belongs to Pino and Franca Passoni, originally from Milan, who pour great enthusiasm and energy into the business. They have created a first-class agriturismo and built a cellar equipped with the latest technology, plus a reception area for visitors. Annual production has reached almost 170,000 bottles but is destined to increase as recently planted vineyards go into production. This year, Paolo Caciornia joins the team as consultant oenologist. The estate already produces some superb labels but Paolo's arrival will undoubtedly inject some extra energy. We particularly liked the Vernaccia di San Gimignano Riserva '04 from the Mormoraia line, which has character, backbone and elegance. It reveals skilled use of new oak barrels and performed very well at our final tastings. Hot on its heels comes the Riserva '04 from the Passoni line with lovely balance and minerality. The Vernaccia '05 is fresh with generous flower and fruit fragrances. The Ostrea Grigia '04, a white obtained from chardonnay and vernaccia, is very interesting. It has elegant character and fresh notes of flowers with a tropical nuance and the palate is fresh-tasting and compact. The fragrant sangiovese-based Neitea '04 shows fruity flesh and richness of extract while the Merlot '04 gives berry fruit, vegetality and pencil lead on both nose and palate. Mitylus '03 from sangiovese, syrah and merlot is very concentrated, soft and pleasantly spicy. The Vernaccia Passoni '05 and Chianti Colli Senesi '05 are both sound.

○	Vernaccia di S. Gimignano Ris. '04	🍷🍷	4
●	Mitylus '03	🍷🍷	5
●	Neitea '04	🍷🍷	4
○	Ostrea Grigia '04	🍷🍷	4
●	San Gimignano Merlot '04	🍷🍷	5
○	Vernaccia di S. Gimignano Passoni Ris. '04	🍷🍷	5
○	Vernaccia di S. Gimignano '05	🍷🍷	3*
●	Chianti Colli Senesi '05	🍷	3
○	Vernaccia di S. Gimignano Passoni '05	🍷	3
●	Mitylus '01	ΥΥ	6
○	Vernaccia di S. Gimignano Ris. '02	ΥΥ	5
○	Vernaccia di S. Gimignano Ris. '03	ΥΥ	4
●	Neitea '01	ΥΥ	5
●	Neitea '03	ΥΥ	4

SAN GIMIGNANO (SI)

Palagetto

via Monteoliveto, 46
53037 San Gimignano (SI)
tel. 0577943090
www.tenuteniccolai.it

Unlike other estates, which have increased their vineyard area and bottle volume in recent years, Palagetto sticks doggedly to a prudent policy that aspires to quality. This year, we have several new developments to report. First, a change of management puts Sabrina Niccolai at the helm; second, the new cellar is up and running; and third, a new label has been released, Uno di Quattro '03, a San Gimignano Rosso based 100 per cent on sangiovese. It's a fine interpretation of the typology that doesn't rely on over-the-top extraction to impress but instead strives for harmony and elegance. Finally, the Sottobosco '02 has passed from IGT to San Gimignano Rosso. The nose offers notes of charred oak and wild berries while the palate offers full body, reasonable balance and tasty tannins. As for the whites, Vernaccia Santa Chiara '05 stands out for its rich aromas of ripe fruit, yellow flowers and measured notes of vanilla. The palate is sweet, full and firmly structured with a faintly mineral finish. Niccolò '05 is every bit as good. It has a nose of fascinating complexity and a substantial palate that is both nicely balanced and leisurely. The Vernaccia Riserva '03 offers flowery, minerally notes on the nose and a solidly built palate with nice acid backbone. The basic Vernaccia is an utterly reliable wine, giving freshness and harmony on the appealing nose. Nor does the Chianti Colli Senesi '04 disappoint with its fruity nose and stylish, layered palate.

●	San Gimignano Uno di Quattro '03	🍷🍷	8
○	Vernaccia di S. Gimignano Ris. '03	🍷🍷	5
○	I'Niccolò '05	🍷🍷	5
○	Vernaccia di S. Gimignano V. Santa Chiara '05	🍷🍷	4
●	San Gimignano Sottobosco '02	🍷	6
●	Chianti Colli Senesi '04	🍷	4
○	Vernaccia di S. Gimignano '05	🍷	4
○	Vernaccia di S. Gimignano Ris. '01	ΥΥ	4
○	Vernaccia di S. Gimignano Ris. '02	ΥΥ	4
●	Sottobosco '00	ΥΥ	5
●	Chianti Colli Senesi Ris. '02	ΥΥ	4
○	I'Niccolò '02	ΥΥ	4
○	I'Niccolò '03	ΥΥ	4
○	I'Niccolò '04	ΥΥ	4

SAN GIMIGNANO (SI)

GIOVANNI PANIZZI
FRAZ. SANTA MARGHERITA
LOC. RACCIANO, 34
53037 SAN GIMIGNANO (SI)
TEL. 0577941576
www.panizzi.it

A deep love of the territory and a great passion for viticulture, especially the challenging, testy vernaccia variety, are the secret of grower Giovanni Panizzi's success. His adherence to these principles and his quality-focused approach enable him to produce consistent vernaccia-based wines of an elegance and style that are quite distinctive in the world of Italian whites. This year, Giovanni did not present his Vernaccia Riserva. By way of compensation, the estate's newest product, Vernaccia Vigna Santa Margherita '05, turned out to be an absolutely superb wine, missing the Three Glass mark by a whisker. It has confident fruit with undertones of attractive, well-integrated oak. The palate is sweet, full and fruity with minerally, almost salty aromas, and the finish is long and leisurely. The new San Gimignano Rubente '04 from 100 per cent cabernet sauvignon put on a fine show, impressing with elegant notes of dark forest fruits, pepper and sweet spice. The palate reveals lovely flesh sustained by fruit and velvety tannins and a sweet, lingering finish. If these characteristics are anything to go by, this is a wine with a rosy future. Giovanni's standard-label Vernaccia '05 is always good. Aromas of flowers and aromatic herbs fill the nose while the palate is sweet, balanced and deliciously acidulous with a classic bitterish note in the finish. The cherry-led aromatics of the Ceraso '05 make it an excellent companion on those scorching midsummer days.

○	Vernaccia di San Gimignano V. Santa Margherita '05	TT	4
●	S. Gimignano Rubente '04	TT	6
○	Vernaccia di S. Gimignano '05	TT	4
●	Ceraso '05	T	4
○	Vernaccia di S. Gimignano Ris. '98	YYY	6
○	Vernaccia di S. Gimignano Ris. '00	YY	6
○	Vernaccia di S. Gimignano Ris. '02	YY	5
○	Vernaccia di S. Gimignano Ris. '99	YY	6
●	S. Gimignano Rosso Folgòre '01	YY	6
○	Vernaccia di S. Gimignano Ris. '01	YY	5

SAN GIMIGNANO (SI)

IL PARADISO
LOC. STRADA, 21A
53037 SAN GIMIGNANO (SI)
TEL. 0577941500
www.telematicaitalia.it/ilparadiso

Il Paradiso continues to make progress by leaps and bounds, expanding its vineyards and increasing the number of labels. Over the last few years, the total number of hectares owned and rented has risen to around 30 and average annual production is now at 150,000 bottles. But don't be fooled. The big numbers have had no effect whatsoever on quality. Quite the opposite. The decision approved by oenologist Paolo Caciorgna to vinify the grapes from different vineyards separately seems to be the right one. The result is prestigious selections such as the latest label presented, the cabernet sauvignon-only Mangiafoco '03 that earned a place in our finals. Its impenetrable ruby red colour announces intense notes of dark berry fruit and liquorice with hints of spice. The palate is concentrated, sustained midway by close-knit tannic texture, but the long finale that is slightly curtailed by its youth. The Paterno II '03 from 100 per cent sangiovese is an elegant wine that merges fruity notes with nuances of coffee and spice on the nose. The softness on the palate is contrasted by smooth tannins. Vinified from sangiovese, merlot and syrah, the Silicum '04 offers aromas of rain-soaked earth and pepper preceding a full, pervasive entry on the palate. The A Filippo '04 was not as invigorating as usual, showing less harmonious and convincing on the palate. From the whites, we liked the Vernaccia Biscondola '04 for its soft, lip-smacking palate and the pleasant Lo Cha '05 from pure chardonnay whose oaky tones are nicely integrated. The rest of the range is correct and well made.

●	Mangiafoco '03	TT	5
●	Paterno II '03	TT	5
●	Silicum '04	TT	5
○	Vernaccia di S. Gimignano Biscondola '04	TT	4
○	Lo Cha '05	TT	4
●	Chianti Colli Senesi Ris. '03	T	4
●	A Filippo '04	T	5
○	Vernaccia di S. Gimignano '05	T	3
●	Saxa Calida '00	YYY	6
●	A Filippo '02	YYY	5
●	Saxa Calida '99	YYY	5
●	Saxa Calida '02	YY	7
●	A Filippo '03	YY	5
●	Saxa Calida '03	YY	7

RAMPA DI FUGNANO

FRAZ. CELLOLE - LOC. FUGNANO
53037 SAN GIMIGNANO (SI)
TEL. 0577941655 - 0041792361784
www.rampadifugnano.it

Since Gisele and her partner Herbert decided to work full-time on their now organic estate, they have made great strides. Over the years, we have been pleasantly surprised by the consistently good quality of their wines. The estate occupies ten hectares of vineyards in the area surrounding the hill of Fugnano, which overlooks a picture-postcard view of San Gimignano's towers. As usual, it was the merlot-only Gisèle '04 that dominated the proceedings in this year's tasting. It is an intense, brilliant ruby with a vivid, reasonably deep nose alternating aromas of forest fruits and spicy notes with vegetal tones. The soft palate is medium dense with restrained acidity and tannins rounded off by good length in the finish. The Chianti Colli Senesi Via dei Franchi '04 is a pleasant wine with a distinctly sangiovese character. It shows lively acid energy and smoothness on the palate. From the whites on offer, the Vernaccia Alata '05 was once more the panel's favourite. The nose is very clean and offers fruity, flowery, vanillaed sensations with faint vegetal nuances. The velvety palate is well supported by fresh acidity and ends in a lip-smacking, leisurely finish. But the Vi ogni è '04 was not on top form. It lacks assertiveness on both nose and palate but is nevertheless well made and agreeable.

●	Gisèle '04	🍷🍷	6
●	Chianti Colli Senesi Via dei Franchi '04	🍷	3
○	Vi ogni è '04	🍷	4
○	Vernaccia di S. Gimignano Alata '05	🍷	3
●	Gisèle '01	🍷🍷🍷	6
●	Gisèle '97	🍷🍷🍷	5
●	Gisèle '00	🍷🍷	7
●	Gisèle '02	🍷🍷	7
●	Gisèle '03	🍷🍷	6
●	Gisèle '99	🍷🍷	6
●	Gisèle '98	🍷🍷	6

SAN GIMIGNANO (SI)

TERUZZI & PUTHOD

LOC. CASALE, 19
53037 SAN GIMIGNANO (SI)
TEL. 0577940143
www.teruzzieputhod.it

To the Teruzzi & Puthod estate goes the honour of having built up the reputation of the vernaccia variety worldwide. After 30 years of activity crowned with success after success, this historic winery has been taken over by the Campari group, bringing with a substantial dowry, given that in recent years production has topped one million bottles a year, quality guaranteed. We can only hope that Campari will not lose sight of what this estate represents for the territory of San Gimignano, Tuscany and Italy. Teruzzi & Puthod played a role in Italy's oenological renaissance and has been featured in our Guide every year since we started publishing, often presenting superb wines. This year's offerings did not impress us particularly but we'd like to think that it's a hiatus caused by the current phase of internal reorganization. The best performance came from estate standard-bearer, Terre di Tufi '05. Rather inexpressive at first, the nose opens out to reveal fine vegetal and flowery aromas and notes of attractive oak. The palate shows medium density, reasonable acidity and decent alcoholic thrust with a faint bitterishness in the uncomplicated finish. The Vermentino '05 performed well, the gusty palate showing fresh and full of flavour to end on a dry, pleasing finish. The Vernaccia Vigna Rondolino '05 has a delicate nose and a simple palate with rather too many acid edges. The Carmen '04 is goodish, nothing more. The nose is subtle and the palate well coordinated but it lacks complexity.

○	Terre di Tufi '05	🍷🍷	5
○	Vermentino '05	🍷🍷	3
○	Carmen Puthod '04	🍷	4
○	Vernaccia di S. Gimignano V. Rondolino '05	🍷	4
○	Terre di Tufi '01	🍷🍷	5
○	Terre di Tufi '99	🍷🍷	5
○	Terre di Tufi '00	🍷🍷	5
○	Terre di Tufi '03	🍷🍷	5
○	Terre di Tufi '04	🍷🍷	5

SAN GIMIGNANO (SI)

Le Tre Stelle
loc. San Benedetto
via Fonte di Campaino, 17b
53037 San Gimignano (SI)
tel. 0577944406
www.letrestelle.com

Le Tre Stelle has finally earned its long-awaited promotion to a full profile. This small, family-run estate was founded as recently as 1998, on the initiative of sisters Antonella and Donatella Rubicini, who are backed up in the running of the business by their strong-willed mother, Maria, and the sound advice of their oenologist father, Francesco Bartoletti. The sisters have 12 hectares planted to vine in good positions facing south and south-east at an altitude of 250 to 300 metres above sea level. The vineyards are planted at a density of 4,000 plants per hectare and Guyot or spurred cordon-trained. The wines we tasted were good and one or two, such as the Ciliegiolo '04, were particularly nice. This well-made red is the estate's key product and ages for a year in barrique. Its dark colour is flecked with purple and the concentrated, complex nose is rich in notes of berry fruit, with raspberry and blueberry to the fore, amid aromas of sweet spice, ground coffee and liquorice. The full, juicy palate has elegant tannins and a fruity, lingering finish. We also liked the merlot-only San Gimignano Doanto '04 for its fresh character and primary aromas. The nose reveals vegetal notes with nuances of pepper and sweet spice while the medium-weight palate has measured acidity and sweet tannins. It's extremely pleasant and drinkable. The ever-reliable Vernaccia '05 offers flowery aromas and hints of grated apple. The palate shows nice harmony and decent backbone, ending in a fresh-tasting, bitterish finish. The Chianti Colli Senesi '05 is fruity, round and nicely tannic.

●	Ciliegiolo '04	🍷🍷	5
●	San Gimignano Doanto '04	🍷🍷	4
●	Chianti Colli Senesi '05	🍷	3*
○	Vernaccia di San Gimignano '05	🍷	3*
●	Ciliegiolo '02	🍷🍷 (white)	5

SAN GIMIGNANO (SI)

F.lli Vagnoni
loc. Pancole, 82
53037 San Gimignano (SI)
tel. 0577955077
www.fratellivagnoni.com

There have been major developments on the Vagnoni brothers' estate. First, work is almost complete on the new, functional cellar that, from next year's harvest, will enable every phase of vinification to be carried out with greater precision; and second, grandson Antonio has been infected with the family's passion and is working in the business. He is already a wine man born and bred and his objective is to improve the estate's quality and reputation even further. The range of wines presented was, as usual, very good. We'll start our notes with the Vernaccia Riserva Mocali '04, still in pole position. It shows less oak than in previous years, its concentrated, seductive nose integrating aromas of apple-like fruit and flowers with attractive oak. The palate has nice flesh, balanced acidity and faint savouriness, leaving a lovely almond aftertaste on the back palate. The Vernaccia '05 is easy-drinking but full of character. The nose reveals fresh notes of flowers and green apple while the palate displays lively acidity, good balance and the classic almondy finish. The Vinbrusco '05 has a soft, dry, full-flavoured palate. As for the reds, the next few vintages will see some major changes. The two versions of I Sodi Lunghi, the '01 and the '03, are interesting. The '01 is mature and mouthfilling with velvety tannins but the '03 is cropped on the palate with tannins that have yet to smooth out. The Chianti Colli Senesi '04 is fruity and approachable.

○	Vernaccia di S. Gimignano Mocali Ris. '04	🍷🍷	4
●	I Sodi Lunghi '01	🍷	4
●	I Sodi Lunghi '03	🍷	4
●	Chianti Colli Senesi '04	🍷	2
⊙	Il Pancolino '05	🍷	2
○	Vernaccia di S. Gimignano '05	🍷	2
○	Vinbrusco '05	🍷	2
○	Vernaccia di S. Gimignano Mocali Ris. '01	🍷🍷 (white)	5
○	Vernaccia di S. Gimignano Mocali Ris. '02	🍷🍷 (white)	5
○	Vernaccia di S. Gimignano Mocali Ris. '03	🍷🍷 (white)	4

SARTEANO (SI)

Tenuta di Trinoro
via Val d'Orcia, 15
53047 Sarteano (SI)
tel. 0578267110
www.trinoro.it

Andrea Franchetti is an unusual sort of wine man who makes regular forays abroad. He lived and worked for a time in Bordeaux, the cradle of great French reds. There he gained a good store of experience, on the basis of which in 1990 he decided to buy an estate in Sarteano in Val d'Orcia, a zone with no great wine tradition. He planted his vines at very high densities, cultivating merlot, cabernet sauvignon and franc, petit verdot and several Italian varieties including cesanese and uva di troia. When they were first released, Andrea's wines achieved instant cult status, partly because of the limited numbers initially produced and partly because of their superb quality. Today, the quantities have increased and Trinoro vinifies about 80,000 bottles a year from its 30 hectares. More impressively, however, the quality has also improved. In 2000, Andrea turned his attention to Sicily where he produces some excellent wines on the Tenuta di Passopisciaro on the slopes of Etna. The Tenuta di Trinoro '04 is a fascinating blend of more than 80 per cent merlot, cabernet franc and sauvignon and petit verdot that repeats the last vintage's extraordinary performance to win Three Glasses. It is a dark, dense, opaque ruby with a complex, concentrated nose whose good depth reveals aromas of ripe red and black berry fruit, tobacco, bitter chocolate, coffee and spice. The palate is full bodied, dense and elegant, with excellent balance and length. The second wine, Le Cupole di Trinoro, is from the same blend. Cincinnato, a cesanese-based red, was not produced in 2004.

●	Tenuta di Trinoro '04	🍷🍷🍷	8
●	Le Cupole di Trinoro '04	🍷🍷	6
●	Tenuta di Trinoro '03	ΥΥΥ	8
●	Tenuta di Trinoro '01	ΥΥ	8
●	Le Cupole di Trinoro '02	ΥΥ	6
●	Le Cupole di Trinoro '03	ΥΥ	6

SCANSANO (GR)

Podere Aia della Macina
loc. Fosso Lombardo
58054 Scansano (GR)
tel. 0577940475 - 3343986357
www.baroncini.it

The estate owned by Bruna Baroncini and Franco Azzara has more than 50 hectares planted to vine plus a further 25 that they rent. Total production is close to 300,000 bottles and seems to have achieved a happy trade-off between quality and quantity. Witness the results obtained by the range of wines presented for tasting this year, wines that year after year demonstrate solid, consistently good quality. From sangiovese, ciliegiolo and merlot, the approachable Morellino Poggio Roggettone '05 is a minor masterpiece of balance and drinkability. Clear, rich notes of fruit emerge on the nose, while the palate shows lovely grip right through to the lip-smacking, intensely fruity finish. The Morellino Poggio Roncone '04 also gave a very fine performance. Obtained mainly from sangiovese with small amounts of ciliegiolo and alicante, it offers an elegant, very clean nose and a mature, juicy palate with good length. Victim of an extremely challenging growing year in the Maremma, the Morellino Terranera Riserva '03 from sangiovese and alicante failed to convince us completely, although it does offer a certain overall enjoyability. The nose is rather veiled and very warm with the odd hint of maturity, while the softness expressed on the palate's entry is gradually eclipsed by the rugged tannins that leave rather a bitterish sensation in the finish. The Labruna '04 from vermentino with a little ansonica is simple but well made. Less challenging in its ambitions, it shows good balance on the palate.

●	Morellino di Scansano Poggio Roncone '04	🍷🍷	4
●	Morellino di Scansano Poggio Roggettone '05	🍷🍷	3
●	Morellino di Scansano Terranera Ris. '03	🍷	5
○	Vermentino Labruna '05	🍷	4
●	Morellino di Scansano Poggio Roggettone '02	ΥΥ	4
●	Morellino di Scansano Poggio Roggettone '03	ΥΥ	3*
●	Morellino di Scansano Poggio Roggettone '04	ΥΥ	4

SCANSANO (GR)

Erik Banti

loc. Fosso dei Molini
58054 Scansano (GR)
tel. 0564508006
www.erikbanti.com

Thanks in part to the renovation of the vineyards begun in 2000, which has seen almost the entire 37-hectare property undergo high-density replanting, the quality of Erik Banti's wines has improved significantly. There is plenty of proof in the excellent results obtained at this year's tastings. The 15,000 bottles of the sangiovese and merlot Poggio Maestrino Anno Sesto '04 are excellent. The nose is complex, showing red berry fruit aromas swathed in sweet spice and pencil lead. The wine is also very full on the palate, showing powerful and generous but not excessive, with more fruit than spice in the finish. The Morellino Ciabatta Riserva '04 from 100 per cent sangiovese has an altogether different style. Produced in around 40,000 bottles, it boasts a more aggressive character but is every bit as fascinating as its stablemate. The nose displays the fruit's lovely freshness, offset by smoky nuances and slight hints of maturation. The palate is tasty and nicely acidic with a deep, lip-smacking finish. The Poggio Maestrino Le Spiaggiole '04 is held back by its notable concentration. This blend of cabernet sauvignon, merlot, syrah, grenache and petit verdot struggles to express its aromas clearly or unbend fully on the palate. It's available in around 7,000 bottles. The Morellino Carato '04, released in 80,000 bottles, is obtained mainly from sangiovese with small additions of cabernet sauvignon, merlot and grenache. It performed well, exhibiting crisp aromas and a no frills palate.

- Poggio Maestrino Anno Sesto '04 — 5
- Morellino di Scansano Ciabatta Ris. '04 — 5
- Morellino di Scansano Carato '04 — 4
- Poggio Maestrino Le Spiaggiole '04 — 4
- Aquilaia '95 — 4
- Aquilaia '96 — 4

SCANSANO (GR)

Cantina Cooperativa Vignaioli del Morellino di Scansano

loc. Saragiolo
58054 Scansano (GR)
tel. 0564507288 - 0564507785
www.cantinadelmorellino.it

The Cantina Cooperativa del Morellino di Scansano is one of the most important producers in the province of Grosseto. As well as owning around 40 hectares of vineyards, it has 158 member growers and its production is in excess of one and a half million bottles a year. Numbers aside, the Morellino winery has also achieved an excellent standard of quality and maintains it consistently year after year. The fine performance given by the range of wines presented for tasting this year is further proof. The Morellino Roggiano '05 and the San Rabano Riserva '02 are both made 100 per cent from sangiovese and are both confident in character. The real strength of the former lies in its clean nose, where crisp aromas of cherry are offset by faint earthy tones. It is lively on the palate with nice sensations and tasty tannins. The San Rabano Riserva has a fairly down-to-earth character. It is produced in just 7,000 bottles and aged for 24 months in big barrels. The nose exhibits flowery notes and some over-evolved nuances, but it's easy to overlook these as the wine enters the palate, where it reveals itself to be full-flavoured, rich and lip-smacking. Intriguing smoky notes flank the intense fruitiness of the Vignabenefizio '04, whose palate is lively and tasty. Morellino Sicomoro '03 was a bit under par, having come from a difficult growing year in Maremma. The nose is dominated by vanilla tones and the palate is held back by rigid tannins.

- Morellino di Scansano San Rabano Ris. '02 — 5
- Morellino di Scansano Vignabenefizio '04 — 4
- Morellino di Scansano Roggiano '05 — 4
- Morellino di Scansano Sicomoro '03 — 5
- Morellino di Scansano Sicomoro '00 — 5
- Morellino di Scansano Vignabenefizio '02 — 4*
- Morellino di Scansano Roggiano '04 — 4*
- Morellino di Scansano Vin del Fattore '04 — 4

SORANO (GR)

SASSOTONDO

LOC. SOVANA
PIAN DI CONATI, 52
58010 SORANO (GR)
TEL. 0564614218
www.sassotondo.it

As well as its dramatic range of temperatures, atypical in comparison to the rest of Maremma, Sovana's tufaceous tableland produces wines of a unique, immediately recognizable character. Carla Benini and Edoardo Ventimiglia have made the most of this distinctive feature by opting for rigorous techniques, such as the almost exclusive use of vines that were cultivated in ancient times, and organic farming methods. They seem to have made the right decisions, given the excellent results obtained over the years by Sassotondo's wines and this year is no exception. Despite the torrid growing year, the ciliegiolo-only San Lorenzo '03 shows all of its customary freshness and easy drinkability. The fruity notes are very clear, free from any hint of overripeness and rendered extremely fresh by undertones of spice. The palate too displays its distinctive style, showing elegant, assertive and effortlessly drinkable. From sangiovese and ciliegiolo, the Sovana Rosso Franze '03 is a well-made wine with ripe aromas and a concentrated, full-flavoured palate. The Pitigliano '05 is an original blend of trebbiano with a little sauvignon and greco di tufo. It is extremely pleasant with a clean, lively nose and an invigorating palate that gives nice acid verve and mineral sensations. The Sassotondo Rosso '05, a blend of ciliegiolo, sangiovese and alicante, is simple, coherent and agreeably grassy. The Numero Sei '03 from greco and sauvignon is full and juicy but a little over-awed by the oak. The estate has 11 hectares planted to vine and annual production of around 40,000 bottles.

●	San Lorenzo '03	▼▼	6
●	Sovana Rosso Sup. Franze '03	▼▼	5
○	Bianco di Pitigliano '05	▼▼	4
○	Numero Sei '03	▼	6
●	Sassotondo Rosso '05	▼	4
●	San Lorenzo '00	▽▽	6
●	Sovana Rosso Sup. Franze '00	▽▽	5
●	San Lorenzo '02	▽▽	6
●	San Lorenzo '99	▽▽	5
●	San Lorenzo '01	▽▽	6
●	Sovana Rosso Sup. Franze '99	▽▽	4

SUVERETO (LI)

LORELLA AMBROSINI

LOC. TABARO, 96
57028 SUVERETO (LI)
TEL. 0565829301

Lorella Ambrosini missed the Three Glass mark yet again, this time by a whisker. Nevertheless, Riflesso Antico '04 is still one of the best versions to come out over the last few years, demonstrating that the estate is growing and moving inexorably towards greater quality. Without a doubt, the generous growing year of 2004 played its part but it was skilfully interpreted in the cellar under the expert guidance of Lorenzo Landi. The wine is obtained from 100 per cent montepulciano and presents a complex nose that is deep and eloquent, intermingling sweet sensations of ripe fruit with balsamic, spicy notes. The full palate has tight-knit, velvety, elegant tannins, measured acid balance and a very long, fruity finish with hints of liquorice. The Val di Cornia Rosso Subertum '04 is less successful. It is obtained from a blend of merlot and syrah in equal parts with 20 per cent petit verdot. The nose is young and complex, offering clear notes of dark forest fruits and faint vegetal aromas and the palate is quite dense, soft and at times juicy, with a fluent progression of medium length. The Val di Cornia Rosso Tabarò '05 never lets us down. It has intense vegetal and spice aromas with earthy nuances and although it may be a bit simple on the palate, it is very well made.

●	Riflesso Antico '04	▼▼	6
●	Val di Cornia Subertum '04	▼	5
●	Val di Cornia Rosso Tabarò '05	▼	4
●	Val di Cornia Subertum '00	▽▽	6
●	Riflesso Antico '01	▽▽	7
●	Riflesso Antico '02	▽▽	6
●	Riflesso Antico '03	▽▽	7
●	Val di Cornia Subertum '01	▽▽	7
●	Val di Cornia Subertum '03	▽▽	7
●	Subertum '99	▽▽	6

SUVERETO (LI)

BULICHELLA

LOC. BULICHELLA, 131
57028 SUVERETO (LI)
TEL. 0565829892
www.bulichella.it

This beautiful estate lies 600 or 700 metres as the crow flies from Montepeloso, one of the most wine-friendly subzones in Val di Cornia. For several years now, it has been working steadily on improving the quality of its production to obtain an increasingly elegant range of wines. To this end, the estate made the drastic decision to skip the 2003 vintage completely as it was not deemed to be of good enough quality. That's why our panel was presented with an array of '04s to taste. But that's not all. Starting this year, the estate's major products, Tuscanio and Coldipietrerosse, will be presented in alternate years. This time round, it was the Coldipietrerosse '04 that garnered highest acclaim for its perfect nose-palate consistency. This blend of 80 per cent cabernet sauvignon and 20 per cent merlot possesses a deep, dark colour and penetrating aromas of red berry fruit enhanced by undertones of spice, balsam and attractive oak. The full, invigorating palate has enveloping tannins and a long, rather intense, finish of spice and fruit. The Val di Cornia Rosso Rubino '05 showed well, too. Crisp, fruity aromas are backed up by flowery sensations on the nose, while the young, fresh-tasting palate displays decent tannic structure, coherent progression and a pleasant finish. The vermentino-based Tuscanio '05 is another well-made wine with a fresh, well-balanced palate that leaves a light, agreeable bitterish aftertaste. And we very much liked the Aleatico '05, a real treat of seductive sweetness for those who are fortunate enough to secure one of its 700 bottles.

●	Val di Cornia Col di Pietre Rosse '04	🍷🍷	7
●	Val di Cornia Aleatico '05	🍷🍷	6
○	Val di Cornia Bianco Tuscanio '05	🍷	4
●	Val di Cornia Rosso Rubino '05	🍷	4
●	Val di Cornia Col di Pietre Rosse '00	🍷🍷	6
●	Val di Cornia Rosso Tuscanio '00	🍷🍷	6
●	Val di Cornia Col di Pietre Rosse '01	🍷🍷	6
●	Val di Cornia Rosso Tuscanio '01	🍷🍷	6
●	Val di Cornia Col di Pietre Rosse '02	🍷🍷	7
●	Val di Cornia Rosso Tuscanio '02	🍷🍷	6

SUVERETO (LI)

GUALDO DEL RE

LOC. NOTRI, 77
57028 SUVERETO (LI)
TEL. 0565829888
www.gualdodelre.it

Long-time grower and member of that hallowed Olympus of the territory's finest producers Nico Rossi inexplicably seems to have veered off course in recent years. He continues to offer well-made wines but to our mind, they don't really do justice to the full potential of this estate. We assume that Nico is just having a bit of an off period and are sure that he will have taken steps to remedy this situation. Of the range he presented for tasting this year, the Federico I '04 and the Gualdo del Re '04 show the most confidence and personality. The former, from cabernet sauvignon only, has a concentrated nose revealing hints of forest fruits and spicy, toasty notes. The juicy, fruity palate reveals nice round tannins and a long, fruity finish. The second, from pure sangiovese, has a deep, intense ruby hue. Varietal notes of violets and cherries form a perfect union with spicy, smoky tones on the nose. The full palate is buttressed and shaped by tight-knit tannic texture, and the lip-smacking finish is leisurely. Perhaps because of its youth, the Rennero '04, the jewel in the estate's crown, is not altogether convincing. As yet, its toasty, spicy aromas have not integrated with the varietal notes. On the palate, its vigour and power promise well but are still very unbalanced. The whites are nice, including the Vermentino Valentina '05, Eliseo Bianco '05 and Strale '04 obtained from pinot bianco. The Aleatico Amansio '05 offers notes of plum and black cherry and an extremely sweet palate with not much acid backbone.

●	Federico Primo '04	🍷🍷	6
●	Val di Cornia Gualdo del Re '04	🍷🍷	6
●	Val di Cornia Rosso I'Rennero '04	🍷🍷	6
○	Strale '04	🍷	5
●	Val di Cornia Aleatico Amansio '05	🍷	5
○	Val di Cornia Bianco Eliseo '05	🍷	3
○	Val di Cornia Vermentino Valentina '05	🍷	4
●	Val di Cornia Rosso I'Rennero '01	🍷🍷🍷	8
●	Federico Primo '00	🍷🍷	6
●	Val di Cornia Gualdo del Re '01	🍷🍷	6
●	Val di Cornia Rosso I'Rennero '00	🍷🍷	8
●	Federico Primo '01	🍷🍷	6
●	Federico Primo '03	🍷🍷	6

SUVERETO (LI)

RUSSO

LOC. PODERE LA METOCCHINA
VIA FORNI, 71
57028 SUVERETO (LI)
TEL. 0565845105

Brothers Antonio and Michele Russo, who hail originally from Campania, run this lovely Suvereto estate with the help of their families. They have 12 hectares planted to vine and only started bottling in 1998. The property is split between Podere Metocchina, the headquarters where vinification takes place, and the south and southeast-facing vineyards of San Giovanni and San Michele. In just a few short years, the Russos have earned a reputation for wines that offer good value for money. This year's range is particularly interesting with the estate's key products earning high marks. We'll start with the leader, Sassobucato '04, a 50-50 blend of merlot and cabernet sauvignon that went all the way to our final selections. It is opaque in colour and discloses notes of ripe fruit led by blackberry, blueberry and morello cherry, laced with spicy, balsamic nuances. On the palate it is powerful, showing concentration, measured acid energy and long, leisurely progression. The Barbicone '04 becomes an IGT this year. Obtained from sangiovese with splashes of colorino, canaiolo and ciliegiolo, it offers elegant, pervasive aromas and a fresh, caressing palate with balanced acidity and dense, lip-smacking tannins. We detected a slight lack of harmony in the extract that we put down to the wine's youth but the finish builds up well and shows nice length. One step below comes the Val di Cornia Ceppitaio '05. The fresh nose reveals fruity, vegetal notes, the palate is reasonably vigorous and strong, but the finish is rather held back by unripe tannins.

● Sassobucato '04	TT	5
● Barbicone '04	TT	5
● Val di Cornia Rosso Ceppitaio '05	T	4
● Val di Cornia Rosso Barbicone '00	YYY	5*
● Sassobucato '00	YY	6
● Val di Cornia Rosso Barbicone '01	YY	5
● Sassobucato '02	YY	6
● Sassobucato '03	YY	5
● Sassobucato '01	YY	5

SUVERETO (LI)

★ TUA RITA

LOC. NOTRI, 81
57025 SUVERETO (LI)
TEL. 0565829237
www.tuarita.it

Three Glasses has become almost a matter of course for Tua Rita, the foremost estate in Val di Cornia. Each year, its excellent, very territorial products conquer yet more fans worldwide. When you visit the cellar it's easy to see why. The stunning vineyard, dense and meticulously tended, that blankets the hill behind the cellar produces wines of great personality. The merlot-only Redigaffi '04 is one of the best versions ever, showing intense, embracing and very firmly structured. The vintage tends towards elegance and helps the wine to attain superb balance. The nose is a riot of aromas in which fresh notes of dark berry fruit, with blueberry and blackberry to the fore, hints of balsam and spice and smoky notes combine to leave no room for intrusive warm notes. Rather unexpectedly for this variety, acidity plays a leading role on the palate, which is full and concentrated but above all long, fresh-tasting and smooth. The ripe tannins are superb and already well-integrated into the structure. This is a wine that should cellar well. The Syrah '04 also excels. It has a wonderfully spicy nose but the tannins have yet to balance out, something that time will resolve. The Giusto di Notri '04 from cabernet sauvignon and merlot is very, very good indeed. Its full, confident, crisp nose sees fruit aromas and vegetal notes vying for supremacy. The palate is long and agreeable with a harmonious profile. The Rosso dei Notri '05, a new wine based mainly on sangiovese, is a personal project of Rita's son, Stefano Frascolla. The Perlato del Bosco '04 and Lodano '04 are both nice.

● Redigaffi '04	TTT	8
● Giusto di Notri '04	TT	8
● Syrah '04	TT	8
● Rosso dei Notri '05	TT	6
○ Lodano '04	T	5
● Perlato del Bosco Rosso '04	T	6
● Redigaffi '00	YYY	8
● Redigaffi '01	YYY	8
● Redigaffi '02	YYY	8
● Redigaffi '03	YYY	8
● Giusto di Notri '94	YYY	5
● Giusto di Notri '95	YYY	5
● Redigaffi '98	YYY	8
● Redigaffi '99	YYY	8

TAVARNELLE VAL DI PESA (FI)

Podere La Cappella

Fraz. San Donato in Poggio
S.da Cerbaia, 10
50020 Tavarnelle Val di Pesa (FI)
tel. 0558072727 - 3396233480
www.poderelacappella.it

There was a fine performance from the Rossini family estate that saw the merlot-only Cantico '03 in our finals again. Bruno Rossini acquired the property in 1979 and spent a few years selling his fruit before deciding in 1995 to vinify his own grapes. Bruno is now flanked by his daughter, Natascia, who looks after the commercial side of things while Luca D'Attoma acts as consultant oenologist. The Rossinis have eight hectares planted to vine and use organic farming methods. The finalist has a very intense colour and a complex nose offering a gorgeous mix of forest fruits, enhanced by hints of spice, notably cinnamon and cloves. Entry on the palate is full and embracing then the very elegant tannins integrate nicely with the alcohol. It's enjoyably fresh but if anything the finish is a little short. We very much liked the Idilio, a sweet wine with no declared vintage. It presents a golden colour with a wealth of aromas including sensations of ripe apricot and peach fruit with nuances of honey and hazelnuts. It's big and dense on the palate and has just the right amount of acidity to make it lively. The finish is long. The only sour note comes from the Chianti Classico Querciolo '03. Its cherry and plum aromas are very concentrated, but the tannins tend to dominate on the palate and curb its length. For those of a cultural bent, the estate has a small church, Santa Maria a Cerbaia, which dates back to 1043 and is open to the public.

●	Cantico '03	TT	8
○	Vin Santo del Chianti Cl. Idilio	TT	7
●	Chianti Cl. Querciolo '03	T	5
●	Corbezzolo '00	YY	7
●	Cantico '01	YY	8
●	Corbezzolo '01	YY	7
●	Chianti Cl. Querciolo Ris. '00	YY	6
●	Corbezzolo '98	YY	5
●	Corbezzolo '99	YY	7

TAVARNELLE VAL DI PESA (FI)

Poggio al Sole

Loc. Badia a Passignano
S.da Rignana, 2
50028 Tavarnelle Val di Pesa (FI)
tel. 0558071850 - 3358117306
www.poggioalsole.com

Giovanni Davaz's wines did not show the continuity that we had expected and failed to match the results attained in recent years. It's a real shame, especially in light of the fact that this estate has even won two Three Glasses in the same edition of the Guide. Our overall impression is that the quest for concentration and fullness has compromised drinkability. The biggest sins are a lack of balance and over-assertive tannins. Giovanni made a major lifestyle choice when he came to live in Tuscany. He left his native Switzerland and bought the estate from a well-known Florentine jeweller who, ironically, had made it famous above all for the white it produced. Sangiovese is now the main variety here but cabernet sauvignon and syrah are also cultivated. These grape types are vinified separately to obtain wines that represent the territory and know how to express its potential in different ways. This is the year of the Chianti Classico '04, object proof of what we were saying earlier. Clean, mineral aromas intermingle with notes of forest fruits on the nose and then the palate is full and balanced, with light tannins and a very tangy finish. The Riserva '03 on the other hand is cowed by the imposing tannins that fail to integrate with the solid, robust body. The finish is full of flavour and leaves a rich, savoury sensation. The Syrah '04 lacks balance because of an excess of concentration on the nose. It has ripe aromas but the palate struggles to unbend.

●	Chianti Cl. '04	TT	5
●	Chianti Cl. Ris. '03	T	6
●	Syrah '04	T	7
●	Chianti Cl. Casasilia '97	YYY	7
●	Chianti Cl. Casasilia '98	YYY	7
●	Chianti Cl. Casasilia '99	YYY	7
●	Syrah '99	YYY	7
●	Syrah '01	YY	7
●	Chianti Cl. Casasilia '00	YY	7
●	Syrah '00	YY	7
●	Chianti Cl. Casasilia '01	YY	7
●	Syrah '03	YY	7

TERRANUOVA BRACCIOLINI (AR)

Cooperativa Agricola Valdarnese
loc. Paterna, 96
52028 Terranuova
Bracciolini (AR)
tel. 055977052

We were delighted to award Three Glasses to Marco Noferi's estate for the Vignanova '03. Marco fully deserves the prize for the consistency of his wines and the unremitting work he has done over the last 20 years to preserve the territory. Paterna was founded in 1977 when a group of young friends decided to set up a co-operative winery and rent 40 hectares of land. Things changed in 1985 when they bought the farm and reduced the size of the estate to 15 hectares, where they cultivated vines, olive trees and various vegetables. At that time, they also went over to organic growing methods. Five of the hectares are planted to vine, mainly sangiovese and varieties native to the territory such as colorino, ciliegiolo and canaiolo. Marco takes care of things in the vineyards himself and Gabriella Tani has been brought in as oenologist. The Vignanova is obtained from a selection of the best fruit harvested from the oldest vines. The '03 presents a lovely rich ruby colour and has a classic nose of cherries, forest fruits, flowery nuances and mineral notes. The palate is nice and fleshy, full and fruity with silky tannic texture, a balanced acid vein and a long, sweet finish. All in all, it's a supremely drinkable wine. The Chianti Colli Aretini '04 is simpler and offers fresh aromas, notably of morello cherry and violet. The solid body flaunts tannins and a lip-smacking finish.

● Vignanova '03	🍷🍷🍷	5
● Chianti Colli Aretini Paterna '04	🍷	3
● Vignanova '00	ᗐᗐ	4
● Vignanova '01	ᗐᗐ	5
● Vignanova '98	ᗐᗐ	4
● Vignanova '99	ᗐᗐ	4

VINCI (FI)

Cantine Leonardo da Vinci
via Provinciale Mercatale, 291
50059 Vinci (FI)
tel. 0571902444
www.cantineleonardo.it

We have high regard for Cantine Leonardo, which manages to produce large numbers of bottles of decent wine at reasonable prices. That said, we would expect to find a little more character and passion in the important selections. The range of labels produced is extensive and some are rather good. The Sant'Ippolito '04, a merlot and syrah blend, made the biggest impression on our judges this year. Its compact appearance announces intense aromas of pepper and ripe red berry fruit. The palate is full and fruity with dynamic acid energy, tanginess and a fresh finish. On a similar level of quality is San Zio '04, from pure sangiovese, showing fruity notes on the nose together with spicy tones and unusual citrus-like nuances. The medium-density palate is consistent with smooth tannins, and develops pleasantly in the finish. The two new reds put on an interesting debut performance. Poggio del Sasso '05 from sangiovese has a solid base of ripe fruit on the nose and a palate displaying lovely tannic texture and vivid acid backbone. Ganzo '05, a 50-50 blend of sangiovese and merlot, charms with its lively acid backbone and fresh aromas. The Chianti Da Vinci '05 and Chianti Leonardo '05 are both quite well made, the former being soft and solidly built while the latter is simple and not very well defined.

● San Zio '04	🍷🍷	4
● Sant'Ippolito '04	🍷🍷	5
● Brunello di Montalcino '01	🍷	7
● Chianti Da Vinci Ris. '03	🍷	4
● Merlot degli Artisti '04	🍷	6
● Chianti Da Vinci '05	🍷	3*
● Chianti Leonardo '05	🍷	3*
● Ganzo '05	🍷	3
● Morellino di Scansano '05	🍷	3*
● Poggio del Sasso '05	🍷	4*
● San Zio '03	ᗐᗐ	4
● Chianti Leonardo Ris. '01	ᗐᗐ	4
● San Zio '02	ᗐᗐ	4
● Sant'Ippolito '03	ᗐᗐ	5

OTHER WINERIES

Fattoria di Gratena

loc. Pieve a Maiano
52100 Arezzo
tel. 0575368664
www.gratena.it

Fattoria di Gratena returns to the Guide, above all for its interesting version of the Siro '04, made from the grapes of a particular sangiovese clone. A complex, nicely firm wine, it has character and good ageing prospects. The Chianti Rapozzo da Maiano '04 is pleasant, too.

● Siro '04	TT	6
● Chianti Rapozzo da Maiano '04	T	4

Fattoria La Striscia

via Dei Cappuccini, 3
52100 Arezzo
tel. 057526740

Fattoria La Striscia continues the work of recent years with a new and impressive Occhini '04 from mainly sangiovese with some merlot. Plum, blackberry jam and spice on the nose precede a well-structured palate with prominent tannins and good acidity. It's a little ruffled but gutsy and sturdy.

● Occhini '04	TT	4*
● Occhini '01	YY	5
● Occhini '03	YY	4

Villa Cilnia

fraz. Bagnoro
loc. Montoncello, 27
52040 Arezzo
tel. 0575365017 - www.villacilnia.com

This Arezzo winery makes dependably good wines, though none stand out. The Cing'Oro '03 is tangy, earthy and rugged with well-judged warmth and a discreetly handled palate. The Chianti Riserva '03 is mature and warm on the nose but slender and edgy. The Vocato '03 shows the effects of the hot year.

● Cign'Oro '03	TT	5
● Chianti Colli Aretini Ris. '03	T	4
● Vocato '03	T	5
● Chianti Colli Aretini Ris. '01	YY	4

Villa La Ripa

loc. Antria, 38
52100 Arezzo
tel. 0575315118 - 057523330
www.villalaripa.it

Quality is steady at this Arezzo winery, which sticks to one wine for now, Tiratari from sangiovese with merlot and syrah. The aromas of the '04 are slightly veiled by charred oak but earthy hints and ripe red berries come through on the nose. The palate is consistent and well textured.

● Tiratari '04	TT	5
● Tiratari '02	YY	5
● Tiratari '03	YY	5

MALENCHINI
LOC. GRASSINA
VIA LILLIANO E MEOLI, 82
50015 BAGNO A RIPOLI (FI)
TEL. 055642602 - www.malenchini.it

The Malenchini family's good performance lacks the glitter we might reasonably expect from years of careful work. The cabernet sauvignon and sangiovese Bruzzico '03 made a good impression again with ripe fruit aromas and a soft, round body. The Chianti Colli Fiorentini '04 is also good.

● Bruzzico '03	🍷🍷	5
● Chianti Colli Fiorentini '04	🍷	4
● Bruzzico '01	🍷🍷 (white)	4
● Bruzzico '02	🍷🍷 (white)	4

CASA EMMA
LOC. CORTINE
S.P. DI CASTELLINA IN CHIANTI, 3
50021 BARBERINO VAL D'ELSA (FI)
TEL. 0558072239

No merlot-based Supertuscan Soloio this year but the Chianti Classicos performed well. The Riserva '03 is characterful with aromatic herbs and ripe fruit on the nose, and an appetizing, gutsy palate with rounded structure. The Chianti Classico '04 is a simpler and more approachable version.

● Chianti Cl. Ris. '03	🍷🍷	6
● Chianti Cl. '04	🍷	4
● Chianti Cl. Ris. '93	🍷🍷🍷 (white)	4
● Chianti Cl. Ris. '95	🍷🍷🍷 (white)	4

CASA SOLA
S.DA DI CORTINE, 5
50021 BARBERINO VAL D'ELSA (FI)
TEL. 0558075028
www.fattoriacasasola.com

Per Gli Amici is the winery's new, fresh-tasting and beautifully drinkable wine, a sort of old-style Chianti with white grapes included in the blend. The cabernet, merlot and sangiovese Montarsiccio '01 is very good, and we also enjoyed the Chianti Classico '04.

● Montarsiccio '01	🍷🍷	6
● Chianti Cl. '04	🍷	4
● Per gli Amici '04	🍷	3

LE FILIGARE
LOC. LE FILIGARE
VIA SICELLE, 35
50020 BARBERINO VAL D'ELSA (FI)
TEL. 0558072796 - www.lefiligare.it

There were gratifying results for Carlo Burchi, even without the winery's Supertuscan, Pietro. The best results came from the rounded, fruity Chianti Classico Lorenzo '04. The Riserva '03 Maria Vittoria is held back by tannin while the Chianti Classico '04 is well typed and nicely drinkable.

● Chianti Cl. Lorenzo '04	🍷🍷	5
● Chianti Cl. Maria Vittoria Ris. '03	🍷	6
● Chianti Cl. '04	🍷	5
● Chianti Cl. Maria Vittoria Ris. '99	🍷🍷 (white)	6

PASOLINI DALL'ONDA
P.ZZA MAZZINI, 10
50021 BARBERINO VAL D'ELSA (FI)
TEL. 0558075019 - 0558066284
www.pasolinidallonda.com

This family also owns property in Emilia Romagna. After many years, they are back in the Guide with a good performance from the Chianti Classico Sicelle '03, with its complex, well-coordinated nose and flavoursome balanced palate unruffled by tannins. The Riserva Sicelle '01 is quite evolved.

● Chianti Cl. Sicelle '03	🍷🍷	4
● Chianti Cl. Sicelle Ris. '01	🍷	5

QUERCIA AL POGGIO
FRAZ. MONSANTO
S.DA QUERCIA AL POGGIO, 4
50021 BARBERINO VAL D'ELSA (FI)
TEL. 0558075278

Only one wine was presented, but we were impressed by the Chianti Classico '03. Its confident impact on the nose has aromas ranging from fruit to leather and animal skins the palate blends its tannins nicely with the alcohol. The nice vein of acidity lengthens the finish.

● Chianti Cl. '03	🍷🍷	4
● Chianti Cl. Ris. '01	🍷🍷 (white)	5
● Chianti Cl. Ris. '00	🍷🍷 (white)	5

LE TORRI
VIA S. LORENZO A VIGLIANO, 3
50021 BARBERINO VAL D'ELSA (FI)
TEL. 0558076161
www.letorri.net

There was a good debut from this Colli Fiorentini winery. The best wine is Magliano '04 with its subtle, aromatic nose and pulpy texture, well-judged tannins and sweet, pleasant finish. The Riserva '03 is also good, showing cherry aromas and a flavoursome palate. The Colli Fiorentini '04 is nice.

● Magliano '04	🍷🍷	5
● Chianti Colli Fiorentini Ris. '03	🍷	4
● Chianti Colli Fiorentini '04	🍷	3

AIA VECCHIA
LOC. CALCINAIOLA
57020 BIBBONA (LI)
TEL. 0586677147

The cabernet sauvignon, merlot and petit verdot Sorugo '03 sailed into the final tastings. Ripe fruit and garden vegetables on the nose usher in a round, lingering palate with slightly rigid tannin. The Lagone '04 is a pleasant blend of merlot, cabernet sauvignon, cabernet franc and sangiovese.

● Sorugo '03	🍷🍷	7
● Lagone '04	🍷	3
● Sorugo '01	🍷🍷 (white)	7

FATTORIA CASA DI TERRA
LOC. LE FERRUGGINI, 162A
57020 BOLGHERI (LI)
TEL. 0565749690

The Frollani brothers' winery made its Guide debut presenting a large number of wines, all good. The Maronea '04 stands out with a warm, enfolding nose and a succulent, enjoyable palate. The Moreccio '05 and the Mosaico '04 are a little affected by the oak.

● Bolgheri Rosso Sup. Maronea '04	🍷🍷	7
● Bolgheri Rosso Mosaico '04	🍷	6
● Bolgheri Rosso Moreccio '05	🍷	4

GIOVANNI CHIAPPINI
LOC. LE PRESELLE
POD. FELCIAINO, 189B
57020 BOLGHERI (LI)
TEL. 0565749665 - 0565765201

We enjoyed another very good cabernet sauvignon and merlot Guado de' Gemoli from Chiappini. The '04 has red berry fruit with grassy hints then a balanced, juicy, long palate although not huge in structure. The oak still needs to fuse in the lovely finish. The Felciaino '05 is nicely drinkable.

● Bolgheri Guado de' Gemoli '04	🍷🍷	7
● Bolgheri Rosso Felciaino '05	🍷	4
● Bolgheri Guado de' Gemoli '03	🍷🍷 (white)	7

TERRE DEL MARCHESATO
LOC. SAN UBERTO, 164
57020 BOLGHERI (LI)
TEL. 0565749752
www.fattoriaterredelmarchesato.it

The Fuselli family winery made its Guide debut with four wines, two of which are particularly outstanding. The cabernet sauvignon, merlot and syrah Emilio Primo and the Syrah del Marchesato, both '04. We also liked the Tarabuso '04 and the Emilio Primo Bianco '05.

● Emilio Primo '04	🍷🍷	4
● Syrah del Marchesato '04	🍷🍷	8
● Tarabuso '04	🍷	6
○ Emilio Primo Bianco '05	🍷	6

CASABIANCA
VIA FROSINI, 14
52021 BUCINE (AR)
TEL. 0559911265

This a first Guide appearance for Casabianca. The sangiovese-only Casino di Bellavista '03 is especially good with clean, crisp red berry fruit, light boisé hints and a balanced, tangily consistent palate. The Chianti Il Leccio and Il Rocolo, both '05, are simple, fresh and drinkable.

● Il Casino di Bellavista '03	🍷🍷	5
● Chianti Il Leccio '05	🍷	4
● Il Rocolo '05	🍷	4

Poggio Molina

Loc. Poggio Molina
52021 Bucine (AR)
tel. 0559789402
www.poggiomolina.it

The leading wine, the merlot and sangiovese Le Caldìe '03, is good again with deep, vibrant aromas of pepper and blueberry jam and a taut, dynamic palate that is still a little tight but echoes the fruit nicely. The tangy, well-coordinated Lo Scopaio '04 also impressed.

● Le Caldie '03	▼▼	6
● Lo Scopaio '04	▼	5
● Vinobono '04	▼	4
● Le Caldie '02	▽▽	6

Prato al Sole

fraz. San Pancrazio
loc. Il Prato,51
52021 Bucine (AR)
tel. 055992821 - www.pratoalsole.it

The range is interesting, especially Orexis '03, almost entirely from canaiolo. The nose is enthralling with floral notes blending with ripe fruit, hints of spice and well-judged wood. The focused palate is flavoursome and balanced. Pause '03 is warmer and marked by oak.

● Orexis '03	▼▼	4
● Plauso '03	▼	5

Cecilia

loc. La Pila - podere La Casina, 8
57034 Campo nell'Elba (LI)
tel. 024989864 - 0565977322
www.aziendacecilia.it

This long-standing Elba winery returns to the Guide with high-quality wines, above all Oglasa '03 from all syrah, which has a spicy nose and succulent, mouthfilling palate. Aleatico '05 shows good balance of acidity and sweetness while we also liked the Elba Ansonica and Zeta del Tucano, both '05.

● Oglasa '03	▼▼	5
● Elba Aleatico '05	▼▼	6
○ Elba Ansonica '05	▼	4
○ Zeta del Tucano '05	▼	4

Tenuta Monteti

s.da della Sgrilla, 6
58011 Capalbio (GR)
tel. 0564896160
www.tenutamonteti.it

We applaud an explosive debut for Paolo Baratta's 25-hectare estate. The complex, enthralling Monteti '04, from cabernet sauvignon, petit verdot, cabernet franc with some alicante and merlot, made it to the finals. The Caburnio '04 is a very nice blend of cabernet sauvignon, alicante and merlot.

● Monteti '04	▼▼	6
● Caburnio '04	▼▼	4

Fattoria Ambra

fraz. Comeana - via Lombarda, 85
59015 Carmignano (PO)
tel. 0558719049 - 055486488
www.fattoriaambra.it

Fattoria di Ambra performed very well. The Vin Santo di Carmignano '99 is good, with a dense but balanced palate. There is less focus in the Carmignanos: Le Vigne Alte di Montalbiolo Riserva '03, Vigna di Montefortini '04 and Elzana Riserva '03, which has a coherent palate with lively tannins.

○ Vin Santo di Carmignano '99	▼▼	7
● Carmignano Elzana Ris. '03	▼	5
● Carmignano Le Vigne Alte di Montalbiolo Ris. '03	▼	5
● Carmignano V. di Montefortini '04	▼	4

Artimino

fraz. Artimino
v.le Papa Giovanni XXIII, 1
59015 Carmignano (PO)
tel. 0558751423 - www.artimino.com

It wasn't a very thrilling performance from Artimino. The Carmignano Villa Artimino '04 is a bit too vegetal on the nose. The palate has good texture but is a little short. Carmignano Villa Medicea Riserva '03 is overripe with a medium-textured, tannic palate. The Rosato '05 is pleasant.

● Carmignano Villa Medicea Ris. '03	▼	5
● Carmignano Villa Artimino '04	▼	4
⊙ Carmignano Rosato Villa Artimino '05	▼	3

ARGENTIERA
LOC. DONORATICO
VIA AURELIA, 410
57024 CASTAGNETO CARDUCCI (LI)
TEL. 0565773176 - www.argentiera.eu

This winery made its debut thanks to a lovely performance from the Bolgheri Superiore Argentiera '03 showing gamey hints and red fruit with light torrefaction on the nose while the palate has elegance, with nicely blended tannin and good acidity. The Villa Donoratico '04 is also good.

- Bolgheri Sup. Argentiera '03 YY 8
- Bolgheri Villa Donoratico '03 Y 5

LA CIPRIANA
LOC. CAMPASTRELLO 176B
57022 CASTAGNETO CARDUCCI (LI)
TEL. 0565775568 - 3385263533
www.lacipriana.it

This winery, owned by the Fabiani brothers, only uses grapes grown on the estate. Alberto Antonini is the consultant winemaker. The Bolgheri Superiore San Martino '03 has beautiful acidity although the tannins are slightly bitter. The Bolgheri Rosso '04 and Scopaio '03 are both very pleasant.

- Bolgheri Rosso Sup. San Martino '03 YY 6
- Bolgheri Rosso Scopaio '03 Y 5
- Bolgheri Rosso '04 Y 4

GREPPI CUPI
LOC. GREPPI CUPI, 212
57024 CASTAGNETO CARDUCCI (LI)
TEL. 0565775272

This small winery northwest of Castagneto Carducci has one and a half hectares of vineyards. The Rubino dei Greppi '03 is a remarkable Bolgheri Rosso Superiore, impressively elegant with black berry fruit and vegetal and balsamic hints on the nose and a long, mouthfilling palate.

- Bolgheri Rosso Sup. Rubino dei Greppi '03 YY 6

VINI MELETTI CAVALLARI
57022 CASTAGNETO CARDUCCI (LI)
TEL. 0565775620
www.vini-meletticavallari.com

This winery, founded in 2002, has ten hectares of vineyards in several different areas. The Impronte '04 is very good. It has a fresh, vibrant nose with hints of blackberries and garden vegetables and a lovely juicy palate that is long and mouthfilling, if not huge in structure.

- Bolgheri Rosso Impronte '04 YY 6

MONTESALARIO
LOC. MONTESALARIO, 27
58040 CASTEL DEL PIANO (GR)
TEL. 0564954173

Mario Pasqui's smallish winery has four and a half hectares and produces 15,000 bottles per year. The Montecucco Sangiovese '04 is particularly enthralling with floral aromas and a tangy, not inelegant flavour. The Riserva '03 performs best on the palate. The Montecucco Rosso '04 is quite simple.

- Montecucco Sangiovese '04 YY 4
- Montecucco Sangiovese Ris. '03 Y 5
- Montecucco '04 Y 4
- Montecucco Sangiovese '02 YY 4

TENUTA DI BIBBIANO
VIA BIBBIANO, 76
53011 CASTELLINA IN CHIANTI (SI)
TEL. 0577743065 - 3355638962
www.tenutadibibbiano.com

It was a transitional year for this territory and traditional variety-focused winery. Generally, aromas are unclear and lack confidence. The standard-label Chianti Classico is enjoyable and the Montornello selection has assertive tannins. The Riserva suffers slightly from the hot growing year.

- Chianti Cl. V. del Capannino Ris. '03 Y 5
- Chianti Cl. '04 Y 4
- Chianti Cl. Montornello '04 Y 4

Concadoro

Loc. Concadoro, 67
53011 Castellina in Chianti (SI)
tel. 0577741285 - 0577740538
www.aziendaconcadoro.it

The Cerasi family gave as sound a performance as ever. The best wine is Riserva Cerasi '03, which is pulpy with good tannic texture and a savoury finish. The Vigna di Gaversa '03 has huge structure but lacks a little balance. The standard-label Chianti Classico is very pleasant.

● Chianti Cl. Cerasi Ris. '03	TT	6
● Chianti Cl. V. di Gaversa '03	T	5
● Chianti Cl. '04	T	4
● Chianti Cl. Ris. '01	YY	5

Tenimenti Angelini - San Leonino

fraz. San Leonino
loc. Cipressi, 49
53011 Castellina in Chianti (SI)
tel. 057780411 - 0577743108

There have been ups and downs here. The Chianti Classico '04 has impressive lively fruit and spice, well-balanced body with tannins nicely tucked in behind the alcohol and a lingering flavour. But the Riserva '03 is too concentrated, like the Salivolpe '01. The Tuttobene '05 is delicious.

● Chianti Cl. '04	TT	4
● Salivolpe '01	T	6
● Chianti Cl. Ris. '03	T	5
● Tuttobene '05	T	4

Podere Tramonti

loc. Tramonti
53011 Castellina in Chianti (SI)
tel. 0577741205

Podere Tramonti's progress is a little muted but no less interesting for it often presents characterful, territory-focused wines. We liked the nose of the Chianti Classico '04, where the aromas range from fruit to light sprinklings of spice. The palate is alluring and flavoursome.

● Chianti Cl. '04	TT	5
● Chianti Cl. '00	YY	5
● Chianti Cl. '01	YY	5

Villa Trasqua

loc. Trasqua
53011 Castellina in Chianti (SI)
tel. 0577743075
www.villatrasqua.it

It was a hesitant performance by the winery, supervised by Stefano Chioccioli. We liked the Riserva '03's cherries and wild berries with hints of leather and pipe tobacco. The palate is succulent, the tannins pleasant and the finish tangy. The Chianti Classico '04 is less complicated.

● Chianti Cl. Ris. '03	TT	4
● Chianti Cl. '04	T	4
● Trasgaia '01	YY	5
● Chianti Cl. '03	YY	4

Borgo Scopeto

loc. Vagliagli
53010 Castelnuovo Berardenga (SI)
tel. 0577848390
www.borgoscopeto.com

We were a little disappointed by the performance of Elisabetta Gnudi Angelini's winery. The Riserva we had to forgo last year was not up to our expectations. It lacks balance in the mouth, where the harder elements are too prominent. The Chianti Classico '04 is very enjoyable drinking, though.

● Chianti Cl. Ris. '03	T	5
● Chianti Cl. '04	T	4
● Chianti Cl. '03	YY	4
● Borgonero '01	YY	6

Fattorie Chigi Saracini

via dell'Arbia, 2
53019 Castelnuovo Berardenga (SI)
tel. 0577355113

This year's results matched last year's at the Monte dei Paschi di Siena bank's winery. The Poggiassai '04 gives prominent charred oak with hints of wild berries. The palate is soft and pleasantly lingering. The Chianti '05 is fresh and appetizing with assertive aromas and excellent flavour.

● Poggiassai '04	TT	5
● Chianti Villa Chigi '05	T	3
● Poggiassai '01	YYY	5
● Poggiassai '02	YY	5

Fornaci di Sotto

loc. Fornaci di Sotto
53019 Castelnuovo Berardenga (SI)
tel. 0577355011

The Chianti Colli Senesi '05 from mainly sangiovese with some cabernet sauvignon is a super wine with outstanding personality and a textbook sensory profile. The winery is also small, with just two hectares of vineyards yielding around 10,000 bottles per year overall.

● Chianti Colli Senesi '05	🍷🍷	3

Pietro e Paolo Losi

fraz. Vagliagli
loc. Pontignanello, 6
53010 Castelnuovo Berardenga (SI)
tel. 0577356842 - 3388672185

The Losi family's winery gave a less impressive performance this year. The Riserva, with its mellow tannic weave, is better than the Millenium selection; both are '03s. The Chianti Classico '04 is slim-bodied with marked acidity. The Vin Santo '97 is not particularly well defined.

● Chianti Cl. Ris. '03	🍷🍷	5
● Chianti Cl. Millenium Ris. '03	🍷	6
● Chianti Cl. '04	🍷	4
○ Vin Santo del Chianti Cl. '97	🍷	5

Cacciagrande

loc. Tirli
s.da Ampio-Tirli
58040 Castiglione della Pescaia (GR)
tel. 0564944168

Bruno Tuccio's winery returns to the Guide after a year with three nice, weighty wines. Cortigiano '05 from syrah and petit verdot has a spicy nose and tangy palate. The syrah and merlot Castiglione '04 is complex with firm follow-through on the palate. The Monteregio '05 is well made.

● Castiglione '04	🍷🍷	6
● Cortigiano '05	🍷🍷	5
● Monteregio di Massa Marittima Rosso '05	🍷	4

Di Fonti

via San Martino a Maiano, 35
50052 Certaldo (FI)
tel. 0571669438
www.agricoladifonti.it

A middling performance put this winery among the short profiles. The best wine is the syrah-only Amorosa Visione '03 with alluring aromas and a succulent, lingering palate. The cabernet sauvignon Il Moro '03 and the Fontirosso '03, from sangiovese, syrah and cabernet sauvignon, are both good.

● Amorosa Visione '03	🍷🍷	5
● Fontirosso '03	🍷	5
● Il Moro '03	🍷	6
● Il Moro '01	🍷🍷 (white)	6

Fattoria di Fiano

loc. Fiano - via Firenze, 11
50050 Certaldo (FI)
tel. 0571669048
www.fattoriadifiano.it

Fattoria di Fiano's wines are less interesting this year. The best is still the Fianesco '04, from mainly sangiovese with dashes of merlot, syrah and colorino. It's soft, fairly dense and supple in the finish. The Chianti Colli Fiorentinis are all enjoyable.

● Fianesco '04	🍷🍷	6
● Chianti Colli Fiorentini '04	🍷	4
● Chianti Colli Fiorentini Ris. '04	🍷	5
● Fianesco '03	🍷🍷 (white)	6

Tenuta della Luia

via Trento, 32
50052 Certaldo (FI)
tel. 3683690957

There was a nice debut from Tenuta della Luia, thanks to the wine of the same name, Luia, a 50-50 blend of merlot and cabernet sauvignon. We tasted three vintages – 2001, 2003 and 2004 – and liked the last one best. It's richly extracted, mouthfilling and has a good long flavour.

● Luia '04	🍷🍷	6
● Luia '01	🍷	6
● Luia '03	🍷	6

Colle Santa Mustiola
via delle Torri, 86a
53043 Chiusi (SI)
tel. 057820525

Fabio Cenni works four hectares of sangiovese with a little colorino at the edge, which is included in the winery's only wine, the Poggio ai Chiari blend. The '04 version shows that this genuine, characterful red that can hold its own against great Sangioveses from classic areas.

● Poggio ai Chiari '04	▼▼	7
● Poggio ai Chiari '01	▽▽	7
● Poggio ai Chiari '02	▽▽	7
● Poggio ai Chiari '03	▽▽	7

Ficomontanino
loc. Ficomontanino
53043 Chiusi (SI)
tel. 0578821180 - 065561283
www.agricolaficomontanino.it

The cabernet sauvignon Lucumone shows a solid tasting profile and although it is from a less than thrilling year, the '03 has distinctively clean aromas and nicely gauged flavour. The Colli Senesi Tutlus '04 is also good and the Chianti Colli Senesi '05 is approachable and enjoyable.

● Lucumone '03	▼▼	6
● Chianti Colli Senesi Tutulus '04	▼	5
● Chianti Colli Senesi '05	▼	4
● Lucumone '02	▽▽	5

Salustri
fraz. Poggi del Sasso
loc. La Cava
58040 Cinigiano (GR)
tel. 0564990529 - www.salustri.it

Lovely delicate aromas and excellent texture are the distinctive features of the Grotte Rosse '04 which took it to the final tastings. This monovarietal Sangiovese in 5,000 bottles aged in barrique for 18 months. The Montecucco Sangiovese Santa Marta '04 is a little huskier and rugged.

● Montecucco Grotte Rosse '04	▼▼	6
● Montecucco Santa Marta '04	▼	5
● Montecucco Grotte Rosse '02	▽▽	6
● Montecucco Marleo '04	▽▽	4

Fattoria Il Palagio
fraz. Castel San Gimignano
loc. Il Palagio
53030 Colle di Val d'Elsa (SI)
tel. 0577953004 - www.ilpalagio.it

The best wine in the range this year is the Sauvignon '05 for its varietal typicity on the nose and the dense, well-balanced palate. Floral aromas blend with bananas in the '05 Chardonnay, with a good mouthfilling palate and sharp notes in the finish. The Vernaccia '05 is fresh but a little lean.

○ Il Palagio Sauvignon '05	▼▼	4
● Chianti Colli Senesi '05	▼	3
○ Il Palagio Chardonnay '05	▼	4
○ Vernaccia di S. Gimignano '05	▼	3

Riccardo Baracchi
loc. Camucia - via Cegliolo, 21
52042 Cortona (AR)
tel. 0575612679
www.baracchiwinery.com

This Cortona winery always presents a good range of technically well-made wines. The Ardito '03 from syrah and cabernet is mature, dense, warm and weighty. The Cortona Smeriglio Sangiovese '04 is less distinct, showing spicier and more mouthfilling than the soft, simple, sweet-toned Merlot.

● Ardito '03	▼▼	6
● Cortona Smeriglio Merlot '04	▼▼	5
● Cortona Smeriglio Sangiovese '04	▼▼	5
○ Astore '05	▼	4

Podere Il Castagno
loc. Il Castagno
52040 Cortona (AR)
tel. 063223541

The 2004 is the second version of Il Castagno's Syrah and it is already considered one of the most interesting wines from the Cortona area. Strongly spicy aromas meld with oak-derived nuances and a soft, well-structured palate, which is slightly stiff in the finish.

● Cortona Syrah '04	▼▼	5
● Cortona Syrah '03	▽▽	5

Il Grillesino

b.go degli Albizi, 14
50122 Firenze
tel. 055243101 - 055245012
www.compagniadelvino.it

Il Grillesino wines are well made with a nice clean palate. Ceccante '04 impressed with fruity balsamic aromas and a lively palate. The juicy, approachable Morellino '05 is also good. The Morellino Riserva '04 is a little edgy and tight. The Ciliegiolo '05 is fresh and straightforward.

●	Ceccante '04	▼▼	6
●	Morellino di Scansano '05	▼▼	4
●	Morellino di Scansano Ris. '04	▼	5
●	Ciliegiolo '05	▼	4

Fattoria Santa Vittoria

loc. Pozzo - via Piana, 43
52042 Foiano della Chiana (AR)
tel. 0575661807
www.fattoriasantavittoria.com

Whites produced the most interesting results this year. As well as liking two excellent Vin Santos – the cellar is a benchmark in the area – we were impressed by the well-structured, tangy and lingering Gaggiole '04 from incrocio Manzoni. The other wines are all good.

○	Valdichiana Vin Santo '01	▼▼	5
○	Le Gaggiole '04	▼▼	3*
○	Conforta '04	▼	5
○	Valdichiana Vin Santo Ris. '99	▼	5

L'Antica Fornace di Ridolfo

fraz. Castagnoli
via della Croce, 17-19
53013 Gaiole in Chianti (SI)
tel. 0577731038 - www.cantalici.it

The Cantalici brothers' winery is on form again. The very nice Chianti Classico Messer Ridolfo '04 has balsamic hints and light fruity aromas before the firm palate shows evenly distributed tannins, fresh acidity and a rising finish. The Chianti Classico '04 is also good.

●	Chianti Cl. Messer Ridolfo '04	▼▼	5
●	Chianti Cl. '04	▼	4
●	Chianti Cl. '03	▽▽	4*

Capannelle

loc. Capannelle, 13
53013 Gaiole in Chianti (SI)
tel. 057774511
www.capannelle.com

We were sorry to find the wines of this prestigious winery well below their usual very high standard. It's hard to see why, although the reds all showed over-evolved aromas and the Chardonnay had a one-dimensional nose and inexpressive palate. It's probably just a hiccup.

●	Capannelle '01	▼	8
●	Chianti Cl. Capannelle '02	▼	7
○	Chardonnay '04	▼	7
●	Chianti Cl. Capannelle '01	▽▽	6

Le Miccine

s.s. Traversa Chiantigiana
53013 Gaiole in Chianti (SI)
tel. 0577749526
www.lemiccine.com

Welcome back to this Gaiole winery and an excellent Vin Santo with honey and dried fruit aromas and a mouthfilling, warm, beautifully rounded palate. The Chianti Classico '03 is also pleasant with ruby red hues, evolved aromas of blackberries and plums and a juicy, taut, characterful palate.

○	Vin Santo del Chianti Cl. La Gloria '00	▼▼	6
●	Chianti Cl. '03	▼	4
●	Chianti Cl. '02	▽▽	5

Rietine

loc. Rietine, 27
53013 Gaiole in Chianti (SI)
tel. 0577731110 - 0577738482
www.rietine.com

The winery owned by Galina Lazarides and Mario Gaffuri returns to the Guide, mainly thanks to the performance of the Chianti Classico '03. Jammy aromas with liquorice spice precede a rounded palate with soft, flavoursome body. The other wines seemed a little tired.

●	Chianti Cl. '03	▼▼	4
●	Chianti Cl. Ris. '00	▼	5
●	Tiziano '01	▼	6
●	Chianti Cl. Ris. '99	▽▽	5

SAN MARTINO
VIA B. BANDINELLI, 13/17
53013 GAIOLE IN CHIANTI (SI)
TEL. 0577749517

It was a good showing by Aldero Montagnani's winery. The Riserva 2003 has good jammy aromas and the tannins fuse nicely with the alcohol on the enjoyable palate. The Chianti Classico 2003, which we reviewed last year by mistake, is even and uncomplicated.

● Chianti Cl. Ris. '03	▼▼	5
● Chianti Cl. '03	▼	4
● Chianti Cl. Ris. '01	▽▽	5

CASTELLO DI SAN SANO
LOC. SAN SANO
53013 GAIOLE IN CHIANTI (SI)
TEL. 0577746056
www.castellosansano.com

Calogero Calì also owns Rocca di Castagnoli. The Chianti Classico '04 has nice fruity aromas with light minerality, tannins and alcohol meld on the well-structured palate and the finish is juicy. The Guarnellotto Riserva '03 is tighter and the Borro al Fumo '03 has an evolved nose.

● Chianti Cl. '04	▼▼	4
● Borro al Fumo '03	▼	6
● Chianti Cl. Guarnellotto Ris. '03	▼	5

I SODI
LOC. MONTI IN CHIANTI
FRAZ.. I SODI
53013 GAIOLE IN CHIANTI (SI)
TEL. 0577747012 - www.agrisodi.com

This Gaiole cellar, which focuses on traditional wines, is back in the Guide. The Chianti Classico Riserva '03 is interesting with an enthralling array of forest floor and ripe fruit aromas followed by a succulent palate. The basic version is more drinkable and the Vin Santo is enjoyable.

● Chianti Cl. Ris. '03	▼▼	4
● Chianti Cl. '04	▼	4
○ Vin Santo del Chianti Cl. '99	▼	5
● Chianti Cl. Ris. '01	▽▽	4

PODERE CONCORI
LOC. FIATTONE
VIA PROVINCIALE, 1
55027 GALLICANO (LU)
TEL. 05836323092

Garfagnana winegrower Gabriele Da Prato gave us a lovely version of Melograno Rosso. Passion, biodynamics and good weather in the impossible vineyards of Podere Concori give this genuine wine an excellent nose and a seductive, well-structured palate. The Melograno Bianco '05 is decent.

● Melograno Rosso '04	▼▼	5
○ Melograno Bianco '05	▼	4

FERTUNA
LOC. GRILLI
VIA AURELIA ANTICA KM 205
58100 GAVORRANO (GR)
TEL. 0392847963 - www.fertuna.it

Ezio Rivella's son Luca manages the family's Maremma winery, which presented two stylish, well-made wines. We just preferred the Lodai '04, which has an elegantly fruity nose and very well-balanced palate. The Messiio '04 is not quite as good. It's got plenty of texture but is slow to open out.

● Lodai '04	▼▼	5
● Messiio '04	▼	6
● Lodai '03	▽▽	5
● Messiio '03	▽▽	7

CARPINETO
LOC. DUDDA, 17B
50022 GREVE IN CHIANTI (FI)
TEL. 0558549086
www.carpineto.com

Carpineto continues steadily on without high notes. The wines are more complex and well typed but a little detached from their territory. The Chianti Classico '04 is delicious but the two Riservas lack balance. Farnito '05 is less drinkable as the oak predominates.

● Chianti Cl. Prebenda Ris. '03	▼	5
● Chianti Cl. Ris. '03	▼	5
● Chianti Cl. '04	▼	4
○ Farnito Chardonnay '05		4

La Presura

Fraz. Strada in Chianti
via della Montagnola, 191
50027 Greve in Chianti (FI)
tel. 0558588859 - www.presura.it

We can report a good showing here, if less thrilling than last year. The best wine was the Chianti Classico '04 with its lively nose and firm but not excessive structure and tasty finish. The Ormato '04 seems a tad too concentrated while the Riserva '03 is slightly overwhelmed by hard components.

● Chianti Cl. '04	🍷🍷	4
● Chianti Cl. Ris. '03	🍷	4
● Ormato '04	🍷	6
● Ormato '03	🥂🥂	5

La Madonnina - Triacca

loc. Strada in Chianti
via Palaia, 39
50027 Greve in Chianti (FI)
tel. 055858003 - www.triacca.com

There was a bit of a hiatus for the Triaccas this year: one selection and the Supertuscan are absent. We liked the Riserva '03 with its fruit and pipe tobacco aromas and good pulpy palate with nicely blended tannin and alcohol. The Chianti Classico Bello Stento '04 is nice but a little too slender.

● Chianti Cl. Ris. '03	🍷🍷	4
● Chianti Cl. Bello Stento '04	🍷	4
● Il Mandorlo '01	🥂🥂	5
● Chianti Cl. Bello Stento '03	🥂🥂	4

Castello di Verrazzano

loc. San Martino in Valle, 12
50022 Greve in Chianti (FI)
tel. 055854243 - 055290684
www.verrazzano.com

Luigi Cappellini's wines put on a rather colourless performance. The Riserva '03 is the best, with typical leather aromas, a well-crafted palate and juicy flavour with a rising finish. The Verrazzano Rosso '04 is simple but pleasant while the Chianti Classico '04 has astringent tannins.

● Chianti Cl. Ris. '03	🍷🍷	5
● Chianti Cl. '04	🍷	4
● Verrazzano Rosso '04	🍷	4

Villa Calcinaia

fraz. Greti - via Citille, 84
50022 Greve in Chianti (FI)
tel. 055854008
www.villacalcinaia.it

Steady good quality but no outstanding peaks sums up Villa Calcinaia. The aromas reflect the territory in fruit that mingles with balsam and slightly unbending, extract-rich body. The Riserva '03 is better than the Chianti Classico '04, which has rather tart acidity.

● Chianti Cl. Ris. '03	🍷🍷	6
● Chianti Cl. '04	🍷	4

Podere Casina

fraz. Istia d'Ombrone
Piagge del Maiano
58040 Grosseto
tel. 0564408210

The Morellino '05 is very good with its clean aromas and a very drinkable palate. The Morellino Marchele '05 is slightly less expressive as the aromas are a little covered by oak sensations. The monovarietal Sangiovese, Aione '04, needs more time to develop for the palate is still clenched.

● Morellino di Scansano '05	🍷🍷	4
● Aione '04	🍷	5
● Morellino di Scansano Marchele '05	🍷	4

Val delle Rose

loc. Poggio La Mozza
58100 Grosseto
tel. 0564409062
www.valdellerose.it

Once again, the 2005 Morellino from this winery is one of the best in its category. A benchmark Morellino, almost, with clean, textbook aromas and dynamic flavour. The Riserva '03 is not far behind with its very spicy nose and flavoursome palate. The Cecchi-label Litorale '05 is well made.

● Morellino di Scansano Ris. '03	🍷🍷	5
● Morellino di Scansano '05	🍷🍷	4
○ Litorale '05	🍷	3

LANCIOLA
VIA IMPRUNETANA, 210
50023 IMPRUNETA (FI)
TEL. 055208324
www.lanciola.net

The Guarneri family are taking what we might call a pause for reflection. In the absence of their most famous Supertuscan, Terricci, the pinot nero Riccionero '04 made a good impression with spicy, wild berry aromas and a supple, balanced body. The Riserva '03 is passably good.

●	Riccionero '04	YY	6
●	Chianti Colli Fiorentini Ris. '03	Y	5
●	Riccionero '03	YY (white)	7

AZ. AGR. I FORNELLI
LOC. MALMANTILE - VIA GAVIGNANO, 1A
50050 LASTRA A SIGNA (FI)
TEL. 0558784558
www.aziendaagricolaifornelli.it

A good range of impressive wines has brought I Fornelli into the Guide this year. Bossù '04, from sangiovese and merlot, is flavoursome and close-knit while the Chianti '05 is pleasant, showing well-judged extract and balanced acidity. Both '05 Fontinos, Bianco and Rosso, are enjoyable.

●	Il Bossù '04	YY	5
●	Chianti '05	Y	3
○	Il Fontino Bianco '05	Y	3
●	Il Fontino Rosso '05	Y	4

TENUTA VITERETA
VIA CASA NUOVA, 108
52020 LATERINA (AR)
TEL. 057589058
www.tenutavitereta.com

Tenuta Vitereta's wines are all well styled and crafted, especially the Villa Bernetti '03. Dark, vibrant fruit with hints of pencil lead and minerals precede the densely textured, pulpy, flavoursome palate. The Trebbiano '04, made with a proportion of part-raisined grapes, has striking aromas.

●	Villa Bernetti '03	YY	5
○	Donna Aurora '04	Y	5
●	Ripa della Mozza '04	Y	5
○	Trebbiano di Toscana '04	Y	5

FATTORIA COLLE VERDE
LOC. MATRAIA
LOC. CASTELLO
55010 LUCCA
TEL. 0583402310 - www.colleverde.it

Consolidated steady quality, year after year, is the keynote at Colle Verde, a benchmark for fine Lucca wines. Brania delle Ghiandaie '03 is very enjoyable with seductive red berry fruit on a tannic, harmonious palate. The Nero della Spinosa is less focused.

●	Colline Lucchesi Rosso Brania delle Ghiandaie '03	YY	5
●	Nero della Spinosa '03	Y	6

FATTORIA SARDI GIUSTINIANI
LOC. MONTE SAN QUIRICO
VIA DELLA MAULINA, 747
55100 LUCCA
TEL. 0583341230

At last something new is emerging from Lucca's wine scene. Fattoria Sardi Giustiniani has fulfilled its potential with the merlot-based Sebastiano '04, which has breadth, succulence and lovely extract. The Colline Lucchesi Quinis '04 is fragrant and lively. The other two wines are pleasant.

●	Colline Lucchesi Quinis '04	YY	4
●	Colline Lucchesi Sebastiano '04	YY	5
○	Colline Lucchesi Quinis Vermentino '05	Y	4
●	Colline Lucchesi Villa Sardi '05	Y	4

FABBRICHE
VIA FABBRICHE, 2-3A
52046 LUCIGNANO (AR)
TEL. 0575836152

Fabbriche is a small winery in the Valdichiana hills between the medieval hamlets of Monte San Savino and Lucignano. We recommend the mainly sangiovese Camargi '04. It's a little reticent on the rugged, temperamental nose and the dynamic, well-structured palate is savoury and well extracted.

●	Camargi '04	YY	5

Poggio Brigante

via Colle di Lupo, 13
58051 Magliano in Toscana (GR)
tel. 0564592507
www.poggiobrigante.it

Poggio Brigante makes good wines. The invigorating, beautifully textured Morellino Arsura '04 has fruity aromas and a tangy, fresh palate supported by well-judged oak. The Morellino '05 is a little more approachable with ripe cherry aromas and a bright palate with very lively acidity.

●	Morellino di Scansano Arsura '04	TT	6
●	Morellino di Scansano '05	TT	4
●	Morellino di Scansano Arsura '03	YY	6
●	Morellino di Scansano '04	YY	4

Tenuta Poggio Verrano

s.da Provinciale n° 9 - Km 4
58052 Magliano in Toscana (GR)
tel. 0564589943
www.poggioverrano.it

There was a well-deserved place in the finals for Dròmos '04, from sangiovese, cabernet sauvignon, cabernet franc and alicante, the only release from Francesco Bolla's winemaking project in Maremma. Above all, it is elegant and balanced on nose and palate, with marked freshness and savouriness.

●	Dròmos '04	TT	8
●	Dròmos '03	YY	8

Montauto

Santa Barbara di Montauto
58014 Manciano (GR)
tel. 3383833928

There was an impressive Guide debut for the 12-hectare estate owned by Riccardo Lepri, a white winemaker at heart. The Sauvignon '05 is very good with fresh, tangy sensations and nice minerality. Bianco di Pitigliano '05 is floral, supple and very drinkable. The Sovana Rosso '04 is also enjoyable.

○	Montauto Sauvignon '05	TT	4
●	Sovana Rosso '04	T	3
○	Bianco di Pitigliano '05	T	3

Poggio Foco

loc. Poggio Fuoco
58014 Manciano (GR)
tel. 0564620537
www.poggiofoco.com

The Sesà '03, cabernet sauvignon and merlot blend aged for 18 months in barrique, gave a good account of itself, showing vibrant, well-focused fruit and a soft, sweet flavour with a slightly astringent finish. The tasty, drinkable Sovana Secondo '04 is also good, albeit obviously simpler.

●	Sesà '03	TT	6
●	Sovana Rosso Sup. Secondo '04	T	4
●	Sesà '02	YY	6

Fattoria Coliberto

fraz. Valpiana
loc. Coliberto
58024 Massa Marittima (GR)
tel. 0566919039 - 0566919337

It was an excellent year for Claudia Reggiannini's winery with its five and a half hectares of vineyards. Monteregio Thesan Riserva '03 got into the finals for its generous, clean aromas and robust, weighty palate. The tasty, succulent Monteregio Laran '03 is also very good.

●	Monteregio di Massa Marittima Rosso Thesan Ris. '03	TT	5
●	Monteregio di Massa Marittima Laran '03	TT	4

La Pieve

loc. La Pieve
via Santo Stefano
50050 Montaione (FI)
tel. 0571697764

La Pieve is proving a dependable winery whose wines are excellent value for money. The leading bottle is still Rosso del Pievano '04, from equal quantities of sangiovese and cabernet sauvignon. The Chianti '05 is quite decent and the Chianti Fortebraccio '04 is pleasant.

●	Rosso del Pievano '04	TT	4
●	Chianti Cl. La Pieve '05	TT	3*
●	Chianti Fortebraccio '04	T	3*
●	Rosso del Pievano '03	YY	4

La Valle

via Sanminiatese, 8
50050 Montaione (FI)
tel. 0571698059
www.agricolalavalle.it

The Bigazzi brothers' small winery made a promising debut. The leading wine is Mandragola '04, from sangiovese, cabernet sauvignon and colorino. Red berry fruit with clean hints of spice introduce its long, well-structured, tannic palate. The two Chiantis, '04 and '05 , are fresh and varietal.

● Mandragola '04	▼▼	4
● Chianti La Valle '04	▼	3*
● Chianti La Valle '05	▼	3*

Abbadia Ardenga

fraz. Torrenieri
via Romana, 139
53028 Montalcino (SI)
tel. 0577834150

This well-established cellar offers very good value for money. The classic Brunello '01 has aromas of tobacco, barley and liquorice on the nose and an elegant palate with dry but balanced extract and rigorously coherent flavour. The balanced, unassuming Rosso di Montalcino '04 is also good.

● Brunello di Montalcino '01	▼▼	6
● Rosso di Montalcino '04	▼	4
● Brunello di Montalcino '00	▽▽	6
● Brunello di Montalcino '99	▽▽	6

Brunelli - Le Chiuse di Sotto

loc. Podernovone
53024 Montalcino (SI)
tel. 0577849337
www.giannibrunelli.it

Gianni divides his time between his Siena osteria and his Montalcino estate, which turns out very fine wines. The Brunello '01 is excellent, showing florality with light oaky spice and classic cherry aromas. The very elegant, classy palate has yet to resolve its tannins. The Rosso '04 is also good.

● Brunello di Montalcino '01	▼▼	7
● Rosso di Montalcino '04	▼	5
● Brunello di Montalcino '00	▽▽	7
● Amor Costante '03	▽▽	6

Camigliano

loc. Camigliano - via d'Ingresso, 2
53024 Montalcino (SI)
tel. 0577816061 - 0577844068
www.camigliano.it

It was a transition year for the Ghezzis, who have now completed their lovely new cellar. The Brunello '01 is good with slightly estery aromas and hints of tobacco and leather emerging after aeration. The tannins are a little sandy and the wine lacks balance overall. The finish is nice and deep.

● Brunello di Montalcino '01	▼▼	6
● Brunello di Montalcino '99	▽▽	6
● Brunello di Montalcino Gualto '99	▽▽	8
● Brunello di Montalcino '00	▽▽	6

Campogiovanni

fraz. Sant'Angelo in Colle
loc. Campogiovanni
53020 Montalcino (SI)
tel. 0577844001

The solid Montalcino branch of San Felice, in Chianti, produces exemplary wines. The Brunello '01 is good, with warm blackcurrant and sour cherry jam on the nose and a flavoursome palate with glossy, pervasive tannins. The Rosso di Montalcino '04 is pleasantly fragrant.

● Brunello di Montalcino '01	▼▼	7
● Rosso di Montalcino '04	▼	4
● Brunello di Montalcino '97	▽▽	7
● Brunello di Montalcino '99	▽▽	7

Canalicchio - Franco Pacenti

via Canalicchio di Sopra, 6
53024 Montalcino (SI)
tel. 0577849277
www.canalicchiofrancopacenti.it

There are good signals from the Brunello '01, which has a vibrant nose of morello and sour cherries and a complex, nicely lingering palate with subtle, balanced extract. Il Bersaglio '04 is simpler but well typed, as is the Rosso di Montalcino '04 with its marked raspberry fruit and balanced palate.

● Brunello di Montalcino '01	▼▼	6
● Il Bersaglio '04	▼	4
● Rosso di Montalcino '04	▼	4
● Brunello di Montalcino '00	▽▽	6*

CANALICCHIO DI SOPRA
LOC. CASACCIA, 73
53024 MONTALCINO (SI)
TEL. 0577848316
www.canalicchiodisopra.com

A good area, reliable cellar and excellent territory focus have given us a good Brunello '01. Its inky colour ushers in a complex nose of vibrant, well-defined fruit that follows through well on the palate in an acidity and extract-led framework. The Rosso di Montalcino '04 is a touch too acidic.

● Brunello di Montalcino '01	TT	6
● Rosso di Montalcino '04	T	4
● Brunello di Montalcino '00	YY	6
● Brunello di Montalcino '99	YY	8

FATTORIA CASISANO COLOMBAIO
LOC. COLLINA POD. COLOMBAIO, 336
53024 MONTALCINO (SI)
TEL. 0577835540 - 3355248626
www.brunello.org

This lovely, all-woman winery is coming on nicely. The Brunello '01 is excellent, giving ripe blackberries, red berries and oak followed by impressive flavour, nice dense structure and restrained tannins. The new Brunello Atreus Riserva '97 is firm and vigorous. The Rosso di Montalcino '04 is nice.

● Brunello di Montalcino '01	TT	6
● Brunello di Montalcino Atreus Ris. '97	TT	8
● Rosso di Montalcino '04	T	4

CERBAIA
LOC. CERBAIA
VIA MOGLIO, 45
53024 MONTALCINO (SI)
TEL. 0577848301 - 066793628

This year, the Brunello '01 is better than the Vigna Cerbaia selection. The former has vibrant pipe tobacco, leather and ripe cherries with a soft, well-crafted palate and juicy, pervasive finish. The selection is less interesting as the vegetal notes disturb the profile and palate is too rigid.

● Brunello di Montalcino '01	TT	7
● Brunello di Montalcino V. Cerbaia '01	T	8
● Brunello di Montalcino V. Cerbaia '99	YY	7

IL COLLE
LOC. IL COLLE 102B
53024 MONTALCINO (SI)
TEL. 0577848295 - 057744578

Improvements in the cellar have brought Il Colle's best-ever Brunello. The excellent '01 reached the national finals with classic aromatics of balsam-tinged white cherry and peach fruit. Its stylish palate has mellow tannins and good supporting acidity. The Rosso '04 is nice, too.

● Brunello di Montalcino '01	TT	6
● Rosso di Montalcino '04	T	4
● Brunello di Montalcino '97	YY	6

COLLELCETO
LOC. CAMIGLIANO - POD. LA PISANA
53024 MONTALCINO (SI)
TEL. 0577816022 - 3496657974
www.collelceto.it

Talented Elia Palazzesi presented us with an excellent Brunello '01 that puts substance before elegance. Vibrant red and black berry fruit mingles with interesting hints of leather and the unusually strong, well-crafted palate supported by nicely acidity and savouriness. The Rosso '04 is good.

● Brunello di Montalcino '01	TT	6
● Rosso di Montalcino '04	T	4
● Brunello di Montalcino '00	YY	6

TENUTA DI COLLOSORBO
FRAZ. CASTELNUOVO DELL'ABATE
LOC. VILLA A SESTA, 25
53020 MONTALCINO (SI)
TEL. 0577835534

This beautiful winery in the Sesta area lacks only an outstanding wine to make its name. The good Brunello '01 has warm fruit, leather and boisé aromas and a subtle, very balanced palate with stylish, well-resolved extract. The good Sant'Antimo Ciacci '04 is long, fresh and very drinkable.

● Brunello di Montalcino '01	TT	6
● Sant'Antimo Ciacci '04	T	4
● Brunello di Montalcino '00	YY	6

Corte Pavone
Loc. Corte Pavone
53024 Montalcino (SI)
tel. 0577848110
www.loacker.net

Corte Pavone has great potential and a promising future. This year, results were uneven. The interesting Brunello '01 has breadth and generous fruit on the nose and a lingering, elegant palate. The excellent Morellino '04 Val di Flaco is from Loacker's Maremma winery.

● Brunello di Montalcino '01	TT	8
● Morellino di Scansano Val di Falco '04	TT	5
● Brunello di Montalcino '99	YY	7

Fattoi
Loc. Santa Restituta
Pod. Capanna, 101
53024 Montalcino (SI)
tel. 0577848613 - www.fattoi.it

We report a good performance from this winery on the western side of town, near the church of Santa Restituta. After a little aeration, the good Brunello '01 presents floral aromas but the well-textured palate is still rather affected by the oak. The Rosso '04 is also pleasant.

● Brunello di Montalcino '01	TT	6
● Rosso di Montalcino '04	T	4

La Fornace
Pod. Fornace, 154a
53024 Montalcino (SI)
tel. 0577848465
www.agricola-lafornace.it

This winery has shown distinct signs of improvement recently. The excellent Brunello '01 reached our finals for its vibrant fruit and spice aromas and austere, complex palate where well-crafted tannins fuse with the alcohol and the finish is nicely textured. The Rosso '04 is good.

● Brunello di Montalcino '01	TT	7
● Rosso di Montalcino '04	T	4
● Brunello di Montalcino Ris. '97	YY	8

Fornacina
Pod. Fornacina, 153
53024 Montalcino (SI)
tel. 0577848464
www.cantinafornacina.it

Simone Biliorsi's winery is in one of the DOCG's best areas and quality is improving yearly. Both wines are good. We just preferred the Brunello '01 for its classic aromas and good dense palate with close-knit and still slightly ruffled tannins. The Rosso '04 is one of the best from its year.

● Brunello di Montalcino '01	TT	7
● Rosso di Montalcino '04	TT	4
● Brunello di Montalcino Ris. '95	YY	6

Fossacolle
Loc. Tavernelle, 7
53024 Montalcino (SI)
tel. 0577816013
www.fossacolle.it

This Tavarnelle winery is steadily improving. The Brunello '01 is well focused and encapsulates the winery's style in bottled red fruit and jam on the nose and a well-crafted palate with complex tannins and a lingering finish. The Bordeaux blend Fossacolle '04 and the Rosso '04 are both good.

● Brunello di Montalcino '01	TT	7
● Fossacolle '04	TT	6
● Rosso di Montalcino '04	T	5
● Brunello di Montalcino '00	YY	7

Innocenti
Fraz. Torrenieri
Loc. Citille di Sotto, 45
53028 Montalcino (SI)
tel. 0577834227 - 3337546139

We note steady progress from this young, promising Terrenieri winery. The excellent Brunello '01 made the finals for generous complex aromas of red and black berry fruit, a hint of charred oak and confident flavour with a broad lingering finish. The Rosso '04 and Vignasole '03 are both well made.

● Brunello di Montalcino '01	TT	6
● Vignalsole '03	T	4
● Rosso di Montalcino '04	T	4
● Vignalsole '02	YY	4

La Lecciaia
loc. Vallafrico
53024 Montalcino (SI)
tel. 0583928366 - 0577849287
www.lecciaia.it

La Lecciaia has made progress in quality and all the wines are well made. We preferred the elegant if not very muscular '01 Brunello to the Manapetra selection as it knits the acidity and extract into the structure better. The Rosso La Lecciaia '02 is very nice.

● Brunello di Montalcino '01	🍷🍷	6
● Brunello di Montalcino Manapetra '01	🍷	6
● Rosso La Lecciaia '02	🍷	4

Luce
loc. Castelgiocondo
53024 Montalcino (SI)
tel. 0577848492

Luce is now run entirely by the Frescobaldi family again after the joint project with the Mondavis. The very good Luce '03 made it to the final tastings with a concentrated, complex nose and rounded, confidently tannic palate. The winery's youngster, Lucente '04, is also good.

● Luce '03	🍷🍷	8
● Lucente '04	🍷🍷	6
● Luce '94	🍸🍸🍸	8

Mocali
loc. Mocali
53024 Montalcino (SI)
tel. 0577849485

This dependable cellar's competitively priced range is just missing a top wine. The '01 Brunellos are well made. We preferred Vigna delle Raunate for its morello cherries and spices on the nose and dense palate, slightly curbed by the extract. The '04 Rosso di Montalcino and I Piaggioni are good.

● Brunello di Montalcino '01	🍷🍷	6
● Brunello di Montalcino V. delle Raunate '01	🍷🍷	7
● I Piaggioni '04	🍷	4
● Rosso di Montalcino '04	🍷	4

Oliveto
fraz. Castelnuovo dell'Abate
loc. Oliveto
53020 Montalcino (SI)
tel. 0577807170 - www.tenutaoliveto.it

The Oliveto style clearly favours overripening since this is a feature of all the wines. Il Leccio '04 is very good, giving quinine, pencil lead and chocolate preceding a generous palate with prominent but slightly aggressive tannins. The other two DOCG wines are a little less focused.

● Il Leccio '04	🍷🍷	6
● Brunello di Montalcino '01	🍷	7
● Rosso di Montalcino Il Roccolo '04	🍷	5

La Palazzetta
fraz. Castelnuovo dell'Abate
via Borgo di Sotto
53020 Montalcino (SI)
tel. 0577835631

Flavio Fanti's wines have become more rigid in recent years. The grapes are excellent, as the Brunello '01 demonstrates with its pipe tobacco, red and black berry fruit on the nose and a gutsy palate with a strong entry and nice progression. The Rosso di Montalcino '04 is very nice.

● Brunello di Montalcino '01	🍷🍷	6
● Rosso di Montalcino '04	🍷	4
● Brunello di Montalcino Ris. '97	🍸🍸🍸	8

Palazzo
loc. Palazzo, 144
53024 Montalcino (SI)
tel. 0577848479
www.aziendapalazzo.it

After the good performances of recent years, Palazzo presented rather anonymous wines. We are sure this is a minor setback. The aromas of the Brunello '01 are dominated by strong incense, which detracts from the fruit. Excessive extract on the palate clenches the finish. The Rosso '04 is better.

● Brunello di Montalcino '01	🍷	7
● Rosso di Montalcino '04	🍷	5
● Brunello di Montalcino '00	🍸🍸	7
● Brunello di Montalcino '99	🍸🍸	7

Pian delle Vigne
Loc. Pian delle Vigne
53024 Montalcino (SI)
tel. 0577816066
www.antinori.it

The Antinori family's Montalcino winery presented a technically flawless Brunello '01, which just lacks a bit of personality. The colour is intense and the nose is overwhelmingly balsamic and vegetal. The concentrated palate has close-knit tannin and a pleasant flavour with quite a long finish.

● Brunello di Montalcino '01	TT	7
● Brunello di Montalcino '00	YY	7
● Brunello di Montalcino '99	YY	7

Piancornello
Loc. Piancornello
53024 Montalcino (SI)
tel. 0577844105

Piancornello makes good wines and Brunello is always one of the best. The '01 has tobacco, yellow peaches, floral hints and eucalyptus on the nose. A good entry on the nicely textured palate takes you through to a round finish, although extract and acidity have yet to knit. The Rosso '04 is good.

● Brunello di Montalcino '01	TT	7
● Rosso di Montalcino '04	T	5
● Brunello di Montalcino '99	YYY	7
● Brunello di Montalcino '00	YY	7

La Pieve
Loc. La Pieve
fraz. Castelnuovo dell'Abate
53020 Montalcino (SI)
tel. 0577835795

The winery's first complex, well-crafted Brunello did very well. After briefly aerating, the nose is mature with leather, tobacco, light boisé and balsamic hints. The complex, nicely lingering palate has tight-knit but subtle tannins and a very long, well-coordinated finish.

● Brunello di Montalcino '01	TT	7

Renieri
loc Renieri
53024 Montalcino (SI)
tel. 0577359330
www.renierimontalcino.com

We applaud the performance from this young, upcoming winery. The excellent Re di Renieri '04 is beautifully made with a generous, well-coordinated palate. The nose has complex aromas of pencil lead, orange peel and black berry fruit. The La Regina '03 is well made and the Rosso '04 is very good.

● Re di Renieri '04	TT	6
● Regina di Renieri '03	TT	6
● Rosso di Montalcino '04	TT	5
● Re di Renieri '03	YY	6

San Giorgio
loc. San Giorgio
fraz. Castelnuovo dell'Abate
53020 Montalcino (SI)
tel. 0577849392

The quality of the wines here has improved. Brunello Ugolforte '01 is good with vibrant floral hints and white cherries introducing a stylish, balanced palate with marked acidity and restrained tannins. The Rosso di Montalcino Ciampoleto '04 is extremely fruity and very drinkable.

● Brunello di Montalcino Ugolforte '01	TT	7
● Rosso di Montalcino Ciampoleto '04	T	5

San Giuseppe
loc. Castelnuovo dell'Abate
Podere San Giuseppe, 35
53020 Montalcino (SI)
tel. 0577835754

There's no doubt: Rosso di Montalcino Stella Viola di Campalto is the best around. Its fruity nose gives cherries nicely fused with spicy hints from the oak and the lovely drinkable palate opens well onto attractively understated extract and a deep, lingering finish worthy of a Brunello.

● Rosso di Montalcino '04	TT	6
● Rosso di Montalcino '02	YY	6
● Rosso di Montalcino '03	YY	6

San Polino
Loc. San Polino
53024 Montalcino (SI)
tel. 0577835775

This organic winery showed off the area's good potential with very interesting wines. The Brunello '01 is good, with a fruity nose, hints of morello cherries and blackberries and a subtle boisé note. The palate is vibrant if still a little harsh. The Rosso '04 is one of the best this year.

● Brunello di Montalcino '01	TT	7
● Rosso di Montalcino '04	TT	5

Santa Lucia
Loc. Santa Lucia
53024 Montalcino (SI)
tel. 0577847156

This winery in upper Montalcino gave us an excellent Brunello '01. The subtle aromas reveal hints of morello cherries and blackberries blending well with the spice, following through well on the freshly drinkable palate with very subtle, mellow tannins and an unusually graceful, vibrant finish.

● Brunello di Montalcino '01	TT	7

Sasso di Sole
Loc. Podere Santa Giulia I, 48a
fraz. Torrenieri
53028 Montalcino (SI)
tel. 0577844238

This small Torrenieri winery marked its Guide debut with an outstanding Brunello '01. The nose is vibrant and clean with clearly defined sour cherries and blackberry jam mixing with attractive florality. The palate is generous, balanced and dynamic, signing of with a lovely reprise of the aromatics.

● Brunello di Montalcino '01	TT	7

La Serena
Loc. Podere Rasa I, 133
53024 Montalcino (SI)
tel. 0577848659

Andrea Mantengoli's winery is expanding with the purchase of new vineyards and a newly built cellar. The nice Brunello '01 has an intensely floral nose that hints at oleander and very clean apple-like fruit. The palate is firm and well-coordinated although the tannins are still a tad harsh.

● Brunello di Montalcino '01	TT	6
● Brunello di Montalcino '00	YY	6

Podere Sesta di Sopra
Loc. Castelnuovo dell'Abate
53020 Montalcino (SI)
tel. 0577835698 - 335464867
www.sestadisopra.it

The vineyards are simply beautiful. The Brunello '01 is as good as ever with aromas of forest floor, liquorice and sour cherries. The subtle, complex palate has slightly rigid tannins that should unbend with age. The very good Rosso '04 has a lively, crisp palate.

● Brunello di Montalcino '01	TT	8
● Rosso di Montalcino '04	T	5
● Brunello di Montalcino '00	YY	7
● Brunello di Montalcino '99	YY	7

Talenti
fraz. Sant'Angelo in Colle
loc. Pian di Conte
53020 Montalcino (SI)
tel. 0577844064

This beautiful classic winery continues to turn out excellent wines. The Brunello '01 has an austere nose with aromas of pipe tobacco, cherry jam and blackberries. The firm, well-coordinated palate satisfies with its substantial texture. The '04 Rosso and Pian di Conte are both good.

● Brunello di Montalcino '01	TT	6
● Pian di Conte '04	T	5
● Rosso di Montalcino '04	T	4
● Brunello di Montalcino Ris. '99	YYY	7

Tornesi
Loc. Le Benducce, 207
53024 Montalcino (SI)
tel. 0577848689

The Brunello '01 is the best wine Maurizio Tornesi has ever presented for the Guide. Intense, clean aromas of chocolate, mint, peaches and flowers on the nose usher in mellow tannins that support the good texture in the mouth. The pervasive finish lingers on the back palate.

● Brunello di Montalcino '01	🍷🍷	6
● Brunello di Montalcino '00	🍸🍸	6

Enzo Carmignani
Loc. Cercatoia Alta
55015 Montecarlo (LU)
tel. 058322463

We note the good performance of this ten-hectare estate in the most prestigious area of Montecarlo, Cercatoia. Whites are to the fore with the Montecarlo '05 showing fruit and mineral aromas followed by a supple, vibrant body. The chardonnay-based La Verruka '03 has breadth and dynamic acidity.

○ La Verruka '03	🍷🍷	5
○ Montecarlo Bianco '05	🍷🍷	4

Fattoria Michi
Via San Martino, 34
55015 Montecarlo (LU)
tel. 058322011

The wines are very good, the highest scores going to the whites. Montecarlo Bianco '05 has fresh pear and almonds followed by a well-poised palate. The Malìe '05 is also nice with pervasive peach and vanilla introducing good acidity to balance out the texture. The Vecchie Vigne '03 is pleasant.

○ Malìe '05	🍷🍷	4
○ Montecarlo Bianco '05	🍷🍷	4
○ Vecchie Vigne '03	🍷	5

Aione
Loc. Aione, 12
56040 Montecatini Val di Cecina (PI)
tel. 058830339

There was an excellent performance from Podere Aione. The well-crafted Aione '03 has vibrant aromas and a juicy, balanced palate. The best features of the good merlot-led Etico '04 are glossy tannins and an elegant flavour. The Salve '04 is also very agreeable.

● Aione '03	🍷🍷	6
● Etico '04	🍷🍷	6
● Salve '04	🍷	6
● Aione '01	🍸🍸	6

Fattoria Sorbaiano
Loc. Sorbaiano
56040 Montecatini Val di Cecina (PI)
tel. 058830243
www.fattoriasorbaiano.it

Fattoria Sorbaiano is back in the Guide after a good all-round performance. Rosso delle Miniere '04 is a nicely put-together wine that shows vigorous and elegant with clean aromas. The red and white Montescudaios are less intense. The Lucestraia '04 is very pleasant.

● Montescudaio Rosso delle Miniere '04	🍷🍷	5
○ Montescudaio Bianco Lucestraia '04	🍷	4
● Montescudaio Rosso '04	🍷	3
○ Montescudaio Bianco '05	🍷	3

Avignonesi
fraz. Valiano di Montepulciano
via Colonica, 1
53040 Montepulciano (SI)
tel. 0578724304 - www.avignonesi.it

The Vin Santo Occhio di Pernice '94 from prugnolo gentile is very appealing, with some huskiness in the aromas but outstanding density and character. The reds gave a colourless performance in comparison to past editions, but the 50 & 50 was missing. The Rosso '05 is attractively approachable.

● Vin Santo Occhio di Pernice '94	🍷🍷	8
● Rosso di Montepulciano '05	🍷	4
● Vin Santo Occhio di Pernice '93	🍸🍸🍸	8

FATTORIA LE CASALTE
FRAZ. SANT'ALBINO
VIA DEL TERMINE, 2
53045 MONTEPULCIANO (SI)
TEL. 0578798246

Quality holds steady at Chiara Barioffi's winery. Despite the hot growing year, Nobile Quercetonda '03 is well made and characterful. The nose is reluctant to open but the palate is gutsy with tannic thrust. The Rosso di Montepulciano '04 is very moreish and the Rosso Le Casalte '04 is coherent.

- Nobile di Montepulciano Quercetonda '03 — 2 glasses (black) — 5
- Nobile di Montepulciano '03 — 1 glass (black) — 4
- Rosso di Montepulciano '04 — 1 glass (black) — 4
- Rosso Le Casalte '04 — 1 glass (black) — 2*

PODERE CASANOVA
LOC. ACQUAVIVA DI MONTEPULCIANO
SS. 326 EST, 196
53040 MONTEPULCIANO (SI)
TEL. 0578766099 - 3332218185

These wines are clean and well made, although they show no great personality. The Nobile '03 has ripe fruit aromas contrasting with good spice and a soft, creamy body. The Rosso '04 is deliciously moreish with subtle but well-defined aromas and a fresh flavour, slightly clenched in the finish.

- Nobile di Montepulciano '03 — 2 glasses (black) — 4
- Rosso di Montepulciano '05 — 2 glasses (black) — 5
- Nobile di Montepulciano Ris. '01 — 2 glasses (white) — 6
- Rosso di Montepulciano '04 — 2 glasses (white) — 4

I CIPRESSI
LOC. GRACCIANO DI MONTEPULCIANO
VIA DELLA CIARLIANA, 4A
53040 MONTEPULCIANO (SI)
TEL. 0578717454

There was a more than satisfactory Guide debut for I Cipressi. The Nobile di Montepulciano '03 has nicely fresh florality and dynamic follow-through on the palate where earthy tannins lead to a fruity finish. The Rosso di Montepulciano '04 is nice, with simple aromas and a full-bodied, even palate.

- Nobile di Montepulciano '03 — 2 glasses (black) — 5
- Rosso di Montepulciano '04 — 1 glass (black) — 4

CORTE ALLA FLORA
FRAZ. ACQUAVIVA
VIA DI CERVOGNANO, 23
53040 MONTEPULCIANO (SI)
TEL. 0578766003 - www.corteallaflora.it

Corte alla Flora's 15 hectares of vineyards are at Cervognano in one of Montepulciano's most interesting zones. The Nobile '03 is good with smoky aromas alongside black berry fruit and vegetal hints. The palate is well made though not very territorial. The Rosso '04 is uncomplicated.

- Nobile di Montepulciano '03 — 2 glasses (black) — 5
- Rosso di Montepulciano '04 — 1 glass (black) — 4
- Nobile di Montepulciano '00 — 2 glasses (white) — 5

IL FAGGETO
FRAZ. SANT'ALBINO
VIA FONTELELLERA
53045 MONTEPULCIANO (SI)
TEL. 0577940600 - 3www.baroncini.it

The Baroncini family's Montepulciano estate has nine hectares under vine. The Nobile Pietra del Diavolo '03 has confident, quite clean aromas and good balance in the mouth. The Rosso di Montepulciano Lupaio '05 is simpler. The nose is fresh and approachable and the supple palate is nice and tangy.

- Nobile di Montepulciano Pietra del Diavolo '03 — 2 glasses (black) — 5
- Rosso di Montepulciano Lupaio '05 — 1 glass (black) — 4
- Nobile di Montepulciano Pietra del Diavolo '02 — 2 glasses (white) — 4

AZIENDA AGRICOLA GODIOLO
VIA DELL'ACQUAPUZZOLA, 13
53045 MONTEPULCIANO (SI)
TEL. 0578757251 - 3387015896

Franco Fiorini's five and half hectare estate made a good debut. The Nobile '03 is characterful and quite complex, especially on the nose, where the perfectly ripe, focused fruit interacts with very pleasant earthy hints. The palate is well-textured, tangy and quite long.

- Nobile di Montepulciano '03 — 2 glasses (black) — 5

Fattoria di Gracciano
Fraz. Gracciano
via Umbria, 63
53040 Montepulciano (SI)
tel. 055859811

Ambrogio and Giovanni Folonari's 20 hectare Montepulciano estate makes about 100,000 bottles a year. The Nobile Torcalvano '03, from sangiovese with some cabernet sauvignon, is impressive with closed but characterful aromas on the nose, emerging confidently sweet and vibrant on the palate.

- Nobile di Montepulciano Torcalvano '03 — TT — 4
- Nobile di Montepulciano Torcalvano Ris. '01 — YY — 5

Lodola Nuova - Tenimenti Ruffino
Fraz. Valiano - via Lodola, 1
53045 Montepulciano (SI)
tel. 0578724032
www.ruffino.com

The Nobile '03 has a nicely complex sensory profile despite the complicated year. Clear aromas of red berry fruit jam lifted by sweet spice usher in a soft palate with firm tannins and an intensely sweet finish. Lorenzo Landi is the winery's consultant winemaker.

- Nobile di Montepulciano '03 — TT — 5
- Rosso di Montepulciano '05 — T — 4
- Nobile di Montepulciano '01 — YY — 4
- Nobile di Montepulciano Ris. '01 — YY — 5

Fattoria di Paterno
Fraz. Sant'Albino
via Fontelellera, 11
53045 Montepulciano (SI)
tel. 0578799194 - 068081881

The Nobile '03 manages to present a tight, well-coordinated sensory profile despite a challenging growing year. Crisp red fruits jam-led aromas are lifted by sweet spice before the soft palate reveals firm extract and an intensely sweet finish. Lorenzo Landi consults.

- Nobile di Montepulciano '03 — TT — 4
- Nobile di Montepulciano Ris. '00 — YY — 5
- Nobile di Montepulciano '01 — YY — 5

Redi
via di Collazzi, 5
53045 Montepulciano (SI)
tel. 0578716092 - 0578716093
www.cantinadelredi.com

The Cantina del Redi-label Nobile di Montepulciano Briareo '03 performed well. The aromas are warm, generous and concentrated, and fruit almost too lively. The well-coordinated palate closes with a warm, deep finale. The Rosso di Montepulciano '05 Vecchia Cantina and Redi are both good.

- Nobile di Montepulciano Briareo '03 — TT — 5
- Rosso di Montepulciano '05 — T — 4
- Rosso di Montepulciano Vecchia Cantina '05 — T — 4

Salcheto
loc. Sant'Albino
via di Villa Bianca, 15
53045 Montepulciano (SI)
tel. 0578799031 - www.salcheto.it

Salcheto's 28 hectares produce about 130,000 bottles under Michele Manelli but the performance was below par. The Nobile '03 stood out for its warm sweet aromas and solid texture on a palate with good, dynamic thrust and an intense finish. The Rosso '05 is uncomplicated and enjoyable.

- Nobile di Montepulciano '03 — TT — 5
- Rosso di Montepulciano '05 — T — 4
- Nobile di Montepulciano '97 — YYY — 5

Villa Sant'Anna
Fraz. Abbadia
via della Resistenza, 143
53040 Montepulciano (SI)
tel. 0578708017 - www.villasantanna.it

The Nobile Poldo '03 from sangiovese with merlot is very good. The aromas are not too mature and offer distinct torrefaction and spices. The very concentrated palate is almost viscous in texture with a warm, lingering finish. The Nobile '03 is less good, showing clean aromas but rigid tannins.

- Nobile di Montepulciano Poldo '03 — TT — 6
- Nobile di Montepulciano '03 — T — 5
- Nobile di Montepulciano Poldo '01 — YY — 6
- Nobile di Montepulciano '02 — YY — 5

SERRAIOLA
FRAZ. FRASSINE
LOC. SERRAIOLA
58025 MONTEROTONDO MARITTIMO (GR)
TEL. 0566910026 - www.serraiola.it

The two red IGTs made by the traditional Serraiola cellar are very interesting. The Shyraz '04 has intensely balsamic aromas and a fresh, tangy flavour. The sangiovese, merlot and syrah Campo Montecristo '04 has excellent texture. Monteregio Bianco Violina '05 is fresh and nicely herbaceous.

● Campo Montecristo '04	▼▼	6
● Shyraz '04	▼▼	5
○ Monteregio di Massa Marittima Violina '05	▼	4

TENUTA LA CIPRESSAIA
VIA ROMITA, 38
50025 MONTESPERTOLI (FI)
TEL. 0571670868
www.tenutalacipressaia.it

This all-female winery did very well, thanks mainly to the sangiovese-only Borgoricco '04 with its austere aromas of plums and blackberries and juicy palate with a long finish. Both Chiantis are good. The '05 is more supple while the Colli Fiorentini has a better orchestrated palate.

● Borgoricco '04	▼▼	5
● Chianti dei Colli Fiorentini '04	▼	3
● Chianti Magolo '05	▼	3

POGGIO CAPPONI
LOC. SAN DONATO A LIVIZZANO
VIA MONTELUPO, 184
50025 MONTESPERTOLI (FI)
TEL. 0571671914

The Poggio Capponi range is interesting. The top wine is Tinorso '04, in a new 70-30 blend this year of merlot and syrah. Its clean nose has hints of fruit and spices and the coherent palate lingers nice. The Chianti Petriccio '04 and the chardonnay-based Sovente '05 are reliably good.

● Tinorso '04	▼▼	5
● Chianti Montespertoli Petriccio '04	▼	4
○ Sovente '05	▼	4
● Tinorso '02	▽▽	5

SONNINO
VIA VOLTERRANA NORD, 6A
50025 MONTESPERTOLI (FI)
TEL. 0571609198 - 0571657481
www.castellosonnino.it

There are encouraging signs at Castello di Sonnino. The sangiovese Cantinino '04 has a floral, fruity nose and a rounded, poised palate. The merlot, sangiovese and petit verdot Sanleone '03 has balsamic notes and a powerful, husky palate with a spicy finish. Chianti Montespertoli '05 is pleasant.

● Cantinino '04	▼▼	5
● Sanleone '03	▼	7
● Chianti Montespertoli '05	▼	3
● Sanleone '01	▽▽	7

MANNUCCI DROANDI
FRAZ. MERCATALE VALDARNO
VIA CAPOSELVI, 61
52020 MONTEVARCHI (AR)
TEL. 0559707276

Roberto Droandi's wines are always impressive. The Campolucci '03 is mature, tangy and well structured. The lovely Chianti Colli Aretini '04 has outstandingly approachable fruit and the rosé Rossinello '05 is enjoyable. The Chianti Classico Ceppeto Riserva '03 is a little affected by the hot year.

● Campolucci '03	▼▼	5
● Chianti Colli Aretini '04	▼▼	3*
● Chianti Cl. Ceppeto Ris. '03	▼	5
⊙ Rossinello '05	▼	3*

VARRAMISTA
LOC. VARRAMISTA
VIA RICAVO
56020 MONTOPOLI IN VAL D'ARNO (PI)
TEL. 057144711 - www.varramista.it

This established winery in the Pisan hills did well. The syrah Varramista '03 has spicy aromas of black pepper on a fruity background of blackberries. The flavour is extremely balanced if not all that complex but this wine is bound to please. The Frasca '04 is uncomplicated but firm-textured.

● Varramista '03	▼▼	7
● Frasca '04	▼	5
● Varramista '00	▽▽▽	7
● Frasca '01	▽▽	4

BRUNI
FRAZ. FONTEBLANDA
LOC. LA MARTA, 6
58010 ORBETELLO (GR)
TEL. 0564885445

Brothers Marco and Moreno Bruni make impressive wines. The sangiovese and syrah Morellino Laire '04 has good personality with generous red berry fruit and a juicy, intensely sweet palate. The Capalbio Bianco Plinio '05 from vermentino with a little viognier is fresh and slightly tangy.

●	Morellino di Scansano Laire '04	🍷🍷	5
○	Capalbio Bianco Vermentino Plinio '05	🍷	4
●	Morellino di Scansano Laire '03	🍷🍷	5
●	Morellino di Scansano Marteto '04	🍷🍷	4

SANTA LUCIA
FRAZ. FONTEBLANDA
VIA AURELIA NORD, 66
58010 ORBETELLO (GR)
TEL. 0564885474 - www.azsantalucia.it

A new wine joins Luciano Scotto's well-stocked range this year, a Cabernet Sauvignon with good temperament, generous aromas and a juicy palate. The Betto '04 from sangiovese, cabernet sauvignon and merlot is good but the aromas are a little confused. The Morellino Tore del Moro '05 is basic.

●	Cabernet Sauvignon '04	🍷🍷	5
●	Betto '04	🍷	4

SANGERVASIO
LOC. SAN GERVASIO
56036 PALAIA (PI)
TEL. 0587483360
www.sangervasio.com

It was an excellent year for Luca Tommasini and his staff, now back in the Guide. Renai '03 sailed into the finals with a fruity, intensely pervasive nose and a generously complex, tannic palate. The moreish whites are both very good and surprisingly fresh. The Sangervasio '05 is very pleasant.

●	I Renai '03	🍷🍷	7
○	Chardonnay '04	🍷🍷	5
○	Sangervasio Bianco '05	🍷🍷	4
●	Sangervasio Rosso '05	🍷	4

TRAVIGNOLI
VIA TRAVIGNOLI, 78
50060 PELAGO (FI)
TEL. 0558361098
www.travignoli.com

Giovanni Busi is back in the Guide with a good performance. The Riserva '03 has fruity aromas, generous, well-balanced body and tannins that blend nicely with the alcohol into a delicious finish. The two Supertuscans are a little too mature on the nose while the Chianti Rufina '04 is very pleasant.

●	Chianti Rufina Ris. '03	🍷🍷	5
●	Calice del Conte '03	🍷	6
●	Tegolaia '03	🍷	5
●	Chianti Rufina '04	🍷	3

SEDIME
POD. SEDIME, 63
53026 PIENZA (SI)
TEL. 0578748436

From five hectares of vineyards Sedime makes just over 10,000 bottles per year of one wine, the mainly sangiovese with a little merlot Orcia Capitoni, which is one of the best of its type. The '04 version is characterful, lively and lingers with on the palate with polished poise.

●	Orcia Rosso Capitoni '04	🍷🍷	4
●	Orcia Rosso Capitoni '02	🍷🍷	5
●	Orcia Rosso Capitoni '03	🍷🍷	4

AZ. AGR. BRANCATELLI
LOC. RIOTORTO - CASA ROSSA, 2
57020 PIOMBINO (LI)
TEL. 056520655
www.brancatelli-toscana.it

There are two very interesting wines in Brancatelli's very extensive range. The Syrah '04 has elegantly exemplary, vibrant varietal aromas and a vigorous, robustly alcoholic palate. The sangiovese Valle del Sogno '04 is concentrated with tasty, close-knit tannins and a bitterish finish.

●	Giuseppe Brancatelli Syrah '04	🍷🍷	7
●	Valle del Sogno '04	🍷	6

TENUTA PODERNOVO
LOC. TERRICCIOLA
VIA PODERNUOVO, 13
56030 PISA
TEL. 0587655173 - 0587658563

The Lunelli family's winery has 40 hectares of vineyards at Pisa and made an excellent debut. The Aliotto '04 has prominent ripe fruit enriching the juicy, broad texture. The Teuto '03 focuses on black berry aromas with a close-knit tannic weave on the very stylish, lingering palate.

● Teuto '03	🍷🍷	5
● Aliotto '04	🍷🍷	4

TENUTA ROCCACCIA
VIA POGGIO CAVALLUCCIO
58017 PITIGLIANO (GR)
TEL. 0564617020 - 0564617976
www.tenutaroccaccia.it

Tenuta Roccaccia, run by brothers Danilo and Rossano Goracci, put on a muted performance. The Chardonnay '05 is clean and well made with light minerality but very simple. The Sovana Rosso '05 from sangiovese, ciliegiolo and alicante is flavoursome but lightweight.

○ Chardonnay '05	🍷	3
● Sovana Rosso La Roccaccia '05	🍷	3

LE FONTI
LOC. SAN GIORGIO
53036 POGGIBONSI (SI)
TEL. 0577935690 - 035711067

Last year, we noted a drop in quality in the Imbeni family's products and again this year there are no outstanding wines. The Chianti Classico '04 is fresh on the fruity nose and on the slender palate. The rest of the wines tend to show flaws on the nose and a lack of balance in the mouth.

● Chianti Cl. Ris. '03	🍷	6
● Chianti Cl. '04	🍷	4
● Sangiovese '04	🍷	3

ACQUABONA
LOC. ACQUABONA
57037 PORTOFERRAIO (LI)
TEL. 0565933013

Acquabona is back in the Guide after a few years' absence. Elba Aleatico '03 is very well made with enfolding black berry fruit and orange peel on the nose and a juicy, elegant palate that lingers. The Voltraio '03 from 50-25-25 sangiovese, merlot and cabernet, is also good.

● Aleatico dell'Elba '03	🍷🍷	6
● Voltraio '03	🍷	5

BORGO SALCETINO
LOC. LUCARELLI
53017 RADDA IN CHIANTI (SI)
TEL. 0577733541 - 0432757173
www.livon.it

The Livon family's Tuscan cellar did itself credit. The flagship Rossole is a blend of sangiovese and merlot with mature aromas the blend nicely with spice. The juicy, rounded palate has fresh, barely perceptible tannins. The Riserva '03 Lucarello has good texture but is uneven and lacks balance.

● Rossole '04	🍷🍷	5
● Chianti Cl. Lucarello Ris. '03	🍷	5
● Rossole '00	🍷🍷 (white)	5
● Rossole '01	🍷🍷 (white)	5

CAPARSA
LOC. CAPARSINO, 48
53017 RADDA IN CHIANTI (SI)
TEL. 0577738174 - 0577738639
www.caparsa.it

Despite the less than thrilling results, we have included this profile of a winery that just two years ago so impressed us. This year, though, the wines disappointed, apart from the Chianti Classico Caparsino '04, which has red berry fruit aromas and a tangy, juicy but slightly short palate.

● Chianti Cl. Caparsino '03	🍷	4
● Chianti Cl. Doccio a Matteo Ris. '00	🍷🍷🍷 (white)	6

FATTORIA DI MONTEMAGGIO
LOC. MONTEMAGGIO
53017 RADDA IN CHIANTI (SI)
TEL. 0577738323
www.montemaggio.com

Welcome back to the Guide for this small Radda winery. The wines are nicely harmonious overall, in particular the merlot Terre di Montemaggio '04 with its tempting nose and soft, nicely extracted body. The gutsy, characterful Riserva '03 is good and the Chianti Classico '04 is refreshing.

●	Torre di Montemaggio '04	▼▼	5
●	Chianti Cl. Ris. '03	▼	5
●	Chianti Cl. '04	▼	4
●	Chianti Cl. Ris. '01	▽▽	5

PODERE L'AJA
LOC. L'AJA
53017 RADDA IN CHIANTI (SI)
TEL. 0577738089
www.poderelaja.com

We report an encouraging showing from the 2003 wines at Ugo Contrino's winery. The Riserva is ruby red with complex aromas ranging from ripe fruit to spice. The juicy palate has good tannic texture and a lingering finish. The basic version is simpler on the nose with slender body and good freshness.

●	Chianti Cl. Ris. '03	▼▼	5
●	Chianti Cl. '03	▼	4

VAL DELLE CORTI
LOC. LA CROCE
FRAZ. CASE SPARSE VAL DELLE CORTI, 144
53017 RADDA IN CHIANTI (SI)
TEL. 0577738215

Roberto Bianchi's small winery has loads of potential. Three of the four hectares under vine are registered as Chianti Classico. The aromas are rich in mineral and fruity sensations while the palate is succulent with nicely resolved tannins and a very satisfying finish.

●	Chianti Cl. '03	▼▼	4
●	Chianti Cl. Ris. '00	▽▽	5

VIGNAVECCHIA
SDRUCCIOLO DI PIAZZA, 7
53017 RADDA IN CHIANTI (SI)
TEL. 0577738090 - 0577738326
www.vignavecchia.com

The Beccari family winery did less well than usual. The Chianti Classico '04 is good and fresh on the palate, proffering well-judged acidity and appealing aromas. The Vin Santo Casuario '97 is well typed but seems a little tired and one-dimensional.

●	Chianti Cl. '04	▼▼	4
○	Vin Santo del Chianti Cl. Casuario '97	▼	6
●	Raddese '03	▽▽	6

CASTELLO DI MODANELLA
LOC. VILLAGGIO DI MODANELLA
53040 RAPOLANO TERME (SI)
TEL. 0577704604
www.modanella.com

This bold winemaking project makes single-variety wines only. The sangiovese Campo d'Aia is firm and succulent. The Poggio l'Aiole '04 from canaiolo is peppery with a fresh-tasting dynamic palate and a little short in the finish. The cabernet sauvignon Le Voliere is less individual but equally good.

●	Campo d'Aia '04	▼▼	5
●	Le Voliere Cabernet Sauvignon '04	▼	5
●	Poggio l'Aiole '04	▼	4
●	Le Voliere Cabernet Sauvignon '01	▽▽	5

LA REGOLA
VIA A. GRAMSCI, 1
56046 RIPARBELLA (PI)
TEL. 0586698145 - 058881363
www.laregola.com

Podere La Regola is back in the Guide with some well-made wines, the cellar now supervised by the talented Luca D'Attoma. We liked Montescudaio La Regola '03 best, with its perfectly blended fruit and oak sensations. Vin Santo Sondrete '01 is also good and has nicely balanced flavour.

●	Montescudaio Rosso La Regola '03	▼▼	6
○	Vin Santo Sondrete '01	▼	5
●	Montescudaio Rosso Vallino '04	▼	5
○	Montescudaio Bianco Lauro '05	▼	4

Ampeleia

Loc. Meleta
58036 Roccastrada (GR)
tel. 0564567155
www.ampeleia.com

It was a convincing debut for Elisabetta Foradori's 50-hectare Maremma property. Ampeleia '04 – the name comes from the Greek word for vine – is a blend of cabernet franc, sangiovese and merlot aged in barrique for 16 months. It has very clean aromas and a dynamic, flavoursome palate.

- Ampeleia '04 🍷🍷 6

Colognole

loc. Colognole
via del Palagio, 15
50068 Rufina (FI)
tel. 0558319870 - www.colognole.it

The Coda Nunziante family is back in the Guide. This year, we liked the Riserva del Don '03, with strong aromas of ripe fruit, leather and tobacco and a good balance of tannin and alcohol on a palate with a long, flavoursome finish. The Chianti Rufina '04 has a tautness that makes it very drinkable.

- Chianti Rufina Ris. del Don '03 🍷🍷 5
- Chianti Rufina '04 🍷 4
- Chianti Rufina '01 🍸🍸 3
- Chianti Rufina '02 🍸🍸 4

Il Pozzo

via Piave, 1
50068 Rufina (FI)
tel. 0558399102

A newcomer from Chianti Rufina, this winery was founded ten years ago and has seven hectares of vineyards, mainly planted to sangiovese. The two wines are both labelled DOCG. The Chianti Rufina '04 has a fresh, supple body and the Riserva '03 has complex aromas, good structure and a long finish.

- Chianti Rufina Ris. '03 🍷🍷 5
- Chianti Rufina '04 🍷 4

Il Borghetto

loc. Montefiridolfi
via Collina Sant'Angelo, 21
50026 San Casciano in Val di Pesa (FI)
tel. 0558244491 - www.borghetto.org

Six of this newcomer's 30 hectares are planted to vine. They gave us an interesting Supertuscan from sangiovese, cabernet sauvignon and merlot that reflects its territory very well indeed. Fruity aromas introduce a powerful, though not excessive, body. The Chianti Classico '04 is appetizing.

- Collina 21 '03 🍷🍷 5
- Chianti Cl. Bilaccio '04 🍷 4

La Loggia

loc. Montefiridolfi
via Collina, 40
50026 San Casciano in Val di Pesa (FI)
tel. 0558244288

This winery in the Florentine part of Chianti Classico presented an impressive '03 which show no ill effects from the hot growing year. The aromas are fresh, almost balsamic, and the generous palate is well structured with confident tannins that meld perfectly with the alcohol.

- Chianti Cl. Terra dei Cavalieri '03 🍷🍷 4
- Chianti Cl. Terra dei Cavalieri '01 🍸🍸 4
- Nearco '00 🍸🍸 6
- Chianti Cl. Terra dei Cavalieri Ris. '01 🍸🍸 5

Machiavelli

loc. Sant'Andrea in Percussina
50026 San Casciano in Val di Pesa (FI)
tel. 055828471
www.giv.it

We can always count on Riserva Vigna di Fontalle, although the '03 version was less impressive than usual, revealing mature aromas redolent of leather and tobacco and a firm, flavoursome palate with rather lively tannins. The Chianti Classico has confident edgy acidity and nicely prominent tannins.

- Chianti Cl. V. di Fontalle Ris. '03 🍷🍷 7
- Chianti Cl. Solatìo del Tani '04 🍷 6
- Il Principe '95 🍸🍸🍸 4
- Chianti Cl. V. di Fontalle Ris. '97 🍸🍸🍸 5

PIEVE DI CAMPOLI
VIA CAMPOLI, 123
50026 SAN CASCIANO IN VAL DI PESA (FI)
TEL. 055821043

The Diocese of Florence is now in the Guide with its one Chianti Classico. The '04 reaps the rewards of hard work in previous years, revealing characteristic cherry-led fruit mingling with florality on the nose and a firm-structured palate with nicely assertive tannins.

●	Chianti Cl. '04	YY	4

VILLA MANGIACANE
VIA FALTIGNANO, 4
50026 SAN CASCIANO IN VAL DI PESA (FI)
TEL. 05588290123
www.mangiacane.it

South African entrepreneur Glynn David Cohen returned to the Guide with a good Chianti Classico '03. Wild berry jam mingles with spice to introduce a generous, juicy palate with nicely defined tannic texture, well-judged acidity and a tangy finish. The drinkable '04 is slimmer and has floral aromas.

●	Chianti Cl. '03	YY	5
●	Chianti Cl. '04	Y	5
●	Chianti Cl. Ris. '01	ΥΥ (outline)	5
●	Chianti Cl. '02	ΥΥ (outline)	5

IL LEBBIO
LOC. SAN BENEDETTO, 11C
53037 SAN GIMIGNANO (SI)
TEL. 0577944725 - 0577944961
www.illebbio.it

This year, Il Lebbio presented very decent wines. The Polito '03 is concentrated but held back by rough-edged tannins. The Grottoni '05 has a juicy, slightly vegetal palate while the Cicogio '05 is supple with an uncomplicated finish. The Lendo '04 has a rich nose but the tannins need smoothing.

●	Polito '03	Y	6
●	Lendo '04	Y	5
●	Cicogio '05	Y	4
●	I Grottoni '05	Y	4

IL PALAGIONE
VIA PER CASTEL SAN GIMIGNANO, 36
53037 SAN GIMIGNANO (SI)
TEL. 0577953134 - 3482653281
www.ilpalagione.com

These wines did not achieve very high scores but they impressed with their reliable quality. The Antajr '03 from sangiovese, cabernet sauvignon and merlot is good and has a firm, slightly rigid palate. The Vernaccia and the Enif are both well made. The Chianti Colli Senesi '04 is fruity.

●	Antajr '03	YY	6
●	Chianti Colli Senesi Caelum '04	Y	4
○	Enif '05	Y	2
○	Vernaccia di S. Gimignano Hydra '05	Y	3

PIETRAFITTA
LOC. CORTENNANO, 54
53037 SAN GIMIGNANO (SI)
TEL. 0577943200
www.pietrafitta.com

This classic winery is back with a good performance from the Vernaccia La Costa Riserva '04. Fruity aromas with prominent hints of torrefaction precede a sweet, full-bodied, mouthfilling palate and a bitterish finish. The excellent Vin Santo di San Gimignano '98 is weighty, balanced and lingering.

○	San Gimignano Vin Santo '98	YY	6
○	Vernaccia di S. Gimignano V. La Costa Ris. '04	Y	5
○	Vernaccia di S. Gimignano V. Borghetto '05	Y	4

FATTORIA SAN DONATO
LOC. SAN DONATO, 6
53037 SAN GIMIGNANO (SI)
TEL. 0577941616
www.sandonato.it

Two sound wines prompted this return to the Guide. The Chianti Colli Senesi Riserva Fede '03 has stylish violets and raspberries and a coherent palate with well-judged tannin and a fruity finish. The Vernaccia Benedetta Riserva '04 has ripe fruit, good pulp and an alcoholic, bitterish flavour.

●	Chianti Colli Senesi Fede Ris. '03	YY	4
○	Vernaccia di S. Gimignano Angelica '04	Y	4
○	Vernaccia di S. Gimignano Benedetta Ris. '04	Y	4

LE SOLIVE
VIA DI SAN BENEDETTO, 11D
53037 SAN GIMIGNANO (SI)
TEL. 0577944909

This debut offers some very expressive wines. Vernaccia Innovazione '04 is very sound with a dynamic balance of structure, depth and pleasant freshness. The Vernaccia Vigna Aprico '05 is fruity and tangy with medium texture. The Connubio '03 is a dynamic, supple San Gimignano Rosso from sangiovese.

○	Vernaccia di S. Gimignano Innovazione '04	▼▼	4
●	S. Gimignano Rosso Connubio '03	▼	4
○	Vernaccia di S. Gimignano V. Aprico '05	▼	3

PIETRO BECONCINI
FRAZ. LA SCALA - VIA MONTORZO, 13A
56020 SAN MINIATO (PI)
TEL. 0571464570 - 3472647861
www.pietrobeconcini.com

Talented Leonardo Beconcini has notched up another success. Reciso '04 is one of the most interesting monovarietals on the Sangiovese-friendly Tuscan coast. Vibrant red berry fruit and spices on the nose introduce a well-balanced, flavoursome body. Just behind is the enjoyable Maurleo '04.

●	Reciso '04	▼▼	6
●	Maurleo '04	▼	4
●	Reciso '03	▽▽	5
●	Maurleo '03	▽▽	4

PODERE SAN MICHELE
VIA CADUTA, 3A
57027 SAN VINCENZO (LI)
TEL. 0565704808 - 05657809879
www.poderesanmichele.it

Podere San Michele is back in the Guide thanks to the Allodio Rosso '03, a blend of 60 per cent sangiovese and 40 per cent syrah. Dark, with a vibrant, spicy nose and soft, concentrated palate, it has a succulent mouthfeel and decent length.

●	Allodio Rosso '03	▼▼	6
●	Allodio Rosso '00	▽▽	5
●	Allodio Rosso '01	▽▽	6
●	Allodio Rosso '99	▽▽	5

SAN MICHELE A TORRI
VIA SAN MICHELE, 36
50020 SCANDICCI (FI)
TEL. 055769111
www.fattoriasanmichele.it

The cabernet sauvignon, sangiovese and colorino Murtas is still the best wine from this steady winery. There are no real stand-outs but general quality us good. The '03 has spicy aromas and a rounded body. The Riserva '03 is powerfully structured and the Chianti Colli Fiorentini is very nice.

●	Murtas '03	▼▼	6
●	Chianti Cl. La Gabbiola Ris. '03	▼	5
●	Chianti Colli Fiorentini '04	▼	3
●	Murtas '02	▽▽	6

POGGIOPAOLI
LOC. POMONTE
VIALE RAGNAIE, 64
58054 SCANSANO (GR)
TEL. 0564599408 - 3388019218

The firs release of Capel Rosso, the '04, is a very interesting blend of sangiovese, ciliegiolo and merlot in only 4,000 bottles. The palate is dense and concentrated with a dynamic, tangy flavour. The two '05 Morellinos are delicious. We preferred the Lorenzolo, which is less oaky than the Pomonte.

●	Capel Rosso '04	▼▼	5
●	Morellino di Scansano Lorenzolo '05	▼▼	4
●	Morellino di Scansano Pomonte '05	▼	4
●	Morellino di Scansano Pomonte '04	▽▽	4

PROVVEDITORE
LOC. SALAIOLO, 174
58054 SCANSANO (GR)
TEL. 0564599237 - 3487018670
www.provveditore.it

This classic Scansano winery manages to keep up to date without straying from tradition. So alongside the modern, beautifully made Campo La Chiesa '05 with its exquisitely soft, balanced palate we tasted the more rugged Morellino Sassato '05. The Bargaglino '05 is unpretentious.

●	Campo La Chiesa '05	▼▼	4
○	Bianco di Pitigliano Bargaglino '05	▼	3
●	Morellino di Scansano Sassato '05	▼	4
●	Campo La Chiesa '01	▽▽	5

Tenuta Farneta

loc. Farneta, 161
53048 Sinalunga (SI)
tel. 0577631025 - 0577631026
www.vignetoitalia.com

The monovarietal Sangiovese Bentivoglio '04 has very clear sweet oaky aromas while the palate is a steady crescendo of fat, sweet tannins. The Bongoverno '04 from sangiovese and merlot is very nice and drinkable but a little light in the finish.

● Bentivoglio '04	TT	4
● Bongoverno '04	T	6
● Bentivoglio '03	YY	4
● Bongoverno '03	YY	6

Incontri

loc. Fossoni, 38
57028 Suvereto (LI)
tel. 0565829401 - 3804138933
www.incontriwine.it

This winery's unquestionable potential is sadly not reflected in all the wines. The best is the Lagobruno '03, a blend of 50 per cent sangiovese with cabernet sauvignon and merlot. Its pulpy, nicely acidic palate has a slightly drying finish. The new red Martellino and the Vignanuova '05 are good.

● Lagobruno '03	TT	5
● Val di Cornia Rosso Martellino '04	T	3
○ Val di Cornia Bianco Vignanuova '05	T	3
● Lagobruno '02	YY	5

Terricciola

loc. Terricciola, 195
57028 Suvereto (LI)
tel. 0565829493

Terricciola's five hectares of vineyards produce wines that have the same name, Antares, but different blends. The '03 and '04 versions of the sangiovese and merlot blend are quite good. The '03 has a sweet, even palate while the '04 is fruity and medium-textured with a well-judged flavour.

● Antares Sangiovese & Merlot '03	T	3
● Antares Sangiovese & Merlot '04	T	3

Casanova della Spinetta

loc. Casanova
56030 Terricciola (PI)
tel. 0141877396
www.la-spinetta.com

The Rivetti family's Tuscan winery presented Nero di Casanova '05, a monovarietal Sangiovese with strawberry fruit on the nose and an enjoyably juicy palate. The other two wines are less focused. Sezzana and Sassontino, both from '03, both show aromas in need of fine-tuning.

● Nero di Casanova '05	TT	4
● Sassontino '03	T	5
● Sezzana '03	T	5
● Nero di Casanova '04	YY	4

Podere La Chiesa

via di Casanova, 13
56030 Terricciola (PI)
tel. 0587653286 - 0587635484
www.sabinianodicasanova.com

Sabiniano di Casanova '04 made the finals as usual with its lovely powerful colour and subtle tannins. The new star of this small but valid winery is Le Redole di Casanova '05 from sangiovese with a little canaiolo. It shows immediate potential, which will surely find fuller expression over time.

● Sabiniano di Casanova '04	TT	5
● Le Redole di Casanova '05	T	3
● Sabiniano di Casanova '01	YY	5
● Sabiniano di Casanova '03	YY	5

Fattoria Dianella Fucini

via Dianella, 48
50059 Vinci (FI)
tel. 0571508166
www.fattoriadianella.it

Forty-five of the 240 hectares are planted to vine, mainly sangiovese. The debut wines impressed. Le Veggie di Neri '04 is good, rounded and mouthfilling with glossy tannins. The Chianti '05 is very well-made and the Matto delle Giungaie '03 is very pleasant.

● Le Veglie di Neri '04	TT	4
● Chianti '05	TT	3*
● Il Matto delle Giungaie '03	T	5

MARCHE

In general 2005 was not an exceptional year for Verdicchio, at least for the standard-label products. For Rosso Piceno and Rosso Conero, it was much the same story, although we tasted very few reds from the vintage and therefore prefer to err on the side of caution. The few whites that we did like came mainly from Matelica, which proved yet again that this area is very well suited to the verdicchio grape. The excellent Verdicchio di Matelica Mirum by La Monacesca is another illustration of the point for it soared away with Three Glasses. The 2005 growing year leads on from 2004, which was originally considered to be a lesser vintage. With hindsight, however, it is beginning to show surprisingly well, especially in the Castelli di Jesi DOC zone. Podium by Garofoli, Balciana by Sartarelli, Le Case di Vallerosa by Bonci and the spectacular Riserva by Villa Bucci all demonstrated just how good 2004 was and picked up Three very well-earned Glasses each. Now that the Verdicchios have sold out, there is very little to talk about regarding whites, with the exception of the superb ageing curve of the heavenly Pecorino from Offida. We just hope that this wine's impressive commercial success does not prompt any producers to cash in unintelligently, thereby jeopardizing the wine's future. The section on reds is full of success stories, albeit with one or two caveats. No Rosso Conero was judged good enough for Three Glasses – the excellent Chaos 2004 from Fattoria Le Terrazze is made in the zone, but is not released as a DOC – even though the average level seems currently to be on better form than Rosso Piceno or Rosso Piceno Superiore. The Three Glasses awarded to Il Maschio da Monte 2004, a Rosso Piceno produced by Santa Barbara, and to Velenosi's Rosso Piceno Superiore Roggio del Filare 2003 would seem to indicate the contrary but sadly they are merely excellent examples of how much unrealized potential there is in the Marche. This is particularly the case for Rosso Piceno Superiore, which has the potential to become the top wine for all Piceno producers but which is often relegated to secondary status. Instead of blending it with sangiovese, as prescribed by the DOC regulations, producers prefer to use the montepulciano grape on its own – as in the Kurni 2004 by Oasi degli Angeli and the Regina del Bosco 2003 by Fattoria Delzi – or blended with cabernet, like Barricadiero 2004 by Aurora. When tasting the results, you cannot blame the producers who do this but it does mean that the future of the Rosso Piceno Superiore denomination needs to be rethought.

Del Carmine

loc. Torrette di Ancona
via del Carmine, 51
60020 Ancona
tel. 071889403
www.aziendadelcarmine.it

The Del Carmine estate belongs to the Roversi family, who have ten hectares of vines in Matelica. Three quarters of the vine stock is verdicchio and the remainder is sangiovese, ciliegiolo and cabernet sauvignon. Even though they have only been bottling for five years, overseen by oenologist Roberto Potentini, this is not a new business. There is a long family tradition of winemaking that goes back into the mists of time. Antonio Roversi is a descendant of the Censi Mancia family whose wines won prizes at the beginning of the 20th century in Paris. The jewels of the range are the two Verdicchio di Matelicas, which are both aged in stainless steel. Aja Lunga 2005 is a selection containing the Roversis' best grapes and consequently has a highly complex nose of almonds, lime blossom, hints of citrus and chamomile. Attractively soft on the palate, it has a full flavour that drives through to an anise-tinged finish. Petrara 2005 is fresher and less complex, but extremely drinkable. Its strong point is the typicity of its aromas of intense lemon peel and almonds, which are then echoed on the palate and sustained by good acid backbone. The two reds from the Colli Maceratesi DOC aren't quite as good. Petrara Rosso 2005 has a nice nose with red fruits but on the palate there are some rough edges of acidity and a slightly bitter note. San Vicino 2003 is a little overripe on the nose and palate and it is already coming towards the end of its ageing curve.

○	Verdicchio di Matelica Aja Lunga '05	🍷🍷	4*
○	Verdicchio di Matelica Petrara '05	🍷🍷	3*
●	Colli Maceratesi Petrara Rosso '05	🍷	3
●	Colli Maceratesi San Vicino '03		4

ANCONA

Lanari

fraz. Varano
via Pozzo, 142
60029 Ancona
tel. 0712861343
www.lanarivini.it

Luca Lanari's estate in the Parco del Monte Conero consists of around 12 hectares of montepulciano. This variety is very well adapted to the chalk and clay soils of these hillsides, where the smells and colours of Mediterranean scrubland, vineyards and olive groves blend together in unique harmony. This is where Luca and his assistant, Giancarlo Soverchia, strive steadfastly to produce wines with personality that reflect their passion for the vineyards. In analysing the range presented to us this year, we'll start with Rosso Conero Fibbio 2004. Densely coloured and at first reluctant on the nose, it then opens out onto notes of sour cherries and morello cherries followed by tobacco and liquorice. It is better on the palate, which echoes the fruit of the nose showing blackberries, morello cherries and notes of sweet spice. Balance is good, the close-knit tannins are assertive and the finish is medium-long. Rosso Conero Clivio 2004 has ripe fruit on the nose, lifted by a slightly vegetal quality and soft spices that are not yet fully integrated. In the mouth, the alcohol and tannins are drying and detract a little from the finish. Rosso Conero 2005 has sweet fragrant fruit and although the alcohol on the palate is exuberant, there is decent overall structure to support it. Lanari Rosa 2005 has slight hints of fruit and flowers and marked freshness in the mouth.

●	Rosso Conero Clivio '04	🍷🍷	5
●	Rosso Conero Fibbio '04	🍷🍷	7
●	Rosso Conero '05	🍷	4
⊙	Lanari Rosa '05		3
●	Rosso Conero Fibbio '99	YYY	6
●	Rosso Conero Aretè '01	YY	6
●	Rosso Conero Fibbio '03	YY	6

ANCONA

Marchetti
Fraz. Pinocchio
via di Pontelungo, 166
60131 Ancona
tel. 071897386
www.marchettiwines.it

Before talking about the real house speciality – wines made with the montepulciano that Maurizio Marchetti grows in a beautiful vineyard on the slopes of Monte Conero – we would like to give the new release of Verdicchio Tenuta del Cavaliere the space it deserves. The 2005 is every bit as aristocratic as the estate's reds, giving lime blossom, hay and ripe apples on the nose before the mouth unveils well-defined flavour, juiciness despite crisp acidity and a finish that ends on a fruit-packed high note. The Marchetti estate can now be said to have a house style, which can be summed up as emphasis on the purity of the fruit. Tasting the two Rosso Coneros illustrates this well. Villa Bonomi 2004 is rich all round. Its very deep purple heralds a nose of morello cherries, blueberries and an elegant touch of balsam. These intense aromas are echoed on the palate and then amplified in a long finish that also showcases the tannic substance of the wine. This all applies to the Rosso Conero 2004 as well, but in a slightly less intense interpretation. But far from being a criticism, the more relaxed texture actually makes for a more easily drinkable wine, which should be enjoyed for its vitality and fruit. The tasting notes ended with a Verdicchio 2005, which was light and citrus-like. It's well made but nothing more.

●	Rosso Conero Villa Bonomi Ris. '04	🍷🍷	5
●	Rosso Conero '04	🍷🍷	4*
○	Verdicchio dei Castelli di Jesi Cl. Tenuta del Cavaliere '05	🍷🍷	4*
○	Verdicchio dei Castelli di Jesi Cl. '05		4
●	Rosso Conero Villa Bonomi Ris. '02	🍷🍷🍷	5
●	Rosso Conero Villa Bonomi Ris. '03	🍷🍷	5
●	Rosso Conero Villa Bonomi Ris. '01	🍷🍷	5

ANCONA

Alessandro Moroder
loc. Montacuto
via Montacuto, 112
60029 Ancona
tel. 071898232
www.moroder-vini.it

The factors that have underpinned the enviable quality of Serenella and Alessandro Moroder's estate for many years can be summed up as: excellent calcareous clay soils for reds; the Monte Conero promontory with its favourable climate; and the oenological assistance of Franco Bernabei. The Moroders also show admirable commitment, as for example when the cellar decided to take the economically painful decision not to produce their top wine, Rosso Conero Riserva Dorico, in the poor 2002 vintage. The 2003 is not ready yet and will only be available at future tastings. But the 2003 version of Ankon, a splendid blend of montepulciano, cabernet and merlot, is a clear success and easily reached the Three Glass final. It opens with elegant vegetal aromas on the nose, followed by pure ripe fruit still slightly masked by wood notes which have not yet been fully absorbed. It is excellent in the mouth, where dense, even tannins and a solid but soft body coat the palate, ensuring good length and a delicately spicy, dry finish. The Moroder Rosso Conero is always scrupulously crafted and a leading example of its type. The 2004 is redolent of raspberries and cherries, has a soft palate with just the right level of tannins, well balanced flavours and good thrust. Rosa di Montacuto 2005 is a blend of montepulciano, alicante and sangiovese with a nose of raspberries and strawberries that reappear on the refreshingly tangy palate. The amber coloured Oro, from moscato, malvasia and trebbiano, shows very ripe fruit, a sweet fat palate and a light finish with a twist of bitterness.

●	Ankon '03	🍷🍷	6
●	Rosso Conero '04	🍷🍷	4*
⊙	Rosa di Montacuto '05	🍷	3
○	Oro		5
●	Rosso Conero Dorico '90	🍷🍷🍷	5
●	Rosso Conero Dorico '93	🍷🍷🍷	5
●	Rosso Conero Dorico Ris. '01	🍷🍷	6
●	Ankon '00	🍷🍷	6
●	Rosso Conero Dorico '00	🍷🍷	5
●	Rosso Conero Dorico '98	🍷🍷	5

ARCEVIA (AN)

CONTI DI BUSCARETO
VIA S. APOLLINARE, 126
60011 ARCEVIA (AN)
TEL. 0717988020 - 0717913180
www.contidibuscareto.com

Conti di Buscareto is a young winery set up by Enrico Giacomelli and Claudio Gabellini, who used to be partners in a software business. A few years ago, they decided to invest in the wine sector and immediately showed that they have very clear ideas and concrete goals. The property now has 65 hectares of vines acquired in several stages at Morro d'Alba and the magnificent Arcevia zone. The grapes are vinified in the new, well-equipped winery in the municipality of Ostra. In setting up the vineyard and winery, they turned to experienced oenologist Giancarlo Soverchia, while the head of day-to-day production is the very professional Vito Camussi. The keenly priced Verdicchio 2005 has great typicity, with a soft attack and good thrust in the mouth, full-flavoured acidity and nice body. Lacrima 2004 is simple, nicely aromatic and has a slightly bitter finish. Crimà 2005 is made with lacrima grapes but released as non-DOC and it would be very enjoyable for immediate consumption as a young everyday wine. Compagnia della Rosa 2003 is a very well-made selection of lacrima grapes with richness, nice structure, intact fruit, creaminess, great balance and convincing complexity. The Lacrima Nicolò di Buscareto 2003 has similar characteristics but the different vinification process has made it a little heavy to the detriment of freshness and fruit. Last but not least, the 2003 Verdicchio Passito has almond and marzipan aromas, good acidity and measured sweetness.

●	Lacrima di Morro d'Alba Compagnia della Rosa '03	🍷🍷	5
○	Verdicchio dei Castelli di Jesi Passito '03	🍷🍷	5
○	Verdicchio dei Castelli di Jesi '05	🍷🍷	3*
●	Lacrima di Morro d'Alba Nicolò di Buscareto '03	🍷	6
●	Lacrima di Morro d'Alba '04	🍷	4
●	Crimà '05	🍷	3
⊙	Rosa '05	🍷	3

ASCOLI PICENO

VELENOSI
LOC. MONTICELLI
VIA DEI BIANCOSPINI, 11
63100 ASCOLI PICENO
TEL. 0736341218
www.velenosivini.com

It will not bother Angela and Ercole Velenosi, or their partner Paolo Garbini, that Roggio di Filare beat Ludi again in the in-house race for Three Glasses. While they are masters of the elegant modern style with intense flavours, as represented by their montepulciano, merlot, cabernet and syrah blend, we know that their hearts beat a little bit faster for Rosso Piceno Superiore, the first wine produced back when they started their quality-improvement plan. The 2003 version of Roggio del Filare comes from an intelligent approach to the hot year, showing intense spice aromas and sumptuous mouthfeel without being in any way too tannic or overripe. This vintage also managed to raise the quality of Brecciarolo to unprecedented levels, thanks to precise morello cherry notes and a fleshy fruit character. Falerio Vigna Solaria and Sauvignon Villa Angela are both ever-dependable fruity, drinkable whites from the most recent vintage. All this would already be a creditable product offering for a company that is expanding in international markets and has just passed the milestone of a million bottles per year. But no, they have also produced two welcome new offerings. A well modulated Verdicchio dei Castelli di Jesi 2005 and Spumante The Rose, a traditional method rosé based on pinot nero with a small amount of chardonnay that shows compact and long with a fragrant fruits of the forest nose, complement the Velenosi Brut, which continues to be very enjoyable and competitive.

●	Rosso Piceno Sup. Roggio del Filare '03	🍷🍷🍷	6
●	Ludi '04	🍷🍷	6
○	Velenosi Brut	🍷🍷	5
●	Rosso Piceno Sup. Il Brecciarolo '03	🍷🍷	3*
○	Falerio dei Colli Ascolani Vigna Solaria '05	🍷🍷	3*
○	Linagre Sauvignon Villa Angela '05	🍷🍷	4
○	Verdicchio dei Castelli di Jesi Cl. '05	🍷🍷	4
⊙	Velenosi Brut The Rose	🍷🍷	6
○	Villa Angela Chardonnay '05	🍷	4
●	Rosso Piceno Sup. Roggio del Filare '02	🍷🍷🍷 (white)	5

BARBARA (AN)

SANTA BARBARA
B.GO MAZZINI, 35
60010 BARBARA (AN)
TEL. 0719674249
www.vinisantabarbara.it

Reading Stefano Antonucci's tasting notes, one gets the suspicion that he was keener to dedicate the name of his estate to the patron saint of artillery than to the local town. Indeed, his cellars are full of explosive wines. The most potent of them all has a peculiar name, Il Maschio da Monte (the male of the mountain). Unsurprisingly, it is mainly montepulciano with the dark power that characterizes the variety's best wines. Now that the marked animal nose of previous years has gone, the 2004 version detonates on the nose with a wide range of smells from black fruits, liquorice and spices. The palate has assertively flavoursome tannins which soon amalgamate with the full, soft body to produce a well-integrated whole. The Stefano Antonucci Rosso 2004 is a well-made Bordeaux blend whose coffee notes are slightly more dominant than its typical green aromas before it expands on the well-integrated palate. Pathos 2004, an equal blend of syrah, cabernet and merlot, has a similar character but more softness. The Riserva di Verdicchio Stefano Antonucci has elegance and good ageing potential. The aromatic contribution of the barriques is still recognizable but is on its way to being integrated and in any case does not overpower the rich vein of fruit on the full-flavoured and full-bodied structure, ending on a fascinating citrus finish. Verdicchio Le Vaglie 2005 is a highly enjoyable drink and Tardivo Ma non Tardo 2003, from overripe grapes with high sugar and aromas of stewed fruit, is a fine dessert wine.

● Rosso Piceno Il Maschio da Monte '04	▼▼▼	5
● Stefano Antonucci Rosso '04	▼▼	4*
○ Verdicchio dei Castelli di Jesi Cl. Stefano Antonucci Ris. '04	▼▼	4*
○ Verdicchio dei Castelli di Jesi Cl. Tardivo Ma non Tardo Ris. '03	▼▼	6
● Pathos '04	▼▼	7
○ Verdicchio dei Castelli di Jesi Cl. Le Vaglie '05	▼▼	4
● Vigna San Bartolo '04	▼	4
○ Verdicchio dei Castelli di Jesi Cl. Pignocco '05	▼	3
○ Verdicchio dei Castelli di Jesi Nidastore '05	▼	3

BELVEDERE OSTRENSE (AN)

LUCIANO LANDI
VIA GAVIGLIANO, 16
60030 BELVEDERE OSTRENSE (AN)
TEL. 073162353
www.aziendalandi.it

Lacrima di Morro d'Alba is an ancient grape variety with distinctive primary aromas but which can be quite awkward to grow. It does not always ripen fully and can therefore yield simple, and sometimes unbalanced, wines that lean towards the unpleasant end of the bitterness spectrum. Luciano Landi, who is an expert in the variety, has always gone for ripeness even if it costs him part of the crop. That's why his Lacrimas are very fruity with less aggressive tannins. The most shining example of his philosophy is Gavigliano 2004. Opaque purple with intense aromas of morello cherries and pot pourri, it is full and balanced on the palate, which progresses to a long finish with that nicely reprises the nose. The basic Lacrima 2005 has pure varietal primary aromas and good balance knitted into a medium-bodied style, in line with the difficult year. But Landi's winemaking skills are not limited to the lacrima grape, so much so that Goliardo 2003 actually turned out to be the best wine from the estate and made it to the Three Glass finals. It is a montepulciano, merlot and cabernet sauvignon blend with enviable concentration of fruit, coffee and sweet spices on the nose. The palate has a powerful structure bolstered by very fine-grained tannins, oak and very pure fruit.

● Goliardo '03	▼▼	6
● Lacrima di Morro d'Alba Gavigliano '04	▼▼	4*
● Lacrima di Morro d'Alba '05	▼	3
● Torre di Re '02	▽▽	4
● Goliardo '02	▽	6

CAMERANO (AN)

SPINSANTI
VIA FONTE INFERNO, 11
60021 CAMERANO (AN)
TEL. 071731797

The scores for this winery have been the same for a few years, as a glance at the table below will show. Sassòne made it to the Three Glass final and Adino and Camars both easily won Two Glasses. However, inertia is not a term you could apply to Catia Spinsanti and her husband Andrea Gaggiotti's small estate. They are so in love with winemaking and their eight-hectare estate that they always seem to be busy in the winery or among the rows. Seen from another perspective, of course, their consistency is a guarantee for the consumer. Hopefully, one day this pattern will be broken, and Sassòne will win our highest national award. The 2004 missed the target by only a whisker, probably as a result of the lack of assurance in the aroma profile, a characteristic of big-bodied Montepulcianos with a lot of personality. This phenomenon, which is usually a passing phase and linked to the variety's marked reductive tendency, takes the edge off the aromas, which range from morello cherries to spices and cocoa. On the other hand, the palate is astounding, showing generous and deep, with an unswervingly intense thrust of flavour and sweet tannins. The purity of the fruit is the defining point of both the Rosso Conero Adino 2005, from 90 per cent montepulciano with sangiovese, and Rosso Conero Camars 2005, a single-variety Montepulciano. The former tastes rounder, has consistent aromas and good drinkability while the latter has a more solid structure, full-flavoured tannins and a good big, fleshy finish reminiscent of liquorice and ripe cherries.

● Sassòne '04	🍷🍷	5
● Rosso Conero Adino '05	🍷🍷	3*
● Rosso Conero Camars '05	🍷🍷	4
● Sassòne '01	YY	5
● Sassòne '03	YY	5
● Sassòne '00	YY	5
● Sassòne '02	YY	5
● Rosso Conero Adino '04	YY	3
● Rosso Conero Camars '04	YY	4

CAMERANO (AN)

SILVANO STROLOGO
VIA OSIMANA, 89
60021 CAMERANO (AN)
TEL. 071731104 - 071732359

Silvano Strologo enjoys creating extreme Montepulcianos. He likes this particular variety for its levels of body and extract, which he tries to push to the limit. His aim is to express the warmth and sunlight of the vineyards, but in his own cool, rational way. This concept is illustrated in Silvano's wines, which all seem to be bear the same imprint, and of course defining a precise style should be a fundamental aim for any self-respecting producer. The only caveat in Silvano's case is that the freshness of the fruit is sometimes sacrificed in favour of extreme extraction, and drinkability suffers as a result. Rosso Conero Riserva Decebalo 2003 is the most integrated and balanced with a nose redolent of animal notes and cherries in alcohol, and a good palate with a decent dose of refreshing acidity. On the other hand, Rosso Conero Traiano 2004 almost exclusively focuses on rich, soft structure shot through with marked notes of cooked prunes and jam. Rosso Conero Julius 2005 is a young wine with a nose that is already mature. The fruit is still fresh on the palate and the relatively long taste profile is reminiscent of herbaceous notes.

● Rosso Conero Decebalo Ris. '03	🍷🍷	6
● Rosso Conero Traiano '04	🍷🍷	5
● Rosso Conero Julius '05	🍷	4
● Rosso Conero Traiano '00	YYY	5
● Rosso Conero Traiano '02	YY	5
● Rosso Conero Traiano '01	YY	5
● Rosso Conero Decebalo Ris. '02	YY	5
● Rosso Conero Traiano '03	YY	5

CASTEL DI LAMA (AP)

Tenuta De Angelis
via San Francesco, 10
63030 Castel di Lama (AP)
tel. 073687429
www.tenutadeangelis.it

Year after year, De Angelis wines line up in a rigid, well thought-out hierarchy. This is made possible by Quinto Fausti's deft handling of the raw material that oenologist Roberto Potentini is then able to vinify with enviable consistency of quality. The weighty Rosso Piceno Oro selection sometimes approaches the quality level of Anghelos, but never quite beats it to the position of the estate's top wine. Both made it to the Three Glass final, where Anghelos 2004 very nearly gained the award. It is a montepulciano, sangiovese and cabernet sauvignon blend, with beautiful fruit on a nose that shows exceptionally intense, clear morello cherries, blueberries and chocolate. The tannins are very sweet in the mouth, where the balanced, full body progresses seamlessly through to a crescendo finish. Oro 2004 may have conceded the top spot but it still manages to give a large dose of ripe red fruits mingled with powerful oaky notes. On the palate, the tannic framework is prominent but integrated into the wine's fleshy structure. Rosso Piceno Superiore 2004 is also highly satisfactory. A marriage of big fruit and tannic austerity, it never descends into heaviness or overripeness. In the presence of so many big hitters, a very keenly priced Rosso Piceno 2005 is not a welcome addition. As usual, there was a little less energy on show from the two young whites, Falerio and Chardonnay Prato Grande, which are both easy-drinking wines with a bitter twist on the finish. We preferred the simple floral and cut grass aromas of the Falerio.

●	Anghelos '04	▼▼	5
●	Rosso Piceno Sup. Oro '04	▼▼	4
●	Rosso Piceno Sup. '04	▼▼	3*
○	Falerio dei Colli Ascolani '05	▼	1*
●	Rosso Piceno '05	▼	2*
○	Prato Grande Chardonnay '05		2
●	Anghelos '01	▽▽▽	5
●	Anghelos '99	▽▽▽	5
●	Anghelos '02	▽▽	5
●	Anghelos '03	▽▽	5
●	Anghelos '00	▽▽	5
●	Rosso Piceno Sup. Oro '03	▽▽	5

CASTELPLANIO (AN)

Fazi Battaglia
via Roma, 117
60032 Castelplanio (AN)
tel. 073181591 - 06844311
www.fazibattaglia.it

An estate's importance is not measured solely by numbers: heritage and product strength are also crucial. Fazi Battaglia is not short of any of the above. With 3,000,000 bottles from 350 hectares under vine, 80 per cent of the estate's production goes into Titulus, the famous amphora-shaped bottle which is still a symbol of Verdicchio in so many parts of the world. The rest is spread across a range that would cover all genres but for a lack of sparkling and fortified wines.
Nevertheless, the cellar has exclusive distribution arrangements with very good Champagne and Port producers to fill the gaps. The Verdicchios are predictably excellent. Masaccio 2004 was similar to previous years, but did not reach Three Glasses as it has in the past. The aroma profile is full and varied with notes of dried fruit and honey, followed by a big-boned palate that is savoury and enveloping at the same time. The oak-aged Verdicchio San Sisto 2003 has good integration of attractive balsamic tones with more harmonious hints of anise and dried flowers before the palate shows fat and attractively nuanced. The aromatic precision of Verdicchio Le Moie and its absolute typicity are really made to sing in the cool 2005 vintage. The reds are also good, the fragrant Rosso Conero 2005 winning plaudits for its precise fruit aromas. Riserva Passo del Lupo 2003 is austere on the palate and the nose shows liqueur cherries. Arkezia 2003 is another excellent wine from dried verdicchio grapes. It is intense and creamy, although lacking in its usual fascinating hint of botrytis.

○	Verdicchio dei Castelli di Jesi Cl. San Sisto Ris. '03	▼▼	5
○	Verdicchio dei Castelli di Jesi Cl. Sup. Massaccio '04	▼▼	4*
○	Arkezia Muffo di S. Sisto '03	▼▼	6
●	Rosso Conero Passo del Lupo Ris. '03	▼▼	5
●	Rosso Conero '05	▼▼	4*
○	Verdicchio dei Castelli di Jesi Cl. Sup. Le Moie '05	▼▼	4*
○	Verdicchio dei Castelli di Jesi Cl. Titulus '05		4
○	Verdicchio dei Castelli di Jesi Cl. Sup. Massaccio '03	▽▽▽	4

CASTELRAIMONDO (MC)

COLLESTEFANO
LOC. COLLE STEFANO, 3
62022 CASTELRAIMONDO (MC)
TEL. 0737640439
www.collestefano.com

Some people think that there is an intrinsic relationship between the quality of a wine and the beauty of its environment, defined as not just aesthetics but rather as an overall vision encompassing all aspects of the land, the suitability of the site climate and local viticultural traditions. If you leave the beaten track to visit the forgotten corner of the world around Castelraimondo and Matelica at the foot of the Apennines, you will see the force of this theory from the evidence before your eyes. Tasting Fabio and Silvia Marchionni's Verdicchio could convince you once and for all. Its pale straw yellow introduces distinct, precise green apples, almonds, grapefruit, acacia flowers and hawthorn. All these elements are perfectly expressed and clearly identifiable yet they meld together magnificently into an intense whole. The palate opens with a decisive attack, progresses aristocratically and shows supple structure. The finish is fascinating. Given that there is only moderate alcohol, the work of drawing out the back palate is left to the lively extract and full flavour profile. It is easy to compare it to a Mosel or Rhine Riesling on this point and another similarity is its impressive minerality, the hallmark of exceptional ageing potential. But the strong varietal typicity is pure Marche.

○	Verdicchio di Matelica Collestefano '05	🍷🍷	4*
○	Verdicchio di Matelica Collestefano '02	YY	4
○	Verdicchio di Matelica Collestefano '03	YY	4
○	Verdicchio di Matelica Collestefano '04	YY	4
○	Verdicchio di Matelica Collestefano '01	YY	4

CINGOLI (MC)

CANTINA COLÒGNOLA
VIA COLÒGNOLA
62011 CINGOLI (MC)
TEL. 0733616438
www.agrarialombardi.it

It is important to have faith in the young. They make mistakes but they do represent the future. And the Cològnola estate is no exception to the rule. Incidentally, the name is the same as a municipality in the Veneto with its own co-operative winery, but the accent is different. The obvious desire here to please shows up some naivety in execution: Verdicchio Labieno 2004 is overpowered by wood, Passito Cingulum 2004 lacks definition and Esino Bianco Condotto 2005 has very little character. But it's nothing that can't be remedied: all that is required is the humility to understand the root causes of problems. Antonietta Lombardi's estate gives no cause for concern on this front. Then there are the positives. The best wine is Verdicchio San Michele della Ghiffa 2004, which comes from a beautiful vineyard surrounded by a small oak wood. It has a tempting aroma profile with dried fruits and almonds knitted together by a touch of botrytis: the grapes were harvested late. Or there is Cantamaggio 2004, which although obtained from the often green and tannic lacrima grape, is fresh, fruity and easy-drinking. The Buraco 2004 is a Montepulciano with uncomplicated drinkability and fragrance balanced by some acidity on mid palate. Finally, Sestriere 2003 is made from a blend of montepulciano and merlot. Balsam on the nose is soon followed by contrasting vegetal notes, medium-bodied structure on the palate and a finish that is not overly long, being held back by tannins that have yet to mature.

●	Buraco '04	🍷🍷	4*
●	Cantamaggio '04	🍷🍷	5
○	Verdicchio dei Castelli di Jesi Cl Sup. S. Michele della Ghiffa '04	🍷🍷	4*
●	Sestiere '03	🍷	4
○	Verdicchio dei Castelli di Jesi Cl. Labieno Ris. '04		5
○	Verdicchio dei Castelli di Jesi Passito Cingulum '04		5
○	Esino Bianco Condotto '05		2

CINGOLI (MC)

TENUTA DI TAVIGNANO
LOC. TAVIGNANO
62011 CINGOLI (MC)
TEL. 0733617303

Cingoli is perched at 600 metres above sea level on the top of a hill halfway between the mountains and the sea. Its stunning views have earned it the nickname of the balcony of the Marche. Tavignano on the other hand is an outlying hamlet towards the Esino river, in the direction of Castelli di Jesi. The view from here is very nearly as good: an irregular series of hills joins the Apennines in the distance in a series of multicoloured humpbacks. Verdicchio has traditionally been grown here and it translates the beauty of the landscape into the glass in brilliant green hues, intense aromas of almonds, apples and anise, and a full-flavoured, concentrated palate. Robust alcohol makes it sweet, and a massive dose of extract worthy of a red wine gives it depth. That was Misco 2005, which is still very youthful and would repay cellaring. Verdicchio Tavignano 2005 is quite similar, but has slightly more direct, varietal tones. It is nicely taut, long and profound. Vigna Verde 2005 is less ambitious and more explicitly fresh with an acid backbone and citrus-flavoured finish. Whereas the great Jesi grape dominates the whites, montepulciano and sangiovese are no less important from the point of view of traditional reds. Those are the grapes in Rosso Piceno Libenter, which we did not taste as the estate has decided to let it age further, and a juicy Rosso Piceno Tavignano 2005 with simple, enjoyable fruitiness.

○	Verdicchio dei Castelli di Jesi Cl. Sup. Misco '05	🍷🍷	4
○	Verdicchio dei Castelli di Jesi Cl. Sup. Tavignano '05	🍷🍷	3*
●	Rosso Piceno Tavignano '05	🍷	4
○	Verdicchio dei Castelli di Jesi Cl. Vigna Verde '05	🍷	2*
●	Rosso Piceno Libenter '03	YY	4
○	Verdicchio dei Castelli di Jesi Cl. Sup. Misco '04	YY	4
○	Verdicchio dei Castelli di Jesi Cl. Sup. Misco '03	YY	4

CIVITANOVA MARCHE (MC)

BOCCADIGABBIA
LOC. FONTESPINA
C.DA CASTELLETTA, 56
62012 CIVITANOVA MARCHE (MC)
TEL. 073370728
www.boccadigabbia.com

For Boccadigabbia's owner, Elvio Alessandri, the art of blending holds little appeal. He does deign to mix montepulciano and sangiovese in the full-bodied, tannic Rosso Piceno 2004. He will add 15 per cent of verdicchio to the maximum possible amount of maceratino in his savoury, evolved Colli Maceratesi Ribona Mont'Anello 2004. But these choices are all about observing the DOC production rules. When he has free rein with French varieties – which have historical links to the area as the estate used to be one of the farms belonging to the Napoleonic administration of Civitanova – he only vinifies single-variety wines. Consequently the Cabernet Sauvignon, Akronte 2003, and the Merlot, Pix 2003, are the purest and most faithful possible renditions of these grapes, showing how they react to being grown a few kilometres from the Adriatic in a sunny climate tempered by warm sea breezes. The characteristic common to both wines is a good integration and structural harmony, with Akronte showing more complex, austere and uncompromising characteristics, while Pix is rounder with a more progressive palate. A number of wines did not have new releases: Saltapicchio Sangiovese, the only varietal wine from a local grape, the international-style Montalperti Chardonnay and the never run-of-the-mill Girone Pinot Nero. In their absence we finished on the La Castelletta Pinot Grigio 2005, which was floral and fresh, with a soft winning style and a delicate twist of bitterness on the finish.

●	Akronte '03	🍷🍷	8
●	Pix Merlot '03	🍷🍷	7
●	Rosso Piceno Boccadigabbia '04	🍷	4
○	La Castelletta Pinot Grigio '05	🍷	4
○	Colli Maceratesi Ribona Mont'Anello '04		4
●	Akronte '93	YYY	7
●	Akronte '94	YYY	7
●	Akronte '95	YYY	7
●	Akronte '97	YYY	7
●	Akronte '98	YYY	7
●	Akronte '01	YY	7
●	Pix Merlot '01	YY	7
●	Saltapicchio Sangiovese '01	YY	6
○	Montalperti Chardonnay '03	Y	5

CIVITANOVA MARCHE (MC)

CANTINE FONTEZOPPA
C.DA SAN DOMENICO, 24
62012 CIVITANOVA MARCHE (MC)
TEL. 0733790504

Cantine Fontezoppa is a new estate set up by the Falc industrial group. The holdings currently consist of around 50 hectares under vine in two areas. One group of vineyards is the Serrapetrona and San Severino Marche zone at around 500 metres above sea level, where there is a wide daytime temperature range. The other vines are on the Adriatic, around Civitanova Alta, where the modern winery is based. The technical director for the whole estate is oenologist Giancarlo Soverchia, who is ably backed up by Giordano Torresi in other areas. The seaside vineyards are planted to sangiovese, cabernet sauvignon, merlot and lacrima whereas in Serrapetrona and San Severino, they have intelligently chosen to grow the local variety, vernaccia nera, which is currently only vinified as still wine. Fontezoppa used this noble grape variety to produce Morò 2003, which is full and fresh, with pure fruit, good progression on the palate, nice dryness, softness and length. Carapetto is a very successful classic Colli Maceratesi Rosso with a good proportion of sangiovese to which some merlot and cabernet has been added. The 2004 is intensely fruity, tasty and drinkable thanks to its round, fresh juiciness and body. Its younger brother Vardò 2004 is forward, simple and well made. Serrapetrona Falcotto 2004 is mainly vernaccia nera with 15 per cent sangiovese, and is a model of balance and vivacity, its rich structure never descending into heaviness. Our final praise goes to the sangiovese, cabernet, merlot and lacrima blend, Piccinì 2005, the region's best rosé.

● Morò '03	🍷🍷	6
● Colli Maceratesi Rosso Carapetto '04	🍷🍷	5
● Serrapetrona Falcotto '04	🍷🍷	5
⊙ Piccinì '05	🍷🍷	4*
● Colli Maceratesi Rosso Vardò '04	🍷	3

CUPRA MARITTIMA (AP)

OASI DEGLI ANGELI
C.DA SANT'EGIDIO, 50
63012 CUPRA MARITTIMA (AP)
TEL. 0735778569
www.kurni.it

There is no doubt that Kurni is a unique wine. Taste it carefully once and you will recognize it anytime. It is impossible to mistake the rich, dense blackberries and blueberries. The palate is distinctively chewy and full yet remains fresh and consistent. All that substance is an excellent illustration of what montepulciano can achieve in this region of Italy. Kurni 2004, Marco Casolanetti and Eleonora Rossi's most recent offering, is the product of a commitment to extremely high quality from vine to winery: very dense planting patterns with over 10,000 vines per hectare, biodynamic viticulture, very low yields and carefully selected wood applied innovatively. It is a wine based on the principle of excess, which is a very difficult goal to achieve. Balance is achieved by adding components, making it a pleasure, not an effort, to drink. It would be easier to work by taking components away but Marco and Eleonora like challenges. We believe that Kurni is also a one-off, in the sense that it would be hard for anyone else to produce a similar style. Imitators run the risk of turning out pumped-up wines from inadequate grapes by using slapdash cellar techniques. The results will almost inevitably be disastrous and more often than not are merely exercises in oenology. Or to put it another way: leave Kurni to Marco, Eleonora and Oasi degli Angeli.

● Kurni '04	🍷🍷🍷	8
● Kurni '00	YYY	8
● Kurni '01	YYY	8
● Kurni '02	YYY	8
● Kurni '03	YYY	8
● Kurni '97	YYY	8
● Kurni '98	YYY	8
● Kurni '99	YY	8

CUPRAMONTANA (AN)

COLONNARA

VIA MANDRIOLE, 6
60034 CUPRAMONTANA (AN)
TEL. 0731780273
www.colonnara.it

This large Cupramontana co-operative was founded in 1959 and supervises its members' 210 hectares, producing around 1,200,000 bottles. Regrettably, it has been several years since it last performed to its full quality potential. We believe that this is just a passing phase that will soon be overcome and we are confident that the new head, Carlo Pigini Campanari, will be able to breathe new life into the winery. For the moment, we will continue to enjoy the attractive Verdicchio Cuprese 2005, where well-applied wood has enriched the fruity, pineapple nose giving it a buttery, hazelnut dimension. The attack on the palate is fine and elegant, followed by confident progression through the taste profile. Lacrima di Morro d'Alba Osiride 2005 is also convincing. Its clean nose, complexity and range transcend mere aromatics preceding a full-bodied palate and a long, dry finish. As the new cuvée of Brut Ubaldo Rosi has not yet been disgorged, the prize for the estate's best sparkling wine goes to the classic Colonnara Brut, which is fresh and vegetal, still fragrant and pleasant to drink. Finally, Rosso Conero Horus 2003 has good fresh fruit on the nose and a well-expressed palate.

●	Lacrima di Morro d'Alba Osiride '05	TT	3*
○	Verdicchio dei Castelli di Jesi Cl. Sup. Cuprese '05	TT	3*
●	Rosso Conero Horus '03	T	4
○	Colonnara Class Dolce	T	3
○	Colonnara Spumante Brut	T	3
●	Tornamagno '01		4
○	Verdicchio dei Castelli di Jesi Cl. Lyricus '05		3
○	Spumante Brut M. Cl. Ubaldo Rosi Ris. '98	YY	5
○	Verdicchio dei Castelli di Jesi Cl. Sup. Tùfico '03	YY	4

CUPRAMONTANA (AN)

VALLEROSA BONCI

VIA TORRE, 13
60034 CUPRAMONTANA (AN)
TEL. 0731789129
www.vallerosa-bonci.com

Wine is a living product. It breathes oxygen, it ages and purple prose terms like soul and character are used to describe it. How can we possibly do justice to the story of Vallerosa Bonci's Le Case 2004, Verdicchio dei Castelli di Jesi? It starts like a trashy novel: one brother, in this case Verdicchio San Michele, kept on winning prizes, was internationally successful and had won the full trust of the people. The other brother, our hero Le Case, never achieved any sort of fame, despite being made with the same high quality fruit and being brought up in the tender care of the Bonci family. Until this summer, that is, when Giuseppe Bonci wisely decided to put back the release of San Michele 2005 by a year for further maturation. At that moment, it seems as if Le Case 2004 lost its inhibitions. It left the shadows to which it had been consigned and took advantage of the occasion to show its accomplished elegance on nose and palate. It has subtle citrus and anise on the nose before the palate offers thrust powered by fullness of flavour, which only well-bred Verdicchios can produce. This time, Le Case is the name that appears on the list of Three Glass wines. We look forward to next year's contest, which will be even more spectacular since there will be new releases of Verdicchios Barré and Pietrone. Meanwhile the very drinkable Casanostra 2003 was fairly vegetal and the simple Verdicchio Viatorre 2005 was nicely bitter but a little thin on the palate. The Verdicchio Brut was very decent, as always.

○	Verdicchio dei Castelli di Jesi Cl. Sup. Le Case '04	TTT	4*
●	Casanostra '03	T	4
○	Verdicchio dei Castelli di Jesi Cl. Viatorre '05	T	3
○	Verdicchio dei Castelli di Jesi Cl. Spumante Brut Charmat	T	4
○	Verdicchio dei Castelli di Jesi Cl. Sup. S. Michele '00	YYY	4
○	Verdicchio dei Castelli di Jesi Cl. Pietrone Ris. '03	YY	5
○	Verdicchio dei Castelli di Jesi Cl. Sup. S. Michele '04	YY	4
○	Verdicchio dei Castelli di Jesi Cl. Manciano '04	YY	4

FERMO (FM)

FAUSTI
C.DA CASTELLETTA, 16
63023 FERMO (FM)
TEL. 0734620492 - 0734621023

Cristina Fausti and Domenico d'Angelo's cellar never rests for a moment. The fact that Vespro 2003 won top honours last year was just a starting point for them, not the end of a long road. This little estate of 11 hectares releasing 70,000 bottles is almost domestic in scale, but it is part of a wider area, Fermano, which is striving to be noticed and where there are new producers every year. The release of the 2004 Vespro can be considered one of the major events in the area. This year's 70-30 montepulciano and syrah blend has its usual power and intensity. Perhaps it is a little overpowered by the wood but at the same time it has an energetic, soft structure underpinned by fleshy fruit, very dense tannins and a long finish with full pepper, cherry and coffee notes. The 20,000 bottles available will walk off the shelves, especially when the wine's ageing potential is taken into account. Rosso Piceno Fausto 2005 on the other hand is more of an early drinker, showing dry and moderately fruity. The Vispo 2005, which is a Falerio for drinking within the year, has a broad fruity palate, with more focus on softness than on the lifted acids suggested by the name: "vispo" is Italian for sprightly.

● Vespro '04	▼▼	5
○ Falerio dei Colli Ascolani Vispo '05	▼	3
● Rosso Piceno Fausto '05	▼	3
● Vespro '03	▽▽▽	4
● Vespro '01	▽▽	4
● Vespro '02	▽▽	4

GROTTAMMARE (AP)

CARMINUCCI
VIA SAN LEONARDO, 39
63013 GROTTAMMARE (AP)
TEL. 0735735869
www.carminucci.com

Pierluigi Lorenzetti, who has long been consultant oenologist to the Carminucci family, is now working this winery on a twin-track strategy: the grapes for the distinctive Naumachos label arrive from hills in the Offida zone, while the flat seaside vineyards around the winery are harvested for the less expensive Grotte sul Mare range. The estate's top wine, Paccaosso 2003 Montepulciano, is distinguished by its intense deep colour. On the nose, the austerity and impenetrability of the fruit only slowly leave space for fresh balsamic notes, whereas the mouth is as hard as granite, and progression is linear through sweet vanilla and liquorice up to a long but slightly dry finish. With slightly more attentive use of wood and less extraction, it would have been a perfect wine. Naumachos 2003 is a benchmark Rosso Piceno Superiore in the old style. It is subtler and slightly evolved with spicy and slightly meaty aromas then a gentle, relatively long body. The chardonnay-based Naumachos 2005 has a nose characterized by vegetal and slightly aromatic notes. It is fairly convincing in the mouth even though it has a slightly over-dry finish. Falerio Naumachos 2005 shows intense white fruit aromas, flowers, sage and tomato leaves which are repeated in their entirety on the fresh palate. The finish is has a pleasant full-flavoured vein. The keenly priced Falerio Grotte sul Mare 2005 is simpler, fairly fruity and very fresh.

● Paccaosso '03	▼▼	8
● Rosso Piceno Sup. Naumachos '03	▼▼	4*
○ Chardonnay Naumachos '05	▼	4
○ Falerio dei Colli Ascolani Grotte sul Mare '05	▼	2*
○ Falerio dei Colli Ascolani Naumachos '05	▼	3
● Rosso Piceno Grotte sul Mare '05		2
● Paccaosso '01	▽▽	7
● Paccaosso '02	▽▽	7
● Rosso Piceno Sup. Naumachos '01	▽▽	4

JESI (AN)

MONTECAPPONE
VIA COLLE OLIVO, 2
60035 JESI (AN)
TEL. 0731205761
www.montecappone.com

Brothers Gianluca and Alessandro Mirizzi, who used to have a wine shop in Rome before becoming full-time producers in the Jesi hills, had never previously presented us with such high-quality wines. An indicator of how well things are going in Montecappone is that care and attention are now lavished on the whole output, and not just on the prestige labels. The most tangible sign of this growth is the development of a distinctive house style based on primary fruit and balanced softness. The impressive Verdicchio Riserva Utopia brings out the best of these characteristics. Aromas of apricots, spun sugar and subtle smokiness explode in the nose and then reappear to envelop the palate with creaminess. Harmony is provided by full flavours and a long finish. The two Tabanos are not far behind. Bianco 2005, from 70-30 verdicchio and sauvignon, has a bouquet that marries ripe apples, tropical fruit and freshness. Progression is good and the finish has an almost salty tang. The Montepulciano, Tabano Rosso 2004, has enveloping fleshy fruit that is barely held back by still fairly assertive but integrated tannins. The finish is intense and redolent of morello cherries and coffee. La Breccia 2005 is a Sauvignon with a lot of typicity. Entry on the palate is opulent but this does not quite hide a vegetal vein that occasionally peeks through those soft folds of fat. Finally, the two Montesecco, a Rosso Piceno and a standard-label Verdicchio, illustrate the house style in a simpler mode.

○	Verdicchio dei Castelli di Jesi Cl. Utopia Ris. '04	▼▼	5
●	Esino Rosso Tabano '04	▼▼	5
○	Esino Bianco Tabano '05	▼▼	5
○	La Breccia Sauvignon '05	▼▼	4*
●	Rosso Piceno Montesecco '05	▼▼	4*
○	Verdicchio dei Castelli di Jesi Cl. Sup. Montesecco '05	▼▼	4*
○	Verdicchio dei Castelli di Jesi Cl. Utopia Ris. '03	▽▽	5
○	Esino Bianco Tabano '04	▽▽	4
●	Esino Rosso Tabano '02	▽▽	5
●	Esino Rosso Tabano '03	▽▽	5

LORETO (AN)

★ GIOACCHINO GAROFOLI
VIA ARNO, 9
60025 LORETO (AN)
TEL. 0717820162 - 0717820163
www.garofolivini.it

It was another excellent year for the Garofoli estate. Brothers Carlo and Gianfranco, who have some free time now their children Beatrice, Gianluca and Caterina have started in the business, showed another flight of impeccable wines, confirming their usual high quality level. We'll start with Verdicchio Podium 2004, which won Three Glasses for its sumptuous elegance, proffering citrus notes, broom, lime blossom, tropical fruits and almonds that alternate unhurriedly on the nose. Perfectly balanced on the palate, its components develop dynamically, leading in to a full-flavoured finish that goes on for ever. The Riserva di Verdicchio Serra Fiorese is as solid as ever. The 2003 has marked menthol notes that develop into ripe fruits and vanilla, ushering in a savoury palate and good mouthfeel harmoniously melding with pineapple, peach and sweet spices through to a long finish. Rosso Conero Agontano is from the torrid 2003 vintage but stands out for its fleshy blackberry fruit, morello cherries and plums, enriched with quinine and liquorice. The palate is supple, never heavy, with fragrant fruit accompanied by silky tannins. Verdicchio Macrina 2005 has delicate aromas of white-fleshed fruits and flowers, good balance and fullness of flavour. Conversely, Rosso Conero Piancarda 2003 has rich, dense and ripe fruit with good drinkability and an enveloping palate. The rest of the range is interesting, with Verdicchio Serra del Conte 2005 particularly good. On retasting, we were delighted by Verdicchio Serra Fiorese 1996, which earned Three retrospective Glasses.

○	Verdicchio dei Castelli di Jesi Cl. Sup. Podium '04	▼▼▼	4*
●	Rosso Conero Grosso Agontano Ris. '03	▼▼	5
○	Verdicchio dei Castelli di Jesi Cl. Serra Fiorese Ris. '03	▼▼	4
○	Brut Riserva M. Cl. '01	▼▼	5
●	Rosso Conero Piancarda '03	▼▼	4
○	Verdicchio dei Castelli di Jesi Cl. Serra del Conte '05	▼▼	2*
○	Verdicchio dei Castelli di Jesi Cl. Sup. Macrina '05	▼▼	3*
○	Brut Charmat	▼	3
○	Verdicchio dei Castelli di Jesi Cl. Serra Fiorese Ris. '96	▽▽▽	5

MAIOLATI SPONTINI (AN)

Monte Schiavo

fraz. Monteschiavo
via Vivaio
60030 Maiolati Spontini (AN)
tel. 0731700385 - 0731700297
www.monteschiavo.it

Since 1995, the Pieralisi family has been managing and continuously adding to an estate which now extends over 115 hectares of vineyards. They offer a wide range with something for every type of consumer. The whites are all Verdicchios and very varied. Without doubt the best of them is Riserva Le Giuncare 2004. The generous nose has elegant notes of citrus, juniper and yellow-fleshed fruits. The palate has evident softness balanced and lifted by nice zest, and the finish shows elegant citrus-veined fruit. Pallio di San Floriano 2005 has peach on the nose, light touches of tropical fruit on the palate and good freshness, which assures enjoyable drinkability and a clean finish. Nativo 2003 was not filtered or cold stabilized. It's themed around aromas of pears, yellow-fleshed fruits and almonds. In the mouth, decent balance is achieved by successfully knitting the body to the flavour profile. Coste di Molino 2005 is fresh with acacia on the nose and almondy flavours on the palate leading to a tangy finish. Ruviano 2005 is clean and enjoyable with simple vegetal and floral notes. Of the reds, the Rosso Conero Adeodato 2004 selection is reminiscent of blackberries, ripe raspberries, plum jam and sweet spices on the nose. The palate starts out smooth but high levels of tannin with the sweetness of the fruit and spices take over on the finish. Ripe red fruits and hints of coffee are to the fore on the nose of the Rosso Conero Conti Cortesi 2004 before the palate shows significant tannin but inadequate fruit.

○ Verdicchio dei Castelli di Jesi Cl. Le Giuncare Ris. '04	🍷🍷	4*
○ Verdicchio dei Castelli di Jesi Cl. Sup. Nativo '03	🍷🍷	4*
● Rosso Conero Adeodato '04	🍷🍷	6
● Rosso Conero Conti Cortesi '04	🍷🍷	4*
○ Verdicchio dei Castelli di Jesi Cl. Sup. Pallio di S. Floriano '05	🍷🍷	4*
○ Verdicchio dei Castelli di Jesi Cl. Coste del Molino '05	🍷	3
○ Verdicchio dei Castelli di Jesi Cl. Ruviano '05	🍷	3
● Lacrima di Morro d'Alba '05		4
● Rosso Conero Adeodato '00	🍷🍷🍷	6
● Rosso Conero Adeodato '03	🍷🍷	6

MAIOLATI SPONTINI (AN)

Pievalta

via Monteschiavo, 18
60030 Maiolati Spontini (AN)
tel. 0309848311
www.baronepizzini.it

The Franciacorta-based Barone Pizzini estate has been for many years. In 2003, it acquired Pievalta in the Marche after a long-term study of the region's potential. And results are already coming through. No doubt one of the factors has been the work carried out in the vineyards, which have all been converted to organic viticulture and planted entirely to verdicchio. That said, the main driving force must have been the skill and positive thinking of Alessandro Fenino, a 30-year old from Milan who has been transplanted to the Marche to run the estate on a day-to-day basis. Currently, there are 27 hectares in production. Five of these are located on the opposite bank of the Esino as seen from the winery, at the village of San Paolo on top of a stunning ridge, and they supply the grapes for the Riserva di Verdicchio 2004. It is a wine with a full, complex bouquet that highlights notes of acacia blossom, orange, grapefruit, medicinal herbs, thyme and a subtle veil of wood. The palate is full and tasty with a long mineral finish. Dominè 2004, another Verdicchio, is intensely perfumed with flowers and citrus, has powerful thrust across the palate and ends on a lip-smacking dry finish. The current Verdicchio Pievalta has good aromas of pears and a supple, attractive body. Our last note is on Curina 2004, which gives toffee apples, measured sweetness and intriguing complexity of flavour. It is a blend of dried-grape wine with wine fermented dry in terracotta amphoras. It's an extremely interesting experiment, which we believe will yield even better results in the future.

○ Verdicchio dei Castelli di Jesi Cl. San Paolo Ris. '04	🍷🍷	4*
○ Verdicchio dei Castelli di Jesi Cl. Sup. Dominè '04	🍷🍷	4
○ Verdicchio dei Castelli di Jesi Passito Curina '04	🍷🍷	5
○ Verdicchio dei Castelli di Jesi Cl. Sup. Pievalta '05	🍷🍷	3*

MATELICA (MC)

Belisario

via Aristide Merloni, 12
62024 Matelica (MC)
tel. 0737787247
www.belisario.it

By now, everyone must know that Verdicchio di Matelica is the Belisario house speciality. A quick look at the score sheet below, and perhaps comparison with previous years' tasting notes, will illustrate that consistency. Doubtless this is partly the result of the seriousness with which chairman Antonio Centocanti runs the business, and the wealth of experience and reliable professionalism contributed by managing director and oenologist Roberto Potentini. But the greatest influence must be the amazing Matelica zone which, when properly understood and cared for, is able to produce extremely high quality grapes with unique characteristics. Verdicchio Riserva Cambrugiano has again proved to be the winery's top product and the 2003 only just missed repeating last year's great result by a whisker. It illustrates mature Verdicchio perfectly, linking a solid structure to an extremely fine, full-flavoured finish. The wood has melded well with the fruity body and the back palate is replete and light. Vigneti Belisario 2005, from organically grown grapes, is more rounded and has fuller fruit, nicely balanced by vivid acidity and a fine vein of minerality. Vigneti del Cerro 2005 is a classic Verdicchio di Matelica offering light fruit, dry flowers and anise on the nose before the tangy, tasty dry palate unfolds. The keenly priced Terre di Valbona 2005 is just as good a wine as its stablemates in terms of its ripe tropical fruit and pretty progression on the palate sustained by fresh acidity.

○	Verdicchio di Matelica Cambrugiano Ris. '03	🍷🍷	4*
○	Verdicchio di Matelica Vign. Belisario '05	🍷🍷	4*
○	Verdicchio di Matelica Terre di Valbona '05	🍷🍷	2*
○	Verdicchio di Matelica Vign. del Cerro '05	🍷🍷	3*
●	Colli Maceratesi Rosso San Leopardo '03	🍷	4
○	Esino Bianco Ferrante '05	🍷	2
●	Esino Rosso Colferraio '05	🍷	2
○	Verdicchio di Matelica Cambrugiano Ris. '02	YYY	4

MATELICA (MC)

La Monacesca

c.da Monacesca
62024 Matelica (MC)
tel. 0733812602
www.monacesca.it

What a surprise! No, we do not mean Mirum winning Three Glasses yet again. That is not at all unexpected if you consider the seriousness with which Aldo Cifola performs his task, his perfectly equipped winery developed with consultancy from Roberto Potentini and Fabrizio Ciufoli, and the stunning vineyards. The only thing that really caught us on the hop was the opportunity to taste the new Ecclesia, a Chardonnay of which 7,000 bottles are produced only in the best vintages. The 2005 has astonishingly fine white peach and pear fruit, delicately woven structure, intense, enveloping flavours and a buttery finish. It is a perfect example of how this international variety can show originality and elegance if grown in the right habitat. Verdicchio Mirum 2004 is even better. Very elegant and restrained, with floral aromas embellished with a note of anise; it opens velvety on the palate, unfolding forcefully on long mineral notes. The absence of any sort of toasted or vanilla component is admirable, as it would have interfered with an otherwise perfect flavour profile, showing that oak has been applied in an optimal manner. As usual, the current Verdicchio La Monacesca is a model of reliability and satisfying drinking. Pretty, rich and tasty, it has impressively precise, confident palate progression.

○	Verdicchio di Matelica Mirum Ris. '04	🍷🍷🍷	5
○	Ecclesia '05	🍷🍷	4*
○	Verdicchio di Matelica La Monacesca '05	🍷🍷	3*
○	Verdicchio di Matelica Mirum Ris. '02	YYY	5
○	Mirus '91	YYY	5
○	Mirum '94	YYY	5
○	Verdicchio di Matelica La Monacesca '94	YYY	4
●	Camerte '99	YYY	5
○	Verdicchio di Matelica Mirum Ris. '03	YY	5

MONDAVIO (PU)

FATTORIA LAILA
VIA S. FILIPPO SUL CESANO, 27
61040 MONDAVIO (PU)
TEL. 0721979353
www.fattorialaila.it

Last year, Lailum Verdicchio 2004 was not reviewed because moving up to the Riserva category meant that it needed a longer period of maturation. This has immensely enhanced its taste-flavour balance. The impact of oak is perceptible but perfectly integrated in a broad swath of aromas which range from floral complexity to soft toffee encompassing intense ripe fruit on the way. The palate has impressively dense flavour continuity and a remarkably coherent finish. We hope that this result bodes well for Rosso Piceno Lailum 2004, which is usually the estate's top wine but which oenologist Lorenzo Landi has decided to postpone for release in a year. We have always praised decisions of this nature as they show that a cellar is prepared to make a financial sacrifice for the benefit of its customers. Rosso Piceno Fattoria Laila 2005 is an exercise in tannins and anthocyanins. It's uncomplicated but nevertheless able to offer a clear nose of morello cherries and a palate with easy-drinking fragrance. The two most recent Verdicchios were very good indeed. Eklektikos 2005 showed more structure but was less ready to drink when we tasted it, citrus dominating the typical bitter almond note on the finish. Fattoria Laila 2005 on the other hand had a more aromatic floral nose and was backed up by considerable fullness of flavour on the uncompromising palate.

○	Verdicchio dei Castelli di Jesi Lailum Ris. '04	▼▼	5
○	Verdicchio dei Castelli di Jesi Cl. Sup. Eklektikos '05	▼▼	4
○	Verdicchio dei Castelli di Jesi Cl. Sup. Fattoria Laila '05	▼▼	3*
●	Rosso Piceno Fattoria Laila '05	▼	4
●	Lailum '01	▽▽	5
●	Lailum '02	▽▽	5
●	Rosso Piceno Lailum '03	▽▽	5
●	Lailum '00	▽▽	5

MONTE ROBERTO (AN)

POGGIO MONTALI
VIA FONTE ESTATE, 6
60030 MONTE ROBERTO (AN)
TEL. 0731702825
www.poggiomontali.it

Carla Panicucci's estate is surrounded by small oak woods and vineyards. The landscape alternates between views visibly affected by human cultivation and other, wilder places of dense vegetation. Carla's welcome is delivered in a noticeable Tuscan accent and it takes us a moment or two to remind ourselves we are not in red wine country, say Chianti. This is the domain of the Marche's white verdicchio. The gaudy buildings, painted bright, cheerful colours, are the farm holiday centre and winery, which has a capacity of 100,000 bottles a year sourced from 12 hectares under vine. We did not manage to taste the last vintages of the estate's basic Rosso Conero or Rosso Conero Riserva Poggio al Cerro because they have been retained for further ageing. But whites did an extremely good job of defending the colours. The Verdicchio Superiore 2005 has a nice hint of lemon zest well integrated with rich fruit on the nose, while the palate develops well without omitting the varietal sweet almond note on the finish. Fontelleccio 2004 is a comprehensive step up in complexity and structure, showing intense apple and yellow plum on the nose. The same notes open the complex profile of the savoury palate, leading in to a delicately mineral finish.

○	Verdicchio dei Castelli di Jesi Cl. Sup. Fontelleccio '04	▼▼	4*
○	Verdicchio dei Castelli di Jesi Cl. Sup. '05	▼▼	4*
○	Verdicchio dei Castelli di Jesi Cl. Sup. Fontelleccio '02	▽▽	4
●	Rosso Conero Poggio al Cerro Ris. '01	▽▽	5
●	Rosso Conero '03	▽▽	4

MONTE URANO (AP)

Maria Pia Castelli
c.da S. Isidoro, 22
63015 Monte Urano (AP)
tel. 0734841774 - 0734840759
www.mariapiacastelli.it

Even though he is very busy with his insurance business, Enrico Bartoletti still finds the time to keep an eye on his winery and vineyards. In fact, he is so conscientious that you might be forgiven for thinking that wine was his only profession. Instead it is still a hobby, albeit one which robs him of all his free time. The wines, which are produced with input from Marco Casolanetti, were original from the start, sometimes in a good way, sometimes less so. In this context, the most successful product is Stella Flora, a white trebbiano, malvasia and pecorino blend whose copper colour betrays its fermentation on the skins. The aromas of meadow grass, mandarins and hazelnuts are echoed on the supple, elegant palate, which leads to a very full-flavoured finish. Erasmo Castelli 2004 is usually the top product. It is a taut and concentrated Montepulciano with considerable extract and lively alcohol. Despite this, a generous helping of tannins gives it balance. It is not built in a round, fruity style, preferring instead to show off its youthful exuberance, which will harmonize with bottle age. Sangiovese Orano 2005 is decidedly unusual on the nose with evolved pepper and spice aromas that turn out to be less precise and fruity than in previous years. Perhaps it pays the price for this vintage's indifferent weather. The 2005 Sant'Isidoro rosé, part barrique-aged, is targeted at customers who appreciate medium dry wines.

●	Erasmo Castelli '04	🍷🍷	6
○	Stella Flora '04	🍷🍷	4
●	Orano '05	🍷	4
⊙	Sant'Isidoro '05		3
●	Erasmo Castelli '02	YY	6
●	Erasmo Castelli '03	YY	6
○	Stella Flora '03	YY	4
●	Orano '04	YY	4

MONTECAROTTO (AN)

Laurentina
via San Pietro 19a
60036 Montecarotto (AN)
tel. 073189435
www.laurentinavini.com

New blood with respect for tradition – this could be the thinking behind recent developments at the attractive Laurentina winery, where the owners have entrusted day-to-day management to brothers Andrea and Alessandro Perticaroli with effect from the 2005 harvest. Alessandro was already a cellarman in the business and is now responsible for production, continuing to display his customary proficiency and spirit of self-sacrifice. Andrea runs the commercial side. Previous to this, there had also been a change on the technical front. Oenologist Giancarlo Soverchia, who had been the guiding hand behind the winery's creation, decided that the person to succeed him should be Aroldo Bellelli, who had previously been his assistant. As a result, Bellelli's work follows the furrow of tradition, in full agreement with Alessandro. The fact that the 11 hectares of vines are in acclaimed wine country is testified by the bottles we tasted, especially the two Verdicchios. The Classico 2005 has textbook richness and fragrance with delicate balsamic and floral aromas and a linear, complex palate. Vigneto di Tobia 2004 has more structure and fuller flavour with a creamy, long palate and decent fresh acidity. Rosso Piceno 2004 has peculiar aromatic, fruity notes and good structure in the mouth while Chioma di Berenice 2005 is a simple early-drinking Lacrima di Morro d'Alba.

○	Verdicchio dei Castelli di Jesi Cl. Il Vigneto di Tobia '04	🍷🍷	3*
○	Verdicchio dei Castelli di Jesi Cl. '05	🍷🍷	2*
●	Rosso Piceno '04	🍷	3
●	Chioma di Berenice '05	🍷	3
○	Verdicchio dei Castelli di Jesi Passito '03		5

MONTECAROTTO (AN)

Fattoria San Lorenzo
via San Lorenzo, 6
60036 Montecarotto (AN)
tel. 073189656

Every year, we expect Natalino Crognaletti to produce something newsworthy and, given his restless character, he comes up trumps every time. This time, he released the first harvest of a Lacrima di Morro d'Alba from a vineyard planted a few years ago. It's along the same lines as all his others with fairly high density, limited yields and near-obsessive focus on the vine's vegetative balance. For the record, this 2003 has a distinctive aroma profile, and some green tannins which still need time to mellow, but it is an encouraging start nonetheless. As we wait for more of the surprises that Natalino is keeping up his sleeve before he releases them to market, we tasted Verdicchio Vigna delle Oche Riserva 2003. It still needs time before reaching its best but it is already able to show off its powerful aromatics and fascinating minerality. The basic Verdicchio Vigna delle Oche 2004 is equally good, showing fresh flower, meadow herb and thyme notes on the nose and an elegant, incisive palate with balance, finesse and full flavour. Verdicchio di Gino 2005 is fragrant, extremely drinkable and uncomplicated. Moving on to the reds, our tasting of Vigneto del Solleone 2002 is very satisfying. A thoroughbred Montepulciano whose only drawback is a little too much extraction, which obscures the freshness and purity of the fruit. The juicy Rosso Conero Vigna la Gattara 2002 is richly spicy on the nose while Rosso Conero 2003 is more restrained and characterized by vegetal notes.

●	Vigneto del Solleone '02	▼▼	6
○	Verdicchio dei Castelli di Jesi Cl. Vigna delle Oche Ris. '03	▼▼	5
○	Verdicchio dei Castelli di Jesi Cl. Sup. Vigna delle Oche '04	▼▼	4*
●	Rosso Conero V. la Gattara '02	▼▼	4
●	Lacrima di Morro d'Alba V. Paradiso '03	▼	5
●	Rosso Conero '03	▼	4
○	Verdicchio dei Castelli di Jesi Cl. di Gino '05	▼	3
○	Verdicchio dei Castelli di Jesi Cl. Vigna delle Oche Ris. '01	▽▽▽	5
●	Vigneto del Solleone '01	▽▽	6

MONTECAROTTO (AN)

Terre Cortesi Moncaro
via Piandole, 7a
60036 Montecarotto (AN)
tel. 073189245
www.moncaro.com

Terre Cortesi Moncaro is a co-operative that releases seven and a half million bottles a year from over 1,600 hectares under vine and three wineries strategically located in Marche's finest wine areas: the hills for verdicchio and Conero and Piceno for reds. With these credentials, the cellar can offer a strong, complete range that has been at the forefront of regional production for years. But this is not a winery that is likely to simply rest on its laurels so there are constant innovations. The first release of Offida Pecorino Ofithe 2005 is richly fruity on the nose without sacrificing varietal richness or depth of flavour. At the moment, only 5,600 bottles are produced, but this will increase from next year. The excellent Verdicchios are benchmark wines. Vigna Novali 2002 easily held onto the top spot thanks to fascinating notes of dried fruit and botrytis on the nose, a fruity, complex palate and a delicious hint of orange peel on the finish. Verde di Ca' Ruptae 2005 has enticing hints of sage and tomato leaves and a savoury body with good balance. Finally, Le Vele 2005 ensures excellent drinkability with classic aromas ranging from ripe fruit to fresher vegetal notes on an attractively nuanced palate. Of the red wines, the cabernet and montepulciano Barocco 2003 shows soft and intense while the 2003 Rosso Conero Riservas share a certain austerity and dense, close-knit tannins. The Vigneti del Parco shows this most clearly. Finally came Tordiruta, a velvety dried-grape Verdicchio which has been made sweet and chewy by the 2003 weather.

○	Verdicchio dei Castelli di Jesi Cl. Vigna Novali Ris. '02	▼▼	4*
●	Rosso Conero Vigneti del Parco Ris. '03	▼▼	5
●	Barocco '03	▼▼	4
●	Rosso Conero Cimerio Ris. '03	▼▼	4
●	Rosso Conero Nerone Ris. '03	▼▼	6
○	Verdicchio dei Castelli di Jesi Passito Tordiruta '03	▼▼	6
○	Offida Pecorino Ofithe '05	▼▼	4
○	Verdicchio dei Castelli di Jesi Cl. Le Vele '05	▼▼	3*
○	Verdicchio dei Castelli di Jesi Cl. Sup. Verde di Ca' Ruptae '05	▼▼	3*
●	Rosso Piceno Roccaviva '03	▼	3

MONTEFANO (MC)

Degli Azzoni Avogadro Carradori

C.so Carradori, 13
62010 Montefano (MC)
tel. 0733850002
www.degliazzoni.it

For around six centuries, the Degli Azzoni Avogadro Carradori family has owned swaths of land in the Recanati hills and the Apennines in the provinces of Macerata and Ancona. Vines alternate with cereals, olives and even a specialized basil crop. For the running of the wine business, Filippo Degli Azzoni relies on the equally young cellarman Lorenzo Gigli, and his new oenologist Salvatore Lovo. This highly competent team processes the estate's best grapes for release as bottled wine while the rest of the production from the 130 hectares is sold unbottled to the many customers who buy direct at the cellars. First up from the bottled wines is Passatempo 2004, a well-made two-thirds montepulciano, one-third merlot and cabernet blend with a lot of body, density, velvety fruit and soft, but not excessive, fullness. Galeotto 2005 is a simple but successful illustration of how to make a simple, early-drinking Montepulciano with good fresh fruit. Rosso di Cantalupo 2004 is an 80-20 merlot and montepulciano mix that shows elegant fruit, a solid balanced structure and a long tasty finish. Rosso Piceno 2004 has good cherry aromas and some slight excess of acidity and tannins but overall is a wine that works enjoyably well. Bianco di Cantalupo 2005, mainly verdicchio with some viognier and sauvignon, is a little too simple while the Grechetto 2005 is linear and enjoyable.

●	Passatempo '04	🍷🍷	5
●	Rosso di Cantalupo '04	🍷🍷	4
●	Rosso Piceno '04	🍷🍷	3*
●	Galeotto '05	🍷🍷	2*
○	Bianco di Cantalupo '05	🍷	4
○	Grechetto '05	🍷	4
○	Colli Maceratesi Bianco '05		4
●	Passatempo '02	🍸🍸	5
●	Passatempo '03	🍸🍸	5
●	Rosso di Cantalupo '03	🍸🍸	4

MONTEGRANARO (AP)

Rio Maggio

C.da Vallone, 41
63014 Montegranaro (AP)
tel. 0734889587
www.riomaggio.it

Montegranaro is well known for its shoe industry and basketball addiction – the local team has just been promoted to the top division. If its name is also familiar in the wine world, this is thanks to the efforts of Simone Santucci. It is not as if there has ever been any lack of vines in these hills, but given its name, the town must have been an arable centre in the past. Traditionally, wine was produced in small quantities, mainly for local consumption. Simone had the courage to give a professional edge to the estate that his father built up out of enthusiasm and these days the vineyards are planted to both traditional and international varieties. Sauvignon Colle Monteverde has always been acknowledged as one of the best whites from Piceno. The 2005 shows intense vegetal aromas of sage, thyme and elderflower leading into a palate that is savoury and hefty, and a smooth-flowing finish. Falerio Telusiano 2005 has different characteristics. It is a traditional blend of trebbiano, passerina and pecorino, and is made more in the soft, fleshy style, with a palate that echoes the ripe fruit of the nose. The alcohol-rich, pervasive Rosso Piceno GrAnarijS 2004 managed to pick up its second Glass with its straightforward montepulciano characteristics – there is also a minimal proportion of sangiovese in the blend, but it is totally overpowered – which compensate for its slightly blurred nose. The 2004 Rossastro's use of wood needs some fine-tuning. A Rosso Piceno released for the first time, it is fairly full-bodied and tannic but dominated by toasty, vanilla notes.

●	Rosso Piceno GrAnarijS '04	🍷🍷	5
○	Colle Monteverde Sauvignon '05	🍷🍷	4*
○	Falerio dei Colli Ascolani Telusiano '05	🍷🍷	4*
●	Rosso Piceno Rossastro '04	🍷	6
○	Colle Monteverde Chardonnay '05		4
○	Falerio dei Colli Ascolani Monte del Grano '05		2
●	Rosso Piceno Rio '05		3
●	Artias Pinot Nero '01	🍸🍸	5
●	Rosso Piceno GrAnarijS '03	🍸🍸	5

MONTEPRANDONE (AP)

IL CONTE
VIA COLLE NAVICCHIO, 28
63030 MONTEPRANDONE (AP)
TEL. 073562593
www.ilcontevini.it

Marino and Emanuel De Angelis' estate is located in the Colli del Piceno, right in the centre of the best area for the production of Rosso Piceno Superiore. Marinus 2004 is representative of the type and showed very well at our tastings, offering clear aromas of cherries and spices shot through with occasional notes of green peppers and a balanced body with thrust on the palate. The estate's top wine, Zipolo 2003 is a blend of montepulciano, sangiovese and merlot. It's much more ambitious and structured. The very ripe grapes and the oak smokiness don't quite manage to mask a marked vegetal character before the palate shows considerable concentration with reasonable suppleness. On the back palate, the return of the greenness spoils the finesse and poise, but there is impressive persistence. The modern style, which characterizes the whole range, is very clearly expressed by Navicchio 2004. It's a successful blend, half of which was provided by equal amounts of two local varieties, malvasia and pecorino, with chardonnay making up the remainder. The elegant aromas of lime blossom and ripe yellow fruits are typical of fully ripe grapes and then a good balance of sweet fruit and acidic backbone on the palate leads into a long, well-sustained finish. Finally, Aurato 2005 is a deliberately soft, enjoyable Falerio. It may not have much personality but it's just the thing if you are looking for upfront, uncomplicated gratification.

● Zipolo '03	🍷🍷	6
○ Navicchio '04	🍷🍷	4*
● Rosso Piceno Sup. Marinus '04	🍷🍷	4*
○ Falerio dei Colli Ascolani Aurato '05	🍷	3
● Zipolo '01	🍷🍷	5
● Rosso Piceno Marinus '02	🍷🍷	4
● Zipolo '02	🍷🍷	5
● Rosso Piceno Marinus '03	🍷🍷	4

MORRO D'ALBA (AN)

STEFANO MANCINELLI
VIA ROMA, 62
60030 MORRO D'ALBA (AN)
TEL. 073163021
www.mancinelli-wine.com

If you are talking about the success of Lacrima di Morro d'Alba, you shouldn't forget Stefano Mancinelli's efforts to bring the wine to the attention of the public. Stefano's dedication, conviction, projects and sheer work ethic make him the unquestioned driving force behind the wine's comeback. The various styles he has coaxed from the lacrima grape, with input from Roberto Potentini, confirm the type's expressive potential. We'll begin with Re Sole 2003, which was produced by drying the grapes on mats. The result is a dark wine with complex, concentrated integrated fresh and preserved sour cherries, blackberry jam, liquorice and chocolate on the nose. The sweet palate with its powerful, balanced tannins is made all the more attractive by a reprise of the red fruit and chocolate, and the finish is long and enjoyable. Terre da Goti 2001 is no less generous. A varietal nose with floral fruity aromas precedes a very rich, drinkable palate that balances extreme softness with opulence, freshness and good tannins. Lacrima Santa Maria del Fiore 2005 is redolent of sweet fruits, raspberry and violets while the palate is balanced, with a delicate fruity finish. Lacrima Sensazioni di Frutto 2005 was vinified with carbonic maceration, and has strawberry aromas and a fresh palate, but has yet to find optimum balance. On the verdicchio side of the estate, we would highlight the Superiore Santa Maria del Fiore 2005 with its sweet, yellow fruit nose and balanced long palate whereas the Classico 2005 shows ripe fruit and light body without much breadth of flavour.

● Terre dei Goti '01	🍷🍷	6
● Lacrima di Morro d'Alba Passito Re Sole '03	🍷🍷	5
○ Verdicchio dei Castelli di Jesi Cl. Sup. S. Maria del Fiore '05	🍷🍷	3*
● Lacrima di Morro d'Alba S. Maria del Fiore '05	🍷	4
● Lacrima di Morro d'Alba Sensazioni di Frutto '05	🍷	4
○ Verdicchio dei Castelli di Jesi Cl. '05	🍷	2
● Lacrima di Morro d'Alba Passito Re Sole '00	🍷🍷	5
● Rubrum '03	🍷🍷	3

MORRO D'ALBA (AN)

MAROTTI CAMPI
VIA S. AMICO, 14
60030 MORRO D'ALBA (AN)
TEL. 0731618027
www.marotticampi.it

The Marotti Campi family's estate looks like a Bordeaux château. It's a fascinating period country house surrounded by lawns and vines in a landscape that descends slowly to the sea in a series of long steps. The estate's 57 hectares under vine have a variety of aspects, but all of them are in the municipality of Morro d'Alba. Obviously, the lacrima grape dominates here but verdicchio is also very important, with some historical justification. The variety always used to be planted in these hills inland from Senigallia. Riserva di Verdicchio Salmariano 2003 shows just how good the area is for the variety. Elegant and muscular, it has perfectly absorbed its three years in barrique, turning a bright gold in the process. The nose has intense aromas of honey and anise veiled by soft toffee that lead to a pervasive palate and a long, salty finish. The fresh, dynamic Verdicchio Luzano 2005 surprised and charmed us with its sweet almond tones. Verdicchio Albiano 2005 is slightly less accomplished and has simpler aromatics. Donderè 2004 is a petit verdot, cabernet sauvignon and merlot blend, and stands out for its round, ripe tannins that back up the remarkable fruit of the palate. Two Lacrimas were on show. Rùbico 2005 has intense floral sweetness on the nose and upfront flavour but some hardness whereas Orgiolo 2004 has greater aromatic intensity, more body and better balance.

○ Verdicchio dei Castelli di Jesi Cl. Salmariano Ris. '03	🍷🍷	4*
● Donderè '04	🍷🍷	5
● Lacrima di Morro d'Alba Orgiolo '04	🍷🍷	4
○ Verdicchio dei Castelli di Jesi Cl. Sup. Luzano '05	🍷🍷	3*
● Lacrima di Morro d'Alba Rùbico '05	🍷	3
○ Verdicchio dei Castelli di Jesi Cl. Albiano '05	🍷	2
● Donderè '03	🍸🍸	5

NUMANA (AN)

CONTE LEOPARDI DITTAJUTI
VIA MARINA II, 24
60026 NUMANA (AN)
TEL. 0717390116
www.leopardiwines.com

Il Coppo is a district of Sirolo nestling at the foot of Monte Conero. The landscape here is not just beautiful to look at – with the greens of the hills and the blue of the sea – but is also exceptional for its climate, which is always sunny and well aired thanks to the sea breezes. Piervittorio Leopardi Dittajuti grows the grapes for his best wines here. Bianco di Coppo is a Sauvignon for early drinking with intense, well-defined varietal notes and a characteristic full flavour. Pigmento 2003 is a Rosso Conero where slightly overripe montepulciano grapes are used to ensure ripe tannins, purity of fruit and pervasive alcohol. All the components are rounded off by unhurried barrique ageing. The 2004 Casirano is part of the Rosso Conero DOC and so the lion's share is montepulciano with the remainder consisting of a pinch of cabernet and syrah. On the nose, there is a light vegetal note with good fruit, which is then echoed on the tannic, full-bodied palate. Vigneti del Coppo 2004 is much more vegetal with a considerably harder palate. Fructus 2005 is the basic Rosso Conero with enjoyable, upfront red fruits and a juicy palate underpinned by good structure. The range is rounded off by a fresh Verdicchio Castelverde 2005 that fuses aromas of almonds, herbs and meadow flowers, and by a brut metodo classico sparkler that makes up for a certain lack of finesse with forthright dollops of supple flavour.

● Rosso Conero Pigmento '03	🍷🍷	5
● Rosso Conero Casirano '04	🍷🍷	4
○ Bianco del Coppo Sauvignon '05	🍷🍷	3*
● Rosso Conero Fructus '05	🍷🍷	4
○ Verdicchio dei Castelli di Jesi Cl. Castelverde '05	🍷🍷	4
● Rosso Conero Vigneti del Coppo '04	🍷	4
○ Villa Marina Brut M. Cl.	🍷	4
● Rosso Conero Vigneti del Coppo '03	🍸🍸	4

NUMANA (AN)

FATTORIA LE TERRAZZE
VIA MUSONE, 4
60026 NUMANA (AN)
TEL. 0717390352
www.fattorialeterrazze.com

It's no longer a surprise that Antonio Terni manages to win Three Glasses every year but it is curious to see that they are awarded to a different wine every time. This might look like a symptom of instability or chance but it is in fact quite the opposite. Antonio's wines are always extremely high quality and the award boils down to tiny nuances, often the result of differences only apparent at specific tastings. This year, Chaos 2004 came out ahead thanks to forwardness and balance that put it ahead of Sassi Neri and Planet Waves, despite the fact that they are a year older. Actually, they reflect the difficulties of managing the heat of the 2003 vintage. Tasting Rosso Conero 2004 is an illustration of how reliable this estate is and how seriously oenologist Attilio Pagli goes about his job. This basic red is one of the best in its class. The impressive fruit is close knit, fresh and intense, the structure is attractively balanced and above all it is a highly drinkable wine. Coming back to the top wine, Chaos 2004 is half montepulciano with the rest merlot and syrah. There is dense, fleshy fruit with freshness on the nose and palate. In fact, this champion is very enjoyable to drink as the rich body works well without being at all tiring. Planet Waves 2003 is three quarters montepulciano and a quarter merlot. It is slightly more structured, and has unstoppable palate progression and a nicely dry finish. Sassi Neri 2003 Montepulciano is in its usual austere style with a terse, intense palate.

● Chaos '04	▼▼▼	6
● Planet Waves '03	▼▼	7
● Rosso Conero Sassi Neri '03	▼▼	6
● Rosso Conero '04	▼▼	4*
○ Chardonnay Le Cave '05	▼	4
● Chaos '01	▽▽▽	7
● Rosso Conero Visions of J '01	▽▽▽	8
● Rosso Conero Sassi Neri '02	▽▽▽	6
● Chaos '97	▽▽▽	7
● Rosso Conero Visions of J '97	▽▽▽	8
● Rosso Conero Sassi Neri '98	▽▽▽	6
● Rosso Conero Sassi Neri '99	▽▽▽	6
● Planet Waves '02	▽▽	7
● Chaos '03	▽▽	6

OFFIDA (AP)

AURORA
LOC. SANTA MARIA IN CARRO
C.DA CIAFONE, 98
63035 OFFIDA (AP)
TEL. 0736810007
www.viniaurora.it

One, two, then three and now four. Barracadeiro has an astonishing record in winning Three Glasses and tasting the 2004 leaves no room for doubt. It shows the rich fruit of a montepulciano combined with the refinement of a cabernet to create an intensely satisfying taste profile without ever going over the top, raising the question of how a wine can be so consistently good with minimal vintage variation year after year. Such small differences is only possible with perfectly balanced vines which are able to produce their best whatever the weather over the season. The importance of this concept has been clearly in the minds of the five partners in the Aurora winery, set up in the 1980s when the prevailing philosophy – especially in this area – was to produce large quantities of low-quality bulk wine for sale in tankers. But Aurora made the courageous decision to go organic and bottle high-quality wine. Now, more than 20 years on, they have the priceless luxury of being able to rely on perfectly grown vines or, to put it differently, their success now is now backed up by a long track record, the only thing that really matters in the quest for top quality. The other wines are in line with this production philosophy and include a soft, full-bodied Rosso Piceno Superiore 2004, a rather lighter Rosso Piceno 2005 and the fresh, immediate Falerio 2005. Finally, we think that the decision to postpone the release of Pecorino 2005 is very praiseworthy. It needs some more time to express the full potential of this great white Piceno grape variety.

● Barricadiero '04	▼▼▼	5
● Rosso Piceno Sup. '04	▼▼	4*
○ Falerio dei Colli Ascolani '05	▼▼	2*
● Rosso Piceno '05	▼	3
● Barricadiero '01	▽▽▽	5
● Barricadiero '02	▽▽▽	5
● Barricadiero '03	▽▽▽	5
○ Offida Pecorino Fiobbo '04	▽▽	4
● Barricadiero '00	▽▽	5

OFFIDA (AP)

Ciù Ciù

Loc. Santa Maria in Carro
c.da Ciafone, 106
63035 Offida (AP)
tel. 0736810001

Massimiliano and Walter Bartolomei's wines are increasingly firm and persuasive. They manage to reconcile a modern style while remaining true to their local roots. Yet again, they just missed out on top honours. The reason is probably that they lack the touch of complexity and elegance needed to bring out the best from the wide range of fruit notes shown at the tastings. The fact is that Oppidum 2002, a Montepulciano made with overripe grapes, has unequalled power and palate progression, and a surprising, enveloping nose but it is just too rich. A wine's balance comes from carefully gauging the relationships of all the ingredients, not merely adding more of them. The same considerations apply to Sangiovese Saggio 2004, which has been improving every year to the point that it is now one of the best versions of this grape variety in the whole region. However, it has a touch too much wood on top of boisterous tannins and its full body. The soft, velvety palate of Esperanto 2003, from montepulciano with 30 per cent cabernet, echoes the intense notes of morello cherries and chocolate on the nose. Le Merlettaie 2005 is a Pecorino with well-defined notes of apples and almonds on the nose. It's a personal take on the variety and benefits from a soft warming palate. The same generosity and high alcohol also show up on the highly fruity San Carro blend of barbera and other red grapes grown on the estate, as well as on the two Rosso Picenos, Gotico 2004 and Orum 2004. The former is bigger and the latter more traditional.

● Oppidum '02	▼▼	5
● Saggio Sangiovese '04	▼▼	5
○ Offida Pecorino Le Merlettaie '05	▼▼	4
● Offida Rosso Esperanto '03	▼▼	5
● Rosso Piceno Sup. Gotico '04	▼▼	4
● Rosso Piceno Sup. Orum '04	▼▼	3*
● San Carro '05	▼▼	3*
○ Falerio dei Colli Ascolani Oris '05	▼	2
● Rosso Piceno Bacchus '05	▼	3
● Offida Rosso Esperanto '01	▽▽	5
● Oppidum '01	▽▽	4
● Offida Rosso Esperanto '02	▽▽	5
● Oppidum '00	▽▽	3

OFFIDA (AP)

San Filippo

c.da Ciafone
63035 Offida (AP)
tel. 0736889828

Brothers Fabrizio and Lino Stracci are young but they know the land well as they have been working it all their lives. In the past, they both worked for estates in the Piceno, gaining hands-on experience in cellar and vineyard. A few years ago, the duo decided to take the big step. They already controlled 28 hectares of good quality organic vineyard, half of which they owned and the rest they were renting from family and friends. Having become tired of sending their grapes to be vinified at various local producers, Fabrizio and Lino started building their small but efficient winery to release their own high-quality estate-bottled wines. Currently production is still limited at barely more than 10,000 bottles but country wisdom dictates that progress is best made by taking small steps. As far as quality goes, however, there is no hesitation apparent: all the wines are enjoyable and well made, thanks in part to the efforts of oenologist Roberto D'Angelo, who helps in the winery. We were particularly struck by the montepulciano and cabernet Lupo del Ciafone 2003, which develops solidly development with rich ripe, candied fruit notes, a balanced palate and great drinkability. Pecorino 2005 is a wine in the modern style that nicely offsets technology and varietal character with fresh floral aromas on the nose, crisp acidity, and a full-flavoured palate. Rosso Piceno Superiore Katharsis 2004 has good, soft, fruity body and Falerio Archè 2005 is fresh and dry on the finish.

● Lupo del Ciafone '03	▼▼	5
○ Offida Pecorino '05	▼▼	4*
● Rosso Piceno Sup. Katharsis '04	▼	4
○ Falerio dei Colli Ascolani Archè '05	▼	3

OFFIDA (AP)

SAN GIOVANNI
C.DA CIAFONE, 41
63035 OFFIDA (AP)
TEL. 0736889032
www.vinisangiovanni.it

Rationalization, small changes and fine tuning make Gianni Di Lorenzo's winery a dynamic enterprise that follows the market intelligently without compromising production. Some of the new watchwords are increased elegance and lower alcohol levels, providing a key to understanding Zeii 2003, which manages to avoid overripe notes despite the particularly hot vintage. It has cherries, capsicum and a hint of talc on the nose while the palate shows soft tannins, a consistently aromatic finish and great drinkability. Rosso Piceno Leo Guelfus was characteristically dense and balanced in 2004 with a focus on redcurrants and morello cherries. Axeé 2003 is also pretty good and just beginning to show some development with a tidy body. We have sympathy with the way in which the cellar has streamlined the range of whites by deciding to follow the single varietal route. This means that Ophites 2005 and Marta 2005 have both been withdrawn from the Falerio dei Colli Ascolani DOC. The former is now a simple, delicate Offida DOC made with passerina grapes for day to day drinking. Marta, which was not produced in 2004, has become a 100 per cent Sauvignon that gives notes of sage and freshly mown grass on an apparently subtle and well-formed body with a slight salty tang. Kiara 2005 has more structure, defined personality and length. An all-pecorino wine, it shows tidy aromas of white-fleshed fruit and sweet almonds.

● Offida Rosso Zeii '03	🍷🍷	5
● Rosso Piceno Sup. Leo Guelfus '04	🍷🍷	4*
○ Offida Pecorino Kiara '05	🍷🍷	4
● Rosso Piceno Sup. Axeé '03	🍷🍷	5
○ Marta '05	🍷🍷	4
○ Falerio dei Colli Ascolani Leo Guelfus '05	🍷	3
○ Offida Passerina Ophites '05	🍷	3
● Rosso Piceno Ophites '05	🍷	3
● Offida Rosso Zeii '02	🍷🍷 (outline)	5
○ Falerio dei Colli Ascolani Marta '03	🍷🍷 (outline)	4
○ Offida Pecorino Kiara '04	🍷🍷 (outline)	4

OFFIDA (AP)

PODERI SAN LAZZARO
C.DA SAN LAZZARO, 65/67
63035 OFFIDA (AP)
TEL. 0736889189

Poderi San Lazzaro is a very new estate. It was founded a few years ago by Paolo Capriotti and Pino Ottavi, two friends with jobs outside the wine world who decided to merge their respective families' vineyards, move up from selling to local co-operatives and produce quality wine instead. Having converted an old country house into a winery, they harvested their first grapes in 2003, taking oenological advice from Marco Casolanetti, the owner of Oasi degli Angeli. The extent of the work undertaken in the vineyard, and Marco's experience – he is good at understanding a site which is different from his own, and acting accordingly – have enabled Paolo and Pino to offer a range of acknowledged quality that beautifully expresses the component grapes. This is especially true of Pistillo Pecorino, which has subtle, delicate aromas, good acidity and good dryness on the palate. Grifola 2004 is also excellent. A montepulciano-only red with pure, powerful fruit, supple complexity and simultaneous sensations of austerity and softness, it is a very fine interpretation of the grape. Podere 72, from vines planted in 1972, is a 50-50 blend of barrique-aged montepulciano and sangiovese that gives a juicy, soft wine with a perfect balance of richness of fruit and elegance, solid body and enjoyable drinking. Sangiovese Polesio 2005 is a little rustic and spicy. This young wine is fermented in stainless steel and earned plaudits for its drinkability and very reasonable price.

● Grifola '04	🍷🍷	5
● Podere 72 '04	🍷🍷	4*
○ Pistillo Pecorino '05	🍷🍷	4*
● Polesio Sangiovese '05	🍷	2

OFFIDA (AP)

Villa Pigna

c.da Ciafone, 63
63035 Offida (AP)
tel. 073687525
www.villapigna.com

Having achieved consistently high quality over the past few years, Annamaria Rozzi is now working on the hard task of honing her wines' individual characters with ever-greater precision. This exercise is made easier by the experience of her consultant oenologist Riccardo Cotarella and by the results already achieved after rationalization of the estate's vineyards in the recent past. Nevertheless, the overall shape of the product range is already well defined and some of the wines clearly outshine the others. Rozzano 2004 is a case in point. A pure Montepulciano. it went on to the Three Glass final for the full-bodied freshness of its fruit and the well-maintained, full-bodied development on the palate. Offida Cabernasco 2003 is a blend of montepulciano, cabernet and merlot in an austere and demanding style. The long maturation demanded by the Offida DOC has perhaps dried the wine out a little. It develops well in the mouth but tends to finish earlier than expected. Rosso Piceno Vergaio 2004 has a complex, supple palate with velvety persistence. Briccaio 2004 is from 100 per cent montepulciano and shows rigid and forbidding on the nose, showing good graphite and liquorice notes that are echoed on the palate with a vein of tannin. Pecorino Rugiasco 2005 proved especially good now that it has finally been given the attention it deserves. It has intense aromas of medicinal herbs and rue with a good crunchy, full-flavoured palate and a long grapefruit finish.

● Rozzano '04	🍷🍷	5
● Offida Rosso Cabernasco '03	🍷🍷	5
● Briccaio '04	🍷🍷	4
● Rosso Piceno Sup. Vergaio '04	🍷🍷	4
○ Offida Pecorino Rugiasco '05	🍷🍷	4
● Rosso Piceno Eliano '05	🍷🍷	3*
● Vellutato '04	🍷	3
○ Falerio dei Colli Ascolani Pliniano '05	🍷	3
○ Offida Passerina Majia '05	🍷	4
● Rozzano '03	YYY	5
● Rozzano '01	YY	5
● Rozzano '00	YY	5

OSIMO (AN)

Umani Ronchi

s.s.16 km 310 + 400, 74
60027 Osimo (AN)
tel. 0717108019 - 0717108716
www.umanironchi.com

Even though this long-established winery's two top reds, Pelago 2004 and Cùmaro 2004, were not presented this year because they require more maturation time, the results achieved were excellent: three wines made it to the final, where one carried off Three Glasses. The champion was Plenio 2003, a textbook Verdicchio where the masterful use of wood has achieved great balance of body with elegance, and of fruit richness with subtle minerality. Congratulations are also due to the Bernetti family and to their oenologist Beppe Caviola for excellent results with the other Verdicchios. Casal di Serra 2005 again shows full, its juicy fruit revealing a wonderful mineral note on the finish. The Vecchie Vigne 2004 selection, made from fully ripened fruit, is even richer and more enveloping in style with a good balance of fullness of flavour and grapefruit-led aromatics. Villa Bianchi 2005 is simple and tasty with a powerful dose of fruit. As for the reds, 2003 was the first year for the Rosso Conero Supra selection, so called because it is sourced from vineyards higher up than those whose fruit goes into Cùmaro. It is an austere, firmly structured wine but the palate is soft, with rich, ripe fruit. The other two Rosso Coneros are also very good. San Lorenzo 2003 is a highly approachable easy drinker while Serrano 2005 is more keenly priced and, with 320,000 bottles available, it is produced in more significant quantities. The result is a fresh, fruity, early drinking wine enhanced on the nose by a faint vegetal note.

○ Verdicchio dei Castelli di Jesi Cl. Plenio Ris. '03	🍷🍷🍷	5
○ Verdicchio dei Castelli di Jesi Cl. Sup. Casal di Serra V. V. '04	🍷🍷	5
○ Verdicchio dei Castelli di Jesi Cl. Sup. Casal di Serra '05	🍷🍷	4*
● Rosso Conero Supra '03	🍷🍷	7
● Rosso Conero S. Lorenzo '03	🍷🍷	4*
● Rosso Conero Serrano '05	🍷🍷	4*
○ Verdicchio dei Castelli di Jesi Cl. Sup. Villa Bianchi '05	🍷🍷	4*
○ Le Busche '04	🍷	5
● Lacrima di Morro d'Alba Fonte del Re '05	🍷	4

OSTRA VETERE (AN)

Bucci

Fraz. Pongelli
via Cona, 30
60010 Ostra Vetere (AN)
tel. 071964179 - 026570558
www.villabucci.com

If you have an empty page in front of you, and are required to write about yet another very well-earned Three Glass award for Verdicchio Villa Bucci, your first thought will probably be jot down a couple of words and let the wine speak for itself. But our duty to our readers is to describe this sublime triumph of winemaking, something we are very happy to do. The 2004 shows vivid freshness with a hint of even finer things to come if allowed to age further. There are aromas of dried flowers, straw and a fine illustration of what is meant by the term "mineral". Are you curious to find out what an ideal Verdicchio tastes like? Here it is. Are you looking for optimal use of large wood vats? Same answer. Thanks are due to Ampelio Bucci for that feeling of anticipation he gives us every time we open a Villa Bucci. Thanks, too, for the amazing experience of finding a few drops left in a bottle a few days later and realizing that the wine is even better than when it was opened and finally thanks for making sure that the lesser labels are almost as exciting. Actually, Villa Bucci Rosso 2003 is incredibly elegant, with French-style delicacy of fruit, sophisticated spice and drinkability in spades. The Verdicchio 2005 also has taste and elegance, bags of floral notes, intense flavours and endless length. Rosso Piceno Tenuta Pongelli 2004 is fresh, direct and light. Bucci wines improve with age and when we retasted the fascinating Villa Bucci 1995, we decided that with hindsight it was worthy of Three Glasses.

○ Verdicchio dei Castelli di Jesi Cl. Villa Bucci Ris. '04	▼▼▼	6
● Rosso Piceno Villa Bucci '03	▼▼	6
○ Verdicchio dei Castelli di Jesi Cl. '05	▼▼	4*
● Rosso Piceno Tenuta Pongelli '04	▼	4
○ Verdicchio dei Castelli di Jesi Cl. Villa Bucci Ris. '95	▽▽▽	6
○ Verdicchio dei Castelli di Jesi Cl. Villa Bucci Ris. '00	▽▽▽	6
○ Verdicchio dei Castelli di Jesi Cl. Villa Bucci Ris. '01	▽▽▽	6
○ Verdicchio dei Castelli di Jesi Cl. Villa Bucci Ris. '03	▽▽▽	6

PESARO

Fattoria Mancini

s.da dei Colli, 35
61100 Pesaro
tel. 072151828
www.fattoriamancini.com

Fattoria Mancini has planted new vines in the heart of one of the Adriatic coastline's most picturesque spots. While waiting for them to come on stream, the cellar continues to produce at an excellent level thanks to ever increasing care and responsible use of technology in the winery, not to mention intense research into the potential of available varieties and terroirs. Our review of the wines begins with the authoritative Focara Pinot Nero Impero 2004, which has poised balance and good complexity of vegetal, fruit, mineral and subtle spice. The Colli Pesaresi Sangiovese 2004 is one of the best of its type. Purple in colour, it gives well-defined fruit, austerity, elegant tannins and youthful verve, which will continue to improve for those who can wait. Next up is Blu 2003, a blend of pinot nero, ancellotta and montepulciano. It is spicy, intense and enveloping in a slightly over-the-top style attributable to the growing year, managing in fact to be a sort of kaleidoscope for the entire region. Of the whites, Roncaglia 2005 is the biggest hit, since every year it manages to bring out the best from the albanella grape, a local variety genetically related to the elbling of the Mosel. Its plus points are subtle, elegant aromatics, a pleasant easy drinking style and a citrus-like, slightly minerally finish. Finally, Impero Bianco 2004 is the best ever version of this wine. A white made with Pinot Nero, it offers a good balance of intense energy and elegance on the palate and intriguing sweet citrus and vanilla hints on the nose.

● Colli Pesaresi Focara Pinot Nero Impero '04	▼▼	6
● Colli Pesaresi Sangiovese '04	▼▼	4*
○ Impero Bianco '04	▼▼	6
○ Colli Pesaresi Roncaglia '05	▼▼	4*
● Blu '03	▼	6
● Blu '00	▽▽	6
● Colli Pesaresi Focara Pinot Nero Impero Ris. '01	▽▽	6
● Blu '01	▽▽	6
● Colli Pesaresi Focara Pinot Nero Impero '01	▽▽	6
● Colli Pesaresi Focara Pinot Nero Impero '03	▽▽	6

POGGIO SAN MARCELLO (AN)

SARTARELLI
VIA COSTE DEL MOLINO, 24
60030 POGGIO SAN MARCELLO (AN)
TEL. 073189732
www.sartarelli.it

Contrada Balciana 1994 showed how a small winery can make strong, terroir-driven wines using practically only artisanal methods and scale. The trick is to get the most out of north-facing, late-ripening verdicchio vines by allowing long hang times to produce amazing fruit and then vinifying only in stainless steel. A style was born, spawning many imitators and amazing commercial success. In ten harvests, the wine has received more honours. On some occasions, it was not produced because of bad weather and some releases have shown excessive generosity with residual sugars and alcohol levels tipping the style into medium, if not outright sweet. The tenth anniversary sees a return to Balciana's best form, which is envelopingly soft and yet balanced, the full flavour hinting at almonds, aromatic herbs, aniseed and orange peel, combining to form a unique wine of great botrytis-enhanced finesse and depth. Balciana 2004 is worth Three resounding Glasses. In the meantime, the winery has grown in size, now producing over 100,000 bottles of Verdicchio Tralivio. Although this selection does not reach the same heights as Balciana, it is a fresher version of the same style. After appropriate bottle ageing, the 2004 is now a perfect model of drinkability and structure. The Verdicchio Classico 2005 wraps up the range. It is a very typical expression of the variety with, almond notes on the nose, a good backbone of flavour and a bitter twist to the finish.

○	Verdicchio dei Castelli di Jesi Cl. Sup. Balciana '04	🍷🍷🍷	6
○	Verdicchio dei Castelli di Jesi Cl. Sup. Tralivio '04	🍷🍷	4*
○	Verdicchio dei Castelli di Jesi Cl. '05	🍷🍷	3*
○	Verdicchio dei Castelli di Jesi Cl. Sup. Contrada Balciana '97	🍸🍸🍸	6
○	Verdicchio dei Castelli di Jesi Cl. Sup. Contrada Balciana '98	🍸🍸🍸	6
○	Verdicchio dei Castelli di Jesi Cl. Sup. Contrada Balciana '01	🍸🍸	6
○	Verdicchio dei Castelli di Jesi Cl. Sup. Contrada Balciana '03	🍸🍸	6

POTENZA PICENA (MC)

SANTA CASSELLA
C.DA SANTA CASSELLA, 7
62018 POTENZA PICENA (MC)
TEL. 0733671507
www.santacassella.it

Reliability and consistency seem to be the distinguishing features that best describe this estate, owned by the Sgarbi and Micheli Gigotti families. The 32 hectares of part native and part French vines are tended by the agronomist, Umberto Santoni, and provide first-class raw material for the cellar, competently run by oenologist Pier Luigi Lorenzetti. The estate's two main reds turned out to be excellent. The Conte Leopoldo 2004 is mainly cabernet sauvignon with a dash of montepulciano and shows austerity with slightly closed, but pure, ripe fruit, dryness and considerable structure emerging on the finish. Cardinal Bonaccorso 2003 is sangiovese with 20 per cent montepulciano in a younger, fresher style, despite the extra year's age and the decidedly warm vintage. It has pretty, aromatic fruit on the palate and a simple but long finish. The Rosso Piceno 2005 is another class act with pure, fleshy cherries, fine spice, nice acidity and a touch too much alcohol. The fresh, almost sweet, aromatic character of malvasia comes out clearly on Donna Angela 2005 while Donna Eleonora 2005 is an intensely fruity, supple blend consisting mainly of chardonnay, with some sauvignon. Colli Maceratesi Bianco 2005 is four-fifths maceratino – a variety only grown in this region – with the rest malvasia, resulting in a simple, fruity wine with good citrus notes and some intriguing aniseed. This bottle got a round of applause from us as it is a territorial wine sold at a reasonable price.

●	Colli Maceratesi Rosso Cardinal Bonaccorso Ris. '03	🍷🍷	4
●	Conte Leopoldo '04	🍷🍷	4
○	Colli Maceratesi Bianco '05	🍷🍷	3*
○	Donna Angela '05	🍷	4
○	Donna Eleonora '05	🍷	4
●	Rosso Piceno '05	🍷	3
○	Giardin Vecchio	🍷	4
●	Conte Leopoldo '03	🍸🍸	4
●	Conte Leopoldo '01	🍸🍸	4
●	Colli Maceratesi Rosso Cardinal Bonaccorso Ris. '02	🍸🍸	4
●	Conte Leopoldo '02	🍸🍸	4

RIPATRANSONE (AP)

Le Caniette

C.da Canali, 23
63038 Ripatransone (AP)
tel. 07359200
www.lecaniette.it

Giovanni Vagnoni has decided to renovate his family's winery to allow for growth and make his space more usable. Once the work is finished, visitors will be able to stand in the tasting room and admire the beautiful scenery with its curving rows of vines swaying in the light sea breezes. The Adriatic seems to be just round the corner but is in fact 500 metres below. Despite the work on this extraordinary project and the concomitant interruptions of the running of the winery, production has not suffered at all and the samples sent for tasting arrived on top form, especially the Rosso Piceno Morellone 2003. This went on to the Three Glass final thanks to its personality, which offers big, juicy purity of fruit and dense, austere tannins that are especially present on the long finish. The Nero di Vite 2003 proved yet again to be a wine of substance with a solid character but perhaps a little too much extract. The excessive body is a little overpowering and works against drinkability and freshness of fruit. This is not a mortal sin considering that the year was so hot and difficult to manage. The Pecorino Iosonogaia non sono Lucrezia 2004 is very interesting and even riper and more evolved than usual, in line with the oxidative style to which it is always made. It has good balance with fresh fruit, lively acidity and substantial, full flavour. Some of the must undergoes limited maceration on the skins, which enhances complexity and adds notes of caramel and dried fruits.

●	Rosso Piceno Morellone '03	🍷🍷	5
●	Rosso Piceno Nero di Vite '03	🍷🍷	7
○	Offida Pecorino Iosonogaia non sono Lucrezia '04	🍷🍷	5
○	Vino Santo di Ripatransone Sibilla Frigia '02	🍷	5
○	Falerio dei Colli Ascolani Lucrezia '04		3
●	Rosso Piceno Nero di Vite '01	YY	7
●	Rosso Piceno Morellone '02	YY	5
●	Rosso Piceno Morellone '00	YY	5
●	Rosso Piceno Nero di Vite '00	YY	7
●	Rosso Piceno Morellone '01	YY	5
●	Rosso Piceno Nero di Vite '02	YY	7
●	Rosso Piceno Morellone '98	YY	5

RIPATRANSONE (AP)

Cocci Grifoni

loc. San Savino
c.da Messieri, 12
63038 Ripatransone (AP)
tel. 073590143
www.tenutacoccigrifoni.it

First of all, Happy 80th Birthday to Guido Cocci Grifoni. He is a winemaker in the old style with the sort of strong-willed, dry character so common among men used to the hard life of the country. Guido's influence was probably the most significant force behind the creation of the Rosso Piceno DOC and he remains a vigorous defender of the denomination. Guido courageously faced down the difficult years which saw the debut of Piceno wine on the world stage and the consequences which that brought: invasion by international grape varieties, overgenerous use of barriques and excessive fruit. He tried everything, without prejudice even if it went against the way he saw the world. Now many people admire him for his intuitions, especially regarding the rediscovery of the pecorino grape. Guido's Colle Vecchio 2005 is still regional leader with intense citrus fruit and fresh flowers on an elegant, enveloping, palate and copious extract. Vigna Messieri is a Rosso Piceno Superiore selection which has always been made in a traditional style. The 2003 is direct and munificent on the palate. On the nose, it shows red fruits and the beginnings of maturity with notes of liquorice and leather. Over the last decade, small barrels have been introduced alongside the existing large wood and they are especially present in the 70-30 montepulciano and cabernet blend, Il Grifone. The 2002 has marked spicy notes, some vegetal hints, a high-energy palate and a solid tannin skeleton. The Passerina Brut is enjoyable and light while Falerio San Basso 2005 is floral with a bitter finish.

○	Offida Pecorino Podere Colle Vecchio '05	🍷🍷	4*
●	Offida Rosso Il Grifone '02	🍷🍷	5
●	Rosso Piceno Sup. V. Messieri '03	🍷🍷	4*
○	Falerio dei Colli Ascolani Vign. San Basso '05	🍷	3
●	Tellus '05	🍷	3
○	Offida Passerina Brut	🍷	4
●	Rosso Piceno Sup. V. Messieri '02	YY	4
○	Offida Pecorino Podere Colle Vecchio '04	YY	4
●	Rosso Piceno Sup. Le Torri '03	YY	3

La Cantina dei Colli Ripani

via Tosciano, 28
63038 Ripatransone (AP)
tel. 07359505
www.colliripani.it

We think that the usually reliable and renowned Ripatransone co-operative has come off the boil slightly, not so much with regard to its top products, which remain good, but regarding the larger output of cheaper wine. The reason is probably the unlucky 2005 harvest, which was not exactly a triumph for all producers. The lion's share of praise – excuse the pun – should go to Leo Ripanus, which is a 2003 Offida Rosso and again the best wine of the estate. The aromatic cabernet character is well integrated into the full, fleshy fruit of the montepulciano with its clean cherry and blackberry flavours. Despite the heat of the growing year, this is an elegant, measured wine that never goes over the top. It has an attractive character and a long, satisfying finish. Rosso Piceno Superiore Castellano 2003 is soft and full with good body but not quite enough freshness, which makes the fruit a little heavy. The rest of the output is reasonably good. Rosso Piceno Transone 2005 has weighty, fruity, vanilla-spiced flavours but it dries the mouth and Offida Pecorino Rugaro 2005 has good, fresh floral aromas on the nose but is let down by a rather tired palate that is not quite up to the same standard.

●	Offida Rosso Leo Ripanus '03	▼▼	4*
●	Rosso Piceno Sup. Castellano '03	▼▼	3*
○	Leukon Chardonnay '04	▼	4
○	Falerio dei Colli Ascolani Brezzolino '05	▼	2
○	Offida Passerina Ninfa Ripana '05	▼	1
○	Offida Pecorino Rugaro '05	▼	3
●	Rosso Piceno Transone '05	▼	1
○	Falerio dei Colli Ascolani Armilla '05		1
●	Offida Rosso Leo Ripanus '02	▽▽	4
●	Khorakhanè '02	▽▽	6

Poderi Capecci - San Savino

loc. San Savino
via Santa Maria in Carro, 13
63038 Ripatransone (AP)
tel. 073590107
www.sansavino.com

Montepulciano, sangiovese, pecorino. Domenico and Simone Capecci eschew French when describing their territory. In fact, they still have not forgotten their local dialect. Their old vines are tended according to the old school and their winery is run on strictly traditional lines. Modern technology is used in the least invasive way possible and barrique maturation is limited. Quinta Regio 2002 is a Montepulciano and contains the estate's best grapes, which are given long fermentation times and several years of maturation in wood and glass. Time is crucial for ensuring that the high-powered tannins are harmonized with the oak aromas and that the alcohol is balanced with the acidity. The result is a complex wine that succeeds in melding together the variety's fruitiness with fascinating cocoa and liquorice notes, which gives intense complexity of flavour and an extremely long, pleasing finish. Pecorino Ciprea 2005 is in the same style: closed in youth but able to open out into fascinating flavour complexity that ranges from salty to a long powerful vein of minerality. In the absence of the Rosso Piceno Picus 2004 and the Sangiovese Fedus 2004, which both performed well in previous Guides, the stage was left open for Ver Sacrum 2005, a steel-vinified Montepulciano with powerful tannins and a well-structured fruit-forward body. The last estate wine on our list was the honest Rosso Piceno Collomura 2005.

●	Quinta Regio '02	▼▼	6
○	Offida Pecorino Ciprea '05	▼▼	4*
●	Ver Sacrum '05	▼▼	4*
●	Rosso Piceno Collemura '05	▼	3
●	Quinta Regio '00	▽▽▽	6
●	Quinta Regio '01	▽▽▽	6
●	Moggio Sangiovese '98	▽▽▽	6
●	Rosso Piceno Sup. Picus '03	▽▽	5
●	Ver Sacrum '03	▽▽	6
●	Fedus Sangiovese '03	▽▽	6

SAN BENEDETTO DEL TRONTO (AP)

VITIVINICOLA COSTADORO
VIA MONTE AQUILINO, 2
63039 SAN BENEDETTO DEL TRONTO (AP)
TEL. 073581781
www.vinicostadoro.com

Giuseppe Costantini Brancadoro manages a large family estate with a correspondingly large winery just outside the centre of San Benedetto del Tronto. They produce almost a million bottles from vineyards perched on the top of long, steep ridges in an area characterized by beautiful sea inlets. Skilful vineyard work and good management in the winery allow the oenologist Nicola Dragani to select grapes for 150,000 bottles released under a range of labels. The best of these is Offida Rosso Diciottoquarantotto 2002, which is mainly montepulciano with 30 per cent cabernet and shows fresh ripe cherries on the nose. These are echoed on the palate, which is supple and enjoyable, if not particularly full-bodied. It's a temptingly easy-drinking wine. Rosso Piceno Superiore La Rocca 2004 is also very well made with simple, effective fresh fruit fragrances and a balanced, satisfying structure. Il Crinale 2003 is a full-bodied, focused Merlot with a rich, airy body that only suffers from the slightly drying effect of the closed tannins. The cellar decided to go down the wood route for Offida Pecorino Danù 2005, which focuses the nose on attractive floral notes but causes the palate to veer from an opening impression of fullness to end on a thin, buttery and faintly bitter finish. Lastly, Offida Passerina La Ferola 2005 is simple and fairly aromatic on the nose but slightly lacking on the palate.

●	Offida Rosso Diciottoquarantotto '02	▼▼	4
●	Rosso Piceno Sup. La Rocca '04	▼▼	4*
●	Il Crinale Merlot '03	▼	5
○	Offida Pecorino Danù '05	▼	4
○	Offida Passerina La Ferola '05		3
●	Offida Rosso Diciottoquarantotto '01	▽▽	5
●	Il Crinale Merlot '02	▽▽	5
●	Rosso Piceno Sup. La Rocca '03	▽▽	4

SENIGALLIA (AN)

PIERGIOVANNI GIUSTI
LOC. MONTIGNANO
VIA CASTELLARO, 97
60019 SENIGALLIA (AN)
TEL. 071918031
www.lacrimagiusti.it

Piergiovanni Giusti only grows and vinifies lacrima di Morro d'Alba but he produces separate bottlings for his different takes on the grape. The driving force behind his range is the 30,000-bottle release of his basic Lacrima, which we tasted in its 2005 incarnation. Despite the far from straightforward year for weather, Giusti has made an intensely perfumed wine with classic notes of violet petals and roses. The balance of ripe tannins, drinkability and nose-palate consistency is perfect. If the Lacrima 2005 is a model to follow, the Rubbjano 2004 selection is on a completely different level of expression again, reaching unscaled heights for this type of wine. The concentrated aromatics are never invasive and manage to encompass vegetal notes with red fruits and candied peel. On the palate, it is creamily intense, smooth and rounded. It is just a shame that with only 3,000 bottles so little of it is made. Luigino 2004 is also just as perfumed but was matured for a good 13 months on the fine lees. This imparts character and complexity but also slightly more stalkiness and bitterness. While waiting for the first dried-grape wine, which should be released next year, Piergiovanni also sent us a rosé, Le Rose di Settembre 2005, which is yet another Lacrima di Morro d'Alba. We liked it for its perfect combination of drinkability and complexity, with fragrant almond and flower notes.

●	Lacrima di Morro d'Alba Rubbjano '04	▼▼	4*
●	Lacrima di Morro d'Alba Luigino '04	▼▼	5
●	Lacrima di Morro d'Alba '05	▼▼	3*
⊙	Le Rose di Settembre '05	▼▼	3*
●	Lacrima di Morro d'Alba Luigino '03	▽▽	4
●	Lacrima di Morro d'Alba Rubbjano '03	▽▽	4

SERRA DE' CONTI (AN)

CASALFARNETO
VIA FARNETO, 16
60030 SERRA DE' CONTI (AN)
TEL. 0731889001
www.togni.it

Modernity and tradition intersect at Casalfarneto. We already pointed out the former in the last edition of the Guide, which was published just in time for the news that the winery had been acquired by the Togni family's large wine and drinks group. As for tradition, this shines through in the fact that the long-standing oenologist Roberto Potentini is remaining in the fold, as is Danilo Solustri who used to be a partner but is now managing the business. Indeed, it looks as having the security of Togni behind them has actually given these two friends extra courage and determination because this year's wines are better and more focused than ever before. We were particularly struck by Verdicchio Fontevecchia 2005 which, although it comes from a growing year that will not exactly be remembered for its generosity, is in fact elegant and well mannered with good palate development through fresh then citrussy notes into a full-flavoured finish. This wine offers enviable value for money and is ideal for daily drinking. Verdicchio Grancasale 2005 is richer bodied, with a punchy fruit burst on the nose that shows citrus, pineapple and grapefruit. The palate offers good minerality in a dry, balanced style. The only red produced on the estate is Rosso Piceno Pitulum 2004, which has notes of fleshy red fruits on the nose and a dry but smooth palate. Finally, the decision to delay the release of Cimaio 2004 by a year is intelligent. This Verdicchio made with overripe grapes cannot fail to benefit from further maturation.

- ● Rosso Piceno Pitulum '04 — 🍷🍷 — 4
- ○ Verdicchio dei Castelli di Jesi Cl. Sup. Fontevecchia '05 — 🍷🍷 — 3*
- ○ Verdicchio dei Castelli di Jesi Cl. Sup. Grancasale '05 — 🍷🍷 — 4
- ○ Verdicchio dei Castelli di Jesi Cl. Sup. Cimaio '03 — ΥΥ — 4
- ○ Verdicchio dei Castelli di Jesi Cl. Sup. Cimaio '01 — ΥΥ — 4
- ○ Verdicchio dei Castelli di Jesi Cl. Sup. Grancasale '04 — ΥΥ — 4

SERRA SAN QUIRICO (AN)

ACCADIA
FRAZ. CASTELLARO
VIA AMMORTO, 19
60048 SERRA SAN QUIRICO (AN)
TEL. 073185172 - 0731859007

Angelo Accadia is a Verdicchio artisan. His five hectares under vine turn out 28,000 bottles a year using exclusively family labour for total control in the vineyard and winery, which also benefits from advice from oenologist Roberto Potentini. Angelo's wines are full bodied and characterful. This is also partly thanks to the altitude of the vineyards, which are in the foothills of the Apennines at around 400 metres above sea level. This gives them plenty of sunlight and a wide range of temperatures. The aromatic intensity of Cantorì 2005 therefore comes as no surprise. It shows delicate notes of flowers and dried fruits followed by a soft, full-flavoured palate with an almondy finish. The 7,000 bottles of Conscio 2005 represent just over twice the production of the Cantorì. Conscio has distinct liveliness that enhances drinkability without losing out on finesse. Consono 2005 has much more aggressive acidity and it plays its varietal card to the full with an almondy, spring flower nose, light palate, a lovely bitterish finish and supple freshness all through. In the middle of all these straw-coloured Verdicchio hues, there is also a ruby-garnet Rosso Piceno Riverbero 2003 blend of montepulciano and sangiovese with a dash of lacrima. Some 3,200 bottles are made, offering intense aromas of flowers, spices and quinine, full flavour and a hint of ripeness.

- ○ Verdicchio dei Castelli di Jesi Cl. Sup. Cantorì '05 — 🍷🍷 — 4
- ○ Verdicchio dei Castelli di Jesi Cl. Sup. Conscio '05 — 🍷🍷 — 3*
- ● Rosso Piceno Riverbero '03 — 🍷 — 4
- ○ Verdicchio dei Castelli di Jesi Cl. Consono '05 — 🍷 — 2
- ○ Verdicchio dei Castelli di Jesi Cl. Sup. Cantorì '04 — ΥΥ — 4
- ○ Verdicchio dei Castelli di Jesi Cl. Sup. Conscio '04 — ΥΥ — 3

SERVIGLIANO (AP)

Fattoria Dezi

via Fonte Maggio, 14
63029 Servigliano (AP)
tel. 0734710090

The Dezi family's wines do not have a single DOC between them. The label clearly says "Contrada Fonte Maggio – Servigliano". This is neither affectation nor a megalomaniac attempt to pass these sunny, round hillsides off as the Richebourg cru at Vosne-Romanée or, to give an Italian example, Cannubi at Barolo. For straightforward farmers Stefano and Davide Dezi, the label is a homage to a land they love like a daughter. As such it requires enormous sacrifices from them, but it also gives back priceless satisfaction. One aspect of this is the first Three Glass award for the montepulciano-only Regina del Bosco, of which just under 9,000 bottles were made. Even in the torrid 2003 vintage, this wine succeeded in marrying finesse on the nose with harmony of structure for an elegant, rounded sensory profile of amazing expressivity. Just below this comes the slightly less complex Sangiovese Solo 2004 with its youthful balsamic, cherry and flower aromas followed by a rounded, accomplished palate with enviable integration of tannins and alcohol. These two characteristics are also the watchwords for Dezio 2004, a blend of montepulciano with some sangiovese. It is so direct that it is almost too much on the palate but it also has a spiciness of the soul that gives the lie to its apparent stylistic simplicity. Finally, we enjoyed the new release of Le Solagne 2004 which has now been accorded longer bottle maturation. It is made with malvasia grapes which are harvested very ripe, giving a velvety, openly aromatic character that signs off on a surprisingly full-flavoured note.

●	Regina del Bosco '03	🍷🍷🍷	6
●	Solo Sangiovese '04	🍷🍷	6
●	Dezio Vign. Beccaccia '04	🍷🍷	4*
○	Le Solagne V. T. '04	🍷🍷	4*
●	Solo Sangiovese '00	🍸🍸🍸	6
●	Solo Sangiovese '01	🍸🍸🍸	6
●	Regina del Bosco '01	🍸🍸	6
●	Regina del Bosco '02	🍸🍸	6
●	Solo Sangiovese '02	🍸🍸	6

SPINETOLI (AP)

Saladini Pilastri

via Saladini, 5
63030 Spinetoli (AP)
tel. 0736899534
www.saladinipilastri.it

"The many faces of Rosso Piceno" could be an advertising slogan for the Saladini Pilastri winery, which specializes in this particular style. Oenologist Alberto Antonini's skill has been to differentiate his wines according to age, crafting a precise character for each. As part of this process, the cellar decided to put back release of the company's two top reds, the 50-50 blends of aglianico and montepulciano, Rosso Piceno Superiore Monteprandone 2004 and Pregio del Conte 2004, as they need a longer maturation period in barrel and bottle. This is a wise decision, which will no doubt pay back consumers who have developed a liking for this estate. But we did manage to taste the new releases of three Rosso Picenos: Vigna Montetinello 2004 is a stiffish, compact wine with a full-bodied, dry palate, good fruit structure, with decent acidity and good development into the finish; Piediprato 2004 is richly fruity with notes of cherry and ripe blackberry followed by a fairly dynamic palate, even though it does tend towards heaviness on the finish; and Parnaso 2004 has an austere style with dense, closed tannins which do then open up a little at the finish. Falerio wines also have a part to play, which is quite important considering that the two versions account for around a half of the winery's production. Vigna Palazzi 2005 is bitter on the finish but more assured than the simple, light basic 2005.

●	Rosso Piceno Sup. V. Montetinello '04	🍷🍷	4
●	Rosso Piceno Piediprato '04	🍷🍷	4*
●	Rosso Piceno Parnaso '04	🍷	4
○	Falerio dei Colli Ascolani V. Palazzi '05	🍷	3
○	Falerio dei Colli Ascolani '05		2
●	Rosso Piceno '05		3
●	Rosso Piceno Sup. V. Monteprandone '00	🍸🍸🍸	5
●	Rosso Piceno Sup. V. Monteprandone '03	🍸🍸	5

STAFFOLO (AN)

CORONCINO
C.DA CORONCINO, 7
60039 STAFFOLO (AN)
TEL. 0731779494

"N'do arivo metto 'n segno" (I leave my mark everywhere I go) is the legend on Fattoria Coroncino's labels in Luca Canestrari's native Roman dialect. And Luca has left a lot of marks these last few years. Above all, he has managed to make his very high quality wines even more focused and seamless. He has achieved this by taking many small steps one at a time and applying his philosophy of living a quiet life, a quality he and his wife Fiorella manage to imbue into their products. We who have known him for many years are sure that Lucio is not going to beat his breast for not winning Three Glasses this year: it is not in his character. Nonetheless, Gaiospino 2004 is a portentously flavoursome and concentrated, following the house style of rich, well-extracted, full-bodied and very long wines. There is an undertone of vanilla that rounds out the full flavour very well. For an example of how barriques and tonneaux leave their mark, look no further than Gaiospino Fumé 2003. The name itself tells you the toastiness of the oak is important before it comes through on the aromatics of the nose and expresses itself on the opulent, smooth, fleshy palate. Everything is taken as far as it will go with Stracacio 2003, which is almost sweet on the palate and has late-harvest fragrances, going way beyond what you expect from the type. It is more of a meditation wine than a wine for food. Coroncino 2004 gives the ultimate expression of verdicchio's varietal character. It has elegant aniseed tones, dried flowers and apricots on a powerful palate with lots of flavour on the finish.

○ Verdicchio dei Castelli di Jesi Cl. Sup. Coroncino '04	🍷🍷	4*
○ Verdicchio dei Castelli di Jesi Cl. Sup. Gaiospino '04	🍷🍷	5
○ Verdicchio dei Castelli di Jesi Cl. Sup. Gaiospino Fumé '03	🍷🍷	6
○ Verdicchio dei Castelli di Jesi Cl. Sup. Stracacio '03	🍷	6
○ Verdicchio dei Castelli di Jesi Cl. Sup. Il Bacco '05	🍷	3
○ Verdicchio dei Castelli di Jesi Cl. Sup. Gaiospino '03	🍷🍷🍷	5
○ Verdicchio dei Castelli di Jesi Cl. Sup. Gaiospino '97	🍷🍷🍷	5

STAFFOLO (AN)

ESTER HAUSER
C.DA CORONCINO, 1A
60039 STAFFOLO (AN)
TEL. 0731770203

Ester Hauser's story started when she left her native Switzerland as a youngster 15 years ago, going to live in Marche with the intention of producing wine on the slightly less than a hectare of vines she had just bought. The place she chose is particularly beautiful and almost wild. Steep sea inlets give way to gentle, mainly unspoilt hills with no warehouses or polluting factories in sight. The backdrop is the blue of the Adriatic, which is only a few kilometres away as the crow flies. Since then, Ester has spent much of her life in the vineyard, which she tends with the knowledge of a farmer and the care of a gardener. Most of the rest of her time is spent in her small winery to see how her wines are developing. This is the story behind Il Cupo 2004, which almost achieved Three Glasses for its dense fruit, closed but well-tempered palate and extraordinarily elegant flavour flaunting balanced, persistent graphite and liquorice notes. The only problem with this wine is the limited run of production, which only stretches to 2,600 bottles. This excellence is all the more significant in that it was produced in a year of change for the winery, which resulted in the decision to call in oenologist Aroldo Bellelli and to produce a second wine to reorganize production. The almost 3,000 bottles of Il Ceppo 2004 follow in the footsteps of its older brother with the same solid, austere style, slightly lighter structure and the same compact fruit.

● Il Cupo '04	🍷🍷	6
● Il Ceppo '04	🍷🍷	5
● Il Cupo Vecchie Vigne '02	🍷🍷	6
● Il Cupo '03	🍷🍷	6

STAFFOLO (AN)

ZACCAGNINI

VIA SALMÀGINA, 9/10
60039 STAFFOLO (AN)
TEL. 0731779892 - 0731705183
www.zaccagnini.it

This winery was founded in 1973 by Mario Zaccagnini and is now managed by his daughter Rosella, who has over 30 hectares of mainly verdicchio in one of the best municipalities of the Castelli di Jesi at an average altitude of almost 500 metres. Verdicchio Salmàgina 2005 is partly made with overripe grapes from the Salmàgina vineyard, and then vinified in stainless steel. It is very persuasive on the nose with its almond, apple and slightly vegetal aromas, which are followed by a subtle palate and a full-flavoured finish. Verdicchio Pier delle Vigne 2004 is on a par now that it is finally free of the oak that overwhelmed it in the past and flaunts rounded fruit intensity. In contrast, Riserva di Verdicchio Maestro di Staffolo 2004 seemed to us to be rather too inclined to a lazy softness. It has aromas of icing sugar and almonds with a slight veil of alcohol which is clearly present in the warmth of the palate. Verdicchio Classico 2005 is much fresher, with precise aromas of citrus peel that are reprised on the supple, easy-drinking palate. The Rosso Conero 2005 is the best of the reds, showing a little vegetal but with good thrust across the palate. Vigna Vescovi 2003 is from 60 per cent cabernet sauvignon with the rest made up of equal parts of pinot nero and montepulciano. It displays ripe fragrances on the nose followed by good structure and a dry, spicy palate. Finally, a few words about Rosella Zaccagnini's other independent estate, Casa Lisà, which produces simple, well-made wines.

● Vigna Vescovi '03	🍷🍷	5
○ Verdicchio dei Castelli di Jesi Cl. Sup. Pier delle Vigne '04	🍷🍷	4
● Rosso Conero '05	🍷🍷	4
○ Verdicchio dei Castelli di Jesi Cl. '05	🍷🍷	3*
○ Verdicchio dei Castelli di Jesi Cl. Sup. Salmàgina '05	🍷🍷	4
○ Verdicchio dei Castelli di Jesi Cl. Maestro di Staffolo Ris. '04	🍷	5
● Casa Lisà '05	🍷	3
○ Casa Lisà Brut	🍷	4
○ Zaccagnini Brut M. Cl. Ris.	🍷	4
● Vigna Vescovi '00	YY	5

TOLENTINO (MC)

IL POLLENZA

VIA CASONE, 4
62029 TOLENTINO (MC)
TEL. 0733961989
www.ilpollenza.it

When an important investment decision is approved, nothing is left to chance. Even more so when the decision is to plant 50 hectares of new vines and build a technologically state-of-the-art winery. Aldo Brachetti Peretti did not follow the Marche traditions he was brought up with, deciding instead – on the advice of an excellent staff led by Giachomo Tachis with Umberto Trombelli in the winery and Vincenzo Melia in the vineyard – to plant a majority of international varieties with very little space for the locals. This wager has yet to pay off completely but the game has only just begun. Pollenza 2002 is now on its second release from vines which are still very young. It is a good blend of cabernet sauvignon and merlot which caresses the nose with balsamic notes followed by a vegetality that is magnified on the palate. It is concentrated without being excessively dense and has suppleness yet lacks the complexity required of a truly fine wine. As neither the Pinot Nero Brachetti nor the Cosmino were sent, the honour of being the second best wine of the estate went to Porpora 2004, an easy-drinking Merlot with a well-gauged nose of tobacco over a background of forest fruits and sweet spice and a palate that is at once soft and powerful. Brianello 2005 is a docile white with a simple, one-dimensional character. In contrast, the sweet, dried-grape Pius IX Mastai 2004, from traminer aromatico and sauvignon, has intense dried figs, caramel and cinnamon on the nose that reappear with velvety opulence on the palate.

● Il Pollenza '02	🍷🍷	7
○ Pius IX Mastai '04	🍷🍷	6
● Porpora '04	🍷🍷	4
○ Brianello '05	🍷	4
● Il Pollenza '01	YY	7
○ Pius IX Mastai '03	YY	6

OTHER WINERIES

VALENTINO FIORINI

VIA GIARDINO CAMPIOLI, 5
61030 BARCHI (PU)
TEL. 072197151
www.fioriniwines.it

Tenuta Campioli 2005 is again the best Bianchello del Metauro of the vintage, a well-deserved feather in Carla Fiorini's cap. It opens softly then grows into a broad, expressive mid palate followed by a very tasty finish. Vigna Sant'Ilario 2005 is simpler and more linear with some fresh fruit.

○ Bianchello del Metauro Tenuta Campioli '05	TT	3*
○ Bianchello del Metauro Vigna Sant'Ilario '05	T	2

CANTINE DI CASTIGNANO

C.DA SAN VENANZO, 31
63032 CASTIGNANO (AP)
TEL. 0736822216
www.cantinedicastignano.com

As several of this large co-operative's wines were not presented this year, we tasted only the good Offida Pecorino Montemisio 2005, with intense flowers and tropical fruits, good citrus acidity on the palate and a flavoursome finish, and the simple, enjoyable Falerio dei Colli Ascolani 2005.

○ Offida Pecorino Montemisio '05	TT	3*
○ Falerio dei Colli Ascolani '05	T	2
● Offida Rosso Gran Maestro '02	YY	4

SAPUTI

C.DA FIASTRA, 2
62020 COLMURANO (MC)
TEL. 0733508137
www.saputi.it

The 2003 is fine comeback for the 70-30 merlot and cabernet Abate Pallia, an austere, toasty wine with good ripe fruit sweetened by balsam and vanilla. Rosso Piceno Castru Vecchiu 2004 is also balsamic. The generous cherry flavour is slightly overpowered by a dry and rather unyielding structure.

● Abate Pallia '03	TT	5
● Rosso Piceno Castru Vecchiu '04	T	4
○ Colli Maceratesi Ribona Castru Vecchiu '05	T	3

LA DISTESA

VIA ROMITA, 28
60034 CUPRAMONTANA (AN)
TEL. 0731781230
www.ladistesa.it

The fly in the ointment here is the tiny production but this is also what allows Corrado Dottori to oversee each detail with care. Verdicchio Gli Eremi 2004 is excellent, its skilful wood maturation giving balance of fullness and elegance. Terre Silvate 2005 has energy and full-flavoured length.

○ Verdicchio dei Castelli di Jesi Cl. Sup. Gli Eremi '04	TT	4
○ Verdicchio dei Castelli di Jesi Cl. Sup. Terre Silvate '05	TT	3*

Sparapani - Frati Bianchi
via Barchio, 12
60034 Cupramontana (AN)
tel. 0731781216 - 0731780303
www.fratibianchi.it

Verdicchio Il Priore di Settimio Sparapani gets better every year. The 2005 went to the Three Glass finals for its impressive fruit and flower progression. The long finish is lifted by subtle minerality while always maintaining perfect balance. Verdicchio Salerna 2005 is lighter and more acid.

○	Verdicchio dei Castelli di Jesi Cl. Sup. Il Priore '05	▼▼	4*
○	Verdicchio dei Castelli di Jesi Cl. Salerna '05	▼	3

Enzo Mecella
via Dante, 112
60044 Fabriano (AN)
tel. 073221680
www.enzomecella.com

Enzo Mecella has three good reds. The stand-out Merlot 2004 has light, enjoyable fruit-driven freshness. The Rosso Conero Rubelliano 2003 is softer at the outset but dries up on the palate because its tannins are still slightly unripe. The Shiraz 2005 is herbaceous and a little dry on the palate.

●	Merlot '04	▼▼	4*
●	Rosso Conero Rubelliano Ris. '03	▼	6
●	Shiraz '05	▼	4

Claudio Morelli
v.le Romagna, 47b
61032 Fano (PU)
tel. 0721823352
www.claudiomorelli.it

Claudio Morelli's Bianchello del Metauro wines are as reliable as ever, especially Borgo Torre 2005, which has subtle fruit and flower notes, freshness and decent flavour intensity. The Sangiovese Sant'Andrea in Villis 2003 is in a structured, slightly drying style with a few too many green notes.

○	Bianchello del Metauro Borgo Torre '05	▼▼	3*
●	Colli Pesaresi Sangiovese Sant'Andrea in Villis '03	▼	4

Madonnabruna
c.da Camera, 100
63023 Fermo (FM)
tel. 0734679500
www.madonnabruna.it

This Fermo estate made its Guide debut with two good reds. Portese 2004 is a cabernet and merlot blend with roundness, austerity and good progression. The all-montepulciano Moresco 2004 has richer, riper fruit and more meatiness. The structure is solid and balanced with a long, enveloping finish.

●	Moresco '04	▼▼	4*
●	Portese '04	▼▼	4*

Mario & Giorgio Brunori
v.le della Vittoria, 103
60035 Jesi (AN)
tel. 0731207213
www.brunori.it

With advice from oenologist Alberto Mazzoni, Carlo and Giorgio Brunori have produced a Verdicchio San Nicolò 2005 with textbook typicity. The subtle fresh flower and straw aromas are elegant, as is the flavour profile which develops well and finishes long. Verdicchio Le Gemme 2005 is simpler.

○	Verdicchio dei Castelli di Jesi Cl. Sup. San Nicolò '05	▼▼	4*
○	Verdicchio dei Castelli di Jesi Cl. Le Gemme '05		3

Bisci
via Fogliano, 120
62024 Matelica (MC)
tel. 0737787490
www.bisciwines.it

Restructuring of the estate's facilities meant that this year we only received the well-defined Verdicchio di Matelica 2004, a wine of fruit-driven finesse with a robust, elegant tasting profile. It is a reminder of the massive potential and expertise here at this long-established Matelica winery.

○	Verdicchio di Matelica '04	▼▼	4*
●	Villa Castiglioni '03	▽▽	5
○	Verdicchio di Matelica Senex '98	▽▽	5

Capinera
c.da Crocette, 12
62010 Morrovalle (MC)
tel. 0733222444
www.capinera.com

Beato Masseo 2003, Capinera's best red, is a 50-50 blend of sangiovese and cabernet. It is still austere, showing dense tannins, pure fruit and a slightly drying finish. Rosso Piceno Duca Guarnerio 2004 is also good while Sauvignon Fontelata 2005 is simple but shows good body and a citrus finish.

● Colli Maceratesi Rosso Beato Masseo Ris. '03	▼▼	5
○ Fontelata Sauvignon '05	▼▼	4*
● Rosso Piceno Duca Guarnerio '04	▼	4

Malacari
via Enrico Malacari, 6
60020 Offagna (AN)
tel. 0717207606

Alessandro Starrabba's Rosso Conero 2004 is an excellent reminder of that this region is exceptionally suitable for growing montepulciano grapes. The fresh, even style is based on aroma-rich, well-ripened fruit and easy drinkability. It's an ideal everyday wine.

● Rosso Conero '04	▼▼	4*
● Rosso Conero Grigiano '03	▽▽	5

Castello Fageto
via Valdaso, 52
63016 Pedaso (AP)
tel. 0734931784
www.castellofageto.it

The beautiful Castello Fageto estate, with its part-terraced 20 hectares, missed a beat this year as some of the range's leading wines were missing. The Pecorino 2005 is very good, with fresh, mineral juiciness. The light, drinkable Falerio is reliable as is the nicely fruit-driven Rosso Piceno.

○ Offida Pecorino Fenèsia '05	▼▼	4*
○ Falerio dei Colli Ascolani '05	▼	3
● Rosso Piceno '05	▼	4

Luca Guerrieri
via San Filippo, 24
61030 Piagge (PU)
tel. 0721890152 - 0721890100
www.aziendaguerrieri.it

The 2004 is the second release for the sangiovese, cabernet and merlot Guerriero Nero. Its attraction lies in soft structure and fresh red fruit aromas. Sangiovese Galileo 2003 is a tad evolved while the Bianchello del Metauro 2005 is fresh with good fruit on the nose.

● Guerriero Nero '04	▼▼	4*
● Colli Pesaresi Sangiovese Galileo Ris. '03	▼	4
○ Bianchello del Metauro '05	▼	3

Casalis Douhet
loc. Porto
via Montecoriolano, 6
62016 Potenza Picena (MC)
tel. 0733688121 - www.coriolano.com

This pretty estate in Potenza Picena produces two excellent reds, now under the Casalis Douhet label. Alberto Mazzoni manages. The 2003 Merlot has good round fruit structure, while the montepulciano and cabernet sauvignon Rosso 2003 has full, enveloping, fleshy fruit at perfect ripeness.

● Rosso '03	▼▼	4
● Merlot '03	▼▼	3*

Croce del Moro
via Tassanare, 4
60030 Rosora (AN)
tel. 0731814158
www.tassanare.it

Verdicchio Crocetta 2004 was the only wine tasted and it easily won Two Glasses. The floral aromas are full and veined with toastiness. Entry on the palate is full-flavoured, leading to a slightly dry mid palate and rounding off with a hazelnut-led finish with a refreshing sweet twist.

○ Verdicchio dei Castelli di Jesi Cl. Sup. Crocetta '04	▼▼	3*
● Rosso Piceno Furtarello '03	▽▽	4

Maurizio Marconi
via Melano, 23
60030 San Marcello (AN)
tel. 0731267223
www.vinoearte.it

Maurizio Marconi's estate has returned to the Guide in style with two really good Verdicchios. Corona Reale 2005 has marked fruit aromas and a fresh tasty mouth livened up by nice grapefruit. Sapore di Generazioni 2005 impressed with vegetal tomato leaves on the nose and a long dry palate.

○ Verdicchio dei Castelli di Jesi Cl. Sup. Corona Reale '05	🍷🍷	4*
○ Verdicchio dei Castelli di Jesi Cl. Sup. Sapore di Generazioni E. N. '05	🍷🍷	4*

Enrico Ceci
via Santa Maria D'Arco, 7
60038 San Paolo di Jesi (AN)
tel. 0731779033
www.verdicchiomarche.it/ceci

Enrico Ceci has come up with another powerful Verdicchio Santa Maria d'Arco. The 2004 has a very elegant nose of fresh flowers and citrus peel with a touch of botrytis to bring out its quality. It is full and warm in the mouth with a very slightly drying finish.

○ Verdicchio dei Castelli di Jesi Cl. Sup. Santa Maria d'Arco '04	🍷🍷	4*
○ Verdicchio dei Castelli di Jesi Cl. Sup. Santa Maria d'Arco '03	🍷🍷 (white)	4

Pontemagno
b.go Santa Maria, 60
60038 San Paolo di Jesi (AN)
tel. 0731703214
www.piersantivini.com

Ottaviano and Silveria Piersanti sent us a white and a red, both good quality and reasonably priced. Rosso Conero Pontelungo 2004 is very fresh, fruity and well made while Verdicchio Ori 2003 has soft sweet notes that contrast with a dry toasty flavour.

○ Verdicchio dei Castelli di Jesi Cl. Sup. Ori '03	🍷🍷	2*
● Rosso Conero Pontelungo '04	🍷🍷	2*

Vignamato
via Battinebbia, 4
60038 San Paolo di Jesi (AN)
tel. 0731779197
www.vignamato.com

Maurizio Ceci's wines have fallen off slightly. Verdicchio Versiano 2005 is still the best with its subtle, well-proportioned structure. Entry is fresh and the finish nicely bitter. Verdicchio Passito Antares 2004 is medium-sweet and alcohol-rich with good body and a bitterish hint on the finish.

○ Verdicchio dei Castelli di Jesi Cl. Sup. Versiano '05	🍷🍷	4*
○ Verdicchio dei Castelli di Jesi Passito Antares '04	🍷	5

Colli di Serrapetrona
via Colli, 7/8
62020 Serrapetrona (MC)
tel. 0733908329
www.collidiserrapetrona.it

The new estate debuted well. We liked the all-vernaccia Robbione 2004, with warm, spicy, sweet and bitter cherries and a fleshy, fruity palate. Sommo 2004 is a characterful still, dried-grape Vernaccia with a nose of ripe cherries firm and measured sweetness. Federico Giotto consults.

● Serrapetrona Robbione '04	🍷🍷	5
● Sommo '04	🍷🍷	5
● Serrapetrona Collequanto '04	🍷	3

Alberto Quacquarini
via Colli, 1
62020 Serrapetrona (MC)
tel. 0733908180 - 0733908790
www.quacquarini.it

The two still reds from vernaccia were back this year but the estate's strong point is the sparkling Vernaccia di Serrapetrona in sweet and dry versions. Petronio 2001 has a good, fresh balsamic nose, even palate and long fruity finish. The Colli della Serra 2001 is simple and dry in the mouth.

● Petronio '01	🍷🍷	5
● Colli della Serra Rosso '01	🍷	3
● Vernaccia di Serrapetrona Secco '05	🍷	3

UMBRIA

Wine is ever more the talking point in Umbria. The huge upturn in quality is no longer news but it still provides food for thought; official bodies put wine at the top of their future socio-economic strategies, tourism included; the number of consumers and lovers of the wines continues to grow; events are mushrooming; and there are an increasing number of tastings, discussions and debates. So things are on the boil. And even though the region produces just 800,000 hectolitres of wine a year, one of the lowest figures in the country, it has nothing to fear when it comes to good drinking. There are 11 DOCs and two DOCGs, Torgiano Rosso Riserva and Sagrantino di Montefalco. This pair is closely linked with Lungarotti and Caprai, two families who have dictated the pace and direction of the region's wine scene. It was they who originally determined the routes to take, and the styles and territories on which to concentrate, so much so that their names are almost synonymous with their DOCGs. Montefalco is the zone that best seems to embody the concept of terroir. Its potential remains as enormous as the advances that have already been made there, in quantity as well as quality. But let's get down to detail, which means taking on board the difficult 2003 vintage. The year was excessively dry almost everywhere but even more fraught in Montefalco where it brought out the extent of the gap between the zone's two qualitative strands. Many of Montefalco's estates are fairly new and young vines have less resistance to excessive heat. Then there's the character of Sagrantino, whose exuberant aromas and weighty structure and tannins certainly aren't helped by high temperatures. What can emerge are convoluted wines with imperfect phenolic ripening that have a sense of warmth and ripeness but lack vibrancy and tannic refinement. So it wasn't the year for newcomers to provide the excitement. As expected, it was the usual two names that emerged: Còlpetrone, whose '03 Sagrantino is a wine of rare balance, and Caprai, who won our top prize for an incredibly refined, complex Collepiano '03 rather than his 25 Anni '03, which is just too big. Such is the irony of the year. Orvieto, Umbria's other classic zone, has still not yet found its true identity but it has given us two outstanding wines in Merlot Gaudio '03 from Tenuta Le Velette, which amply rewards the estate's work in recent years, and a sumptuous '04 Cervaro della Sala, possibly the best release ever. Then another Merlot, from Castello delle Regine, in Amelia in the province of Terni won Three Glasses for the fourth year running. Heading north to Trasimeno we find a terrific Campoleone '04, a sangiovese-merlot blend from Lamborghini made by Cotarella. That brings the Three Glasses tally to six. But there's also one assigned retrospectively to Lungarotti's '88 Vigna Monticchio. So things aren't so bad after all.

ALLERONA (TR)

TENUTA POGGIO DEL LUPO
VIA VOCABOLO BUZZAGHETTO, 100
05011 ALLERONA (TR)
TEL. 0763628350
www.tenutapoggiodellupo.it

Once the Polato family made the decision to invest resources and energy into their Poggio del Lupo estate, the wines started to improve by leaps and bounds. And in the last two years, a further change of pace has become apparent, turning Poggio del Lupo into one of the region's most distinctive wineries. It lies in Allerona, a short hop from Orvieto, and has 116 hectares of land all in one block, with 40 or so of vineyard. The care taken in the vineyards and cellar, not to mention the reliability given by consultancy from Cotarella, has led to another excellent range of wines this year. Il Silentis '04, from all montepulciano, sailed into the finals with its incredibly intense, complex aromas, ranging from small black berry fruits and aromatic herbs to toasty, balsamic sensations. Its vigorous, savoury, juicy palate lacks nothing in terms of liveliness, depth or tannic weight. We also found excellence from Màrneo '05, a blend of grechetto, chardonnay and sauvignon, which gives intriguing mineral and tropical fruits notes. Lupiano '05 and Novilunio '05 were surprisingly good for their category. The former blends vegetal hints with a firm, ripe, intense fruitiness, is beautifully clean and holds together well whereas Novilunio is an Orvieto of personality which has chalky minerality, citrus, aromatic herbs and a subtle white peachiness.

●	Rosso Silentis '04	🍷🍷	6
●	Rosso Orvietano Lupiano '05	🍷🍷	3*
○	Màrneo '05	🍷🍷	5
○	Orvieto Novilunio '05	🍷🍷	4*
●	Rosso Silentis '03	YY	5
●	Rosso Silentis '02	YY	5
○	Màrneo '04	YY	4*

AMELIA (TR)

CANTINA DEI COLLI AMERINI
LOC. FORNOLE
ZONA INDUSTRIALE
05022 AMELIA (TR)
TEL. 0744989721
www.colliamerini.it

The Colli Amerini co-operative is responsible for bringing lustre to the zone, one that is visually stunning and has a centuries-old viticultural tradition. And it's all change this year, with a new look to the wines, both in style and presentation. They benefit from an ideal mix of heights, site climates and soils across the more than 700 hectares of vineyard carefully worked by its 350-plus members. There is also an excellent team of agronomists and winemakers to back them up. Quality is consistently high and one wine, Carbio, the estate's emblem, is truly starry once more. Indeed, the '04 of this fine blend of merlot, sangiovese, ciliegiolo and montepulciano, flew right into the finals. It is deep in hue. There is a fruity, smoky nose with hints of pink pepper and a touch of tarriness, and the palate, sweet, succulent and deep, is just as good, its acidity perfectly melded into the wine's body, followed by a long aftertaste of black cherry. The real interest this year, though, comes from Ciliegiolo di Narni 30 Anni. This is the result of a long process of research and development, and undergoes six months' barrique ageing. It has vegetal hints and aromas of ashes underlying sweet scents of red berry fruits, mainly raspberries. The palate is lively, full of fruit and finishes well. Finally come Olmeto '05, a good monovarietal Merlot which is not, though, as good as the '04, and Rocca Nerina '05, from malvasia and a little chardonnay, which has sweet, ripe fruit on both nose and palate.

●	C. Amerini Rosso Sup. Carbio '04	🍷🍷	5
●	Ciliegiolo di Narni 30 Anni '05	🍷🍷	4*
●	Olmeto '05	🍷	4
○	Rocca Nerina '05	🍷	4
●	Olmeto '04	YY	4*
●	C. Amerini Rosso Sup. Carbio '00	YY	5
●	C. Amerini Rosso Sup. Carbio '01	YY	5
●	Olmeto '02	YY	4*
●	C. Amerini Rosso Sup. Carbio '03	YY	5
●	Olmeto '98	YY	3
●	C. Amerini Rosso Sup. Carbio '99	YY	5

AMELIA (TR)

CASTELLO DELLE REGINE
LOC. LE REGINE
VIA DI CASTELLUCCIO
05022 AMELIA (TR)
TEL. 0744702005
www.castellodelleregine.com

This fabulous mixed-crop estate, straddling the townships of Narni and Amelia, is owned by the Nodari family who have worked incessantly to elevate it to the position of one of the brightest stars in Italy's agricultural firmament, with wine their priority. It spans 400 hectares, 50 of which are under vine, and a further 30 are being planted. The soils are clayey-sandy and lie at 180 to 280 metres, the vinification cellar is brand new, Franco Bernabei is consultant and the owners put great passion into everything they do. All this leads to superb wines, and this year's offerings are no let-down. The '04 Merlot, after its masterful showing in the difficult '02 and '03 vintages, is simply stunning and worthily earned Three Glasses. Notes of quinine and black berry fruit play around spices and oriental woods. These scents also come through on the creamy, well balanced and supremely elegant palate, where blueberry and blackcurrant intermingle with a hint of caramel and silky tannins give way to an intense aftertaste of fruit and fresh mint leaves: a masterpiece. The '01 Sangiovese Selezione del Fondatore, is more austere and a touch edgy but deep and fascinating, easily good enough for a place in the finals once more. Princeps '03, from carefully selected cabernet, sangiovese and merlot grapes, is a cohesive wine with a spicy, clove-like nose, and a zesty, steely palate. Bianco delle Regine '05 is aromatic and full of tropical fruit. Both showed well.

●	Merlot '04	▼▼▼	7
●	Sangiovese Sel. del Fondatore '01	▼▼	6
●	Princeps '03	▼▼	6
○	Bianco delle Regine '05	▼▼	4*
●	Merlot '01	▽▽▽	7
●	Merlot '02	▽▽▽	6
●	Merlot '03	▽▽▽	7
●	Merlot '00	▽▽	7
●	Podernovo '00	▽▽	4
●	Princeps '00	▽▽	6

BASCHI (TR)

TENUTA DI SALVIANO
LOC. CIVITELLA DEL LAGO
VOC. SALVIANO, 44
05020 BASCHI (TR)
TEL. 0744950459

The castles of Titignano and Salviano mirror each other across the right and left banks of Lake Corbara respectively in a natural landscape of amazing splendour. The property has been owned by the Corsini families since the end of the 17th century and now forms a modern estate and has 70 hectares of vines, all lying between 150 and 500 metres. The wines again follow their usual pecking order, with top of the tree Lago di Corbara Turlò '04, from sangiovese, cabernet sauvignon and merlot. There is a deep ruby colour, a well-defined, nicely cohesive, spicy nose with hints of balsam and a palate of personality, with good texture and crisp fruit, one suggesting long-ageing potential. Lago di Corbara Solideo '03, from cabernet sauvignon and merlot, is also good but reflects the dry year. It shows some over-development right from the first sniff and its initial fruit rapidly gives way to sponge cake, cinnamon and cloves. The palate is round, warm and chocolatey and the tannic weave is dense but a little tight. In short, it's a classic 2003. Orvieto Classico Superiore '05 has very good style. It's lightly citrussy, with hints of citron leaves and lemon, and has a good acid backbone.

●	Lago di Corbara Solideo '03	▼▼	4
●	Lago di Corbara Turlò '04	▼▼	4
○	Orvieto Cl. Sup. '05	▼	4
●	Lago di Corbara Solideo '01	▽▽	4
●	Lago di Corbara Solideo '02	▽▽	4
●	Lago di Corbara Turlò '02	▽▽	4
○	Orvieto Cl. Sup. '04	▽▽	4

BEVAGNA (PG)

ADANTI

LOC. ARQUATA
06031 BEVAGNA (PG)
TEL. 0742360295
www.cantineadanti.com

The history of Adanti dates from 1960 when the family converted an old Celestine friary into a cellar and started to replant vineyards. The territories of Arquata and Colcimino in Bevagna, suited as they are to viticulture, have been of fundamental importance to the winery's development, but those who have dedicatedly worked daily towards the realization of the dream have been even more pivotal. These include Adanti himself, now more active than ever, right down to Pavini, the long-standing cellarman, and his son Daniele, and include oenologist Graziana Grassini to whom falls the difficult task of making ever greater wines without ever losing sight of tradition. This means wines of elegance, maybe with a little austerity: wines that are never simplistic, never forced into roundness. They are led by the Sagrantino which, despite the difficult 2002 vintage, has a wealth of fascination. The colour is ruby-garnet and the nose is intriguing, with briary fruit, spiciness and pencil lead-like mineral scents. The palate is awesome, reflecting its provenance with wonderful liveliness, finesse and a delightful citrus finish. The '04 Rosso di Montefalco runs along similar lines, although is more directed towards mainly damson and strawberry red berry fruit and, naturally, easier drinking. The Sagrantino Passito '03 is one of the best in the zone, with blackberry and chocolate leaping out, yet lacking neither varietal definition nor the Adanti style. The two young whites are also pleasing.

●	Montefalco Sagrantino Arquata '02	🍷🍷	6
●	Montefalco Sagrantino Passito Arquata '03	🍷🍷	7
●	Montefalco Rosso Arquata '04	🍷🍷	4
○	Colli Martani Grechetto Arquata '05	🍷	3
○	Montefalco Bianco Arquata '05	🍷	3
●	Montefalco Sagrantino Arquata '01	YY	6
●	Montefalco Sagrantino Arquata '00	YY	6
●	Montefalco Sagrantino Passito '01	YY	6
●	Montefalco Sagrantino Passito '02	YY	7
●	Montefalco Sagrantino Passito '99	YY	7

BEVAGNA (PG)

FATTORIA COLLE ALLODOLE

LOC. COLLE ALLODOLE
06031 BEVAGNA (PG)
TEL. 0742361897 - 0742360371

Francesco Antano is a young, enthusiastic wine man in the highest, truest sense of the term, who has taken up the difficult task of carrying forward his family's traditions. This means producing individual wines that are rooted in the area's traditions yet have strong personality and great quality. His efforts seem to be leading him in the right direction and, year by year, his wines become more impressive, especially after a little bottle age. After a necessary pause with the '02 vintage, he's back on track with a great Sagrantino di Montefalco Colleallodole '03, a cru made entirely with grapes from the Colleallodole vineyard. It is superb from the first glance. The aromas of blackberry and liqueur cherries are impressive, there are intriguing balsamic flashes, and the palate is deep and cohesive, finishing on youthful but well-gauged tannins. All in all, it's a close-knit but racy wine that well reflects its provenance. The Montefalco Rosso Riserva '03 is in similar style, despite the necessary difference in the grape blend. It offers impressive warmth and ripeness, yet remains lively and spirited, and finishes on spices and tobacco. Also good are the young Rosso di Montefalco '04, the winery's battle horse, which has its habitual style, and Sagrantino Passito '03, which practically bursts with jammy fruit but is just a touch too sweet and lacks lift on the palate. Finally, we have the basic Sagrantino '03, a pleasant wine but one that has been affected by the dry year.

●	Montefalco Sagrantino Colle delle Allodole '03	🍷🍷	7
●	Montefalco Rosso Ris. '03	🍷🍷	6
●	Montefalco Sagrantino Passito '03	🍷🍷	5
●	Montefalco Rosso '04	🍷🍷	5
●	Montefalco Sagrantino '03	🍷	6
●	Montefalco Sagrantino '01	YY	6
●	Montefalco Sagrantino '98	YY	5
●	Montefalco Sagrantino Colle delle Allodole '98	YY	6

CASTEL VISCARDO (TR)

CANTINA MONRUBIO
FRAZ. MONTERUBIAGLIO
LOC. LE PRESE, 22
05010 CASTEL VISCARDO (TR)
TEL. 0763626064

Another fine set of results for Monrubio shows once again how it is possible to have good quality across the board while making wines in large quantities and selling them at very fair prices. In the case of this long-standing co-operative from a part of Orvieto dominated by vines and olives, the achievement is down to good internal organization and tip-top technical supervision: Riccardo Cotarella has been consultant here for a good number of years. All this brings assurance not just to its numerous grape-supplying members but also to the steadily growing band of Monrubio admirers. Our tastings again rated Palaia, from merlot and cabernet, as the best of the broad range. The '04 has a complex nose that happily integrates forest fruits, mostly blackberries and blueberries, with toastiness and spiciness. The inviting palate is equally fine, with excellent underlying texture and just a hint of over-firmness on the tannic weave. There is also good nose-palate consistency. Red Monrubio '05 is quite different in style, but incredibly enjoyable. It's young, hugely attractive and spot-on value for money, an archetype of the less multi-faceted, less complicated styles. The nose centres on black berry fruit and has fresh vegetal hints. The palate is low-key but round, soft and fresh, with overt yet gentle tannins. All the whites, from Orvieto Macchia del Pozzo '05, Orvieto Classico Salceto '05 and Orvieto Classico Roio '05, to Le Coste '05 and Campo della Casa '05, this last from grechetto, are well up to speed.

●	Palaia '04	🍷🍷	5
●	Monrubio '05	🍷🍷	3*
○	Campo della Casa '05	🍷	3
○	Le Coste '05	🍷	1*
○	Orvieto Cl. Macchia del Pozzo '05	🍷	2*
○	Orvieto Cl. Roio '05	🍷	2*
○	Orvieto Cl. Salceto '05	🍷	3
●	Nociano '03	🍷🍷 (outline)	4*
●	Palaia '03	🍷🍷 (outline)	5
●	Monrubio '04	🍷🍷 (outline)	3*

CASTIGLIONE DEL LAGO (PG)

DUCA DELLA CORGNA
VIA ROMA, 236
06061 CASTIGLIONE DEL LAGO (PG)
TEL. 0759652493
www.ducadellacorgna.it

No, there's nothing out of the ordinary here this year. Corniolo '04 is naturally more backward that the more opulent '03 and doesn't as yet make as good an impression, as it's still rather too tight. The nose has black cherry and almond surrounding a youthful lactic note. The palate is lively and holds together well, although the flavours are not yet fully developed and distinct. Don't misunderstand us, Corniolo certainly hits the mark as a wine, and we don't feel that it's inferior to previous vintages: its score confirms that. No, we just feel that it probably needs a few months' more bottle age so that when it goes on sale its character will be more fully developed. We shall see. For now, we have the rest of the range to enjoy, this year's wines again showing that Duca della Corgna has few rivals in the region when it comes to value for money. For example, we really liked Divina Villa Etichetta Nera '04, mentioned erroneously in last year's Guide, a Gamay Perugino given a few months' barrique ageing. Rich scents of sponge cake and rose water lead to a ripe, lightly spicy palate which tapers off slowly. And what can we say about Baccio del Rosso '05? Only that it continues to amaze us with its fruity intense nose and its easy-drinking style. Divina Villa Etichetta Bianca '05, Baccio del Bianco '05 and Grechetto Nuricante '05, the last still rather over-oaky, bring the range to a close.

●	C. del Trasimeno Gamay Divina Villa Et. Nera '04	🍷🍷	4
●	C. del Trasimeno Rosso Corniolo '04	🍷🍷	4
●	C. del Trasimeno Baccio del Rosso '05	🍷🍷	3*
○	C. del Trasimeno Baccio del Bianco '05	🍷	2*
●	C. del Trasimeno Gamay Divina Villa Et. Bianca '05	🍷	4
○	C. del Trasimeno Grechetto Nuricante '05	🍷	3
●	C. del Trasimeno Rosso Corniolo '03	🍷🍷 (outline)	4
●	C. del Trasimeno Baccio del Rosso '04	🍷🍷 (outline)	3*
●	C. del Trasimeno Gamay Divina Villa Et. Bianca '04	🍷🍷 (outline)	4*

CASTIGLIONE DEL LAGO (PG)

POGGIO BERTAIO
FRAZ. CASAMAGGIORE
VIA FRATTAVECCHIA, 29
06061 CASTIGLIONE DEL LAGO (PG)
TEL. 075956921

Who knows how many oenological consultants, folk whose life is dedicated to bringing success to others, have thought to have a go at making wine for themselves, building their own cellar and giving form to their own ideas on wine, without need for discussion or compromise? Fabrizio Ciufolo is certainly one and some years ago, he set up Poggio Bertaio on the Tuscan border, in tandem with his agronomist brother, Ugo. The enterprise immediately started to make waves for its impeccable working methods and the quality of the results. This translates as beautiful vineyards looked after with care and devotion, a new cellar fitted out with every possible bit of equipment, and superb wines full of stuffing and complexity. The style, for want of a better word, is "modern". Given that we couldn't taste the '04 Crovello, the estate's Bordeaux-style flagship, because the estate had decided to give it a further year's bottle age, our comments start with the muscular Cimbolo '04, from sangiovese. It is deep in colour. First impressions on the nose are of an intense fruitiness that ranges from cherry to blueberry, accompanied by clear toasty hints which recall coffee and caramel. The oaking is certainly elegant but currently covers the fruit a little too much. The real interest this year, though, is Stucchio '03. This is also from sangiovese and has a spicy, slightly toasty nose followed by an attractive, clean, tangy palate, and is good drinking.

● Stucchio '03	▼▼	4
● Cimbolo '04	▼▼	6
● Crovello '01	▽▽▽	8
● Cimbolo '02	▽▽	6
● Crovello '02	▽▽	8
● Crovello '03	▽▽	7
● Cimbolo '01	▽▽	6
● Cimbolo '03	▽▽	6

FICULLE (TR)

★ CASTELLO DELLA SALA
LOC. SALA
05016 FICULLE (TR)
TEL. 076386051
www.antinori.it

There have been changes afoot at Antinori's Castello della Sala. Work on the new cellar having now been completed, attention has turned to revamping some of the wines, changing their names and presentation. The top wine, though, Cervaro della Sala, hasn't been touched by this and retains the complexity and ageing capacity that has made it a legend among Italy's white wines. The grapes come from clayey and sandy soils, so rich in minerals and limestone that it's not unusual for shells to be unearthed, and its makers don't rest on their laurels but are always looking for new stimuli and ways to give it extra bursts of quality. Which is how the '04, even though along similar lines to previous vintages, has turned out as one of the best ever. It is bright straw with green-gold highlights. The nose is an explosion of tropical fruit, citrus and mint leaves, all perfectly interwoven with toasty, smoky aromas. The palate is quite simply monumental, showing opulent and deep without being heavy, full of youth, spicy, and with minerals, aromatic herbs and spring flowers on the infinite finish. Conte della Vipera '04, from sauvignon with a little chardonnay, is very fine, too. It initially gives herbaceous and balsamic streaks which are supported by citron and peach, the structure is multi-faceted and there is plenty of verve. The new Bramito del Cervo '05, from chardonnay, and the '04 release of the well-known Muffato della Sala are both excellent while Orvieto Classico Superiore San Giovanni della Sala '05 is excellently styled.

O Cervaro della Sala '04	▼▼▼	6
O Conte della Vipera '04	▼▼	5
O Muffato della Sala '04	▼▼	6
O Bramito del Cervo '05	▼▼	4
O Orvieto Cl. Sup. San Giovanni della Sala '05	▼	4
O Cervaro della Sala '00	▽▽▽	6
O Cervaro della Sala '01	▽▽▽	6
O Cervaro della Sala '02	▽▽▽	6
O Cervaro della Sala '03	▽▽▽	6
O Cervaro della Sala '95	▽▽▽	6
O Cervaro della Sala '96	▽▽▽	6

FOLIGNO (PG)

TERRE DE' TRINCI
VIA FIAMENGA, 57
06034 FOLIGNO (PG)
TEL. 0742320165
www.terredetrinci.com

Take 300 hectares of vineyard, 350 grape-supplying members and an annual output of 500,000 bottles, and you will immediately have an idea of the sphere in which this noted co-operative, situated just outside Foligno, moves. With Ludovico Mattoni, who now also leads the Consorzio di Tutela dei Vini di Montefalco, as president, Maurilio Chioccia as winemaking consultant and a reliable team of personnel, high quality throughout the range can be practically guaranteed, and the future seems assured. The wine that showed best at this year's tasting was the '03 release of Sagrantino di Montefalco Ugolino, which rightly returns to its flagship role. The colour is a deep ruby, the nose recalls ripe forest fruits, and the palate is supple and nicely deep, with a good, if slightly tight, tannic weave. The basic Sagrantino '03 is simpler, with youthful aromas of red berry fruits and flowers, and a slim-bodied but decidedly tannic palate. Cajo '05, from equal amounts of cabernet sauvignon, sagrantino and merlot, is pleasant but very closed-in, a mix of wild cherry fruit and firm tannicity. Luna '05 isn't bad at all. Made from grechetto with 15 per cent chardonnay, there is peach interwoven with banana on the rather ripe nose. The palate echoes this well, is similarly attractive and has good underlying balance.

●	Montefalco Sagrantino Ugolino '03	🍷🍷	7
●	Montefalco Sagrantino '03	🍷	6
●	Cajo '05	🍷	4
○	Luna '05	🍷	4
●	Montefalco Sagrantino '02	🥂🥂	6
●	Montefalco Sagrantino Ugolino Ris. '01	🥂🥂	7

GUALDO CATTANEO (PG)

CÒLPETRONE
LOC. MARCELLANO
VIA PONTE LA MANDRIA, 8/1
06035 GUALDO CATTANEO (PG)
TEL. 057899827
www.saiagricola.it

The new cellar here is not just beautifully designed; it is set in a natural cleft that encapsulates the perfection of the gentle Umbrian landscape. "Here" is Marcellano, in the municipality of Gualdo Cattaneo, and this is where, back in 1985, the Saiagricola group planned and then carried out its decision to enter the world of Sagrantino. Their success has been such that Còlpetrone is now a cornerstone of the zone. Its fame is well deserved and it swept home once more to win Three Glasses for its Sagrantino, despite the difficulties of the '03 vintage. A deep-coloured wine, it releases a sensational burst of fruit, giving blackberry, blueberry and blackcurrant, rendered complex by intense, elegant nuances of spices and balsam. There follows a stylish palate which is broad and deep yet avoids all heaviness while the tannic weave remains tight. The '03 Passito is also a thoroughly enjoyable wine and perhaps the best of recent releases since it has gained new balance, most notably of sweetness and acidity. It therefore has richness without cloying. Finally, we have an excellent Montefalco Rosso '04, which alternates black and red berry fruits and sweet spices on the nose, and whose sound, savoury palate extends to a lively, citrus-like finish. It's a very fine example of its type.

●	Montefalco Sagrantino '03	🍷🍷🍷	6
●	Montefalco Sagrantino Passito '03	🍷🍷	6
●	Montefalco Rosso '04	🍷🍷	4
●	Montefalco Sagrantino '00	🥂🥂🥂	6
●	Montefalco Sagrantino '01	🥂🥂🥂	6
●	Montefalco Sagrantino '02	🥂🥂🥂	6
●	Montefalco Sagrantino '96	🥂🥂🥂	4
●	Montefalco Sagrantino '97	🥂🥂🥂	5
●	Montefalco Sagrantino '98	🥂🥂🥂	5
●	Montefalco Sagrantino '99	🥂🥂🥂	6

GUALDO CATTANEO (PG)

PERTICAIA
VIA E. CATTANEO, 39
06035 GUALDO CATTANEO (PG)
TEL. 0742379014 - 0742920328
www.perticaia.it

Guido Guardigli was previously a top-level manager of numerous wine estates around Italy but then decided to abandon this career and take on the much harder but far more fascinating task of creating his own. He was born in Romagna but considers himself an adopted Umbrian, having been literally spellbound by the Sagrantino area. So he bought his property there, at Casale di Montefalco, and has rapidly transformed it into one of the most distinctive in the zone. His first move was to renew the vineyards. Now there is also a new, modern vinification and ageing cellar, which includes a good tasting room. And that's the basis of today's Perticaia. Guardigli didn't release the '02 Sagrantino di Montefalco because it wasn't up to his standards but he's back in force with the '03, a very fine wine that has striking balance and the finesse that is the estate's hallmark, no mean feat in such a hot year. There is bramble and cherry on the nose, alternating with spice and tobacco. The palate is deeply fruity, decidedly complex and has an excellent tannic presence. The Rosso di Montefalco is, as usual, excellent. The '04's habitual aromas of plum and red berry fruits are accompanied by slight greenness while the palate is beautifully crafted and has that rare quality of combining structure with drinkability. The newest wine in the range, Umbria Rosso '05, appears to have already developed its own stylistic imprint. It's simple without being simplistic, juicy, supple and just begging to be drunk.

● Montefalco Sagrantino '03	🍷🍷	6
● Montefalco Rosso '04	🍷🍷	4
● Umbria Rosso '05	🍷🍷	3*
● Montefalco Sagrantino '01	YY	6
● Montefalco Sagrantino '00	YY	6

MAGIONE (PG)

CASTELLO DI MAGIONE
VIA DEI CAVALIERI DI MALTA, 31
06063 MAGIONE (PG)
TEL. 075843547
www.castellodimagione.it

From bastion of Christianity to custodian of variety: grape varieties that is. The Sovereign Military Order of the Knights of Malta, which guards Castello di Magione's splendid cellar, seems to have a new mission. It has 30 hectares of vineyard, all high-density plantings and all split into "mezzadrie", or crus, from which the wines often take their name. We found the most interesting, the one which best embodies the variables of climate, soil, grape variety and man's labour, to be Monterone. This plot regularly gives a fabulous Grechetto and 2005 was no exception: it has such a wealth of qualities that it went straight into the finals. It may seem subtle, on both nose and palate, but actually has great class and complexity, hinging on finesse and elegance more than muscle and roundness. Citron and citrus on the nose interweave with evident mineral scents, which are clearly perceptible on the taut palate, supported by deep, youthfully vibrant acidity. The more basic Grechetto '05 is less complex but highly enjoyable, offering peach and melon fruitiness, with lively shots of sage. The palate is savoury and has a typical lightly bitter finish. Albaneta '05, from a broad-based blend of chardonnay, sauvignon and grechetto, is another fine wine, with broom, banana and hints of white pepper on the nose, and a full, harmonious palate. We'd still like to see a step-up in quality with the reds. Morcinaia '03, which has a fruity and spicy range of aromas, is the best of them, although it is not without herbaceousness.

○ Colli del Trasimeno Grechetto Monterone '05	🍷🍷	3*
○ Colli del Trasimeno Albaneta '05	🍷🍷	4*
○ Grechetto '05	🍷🍷	2*
● Colli del Trasimeno Rosso Morcinaia '03	🍷	5
○ Colli del Trasimeno Grechetto Monterone '04	YY	2*

ANTONELLI - SAN MARCO

LOC. SAN MARCO, 59
06036 MONTEFALCO (PG)
TEL. 0742379158
www.antonellisanmarco.it

The fact of running one of the few estates in Sagrantino with a history and traditions going back to the end of the 19th century has not prevented Filippo Antonelli from wanting to experiment. He continues to question the status quo, searching for approaches more suited to the times. The result is an estate of dynamism, one that is watchful of change without necessarily succumbing to it, and one that remains faithful to clear stylistic parameters. This is probably why Antonelli's wines are sought out by large numbers of dedicated admirers. But let's go straight to this year's tastings. We really liked the Sagrantino '03. The heat of the year, far from compromising its excellently constructed profile, has actually given it something in terms of flesh and underlying substance. Thus the red and black berry fruits are accompanied by grace notes of oriental spices and the velvetiness of the palate broadens into depth, held in check only lightly by the tannic weave. As with previous vintages, it will doubtless repay keeping a few years. The Rosso di Montefalco Riserva '03 has also lived up to expectations and is a wine of distinction. It has shots of minerals and hints of leather and spice that notch into a firm structure, although it's a touch warm on the finish. There were also high scores for Sagrantino Passito '03, where coffee and cocoa powder play over the fruit, for the great Montefalco Rosso '04, and for the basic Grechetto '04 which, like last year, impressed us more than its big brother, Vigna Tonda '04. Baiocco '04, from sangiovese, is good drinking.

●	Montefalco Rosso Ris. '03	▼▼	5
●	Montefalco Sagrantino '03	▼▼	6
●	Montefalco Sagrantino Passito '03	▼▼	6
●	Montefalco Rosso '04	▼▼	4
○	Colli Martani Grechetto '05	▼▼	3*
●	Baiocco '04	▼	3
○	Colli Martani Grechetto Vigna Tonda '04	▼	4
●	Montefalco Sagrantino '00	▽▽	7
●	Montefalco Rosso Ris. '01	▽▽	5
●	Montefalco Sagrantino '01	▽▽	7
●	Montefalco Sagrantino '02	▽▽	6

MONTEFALCO (PG)

★ ARNALDO CAPRAI - VAL DI MAGGIO

LOC. TORRE
06036 MONTEFALCO (PG)
TEL. 0742378802
www.arnaldocaprai.it

So, how would you react? Would you delight in the fact that four wines of your six reached the finals, thus reaffirming your leadership position, or regret more that only one of them achieved the ultimate accolade, and not the one generally considered the flagship? It's the old story of the glass – of Sagrantino, in this case – being half full or half empty. From our side it's obvious, we see another top-notch performance but knowing Marco Caprai, we reckon he'll feel the disappointment more keenly. And it will start him working to do even better next time round. This is the second year running that Sagrantino di Montefalco Collepiano '03 has hit the big time, almost as if, after an eternity in second place, it has acquired a taste for a solitary moment of glory. This wine truly deserves its applause, so well does it ride the difficulties of the hot year, emerging with a profile that remains fresh yet has complexity. The nose immediately inspires interest and in no time glorious aromas of briary fruit start to intermingle with liqueur chocolates and oriental spices, all of great elegance. The palate has considerable body but this is so well managed that there is even grace and velvetiness to the tannins. The Sagrantino 25 Anni '03 is a very fine wine but possibly a touch over-extracted and over-opulent. So it was "only" a finalist, along with a glorious Passito '03, without doubt the best in the zone, and the '04 Rosso Outsider, a Bordeaux blend that appears perfectly at home in the Montefalco hills, confirming last year's performance.

●	Montefalco Sagrantino Collepiano '03	▼▼▼	7
●	Montefalco Sagrantino Passito '03	▼▼	7
●	Montefalco Sagrantino 25 Anni '03	▼▼	8
●	Rosso Outsider '04	▼▼	7
●	Montefalco Rosso '04	▼▼	5
○	Colli Martani Grechetto Grecante '05	▼▼	4*
●	Montefalco Sagrantino 25 Anni '00	▽▽▽	8
●	Montefalco Sagrantino 25 Anni '01	▽▽▽	8
●	Montefalco Sagrantino Collepiano '02	▽▽▽	7
●	Montefalco Sagrantino 25 Anni '95	▽▽▽	8
●	Montefalco Sagrantino 25 Anni '96	▽▽▽	8
●	Montefalco Sagrantino 25 Anni '97	▽▽▽	8
●	Montefalco Sagrantino 25 Anni '98	▽▽▽	8
●	Montefalco Sagrantino 25 Anni '99	▽▽▽	8

MONTEFALCO (PG)

Madonna Alta
via Piceni, 14
06036 Montefalco (PG)
tel. 0742378568
www.madonnalta.it

We have been following the progress of Madonna Alta for a while now and finally, after the appropriate running-in period, the time has come to give it the full entry it deserves. The owners, the Ferrero family, originally from Campania but now adopted Umbrians, named the estate after the 16th-century church which lies close to Montefalco's medieval walls thus, seemingly, cementing the bond between the family and the area. Much of the property's 50 hectares is vineyard or olive grove and in 2001 a new, modern cellar was built. From the wines we tasted, we particularly liked Rosso di Montefalco '04 whose classic aromas of red and black berry fruits alternate with alluring spicy nuances evoking curry powder and nutmeg. The wine is modern in style and the fruit is partnered by oaky notes on both nose and palate. Falconero '05, a white, despite its name, which means "black falcon", is from grechetto and chardonnay. It's not at all bad, with jasmine and white peach aromas, intriguing vegetal and balsamic hints, and a juicy, zesty palate. We particularly liked the Sagrantino Passito '03. Wild berry fruit jam is well in evidence on the nose, as are sweet notes of chocolate and liquorice. The palate, despite its excellent structure, remains fresh and supple. The Sagrantino '03 comes one Glass down because the oak tends to dominate and the tannin seems a bit out of place. Falconero Rosso '05 and Colli Martani Grechetto '05 scored similarly.

● Montefalco Sagrantino Passito '03	▼▼	6
● Montefalco Rosso '04	▼▼	4
○ Falconero Bianco '05	▼▼	3*
● Montefalco Sagrantino '03	▼	6
○ Colli Martani Grechetto '05	▼	4
● Falconero Rosso '05	▼	3
● Montefalco Sagrantino '02	▽▽	6
● Montefalco Rosso '03	▽▽	4

MONTEFALCO (PG)

F.lli Pardi
via Giovanni Pascoli, 7/9
06036 Montefalco (PG)
tel. 0742379023
www.cantinapardi.it

Human history is made up of cycles, recurrent themes and passions that pass down generations or that disappear and re-emerge when the moment is right, and the wine world is no exception. So it seems only right that after brothers Alberto, Alfredo and Francesco Pardi had worked their family vineyards by hand during the first half of the 20th century to produce and sell wine throughout Umbria, in 2002 their great-grandchildren, Francesco, Gianluca Rio and Alberto Mario Pardi should picked up the threads of history and restart their ancestors' old cellar. The results, at least so far, are more than encouraging. The '03 Sagrantino, the first release from the relaunched estate, homes in on hints of wild strawberries, raspberries and blackberries, integrated into aromas of Mediterranean scrubland and rain-soaked earth. The palate is racy yet deep and has good acidity, resulting in a wine that is full but makes for good drinking. Rosso di Montefalco '04 is a similar prospect and in fact one of the best in the zone for liveliness, fruit definition and depth of flavour. This comes through primarily in terms of small red berry fruit, shot through with some flashes of green and interwoven with a light smokiness. There's good backbone on the finish, too, making the wine a delight to drink. Sagrantino Passito '03 also showed well. Chocolate and tertiary aromas alternate on the nose while the palate is juicy and has a craft-made feel.

● Montefalco Sagrantino '03	▼▼	6
● Montefalco Sagrantino Passito '03	▼▼	6
● Rosso di Montefalco '04	▼▼	4
● Rosso di Montefalco '03	▽▽	4*

MONTEFALCO (PG)

ROCCA DI FABBRI
LOC. FABBRI
06036 MONTEFALCO (PG)
TEL. 0742399379
www.roccadifabbri.com

Rocca di Fabbri is one of the most illustrious wine names at Montefalco and belongs to a restricted circle of estates that bring historical continuity to Sagrantino production. The winery was started up in conjunction with the restoration of the glorious 14th-century Rocca (fortress). Production commenced in 1984 and is currently managed with skill by sisters Roberta and Simona Vitali. After a few years of ups and downs, the wines are now back in splendid form. The best of the lot, we felt, was once more the Sagrantino, the '03. This shines through on the nose, which is centred on intense, ripe fruit, ranging from plum to blood oranges, with peripheral hints of chocolate and cocoa powder. It is greatly enjoyable on the palate too, which has a fine piquancy, richness of extract and delightful sensations of leather and tobacco on the finish. In short, it's balanced and full of structure but neither heavy nor overblown. The estate decided to give the '04 Faroaldo, made from cabernet and sagrantino, additional bottle age so we will taste it next year. Instead we took a second look at the '03 and found it still has good ageing potential. This brings us to the whites, the best of which is again the Chardonnay. The '05 is bright straw. The nose has ripe, apricot and peachy fruit preceding a palate that is juicy, full of flavour and long. Montefalco Rosso '04 gained just one Glass since there's a slight lack of complexity and definition.

● Montefalco Sagrantino '03	🍷🍷	7
○ Chardonnay '05	🍷🍷	3*
● Montefalco Rosso '04	🍷	5
○ Colli Martani Grechetto '05	🍷	4
● Montefalco Sagrantino '02	ŸŸ	7
● Montefalco Sagrantino '00	ŸŸ	7
● Montefalco Sagrantino '01	ŸŸ	7
● Faroaldo '03	ŸŸ	6

MONTEFALCO (PG)

SCACCIADIAVOLI
LOC. CANTINONE, 31
06036 MONTEFALCO (PG)
TEL. 0742371210 - 0742378272

After the fall of a number of giants into the netherworld of the Other Wineries, the affable Amilcare Pambuffetti will surely be relieved that at least his winery has been restored to a full entry. For down in the depths is not where Scacciadiavoli feels at home. After all, the name means "devil-buster". Puns aside, this year's wines were the first to have been followed from beginning to end by Stefano Chioccioli and it seems he has hit the spot, promising well for the future of this superb winery. The most impressive bottle on the list is Sagrantino '03. It is a beautiful deep ruby. The nose is lively and inviting, with aromas of briary fruit and sweet spices. It is the palate, though, that brings the whole thing together with a well-delineated framework and excellent complexity of flavour, despite being a little overwhelmed by oak that gives the tannins a sensation of slight roughness. Sagrantino Passito '03, with its melted chocolate and black berry fruit flavours, scored similarly, although a touch more dynamism would not have been out of place. We were also hoping that there would have been more improvement in the Montefalco Rosso. Instead, the '04 seems a bit overweening, all sweetness and toastiness, which tends to overwhelm the rather slim fruit.

● Montefalco Sagrantino '03	🍷🍷	6
● Montefalco Sagrantino Passito '03	🍷🍷	6
● Montefalco Rosso '04	🍷	4
● Montefalco Sagrantino '00	ŸŸ	6
● Montefalco Sagrantino '01	ŸŸ	6
● Montefalco Sagrantino Passito '01	ŸŸ	6

MONTEFALCO (PG)

TABARRINI
FRAZ. TURRITA
06036 MONTEFALCO (PG)
TEL. 0742379351 - 3281599119
www.tabarrini.com

We are happy to report another excellent showing for this estate which, despite fierce competition, has taken its place among the best in Sagrantino, and in a remarkable short space of time. It is run by the young, bright Giampaolo Tabarrini, a lad full of enthusiasm and desire to do well. Tabarrini has about 22 hectares of land, eight of them under vine, there's a superb cellar at the heart of the property and Emiliano Falsini is the consultant oenologist. None of the wines is less than very good, showing that Tabarrini has been concentrating hard on achieving a maturity and an individuality of style. It has succeeded. The style is based on using perfectly ripe grapes and maximizing the fruit in the wines, giving them abundant but not exaggerated flavour. As a result they need time to find their balance and for their youthful exuberance to settle down. These are wines that usually come together at least a year after release. Still, the growing numbers of fans are prepared to wait. Sagrantino di Montefalco Colle Grimaldesco '03 was in the running for Three Glasses. Its intense, deep nose has aromas ranging from briary fruit to ink and from barbecue notes to balsam. The palate, as usual, is full of stuffing although not yet perfectly balanced so we shall see. Sagrantino Passito '03 is full of chocolate, dried figs and honey. Rosso di Montefalco '04 is characterized by wild berries. And the citrus-like Adarmando '05, from trebbiano spoletino, has firm body and long, clean finish. All three are good and you don't need to wait for them.

● Montefalco Sagrantino Colle Grimaldesco '03	▼▼	6
● Montefalco Sagrantino Passito '03	▼▼	7
● Montefalco Rosso '04	▼▼	4
○ Adarmando '05	▼▼	4*
● Il Padrone delle Vigne '05	▼	3
● Montefalco Sagrantino Colle Grimaldesco '01	▽▽▽	6
● Montefalco Sagrantino Colle Grimaldesco '02	▽▽	6
● Montefalco Rosso '03	▽▽	4
○ Adarmando '04	▽▽	3*

MONTEGABBIONE (TR)

TENUTA CORINI
VOC. CASINO, 53
05010 MONTEGABBIONE (TR)
TEL. 0763837535 - 3355486714
www.tenutacorini.it

The Corini husband-and-wife team are distinctly out of the ordinary but sunny in disposition and really nice. After a long period abroad, they decided to return to Umbria and invest their life savings in a wine estate. Judging by what they've done to the vineyards, cellar and the property in general, they didn't count the pennies. Part of their aim is to bring greater renown to Montegabbione as a wine zone. So far, it's been considered one of promise, but mainly for international varieties and international tastes. Frabusco, from sangiovese, montepulciano and merlot, takes its name from the initials of the estate's partners and the '04 really does reflect their ebullience. It is complex throughout. The nose has an intense, rounded fruitiness, well knit into bell pepper vegetal notes. There's no initial let-down on the palate, which is soft but not too soft, but it then slims down and the final sensation is that it's a touch thin and could do with a tiny bit more stuffing. Pinot Nero Camerti '04 is admirable – not a complete surprise – and one of the best examples from Umbria of this fabulous but hugely complicated variety. The colour is, rightly, pale. The nose has subtle, delicate fruit and appreciable elegance before the palate shows low-key but juicy, savoury and cool, pervaded by enlivening sweet spices and discreet gamey notes. Sauvignon Casteldifiori '05 is just as fine and fills the glass with inviting aromas of white peach, pineapple and grapefruit, followed by a palate of crisp, sweet fruitiness and well-restrained opulence.

● Frabusco '04	▼▼	6
● Pinot Nero Camerti '04	▼▼	6
○ Casteldifiori '05	▼▼	4
● Frabusco '01	▽▽	6
● Frabusco '03	▽▽	6
● Pinot Nero Camerti '01	▽▽	6

ORVIETO (TR)

BARBERANI - VALLESANTA

LOC. CERRETO
05023 ORVIETO (TR)
TEL. 0763341820
www.barberani.it

Barberani is one of the most dependable estates in the region, with an innovative spirit and great consistency of quality, which has remained undiminished over the years. This is all down to the family, all of whom work full-time for the estate in one way or another, and whose constant aim is to bring ever greater lustre to Orvieto's wines. Such endeavours would naturally have brought Orvieto Classico Superiore Calcaia, their most distinct wine, to the fore sooner or later. This is a botrytis wine, the necessary humidity deriving from the estate's vicinity to Lake Corbara. And with 2003 being a fabulous year for noble rot, it shot straight into the finals. The aromatic spectrum and the bouquet of this amazing sweet wine is complex to say the least. The deep gold of its colour frames aromas of tropical fruit, hazelnut, dried figs and musk, complemented by the most elegant nuances of minerals and botrytis. The palate too is endlessly deep, vibrant and marked out by a stimulating echo of Mediterranean scrubland. This is a great example of the style, possibly one of the best ever. Despite initial announcements to the contrary, in the end a small amount of Lago di Corbara Rosso Villa Monticelli '02 was produced, although it certainly reflects the difficult vintage. The other Lago di Corbara Rosso, Foresco '03, is showing well, as are Grechetto '05, Orvieto Classico Superiore Castagnolo '05, Moscato Passito Villa Monticelli '04 and Rosato Vallesanta '05.

○ Orvieto Cl. Sup. Calcaia '03	TT	6
● Lago di Corbara Rosso Villa Monticelli '02	T	5
● Lago di Corbara Foresco '03	T	4
○ Moscato Passito Villa Monticelli '04	T	6
○ Grechetto '05	T	4
○ Orvieto Cl. Sup. Castagnolo '05	T	4
⊙ Vallesanta Rosato '05	T	2
● Lago di Corbara Rosso Villa Monticelli '01	YY	5
○ Orvieto Cl. Sup. Calcaia '00	YY	6
○ Orvieto Cl. Sup. Calcaia '93	YY	5
○ Orvieto Cl. Sup. Calcaia '95	YY	5
○ Orvieto Cl. Sup. Calcaia '97	YY	5

ORVIETO (TR)

BIGI

LOC. PONTE GIULIO
05018 ORVIETO (TR)
TEL. 0763315888
www.giv.it

Bigi, now in the hands of Gruppo Italiano Vini, has been active in Orvieto since the 1800s. Its dependability and qualitative consistency are there for all to see, and this year's tastings do nothing to dispel that impression. In fact, the qualitative batting order of the wines remains substantially the same as last year: Tamante '05 is first out, followed by Grechetto '05, Orvieto Classico '05 and Orvieto Classico Vigneto Torricella '05. But let's go one step at a time. Tamante, the winery's sole red, at least this year, has a lively nose of raspberry and red berry fruit. There is depth and balance along the attractively slim, zesty palate and just a hint of citrus on the finish. We found the Grechetto extremely interesting, too. Initial hesitance soon gives way to more confident banana and pineapple aromas, these then forming an attractive prelude to the succulent, savoury palate, characterized by the acidity typical of the variety. Orvieto Classico Vigneto Torricella is not only good but value for money is spot-on. The straw hue leads to floral aromas of sycamore and broom, which also weave around the tropical fruit sweetness on the front palate, before a gentle sensation of barley sugar appears and marks out the finish. Finally, the uncomplicated Orvieto Classico has a good lively aroma, giving apple and lemon on the palate and finishing well with a pleasant touch of bitterness.

○ Grechetto '05	TT	3*
● Tamante '05	TT	3*
○ Orvieto Cl. '05	T	3
○ Orvieto Cl. Vigneto Torricella '05	T	3*
● Sartiano '01	YY	4
○ Grechetto '04	YY	3*
● Tamante '04	YY	3*

ORVIETO (TR)

Cardeto

fraz. Sferracavallo
loc. Cardeto
05010 Orvieto (TR)
tel. 0763341286 - 0763343189
www.cardeto.com

The quality of Orvieto has not always matched the fame of its name. But there are those who have consistently achieved satisfyingly good wines while producing them in large quantities and the Cardeto co-operative, with 2,000,000 bottles a year, is certainly one. It has 350 members who supply grapes from more than 1,000 hectares of vineyard, most of it in the Orvieto and Orvieto Classico DOC zones, even though some of the output is a range of very encouraging high-quality reds. There is also a first-rate team of technical staff, led by oenologist Maurilio Chioccia. The results are there for all to see. This year's tastings confirm that quality continues to improve and the wines' scores are heading towards higher bandings. Nero della Greca '04 reached the finals. This is from sangiovese with some merlot and is aged 12 months in small oak casks. The complex nose has ripe red berry fruit and bell pepper, well integrated into toasty notes. The palate is supple but has substance, and is rounded, refreshingly fruity, and deeply flavoured. Arciato '04, though not a finalist, is still a truly admirable wine. Made in the classic Bordeaux mould, the nose is intense and full of black berry fruit and minerality introducing a palate that is lively, elegant and highlighted with balsam. We also liked Colbadia '05 and Rupestro '05, the latter a less complex but great-drinking wine from sangiovese and montepulciano with traces of canaiolo and ciliegiolo. Alborato '05 and the whites Grechetto '05, Pierleone '05 and Febeo '05 are all attractive.

●	Nero della Greca '04	YY	4*
○	Arciato '04	YY	4
○	Colbadia '05	YY	3*
●	Rupestro '05	YY	2*
●	Alborato '05	Y	3
○	Grechetto '05	Y	2*
○	Orvieto Cl. Pierleone '05	Y	1*
○	Orvieto Cl. Sup. Febeo '05	Y	3
●	Nero della Greca '01	YY	5
●	Rupestro '04	YY	3*
●	Arciato '03	YY	6

ORVIETO (TR)

La Carraia

loc. Tordimonte, 56
05018 Orvieto (TR)
tel. 0763304013

There may not have been a winner this year but there is certainly nothing to complain about in La Carraia's wines. The estate was set up in 1988 as a joint project of the Gialletti family, expert Orvieto grape-growers, and the Cotarella family, who were then go-getting winemakers and are now internationally famous oenologists. It comprises several plots, all in areas highly suited to viticulture, and a cellar that has been renovated to operate highly efficiently. But let's move on to this year's tastings, which saw two wines in the finals, one up on last year. Fobiano '04, from merlot with 30 per cent cabernet sauvignon, may have a touch less stuffing than the sumptuous '03 but is still highly impressive. The aromas are clean and well orchestrated, initially giving a complex fruitiness before turning confidently to rose water, leather and animal hide. The palate is still a little closed in but its florality, its hints of black pepper and, especially, its beautiful freshness and good tannin should ensure it develops well. Giro di Vite '04 scored similarly. This is an inky deep, monovarietal Montepulciano, with flavours of coffee, black cherry and printer's ink, and with tight-knit but finely grained tannins. The rest of the range is dependable too, especially the reds Tizzonero '04 and Sangiovese '05. The two '05 Orvieto Classicos, the basic version and the Poggio Calvelli, are both excellently styled.

●	Fobiano '04	YY	5
●	Giro di Vite '04	YY	5
●	Tizzonero '04	YY	4
●	Sangiovese '05	YY	3*
○	Orvieto Cl. '05	Y	2*
○	Orvieto Cl. Poggio Calvelli '05	Y	3*
●	Fobiano '03	YYY	5
●	Fobiano '98	YYY	5
●	Fobiano '99	YYY	6
●	Giro di Vite '03	YY	5

ORVIETO (TR)

Castello di Corbara

Loc. Corbara, 7
05019 Orvieto (TR)
tel. 0763304035 - 0763304003
www.castellodicorbara.it

Castello di Corbara wines are improving so much it's as if they had been playing second fiddle and have now decided to aim for roles as soloists. The estate lies at the confluence of the Tevere and Paglia rivers and extends over 1,100 hectares, all cultivated organically and thus pesticide-free. Lago di Corbara Merlot De Coronis '03, named after the plot of land where its grapes grow, was a finalist. There is a good shower of fruit on the nose, although it's a little squashed by dominant new oak. The palate shows better, developing well throughout the mouth and is nicely savoury, with an impressive acid backbone and mellow tannins. But, as we said, the whole range impressed us. Lago di Corbara Rosso '04 has aromas of toasted bread and good black berry fruitiness. The inviting Cabernet Sauvignon '04 evokes melted chocolate, black cherry and slight sensations of greenness, and is deep and firm-bodied. The attractively raspberry-like Caio '05, from sangiovese, merlot and cabernet; and, despite the vintage, the lively, juicy Calistri '03, from sangiovese, are both very well made although quite different in style. All in all, it's a great range and confirms once and for all that this is a fine estate of high standing.

●	Lago di Corbara De Coronis '03	TT	5
●	Calistri '03	TT	5
●	Lago di Corbara Cabernet Sauvignon '04	TT	5
●	Lago di Corbara Rosso '04	TT	4
●	Podere Il Caio Rosso '05	TT	4*
●	Lago di Corbara Rosso '02	YY	5
●	Lago di Corbara Rosso '03	YY	4
●	Podere Il Caio Rosso '04	YY	3

ORVIETO (TR)

Decugnano dei Barbi

Loc. Fossatello, 50
05019 Orvieto (TR)
tel. 0763308255
www.decugnanodeibarbi.com

It's been a year of light and shade for Decugnano dei Barbi, a property set in a glorious position looking onto both the crag of Orvieto and Lake Corbara, and immersed in a fascinating natural landscape. Moreover, there have been ups and downs in previous years, at least compared with what would be expected of an estate of this importance, which inevitably leads to some concerns. There are, of course, mitigating circumstances. Firstly there's the type of wines produced. These centre on elegance and aromatic depth rather than body and overall structure. Then there's the time of bottling, often just prior to our tastings, which means the wines we receive are not always ready to communicate. And this year, there's also the absence of Lago di Corbara Rosso "IL", the wine that has come to be known as the estate's standard bearer, and which won Three Glasses some years ago. Still, it's bound to be back on form before too long and we already have high hopes for the '03. We felt that Orvieto Classico Superiore "IL" Selezione '04 was the wine that showed best this year. It is still in development and is slightly opalescent in appearance but already has rare complexity. Aromas of yeast and wheat alternate with scents of flowers, white-fleshed fruit and barley sugar. The palate is broad and savoury, complex in flavour and has excellent supporting acidity. Just One Glass was awarded to Lago di Corbara Pinot Nero '03, the dryness of the year not being best suited to the variety's characteristics, and to Orvieto Classico Superiore Pourriture Noble '03.

○	Orvieto Cl. Sup. "IL" Sel. '04	TT	5
●	Lago di Corbara Pinot Nero '03	T	6
○	Orvieto Cl. Sup. Pourriture Noble '03	T	6
●	Lago di Corbara Decugnano Rosso '04		4
●	"IL" Rosso '98	YYY	5
●	Lago di Corbara "IL" '01	YY	6
●	Lago di Corbara "IL" '02	YY	6
●	"IL" Rosso '99	YY	6
○	Orvieto Cl. Sup. Pourriture Noble '01	YY	6

ORVIETO (TR)

PALAZZONE

LOC. ROCCA RIPESENA, 68
05018 ORVIETO (TR)
TEL. 0763344921
www.palazzone.com

It is certainly not easy giving a definitive judgement on the wines of historian and dedicated winemaker Giovanni Dubini, whose vineyards lie on some of Orvieto's best sites. The difficulty comes from the nature of his straight-down-the-line production philosophy. He doesn't go for compromise, avoids tastes that are commonplace or typecast, and sends us wines that are still gaining definition and settling down at the time we taste them. Moreover, they're complex wines that need time to express their characteristics to the full and realize their full potential. A taste of the '90 Campo del Guardiano, made mostly from grechetto, or the '94 Muffa Nobile will explain what we mean better than any words can. And really, this is what wine is all about. wine is alive; it is something that can evolve, surprise, arouse emotion, confirm ideas or blow them apart. That said, Campo del Guardiano '03 defied the year's hot weather to develop a stylish nose, with broom and chamomile flowers, and a minerally, slightly peppery palate of good elegance. Orvieto Classico Superiore Terre Vineate '05 is an equally fine wine. It has aromas of fresh and sugared almonds which notch perfectly into its baseline fruit and balance, followed by a cohesive, taut, long palate that is already bedding down. One Glass down come the substantial, slightly tannic Grechetto '05 and oak-free L'Ultima Spiaggia '05, from 100 per cent viognier.

○ Orvieto Cl. Campo del Guardiano '03	TT	5
○ Orvieto Cl. Sup. Terre Vineate '05	TT	4
○ Grechetto '05	T	4
○ L'Ultima Spiaggia '05	T	5
● Armaleo '00	YYY	6
● Armaleo '95	YYY	6
● Armaleo '97	YYY	6
● Armaleo '98	YYY	6
○ Muffa Nobilis '03	YY	6
● Armaleo '99	YY	5

ORVIETO (TR)

TORDIMARO

LOC. TORDIMONTE, 37
05019 ORVIETO (TR)
TEL. 0763304227
www.tordimaro.com

The Tordimaro estate is run with commitment and tender loving care by Reinmar and Caterina Fullemann, a Swiss couple now settled in Orvieto. The property lies in glorious hillside and extends over 24 hectares, 11 of them specialized vineyard plus a fair portion given over to olive grove. The altitudes and soil types, combined with the skills of the owners and their brilliant oenologist Emiliano Falsini, have led to swift improvements in the wines. Our top choice this year is Rosso Orvietano Sangiovese '04. The colour is a deep ruby. The nose is well sustained by black cherry and spice, and is incredibly vivacious, while the palate is juicy, tasty and full, yet fresh, supple and balanced in its flavours. Rosso Orvietano Cabernet '04 is roughly on a par with last year's release, which means it's very good. The deep ruby colour is the right start to a wine of this complexity, which gives blackberries, blueberries and a swath of balsam. Only the tannin, which seems a tad drying, risks tarnishing the overall roundness. The youthful Torrello '05, from sangiovese, barbera, montepulciano and canaiolo, is simpler but extremely attractive and all too drinkable, just as is Rosato Saignée '05, with its pale coppery colour and its pleasing tangerine flavours.

● Rosso Orvietano Cabernet '04	TT	5
● Rosso Orvietano Sangiovese '04	TT	5
⊙ Saignée '05	T	2*
● Torrello '05	T	3*
● Rosso Orvietano Cabernet '03	YY	5
● Torrello '04	YY	3*

ORVIETO (TR)

Tenuta Le Velette

Fraz. Canale di Orvieto
loc. Le Velette, 23
05019 Orvieto (TR)
tel. 076329090 - 076329144
www.levelette.it

Corrado and Cecilia Bottai's estate must be one of the most scenically stunning in Orvieto. If we then add that the wines are among those that best express the zone's potential, having impeccable styling, a wealth of personality and their soul rooted in the territory, the winery's standing in the Guide becomes obvious. After a marvellous showing by Calanco '01 last year, Three Glasses were in the air somewhere or other and this year they've arrived, for a stupendous Gaudio '04. The year's mild weather has given this single-variety Merlot the densest of noses, with black cherry perfectly integrated into new oak, and intriguing notes of mint chocolate along with elegant spiciness. And the taste? Even better. It presents a wealth of energy and complexity, doesn't lack minerality and is supported throughout by a silky tannic weave. But it's the depth of the wine that is so outstanding, that and an unwavering underlying balance. Coming back down to earth, Sangiovese Accordo '04 is not bad at all. It has raspberry and other forest fruits mingling with hints of black pepper and balsam, thereby gaining finesse and complexity. Finally comes the usual round-up of the rest. There's an extremely attractive Rosso di Spicca '05, from sangiovese and canaiolo, a refreshing, confident Velico '05, from a wide-ranging blend of grechetto, chardonnay, trebbiano, verdello, drupeggio and malvasia, and the Orvieto Classico Berganorio '05, which has pleasing notes of white-fleshed fruit.

●	Gaudio '03	🍷🍷🍷	5
●	Accordo '04	🍷🍷	4
○	Orvieto Cl. Berganorio '05	🍷	3
●	Rosso Orvietano Rosso di Spicca '05	🍷	3
○	Velico '05	🍷	4
●	Calanco '01	ΥΥ	5
●	Gaudio '01	ΥΥ	5
●	Gaudio '98	ΥΥ	5
●	Gaudio '00	ΥΥ	5
●	Gaudio '99	ΥΥ	5

PANICALE (PG)

Lamborghini

loc. Soderi, 1
06064 Panicale (PG)
tel. 0758350029
www.lamborghinionline.it

Lamborghini's Campoleone, a sangiovese-merlot blend from the Trasimeno hills, is a wine of pedigree which, like all thoroughbreds, can perform erratically. There's genius on the one hand and decadence on the other. When the year is right, the wine has few equals and goes beyond being impressive to take you by storm, and sometimes even knock you sideways. But then, there are all the prerequisites for making great reds at its disposal, including the property itself, with 32 hectares of vineyard currently undergoing replanting, and its management, in the hands of the youthfully determined Patrizia Lamborghini. Then there's the estate's consultant, Riccardo Cotarella, one of the best oenologists around. But let's get to that wine which struck us so forcibly. The '04 Campoleone is a deep ruby colour. The nose has extreme complexity and refinement, with small red and black berry fruit, nuances of new oak and swaths of balsam, all of which continually alternate and intermingle, to glorious effect. The palate is full of flesh, showing vibrant and deeply fruity, with a superb tannic weave. It has a clear stamp of Bordeaux about it. We thought Torami '04, from montepulciano, was the best of the rest. It is deeply hued and has scents of cherry jam and spices, although the oak is a little invasive. Trescone '04, from sangiovese, ciliegiolo and merlot, has forest fruits on both nose and palate but is less complex and less supple.

●	Campoleone '04	🍷🍷🍷	6
●	Torami '04	🍷🍷	5
●	Trescone '04	🍷	4
●	Campoleone '00	ΥΥΥ	6
●	Campoleone '01	ΥΥΥ	6
●	Campoleone '99	ΥΥΥ	6
●	Campoleone '02	ΥΥ	6
●	Campoleone '03	ΥΥ	6

PERUGIA

BROGAL VINI
LOC. BASTIA UMBRA
VIA DEGLI OLMI, 9
06083 PERUGIA
TEL. 0758001501 - 0758000525
www.brogalvini.com

Brogal Vini has its logistical base at Bastia Umbra but its properties, cellars and vineyards are in Torgiano, with more than 50 hectares, and Montefalco, where there are about 30 hectares. It hardly needs saying that these two zones lead those that have brought Umbria its renown, although we should confirm that all the Brogal vines lie in DOC or DOCG areas. This year's wines retain their high quality standards and form an admirable batch, even though there are no outstanding peaks, but then they had the terrible 2002 vintage to contend with. Even so, Torgiano Rosso Riserva Santa Caterina '02 is a wine of excellent promise, despite being a touch less assured than previous vintages. The nose is vegetal and spicy, with black berry fruit and chocolate, the palate is slimmer than usual and a touch over-firm on the finish. Torgiano Rosso '03 is a terrific wine, with a great burst of ripe fruit and black pepper on the nose, and a deep, tangy, exuberantly youthful palate of firm tannic weight and good length. Cabernet Sauvignon '03 is similarly good, all pink pepper and herbaceousness, with a juicy, sweetly fruity, flavoursome palate. There is good news too from the '05 Grechetto, which has a straw colour. The most delicate aromas of banana, sage and mint usher in a fresh palate with supple body and a tasty grapefruit-like finish. Torgiano Bianco Antigniano '05 is less complex, less concentrated and comes one Glass down. Neither was there anything truly exciting from the Montefalco range.

●	Torgiano Rosso Santa Caterina Ris. '02	2 Glasses (black)	6
●	Torgiano Cabernet Sauvignon '03	2 Glasses (black)	5
●	Torgiano Rosso '03	2 Glasses (black)	4
○	Grechetto '05	2 Glasses (black)	4*
●	Montefalco Sagrantino '03	1 Glass (black)	7
●	Montefalco Rosso '04	1 Glass (black)	5
○	Torgiano Bianco Antigniano '05	1 Glass (black)	4
●	Umbria Rosso '05	1 Glass (black)	3
●	Torgiano Rosso Ris. Santa Caterina '00	2 Glasses (white)	6
●	Torgiano Rosso Santa Caterina Ris. '01	2 Glasses (white)	6
●	Torgiano Rosso Santa Caterina Ris. '99	2 Glasses (white)	6

PERUGIA

CARINI
FRAZ. COLLE UMBERTO
S.DA DEL TEGOLARO
06070 PERUGIA
TEL. 0755829102 - 3476303781
www.agrariacarini.it

Our more assiduous readers will probably recall some of our comments last year on the model Carini estate, situated half way between Mount Tezio and Lake Trasimeno. We were talking about Tegolaro, its top wine, which comes from merlot, cabernet and sangiovese, and about the '03 not being one of the best releases as there were hints of overripeness and over-development. We reported what we felt, especially considering the class and promise of earlier vintages, and the far greater vitality we were sensing from early cask tastings of the '04. At that stage, of course, those sensations were simply sensations. The wine had not been bottled and still had a long way to go. But now we can really say what sort of a wine Tegolaro '04 is, and it's superb, the best ever. Initial hints of forest fruits and violet on the nose are soon joined by elegant notes of liquorice and pink pepper that imbue it with complexity and a light smokiness. The palate is exemplary, with balance, breadth, richness of flavour, an excellent level of acidity, silky tannins and a long finish. Colli del Trasimeno Oscano '05, from sangiovese with 30 per cent ciliegiolo, is also very good. There are black berry fruits and tar on the nose, and it has a fresh, attractive palate full of red berry fruits, although the tannins are a little too evident. Poggio Canneto '05, from chardonnay and pinot bianco, with ten per cent grechetto, is of similar quality. This has tropical fruit on nose and palate, and a good acid backbone that adds depth of flavour and length.

●	Tegolaro '04	2 Glasses (black)	6
●	Colli del Trasimeno Oscano '05	2 Glasses (black)	4*
○	Poggio Canneto '05	2 Glasses (black)	4
●	Tegolaro '01	2 Glasses (white)	6
●	Tegolaro '02	2 Glasses (white)	6
●	Tegolaro '03	2 Glasses (white)	6

PERUGIA

GORETTI
LOC. PILA
S.DA DEL PINO, 4
06070 PERUGIA
TEL. 075607316
www.vinigoretti.com

Brothers Stefano and Gianluca Goretti, and their solidly-based estate, are an example to the whole sector. They bring commitment, skill, well-directed investment proportional to their means, an ability to innovate without turning everything upside down and moreover offer well-priced wines that are always well made. In short, theirs is a well-oiled machine that from time to time can really pull out the stops. It won't be a surprise that the estate has always had a place in our Guide, nor that the Gorettis have at last got a wine into the finals, their Grechetto '05. It hardly matters that it just scraped in: what counts is that it's there. The result rewards a great team effort and interestingly the team has recently gained further strength with Vittorio Fiore and Barbara Tamburini now also supplying technical input. The wine is a deep straw with bright green highlights. The nose erupts in a surge of white peach, flowers and aromatic herbs yet the palate is where it really scores, with citrus hints, great texture and a perfectly balanced acid backbone. L'Arringatore '03, from sangiovese and merlot, has been carefully moulded to cope with the year's heat and showed well. Both nose and palate give sensations running from black cherry to spices and there is a firm stamp of new oak, caramel and coffee throughout. Such sensations are not always elegant and, we have to say, are to some extent present on all the estate's barrique-aged wines. It's a small black mark but it's one that needs remedying as soon as possible.

○	Colli Perugini Grechetto '05	TT	3*
●	Colli Perugini Rosso L'Arringatore '03	TT	5
●	Montefalco Sagrantino Le Mure Saracene '01	T	6
○	Colli Perugini Chardonnay '05	T	3
●	Fontanella Rosso '05	T	3
●	Colli Perugini Rosso L'Arringatore '00	YY	5
●	Montefalco Sagrantino Le Mure Saracene '00	YY	6
●	Colli Perugini Rosso L'Arringatore '01	YY	5
●	Colli Perugini Rosso L'Arringatore '98	YY	4
●	Montefalco Sagrantino Le Mure Saracene '99	YY	6

SPELLO (PG)

SPORTOLETTI
LOC. CAPITAN LORETO
VIA LOMBARDIA, 1
06038 SPELLO (PG)
TEL. 0742651461
www.sportoletti.com

The Sportoletti family has been growing grapes and producing wine with love and dedication for a long time now. They started to sell their wine in bottle at the end of the 1970s but it was 20 years later when quality really took a leap. The turn-around came from the sheer passion of brothers Remo and Ernest, which led to a new direction in grape-growing and winemaking, including the arrival of Riccardo Cotarella. The results carried Sportoletti on to become one of the beacons of Umbrian winemaking. There are now 20 hectares of vineyard and varieties range from the traditional grechetto and sangiovese to the major international grapes, primarily chardonnay, merlot and cabernet. And, pivotally, there's a new, efficiently planned cellar able to maximize what the fruits of the vine can give. This year, we again found that Villa Fidelia Rosso, from merlot, cabernet sauvignon and cabernet franc, led the range. The '04 showed so magnificently that it very nearly took home Three Glasses. Its toastiness forms a perfect complement to its blackberry, blueberry and cherry fruitiness, giving overall sweetness without excesses and without looseness. These aromas are reflected on the firm, dense palate which develops confidently to a long finish. The rest of the range also impresses, from an intense, spicy, floral, Villa Fidelia Bianco '04, from chardonnay and grechetto, which gets better every year, to an ultra-fruity, ultra-sound Grechetto, and a soft, highly attractive, cherry and tobacco-like Assisi Rosso '05, from merlot, sangiovese and cabernet.

●	Villa Fidelia Rosso '04	TT	6
○	Villa Fidelia Bianco '04	TT	5
○	Assisi Grechetto '05	TT	3*
●	Assisi Rosso '05	TT	4*
●	Villa Fidelia Rosso '98	YYY	6
●	Villa Fidelia Rosso '00	YY	7
●	Villa Fidelia Rosso '03	YY	6
●	Villa Fidelia Rosso '99	YY	6
●	Villa Fidelia Rosso '01	YY	7
●	Villa Fidelia Rosso '02	YY	6
●	Villa Fidelia Rosso '97	YY	4

STRONCONE (TR)

LA PALAZZOLA
LOC. VASCIGLIANO
05039 STRONCONE (TR)
TEL. 0744609091 - 0744272357

Stefano Grilli proceeds apace with his innovative approach, one that would even be slightly over-the-top were it not for the type of wines he's producing and the direction in which he's heading. His fascinating character means that each year brings surprises. This year is no exception, and without doubt there are all sorts of new ideas for the future already spinning round his head. So what's this year's news? The most important item is the return of the Merlot after several years out in the wilderness. It's a wine that has brought the estate accolades on more than one occasion. And the new '04 is right up there at the level that brought fame to its predecessors. Touches of greenness on the nose weave into a remarkably full fruity framework highlighted by clear smoky nuances. These sensations come through on the palate, too, which is taut, deep and nicely complex. It's a fine wine indeed. The sparkling Riesling Brut '01 isn't at all bad either. Its appearance is flecked with gold, the nose has ripe yellow-fleshed fruit, citrus and sage leaves while the palate is petrolly, and has a glorious acid backbone and plenty of length. The Vendemmia Tardiva da Uve Muffate '04 scored similarly, and has aromas of peaches in syrup and honey, and an elegantly sweet yet dynamic palate, giving a good interplay between supporting sweetness and shots of liveliness. The other sparkler, Gran Cuvée Brut '02, gained just One Glass, but is still a distinctive wine which has aromas of apricot and tropical fruit and a full, zesty palate with a chestnut honey finish.

○ Riesling Brut M. Cl. '01	TT	5
○ V. T. da Uve Muffate '04	TT	4
● Merlot '04	TT	5
○ Gran Cuvée Brut '02	T	5
● Merlot '97	YYY	5
● Merlot '99	YY	5
● Rubino '00	YY	5
○ Vin Santo Passito '00	YY	5
○ Gran Cuvée Brut '01	YY	5
● Rubino '01	YY	5
○ Vin Santo Passito '01	YY	5
● Rubino '02	YY	5
● Syrah '03	YY	4
○ Riesling Brut M. Cl. '99	YY	4
● Rubino '99	YY	5

TODI (PG)

TODINI
FRAZ. COLLEVALENZA
06050 TODI (PG)
TEL. 075887122 - 075887222
www.cantinafrancotodini.com

The countryside around Todi is full of fascination, historically, culturally and visually, and in the last few years, viticulture has joined the list of attractions. Agricola Todini is a good example. It spans 300 hectares, with about 30 under vine, and is dominated by a superb period residence which includes a restaurant. A new cellar will shortly be appearing. A long list of wines is produced under the supervision of oenologist Maurilio Chioccia, ranging from great international-style reds to the most traditional of local whites, with Grechetto prominent. But let's take this one step at a time. Nero della Cervara '04, a cabernet sauvignon-merlot blend aged in French oak barriques, is the wine tipped to be the estate's flagship. Everything hangs on the balance of fruit ripeness and the use of oak. The nose has blackberries and cherry followed by clear caramel hints, the palate is full, round, juicy and cohesive and develops evenly although, to be really starry, there would have to be an extra boost of personality. Rubro '04, made mainly from sangiovese, is similarly styled, and scored similarly, too. Oak and caramel notes weave through its fruit and the palate is savoury and wonderfully deep. The classic Grechetto di Todi '05, fresh, vegetal, slightly balsamic and full of grip, is also good.

● Colli Martani Sangiovese Rubro '04	TT	5
● Nero della Cervara '04	TT	6
○ Colli Martani Grechetto di Todi '05	TT	4*
● Colli Martani Sangiovese Rubro '01	YY	6
● Nero della Cervara '03	YY	6
○ Colli Martani Grechetto di Todi '04	YY	4

TODI (PG)

TUDERNUM
PIAN DI PORTO, 146
06059 TODI (PG)
TEL. 0758989403
www.tudernum.it

This co-operative, lying below the glorious town of Todi, once produced wines that were little more than anonymous but changed direction and is now steaming ahead. There have been improvements in the vineyards, considerable investment in the cellar and winemaking was passed to Emiliano Falsini and a group of reliable, well-trained technical staff. Indeed, it took hardly any time before Tudernum, literally transformed, became one of the most noteworthy wineries in the region. The Merlot '05 reached the finals with its purple-ruby colour. It has aromas of morello cherry and printer's ink and the palate is monumental, both broadly and deeply fruity yet elegant and with a well-judged tannin level. It is even more applause-worthy when you take the price tag into account. Sangiovese Belforte '05 is excellent, too, uniting rose water-like and cherry aromas, enclosed in a rich yet extremely lively structure of great appeal. Also good is the elegant, spicy Cabernet Sauvignon '05, which is free of any clumsy herbaceousness. Two Glasses also went to the Sagrantino '03, all sweet fruit and oak, and the two incredibly elegant Grechettos with their deep straw and gold colours. The straight '05 is an early-drinking, almost salty, wine of attack. Colle Nobile '05 has complexity and smoothness from its short time in barrique but has not lost its fruit freshness. In short, there isn't a single wine which isn't at least admirable. Long may it last.

●	Merlot '05	TT	3*
●	Montefalco Sagrantino Tudernum '03	TT	6
●	Cabernet Sauvignon '05	TT	3*
○	Colli Martani Grechetto di Todi '05	TT	3*
○	Colli Martani Grechetto di Todi Colle Nobile '05	TT	4
●	Colli Martani Sangiovese Belforte '05	TT	3*
●	Montefalco Sagrantino Tudernum '01	YY	5
●	Roiano '03	YY	4*

TORGIANO (PG)

LUNGAROTTI
VIA MARIO ANGELONI, 16
06089 TORGIANO (PG)
TEL. 075988661
www.lungarotti.it

When, in the mid 1960s, Giorgio Lungarotti started to think about the wine that would embody the soul of his estate, he had no doubts. It needed to be a Riserva, made with grapes from a single vineyard, in other words a cru, and produced only in the best vintages. The wine, Torgiano Rosso Riserva Vigna Monticchio, is now legendary. The tradition has naturally been maintained by Giorgio's two daughters Chiara and Teresa, who now head the estate. The '02 vintage was not considered outstanding and so wasn't produced. But there is consolation. Three Glasses have been awarded, even if rather later than usual, to the stunning '88 vintage. This has been retasted over the years and remains elegant and deep, and still has ages to go. Moving back to the newer wines, San Giorgio '03 reached the finals. It comes from barrique-aged sangiovese, canaiolo and cabernet sauvignon, and has huge fascination with ripe black cherry and sweet spiciness on the nose, and a silky, round palate of innumerable flavours and incredibly firm character. Other sure finalists were Aurente '04, made from oak-fermented chardonnay and grechetto, which has gained benefit from extended bottle ageing, and the highly promising Torgiano Bianco Riserva Vigna il Pino '04, which has fascinating limestone and mineral hints. The '04 Giubilante, from syrah, merlot and sangiovese, is as good as ever, as is the classic Rubesco '03 and the white Torre di Giano '05. And what's new this year? The first release of an excellent Sagrantino, the '03, from the new holding in Montefalco. We look forward to developments.

●	San Giorgio '03	TT	6
○	Aurente '04	TT	5
○	Torgiano Bianco Torre di Giano V. il Pino Ris. '04	TT	4*
●	Montefalco Sagrantino '03	TT	5
●	Torgiano Rosso Rubesco '03	TT	4*
●	Giubilante '04	TT	4
○	Torgiano Bianco Torre di Giano '05	TT	3*
●	Torgiano Rosso Vigna Monticchio Ris. '01	YYY	6
●	Torgiano Rosso Vigna Monticchio Ris. '78	YYY	6
●	Torgiano Rosso Vigna Monticchio Ris. '88	YYY	5
●	San Giorgio '01	YY	6

OTHER WINERIES

BENINCASA
LOC. CAPRO, 99
06031 BEVAGNA (PG)
TEL. 0742361307
www.aziendabenincasa.com

There's plenty of promise at Benincasa; all that's needed is a bit more consistency. The best wine this year is the clean, enjoyable Montefalco Rosso '04 with its multi-faceted, intense nose of blackberry and red fruits. Sagrantino '02, though, is far less impressive than the '01.

●	Montefalco Rosso '04	▼▼	4
●	Montefalco Sagrantino '02		6
●	Vigna La Fornace '00	▽▽	5
●	Montefalco Sagrantino '01	▽▽	6
●	Montefalco Rosso '03	▽▽	4

FATTORIA COLSANTO
LOC. CANTALUPO - MONTARONE
06031 BEVAGNA (PG)
TEL. 0742360412 - 0432757173
www.livon.it

This 20-hectare estate is owned by the Livon family. The wines get better each year, especially the Sagrantino. The '03 has a citrus and dried flowers nose and a piquant, juicy, palate with a good tannic weave. Rosso di Montefalco '04 is a touch edgy but good. Rosso Ruris '04 is good, too.

●	Montefalco Sagrantino '03	▼▼	6
●	Montefalco Rosso '04	▼	4
●	Ruris Rosso '04	▼	4

MARTINELLI
LOC. SASSO, 12A
06031 BEVAGNA (PG)
TEL. 0742362124
www.cantinemartinelli.com

The Martini brothers' winery is still one to watch. This year, there's an impressive new selection, Soranna '03, alongside the basic Sagrantino. It has a nose of chocolate, spices and briary fruit, and a warm, sturdy palate with good tannin and plenty of length.

●	Montefalco Sagrantino '03	▼▼	6
●	Montefalco Sagrantino Sel. Soranna '03	▼▼	7
●	Montefalco Sagrantino '02	▽▽	6

ITALO DI FILIPPO
VIA CONVERSINO, 153
06033 CANNARA (PG)
TEL. 0742731242
www.vinidifilippo.com

This organic estate often has excellent wines but hasn't yet achieved any real consistency. The best this year are Montefalco Rosso Sallustio '04, Colli Martani Grechetto '05 and Bianco Villa Conversino '05, this last from grechetto and trebbiano.

●	Montefalco Rosso Sallustio '04	▼	4
○	Colli Martani Grechetto '05	▼	3
○	Villa Conversino Bianco '05	▼	2*

Tenuta Vitalonga
loc. Montiano
05016 Ficulle (TR)
tel. 0763836722
www.vitalonga.it

Riccardo Cotarella now consults at the Maravalle family's property. Elcione '04, from merlot and cabernet, is spicy and mouthfilling with velvety tannins. Terra di Confine '04, montepulciano and merlot, is a little too oaky but has class with rounded fruit, intensity and supple freshness.

● Elcione '04	🍷🍷	4
● Terra di Confine '04	🍷🍷	5

Terre De La Custodia
loc. Palombara
06035 Gualdo Cattaneo (PG)
tel. 0742929595

This estate was set up by the Farchioni family, successful oil merchants. Sagrantino di Montefalco Exubera '03 impresses for the intensity of its spicy and forest fruit jam nose, and its well-defined structure, although the tannins are a bit edgy. Sagrantino di Montefalco '03 is well styled.

● Montefalco Sagrantino Exubera '03	🍷🍷	7
● Montefalco Sagrantino '03	🍷	8

Pucciarella
loc. Villa di Magione
06063 Magione (PG)
tel. 0758409147
www.FondoPensioniCariplo.it

Pucciarella returns! Riccardo Cotarella has inspired a great Empireo '04. From merlot, sagrantino and cabernet sauvignon, it offers sweet spice, oak toast and fruit, showing a full yet stylish palate and perfect tannic weave. Vin Santo Eletto '01 is most successful. Chardonnay Arsiccio '05 is good.

○ C. del Trasimeno Vin Santo Eletto '01	🍷🍷	4
● Empireo '04	🍷🍷	4
○ Chardonnay Arsiccio '05	🍷	4

Flavio Busti
fraz. Sant' Elena
06052 Marsciano (PG)
tel. 075879458 - 34708070455
www.cantinebusti.it

Quality here has made rapid progress. The wines are very well made and starting to gain character. Merlot Castel Sant'Elena '05, fresh and floral with quinine and black berries, is excellent. Grechetto '05 is one of the best in the area and Sangiovese '05 is enjoyable.

● Castel Sant'Elena '05	🍷🍷	4
○ Grechetto '05	🍷🍷	3*
● Sangiovese '05	🍷	3

Cantina La Spina
fraz. Spina
via Emilio Alessandrini, 1
06050 Marsciano (PG)
tel. 0758738120 - www.cantinalaspina.it

There is more good news from Moreno Peccia. Work on the cellar is finished and the potential of the wines is more apparent. Merlato '05 is spot on, with depth and flavour, despite a slimmer profile than in '04. Rosso Spina '04 is very good. Polimante '04 has improved but still needs some tinkering.

● Rosso Spina '04	🍷🍷	5
● Merlato '05	🍷🍷	4*
● Polimante '04	🍷	5
● Rosso Spina '03	🍷🍷 (white)	5

Opinioni
loc. San Pietro
05020 Montecchio (TR)
tel. 07449556

Opinioni is Riccardo and Renzo Cotarella's kosher wine estate and very good it is, too. Verdetto, from merlot, cabernet and sangiovese, is intense and velvety. Monte Olivo Bianco, from chardonnay and trebbiano, is fresh and aromatic. Monte Olivo Rosé is a perfect partner to the local cured meats.

○ Monte Olivo Bianco '05	🍷🍷	3*
⊙ Monte Olivo Rosé '05	🍷🍷	3*
● Verdetto '05	🍷🍷	4

Tenuta Alzatura

loc. Fratta - Alzatura, 108
06036 Montefalco (PG)
tel. 0742399435
www.tenuta-alzatura.it

The Cecchi brothers have made small but perceptible improvements here. Rosso di Montefalco '04 is impressive. Dark ruby with aromas ranging from black cherry to herbaceous and spicy, it has a confident palate of depth. Sagrantino '03, a One Glass wine, has a less defined nose and greener tannin.

- ● Montefalco Rosso '04 ŶŶ 4
- ● Montefalco Sagrantino Uno di Sei '03 Ŷ 6

Ruggeri

via Montepennino, 5
06036 Montefalco (PG)
tel. 0742379294

There's plenty of dynamism in the Sagrantino zone. Ruggeri is not a new name but is now back in the Guide with a Sagrantino '03 of excellent balance, poised between oak toast and fruit intensity. The Rosso di Montefalco '04 is admirable but we found the Passito '03 a little less impressive.

- ● Montefalco Sagrantino '03 ŶŶ 6
- ● Montefalco Rosso '04 ŶŶ 4
- ● Montefalco Sagrantino Passito '03 Ŷ 6

Tiburzi

loc. Montepennino
06036 Montefalco (PG)
tel. 0742379203 - 3357758002
www.tiburzicantine.com

There's been a slight fall from grace here. The wines are still sound but nothing stands out and they're all around the One Glass mark. Sagrantino Taccalite '03 is too sweet and ripe, Rosso di Montefalco Santambrà '04 is decent and Colle Scancellato '05, from sangiovese, is pleasant.

- ● Montefalco Sagrantino Taccalite '03 Ŷ 6
- ● Montefalco Santambrà '04 Ŷ 4
- ● Colle Scancellato '05 Ŷ 2*
- ● Montefalco Sagrantino Taccalite '02 YY 6

Brugnoli

via Poggente, 46
05019 Orvieto (TR)
tel. 0763215052

The '03 Cavalmoro, the most interesting wine here, is again splendid. An initial herbaceousness with bell pepper is quickly followed by tobacco and great fruitiness. The palate is succulent, tangy and tight woven. Rosso Orvietano Sesil '03 is unbalanced and too sweet, winning just One Glass.

- ● Cavalmoro '03 ŶŶ 2*
- ● Rosso Orvietano Sesil '03 Ŷ 4

Chiorri

loc. Sant' Enea
via Todi, 98/100
06070 Perugia
tel. 075607141 - www.chiorri.it

The news here is that the new cellar is almost finished giving Mariotti Tito and his daughters more space in which to work. Sangiovese '05 is as enjoyable as ever. Cabernet Selezione Antonio Chiorri '04 has depth and flavour. Rosato '05 is fresh and juicy. All have a comforting "handmade" feel.

- ● Cabernet Sel. Antonio Chiorri '04 ŶŶ 5
- ● Sangiovese '05 ŶŶ 3*
- ⊙ Colli Perugini Rosato '05 Ŷ 3

Spoletoducale

loc. Petrognano, 54
06049 Spoleto (PG)
tel. 074356224
www.spoletoducale.it

There are ups and downs at this co-operative. The most striking wine is Montefalco Rosso Spoletoducale '04. Cherry and ripe blackberry meld into deep scents of black pepper accompanied by a welcome light balsamic tone. It's an early drinker, full and with softish tannins on the palate.

- ● Montefalco Rosso Spoletoducale '04 ŶŶ 3
- ● Montefalco Sagrantino Casale Triocco '03 Ŷ 5
- ● Montefalco Rosso Casale Triocco '04 Ŷ 4
- ○ Trebbiano Spoletino '05 Ŷ 2*

LAZIO

If Lazio could have a motto for its wines this year, it should probably be "slow ahead". The region can at last boast two Three Glass wines rather than one, but their artificers remain Lazio's same leading players, Falesco, whose Marciliano takes the honours instead of the multiple prizewinner Montiano, and Sergio Mottura. His Three Glasses naturally went to Latour a Civitella which is steadily becoming one of Italy's most distinctive white wines and so is doing much to raise the profile of grechetto. But when you consider that this is probably the last year that Falesco will be listed under Lazio as the estate is progressively shifting into Umbria, you can see that the Three Glass situation is still precarious. Yet judging the region solely by the number of its Three Glass wines gives an unbalanced picture, for two reasons. The first is that the number of wines in the finals has increased, which augurs very well for the future. The second is that there is a huge, growing disparity between the development going on in some provinces and the difficulties bedevilling the others. Progress in the province of Latina is driven by a group of wineries including Casale del Giglio, Sant'Andrea and Marco Carpineti, all very diverse in their background and their way of expressing provenance, and we are seeing a highly promising, rapid growth in quality. Viterbo may be home to our two top wineries but it hasn't yet developed a clear identity and forms a sort of buffer zone with wines from indigenous grapes on the one side and all sorts of experiments on the other. But producers are beginning to work together and build on the idea of provenance which, together with the undoubted potential of its lands, is highly promising. When it comes to Frosinone, although there is much work going on into producing great reds from cesanese, we don't feel that most people are on the right track yet. Nevertheless, we are optimistic here too. Two Cesaneses reached the finals this year and producers' determination to nail the variety is so strong that we would be surprised if a real stunner didn't emerge within the next two to three years. It's also good to see Santa Lucia, a winery from the province of Rieti, at last gaining a full entry in the Guide. But that brings us to our sore spot, the province of Rome, whose producers seem not to know how to handle the huge potential they have at their fingertips in the Castelli Romani. But even here something is moving and alongside the clutch of reliable co-operatives and long-standing leading names, such as Paola di Mauro, Castel de Paolis and Villa Simone, there are wineries – Poggio Le Volpi and Pallavicini, for instance – which are investing in quality-directed research. If they haven't yet achieved their aims, at least they are headed in the right direction.

ACUTO (FR)

CASALE DELLA IORIA
P.ZZA REGINA MARGHERITA, 1
03010 ACUTO (FR)
TEL. 077556031 - 3356403074
www.casaledellaioria.com

Sometimes financial investment, productive strength and constant effort aren't enough. If the weather goes pear-shaped, then woe ensues and it always shows somewhere. Please excuse this preamble but it is a necessary prelude to looking at the '04 vintage of a wine that has always received unanimous acclaim, the renowned Cesanese del Piglio Torre del Piano. To its producers' credit, the wine has managed to achieve a certain complexity and elegance, despite the miserable vintage, but it lacks a bit of focus. As a consequence, it is Casale della Ioria '05, the more basic Cesanese del Piglio formulated by owner Paolo Perinelli and oenologist Roberto Mazzer, that obtained our highest score and Two well-deserved Glasses. It has a rich nose, full of pervasive hints of warm red fruit. There is plentiful but not excessive alcohol, balanced by good depth and richness of flavour, and it finishes long. Passerina del Frusinate, conceived as a means of reflecting the territory through a white wine, has never gained much favour with the general public and is generally treated as little more than something to accompany the more serious red. But the '05 version from Casale della Ioria, with its lively note of slightly bitterish apples, has a bit more to offer.

● Cesanese del Piglio Casale della Ioria '05	🍷🍷	4
● Cesanese del Piglio Torre del Piano '04	🍷	5
○ Passerina del Frusinate Colle Bianco '05	🍷	3
● Cesanese del Piglio Torre del Piano '01	YY	5
● Cesanese del Piglio Torre del Piano '03	YY	5
● Cesanese del Piglio Torre del Piano '00	YY	5

ANAGNI (FR)

COLACICCHI
VIA ROMAGNANO, 2
03012 ANAGNI (FR)
TEL. 064469661

If popes still resided at Anagni, they wouldn't lack for fine drinking. Never has there been such a spectrum of high quality wines in the area. The estate spearheading this revival is indisputably Colacicchi, which for some time now has been masterfully run by the Trimani family, who acquired it from Luigi Colacicchi. The most renowned of its wines is Torre Ercolana, made from cabernet and merlot with the indigenous cesanese. Year after year, the odd slip-up apart, it has supreme elegance and class, and the '03 is again beautifully stylish. The Bordeaux grapes give the nose a spicy, vegetal richness that melds effortlessly into the red berry fruits aromas of the cesanese. The palate is long, soft yet powerful, and deeply satisfying. Romagnano Rosso '04 comes from the same grapes but with cesanese taking the lion's share. It's a tighter, slimmer version of its big brother but has good body. Schiaffo, which means "slap", was named in memory of a medieval insult. It again comes from the same three varieties but is oak-free, producing a more enticing, easy-drinking style, hinged on softness, immediacy and fruit. The '05 is a typical example. The sole white, Romagnano Bianco '05 made from malvasia del Lazio and other indigenous varieties, also showed well. It's a sound example of a wine straddling tradition and modernity, and has good overall harmony, firm structure and good supporting acidity. Even so, there's a touch of the flabbiness that is typical of wines from central Lazio.

● Torre Ercolana '03	🍷🍷	7
● Romagnano Rosso '04	🍷	5
○ Romagnano Bianco '05	🍷	5
● Schiaffo '05	🍷	5
● Torre Ercolana '01	YY	6
● Torre Ercolana '97	YY	6
● Torre Ercolana '98	YY	6

ANAGNI (FR)

Antonello Coletti Conti
via Vittorio Emanuele, 116
03012 Anagni (FR)
tel. 0775728610
www.coletticonti.it

Anton Maria Coletti Conti, scion of an ancient Anagni family which once gave birth to a pope, inherited his family estate in the southern part of the Cesanese del Piglio zone some time ago and is now dedicating himself to winemaking full time. Having made the decision to renovate the vineyards and the cellar, he first worked on determining the plant spacing and the rootstocks, which he chose with great care. He then moved on to select his varieties and carried out a series of microvinifications to find the wine styles giving most character. Finally, he created a small but efficient vinification cellar and adjacent barrel cellar, where two wines not yet on the market, Cosmato '05 and Romanico '05, are currently ageing. This year, he submitted two wines to our tastings, Cesanese del Piglio Hernicus '05 and, for the first time, the white Arcadia '05, from 80 per cent incrocio Manzoni with passerina. The former is part barrique-aged which has softened out any sharp edges and broadened out the aromas, giving spiciness, black berry fruit and leather. Rich, powerful and assertive, it justifiably gained a place in the finals. The most impressive aspects of the white are its originality and a stylistic verve that emphasizes its ageing potential. The nose is intense and complex with citrus and balsam, and the palate has great structure although isn't yet fully balanced. Time will tell if our enthusiasm is justified.

● Cesanese del Piglio Hernicus '05	**YY**	4
○ Arcadia '05	**YY**	4
● Cosmato '03	YY	6
● Cesanese del Piglio Hernicus '04	YY	4

ANAGNI (FR)

Marcella Giuliani
loc. Vico
via Anticolana, km 5
03012 Anagni (FR)
tel. 0644235908 - 3358219504

For the first time Cesanese del Piglio Dives, Marcella Giuliani's top wine, won a place in the finals. And it very nearly went the whole distance to pick up Three Glasses. The credit for this success naturally belongs to its producer but also to high-ranking consultant Riccardo Cotarella. Indeed, year by year they have been gradually honing the wine's character into ever classier form. This year's '04 has a wide spectrum of aromas, with top notes of coffee and spices that meld into more mineral, vegetal sensations. Given its youth, the tannin is still evident but it's well integrated because there is a denser weave and more complexity than usual while the finish is warm, cohesive and long. The other Cesanese, Alagna '05, is also well up to expectations. It's traditionally styled, bringing out the fruit of the variety more than spiciness, and has developed some complexity. The nose has red berry fruit and the palate is medium-bodied but avoids being overwhelmed by an excess of alcohol, as can happen with wines from cesanese. Finally, we have the '05 release of Alagna Bianco '05, made solely from passerina del Frusinate, a wine that always helps shape the Ciociara area's range. The Giuliani style is to bring out the softness of the variety, its swath of gentle acidity and its buttressing of moderate alcohol, resulting in a coherent, clean wine of fair length.

● Cesanese del Piglio Dives '04	**YY**	5
○ Alagna Bianco '05	**Y**	3
● Cesanese del Piglio Alagna '05	**Y**	3
● Cesanese del Piglio Dives '02	YY	5
● Cesanese del Piglio Dives '03	YY	5

APRILIA (LT)

CASALE DEL GIGLIO

LOC. LE FERRIERE
S.DA CISTERNA-NETTUNO, KM 13
04010 APRILIA (LT)
TEL. 0692902530 - 065745717
www.casaledelgiglio.it

Twenty years ago, Antonio Santarelli wanted to fulfil his dream of making top-quality wine on the Pontine plains, where there was no tradition. But research revealed that the area had affinities with the Napa valley, Santarelli took on top oenologist Paolo Tiefenthaler, and Casale del Giglio is now one of Lazio's top estates. Mater Matuta and Antinoo are habitual finalists and again reached the podium. The former, '03 and from shiraz and petit verdot, is its usual self. A broad, rich, cohesive, balanced red with tertiary leather notes offsetting silky, ripe tannins. The '04 Antinoo has also retained its standard format: chardonnay and viognier, finely judged use of barriques and elegance, balance and length providing great drinkability. A note of praise goes to all the reds en bloc after their release was held back for a year, especially the '03s, Madreselva and Cabernet Sauvignon. The former, from cabernet and merlot, has great softness and appeal while the latter is in more serious style, with more structure and tannin. The trio of monovarietal '04s, Merlot, Shiraz and Petit Verdot, are showing better than ever, with focus on the balance for the first, richness and breadth characterizing the second and the third showing youthful, red berry fruitiness. The '05 whites are also generally up to scratch. There's a vanillaed Chardonnay, a fresh, varietal Sauvignon and a well-styled, attractive Satrico. Finally comes just a quick mention for Albiola '05 and a cheer for Aphrodisium '05, which has even better defined notes of apricot, acacia blossom and honey.

● Mater Matuta '03	🍷🍷	6
○ Antinoo '04	🍷🍷	4*
● Cabernet Sauvignon '03	🍷🍷	5
● Madreselva '03	🍷🍷	5
● Merlot '04	🍷🍷	4*
● Shiraz '04	🍷🍷	4
○ Aphrodisium '05	🍷🍷	6
⊙ Albiola '05	🍷	3
○ Chardonnay '05	🍷	3
○ Satrico '05	🍷	2
○ Sauvignon '05	🍷	3
● Mater Matuta '00	ΥΥ	6
● Mater Matuta '01	ΥΥ	6
○ Antinoo '03	ΥΥ	4*

CASTIGLIONE IN TEVERINA (VT)

ALESSIA

FRAZ. VAIANO
LOC. PALOMBARO
01024 CASTIGLIONE IN TEVERINA (VT)
TEL. 0761948034 - 0684561471
www.paoloenoemiadamico.it

The wines from this splendid estate overlooking the Viterbo ravines have become some of the most distinctive and reliable in the region. The D'Amico husband-and-wife team have 21 hectares under vine, giving 60,000 bottles, and the well-coordinated team of manager Enrico Peyron, oenologist Carlo Corino and agronomist Fabrizio Moltard ensures that everything is good quality. Calanchi di Vaiano '05, from 100 per cent stainless-steel aged chardonnay is like a surge of summer sun, all richness and tropical fruits that captivate the nose and fill the mouth in a continuing silky harmony. But if we are to nit-pick, the palate tails off a touch at the finish. Falesia '04 scored almost as well. This, too, is from chardonnay but ages eight months in barrique. It's a golden straw with a nose typical of oak-aged chardonnay with overt butteriness. The palate is full, rich and gutsy, with good backbone and length, but it lacks a touch of elegance, as if the vinification or ageing had given it too much weight. The last white of the threesome is Orvieto Noe '05. This has pleasant aromas of fresh fruit and white flowers, and a racy palate of verve and zest, tempered by a sheath of softness. The new vintage of Villa Tirrena, from 100 per cent merlot, is the estate's only red. It was not submitted to our tastings as it is being left to age for another few months.

○ Falesia '04	🍷🍷	5
○ Calanchi di Vaiano '05	🍷🍷	4*
○ Orvieto Noe '05	🍷	3
○ Falesia '01	ΥΥ	5
○ Falesia '03	ΥΥ	5

CASTIGLIONE IN TEVERINA (VT)

TRAPPOLINI
VIA DEL RIVELLINO, 65
01024 CASTIGLIONE IN TEVERINA (VT)
TEL. 0761948381 - 3356261303

We always follow the wines of Trappolini brothers Roberto and Paolo with great interest. Unfortunately, a slip-up last year left their entry out of the Guide. So this year, we are making amends and including comments on last year's best two wines too, which are not only still drinkable but have improved. Let's start at the top of the range with Paterno, from 100 per cent sangiovese. Last year's '03 is fabulous, and was a finalist. Close knit, full and elegant all at once, it's a wine that has nothing to fear from other Sangioveses from anywhere in Italy. This year's '04 is not quite as starry. There's blueberry and cassis, and the tannin is soft, making its presence felt without being overly invasive and providing excellent buttressing to the wine's good structure. But it's a touch shorter and less concentrated than the '03. Brecceto comes from equal parts of chardonnay and grechetto and aged in small oak barrels. Both the '04 and the '05 are admirable. The former is refined, soft and velvety, with good body and a fine fruit-vanilla balance. The '05 has elegant wafts of fruitiness that meld nicely into the toasty notes from its oaking. Moving on to the other wines, the varietal aromas on Sartei '05, a 50-50 blend of malvasia and trebbiano, are fairly pronounced and the wine holds together reasonably well. Est Est Est di Montefiascone '05 is fresh, clean and well styled, as is the '05 Orvieto, and both are remarkably well priced. Aleatico Idea '05 is also good and ideal for partnering chocolate-based desserts.

●	Paterno '03	🍷🍷	4*
○	Brecceto '04	🍷🍷	4*
●	Paterno '04	🍷🍷	4
○	Brecceto '05	🍷🍷	4*
○	Est Est Est di Montefiascone '05	🍷	2
●	Idea '05	🍷	4
○	Orvieto '05	🍷	2
○	Sartei '05	🍷	2

CIVITELLA D'AGLIANO (VT)

SERGIO MOTTURA
LOC. POGGIO DELLA COSTA, 1
01020 CIVITELLA D'AGLIANO (VT)
TEL. 0761914533
www.motturasergio.it

Sergio Mottura can boast a first. He's the first producer in the region to have gained Three Glasses for a white wine and he's done it not once but twice. Yes, Latour a Civitella again takes top honours, this time with the '04. You can't remain indifferent to a wine that takes the upper Lazio native grechetto, from which it's produced 100 per cent, out of its stereotype as a grape suited for no more than well-made but straightforward wines and turns it into something far, far greater. If you doubt us, just try it. You are bound to be struck by the breadth of the nose, the richness of its tropical fruit aromas, the marvellous nose-palate harmony and the subtlety of the discreet, refined oaking. And all this comes despite the fact that the wine is still very young and far from revealing its full potential. If you take our advice, you'll keep it for five to ten years and if you do, you'll then have one of Italy's greatest whites in your glass. Mottura's other monovarietal Grechetto, the citrus-veined, mineral, taut, austere Poggio della Costa '05, is also first rate and best left to age for a few years. Magone '04 is just as good. It comes from pinot nero, a notoriously tetchy grape, and yet the wine has firmness, grip and elegance. The pervasive, long palate unveils impressive cleanliness and richness of fruit. Finally, the basic-level Orvieto '05 deserves a word. It's light but not simplistic and keeps its promise to be a racy easy drinker.

○	Grechetto Latour a Civitella '04	🍷🍷🍷	5*
●	Magone '04	🍷🍷	5
○	Grechetto Poggio della Costa '05	🍷🍷	4
○	Orvieto '05	🍷	4
○	Grechetto Latour a Civitella '01	☐☐☐	4
○	Grechetto Latour a Civitella '02	☐☐	5
○	Grechetto Latour a Civitella '00	☐☐	5
○	Grechetto Latour a Civitella '03	☐☐	5
●	Magone '03	☐☐	5
○	Grechetto Latour a Civitella '96	☐☐	4
○	Grechetto Latour a Civitella '99	☐☐	4

COLONNA (RM)

PALLAVICINI
VIA CASILINA, KM 25,500
00030 COLONNA (RM)
TEL. 069438816 - 069438027
www.vinipallavicini.com

Ongoing organizational and technical improvements at this Castelli Romani winery have yielded a number of distinctive and at times superb wines, and swept it back to a full entry. The impetus comes from the growing confidence of the Pallavicini family and the commitment of three important figures: experienced oenologist Carlo Roveda, tenacious agronomist Mauro De Angelis and the estate's tireless ambassador, Giovanna Trisorio. There are 80 hectares of vines, some in Colonna, some in Cerveteri, and the estate is also set up to receive groups of wine lovers and organize various tasting events. Let's go straight to the reds and the elegant Moroello '03, from sangiovese grosso and merlot. The nose has wild cherry and fresh tobacco and the palate is harmonious with good body and just a touch of leanness on the finish. Amarasco '03 is quite different in style. Here the base is ripe cesanese, which gives aromas of red berry fruit jam and a palate of notable depth and length. Pagello '05, from greco, grechetto and falanghina, heads the whites with its clear citrus aromas and attractively fruity palate. La Giara '05, a stylish wine made solely from malvasia puntinata, is less rich but fragrant and expressive. The typically styled Frascati Superiore Poggio Verde '05 showed well, with a clear-cut, floral finish. Finally, Stillato an excellent dried-grape passito made solely from malvasia puntinata is becoming the estate's standard-bearer. The '05 has a complex nose that marries the penetrating freshness of lavender flowers with the richness of candied apricots.

● Amarasco '03	🍷🍷	4
● Moroello '03	🍷🍷	6
○ Stillato '05	🍷🍷	5
○ Frascati Sup. Poggio Verde '05	🍷	3
○ La Giara '05	🍷	2
○ Pagello '05	🍷	4

CORI (LT)

MARCO CARPINETI
LOC. CAPO LE MOLE
S.P. VELLETRI-ANZIO, 1
04010 CORI (LT)
TEL. 069679860
www.marcocarpineti.it

It is always a pleasure to record success for good, young, enthusiastic wine producers. Marco Carpineti, a man who is consistent to the point of obstinacy, is one such and, having worked consistently for some time, this year he finally had the satisfaction of seeing a wine in the finals. It's the best release ever of Dithyrambus '03, made from nero buono di Cori and montepulciano. There is a nose of great intensity and breadth, ranging from forest fruits to pepper and clove, and a distinguished palate with just enough astringency well offset by alcohol. Then comes another pleasant surprise, in the form of the unoaked Rosso Tufaliccio '05, from montepulciano and cesanese. The nose is cherry-like and extremely youthful, and both nose and palate are highly attractive. Good style is also the hallmark of Cori Rosso Capolemole '04, from nero buono with a little cesanese. Moving on to the whites, the '05 Moro, from a local clone of greco bianco, is up to its usual standards with intense aromas of summer flowers and tropical fruits, and an unusual but pleasantly rustic note to the palate. Cori Bianco Capolemole '05, from malvasia, trebbiano and cacchione, scored similarly. The nose is broad and elegant while the palate strongly assertive. Finally, we have Ludum '04, a dried-grape passito from arciprete, which is shaped by its aromas of tobacco and honey, and its lively palate.

● Dithyrambus '03	🍷🍷	6
○ Cori Bianco Capolemole '05	🍷🍷	4*
○ Moro '05	🍷🍷	4*
● Rosso Tufaliccio '05	🍷🍷	3*
● Cori Rosso Capolemole '04	🍷	4
○ Ludum '04	🍷	6
○ Collesanti '05	🍷	4
● Dithyrambus '00	🍸🍸	5
● Dithyrambus '01	🍸🍸	5
○ Moro '04	🍸🍸	3*

CORI (LT)

CANTINA AGRICOLA CINCINNATO
VIA CORI - CISTERNA, KM 2
04010 CORI (LT)
TEL. 069679380
www.cantinacincinnato.it

In wine, as in other fields, it is usually easier to attain a certain level than maintain it. But that, we believe, is the goal of the Cincinnato co-operative and it seems to have gone some way towards achieving it, helped by a united, motivated staff, headed by president Nazareno Milita and oenologist Carlo Morettini. As we predicted last year, Nero Buono, now at its second release and with its style reflecting the better '03 vintage, has risen to take on the role of flagship wine for which it is cut out. Careful winemaking has drawn out all the characteristics of this indigenous variety, producing a wine with an intense, complex nose of red berry fruits and tobacco, and a lively palate with soft tannins and fair length. The other two reds, Rosso dei Dioscuri '04 and Cori Raverosse '03, also showed well. The latter is from nero buono, montepulciano and cesanese, and there are the beginnings of tertiary aromas of spices and vanilla, as well as just a hint of bitterness on the finish. Both Bianco dei Dioscuri '05, from 100 per cent bellone, and Cori Bianco Illirio '05, mostly from malvasia puntinata, are well-made wines that offer excellent value for money. The former has attractive aromas of flowers and white-fleshed fruit while the Cori has a more complex array of aromatics, ranging from lavender flowers to white chocolate. The '04 Bellone comes from very low-yielding vines and spent six months in oak on its lees. Even so, it can't match the fabulous '03 but it is still a wine of great potential and one to watch.

● Nero Buono '03	🍷🍷	4
● Cori Rosso Raverosse '03	🍷	3
○ Bellone '04	🍷	4
● Rosso dei Dioscuri '04	🍷	2*
○ Bianco dei Dioscuri '05	🍷	2*
○ Cori Bianco Illirio '05	🍷	3
● Cori Rosso Raverosse '02	ΥΥ	3*
○ Bellone '03	ΥΥ	3*

GROTTAFERRATA (RM)

CASTEL DE PAOLIS
VIA VAL DE PAOLIS
00046 GROTTAFERRATA (RM)
TEL. 069413648
www.casteldepaolis.it

Like every top squad with a large number of talented players that enable it to field a strong side for every game even when some are absent, Castel de Paolis continues to provide a great range of wines, even in years when its top reds are not released. The operation is run by Fabrizio Santarelli, who now also manages the Strada dei Vini dei Castelli Romani, and his father Giulio. Maybe they're a little disappointed that, with two wines in the finals, both stopped there but we are sure that Three Glasses are just around the corner. The estate owns 12 hectares of vineyard and annual production is almost 100,000 bottles. Recent now completed building works have created a new vinification cellar and areas for receiving visitors, an activity in which the family believes strongly. The '05 Vigna Adriana, a refined blend of malvasia puntinata with viognier and sauvignon, is once more absolutely fabulous. This wine has great personality, with deep, captivating aromas of apple and spring flowers, and a rich palate of length. The stylish Muffa Nobile is also back in the fray after some years of absence. Made from 80 per cent sémillon with sauvignon, it is fermented and aged in barrique, giving a generous, balanced wine with clean, pervasive notes of dried apricot and a savoury, mineral palate. The other whites, Frascati Superiore and Campo Vecchio, are satisfyingly harmonious, the former more fragrant and fruity, the latter showing more structure and length. The delicate, aromatic Rosathea from moscato rosa is another of the fine wines developed at this excellent winery.

○ Muffa Nobile '05	🍷🍷	6
○ Vigna Adriana '05	🍷🍷	5
○ Campo Vecchio Bianco '05	🍷	4
○ Frascati Sup. '05	🍷	4
● Rosathea '05	🍷	5
● Quattro Mori '00	ΥΥ	6
● Quattro Mori '01	ΥΥ	6
○ Vigna Adriana '01	ΥΥ	5
○ Vigna Adriana '02	ΥΥ	5
● Campo Vecchio Rosso '01	ΥΥ	4
● Quattro Mori '03	ΥΥ	6
○ Vigna Adriana '03	ΥΥ	5
○ Vigna Adriana '04	ΥΥ	5

MARINO (RM)

PAOLA DI MAURO
LOC. FRATTOCCHIE
VIA COLLE PICCHIONE, 46
00040 MARINO (RM)
TEL. 0693546329 - 0693541012
www.collepicchioni.it

Yet again, Vigna del Vassallo has impeccable style. This wine is the enduring emblem of this small, delightful estate where the family's instinctive affectionate warmth and their desire for unmitigated quality and personality in their wines comes through in everything they do. The wine, a Bordeaux blend, fills the nose with stylish aromas of morello cherry and wild rose, and grows across the palate, with increasing elegance, generosity and balance until it comes to a dry finish. The experience of Armando Di Mauro and the energy of his talented son Valerio are driven by passion, forming the perfect counterpoint to the stable figure of the tireless Paola. The result is sound wines of indubitable class. The standards they set themselves are difficult to achieve but support comes from Riccardo Cotarella, high-ranking consultant oenologist and great family friend. Works to modernize the vineyards and the vinification cellar are still in hand and when completed, management of the annual production 120,000 bottles will be greatly facilitated. In the meantime, two styles of Marino, both of great typicity, dominate the range. The silky, rounded Donna Paola '05 has subtle peachiness and the inviting Coste Rotonde '05 is delicately fresh and balanced. Perlaia '05 is a most attractive wine, with roses and raspberries on the graceful, floral nose and well-balanced tannin on the palate. Finally comes the oak-aged, elegant Le Vignole, from a blend of white grapes. The '04 has overt acacia blossom and good structure but more sauvignon in the blend would not have come amiss.

●	Vigna del Vassallo '04	🍷🍷	6
○	Le Vignole '04	🍷	4
○	Marino Coste Rotonde '05	🍷	3
○	Marino Donna Paola '05	🍷	4
●	Perlaia '05	🍷	4
●	Vigna del Vassallo '00	YYY	6
●	Vigna del Vassallo '01	YYY	6
●	Vigna del Vassallo '88	YYY	5
●	Vigna del Vassallo '02	YY	6

MONTE PORZIO CATONE (RM)

FONTANA CANDIDA
VIA FONTANA CANDIDA, 11
00040 MONTE PORZIO CATONE (RM)
TEL. 069401881
www.giv.it

It's almost a case of "no news is good news" at this nearly 50-year-old Castelli Romani winery, which manages 100 hectares of vineyard and turns out 8,000,000 bottles. It's one of the biggest in the area and one of the most important in the Gruppo Italiano Vini. But there is a bit of news and that's the return to form of the winery's two leading lights, Frascati Superiore Santa Teresa, with the '05, and Kron, from merlot and sangiovese, with the '04. The nose on the Frascati is youthfully fragrant and has clear citrus tones introducing a palate with perfect balance and a beautifully aromatic finish. Kron has a penetrating nose of black berry jam and fresh spices, and an intensely fruity palate of notable harmony with a tannic weave of great finesse. Skilled oenologist Francesco Bardi should be well pleased. He should also be pleased with Togale '05, made solely from merlot, which has well-defined aromas of mature oak and tobacco before the pervasive palate reprises all its sensations on the long finish. Finally come two attractive, well-made wines from the Terre dei Grifi line. Frascati Superiore '05 has a youthful, fresh nose and a good, zesty palate and Malvasia del Lazio '05 has florality, tropical fruits and attractive flavours that grow through the mouth.

●	Kron '04	🍷🍷	6
○	Frascati Sup. Santa Teresa '05	🍷🍷	5
○	Frascati Sup. Terre dei Grifi '05	🍷	4
○	Malvasia del Lazio Terre dei Grifi '05	🍷	4
●	Togale '05	🍷	3*
●	Kron '01	YY	6
●	Kron '02	YY	5

MONTE PORZIO CATONE (RM)

Poggio Le Volpi

via Colle Pisano, 27
00040 Monte Porzio Catone (RM)
tel. 069426980
www.poggiolevolpi.it

Skilled Felice Mergè and his staff have invested great effort at this newish estate and the wines have palpably improved each year since it first entered the Guide four years ago. Under the attentive supervision of consultant Riccardo Cotarella, work has gone into the vineyards and the winemaking, bringing improved grape quality and refining the character of everything in the range. The result is two wines in our finals and the sense that future releases will be even better. So let's give a round of applause in the hope it will encourage the team to carry on applying their commitment and skills. First of the two finalists is the memorable Baccarossa '04, from montepulciano and merlot, a vibrant, tight-knit wine with pervasive aromas of plum and violet, and a harmonious palate that marries body and flavour, exuding class from start to finish. The other, Donnaluce '05, is a compelling wine, with the stamp of high-quality chardonnay giving stylish aromas of flowers and tropical fruits, and a long, balanced palate that shows a wealth of restrained expressivity and good follow-through. Frascati Superiore Epos '05 also performed very well. It's possibly not very typical but it is beautifully made, its carefully selected malvasia grapes giving pervasive tones of yellow-fleshed fruit and notable structure. Frascati Superiore People and the dried-grape passito Odos were not submitted so we'll close with the attractively approachable Frascati Superiore Cannellino which, as usual, has candied and dried fruit aromas of good richness.

● Baccarossa '04	TT	6
○ Donnaluce '05	TT	5
○ Frascati Sup. Epos '05	TT	5
○ Frascati Cannellino '05	T	5
● Baccarossa '03	YY	5

MONTE PORZIO CATONE (RM)

Villa Simone

via Frascati Colonna, 29
00040 Monte Porzio Catone (RM)
tel. 069449717
www.pierocostantini.it

Life progresses calmly from vintage to vintage at Villa Simone, the well-known estate owned by the astute Piero Costantini. Piero also runs a well-known wine shop in Rome so he's never short of things to do, but even so each year his range comes up to the same high standards. Experienced management of the grapes from his almost 30 hectares of vineyard means he can produce 300,000 bottles of classically styled Frascatis and elegant reds. And it is the reds that have truly distinguished themselves this year. Ferro e Seta '04, from cesanese and sangiovese, has concentrated, deep aromas of ripe red berry fruit and soft leather. The palate is full, rich and harmonious, with fleshy black berry fruit and a tight tannic weave leading it to a graceful finish. Torraccia '05 is from the same grape blend and is an equally good wine but quite different in style. The nose gives plum, quinine, liquorice and blackberries before the even-bodied palate shows good dynamism and backbone, finishing pleasantly lean. Best of the Frascatis is the Superiore Villa dei Preti '05, which has delicate fruitiness and light vegetal tones, and a fragrant, well-structured palate. Vigneto Filonardi '05 is a little riper and warmer while Villa Simone '05 is fragrant, open and a sheer joy to drink.

● Ferro e Seta '04	TT	6
● Torraccia '05	TT	4
○ Frascati Sup. Vign. Filonardi '05	T	4
○ Frascati Sup. Villa dei Preti '05	T	4
○ Frascati Sup. Villa Simone '05	T	3
● Ferro e Seta '00	YY	6
● Ferro e Seta '01	YY	6
● Ferro e Seta '03	YY	6
● Torraccia '04	YY	4

MONTEFIASCONE (VT)

★ Falesco

via Cassia, km 94,155
01127 Montefiascone (VT)
tel. 074495561 - 0761827032
www.falesco.it

The consistency and remarkable quality of practically everything Riccardo Cotarella makes continues to amaze us, from his celebrated reds from international grapes to his indigenous whites and the new sweet wine Passirò. In fact, five of his wines reached the finals. At times, it is mere nuances that lead us to prefer one wine over another and we end up in long discussions over which to choose. This year, after long debate, we gave Three Glasses to Marciliano '04, a 70-30 blend of cabernets sauvignon and franc, grown and vinified in Umbria but listed here because Falesco is still based in Lazio. The wine is quite exemplary, a cut above the rest for richness of fruit, complexity, structure and softness. Montiano '04, from monovarietal merlot, comes barely a whisker behind, showing soft and full of appeal in its notes of tobacco and sweet spices. Tellus '05 is a highly impressive, complex wine from merlot and shiraz, full of fruit, densely woven, savoury and taut. Pesano '05, from merlot, is warm, silky, immediate and mouthfilling. The '05 Vitiano, a Bordeaux blend with some sangiovese, is as delightful as ever and now there's rosé version, too. Ferentano, from the roscetto variety, is becoming the classiest of the whites on the list. The '04 has a floral nose and a long, complex palate. Poggio dei Gelsi '05, savoury and full of citrus, showed well too. For sweet wines, there's the impressive new Passirò '04, from dried and partially botrytized roscetto, which is creamy and full of candied fruits; and the fast-improving Pomele '05, from aleatico. It's quite a line-up.

● Marciliano '04	🍷🍷🍷	6
○ Ferentano '04	🍷🍷	4*
● Montiano '04	🍷🍷	6
○ Passirò '04	🍷🍷	5*
● Tellus '05	🍷🍷	4*
● Pesano '05	🍷🍷	4
● Vitiano '05	🍷🍷	3*
○ Poggio dei Gelsi '05	🍷	3
● Pomele '05	🍷	5
⊙ Vitiano Rosato '05	🍷	2*
● Montiano '00	YYY	6
● Montiano '01	YYY	6
● Montiano '03	YYY	6

POGGIO MIRTETO (RI)

Tenuta Santa Lucia

loc. Santa Lucia
02047 Poggio Mirteto (RI)
tel. 076524616 - 3482644439
www.tenutasantalucia.com

Last year, this estate appeared as a promising newcomer. Now, we're pleased to see that it's fulfilling its promise for Mario and Gabriella Colantuono have produced a range of wines of elegance and character. They started growing grapes in 1979 but things took off 17 years later, first with new plantings then with a modern, welcoming vinification cellar, which was inaugurated in 2005. They now have around 40 hectares, producing 100,000 bottles, and are closely followed by two top-notch oenologists, Franco and Marco Bernabei. First up is Elodia '04 made from equal parts of falanghina, sauvignon and barrique-fermented malvasia puntinata. The nose is stylish with ripe white peach and spring and summer flowers, and the pervasive palate has depth, harmony and length. Collis Pollionis Bianco '05 comes from the same grapes but the blend contains a far greater proportion of malvasia. It is less incisive but still distinctive, showing more perfume but a touch of pungency. Its red partner is from sangiovese and montepulciano with a little merlot and has more lift to its personality. There is overt, pervasive fruit and refined spiciness. The palate is impressively individual with roundness and a harmonious expansiveness leading to a pleasingly intense finish. Otio '04 is from montepulciano, cabernet sauvignon and merlot which are vinified separately and aged in barrique for up to six months. It's a zesty, balanced wine with morello cherry and liquorice aromas and a slim-bodied, dynamic palate of good tannic weave.

○ Elodia '04	🍷🍷	5
● Colli della Sabina Collis Pollionis Rosso '05	🍷🍷	4*
● Otio '04	🍷	5
○ Colli della Sabina Collis Pollionis Bianco '05	🍷	4

SPIGNO SATURNIA (LT)

TERRA DELLE GINESTRE
LOC. CAMPOLUNGO
VIA FORNELLO, 94
04020 SPIGNO SATURNIA (LT)
TEL. 0771700297
http://member.xoom.it/ginestravini

Eight years ago, a group of wine lovers decided to take a punt at making wine almost for fun. But gradually, the venture turned into a far more serious, full-time activity, involving an oenologist, Maurizio De Simone, and a consultant, Roberto Cipresso. At the moment, whites lead the field, mostly because of the use of indigenous varieties and well thought-out vinification techniques. Lentisco '04, for instance, comes from 100 per cent bellone which is fermented in 300-litre chestnut casks and remains on its lees for about six months. The result is an intense, floral, slightly nutty nose and an enjoyably savoury palate. There are three versions of Moscato di Terracina, Invito '05, Stellaria '05 and Promessa '04, all from the top vineyard area of Vallemarina. Invito is vinified traditionally to bring out the variety's typical perfume and florality, its balanced palate and its slightly tart finish. Stellaria undergoes barrique ageing and the results are interesting but still need tweaking. The nose is so intense as to seem forced and the palate's alcohol and acid backbone are not yet in balance. Promessa is quite different, coming from grapes that are left to dry until November. Fermentation is in barrique and the wine remains in contact with its lees for a year. Orange blossom and honey make for a fine nose but we'd have preferred greater freshness on the palate to counterbalance the notable sweetness. Il Generale '03, from metolano, primitivo and aglianico, brings the range to a close with clean, balsamic oakiness that tends slightly to outweigh the fruit.

○	Lentisco '04	🍷🍷	3*
○	Invito '05	🍷🍷	2*
●	Il Generale '03	🍷	4
○	Promessa Passito Dolce '04	🍷	4
○	Stellaria '05	🍷	4

TERRACINA (LT)

SANT'ANDREA
LOC. BORGO VODICE
VIA RENIBBIO, 1720
04010 TERRACINA (LT)
TEL. 0773755028
www.cantinasantandrea.it

Last year, Sant'Andrea sent its first wine – the white Dune – to the finals. This time there were two finalists, one red and one a dried-grape passito. The obvious conclusion is that quality is high across the board and Gabriele Pandolfo and his son Andrea should be very proud of their range. Let's start with Circeo Il Sogno '03, from barrique-aged merlot and cesanese. An intense nose ranges from forest fruits to bell pepper with a hint of vanilla. There is still marked tannin on the palate but it shows ripe with no harshness. The winery helped Moscato di Terracina become DOC, which it did in 2006, and Capitolium Passito '04 shows exactly why the denomination is justified. There's peach and apricot, it's sweet without cloying and candied orange peel enlivens the finish. Oppidum Secco '05 is the more interesting of the other two Moscato di Terracinas, showing personality in a nose of tropical fruit, sweet tobacco and even honey, and a lively, zesty palate. The third, Templum Amabile '05, has the variety's typical perfume but is better on the nicely balanced palate. The '04 Circeo Dune again showed excellently. The oak is not excessive, there is aroma from the malvasia puntinata in the blend and an alluring huskiness to the palate from the trebbiano. The two '05 Circeo Riflessi wines are also attractive. The white is cohesive, even and easy drinking while the red, made solely from merlot, is beautifully clean. Finally comes Circeo Preludio alla Notte '04, from merlot with 15 per cent sangiovese, which has red berry fruit and rhubarb, and a slightly bitterish finish.

●	Circeo Rosso Il Sogno '03	🍷🍷	4*
○	Moscato di Terracina Passito Capitolium '04	🍷🍷	3*
○	Circeo Bianco Dune '04	🍷🍷	4
○	Moscato di Terracina Secco Oppidum '05	🍷🍷	3*
●	Circeo Rosso Preludio alla Notte '04	🍷	3
○	Circeo Bianco Riflessi '05	🍷	2*
●	Circeo Rosso Riflessi '05	🍷	2*
○	Moscato di Terracina Amabile Templum '05	🍷	3
○	Circeo Bianco Dune '03	YY	4*
○	Moscato di Terracina Secco Oppidum '04	YY	3*

OTHER WINERIES

Donnardea

Loc. Santa Palomba
via Fosso di Valle Caia, 7
00040 Ardea (RM)
tel. 069115435 - www.donnardea.it

This is a fine start in the Guide for a much-visited 80-hectare winery lying south of Rome. Best of the wines tasted was a classy, long Syrah '04, which has pervasive tobacco and rhubarb aromas. Lazio Rosso and the pleasant Rosato showed well. Colli Albani Sup. Bianco has an elegant nose.

● Donnardea Syrah '04	🍷🍷	4*
● Donnardea Rosso '04	🍷	3
○ Colli Albani Sup. Donnardea '05	🍷	3
⊙ Donnardea Rosato '05	🍷	3

Fontana di Papa

via Nettunense, km 10,800
00040 Ariccia (RM)
tel. 06934781
www.fontanadipapa.it

Founded half a century ago, this Castelli Romani winery is now in the Guide. Fontana di Papa groups 400 small and medium-sized growers with 700 hectares. Best of the wines is a distinctive, white Colli Albani Poggio del Cardinale '05 of good fragrance and harmony. Calathus '05 is firm and clean-cut.

○ Colli Albani Poggio del Cardinale Sup. '05	🍷	3
● Calathus '05		3

Giovanni Palombo

Loc. Ponte Melfa
c.so Munanzio Planco
03042 Atina (FR)
tel. 0776610200

Giovanni's son Stefano now runs the estate. He starts well with the cabernet-only Duca Cantelmi '03, a stylish, powerful wine with enough stuffing for long ageing. Its only good partner this year is the pleasant, uncomplicated, easy-drinking Malvasia del Lazio, Bianco delle Chiaie '05.

● Atina Cabernet Duca Cantelmi Ris. '03	🍷🍷	6
○ Bianco delle Chiaie '05	🍷	3

Mazziotti

Loc. Melona Bonvino
via Cassia, km 110
01023 Bolsena (VT)
tel. 0644291377

This wasn't a great year for Valeria Mazziotti. The classic Est Est Est '05 has appealing freshness underlying intense fragrance. Canuleio '05, from chardonnay, sauvignon and malvasia, is complex and pervasive. Volgente '04, an astute blend of merlot, cabernet and sangiovese, is well styled.

● Volgente Rosso '04	🍷	4
○ Canuleio '05	🍷	3
○ Est Est Est di Montefiascone '05	🍷	3
● Volgente Rosso '02	ΥΥ	5

VILLA PURI
LOC. VILLA PURI
01023 BOLSENA (VT)
TEL. 0761799190

We're pleased to see Vittorio Puri and his wines back in the Guide after a long absence. Est Est Est '04 has hints of ripe, warm fruit, the fragrance of spring flowers and minerality. Moscatello '04 and the sweetish red Cannaiola '04 are both good choices for a chat with friends.

○ Est Est Est di Montefiascone Scelta Vendemmiale '04	🍷🍷	3*
● C. E. V. Cannaiola '04	🍷	3
○ C. E. V. Moscatello '04	🍷	3

CASALE DEI CENTO CORVI
VIA AURELIA KM 45,500
00052 CERVETERI (RM)
TEL. 069903902
www.casalecentocorvi.com

We hope Cento Corvi's drop to a short profile will soon be reversed. The '04 of the unusual red Giacché has some complexity. Kottabos Rosso '04, from merlot and sangiovese, has complexity and a good weave. The '05 Bianco, from chardonnay with ten per cent trebbiano, is floral and well-structured.

● Giacché '04	🍷	8
○ Kottabos Bianco '04	🍷	4
● Kottabos Rosso '04	🍷	4
● Giacché '03	🍷🍷 (white)	8

CANTINA CERVETERI
VIA AURELIA, KM 42,700
00052 CERVETERI (RM)
TEL. 06994441
www.cantinacerveteri.it

Only inconsistent quality caused the Cerveteri co-operative to drop to this section. Malvasia Novae '05 is pleasant, fresh and lightly aromatic. Cerveteri Rosso Viniae Grande '04, from cabernet, montepulciano and merlot, is full. Tertium '04, from montepulciano and sangiovese, is well made.

● Cerveteri Rosso Viniae Grande '04	🍷	4
● Tertium '04	🍷	4
○ Novae '05	🍷	3
● Tertium '99	🍷🍷 (white)	4

IL QUADRIFOGLIO
LOC. DOGANELLA DI NINFA
VIA ALESSANDRO III, 5
04012 CISTERNA DI LATINA (LT)
TEL. 069601530

The De Gregorio siblings' top wine Ottavione is still ageing but both Muro Pecoraro '05, from cabernet and montepulciano, and the syrah and merlot Perazzeto '05 are excellent, showing clean, long and with ripe tannins. Chardonnay Pezze di Ninfa has hawthorn and yellow-fleshed fruit.

● Muro Pecoraro '05	🍷🍷	4*
● Perazzeto '05	🍷🍷	3*
○ Pezze di Ninfa '05	🍷	3

PIETRA PINTA
S.P. PASTINE KM. 20.300
04010 CORI (LT)
TEL. 069678001
www.pietrapinta.it

The Ferretti siblings are quality pioneers in Cori and the wines have returned to good levels this year. Colle Amato '03 has a nice oak-fruit balance. Chardonnay '05 is lively. Shiraz '03, all red berry fruit, and Falanghina '05, still a touch shaky but promising well long term, scored similarly.

● Colle Amato '03	🍷	5
● Shiraz '03	🍷	4
○ Chardonnay '05	🍷	4
○ Falanghina '05	🍷	4

CASALE MARCHESE
VIA DI VERMICINO, 68
00044 FRASCATI (RM)
TEL. 069408932
www.casalemarchese.it

The new Carletti cellar and guest areas are ready. Clemens, from chardonnay and malvasia puntinata, has flesh, fragrance, grapefruit and spring flowers while the cesanese and cabernet sauvignon Novum has good grip. Both are new. The Rosso is sound. Marchese dei Cavalieri is nice but a touch simple.

○ Clemens '05	🍷🍷	5
● Marchese dei Cavalieri '03	🍷	5
● Novum '05	🍷	4
● Rosso di Casale Marchese '05	🍷	4

L'OLIVELLA
VIA DI COLLE PISANO, 5
00044 FRASCATI (RM)
TEL. 069424527
www.racemo.it

Once more, Racemo Rosso is this organic estate's best wine. The difficult '02 vintage has toned down its fruit and spice without removing warmth and density from the palate. Tre Gomme has great typicity, as does the passito version. The soft, citrus-like monovarietal Bombino is again intriguing.

● Racemo Rosso '02	🍷🍷	4
○ Passito Tre Grome '02	🍷	6
○ Bombino '05	🍷	4
○ Tre Grome '05	🍷	5

CANTINE SAN MARCO
LOC. VERMICINO
VIA DI MOLA CAVONA, 26/28
00044 FRASCATI (RM)
TEL. 069409403 - 069422689

This major winery is always trying out new ideas while keeping close ties with its territory. The new, well-made cesanese One '04 has plenty on the nose. Meraco Rosso is mouthfilling and more mature. The tangy, mineral Solomalvasia and bright Frascati Meraco with white-fleshed fruit lead the whites.

● Meraco Rosso '02	🍷	4
● One '04	🍷	4
○ Frascati Sup. Meraco '05	🍷	4
○ Solomalvasia '05	🍷	4

CASALE VALLECHIESA
VIA PIETRA PORZIA, 19/23
00044 FRASCATI (RM)
TEL. 069417270
www.casalevallechiesa.it

Wines from this admirable Castelli Romani winery are reliable and good value for money. The reds are characterful. Cesanese is well-defined, with pleasing ripe cherry and coffee notes. Syrah is lean, broad and long. Merlot is soft with a tight finish. Frascati Le Rubbie is gently fragrant.

● Cesanese '03	🍷	4
● Merlot '03	🍷	4
● Syrah '03	🍷	4
○ Frascati Sup. Le Rubbie '05	🍷	1*

CAMPONESCHI
VIA PIASTRARELLE, 14
00040 LANUVIO (RM)
TEL. 069374390
www.collilanuvini.it

The Camponeschi family are leaders in this small but worthy DOC, assuring typicity and consistent quality. They again have two pleasing whites. Malvasia '05 is open and soft with delicate aromas and Colli Lanuvini '05 is piercing and subtly floral on the nose, savoury and mineral on the palate.

○ Colli Lanuvini Sup. '05	🍷	4
○ Malvasia '05	🍷	4

GOTTO D'ORO
LOC. FRATTOCCHIE
VIA DEL DIVINO AMORE, 115
00040 MARINO (RM)
TEL. 0693022211 - www.gottodoro.it

With a potential 8,000,000 bottle output, there is something of note every year at this winery. This time, it's the crisp, deeply fruity Marino, the open, attractive, firm-finishing Castelli Romani Rosso, and the intriguing, savoury, clean-cut Mithra, from sangiovese, merlot and syrah.

● Castelli Romani Rosso '05	🍷	2*
○ Marino Sup. '05	🍷	2*
● Mitreo Mithra '05	🍷	4

CANTINA CERQUETTA
VIA DI FONTANA CANDIDA, 20
00040 MONTE PORZIO CATONE (RM)
TEL. 069424147
www.cantinacerquetta.it

The Ciuffa family's dynamic winery, now with a stylish sales and visitor area, is making headway. Fulgor from cesanese is crisp and firm. Grotta del Cenacolo is softer and more intriguing. The coherent Frascati Superiore is well typed and Cannellino also has an attractively pervasive nose.

● Fulgor '04	🍷	3
● Grotta del Cenacolo '04	🍷	4
○ Frascati Cannellino '05	🍷	4
○ Frascati Sup. '05	🍷	3

CASALE MATTIA
LOC. COLLE MATTIA
VIA MONTE MELLONE, 19
00040 MONTECOMPATRI (RM)
TEL. 069426249 - www.casalemattia.it

Roberto Rotelli's wines are stylish. Merlot Terre Laviche '05, deep and rich, with coffee and morello cherry, tops the range, followed by a fruity, acidulous Costamagna. Frascati Superiore is fresh and attractive while fruit zest and breadth are in greater harmony on the Terre Laviche selection.

● Merlot Terre Laviche '05	🍷🍷	4*
○ Frascati Sup. '05	🍷	3
○ Frascati Sup. Terre Laviche '05	🍷	4
● Merlot Costamagna '05	🍷	4

ANTICA CANTINA LEONARDI
VIA DEL PINO, 12
01027 MONTEFIASCONE (VT)
TEL. 0761826028
www.cantinaleonardi.it

This winery performed well. Est Est Est Poggio del Cardinale '05 has verve and fragrance in its aromatics. Pensiero '05, from 100 per cent grechetto, is floral, supple and easy drinking. But the merlot and cabernet '04 Don Carlo is a little under par, with less elegance than usual.

● Don Carlo '04	🍷	4
○ Est Est Est di Montefiascone Poggio del Cardinale '05	🍷	3
○ Pensiero '05	🍷	3
● Don Carlo '03	ΥΥ	4

TENUTA RONCI DI NEPI
LOC. VALLE RONCI
01036 NEPI (VT)
TEL. 0761555125
www.roncidinepi.com

After a great first showing last time, this year's wines are in lower key. We preferred Oro di Corte '05 of the two Chardonnays, the lack of oak allowing its cleanliness and fruit quality to come through. On Vigna Manti '05 the oak tends to dominate the nose, although the palate has fair balance.

○ Oro di Corte '05	🍷	4
○ Vigna Manti '05	🍷	5
● Veste Porpora '03	ΥΥ	4
○ Vigna Manti '04	ΥΥ	6

CANTINE CIOLLI
VIA DEL CORSO
00035 OLEVANO ROMANO (RM)
TEL. 069564547

Olevano's repute as a wine zone comes from dynamic, spunky producer Damiano Ciolli. He makes less than 15,000 bottles, a third of them the powerful, elegant selection Cirsium '04. Silene '04 is in more traditional style, with good varietal aromas and a close-knit, firm structure.

● Cesanese di Olevano Cirsium '04	🍷🍷	5
● Cesanese di Olevano Silene '04	🍷	4
● Cesanese di Olevano Cirsium '01	ΥΥ	6
● Cesanese di Olevano Cirsium '03	ΥΥ	5

RISERVA DELLA CASCINA
LOC. FIORANO
VIA APPIA ANTICA
00043 ROMA
TEL. 067917221 - 3393759069

Disruptive cellar works have not dimmed the Brannetti couple's enthusiasm and the quality of their wines remains good. Marino is again very well typed although less assertive than usual. Castelli Romani Rosso, from cabernet and sangiovese, has more appeal, with plentiful aroma and a sound balance.

● Castelli Romani Rosso '05	🍷🍷	3*
○ Marino Sup. '05	🍷	2*

CHRISTINE VASELLI
P.ZZA DEL PARLAMENTO, 14
00186 ROMA
TEL. 0668805128
www.christinevaselli.it

Christine Vaselli keeps her eye on the ball and it shows. Le Poggere, from barrique-aged cabernet sauvignon and merlot, never fails. The '04 is robust yet elegant. Appunto '05, from canaiolo and ciliegiolo, is fairly complex and the malvasia and bombino Accenno '05 is floral and delicately fruity.

● Le Poggere '04	🍷🍷	6
○ Accenno '05	🍷	3
● Appunto '05	🍷	4
● Le Poggere '01	ΥΥ	5

Conte Zandotti

via Vigne Colle Mattia, 8
00132 Roma
tel. 0620609000 - 066160335
www.cantinecontezandotti.it

Despite vines of great potential, we're still waiting for a well-typed Frascati from Zandotti that enthrals. But La Petrosa '02, from sangiovese, cabernet and ottonese nero, has character and balance, and Malvasia Rumon is delicately fruity and typically almondy.

●	La Petrosa '02	▼	5
○	Malvasia del Lazio Rumon '05	▼	4

Villa Gianna

loc. B.go San Donato
s.da Maremmana
04010 Sabaudia (LT)
tel. 077350757 - www.villagianna.it

The Gianni family's wines are again good. Vigne del Borgo Cabernet Sauvignon '04 is all spice, juniper berries and rhubarb. Barriano '03 is an attractive blend of merlot, cabernet sauvignon and montepulciano. Circeo Bianco '05 is fragrant. Vigne del Borgo Sauvignon '05 is varietal and intense.

○	Vigne del Borgo Cabernet Sauvignon '04	▼▼	4
●	Barriano '03	▼	4
○	Circeo Bianco '05	▼	2*
○	Vigne del Borgo Sauvignon '05	▼	3

Puri Charlotte

via Cassia, Km 119,7
01020 San Lorenzo Nuovo (VT)
tel. 0763727160 - 0763727632

Overall, Charlotte Puri's range is sound. Calenne '05, from trebbiano with some chardonnay, sauvignon and roscetto, is full of fruit and supported by lively piquancy. But the sangiovese, montepulciano and merlot '04 Montemoro, medium bodied and with red berries and balsam, is a touch under par.

●	Montemoro '04	▼	4
○	Calenne '05	▼	3
●	Montemoro '03	▽▽	5

Giovanni Terenzi

loc. La Forma
via Prenestina, 140
03010 Serrone (FR)
tel. 0775594286 - 0775595466

There have been a few wobbles here but nothing major. The '05 Cesanese Velobra maintains firm, cohesive style. The '04 Cesanese Colle Forma is a touch under par with attractive red berry fruit but a bit of rusticity. Villa Santa '05, from passerina del frusinate, is fresh, fruity and well made.

●	Cesanese del Piglio Colle Forma '04	▼	5
●	Cesanese del Piglio Velobra '05	▼	3
○	Passerina Villa Santa '05	▼	3
●	Cesanese del Piglio Velobra '04	▽▽	3*

Sant'Isidoro

loc. Portaccia
01016 Tarquinia (VT)
tel. 0766869716 - 3478817545
www.santisidoro.net

With the '04, the muscular, montepulciano-based Soremidio is back, full of pervasive spice and roasted coffee beans aromas. Corithus '05, from sangiovese, montepulciano and merlot, is sound but a touch heavy in the mouth. Chardonnay Forca di Palma '05, aromatic and with backbone, showed better.

●	Soremidio '04	▼▼	5
●	Corithus '05	▼	4
○	Forca di Palma '05	▼	3
●	Soremidio '02	▽▽	5

Colle di Maggio

via Passo dei Coresi, 25
00049 Velletri (RM)
tel. 0696453072 - 3489126114
www.colledimaggio.com

Management and style have changed for the good. Porticato Bianco is back on form, showing characterful, full of tropical fruit and densely structured. From the reds, Tulino Syrah is soft, Porticato Rosso is easily approachable and Cesare Ottaviano Augusto, from syrah and merlot, is spicy and oaky.

○	Porticato Bianco '05	▼▼	4
●	Cesare Ottaviano Augusto '04	▼	6
●	Porticato Rosso '04	▼	4
●	Tulino Syrah '04	▼	4

ABRUZZO

As we were tasting the wines of Abruzzo this year, we gradually began to realize that something had changed. We had never before been confronted with such a large group of high-quality wines from this region. The fact that we were dealing with vintages that were admittedly superior did not go far enough to explain the phenomenon, since the wines we were sampling ranged from 2000 to 2005, and not all of these vintages offered identical levels of quality. What is changing in Abruzzo has more to do with a new awareness on the part of many producers and their belief that Abruzzo can take advantage of its traditional varieties, trebbiano and montepulciano, to make wines that impress both for their inherent quality and for the value for money that they offer. We could not help remembering the words of Edoardo Valentini, who had for decades served effectively as the mentor for Abruzzo winemaking and who unfortunately passed away in April 2006. Valentini would always remind us that it was not he who was making the wines: it was Abruzzo itself that was crafting them into their final form. His words served to remind producers that with closer attention, and with a bit more ability and experience, truly wonderful wines would flow from this region, which is precisely what is beginning to happen. Because alongside the wines of Edoardo and Francesco Valentini, and of Gianni and Marina Masciarelli, so different but equally remarkable, we now are witnessing the grand entrance onto the stage of the reds of Luigi Cataldi Madonna, who is finally achieving results worthy of this long-respected name in Abruzzo viticulture. And we can add the continued validation of another highly respected producer, Dino Illuminati. The list continues, with the success of two younger lions, Federica Morricone and Leonardo Pizzolo, of Villa Medoro and Valle Reale respectively. This is fitting since in this edition we have nominated Morricone the Up-and-Coming Winery of the Year. Abruzzo also racked up a total of nine Three Glass awards, more than in any of our previous nineteen editions. And this is far from being the end of the line for many more awards will come in future editions. Abruzzo boasts a fabric of producers that has few equals in other regions of Italy, comprising wineries such as the tiny Le Querce, Valori, Monti, Nicodemi and Centorame, all of them in the new Colline Teramane DOCG, as well as Zaccagnini, Pasetti, Filomusi Guelfi and the larger producers such as Farnese, not to mention co-operatives like Tollo, Frentana and Citra. Abruzzo can also point to an extensive presence in the market at all levels, from the most standard offerings all the way up to the stars. Nor should it be forgotten, although few realize it, that Abruzzo turns out almost 4,000,000 hectolitres of wine each year, more or less the same as Chile.

ATESSA (CH)

Terra d'Aligi
Loc. Piazzano
via Piana La Fara, 90
66041 Atessa (CH)
tel. 0872897916
www.terradaligi.it

In an area that has not hitherto witnessed premium-quality viticulture, the Strappelli brothers are offering proof that there is some fascinating potential. Terra d'Aligi has restructured its vineyards, amounting to some 60 hectares sited on various slopes of the Monti dei Frentani foothills southeast of Chieti. The vines yield an impressive portfolio of wines that are pleasurable, well made and even formidable even at times, all with the invaluable assistance of oenologist Riccardo Brighigna. Let's begin with the impressive Montepulciano Tolos '03, which this year went to our national finals thanks to vibrant tonality, solid, complex varietal aromas and an expansive palate that is just tannic to taste and unmarred by too much barrique. We also liked the more straightforward Montepulciano '04, which serves up traditional varietal fruit with no pretensions and unveils progression that may not be huge but does demonstrate some real finesse. Montepulciano Tatone '03 bears the local dialect name for grandfather. It's a red that shows some maturity, with slightly overripe fruit in the mouth and tannins that are a shade too bitter. From the whites, Trebbiano '05 stands out for its notable savouriness on the palate, although this is muffled somewhat by still obstreperous new oak. Terra d'Aligi is worth watching as a winery that is carving out for itself a niche of some importance in the dynamic world of Abruzzo winemaking.

●	Montepulciano d'Abruzzo Tolos '03	▼▼	5
●	Montepulciano d'Abruzzo '04	▼▼	3*
●	Montepulciano d'Abruzzo Tatone '03	▼	4
○	Trebbiano d'Abruzzo Terra d'Aligi '05	▼	2
●	Montepulciano d'Abruzzo Tolos '01	▽▽	5
●	Montepulciano d'Abruzzo Tatone '00	▽▽	4
●	Montepulciano d'Abruzzo Tolos '00	▽▽	5
●	Montepulciano d'Abruzzo Tatone '01	▽▽	4
●	Montepulciano d'Abruzzo Tolos '02	▽▽	4

ATRI (TE)

Centorame
Loc. Casoli di Atri
via delle Fornaci, 15
64030 Atri (TE)
tel. 0858709115
www.centorame.it

In just a handful of years, Centorame has emerged as one of the benchmarks in the Abruzzo wine world. Since construction of the new cellar in 2002, an impressive amount of ground has been covered. With the passionate commitment of a young enthusiast, Lamberto Vannucci has grasped the reins of this delightful small family winery and has put in a new vineyard, refitted the cellar and brought in new casks, both large and small, following a carefully devised plan. With the assistance of oenologist Loriano di Sabatino, he has introduced a series of wines that demonstrate his love for the beautiful area of Atri. Impressive results did not take long to emerge. Already at our tastings last year, we were struck by the wines' eloquent expression of their terroir, by the thankfully judicious use of oak and by the overall quality of the fruit they displayed. This year opened our eyes even wider, so much so that two of the wines actually went to our national finals, Montepulciano Colline Teramane '04 and Trebbiano '04, both from the Castellum Vetus line and both imposing, masterfully crafted contributions. Even the less complex San Michele line boasts wines that are sound, exhibit enviable typicity and are absolutely delicious. Enthusiastic plaudits to Vannucci for the uncompromising, passionate work that has brought him these achievements and that will bring us more delights over the years to come.

●	Montepulciano d'Abruzzo Colline Teramane Castellum Vetus '04	▼▼	5
○	Trebbiano d'Abruzzo Castellum Vetus '04	▼▼	4
●	Montepulciano d'Abruzzo San Michele '04	▼▼	3*
○	Trebbiano d'Abruzzo San Michele '05	▼	3
●	Montepulciano d'Abruzzo Colline Teramane Castellum Vetus '03	▽▽	5
●	Montepulciano d'Abruzzo San Michele '03	▽▽	5

ATRI (TE)

Villa Medoro
fraz. Fontanelle
64030 Atri (TE)
tel. 0858708142
www.villamedoro.it

Villa Medoro has been steadily growing in stature as a producer in the Colline Teramane denomination. This year, the winery made a grand entrance into the nobility of Abruzzo winemaking with one bottle that captured our Three Glass award and a second that went through to the national finals. The trophy winner was Adrano '04, an elegant, captivating Montepulciano that bespeaks splendid fruit and a fine hand with the oak. Closely following it was the second Montepulciano, Rosso del Duca '04, a finalist for its ultra-savoury fruit and the elegant typicity of its aromas. In the very few years it has been active, Villa Medoro has achieved great things, evidence that when passion and dedication are in play, the sky is the limit. The passion and dedication here belong to Federica Morricone, the young dynamo who manages this operation and one of the youngest women professionals in Italian winemaking. In another age, she would be described as having quicksilver in her veins, so active is she in her work and love for her wines. Federica has some 60 hectares in the Atri area, rigorous discipline in vineyard practices, meticulous attention in the cellar, the crucial assistance of a prestigious consultant in Riccardo Cotarella and the contagious passion of the winery owner as well as of the entire staff, ably led by cellarmaster Casto. With all this behind her, it is no wonder that Federica's reds are so impressive for their elegance, typicity and harmony. We thought these were well-founded reasons to assign to Villa Medoro our award as Up-and-Coming Winery of the Year.

●	Montepulciano d'Abruzzo Colline Teramane Adrano '04	🍷🍷🍷	6
●	Montepulciano d'Abruzzo Rosso del Duca '04	🍷🍷	4*
○	Chimera Bianco '05	🍷	4
○	Trebbiano d'Abruzzo '05	🍷	3
●	Montepulciano d'Abruzzo Colline Teramane Adrano '03	YYY	6
●	Montepulciano d'Abruzzo Colline Teramane Adrano '01	YY	6
●	Montepulciano d'Abruzzo '03	YY	3*
●	Montepulciano d'Abruzzo Rosso del Duca '03	YY	4
●	Montepulciano d'Abruzzo Colline Teramane Adrano '98	YY	5

BOLOGNANO (PE)

Ciccio Zaccagnini
c.da Pozzo
65020 Bolognano (PE)
tel. 0858880195
www.zaccagninivini.it

Ciccio Zaccagnini's winery at Bolognano marches on like an irresistible phalanx, balancing high production against fine quality while almost instinctively hitting that perfect equilibrium between integrity of product and satisfaction of the market. Zaccagnini shows that in a region like Abruzzo, but certainly in others as well, such balancing acts are feasible, if only the will and hard work are there. Ciccio's wines represent almost a map of the entire area, and we are repeatedly struck by their high quality and integrity. Sadly, they stopped just shy of Three Glasses but San Clemente '04, an outstanding Montepulciano, is a perennial competitor in our final round. Its soundness and power have always impressed us and the only thing it lacks is perhaps a tad more time in the bottle. Montepulciano Tralcetto is produced in large quantities and at a truly affordable price. The '04 version has typicity, good varietal expression and delicious, succulent fruit. The internationally styled Trebbiano San Clemente '05 is worth noting for the elegance of its rich, fruited aromas. Ciccio Zaccagnini has every reason to be proud of these performances and we look forward to tasting many more fine wines in the years ahead.

●	Montepulciano d'Abruzzo S. Clemente '04	🍷🍷	6
●	Capsico Rosso '02	🍷🍷	5
●	Montepulciano d'Abruzzo Cuvée dell'Abate '04	🍷🍷	3*
●	Montepulciano d'Abruzzo Tralcetto '04	🍷🍷	3*
○	Plaisir Bianco '05	🍷🍷	4
○	Trebbiano d'Abruzzo S. Clemente '05	🍷🍷	5
⊙	Ibisco Rosa '05	🍷	3
●	Plaisir Rosso '05	🍷	4
●	Montepulciano d'Abruzzo Abbazia S. Clemente '02	YY	6
●	Montepulciano d'Abruzzo S. Clemente '03	YY	6
●	Capsico Rosso '01	YY	5

CASTILENTI (TE)

San Lorenzo

C.da Plavignano, 2
64035 Castilenti (TE)
tel. 0861999325
www.sanlorenzovini.com

San Lorenzo is a substantial operation in the Colline Teramane denomination, between Pescara and Teramo. With more than 150 hectares, the estate is serious in its efforts and obtains fine results. Gianluca Galasso complements his youthful enthusiasm with the shrewd assistance of Abruzzo oenologist Riccardo Brighigna to produce the series of ambitiously elegant offerings that we looked forward to this year. Escol Riserva '03 is in fact a fine Montepulciano, full-bodied and confident with generous, full-fruited fragrances and a palate of excellent typicity and breadth. We particularly liked the lively acidity that enlivens its dense texture. Complex, pungent balsam infuses Colline Teramane Oinos '03, while the concentrated, complex palate is just slightly blurred by bitterish tannins. Sirio '04 is a simple, clean Montepulciano that presents youthful, zesty and pleasurable. Moving on to the whites, we noted the exuberant acidity that marks Trebbiano Sirio '05, which shows satisfying varietal qualities and typicity. Bianco di Luce '04 is an imaginative 80-20 blend of trebbiano and montonico that flaunts generous aromas of spicy aniseed and toasty oak before developing crisp and sapid in the mouth. Pecorino '05 makes its San Lorenzo debut, another example of the widespread Abruzzo enthusiasm for this native variety. Simple it may be but it is so likeably fresh and easy drinking that it is hard to stop after just one glass. Summing up, San Lorenzo is a fine winery and already plays an important role but we feel that it has the potential to perform even better in the future.

●	Montepulciano d'Abruzzo Colline Teramane Escol Ris. '03	▼▼	5
●	Montepulciano d'Abruzzo Colline Teramane Oinos '03	▼	5
○	Bianco Luce '04	▼	5
●	Montepulciano d'Abruzzo Sirio '04	▼	2
○	Chardonnay Chioma di Berenice '05	▼	4
○	Il Pecorino '05	▼	4
○	Trebbiano d'Abruzzo Sirio '05	▼	2*
●	Montepulciano d'Abruzzo Colline Teramane '03	▽▽	5
●	Montepulciano d'Abruzzo Colline Teramane Escol Ris. '01	▽▽	6
●	Montepulciano d'Abruzzo Colline Teramane Escol Ris. '02	▽▽	5

CONTROGUERRA (TE)

Dino Illuminati

C.da San Biagio, 18
64010 Controguerra (TE)
tel. 0861808008
www.illuminativini.it

Illuminati enjoys a solid reputation in Abruzzo and has long been synonymous here and farther afield with quality and typicity. The winery has put in long years of dedicated effort to the development and promotion of the Teramo area, with an unshakeable belief in its potential and in its unique qualities. Illuminati helped draw up, and sponsored, the Colline Teramane DOCG, pressing hard for its approval. This wonderful Controguerra operation offered us a line-up of wines that again impressed our tasters. Leading the field was a superb performance from the wonderful Zanna Montepulciano Colline Teramane Riserva '01. An easy Three Glasses went to this offering characterized by acidic grip, transparent typicity and a traditional style that should serve as a model. Lumen '03 is another true thoroughbred that went through to our national finals for its appealing, complex fruit but it is perhaps just a tad too dense. We very much appreciated Montepulciano Riparosso '05 for its crisp, refreshing drinkability, quite remarkable for a standard version at such a reasonable price. Among the whites, we would point out Controguerra Costalupo '05. Simple, clean and uncomplicated add up to a wine that is far from banal for this is a pleasurable, distinctive effort. The more challenging Daniele '04, on the other hand, is too encumbered by its weight of oak. Finally, Metodo Classico Brut, practically the only sparkler in the region, is a talented entertainer, showing delicious and savoury.

●	Montepulciano d'Abruzzo Colline Teramane Zanna Ris. '01	▼▼▼	5
●	Controguerra Rosso Lumen '03	▼▼	6
○	Illuminati Brut '03	▼	5
○	Controguerra Bianco Daniele '04	▼	5
○	Controguerra Bianco Ciafré '05	▼	4
○	Controguerra Bianco Costalupo '05	▼	2
●	Montepulciano d'Abruzzo Riparosso '05	▼	3*
○	Brut M. Cl.	▼	5
●	Controguerra Rosso Lumen '97	▽▽▽	6
●	Controguerra Rosso Lumen '00	▽▽	8
●	Controguerra Rosso Lumen '01	▽▽	6
●	Montepulciano d'Abruzzo Riparosso '04	▽▽	3*

CONTROGUERRA (TE)

Antonio e Elio Monti
via Pignotto, 62
64010 Controguerra (TE)
tel. 086189042
www.vinimonti.it

The Antonio e Elio Monti winery is located on one of the most sun-blest and viticulturally suited of Controguerra's hills. This historic Abruzzo wine enterprise is going through some heady times with the arrival of a new generation in the winery and the crucial influence of consultant Riccardo Cotarella. The 13 hectares of estate vineyards produce a wide range of wines that vary in category and price, with a preference for reds "with plenty of thrust". We were not able to taste the steel-fermented Senior, a Monti favourite, which was so impressive last year that it competed in our finals. But Pignotto Riserva '03 Montepulciano Colline Teramane went to the finals in its stead. Its modernist slant certainly relies on the barrique but we couldn't but be impressed by the impact of its fruit, its well-typed qualities and judicious level of oak, all of which exemplifies the maturity that the Monti operation has now attained. The "Superabruzzan" Rio Moro Riserva '04, an assemblage of merlot, cabernet and sangiovese, deserves separate comment. Matured in barriques, it is unabashedly and ambitiously international but, we would say, decidedly off the beaten path for its excessively soft sheen of oak. At the end of the day, Antonio e Elio Monti remains a fascinating winery for its intriguingly individual search for a balanced position between modernity and tradition.

●	Montepulciano d'Abruzzo Colline Teramane Pignotto Ris. '03	▼▼	5
●	Controguerra Rosso Rio Moro Ris. '04	▼	5
●	Montepulciano d'Abruzzo Senior '03	▽▽	4*
●	Montepulciano d'Abruzzo Pignotto '00	▽▽	5
●	Montepulciano d'Abruzzo Colline Teramane Pignotto '03	▽▽	6

CONTROGUERRA (TE)

Camillo Montori
loc. Piane Tronto
64010 Controguerra (TE)
tel. 0861809900
www.montorivini.it

Camillo Montori has been around so long in Abruzzo that he is a true senator of wine in the region. His lovely winery at Controguerra in the Teramo hills is ample evidence of his sure hand and commitment. Along with his friend and rival Dino Illuminati, Montori was a strong proponent of the Colline Teramane DOCG, convinced as he was of the unique qualities of this striking area. He then assumed the vice-presidency of the local Consorzio di Tutela and was generous with his time and energy on its behalf. Turning to the wines we tasted, we want to draw merited attention to his Montepulciano Colline Teramane Fonte Cupa '02, a thoroughbred in every sense. We were most impressed by a nose that releases aromas of considerable elegance and delicacy, as well as by its self-confident, spacious palate, which is perhaps a shade less complex this year than previous versions. From the whites, Trebbiano '05 comes across as crisp, refreshing and well delineated on the nose, with fine typicity. The palate, too, is savoury and nicely varietal, showing uncomplicated but with impressive breadth in the mouth. Pecorino '05 opens to tasty yeast and fresh bread but the zesty acidity typical of this native grape is here too emphatic.

●	Montepulciano d'Abruzzo Colline Teramane Fonte Cupa '02	▼▼	5
○	Trebbiano d'Abruzzo '05	▼▼	2*
○	Pecorino '05	▼	4
●	Controguerra Leneo Moro '00	▽▽	5
○	Controguerra Leneo d'Oro '00	▽▽	5
●	Montepulciano d'Abruzzo Colline Teramane Fonte Cupa '00	▽▽	5
●	Montepulciano d'Abruzzo Colline Teramane Fonte Cupa '01	▽▽	5
○	Trebbiano d'Abruzzo Fonte Cupa '02	▽▽	4*
○	Trebbiano d'Abruzzo '03	▽▽	3
○	Pecorino '04	▽▽	4

FOSSACESIA (CH)

Cantina Sangro
via per Santa Maria Imbaro, 1
66022 Fossacesia (CH)
tel. 087257412 - 087257723
www.cantinasangro.it

Cantina Sangro made its debut this year in the Guide and immediately earned a full profile. This feat is the result of the remarkable performance of its most ambitious Montepulciano, Terra Regia '03. This wine went through to our final tastings thanks to its well-defined, elegant aromas of roasted coffee and subtle smoke, and to a palate that steadily builds to impressive depth and breadth, all the while displaying rich fruit. This offering is convincing proof of the overall level of quality achieved by what is a venerable co-operative winery. The tiles that have built up this complex mosaic of quality include an able new oenologist, Goffredo Albanese. A zonation study has been launched in collaboration with the University of Ancona and the Institute of Oenology at Lana d'Adige to identify the best viticultural sites in the Sangro hill country. And 300 member growers contribute their dedicated labour. All this has led to the success of Cantina Sangro, which means not simply the performance of its blue-eyed boy, Terra Regia, but also of its simpler sibling, Colle Cesi '05. The latter is a traditional Montepulciano of considerable character with a dark, brooding nose and excellent progression and depth in the mouth. Pecorino Kaleo '05 is crisp and clean throughout, releasing appealing varietal fragrances and then a compelling, tasty progression. The bottom line is that in Cantina Sangro we have another co-operative that thanks to dedicated, continuous effort has courageously taken the path to better quality, and succeeded.

● Montepulciano d'Abruzzo Terra Regia '03	🍷🍷	4*
● Montepulciano d'Abruzzo Colle Cesi '05	🍷🍷	1*
○ Pecorino Kaleo '05	🍷	2
● Montepulciano d'Abruzzo Colle Cesi '03	ꝏ	1*

FRANCAVILLA AL MARE (CH)

Franco Pasetti
c.da Pretaro
via San Paolo, 21
66023 Francavilla al Mare (CH)
tel. 08561875
www.pasettivini.it

These are crucial years for Franco Pasetti's winery. They are years full of ceaseless labour and attention, of new wines and new sites, of steady growth that will, we are certain, bring remarkable results. Indeed, the first results are already coming through. Franco and Mimma Pasetti are a husband and wife team that does not begrudge the considerable efforts necessary to turn out a range of wines whose average quality delighted us at our tastings. The standard Montepulciano, the '04, seems simple when you look at its technical data but in the glass it reveals complexity and impressive distinctiveness. The youngster of the line-up, Harimann '01, is a Montepulciano with pretensions. The fruit was harvested daringly late and barrique conditioning was laid on with a trowel but the wine has emerged wondrously unscathed, showing generous and well balanced. Montepulciano Testarossa '02 is by now a favourite competitor and as good here as always. In fact, it even shows a bit more spirited and varietal. Turning to the whites, Pecorino '05 stands out from the many versions of this grape that today seems a fixture in Abruzzo and elsewhere. Its varietal crispness and bitter almonds are in bountiful evidence here, as is a zesty savouriness that energizes the entire palate. Cerasuolo is exactly what is should be: refreshing and delicious, with a lovely bitterish finish, for an elegant, country-style pleaser. Thus, the Pasettis' operation lacks just that final push, that last flick of the maestro's baton, which we are sure will come very soon. We wish them well.

● Montepulciano d'Abruzzo Harimann '01	🍷🍷	7
● Montepulciano d'Abruzzo Tenuta di Testarossa '02	🍷🍷	5
● Montepulciano d'Abruzzo Fattoria Pasetti '04	🍷🍷	4*
○ Pecorino Pasetti '05	🍷🍷	4
○ Tenuta di Testarossa Bianco '04	🍷	5
● Diecicoppe '05	🍷	4
⊙ Montepulciano d'Abruzzo Cerasuolo '05	🍷	3
○ Trebbiano d'Abruzzo Zarachè '05	🍷	4
● Montepulciano d'Abruzzo Harimann '00	ꝏ	7
● Montepulciano d'Abruzzo Tenuta di Testarossa '00	ꝏ	5
● Montepulciano d'Abruzzo Tenuta di Testarossa '01	ꝏ	5

LORETO APRUTINO (PE)

TORRE DEI BEATI

C.DA POGGIORAGONE, 56
65014 LORETO APRUTINO (PE)
TEL. 085 8289490 - 3333832344

Torre dei Beati, located in Loreto Aprutino, makes its first appearance in these pages and impresses from the off. Husband and wife team Adriana Galasso and Fausto Albanesi lavish passionate care on this fairly new winery, assisted by oenologist Giancarlo Soverchia. In the vineyards, their management is traditional and non-invasive to an extreme, even, but always inspired solely by love for their land and for traditional winemaking. This alchemy yields distinctive creations, uncompromising characterful wines that seem almost Burgundian in their individuality and stand apart from others in the region. Cocciapazza '03 is a challenging Montepulciano that easily secured a place in our national finals, thanks to its balsam-led, multi-faceted aromas and a supple palate that showcases rich, dark fruit. The less complicated Montepulciano '04 is still very impressive with a nose that lays out straightforward varietal fragrances, followed by balance and finesse in the mouth. Rosae '04 is an intriguing Cerasuolo and a bit of a one-off. Its sparkling tonality leads to a mineral-laced palate that serves up lean fruit pleasantly burred by fairish tannins. All in all, we recommend that you keep an eye on Torre dei Beati, since these solid performances portend an even brighter future.

● Montepulciano d'Abruzzo Cocciapazza '03	🍷🍷	5
● Montepulciano d'Abruzzo '04	🍷🍷	4*
⊙ Montepulciano d'Abruzzo Cerasuolo Rosae '05	🍷	3*

LORETO APRUTINO (PE)

★ VALENTINI

VIA DEL BAIO, 2
65014 LORETO APRUTINO (PE)
TEL. 0858291138

Over our 20 years of publishing this Guide, we have often had to mark sad events and to write of the passing of many winemakers who have themselves been the history of Italian wine. We never thought that we would be doing so for Edoardo Valentini, who left us in April 2006 at just 74 years of age, 52 of which he spent as grower. Valentini was a great maestro of the vineyard, besides being scrupulous, talented and committed in his work. He leaves a void in all of us but his son is carrying on his tradition. Francesco has worked the last 25 harvests alongside his father and has for some years now largely run the operation, so he won't be changing his father's philosophy. The wines from this famous and tradition-minded winery will continue as we've known them. Montepulciano d'Abruzzo, for instance, in an absolutely magisterial '01 version that does full honours to an impressive year. Here are all of the characteristics classic to this wine, plus even a shade more elegance. Sinew and cellarability are the hallmarks of Trebbiano '02, on the other hand. The 2002 growing season was rather cool and rainy, but it produced some fine white wines, and this is definitely one of them. Both of these wines betray slight, initial carbon dioxide, particularly if opened during the harvest season when the yeast-laden air affects the wine. Valentini referred to these slight refermentations as the "breathing" and the effects will clear up if the wine is allowed to air for a moment or if, as we advise, the bottle is consigned to the cellar for a good long while.

● Montepulciano d'Abruzzo '01	🍷🍷🍷	8
○ Trebbiano d'Abruzzo '02	🍷🍷🍷	7
● Montepulciano d'Abruzzo '00	🍷🍷🍷 (white)	8
○ Trebbiano d'Abruzzo '00	🍷🍷🍷 (white)	6
○ Trebbiano d'Abruzzo '01	🍷🍷🍷 (white)	6
● Montepulciano d'Abruzzo '77	🍷🍷🍷 (white)	6
● Montepulciano d'Abruzzo '85	🍷🍷🍷 (white)	6
● Montepulciano d'Abruzzo '88	🍷🍷🍷 (white)	6
● Montepulciano d'Abruzzo '90	🍷🍷🍷 (white)	6
○ Trebbiano d'Abruzzo '92	🍷🍷🍷 (white)	5
● Montepulciano d'Abruzzo '95	🍷🍷🍷 (white)	6
○ Trebbiano d'Abruzzo '95	🍷🍷🍷 (white)	5
● Montepulciano d'Abruzzo '97	🍷🍷🍷 (white)	7
○ Trebbiano d'Abruzzo '99	🍷🍷🍷 (white)	8

MORRO D'ORO (TE)

LA QUERCIA

C.DA COLLE CROCE
64020 MORRO D'ORO (TE)
TEL. 0858959110
www.vinilaquercia.it

La Quercia debuts in this Guide, meriting a full profile right away thanks to fine performances by its wines, particularly Colline Teramane Riserva '02, which went through to the national finals. This young operation, located at Morro d'Oro in the lovely hills inland from Roseto degli Abruzzi, is the love-child of three partners with experience in the regional wine world. Partner Antonio La Mona, the oenologist, consulted to some of the longest-established wineries in the area but he decided to devote all his time to this new adventure at La Quercia. The philosophy here embraces uncompromising practices in the vineyard, the use of large casks exclusively, traditional grape varieties and tons of passionate commitment. The results are elegant wines with eloquent typicity that impressed our tasters. Let's begin with Colline Teramane Riserva '02, a sturdy Montepulciano that has plenty of grace notes. It releases pungent spice essences and then builds a palate of extraordinary, solid fruit, showing varietal to a fault. Montepulciano '03 is straightforward and traditional, giving rich, textbook fruit on the nose while a crisp vein of acidity and crackling tannins make for a delicious, easy-drinking quaffer. Rich strawberry opens Cerasuolo '05, which then unfurls a marvellously fluid, nervy palate. Trebbiano '05 is uncomplicated and clean but has much to offer, with a generous, spacious palate loaded with crisp, dense fruit. We look forward to a bright future for La Quercia.

● Montepulciano d'Abruzzo Colline Teramane La Quercia Ris. '02	🍷🍷	5
● Montepulciano d'Abruzzo '03	🍷🍷	4*
⊙ Montepulciano d'Abruzzo Cerasuolo '05	🍷🍷	3*
○ Trebbiano d'Abruzzo '05	🍷	3

NOCCIANO (PE)

NESTORE BOSCO

C.DA CASALI, 147
65010 NOCCIANO (PE)
TEL. 085847345 - 085847139
www.nestorebosco.com

In Abruzzo, Nestore Bosco means history and specifically wine history going back to the late 19th century. This is a winery with a long, illustrious tradition, highly respected in other countries, and over the last few years it has seen a wealth of changes and new developments, thanks to the arrival of a new generation. Talented cousins Nestore and Stefania Bosco have thrown themselves with enthusiasm into managing the 60 hectares of estate vineyards lying in the pleasant hills of Nocciano upland from Pescara. Bosco is thus a winery with a double soul and twin styles. One side emphasizes the traditional and the typical, offering uncomplicated, country-style wines, but certainly not devoid of elegance. The other side is more modern and creative, bringing out ambitious, imaginative wines with trendy labels and fantasy names. Don Bosco '01 is quite impressive. It's a traditional-style Montepulciano matured in large casks that you appreciate for its sinewy, full body and appealing balsam scents. Every bit as impressive is Linfa '02, a "Superabruzzan" that flaunts elegant, delicate aromas, again scented with nicely pungent balsam, and develops excellent progression with a full, expansive palate. Pan '03's label signals that this will be a modern, daring effort but it doesn't quite make the grade, since both oak and alcohol are too abundant. All of the standard Nestore Bosco offerings are more than pleasurable, each showing sound typicity and hewing beautifully to local traditions.

● Montepulciano d'Abruzzo Don Bosco '01	🍷🍷	5
● Linfa '02	🍷🍷	4
● Montepulciano d'Abruzzo Pan '03	🍷	5
○ Trebbiano d'Abruzzo '05	🍷	3

NOTARESCO (TE)

BRUNO NICODEMI

C.DA VENIGLIO
64024 NOTARESCO (TE)
TEL. 085895493
www.nicodemi.com

A new generation of wine entrepreneurs characterized by passion, seriousness and commitment is emerging in the Abruzzo wine world. Some are founding new operations; others are bringing new life to long-established, influential wineries. Among the revivalists are Alessandro and Elena Nicodemi, who for awhile now have been managing their family's 30 hectares pouring in investments and passionate commitment. Surrounding themselves with talented collaborators, they are tirelessly blazing their own trail, firmly convinced of the qualities rooted in their lovely Notaresco area. And they have certainly divined correctly, judging from the wines they have brought forth and which we tasted this year. Montepulciano '04 is both thoroughly typical and pleasingly complex, showing full and concentrated in the mouth and displaying an overall refined rusticity that makes it an impressive offering. Clean, uncomplicated fragrances open Trebbiano '05 but it develops compelling, well-structured concentration in the mouth. Trebbiano Notàri '05 shows true elegance, with its lively savouriness complemented by judicious oak and a structure worthy of a great white wine. We had been looking forward eagerly to the ambitious Montepulciano Notàri '03 but it is still closed in and hobbled by tannins so predominant that they will remain untamed, we fear.

●	Montepulciano d'Abruzzo '04	🍷🍷	4*
○	Trebbiano d'Abruzzo '05	🍷🍷	3*
○	Trebbiano d'Abruzzo Notàri '05	🍷🍷	4
●	Montepulciano d'Abruzzo Colline Teramane Notari '03	🍷	5
●	Montepulciano d'Abruzzo Colline Teramane Ris. '00	YY	5
●	Montepulciano d'Abruzzo '01	YY	4
●	Montepulciano d'Abruzzo Colline Teramane Neromoro Ris. '02	YY	5
●	Montepulciano d'Abruzzo '03	YY	4*
○	Trebbiano d'Abruzzo Sel. '03	YY	4*

OFENA (AQ)

LUIGI CATALDI MADONNA

LOC. PIANO
67025 OFENA (AQ)
TEL. 0862954252

The Radetzsky March could be the sound track of this profile, since our "peasant philosopher" has achieved a memorable victory. Last year, he began his march with Three Glasses going to the superb Montepulciano Malandrino '03. Then he won our Rosé of the Year award for Cerasuolo Piè delle Vigne '04, a monument to Cerasuolo d'Abruzzo. The finale, for now, is Three Glasses for both the '04 edition of Montepulciano Malandrino and for the historic Montepulciano Tonì '03. It was a triumphal year, then, with a number of contributing factors. First, the magnificent and formidable Ofena territory, the "furnace of Abruzzo", whose mountains close it round and provide its dramatic diurnal temperature ranges. The winery itself boasts many years and generations, perfectly summed up in Cataldi Madonna himself, with his deep culture and fierce attachment to wine. And there is the shrewd appointment of a dedicated, refined oenologist like Lorenzo Landi, who has gently sanded off the rough edges yet keeps the wines faithful to a traditional, almost Burgundian, style. These are some of the factors that have led to a wealth of awards, and not only ours, of course. Our thoughts at such a moment cannot help but turn to winery founder Tonino, a man of few words and an ironic smile, who dedicated long years of effort to this winery that he loved so much. It would be fascinating to know what he might be thinking about the wonder that is the '03 edition of his own Tonì. And the wine descriptions? We have run out of space, so just enjoy them at every possible opportunity. That's what we do.

●	Montepulciano d'Abruzzo Tonì '03	🍷🍷🍷	6
●	Montepulciano d'Abruzzo Malandrino '04	🍷🍷🍷	5*
⊙	Montepulciano d'Abruzzo Cerasuolo Piè delle Vigne '04	🍷🍷	4*
○	Pecorino '05	🍷🍷	6
○	Trebbiano d'Abruzzo '05	🍷🍷	3*
●	Montepulciano d'Abruzzo '04	🍷	3
●	Montepulciano d'Abruzzo Malandrino '03	YYY	5
●	Montepulciano d'Abruzzo '03	YY	4*
●	Montepulciano d'Abruzzo Tonì '02	YY	6
⊙	Montepulciano d'Abruzzo Cerasuolo Piè delle Vigne '03	YY	4

OFENA (AQ)

Gentile

via del Giardino, 7
67025 Ofena (AQ)
tel. 0862956138 - 3471362082
www.gentilevini.it

Another Ofena winery, near the picturesque river Tirino, appears for the first time in the Guide and the results of our tasting were so impressive that it receives a full-scale profile. Riccardo Gentile relies on ten hectares of vineyard in this "furnace of Abruzzo", next door to the Cataldi Madonna operation. Assisted by his father and by consulting oenologist Vittorio Festa, Riccardo produces Montepulciano and Trebbiano with classic, traditional traits, all of them taking advantage of wonderfully sound, complex fruit. Let's begin with Orfeo '04, an ambitious Montepulciano that earned a place in our national final taste-off. We liked its rich varietal fragrances and a full-fruited, but refined, palate which owed not a little elegance to a restrained use of the barrique. Zefiro '01, in contrast, is a more traditional-style Montepulciano that matured in large casks, where it built up a varietally faithful medley of complex, appealing fragrances. The palate may not exhibit much complexity but its volume certainly impresses, as does the supremely savoury fruit that is well in evidence. Trebbiano Adone '05 is true to class, showing uncomplicated, clean, fresh and classic. All told, Gentile has provided us a welcome surprise, and we expect to hear more from this modest, hard-working enterprise.

● Montepulciano d'Abruzzo Orfeo '04	🍷🍷	3*
● Montepulciano d'Abruzzo Zefiro '01	🍷🍷	4
○ Trebbiano d'Abruzzo Adone '05	🍷	2

ORTONA (CH)

Agriverde

loc. Caldari
via Stortini, 32a
66020 Ortona (CH)
tel. 0859032101
www.agriverde.it

Agriverde boasts 75 hectares of vines in the Chieti countryside and vine stock caressed by the sun and breezes from the nearby sea. Besides an avant-garde cellar built according to bio-architectural canons, the estate runs a stylish health centre that offers oenotherapy with massages and must and wine-based treatments. There is also a modest but tastefully appointed hôtel de charme, offering a line of organic products. Dynamic Giannicola Di Carlo directs this fine Ortona-based operation, ably assisted by winemaker Riccardo Brighigna. Their Plateo, an elegant, complex Montepulciano, has been winning plaudits for years, of course, but it wasn't presented this year so Trebbiano Solarea '04 graciously stepped up and went to our final tasting round instead. The nose shows an impressive, well-integrated complex of fine fruit and toasty oak while tangy acidity makes for appealing savouriness and a supple palate. Riseis di Recastro 04 is a sinewy, traditional Montepulciano, all the more impressive for being uncomplicated in both character and price. Pecorino '05, from the same reasonably priced line, is outstanding with a tangy, varietal acidity that beautifully supports dense, full fruit in the mouth. A tip of the hat goes to all of the wines of the Natum Bio line, which are clean, straightforward products from organic grapes. We are pleased to see that Agriverde skilfully combines the best in traditional Abruzzo winemaking with a modern eye on new markets. There are plenty of arrows in the Agriverde quiver.

○ Trebbiano d'Abruzzo Solarea '04	🍷🍷	4
● Montepulciano d'Abruzzo Riseis di Recastro '04	🍷🍷	4*
○ Pecorino Riseis di Recastro '05	🍷🍷	3*
○ Chardonnay Riseis di Recastro '05	🍷	3
○ Trebbiano d'Abruzzo Natum '05	🍷	3
○ Trebbiano d'Abruzzo Riseis di Recastro '05	🍷	3
● Montepulciano d'Abruzzo Plateo '98	🍷🍷🍷	6

ORTONA (CH)

Farnese
loc. Castello Caldora
via dei Bastioni
66026 Ortona (CH)
tel. 0859067388
www.farnese-vini.com

Farnese by numbers tots up to a truly impressive set of figures. The cellar produces millions upon millions of bottles, with well-fed distribution networks both in Italy and abroad, and in styles carefully calibrated to the demands of many different markets. The various lines run the gamut from the simplest of quaffers to the most refined and international, including top-ranked champions. This year, we were again faced with a formidable line-up to taste, all of the wines being extremely well executed with attention given to every contour. Details are perhaps taken to extremes, given the current Italian market, which tends to straightforward, uncomplicated versions. Montepulciano Colline Teramane Opis Riserva '03 stood out easily from the crowd. It's a powerful, impressive wine with fine varietal expression and compelling complexity in the mouth. We liked the rich, balsam-laced aromas on Montepulciano Colline Teramane '03 and the inviting, dense fruit that abounds on the palate. Casale Vecchio '05 bears a considerable load of oak but that doesn't mar its elegance nor its vein of vibrant, zesty acidity. From the whites, Trebbiano '05 in the Farneto Valley line, stood out for its refreshing, crisp fragrances and tasty, full flavours on the palate. Pecorino '05 is uncomplicated and delicious.

●	Montepulciano d'Abruzzo Opis Ris. '03	▼▼	6
●	Montepulciano d'Abruzzo Colline Teramane '03	▼▼	5
●	Montepulciano d'Abruzzo Casale Vecchio '05	▼▼	4*
○	Trebbiano d'Abruzzo Farneto Valley '05	▼▼	3*
●	Montepulciano d'Abruzzo Farneto Valley '05	▼	3
○	Pecorino Casale Vecchio '05	▼	4
●	Sangiovese Don Camillo '05	▼	4
●	Edizione 5 Autoctoni '03	▽▽	6
●	Montepulciano d'Abruzzo Casale Vecchio '03	▽▽	4*

PIANELLA (PE)

Chiarieri
via Sant'Angelo, 20
65019 Pianella (PE)
tel. 085971365 - 085973313
www.chiarieri.com

Chiarieri is located in Pianella, in the hill country inland of Pescara, on sun-drenched slopes that seem to have been producing prized fruit forever. The 35 hectares of estate vines, planted to montepulciano and trebbiano, are farmed according to traditional local methods and the wines they yield are clean and straightforward. Father and son Giovanni and Ciriaco Chiarieri are in charge, ably assisted by oenologist Vittorio Festa. Hannibal is what the name suggests, an imposing, ambitious Montepulciano, and this '02 edition opens with plenty of complexity and typicity, and then develops compelling consistency across the palate, which is well delineated and full of tasty, crisp fruit. Granaro '05 has no aspirations to complexity but it opens to crisp draughts of spicy balsam before revealing itself as a delightfully sound Montepulciano. Cerasuolo Granaro '05 is appealingly typical, with textbook cherry and strawberry fragrances smoothed out by just a hint of grassiness. The palate is saved from too much sweetness by ringingly crisp, delicious acidity. Trebbiano Granaro '05 is a country-style pleaser that releases delicious fresh bread and ripe fruit. In short, Chiarieri is a hardworking, meticulous family enterprise that embodies the noblest farming ethos.

●	Montepulciano d'Abruzzo Hannibal '02	▼▼	5
⊙	Montepulciano d'Abruzzo Cerasuolo Granaro '05	▼	3
●	Montepulciano d'Abruzzo Granaro '05	▼	3*
○	Trebbiano d'Abruzzo Granaro '05	▼	4
●	Montepulciano d'Abruzzo Hannibal '97	▽▽	4
●	Montepulciano d'Abruzzo Hannibal '01	▽▽	5
●	Montepulciano d'Abruzzo Hannibal '98	▽▽	4
●	Montepulciano d'Abruzzo Hannibal '99	▽▽	5

PINETO (TE)

F.lli Barba
loc. Scerne
s.da rotabile per Casoli
64025 Pineto (TE)
tel. 0859461020 - 0858990104
www.fratellibarba.it

Fratelli Barba is one of the largest wineries in Abruzzo, with 75 hectares at Pineto, southeast of Teramo. It has been experiencing something of a renaissance lately under the serious, forward-looking Giovanni Barba, who has talented help from consulting oenologist Stefano Chioccioli. Results are already emerging from the cellar, restructured in the 1990s, and the wines are all good, with some terrific products. These are soundly crafted offerings with impressive structure and body that solidly reflect local traditions. Montepulciano Vignafranca '03 is one of the most compelling and it went through to compete in our national finals. Toasty oak complements dense fruit to create an appealing complexity on the nose while savoury flavours expand on the palate into an almost endless finish. Montepulciano Colle Morino '05 may not be as ambitious but it shows excellent varietal qualities on the nose. The palate may only be medium bodied but it is nonetheless pleasurable. Trebbiano Colle Morino '05 is uncomplicated but admirably clean edged and offers plenty of rich, savoury fruit. Passerina '05 will be of interest to those who appreciate native grapes as it is from 100 per cent passerina. Its intriguing minerally essences on the nose precede a fluid, crisp palate. It's a line-up that puts Barba in the front rank and there is surely more to come.

●	Montepulciano d'Abruzzo Vignafranca '03	YY	4*
●	Montepulciano d'Abruzzo Colle Morino '05	Y	2
○	Passerina Bianco '05	Y	2
○	Trebbiano d'Abruzzo Colle Morino '05	Y	2
●	Montepulciano d'Abruzzo Vignafranca '01	YY	4*
●	Montepulciano d'Abruzzo Vignafranca '00	YY	4

POPOLI (PE)

Valle Reale
loc. San Calisto
65026 Popoli (PE)
tel. 0859871039
www.vallereale.it

We began last year's comments about Valle Reale by saying that we would be hearing impressive things about this winery in the future. Little did we know how prophetic those words were. This year, the champion Montepulciano, San Calisto '04, so impressed us with its elegance and richness that it was awarded Three Glasses, a fitting crown to years of hard, steady efforts. Leo Pizzolo, the young owner of this dynamic winery at Popoli, implemented the difficult measures required to adapt his operation to his mountainous terrain. With the help of his young cellar staff and a strong hand from oenologist Carlo Ferrini, Pizzolo crafted a series of truly remarkable wines. The power and genuineness of San Calisto '04 won it our top prize but Leo's Montepulciano '04 was behind by only a hair and also took part in our final taste-offs. We were mightily impressed by the graceful, varietal character of its nose and by the quality of the vibrant fruit on a palate that stood out for its elegance. Montepulciano Vigne Nuove '05 shines for its typicity and straightforwardness, not to mention its appealing price. Valle Reale's Cerasuolo '05 is simply one of the best in this category in the region. It offers an intriguing blend of cassis and strawberry on the nose, followed by smooth fruit and a zesty acidity that contributes to an impressively structured and absolutely delicious palate. Eyes on this winery, then, and on its staff as well. Their journey, we are sure, will be taking them to important places.

●	Montepulciano d'Abruzzo San Calisto '04	YYY	6
●	Montepulciano d'Abruzzo Valle Reale '04	YY	4
⊙	Montepulciano d'Abruzzo Cerasuolo Vigne Nuove '05	Y	2*
●	Montepulciano d'Abruzzo Vigne Nuove '05	Y	2*
○	Trebbiano d'Abruzzo Vigne Nuove '05	Y	2
●	Montepulciano d'Abruzzo San Calisto '03	YY	5
●	Montepulciano d'Abruzzo San Calisto '01	YY	5
●	Montepulciano d'Abruzzo Vigne Nuove '04	YY	2*

ROCCA SAN GIOVANNI (CH)

Cantina Frentana

via Perazza, 32
66020 Rocca San Giovanni (CH)
tel. 087260152
www.cantinafrentana.it

Cantina Frentana continues to reap good results. This co-operative, which has many member growers in the Chieti area, decided a number of years ago to take the sometimes difficult path to quality and better expression of this outstanding terroir. Huge investments and many sacrifices followed but thanks to the efforts of president Carlo Romanelli, with oenologist Gianni Pasquale and agronomist Maurizio Gily, Cantina Frentana succeeded in creating a line-up of wines that reflect true excellence. The standard-bearer remains Panarda, a sturdy Montepulciano, as fulsomely opulent as the traditional Abruzzo banquet it is named after. The '03 is not quite as impressive as last year's version, showing a shade too dense on the palate and too assertive on the nose. Montepulciano Terre Valse '05 is far less complex but cleanness is a virtue here, as is its smooth, rounded palate, which makes for a very pleasant varietal wine. Turning to the whites, Pecorino '05 adds smoky nuances to varietal fruit on the nose and then displays tangy acidity and a palate that is appealing for its verve and lively flavours. Trebbiano Terre Valse '05 is straightforward but its clean, crisp fruit is attractive and tasty.

●	Montepulciano d'Abruzzo Panarda '03	🍷🍷	4
●	Montepulciano d'Abruzzo Frentano '05	🍷	1*
●	Montepulciano d'Abruzzo Terre Valse '05	🍷	2*
○	Pecorino '05	🍷	2*
○	Trebbiano d'Abruzzo Frentano '05	🍷	1*
○	Trebbiano d'Abruzzo Terre Valse '05	🍷	2*
●	Montepulciano d'Abruzzo Panarda '01	🍷🍷 (white)	4

SAN MARTINO SULLA MARRUCINA (CH)

★ Masciarelli

via Gamberale, 1
66010 San Martino sulla Marrucina (CH)
tel. 087185241 - 087182333
www.masciarelli.it

It is hard to say anything new about Gianni Masciarelli. He is one of Italy's finest winemakers and has done much to improve Abruzzo's wines. Gianni is also a shrewd businessman and has succeeded in under two decades in doing what others have failed to achieve in over two centuries. Assisting him is his wife Marina Cvetic, originally from Serbia but now a naturalized Italian, who directs marketing with great competence. We witnessed a superb performance from Montepulciano d'Abruzzo Villa Gemma '03. Always magnificent and powerful, in this edition the wine benefits from spicy nuances that add special richness. Less predictable, but not surprising, were the Three Glasses for Montepulciano d'Abruzzo Marina Cvetic '03. Emerging from its "younger sibling" status, this bottle has the noble elegance of a true thoroughbred and at a very nice price to boot. The '04 editions of the two main whites, Trebbiano d'Abruzzo and Chardonnay Marina Cvetic, are impressive, although the oak seems to intrude. We gave a slight edge to the Chardonnay for its sinewy acidity. Performing almost as well was the new all-steel Trebbiano d'Abruzzo Castello di Semivicoli '04. Iskra '03 is the other debutante, a montepulciano-based IGT Rosso and the first wine from a brand-new facility near Teramo. Closing our review are Villa Gemma Bianco '05, from trebbiano and cococciola, Montepulciano Cerasuolo Villa Gemma '05 and the standard Montepulciano d'Abruzzo '04, all superlative Two Glass efforts, plus the Trebbiano d'Abruzzo '05, which is also fine. And the legend continues.

●	Montepulciano d'Abruzzo Marina Cvetic '03	🍷🍷🍷	5*
●	Montepulciano d'Abruzzo Villa Gemma '03	🍷🍷🍷	8
●	Iskra '03	🍷🍷	5
○	Chardonnay Marina Cvetic '04	🍷🍷	6
○	Trebbiano d'Abruzzo Castello di Semivicoli '04	🍷🍷	6
○	Trebbiano d'Abruzzo Marina Cvetic '04	🍷🍷	6
●	Montepulciano d'Abruzzo '04	🍷🍷	3*
⊙	Montepulciano d'Abruzzo Cerasuolo Villa Gemma '05	🍷🍷	4*
○	Villa Gemma Bianco '05	🍷🍷	4*
○	Trebbiano d'Abruzzo '05	🍷	3
●	Montepulciano d'Abruzzo Villa Gemma '00	🍷🍷🍷 (white)	8
●	Montepulciano d'Abruzzo Villa Gemma '01	🍷🍷🍷 (white)	8

SANT'OMERO (TE)

VALORI

via Torquato al Salinello, 8
64027 Sant'Omero (TE)
tel. 086188461

This successful, long-standing Teramo-area winery now counts Gianni Masciarelli among its partners. Valori relies on some eight hectares of vineyards in its two estates at Sant'Omero and Controguerra, and the wines bear witness to one of the most capable of Italy's producers. Vigna Sant'Angelo, sourced from a vineyard of the same name, is an ambitious, broad-shouldered Montepulciano and the 2004 growing season may be one reason why the '04 is down just a rung from last year, a hair's breadth short of the trophy. But there is nothing not to like in its complex aromas subtly infused with smoky notes, or in its power and impressive texture in the mouth, although the tannins may be attracting a tad too much attention just now. But the standard Montepulciano is the real eye-opener. The '05 is a stand-out for its expansive, opulent aromas and a supple, measured palate that unveils plenty of crisp, savoury fruit. Not only did it go effortlessly into the national finals but its production is in the tens of thousands of bottles, and at irresistible value for the price. There is plenty of Trebbiano '05 produced, too, and it is just what one would expect: straightforward, clean as a whistle and delicious to a fault.

● Montepulciano d'Abruzzo Vigna S. Angelo '04	5
● Montepulciano d'Abruzzo '05	3*
○ Trebbiano d'Abruzzo '05	3
● Montepulciano d'Abruzzo Vigna S. Angelo '03	5
● Montepulciano d'Abruzzo Vigna S. Angelo '01	5
● Montepulciano d'Abruzzo Vigna S. Angelo '99	5

SPOLTORE (PE)

FATTORIA LA VALENTINA

via Torretta, 52
65010 Spoltore (PE)
tel. 0854478158
www.fattorialavalentina.it

Sabatino Di Properzio is the true guiding spirit behind La Valentina. Though not exactly venerable, this well-established operation was among the first to benefit from an injection of the new energy that is now bringing the region so many top-quality achievements. We were therefore very pleased that the standard-level wines did so well at our tastings. We liked the crisp, delicate citrus notes that Montepulciano '04 displays, as well as the varietal quality of its palate, which expands nicely and shows admirable finesse. Trebbiano '05 is fine too, with nicely honed varietal fragrances, excellent heft in the mouth and vibrant, succulent flavours. But the wines from which we hoped more were not up to our expectations, perhaps because we tasted them too soon in careers meant to develop over more years. Bellovedere '03 returns after last year's absence but oak infuses the nose all too liberally. The palate seems somewhat one-dimensional, and the tannins a tad burred, but it offers fruit that is smooth and tasty enough. Binomio '03 is an intriguing experiment by white-wine oenologist Stefano Inama and his team. Full aromas and smooth oak on the palate, however, don't add up yet to an impressive wine. We've always had a soft spot for Spelt but this '02 comes across as somewhat blurred and too countryish. It has to be said that the 2002 season was unhelpful. Overall, enthusiasm seems to have resulted in some stubbed toes but this is probably a passing phase, and better performances are around the corner.

● Montepulciano d'Abruzzo '04	3*
○ Trebbiano d'Abruzzo '05	3
● Montepulciano d'Abruzzo Spelt '02	5
● Montepulciano d'Abruzzo Bellovedere '03	7
● Montepulciano d'Abruzzo Binomio '03	6
● Montepulciano d'Abruzzo Bellovedere '00	7
● Montepulciano d'Abruzzo Bellovedere '01	7
● Montepulciano d'Abruzzo Spelt '97	4
● Montepulciano d'Abruzzo Spelt '98	5
● Montepulciano d'Abruzzo Spelt '99	5
● Montepulciano d'Abruzzo Spelt '00	5
● Montepulciano d'Abruzzo '01	3
● Montepulciano d'Abruzzo Spelt '01	5
● Montepulciano d'Abruzzo '03	3*

TERAMO

Emidio Pepe
loc. Torano Nuovo
via Chiesi, 10
64010 Teramo
tel. 0861856493 - 3357730052
www.emidiopepe.com

The return of this long-established winery to a full profile is deeply satisfying, as are the two wines that competed in our final round. In Abruzzo, Emidio Pepe has always been synonymous with wine. His fine cellar at Torano Nuovo north of Teramo has for many years been turning out traditional wines, those of the old-style, small farmer with distinctive aromas that are at times, particularly lately, somewhat too pronounced: these are wines needing lengthy cellaring. But they are also wines that spring from a deep love of the land and an adherence to traditional winemaking canons. They have always shown an unquestioning conviction in the qualities of the local terrain. In consequence, they have been very personal, instantly recognizable products, even if at times just a tad over the top. This year, to the contrary, the wines presented were cleaner and more elegant, which we hope will be a more stable style. Montepulciano Colline Teramane debuted in this '03. With a dark, brooding, almost Gothic character, it opens to a complex, varietal nose then exhibits a denseness and superb suite of tannins that will ensure it years of maturation. The classic-style Montepulciano '04 is a country wine at heart but in an elegant key, with sound varietal qualities joined to rich, juicy fruit. In these times, when you hear so much about terroir and organic farming, Emidio Pepe harmonizes the two within the context and limits of its actual situation, still producing wines that are always sound and unfailingly distinctive.

●	Montepulciano d'Abruzzo Colline Teramane '03	🍷🍷	7
●	Montepulciano d'Abruzzo '04	🍷🍷	5
●	Montepulciano d'Abruzzo '01	ΥΥ	6
○	Trebbiano d'Abruzzo '02	ΥΥ	5

TOCCO DA CASAURIA (PE)

Filomusi Guelfi
via F. Filomusi Guelfi, 11
65028 Tocco da Casauria (PE)
tel. 085986908

The results this year for Filomusi Guelfi are somewhat below expectations. At the time of our tastings in summer 2006, only three wines were ready, none of them the cellar's top wines. Part of the blame goes to the unfavourable 2004 year, of course. We had been used to welcoming from this fine estate winery, with its ten hectares of vineyards at Ceppete near Tocco Casauria, a line-up of offerings that were varietal, distinctive and deliciously traditional. In past editions of the Guide, these wines had all but garnered the top trophy, particularly Montepulciano Fonte Dei. No such luck this year, but only because of the paucity of wines available. From the wines we tasted, Montepulciano '04 had only recently been bottled so it was reticent. Still, we noted good fruit and nice typicity. Cerasuolo '05 lived up to its billing as one of the most highly regarded in the region, a solidly traditional, clean-edged rosé that is delicious, unfussy and uncomplicated. Le Scuderie del Cielo '05 is a creative assemblage of chardonnay, sauvignon and cococciola, with clean aromas and abundant crisp, savoury fruit on the palate, an eminently pleasurable creation. This year's small band of wines was too limited for a comprehensive judgement but the reliability and dedicated efforts that we know have always been characteristic of Lorenzo Filomusi give us hope for next year.

○	Le Scuderie del Cielo '05	🍷	4
⊙	Montepulciano d'Abruzzo Cerasuolo '05	🍷	4*
●	Montepulciano d'Abruzzo '04		4
●	Montepulciano d'Abruzzo V. Fonte Dei '00	ΥΥ	6
●	Montepulciano d'Abruzzo Fonte Dei '01	ΥΥ	6
●	Montepulciano d'Abruzzo '02	ΥΥ	4*
⊙	Montepulciano d'Abruzzo Cerasuolo '04	ΥΥ	3*

TOLLO (CH)

CANTINA TOLLO
VIA GARIBALDI, 68
66010 TOLLO (CH)
TEL. 087196251 - 08719625201
www.cantinatollo.it

Cantina Tollo is a truly impressive operation, a co-operative that relies on thousands of member growers in the Chieti area, from the slopes of the Maiella down to the shores of the Adriatic. The talented winemaking staff, headed by Riccardo Brighigna, harnesses this synergy and range of territories to produce a fine group of wines that impressed our tasters. Our vote went to the intriguing Trebbiano Aldiano '05, which by common consent went on to the national finals. We liked its straightforward but exquisitely varietal aromas, its spaciousness on the palate and its finely-crafted fruit. Montepulciano '04 Aldiano too displays excellent varietal faithfulness and steady progression for a fine overall example of typicity. Pecorino '05 has considerable power and body for a white monovarietal but it is pleasurable from beginning to end. Trebbiano '04 Menir aspires to complexity, opening to measured toasty oak and emphatic tropical fruit, and then develops impressive depth and drive. The Colle Secco line merits positive comment. The numerous wines and big production numbers make this a formidable range but the quality is undeniably high and these are delicious wines at very affordable prices. Cantina Tollo, then, is an operation that has been successful in walking the fine line between, on the one hand, the economic pressures facing a large enterprise and, on the other, a well-focused dedication to unique terroirs and high quality. They have succeeded brilliantly and we hope they will go on to even greater achievements.

○	Trebbiano d'Abruzzo Aldiano '05	▼▼	4*
○	Chardonnay Cretico '04	▼▼	5
●	Montepulciano d'Abruzzo Aldiano '04	▼▼	4*
●	Montepulciano d'Abruzzo Valle d'Oro '04	▼▼	2*
○	Trebbiano d'Abruzzo Menir '04	▼▼	5
○	Pecorino '05	▼▼	4
○	Trebbiano d'Abruzzo Colle Secco '05	▼▼	3*
●	Montepulciano d'Abruzzo Cagiòlo '03	▼	5
●	Montepulciano d'Abruzzo Colle Secco '03	▼	3
●	Montepulciano d'Abruzzo Colle Secco Rubino '03	▼	3
○	Trebbiano d'Abruzzo Valle d'Oro '05	▼	2*
●	Montepulciano d'Abruzzo Aldiano '03	▽▽	4*

TORANO NUOVO (TE)

BARONE CORNACCHIA
VIA LE TORRI, 20
64010 TORANO NUOVO (TE)
TEL. 0861887412
www.baronecornacchia.it

We are delighted to welcome back into the main section the long-respected Barone Cornacchia winery. The 42-hectare estate at Torano Nuovo is the remnant of a Bourbon feudal estate at Teramo, which we mention only to indicate how far back in time the origins of this cellar extend. Many consider Barone Cornacchia the finest producer in the region, with its tradition of straightforward, always well executed, typical wines. The recent participation of a new generation, with its understandable enthusiasm and dedication, has brought us a bevy of intriguing wines this year. Rich, opulent aromas lead off in Vigna Le Coste '03, with its full-bodied palate offering a balanced duet of oak-laced fruit and tangy acidity. Montepulciano Poggio Varano '03, in the new Antico Feudo line, releases rich varietal fruit on the nose but is slightly muffled by emphatic oak tones, and impresses with a supple, energy-laden palate that shows beautiful balance. Montepulciano '04 is uncomplicated and pleasant, smooth and full in the mouth, but doesn't seem to grab attention in any way. Trebbiano '05 leads the whites. A consistent wine, with appreciable varietal character, and zingy acidity that instantly suggests a second glass. We hope that Barone Cornacchia continues down the path of renewal that they have obviously chosen, and continues the present sequence of excellent performances.

●	Montepulciano d'Abruzzo Poggio Varano '03	▼▼	4
●	Montepulciano d'Abruzzo V. Le Coste '03	▼▼	4
●	Controguerra Rosso Villa Torri '02	▼	4
●	Montepulciano d'Abruzzo '04	▼	3
○	Trebbiano d'Abruzzo '05	▼	3
●	Montepulciano d'Abruzzo Poggio Varano '01	▽▽	4
●	Montepulciano d'Abruzzo '03	▽▽	3*

TORANO NUOVO (TE)

STRAPPELLI

LOC. TORRI
VIA TORRI, 15
64010 TORANO NUOVO (TE)
TEL. 0861887402
www.cantinastrappelli.it

Guido Strappelli directs a modest estate at Torano Nuovo whose seven hectares are cultivated organically and in compliance with the local traditions. Guido's wines are faithful reflections of those traditions, as well as of the fine local territory. Following the usage of the best local growers, Strappelli produces his wines only in the better years since they must have sufficient character to last over many years. This year's wines were few in number but we were impressed by their quality. Let's begin with Montepulciano Colline Teramane Riserva Celibe '03, a wine that we immediately sent to the national taste-offs. Its complexity is signalled by its almost opaque hue and by the thoroughgoing varietal characteristics of the nose. A crisp vein of tasty acidity makes itself felt and nicely bolsters the imposing denseness of the fruit on the palate. The simpler Montepulciano '04 shows a subtle toasty oak on the nose but the barrique's contribution creates bitterish tannins that intrude on the palate and mar the varietal character. Pecorino Soprano '05 is the only white we tasted. Unpretentious and clean, it nonetheless offers good varietal faithfulness while the palate displays the delicious acidity typical of pecorino and supple, toothsome fruit. Modest in size though it is, Strappelli takes its work seriously, and its wines show this.

●	Montepulciano d'Abruzzo Colline Teramane Celibe Ris. '03	🍷🍷	5
●	Montepulciano d'Abruzzo '04	🍷🍷	4*
○	Pecorino Soprano '05	🍷	4
●	Montepulciano d'Abruzzo Colline Teramane Celibe Ris. '01	♡♡	5

VILLAMAGNA (CH)

TORRE ZAMBRA

V.LE REGINA MARGHERITA, 18
66010 VILLAMAGNA (CH)
TEL. 0871300121
www.torrezambra.it

Riccardo and Vincenzo De Cerchio farm some 40 hectares on the gentle slopes of Villamagna and Miglianico. With the invaluable assistance of oenologist Romeo Taraborelli, they produce impressive wines that nicely express the qualities of the local area, and which they release at ultra-reasonable prices. Once again, we were impressed by the wines presented, Montepulciano and Trebbiano naturally, in line with tradition, but a sound Pecorino as well that fits in nicely with current interest in native varieties. Montepulciano Colle Maggio '03 is straightforward and well crafted but it offers quite a bit more. The nose features rich, dense fruit and a lean, vibrant palate completes a red that is varietally faithful and reassuringly traditional. Montepulciano Brune Rosse '01 is more ambitious, with riper and more evolved fruit on the nose, followed by dense texture and concentrated fruit in the mouth, although it seems weighed down by excessive oak influence. Trebbiano '05, from the Colle Maggio line, opens with striking finesse and elegance, and then turns to nervy acidity to enliven crisp, tasty fruit. All in all, a straightforward wine with a very modest price tag. From the same line, Pecorino '05 likewise offers complex, lively fruit and that lovely acidity typical of pecorino but some oak tannins, although not exactly heavy, do throw off the overall balance. Taking everything into account, though, Torre Zambra is a fine operation that does credit to one of the Abruzzo's finest growing areas.

●	Montepulciano d'Abruzzo Colle Maggio '03	🍷🍷	4*
●	Montepulciano d'Abruzzo Brune Rosse '01	🍷	5
○	Chardonnay Colle Maggio '05	🍷	2
⊙	Montepulciano d'Abruzzo Cerasuolo '05	🍷	1
⊙	Montepulciano d'Abruzzo Cerasuolo Colle Maggio '05	🍷	2
●	Montepulciano d'Abruzzo Diomede '05	🍷	3
○	Pecorino Colle Maggio '05	🍷	3
○	Trebbiano d'Abruzzo Colle Maggio '05	🍷	2
●	Montepulciano d'Abruzzo Brune Rosse '00	♡♡	5
●	Montepulciano d'Abruzzo Colle Maggio '01	♡♡	4*
●	Montepulciano d'Abruzzo Brume Rosse '98	♡♡	5

OTHER WINERIES

Podere Castorani

C.da Oratorio, 100
65020 Alanno (PE)
tel. 3355312961
www.poderecastorani.it

Iarno Trulli and his family, assisted by oenologist Luca Patricelli, are deeply attached to their terroir. They cultivate some 60 hectares in the Pescara mountains, producing complex, if at times inconsistent, wines. Montepulciano '03 is opulent and complex with an elegant, full-bodied palate.

- ● Montepulciano d'Abruzzo Podere Castorani '03 — 🍷🍷 — 6
- ● Montepulciano d'Abruzzo Costa delle Plaie '05 — 🍷 — 4

Col Del Mondo

C.da Campotino, 35c
65010 Collecorvino (PE)
tel. 0858207831 - 3388367677
www.coldelmondo.com

A new generation is energizing this winery in the Pescara hills. We liked Sunnae '04 for its complex, Bordeaux-like nose and its savoury, though somewhat unusual, palate. The more straightforward Montepulciano '03 shows balanced oak nuances and develops full and sinewy in the mouth.

- ● Montepulciano d'Abruzzo '03 — 🍷🍷 — 4
- ● Montepulciano d'Abruzzo Sunnae '04 — 🍷🍷 — 3*
- ● Montepulciano d'Abruzzo Kerrias '02 — 🍷 — 5

Contesa di Rocco Pasetti

C.da Caparrone, 9
65100 Collecorvino (PE)
tel. 0854549622
www.contesa.it

Rocco Pasetti owns a dynamic, forward-looking operation above Pescara, making challenging and often delightful wines. His Trebbianos impressed us this year. Vigna Corvino '05 is assertive with full, tangy flavours while the nicely complex Trebbiano '04 flaunts appealing, dense aromas.

- ○ Trebbiano d'Abruzzo '04 — 🍷🍷 — 4
- ○ Trebbiano d'Abruzzo Vigna Corvino '05 — 🍷🍷 — 3*

Lepore

C.da Civita, 29
64010 Colonnella (TE)
tel. 086170860
www.vinilepore.it

We had hoped last year for better results from Gaspare Lepore. They did not materialize and the same is true this year, unfortunately. We did like his Luigi Lepore '02, however, an ambitious Montepulciano with pleasantly rustic fragrances and an expansive palate displaying lovely, savoury fruit.

- ● Montepulciano d'Abruzzo Colline Teramane Luigi Lepore Ris. '02 — 🍷 — 5

Faraone
loc. Colleranesco
via Nazionale per Teramo, 290
64020 Giulianova (TE)
tel. 0858071804 - www.faraonevini.it

Faraone practises organic farming and traditional winemaking, turning out distinctive and occasionally uneven wines. We liked best Montepulciano '01 dal Podere Santa Maria in Arco, which shows country-style appealing aromas of great varietal character, freshness and marked fruit.

- ● Montepulciano d'Abruzzo S. Maria dell'Arco '01 🍷 5

Nicola Santoleri
via dei Cavalieri, 20
66016 Guardiagrele (CH)
tel. 0871893301

We didn't receive any wines to taste this year from Nicola Santoleri, whether by their own decision or because no wines were ready. We are sorry about this but we are keeping the profile active since the cellar is such a key player in the Abruzzo wine world. We send Santoleri our best wishes.

- ● Montepulciano d'Abruzzo Crognaleto '00 🍷 6
- ● Montepulciano d'Abruzzo '01 🍷 5
- ○ Trebbiano d'Abruzzo Crognaleto '03 🍷 4

Cantine Talamonti
c.da Palazzo
65014 Loreto Aprutino (PE)
tel. 0858289039
www.cantinetalamonti.it

Young, motivated professionals drive this forward-looking operation, releasing crisp, refreshing wines that are eminently drinkable. Modà '04 impressed us. It's a seductive, elegant Montepulciano with a lively vein of acidity that bolsters wonderful fruit on the palate.

- ● Montepulciano d'Abruzzo Modà '04 🍷🍷 3*
- ● Montepulciano d'Abruzzo Tre Saggi '04 🍷 4
- ○ Trebbiano d'Abruzzo Aternum '05 🍷 4
- ○ Trebbiano d'Abruzzo Trebì '05 🍷 3

Giuseppe Ciavolich
loc. Quattro Strade
c.da Cerreto, 18
66010 Miglianico (CH)
tel. 0871958797 - www.ciavolich.com

This long-respected winery has operated in Miglianico and Loreto Aprutino since 1852, producing traditional wines with an elegantly rustic edge. Pecorino Aries '05 is one of the best in the region from this native grape, showing dense, minerally aromas and fine varietal fruit in the mouth.

- ○ Pecorino Aries '05 🍷🍷 4
- ● Montepulciano d'Abruzzo Divus '04 🍷 4
- ● Cabernet Sauvignon '05 🍷 3
- ● Montepulciano d'Abruzzo '05 🍷 2

Cantina Sociale Miglianico
via San Giacomo, 40
66010 Miglianico (CH)
tel. 087195831 - 0871958321
www.cantinamiglianico.it

This co-operative that has been producing impressive wines from traditional varieties debuts in the Guide this year. The wines are sincere, varietal, attractively traditional and reasonably priced. Murelle '04 is a classic-style Montepulciano with appealing balsam and sound, savoury fruit.

- ● Montepulciano d'Abruzzo Murelle '04 🍷🍷 2*
- ○ Trebbiano d'Abruzzo Murelle '05 🍷 1

Il Feuduccio di Santa Maria d'Orni
via Feuduccio, 1a
66036 Orsogna (CH)
tel. 0871891646
www.ilfeuduccio.it

The 2002 versions of Il Feuduccio's star performers, Ursonia and Margae, were not released as the vintage was not up to winery standards. We look forward to next year's offerings. In the meantime, we will be enjoying glasses of their scrumptious Pecorino '05.

- ● Montepulciano d'Abruzzo Fonte Venna '03 🍷 2
- ○ Pecorino '05 🍷 2

Citra
c.da Cucullo
66026 Ortona (CH)
tel. 0859031342
www.citra.it

The Citra co-operative numbers over 5,000 growers and relies on oenologist Romeo Taraborelli. Its wines are at times complex and ultra-refined oenologically but always pleasurable and with good price tags. The stand-out Montepulciano Palio '04 is nicely traditional with rich varietal fragrances.

●	Montepulciano d'Abruzzo Palio '04	🍷🍷	3*
●	Montepulciano d'Abruzzo Laus Viate '02	🍷	6
●	Montepulciano d'Abruzzo Caroso '03	🍷	4
○	Trebbiano d'Abruzzo Citra '05	🍷	2*

Dora Sarchese
c.da Caldari Stazione, 65
66026 Ortona (CH)
tel. 0859031249
www.dorasarchese.it

The D'Auria brothers preside over 17 hectares of vines overlooking the Adriatic and produce unpretentious but alluring wines. Pronounced varietal aromas stand out in their Montepulciano Pietrosa '04, which builds an impressive progression featuring zesty, deliciously opulent fruit.

●	Montepulciano d'Abruzzo Pietrosa '04	🍷🍷	4
○	Bianco della Rocca '05	🍷	4
○	Pecorino Dora D'Or '05	🍷	4

Orlandi Contucci Ponno
loc. Piana degli Ulivi, 1
64026 Roseto degli Abruzzi (TE)
tel. 0858944049
www.orlandicontucci.com

This winery has over 30 hectares of vines on the coast east of Teramo and puts out ambitious, often internationally styled, wines of uneven quality at times. This year, we liked Cabernet Colle Funaro '03 with good complexity on the nose and savoury, dynamic palate, although the oak intrudes.

●	Cabernet Sauvignon Colle Funaro '03	🍷🍷	5
●	Liburnio '03	🍷	6
●	Montepulciano d'Abruzzo Colline Teramane Ris. '03	🍷	6
○	Trebbiano d'Abruzzo Colle della Corte '05	🍷	4

Tommaso Olivastri
c.da Quercia del Corvo, 37
66038 San Vito Chietino (CH)
tel. 087261543

This family winery on the Adriatic south of Ortona cultivates ten hectares. Its wines are largely complex, cellarable Montepulcianos that sometimes lack consistency. La Carraia '02 is impressive with a complex nose of smoky essences and toasty oak followed by an even, textbook palate.

●	Montepulciano d'Abruzzo La Carraia '02	🍷	5

Villa Bizzarri
loc. Villa Bizzarri
64010 Torano Nuovo (TE)
tel. 0861856933

Good performances by the reds brought a Guide debut for this winery, located north of Teramo. Controguerra Ferro di Re '03 boasts rich balsamic aromas and a full-bodied, elegantly balanced palate. Dense fruit marks the nose of the tangy, dynamic Montepulciano Sasso Arso '03.

●	Controguerra Ferro di Re '03	🍷🍷	5
●	Montepulciano d'Abruzzo Girone dei Folli '03	🍷	3
●	Montepulciano d'Abruzzo Sasso Arso '03	🍷	3
○	Trebbiano d'Abruzzo Antigo '05	🍷	3

Pietrantonj
via San Sebastiano, 38
67030 Vittorito (AQ)
tel. 0864727102 - 0864727251
www.vinipietrantonj.it

The traditional country winemaking here is responsible for wines that show good typicity, soundness and elegant rusticity. Montepulciano Arboreo '03 is appealingly tannic and savoury while Montepulciano Cerano '02 is sound and well-crafted, boasting a spacious palate with crisp fruit.

●	Montepulciano d'Abruzzo Cerano '02	🍷🍷	4
●	Montepulciano d'Abruzzo Arboreo '03	🍷🍷	2*
○	Trebbiano d'Abruzzo Cerano '05	🍷	4

MOLISE

Modest-sized Molise brought home Three Glass honours for the third time in the two decade-long history of the Guide. The champion is Alessio Di Majo's 2003 edition of Molise Aglianico Contado, a wine by no means unaccustomed to our laurels, since the 1999 vintage also wore the crown. Such performances simply confirm yet again that even the admittedly tiny vinous output of this region can provide wines of considerable character and, as in this case, at decidedly surprising prices for the quality. Molise has shown itself to be an area with a particular oenological physiognomy. It has its own traditional grape, tintilia, which is beginning to shine in some versions. Then there are varieties that are common in contiguous regions but that here yield versions that are distinctive. That list would include aglianico, montepulciano, trebbiano, greco and even falanghina, which here expresses itself differently tending more to citrus, perhaps because of the wide-ranging diurnal temperature variations during the harvest period. Physically, Molise is a vast, undulating high plateau surrounded by mountain chains and by massifs such as the Mainarde and the Matese. The region slopes very gradually east towards the Adriatic, presenting rather dramatic climatic variations at even relatively short distances. Producers are still somewhat thin on the ground. In addition to Di Majo Norante, there are only a few others, in particular Borgo di Colloredo, Fattoria di Vaira, Masseria Flocco and D'Uva, which are the most representative of Molise wine production. Given their small number, Molise still lacks a critical mass, so to speak, and the risk of being considered simply marginal in wine production is a real one. To forestall unfavourable judgments, and also to promote a sense of identity, the region should continue to develop the potential of tintilia. It should also develop a winemaking style that will identify and encourage the traditions peculiar to the various locales, rather than standardize them in any single direction. The oenological globalization of Molise would only play into the hands of neighbouring regions, such as Abruzzo and Puglia, which can rely on a far larger number of producers and broader marketing networks. Adequate foundations have been laid here, however, and in some instances the business structures as well. This should be sufficient to form a core of Molise producers capable of drawing attention to themselves for the distinctive and unique qualities of their wines. It is a game that will have to be played out in the coming years but Molise already has all it takes to emerge a winner.

BORGO DI COLLOREDO

LOC. NUOVA CLITERNIA
86042 CAMPOMARINO (CB)
TEL. 087557453
www.borgodicolloredo.com

Borgo di Colloredo is a young operation, founded in 1994, and comprises some 70 hectares of vineyards planted in the attractive hills that descend steeply from Campobasso towards the Adriatic. Owners Enrico and Pasquale Di Giulio have poured ten years' worth of investments and dedication into their winery, which has now become one of the most closely watched cellars in the region. With an annual production of some 300,000 bottles, they release a number of intriguing wines and the batch they sent us this year pleasantly surprised our tasting panel. This was in spite of the absence of the winery's star, Gironia Rosso, which generally scores very high marks. We can recommend two whites. More specifically, we consider Falanghina '05 to be simply the finest white wine in the region. The nose flaunts complex, crisp, flint-mineral essences while the palate is expansive and densely textured. Biferno Bianco Gironia '05, largely from trebbiano with dollops of bombino and malvasia, is an ambitious and distinctly challenging white. Still slightly closed in, it nonetheless offers dense aromas, expanding beautifully on the palate into very concentrated, crisp fruit.

○ Biferno Bianco Gironia '05	▼▼	3
○ Molise Falanghina '05	▼▼	4*
● Aglianico '00	▽▽	4
● Biferno Rosso Gironia '00	▽▽	4
● Molise Montepulciano '00	▽▽	2*
● Molise Montepulciano '01	▽▽	3*
○ Biferno Bianco Gironia '04	▽▽	3*
● Biferno Rosso Gironia '98	▽▽	4

CAMPOMARINO (CB)

DI MAJO NORANTE

FRAZ. NUOVA CLITERNIA
VIA RAMITELLI, 4
86042 CAMPOMARINO (CB)
TEL. 087557208
www.dimajonorante.com

In Molise, the name of Di Majo Norante is synonymous with wine. Certainly the most highly respected winery in Molise, it has been a leader in implementing the changes that are sweeping through the region. Luigi Di Majo founded and led the winery in its early years and it is now firmly and confidently directed by his son Enrico, with the help of the well-known consultant, Riccardo Cotarella. The 80 and more hectares of vineyards in Campomarino yield impressive, modern-style wines that are still fully respectful of local traditions. Don Luigi '04, the winery's true champion, all but took our top award. The nose offers attractive nuances of smoke and toasty oak before the palate shows profound and complex, with generous yet appealing tannins. The polished Aglianico Contado '03 unsurprisingly took our Three Glasses trophy. Elegant, rich aromas abound on the nose and few wines can match its superlative, balanced progression on the palate. We were equally impressed by its reasonable price tag. Prugnolo '03 is a fetching offering that opens to measured oak influence and develops complex, rich fruit in the mouth. Biblos '04, a greco and falanghina blend, stands out among the whites for its delicious citrus fragrance and crisp, refreshing fruit, all in all a delicious wine. Beyond such line-up leaders, Di Majo Norante's entire wine portfolio is remarkable for its consistency and for its overall high quality.

● Molise Aglianico Contado '03	▼▼▼	4*
● Molise Don Luigi '04	▼▼	6
● Prugnolo '03	▼▼	4*
○ Biblos '04	▼▼	4*
● Biferno Rosso Ramitello '03	▼	4
○ Molì Bianco '05	▼	2
● Molì Rosso '05	▼	3
○ Molise Falanghina Ramì Bianco '05	▼	3
○ Molise Greco '05	▼	4
● Molise Aglianico Contado '99	▽▽▽	4*
● Molise Don Luigi '99	▽▽▽	5
● Molise Aglianico Contado '00	▽▽	4
● Molise Don Luigi '02	▽▽	6
● Molise Aglianico Contado '02	▽▽	4*

PETACCIATO (CB)

FATTORIA DI VAIRA
TERRA DI SOLIDARIETÀ
C.DA COLLECALCIONI
86038 PETACCIATO (CB)
TEL. 087567304

Stories such as that of Fattoria di Vaira-Terra di Solidarietà still bear telling today since they add to our appreciation of wine, that noble food which is such a basic element in our Mediterranean culture. The origins of this winery lie in the more than 100 hectares that were the property of the Ente di Beneficenza Cavaliere del Lavoro Francesco Di Vaira. The foundation concerned itself with social work from 1952 on, assisting disadvantaged youngsters in collaboration with Caritas. But it has been bottling premium wine for only for a few years, since the arrival of Pasquale Di Lena, himself Molise-born. One of the old lions of Italian wine, Pasquale was in charge of the Enoteca Nazionale in Siena before returning to his home region to direct this worthy enterprise. The 2002 harvest was the first to be produced and the results have been steadily improving. The all-montepulciano Monsignore 2003 is a fine red, with resplendent, rich aromas and a powerful dense-textured palate showcasing a tasty suite of tannins. Cavalier Francesco 2005 is a blend of montepulciano and aglianico but not quite as complex. The aromas are straightforward on the nose but with a nice citrussy tang and it develops full and smooth in the mouth. For the whites, the Falanghina Signora Francesca that so impressed us last year is not quite as interesting in its '05 edition, coming across as a tad too slender. Fattoria di Vaira is an admirable operation with an inspiring history behind it and one that is demonstrating the impressive achievements that are possible in this region.

● Molise Rosso Il Monsignore Ris. '03	🍷🍷	4
● Molise Rosso Cavalier Francesco '05	🍷🍷	3*
○ Molise Falanghina Signora Francesca '05	🍷	3*
● Molise Rosso Il Monsignore Ris. '02	🍸🍸	4
○ Molise Falanghina Signora Francesca '04	🍸🍸	3*

SAN FELICE DEL MOLISE (CB)

CIPRESSI
C.DA MONTAGNA
86030 SAN FELICE DEL MOLISE (CB)
TEL. 0874874535
www.cantinecipressi.it

In last year's edition, we introduced a promising new development, the Cipressi family's Cantine Cipressi. Today, we can describe it as a going concern that puts out ambitious, complex Molise wines, all of them well made and all at consumer-friendly prices. The Cipressis cultivate about 25 hectares of vineyards, divided between the two areas of Guaglionesi and of San Felice in Molise, above the Trigno river, in the north-eastern corner of the region. Besides the grapes traditional to the area, the estate also grows the internationals chardonnay and merlot. Molise Rosso Mekan '04 impressed us the most, with striking, very pleasurable aromas and a palate marked by crisp fruit and a steady progression. No less fine is Rumen '04, where rich fruit is nicely offset by toasty oak, although slightly blurred by gamey notes in the background. The depth on the palate is considerable, however, and this is a chewy, full-textured red. From the whites, we preferred Chardonnay Voira '05, which sports complex varietal fruit on a nose enhanced by mineral and toasty oak nuances while plenty of dense fruit in the mouth makes for an appealing, stylish international pleaser. Cipressi is a youthful winery that is quickly creating its own unique style on the Molise winescape.

○ Chardonnay Voira '04	🍷	3
● Molise Rosso Mekan '04	🍷	4
● Molise Rosso Rumen '04	🍷	3
○ Venas Bianco '05	🍷	2*
● Molise Rosso Rumen '03	🍸🍸	3*

OTHER WINERIES

D'Uva
C.DA RICUPO, 13
86035 LARINO (CB)
TEL. 0874822320 - 3383498632
www.cantineduva.com

This prominent producer has won attention for its work with tintilia, a variety native to Molise that is starting to enjoy a renaissance. Its Tintilia '05 has zesty acidity that helps forge a delicious palate. The straightforward Kantharos '05 is fine; the Trebbiano elegantly rustic and tasty.

● Molise Tintilia '05	🍷	6
○ Molise Trebbiano Kantharos '05	🍷	4

Masserie Flocco
C.DA DIFENSOLA
86045 PORTOCANNONE (CB)
TEL. 0875590032
www.masserieflocco.com

We've had many a pleasurable, well-executed wine from Flocco. Tintilia '04 offers dense aromas and a savoury, complex palate. Podere di Sot '05 is an expansive Montepulciano with zesty fruit. Appealing minerally notes open Trebbiano Terre Scure '05, which develops complexity and full flavours.

● Molise Tintilia '04	🍷	4
● Molise Rosso Podere di Sot '05	🍷	4
○ Trebbiano Terre Scure '05	🍷	2*

I.A.C. - Catabbo
C.DA PETRIERA
86046 SAN MARTINO IN PENSILIS (CB)
TEL. 0875604945
www.catabbo.it

Catabbo's fine group of wines this year includes Petriera '05, a succulent, dense Montepulciano with an expansive palate. Molise Rosso '04 is a crisp Montepulciano that is supple and delicious. Falanghina Caratus '05 shows delicate oak nuances and turns rich and deep in the mouth.

● Petriera Rosso '05	🍷🍷	2*
● Molise Rosso '04	🍷	4
○ Caratus '05	🍷	2

CAMPANIA

Campania's role in the history of wine is both important and challenging. Italian viticulture has its roots here, but the land of the Samnites has been slow to move into 21st-century grape-growing and wine-producing. There's a gap of almost 2,000 years between the last imperial banquet and recent successes: the region's modern wine history spans fewer than 15 harvests. Campania needs time and patience to develop but local producers are making up for lost time and progress is faster than in most other zones. In three years, the number of Three Glass awards has more than doubled and finalists have quadrupled, involving estates large and small and coinciding with vintages that have been little more than average. Cool and inaccessible, Irpinia is the leader of this trend, thrilling us with its severe, aglianico-based reds and its austere, mineral whites that all too often suffer at the impatient hands of producers, restaurateurs and consumers. After taking the prize for best red in 2006, the province of Avellino presented another champion. Cupo '05 is a steel-aged Fiano selection sourced from vineyards at Montefredane from the colourful Sabino Loffredo of Pietracupa, who won our special prize for White of the Year. The 2005 vintage was excellent for Irpinia's variety and the Fiano di Avellino '05 from Colli di Lapio gave a splendid encore of last year's Three Glass performance. Another great classic of the typology, Fiano di Avellino Vigna della Congregazione '04, scored its first Three Glasses alongside Mastroberardino's Fiano di Avellino Radici '05, a masterpiece of elegance and minerality. This historic Atripalda estate chalked up a fine double – actually, triple – crown, thanks to a classic version of Taurasi Radici Riserva '00 and a retrospective award for the Taurasi Radici Riserva '99. There were no surprises from the Serpico and Patrimo '04 double-act that gave Feudi in San Gregorio a total of 17 Three Glasses in less than ten years. Salvatore Molettieri's second consecutive win is hardly unexpected, as the wine in question is the Riserva '01 edition of his Taurasi Cinque Querce. But Campania doesn't stop at Irpinia. Sannio is showing every sign of recovery and the province of Caserta is also making headway. Villa Matilde's compact range caught us almost unawares with a magnificent Falerno del Massico Caracci '04, which won its first Three Glasses. Terra di Lavoro '04 put on another outstanding performance. But Salerno is a different kettle of fish. The last few harvests have produced little of note from Cilento to the Amalfi coast, but in compensation the veterans in the field are forging ahead at full speed. The Montevetrano '04 is a perfect example of its style, Marisa Cuomo scored again with her Fiorduva '05 and Luigi Maffini wowed the crowd with his Pietraincatenata '04, an eloquent, modern Fiano.

ATRIPALDA (AV)

MASTROBERARDINO
VIA MANFREDI, 75/81
83042 ATRIPALDA (AV)
TEL. 0825614111
www.mastroberardino.com

It was another fine performance from this Atripalda estate. The starting point for what today is one of the most interesting subzones, Mastroberardino has gone beyond making news for its past exploits or the odd legendary bottle. Today's news is tomorrow's history and we have the sneaking suspicion that the champions presented this year by the highly talented Vincenzo Mercurio may well be the great classics of the future. The top contender is without a doubt the Taurasi Radici Riserva '00, a moving interpretation that exalts tradition in a sound, austere profile to win Three effortless Glasses. We also gave a retrospective Three Glasses to the Taurasi Radici Riserva '99. Nor were there any doubts about Fiano di Avellino Radici '05 either, with its Chablis aromas and Apennine fullness. The nose opens on clean notes of minerals, rain-washed stone and ash and goes on to reveal aromas of thyme, aniseed and iodine. The fine, balanced palate changes gear midway thanks to perfect integration of backbone and acidity, the very long finish suggesting iodine and mint. The rest of the range is solid across the board. Greco di Tufo Novaserra '05 feels the effects of a vintage that didn't exactly favour the variety but it's still one of the most elegant versions we have tasted. The Fiano di Avellino '05 and the basic Greco di Tufo '05 cruised past the Two Glass mark. Taurasi Radici '03 is good and the fiano-based Melizie '04 is the best sweet wine to come out of Campania. The Falanghina del Sannio '05 is tasty and succulent but the Lacrimarosa '05 is a bit low-key.

●	Taurasi Radici Ris. '00	🍷🍷🍷	6
○	Fiano di Avellino Radici '05	🍷🍷🍷	4*
●	Taurasi Radici '03	🍷🍷	5
○	Melizie '04	🍷🍷	5
○	Greco di Tufo Novaserra '05	🍷🍷	4*
○	Fiano di Avellino More Maiorum '03	🍷🍷	5
●	Aglianico '04	🍷🍷	4*
○	Fiano di Avellino '05	🍷🍷	4*
○	Greco di Tufo '05	🍷🍷	4*
○	Sannio Falanghina '05	🍷🍷	4*
⊙	Lacrimarosa '05	🍷	4
●	Taurasi Radici '00	🍷🍷🍷 (white)	5
●	Taurasi Radici '01	🍷🍷🍷 (white)	5
○	Greco di Tufo Novaserra '04	🍷🍷🍷 (white)	4*
●	Taurasi Radici '90	🍷🍷🍷 (white)	8

CARINARO (CE)

CAPUTO
VIA CONSORTILE
81032 CARINARO (CE)
TEL. 0815033955
www.caputo.it

When all an estate's labels effortlessly and consistently outperform the average, you know things are going well. It's particularly impressive when you consider that the estate in question regularly produces up to a million bottles a year and operates in an area whose viticultural history and suitability is not of the best. Over the years, however, the Cantine Caputo at Carinaro has so accustomed us to wines of quality that we now expect to be awed, not just reassured, by its performance. Although the range presented for this year's edition of the Guide is as reliable as ever, it failed to produce a heavyweight to match the other champions that emerged across Campania. We were particularly disappointed by the Aglianico Zicorrà '04. Its very fine, elegant nose blends fruity notes of blackberry and mulberry blossom with hints of ink and white pepper. But the palate lacks the support necessary to give consistency to the smooth, juicy entry. Asprinio d'Aversa Fescine '05 continues to rise up through the ranks of the estate's hierarchy and is easily the best interpretation of the typology. Fresh notes of citrus fruit and tropical nuances emerge on the nose, announcing a full, edgy palate that gets better with every passing season in terms of weight and complexity. The Sannio Aglianico Clanius '05 showed well but is not at its best. The Taurasi '02 and Greco di Tufo Vigne dei Lupi '05 are goodish, nothing more. They offer full and eloquent but rather uncharacteristic interpretations.

●	Zicorrà '04	🍷🍷	5
○	Asprinio d'Aversa Fescine '05	🍷🍷	4
●	Taurasi '02	🍷	6
○	Campi Flegrei Falanghina Vigne del Fuoco '05	🍷	4
○	Greco di Tufo Vigne dei Lupi '05	🍷	4
●	Sannio Aglianico Clanius '05	🍷	4
●	Sannio Aglianico Clanius '02	🍷🍷 (white)	5
●	Zicorrà '02	🍷🍷 (white)	5
●	Sannio Aglianico Clanius '03	🍷🍷 (white)	4*
●	Zicorrà '03	🍷🍷 (white)	5
●	Sannio Aglianico Clanius '04	🍷🍷 (white)	4*

CASTEL CAMPAGNANO (CE)

Terre del Principe

fraz. Squille
via s.s. Giovanni e Paolo, 30
81010 Castel Campagnano (CE)
tel. 0823867126 - 0818541125
www.terredelprincipe.com

This year's results from Terre del Principe lay to rest any doubts we may have had in the 2006 edition of the Guide. The estate belongs to Giuseppe Mancini and Manuela Piancastelli and came into being after they separated from Vestini Campagnano. Much of their land is given over to experimentation with pallagrello and casavecchia, varieties indigenous to the Caserta area that are seeking to establish themselves. With the support of Luigi Moio, this Castel Campagnano cellar presents several wines that attest to the potential of these two varieties. The Pallagrello Nero Ambruco '04 offers sensations derived from its sojourn in new oak with undertones of ripe blackcurrant and pencil lead that are consistently mirrored on the full, tidy palate. Vigna Piancastelli '03, a blend of casavecchia and pallagrello nero, has a similar profile but is smoother and rounder, thanks in part to the hot vintage. The Castello delle Femmine '04, another 50-50 blend, is more supple yet also a bit simpler and lethargic. But Casavecchia Centomoggia '04 towers head and shoulders above the rest and earned a place in our finals. The nose starts out hesitantly but gradually opens up to reveal fabulous, crisp aromas of blackberry, orange peel and camphor with very smoky, almost volcanic undertones. Entry on the palate is soft but not ingratiating, creamy and complex with a prolonged, radiant finish. Of the two Pallagrello Biancos, the barrique-aged Le Serole '05 is fuller and more substantial but we also found the chewy, racy Fontanavigna attractive.

●	Centomoggia '04	▼▼	6
●	Vigna Piancastelli '03	▼▼	7
●	Ambruco '04	▼▼	6
○	Fontanavigna Pallagrello Bianco '05	▼▼	4
○	Le Serole Pallagrello Bianco '05	▼▼	5
●	Castello delle Femmine '04	▼	4
○	Le Serole Pallagrello Bianco '03	▽▽	5
●	Castello delle Femmine '03	▽▽	4*
○	Fontanavigna Pallagrello Bianco '03	▽▽	4

CASTELFRANCI (AV)

Colli di Castelfranci

c.da da Braudiano
83040 Castelfranci (AV)
tel. 082772392
www.collidicastelfranci.com

When a new estate explodes onto the scene, our delight at the discovery of a new talent is often shadowed by doubt. But when the debut performance is backed up by maturity and authority, our doubts swiftly disappear. And this is exactly what happened in the case of Colli di Castelfranci, the small estate belonging to Luciano Gregorio and Gerardo Colucci. What does it matter if none of their wines made our final selections this year? They continue to progress in leaps and bounds, garnering acclaim along the way. The whites all scored high in the Two Glass band, further tribute to the skilled hand of oenologist Giuseppe Mancini. The Greco di Tufo Grotte '05 offers its usual consistent and eloquent interpretation. It displays notes of citron and white peach with faint sulphurous nuances and a palate that is caressing yet vigorous thanks to the perfect integration of glycerine and acidity. Fiano di Avellino Pendino '05 also offers a very faithful rendering of the type. It's less mouthfilling and still developing, but very tasty and full of citrus-like sensations. Obtained from late-harvested fiano grown outside the DOC zone, Paladino '05 didn't number among the finalists this year. Nonetheless, it's still an original wine that offers anything but a strained interpretation and manages to maintain surprising suppleness. The Taurasi '02 debuted well, Gagliardo (spirited) by name and nature. Rather than attempting to disguise the shortcomings of the vintage, it channels them into sound, elegantly edgy drinkability. The other labels are all very good.

●	Taurasi Gagliardo '02	▼▼	6
○	Fiano di Avellino Pendino '05	▼▼	4*
○	Greco di Tufo Grotte '05	▼▼	4
○	Paladino V.T. '05	▼▼	5
●	Candriano '04	▼	4
●	Vadantico '04	▼	4
○	Sannio Falanghina Falangò '05	▼	4
○	Paladino V.T. '04	▽▽	4
○	Fiano di Avellino Pendino '03	▽▽	4
○	Greco di Tufo Grotte '03	▽▽	4
○	Fiano di Avellino Pendino '04	▽▽	4
○	Greco di Tufo Grotte '04	▽▽	4

CASTELFRANCI (AV)

Perillo

C.da Valle, 19
83040 Castelfranci (AV)
tel. 082772252

At times, Michele Perillo resembles nothing so much as a small, determined ant as he goes about his work silently and without pause. We are sure that one of these days his Castelfranci storehouse will be besieged by all those happy-go-lucky crickets who have no idea as yet what a treasure trove he is constructing. He's not quite there but with the support of Carmine Valentino Michele he is creeping inexorably towards Three Glass level and this year the Taurasi Riserva '01 comes very close. This is a wine strongly rooted in its subzone of origin, Castelfranci, whose terrains are largely clay-based and rich in limestone. Chewy and powerful but austere, it opens out gradually to reveal notes of pencil lead and liquorice, tobacco, balsamic nuances and hints of rich, ripe plum. The oak is balanced but still evident on the palate, which is dense, close-knit, extremely tangy, severe and slightly tart in the finish. But more than the hardness, which is perfectly in keeping with the character of this zone, it's the texture of the tannins that failed to convince us fully. We must confess that we expected greater things of the Taurasi '02. Even taking into account the limits of the vintage, its development is curbed by the alcohol, especially on the palate, and the nose takes time to show its potential. Aglianico Castelfranci '02 is more subdued than usual but that's not necessarily a bad thing. Previous versions have tended to be a tad too challenging, rather like a Taurasi. The '02 shows the uninhibited suppleness that is more characteristic of this typology.

●	Taurasi Ris. '01	2 glasses (black)	6
●	Taurasi '02	2 glasses (black)	6
●	Castelfranci '02	1 glass (black)	5
●	Taurasi '00	2 glasses	6
●	Taurasi '01	2 glasses	6
●	Castelfranci '00	2 glasses	5
●	Castelfranci '01	2 glasses	5
●	Taurasi '99	2 glasses	6

CASTELLABATE (SA)

Luigi Maffini

fraz. San Marco
loc. Cenito
84071 Castellabate (SA)
tel. 0974966345
www.maffini-vini.com

It's not wise to down the gauntlet to Luigi Maffini and Luigi Moio. While congratulating them on their first Three Glass Cenito in last year's edition of the Guide, we needled them about their Pietraincatenata, which was good but not excellent. So what did they do? They rose to the challenge, transforming this wine obtained from pure, barrique-matured fiano into the first Cilento white to obtain our top prize. It's a modern wine, ambitious in both form and substance, and completely different in style from more traditional Irpinia interpretations but absolutely complete. The nose is a symphony of tropical nuances, mingling mango, kiwi and passion fruit lifted by smoky, spicy notes and hints of cakes. The palate is round, concentrated and opulent, showing astonishingly nonchalant savouriness in the finish. It is still developing, and the oak is not yet fully integrated, but the end result is absolutely stunning. Cenito has little to envy this champion. The nose is a fabulous fusion of flowery, fruity sensations with balsamic undertones and has a vivid, continuous profile that shows not the slightest hint of overripeness. Entry on the palate is confident and engaging, displaying aromas of mint and liquorice before ending in a soft – perhaps too soft – finish. The fiano-based Kràtos '05 is another wonderful wine that offers a tantalizing glimpse of what its elder brother may offer next year. The Kléos, also '05, is simpler and a bit dilute in the finish.

○	Pietraincatenata '04	3 glasses (black)	5
●	Cilento Aglianico Cenito '04	2 glasses (black)	6
○	Kràtos '05	2 glasses (black)	4
●	Kléos '05	1 glass (black)	4
●	Cilento Aglianico Cenito '03	3 glasses	6
●	Cenito '00	2 glasses	7
●	Cenito '01	2 glasses	7
●	Cenito '99	2 glasses	7
○	Pietraincatenata '02	2 glasses	5
○	Pietraincatenata '03	2 glasses	5
●	Kléos '04	2 glasses	4

CELLOLE (CE)

Villa Matilde
s.s. Domitiana, km. 4,700
81030 Cellole (CE)
tel. 0823932088
www.fattoriavillamatilde.com

In Roman times, Falerno apparently enjoyed a status similar to that of Bordeaux or Burgundy wines today in terms of taste and cost. Two thousand years on, the wine of emperors is reliving its former glory not least in the bottles produced by Villa Matilde over the last few years. Flanked by Riccardo Cotarella, the Avallone family has repeatedly shown just how good a red Falerno made from aglianico grown in the Camarato vineyard can be. This time round, however, it was the Falerno del Massico Bianco Caracci that triumphed to take the Three Glass crown with what is without a doubt the best falanghina-based wine to come out of Campania in recent years. The '04 version stands out for its scintillating nose of balsamic notes and spicy aromas of mint and cumin with undertones of apricot. The palate is caressing, full flavoured and taut and the wine's maturation in new oak helps to measure and moderate its impetuous development in which almost gamey sensations emerge. This absolutely superb performance ran the risk of eclipsing the very decent Falerno del Massico Camarato '03, which feels the effects of the torrid vintage that deprives it of depth, especially on the palate. The nose, however, is very intriguing thanks to its notes of gunpowder and raspberry jam. The Cecubo '04, a blend of aglianico, primitivo and abbuoto also did very well. While the rich nose profile of cocoa powder, almond and tobacco is par for the course, the close-knit, austere palate with marked tannins came as more of a surprise. The rest of the range is impressively consistent.

○	Falerno del Massico Bianco V. Caracci '04	YYY	4*
●	Falerno del Massico Camarato '03	YY	6
●	Cecubo '04	YY	5
○	Falerno del Massico Cl. '04	YY	4*
○	Falanghina del Beneventano '05	YY	3
○	Greco di Tufo Tenute di Altavilla '05	YY	4
○	Falanghina di Roccamonfina '05	Y	3*
○	Falerno del Massico Bianco '05	Y	3
●	Falerno del Massico Rosso V. Camarato '00	YYY	6
●	Falerno del Massico Camarato '01	YYY	6
●	Vigna Camarato '95	YYY	5
●	Falerno del Massico Rosso V. Camarato '97	YYY	6
●	Falerno del Massico Rosso V. Camarato '98	YYY	6

FOGLIANISE (BN)

Cantina del Taburno
via Sala
82030 Foglianise (BN)
tel. 0824871338
www.cantinadeltaburno.it

We like to think of wine as a fascinating universe with its own intrinsic logic, psychology and even its own sociology. Considered in these terms, the results obtained by the Cantina del Taburno are enlightening. After a couple of low-key years this big Foglianise co-operative is back on top form. Perhaps it's no surprise that this coincides with the return of its most representative label, Aglianico del Taburno Bue Apis, which has been conspicuous by its absence at our last two tastings. It's almost as if the return of the big boy has galvanized the whole range, starting with Falanghina del Taburno '05, Campania's version of the quintessential good-value-for-money wine. The Cesco dell'Eremo '03 from late-harvested falanghina is excellent. In addition to the sweetness and concentration of a hot growing year, it offers grip and richness of flavour. A placidly tidy, reasonable wine, the Aglianico del Taburno Fidelis '03 never disappoints. Delius '03 is enveloped in dark tones that are as yet imperfectly defined. This modern Aglianico lacks neither fullness nor density but further ageing would release the fruit and tame the very oaky tannins. The Aglianico del Taburno Bue Apis '03 has the same limits but possesses altogether different body and complexity. At the moment, toasty notes of liquorice and coffee hold sway, but enormous mineral energy is discernible in the background. This also comes through on a palate that is big and full but still too severe in the finish. It may yet balance out but for the moment got no further than the finals.

●	Aglianico del Taburno Bue Apis '03	YY	8
●	Aglianico del Taburno Delius '03	YY	5
○	Falanghina Cesco Dell'Eremo V.T. '03	YY	4*
○	Taburno Falanghina '05	YY	4*
○	Ruscolo '02	Y	6
●	Aglianico del Taburno Fidelis '03	Y	4
●	Bue Apis '00	YYY	7
●	Bue Apis '99	YYY	7
●	Delius '00	YY	6
●	Bue Apis '01	YY	8
●	Delius '02	YY	5
●	Delius '99	YY	6

FONTANAROSA (AV)

Di Prisco

c.da Rotole, 37
83040 Fontanarosa (AV)
tel. 0825475738

If you don't know Pasqualino Di Prisco well, it's easy to see him as a shy, modest person who takes pride in his work but doesn't have too much ambition. This is true but only in part. Behind that quiet, reserved exterior lies the passion of the true viticulturist who burns to be better than average and is prepared to take the necessary risks to achieve his goals. For this edition of the Guide, Pasqualino presented us with just half of his usual range, as he left out the wines he felt needed longer ageing, notably the Greco di Tufo Pietra Rosa. By way of compensation, we tasted a trio of very high quality products, the finest of which is the Taurasi '02. Despite the appalling growing year, it managed to achieve two major objectives: it offers a vigorous, graceful interpretation of Pasquale's most prestigious label; and it has made an important contribution to defining the typically chalky character of the Fontanarosa terrain. This is in many ways a separate subzone within the production area and we are confident that we shall see some excellent wines coming out of here in a few years' time, especially for those who like their Taurasi lighter and smoother. In the absence of the Pietra Rosa, we tasted a well-made standard label Greco di Tufo '05. Although still very closed on the nose, it hints at the great power of the fruit to come, showing sound and balsamic. The palate, too, is still a bit muddled and skittish but does have breadth and an unusually gutsy character. Fiano di Avellino '05 requires patience but is already full, delicious and slightly salty in the mouth.

●	Taurasi '02	▼▼	6
○	Fiano di Avellino '05	▼▼	4
○	Greco di Tufo '05	▼▼	4
●	Aglianico '03	∇∇	4
○	Greco di Tufo '03	∇∇	4*
○	Greco di Tufo Pietrarosa '04	∇∇	4
●	Taurasi '01	∇∇	6
○	Greco di Tufo '04	∇∇	4*

FORINO (AV)

Urciuolo

fraz. Celzi
via Due Principati, 9
83020 Forino (AV)
tel. 0825761649
www.fratelliurciuolo.it

Ciro is lean and Antonello looks like an urchin but this duo differs more in character than in appearance. As in all successful partnerships, their differences are complementary. They are a couple of extroverts with a shared passion who like to laugh and joke but who take their wine very seriously. This year, the egregious Urciuolo brothers placed three wines in our finals, one for each of Irpinia's designated areas. This is no mean feat but given the recent investments in vineyards and cellar, we have a strong suspicion that the best has yet to come. To give you an idea of how impressive this is, the Urciuolos' Taurasi was the only 2002 to reach our finals. It showed remarkably well thanks to the rich minerality on the nose flanked by fresh nuances of raspberry and bay leaf and the palate that injects personality into a tight-knit body whose only weak point is the vintage. The Greco di Tufo took a significant stride forward in quality. The '05 exhibits that extractive, opulent style that Ciro and Antonello are so fond of but this time it offers an extra mineral boost that lends the palate satisfaction and consistency. In spite of the smooth finish, we weren't altogether convinced by the Fiano di Avellino Faliesi '05. The nose starts out rather muddled and reveals very unbalanced notes of hazelnut, pear and honey. The palate's a bit overripe and although the body is irreproachable, it lacks the depth of the more classic Fianos. The Fiano di Avellino '05 and the Aglianico '04 are both excellent.

●	Taurasi '02	▼▼	6
○	Fiano di Avellino Faliesi '05	▼▼	4*
○	Greco di Tufo '05	▼▼	4*
●	Aglianico '04	▼▼	3*
○	Fiano di Avellino '05	▼▼	4*
●	Taurasi '01	∇∇	5*
○	Fiano di Avellino '03	∇∇	4*
○	Fiano di Avellino Faliesi '04	∇∇	4*
●	Aglianico '03	∇∇	4*
○	Fiano di Avellino '04	∇∇	4*
●	Taurasi '99	∇∇	6

FORIO (NA)

D'AMBRA VINI D'ISCHIA
FRAZ. PANZA
VIA MARIO D'AMBRA, 16
80075 FORIO (NA)
TEL. 081907210 - 081907246
www.dambravini.com

Mention Ischia and Vigna Frassitelli immediately springs to mind with its tiny terraces perched over the sea, the monorail and the heroic working conditions. Over the last few years, this most famous of Biancolella crus has taken top prize for most beautiful label, but we're convinced that sooner rather than later the wine inside the bottle will tempt us more than the views of the local woods. The talented Andrea D'Ambra almost convinced us in this edition of the Guide with a gutsier than usual version of the Frassitelli that just missed out on our final selections. The '05 presents delicate nuances of melon and fresh hazelnut and a fine, fragrant palate with a typical finish hinting pleasantly at almond. The Ischia Forastera Euposia '05 showed very well. Generally considered to be a poor relation of the Biancolella, it is actually acquiring more and more character of its own. Notes of yeast are the prelude to undertones of citrus fruit and unusual hints of ripe watermelon. The palate is savoury, racy, sound and consistent, betrayed only by slightly jarring alcohol in the finish. Kyme never ceases to astonish. It is obtained from varieties native to the Aegean islands that Andrea selected during a visit and planted on Ischia. The '04 flags somewhat on the nose and the finish is slightly dilute, but overall it still manages to offer a wonderful combination of tertiary sensations and mineral notes. Ischia Biancolella '05 rises to the occasion, showing light, well-defined, smooth and easy all at the same time.

○ Ischia Bianco Kyme '04	TT	5
○ Ischia Biancolella '05	TT	4*
○ Ischia Biancolella Tenuta Frassitelli '05	TT	5
○ Ischia Forastera Euposia '05	TT	4
○ Ischia Biancolella Tenuta Frassitelli '90	YYY	4
○ Ischia Biancolella Tenuta Frassitelli '01	YY	5*
○ Ischia Bianco Kyme '02	YY	5
○ Ischia Biancolella Tenuta Frassitelli '04	YY	5
○ Ischia Forastera Euposia '04	YY	4

FURORE (SA)

CANTINE GRAN FUROR
DIVINA COSTIERA
VIA G. B. LAMA, 16/18
84010 FURORE (SA)
TEL. 089830348 - 3356886793
www.granfuror.it

Every day of the year, a blustering wind sweeps up from the inlet and across the terraces hewn from the rock, a salty blast laden with sea water but never rain. It has shaped this town that does not have a single square. It's not called Furore for nothing. In these parts, the wind is the harbinger of good and bad news but for the last couple of years it has heralded the repeated triumphs of Marisa Cuomo and Andrea Ferraioli. Furore has seen its fair share of extraordinary couples but these two are the perfect ambassadors for this unique land. Their flagship wine, Fiorduva, has carved a niche for itself among the oenological jet set. Under the watchful eye of Professor Luigi Moio, this peerless wine continues to improve with every passing harvest. In the glass, the '05 offers an intense buttery sensation of shortbread and confectioner's cream that expands, sustained by fresh notes of aromatic herbs and citrus peel and a fascinating nuance of botrytis. The palate impresses with its weight and power and the iodine element triggers a crescendo in the finish that is both velvety and lingering. Those who harbour doubts about the quality of the vintage must try the Furore Bianco '05. We gave it Two full Glasses for the balsamic compactness of its nose, oscillating between notes of citron and rosemary, and its full, chewy palate. The torrid vintage deprived the Furore Rosso Riserva '03 of energy and depth, characteristics that the lighter but confident Furore Rosso '05 has in spades. The Ravello wines are a bit below par but we have no time or space here for despondency.

○ Costa d'Amalfi Furore Bianco Fiorduva '05	TTT	7
● Costa d'Amalfi Furore Rosso Ris. '03	TT	7
○ Costa d'Amalfi Furore Bianco '05	TT	5
● Costa d'Amalfi Furore Rosso '05	TT	5
○ Costa d'Amalfi Ravello Bianco '05	T	5
○ Costa d'Amalfi Furore Bianco Fiorduva '04	YYY	7
○ Costa d'Amalfi Furore Bianco Fiorduva '00	YY	7*
● Costa d'Amalfi Furore Rosso Ris. '02	YY	7
○ Costa d'Amalfi Furore Bianco Fiorduva '01	YY	7
○ Costa d'Amalfi Furore Bianco Fiorduva '03	YY	7

LAPIO (AV)

COLLI DI LAPIO
VIA ARIANIELLO
83030 LAPIO (AV)
TEL. 0825982184

Around 95 per cent of the white wines produced in Italy are sold and drunk within the year. It is our fervent hope that the remaining five per cent includes a lot of Colli di Lapio's Fiano di Avellino '05, the result of a collaboration between Clelia Romano and oenologist Angelo Pizzi. While this stupendous wine comes from a controversial year, it also hails from one of the best zones for the Irpinia variety. At this phase of its development, however, it only expresses a minimal part of its potential. Colli di Lapio's Fianos, particularly those from northeast-facing vineyards, are rather recalcitrant wines that age extremely well. After a fairly rigid, restrained start, Fiano di Avellino '05 came on in leaps and bounds during our tastings to take an easy Three Glasses for the second year in a row. Still rather reduced on the nose, it opens out gradually to reveal mountain aromas and notes of citron and marjoram, evolving towards unusual sensations of raspberry and liquorice with chalk and flint peeking through. Vibrant and sharp, with intense minerality, it is well buttressed by the delightfully broad mid palate, which is weighty right through a long finish still in search of definition. It's readier than the equally wonderful Fiano di Avellino '04 and reminds us very much of the '99, which today is on top form. The Taurasi Vigna Andrea '02 is very decent. It presents garnet ruby, with a dense, chewy bouquet of pencil lead, cherry and cocoa powder, and a simpler, linear palate capped by a slightly dilute finish.

○	Fiano di Avellino '05	🍷🍷🍷	5
●	Taurasi Vigna Andrea '02	🍷	6
○	Fiano di Avellino '04	YYY	5
●	Taurasi Vigna Andrea '01	YY	6
○	Fiano di Avellino '03	YY	5
○	Fiano di Avellino '00	YY	4*
○	Fiano di Avellino '01	YY	5
○	Fiano di Avellino '02	YY	5
○	Fiano di Avellino '95	YY	4
○	Fiano di Avellino '96	YY	4
○	Fiano di Avellino '97	YY	4

LUOGOSANO (AV)

TENUTA PONTE
VIA CARAZITA, 1
83040 LUOGOSANO (AV)
TEL. 082773564
www.tenutaponte.it

There's a lot of solid work behind Tenuta Ponte at Luogosano, one of the most reliable, consistent estates in Irpinia and one whose results this year are in inverse proportion to its low profile. The Taurasi returned to our final tasting table in an '01 version that flaunts an extremely fascinating personality. It's earthy, dynamic and rigorous and anything but approachable. That said, the dark tones tend to dominate and the palate lacks the consistency required to minimize the contrast with the alcoholic, astringent finish. It's a real shame because the wine has an eclectic style that is most intriguing. The whites also offer a good compromise between fullness and minerality. Fiano di Avellino '05 has a very varietal nose showing notes of pear and golden delicious apples enhanced by balsamic, smoky tones. Big, vibrant and lingering, it's still a bit unruly in the finish, indicating that it needs a bit more time. Greco di Tufo '05 is a readier wine, almost Fiano-esque in its nuances of sage, hazelnut and white damson. It's robust and edgy on the palate and even aromatic in the finish. Obtained from pure merlot grown in vineyards next to the river Calore, the Cossano gave a solid performance, the '03 bursting with fruit and sweetness without going over the top. Carazita '03, a blend of aglianico, sangiovese and merlot matured in stainless steel, is the archetypal everyday wine. It has aromas of morello cherry and tobacco with vegetal undertones and measured body. Best of all, it's a snip at the price.

●	Taurasi '01	🍷🍷	6
●	Cossano '03	🍷🍷	6
○	Fiano di Avellino '05	🍷🍷	4
○	Greco di Tufo '05	🍷🍷	4*
●	Carazita '03	🍷	3*
●	Taurasi '00	YY	5*
○	Fiano di Avellino '04	YY	4*
●	Cossano '01	YY	7
○	Coda di Volpe '04	YY	3*

MONDRAGONE (CE)

MICHELE MOIO
V.LE REGINA MARGHERITA, 6
81034 MONDRAGONE (CE)
TEL. 0823978017
www.cantinemoio.it

It is quite incredible the pace at which new estates are springing up all over Campania – there are now over 300. Many are determined and raring to go, happy to elbow others out of the way to create a space for themselves. But a word of warning. The old lions still rule the region and these young cubs will have to contend with them. A case in point are the wines of that monumental Campania winemaker, Michele Moio. The great man has no time to stop and enjoy his well-deserved fame, but marches on apace, astonishing us anew with each harvest. This year, the king of primitivo bowled us over with two voluptuous, fascinating whites. The Falerno del Massico Bianco '05 is about as far as you can get from an easy-going glass of wine. Intense notes of peach and apricot are buttressed by vegetal-balsamic aromas and echo consistently across the palate that develops weighty and dynamic all the way to the apricot finish. Our only criticism is the final alcoholic note. The Falerno del Massico Aloara '04 is its oak-aged alter ego. Toasty notes emerge at the beginning and the end but are integrated mid palate with the variety's acidulous elements. The two Falerno del Massicos took home Two Glasses apiece. Hats off to the Primitivo '04, which refuses to succumb entirely to the roundness of its ripe fruit, managing to hold on to its vigour and mineral character. The Maiatico '03 bears the indelible stamp of its sojourn in new oak but this gradually fades, showing that it still has room to grow. Table wines Gaurano and Moio '57 are quintessentially Moio-ish.

●	Falerno del Massico Maiatico '03	TT	6
○	Falerno del Massico Alaora '04	TT	5
●	Falerno del Massico Primitivo '04	TT	4
○	Falerno del Massico Bianco '05	TT	4*
●	Gaurano '03	T	4
●	Moio 57 '03	T	4
●	Falerno del Massico Primitivo '01	YY	5
●	Moio 57 '01	YY	4
●	Gaurano '02	YY	4
●	Moio 57 '02	YY	4

MONTEFREDANE (AV)

PIETRACUPA
C.DA VADIAPERTI, 17
83030 MONTEFREDANE (AV)
TEL. 0825607418

His friends know that the last thing they should do is take Sabino Loffredo literally. "Permanently closed" reads the sign at the entrance to his estate, when his small cellar is in fact a gathering place open all hours to friends and producers. Cupo (dark) is the name blazoned across his most important label but it contains a brilliant, radiant, steel-aged Fiano. Loffredo learned his craft from Professor De Magistris and now works with the talented Carmine Valentino. The most impressive thing about him is his ability to transfer his experience and his own contradictions into his wines. Especially when young, they can be as challenging and inscrutable as he is open and extrovert but their immense vital energy is all his. The Cupo '05 emerged as the front runner of this year's tastings, coasting across the finishing line to take its second Three Glass trophy. It also went home with a special award for White of the Year in this 2007 edition of the Guide. A highly territorial wine, it has confident smoky aromas sustaining deep, penetrating notes of balsam and citrus fruit. But it really comes into its own on the palate, where it displays greater fullness and superb mineral verve. The Fiano di Avellino '05 also did very well. Restrained yet powerful and vibrant on the nose, it will only improve with cellaring. Time should also help the Greco di Tufo '05 to unbend. Although finer than usual, this is one of the more vibrantly richer versions we have tasted. The Taurasi '02 excels in its restraint and minerality and the Quirico '04 is just as good.

○	Cupo '05	TTT	5
○	Fiano di Avellino '05	TT	4*
○	Greco di Tufo '05	TT	4*
●	Taurasi '02	TT	6
●	Quirico '04	TT	5
○	Cupo '03	YYY	4*
●	Taurasi '00	YY	6
○	Fiano di Avellino '03	YY	4
○	Greco di Tufo "G" '03	YY	4
○	Fiano di Avellino '04	YY	4
○	Greco di Tufo '04	YY	4
○	Greco di Tufo "G" '01	YY	4*
●	Taurasi '01	YY	6

MONTEFREDANE (AV)

VADIAPERTI
C.DA VADIAPERTI
83030 MONTEFREDANE (AV)
TEL. 0825607270
www.vadiaperti.it

Vadiaperti in Montefredane was founded in 1984 by Antonio Troisi. Antonio was much more than a great producer. He had a major influence on many people, wine lovers and others alike. Since he passed away in 1998, his son Raffaele has carried the torch not only on the estate but also, and more importantly, for his aesthetics and philosophy. The estate continues to offer what is in many ways an extreme interpretation of Irpinia wines: unruly, impetuous, sometimes unapproachable when young, but capable of enhancing the natural cellarability that distinguishes Grecos and Fianos. Then there is Coda di Volpe, which in the '05 version showed its best ever form to earn a place in our finals. Hints of flint intermingle with aromas of citrus peel and ripe pear on the nose while the palate displays power and energy worthy of a Greco, finishing on a lovely iodine note. The Fiano di Avellino '05 flaunted the classic style and character of the Montefredane slopes to stride into our finals. It is penalized by its extreme youth but promises great things over the next ten years. Reticent at the outset, the nose gradually opens up to reveal nuances of grapefruit and green apple with distinctly smoky undertones. A sharp, edgy palate shows more than enough flesh but is too aggressive in the finish. The Greco di Tufo '05 is more open but also has a long way to go. It offers a virile interpretation of one of the steepest slopes in Montefusco. The Falanghina del Beneventano '05 and the Aglianico '02 are both worth investigating.

○	Coda di Volpe '05	🍷🍷	2*
○	Fiano di Avellino '05	🍷🍷	4
○	Greco di Tufo '05	🍷🍷	4*
●	Aglianico '02	🍷	4
○	Falanghina '05	🍷	4
○	Greco di Tufo '04	(🍷🍷)	4*
○	Coda di Volpe '04	(🍷🍷)	2
○	Fiano di Avellino '04	(🍷🍷)	4
○	Fiano di Avellino '93	(🍷🍷)	4
○	Fiano di Avellino '94	(🍷🍷)	4
○	Fiano di Avellino '95	(🍷🍷)	4
○	Fiano di Avellino '96	(🍷🍷)	4

MONTEFREDANE (AV)

VILLA DIAMANTE
VIA TOPPOLE, 16
83030 MONTEFREDANE (AV)
TEL. 0825670014

Villa Diamante is a tiny estate that has managed to carve an important role for itself in the largely unknown world of Fiano di Avellino. Most of those who have ventured into this unknown territory are explorers, enthusiasts who will go to the ends of the earth to discover a niche product. We were given just one wine to taste this year, a hand-crafted product matured in stainless steel and bottled almost a year after harvesting. Thanks to some mixed performances and a tendency to vary from bottle to bottle, it has gained a bit of a dubious reputation but there is nothing at all ambiguous about the '04 edition. Fiano di Avellino Vigna della Congregazione won a resounding Three Glasses. This prize is a tribute to the passion and skill of its authors, Antoine Gaita and Diamante Renna, and their inspired decision to extend the ageing period for a variety that needs plenty of time to realize its full potential. It's also a nod to the Montefredane subzone, which is beginning to emerge as a bit of a grand cru in the Fiano di Avellino area, as witnessed also by other major makers. With an altitude of around 400 metres, south-eastern exposure and a clayey, chalky base with lots of shale, this slope produces wines of a very minerally, smoky character, with the vigour and lifespan embodied in Vigna della Congregazione '04. After rather a closed start, it reveals crisp sulphurous notes accompanied by hints of citrus fruit and medicinal herbs. The palate is broad, vibrant, austere and deep, and while the finish may not be perfect, this is a wine brimming with personality.

○	Fiano di Avellino Vigna della Congregazione '04	🍷🍷🍷	5

MONTEFUSCO (AV)

TERREDORA
VIA SERRA
83030 MONTEFUSCO (AV)
TEL. 0825968215
www.terredora.com

The results achieved by Terredora over the last few years remind us of those rare athletes who perform at the peak of their condition in every major race, winning medal after medal, but who never quite manage to clinch the gold. It's a shame, though, because this year the great Montefusco estate came as close as it's ever been to a Three Glass trophy. The contenders were the Greco di Tufo Terre degli Angeli and the Greco di Tufo Loggia della Serra, Terradora's two most important products. The first is gentler and more reassuring, the second gutsier and more mineral in tone. Despite rather a difficult year for the greco variety, they are both very open and convincing with the generosity of their lively profiles. That said, they lack the verve necessary to carry them right through to the finish where the variety's typical acidity is thrown into relief by rather excessive sweetness. Fiano di Avellino Terre di Dora '05 is on its usual splendid form. It's extremely flowery with loads of citrus on the nose but not quite integrated on the palate yet, which is caressing on entry but rather aggressive in the finish. We also gave Two Glasses to the '05 Falanghina, one of the best editions of this type we tasted for weight and character. The Aglianico '05 is a sure bet with an exemplary price tag and a wholly reliable palate. The Vesuvio Lacryma Christi Bianco '05 is one of the few to be reviewed in the Guide. But we were a bit disappointed by Principio '03, a modern Aglianico that's a bit short on flesh and rather dusty on the back palate.

○	Greco di Tufo Loggia della Serra '05	▼▼	4*
○	Greco di Tufo Terra degli Angeli '05	▼▼	4*
○	Falanghina '05	▼▼	4*
○	Fiano di Avellino Terre di Dora '05	▼▼	4
●	Aglianico Il Principio '03	▼	5
○	Passito Fiano '04	▼	5
●	Aglianico '05	▼	4
○	Vesuvio Lacryma Christi Bianco '05	▼	4
○	Fiano di Avellino Terre di Dora '03	▽▽	4*
○	Fiano di Avellino Terre di Dora '04	▽▽	4*
○	Greco di Tufo Loggia della Serra '04	▽▽	4*
○	Greco di Tufo Terra degli Angeli '04	▽▽	4*

MONTEMARANO (AV)

SALVATORE MOLETTIERI
C.DA MUSANNI, 19B
83040 MONTEMARANO (AV)
TEL. 082763722 - 082763624
www.salvatoremolettieri.it

Salvatore Molettieri and his family won't forget this vintage in a hurry. Just as they were engulfed by snow on the eve of Easter in 2001, today they are being showered with awards and prizes. Salvatore took the loss of almost half of his crop in his stride, reasoning that rightly or wrongly what nature takes away with one hand it gives back with the other. And he was right. After the Taurasi Cinque Querce '01's spectacular Three Glass performance, the Riserva followed up with a perfect encore. The wine is obtained from the grapes grown in the highest part of the vineyard at an altitude of around 600 metres, where the compact clay base contains a large amount of crushed reddish-grey volcanic stone. These are the last grapes to be harvested, very often as late as November, and the wine they produce has tended to show signs of being over-evolved. Not this time, though. This version offers a fabulous combination of weight, character, fullness and austerity. Aromas of topsoil, pencil lead and chlorophyll seem to huddle round the fruit, which is partially hidden but ready to make a burst when the time is right, rather like a mountaineer on the final stretch of a climb. The palate has wonderful density and energy, revealing hints of liquorice and cocoa powder midway and a flurry of first-class tannins. The Taurasi Cinque Querce '02 is about as good as it gets, but the Aglianico Cinque Querce '04 was a bit disappointing. There was an extraordinary debut from the Fiano di Avellino and the Greco di Tufo '05, both of which impressed us almost as much as the Three Glass reprise.

●	Taurasi Vigna Cinque Querce Ris. '01	▼▼▼	8
●	Taurasi Vigna Cinque Querce '02	▼▼	7
●	Ischia Piana '04	▼▼	4
○	Fiano di Avellino Apianum '05	▼▼	5
○	Greco di Tufo '05	▼▼	5
●	Aglianico Cinque Querce '04	▼	5
●	Taurasi Vigna Cinque Querce '01	▽▽▽	6
●	Taurasi Vigna Cinque Querce '00	▽▽	6
●	Taurasi Vigna Cinque Querce Ris. '00	▽▽	7
●	Aglianico Cinque Querce '03	▽▽	5
●	Taurasi Vigna Cinque Querce '97	▽▽	7
●	Taurasi Vigna Cinque Querce '98	▽▽	7
●	Taurasi Vigna Cinque Querce '99	▽▽	7

PONTELATONE (CE)

ALOIS
LOC. AUDELINO
VIA REGAZZANO
81040 PONTELATONE (CE)
TEL. 0823876710
www.vinialois.it

It may not be the best performance we've seen, but this young estate belonging to Michele Alois and his son Massimo remains a point of reference for the production area north of Caserta. The zone is making a concerted effort to salvage several varieties that have all but disappeared, such as pallagrello and casavecchia, but it also shows great potential for aglianico-based wines in particular. Witness Campole '05, the wine that best represents the hard work of the Alois family and their consultant oenologist Riccardo Cotarella in this edition of the Guide. Basic in nothing but price, it debunks the myth that a standard-label Aglianico must be pleasant but ordinary. The rich ruby introduces an ambitious, multi-faceted range of aromas with notes of ripe red cherry lifted by flowery nuances of rose and spicy hints of cinnamon. The broad, compelling palate is savoury and confident, building up to a finish that hints at wonderfully smooth tannins. We weren't particularly impressed by Trebulanum, which is derived from pure casavecchia grown in vineyards at Pontelatone near the estate. The previous version knocked our socks off with its measured fullness and perfect combination of precision and varietal character. In comparison, the '04 is already rather evolved and shows notes of overripeness. The palate is quite traditional, unpolished, a bit mouth-drying and seems to lack weight. Finally, the coherent, very well-managed Caulino '05 is a supple, full-flavoured Campania Falanghina.

● Campole '05	🍷🍷	4
● Trebulanum '04	🍷	5
○ Caulino '05	🍷	4
● Campole '03	YY	3*
● Trebulanum '03	YY	5
● Trebulanum '02	YY	5
● Campole '04	YY	4

PRATOLA SERRA (AV)

LA CASA DELL'ORCO
FRAZ. SAN MICHELE
VIA LIMATURO, 52
83039 PRATOLA SERRA (AV)
TEL. 082537247 - 0825967038
www.lacasadellorco.it

We have been following the fortunes of La Casa dell'Orco for several years now. The estate has the most monstrous name – the Ogre's Den – in Irpinia and if the magic woven here over the last few seasons is anything to go by, then it would seem that there actually is something enchanted about San Michele in Pratola. It's the giant talent of Massimiliano Musto, the oenologist and son of owner Pellegrino, whose Fiano di Avellino '05 appeared in our finals again this year. Again, it fell just short of Three Glasses for the same reasons that have held it back in previous editions. It shows fabulous intensity and fullness on both nose and palate but we'd like to see these qualities develop more vibrantly and multi-dimensionally. The nose is rather stuck on aromatic, slightly fermentative notes and the palate needs a good shove and a bit more character. All told, however, it's still one of the best examples from the vintage. The Coda di Volpe '05 also took Two comfortable Glasses. This lively, full wine mingles wonderful warm, exotic aromas with notes of sage and rosemary and the palate is full despite unruly acidity. The Taurasi '02 is very good, offering a skilful interpretation of a difficult year. We'll need to retaste the Greco di Tufo '05, as it's currently suffering from a very reduced nose and rather an edgy palate that still has along way to go. The Incontri line produced by Agricola Irpina, the Musto family's second estate, debuted in great style. Its image is very similar to that of the main estate, as are the results.

○ Fiano di Avellino '05	🍷🍷	4
○ Coda di Volpe '05	🍷🍷	3*
○ Fiano di Avellino Incontri '05	🍷🍷	4
○ Greco di Tufo Incontri '05	🍷🍷	4
● Taurasi '02	🍷	6
● Taurasi Incontri '02	🍷	6
○ Greco di Tufo '05	🍷	4
○ Greco di Tufo '03	YY	4*
○ Greco di Tufo '04	YY	4
● Taurasi '00	YY	6
○ Coda di Volpe '04	YY	3*

PRIGNANO CILENTO (SA)

VITICOLTORI DE CONCILIIS
LOC. QUERCE, 1
84060 PRIGNANO CILENTO (SA)
TEL. 0974831090
www.viticoltorideconciliis.it

We don't know where he gets his inspiration from, but to us Rà! sounds like the battle cry of Bruno De Conciliis, the grand old samurai of Cilento and Campania viticulture. This year the Naima '04 is missing from the ranks, as he has left it to age for longer than usual and will present it for next year's edition of the Guide. Bereft of his katana, the sword that has helped him in his greatest triumphs, our hero did not commit hara-kiri. Quite the opposite. He revealed a whole new dimension of his fighting spirit. And leading the attack is Rà!, an archetypal meditation wine based on aglianico that is one of the best of its type in Campania. It presents pungently estery sensations on the nose but behind the brandied cherries lie spicy, earthy notes of cinchona, cinnamon and even gamey nuances. The palate is sweet but not too sweet, enlivened by rather excessive acidity and tannins that although not perfect are mineral in tone and tasty. The Aglianico Donnaluna is every bit as good, a plucky warrior enlisted to fight the good fight of the everyday wine and the '05 is well-equipped to win. It's alcohol-rich, full and attractive and complements these youthful qualities with attractive oaky sensations. The palate is dense and racy, convincing even if not particularly long. The Donnaluna Fiano '05 lacks character, especially on the nose. The Fiano Perella '04 makes a much bigger impression with its aromas of roast hazelnut and ripe pear but the palate is a bit big and overweight.

●	Donnaluna Aglianico '05	**YY**	4
○	Donnaluna Fiano '05	**YY**	4
●	Rà!	**YY**	7
○	Perella Fiano '04	**Y**	5
●	Naima '01	YYY	6
●	Naima '00	YY	6
●	Naima '02	YY	7
○	Naima '03	YY	7
●	Naima '99	YY	6
●	Donnaluna Aglianico '04	YY	4
○	Donnaluna Fiano '04	YY	4

QUARTO (NA)

CANTINE GROTTA DEL SOLE
VIA SPINELLI, 2
80010 QUARTO (NA)
TEL. 0818762566 - 0818761320
www.grottadelsole.it

There are new labels but the same results from Grotta del Sole, a battleship in the fleet of Neapolitan and Campanian wine. This huge Quarto cellar gave us another extremely comprehensive range of labels to taste for this edition of the Guide. We can't possibly review them all here so let's take a quick look at the region's best fizz, the Charmat method Asprinio d'Aversa Brut and the Asprinio d'Aversa Extra Brut '97, a metodo classico that is much more tertiary and complex in its aromas. Then there's the Penisola Sorrentina Gragnano and Lettere, both '05s, which are much more than just traditional wines for they are peerless accompaniments to a whole host of Neapolitan dishes. The Falanghina dei Campi Flegrei '05 is an impressively consistent wine that combines the salty minerality of the terroir with the eloquent solemnity of a producer that takes winemaking seriously. The Quarto di Luna '04 recaptured its Two Glass form with an unusual interpretation of Cuma-grown falanghina. It has an elegant, confident nose but the finish is slightly dried by the alcohol. The Aglianico and Vesuvio Lacryma Christi, both Bianco and Rosso, are stalwart everyday wines in the '05 editions. But without a doubt, the cream of this year's crop is the Quarto di Sole '04, an elegant blend of piedirosso and aglianico that reached our finals and made quite an impression with its big character. Unlike so many opulent, muscle-bound Supercampanians, Quarto di Sole is harmonious, consistent and nicely acidic.

●	Quarto di Sole '04	**YY**	5
○	Quarto di Luna '04	**YY**	5
○	Campi Flegrei Falanghina '05	**YY**	4*
●	Penisola Sorrentina Gragnano '05	**YY**	4*
●	Penisola Sorrentina Lettere '05	**YY**	4*
○	Asprinio d'Aversa Extra Brut '97	**YY**	5
○	Asprinio d'Aversa Brut	**YY**	4*
●	Campi Flegrei Piedirosso Passito '01	**Y**	6
○	Campi Flegrei Falanghina Coste di Cuma '04	**Y**	4
●	Aglianico '05	**Y**	4
○	Vesuvio Lacryma Christi Bianco '05	**Y**	4
●	Vesuvio Lacryma Christi Rosso '05	**Y**	4

SALZA IRPINA (AV)

Di Meo

c.da Coccovoni, 1
83050 Salza Irpina (AV)
tel. 0825981419
www.dimeo.it

OK, we admit it. We've been extremely difficult to please in our reviews of the wines produced by Roberto, Erminia and Generoso Di Meo. It's just that with their magnificent cellar and those vineyards situated in Irpinia's best zones, we expect at least one of their wines to win our top award. This year, though, the Di Meos have reason to be proud. To our minds their wines have given one of the best performances we've seen for quite some time in these parts. Five labels in the Two Glass category and a very promising Taurasi Riserva '01 that we were only able to sample from the barrel – we'll come back to it next year. The humblest of the five is Greco di Tufo '05, an intense, solid wine that is very well-made but rather atypical, dominated as it is by tropical hints of pineapple and honeydew melon that also emerge strongly on the palate. Fiano di Avellino '05 is also soft and full but doesn't have a great deal of depth. It's a little too fruity and its energy flags as it develops. There's a lot more character and complexity in the Fiano di Avellino Alessandra '04, a selection matured in stainless steel that in time expresses the potential of the Irpinia variety more fully. This is a typical, solid interpretation whose aromas range from lemon leaf to apple-like fruit with smoky undertones. The palate is graceful and measured but could do with a bit more body. Close-knit and lively, the very elegant Aglianico '04 shows earthy notes of autumn leaf. The '04 Don Generoso is a step up on previous versions, showing balsamic and flowery with a linear but smooth palate.

●	Aglianico '04	**YY**	4
●	Don Generoso '04	**YY**	8
○	Fiano di Avellino Alessandra '04	**YY**	5
○	Fiano di Avellino '05	**YY**	4
○	Greco di Tufo '05	**YY**	4
○	Coda di Volpe '05	**Y**	4
○	Fiano di Avellino Colle dei Cerri '05	**Y**	5
○	Fiano di Avellino Alessandra '03	YY	5
●	Taurasi Ris. '00	YY	6
●	Taurasi Ris. '97	YY	6
●	Taurasi Ris. '98	YY	6

SAN CIPRIANO PICENTINO (SA)

★ Montevetrano

loc. Nido
via Montevetrano, 3
84099 San Cipriano Picentino (SA)
tel. 089882285
www.montevetrano.it

It's a very fine line that separates a simple wine from an elegant one, especially when you're doing a blind tasting and the range includes some good weighty specimens. When the wine is question is a Montevetrano, however, this fine line suddenly stretches into a wide chasm because what the senses recognize as lightness and essentiality, the heart reads as pure, unadulterated emotion. We've already said all there is to say about Montevetrano: the distinctive Mediterranean Bordeaux profile, the silky mineral development and the brilliant expansion in the finish. And yet we never cease to be amazed by the way in which Silvia Imparato's and Riccardo Cotarella's creation manages to thrill us time after time. This wine positively radiates charisma before we even get to its organoleptic excellence, and steals the show with a crisp, complex performance like those characters in Dostoevsky whose silent aura draws everyone's attention. The fresh but full 2004 vintage combines seductive classicism with astonishingly graceful definition. Notes of freshly mown grass and minty talc are the prelude to an inexorable crescendo of aromas that run the gamut from blueberry to musk, black pepper and bitter herbs. The palate displays its usual spectacular grace and harmony with masterful acidity and a textbook dose of oak. The stronger than usual, almost salty, iodine note will mark this vintage out in years to come. Just the vintage, though, because Montevetrano is already unique.

●	Montevetrano '04	**YYY**	8
●	Montevetrano '00	YYY	8
●	Montevetrano '01	YYY	8
●	Montevetrano '02	YYY	8
●	Montevetrano '03	YYY	8
●	Montevetrano '93	YYY	8
●	Montevetrano '95	YYY	8
●	Montevetrano '96	YYY	8
●	Montevetrano '97	YYY	8
●	Montevetrano '98	YYY	8
●	Montevetrano '99	YYY	8

SERINO (AV)

VILLA RAIANO
VIA PESCATORE, 19
83028 SERINO (AV)
TEL. 0825595663
www.villaraiano.it

This year's showing by the Basso brothers' beautiful estate is rather low-key compared to usual, even if a quick glance at the results below would seem to belie this. The fact is, we've been anticipating a Three Glass winner from Villa Raiano for a couple of years now and although two of this year's offerings reached the finals, the coveted prize seems more elusive than ever. Their Fiano di Avellino '05 is a wonderful combination of softness and austerity with fresh undertones of aromatic herbs that enliven its fleshier notes of white peach and pineapple. The palate has a very sweet entry that tends to render its development rather one-dimensional even in the face of the sound body. The Greco di Tufo '05 is along the same lines. It's more fermentative in its notes of banana and peppermint, showing graceful and caressing, but fails to find the depth we would expect. The Taurasi '03 did well, offering a solid, pragmatic interpretation of a difficult vintage that sacrifices some of its concentration to preserve its sound, juicy fruit. Nuances of blackberry, liquorice and nutmeg emerge on the nose and are mirrored on the measured, well-balanced palate that never turns bitter. The barrique-aged Fiano di Avellino Ripa Alta '05 defies description at this moment in time. Time will work its magic but it promises well given the fullness, width, glycerine and good supporting acidity it already displays. The Falanghina del Beneventano '05 stands out for its concentration and elegance. The Orano '05, a rosé obtained from aglianico, is fair.

○	Fiano di Avellino '05	2 glasses (black)	4*
○	Greco di Tufo '05	2 glasses (black)	4
●	Taurasi '03	2 glasses (black)	6
○	Falanghina Beneventano '05	2 glasses (black)	4*
○	Fiano di Avellino Ripa Alta '05	2 glasses (black)	5
⊙	Orano '05	1 glass (black)	4
●	Taurasi '01	2 glasses (white)	6
○	Fiano di Avellino '03	2 glasses (white)	4*
○	Fiano di Avellino '04	2 glasses (white)	4
○	Greco di Tufo '04	2 glasses (white)	4
○	Fiano di Avellino Ripa Alta '03	2 glasses (white)	5

SESSA AURUNCA (CE)

GALARDI
FRAZ. SAN CARLO
S.P. SESSA-MIGNANO
81030 SESSA AURUNCA (CE)
TEL. 0823925003 - 0823708900
www.terradilavoro.com

One love, one wine. We openly declare our passion for Terra di Lavoro with a phrase adapted from U2's greatest love song. We flirted with this charmer when it was first released and forgave its occasional youthful peccadilloes even when we were the first to recognize them. But now that our head is telling us what our heart has always known, we have put the wine on a pedestal and bow down before it. The object of our abject affection is the '04 edition of this famous blend of aglianico with small additions of piedirosso, sourced from the volcanic terrain of San Carlo at Sessa Aurunca. In our opinion, this is the best version ever made. It's an absolute thoroughbred, full of minerality and above all restrained power that combine to support astonishing suppleness. That unique smoky note is still there but with each vintage it becomes more and more integrated with the cornucopia of forest floor aromas, ranging through briary fruit, cinchona root, wet leaves, gamey notes and others too varied to mention. Entry on the palate is gripping, creamy and velvety, intensified by a wonderful earthiness that seems to augment these sensations. The finish is multi-faceted and deep, buttressed by a multitude of luxuriant, very dense, perfectly smooth tannins. For this, one of the great wines of Italy, our heartfelt thanks go to Luisa Murena, Arturo Celentano, Francesco and Dora Catello and their friend and consultant oenologist, Riccardo Cotarella.

●	Terra di Lavoro '04	3 glasses (black)	7
●	Terra di Lavoro '02	3 glasses (white)	7
●	Terra di Lavoro '03	3 glasses (white)	7
●	Terra di Lavoro '99	3 glasses (white)	7
●	Terra di Lavoro '00	2 glasses (white)	7
●	Terra di Lavoro '01	2 glasses (white)	7
●	Terra di Lavoro '94	2 glasses (white)	7
●	Terra di Lavoro '95	2 glasses (white)	7
●	Terra di Lavoro '97	2 glasses (white)	7
●	Terra di Lavoro '98	2 glasses (white)	7

SORBO SERPICO (AV)

★ Feudi di San Gregorio
loc. Cerza Grossa
83050 Sorbo Serpico (AV)
tel. 0825986611
www.feudi.it

We applaud another brace of Three Glass trophies and, more important, another stunning performance from the powerhouse of Sorbo Serpico. The metodo classico Irpinias created with the exceptional support of Anselme Selosse are not yet ready but the estate placed no less than six wines in our final selections. The Rubrato '04 is one of the best and most reasonably priced versions of aglianico to come out of Irpinia. The Fiano di Avellino Pietracalda '05 and Greco di Tufo Cutizzi '05 are intense and full but they both lack complexity and eloquence in the finish. The superb Fiano di Avellino Campanaro '05 came within a hair's breadth of Three Glasses for its sweet, fermentative entry on the palate followed by a varied, lively profile of pink grapefruit and white pepper. Big and wide, it even shows a certain austerity in the finish and we have great hopes for its future development. A measured, patient approach will also help to reveal the full fabulous density of the Serpico and Pàtrimo, a classic couple like the '04 vintage that created them. The first offers a very ripe, fleshy nose of jam and brandied fruit but the clenched, vigorous palate sweeps away any doubts about its soundness and ageing potential. Pàtrimo is a more challenging wine. The nose is inscrutable, but the weight and power displayed on the palate don't require much interpretation. The Fiano di Avellino and the Greco di Tufo '05 cruise past the Two Glass line alongside the Sannio Falanghina Serrocielo '05.

● Pàtrimo '04	🍷🍷🍷	8
● Serpico '04	🍷🍷🍷	8
● Rubrato '04	🍷🍷	5
○ Fiano di Avellino Campanaro '05	🍷🍷	7
○ Fiano di Avellino Pietracalda '05	🍷🍷	6
○ Greco di Tufo Cutizzi '05	🍷🍷	6
○ Fiano di Avellino '05	🍷🍷	5
○ Greco di Tufo '05	🍷🍷	5
○ Sannio Falanghina Serrocielo '05	🍷🍷	4
○ Sannio Falanghina '05	🍷	5
⊙ Sannio Rosato '05	🍷	4
● Pàtrimo '02	YYY	8
○ Greco di Tufo Cutizzi '03	YYY	5*
● Serpico '03	YYY	8
○ Fiano di Avellino Pietracalda '04	YYY	5

SUMMONTE (AV)

Guido Marsella
via Marone, 2
83010 Summonte (AV)
tel. 0825626555 - 3484777019

He worked in bitumen and asphalt before the oenology bug hit him and the pursuit of the perfect wine became his mission in life. He is a unique character who keeps a low profile and feels enormous passion for the lamentably few bottles he produces. We're talking about Guido Marsella, winemaker in Summonte, as he likes to describe himself on the labels of his Fiano di Avellino. This is one of those wines that fans of the type are called upon to reckon with. Full, powerful, alcoholic and rich in tropical fruit sensations, it can prompt those unfamiliar with the diversities of this production area to view it as an atypical Fiano. In fact, the soil and climate at Summonte are completely different from the more classic zones of Montefredane, Lapio or Candida. At an altitude of around 600 metres, Marsella's vineyards are some of the highest in the DOC and lie on the foothills of Monte Partenio in a stony, rocky zone that has shallow, fossil-rich soil. These conditions produce very fresh, concentrated wines with less minerally character but they still need time to attain perfect balance. A classic example is the Fiano di Avellino '04, a blue-blooded finalist that would merit Three Glasses if it just bared its teeth a bit more. The generous, fascinating nose offers notes of mango and papaya enhanced by smoky tones and unexpected veins of freshness. Sumptuous and rich in extract, the palate seems to promise an explosive finish but it doesn't quite go the distance.

○ Fiano di Avellino '04	🍷🍷	4
○ Fiano di Avellino '03	YY	4

TAURASI (AV)

Antonio Caggiano

C.DA SALA
83030 TAURASI (AV)
TEL. 082774723 - 082774043
www.cantinecaggiano.it

With Antonio Caggiano, ex-globetrotting photographer with a passion for wine, it's always a question of perspective. If you look at the subject close up, you are fascinated by its elegance and personality. If you stand back and view it from a distance, you begin to notice the figures in the background rather than what's in the foreground. There's no point repeating that the Taurasi Macchia dei Goti still plays the starring role here. The '03 was a strong contender at our final tastings but just fell short of the Three Glass mark. The multi-faceted nose is still in thrall to the oak but underneath unusual gamey notes emerge, flanked by earthy aromas and elegant touches of spice. The effects of the torrid growing year also seem to have been kept under control on the palate. It shows more continuity than impact and only the tannins seem to suffer, being rather dusty. Salae Domini '04 gives a fairly satisfactory performance but it's still a long way from those versions that made such a splash in past finals. Sweet notes of oak emerge on the nose and in the quite bitterish finish, but the palate is broad and full. The Taurì '04 is finer and more delicate, if not quite up to the same standard. It's enlivened by flowery notes and the palate is lean and perhaps a touch too light. The estate's two main whites are still quite difficult to define, as they offer both the youthful sensations from their sojourn in new oak and hints of development that emerge in the rather burning finish, which lacks thrust. The Fiagre '05 is not as weighty but the interpretation is very well done.

●	Taurasi V. Macchia dei Goti '03	TT	6
●	Salae Domini '04	TT	6
●	Taurì '04	T	4
○	Fiagre '05	T	4
○	Fiano di Avellino Béchar '05	T	5
○	Greco di Tufo Devon '05	T	5
●	Taurasi V. Macchia dei Goti '99	YYY	7
●	Taurasi V. Macchia dei Goti '00	YY	7
●	Taurasi V. Macchia dei Goti '01	YY	7
●	Salae Domini '01	YY	6

TORRECUSO (BN)

Fattoria La Rivolta

C.DA RIVOLTA
82030 TORRECUSO (BN)
TEL. 0824872921
www.fattorialarivolta.com

The wonderful thing about wine is that you can never take anything for granted. Things can change at the drop of a hat. Ask Paolo Cotroneo, the driving force behind the Fattoria La Rivolta, for his estate dropped out of the Guide in 2006 but is back with a vengeance this year. The Aglianico del Taburno Terra di Rivolta Riserva came excruciatingly close to winning our top prize with a masterful interpretation of the scorching '03 vintage. It offers a nose of rare beauty with aromas of eucalyptus, wood resin and even gamey notes and tar. Mid palate is wide and embracing, ceaselessly changing, even revealing notes that hint at camphor. Anything missing? Probably not, although more solid, smoother tannic support would have dismissed any lingering doubts we might have entertained about its ageing potential. As usual, the '04 Aglianico del Taburno showed well. It's an approachable, fruitily pleasant wine despite its vegetal tones. The whites are an altogether different matter. Their quest for originality is reflected in a style similar to that of what are commonly – and wrongly – defined as biodynamic wines, but they don't always achieve the same results as the best in this class. The most successful is Sogno di Rivolta '04, a blend of falanghina, greco and fiano. It presents unusual tertiary sensations of peach tea, dried grape skins and carob, and its oxidative but lively character also comes through on the concentrated, astringent, alcohol-rich palate. The Sannio Fiano '05 is built on similar lines but less complex and we must confess that we expected a bit more from it.

●	Aglianico del Taburno Terra di Rivolta Ris. '03	TT	6
●	Aglianico del Taburno '04	TT	4*
○	Sogno di Rivolta '04	TT	4
○	Sannio Fiano '05	T	4
●	Aglianico del Taburno Terra di Rivolta Ris. '00	YY	6
●	Aglianico del Taburno '01	YY	4

TUFO (AV)

Benito Ferrara

fraz. San Paolo, 14a
83010 Tufo (AV)
tel. 0825998194
www.benitoferrara.it

Three out of three wines in the Two Glass category would be a more than gratifying result for most Campania estates, old or new, but it's not enough to satisfy Gabriella Ferrara and her husband, Sergio. Their Greco di Tufo Vigna Cicogna selection is a benchmark for the entire production zone. The vineyard is at an altitude of 500 metres and has a compact, sound clayey base on slopes that are steep enough to bring on an attack of vertigo. For these and other reasons, not least the passion of its creators, we expect mega-results from this small San Paolo cellar every year. But once more, it lacks the wow factor that would put it at the top of Irpinian winemaking. Gabriella Ferrara's wines are all highly distinctive with a style that favours the opulence, extract and ripeness of the fruit over the elegance, mineral verve and above all the soundness and freshness of the aromas. It's an extremely fascinating style, deeply rooted in the vinification traditions of this small mining town, but it doesn't altogether convince us, especially when dominated by hints of development. The Vigna Cicogna '05 is the weightier of the two Grecos but the basic version currently shows greater complexity and smoother integration of glycerine and acidity. The Fiano di Avellino '05 is a more versatile wine that also possesses a full palate and already shows very tertiary aromas of dried fruit and almost toasty nuances that crimp its liveliness.

O Fiano di Avellino '05	🍷🍷	5
O Greco di Tufo '05	🍷🍷	4
O Greco di Tufo Vigna Cicogna '05	🍷🍷	5
O Greco di Tufo Vigna Cicogna '04	🍷🍷 (white)	5
O Greco di Tufo Vigna Cicogna '01	🍷🍷 (white)	5
O Greco di Tufo Vigna Cicogna '02	🍷🍷 (white)	5
O Greco di Tufo Vigna Cicogna '03	🍷🍷 (white)	5
O Greco di Tufo Vigna Cicogna '99	🍷🍷 (white)	4

TUFO (AV)

Torricino

loc. Torricino, 5
83010 Tufo (AV)
tel. 0825998119
www.torricino.com

Greco comes from Tufo but its best producers rarely do. The little town that gives its name to the DOC was in dire need of reinforcements when young Stefano Di Marzo, oenologist and owner of Torricino, came along. His wines are not just excellent; they are also highly distinctive, richly extracted, full and often tertiary, whether you like their style or not you have to admit that it's anything but standardized. In the case of Di Marco's wines, sweetness and fullness do not constitute a quick, easy route to simple tastes but seek to add something new in the context of the everyday vinifications traditional to Tufo's viticulturists. His Greco di Tufo '05 is a perfect example, winning a place in our finals for its apparently evolved notes of honey, nougat and candied citrus fruit unexpectedly enlivened by hints of basil and pepper. The sulphurous character of the Tufo terrain comes through more strongly on the palate, which expands powerfully and vigorously to end in an almost tannic finish whose only fault is its slightly excessive alcohol. It's almost impossible to detect the fine rocky elegance of those Fianos produced in steeper zones in Stefano's '05. It focuses more on sweet notes of acacia, bitter orange and pistachio and shows impressive backbone that loosens up a bit under the influence of the supporting acidity. Greco di Tufo Raone '04 isn't perfect but it is delightful and offers an interesting opportunity to explore the potential of the variety when aged in oak.

O Fiano di Avellino '05	🍷🍷	4*
O Greco di Tufo '05	🍷🍷	4*
O Greco di Tufo Raone '04	🍷🍷	4
O Greco di Tufo '04	🍷🍷 (white)	4*

OTHER WINERIES

Fattoria Selvanova
via Selvanova
81010 Castel Campagnano (CE)
tel. 0823867261 - 0823867025
www.fattoriaselvanova.com

Antonio Buono's is one of the new, emerging estates to the north of Caserta. The Aglianico Selvanova '04 is absent but the Cabernet Sopralago '04 shows unexpected character. The reasonably priced Aglianico Vignantica '05 is much more than an easy-drinker and the Aglianico Silicata '04 debuted well.

● Sopralago '04	🍷🍷	4
● Silicata '04	🍷	5
● Aglianico Vignantica '05	🍷	3*

Fattoria Ciabrelli
via Italia, 3
82037 Castelvenere (BN)
tel. 0824940565
www.ciabrelli.it

The historic Ciabrelli estate in Benevento did well. Sannio Coda di Volpe '05 has lots of body and personality with notes of ripe pear and even lavender announcing a lively, pervasive palate. The robustly vigorous Aglianico '03 has a well-defined palate. It's substantial, like its creator.

○ Sannio Coda di Volpe '05	🍷🍷	4
● Aglianico '03	🍷	5

Aminea
via Santa Lucia
83040 Castelvetere sul Calore (AV)
tel. 082765787

Mimì Mongiello's Irpinia estate is very reliable, even if its wines don't have that wow factor. This year our vote went to Greco di Tufo '05, a ripe fruity wine with good consistency. The Fiano di Avellino '05 is grassier and the severe, mouth-drying Taurasi Baiardo '01 is a bit more developed.

● Taurasi Baiardo '01	🍷	5
○ Fiano di Avellino '05	🍷	4
○ Greco di Tufo '05	🍷	4

I Favati
p.zza Di Donato
83020 Cesinali (AV)
tel. 0825666898
www.cantineifavati.it

Rosanna and Piersabino Favati's small estate is ready for the big step. The Pietramara '05 is very elegant but lacks weight. Similarly, Greco di Tufo Terrantica '05 is very minerally, vibrant and full but not very long. The Aglianico Cretarossa '04 is over-firm but typical and eloquent.

● Aglianico Cretarossa '04	🍷🍷	4
○ Fiano di Avellino Pietramara '05	🍷🍷	4
○ Greco di Tufo Terrantica '05	🍷🍷	4

MACCHIALUPA
FRAZ. SAN PIETRO IRPINO
VIA FONTANA
83010 CHIANCHE (AV)
TEL. 0825996396 - www.macchialupa.it

Angelo Valentino missed our top prize but three Two Glasses is a major result. The Greco di Tufo '05 is a bit too fruit-centric but has exemplary weight. Keep an eye on the Fiano di Avellino '05. It's sharp and still quite hard but robust. The Taurasi '02 is a brave interpretation of a poor vintage.

● Taurasi Le Surte '02	🍷🍷	6
○ Fiano di Avellino '05	🍷🍷	4
○ Greco di Tufo '05	🍷🍷	4
● Campania Aglianico '04	🍷	4

COLLE DI SAN DOMENICO
S.S. OFANTINA KM 7,500
83040 CHIUSANO DI SAN DOMENICO (AV)
TEL. 0825985423 - 082539554
www.cantinecolledisandomenico.it

In all the years we've tasted Colle di San Domenico wines, this is the best showing we've seen from this Chiusano cellar. Despite their age, the two Taurasis are dynamic and elegant. The Falanghina del Sannio '05 is fruity and the Aglianico performs to type.

● Taurasi Ris. '98	🍷🍷	6
● Taurasi '99	🍷🍷	5
● Aglianico '04	🍷	3
○ Sannio Falanghina '05	🍷	4

GENNARO PAPA
P.ZZA LIMATA, 2
81030 FALCIANO DEL MASSICO (CE)
TEL. 0823931267

Falerno's recent history sees the austerity of aglianico set against the exuberant sweetness of primitivo. Those who prefer the latter will enjoy the new Falerno del Massico Primitivo Campantuono '04 produced by Papa, a small Caserta estate where Maurilio Chioccia is consultant oenologist.

● Falerno del Massico Primitivo Campantuono '04	🍷🍷	6

PIETRATORCIA
FRAZ. CUOTTO
VIA PROVINCIALE PANZA, 309
80075 FORIO (NA)
TEL. 081908206 - www.pietratorcia.it

You either love or hate Pietratorcia's wines. We like their originality but believe there's significant room for improvement. The Scheria Bianco '03 has tertiary notes of macerated flowers and ripe figs, and a big, edgy palate. The Scheria Rosso '03 shows potential despite its rather muddled nose.

○ Scheria Bianco '03	🍷🍷	6
● Scheria Rosso '03	🍷	6
○ Ischia Bianco Sup. Vigne del Cuotto '05	🍷	4

TENUTA ADOLFO SPADA
LOC. FONTANA DI TEANO
FRAZ. VAGLIE - VIA S. GIACOMO
81045 GALLUCCIO (CE)
TEL. 0823925709 - www.tenutaspada.it

Galluccio is not yet a terroir of reference for Campania but Adolfo Spada's wines may well turn it into one. The cream of the crop is the Gladius '04, a measured, elegant wine that is a little tight in the finish. The Gallicius debuted well, showing supple and racy but never forced.

● Gladius '04	🍷🍷	5
● Gallicius Rosso '05	🍷	2

TELARO
LOC. CALABRITTO
VIA CINQUE PIETRE, 2
81045 GALLUCCIO (CE)
TEL. 0823925841 - www.vinitelaro.it

Telaro wines are good and reasonably priced but we can't review them all here. Falanghina di Roccamonfina V.T. '05 is seductive, Falanghina Brut Tefrite is one of Campania's best fizzes and Galluccio Falanghina Ripa Bianca '04 did well but the Galluccio Aglianico Montecaruso lacks support.

○ Falanghina di Roccamonfina V.T. '05	🍷🍷	4*
○ Falanghina Tefrite Brut	🍷🍷	4*
● Galluccio Montecaruso '04	🍷	4
○ Galluccio Falanghina Ripa Bianca '05	🍷	3

CANTINE FEDERICIANE
FRAZ. MARANO
VIA TOSCANA, 2
80016 LETTERE (NA)
TEL. 0815764153

Cantine Federiciane manages to combine volume with reasonable prices. A fine example is the Gragnano della Penisola Sorrentina '05, much more than just an enjoyable wine. The Greco di Tufo '05 is well made, the Fiano di Avellino '05 is simpler and the Falanghina dei Campi Flegrei '05 is typical.

○ Campi Flegrei Falanghina '05	🍷	3
○ Fiano di Avellino '05	🍷	3
○ Greco di Tufo '05	🍷	3
● Penisola Sorrentina Gragnano '05	🍷	3*

D'ANTICHE TERRE - VEGA
C.DA LO PIANO - S.S. 7 BIS
83030 MANOCALZATI (AV)
TEL. 0825675689 - 0825675358
www.danticheterre.it

This Manocalzati cellar is one of the oldest in Irpinia and offers a reliable, compact range. The Greco di Tufo '05 is excellent, as soft and embracing as ever but not terribly deep. We liked both the warm, smooth Aglianico '03 and the solid, persistent Coda di Volpe '05.

○ Greco di Tufo '05	🍷🍷	4
● Aglianico '03	🍷	4
○ Coda di Volpe '05	🍷	3
○ Fiano di Avellino '05	🍷	4

QUINTODECIMO
VIA SAN LEONARDO
83036 MIRABELLA ECLANO (AV)
TEL. 0825449321
www.quintodecimo.it

We'll fess up. We were very curious to taste the first offerings from the new estate set up by Luigi Moio, a leading light in recent Campania and Basilicata wine production. The Terra d'Eclano '04 is excellent. The notes of new oak are strong but the body is sound and compact and promises well.

● Terra d'Eclano '04	🍷🍷	6

LUNA ROSSA
VIA ANDREA MEO, 1
84096 MONTECORVINO ROVELLA (SA)
TEL. 0898021016
www.combination.it

What a Combination! This Salerno blend of aglianico and merlot is a very pragmatic interpretation of the torrid summer of '03. Warm but not overripe notes of pepper and cinnamon have undertones of cherry and liquorice. The palate rather lacks concentration and intensity but is surprisingly supple.

● Combination '03	🍷🍷	5

COLLI IRPINI
LOC. SERRA DI MONTEFUSCO
VIA SERRA
83030 MONTEFUSCO (AV)
TEL. 0825963972 - www.montesole.it

Colli Irpini presented around ten labels this year but we can't review them all here. Once more, the fragrant, tasty Greco di Tufo '05 is in pole position. It's not huge but behaves well on the palate. Greco Brut is surprising, Taurasi '00 convincing and Falanghina Simposium '05 has improved.

○ Greco di Tufo '05	🍷🍷	4
● Taurasi Montesolae '00	🍷	4
○ Simposium Bianco '05	🍷	4
○ Greco Brut	🍷	4

CANTINA FARRO
LOC. FUSARO - FRAZ. BACOLI
VIA VIRGILIO, 16/24
80070 NAPOLI
TEL. 0818545555 - www.cantinefarro.it

Delicate, continuous notes of apple and broom with iodine hints, a caressing, tasty almost salty palate and a fine, acidulous finish. Michele Farro's Falanghina dei Campi Flegrei is an '05 in spades. Cigliate '04 has more tertiary notes and Piedirosso dei Campi Flegrei '05 is supple but vibrant.

○ Campi Flegrei Falanghina '05	🍷🍷	4*
○ Campi Flegrei Le Cigliate '04	🍷	4
● Campi Flegrei Piedirosso '05	🍷	4

Manimurci

via Casale, 9bis
83052 Paternopoli (AV)
tel. 0827771012 - 0827771977
www.cantinemanimurci.com

We have another new entry from Irpinia. In pride of place is the Rossocupo '04, an extrovert Aglianico that develops vigorously without going over the top. The Greco di Tufo '05 is excellent, soft and full-flavoured. The Aglianico Quattro Contrade '04 and the Coda di Volpe '05 are both decent.

● Rossocupo '04	🍷🍷	4
○ Greco di Tufo '05	🍷🍷	4
● Quattro Contrade '04	🍷	4
○ Coda di Volpe '05	🍷	4

Lorenzo Nifo Sarrapochiello

via Piana
82030 Ponte (BN)
tel. 0824876450

Passionate Ponte viticulturist Lorenzo Nifo Sarrapochiello produces Falanghinas with a difference. He transforms the flowers-fruit-acidity trio into an unusual mix of ripe notes of honey and candied citrus fruit and weight. The wine avoids excess, thanks to its lively, lingering palate.

○ Sannio Falanghina '05	🍷🍷	3*
○ Sannio Falanghina Alenta '05	🍷🍷	3*

Ocone

loc. La Madonnella
via del Monte, 56
82030 Ponte (BN)
tel. 0824874040 - www.oconevini.it

Results apart, producers like Domenico Ocone leave a mark. His Falanghina del Taburno '05 is seductively golden and unashamedly tertiary with notes of dried fruit and fresh veins of thyme and rosemary. The Taburno Coda di Volpe '05 and the Aglianico del Taburno Vigna Pezza la Corte '02 are correct.

○ Taburno Falanghina '05	🍷🍷	3*
● Aglianico del Taburno V. Pezza la Corte '02	🍷	4
○ Taburno Coda di Volpe '05	🍷	3*

Viticoltori del Casavecchia

via Madonna delle Grazie, 28
81040 Pontelatone (CE)
tel. 0823659198

This was a good year for casavecchia. Many Caserta producers are recovering the variety, not least this Pontelatone co-operative whose Corte Rosa '04 is a fine compromise of approachability and complexity. The Erta dei Ciliegi '05 is simpler but intriguing and the Vigna Prea '04 is more linear.

● Corte Rosa '04	🍷🍷	4*
● Vigna Prea '04	🍷	5
● Erta dei Ciliegi '05	🍷	3

Giulia

via Boschetto, 42
83030 Prata di Principato Ultra (AV)
tel. 0825961219
www.giuliaonline.com

Prata is one of the eight Greco di Tufo production areas and Giulia, property of the Freda family, is the only cellar here. Its wines are distinctive. They may not be perfect but they are assertive. The Fiano di Avellino '05 is well defined, the Greco di Tufo '05 and Taurasi '01 decent.

○ Fiano di Avellino '05	🍷🍷	4
● Taurasi '01	🍷	5
○ Greco di Tufo '05	🍷	4

Ettore Sammarco

via Civita, 9
84010 Ravello (SA)
tel. 089872774
www.ettoresammarco.it

Sammarco's Ravello Bianco Selva delle Monache '05 has character, guts and a minty finish. It's more complex than the Vigna Grotta Piana '05. From the reds, we liked Ravello Selva delle Monache '04 for its crisp, fleshy citrus nose and taut if rather rigid palate. The other labels are decent.

● Costa d'Amalfi Ravello Rosso Selva delle Monache '04	🍷🍷	4
○ Costa d'Amalfi Ravello Bianco Selva delle Monache '05	🍷🍷	4

De Falco
via Figliola
80040 San Sebastiano al Vesuvio (NA)
tel. 0817713755
www.defalco.it

San Sebastiano al Vesuvio is a reliable estate. The Falanghina '05 offers one of the best interpretations of the type from a controversial but positive year. The Gragnano della Penisola Sorrentina '05 is its usual vital self while the Greco di Tufo '05 and Taurasi '01 show well.

○	Falanghina del Beneventano '05	🍷🍷	3*
●	Taurasi '01	🍷	5
○	Greco di Tufo '05	🍷	4
●	Penisola Sorrentina Gragnano '05	🍷	4

Cantina dei Monaci
fraz. Santa Lucia, 206
83030 Santa Paolina (AV)
tel. 0825964350

It wasn't the best year for Greco di Tufo but we expected more of Angelo Carpenito's and Maria Coppola's keynote wine. The '05 is quite aggressive, despite very decent body and nice full flavour. The Fiano di Avellino '05 did much better with its fascinating notes of rain-washed stone and sage.

○	Fiano di Avellino '05	🍷🍷	4
○	Greco di Tufo '05	🍷	4

Mustilli
via Caudina, 10
82019 Sant'Agata de' Goti (BN)
tel. 0823718142 - 0823717433
www.mustilli.com

This historic Sant'Agata dei Goti estate showed well but not brilliantly. Our vote goes to the delicately flowery Sannio Fiano '05. The Sannio Greco Vigna Fontanella '05 and Conte Artus '04 did well but Campania's emblematic Sant'Agata dei Goti Falanghina '05 was below par.

●	S. Agata dei Goti Rosso Conte Artus '04	🍷	4
○	S. Agata dei Goti Falanghina '05	🍷	4
○	Sannio Fiano '05	🍷	4
○	Sannio Greco V. Fontanella '05	🍷	4

Masseria Felicia
fraz. Carano di Sessa Arunca
via Prov. Appia Carano
81030 Sessa Aurunca (CE)
tel. 0823935095

Masseria Felicia, a innovative force in Caserta winemaking, is back in the Guide. Falerno del Massico Etichetta Bronzo '03 has chocolate and plum notes and a very full palate but lacks continuity. Falerno del Massico Ariapetrina '04 is lovely and earthy but is curbed by its over-assertive tannins.

●	Falerno del Massico Rosso Etichetta Bronzo '03	🍷🍷	6
●	Falerno del Massico Rosso Ariapetrina '04	🍷	4

De Angelis
via Marziale, 14
80067 Sorrento (NA)
tel. 0818781648

It was a low-key year for the De Angelis estate. The '04 version of Nero del Tasso, its leading label, is rather disappointing but by way of compensation the Lacryma Christi Bianco '05 and the Sorrento della Penisola Sorrentina '05 performed extremely well.

●	Aglianico del Beneventano '04	🍷	4
●	Nero del Tasso '04	🍷	6
○	Penisola Sorrentina Sorrento Bianco '05	🍷	3
○	Vesuvio Lacryma Christi Bianco '05	🍷	4*

Antica Hirpinia
c.da Lenze, 10
83030 Taurasi (AV)
tel. 082774730
www.anticahirpinia.it

This big Taurasi co-operative has made its move. Reorganization of the vineyards and cellar is having an effect, especially on the lively, extrovert Greco di Tufo '05. The Taurasi Riserva '00 is good and full, if a little over-extracted. Don Gesualdo '03 is ambitious but rather sedentary.

●	Taurasi Ris. '00	🍷🍷	6
○	Greco di Tufo '05	🍷🍷	4
●	Don Gesualdo '03	🍷	5

CANTINE CASPARRIELLO
C.DA SAN PIETRO
83030 TAURASI (AV)
TEL. 082774793
www.cantinecasparriello.it

Michele Casparriello failed to encore last year's superb results. Of the rather too many wines presented, Taurasi Riserva '00 has a very interesting tertiary yet sound style. The excellent Aglianico '03 is well priced, the Platinum '01 is more linear and the Fiano di Avellino '05 is goodish.

● Taurasi Ris. '00	🍷🍷	4
● Aglianico '03	🍷🍷	3*
● Platinum '01	🍷	3
○ Fiano di Avellino '05	🍷	3

CONTRADE DI TAURASI
VIA MUNICIPIO, 39
83030 TAURASI (AV)
TEL. 0815442457
www.contradeditaurasi.it

Enza Lonardo's Taurasis guarantee quality, especially to those fans who seek an eclectic, modern, elegant style. The Taurasi Riserva '01 performed confidently in our finals, showing notes of liquorice, blackberry and cocoa powder and a concentrated palate, although the finish is still over-firm.

● Taurasi Ris. '01	🍷🍷	7
● Aglianico '04	🍷	4

I CAPITANI
VIA BOSCO FAIANO, 15
83030 TORRE LE NOCELLE (AV)
TEL. 0825969182 - 082522624
www.icapitani.com

This is the first entry for Ciriaco Cefalo's estate, one of Avellino's loveliest. We enjoyed a superb Fiano di Avellino Gaudium '05, full and fleshy with a pleasant citrus finish. The Jumara '03 is a very convincing Irpinia Rosso, continuous and sustained by lovely tannic texture.

● Jumara '03	🍷🍷	4
○ Fiano di Avellino Gaudium '05	🍷🍷	4
● Taurasi '01	🍷	6

FONTANAVECCHIA
VIA FONTANAVECCHIA
82030 TORRECUSO (BN)
TEL. 0824876275
www.fontanavecchia.info

No offence to the talented Libero Rillo. His wines are good but not quite good enough to withstand the competition in Campania. The Orazio '03 did well but not so the Grave Mora '04. It's closed on the nose and the palate shows excessive extract. The Aglianico del Taburno '04 is solid and vigorous.

● Orazio '03	🍷🍷	5
● Aglianico del Taburno '04	🍷	4
● Aglianico del Taburno Grave Mora '04	🍷	6
○ Taburno Falanghina '05	🍷	3*

IANNELLA
VIA TORA
82030 TORRECUSO (BN)
TEL. 0824872392
www.cantineiannella.it

Keep an eye on Antonio Iannella's small estate. Despite the year, his Aglianico '02 shows style and substance. The Don Nicola 'U Signore Riserva '01 is even better, not far off Campania's weightiest aglianico-based wines. The very well-made Falanghina del Taburno '05 is full on the palate.

● Taburno Don Nicola Ris. '01	🍷🍷	6
● Taburno Aglianico '02	🍷🍷	4*
○ Taburno Falanghina '05	🍷	4*

GIUSEPPE APICELLA
FRAZ. CAPITIGNANO
VIA CASTELLO SANTA MARIA, 1
84010 TRAMONTI (SA)
TEL. 089856209 - www.viniapicella.com

Giuseppe Apicella's day will come. His century-old, terraced vineyards of tintore vines come up with the goods. Costa d'Amalfi Tramonti 'A Scippata Riserva '03 has great weight, if not the depth, Tramonti Bianco '05 is crisp and jolly and the Costa d'Amalfi Rosato '05 is fair.

● Costa d'Amalfi Tramonti Rosso A' Scippata Ris. '03	🍷🍷	6
○ Costa d'Amalfi Tramonti Bianco '05	🍷	4
⊙ Costa d'Amalfi Tramonti Rosato '05	🍷	4

BASILICATA

After a dearth of Three Glass wines last time, this year Basilicata returned to take its share of the honours and we have two wines new to the accolade to celebrate. The first is Aglianico del Vulture Vigna Caselle Riserva '01, a classically restrained example from the renowned D'Angelo winery, which is led by highly talented oenologist Donato D'Angelo. The other is Aglianico del Vulture Nibbio Grigio Etichetta Nera '03, an enticing, modern-style version from the Di Palma family. Their different approaches are two sides of the same coin – a wine of outstanding appeal which comes from some of the best grape-growing land in southern Italy. To celebrate our 20th edition, we've added one more, a wine that was not awarded Three Glasses when it was first released but which over the years has proved to be quite superb, Aglianico del Vulture Don Anselmo '04 from the renowned Paternoster cellar. Then it's important to remember that there were over 15 wines in the finals which, given the small number of producers in the region, says much for overall quality levels. The volcanic lands of Basilicata would have been long forgotten had it not been for the great reds of D'Angelo, Paternoster and a couple of others but today, they form the backdrop to what amounts to a winemaking renaissance, one that has attracted outside investors and given its traditional producers the spur to take on ever more competitive markets. The results are there for all to see. Tourists no longer come to Basilicata simply for the Roman remains at Venosa, the castles of Frederick II or the splendours of Matera but also for the region's food and wines. Then just look at how vineyards are burgeoning, covering ever more of Vulture's best slopes. Yet just a few years ago, much of the land was lying abandoned, unless as often happens in top vineyard areas it was suitable for other crops. The Vulture zone is not yet at critical mass like that other great bastion of Aglianico, Taurasi, or the Sannio, but its new estates have started off on the right foot. They've planted their vines to quality-led criteria, their equipment is modern and they've taken on high-ranking viticultural and winemaking consultants. And if giants of the calibre of Gruppo Italiano Vini or Feudi di San Gregorio are investing in the area, then it's fair to say that Basilicata has arrived. The proof of the pudding is in the excellent wines of Paternoster, Fucci, Macarico, Basilisco, Eubea, Tenuta Le Querce, Terra dei Re, Cantine del Notaio, Bisceglia and Terre degli Svevi, as well as in those from the Cantina di Venosa and Consorzio Viticoltori Associati del Vulture co-operatives. But the province of Matera is also coming on, although average quality is well behind that of Vulture. Indeed, the speed and the commitment with which Matera producers are moving forward makes us highly optimistic for its future.

BARILE (PZ)

Consorzio Viticoltori Associati del Vulture

S.S. 93
85022 Barile (PZ)
tel. 0972770386

This co-operative was set up in 1977 and its members currently have vineyards in every part of the Vulture denomination. The president is Pasquale Pellegrino and winemaking is overseen by Sergio Paternoster, a highly experienced oenologist and an expert on Aglianico. Production is now around 250,000 bottles a year of wines that have attracted much praise. The workhorse of the range is, naturally, the basic Aglianico. The '04 is a good deep ruby. There are gentle aromas of ripe cherry and plum with floral nuances and the palate is clear-cut, fleshy and dense. The '04 Carpe Diem selection has more complex, more multi-faceted aromas, with forest fruits and blackberry jam laced with smoky and spicy notes of some finesse. The palate has good backbone, sound fruit and close-knit tannins, and reveals good use of new oak. But the top wine is Vetusto. The '04 has abundant structure and depth. Its colour is a deep, dense ruby. There are initial aromas of morello cherry and red berry fruit jam, followed by more complex, tobacco and oak toast notes, and the palate is soft and full, with clean, fleshy fruit underpinned by notable freshness and smooth, elegant tannins. Elegant peaty and oaky notes emerge on the assertive, long finish. Finally comes the fragrant Ellenico, a sweet sparkling wine made from aglianico, which has blackberry and dried rose on the nose, and is pleasantly soft and fresh.

● Aglianico del Vulture Carpe Diem '04	🍷🍷	6
● Aglianico del Vulture Vetusto '04	🍷🍷	8
● Aglianico del Vulture '04	🍷	4
● Ellenico	🍷	3
● Aglianico del Vulture Carpe Diem '00	YY	6
● Aglianico del Vulture Vetusto '00	YY	6
● Aglianico del Vulture Carpe Diem '01	YY	4
● Aglianico del Vulture Vetusto '01	YY	6
● Aglianico del Vulture Carpe Diem '99	YY	4*
● Aglianico del Vulture Vetusto '99	YY	6
● Aglianico del Vulture Carpe Diem '03	YY	4
● Aglianico del Vulture Vetusto '03	YY	6

BARILE (PZ)

Elena Fucci

C.da Solagna del Titolo
85022 Barile (PZ)
tel. 0972770736

Salvatore Fucci's first release was in 2000 although his family has long had close ties with the land. Quantities are certainly not huge but even so this small, family-run estate has carved out an important place for itself in the region. Salvatore's wife Carmela and his daughter Elena, an oenology graduate, work with him and in the few years since they started, they have increased the vineyard area to over six hectares and brought output to 16,000 bottles. The vines lie on the southern slopes of Vulture and are cultivated manually by the family. Oenological consultancy comes from a real specialist in Aglianico, Sergio Paternoster. As well as the new plantings, there has been work to enlarge and modernize the cellar, which has just finished. With everything now in place, Fucci has the look and feel of a real boutique winery. The Fuccis produce just one wine, Aglianico del Vulture Titolo, Titolo being a zone that merits cru status. The '04 came dangerously close to repeating the Three Glass success of the '02. It's a deep, dense ruby. The intense, elegant nose has red and black berries, and hints of oak and spiciness. The palate is firm and deep, with good grip, and is full of fruit and soft tannins. No doubt further top honours are just around the corner.

● Aglianico del Vulture Titolo '04	🍷🍷	6
● Aglianico del Vulture Titolo '02	YYY	6
● Aglianico del Vulture Titolo '00	YY	5
● Aglianico del Vulture Titolo '01	YY	6
● Aglianico del Vulture Titolo '03	YY	6

BARILE (PZ)

PATERNOSTER
C.SO A. DE GASPERI, 86
85022 BARILE (PZ)
TEL. 0972770224
www.paternostervini.it

Paternoster's name has been associated with Aglianico del Vulture since 1925 but the estate has risen to renown in the last few years. It has increased its vineyard holding and built a state-of-the-art cellar, which dominates the valley right in the heart of the Rotondo vineyard, the pride of the Paternoster holdings. Flanking the patriarchal figure of Pino Paternoster are his sons Vito, who manages the winery, and Sergio and Anselmo, both oenologists. Together they make a formidable team and ensure that quality remains high. This year, the wines are again admirable. The '04 release of Rotondo, a past Three Glass winner, is tight-knit and dense, with a glorious, super-smooth, close tannic weave, and great presence, but it's a little drying on the back palate. It probably needs a few more years to soften out. Don Anselmo '03 is more classically styled. It has fine fruit richness, the oak is well tempered and there is great overall complexity but the tannins are a touch too firm. Aglianico Synthesi '04 has clear, inviting aromas of red berry fruit and spice and, although still young, is succulent and enjoyable. Clivus '05, from the Casano vineyard, is highly impressive, showing sweet and balanced, with opulent notes of sage, melon and tropical fruit. The slightly sparkling Barigliòtt '05, from aglianico, and Bianco di Corte '05, from fiano, are attractive and well made. Finally, we gave Three retrospective Glasses to Don Anselmo '94, a wine that has developed amazing elegance over the years, astounding us anew every time we taste it.

●	Aglianico del Vulture Don Anselmo '03	TT	6
●	Aglianico del Vulture Rotondo '04	TT	6
●	Aglianico del Vulture Synthesi '04	TT	4*
○	Clivus '05	TT	3*
●	Barigliòtt '05	T	3
○	Bianco di Corte '05	T	4
●	Aglianico del Vulture Rotondo '00	YYY	6
●	Aglianico del Vulture Rotondo '01	YYY	6
●	Aglianico del Vulture Don Anselmo '94	YYY	5
●	Aglianico del Vulture Don Anselmo '00	YY	6
●	Aglianico del Vulture Don Anselmo '01	YY	6
●	Aglianico del Vulture Rotondo '03	YY	6
●	Aglianico del Vulture Don Anselmo '98	YY	6
●	Aglianico del Vulture Don Anselmo '99	YY	6

BARILE (PZ)

TENUTA LE QUERCE
C.DA LE QUERCE
85022 BARILE (PZ)
TEL. 0971725102 - 0971470709
www.tenutalequerce.com

In 1995, the Pietrafesa family purchased the property and label of Sasso, a winery founded in 1922, and started to build up what has become one of the most distinctive estates in Vulture. The estate now has 70 hectares of well-tended vines in Barile and produces 650,000 bottles a year, 300,000 of them for the Sasso line. Leonardo Valenti from the University of Milan oversees both the vineyards, where he set in place a planting density of over 6,000 vines per hectares, and winemaking, which takes place in a very modern, well-equipped cellar. Pride of place goes to Vigna della Corona, an Aglianico selection. Although the '04 lacks the huge concentration of previous vintages, it does have great overall balance and harmony and is a clean, dense, complex, lively wine full of fruit. Aglianico Rosso di Costanza '04 has a wealth of fruit on the nose, interwoven with spiciness and notes of Mediterranean scrubland. The palate is cleanly textured with just the right touch of oak. We thoroughly enjoyed the more immediate Aglianico Il Viola, also '04, with its exuberant black berry fruit and soft tannins. Tamurro Nero '04 is an unusual wine from the indigenous grape of the same name, which Valenti has selected and propagated. It has powerful structure and great fruit richness. Best of the Sasso line are the full Aglianico Minorco '03, which has a tobacco-like nose and good grip, and the simpler, Aglianico '04, which is well-styled and supple.

●	Aglianico del Vulture Rosso di Costanza '04	TT	6
●	Aglianico del Vulture V. della Corona '04	TT	8
●	Aglianico del Vulture Minorco Sasso '04	TT	8
●	Tamurro Nero '04	TT	8
●	Aglianico del Vulture Il Viola '04	T	4
●	Aglianico del Vulture Sasso '04	T	4
●	Aglianico del Vulture V. della Corona '00	YY	8
●	Aglianico del Vulture Rosso di Costanza '01	YY	6
●	Aglianico del Vulture V. della Corona '01	YY	8
●	Aglianico del Vulture Rosso di Costanza '02	YY	6
●	Aglianico del Vulture V. della Corona '02	YY	8
●	Aglianico del Vulture V. della Corona '03	YY	8
●	Aglianico del Vulture Rosso di Costanza '00	YY	6
●	Aglianico del Vulture Rosso di Costanza '03	YY	6

LAVELLO (PZ)

BISCEGLIA
C.DA FINOCCHIARO
85024 LAVELLO (PZ)
TEL. 097288409 - 3394246074
www.agricolabisceglia.com

Mario Bisceglia was working as a successful manager when he decided to set up his own wine estate, investing resources and, vitally, his managerial know-how. He bought 30 hectares around Lavello and leased a further 15, replanting them to strict criteria. He has built a state-of-the-art cellar and also opened an elegant country hotel. The production is certified organic and currently reaches 200,000 bottles but that figure is due to increase considerably. The range includes not just the Basilicata classics but also wines from Puglian and Campanian grapes. Winemaking is in the hands of expert Sergio Paternoster. The wine we liked best was the '01 Aglianico Riserva. Its deep, dense ruby introduces a nose with aromas that evoke the Mediterranean, along with ripe cherry, liqueur fruits and roasted coffee beans. The palate is structured and harmonious, and finishes long with attractive hints of balsam. The '03 Aglianico from the Terra di Vulcano line is also first-rate. It's a wine of presence with good fruit, backbone and definition, and refined tannins. Fiano di Avellino '05 impresses with taut freshness supporting ripe fruit, which gives way to minerality on the back palate. Tréje, from aglianico, merlot and syrah; and Armille '04, from aglianico and merlot, are both good. Everything else, from Terra di Vulcano Negroamaro Rosato '05 to Terra di Vulcano Falanghina '05 and Terra di Vulcano Primitivo'05, is well made.

● Aglianico del Vulture Ris. '01	🍷🍷	7
● Aglianico del Vulture Terra di Vulcano '03	🍷🍷	4
○ Fiano di Avellino '05	🍷🍷	6
● Armille '04	🍷	7
● Tréje '04	🍷	5
○ Chardonnay '05	🍷	5
● Terra di Vulcano Falanghina '05	🍷	4
⊙ Terra di Vulcano Negroamaro Rosato '05	🍷	4
● Terra di Vulcano Primitivo '05	🍷	4

RIONERO IN VULTURE (PZ)

BASILISCO
VIA UMBERTO I, 129
85028 RIONERO IN VULTURE (PZ)
TEL. 0972725477

Some years ago Michele Cutolo, a doctor, and his wife Nunzia decided to start producing wine, a venture that is proceeding with great success. Their estate has 20 hectares, ten of them now under vines, and their Basilisco, with a production run of 20,000 bottles, continues to be one of the best Aglianicos in the DOC. The '03 came perilously close to sharing the '01's Three Glass triumph. It is a dark, inky-deep ruby and the nose is full of ripe red and black berry fruit. There are also notes of pencil lead, roasted coffee beans and new oak, and delicate hints of balsam before the rich palate shows concentrated, warm and noticeably alcoholic, its wealth of refined tannins just teetering on the edge of over-assertiveness. Cutolo and his consultant Lorenzo Landi have now agreed to produce a second wine, in the French sense of the term. This will bring further lustre to Basilisco as it will be made from more tightly selected grapes. The first vintage, '04, of this new wine, Aglianico Teodosio, has been released. It gives an excellent preview of what Basilisco will be like next year: concentrated and tight-knit. The colour is a dense, almost black, purple colour. The nose has intense cherry, tobacco and oak despite being a bit closed when we tasted it but the palate has great depth of expression, invigorating, lively fruitiness, elegant tannins and great length. The icing on the cake is that the price is remarkably good.

● Aglianico del Vulture Basilisco '03	🍷🍷	6
● Aglianico del Vulture Teodosio '04	🍷🍷	4
● Aglianico del Vulture Basilisco '01	ꙮꙮꙮ (outline)	6
● Aglianico del Vulture Basilisco '00	ꙮꙮ (outline)	6
● Aglianico del Vulture Basilisco '02	ꙮꙮ (outline)	6
● Aglianico del Vulture Basilisco '99	ꙮꙮ (outline)	5
● Aglianico del Vulture Basilisco '98	ꙮꙮ (outline)	5

D'Angelo

via Provinciale, 8
85028 Rionero in Vulture (PZ)
tel. 0972721517

We've been dying to be able to write a report like this on the D'Angelo wines for years. The winery dates from the 1930s when it carried the flag for Vulture and its Aglianico throughout Italy and worldwide, and brothers Donato and Lucio D'Angelo continue to maintain its heritage. Donato, an oenologist, has always handled the winemaking himself. His wines eschew current fashions and trends and have the character and finesse of true classics. This year the most traditional wine of the range, Riserva Vigna Caselle '01, which ages two years in large, old "botti", simply took us by storm. The colour is a bright, intense ruby. The nose is deep and intricate, with red and morello cherries which meld into scents of the Mediterranean, liquorice, tar and a complex minerality. The palate is almost austere but has elegance, velvetiness and astounding length. It's warm and pervasive with plentiful backbone and the most elegant tannins. And there are 60,000 bottles of it! Alongside this stunner come two excellent '04 Aglianicos. Donato D'Angelo ages in small barrels and is a good deep ruby, with elegant aromas of small red berry fruits, vanilla and spices. In the mouth, it is soft and pervasive. Valle del Noce, which ages for 18 months in large casks, has good concentration, a wide spectrum of fruit and tannins that while elegant are still young and a little edgy. The straight Aglianico del Vulture '04, Canneto '04, also aglianico, and the white Vigna dei Pini '05, from chardonnay, incrocio Manzoni and pinot bianco, are as ever well made and attractive.

●	Aglianico del Vulture V. Caselle Ris. '01	🍷🍷🍷	4*
●	Aglianico del Vulture Donato D'Angelo '04	🍷🍷	5
●	Aglianico del Vulture Valle del Noce '04	🍷🍷	6
●	Canneto '04	🍷🍷	5
●	Aglianico del Vulture '04	🍷	4
○	Vigna dei Pini '05	🍷	4
●	Aglianico del Vulture Donato D'Angelo '00	♀♀	5
●	Aglianico del Vulture Donato D'Angelo '01	♀♀	5
●	Aglianico del Vulture Valle del Noce '03	♀♀	4
●	Aglianico del Vulture V. Caselle Ris. '00	♀♀	4
●	Aglianico del Vulture Donato D'Angelo '03	♀♀	5

Cantine Di Palma

c.da Scavoni
85028 Rionero in Vulture (PZ)
tel. 0972722891
www.cantinedipalma.com

Antonio Di Palma is a successful engineer with a great passion for viticulture and for wine. His family has been growing grapes in Rionero for generations and ten years ago he felt the call of the land becoming ever stronger. So he set up his own estate. Working alongside his brother Giuseppe and sister Caterina, and with support from his parents Achille and Filomena, he has built up 15 hectares of fine vineyard, much of it newly planted and still to come into production. The leitmotif of his endeavours is respect for provenance and faith in the qualities of aglianico, his principal grape. The vines are grown organically and yield an excellent range of wines. The style is now being tweaked by Di Palma's new consultant, Stefano Chioccioli, and the first result of his input can be seen on Aglianico del Vulture Nibbio Grigio Etichetta Nera '03, which has a production run of 20,000. It was the only wine to be submitted to our tastings this year and it has superb character. Still at the beginning of its long life, it is already refined, rich and structured, yet not overly so. It's full of fruit and spiciness, and there is a long, elegant finish with blackberry jam, tobacco and cocoa powder, all of which earned it a thoroughly deserved Three Glasses. The award projects the estate into the select band of Italy's elite and is, no doubt, just only first in a long line of similar successes.

●	Aglianico del Vulture Il Nibbio Grigio Et. Nera '03	🍷🍷🍷	6
●	Aglianico del Vulture Il Nibbio Grigio '00	♀♀	6
●	Aglianico del Vulture Il Nibbio Grigio '02	♀♀	6
●	Aglianico del Vulture Tenuta San Savino '02	♀♀	5
●	Aglianico del Vulture Tenuta Piano Regio '03	♀♀	4
●	Aglianico del Vulture Il Nibbio Grigio '97	♀♀	5
●	Aglianico del Vulture Il Nibbio Grigio '98	♀♀	4

RIONERO IN VULTURE (PZ)

Cantine del Notaio

via Roma, 159
85028 Rionero in Vulture (PZ)
tel. 0972723689
www.cantinedelnotaio.com

With less than ten years behind it, Cantine del Notaio has already become a landmark winery in Vulture. It is skilfully run by agronomist Gerardo Giuratrabocchetti who invests great passion into the undertaking, Professor Luigi Moio is oenological consultant, and there are 22 hectares of beautifully tended vineyard, all cultivated organically. Construction works on a new, modern cellar have recently started, leaving the old one to be used for barrel ageing. This dates from medieval times and is a fascinating structure with various different areas, all hewn from the tufa rock face. The '04 release of the flagship wine Aglianico del Vulture La Firma is one of the most impressive aglianicos of the vintage and came within a hair of Three Glasses. It is a deep, dark, dense ruby; the soft, complex nose is alluring with red berry fruit followed by aromatic herbs which then give way to spicy oak tones; the palate is invigorating, concentrated, fully structured and long. Aglianico Il Repertorio '04 has a weighty muscularity, good overall balance, and a long finish with forest fruits and new oak. The successful Autentica '04 is a sweet wine based on malvasia bianca. The nose has candied citrus peel and dried roses, and there is apricot jam on the sweet, fresh, fragrantly nuanced palate. The lively rosé Il Rogito '05 is well styled.

●	Aglianico del Vulture La Firma '04	▼▼	7
●	Aglianico del Vulture Il Repertorio '04	▼▼	5
○	L'Autentica '04	▼▼	6
⊙	Il Rogito '04	▼	5
●	Aglianico del Vulture La Firma '00	▽▽▽	6
●	Aglianico del Vulture La Firma '01	▽▽	6
●	Aglianico del Vulture La Firma '02	▽▽	6
●	Aglianico del Vulture La Firma '03	▽▽	6
●	Aglianico del Vulture La Firma '99	▽▽	6
○	L'Autentica '01	▽▽	6
○	L'Autentica '02	▽▽	6
○	L'Autentica '03	▽▽	6

RIONERO IN VULTURE (PZ)

Terra dei Re

via Monticchio s. s. 167 Km 2700
85028 Rionero in Vulture (PZ)
tel. 0972725116
www.terradeire.com

With Vulture being one of the most innovative, dynamic zones in southern Italy, recent years have seen the burgeoning of numerous new estates determined to make fine wines which reflect their provenance. One of the most interesting of these is Terra dei Re, owned by the De Sio and Leone families. It was set up in 2002 and has rapidly risen to become one of the region's best. There are 30 hectares of vineyard, cultivated organically, and much of it already in production, located in various excellently aspected sites in Barile, and in Rionero, Rapolla, Ginestra and Ripacandida. Paride Leone and Michele De Sio also benefit by expert advice from consultant oenologist and Aglianico specialist, Sergio Paternoster. Their cellar in Rionero is brand-new and ultra-modern, and is used to make two styles of Aglianico del Vulture, giving a total production of 135,000 bottles a year. The better of the two is Divinus, and the absolutely fascinating '03 is one of the best of the vintage. It has a dense, dark ruby colour; there are elegant, deep aromas of fully ripe black and red berry fruit, pencil lead and tobacco, and elegant touches of minerality and oak toast. The palate is richly opulent but kept in balance by a fine swath of acidity. It's richly fruity but without over-extraction, the tannins are elegant, and it develops evenly throughout the mouth to a long finish with blackberry jam, aromatic herbs and vanilla. Vultur '04 as not as successful as the fine '01. It's attractive and well-made but a touch rustic in style and has rather overt tannin.

●	Aglianico del Vulture Divinus '03	▼▼	5
●	Aglianico del Vulture Vultur '04	▼	4
●	Aglianico del Vulture Divinus '01	▽▽	5
●	Aglianico del Vulture Vultur '01	▽▽	4

VENOSA (PZ)

TERRE DEGLI SVEVI
LOC. PIANI DI CAMERA
85029 VENOSA (PZ)
TEL. 097231263 - 0577998511
www.giv.it

Terre degli Svevi, which comes under the Gruppo Italiano Vini umbrella, was founded in 1998 and has a solid base. Its wines come from 105 hectares of well-tended vines around Piani di Camera at Venosa, where it has a modern, well-equipped cellar. Management of the estate and winemaking are in the hands of Nunzio Capurso, one of Italy's best oenologists, and annual production is around 230,000 bottles, a figure that is due to rise considerably when new vineyards come into production. Aglianico del Vulture Re Manfredi '04 was still in ageing at the time of our tastings but Aglianico del Vulture Vigneto Serpara '01 has now been released and strode confidently into the finals. Although it has firm structure, good concentration and good extractive weight, like all the wines here its real plus-point is refinement. This comes through both on the nose, where initial ripe cherry aromas give way to tobacco and balsamic tones, and on the beautifully balanced palate, which has clean, lively fruit and, especially, elegant tannins. It is already drinking but will repay keeping for many years more. A special mention goes to Re Manfredi Bianco '05, a delicious but atypical white from 70 per cent müller thurgau with gewürztraminer. Both the nose and the fresh, juicy palate are particularly fruity, abundantly floral, mostly lavender and orange blossom, and have medicinal herbs. Re Manfredi Rosato '05, again from aglianico, is well-styled, supple and fresh.

●	Aglianico del Vulture Vign. Serpara '01	▼▼	7
○	Re Manfredi '05	▼▼	4
⊙	Re Manfredi Rosato '05	▼	5
●	Aglianico del Vulture Re Manfredi '99	▽▽▽	5*
●	Aglianico del Vulture Re Manfredi '00	▽▽	5
●	Aglianico del Vulture Re Manfredi '01	▽▽	5
●	Aglianico del Vulture Re Manfredi '03	▽▽	7

VENOSA (PZ)

CANTINA DI VENOSA
LOC. VIGNALI
VIA APPIA
85029 VENOSA (PZ)
TEL. 097236702
www.cantinadivenosa.it

The Venosa co-operative was founded in 1957 and, at 50 years of age, is in excellent health. Its original 27 members have grown to over 500 and they farm around 900 hectares of vineyard on some of the best sites in the area. The president is Teodoro Palermo, winemaking is managed by Luigi Cantatore and they have helped Cantina di Venosa become a landmark winery for all of southern Italy, as well as Basilicata. The wines are available in export markets worldwide. The most impressive product this year was Aglianico Carato Venusio Riserva '01, a wine that is only made in better vintages. It is a dark, dense ruby with a pale orange rim. The nose is complex with hints of curry-led spiciness, threaded through with plum and ripe, small black berry fruitiness. In the mouth, it is assertive and creates breadth as it moves across the palate, where the austerity of its tannins is tempered by the richness of its fruit and its elegant vanilla and tobacco tones. Aglianico Bali'Aggio '03 is rather quiet on the nose but the palate reveals great freshness, despite the hot vintage. It reveals lively fruit and elegant tannins that persist on the long finish and make for highly attractive drinking. Aglianico Vignali '04 is balanced and soft, with good structure, and gives an excellent idea of what the '04 selections will be like when they're released. Despite this being red wine territory, there are also some good whites, most notably the attractively aromatic Dry Muscat Terre d'Orazio '05. Rosso Vignali '05 is sound, with lively red berry fruits and aromatic herbs.

●	Aglianico del Vulture Carato Venusio Ris. '01	▼▼	6
●	Aglianico del Vulture Bali'Aggio '03	▼▼	3*
○	Dry Muscat Terre di Orazio '05	▼▼	3*
●	Aglianico del Vulture Vignali '04	▼	3
●	Rosso Vignali '05	▼	3
●	Aglianico del Vulture Carato Venusio '01	▽▽	5
●	Aglianico del Vulture Carato Venusio '03	▽▽	5
●	Aglianico del Vulture Carato Venusio '99	▽▽	5

OTHER WINERIES

WINERS BASILIUM
C.DA PIPOLI
85011 ACERENZA (PZ)
TEL. 0971741449
www.basilium.it

Basilium has 80 members supplying grapes from 350 hectares of vines. Heading the vast range are the fruity, slim-bodied Aglianico I Portali '04, the floral, almondy, Albula '04, a white from aglianico, and the lively Greco I Portali '05, which has inviting ripe apple notes.

- Aglianico del Vulture I Portali '04 — 4
- Le Gastaldie Albula '04 — 4
- Greco I Portali '05 — 3

SOLIVO
VIA VITTORIO EMANUELE, 23
85010 BANZI (PZ)
TEL. 0971947631 - 3485810678
www.solivoitalia.it

Solivo is situated in the glorious countryside of Banzi, in the province of Potenza, and makes a good Aglianico, Il Rapace '04. It is a deepish ruby and the intense nose is fairly refined, giving ripe red berry fruit laced with printers' ink. The palate has good body and respectable balance.

- Il Rapace '04 — 4

ALLEGRETTI
P.ZZA CARACCIOLO, 4
85022 BARILE (PZ)
TEL. 0972770549
www.aglianicodelvulture.it

Francesco Allegretti makes sound aglianico-based wines from his Barile vineyards. Barile Vecchio '03 has good structure, juicy fruit and smooth tannins. Barile '04 has less body but is clean-cut and supple. Castello Svevo '05 is well-styled and lively with forest fruits.

- Aglianico del Vulture Il Barile Vecchio '03 — 5
- Aglianico del Vulture Il Barile '04 — 4
- Castello Svevo '05 — 4

GIANNATTASIO
P.ZZA ANGELO BOZZA, 5
85022 BARILE (PZ)
TEL. 0972770571 - 068083255
www.giannattasio.net

Although Arcangelo Giannattasio's estate has only five hectares, it is regarded as one of the best in the area. Aglianico Arcà '04 has a good deep ruby colour and an intense, complex nose with black berry fruit, tobacco and spices, followed by a deep, soft palate with complexity and length.

- Aglianico del Vulture Arcà '04 — 5
- Aglianico del Vulture Arcà '03 — 5

LELUSI VITICOLTORI
VIA CROCE, 3
85022 BARILE (PZ)
TEL. 024043805 - 3356170257

Letizia, Luca and Simona Labarbuta tend four and a half hectares of land in Lavello, producing two excellent Aglianicos. Shesh '04 is full and balanced with austere tannins and the '04 IGT has a full, complex nose and a soft, juicy palate with black berry fruits on its long finish.

- ● Aglianico '04 ▼▼ 5
- ● Aglianico del Vulture Shesh '04 ▼▼ 4
- ● Aglianico '03 ▽▽ 5

MACARICO
P.ZZA CARACCIOLO, 7
85022 BARILE (PZ)
TEL. 0972771051 - 3355937346
www.macaricovini.it

With Macario '04 ageing, it's been a subdued showing for Rino Botte and Vito Paternoster. Still, their second wine, Macarì, also '04, is crisp and juicy, with blackcurrant and blackberry. The palate is just as satisfying as the nose, showing good structure, elegant tannin and attractive oakiness.

- ● Aglianico del Vulture Macarì '04 ▼▼ 5
- ● Aglianico del Vulture Macarico '03 ▽▽ 6
- ● Aglianico del Vulture Macarì '03 ▽▽ 5

TENUTA DEL PORTALE
LOC. LE QUERCE
85022 BARILE (PZ)
TEL. 0972724691

Filena Ruppi puts body and soul into her 20-hectare property, which she runs with her oenologist husband Donato D'Angelo. The '01 Aglianico Riserva is firm, balanced and nicely complex even though it's a touch over-evolved. The oaky Pian del Carro '04 and the basic Aglianico '04 are interesting.

- ● Aglianico del Vulture Ris. '01 ▼▼ 4
- ● Aglianico del Vulture '04 ▼ 4
- ● Aglianico del Vulture Pian del Carro '04 ▼ 5

VIGNE DI MEZZO
P.ZZA CARACCIOLO, 7
85022 BARILE (PZ)
TEL. 0972771051
www.feudi.it

Feudi di San Gregorio have now bought a fine establishment at Barile, where they can vinify the grapes from their 32 hectares of vines. The only release this year was Aglianico '04. It has good concentration, cherry and blackberry fruit on both nose and palate, soft tannins and overall elegance.

- ● Aglianico del Vulture '04 ▼▼ 5
- ● Aglianico del Vulture '03 ▽▽ 5
- ● Aglianico del Vulture Efesto '03 ▽▽ 7

ALOVINI
VIA GRAMSCI, 30
85013 GENZANO DI LUCANIA (PZ)
TEL. 0971776372
www.alovini.it

This is respected consultant oenologist Oronzo Alò's own winery where he makes carefully crafted wines like the complex, elegant spicy Aglianico Al Volo '01 and the soft, graceful Aglianico Armànd '01. Aglianico Le Ralle '04 is fresh and vegetal but the tannins are a little too overt.

- ● Aglianico del Vulture Al Volo '01 ▼▼ 5
- ● Aglianico del Vulture Armand '01 ▼ 4
- ● Aglianico del Vulture Le Ralle '04 ▼ 3

MICHELE LALUCE
VIA ROMA, 21
85020 GINESTRA (PZ)
TEL. 0972646145 - 3336879574
www.vinilaluce.it

Michele Laluce personally takes care of his six hectares of vineyard in the excellent grape-growing area of Ginestra. The full-bodied, slightly rustic Aglianico del Vulture Zimberno '04 is worth investigating, as is the fruity, supple Colle del Tesoro '05, this too from Aglianico.

- ● Aglianico del Vulture Zimberno '04 ▼ 4
- ● Colle del Tesoro '05 ▼ 4

Dragone

loc. Pietrapenta
p.zza degli Olmi, 66
75100 Matera
tel. 0835261740 - www.dragonevini.it

Michele and Cataldo Dragone are serious about cultivating their 27 hectares of vineyard outside Matera. This year, we were highly impressed by Brut Ego Sum Rosé, a classic method sparkler. Pietrapenta '04 is a nicely fruity, spicy wine. Both are based on primitivo.

⊙	Ego Sum Rosé	🍷🍷	4*
●	Pietrapenta '04	🍷	4
●	Pietrapenta '03	🍸🍸	4*

Colli Cerentino

trav. via Sanremo, 26
85025 Melfi (PZ)
tel. 0972237587 - 0972720329
www.collicerentino.com

Colli Cerentino produces two excellent DOC Aglianicos from vines at Maschito. Cerentino '04 is full of fruit and has balsamic tones and soft tannins while Masquito '04 is meaty and spicy, has notable concentration and reveals careful use of new oak. Both will age well.

●	Aglianico del Vulture Cerentino '04	🍷🍷	6
●	Aglianico del Vulture Masquito '04	🍷🍷	7
●	Aglianico del Vulture Masquito '03	🍸🍸	7

Lucania

via Aldo Moro, 5
85025 Melfi (PZ)
tel. 0578717256

Having sold their Salcheto estate at Montepulciano, Fabrizio Piccin and Cecilia Naldoni are putting everything into their 16 hectares here. Aglianico Grifalco '04 is first-rate, with a good, deep ruby colour, a nose full of red and black berry fruits and spices, and a fleshy, assertive palate.

●	Aglianico del Vulture Grifalco '04	🍷🍷	4*

Taverna

c.da Taverna, 15
75020 Nova Siri (MT)
tel. 0835877083
www.aataverna.com

The Lunati family, in liaison with oenologist Oronzo Alò, make good wines from their 24 hectares of vineyard. Aglianico '03 has depth, good concentration, red and black berry fruit, and hints of tobacco, pepper and bitter chocolate on both the nose and the firm, rounded palate.

●	Aglianico del Vulture '03	🍷🍷	3*
●	Syrah '04	🍸🍸	2*

Camerlengo

via T. Tasso, 3
85027 Rapolla (PZ)
tel. 335251885 - 335254885
www.camerlengodoc.com

Oenologist Sergio Paternoster helps Biagio Cristofaro groom his ten hectares of aglianico into excellent wines. Aglianico Camerlengo '04 is deep ruby. Intense, very ripe red and black berries, pencil lead and vanilla lead to a well-structured, long palate with clean fruit and elegant tannins.

●	Aglianico del Vulture Antelio '04	🍷🍷	4
●	Aglianico del Vulture Camerlengo '04	🍷🍷	5
●	Aglianico del Vulture Camerlengo '03	🍸🍸	5

Eleano

c.da Piazzolla, snc
85028 Rionero in Vulture (PZ)
tel. 0972722273
www.eleano.it

Alfredo Cordisco and Francesca Greco have four hectares of vines at Pian dell'Altare and make two wines, the attractively balanced but slightly over-evolved Aglianico Eleano '02 and the pleasant Moscato Passito Ambra '05, which is sweet, with lavender and sage aromas, and good acid backbone.

●	Aglianico del Vulture '02	🍷	6
○	Ambra '05	🍷	5

EUBEA
VIA ROMA, 209
85028 RIONERO IN VULTURE (PZ)
TEL. 0972723574
www.sacavid.com

The '04 reds were still ageing at the time of our tastings but Eugenia Sasso submitted an excellent Covo dei Briganti '03, which has concentrated, refined aromas of ripe plum and blackberry. The structured, harmonious palate gives supremely elegant fruit, tobacco and oak on the long finish.

● Aglianico del Vulture Il Covo dei Briganti '03	▼▼	6
● Aglianico del Vulture Roinos '01	▽▽▽	8
● Aglianico del Vulture Il Covo dei Briganti '01	▽▽	7

OFANTO
C.DA PADURI
85020 RIONERO IN VULTURE (PZ)
TEL. 097223320 - 3289731613
www.ofantovini.it

This estate, run by Potito Ruggiero, submitted two Aglianico del Vultures. We preferred the juicy, close-knit Inatteso '04 with its spicy character and its smooth tannins. Emozioni '03, although interesting, is rather evolved and appears already mature.

● Aglianico del Vulture L'Inatteso '04	▼▼	5
● Aglianico del Vulture Emozioni '03	▼	5

CANTINA DEL VULTURE
VIA SAN FRANCESCO
85028 RIONERO IN VULTURE (PZ)
TEL. 0972721062

This co-operative, founded in the 1950s, produces sound Aglianico. This year, it was Don Giustino '04 that stood out, a stylish wine showing well on both nose and palate, with red berry fruit and smooth tannins. Carteggio '04 is well made but rather overt vegetal notes detract from its appeal.

● Aglianico del Vulture Don Giustino '04	▼▼	4*
● Aglianico del Vulture Carteggio '04	▼	4
● Aglianico del Vulture Carteggio '03	▽▽	4

FONTANAROSA
LOC. TERZO CAVONE
VIA ROMA, 14
75020 SCANZANO JONICO (MT)
TEL. 0835971368 - www.fontanarosavini.it

Filomena Fontanarosa runs her small estate determinedly and her reds are again looking good. Portogreco '05, from aglianico, merlot and sangiovese, has concentration, soft fruit and coffee. Achelandro '05, from sangiovese and montepulciano, and the sangiovese and merlot Molosso '05, are both good.

● Achelandro '05	▼	3
● Il Molosso '05	▼	3
● Portogreco '05	▼	4

CASTELLUCCIO
C.DA CHIANIZZI
85038 SENISE (PZ)
TEL. 097358416 - 3471375769
www.castelluccioviní.it

Raffaele and Amedeo Castellucio own ten hectares of organically cultivated vineyard in Senise. We picked out a pleasant Senisium '04, from montepulciano, which is well structured and savoury, and Massanova Rosso '04, from sangiovese, which is slim bodied but nicely styled.

● Massanova Rosso '04	▼	4
● Senisium '04	▼	4
● Massanova Rosso '02	▽▽	4

SALVATORE ACINAPURA
C.DA ANGLONA, 5
75028 TURSI (MT)
TEL. 0835810035 - 3932580961
www.viniacinapura.it

Salvatore Acinapura and his son Roberto make several good wines, most notably the fresh, supple Chardonnay Campofreddo; Pandosia '05, from sangiovese and aglianico, which is fresh, with plum and bay leaf, and the ripe cherry-like Rosso d'Anglona '05 from aglianico and cabernet.

○ Campofreddo Chardonnay '05	▼	4
● Pandosia '05	▼	3
● Rosso d'Anglona '05	▼	4

Francesco Bonifacio

c.da Piani di Camera
85029 Venosa (PZ)
tel. 097231436 - 3392226337
www.cantinebonifacio.it

While awaiting the release of the new vintage of La Sfida, Franceso Bonifacio submitted his basic '05 Aglianico, a fresh, uncomplicated, supple red. Miky Bì '05, a lively, strongly aromatic dry Moscato, is attractive and good drinking.

● La Sfida '05	Y	2
○ Miky Bì '05	Y	3

Viticoltori in Vulture Lagala

c.da La Maddalena
85029 Venosa (PZ)
tel. 0972375007 - 3355617939
www.lagala.it

Antonio Lagala makes carefully crafted wines from his seven hectares of vines. Nero degli Orsini has ripe plum and cherry aromas, and a dense palate enlivened by aromatic herbs and black berry fruit. Rosso del Balzo '05 is simpler but lively, attractive and full of fruit. Both are from aglianico.

● Aglianico del Vulture Nero degli Orsini '04	YY	5
● Rosso del Balzo '05	Y	3
● Rosso del Balzo '04	YY	4*

Agricola Regio

loc. Piano Regio
85029 Venosa (PZ)
tel. 0824381021 - 3341063188
www.agricolaregio.com

This is a new estate with nine hectares in the Piano Regio area of Venosa and produces 80,000 bottles a year. Aglianico Donpà '03 has concentration, fruit, ripe tannins and a firm, long, spicy finish. Aglianico Genesi '04 is more straightforward but nicely supple.

● Aglianico del Vulture Donpà '03	YY	5
● Aglianico del Vulture Genesi '04	Y	4

Pisani

c.da San Lorenzo
85059 Viggiano (PZ)
tel. 0975314663
www.vinibiologicipisani.it

Vincenzo Pisani has 20 hectares of organically cultivated vineyard in the Terre dell'Alta Valdagri DOC zone. The '03 Concerto, a Bordeaux blend, has suffered from the heat of the vintage and, while well made, lacks the attack and the liveliness of earlier releases.

● Terre dell'Alta Val d'Agri Concerto '03	Y	5
● Selvaggio '00	YY	4
● Terre dell'Alta Val d'Agri Fantasia '03	YY	4*

PUGLIA

So what are the main developments on Puglia's current wine scene? The first thing is that there has been no lessening of the region's role or its importance, as the following pages will demonstrate. And that is no insignificant matter given the difficulties of the past few years, both weather-wise – at least as regards the higher quality wines – and in terms of sales. Next is that all that development we have long been talking about is at last bearing fruit: just look at proportion of the Puglian estates we list that are new to the scene and have been set up solely for quality production. Their influence is changing the face of the entire region: viticulturally, with vineyards planted at densities previously unheard of; in respect of cellar techniques, where temperature control is in prime place; and in instilling a new mentality. No part of the region is immune from the changes, which are also reflected in this year's Three Glass awards. The total is the same as last year at five but three of them went to wines from estates set up for premium production: Cotinone '05 from Tenuta Coppadoro, Masseria Maime '04 from Tormaresca and Artas '04 from the GIV-owned Castello Monaci estate. The third point to consider is that the increased emphasis on indigenous varieties has led to a far more prominent role for nero di Troia, especially in the Castel del Monte zone. Indeed, the increasing number of serious Castel del Monte DOC wines made solely from this grape has led to a renaissance for the denomination, giving it the clear identity that we have often felt it lacked. And we have a perfect example of this that we are delighted to announce: Puer Apuliae from Rivera, which earned its second consecutive Three Glass award, this time for the '03. The fourth development is that Puglia is the perfect example of how well modernity and tradition can combine without one having to exclude the other. The old bush training system is becoming ever more central to production and maintenance of a recognizable style is increasingly focal to Puglian viticulture's common heritage. But it is now sought in different ways, without recourse to standardization. The aim is for wines with ancient aromas and flavours but ever-higher quality. That said, it cannot be too great a surprise that the fifth Three Glass prize went to Vallone's Graticciaia '01. It is totally different in style from its peers but just as valid and just as exciting. Finally, our hope is that next year will not only see all these achievements being consolidated but will also bring Three Glass awards for wines reflecting both the old and new identities that we all now realize are intrinsic to Puglia.

ALBEROBELLO (BA)

CANTINA ALBEA
VIA DUE MACELLI, 8
70011 ALBEROBELLO (BA)
TEL. 0804323548
www.albeavini.com

Albea is a splendid winery, built at the start of the 20th century by Luigi Lippolis, all in stone and with its vats built into the rock face, just as were the water tanks for conical "trulli" homes in times past. Its wines again showed well but this was no surprise, given the quality of the technical team, led by Claudio Sisto and overseen by consultant Riccardo Cotarella. The '04 is the second release of Lui, a monovarietal Nero di Troia, and its second time in the finals. The colour is purplish. The nose has balsam, red fruits jam and pepper and the palate is long, vigorous and richly fruity, although the tannins still have to knit together. Raro '05, from negroamaro and primitivo, is very fine, too. Its red and black berry fruits nose, with touches of spice and oak toast, is followed by a clean palate of good body, well supported by acidity, which finishes on sweet black berry fruit. Further good news came from Petranera '04, made from primitivo, which is full of strongly balsamic aromas of eucalyptus and mint, and has a still youthful, balanced, fruity, succulent palate, although it is still a bit too oaky and the finish tends to be drying. Locorotondo Il Selva '05 is well styled with an aromatic nose and an uncomplicated palate full of white-fleshed fruit.

●	Lui '04	🍷🍷	6
●	Petranera '04	🍷🍷	4
●	Raro '05	🍷🍷	5
○	Locorotondo Il Selva '05	🍷	3
●	Lui '03	🍷🍷 (outline)	6
●	Raro '03	🍷🍷 (outline)	5

ALEZIO (LE)

ROSA DEL GOLFO
VIA GARIBALDI, 56
73011 ALEZIO (LE)
TEL. 0833281045 - 0331993198
www.rosadelgolfo.com

Damiano Calò and his supportive consultant oenologist Angelo Solci have come up with a completely new rosé. It's a classic-method brut sparkler from 90 per cent negroamaro with chardonnay. Its addition to the range means that rosé now forms half the winery's entire output of 120,000 bottles. It has fine, long-lasting bubbles, the nose is complex, with yeast and small red berry fruits, and the palate is rounded and full of fruit, with zip and backbone too. It is unique in that the liqueur d'expédition comes from the same selection of negroamaro grapes used for Vigna Mazzi and it is the only classic-method sparkling rosé in central-southern Italy made from indigenous grapes. There are a further three wines at Two Glass level. Scaliere '05, from negroamaro, has a dark nose all intense aromas of coffee and red berries, and a palate that is fresh, supple and attractive. The rich, full Vigna Mazzi '05 is a one-off rosé with scents of pennyroyal and red fruits, although it hasn't quite found its feet yet and is still a bit oaky. Rosa del Golfo '05, this too solely from negroamaro, with spicy aromas of Mediterranean scrubland and hints of flowers and strawberries, and a clean palate finishing on bitter almonds. Quarantale '03, from 70 per cent negroamaro with primitivo and aglianico, is one level down but very well made: the fairly complex nose has aromas of black berry fruits and sweet spice, and vegetal hints; the palate is still difficult to judge, being closed and very youthful, but finishes on wild herbs. Similar quality comes from the fruity, balsamic Primitivo '04.

⊙	Rosa del Golfo '05	🍷🍷	3
●	Scaliere '05	🍷🍷	2*
⊙	Vigna Mazzì '05	🍷🍷	4
⊙	Brut Rosé	🍷🍷	5
●	Quarantale '03	🍷	6
●	Primitivo '04	🍷	4
⊙	Vigna Mazzì '02	🍷🍷 (outline)	4*

ANDRIA (BA)

Maria Marmo
c.da Cocevola
s.s. 170
Castel del Monte-Andria, km 9.9
70031 Andria (BA)
tel. 0883566945 - 0883556006

Tenuta Cocevola is a newcomer to the Guide and makes only Castel del Monte, using nero di Troia only, a further sign of the revival of both the DOC and the variety. It was 2000 when the Marmo family, advised by Luigi Moio, decided to plant seven hectares, all with nero di Troia, and push for top quality. The concentration on a single variety was very unusual for Puglia where wineries seem to compete to make every single variation on every single theme, often resulting in an unmanageably large range. But the Cocevola policy of keeping the range small and thereby ensuring high quality throughout has led it straight to a full entry in the Guide. The best wine was the '04 Castel del Monte Nero di Troia Vandalo, named after a 19th-century thoroughbred racehorse and it reached our final taste-off. The colour is a pale ruby and the nose has white-fleshed fruit, hints of vanilla and liquorice, with florality. On the rich palate, which well echoes the nose, overt but well balanced tannins take you into a long, firm, liquorice-and-tar finish. The aromas on Castel del Monte Nero di Troia Rosso Cocevola '04 are more inclined to ripe red berry fruits and printers' ink while the medium-bodied palate is less complex but has cherries and vegetal hints. Finally comes Castel del Monte Rosato '05, which has intense aromas of blueberry, raspberry and dried flowers introducing a full-bodied palate finishing on spiciness that makes for enjoyable drinking.

●	Castel del Monte Nero di Troia Vandala '04	🍷🍷	7
●	Castel del Monte Nero di Troia Rosso Cocevola '04	🍷🍷	4
⊙	Castel del Monte Rosato '05	🍷🍷	4

ANDRIA (BA)

Rivera
fraz. c.da Rivera
s.p. 231, km 60.500
70031 Andria (BA)
tel. 0883569501 - 0883569510
www.rivera.it

The De Corato family continues to lead an enchanted life, winning Three Glasses for the second year running for Puer Apuliae, a wine that has become the benchmark in Puglia for Nero di Troia. And they've managed it while also dedicating energy to the rest of the range, from old-timers like Il Falcone right through to newcomers such as Violante and Pungirosa. The credit for this extends through to its personnel, especially oenologist Leonardo Palumbo and consultant Attilio Scienza. So what of this Puer Apuliae '04? Well, it has an elegant, intense, mineral nose, full of fresh black berry fruits, and a concentrated, austerely taut yet deep palate whose fruit remains through to the long finish. Then comes a flock of reliable, high-quality wines. Il Falcone, from 70 per cent nero di Troia with montepulciano, the estate's classic, has a broad array of aromas and a well-structured palate. Triusco Primitivo '05, gives scents of black berry fruits, violets and aromatic herbs and a full, long, cohesive palate. Violante '05, is lively on both nose and palate, with red fruits and liquorice. Lama di Corvo Chardonnay '05 has a spicy nose, threaded through with vanilla and pink grapefruit and a fat yet vigorous palate. Moscato di Trani Piani di Tufara '04, all apricot and dried figs, has good body, and is clean, varietal and non-cloying. From the rest of the range, we particularly liked the two rosés, Pungirosa and Rosé, both from bombino nero and both nicely savoury: the attractive, citrus-like Terre al Monte Sauvignon '05; and the floral, well-made Preludio n.1 Chardonnay '05.

●	Castel del Monte Nero di Troia Puer Apuliae '04	🍷🍷🍷	7
●	Castel del Monte Rosso Il Falcone Ris. '03	🍷🍷	5
○	Moscato di Trani Piani di Tufara '04	🍷🍷	4*
○	Castel del Monte Chardonnay Lama di Corvo '05	🍷🍷	5
●	Castel del Monte Violante '05	🍷🍷	3*
●	Triusco Primitivo '05	🍷🍷	4
○	Castel del Monte Chardonnay Preludio n.1 '05	🍷	3
⊙	Castel del Monte Pungirosa '05	🍷	3
⊙	Castel del Monte Rosé '05	🍷	2*
○	Castel del Monte Sauvignon Terre al Monte '05	🍷	3

BARI

TORMARESCA
VIA AMENDOLA, 201/9
70126 BARI
TEL. 0805486943
www.tormaresca.it

The Marchesi Antinori continue to produce top-quality wines from their two splendid Puglian properties: Bocca di Lupo in Murgia in the province of Bari and Masseria Maime in the upper Salento. The entire complex dates from 1998 and comprises 600 hectares, 350 of them under vine, with an annual output of a million bottles. Renzo Cotarella is the consultant, here working with Davide Sarcinella. We weren't really surprised by the return to Three Glass stardom for Masseria Maime, which comes solely from negroamaro grown on old bush-trained vines on the Masseria Maime property. The '04 has intense, deep aromas led by coffee, pepper and black berry fruits with a touch of oak toast, followed by a clean, close-knit, nicely firm palate with a pleasantly aromatic finish giving, again, coffee and black berries. Castel del Monte Chardonnay PietraBianca '05, from the Bocca di Lupo holding, also showed well and almost made it to the finals. It has stylish, elegant aromas of apricot and aromatic herbs lifted by butter and almond milk. The clean, balanced, palate has similar characteristics, good acid backbone and good length. None of the other wines fell short of good, from Fichimori '05, a Negroamaro made for drinking chilled, which has youthful, primary, strawberry-like aromas and an attractive, fresh palate with soft tannins, to the slightly evolved, liquorice-like Neprica '05 from a 65-25-10 blend of negroamaro, cabernet sauvignon and primitivo, and Tormaresca Chardonnay '05 with tropical fruits aromas and an uncomplicated, citrus-like palate.

●	Masseria Maime '04	TTT	5*
○	Castel del Monte Chardonnay PietraBianca '05	TT	5
●	Fichimori '05	T	4
●	Neprica Rosso '05	T	3
○	Tormaresca Chardonnay '05	T	3
●	Masseria Maime '00	YYY	5*
●	Torcicoda '01	YYY	5*
●	Masseria Maime '02	YYY	5
●	Masseria Maime '01	YY	5
●	Torcicoda '03	YY	5*
○	Castel del Monte Chardonnay PietraBianca '04	YY	5

BRINDISI

TENUTE RUBINO
VIA E. FERMI, 50
72100 BRINDISI
TEL. 0831571955 - 0831502912
www.tenuterubino.it

The Tenute Rubino wines are back up to speed. Nothing won Three Glasses but quality overall has now returned to the levels we had come to expect. Meanwhile the estate has been growing. The area under vine has reached 200 hectares, production is up to 700,000 bottles a year and there is a new cellar in operation. The team, though, remains unchanged, from oenologist Luca Petrelli to consultant Riccardo Cotarella. There was much excitement from the '04 Torre Testa, made from sussumaniello, the nose giving balsam, blueberry jam and a light waft of oak toast before the palate shows balance, backbone and length with fresh black berry fruits, liquorice and printers' ink. It reached the finals, as did Visellio '04, a Primitivo with aromas of eucalyptus, incense and black berry fruits and a rich, tight-knit palate full of plum and tobacco. Best of the rest were Brindisi Rosso Jaddico '04, which has florality and black cherry jam on both its nose and its compact, cleanly defined palate, and Marmorelle Rosso '05, from negroamaro and malvasia nera, which has aromas of violet and sweet spices, and a modern-style, closely-knit, richly-fruited, long, clean palate. We were also intrigued by Giancola '05, previously called Sedna, a Malvasia Bianca with a typically varietal nose of white-fleshed fruit nuanced with minerals, and a fresh, floral palate that still needs time to come round. Everything else is well made, from the attractively zesty rosé Saturnino '05 to the spicy, mid-bodied Primitivo Punta Aquila '05 and the crisp, citrus-like Marmorelle Bianco '05.

●	Primitivo Visellio '04	TT	5
●	Torre Testa '04	TT	6
●	Brindisi Rosso Jaddico '04	TT	5
○	Giancola '05	TT	4
●	Marmorelle Rosso '05	TT	3*
○	Marmorelle Bianco '05	T	3
●	Primitivo Punta Aquila '05	T	4
⊙	Salento Rosato Saturnino '05	T	3
●	Torre Testa '01	YYY	6
●	Torre Testa '02	YYY	6
●	Brindisi Rosso Jaddico '01	YY	5
●	Primitivo Visellio '03	YY	5
●	Torre Testa '03	YY	6

CARMIANO (LE)

GIOVANNI PETRELLI
VIA VILLA CONVENTO, 33
73041 CARMIANO (LE)
TEL. 0832603051
www.cantinapetrelli.com

This is the third year this estate has appeared in the Guide and it now has a full entry. It is owned by Giovanni Petrelli who is also its agronomist and oenologist. His 15 hectares of vineyard give almost 100,000 bottles a year of reliably sound, high-quality wine. This time, it was the Don Pepè '02 that stood out. Obtained from negroamaro with ten per cent malvasia nera di Lecce and five per cent montepulciano, it gives ultra-ripe fruit and tobacco with vegetal touches before the palate shows good definition and liveliness, soft tannins and red berry fruitiness. Diecimila '03, from 60 per cent cabernet sauvignon with montepulciano, is also very good. It's a deep wine with tertiary aromas of liquorice, leather and tobacco. These are echoed on the close-knit palate, which has firm acidity and a chocolate-like finish. Similar interest comes from Primiero Primitivo '04. Its youthful, intense nose is redolent of red berry fruits and the attractive, cohesive, medium-bodied palate unveils good acidity to support it through to a fresh finish. Best of the rest was Salice Salentino Rosso Centopietre '04, with a fruity nose and an uncomplicated vegetal and red berry fruits palate.

●	Salento Don Pepè Rosso '02	**YY**	5
●	Diecimila '03	**YY**	5
●	Primiero Primitivo '04	**YY**	4*
●	Salice Salentino Centopietre '04	**Y**	4
●	Salento Don Pepè Rosso '00	YY	5
●	Primiero '03	YY	4*

CELLINO SAN MARCO (BR)

AZIENDA VINICOLA ALBANO CARRISI
C.DA BOSCO
72020 CELLINO SAN MARCO (BR)
TEL. 0831619211
www.albanocarrisi.com

Although we still feel that the potential of this estate has yet to be fully realized, its leading wines are certainly looking better this year. It would have been even more welcome had there been similar improvements throughout the range, especially since there are 65 hectares under vine and an output of 350,000 bottles a year, offering sufficient quantity to make reliably high quality perfectly feasible. Nevertheless, there was a return to the finals for Platone, a 50-50 blend of negroamaro and primitivo, with the '03 vintage. This is a deep ruby. The nose is primarily balsamic, with supporting notes of caramelized cherry and printers' ink, and balsam comes through again on the soft palate, along with fresh black berry fruits. The tannins are dense and tight and the finish is nicely clean. Taras '04, a monovarietal Primitivo, also showed well, with a floral nose and a full-bodied yet soft palate, although we'd have liked a bit more grip on the finish. More good news came from Don Carmelo Rosso '04, from negroamaro with 15 per cent primitivo, which has cherry jam and spices on the nose, and an attractive but somewhat simple, nicely fruited palate. Also good was Il Basiliano '05, from negroamaro, which has red berry fruits and nuts on both nose and palate but finishes a mite too tannic. Finally came the more than decent Aleatico Passito '03, with spicy and quinine aromas, and a cohesive, well-knit, black cherry-like palate which is not too sweet and has a strongly tannic finish.

●	Platone '03	**YY**	8
●	Taras '04	**YY**	6
●	Aleatico '03	**Y**	5
●	Don Carmelo Rosso '04	**Y**	4
●	Il Basiliano '05	**Y**	4
●	Platone '98	YYY	8
●	Platone '00	YY	8
●	Platone '02	YY	8

CELLINO SAN MARCO (BR)

CANTINA DUE PALME
VIA SAN MARCO, 130
72020 CELLINO SAN MARCO (BR)
TEL. 0831617909 - 0831617865
www.cantineduepalme.it

We are particularly pleased to see some stylistic changes emerging at this large co-operative. Naturally, the large quantities involved, with grapes coming from 2,000 hectares and going into a good 3,500,000 bottles, mean that Angelo Maci has to concentrate on attractiveness and drinkability. Part of this is good use of wood, especially French barriques. But it seems that Angelo is now paying greater attention to liveliness and achieving good acid backbone, thereby reducing the tendency to sweetness that has often concerned us. The first result of this change was a place in the finals for Salice Salentino Selvarossa Riserva '03, the winery's flagship. It has a pervasive, complex nose with black berry fruits, coffee and chocolate. The palate echoes these sensations, and is balanced and soft, mouthfilling yet lively, deep and long. Just below it come a number of well-made and highly attractive if less complex wines. Squinzano Rosso '05 has fruity aromas of plum and blackberry, and a dense, richly fruited palate, here too well supported by acidity. Tenuta Albrizzi '05, a 50-50 blend of cabernet sauvignon and primitivo, is a touch vegetal on the nose and then fruity and richly extracted on the palate. Salice Salentino Rosso '05 abounds in oak toast and has a dense, close-knit palate giving black berry fruit. The rest of the range, from the simple, fruity Primitivo '05 to the supple, more vegetal Brindisi Rosso '05 and the clean, highly drinkable Negroamaro, Canonico '05, are all well up to snuff.

● Salice Salentino Rosso Selvarossa Ris. '03	🍷🍷	6
● Salice Salentino Rosso '05	🍷🍷	4
● Squinzano Rosso '05	🍷🍷	4
● Tenuta Albrizzi '05	🍷🍷	4
● Brindisi Rosso '05	🍷	4
● Canonico '05	🍷	3
● Primitivo '05	🍷	4

CERIGNOLA (FG)

PARADISO
VIA MANFREDONIA, 39
71042 CERIGNOLA (FG)
TEL. 0885428720
www.cantineparadiso.it

The Paradiso wines have been a bit up and down this year. One reason, of course, is that Angelo Paradiso and his oenologist Luigi Cantatore have had to grapple with a series of tetchy vintages, and just remaining alongside Puglia's best wineries is a laudable result in itself. Yet we thought that the wines would be even better, so convinced were we by the quality of the work on the estate and the efforts that everyone there has been making to move things forward and achieve ever higher quality. It was again Belmantello, made solely from nero di Troia, that shone out. The '04 is a bright ruby with a pervasive, intense nose, giving Mediterranean scrubland, liqueur cherries, mint and chocolate, these last two balsam-like. The palate is rounded and full of ripe red berry fruitiness, with a good acid backbone taking it through to a long finish. Primitivo '04, a wine of great typicity, scored similarly. It has aromas of plum, small red berry fruits and pepper, giving a slight sense of sweetness. The remarkably vibrant, fresh, balanced palate has good definition and returns to echo the nose on the finish. The '05s from the Podere Sant'Andrea line are sound but less exciting than the '04s. The Primitivo is ripe and fruity with hints of coffee, the Uva di Troia is uncomplicated and easy drinking, the Bombino is floral but a touch dumb, but the Rosato, from a 50-50 mix of nero di Troia and negroamaro, is better, with florality, a touch of spice, nice structure and good length.

● Belmantello '04	🍷🍷	3*
● Primitivo '04	🍷🍷	3*
○ Bombino Podere Sant'Andrea '05	🍷	2
● Primitivo Podere Sant'Andrea '05	🍷	2
⊙ Rosato Podere Sant'Andrea '05	🍷	1*
● Uva di Troia Podere Sant'Andrea '05	🍷	2
● Belmantello '03	🍷🍷 (white)	3*
● Primitivo '03	🍷🍷 (white)	3*

CERIGNOLA (FG)

Torre Quarto
c.da Quarto, 5
71042 Cerignola (FG)
tel. 0885418453 - 0885418456
www.torrequartocantine.it

Stefano Cirillo Farrusi is continuing to work on his vineyard conversion and has so far reduced his tendone-trained vines to 30 per cent of the total. This total is 40 hectares, 30 of which Farrusi owns outright, and annual production is 400,000 bottles. The last two vintages were not particularly brilliant for quality, mostly because of weather conditions, but it is when the chips are down that you can judge real worth and, thanks to oenologist Cristoforo Pastore's excellent work, that worth has again shone through. The wine that showed best was Bottaccia '05, a monovarietal Nero di Troia which, after a couple of years in the doldrums, is now back on form. Aromas of fresh red berries with hints of flowers and liquorice are followed by a palate of good texture, good immediacy and good nose-palate consistency. Tarabuso, a monovarietal Primitivo, was a little less successful this year. The '05 is fruity, with quince and strawberry, but the palate, although vigorous and long, has previously had greater complexity. Guappo '05, from sangiovese, nero di Troia, primitivo and ten per cent montepulciano, is an attractively fresh, citrussy, zesty rosé with notes of white cherry, as is the clean, medium-bodied Nina '05, from falanghina, although here the oak tends still to dominate, giving vanilla, butter and banana. The other two whites, Claire '05, a floral Chardonnay with a tart finish, and the fresh, citrus-like Hirondelle '05, from greco, are both well made.

●	Bottaccia '05	▼▼	4
●	Tarabuso Primitivo '05	▼▼	4
○	Claire '05	▼	3
⊙	Guappo '05	▼	3
○	Hirondelle '05	▼	3
○	Nina '05	▼	3
●	Tarabuso Primitivo '03	▽▽	3*
●	Tarabuso Primitivo '04	▽▽	3*

COPERTINO (LE)

Azienda Monaci
loc. Tenuta Monaci
73043 Copertino (LE)
tel. 0832947512
www.masseriamonaci.com

This estate, owned by Severino Garofano and his family, has 36 hectares of vines, 80 per cent of them traditionally bush-trained, and for some years now has been making some of the best wines in Puglia. Their leading wine is Le Braci, a Negroamaro, and, having skipped the '02, it was back this year in the '03 edition, which reached the finals. Its garnet ruby introduces a nose of good breadth, with red berry fruit jam and pepper, aromas that are echoed on the warm, full palate. Had it just had a bit more depth, it would have joined its two predecessors in taking home Three Glasses. Girofle '05 proved a pleasant surprise. This really lively rosé from negroamaro has a nose of citrus peel and cherry, and an attractively rich palate. Equally rewarding is Sine Pari '04, from nero di Troia with ten per cent negroamaro, which has aromas of liquorice, dried flowers and plum, and a full, fleshy, fruity palate with good acidity to hold up the finish. The dry version of Le Briciole, from '05, a blend of 80 per cent chardonnay with sauvignon, showed well. It's a little dumb on the nose but more open on the palate, which is fresh, clean and savoury with good length. But Le Briciole Passito '03, from malvasia and chardonnay, is less successful than previous vintages. Its aromas of mixed flower honey and dried apricot lead to a palate that is sweet but lacks a bit of backbone. I Censi '03, a straightforward, clean Negroamaro, and the traditionally-styled, liqueur cherry-like Copertino Rosso Eloquenzia '03 are both well made.

●	Le Braci '03	▼▼	7
●	Sine Pari '04	▼▼	4*
⊙	Girofle '05	▼▼	3*
●	Copertino Rosso Eloquenzia '03	▼	3
●	I Censi '03	▼	3
○	Le Briciole Passito '03	▼	5
○	Le Briciole '05	▼	3
●	Le Braci '00	▽▽▽	7*
●	Le Braci '01	▽▽▽	7

CORATO (BA)

TORREVENTO
LOC. CASTEL DEL MONTE
S.P. 234, KM 10,600
70033 CORATO (BA)
TEL. 0808980923 - 0808980929
www.torrevento.it

After a year's relegation to the Other Wineries section, Torrevento has regained a full entry for not just the best Kebir ever – so good it reached the finals – but a really impressive range throughout. Grapes come from 150 hectares of directly owned vineyard and a further 250 in the hands of growers who are followed throughout the year by oenologist Pasquale Carparelli and agronomist Luigi Tarricone. Overall output is 2,500,000 bottles, spanning 22 different wines. But let's get back to Kebir, the '02, a 50-50 blend of nero di Troia and cabernet sauvignon, which has pervasive aromas of Mediterranean scrubland and red fruits, and a full, tightly-knit, still youthful but attractive, fresh, clean palate giving crisp black berry fruitiness plus coffee and liquorice on the finish. As we've already said, there are lots of good wines this year, most notably Castel del Monte Rosso Riserva Vigna Pedale '03, a monovarietal Nero di Troia, whose violet-like nose leads to an expansive, supple palate, which has surprising freshness for the vintage. Torre del Falco '04 is also noteworthy. This, too, is from nero di Troia and is slightly vegetal on both nose and palate but nicely dense and full of fruit. Best of the rest are Madrevite Negroamaro '04 which has a nose of small black berry fruits and a clean, attractive palate, the immediate, simply fruity Castel del Monte Rosso Bolonero '04, from nero di Troia with 30 per cent aglianico, and the floral Castel del Monte Bianco Pezzapiana '05, from 70 per cent bombino with pampanuto, which is full of white-fleshed fruit.

● Kebir '02	🍷🍷	5
● Castel del Monte Rosso V. Pedale Ris. '03	🍷🍷	4*
● Torre del Falco '04	🍷🍷	4*
● Castel del Monte Rosso Bolonero '04	🍷	3
● Madrevite Negroamaro '04	🍷	3
○ Castel del Monte Bianco Pezzapiana '05	🍷	2*
● Kebir '00	🍷🍷 (white)	6
● Castel del Monte Rosso V. Pedale Ris. '01	🍷🍷 (white)	4*

GUAGNANO (LE)

ANTICA MASSERIA DEL SIGILLO
VIA PROVINCIALE, 196
73010 GUAGNANO (LE)
TEL. 0832706331
www.vinisigillo.net

Year after year, we find ourselves saying the same thing about this estate: it has competence and quality aplenty, making reliability a major attraction. There are 30 hectares of vineyard, ten of them owned directly, and we can recommend every single one of the wines, which is really something for a winery producing 200,000 bottles a year. The top wine is again Terre del Guiscardo, a 60-20-20 blend of primitivo, merlot and cabernet sauvignon, this year the '04. The nose is clean, fresh and floral, with red fruits, sensations that come through too on the well-knit, well-defined palate. Sigillo Primo Chardonnay '05 is similarly impressive. Intense aromas of white-fleshed fruit and hints of florality lead to a savoury, fresh, succulent palate of good body and length, with distinct notes of peach and apricot on the finish. All the other wines submitted showed well too. Sigillo Primo Primitivo '05 has medicinal herbs on the nose and a well-knit palate giving black berry fruits and calisaya bark. Salice Salentino Rosso Il Secondo '04 is in more traditional vein, with liqueur cherries and liquorice. Salice Salentino Rosso Hilliryos '03 has mostly coffee-like tertiary aromas, with hints of printers' ink and rhubarb, followed by similar sensations on the dense palate, which finishes on black berry fruits.

● Terre del Guiscardo '04	🍷🍷	5
○ Sigillo Primo Chardonnay '05	🍷🍷	4
● Salice Salentino Hilliryos '03	🍷	4
● Salice Salentino Il Secondo '04	🍷	3
● Primitivo Sigillo Primo '05	🍷	4
● Terre del Guiscardo '01	🍷🍷 (white)	4*
● Terre del Guiscardo '03	🍷🍷 (white)	5

GUAGNANO (LE)

CANTELE
S.P. SALICE SALENTINO-SAN DONACI, KM 35,6
73010 GUAGNANO (LE)
TEL. 0832705010
www.cantele.it

Things continue to progress with the Cantele family, who divide their time between producing 2,000,000 bottles of wine a year from bought-in grapes and making top-end wines from their own 30 hectares. Three Glasses went to the '03 Amativo last year and the '04 is again a great wine, good enough to be the sixth successive release in the finals. It comes from 60 per cent primitivo with negroamaro and initially gives lavender-like florality, followed by balsam and lively black berry fruit. These aromas are echoed on the palate, which has a good acid backbone, plentiful soft, well-meshed tannin and aromatic herbs on the finish. The two wines in the Teresa Manara line are excellent. The Negroamaro '03 has a nose of black cherry, chocolate and coffee, and a modern, attractive, well-knit palate with crisp fruit, good backbone and great length and the '05 Chardonnay is one of the best in the region. Here, a light oakiness underlies a pineapple and banana nose, and there are similar sensations on the full palate, which also has white-fleshed fruit, and good acidity and length. Varius '04, a 50-30-20 blend of negroamaro, cabernet sauvignon and montepulciano, scored similarly. Its nose is still a little closed but nevertheless gives raspberry and blueberry. The palate is fresh, attractive and sweetly fruity. Salice Salentino Riserva '03 is a touch over-evolved on the nose but has a lively, supple palate and showed well, as did the floral, savoury Negroamaro Rosato '05 and the citrus-like, perfumed Alticelli '05 from fiano, with its gently sweet finish.

●	Amativo '04	▼▼	5*
●	Teresa Manara Negroamaro '03	▼▼	4
●	Varius '04	▼▼	4*
○	Teresa Manara Chardonnay '05	▼▼	4
●	Salice Salentino Rosso Ris. '03	▼	3
○	Alticelli '05	▼	3
⊙	Negroamaro '05	▼	3
●	Amativo '03	▽▽▽	5*
●	Amativo '00	▽▽	4*
●	Amativo '01	▽▽	5*
●	Amativo '02	▽▽	5

GUAGNANO (LE)

COSIMO TAURINO
S.S. 605
73010 GUAGNANO (LE)
TEL. 0832706490
www.taurinovini.it

Francesco and Rosanna Taurino, overseen by oenologist Severino Garofano, continue in the direction of their late father Cosimo. The grapes come from 150 hectares of vineyard, 130 of them owned directly and almost all of them planted with indigenous red varieties. Production is around 1,500,000 bottles and the wines remain traditional in conception and approach, all too rare in a world that is often so easily swayed by passing trends and fashions. We liked A Cosimo Taurino '03, negroamaro-based with 15 per cent cabernet sauvignon from 20-year-old vines. The aromas of leather, spices and tobacco are traditional while the palate is attractive, balanced and savoury, with black berry fruit and tobacco, and a good acid backbone supporting it through to a long, tight finish. The '00 Patriglione, though, isn't quite as stunning as in the past, perhaps because of the particularly hot year. There is black fruit jam and leather on the nose. The palate is certainly full and rich but less dynamic and complex than previous releases and the overripe plum and tobacco finish falls a bit flat. There was no Notarpanaro to assess but we liked the '03 Salice Salentino Rosso Riserva with its mature garnet-ruby hue, its leather, walnutskin and generally nutty aromas, and its cohesive, soft, forward, attractive palate. The dried-grape passito Le Ricordanze '02, from sémillon and riesling, also showed well. The nose is perfumed, lightly resinous and has acacia honey and tea biscuits. The palate is less complex than the nose leads you to expect but echoes it well and is attractive.

●	A Cosimo Taurino '03	▼▼	5
●	Patriglione '00	▼▼	8
●	Salice Salentino Rosso Ris. '03	▼▼	5
○	Le Ricordanze Passito '02	▼	6
●	Patriglione '85	▽▽▽	5
●	Patriglione '88	▽▽▽	5
●	Patriglione '94	▽▽▽	6
●	Patriglione '99	▽▽	8

LATIANO (BR)

LOMAZZI & SARLI
LOC. PARTEMIO
C.DA PARTEMIO, S.S. 7
72022 LATIANO (BR)
TEL. 0831725898 - 337282775
www.vinilomazzi.it

The Dimastrodonato family produce around 700,000 bottles from 108 hectares of vineyard, some owned and some leased. A good 90 of them are planted with the region's traditional red varieties, including negroamaro, primitivo, malvasia nera and sussumaniello. The arrival of consultants Marco and Franco Bernabei to work alongside oenologist Davide Terlizzi is bearing fruit and the wines are gaining in definition, backbone and freshness. Let's start with Nomas '03, made from 100 per cent sussumaniello. This has intense aromas of chocolate, black berry fruit and figs, and a full, soft, nicely fruity palate with a long, tobacco-and-coffee finish. Latias '04 is a Primitivo with a slightly balsamic nose, sensations of small black berry fruit, printers' ink and tobacco, and medicinal herbs on the finish. Salice Salentino Rosso Irenico '04, from negroamaro with a little malvasia nera, is soft and fruity, giving aromas of black cherry and liquorice, and an easy-going, attractive, typically plum-like palate. Both are very good. Brindisi Riserva Solise '03 is not quite as good but still very sound. It is a monovarietal Negroamaro and is still a bit too oaky on its ripe-cherry nose but its palate is balanced, it has backbone and it finishes on a rich mix of plum, liquorice and tobacco.

●	Nomas '03	▼▼	6
●	Latias '04	▼▼	4
●	Salice Salentino Irenico '04	▼▼	4
●	Brindisi Rosso Solise Ris. '03	▼	4

LECCE

AGRICOLE VALLONE
VIA XXV LUGLIO, 5
73100 LECCE
TEL. 0832308041
www.agricolevallone.it

When Graticciaia is vying for Glasses at our finals, opinions are always fiercely held and clear-cut. The jury is split right down the middle. There are those who condemn it as from another age, an archetype of that world of badly made sweet, almost oxidized, wines from overripe grapes that is quite rightly disappearing. And there are those who see it as a successful, modern incarnation of tradition with all the good points of wines from the past but none of the defects. The tasting usually finishes with the majority saying something like, "We can see the idea behind the wine but we don't share it". This year, the vote went the other way and so, for the first time, Graticciaia gained Three Glasses. There is no doubt that the '01 is an excellent release, and possibly the best ever, but we feel that the award also recognizes a way of conceiving wine that is rooted in Italian – not just Puglian – wine culture and which perhaps we risk losing for ever. The wine is garnet ruby. The nose is evolved, with plum jam, spice and tobacco, and the palate follows on in similar vein, giving ultra-ripe black berry fruit. It's soft, silky and mouthfilling, finishing clean, tight and sweet. It would seem, though, that almost all efforts at Vallone are concentrated on Graticciaia because the other wines disappoint. Interest came in particular from the attractive, cherry-like Brindisi Rosato Vigna Flaminio '05 and the rather simple, dried-flowers-like Brindisi Rosso Vigna Flaminio '04, both of them oxidative in style.

●	Graticciaia '01	▼▼▼	7
●	Brindisi Rosso V. Flaminio '04	▼	3
⊙	Brindisi Rosato V. Flaminio '05	▼	3
●	Graticciaia '00	▽▽	7
●	Graticciaia '96	▽▽	6
●	Graticciaia '97	▽▽	7
●	Graticciaia '98	▽▽	7
○	Passo delle Viscarde '00	▽▽	6

LEVERANO (LE)

CONTI ZECCA
VIA CESAREA
73045 LEVERANO (LE)
TEL. 0832925613
www.contizecca.it

Although Nero has won Three Glasses six years running for the vintages 1998 to 2003, making it Puglia's top award-winner, this year it pulled up at the finals. No doubt the Zecca family and Romano, their oenologist, will be disappointed but we hope not too much. After all, Nero '04 is still top-notch and there is nothing to complain about anywhere in the excellent range. But let's go into detail. Nero '04 is from negroamaro with 30 per cent cabernet sauvignon. There is black berry fruit and chocolate on the nose. The palate is balanced, well-textured and long, with blackberry jam and smoky notes. Leverano Terra Riserva '03, from negroamaro with 30 per cent aglianico, is also a very fine wine, its aromas balsamic and spicy, and more spice on its complex, crisply fruity palate. Donna Marzia Rosato '05 has intense aromas of Mediterranean scrubland, followed by a fresh, firm palate full of flesh. It is surprisingly good, as is Donna Marzia Rosso '04, which has aromas of black berry fruit and aromatic herbs, and a clean, attractive palate with tobacco and more black berries. Both are from negroamaro-based blends. Salice Salentino Cantalupi Riserva '03 is equally good. This has aromatic Mediterranean herbs nuanced with chocolate and cherry jam, and a palate that balances suppleness with body. Indeed, it is difficult not to mention all the wines, so good are they, but we'll simply finish by highlighting the soft, full, fruity Primitivo '04; the fresh, red-fruits Leverano Rosato Saraceno '05 and the relaxed, traditional-style Salice Salentino Cantalupi '03.

● Nero '04	🍷🍷	6
● Leverano Rosso Terra Ris. '03	🍷🍷	4
● Salice Salentino Rosso Cantalupi Ris. '03	🍷🍷	4
● Donna Marzia Rosso '04	🍷🍷	2*
⊙ Donna Marzia Rosato '05	🍷🍷	2*
● Salice Salentino Rosso Cantalupi '03	🍷	3
● Primitivo '04	🍷	4
⊙ Leverano Rosato V. del Saraceno '05	🍷	2*
● Nero '00	🍷🍷🍷	6
● Nero '01	🍷🍷🍷	6
● Nero '02	🍷🍷🍷	6
● Nero '03	🍷🍷🍷	6

MANDURIA (TA)

ACCADEMIA DEI RACEMI
VIA SANTO STASI PRIMO - Z. I.
74024 MANDURIA (TA)
TEL. 0999711660
www.accademiadeiracemi.it

It would be hard to add anything new to what we have already said over the years on Gregory Perrucci's vision were we not so firmly convinced that this galaxy of estates is not only the most significant development in Puglia this decade but also crucial to the survival of winemaking conceived as a fusion of ancient techniques and modern interpretation. The ability to achieve this mix is revealed perfectly in Primitivo di Manduria Zinfandel Sinfarosa '05, for instance. This reached the finals with its intense nose full of black berry fruit and aromatic herbs, and its tight-knit, cohesive, long palate with good backbone and a tobacco-like finish. It is followed by a whole raft of excellent wines. Njùru '05 is new, a clean, fresh, soft wine from negroamaro which has attractive sensations of ripe red fruitiness. Dedalo Torre Guaceto '05 is100 per cent ottavianello and has a chocolate, tobacco and black cherry jam nose, and a deep, dense, well-fruited palate. Primitivo di Manduria Giravolta Tenuta Pozzopalo '05 is floral, slightly vegetal, and has wafts of ultra-ripe red berry fruit and coffee. The palate is full, round, fresh and attractive. Pietraluna Torre Guaceto '05 is a floral, fruity Negroamaro with a liquorice-like finish. Then we have an even fruitier, spicy, fresh, attractive Anarkos '05. On One Glass, we find Sinfarosa Primitivo '05, with its black cherries and firm palate, and the more traditional Salice Salentino Te Deum Laudamus Casale Bevagna '05, which mainly gives dried flowers.

● Primitivo di Manduria Zinfandel Sinfarosa '05	🍷🍷	5
● Anarkos '05	🍷🍷	3*
● Dedalo Torre Guaceto '05	🍷🍷	4
● Njùru '05	🍷🍷	2
● Pietraluna Torre Guaceto '05	🍷🍷	2*
● Primitivo di Manduria Giravolta Tenuta Pozzopalo '05	🍷🍷	4
● Salice Salentino Rosso Te Deum Laudamus Casale Bevagna '05	🍷	4
● Sinfarosa Primitivo '05	🍷	4

MANDURIA (TA)

FELLINE - PERVINI

VIA SANTO STASI PRIMO - Z. I.
74024 MANDURIA (TA)
TEL. 0999711660
www.accademiadeiracemi.it

Gregory Perrucci continues to work successfully on two fronts, Accademia dei Racemi and his "home" estate, Felline - Pervini. The second estate, where Cosimo Spina works as oenologist and Salvatore Mero as agronomist, always has a wine in our finals while also managing to achieve high quality across the range submitted. For instance, Vigna del Feudo, from equal parts of primitivo, malvasia nera and ottavianello – the last is the Puglian version of the French cinsault grape – again displays its usual top-notch quality with the '05 vintage, The nose is pervasive and complex, and has black berry fruit nuanced with oak toast. The fresh palate has backbone, its crisp black berry fruit ties in with the nose and there is a firm finish with hints of rhubarb. The '05 Alberello is as attractive as ever, managing to marry the breadth of its spicy aromas with a rich, mouthfilling palate that finishes long and fresh. There was a lovely surprise in Primitivo di Manduria Dolce Naturale Primo Amore '05, which has a black cherry and coffee nose, a palate with both sweetness and backbone, and a well-defined, fresh finish. Everything else is reliably good. Primitivo Felline '05 has black cherry on both nose and palate. It's a bit rustic but attractive. Bizantino Rosso '05 is packed with fruit and ready to drink. Primitivo di Manduria Paesaggio '05 remains a bit astringent under its flavours of bitter orange, plum and black cherry, and the uncomplicated, supple Primitivo di Manduria Segnavento '05 is still closed but supple and delicately fruity.

●	Vigna del Feudo '05	🍷🍷	5
●	Alberello '05	🍷🍷	3*
●	Primitivo di Manduria Dolce Naturale Primo Amore '05	🍷🍷	3*
●	Bizantino Rosso '05	🍷	3
●	Primitivo di Manduria Paesaggio '05	🍷	3
●	Primitivo di Manduria Segnavento '05		3
●	Primitivo Felline '05	🍷	3
●	Vigna del Feudo '02	🍸🍸	5*
●	Vigna del Feudo '04	🍸🍸	5

MANDURIA (TA)

MORELLA

VIA SAN PIETRO, 65
74024 MANDURIA (TA)
TEL. 0999791482

Australian Lisa Gilbee's Puglian baby has confidently retained its standing this year. Output is still small, at 10,000 bottles, despite the area under vine having increased to seven hectares, but all the vines are bush-trained and, in the case of the primitivo, range from 25 to 70 years old. The other variety is malbec. This year's results are just as good as last year's. Doubtless scrupulously keeping yields down to below 2,500 kilograms per hectare has had its effect. Primitivo Old Vines again reached the finals, this year with the '04. Oakiness and toastiness from its 14 months in barrique meld beautifully with its black cherry fruitiness, caramel undertones and nicely full, broad, balsamic palate, which finishes with overt sweet fruit. Primitivo La Signora '04 came quite close. Its style is very similar but there's more cherry fruit and Mediterranean scrubland on the nose, which also has balsamic notes and sweet spice. The full, well-textured palate turns more on fresh cherry and blackberry fruit, and finishes long but a bit sweet. Finally comes Primitivo Malbek Terre Rosse '04, which has 15 per cent of malbec alongside the primitivo. The nose is a touch vegetal and it's still a bit oaky on the palate, and gives butter and overripe fruit.

●	Primitivo Old Vines '04	🍷🍷	6
●	Primitivo La Signora '04	🍷🍷	6
●	Primitivo Malbek Terre Rosse '04	🍷	5
●	Old Vines Primitivo '03	🍸🍸	6
●	Malbek Terre Rosse '01	🍸🍸	4
●	Primitivo Terre Rosse '01	🍸🍸	4
●	Primitivo Malbek '03	🍸🍸	5

SALICE SALENTINO (LE)

Leone de Castris
via Senatore de Castris, 26
73015 Salice Salentino (LE)
tel. 0832731112 - 0832731113
www.leonedecastris.com

Leone De Castris continues unperturbed to plough its furrow of quality, concern for provenance, technical forward-thinking and attentiveness to all markets, domestic and non-domestic. Salice Salentino Rosso Riserva Donna Lisa did not gain Three Glasses this year, probably because of problems with the 2002 vintage, but our opinion of the estate remains extremely high. The nose gives Mediterranean scrubland, with vegetal and marzipan hints. The palate is medium-bodied, balanced and attractive, and has a good, black fruits finish. Both Five Roses wines, the Anniversario 62° Anno, from negroamaro with 20 per cent malvasia nera di Lecce, and the standard version, with just ten per cent malvasia, are among Italy's best rosés. The latter, all red berry fruit, is attractive, balanced and long. The Anniversario has a complex nose with floral, citrus and spicy aromas, and similar sensations come across on the nicely full and gentle but firm palate, which has good backbone. There is great interest to be found on the fruity, fleshy Salice Salentino Bianco Donna Lisa '05, solely from chardonnay, which is lively, piquant and very well made, although still quite oaky. Also of note are the more traditional Copertino Rosso '04, with its plum and printers' ink nose and its full, long palate; the intense, black cherry-like Illemos '02, from a 50-20-20-10 blend of primitivo, montepulciano, merlot and negroamaro; and the smoky Salice Salentino Rosso Riserva '03 which has lively, crisp, black berry fruit. Finally comes the floral Brut Rosé Donna Lisetta with its taut palate.

● Salice Salentino Rosso Donna Lisa Ris. '02	TT	6
● Illemos '02	TT	5
● Salice Salentino Rosso Ris. '03	TT	4
● Copertino Rosso '04	TT	2*
⊙ Five Roses '05	TT	3
⊙ Five Roses Anniversario 62° Anno '05	TT	4
○ Salice Salentino Bianco Donna Lisa '05	TT	5
⊙ Donna Lisetta Brut Rosé	TT	4
● Salice Salentino Rosso Donna Lisa Ris. '00	YYY	6
● Salice Salentino Rosso Donna Lisa Ris. '01	YYY	6
● Salice Salentino Rosso Donna Lisa Ris. '99	YYY	6

SALICE SALENTINO (LE)

Castello Monaci
c.da Monaci
73015 Salice Salentino (LE)
tel. 0831665700
www.giv.it

And now Artas has finally made it. At its fourth appearance in the finals, it finally emerged with Three Glasses. The estate is part of the Gruppo Italiano Vini stable and has 150 hectares under vine with quality improvements regularly apparent. The '04 Artas is the best ever. The wine comes from primitivo with 15 per cent negroamaro, and reflects a perfect balance of tradition and innovation. There are aromas of tobacco, black berry fruits, vanilla and antique wood. The elegant, soft palate is rich and full, and has flavours of liqueur cherries and chocolate, good backbone and a well-defined finish that makes for suppleness and attractive drinking. But this year's quality improvements spread further. We were also particularly struck by Salice Salentino Aiace Riserva '03, where the cherry, cinnamon, other spices and balsamic hints on the nose are echoed on a clean attractive palate with a firm, long finish. Then came the rather more traditional Salice Salentino Rosso '05, which has an evolved nose of ripe cherry and damson, and an easy-going palate where the same fruit characteristics return on the finish. It's another wine with good things to offer, as is the attractive, bright pink, minerally rosé Kreos '05, from negroamaro and a touch of malvasia nera, which has delicate morello cherry and blackcurrant.

● Artas '04	TTT	5*
● Salice Salentino Aiace Ris. '03	TT	4
⊙ Kreos '05	T	3
● Salice Salentino Rosso '05	T	3
● Artas '01	YY	5*
● Artas '02	YY	5
● Artas '03	YY	5*

SAN DONACI (BR)

Francesco Candido

via A. Diaz, 46
72025 San Donaci (BR)
tel. 0831635674 - 0831635675
www.candidowines.it

A Candido wine reached the finals this year after several years' absence, but it wasn't their most famous one. Out of the 2,000,000 bottles produced from their 160 hectares of vines and additional selected grapes bought in from a fixed group of growers, the wine that emerged as top of the tree this year was Immensum '04. It is made from 70 per cent negroamaro with cabernet sauvignon and the nose is complex, with tertiary notes of coffee, cocoa powder and tobacco alongside Mediterranean scrubland and plum. The palate has body, depth, length and attractiveness. But the whole range is impressive. The '01 vintage of the historic Cappello di Prete, a monovarietal Negroamaro, has a nose of liquorice with balsamic hints, and an expansive, medium-bodied palate with a nutty finish. Next comes the more traditional Salice Salentino Riserva '01, which has dried flowers and ripe black berry fruits aromas followed by a soft, rich palate giving ripe red fruits flavours and a relaxed finish. Salice Salentino Bianco Portafalsa '05, exclusively from chardonnay, is full of yellow-fleshed fruit and vanilla, and is cohesive, of good substance and fresh on its apricot-like finish. The classic Paule Calle '03 is a dried-grape passito from chardonnay and malvasia bianca. It is floral, has aromas of apricot and dried figs, and is well-made, clean and attractive. The sound rosé Piccoli Passi '05 has citrus peel fruitiness.

●	Immensum '04	🍷🍷	5*
●	Cappello di Prete '01	🍷🍷	4*
●	Salice Salentino Rosso Ris. '01	🍷🍷	3*
○	Paule Calle '03	🍷🍷	4
○	Salice Salentino Bianco Portafalsa '05	🍷🍷	3*
⊙	Piccoli Passi '05	🍷	3
●	Duca d'Aragona '96	🍸🍸	5
●	Cappello di Prete '00	🍸🍸	4*
●	Immensum '01	🍸🍸	4
○	Paule Calle '02	🍸🍸	4*
●	Cappello di Prete '99	🍸🍸	4*

SAN PIETRO VERNOTICO (BR)

Santa Barbara

via Maternità e Infanzia, 23
72027 San Pietro Vernotico (BR)
tel. 0831652749

After a few years' absence, a range of good quality wines has brought the Santa Barbara co-operative back into the Guide with a full entry. Founded in 1983, it is directed by oenologist Pietro Giorgiani and has 150 members supplying grapes from 150 hectares of vineyard, almost all bush-trained, in and around San Pietro Vernotico. Annual production is 2,000,000 bottles. Most interest this year came from two wines. The well-made, traditionally styled Barbaglio '01, from negroamaro with 20 per cent primitivo, has a deep nose of oriental spices, bottled red fruits, printer's ink, leather and tobacco introducing a soft, expansive palate with overripe red berry fruit and an attractive, firm finish. The other stand-out was Salento Bianco '05, from 100 per cent chardonnay, which has overt aromas of citrus and spring flowers, light smoky, mineral notes, and a cohesive, nicely acidic, long, lively palate with a grapefruit and pineapple finish. All the other wines submitted also showed well. Brindisi Rosso '03 has the dried figs, liquorice and leather nose typical of the wine, and an attractive, cohesive, soft – perhaps too soft – palate that just begs to be drunk. Cantamessa '05 is a clean, highly aromatic, floral Sauvignon with good texture. Sumanero '02, from 60 per cent sussumaniello with negroamaro and malvasia nera, has a slightly over-evolved, liqueur cherries and chocolate nose but is nevertheless highly attractive, mouthfilling and ready for the corkscrew.

●	Il Barbaglio '01	🍷🍷	4
○	Salento Bianco '05	🍷🍷	5*
●	Sumanero '02	🍷	4
●	Brindisi Rosso '03	🍷	3
○	Cantamessa '05	🍷	3

SAN SEVERO (FG)

TENUTA COPPADORO
S.DA PROVINCIALE, 35
71016 SAN SEVERO (FG)
TEL. 0882242301 - 0882242311
www.tenutacoppadoro.it

Director Luigi Albano, agronomist Giuseppe Pisante and oenologist Riccardo Cotarella have lost no time in picking up the knack of producing outstanding wines here. Cotinone has taken Three Glasses for the second year running and everything else is showing excellently, too. And for a winery at only its third vintage, that is really something. The enterprise has 20 members who own 120 hectares of vine, all cordon spur-trained and with densities exceeding 6,000 plants per hectare. Output is nearly 500,000 bottles a year so there is quantity as well as quality, including 75,000 bottles of Cotinone. This is a blend of equal parts of montepulciano, aglianico and cabernet sauvignon, and the '05 majors on freshness, both on its youthful, black berry fruits nose with hints of vanilla and liquorice, and on its balanced, nicely full, long palate with clean tannins and a highly attractive finish. Radicosa '04 comes from 100 per cent montepulciano. This is deeper on the nose, with liqueur fruits, coffee and cocoa powder. The palate is more compact, fleshy and austere, with black berry fruitiness and a long but not yet clearly defined finish. The floral and black berry fruits Pescorosso '04, from nero di Troia with 25 per cent aglianico, is very good as is Rosa di Salsola '05, whose intense cherry and raspberry nose leads to a lively, spicy, savoury palate. We finish with Ratino '05, from 60 per cent bombino and equal quantities of chardonnay, sauvignon and moscato, which has white-fleshed fruit on the nose and a fleshy palate giving flavours of sweet pineapple and citrus.

● Cotinone '05	🍷🍷🍷	5*
● Radicosa '04	🍷🍷	7
● Pescorosso '04	🍷🍷	4
⊙ Rosa di Salsola '05	🍷🍷	4
○ Ratino '05	🍷	4
● Radicosa '03	YYY	7
● Radicosa '02	YY	8
● Cotinone '03	YY	5*
● Cotinone '02	YY	5
● Pescorosso '03	YY	4*

SAN SEVERO (FG)

D'ALFONSO DEL SORDO
C.DA SANT'ANTONINO
71016 SAN SEVERO (FG)
TEL. 0882221444 - 0882335588
www.dalfonsodelsordo.it

D'Alfonso del Sordo has been a landmark winery in San Severo and indeed the province of Foggia for almost 50 years, and currently has 90 hectares of vineyard with an output of almost 350,000 bottles. Gianfelice d'Alfonso del Sordo hasn't looked back since he handed over the winemaking to Luigi Moio in 2001. Qualitative consistency is now at levels that are rare, especially for Puglia, even in difficult vintages like the recent ones. Four wines particularly impressed us this year. First up is Montero '05, from montepulciano with cabernet sauvignon. The nose is fresh and floral with red berries. The palate is in similar vein and shows clean, attractive and long. Cava del Re Cabernet Sauvignon '05 is on a par. Its deep complex nose is dominated by coffee and incense. The palate is more open, showing mid-bodied and supple, and has a varietally vegetal finish. Next come Doganera '05, a spicy Merlot with liqueur cherries, oak toast, cinnamon, clove and tobacco, and a nicely full, soft, easy-going, multi-faceted palate and San Severo Rosso Posta Arignano '05, from montepulciano with 30 per cent sangiovese, which has fresh cherry and balsamic aromas shot through with vegetal hints, and a cohesive, well-defined palate with good backbone. Everything else is very well made, notably the ripe, soft, long Casteldrione '04 with its red fruits jam flavours, the immediate, floral San Severo Rosato Posta Arignano '05, and Catapanus '05, from bombino, which has broom flowers on the nose and white-fleshed fruit on the palate.

● Cava del Re Cabernet Sauvignon '05	🍷🍷	6
● Doganera Merlot '05	🍷🍷	6
● Montero '05	🍷🍷	4*
● Casteldrione '04	🍷	3
○ Catapanus '05	🍷	3
⊙ San Severo Rosato Posta Arignano '05	🍷	2*
● San Severo Rosso Posta Arignano '05	🍷	2*
● Cava del Re Cabernet Sauvignon '02	YY	6
● Cava del Re Cabernet Sauvignon '03	YY	6
● Cava del Re Cabernet Sauvignon '04	YY	6

TARANTO

Fusione

LOC. CASTELLANETA
C.DA CACCAMONE
MASSERIA SIGNORELLA
74011 TARANTO
TEL. 0998493770

Some see Elvezia Sbalchiero from Friuli and Mark Shannon, a California winemaker, as an odd couple. They came to Puglia nine years ago and started to search out old vineyards and make contact with small owners with the aim of making fine wine. They were received with no little mistrust. But time has gone on and the couple have established themselves as grower producers releasing 150,000 bottles a year. Their grapes come from various zones. The primitivo is from Manduria, Sava, Torricella and Maruggio, the negroamaro is from San Pietro Vernotico, and there is also greco and fiano, grown south of Bari, at Putignano and Acquaviva, for a new white. This mosaic comes together only because the pair take huge care throughout the year to follow the vines and growers, and dedicate great commitment to winemaking. But let's have a look at the wines themselves. Prima Mano is an excellent Primitivo produced only in the better years. The grapes come from two old vineyards at Torricella, close to the sea. The nose on the '03 has plum syrup, eucalyptus and a light spiciness. The palate is tightly knit with good body and has fragrant black berry fruitiness but is still rather dominated by its oak. Promessa Negroamaro '05 showed almost as well. Its lively red berry fruit, black cherry and vanilla lead to a clean, fresh, fruity, highly attractive palate. A Mano Primitivo '03, which has liquorice, black cherry and a simple, open palate, and A Mano Bianco '05, from equal parts of fiano and greco, with pear, lemon and floral aromas and a soft, mouthfilling palate, both scored well.

●	Prima Mano '03	🍷🍷	5
●	Promessa Negroamaro '05	🍷🍷	3*
●	A Mano Primitivo '03	🍷	3
○	A Mano Bianco '05	🍷	3

TARANTO

Vetrere

FRAZ. VETRERE
S.P. MONTEIASI - MONTEMESOLA KM. 16
74020 TARANTO
TEL. 0995661054 - 3402977870
www.vetrere.it

This 300-hectare property, owned by the Bruni sisters, has 37 hectares under vine with a further eight hectares leased. Annual output is 150,000 bottles. Vincenzo Laera has now joined oenologist Giuseppe Caragnulo and agronomist Annamaria Bruni, bringing additional strength to an estate that has already achieved qualitative consistency and acquired a stable position among the region's best. This year, we really liked the unoaked Tempio di Giano '05, from 100 per cent negroamaro, which is all liveliness and attractiveness. Fresh small red berry fruits and liquorice and liquorice on the nose leads to a clean, cohesive palate with good backbone. The '04 Barone Pazzo, from primitivo, is as good as ever, a year in barrique giving complexity to its nose, even though the oak still outweighs the aromas of Mediterranean herbs, and to the soft, mouthfilling palate with its ripe black berry fruit finish. Further excellence is found on Taranta '05, a fruity rosé from 85 per cent negroamaro with malvasia nera, which has vegetal and pencil lead notes and a velvety yet refreshing palate. The other wines are also good. The nicely firm Finis Terrae '05, from chardonnay with some malvasia and verdeca, has white-fleshed and tropical fruits. Lago della Pergola '04 comes from a 75-15-10 blend of negroamaro, cabernet and aglianico but doesn't quite seem full and dense enough to cope with its year in barrique. Livruni '05 is a simple, youthful Primitivo full of lively red berries. Finally, Laureato '05, from a 55-25-20 blend of chardonnay, malvasia and fiano, is floral and citrus-like.

●	Barone Pazzo '04	🍷🍷	4
⊙	Taranta '05	🍷🍷	3*
●	Tempio di Giano '05	🍷🍷	3*
●	Lago della Pergola '04	🍷	4
○	Finis Terrae '05	🍷	3
○	Laureato '05	🍷	4
●	Livruni '05	🍷	3
●	Barone Pazzo '02	ΥΥ	4
●	Barone Pazzo '03	ΥΥ	4

OTHER WINERIES

Giancarlo Ceci

C.da Sant'Agostino
70031 Andria (BA)
tel. 0883564938

Giancarlo Ceci first vinified his 65 hectares of vines a couple of years ago, with Lorenzo Landi as consultant, and the estate now debuts in the Guide. Parco Marano '04, from nero di Troia, is very good with red and black berries and a fresh, balanced palate. Parco Grande '05 is attractively fruity.

●	Castel del Monte Rosso Parco Marano '04	🍷🍷	4
●	Castel del Monte Rosso Parco Grande '05	🍷	3

Conte Spagnoletti Zeuli

fraz. Montegrosso
s.p. 231 km. 21,00
70031 Andria (BA)
tel. 0883569511

This has been a low-key year for the estate. Castel del Monte Rosato Mezzana'05 is very good with raspberry and blackcurrant fruit, and a lively, full palate. Jody '05, from fiano, has good style, with white-fleshed fruit, and an uncomplicated, well-textured palate.

⊙	Castel del Monte Rosato Mezzana '05	🍷🍷	4*
○	Jody '05	🍷	4

Sergio Botrugno

loc. Casale - via Arcione, 1
72100 Brindisi
tel. 0831555587 - 3200797738
www.vinisalento.com

A full entry beckons here. Seno di Ponente '05, from negroamaro with 20 per cent malvasia nera, has a vanilla and plum nose, and a soft, creamy palate with a nutty finish. Ottavianello '04 is fresh, fruity and attractive. Black berry fruit jam marks out Brindisi Rosso Arcione '04.

●	Ottavianello '04	🍷🍷	4*
●	Seno di Ponente Rosso '05	🍷🍷	3*
●	Brindisi Rosso Arcione '04	🍷	4

Cefalicchio

c.so San Sabino, 6
70053 Canosa di Puglia (BA)
tel. 0833617601
www.cefalicchio.it

Fabrizio Rossi's biodynamic estate again showed well. The fine Romanico '04, from uva di Troia, has Mediterranean scrubland and balsam, and is clean, soft and balanced. Ponte della Lama '05 is a fresh, attractive rosé. Vigne Alte '03, from 65 per cent uva di Troia and montepulciano, is also good.

●	Rosso Canosa Romanico '04	🍷🍷	3*
●	Rosso Canosa Vigne Alte '03	🍷	3
⊙	Ponte della Lama Rosato '05	🍷	3

MASSERIA LI VELI
S.P. CELLINO-CAMPI, KM 1
72020 CELLINO SAN MARCO (BR)
TEL. 0831617906
www.liveli.it

This estate, founded in 1999 and with 51 hectares under vine, remains a bit middle of the road. Passamante '04, from negroamaro only, has a broad, complex nose and an attractive but rather simple palate. The mid-bodied Orion '05, from primitivo, and the clean, floral Rosato '05 are both good.

● Passamante '04	🍷🍷	3*
● Orion '05	🍷	4
⊙ Rosato '05	🍷	3

ANTICA ENOTRIA
C.DA POSTA UCCELLO
71042 CERIGNOLA (FG)
TEL. 0885418462
www.anticaenotria.it

This splendid estate seems to be in a transitional state with new oenologist Giuseppe Dambra just arrived. For now, the best wines are Nero di Troia '05, which has a smoky, red fruits nose and a lively, well-structured palate, and the well-styled Falù '04, a fruity, supple Montepulciano.

● Nero di Troia '05	🍷🍷	4*
● Falù '04	🍷	4

CANTINE DE LA MANNA
LOC. BORGO LIBERTÀ
VIA MONTANARA, 1
71040 CERIGNOLA (FG)
TEL. 0885447144 - www.blibcoop.it

This 1,000-member co-operative submitted some excellent wines, especially Teutonico '04, from nero di Troia, which is full, long and with black berry fruit. The fresh, floral Rosato '05, the nice, uncomplicated Rosso '04 and the aromatic, firmly acidic Greco '05 from the Turris line are all good.

● Teutonico '04	🍷🍷	4*
● Turris Rosso '04	🍷	2
○ Turris Greco '05	🍷	2
⊙ Turris Rosato '05	🍷	1*

CANTINE CARPENTIERE
C.DA BAGNOLO
70033 CORATO (BA)
TEL. 0883341104
www.cantinecarpentiere.it

Oenologist Franco Pastore's work on Enzo and Luigi Carpentiere's lovely property in the Murgia parkland shows. Esordio '05, from nero di Troia, is one of Puglia's best rosés, with florality, intensity and backbone. The fruity Colle dei Grillai '05, from cabernet, merlot and nero di Troia, is good.

● Castel del Monte Colle dei Grillai '05	🍷🍷	3
⊙ Castel del Monte Rosato Esordio '05	🍷🍷	4

SANTA LUCIA
S.DA SAN VITTORE, 1
70033 CORATO (BA)
TEL. 0817642888
www.vinisantalucia.com

Perrone Capano's estate remains a focal point in Castel del Monte, especially for its wines from nero di Troia. Vigna del Melograno '04 has tobacco and red fruits and a full, fresh palate of backbone. Riserva Le More '04 has quinine notes and a soft, medium-bodied palate.

● Castel del Monte Le More Ris. '04	🍷🍷	6
● Castel del Monte Rosso V. del Melograno '04	🍷🍷	4*

COSIMO PALAMÀ
VIA A. DIAZ, 6
73020 CUTROFIANO (LE)
TEL. 0836542865
www.vinicolapalama.com

This winery returns to the Guide thanks to its flagship Mavro, from 80 per cent negroamaro with malvasia nera. The '04 has a broad, floral, spicy nose and a soft palate with ripe black berry fruit that ends on coffee and pepper. Albarossa Primitivo '04 is pleasantly fruity.

● Mavro '04	🍷🍷	3*
● Albarossa Primitivo '04	🍷	2*
● Mavro '01	🍷🍷 (white glasses)	4*

SANTA MARIA DEL MORIGE
FRAZ. CARPIGNANA - VIA DEL MARE, KM 2
73044 GALATONE (LE)
TEL. 0833864525
www.santamariadelmorige.com

This new estate, owned by the Conserva family, debuted in the Guide thanks to Cinabro '03, made solely from 30-year-old bush-trained negroamaro. It's all blackberry, plum and coffee, with a clean, long, fruity palate of good substance.

- ● Cinabro '03 — 🍷🍷 4

GUTTAROLO
LAMIE DI FATALONE, KM 2,385
70023 GIOIA DEL COLLE (BA)
TEL. 089236612 - 3384090058

Cristiano Guttarolo and oenologist Antonio Di Gruttola did well with their stylish Mediterranean scrubland and spice Primitivo '04 with its full, fruity palate. The weightier, more concentrated Antello delle Murge '04, also primitivo, is nice if less balanced. Fewer than 10,000 bottles are released.

- ● Primitivo '04 — 🍷🍷 4*
- ● Antello delle Murge '04 — 🍷🍷 4

CANTINE BOTROMAGNO
LOC. ZONA PIP
VIA ARCHIMEDE, 20/22/24
70024 GRAVINA IN PUGLIA (BA)
TEL. 0803265865 - www.botromagno.it

The 2001 vintage was difficult for Pier delle Vigne, which is pleasant but a bit over-evolved. Gravisano '03, though, is up to speed. The nose has confectioners' cream and candied orange peel, the palate doesn't cloy and is nicely full and soft, well supported by acidity, finishing fresh.

- ○ Gravisano '03 — 🍷🍷 5
- ● Pier delle Vigne '01 — 🍷 4
- ● Pier delle Vigne '00 — 🍷🍷 (white) 4*

VIGNE & VINI
VIA AMENDOLA, 36
74020 LEPORANO (TA)
TEL. 0995332254 - 0995334116
www.vigneevini.it

There are 500,000 bottles here and a good range of Primitivos, led by the fruity, clean, balanced Papale '04. Chicca '03, which is medium-bodied and sweet but not cloying, and Tatù '05, a bit closed on the nose but with good fruit on the palate, also showed well.

- ● Primitivo di Manduria Papale '04 — 🍷🍷 4
- ● Primitivo di Manduria Dolce Naturale Chicca '03 — 🍷 4
- ● Tatù '05 — 🍷 4

CANTINA SOCIALE COOPERATIVA VECCHIA TORRE
VIA MARCHE, 1
73045 LEVERANO (LE)
TEL. 0832925053 - 0832921985

Wines from this long-standing co-operative showed well although last year's peak was not repeated. Primitivo '03 has red berry fruit and a cohesive, poised palate of good weight. A fruity, slightly spicy, nicely soft Salice Salentino Rosso '03 and a floral, citrus Chardonnay '05 scored similarly.

- ● Primitivo '03 — 🍷 3
- ● Salice Salentino Rosso '03 — 🍷 2*
- ○ Chardonnay '05 — 🍷 2*

MILLE UNA
L.GO CHIESA, 11
74020 LIZZANO (TA)
TEL. 0999552638 - 3939615067
www.milleuna.it

There are still ups and downs here as the wines remain very sensitive to vintage variations. We best liked the floral, varietal Ori di Taranto Chardonnay '05 with its long, full, firmly acidic palate, and D. Mero '04, a plum jam-like Primitivo Passito from 70-year-old vines.

- ● D. Mero Passito '04 — 🍷 7
- ○ Ori di Taranto Chardonnay '05 — 🍷 4
- ● Tre Tarante '03 — 🍷🍷 (white) 8

VINI CLASSICI CARDONE

VIA MARTIRI DELLA LIBERTÀ, 32
70010 LOCOROTONDO (BA)
TEL. 0804311624 - 0804312561
www.cardonevini.com

The 2005 vintage challenged many Puglian wineries and Cardone was no exception. The best wines are the citrus-like Locorotondo Il Castillo with an attractive palate of backbone, Placeo, a citron-like Chardonnay with a little residual sugar, and the supple Primitivo Primaio with aromatic herbs.

○ Locorotondo Il Castillo '05	🍷	4
○ Placeo '05	🍷	4
● Primaio '05	🍷	4

CANTINA LOCOROTONDO

VIA MADONNA DELLA CATENA, 99
70010 LOCOROTONDO (BA)
TEL. 0804311644 - 0804311850
www.locorotondodoc.com

Reds give consistent quality here. Cummerse Rosso '03, from aglianico, nero di Troia and cabernet sauvignon, is fresh and attractive. The negroamaro, montepulciano and malvasia nera Roccia Rosso '05 has violets and black berries. Casale San Giorgio Rosato '05, a Montepulciano, is full and intense.

● Cummerse Rosso '03	🍷	4
⊙ Casale San Giorgio Rosato '05	🍷	4
● Roccia Rosso '05	🍷	4

I PASTINI - CARPARELLI

VIA ITALO BALBO, 22/24
70010 LOCOROTONDO (BA)
TEL. 0804313309

Nicola and Pasquale Carparelli continue to produce high-quality wines from their 21 hectares of vines. The fine Vigna Rampone '05, from fiano minutolo, is intensely floral, mineral, and long, with a fruity, nicely fresh palate. Arpago '04, from primitivo, is balsamic, attractive and uncomplicated.

○ Vigna Rampone '05	🍷🍷	4
● Arpago '04	🍷	3

ALBERTO LONGO

LOC. C.DA PADULECCHIA
S.P. PIETRAMONTECORVINO, KM 4
71036 LUCERA (FG)
TEL. 0881539057 - www.albertolongo.it

This newcomer to the Guide has 35 hectares planted at an unusually high density for Puglia. The best wines are the fruity, mouthfilling nero di Troia Le Cruste '04 and the floral, well-structured Rosato Donnadele '05, from negroamaro. The plums and tobacco Cacc'e Mmitte '04 is also noteworthy.

● Le Cruste '04	🍷🍷	5
⊙ Donnadele '05	🍷🍷	4
● Cacc'e Mmitte di Lucera '04	🍷	4

PAOLO PETRILLI

LOC. MOTTA DELLA REGINA
71036 LUCERA (FG)
TEL. 0881523980 -
3483383283285

Just 15,000 bottles are made, all top quality. Guerro '04 is nero di Troia only, full of violet, liquorice and plum, and with a deep, well-sustained palate. Ferraù '04, from equal parts of nero di Troia and sangiovese, is just as good, showing all red fruits and spices. Long may it last.

● Ferraù '04	🍷🍷	5
● Il Guerro '04	🍷🍷	5
● Ferraù '02	🍷🍷 (white)	5

CONSORZIO PRODUTTORI VINI E MOSTI ROSSI

VIA FABIO MASSIMO, 19
74024 MANDURIA (TA)
TEL. 0999735332 - www.cpvini.com

It's been a low-key year at this major co-operative, especially for its Primitivo di Mandurias. The best wines are the fresh, pear-like Calice '05, from chardonnay and verdeca, the clean rosé Riflesso '05, all red berry fruit, and the uncomplicated, plum-like Primitivo di Manduria Il Madrigale '04.

● Primitivo di Manduria Dolce Naturale Il Madrigale '04	🍷	4
○ Calice '05	🍷	3
⊙ Riflesso '05	🍷	3

Apollonio
via San Pietro in Lama, 7
73047 Monteroni di Lecce (LE)
tel. 0832327182
www.apolloniovini.it

Apollonio has been in the doldrums, suffering more than most from recent poor vintages. Relief comes from an attractive, floral, fresh, negroamaro-based Elfo Rosato '05; a pear-and-citrus, bombino-based Elfo Bianco '05, and a chocolate-veined, negroamaro-based dried-grape passito, Mater Terra '03.

● Mater Terra '03	🍷	5
○ Elfo Bianco '05	🍷	2
⊙ Elfo Rosato '05	🍷	2

Mocavero
c.da Mallacca Zummari
73010 Monteroni di Lecce (LE)
tel. 0832327194
www.mocaverovini.it

There have been ups and downs this year on this 35-hectare estate producing 400,000 bottles. The best wines are the primitivo-only Santufili '03 with its deep aromas, warmth and black berry fruit, the ripe, quinine-like Negroamaro '05, and the clean, uncomplicated Chardonnay '05.

● Santufili '03	🍷	5
○ Chardonnay '05	🍷	2
● Negramaro '05	🍷	3

La Corte
via Trepuzzi
73051 Novoli (LE)
tel. 0559707594
www.renideo.com

This year La Corte submitted only its two base-level wines. Anfora Primitivo '05 showed excellently, with toasty, coffee-like aromas, hints of cherry and plum, and a fresh, supple, balanced palate. Solyss Negroamaro '05 is attractive, well-made, floral, clean and full of red berry fruit.

● Anfora Primitivo '05	🍷🍷	4
● Solyss Negroamaro '05	🍷	4
● Negroamaro Vigne Vecchie '03	🍷🍷 (white)	5*
● Primitivo Vigne Vecchie '03	🍷🍷 (white)	5*

De Falco
via Milano, 25
73051 Novoli (LE)
tel. 0832711597
www.cantinedefalco.it

The De Falco wines again showed well this year. Artiglio '03, from 60 per cent montepulciano with primitivo, is fruity, spicy and full of lively, black berry fruit. Squinzano Rosso Serre di Sant'Elia '04 is firm, with cinnamon and clove. Bocca della Verita '04 is a clean, uncomplicated Primitivo.

● Artiglio '03	🍷🍷	5
● Squinzano Rosso Serre di Sant'Elia '04	🍷🍷	3*
● Bocca della Verità '04	🍷	4

Ognissole
via Luigi di Savoia, 3
74026 Pulsano (TA)
tel. 0825986611
www.feudi.it

Feudi di San Gregorio's Puglian winery is almost up to cruising speed with 32 hectares giving 100,000 bottles. Primitivo di Manduria '05 has a slightly vegetal nose, with red berry fruits, and an attractive, nicely savoury palate. Verdeca Medico di Maglie '05 is fruity and supple.

● Primitivo di Manduria '05	🍷🍷	5
○ Verdeca Medico di Maglie '05	🍷	5
● Primitivo di Manduria '03	🍷🍷 (white)	4

Vinagri
via Tuturano, 21
72025 San Donaci (BR)
tel. 0831635073
www.vinagripuglia.it

Paolo Leo continues to produce good quality wines. This year's best was the basic Negroamaro '05 with fresh cherry and raspberry, and an elegant, attractive palate. Orfeo '03, with oak toast and black berry fruits, and the soft, well-defined Limitone dei Greci Primitivo '04, are also well made.

● Negroamaro '05	🍷🍷	2*
● Orfeo '03	🍷	4
● Limitone dei Greci Primitivo '04	🍷	4

VINICOLA RESTA
VIA CAMPI, 7
72027 SAN PIETRO VERNOTICO (BR)
TEL. 0831671182
www.vinicolaresta.it

Quality remains good here. The admirable Salice Salentino Rosso Riserva Torre Saracena '03 has a wealth of balsamic notes and a close-knit palate of backbone. The basic Salice Salentino Rosso '03, soft, with plum and tobacco, showed well, as did the simple, attractive Squinzano Rosso '03.

● Salice Salentino Rosso Torre Saracena Ris. '03	🍷🍷	4
● Salice Salentino Rosso '03	🍷	4
● Squinzano Rosso '03	🍷	4

VINICOLA MEDITERRANEA
VIA MATERNITÀ INFANZIA, 22
72027 SAN PIETRO VERNOTICO (BR)
TEL. 0831676323 - 0831659329
www.vinicolamediterranea.it

The low-key wines here reflect the 2005 vintage. Primitivo Scalee is clean with small red berry fruit. Chardonnay Nature is well-made and citrus-like. Negroamaro Emozione is more complex on the nose than the palate; Don Vito, from negroamaro and primitivo, has good fruit but is a bit too sweet.

○ Chardonnay Nature '05	🍷	2
● Don Vito '05	🍷	2*
● Negroamaro Emozione '05	🍷	5
● Primitivo Scalee '05	🍷	3

GIANFRANCO FINO
LOC. LAMA - VIA FIOR DI SALVIA, 8
74020 TARANTO
TEL. 0997773970 - 3488838639
www.gianfrancofino.com

Fino has just one hectare, planted more than 50-year-old bush-trained primitivo, and produces no more than 3,000 bottles. But the resulting wine, Es, impresses. The '04 has a broad, complex nose, a full, long palate and 18 per cent alcohol, which is apparent on the finish.

● Primitivo di Manduria Es '04	🍷🍷	6

CASTEL DI SALVE
FRAZ. DEPRESSA - VIA SALVEMINI, 32
73026 TRICASE (LE)
TEL. 0833771041 - 0833771012
www.casteldisalve.com

This has not been the happiest of years here. Lama del Tenente, a 40-40-10 blend of primitivo, montepulciano and malvasia nera, is very good, with Mediterranean scrubland, red berry fruits, structure and backbone. A fresh, zesty Santi Medici Bianco and a youthful, fruity Armecolo are well made.

● Lama del Tenente '03	🍷🍷	5
● Armecolo '05	🍷	4
○ Santi Medici Bianco '05	🍷	3

MICHELE CALÒ & FIGLI
VIA MASSERIA VECCHIA, 1
73058 TUGLIE (LE)
TEL. 0833596242 - 0833381612
www.mjere.it

This is one of Puglia's leading estates and the Mjère line retains its high-quality imprint. The '05 Rosato, from negroamaro and malvasia nera, is nice, showing citrus-like, rich and fruity. Also good are the vigorous, nutty '05 Bianco, verdeca and the negroamaro '04 Rosso with ultra-ripe fruit.

● Mjère Rosso '04	🍷	4
⊙ Alezio Rosato Mjère '05	🍷	4
○ Mjère Bianco '05	🍷	4

C.A.L.O.S.M.
VIA PIETRO SICILIANI
73058 TUGLIE (LE)
TEL. 0833598051 - 3475946330

Quality levels at C.a.l.o.s.m are epitomized by an excellent Primitivo Villa Valentino '05. The broad, floral nose has red berry fruits and the long palate is lively and elegant. The nice, fruity Tisciano '04, and the balanced, citrussy rosé Salmace '05, are both from negroamaro and malvasia nera, and both good.

● Primitivo Villa Valentino '05	🍷🍷	2*
● Tisciano '04	🍷	4
⊙ Salmace '05	🍷	4

CALABRIA

At last Calabria can again boast a Three Glass wine, the fabulous '03 Scavigna Vigna Garrone from Odoardi. And curiously it was the '99 vintage of the same wine which was the region's previous Three Glass winner in our 2003 edition. But this is not the only good news from Italy's toe. For the second year running, we have noted an improvement in quality across the board in the region which, as we have said for years, has ideal natural conditions for top-quality wine production. It just seems, or seemed, that producers were happier ignoring them. There's been an absence this year of the stop-go that has previously plagued many of the wines and we sincerely hope that the phenomenon now disappeared once and for all. It seems quite likely, judging by our tastings. Admittedly Vigna Garrone '03 is the only wine to be awarded Three Glasses but there are numerous other fabulous wines, some of them only a whisper away from top honours. There's Moscato di Saracena '04, for instance, from Luigi Viola, a real wine artisan of great skill who has revived the ancient tradition of making this wine and thereby revitalized his entire zone. Then again, there's Librandi's Gravello which, with the '04 vintage, has acquired even greater elegance and stylistic maturity. There were compliments all round for finalist Terraccia '03, from Demetrio Stancati's small estate. This terrific red comes from the rare magliocco dolce variety, which is found only in the area of Bisignano in the province of Cosenza, and is currently being entered in the national register of vine varieties. The wines from the Cirò zone generally showed creditably with the usual high spot: the brilliant wines of Nicodemo and Antonio Librandi, who continue relentlessly to recover indigenous Calabrian varieties. There have also been great strides forward around Lamezia and a notable upswing at its two leading wineries. The Lento family's wines seem to have regained the sparkle of earlier years and those of the Statti brothers have risen to the region's top rank. It would be good to see at least one really exceptional wine here but that surely is only a matter of time. In the province of Catanzaro there is, of course, Odoardi, whose praises we never tire of singing. But other producers are gradually emerging and from this year, the Savuto DOC is no longer an Odoardi monopoly. There are also great developments in the province of Cosènza. The two estates that have guided its fortunes, Serracavallo and Terre di Balbia, are now surrounded by some promising newcomers. We'll update you next year. It is only in the far south of the region that things haven't really moved much. The excellent work of the Stelitano siblings in restoring Greco di Bianco to its ancient renown goes on but there is little else to report.

ALTOMONTE (CS)

TERRE DI BALBIA

LOC. MONTINO
87042 ALTOMONTE (CS)
TEL. 048161264 - 0981948339
www.terredibalbia.it

Gianni Venica and Silvio Caputo have been friends for many years. Both are important names in the wine world for Venica is a renowned producer in Friuli while Caputo is from Calabria and made his name importing Italy's top wines into California. On one of his periodic trips back home, Silvio heard from friends that there was a fabulous ten-hectare plot near Altomonte for sale. He went to have a look and liked what he saw but was undecided what to do. After all, he'd always been on the other side, the one who niggled producers if he wasn't totally convinced by a wine he had to distribute and he felt happy in that role. But then there was that remarkable vineyard and with it a chance to return to his beloved Calabria. He decided he needed some expert advice and there was no-one better than his friend Gianni Venica. You know the rest. The two formed a partnership and the Terre di Balbia estate was formed, its title taken from the old Roman name for Altomonte. SerraMonte '02, erroneously printed as '03 last year, is maturing well but the real '03 is a fine wine too. It comes from sangiovese, magliocco and a little gaglioppo, and has a complex nose and an elegant, fleshy palate. The '03 Balbium, from gaglioppo and magliocco, is simpler. It's the wine from those submitted that has suffered most from the rather uninspiring vintage. The new Montino 101, from 100 per cent magliocco and also from '03, made an excellent start, revealing good stuffing and remarkable balance of fruit and tannin.

● Balbium '03	▼▼	4
● Montino 101 '03	▼▼	5
● SerraMonte '03	▼▼	7
● SerraMonte '02	▽▽	7
● SerraMonte '01	▽▽	5
● Balbium '02	▽▽	4

CIRÒ (KR)

SANTA VENERE

LOC. TENUTA VOLTAGRANDE
S.P. 04, KM 10,00
88813 CIRÒ (KR)
TEL. 096238519 - 09621876256
www.santavenere.com

Santa Venere is a fine 150-hectare estate, 25 of them planted with vines, and was one of the first in Calabria to convert to organic viticulture. Hence no chemical treatments are used at any point on the grapes or their juice. Both viticulture and winemaking are managed by Federico Scala, representing the current generation of the family that has owned the property for over four centuries. For many years, the Scalas, like most local growers, preferred to sell their grapes rather than vinifying and bottling themselves. The change occurred only recently, in 1997 when Federico arrived at the estate. His input has been crucial. It took him just a few years to increase the area under vine and set up a large experimental plot for selection of indigenous varieties. And when he had the viticultural side as he wanted it, he managed to persuade leading consultant oenologist Riccardo Cotarella to come and work in Calabria. Cirò Classico Superiore Federico Scala Riserva '02, made solely from gaglioppo, is excellent. Full of citrus and aromatic herbs, it is well structured with plentiful tannin in the mouth. The other wines submitted were from '05 and a little low-key because of the year's unstable weather conditions. Cirò Rosato has a nice coral colour and is fresh and fragrant, with wild rose and cherry. Vurgadà, from equal parts of nerello cappuccio, merlot and gaglioppo, has a good, assertive tannic weave but we found a little too much youthful hesitancy. Chardonnay Vescovado '05 is well made and attractive.

● Cirò Rosso Cl. Sup. Federico Scala Ris. '02	▼▼	5
○ Cirò Bianco '05	▼	3
⊙ Cirò Rosato '05	▼	3
○ Vescovado '05	▼	4
● Vurgadà '05	▼	4
● Cirò Rosso Cl. Sup. Federico Scala Ris. '01	▽▽	5
● Vurgadà '04	▽▽	4

CIRÒ MARINA (KR)

Librandi

Loc. C.da San Gennaro
S.S. Jonica 106
88811 Cirò Marina (KR)
tel. 096231518
www.librandi.it

The Librandi brothers' winery has grown into quite an undertaking. As well as its nucleus at Cirò Marina, it now has two other large properties. The first, Critone, extends over 51 hectares. It was bought for the production of international varieties but there has now been a rethink and, under the direction of agronomist Andrea Paoletti who has worked with Librandi for years and followed the project for some time, both the planting layout and the grapes grown will soon be changed. The second, the 250-hectare Rosaneti, is for the research and experimentation into indigenous Calabrian varieties that is so important to the Librandis. Actually, Rosaneti has the largest experimental plot in Italy, growing nothing but indigenous stocks. It's all worthily far-sighted but, with the selection of clones, experimental plantings and microvinifications, it requires an astounding amount of work. Even with the help of oenologist Donato Lanati, it creates a huge burden for a single winery. Nevertheless, Librandi wines are still impeccable. For instance, the '04 vintage of the celebrated Gravello, from gaglioppo and cabernet sauvignon, is a bottle of rare elegance and complexity. The '05 Efeso, from mantonico, is again Calabria's best white. It's zesty, minerally and rich and will improve with age, as will the stylish, fresh, fruity Magno Megonio '04 from magliocco. The '03 Cirò Rosso Duca San Felice is a great wine, with a deep, multi-faceted nose and lovely balance on the palate. The '04 Mantonico Passito Le Passule is again a wine of great character and complexity.

●	Gravello '04	🍷🍷 (grey)	6
○	Efeso '05	🍷🍷 (grey)	6
●	Cirò Rosso Duca Sanfelice Ris. '03	🍷🍷	4*
○	Le Passule '04	🍷🍷	5
●	Magno Megonio '04	🍷🍷	6
○	Critone '05	🍷🍷	4
⊙	Terre Lontane '05	🍷🍷	4*
○	Cirò Bianco '05	🍷	3
⊙	Cirò Rosato '05	🍷	3
○	Melissa Asylia Bianco '05	🍷	4
●	Melissa Asylia Rosso '05	🍷	4
●	Gravello '98	YYY	5
●	Gravello '01	YY	6
●	Gravello '03	YY	6
○	Efeso '04	YY	6

COSENZA

Serracavallo

C.da Serracavallo
87043 Cosenza
tel. 098421144 - 3355272586
www.viniserracavallo.com

Demetrio Stancati believes that there is not a great deal of difference between his previous work as a doctor and his current occupation as a winemaker. For both, you need experience, dedication and intuition. When that's not enough, you need to turn to the analysis sheets. For a couple of years now, Demetrio's wines have been classy, especially the reds, to the extent that his Serracavallo estate, its name taken from the hill on which it sits, is now considered to be in Calabria's front rank. It seems like ancient history when wine here was produced simply for the family – the Stancatis have owned it for ages – and their friends. Yet it's actually been just a decade, the time it has taken Demetrio to transform its 20 hectares. The vineyards, which lie at an average height of 600 metres on hills overlooking the ancient village of Bisignano, have all been replanted at a much higher density and are kept in immaculate condition. The ancient farmhouses have been totally restored and now house the cellar and estate offices. Terraccia '03, from magliocco dolce, a variety grown only in this part of Calabria, tops the range. It's a close-knit yet succulent wine that manages to marry power with elegance. It went through to the finals where it held its ground well. Sette Chiese '05, from magliocco and cabernet sauvignon, is certainly less complex but admirably fruity and invigorating, and has great drive. Besiadae '05, from high-altitude riesling and sauvignon, is zippy, delicately aromatic, and has a good sage and mint finish.

●	Terraccia '03	🍷🍷 (grey)	5
●	Sette Chiese '05	🍷🍷	4*
○	Besidiae '05	🍷	3
●	Terraccia '00	YY	4
●	Terraccia '01	YY	5
●	Terraccia '02	YY	5
●	Sette Chiese '04	YY	4*

LAMEZIA TERME (CZ)

CANTINE LENTO
VIA DEL PROGRESSO, 1
88046 LAMEZIA TERME (CZ)
TEL. 096828028 - 096823804
www.cantinelento.it

The Lento family was the first, 30 years ago, to reveal the high potential of the area around Lamezia for wine. Well, the first in recent times, because it was the Greeks 2000 years ago, who realized that the geographical position of this corner of Calabria was ideal for viticulture. This year's wines show no dip in the quality that we have become used to from the estate; indeed it continues to rise. This must be hugely satisfying for the Lentos, who not only do everything themselves but have recently invested heavily in their vineyards and cellar. It is the women of the family, Giovanna and daughters Danila and Manuela, who handle sales and public relations, while Salvatore and his brother-in-law Antonio Zaffina take care of the grape-growing and winemaking. Now that the vines at the new Tenuta Galati di Amato holding have reached maturity, the future is looking increasingly serene, especially in terms of consistency. The family has also brought out a new wine, the successful Tisaloro '03, made from a 50-50 blend of greco bianco and chardonnay, which has great structure and is firmly underpinned by good acidity. Lamezia Riserva '01, from the indigenous varieties magliocco, greco nero and nerello, is a complex, elegant wine of notable structure, with ripe tannins and good length. The other wines submitted also showed well overall, especially Contessa Emburga '04, from sauvignon, and the classic Federico II '03, a robust Cabernet Sauvignon.

● Lamezia Rosso Ris. '01	TT	5
○ Tisaloro '03	TT	5
○ Contessa Emburga Capsula Nera '04	TT	4
● Federico II '03	T	5
● Lamezia Rosso Dragone '04	T	4
⊙ Lamezia Rosato Romeo '05	T	4
● Lamezia Rosso Tenuta Romeo '05	T	4
● Federico II '00	YY	5
● Federico II '01	YY	5
● Federico II '02	YY	5

LAMEZIA TERME (CZ)

STATTI
TENUTA LENTI
88046 LAMEZIA TERME (CZ)
TEL. 0968456138 - 0968453655
www.statti.com

It hasn't taken long for Alberto and Antonio Statti to show that their initial success was no shot in the dark, and that their place in the top band of Calabrian producers is fully justified. They haven't yet come up with anything absolutely outstanding – the sort of wine that blows your socks off – but you can sense the way the brothers are working from this year's terrific range, so maybe before too long... Their 500-hectare property is one of the largest in the region. Currently, they have 55 hectares under vine but now that the new cellar is operational this is due to rise to 100 hectares. The Stattis are giving prominence to magliocco, gaglioppo and mantonico, a concentration on indigenous varieties that shows far-sighted thinking. Consultancy comes from two Sicilian oenologists, Nicola Bambina and Vincenzo Centonze, and to judge by the wines, their skills are equally effective either side of the Straits of Messina. Nosside '05, a dried-grape passito from mantonico, came within a hair of the finals for its captivating nose, all orange blossom and aromatic herbs, which leads to a fresh palate full of life. Arvino '04, from a finely-honed blend of gaglioppo and cabernet sauvignon, also fully merits its Two Glasses. It's a lively, soft wine of good length. I Gelsi '05, from gaglioppo, merlot and cabernet sauvignon, is surprisingly good and excellent value for money. Both the long, fleshy Cauro '04, from gaglioppo, magliocco and cabernet, and the lively, supple Ligeia '05, from chardonnay and mantonico, are well-made, attractive wines.

○ Nosside '05	TT	5
● Arvino '04	TT	3*
● Cauro '04	TT	5
○ I Gelsi Bianco '05	TT	2*
● Gaglioppo '05	T	3
○ Lamezia Bianco '05	T	3
○ Lamezia Greco '05	T	3
● Lamezia Rosso '05	T	3
○ Ligeia '05	T	3*
● Arvino '03	YY	3*
● Cauro '03	YY	5
○ Nosside '04	YY	5

NOCERA TERINESE (CZ)

G.B. Odoardi
c.da Campodorato
88047 Nocera Terinese (CZ)
tel. 098429961
'

Odoardi is a historic name in southern Italian winemaking. The 270-hectare estate has belonged to the family for over five centuries and has always produced wine. In times past, the robust, alcoholic wines from Nocera Torinese were sold in bulk, but in the middle of the 20th century, Giovambattista Odoardi started to market wine in bottles under his own name. That was a major move but an even more important development has come in the last decade, bringing the Odoardi brothers' wines to levels of quality that would have previously been unimaginable. Gregorio and Giovambattista's enthusiasm has now found the perfect foil in consultant Stefano Chioccioli. The '03 vintage returned Three Glass stardom to Scavigna Vigna Garrone, a marvellous blend of gaglioppo with small amounts of nerello cappuccio, cabernet franc, cabernet sauvignon and merlot. It has wonderful complexity and elegance, unveiling beautifully clean, intense fruit, which is well supported by imposing alcohol and smooth tannins to finish sweet and very long. The other finalist, Polpicello '03, from gaglioppo, nocera, magliocco and nerello cappuccio, is a close-knit, fleshy wine of length. Vigna Mortilla '03, from 50 per cent gaglioppo with greco nero, magliocco canino, nerello cappuccio and sangiovese, has crisp fruit and good backbone. The same blend is used in Mortilla Per Il Savuto '04, a wine that is nicely fresh and has elegant tannins but is a little less complex than the others. But everything is good here.

●	Scavigna Vigna Garrone '03	🍷🍷🍷	6
●	Scavigna Polpicello '03	🍷🍷	7
●	Savuto Sup. V. Mortilla '03	🍷🍷	5
●	Savuto '04	🍷🍷	4*
○	Scavigna Pian della Corte '05	🍷	4
●	Scavigna Vigna Garrone '99	YYY	8
●	Scavigna Polpicello '01	YY	7
●	Scavigna Vigna Garrone '01	YY	6
●	Scavigna Polpicello '02	YY	7
●	Savuto '03	YY	4*
●	Savuto Sup. V. Mortilla '01	YY	5
●	Savuto Sup. V. Mortilla '02	YY	5
●	Scavigna Vigna Garrone '02	YY	6

SARACENA (CS)

Luigi Viola
via Roma, 18
87010 Saracena (CS)
tel. 098134071
www.cantineviola.it

Saracena is a village of 5,000 inhabitants at an altitude of 650 metres inside the Pollino nature reserve. Sweet wine, or meditation wine as it is now termed, has been made at Saracena for centuries, although it has had mixed fortunes. It was produced regularly until the early 20th century and had admirers throughout Europe. But then there was a progressive abandonment of the countryside, leaving Saracena few souls to grow grapes and its Moscato slowly slid into oblivion. So it remained, with just a few growers producing just a few bottles, made following techniques passed down from father to son, and drunk by the families or some lucky tourist – until a decade ago. That's when Luigi Viola, a grower who is self-effacing and strong-willed as only a Calabrian can be, got it into his head to restore the wine to its ancient splendour. When we first met Luigi, he was practically the only producer left but he never lost heart and carried on making his nectar regardless. Now, just in time, he's managed to set in place a virtuous circle, bringing about the restoration of this unique wine and its resonantly named grapes, guarnaccia, malvasia and odoacra. Moscato di Saracena has become a Slow Food Presidium, DOC is on its way and other young growers have taken up producing the wine. Luigi should be well pleased. Naturally he's still producing his own Moscato and it's as fine as ever, the '05 again nudging Three Glasses. It's fragrant with lavender and apricot, close-knit, invigorating, sweet and very, very, long. In short, another minor masterpiece.

○	Moscato di Saracena '05	🍷🍷	7
○	Moscato di Saracena '03	YY	6
○	Moscato di Saracena '04	YY	7
○	Moscato di Saracena '00	YY	4
○	Moscato di Saracena '01	YY	4

OTHER WINERIES

EREDI BOSCARELLI

VIA VITTORIO VENETO,86
87043 BISIGNANO (CS)
TEL. 0984951012 - 098471448
www.viniboscarelli.it

The Boscarelli family's vines and cellar lie above the Crati valley, north of Cosenza. We liked the well-structured gaglioppo, aglianico and cabernet sauvignon Valle del Crati Rosso '05. Valle dei Crati Rosso del Castello '05 and Rosato '05, from gaglioppo, sangiovese and cabernet, are good.

⊙	Valle dei Crati Rosato '05	🍷	3
●	Valle dei Crati Rosso '05	🍷	3
●	Valle dei Crati Rosso del Castello '05	🍷	3

STELITANO

LOC. PALAZZI DI CASIGNANA
C.DA PALAZZI, 1
89030 CASIGNANA (RC)
TEL. 0964913023 - 3491554481'

Siblings Francesco and Angela Stelitano are among the few maintaining the tradition of Greco di Bianco production. Their elegant '04 showed very well with apricot and quince on the nose, and a fresh, well-structured palate finishing on a note of dried figs. Mantonico '04 is nice and fruity.

○	Greco di Bianco '04	🍷🍷	7
○	Mantonico '04	🍷	6

VIGNAIOLI DEL POLLINO

C.DA FERROCINTO, 151
87012 CASTROVILLARI (CS)
TEL. 098138035
www.vinopollino.com

The Braile family's vines lie at 500 metres in Pollino, the natural border between Calabria and Basilicata. Harè '03, from magliocco canino, is complex and structured, with red berry fruit, Mediterranean herbs and chocolate. Ceraso '05, from magliocco canino, is lively, juicy and good drinking.

⊙	Ceraso '05	🍷	3
●	Pollino Sup. Harè '05	🍷	4

FATTORIA SAN FRANCESCO

LOC. QUATTROMANI - S.S. JONICA 106
88813 CIRÒ (KR)
TEL. 096232228
www.fattoriasanfrancesco.it

This year we really liked the fresh, savoury, minerally Fata Morgana Greco '05 with its nicely fruity finish but we found the dried-grape Brisi '03 from greco and Ronco dei Quattro Venti '04 disappointing compared with previous releases. Cirò Rosato '05 is a well-made, fresh, early drinker.

○	Brisi '03	🍷	7
●	Cirò Rosso Cl. Ronco dei Quattro Venti '04	🍷	6
⊙	Cirò Rosato '05	🍷	4
○	Fata Morgana '05	🍷	5

Caparra & Siciliani

bivio S.S. Jonica 106
88811 Cirò Marina (KR)
tel. 0962371435
www.caparraesiciliani.it

This estate makes well-typed wines that reflect their provenance. Cirò Riserva '03 is a case in point: clean, attractive and supported by good acidity. Cirò Volvito Riserva '03 has good texture and close-knit tannins. Cirò Rosato '05 and Mastro Giurato '03, from gaglioppo and greco nero, are sound.

- ● Cirò Rosso Cl. Sup. Ris. '03 🍷 4
- ● Cirò Rosso Cl. Sup. Volvito Ris. '03 🍷 4
- ● Mastro Giurato '03 🍷 5
- ⊙ Cirò Rosato '05 🍷 3

Cantina Enotria

loc. San Gennaro
S.S. Jonica 106
88811 Cirò Marina (KR)
tel. 0962371181

This is Calabria's leading co-operative, controlling 150 hectares of vineyard. Its best wine this year is the clean, varietal Cirò Riserva Piana delle Fate '02 with its good tannins. Cirò Bianco '05, made solely from greco bianco, is floral and citrus-like; Cirò Rosato '05 is attractive.

- ● Cirò Rosso Cl. Sup. Piana delle Fate Ris. '02 🍷🍷 5
- ○ Cirò Bianco '05 🍷 3
- ⊙ Cirò Rosato '05 🍷 3

Ippolito 1845

via Tirone, 118
88811 Cirò Marina (KR)
tel. 096231106
www.ippolito1845.it

Having passed its 150th anniversary, Ippolito is now looking forward, adding a range of modern-styled wines to its more classic line. We liked the fruity, spicy Cirò Liber Pater '04, and the good-drinking, varietal Cirò Colli del Mancuso '03. Rosé Mabilia '05 is fresh and supple.

- ● Cirò Rosso Cl. Sup. Colli del Mancuso Ris. '03 🍷 4
- ● Cirò Rosso Cl. Sup. Liber Pater '04 🍷 3
- ⊙ Cirò Rosé Mabilia '05 🍷 3

Malena

loc. Petraro
S.S. Jonica 106
88811 Cirò Marina (KR)
tel. 096231758 - www.malena.it

Cataldo and Antonio Malena's new Cutura del Marchese '03, from equal parts of gaglioppo and cabernet sauvignon, has good structure and concentration, a close-knit nose with nice balsam and a long, fruity finish. The sweet greco bianco Passus '04 and gaglioppo-only Rosato Bacco '05 are sound.

- ● Cutura del Marchese '03 🍷🍷 4
- ● Cirò Rosso Cl. Sup. '04 🍷 3
- ○ Passus Greco Passito '04 🍷 5
- ⊙ Bacco Rosato '05 🍷 3

Parrilla

via Cesare Battisti, 83
88811 Cirò Marina (KR)
tel. 096231927

After a good start last year, this year's wines are in lower key, probably due to the troublesome '04 vintage. Cirò Rosato '05 is supple and well made. Cirò Bianco '05, from greco bianco, is fresh and easy drinking, with a nice almondy finish.

- ○ Cirò Bianco '05 🍷 3
- ⊙ Cirò Rosato '05 🍷 3

Vinicola Zito

via Scalaretto
88811 Cirò Marina (KR)
tel. 096231853
www.zito.it

All the wines submitted by Zito, one of the longest standing wineries in the region, were sound. Cirò Bianco Nosside '05 is fresh and attractive. Cirò Rosato '05 Imerio is supple and fruity. Cirò Rosso Krimisa '04 is floral on the nose, savoury on the palate and as enjoyable as Cirò Alceo '04.

- ● Cirò Rosso Cl. Alceo '04 🍷 2
- ● Cirò Rosso Cl. Krimisa '04 🍷 4
- ○ Cirò Bianco Nosside '05 🍷 2
- ⊙ Cirò Rosato Imerio '05 🍷 2

TENUTA TERRE NOBILI
LOC. MONTALTO UFFUGO
C.DA CARIGLIALTO
87046 COSENZA
TEL. 0984934005 - 333645351'

Lidia Matera submitted a good range. Cariglio '05, from magliocco with 20 per cent merlot, has a good tannic weave and fair length. Santa Chiara '05, from greco and chardonnay, is clean and lively. Aglianico Alarico '05 and the rosé Donna Eleonora '05, from nerello and magliocco, are sound.

● Alarico '05	🍷	4
● Cariglio '05	🍷	3
⊙ Donna Eleonora '05	🍷	3
○ Santa Chiara '05	🍷	3

LUIGI VIVACQUA
C.DA SAN VITO
87040 LUZZI (CS)
TEL. 0984543404 - 098428815
'

San Vito di Luzzi Rosso '04, based on gaglioppo and greco nero, tops the Vivacqua range this year. A deep, concentrated nose leads to a fruity palate supported by a good tannic weave. The long, minerally Chardonnay Donna Aurelia '05 and Marinò '03, from gaglioppo and merlot, are also good.

● San Vito di Luzzi Rosso '04	🍷🍷	3*
● Marinò Rosso '03	🍷	3
○ Chardonnay Donna Aurelia '05	🍷	4

DOMENICO SPADAFORA
ZONA INDUSTRIALE, 18
87050 MANGONE (CS)
TEL. 0984969080
www.cantinespadafora.it

Some years ago, Ippolito Spadafora took over running his family's estate and is maintaining its traditions. This year, our interest was taken by Donnici Rosato Vigna Fiego '05, despite its unusually deep colour, and by the dried-grape passito Solarys, from greco bianco and malvasia.

⊙ Donnici Rosato V. Fiego '05	🍷	3
○ Solarys	🍷	4

VAL DI NETO
FRAZ. CORAZZO - VIA NAZIONALE
88831 SCANDALE (KR)
TEL. 096254079
www.cantinavaldineto.com

Nicola Cappa has around 30 hectares of vineyard, all farmed organically. Melissa Mutrò '04 showed very well, with violets and red and black cherry on the nose and a fruit-forward palate supported by elegant, dense tannins. Arkè, from gaglioppo, greco nero and aglianico, is sound.

● Melissa Rosso Sup. Mutrò '04	🍷🍷	4*
● Rosso Arkè '04	🍷	4

SICILY

This is a year to remember for Sicilian wine, firstly because there are 15 Three Glasses wines, equalling the region's highest ever achieved. But we can add Three Glasses assigned retrospectively to Giuseppe Benanti's amazing Pietramarina '97, a fabulous Etna Bianco that we have had the pleasure of tasting often over the years and that brings the total to 16, a new record. Next, this year's Winery of the Year is from Sicily and it's... Benanti, with two top-scoring wines and a retrospective Three Glasses making a triple jackpot. There's another related aspect to consider. Etna has really shone in our tastings this year. It's not just the Three Glasses for Andrea Franchetti's Passopisciaro, Benanti's Serra della Contessa and Marc de Grazia's Feudo di Mezzo Il Quadro delle Rose. It's the dozens of other fascinating wines from the slopes of the volcano. They are wines driven by elegance, complexity and balance, rather than the extractive weight, fruit and oak that used to be the stereotype of quality Sicilian offerings. Before, only Salvatore Geraci and his Faro Palari seemed to embrace the philosophy and maybe he's had a seminal role in this stylistic turn-around. And now, as our tastings show, the change is spreading through the whole region. It is the east of the island, though, that is the linchpin. There are the volcanic soils and the high-altitude vineyards, sometimes over 1,000 metres above sea level. There are the excellent indigenous varieties, such as nerello mascalese and nerello cappuccio. But most of all, there is the innovative mindset of its top producers. Sicilian winemakers are learning to anticipate future taste trends. To understand the reach of this, just try one of the island's international wines such as Planeta's elegant, lively, varietal '04 Merlot. Similar considerations apply to the other top-ranking wines, from Donnafugata's Milleunanotte '03 and Corvo's Duca Enrico '03 to Foraci's Tenuta Dorrasita Nero d'Avola, the excellent Rosso del Conte '03 from Tasca d'Almerita and the equally excellent Ribeca '04 from Firriato, this latter from nero d'Avola and perricone. But the groundswell of change has spread beyond the Nero d'Avolas, and the great nerello mascalese wines of Etna. Even blends of indigenous and international varieties such as Cusumano's Benuara '05, from nero d'Avola and syrah, and Santa Anastasia's Montenero '04, from cabernet, merlot and nero d'Avola, seem to be falling in line with the new stylistic direction. Cusumano, for instance, has delayed the release of Noà and Sagana '05. While opulent fruit remains a keynote, he is working towards a different balance-point. The seal is set on this exciting year for Sicily by our final two Three Glasses wines, which are two classics: Planeta's Cometa '05 and, naturally, a Passito di Pantelleria from Salvatore Murana, this year the '04 Mueggen.

ACATE (RG)

VALLE DELL'ACATE
C.DA BIDINI
97011 ACATE (RG)
TEL. 0932874166
www.valledellacate.com

Valle dell'Acate is an extensive property which has been owned by the Jacono family for more than two centuries. It lies between Acate and Vittoria, in hilly, vine-dominated countryside, cut through by the river Dirillo. The winery is fitted out with the most up-to-date equipment, allowing the grapes' aromatics to be preserved despite the high temperatures during the harvest period. What emerges is impeccable, both the wines from indigenous varieties and those from international grapes, in a range widely admired in Italy and further afield and which gets better every year. Much is down to the fine work of the winemaking personnel, not to mention the skills and dedication of Gaetana Jacono, who handles marketing and communications. This year saw Tanè '03, from nero d'Avola and syrah, in the finals. It's a concentrated, rich wine, full of aroma and intense, clean fruit. Bidis, from chardonnay and inzolia, never disappoints. This year's '04 is attractively floral and there's an intriguing swath of minerality on both nose and palate. The delicious '05 Frappato is archetypal, full of its customary fragrance and liveliness. Moro '04, a monovarietal nero d'Avola, is a touch overripe but interesting nonetheless, with red cherry aromas and good varietal style. The sound Cerasuolo di Vittoria '04, from nero d'Avola and frappato, has good typicity and admirably unites drinkability with sense of provenance. The fresh Zagra '05, from inzolia, is zesty and minerally, and evokes orange and lemon blossom.

●	Tanè '03	🍷🍷	6
○	Bidis '04	🍷🍷	5
●	Il Moro '04	🍷🍷	4
●	Il Frappato '05	🍷🍷	4*
●	Cerasuolo di Vittoria '04	🍷	4
○	Insolia '05	🍷	3
○	Zagra '05	🍷	4
●	Tanè '00	YY	6
○	Bidis '03	YY	4
●	Cerasuolo di Vittoria '02	YY	4
●	Cerasuolo di Vittoria '03	YY	4
●	Il Frappato '03	YY	4
●	Il Moro '03	YY	4
●	Il Frappato '04	YY	4

ALCAMO (TP)

CEUSO
VIA ENEA, 18
91013 ALCAMO (TP)
TEL. 092422836
www.ceuso.it

The Melia brothers' well-cared-for property, extending over 50 hectares, lies just a few kilometres from the stunning Doric temple of Segesta. Recent plantings of grillo and chardonnay have brought the area under vine to 45 hectares. The next move will be to improve the one white wine so far produced. The brothers, who come from a family which has been growing grapes for generations, are close and do everything themselves. Vincenzo competently looks after the viticultural side while Giuseppe just as skilfully manages the winemaking. This year saw the return of Fastaia, the '04, which had been absent from our tastings for some years. It was so impressive that it simply strode into the finals and came within an ace of Three Glasses. It is made from practically equal amounts of cabernet sauvignon and merlot with a little petit verdot. The colour is a dark, almost opaque ruby. There is a burst of red berry fruit on the nose, which is nicely interwoven with tobacco and chocolate, and with the spiciness that comes from fine quality, well-integrated oak. The palate is soft and rounded with a long finish and there is perfect nose-palate harmony. The '04 vintage of the estate's top-notch Ceuso Custera, from nero d'Avola, cabernet sauvignon and merlot, was still youthfully impetuous at the time of our tastings but it will surely gain elegance with time. It has small red berry fruit aromas and a sturdy palate fully supported by tannin. Scurati '05, from 100 per cent nero d'Avola, is a good wine and excellent value for money.

●	Fastaia '04	🍷🍷	4
●	Ceuso Custera '04	🍷🍷	6
●	Scurati Rosso '05	🍷🍷	4*
●	Ceuso Custera '01	YYY	6
●	Fastaia '01	YY	5
●	Ceuso Custera '03	YY	6
●	Ceuso Custera '99	YY	6
●	Scurati Rosso '04	YY	4*

BUTERA (CL)

FEUDO PRINCIPI DI BUTERA
C.DA DELIELLA
93011 BUTERA (CL)
TEL. 0934347726 - 0934346766
www.feudobutera.it

This year, Franco Giacosa, brilliant oenologist and Zonin's technical director, didn't feel that the top wines here would be ready by the time of our tastings so he didn't submit them. That couldn't have been an easy decision but was certainly one that is in line with the Zonin philosophy and the professionalism that marks out its Sicilian operation. The property extends over 200 hectares of attractive countryside in Riesi and Butera with its vineyards lying at an average height of 350 metres. The best way to see it is from the top of the tower that dominates the property. The landscape is fabulous: a magical, almost dreamlike, a huge rectangle of bright green, so beautifully tended that you can look for ever without catching an imperfection. It's the sun that makes everything so verdant. Sunlight reflects off the characteristic white soil, full of limestone and quartz, and gives the vines tremendous vigour. But vigour can be a double-edged sword. If not properly harnessed, it can become exaggerated and create problems during ripening. Even without the flagship wines, a wide range was submitted, and everything was well made and well styled. Riesi '04, from nero d'Avola with a touch of syrah, is the first release of the company's first DOC wine, and it showed well, being ripe and well balanced. Nero d'Avola '04 is also first-rate. It's varietal and has a pervasive, captivating minerality. The fresh, balanced Chardonnay '05 is very fine, too. Syrah '04 is mouthfilling and spicy, Merlot '04 has sweet ripe fruit on the nose and a soft, dry palate. Both are noteworthy.

●	Merlot '04	🍷🍷	4
●	Nero d'Avola '04	🍷🍷	4
●	Riesi '04	🍷🍷	4
●	Syrah '04	🍷🍷	4
○	Chardonnay '05	🍷🍷	4
●	Cabernet Sauvignon '04	🍷	4
○	Inzolia '05	🍷	4*
●	Cabernet Sauvignon '00	YYY	7
●	Deliella '00	YYY	6
●	Deliella '02	YYY	8
●	Deliella '01	YY	8
●	San Rocco '02	YY	7
●	Calat '03	YY	7
●	Deliella '03	YY	8
●	San Rocco '03	YY	7

CAMPOREALE (PA)

TENUTE RAPITALÀ
C.DA RAPITALÀ
90043 CAMPOREALE (PA)
TEL. 092437233
www.rapitala.it

The joint venture between the De La Gatinais family and Gruppo Italiano Vini, the largest producer of Italian wines, is going swimmingly. The property has 145 hectares of attractive vineyard stretching over the Camporeale hillsides at altitudes of 300 to 600 metres. This, plus carefully selected bought-in grapes, allows annual production to top 3,000,000 bottles. The elegant, deep Solinero, from syrah, is again the top wine. Actually, the '04 very nearly followed last year's '03 onto the Three Glass podium. The colour is a deep ruby. The nose is complex, redolent of red and black berries, white pepper and Mediterranean scrubland and the structured, lively palate is full of soft tannin, finishing long with briary fruit. Hugonis '04, named after Conte Hugues, is a highly successful, attractive blend of cabernet sauvignon and nero d'Avola, with ripe black berries, tobacco and chocolate, enlivened by a tangy vegetal note, and good body. Conte Hugues also named an excellent Chardonnay, made from the estate's highest growing grapes, after himself, Conte Hugues Bernard de la Gatinais, but it's better known as Grand Cru. The '04 is a deep straw with golden highlights. There are plentiful nuances of white-fleshed and citrus fruit on both nose and palate, the latter showing good texture, liveliness and clean fruit. Nuhar '04 is an excellent nero d'Avola and pinot nero blend, full of ripe cherry and balsam. Nadir Syrah '04, like Casalj '05 from catarratto and chardonnay and the sweet Cielo d'Alcamo from catarratto and sauvignon, is distinctive and well made.

●	Solinero '04	🍷🍷	6
○	Conte Hugues Bernard de la Gatinais Grand Cru '04	🍷🍷	5
●	Hugonis '04	🍷🍷	6
●	Nuhar '04	🍷🍷	4
○	Cielo d'Alcamo '04	🍷	6
●	Nadir '04	🍷	4
○	Casalj '05	🍷	4
●	Solinero '00	YYY	6
●	Hugonis '01	YYY	7
●	Solinero '03	YYY	6
●	Solinero '01	YY	8
○	Conte Hugues Bernard de la Gatinais '02	YY	4
●	Nadir '03	YY	4

CASTELBUONO (PA)

Abbazia Santa Anastasia

C.da Santa Anastasia
90013 Castelbuono (PA)
tel. 0916932060
www.abbaziasantanastasia.it

We've grown used to surprises from Francesco Lena. It's taken him no time to realize his dream of turning his glorious property on the slopes of the Madonia mountains into an exclusive, luxurious Relais hotel. Meanwhile he's also moved from organic to biodynamic agriculture, showing how deeply he cares about quality, from the soil up. There's another surprise. Cabernet Sauvignon Litra '04, like all the wines under the supervision of Riccardo Cotarella, was aged longer before release so we'll be tasting it next year. But the best surprise of all is Montenero '04, which stood out in the finals and took home Three Glasses. The name comes from the 500-metre hill where the grapes grow. These are nero d'Avola, cabernet sauvignon and merlot, used in a 60-20-20 ratio. The wine has mind-blowing density and concentration but there's no lack of finesse or lift, and it expresses its character as a great Mediterranean red with ineffable elegance. Is anything else new? Yes, Zahir '04 from 100 per cent nero d'Avola, which is extremely promising. It's direct yet multi-faceted and has distinct varietal character. The whites, as ever, are firing on all cylinders. Sinestesìa '05, for example, from sauvignon blanc and inzolia, has a delightful nose of tomato leaf and peach, and a good, taut, fruity palate. The grillo-chardonnay blend Baccante '05 is a wealth of aroma and freshness. The two mid-range wines, the red Passomaggio, from nero d'Avola with a touch of merlot, and the white, from inzolia and chardonnay, are great. The basic range is nice too, especially Contempo Nero d'Avola '05.

●	Montenero '04	🍷🍷🍷	5
●	Passomaggio '04	🍷🍷	4
●	Zahir '04	🍷🍷	6
○	Baccante '05	🍷🍷	5
○	Bianco di Passomaggio '05	🍷🍷	3*
●	Contempo Nero d'Avola '05	🍷🍷	3*
○	Sinestesìa '05	🍷🍷	4
○	Contempo Grillo '05	🍷	3
○	Gemelli '05	🍷	5
○	Inzolia Contempo '05	🍷	3
●	Litra '00	🍸🍸🍸	7
●	Litra '01	🍸🍸🍸	8
●	Litra '96	🍸🍸🍸	7
●	Litra '97	🍸🍸🍸	7
●	Litra '99	🍸🍸🍸	7

CASTELDACCIA (PA)

Duca di Salaparuta - Vini Corvo

via Nazionale s.s. 113
90014 Casteldaccia (PA)
tel. 091945201
www.vinicorvo.it

With the excellent '03, the nero d'Avola Duca Enrico, one of the island's long-standing greats, regains the standing it deserves. But there is a sense of enthusiasm and creativity throughout the whole company. This, like Florio, is part of the ILLVA Saronno group, and it is skilfully led by oenologist and general manager, Carlo Casavecchia. With almost 180 years of history behind it, Duca di Salaparuta is currently enjoying a growth period. Its vineyard holding is 120 hectares, split across several properties, but is due to increase. Grapes are also bought in from every viticultural area in Sicily and the range of wines produced is huge. But Duca Enrico '03 marks out the year. The colour is a deep ruby. The nose is outstanding, with great depth, its aromas evoking the Mediterranean, the sun and fruit. Full and mouthfilling on the palate, it has authoritative backbone and ripe, elegant tannins. Alongside it come Bianca di Valguarnera '04, a soft, opulent monovarietal Inzolia, and Grillo Kados '05, full of tropical fruit and tangy minerality. Other outstanding reds are Passo delle Mule '04, a structured, varietal Nero d'Avola from the Suor Marchesa property near Butera, and the balsamic, elegant Lavico '03, from nerello mascalese and merlot, from the Vajasindi holding on Etna. Triskelè '04, a full-bodied blend of nero d'Avola, cabernet and merlot, has elegant red and black berry fruit aromas interwoven with spiciness. From the vast Corvo range, we particularly liked Sciaranèra '05, from nero d'Avola and frappato, and Colomba Platino '05, from inzolia.

●	Duca Enrico '03	🍷🍷🍷	7
●	Lavico Tenuta Vajasindi '03	🍷🍷	4
○	Bianca di Valguarnera '04	🍷🍷	6
●	Passo delle Mule '04	🍷🍷	4
●	Triskelè '04	🍷🍷	5
●	Corvo Rosso '04	🍷	3*
●	Megara '04	🍷	4
○	Corvo Bianco '05	🍷	3
○	Corvo Colomba Platino '05	🍷	4
○	Corvo Glicine '05	🍷	3
○	Corvo Oniris '05	🍷	4
⊙	Corvo Rosa '05	🍷	3
●	Corvo Sciaranera '05	🍷	4*
○	Kados '05	🍷	4
●	Duca Enrico '01	🍸🍸🍸	7

COTTANERA

LOC. IANNAZZO
S.P. 89
95030 CASTIGLIONE DI SICILIA (CT)
TEL. 0942963601
www.cottanera.it

Terroir, that special combination of soil, aspect and climate, is king on Etna with its unique environment for grape cultivation. Proof comes from the Cottanera wines, produced from a 50-hectare garden-vineyard 700 metres high overlooking the Ionian sea. Running the estate along with Enzo and Guglielmo Cambria are Guglielmo's children Francesco and Mariangela, and winemaking is in the hands of the skilled Michele Bean under the competent guidance of consultant Lorenzo Landi. Even if the '04 vintage did not bring Three Glasses, there is ongoing improvement across the whole range, which has increasing stylistic harmony and cohesion. Just take a look at Fatagione, from 85 per cent nerello mascalese with nero d'Avola, a wine which has rapidly gained in class. The '04, a finalist, is authoritative, full of personality, intense, stylish, concentrated and long, and is a fine example of the estate's unwavering commitment to indigenous varieties. Indeed, we wouldn't be surprised to see the wine making it really big. Mondeuse L'Ardenza '04 was also in the finals. Here too Etna spun its magic. The mineral finesse, the intensity of fruit and the generosity on this red make it simply irresistible. The other non-indigenous reds also retain their fascination. Syrah Sole di Sesta '04 is best summed up as "sauvage", Merlot Grammonte '04 is fully ripe and Cabernet Nume '04 encapsulates elegance over power. Finally, we cannot fail to mention the excellent showing of the fruit-filled, vigorous Barbazzale Rosso '05, made almost entirely from nerello mascalese.

●	Fatagione '04	▼▼	5*
●	L'Ardenza '04	▼▼	6
●	Grammonte '04	▼▼	6
●	Nume '04	▼▼	6
●	Sole di Sesta '04	▼▼	6
●	Barbazzale Rosso '05	▼▼	3*
○	Barbazzale Bianco '05	▼	3*
●	Sole di Sesta '00	▽▽▽	7
●	Grammonte '00	▽▽	7
●	L'Ardenza '01	▽▽	6
●	Sole di Sesta '01	▽▽	6
●	L'Ardenza '03	▽▽	6
●	Sole di Sesta '03	▽▽	6
●	Grammonte '99	▽▽	5
●	Fatagione '03	▽▽	5

PASSOPISCIARO

LOC. LA GUARDIOLA
95030 CASTIGLIONE DI SICILIA (CT)
TEL. 0578267110
www.passopisciaro.com

Andrea Franchetti owns and inspires Tuscany's Tenuta di Trinoro. Then in 2000, which is before Etna and its ancient vine varieties became the Mecca of a new young generation of winemakers, he decided to set up a new estate on the slopes of the volcano. A lot has happened since then. Andrea found and bought a 40-hectare property with 15 hectares of vineyard, the rest being woodland and "sciara", solidified lava from recent eruptions that has not yet become fertile. He then replanted the vineyards and he's now started to restore the press-house cum villa which he hopes to be able to move into shortly. The new plantings are mostly cabernet, merlot, cesanese and petit verdot, bush-trained – naturally – and with a density of 12,000 vines per hectare. Some came into production in 2005, the others, including some experimental whites, most notably viognier, are following. In the meantime, Andrea is buying in and vinifying grapes from old and very old local vineyards so he can get a feel of the territory, The '04 Passopisciaro, from nerello mascalese, reflects the excellent vintage and is now at a perfect peak of eloquence. The colour is a bright ruby. The nose is irresistible with great depth and elegance as healthy, ripe, red and black berry fruit interweaves with elegant notes of balsam and mountain herbs before the palate shows full and powerful, as you would expect from Andrea, with plenty of fruit and sinew, but it also has that amazing mineral depth which epitomizes Etna. And when you think that we are just at the beginning of this venture...

●	Passopisciaro '04	▼▼▼	6
●	Passopisciaro '01	▽▽	6
●	Passopisciaro '03	▽▽	6

CHIARAMONTE GULFI (RG)

Gulfi

Loc. c.da Roccazzo
via Maria Santissima del Rosario, 90
97012 Chiaramonte Gulfi (RG)
tel. 0932921654 - 0396134
www.gulfi.it

We wouldn't be surprised if one day Vito Catania decided to settle permanently in Sicily. He loves the island. It seems strange to think that when he first decided to produce wine here, in the land of his birth, he viewed it as a relaxing hobby, one that would give him a few days a month in the sun, away from his demanding career as an industrialist in the Po Valley fogs. And it would have been so easy for him to have simply produced charming, international-style wines, the sort that sell on any market without difficulty. Instead he entrusted his project to academic-oenologist Salvo Foti, an expert on Sicilian vine varieties. The plan was complex. For a start, the emphasis was on indigenous grapes, this in memory of his father who had owned a small nero d'Avola vineyard in Chiaramonte Gulfi, but also because he recalled hearing discussions as a child on the merits of the variety in this or that small area. As he was building up the estate, the names of these places became etched large in his memory: Maccari, Bufaleffi, Baroni and San Lorenzo. It prompted him to make four crus, one for each of these erstwhile renowned spots. Of these, it was Nerobaronj '03 that led the range this year, reaching the finals. This solid, well-structured yet complex wine that shows perfectly why nero d'Avola is king in eastern Sicily. The other selections followed close behind, especially the intriguing '03 crus Neromaccarj and Nerobufaleffj. Carjcanti '04, from bush-trained carricante grown on Etna is also first-rate, showing savour, minerality, stuffing and depth.

● Nerobaronj '03	▼▼	7
● Nerobufaleffj '03	▼▼	6
● Neromaccari '03	▼▼	6
○ Carjcanti '04	▼▼	5
● Nerojbleo '04	▼▼	4*
○ Valcanzjria '05	▼▼	4*
● Nerosanlorenzj '03	▼	7
● Cerasuolo di Vittoria '05	▼	4
● Rossojbleo '05	▼	4*
● Nerobaronj '02	▽▽	7
● Nerobufaleffj '02	▽▽	6
○ Valcanzjria '04	▽▽	4*

GROTTE (AG)

Morgante

c.da Racalmare
92020 Grotte (AG)
tel. 0922945579
www.morgantevini.it

Antonio Morgante is one of the most outstanding of the new wave of Sicilian winemakers. His family has been linked with viticulture for five generations but it was 1998 before he decided to vinify and bottle. Thanks to his fine vineyards – now over 60 hectares of them – lying close to his property, the dedicated involvement of his sons Carmelo and Giovanni, and technical consultancy from the high-calibre Riccardo Cotarella, it took just a few years for his wines to become new Sicilian classics. Morgante specializes in nero d'Avola, making two wines from the grape. Don Antonio is the grander one. The '04 again has the fascination and opulence of fruit that typifies the wine, but the problematical vintage has had its effect and there is a touch less purity on the nose and a touch less definition to the tannic weave than on the finest examples. It is still excellent, though, full of red and black berry fruit with swaths of Mediterranean scrubland, but just not quite up to Three Glass level. It will be back there, though, for sure. The more straightforward Nero d'Avola has regularly shown that it has nothing to fear from its big brother and the excellent '05 is no exception. It is a deep ruby introducing intense, vital aromas of blackberry jam and spice, and fresh, delicate vegetal hints. The palate is full, succulent, vigorous and long, boding well for next year's Don Antonio. Both wines are also excellent value for money.

● Don Antonio '04	▼▼	5
● Nero d'Avola '05	▼▼	3*
● Don Antonio '00	▽▽▽	6
● Don Antonio '01	▽▽▽	5
● Don Antonio '02	▽▽▽	5
● Don Antonio '03	▽▽▽	5
● Don Antonio '98	▽▽▽	5
● Don Antonio '99	▽▽▽	5
● Nero d'Avola '03	▽▽	3*
● Nero d'Avola '04	▽▽	3*

ISPICA (RG)

MARABINO

C.DA MARABINO C.P. 19
97014 ISPICA (RG)
TEL. 0932955696

Sebastiano Messina is a successful businessman who has diverted part of his energies into agriculture. So far that's nothing unusual. But Natura Iblea is rather different. It extends over 100 hectares or so of the province of Ragusa in south-eastern Sicily and also takes produce from other growers, making it one of Europe's largest certified organic fruit and vegetable undertakings. The produce is sold throughout Italy and has a high reputation. But Sebastiano is also a great wine lover, so sooner or later grapes and wine had to become part of his endeavours. They did so in 2001. There are currently ten hectares under vine. Grapes are also bought in, giving a total annual production of 180,000 bottles. This wine arm has now become separate, under the title Marabino, the name of the small area of Ispica where the estate is based, and is beginning to concentrate on quality in a way that we are sure will soon bring the wines to high renown. Already, the elegant Moscato di Noto Moscato della Torre '05 is classy enough for our finals. It has an intense, elegant nose of ripe pear, aromatic herbs and Mediterranean scrub, and is delicately sweet and aromatic on the palate, which is balanced and long. We also enjoyed Eloro Archimede '03, which has the aromatic complexity and the elegant, firm structure of nero d'Avola grown on ideal sites. Nero d'Avola Carmen '05 is lively, succulent and deep. To finish come two intriguing whites, Impronta '05, from inzolia and chardonnay, which is fresh and minerally, and a juicy, zesty Chardonnay, Eureka '05.

○	Moscato di Noto Moscato della Torre '05	**YY**	6
●	Eloro Archimede '03	**YY**	5
●	Carmen '05	**YY**	3*
●	Eloro Don Pasquale '05	**Y**	4
○	Eureka '05	**Y**	4
○	Impronta '05	**Y**	3*

MARSALA (TP)

MARCO DE BARTOLI

C.DA FORNARA SAMPERI, 292
91025 MARSALA (TP)
TEL. 0923962093
www.marcodebartoli.com

At the start of the 1980s, Marco De Bartoli created an explosion in the then sleepy world of Sicilian wine. Passionate, iconoclastic and often unsettling, he played a major part in bringing about the changes that have led to the new Sicilian wine scene. In the past 20 years, he has produced some masterpieces, wines that are incredibly complex, deep, assertive, elegant and often courageously experimental, like the man himself. His Marsala and Vecchio Samperi are known and revered worldwide, and his other wines are greatly admired too, those from Samperi, near Marsala, and those from Pantelleria, where Marco now spends most of his time. This year, he has a glorious Passito di Pantelleria Bukkuram '03. It comes from Marco's five hectares of vineyard in the small area of Bukkuram, with the grapes being left to dry on the ground in the traditional manner. It has an attractive deep amber hue flecked with orange and the nose is full of apricot jam and figs, with wafts of balsam and the herbs native to Mediterranean scrubland. It is dense, fleshy and intensely sweet, yet also stylish, full of fresh acidity and long. Pietra Nera '05, a dry Zibibbo, has an exuberant array of aromas and an intensely flavoured palate full of rich fruit freshness. Grappoli del Grillo '05 is a wine of great character that shows structured, harmonious, fruit-rich and with mineral savouriness. Sole e Vento '05 comes from grillo and zibibbo, and is dry, supple and full of freshness and varietal aromas. Finally comes Vigna La Miccia, a sweet, opulent Marsala Superiore Oro of impeccable quality.

○	Passito di Pantelleria Bukkuram '03	**YY**	8
○	Grappoli del Grillo '05	**YY**	5
○	Pietra Nera '05	**YY**	5
○	Sole e Vento '05	**YY**	4
○	Marsala Sup. Oro Vigna La Miccia	**YY**	4
○	Marsala Sup. Ris. 10 Anni	YYY	7
○	Marsala Sup. Vintage '86	YY	8
○	Marsala Sup. Ris. 20 Anni	YY	6
○	Passito di Pantelleria Bukkuram '01	YY	8

MARSALA (TP)

DONNAFUGATA
VIA SEBASTIANO LIPARI, 18
91025 MARSALA (TP)
TEL. 0923724200
www.donnafugata.it

From its first appearance with the '96 vintage, Milleunanotte, from nero d'Avola with small amounts of other indigenous grapes, has always been one of Sicily's most fascinating and elegant reds. Its fame and its quality now go without saying, which is quite remarkable when you consider that by 2003 a good 45,000 bottles were being made. So our congratulations to Giacomo Rallo and his wife Gabriella, who helped pioneer the Sicilian wine revival, and to their children Antonio and Josè, who work on the estate with such enthusiasm and creativity. From the tone of these comments, you may have guessed that there is something to celebrate. Well, there is. Milleunanotte '03 earned Three Glasses. It's a fascinating wine that presents complex, compact, meaty and austere, with clean fruit, smooth tannins and elegant touches of balsam that lead on to sensations of Mediterranean scrubland. The succulent, opulent, deep Tancredi '04, made from 70 per cent nero d'Avola with cabernet has almost as much to offer. The Rallos also have vineyards on Pantelleria that provide fruit for Ben Ryé, a DOC Passito, or dried-grape wine. The '05, like previous vintages, is full of aroma and dried apricot fleshiness. Chiarandà '04, from chardonnay and inzolia, aged in new oak, is an imposing wine but also a supple, fruit-rich one. Angheli '04 is from merlot and nero d'Avola, and is as intense and multi-faceted as ever, full of red berry fruit, tobacco and oak. There are also numerous other, simpler wines, together forming an excellent overall range, one that cements Donnafugata as a top-notch estate.

●	Contessa Entellina Milleunanotte '03	▼▼▼	7
●	Tancredi '04	▼▼	5
○	Passito di Pantelleria Ben Ryé '05	▼▼	7
●	Angheli '04	▼▼	5
○	Contessa Entellina Chiarandà '04	▼▼	6
●	Sedàra '05	▼▼	4*
○	Anthìlia '05	▼	3*
○	Contessa Entellina Chardonnay La Fuga '05	▼	4
○	Contessa Entellina Vigna di Gabri '05	▼	4
○	Lighea '05	▼	4
●	Contessa Entellina Milleunanotte '00	▽▽▽	7
●	Contessa Entellina Milleunanotte '01	▽▽▽	7
●	Contessa Entellina Milleunanotte '02	▽▽▽	7

MARSALA (TP)

CANTINE FLORIO
VIA VINCENZO FLORIO, 1
91025 MARSALA (TP)
TEL. 0923781111
www.cantineflorio.it

Cantine Florio is emblematic of continuity in the Italian wine world. It looks back over 170 years of history, its name is renowned worldwide and, since 2003, it has been linked with another longstanding Sicilian wine name, that of Duca di Salaparuta. The winery is active in Sicily's three most important areas for sweet and meditation wines, Marsala, Pantelleria and Salina. And the guiding hand of Carlo Casavecchia, from Piedmont, an oenologist of great experience, ensures wines of distinction emerge from all of them, as our tastings reveal. Malvasia delle Lipari Passito '05 isn't quite up to the heights of the '03 but the overall characteristics are similar. The nose abounds in Mediterranean scrubland and apricot jam, and the palate is full of succulence. Marsala Vergine Baglio Florio '03 came very close to reaching the finals with its complex, aristocratic nose, its warmth and its exemplary length. The soft, elegant Marsala Vergine Terre Arse '98 scored similarly and has notes of dried aromatic herbs and walnutskin. Passito di Pantelleria '04 stands out for the cleanliness of its apricot jam-like nose, its eloquence and its typicity. Marsala Superiore Ambra Secco Vecchioflorio '03 is a true classic. The two Zibibbo wines, the fortified, barrique-aged Morsi di Luce '04 and the more immediate Grecale '05, are as good as ever. Since 2003, the latter has had a red partner, made from pignatello, a synonym of perricone. This, too, is sweet and fortified and the '05 has good cherry fruit and a pleasing astringency on the finish.

○	Marsala Vergine Baglio Florio '03	▼▼	6
○	Passito di Pantelleria '04	▼▼	6
○	Malvasia delle Lipari Passito '05	▼▼	7
○	Marsala Terre Arse '98	▼▼	5
○	Marsala Sup. Vecchioflorio '03	▼	3*
○	Morsi di Luce '04	▼	5
○	Grecale Vino Liquoroso '05	▼	4
●	Grecale Vino Liquoroso Rosso '05	▼	4
○	Malvasia delle Lipari Passito '03	▽▽	6
○	Marsala Vergine Baglio Florio Oro '88	▽▽	6
○	Passito di Pantelleria '02	▽▽	6

MARSALA (TP)

CARLO PELLEGRINO
VIA DEL FANTE, 39
91025 MARSALA (TP)
TEL. 0923719911
www.carloperllegrino.it

Pellegrino, a long-standing Marsala estate, has learnt how to move with the times and to anticipate change and its challenges, while preserving the essential values of its geographical identity. Proof comes from two amazing wines, each a snapshot of soulful beauty, each very different, but each with recognizable common traits: Marsala Vergine Riserva '62 and Riserva del Centenario '80. The former is almost esoteric so subtle are its finesse and complexity, but there is also surprising firmness and length, especially for a 44-year-old wine. Riserva del Centenario has just as much class but is racier and tauter, showing wonderfully clean and full of the sun, all aspects that took it close to Three Glasses. Leading the rest of the Marsalas are the impeccable Vergine Soleras with its elegant, harmonious palate and attractive quinine and coffee finish. The modern-style Superiore Riserva Oro Dolce has a pleasantly nutty nose and well-judged sweetness. And the cheery Rubino, from nero d'Avola, evokes liqueur cherries and almond brittle. Moving on to the Duca di Castelmonte line, Tripudium, a blend of nero d'Avola, syrah and cabernet sauvignon, remains a reliably fine wine, the '03 giving very ripe fruit, refined spicy and gamey notes, nicely assertive tannins and a long finish. Gorgo Tondo '05, from grillo and chardonnay, also showed very well, with alluring hints of peach and spring flowers on the nose, and enlivening acidity on the palate. We close with the well-balanced Grillo '05, which is attractively fruity and nuanced with fresh almond.

○	Marsala Vergine Ris. del Centenario '80	2 black glasses	5
●	Tripudium '03	2 black glasses	5
○	Gorgo Tondo Bianco '05	2 black glasses	4
○	Grillo '05	2 black glasses	4*
○	Marsala Vergine Ris. '62	2 black glasses	5
○	Marsala Ruby	2 black glasses	2*
○	Marsala Vergine Soleras	2 black glasses	4
●	Nero d'Avola '03	1 black glass	3
○	Delia Nivolelli Chardonnay '05	1 black glass	4
○	Marsala Sup. Ris. Oro Dolce	1 black glass	5
●	Tripudium '02	2 white glasses	5
●	Gorgo Tondo Rosso '02	2 white glasses	4

MAZARA DEL VALLO (TP)

AJELLO
C.DA GIUDEO
91025 MAZARA DEL VALLO (TP)
TEL. 091309107 - 0923941218
www.ajello.info

Salvatore Ajello's property surrounds a fascinating 19th-century enclosed farmstead and his equally fascinating wines demonstrate that a quality-conscious attitude, respect for provenance and, especially, intelligence and care in tending vines are prerequisites for excellence. This year's offerings are no exception. Furat, from nero d'Avola, cabernet sauvignon, syrah and merlot, is the landmark wine, the estate's flagship and the wine that most impressed us. The '04 is intriguing with a delicious nose of blackcurrant, plum and bitter chocolate preceding a vigorous, close-knit, soft and highly attractive palate. There is plentiful quality on the dense Majus Nero d'Avola '04, too, with its attractive deep ruby colour and its complex aromatic spectrum evoking blueberry-like fruit and spiciness. Bizir, a well-judged blend of chardonnay, grillo and inzolia, is always first-rate, and the golden-hued '05 is marked by pervasive, seductive, ripe, white-fleshed and tropical fruit. Further excellence is found from Majus Grillo Catarratto '05, which has aromatic herbs on the nose and a fresh, balanced palate. Shams '05, a sweet wine from moscato, catarratto, grillo and inzolia grapes left to concentrate on the vine, is a tad less impressive than previous vintages but still has gentle sweetness and good balance of acidity and softness.

●	Furat '04	2 black glasses	5
●	Majus Nero d'Avola '04	2 black glasses	3*
○	Bizir '05	2 black glasses	5
○	Majus Grillo Catarratto '05	2 black glasses	4*
○	Shams '05	1 black glass	5
●	Furat '01	2 white glasses	5
●	Furat '03	2 white glasses	5
○	Bizir '03	2 white glasses	5
●	Majus Nero d'Avola '03	2 white glasses	3
○	Shams '03	2 white glasses	5
○	Bizir '04	2 white glasses	4
○	Shams '04	2 white glasses	6

MAZARA DEL VALLO (TP)

CANTINE FORACI
C.DA SERRONI
91026 MAZARA DEL VALLO (TP)
TEL. 0923934286
www.foraci.it

The Three Glasses that the Foraci family take home this year sets the seal on a process initiated by founder Pietro Foraci in 1936, followed by his pivotal decision in 1992 to become completely, scrupulously organic. This means not just that the property's 75 hectares, situated in the township of Partanna and the Giudeo Minore zone of Mazara del Vallo, are subject to the strict controls necessary for organic certification but that the vineyards of their grape suppliers are, too. The Three Glass wine, Tenute Dorrasita Nero d'Avola '04, pips the two previous vintages, which were finalists. It comes from an enlightened marriage between ancient cultivation traditions and modern technology, the latter in Sicily meaning protecting the grapes from the effects of the extreme heat of the delicate vintage period, thus safeguarding their characteristics. It is elegant, varietal and has outstanding personality, with a complex, multi-faceted aromatic spectrum, a wealth of expressivity, vitality and great length. Tenute Dorrasita Grillo '05 reached the finals. We were highly impressed by its nose full of white peach and Mediterranean herbs, and its succulent, tangy palate. Satiro Danzante Nero d'Avola '04, dedicated to the statue of the same name, is also worthy of note, and the rest of the range is exemplary, on all counts, from Alcamo '05 through to the Galhasi range, sold at laudably low prices. The team making these starry wines is led by Riccardo Cottarella.

●	Tenute Dorrasita Nero d'Avola '04	🍷🍷🍷	5
○	Tenute Dorrasita Grillo '05	🍷🍷	5
●	Le Gioie '04	🍷🍷	5
●	Nero d'Avola Satiro Danzante '04	🍷🍷	5
●	Galhasi Nero d'Avola '04	🍷	3*
●	Galhasi Nero d'Avola Syrah '04	🍷	4
○	Alcamo Conte Ruggero '05	🍷	3*
○	Galhasi Inzolia Catarratto '05	🍷	3*
○	Galhasi Inzolia Chardonnay '05	🍷	3
●	Tenute Dorrasita '02	🍸🍸	5
●	Tenute Dorrasita Nero d'Avola '03	🍸🍸	5
●	Galhasi Nero d'Avola Syrah '03	🍸🍸	4*

MENFI (AG)

★ PLANETA
C.DA DISPENSA
92013 MENFI (AG)
TEL. 091327965
www.planeta.it

Planeta did as spectacularly well as ever. Two wines picked up Three Glasses – Fiano Cometa '05 and Merlot '04 – and a further three reached the finals. This is ample proof that Diego Planeta's intuition was spot on when, in the early 1990s, while president of the huge Settesoli co-operative, he set up his own estate, entrusting winemaking to oenologist Carlo Corino. The work that his daughter Francesca and nephews Alessio and Santi have put in is just as admirable. Planeta now controls 350 hectares of vineyard spanning four properties and produces more than 2,200,000 bottles a year. Cometa has become a classic. The '05 is a voluptuous white of great concentration and extraordinary complexity on both nose and palate, giving ripe tropical and citrus fruit shot through with minerality and underpinned by a fresh swath of acidity. Then there is the varietal Merlot '04, all refinement and perfect definition in its small red berry fruits, pencil lead and herbaceous nuances, and its firm, elegant palate with abundant smooth tannin. We were bowled over by Nero d'Avola Santa Cecilia '04, which is intense, spicy and truly Mediterranean, and by the very fine Syrah '04 with its hallmark notes of pepper and blackberry jam. The international-style '05 Chardonnay is again outstanding and the '04 release of the Bordeaux blend Burdese has its habitual full structure and clean, sound, well-defined fruit. The delightfully vital, "sauvage" Cerasuolo di Vittoria '04 and the fleshy, sweet Moscato di Noto '05 are both excellent, while the basic range wines are attractive and inexpensive.

●	Merlot '04	🍷🍷🍷	5
○	Cometa '05	🍷🍷🍷	5
●	Santa Cecilia '04	🍷🍷	5
●	Syrah '04	🍷🍷	5
○	Chardonnay '05	🍷🍷	5
●	Burdese '04	🍷🍷	5
○	Alastro '05	🍷🍷	4
●	Cerasuolo di Vittoria '05	🍷🍷	4
○	La Segreta Bianco '05	🍷🍷	3*
○	Moscato di Noto '05	🍷🍷	6
●	La Segreta Rosso '05	🍷	3*
●	Syrah '02	🍸🍸🍸	5
●	Burdese '03	🍸🍸🍸	5
○	Cometa '04	🍸🍸🍸	5

MENFI (AG)

SETTESOLI
S.S. 115
92013 MENFI (AG)
TEL. 092577111
www.mandrarossa.it

Settesoli, with its 2,300 members, over 6,000 hectares of vineyard and an annual turnover exceeding 34,000,000 euros, is one of the largest co-operatives in Europe. Its success derives from the vision of its president Diego Planeta, who has led it on a path to quality that extends from the growers through to the cellar, which is directed by the internationally experienced Carlo Corino. The Mandrarossa range tops the pyramid of product lines and is unbeatable value for money. It's perceived by many consumers as an independent marque but actually comes from a rigorous selection of the grapes from the best ten per cent of the vineyards. This year, a monovarietal Nero d'Avola, Cartagho '04, has been added to the range and its varietal elegance shot it straight to the finals. There is magnificent plum jam fruitiness given emphasis by the most refined of balsamic notes, and the palate is beautifully incisive. The '04 release of the full-bodied nero d'Avola, merlot and syrah blend Bendicò is austere yet ripe, with intriguing gamey hints. Furetta '05, from chardonnay and fiano, is close-knit and succulent with a nose that will be adored by fans of barrique-aged whites. But there's excellent news too for those who prefer the clear-cut fruitiness and immediacy of non-oaked wines. The range includes a rich, ripely fruity Cabernet Sauvignon, a rounded Nero d'Avola of good character, and a spicy, attractively easy-drinking Syrah, all '05. Fiano '05, with fascinating aromas of peach and mint, and the lively Grecanico '05, characterized by elegant minerality, stand out among the whites.

●	Mandrarossa Cartagho '04	TT	4
●	Bendicò Mandrarossa '04	TT	4
●	Cabernet Sauvignon Mandrarossa '05	TT	3*
○	Fiano Mandrarossa '05	TT	3*
○	Furetta Mandrarossa '05	TT	4*
○	Grecanico Mandrarossa '05	TT	3*
●	Nero d'Avola Mandrarossa '05	TT	3*
●	Syrah Mandrarossa '05	TT	3*
○	Chardonnay Mandrarossa '05	T	3
○	Feudo dei Fiori Mandrarossa '05	T	3*
●	Merlot Mandrarossa '05	T	3*
○	Viogner Mandrarossa '05	T	3
●	Bendicò Mandrarossa '03	YY	4

MESSINA

PALARI
LOC. SANTO STEFANO BRIGA
C.DA BARNA
98137 MESSINA
TEL. 090630194 - 0906406221
www.palari.it

Salvatore Geraci, owner of this attractive estate in the hills overlooking the town and the straits of Messina, is not just an excellent wine producer. He's also an architect and has at least two other great merits. The first is to have saved Faro from extinction. It's a wine of ancient tradition but one that had almost disappeared by the mid 1980s, leaving practically all its vineyards abandoned. His second, even more important merit is that in recreating this great wine – well, two wines really – and turning it into a new classic, Geraci has never had an eye to fashion. Indeed, Faro Palari, which is made under Donato Lanati's consultancy, is far more than the sum of its parts, a multi-grape blend dominated by nerello mascalese and nerello cappuccio, with smaller quantities of nocera, cappuccio tignolino, cor 'e palumba, acitana, galatena, calabrese (or nero d'Avola) and more. No, it's a wine that goes straight to your heart, captivates you and sets you dreaming. The '04 runs along similar lines to previous vintages but is, if anything, better. It is a bright intense ruby. The nose is elegant and complex, forming a refined encounter of red berries, spices and Mediterranean-type aromas and the palate has great structure but astounding finesse and the minerality and elegance that makes you think more of Burgundy than Sicily. Hence Faro again won Three Glasses. The second wine, Rosso del Soprano '04, is starry too. Never before has it been so sharply defined, full and all-embracing.

●	Faro Palari '04	TTT	7
●	Rosso del Soprano '04	TT	5
●	Faro Palari '00	YYY	7
●	Faro Palari '01	YYY	7
●	Faro Palari '02	YYY	7
●	Faro Palari '03	YYY	7
●	Faro Palari '96	YYY	7
●	Faro Palari '98	YYY	7

PACECO (TP)

FIRRIATO
VIA TRAPANI, 4
91027 PACECO (TP)
TEL. 0923882755
www.firriato.it

This estate, owned by Salvatore and Vinzia Di Gaetano, is still young but has already reached starry heights, the wines reflecting the degree to which the Di Gaetanos understand the exigencies of modern times and interpret them with sensitivity. It took them just a few years to attain full ownership of the property, to renovate the cellar, equip it with the most up-to-date technological resources, and buy over 300 hectares of prime vineyards. As a result, Firriato is now probably the estate that best reveals the huge viticultural potential of the province of Trapani. This is an area of strategic importance to the island, and not just for the huge quantities for which it's best known. Pivotally, Firriato's prominence has not come simply from the use of international varieties but primarily from traditional grapes. The lessons learnt from the Australian winemaking team that gave the winery its kick start were well absorbed. Now they are intrinsic to the new team, led by skilled house oenologist Peppe Pellegrino, which has been in place now for over two years. The marvellous '04 Ribeca, which picked up Three Glasses for the first time, is a perfect example of all this. It's a wine that has a very recognizable sense of provenance, made from the vigorous nero d'Avola and the delicate yet decisive perricone, a grape so often unjustifiably overlooked. The rest of the range is also excellent in all respects, from the great reds such as the nero d'Avola-based Harmonium '04 and the Bordeaux blend Camelot '04, both of them finalists, down to the simplest base-level wines.

● Ribeca '04	🍷🍷🍷	6
● Camelot '04	🍷🍷	7
● Harmonium '04	🍷🍷	6
● Altavilla della Corte Rosso '04	🍷🍷	4*
● Chiaramonte Rosso Nero d'Avola '04	🍷🍷	4*
● Epoca Rosso '04	🍷🍷	4*
● Santagostino Rosso Baglio Sorìa '04	🍷🍷	5
○ Altavilla della Corte Bianco '05	🍷🍷	4
○ Santagostino Bianco Baglio Sorìa '05	🍷🍷	5
○ Chiaramonte Ansonica Bianco '05	🍷	4
○ Epoca Bianco '05	🍷	4
● Harmonium '00	YYY	5
● Camelot '01	YYY	7
● Harmonium '02	YYY	6
● Harmonium '03	YYY	6

PALERMO

SPADAFORA
VIA AUSONIA, 90
90144 PALERMO
TEL. 091514952 - 0916703322
www.spadafora.com

When the Spadafora family decided some years ago that it was time to move from simply growing grapes to making their own wines, they were one of the earliest estates in Sicily to do so. Francesco Spadafora already had a clear plan in his head. His aim was to put into action all he had learnt during his many years' study and the many months he'd spent at leading châteaux in France following the vintage and the winemaking. To the amazement of the farmers who had always worked on the property – and who thought he'd gone mad – he started to uproot, substituting the old, high-yielding vines with new ones set on a much tighter planting grid. When the work was finished the property had been completely transformed, and there was the chardonnay, cabernet and syrah that Francesco had fallen in love with in France sitting alongside the indigenous grapes. The hardest thing was – and still is – convincing his growers that low yields are the mainstay of high quality. More recent projects have involved the small houses around the winery which have been made over and now provide welcoming on-site holiday accommodation. This year, Spadafora's top wines, Schietto Syrah '04 and the also syrah-based Sole dei Padri '04, were not available for tasting as he'd sensibly left them to age longer before release. We'll review them next year. But intense, firm and fresh Schietto Chardonnay '05 was submitted and it leapt into the finals. The spicy, elegant Schietto Cabernet Sauvignon '04 is also admirable. The more basic wines are, as usual, reliably well made.

○ Schietto Chardonnay '05	🍷🍷	5
● Don Pietro Rosso '04	🍷🍷	4
● Schietto Cabernet Sauvignon '04	🍷🍷	6
● Monreale Syrah '05	🍷🍷	4*
○ Don Pietro Bianco '05	🍷	4
○ Monreale Alhambra '05	🍷	3*
● Schietto Syrah '01	YY	6
● Sole dei Padri '01	YY	8
● Schietto Cabernet Sauvignon '02	YY	6
● Sole dei Padri '02	YY	8
● Schietto Syrah '03	YY	6
● Sole dei Padri '03	YY	8

PALERMO

★ TASCA D'ALMERITA
LOC. SCLAFANI BAGNI
C.DA REGALEALI
90020 PALERMO
TEL. 0916459711 - 0921544011
www.tascadalmerita.it

The Conti Tasca have owned land and produced wine since the first half of the 19th century and their huge property, straddling the provinces of Palermo and Caltanissetta, is one of the most impressive on the island. Lucio Tasca works with his sons Giuseppe and Alberto and consultant Carlo Ferrini to produce a vast range of wines, from the famous Cabernet Sauvignon, Chardonnay and Rosso del Conte to more immediate wines made in larger quantities. Indeed, the estate has over 450 hectares of vineyard and has for some years now been producing over 3,000,000 bottles annually of wines that are successfully exported all over the world. This year, it was Rosso del Conte '03, made from nero d'Avola with small amounts of other indigenous grapes, which stole the show. It is a dark ruby colour and its nose is deep and complex, with ripe red and morello cherries, accompanied by elegant balsamic and oaky notes. The palate has elegance, finesse, balance and a long, impressive finish: in short, it's in a class of its own. Beside it sits a fabulous Cabernet Sauvignon '04 that is close-knit, elegant and varietal and a powerful, minerally, rich Chardonnay '04 of great balance, both of them among the best of recent releases. From the numerous other wines, we liked the richly fruity, spicy Cygnus '04, from nero d'Avola and cabernet sauvignon, the elegant yet opulent, Mediterranean-style Almerita Brut '03, from Chardonnay, and Tenuta Capofaro Malvasia '05, a fascinating sweet wine from the family's holding on the island of Salina.

●	Contea di Sclafani Rosso del Conte '03	🍷🍷🍷	6
●	Contea di Sclafani Cabernet Sauvignon '04	🍷🍷	6
O	Contea di Sclafani Chardonnay '04	🍷🍷	6
O	Contea di Sclafani Almerita Brut '03	🍷🍷	6
●	Cygnus '04	🍷🍷	5
●	Lamùri '04	🍷🍷	4*
O	Diamante d'Almerita '05	🍷🍷	6
O	Regaleali Bianco '05	🍷🍷	4*
●	Regaleali Nero d'Avola '05	🍷🍷	4*
O	Tenuta Capofaro Malvasia di Salina '05	🍷🍷	6
●	Camastra '04	🍷	5
O	Contea di Sclafani Nozze d'Oro '05	🍷	5
O	Leone d'Almerita '05	🍷	4
●	Contea di Sclafani Cabernet Sauvignon '02	🍷🍷🍷 (white)	6
●	Contea di Sclafani Cabernet Sauvignon '03	🍷🍷🍷 (white)	6

PANTELLERIA (TP)

SALVATORE MURANA
C.DA KHAMMA, 276
91017 PANTELLERIA (TP)
TEL. 0923915231
www.salvatoremurana.com

Every year without fail, Salvatore Murana takes home Three Glasses, and this year is no exception. Last year, it was the unique Creato '76 that literally set our hearts racing, this year the honours go to Moscato di Pantelleria Mueggen '04. Like Salvatore's other wines, it is made from low, bush-trained vines, most of them grown on steep terraced slopes surrounded by dry stone walls to protect them from the strong winds that batter the island all year round. This is what we call heroic viticulture, labour-intensive grape-growing based on ritual and knowledge accumulated over more than 2,000 years, where modern techniques count for little or nothing. The annual miracle that is the wines depends on the lava rock where the grapes are planted, the strong Mediterranean sun and Salvatore's expert ministrations, The grapes, once picked, are left to dry in the open air, lying on stone, a technique that has been passed down from generation to generation, since the early Phoenician colonists passed it on to the Greeks. Mueggen '04 comes from grapes grown in the small area of the same name. It has a glorious, bright, deep amber hue. The nose bursts with ultra-ripe apricot, peach and fig, interwoven with Mediterranean-type aromas and the palate is sumptuous, harmonious and perfectly balanced, filling the mouth with sweetness and lingering endlessly. Khamma and Martingana were not submitted this year but Gadì '05, a perfumed dry Zibibbo from vines on the island's northern slopes, was, as was the sweet Turbè '04, which has candied citrus peel, apricot and almond.

O	Moscato di Pantelleria Mueggen '04	🍷🍷🍷	7
O	Moscato di Pantelleria Turbè '04	🍷🍷	5
O	Gadì '05	🍷🍷	4
O	Moscato Passito di Pantelleria Martingana '00	🍷🍷🍷 (white)	8
O	Moscato Passito di Pantelleria Creato '76	🍷🍷🍷 (white)	8
O	Moscato Passito di Pantelleria Martingana '93	🍷🍷🍷 (white)	6
O	Moscato Passito di Pantelleria Martingana '94	🍷🍷🍷 (white)	6
O	Moscato Passito di Pantelleria Martingana '96	🍷🍷🍷 (white)	6
O	Moscato Passito di Pantelleria Martingana '98	🍷🍷🍷 (white)	8

PARTINICO (PA)

Cusumano

C.da San Carlo - s.s. 113
90047 Partinico (PA)
tel. 0918903466 - 0918908713
www.cusumano.it

Dynamic brothers Diego and Alberto Cusumano continue to bestride the peaks of quality winemaking with unchanging success. Their seven holdings span over 400 hectares and are strategically located in areas ideal for viticulture, such as Alcamo, Monreale, Partinico, Ficuzza and Butera. The nucleus is at Partinico where a new cellar, fitted out with the best of modern equipment, is almost ready, while the wineries at Butera and Ficuzza are now operational. Ficuzza is a nature reserve area with extensive woodland. It has large day-night temperature swings, tempered by the presence of Lake Gorgo Tondo and is also blessed by excellent terroir. It is here that the Cusumanos produce their top whites. Alberto manages the winemaking team, led by oenologist Giuseppe Clemente and Piedmontese consultant Mario Ronco, while Diego takes care of sales and is frequently off travelling the world. This year, the brothers took the sensible decision not to submit their top wines, Sagana and Noà '05, as they did not feel they were ready at the time of our tastings. But there were other family jewels to assess and the diamond was Benuara '05, from 75 per cent nero d'Avola from Butera and 25 per cent syrah from Monreale. Its intense, ripe fruit and seductive tannin swept it straight to Three Glasses. Cubìa '05, from inzolia, is fleshy and full of aroma. The classy Jalé '05, from chardonnay, scored similarly. The rest of the range is excellent too, from the fruity, fragrant Angimbè '05, from inzolia and chardonnay, to the simpler Alcamo Rosato '05 and everything is very well priced.

●	Benuara '05	TTT	4*
○	Cubìa '05	TT	5
○	Jalé '05	TT	5
○	Angimbè '05	TT	4*
●	Merlot '05	TT	3*
●	Nero d'Avola '05	TT	3*
●	Syrah '05	TT	3*
○	Alcamo '05	T	3
○	Inzolia '05	T	3
⊙	Rosato '05	T	3
●	Noà '00	YYY	5
●	Noà '03	YYY	5
●	Noà '04	YYY	5
●	Sàgana '04	YYY	5
●	Benuara '04	YY	4*

PIAZZA ARMERINA (EN)

Maurigi

C.da Budonetto
94015 Piazza Armerina (EN)
tel. 091321788 - 093585240
www.maurigi.it

Francesco Maurigi, a plucky type with a businessman's approach, took on what many felt to be a risky venture: growing grapes in the province of Enna, which has no viticultural traditions, and he has succeeded. His reasoning back in 1996 was simple. The lands around Piazza Armerina are fertile, look good and have shown to be suitable for growing many other types of produce so why not grapes? Not being the sort of guy to do things by halves, Maurigi wasted no time in planting 40 hectares, going for international varieties since the area had no traditions to guide him. He sympathetically restored the property's 18th-century convent, which became the estate's centre of operations, and built a large, modern, well-planned cellar. The rest, as they say, is history. The wines had amazing elegance and modernity, and quickly shot to prominence. A case in point this year is the delicious new Le Chiare '05, from 100 per cent viognier, which soared straight into the finals. It is a bright deep straw and the nose is nuanced with white peach and apricot. The palate is fresh and invigorating and it's a wine that is sure to get people talking, even more so since it's so well priced. The other newcomer to Maurigi's range is Lù '02, a meaty, close-knit Petit Verdot, which also promises well. Terre di Sofia '04, an attractively floral and mineral Chardonnay, almost reached the finals. Finally, we have Saia Grande '04, from syrah, merlot and pinot nero, another first-rate wine that combines fruit, balance and personality.

○	Le Chiare '05	TT	4*
●	Lù '02	TT	6
●	Terre di Ottavia '03	TT	6
●	Saia Grande '04	TT	5
○	Terre di Sofia '04	TT	5
○	Bacca Bianca '05	T	4
●	Bacca Rossa '05	T	4
○	Coste all'Ombra '05	T	5
●	Terre di Maria '01	YY	6
○	Terre di Sofia '01	YY	5
●	Terre di Ottavia '02	YY	6
●	Terre di Maria '02	YY	6
○	Terre di Sofia '03	YY	5

RANDAZZO (CT)

Tenuta delle Terre Nere

C.da Calderara
95036 Randazzo (CT)
tel. 095924002

Cosmopolitan Marc De Grazia, originally from Florence, has been an important name on the Italian wine scene for 20 years. He has unearthed talented producers all over Italy and brought them to the world's notice. And now Etna has given him what he had been seeking for some time: a place that inspired him to make wine for himself, rather than simply judging those of others. It happened on a visit to Benanti, one of his clients. Marc was drinking a local grower's wine and found it not just excellent but endowed with a clear sense of place. His plans took shape in 2002 and he went live in 2004 after two trial vintages. At that point, he had around 15 hectares, scattered across Etna's northern slopes in Randazzo and Castiglione, and had equipped his cellar, which he'd created by renovating an ancient wine-press area. We had high expectations for his three reds, all exclusively from nerello mascalese, but they well exceeded them. Feudo di Mezzo Il Quadro dell Rose '04, the most extrovert and forward of the threesome, sailed confidently to a well-deserved Three Glasses. It's a bright, deep ruby. The elegant, complex nose gives a weave of small red berry fruit and aromatic herbs well integrated into the aromas of new oak and the palate is generous, mouthfilling, firmly structured, elegantly fruity, satisfying and very long. But the slightly more austere Guardiola '04, with rarefied elegance and wonderful harmony on the palate, also nearly gained Three Glasses. Calderara Sottana '04, was also highly impressive, with a firm mesh, elegant minerality and great overall harmony.

●	Etna Rosso Feudo di Mezzo Quadro delle Rose '04	▼▼▼	6
●	Etna Rosso Calderara Sottana '04	▼▼	6
●	Etna Rosso Guardiola '04	▼▼	6
●	Etna Rosso Guardiola '03	▽▽	6
●	Etna Rosso Calderara Sottana '03	▽	5

SAN CIPIRELLO (PA)

Vinicola Calatrasi

C.da Piano Piraino
90040 San Cipirello (PA)
tel. 0918576767
www.calatrasi.it

Calatrasi is an enterprise in continuous evolution that moves with surprising dexterity in the global market. It currently has three wineries, in Sicily, the Salento area of Puglia and Tunisia, makes almost 10,000,000 bottles a year and has a turnover of more than 15,000,000 euros. Credit goes to the entrepreneurial acumen of Maurizio Micciché, who founded the company along with his brother Giuseppe. He's a great motivator and unusually skilled at transmitting his philosophy to those with whom he works. A new oenologist, Piergiorgio Berta, from Piedmont, took over in March 2006 but the wines we tasted came from his predecessor, New Zealander Tamra Washington, and showed the classic Calatrasi style, that careful mix of New World winemaking and Mediterranean warmth. Heading the range are two wines smartly dubbed "Super Sicilians", D'Istinto Magnifico '04, from cabernet sauvignon and merlot, and the Terre di Ginestra 651 Nero d'Avola/Shiraz '04. The former has a super-clean nose, all small red berry fruit and elegant herbaceous hints, and shows deep, powerful yet smooth. It lives up to the "magnificent" of its name and, like previous vintages, took its place in the finals, as did the 651. This is full of spicy, balsamic aromas, has well-integrated oak and considerable body. Everything else is very good too, especially the attractive Nero d'Avola-Petit Verdot D'Istinto Bathéos '05. Terre di Ginestra 651 Chardonnay, the two Baglio Badami wines and some of the wines from the D'Istinto range had not been released by the time of our tastings. We'll look at them once they're ready.

●	D'Istinto Magnifico '04	▼▼	6
●	Terre di Ginestra 651 '04	▼▼	6
●	D'Istinto Batheos '05	▼▼	3*
○	D'Istinto Ljetas Bianco '05	▼▼	3*
●	Accademia del Sole Merlot '04	▼	4
○	Accademia del Sole Viogner '05	▼	4
○	D'Istinto Catarratto-Chardonnay '05	▼	4
○	D'Istinto Chardonnay '05	▼	4
○	D'Istinto Grillo '05	▼	4*
⊙	D'Istinto Rosato '05	▼	4
○	Terre di Ginestra Catarratto '05	▼	4
●	Terre di Ginestra 651 '02	▽▽	7
●	D'Istinto Magnifico '03	▽▽	7
●	D'Istinto Batheos '04	▽▽	3*

TRAPANI

ADRAGNA
VIA REGINA ELENA, 4
91100 TRAPANI
TEL. 092326401
www.classica.it

The province of Trapani has always been a major grape-growing zone and it has one of the most extensive surface areas under vine in Europe. From Trapani to Mazara del Vallo, including the famous Marsala zone and the Salemi countryside, is one vast, luxuriant vineyard, interspersed with wineries of high renown, some enjoying international repute. The Rocca di Giglio vineyards lie right at its heart, on the slopes of Monte San Giuliano, better known as Mount Erice, in the township of Valderice. They have been owned by the Adragna family for over 200 years. Roberto, the current head of the family, is passionate about viticulture and is also president of the highly regarded Cantina Sociale di Trapani. This part of western Sicily has specific soil and climate conditions that benefit the grapes produced. Proof comes in the form of Roccagiglio, a successful blend of cabernet sauvignon and merlot and the sort of wine that never passes unnoticed at our tastings. This year the '04 simply flew into the finals. It is stylish and intense, and shrieks quality throughout, from its nose of small red berries and chocolate onwards. Another wine that never disappoints is the monovarietal Nero d'Avola. The '05 is surprisingly good in its fine mix of great richness of flavour and attractive drinkability. The '05 Grillo is not monovarietal for it includes a little chardonnay. This is the second release of the wine and it has all the freshness, fragrance and delicate citrus-like character of its predecessor.

●	Roccagiglio '04	▼▼	6
●	Nero d'Avola '05	▼▼	4*
○	Grillo '05	▼	4
●	Roccagiglio '01	▽▽	6
●	Roccagiglio '02	▽▽	5
●	Roccagiglio '03	▽▽	5
○	Chardonnay '03	▽▽	5
●	Nero d'Avola '03	▽▽	4
●	Nero d'Avola '04	▽▽	4*

TRAPANI

CANTINA SOCIALE DI TRAPANI
LOC. FONTANELLE
C.DA OSPEDALETTO
91100 TRAPANI
TEL. 0923539349
www.cantinasocialetrapani.com

This co-operative was founded half a century ago but it is only in the last ten years that the wish of a small number of members for a more forward-looking, quality-led policy has prevailed. Since then, there have been increases in sales and, vitally, credibility, and it now stands out as one of Sicily's leading wineries. But let's move straight on to the wines. The flagship, Forti Terre di Sicilia Cabernet Sauvignon, which a two-time Three Glass winner and frequent finalist, was not available for tasting since the co-operative's dynamic president Roberto Adragna and his oenologist Nicola Centonze did not feel it was ready for release. But the other wines were submitted and were as good as ever. The excellent Forti Terre di Sicilia Rocche Rosse '05, from syrah, merlot and cabernet sauvignon, has aromas of ripe red and morello cherries and a palate of rich, opulent fruitiness. Forti Terre di Sicilia Nero d'Avola '04 is attractively firm, spicy and varietal. Chardonnay '05, again from the Forti Terre line, is another highly successful wine, with an intense green-apple nose and a smooth, supple, varietal palate. Forti Terre Il Rosso '05, from nero d'Avola and cabernet sauvignon, has a racy palate of good weight. There were more good results from the more basic Drepanum line, which offers impeccably made wines at good prices. The best of these is the vibrant, clean Nero d'Avola '05, which has plum and small red berry fruit.

●	Forti Terre di Sicilia Nero d'Avola '04	▼▼	4
○	Forti Terre di Sicilia Chardonnay '05	▼▼	4
●	Forti Terre di Sicilia Rocche Rosse '05	▼▼	4
○	Drepanum Bianco '05	▼	2*
●	Drepanum Nero d'Avola '05	▼	2*
⊙	Drepanum Rosato '05	▼	2*
○	Forti Terre di Sicilia Il Bianco '05	▼	3*
●	Forti Terre di Sicilia Il Rosso '05	▼	3*
●	Forti Terre di Sicilia Cabernet Sauvignon '01	▽▽▽	5
●	Forti Terre di Sicilia Cabernet Sauvignon '02	▽▽	5
●	Forti Terre di Sicilia Cabernet Sauvignon '03	▽▽	5

VIAGRANDE (CT)

BENANTI
VIA G. GARIBALDI, 475
95029 VIAGRANDE (CT)
TEL. 0957893438 - 0957893533
www.vinicolabenanti.it

The awesome showing by Giuseppe Benanti's wines this year didn't surprise us. We have followed the progress of his winery closely since its first entry to the Guide in 1995. Even then, Giuseppe had been making wine for many years, having continued an old family tradition. He set his sights on conquering the difficult Etna conditions and its low pH, high malic acid wines, selecting the best soils, identifying the best clones and refining cellar techniques. Time is kind to those who labour with love and tenacity. So Giuseppe, with his sons Salvino and Antonio, is at last reaping his well-deserved success. Oenologist Salvo Foti, probably the greatest expert on Sicily's indigenous varieties, has also had important input. Two wines this year won Three Glasses. Etna Bianco Superiore Pietramarina '02, from carricante, a completely unique wine is crystal-clean, minerally, long-lived and absolutely fascinating, and Serra della Contessa '03 presents a deep, sensual red of great character and elegance, and beautifully defined aromas. From a more recently acquired property at Noto, in the homeland of at nero d'Avola in Avola and Pachino, comes an imposing, varietal Nero d'Avola '03, a wine that combines structure with great elegance and has supreme balance and harmony. We almost forgot: the quality of everything else is stunning. Finally, we had to award Three Glasses to Pietramarina '97, albeit retrospectively, in honour of all those early wines. If you're lucky enough to find a bottle you'll understand why. At this point, the title Winery of the Year is no less than Benanti's due.

○	Etna Bianco Sup. Pietramarina '02	▼▼▼	6
●	Etna Rosso Serra della Contessa '03	▼▼▼	7
●	Nerello Mascalese '03	▼▼	6
●	Nero d'Avola '03	▼▼	5
●	Etna Rosso Rovittello '02	▼▼	6
●	Lamorèmio '02	▼▼	6
●	Etna Rosso Rosso di Verzella '03	▼▼	4
●	Majora '03	▼▼	4
●	Nerello Cappuccio '03	▼▼	6
○	Etna Bianco Bianco di Caselle '05	▼▼	4
○	Minnella '05	▼▼	6
○	Etna Bianco Sup. Pietramarina '00	▽▽▽	6
○	Etna Bianco Sup. Pietramarina '01	▽▽▽	6
○	Etna Bianco Sup. Pietramarina '97	▽▽▽	5

VITTORIA (RG)

COS
P.ZZA DEL POPOLO, 34
97019 VITTORIA (RG)
TEL. 0932876145
www.cosvittoria.it

Having galloped through the landmark event of their 25th vintage with their usual enthusiasm, the two eternal youngsters of COS, Titta Cilia and Giusto Occhipinti, both successful architects, are now back pursuing their great love of winemaking, a vocation that has led them to become some of Italy's leading exponents of biodynamic agriculture. For Cilia and Occhipinti, this was a natural development from the deep respect for mother earth and all it produces that they had always held. The basics of biodynamics lie in safeguarding the vitality of the soil and the micro-organisms that live in it. With wine, this leads automatically to using indigenous yeasts and keeping sulphur additions to the minimum. The estate and its cellar are located in Bastonaca, in the Vittoria zone. It was founded in 1980 and now comprises around 47 hectares, 22 of them beautifully tended vineyard. There is also a delightful 19th-century farmhouse which has been tastefully restored to form an area for welcoming guests. All the wines that were ready in time for our tastings were showing very well. There was the mineral, fruity, zesty Ramì '05, from inzolia and grecanico. The classic Cerasuolo di Vittoria '04, a delicious frappato-nero d'Avola blend, is all ripe cherry and spiciness, which this year takes the name Venticinquesima Vendemmia (25th vintage). Finally, Pojo di Lupo '04 is a weighty, deep Nero d'Avola.

●	Cerasuolo di Vittoria Venticinquesima Vendemmia '04	▼▼	4
●	Pojo di Lupo '04	▼▼	4
○	Ramì '05	▼▼	4
●	Contrade Labirinto '01	▽▽	8
●	Scyri '00	▽▽	6
●	Cerasuolo di Vittoria V. di Vastunaca '02	▽▽	4
●	Cerasuolo di Vittoria '03	▽▽	4
●	Cerasuolo di Vittoria Pithos '03	▽▽	5
●	Pojo di Lupo '03	▽▽	4
○	Ramì '03	▽▽	4
○	Ramì '04	▽▽	4
●	Contrade - Dedalo '98	▽▽	8

OTHER WINERIES

Geraci

C.da Tarucco, SP 12 km 5,3
90146 Bisacquino (PA)
tel. 091306596
www.tarucco.com

Antonella and Stefano Geraci's two basic blends, the elegant, mineral, fresh Colonna '05, from chardonnay, grillo and greco dorato, and the intense, fragrant, structured Gioeni '05, from cabernet, alicante and merlot, are great. The top wines, Nero d'Avola '04 and Chardonnay '05, showed excellently.

●	Tarucco Nero d'Avola '04	🍷🍷	3*
○	Tarucco Chardonnay '05	🍷🍷	4
○	Tarucco Colonna Bianco '05	🍷	3*
●	Tarucco Gioeni '05	🍷	3*

Tenuta dell' Abate

via Kennedy, 46
93100 Caltanissetta
tel. 0934584188 - 3355388549

Luigi Romano makes good wines, especially the concentrated, savoury, light spice and balsam Giffarrò '04, from cabernet sauvignon and syrah. Monte Palco '05, a Nero d'Avola, is structured, fragrant and attractive. Lissandrello '05, from inzolia, and Monte Palco Chardonnay '05 are well styled.

●	Giffarrò '04	🍷🍷	5
○	Lissandrello '05	🍷	3
○	Monte Palco Chardonnay '05	🍷	4
●	Monte Palco Nero d'Avola '05	🍷	4

Masseria Feudo Grottarossa

C.da Grottarossa
93100 Caltanissetta
tel. 0934856575
www.masseriadelfeudo.it

The concentrated Rosso delle Rose '04, from nero d'Avola and syrah, has red fruits and spices, and is siblings Francesco and Caterina Cucurullo's best wine this year. Chardonnay Haermosa '05, Giglio Bianco '05, from grillo and inzolia, and Il Giglio Rosso '05, nero d'Avola, all showed well.

●	Rosso delle Rose '04	🍷🍷	4
○	Haermosa '05	🍷	5
○	Il Giglio Bianco '05	🍷	3*
●	Il Giglio Rosso '05	🍷	3*

Feudo San Martino

C.da San Martino
93100 Caltanissetta
tel. 0934568817
www.feudosanmartino.it

The '03 Mon Roy, a structured Cabernet Sauvignon, is again the top wine from this promising estate. It's full of fruit, balanced and attractive, with fat tannins. Yerax '03 is a successful blend of nero d'Avola, cabernet sauvignon and syrah. Nero d'Avolas Mons Mellis '03 and Signoria '04 are sound.

●	Cabernet Mon Roy '03	🍷🍷	5
●	Yerax '03	🍷🍷	5
●	Nero d'Avola Mons Mellis '03	🍷	5
●	Nero d'Avola Signoria '04	🍷	4

FEUDO MONTONI

C.DA MONTONI VECCHI
92022 CAMMARATA (AG)
TEL. 091513106
www.feudomontoni.it

Fabio Sireci continues to produce some of the most characterful wines from the complex nero d'Avola variety. Selezione Speciale Vrucara '04 is austere and intense, with great personality. The nose has red berry fruit while the palate has considerable structure and beguiling tannin.

●	Nero d'Avola '04	YY	4
●	Nero d'Avola Sel. Speciale Vrucara '04	YY	6

BAGLIO DELLE CICALE

S.DA PROVINCIALE PER GRANITOLA, 282
91021 CAMPOBELLO DI MAZARA (TP)
TEL. 092440450
www.bagliodellecicale.it

This new estate, owned by Varese textile producer Giampiero Ielmini and a group of friends, has fine wines, led by Merlot '04, with a complex nose, rounded palate, and long, fruity finish. Syrah '05 is spicy and charming. Uzeda '04, from nero d'Avola and cabernet, and grillo-only Iddu '05 are sound.

●	Baglio delle Cicale Merlot '04	YY	5
●	Syrah '05	YY	4
●	Uzeda '04	Y	4
○	Iddu '05	Y	4

ALESSANDRO DI CAMPOREALE

C.DA MANDRANOVA
90043 CAMPOREALE (PA)
TEL. 092437038 - 3339008696
www.alessandrodicamporeale.it

Syrah Kaid '04, has a well-expressed varietal nose, ethery hints and dense tannins. Nero d'Avola DonnaTá '05 has much to offer, especially considering its price, and reveals a rich, elegant, ripely fruity nose and a round, full palate. Benedè '05, from catarratto, is varietal and fresh.

●	Kaid '04	YY	4
●	DonnaTá '05	YY	3*
○	Benedè '05	Y	3*

FATTORIE AZZOLINO

C.DA AZZOLINO
90043 CAMPOREALE (PA)
TEL. 092436123 - 0464834195
www.athesiavini.it

Franco Sacco's elegant, intense '04 Chardonnay nearly reached the finals. The nose has tropical fruit well integrated with oak and the palate is fresh, buttery and deep. The varietal, fragrant Nero d'Avola '04 and Tranùi '05, this a fruity blend of catarratto, inzolia and chardonnay, are good too.

○	Chardonnay '04	YY	5
●	Nero d'Avola '04	YY	4*
○	Tranui '05	YY	4*
●	Monreale Nero d'Avola Notturno '05	Y	4

CANTINA VITICOLTORI ASSOCIATI CANICATTÌ

C.DA AQUILATA
92024 CANICATTÌ (AG)
TEL. 0922829371 - www.viniaquilae.it

The work of oenologist Tonino Guzzo and the co-operative staff is bearing fruit and the high quality of the wines is attracting attention. Proof comes from Aynat '04, an elegant monovarietal Nero d'Avola that reached the finals. The complex Aquilae Cabernet Sauvignon '05 is also good.

●	Aynat '04	YY	4*
●	Aquilae Cabernet Sauvignon '05	YY	3*
●	Aquilae Syrah '05	Y	3*

ZENNER

VIA PIETRO MASCAGNI, 72
95131 CATANIA
TEL. 095530560
www.terradellesirene.com

Terre delle Sirene '04, from nero d'Avola grown at Bufaleffi, near Pachino, flew into the finals. It's intense, varietal, full of ripe fruit and elegantly tannic. The Zenner family, German but in Sicily since 1975, make just small quantities, from organically grown grapes and with great love.

●	Terra delle Sirene '04	YY	5

Rizzuto
c.da Piconello
92011 Cattolica Eraclea (AG)
tel. 0922847593 - 091333081
www.rizzutoguccione.com

The '03 release of the estate's classic, Ibisco, from nero d'Avola, cabernet sauvignon and merlot, is excellent. Piconello Cabernet Sauvignon Chiaro '05, is a firm, fruity rosé with attractive aromas of small red berries. Merlot Statale 115 '04 and Piconello Grillo '05 are also sound.

● Ibisco '03	ŸŸ	5
⊙ Piconello Cabernet Sauvignon Chiaro '05	ŸŸ	4*
● Statale 115 '04	Ÿ	4
○ Piconello Grillo '05	Ÿ	4

Poggio di Bortolone
loc. Roccazzo - c.da Bortolone, 19
97010 Chiaramonte Gulfi (RG)
tel. 0932921161
www.poggiodibortolone.it

Ignazio Cosenza, working with his son Gianluigi, has made a first-rate Cerasuolo di Vittoria '03 from the Para Para vineyard. It's deep and complex, and stood out in our finals. Cerasuolo '04 and the two reds Pigi '02, from syrah and cabernet, and the petit verdot Kiron '03 are all excellent.

● Cerasuolo di Vittoria V. Para Para '03	ŸŸ	5
● Pigi Rosso '02	ŸŸ	6
● Kiron '03	ŸŸ	6
● Cerasuolo di Vittoria '04	ŸŸ	4*

Avide
c.da Mastrella, 346
97013 Comiso (RG)
tel. 0932967456
www.avide.it

Our first choice from the ever-dependable range of wines was Cerasuolo di Vittoria Etichetta Nera '04. The colour is deep ruby, the nose is fruity with spicy hints and there is attack on the fruity, full palate. Sigillo '03, from nero d'Avola and cabernet, and Frappato Herea '05 are both very good.

● Cerasuolo di Vittoria Etichetta Nera '04	ŸŸ	4*
● 3 Carati '04	ŸŸ	5
● Herea Frappato '05	ŸŸ	3*
● Sigillo '03	Ÿ	6

Curto
c.da Sulla s.s.115 Ispica-Rosolini
via G. Galilei, 4
97014 Ispica (RG)
tel. 0932950161 - www.curto.it

Fontanelle '03, from 100 per cent nero d'Avola, has great personality. It's spicy, complex and balanced, with plentiful soft tannins and good alcohol. Oenologist Francesca Curto also submitted a fine Ikano '04, from nero d'Avola, syrah and merlot, and a very good Eloro Nero d'Avola '04.

● Eloro Fontanelle '03	ŸŸ	5
● Curto Ikano '04	ŸŸ	4
● Eloro Curto Rosso '04	Ÿ	3*

Tenute Chiuse del Signore
loc. Alboretto
s. p. Linguaglossa-Zafferana
95015 Linguaglossa (CT)
tel. 094221165 - www.gaishotels.com

Taormina hotel owner Sergio De Luca now works full time on Etna on his estate, with consultants Paolo Peira for winemaking and Lucio Brancadoro for viticulture. Serrantico '04, a lively, clean merlot-syrah blend, made the finals. Rasule Alte '05, from nerello mascalese and merlot, is very good.

● Serrantico '04	ŸŸ	6
● Rasule Alte '05	ŸŸ	4*

Tenuta Scilio di Valle Galfina
c.da Arrigo
95015 Linguaglossa (CT)
tel. 095932822 - 095647789
www.scilio.com

Sikélios '03, a sweet red from nerello mascalese and other local grapes grown in an old vineyard on the family estate, is the most interesting of the wines. But all have good style, most notably Rubé Bianco '05 and Etna Bianco '05, both from carricante and catarratto, both with fresh minerality.

● Sikélios Rosso '03	Ÿ	5
○ Etna Bianco '05	Ÿ	4*
○ Rubé Bianco '05	Ÿ	3*

HAUNER
LOC. SANTA MARIA
VIA UMBERTO I
98050 LIPARI (ME)
TEL. 0909843141 - 0906409427

Best this year is Malvasia delle Lipari Passito Carlo Hauner '03, elegant, invigorating and full of nuances of Mediterranean scrubland. The fruity nero d'Avola and nerello mascalese Salina Rosso '04 and Malvasia Passito '05 are on a par. Salina Bianco '05, from inzolia and catarratto, is good.

○	Malvasia Passito Carlo Hauner '03	🍷🍷	7
●	Salina Rosso '04	🍷🍷	4
○	Malvasia delle Lipari Passito '05	🍷	6
○	Salina Bianco '05	🍷	4

BAGLIO HOPPS - JOHN HOPPS & SONS
C.DA BIESINA - VIA SALEMI KM 12.220
91025 MARSALA (TP)
TEL. 0923967020
www.bagliohopps.com

We particularly liked Hopps' Merlot '03 from this year's wines. It has clean fruit and good balance despite the troublesome vintage. The Chardonnay '05 is fresh, clean and supple. Contrasti '05, from nero d'Avola, and Diana '03, a nero d'Avola and cabernet mix, are both good.

●	Merlot '03	🍷🍷	5
●	Diana '03	🍷	4
○	Chardonnay '05	🍷	4
●	Contrasti '05	🍷	4

BARRACO
C.DA FONTANELLE, 252
91025 MARSALA (TP)

Wine artisan Antonino looks after his estate himself, uses indigenous yeasts and avoids all invasive cellar techniques. His Catarratto '05 has a surprising earthy minerality. Zibibbo Secco '05 fascinates with roses and peaches. Grillo '04 has a highly refined nose, an oxidative touch and great zip.

○	Grillo '04	🍷🍷	4
○	Catarratto '05	🍷🍷	4
○	Zibibbo '05	🍷🍷	4
●	Nero d'Avola '04	🍷	4

CANTINE BUFFA
VIA VINCENZO FLORIO, 31
91025 MARSALA (TP)
TEL. 0923982444

Buffa, founded in 1931, has a long history behind it. We tasted the fine, deep amber Marsala Superiore Secco with its dried fruit and candied orange peel nose and dry, soft, long palate. Marsala Vergine is complex and full but a touch rustic.

○	Marsala Sup. Secco	🍷🍷	5
○	Marsala Vergine	🍷	6

CANTINE MOTHIA
VIA GIOVANNI FALCONE, 22
91025 MARSALA (TP)
TEL. 0923737295
www.cantine-mothia.com

This is owned by the Bonomo family and quality is improving. The elegant, structured Hammon '02, from cabernet sauvignon and nero d'Avola, is good, as is the nice, complex Mulsum '05, from semi-dried grillo. Vela Latina '05, from grillo and chardonnay, and Inzolia Saline '05 are both good.

●	Hammon '02	🍷🍷	4
○	Mulsum '05	🍷🍷	5
○	Saline '05	🍷	2*
○	Vela Latina '05	🍷	4

CANTINE RALLO
VIA VINCENZO FLORIO, 2
91025 MARSALA (TP)
TEL. 0923721633 - 0923721634
www.cantinerallo.it

Andrea Vasco's winery was one of the first to go organic in Sicily and is showing well. Passito di Pantelleria '04 captivates, its gentle sweetness mitigated by a fresh swath of acidity. The fruity Alcamo Nero d'Avola '05, the complex Marsala Soleras and the fragrant Chardonnay '05 are all good.

○	Passito di Pantelleria '04	🍷🍷	6
●	Alcamo Nero d'Avola '05	🍷🍷	4*
○	Marsala Vergine Soleras Ris. Venti Anni	🍷🍷	6
○	Chardonnay '05	🍷	4

Cantine Barbera
C.da Torrenova, s. p. 79
92013 Menfi (AG)
tel. 0925570442
www.cantinebarbera.it

The excellent Coda della Foce '04, from merlot, petit verdot and nero d'Avola, is deep and concentrated, with elegant notes of roasted coffee beans and tobacco. The '03 is also attractive and has lingering flavours. Chardonnay Piana del Pozzo '05 is all tropical fruit, freshness and zest.

● Coda della Foce '04	🍷🍷	5
○ Piana del Pozzo '05	🍷🍷	4
● Coda della Foce '03	🍷	5
● Nero d'Avola V. La Costa '05	🍷	4

Barone di Villagrande
via del Bosco, 25
95025 Milo (CT)
tel. 0957082175 - 0957494339
www.villagrande.it

Carlo and Maria Nicolosi Asmundo's wines fully reflect the character of the Etna terrain. The merlot and nerello mascalese Sciara '03 is fragrant and well structured. Etna Rosso '04 is deep and concentrated. Etna Bianco Superiore '05 and Fiore '05, from catarratto and chardonnay, are well made.

● Sciara '03	🍷🍷	5
● Etna Rosso di Villagrande '04	🍷🍷	4*
○ Etna Bianco Sup. Villagrande '05	🍷	4*
○ Fiore '05	🍷	5

Pollara
s.p. 4 bis, km 2, c.da Malvello
90046 Monreale (PA)
tel. 0918462922 - 0918463512
www.principedicorleone.it

The wines from the Principe di Corleone line are well styled and attractive, especially the Rosso '04, from nero d'Avola and merlot, with its fruity nose and good structure. The soft Nero d'Avola Narciso '05 and Cabernet Sauvignon Monreale '02 were not far from Two Glasses.

● Principe di Corleone Rosso '04	🍷🍷	4*
● Principe di Corleone Monreale '02	🍷	5
● Principe di Corleone Narciso '05	🍷	3

Sallier de la Tour
c.da Pernice
90144 Monreale (PA)
tel. 092436797
www.sallierdelatour.it

There is very high quality at Principe Filiberto Sallier de la Tour's winery. Sallier de la Tour Rosso '03, an elegant, intense wine from merlot, cabernet sauvignon, syrah and nero d'Avola, simply flew into the finals. The other wines submitted are pleasing, especially Syrah '03 and Merlot '03.

● Sallier de la Tour Rosso '03	🍷🍷	5
● Merlot '03	🍷🍷	4
● Syrah '03	🍷🍷	4
● Cabernet '03	🍷	4

Tamburello
c.da Pietragnella
90144 Monreale (PA)
tel. 0918465272

Mirella Tamburello's best wine is Perricone Pietragavina '04 with its multi-faceted, stylish aromatic spectrum and good depth. Nero d'Avola Pietragavina '03, with its ripe cherry nose, Dagala Bianco '05, from inzolia and catarratto, and the nero d'Avola and cabernet Dagala Rosso '03 are attractive.

● Monreale Pietragavina Perricone '03	🍷🍷	4*
● Dagala Rosso '03	🍷	3
● Monreale Pietragavina Nero d'Avola '03	🍷	4
○ Dagala Bianco '05	🍷	2

Feudo Maccari
c.da Maccari
s. p. Pachino-Noto, km 13,5
96017 Noto (SR)
tel. 0931596894 - www.feudomaccari.it

Tuscan businessman Antonio Moretti, ably assisted by consultant Carlo Ferrini, continues to submit very good wines. The richness and concentration of Saia '04, from nero d'Avola, and the cleanliness of its fruit, took it to our finals. The other Nero d'Avola, ReNoto '05, also impressed.

● Saia '04	🍷🍷	5
● ReNoto '05	🍷🍷	4*

Zisola

C.da Zisola
96017 Noto (SR)
tel. 057773571
www.zisola.it

The Mazzei family's Sicilian estate lies near Noto, one of the island's loveliest areas. The vineyards, all nero d'Avola, and the winemaking are followed by top consultant Carlo Ferrini. Zisola '04, a monovarietal Nero d'Avola, is excellent, showing powerful and soft with alluring chocolate aromas.

● Nero d'Avola '04	YY	4*

Barone Sergio

via Cavour, 29
96018 Pachino (SR)
tel. 0902927878
www.baronesergio.it

Long-time farmers, the Sergio family set up this winery in 2002. Kalùri '04, a Passito from moscato bianco, is complex, intense and fruity with mineral hints. Petit Verdot Verdò '05 is nicely herbaceousness. Eloro Nero d'Avola Barone Sergio '05 is pleasantly varietal and almost overripe.

○ Kalùri '04	YY	6
● Eloro Nero d'Avola Barone Sergio '05	Y	4
● Verdò '05	Y	4

Rudinì

C.da Camporeale
96018 Pachino (SR)
tel. 0931595333
www.vinirudini.it

This estate, run by Giuseppe Di Pietro, has two highly typical Eloros, with the unmistakeable traits of nero d'Avola from Pachino, including a full, pervasive iodine minerality. Saro '04 comes from old vines and has a touch more finesse. Moscato di Noto Baroque '05 is attractively green.

● Eloro Pachino '03	YY	4
● Eloro Pachino Saro '04	YY	5
○ Moscato di Noto Baroque '05	YY	4

Fatascià

via Mazzini, 40
90139 Palermo
tel. 091332505
www.fatascia.it

Stefania Lena's dense Rosso del Presidente '04, a well-judged cabernet franc and nero d'Avola blend, and her fresh, sweet, floral Ylenia '04, from grillo, traminer and sauvignon blanc, are very fine wines. The nero d'Avola Almanera '04 and Alirè '04 from syrah and nero d'Avola have character.

● Rosso del Presidente '04	YY	5
○ Ylenia '04	YY	6
● Aliré '04	Y	4
● Almanera '04	☐Y	4

Solidea

C.da Kaddiuggia
91017 Pantelleria (TP)
tel. 0923913016
www.solideavini.it

The 2005 vintage was good for Pantelleria and the D'Ancona family. The Passito has an exemplary, clean nose, full of dried fig and apricot, attractive minerality and length. Freshness and immediacy of aroma mark out the Moscato and the dry Zibibbo Ilios.

○ Moscato di Pantelleria '05	YY	5
○ Passito di Pantelleria '05	YY	6
○ Ilios '05	Y	4

Cossentino

via P.pe Umberto, 241
90047 Partinico (PA)
tel. 0918782569
www.cossentino.it

This organic estate is in the Alcamo DOC, inland from the Gulf of Castellammare. Merlot '03 has personality, morello cherry aromas with hints of tobacco and earth, and a warm, softly tannic palate. Syrah '04 has similar minerality but is a touch rustic. Catarratto Gadì '05 is intense and varietal.

● Merlot '03	YY	4*
● Syrah '04	Y	3
○ Gadì Catarratto '05	Y	4

Di Giovanna
c.so Umberto I, 137
92017 Sambuca di Sicilia (AG)
tel. 0925941086 - 3298355523
www.digiovanna-vini.it

Gunther and Klaus di Giovanna's wines come from organic grapes. Overseen by Riccardo Cotarella, they get better each year. Nero d'Avola '05 has a good varietal profile and notable depth. Gerbino Cabernet Sauvignon '04 is equally successful. Chardonnay '05 is good, Grillo '05 well styled.

● Gerbino Cabernet Sauvignon '04	🍷🍷	3*
● Nero d'Avola '05	🍷🍷	4*
○ G e K Grillo '05	🍷	4
○ Gerbino Chardonnay '05	🍷	3

Gaspare Di Prima
via G. Guasto, 27
92017 Sambuca di Sicilia (AG)
tel. 0925941201 - 0925941279
www.diprimavini.it

Syrah Villamaura '03 reached the finals and showed well there with its pervasive notes of balsam, elegance and notable depth. The intense, structured Gibilmoro Nero d'Avola '04 and the pleasant Pepita Rosso '05, from syrah and nero d'Avola, are also up to speed. Gibilmoro Merlot '04 is sound.

● Villamaura Syrah '03	🍷🍷	6
● Gibilmoro Nero d'Avola '04	🍷🍷	4
● Gibilmoro Merlot '04	🍷	4
● Pepita Rosso '05	🍷	4

Feudo Arancio
c.da Portella Misilbesi
92017 Sambuca di Sicilia (AG)
tel. 0925579000
www.feudoarancio.it

In 2001, Mezzacorona arrived on the shores of Lake Arancio to make good-value wine in large quantities. Mission accomplished. The results are great, from the nice, fleshy Merlot, to the fruity, zesty Chardonnay and the floral, dried-grape wine Hekate '04, made from non-specified aromatic grapes.

● Merlot '03	🍷🍷	4*
○ Hekate '04	🍷🍷	5
● Cabernet Sauvignon '03	🍷	4
○ Chardonnay '04	🍷	4

Feudo Zirtari
c.da Portella Misilibesi
92017 Sambuca di Sicilia (AG)
tel. 0421246281
www.feudozirtari.com

This independent estate within the Silene group gave us two superb-value blends: the easy-drinking, pleasantly fruity Feudo Zirtari Rosso '04, from equal parts of nero d'Avola, cabernet sauvignon, merlot and syrah; and the floral, fresh Feudo Zirtari Bianco '05, from grillo, inzolia and chardonnay.

● Feudo Zirtari Rosso '04	🍷	3
○ Feudo Zirtari Bianco '05	🍷	3

Terreliade
loc. Silene
c.da Portella Misilbesi
92017 Sambuca di Sicilia (AG)
tel. 0421246281 - www.terreliade.com

This Santa Margherita-owned winery has come on fast. Nero d'Avola-Syrah (Utti) Majuri '04, with depth and delicate streaks of balsam, reached the finals. Merlot-Nero d'Avola Musía '04 has a nose of finesse and good grip. Grillo Timpa Giadda '05 and Nero d'Avola Nirà '04 also showed well.

● (Utti) Majuri '04	🍷🍷	5
● Musìa '04	🍷🍷	4
● Nirà '04	🍷	4
○ Timpa Giadda '05	🍷	4*

Alto Belice
v.le Enrico Berlinguer, 2
90040 San Cipirello (PA)
tel. 0918573558
www.cantinasocialealtobelice.it

The wines from this co-operative, run by the skilled Nino Inzirillo, again bring reassurance. All those submitted were well made, well styled and clean; and good value, too. The lively, attractive Monreale Catarratto Trerrè '05 is particularly good.

● Monreale Nero d'Avola Trerrè '04	🍷	4
○ Monreale Catarratto Trerrè '05	🍷	4
○ Tre Feudi Catarratto '05	🍷	4
● Tre Feudi Nero d'Avola '05	🍷	4

TENUTA MARIANO
C.DA MARIANO
90100 SAN CIPIRELLO (PA)
TEL. 091324002

It's a great start for the two wines from lawyer Calogero Leone's estate. Rubro di Leone '03, from nero d'Avola, cabernet sauvignon and petit verdot, is elegant, warm and deep, and has intense red berry fruit jam. Rosso di Mariano, a cabernet franc, merlot and petit verdot mix, is intriguing.

●	Rosso di Mariano '03	🍷🍷	5
●	Rubro di Leone '03	🍷🍷	5

FEOTTO DELLO JATO
C.DA FEOTTO
90048 SAN GIUSEPPE JATO (PA)
TEL. 0918572650 - 0918579729
www.feottodellojato.it

An elegant, balsamic Syrah Sirae '04 from this new estate run by Calogero Todaro reached the finals. The solid Merlot Rosso di Turi '03, marked by ripe red fruits, also impressed. Vigna Curria, from perricone, and the nero d'Avola, merlot and syrah Terre di Giulia are fleshy and distinctive.

●	Monreale Sirae '04	🍷🍷	5
●	Monreale Rosso di Turi '03	🍷🍷	5
●	Vigna Curria '03	🍷🍷	6
●	Terre di Giulia '04	🍷	5

BAGLIO DI PIANETTO
VIA FRANCIA
90030 SANTA CRISTINA GELA (PA)
TEL. 0918570002
www.bagliodipianetto.com

Paolo Marzotto's Sicilian estate did well. Chianu Carduni '04, from petit verdot, is a solid wine with nice balsamic notes. The spicy, elegantly tannic Shymer '04 is from syrah and merlot and the inzolia and viognier Ficiligno '05 is equally admirable. The new Moscato di Noto Ra'is '05 beguiles.

●	Chianu Carduni '04	🍷🍷	7
●	Shymer '04	🍷🍷	4*
○	Ficiligno '05	🍷🍷	4*
○	Ra'is '05	🍷🍷	5

FERRERI
C.DA SALINELLA
91029 SANTA NINFA (TP)
TEL. 092461871 - 3473205627
www.ferrerivini.it

There are 50 hectares of vineyard here, stretching between Gibellina and Santa Ninfa, one of the most beautiful parts of Belice. The top wine this year is Cabernet Sauvignon Karren '04, which is ripe, sunny and has a distinctive character. Catarratto '05 is attractive.

●	Karren '04	🍷🍷	5
●	Al Merat '04	🍷	5
●	Brasi '04	🍷	5
○	Catarratto '05	🍷	4

EMANUELE SCAMMACCA DEL MURGO
VIA ZAFFERANA, 13
95010 SANTA VENERINA (CT)
TEL. 095950520
www.murgo.it

Cabernet Sauvignon Tenuta San Michele '03 is classy, with a ripe, mineral, balsamic nose and good structure. The fresh, exuberant nerello mascalese Murgo Extra Brut '00 reflects the volcanic terrain, as does the ripe Chardonnay Arbiato '03 with its elegant citrus. Etna Rosso '04 is sound.

○	Arbiato '03	🍷🍷	4
●	Tenuta San Michele '03	🍷🍷	4
○	Murgo Extra Brut '00	🍷	4
●	Etna Rosso '04	🍷	3*

AZIENDE VINICOLE MICELI
C.DA PIANA SCUNCHIPANI, 190
92019 SCIACCA (AG)
TEL. 092580188 - 0916759411
www.miceli.net

The most interesting of the numerous wines submitted is the new Merlot Nia Maro '04, which is powerful, complex and elegant. Ymm '05, a dry Zibibbo, is concentrated, aromatic and long. Nero d'Avola 'U Nicu and Salgalaluna, from grillo, are both '05s and both showed well.

●	Nia Maro '04	🍷🍷	5
○	Moscato di Pantelleria Yrnm '05	🍷🍷	5
○	Salgalaluna Bianco '05	🍷	4
●	'U Nicu '05	🍷	4

PUPILLO
C.DA LA TARGIA
96100 SIRACUSA
TEL. 0931494029 - 3395700843
www.solacium.it

Nino Pupillo has re-established the once forgotten Moscato di Siracusa. Solacium '05 is first-rate, showing fresh and sweet with elegant yellow-fleshed fruit and aromatic herbs. Cyane '05, a dry Moscato, is intriguing. Nero d'Avola Re Federico '05 and Moscato di Siracusa Pollio '05 are well styled.

○ Cyane '05	🍷🍷	4
○ Moscato di Siracusa Solacium '05	🍷🍷	6
○ Moscato di Siracusa Pollio '05	🍷	6
● Re Federico '05	🍷	4

CAPO CROCE - VINI GANCIA
C.DA CASTELLAZZO
91027 TRAPANI
TEL. 03489999382
www.gancia.it

Addumari '04, shaped by oenologist Beppe Caviola and agronomist Federico Curtaz, is a gem, a superb, elegant cabernet sauvignon and syrah mix which almost won Three Glasses. Pulpito '04 is a fine, dense, varietal Nero d'Avola. Nero d'Avola Nartece '05 and Grillo Pulvino '05 are both very good.

● Addumari '04	🍷🍷	5
● Pulpito '04	🍷🍷	5
● Nartece '05	🍷	4
○ Pulvino '05	🍷	4

FONDO ANTICO
FRAZ. RILIEVO - VIA FIORAME, 54A
91020 TRAPANI
TEL. 0923864339 - 0923865151
www.fondoantico.it

The wines submitted were classy and good value. Grillo Parlante '05, from grillo, is fresh and fruity with underlying aromatic herbs. Canto '04, from nero d'Avola and cabernet, Coro '05, from grillo and chardonnay, and Boccadoro '05, a grillo-based, late-harvest wine are all good.

○ Baccadoro '05	🍷🍷	4
○ Grillo Parlante '05	🍷🍷	4*
● Il Canto di Fondo Antico '04	🍷	5
○ Il Coro '05	🍷	4

VINI BIONDI
C.SO SICILIA, 20
95039 TRECASTAGNI (CT)
TEL. 3928191538
www.vinibiondi.it

We are on Etna's eastern flank. At 550 metres are the nerello mascalese and nerello cappuccio used for the minerally, elegant Outis '03 while at 700 metres are the carricante, minnella and other local grapes used in Gurna '05, which has fruit of crystalline finesse, minerality and fabulous acidity.

● Outis '03	🍷🍷	5
○ Gurna Bianco '05	🍷🍷	4

TENUTA DI SERRAMARROCCO
LOC. FONTANELLE - C.DA OSPEDALETTO
91100 VALDERICE (TP)
TEL. 063220973 - 3487308270
www.serramarrocco.com

Massimiliano and Marco Marrocco Trischitta, cardiologist and multinational executive respectively, can be well pleased with the wines of their family estate. Serramarrocco '04, a Bordeaux blend, has captivating elegance. The two Nero d'Avolas are both excellent. Grillo '05 is fresh and zesty.

● Serramarrocco '04	🍷🍷	6
● Nero di Serramarrocco '04	🍷🍷	5
● Baglio di Serramarrocco '05	🍷	3
○ Grillo del Barone '05	🍷	3

CASTELLUCCI MIANO
VIA SICILIA, 1
90029 VALLEDOLMO (PA)
TEL. 0921542385

This co-operative, overseen by oenologist Tonino Guzzo, is fully equipped to modern standards and its carefully tended vineyards reach 900 metres. From this height cómes the excellent catarratto used exclusively in the fruity, attractively mineral Shiarà '05. The other wines are good, too.

○ Catarratto Inzolia '05	🍷🍷	3*
● Nero d'Avola '04	🍷	3
○ Shiarà '05	🍷	3

SARDINIA

The main news from Sardinia this year is the emergence of many new estates, most small or medium-sized. The number in the Guide has also grown to 58 compared with 15 in the first edition. The larger ones often set out with an awareness of market situations and lay down a clear, quality-led development plan from square one. The smaller ones are sometimes simply content to see their name on a bottle and go ahead, unaware of the risks lying in wait for those who lack winemaking or commercial nous. The other aspect of note, which isn't really news, is the continued success of the island's reds. We tasted many truly excellent wines, from north to south, most based on cannonau or carignano, or various blends of indigenous varieties. Let's start with the enfant terrible of Sardinian winemaking, Alessandro Dettori, who picked up his first Three Glasses, for Cannonau Tenores '03. Three Glasses also deservedly went to Sella & Mosca's fabulous Cabernet, Marchese di Villamarina '01, and to Argiolas' Turriga '02, bringing Argiolas' Three Glass total to 12. It then gives us huge satisfaction to announce top honours for Terras, made from nieddera, sangiovese and carignano by Josto Puddu, a Vernaccia producer of long-standing renown. There are also many runners-up to these top wines; some are well-known names, others less so. Leading the newcomers here are Mesa, a Sulcis estate producing excellent reds, and Olbios, concentrating on classic Vermentino di Gallura. Most of the best whites still come from Gallura and the list is topped by Genesi '05, from Cantina Gallura in Tempio, which very nearly clinched Three Glasses. Dessert wines aside, only one other white reached the finals, Alba Nora '04 from Feudi della Medusa. But the Ragnedda brothers' Capichera wines weren't in the running as they had decided to leave them to age a further year. We support this sensible move as we have long said that many whites improve after an extra year's ageing, especially those from Gallura. The market, though, often imposes other rules – to the detriment of the wines. Nevertheless, most of the '05 Vermentino di Sardegnas put on a good showing, especially Cherchi's Tuvaoes and Pala's Stellato. We also had a great series of IGT wines to taste, most notably Alba Nora '04 from Feudi della Medusa, Entemari '05 from Pala and Montesicci '05 from Cantine di Dolianova. Then came large numbers of very sound wines in the medium-low price band, leading us to conclude that wineries are becoming more adept at providing the consumer with wines they can trust while still balancing the books. There are even improvements on the dessert wine front: Fratelli Porcu's Malvasia di Bosa '02, Soletta's Dolce Valle '03, Contini's Vernaccia di Oristano Riserva '87 and Feudi della Medusa's Aristeo '04 all joined Argiolas' '03 Angialis on the Three Glass threshold.

ALGHERO (SS)

CANTINA SOCIALE SANTA MARIA LA PALMA

LOC. SANTA MARIA LA PALMA
07041 ALGHERO (SS)
TEL. 079999008 - 079999044
www.santamarialapalma.it

For some years now, there has been a quality plan in action here for vineyard selections, harvesting decisions and reductions in yields. Reception facilities in the cellar have been expanded, equipment is being modernized and there will soon be a new barrel storage area. This has all required huge investment but should lead to more consistently high quality, at least we hope so. There are currently four production lines, ranging from the sparkling wines to the crus. The range of varieties has been increased, with chardonnay, sauvignon, cabernet, monica, cagnulari and carignano now planted alongside the cannonau, vermentino and sangiovese. Our tastings revealed improvements in the reds and a stable situation with the whites. Vermentino di Sardegna Blu '05 is a new wine that has made a promising start. It's fresh, uncomplicated, easy-drinking and aimed at younger drinkers who like wines that are simple but not frivolous. Vermentino I Papiri '05 is also attractive, with vegetal notes and a fresh, savoury palate. Cannonau di Sardegna Le Bombarde stands out among the reds as usual. The '05 is balanced, harmonious and excellent value for money. Cagnulari '04 is enjoyable for its fruit, softness and good nose-palate harmony. But Cannonau Riserva '02 steps up the pace, with fine structure and blackberry jam fruitiness. The new Monica di Sardegna '05 is a pleasant wine with delicate aromas and good harmony on the palate.

●	Cannonau di Sardegna Ris. '02	🍷🍷	5
●	Alghero Cagnulari '04	🍷🍷	5
●	Cannonau di Sardegna Le Bombarde '05	🍷	4*
●	Monica di Sardegna '05	🍷	3*
○	Vermentino di Sardegna Blu '05	🍷	3
○	Vermentino di Sardegna I Papiri '05	🍷	4
●	Cannonau di Sardegna '01	🍸🍸	4
○	Vermentino di Sardegna Palmador '01	🍸🍸	5
●	Alghero Cagnulari '03	🍸🍸	5

ALGHERO (SS)

TENUTE SELLA & MOSCA

LOC. I PIANI
07041 ALGHERO (SS)
TEL. 079997700
www.sellaemosca.com

Let's go straight to Marchese di Villamarina, the winery's flagship, which this year again won Three Glasses. It's made solely from cabernet sauvignon and has two years in wood, one in barrique and one in large old botti, followed by at least another two years in bottle. This ageing period depends mainly on the characteristics of the year and is kept under close observation. This year's '01 is drinking well now but has clear potential for further improvement. The nose reflects the characteristics of the variety, with vegetal notes and ripe fruit. The palate is dense and full, and is tending towards softness despite still rather dominant tannin, and the finish is long and clean. Tanca Farrà '02, from cabernet sauvignon and cannonau, is another fine red. It underwent a similar two-stage oak-ageing process but for shorter periods. Terre Rare '02, Carignano del Sulcis, is impressive but not as impressive as last year's. There's good structure, a touch of overripeness and a slightly bitter finish. Rosato Oleandro '05, from cabernets franc and sauvignon, is attractively fruity. Moving on to the whites, Vermentino di Gallura Monteoro '05 has a nose of ripe fruit with touches of almond blossom, and a pleasantly savoury palate. There is a fresh, delicate nose on Terre Bianche '05, from torbato, but it has more to offer on the palate. Even so, we feel that its real character will emerge after another year in bottle.

●	Alghero Marchese di Villamarina '01	🍷🍷🍷	7
●	Alghero Tanca Farrà '02	🍷🍷	5
●	Carignano del Sulcis Terre Rare '02	🍷🍷	4
○	Vermentino di Gallura Sup. Monteoro '05	🍷🍷	5
⊙	Alghero Oleandro '05	🍷	4
○	Alghero Torbato Terre Bianche '05	🍷	4
●	Alghero Marchese di Villamarina '00	🍸🍸🍸	7
●	Alghero Marchese di Villamarina '95	🍸🍸🍸	7
●	Alghero Marchese di Villamarina '97	🍸🍸🍸	6
●	Alghero Marchese di Villamarina '99	🍸🍸🍸	6

BERCHIDDA (OT)

Cantina del Giogantinu
via Milano, 30
07022 Berchidda (OT)
tel. 079704163 - 079704938
www.giogantinu.it

There are signs of improved consistency here. We have often stressed the winery's potential, feeling that it hasn't always been fully exploited, and we appreciate the efforts that are being taken to retain competitiveness on major markets. We are also aware that greater attention is being paid to details and quality levels have generally increased, especially with the vermentino-based whites. Vermentino di Gallura Lughente '05 is excellent. The nose is fruity and has almondy notes while the palate has good structure and a pleasing savoury freshness. The vines for Vermentino di Gallura Superiore Karenzia Vigne Storiche '05 are mostly bush trained and the nose has complexity over and above the classic almondy note, while there is fullness accentuated by softness on the palate. The Vermentino di Sardegna Superiore, the most traditional of the range, again showed very well, the '05 offering a nose full of fruit and softness in the mouth. The most interesting of the reds was Terra Mala Vigne Storiche '03, from carignano and muristellu. The nose is still closed but scents of Mediterranean scrubland, most notably ripe arbutus berries, come through and the palate is also evolving. Tannin and acidity still dominate but the structure is good. Terra Saliosa '05, from cabernet, merlot and muristellu, is simpler and more immediate, with a vegetal nose and good harmony on the palate. Finally comes Lughente Vendemmia Tardiva '03, which has aromas of hay and dried fruit, and a sweet, lively palate which finishes very long.

○	Lughente V. T. '03	**YY**	5
●	Terra Mala Vigne Storiche '03	**YY**	6
○	Vermentino di Gallura Lughente '05	**YY**	4*
○	Vermentino di Gallura Sup. '05	**YY**	3*
○	Vermentino di Gallura Sup. Karenzia Vigne Storiche '05	**YY**	5
●	Terra Saliosa '05	**Y**	4
●	Terra Saliosa '04	YY	4*
○	Vermentino di Gallura Sup. '04	YY	3*

CABRAS (OR)

Attilio Contini
via Genova, 48/50
09072 Cabras (OR)
tel. 0783290806
www.vinicontini.it

Paolo Contini has moved things along well in the past few years, helped by his offspring who are now dedicating more time to the winery. High quality remains the aim and there is no lack of enthusiasm. The Continis have increased their range but they haven't forgotten provenance. Although Vernaccia di Oristano was the wine that for a century was the winery's hallmark, more emphasis is now being placed on other indigenous varieties that previously had a minor role, such as nieddera and caddiu. And it was Nieddera '04 that not just topped the range this year but also turned out to be one of the island's best wines, very nearly winning Three Glasses. It is not simply the broad array of aromas on the lively, youthful nose that amazes, but the wine's structure, which gives the palate fullness and balance despite its still-evolving acidity and tannin. Barrile '03 is another fine red, also from nieddera but with some caddiu, and aged in barrique for about a year. There is notable breadth on the ripe blackberry and plum nose then the palate is soft and finishes long. Vernaccia di Oristano Riserva '87 is a remarkable wine, 15 years in oak having given it an amber hue, an almondy nose with notes of coffee, and a warm, soft palate that goes on for ever. The '03 release of Pontis, a warm, soft, nuts-and-honey Vernaccia with some residual sugar, is not as good as last year's but still a great little wine. Cannonau di Sardegna Inu Riserva '03 is very nice. Karmis '05, based on vernaccia, and Vermentino di Sardegna '05 are both attractive.

●	Nieddera Rosso '04	**YY**	4*
●	Barrile '03	**YY**	7
●	Cannonau di Sardegna Inu Ris. '03	**YY**	5
○	Pontis '03	**YY**	5
○	Vernaccia di Oristano Ris. '87	**YY**	6
○	Karmis '05	**Y**	4
○	Pontis '00	YYY	5
○	Vernaccia di Oristano Antico Gregori	YY	7
●	Cannonau di Sardegna Inu Ris. '01	YY	5
●	Nieddera Rosso '03	YY	4*
○	Vernaccia di Oristano Ris. '85	YY	6

CARDEDU (NU)

ALBERTO LOI
S.S. 125, KM. 124,2
08040 CARDEDU (NU)
TEL. 070240866 - 078275807
www.cantina.it/albertoloi

Cannonau was once considered one of the varieties least suitable for high-quality wines. But to harness its potential, all that was needed was to look at producers like Alberto Loi, who take great care in selection, in aspect, in yield and in not skimping maceration times. Alberto's estate has now passed to his children, who have smartened up the cellar and renewed its equipment. They've also increased the area under vine, adding small quantities of other varieties, both indigenous and international. Nevertheless, cannonau remains their greatest point of strength and with small amounts of muristellu, carignano and cabernet sauvignon, it shapes Loi Corona '02, which ages for around 20 months in barrique and a further 12 in bottle. It is full and pervasive on the nose with aromas of morello cherry and blackberry jam. These sensations are echoed on the ripely fruited palate which is warm and soft, tending to roundness, and has good length. Tuvara '02 comes entirely from indigenous grapes, cannonau, muristellu and carignano. It too impressed as a close-knit wine of character with richness and ripe fruit. The attraction of Astangia '03, from cannonau, muristellu, carignano and bovale, is the way it successfully retains zest and youthful vinosity alongside notable body and structure. Cannonau di Sardegna Alberto Loi Riserva '02, Cardedo Riserva '03 and Sa Mola '04 are all up to their usual standards. The unusual white Leila '04 from cannonau – a red grape – and some local white varieties is another successful wine.

● Cannonau di Sardegna Jerzu Alberto Loi Ris. '02	🍷🍷	5
● Loi Corona '02	🍷🍷	6
● Tuvara '02	🍷🍷	6
● Astangia '03	🍷🍷	5
● Cannonau di Sardegna Jerzu Cardedo Ris. '03	🍷	4
● Cannonau di Sardegna Jerzu Sa Mola '04	🍷	4*
○ Leila '04	🍷	5
● Tuvara '01	🍷🍷 (white)	6
● Tuvara '98	🍷🍷 (white)	6
● Cannonau di Sardegna Jerzu Alberto Loi Ris. '01	🍷🍷 (white)	5
● Loi Corona '01	🍷🍷 (white)	6
● Astangia '99	🍷🍷 (white)	4

CODRONGIANOS (SS)

TENUTE SOLETTA
LOC. SIGNOR'ANNA
07040 CODRONGIANOS (SS)
TEL. 079435067
www.tenutesoletta.it

The Soletta siblings are true to their belief that viticulture is one of Sardinia's primary resources. The success that they are obtaining, on the island and beyond, is thoroughly deserved for the quality of their wines continues to rise and the new products emerging are not simply there to spice up their list. They emphasize the strong ties Tenute Soletta wines have with their provenance. The estate concentrates mainly on vermentino and cannonau but also grows small quantities of cabernet sauvignon, chardonnay, incrocio Manzoni and tocai. The newest wine, Kianos '04, is from 40 per cent vermentino with pinot bianco and riesling renano, and is barrique aged, giving it a more international feel. It's highly appealing, especially on the nose, despite oak still dominating the ripe fruit. Oak is also still rather marked on the slightly bitterish finish but the palate is otherwise full and fleshy. Vermentino di Sardegna Prestizu '05 is a touch low-key but still attractive, and clean, uncomplicated and fresh on both nose and palate. Turning to the reds, Cannonau di Sardegna Riserva '03 has ripe fruit, most notably black cherry. The fruit also comes through on the balanced, still-youthful palate. The rosé Petalo '05 is lively and attractive. But the best wine is still Dolce Valle and the '03 again came close to Three Glasses. Made solely from moscato grapes left to dry on the vine and on rush matting, it has a richly fruity nose, full of apricot, with some balsamic hints. The palate is soft, sweet and finely balanced, it also has great body and an attractive long finish.

○ Dolce Valle Moscato Passito '03	🍷🍷	4*
● Cannonau di Sardegna Ris. '03	🍷🍷	4
○ Kianos '04	🍷🍷	5
⊙ Petalo Rosato '05	🍷	3
○ Vermentino di Sardegna Prestizu '05	🍷	4
● Cannonau di Sardegna Firmadu '00	🍷🍷 (white)	3*
○ Dolce Valle Moscato Passito '01	🍷🍷 (white)	4
● Cannonau di Sardegna Firmadu '02	🍷🍷 (white)	4*
○ Dolce Valle Moscato Passito '02	🍷🍷 (white)	4
● Cannonau di Sardegna Firmadu '03	🍷🍷 (white)	4*
○ Vermentino di Sardegna Barriques '03	🍷🍷 (white)	4
○ Vermentino di Sardegna Prestizu '04	🍷🍷 (white)	4*

DOLIANOVA (CA)

CANTINE DOLIANOVA
LOC. SAN'ESU
S.S. 387, KM. 17,150
09041 DOLIANOVA (CA)
TEL. 070744101 - 07074410226
www.cantinedolianova.com

The experience gained over the last decade by technical and administrative personnel has brought Dolianova success on markets worldwide. It was not unrealistic to take a quality-led direction here, because the lands easily yield wines of good typicity at low cost, and this has been the estate's winning formula. Annual production is around 4,000,000 bottles, mostly from indigenous varieties, although there are a few hectares of international varieties, used in small proportions in some of the wines. This year, we really liked Terresicci '03, from 85 per cent barbera sarda with syrah and montepulciano. Ripe red fruits dominate the nose and then the palate starts softly before rounding out and finishing long. Montesicci '05, from 75 per cent vermentino with malvasia and nasco, is another fine wine with finesse and elegance on the nose, and an attractive roundness to the palate. Blasio '03 is a Cannonau di Sardegna Riserva that displays the typical characteristics of the variety and has a full, pervasive nose followed by a palate that balances notable acidity and tannin with softness. The '05 Monica di Sardegna Arenada is as good as ever. It's youthful and lively on both nose and palate, and finishes clean. The whites, Nuragus di Cagliari Perlas '05, Vermentino di Sardegna Prendas '05 and Vermentino di Sardegna Naèli '05, are all attractive but especially the last of the three, which has greater structure and is full of fruit and vegetal hints. Finally comes a good rosé, Sibiola '05, from cannonau, sangiovese and montepulciano.

●	Cannonau di Sardegna Blasio Ris. '03	🍷🍷	4
●	Terresicci '03	🍷🍷	6
●	Monica di Sardegna Arenada '05	🍷🍷	3*
○	Montesicci '05	🍷🍷	4
○	Nuragus di Cagliari Perlas '05	🍷	3*
⊙	Sibiola Rosato '05	🍷	3*
○	Vermentino di Sardegna Naèli '05	🍷	4
○	Vermentino di Sardegna Prendas '05	🍷	3
●	Cannonau di Sardegna Blasio Ris. '00	ϒϒ	4
●	Falconaro '03	ϒϒ	5
○	Montesicci '04	ϒϒ	4

JERZU (NU)

ANTICHI PODERI JERZU
VIA UMBERTO I, 1
08044 JERZU (NU)
TEL. 078270028 - 078270557
www.jerzuantichipoderi.it

Ogliastra is one of the best and most attractive areas for cannonau production, and offers considerable variation in aspect, altitude and microclimate. In fact, for some years now work has been going on to identify sites that will be able to reinforce the character of the area's wines. The winery has also been investing in renovating its winemaking and administrative areas, and its facilities for guests. This work is essential to its smooth running, especially considering its hefty output of over 2,000,000 bottles a year. The range continues to grow and now includes a few well-made whites, most notably Vermentino di Sardegna Lucean Le Stelle. The '05 has an intense nose, with broom-like florality and a clean, soft palate. Radames '00 is a cannonau, cabernet and carignano blend aged in oak for a year. Its nose is still lively and herbaceous, with Mediterranean scrubland and sweet oakiness. There is more liveliness on the palate, together with soft tannin and a long, pleasant finish. Cannonau di Sardegna Marghìa '04 is an attractive wine that has still to come round. Its pleasing aromas of blackberries and jam usher in overt but not excessive acidity and tannin. Akratos '03, made mostly from cannonau grapes allowed to dry out on the vine, has good concentration on the nose, with prune jam followed by blackberry and morello cherry. The palate is sweet but not cloying, soft and enticing, and has a long, velvety finish.

●	Radames '00	🍷🍷	6
●	Akratos '03	🍷🍷	5
●	Cannonau di Sardegna Marghìa '04	🍷🍷	4
○	Vermentino di Sardegna Lucean Le Stelle '05	🍷	5
●	Cannonau di Sardegna Josto Miglior Ris. '01	ϒϒ	5
●	Cannonau di Sardegna Ris. Chuerra '01	ϒϒ	5

NUORO

Giuseppe Gabbas

via Trieste, 65
08100 Nuoro
tel. 078433745

Cannonau is the love of Giuseppe Gabbas' life. He has almost 20 hectares of vines in a fine area straddling Oliena and Orgosolo, where he's built a new cellar. He's planted some cabernet, merlot, sangiovese and syrah too, for use solely in blends. He makes the type of wines that he likes himself, although they also appeal to a broad band of consumers, the sort who want to be able to enjoy a bottle of wine without having to wait years for it to come round. Now that the new cellar is operational, it is more feasible to undertake the research that Gabbas has been keen to carry out, primarily on cannonau, in its ideal habitat around here. A considerable part of the character of the wines comes from the high-altitude vineyards and strong day-night temperature swings. When you add the consummate professionalism of the entire team here, high quality is practically guaranteed. A perfect example is Cannonau di Sardegna Lillové '05, which is youthful with cherry fruitiness on both nose and palate, and leaves the mouth fresh and clean. Cannonau di Sardegna Dule Riserva '03 is a touch low-key. The nose is full of Mediterranean scrubland and chocolate, and the palate is harmonious and balanced, but the structure is a little slim. Finally comes Arbeskia, from cannonau and cabernet aged almost two years in barrique, which again reached the finals, this year with the '03. Balsamic and mineral notes dominate the broad, complex nose and the palate has good acidity and a long, savoury finish.

●	Arbeskia '03	▼▼	5
●	Cannonau di Sardegna Lillové '05	▼▼	4*
●	Cannonau di Sardegna Dule Ris. '03	▼	4
●	Arbeskia '00	▽▽	5
●	Cannonau di Sardegna Dule Ris. '01	▽▽	4*
●	Arbeskia '02	▽▽	5
●	Arbeskia '01	▽▽	5
●	Avra '01	▽▽	4
●	Dule '01	▽▽	4
●	Cannonau di Sardegna Dule Ris. '02	▽▽	4*
●	Cannonau di Sardegna Lillové '02	▽▽	4
●	Cannonau di Sardegna Lillové '03	▽▽	4*
●	Cannonau di Sardegna Lillovè '98	▽▽	3

OLBIA

Piero Mancini

loc. Cala Saccaia
07026 Olbia
tel. 078950717
www.pieromancini.it

There have been no great developments here since last year, so let's spend a moment simply reporting quantities, which require no comment. There are 800 hectares of vineyard spread across the Gallura and annual production reaches 1,500,000 bottles with sales rising worldwide. There are no particular secrets to the winery's success, either. It has simply concentrated on classic regional wine styles and kept its prices fair. There's no real stunner yet, the sort of wine that drags everything along in its wake, as can be found at many other Italian estates, but there's no lack of potential so maybe it's only a matter of time. In general, the wines performed well across the board, with fewer ups and downs than previously. Wine types were also clearly identifiable. These are all good signs. Although still young, Antiche Cussorgie '04, from cabernet, cannonau and merlot, was impressive, displaying a wide array of aromas that range from vinous to vegetal and from red berry fruits to balsam. Hints of balsam also come through on the rich, full, long palate. The other top reds are the harmonious, balanced Cannonau di Sardegna, and Saccaia, from cabernet sauvignon and cannonau, which is also excellent value for money. Standing out among the whites is the fresh, aromatic Vermentino di Gallura Saraìna '05, which has a pleasantly savoury palate and an almondy finish. Vermentino di Gallura Cuccaione '05, the simpler, more immediate Vermentino di Sardegna '05 and the rosé Montepino '05 are all good.

●	Antiche Cussorgie '04	▼▼	6
●	Cannonau di Sardegna '04	▼▼	4*
○	Vermentino di Gallura Saraina '05	▼▼	5
⊙	Montepino '05	▼	4
○	Vermentino di Gallura '05	▼	4
○	Vermentino di Gallura Cucaione '05	▼	4
●	Saccaia	▼	4*
●	Saccaia '00	▽▽	3*
●	Saccaia '01	▽▽	3*
●	Saccaia '02	▽▽	3*
●	Antiche Cussorgie '03	▽▽	6
○	Vermentino di Gallura Saraina '04	▽▽	5

OLBIA

MASONE MANNU
C.SO UMBERTO, 46
07026 OLBIA
TEL. 0789846002

We often recall Michele Ghirra, who passed away prematurely, and with pleasure because it was he who was behind this new estate just outside Olbia. The partners shared his passion and are applying the same enthusiasm to carrying the estate forward. Piero Cella, who worked for many years with Giacomo Tachis, is consultant oenologist. It goes without saying that it is the vine that makes the wine but here the viticultural side is followed particularly closely to ensure that healthy grapes with the right degree of ripeness arrive in the cellar, thereby making Piero's life easier. Our highest score this year went to Ammentu '04, a sweet wine from vermentino and malvasia with damson jam on the nose and enough sweetness on the palate to emphasize the slight lack of acidity and backbone. Mannu '04 is a barrique-aged blend of cannonau, carignano and muristellu which is still young but has good ageing potential. Morello cherry, plum and mineral notes mark out the nose and the palate is full-bodied and rounded but the finish is a little disappointing. The other red, Entu '05, from carignano, cannonau and syrah, has notable breadth of aromas, which range from jam to sweet vanilla and ripe red fruits. The palate has softness, attenuating its tannin and acidity, and finishes long. The whites were generally impressive, especially Costarenas '05, based on vermentino with some malvasia. The nose is fruity with hints of perfume and the palate is soft and warm. Vermentino Petrizza '05 is simple but not simplistic: a nice fresh, harmonious wine with elegant aromas and a clean finish.

○ Ammentu '04	🍷🍷	5
● Mannu '04	🍷🍷	7
○ Costarenas '05	🍷🍷	5
● Entu '05	🍷🍷	4
○ Vermentino di Sardegna Petrizza '05	🍷🍷	4
● Entu '04	YY	4
○ Costarenas '03	YY	5
● Mannu '03	YY	5
○ Costarenas '04	YY	5
○ Vermentino di Sardegna Petrizza '04	YY	4

OLBIA

PEDRES
Z.I. SETTORE 7
07026 OLBIA
TEL. 0789595075
www.cantinapedres.it

This Gallura estate, nestling in the Monti and Calangianus hills, has around 40 hectares of vines planted on sandy and granitic soils. Vermentino takes the lion's share, followed by moscato, and there are smaller amounts of cannonau and several international grapes. The range grows each year and production currently stands at 300,000 bottles. The year's top wine for us was Moscato di Sardegna Spumante Dolce. There is good peachy fruit and sage on the nose. The palate is elegant, harmonious and delicately sweet, acidity bringing good balance. Most noteworthy of the new wines is Muros '03, from 80 per cent cabernet sauvignon with merlot and syrah. It has a broad array of aromas, with alternating sensations of liquorice, tobacco and coffee. The palate is highly concentrated but has a roundness that attenuates the tannins and lends drinkability. Maranto '02, from a 50-25-25 blend of sangiovese, cabernet and syrah, is well styled and fruity but a touch over-evolved. The whites seemed a little subdued compared with last year although Vermentino di Gallura Plebi '05 almost gained Two Glasses for its delicately fruity nose and soft, attractive palate. In comparison, Vermentino Thilibas '05 is far more acidic and therefore stalkier. Greater pleasure comes from the intense nose. Vermentino di Gallura Jaldinu '05 is more straightforward and has better balance. Lu Gadduresu, a brut sparkler from vermentino, is also good.

● Muros '03	🍷🍷	4
○ Moscato di Sardegna '05	🍷🍷	5
● Maranto '02	🍷	4
○ Vermentino di Gallura Jaldinu '05	🍷	4*
○ Vermentino di Gallura Plebi '05	🍷	4
○ Vermentino di Gallura Sup. Thilibas '05	🍷	4
○ Lu Gadduresu Spumante Brut	🍷	4
○ Moscato di Sardegna '04	YY	4
○ Vermentino di Gallura Sup. Thilibas '04	YY	4

PULA (CA)

FEUDI DELLA MEDUSA
LOC. SANTA MARGHERITA
P.RE SAN LEONARDO,15
09010 PULA (CA)
TEL. 0709259019 - 0636006182
www.feudidellamedusa.it

This estate has only been producing for two years yet had three wines in the finals. Grapes come both from the estate's 40 hectares or so of vineyard and from various other parts of the island. For instance, the monovarietal Cannonau di Sardegna '04 comes from grapes grown at Jerzu and has ripe fruit, freshness and vivacity throughout. But the wine that gave us greatest satisfaction was Biddas Arrubias '04, a fine red from low-yielding cannonau, bovale and cagnulari that sees no oak. It has a rich, intense nose full of ripe red berry fruit and the palate is a touch less complex but has elegance, softness and balance, with well-meshed tannins. There are a further two reds of interest, both still young and needing time to come round. Norace '04, from bovale, cannonau and syrah, is rich and tobacco-like on the nose, and has notable structure while Cagnulari '05, from bush-trained vines, is a vegetal, slightly rustic wine but one that has lots of personality and a lively, still-tannic palate. Alba Nora '04 leads the whites. It's a monovarietal Chardonnay, aged nine months in barrique, and has a nice touch of oakiness on its broad, intense nose. The palate is well-defined, fresh, tangy and long. The trio of finalists is completed by Aristeo '04, a dessert wine from malvasia and nasco. This has marked aromas of Mediterranean scrubland, especially helichrysum, followed by candied citrus peel and jam. The palate is warm and soft with a long-lasting velvetiness. The rosé Bithia '04 and the whites Sa Perda Bianca '04 and Vermentino di Sardegna '05 are all nice.

○	Alba Nora '04	▼▼	6
○	Aristeo '04	▼▼	6
●	Biddas Arubbias '04	▼▼	4*
●	Cannonau di Sardegna '04	▼▼	5
●	Cagnulari '05	▼▼	7
⊙	Bithia '04	▼	4
●	Norace '04	▼	8
○	Sa Perda Bianca '04	▼	5
○	Vermentino di Sardegna '05	▼	5
●	Gerione '03	▽▽	8
●	Norace '03	▽▽	8
○	Alba Nora '03	▽▽	6
●	Biddas Arubbias '03	▽▽	5
○	Sa Perda Bianca '03	▽▽	6
●	Cagnulari '04	▽▽	7

SAN VERO MILIS (OR)

JOSTO PUDDU
VIA SAN LUSSORIO, 1
09070 SAN VERO MILIS (OR)
TEL. 078353329
www.cantinapuddu.it

Josto Puddu is a wine man through and through. He grew up surrounded by the aromas of Vernaccia di Oristano and that is the wine that brought him his greatest rewards. Until, that is, unscrupulous merchants came along, creating problems for more honest producers and ruining sales of one of the world's most individual wines. But Puddu wouldn't let himself be beaten. He kept on producing and, like many others, diversified his range. He now owns 30 hectares of vines and leases a further 12, giving him an annual production of 300,000 bottles, mostly white. The range is large – maybe even too large – and not all of the wines are strictly territory-based but sometimes you need to follow market demands to keep afloat. Josto now benefits from having his children Rita and Alberto at his side. They share his tenacity and passion for both know full well that making and selling wine involves sacrifice. Their efforts this year have been rewarded by Three Glasses, which went to Terras '04, a wine made mostly from nieddera, with 20 per cent of carignano and small amounts of bovale and sangiovese, and aged one year in barrique and three months in bottle. The nose has intense, elegant aromas of ripe fruit and tempting touches of vanilla that take you into a palate that is full, warm, fragrant and attractively long. The classic Vernaccia di Oristano Riserva '99, a long wine, has pervasive dried fruit and toasted hazelnuts while the Vermentino di Sardegna Maris '05 is bright and lively. Both are very fine.

●	Terras Rosso '04	▼▼▼	6
○	Vermentino di Sardegna Maris '05	▼▼	4*
○	Vernaccia di Oristano Ris. '99	▼▼	4*
●	Terras Rosso '01	▽▽	6
●	Terras Rosso '02	▽▽	6
○	Vernaccia di Oristano '80	▽▽	6
○	Vernaccia di Oristano '98	▽▽	4*

SANTADI (CI)

CANTINA SOCIALE DI SANTADI
VIA CAGLIARI, 78
09010 SANTADI (CI)
TEL. 0781950127 - 0781953007
www.cantinadisantadi.it

This is the winery that deserves the credit for rediscovering and the ancient carignano variety and introducing it to a wider public. The variety has now inspired great interest among other producers, some of them from outside Sardinia, who continue to buy vineyards and build cellars in the district. This has brought great benefits to the entire Sulcis area, both financially and in terms of image. The wines from the Santadi co-operative have now achieved high levels of quality and can be found on all the world's most important markets. The '02 Carignano del Sulcis Superiore Terre Brune was not as good as previous vintages but still has terrific structure. It also needs more bottle age for it is still a bit vegetal, oak dominating both nose and palate, and the acidity and tannin are fairly pronounced. Araja '04, from bush-trained carignano and sangiovese, doesn't see any oak and is a great little wine with lovely blackberry and cherry jam fruit on the nose followed by a warm, elegant palate of great structure and length. Monica di Sardegna Antigua '05 also stands out and is one of the best examples of the wine we tasted this year. Its vegetal nose is followed by a well-balanced palate backed by good structure. Fine impressions came too from the soft, fleshy, mouthfilling Rocca Rubia Riserva '03 and the more vegetal Grotta Rossa '04, both Carignano del Sulcis. Leading the whites is Vermentino di Sardegna Villa Solais '05, which has a sweet fruitiness on the nose and a full, soft palate. Both the fresh Nuragus di Cagliari Pedraia '05 and Vermentino Cala Silente '05 are good.

●	Carignano del Sulcis Sup. Terre Brune '02	ΨΨ	7
●	Araja '04	ΨΨ	4*
●	Carignano del Sulcis Rocca Rubia Ris. '03	ΨΨ	5
●	Carignano del Sulcis Grotta Rossa '04	ΨΨ	3*
●	Monica di Sardegna Antigua '05	ΨΨ	3*
○	Vermentino di Sardegna Villa Solais '05	ΨΨ	3*
○	Nuragus di Cagliari Pedraia '05	Ψ	3
○	Vermentino di Sardegna Cala Silente '05	Ψ	4
●	Carignano del Sulcis Sup. Terre Brune '00	YYY	7
●	Carignano del Sulcis Sup. Terre Brune '01	YYY	7
○	Latinia '01	YYY	5
●	Terre Brune '93	YYY	6
●	Terre Brune '94	YYY	6
●	Carignano del Sulcis Sup. Terre Brune '98	YYY	6

SANT'ANNA ARRESI (CI)

MESA
LOC. SU BARONI
09010 SANT'ANNA ARRESI (CI)
TEL. 0781689390

Mesa is a new Sulcis estate of over 100 hectares, 50 of them under vine, and it made a stunning debut in the Guide. The winery was started by Gavino Sanna, a noted Sardinia-born advertising agent, and Giuseppe Mele, president of the Sassari young industrialists, and the vineyards and winemaking are taken care of by Emanuele Porcina and Daniele Pintus. Together, the four have created a synergy which has already led to some excellent wines, even more so thanks to guidance from young, skilled oenologist Piero Cella. Carignano is undisputed king of the vineyards, followed by cannonau, syrah, vermentino and chardonnay. The cellar is still being completed and will be both attractive and functional, easing all stages of winemaking and looking after guests. Image communication is naturally in Sanna's hands. We were pleasantly surprised by it all, especially since two wines, Malombra '04 and Buio Buio '04, reached the finals. The former is from 85 per cent carignano with syrah and ages one year in barrique. The nose is intense and complex with ripe fruit and sweet oakiness. The palate has great structure, showing full and juicy, and giving vanilla on its long, attractive finish. Buio Buio instead comes from 100 per cent carignano and is concentrated on the nose with blackberry and balsamic hints. Similar sensations come through on the palate, which is warm and soft. Cannonau di Sardegna Moro '05 is an excellent wine. Lively and vegetal, with Mediterranean herbs on the nose, it has a round, pervasive palate. Buio '04, Opale '05 and Giunco '05 are also good.

●	Buio Buio '04	ΨΨ	5
●	Malombra '04	ΨΨ	7
●	Cannonau di Sardegna Moro '04	ΨΨ	5
●	Buio '04	Ψ	4
○	Giunco '05	Ψ	4
○	Opale '05	Ψ	5

SANT'ANTIOCO (CI)

Sardus Pater

via Rinascita, 46
09017 Sant'Antioco (CI)
tel. 0781800274 - 078183937
www.cantinesarduspater.com

This is one of the leading wineries in Sulcis, especially for carignano and monica production, many of the grapes coming from ungrafted vines grown on sandy soils close to the sea. For many years, these grapes were used to make highly concentrated bulk wines which were in great demand from producers in other regions. But some years ago, the winery managers decided to change over to quality production and bottled wines – to good effect. They have now taken on Riccardo Cottarella, who needs no introduction, as consultant oenologist. We found the reds again on good form this year but there's also interesting news from two new whites. Lugore '05, Vermentino di Sardegna, is one of them. It has an intense, fruity nose, good body, freshness from its overt acidity and a long, clean finish. The other is Moscato di Cagliari Amentos '05. This has a fresh, vegetal nose with notes of basil and sage. The palate is sweet and soft, revealing candied fruit on its long finish. Carignano Kanai Riserva '03 is a great glass of wine, with red berry fruit and spices on the nose and a warm, mouthfilling palate. Monica di Sardegna Insula '05 is also excellent. There is good concentration on the nose, which is fruity and has vegetal hints, preceding a full-bodied, well-structured palate with marked acidity and tannin that underline its youth. Finally comes the admirable Carignano Is Solus '05 which has a broad, complex array of jammy, ultra-ripe aromas. The warm, soft palate discloses assertive tannin and a touch of bitterness on the finish.

●	Carignano del Sulcis Kanai Ris. '03	🍷🍷	4
●	Carignano del Sulcis Is Solus '05	🍷🍷	4
●	Monica di Sardegna Insula '05	🍷🍷	3
○	Moscato di Cagliari Amentos '05	🍷🍷	5
○	Vermentino di Sardegna Lugore '05	🍷🍷	4
●	Carignano del Sulcis Issolus '01	YY	3*
●	Carignano del Sulcis Kanai Ris. '01	YY	4
○	Kermy '01	YY	6
○	Naam '01	YY	5
●	Sardus Pater Rosso '01	YY	3*
●	Sulky '99	YY	6

SELARGIUS (CA)

Meloni Vini

via Gallus, 79
09047 Selargius (CA)
tel. 070852822
www.melonivini.com

The size and set-up of Meloni Vini enables it to carry out research and experimentation on new wines, which is done with an eye to keeping abreast of market developments. Although there are usually numerous dessert wines in the large range, none of them was submitted this year but we did taste an impressive Moscato di Sardegna Spumante. The aromas are varietal, foregrounding raisined grapes and honey, while the palate is fruity and sweet. On a par is the organic Cannonau di Sardegna Le Sabbie '04, which also has a little barbera and syrah. The nose is fairly open and proffers chocolate and oak. The palate is soft with good structure but the tannins, which taper off on the finish, are a touch bitterish. Cannonau di Sardegna Terreforru '03 is a most pleasing wine whose herbaceousness gives it liveliness and grip. There is very ripe fruit on the nose of Monica di Sardegna Jaccia '04, whose palate is lively and flaunts fair balance. Most of the whites are vermentino based. We enjoyed the gently perfumed but primarily vegetal Salike '05 with its aromas of fresh-cut grass and tomato leaf, its refreshing palate and its almondy finish. Vermentino di Sardegna Le Sabbie '05 has elegant touches of perfume on the nose but is little more than straightforward on the palate. Vermentino di Sardegna Omarus '05 is more balanced and harmonious, with attractive aromatics, good nose-palate harmony and an almondy finish.

●	Cannonau di Sardegna Le Sabbie '04	🍷🍷	4*
○	Moscato di Sardegna Spumante	🍷🍷	4
●	Cannonau di Sardegna Terreforru '03	🍷	3*
○	Vermentino di Sardegna Le Sabbie '05	🍷	4
○	Vermentino di Sardegna Omarus '05	🍷	4
○	Vermentino di Sardegna Salike '05	🍷	3*
●	Monica di Sardegna Jaccia '98	🍷	3*
○	Nasco di Cagliari Donna Jolanda '03	YY	5
○	Malvasia di Cagliari Donna Jolanda '98	YY	4
●	Girò di Cagliari Donna Jolanda '99	YY	4

SENNORI (SS)

TENUTE DETTORI
LOC. BADDE NIGOLOSU
S.DA PROVINCIALE 29 KM 10
07036 SENNORI (SS)
TEL. 079514711
www.tenutedettori.it

We are now appreciating Alessandro Dettori's philosophy just as much as his wines. Having started out in a burst of impetuousness, he now reflects as he moves through his vines, thinking about what he wants to achieve from the grapes. At each vintage, he weighs up the risks involved. He doesn't particularly choose to go against the stream but he prefers to stay out of the DOC system, which he feels tends to flatten out the individualities of terroir. And yet Alessandro's lands have long been famed for great reds, primarily Cannonau. Maybe he would change his mind if the DOC provided for subzones. That aside, he can take pleasure from having achieving an objective he's been chasing for a couple of years: our Three Glasses. The well-deserved award goes to Tenores '03, made from bush-trained cannonau. The wine itself was not clarified, or filtered or stabilized, and was aged solely in concrete vats and bottle. The nose is intense and recalls blackberry and morello cherry and there is considerable structure on the palate, underpinned by a good 17 per cent alcohol, which is delightfully balanced by softness and acidity. Tuderi '03, from cannonau, is also first-rate, albeit a tad rustic, and has red berry fruits aromas and notable fullness on the palate. Chimbanta '04, from monica, is concentrated and even a touch pungent on its dried rose-themed nose. The palate is warm and full, leading to a long, complex finish. Dettori Bianco '04 is from 100 per cent vermentino but still bottled as IGT. It's attractive on the nose but even better on the fleshy, full-bodied palate.

●	Tenores '03	**YYY**	8
●	Tuderi '03	**YY**	6
●	Chimbanta '04	**YY**	6
○	Dettori Bianco '04	**YY**	5
●	Chimbanta '03	YY	6
●	Ottomarzo '03	YY	6
○	Dettori Bianco '03	YY	5

SENORBÌ (CA)

CANTINA TREXENTA
V.LE PIEMONTE, 40
09040 SENORBÌ (CA)
TEL. 0709808863 - 0709809005
www.cantina-trexenta.it

The Trexenta co-operative started with 23 members 50 years ago and now has over 200, farming 350 hectares of vines. This growth resulted from a natural generation change and because viticulture remains a linchpin of the local economy, also accounting for the preservation of much of the landscape. Trexenta managers have long been aware that success can only come through quality wines and for some years now they have been persuading their members to go back to using bush-training systems and the more renowned indigenous varieties. There is a large range of wines, all good value for money, embracing almost all the available styles. Our first comment on the wines themselves has to be that the '02 release of Alter Nos, made from 50 per cent cannonau and 30 per cent carignano plus other reds, is good but not as good as previous vintages. Moving on to the barrique-aged Tanca Su Conti '02, from equal parts of carignano and cannonau, things started looking better. Here, we found aromas of plum and blackberry jam. The palate is soft, almost round, the oak does not overwhelm the ripe fruitiness and the finish is long. Cannonau di Sardegna Baione '04, from bush-trained vines, is admirable, its varietal characteristics enhanced by its ageing in large old barrels. There is red berry fruit and a touch of balsam and similar fruitiness also appears on the soft, rounded palate. The attractive, immediate Vermentino Donna Leonora '05, the fresh, elegant Tanca Sa Contissa '05 and Nuragus Tenute San Mauro '05 are all as good as ever.

●	Tanca Su Conti '02	**YY**	5
●	Cannonau di Sardegna Baione '04	**YY**	3
○	Vermentino di Sardegna Tanca Sa Contissa '05	**YY**	2*
●	Alter Nos '02	**Y**	6
●	Cannonau di Sardegna Corte Adua '04	**Y**	2*
○	Nuragus di Cagliari Tenute San Mauro '05	**Y**	1*
○	Vermentino di Sardegna Donna Leonora '05	**Y**	1*
●	Tanca Su Conti '00	YY	5
●	Alter Nos '01	YY	6
●	Cannonau di Sardegna Baione '03	YY	3*
●	Monica di Sardegna Duca di Mandas '04	YY	2*

SERDIANA (CA)

★ ANTONIO ARGIOLAS
VIA ROMA, 56/58
09040 SERDIANA (CA)
TEL. 070740606
www.cantine-argiolas.it

People often overreact to sudden fame but when success comes slowly it's easier to savour and encourages the spirit to aim even higher. That's what's happened with the Argiolas family, who now have another Three Glass wine to add to their tally, the flagship '02 Turriga. It has remarkable breadth and complexity on the nose, with distinct scents of blackberry and morello cherry, followed by a well-judged touch of sweet oakiness. The palate is soft, generous and gently tannic. Already drinking beautifully, it should improve considerably over the next few years. Korem '04, from bovale, bovaleddu, cannonau and carignano, very nearly gained Three Glasses too. It's characterful, deep and pervasive, and threaded through with balsam. The '03 vintage of the renowned Angialis has tremendous finesse and elegance, and is one of the best nasco-based wines around. Cerdena, from vermentino and other local grapes, confirmed its standing, the '04 being full, rounded and decisive, with beautiful fruit and vanilla scents. Vermentino di Sardegna Is Argiolas '05 is another first-rate wine, showing harmonious, fresh and floral on both nose and palate. The 2005 vintage was memorable for Monica di Sardegna Perdera, which has distinct vegetal aromas and a palate characterized by good structure, liveliness and vigour. Costera '05 is still young but already goes to the heart of Cannonau di Sardegna in its intense aromas, concentrated palate and ripe fruitiness. The '05 releases of Nuragus di Cagliari S'Elegas, Vermentino di Sardegna Costamolino and Serralori are all well up to speed.

●	Turriga '02	▼▼▼	8
○	Angialis '03	▼▼	6
●	Korem '04	▼▼	6
○	Cerdeña '04	▼▼	7
●	Cannonau di Sardegna Costera '05	▼▼	4
●	Monica di Sardegna Perdera '05	▼▼	4
○	Nuragus di Cagliari S'Elegas '05	▼▼	3
⊙	Serralori Rosato '05	▼▼	3
○	Vermentino di Sardegna Costamolino '05	▼▼	4
○	Vermentino di Sardegna Is Argiolas '05	▼▼	4
●	Turriga '00	▽▽▽	8
○	Angialis '01	▽▽▽	6
●	Turriga '01	▽▽▽	8

SERDIANA (CA)

F.LLI PALA
VIA VERDI, 7
09040 SERDIANA (CA)
TEL. 070740284
www.pala.it

The Pala brothers' estate is small but dynamic, a place where growth means higher quality not greater quantity, and where quality comes primarily from selection, first in the vineyard and then through microvinifications. There is a new wine this year, Vermentino di Sardegna Stellato '05, which remains on its lees for three months. It has a pleasant nose of almond and apricot jam. The palate is fresh, savoury and supple, finishing clean and long. The estate's leading white, though, is Entemari, made from vermentino, malvasia and chardonnay. The '05 has freshness, structure and elegance, as well as plenty of fragrance which comes through on both the nose and the full, round palate. The much-acclaimed S'Arai, from carignano, cannonau, bovale and barbera sarda, is another top-ranking wine. The '03 has an alluring nose of blackberry, sweet oak and balsamic hints that meld beautifully into a full, round palate. Assoluto '05, the estate's only dessert wine, made from nasco with some vermentino, is another very fine product. The nose is not overly intense but still nicely forthcoming, giving citrus, honey and nuts. The fleshy palate is sweet without being cloying and there is additional fruit on its long finish. The '04 Essentija, from 100 per cent bovale, fell short of last year's release but still showed good personality. It is not yet ready, its marked acidity making it a bit edgy and stalky, but it is bound to improve. All the traditional-style wines from vermentino, cannonau, monica and nuragus showed well.

●	S'Arai '03	▼▼	5
○	Assoluto '05	▼▼	5
○	Entemari '05	▼▼	5
○	Vermentino di Sardegna Stellato '05	▼▼	4*
●	Essentija '04	▼	4
●	Cannonau di Sardegna Triente '05	▼	4
●	Monica di Sardegna Elima '05	▼	3*
○	Nuragus di Cagliari Sálnico '05	▼	2*
○	Vermentino di Sardegna Crabilis '05	▼	3*
●	S'Arai '00	▽▽	5
●	S'Arai '01	▽▽	6
○	Entemari '02	▽▽	6
●	S'Arai '02	▽▽	5
○	Assoluto '03	▽▽	5
○	Entemari '03	▽▽	5

SETTIMO SAN PIETRO (CA)

Ferruccio Deiana

via Gialeto, 7
09040 Settimo San Pietro (CA)
tel. 070749117 - 070767960
www.ferrucciodeiana.it

Ferruccio Deiana is a retiring soul but a notable personality in the insular world of wine. It was he who many years ago first accompanied Giacomo Tachis around Sardinia's vineyards and wineries. A skilled oenologist, Ferruccio used to select the bulk wines to send to mainland Italy and abroad. Now he can take pride in his ownership of a 40-hectare estate and in making high-quality wines. This year's '03 Ajana, from cannonau, carignano and bovale, almost picked up Three Glasses. There is great concentration on the nose, which opens slowly, a sign that the wine is not yet ready for the corkscrew. This is confirmed by notable acidity and tannin on the otherwise rich, soft, balanced and harmonious palate. Monica di Sardegna Karel '05 is also top quality and also not yet mature, especially on the nose which is very vegetal, although the palate is rich and soft. Cannonau di Sardegna Sileno '04 is highly successful, with a beautifully clean nose of blackberry with hints of balsam throughout. Vermentino and chardonnay both went into Plurimus '05, which was fermented and aged six months in barrique. The nose has fair breadth and complexity, with sweet oakiness and ripe tropical fruits, but the wine's structure and the richness of its fruit comes through more on the full, elegant palate. Vermentino di Sardegna Arvali '05 and Donnikalia '05 are also good. Finally comes Oirad '05, from moscato and malvasia, one of the best dessert wines on the island. The nose is rich and aromatic, the palate austere yet warm, and the finish long and attractive.

● Ajana '03	▼▼	7
● Monica di Sardegna Karel '05	▼▼	4
○ Oirad '05	▼▼	6
○ Pluminus '05	▼▼	7
● Cannonau di Sardegna Sileno '04	▼	4
○ Vermentino di Sardegna Arvali '05	▼	4
○ Vermentino di Sardegna Donnikalia '05	▼	4
● Ajana '02	▽▽▽	7
● Ajana '01	▽▽	7
● Ajana '00	▽▽	7
○ Vermentino di Sardegna Arvali '02	▽▽	4*
○ Oirad '03	▽▽	6
● Monica di Sardegna Karel '04	▽▽	4*
○ Oirad '04	▽▽	6
○ Pluminus '04	▽▽	7

TEMPIO PAUSANIA (OT)

Cantina Sociale Gallura

via Val di Cossu, 9
07029 Tempio Pausania (OT)
tel. 079631241
www.cantinagallura.com

A history spanning 50 years, 135 members, 350 hectares of vines at altitudes from 250 to over 500 metres, 70 per cent of them vermentino, the rest moscato and local red varieties, and 1,300,000 bottles. That, in a nutshell, is what Dino Addis has built up at this co-operative. But there's more. He's made considerable improvements to quality while maintaining value for money, thereby establishing the cellar in many important markets. Indeed quality is such that for several years now, Dino has had wines in the finals. This year's finalist is Vermentino di Gallura Superiore Genesi '05. It underwent brief skin maceration, which has given it an accentuated colour. The intense aromas span broom, tropical fruit and minerality, and the full, close-knit palate has a well-integrated acid backbone. The other Vermentino Superiore, Canayli '05, also has breadth on its elegantly fruity, floral nose, followed by a palate with grip and vigour. Piras '05, a Vermentino but not Superiore, is aromatic and pleasantly fresh. The other non-Superiore Vermentinos, Gemellae '05 and Mavriana '05, are both excellent. Moving on to the reds, the '04 Cannonau di Sardegna Templum has stolen a march on the '03. It's more concentrated on the nose, with ultra-ripe fruit, and clean and full on the palate. The '05 Karana and the Moscato Spumante are well up to their usual standards.

○ Vermentino di Gallura Sup. Genesi '05	▼▼	6
● Cannonau di Sardegna Templum '04	▼▼	4*
● Karana Nebbiolo dei Colli del Limbara '05	▼▼	3*
○ Moscato di Tempio Pausania '05	▼▼	4*
○ Vermentino di Gallura Gemellae '05	▼▼	3*
○ Vermentino di Gallura Mavriana '05	▼▼	3
○ Vermentino di Gallura Piras '05	▼▼	3*
○ Vermentino di Gallura Sup. Canayli '05	▼▼	4*
⊙ Campos '05	▼	3*
○ Vermentino di Gallura Sup. Canayli '03	▽▽	4*
○ Vermentino di Gallura Sup. Genesi '04	▽▽	6
○ Balajana '02	▽▽	4
● Dolmen '03	▽▽	5
○ Vermentino di Gallura Sup. Canayli '04	▽▽	4*

USINI (SS)

CARPANTE
VIA GARIBALDI, 151
07049 USINI (SS)
TEL. 079380614 - 3351318373

This small, new estate, run by three friends who fell in love with viticulture, now takes its place among the great and the good. It has little more than ten hectares, with plots in the best parts of Usini. The vines are still bush-trained and most are indigenous varieties, primarily cagnulari, a grape that has gone from the edge of extinction to become the area's leading grape. The work going on at Carpante is leading to improved understanding and appreciation of the variety and its potential. Dino Addis is consultant, a diligent researcher who hates top-of-the-head decisions and likes to formulate his wines while in the vineyards. Such was the gestation of Carpante, a wine from cagnulari with a little bovale and pascale, which aged one year in barrique and six months in bottle. The '03 has notable concentration of aroma, mainly ripe blackberry but also tobacco, spice and sweet oakiness. Tannins are still evident on the palate but it is soft and mouthfilling, with a long, attractive finish. Cagnulari '05 has the intense vegetal aromas characteristic of young wines, and is medium-bodied and slightly tannic but balanced. Cannonau di Sardegna '05 is also still young. There is ripe fruit on the nose preceding a rich, well-structured palate, with overt but not aggressive tannins and a slightly bitterish finish. Vermentino di Sardegna Frinas '05 is a distinctive wine, showing more close-knit and structured than its partner Vermentino, Longhera '05, which has a fresh, aromatic, citrus nose, and a soft, savoury palate with an attractive finish.

● Carpante '03	TT	5
● Cagnulari '05	TT	4
● Cannonau di Sardegna '05	TT	4
○ Vermentino di Sardegna Frinas '05	TT	5
○ Vermentino di Sardegna Longhera '05	T	4

USINI (SS)

GIOVANNI CHERCHI
LOC. SA PALA E SA CHESSA
07049 USINI (SS)
TEL. 079380273

The generation change at Cherchi is beginning to bear fruit. Giovanni Cherchi, though still active, is getting on and managing almost 30 hectares of vines plus the new cellar would have been too much for him. His sons, though, work assiduously and their motivation is ever stronger. This has been further stimulated by the acclaim that, after a period of ups and downs, is now beginning to come their way. Soberanu '03, a superb barrique-aged red from selected cagnulari grapes and sold only in magnums, came within a hair of Three Glasses. Putting your nose in the glass is like diving into Mediterranean scrubland while scenting morello cherries and jam. These same sensations come through on the full, long palate. Luzzana '04, from cannonau and cagnulari, is another admirable wine, with red berry fruit and balsamic notes dominating the nose, and great structure and elegant softness marking out the palate. Cagnulari '05 is still young but its lively, youthful nose and its palate full of promise, together with a strong, clear-cut personality, makes it most impressive. Moving on to the whites, Vermentino di Sardegna Tuvaoes '05 has good breadth on the nose, with distinct tropical fruits and tomato leaf-like vegetal notes. The palate is fresh and clean, gaining distinction and attraction from its fine balance of softness and acidity. The '05 Boghes, a Vermentino aged in new barriques, is vegetal, attractive but still young. Good as it is, we preferred last year's. Vermentino di Sardegna Pigalva '05 has a clean nose and a pleasant palate.

● Soberanu '03	TT	8
● Luzzana '04	TT	6
○ Boghes '05	TT	6
● Cagnulari '05	TT	5
○ Vermentino di Sardegna Tuvaoes '05	TT	5
○ Vermentino di Sardegna Pigalva '05	T	4
● Luzzana '01	YY	6
● Luzzana '02	YY	6
○ Boghes '03	YY	6
● Luzzana '03	YY	6
○ Vermentino di Sardegna Tuvaoes '04	YY	5

OTHER WINERIES

Antonella Ledà d'Ittiri

via Manno, 12
07100 Alghero (SS)
tel. 079233304
www.margallo.it

This is the first time this estate appears in the Guide. It has six hectares of vineyard, two of them newly planted, growing merlot, sangiovese and cabernet franc. The result is Margallò '04, a fruity, fully-structured, soft, mouthfilling wine with an attractive, long finish.

- ● Margallò '04 — 🍷🍷 4

Fradiles

via Sandro Pertini, 2
08030 Atzara (NU)
tel. 0784659010

Fradiles is a small, new property making classic Mandrolisai DOC wines. It produces two styles, the more impressive of which is Antiogu, from bush-trained cannonau, monica, bovale and muristellu. The '04 has ripe fruit aromas and a warm, full palate.

- ● Mandrolisai Antiogu '04 — 🍷🍷 5

Li Duni

loc. Li Parisi
07030 Badesi (SS)
tel. 079585844 - 3460051776
www.cantinaliduni.it

This small winery is valiantly producing wines that need considerable maturation. Vermentino di Gallura Renabianca '04 has an evolved, lightly fruity nose. Its warm palate evokes hay and signs off with a slightly almondy finish.

- ○ Vermentino di Gallura Renabianca '04 — 🍷 5
- ● Tajanu '03 — ΥΥ 5

Li Seddi

via Mare, 29
07030 Badesi (SS)
tel. 079683052 - 079684121
www.cantinaliseddi.it

This first-ever releases here are two promising but still youthful wines. Lu Ghiali '05, from cannonau and muristeddu, has a vegetal, balsamic nose and a lively, slightly tannic palate. The cannonau, monica, girò and muristeddu Petra Ruja '05 is easy-drinking, fresh and medium-bodied.

- ● Lu Ghiali '05 — 🍷🍷 5
- ● Petra Ruja '05 — 🍷 4

Cantina Arvisionadu
via Lodi, 4
07010 Benetutti (SS)
tel. 079796947

This new entry is recovering the ancient native arvisionadu white grape, which goes into its best wine, the single-variety Lesitanus '05. Labirintu '05, from arvisionadu with vermentino and caricatola, and the red Contraruia '05, from muristellu, cannonau, cagnulari and carignano, are good.

○	Lesitanus '05	YY	5
●	Contraruia '05	Y	4
○	Labirintu '05	Y	4

Columbu
via Marconi, 1
08013 Bosa (NU)
tel. 0785373380 - 0785359190
www.vinibosa.com

This year, Columbu submitted two styles of Malvasia di Bosa, one traditional, DOC and from '01, the other youthful, an '05 Planargia Alvarega IGT. The former has an ethery, evolved nose, and a warm, well-structured, long palate while the latter is apricot-themed, intense and pleasing.

○	Malvasia di Bosa '01	YY	6
○	Planargia Alvarega '05	YY	5

Manconi - Mura
via G. Ibba Piras, 20
08015 Bosa (NU)
tel. 0785374904

This small estate, another new Guide entry, has just three hectares, all planted with malvasia. The Terra Antiga '03 selection is a fine example of the sweet style of Malvasia di Bosa. The nose evokes dried fruit and apricot before the palate shows warm, harmoniously sweet, pervasive and long.

○	Malvasia di Bosa Terra Antiga '03	YY	6

Cantina Tondini
loc. San Leonardo
07023 Calangianus (OT)
tel. 079661359

The family have long been growing grapes on the Limbara slopes in the Gallura but are new to winemaking and have just two wines. Taroni '05 is a lively, youthful blend of nebbiolo and cannonau and the Vermentino di Gallura Karagnani '05 is fruity and soft.

●	Taroni '05	Y	4
○	Vermentino di Gallura Karagnani '05	Y	5

Cantina di Calasetta
via Roma, 134
09011 Calasetta (CI)
tel. 078188413
www.cantinacalasetta.com

This winery, more than half a century old, is in the Guide for the first time with two Carignano del Sulcis wines. Tupei '05 ages six months in barrique and has a balsamic, lightly oaky nose, and a full, fleshy palate. Piede Franco '05 is less elegant on the nose and a touch thin.

●	Carignano del Sulcis Tupei '05	YY	5
●	Carignano del Sulcis Piede Franco '05	Y	5

Cantina Sociale di Castiadas
loc. Olia Speciosa
09040 Castiadas (CA)
tel. 0709949004
www.castiadasonline.it

We were more impressed by the reds and whites than the rosés here. Parolto '02, from cabernet, carignano and cannonau, is fruity on the nose and soft on the palate. Cannonau di Sardegna Riserva '02 is soft and full, with blackberry and morello cherry. Praidis '05 is straightforward but well made.

●	Cannonau di Sardegna Ris. '02	YY	4*
●	Parolto '02	YY	4*
○	Vermentino di Sardegna Praidis '05	Y	3*

Cantina Sociale Dorgali
via Piemonte, 11
08022 Dorgali (NU)
tel. 078496143
www.csdorgali.com

A warm, savoury Cannonau di Sardegna Riserva Vinìola '02, with a concentrated, red berry fruits nose and an almondy finish, shows that great reds can come from Baronia, too. Vigna di Isalle '04 is still youthfully vinous and vegetal, with distinct tannin and acidity, but is harmonious and long.

●	Cannonau di Sardegna Vinìola Ris. '02	YY	5
●	Cannonau di Sardegna V. di Isalle '04	YY	4*

Lisca
via Delogu, 89
07025 Ittiri (SS)
tel. 079442612

Boldly, this family-run winery is now making a classic method brut sparkler, using vermentino and cannonau. Results are encouraging, especially for a small estate, for the nose is nicely fruity and the palate fresh. Carignos '05, from vermentino, vernaccia, torbato and tocai, is clean and tidy.

○	Lisca Brut '01	Y	5
○	Carignos '05	Y	4

Mura
loc. Azzanido, 1
07020 Loiri Porto San Paolo (OT)
tel. 078941070
www.vinimura.it

The Mura siblings submitted two characterful Vermentinos. Superiore Sienda '05 is fresh, fruity and alluring on the nose and the palate is attractive, full, firm and fleshy, finishing long. Cheremi '05 is livelier and more immediate, with a tropical fruits nose and a balanced, savoury palate.

○	Vermentino di Gallura Cheremi '05	YY	4*
○	Vermentino di Gallura Sup. Sienda '05	YY	4

Paolo Depperu
loc. Sas Ruinas
07025 Luras (OT)
tel. 079647314

The Depperu siblings are indefatigable grape-growers. They have decided to leave the DOCG but their Ruinas '05 has all the characteristics of a great Vermentino. It's fresh and floral on the nose, juicy and fleshy on the palate, and has great structure and lively, well-integrated acidity.

○	Ruinas '05	YY	5
○	Vermentino di Gallura Sup. Ruinas '04	YY (white)	6

Zarelli Vini
via Vittorio Emanuele, 36
08010 Magomadas (NU)
tel. 078535311

The range has increased at this small, primarily malvasia-based winery. Licoro '05 is a sweetish Malvasia with lightly fruity aromas and a clean finish. The pleasant, vegetal Turudas '04, from cabernet, cannonau and sangiovese, has more interest on the palate than the nose.

○	Licoro '05	Y	5
●	Turudas '05	Y	4

Giampietro Puggioni
via Nuoro, 11
08024 Mamoiada (NU)
tel. 0784203516 - 3496406261
www.cantinagiampietropuggioni.it

With 15 hectares of low-yielding cannonau vines, this estate produces concentrated wines of depth. We liked two Cannonau di Sardegnas in particular, the warm, fruity Lakana '04 and Mamuthone '04 with its ripe blackberry and plum aromas.

●	Cannonau di Sardegna Lakana '04	YY	4
●	Cannonau di Sardegna Mamuthone '04	YY	4
●	Cannonau di Sardegna Ilisi '03	YY (white)	6

Giuseppe Sedilesu

via Adua, 2
08024 Mamoiada (NU)
tel. 078456333 - 078456791

This is a year of transition for this newish Barbagia estate, which has gained a reputation for full-bodied, alcoholic reds from cannonau. The fruit of the Carnevale '04 is still dominated by oak and balsam on the nose while the palate is warm and soft but falls a little short.

●	Cannonau di Sardegna Carnevale '04	▼	6
●	Cannonau di Sardegna Carnevale '03	▽▽	6
●	Cannonau di Sardegna Mamuthone '04	▽▽	4

F.lli Porcu

loc. Su e Giagu
08019 Modolo (NU)
tel. 078535420

Young, ambitious Carlo Porcu has now taken over at this small estate and has already produced an excellent Malvasia di Bosa '02, which almost secured Three Glasses. The nose is broad, intense and citrus-like, the palate is soft and warm, and there is good nose-palate consistency.

○	Malvasia di Bosa '02	▼▼	5
○	Malvasia di Bosa '00	▽▽	5

Cantina Sociale Il Nuraghe

s.s. 131, Km 62
09095 Mogoro (OR)
tel. 0783990285
www.ilnuraghe.it

One of the new wines from a growing range at this co-operative is a fresh, herbaceous, bovale-based Campidano di Terralba Tiernu '05. Monica Nabui '02, with a vegetal nose and a ripely fruited palate, is also good. The honeyed Moscato Capodolce '04 and Semidano Anastasia '05 are both enjoyable.

●	Monica di Sardegna Nabui '02	▼	6
○	Moscato di Cagliari Capodolce '04	▼	4
●	Campidano di Terralba Tiernu '05	▼	4
○	Sardegna Semidano Anastasia '05	▼	4

Pedra Majore

via Roma, 106
07020 Monti (OG)
tel. 078943185

This winery, which produces large quantities of Vermentino di Gallura, comes and goes in our Guide. The Superiore Hysonj '05 has an elegant nose, and is rich and mouthfilling. I Graniti '05 and Le Conche '05 are good. The very fine Mirju '04, from semi-dried moscato, is concentrated yet elegant.

○	Mirju '04	▼▼	5
○	Vermentino di Gallura I Graniti '05	▼▼	4
○	Vermentino di Gallura Sup. Hysonj '05	▼	5
○	Vermentino di Sardegna Le Conche '05	▼	4

Cantina del Vermentino

via San Paolo, 1
07020 Monti (OG)
tel. 078944012 - 078944631
www.vermentinomonti.it

It is Funtanaliras that again stands out here. The '05 has pleasing apricot and rose aromas, and is attractively harmonious on the palate. Aghiloia '05 can't match it, even though it is a good wine. Arakena '04, this too from Vermentino di Gallura Superiore, is better on the palate than the nose.

○	Vermentino di Gallura Funtanaliras '05	▼▼	5
○	Vermentino di Gallura Sup. Arakena '04	▼	6
○	Vermentino di Gallura Sup. Aghiloia '05	▼	3

Tenute Olbios

loc. Venafiorita
via Loiri, 83
07026 Olbia
tel. 0789641003 - 0789641003

This is a new estate owned by young growers with 50 hectares of vineyard, mostly planted with vermentino. Vermentino di Sardegna Lupus in Fabula '05 is attractive, though rather alcoholic, and has a nicely fruity nose and a lively palate.

○	Vermentino di Sardegna Lupus in Fabula '05	▼	5

Gostolai
via Friuli Venezia Giulia, 24
08025 Oliena (NU)
tel. 0784288417

Tonino Arcadu produces ten wines from ten hectares. The best of them is once more Puer sed Formosus, made from cannonau, cabernet and carignano. The '04 has a blackberry nose with balsamic hints and a harmonious palate. The other Cannonau di Sardegnas are also good.

- ● Puer sed Formosus '04 — 4*
- ● Cannonau di Sardegna Nepente di Oliena Sos Usos '04 — 4
- ● Cannonau di Sardegna Sonazzos '04 — 4

Cantina Cooperativa di Oliena
via Nuoro, 112
08025 Oliena (NU)
tel. 0784287509
www.cantinasocialeoliena.it

We are in Cannonau country, in the Oliena subzone, also called Nepente di Oliena. The latest release from this co-operative, the '05, has a youthful, vegetal nose and a full, balanced palate. But alcohol predominates on the '03 Riserva, coming through on both nose and palate.

- ● Cannonau di Sardegna Nepente di Oliena '05 — 4*
- ● Cannonau di Sardegna Corrasi Nepente di Oliena Ris. '03 — 5

Cantina di Quartu
via Nazionale
09045 Quartu Sant'Elena (CA)
tel. 070789865
www.cantinadiquartu.it

It is a joy to see the achievements of this co-operative in the difficult task of making good dessert wines. Nasco Apassili '04 is nutty, with a warm yet elegant palate. The simple, fresh Nuragus di Cagliari Nuraghe Lua '05 and the clean, well-made Monica Tuerra '04 are very successful.

- ○ Nasco di Cagliari Apassili '04 — 3*
- ● Monica di Sardegna Tuerra '04 — 3*
- ○ Nuragus di Cagliari Nuraghe Lua '05 — 2*

Villa di Quartu
via G. Garibaldi, 90
09045 Quartu Sant'Elena (CA)
tel. 070826997 - 070820947
www.villadiquartu.ory.it

Improvements here are such that more Guide space may be due. Maripintau, a barrique-aged Vermentino, again stands out with a fruity, fleshy, pervasive '05. Cepola Rosso '04, from cannonau, bovale, monica and barbera, has a broad, complex nose and a soft palate. Monica '04 is uncomplicated.

- ● Cepola Rosso '04 — 4
- ○ Maripintau '05 — 5
- ● Monica di Sardegna '04 — 4

Compagnia delle Figlie del Sacro Cuore Evaristiane
loc. Putzu Idu
09070 San Vero Milis (OR)
tel. 078352007 - www.vinievaristiano.com

The estate is part of an organic farming community. Some wines are from local grapes, others not. Our favourites were the youthful, fresh, savoury Tharros '04, from sangiovese, cabernet, barbera and cannonau, and the well-made, balanced Monica di Sardegna Flora '04, evoking Mediterranean scrubland.

- ● Evarstiano Rosso '04 — 4
- ● Monica di Sardegna Flora '04 — 4
- ● Tharros '04 — 4

Agricola Punica
loc. Barrua
09810 Santadi (CI)
tel. 0781950127

The '03 is only the second release of Barrua but it is clearly a wine of great structure and personality. It comes from Sulcis-grown carignano, cabernet and merlot. The nose has good jammy fruit and, despite its youth, as manifested by marked acidity and tannin, the palate is impressive.

- ● Barrua '03 — 8

Deidda

S. S. 388 km 7.200
09088 Simaxis (OR)
tel. 0783406142
www.cantinadeidda.it

You need tremendous dedication and determination to produce classic method sparkling wine in small quantities. Giampiero Deidda says, jokingly, that you also need to be foolhardy. But that's what he's been doing and the results are good, especially the fresh, fruity Marzani Brut.

○ Marzani Brut M. Cl.	🍷	4

Cantina Sociale del Mandrolisai

c.so IV Novembre, 20
08038 Sorgono (NU)
tel. 078460113
www.mandrolisai.com

Things are up and down at this co-operative despite its high potential. The reds are all cannonau-based blends. The concentrated Mandrolisai Superiore '03 is warm and full with overripe notes while Kent'Annos '01 also has firm, compact structure and red berry fruit.

● Mandrolisai Kent'Annos '01	🍷🍷	6
● Mandrolisai Rosso Sup. '03	🍷	4

Cooperativa Romangia

via Marina, 5
07037 Sorso (SS)
tel. 079351666
www.vinidellaromangia.it

As its range of wines continues to grow, Romangia is starting to look like a major winery. The best of the wines tasted was Tres Montes, a honey-nosed Moscato with a soft, balanced palate. Both Monica '05 and Cannonau Jennos '05 are good, attractively fresh and youthful.

○ Moscato di Sorso Sennori Tres Montes '05	🍷🍷	5
● Cannonau di Sardegna Jennos '05	🍷	4
● Monica di Sardegna '05	🍷	3

Melis

via Santa Suina, 20
09098 Terralba (OR)
tel. 0783851090 - 0783850751

This new estate is new to the Guide. The range is fairly wide. Moscato di Cagliari Lauretum '03 stands out, with a nose of Mediterranean scrubland, sage and orange blossom, and a majestic, warm palate with a long, aromatic finish. Terralba Nabj '03, mostly bovale and sangiovese, also showed well.

○ Moscato di Cagliari Lauretum '04	🍷🍷	5
● Terralba Nabj '03	🍷	5

Virdis

via J. F. Kennedy, 6
07049 Usini (SS)
tel. 079380133

There is a Guide debut for this small, new estate with just two hectares under vine. Its white, vermentino-based Su Monte de S'Ulimu '03, is soft, warm and slightly rustic. The red, Monte Alvanu '03, from cagnulari only, is sweet. It has red berry fruit, great structure and 18 per cent alcohol.

● Virdis Rosso Monte Alvanu '03	🍷🍷	7
○ Virdis Bianco Su Monte de S'Ulimu '03	🍷	5

F.lli Serra

via Garibaldi, 25
09070 Zeddiani (OR)
tel. 0783418276
www.vernacciaserra.it

This small estate, best known for Vernaccia di Oristano, is in and out of the Guide. Its Riserva '00 has intense aromas of almond and a warm, pervasive palate. Kora Kodes '04 blends cabernet sauvignon with indigenous grapes. It's vegetal and balsamic on the nose then savoury and lively in the mouth.

○ Vernaccia di Oristano Ris. '00	🍷🍷	4
● Kora Kodes Rosso '04	🍷	4*

INDEX OF WINES

INDEX OF PRODUCERS

Locanda nel Borgo Antico:

Tele

Barolo: Angelo Gaja 'Gromis' 2000

- Amuse bouche of soft white cheese w. herbs on spoon, cod puff. ?potato puff?!
- Amuse II: pasta plin, ?veal-filled?
- Quail, foie gras sauce, heart of, [illegible], fried leave, leg in tempura batter
- Pasta filled w. Ricciola? w. prawn sauce & broccoli
- Maiale, baton, stuffed w. pork sausage & sage - turned veal.
- Cheese
- Yoghurt ice cream, blackcherries, mango coulis, s'thing banana, poached pear
- Petit fours inc. mascarpone cream w. raspberry sauce, [illegible], choc...